The HAMMOND ALMANAC

of a million facts records forecasts

1980

Martin A. Bacheller, Editor in Chief

Hammond Almanac, Inc.

Maplewood, N. J. 07040

Martin A. Bacheller, Editor in Chief

Dorothy C. Bacheller, Ernest J. Dupuy, Jonathan F. Erway, Marjorie Joyce, Charles G. Lees, Jr. (Sports), **Maria Maggi, Alice Melillo, W. Z. Myers,** Editors

Harvey Brittle, Director of Production

Drew Kuber, Director of Creative Operations

William A. DeGregorio, William E. Kennedy, Bob Perlongo, Charles Johnson Taggart, Contributing Editors

---

Laurence Urdang, Contributing Editor

John Daintith, Editor, Science

Edward R. Brace, Editor, Medicine

William H. Pinson, Jr., Editor, Astronomy

Elizabeth Martin, Editor, Earth Sciences

Alan Isaacs, Advisory Editor, Science

Bill Carter, *Television Review*

Robert Dahlin, *Book Review*

Mel Gussow, *Theater Review*

Stephen Handzo, *Film Review*

Henry T. Wallhauser, *Music Review*

THE FUTURE *section appearing on pages 16–48 was prepared by the World Future Society, 4916 St. Elmo Avenue, Washington, D.C. 20014; Edward S. Cornish, President.*

Data for the Index of U.S. Colleges and Universities found on pages 739–757 were supplied by Peterson's Guides, 228 Alexander St., Princeton, N.J. 08540, a communications company specializing in higher educational data.

The Hammond Almanac is the successor to The New York Times Encyclopedic Almanac.

Library of Congress Catalog Card Number: 79-642716

Published simultaneously in the United States and Canada   ISBN 0-451-82057-2 395 (Soft-cover)

Printed in the United States of America   ISBN 0-8437-4017-5 (Hard-cover)

HAMMOND ALMANAC, INC.
Maplewood, New Jersey 07040
HUGH JOHNSON, *President*

CONTENTS

U.S. CRIME SUMMARY 261–263

CIVIL RIGHTS/RACE 264–268

PUBLIC HEALTH/MEDICINE 269–283

EARTH: FACTS/FIGURES 284–313

THE 1980 OLYMPICS

A Tale of Two Cities
by Bob Perlongo

Citius — Altius — Fortius
("Faster — Higher — Stronger")

— Olympic motto

The fame of the Olympic festivals
Shines from afar amid the race-courses . . .
The victor all his remaining days
Breathes a delicious and serene air
When he remembers the Games.

— Pindar
(from *Olympian Odes* I, 476, B.C.)

In *these* particular best and worst of times, a fairly safe prediction: the 1980 Olympics, to be held in Moscow and Lake Placid, New York, will be one of the year's biggest — and most controversial — happenings, a kaleidoscope of substance and symbol in which amateur athletics, superpower politics and near-rampant commercialism all will play a part.

It's not a new mixture, of course — politics, for instance, has been a factor in the Games since they began — but this Olympiad promises to epitomize this aspect, with many a drama and confrontation in store, and not all on the field of sport.

The main event will be Moscow, principal site of the July 19-August 3 Summer Games (some events will be held in Leningrad, Kiev, Minsk and Tallinn). But while Moscow continues its roughly $330-million preparations for the Games, the immediate focus for Olympics-watchers will be Lake Placid, an idyllic resort town set in a wilderness area in upstate New York's Adirondack Mountains. On February 13, 1980, Lake Placid will become the first modern site to host two Winter Olympic celebrations (the first Lake Placid Games were in 1932). The Games, which will run through February 24, are expected to draw 51,000 on peak competition days — the maximum that will be allowed for environmental reasons.

Emblems for 1980 Olympics.

Planning Ahead

Businessmen are hoping the Games will restore Lake Placid to its one-time prominence as a winter sports center, an away-from-it-all place where people come to play and spend. The latest, revised budget for the Games stands at about $150 million — three-fifths for construction, the rest for operation. State funds, corporate donations and the sale of TV rights are helping to meet the cost. The U.S. Department of Commerce has also provided $57 million of economic development funds, but to justify the funding, federal regulations require that the facilities must have a long-term "secondary purpose."

Contributing Editor Bob Perlongo is a free-lance writer/editor whose work has appeared in a number of periodicals including The New York Times, Playboy *and* Rolling Stone.

U.S. Prison Director Norman A. Carlson has been pushing a plan to turn the site into a minimum-security prison, but this is being strongly opposed by church groups, black state legislators and Chicago's John Howard Association, one of the nation's leading prison-reform groups. Proposed alternate uses for the site include a permanent training center for future Olympic athletes, a youth hostel or campground — or, more mundanely, public housing, which is much needed in the Adirondacks, where unemployment runs high.

Meanwhile, as the debate continues, there has come a twist of the twine from the never-far-absent world of politics: the Soviets have proudly announced that *their* Olympic Village will be converted after the Games into a housing project for some 12,000 Muscovites. One can almost see now the Russian headlines to come: A Prison for Placid, Happy Homes for Moscow!

Of more immediate concern, of course, are the Games themselves and the training of those who will be taking part in them. A big help here is the fact that the U.S. Olympic Committee (USOC) is having little trouble, for a change, funding its budget, pegged at about $26 million. Aiding its efforts has been an advertising campaign consisting of a series of TV and radio spots delivered by Olympic winners and aspirants who have donated their services. "Without your help," they say, "we can't afford to win." The Olympic Committee has sought Federal funds for the first time, collecting $16 million.

Jeans for the People

In addition, the USOC has received over $7 million in cash and services from corporations, from auto makers to fast-food chains and manufacturers of photographic equipment to name just a few sponsors. One of the fast-food chains has contributed $2 million toward the U.S. Olympic Training Centers in Colorado Springs and Squaw Valley, California. Other corporations are sponsoring the AAU's track and field program. Somewhat surprisingly, in a year when the oil industry is seeking to improve its public image, one oil company is keeping a low profile concerning its support of a national wrestling coach and staff — support which has in a short time greatly helped amateur wrestling.

*Above: Crab-shaped volleyball arena in Moscow
in final stage of construction.
Left: Bobsled run at Lake Placid being tested.*

Much more publicly, in return for a goodwill investment of $1 million, a prestigious maker of sportswear stands to gain "free" advertising worth many times that amount. (The $1 million will be used for the manufacture of travel and parade uniforms for the U.S. Olympic athletes at Moscow and Lake Placid and to supply thousands of pairs of jeans to be distributed free to Russians involved with running the Olympics — a display of generosity not apt to go unnoticed on the air waves.) And $8 million worth of the manufacturer's ads will be aired on NBC during the Summer Games. Corporate gifts to the Olympic Committee earn an exclusivity clause barring competitors from promoting similar products in the same way.

Few in or out of the Olympic movement see anything wrong with the increased funds from corporations, or the newly relaxed strictures against the appearance of Olympic athletes in commercials — now O.K. as long as the fee goes to the individual's governing body. As has been copiously pointed out in the media, the United States is the exception among nations in that the government doesn't subsidize sports. And in any case, all Olympic sponsors are required to submit ads and releases to the USOC for screening.

According to U.S. pole vaulter Mike Tully, a possible Olympic gold medalist, top track athletes have for some time now been wondering why they haven't been getting paid to train, especially when they read of the houses and cars their European counterparts get when training under the same international rules of amateurism that apply to Americans. Veteran Olympic hurdler Willie Davenport thinks the answer is providing athletes with jobs where performance, but not necessarily a strict schedule, counts: "There's no way a person can have an 8-to-5 clock-punching job to support his family and still be a 'world class' athlete." Most folks, these inflationary days, are inclined to agree. The purists may squawk and balk, but purists, for better or worse seem now a dwindling breed: and the bottom line is that time and training and adequate facilities, like most all else, take boodles of rubles.

Selling the Athletes

One can expect to see the United States Olympic logo adorning everything from jeans to frisbees as merchants enjoy a marketing bonanza while helping sponsor the 1980 Olympic team. However, some feel that the new fund raising allowing athletes to endorse products blurs the boundary between amateur and professional sports. For the first time the committee permits athletes to appear in commercials without forfeiting their amateur status — so long as amateur sports associations get the proceeds. In one case under the new rule-loosening, the AAU has allowed a track star to endorse a major hotel chain because it is paying the AAU a $25,000 "sponsorship fee." No fee goes to the athlete — but he has been employed by the chain as a consultant. "So what we have here," writes Bert Nelson of *Track and Field News,* "is the AAU literally selling the services of the athlete and taking its cut. In some professions that is called pimping. Here it's wrapped in a protective mantle of press releases extolling the virtues of aiding amateur sports."

Amateur or semi-professional, however the Olympic Games now classify, the big-stakes player will be NBC, which has paid the Russians $85 million for exclusive rights to televise 150 hours worth of events in Moscow — $60 million more than what ABC paid to cover the 1976

U.S. Olympic training center at Squaw Valley.

Games in Montreal. Perhaps hoping for the Olympics to generate enough excitement and momentum to pull it out of the ratings basement, the network is sparing no expense in its preparatory endeavors: "making sure" at the pre-Olympic Spartakiad Games in Moscow this past summer were 45 NBC production officials, scouting the sites and presumably amassing mountains of memos.

One thing NBC can count on at the Games is that the ever-present question of politics will certainly, to some extent or other, prove a distraction if not an outright disruption. Politics being only human, and humans being what we are, there has been some understandable concern that NBC may unavoidably lend itself to Soviet manipulation.

The big question many have asked — including a Congressional subcommittee — is: "Will NBC's coverage be censored in any way?"

Replied network President Robert Mulholland: "We've told them that we'll cover anything that happens, and they've understood that from Day One. But it's their house and they own the electricity" — apparently meaning the Russians can "pull the plug" if they dislike what they see.

Spartakiad, Prelude to the 1980 Games

A good, long look at just what we might expect in Moscow was provided by the two-week Soviet Spartakiad Games, the most important of several pre-Olympic meets held in 1979. (Among the others were the Pan American Games in San Juan, Puerto Rico, and the National Sports Festival in Colorado Springs.) The quadrennial Spartakiad Games, held first in 1951 (always a year before the Olympics) are the Russian national finals, comparable to those of the AAU; they cap a process that winnows out the best in mass competitions in all the Soviet republics, and in separate preliminaries in Moscow and Leningrad. The winners become the country's contenders in the Olympics.

As a dress rehearsal for 1980, with foreign athletes taking part for the first time, Spartakiad drew mixed reviews. On the whole, the stage and sets — such as Lenin Stadium, site of the Olympic track and field events — were judged impressive by the U.S. and 83 other foreign teams, whose members were also delighted at the chance to size up potential opponents. Amid the pageantry, however, were some Soviet snafus — harbingers, perchance, of hassles ahead. Complaints included stalled visas, scheduling screwups and unsanitary toilet conditions at the arenas. One reporter laid the blame on "the Russian proclivity for excelling at pomp and fouling up circumstance." To be fair, there was still nearly a year between Spartakiad and The Big One, and — with all the manpower — and womanpower — the Soviets have to work with, few doubt that the construction will be finished on time and that most, if not all, the glitches will be gone by the time the games begin.

In their spare time at Spartakiad, Americans indulged in some free-lance cultural exchange activity. "This is not fun city," noted the physician for the U.S. track and field squad. "I hope they have a disco at the Olympic Village." (The Russians have, in fact, promised there will be one, along with English signs in the subway system. Other Olympian projects include a complete face-lift for Red Square.)

Lenin Stadium in Moscow during Spartakiad Games.

A principal pastime was sampling what Olympic spectators will be downing — smoked salmon, caviar or sliced sausages; hot tea, vodka or Coca-Cola (along with sister-drink, Fanta.) Perhaps inevitably, a casual kind of black market developed, as austerity-surfeited Soviets plied athletes with "plenty rubles" for such capitalistic contraband as American-brand sweatsocks or chewing gum, the latter at a very neat ruble — or $1.53 a pack. "Are you going to sell your uniform before you leave the Soviet Union?" one track athlete was asked. "Of course," was the ready reply. "I have more back home."

Big Misha is Watching You

One surprise: though there were some 103,000 spectators on hand for Spartakiad's opening day, Olympic-like ceremonies, attendance thereafter was surprisingly poor, with seas of empty seats in Lenin Stadium — most Muscovites apparently preferring to watch the proceedings on TV in the privacy of their own homes. A hearty dash of propaganda marked the celebration as a huge card section in the stands simulated the fiery explosion of an H-bomb to appropriate sound effects from loudspeakers. Then, as the crowd burst into applause, the mushroom cloud was crossed out and replaced by "mir," the Russian word for "peace," and the cards spelled out: "Glory to the Communist Party of the Soviet Union."

Still, there *were* lighter Soviet images for visitors to carry away from Spartakiad, images soon to be familiar to the TV millions. Chief among these may well be the winsome and utterly ubiquitous mug of the Olympic mascot, Misha the bear — a kind of Soviet counterpart of Winnie the Pooh. (The idea of an Olympic mascot is not new: Munich had a dachshund, Montreal a beaver.)

Those who feel that politics have been a corruptive influence on recent Games — and many there are who do — should realize that politics have *always* played their part. For to the Greek city-states that were the jealous nations of their time, victory upon Olympia's sacred grass was as dear, if not seemingly dearer betimes, as victory upon the battlefield. Winners were national heroes, crowned with laurel and wild olive, and poets and musicians sang their praises.

Zeus Was the Juice

While the exact origin of the Games lies forever befogged by the fancies of myth, it is fairly certain that some sort of athletic contests took place for centuries before their recorded beginning in 776 B.C. One legend suggests that

U.S. figure skating duo, Tai Babilonia and Randy Gardner.   *Britain's Sebastian Coe setting record mile run.*

Zeus was the juice from whence the original Games began, following a battle for possession of the earth between Zeus and Kronos in the mountains surrounding Olympus: when Zeus, a kind of pre-Paramount godfather of the gods, triumphed, celebratory games were held upon a fertile plain in the valley below, at Olympia. Hercules, the Hulk of his fabled day, also figures in some of these lofty legends. Yet whatever their real seed, there in the center of Olympia, in the hallowed grove of Zeus, the Games were held every four summers for over a thousand years.

The Greek lyric poet Pindar (518-438 B.C.) believed that the Games were "the peak of contests," providing a means by which a man's worth might be tested in action. The delight of winning, he felt, was all the dearer for the pain preceding and attending it: "Where toil has been, greater is the delight that follows" — a sentiment often voiced by modern Olympic winners.

Through the fifth and fourth centuries B.C. the Games constituted the Greek world's grandest festival, but then began a gradual decline that paralleled the decline of Greek supremacy in the region, as the Roman Empire continued to grow. Commercialism started to erode the original purity of the Games, as the large cities began to hire professional athletes, many of whom were not native-born but who were quickly nationalized to comply with the rules. The Emperor Nero, no less, had a hand in making a mockery of the Games of A.D. 66, entering several events and breaking rules to win. Finally, in A.D. 393, the Emperor Theodosius I, a Christian, abolished the Games on the grounds of paganism.

The Modern Revival

The modern revival of the Games at the end of the nineteenth century was due largely to the efforts of a Parisian scholar, Pierre de Fredy, Baron de Coubertin, who was fervent in his belief that through the Games a genuine contribution to World Peace could be made. Addressing a meeting of the Union des Sports Athlétiques in Paris in 1892, Baron de Coubertin exhorted: "Let us export our oarsmen, our runners, our fencers into other lands. That is the true Free Trade of the future; and the day it is introduced into Europe the cause of Peace will have received a new and strong ally."

Alas, the cause of Peace was destined for a couple of particularly hard falls — with or without Olympic influence — but meanwhile de Coubertin managed to realize his dream. In 1896, after many an obstacle had been surmounted, the Games were held in Athens, under the patronage of the King of Greece, with 13 nations taking part. The modern Olympic era had begun.

The first three of these celebrations lacked sufficient organization and worldwide representation (only 11 nations made it to St. Louis in 1904), and not until 1908 in London did the Games truly begin to establish themselves.

As for U.S. prospects in the 1980 Games, they are generally good, with much metal apparently in the offing. At Lake Placid, Linda Fratianne and Lisa-Marie Allen should be at or near the top in figure skating, while fourteen-year-old Elaine Zayak of Paramus, N.J., will definitely win hearts if not gold — providing, of course, she first wins an Olympic berth. (These and other prognostications are, of course, based on the assumption that those named will make the upcoming Olympic Trials, an accomplishment never, quite, to be taken for granted.) Another crowd-pleaser, and probable medal winner, will be the class-act U.S. figure-skating duo of Tai Babilonia and Randy Gardner.

Fans should also be gladdened by the grit and drive of this Olympiad's U.S. hockey squad, which will be the best prepared we've ever sent, and probably the youngest of any team in the entire Winter Games. They'll need everything they can muster when they go against the Soviet team that routed some of the National Hockey League's best players in the recent Challenge Cup series at Madison Square Garden.

Dashing Sebastian

Track and field has always been the heart of the Summer Games, and in 1976 U.S. men won

UPI   UPI

U.S. hurdler Renaldo Nehemiah.

Nineteen-year-old U.S. diver Greg Louganis.

more gold medals (six) than any other nation; we were, in fact, the only nation to win more than two. In 1980 wins may come harder, as European runners have recently been rocking the timer's clock. Striding swiftest of all has been Britain's twenty-two-year-old son of a Sheffield cutler, Sebastian Coe. Within the space of six weeks this past summer, Coe busted world marks in the 800-meter (1:42.4) and the mile (3:49), and the 1500-meter (3:21.1) a feat that has made him an early favorite in the 800- and 1500-meter in Moscow.

Chasing Coe will be Cuba's Alberto Juantorena, the man who holds Olympic gold in both events and whose record in the 800 Coe bettered by over a second. The best U.S. hope here seems to be James Robinson, who has beaten Juantorena twice, most recently in the Pan Am Games. Those to watch in the 1500, besides Coe and Juantorena, will be former record-miler John Walker of New Zealand, Steve Scott and Don Paige of the United States and Eamonn Coghlan of Ireland, who just missed metal in Montreal and who should bag at least bronze this time around. In the 400, Americans Tony Darden, Willie Smith and Herman Frazier have been running well of late, with the twenty-one-year-old Darden emerging as the best prospect for gold.

James Sanford is among the favorites in the 200-meter, as is Wardell Gilbreath, who won gold at Spartakiad. In the 100, Silvio Leonard of Cuba, who missed Montreal but won in both the Pan Am and Spartakiad Games this summer, is the clear favorite. Harvey Glance and Houston McTear of the United States also figure to do well.

At twenty-four, Craig Virgin is the best and youngest of the U.S. long-distance runners. He recently broke the U.S. record in the 10,000 meters, but the marathon remains his best chance for metal in Moscow. Another marathon man, Frank Shorter, is working hard to regain the form that won him Olympic gold in 1972.

American hurdlers Renaldo Nehemiah and Edwin Moses and relay runners Don Coleman

and Stan Vinson have also been doing well of late — as have triple jumper Milan Tiff and decathlon hopeful Fred Dixon. In the discus throw, veteran Olympic medalists Mac Wilkins, Al Oerter and John Powell are all thought to have a reasonable fling at silver or gold.

Women's track and field, this Olympiad, will be mainly a matter of gaining some kind of toehold against the dominant Europeans (especially East Germans). There *are* some rays of hope. Among them: Sheree Howard in the 400-meter; Essie Kelley, perhaps our best hope in the 800; and Darlene Beckford, who won the 1500 at the National Sports Festival. In the 100-meter hurdles, AAU champion Deby LaPlante, who excelled at Spartakiad, could win a bronze; in the same event, Patty Van Wolvelaere is looking for a comeback after a foot injury kept her out of the 1976 Games. Candy Young is another who looks good in this event.

In the 400-meter dash, the woman to beat will be world record-holder Marita Koch of East Germany. In the 400-meter hurdles, the big threat will be Marina Makeeva of the Soviet Union. In the javelin throw, 1976 bronze medalist Kathy Schmidt will be seeking to out-toss the reigning champ, Ruta Fuchs of East Germany.

American swimmers and divers, who won big in the Pan Am Games should continue their winning ways in Moscow. Brian Goodell, Steve Lundquist and Jesse Vassallo are shaping up well and could prove winners. One performer rated almost a sure thing for gold is nineteen-year-old diver Greg Louganis, considered by many to be the world's very best. The women's swimming team, which had blitzed every Olympic meet since 1956, was outclassed in 1976 by the East Germans; but now youthful speedsters such as Tracy Caulkins, Cynthia Woodhead and Mary T Meagher seem set on redemption.

Canary on the Wing?

The Soviets and Romanians are odds-on to continue their general supremacy in gymnastics, but this time many see the American team as making quite a stir. Kurt Thomas and Bart Conner should finish among the leaders, while in the woman's division three of the brightest stars are three of the youngest: Jackie Cassello (thirteen), Tracee Talavera (twelve) and Christa Canary (seventeen), whose vaulting could send her soaring at least a 9.3 for that incredible name. All three, if they

Wide World

U.S. gymnast Christa Canary.

get to Moscow to begin with, have a more-than-fair chance to win metal — and lots of hearts — there.

Stevenson Speaks

The U.S. boxing squad may not repeat its sterling 1976 performance, but it should end up at or near the top in several divisions. Among the promising new faces are light heavyweights Tony Tucker and Lemuel Steeples, lightweight Robert Hines and bantamweight Jackie Beard. At present there aren't any heavyweights — American or otherwise — around to pose a serious threat to the twenty-seven-year-old Cuban, Tefilo Stevenson, who has reigned for seven years as the top amateur heavyweight. Many feel Stevenson could succeed Muhammad Ali, were he to turn pro, but he says proudly, "If you are a professional, you are not an athlete" — an extreme view, perhaps, in these days of Big-Buck Sports, but an utterance somehow appropriate for an Olympian.

For whatever the hassles, however sullied by politics and commerce the Games may sometimes be, they do after all have something of idealism and brotherhood about them, as well as providing a terrific test for raw physical prowess. They are certainly a whole lot better than, say, war. And when the trumpet fanfares signal the raising of the five-ringed Olympic flag and the release of thousands of pigeons to symbolically fly to the nations with the news of the Games, who's to say that such antique notions as mutual respect and peaceful competition may not yet have a chance?

Or, as one of our Summer Games hosts might put it: "Mozhno."

"It is possible."

Schedule of Events 1980 Winter Games - Lake Placid

Event	Tu 12	We 13	Th 14	Fr 15	Sa 16	Su 17	Mo 18	Tu 19	We 20	Th 21	Fr 22	Sa 23	Su 24
Opening ceremony		●											
1. Figure skating						●		●		●		●	
2. Figure skating, pairs					●			●					
3. Speed skating				●	●	●	●	●	●	●			
4. Ski jumping						●				●		●	
5. Downhill skiing			●			●			●				
6. Cross-country			●		●		●		●			●	
7. Biathlon				●				●			●		
8. Slalom			●								●		
9. Giant slalom							●		●				
10. Bobsledding, four-man / two-man					●							●	●
11. Luge, single / double			●	●	●								
12. Ice hockey			●		●	●		●		●	●		
Closing ceremony													●

Schedule of Events 1980 Summer Games - Moscow

Event	Sa 19	Su 20	Mo 21	Tu 22	We 23	Th 24	Fr 25	Sa 26	Su 27	Mo 28	Tu 29	We 30	Th 31	Fr 1	Sa 2	Su 3
	July													August		
Opening ceremony	•															
1. Athletics							•	•	•	•	•	•	•	•		
2. Rowing		•	•	•	•		•	•								
3. Basketball		•	•	•	•	•	•	•	•	•	•					
4. Boxing			•	•	•		•		•	•	•	•	•		•	
5. Canoeing												•	•	•	•	
6. Cycling, track road		•														
7. Fencing			•	•	•	•	•	•	•	•	•	•				
8. Football (Soccer)		•	•				•					•	•	•	•	
9. Gymnastics		•	•	•	•	•	•									
10. Weightlifting		•	•	•	•	•	•	•								
11. Handball		•	•	•	•	•	•	•	•	•	•	•				
12. Hockey		•	•	•	•	•	•	•	•	•	•	•	•			
13. Judo									•	•	•	•	•		•	
14. Wrestling, freestyle							•	•	•	•		•	•			
Greco-Roman		•	•	•	•	•										
15. Swimming		•	•	•	•	•	•	•	•	•						
16. Modern pentathlon		•	•	•	•	•										
17. Equestrian sports		•				•			•			•	•	•	•	
18. Shooting		•	•	•	•	•	•	•	•	•		•	•			
19. Archery													•	•	•	
20. Volleyball		•	•	•	•	•	•	•	•	•	•	•	•			
21. Yachting			•	•	•	•	•	•	•	•	•					
Closing ceremony																•

U.S. swimmer Steve Lundquist, world record holder for 200-meter individual medley.

Defending heavyweight world boxing champion, — Teofilo Stevenson of Cuba.

Wide World

Wide World

THE FUTURE

A special report prepared for the Hammond Almanac by the staff of the World Future Society.

A look ahead on the U.S. Economy and what to expect in the 1980s on —

- Inflation
- Work and careers
- Energy
- Automobiles
- Housing
- Technology
- Food and agriculture

Geothermal experimental facility

SDG&E

Homes For Living Inc.

Salt box solar house

Below: Automatic transport vehicle
Bottom: Laser fusion research

Ford Motor Corp.

Electricar

Above: Electric car being charged

Lawrence Livermore Lab.

The World Future Society is a nonprofit, non-partisan association of scholars, scientists and others interested in forecasts of what may happen in technology, society, human values and other fields during the coming years. The Society's headquarters are at 4916 St. Elmo Avenue, Washington, D.C. 20014.

The U.S. Economy in the 1980s

Economic Forecast: Things won't get much better or much worst — maybe.

by **Edward Cornish**,

President of the
World Future Society
Washington, D.C.

Energy shortages and persistent inflation were the big worries of the 1970s: Twice during the decade motorists experienced aggravating periods during which they had to spend hours waiting in line at gasoline stations. But even worse than that was the relentless increase in the price of almost everything. Inflation — even more than the energy shortages — was the great economic agony of the 1970s.

But what about the 1980s? Will there be relief from inflation? Will energy crises become normal? Just what will the economy be like during the years ahead?

The consensus of the experts seems to be that the current malaise will continue in the foreseeable future — things won't get much better or much worse — but that is only the consensus. Some experts foresee considerable improvement in the economic picture, while others believe things are likely to get much worse — that we might even have another depression! The division of opinion suggests that the 1980s will be a period of surprises — at least for some of the experts!

To generalize a bit, there appear to be three views of the future of the U.S. economy: the optimistic, the pessimistic, and the middle-of-the-road viewpoints. Let's look at each in turn, starting with the middle-of-the-road view, since that appears to be the outlook of most economists:

Standard or "middle-of-the-road" Forecast:

Inflation will continue to be a serious problem during the 1980s: There will be periods when it will get better but there will also be periods when it will get worse. However, it is unlikely to read the horrendous levels experienced by some foreign nations. Unemployment will remain troublesome, especially for certain disadvantaged groups like young blacks, but new government programs should keep unemployment from rising to anything approaching the levels reached during the Great Depression. The standard of living will continue to rise, but not at the brisk rate of the 1950s and 1960s. In short, the 1980s will see a continuation of the economy of the 1970s — continued but modest growth, inflation, and persistent unemployment among some groups, but with a continued high standard of living for most Americans.

Optimistic Forecast:

The economy will soon begin to shake off the troubles it experienced during the 1970s and enter a new period of prosperity. Inflation may continue but it will not get out of control; business will grow steadily, though there may not be an outright boom. There will be all kinds of jobs for people who want work. Population will grow somewhat faster and there will be the largest increases in individual households in history. A whole raft of exciting new products and technological innovations will enter the marketplace, and these will stimulate innumerable new business opportunities and jobs.

Pessimistic Forecast:

The economy will experience a major slump in the 1980s with waves of bank failures and business bankruptcies and skyrocketing unemployment rates. Inflation might come to an end as prices collapse in one area after another — stocks, housing, commodities, etc. As inflation gives way to deflation and dollars start becoming more rather than less valuable, many people will have great difficulty meeting heavy mortgage payments — and may face foreclosure. The most pessimistic of the pessimists foresee a widespread breakdown of social and political structures as the economy deteriorates, wtih possible violence or even civil war.

Generally speaking, professional economists and businessmen seem to accept the "middle-of-the-road" forecast. U.S. Government officials and journalists closely associated with the government often favor the optimistic forecast, while the pessimistic view is expressed by a number of widely scattered experts, who tend to work independently of both government and the economics profession. In 1978 a book expressing the pessimistic view, *How to Prosper During the Coming Bad Years* by financial analyst Howard Ruff, became a best seller across the nation.

Only time will tell who is the closest to being right. In the meantime, valuable insights into the world of the future can be gained by looking at the recent history of the U.S. economy and some of the most significant aspects of today's economy.

Recent Trends

The United States emerged from World War II as the world's wealthiest and most powerful nation. Its workforce had performed prodigies during the war. The products of U.S. technology could be seen everywhere, from Siberian steppes to Pacific atolls. Millions of people lived as beneficiaries of U.S. largesse. Everywhere the U.S. dollar commanded a respect bordering on awe.

The economic pre-eminence of the United States, which had just emerged from the worst depression in its history, arose from certain specific circumstances:

1. The destruction of its economic competitors: Much of Europe and Japan lay in ruins. Countless factories of major nations lay in ruins; the prewar colonial empires had loosened their ties to the mother countries. Of the major nations, only the U.S. had factories untouched by wartime destruction. Under these circumstances, America could buy cheaply from distressed foreigners and sell U.S. products to them at high prices.

2. Hard-working people: The Great Depression had taught the American people the value of having a job. Hard work was vital both for survival and for getting ahead. During the war, many Americans worked 50, 60, or more hours a week for low wages and few fringe benefits.

3. Accumulated gold reserves and other assets: Desperate Europeans had transferred many assets to America. Vast amounts of gold stored in Fort Knox, Kentucky, provided solid backing for the dollar, making it "as good as gold."

4. Vast amounts of savings: During the war, the American people had accumulated enormous savings because they had faith in financial instruments. Unlike the Germans, who had the experience of seeing their bonds and paper money lose their value, Americans had seen paper money increase in value, so they willingly loaned their money to the government, accumulating large holdings of U.S. bonds. After the war, these savings provided the stimulus for a boom in the sale of automobiles, homes, and appliances.

But even as Americans relaxed in their unprecedented prosperity during the 1950s, forces were at work to undermine it. The Europeans and Japanese rebuilt their industrial plant and began producing enough goods not only to meet their own requirements but to export around the world. During the years of quasi-monopoly in many industrial fields, U.S. workers succeeded in obtaining very high wages — thus pushing up the cost of U.S. goods. European and Japanese producers — whose workers received far less pay — found it relatively easy to undersell U.S. goods and still make a profit. The Europeans and Japanese also began bidding up the prices of raw materials, forcing American producers to pay more.

After World War II, American workers began to take life easier. Hours were trimmed at factories; women left their jobs and began keeping house. At the same time, American workers went on the greatest binge of consumer spending the world has ever known. The American standard of living bounded upward. People who had once lived in shacks without electricity or plumbing moved into homes with beautifully appointed kitchens, indoor plumbing, and everything else. The education level of young Americans soared: where once college was the domain of the privileged, it now became a part of normal expectations. Young people whose parents were laborers and shopkeepers now trained for high-prestige, high-paying professional positions. At the same time, older people were pensioned off ever more generously so that they could enjoy their golden years without having to work.

By the late 1960s, it had become clear that the American people were on a collision course between their skyrocketing expectations of the good life — and the growing inability of the economy to meet them. The U.S. simply could no longer afford to provide its citizens with a rapidly rising standard of living when its citizens were working less, domestic supplies of raw materials like petroleum were being used up, and foreign competition was intensifying.

The crisis built up steadily during the 1960s and intensified by the economically debilitating and divisive Vietnam War. As so often happens, the cracks in the economy resounded on Wall Street. In 1966, the Great Bull market faltered, a victim of the declining prospects for American business; stock prices have never regained — in real dollars — the levels they reached in the mid 1960s; since then real prices have declined steadily, though erratically, and the "soaring Sixties" have become the "slumping Seventies."

Gary Gappert, a University of Wisconsin economist, has summed up the postwar era in these words:

"Future historians will likely characterize the 25 years from 1945 to 1970 in American society as a period of foolish affluence fueled by borrowed money.

"During these decades, American society, after years of deprivation during the Depression of the 1930s and World War II, attempted to buy back the lost time by becoming the most lavish consumer society in history. The spending spree was financed in large measure by an explosion of personal credit, by federal subsidies for home ownership and highway construction, and through the floating of local bond issues to build the schools, sewers, hospitals, and other infrastructure for the thousands of growing suburbs."

Gappert's book *Post Affluent America: The Social Economy of the Future* (1979) forecasts rising inflation and unemployment, and falling living standards as more and more income is redistributed abroad due to the rising cost of raw materials like petroleum.

Weakness of the Dollar

During the great boom years from 1950 to 1966, the world operated on the basis of a sound U.S. dollar, which the U.S. Treasury promised to redeem at the rate of $35 per ounce of gold. Billions of billions of dollars of gold were held in reserve at Fort Knox, Kentucky. But as the years passed, the U.S. sold off much of its gold. At the same time, the U.S. dollar became subject to rapid inflation, especially after President Johnson stepped up the Vietnam War and tried to pay for it without raising taxes.

Many people recognized that the U.S. could no longer keep its pledge to redeem dollars at the $35 per ounce rate because it simply didn't have anywhere near enough gold to back all the paper dollars with which it had flooded the world. So foreigners began demanding gold and the U.S. Government was forced to revoke its long-standing promise to redeem dollars with gold. Since 1971, the U.S. dollar has had no gold behind it. Earlier, in 1964, the U.S. stopped minting silver coins. So the U.S. dollar today is no longer backed by precious metals. It doesn't promise to pay the bearer anything at all — except more paper money.

Paper dollars continue to function as currency, but both Americans and non-Americans are increasingly suspicious of them, especially since inflation steadily gnaws away their value. A stupendous amount of dollars — estimated at perhaps $400 to $700 billion — now exists *outside* the United States. This huge sum hangs over the U.S. economy like a sword of Damocles. Sudden movements of these dollars between banks and nations can create major financial tremors, and the movements are largely unpredictable, often secret, and potentially disastrous. In 1978 a "run" on the dollar caused it to plunge in value; to head off catastrophe, President Carter and Secretary of the Treasury Michael Blumenthal organized a major "rescue" operation (issuing bonds denominated in German marks and Swiss francs, doubling gold sales, etc.). The operation halted the decline of the dollar, but did not cure the basic problem of financial instability. Since the dollar is no longer "as good as gold," the world now has no fixed standard of value: the dollar is a paper "I.O.U."

The disappearance of a stable dollar is today a critical problem for the world economy. John Exter, a retired senior vice president of the Citibank who earlier served as vice president of the Federal Reserve Bank of New York, says the world now has the most disorderly monetary system it has ever known. "Every currency in the world is fiat paper money, not a promise to pay anything," says Exter. "There are no hard currencies in the world today."

The lack of a stable dollar of value has led to enormous uncertainty and risk in business, especially in international operations. A businessman may find that his anticipated profit has disappeared because of an unexpected change in the the exchange rates. Today many large U.S. corporations report major alterations to their balance sheets due to unforseen shifts in the value of currencies.

Monetary chaos leads to speculation because shifts in the value of a currency means that a businessman must either take the risk himself or pay a speculator to take that risk for him. Thus, there now is a major market for currency futures — which in effect allows a businessman to hedge against a major shift in the value of a currency — by placing a wager so that if the feared change occurs his loss will be offset by his winnings from the wager. But buying such a futures contract adds to the cost of business and thereby reduces profits; in effect the speculator syphons off much of the profit from business transactions. At the same time, the transactions themselves become increasingly uncertain, risky, and time-consuming.

The weakest link in the international banking system, Exter suggests, may be the Eurodollar market. The non-American banks who deal in U.S. dollars are freed from the requirements of the U.S. banking system, such as having large reserves and not paying interest on very short-term deposits. As a consequence of its freedom from regulation, the Eurodollar market has grown like Topsy; dollars are flashed electronically around the world in bewildering patterns: a dollar may be in New York on Monday, Nassau on Tuesday, and Paris on Wednesday. It may be loaned out overnight by a bank in Hong Kong to a bank in Amsterdam. Furthermore, the "dollar" may change into Swiss francs, then metamorphose into Dutch guilders or British pounds, before reappearing as a dollar in Afghanistan. The exchange rates between the dollar

and other currencies now "float" — change from day to day — which means that money handlers stand to win or lose substantial amounts of money depending on when they buy or sell dollars. It was the ability of traders to make money by "shorting" the dollar—selling dollars that they were not actually holding — that led to the steady decline of the dollar and the resulting rescue operation of 1978.

Financial Terrorism

An international financial castastrope is now possible, especially since nations have come to recognize that they can use financial and economic power for political gain. Just how much of total U.S. assets is already in OPEC hands is unknown. The Ford Administration, as part of a campaign to attract foreign investment in the United States, entered into secret agreements with several Middle East governments to protect the confidentiality of those investments, and the practice has been continued by the Carter Administration, according to a report by the U.S. General Accounting Office.

The GAO report, made public on July 16, 1979, by the House of Representatives' government affairs subcommittee which has been investigating OPEC investments in the U.S., called the agreements "unique" and "not consistent with our treatment of other nations." Subcommittee chairman Benjamin S. Rosenthal, a New York Democrat, said "the secrecy surrounding OPEC investment and the refusal by Federal agencies to provide detailed and meaningful information on the nature and extent of such investment compounds public concern and inhibits congressional and public consideration of this vital issue."

Since the extent of OPEC holdings in the U.S. is uncertain, it is very difficult to do much more than make an educated guess as to how great the dangers may be. But Senator Jacob Javits of New York, who has warned — in speech after speech — about the dangerous international financial situation created by the recycling of OPEC dollars through U.S. banks, said in a 1977 speech:

"The pivotal role played by our private commercial banks is successfully helping to recycle the massive amounts of petro-dollars from their OPEC depositors to their oil-importing customers must not obscure the fragile basis on which the financial arrangements have been built. The

Continued on page 21

UPI

The U.S. dollar is no longer "as good as gold."

UPI

Tokyo monetary shifts reflect worldwide instability.

How to Prosper in Good Times and Bad

Economic prosperity causes most business to improve — but some businesses actually decline during a boom — and revive during the next slump. Here are some suggestions for making the most of whatever phase the economy happens to be in.

Good Times

Bad Times

Businesses Likely to Prosper

Hotels and motels • night clubs • resorts • cocktail lounges • fancy restaurants • new automobiles • real estate • hairstyling • travel bureaus • "fat farms" (weight reduction centers) • home furnishings (new) • swimming pool and tennis court construction • home building • airlines • art galleries • plastic surgery • saunas and jacuzzi baths • ballet schools • interior decorating • fashion dressmaking • poodle parlors

Shoe repair • pawnbroker • junkyard • used automobiles • milk delivery • garment repair • barbering • home delivery services • bus driving • millinery repair • boardinghouses • used furniture • door-to-door selling • used clothing • seeds and fertilizer • second-hand books • bowling and billiards

Survival Skills

Keeping one's weight down • having excuses for passing up a lunchtime martini • proper tipping • knowing the best schools • finding a maid

Using public transportation • fending off panhandlers • sewing • home repairs (do it yourself) • coping with poor relations • trading goods and services • eating more grains and vegetables, less meat • renting rooms in one's home • gardening • canning fruits & vegetables • imaginative substitutions — using newspaper to wrap presents, etc.

Recreation

Country clubs • golf • tennis • foreign travel • fancy bars and restaurants • exotic sports (hang-gliding, parachute jumping) • skiing • surfing • catered parties • theater, concerts and the opera

Hunting and fishing • hiking and city walks • church suppers • window-shopping • parlor games (e.g., charades) • card games • home baking • backyard picnics • visiting neighbors • radio and TV • going to local bar • jigsaw and crossword puzzles • reading

Good Times Menu

Bad Times Menu

appetizers

oysters Rockefeller
shrimp
honeydew melon
caviar canapes

entrees

filet mignon
lobster tails
veal scalloppini
salmon
rack of lamb

appetizers

tomato juice
vegetable soup
raw vegetables

entrees

pork and beans
macaroni and cheese
chipped beef on toast
Spanish rice
potatoes and gravy
casseroles (noodles plus
    whatever is cheap)

desserts

peach melba
crepes suzettes
cheese cake

beverages

mineral water
cocktails
vintage wines
liqueurs

desserts

applesauce
apple pie
bread pudding

beverages

tap water
soft drinks
beer
jug wines

essential weakness of this system is in the short-term structure of OPEC deposits and the longer-term nature of the credit that the banks extend to the deficit countries. The dependence of the banking system on the goodwill of a small group of depositors makes the banks 'hostages' to the threat of sudden withdrawals."

As Javits suggests, much danger arises from the fact that many U.S. banks have lent large amounts of money to developing countries who are no longer able to pay off the loans as originally scheduled. Big U.S. banks are reported to have billions of dollars outstanding in bad loans to developing countries as well as to other poor risks. The failure of the Franklin National Bank, one of the biggest in the United States, came at a time when the strains on the international monetary system were far less than they appear to be now. A failure by other major banks could set off a chain-reaction of business failures.

Looking forward to the 1980s, optimists can point to the continued strength of the U.S. economy as demonstrated by its ability to provide most Americans with a standard of living that would have seemed incredible in past eras. At the same time, many new technologies are coming on strong and there are innumerable ideas about how to solve the energy problems through conservation and new sources of power. Pessimists, however, stress the new dangers involved in the world's tangled financial networks as well as the inability of the government to curb inflation, which constantly threatens to get totally out of control. One thing both optimists and pessimists can agree on: the economy of the 1980s seems certain to offer surprises.

The Inflation Game: Will It Ever Stop?

Inflation is a game that everybody plays — but most people think they lose. In recent years, the game has become increasingly intense and has almost replaced the weather as a popular topic of conversation. And, like the weather, inflation seems to be something nobody ever does anything about.

Inflation is fairly easy to define: It is a general rise in the prices that people must pay for goods and services. Since the Great Depression of the 1930s, average prices in the United States have moved steadily upward, almost never downward. The rate of inflation was relatively modest during the 1940s and 1950s, but in the 1960s and 1970s prices bounded higher. The cost of most goods and services today is very roughly 10 times higher than it was during the 1930s and 1940s. Back then a haircut cost about 75 cents — and the barber would be happy with a dime tip. A meal in a restaurant might be bought for 50 cents. A cup of coffee cost a nickel; a hamburger 15 cents. A pair of really good shoes was $4.95; a paperback book, 25 cents.

But there was another side to it: During the 1930s, grown men were often grateful to get a dollar for working a whole day. People had little money to spend, because their wages were so low.

During the 1970s, the increase in prices has accelerated. In 1974 their rise over the previous year hit 12%; in 1979 inflation again soared above the 12% mark during the beginning months, though the recession was expected to bring the rate down during the final months of the year.

As the 1970s came to an end, most people seem to agree that inflation is the number-one economic problem that the United States faces. But the causes — and appropriate remedies — for this malady cause sharp disputes among economists, politicians, and almost everybody else.

What causes prices to rise? Clearly, most people would like to receive more money for the goods and services they produce, so it's not surprising if they try to charge more. But they couldn't get away with charging more if people refused to buy or switched to another supplier who charged less. So the first question is why do people continue to buy? They will say that they haven't much choice. Prices everywhere go up more or less simultaneously. Meanwhile the businessman who raises his prices will say that he was forced to because he had to give his workers a wage increase even though they are not producing any more goods than previously, and the workers, of course, say that they must have the wage increase to "keep up" with inflation. Clearly, one cause of inflation is inflation itself: once inflation has started, people assume that it will continue and therefore demand higher wages which must be paid for by raising prices. And once the inflation rate speeds up, workers are likely to ask for still higher wage increases, causing a further increase in inflation.

The causes often given for inflation include:

Falling productivity. During the 1950s and early 1960s, U.S. wages rose rapidly—well ahead of the rise in prices, giving workers a rapidly improving standard of living. One reason for this happy situation was that workers were increasingly productive, thanks to new machines and systems that enabled each worker to produce more per hour worked.

During the 1970s, productivity ceased to rise rapidly and even fell at times. For instance, in the second quarter of 1979, productivity actually declined at an annual rate of 3.3%, the Labor Department reported. The reasons for faltering productivity are a subject of much dispute. Some experts attribute it to the influx of inexperienced workers — women, young people, minorities, etc.; other observers believe that workers' attitudes have changed, and they no longer are willing to work as diligently as before.

Government's fear of unemployment. Government leaders influenced by British economist John Maynard Keynes and his followers have sought to minimize unemployment by accelerating government spending during periods of low demand for labor. One effect of this is to keep the demand for labor high — and that means wages are not reduced as they were in the past during periods of slack demand for workers.

Energy: The exhaustion of the richest and most convenient sources of petroleum in the United States is another important factor. Today oil men must go deeper or farther to find oil — and the costs go up. Furthermore, much of the petroleum and natural gas must come from out-

Many of the nation's 6 million unemployed — often blacks and Hispanics — lack marketable skills.

The 1978 prices on this fruit stand look like today's bargains in a time of unending inflation.

side the U.S., causing a persistent trade deficit. The rising cost of energy pushes up the cost of virtually everything.

Expansion of the money supply. Through the Federal Reserve System, the U.S. government tries to regulate the amount of money in circulation. Between 1960 and 1979, the U.S. money supply (broadly defined) surged nearly 380% — from less than $320 billion to about $1.5 *trillion*. During the same time, the real gross national product grew less than 90%, which means that in 1979 there was far more money around in relation to the available goods and services than there was in 1960. The extra money made available by the Federal government has pushed up the price of goods, many economists think.

Protectionism. U.S. manufacturers can raise prices partly because the government restricts imported goods. Without duties and quotas imposed by the government, consumers could buy cheaper goods produced in foreign nations, and domestic producers could not raise their prices.

Monopoly power. Some companies can raise prices and force consumers to pay them because there is little or no effective competition. Many labor unions also have the power to force companies to grant wage increases even when the workers are producing no more than before.

Minimum wage laws. Both Federal and state officials have regularly raised the minimum wage. When workers at the bottom of the wage scale are raised, workers receiving higher pay demand that their wages also be raised. As a result, most wages are pushed upward, and the prices of the goods the workers produce must be pushed up so that the wages can be paid. Minimum wage laws may also increase inflation by making it difficult for employers to hire certain workers — such as ghetto youths, who then turn to crime, which increases the cost of goods indirectly.

Welfare and unemployment compensation. Economists ave recently become concerned that the benefits granted people who are not working are encouraging large numbers of people not to work. The burden of supporting the nonworkers must be borne by the companies and workers producing goods and services, and the added cost is reflected in the prices of goods and services.

But the ultimate causes of inflation may lie even deeper. Alfred Kahn, President Carter's

chief inflation fighter, has said that the root cause of the current high inflation rate is the insistence of Americans on a constantly rising standard of living: "I think it comes down to the nature of our society, to the commitments that we have made to ourselves to maintain full employment or something very close to it, to the general expectation on the part of all of us that we are entitled every year to an increase in our real incomes so that, if the cost of living has increased, we are entitled to get the cost of living back — plus something." In recent years, many people have developed a disdain for many types of work — especially the menial humdrum tasks that are often scorned as "dead-end jobs" and "grundge work." At the same time, people who work hard are labeled "workaholics" and urged to join the leisure crowd. Such attitudes toward work clearly do not contribute to productivity and therefore add to inflation.

Although many people complain about inflation, few complain when their own wages are inflated: That is generally viewed as simply enabling them to "keep up with inflation." It is not always clear whether people really mind inflation as long as their own wages are inflated a little faster. Many groups of people actually benefit from inflation. For instance, homeowners find that inflation increases the value of their homes — but reduces the burden of their mortgage payments. On the other hand, buyers of bonds paying 3% or 5% have suffered monstrous losses as the inflation rate skyrocketed upward to 10% and higher.

Inflation naturally leads to higher interest rates since lenders realize that they will probably be paid back in dollars that will have declined in value. This rise in interest costs shuts off long-term investment, because a borrower must pay back so much so quickly that he cannot risk a long-range project. For example, if the interest rate is 1%, it will take about seventy years for the accumulated interest to equal the principal; at 7%, the time-interval drops to 10 years; at 10%, only seven; at 12%, only six.

Inflation penalizes savers. Many people with hard-ingrained habits of saving for a rainy day have found that their savings are so eroded by inflation and taxes that they have stopped saving money and instead are buying things likely to hold their value — gold, silver coins, rare postage

UPI

Shopping for no-name canned goods is one way consumers can cut high grocery bills.

stamps, antiques, etc. The rich are often thought of as escaping the ravages of inflation through various hedges, but a study by Joseph J. Minarik of the Brookings Institution in Washington concluded that inflation reduces the real income of the rich even more than it does that of the poor and middle-income groups. For the bulk of the population, the effects of inflation are relatively modest, Minarik claimed. Some groups now are substantially protected against inflation; for example, social security recipients, whose income is regularly adjusted upward in line with the cost of living.

Many economists have sought to find painless cures for inflation, but there do not appear to be any. If the money supply is reduced, the result could be a recession in which many people will lose their jobs. If government regulations are cut back, workers may have to work in less-safe conditions and pollution may increase. If minimum wage laws, welfare payments, and unemployment benefits are reduced, many unemployed people will suffer, and some workers will receive less in wages. President Carter has proposed voluntary wage-price controls, but controls often prove largely ineffective.

So what will happen in the years ahead? Will inflation abate — or get worse? Here are four scenarios suggesting how things might go:

Scenario One: A Slowdown in Inflation. During the summer of 1979, a number of economists reported that inflation seemed to be showing signs of slowing from the horrendous rates earlier in the year. Many of the factors that pushed inflation so high — the OPEC boost in energy and the severe winter which hit food prices — had abated. Clearly, the government had identified inflation as the number one economic problem facing the U.S. and seemed prepared to do whatever might be necessary to slow the inflation rate. Thus it is possible to imagine that the government will gradually tame the inflation monster and get it back into its cage — perhaps with the help of a recession or two.

Scenario Two: Inflation Continues at the Present High Rate. Inflation may prove very difficult to bring down, partly because people now expect more and more inflation and will insist on wage hikes and tolerate higher prices. Thus despite government efforts, inflation may persist for years at approximately the same levels as now.

Scenario Three: Inflation Speeds Up. In some countries, inflation has become far worse than in the United States. During the first half of 1979, consumer prices in Israel rose by about 41% and economists were predicting that the rate for the entire year would be about 80%; Israelis began talking about the possibility of triple-digit inflation. Argentina already has triple-digit inflation, and can claim the distinction of having the highest inflation rate in the world — 170% in 1978.

Israel and Argentina are able to cope with their extraordinarily high inflation rates by such techniques as indexing pensions, bonds, and interest rates on savings accounts. Even so, people in these nations strive mightily to invest their money in things likely to maintain their value. For instance, many Israelis buy expensive color television sets even though the nation has no color television.

The United States already has shown some signs of indexing: variable-rate mortgages are available in some areas, such as California, and there is talk of eliminating the taxes on bank interest rates, which are taxed as if the savings had gained in value, whereas they actually have declined due to inflation.

Indexing may make inflation more bearable, but it does not cure the problems that inflation causes. The uncertainty caused by inflation leads to a general lack of long-term investment, stagnant productivity, energy-wasting speculation, and political instability. Furthermore, there is always the danger that the inflation rate will move into the hyperinflation that destroys a currency beyond repair. The best known of the hyperinflations occurred in Germany in 1923. By October 1923, trillions of marks were required to buy a loaf of bread and the interest rate reached 10,000%.

Scenario IV: Deflation. Hard as it may be for people today to believe, paper money can gain as well as lose in value. That happened in 1929 in the United States, when a stock that had been worth $400 might suddenly be available for $100. People generally think of the stock as losing value, but it would be equally true to say that the money gained in value. John Exter, former vice-president of Citibank, says that the sequence of falling prices during a deflation is likely to be as follows: falling stock and bond markets, falling commodity prices, falling real estate markets, eventually falling consumer prices, and lastly falling wage rates.

A shift from inflation to deflation would, of course, cause considerable hardship for certain groups. Homeowners with large mortgages, for example, would find their payments increasingly burdensome, and many might face foreclosure. Deflation also would mean that fewer people could afford to buy goods, so sales would slump and many people would lose their jobs.

Only time will tell which of these scenarios best represents what will happen in the 1980s. But one thing is certain: the rate of inflation (or deflation) will be a crucial indicator of economic life during the coming decade: Deflation — and hyperinflation — suggests a decade marked by skyrocketing unemployment and social disorder. A slowdown in inflation (but no deflation) suggests an economy of stable prosperity; many people would probably view that as the most desirable outcome.

Work and Careers

The Good and the Bad News in Job Futures

Once upon at time, a young man who marched through the front doors of a company to begin his career might expect to emerge forty years later with best wishes and a gold watch. Today, everything is different — including the fact that the young "man" is often a young woman. A career is no longer conceived of as occurring in one company where one gradually climbs the ladder. Instead, the concept of a career has broadened to involve different companies and often different fields.

Management and career specialist Andrew H. Souerwine summarizes the attitude of today's younger worker by offering this typical scenario: "I'll work as a systems analyst until I'm about 30; then I'll see what happens. I have interests in other areas, and I think I'd like to get involved directly with the sales operations and try that out. Hopefully, by the time I'm 50 or 55 I can think of leaving all of this and maybe go into teaching, or perhaps open up my own small business. We'll see how things develop."

A "new breed" of workers is seeking careers that fulfill psychological needs and nourish self-esteem. The generation of income has been losing ground as the prime motive for working. And as Souerwine notes, "loyalty to a firm for a lifetime is giving way to mobility when interests are not satisfied by the work situation."

The rising tide of younger, more educated workers has widened expectations, including what sociologist Rosabeth Moss Kanter calls a growing "rights consciousness." Many young people believe they are entitled to a job "as a social right" — and not just a job but a *good* job, that is, one that is highly rewarding, psychically as well as financially. Furthermore, an anti-authority attitude has entered the workplace. Many young workers believe they have the right of "conscientious objection" to employer demands.

Many of today's workers expect a wide array of fringe benefits. College graduates often anticipate starting with a high-level job. In the past, a degree was a passport to white collar success, but now there are too many graduates for the available prestige openings. College students now are extending their educations in the belief that a more advanced degree will guarantee a good position complete with psychic fulfillment, prestige and "perks" in addition to money.

Dreams vs. Realities

A number of harsh realities are now intruding on the rosy dreams and inflated expectations of those seeking careers in the 1980s. For one thing, the economy is displaying a number of disturbing symptoms. A slackening in the demand for goods and services could darken the general employment picture. Many economic observers foresee continuing inflation that will result in a reduction in real income. Premium pay for new college graduates is declining, due to the increasing competition for jobs caused by the excessive availability of applicants. Fulfillment and extra benefits could pale in importance as wages once again become the foremost aspect of one's job in the coming decade.

Energy shortages are a distinct possibility and may cause disruptions in many economic sectors. Booming career areas — such as airline jobs — may suffer severe cutbacks if energy becomes too expensive and too scarce.

Technology's continued expansion has already changed the employment emphasis from production to service, but its relentless forward march now appears to be on the verge of engulfing the largest area of employment — the burgeoning service economy. Automation has been displacing workers from the production of goods and is now on the brink of affecting many of those who perform services.

Microprocessors may revolutionize employment prospects. These "computers on chips" are smaller than a fingertip, yet contain all the complex circuitry needed to perform a myriad of duties and will take the place of many humans who type, mail, bill, file and perform other routine tasks.

The U.S. government has not yet published a study of the impending impact of this technology, but studies in other countries indicate massive job losses in the 1980s, according to Jon Stewart, writing in *Saturday Review*. A West German study predicts that about 40% of the secretaries will lose their jobs and a French report foresees job losses for about 30% of those performing routine computing and service tasks in the banking and insurance industries.

A major U.S. bank has already begun the installation of these computers — linked by instant telecommunication — in its offices around the world. Where the new systems are already in operation, production is up about 50% while staff size is down 40%. Tens of thousands of telephone operators are due to be replaced by automated systems in the next decade.

Continued on page 26

UPI

Bubbly bliss of graduation day, Columbia Univ., 1979.

Career Prospects — The Bright and Gloomy

Considering the shifting sands of the employment picture, it is difficult to make career decisions. However, the Bureau of Labor Statistics at the U.S. Department of Labor makes surveys of expected employment opportunities based mainly on projected openings, and their latest report contains projections through 1985. The Bureau adds a caveat: The projections assume a steady improvement in the economy, without radical technological changes, war, or serious energy shortages.

Opportunities characterized below as "bright" are those for which the Bureau foresees faster than average growth without excessive competition; the "gloomy" occupations are areas for which the Bureau foresees keen competition or declining or slower than average growth.

Industrial production and related occupations: Bright — lithographers, assemblers, boilermakers, inspectors, opthalmic and photographic laboratory technicians, welders, and wastewater treatment plant operators. Gloomy — compositors and photoengravers, bookbinders, printing press operators, and forge shop workers.

Office occupations: Bright — collection workers, secretaries, bank tellers and officers, market researchers, urban planners, purchasing agents, computer programmers, and systems analysts. Gloomy — bookkeepers, office machine operators, and postal clerks.

Service occupations: Bright — cooks and chefs, dining room and food counter workers, pest controllers, guards, police officers, and construction, health, and regulatory inspectors. Gloomy — telephone operators and hotel housekeepers and assistants.

Education and library occupations: Bright— teachers aides and library assistants. Gloomy — teachers and librarians.

Construction occupations: Bright—cement and terrazzo workers, drywall workers, electricians, elevator constructors, glaziers, insulation workers, ironworkers, operating engineers, paperhangers, plumbers and pipefitters, and roofers. Gloomy — none.

Sales occupations: Bright — automobile and automobile parts salespersons. Gloomy —gasoline service station attendants and retail trade sales workers.

Transportation occupations: Bright — local truckdrivers. Gloomy—long-distance truckdrivers, merchant marine crews, railroad conductors, engineers, and station agents.

Scientific and technical occupations: Bright —range managers, geologists, geophysicists, life scientists, technicians, and surveyors, plus a variety of engineers—agricultural, biomedical, ceramic, industrial, metallurgical, mining, and petroleum. Gloomy — aerospace engineers, mathematicians, astronomers and physicists.

Mechanics and repairers: Bright — air-conditioning, refrigeration, heating, motorcycle and diesel mechanics, business machine and industrial machinery repairers, computer, television and radio service technicians, and locksmiths. Gloomy — bowling-pin-machine mechanics, jewelers, watch repairers, and central telephone office equipment installers.

Health occupations: Bright — dental assistants, hygienists, and laboratory technicians, physicians and veterinarians, medical technicians and assistants, nurses and assistants, therapy and rehabilitation professionals and assistants, health service and medical record administrators. Gloomy — none.

Social scientists: Bright — economists and geographers with advanced degrees, but not in academia. Gloomy — historians, political scientists, and sociologists.

Social service occupations: Bright — homemaker-home health aides, park, recreation, and leisure workers, social workers and aides, and Roman Catholic priests. Gloomy — Protestant ministers and rabbis, cooperative extension service workers.

Art, design, and communications-related occupations: Bright — floral designers and landscape architects. Gloomy — industrial designers, photographers, and newspaper reporters.

LLL Photo   Charles Tidd   Charles Tidd

Job prospects are bright for scientists, nurses and plumbers of both sexes.

The microprocessor revolution is expected to extend far beyond the office. At General Motors plants, for instance, production workers will soon be working alongside robots that can assemble carburetors and alternators. "The robots of industry may not do the job better than their human counterparts, but they are not subject to health and safety legislation, do not go on strike, and pay for themselves (in terms of worker salaries) in about two years, after which they are free," notes Stewart. Microprocessor specialist Jon Roland in *The Futurist* predicts that "in the not too distant future" microcomputers will replace air traffic controllers, train, ship and plane crews, truckdrivers and subway operators.

The impact of the mircroprocessor revolution will be so sweeping, says Roland, that more than half of the occupations listed in the yellow pages of any large metropolitan directory will cease to exist. The dilemma of displacement is not likely to be solved by involving the overflow in the manufacturing of these computers, since most of those jobs are outside the U.S., where workers assemble components for low wages.

The microprocessor's development has serious implications for women, according to Irving Leveson, director of economic studies at the Hudson Institute. He points out that "the result of these technological changes will be weak demand for labor in the occupations in which females still tend to be most highly concentrated," and he foresees a dramatic slowdown in the rate of growth of female employment and the creation of "numerous pressures for women to move into traditionally male areas or be upgraded within their current work environments."

Mortarboards and Blue Collars

The big jump in job offers for last year's June college graduates was a "fluke," says Jeremy Main, an economic specialist writing in the *Washington Post*. The surplus of college degree holders has been steadily building and will persist well into the 1980s.

The Bureau of Labor Statistics estimates that one out of every four of those graduating between 1976 and 1985 will have to settle for jobs not previously filled by college graduates — such as retail sales, clerical, or blue-collar jobs — or face unemployment.

With a more highly educated pool from which to draw workers, employers can upgrade their requirements. "You need a college degree more than ever but it guarantees less than ever," says Main. Patrick Montana and Margaret Higginson point out in *Career Life Planning for Americans* that "employers often raise education requirements, despite their lack of evidence that they are deriving any benefit from doing so."

The outlook is brightest for skilled craft workers — electricians, carpenters, plumbers, and similar occupations. The demand for this group will be above average, says Main, because "like doctors, craft workers are protected by a bottleneck." Currently there are ten applicants for every three apprentice-level openings. During economic downturns, blue-collar workers have less security than professionals. The number of professional jobs rose during the last recession, according to Main, while the amount of blue-collar jobs declined by several million.

The prospects for semi- and unskilled workers are not good. Employment for this segment of the work force is not expected to grow as fast in the 1980s as employment as a whole. In addition technological progress may act as a double-edged sword against this group both eliminating jobs through automation and placing jobs beyond the reach of the "underclass" unable to benefit from the new technology.

Coping with "Career Shock"

"Living with the future is like sleeping with an elephant," says futurist author Gary Gappert, in that "you run the risk that it will roll over upon you."

Anyone planning a future career will need to keep informed about the changing outlook. Technological, economic, demographic, and environmental changes both create and eliminate opportunities. For example, careers in the medical field look very promising, due to the increasing concern over health, the growing elderly population, and the increasing number of dangerous environmental factors. On the other hand, office work — listed as one of the best areas of growth in a report dealing with opportunities up to 1985 — may become one of the worst after 1985 if microprocessor technology lives up to its promise. Knowledge of trends will be the key to preparing to make a move "before the elephant rolls over."

Mobility will be an important aid in coping with shifts in the work environment. People will need to be prepared to move both mentally — from one field to another — as well as physically, from one area to another.

Lifelong education will become increasingly important. Montana and Higginson estimate that now "approximately 80% of what is learned in college is obsolete 15 years after graduation." In some technical fields similar obsolescence is telescoped into less than five years. Roland warns that "within a few years, the ability to program and use microcomputers will be as important as being able to read, write, type, drive, or use the telephone."

A flexible attitude will be another useful attribute. A Bureau of Labor Statistics report cites a study which found that more and more graduates see jobs as craft workers, farmers, and self-employed retail store managers, those associated with "alternative life styles," as more desirable than the traditional jobs chosen by graduates. "This shift in attitudes eases the problems of underemployment and job dissatisfaction for many college graduates," the Bureau says.

The Work Force of the Future

Many observers anticipate a growing dichotomy in the work force. Sociologist Suzanne Keller of Princeton sees a shift to jobs requiring more professional skills and technical expertise, leaving in its wake a pool of workers with unrewardable skills. She predicts "the rise of a super-trained, well-paid, relatively contented class of technicians, service workers and professionals and an underclass of unemployed and perhaps unemployables."

There may be "enormous" competition for the shrinking number of "desirable" jobs, according to Kanter, who foresees a "bump phenomenon": Those who would normally have obtained "elite" jobs take lesser jobs, pushing the normal occupants of those jobs down to the next level.

The path does not look easy for those pursuing a career in the 1980s. Agility, resourcefulness, and unique skills will be needed to adapt to the rapid changes expected in the world of work.

Energy and the Economy

America's Energy Future—Three Speculations

With gas lines snaking around corners, the OPEC nations threatening to further increase oil prices, and concern growing about imminent shortages of home heating fuel, President Nixon on November 7, 1973, asked the nation to commit itself to the goal of energy independence by 1980. At the time the United States imported 35% of its petroleum, a little over six million barrels per day.

The target date for Project Independence has arrived, and it finds the U.S. importing 44% of its oil, about eight million barrels per day. President Nixon's calls ,for energy self-sufficiency were not taken seriously for long, even within his own administration. But they stand as an ominous reminder of how little policymakers can control the energy juggernaut.

Since the beginning of the industrial revolution, evolving technologies have been weaving energy and the economy into a closely linked complex. Especially during the age of oil, beginning at the end of the nineteenth century, economic growth and energy use have moved in lockstep. Changes, either up or down, in one measure have always accompanied similar changes in the other.

Most of the economic expansion in the U.S. since World War II has been fueled by additional supplies of cheap, clean, and convenient petroleum. The result has been an even closer tie between energy and the economy. The ratio of energy used to the gross national product was the same in 1974 as it was in 1953, even though both quantities had more than doubled.

The interconnections between energy and the economy are complex, at various times making themselves felt through prices, political decisions, technological constraints, and public attitudes. But with supplies of energy beginning to dwindle, the historical correspondence between the two foreshadows a difficult time ahead for the economy.

The End of an Era

Estimates of how much oil, natural gas, and coal remain in the earth vary widely, and predicting when these resources will begin to run out is an exercise in uncertainty. A much more useful measurement is the level of production. In the United States, the production of crude oil peaked and began to decline in 1970. The production of natural gas went through a similar turning point in 1973.

These declines may still reverse themselves. The flow of crude oil from Alaska, beginning in 1977, has propped up domestic supplies. And President Carter's decontrol of domestic oil prices by next year may boost production in the rest of America. But few people expect domestic production of oil ever again to exceed its 1970 maximum.

Because the expanding economy of the late 1970s has demanded ever greater influxes of energy, imports of oil have risen precipitously. But many of the experts who predicted the decline of domestic oil production foresee the same fate for world production sometime within the next two decades.

On a global scale, predictions of declining production are highly tentative. Many areas of the world, whether because of hostile climates or hostile governments, have yet to be explored. But because production from new fields cannot start immediately, decisions being made now will largely determine how much oil will be available during the 1980s. Many of these decisions could mean trouble for the United States and its energy-dependent economy.

One of the most authoritative studies of petroleum for the coming two decades, and one of the most alarming, was done several years ago by the Workshop on Alternative Energy Strategies (WAES). Projecting future economic growth, oil prices, and energy supplies in several scenarios, the WAES researchers found that the demand for oil will begin to exceed the supply sometime during the 1980s or early 1990s. By the year 2000, they concluded, oil supplies will amount to only two-thirds to three-fourths of the total demand.

Unless coal and nuclear energy are ready to pick up where oil lets off, the WAES report warns, the transition between sources of energy could devastate the industrialized countries. "What is at stake is world economic stability," the report says. "Nations will have to decrease dependence on oil and shift to other energy sources in order to sustain economic and energy systems into the 21st century."

Other studies cast a brighter picture of future energy supplies, contending that even increased levels of production can continue for decades. But all agree that the U.S. walks a dangerous path in relying on volatile foreign governments for its day-to-day supplies of liquid energy. And all acknowledge that the shift to other forms of energy must begin soon, and that it won't be easy.

The Coming Transition

Immense gaps between global supply and demand, such as those foreseen by the WAES report, are a statistician's fancy; they cannot really occur. If oil supplies cannot keep pace with a steadily increasing global demand, prices will tend to rise. Eventually oil consumers will begin to look elsewhere for their energy supplies, and producers will find the profits in increased production irresistible.

In the coming decade of skyrocketing prices for oil, much will depend on how the increases

DOE Photo

8 million barrels of oil arrive in U.S. each day.

19 million barrels of oil are used in U.S. each day.

take place. Sudden jumps in prices can prove disastrous, even for countries wealthy enough to sustain the blow. (As painful as OPEC's decisions are in the U.S., they are much worse in developing countries.)

Government analysts have concluded that the sudden quadrupling of oil prices in 1973-74 slashed several percentage points off the rate of economic growth for several years. Coming at what was a bad time for the economy anyway, the increases forced up inflation, caused hundreds of thousands of layoffs, and cost Americans tens of billions of dollars.

Though the circumstances differ, the recent surge in energy prices will have a similar effect on the American economy. Economists estimate that economic growth last year was half of what it would have been without the increases. With the economy again teetering on the brink of a slump, the shocks of the recent price increases could reverberate through the industrialized world for years.

There is no reason, though, why the U.S. economy cannot prosper with high prices for energy. The problems all come in the transition. If, when prices for oil suddenly spurt up, other forms of energy are not immediately available, consumers have no choice. They pay the higher prices, scale back their expectations, and grumble about the inconvenience.

Because of the inevitable lag between price increases and the availability of other forms of energy, many people have questioned the ability of the free market to manage the coming transition. Government policies, which usually act to supersede the market, have thus come into play.

Foresight is a scarce commodity in both public and private decisions. But government policies, in conjunction with market forces, will largely determine what mix of fuels will eventually replace petroleum. The outcome could affect nearly every aspect of the economic life and social structure of the future.

Alternatives to Oil

At once the most preferable, obvious, and ignored alternative to oil is conservation. Its advantages are numerous and substantial; properly done, it can reduce America's dependence on all forms of energy without crippling the economy.

Conservation is a prime example of an energy alternative that may be uneconomical in today's marketplace, but extremely valuable in the long run. Consequently, government policies and individual initiative are now the prime movers behind conservation. Already the effort to drive smaller cars, insulate houses, build more efficient factories, and eliminate wasteful habits is having an effect. Energy use grew 170% faster than GNP between 1966 and 1970, but since then it has grown only 61% as fast.

However, conservation is by no means the entire cure for America's energy addiction. Many of the initial savings may already have been made, with additional measures both costing more and having less effect. Also, conservation, as with other energy technologies, entails certain unavoidable lead times. Replacing an entire fleet of cars or industrial equipment takes at least a decade. In some cases, fostering new habits can take a generation. Building a new stock of energy-efficient homes can take a century. Conservation can soften, but it cannot eliminate, any energy crunches during the 1980s.

America can also lessen its dependence on imported oil by encouraging the use of those fossil fuels that have lately taken a back seat to oil — natural gas and coal. Most experts agree that reserves of natural gas are large and will not run dry before the end of the century. The problem is that these reserves are often in the wrong places. Moving the gas to where it is needed will require extensive and costly transportation networks, generally pipelines or liquefied natural gas facilities. The difficulties that

Energy by the Numbers

Energy is a game of numbers, and it's easy to get lost among the barrels, quads, and Btu's. Most of today's debate, however, employs only two indispensable terms. The most important is million barrels per day, generally abbreviated MMBD. A barrel of oil consists of 42 gallons, weighing up to 310 pounds for the heaviest kinds of oil.

America's use of oil now amounts to about 19 MMBD, a little less than half of which is imported. With the use of a conversion table, 19 million barrels of petroleum turns out to take up 110 million cubic feet. In other words, the U.S. uses enough petroleum in its cars, factories, and buildings to fill the entire Empire State Building three times over each day.

The other important measurement is the quad, which is an abbreviation for quadrillion British thermal units (Btu's). One Btu is the amount of heat needed to raise the temperature of one pound of water by one degree Fahrenheit, so a quad is the amount of energy needed to raise 1,000,000,000,000,000 pounds of water by one degree.

The U.S. now uses around 75 quads of energy per year. In the heyday of nuclear optimism, some projections saw the U.S. using over 200 quads per year by the turn of the century. These forecasts have since proven laughable, but most experts still believe that America will need around 100 quads by the year 2000, even with reduced economic growth and widespread conservation.

DOE Photo

Strip mining of coal is not without its problems.

C-E Power Systems

Nuclear plants, even if approved, take time to build.

long and costly pipelines cause are well known to Americans. A tanker of liquefied natural gas, moreover, could prove the vehicle to turn a small fire into one of the most spectacular man-made disasters in history.

The flip side of clean and evanescent natural gas is coal, the drudge of the energy world. Coal's contribution to America's energy has dropped during this century for very good reasons. It is dirty to burn, awkward to handle, and, at least so far, the most dangerous form of energy to obtain. A satellite photograph taken in 1979 shows a swath of haze stretching from the central Midwest across the eastern seaboard and up through New England. The haze, which reduces visibility by half, comes from coal-fired power plants, which emit sulfates into the air around which water condenses.

To reduce oil imports without shackling the economy will require greatly expanded mining of coal — perhaps twice or three times the amount mined today. Because more coal comes from strip mining than underground mining, this will disrupt vast tracts of land in the western United States, requiring costly and controversial measures to reclaim the violated earth.

The amount of upheaval to strike the West will also depend on the eventual fate of today's prospective energy wunderkind — synthetic fuels. Gradually acquiring the name synfuels, these liquids can be made from domestic supplies of coal, shale oil, or natural gas. Since transportation in this country relies almost exclusively on liquid fuels, the mobility of Americans in the future will hinge to a great extent on the success or failure of synthetic fuels.

Today all of the synfuels cost more than imported petroleum, and none is yet being produced commercially. But synthetic crude oil from shale oil could become competitive in the 1980s, given enough investment in the technology now. Oil can be extracted from shale either by mining the shale and heating (retorting) it, or by igniting the shale underground (in situ) and pumping out the oil that accumulates. Getting liquid fuels from coal, in contrast, requires a more complex and costly process: synfuels from coal will probably not become competitive until the 1990s.

Despite their present popularity among policymakers, synfuels face a number of environmental barriers that could obstruct full-scale production. To produce between three and five million barrels of synfuels per day, the goal now being aired for the year 2000, would require as many as 100 gigantic plants, bringing to an area already burdened with great increases in mining all of the economic dislocations caused by sudden boom towns.

Making synthetic fuels would also require large amounts of water — a resource in perilously short supply in the West. Removing deadly contaminants from the water would be difficult and costly, as would cleaning the air emitted from synfuel plants. Finally, synthetic fuels, in their production and their use, release two to three times more carbon dioxide than conventional fossil fuels do. Many scientists fear that the accumulation of carbon dioxide from fossil fuels in the atmosphere will soon begin to raise the temperature of the earth.

Because synthetic fuels now cost more than natural oil, private industry will not develop the technology without government backing. Such governmental aid appears certain, but many people worry that it will drain vital funds away from other, more proven energy technologies. Lead times, too, are a problem. The U.S. cannot expect synfuels to offer much relief from imports for more than a decade.

For that part of its energy consumed as electricity, the U.S. could turn once again to the construction of new nuclear power plants. However, no conclusions seem yet to have emerged from the nuclear controversy, except for the decision by default to postpone the nuclear option. The uncertainties and ideological counterpoint inherent within nuclear power will undoubtedly prolong the debate for years.

Prospects for the Future

Both in the short term and in the long term, the future of energy in the United States is fraught with uncertainties. The problem is further compounded because of its complexity. Energy comes from so many different and complicated sources, and it goes to such a wide variety of uses, that forming a coherent energy policy is somewhat like managing a national economy.

Nevertheless, certain extreme cases can be staked out, within which future developments are likely to fall. Following are two such extreme scenarios, combining different measures of optimism and pessimism, along with a look at what current trends might bring in the 1980s.

Speculation I: Toward a High-Energy Future

Suppose that sometime within the next decade oil suddenly becomes overabundant and the price drops, with these conditions lasting for several years. Though unlikely, such a situation is far from impossible. The OPEC cartel, which now sets the global price for oil, consists of

Energy for a Self-Sustaining Future

Renewable sources of energy, those not dependent on fossil fuels or nuclear power, today supply only 6% of America's energy needs, mostly from immense dams and the burning of wood. But as fossil fuels become scarce, and if nuclear power proves too technologically difficult or dangerous to use, renewable energy sources will assume a major role in shaping the societies of the future. Among the sources and technologies now being studied are:

Biomass—Besides directly burning wood or agricultural residues, organic materials can be converted into high-energy alcohols. Two kinds of "biofuels" now appear promising. In large industrial plants, biomass can be converted into methanol. On a much smaller, even backyard scale, biomass can be fermented to produce ethanol, the substance that is already being added to gasoline to make gasohol.

Wind Power—Windmills either on land or at sea could generate an indirect form of solar energy through the movements of the air. Another possibility is the return of sail-driven oceangoing ships.

Geothermal—Several locations around the world already provide electricity from hot water or steam trapped close to the earth's surface. But only if scientists perfect a way to tap the virtually unlimited heat of the earth's core, can geothermal energy provide a significant proportion of the world's energy.

Solar—Sunlight, the original source of fossil fuels, can also be converted directly into heat, electricity, or chemical energy (in the form of energy stored in batteries). The most immediately promising renewable energy source, solar energy, has already become a prominent consideration in residential and industrial applications.

SOLAR ENERGY

Water Power—Only about 10% of the potential hydroelectric power around the world has yet been exploited. In this country, the large sites have already been developed, but smaller dams could still provide electricity for local use if generators were installed. Unfortunately, over a period of time, dams silt up. Other forms of water power include energy from the waves, the tides, or ocean currents.

Ocean Thermal Energy Conversion (OTEC)—Using large floating power plants, the temperature difference between warm upper layers of water and cool lower layers of water can generate electricity. Pilot plants have already shown the way.

Most forecasts expect little expansion of these sources of energy by the year 2000. But some projections, realizing the appeal of renewable energies to people proud of their independence, contend that they could provide 20-25% of America's energy by the turn of the century.

All DOE Photos

widely varying countries, from arid and sparsely populated Saudi Arabia to tropical, densely populated Venezuela. Disagreements over production levels and prices, as well as simple international animosity, could strain the cartel to the breaking point.

Oil could also become more plentiful through unexpected discoveries of new fields or through technological breakthroughs in recovering oil from existing fields. Several oil companies will soon drill exploratory wells off the shores of China, a nation desperate for foreign exchange. Similarly, Mexico or several South American countries could opt to quickly produce and export their reserves.

Awash once again in abundant, cheap petroleum, the American economy could avoid the shocks that energy shortages have caused in the past. Conservation would again become simply preferable rather than essential; the suburbanization of America could continue unabated; pressure would grow on Congress to ease mileage standards and sanction bigger cars.

Of course, a period of plentiful oil would only be a reprieve from the eventual crunch. But it might give the U.S. time to develop its own sources of energy. With careful management and planning, the shift from oil need not have the economic consequences it is having today.

In the long run, well beyond the next decade, only technoligical innovation and development can continue to guarantee a high-energy future. No law known to science says that it is impossible to generate cheap, abundant, and virtually limitless forms of energy. Perhaps scientists will master fusion, or learn how to tap the energy seething in the earth's molten core, or develop an efficient way to convert sunlight into electricity. Perhaps America will turn to breeder reactors, which could supply electricity for tens of thousands of years.

Technological innovation could allow societies to sidestep the problems caused by dwindling supplies of oil. But people cannot let technology's allure blind them to the pressing dilemmas of the day. As Earl Cook says in *Man, Energy, Society,* "The claim that the 'unlimited ingenuity' of man will overcome physical obstacles as they are perceived in the road of progress is a myth that tranquilizes concern, numbs responsibility, and defeats planning."

Speculation II: Muddling Through the 80s

With the energy shortage in 1979-80 so similar to the shortage in 1973-74, one of the most likely prospects for the 1980s calls for more of the same. Prices of oil and natural gas would continue to increase, hopefully without disruptive suddenness, eventually reaching $40 to $60 per barrel in the 1990s (assuming continued inflation).

Occasional shortages would recur throughout the decade. Alternative sources of energy would assume a greater burden, aided by conservation meant to cut down America's need for imports. The economy, along with its customary ebbs and flows, would painfully adjust to the higher prices. It might even find the technologies designed to replace oil a source of needed vigor.

High energy prices don't have to permanently cripple the economy. With minor adjustments, most Americans could lead the same lives they do today while using much less energy. Perhaps some of the agreeable trends that have marked past energy crises would intensify: fewer fatal accidents on America's highways, greater sales of books in many cities, a healthy criticism of the forces and institutions in this country that hinder change, and a new spirit of cooperation in meeting the challenge of an austere future.

Speculation III: A Massive Energy Crunch

Unexpected political, social, or economic upheavals anywhere in the world could wreak havoc on energy supplies in this country. A sudden interruption of the flow of oil through the Persian Gulf could send the economies of the Western world into a tailspin. Governments would simultaneously have to shore up economies reeling from their partial withdrawal from oil and somehow mobilize their citizens to meet an energy crisis of unprecedented severity. The combination could be devastating.

For a few months, the U.S. could fall back on its Strategic Petroleum Reserve, which could reach one billion barrels in the 1980s. But soon other sources of energy would have to replace the loss of oil. Domestic production of fossil fuels would strain at its technological limits. Environmental restrictions would probably be relaxed to permit the burning of additional coal. New and untested technologies would be pressed into service, and everywhere people would have to closely control their use of energy.

International tensions would increase. The U.S. might be tempted to use its food exports as a weapon, offering them in exchange for energy. Talk of invading any recalcitrant oil producers would appear. The American people would band together to protect their interests, as in past crises, and the government would reflect this darkened mood.

Suppose this situation were to stabilize, through some combination of environmental limits, exhausted supplies, and technological constraints. Gradually America would head back toward a low-energy society. Teams of workers would reappear on farms, mobility would be highly restricted, and service jobs would largely disappear. The suburbs would soon atrophy, beginning at the edges and working in towards the city. Perhaps telecommunications would thrive in a society now deprived of many of its former activities.

In the long run, this transition could lead to a steady-state society, one with a very low level of energy use. Many features of modern life that are now in constant flux would have to stabilize. Quite likely, perceptions of the world would change radically. The mentality of a steady-state society might be as different from ours as was the mentality of the European Middle Ages.

Energy for the Future

Many of the long-term speculations about America's energy future may seem remote. But they will not remain so for long: experts say that we have between 25 and 50 years to make most of the decisions that will determine what kinds of energy, and what kinds of societies, will characterize the distant future.

The responsibility is an awesome one. We decide today not only for ourselves, but for generations to come. Perhaps the ability to make such decisions is beyond the ken of our intellects and imagination. But at least the challenge has presented itself, fully and clearly. It is the privilege of the future to be the judge of our wisdom.

The Automobile, the Economy, and the Future

"Americans are in the habit of never walking if they can ride."

— Louis Philippe, Duc d'Orleans, 1798

Throughout the history of the United States, Americans have prized their mobility. The freedom to move about and make changes, whether socially, economically, politically, or personally, has been a mainstay of American life.

For much of the twentieth century, personal mobility in the U.S. has largely meant automobility. Today, over 100 million cars are at the beck and call of America's 130 million licensed drivers. All together, the automobiles in this country log over 1 trillion miles of travel every year. They account for more than 90% of all personal transportation.

Over the years, Americans have spent literally trillions of dollars shaping the land to suit the automobile. Cars have flung cities across the countryside even more dramatically than elevators have drawn cities toward the sky. Over four million miles of paved roads crisscross the country; they (along with their rights of way) cover an area equal to the size of West Virginia.

Governments at all levels have played pivotal roles in this development of a mobile America. The federal government, besides supplementing state and local road-building, has subsidized suburban and exurban development through its mortgage assistance policies. It has also, until recently, ignored public transportation. Without federal support, most mass transit systems long ago fell into disuse and disrepair. Local governments and shaky private companies were left to shore up the remains.

America's commitment to the automobile has transformed a handful of tinkerers and entrepreneurs into a massive industrial complex. Watched over by politicians, alternately loved and hated by the American public, and driven by its own economic logic, the auto industry in its broadest sense produces some 10% of America's gross national product. It directly employs five million workers, about 5% of all those in the U.S. When all the businesses related to the automobile — the insurance and tourist industries, for instance — are added to the total, the automobile becomes the source of one out of every six to eight American jobs.

As with any innovation as radical and far-reaching as the automobile, the system has always had its critics. But beginning at the end of the 1950s, a groundswell of anti-auto sentiment started to grow, led by such critics as Lewis Mumford, Ralph Nader, and Daniel P. Moynihan. In the two decades since, the list of problems attributable to the automobile has both lengthened and become widely known.

The most immediate problem concerns safety. Traffic accidents kill approximately 50,000 people every year. They injure millions more. The number of people killed by traffic accidents in this country since 1900 — 2 million — is over three times the number of battle deaths suffered by the U.S. in all of its wars — 625,000.

Cars are also responsible for about half of the air pollution that hounds many American cities. Scientists are sharply divided on the actual harms of air pollution, but it is blamed for thousands of deaths and inestimable suffering.

Junked cars, furthermore, constitute about 7% of all solid waste in the U.S., and their lubricants, fuels, and various other fluids pollute roadsides, junkyards, and the water underneath them all.

The obvious problems and less obvious fears of the automobile have troubled many people for years. But it has taken the greatest challenge to the automobile's existence to draw them fully into the public eye. In the summer of 1979, gas lines reappeared in some of the nation's more heavily populated areas, and this time motorists could not shift the blame from the automobile's avarice to a petroleum boycott.

Suddenly the general public realized that unlimited automobility would not necessarily last forever. The outcome could be a general reappraisal of transportation in American society, resulting in new directions for the automobile in the future.

Cars in the Year 2000

Several months before the summer of 1979, the Congressional Office of Technology Assessment released the most comprehensive study of the automobile's future ever done. Entitled "Changes in the Future Use and Characteristics of the Automobile Transportation System," the report carefully details the options available to policymakers in meeting the needs and solving the problems of the automobile's next two decades.

The OTA researchers begin their analysis by developing what they call a no-policy-change base case. This scenario assumes that the government will freeze all of its policies affecting the automobile in their present form. For instance, it foresees no changes in the law requiring Detroit to produce fleets that average 27.5 miles per gallon (mpg) by 1985. By incorporating several other assumptions about the economy, the auto industry, and consumer preferences, the base case then outlines the status of the automobile in the years 1985 and 2000.

The OTA researchers emphasize, however, that the base case is more of a tool than an actual forecast. The government will quite likely act to lessen the adverse conditions foreseen in the base case. Furthermore, many of the assumptions underlying the base case are likely to prove mistaken.

The overall message of the base case is that, provided there are no severe shortages of petroleum or alternative fuels, automobiles will continue their domination of American travel through the year 2000. With a greatly expanded economy, a thriving auto industry, and relatively cheap fuels, there will be more cars on the road driving more miles in the year 2000, and they will be using less fuel and emitting less emissions than today. (See table.)

The automobile presently consumes about 5.2 million barrels of oil per day (MMBD), about 30% of the 19 MMBD burned in this country. Under present policies, the automobile will burn only 4.8 MMBD in the year 2000, despite an increase of 75% in the total number of miles that automobiles travel. According to OTA projections, the automobile will then be using only about 20% of the petroleum consumed in this country. (See chart.)

The base case draws several other important conclusions about today's governmental policies. With no changes in current laws, fatalities from traffic accidents will rise from 50,000 today to 64,000 in the year 2000, even though air bags and shoulder harnesses will become mandatory equipment in all cars between 1983 and 1985. The increase will come about largely because of the greater number of miles that people will be traveling, but also because cars will have to be smaller to meet fuel economy standards.

Congestion in urban areas will become much worse in the next two decades, according to the base case. Average highway speeds in urban areas will drop from about 50 mph to about 35 mph, and drivers will encounter congested conditions in cities about three times as often as today. This continued crowding will partially offset some of the progress made in fighting air pollution. The air in most cities will be cleaner, but greater numbers of cars and stationary sources of pollution will combine to keep pollution a significant problem.

Roadways and bridges will continue to deteriorate faster than they can be repaired, under OTA's base case. Without additional outlays, most of the money going for new roads today will have to go for repairs at the turn of the century, and even that won't be enough to win the battle against disintegrating pavement.

In addition to the above dire projections, the base case has some bright spots for the auto industry. Sales of new cars could nearly double in the next 20 years. The OTA researchers also believe that the industry will be able to reach the mileage and emissions standards that the government has already set.

The uncertainty surrounding several of the base case's assumptions, however, casts doubt especially on these projections for the auto industry. The fates of the industry and of the economy in general are closly intertwined, and unexpected economic events could make the base case a much rosier future than may actually occur.

Assumptions Gone Awry: The Oil Supply

Two particular assumptions that underlie OTA's base case are starting to look less and less likely as time goes on. The first concerns the supply of natural petroleum. The researchers acknowledge that oil will become increasingly scarce during the next 20 years, but for the purposes of the base case they assume there will be no interruptions in the supply of petroleum or alternative fuels. Their second questionable assumption concerns the economy. Throughout their entire report, the researchers assume the economy will grow at an average of 3.5% from now to the year 2000. There are good reasons to believe that this assumption, too, will prove overly optimistic.

The gasoline shortage of 1979 reinforced many people's belief that the global supply of oil will soon begin to fall behind the global demand. Several recent studies indicate that the shortfall may become severe even within the next decade. One of the most authoritative of these studies, prepared by the Workshop on Alternative Energy Strategies (WAES), predicts that a gap between supply and demand will appear and begin to grow sometime during the 1980s. By the year 2000, according to the WAES report, the world supply of oil will amount to only two-thirds to three-fourths of the overall demand.

Gaps between supply and demand generally cause prices to change until the two return to a

Base Case Projections	1975	1985	2000
Mobility			
Automobiles in operation (millions)	95	118	148
Automobile vehicle miles (trillions)	1.03	1.43	1.80
Urban auto travel in congested conditions (percent)	10	14	24
Transit vehicle miles traveled (billions) ..	2.0	2.3	3.0
Transit ridership (billions)	5.6	6.5	6.5
Energy			
Fleet fuel economy (miles per gallon)[a] ..	13.6	19.4	24.6
Automobile fuel demand (MMBD)	5.0	4.8	4.8
Petroleum imports (MMBD)	7.4	10.0	8.8[b]
Enviornment			
Automobile air pollutant emissions (millions of tons per year)			
Carbon monoxide	69.3	32.6	27.3
Hydrocarbons	7.9	3.5	2.9
Oxides of nitrogen	4.0	2.7	2.9
Safety			
Highway fatalities (thousands)	46.0	58.4	64.0
Highway fatality rate (per 100 million miles)	3.4	3.1	2.8
Cost and capital			
New car sales (millions)	8.6	13.1	16.4

[a] Fuel economy under actual driving conditions; EPA procedures yield estimates 10 to 20 percent higher.
[b] Assumes 2.75 MMBD domestic production of alternate fuels.

U.S. Petroleum Demand (Millions barrels per day, MMBD)

	1976 (17.5 MMBD)	1985 (20.1 MMBD)	2000 (22.4 MMBD)
			0.6
Electrical	1.6	1.5	3.1
Residential & commercial	3.5	2.7	6.1
Industrial	3.2	5.6	3.9
Rail, air, water	2.1	2.9	3.9
Truck	1.9	2.6	3.9
Auto	5.2	4.8	4.8

AiResearch Manufacturing Co.

General Motors Corp.

Electric auto design features a flywheel booster.

Cars have trip computers for programmed driving.

rough equilibrium. The OTA report clearly recognizes the implications of this economic law for petroleum: "In the case of a decreasing supply of a nonrenewable resource such as oil, the price necessary to equate supply and demand will become so high as to price millions of former users out of the market." Because at least for the present petroleum in the American economy is in many cases irreplaceable, higher prices result in a slowdown of the economy. The general consensus among economists is that the economies of the industrialized countries will grow at about half of what they would have without the recent surge in energy prices.

As gloomy as the petroleum production-consumption ratio is abroad, it is even worse in the U.S. Currently, we import about half of the petroleum we consume. By the year 2000, according to the OTA report, this proportion could go up to around 70% (although this will depend on the success or failure of President Carter's ceiling on petroleum imports).

Even with only moderate price increases over the next 20 years, petroleum imports of as much as 70% could decimate the American economy. They would more than triple the sum that American consumers now pay to foreign producers, pushing up a trade deficit that some claim is already dangerously high.

Economists differ in their interpretations of how a steadily increasing trade deficit harms the U.S. economy. But it has been blamed for a number of economic ills, including . inflation, unemployment, and reduced economic growth. Another consideration is the dislocation of the world financial system caused by the power of the burgeoning "petrodollars" in foreign hands.

Assumptions Gone Awry: The Auto Industry

The auto industry has traditionally taken a conservative approach to its business strategies. But during the next several years it will have to undergo a transition that would be considered risky in any business. The reason lies partly in the relationship between federal regulators and the industry. Generally, federal agencies have limited their role in the auto industry to setting standards that future automobiles must meet. Auto makers must then comply with the federal regulations, raising the capital and developing the technologies needed to make any changes.

Within the next several years, the auto industries will have to alter their production lines significantly to meet mileage, safety, and emissions standards already set by the government. The most important change they will make is known as downsizing — reducing the sizes of their cars to achieve a higher fleet mileage with lower emission levels. But retooling assembly

lines to produce smaller cars is an expensive process, and it comes at a time when policies designed to slow inflation have made investment capital especially dear.

A prolonged petroleum shortage could make the economic crunch on the auto industry much more acute. Whenever gasoline has been in short supply in the U.S., sales of new cars have tended to slump. If this trend were sustained over an extended petroleum shortfall, the auto industry could head into a major downturn.

A sudden slowdown in the auto industry could have drastic effects on the economy as a whole. Industry sources claim that, for every 250,000 new-car sales lost, they must lay off 21,000 workers and related industries must lay off 41,000 workers. Regardless of the accuracy of these figures, a slump in the auto industry could radiate into other economic sectors.

Government decisions over the next several years will greatly influence how such economic pressures actually will affect the auto industry. The larger auto companies demand that the government postpone or cancel many of their existing regulations, claiming that they need more time to develop a fuel-efficient and salable car. The smaller auto firms, the automotive unions, and people less wary of sacrificing economic growth to environmental concerns urge more government participation in the industry. They would like to see the federal government help to both raise the needed capital, through loans and loan guarantees, and develop the technologies needed to guarantee the automobile's survival.

Options for the 80s

Even direct federal intervention in the auto industry may not be enough to stave off the effects of future petroleum shortages. Given shortfalls as large as those foreseen by the WAES study, the government will have to take much more forceful steps to prevent substantial cutbacks in America's mobility.

One option that that government might choose is to further tighten future mileage standards. The OTA report estimates that by combining a 40-mpg mileage standard by 2000, a large tax on gas guzzlers, an increased tax on gasoline, and a ban on new cars getting less than 25 mpg after 1985, gasoline consumption by new cars in this country could drop to just 3.4 MMBD in the year 2000 with only a minimal effect on driving habits. It is important to note that present energy policies should lead to the production of about 3.0 MMBD of synthetic fuels by the year 2000, and many people feel that the level of production could be closer to the year 2000 consumption figure.

An even more forceful response to a petroleum crisis would be a long-term rationing program. If cars could use only six gallons of gas per week — today they use an average of fifteen gallons per week — automobiles would consume only about 3.0 MMBD of gas in the year 2000, over 40% less than they do today. This strategy, as well as the ones above, would greatly increase the demand for small cars. The auto industry would have to adapt its production lines, but the demand for fuel-efficient cars could, in the long run, bring a profitable return on the industry's investments.

If petroleum does become increasingly scarce, synthetic fuels, or synfuels, will have to take up much of the slack. Already the federal government is increasing its commitment to synfuels. With immediate development, they could come into widespread use sometime during the 1980s.

Synthetic fuels fall into two broad categories. The first includes those that would require no changes in today's conventional auto engines. These include synthetic gasolines made from shale oil, coal, and tar sands, plus blends of gasoline and alcohol (gasohol). The second category includes those synfuels that would require substantial modifications of today's engines.

At this time, none of the synfuels has yet entered the commercial stage. However, as prices for natural petroleum continue to rise, and as the production technologies evolve, synthetic gasolines are rapidly becoming competitive. But the lead times for these plants are on the order of five to fifteen years.

Finally, synthetic gasolines could further degrade the quality of the air, both in their production and in their use. Producing the fuels will require extensive and costly pollution control devices in order to contain gaseous emissions and to clean contaminants from the processed water. Also, using synthetic fuels produces overall about two and one-half to three times the amount of carbon dioxide than does burning natural fossil fuels. Many scientists fear that the buildup of carbon dioxide in the atmosphere could trigger a global warming trend.

To avoid some of these environmental problems, cars in the future may run on a number of new and different fuels and engines. Pure alcohols produced from biomass or fossil fuels are one promising possibility. Although they require modifications of today's engine, they offer greater energy efficiency, generally reduced emissions, and tremendous versatility of production. Along with synthetic gasolines, they stand as the best candidates to begin replacing natural gasoline sometime during the 1980s.

Electric vehicles are another possibility. The low power densities of today's batteries now limit the range and performance of electric cars. But the federal government has given its backing to the needed technological development and hopes to have thousands of electric vehicles on the roads for testing and demonstration in the next few years.

Perhaps the ideal automotive fuel, but technically the most distant, is hydrogen. Burned with oxygen, it releases high amounts of energy with essentially no harmful emissions. But storing hydrogen, both during distribution and in cars, presents great difficulties. And no one has yet invented an inexpensive way of extracting hydrogen from water.

Besides investigating alternative sources of fuel, researchers are looking into several new kinds of engines that could stretch gasoline supplies and run on alternative fuels. Gas turbines, which use expanding gases to drive a turbine, are a favorite technology. Unfortunately, they run only at very high temperatures. Until scientists develop new alloys or ceramics that can withstand intense heat, gas turbines cannot be used in automobiles.

Another possibility is the Stirling engine. These engines use an independent source of heat to expand a sealed, internal working fluid which drives a piston and powers the vehicle. The technology to produce Stirling engines is still distant, but they also hold out the promise of very high efficiencies with greatly reduced emissions.

The Retooling of America

The fortunes of the alternative fuels and new technologies now under study will powerfully influence the future mobility of Americans. Indirectly, these innovations will affect mobility through their impact, or lack of impact, on the economy. With a petroleum crisis looming on the horizon, the lead times for these technologies will be a crucial factor.

If developed in time, though, they could rejuvenate the auto industry, creating a strong demand for new kinds of cars that could pull the entire economy into a new age of technological advancement. One likely result would be an increased specialization of automobiles. People might use small electric vehicles for city travel and short trips, saving their larger and more powerful cars for extended journeys. Tomorrow's engines may possibly have to be appreciably larger than today's, making mass transit the only option for many former motorists.

Studies have shown, however, that mass transportation has only a limited capacity to replace the automobile. As Barry Bruce-Briggs reminds his readers in *The War Against the Automobile,* America's network of roads and personal automobiles is the best mass transportation system in the world. It is difficult to envision a system that could simultaneously deliver the versatility, convenience, and efficiency of the automobile.

As the threats to the automobile grow stronger, Americans will have to make some unpleasant choices. But they will undoubtedly decide that the automobile is worth saving. They will then just have to hope that the environment, the earth's resources, and the vagaries of technology will all cooperate in the struggle.

Concept of a van or utility vehicle of the future.

General Motors Corp.

The Gas Crunch and the 1980s

The immediate consequences of a gasoline shortage are now painfully apparent to most Americans. The gas crunch of 1979 jolted millions of Americans out of their daily routines, cost them millions of dollars, and changed the way many people lead their everyday lives. Tighter gas supplies may be the rule in the years ahead—certainly higher gas prices will—and even if shortages do not occur in the next decade, changes brought about by tighter gas supplies and higher prices may well permanently alter the fabric of American society.

The gas shortage of 1979 produced gas lines over three miles long, odd-even rationing plans, and maximum and minimum limits on gas sales. Owners of gasoline stations were forced to curtail hours, turn away thousands of desperate motorists, and break up all-too-common gas line fistfights. Millions of commuters left their automobiles at home and rode buses and subways to work. Planes, trains, and buses in intercity travel have enjoyed a burst of new business as a result of the gas shortage.

Outside the transportation industry, the effects of the gas shortage were equally acute. America's $110 billion-a-year vacation industry suffered because many people were afraid to take long trips without being sure of an adequate supply of gas. Restaurants, motels and service-oriented firms of all kinds endured a loss of business.

What do the effects of the gasoline shortage of 1979 suggest for the 1980s? In general terms, a long period of readjustment probably lies ahead, more painful for some than others, and more or less severe, depending on the price and availability of gasoline. In a recent *Washington Post* article (August 17, 1979), Robert Landmann, a researcher with the Community Services Administration in Washington, D.C., says that as with higher prices for any basic commodity, the poor "are getting hurt first and worst." Higher gas prices mean higher food and clothing prices, since roughly 80% of all foods and fabrics are shipped by truck. Tight gas supplies could mean curtailing outreach programs for senior citizens, the handicapped, and the rural poor, since fewer volunteers will be willing to drive long distances. The poor would also suffer if gas supplies are tight due to difficulties in both looking for jobs and getting to distant workplaces.

Of course, the economic and social effects of tight gas supplies are not confined to the poor. Nor are they necessarily bad for all businesses. Bicycle and motorcycle manufactures could have some good years ahead. Mass transit companies will probably get both new customers and additional funds to help expand their services.

Neighborhood stores could enjoy a comeback as people try to conserve gas by driving fewer miles. More backyard swimming pools may be built as people try to relax in the water without having to drive to it. In the recent gas crunch, bowling alleys and local movie theaters enjoyed new popularity, and in the next decade, local businesses of all sorts could enjoy a renaissance as more people try to stay closer to home.

Staying closer to home, in fact, may be an increasingly frequent practice in the future. Modern telecommunications make shopping by phone possible, and more and more workers may use computer terminals in their homes to avoid the expense of driving to work. People may stock up more on frozen and canned foods to save trips to the supermarket. Cable television, videocassette recorders and electronic games could enjoy even greater popularity as alternatives to entertainment away from home. People may also watch more television and read more than they do today.

But although certain sectors of the economy may benefit, a decade of tight gas supplies and high prices will almost certainly foster major and sometimes painful changes in the economy in general. The automobile industry, already forced to build smaller, more efficient cars, may find fewer customers for their cars. Tire companies could be doubly hurt because not only might people be driving less but the oil used to make tires will cost more. Sales of camping, hunting, fishing, and skiing equipment may fall off, and powerboats may be harder to sell. A further decline in tourism may well occur, and remote ski resorts could be particulaly hard hit. Sales of recreational vehicles may continue to slump.

In broader terms, what continued gasoline shortages could cost Americans is one of their most prized freedoms — mobility. And this loss of mobility may well mean that people's decisions about how to spend their time and money may be both more difficult and more important. With less eating out, working women, for example, could be put in a double bind by having to shop for and cook more meals at home. At the same time the need for a second income in many families could become more acute. As higher gasoline prices drive up prices in general, economic choices could be more limited and their consequences more severe, and tight gas supplies could limit people's ability to travel.

These kinds of decisions may mean that the 1980s will be a decade where cooperation — between commuters, husbands and wives, gas station owners and motorists, retailers and customers, and government and businesses — may be more important than ever. But in a century where mobility and the independence it brings have been increasing almost decade by decade, the loss of much of that mobility and independence could breed frustrations that make cooperation that much harder.

Gas rationing coupons available if needed.

Houses: More Boom — or a Bust?

For Many a Rude Awakening To the American Dream

A home of one's own has long been an essential feature of the American dream. The good news today is that more and more Americans are in fact realizing that dream; the bad news is that they have gone heavily in debt to do so and many others still cannot afford a home of their own.

Besides increasing in number, homes are continuing to get bigger. At the end of World War II, the average house had a living area of less than 1,000 square feet. By early 1972, the average size of a new detached home had reached 1,700 square feet. Just in the past four years, the average size of a house increased by 112 square feet, the equivalent of a 10 by 11-foot room, according to the Home Owners Warranty program. In 1950 only 1% of homes had four or more bedrooms; by 1978; 26% of new detached homes had at least four bedrooms.

While the home was getting bigger, the number of people living in it was getting smaller — from 3.37 persons in 1950 to 2.8 persons today. One reason for this trend is that buying a home has become "in" for singles. Between 1970 and 1976, homeownership of single male homeowners under 35 rose 213%, according to the U.S. Department of Housing and Urban Development. Single females under 35 who own homes jumped 141%. Single people are buying homes partly to beat inflation and for the sense of belongingness and security that homeownership gives. Then, too, there are simply more under-35 single adults around due to the postponement of marriage and the prevalence of divorce.

The total number of Americans living alone has boomed upward from about eight million in 1960 to nearly 16 million in 1975. Young people break away from their parents earlier to establish their own households. In addition, many older people find themselves again living alone due to rising rates of divorce and separation.

The conventional single-family residence remains the dream of most Americans, but many have found a satisfactory form of homeownership in townhouses, mobile homes, and condominium apartments. Many renters are forced to become owners when their apartment buildings are converted from rental property to condominiums.

House Prices Escalate

The price of housing has increased rapidly in recent years. The median value of owner-occupied, single-family homes climbed 53% between 1973 and 1977, reaching $36,900, according to a joint report by the U.S. Department of Housing and Urban Development and the Bureau of the Census. The increase was most apparent in the South and West. Homeowners in the West saw the median value of their housing rise 76% in four years to $48,800; while the value of homes in the South rose 59% to $31,400. The report, based on data collected in the 1977 Annual Housing Survey conducted by the Census Bureau for HUD, also shows that the median value of owner-occupied, single-family homes rose faster during the period than the median income of the homeowners. While the value of an owner-occupied single family went up 53%, the owner's income increased only 39%. This discrepancy suggests that many Americans have stretched themselves to the limit to attain the status of single-family homeownership.

The rapid increase in home prices has created something of a buying "panic" among some young couples. Many couples fear that unless they buy immediately they will miss "the last boat' to the middle class." A new median-priced home bought in 1966 and sold in 1976 would have yielded an average annual pre-tax gain of 18.5%, says Michael Sumichrast, chief economist of the National Association of Home Builders. Salomon Brothers has calculated that over the past 10 years, an investment in housing brought a return of 9.6% while stocks brought in only 3.1%. During the same period, consumer prices rose at the rate of 6.5%.

Heavy speculation in house prices has been greatest perhaps in California. In the Beverly Hills area, prices of many homes have jumped 100% to 250% in the past few years. Many houses are bought by Europeans and by oil-rich mideasterners.

DOE Photo

Demonstration homes in California were designed to use less energy. Features include solar heating, double-paned windows and extra thick insulation.

Traditional house construction board-by-board, above, is time consuming and expensive. Modular building technique, right, allows quick assembly of segments at the building site.

If housing costs and inflation keep soaring, an American home now costing $50,000 will cost $115,000 by 1985, according to Don Hovde, president of the National Association of Realtors. Middle-class homeowners as well as the elderly would be priced out of the market. Hovde blames much of this increase on moratoriums and local restrictions that have driven up the cost of land to the point where a building plot now is 25% of the cost of the new home.

A "Crash" in Real Estate Prices?

Will house prices continue to rise? Will Americans continue to be able to afford them? Yes, says economist Sumichrast in his book *The Complete Book of Home-Buying* (Dow-Jones, 1979). With rising incomes and smaller families, Americans will have more money to spend on housing. No real drop in housing demand is expected before 1990 due to the baby-boom generation's huge need for housing, Sumichrast argues. And many other authorities agree: For instance, Austin H. Kiplinger and Arnold Barach in their book *The Exciting '80s* (Kiplinger Editors, 1979) say that "the direction of house prices in the '80s is expected to be up."

But a few authorities disagree strongly. Two investment counselors, Gray Emerson Cardiff and John Wesley English, have argued that there will be a sharp downturn in housing prices. In their book *The Coming Real Estate Crash* (Arlington House, 1979), Cardiff and English compare the current speculation in real estate with earlier real estate booms in the United States — the Chicago real estate boom of the 1830s, the California boom of the 1860s, and the Florida boom of the 1920s.

In each case, speculation began when people recognized that the real estate in question would likely appreciate rapidly in value because of certain favorable features, Cardiff and English report. As investors bought property, prices began to rise, and as the price rise was observed, more investors rushed to buy on the basis of the established upward trend. The new group of investors naturally bid prices up still further, attracting still more investors, who in turn bid

prices to still higher levels. The rapid rise of the prices soon attracted people who bought only in the hope that they could soon sell at a higher price, and these speculators naturally pushed prices still further upward.

But the process cannot go on indefinitely. At some point, the prices will start declining again. Typically, the decline is very rapid — because speculators, who may have bought property on margin, see ruin ahead if prices start to decline and they panic, selling quickly at whatever price they can get. Panicky selling pushes prices down rapidly, especially when potential buyers — recognizing the downward trend — decide to postpone their purchases in order to buy at the lowest possible price.

But what about the *real* value of the property. After all, aren't we talking about *real* estate? The property may be real all right, but its dollar value is not fixed. Any piece of property is worth only what someone will pay. A serious downturn in the economy can make it difficult for people to buy houses, but very eager to sell; thus prices can fall rapidly.

Housing was a very good investment during the 1950s and 1960s, Cardiff and English say, but during the late 1970s there are clear signs it is becoming much less so. Most obviously, the steep increase in prices has made housing so expensive that more and more people simply cannot afford it: The house may still be viewed as a "good investment," but its price cannot exceed people's ability to pay for it.

English and Cardiff carefully review a number of the factors that are widely assumed to insure the continuance of high real estate prices and find that many are losing their force:

Population: The U.S. birth rate declined rapidly after the baby boom and there will be fewer people coming into the home-buying age. Based on the 1970 census, a straightforward calculation reveals demand increasing through 1984 and declining sharply thereafter.

Land: Many homebuyers feel that land is in limited supply and will inevitably become more valuable, but on a national basis there is not

Grumman

New house designs increasingly include clusters of rooftop solar collectors to use the sun's rays for heating.

now, nor has there ever been, a physical shortage of land for real estate activities. According to the 1970 census only 10% of the land within U.S. metropolitan areas had been developed.

Recent land prices have resulted not from physical shortages, say English and Cardiff, but from temporary distortions in supply and demand patterns. Environmental regulations have restricted supply in the face of unparalleled demand resulting from the post-war generation. Most environmental regulation did not disallow development, but merely imposed an additional lead time for builders. This regulated supply of land is just becoming available.

Inflation: Constantly rising prices are widely assumed to be part of the eternal order of things, but they are not. The historical record suggests that inflation is high for several years after an expensive war and then begins to abate, with deflation actually occurring. If inflation abates, housing will lose its value as an inflation hedge, and fewer people will find it an attractive investment.

Taxation: Housing has long enjoyed favorable tax treatment: Homeowners can deduct their real estate taxes on their income tax returns. But the 1978 Congress witnessed a political swing against tax favoritism for real estate. If real estate loses some of its tax advantages, house prices will suffer. The taxpayer's revolt, symbolized by California's passage of Proposition 13, suggests a trimming of governmental expenditures. On a national basis, less government and lower taxes will be deflationary and may lead to lower home prices, English and Cardiff argue.

When prices start spiraling upward, the boom develops a life of its own, feeding on itself. Prices go up because they are expected to go up.

But just as a boom feeds on itself, so does a bust, say English and Cardiff. When people perceive prices are going down, they are likely to rush madly to unload, thus causing prices to plunge downward sharply rather than decline gracefully.

"House-Poor" Americans

Whatever the future of house prices, there is

little doubt that Americans have strained to the utmost to buy houses. The old rule of thumb that one should not buy a house costing more than twice one's annual income has gone by the boards. People now buy houses that cost three or more times their annual income and take out second mortgages so as to come up with the downpayment. These "house-poor" Americans find that they have little money left after they make their mortgage payments. Furthermore, many are extremely vulnerable financially if they lose their jobs. If they can hold on for a couple of years, however, homeowners may find that inflation has greatly reduced their mortgage burden.

Financial agencies have constantly sought ways to provide more money for mortgages. In 1979, the Federal Home Loan Bank Board advanced a plan that would allow savings and loan associations to raise funds in the Eurodollar market, where money often can be obtained more cheaply than in the United States. Already many foreign investors are putting up money for U.S. homes. U.S. real estate investment trusts (REITs) proved popular with foreign investors in 1979. OPEC nations are reported to hold about 80% of the bonds issued by the Federal National Mortgage Association (Fannie Mae); the second-largest issuer of government debt instruments after the U.S. Treasury.

Some local jurisdictions are issuing tax-exempt bonds to finance home mortgages. Proponents of these bond issues argue that they make home-ownership possible for families who can't afford the 20% to 30% downpayments being charged in 1979. Another popular way around the down-payment problem is for the seller to let the buyer pay the downpayment in installments, using a second mortgage as security. Thanks partly to these new arrangements — and the soaring price of houses — mortgage debt in the U.S. has nearly doubled over the past five years.

Ways for Housing to Go

Most experts expect inflation to continue during the 1980s and for housing to continue to be one of the best hedges against its ravages. But the high cost of housing and the dwindling percentage of Americans who can afford the downpayment and/or mortgage are worrisome. Thus the experts' consensus for housing during the 1980s seems to be as follows: Housing will continue to rise in price but will remain a good hedge against inflation for those who can afford the initial outlay. In general, the industry will continue strong, but there will be weak periods. Many young people will find it very difficult to get their starter home, although mobile homes may help along with new financial instruments such as variable-rate mortgages.

An alternative forecast is for a "crash" in the price of houses. If such were to occur, many people would find themselves with little or no equity in their homes — and might decide to allow the mortgagor to foreclose.

Clearly, millions of Americans want homes of their own. Perhaps government, financial institutions, and the people themselves will be able to come up with new devices to enable a growing proportion of Americans to participate in the dream of homeownership. But the clouds on the housing horizon suggest that many people will find the forecast on their chances for homeownership is still less than bright.

Technology in the Economy of the 1980s

"Science explores; Technology executes; Man conforms."

—Inscription above portals of the 1933 Chicago World's Fair.

Few could have realized, in the midst of the Great Depression, how accurate their welcome to Chicago's fair would prove. From mechanical adders to hand-held computers, from model A's to atomic power, from barnstormers to moon landings, the union of science and technology has touched almost every aspect of American life.

In the process it has made widespread affluence possible for the first time in history. Brookings Institute researcher Ed Denison has calculated that nearly half of the increase in national income between 1929 and 1969 came from "advances in knowledge" — technology.

Of course, any term that can include the family car, the lessons of a business school, miracle vaccines, and offshore drilling platforms is an open invitation to oversimplification. Even economists have difficulty disaggregating the blanket term, technology. They have to measure technological progress indirectly, through increases in productivity. Defined as economic output per unit of input, productivity indicates how many goods and services are optimally available for each worker.

One way to measure America's tremendous economic expansion after World War II is through productivity. Between 1948 and 1966, the productivity of the American worker grew at an average rate of 2.5% per year. Since 1966, however, in a trend that has been widely noted and lamented, productivity increases have fallen well below the postwar average. Between 1966 and 1973, productivity in America grew at only 1.6% per year. Since 1973, it has fallen even lower. President Carter's Council of Economic Advisors has calculated that private non-farm productivity grew only 0.8% in 1978. With the economy again on the verge of hard times, the rate could drop even below that.

In a society committed to economic growth, slackening productivity inevitably frustrates many people's economic aspirations. It also harms America's position with respect to international trade. U.S. workers overall are still the most productive in the world, a distinction they have held for decades. But America's rate of productivity growth has fallen below the rates of every other major industrial nation. With surprising rapidity, other nations are erasing America's traditional lead and even surpassing the productivity of some American industries. The result has been a weakening of America's trading stance, and just at a time when the United States needs to boost its exports to make up for the cost of imported oil.

Declining Productivity

Many economists have puzzled over the drop in productivity since 1966, wondering if the long-term trend will ever reappear. To account for the drop, they cite several factors. First of all, this period saw many women, youths, and minorities enter the labor market. Because these workers were theoretically less skilled, productivity fell. This theory does not explain why productivity has continued to fall, however, since by now most of these workers have melted into the economic mainstream.

Another theory looks towards the continuing shift from manufacturing jobs to service jobs in the U.S. Service jobs have traditionally generated lower increases in productivity, but most economists don't believe that this trend alone could account for the dramatic falloff.

Failing to find an adequate explanation in the composition of the labor force, many economists have turned their attention to technology. If technological innovation, the process whereby scientific or technological insights are applied to the production of goods and services, has fallen off, this could account for the slowing of the productivity growth rate.

However, the connection between basic discoveries and economic progress is long and tenuous. In general, technological innovations can affect the economy in two different ways. Firstly, they can increase the efficiency of the

UPI

Hand labor skills are still an advantage in Japan as in this Sony plant assembly line.

General Motors

Robot assembly machine by General Motors can install lightweight automotive parts.

processes by which goods are manufactured. This lowers the price of the good and releases some of the raw materials that had previously gone into the good to other parts of the economy. Both of these effects spur economic growth, by increasing the demand for the good and making the overall economy more efficient.

Technological innovation can also affect the economy by providing entirely new goods. In this case, the implications are more complex and dramatic. New products, by changing people's demands, can displace older products, possibly shutting down entire industries. New products can also change the demand for raw materials, and they can increase the efficiency of other processes, as above.

Since the industrial revolution, new products have been a powerful force behind economic growth. But they can also have harmful consequences, putting people out of work and ruining once-thriving industries. In addition, new products can have many effects that don't show up in the gross national product. Essentially, the harmful non-economic effects of new products are what have caused today's crisis of confidence in technology. The resolution of this crisis will greatly influence the directions that technology takes in the future.

R & D and Productivity

With the rise of big science, the day when an individual could come up with inventions powerful enough to shake the economy has long since passed. Today most technological innovations come from private, governmental, or university research departments, and the amount of money financing such projects is a good measure of a nation's commitment to its technological future.

Many people have blamed the drop in productivity growth since 1966 on substantial cutbacks by the federal government of its research and development (R&D). At the end of the 1960s, with the approaching completion of the Apollo program and the Vietnam War, the federal government began to reduce its backing of new military and space research. The economic stagnation of the 1970s brought further cutbacks, as the government concentrated on programs that would have more immediate effects.

Private industry has increased its funding of R&D over the last decade, but not enough to compensate for the government's cutbacks. Overall, the proportion of the GNP devoted to R&D fell from 3.0% in 1964 to 2.2% in 1976. Meanwhile, this proportion has been rising in most of the other industrialized countries.

Even the increased R&D by private industry in the U.S. may have less of an effect than private R&D has had in the past. Studies are rare, but sources within the industry claim that most R&D now goes towards "defensive" projects. The emphasis is on improving old products and making short-term gains in the marketplace rather than on taking the risks necessary to ensure the economy's continued growth.

Industrial leaders give several reasons for this redirection of private R&D. The most important factor they cite is uncertainty about the future. In a period of economic and political instability, industries have felt unable to see far enough into the future to begin research projects that would not pay off for years. Investments are now geared towards the near and more certain future.

Many industries also claim that increased governmental regulations have hampered their ability to innovate. Regulations governing pollution, the safety of workers and products, and other social concerns drain time and money away from the traditional pursuit of increased efficiency, according to these industries. A favorite example comes from the pharmaceutical industry. In the 1950s, the application required by the Food and Drug Administration for a new drug consisted of only a few hundred pages. In the 1970s, applications for drugs could run to tens of thousands of pages.

No one faults the general intent of the regulations that have been established. But industries emphasize that regulations cost much more than just the payroll of the regulators. Decreasing pollution, making safe products, or guaranteeing safe working conditions entails certain costs in economic output (and in company profits). Calculating the full cost of a given regulation must take all these losses into account.

Stagnating Technology

In contract to the complaints of industry, some economists fear that the slowdown in technological innovation may not arise just from the short-term conditions of increased regulation, tight money markets, and economic uncertainties. They suspect that the slowdown may reflect a much more fundamental aspect of technological progress, a structural flaw that could have the potential to cripple the economies of the industrialized world.

Orio Giarini and Henri Louberge, in *The Diminishing Returns of Technology*, argue that economic growth has slowed because of a decline in the effectiveness of scientific and technological progress. Applying the theory of diminishing returns to the entire area of technology, they conclude that the union of science and technology, the catalyst behind economic growth in this century, has run its course. The potential for major technological breakthroughs in many of the industries that have traditionally fueled economic growth — metallurgy, agriculture, artificial fibers, chemistry, aviation, and so on — has been exhausted. No significant developments can be expected in these fields in the near future.

Giarini and Louberge contend that this inherent decline of scientific and technological progress has caused the economic sluggishness of the 1970s. They also say that it has caused the economic system to become inflexible, because technological barriers now limit the possible responses to crises, such as increases in oil prices. "It becomes increasingly difficult for the system to react spontaneously to an emergency because the market system is held back by technological delays," they say. "And the increased vulnerability of the economic system makes it increasingly necessary to resort to planning, both at the company level and at the national level."

Other economists have proposed similar theories about technology and the economy. Joseph Schumpeter in the 1950s and 1960s forwarded the idea that clusters of technological innovation are the driving force behind long-term waves in the economy. Thus the end of the technological innovation that swelled around the turn of the century, yielding the telephone, the automobile, airplanes, radio, and filament lamps, led to the Great Depression. Another wave of technological innovation, bringing television, computers, medical technologies, jets, and nuclear power, helped pull the economy out of the Great Depression, but this wave is now faltering itself.

Many economists have faulted Schumpeter for his simplification of technological evolution. But if the economy is indeed suffering from a lack of technological innovation, the future could be much different than the recent past. Either technology must expand into new and perhaps unanticipated areas, or growth will gradually subside and the developed world will have to struggle to adjust.

Prods to Innovation

The lack of technological innovation has not gone unnoticed by policymakers and politicians, those invested with sustaining the growth state. President Carter has often shown a strong concern for U.S. science and technology, and even in a time of tight federal budgets the real outlays for R&D have started to inch back towards previous levels.

But Willis Shapley, a consultant to the American Association for the Advancement of Science, echoes the warnings of many scientists that politicians should not expect immediate payoffs from basic research. In his analysis of R&D in the 1979 federal budget, Shapley says that "except perhaps in a few cases where potential new applications are clearly seen in advance, one should not count on current decisions on basic research to have an appreciable impact on near-term problems in the economy. To claim too much too soon for basic research could undermine the credibility of its legimate and essential longer-term claims."

Because of the lag between basic research and technological innovation, many economists feel that the federal government should concentrate on the actual process whereby scientific discoveries become economic gains. Many other industrialized countries have had great success funding university engineering departments that specialize in increasing industrial productivity.

The federal government could also use its tax policies to foster industrial R&D, or it could ease some regulations and look for industry's response. Some people have also advocated reforming the patent system, contending that industries are underinvesting in R&D because they do not reap enough profits from their inventions.

To protect America's traditional trading advantage, some groups have called for the government to limit the movement of technical expertise out of the country. This course of action appears unlikely, though, partially because the multinational corporations are the primary exporters of technology. Also, the U.S. has been a staunch defender of free trade, and moving to block the flow of something as volatile as information would require a significant departure from this position.

Some economists have suggested that the U.S. should forfeit its technological leadership in certain areas but maintain its lead in high technology fields. In this way, the U.S. could take advantage of technology developed abroad, as many countries do today, while not seriously worsening its present trade deficit.

Another possibility is for technological progress to veer into wholly new areas in the future. Calls for "soft" or "appropriate" technologies, ones that recognize the importance of other factors than the gross national product, could prove the source of the important breakthroughs of the future. Such a movement would have the potential to both ease America's present technological problems and improve its balance of trade. But because productivity, as traditionally measured, would tend to be lower for many such technologies, the traditional concern associated with economic growth would have to soften. It remains to be seen if such a transition can be made smoothly, or if it would come only after severe technological crises.

Possible Technological Breakthroughs

Because the historical connection between technology and the economy is so unclear, speculating how about future inventions could affect the economy is doubly difficult. Nevertheless, many of the technological breakthroughs that may occur in the near future could cause major changes in the economy. Following are some of the fields where the prospects for technological change look especially promising in the 1980s.

Hybrid circuit, the latest in U.S. miniaturization.

Microprocessors can bill, update, store and print.

Electronics and Communications

The continued evolution and spread of micro-processors and other electronic technologies could have the most dramatic impact in the near-term future. Many experts believe that the next decade will see the first step towards establishing regional or national data banks connected to home computers. Such a development, if widespread, could bring a number of changes to American life: improvements in education, easier access to information, improved communications, and on the debit side, greater threats to personal privacy, a potential increase in computer crime, and so on.

Such changes would affect the economy both directly and indirectly. The application of computer technologies could greatly increase the productivity of workers in the services, a sector of the economy that many economists feel has held back productivity. Moreover, the demand for these technologies could make the computer industry itself into an even larger and healthier industry than it already is.

Computer technologies could also have negative effects on the economy. Although conclusions are still scarce, cybernation has long been blamed for excessive unemployment. If the use of computers were to replace other activities that now bolster the economy (such as transportation), overall economic growth could slow.

Biomedicine

The pace of biomedical progress has been accelerating for decades, and the 1980s could see developments even more radical than the miracles of the past. Researchers could learn how to control some of the remaining unconquered diseases. Perhaps they will master the process of aging itself. The 1980s could see a cheap and perfectly safe contraceptive, or ways to control the sex of a child, or methods by which to control behavior through the direct manipulation of the brain.

Any of these breakthroughs could transform many long-standing social institutions, as well as the economy. In the area of genetics, for example, the further development of cloning and recombinant DNA could prolong the faltering Green Revolution. It could also wreak much more fundamental changes in humanity's control over life. Such development would change the world in unforeseeable ways.

Transportation

As fossil fuels become increasingly scarce and costly, the demand for new kinds of transportation could boost the economy. Smaller cars are already in high demand, and the automakers are hurrying to adjust their assembly lines to take advantage of the trend. Other vehicles will undergo similar transformations. In what a metaphor for the entire history of technology after World War II, the evolution of jets will take new directions in the future. After the steady growth of jets that culminated in the Boeing 747, the Boeing 767 will be smaller, lighter, quieter, and more fuel efficient.

Traveling by train should become more popular, and the demand for higher rail speed will once again become important. Trains in the Northeast Corridor of the U.S. will soon run well in excess of 100 mph, and the 200-mph train may not be far away. New mass transportation systems will also be a powerful source of economic growth. Several cities may plan new subway systems, and bus travel has already started to increase.

In the longer term, the drive to conquer space may intensify. The Space Shuttle will make space industrialization a commercial venture, and it may be the stepping-stone to even bigger projects within the next several decades. Although impossible without a greatly expanded economy here on earth, giant orbiting space stations could prove to be the growth industry of the distant future.

Energy

Because almost every sector of the economy now relies to some extent on fossil fuels, the imminent shift of our energy sources could refashion the entire economy. None of the long-term sources of energy — fusion, breeder reactors, geothermal or solar power — will likely play a sizable role in the economy of the 1980s. But solar power could turn into a major industry, especially given technological breakthroughs in converting energy from the sun into other, more usable forms. The eventual impact of energy on the economy will depend on the extent to which technological breakthroughs can counteract the negative effects of rising energy prices through the 1980s.

Towards the Future

Over the past several decades, people have begun to realize that technology has its dangers as well as its promises. Many claim that, instead of being the mediator between science and man, technology has taken on a life of its own. It no longer takes notice of the needs of man, and it has become too entrenched to heed the warnings of science.

If technological innovation has indeed slowed down, perhaps the 1980s will offer a chance to recover from future shock. But the shocks of technological stagnation may prove no less disruptive.

Commentators on technology's relation to society often say that only if people reestablish their control over technology can it be made both balanced and humane in the future. Global movements such as technology assessment, and futurism in general, offer one way to gain this control. But public concern is the only human force powerful enough to bring about major changes. At a basic level, everyone bears the burdens and enjoys the benefits of technology. So everyone has a stake in its future.

Combustion Engineering, Inc.

Fuel loading operation in a nuclear power plant.

Food and Agriculture in the 1980s

World Food Needs Outpace Gains Made by the Green Revolution

Agriculture today is far and away the biggest industry in the United States, with assets of some $671 billion in 1977. Agriculture is also the country's largest employer — somewhere between 14 and 17 million people share in getting food from the farm to the table. Farming itself uses 4.4 million workers — more than the transportation, steel, and auto industries combined. In 1974, consumers spent over $180 billion for food, and according to U.S. Department of Agriculture (USDA) estimates, 24% of the nation's gross business activity was generated directly or indirectly by agriculture in 1973. In a world where millions of people in affluent countries take three meals a day for granted, few people seem to spend much time reflecting on all the energy, resources, dollars, and labor required to put those three meals on the table. In the last decade, however, inflation, population pressures, and poor harvests have begun to draw food and agriculture into the spotlight. The economics of keeping the population of the U.S. and the entire world fed is now a topic commanding the attention of farmers, governments, and people everywhere. Food is big business — in fact, the biggest — and the way in which the U.S. and other nations manage the production, distribution, and consumption of food in the next decade could profoundly affect the well-being of the world's nations and citizens.

A Brief Look Back — The Green Revolution

Until the widespread use of fertilizers, improved plant strains, and farm machinery began, the only way to get more food was to cultivate more land. In Food for the Future, Keith O. Campbell, Professor of Agricultural Economics at the University of Sydney, points out that, in fact, "it was not until about 1950 that, on a world basis, the predominant source of additional food output became that of increased yields rather than the expansion of the area under cultivation."

But with the 1950s began the "Green Revolution," a series of unprecedented agricultural achievements that enabled farmers around the world to increase dramatically the amount of food that they could coax from the land.

The Green Revolution began at the International Maize and Wheat Improvement Center in Mexico, with the financial support of the Rockefeller Foundation. The development of the first high-yielding varieties (HYVs) of wheat in the late 1940s led to the doubling of wheat yields in in Mexico in the space of ten years. The introduction of semidwarf wheats, which responded well to fertilizer without growing too tall and toppling over before they could be harvested as did some other hybrids, led to another doubling of yields in the 1960s. The success of high-yielding varieties of wheat prompted the establishment of the International Rice Research Institute in the Philippines in 1960, and attempts to crossbreed semidwarf strains of rice met similar exhilarating successes. "During the late 1960s," reports food expert Lester Brown of the Worldwatch Institute, "the Philippines were able to achieve self-sufficiency in rice, ending a half century of dependence on imports." Brown continues: "Over a period of only seven years, 1965 to 1972, India expanded its wheat production from 11 million tons to 26 million tons — an increase in production of a food staple unmatched by any other country in history." In The Food in Your Future, agricultural technologist Keith C. Barrons says that "Pakistan's 1971 wheat production was up 76% from its 1961-1965 average, while Latin American corn production was up over 50%." Between 1961 and 1971, total world food production grew more than 26%. Prices were low and grain surpluses enormous in the United States. Fertilizer, a crucial ingredient in the success of high-yielding varieties of rice and wheat, was plentiful. At the beginning of the 1970s, the Green Revolution seemed to many to have all but solved the world food problem.

In the early 1970s, however, a combination of factors including poor harvests, increasing affluence in some countries, rising energy prices, tightening supplies of fertilizer, and most importantly, the relentless growth of population in the developing world, combined to all but obliterate the gains made in the previous fifteen years of the Green Revolution.

"World food production declined modestly in 1972 — only 1.6% at the world level — but the impact of this decline on some countries, commodities, trade patterns, prices, and per capita food production levels was serious," reports the U.S. Department of Agriculture's Economic Research Service in The World Food Situation and Prospects to 1985. "The crop shortfalls were particularly unsettling because they broke the growing confidence about overcoming the world food problem that had emerged in the period after 1966." Mexico, which had exported 10% of its grain between 1965 and 1969, found it necessary to import 20% of its grain by the mid-1970s, according to Brown. The Philippines went from independence back to dependence on rice in less than ten years. "The USSR, customarily a net grain exporter," reports the Department of Agriculture, "became the world's largest importer of grain, importing a total of 30 million tons (net), in 1972 and 1973, compared with total net exports of 8.6 million tons in the previous two years." The price of wheat according to USDA statistics, rose from $60 per ton in the second quarter of 1972 to $210 per ton in the first quarter of 1974, an increase of 250%. The price of rice rose over 300%, from $132 to $570 per ton, in the same period. Grain reserves around the world plummeted from 259 million metric tons in 1970 to 100 million metric tons in 1976.

The effects of increasing demand for food throughout the world were to drive food prices up everywhere, including the United States, and, according to Selwyn Enzer, Richard Drobnick, and Steven Alter of the University of Southern California in their book Neither Feast Nor Famine, to transform American agriculture "from a highly subsidized sector to one that is being called upon to bail out the national economy and to contribute significantly to U.S. political clout in international circles." The food grown on one out of every three acres in the United States was exported in 1977, and this massive agricultural trade contributed $10 billion to the U.S. balance of trade in 1977, thus making it extremely important in offsetting the cost of oil imports.

In his monograph *The Politics and Responsibility of the North American Breadbasket,* Lester Brown says that as a result of increasing worldwide demand for food, rising affluence in OPEC countries and some other nations, high energy prices, and agricultural mismanagement in some parts of the world. "North America today finds itself with an almost monopolistic control of the world's exportable grain supplies, a situation for which there is no historical precedent." This unprecedented situation is what makes the future of American agriculture so critically important.

Agriculture and Economics

Agriculture in the United States, as noted earlier, is big business. And today's farmer, big or small, is perhaps best described as a businessman. The days when the farmer produced everything he needed from potatoes to pork chops, kept what he had to and sold what was left are long gone. A farm today is much like a factory: the farmer buys raw materials like seed and feed, enormously expensive tools such as tractors and milking machines, chemicals in the form of fertilizers and pesticides, and uses them plus his land to turn out a vast array of agricultural products. Owning a farm is just as expensive a proposition as owning and running a small business, since the value of the land alone on the average farm today is $200,000 (up from $63,000 ten years ago). For years, as many people know and some lament, the number of farms in the U.S. has been declining and the average size increasing. Many small farmers today are faced with the ultimatum: "Get big or get out."

The remarkable productive capacity of America's farmers is the cornerstone of the U.S. economy and is largely responsible for the country's current position as the world's biggest granary. The tremendous increase in the value of U.S. agricultural products in the last decade would seem to bode well for the future of U.S. agriculture. And, indeed, most experts agree that the U.S. is completely capable of producing enough food to feed all of its citizens, and to feed almost all of them well, for as many years ahead as anyone can see. But the peculiar nature of food as a commodity, rising energy and fertilizer prices, urban pressures on cropland, competing demands for water, and most importantly the rest of the world's desperate need for U.S. agricultural products could all pose serious problems for agriculture and the economy in the 1980s.

The Demand for Food

As the remarkable jump in wheat and rice prices between 1972 and 1974 graphically demonstrates, huge price fluctuations are part and parcel of the world food problem. One reason that food prices can jump so quickly is that even in times of scarcity, people still want to eat as much as during periods of abundance. In economic terms, the demand for food is relatively inelastic: Demand stays pretty much the same in times of both surplus and shortage.

Today, the enormous international demand for U.S. agricultural products puts the United States in a profitable but difficult position. High demand abroad means high food prices at home, which contribute to inflation, make agricultural

UPI

High yield varities of wheat plus efficient combines have made U.S. the world's biggest granary.

World Bank

Improved rice strains in Bangladesh are also part of the "Green Revolution."

USIA

Indian children with bare subsistence rations.

UPI

The new pattern — U.S. wheat going to the U.S.S.R.

land more valuable, and thus make food more expensive to produce. But exporting less food to keep domestic prices down means a worsening balance of trade. And perhaps most troubling of all, as the world's largest exporter of food, the U.S. must adjudicate between the demands of affluent countries that can afford to pay high prices for U.S. agricultural products, and the needs of impoverished countries that can afford to pay little or nothing for desperately needed food imports, and whose steadily increasing populations continually erode their ability to pay for food.

The Most Tragic Problem: Poverty

The distribution of food is not really a problem for farmers, or the agricultural community, but rather part of the broader problem of income distribution. Food is almost always available for people who can pay for it. The developing nations as a whole do not produce enough food to feed themselves and often cannot afford to buy all the food they need. The U.S. has sold vast amounts of food at concessional prices to poor nations in the past, but there is no guarantee that the U.S. can continue to do so indefinitely. Some experts state flatly that the rising level of food imports by poor regions will not be sustained over the next twenty years. Keith Barrons warns that "India, Bangladesh, and China are especially vulnerable because they feed so little livestock and there is thus little grain to be diverted to human use. Don't be surprised if the greatest famine in history occurs somewhere in the next decade." The problem facing the U.S. in this regard is twofold: in times of economic problems or food shortages, when so many other countries are willing to buy U.S. agricultural products, can the U.S. afford to support millions of people who cannot pay for the food they receive? and, in the eyes of the rest of the world, can the U.S. afford not to?

Energy and Fertilizers

The increase in the world's food supply since World War II has been achieved largely through increased consumption of fossil fuels and fossil fuel derivatives, which are used not only to power equipment but as raw material for making fertilizer. Hence, the rising prices of energy and fertilizer could have a significant influence on U.S. agriculture in the 1980s. Nations which must import both oil and fertilizers are doubly damned. Since fertilizers are in large part responsible for the productivity of high-yielding varieties of rice and wheat, a fertilizer shortage in developing countries is especially crippling. And developing countries may not get enough fertilizer to expand food production in times of shortages.

Can Organic Farming Reduce Food Costs?

The use of chemical fertilizers, insecticides, and herbicides, advanced farm machinery, and new hybrid grain varieties fostered an unprecedented boom in agricultural productivity in the U.S. in the last four decades. Between 1950 and 1970, corn production almost tripled in the U.S., and according to the U.S. Department of Agriculture, "American farmers today produce over 54% more crop on 3% fewer acres than did their fathers." The use of chemical fertilizers, insecticides, and herbicides has proved so successful that the organic farmer, who avoids the use of chemicals, has been swept into agriculture's backwaters. The orthodox agriculture of today is inorganic farming; organic farmers and their supporters are widely viewed as heretics.

But in the eyes of a growing number of farmers and agronomists, the heresy of organic farming is beginning to make at least a little sense. The enormous success of chemical fertilizers and other modern farming tools obscured for a time some of their weaknesses. The toxicity of a few insecticides and herbicides is now well known, and many farmers have learned to use them carefully and selectively to minimize environmental hazards. But perhaps the single most important criticism by organic farming enthusiasts of modern agricultural methods is their effect on the soil. Nothing, in fact, separates the orthodox farmer from the organic heretic in modern agriculture so clearly as their differing views on the ground that they farm.

"Much of America's exemplary record for food production has come at the expense of America's soil," says William Tucker in a recent article in The Atlantic magazine entitled, "The Next American Dust Bowl — And How to Avert It." In The Unsettling of America: Culture and Agriculture, ecologist Wendell Berry puts the point even more bluntly. Today's tremendous agricultural production, he says, "is being paid for, not just with labor, money, and fuel, but with land." The use of chemical fertilizers makes it possible, and even profitable, to avoid spreading manure and rotating crops to keep the soil fertile and to practice instead what is known as continuous cropping — planting the most profitable crop on the same soil year after year. Tucker says, in fact, that "some scientists in agricultural schools are now taking the extreme position that 'the soil is there simply to hold up the plant while the farmer feeds it nutrients.'" The problem with this position, is, first, that without adequate soil conservation measures, some areas may eventually not even have soil to hold up the plants, and, second, that the price of inorganic nutrients is rising with the cost of fossil fuels, from which many chemical fertilizers are made. In addition, heavy farm machinery makes the soil harder and harder to work. In Our Synthetic Environment, professor of social ecology Murray Bookchin says that, "data from Texas indicate that crop yields of compacted soils there have fallen off from 40 to 50%, and commercial fertilizers have not been able to increase the yields to any great extent."

Instead of seeing the soil as a something to hold the plants upright while they are being fed, organic farmers take the position that "if a farmer keeps his soil in good condition, the plants will pretty much take care of themselves," says Tucker. The view of the soil held

Water and Land Use

Today almost one-seventh of the total cultivated area (about 500 million acres) is irrigated, and roughly 30% of the world's food is produced on irrigated land. But competing demands for water from urban areas and hydroelectric power could limit the amount of water available for irrigation in the 1980s. The inefficiency of some irrigation systems, some of which waste 50% of the water they use, also hampers food production. According to the U.S. Department of Agriculture, water supplies around the U.S. are such that "shortages could occur in any region in any year."

Perhaps more serious than competing demands for water are the growing pressures on cropland both in the U.S. and around the world. Overgrazing, poor agricultural practices, overcultivation of marginal land, erosion, deforestation, and the expansion of deserts are steadily impinging upon the cropland of developing nations at a time when their populations need more land to grow food on.

In the United States, urban sprawl, increasing amounts of land needed to produce energy, and other factors have combined to put more pressure on cropland. According to the Department of Agriculture, in recent years about 2 million acres of rural land have been converted annually

"New Look" on American farms —women in increasing numbers with agriculture degrees.

to urban, transportation, and other intensive uses. About one-quarter of this land is cropland. In *The Worldwide Loss of Cropland,* Lester Brown reports that "although the strong world demand for U.S. grain has made the continuous cropping of corn profitable, it has also led to an unacceptable level of soil erosion in many parts of the corn belt."

Another crucial factor in the use of land deserves mention: in the advanced countries

---

by some organic farming adherents might, in fact, almost be described as reverential. Bookchin writes: "The soil is a palpitating sheet of life, varying in composition not only from one part of a country to another but from acre to acre. Man can analyze the soil, but he cannot manufacture it. The first difficulty he encounters is its highly dynamic character and its remarkable complexity. The soil is a highly differentiated world of living and inanimate things, of vegetable and animal matter in various stages of decomposition, and of rock particles, minerals, water, and air. Soil is always in the process of formation. It gives its nutrients to the wind, rain, and plants, and is replenished by the breakdown of rocks, the putrefaction of dead animals and plants, and the never-ending activities of microscopic life. The soil is the dramatic arena where life and death complement each other, where decay nourishes regeneration."

Successful organic farming involves putting this kind of knowledge and concern for the soil to hard-headed, practical use. Organic farming on a large scale is a subtle and complex combination of agricultural techniques that demand much of a farmer, not a throwback to antiquated and unproductive farming. It involves rotating crops so that nitrogen-fixing legumes such as clover and soybeans help leave the ground more fertile for subsequent corn or wheat crops. Organic farmers also make extensive use of animal manure and many, if not most, have their own herds of livestock. Many organic farmers rely on extra cultivation rather than herbicides to take care of weeds, and on insect predators and wildlife to keep down insect pests.

Studies by Barry Commoner show that organic agriculture is highly productive and, because it requires less energy in the form

of chemical fertilizers, is cheaper than conventional farming methods. Commoner's studies show that organic farms sometimes do experience a slight reduction in yields per acre, but the decline is compensated for by decreased costs to the farmer and a much healthier soil.

Organic farmers are also less vulnerable to fluctuations in the price of fertilizers and insecticides, which can have a devastating effect on some farmers, as they did between 1971 and 1974 when the price of some kinds of fertilizers jumped over 700%. It may be the economics of organic farming that will make it more attractive in the future. Tucker quotes microbiologist Robert Pettit of Texas A & M: "There's absolutely nothing sacred about having organic matter and humus in your soil. You can grow the same plants in water if you want to add enough chemical fertilizers. There's only one advantage to organic farming and that is that it's *cheaper.* And it's going to get cheaper still as the price of natural gas [from which chemical fertilizers are made] goes up. Plus organic farming is easier on your soils and keeps them healthy and that's really going to make the difference in the long, long run."

Neither organic farming nor orthodox agriculture are panaceas. And if organic farming is to prove itself, it must do so in the fields and in the marketplace, as orthodox farming did. But the success of today's organic farmers suggests that such proof is very possible. And even more importantly, high energy prices and the possibility that orthodox farming methods might be buying agricultural productivity at the price of declining soil fertility and increased erosion make organic farming an alternative too potentially valuable to ignore.

especially, but also in many of the world's impoverished regions, the best land is already being cultivated, and the acres brought under the plow in the years ahead are likely to be less productive than those being farmed today. As Barrons notes, "land resources are finite, they stopped making land some time ago."

Stability: A Goal for the 1980s

Stabilizing the production and demand of food around the world could be an enormous blessing for developed and developing nations alike, but it will not be easy, if it is possible at all. Some observers believe it is unlikely that the world will again see a long period of surpluses such as it experienced in the 1950s and 1960s. Many growers will find it difficult and sometimes costly to increase yields further.

Since the demand for food appears certain to increase in the next decade, the only way to keep prices from soaring is to better control supply. Rebuilding international grain reserves is an important step toward stabilizing the world food economy and mitigating the effect of price fluctuations that can wreak havoc on the economies of rich and poor nations alike. But with worldwide demand for food so closely matching supply, reserves will not accumulate easily.

Although the policy decisions necessary to rebuilding grain reserves may meet with disapproval from some quarters, many food experts think that adequate grain reserves are well worth the effort. The United Nations Food and Agriculture Organization (FAO), for example, has called for a system of nationally held grain reserves plus an exchange of information and international consultation. Because grain reserves, and the rates at which they are filled and emptied, can cause price changes, the USDA notes that "the management of stocks is a political issue influenced by pressures from consumers, producers, taxpayers, exporters, and importers." But researchers from the Department of Agriculture's Economic Research Service argue that "in the present situation of rapidly growing population, high food prices, high rates of inflation, and increasing international interdependence, the world clearly has a vested interest in producing and distributing food in adequate quantities and at prices that stimulate needed production and reduce wasteful uses."

Safeguarding the world's cropland from urban encroachment and soil erosion will also be extremely important in ensuring agricultural production in the 1980s and beyond. Lester Brown argues that as cropland becomes more scarce,

"it can be protected from competing nonfarm demands only through some form of land-use planning," and he suggests that this planning be undertaken at all levels, from local to national. Halting soil erosion requires investments in land improvements and changes in cropping practices, but delaying attention to soil erosion could result in the steady deterioration of agricultural productivity.

Managing agricultural water supplies, and protecting them from competing urban demands, is also important for the future of U.S. agriculture. Keith Campbell argues that many irrigation projects already in use could be greatly improved, and stresses that "the importance of carrying out benefit-costs studies of projected irrigation and drainage works cannot be overemphasized. Too many irrigation schemes even in developed countries cannot be justified on economic grounds. Because of the irreversible nature of many water resource developments, it is imperative that they be carefully planned in advance."

Science and technology offer a key to achieving the increased food output. Further improvements in plant breeding, more research into integrated pest management and the biological control of insects, further efforts to make crop and other wastes more digestible for livestock, better agricultural equipment for small-scale farming in developing nations, more governmental support for agricultural research, and many other scientific and technological efforts could further enhance mankind's ability to feed itself.

Agriculture and the 1980s: A Glimpse Ahead

The 1980s may well be a decade of increasing food prices for reasons mentioned earlier: high energy and fertilizer prices, increasing production costs on U.S. farms, higher prices for farmland, the steadily increasing worldwide demand for food, inflation, and other factors. Barrons asserts that people in the U.S. "will not go hungry, but there will be shortages of some things at certain times, a situation the affluent world is going to have to learn to live with."

Because high grain prices will drive up the price of meat, more meat substitutes and extenders made directly from cereals or legumes will probably appear on the market. Backyard gardens may enjoy a renaissance, and beef may be a little tougher, since more of it may be fed with roughage rather than grain. But despite changes in some foods and in consumption patterns, most Americans are all but assured an adequate diet in the 1980s.

The most important change fostered by agriculture in the 1980s, in fact, may have more to do with people's attitudes than their diets. The significance of the position of the U.S. as the cornerstone of world food production may come to be more keenly felt not only by farmers and politicians but by the average citizen. Agriculture is so important to the U.S. economy, and to world economy as a whole, that a more acute awareness of the workings of agriculture, the impact of food policies, the effects of overconsumption in the affluent nations, the desperate need to foster food production in developing nations, the plight of malnourished peoples, and a host of other concerns may be the most significant "products" of agriculture in the decade ahead.

UPI

IF IT'S ALL ASPHALT IT'S NOT *OUR* FAULT!   New Jersey Farmers

Appeal against encroachment of agricultural land.

'78/'79 MONTH-BY-MONTH CHRONOLOGY

OCTOBER 1978

NATIONAL

1 / Senator Edward M. Kennedy (D.-Mass.) unveils his proposals for a national health insurance plan; companies would pay the major share of their employees' coverage, with the Federal government to bear the cost for the poor and unemployed.

2 / Supreme Court upholds a lower court's ruling that the Labor Department cannot force employers not to penalize workers who refuse to do work they consider dangerous.

3 / William and Emily Harris are sentenced in San Francisco to a minimum 10-year jail term for the 1974 abduction of heiress Patricia Hearst.

4 / House Ethics Committee clears Rep. Edward J. Patten (D.-N.J.) of all charges of campaign fraud in his dealings with South Korean influence-peddler Tongsun Park.

Council on Wage and Price Stability reports inflation reached 7 percent for the year ending August, 1978; the average American worker's purchasing power also fell by 2.5 percent, despite a 9.2 percent increase in real wages.

5 / House upholds President Carter's veto of $10.2-billion public works bill he termed "inflationary"; action is major victory for the White House's anti-inflation policy.

Senate votes to approve $116.3-billion military appropriations bill, the largest budget item passed in congressional history.

6 / Senate votes 60-36 to extend the ratification deadline for Equal Rights Amendment by 39 months from original March 22, 1979 date; passage seen as victory for feminists and the Carter Administration.

7 / Charles C. Diggs Jr. (D.-Mich.), a 12-term veteran of the House of Representatives and founder of the Congressional Black Caucus, is convicted in Washington on Federal charges of mail fraud and falsification of payroll records.

9 / Senate in a 65-20 vote approves a $142-billion across-the-board tax cut over the next five years, in addition to the $23 billion tax cut passed by the Senate finance panel; move mandates reduced Federal spending and a balanced budget by 1982.

11 / The 280,000-member American Postal Workers union votes to accept new wage pact, ending a six-month labor dispute that threatened to snowball into a nationwide mail strike.

12 / Rep. Daniel J. Flood (D.-Pa.) is indicted by a federal grand jury in Washington on 10 counts of conspiracy and bribe-taking to influence the awarding of Federal aid.

NY Times reporter Myron Farber returns to Bergen County, New Jersey jail after again refusing to turn over his files to the judge in the curare murder trials.

13 / Two Soviet employees of the United Nations are convicted in a Newark, N.J. trial of paying an undercover U.S. agent for top-secret defense documents.

14 / Senate passes energy tax bill by a 60-11 vote, after 15-hour filibuster by Sen. James Abourezk (D.-S. Dak.).

15 / House votes 337-38 to approve $18.7-billion compromise tax-cut bill, in a marathon session prior to adjournment of the 95th Congress; Senate had passed same bill previously.

Both houses of Congress approve Administration's national energy plan first sent to Capitol Hill 18 months ago; it is President Carter's biggest legislative victory since he took office.

House passes compromise version of the Humphrey-Hawkins full employment bill, setting as a national priority the reduction of unemployment to 4 percent by 1983.

16 / Supreme Court lets stand lower court ruling that free-speech guarantees allows Nazi groups to march in Skokie, Illinois, home of many World War II concentration camp survivors.

18 / President Carter announces that U.S. will begin production of the neutron bomb; but White House sources say decision has yet to be made on whether or not to deploy weapon, which kills by radiation but leaves buildings unharmed.

20 / The Firestone Tire Co. agrees to recall nearly 7.5 million of its "500" steel-belted radial tires, after structural failure allegedly resulted in 41 deaths.

24 / New Jersey jury acquits Dr. Mario E. Jascalevich of all charges in the deaths of three of his patients, allegedly by curare poisoning. Court suspends contempt citations against the New York Times and reporter Myron Farber for refusing to turn over his notes to defense attorneys.

President Carter announces Administration's voluntary anti-inflation program, which calls for a 7 percent limit to wage increases and a 5.75 percent ceiling on prices; formula will hopefully slow the annual inflation to 6.5 percent in 1979.

25 / President Carter names Civil Aeronautics Board chief Alfred Kahn to succeed Robert Strauss as head of the Administration's anti-inflation drive.

27 / President Carter signs Humphrey-Hawkins full-employment bill into law, designed to cut the jobless rate to 4 percent by 1983 and reduce inflation to 3 percent.

30 / Federal district court judge in Newark, New Jersey, sentences two Soviet UN employees to up to 50 years apiece for espionage.

INTERNATIONAL

2 / Syrian peace-keeping forces battle Christian rightists in Beirut, Lebanon, in some of the most savage fighting in the three years of civil strife.

Vietnam rejects Cambodian offer of peace talks to settle border disputes, branding Phnom Penh a "reactionary" and "anti-Communist" regime guilty of mass murder.

4 / Over 100,000 attend simple funeral services for Pope John Paul I in the Vatican's St. Peter's Square.

5 / Israeli gunboats shell Syrian positions in and around Beirut, in move to lift siege of Christian military forces.

6 / UN Security Council calls for a cease-fire between Syrian and Christian forces in Lebanon; move backed by U.S., which fears fighting may jeopardize Camp David accords.

7 / Talks in Damascus between Syrian President Hafez al-Assad and Lebanese President Elias Sarkis result in new cease-fire between Syrian-dominated Arab League troops and Christian militia forces.

8 / Israel's Cabinet names Foreign Minister Moshe Dayan and Defense Minister Ezer Weizman to head that nation's delegation to the Washington peace talks with Egypt.

9 / Secretary of State Cyrus Vance meets with Rhodesia's Prime Minister Ian Smith in Washington; but talks fail to gain U.S. backing for Smith's interim government.

12 / Mideast peace talks between Egypt and Israel open in Washington under U.S. auspices; progress reported in initial talks between Secretary Vance and Israeli and Egyptian negotiators.

13 / Lebanese army units enter Christian suburbs of Beirut, taking up buffer positions between Syrian and rightist Christian forces in attempt to enforce cease-fire plan.

14 / President Carter assails Arab states withholding support for Camp David accords, saying they seek to block a separate peace treaty between Egypt and Israel.

15 / College of Cardinals meet in Rome conclave to elect a new Pope, but fail after two ballots to quickly name successor to the late Pope John Paul I.

16 / Karol Cardinal Wojtyla, 58, Archbishop of Cracow, is chosen by College of Cardinals in Rome as the 264th Pope of the Roman Catholic Church, the first Polish Pontiff and the first non-Italian elected Pope in 455 years. A moderate prelate known for his strong anti-Communist views and pastoral and administrative abilities, he assumes the papal title of Pope John Paul II.

17 / Foreign ministers of the Arab League states agree on 8-point plan for a cease-fire in Beirut, Lebanon; terms include withdrawal of Syrian units of Arab peace-keeping force and their replacement by Saudi troops.

Pope John Paul II in first policy statement of his Vatican reign, pledges to carry on reforms of Vatican Council II, but warns he will not permit basic doctrines to be undermined.

19 / South Africa agrees to compromise in pre-independence elections for Namibia (South-West Africa), which are to include two ballots: a Dec. 4 South African-sponsored election and a UN-supervised poll in the near future.

Rhodesian warplanes strike at nationalist guerrilla bases near Lusaka, Zambia; guerrilla leader Joshua Nkomo claims raid "kills hundreds," mostly civilians.

20 / Biracial transition government in Salisbury agrees to joint U.S.-British plan to discuss majority rule government with leaders of the Patriotic Front guerrillas.

22 / Israeli and Egyptian negotiators announce tentative agreement on the text of a Middle East peace treaty.

Deputy Premier Deng Xiaoping arrives in Tokyo for formal ratification of the Sino-Japanese friendship treaty, the first top-ranking Chinese Communist leader to visit Japan.

23 / U.S. Secretary of State Cyrus R. Vance and Soviet Foreign Minister Andrei Gromyko end two days of talks on strategic arms limitations; both sides term meeting as "constructive."

25 / Israeli Cabinet approves tentative peace treaty with Egypt, in accordance with proposed modifications outlined by Prime Minister Menachem Begin.

26 / Syria and Iraq sign a "charter for joint national action" in Baghdad, pledging opposition to proposed Egyptian-Israeli peace agreement.

Israeli government reveals plans to expand Jewish settlements in the occupied West Bank of the Jordan, raising new obstacles to concluding peace treaty with Egypt.

27 / Nobel Committee in Oslo, Norway, awards the 1978 Nobel Peace Prize jointly to President Anwar Sadat and Prime Minister Menachem Begin; committee notes President Carter's "great role" in promoting Middle East peace.

28 / Foreign Minister of the German Democratic Republic Oskar Rischer meets with Pope John Paul II in Rome, the first visit by an East German official to the Vatican.

31 / Tanzania claims Ugandan troops have invaded its territory in the Lake Victoria region, penetrating 18 miles to the town of Kyanka.

Spain's Cortes (parliment) approves by overwhelming margin a new Constitution — that nation's tenth since 1808 — for voter ratification by a national referendum due in December.

NOVEMBER 1978

NATIONAL

1 / White House unveils plan to bolster falling exchange rate of the U.S. dollar; proposals include an increase in the Federal Reserve Board discount rate, a $30 billion currency support program, and expanded sale of Treasury gold reserves.

6 / The *New York Times* and *Daily News* resume publication after an 89-day strike by pressmen; union accepts cut in manning in exchange for wage increases and job security guarantees.

7 / Republicans score modest gains in Congressional elections, gaining 12 House and three Senate seats; Democrats retain control of Congress with a 276-159 majority in the House and a 59-41 edge in the Senate. Republicans win six new governorships to increase their total to 18; Democrats retain control of 32 remaining state houses. Voter turnout around the nation is light; local referenda for ERA and gay rights provisions are defeated. Philadelphia voters reject proposed charter revision that would allow Mayor Frank L. Rizzo a third term.

8 / Investigations into mismanagement in the Small Business Administration reveal poor fiscal management has cost $3.5 million in unrecoverable revenue, and may jeopardize $50 million designated for minority businesses.

9 / President Carter says he will boost the defense budget three percent but cut overall Federal spending in fiscal 1980; projected deficit woud be trimmed by $10 billion, to just under $30 billion for 1980.

AFL-CIO president George Meany assails President Carter as "the most conservative President I have seen in my lifetime," accusing him of combating inflation by promoting increased unemployment.

12 / President Carter tentatively approves plan to strengthen U.S. civil defense preparedness, designed to protect up to 140 million Americans in case of a nuclear attack; the new program would cost $2 billion by 1984.

13 / National Cancer Institute study shows ethylene dibromide, a gasoline additive also used in crop fumigants, to be the most carcinogenic substance yet found, indicating it poses a potential threat to human health.

15 / President Carter approves a $123.8 billion defense budget for fiscal 1980; the three percent increase over 1979 spending is designed to strengthen NATO and U.S. forces in Europe.

17 / Ex-CIA employee William Kampiles, 23, is convicted of selling top-secret government documents to the Soviet Union; Kampiles faces a possible life prison sentence.

20 / White House science panel urges President Carter to adopt program for development of a mobile, airborne intercontinental missile system which would cost $40-50 billion by the mid-1980s.

Representative Charles C. Diggs Jr. (D.-Mich.), is sentenced to three years imprisonment for defrauding the government in an employee kickback scheme; a senior black Congressman who is appealing his conviction, Diggs was overwhelmingly re-elected by his Detroit constituency November 7.

22 / President Carter is said to criticize U.S. intelligence agencies for their apparent failure to foresee foreign political crises; comments are prompted by the CIA's inability to predict widespread unrest in Iran or to provide information on the anti-Shah opposition.

23 / Fifteen prominent black leaders call on President Carter to discuss their concerns with reports that social programs to aid minorities are to be sharply cut in the 1980 Federal budget.

24 / Peace Corps director Dr. Carolyn R. Payton, 53, the first black to head that agency, resigns after policy disputes with her boss, Sam Brown, who heads ACTION, the umbrella agency for volunteer Federal social programs.

27 / San Francisco Mayor George Moscone and supervisor Harvey Milk are shot to death in their City Hall offices; former supervisor Dan White, an ex-fireman and police officer, is later charged with both murders.

U.S. Supreme Court declines to review contempt convictions of the *New York Times* and reporter Myron Farber, for refusal to surrender his notes to defense attorneys in the New Jersey murder trial of Dr. Mario Jascalevich; decision upholds lower court ruling that reporters have no absolute Constitutional privilege to withhold information demanded in a criminal case.

29 / President Carter announces a new ceiling of $8.43 billion on U.S. arms sales to non-U.S.-allied countries for fiscal 1979 — a cut of 8 percent.

Commerce Department reports that October's trade deficit reached $2.13 billion, bringing the overall U.S. trade deficit for 1978 to $24.8 billion so far.

30 / President Carter in a White House press conference concedes that U.S. economic growth for 1979 might fall below the three percent rate predicted by Administration economists, but says that problem alone will not lead to another recession in 1979.

INTERNATIONAL

1 / President Idi Amin says Uganda has annexed a 710-square mile strip of Tanzanian territory, bordering the western shore of Lake Victoria and the Kagera River.

2 / Arab League states — excluding Egypt — hold summit conference in Baghdad, Iraq to discuss a unified strategy vis-a-vis the imminent Egyptian-Israeli peace accord.

Chile and Argentina end six-month negotiations on contested islands in the Beagle Channel deadlocked; although both sides have mobilized militarily, both pledge to continue to seek a peaceful settlement.

3 / Vietnam and Soviet Union sign friendship and mutual cooperation treaty in Moscow; Hanoi reports border clash with Chinese troops in the disputed Friendship Pass area.

5 / The Shah of Iran places nation under military rule after Premier Jaafar Sharif Emani resigns under pressure of continuing anti-Shah demonstrations.

Austrian voters by a narrow margin halt opening of the country's first nuclear power plant, built in the Danube River basin 25 miles northwest of Vienna.

Chinese Deputy Premier Deng Xiaoping arrives in Bangkok for talks with Thai government, beginning a three-nation tour of Southeast Asia in effort to counter Soviet and Vietnamese influence in that region.

6 / Shah Mohammad Reza Pahlavi appoints army chief Gen. Gholam Reza Azhari to head military government in Iran; the Ayatollah Khomeini, exiled Shi'ite Muslim leader, says in Paris he will call on his supporters to stage "civil war" to overthrow the Shah.

7 / Former prime minister Indira Gandhi wins parliamentary seat in southern Indian state of Karnataka, signaling a possible comeback for her Congress party faction.

South Africa's Black Affairs Minister Cornelius Mulder resigns amid scandal involving misappropriation of government funds and other abuses within the Information Ministry which he headed.

8 / Israeli Cabinet rejects "linkage" between the tentative peace treaty with Egypt and future steps towards an overall Arab-Israeli peace settlement.

Shah of Iran orders the arrest of former premier Amir Abbas Hoveida and calls for top-level inquiry into the business dealings of the imperial family.

Argentina accepts Chilean proposal to seek third-party mediation in dispute over Beagle Channel islands.

11 / Iran's military regime arrests opposition National Front leader Karim Sanjabi, who has repeatedly refused to cooperate with the present government.

Nicaragua's President Anastasio Somoza Debayle calls for national plebiscite to test electoral strength of anti-government forces; Broad Opposition Front rejects bid because it does not include Somoza's resignation.

Tanzanian forces counterattack against Ugandan troops in the Kagera River area.

12 / Government orders 35,000 striking Iranian oil workers to return to work or face dismissal; strikers, who had demanded higher wages and freedom for all political prisoners, return to work under military pressure.

Deng Xiaoping arrives in Singapore on last stop of his Southeast Asian tour, after receiving a chilly official reception in Malaysia Nov. 9.

13 / UN Security Council votes censure of South Africa, warning Pretoria that it will face sanctions unless it agrees to UN-supervised elections in South-West Africa (Namibia).

14 / South African Prime Minister P. W. Botha appoints a moderate, Pieter G. Koornhof, to succeed Cornelius Mulder as Black Affairs minister.

16 / Rhodesia's biracial government postpones scheduled Dec. 31 elections for majority rule until April 20, 1979, in order to draft a new constitution.

Officials of both Germanys in East Berlin conclude $2 billion agreement allowing uninterrupted access between West Berlin and the Federal Republic.

17 / Soviet President Leonid I. Brezhnev tells visiting U.S. Senators that the USSR tested a neutron weapon "many years ago," but that it was never put into production.

Inter-American Commission on Human Rights accuses Nicaraguan government of flagrant rights violations, including the torture and execution of its political opponents.

18 / Congressman Leo Ryan (D.-California) and four members of his party are killed in ambush at a jungle airstrip in northern Guyana; group was departing from an investigation into Jonestown, a religious commune run by the San Francisco-based People's Temple.

19 / Wall posters in Peking accuse the late Chairman Mao Zedong of supporting the "Gang of Four," the first time the Chinese Communist leader has been linked to that hard-line group.

20 / Guyanese troops find 300 to 400 bodies of Jonestown cultists at that jungle settlement, all apparent suicides in a bizarre mass ritual, including leader Rev. Jim Jones.

21 / Israeli Cabinet approves draft peace treaty with Egypt, but rejects President Sadat's demands that it be linked to a timetable for Palestinian autonomy in the West Bank and Gaza.

Costa Rica severs diplomatic relations with Nicaragua after border clash kills one Costa Rican security guard and leaves two wounded.

22 / Cuban President Fidel Castro tells exile representatives he will release 3,000 political prisoners providing the U.S. will accept all those released; U.S. promises to speed up processing of Cuban emigres.

Portugal's President Ramahlo Eanes swears in Carlos Mota Pinto as the country's new prime minister; Mota will head 15-member cabinet composed mostly of independents.

24 / Bolivian army ousts four-month government of Gen. Juan Pereda Asbun; Army chief Gen. David Padilla Aranciba heads three-man junta, which promises prompt elections and a return to civilian rule.

25 / Death toll estimate for Jonestown mass suicide rises to final count of over 900; U.S. authorities say lack of autopsies leaves exact cause of death unclear, with the possibility of deaths having been coerced remaining.

28 / Romanian President Nicolae Ceausescu rejects bid by Soviets to join six other Warsaw Pact nations in raising military spending.

Vietnamese troops continue to advance into Cambodian territory, with a major offensive against Phnom Penh likely.

30 / Chinese leaders order crackdown on Peking wall poster campaign, that has demanded more democracy and criticized Communist Party Chairman Hua Guofeng and the late Mao Zedong.

The *Times* of London suspends publication after contract talks with rebellious employees is stalemated; management says presses will not roll until all 65 bargaining units of the nine employee unions agree to an end to work stoppages as part of the new contract.

DECEMBER 1978

NATIONAL

1 / President Carter by executive order turns over 56 million acres of Federal land in Alaska to the National Park system, barring development of oil or mineral deposits without Congressional authorization; it is largest conservation move undertaken by a President.

4 / Black leaders warn Pres. Carter in White House meeting they are "distressed" that the Administration's anti-inflation fight will mean cuts in social programs; Carter says he intends to continue Federal programs that stress economic progress for minorities.

5 / FBI director William H. Webster dismisses two bureau supervisors involved in illegal surveillance of fugitive radicals in the 1970s, but rules out action against 59 agents involved in those activities who believed they were following legitimate orders.

7 / Federal appeals court in Washington rules against the arbitrary dismissal of homosexuals from the armed forces "without . . . explanation;" Pentagon legal experts say ruling complicates problem by failing to overturn statutes barring homosexuals from military service.

10 / President Carter wins party backing for his budgetary plans at midterm Democratic convention in Memphis; liberal criticisms of Administration spending cuts are muted when Vice-President Walter Mondale promises close scrutiny of Pentagon budgetary increases.

11 / President Carter tells nine Black leaders that budget cuts in social programs that aid minorities have not been finalized, holding out hopes that cuts in domestic spending will not be drastic.

12 / Cleveland's Mayor Dennis J. Kucinich presents city banks with fiscal reorganization designed to keep the city from defaulting on $15.5 million in debt payments due by Dec. 15; proposals include a 50 percent hike in city income taxes, and issuing $90 million in city bonds by 1979.

13 / Administration asks Congress for legislation to bar surprise police searches of news offices for materials intended for publication.

16 / Cleveland's Mayor Kucinich announces plans to lay off 3,000-5,000 city employees following municipal default on $15.5 million in loan repayments; cutbacks follow refusal by the city council and Cleveland's main creditors to back Kucinich's financial rescue plan.

17 / Defense Secretary Harold Brown proposes overhaul of the military pension system to limit the amounts retirees may receive after 20 years' service, as a first step towards trimming the rapidly expanding Pentagon budget.

Cleveland's major unions threaten a possible general strike if Mayor Dennis Kucinich proceeds with drastic cuts in the city's workforce to reverse default.

19 / Cleveland's Mayor Kucinich, attempting to forestall city bankruptcy, offers to place sale of municipally-owned electric light plant to a public vote if the city council agrees to a referendum on raising city income taxes.

20 / National Conference of Democratic Mayors sharply criticizes White House budget plans to cut domestic programs to reduce the Federal deficit to $30 billion.

21 / House assassination panel sources reveal that committee has received additional evidence that more than one gunman was involved in the 1963 assassination of President John F. Kennedy.

22 / President Carter restores $2 billion to the social welfare budget, responding to appeals from urban mayors and minority groups that those programs not be cut in the next fiscal year.

Cleveland's city council approves a February 27 referendum on emergency revenue measures in a compromise with Mayor Dennis Kucinich.

27 / President Carter cuts budget for proposed expansion of civil defense programs to $115 million — down from a projected $2 billion and Administration doubts that programs could effectively protect most Americans.

28 / Administration sets voluntary goal to limit rate increases in patient charges for hospital costs to 9.7 percent in 1979, with mandatory controls on hospital operating costs to be sought.

Mayor Kucinich cancels layoff of 2,000 Cleveland municipal workers slated for January 1979, after the city's biggest creditor agrees not to seek payment on a defaulted $5 million loan until after the Feb. 27 referendum on city funding measures.

30 / The House Select Committee on Assassinations reports its conclusions, that both President Kennedy and the Rev. Dr. Martin Luther King Jr. were killed "as a result of a conspiracy."

President Carter proposes cutbacks in some future Social Security benefits to trim the 1980 Federal budget; elimination of lump-sum death benefits and other cuts would save $900 million that year, and $5 billion annually by 1985.

INTERNATIONAL

2 / Riots break out in Iran at start of the holy month of Moharram; troops fire on massive demonstrations, killing as many as 67.

Boat packed with Vietnamese refugees sinks off Malaysia, drowning 143; Kuala Lumpur allows 2,500 "boat people" to move into temporary camps after U.S. offers to accept those unable to find permanent refuge elsewhere.

3 / Radio Hanoi announces formation of the Kampuchean United Front for National Salvation in the "liberated" zone of Cambodia, which calls for the overthrow of the present Khmer Rouge government in Phnom Penh.

4 / Israel rejects any renegotiation of current draft peace treaty with Egypt; but Prime Minister Begin says Jerusalem would consider talks on accompanying protocols dealing with the status of the West Bank and Gaza.

5 / Afghanistan and the Soviet Union sign a 20-year treaty of friendship and cooperation that promises closer economic and military ties between the two countries.

6 / Spanish voters approve nation's first democratic constitution in 40 years by a 2-to-1 margin; referendum is marred by separatist violence in northwestern Basque provinces and low voter turnouts there and in Catalonia, where nationalist sentiment is also strong.

7 / Masayoshi Ohira is elected Prime Minister by Japan's parliament, following bitter conflict within ruling Liberal Democratic party over Ohira's patronage appointments to important party posts.

8 / Golda Meir, 80, a founder and major leader of Israel's Labor party who served as that country's Prime Minister in 1969-74, dies in Jerusalem after being hospitalized for liver failure.

10 / Secretary of State Cyrus Vance and Egypt's President Anwar Sadat meet near Cairo in first round of talks designed to restart stalled Egyptian-Israeli peace talks.

Opponents of the Shah of Iran march by the hundreds of thousands in mourning procession in Tehran; demonstration is allowed by authorities to avoid violence.

11 / Rhodesia launches air strikes on guerrilla arms depot in Mozambique; Maputo radio claims 26 killed, including many civilians.

12 / Clashes between anti-Shah demonstrators and troops leave 40 dead in Isfahan as widespread strike in Iran's southern oil fields brings production to a near-halt.

14 / Vietnamese forces invade Cambodia, advancing 70 miles into Kehmer Rouge territory and threatening to cut Phnom Penh's vital supply link to China by severing the highway connecting the capital to major port of Kompong Som.

15 / President Carter announces U.S. will establish full diplomatic relations with China on Jan. 1; recognition of Peking will mean terminating relations with Taiwan and abrogation of the U.S.-Taiwan mutual defense treaty.

Israeli Cabinet rejects newest U.S.-backed Egyptian peace proposals, but leaves open the possibility of resuming negotiations at a later date.

16 / Congressional conservatives blast President Carter's decision to sever U.S.-Taiwan defense treaty; opposition is likely to hinder Senate approval of the SALT-II accord with the Soviet Union.

19 / President Carter says that Moscow supports U.S. move to normalize relations with China, and that Soviet Pres. Leonid Brezhnev considers it "positive," despite negative articles in the official Soviet press.

Indira Gandhi is jailed by India's Parliament after being expelled from its current session, over charges that while Prime Minister she harassed officials during a 1975 investigation into her son Sanjay's business dealings.

20 / Two armed men hijack airliner in northern India, demanding the release of Indira Gandhi, as thousands protest against the former Prime Minister's arrest.

Israeli jets attack Palestinian bases in and around the southern Lebanese port of Tyre, in response to recent terrorist attacks inside Israel.

21 / Palestinian guerrillas launch rocket attack on northern Israeli settlement of Qiryat Shemona in retalia-

tion for air strikes against their bases in southern Lebanon.

22 / South Korea announces amnesty for 4,000 prisoners; list includes opposition leader Kim Dae Jung and 106 other political detainees.

23 / U.S.-Soviet arms limitation talks end in Geneva with some progress reported but no final agreement on the terms of the final SALT-II accords.

Argentina and Chile accept mediation of a papal envoy to settle the dispute over possession of three islands in the Beagle Channel.

24 / Efforts to revive stalled Mideast peace talks fail in Brussels, but U.S., Israel and Egypt agree to maintain contacts and avoid counterproductive rhetoric.

26 / Moscow denies allegation that it has delayed conclusion of SALT-II agreement with the U.S. because of its concern over American recognition of China.

Turkey's parliament imposes martial law in 13 southeastern cities after clashes between rival Muslim sects leave 97 dead and over 1,000 injured.

27 / U.S. mission to discuss future relations with Taiwan is attacked by anti-American mobs upon arrival in Taipei; delegation lead by State Department official William Christopher will seek a framework for nonofficial ties with Nationalist China after termination of diplomatic relations.

South Africa agrees to cooperate with a United Nations plan for Namibian independence by 1979; agreement includes a UN peacekeeping force to supervise pre-independence elections.

Algeria's President Houari Boumediene, spokesman for the third world who ruled Algeria since 1965, dies in Algiers after nearly six weeks in a coma.

28 / Strikes and demonstrations paralyze Iran as the government institutes fuel rationing caused by the total shutdown of production by oil workers.

29 / Shah of Iran empowers long-time opponent Shahpur Bakhtiar to form a civilian coalition government.

U.S. orders a Navy task force out of the Philippines in preparation for move into the Persian Gulf if political situation in Iran warrants; action seen to counter possible Soviet actions.

Talks in Taipei fail to achieve agreement on framework for future U.S.-Taiwan relations.

30 / Iran's premier-designate Shahpur Bakhtiar says a new civilian government will be formed by next week, after which the Shah of Iran will then leave Iran for an extended period, turning power over to a regency council.

31 / Washington denies that American citizens in Iran have been ordered "evacuated," after U.S. Ambassador William Sullivan recommends that U.S. dependents return home at least temporarily.

Communist China calls on Taiwan to establish commercial and other ties with the mainland as a first step towards eventual reunification of the two Chinas.

JANUARY 1979

NATIONAL

2 / White House says President Carter will resubmit to Congress a bill providing $150 million in counter-cyclical revenue-sharing aid to cities with high unemployment.

3 / White House restores cuts in Federal health programs following appeals from HEW officials and public criticism by Senator Edward M. Kennedy.

4 / Civil damage suit in the 1970 shooting of thirteen students at Kent State University is settled out of court, with Ohio authorities to pay $675,000 to victims and surviving relatives. Gov. James Rhodes and 27 National Guardsmen also sign statement regretting incident during protests against the U.S. invasion of Cambodia in which four died.

5 / Energy Department sues the nation's nine largest oil companies, alleging they had overcharged consumers by nearly $1 billion since 1973; companies claim they followed regulations and deny price-gouging charges.

6 / Interior Secretary Cecil D. Andrus announces a six-month delay in implementing environmental controls on strip mining; delay is opposed by environmentalists.

8 / President Carter rejects request by Defense Secretary Harold Brown for construction of a new 90,000-ton supercarrier, and orders Pentagon officials to begin plans for building a new fleet of smaller carriers.

9 / Supreme Court rules 6-3 to overturn as "unconstitutionally vague" a Pennsylvania abortion law requiring doctors to select procedures most likely to preserve viable fetal life or face criminal penalties.

11 / U.S. Surgeon General Dr. Julius B. Richmond issues massive report citing "overwhelming proof" that links smoking to such health hazards as lung cancer, heart disease and possible fetal deformities.

Federal appeals court overturns conviction of Maryland Governor Marvin Mandel and five co-defendants on bribery and mail fraud charges.

White House disassociates President Carter from brother Billy's "embarrassing" public statements as host to touring Libyan businessmen.

Major oil producers and the Oil, Chemical and Atomic Workers union reach agreement on new contract, which incorporates Federal guidelines limiting overall wage increases to an annual 7 percent.

12 / President Carter dismisses Bella S. Abzug as co-chairwoman of the National Advisory Committee on Women, after its members had criticized Administration policies; 23 of NACW's 39 members resign in show of support for Mrs. Abzug.

14 / President Carter, speaking at Atlanta commemorative on the 50th birthday of slain civil rights leader Dr. Martin Luther King Jr., calls on Congress to designate King's birthday — Jan. 15 — a national holiday.

16 / President Carter names Marjorie Bell Chambers to replace Bella Abzug as head of the National Advisory Committee on Women.

17 / Governor-elect Lamar Alexander of Tennessee is sworn into office three days early, after a Federal probe implicates outgoing Gov. Ray Blanton in an alleged pardon-selling scheme; Blanton had recently pardoned 52 convicts.

18 / Dealings between President Carter's peanut business and the Georgia bank once headed by Bert Lance are questioned; report discloses that in 1975 the Carter warehouse retained assets while remaining delinquent on loans that should have been repaid to the bank. White House spokesmen say Carter was unaware of those practices.

19 / Nuclear Regulatory Commission withdraws support for a 1975 study minimizing the possibility of serious nuclear reactor accidents, calling it "unreliable."

22 / President Carter submits "lean" Federal budget to Congress that includes cuts in social programs and a 3 percent increase in defense spending, warning that "real sacrifices" are needed to slow inflation.

23 / President Carter in his State of the Union address urges Congress to help his Administration build a "new foundation" for the future by controlling inflation and supporting the projected SALT-II pact with the U.S.S.R.

Republican National Committee picks Detroit as site for party's 1980 convention; chairman Bill Brock says choice emphasizes the GOP's campaign to win over urban and black voters.

24 / John B. Connolly, former Texas governor and Secretary of the Treasury, announces his candidacy for the Republican Presidential nomination in 1980.

26 / Nelson A. Rockefeller, former U.S. Vice-President and Governor of New York, scion of the Rockefeller fortune who had long sought the nation's highest office, dies of a heart attack in his Manhattan (N.Y.) townhouse.

30 / Poll conducted by the *New York Times* and CBS News shows Americans support President Carter's trim budget by a two-thirds margin, but that only an even majority see Carter as a strong President.

INTERNATIONAL

1 / Resumption of formal diplomatic relations between the U.S. and China is celebrated in both Washington and Peking.

2 / Iranian troops replace striking air traffic controllers in Tehran, allowing exit of over 2,000 stranded foreigners from the country.

3 / U.S. State Department announces backing for Cambodia's request for a meeting of the UN Security Council to discuss Vietnam's invasion of its territory.

5 / China moves troops and fighter planes to border with Vietnam in response to Hanoi's continued invasion of Cambodia.

Shah of Iran installs new civilian government in Tehran with Shahpur Bakhtiar as premier; oil shipments begin to increase after weeks of virtually no production.

Prime Minister James Callaghan tells four-power summit on world affairs in Guadeloupe that Britain is to sell China jet fighters as part of a $2 billion trade package.

6 / Joint statement by leaders of U.S., France, Britain and West Germany concluding Guadeloupe conference reassures the Soviet Union that normalization of U.S.-China relations will not threaten commitment to detente.

7 / Hanoi radio announces the capture of Phnom Penh by anti-Khmer Rouge forces backed by regular Vietnamese troops.

Rioting continues in Iran despite the coming to power of the new civilian government; soldiers battle followers of exiled Muslim leader Khomeini.

8 / Prince Norodom Sihanouk in Peking calls for UN intervention to expel Vietnamese troops from Cambodia; a prisoner of the Khmer Rouge for three years, he says all Cambodians now face common threat from Vietnam.

9 / China's Deputy Premier Deng Xiaoping pledges to allow Taiwan full autonomy in any future unification with the mainland, in return for Taipei's renunciation of Taiwan's sovereignty.

10 / U.S. dispatches a dozen advanced F-15 fighters and a 300-man Air Force contingent to Saudi Arabia at Riyadh's request, in response to Saudi fears of instability in Iran and growing Soviet influence in the region.

Romania splits with Soviet bloc and denounces the Vietnamese invasion of Cambodia, branding it "a heavy blow for the prestige of socialism" and a threat to detente.

11 / Premier Shahpur Bakhtiar says Iran's new government will seek stronger ties with the Arab world and will support Palestinian self-determination; he also pledges to ease martial law, grant more political freedoms and schedule early elections for full civilian rule.

Prince Sihanouk appeals to the UN Security Council for help against the Vietnamese invasion of Cambodia.

14 / Washington sources disclose that U.S. will continue unofficial relations with Taiwan through the newly-established American Institute in Taipei.

15 / Israel establishes three new military settlements in the occupied territories, despite U.S. and Egypt's protests that move jeopardizes resumption of Mideast peace talks.

Soviet Union vetoes a UN Security Council resolution calling for Vietnamese withdrawal from Cambodia.

16 / Shah Mohammad Reza Pahlavi leaves Iran for "extended vacation" viewed as virtual permanent exile. Hundreds of thousands throng Tehran to celebrate Shah's departure.

17 / President Carter endorses Iran's new civilian government, calling on exiled opposition leader Ayatollah Khomeini to give present government a chance to rule.

18 / Ayatollah Khomeini rejects White House appeal to work with Iran's new government, ruling out any future negotiations with the Bakhtiar regime.

19 / Israeli troops attack PLO bases in Lebanon in retaliation for Jan. 18 terrorist bombing in Jerusalem; guerrillas reply by shelling two northern Israeli towns.

21 / Inter-American Human Rights Commission accuses El Salvador's military regime with murdering and torturing its opponents and of "persecuting" the Roman Catholic Church.

22 / Palestinian terrorist leader Ali Hassan Salemeh—regarded as the mastermind of the "Black September" attack on the Israeli Olympic team in 1972—dies in a bomb explosion in Beirut which claims nine other lives.

British municipal workers stage a 24-hour walkout; strike increases the disruption begun Jan. 8 by a nationwide truck drivers' strike, which had plunged Britain into its worst labor unrest since 1974.

23 / Israelis fire on guerrilla bases in Lebanon, in the heaviest shelling there since invasion of March, 1978.

25 / 250,000 attend outdoor mass as Pope John Paul II arrives in Santo Domingo on his way to open conference of Latin American bishops in Mexico City.

26 / Troops in Tehran fire on pro-Khomeini marchers; 15 are killed as army tries to enforce ban on demonstrations.

27 / Pope John Paul II opens Latin American bishop's conference, calling for a more traditional direction for hemisphere's Roman Catholics.

28 / Ayatollah Khomeini again rejects overtures by Premier Bakhtiar to settle differences between Iran's government and the religious opposition; troops fire on student demonstrators at Tehran University, killing 28.

Special Mideast envoy Alfred Atherton returns to Washington after negotiations fail to break impasse in Egyptian-Israeli peace talks.

29 / Talks open in Washington between China's Deputy Premier Deng Xiaoping and President Carter; discussions focus on China's concerns over U.S.-Soviet relations and the SALT-II treaty. Former President Richard M. Nixon attends White House dinner honoring Deng, at the behest of President Carter.

Pope John Paul II vows to speak for the world's poor and oppressed in address before audience of 15,000 Indians in Oaxaca, Mexico.

30 / Iranian government authorizes the return of Ayatollah Khomeini from exile; U.S. orders evacuation of all American dependents and non-essential U.S. personnel from Iran.

White Rhodesians vote to accept limited black-majority rule by April, 1979; approval of new constitution will allow for a freely elected black-led government with extensive built-in safeguards for whites.

31 / President Carter and Vice-Premier Deng sign two U.S.-Chinese accords on scientific and cultural exchanges, indicating what Carter calls "a new and irreversible course" in Washington-Peking relations.

Algeria's ruling Revolutionary Council names acting Defense Minister Col. Benjedid Chadli, a moderate, to succeed the late President Houari Boumediene.

FEBRUARY 1979

NATIONAL

1 / Patricia Hearst is released from Federal prison near San Francisco under clemency order by President Carter, after serving 22 months of her seven-year sentence.

3 / Mistrial is declared in the case of Representative Daniel J. Flood (D.-Pa.) in a Washington, D.C. federal trial on bribery, conspiracy and perjury charges after a deadlocked jury fails to return a verdict.

5 / Farmers demonstrate in Washington to press demands for increased Federal price supports, and clash with police as their tractor caravan stalls city traffic.

6 / Sara Jane Moore, serving a life sentence for her 1975 assassination attempt on President Ford, escapes from a Federal prison in Anderson, W. Va., but is quickly recaptured.

8 / Justice Department drops perjury charges against a former executive of I.T.T. involving that corporation's alleged bid to block Salvadore Allende's election as President of Chile in 1970, fearing possible disclosures regarding U.S. intelligence activities.

10 / Federal grand jury hears details of President Carter's family business from financial trustee Charles Kirbo; probe into possible campaign irregularities discloses that the Carter peanut warehouse received large loans from the National Bank of Georgia in 1975 and 1976, then headed by Bert Lance. White

House spokesmen deny that any of the borrowed money found its way into Carter's Presidential campaign.

14 / Two Cuban exiles are convicted in Miami for murder in the 1976 Washington slaying of Orlando Letelier, a former Chilean official in the Allende government who was a leading opponent of Chile's military regime.

15 / Justice Department affirms it will seek a retrial of the bribery-perjury case of 16-term Congressman Daniel Flood, after his first trial ended in a hung jury amid widening reports of possible jury-tampering.

HEW Secretary Joseph Califano backs study proposing reforms in the Social Security benefits system to eliminate sex discrimination.

16 / New Orleans police vote to resume strike that had ended earlier this month, threatening cancellation of Mardi Gras festivities; court bars walkout by 1,350 unionized police officers.

GAO report to Senator Alan Cranston's inquiry into Jonestown massacre reveals that as many as 17 of the children placed in People's Temple foster homes by California authorities died in the Guyana commune.

19 / Unexpected snowstorm strikes the East Coast, dumping 13-30 inches on New York-New Jersey area and burying Washington under nearly two feet of snow, shutting down the nation's capital.

22 / AFL-CIO officials say the federation plans to challenge the Carter Administration's voluntary wage-price controls in court, contending they force companies to hold down real wages.

23 / Consumer prices are reported to have risen .9 percent in January, averaging a 12 percent annual hike in the cost of living, indicating that Federal wage-price guidelines have not halted the tide of inflation.

Files of the White House's Office of Telecommunications from 1969 to 1974 — released under Freedom of Information Act — reveal a concerted campaign by the Nixon Administration to politically control public broadcasting.

24 / Joshua Eilberg, former Democaric congressman from Pennsylvania, is sentenced to five years probation and fined $10,000 after pleading guilty to charges that while in office he illegally accepted money for helping his former law firm obtain a $14.5 million grant for a Philadelphia hospital.

25 / President Carter disavows comments made recently by brother Billy, widely regarded as anti-Semitic, saying he regrets them and that they do not reflect his views.

26 / Republican caucus at National Governors Association meeting calls for a balanced Federal budget, and asks Congress to study proposals for a constitutional amendment to limit spending.

27 / Cleveland voters approve a 50 percent increase in city taxes to bail out the financially strapped city government and the retention of the city-owned municipal electrical utility; results seen as victory for Mayor Dennis J. Kucinich, who campaigned for both measures.

Study by the National Academy of Sciences recommends restrictions but no ban on use of the artificial sweetener Saccharin, which has caused cancer in laboratory rats.

28 / Jane M. Byrne defeats incumbent Michael A. Bilandic in Chicago's Democratic primary for Mayor, a major upset for the old-line Daley political machine.

INTERNATIONAL

1 / The Ayatollah Khomeini returns to Iran after 15 years of exile; he denounces Bakhtiar government as nearly three million flock to greet him in Tehran.

3 / Republican leaders at national conference vote to drop bipartisan foreign policy stance and make Soviet conduct a key issue in negotiating a new SALT agreement.

4 / China and Vietnam reinforce border patrols with regular troops and armored units, in preparation for possible stepped-up clashes in the Friendship Pass area.

5 / Ayatollah Khomeini names opposition figure Mehdi Bazargan as head of a "provisional government," and calls for elections to a new constituent assembly as a step towards making Iran an Islamic republic.

Chinese Deputy Premier Deng Xiaoping ends nine-day U.S. tour, asserting that expanded cooperation between the two countries will be forthcoming.

6 / Pakistan's Supreme Court upholds the death sentence of former Premier Zulfikar Ali Bhutto, convicted of complicity in a 1974 political murder.

7 / State Department report to Congress claims Israel has suspended some human-rights guarantees in the occupied Arab territories, with some political detainees being mistreated; Israel denies allegations.

8 / One million march in Tehran to demand ouster of Premier Shahpur Bakhtiar; Bakhtiar vows not to accede to opposition demands for his resignation.

Washington terminates military ties with Nicaragua because of Pres. Anastasio Somoza's refusal to accept U.S. or OAS mediation of that country's civil strife.

10 / Iran edges closer to all-out civil war after air force cadets and technicians outside Tehran defect to the opposition; over 100 are killed in fighting between military and armed civilians.

11 / Premier Bakhtiar resigns as head of Iran's government after the army declares its neutrality in the current political crisis; over 200 die as loyal government troops continue to battle supporters of the Ayatollah Khomeini.

Defense Secretary Harold Brown tells Saudi Arabian leaders that the U.S. will send more arms to Yemen and Sudan to help stabilize the military balance of power in the Persian Gulf and the Middle East.

12 / Pro-Khomeini forces seize major military bases in Tehran, effectively gaining control of Iran after two days of heavy fighting; the Ayatollah broadcasts appeal for an end to violence and a return to order.

13 / Conference of Roman Catholic bishops ends in Puebla, Mexico with call for increased social activism on behalf of Latin America's poor, and plea for the peaceful resolution of inter-American disputes.

14 / U.S. Ambassador to Afghanistan Adolph Dubs is slain after his abduction by right-wing Muslim terrorists results in shootout between terrorists and government security forces in Kabul.

Guerrillas attack American Embassy in Tehran, trapping Ambassador William H. Sullivan and staff inside; pro-Khomeini forces free captives after brief gun battle. Washington announces evacuation of 7,000 remaining Americans in Iran.

15 / Iran's provisional government accuses leftist People's Fedayeen guerrillas of attacks on government installations and foreign embassies in attempt to destabilize regime.

16 / Ambassador Sullivan requests meeting with Iran's new premier, Mehdi Bazargan, implying that Washington will maintain relations with the provisional government. Four generals loyal to the Shah are executed in Tehran after trial by "revolutionary Islamic court."

President Carter and Mexico's Pres. Jose Lopez Portillo agree to state-to-state negotiations for American purchase of Mexican natural gas, after two days of talks covering trade and immigration problems that have strained U.S.-Mexican relations for the past two years.

17 / China invades Vietnam in response to what Peking calls "incessant encroachments" on its territory; Vietnam accuses China of aggression in the UN General Assembly, asking that body to take steps to force China's withdrawal.

18 / Soviet Union demands that China withdraw immediately from Vietnam "before it is too late," and pledges to come to Hanoi's aid.

19 / Pres. Ziaur Rahman's Nationalist Party wins a two-thirds majority in first parliamentary elections in Bangladesh since martial lay was declared in 1975.

20 / President Carter says turmoil in the Middle East and Indochina will not deter U.S. efforts to conclude a new SALT agreement with the U.S.S.R., but warns Moscow to respect Iran's independence or face possibly unfavorable consequences.

21 / Secretary of State Cyrus Vance and Egyptian and Israeli negotiators meet at Camp David to resume stalled Mideast peace talks.

22 / Soviet Union begins military airlift to Vietnam; Moscow officials say they foresee no Soviet military intervention into China-Vietnam conflict as long as its scope remains limited.

President Carter orders most U.S. aid to Afghanistan cut off in wake of the Feb. 14 slaying of U.S. Ambassador Dubs in government shootout with terrorists.

23 / U.S. envoy to the UN Andrew Young urges end to fighting in Indochina, asking that Security Council call for a withdrawal of Chinese troops from Vietnam and of Vietnamese forces from Cambodia.

24 / President Carter names Army Chief of Staff Gen. Bernard H. Rogers to succeed Gen. Alexander M. Haig as commander of U.S. forces in Europe and Supreme Commander of NATO forces.

25 / President Carter invites Israel's Prime Minister Menachem Begin to join him and Egypt's Premier Mustafa Khalil at Camp David peace talks, in bold move to hasten efforts to conclude a peace treaty.

Heavy fighting continues on the northern border between Vietnam and China; Peking's Deputy Premier Wang Chen claims China's invasion into Vietnamese territory will be "limited in scope and duration."

Fighting erupts along border between Yemen and Southern Yemen as both nations accuse each other of staging an invasion.

27 / Prime Minister Menachem Begin agrees to meet with President Carter to discuss proposed Mideast peace agreement; but Israeli Cabinet vetoes Begin's return to Camp David to conclude treaty negotiations with Egypt.

28 / U.S. abandons electronic listening post on U.S.S.R.-Iran border after it is shut down by Iranian employees in a dispute over severance pay.

Saudi Arabia puts armed forces on alert in response to continued fighting between the two Yemens, as Riyadh calls for Arab League meeting to resolve the dispute.

MARCH 1979

NATIONAL

3 / President Carter authorizes fundraising committee for his 1980 reelection bid, to be headed by Democratic National Committee treasurer Evan Dobelle.

4 / New Orleans police return to work despite rejection of the city's contract offer, ending a two-week strike; Mayor Ernest N. Morial says city will no longer recognize policemen's union as a bargaining agent.

Torrential rainfall causes flash floods in Southeast and Gulf states, claiming several lives.

5 / Supreme Court rules 6-to-3 that state laws requiring only men to pay alimony violate the equal protection statutes of the Constitution.

Study of Chicago's public school system reveals that a $35 million "access to excellence" desegregation program has failed to significantly alter previous racial patterns in the city's 600 schools.

8 / Senate votes to postpone until 1983 a rule limiting Senators' outside income over and above annual $57,500 salary to $8,625, which had taken effect Jan. 1.

12 / Resumption of a limited military draft is proposed in Congressional debate over solution to critical manpower shortages faced by the armed services.

Senator Lowell P. Weicker, Jr. (R.-Connecticut), who gained national prominence as a chief inquisitor on the Senate Watergate committee, declares his candidacy for the 1980 Republican Presidential nomination.

13 / Nuclear Regulatory Commission orders five nuclear power plants closed within 48 hours because of a deficient analysis of their ability to withstand earthquakes.

Teachers in St. Louis end eight-week strike after approving a new contract; make-up classes are scheduled to run through July 20.

15 / House approves increase in the national debt limit by $32 billion to $830 billion total; but close 201-199 vote shows growing support for a balanced Federal budget.

19 / Attorney General Griffin Bell wins reversal in Federal appellate court of contempt citation in suit by the Socialist Workers Party seeking confi-

dential files on 18 informers who had spied on that group.

20 / Attorney General Griffin Bell appoints former Federal attorney Paul J. Curran as special counsel to investigate practices by Bert Lance's National Bank of Georgia involving $7 million in loans to President Carter's family business.

Commerce Department announces that corporate profits rose 26 percent in 1978, posing a serious challenge to President Carter's anti-inflation drive.

22 / White House announces that Rear Admiral Rowland G. Freeman III will succeed Jay Solomon as head of the scandal-plagued General Services Administration.

23 / Attorney General Bell confers full powers of a special prosecutor to special counsel Paul Curran, amid Republican criticisms that Curran had not been given sufficient authority to conduct a thorough investigation.

25 / A bomb explodes in the baggage-loading area of JFK International Airport in New York, injuring four; bomb had been set to explode aboard a Los Angeles-bound flight. Anti-Castro Cuban group claims responsibility.

26 / Federal judge in Milwaukee grants a government motion to bar *The Progressive* magazine's publication of an article describing how a hydrogen bomb works, in the first such injunction to impose prior restraint in the name of national security.

27 / Court order halts municipal elections in Houston and Dallas, Texas, as Justice Department and Federal courts investigate the apparent failure of those cities to enforce the Federal Voting Rights Act.

28 / Accident causes release of radiation from the three-month-old Three Mile Island nuclear power plant, 11 miles south of Harrisburg, Pa.; Nuclear Regulatory Commission initially minimizes danger from radiation leak.

29 / Radiation leak continues at the Three Mile Island nuclear power plant, releasing unspecified levels of radiation over a four-county area, and prompting angry anti-nuclear protests and demands by public officials that emergency steps be taken to safeguard the public.

30 / Pennsylvania Governor Richard Thornburgh issues emergency warning that children and pregnant women should be evacuated from the vicinity of the Three Mile Island nuclear accident; NRC warns Congress that a core meltdown is still possible at the crippled reactor.

Teamsters reach tentative accord with the trucking industry on wage issues in proposed three-year master freight contract, which covers 300,000 union members; present contract expires April 1.

31 / Federal inspectors at Three Mile Island say damaged reactor is cooling down, but that "crisis" and the possibility of a non-nuclear pressure explosion still exists. Leading Congressional figures demand tighter Federal controls over the nuclear industry.

INTERNATIONAL

1 / Israel rejects U.S. proposals for a peace treaty with Egypt; Prime Minister Menachem Begin arrives in Washington for talks with President Carter.

U.S. Treasury Secretary W. Michael Blumenthal signs accord in Peking in which China agrees to settle U.S. claims on $196.6 million in assets confiscated in 1949.

2 / Spain's ruling Center Democrats win a 167-seat majority in general elections to the 350-member Congress of Deputies, decisively beating opposition Socialists.

Scottish voters approve referendum on limited self-rule by a slim margin, but short of the absolute majority required for passage; a similar home-rule referendum is defeated in Wales.

3 / Yemen and South Yemen agree to cease-fire mediated by Syria and Iraq.

4 / Tanzanian troops invade Uganda, penetrating to within 50 miles of the capital of Kampala.

5 / White House announces President Carter will fly to the Middle East in a personal effort to negotiate the final terms of an Egyptian-Israeli peace treaty.

China declares it has begun withdrawing its troops from Vietnam, stating it had gained all its objectives in the 17-day invasion.

6 / South African forces attack guerrilla bases in Angola to halt incursions into South-West Africa

(Namibia); action coincides with Pretoria's rejection of a UN-sponsored cease-fire to aid transition to majority rule.

800 Moslems are reported killed by angry blacks in Chad, in ethnic strife following a February 1979 abortive coup by Islamic separatists.

8 / President Carter confers with Egypt's Pres. Sadat in Cairo, but meeting fails to resolve issues blocking peace accord with Israel.

10 / President Carter tells Israelis upon arrival in Jerusalem that he believes a peace treaty can be concluded soon, despite remaining differences with Egypt on the future status of the occupied Arab territories.

11 / Israeli Cabinet approves newly revised language in U.S. - proposed Mideast peace treaty; Secretary of State Vance arrives in Jerusalem to continue negotiations.

Colombia's military arrests 1,000 persons in crackdown against terrorists; opponents protest that government is violating human rights by illegal detentions and the use of torture in interrogating prisoners.

12 / 15,000 Iranian women march through Tehran in continuing protests against the government's traditionalist Islamic policies toward women.

13 / Dramatic shift in course of Mideast peace talks develops as President Carter announces in Cairo Egypt's approval of the bulk of treaty provisions with Israel.

14 / Israeli Cabinet approves last provisions to Mideast peace treaty; Egypt follows suit March 15.

15 / Pope John Paul II, in his first papal encyclical, declares his theological conservatism and his concerns for the world's poor.

17 / U.S. and Britain appeal to Patriotic Front guerrillas to resume negotiations with Salisbury regime for a peaceful transition to majority rule in Rhodesia-Zimbabwe that would include UN-supervised elections.

18 / Jordan's King Hussein and Saudi Arabian leaders decline to back Mideast peace treaty after separate talks with U.S. envoy Zbigniew Brzezinski; but Saudis pledge not to join any anti-Egypt economic boycott.

19 / Carter Administration pledges $2 billion in arms aid to Egypt and $3 billion towards cost of Sinai disengagement to Israel after Mideast peace treaty is signed.

Kurds demanding autonomy in southwestern Iran clash with government troops in Sanadaj, which suffer heavy losses.

20 / Prime Minister Begin in Knesset debate on treaty with Egypt vows not to allow a Palestinian state to be established in the West Bank or Gaza.

France withdraws its troops from Chad after peace accord between warring factions in the former French colony is announced in Paris.

21 / Israel's Knesset endorses peace treaty with Egypt, clearing way for signing ceremonies in Washington March 26; U.S. is expected to pledge support for Israel in event pact with Egypt is violated.

South African bribery scandal widens as ex-Information Ministry figure Eschel Rhoodie says that the U.S. was main target of Pretoria's bid to influence press and government figures to support its racial policies.

Pres. Mobutu Sese Seko announces the International Monetary Fund has pledged $150 million in aid to Zaire, in exchange for his government's pledge to cut public spending by two-thirds.

22 / White House says U.S. will continue surveillance flights over the Sinai — begun secretly in 1974 at Israeli and Egyptian request — for three years to verify both sides' compliance with Mideast peace treaty.

Britain's Ambassador to the Netherlands is slain outside his home in The Hague; assassination is believed work of a faction of the provisional Irish Republican Army.

23 / Over 60,000 steelworkers march in Paris against unemployment, layoffs and the possible shutdown of France's steel industry.

Guatemala is shaken by terrorist campaign against the moderate opposition; military government denies involvement, but moderate leaders say rightists are tied to elements within the police and the armed forces.

25 / Israeli and Egyptian leaders in Washington agree on timetable for scheduled return by Israel of Sinai oil fields to Egypt, the last issue blocking a comprehensive peace treaty.

26 / Egypt's President Anwar Sadat and Israel's Prime Minister Menachem Begin sign joint peace treaty in Washington, ending nearly 31 years of hostilities; President Jimmy Carter signs as witness for the U.S.

27-28 / Arab League conference in Baghdad agrees to limited political boycott against Egypt; but Libya and the P.L.O. walk out after moderates, led by Saudi Arabia, refuse to go beyond minimum sanctions.

28 / Britain's Labour government loses by 310-to-311 a no confidence vote in Parliament; general elections are set for early May, with Conservatives given the edge.

29 / Argentina's military regime allows the Inter-American Human Rights Commission to investigate charges that it has violently repressed suspected "subversives," indicating a letup in the general crackdown against leftists.

30 / Airey M. S. Neave, a Tory MP and close advisor to Conservative leader Margaret Thatcher, is killed by a bomb in London believed planted by IRA terrorists.

31 / Foreign ministers of 18 Arab nations plus the PLO announce severing of relations with Egypt and imposition of a total economic boycott against Cairo.

Iranians overwhelmingly support Islamic republic favored by the Ayatollah Khomeini in initial returns of a nationwide referendum.

APRIL 1979

NATIONAL

1 / Trucking industry locks out 300,000 Teamsters as union calls selective nationwide strike after rejecting a tentative three-year contract.

President Carter visits the Three Mile Island nuclear plant; he and advisors stress situation is stable, but evacuation remains a possibility.

Former Congressman Otto Passman is found not guilty by a Monroe, Louisiana jury of accepting bribes from South Korean rice dealer Tongsun Park.

3 / Jane M. Byrne is elected Mayor of Chicago, Ill., by a landslide 82 percent margin to become the Windy City's first woman chief executive.

4 / Federal investigators report to the Nuclear Regulatory Commission that a combination of human, mechanical and design errors were responsible for near-disaster at the Three Mile Island nuclear facility.

House ethics panel charges Rep. Charles Diggs (D.-Mich.), with 18 counts of violating House rules; Diggs had been convicted on Federal charges of payroll padding and accepting kickbacks from his staff.

5 / President Carter announces he will seek to gradually phase out price controls on domestic oil production by July 1, in effort to spur U.S. production and curb consumption.

6 / NRC turns down request by California's Gov. Edmund G. Brown, Jr. to temporarily close the Rancho Seco nuclear plant near Sacramento — a twin of the Three Mile Island facility.

7 / Three thousand anti-nuclear demonstrators protest launching of first Trident-missile nuclear submarine in Groton, Connecticut.

8 / Thousands are evacuated near Crestview, Florida, after a freight train carrying toxic chemicals derails, threatening an 80-square-mile area with deadly fumes.

Austin, Texas voters approve bond issue for construction of a local nuclear power plant, in first test of public opinion on nuclear power since the Three Mile Island accident.

9 / NRC announces crisis at the Three Mile Island power plant is over as the crippled reactor is brought towards a cold shutdown.

10 / Tentative settlement is reached in 10-day strike by 300,000 Teamsters that had idled most of the nation's trucking industry.

Senate Budget committee approves five-year fiscal plan mandating a balanced Federal budget by 1981; bill also calls for substantial tax cuts in 1982.

11 / President Carter appoints 11-member panel to determine the causes of the Three Mile Island nuclear accident and to recommend safeguards against future mishaps.

Sixty die and over 800 are injured as tornadoes sweep across northern Texas and southern Oklahoma, devastating four communities.

14 / Flash floods in the Southeast claim nine lives as river banks overflow, forcing 5,000 to flee their homes in Alabama and Mississippi.

Pennsylvania State House subcommittee charges that "police lawlessness" in Philadelphia sometimes reaches "homicidal" levels; U.S. Civil Rights Commission sets early hearings on police brutality.

15 / Flooding along a 15-mile stretch of the Pearl River inundates Jackson, Miss.; 15,000 are left homeless.

17 / United Auto Workers president Douglas A. Fraser blasts Federal wage guidelines, saying they do not require equal sacrifices from employers, suggesting the union not consider them in upcoming contract talks.

18 / Supreme Court ruling allows plaintiffs in press libel suits to inquire as to a reporter's "state of mind," judgments and opinions while preparing material for publication.

Air crash at Newark International Airport of a New York Airways helicopter kills three, injures 12 of the remaining 15 survivors.

19 / Disclosure of Atomic Energy Commission records reveal that the Eisenhower Administration told the AEC in 1953 to confuse the public about the possible consequences of fallout from nuclear testing in southern Utah.

Federal safety officials ground 1,000 Sikorsky S-61 helicopters worldwide, after evidence in Newark, N.J. crash involving that model shows mechanical defect was responsible for accident.

27 / Nuclear Regulatory Commission orders the temporary closing of all operating reactors designed by Babcock & Wilcox, manufacturers of the Three Mile Island nuclear plant; ruling allows two plants in the Southeast to remain in operation to forestall widespread power shortages.

29 / National Academy of Sciences study predicts 2,000 fatalities linked to atomic energy in the U.S. by the year 2000, with one in every 1,000 Americans likely to develop cancer from combined radiation sources.

30 / Senator Herman E. Talmadge (D.-Ga.) professes his innocence in Senate hearings to five charges of mishandling his financial affairs and thus breaching the Senate's code of ethics.

Senate approves Administration bill creating a new Department of Education; but measure faces stiff House opposition.

INTERNATIONAL

1 / Israeli Cabinet formally ratifies treaty with Egypt; Prime Minister Menachem Begin makes first state visit to Cairo (April 2).

3 / Zulfikar Ali Bhutto is executed in Pakistan; the former Prime Minister had been convicted of plotting the murder of a political opponent in 1974.

Prime Minister Begin announces in Cairo that Egyptian-Israeli border will be opened after Sinai capital of El Arish is returned to Egyptian control May 26.

4 / Anti-Amin exile forces and their Tanzanian allies continue invasion of Uganda, assaulting capital of Kampala.

Vietnam requests peace talks with China to seek resumption of normal relations, dropping demand that Peking must withdraw its troops before negotiations could start.

5 / Violence erupts in Pakistan as demonstrators protesting the execution of ex-premier Ali Bhutto clash with police.

6 / U.S. cuts off all aid to Pakistan after intelligence sources report that Islamabad is acquiring the capability to build nuclear weapons.

7 / Amir Abbas Hoveida is executed in Tehran after a summary trial by Islamic court; Hoveida had served as Premier during the Shah of Iran's reign.

8 / Palestine Liberation Organization vows stepped-up campaign of military and political actions against Egypt and Israel — especially within the occupied Arab territories — in retaliation for the Mideast peace treaty.

9 / Pakistan denies charges by Afghanistan that its troops had crossed over their mutual border, as widespread Muslim insurgency continues against pro-Soviet regime in Kabul.

Pope John Paul II in ecclesiastic letter to the Catholic clergy stresses celibacy as prerequisite for the priesthood, affirming traditional church doctrines.

10 / A terrorist bomb explodes in Tel Aviv, killing one and injuring 36 on Passover eve; Israeli jets retaliate against two guerrilla bases in Lebanon.

11 / Kampala falls to Tanzanian and Ugandan exile troops; residents cheer liberators as Pres. Idi Amin is reported fleeing east with the remnants of his army.

12 / South Africa's Prime Minister P. W. Botha orders expulsion of several American embassy staffers, charging them with espionage.

Tanzania recognizes new government in Kampala, composed solely of exiled opponents of dictator Idi Amin.

13 / U.S. retaliates against Pretoria's expulsion of three American officials by ordering two South African military attaches to leave Washington.

Rhodesian commandos raid Lusaka, Zambian headquarters of the Patriotic Front, in attempt to kill or kidnap guerrilla leader Joshua Nkomo; 10 die in raid.

14 / Chinese delegation flies to Hanoi in attempt to settle issues that led to border war with Vietnam.

15 / An earthquake in southern Yugoslavia — the strongest ever recorded there — razes 13 villages along the Adriatic coast, killing and injuring hundreds.

Wallposters in Chinese city of Shanghai demand human rights and protest recent arrest of activists there, challenging a Peking directive banning such activities in March 1979.

16 / Palestinian terrorists attempt to hijack an El Al airliner at Brussels airport, but are thwarted by police.

Iran's Foreign Minister Karim Sanjabi resigns amid mounting "trials" and executions of former pro-Shah officials.

CIA director Adm. Stansfield Turner says in Senate testimony that the loss of two listening posts in Iran would set U.S. back five years in ability to monitor Soviet missile tests and development.

17 / Defense Secretary Harold Brown tells Senate that despite loss of U.S. listening posts in Iran, Soviet compliance with a new SALT pact could be "adequately" verified within a year.

19 / Israeli units and Palestinian guerrillas clash along Lebanese border; right-wing Lebanese militia attacks UN peacekeeping forces in area.

20 / Terrorists bomb Rome's Palace of Senators — designed by Michelangelo; both left- and right-wing groups claim responsibility.

21 / Moderates are big winners in five-day Rhodesian elections for black majority rule; Bishop Abel T. Muzorewa's party wins a 51-seat majority in the new Black-dominated parliament.

22 / Israeli gunboats shell guerrilla bases in southern Lebanon after terrorists kill four Israelis in northern town of Hahariya.

Twenty thousand Cambodian refugees enter Thailand, fleeing continued Vietnamese offensive against remaining Khmer Rouge forces along the Thai-Cambodian border.

23 / Saudi Arabia severs diplomatic and political ties with Egypt; but Riyadh — which remains Cairo's financial backer — backs off from a complete economic break.

Rev. Ndabaningi Sithole, defeated by Bishop Muzorewa in Rhodesian elections, calls vote fraudulent, says his party will not accept results due to "gross irregularities" in the balloting.

24 / President Carter appoints former special trade representative Robert S. Strauss as chief U.S. envoy to Mideast negotiations on Palestinian self-rule.

Iran's Premier Medhi Bazargan blasts Islamic committees linked to the Ayatollah Khomeini, calling for an end to anarchy and the "rule of revenge."

26 / UN peace forces arrange cease-fire between Israelis and Palestinian guerrillas in southern Lebanon, halting four days of intense fighting.

UN Secretary-General Kurt Waldheim arrives in Hanoi to aid negotiations for Vietnam-China disengagement.

27 / Soviet Union frees five prominent dissidents in exchange for two Russian spies held by the U.S.; Aleksandr Ginzburg, Valentin Moroz, Eduard Kuznetsov, Mark Dymshits and Georgi Vins are then flown to New York.

28 / Administration discloses that two Americans convicted in 1976 of selling government secrets to the USSR had given Soviets information on the satellite systems the U.S. expected to use in monitoring Russian compliance with the SALT-II agreement.

29 / Left-center candidate Jaime Roldos is elected President of Ecuador in that country's first free elections since imposition of military rule in 1972.

30 / President Carter defends proposed strategic arms limitation treaty, saying Moscow would not violate SALT-II for fear of U.S. rejection of the entire pact, and the resultant threat to U.S.-Soviet relations.

MAY 1979

NATIONAL

1 / House votes to end Administration program giving $250 million in Federal aid to cities with high unemployment.

Former C.I.A. director George Bush, a moderate Republican, announces his candidacy for the 1980 GOP Presidential nomination.

3 / HEW Secretary Joseph Califano says in Senate testimony that radiation danger from the Three Mile Island accident was twice as high as original estimates, and could account for one to ten cancer deaths in the future for area residents.

6 / Over 65,000 antinuclear protesters march on the Capitol in Washington, D.C., the largest antinuclear demonstration ever held; speakers include actress Jane Fonda, physicist Dr. John Gofman, consumer advocate Ralph Nader and California's Gov. Jerry Brown.

8 / Gov. Jerry Brown signs emergency gas-rationing law, strictly limiting auto fuel consumption and mandating odd-even gas supply days throughout California.

9 / House Interior committee approves six-month moratorium on construction permits for nuclear reactors, and bans operations at new plants until Federal authorities approve emergency contingency plans for all nuclear plants.

11 / Offshore oil-drilling rig collapses in Gulf of Mexico off Galveston, Texas; 24 crewmen are rescued, eight others are missing and presumed dead.

NRC reports that the Three Mile Island disaster occurred because a minor malfunction was misdiagnosed by plant operators, who were unable to monitor exactly what was happening inside the reactor's core, thus compounding the initial breakdown.

12 / Documents released under the Freedom of Information Act reveal that it was Federal policy in the 1950's to downplay the possible dangers of radioactive fallout from atomic testing in Nevada in the interest of national security.

14 / Supreme Court rules 6-3 to allow individuals to bring sex-bias suits against schools and colleges.

Senator Robert Dole of Kansas, President Ford's running mate in 1976, announces his candidacy for the GOP's 1980 Presidential nomination.

15 / Sears, Roebuck Company's suit challenging Federal equal employment programs is dismissed by a Washington, D.C. district court judge.

16 / House approves by a 268-157 vote bill to preserve over 125 million acres of Federal land in Alaska from commercial development.

18 / House-Senate conferees approve a projected $23-billion Federal budget deficit for 1980, $5 billion less than amount estimated by the White House.

Federal jury awards $10.5 million in damages to estate of Karen Silkwood, an employee at the Kerr-McGee plutonium processing plant near Oklahoma City, who died in a suspicious auto crash in 1974 while on her way to expose unsafe plant conditions to a NY Times reporter.

19 / United Airlines and striking machinists reach tentative accord on a new contract, ending a 50-day strike against the nation's largest air carrier.

21 / Former San Francisco supervisor Dan White is convicted of voluntary manslaughter in the November 1978 slaying of Mayor George Moscone and Supervisor Harvey Milk; pleading diminished capacity, White later receives maximum sentence of seven years and eight months.

22 / San Francisco's gay community protests "lenient" verdict against Dan White in the killing of Moscone and Supervisor Milk – a self-described homosexual; angry demonstrators clash with police.

23 / Bert Lance is indicted in Atlanta on Federal charges of filing false financial statements, misleading regulatory agencies and using bank funds to pay his personal bills, alleging that these activities continued while Lance was director of the Office of Management and Budget. Lance and three business associates later plead not guilty to charges.

24 / Proposed Federal budget narrowly passes House; 202-196 vote comes after liberal Democrats accept Senate compromise of $350 million in additional funds for social programs.

25 / American Airlines DC-10 crashes on take-off from Chicago's O'Hare International Airport, killing all 273 persons aboard; the worst U.S. air disaster in history, it prompts investigation into apparent defect in the wing-engine assembly.

John Spenkelink is executed in Florida after his appeal to the Supreme Court is turned down; the first convicted murderer to suffer the death penalty since Gary Gilmore in 1977, he is first since 1967 to be put to death against his wishes.

29 / Federal authorities order all DC-10's grounded after inspections prove structural problems in that model's engine mounts are more widespread than first believed.

Federal judge John H. Wood, Jr. is fatally shot as he leaves his home in San Antonio, Texas; scheduled to preside over a major narcotics case, he is first Federal judge to be murdered.

31 / Inspection of 37 DC-10's finds "problems" in engine mounts similar to that thought responsible for the May 25 airline disaster near Chicago.

INTERNATIONAL

1 / Islamic guerrillas opposed to "fanatic mullahs," assassinate Ayatollah Morteza Motahari in Tehran; he had been a member of Iran's ruling Revolutionary Council.

Deputy Premier Deng Xiaoping tells UN Secretary-General Kurt Waldheim in Peking that China will attack Vietnam again if Hanoi "continues it provocations."

2 / Prime Minister Menachem Begin, on 31st anniversary of independence, affirms government's stance that Israel will make no further withdrawals from occupied Arab territory in exchange for an overall Mideast settlement.

Peking reports losses during four-week war against Vietnam included 20,000 Chinese and 50,000 Vietnamese killed or wounded; but U.S. estimates set Chinese casualties as much higher.

3 / Conservatives claim victory in British general elections, winning a 43-seat majority in Parliament; Tory leader Margaret Thatcher takes office as Prime Minister May 4, the first woman head of state of a major European country.

4 / Leftists seize the French and Costa Rican embassies in capital of El Salvador and hold ambassadors hostage for release of five comrades jailed May 1.

6 / Austrian Premier Bruno Kreisky is returned to office after his Socialist party wins a narrow majority in parliament, after government setback caused by the April 1979 Danube nuclear plant referendum defeat.

7 / Israel's Prime Minister Begin proposes to Knesset that a peace treaty be signed with Lebanon, but

rules out halting retaliatory raids against PLO bases there.

8 / Murder-conspiracy trial of Jeremy Thorpe, former Liberal party leader defeated in May 3 elections, begins in London.

Twenty-three die in El Salvador as police fire on supporters of the Popular Revolutionary Bloc (BPR) outside San Salvador Cathedral, which the BPR occupied May 4.

9 / U.S. Secretary of State Cyrus Vance announces basic agreement has been reached with the Soviet Union on SALT-II treaty; President Carter and Premier Brezhnev scheduled to sign accords in June.

Israeli troops attack southern Lebanon in force, in retaliation for PLO raid on northern Israeli kibbutz.

11 / South African court finds 11 Black students guilty of organizing protests that erupted into riots in Soweto in 1976 and 1977, but most receive suspended sentences.

13 / Chief of Iran's revolutionary courts calls for the assassination of the deposed Shah, his family and former political leaders under his regime; other Islamic leaders limit death sentences to those "proved to have killed others."

14 / Arms accord faces new hitch as Turkey says it will not allow U.S. overflights of its territory to verify Soviet compliance with SALT-II unless Moscow agrees to them.

Chile's Chief Justice rejects U.S. request to extradite three military officers indicted in Washington for the 1976 murder of anti-junta figure Orlando Letelier; U.S. plans appeal.

15 / U.S. Senate in a non-binding resolution calls for lifting sanctions against Rhodesia 14 days after black-majority rule takes effect, a rebuff to the White House's southern Africa policy.

16 / Hanoi admits that 400-600,000 Vietnamese, most ethnic Chinese from the South, seek to emigrate, but warns that refugees will not be allowed out until other nations accept them.

West German government postpones indefinitely construction of a planned nuclear fuel re-processing plant, in the face of growing resistance to nuclear power.

17 / Fidel Castro arrives in Mexico for official state talks, his first visit there since he came to power in Cuba in 1959; Pres. Castro later assails continued U.S. economic blockade of Cuba.

20 / Islamic regime asks U.S. to delay replacement of Ambassador to Tehran, after the Ayatollah Khomeini denounces a Senate resolution condemning recent executions as "interference" in Iran's internal affairs.

Swiss voters overwhelming approve referendum on nuclear power that tightens controls on existing nuclear plants and mandates stricter construction requirements.

21 / Israeli government approves plan for limited Arab self-rule in the occupied West Bank and Gaza Strip.

22 / U.S. Senate backs White House in voting a $50 million arms grant to Turkey, after four-year ban on military aid to Ankara for its 1974 invasion of Cyprus.

23 / West Germany's legislature elects ex-Nazi Party member Karl Carstens, 64, a Christian Democrat, President of the Federal Republic; choice is opposed in nationwide demonstrations.

Three die and 13 are hurt as terrorist bomb explodes outside Jerusalem; Israeli warplanes retaliate against PLO-occupied areas of southern Lebanon.

25 / Israel returns Sinai capital of El Arish to Egypt after 12 years of occupation, as talks open in Beersheba between U.S., Egypt and Israel on Palestinian autonomy.

26 / Secretary of State Vance pledges support for Palestinian cause in Beersheba talks, in hopes of bringing West Bank and Gaza leaders into the negotiations.

28 / Greece becomes the 10th member of the European Economic Community, a goal long sought by successive governments in Athens.

29 / Bishop Abel T. Muzorewa is sworn in as first black Prime Minister of Zimbabwe Rhodesia; he later appoints new Cabinet which includes outgoing Prime Minister Ian Smith as third-highest government minister. Nigeria and Ghana denounce new government (May 31), and seek continued sanctions against Salisbury.

30 / Arabs in Iran's Khuzistan province attack government troops in bid for increased autonomy for the oil-rich region from Tehran; 21 are killed, 71 wounded.

Defense Secretary Harold Brown says that the USSR continues to seek a first-strike capability against U.S. land-based missiles, saying that the new missiles Moscow is developing could, by the 1980's, enable the Soviets to destroy existing American ICBM's.

31 / Former Khmer Rouge foreign minister Ieng Sary calls for coalition with former foes in the Lon Nol regime to roll back the Vietnamese occupation of Cambodia.

JUNE 1979

NATIONAL

1 / Labor Department reports no rise in jobless rate for May, 1979, indicating current slowdown in the nation's economy may not adversely affect employment.

2 / House Select Committee on Assassinations issues final report, in line with previous assertions that President Kennedy's death was probably the result of conspiracy.

5 / Supreme Court rules 7-2 to uphold job preference requirements for veterans as not constituting discrimination against women; justices also act to reaffirm ban against use of illegally obtained evidence in trials.

8 / Rep. John B. Anderson (R.-Ill.), a moderate liberal announces he will seek the GOP's 1980 Presidential nomination, the seventh to enter the race officially (Sen. Lowell Weicker had dropped out on May 16).

9 / NY Times-CBS-TV News poll shows President Carter's popularity at a low ebb; overall public approval of his performance dropped from 42 percent in March to 30 percent in June.

11 / Supreme Court rules that Federal laws barring discrimination against the handicapped does not require colleges to accept students whose disability may prevent them from fulfilling the requirements of a particular degree program.

John Wayne, 72, the "Duke" who appeared in over 200 films and was one of America's best-loved actors, dies of cancer at the U.C.L.A. Medical Center in California.

12 / Conflicting national health care bills are proposed to Congress by President Carter and Senator Edward Kennedy; bills differ on provisions and cost to the Federal government if enacted.

13 / President Carter is reported to say that he would "whip" Sen. Ted Kennedy if the Massachusetts Democrat opposed him for the party's Presidential nomination in 1980.

15 / Federal judge in Milwaukee denies Progressive magazine's bid to vacate an injunction prohibiting its publication of controversial article about the hydrogen bomb.

18 / Supreme Court rules that Laetrile, used by some as a cancer cure, can be banned by the Federal government.

Uniroyal and the United Rubber Workers union reach accord on a three-year contract, ending a six-week strike and paving the way for an industry-wide settlement.

19 / Gasoline sales on odd-even days begin on New Jersey's Garden State Parkway; allocation plan is imposed in the entire tristate Metropolitan area June 20.

20 / Independent truckers stage nationwide work stoppage to protest fuel prices and inadequate Federal allocations, after weeks of escalating wildcat slowdowns.

Serbian nationalist Nikola Kavaja hijacks Chicago-bound American Airlines jet in New York; Kavaja had been convicted of bombing attempts in New York. He later releases all passengers in Chicago and orders plane to Ireland, where he surrenders June 21.

21 / Truckers' strike idles 40 percent of freight-hauling industry; energy officials plan to end farmers' fuel preference to free diesel oil for trucks. President Carter proposes deregulation of the industry to spur competition and help save energy.

24 / Americans for Democratic Action vote to "dump" President Carter and support Sen. Edward Kennedy for the 1980 Democratic nomination.

26 / Supreme Court eases restrictions in libel cases, ruling that individuals who do not by choice become involved in public controversy are not public figures, and thus need not prove malice in such civil suits.

27 / Supreme Court rules 5-2 to uphold voluntary affirmative action plans in the "Webber" case, allowing companies to give special preference to blacks to eliminate past "racial imbalance" in job classifications.

29 / White House asks truckers to return to work, having made all possible commitments to them; Interstate Commerce Commission says strike is virtually over, with most affected shipments already being resumed.

Rep. Charles C. Diggs, Jr. (D.-Mich.) admits in House ethics hearing that he used Federal funds to pay over $40,000 in personal bills, and agrees to repay that amount and accept censure in return for dropping of any further investigation.

INTERNATIONAL

1 / Heavy fighting erupts in Nicaragua as guerrillas of the Sandinista National Liberation Front (FSLN) open new offensive against the regime of Pres. Anastasio Somoza Debayle.

2 / Pope John Paul II receives tumultuous welcome in his native Poland, at start of first visit by a Pope to a Communist state.

3 / Israeli Cabinet approves new settlements in the West Bank; U.S. and Egypt protest that such colonization of the occupied territories is illegal.

4 / Junior officers led by Flight Lt. Jerry Rawlings overthrow military regime in Ghana headed by Gen. Fred Akuffo.

Parliamentary elections in Italy result in losses for both the ruling Christian Democrats and the opposition Communist Party, with gains for smaller centrist and far left parties.

Johannes Vorster resigns as President of South Africa amid widening scandal involving government funds spent on propaganda abroad, which Vorster is accused of lying about when he denied knowledge while Prime Minister.

5 / Pope John Paul II appeals to Poland's regime to recognize "fundamental human rights and religious liberty," and urges Church leaders to seek normalization of relations with the Communist government.

7 / President Carter says U.S. will not lift sanctions against Zimbabwe Rhodesia despite Congressioanl mandate to do so because it would damage American foreign relations to act unilaterally.

9 / Sandinista uprising in Nicaragua spreads to capital of Managua, where rebels seize several outskirts areas, inflicting heavy losses on the National Guard.

10 / Results of two-day voting in nine Common Market countries for popularity-elected European Parliament show major setback for Socialists and Communists, with a plurality of seats won by center-right parties.

Pope John Paul II celebrates mass for one million in Cracow, and ends his trip to Poland with a plea for renewed strength of that nation's Christians.

11 / Prime Minister Menachem Begin denounces critics of his government's settlement policy, reiterating Israel's right to build new communities in occupied Arab lands.

Thailand expels 30,000 refugees from Cambodia back across the border, and warns it will soon eject 50,000 more.

12 / Senate hands President Carter stinging rebuke on policy towards Zimbabwe Rhodesia by voting 52-41 to lift the U.S. economic embargo of the Salisbury government.

Britain's Conservative government presents proposed national budget to Parliament, which cuts state spending and personal income taxes while imposing large increases in sales taxes and interest rates.

15 / President Carter arrives in Vienna for summit conference on strategic arms limitations with Soviet leader Leonid Brezhnev that is to conclude a U.S.-USSR accord.

House Foreign Affairs panel votes 26-0 to allow President Carter to maintain economic sanctions against Zimbabwe Rhodesia if he determines that that to do so would be in the national interest.

16 / Ghana's head of state from 1972 to 1978, Ignatius K. Acheampong, 47, is executed after a military tribunal finds him guilty of squandering government funds.

17 / Soviet leader Leonid I. Brezhnev warns that proposed SALT-II agreement would collapse if it is amended by Congress prior to ratification, with "grave consequences" held for U.S.-Soviet relations and world peace.

Sandinistas announce composition of a provisional Nicaraguan government to succeed Pres. Somoza; junta is mainly moderate, with few — but important — FSLN representatives.

18 / Strategic arms treaty is signed in Vienna by President Carter and Soviet chief Brezhnev; in televised address to a joint session of Congress, Carter asserts that pact "will withstand . . . scrutiny" and help prevent "an uncontrolled arms race."

20 / American reporter for ABC-TV Bill Stewart and his interpreter are summarily shot to death by National Guardsmen at the scene of recent fighting between government and rebel forces in Nicaragua.

Zimbabwean Prime Minister Abel Muzorewa loses his parliamentary majority as eight leaders of his own party defect and form their own faction; governing coalition remains shaky in the face of continued war with Patriotic Front guerrillas.

21 / Secretary of State Cyrus Vance urges formation of a new government in Nicaragua — implicitly, without Somoza — and calls for an inter-American peace force to restore order there.

22 / Sandinistas reject U.S. intervention to force Somoza's ouster; Washington's proposals fail to gain backing at emergency OAS meeting.

Jeremy Thorpe, former leader of Britain's Liberal Party, is acquitted along with three co-defendants in London trial on charges that they conspired to kill Norman Scott, a male model who claimed to have been Thorpe's "lover."

23 / Organization of American States agrees to press for "the immediate and definitive replacement" of the Somoza regime by a broadly based democratic government.

24 / Pres. Somoza ignores call by OAS for his resignation, vowing to continue his fight against Sandinista rebels.

25 / NATO commander Gen. Alexander M. Haig, Jr., narrowly escapes assassination attempt when a bomb explodes near his car outside Casteau, Belgium, demolishing an accompanying vehicle.

27 / Syrian MIGs dogfight with Israeli jets over southern Lebanon, in first aerial combat between the two countries in five years; Israelis had been attacking PLO bases.

Washington sends special envoys to Nicaragua in attempt to persuade Pres. Anastasio Somoza to step down in favor of a provisional government that would include Sandinista elements.

28 / Meeting by member states of the Organization of Petroleum Exporting Countries sets new price increases on OPEC-produced crude oil; two-tiered system will raise price from $18 to $23.50 a barrel, averaging a 16 percent increase in the price customer nations must pay.

Economic summit meeting of the seven leading industrial democracies opens in Tokyo; conference hopes to reach agreement on freezing oil imports and reduce energy consumption and Western reliance on OPEC.

29 / Economic summit in Tokyo agrees to ceiling on oil imports up to 1985; U.S. agrees to seek to keep imports down to 8.5 million barrels a day.

Both moderate and leftist opponents of Pres. Somoza reject U.S. proposals to end Nicaragua's civil war, aimed at installing an interim government more conservative than the Sandinista's provisional junta.

30 / President Carter and South Korea's Pres. Park Chung Hee meet in Seoul for talks on future U.S. presence in that country; talks result in call for discussions with North Korea on easing border tensions and negotiations for eventual reunification of the two Koreas.

JULY 1979

NATIONAL

1 / President Carter blasts recent OPEC price increase, saying it will cause the loss of 800,000 jobs and is likely to raise inflation 2.5 percent by 1980.

2 / Supreme Court ruling gives local judges greater discretion in closing pretrial hearings to the press and public. Other rulings uphold court-ordered busing in Columbus and Dayton, Ohio, and strike down a Massachusetts law requiring parental or court consent for abortions involving minors.

6 / President Carter calls top aides and energy advisors to Camp David "weekend summit" after cancelling (July 4) a major address on Administration energy policy.

10 / Federal report on the May 25 DC-10 disaster points to poor maintenance and poor training of mechanics as largely to blame for crash of the American Airlines jet near Chicago which claimed 275 lives.

11 / President Carter ends domestic summit with top advisors and other national political leaders at Camp David.

House passes by 210-206 vote bill authorizing the creation of a Cabinet-level Education Department, a victory for the White House.

13 / Government lifts ban on DC-10 flights, after ordering manufacturer — the McDonnell Douglas Company — to redesign vital components of the aircraft within two years.

15 / President Carter proposes bold energy program to conserve 4.5 million barrels of oil daily by 1990; in nationally televised address, Carter says U.S. must develop alternative energy sources and cut dependence on foreign oil in order to overcome nation's current "crisis of confidence."

16 / In follow-up energy speech, President Carter says the Federal government will spend $140 billion by 1990 to end U.S. dependence on imported oil, to be financed entirely by a "windfall" profits tax on oil companies.

Final House Assassinations Committee report concludes that the murders of President Kennedy and Dr. Martin Luther King, Jr., "likely" resulted from conspiracies not fully explored by either the Warren Commission or the F.B.I.

17 / Administration shake-up follows President Carter's energy declarations; Cabinet and senior White House staffers tender their resignations en masse.

18 / Presidential aide Hamilton Jordan is named White House chief of staff; Jordan then orders senior White House and Cabinet-level appointees to conduct evaluations of their staffs to clear 'dead wood.'

19 / Cabinet is reshuffled as President Carter accepts resignations of HEW Secretary Joseph A. Califano, Jr., Treasury Secretary W. Michael Blumenthal, and Attorney General Griffin B. Bell. HUD Secretary Patricia R. Harris is tapped to replace Califano, Federal Reserve Board chairman G. William Miller is named to replace Blumenthal, and Bell — who announced his intention to step down last year — is succeeded by his deputy, Benjamin R. Civiletti.

20 / President Carter accepts resignations of Energy Secretary James R. Schlesinger and Transportation Secretary Brock Adams, who is to be succeeded by deputy Defense Secretary Charles W. Duncan, Jr.

Federal Court of Appeals upholds the 1977 conviction of Maryland Governor Marvin Mandel and five co-defendants on mail fraud and racketeering charges, reversing its previous ruling that overturned that verdict.

24 / House in 216-209 vote narrowly rejects proposed constitutional amendment to ban forced busing to achieve school integration.

25 / President Carter names Paul A. Volker, head of New York's Federal Reserve bank and an expert on international finances, to replace G. William Miller as head of Federal Reserve Board; Hedley Donovan,

head of Time-Life, Inc., is appointed special White House advisor.

House authorizes a three-year, $2.7 billion operating budget for Amtrak; 20 percent cut in annual funding is less than the 43 percent urged by Administration.

26 / House votes 237-182 to continue the Clinch River nuclear breeder reactor project in Tennessee, which the White House had favored terminating.

27 / President Carter appoints Moon Landrieu, former Mayor of New Orleans credited with opening city government to blacks, as Secretary of Housing and Urban Development; Carter also names Neil E. Goldschmidt, Mayor of Portland, Ore., to head the Department of Transportation.

General Motors lays off 12,000 workers and announces cutback in 1980 production, after prolonged slump in sales due to the recent gas shortage and OPEC price increases.

30 / California's Gov. Jerry Brown authorizes "exploratory" campaign committee, his first formal challenge to President Carter for the 1980 Democratic Presidential nomination.

31 / House votes to authorize President Carter to draft a standby gas rationing plan, reversing a July 25 vote calling for a Congressional veto over any such program.

House votes unanimously to censure Rep. Charles C. Diggs, Jr. (D.-Mich.) for padding his office payroll and using public funds to pay off his debts; the senior black Democrat in the House agrees to repay $40,000 in misappropriated funds to the Federal government.

Chrysler Corporation reports a record quarterly deficit of $207.1 million; officials of nation's third-ranking auto manufacturer announce they have asked Washington for $1 billion in aid to see the company through its financial crisis.

INTERNATIONAL

1 / U.S. requests Seoul to release up to 100 political prisoners as President Carter concludes trip to South Korea; government later releases 86 detainees July 17.

2 / Returns from July 1 Bolivian elections — the first since imposition of military rule in 1969 — show none of the candidates received the majority of popular votes required to be elected President; newly-elected Congress is empowered to elect new chief executive.

3 / West Germany's Bundestag (lower house) votes to lift statute of limitation on murder, allowing prosecution of Nazi war criminals beyond previous 1979 limit.

4 / Algeria announces the release of former president Ahmed Ben Bella after 14 years under house arrest.

5 / American envoys in Nicaragua obtain Pres. Somoza's promise to resign; U.S. also seeks to assure a moderate role for future Sandinista-backed government.

6 / Egypt and Israel agree to plan by U.S. Mideast envoy Robert S. Strauss to form "working groups" to hammer out issues in stalemated talks on Palestinian self-rule in the West Bank and Gaza.

7 / China and U.S. sign three-year trade pact in Peking, potentially doubling the present volume of trade; China also seeks lower tariffs under most-favored nation status.

8 / Vienna parley ends between Austrian Chancellor Bruno Kreisky, former West German leader Willy Brandt and PLO chief Yasir Arafat; joint statement expresses "concern" over Israeli settlements in the occupied territories, and cites Palestinian issue as "the central problem of the Middle East conflict."

9 / Secretary of State Cyrus Vance defends SALT-II treaty as U.S. Senate hearings on arms pact with the USSR begin; Vance says "we cannot expect to shift the bargin more to our favor."

Ayatollah Khomeini declares a general amnesty for "offenses committed under the past regime," except for murder and torture; decree effects some 3,000 political prisoners now held in Iran.

11 / U.S. space station Skylab falls back to Earth, breaking up over the Indian Ocean and showering debris over the Australian desert; no injuries reported.

U.S. Joint Chiefs of Staff endorse the strategic arms limitations treaty, but say pact with Soviet Union may be a "net loss" unless Washington increases defense spending.

13 / Palestinians raid Egypt's embassy in Ankara, Turkey, killing two guards and holding the Ambassador and 19 others hostage to demand release of jailed terrorists; condemned by the PLO, they later surrender (July 15).

14 / Nicaragua's provisional junta announces Cabinet to oversee transition government, representing a broad spectrum of moderate-to-radical anti-Somoza forces.

15 / Morarji R. Desai resigns as India's Prime Minister after 12-day parliamentary crisis that threatened to plunge India into political chaos.

17 / Gen. Anastasio Somoza Debayle resigns as President of Nicaragua and flies to exile in Miami; his successor, Francisco Urcoyo Maleanos, says he will stay in office, despite U.S. assurance to rebels that he was only an interim head of state.

CIA director Adm. Stansfield Turner says in closed Senate testimony on SALT-II that the Soviet Union could deploy five new missile systems under the terms of the treaty; Senate had been informed that Moscow was allowed deployment of only one missile system.

18 / Acting president Urcoyo flees Nicaragua, apparently as a result of U.S. pressure on the exiled Somoza to keep his agreement on a transfer of power; National Guard crumbles, leaving power to the rebel provisional junta.

19 / FSLN forces take control of capital of Managua, ending civil war in Nicaragua; 5-member ruling junta takes control July 20, expropriates all Somoza family holdings and dissolves Congress and the National Guard.

20 / UN conference on Indochinese refugees opens in Geneva, with Vietnam urging Western nations to accept more refugees from crowded Southeast Asian camps.

President Carter postpones withdrawal of U.S. combat forces from South Korea until at least 1981.

Two supertankers collide off Tobago July 19 in the West Indies, resulting in 10-square-mile oil spill; 26 of 70 crewmen aboard are missing, and presumed dead.

21 / UN Secretary-General Kurt Waldheim says in Geneva that Vietnam has agreed to halt the current exodus of refugees from that country, at least for the present.

22 / Israeli warplanes bomb three coastal villages in Lebanon; Beirut sources claim 15 civilians are killed. U.S. criticizes Jerusalem for the attacks (July 23).

Revolutionary junta in Nicaragua announces it will try former members of Somoza's military and government for war crimes, but that no executions are planned.

23 / U.S. and Vietnam reach accord on aiding refugees, allowing American consular officials into Ho Chi Minh City (Saigon) to process those seeking to enter the United States.

24 / UN Security Council agrees to withdraw its peace-keeping forces from the Sinai after USSR refuses to extend mandate, but acts to retain unarmed observer posts to monitor Israeli withdrawal.

25 / Israel turns over 2,500-square miles of Sinai territory to Egypt in second phase of planned withdrawal.

U.S. Senator Sam Nunn (D.-Ga.) says he will oppose the proposed arms treaty with the USSR unless the Carter Administration agrees to substantially raise military spending.

26 / India's President N. Sanjiva Reddy names C. Charan Singh — former deputy to Morarji Desai who led move to oust him — as Prime Minister.

Retired NATO commander Gen. Alexander M. Haig, Jr. tells Senate in SALT-II hearings to delay ratification until treaty's "flaws" are resolved and an assessment is made of future Administration spending programs.

28 / Iraq's Pres. Saddam Hussein orders arrest of five members of ruling Revolutionary Council on charges of conspiring against his regime; purge of officials follows July 16 resignation of Pres. Ahmed Hassan al-Bakr.

29 / Israel and Egypt both agree to send representatives to Washington for talks on U.S. proposal for an expanded UN truce monitoring team in the Sinai.

Basque separatists bomb main airport and two railway stations in Madrid, Spain, killing two and injuring over 100 in terror campaign to demand release of political prisoners.

30 / Secretary of State Vance says that U.S. will honor a 1977 pledge to NATO alliance to raise military spending by 3 percent annually; statement seen as attempt to placate Senate critics of SALT-II who seek to link arms agreement to increased defense spending.

31 / Former premier Shahpur Bakhtiar emerges from silent exile in Paris to denounce rule of the Ayatollah Khomeini, saying that his Islamic regime has brought "chaos and dictatorship" to Iran.

AUGUST 1979

NATIONAL

1 / House approves Administration's standby gas rationing plan, but White House fears that amendments included will dilute its effectiveness; Senate panel cuts proposed $22-billion allocation for synthetic fuel development to $3 billion for 1980.

3 / Chrysler is rebuffed by UAW leaders on proposed 2-year wage freeze to bail out financially stricken company.

5 / Chief Justice Warren E. Burger tells meeting of state chief judges that jury trials should be forgone in civil cases that are too technical for most laymen.

6 / AFL-CIO Executive Council calls for nationalization of U.S. oil companies unless they improve current practices to better serve the public.

7 / Massive oil slick from possibly the worst oil spill in history — a Mexican oil well that blew out August 1 — pollutes south Texas beaches.

8 / Senate confirmation panel will probe a possible conflict-of-interest that HUD Secretary-designate Moon Landrieu reportedly had while he was Mayor of New Orleans.

9 / Three F.B.I. agents are slain in unrelated incidents in Cleveland, Ohio and El Centro, Calif., the greatest loss of life in a single day in the Bureau's 71 years.

10 / White House counsel Robert J. Lipshutz resigns, the first Carter aide from Georgia to leave since July Cabinet shake-up; Presidential assistant Timothy Kraft resigns to head Carter-Mondale re-election committee. Personnel consultant Daniel W. Horgan resigns after his name is linked to probe of a New Jersey housing agency which had been under his supervision.

13 / Justice Department in suit charges Philadelphia's police with widespread and systematic brutality against minority groups; Mayor Frank L. Rizzo and police officials deny charges.

14 / White House says recent Energy Department study absolving oil companies of responsibility for summer fuel crisis will be reexamined, amid charges that report relied exclusively on unverified industry figures.

Outgoing Attorney General Griffin Bell chides friend, President Carter, as "trivializing" the Presidency by working on too many minor problems and acting "like he wasn't the President."

16 / White House taps John C. Sawhill, top-ranking energy official under Nixon and Ford administrations, as Deputy Secretary of Energy.

Korean influence-buying probe ends as Tongsun Park returns to Washington to testify in inquiry, after the Justice Department drops all charges pending against him.

17 / President Carter appoints Lloyd N. Cutler as White House counsel, replacing the resigning Robert Lipshutz.

President Carter and family leave on a one-week vacation by paddle-wheel steamer down the Mississippi, which is also viewed as an unofficial campaign tour.

21 / Federal Elections Commission report concludes that Gerald Rafshoon's advertising agency did not make any illegal contributions to President Carter's 1976 campaign; but Justice Department continues

probe of Presidential primaries, in which Rafshoon extended credit to Carter campaign committees.

22-23 / Nuclear Regulatory Commission resumes licensing of nuclear plants, then reverses itself after it is criticized by Presidential panel studying Three Mile Island.

24 / Hamilton Jordan denies allegations by owners of New York's Studio 54 disco that he used cocaine there last year; Justice Department will investigate charges.

27 / Teachers strike across the nation as students return from vacation; disputes reported from six Midwestern states, New Orleans and Oklahoma City, where it was the first job action by teachers in memory.

29 / Jeffrey R. MacDonald, 35, physician and a former Green Beret captain, is convicted in Fort Bragg, N.C., of killing his wife and two young daughters in 1970; Army had cleared MacDonald, who claims a "hippie" gang murdered his family.

30 / Presidential aide Richard M. Harden is alleged to have perjured himself in testimony to the grand jury investigating a supposed plan to fix the legal problems of fugitive financier Robert L. Vesco; Assistant Attorney General Philip B. Heymann later denies he leaked the story.

UAW picks General Motors as "target company" in negotiations for a new contract that would set the pace for other auto industry agreements in the fall.

INTERNATIONAL

1 / Britain's Prime Minister Margaret Thatcher hits recent Nigerian takeover of British oil companies at Commonwealth leaders' conference in Lusaka, Zambia; Lagos had accused companies of selling oil to South Africa.

2 / Anti-SALT Senators Sam Nunn (D.-Ga.), John Tower (R.-Tex.) and Henry Jackson (D.-Wash.) demand commitment from President Carter to increase defense spending before the Senate considers the arms accord with Moscow; Henry A. Kissinger says he will urge the Senate to reject the pact if such a commitment is not met.

4 / Christian Democratic leader Francesco Cossiga forms new three-party coalition government in Italy, after a month-long minority Socialist government falls.

5 / Commonwealth leaders in Lusaka approve new Zimbabwe peace plan; pact includes a cease-fire between Salisbury and guerrillas, drafting of a new constitution, and British supervision of new elections.
Pres. Nguema Biyoto Masie — whose 11-year reign of Equatorial Guinea had been called one of the most brutal in Africa — is overthrown (August 3) in a bloodless coup.

6 / Bolivia's Congress elects Walter Guevara Arze interim President after month-long electoral deadlock; he will serve until new elections are held in May, 1980.

7 / Carter Administration says in report to Congress that Israel may have violated agreement with the U.S. when it used American-supplied jets against Lebanon in July.

8 / Iraqi regime executes 21 persons found guilty of treason in recent secret trial, including five members of ruling Revolutionary Council.

11 / President Carter affirms to Israel his continued opposition to a Palestinian state and pledges no change in U.S. policy towards the PLO.

12 / Islamic militants attack Iranian leftists protesting recent press restrictions by the Bazargan government, and later ransack offices of left-wing parties and newspapers.

14 / State Department discloses that UN Ambassador Andrew Young held an unauthorized meeting in July with a representative of the Palestine Liberation Organization and later gave a false account of it to his superiors; Young admits meeting, stating he acted alone and was of limited scope.
Roaring seas and gale-force winds swamp competitors in the Fastnet yachting race in the English Channel and Irish Sea; as many as 17 persons are reported drowned.

15 / Andrew Young resigns as U.S. delegate to the United Nations after official reprimand for his unauthorized meeting with a PLO representative.

19 / Andrew Young calls U.S. policy of shunning contacts with the PLO "foolish;" intelligence sources say State Department knew of Young's meeting with the PLO and the gist of the discussion four days after they occurred.

India's Prime Minister Charan Singh quits after one-month-old government loses a parliamentary vote of confidence; Singh appointed to head new interim government.

Iran's Ayatollah Khomeini orders a general offensive to crush recent Kurdish rebellion; government troops surround Kurdistan capital of Sanandaj.

21 / Islamic government in Iran executes 18 Kurdish rebels; Western reporters are ordered expelled and regime announces closing of 26 newspapers and magazines in crackdown on critics of Iran's Islamic revolution.

22 / Mideast envoy Robert S. Strauss announces that President Carter has agreed to drop sponsorship of a resolution in the UN Security Council on Palestinian autonomy which had been rejected by Egypt and Israel.

23 / Eschel M. Rhoodie, central figure in the South African influence-buying scandal, is extradited by France to Johannesburg, where he faces charges of misappropriating part of the secret $75-million fund used to seek Western support for Pretoria's apartheid policies.
Aleksandr Godunov, a leading Soviet dancer, defects in New York, where he had been on tour with the Bolshoi Ballet.

24 / U.S. succeeds in delaying a UN vote on resolution calling for Palestinian self-determination.
U.S. immigration authorities delay takeoff of a Moscow-bound Aeroflot jetliner in New York carrying Ludmilla Vlasova, wife of defector Aleksandr Godunov; airliner departs (August 27) after Vlasova assures U.S. officials that she is leaving voluntarily.

25 / U.S. Vice-President Walter Mondale arrives in Peking for weeklong visit to cement Chinese-American relations.

27 / British World War II hero Earl Mountbatten and three companions are killed when a bomb destroys his fishing boat in Donegal Bay off Ireland; outlawed Irish Republican Army later claims responsibility for the slayings.

29 / U.S. calls on Israel to halt its pre-emptive strikes against southern Lebanon, calling on the PLO to also end its attacks on Israel and withdraw from the border area.

30 / Flap emerges over U.S. sale of 2 million gallons of diesel oil and kerosene to Iran, as chief of the national oil company in Tehran says shipment wasn't needed, and will instead be sold at a higher price on the world market.

31 / State Department discloses that 3,000 Soviet combat troops are currently stationed in Cuba; U.S. asks for explanation from Moscow.

SEPTEMBER 1979

NATIONAL

3-4 / Hurricane David strikes Florida's Atlantic coast causing severe damage but bypassing Miami; storm later buffets rest of Southeast coastal states.

6 / President Carter frees four Puerto Rican nationalists — Oscar Collazo, Irving Flores, Lolita Lebrón and Raphael Cancel-Miranda — imprisoned for terrorist activities, citing "humanitarian" reasons.
Secretary-designate of HUD Moon Landrieu admits in Senate confirmation hearings that he was the partner of a real estate developer who had done business with the city of New Orleans while Landrieu was Mayor, but says he did nothing improper.

10 / House Budget panel approves a $1.6 billion increase in arms spending for 1980, but defeats a $2-billion tax cut in the proposed 1980 Federal budget.

11 / President Carter submits $130.6 billion military budget to Congress that boosts arms spending by

percent; version is $2 billion more than spending bill passed by the House Budget committee.

12 / House rejects 259-155 bill reinstituting draft registration for 18-year-old males, and instead asks a Presidential study of military-manpower options.

Hurricane Frederic — the second major tropical storm of the season — hits the Gulf Coast area, causing over 500,000 people to flee inland; storm claims eight lives, causes nearly $1 billion in property loss.

14 / Senate Ethics Committee's investigation of alleged misfeasance by Senator Herman E. Talmadge (D.-Ga.) concludes by recommending that the Senate "denounce" Talmadge for "reprehensible" conduct, and that he reimburse the Senate $13,000 in misappropriated expenses.

United Auto Works and General Motors reach tentative agreement on a three-year contract that will set the tone for upcoming industry-labor negotiations.

15 / President Carter drops out of jogging race near Camp David from exhaustion; White House physician Dr. William Lukash says there is "no reason" to worry.

16 / Data on the hydrogen bomb is published in the Madison (Wis.) Press Connection after a court order barred its publication in a Berkeley, California newspaper.

17 / Justice Department drops effort to ban publication of articles on the hydrogen bomb by The Progressive magazine, after the Madison Press Connection printed a letter disclosing the same information.

Air Canada DC-9 jetliner returns to Boston after losing its rear door and part of its tail over the Atlantic; accident prompts investigation of DC-9's for possible structural defects.

19 / House votes 213-192 to reject proposed 1980 Federal budget; Senate had passed a $546.3 billion budget which included a deficit of $31.6 billion.

20 / President Carter orders Secret Service protection for Senator Edward Kennedy, shortly before Kennedy discloses plans to form an exploratory campaign committee for the 1980 elections.

23 / Over 200,000 gather in New York City to protest the continued use of atomic power, the largest anti-nuclear rally ever held in the United States.

24 / Carter appointees Moon Landrieu and Neil E. Goldschmidt take office as the respective chiefs of the Department of Housing and Urban Development and the Department of Transportation.

25 / House approves 5.5 percent pay increase for Congress and most top-level Federal employees, after defeating a proposed 7 percent raise Sept. 19.

27 / House by 215-to-210 approves final authorization for a Cabinet-level Department of Education.

House approves a $548 billion Federal budget for 1980 — including a $29 billion deficit — after rejecting a similar spending package Sept. 19.

28 / Senate rejects House-approved budget 59-9, objecting to restrictive language on abortion funding and a 5.5 percent pay increase for Congress and senior Federal officials.

George Meany, 85, announces he will step down in November as president of the powerful AFL-CIO labor federation; current secretary-treasurer Lane Kirkland, a long-time Meany aide, is expected to succeed the ailing labor leader.

INTERNATIONAL

1 / Dominican Republic is battered by Hurricane David; death toll is reported at over 1,000.

3 / Fidel Castro opens non-aligned conference in Havana with denunciation of both Washington and Peking as being chiefly responsible for global conflicts.

4 / Yugoslavia's President Tito urges third-world nations to remain independent of the superpowers at non-aligned conference, implicitly criticizing Cuba's pro-Soviet stance.

5 / Egypt and Israel agree to joint patrols in the Sinai to monitor compliance with Mideast peace agreement after withdrawal of UN peacekeeping force.

7 / President Carter warns Moscow that its relations with the U.S. will be "adversely affected" if it does not respond to Washington's concerns over Soviet troops in Cuba.

President Carter announces plans to deploy 200 MX missiles — mobile-based ICBMs with multiple silos to confuse the Russians — by 1989.

8 / President Carter says the Senate should approve the arms treaty with the Soviet Union "on its own merits," and not link it to Russian activity in Cuba.

9 / Senator Frank Church (D.-Idaho) demands USSR recall troops now in Cuba; Soviets deny that Russian combat troops are stationed in Cuba (Sept. 10).

Non-aligned conference ends in Havana with the delegates reaffirming movement's neutrality. Fidel Castro is elected coordinator of the 95-member body, but promises not to use position to further his own pro-Soviet views.

10 / Constitutional conference on Zimbabwe opens in London; Britain will seek a peaceful resolution to continued war between Prime Minister Abel Muzorewa's government and the Patriotic Front led by Robert Mugabe and Joshua Nkomo.

12 / Patriotic Front leaders accept British proposal on a new constitution for increased Black power in Zimbabwe as first order of business at London parley.

14 / Zimbabwe's Prime Minister Muzorewa accepts British proposal for a new constitution at London meeting; but Salisbury representative Ian Smith rejects new charter, which reduces white privileges.

16 / Israel lifts ban on purchase of land in the occupied territories by private Israeli citizens; move is later criticized by both U.S. and Egypt.

Afghanistan's Pres. Noor Mohammed Taraki resigns in favor of hard-line Premier Hafizullah Amin; Amin is reported to have staged a coup against Taraki, and to have "eliminated" many of his political opponents.

17 / Cuba frees the last four Americans held there on political charges; State Department denies "exchange" for four Puerto Rican nationalists, but release is seen as reciprocal gesture by Pres. Fidel Castro.

19 / Tentative accord is reached on expansion of a U.S. surveillance team in the Sinai, which will monitor Israeli-Egyptian compliance with the Mideast peace treaty.

Moderate parties narrowly retain power in Sweden's Sept. 16 elections, after mail balloting cancels an earlier lead by the Socialist-Communist coalition.

20 / Argentina's Supreme Court orders the release of La Opinión publisher Jacobo Timerman, who had been detained without charges by the military regime for 29 months; he is later expelled from Argentina (Sept. 25).

21 / Emperor Jean-Bedel Bokassa I of the Central African Empire is overthrown in a bloodless coup; new chief of state, former Pres. David Dacko, declares nation a republic.

UN General Assembly votes by 2-to-1 margin to retain Pol Pot's representative as Cambodia's official delegate, a defeat for the USSR and a victory for China and the non-Communist nations of Southeast Asia.

23 / China's Deputy Foreign Minister Wang Youping arrives in Moscow for talks aimed at easing Sino-Soviet tensions, the first such meeting since 1969.

24 / Patriotic Front leaders formally agree in London to guarantee 20 percent of the seats in Zimbabwe's parliament to whites under a new constitution.

25 / Soviet Foreign Minister Andrei Gromyko at the UN dismisses U.S. charges on Soviet combat troops in Cuba as "artificial;" statement is challenged by the White House.

26 / House votes 232-188 to approve the implementation of the Panama Canal treaty, scheduled to take effect on Oct. 1.

27 / Secretary of State Vance meets with Soviet Foreign Minister Gromyko in New York, but talks fail to resolve U.S. concerns over Soviet presence in Cuba.

28 / Fidel Castro accuses President Carter of creating "artificial" crisis over Soviet combat troops in Cuba, which Castro insists are advisors at a "training center" that has been in Cuba for 17 years.

President Carter meets with Mexico's Pres. Jose Lopez Portillo in Washington to discuss issues affecting future U.S.-Mexican relations, including illegal aliens and Mexico's new oil reserves.

29-30 / Pope John Paul II begins two-day visit to Ireland by calling on both sides of the conflict in Northern Ireland to "desist from hatred and violence;" nearly two million greet Pontiff in Drogheda, Galway and Dublin. On Oct. 1, he arrives in the U.S.

THE UNITED STATES

OUTLINE OF UNITED STATES HISTORY

16TH CENTURY

1564 French Huguenots failed in attempts to establish settlements in present-day South Carolina and Florida.

1565 Spaniards built fort at St. Augustine, Florida, first permanent white colony in present-day United States.

1585 Sir Walter Raleigh dispatched expedition to Roanoke Island, Virginia; settlement abandoned (1586).

1590 No traces found of second Roanoke settlement—the Lost Colony (established 1587)—and birthplace of Virginia Dare, first English child born (1587) in America.

1598 Juan de Oñate began settlement in New Mexico.

17TH CENTURY

1607 Colony established at Jamestown, Virginia; Captain John Smith elected (1608) head of group.
Pocahontas, daughter of Powhatan, head of an Indian confederacy in that region, rescued John Smith after Indian capture.

1612 John Rolfe developed effective method of curing tobacco; later (1614) married Pocahontas.

1614 Dutch established trading post in what is now New York State.

1619 House of Burgesses, first representative assembly in America, met at Jamestown.
The first 20 blacks arrived in Virginia as indentured servants.

1620 Pilgrims arrived from England in *Mayflower* and founded colony at Plymouth, Massachusetts; signed Mayflower Compact, first written constitution in colonies.

1626 Peter Minuit bought Manhattan Island from Indians for the equivalent of $24 and named it New Amsterdam.

1629 Massachusetts Bay Company formed; John Winthrop elected governor.

1630 Settlement established at Boston, Massachusetts.

1630–1640 "Great Migration" of Puritans from England settled Massachusetts and Connecticut.

1632 Cecilius Calvert, 2d Lord Baltimore, established Roman Catholic colony in Maryland.

1636 Banished (1635) from Massachusetts Bay colony, Roger Williams founded Providence, Rhode Island, first English colony to grant religious freedom.
Harvard College founded.

1638 First printing press established in Cambridge, Massachusetts; printed (1640) *Bay Psalm Book*.

1647 Peter Stuyvesant became head of New Netherlands; his dictatorial rule was resented.

1655 Stuyvesant seized Swedish forts on Delaware, ending Swedish rule in North America.

1662 Virginia became the first colony to declare slavery hereditary.

1664 English took New Amsterdam, changing name to New York.

1676 Nathaniel Bacon led Virginia frontiersmen against raiding Indians and then against Governor Berkeley; Bacon's death virtually ended rebellion.

1677 William Penn framed first charter separating church and state at the Quaker colony of West Jersey.

1680 New Hampshire became separate province.

1682 La Salle reached mouth of Mississippi and claimed area from Quebec to Gulf Coast—Louisiana—for France.
William Penn founded Philadelphia for Quakers.

1686 New England made a royal dominion; tyrannical rule of Edmund Andros ended in 1689 when England's "Glorious Revolution" spread to the colonies.

1689 King William's War between French and English began as part of greater European war; Treaty of Ryswick (1697) restored prewar positions.

1690 Benjamin Harris published first newspaper, in Boston, that was suppressed after one issue for criticizing conduct of war.

1692 Witch trials began in Salem, Massachusetts; 20 "witches" executed before hunt ended (1693).

1693 William and Mary College founded in Williamsburg, Virginia.

1699 Sieur d'Iberville founded Old Biloxi (now Ocean Springs) on Biloxi Bay, first permanent settlement in Louisiana Territory.

18TH CENTURY

1700 By this date, shipbuilding and whaling industries had developed in New England; plantation system in Virginia, Maryland, and Carolina fully established.

1704 Boston *News-Letter*, first continuous colonial newspaper, was started.

1716 First American theater built, in Williamsburg.

1724 English established Fort Dummer near site of Brattleboro, considered first permanent Vermont settlement.

1732–1757 Benjamin Franklin annually published *Poor Richard's Almanack*.

1733 James Oglethorpe founded colony in Savannah, Georgia, last of the original 13 colonies to be settled.

1734–1735 John Peter Zenger, editor and publisher of *New-York Weekly Journal*, tried for sedition; acquittal was landmark in assuring freedom of press in America.

1734–1750 Jonathan Edwards, in New England, and George Whitefield, in Georgia, led Great Awakening, a series of religious revivals.

1741 Captain Vitus Bering discovered Alaska and claimed it for Russia.

1744 King George's War, extension in America of War of the Austrian Succession in Europe, began; Treaty of Aix-la-Chapelle (1748) restored prewar position.

1754 French erected Fort Duquesne, on site of Pittsburgh, Pennsylvania.
George Washington's fight with French in Ohio territory became first skirmish of French and Indian War, which spread (1756) to Europe and became known as the Seven Years War.

1763 Treaty of Paris ended French control east of Mississippi; Spain ceded Florida to England in return for Cuba.

1764 Parliament passed the Sugar Act, first law to raise money for crown in the colonies, and Currency Act, which forbade all colonies to issue paper money.
James Otis denounced acts in pamphlet, noting British offense of taxation without representation.

1765 College of Philadelphia (later part of University of Pennsylvania) offered first professional medical training in colonies.
Parliament issued Stamp Act, first direct tax levied by crown on American colonies.
Colonials convoked Stamp Act Congress; organized Sons of Liberty.

1766 Stamp Act repealed, but Parliament passed Declaratory Act, affirming its right to legislate for colonies.

1767 Townshend Acts passed by Parliament, imposing import duties; many colonies enacted nonimportation agreements.

1769–1782 Fray Junípero Serra founded nine Franciscan missions in California.

1770 In Boston, several colonists were killed by English soldiers in a melee, later known as the Boston Massacre.
Townshend Acts repealed, except for tea tax; colonial merchants worked for conciliation.

1773 Parliament passed Tea Act granting East India Company full remission of all tea duties.
Boston Tea Party occurred, when patriots dressed

as Indians dumped tea shipment into Boston Harbor.

1774 First Continental Congress met in Philadelphia, with representatives from all colonies except Georgia.

1775 Patrick Henry made his "Liberty or Death" speech before Virginia Assembly.

Parliament passed New England Restraining Act, forbidding colonies to trade with any nation except Britain and British West Indies.

Minutemen fought British at Lexington and Concord, signaling start of American Revolution's military phase.

Second Continental Congress met in Philadelphia and appointed Washington chief of Continental forces.

The first abolitionist society in America was established in Philadelphia.

British defeated Americans at Bunker Hill and attacked Boston; city under siege until March 1776.

1776 Thomas Paine's *Common Sense* published, calling for American independence.

Declaration of Independence adopted by Congress.

Nathan Hale ("I only regret that I have but one life to lose for my country") executed by British as American spy.

Washington, leading troops across Delaware River, made surprise attack on British at Trenton, New Jersey.

1777 General Burgoyne's defeat at Saratoga was major American victory.

Articles of Confederation adopted by Congress (ratified by all colonies by 1781).

Congress recommended that colonial governments appropriate Loyalist property.

Washington and troops took up winter quarters at Valley Forge, Pennsylvania.

1778 Americans and French signed Treaty of Alliance.

British took Savannah, Georgia.

1779 John Paul Jones ("I have not yet begun to fight"), commanding *Bon Homme Richard*, defeated British frigate *Serapis*, off coast of England.

1780 Washington's troops mutinied at Morristown, New Jersey, because of sparse supplies and delayed salaries.

Benedict Arnold's treason exposed.

1781 Washington and Rochambeau planned joint Franco-American Yorktown (Va.) campaign, which brought surrender of Cornwallis and virtually ended hostilities.

Congress chartered Bank of North America to supply government with money.

1782 John Adams, Benjamin Franklin, and John Jay negotiated peace treaty with British in Paris.

1783 Treaty of Paris acknowledged independence of the United States.

Almost the entire American army disbanded without authority and Congress fled Philadelphia to escape discontented soldiers.

Last of 100,000 Loyalists fled country.

General Washington bade farewell to his officers at Fraunces Tavern, New York City.

1786 Daniel Shays led discontented Massachusetts farmers in armed rebellion; insurrection crushed (1787) and later Massachusetts enacted more liberal legislation.

1787 Constitutional Convention held in Philadelphia.

Congress adopted the Northwest Ordinance creating and providing a government for the Northwest Territory; slavery in region was prohibited.

Alexander Hamilton, James Madison, and John Jay began writing *The Federalist Papers*, which urged acceptance of Constitution.

Delaware was first state to ratify Constitution.

1788 New Hampshire ratified the Constitution, thereby achieving the necessary nine-state acceptance.

1789 George Washington elected nation's first President and John Adams became Vice-President.

First Congress met in New York, nation's first capital.

Federal Judiciary Act provided for organization of Supreme Court, 13 district courts, and three circuit courts; John Jay became first Chief Justice.

1790 Hamilton organized national fiscal program.

First census recorded American population as **3,929,214.**

Capital temporarily moved to Philadelphia.

1791 Bill of Rights became part of Constitution.

Bank of the United States established.

1793 Washington declared American neutrality vis-à-vis France and Britain.

Citizen Genêt, Minister of French Republic to the United States, asked to leave because of his conduct; later became American citizen.

The Fugitive Slave Act was passed, making it illegal to give comfort to or prevent the arrest of a runaway slave.

Eli Whitney invented cotton gin.

1794 Federal troops put down Whisky Rebellion in western Pennsylvania.

Jay's treaty with Britain concluded; provision included British agreement to withdraw from Northwest posts; ratified (1795).

1795 11th Constitutional Amendment is ratified: a state cannot be sued by citizen of another state.

1796 In his Farewell Address, Washington warned of permanent foreign alliances and encouraged temporary ones in times of emergency.

John Adams (Federalist) elected President; Thomas Jefferson (Democratic-Republican) elected Vice-President.

1797 Affairs with France deteriorated, especially after the XYZ Affair: Talleyrand's agents tried to extort bribes from American commissioners in Paris.

1798–1800 Americans fought undeclared naval war with France; Convention of 1800 released United States from alliance with France.

1798 Alien and Sedition Acts passed by Federalists to repress political opposition.

Kentucky and Virginia Resolutions maintained unconstitutionality of Alien and Sedition Acts; expressed early states rights theory.

1799 Washington died at Mount Vernon.

19TH CENTURY

1800 Washington, D.C., became nation's capital.

1801 House of Representatives chose Jefferson for President and Aaron Burr Vice-President after electoral tie; Jefferson was first President inaugurated in new capital.

1802 Congress established U.S. Military Academy at West Point, New York.

1803 In *Marbury* v. *Madison*, Chief Justice Marshall established principle of judicial review.

United States purchased Louisiana from France for about $15 million, doubling nation's area.

Meriwether Lewis and William Clark began their westward expedition.

1804 Hamilton killed in duel with Aaron Burr.

1807 Congress enacted law prohibiting importation of slaves after January 1, 1808.

Embargo enacted because of British harassment on seas; repealed (1809), but trade with France and Great Britain still prohibited.

1808 Congress prohibited the admission of any new slaves into the United States.

1809 James Madison sworn in as President with George Clinton as Vice-President.

1811 General William Henry Harrison defeated Tecumseh's forces at Battle of Tippecanoe.

1812 War declared on Great Britain for impressing U.S. seamen, blockading, and violating neutrality; Americans suffered setbacks on land, but naval successes boosted low morale.

1813 British blockaded coast, but Captain Oliver Hazard Perry's naval victory secured Lake Erie for United States.

1814 British took offensive, capturing and burning Washington, but suffered losses in attempt to invade New York from Canada.

Francis Scott Key wrote lyrics of "Star-spangled Banner."

At Hartford Convention, New England delegates met to revise Constitution and oppose war.

Treaty of Ghent ended war.

1815 Andrew Jackson defeated British at New Orleans before news of peace arrived.

Fleet under Stephen Decatur ended Barbary states' imposition of tribute on American merchant vessels.

1816 James Monroe elected President and Daniel D. Tompkins, Vice-President.

First protective tariff enacted.

1817 New York State legislature authorized construction of Erie Canal; it opened in 1825.

1818 U.S.-Canadian boundary to Rockies fixed; United States and Britain agreed to occupy Oregon Territory jointly.

1819 Financial panic seized nation.

Adams-Onis Treaty, ceding Spain's Florida holding to the United States, signed; Andrew Jackson became (1821) Florida's first governor.

1820 Missouri Compromise prohibited slavery in Louisiana Territory north of Missouri's southern border; Missouri admitted to Union as slave state and Maine as free state.

First American missionaries arrived in Hawaii.

1821 Spain granted Moses Austin land in Texas for settlement.

1822-1826 U.S. government recognized newly independent Latin American republics.

1823 Monroe Doctrine promulgated: any further European effort to colonize the Americas or interfere in their affairs would be considered a hostile act.

1824-1825 Presidential election resulted in no candidate having a majority; House chose John Quincy Adams President after much bargaining between candidates.

1828 Congress passed protectionist "Tariff of Abominations."

Andrew Jackson elected first Democratic President; introduced spoils system on national level; Calhoun reelected Vice-President.

1829 David Walker, a free black, published his famous "Appeal," one of the most militant antislavery documents.

1830 Senators Daniel Webster (Mass.) and Robert Y. Hayne (S.C.) engaged in historic states' rights debate.

1831 William Lloyd Garrison began to publish *The Liberator.*

Nat Turner led major slave insurrection in Virginia.

1832 President Jackson vetoed renewal of National Bank.

South Carolina nullified U.S. tariff laws; Jackson declared action was rebellion and ordered Forts Moultrie and Sumter reinforced.

1833 Jackson began second term; ordered public deposits withdrawn from Bank of the United States and put into state banks; Secretary of the Treasury Taney deposited funds in "pet banks."

American Anti-Slavery Society founded at Philadelphia as abolitionist movement grew more vocal.

1834 Whig party had come into being; Henry Clay led group formed by National Republicans, states' righters, and dissident Democrats.

1835 Seminoles in Florida resisted forced transportation West; despite capture (1837) of their leader Osceola, resistance continued until 1842.

1836 Mexican leader Santa Anna captured fort of Alamo at San Antonio, Texas; Sam Houston later led American victory at Battle of San Jacinto.

Texas declared its independence from Mexico; Houston became president of independent republic.

1837 Martin Van Buren inaugurated as President.

Panic of 1837 depressed economy.

1840 By this time, Underground Railroad was fully organized to rescue fugitive slaves.

1841 President William Henry Harrison died a month after inauguration; John Tyler became first Vice-President to succeed to Presidency as a result of incumbent's death.

Horace Greeley founded the New York *Tribune.*

1842 Webster-Ashburton Treaty with Britain settled northeastern U.S. boundary.

1843 United States recognized independence of Hawaii.

1844 James K. Polk elected President; George M. Dallas elected Vice-President.

1845 Texas agreed to join Union and was annexed.

Mexico broke off diplomatic relations with United States.

U.S. Naval Academy established at Annapolis, Maryland.

1846 Mexican War broke out after Mexican troops crossed Rio Grande; Zachary Taylor led American victory at Battles of Palo Alto, Resaca de la Palma, Monterrey, and Buena Vista.

Oregon boundary established by treaty with Great Britain.

Wilmot Proviso, banning slavery in territory acquired from Mexican War, failed to pass (1846, 1847) Congress.

1847 General Winfield Scott captured Mexico City.

Led by Brigham Young, the Mormons settled at Salt Lake City, Utah.

1848 Treaty of Guadalupe Hidalgo signed by the United States and Mexico; established Rio Grande as boundary; Mexico recognized U.S. claim to Texas and ceded New Mexico and California in return for $15 million.

First Women's Rights Convention, led by Lucretia Mott and Elizabeth Cady Stanton, held at Seneca Falls, New York.

Discovery of gold in California touched off "Gold Rush."

1849 Zachary Taylor (Whig) was inaugurated.

The first school integration lawsuit was filed by Benjamin Roberts against the City of Boston. The Massachusetts Supreme Court rejected the suit, setting the groundwork for the "separate but equal" doctrine.

1850 Vice-President Millard Fillmore (Whig) succeeded to the Presidency after Taylor died of cholera.

Congress passed Henry Clay's Compromise of 1850: California admitted as free state; remainder of Mexican territory divided into New Mexico and Utah, without prior decision on slavery; more effective Fugitive Slave Law enacted; slave trade abolished in capital.

Clayton-Bulwer Treaty, concerning freedom of future canal zone, signed with Britain; abrogated (1901).

1852 Harriet Beecher Stowe's *Uncle Tom's Cabin* published.

1853 Commodore Matthew C. Perry visited Japan and obtained (1854) trade agreement.

Gadsden Purchase: land now included in New Mexico and Arizona purchased from Mexico.

1854 Congress enacted Kansas and Nebraska Act, sponsored by Stephen A. Douglas; repealed Missouri Compromise and provided that people in states would decide slavery issue.

1854-1856 Settlement of Kansas brought bloody fighting; U.S. Senate engaged in violent debates.

1856 Republican party, formed in large part by Northern Whigs, held its first convention.

1857 Supreme Court's Dred Scott decision ruled Missouri Compromise unconstitutional, holding that a slave's residence in free territory did not make him free and denying citizenship rights to descendants of slaves.

1858 Abraham Lincoln debated Senator Douglas on slavery issue and became national figure.

1859 John Brown, Kansas abolitionist, unsuccessfully tried to seize federal arsenal at Harpers Ferry, Virginia, to start slave insurrection; captured, he was hanged for treason.

First oil well drilled at Titusville, Pa., by Col. Edwin L. Drake.

1860 Lincoln elected President; South Carolina passed ordinance of secession.

1861 Mississippi, Florida, Alabama, Georgia, Louisiana, and Texas seceded from Union; Confederate States of America formed with Jefferson Davis (Miss.) as president; constitution based on states' rights doctrine.

South Carolina troops fired on Fort Sumter (April 12), forcing Union troops to evacuate; signaled start of Civil War.

Lincoln proclaimed blockade of Confederate states.

Virginia, Arkansas, Tennessee, and North Carolina joined Confederacy.

Robert E. Lee and Joseph E. Johnston resigned from U.S. Army.

West Virginia broke away from Virginia; admitted to Union in 1863.

1862 Lincoln issued Emancipation Proclamation to take effect January 1863.

Major Civil War battles of Shiloh, *Monitor* and *Merrimack*, Peninsular Campaign, Second Bull Run, Antietam, and Fredericksburg occurred.

1863 First national conscription act enacted; draft riots exploded in New York City.

General George Meade's Union forces defeated General Lee's army at Gettysburg; Lincoln delivered famous address at dedication of Gettysburg Cemetery.

1864 General Ulysses S. Grant became commander of Union armies.

General William Tecumseh Sherman marched through Georgia to the sea; captured Atlanta and Savannah.

1865 13th Amendment abolishing slavery was ratified.

Lee surrendered (April 9) at Appomattox (Va.) Courthouse.

Lincoln assassinated (April 14) by John Wilkes Booth at Ford's Theater, Washington, D.C.; Vice-President Andrew Johnson became President.

1866 Ku Klux Klan formed in Tennessee.

Civil Rights Act, bestowing citizenship on blacks passed over Johnson's veto.

Congress adopted the 14th Amendment containing "due process" and "equal protection" clauses guaranteeing civil rights of blacks.

1867 Three Reconstruction Acts passed over Johnson's vetoes; divided South into military districts and abolished qualifications for Confederate States' readmission to Union.

Secretary of State William H. Seward purchased Alaska from Russia for $7.2 million.

Northerners, called "carpetbaggers," participated in Southern Reconstruction; Southern whites allying themselves with Radicals were called "scalawags."

1868 Andrew Johnson was impeached by House and tried by Senate; two-thirds vote required for conviction failed by one vote.

Seven former Confederate states readmitted to Union.

14th Amendment was ratified.

The transcontinental railroad was completed.

1869 15th Amendment, giving blacks right to vote, proposed; ratified (1870).

1870 *New York Times* began exposé of Tammany Hall corruption; led to eventual imprisonment of Boss Tweed.

Joseph H. Rainey of South Carolina became the first black to sit in the House of Representatives after election to the 41st Congress; he subsequently was reelected four times.

General Robert E. Lee died.

The 15th Amendment was adopted, guaranteeing the right to vote to all U.S. citizens.

1871 Civil service reform began with establishment of first Civil Service Commission.

Disastrous fire destroyed most of Chicago.

1872 New York *Sun* charged prominent Republicans with taking bribes in Crédit Mobilier scandal (corruption in building Union Pacific railroad); resulted (1873) in Congressional investigation.

1873 Financial panic developed into five-year depression, worst to date.

1875 Civil Rights Act was passed forbidding discrimination against blacks in public facilities.

1876 General Custer and his troops were massacred by Sitting Bull's Sioux Indians at the Little Bighorn.

Presidential election contest between Samuel Tilden and Rutherford B. Hayes disputed; special electoral commission declared (1877) Hayes President.

1877 Reconstruction Era officially ended.

Federal troops put down a series of railroad strikes.

1878 Bland-Allison Act, passed over Hayes's veto, required government to purchase silver.

1881 President James A. Garfield was shot; succeeded by Chester A. Arthur.

1882 Chinese Exclusion Act barred immigration of Chinese laborers for 10 years; later legislation continued policy until 1943.

1883 Pendleton Act established civil service system.

Supreme Court ruled antidiscrimination portions of 1875 Civil Rights Act invalid, opening the way for repassage of Jim Crow laws.

1886 American Federation of Labor organized with Samuel Gompers as first president.

Statue of Liberty unveiled in New York harbor.

Capture of Apache chief Geronimo ended Southwest Indian warfare.

Anarchists convicted of Haymarket Massacre.

1889 Oklahoma "land rush" opened all but panhandle of Oklahoma Territory for settlement.

U.S.-Latin American conference established (1890) body later called Pan American Union.

1890 Sherman Anti-Trust Act became law.

Highly protective McKinley Tariff adopted.

1891 Populist party formed as part of agrarian protest movement.

1893 Financial panic caused partly by severe gold drain began; thousands of banks and commercial institutions failed before economy recovered (1897).

World's Columbian Exposition held in Chicago.

1894 Unemployment became widespread; "Coxey's Army" of the jobless marched on Washington to demand public works program.

Pullman strike brought federal intervention.

1895 Southern states inaugurated "grandfather" clauses as part of program (including literacy tests and poll taxes) to disfranchise blacks.

U.S. involvement in British-Venezuelan dispute led to broad construction of Monroe Doctrine, stressing right of the United States to intercede in hemispheric disputes.

1896 Supreme Court in *Plessy* v. *Ferguson* upheld Louisiana law requiring segregated railroad facilities, under "separate but equal" doctrine.

1897 Gold rush in Klondike began.

1898 Spanish-American War broke out after battleship *Maine* exploded in harbor of Havana, Cuba; in Treaty of Paris Spain granted Cuba independence, ceded Puerto Rico, Guam, and Philippines to United States in return for payment of $20 million; Cuba came under U.S. military control, headed by General Leonard Wood.

United States annexed Hawaii.

1899 United States participated in first Hague Conference, which established Permanent Court of Arbitration.

20TH CENTURY

1900 United States expressed its commitment to Chinese Open Door policy.

U.S. troops helped relieve Peking during Boxer Rebellion.

Samoan Islands were divided between the United States and Germany.

1901 U.S. military rule of Philippines ended and civil government organized; islands became territory (1902).

Platt amendment, which Cubans had to incorporate (1902) in their constitution and recognize (1903) in treaty, made island virtual American protectorate; abrogated (1934).

Second Hay-Pauncefote Treaty gave Americans free hand in Isthmian canal.

President McKinley was shot in Buffalo; Theodore Roosevelt became President.

1902 Roosevelt pledged "Square Deal" for both labor and industry; began "trust-busting" with prosecution of the Northern Securities Company.

1903 Wright brothers flew first successful heavier-than-air machine.

1904 Roosevelt's annual message contained his "Corollary" to the Monroe Doctrine: United States' obligation to maintain order in Latin America.

1905 Russo-Japanese peace treaty signed at Portsmouth, New Hampshire; Roosevelt's role of mediator brought him (1906) Nobel Peace Prize.

Industrial Workers of the World, radical labor organization, founded in Chicago.

1906 Earthquake and fire destroyed San Francisco.

Pure Food and Drug and Meat Inspection Acts signed.

1907 "Gentlemen's Agreement": Japan agreed not to allow laborers to migrate to America.

1908 William Howard Taft elected President.

1909 Payne-Aldrich Tariff set high protective rates.

Robert E. Peary discovered North Pole.

1912 Roosevelt bolted Republican party and was Progressive (Bull Moose) party's candidate for President.

Woodrow Wilson won three-way Presidential race.

U.S. marines landed in Nicaragua to protect American interests during revolt.

1913 The 16th (income tax) and 17th (popular election of U.S. Senators) Amendments ratified.

Federal Reserve System established national banking and currency system.

United States began intervention in Mexican Revolution.

1914 Federal Trade Commission established.

Clayton Anti-Trust Act supplemented and strengthened Sherman Anti-Trust Act.

United States proclaimed its neutrality in World War I.

U.S. naval forces bombarded and occupied Vera Cruz, Mexico.

Panama Canal opened.

1915 *Lusitania* and *Arabic* sinkings brought strong protest notes from Wilson and modification of German submarine warfare.

1916 General John J. Pershing's troops pursued Pancho Villa 200 miles into Mexico without success.

1916–1924 U.S. troops occupied Santo Domingo.

1917 United States severed relations with Germany.

Publication of secret Zimmermann note, proposing German-Mexican alliance, helped Wilson gain House approval for arming merchantmen.

Congress declared war on Germany (April 6); General Pershing appointed head of American Expeditionary Force (AEF).

Congress passed Selective Service Act; Espionage Act; and Trading with the Enemy Act, forbidding commerce with enemy nations.

United States purchased Virgin Islands from Denmark.

1918 Wilson announced his "Fourteen Points" for peace.

Germany surrendered and armistice signed (November 11); U.S. war deaths, 112,432, many from disease.

Sedition Act passed; many Socialist and pacifist leaders imprisoned during next few years.

1919 Wilson toured country on behalf of League of Nations; awarded Nobel Peace Prize; suffered stroke.

18th Amendment (Prohibition) ratified.

1920 19th Amendment (women's suffrage) ratified.

Socialist Presidential candidate Eugene Debs, in prison, polled almost a million votes.

A. Mitchell Palmer ordered mass arrests of agitators during "Red scare" period.

Senate refused to ratify Versailles Treaty, ending World War I.

Warren G. Harding (Republican) and Calvin Coolidge elected President and Vice-President.

1922 Leading powers agreed to limit naval forces at Washington Arms Conference.

1923 Harding died; Coolidge became President.

1923–1924 Knowledge that Secretary of the Interior Albert B. Fall had secretly leased Teapot Dome oil reserves to Harry F. Sinclair was one of many Harding administration scandals made public.

1924 Soldiers Bonus Act compensated veterans for overseas duty.

1925 John Scopes, Tennessee schoolteacher, was defended by Clarence Darrow and prosecuted by William Jennings Bryan; Bryan secured the conviction of Scopes for teaching evolution.

1926 Richard Byrd and Floyd Bennett became first men to fly over North Pole.

U.S. troops landed in Nicaragua to quell rebellion; troops finally withdrawn in 1933.

1927 Charles A. Lindbergh made first nonstop solo flight from New York to Paris, becoming an international hero overnight.

1928 Kellogg-Briand Pact, outlawing war, signed by the United States; ratified by Senate (1929).

Al Smith, a Roman Catholic, ran as Democratic Presidential candidate.

Herbert C. Hoover and Charles Curtis elected President and Vice-President.

1929 Stock Market crash grew into worldwide Great Depression; low point came 1932–1933.

St. Valentine's Day massacre in Chicago marked peak of gangster wars.

1930 United States, Great Britain, and Japan agreed to limit navies at London Naval Conference.

Hawley-Smoot Tariff brought duty level to an all-time high.

1931 Hoover proposed one-year moratorium on inter-allied debts and reparations because of worldwide economic crisis.

1932 Reconstruction Finance Corporation established.

Lindbergh's son kidnapped and slain.

"Bonus Army," camped in Washington seeking early payment of veterans' benefits, was dispersed by Army troops led by Douglas MacArthur.

Franklin Delano Roosevelt and John Nance Garner were elected President and Vice-President.

1933 Roosevelt's "New Deal" began with bank holiday

to lessen severe economic crisis; later he took nation off gold standard and delivered his radio "fireside chats."

"Hundred Days" session of Congress produced Emergency Banking Relief Act, Agricultural Adjustment Act, Federal Emergency Relief Act, and established Civilian Conservation Corps, Civil Works Administration, and Federal Bank Deposit Insurance Corporation. Supreme Court later declared several New Deal Acts unconstitutional.

Congress created Tennessee Valley Authority and established Commodity Credit Corporation.

21st Amendment repealed Prohibition.

Roosevelt's "Good Neighbor Policy" included opposition to armed intervention in Latin America.

1933–1936 Severe drought converted Great Plains into "Dust Bowl."

1934 Export-Import Bank established.

Congress passed Securities Exchange Act and established Federal Communications Commission and Federal Housing Administration.

John Dillinger slain by FBI agents in Chicago.

1935 Additional New Deal agencies created included Works Progress Administration, with Harry L. Hopkins as head; Resettlement Administration, directed by Rexford G. Tugwell; Rural Electrification Administration; and a new National Labor Relations Board.

Social Security Act created federal-state system of unemployment and old-age compensation.

1937 Supreme Court upheld New Deal legislation such as N.L.R.A. and Social Security; Roosevelt allowed "Court packing" plan to drop.

Relations with Japan started to deteriorate after sinking of U.S. gunboat *Panay*.

1938 Congress voted billion-dollar naval building program.

Fair Labor Standards Act (Wages and Hours Law) set up minimum wage and maximum hours for companies connected with interstate commerce.

Mexican expropriation of U.S. oil property caused long controversy.

1939 American neutrality pledged after war broke out in Europe; but "cash and carry" policy allowed for exports of arms to belligerent powers.

Albert Einstein and other scientists told Roosevelt of possibilities of developing atomic bomb.

1940 Smith Act (Alien Registration Act) included provisions that made it unlawful to advocate or teach the overthrow or destruction of any government in the United States by force and to be a member of any group dedicated to such a policy.

Selective Training and Service Act (Burke-Wadsworth Bill), nation's first peacetime program of compulsory military service was enacted.

1941 Roosevelt delivered Four Freedom's speech.

Lend-Lease Act allowed friendly nations to secure arms without cash.

Atlantic Charter, joint statement of postwar aims, issued by Roosevelt and Prime Minister Churchill.

Japanese attacked (December 7) Pearl Harbor; Congress declared war on Japan.

Germany and Italy declared war (December 11) on United States.

1942 Pacific Coast Japanese-Americans were relocated to Western detention camps; released in 1944; action upheld by Supreme Court.

In Pacific, Bataan and Corregidor fell to Japanese; U.S. Marines won major victory at Guadalcanal; U.S. planes, led by Major General James H. Doolittle, raided Tokyo.

First self-sustaining nuclear reaction achieved at the University of Chicago.

United Nations Pact signed by 26 nations at Washington.

1943 American forces helped drive Germans from North Africa and invaded Italy, which surrendered to Allies.

U.S. troops in the Pacific began island-hopping operations and combined with ANZAC troops to force retreat of Japanese in New Guinea.

Roosevelt attended conferences in Casablanca, Quebec, Cairo, and Teheran.

1944 Dwight D. Eisenhower became Supreme Commander of American Expeditionary Forces.

Allies invaded Europe and liberated France, Belgium, and Luxembourg.

Bretton Woods Conference set up International Monetary Fund and International Bank for Reconstruction and Development.

Roosevelt defeated Thomas E. Dewey and won fourth term; Harry S. Truman elected Vice-President.

1945 U.S. troops recaptured Philippines from Japanese.

Churchill, Roosevelt, and Stalin met at Yalta.

Roosevelt died (April 12); succeeded by Truman.

United Nations established in San Francisco.

Germany surrendered (May 7) unconditionally.

United States dropped atomic bombs on Japanese cities of Hiroshima and Nagasaki; Japan surrendered (August 14).

Potsdam Conference, to plan occupation and settlement of Europe, attended by Truman, Churchill (succeeded by Clement Attlee), and Stalin.

1946 Philippines gained independence from U.S.

United States set up Atomic Energy Commission for civilian control of atomic energy.

United Nations established permanent headquarters in New York City.

Churchill delivered his "Iron Curtain" speech at Fulton, Missouri; marked beginning of Cold War.

1947 "Truman Doctrine," economic and military assistance, began with aid to Greece and Turkey; doctrine was part of policy to contain Communism.

General George C. Marshall proposed plan for European recovery.

Taft-Hartley Act, limiting power of labor, passed over Truman's veto.

1948 Whittaker Chambers accused Alger Hiss of transmitting documents to Russians; Hiss denied charges, was indicted for perjury, and convicted (1950).

Truman issued Executive Order ending segregation in the armed forces.

U.S. airlift frustrated Soviet blockade of Berlin.

Truman defeated Dewey in upset election.

1949 Truman outlined his Point Four program of technical assistance to aid world peace.

North Atlantic Treaty Organization approved.

1950 South Korea invaded by North Korean troops; Truman ordered U.S. forces into area.

Senator Joseph McCarthy charged that the State Department was infiltrated by Communists.

1951 22d Amendment, limiting President to two terms, ratified.

Truman recalled General MacArthur from Korea for insubordination.

1952 Supreme Court declared Truman's seizure of steel mills during strike unconstitutional.

McCarran-Walter Bill restricted immigration.

General Dwight D. Eisenhower became first Republican to win Presidency since 1928.

1953 Korean armistice signed.

1954 *Brown* v. *Board of Education of Topeka:* Supreme Court outlawed racial segregation in public schools, as "inherently unequal."

United States commitment in Southeast Asia began with formation of SEATO and financial aid to Indo-China (Vietnam, Laos, and Cambodia).

1955 Supreme Court ordered school desegregation to proceed "with all deliberate speed."

AFL and CIO merged into one labor organization.

1956 Arrest of seamstress Rosa Parks for refusing to give her seat to a white man on a bus in Montgomery, Alabama, resulted in a bus boycott led by Martin Luther King, Jr.

1957 Eisenhower extended Truman Doctrine to Middle East with aid to Jordan.

Governor Orval Faubus called out Arkansas National Guard to prevent integration of Little Rock schools; Eisenhower sent federal troops to protect rights of black students.

Civil Rights Act was passed—the first such legislation since Reconstruction.

1958 First U.S. Earth satellite was launched.

Eisenhower sent marines to Lebanon during civil insurrection.

1959 Alaska and Hawaii admitted to Union.

Soviet Premier Khrushchev met with Eisenhower at Camp David, Maryland.

1960 American U-2 reconnaissance plane shot down over Soviet territory; Francis Gary Powers, pilot, exchanged for Rudolf Abel in 1962.

John F. Kennedy elected President with Lyndon B. Johnson as Vice-President.

1961 Anti-Castro invasion at Bay of Pigs failed.

Kennedy established Peace Corps and proposed Alliance for Progress.

Alan B. Shepard, Jr.; first American in space.

1962 After bloody campus clashes, James H. Meredith became the first black to enter the University of Mississippi.

John H. Glenn, Jr.; first American to orbit Earth.

Kennedy protested presence of Russian missiles on Cuba; danger of nuclear war ended with Soviet dismantling of weapons.

1963 Racial violence broke out in Birmingham, Ala.

United States, Britain, and Soviet Union signed treaty barring atmospheric nuclear testing.

Washington and Moscow opened "hot line" phone connection to reduce risk of accidental war.

Martin Luther King led "March on Washington."

Kennedy assassinated in Dallas; Lyndon B. Johnson became President.

1964 Civil Rights Act strengthened voting guarantee, prohibited segregation in public accommodations and facilities.

24th Amendment, abolishing poll tax, ratified.

Johnson won landslide victory over Barry Goldwater in Presidential election.

1965 Large-scale antiwar demonstrations developed after Johnson announced Vietnam troop build-up.

Race riot erupted in Watts section of Los Angeles.

Johnson sent troops to Dominican Republic to put down "revolution."

1966 Medicare program went into effect.

Chicago, Cleveland, and other Northern cities experienced major race riots.

1967 Antiwar, antidraft, and race riots increased.

Johnson and Premier Kosygin met at Glassboro, New Jersey.

Thurgood Marshall; first black on Supreme Court.

25th Amendment, providing continuity in case of Presidential disability, ratified.

Treaty pledging peaceful uses of outer space signed with Soviet Union and Great Britain.

1968 North Korea seized U.S. Navy intelligence ship *Pueblo;* men released 11 months later.

Reverend Martin Luther King, Jr. and Senator Robert F. Kennedy assassinated.

Delegates from Washington and Hanoi met in Paris for preliminary Vietnam peace talks.

Richard M. Nixon won Presidential election; Spiro Agnew became Vice-President.

1969 Americans Neil A. Armstrong and Edwin E. Aldrin, Jr., were first men to land on Moon.

1970 U.S. and South Vietnamese troops enter Cambodia.

1971 26th Amendment grants voting rights to 18-year-olds. Nixon froze wages and prices; devalued dollar by 8.57%.

1972 Nixon visited Russia and China.

"Watergate Burglars" caught inside Democratic party's national headquarters.

Richard M. Nixon and Spiro T. Agnew reelected President and Vice-President.

1973 "Watergate" dominated American political scene.

Spiro T. Agnew resigned vice-presidency; Gerald R. Ford replaced him.

1974 President Nixon resigned and Gerald Ford became the 38th president.

1975 The Vietnam war ended. Unemployment reached 9.2%, highest since 1941.

1976 Jimmy Carter defeated Ford in Presidential election; Walter F. Mondale elected Vice-President.

1977 Carter established "human rights" as a key element in U.S. foreign policy.

1978 U.S. dollar fell in value against Western European and Japanese currencies.

1979 U.S. recognized the People's Republic of China.

Gasoline and fuel oil prices rose sharply.

Canal Zone ceded to Panama.

In CONGRESS, July 4, 1776

A DECLARATION

By the REPRESENTATIVES of the UNITED STATES OF AMERICA,

In GENERAL CONGRESS assembled.

WHEN in the Course of human Events, it becomes necessary for one People to dissolve the Political Bands which have connected them with another, and to assume among the Powers of the Earth, the separate and equal Station to which the Laws of Nature and of Nature's God entitle them, a decent Respect to the Opinions of Mankind requires that they should declare the causes which impel them to the Separation.

WE hold these Truths to be self-evident, that all Men are created equal, that they are endowed by their Creator with certain unalienable Rights, that among these are Life, Liberty, and the Pursuit of Happiness—That to secure these Rights, Governments are instituted among Men, deriving their just Powers from the Consent of the Governed, that whenever any Form of Government becomes destructive of these Ends, it is the Right of the People to alter or to abolish it, and to institute new Government, laying its Foundation on such Principles, and organizing its Powers in such Form, as to them shall seem most likely to effect their Safety and Happiness. Prudence, indeed, will dictate that Governments long established should not be changed for light and transient Causes; and accordingly all Experience hath shewn, that Mankind are more disposed to suffer, while Evils are sufferable, than to right themselves by abolishing the Forms to which they are accustomed. But when a long Train of Abuses and Usurpations, pursuing invariably the same Object, evinces a Design to reduce them under absolute Despotism, it is their Right, it is their Duty, to throw off such Government, and to provide new Guards for their future Security. Such has been the patient Sufferance of these Colonies; and such is now the Necessity which constrains them to alter their former Systems of Government. The History of the present King of Great-Britain is a History of repeated Injuries and Usurpations, all having in direct Object the Establishment of an absolute Tyranny over these States. To prove this, let Facts be submitted to a candid World.

HE has refused his Assent to Laws, the most wholesome and necessary for the public Good.

HE has forbidden his Governors to pass Laws of immediate and pressing Importance, unless suspended in their Operation till his Assent should be obtained; and when so suspended, he has utterly neglected to attend to them.

HE has refused to pass other Laws for the Accommodation of large Districts of People, unless those People would relinquish the Right of Representation in the Legislature, a Right inestimable to them, and formidable to Tyrants only.

HE has called together Legislative Bodies at Places unusual, uncomfortable, and distant from the Depository of their public Records, for the sole Purpose of fatiguing them into Compliance with his Measures.

HE has dissolved Representative Houses repeatedly, for opposing with manly Firmness his Invasions on the Rights of the People.

HE has refused for a long Time, after such Dissolutions, to cause others to be elected; whereby the Legislative Powers, incapable of Annihilation, have returned to the People at large for their exercise; the State remaining in the mean time exposed to all the Dangers of Invasion from without, and Convulsions within.

HE has endeavoured to prevent the Population of these States; for that Purpose obstructing the Laws for Naturalization of Foreigners; refusing to pass others to encourage their Migrations hither, and raising the Conditions of new Appropriations of Lands.

HE has obstructed the Administration of Justice, by refusing his Assent to Laws for establishing Judiciary Powers.

HE has made Judges dependent on his Will alone, for the Tenure of their Offices, and the Amount and Payment of their Salaries.

HE has erected a Multitude of new Offices, and sent hither Swarms of Officers to harass our People, and eat out their Substance.

HE has kept among us, in Times of Peace, Standing Armies, without the consent of our Legislatures.

HE has affected to render the Military independent of and superior to the Civil Power.

HE has combined with others to subject us to a Jurisdiction foreign to our Constitution, and unacknowledged by our Laws; giving his Assent to their Acts of pretended Legislation:

FOR quartering large Bodies of Armed Troops among us:

FOR protecting them, by a mock Trial, from Punishment for any Murders which they should commit on the Inhabitants of these States:

FOR cutting off our Trade with all Parts of the World:

FOR imposing Taxes on us without our Consent:

FOR depriving us, in many Cases, of the Benefits of Trial by Jury:

FOR transporting us beyond Seas to be tried for pretended Offences:

FOR abolishing the free System of English Laws in a neighbouring Province, establishing therein an arbitrary Government, and enlarging its Boundaries, so as to render it at once an Example and fit Instrument for introducing the same absolute Rule into these Colonies:

FOR taking away our Charters, abolishing our most valuable Laws, and altering fundamentally the Forms of our Governments:

FOR suspending our own Legislatures, and declaring themselves invested with Power to legislate for us in all Cases whatsoever.

HE has abdicated Government here, by declaring us out of his Protection and waging War against us.

He has plundered our Seas, ravaged our Coasts, burnt our Towns, and destroyed the Lives of our People.

He is, at this Time, transporting large Armies of foreign Mercenaries to compleat the Works of Death, Desolation, and Tyranny, already begun with circumstances of Cruelty and Perfidy, scarcely paralleled in the most barbarous Ages, and totally unworthy the Head of a civilized Nation.

He has constrained our fellow Citizens taken Captive on the high Seas to bear Arms against their Country, to become the Executioners of their Friends and Brethren, or to fall themselves by their Hands.

He has excited domestic Insurrections amongst us, and has endeavoured to bring on the Inhabitants of our Frontiers, the merciless Indian Savages, whose known Rule of Warfare, is an undistinguished Destruction of all Ages, Sexes and Conditions.

In every stage of these Oppressions we have Petitioned for Redress in the most humble Terms: Our repeated Petitions have been answered only by repeated Injury. A Prince, whose Character is thus marked by every act which may define a Tyrant, is unfit to be the Ruler of a free People.

Nor have we been wanting in Attentions to our British Brethren. We have warned them from Time to Time of Attempts by their Legislature to extend an unwarrantable Jurisdiction over us. We have reminded them of the Circumstances of our Emigration and Settlement here. We have appealed to their native Justice and Magnanimity, and we have conjured them by the Ties of our common Kindred to disavow these Usurpations,

which, would inevitably interrupt our Connections and Correspondence. They too have been deaf to the Voice of Justice and of Consanguinity. We must, therefore, acquiesce in the Necessity, which denounces our Separation, and hold them, as we hold the rest of Mankind, Enemies in War, in Peace, Friends.

We, therefore, the Representatives of the UNITED STATES OF AMERICA, in General Congress, Assembled, appealing to the Supreme Judge of the World for the Rectitude of our Intentions, do, in the Name, and by Authority of the good People of these Colonies, solemnly Publish and Declare, That these United Colonies are, and of Right ought to be, Free and Independent States; that they are absolved from all Allegiance to the British Crown, and that all political Connection between them and the State of Great-Britain, is and ought to be totally dissolved; and that as Free and Independent States, they have full Power to levy War, conclude Peace, contract Alliances, establish Commerce, and to do all other Acts and Things which Independent States may of right do. And for the support of this Declaration, with a firm Reliance on the Protection of divine Providence, we mutually pledge to each other our Lives, our Fortunes, and our sacred Honor.

Signed by Order *and in* Behalf *of the* Congress,

JOHN HANCOCK, President

Attest.

CHARLES THOMSON, Secretary.

SIGNERS OF THE DECLARATION OF INDEPENDENCE: 1776

Name	Age	Occupation	Education	Representing	Birthplace	Born	Died
John Adams	40	Lawyer	Harvard	Massachusetts	Braintree, Mass.	1735	1826
Samuel Adams	53	Politician	Harvard	Massachusetts	Boston, Mass.	1722	1803
Josiah Bartlett	46	Physician	Private tutors	New Hampshire	Amesbury, Mass.	1729	1795
Carter Braxton	39	Planter	William & Mary	Virginia	Newington, Va.	1736	1797
Charles Carroll	38	Planter	Educated in Europe	Maryland	Annapolis, Md.	1737	1832
Samuel Chase	35	Lawyer	Private tutors	Maryland	Somerset Co., Md.	1741	1811
Abraham Clark	40	Lawyer-Farmer	Self-educated	New Jersey	Elizabethtown, N.J.	1726	1794
George Clymer	37	Merchant	Self-educated	Pennsylvania	Philadelphia, Pa.	1739	1813
William Ellery	48	Lawyer	Harvard	Rhode Island	Newport, R.I.	1727	1820
William Floyd	41	Farmer	Private tutors	New York	Brookhaven, N.Y.	1734	1821
Benjamin Franklin	71	Public servant	Grammar school	Pennsylvania	Boston, Mass.	1706	1790
Elbridge Gerry	31	Merchant	Harvard	Massachusetts	Marblehead, Mass.	1744	1814
Button Gwinnett	c. 41	Planter	Preparatory studies	Georgia	Gloucestershire, England	c. 1735	1777
Lyman Hall	52	Physician	Yale	Georgia	Wallingford, Conn.	1724	1790
John Hancock	39	Merchant	Harvard	Massachusetts	Braintree, Mass.	1737	1793
Benjamin Harrison	c. 50	Planter	Attended William & Mary	Virginia	Charles City Co., Va.	c. 1726	1791
John Hart	c. 65	Farmer	Self-educated	New Jersey	Stonington, Conn.	c. 1711	1779
Joseph Hewes	46	Merchant	Grammar school	North Carolina	Kingston, N.J.	1730	1779
Thomas Heyward	29	Lawyer	Studied law in England	South Carolina	St. Helena's Parish, S.C.	1746	1809
William Hooper	34	Lawyer	Harvard	North Carolina	Boston, Mass.	1742	1790
Stephen Hopkins	70	Public servant	Self-educated	Rhode Island	Providence, R.I.	1707	1785
Francis Hopkinson	38	Lawyer	College of Philadelphia[1]	New Jersey	Philadelphia, Pa.	1737	1791
Samuel Huntington	45	Lawyer	Self-educated	Connecticut	Windham, Conn.	1731	1796
Thomas Jefferson	33	Lawyer-Planter	William & Mary	Virginia	Goochland Co., Va.	1743	1826
Richard Henry Lee	44	Planter	Private tutors	Virginia	Westmoreland Co., Va.	1732	1794
Francis Lightfoot Lee	41	Planter	Private tutors	Virginia	Westmoreland Co., Va.	1734	1797
Francis Lewis	63	Merchant	Grammar school	New York	Llandaff, Wales	1713	c. 1802
Philip Livingston	60	Merchant	Yale	New York	Albany, N.Y.	1716	1778
Thomas Lynch	26	Planter	Studied law in England	South Carolina	Prince George's Parish, S.C.	1749	1779
Thomas McKean	42	Lawyer	Preparatory studies	Delaware	New London Township, Pa.	1734	1817
Arthur Middleton	34	Planter	Studied law in England	South Carolina	near Charlestown, S.C.	1742	1787
Lewis Morris	50	Landowner	Yale	New York	Morrisania, N.Y.	1726	1798
Robert Morris	42	Merchant	Self-educated	Pennsylvania	Liverpool, England	1734	1806
John Morton	c. 42	Surveyor	Private tutors	Pennsylvania	Ridely, Pa.	c. 1724	1777

Name	Age	Occupation	Education	Representing	Birthplace	Born	Died
Thomas Nelson	41	Planter	Educated in England	Virginia	Yorktown, Va.	1738	1789
William Paca	37	Lawyer	College of Philadelphia;[1] attended schools in England	Maryland	near Abingdon, Md.	1740	1799
Robert Treat Paine	45	Lawyer	Harvard	Massachusetts	Boston, Mass.	1731	1814
John Penn	c. 36	Lawyer	Self-educated	North Carolina	Caroline Co., Va.	c. 1740	1788
George Read	42	Lawyer	Preparatory studies	Delaware	near Northeast, Cecil Co., Md.	1733	1798
Caesar Rodney	48	Landowner	Private tutors	Delaware	near Dover, Del.	1728	1784
George Ross	46	Lawyer	Preparatory studies	Pennsylvania	New Castle, Del.	1730	1779
Benjamin Rush	30	Physician	College of New Jersey;[2] medical education, Univ. of Edinburgh	Pennsylvania	Byberry, Pa.	1745	1813
Edward Rutledge	26	Lawyer	Studied law in England	South Carolina	Charleston, S.C.	1749	1800
Roger Sherman	55	Merchant	Self-educated	Connecticut	Newton, Mass.	1721	1793
James Smith	c. 57	Lawyer-Iron master	Preparatory studies	Pennsylvania	Ireland	c. 1719	1806
Richard Stockton	46	Lawyer	College of New Jersey[2]	New Jersey	Princeton, N.J.	1730	1781
Thomas Stone	c. 33	Lawyer-Planter	Private tutors	Maryland	Charles Co., Md.	1743	1787
George Taylor	c. 60	Iron master	Preparatory studies	Pennsylvania	Ireland	1716	1781
Matthew Thornton	c. 62	Physician	Preparatory studies	New Hampshire	Ireland	c. 1714	1803
George Walton	c. 35	Lawyer	Self-educated	Georgia	Prince Edward Co., Va.	c. 1741	1804
William Whipple	46	Merchant	Grammar school	New Hampshire	Kittery, Me.	1730	1785
William Williams	45	Public servant-Merchant	Harvard	Connecticut	Lebanon, Conn.	1731	1811
James Wilson	33	Lawyer	Educated in Scotland	Pennsylvania	near St. Andrews, Scotland	1742	1798
John Witherspoon	53	College president-Clergyman	Univ. of Edinburgh	New Jersey	Gifford, Haddingtonshire, Scotland	1723	1794
Oliver Wolcott	49	Lawyer	Yale	Connecticut	Windsor, Conn.	1726	1797
George Wythe	c. 50	Lawyer	Attended William & Mary	Virginia	Elizabeth City Co., Va.	1726	1806

[1] now University of Pennsylvania. [2] now Princeton University.

THE CONSTITUTION

WE, the People of the United States, in order to form a more perfect union, establish justice, insure domestic tranquility, provide for the common defence, promote the general welfare, and secure the blessings of liberty to ourselves and our posterity, do ordain and establish this Constitution for the United States of America.

ARTICLE I.

Sect. 1. A L L legislative powers herein granted shall be vested in a Congress of the United States, which shall consist of a Senate and House of Representatives.

Sect. 2. The House of Representatives shall be composed of members chosen every second year by the people of the several states, and the electors in each state shall have the qualifications requisite for electors of the most numerous branch of the state legislature.

No person shall be a representative who shall not have attained to the age of twenty-five years, and been seven years a citizen of the United States, and who shall not, when elected, be an inhabitant of that state in which he shall be chosen.

[1][Representatives and direct taxes shall be apportioned among the several states which may be included within this Union, according to their respective numbers, which shall be determined by adding to the whole number of free persons, including those bound to service for a term of years, and excluding Indians not taxed, three-fifths of all other persons.] The actual enumeration shall be made within three years after the first meeting of the Congress of the United States, and within every subsequent term of ten years, in such manner as they shall by law direct. The number of representatives shall not exceed one for every thirty thousand, but each state shall have at least one representative; and until such enumeration shall be made, the state of New-Hampshire shall be entitled to chuse three, Massachusetts eight, Rhode-Island and Providence Plantations one, Connecticut five, New-York six, New-Jersey four, Pennsylvania eight, Delaware one, Maryland six, Virginia ten, North-Carolina five, South-Carolina five, and Georgia three.

When vacancies happen in the representation from any state, the Executive authority thereof shall issue writs of election to fill such vacancies.

The House of Representatives shall chuse their Speaker and other officers; and shall have the sole power of impeachment.

Sect. 3. The Senate of the United States shall be composed of two senators from each state, [2][chosen by the legislature thereof,] for six years; and each senator shall have one vote.

Immediately after they shall be assembled in consequence of the first election, they shall be divided as equally as may be into three classes. The seats of the senators of the first class shall be vacated at the expiration of the second year, of the second class at the expiration of the fourth year, and of the third class at the expiration of the sixth year, so that one-third may be chosen every second year; [3][and if vacancies happen by resignation, or otherwise, during the recess of the

[1] The part enclosed by brackets was changed by section 2 of Amendment XIV. [2] The clause enclosed by brackets was changed by clause 1 of Amendment XVII. [3] The part enclosed by brackets was changed by clause 2 of Amendment XVII.

Legislature of any state, the Executive thereof may make temporary appointments until the next meeting of the Legislature, which shall then fill such vacancies.]

No person shall be a senator who shall not have attained to the age of thirty years, and been nine years a citizen of the United States, and who shall not, when elected, be an inhabitant of that state for which he shall be chosen.

The Vice-President of the United States shall be President of the Senate, but shall have no vote, unless they be equally divided.

The Senate shall chuse their other officers, and also a President pro tempore, in the absence of the Vice-President, or when he shall exercise the office of President of the United States.

The Senate shall have the sole power to try all impeachments. When sitting for that purpose, they shall be on oath or affirmation. When the President of the United States is tried, the Chief Justice shall preside: And no person shall be convicted without the concurrence of two-thirds of the members present.

Judgment in cases of impeachment shall not extend further than to removal from office and disqualification to hold and enjoy any office of honor, trust or profit under the United States; but the party convicted shall nevertheless be liable and subject to indictment, trial, judgment and punishment, according to law.

Sect. 4. The times, places and manner of holding elections for senators and representatives, shall be prescribed in each state by the legislature thereof; but the Congress may at any time by law make or alter such regulations, except as to the places of chusing Senators.

The Congress shall assemble at least once in every year, and such meeting shall [be on the first Monday in December,] unless they shall by law appoint a different day.

Sect. 5. Each house shall be the judge of the elections, returns and qualifications of its own members, and a majority of each shall constitute a quorum to do business; but a smaller number may adjourn from day to day, and may be authorized to compel the attendance of absent members, in such manner, and under such penalties as each house may provide.

Each house may determine the rules of its proceedings, punish its members for disorderly behaviour, and, with the concurrence of two-thirds, expel a member.

Each house shall keep a journal of its proceedings, and from time to time publish the same, excepting such parts as may in their judgment require secrecy; and the yeas and nays of the members of either house on any question shall, at the desire of one-fifth of those present, be entered on the journal.

Neither house, during the session of Congress shall, without the consent of the other, adjourn for more than three days, nor to any other place than that in which the two houses shall be sitting.

Sect. 6. The senators and representatives shall receive a compensation for their services, to be ascertained by law, and paid out of the treasury of the United States. They shall in all cases, except treason, felony and breach of the peace, be privileged from arrest during their attendance at the session of their respective houses, and in going to and returning from the same; and for any speech or debate in either house, they shall not be questioned in any other place.

No senator or representative shall, during the time for which he was elected, be appointed to any civil office under the authority of the United States, which shall have been created, or the emoluments whereof shall have been encreased during such time; and no person holding any office under the United States, shall be a member of either house during his continuance in office.

Sect. 7. All bills for raising revenue shall originate in the house of representatives; but the senate may propose or concur with amendments as on other bills.

Every bill which shall have passed the house of representatives and the senate, shall, before it become a law, be presented to the president of the United States; if he approve he shall sign it, but if not he shall return it, with his objections to that house in which it shall have originated, who shall enter the objections at large on their journal, and proceed to reconsider it. If after such reconsideration two-thirds of that house shall agree to pass the bill, it shall be sent, together with the objections, to the other house, by which it shall likewise be reconsidered, and if approved by two-thirds of that house, it shall become a law. But in all such cases the votes of both houses shall be determined by yeas and nays, and the names of the persons voting for and against the bill shall be entered on the journal of each house respectively. If any bill shall not be returned by the President within ten days (Sundays excepted) after it shall have been presented to him, the same shall be a law, in like manner as if he had signed it, unless the Congress by their adjournment prevent its return, in which case it shall not be a law.

Every order, resolution, or vote to which the concurrence of the Senate and House of Representatives may be necessary (except on a question of adjournment) shall be presented to the President of the United States; and before the same shall take effect, shall be approved by him, or, being disapproved by him, shall be repassed by two-thirds of the Senate and House of Representatives, according to the rules and limitations prescribed in the case of a bill.

Sect. 8. The Congress shall have power

To lay and collect taxes, duties, imposts and excises, to pay the debts and provide for the common defence and general welfare of the United States; but all duties, imposts and excises shall be uniform throughout the United States;

To borrow money on the credit of the United States;

To regulate commerce with foreign nations, and among the several states, and with the Indian tribes;

To establish an uniform rule of naturalization, and uniform laws on the subject of bankruptcies throughout the United States;

To coin money, regulate the value thereof, and of foreign coin, and fix the standard of weights and measures;

To provide for the punishment of counterfeiting the securities and current coin of the United States;

To establish post offices and post roads;

To promote the progress of science and useful arts, by securing for limited times to authors and inventors the exclusive right to their respective writings and discoveries;

4 The clause enclosed by brackets was changed by section 2 of Amendment XX.

To constitute tribunals inferior to the supreme court;

To define and punish piracies and felonies committed on the high seas, and offences against the law of nations;

To declare war, grant letters of marque and reprisal, and make rules concerning captures on land and water;

To raise and support armies, but no appropriation of money to that use shall be for a longer term than two years;

To provide and maintain a navy;

To make rules for the government and regulation of the land and naval forces;

To provide for calling forth the militia to execute the laws of the union, suppress insurrections and repel invasions;

To provide for organizing, arming, and disciplining, the militia, and for governing such part of them as may be employed in the service of the United States, reserving to the States respectively, the appointment of the officers, and the authority of training the militia according to the discipline prescribed by Congress;

To exercise exclusive legislation in all cases whatsoever, over such district (not exceeding ten miles square) as may, by cession of particular States, and the acceptance of Congress, become the seat of the government of the United States, and to exercise like authority over all places purchased by the consent of the legislature of the states in which the same shall be, for the erection of forts, magazines, arsenals, dock-yards, and other needful buildings;—And

To make all laws which shall be necessary and proper for carrying into execution the foregoing powers, and all other powers vested by this constitution in the government of the United States, or in any department or officer thereof.

Sect. 9. The migration or importation of such persons as any of the states now existing shall think proper to admit, shall not be prohibited by the Congress prior to the year one thousand eight hundred and eight, but a tax or duty may be imposed on such importation, not exceeding ten dollars for each person.

The privilege of the writ of habeas corpus shall not be suspended, unless when in cases of rebellion or invasion the public safety may require it.

No bill of attainder or ex post facto law shall be passed.

No capitation, or other direct, tax shall be laid, unless in proportion to the census or enumeration herein before directed to be taken.[5]

No tax or duty shall be laid on articles exported from any state. No preference shall be given by any regulation of commerce or revenue to the ports of one state over those of another: nor shall vessels bound to, or from, one state, be obliged to enter, clear, or pay duties in another.

No money shall be drawn from the treasury, but in consequence of appropriations made by law; and a regular statement and account of the receipts and expenditures of all public money shall be published from time to time.

No title of nobility shall be granted by the United States:—And no person holding any office of profit or trust under them, shall, without the consent of the Congress, accept of any present, emolument, office, or title, of any kind whatever, from any king, prince, or foreign state.

Sect. 10. No state shall enter into any treaty, alliance, or confederation; grant letters of marque and reprisal; coin money; emit bills of credit; make any thing but gold and silver coin a tender in payment of debts; pass any bill of attainder, ex post facto law, or law impairing the obligation of contracts, or grant any title of nobility.

No state shall, without the consent of the Congress, lay any imposts or duties on imports or exports, except what may be absolutely necessary for executing its inspection laws; and the net produce of all duties and imposts, laid by any state on imports or exports, shall be for the use of the Treasury of the United States; and all such laws shall be subject to the revision and controul of the Congress. No state shall, without the consent of Congress, lay any duty of tonnage, keep troops, or ships of war in time of peace, enter into any agreement or compact with another state, or with a foreign power, or engage in war, unless actually invaded, or in such imminent danger as will not admit of delay.

II.

Sect. 1. The executive power shall be vested in a president of the United States of America. He shall hold his office during the term of four years, and, together with the vice-president, chosen for the same term, be elected as follows.

Each state shall appoint, in such manner as the legislature thereof may direct, a number of electors, equal to the whole number of senators and representatives to which the state may be entitled in the Congress: but no senator or representative, or person holding an office of trust or profit under the United States, shall be appointed an elector.

[6][**The electors shall meet in their respective states, and vote by ballot for two persons, of whom one at least shall not be an inhabitant of the same state with themselves. And they shall make a list of all the persons voted for, and of the number of votes for each; which list they shall sign and certify, and transmit sealed to the seat of the government of the United States, directed to the president of the senate. The president of the senate shall, in the presence of the senate and house of representatives, open all the certificates, and the votes shall then be counted. The person having the greatest number of votes shall be the president, if such number be a majority of the whole number of electors appointed; and if there be more than one who have such majority, and have an equal number of votes, then the house of representatives shall immediately chuse by ballot one of them for president; and if no person have a majority, then from the five highest on the list the said house shall in like manner chuse the president. But in chusing the president, the votes shall be taken by states, the representation from each state having one vote; a quorum for this purpose shall consist of a member or members from two-thirds of the states, and a majority of all the states shall be necessary to a choice. In every case, after the choice of the president, the person having the greatest number of votes of the electors shall be the vice-president. But if there should remain two or more who have equal votes, the senate shall chuse from them by ballot the vice-president.**]

The Congress may determine the time of chusing the electors, and the day on which they shall give their votes; which day shall be the same throughout the United States.

[5] See also Amendment XVI.   [6] This paragraph has been superseded by Amendment XII.

No person except a natural born citizen, or a citizen of the United States, at the time of the adoption of this constitution, shall be eligible to the office of president; neither shall any person be eligible to that office who shall not have attained to the age of thirty-five years, and been fourteen years a resident within the United States.

[7]In case of the removal of the president from office, or of his death, resignation, or inability to discharge the powers and duties of the said office, the same shall devolve on the vice-president, and the Congress may by law provide for the case of removal, death, resignation or inability, both of the president and vice-president, declaring what officer shall then act as president, and such officer shall act accordingly, until the disability be removed, or a president be elected.

The president shall, at stated times, receive for his services, a compensation, which shall neither be encreased nor diminished during the period for which he shall have been elected, and he shall not receive within that period any other emolument from the United States, or any of them.

Before he enter on the execution of his office, he shall take the following oath or affirmation:

"I do solemnly swear (or affirm) that I will faithfully execute the office of president of the United States, and will to the best of my ability, preserve, protect and defend the constitution of the United States."

Sect. 2. The president shall be commander in chief of the army and navy of the United States, and of the militia of the several States, when called into the actual service of the United States; he may require the opinion, in writing, of the principal officer in each of the executive departments, upon any subject relating to the duties of their respective offices, and he shall have power to grant reprieves and pardons for offences against the United States, except in cases of impeachment.

He shall have power, by and with the advice and consent of the senate, to make treaties, provided two-thirds of the senators present concur; and he shall nominate, and by and with the advice and consent of the senate, shall appoint ambassadors, other public ministers and consuls, judges of the supreme court, and all other officers of the United States, whose appointments are not herein otherwise provided for, and which shall be established by law. But the Congress may by law vest the appointment of such inferior officers, as they think proper, in the president alone, in the courts of law, or in the heads of departments.

The president shall have power to fill up all vacancies that may happen during the recess of the senate, by granting commissions which shall expire at the end of their session.

Sect. 3. He shall from time to time give to the Congress information of the state of the union, and recommend to their consideration such measures as he shall judge necessary and expedient; he may, on extraordinary occasions, convene both houses, or either of them, and in case of disagreement between them, with respect to the time of adjournment, he may adjourn them to such time as he shall think proper; he shall receive ambassadors and other public ministers; he shall take care that the laws be faithfully executed, and shall commission all the officers of the United States.

Sect. 4. The president, vice-president and all civil officers of the United States, shall be removed from office on impeachment for, and convicted of, treason, bribery, or other high crimes and misdemeanors.

III.

Sect. 1. The judicial power of the United States, shall be vested in one supreme court, and in such inferior courts as the Congress may from time to time ordain and establish. The judges, both of the supreme and inferior courts, shall hold their offices during good behaviour, and shall, at stated times, receive for their services, a compensation, which shall not be diminished during their continuance in office.

Sect. 2. The judicial power shall extend to all cases, in law and equity, arising under this constitution, the laws of the United States, and treaties made, or which shall be made, under their authority; to all cases of admiralty and maritime jurisdiction; to controversies to which the United States shall be a party; to controversies between two or more States, between a state and citizens of another state,[8] between citizens of different States, between citizens of the same state claiming lands under grants of different States, and between a state, or the citizens thereof, and foreign States, citizens or subjects.

In all cases affecting ambassadors, other public ministers and consuls, and those in which a state shall be party, the supreme court shall have original jurisdiction. In all the other cases before mentioned, the supreme court shall have appellate jurisdiction, both as to law and fact, with such exceptions, and under such regulations as the Congress shall make.

The trial of all crimes, except in cases of impeachment, shall be by jury; and such trial shall be held in the state where the said crimes shall have been committed; but when not committed within any state, the trial shall be at such place or places as the Congress may by law have directed.

Sect. 3. Treason against the United States, shall consist only in levying war against them, or in adhering to their enemies, giving them aid and comfort. No person shall be convicted of treason unless on the testimony of two witnesses to the same overt act, or on confession in open court.

The Congress shall have power to declare the punishment of treason, but no attainder of treason shall work corruption of blood, or forfeiture except during the life of the person attainted.

IV.

Sect. 1. Full faith and credit shall be given in each state to the public acts, records, and judicial proceedings of every other state. And the Congress may by general laws prescribe the manner in which such acts, records and proceedings shall be proved, and the effect thereof.

Sect. 2. The citizens of each state shall be entitled to all privileges and immunities of citizens in the several states.

A person charged in any state with treason, felony, or other crime, who shall flee from justice, and be found in another state, shall, on demand of the executive authority of the state from which he fled, be delivered up, to be removed to the state having jurisdiction of the crime.

[9][No person held to service or labour in one state, under the laws thereof, escaping into another, shall, in consequence of any law or regulation therein, be discharged from such service or labour, but shall be delivered up on claim of

---

[7] Affected by Amendment XXV. [8] Affected by Amendment XI. [9] Superseded by Amendment XIII.

the party to whom such service or labour may be due.]

Sect. 3. New states may be admitted by the Congress into this union; but no new state shall be formed or erected within the jurisdiction of any other state; nor any state be formed by the junction of two or more states, or parts of states, without the consent of the legislatures of the states concerned as well as of the Congress.

The Congress shall have power to dispose of and make all needful rules and regulations respecting the territory or other property belonging to the United States; and nothing in this Constitution shall be so construed as to prejudice any claims of the United States, or of any particular state.

Sect. 4. The United States shall guarantee to every state in this union a Republican form of government, and shall protect each of them against invasion; and on application of the legislature, or of the executive (when the legislature cannot be convened) against domestic violence.

V.

The Congress, whenever two-thirds of both houses shall deem it necessary, shall propose amendments to this constitution, or, on the application of the legislatures of two-thirds of the several states, shall call a convention for proposing amendments, which, in either case, shall be valid to all intents and purposes, as part of this constitution, when ratified by the legislatures of three-fourths of the several states, or by conventions in three-fourths thereof, as the one or the other mode of ratification may be proposed by Congress; Provided, that no amendment which may be made prior to the year one thousand eight hundred and eight shall in any manner affect the first and fourth clauses in the ninth section of the first article; and that no state, without its consent, shall be deprived of its equal suffrage in the senate.

VI.

All debts contracted and engagements entered into, before the adoption of this Constitution, shall be as valid against the United States under this Constitution, as under the confederation.

This constitution, and the laws of the United States which shall be made in pursuance thereof; and all treaties made, or which shall be made, under the authority of the United States, shall be the supreme law of the land; and the judges in every state shall be bound thereby, any thing in the constitution or laws of any state to the contrary notwithstanding.

The senators and representatives beforementioned, and the members of the several state legislatures, and all executive and judicial officers, both of the United States and of the several States, shall be bound by oath or affirmation, to support this constitution; but no religious test shall ever be required as a qualification to any office or public trust under the United States.

VII.

The ratification of the conventions of nine States, shall be sufficient for the establishment of this constitution between the States so ratifying the same.

[Done in Convention, by the unanimous consent of the States present, the seventeenth day of September, in the year of our Lord one thousand seven hundred and eighty-seven, and of the Independence of the United States of America the twelfth. In witness whereof we have hereunto subscribed our Names.]

SIGNERS OF THE CONSTITUTION: 1787

Name	Age	Occupation	Education	Representing	Birthplace	Born	Died
Abraham Baldwin	32	Lawyer	Yale	Georgia	Guilford, Conn.	1754	1807
Richard Bassett	42	Lawyer	Private tutors	Delaware	Cecil Co., Md.	1745	1815
Gunning Bedford	c. 40	Lawyer	College of New Jersey[1]	Delaware	Philadelphia, Pa.	1747	1812
John Blair	c. 55	Jurist	Studied law in England	Virginia	Williamsburg, Va.	1732	1800
William Blount	38	Public servant	Private tutors	North Carolina	Bertie Co., N.C.	1749	1800
David Brearley	42	Jurist	Private tutors	New Jersey	Spring Grove, N.J.	1745	1790
Jacob Broom	35	Businessman	Preparatory studies	Delaware	Wilmington, Del.	1752	1810
Pierce Butler	43	Planter	Private tutors	South Carolina	Co. Carlow, Ireland	1744	1822
Daniel Carroll	57	Planter-Businessman	Educated at Jesuit schools in Maryland and France	Maryland	Upper Marlboro, Md.	1730	1796
George Clymer	48	Merchant	Self-educated	Pennsylvania	Philadelphia, Pa.	1739	1813
Jonathan Dayton	26	Lawyer	College of New Jersey[1]	New Jersey	Elizabeth-Town, N.J.	1760	1824
John Dickinson	55	Public servant	Studied law in England	Delaware	Talbot Co., Md.	1732	1808
William Few	39	Lawyer	Self-educated	Georgia	near Baltimore, Md.	1748	1828
Thomas Fitzsimons	c. 46	Businessman	Self-educated	Pennsylvania	Ireland	1741	1811
Benjamin Franklin	81	Public servant	Grammar school	Pennsylvania	Boston, Mass.	1706	1790
Nicholas Gilman	32	Public servant	Grammar school	New Hampshire	Exeter, N.H.	1755	1814
Nathaniel Gorham	49	Businessman	Private tutors	Massachusetts	Charlestown, Mass.	1738	1796
Alexander Hamilton	32	Lawyer	King's College[2]	New York	West Indies	1755	1804
Jared Ingersoll	37	Lawyer	Yale; studied law in England	Pennsylvania	New Haven, Conn.	1749	1822
Daniel of St. Thomas Jenifer	c. 64	Planter-Public servant	Preparatory studies	Maryland	Charles Co., Md.	1723	1790
William Samuel Johnson	59	Lawyer-College president	Yale; A.M., Harvard	Connecticut	Stratford, Conn.	1727	1819
Rufus King	32	Lawyer	Harvard	Massachusetts	Scarboro, Mass.	1755	1827
John Langdon	46	Businessman	Grammar School	New Hampshire	Portsmouth, N.H.	1741	1819
William Livingston	53	Public servant	Yale	New Jersey	Albany, N.Y.	1723	1790
James Madison	36	Lawyer	College of New Jersey[1]	Virginia	Port Conway, Va.	1751	1836
James McHenry	c. 34	Businessman	Educated in Ireland and Delaware; studied medicine under Benjamin Rush	Maryland	Ireland	c. 1753	1816
Thomas Mifflin	33	Merchant	College of Philadelphia[3]	Pennsylvania	Philadelphia, Pa.	1744	1800
Gouverneur Morris	35	Lawyer	King's College[2]	Pennsylvania	Morrisania, N.Y.	1752	1816
Robert Morris	53	Merchant	Self-educated	Pennsylvania	Liverpool, England	1734	1806
William Paterson	31	Lawyer	College of New Jersey[1]	Maryland	Co. Antrim, Ireland	1745	1806

Name	Age	Occupation	Education	Representing	Birthplace	Born	Died
Charles Pinckney	29	Lawyer	Preparatory studies	South Carolina	Charleston, S.C.	1757	1824
Charles Cotesworth Pinckney	41	Lawyer	Oxford	South Carolina	Charleston, S.C.	1746	1825
George Read	53	Lawyer	Preparatory studies	Delaware	near Northeast, Cecil Co., Md.	1733	1798
John Rutledge	c. 58	Public servant	Studied law in England	South Carolina	Charleston, S.C.	1739	1800
Roger Sherman	66	Businessman	Self-educated	Connecticut	Newton, Mass.	1721	1793
Richard Dobbs Spaight	29	Planter	Educated in Ireland and Scotland	North Carolina	New Bern, N.C.	1758	1802
George Washington	55	Planter	Private tutors	Virginia	Westmoreland Co., Va.	1732	1799
Hugh Williamson	41	Businessman-Physician	College of Philadelphia;[3] M.D., Univ. of Utrecht	North Carolina	West Nottingham, Pa.	1735	1819
James Wilson	44	Lawyer	Educated in Scotland	Pennsylvania	Scotland	1742	1798

[1] now Princeton University. [2] now Columbia University. [3] now University of Pennsylvania.

THE CONSTITUTIONAL AMENDMENTS

The first ten amendments* to the original Constitution are known as the Bill of Rights.

AMENDMENT [I]

Congress shall make no law respecting an establishment of religion, or prohibiting the free exercise thereof; or abridging the freedom of speech, or of the press; or the right of the people peaceably to assemble, and to petition the Government for a redress of grievances.

AMENDMENT [II]

A well regulated Militia, being necessary to the security of a free State, the right of the people to keep and bear Arms, shall not be infringed.

AMENDMENT [III]

No Soldier shall, in time of peace be quartered in any house, without the consent of the Owner, nor in time of war, but in a manner to be prescribed by law.

AMENDMENT [IV]

The right of the people to be secure in their persons, houses, papers, and effects, against unreasonable searches and seizures, shall not be violated, and no Warrants shall issue, but upon probable cause, supported by Oath or affirmation, and particularly describing the place to be searched, and the persons or things to be seized.

AMENDMENT [V]

No person shall be held to answer for a capital, or otherwise infamous crime, unless on a presentment or indictment of a Grand Jury, except in cases arising in the land or naval forces, or in the Militia, when in actual service in time of War or public danger; nor shall any person be subject for the same offence to be twice put in jeopardy of life or limb; nor shall be compelled in any criminal case to be a witness against himself, nor be deprived of life, liberty, or property, without due process of law; nor shall private property be taken for public use, without just compensation.

AMENDMENT [VI]

In all criminal prosecutions, the accused shall enjoy the right to a speedy and public trial, by an impartial jury of the State and district wherein the crime shall have been committed, which district shall have been previously ascertained by law, and to be informed of the nature and cause of the accusation; to be confronted with the witnesses against him; to have compulsory process for obtaining witnesses in his favor, and to have the Assistance of Counsel for his defence.

AMENDMENT [VII]

In Suits at common law, where the value in controversy shall exceed twenty dollars, the right of trial by jury shall be preserved, and no fact tried by a jury, shall be otherwise re-examined in any Court of the United States, than according to the rules of the common law.

AMENDMENT [VIII]

Excessive bail shall not be required, nor excessive fines imposed, nor cruel and unusual punishments inflicted.

AMENDMENT [IX]

The enumeration in the Constitution, of certain rights, shall not be construed to deny or disparage others retained by the people.

AMENDMENT [X]

The powers not delegated to the United States by the Constitution, nor prohibited by it to the States, are reserved to the States respectively, or to the people.

AMENDMENT [XI][1]

The Judicial power of the United States shall not be construed to extend to any suit in law or equity, commenced or prosecuted against one of the United States by Citizens of another State, or by Citizens or Subjects of any Foreign State.

AMENDMENT [XII][2]

The Electors shall meet in their respective states, and vote by ballot for President and Vice-President, one of whom, at least, shall not be an inhabitant of the same state with themselves; they shall name in their ballots the person voted for as President, and in distinct ballots the person voted for as Vice-President, and they shall make distinct lists of all persons voted for as President, and

---

* The first 10 amendments, together with 2 others that failed of ratification, were proposed to the several States by resolution of Congress on September 25, 1789. The ratifications were transmitted by the Governors to the President and by him communicated to Congress from time to time. The first 10 amendments were ratified by 11 of the 14 States. Virginia completed the required three fourths by ratification on December 15, 1791, and its action was communicated to Congress by the President on December 30, 1791. The legislatures of Massachusetts, Georgia, and Connecticut ratified them on March 2, 1939, March 18, 1939, and April 19, 1939, respectively.

[1] The Eleventh Amendment was proposed by resolution of Congress on March 4, 1794. It was declared by the President, in a message to Congress dated January 8, 1798, to have been ratified by three fourths of the several States. Records of the National Archives show that the 11th Amendment was ratified by 13 of the 16 States. It was not ratified by New Jersey or Pennsylvania.

[2] The Twelfth Amendment was proposed in lieu of the original third paragraph of section 1 of article II, by resolution of Congress on December 9, 1803. It was declared in a proclamation of the Secretary of State, dated September 25, 1804, to have been ratified by three fourths of the States. Records of the National Archives show that it was ratified by 14 States and rejected by Connecticut and Delaware.

of all persons voted for as Vice-President, and of the number of votes for each, which lists they shall sign and certify, and transmit sealed to the seat of the government of the United States, directed to the President of the Senate;—The President of the Senate shall, in the presence of the Senate and House of Representatives, open all the certificates and the votes shall then be counted;—The person having the greatest number of votes for President, shall be the President, if such number be a majority of the whole number of Electors appointed; and if no person have such majority, then from the persons having the highest numbers not exceeding three on the list of those voted for as President, the House of Representatives shall choose immediately, by ballot, the President. But in choosing the President, the votes shall be taken by states, the representation from each state having one vote; a quorum for this purpose shall consist of a member or members from two-thirds of the states, and a majority of all the states shall be necessary to a choice. ³[And if the House of Representatives shall not choose a President whenever the right of choice shall devolve upon them, before the fourth day of March next following, then the Vice-President shall act as President, as in the case of the death or other constitutional disability of the President.]—The person having the greatest number of votes as Vice-President, shall be the Vice-President, if such number be a majority of the whole number of Electors appointed, and if no person have a majority, then from the two highest numbers on the list, the Senate shall choose the Vice-President; a quorum for the purpose shall consist of two-thirds of the whole number of Senators, and a majority of the whole number shall be necessary to a choice. But no person constitutionally ineligible to the office of President shall be eligible to that of Vice-President of the United States.

AMENDMENT [XIII]⁴

Section 1. Neither slavery nor involuntary servitude, except as a punishment for crime whereof the party shall have been duly convicted, shall exist within the United States, or any place subject to their jurisdiction.

Section 2. Congress shall have power to enforce this article by appropriate legislation.

AMENDMENT [XIV]⁵

Section 1. All persons born or naturalized in the United States, and subject to the jurisdiction thereof, are citizens of the United States and of the State wherein they reside. No State shall make or enforce any law which shall abridge the privileges or immunities of citizens of the United States; nor shall any State deprive any person of life, liberty, or property, without due process of law; nor deny to any person within its jurisdiction the equal protection of the laws.

Section 2. Representatives shall be apportioned among the several States according to their respective numbers, counting the whole number of persons in each State, excluding Indians not taxed. But when the right to vote at any election for the choice of electors for President and Vice President of the United States, Representatives in Congress, the Executive and Judicial officers of a State, or the members of the Legislature thereof, is denied to any of the male inhabitants of such State, being twenty-one years of age, and citizens of the United States, or in any way abridged, except for participation in rebellion, or other crime, the basis of representation therein shall be reduced in the proportion which the number of such male citizens shall bear to the whole number of male citizens twenty-one years of age in such State.

Section 3. No person shall be a Senator or Representative in Congress, or elector of President and Vice President, or hold any office, civil or military, under the United States, or under any State, who, having previously taken an oath, as a member of Congress, or as an officer of the United States, or as a member of any State legislature, or as an executive or judicial officer of any State, to support the Constitution of the United States, shall have engaged in insurrection or rebellion against the same, or given aid or comfort to the enemies thereof. But Congress may by a vote of two-thirds of each House, remove such disability.

Section 4. The validity of the public debt of the United States, authorized by law, including debts incurred for payment of pensions and bounties for services in suppressing insurrection or rebellion, shall not be questioned. But neither the United States nor any State shall assume or pay any debt or obligation incurred in aid of insurrection or rebellion against the United States, or any claim for the loss or emancipation of any slave; but all such debts, obligations and claims shall be held illegal and void.

Section 5. The Congress shall have power to enforce, by appropriate legislation, the provisions of this article.

AMENDMENT [XV]⁶

Section 1. The right of citizens of the United States to vote shall not be denied or abridged by the United States or by any State on account of race, color, or previous condition of servitude.

Section 2. The Congress shall have power to enforce this article by appropriate legislation.

AMENDMENT [XVI]⁷

The Congress shall have power to lay and collect taxes on incomes, from whatever source de-

---

3 The part enclosed by brackets has been superseded by section 3 of Amendment XX.

4 The Thirteenth Amendment was proposed by resolution of Congress on January 31, 1865. It was declared in a proclamation of the Secretary of State, dated December 18, 1865, to have been ratified by 27 States. Subsequent records of the National Archives show that the 13th Amendment was ratified by 7 additional States. It was rejected by Kentucky and Mississippi.

5 The Fourteenth Amendment was proposed by resolution of Congress on June 13, 1866. By a concurrent resolution of Congress adopted July 21, 1868, it was declared to have been ratified by "three fourths and more of the several States of the Union," and the Secretary of State was required duly to promulgate the amendment as a part of the Constitution. He accordingly issued a proclamation, dated July 28, 1868, declaring the amendment to have been ratified by 30 States, "being more than three fourths." Records of the National Archives show that the 14th Amendment was subsequently ratified by 8 additional States. It was rejected by Kentucky.

6 The Fifteenth Amendment was proposed by resolution of Congress on February 26, 1869. It was declared in a proclamation of the Secretary of State, dated March 30, 1870, to have been ratified by 29 States, which "constitute three fourths." Records of the National Archives show that the 15th Amendment was subsequently ratified by 6 more of the States. It was rejected by Kentucky, Maryland, and Tennessee.

7 The Sixteenth Amendment was proposed by resolution of Congress on July 12, 1909. It was declared in a proclamation of the Secretary of State, dated February 25, 1913, to have been ratified by 38 States, which "constitute three fourths." Subsequent records of the National Archives show that the 16th Amendment was ratified by 4 additional States. It was rejected by Connecticut, Florida, Rhode Island, and Utah.

rived, without apportionment among the several States, and without regard to any census or enumeration.

AMENDMENT [XVII][8]

The Senate of the United States shall be composed of two Senators from each State, elected by the people thereof, for six years; and each Senator shall have one vote. The electors in each State shall have the qualifications requisite for electors of the most numerous branch of the State legislatures.

When vacancies happen in the representation of any State in the Senate, the executive authority of such State shall issue writs of election to fill such vacancies: *Provided*, That the legislature of any State may empower the executive thereof to make temporary appointments until the people fill the vacancies by election as the legislature may direct.

This amendment shall not be so construed as to affect the election or term of any Senator chosen before it becomes valid as part of the Constitution.

AMENDMENT [XVIII][9]

[Section 1. After one year from the ratification of this article the manufacture, sale, or transportation of intoxicating liquors within, the importation thereof into, or the exportation thereof from the United States and all territory subject to the jurisdiction thereof for beverage purposes is hereby prohibited.

[Sec. 2. The Congress and the several States shall have concurrent power to enforce this article by appropriate legislation.

[Sec. 3. This article shall be inoperative unless it shall have been ratified as an amendment to the Constitution by the legislatures of the several States, as provided in the Constitution, within seven years from the date of the submission hereof to the States by the Congress.]

AMENDMENT [XIX][10]

The right of citizens of the United States to vote shall not be denied or abridged by the United States or by any State on account of sex.

Congress shall have power to enforce this article by appropriate legislation.

AMENDMENT [XX][11]

Section 1. The terms of the President and Vice President shall end at noon on the 20th day of January, and the terms of Senators and Representatives at noon on the 3d day of January, of the years in which such terms would have ended if this article had not been ratified; and the terms of their successors shall then begin.

Sec. 2. The Congress shall assemble at least once in every year, and such meeting shall begin at noon on the 3d day of January, unless they shall by law appoint a different day.

Sec. 3. If, at the time fixed for the beginning of the term of the President, the President elect shall have died, the Vice President elect shall become President. If a President shall not have been chosen before the time fixed for the beginning of his term, or if the President elect shall have failed to qualify, then the Vice President elect shall act as President until a President shall have qualified; and the Congress may by law provide for the case wherein neither a President elect nor a Vice President elect shall have qualified, declaring who shall then act as President, or the manner in which one who is to act shall be selected, and such person shall act accordingly until a President or Vice President shall have qualified.

Sec. 4. The Congress may by law provide for the case of the death of any of the persons from whom the House of Representatives may choose a President whenever the right of choice shall have devolved upon them, and for the case of the death of any of the persons from whom the Senate may choose a Vice President whenever the right of choice shall have devolved upon them.

Sec. 5. Sections 1 and 2 shall take effect on the 15th day of October following the ratification of this article.

Sec. 6. This article shall be inoperative unless it shall have been ratified as an amendment to the Constitution by the legislatures of three-fourths of the several States within seven years from the date of its submission.

AMENDMENT [XXI][12]

Section 1. The eighteenth article of amendment to the Constitution of the United States is hereby repealed.

Sec. 2. The transportation or importation into any State, Territory, or possession of the United States for delivery or use therein of intoxicating liquors, in violation of the laws thereof, is hereby prohibited.

Sec. 3. This article shall be inoperative unless it shall have been ratified as an amendment to the Constitution by conventions in the several States, as provided in the Constitution, within seven

---

[8] The Seventeenth Amendment was proposed by resolution of Congress on May 13, 1912. It was declared in a proclamation of the Secretary of State, dated May 31, 1913, to have been ratified by 36 States, which "constitute three fourths." Records of the National Archives show that the 17th Amendment was subsequently ratified by 1 additional State. It was rejected by Utah and Delaware.

[9] The Eighteenth Amendment was proposed by resolution of Congress on December 18, 1917. It was declared in a proclamation of the Acting Secretary of State, dated January 29, 1919, to have been ratified by 36 States, which "constitute three fourths." Subsequent records of the National Archives show that the 18th Amendment was ratified by 10 additional States. It was rejected by Rhode Island. By its own terms the 18th Amendment became effective one year after its ratification, which was consummated on January 16, 1919, and therefore went into effect on January 16, 1920.
Repeal of the 18th Amendment on December 5, 1933, was proclaimed by the President in his proclamation of that date, when the ratification of the 21st Amendment was certified by the Acting Secretary of State.

[10] The Nineteenth Amendment was proposed by resolution of Congress on June 4, 1919. It was declared in a proclamation of the Secretary of State, dated August 26, 1920, to have been ratified by 36 States, which "constitute three fourths." Subsequent records of the National Archives show that the 19th Amendment was ratified by 5 additional States. It was rejected by Georgia, South Carolina, Mississippi, Delaware, and Louisiana.

[11] The Twentieth Amendment was proposed by resolution of Congress on March 2, 1932. It was declared in a proclamation of the Secretary of State, dated February 6, 1933, to have been ratified by 39 States, which "constitute more than the requisite three fourths." Subsequent records of the National Archives show that the 20th Amendment was ratified by all 48 States before sections 1 and 2 became effective on October 15, 1933. The other sections of the amendment became effective on January 23, 1933, when its ratification was consummated by three fourths of the States.

[12] The Twenty-first Amendment was proposed by resolution of Congress on February 20, 1933. It was certified in a proclamation of the Acting Secretary of State dated December 5, 1933, to have been ratified by conventions of 36 States, which "constitute the requisite three fourths of the whole number of States." Subsequent records of the National Archives show that the 21st Amendment was ratified by 2 additional States. It was rejected by the convention of South Carolina. North Carolina voted against holding a convention.

years from the date of the submission hereof to the States by the Congress.

AMENDMENT [XXII][13]

Section 1. No person shall be elected to the office of the President more than twice, and no person who has held the office of President, or acted as President, for more than two years of a term to which some other person was elected President shall be elected to the office of the President more than once. But this Article shall not apply to any person holding the office of President when this Article was proposed by the Congress, and shall not prevent any person who may be holding the office of President, or acting as President, during the term within which this Article becomes operative from holding the office of President or acting as President during the remainder of such term.

Sec. 2. This article shall be inoperative unless it shall have been ratified as an amendment to the Constitution by the legislatures of three-fourths of the several States within seven years from the date of its submission to the States by the Congress.

AMENDMENT [XXIII][14]

Section 1. The District constituting the seat of Government of the United States shall appoint in such manner as the Congress may direct:

A number of electors of President and Vice President equal to the whole number of Senators and Representatives in Congress to which the District would be entitled if it were a State, but in no event more than the least populous State; they shall be in addition to those appointed by the States, but they shall be considered, for the purposes of the election of President and Vice President, to be electors appointed by a State; and they shall meet in the District and perform such duties as provided by the twelfth article of amendment.

Section 2. The Congress shall have power to enforce this article by appropriate legislation.

AMENDMENT [XXIV][15]

Section 1. The right of citizens of the United States to vote in any primary or other election for President or Vice President, for electors for President or Vice President, or for Senator or Representative in Congress, shall not be denied or abridged by the United States or any State by reason of failure to pay any poll tax or other tax.

Section 2. The Congress shall have power to enforce this article by appropriate legislation.

AMENDMENT [XXV][16]

Section 1. In case of removal of the President from office or of his death or resignation, the Vice President shall become President.

Sec. 2. Whenever there is a vacancy in the office of the Vice President, the President shall nominate a Vice President who shall take office upon confirmation by a majority vote of both Houses of Congress.

Sec. 3. Whenever the President transmits to the President pro tempore of the Senate and the Speaker of the House of Representatives his written declaration that he is unable to discharge the powers and duties of his office, and until he transmits to them a written declaration to the contrary, such powers and duties shall be discharged by the Vice President as Acting President.

Sec. 4. Whenever the Vice President and a majority of either the principal officers of the executive departments or of such other body as Congress may by law provide, transmit to the President pro tempore of the Senate and the Speaker of the House of Representatives their written declaration that the President is unable to discharge the powers and duties of his office, the Vice President shall immediately assume the powers and duties of the office as Acting President.

Thereafter, when the President transmits to the President pro tempore of the Senate and the Speaker of the House of Representatives his written declaration that no inability exists, he shall resume the powers and duties of his office unless the Vice President and a majority of either the principal officers of the executive department or of such other body as Congress may by law provide, transmit within four days to the President pro tempore of the Senate and the Speaker of the House of Representatives their written declaration that the President is unable to discharge the powers and duties of his office. Thereupon Congress shall decide the issue, assembling within forty-eight hours for that purpose if not in session. If the Congress, within twenty-one days after receipt of the latter written declaration, or, if Congress is not in session, within twenty-one days after Congress is required to assemble, determines by two-thirds vote of both Houses that the President is unable to discharge the powers and duties of his office, the Vice President shall continue to discharge the same as Acting President; otherwise, the President shall resume the powers and duties of his office.

AMENDMENT [XXVI][17]

Section 1. The right of citizens of the United States, who are eighteen years of age or older, to vote shall not be denied or abridged by the United States or by any State on account of age.

Sec. 2. The Congress shall have power to enforce this article by appropriate legislation.

---

[13] The Twenty-second Amendment was proposed by resolution of Congress on March 24, 1947. Ratification was completed on February 27, 1951, when the thirty-sixth State (Minnesota) approved the amendment. On March 1, 1951, the Administrator of General Services certified that "the States whose Legislatures have so ratified the said proposed Amendment constitute the requisite three-fourths of the whole number of States in the United States." Records of the National Archives show that the 22d Amendment was subsequently ratified by 5 additional States.

[14] The Twenty-third Amendment was proposed by resolution of Congress on June 16, 1960. The Administrator of General Services certified the ratification and adoption of the amendment by three-fourths of the States on April 3, 1961. It was rejected by Arkansas.

[15] The Twenty-fourth Amendment was proposed by resolution of Congress on August 27, 1962. It was declared in a Proclamation of the Administrator of General Services dated February 4, 1964, to have been ratified by three-fourths of the States. It was rejected by the legislature of Mississippi on December 20, 1962.

[16] The Twenty-fifth Amendment to the Constitution was proposed by the Congress on July 6, 1965. It was declared in a certificate of the Administrator of General Services, dated February 23, 1967, to have been ratified by the legislatures of 39 of the 50 States. Ratification was completed on February 10, 1967.

[17] The Twenty-sixth Amendment was proposed by resolution of Congress on March 23, 1971. On July 5, 1971, the Administrator of General Services certified the ratification and adoption of the amendment by three fourths of the states.

ADMINISTRATIONS, CABINETS, AND CONGRESSES
SOURCE: *Biographical Directory of the American Congress* and other sources

A cabinet officer is not appointed for a fixed term and does not necessarily go out of office with the President who appointed him; while it is customary to tender his resignation at the time a change of administration takes place, he remains formally at the head of his department until a successor is appointed. Subordinates acting temporarily as heads of departments are not considered cabinet officers; in the earlier period of the nation's history, not all cabinet officers were heads of departments.

The dates immediately following the names of executive officers are those upon which commissions were issued, unless otherwise specifically noted. Where periods of time are indicated by dates as, for instance, March 4, 1793–March 3, 1797, both such dates are included as portions of the time period.

The National Security Act of 1947 (Pub. Law 253, 80th Cong., 1st sess.), approved July 26, 1947, created the office of Secretary of Defense and merged the War and Navy Departments into the National Military Establishment. The act was subsequently amended (Pub. Law 216, 81st Cong., 1st sess.): Section 201. (a) There is hereby established, as an executive department of the Government, the **Department of Defense.**

The Reorganization Plan Number 1 of 1953 (Pub. Law 13, 83d Cong., 1st sess.), approved April 1, 1953, abolished the Federal Security Agency and created the **Department of Health, Education, and Welfare,** which was renamed the **Department of Health and Human Services** in 1979.

The **Department of Housing and Urban Development** was established by the Department of Housing and Urban Development Act of September 9, 1965 (79 Stat. 667; 5 U.S.C. 642).

The **Department of Transportation** was established by the Department of Transportation Act of October 15, 1966 (80 Stat. 931; 49 U.S.C. 1681).

As of July 1, 1971, the Post Office Department became **The U.S. Postal Service,** a quasi-independent nonprofit corporation. The Postmaster General ceased to be a member of the cabinet.

The **Department of Energy** was established by the bill, S. 826, Department of Energy Organization Act, approved by Congress on August 2, 1977.

The **Department of Education** was established by the Bill to Establish a Department of Education on September 27, 1979.

Congressional vacancies are not noted below.

First Administration of GEORGE WASHINGTON
APRIL 30, 1789, TO MARCH 3, 1793

PRESIDENT—George Washington, of Virginia (Federalist). VICE-PRESIDENT—John Adams, of Massachusetts. SECRETARY OF STATE—John Jay, of New York, was Secretary for Foreign Affairs under the Confederation, and continued to act, at the request of Washington, until Jefferson took office. Thomas Jefferson, of Virginia, September 26, 1789; entered upon duties March 22, 1790. SECRETARY OF THE TREASURY—Alexander Hamilton, of New York, September 11, 1789. SECRETARY OF WAR—Henry Knox, of Massachusetts, September 12, 1789. ATTORNEY GENERAL—Edmund Randolph, of Virginia, September 26, 1789; entered upon duties February 2, 1790. POSTMASTER GENERAL—Samuel Osgood, of Massachusetts, September 26, 1789. Timothy Pickering, of Pennsylvania, August 12, 1791; entered upon duties August 19, 1791.

1st Congress

1st Session: Mar. 4, 1789–Sept. 29, 1789[1]; 2d Session: Jan. 4, 1790–Aug. 12, 1790; 3d Session: Dec. 6, 1790–Mar. 3, 1791.

President pro tempore of the Senate: John Langdon, of New Hampshire (elected Apr. 6, 1789). Speaker of the House: Frederick A. C. Muhlenberg, of Pennsylvania (elected Apr. 1, 1789).
Senate: 17 pro-administration; 9 opposition
House: 38 pro-administration; 26 opposition

2d Congress

1st Session: Oct. 24, 1791–May 8, 1792; 2d Session: Nov. 5, 1792–Mar. 2, 1793; Special Session of the Senate: Mar. 4, 1791.

President pro tempore of the Senate: Richard H. Lee, of Virginia (elected Apr. 18, 1792); John Langdon, of New Hampshire (elected Nov. 5, 1792 and Mar. 1, 1793). Speaker of the House: Jonathan Trumbull, of Connecticut (elected Oct. 24, 1791).
Senate: 16 Federalist; 13 Democratic-Republican
House: 37 Federalist; 33 Democratic-Republican

Second Administration of GEORGE WASHINGTON
MARCH 4, 1793, TO MARCH 3, 1797

PRESIDENT—George Washington, of Virginia (Federalist). VICE-PRESIDENT—John Adams, of Massachusetts. SECRETARY OF STATE—Thomas Jefferson, of Virginia, continued from preceding administration. Edmund Randolph, of Virginia, January 2, 1794. Timothy Pickering, of Pennsylvania (Secretary of War), ad interim, August 20, 1795. Timothy Pickering, of Pennsylvania, December 10, 1795. SECRETARY OF THE TREASURY—Alexander Hamilton, of New York, continued from preceding administration. Oliver Wolcott, Jr., of Connecticut, February 2, 1795. SECRETARY OF WAR—Henry Knox, of Massachusetts, continued from preceding administration. Timothy Pickering, of Pennsylvania, January 2, 1795. Timothy Pickering, of Pennsylvania (Secretary of State), ad interim, December 10, 1795, to February 5, 1796. James McHenry, of Maryland, January 27, 1796; entered upon duties February 6, 1796. ATTORNEY GENERAL—Edmund Randolph, of Virginia, continued from preceding administration. William Bradford, of Pennsylvania, January 27, 1794; entered upon duties January 29, 1794. Charles Lee, of Virginia, December 10, 1795. POSTMASTER GENERAL—Timothy Pickering, of Pennsylvania, continued from preceding administration. Timothy Pickering, of Pennsylvania, recommissioned June 1, 1794. Joseph Habersham, of Georgia, February 25, 1795.

3d Congress

1st Session: Dec. 2, 1793–June 9, 1794; 2d Session: Nov. 3, 1794–Mar. 3, 1795; Special Session of the Senate: Mar. 4, 1793.

President pro tempore of the Senate: Ralph Izard, of South Carolina (elected May 31, 1794); Henry Tazewell, of Virginia (elected Feb. 20, 1795). Speaker of the House: Frederick A. C. Muhlenberg, of Pennsylvania (elected Dec. 2, 1793).
Senate: 17 Democratic-Republican; 13 Federalist
House: 57 Democratic-Republican; 48 Federalist

4th Congress

1st Session: Dec. 7, 1795–June 1, 1796; 2d Session: Dec. 5, 1796–Mar. 3, 1797; Special Session of the Senate: June 8, 1795–June 26, 1795.

President pro tempore of the Senate: Henry Tazewell, of Virginia (elected Dec. 7, 1795), Samuel Livermore, of New Hampshire (elected May 6, 1796), William Bingham, of Pennsylvania (Feb. 16, 1797). Speaker of the House: Jonathan Dayton, of New Jersey (elected Dec. 7, 1795).
Senate: 19 Federalist; 13 Democratic-Republican
House: 54 Federalist; 52 Democratic-Republican

Administration of JOHN ADAMS
MARCH 4, 1797, TO MARCH 3, 1801

PRESIDENT—John Adams, of Massachusetts (Federalist). VICE-PRESIDENT—Thomas Jefferson, of Virginia. SECRETARY OF STATE—Timothy Pickering, of Pennsylvania, continued from preceding administration; resignation requested May 10, 1800, but declining to resign, he was dismissed May 12, 1800. Charles Lee, of Virginia (Attorney General), ad interim, May 13, 1800. John Marshall, of Virginia, May 13, 1800; entered upon duties June 6, 1800. John Marshall, of Virginia (Chief Justice of the United States), ad interim, February 4, 1801, to March 3, 1801. SECRETARY OF THE TREASURY—Oliver Wolcott, Jr., of Connecticut, continued from preceding administration. Samuel Dexter, of Massachusetts, January 1, 1801. SECRETARY OF WAR—James McHenry, of Maryland, continued from preceding administration. Benjamin Stoddert, of Maryland (Secretary of the Navy), ad interim, June 1, 1800, to June 12, 1800. Samuel Dexter, of Massachusetts, May 13, 1800; entered upon duties June 12, 1800. Samuel Dexter, of Massachusetts (Secretary of the Treasury), ad interim, January 1, 1801. ATTORNEY GENERAL —Charles Lee, of Virginia, continued from preceding administration. POSTMASTER GENERAL—Joseph Habersham, of Georgia, continued from preceding administration. SECRETARY OF THE NAVY—Benjamin Stoddert, of Maryland, May 21, 1798; entered upon duties June 18, 1798.

5th Congress

1st Session: May 15, 1797–July 10, 1797; 2d Session: Nov. 13, 1797–July 16, 1798; 3d Session: Dec. 3, 1798–Mar. 3, 1799; Special Sessions of the Senate: Mar. 4, 1797; July 17, 1798–July 19, 1798.

President pro tempore of the Senate: William Bradford, of Rhode Island (elected July 6, 1797); Jacob Read, of South Carolina (elected Nov. 22, 1797); Theodore Sedgwick, of Massachusetts (elected June 27, 1798); John Laurence, of New York (elected Dec. 6, 1798); James Ross of Pennsylvania (elected Mar. 1, 1799). Speaker of the House: Jonathan Dayton, of New Jersey (reelected May 15, 1797); George Dent, of Maryland served as Speaker pro tempore Apr. 20, 1798, and May 28, 1798.
Senate: 20 Federalist; 12 Democratic-Republican
House: 58 Federalist; 48 Democratic-Republican

---

[1] Both houses met for the first time on Mar. 4, 1789, but each lacked a quorum. They met from day to day until the House attained a quorum on Apr. 1, 1789, and the Senate on Apr. 6, 1789.

6th Congress

1st Session: Dec. 2, 1799–May 14, 1800; 2d Session: Nov. 17, 1800–Mar. 3, 1801.

President pro tempore of the Senate: Samuel Livermore, of New Hampshire (elected Dec. 2, 1799); Uriah Tracy, of Connecticut (elected May 14, 1800); John E. Howard, of Maryland (elected Nov. 21, 1800); James Hillhouse, of Connecticut (elected Feb. 28, 1801). Speaker of the House: Theodore Sedgwick, of Massachusetts (elected Dec. 2, 1799).

Senate: 19 Federalist; 13 Democratic-Republican
House: 64 Federalist; 42 Democratic-Republican

First Administration of THOMAS JEFFERSON
MARCH 4, 1801, TO MARCH 3, 1805

PRESIDENT—Thomas Jefferson, of Virginia (Democratic-Republican). VICE-PRESIDENT—Aaron Burr, of New York. SECRETARY OF STATE—John Marshall, of Virginia (Chief Justice of the United States), for one day (March 4, 1801), and for a special purpose. Levi Lincoln, of Massachusetts (Attorney General), ad interim, March 5, 1801. James Madison, of Virginia, March 5, 1801; entered upon duties May 2, 1801. SECRETARY OF THE TREASURY—Samuel Dexter, of Massachusetts, continued from preceding administration to May 6, 1801. Albert Gallatin, of Pennsylvania, May 14, 1801. SECRETARY OF WAR—Henry Dearborn, of Massachusetts, March 5, 1801. ATTORNEY GENERAL—Levi Lincoln, of Massachusetts, March 5, 1801, to December 31, 1804. POSTMASTER GENERAL—Joseph Habersham, of Georgia, continued from preceding administration. Gideon Granger, of Connecticut, November 28, 1801. SECRETARY OF THE NAVY—Benjamin Stoddert, of Maryland, continued from preceding administration. Henry Dearborn, of Massachusetts (Secretary of War), ad interim, April 1, 1801. Robert Smith, of Maryland, July 15, 1801; entered upon duties July 27, 1801.

7th Congress

1st Session: Dec. 7, 1801–May 3, 1802; 2d Session: Dec. 6, 1802–March 3, 1803; Special Session of the Senate: Mar. 4, 1801–Mar. 5, 1801.

President pro tempore of the Senate: Abraham Baldwin, of Georgia (elected Dec. 7, 1801; Apr. 17, 1802); Stephen R. Bradley, of Vermont (elected Dec. 14, 1802; Feb. 25, 1803; Mar. 2, 1803). Speaker of the House: Nathaniel Macon, of North Carolina (elected Dec. 7, 1801).

Senate: 18 Democratic-Republican; 14 Federalist
House: 69 Democratic-Republican; 36 Federalist

8th Congress

1st Session: Oct. 17, 1803–Mar. 27, 1804; 2d Session: Nov. 5, 1804–Mar. 3, 1805.

President pro tempore of the Senate: John Brown, of Kentucky (elected Oct. 17, 1803; Jan. 23, 1804); Jesse Franklin, of North Carolina (elected Mar. 10, 1804); Joseph Anderson, of Tennessee (elected Jan. 15, 1805; Feb. 28, 1805; Mar. 2, 1805). Speaker of the House: Nathaniel Macon, of North Carolina (reelected Oct. 17, 1803).

Senate: 25 Democratic-Republican; 9 Federalist
House: 102 Democratic-Republican; 39 Federalist

Second Administration of THOMAS JEFFERSON
MARCH 4, 1805, TO MARCH 3, 1809

PRESIDENT—Thomas Jefferson, of Virginia (Democratic-Republican). VICE-PRESIDENT—George Clinton, of New York. SECRETARY OF STATE—James Madison, of Virginia, continued from preceding administration. SECRETARY OF THE TREASURY—Albert Gallatin, of Pennsylvania, continued from preceding administration. SECRETARY OF WAR—Henry Dearborn, of Massachusetts, continued from preceding administration. John Smith (chief clerk), ad interim, February 17, 1809. ATTORNEY GENERAL—John Breckinridge, of Kentucky, August 7, 1805 (died December 14, 1806). Caesar A. Rodney, of Delaware, January 20, 1807. POSTMASTER GENERAL—Gideon Granger, of Connecticut, continued from preceding administration. SECRETARY OF THE NAVY—Robert Smith, of Maryland, continued from preceding administration.

9th Congress

1st Session: Dec. 2, 1805–Apr. 21, 1806; 2d Session: Dec. 1, 1806–Mar. 3, 1807; Special Session of the Senate: Mar. 4, 1805.

President pro tempore of the Senate: Samuel Smith, of Maryland (elected Dec. 2, 1805; Mar. 18, 1806; Mar. 2, 1807). Speaker of the House: Nathaniel Macon, of North Carolina (reelected Dec. 2, 1805).

Senate: 27 Democratic-Republican; 7 Federalist
House: 116 Democratic-Republican; 25 Federalist

10th Congress

1st Session: Oct. 26, 1807–Apr. 25, 1808; 2d Session: Nov. 7, 1808–Mar. 3, 1809.

President pro tempore of the Senate: Samuel Smith, of Maryland (elected Apr. 16, 1808); Stephen R. Bradley, of Vermont (elected Dec. 28, 1808); John Milledge, of Georgia (elected Jan. 30, 1809). Speaker of the House: Joseph B. Varnum, of Massachusetts (elected Oct. 26, 1807).

Senate: 28 Democratic-Republican; 6 Federalist
House: 118 Democratic-Republican; 24 Federalist

First Administration of JAMES MADISON
MARCH 4, 1809, TO MARCH 3, 1813

PRESIDENT—James Madison, of Virginia (Democratic-Republican). VICE-PRESIDENT—George Clinton, of New York. (Died April 20, 1812.) SECRETARY OF STATE—Robert Smith, of Maryland, March 6, 1809. James Monroe, of Virginia, April 2, 1811; entered upon duties April 6, 1811. SECRETARY OF THE TREASURY—Albert Gallatin, of Pennsylvania, continued from preceding administration. SECRETARY OF WAR—John Smith (chief clerk), ad interim, continued from preceding administration. William Eustis, of Massachusetts, March 7, 1809; entered upon duties April 8, 1809; served to December 31, 1812. James Monroe, of Virginia (Secretary of State), ad interim, January 1, 1813. John Armstrong, of New York, January 13, 1813; entered upon duties February 5, 1813. ATTORNEY GENERAL—Caesar A. Rodney, of Delaware, continued from preceding administration; resigned December 5, 1811. William Pinkney, of Maryland, December 11, 1811; entered upon duties January 6, 1812. POSTMASTER GENERAL—Gideon Granger, of Connecticut, continued from preceding administration. SECRETARY OF THE NAVY—Robert Smith, of Maryland, continued from preceding administration. Charles W. Goldsborough (chief clerk), ad interim, March 8, 1809. Paul Hamilton, of South Carolina, March 7, 1809; entered upon duties May 15, 1809; served to December 31, 1812. Charles W. Goldsborough (chief clerk), ad interim, January 7, 1813, to January 18, 1813. William Jones, of Pennsylvania, January 12, 1813; entered upon duties January 19, 1813.

11th Congress

1st Session: May 22, 1809–June 28, 1809; 2d Session: Nov. 27, 1809–May 1, 1810; 3d Session: Dec. 3, 1810–Mar. 3, 1811; Special Session of the Senate: Mar. 4, 1809–Mar. 7, 1809.

President pro tempore of the Senate: Andrew Gregg, of Pennsylvania (elected June 26, 1809); John Gaillard, of South Carolina (elected Feb. 28, 1810; Apr. 17, 1810); John Pope, of Kentucky (elected Feb. 23, 1811). Speaker of the House: Joseph B. Varnum, of Massachusetts (reelected May 22, 1809).

Senate: 28 Democratic-Republican; 6 Federalist
House: 94 Democratic-Republican; 48 Federalist

12th Congress

1st Session: Nov. 4, 1811 to July 6, 1812; 2d Session: Nov. 2, 1812–Mar. 3, 1813.

President pro tempore of the Senate: William H. Crawford, of Georgia (elected Mar. 24, 1812). Speaker of the House: Henry Clay, of Kentucky (elected Nov. 4, 1811).

Senate: 30 Democratic-Republican; 6 Federalist
House: 108 Democratic-Republican; 36 Federalist

Second Administration of JAMES MADISON
MARCH 4, 1813, TO MARCH 3, 1817

PRESIDENT—James Madison, of Virginia (Democratic-Republican). VICE-PRESIDENT—Elbridge Gerry, of Massachusetts (died November 23, 1814). SECRETARY OF STATE—James Monroe, of Virginia, continued from preceding administration. James Monroe, of Virginia (Secretary of War), ad interim, October 1, 1814. James Monroe, of Virginia, February 28, 1815. SECRETARY OF THE TREASURY—Albert Gallatin, of Pennsylvania, continued from preceding administration. William Jones, of Pennsylvania (Secretary of the Navy), performed the duties of the Secretary of the Treasury during the absence of Mr. Gallatin in Europe (April 21, 1813, to February 9, 1814). George W. Campbell, of Tennessee, February 9, 1814. Alexander J. Dallas, of Pennsylvania, October 6, 1814; entered upon duties October 14, 1814. William H. Crawford, of Georgia, October 22, 1816. SECRETARY OF WAR—John Armstrong, of New York, continued from preceding administration. James Monroe, of Virginia (Secretary of State), ad interim, August 30, 1814. James Monroe, of Virginia, September 27, 1814; entered upon duties October 1, 1814. James Monroe, of Virginia (Secretary of State), ad interim, March 1, 1815. Alexander J. Dallas, of Pennsylvania (Secretary of the Treasury), ad interim, March 14, 1815, to August 8, 1815. William H. Crawford, of Georgia, August 1, 1815; entered upon duties August 8, 1815. George Graham (chief clerk), ad interim, October 22, 1816, to close of administration. ATTORNEY GENERAL—William Pinkney, of Maryland, continued from preceding administration. Richard Rush, of Pennsylvania, February 10, 1814; entered upon duties the day following. POSTMASTER

GENERAL—Gideon Granger, of Connecticut, continued from preceding administration. Return J. Meigs, Jr., of Ohio, March 17, 1814; entered upon duties April 11, 1814. SECRETARY OF THE NAVY—William Jones, of Pennsylvania, continued from preceding administration. Benjamin Homans (chief clerk), ad interim, December 2, 1814. Benjamin W. Crowninshield, of Massachusetts, December 19, 1814; entered upon duties January 16, 1815.

13th Congress
1st Session: May 24, 1813–Aug. 2, 1813; 2d Session: Dec. 6, 1813–Apr. 18, 1814; 3d Session: Sept. 19, 1814–Mar. 3, 1815.

President pro tempore of the Senate: Joseph B. Varnum, of Massachusetts (elected Dec. 6, 1813); John Gaillard, of South Carolina (elected Apr. 18, 1814; Nov. 25, 1814). Speaker of the House: Henry Clay, of Kentucky (reelected May 24, 1813); Langdon Cheves, of South Carolina (elected Jan. 19, 1814).

Senate: 27 Democratic-Republican; 9 Federalist
House: 112 Democratic-Republican; 68 Federalist

14th Congress
1st Session: Dec. 4, 1815–Apr. 30, 1816; 2d Session: Dec. 2, 1816–Mar. 3, 1817.

President pro tempore of the Senate: John Gaillard, of South Carolina (continued from preceding Congress). Speaker of the House: Henry Clay, of Kentucky (reelected Dec. 4, 1815).

Senate: 25 Democratic-Republican; 11 Federalist
House: 117 Democratic-Republican; 65 Federalist

First Administration of JAMES MONROE
MARCH 4, 1817, TO MARCH 3, 1821

PRESIDENT—James Monroe, of Virginia (Democratic-Republican). VICE-PRESIDENT—Daniel D. Tompkins, of New York. SECRETARY OF STATE—John Graham (chief clerk), ad interim, March 4, 1817. Richard Rush, of Pennsylvania (Attorney General), ad interim, March 10, 1817. John Quincy Adams, of Massachusetts, March 5, 1817; entered upon duties September 22, 1817. SECRETARY OF THE TREASURY—William H. Crawford, of Georgia, continued from preceding administration. William H. Crawford, of Georgia, recommissioned March 5, 1817. SECRETARY OF WAR—George Graham (chief clerk), ad interim, March 4, 1817. John C. Calhoun, of South Carolina, October 8, 1817; entered upon duties December 10, 1817. ATTORNEY GENERAL—Richard Rush, of Pennsylvania, continued from preceding administration to October 30, 1817. William Wirt, of Virginia, November 13, 1817; entered upon duties November 15, 1817. POSTMASTER GENERAL—Return J. Meigs, Jr., of Ohio, continued from preceding administration. SECRETARY OF THE NAVY—Benjamin W. Crowninshield, of Massachusetts, continued from preceding administration. John C. Calhoun, of South Carolina (Secretary of War), ad interim, October 1, 1818. Smith Thompson, of New York, November 9, 1818; entered upon duties January 1, 1819.

15th Congress
1st Session: Dec. 1, 1817–Apr. 20, 1818; 2d Session: Nov. 16, 1818–Mar. 3, 1819; Special Session of the Senate: Mar. 4, 1817–Mar. 6, 1817.

President pro tempore of the Senate: John Gaillard, of South Carolina (continued from preceding Congress; elected Mar. 6, 1817; Mar. 31, 1818). James Barbour, of Virginia (elected Feb. 15, 1819). Speaker of the House: Henry Clay, of Kentucky (reelected Dec. 1, 1817).

Senate: 34 Democratic-Republican; 10 Federalist
House: 141 Democratic-Republican; 42 Federalist

16th Congress
1st Session: Dec. 6, 1819–May 15, 1820; 2d Session: Nov. 13, 1820–Mar. 3, 1821.

President pro tempore of the Senate: James Barbour, of Virginia (continued from preceding Congress); John Gaillard, of South Carolina (elected Jan. 25, 1820). Speaker of the House: Henry Clay, of Kentucky (reelected Dec. 6, 1819); John W. Taylor, of New York (elected Nov. 15, 1820).

Senate: 35 Democratic-Republican; 7 Federalist
House: 156 Democratic-Republican; 27 Federalist

Second Administration of JAMES MONROE
MARCH 4, 1821, TO MARCH 3, 1825

PRESIDENT—James Monroe, of Virginia (Democratic-Republican). VICE-PRESIDENT—Daniel D. Tompkins, of New York. SECRETARY OF STATE—John Quincy Adams, of Massachusetts, continued from preceding administration. SECRETARY OF THE TREASURY—William H. Crawford, of Georgia, continued from preceding administration. SECRETARY OF WAR—John C. Calhoun, of South Carolina, continued from preceding administration. ATTORNEY GENERAL—William Wirt, of Virginia, continued

from preceding administration. POSTMASTER GENERAL—Return J. Meigs, Jr., of Ohio, continued from preceding administration. John McLean, of Ohio, commissioned June 26, 1823, to take effect July 1, 1823. SECRETARY OF THE NAVY—Smith Thompson, of New York, continued from preceding administration. John Rodgers (commodore, United States Navy, and President of the Board of Navy Commissioners), ad interim, September 1, 1823. Samuel L. Southard, of New Jersey, September 16, 1823.

17th Congress
1st Session: Dec. 3, 1821–May 8, 1822; 2d Session: Dec. 2, 1822–Mar. 3, 1823.

President pro tempore of the Senate: John Gaillard, of South Carolina (elected Feb. 1, 1822; Feb. 19, 1823). Speaker of the House: Philip P. Barbour, of Virginia (elected Dec. 4, 1821).

Senate: 44 Democratic-Republican; 4 Federalist
House: 158 Democratic-Republican; 25 Federalist

18th Congress
1st Session: Dec. 1, 1823–May 27, 1824; 2d Session: Dec. 6, 1824–Mar. 3, 1825.

President pro tempore of the Senate: John Gaillard, of South Carolina (elected May 21, 1824). Speaker of the House: Henry Clay, of Kentucky (elected Dec. 1, 1823).

Senate: 44 Democratic-Republican; 4 Federalist
House: 187 Democratic-Republican; 26 Federalist

Administration of JOHN QUINCY ADAMS
MARCH 4, 1825, TO MARCH 3, 1829

PRESIDENT—John Quincy Adams, of Massachusetts (Democratic-Republican). VICE-PRESIDENT—John C. Calhoun, of South Carolina. SECRETARY OF STATE—Daniel Brent (chief clerk), ad interim, March 4, 1825. Henry Clay, of Kentucky, March 7, 1825. SECRETARY OF THE TREASURY—Samuel L. Southard, of New Jersey (Secretary of the Navy), ad interim, March 7, 1825. Richard Rush, of Pennsylvania, March 7, 1825; entered upon duties August 1, 1825. SECRETARY OF WAR—James Barbour, of Virginia, March 7, 1825. Samuel L. Southard, of New Jersey (Secretary of the Navy), ad interim, May 26, 1828. Peter B. Porter, of New York, May 26, 1828; entered upon duties June 21, 1828. ATTORNEY GENERAL—William Wirt, of Virginia, continued from preceding administration. POSTMASTER GENERAL—John McLean, of Ohio, continued from preceding administration. SECRETARY OF THE NAVY—Samuel L. Southard, of New Jersey, continued from preceding administration.

19th Congress
1st Session: Dec. 5, 1825–May 22, 1826; 2d Session: Dec. 4, 1826–Mar. 3, 1827; Special Session of the Senate: Mar. 4, 1825–Mar. 9, 1825.

President pro tempore of the Senate: John Gaillard, of South Carolina (elected Mar. 9, 1825). Nathaniel Macon, of North Carolina (elected May 20, 1826; Jan. 2, 1827; Mar. 2, 1827). Speaker of the House: John W. Taylor, of New York (elected Dec. 5, 1825).

Senate: 26 pro-administration; 20 opposition
House: 105 pro-administration; 97 opposition

20th Congress
1st Session: Dec. 3, 1827–May 26, 1828; 2d Session: Dec. 1, 1828–Mar. 3, 1829.

President pro tempore of the Senate: Samuel Smith, of Maryland (elected May 15, 1828). Speaker of the House: Andrew Stevenson, of Virginia (elected Dec. 3, 1827).

Senate: 20 pro-administration; 26 opposition
House: 94 pro-administration; 119 opposition

First Administration of ANDREW JACKSON
MARCH 4, 1829, TO MARCH 3, 1833

PRESIDENT—Andrew Jackson, of Tennessee (Democratic). VICE-PRESIDENT—John C. Calhoun, of South Carolina (resigned December 28, 1832). SECRETARY OF STATE—James A. Hamilton, of New York, ad interim, March 4, 1829. Martin Van Buren, of New York, March 6, 1829; entered upon duties March 28, 1829. Edward Livingston, of Louisiana, May 24, 1831. SECRETARY OF THE TREASURY—Samuel D. Ingham, of Pennsylvania, March 6, 1829. Asbury Dickins (chief clerk), ad interim, June 21, 1831. Louis McLane, of Delaware, August 8, 1831. SECRETARY OF WAR—John H. Eaton, of Tennessee, March 9, 1829. Philip G. Randolph (chief clerk), ad interim, June 20, 1831. Roger B. Taney, of Maryland (Attorney General), ad interim, July 21, 1831. Lewis Cass, of Ohio, August 1, 1831; entered upon duties August 8, 1831. ATTORNEY GENERAL—John M. Berrien, of Georgia, March 9, 1829, to June 22, 1831. Roger B. Taney, of Maryland, July 20, 1831. POSTMASTER GENERAL—John McLean, of Ohio, continued from preceding administration. William T. Barry, of Kentucky, March 9, 1829; entered upon duties April 6, 1829. SECRETARY OF THE NAVY—Charles Hay (chief clerk), ad interim, March 4, 1829. John Branch, of North Carolina, March 9, 1829. John Boyle (chief clerk), ad interim, May 12, 1831. Levi Woodbury, of New Hampshire, May 23, 1831.

21st Congress

1st Session: Dec. 7, 1829–May 31, 1830; 2d Session: Dec. 6, 1830–Mar. 3, 1831; Special Session of the Senate: Mar. 4, 1829–Mar. 17, 1829.

President pro tempore of the Senate: Samuel Smith, of Maryland (elected Mar. 13, 1829; May 29, 1830; Mar. 1, 1831). Speaker of the House: Andrew Stevenson, of Virginia (reelected Dec. 7, 1829).

Senate: 26 Democratic; 22 National Republican

House: 139 Democratic; 74 National Republican

22d Congress

1st Session: Dec. 5, 1831–July 16, 1832; 2d Session: Dec. 3, 1832–Mar. 2, 1833.

President pro tempore of the Senate: Littleton W. Tazewell, of Virginia (elected July 9, 1832); Hugh L. White, of Tennessee (elected Dec. 3, 1832). Speaker of the House: Andrew Stevenson of Virginia (reelected Dec. 5, 1831).

Senate: 25 Democratic; 21 National Republican

House: 141 Democratic; 58 National Republican

Second Administration of ANDREW JACKSON
MARCH 4, 1833, TO MARCH 3, 1837

PRESIDENT—Andrew Jackson, of Tennessee (Democratic). VICE-PRESIDENT—Martin Van Buren, of New York. SECRETARY OF STATE—Edward Livingston, of Louisiana, continued from preceding administration. Louis McLane of Delaware, May 29, 1833. John Forsyth, of Georgia, June 27, 1834; entered upon duties July 1, 1834. SECRETARY OF THE TREASURY—Louis McLane, of Delaware, continued from preceding administration. William J. Duane, of Pennsylvania, May 29, 1833; entered upon duties June 1, 1833. Roger B. Taney, of Maryland, September 23, 1833. McClintock Young (chief clerk), ad interim, June 25, 1834. Levi Woodbury, of New Hampshire, June 27, 1834; entered upon duties July 1, 1834. SECRETARY OF WAR—Lewis Cass, of Ohio, continued from preceding administration. Carey A. Harris, of Tennessee (Commissioner of Indian Affairs), ad interim, October 5, 1836. Benjamin F. Butler, of New York (Attorney General), ad interim, October 26, 1836. Benjamin F. Butler, of New York, commissioned March 3, 1837, ad interim, "during the pleasure of the President, until a successor, duly appointed, shall accept such office and enter upon the duties thereof." ATTORNEY GENERAL—Roger B. Taney, of Maryland, continued from preceding administration to September 23, 1833. Benjamin F. Butler, of New York, November 15, 1833; entered upon duties November 18, 1833. POSTMASTER GENERAL—William T. Barry, of Kentucky, continued from preceding administration. Amos Kendall, of Kentucky, May 1, 1835. SECRETARY OF THE NAVY—Levi Woodbury, of New Hampshire, continued from preceding administration. Mahlon Dickerson, of New Jersey, June 30, 1834.

23d Congress

1st Session: Dec. 2, 1833–June 30, 1834; 2d Session: Dec. 1, 1834–Mar. 3, 1835.

President pro tempore of the Senate: Hugh L. White, of Tennessee (continued from the previous Congress); George Poindexter, of Mississippi (elected June 28, 1834); John Tyler, of Virginia (elected Mar. 3, 1835). Speaker of the House: Andrew Stevenson, of Virginia (reelected Dec. 2, 1835); John Bell, of Tennessee (elected June 2, 1834); Henry Hubbard, of New Hampshire served as Speaker pro tem May 16, 1834.

Senate: 20 Democratic; 20 National Republican

House: 147 Democratic; 113 various parties

24th Congress

1st Session: Dec. 7, 1835–July 4, 1836; 2d Session: Dec. 5, 1836–Mar. 3, 1837.

President pro tempore of the Senate: William R. King, of Alabama (elected July 1, 1836; Jan. 28, 1837). Speaker of the House: James K. Polk, of Tennessee (elected Dec. 7, 1835).

Senate: 27 Democratic; 25 Whig

House: 145 Democratic; 98 Whig

Administration of MARTIN VAN BUREN
MARCH 4, 1837, TO MARCH 3, 1841

PRESIDENT—Martin Van Buren, of New York (Democratic). VICE-PRESIDENT—Richard M. Johnson, of Kentucky. SECRETARY OF STATE—John Forsyth, of Georgia, continued from preceding administration. SECRETARY OF THE TREASURY—Levi Woodbury, of New Hampshire, continued from preceding administration. SECRETARY OF WAR—Benjamin F. Butler, of New York, ad interim, continued from preceding administration. Joel R. Poinsett, of South Carolina, March 7, 1837; entered upon

---

duties March 14, 1837. ATTORNEY GENERAL—Benjamin F. Butler, of New York, continued from preceding administration. Felix Grundy, of Tennessee, July 5, 1838, to take effect September 1, 1838. Henry D. Gilpin, of Pennsylvania, January 11, 1840. POSTMASTER GENERAL—Amos Kendall, of Kentucky, continued from preceding administration. John M. Niles, of Connecticut, May 19, 1840, to take effect May 25, 1840; entered upon duties May 26, 1840. SECRETARY OF THE NAVY—Mahlon Dickerson, of New Jersey, continued from preceding administration. James K. Paulding, of New York, June 25, 1838, to take effect "after the 30th instant"; entered upon duties July 1, 1838.

25th Congress

1st Session: Sept. 4, 1837–Oct. 16, 1837; 2d Session: Dec. 4, 1837–July 9, 1838; 3d Session: Dec. 3, 1838–Mar. 3, 1839; Special Session of the Senate: Mar. 4, 1837–Mar. 10, 1837.

President pro tempore of the Senate: William R. King, of Alabama (elected Mar. 7, 1837; Oct. 13, 1837; July 2, 1838; Feb. 25, 1839). Speaker of the House: James K. Polk, of Tennessee (reelected Sept. 4, 1837).

Senate: 30 Democratic; 18 Whig; 4 other

House: 108 Democratic; 107 Whig; 24 other

26th Congress

1st Session: Dec. 2, 1839–July 21, 1840; 2d Session: Dec. 7, 1840–Mar. 3, 1841.

President pro tempore of the Senate: William R. King, of Alabama (continued from the preceding Congress; reelected July 3, 1840; Mar. 3, 1841). Speaker of the House: Robert M. T. Hunter, of Virginia (elected Dec. 16, 1839).

Senate: 28 Democratic; 22 Whig

House: 124 Democratic; 118 Whig

Administration of WILLIAM HENRY HARRISON
MARCH 4, 1841, TO APRIL 4, 1841

PRESIDENT—William Henry Harrison, of Ohio (Whig) (died April 4, 1841). VICE-PRESIDENT—John Tyler, of Virginia. SECRETARY OF STATE—J. L. Martin (chief clerk), ad interim, March 4, 1841. Daniel Webster, of Massachusetts, March 5, 1841. SECRETARY OF THE TREASURY—McClintock Young (chief clerk), ad interim, March 4, 1841. Thomas Ewing, of Ohio, March 5, 1841. SECRETARY OF WAR—John Bell, of Tennessee, March 5, 1841. ATTORNEY GENERAL—John J. Crittenden, of Kentucky, March 5, 1841. POSTMASTER GENERAL—Selah R. Hobbie, of New York (First Assistant Postmaster General), ad interim, March 4, 1841. Francis Granger, of New York, March 6, 1841; entered upon duties March 8, 1841. SECRETARY OF THE NAVY—John D. Simms (chief clerk), ad interim, March 4, 1841. George E. Badger, of North Carolina, March 5, 1841.

Administration of JOHN TYLER
APRIL 6, 1841, TO MARCH 3, 1845

PRESIDENT—John Tyler, of Virginia (Whig). SECRETARY OF STATE—Daniel Webster, of Massachusetts, continued from preceding administration. Hugh S. Legaré, of South Carolina (Attorney General), ad interim, May 9, 1843. William S. Derrick (chief clerk), ad interim, June 21, 1843. Abel P. Upshur, of Virginia (Secretary of the Navy), ad interim, June 24, 1843. Abel P. Upshur, of Virginia, July 24, 1843 (killed by the explosion of a gun on the U.S.S. Princeton February 28, 1844). John Nelson, of Maryland (Attorney General), ad interim, February 29, 1844. John C. Calhoun, of South Carolina, March 6, 1844; entered upon duties April 1, 1844. SECRETARY OF THE TREASURY—Thomas Ewing, of Ohio, continued from preceding administration. McClintock Young (chief clerk), ad interim, September 13, 1841. Walter Forward, of Pennsylvania, September 13, 1841. McClintock Young (chief clerk), ad interim, March 1, 1843. John C. Spencer, of New York, March 3, 1843; entered upon duties March 8, 1843. McClintock Young (chief clerk), ad interim, May 2, 1844. George M. Bibb, of Kentucky, June 15, 1844; entered upon duties July 4, 1844. SECRETARY OF WAR—John Bell, of Tennessee, continued from preceding administration. Albert M. Lea, of Maryland (chief clerk), ad interim, September 12, 1841. John C. Spencer, of New York, October 12, 1841. James M. Porter, of Pennsylvania, March 8, 1843. William Wilkins, of Pennsylvania, February 15, 1844; entered upon duties February 20, 1844. ATTORNEY GENERAL—John J. Crittenden, of Kentucky, continued from preceding administration. Hugh S. Legaré, of South Carolina, September 13, 1841; entered upon duties September 20, 1841 (died June 20, 1843). John Nelson, of Maryland, July 1, 1843. POSTMASTER GENERAL—Francis Granger, of New York, continued from preceding administration. Selah R. Hobbie, of New York (First Assistant Postmaster General) ad interim, September 14, 1841. Charles A. Wickliffe, of Kentucky, September 13, 1841; entered upon duties October 13, 1841. SECRETARY OF THE NAVY—George E. Badger, of North Carolina, continued from preceding administration. John D. Simms (chief clerk), ad interim, September 11, 1841. Abel P. Upshur, of Virginia, September 13, 1841; entered upon duties October 11, 1841. David Henshaw, of Massachusetts, July 24, 1843. Thomas W. Gilmer, of Virginia, February 15, 1844; entered upon duties February 19, 1844 (killed by the explosion of a gun on the U.S.S. Princeton February 28, 1844). Lewis Warrington (captain, United States Navy), ad interim, February 29, 1844. John Y. Mason, of Virginia, March 14, 1844; entered upon duties March 26, 1844.

27th Congress

1st Session: May 31, 1841–Sept. 13, 1841; 2d Session: Dec. 6, 1841–Aug. 31, 1842; 3d Session: Dec. 5, 1842–Mar. 3, 1843; Special Session of the Senate: Mar. 4, 1841–Mar. 15, 1841.

President pro tempore of the Senate: William R. King, of Alabama (elected Mar. 4, 1841); Samuel L. Southard, of New Jersey (elected Mar. 11, 1841); Willie P. Mangum, of North Carolina (elected May 31, 1842). Speaker of the House: John White, of Kentucky (elected May 31, 1841).

Senate: 28 Whig; 22 Democratic; 2 other
House: 133 Whig; 102 Democratic; 6 other

28th Congress

1st Session: Dec. 4, 1843–June 17, 1844; 2d Session; Dec. 2, 1844–Mar. 3, 1845.

President pro tempore of the Senate: Willie P. Mangum, of North Carolina (continued from the preceding Congress). Speaker of the House: John W. Jones, of Virginia (elected Dec. 4, 1843); George Hopkins acted as Speaker for part of the day Feb. 28, 1845.

Senate: 28 Whig; 25 Democratic; 1 other
House: 115 Whig; 108 Democratic; 4 other

Administration of JAMES K. POLK
MARCH 4, 1845, TO MARCH 3, 1849

PRESIDENT—James K. Polk, of Tennessee (Democratic). VICE-PRESIDENT—George M. Dallas, of Pennsylvania. SECRETARY OF STATE—John C. Calhoun, of South Carolina, continued from preceding administration. James Buchanan, of Pennsylvania, March 6, 1845; entered upon duties March 10, 1845. SECRETARY OF THE TREASURY—George M. Bibb, of Kentucky, continued from preceding administration. Robert J. Walker, of Mississippi, March 6, 1845; entered upon duties March 8, 1845. SECRETARY OF WAR—William Wilkins, of Pennsylvania, continued from preceding administration. William L. Marcy, of New York, March 6, 1845; entered upon duties March 8, 1845. ATTORNEY GENERAL—John Nelson, of Maryland, continued from preceding administration. John Y. Mason, of Virginia, March 6, 1845; entered upon duties March 11, 1845. Nathan Clifford, of Maine, October 17, 1846, to March 18, 1848, when he resigned. Isaac Toucey, of Connecticut, June 21, 1848; entered upon duties June 29, 1848. POSTMASTER GENERAL—Charles A. Wickliffe, of Kentucky, continued from preceding administration. Cave Johnson, of Tennessee, March 6, 1845. SECRETARY OF THE NAVY—John Y. Mason, of Virginia, continued from preceding administration. George Bancroft, of Massachusetts, March 10, 1845. John Y. Mason, of Virginia, September 9, 1846.

29th Congress

1st Session: Dec. 1, 1845–Aug. 10, 1846; 2d Session: Dec. 7, 1846–Mar. 3, 1847; Special Session of the Senate: Mar. 4, 1845–Mar. 20, 1845.

President pro tempore of the Senate: Ambrose H. Sevier, of Arkansas (under designation of the Vice-President served Dec. 27, 1845); David R. Atchison, of Missouri (elected Aug. 8, 1846; Jan. 11, 1847; Mar. 3, 1847). Speaker of the House: John W. Davis, of Indiana (elected Dec. 1, 1845).

Senate: 31 Democratic; 25 Whig
House: 143 Democratic; 77 Whig; 6 other

30th Congress

1st Session: Dec. 6, 1847–Aug. 14, 1848; 2d Session: Dec. 4, 1848–Mar. 3, 1849.

President pro tempore of the Senate: David R. Atchison, of Missouri (elected Feb. 2, 1848; June 1, 1848; June 26, 1848; July 29, 1848; Dec. 26, 1848; Mar. 2, 1849). Speaker of the House: Robert C. Winthrop, of Massachusetts (elected Dec. 6, 1847); Armistead Burt served as Speaker pro tem June 19–22, 1848.

Senate: 36 Democratic; 21 Whig; 1 other
House: 115 Whig; 108 Democratic; 4 other

Administration of ZACHARY TAYLOR
MARCH 4, 1849, TO JULY 9, 1850

PRESIDENT—Zachary Taylor, of Louisiana (Whig). (Oath administered March 5, 1849. Died July 9, 1850.) VICE-PRESIDENT

—Millard Fillmore, of New York. SECRETARY OF STATE—James Buchanan, of Pennsylvania, continued from preceding administration. John M. Clayton, of Delaware, March 7, 1849. SECRETARY OF THE TREASURY—Robert J. Walker, of Mississippi, continued from preceding administration. McClintock Young (chief clerk), ad interim, March 6, 1849. William M. Meredith, of Pennsylvania, March 8, 1849. SECRETARY OF WAR—William L. Marcy, of New York, continued from preceding administration. Reverdy Johnson, of Maryland (Attorney General), ad interim, March 8, 1849. George W. Crawford, of Georgia, March 8, 1849; entered upon duties March 14, 1849. ATTORNEY GENERAL—Isaac Toucey, of Connecticut, continued from preceding administration. Reverdy Johnson, of Maryland, March 8, 1849. POSTMASTER GENERAL—Cave Johnson, of Tennessee, continued from preceding administration. Selah R. Hobbie, of New York (First Assistant Postmaster General), ad interim, March 6, 1849. Jacob Collamer, of Vermont, March 8, 1849. SECRETARY OF THE NAVY—John Y. Mason, of Virginia, continued from preceding administration. William B. Preston, of Virginia, March 8, 1849. SECRETARY OF THE INTERIOR—Thomas Ewing, of Ohio, March 8, 1849.

Administration of MILLARD FILLMORE
JULY 10, 1850, TO MARCH 3, 1853

PRESIDENT—Millard Fillmore, of New York (Whig). SECRETARY OF STATE—John M. Clayton, of Delaware, continued from preceding administration. Daniel Webster, of Massachusetts, July 22, 1850 (died October 24, 1852). Charles M. Conrad, of Louisiana (Secretary of War), ad interim, October 25, 1852. Edward Everett, of Massachusetts, November 6, 1852. SECRETARY OF THE TREASURY—William M. Meredith, of Pennsylvania, continued from preceding administration. Thomas Corwin, of Ohio, July 23, 1850. SECRETARY OF WAR—George W. Crawford, of Georgia, continued from preceding administration. Samuel J. Anderson (chief clerk), ad interim, July 23, 1850. Winfield Scott (major general, U.S. Army), ad interim, July 24, 1850. Charles M. Conrad, of Louisiana, August 15, 1850. ATTORNEY GENERAL—Reverdy Johnson, of Maryland, continued from preceding administration, served to July 22, 1850. John J. Crittenden, of Kentucky, July 22, 1850; entered upon duties August 14, 1850. POSTMASTER GENERAL—Jacob Collamer, of Vermont, continued from preceding administration. Nathan K. Hall, of New York, July 23, 1850. Samuel D. Hubbard, of Connecticut, August 31, 1852; entered upon duties September 14, 1852. SECRETARY OF THE NAVY—William B. Preston, of Virginia, continued from preceding administration. Lewis Warrington (captain, U.S. Navy), ad interim, July 23, 1850. William A. Graham, of North Carolina, July 22, 1850; entered upon duties August 2, 1850. John P. Kennedy, of Maryland, July 22, 1852; entered upon duties July 26, 1852. SECRETARY OF THE INTERIOR—Thomas Ewing, of Ohio, continued from preceding administration. Daniel C. Goddard (chief clerk), ad interim, July 23, 1850. Thomas M. T. McKennan, of Pennsylvania, August 15, 1850. Daniel C. Goddard (chief clerk), ad interim, August 27, 1850. Alexander H. H. Stuart, of Virginia, September 12, 1850; entered upon duties September 16, 1850.

31st Congress

1st Session: Dec. 3, 1849–Sept. 30, 1850; 2d Session: Dec. 2, 1850–Mar. 3, 1851; Special Session of the Senate: Mar. 5, 1849–Mar. 23, 1849.

President pro tempore of the Senate: David R. Atchison, of Missouri (elected Mar. 5, 1849; Mar. 16, 1849). William R. King, of Alabama (elected May 6, 1850, July 11, 1850). Speaker of the House: Howell Cobb, of Georgia (elected Dec. 22, 1849), Robert C. Winthrop, of Massachusetts, served as Speaker pro tem April 19, 1850.

Senate: 35 Democratic; 25 Whig; 2 other
House: 112 Democratic; 109 Whig; 9 other

32d Congress

1st Session: Dec. 1, 1851–Aug. 31, 1852; 2d Session: Dec. 6, 1852–Mar. 3, 1853; Special Session of the Senate: Mar. 4, 1851–Mar. 13, 1851.

President pro tempore of the Senate: William R. King, of Alabama (continued from preceding Congress); David R. Atchison, of Missouri (elected Dec. 20, 1852). Speaker of the House: Linn Boyd, of Kentucky (elected Dec. 1, 1851).

Senate: 35 Democratic; 24 Whig; 3 other
House: 140 Democratic; 88 Whig; 5 other

Administration of FRANKLIN PIERCE
MARCH 4, 1853, TO MARCH 3, 1857

PRESIDENT—Franklin Pierce, of New Hampshire (Democratic). VICE-PRESIDENT—William R. King, of Alabama (died April 18, 1853). SECRETARY OF STATE—William Hunter (chief clerk), ad interim, March 4, 1853. William L. Marcy, of New York,

March 7, 1853. SECRETARY OF THE TREASURY—Thomas Corwin, of Ohio, continued from preceding administration. James Guthrie, of Kentucky, March 7, 1853. SECRETARY OF WAR—Charles M. Conrad, of Louisiana, continued from preceding administration. Jefferson Davis, of Mississippi, March 7, 1853. Samuel Cooper (Adjutant General, U.S. Army), ad interim, March 3, 1857. ATTORNEY GENERAL—John J. Crittenden, of Kentucky, continued from preceding administration. Caleb Cushing, of Massachusetts, March 7, 1853. POSTMASTER GENERAL—Samuel D. Hubbard, of Connecticut, continued from preceding administration. James Campbell, of Pennsylvania, March 7, 1853. SECRETARY OF THE NAVY—John P. Kennedy, of Maryland, continued from preceding administration. James C. Dobbin, of North Carolina, March 7, 1853. SECRETARY OF THE INTERIOR—Alexander H. H. Stuart, of Virginia, continued from preceding administration. Robert McClelland, of Michigan, March 7, 1853.

33d Congress

1st Session: Dec. 5, 1853–Aug. 7, 1854; 2d Session: Dec. 4, 1854–Mar. 3, 1855; Special Session of the Senate: Mar. 4, 1853–Apr. 11, 1853.

President pro tempore of the Senate: David R. Atchison, of Missouri (elected Mar. 4, 1853); Lewis Cass, of Michigan (elected Dec. 4, 1854); Jesse D. Bright, of Indiana (elected Dec. 5, 1854). Speaker of the House: Linn Boyd, of Kentucky (re-elected Dec. 5, 1853).

Senate: 38 Democratic; 22 Whig; 2 other
House: 159 Democratic; 71 Whig; 4 other

34th Congress

1st Session: Dec. 3, 1855–Aug. 18, 1856; 2d Session: Aug. 21, 1856–Aug. 30, 1856; 3d Session: Dec. 1, 1856–Mar. 3, 1857.

President pro tempore of the Senate: Jesse D. Bright, of Indiana (continued from preceding Congress; elected June 11, 1856); Charles E. Stuart, of Michigan (served June 5, 1856; elected June 9, 1856); James M. Mason, of Virginia (served Jan. 5, 1857; elected Jan. 6, 1857). Speaker of the House: Nathaniel, P. Banks, of Massachusetts (elected Feb. 2, 1856).
Senate: 40 Democratic; 15 Republican; 5 other
House: 108 Republican; 83 Democratic; 43 other

Administration of JAMES BUCHANAN
MARCH 4, 1857, TO MARCH 3, 1861

PRESIDENT—James Buchanan, of Pennsylvania (Democratic). VICE-PRESIDENT—John C. Breckinridge, of Kentucky. SECRETARY OF STATE—William L. Marcy, of New York, continued from preceding administration. Lewis Cass, of Michigan, March 6, 1857. William Hunter (chief clerk), ad interim, December 15, 1860. Jeremiah S. Black, of Pennsylvania, December 17, 1860. SECRETARY OF THE TREASURY—James Guthrie, of Kentucky, continued from preceding administration. Howell Cobb, of Georgia, March 6, 1857. Isaac Toucey, of Connecticut (Secretary of the Navy), ad interim, December 10, 1860. Philip F. Thomas, of Maryland, December 12, 1860. John A. Dix, of New York, January 11, 1861; entered upon duties January 15, 1861. SECRETARY OF WAR—Samuel Cooper (Adjutant General, U.S. Army), ad interim, March 4, 1857. John B. Floyd, of Virginia, March 6, 1857. Joseph Holt (Postmaster General), ad interim, January 1, 1861. Joseph Holt, of Kentucky, January 18, 1861. ATTORNEY GENERAL—Caleb Cushing, of Massachusetts, continued from preceding administration. Jeremiah S. Black, of Pennsylvania, March 6, 1857; entered upon duties March 11, 1857. Edwin M. Stanton, of Pennsylvania, December 20, 1860; entered upon duties December 22, 1860. POSTMASTER GENERAL—James Campbell, of Pennsylvania, continued from preceding administration. Aaron V. Brown, of Tennessee, March 6, 1857 (died March 8, 1859). Horatio King, of Maine (First Assistant Postmaster General), ad interim, March 9, 1859. Joseph Holt, of Kentucky, March 14, 1859. Horatio King, of Maine (First Assistant Postmaster General), ad interim, January 1, 1861. Horatio King, of Maine, February 12, 1861. SECRETARY OF NAVY—James C. Dobbin, of North Carolina, continued from preceding administration. Isaac Toucey, of Connecticut, March 6, 1857. SECRETARY OF THE INTERIOR—Robert McClelland, of Michigan, continued from preceding administration. Jacob Thompson, of Mississippi, March 6, 1857; entered upon duties March 10, 1857. Moses Kelly (chief clerk), ad interim, January 10, 1861.

35th Congress

1st Session: Dec. 7, 1857–June 14, 1858; 2d Session: Dec. 6, 1858–Mar. 3, 1859; Special Sessions of the Senate: Mar. 4, 1857–Mar. 14, 1857; June 15, 1858–June 16, 1858.

President pro tempore of the Senate: James M. Mason, of Virginia (elected Mar. 4, 1857); Thomas J. Rusk, of Texas (elected Mar. 14, 1857); Benjamin Fitzpatrick, of Alabama (elected Dec. 7, 1857; Mar. 29, 1858; June 14, 1858; Jan. 25, 1859). Speaker of the House: James L. Orr, of South Carolina (elected Dec. 7, 1857).

Senate: 36 Democratic; 20 Republican; 8 other
House: 118 Democratic; 92 Republican; 26 other

36th Congress

1st Session: Dec. 5, 1859–June 25, 1860; 2d Session: Dec. 3, 1860–Mar. 3, 1861; Special Sessions of the Senate: Mar. 4, 1859–Mar. 10, 1859; June 26, 1860–June 28, 1860.

President pro tempore of the Senate: Benjamin Fitzpatrick, of Alabama (elected Mar. 9, 1859; Dec. 19, 1859; Feb. 20, 1860; June 26, 1860); Jesse D. Bright, of Indiana (June 12, 1860); Solomon Foot, of Vermont (elected Feb. 16, 1861). Speaker of the House: William Pennington, of New Jersey (elected Feb. 1, 1860).

Senate: 36 Democratic; 26 Republican; 4 other
House: 114 Republican; 92 Democratic; 31 other

First Administration of ABRAHAM LINCOLN
MARCH 4, 1861, TO MARCH 3, 1865

PRESIDENT—Abraham Lincoln, of Illinois (Republican). VICE-PRESIDENT—Hannibal Hamlin, of Maine. SECRETARY OF STATE—Jeremiah S. Black, of Pennsylvania, continued from preceding administration. William H. Seward, of New York, March 5, 1861. SECRETARY OF THE TREASURY—John A. Dix, of New York, continued from preceding administration. Salmon P. Chase, of Ohio, March 5, 1861; entered upon duties March 7, 1861. George Harrington, of the District of Columbia (Assistant Secretary), ad interim, July 1, 1864. William P. Fessenden, of Maine, July 1, 1864; entered upon duties July 5, 1864. SECRETARY OF WAR—Joseph Holt, of Kentucky, continued from preceding administration. Simon Cameron, of Pennsylvania, March 5, 1861; entered upon duties March 11, 1861. Edwin M. Stanton, of Pennsylvania, January 15, 1862; entered upon duties January 20, 1862. ATTORNEY GENERAL—Edwin M. Stanton, of Pennsylvania, continued from preceding administration. Edward Bates, of Missouri, March 5, 1861. James Speed, of Kentucky, December 2, 1864; entered upon duties December 5, 1864. POSTMASTER GENERAL—Horatio King, of Maine, continued from preceding administration. Montgomery Blair, of the District of Columbia, March 5, 1861; entered upon duties March 9, 1861. William Dennison, of Ohio, September 24, 1864; entered upon duties October 1, 1864. SECRETARY OF THE NAVY—Isaac Toucey, of Connecticut, continued from preceding administration. Gideon Welles, of Connecticut, March 5, 1861; entered upon duties March 7, 1861. SECRETARY OF THE INTERIOR—Moses Kelly (chief clerk), ad interim, March 4, 1861. Caleb B. Smith, of Indiana, March 5, 1861. John P. Usher, of Indiana (Assistant Secretary), ad interim, January 1, 1863. John P. Usher, of Indiana, January 8, 1863.

37th Congress

1st Session: July 4, 1861–Aug. 6, 1861; 2d Session: Dec. 2, 1861–July 17, 1862; 3d Session: Dec. 1, 1862–Mar. 3, 1863; Special Session of the Senate: Mar. 4, 1861–Mar. 28, 1861.

President pro tempore of the Senate: Solomon Foot, of Vermont (elected Mar. 23, 1861; July 18, 1861; Jan. 15, 1862; Mar. 31, 1862; June 19, 1862; Feb. 18, 1863). Speaker of the House: Galusha A. Grow, of Pennsylvania (elected July 4, 1861).

Senate: 31 Republican; 10 Democratic; 8 other
House: 105 Republican; 43 Democratic; 30 other

38th Congress

1st Session: Dec. 7, 1863–July 4, 1864; 2d Session: Dec. 5, 1864–Mar. 3, 1865; Special Session of the Senate: Mar. 4, 1863–Mar. 14, 1863.

President pro tempore of the Senate: Solomon Foot, of Vermont (elected Mar. 4, 1863; Dec. 18, 1863; Feb. 23, 1864; Mar. 11, 1864; Apr. 11, 1864); Daniel Clark, of New Hampshire (elected Apr. 26, 1864; Feb. 9, 1865). Speaker of the House: Schuyler Colfax, of Indiana (elected Dec. 7, 1863).

Senate: 36 Republican; 9 Democratic; 5 other
House: 102 Republican; 75 Democratic; 9 other

Second Administration of ABRAHAM LINCOLN
MARCH 4, 1865, TO APRIL 15, 1865

PRESIDENT—Abraham Lincoln, of Illinois (Republican) (died April 15, 1865). VICE-PRESIDENT—Andrew Johnson, of Tennessee. SECRETARY OF STATE—William H. Seward, of New York, continued from preceding administration. SECRETARY OF THE TREASURY—George Harrington, of the District of Columbia (Assistant Secretary), ad interim, March 4, 1865. Hugh McCulloch, of Indiana, March 7, 1865; entered upon duties March 9, 1865. SECRETARY OF WAR—Edwin M. Stanton, of Pennsylvania, continued from preceding administration. ATTORNEY GENERAL—James Speed, of Kentucky, continued from preceding administration. POSTMASTER GENERAL—William Dennison, of Ohio, continued from preceding administration. SECRETARY OF THE NAVY—Gideon Welles, of Connecticut, continued from preceding administration. SECRETARY OF THE INTERIOR—John P. Usher, of Indiana, continued from preceding administration.

Administration of ANDREW JOHNSON
APRIL 15, 1865, TO MARCH 3, 1869

PRESIDENT—Andrew Johnson, of Tennessee (Republican). SEC-RETARY OF STATE—William H. Seward, of New York, continued from preceding administration. SECRETARY OF THE TREASURY—Hugh McCulloch, of Indiana, continued from preceding administration. SECRETARY OF WAR—Edwin M. Stanton, of Pennsylvania, continued from preceding administration; suspended August 12, 1867. Ulysses S. Grant (General of the Army), ad interim, August 12, 1867. Edwin M. Stanton, of Pennsylvania, reinstated January 13, 1868, to May 26, 1868. John M. Schofield, of Illinois, May 28, 1868; entered upon duties June 1, 1868. ATTORNEY GENERAL—James Speed, of Kentucky, continued from preceding administration. J. Hubley Ashton, of Pennsylvania (Assistant Attorney General), acting, July 17, 1866. Henry Stanbery, of Ohio, July 23, 1866. Orville H. Browning, of Illinois (Secretary of the Interior), ad interim, March 13, 1868. William M. Evarts, of New York, July 15, 1868; entered upon duties July 20, 1868. POSTMASTER GENERAL—William Dennison, of Ohio, continued from preceding administration. Alexander W. Randall, of Wisconsin (First Assistant Postmaster General), ad interim, July 17, 1866. Alexander W. Randall, of Wisconsin, July 25, 1866. SECRETARY OF THE NAVY—Gideon Welles, of Connecticut, continued from preceding administration. SECRETARY OF THE INTERIOR—John P. Usher, of Indiana, continued from preceding administration. James Harlan, of Iowa, May 15, 1865. Orville H. Browning, of Illinois, July 27, 1866, to take effect September 1, 1866.

39th Congress
1st Session: Dec. 4, 1865–July 28, 1866; 2d Session: Dec. 3, 1866–Mar. 3, 1867; Special Session of the Senate: Mar. 4, 1865–Mar. 11, 1865.

President pro tempore of the Senate: Lafayette S. Foster, of Connecticut (elected Mar. 7, 1865); Benjamin F. Wade, of Ohio (elected Mar. 2, 1867). Speaker of the House: Schuyler Colfax, of Indiana (reelected Dec. 4, 1865).

Senate: 42 Union; 10 Democratic
House: 149 Union; 42 Democratic

40th Congress
1st Session: Mar. 4, 1867–Mar. 30, 1867; July 3, 1867–July 20, 1867; Nov. 21, 1867–Dec. 1, 1867; 2d Session: Dec. 2, 1867–July 27, 1868; Sept. 21, 1868; Oct. 16, 1868; Nov. 10, 1868; 3d Session: Dec. 7, 1868–Mar. 3, 1869; Special Session of the Senate: Apr. 1, 1867–Apr. 20, 1867.

President pro tempore of the Senate: Benjamin F. Wade, of Ohio (continued from the preceding Congress). Speaker of the House: Schuyler Colfax, of Indiana (reelected Mar. 4, 1867); Theodore M. Pomeroy, of New York (elected Mar. 3, 1869).

Senate: 42 Republican; 11 Democratic
House: 143 Republican; 49 Democratic

First Administration of ULYSSES S. GRANT
MARCH 4, 1869, TO MARCH 3, 1873

PRESIDENT—Ulysses S. Grant, of Illinois (Republican). VICE-PRESIDENT—Schuyler Colfax, of Indiana. SECRETARY OF STATE—William H. Seward, of New York, continued from preceding administration. Elihu B. Washburne, of Illinois, March 5, 1869. Hamilton Fish, of New York, March 11, 1869; entered upon duties March 17, 1869. SECRETARY OF THE TREASURY—Hugh McCulloch, of Indiana, continued from preceding administration. John F. Hartley, of Maine (Assistant Secretary), ad interim, March 5, 1869. George S. Boutwell, of Massachusetts, March 11, 1869. SECRETARY OF WAR—John M. Schofield, of Illinois, continued from preceding administration. John A. Rawlins, of Illinois, March 11, 1869. William T. Sherman, of Ohio, September 9, 1869; entered upon duties September 11, 1869. William W. Belknap, of Iowa, October 25, 1869; entered upon duties November 1, 1869. ATTORNEY GENERAL—William M. Evarts, of New York, continued from preceding administration. J. Hubley Ashton, of Pennsylvania (Assistant Attorney General), acting, March 5, 1869; entered upon duties March 11, 1869. Ebenezer R. Hoar, of Massachusetts, March 5, 1869; entered upon duties March 11, 1869. Amos T. Akerman, of Georgia, June 23, 1870; entered upon duties July 8, 1870. George H. Williams, of Oregon, December 14, 1871, to take effect January 10, 1872. POSTMASTER GENERAL—St. John B. L. Skinner, of New York (First Assistant Postmaster General), ad interim, March 4, 1869. John A. J. Creswell, of Maryland, March 5, 1869. SECRETARY OF THE NAVY—William Faxon, of Connecticut (Assistant Secretary), ad interim, March 4, 1869. Adolph E. Borie, of Pennsylvania, March 5, 1869; entered upon duties March 9, 1869. George M. Robeson, of New Jersey, June 25, 1869. SECRETARY OF THE INTERIOR—William T. Otto, of Indiana (Assistant Secretary), ad interim, March 4, 1869. Jacob D. Cox, of Ohio, March 5, 1869; entered upon duties March 9, 1869. Columbus Delano, of Ohio, November 1, 1870.

41st Congress
1st Session: Mar. 4, 1869–Apr. 10, 1869; 2d Session: Dec. 6, 1869–July 15, 1870; 3d Session: Dec. 5, 1870–Mar. 3, 1871; Special Session of the Senate: Apr. 12, 1869–Apr. 22, 1869.

President pro tempore of the Senate: Henry B. Anthony, of Rhode Island (elected Mar. 23, 1869; Apr. 9, 1869; May 28, 1870; July 1, 1870; July 14, 1870). Speaker of the House: James G. Blaine, of Maine (elected Mar. 4, 1869).

Senate: 56 Republican; 11 Democratic
House: 149 Republican; 63 Democratic

42d Congress
1st Session: Mar. 4, 1871–Apr. 20, 1871; 2d Session: Dec. 4, 1871–June 10, 1872; 3d Session: Dec. 2, 1872–Mar. 3, 1873; Special Session of the Senate: May 10, 1871–May 27, 1871.

President pro tempore of the Senate: Henry B. Anthony, of Rhode Island (elected Mar. 10, 1871; April 17, 1871; May 23, 1871; Dec. 21, 1871; Feb. 23, 1872; June 8, 1872; Dec. 4, 1872; Dec. 13, 1872; Dec. 20, 1872; Jan. 24, 1873). Speaker of the House: James G. Blaine, of Maine (reelected Mar. 4, 1871).

Senate: 52 Republican; 17 Democratic; 5 other
House: 134 Democratic; 104 Republican; 5 other

Second Administration of ULYSSES S. GRANT
MARCH 4, 1873, TO MARCH 3, 1877

PRESIDENT—Ulysses S. Grant, of Illinois (Republican). VICE-PRESIDENT—Henry Wilson, of Massachusetts (died November 22, 1875). SECRETARY OF STATE—Hamilton Fish, of New York, continued from preceding administration. Hamilton Fish, of New York, recommissioned March 17, 1873. SECRETARY OF THE TREASURY—George S. Boutwell, of Massachusetts, continued from preceding administration. William A. Richardson, of Massachusetts, March 17, 1873. Benjamin H. Bristow, of Kentucky, June 2, 1874; entered upon duties June 4, 1874. Charles F. Conant, of New Hampshire (Assistant Secretary), ad interim, June 21, 1876, to June 30, 1876. Lot M. Morrill, of Maine, June 21, 1876; entered upon duties July 7, 1876. SECRETARY OF WAR—William W. Belknap, of Iowa, continued from preceding administration. William W. Belknap, of Iowa, recommissioned March 17, 1873. George M. Robeson, of New Jersey (Secretary of the Navy), ad interim, March 2, 1876. Alphonso Taft, of Ohio, March 8, 1876; entered upon duties March 11, 1876. James D. Cameron, of Pennsylvania, May 22, 1876; entered upon duties June 1, 1876. ATTORNEY GENERAL—George H. Williams, of Oregon, continued from preceding administration. George H. Williams, of Oregon, recommissioned March 17, 1873. Edwards Pierrepont, of New York, April 26, 1875, to take effect May 15, 1875. Alphonso Taft, of Ohio, May 22, 1876; entered upon duties June 1, 1876. POSTMASTER GENERAL—John A. J. Creswell, of Maryland, continued from preceding administration. John A. J. Creswell, of Maryland, recommissioned March 17, 1873. James W. Marshall, of Virginia, July 3, 1874; entered upon duties July 7, 1874. Marshall Jewell, of Connecticut, August 24, 1874; entered upon duties September 1, 1874. James N. Tyner, of Indiana, July 12, 1876. SECRETARY OF THE NAVY—George M. Robeson, of New Jersey, continued from preceding administration. George M. Robeson, of New Jersey, recommissioned March 17, 1873. SECRETARY OF THE INTERIOR—Columbus Delano, of Ohio, continued from preceding administration. Columbus Delano, of Ohio, recommissioned March 17, 1873. Benjamin R. Cowen, of Ohio (Assistant Secretary), ad interim, October 1, 1875. Zachariah Chandler, of Michigan, October 19, 1875.

43d Congress
1st Session: Dec. 1, 1873–June 23, 1874; 2d Session: Dec. 7, 1874–Mar. 3, 1875; Special Session of the Senate: Mar. 4, 1873–Mar. 26, 1873.

President pro tempore of the Senate: Mathew H. Carpenter, of Wisconsin (elected Mar. 12, 1873; Mar. 26, 1873; Dec. 11, 1873; Dec. 23, 1874); Henry B. Anthony, of Rhode Island (elected Jan. 25, 1875; Feb. 15, 1875). Speaker of the House: James G. Blaine (reelected Dec. 1, 1873).

Senate: 49 Republican; 19 Democratic; 5 other
House: 194 Republican; 92 Democratic; 14 other

44th Congress
1st Session: Dec. 6, 1875–Aug. 15, 1876; 2d Session: Dec. 4, 1876–Mar. 3, 1877; Special Session of the Senate: Mar. 5, 1875–Mar. 24, 1875.

President pro tempore of the Senate: Thomas W. Ferry, of Michigan (elected Mar. 9, 1875; Mar. 19, 1875; Dec. 20, 1875). Speaker of the House: Michael C. Kerr, of Indiana (elected Dec. 6, 1875); Samuel J. Randall, of Pennsylvania (elected Dec. 4, 1876).

Senate: 45 Republican; 29 Democratic; 2 other
House: 169 Democratic; 109 Republican; 14 other

Administration of RUTHERFORD B. HAYES
MARCH 4, 1877, TO MARCH 3, 1881

PRESIDENT—Rutherford B. Hayes, of Ohio (Republican) (oath administered March 5, 1877). VICE-PRESIDENT—William A. Wheeler, of New York. SECRETARY OF STATE—Hamilton Fish, of

New York, continued from preceding administration. William M. Evarts, of New York, March 12, 1877. SECRETARY OF THE TREASURY—Lot M. Morrill, of Maine, continued from preceding administration. John Sherman, of Ohio, March 8, 1877; entered upon duties March 10, 1877. SECRETARY OF WAR—James D. Cameron, of Pennsylvania, continued from preceding administration. George W. McCrary, of Iowa, March 12, 1877. Alexander Ramsey, of Minnesota, December 10, 1879; entered upon duties December 12, 1879. ATTORNEY GENERAL—Alphonso Taft, of Ohio, continued from preceding administration. Charles Devens, of Massachusetts, March 12, 1877. POSTMASTER GENERAL—James N. Tyner, of Indiana, continued from preceding administration. David M. Key, of Tennessee, March 12, 1877; resigned June 1, 1880; served to August 24, 1880. Horace Maynard, of Tennessee, June 2, 1880; entered upon duties August 25, 1880. SECRETARY OF THE NAVY—George M. Robeson, of New Jersey, continued from preceding administration. Richard W. Thompson, of Indiana, March 12, 1877. Alexander Ramsey, of Minnesota (Secretary of War), ad interim, •December 20, 1880. Nathan Goff, Jr., of West Virginia, January 6, 1881. SECRETARY OF THE INTERIOR—Zachariah Chandler, of Michigan, continued from preceding administration. Carl Schurz, of Missouri, March 12, 1877.

45th Congress

1st Session: Oct. 15, 1877–Dec. 3, 1877; 2d Session: Dec. 3, 1877–June 20, 1878; 3d Session: Dec. 2, 1878–Mar. 3, 1879; Special Session of the Senate: Mar. 5, 1877–Mar. 17, 1877.

President pro tempore of the Senate: Thomas W. Ferry of Michigan (elected Mar. 5, 1877; Feb. 26, 1878; Apr. 17, 1878; Mar. 3, 1879). Speaker of the House: Samuel J. Randall, of Pennsylvania (reelected Oct. 15, 1877).

Senate: 39 Republican; 36 Democratic; 1 other
House: 153 Democratic; 140 Republican

46th Congress

1st Session: Mar. 18, 1879–July 1, 1879; 2d Session: Dec. 1, 1879–June 16, 1880; 3d Session: Dec. 6, 1880–Mar. 3, 1881.

President pro tempore of the Senate: Allen G. Thurman, of Ohio (elected Apr. 15, 1879; Apr. 7, 1880, May 6, 1880). Speaker of the House: Samuel J. Randall, of Pennsylvania (re-elected Mar. 18, 1879).

Senate: 42 Democratic; 33 Republican; 1 other
House: 149 Democratic; 130 Republican; 14 other

Administration of JAMES A. GARFIELD
MARCH 4, 1881, TO SEPTEMBER 19, 1881

PRESIDENT—James A. Garfield, of Ohio (Republican) (died September 19, 1881). VICE-PRESIDENT—Chester A. Arthur, of New York. SECRETARY OF STATE—William M. Evarts, of New York, continued from preceding administration. James G. Blaine, of Maine, March 5, 1881; entered upon duties March 7, 1881. SECRETARY OF THE TREASURY—Henry F. French, of Massachusetts (Assistant Secretary), ad interim, March 4, 1881. William Windom, of Minnesota, March 5, 1881; entered upon duties March 8, 1881. SECRETARY OF WAR—Alexander Ramsey, of Minnesota, continued from preceding administration. Robert T. Lincoln, of Illinois, March 5, 1881; entered upon duties March 11, 1881. ATTORNEY GENERAL—Charles Devens, of Massachusetts, continued from preceding administration. Wayne MacVeagh, of Pennsylvania, March 5, 1881; entered upon duties March 7, 1881. POSTMASTER GENERAL—Horace Maynard, of Tennessee, continued from preceding administration. Thomas L. James, of New York, March 5, 1881; entered upon duties March 8, 1881. SECRETARY OF THE NAVY—Nathan Goff, Jr., of West Virginia, continued from preceding administration. William H. Hunt, of Louisiana, March 5, 1881; entered upon duties March 7, 1881. SECRETARY OF THE INTERIOR—Carl Schurz, of Missouri, continued from preceding administration. Samuel J. Kirkwood, of Iowa, March 5, 1881; entered upon duties March 8, 1881.

Administration of CHESTER A. ARTHUR
SEPTEMBER 20, 1881, TO MARCH 3, 1885

PRESIDENT—Chester A. Arthur, of New York. SECRETARY OF STATE—James G. Blaine, of Maine, continued from preceding administration. Frederick T. Frelinghuysen, of New Jersey, December 12, 1881; entered upon duties December 19, 1881. SECRETARY OF THE TREASURY—William Windom, of Minnesota, continued from preceding administration. Charles J. Folger, of New York, October 27, 1881; entered upon duties November 14, 1881 (died September 4, 1884). Charles E. Coon, of New York (Assistant Secretary), ad interim, September 4, 1884. Henry F. French, of Massachusetts (Assistant Secretary), ad interim, September 8, 1884. Charles E. Coon, of New York (Assistant Secretary), ad interim, September 15, 1884. Walter Q. Gresham, of Indiana, September 24, 1884. Henry F. French, of Massachusetts (Assistant Secretary), ad interim, October 29, 1884. Hugh McCulloch, of Indiana, October 28, 1884; entered upon duties

October 31, 1884. SECRETARY OF WAR—Robert T. Lincoln, of Illinois, continued from preceding administration. ATTORNEY GENERAL—Wayne MacVeagh, of Pennsylvania, continued from preceding administration. Samuel F. Phillips, of North Carolina (Solicitor General), ad interim, November 14, 1881. Benjamin H. Brewster, of Pennsylvania, December 19, 1881; entered upon duties January 3, 1882. POSTMASTER GENERAL—Thomas L. James, of New York, continued from preceding administration. Thomas L. James, of New York, recommissioned October 27, 1881. Timothy O. Howe, of Wisconsin, December 20, 1881; entered upon duties January 5, 1882 (died March 25, 1883). Frank Hatton, of Iowa (First Assistant Postmaster General), ad interim, March 26, 1883. Walter Q. Gresham, of Indiana, April 3, 1883; entered upon duties April 11, 1883. Frank Hatton, of Iowa (First Assistant Postmaster General), ad interim, September 25, 1884. Frank Hatton, of Iowa, October 14, 1884. SECRETARY OF THE NAVY—William H. Hunt, of Louisiana, continued from preceding administration. William E. Chandler, of New Hampshire, April 12, 1882; entered upon duties April 17, 1882. SECRETARY OF THE INTERIOR—Samuel J. Kirkwood, of Iowa, continued from preceding administration. Henry M. Teller, of Colorado, April 6, 1882; entered upon duties April 17, 1882.

47th Congress

1st Session: Dec. 5, 1881–Aug. 9, 1882; 2d Session: Dec. 4, 1882–Mar. 3, 1883; Special Sessions of the Senate: Mar. 4, 1881–May 20, 1881; Oct. 10, 1881–Oct. 29, 1881.

President pro tempore of the Senate: Thomas F. Bayard, of Delaware (elected Oct. 10, 1881); David Davis, of Illinois (elected Oct. 13, 1881); George F. Edmunds, of Vermont (elected Mar. 3, 1883). Speaker of the House: J. Warren Keifer, of Ohio (elected Dec. 5, 1881).

Senate: 37 Republican; 37 Democratic; 1 other
House: 147 Republican; 135 Democratic; 11 other

48th Congress

1st Session: Dec. 3, 1883–July 7, 1884; 2d Session: Dec. 1, 1884–Mar. 3, 1885.

President pro tempore of the Senate: George F. Edmunds, of Vermont (reelected Jan. 14, 1884). Speaker of the House: John G. Carlisle, of Kentucky (elected Dec. 3, 1883).

Senate: 38 Republican; 36 Democratic; 2 other
House: 197 Democratic; 118 Republican; 10 other

First Administration of GROVER CLEVELAND
MARCH 4, 1885, TO MARCH 3, 1889

PRESIDENT—Grover Cleveland, of New York (Democratic). VICE-PRESIDENT—Thomas A. Hendricks, of Indiana (died November 25, 1885). SECRETARY OF STATE—Frederick T. Frelinghuysen, of New Jersey, continued from preceding administration. Thomas F. Bayard, of Delaware, March 6, 1885. SECRETARY OF THE TREASURY—Hugh McCulloch, of Indiana, continued from preceding administration. Daniel Manning, of New York, March 6, 1885; entered upon duties March 8, 1885. Charles S. Fairchild, of New York, April 1, 1887. SECRETARY OF WAR—Robert T. Lincoln, of Illinois, continued from preceding administration. William C. Endicott, of Massachusetts, March 6, 1885. ATTORNEY GENERAL—Benjamin H. Brewster, of Pennsylvania, continued from preceding administration. Augustus H. Garland, of Arkansas, March 6, 1885; entered upon duties March 9, 1885. POSTMASTER GENERAL—Frank Hatton, of Iowa, continued from preceding administration. William F. Vilas, of Wisconsin, March 6, 1885. Don M. Dickinson, of Michigan, January 16, 1888. SECRETARY OF THE NAVY—William E. Chandler, of New Hampshire, continued from preceding administration. William C. Whitney, of New York, March 6, 1885. SECRETARY OF THE INTERIOR—Merritt L. Joslyn, of Illinois (Assistant Secretary), ad interim, March 4, 1885. Lucius Q. C. Lamar, of Mississippi, March 6, 1885. Henry L. Muldrow, of Mississippi (First Assistant Secretary), ad interim, January 11, 1888. William F. Vilas, of Wisconsin, January 16, 1888. SECRETARY OF AGRICULTURE—Norman J. Colman, of Missouri, February 13, 1889.

49th Congress

1st Session: Dec. 7, 1885–Aug. 5, 1886; 2d Session: Dec. 6, 1886–Mar 3, 1887; Special Session of the Senate: Mar. 4, 1885–Apr. 2, 1885.

President pro tempore of the Senate: John Sherman, of Ohio (elected Dec. 7, 1885); John J. Ingalls, of Kansas (elected Feb. 25, 1887). Speaker of the House: John G. Carlisle, of Kentucky (reelected Dec. 7, 1885).

Senate: 43 Republican; 34 Democratic
House: 183 Democratic; 140 Republican; 2 other

50th Congress

1st Session: Dec. 5, 1887–Oct. 20, 1888; 2d Session: Dec. 3, 1888–Mar. 3, 1889.

President pro tempore of the Senate: John J. Ingalls, of Kansas (continued from the preceding Congress). Speaker of the House: John G. Carlisle, of Kentucky (reelected Dec. 5, 1887).

Senate: 39 Republican; 37 Democratic
House: 169 Democratic; 152 Republican; 4 other

Administration of BENJAMIN HARRISON
MARCH 4, 1889, TO MARCH 3, 1893

PRESIDENT—Benjamin Harrison, of Indiana (Republican). VICE-PRESIDENT—Levi P. Morton, of New York. SECRETARY OF STATE—Thomas F. Bayard, of Delaware, continued from preceding administration. James G. Blaine, of Maine, March 5, 1889; entered upon duties March 7, 1889. William F. Wharton, of Massachusetts (Assistant Secretary), ad interim, June 4, 1892. John W. Foster, of Indiana, June 29, 1892. William F. Wharton, of Massachusetts (Assistant Secretary), ad interim, February 23, 1893. SECRETARY OF THE TREASURY—Charles S. Fairchild, of New York, continued from preceding administration. William Windom, of Minnesota, March 5, 1889; entered upon duties March 7, 1889 (died January 29, 1891). Allured B. Nettleton, of Minnesota (Assistant Secretary), ad interim, January 30, 1891. Charles Foster, of Ohio, February 24, 1891. SECRETARY OF WAR—William C. Endicott, of Massachusetts, continued from preceding administration. Redfield Proctor, of Vermont, March 5, 1889. Lewis A. Grant, of Minnesota (Assistant Secretary), ad interim, December 6, 1891. Stephen B. Elkins, of West Virginia, December 22, 1891; entered upon duties December 24, 1891. ATTORNEY GENERAL—Augustus H. Garland, of Arkansas, continued from preceding administration. William H. H. Miller, of Indiana, March 5, 1889. POSTMASTER GENERAL—Don M. Dickinson, of Michigan, continued from preceding administration. John Wanamaker, of Pennsylvania, March 5, 1889. SECRETARY OF THE NAVY—William C. Whitney, of New York, continued from preceding administration. Benjamin F. Tracy, of New York, March 5, 1889. SECRETARY OF THE INTERIOR—William F. Vilas, of Wisconsin, continued from preceding administration. John W. Noble, of Missouri, March 5, 1889; entered upon duties March 7, 1889. SECRETARY OF AGRICULTURE.—Norman J. Colman, of Missouri, continued from preceding administration, Jeremiah M. Rusk, of Wisconsin, March 5, 1889; entered upon duties March 7, 1889.

51st Congress
1st Session: Dec. 2, 1889–Oct. 1, 1890; 2d Session: Dec. 1, 1890–Mar. 2, 1891; Special Session of the Senate: Mar. 4, 1889–Apr. 2, 1889.

President pro tempore of the Senate: John J. Ingalls, of Kansas (reelected Mar. 7, 1889; Apr. 2, 1889; Feb. 28, 1890; Apr. 3, 1890); Charles F. Manderson, of Nebraska (elected Mar. 2, 1891). Speaker of the House: Thomas B. Reed, of Maine (elected Dec. 2, 1889).

Senate: 39 Republican; 37 Democratic
House: 166 Republican; 159 Democratic

52d Congress
1st Session: Dec. 7, 1891–Aug. 5, 1892; 2d Session: Dec. 5, 1892–Mar. 3, 1893.

President pro tempore of the Senate: Charles F. Manderson, of Nebraska (continued from preceding Congress). Speaker of the House: Charles F. Crisp, of Georgia (elected Dec. 8, 1891).

Senate: 47 Republican; 39 Democratic; 2 other
House: 235 Democratic; 88 Republican; 9 other

Second Administration of GROVER CLEVELAND
March 4, 1893, TO MARCH 3, 1897

PRESIDENT—Grover Cleveland, of New York (Democratic). VICE-PRESIDENT—Adlai E. Stevenson, of Illinois. SECRETARY OF STATE—William F. Wharton, of Massachusetts (Assistant Secretary), ad interim, continued from preceding administration. Walter Q. Gresham, of Illinois, March 6, 1893 (died May 28, 1895). Edwin F. Uhl, of Michigan (Assistant Secretary), ad interim, May 28, 1895. Alvey A. Adee, of the District of Columbia (Second Assistant Secretary), ad interim, May 31, 1895. Edwin F. Uhl, of Michigan (Assistant Secretary), ad interim, June 1, 1895. Richard Olney, of Massachusetts, June 8, 1895; entered upon duties June 10, 1895. SECRETARY OF THE TREASURY—Charles Foster, of Ohio, continued from preceding administration. John G. Carlisle, of Kentucky, March 6, 1893. SECRETARY OF WAR—Stephen B. Elkins, of West Virginia, continued from preceding administration. Daniel S. Lamont, of New York, March 6, 1893. ATTORNEY GENERAL—William H. H. Miller, of Indiana, continued from preceding administration. Richard Olney, of Massachusetts, March 6, 1893. Judson Harmon, of Ohio, June 8, 1895; entered upon duties June 11, 1895. POSTMASTER GENERAL—John Wanamaker, of Pennsylvania, continued from preceding administration. Wilson S. Bissell, of New York, March 6, 1893. William L. Wilson, of West Virginia, March 1, 1895; entered upon duties April 4, 1895. SECRETARY OF THE NAVY—Benjamin F. Tracy, of New York, continued from preceding administration. Hilary A. Herbert, of Alabama, March 6, 1893. SECRETARY OF THE INTERIOR—John W. Noble, of Missouri, continued from preceding administration. Hoke Smith, of Georgia, March 6, 1893. John M. Reynolds, of Pennsylvania (Assistant Secretary), ad interim, September 1, 1896. David R. Francis, of Missouri, September 1, 1896; entered upon duties September 4, 1896. SECRETARY OF AGRICULTURE—

Jeremiah M. Rusk, of Wisconsin, continued from preceding administration. Julius Sterling Morton, of Nebraska, March 6, 1893.

53d Congress
1st Session: Aug. 7, 1893–Nov. 3, 1893; 2d Session: Dec. 4, 1893–Aug. 28, 1894; 3d Session: Dec. 3, 1894–Mar. 3, 1895; Special Session of the Senate: Mar. 4, 1893–Apr. 15, 1893.

President pro tempore of the Senate: Charles F. Manderson, of Nebraska (continued from preceding Congress); Isham G. Harris, of Tennessee (elected Mar. 22, 1893; Jan. 10, 1895); Matt W. Ransom, of North Carolina (elected Jan. 7, 1895). Speaker of the House: Charles F. Crisp, of Georgia (reelected Aug. 7, 1893).

Senate: 44 Democratic; 38 Republican; 3 other
House: 218 Democratic; 127 Republican; 11 other

54th Congress
1st Session: Dec. 2, 1895–June 11, 1896; 2d Session: Dec. 7, 1896–Mar. 3, 1897.

President pro tempore of the Senate: William P. Frye, of Maine (elected Feb. 7, 1896). Speaker of the House: Thomas B. Reed, of Maine (elected Dec. 2, 1895).

Senate: 43 Republican; 39 Democratic; 6 other
House: 244 Republican; 105 Democratic; 7 other

First Administration of WILLIAM McKINLEY
MARCH 4, 1897, TO MARCH 3, 1901

PRESIDENT—William McKinley, of Ohio (Republican). VICE-PRESIDENT—Garret A. Hobart, of New Jersey (died November 21, 1899). SECRETARY OF STATE—Richard Olney, of Massachusetts, continued from preceding administration. John Sherman, of Ohio, March 5, 1897. William R. Day, of Ohio, April 26, 1898; entered upon duties April 28, 1898. Alvey A. Adee (Second Assistant Secretary), ad interim, September 17, 1898. John Hay, of the District of Columbia, September 20, 1898; entered upon duties September 30, 1898. SECRETARY OF THE TREASURY—John G. Carlisle, of Kentucky, continued from preceding administration. Lyman J. Gage, of Illinois, March 5, 1897. SECRETARY OF WAR—Daniel S. Lamont, of New York, continued from preceding administration. Russell A. Alger, of Michigan, March 5, 1897. Elihu Root, of New York, August 1, 1899. ATTORNEY GENERAL—Judson Harmon, of Ohio, continued from preceding administration. Joseph McKenna, of California, March 5, 1897; entered upon duties March 7, 1897. John K. Richards, of Ohio (Solicitor General), ad interim, January 26, 1898. John W. Griggs, of New Jersey, January 25, 1898; entered upon duties February 1, 1898. POSTMASTER GENERAL—William L. Wilson, of West Virginia, continued from preceding administration. James A. Gary, of Maryland, March 5, 1897. Charles Emory Smith, of Pennsylvania, April 21, 1898. SECRETARY OF THE NAVY—Hilary A. Herbert, of Alabama, continued from preceding administration. John D. Long, of Massachusetts, March 5, 1897. SECRETARY OF THE INTERIOR—David R. Francis, of Missouri, continued from preceding administration. Cornelius N. Bliss, of New York, March 5, 1897. Ethan A. Hitchcock, of Missouri, December 21, 1898; entered upon duties February 20, 1899. SECRETARY OF AGRICULTURE—Julius Sterling Morton, of Nebraska, continued from preceding administration. James Wilson, of Iowa, March 5, 1897.

55th Congress
1st Session: Mar. 15, 1897–July 24, 1897; 2d Session: Dec. 6, 1897–July 8, 1898; 3d Session: Dec. 5, 1898–Mar. 3, 1899; Special Session of the Senate: Mar. 4, 1897–Mar. 10, 1897.

President pro tempore of the Senate: William P. Frye, of Maine (continued from preceding Congress). Speaker of the House: Thomas B. Reed, of Maine (reelected Mar. 15, 1897).

Senate: 47 Republican; 34 Democratic; 7 other
House: 204 Republican; 113 Democratic; 40 other

56th Congress
1st Session: Dec. 4, 1899–June 7, 1900; 2d Session: Dec. 3, 1900–Mar. 3, 1901.

President pro tempore of the Senate: William P. Frye, of Maine (continued from preceding Congress). Speaker of the House: David B. Henderson, of Iowa (elected Dec. 4, 1899).

Senate: 53 Republican; 26 Democratic; 8 other
House: 185 Republican; 163 Democratic; 9 other

Second Administration of WILLIAM McKINLEY
MARCH 4, 1901, TO SEPTEMBER 14, 1901

PRESIDENT—William McKinley, of Ohio (Republican) (died September 14, 1901). VICE-PRESIDENT—Theodore Roosevelt, of New York. SECRETARY OF STATE—John Hay, of the District of Columbia, continued from preceding administration. John Hay, of the District of Columbia, recommissioned March 5, 1901. SECRETARY OF THE TREASURY—Lyman J. Gage, of Illinois, continued from preceding administration. Lyman J. Gage, of

Illinois, recommissioned March 5, 1901. SECRETARY OF WAR—Elihu Root, of New York, continued from preceding administration. Elihu Root, of New York, recommissioned March 5, 1901. ATTORNEY GENERAL—John W. Griggs, of New Jersey, continued from preceding administration. John W. Griggs, of New Jersey, recommissioned March 5, 1901. John K. Richards, of Ohio (Solicitor General), ad interim, April 1, 1901. Philander C. Knox, of Pennsylvania, April 5, 1901; entered upon duties April 10, 1901. POSTMASTER GENERAL—Charles Emory Smith, of Pennsylvania, continued from preceding administration. Charles Emory Smith, of Pennsylvania, recommissioned March 5, 1901. SECRETARY OF THE NAVY—John D. Long, of Massachusetts, continued from preceding administration. John D. Long, of Massachusetts, recommissioned March 5, 1901. SECRETARY OF THE INTERIOR—Ethan A. Hitchcock, of Missouri, continued from preceding administration. Ethan A. Hitchcock, of Missouri, recommissioned March 5, 1901. SECRETARY OF AGRICULTURE—James Wilson, of Iowa, continued from preceding administration. James Wilson, of Iowa, recommissioned March 5, 1901.

First Administration of THEODORE ROOSEVELT
SEPTEMBER 14, 1901, TO MARCH 3, 1905

PRESIDENT—Theodore Roosevelt, of New York (Republican). SECRETARY OF STATE—John Hay, of the District of Columbia, continued from preceding administration. SECRETARY OF THE TREASURY—Lyman J. Gage, of Illinois, continued from preceding administration. Leslie M. Shaw, of Iowa, January 9, 1902; entered upon duties February 1, 1902. SECRETARY OF WAR—Elihu Root, of New York, continued from preceding administration. William H. Taft, of Ohio, January 11, 1904, to take effect February 1, 1904. ATTORNEY GENERAL—Philander C. Knox, of Pennsylvania, continued from preceding administration. Philander C. Knox, of Pennsylvania, recommissioned December 16, 1901. William H. Moody, of Massachusetts, July 1, 1904. POSTMASTER GENERAL—Charles Emory Smith, of Pennsylvania, continued from preceding administration. Henry C. Payne, of Wisconsin, January 9, 1902. Robert J. Wynne, of Pennsylvania, October 10, 1904. SECRETARY OF THE NAVY—John D. Long, of Massachusetts, continued from preceding administration. William H. Moody, of Massachusetts, April 29, 1902; entered upon duties May 1, 1902. Paul Morton, of Illinois, July 1, 1904. SECRETARY OF THE INTERIOR—Ethan A. Hitchcock, of Missouri, continued from preceding administration. SECRETARY OF AGRICULTURE—James Wilson, of Iowa, continued from preceding administration. SECRETARY OF COMMERCE AND LABOR—George B. Cortelyou, of New York, February 16, 1903. Victor H. Metcalf, of California, July 1, 1904.

57th Congress
1st Session: Dec. 2, 1901–July 1, 1902; 2d Session: Dec. 1, 1902–Mar. 3, 1903; Special Session of the Senate: Mar. 4, 1901–Mar. 9, 1901.
President pro tempore of the Senate: William P. Frye, of Maine (reelected Mar. 7, 1901). Speaker of the House: David B. Henderson, of Iowa (reelected Dec. 2, 1901).
Senate: 55 Republican; 35 Democratic; 4 other
House: 197 Republican; 151 Democratic; 9 other

58th Congress
1st Session: Nov. 9, 1903–Dec. 7, 1903; 2d Session: Dec. 7, 1903–Apr. 28, 1904; 3d Session: Dec. 5, 1904–Mar. 3, 1905; Special Session of the Senate: Mar. 5, 1903–Mar. 19, 1903.
President pro tempore of the Senate: William P. Frye, of Maine (continued from preceding Congress). Speaker of the House: Joseph G. Cannon, of Illinois (elected Nov. 9, 1903).
Senate: 57 Republican; 33 Democratic
House: 208 Republican; 178 Democratic

Second Administration of THEODORE ROOSEVELT
MARCH 4, 1905, TO MARCH 3, 1909

PRESIDENT—Theodore Roosevelt, of New York (Republican). VICE-PRESIDENT—Charles Warren Fairbanks, of Indiana. SECRETARY OF STATE—John Hay, of the District of Columbia, continued from preceding administration. John Hay, of the District of Columbia, recommissioned March 6, 1905 (died July 1, 1905). Francis B. Loomis, of Ohio (Assistant Secretary), ad interim, July 1, 1905, to July 18, 1905. Elihu Root, of New York, July 7, 1905; entered upon duties July 19, 1905. Robert Bacon, of New York, January 27, 1909. SECRETARY OF THE TREASURY—Leslie M. Shaw, of Iowa, continued from preceding administration. Leslie M. Shaw, of Iowa, recommissioned March 6, 1905. George B. Cortelyou, of New York, January 15, 1907, to take effect March 4, 1907. SECRETARY OF WAR—William H. Taft, of Ohio, continued from preceding administration. William H. Taft, of Ohio, recommissioned March 6, 1905. Luke E. Wright, of Tennessee, June 29, 1908; entered upon duties July 1, 1908. ATTORNEY GENERAL—William H. Moody, of Massachusetts, continued from preceding administration. William H. Moody, of Massachusetts, recommissioned March 6, 1905. Charles J. Bonaparte, of Maryland, December 12, 1906; entered upon duties December 17, 1906. POSTMASTER GENERAL—Robert J.

Wynne, of Pennsylvania, continued from preceding administration. George B. Cortelyou, of New York, March 6, 1905. George von L. Meyer, of Massachusetts, January 15, 1907, to take effect March 4, 1907. SECRETARY OF THE NAVY—Paul Morton, of Illinois, continued from preceding administration. Paul Morton, of Illinois, recommissioned March 6, 1905. Charles J. Bonaparte, of Maryland, July 1, 1905. Victor H. Metcalf, of California, December 12, 1906; entered upon duties December 17, 1906. Truman H. Newberry, of Michigan, December 1, 1908. SECRETARY OF THE INTERIOR—Ethan A. Hitchcock, of Missouri, continued from preceding administration. Ethan A. Hitchcock, of Missouri, recommissioned March 6, 1905. James R. Garfield, of Ohio, January 15, 1907, to take effect March 4, 1907. SECRETARY OF AGRICULTURE—James Wilson, of Iowa, continued from preceding administration. James Wilson, of Iowa, recommissioned March 6, 1905. SECRETARY OF COMMERCE AND LABOR—Victor H. Metcalf, of California, continued from preceding administration. Victor H. Metcalf, of California, recommissioned March 6, 1905. Oscar S. Straus, of New York, December 12, 1906; entered upon duties December 17, 1906.

59th Congress
1st Session: Dec. 4, 1905–June 30, 1906; 2d Session: Dec. 3, 1906–Mar. 3, 1907; Special Session of the Senate: Mar. 4, 1905–Mar. 18, 1905.
President pro tempore of the Senate: William P. Frye, of Maine (continued from preceding Congress). Speaker of the House: Joseph G. Cannon, of Illinois (reelected Dec. 4, 1905).
Senate: 57 Republican; 33 Democratic
House: 250 Republican; 136 Democratic

60th Congress
1st Session: Dec. 2, 1907–May 30, 1908; 2d Session: Dec. 7, 1908–Mar. 3, 1909.
President pro tempore of the Senate: Willliam P. Frye, of Maine (reelected Dec. 5, 1907). Speaker of the House: Joseph G. Cannon, of Illinois (reelected Dec. 2, 1907).
Senate: 61 Republican; 31 Democratic
House: 222 Republican; 164 Democratic

Administration of WILLIAM H. TAFT
March 4, 1909, TO MARCH 3, 1913

PRESIDENT—William H. Taft, of Ohio (Republican). VICE-PRESIDENT—James S. Sherman, of New York (died October 30, 1912). SECRETARY OF STATE—Robert Bacon, of New York, continued from preceding administration. Philander C. Knox, of Pennsylvania, March 5, 1909. SECRETARY OF THE TREASURY—George B. Cortelyou, of New York, continued from preceding administration. Franklin MacVeagh, of Illinois, March 5, 1909; entered upon duties March 8, 1909. SECRETARY OF WAR—Luke E. Wright, of Tennessee, continued from preceding administration. Jacob M. Dickinson, of Tennessee, March 5, 1909; entered upon duties March 12, 1909. Henry L. Stimson, of New York, May 16, 1911; entered upon duties May 22, 1911. ATTORNEY GENERAL—Charles J. Bonaparte, of Maryland, continued from preceding administration. George W. Wickersham, of New York, March 5, 1909. POSTMASTER GENERAL—George von L. Meyer, of Massachusetts, continued from preceding administration. Frank H. Hitchcock, of Massachusetts, March 5, 1909. SECRETARY OF THE NAVY—Truman H. Newberry, of Michigan, continued from preceding administration. George von L. Meyer, of Massachusetts, March 5, 1909. SECRETARY OF THE INTERIOR—James R. Garfield, of Ohio, continued from preceding administration. Richard A. Ballinger, of Washington, March 5, 1909. Walter Lowrie Fisher, of Illinois, March 7, 1911. SECRETARY OF AGRICULTURE—James Wilson, of Iowa, continued from preceding administration. James Wilson, of Iowa, recommissioned March 5, 1909. SECRETARY OF COMMERCE AND LABOR—Oscar S. Straus, of New York, continued from preceding administration. Charles Nagel, of Missouri, March 5, 1909.

61st Congress
1st Session: Mar. 15, 1909–Aug. 5, 1909; 2d Session: Dec. 6, 1909–June 25, 1910; 3d Session: Dec. 5, 1910–Mar. 3, 1911; Special Session of the Senate: Mar. 4, 1909–Mar. 6, 1909.
President pro tempore of the Senate: William P. Frye, of Maine (continued from preceding Congress). Speaker of the House: Joseph G. Cannon, of Illinois (reelected Mar. 15, 1909).
Senate: 61 Republican; 32 Democratic
House: 219 Republican; 172 Democratic

62d Congress
1st Session: Apr. 4, 1911–Aug. 22, 1911; 2d Session: Dec. 4, 1911–Aug. 26, 1912; 3d Session: Dec. 2, 1912–Mar. 3, 1913.
President pro tempore of the Senate: William P. Frye, of Maine (continued from preceding Congress). Charles Curtis, of Kansas (elected to serve Dec. 4–12, 1911). Augustus O. Bacon, of Georgia (elected to serve Jan. 15–17, 1912; Mar. 11–12, 1912; Apr. 8, 1912; May 10, 1912; May 30–June 3, 1912; June 13–July 5, 1912; Aug. 1–10, 1912; Aug. 27–Dec. 15, 1912; Jan. 5–18, 1913; Feb. 2–15, 1913). Jacob H. Gallinger, of New

Hampshire (elected to serve Feb. 12–14, 1912; April 26–27, 1912; May 7, 1912; July 6–31, 1912; Aug. 12–26, 1912; Dec. 16, 1912–Jan. 4, 1913; Jan. 19–Feb. 1, 1913; Feb. 16–Mar. 3, 1913). Henry C. Lodge, of Massachusetts (elected to serve Mar. 25–26, 1912). Frank B. Brandegee, of Connecticut (elected to serve May 25, 1912). Speaker of the House: James B. Clark, of Missouri (elected Apr. 4, 1911).

Senate: 51 Republican; 41 Democratic
House: 228 Democratic; 161 Republican; 1 other

First Administration of WOODROW WILSON
MARCH 4, 1913, TO MARCH 3, 1917

PRESIDENT—Woodrow Wilson, of New Jersey (Democratic). VICE-PRESIDENT—Thomas R. Marshall, of Indiana. SECRETARY OF STATE—Philander C. Knox, of Pennsylvania, continued from preceding administration. William Jennings Bryan, of Nebraska, March 5, 1913. Robert Lansing, of New York (counselor), ad interim, June 9, 1915. Robert Lansing, of New York, June 23, 1915. SECRETARY OF THE TREASURY—Franklin MacVeagh, of Illinois, continued from preceding administration. William Gibbs McAdoo, of New York, March 5, 1913; entered upon duties March 6, 1913. SECRETARY OF WAR—Henry L. Stimson, of New York, continued from preceding administration. Lindley M. Garrison, of New Jersey, March 5, 1913. Hugh L. Scott (United States Army), ad interim, February 12, 1916; served from February 11 to March 8, 1916. Newton D. Baker, of Ohio, March 7, 1916; entered upon duties March 9, 1916. ATTORNEY GENERAL—George W. Wickersham, of New York, continued from preceding administration. James Clark McReynolds, of Tennessee, March 5, 1913; entered upon duties March 6, 1913. Thomas Watt Gregory, of Texas, August 29, 1914; entered upon duties September 3, 1914. POSTMASTER GENERAL—Frank H. Hitchcock, of Massachusetts, continued from preceding administration. Albert Sidney Burleson, of Texas, March 5, 1913. SECRETARY OF THE NAVY—George von L. Meyer, of Massachusetts, continued from preceding administration. Josephus Daniels, of North Carolina, March 5, 1913. SECRETARY OF THE INTERIOR—Walter Lowrie Fisher, of Illinois, continued from preceding administration. Franklin Knight Lane, of California, March 5, 1913. SECRETARY OF AGRICULTURE—James Wilson, of Iowa, continued from preceding administration. David Franklin Houston, of Missouri, March 5, 1913; entered upon duties March 6, 1913. SECRETARY OF COMMERCE—Charles Nagel, of Missouri (Secretary of Commerce and Labor), continued from preceding administration. William C. Redfield, of New York, March 5, 1913. SECRETARY OF LABOR—Charles Nagel, of Missouri (Secretary of Commerce and Labor), continued from preceding administration. William Bauchop Wilson, of Pennsylvania, March 5, 1913.

63d Congress
1st Session: Apr. 7, 1913–Dec. 1, 1913; 2d Session: Dec. 1, 1913–Oct. 24, 1914; 3d Session: Dec. 7, 1914–Mar. 3, 1915; Special Session of the Senate: Mar. 4, 1913–Mar. 17, 1913.
President pro tempore of the Senate: James P. Clarke, of Arkansas (elected Mar. 13, 1913). Speaker of the House: James B. Clark, of Missouri (reelected Apr. 7, 1913).
Senate: 51 Democratic; 44 Republican; 1 other
House: 291 Democratic; 127 Republican; 17 other

64th Congress
1st Session: Dec. 6, 1915–Sept. 8, 1916; 2d Session: Dec. 4, 1916–Mar. 3, 1917.
President pro tempore of the Senate: James P. Clarke, of Arkansas (reelected Dec. 6, 1915); Willard Saulsbury, of Delaware (elected Dec. 14, 1916). Speaker of the House: James B. Clark, of Missouri (reelected Dec. 6, 1915).
Senate: 56 Democratic; 40 Republican
House: 230 Democratic; 196 Republican; 9 other

Second Administration of WOODROW WILSON
MARCH 4, 1917, TO MARCH 3, 1921

PRESIDENT—Woodrow Wilson, of New Jersey (Democratic). (Oath administered March 5, 1917.) VICE-PRESIDENT—Thomas R. Marshall, of Indiana. SECRETARY OF STATE—Robert Lansing, of New York, continued from preceding administration. Frank L. Polk, of New York (Under Secretary) ad interim, February 14, 1920, to March 13, 1920. Bainbridge Colby, of New York, March 22, 1920; entered upon duties March 23, 1920. SECRETARY OF THE TREASURY—William Gibbs McAdoo, of New York, continued from preceding administration. Carter Glass, of Virginia, December 6, 1918; entered upon duties December 16, 1918. David F. Houston, of Missouri, January 31, 1920; entered upon duties February 2, 1920. SECRETARY OF WAR—Newton D. Baker, of Ohio, continued from preceding administration. ATTORNEY GENERAL—Thomas Watt Gregory, of Texas, continued from preceding administration. A. Mitchell Palmer, of Pennsylvania, March 5, 1919. POSTMASTER GENERAL—Albert Sidney Burleson, of Texas, continued from preceding administration. Albert Sidney Burleson, of Texas, recommissioned January 24, 1918. SECRETARY OF THE NAVY—Josephus Daniels, of North Carolina, continued from preceding administration. SECRETARY OF THE INTERIOR—Franklin Knight Lane, of California, continued from preceding administration. John Barton Payne, of Illinois, February 28, 1920; entered upon duties March 13, 1920. SECRETARY OF AGRICULTURE—David Franklin Houston, of Missouri, continued from preceding administration. Edwin T. Meredith, of Iowa, January 31, 1920; entered upon duties February 2, 1920. SECRETARY OF COMMERCE—William C. Redfield, of New York, continued from preceding administration. Joshua Willis Alexander, of Missouri, December 11, 1919; entered upon duties December 16, 1919. SECRETARY OF LABOR—William Bauchop Wilson, of Pennsylvania, continued from preceding administration.

65th Congress
1st Session: Apr. 2, 1917–Oct. 6, 1917; 2d Session: Dec. 3, 1917–Nov. 21, 1918; 3d Session: Dec. 2, 1918–Mar. 3, 1919; Special Session of the Senate: Mar. 5, 1917–Mar. 16, 1917.
President pro tempore of the Senate: Willard Saulsbury, of Delaware (continued from preceding Congress). Speaker of the House: James B. Clark, of Missouri (reelected Apr. 2, 1917).
Senate: 53 Democratic; 42 Republican
House: 216 Democratic; 210 Republican; 6 other

66th Congress
1st Session: May 19, 1919–Nov. 19, 1919; 2d Session: Dec. 1, 1919–June 5, 1920; 3d Session: Dec. 6, 1920–Mar. 3, 1921.
President pro tempore of the Senate: Albert B. Cummins, of Iowa (elected May 19, 1919). Speaker of the House: Frederick H. Gillett, of Massachusetts (elected May 19, 1919).
Senate: 49 Republican; 47 Democratic
House: 240 Republican; 190 Democratic; 3 other

Administration of WARREN G. HARDING
MARCH 4, 1921, TO AUGUST 2, 1923

PRESIDENT—Warren G. Harding, of Ohio (Republican) (died August 2, 1923). VICE-PRESIDENT—Calvin Coolidge, of Massachusetts. SECRETARY OF STATE—Bainbridge Colby, of New York, continued from preceding administration. Charles Evans Hughes, of New York, March 4, 1921; entered upon duties March 5, 1921. SECRETARY OF THE TREASURY—David F. Houston, of Missouri, continued from preceding administration. Andrew W. Mellon, of Pennsylvania, March 4, 1921; entered upon duties March 5, 1921. SECRETARY OF WAR—Newton D. Baker, of Ohio, continued from preceding administration. John W. Weeks, of Massachusetts, March 5, 1921. ATTORNEY GENERAL—A. Mitchell Palmer, of Pennsylvania, continued from preceding administration. Harry M. Daugherty, of Ohio, March 5, 1921. POSTMASTER GENERAL—Albert Sidney Burleson, of Texas, continued from preceding administration. Will H. Hays, of Indiana, March 5, 1921. Hubert Work, of Colorado, March 4, 1922. Harry S. New, of Indiana, February 27, 1923; entered upon duties March 5, 1923. SECRETARY OF THE NAVY—Josephus Daniels, of North Carolina, continued from preceding administration. Edwin Denby, of Michigan, March 5, 1921. SECRETARY OF THE INTERIOR—John Barton Payne, of Illinois, continued from preceding administration. Albert B. Fall, of New Mexico, March 5, 1921. Hubert Work, of Colorado, February 27, 1923; entered upon duties March 5, 1923. SECRETARY OF AGRICULTURE—Edwin T. Meredith, of Iowa, continued from preceding administration. Henry C. Wallace, of Iowa, March 5, 1921. SECRETARY OF COMMERCE—Joshua Willis Alexander, of Missouri, continued from preceding administration. Herbert C. Hoover, of California, March 5, 1921. SECRETARY OF LABOR—William Bauchop Wilson, of Pennsylvania, continued from preceding administration. James J. Davis, of Pennsylvania, March 5, 1921.

First Administration of CALVIN COOLIDGE
AUGUST 3, 1923, TO MARCH 3, 1925

PRESIDENT—Calvin Coolidge, of Massachusetts (Republican). SECRETARY OF STATE—Charles Evans Hughes, of New York, continued from preceding administration. SECRETARY OF THE TREASURY—Andrew W. Mellon, of Pennsylvania, continued from preceding administration. SECRETARY OF WAR—John W. Weeks, of Massachusetts, continued from preceding administration. ATTORNEY GENERAL—Harry M. Daugherty, of Ohio, continued from preceding administration. Harlan F. Stone, of New York, April 7, 1924; entered upon duties April 9, 1924. POSTMASTER GENERAL—Harry S. New, of Indiana, continued from preceding administration. SECRETARY OF THE NAVY—Edwin Denby, of Michigan, continued from preceding administration. Curtis D. Wilbur, of California, March 18, 1924. SECRETARY OF THE INTERIOR—Hubert Work, of Colorado, continued from preceding administration. SECRETARY OF AGRICULTURE—Henry C. Wallace, of Iowa, continued from preceding administration (died October 25, 1924). Howard M. Gore, of West Virginia (Assistant Secretary), ad interim, October 26, 1924, to November 22, 1924. Howard M. Gore, of West Virginia, November 21, 1924; entered upon duties November 22, 1924. SECRETARY OF COMMERCE—

Herbert C. Hoover, of California, continued from preceding administration. SECRETARY OF LABOR—James J. Davis, of Pennsylvania, continued from preceding administration.

67th Congress
1st Session: Apr. 11, 1921–Nov. 23, 1921; 2d Session: Dec. 5, 1921–Sept. 22, 1922; 3d Session: Nov. 20, 1922–Dec. 4, 1922; 4th Session: Dec. 4, 1922–March 3, 1923; Special Session of the Senate: Mar. 4, 1921–Mar. 15, 1921.

President pro tempore of the Senate: Albert B. Cummins, of Iowa (reelected Mar. 7, 1921). Speaker of the House: Frederick H. Gillett, of Massachusetts (reelected Apr. 11, 1921).

Senate: 59 Republican; 37 Democratic
House: 303 Republican; 131 Democratic; 1 other

68th Congress
1st Session: Dec. 3, 1923–June 7, 1924; 2d Session: Dec. 1, 1924–Mar. 3, 1925.

President pro tempore of the Senate: Albert B. Cummins, of Iowa (continued from preceding Congress). Speaker of the House: Frederick H. Gillett, of Massachusetts (reelected Dec. 3, 1923).

Senate: 51 Republican; 43 Democratic; 2 other
House: 225 Republican; 205 Democratic; 5 other

Second Administration of CALVIN COOLIDGE
MARCH 4, 1925, TO MARCH 3, 1929

PRESIDENT—Calvin Coolidge, of Massachusetts (Republican). VICE-PRESIDENT—Charles G. Dawes, of Illinois. SECRETARY OF STATE—Charles Evans Hughes, of New York, continued from preceding administration. Frank B. Kellogg, of Minnesota, February 16, 1925; entered upon duties March 5, 1925. SECRETARY OF THE TREASURY—Andrew W. Mellon, of Pennsylvania, continued from preceding administration. SECRETARY OF WAR—John W. Weeks, of Massachusetts, continued from preceding administration. Dwight F. Davis, of Missouri, October 13, 1925; entered upon duties October 14, 1925. ATTORNEY GENERAL—James M. Beck, of Pennsylvania (Solicitor General), ad interim, March 4, 1925, to March 16, 1925. John G. Sargent, of Vermont, March 17, 1925; entered upon duties March 18, 1925. POSTMASTER GENERAL—Harry S. New, of Indiana, continued from preceding administration. Harry S. New, of Indiana, recommissioned March 5, 1925. SECRETARY OF THE NAVY—Curtis D. Wilbur, of California, continued from preceding administration. SECRETARY OF THE INTERIOR—Hubert Work, of Colorado, continued from preceding administration. Roy O. West, of Illinois, ad interim, July 25, 1928, to January 21, 1929. Roy O. West, January 21, 1929. SECRETARY OF AGRICULTURE—Howard M. Gore, of West Virginia, continued from preceding administration. William M. Jardine, of Kansas, February 18, 1925; entered upon duties March 5, 1925. SECRETARY OF COMMERCE—Herbert C. Hoover, of California, continued from preceding administration. William F. Whiting, of Massachusetts, ad interim, August 21, 1928, to December 11, 1928. William F. Whiting, December 11, 1928. SECRETARY OF LABOR—James J. Davis, of Pennsylvania, continued from preceding administration.

69th Congress
1st Session: Dec. 7, 1925–July 3, 1926; Nov. 10, 1926; 2d Session: Dec. 6, 1926–Mar. 3, 1927; Special Session of the Senate: Mar. 4, 1925–Mar. 18, 1925.

President pro tempore of the Senate: Albert B. Cummins, of Iowa (continued from preceding Congress); George H. Moses, of New Hampshire (elected Mar. 6, 1925). Speaker of the House: Nicholas Longworth, of Ohio (elected Dec. 7, 1925).

Senate: 56 Republican; 39 Democratic; 1 other
House: 247 Republican; 183 Democratic; 4 other

70th Congress
1st Session: Dec. 5, 1927–May 29, 1928; 2d Session: Dec. 3, 1928–Mar. 3, 1929.

President pro tempore of the Senate: George H. Moses, of New Hampshire (reelected Dec. 15, 1927). Speaker of the House: Nicholas Longworth, of Ohio (reelected Dec. 15, 1927).

Senate: 49 Republican; 46 Democratic; 1 other
House: 237 Republican; 195 Democratic; 3 other

Administration of HERBERT C. HOOVER
MARCH 4, 1929, TO MARCH 3, 1933

PRESIDENT—Herbert C. Hoover, of California (Republican). VICE-PRESIDENT—Charles Curtis, of Kansas. SECRETARY OF STATE—Frank B. Kellogg, of Minnesota, continued from preceding administration. Henry L. Stimson, of New York, March 4, 1929; entered upon duties March 29, 1929. SECRETARY OF THE TREASURY—Andrew W. Mellon, of Pennsylvania, continued from preceding administration. Ogden L. Mills, of New York, February 10, 1932; entered upon duties February 13, 1932. SECRETARY OF WAR—Dwight F. Davis, of Missouri, continued from preceding administration. James W. Good, of Illinois, March 5, 1929; entered upon duties March 6, 1929. Patrick J. Hurley, of Oklahoma, December 9, 1929. ATTORNEY GENERAL—John G. Sargent, of Vermont, continued from preceding administration. James DeWitt Mitchell, of Minnesota, March 5, 1929; entered upon duties March 6, 1929. POSTMASTER GENERAL—Harry S. New, of Indiana, continued from preceding administration. Walter F. Brown, of Ohio, March 5, 1929; entered upon duties March 6, 1929. SECRETARY OF THE NAVY—Curtis D. Wilbur, of California, continued from preceding administration. Charles F. Adams, of Massachusetts, March 5, 1929. SECRETARY OF THE INTERIOR—Roy O. West, of Illinois, continued from preceding administration. Ray L. Wilbur, of California, March 5, 1929. SECRETARY OF AGRICULTURE—William M. Jardine, of Kansas, continued from preceding administration. Arthur M. Hyde, of Missouri, March 5, 1929; entered upon duties March 6, 1929. SECRETARY OF COMMERCE—William F. Whiting, of Massachusetts, continued from preceding administration. Robert P. Lamont, of Illinois, March 5, 1929. Roy D. Chapin, of Michigan, ad interim, August 8, 1932, to December 14, 1932. Roy D. Chapin, of Michigan, December 14, 1932. SECRETARY OF LABOR—James J. Davis, of Pennsylvania, continued from preceding administration. William N. Doak, of Virginia, December 8, 1930; entered upon duties December 9, 1930.

71st Congress
1st Session: Apr. 15, 1929–Nov. 22, 1929; 2d Session: Dec. 2, 1929–July 3, 1930; 3d Session: Dec. 1, 1930–Mar. 3, 1931; Special Sessions of the Senate: Mar. 4, 1929–Mar. 5, 1929; July 7, 1930–July 21, 1930.

President pro tempore of the Senate: George H. Moses, of New Hampshire (continued from preceding Congress). Speaker of the House: Nicholas Longworth, of Ohio (reelected Apr. 15, 1929).

Senate: 56 Republican; 39 Democratic; 1 other
House: 267 Republican; 167 Democratic; 1 other

72d Congress
1st Session: Dec. 7, 1931–July 16, 1932; 2d Session: Dec. 15, 1932–Mar. 3, 1933.

President pro tempore of the Senate: George H. Moses, of New Hampshire (continued from preceding Congress). Speaker of the House: John N. Garner, of Texas (elected Dec. 7, 1931).

Senate: 48 Republican; 47 Democratic; 1 other
House: 220 Democratic; 214 Republican; 1 other

First Administration of FRANKLIN DELANO ROOSEVELT
MARCH 4, 1933, TO JANUARY 20, 1937

PRESIDENT—Franklin Delano Roosevelt, of New York (Democratic). VICE-PRESIDENT—John N. Garner, of Texas. SECRETARY OF STATE—Cordell Hull, of Tennessee, March 4, 1933. SECRETARY OF THE TREASURY—William H. Woodin, of New York, March 4, 1933. Henry Morgenthau, Jr., of New York (Under Secretary), ad interim, January 1, 1934, to January 8, 1934. Henry Morgenthau, Jr., of New York, January 8, 1934. SECRETARY OF WAR—George H. Dern, of Utah, March 4, 1933. ATTORNEY GENERAL—Homer S. Cummings, of Connecticut, March 4, 1933. POSTMASTER GENERAL—James A. Farley, of New York, March 4, 1933. SECRETARY OF THE NAVY—Claude A. Swanson, of Virginia, March 4, 1933. SECRETARY OF THE INTERIOR—Harold L. Ickes, of Illinois, March 4, 1933. SECRETARY OF AGRICULTURE—Henry A. Wallace, of Iowa, March 4, 1933. SECRETARY OF COMMERCE—Daniel C. Roper, of South Carolina, March 4, 1933. SECRETARY OF LABOR—Frances Perkins, of New York, March 4, 1933.

73d Congress
1st Session: March 9, 1933–June 15, 1933; 2d Session: Jan. 3, 1934–June 18, 1934; Special Session of the Senate: Mar. 4, 1933–Mar. 6, 1933.

President pro tempore of the Senate: Key Pittman, of Nevada (elected Mar. 9, 1933). Speaker of the House: Henry T. Rainey, of Illinois (elected Mar. 9, 1933).

Senate: 60 Democratic; 35 Republican; 1 other
House: 310 Democratic; 117 Republican; 5 other

74th Congress
1st Session: Jan. 3, 1935–Aug. 26, 1935; 2d Session: Jan. 3, 1936–June 20, 1936.

President pro tempore of the Senate: Key Pittman, of Nevada (reelected Jan. 7, 1935). Speaker of the House: Joseph W. Byrnes, of Tennessee (elected Jan. 3, 1935); William Bankhead, of Alabama (elected June 4, 1936).

Senate: 69 Democratic; 25 Republican; 2 other
House: 319 Democratic; 103 Republican; 10 other

Second Administration of FRANKLIN DELANO ROOSEVELT
JANUARY 20, 1937, TO JANUARY 20, 1941

PRESIDENT—Franklin Delano Roosevelt, of New York (Democratic). VICE-PRESIDENT—John N. Garner, of Texas. SECRETARY OF STATE—Cordell Hull, of Tennessee, continued from preceding administration. SECRETARY OF THE TREASURY—Henry Morgenthau, Jr., of New York, continued from preceding administration. SECRETARY OF WAR—George H. Dern, of Utah, continued from preceding administration (died August 27, 1936). Harry H. Woodring, of Kansas (Assistant Secretary), ad interim, September 25, 1936, to May 6, 1937. Harry H. Woodring, of Kansas, May 6, 1937. Henry L. Stimson, of New York, July 10, 1940. ATTORNEY GENERAL—Homer S. Cummings, of Connecticut, continued from preceding administration. Frank Murphy, of Michigan, ad interim, January 2, 1939, to January 17, 1939. Frank Murphy, of Michigan, January 17, 1939. Robert H. Jackson, of New York, January 18, 1940. POSTMASTER GENERAL—James A. Farley, of New York, continued from preceding administration. James A. Farley, of New York, recommissioned January 22, 1937. Frank C. Walker, of Pennsylvania, September 10, 1940. SECRETARY OF THE NAVY—Claude A. Swanson, of Virginia, continued from preceding administration (died July 7, 1939). Charles Edison, of New Jersey, Acting Secretary from August 5, 1939, to December 30, 1939. Charles Edison, of New Jersey (Assistant Secretary), ad interim, December 30, 1939, to January 11, 1940. Charles Edison, of New Jersey, January 11, 1940. Frank Knox, of Illinois, July 10, 1940. SECRETARY OF THE INTERIOR—Harold L. Ickes, of Illinois, continued from preceding administration. SECRETARY OF AGRICULTURE—Henry A. Wallace, of Iowa, continued from preceding administration. Claude R. Wickard, of Indiana, August 27, 1940; entered upon duties September 5, 1940. SECRETARY OF COMMERCE—Daniel C. Roper, of South Carolina, continued from preceding administration. Harry L. Hopkins, of New York, ad interim, December 24, 1938, to January 23, 1939. Harry L. Hopkins, of New York, January 23, 1939. Jesse H. Jones, of Texas, September 16, 1940; entered upon duties September 19, 1940. SECRETARY OF LABOR—Frances Perkins, of New York, continued from preceding administration.

75th Congress
1st Session: Jan. 5, 1937–Aug. 21, 1937; 2d Session: Nov. 15, 1937–Dec. 21, 1937; 3d Session: Jan. 3, 1938–June 16, 1938.

President pro tempore of the Senate: Key Pittman, of Nevada (continued from preceding Congress). Speaker of the House: William B. Bankhead, of Alabama (reelected Jan. 5, 1937).

Senate: 76 Democratic; 16 Republican; 4 other
House: 331 Democratic; 89 Republican; 13 other

76th Congress
Jan. 3, 1939–Aug. 5, 1939; 2d Session: Sept. 21, 1939–Nov. 3, 1939; 3d Session: Jan. 3, 1940–Jan. 3, 1941.

President pro tempore of the Senate: Key Pittman, of Nevada (continued from preceding Congress); William H. King, of Utah (elected Nov. 19, 1940). Speaker of the House: William B. Bankhead, of Alabama (reelected Jan. 3, 1940); Sam Rayburn, of Texas (elected Sept. 16, 1940).

Senate: 69 Democratic; 23 Republican; 4 other
House: 261 Democratic; 164 Republican; 4 other

Third Administration of FRANKLIN DELANO ROOSEVELT

JANUARY 20, 1941, TO JANUARY 20, 1945

PRESIDENT—Franklin Delano Roosevelt, of New York (Democratic). VICE-PRESIDENT—Henry A. Wallace, of Iowa. SECRETARY OF STATE—Cordell Hull, of Tennessee, continued from preceding administration. Edward R. Stettinius, of Virginia, November 30, 1944; entered upon duties December 1, 1944. SECRETARY OF THE TREASURY—Henry Morgenthau, Jr., of New York, continued from preceding administration. SECRETARY OF WAR—Henry L. Stimson, of New York, continued from preceding administration. ATTORNEY GENERAL—Robert H. Jackson, of New York, continued from preceding administration. Francis Biddle, of Pennsylvania, September 5, 1941. POSTMASTER GENERAL—Frank C. Walker, of Pennsylvania, continued from preceding administration. Frank C. Walker, of Pennsylvania, recommissioned January 27, 1941. SECRETARY OF THE NAVY—Frank Knox, of Illinois, continued from preceding administration (died April 28, 1944). James V. Forrestal, of New York, May 18, 1944. SECRETARY OF THE INTERIOR—Harold L. Ickes, of Illinois, continued from preceding administration. SECRETARY OF AGRICULTURE—Claude R. Wickard, of Indiana, continued from preceding administration. SECRETARY OF COMMERCE—Jesse H. Jones, of Texas, continued from preceding administration. SECRETARY OF LABOR—Frances Perkins, of New York, continued from preceding administration.

77th Congress
1st Session: Jan. 3, 1941–Jan. 2, 1942; 2d Session: Jan. 5, 1942–Dec. 16, 1942.

President pro tempore of the Senate: Pat Harrison, of Mississippi (elected Jan. 6, 1941); Carter Glass, of Virginia (elected July 10, 1941). Speaker of the House: Sam Rayburn, of Texas (reelected Jan. 3, 1941).

Senate: 66 Democratic; 28 Republican; 2 other
House: 268 Democratic; 162 Republican; 5 other

78th Congress
1st Session: Jan. 6, 1943–Dec. 21, 1943; 2d Session: Jan. 10, 1944–Dec. 19, 1944.

President pro tempore of the Senate: Carter Glass, of Virginia (continued from preceding Congress). Speaker of the House: Sam Rayburn, of Texas (reelected Jan. 6, 1943).

Senate: 57 Democratic; 38 Republican; 1 other
House: 222 Democratic; 208 Republican; 5 other

Fourth Administration of FRANKLIN DELANO ROOSEVELT

JANUARY 20, 1945, TO APRIL 12, 1945

PRESIDENT—Franklin Delano Roosevelt, of New York (Democratic) (died April 12, 1945). VICE-PRESIDENT—Harry S. Truman, of Missouri. SECRETARY OF STATE—Edward R. Stettinius, of Virginia, continued from preceding administration. SECRETARY OF THE TREASURY—Henry Morgenthau, Jr., of New York, continued from preceding administration. SECRETARY OF WAR—Henry L. Stimson, of New York, continued from preceding administration. ATTORNEY GENERAL—Francis Biddle, of Pennsylvania, continued from preceding administration. POSTMASTER GENERAL—Frank C. Walker, of Pennsylvania, continued from preceding administration. Frank C. Walker, of Pennsylvania, recommissioned February 6, 1945. SECRETARY OF THE NAVY—James V. Forrestal, of New York, continued from preceding administration. SECRETARY OF THE INTERIOR—Harold L. Ickes, of Illinois, continued from preceding administration. SECRETARY OF AGRICULTURE—Claude R. Wickard, of Indiana, continued from preceding administration. SECRETARY OF COMMERCE—Jesse H. Jones, of Texas, continued from preceding administration. Henry A. Wallace, of Iowa, March 1, 1945; entered upon duties March 2, 1945. SECRETARY OF LABOR—Frances Perkins, of New York, continued from preceding administration.

First Administration of HARRY S TRUMAN

APRIL 12, 1945, TO JANUARY 20, 1949

PRESIDENT—Harry S Truman, of Missouri (Democratic). SECRETARY OF STATE—Edward R. Stettinius, of Virginia, continued from preceding administration. James F. Byrnes, of South Carolina, July 2, 1945; entered upon duties July 3, 1945. George C. Marshall, of Pennsylvania, January 8, 1947; entered upon duties January 21, 1947. SECRETARY OF THE TREASURY—Henry Morgenthau, Jr., of New York, continued from preceding administration. Fred M. Vinson, of Kentucky, July 18, 1945; entered upon duties July 23, 1945. John W. Snyder, of Missouri, June 12, 1946; entered upon duties June 25, 1946. SECRETARY OF DEFENSE—James Forrestal, of New York, July 26, 1947; entered upon duties September 17, 1947. SECRETARY OF WAR—Henry L. Stimson, of New York, continued from preceding administration. Robert Porter Patterson, of New York, September 26, 1945; entered upon duties September 27, 1945. Kenneth C. Royall, of North Carolina, July 21, 1947; entered upon duties July 25, 1947, and served until September 17, 1947. ATTORNEY GENERAL—Francis Biddle, of Pennsylvania, continued from preceding administration. Tom C. Clark, of Texas, June 15, 1945; entered upon duties September 27, 1945. POSTMASTER GENERAL—Frank Walker, of Pennsylvania, from preceding administration. Robert E. Hannegan, of Missouri, May 8, 1945; entered upon duties July 1, 1945. Jesse M. Donaldson, of Missouri, December 16, 1947. SECRETARY OF THE NAVY—James V. Forrestal, of New York, continued from preceding administration; served until September 17, 1947. SECRETARY OF THE INTERIOR—Harold L. Ickes, of Illinois, continued from preceding administration. Julius A. Krug, of Wisconsin, March 6, 1946; entered upon duties March 18, 1946. SECRETARY OF AGRICULTURE—Claude R. Wickard, of Indiana, continued from preceding administration. Clinton P. Anderson, of New Mexico, June 2, 1945; entered upon duties June 30, 1945. Charles F. Brannan, of Colorado, May 29, 1948; entered upon duties June 2, 1948. SECRETARY OF COMMERCE—Henry A. Wallace, of Iowa, continued from preceding administration. William Averell Harriman, of New York, ad interim, September 28, 1946, to January 28, 1947. William Averell Harriman, of New York, January 28, 1947. Charles Sawyer, of Ohio, May 6, 1948. SECRETARY OF LABOR—Frances Perkins, of New York, continued from preceding administration. Lewis B. Schwellenbach, of Washington, June 1, 1945; entered upon duties July 1, 1945 (died June 10, 1948). Maurice J. Tobin, of Massachusetts, ad interim, August 13, 1948.

79th Congress
1st Session: Jan. 3, 1945–Dec. 21, 1945; 2d Session: Jan. 14, 1946–Aug. 2, 1946.

President pro tempore of the Senate: Kenneth McKellar, of Tennessee (elected Jan. 6, 1945). Speaker of the House: Sam Rayburn, of Texas (reelected Jan. 3, 1945).

Senate: 56 Democratic; 38 Republican; 1 other
House: 242 Democratic; 190 Republican; 2 other

80th Congress
1st Session: Jan. 3, 1947–Dec. 19, 1947; 2d Session: Jan. 6, 1948–Dec. 31, 1948.

President pro tempore of the Senate: Arthur H. Vandenberg, of Michigan (elected Jan. 4, 1947). Speaker of the House: Joseph W. Martin, Jr., of Massachusetts (elected Jan. 3, 1947).
Senate: 51 Republican; 45 Democratic
House: 245 Republican; 188 Democratic; 1 other

Second Administration of HARRY S TRUMAN

JANUARY 20, 1949, TO JANUARY 20, 1953

PRESIDENT—Harry S Truman, of Missouri (Democratic). VICE-PRESIDENT—Alben W. Barkley, of Kentucky. SECRETARY OF STATE—Dean G. Acheson, of Connecticut, January 19, 1949; entered upon duties January 21, 1949. SECRETARY OF THE TREASURY—John W. Snyder, of Missouri, continued from preceding administration. SECRETARY OF DEFENSE—James V. Forrestal, of New York, continued from preceding administration. Louis A. Johnson, of West Virginia, March 23, 1949; entered upon duties March 28, 1949. George C. Marshall, of Pennsylvania, September 20, 1950; entered upon duties September 21, 1950. Robert A. Lovett, of New York, September 14, 1951; entered upon duties September 17, 1951. ATTORNEY GENERAL —Tom C. Clark, of Texas, continued from preceding administration. J. Howard McGrath, of Rhode Island, August 19, 1949; entered upon duties August 24, 1949. James P. McGranery, of Pennsylvania, May 21, 1952; entered upon duties May 27, 1952. POSTMASTER GENERAL—Jesse M. Donaldson, of Missouri, continued from preceding administration. Jesse M. Donaldson, of Missouri, recommissioned February 8, 1949. SECRETARY OF THE INTERIOR—Julius A. Krug, of Wisconsin, continued from preceding administration. Oscar L. Chapman, of Colorado (Under Secretary), ad interim, December 1, 1949, to January 19, 1950. Oscar L. Chapman, of Colorado, January 19, 1950. SECRETARY OF AGRICULTURE—Charles F. Brannan, of Colorado, continued from preceding administration. SECRETARY OF COMMERCE—Charles Sawyer, of Ohio, continued from preceding administration. SECRETARY OF LABOR—Maurice J. Tobin, of Massachusetts, ad interim, continued from preceding administration. Maurice J. Tobin, of Massachusetts, recommissioned February 1, 1949.

81st Congress

1st Session: Jan. 3, 1949–Oct. 19, 1949; 2d Session: Jan. 3, 1950–Jan. 2, 1951.
President pro tempore of the Senate: Kenneth D. McKellar, of Tennessee (elected Jan. 3, 1949). Speaker of the House: Sam Rayburn, of Texas (elected Jan. 3, 1949).
Senate: 54 Democratic; 42 Republican
House: 263 Democratic; 171 Republican; 1 other

82d Congress

1st Session: Jan. 3, 1951–Oct. 20, 1951; 2d Session: Jan. 8, 1952—July 7, 1952.
President pro tempore of the Senate: Kenneth D. McKellar, of Tennessee (continued from preceding Congress). Speaker of the House: Sam Rayburn, of Texas (reelected Jan. 3, 1951).
Senate: 49 Democratic; 47 Republican
House: 234 Democratic; 199 Republican; 1 other

First Administration of DWIGHT D. EISENHOWER

JANUARY 20, 1953, TO JANUARY 20, 1957

PRESIDENT—Dwight D. Eisenhower, of New York (Republican). VICE-PRESIDENT—Richard M. Nixon, of California. SECRETARY OF STATE—John Foster Dulles, of New York, January 21, 1953. SECRETARY OF THE TREASURY—George M. Humphrey, of Ohio, January 21, 1953. SECRETARY OF DEFENSE—Charles E. Wilson, of Michigan, January 26, 1953; entered upon duties January 28, 1953. ATTORNEY GENERAL—Herbert Brownell, Jr., of New York, January 21, 1953. POSTMASTER GENERAL—Arthur E. Summerfield, of Michigan, January 21, 1953. SECRETARY OF THE INTERIOR—Douglas McKay, of Oregon, January 21, 1953. Frederick A. Seaton, of Nebraska, June 6, 1956; entered upon duties June 8, 1956. SECRETARY OF AGRICULTURE—Ezra Taft Benson, of Utah, January 21, 1953. SECRETARY OF COMMERCE—Sinclair Weeks, of Massachusetts, January 21, 1953. SECRETARY OF LABOR—Martin P. Durkin, of Maryland, January 21, 1953. James P. Mitchell, of New Jersey, ad interim, October 9, 1953, to January 19, 1954. James P. Mitchell, of New Jersey, January 19, 1954. SECRETARY OF HEALTH, EDUCATION, AND WELFARE—Oveta Culp Hobby, of Texas, April 10, 1953; entered upon duties April 11, 1953. Marion B. Folsom, of New York, July 20, 1955; entered upon duties August 1, 1955.

83d Congress

1st Session: Jan. 3, 1953—Aug. 3, 1953; 2d Session: Jan. 6, 1954—Dec. 2, 1954.
President pro tempore of the Senate: Styles Bridges, of New Hampshire (elected Jan. 3, 1953). Speaker of the House: Joseph W. Martin, Jr., of Massachusetts (elected Jan. 3, 1953).

Senate: 48 Republican; 47 Democratic; 1 other
House: 221 Republican; 211 Democratic; 1 other

84th Congress

1st Session: Jan. 5, 1955–Aug. 2, 1955; 2d Session: Jan. 3, 1956–July 27, 1956..
President pro tempore of the Senate: Walter F. George, of Georgia (elected Jan. 5, 1955). Speaker of the House: Sam Rayburn, of Texas (elected Jan. 5, 1955).
Senate: 48 Democratic; 47 Republican; 1 other
House: 232 Democratic; 203 Republican

Second Administration of DWIGHT D. EISENHOWER

JANUARY 20, 1957, TO JANUARY 20, 1961

PRESIDENT—Dwight D. Eisenhower, of Pennsylvania (Republican). VICE-PRESIDENT—Richard M. Nixon, of California. SECRETARY OF STATE—John Foster Dulles, of New York, continued from preceding administration. Christian A. Herter, of Massachusetts, April 21, 1959; entered upon duties April 22, 1959. SECRETARY OF THE TREASURY—George M. Humphrey, of Ohio, continued from preceding administration. Robert Bernerd Anderson, of Connecticut, July 2, 1957; entered upon duties July 29, 1957. SECRETARY OF DEFENSE—Charles E. Wilson, of Michigan, continued from preceding administration. Neil H. McElroy, of Ohio, August 19, 1957; entered upon duties October 9, 1957. Thomas S. Gates, Jr., of Pennsylvania, ad interim, December 1, 1959, to January 26, 1960. Thomas S. Gates, Jr., of Pennsylvania, January 26, 1960. ATTORNEY GENERAL—Herbert Brownell, Jr., of New York, continued from preceding administration. William P. Rogers, of Maryland, ad interim, November 8, 1957, to January 27, 1958. William P. Rogers, of Maryland, January 27, 1958. POSTMASTER GENERAL—Arthur E. Summerfield, of Michigan, continued from preceding administration. Arthur E. Summerfield, of Michigan, recommissioned February 4, 1957. SECRETARY OF THE INTERIOR—Frederick A. Seaton, of Nebraska, continued from preceding administration. SECRETARY OF AGRICULTURE—Ezra Taft Benson, of Utah, continued from preceding administration. SECRETARY OF COMMERCE—Sinclair Weeks, of Massachusetts, continued from preceding administration. Lewis L. Strauss, of New York, ad interim, November 13, 1958, to June 27, 1959. Frederick H. Mueller, of Michigan (Under Secretary), ad interim, July 21, 1959, to August 6, 1959. Frederick H. Mueller, of Michigan, August 6, 1959. SECRETARY OF LABOR—James P. Mitchell, of New Jersey, continued from preceding administration. SECRETARY OF HEALTH, EDUCATION, AND WELFARE—Marion B. Folsom, of New York, continued from preceding administration. Arthur S. Flemming, of Ohio, July 9, 1958; entered upon duties August 1, 1958.

85th Congress

1st Session: Jan. 3, 1957–Aug. 30, 1957; 2d Session: Jan. 7, 1958–Aug. 24, 1958.
President pro tempore of the Senate: Carl Hayden, of Arizona (elected Jan. 3, 1957). Speaker of the House: Sam Rayburn, of Texas (reelected Jan. 3, 1957).
Senate: 49 Democratic; 47 Republican
House: 233 Democratic; 200 Republican

86th Congress

1st Session: Jan. 7, 1959–Sept. 15, 1959; 2d Session: Jan. 6, 1960–Sept. 1, 1960.
President pro tempore of the Senate: Carl Hayden, of Arizona (continued from preceding Congress). Speaker of the House: Sam Rayburn, of Texas (reelected Jan. 7, 1959).
Senate: 64 Democratic; 34 Republican
House: 283 Democratic; 153 Republican

Administration of JOHN F. KENNEDY

JANUARY 20, 1961, TO NOVEMBER 22, 1963

PRESIDENT—John F. Kennedy, of Massachusetts (Democratic) (died November 22, 1963). VICE-PRESIDENT—Lyndon B. Johnson, of Texas. SECRETARY OF STATE—Dean Rusk, of New York, January 20, 1961. SECRETARY OF THE TREASURY—C. Douglas Dillon, of Washington, D.C., January 20, 1961. SECRETARY OF DEFENSE—Robert S. McNamara, of Michigan, January 20, 1961. ATTORNEY GENERAL—Robert F. Kennedy, of Massachusetts, January 20, 1961. POSTMASTER GENERAL—J. Edward Day, of California, January 20, 1961, to August 9, 1963. John A. Gronouski of Wisconsin, September 10, 1963. SECRETARY OF THE INTERIOR—Stewart L. Udall, of Arizona, January 20, 1961. SECRETARY OF AGRICULTURE—Orville L. Freeman, of Minnesota, January 20, 1961. SECRETARY OF COMMERCE—Luther H. Hodges, of North Carolina, January 20, 1961. SECRETARY OF LABOR—Arthur J. Goldberg, of Washington, D.C., January 20, 1961. W. Willard Wirtz, of Illinois, September 25, 1962. SECRETARY OF HEALTH, EDUCATION, AND WELFARE—Abraham A. Ribicoff, of Connecticut, January 21, 1961, to July 13, 1962. Anthony J. Celebrezze, of Ohio, July 31, 1962.

First Administration of LYNDON B. JOHNSON
NOVEMBER 22, 1963, TO JANUARY 20, 1965

PRESIDENT—Lyndon B. Johnson, of Texas (Democratic). SECRETARY OF STATE—Dean Rusk, of New York, continued from preceding administration. SECRETARY OF THE TREASURY—C. Douglas Dillon, of Washington, D.C., continued from preceding administration. SECRETARY OF DEFENSE—Robert S. McNamara, of Michigan, continued from preceding administration. ATTORNEY GENERAL—Robert F. Kennedy, of Massachusetts, continued from preceding administration. Nicholas Katzenbach, of Illinois, ad interim, Sept. 4, 1964. POSTMASTER GENERAL—John S. Gronouski, of Wisconsin, continued from preceding administration. SECRETARY OF THE INTERIOR—Stewart L. Udall, of Arizona, continued from preceding administration. SECRETARY OF AGRICULTURE—Orville L. Freeman of Minnesota, continued from preceding administration. SECRETARY OF COMMERCE—Luther H. Hodges, of North Carolina, continued from preceding administration to January 15, 1965. John T. O'Connor, of New Jersey, January 15, 1965. SECRETARY OF LABOR—W. Willard Wirtz, of Illinois, continued from preceding administration. SECRETARY OF HEALTH, EDUCATION, AND WELFARE—Anthony J. Celebrezze, of Ohio, continued from preceding administration.

87th Congress

1st Session: Jan. 3, 1961—Sept. 27, 1961; 2d Session: Jan. 10, 1962—Oct. 13, 1962.

President pro tempore of the Senate: Carl Hayden, of Arizona (continued from preceding Congress). Speaker of the House: Sam Rayburn, of Texas (reelected Jan. 3, 1961); John W. McCormack, of Massachusetts (elected Jan. 10, 1962).

Senate: 65 Democratic; 35 Republican
House: 263 Democratic; 174 Republican

88th Congress

1st Session: Jan. 9, 1963—Dec. 30, 1963; 2d Session: Jan. 7, 1964—Oct. 3, 1964.

President pro tempore of the Senate: Carl Hayden, of Arizona (continued from preceding Congress). Speaker of the House: John W. McCormack (reelected Jan. 9, 1963).

Senate: 67 Democratic; 33 Republican
House: 258 Democratic; 177 Republican

Second Administration of LYNDON B. JOHNSON
JANUARY 20, 1965 TO JANUARY 20, 1969

PRESIDENT—Lyndon B. Johnson, of Texas (Democratic). VICE-PRESIDENT—Hubert H. Humphrey, of Minnesota. SECRETARY OF STATE—Dean Rusk, of New York, continued from preceding administration. SECRETARY OF THE TREASURY—C. Douglas Dillon, of Washington, D.C., continued from preceding administration to March 31, 1965. Henry H. Fowler, of Virginia, April 1, 1965 to December 20, 1968. Joseph W. Barr, of Indiana, December 23, 1968. SECRETARY OF DEFENSE—Robert S. McNamara, continued from preceding administration. Clark Clifford, of Maryland, January 19, 1968. ATTORNEY GENERAL—Nicholas Katzenbach, of Illinois, ad interim, continued from preceding administration, confirmed on Feb. 10, 1965. Ramsey Clark, of Texas, March 2, 1967. POSTMASTER GENERAL—John A. Gronouski, of Wisconsin, continued from preceding administration. Lawrence O'Brien, of Massachusetts, August 29, 1965, to April 10, 1968. Marvin Watson, of Texas, April 10, 1968. SECRETARY OF THE INTERIOR—Stewart L. Udall, of Arizona, continued from preceding administration. SECRETARY OF AGRICULTURE—Orville L. Freeman, of Minnesota, continued from preceding administration. SECRETARY OF COMMERCE—John T. O'Connor, of New Jersey, continued from preceding administration to January 18, 1967. Alexander B. Trowbridge, of New York, May 23, 1967, to February 16, 1968. C. R. Smith, of New York, March 1, 1968. SECRETARY OF LABOR—W. Willard Wirtz, of Illinois, continued from preceding administration. SECRETARY OF HEALTH, EDUCATION, AND WELFARE—Anthony J. Celebrezze, of Ohio, continued from preceding administration. John W. Gardner, of New York, July 27, 1965. Wilbur J. Cohen, of Michigan, May 16, 1968. SECRETARY OF HOUSING AND URBAN DEVELOPMENT—Robert C. Weaver, of Washington, D.C., January 18, 1966 to January 1, 1969. Robert C. Wood, of Massachusetts, January 2, 1969. SECRETARY OF TRANSPORTATION—Alan S. Boyd, of Florida, January 16, 1967.

89th Congress

1st Session: Jan. 4, 1965—Oct. 23, 1965; 2d Session: Jan. 10, 1966—Oct. 22, 1966.

President pro tempore of the Senate: Carl Hayden, of Arizona (continued from preceding Congress). Speaker of the House: John W. McCormack, of Massachusetts (reelected Jan. 4, 1965).

Senate: 68 Democratic; 32 Republican
House: 295 Democratic; 140 Republican

90th Congress

1st Session: Jan. 10, 1967—Dec. 15, 1967; 2d Session: Jan. 15, 1968—Oct. 14, 1968.

President pro tempore of the Senate: Carl Hayden, of Arizona (continued from preceding Congress). Speaker of the House: John W. McCormack, of Massachusetts (reelected Jan. 10, 1967).

Senate: 64 Democratic; 36 Republican
House: 248 Democratic; 187 Republican

First Administration of RICHARD M. NIXON
JANUARY 20, 1969, TO JANUARY 20, 1973

PRESIDENT—Richard M. Nixon, of California (Republican). VICE-PRESIDENT—Spiro T. Agnew, of Maryland. SECRETARY OF STATE—William P. Rogers, of New York, January 22, 1969. SECRETARY OF THE TREASURY—David M. Kennedy, of Illinois, January 22, 1969 to February 10, 1971. John B. Connally, of Texas, February 11, 1971. George P. Shultz of Illinois, June 12, 1972. SECRETARY OF DEFENSE—Melvin R. Laird, of Wisconsin, January 22, 1969. ATTORNEY GENERAL—John N. Mitchell, of New York, January 22, 1969. Richard G. Kleindienst, of Arizona, ad interim, Feb. 15, 1972; took office June 12, 1972. POSTMASTER GENERAL—Winton M. Blount, of Alabama, January 22, 1969 to July 1, 1971. This office was then abolished as a cabinet post. SECRETARY OF THE INTERIOR—Walter J. Hickel, of Alaska, January 23, 1969. Fred J. Russell, of California, ad interim, Nov. 26, 1970. Rogers C. B. Morton, of Maryland, Jan. 29, 1971. SECRETARY OF AGRICULTURE—Clifford M. Hardin, of Nebraska, Jan. 22, 1969. Earl L. Butz, of Indiana, Dec. 2, 1971. SECRETARY OF COMMERCE—Maurice H. Stans, of New York, Jan. 22, 1969. Peter G. Peterson, of Illinois, Feb. 21, 1972. SECRETARY OF LABOR—George P. Shultz, of New York, Jan. 22, 1969. James D. Hodgson, of California, July 2, 1970. SECRETARY OF HEALTH, EDUCATION, AND WELFARE—Robert H. Finch, of California, Jan. 22, 1969. Elliot L. Richardson, of Massachusetts, June 15, 1970. SECRETARY OF HOUSING AND URBAN DEVELOPMENT—George W. Romney, of Michigan, Jan. 22, 1969. SECRETARY OF TRANSPORTATION—John A. Volpe, of Massachusetts, Jan. 22, 1969.

91st Congress

1st Session: Jan. 3, 1969—Dec. 23, 1969; 2d Session: Jan. 19, 1970—Jan. 2, 1971.

President pro tempore of the Senate: Richard B. Russell, of Georgia (elected Jan. 3, 1969). Speaker of the House: John W. McCormack, of Massachusetts (reelected Jan. 3, 1969).

Senate: 57 Democratic; 43 Republican
House: 244 Democratic; 191 Republican

92d Congress

1st Session: Jan. 21, 1971—Dec. 17, 1971; 2d Session: Jan. 18, 1972—Oct. 18, 1972

President pro tempore of the Senate: James O. Eastland of Mississippi (elected July 28, 1972). (Richard B. Russell, continued from preceding Congress, died in office. Allen J. Ellender of Louisiana, who was elected Jan. 22, 1971, died in office.) Speaker of the House: Carl Albert, of Oklahoma (elected Jan. 21, 1971). Senate: 54 Democratic; 44 Republican; 1 Independent-Democratic; 1 Conservative-Republican.
House: 255 Democratic; 180 Republican

Second Administration of RICHARD M. NIXON
JANUARY 20, 1973, TO AUGUST 9, 1974

PRESIDENT—Richard M. Nixon, of California (Republican). Resigned August 9, 1974. VICE PRESIDENT—Spiro T. Agnew, of Maryland. Resigned October 10, 1973. Gerald R. Ford, Jr., of Michigan, December 6, 1973. SECRETARY OF STATE—William P. Rogers, of Maryland, continued from preceding administration. Kenneth Rush, of New York (Deputy Secretary of State), ad interim, September 4, 1973. Henry A. Kissinger, of the District of Columbia, September 21, 1973. SECRETARY OF THE TREASURY—George P. Shultz, of Illinois, continued from preceding administration. William E. Simon, of New Jersey, April 30, 1974. SECRETARY OF DEFENSE—Melvin R. Laird, of Wisconsin, continued from preceding administration. Elliot L. Richardson, of Massachusetts, January 29, 1973. William P. Clements, Jr., of Texas, ad interim, May 26, 1973. James R. Schlesinger, of Virginia, June 28, 1973. ATTORNEY GENERAL—Richard G. Kleindienst, of Arizona, continued from preceding administration. Elliot L. Richardson, of Massachusetts, May 23, 1973. Robert H. Bork, of Pennsylvania (Solicitor General), ad interim, October 20, 1973. William B. Saxbe, of Ohio, Feb. 4, 1974. SECRETARY OF THE INTERIOR—Rogers C. B. Morton, of Maryland, continued from preceding administration. SECRETARY OF AGRICULTURE—Earl L. Butz, of Indiana, continued from preceding administration. SECRETARY OF COMMERCE—Frederick B. Dent, of South Carolina, ad interim, Jan. 18, 1973; took office Feb. 2, 1973. SECRETARY OF LABOR—James D. Hodgson, of California, continued from preceding administration. Peter J. Brennan, of New York, January 31, 1973. SECRETARY OF HEALTH, EDUCATION, AND WELFARE—Elliot L. Richardson, of Massachusetts, continued from preceding administration. Caspar W. Weinberger, of California, February 8, 1973. SECRETARY OF HOUSING AND URBAN DEVELOPMENT—George Romney, of Michigan, continued from preceding administration. James T. Lynn, of Ohio, January 31, 1973. SECRETARY OF TRANSPORTATION—John A. Volpe, of Massachusetts, continued from preceding administration.

Claude S. Brinegar, of California, January 18, 1973.

93rd Congress

1st Session: Jan. 3, 1973-Dec. 22, 1973; 2nd Session: Jan. 21, 1974-Dec. 20, 1974.

President pro tempore of the Senate: James O. Eastland of Mississippi (continued from preceding Congress). Speaker of the House: Carl Albert, of Oklahoma (continued from preceding Congress).

Senate: 56 Democratic; 42 Republican; 1 Conservative-Republican; 1 Independent

House: 244 Democratic; 191 Republican; 1 Independent

Administration of GERALD R. FORD, JR.

AUGUST 9, 1974 TO JANUARY 20, 1977

PRESIDENT—Gerald R. Ford, Jr., of Michigan. VICE PRESIDENT—Nelson A. Rockefeller, of New York, December 19, 1974. SECRETARY OF STATE—Henry A. Kissinger, of the District of Columbia, continued from preceding administration. SECRETARY OF THE TREASURY—William E. Simon, of New Jersey, continued from preceding administration. SECRETARY OF DEFENSE—James R. Schlesinger, of Virginia, continued from preceding administration. Donald H. Rumsfeld, of Illinois, November 18, 1975. ATTORNEY GENERAL—William B. Saxbe, of Ohio, continued from preceding administration. Edward H. Levi, of Illinois, February 5, 1975. SECRETARY OF THE INTERIOR—Rogers C.B. Morton, of Maryland, continued from preceding administration. D. Kent Frizzell, of Kansas (Solicitor), ad interim, May 1, 1975. Stanley K. Hathaway of Wyoming, June 11, 1975. D. Kent Frizzell, of Kansas (Solicitor), ad interim, July 25, 1975. Thomas S. Kleppe, of North Dakota, October 9, 1975. SECRETARY OF AGRICULTURE—Earl L. Butz, of Indiana, continued from preceding administration. John A. Knebel, of Oklahoma, ad interim, October 4, 1976. John A. Knebel, November 5, 1976. SECRETARY OF COMMERCE—Frederick B. Dent, of South Carolina, continued from preceding administration. John K. Tabor, of Pennsylvania (Under Secretary), ad interim, March 12, 1975. Rogers C.B. Morton, of Maryland, April 25, 1975. Elliot L. Richardson, of Massachusetts, December 11, 1975. SECRETARY OF LABOR—Peter J. Brennan, of New York, continued from preceding administration. John T. Dunlop, of Massachusetts, March 6, 1975. Willie J. Usery, Jr., of Georgia, February 4, 1976. SECRETARY OF HEALTH, EDUCATION, AND WELFARE—Caspar W. Weinberger, of California, continued from preceding administration. Forrest David Mathews, of Alabama, June 26, 1975. SECRETARY OF HOUSING AND URBAN DEVELOPMENT—James T. Lynn, of Ohio, continued from preceding administration. Carla A. Hills, of California, March 5, 1975. SECRETARY OF TRANSPORTATION—Claude S. Brinegar, of California, continued from preceding administration. William T. Coleman, Jr., of Pennsylvania, March 3, 1975.

94th Congress

1st Session: Jan. 14, 1975-Dec. 19, 1975; 2nd Session: Jan. 19, 1976-Oct. 1, 1976.

President pro tempore of the Senate: James O. Eastland, of Mississippi (continued from preceding Congress). Speaker of the House: Carl Albert, of Oklahoma (continued from preceding Congress).

Senate: 61 Democratic; 37 Republican; 1 Conservative-Republican; 1 Independent

House: 291 Democratic; 144 Republican

Administration of JIMMY CARTER

FROM JANUARY 20, 1977

PRESIDENT—Jimmy (James E.) Carter, of Georgia. VICE PRESIDENT—Walter F. Mondale, of Minnesota. SECRETARY OF STATE—Cyrus R. Vance, of New York, January 23, 1977. SECRETARY OF THE TREASURY—W. Michael Blumenthal, of Michigan, January 23, 1977. G. William Miller, of Oklahoma, August 6, 1979. SECRETARY OF DEFENSE—Harold Brown, of California, January 21, 1977. ATTORNEY GENERAL—Griffin B. Bell, of Georgia, January 26, 1977. Benjamin R. Civiletti, of Maryland, August 16, 1979. SECRETARY OF THE INTERIOR—Cecil R. Andrus, of Idaho, January 23, 1977. SECRETARY OF AGRICULTURE—Robert S. Bergland, of Minnesota, January 23, 1977. SECRETARY OF COMMERCE—Juanita M. Kreps, of North Carolina, January 23, 1977. SECRETARY OF LABOR—F. Ray Marshall, of Texas, January 27, 1977. SECRETARY OF HEALTH, EDUCATION, AND WELFARE—Joseph A. Califano, Jr., of the District of Columbia, January 25, 1977. Patricia R. Harris, of the District of Columbia, August 3, 1979. (On Sept. 27, 1979 Congress gave final approval to a bill establishing a cabinet-level Department of Education; the Department of Health, Education and Welfare is to be renamed the Department of Health and Human Resources) SECRETARY OF HOUSING AND URBAN DEVELOPMENT—Patricia R. Harris, of the District of Columbia, January 23, 1977. Moon Landrieu, of Louisiana, September 24, 1979. SECRETARY OF TRANSPORTATION—Brockman Adams, of Washington, January 23, 1977. Neil E. Goldschmidt, of Oregon, August 15, 1979. SECRETARY OF ENERGY—James R. Schlesinger, of Virginia, August 5, 1977. Charles W. Duncan of Texas, August 24, 1979.

95th Congress

1st Session: Jan. 4, 1977-Dec. 15, 1977; 2nd Session: Jan. 19, 1978-Oct. 15, 1978

President pro tempore of the Senate: James O. Eastland, of Mississippi (continued from preceding Congress). Deputy President pro tempore of the Senate: Hubert H. Humphrey,[1] of Minnesota. Speaker of the House: Thomas P. O'Neill, Jr., of Massachusetts.

Senate: 61 Democratic; 38 Republican; 1 Independent
House: 290 Democratic; 145 Republican

96th Congress

1st Session: January 15, 1979

President pro tempore of the Senate: Warren G. Magnuson, of Washington. Speaker of the House: Thomas P. O'Neill, Jr., of Massachusetts. Senate: 58 Democratic; 41 Republican; 1 Independent. House: 276 Democratic; 159 Republican.

[1]Office of Deputy President pro tempore was established January 5, 1977, pursuant to Senate Resolution 17, Ninety-fifth Congress. This office no longer exists since the death of Hubert H. Humphrey, Jan. 13, 1978.

LINCOLN'S GETTYSBURG ADDRESS

Four score and seven years ago our fathers brought forth on this continent, a new nation, conceived in Liberty, and dedicated to the proposition that all men are created equal.

Now we are engaged in a great civil war, testing whether that nation, or any nation so conceived and so dedicated, can long endure. We are met on a great battle-field of that war. We have come to dedicate a portion of that field, as a final resting place for those who here gave their lives that that nation might live. It is altogether fitting and proper that we should do this.

But, in a larger sense, we can not dedicate—we can not consecrate—we can not hallow—this ground. The brave men, living and dead, who struggled here, have consecrated it, far above our poor power to add or detract. The world will little note, nor long remember what we say here, but it can never forget what they did here. It is for us the living, rather, to be dedicated here to the unfinished work which they who fought here have thus far so nobly advanced. It is rather for us to be here dedicated to the great task remaining before us—that from these honored dead we take increased devotion to that cause for which they gave the last full measure of devotion—that we here highly resolve that these dead shall not have died in vain—that this nation, under God, shall have a new birth of freedom—and that government of the people, by the people, for the people, shall not perish from the earth.

THE PRESIDENTIAL BIOGRAPHIES

George Washington

George Washington, 1st President (1789–1797), son of Augustine and Mary (Ball) Washington, was born on February 22, 1732, in Westmoreland County, Virginia. Of a family that migrated from England in 1658, George's father was a moderately well-to-do planter. He died when George was 11, and young Washington was brought up by his half-brother, Lawrence, whom he idolized and who took over the estate and functioned as a surrogate father.

George received a simple education at the parish church and at 16 entered the employ of Lord Thomas Fairfax as a land surveyor. Adept at mathematics and athletics, Washington in surveying Fairfax's vast holdings in mountainous western Virginia, learned to live in the wilderness, govern his helpers, and maintain accurate survey records on which land titles were based. In 1752, Lawrence Washington died. George inherited a share of Lawrence's lands, and he was commissioned (1753) a major and put in charge of training militia in southern Virginia. He immediately began to study histories of wars and books on military tactics.

Soon after, Washington emerged into public view when he volunteered for a hazardous and vital mission. Governor Robert Dinwiddie of Virginia was eager to warn the French that they must withdraw their troops from the Ohio River Valley, which the British hoped to settle. Bearing Dinwiddie's message, Washington, prudent and an excellent horseman, led a small party through the snow-covered wilderness to the successful completion of the mission.

At 22, Washington was promoted to lieutenant colonel as the French and Indian Wars commenced and was assigned as aide to British General Edward Braddock, a respected professional soldier, who led a disastrous expedition against the French at Fort Duquesne. Washington's personal skill in the battle was widely praised, and he was appointed (1755) colonel and entrusted with the defense of Virginia's 350-mile western frontier. At his urging, a new attack was made upon Fort Duquesne, and he again distinguished himself by capturing the French stronghold. With the French retreating into Canada, the fighting ceased, and Washington, now the most famous American-born soldier, retired to private life.

At Mount Vernon, which initially he leased from Lawrence's widow, he became at the age of 26, a country gentleman and successful businessman. He also commenced his political career by serving from 1759 to 1774 as a member of Virginia's House of Burgesses. This legislative background stood him well. A leader in opposition to British policy, Washington was a delegate to the First Continental Congress (1774-75) and, with the outbreak of the Revolutionary War, he was named commander-in-chief of the Continental forces.

Beset with obstacles seldom faced by military commanders, Washington described his troops as "raw militia, badly officered, and with no government." Since his troops preferred short-term enlistments and summer fighting to winter, he seldom commanded 10,000 men at one time. Weak in power, Congress supported Washington poorly, sometimes leaving him without adequate funds to pay his troops. Many subordinate officers were preoccupied with jealousies and intrigues.

Yet by ingenious retreats and thrusts, Washington kept his army afield, survived defeat at Germantown, a cruel winter at Valley Forge, and built up an able force that entrapped Cornwallis's army at Yorktown and forced its surrender. Washington emerged from the Revolution as the unrivaled hero and symbol of the new nation.

In 1783, he again retired to Mount Vernon, where life was pleasantly calm. However, by 1786, he like other leaders was distressed by the weaknesses of American government under the Articles of Confederation. When the Constitutional Convention gathered at Philadelphia in 1787, Washington received a hero's welcome as head of the Virginia delegation, and he was promptly elected president of the convention. In fashioning a strong Presidency, the convention, Pierce Butler wrote, "cast their eyes toward General Washington . . ."

After the Constitution was ratified, the first Electoral College met on February 4, 1789, and unanimously elected Washington President. On April 30, he was inaugurated at Federal Hall, in New York City, the capital. "I walk on untrodden ground," Washington said soon after beginning his new responsibilities. "There is scarcely any part of my conduct that may not hereafter be drawn into precedent."

Facing times that overflowed with crises, Washington left the republic far stronger and more confident than when he took office. An output of measures, highly impressive by today's standards, flowed from his administration. The Revolutionary debts of the states were assumed by the national government, a national currency was issued, and a Bank of the United States established to provide credit. Manufacture and trade were promoted by tariffs and bounties; inventions were protected by patent and copyright laws. A postal system was established; national security was improved by the reorganization of the army and the navy, the founding of West Point, and the construction of fortifications on the eastern seaboard and in the West. In the development of many of these measures, Washington was aided by his brilliant Secretary of the Treasury, Alexander Hamilton.

Hamilton's advocacy of a Bank of the United States touched off a dispute with Secretary of State Thomas Jefferson and Attorney General Edmund Randolph, who considered the bank unconstitutional because express authorization was not provided in the fundamental law. Washington sided with Hamilton, who argued that the national government could use all powers, except those denied by the Constitution. Time and again, where the Constitution was unclear, Washington exercised executive authority.

The President truly dominated the executive branch. With few exceptions, he prescribed the duties of his department heads and kept abreast of daily detail. So confident was he of his mastery that he brought together two of the most gifted and assertive department heads the nation has ever known—Jefferson and Hamilton. Washington succeeded outstandingly, where many of his successors have failed, in relations with Congress. He converted his popularity into major laws without tarnishing his prestige in political struggles. He prized the intrinsic dignity of the Presidency and gave the office a regal quality.

In 1793, Washington was reelected again by a unanimous electoral vote; his second term was to be more difficult than the first. War now raged between England and France, growing out of the French Revolution. Hamilton and Jefferson, in conflict over domestic questions, were also bitterly divided over the war. Each led a party reflecting his views: Hamilton—the Federalists, Jefferson—the Anti-Federalists (Democratic-Republicans). Hamilton's party sympathized with Britain and Jefferson's with France. As usual, Washington tried to be a moderating influence between his two strong secretaries. In weighing policy toward the war, he found convenience in meeting with all his secretaries simultaneously; and the institution known as the Cabinet was born.

On April 22, 1793, Washington issued a neutrality proclamation calling for "conduct friendly and impartial" to the warring nations. American vessels were barred from carrying war supplies to the belligerents. When the French minister to the United States, Citizen Genêt, attempted to outfit warships in American ports and to send them against the British, Washington requested that France recall its representative, because of his threat to American neutrality.

American relations with Britain also were badly deteriorating. British warships intercepted United States' vessels bearing food supplies to France, seizing their cargoes and impressing their seamen into the British navy. The British also refused to give up western frontier forts as they were obligated to under the treaty ending the Revolutionary War; instead, they stirred up the Indians in the surrounding area. To resolve these prickly questions, Washington dispatched Chief Justice John Jay to Britain. The resulting Jay Treaty dealt with trade and the frontier forts, but not with Britain's halting of American ships and seizure of seamen. Senate consideration of the treaty occasioned a bitter fight between the Federalists who supported it and the Anti-Federalists. Hostile newspapers called for Washington's impeachment. And some denounced him as an aristocrat and an enemy of true democracy. The Senate eventually approved the treaty.

In 1794, Washington demonstrated that he could enforce federal laws in the states when he put down the Whisky Rebellion by dispatching troops against farmers in western Pennsylvania who refused to pay federal taxes on whisky.

Declining to serve a third term, Washington issued his Farewell Address in 1796, announcing his retirement and warning against "permanent alliances" with foreign powers. Washington had gotten the U.S. Presidency off to a strong start, perhaps most fundamentally because of the bold, enterprising view he took of his office and his inspiring personal qualities. Washington retired to Mount Vernon, where he died on December 14, 1799.

John Adams

John Adams, 2d President (1797–1801), was born October 30, 1735, in Braintree (now Quincy), Massachusetts. The son of a Puritan farmer, Adams was graduated (1755) from Harvard College. After teaching briefly, he read law, was admitted (1758) to the bar.

An opponent of the Stamp Act, he was elected (1771) to the Massachusetts colonial legislature. There he steadily resisted British colonial policies and in 1774, just prior to the American Revolution, he was chosen a delegate to the First Continental Congress. At the Second Continental Congress (1775), he pressed for American independence and persuaded Congress to organize the Continental Army and to appoint George Washington as commander-in-chief. Adams helped draft and defend the Declaration of Independence amid turbulent Congressional debates.

In 1778 Adams was dispatched to Paris to build ties between France and the struggling new nation, but his impatience, ready candor, and pride served him ill in diplomacy, and he returned home. A year later, he was elected to the convention that prepared the important Massachusetts state constitution. He returned (1780) to diplomacy as minister to the Netherlands, where he won recognition for the United States and, more important, negotiated a loan. With John Jay and Benjamin Franklin, Adams negotiated (1782) the Treaty of Paris with Great Britain that ended the American Revolution. Three years later, Congress named him the first United States minister to Britain. He was rebuffed by the British, and in 1788 he asked to be recalled.

Soon after his return to America, he was elected Vice-President under George Washington. Despite his characterization of his new post as "the most insignificant office that ever the invention of man contrived or his imagination conceived," Adams was a constructive influence in filling his duties in the Senate.

When Washington declined (1796) to serve a third Presidential term, the Federalists, led by Alexander Hamilton, supported Adams for the Presidency, while the Democratic-Republicans turned to Thomas Jefferson. Adams won by three votes.

At the outset, Adams stressed that his Presidency would be an extension of Washington's. He retained his predecessor's entire cabinet and, in his inaugural address, promised to continue the Washington policies. Despite these reassurances, Federalists became distrustful when Adams, deeming it necessary to improve relations with France, offered the ministry to that country to Jefferson.

When Jefferson declined, Adams was on the point of conferring the post upon another Democratic-Republican leader, James Madison. However, a cabinet upheaval loomed over the step, and Adams reconsidered. Although President, Adams was not leader of his party. Alexander Hamilton, who held no government post was the Federalist leader, and the loyalties of some cabinet members ran to him rather than to Adams.

The central problems and policies of the Adams administration derived from the French Revolution and the ensuing war between France and Britain. Both countries claimed the right to seize American vessels, and the French Directory went so far as to declare that all Americans serving on British vessels were pirates. Adams sought to steer a middle course between Hamilton and his strong partiality toward Britain and Jefferson's similar disposition toward France.

The President called Congress into special session to consider ways of keeping peace. To his cabinet he distributed a series of questions on the Franco-British situation, seeking advice before framing his message to Congress. The questions were leaked to Hamilton, who prepared replies that were submitted through the cabinet to Adams, who accepted their substance, proposing that defenses be strengthened.

Simultaneously, the President dispatched ministers to France to arrange a treaty. The French representatives demanded a bribe and a loan, touching off the sensational episode that became known as the XYZ Affair. Adams again asked his cabinet for advice, and again Hamilton surreptitiously supplied it, proposing a more vigorous policy toward France and closer ties with Britain. Adams accepted the former, but not the latter. Congress responded with actions just short of war, by declaring all treaties with France null and void, creating a Navy Department, and increasing the army and authorizing new ships.

Eager to keep peace, Adams moved to restore diplomatic relations with France. (Adams first nominated W. Vans Murray to become minister to France. The President acted without consulting the cabinet, which enraged the Hamiltonians in it. Federalists in the Senate raised various objections as a prelude to rejecting it. In a bold move, Adams replaced the Murray nomination with the proposal of a three-member peace commission. The step brought press and public opinion so strongly to the President's side that the commission was approved.) Fearful of an Anglo-American alliance, the French this time were cooperative and war was averted. Adams achieved his supreme goal of maintaining peace, but at the high price of alienating his ardently pro-British Federalist party.

In 1798, smarting under criticism of their opposition to France, the Federalists passed the repressive Alien and Sedition laws that were designed to limit and punish criticism of the government and its officers. Adams neither supported the laws' passage nor applied them. Nevertheless, anti-Federalist journalists were arrested and sentiment turned against the administration.

His successful avoidance of war with France alienated Federalist leaders who deemed Adams a traitor to his party. Jefferson, leader of the Democratic-Republicans, observed that the followers of Hamilton were only "a little less hostile" to Adams than to himself. After long, calculated delay, Adams dealt with his cabinet secretaries who, in effect, were Hamilton's spies. One, James McHenry, resigned after a stormy confrontation with Adams, and another, Timothy Pickering, was dismissed.

Without a party behind him, Adams made a poor showing in seeking reelection in 1800. Both Jefferson and Aaron Burr exceeded him in electoral votes (73 each), while Adams received 65. The election was ultimately decided by the House of Representatives.

So aggrieved was Adams by his defeat that he refused to remain in Washington for Jefferson's inauguration and returned home to Quincy. Subsequently the two Presidents—Jefferson and Adams—renewed their friendship. Adams lived longer than any other President, dying on July 4, 1826, a few months before his 91st birthday.

Thomas Jefferson

Thomas Jefferson, 3d President (1801–1809), was born at Shadwell in Goochland County, Virginia, on April 13, 1743. His father was a planter, scholar, militia colonel, and a member of the House of Burgesses; his mother was a Virginia Randolph. Something of Jefferson's democratic impulse doubtless derived from the frontier influences of the Blue Ridge region in which he was reared. Educated by tutors and in local schools, Jefferson studied at William and Mary College, from which he was graduated (1762).

After leaving college, Jefferson studied law under George Wythe and was admitted (1767) to the bar. His practice was soon very successful, and in 1769, his political career began with his election to the House of Burgesses, in which he served until 1774. Not a brilliant speaker (later, as President, he abandoned the practice of delivering Congressional messages in person), Jefferson was brilliant at drafting laws and resolutions. As relations with the British deteriorated, Jefferson on the eve of the Revolution was a busy draftsman of protest documents. A triumph of revolutionary logic was his pamphlet "A Summary View of the Rights of British America," printed in 1774.

A year later, Jefferson was sent as a delegate to the Continental Congress. Always standing with those who were resolved to resist Great Britain, he was deputed to draft the Declaration of Independence, which with few changes Congress adopted on July 4, 1776.

Two months later, Jefferson resigned from Congress and returned to the Virginia House of Delegates, in which he served until 1779 when he was elected governor of Virginia, succeeding Patrick Henry. Disinclined toward the military life, he did not fight in the Revolutionary War. As a Virginia lawmaker, Jefferson was a powerful democratizing influence who moved his state away from virtual control by a few wealthy slaveholders. By amendment of the Virginia land laws, he effected a more equitable land distribution, which was the key to voting rights and educational opportunity. Even more important were his bills to assure religious freedom. Although he failed in his attempt to pass laws that would have gradually abolished slavery in Virginia, he remained opposed to that institution.

Jefferson resigned (1781) as governor, believing that the British army's threat to his state necessitated a military man to serve as chief executive. During a brief interval of private life, Jefferson began writing his *Notes on Virginia*, an extended statement of his beliefs.

He served (1784–89) in several diplomatic assignments and replaced Benjamin Franklin as minister to France. Jefferson sympathized openly with the French Revolution, believing it similar in essence to the American rebellion. His wide travel in Europe broadened his interests, particularly in architecture and agriculture.

Jefferson was abroad and did not participate in the Constitutional Convention of 1787, but his influence was felt in the quick preparation of the Bill of Rights; its omission from the original Constitution he had considered intolerable. He served as Secretary of State in Washington's first administration.

Jefferson was soon sharply at odds with the Secretary of the Treasury, Alexander Hamilton. After supporting several of Hamilton's early financial measures for the sake of unity, Jefferson, preferring an agricultural society, opposed Hamilton's plans to encourage manufacturing and trade and to found a national bank. In resisting Hamilton's broad interpretation of the Constitution to justify these measures, Jefferson advocated states' rights and "strict construction" of the Constitution, limiting the federal government's powers to those that the document specifically granted. Jefferson and Hamilton fought bitterly over foreign policy. Jefferson and the "Democratic-Republicans" who gathered as a party around him (and who were precursors of today's Democratic party) favored France, while Hamilton and the Federalists favored England. Late in 1793 their differences became so acute that Jefferson resigned.

He was elected (1796) Vice-President, with the Federalist John Adams as President. After four years of bitter party strife, Jefferson was elected (1800) President. His Vice-Presidential running mate, Aaron Burr, received the same number of electoral votes, and the election was referred to the House of Representatives. Thanks to the intervention of Hamilton, who advised Federalists to support Jefferson, the sage of Monticello won.

The first President to be inaugurated in Washington, Jefferson quickly set an example of simplicity. His inaugural address was an appeal for bipartisan cooperation—"We are all Republicans —we are all Federalists"—and his conception of government was largely negative, in the sense that he believed the federal government should deal chiefly with foreign affairs, leaving local matters to the states. Jefferson's view was that government should restrain men from harming one another, but otherwise leave them to their own concerns. Federal expenditures should be curtailed and excise taxes repealed.

Although Jefferson appointed followers such as James Madison as Secretary of State and Albert Gallatin as Secretary of the Treasury, he found the lesser offices, the infant bureaucracy, filled with Federalists. Noting that vacancies "by death are few; by resignations none," Jefferson foreshadowed the spoils system by replacing some Federalists in lesser offices with Democratic-Republicans. He refused to honor the Federalist appointment of "midnight judges" in the outgoing Adams' administration. Near the close of his Presidential tenure, Republicans held a majority of executive-branch appointments.

Through his party, Jefferson exerted strong control over Congress and accomplished the repeal of major Federalist statutes, including the Judiciary Act of 1801. His action was rebuked in *Marbury* v. *Madison*, the principle of which was that the Supreme Court may invalidate an act of Congress; Jefferson never accepted this principle. In pardoning those convicted of violating the Alien and Sedition laws, he asserted Presidential power over Congressional law. Heartily approving the use of the impeachment power against partisan Federalist judges, he was regretful of its failure when it was directed against Justice Samuel Chase, who had been impeached (1804) for discrimination against Jeffersonians.

The extraordinary diplomatic achievement of Jefferson's Presidency was the Louisiana Purchase (1803), which was negotiated by Robert Livingston and James Monroe. The temptation of acquiring a vast territory under favorable terms and of protecting the Mississippi's freedom of navigation overwhelmed Jefferson's devotion to strict Constitutional construction. Observing later that he "stretched the Constitution till it cracked," Jefferson submitted the purchase treaty to the Senate which readily approved it.

Jefferson was unsuccessful in seeking to acquire West Florida, chiefly because his lack of candor offended Congress. His reliance on diplomacy collapsed against the depredations of the Barbary pirates off North Africa. Ultimately, he dispatched a naval force and blockaded ports, and later he ordered frigates into action against the sultan of Morocco.

Aided by economic prosperity as well as political achievement, Jefferson was reelected in 1804 by an overwhelming majority. A major event in the second term was the trial of former Vice-President Aaron Burr, who was suspected by Jefferson of having politicked for the Presidency and now was accused of treasonable plottings. Burr's trial became a contest of wits between Jefferson and Chief Justice John Marshall. The latter's definition of treason made Burr's conviction impossible, to Jefferson's disgust.

Jefferson's diplomatic skill at peace-keeping was severely tested by the pressures of European war upon American neutrality. The Napoleonic decrees, British impressment of American seamen, and the audacity of a British frigate in firing on the United States' *Chesapeake*, combined to drive Jefferson to issue a proclamation denying British armed vessels the hospitality of United States waters.

In December 1807, Jefferson forced the Embargo Act through Congress; it prohibited exporting any produce from an American port or sailing any American ship to a foreign port. Enforcement of the act cast the administration in the role of exercising arbitrary power against key rights of the individual. Ironically, the exigencies of the Presidency brought Jefferson to violate the very values with which he was so long and so thoroughly identified—the sanctity of individual rights against governmental encroachment.

The embargo fell more heavily and injuriously upon the United States than upon France and England. Idle ships, unsold goods, and commercial unemployment fired opposition in New England, embittered the sections most loyal to Jefferson, and brought Congress to rebel against the President. Ultimately, Jefferson retreated by approving the Non-Intercourse Act of 1809 under which the embargo was partially raised.

Despite the rocky conclusion of his tenure, Jefferson handpicked his successor, Madison. He retired to Monticello, pursued scientific farming, counseled Presidents Madison and Monroe, and kept in touch with public affairs through a large correspondence. He died on July 4, 1826, on the same day as John Adams and on the 50th anniversary of the adoption of the Declaration of Independence.

James Madison

James Madison, 4th President (1809–1817), was born on March 16, 1751, in Port Conway, Virginia, the son of a planter and justice of the peace, whose forebears had settled in Virginia in the 1600s. A frail and sickly child, Madison was educated by private tutors and graduated (1771) from the College of New Jersey (now Princeton). A year of postgraduate study there was devoted to Hebrew, history, and law.

Torn between the ministry and politics, he chose the latter and was elected (1774) to the Committee of Safety in Orange County, Virginia, an important organ of local government in the twilight of the colonial period. In 1776, Madison was a delegate to the Williamsburg convention that declared for independence and established a state government. Serving in Virginia's first legislative assembly, Madison met Thomas Jefferson and began a lifelong friendship. In 1778, Madison was a member of the executive council, and in 1779 the state legislature elected him to the Continental Congress.

Until 1788, Madison served either in the Virginia legislature or in Congress, where he quickly became convinced that the Continental Congress needed more power, particularly in financial affairs. Although only 36 years old, Madison represented (1787) Virginia at the Constitutional Convention in Philadelphia and took a leading part in the deliberations. Champion of a strong central government, he drafted the "Virginia Plan" on which the Constitution was based. Known as the "Father of the Constitution," Madison kept a journal of the convention—the most complete record available of the proceedings—and his knowledge of past governments and the inherent problems of federalism was invaluable. Madison was a member of the Virginia ratifying convention and, with John Jay and Alexander Hamilton, wrote The Federalist, a series of newspaper essays that are regarded as the best explanation of the American constitutional system.

In 1789, Madison defeated James Monroe for election to the new U.S. House of Representatives. One of its most able members, Madison drafted key legislation and played a leading part in preparing the first 10 amendments to the Constitution, known as the Bill of Rights. Soon convinced that Hamilton's policies were hurtful to farmers in the South and West, Madison joined Jefferson in founding the Democratic-Republican party. In 1797, Madison retired, briefly, from politics; however, outraged by the repressive Alien and Sedition Acts (1798), he drafted the Virginia Resolutions, condemning the acts and holding that the states could declare them unconstitutional.

Upon becoming President in 1801, Jefferson appointed Madison Secretary of State. He passed a busy apprenticeship in an administration that, like his own would be, was preoccupied with foreign affairs and the problems of European war. In 1808, after two Presidential terms, Jefferson, following the tradition of George Washington, declined a third term. He chose Madison to be his successor. Madison received 122 electoral votes to 47 for Federalist C. C. Pinckney.

Small and unimpressive in person, Madison at his inaugural, wrote Washington Irving, looked like "a withered little apple-John."

In its early months, Madison's administration was largely an inherited Presidency. He made no changes in Jefferson's cabinet, except to move Robert Smith from the Navy to the State Department. The cabinet, however, had an additional heritage, an old feud between Smith and Treasury Secretary Albert Gallatin. Eventually, Madison dismissed Smith and made Monroe his Secretary of State.

The war between Britain and France was continuing as were their depredations upon American shipping, despite Jefferson's policy of neutrality. In 1810, an act of Congress called for the resumption of trade with both France and Britain, but warned of American withdrawal if either power resumed shipping violations. France soon began such violations, and Britain stirred up the Indians in the West. In the House of Representatives, "hawks" such as Henry Clay and John Calhoun clamored for a war which, they believed would result in the annexation of Canada and Spanish Florida. New England was opposed to war; the rest of the nation demanded it; ultimately Madison called for war against Great Britain, and Congress declared it on June 18, 1812.

Later that year Madison was reelected President by 128 electoral votes to 89 for Mayor De Witt Clinton of New York City.

Both by his contemporaries and by historians, Madison is not rated as a good war President. Calhoun wrote of him, "Our President though a man of amiable manners and great talents has not I fear those commanding talents, which are necessary to control those about him." Madison was handicapped by poor field commanders and by acute sectional and factional differences. Northern Republicans hobbled his efforts to seize the remainder of the Floridas, and Southern Republicans were unenthusiastic about conquering Canada. Each party faction feared that out of conquered territory might come new states favoring the other. Federalists generally opposed "Mr. Madison's War."

In its early stage the war went badly for the United States. For two years, every thrust into Canada was foiled. Britain clamped a tight blockade upon the eastern coast. On August 24, 1814, British forces occupied and burned Washington, and the Madisons fled the White House. But then American fortunes brightened. A British thrust down Lake Champlain was repulsed, and Andrew Jackson won a thrilling victory at New Orleans. In the Treaty of Ghent, however, signed December 24, 1814, not a single U.S. war aim was achieved. At Madison's direction, the demand upon Britain to renounce impressments was dropped. The only demand imposed was that Britain leave occupied American territory.

The war's close saw the decline of the Federalist party, a decline speeded by Madison's adopting its key principles. He approved a new bank of the United States, a tariff act of 1816 to protect "infant industries," and the establishment of substantial military and naval forces on a permanent basis. However, Madison did not accept the Federalist plank of internal domestic improvements to be undertaken by the national government. Such ventures, he thought, necessitated a constitutional amendment.

After leaving the Presidency, Madison lived in retirement on his estate at Montpelier, Virginia. He was a member of the Virginia Constitutional Convention of 1829 and occasionally offered counsel to his successor, James Monroe. Madison died at Montpelier on June 28, 1836, and is buried nearby.

James Monroe

James Monroe, 5th President (1817–1825), was born April 28, 1758, in Westmoreland County, Virginia, the eldest of five children of a circuit judge and planter. A student at William and Mary College when the Revolution broke out, Monroe joined the army, fought in major battles, and was wounded at Harlem Heights in New York and at the Battle of Trenton.

After the Revolution, Monroe studied law under Thomas Jefferson, then the governor of Virginia, and an important friendship between the two began. Monroe's political career commenced with his election (1780) to the Virginia legislature. Three years later he was elected to the Continental Congress, in which he opposed a highly centralized government but supported tariff-making by Congress. In 1786, he returned from Congress to serve in the Virginia Assembly.

Monroe was a state delegate to the Virginia convention that was called to ratify the new U.S. Constitution. So strong was his admiration for Jefferson that he moved to Charlottesville, Virginia, where he built Ash Lawn, not far from Jefferson's estate, Monticello.

Monroe ran unsuccessfully against James Madison for the first U.S. House of Representatives; however, the Virginia legislature elected him (1790) to the U.S. Senate. Allied with Jefferson and Madison, Monroe opposed the centralizing policies of Alexander Hamilton and, aided by Albert Gallatin and Aaron Burr, shared in the founding of the Democratic-Republican party. In 1794, Washington appointed Monroe minister to France, a country he deeply admired. He criticized Jay's (Anglo-American) Treaty so severely, however, that Washington, with whom he had previously clashed, recalled him in 1796.

From 1799 to 1802, Monroe was governor of Virginia. During Jefferson's Presidency, he was dispatched (1802) to Paris to help Robert R. Livingston arrange the Louisiana Purchase; the next year in Spain he aided in the unsuccessful negotiations for the purchase of the Floridas. In 1803 Jefferson named Monroe minister to Britain. From 1811 to 1816, he was Madison's Secretary of State.

In 1816, Monroe was elected President, winning easily over his Federalist opponent, Senator Rufus King of New York. He was reelected in 1820, with only one electoral vote cast against him.

Monroe's Presidency coincided with "the era of good feeling." After the election of 1816, the Federalist party disappeared and the Democratic-Republicans flourished as the country's only party. Thanks to fast developing industry and western settlement, the country prospered. Not even the depression of 1818 dampened the good feeling.

Few disturbing domestic political issues troubled Monroe's first Presidential years. He opposed "the American System" of House Speaker Henry Clay, who demanded internal domestic improvements and a protective tariff. A strict constructionist, Monroe in his first annual message declared that Congress lacked the constitutional power to establish a system of internal improvements. Subsequently, however, he modified his position by granting an appropriation to repair the Cumberland Road and approving the first harbor act. He also approved the 1824 tariff act and moved to a middle-of-the-road position on tariffs and domestic improvements.

In 1819, Missouri applied for admission to the Union as a slave state. A bitter legislative struggle followed on the questions of limiting slavery in Missouri and in the remainder of the Louisiana Purchase. Although sympathetic to the South, Monroe, in keeping with his view of the Presidency, did not involve himself in the struggle until a bill reached him. It provided for the admission of Missouri as a slave state, while banning slavery from much of the rest of the Louisiana Purchase.

Monroe doubted that Congress could constitutionally impose such a ban. His cabinet also had doubts but, ultimately, he decided to leave the question unresolved, signing the act that became known as the Missouri Compromise of 1820.

Attentive to the public's attitude toward his administration, Monroe traveled through the Northeast—a venture that increased his popularity —and later toured the South and Southwest. Monroe demonstrated unusual personal growth in the Presidency by moving away from the evident sectionalism of his first years toward national perspectives. With breadth of vision and a talent for conciliation, Monroe led a cabinet of strong personalities drawn from the country's major regions: John Quincy Adams (Secretary of State), John Calhoun (War), William Wirt (Attorney General), and William H. Crawford (Treasury).

In foreign affairs, the Monroe administration arranged with Great Britain to limit armaments on the Great Lakes and resolved a long-standing dispute with Newfoundland and Labrador over fishing rights. Monroe acquired (1819) Florida from Spain by the Adams-Onís Treaty, even though midway in the negotiations Andrew Jackson had invaded Florida (1818). Monroe also approved of the American Colonization Society settling Liberia; Monrovia was named for him.

A triumph of skillful Presidential leadership, the Monroe Doctrine began its evolution with the clamors for recognition by Spain's former Latin American colonies. Monroe dispatched special agents to those emerging countries and sought to associate Congress with his eventual policy. He recognized the former colonies and, on learning that European powers contemplated a reconquest of them, he and his cabinet developed the message to Congress of December 2, 1823, that set forth the doctrine. In effect, it threatened war against European powers that attempted to "extend their system to any portion of this hemisphere." Although Secretary of State Adams played an important part in the formulation of the doctrine, Monroe conceived the idea of a legislative message to convey it and drafted its central paragraphs.

After leaving office, Monroe retired to his estate near Leesburg, Virginia. He served as regent of the University of Virginia and was presiding officer of the Virginia Constitutional Convention in 1829. Financial distress, stemming from long years of public service, forced Monroe to move (1830) to New York City to live with his married daughter. He died there on July 4, 1831. Subsequently his remains were moved to Richmond, Virginia.

John Quincy Adams

John Quincy Adams, 6th President (1825–1829), was born July 11, 1767, in Braintree (now Quincy), Massachusetts, the eldest son of the 2d President of the United States. Because his father had served as American diplomatic representative to several European countries during the Revolution, Adams received his early schooling abroad. His advanced learning enabled him to enter Harvard College as a junior and graduate in 1787. After reading law for three years, he was admitted to the bar.

But having few clients, Adams took up political journalism. He wrote articles replying to Tom Paine's *The Rights of Man*, which he considered too radical, and attacked the French Minister Edmond Genêt, who during the Washington administration urged the United States to join France in her war with Great Britain. In 1794, George Washington appointed the 27-year-old Adams minister to the Netherlands and, two years later, to Portugal. He served as minister to Prussia after his father became (1797) President.

With the advent (1801) of the Jefferson administration, Adams abandoned diplomacy and turned to politics as a Federalist; he was elected (1802) to the Massachusetts Senate but the Federalist leader there soon considered Adams "too unmanageable." A year later he was elected to the U.S. Senate from Massachusetts. In the Senate, he often voted with the Democratic-Republicans, although a Federalist, and he supported Jefferson's embargo policy to which other New England Federalists were bitterly opposed. When the end of Adams' term approached, the Federalists, feeling betrayed, elected (1808) another man to his place, and Adams immediately resigned.

He returned (1809) to diplomacy under James Madison, who appointed him minister to Russia. Near the end of his service there (1814), he became one of the U.S. commissioners who negotiated the Treaty of Ghent ending the War of 1812. In 1815 Madison appointed Adams minister to Britain; in 1817 James Monroe named him Secretary of State. Adams was a leading influence in the formulation of the Monroe Doctrine.

Just as Madison and Monroe had risen to the Presidency from the post of Secretary of State, Adams considered himself qualified for a similar ascent in the election of 1824. Proud, high-minded, and an independent in politics (which made party men look askance at him), Adams made little effort to obtain votes. Moreover, he faced formidable opponents: John Calhoun, Henry Clay, Andrew Jackson, and William Crawford. Calhoun soon withdrew from the Presidential race and was elected Vice-President. For President, Jackson received 99 electoral votes; Adams, 84; Crawford, 41; and Clay, 37. Since none of the candidates had won a majority, the House of Representatives had to choose among the three leading candidates.

Before the House voted, however, Jackson's followers charged that Adams had promised Clay a cabinet post in exchange for his support. Following his election, Adams appointed Clay Secretary of State, prompting Jacksonians in Congress to cry that Adams and Clay had made "a corrupt bargain." These circumstances assured Adams of unrelenting Jacksonian hostility.

In his inaugural address, Adams advocated an ambitious program of domestic improvements and, in his first annual message, he called for federal promotion of the arts and sciences, establishment of a national university and astronomical observatories, and support for scientific enterprises. Strict Northern constructionists were distressed by Adams' liberal interpretations of the Constitution, while Southerners were fearful that the logic of these Constitutional views might lead to federal abolition of slavery.

Neither by personality nor by circumstance was Adams sufficiently endowed to excel in two critical Presidential roles: as party leader and as legislative leader. Although his party controlled the House, the opposition ruled the Senate. Adams himself had little faith in his ability to command success in Congress. A simple proposal, such as his request for authority to dispatch a mission to the Panama Congress of Latin American states, encountered rough trouble in the legislature. A master of diatribe, John Randolph, launched a pointed attack on the supposed Adams-Clay "deal." Worse than Randolph's attack was the failure of anyone in the President's own party to defend him.

Adams made no attempt to soften Congressional opposition by the adroit use of patronage. Seemingly self-obstructive, his principles took precedence over party claims. His administration made only 12 removals from office, a degree of restraint that alienated friends and encouraged enemies. In other ways, too, Adams demonstrated that he was very little of a politician. His cabinet contained no one who had openly supported him for President. He even countenanced the aid openly given by one cabinet secretary to the future Presidential candidacy of Jackson.

The midterm Congressional elections went against Adams' interests, and for the first time in the history of the Presidency a large majority of Congress opposed the administration.

Adams' chief legislative success was the enactment (1828) of the "tariff of abominations," the high rates of which favored New England manufacturers and hurt Southern farmers, who had to pay more for imports. Southern resentment endangered Adams' chances for reelection.

The 1828 Presidential campaign was one of unparalleled bitterness. Adams did not answer—although his supporters did—the attacks of Jackson and his followers. Adams believed it beneath the dignity of the President to engage in political debate. Adams had no party of his own to cope with the well-organized opposition, and Jackson won an overwhelming victory: 178 electoral votes to 83 for Adams. But Adams did not regret leaving the Presidency.

After his Presidential term, Adams briefly enjoyed political retirement, until his election to the House of Representatives. Taking his seat in 1831, he served there for 17 years. He was the first Congressman to argue that slaves could be freed in time of war, an argument that Lincoln was to utilize in the Emancipation Proclamation.

Adams died of a paralytic stroke in the Speaker's Room of the House of Representatives on February 23, 1848. He is buried in Quincy, Massachusetts.

Andrew Jackson

Andrew Jackson, 7th President (1829–1837), was born on March 15, 1767, in Waxhaw, South Carolina, the son of a linen weaver who, upon migrating to the United States from Ireland, became a farmer. Jackson's mother, too, was born in Ireland. In the frontier wilderness of the Carolinas, Jackson grew up with little education or refinement, and with a combative nature. But he was also energetic, self-confident, honest, and straightforward. He was genuinely the first of the "log-cabin" Presidents.

In the American Revolution, Jackson at 13 joined the South Carolina militia and was captured (1781) by the British. After the war, he read law and was admitted (1787) to the bar at the age of 20. In 1788, he became solicitor of the western district of North Carolina (now Tennessee) and soon excelled at sending law violators and debtors to jail. His success in public office rapidly enlarged his private law practice. Through successful land speculation, Jackson also increased his fortune, and he acquired the Hermitage, a plantation near Nashville.

Later that year, he was elected to the U.S. House of Representatives. His rough frontier manners won him attention and popularity, and he was appointed (1797) to the U.S. Senate at the age of 30. But impatient of the slow pace of life in Philadelphia (then the capital) and eager to care for his private affairs, Jackson resigned from the Senate the following year. The Tennessee legislature made his political retirement short lived by making him justice of the state supreme court (July 1798), and he served in that capacity until 1804. The pressures of creditors forced him to resign and devote himself to private affairs. By selling off land and winning steadily on his horses, Jackson withstood his creditors.

His already substantial public service had not compensated for his scanty formal education. A critic said that "his letters, with their crudities in spelling and grammar, would make the better educated angels weep." Nor did his temper diminish; he was party to many duels.

His service in the War of 1812 established him as a national military hero and a popular idol of the West. His best-known victory, at New Orleans, was gained after the treaty of peace had been signed, but before he had learned of it. In 1817 Jackson led a military expedition to Florida to guard the border, but he engaged and defeated the Seminole Indians in battle, pursuing them into northwest Florida. He ordered two British subjects, accused of inciting the Seminoles, hanged, thus precipitating diplomatic crises with Britain and Spain.

As a war hero, Jackson was attractive to politicians, and they began to talk of electing him President. In 1822 the Tennessee legislature nominated him to run for President in 1824 and, as a step in that direction, the legislature elected him to the U.S. Senate in 1823. Jackson again favorably impressed the Washington political community.

In the bitterly fought Presidential election of 1824, Jackson was one of five major candidates. Although he received more electoral votes than any of his rivals, he lacked a majority and the choice went to the House of Representatives. Supporters of Henry Clay in the House gave their votes to John Quincy Adams, who was elected. When Adams appointed Clay as Secretary of State, Jackson was convinced that he had been cheated out of the Presidency by "a corrupt bargain" between his two rivals.

The Presidential election of 1828 was even more bitter. It was the first election in which each Presidential nomination was made by state legislatures and mass meetings, instead of the traditional Congressional caucuses. Seeking reelection, Adams was the "National Republican" or Whig candidate. Jackson won easily, with 178 electoral votes to 83 for Adams.

His inaugural address was a true harbinger of Jackson's future policies. "The Federal Constitution," he said, "must be obeyed, state rights preserved, our national debts must be paid, direct taxes and loans avoided, and the Federal Union preserved." Jackson, who expressed and believed in the phrase "Let the people rule," invited the inaugural crowd into the White House. The results were disastrous: people grabbed up food and punch, stood on chairs, tore draperies, and broke china. The crowd's pressure endangered Jackson, who gladly escaped through a window.

Consistent with his desire for popular rule, Jackson became the first President to use the spoils system on a substantial scale. To Jackson's friend, Senator William L. Marcy of New York, is credited the slogan, "to the victor belong the spoils." Under the Jacksonian conception of spoils, experts were unnecessary for the conduct of government. The people could do its tasks and, best of all, members of the victorious party.

Although Jackson extolled popular rule, he also maximized his own personal rule as President, sometimes to the point of arbitrary power. He developed what became known as the "kitchen cabinet," a small group of personal advisers who were not in the cabinet but, in some cases, occupied subcabinet positions. The kitchen cabinet advised on policies and helped implement them; it tended to supplant the regular cabinet with which Jackson was chronically dissatisfied.

Jackson's revulsion to anything smacking of class privilege led him to attack the Bank of the United States. Although privately owned and managed, the bank, as chartered by Congress, had control over the nation's currency system. Jackson considered the act of Congress that had created the bank unconstitutional. On economic grounds, also, he opposed the bank. Jackson criticized it for failing to establish a "uniform and sound" currency, since he favored a "hard money" policy—one in which paper money would be based on specie (gold and silver).

In 1832 when Congress passed a bill rechartering the bank, Jackson vetoed it. Hitherto Presidents had restricted their use of the veto to constitutional grounds, but Jackson broke new ground by elaborating on the policy considerations prompting his action.

The election of 1832 was a landmark in Presidential history. For the first time, Presidential nominees were chosen by national conventions. The Democratic-Republican party broke into two parties. Jackson's opponents, who called themselves "National Republicans," nominated Henry Clay, while Jackson's followers continued to style themselves as "Republicans" or "Democratic-Republicans." The election was fought on the issue "Jackson or the Bank," and Jackson again won easily, with 219 electoral votes to 49 for Clay.

Spurred by his victory, Jackson continued to move against the Bank of the United States. He directed that government funds deposited with it be removed and placed in state banks, which opponents called "pet banks." "The dying monster," as Jackson called the Bank of the United States, was defeated after a savage fight and transformed itself into a state bank of Pennsylvania.

Meanwhile, banks having the use of government funds issued paper money in enormous quantities, prompting wild speculation. In 1836, Jackson suddenly issued his "specie circular," declaring that the government would accept only gold or silver in payment for public lands. He also required these banks to give up the money deposited with them, so that he might lend it to the states. The result was a disastrous panic that reached full force in the administration of his successor, Martin Van Buren.

Jackson also enhanced Presidential influence by his firm handling of the nullification crisis. In November 1832, South Carolina declared the high tariff acts of 1828 and 1832 null and void and threatened to secede. By proclamation, Jackson warned South Carolina that the law would be enforced and ordered troops and warships concentrated near Charleston. Congress passed a force bill, authorizing the President to employ the armed forces to collect tariffs. Eventually a new compromise tariff law was passed, and South Carolina withdrew its nullification of the tariff laws.

Jackson took a different course when Georgia disregarded the authority of the United States, as expressed by the Supreme Court. The Court had held unconstitutional a Georgia law concerning lands which by treaties had been given to the Indians. When Georgian authorities imprisoned a violator of the state law, Jackson refused to use the executive power to uphold the decision of the Supreme Court, and merely remarked, "John Marshall has made the decision; now let him enforce it." Some explain Jackson's position as one motivated by his long-standing distaste for Indians and for Marshall.

The audacious, enterprising, politically skillful Jackson remade the Presidency. His unprecedented use of spoils and the national nominating convention made it a party office. As a popular President and effective party leader, he became the first President to appeal to the people over the heads of their legislative representatives.

After leaving the Presidency, Jackson retired to the Hermitage and supported the Presidencies of his protégés—Van Buren and Polk. He died on June 8, 1845, and is buried at the Hermitage.

Martin Van Buren

Martin Van Buren, 8th President 1837–1841), was born on December 5, 1782, in Kinderhook, New York, the son of a truck-farmer who was also tavern keeper. As a child, Van Buren enjoyed listening to his father's patrons discuss politics. At the age of 14, he left school to serve an apprenticeship in law offices at Kinderhook and Albany and was admitted to the bar in 1803.

While practicing in Kinderhook, he gained (1808) his first public office, being appointed surrogate of Columbia County by Gov. Daniel D. Tompkins. Van Buren rose rapidly in his New York political career, serving as state senator, attorney general, U.S. Senator, and delegate to the New York constitutional convention of 1821. An admirer of the ideas of Thomas Jefferson, Van Buren was a Democratic-Republican. As U.S. Senator (1821–28), he led in the fight against imprisonment for debt and the extension of the slave trade.

In 1828, Van Buren was elected governor of New York and gave invaluable support to the Presidential race of Andrew Jackson. A grateful Jackson named him Secretary of State but, more important, Van Buren rose to primacy among Jackson's advisers. Completely in accord with Jackson's policies, Van Buren in 1832 ran successfully for Vice-President, Jackson being elected. As Jackson's chosen successor, Van Buren received the Democratic Presidential nomination in 1836 and won the election virtually unopposed.

Van Buren entered office pledged to follow the footsteps of his predecessor. The new President inherited not only policies but a legacy of problems as well. The worst of these was the feverish speculation in public lands that had developed in the latter days of the Jackson administration. Rich and poor alike, banks and their branches had all indulged in speculation. To check it, Jackson had issued the Specie Circular of July 1, 1836, that stipulated the government need only accept gold and silver in payment for public lands. Despite this restraint and others, a financial crash occurred (May 10, 1837) on Van Buren's 36th day in office. Bank closings and failures spread like plague, the nation having begun its first great depression.

Van Buren perceived neither the power nor the duty of the Presidency to help the people in their economic plight. Despite loud clamors of opposition, Van Buren held to Jackson's Specie Circular. His financial policies alienated conservative (or "bank") Democrats, especially in the politically important states of Virginia and New York. The rival Whig party denounced Van Buren for indifference and "heartlessness," pointing to his failure to issue paper money and resort to other relief measures that might have benefited the people and the economy. Van Buren, whose talents lay more in political manipulation than in persuasive public leadership, followed the practice of ignoring his critics. At this time, as throughout his political career, he was confident that "the sober second thought" of the people would support him.

Another Jacksonian inheritance was America's fiercest and costliest Indian war, the Seminole War in Florida. The great treasure of lives and money required to prosecute the eight-year war further diminished Van Buren's popularity. Even more costly, politically, was his policy toward Canada, since Americans sympathized with the Canadian rebellion of 1837. When British authorities seized an insurgent vessel in American waters, Van Buren resisted vociferous opinion that the country go to war with Great Britain. The President and his administration were derided as "tools of Victoria." In 1839, a border dispute between Maine and New Brunswick erupted, threatening war again, but Van Buren prevailed for peace with patience and tact.

Foreign policy, however, damaged his standing with the Southern base of his party. Facing pressures to annex the now independent Texas, he resisted because he did not want war with Mexico. He also opposed the extension of slavery, which the acquisition of Texas augured.

Dignified, courtly, and given to dandified dress and expensive tastes, Van Buren was a cartoonist's delight. But he was a leader with principles and convictions that he held to at the price of unpopularity and failure of reelection. His party bravely renominated him in 1840. In the boisterous "hard-cider" campaign of 1840, the Whigs delighted to chant that "Little Van" was "a used-up man." In his overwhelming defeat, Van Buren even lost his own state of New York.

Although driven from the Presidency, Van Buren remained active in politics for the next two decades. He continued to oppose annexation of Texas and approved the Wilmot Proviso, which barred slavery in territory acquired from Mexico. In 1848, he was the Presidential nominee of the Free-Soil party. Although defeated, he took so many votes in New York from the Democratic nominee, Lewis Cass, that the Whigs' Zachary Taylor was elected. Van Buren supported Democratic Presidents Pierce and Buchanan, as well as the prosecution of the Civil War. He died at his country estate of Lindenwald, near his birthplace, July 24, 1862.

William Henry Harrison

William Henry Harrison, 9th President (March 4–April 4, 1841), was born at Berkeley, Charles City County, Virginia, on February 9, 1773. His father, a plantation owner and member of the Virginia aristocracy, was a signer of the Declaration of Independence.

Harrison attended Hampden-Sydney College and studied medicine in Philadelphia. Unattracted by the medical profession, he accepted an appointment by President Washington to the army as ensign in 1791.

Harrison served with distinction in the Indian campaigns of the Northwest Territory, rose to a captaincy, and in 1798 resigned his commission to settle at North Bend, Ohio, near Cincinnati. President John Adams appointed him secretary of the Northwest Territory. In 1799, he became the first territorial delegate to Congress.

For 12 years Harrison was territorial governor of Indiana and superintendent of Indian affairs. By negotiating vast land cessions from the Indians, he opened Ohio and Indiana to American settlement. When Tecumseh, a chieftain of the Shawnee Indians, and his brother the Shawnee Prophet objected to the land cessions, Harrison in November 1811 defeated the Indians in a formidable battle at Tippecanoe on the Wabash River. The battle made Harrison a national hero, admiringly called "Old Tippecanoe."

In the War of 1812, Harrison was commissioned a major general in command of forces in the Northwest. He took Detroit in September 1813, and in early October he established American hegemony in the West, when he defeated the combined Indian and British forces at the Thames River in Ontario, where Tecumseh was finally killed.

Harrison resigned his commission and as a war hero was elected in 1816 to the U.S. House of Representatives. He subsequently served in the Ohio Senate and in the U.S. Senate. Appointed minister to Colombia by President John Quincy Adams, Harrison was recalled when Andrew Jackson came to power. He retired to his farm at North Bend, and, to supplement his income, served as county recorder and clerk of the county court.

In 1836, Harrison's political fortunes recovered dramatically when the Whigs nominated him for President. Although defeated by Martin Van Buren, the Democratic candidate, Harrison ran an impressive race, carrying seven states. In 1840, the Whigs, including Daniel Webster and Henry Clay, nominated Harrison for President and John Tyler for Vice-President.

The 1840 Presidential campaign, famous for its slogan "Tippecanoe and Tyler too," is a classic of political demagoguery. Harrison's standing as a war hero, the absence of a platform, and diversionary political propaganda, enabled the Whigs to avoid the emerging issue of slavery. Van Buren, the incumbent, was portrayed drinking champagne from a crystal goblet at a table laden with costly viands and dinnerware. Harrison was seen content with a log cabin and hard cider. Aided also by the suffering of the Panic of 1837, Harrison scored an overwhelming victory.

His inaugural stirred enormous enthusiasm. His address, partly the work of Webster, prolix and abounding in classical allusions, was an extended statement of the Whig doctrine of the Presidency. Deferential to Congress, it viewed the legislators as the center of decision.

Harrison appointed a cabinet of high quality, headed by Daniel Webster as Secretary of State. On March 17, the President called a special session of Congress to meet on May 31 to act on the country's continuing financial distress. A week later, he took ill, developed pneumonia, and died, a month after his inauguration. Harrison was the first of our Presidents to die in office.

John Tyler

John Tyler, 10th President (1841–1845), was born on March 29, 1790, in Charles City County, Virginia, the son of Judge John Tyler, a distinguished lawyer and governor of Virginia. Young Tyler graduated from William and Mary College at 17, was admitted to the bar at 19, and at 21 his public career began with his election to the Virginia House of Delegates.

Tyler moved steadily through a political career of remarkable breadth, as U.S. Congressman, Senator, governor of Virginia, and delegate to the important Virginia constitutional conventions of 1829 and 1830. In 1836, he was an unsuccessful candidate for the Vice-Presidency, but in the "Tippecanoe and Tyler too" campaign of 1840, with William Henry Harrison heading the Whig ticket, he ran again, this time successfully. Harrison died a month after his inauguration, and on April 4, 1841, Tyler became the first Vice-President to succeed to the Presidency.

Some chose to interpret the succession provision of the Constitution to mean that Tyler was only "Acting President," but he insisted upon the office's full title and powers. The reluctance to grant Tyler recognition was partly rooted in the unusual circumstances of his nomination. Tyler was an ex-Democrat who, as a legislator, had been a stubborn advocate of states' rights and consequently opposed to nationalistic Whig policies. The Whigs had nonetheless nominated him for the Vice-Presidency to attract Southern votes. They reasoned that, as Vice-President, Tyler would command no influence in the Harrison administration.

After Tyler became President, his ambiguous situation was further complicated by the presence in the Senate of Henry Clay, the heavy-handed but powerful leader of the Whig party. Clay was soon scornfully speaking of Tyler as "a President without a party." Tyler was also an obstacle to Clay's driving ambition to become President; if Tyler could be discredited to the point of being denied renomination, Clay might himself seize the prize.

Tyler, in a conciliatory step, retained the entire Harrison cabinet, which presumably should have satisfied the Whigs and Clay, but they were irreconcilable. A rift quickly developed over the Whig measure to reestablish a national bank. Twice Tyler vetoed the national bank bill. As a strict constitutionalist, he argued that a national bank must not be permitted to establish branches in the states without their prior consent. After the second bank veto, Tyler's entire cabinet resigned, with the exception of Daniel Webster, the Secretary of State. Webster remained only long enough to complete a treaty with Canada setting the northeast boundary of the United States.

With Clay now openly saying of the President that "I'll drive him before me," Tyler's own measures encountered rough treatment in Congress and his nominations to office were usually blocked.

Despite the deadlock with his own party, Tyler brought off some substantial achievements. He was adept at seizing upon issues that by their merit or popularity transcended partisanship. He was not unskilled at political maneuver and when a favorite project to annex Texas by treaty was lost—with every Whig but one voting against it—Tyler outmaneuvered his opponents and arranged for annexation by joint resolution.

A cultivated Southern gentleman, master of the good story and easy conversation, Tyler was attractive to Congressmen and, as a veteran legislator, experienced in dealing with them. Under his evident influence Congress passed a number of constructive laws. The Navy was thoroughly reorganized. A bureau was established for nautical charts and instruments, which later developed into the Naval Observatory. An act opening the way to initiating a national telegraphic system was passed, a step leading to the development of the Weather Bureau.

As President, Tyler excelled as an administrator and in employing his powers in foreign affairs. He conducted the government with a minimum of waste, although Congress provided no system for controlling public funds. Tyler brought the Seminole War to an end, entered into a treaty with China opening the doors of the Orient for the first time, and applied the Monroe Doctrine to Texas and Hawaii.

Despite his achievements, Tyler could muster only minor factional support for renomination in 1844. Withdrawing from the Presidential race, he retired to his estate, Sherwood Forest, in Virginia on the James River. There he lived in virtual retirement for 14 years, except for service as chancellor of the College of William and Mary from 1859 to 1861. In 1861, he proposed and presided over the secret North-South Conference held at Washington in an eleventh-hour effort to prevent the Civil War. When this failed, he advocated immediate secession and was elected a member of the congress of the Confederacy, but he died on January 18, 1862, before he could take his seat in that body.

James Knox Polk

James Knox Polk, 11th President (1845–1849) was born on November 2, 1795, near Pineville in Mecklenburg County, North Carolina. Polk was of Scots-Irish stock, and his father soldiered in the Revolution. In 1806, the large and growing Polk family moved to central Tennessee, and Polk's schooling in that frontier district was fragmentary. Nevertheless, he entered the University of North Carolina at the age of 20, compiled an impressive record, and graduated in 1818. He studied law under Felix Grundy, the politician

and noted criminal lawyer, was admitted to the bar, and practiced in Columbia, Tennessee.

An able orator in demand at political meetings, Polk became known as "the Napoleon of the Stump." This talent, as well as his friendship with Andrew Jackson, propelled him into a political career. In 1823 he was elected to the Tennessee House of Representatives, and in 1825 to the U.S. Congress, where he served seven consecutive terms, the last two as Speaker.

In 1839, he was elected governor of Tennessee. Although an ardent Jacksonian Democrat, he was defeated for reelection in 1841 and again in 1843.

Polk then turned to national politics, and when the Democratic national convention gathered in Baltimore in 1844, he was considered a serious candidate for the Vice-Presidency, but was unthought of for the Presidency. Circumstances, however, brought him an unexpected Presidential nomination: the first successful "dark horse" candidate in the history of the office.

Just before the convention met, former President Martin Van Buren issued a statement opposing the annexation of Texas, which offended both Western and Southern interests. This position eliminated Van Buren, the leading contender for the Democratic nomination. Polk's stand on Texas and the disputed territory of Oregon—"Reannexation of Texas and Reoccupation of Oregon" —won him the nomination and the election. Since Polk lacked national prominence, the rival Whig party's campaign slogan was, "Who is James Polk?" The Democrats countered with "54–40 or Fight!", a reference to the entire Oregon territory, which the United States, it was felt, should possess even at the price of war with Great Britain. In the election Polk narrowly defeated Henry Clay, the Whig candidate, by winning New York State.

His inaugural address exalted the Union and deplored sectional discord. More specifically, he opposed a tariff "for protection merely" and asserted uncompromisingly that the United States' title to Oregon was "clear and unquestionable."

The independent treasury bill of 1846, which he adroitly shepherded through Congress, reestablished a financial system that endured, with only minor modification, until the Federal Reserve System was established during Woodrow Wilson's administration.

The Walker Tariff Act of 1846, true to Polk's purpose, put most tariff duties on a revenue basis and used ad valorem in place of specific duties. Polk prevailed against political foes who foresaw only ruination for manufacturing and the public treasury.

Oregon proved a more difficult issue. Aided by Secretary of State James Buchanan and after long negotiations with Great Britain, Polk won a settlement that was something less than his campaign slogan had demanded. Buchanan proposed that the Oregon Territory be divided by extending to the Pacific coast the boundary provided by the 49th parallel. When Britain rejected the compromise, Polk boldly reasserted his claim to the entire Oregon Territory. Britain then acquiesced to the 49th parallel line, except for Vancouver Island, and the treaty that was signed (1846) incorporated this division.

The acquisition of California was a severe test of Polk's political skills. Aiming to secure the territory by purchases, he reasserted some longstanding damage claims against Mexico. Certain that Mexico could not pay her debt, he expected her to cede the territory. Mexico rejected any kind of bargain, and American troops under Gen. Zachary Taylor provoked hostilities along the Rio Grande. Polk asked Congress on May 9, 1846, for a declaration of war because of the unpaid claims and because Mexico had invaded American soil. The treaty at the end of the Mexican War ceded California and New Mexico to the United States, for which Mexico was paid $15 million, and the old damage claims were assumed by the United States. Polk's opponents charged that he had forced the war upon Mexico to extend slavery.

To induce Mexico to accept the treaty, Polk had asked Congress for $2 million to be used for "diplomatic purposes." The sum was to be devoted to paying the Mexican army, a step that was indispensable to acceptance of the treaty. David Wilmot offered a proviso to the appropriation, directing that slavery be excluded from any territory acquired through use of the funds made available to the President. Polk angrily termed Wilmot's proviso "a mischievous and foolish amendment," aimed at diplomatic embarrassment. After Polk threatened to veto it, the proviso was defeated, but it brought the building conflict between North and South into the open.

In foreign affairs, Polk extended the reach of the Monroe Doctrine from a prohibition of forcible foreign interference to any kind of interference in American affairs. He effectively opposed an invitation by the people of Yucatán in Mexico for Britain or Spain to exert sovereignty over their territory.

Polk was an exacting administrator who closely supervised the affairs of his departments. He bore ungladly the less palatable aspects of politics. He was contemptuous of the spoils system and, in a rare act for a President, vetoed two river-and-harbor bills, Congress's traditional and politically sacred pork-barrel method of legislation.

Serious and diligent almost to a fault, Polk had little time for pleasure and small talk. Secretive, particularly in dealing with Congress, he offended many by his reticence and sly maneuvers. He was lacking in personal magnetism and had few intimate friends, although Bancroft deemed him "generous and benevolent."

Just before taking office, Polk declared he would not be a candidate for reelection. He died on June 15, 1849, shortly after leaving office.

Zachary Taylor

Zachary Taylor, 12th President (March 4, 1849– July 9, 1850) was born November 24, 1784, at Montebello, Orange County, Virginia. His father was a farmer and a colonel in the Revolution. When he was less than a year old, Taylor and his family migrated to Kentucky. There on the frontier, schools were little known, and Taylor absorbed a sketchy education from tutoring.

In 1808, he obtained a commission as first lieutenant in the army. During 40 years of military service, which ended when he was nominated for President, Taylor fought in the War of 1812, against the Indians in the Northwest and in Florida, and in the Mexican War. In the Seminole Indian War in Florida, the muscular, stocky Taylor became known as "Old Rough and Ready" to troops who admired his valor and candor. His dis-

tinction at the battle of Okeechobee against the Seminoles won him the rank of brevet brigadier general.

Taylor commanded the army in Texas, and a Mexican attack upon his forces in 1846 was used by Congress as justification for declaring war. After Taylor's victory at Monterrey, Mexico, President James K. Polk, distrustful of Taylor's independent spirit and his potential as a political rival, turned over most of Taylor's troops to a new commander. Santa Anna, the Mexican commander, learning of Taylor's weakened forces, attacked him at Buena Vista with troops that were numerically far superior. A stunning victory in an all-day battle made Taylor a national hero and immediately inspired both leading parties, the Democrats and the Whigs, to consider him as a candidate for the Presidential election of 1848.

As a lifelong soldier, Taylor had never voted, and his political views, if any existed, were unknown. Mindful of their victory with another military hero, W. H. Harrison in 1840, the Whigs in 1848 chose Taylor as their nominee over such other formidable contenders as Henry Clay and Daniel Webster.

Stressing that his administration would be nonpartisan and free from party pledges, Taylor defeated his Democratic opponent, Lewis Cass, and the Free-Soil nominee, Martin Van Buren, in the first election to be held simultaneously in all the states.

As President, Taylor was a potential force to check the widening breach between the North and South over slavery. He was a slave owner, but numbered among his closest counselors the antislavery Whig, Senator William H. Seward of New York. In addition, his electoral victory was fashioned by substantial support from both sections; he carried seven Northern and eight Southern states. His inaugural address urged Congress to work for conciliation of sectional controversies and offered a program no one could criticize: friendly relations in foreign affairs, an efficient army and navy, and encouragement of agriculture, commerce, and manufacture.

For all of this political insulation, Taylor had to face the fiery issue of the admission of new states to the Union on a free or slave basis. Thanks largely to his overriding nationalistic sentiment, Taylor quickly took an antislavery position, for above all he wanted to annex the territories won in the Mexican War. He wrote to Jefferson Davis that nature had excluded slavery from the new Southwest, and, in a Pennsylvania address, he assured Northerners they "need have no apprehension of the further extension of slavery."

Taylor dispatched a special emissary, Thomas Butler King, to counsel Californians in forming a constitution and applying for statehood. Similar assistance was given New Mexico. In special messages to Congress in 1850, he urged unconditional admission for California and statehood for New Mexico.

In a counterthrust, Southern legislators filibustered against the admission of California and insisted that all measures concerning territories ceded by Mexico be taken up in a single bill. Southern Whigs withdrew their support of Taylor, and such Southern leaders as Alexander Stephens and Robert Tombs threatened the President with secession.

In Congress, Henry Clay framed a series of bills known collectively as the Compromise of 1850 in an effort to placate both the North and the South. Taylor would doubtless have opposed the compromise, but following ceremonies connected with building the Washington Monument, he was stricken with cholera and died after a Presidential tenure of only 16 months.

In foreign affairs, Taylor's Secretary of State, John M. Clayton, negotiated the Clayton-Bulwer Treaty with Great Britain which guaranteed the neutrality of an isthmian canal. (The previous Polk administration had secured rights to build a canal across Nicaragua.)

Millard Fillmore

Millard Fillmore, 13th President (July 10, 1850–March 3, 1853), was born in Locke (now Summerhill) in Cayuga County, New York, on January 7, 1800. The son of a frontier farmer who had migrated from Vermont, young Fillmore had scant schooling and was apprenticed to a wool carder. Intent upon studying law, he migrated to Buffalo, where he worked in a lawyer's office for room and board. In 1823, he was admitted to the bar and began practice in East Aurora, New York.

Fillmore's political career began with his election in 1828 to the New York State Assembly on an Anti-Mason ticket. He secured the passage of a law that abolished imprisonment for debt and formed a friendship with the Albany publisher and political leader, Thurlow Weed. In 1830, Fillmore moved back to Buffalo and a year later was elected to the first of four terms in the U.S. Congress. He supported the emerging Whig party and the nationalistic policies of Henry Clay. As chairman of the powerful Ways and Means Committee, he oversaw the 1842 tariff act that raised duties on manufactured goods. On the burning issue of slavery, he was a moderate.

In 1844, Fillmore ran as the Whig candidate for governor of New York but was unsuccessful and returned to his law practice. In 1846, he became the first chancellor of the University of Buffalo. A year later, he was elected comptroller of New York.

Fillmore's acceptability to both Northern and Southern Whigs and his backing by Henry Clay resulted in his election as Vice-President with Zachary Taylor in 1848. As Vice-President, he presided over the bitter Senate debates on the slavery compromise measures of 1850 with notable fairness. Midway in this political turbulence President Taylor died, and Fillmore became the second "accidental President."

The Taylor Cabinet promptly resigned. Fillmore's nomination of Daniel Webster of New Hampshire as Secretary of State and John Crittenden of Kentucky as Attorney General was indicative of the new President's preference for a moderate Whig position and his readiness to compromise in the growing conflict between North and South. In his message to Congress of August 6, 1850, Fillmore made a compelling plea for settlement by compromise. An opponent, Salmon Chase, credited the Presidential message with winning over six New England votes in the Senate and moving Congress down the compromise road.

Clay's "omnibus" compromise bill, unable to be passed as a whole, was separated into its several parts. These sections were soon enacted, and the President approved them believing that only through them could the Union be saved. Fillmore

and Clay led not a united party, but rather one that represented a bipartisan coalition of Northern Democrats and Southern Whigs. To Southerners, a key element of the compromise was the new Fugitive Slave Law; Fillmore's approval of it cost him the support of Northern Whigs. Since the Presidency was Whig and Congress Democratic, little important legislation was passed, other than the Compromise of 1850.

In seeking renomination as the Whig standard-bearer in 1852, Fillmore enjoyed support from Southern Whigs. His rival, Webster, was backed by New Englanders, and another rival, General Winfield Scott, by an extreme antislavery group. When the Fillmore-Webster factions failed to unite, the nomination passed to Scott. Like other Presidents from Jackson to Lincoln, Fillmore was limited to one Presidential term by the slavery dispute, which prevented the Chief Executive from satisfying both the Northern and Southern wings of his party.

As President, Fillmore presented an image of cool-headedness and caution. His paramount political value was preservation of the Union, a goal to which he subordinated any specific interest or issue in the slavery controversy. From his deathbed, Henry Clay urged Fillmore's renomination, while Webster hailed his administration as one of the ablest.

Fillmore's advent to politics coincided with the emergence of the Whig party, and his departure with its demise. The 1852 elections were the last national campaign in which the Whigs were active. In 1856, Fillmore was the Presidential nominee of the American, or Know-Nothing, party. Stressing the value of unity and the dangers of sectionalism, he ran last in a three-way race. Always preferring conciliation to coercion, Fillmore opposed Lincoln's policies in the Civil War and supported Andrew Johnson's stand against radical reconstruction.

For all his lack of early advantages, Fillmore, according to a contemporary, possessed "a grace and polish of manner which fitted him for the most refined circles of the metropolis." Fillmore's political activities ended with the Reconstruction. He died on March 8, 1874. In 1969, a substantial body of Fillmore papers was discovered.

Franklin Pierce

Franklin Pierce, 14th President (1853–1857), was born on November 23, 1804, in Hillsboro, New Hampshire. His father, Benjamin Pierce, served in the Revolution and later was a brigadier general in the state militia. He was also a two-term governor of New Hampshire and left a valuable heritage of political connections for his son, who, after study at nearby academies and at Phillips Exeter, entered Bowdoin College in Maine.

After graduating from Bowdoin in 1824, Pierce read law and was admitted to the bar in 1827. He began practice in Hillsboro and two years later commenced his political career by winning election as a Jacksonian Democrat to the New Hampshire House of Representatives. Reelected two years later, he also began as Speaker. In 1833, he began a term in the U.S. House of Representatives and after a second term was elected to the U.S. Senate. He was the youngest member of that body, which then included such giants as Webster, Clay, and Calhoun. Because of his wife's poor health, Pierce resigned from the Senate in 1842 and resumed law practice in Concord, New Hampshire.

When the Mexican War broke out, Pierce, a staunch nationalist, inspired by his father's record in the Revolution, enlisted as a private. He advanced rapidly to brigadier general and served in key battles. In 1848, he resigned from the army, and two years later he became president of New Hampshire's Fifth State Constitutional Convention.

In 1852, Pierce became the Democratic Presidential nominee, a classic instance of a successful "dark horse" candidate. He received no votes until the 35th ballot and won on the 49th, as an acceptable compromise candidate in the deepening North-South split over slavery. An advocate of the Compromise of 1850, Pierce was regarded as a Northerner with Southern sympathies. Pierce was victorious over his Whig opponent, General Winfield Scott, by carrying every state but four, although with less than a 50,000 plurality.

By having avoided issues in his campaign, Pierce hoped to make his administration one of harmony. His cabinet was a perfect political balance of two conservative Southerners, two conservative Northerners, an antislavery Northerner, a states' rights Southerner, and a New England Whig. His inaugural address and early actions stressed objectives of general appeal. He promised a vigorous foreign policy and an economical and efficient administration. He called for a larger and better army and navy and reduction of the debt through use of the Treasury surplus. But Pierce's strategy of harmony was bedeviled by rising Northern sentiment against slavery and its expansion.

In foreign affairs, Pierce was an expansionist. His policies reflected his nationalism and, presumably, were designed to divert attention from domestic issues and gratify Southern hopes of introducing the slave economy into new territories. Accordingly, Pierce sought to convince Great Britain that under the Clayton-Bulwer Treaty she ought to withdraw from Nicaragua and Honduras. When negotiations failed, he tacitly supported a proslavery "filibustering" expedition against Nicaragua.

Pierce negotiated to acquire Hawaii, but the venture failed when the king of the islands died. Pierce's overtures to the Russians for the purchase of Alaska were unavailing. His administration's most brazen move was the Ostend Manifesto, a declaration by three proslavery American ministers calling for the annexation of Cuba. The public, the Senate, and the President's own party reacted indignantly to this move.

Pierce's foreign policies were not altogether blanketed with failure. A treaty was made with Japan in 1854, opening that country to American trading interests. James Gadsden, a special Presidential emissary, negotiated the purchase of land from Mexico that settled a boundary dispute and secured right-of-way for a southern railroad to the Pacific.

The President's preoccupation with foreign policy could not forestall a sudden, unexpected upsurge of the slavery issue. Leading Democratic Senators brought up a bill to organize Kansas and Nebraska as new territories out of the Indian lands, thus threatening the slender slavery truce.

When the Kansas-Nebraska Bill became law in 1854, both proslavery and antislavery settlers poured into the territory, and trouble quickly developed as both factions vied for control. Civil war erupted in Kansas when a free-soil group organized a government independent of the President's. Ultimately, Pierce ordered the free-soil government to cease and put federal troops at the disposal of the governor of Kansas. The Kansas experience served to reinforce the Democratic party's identification with slavery and to spur the rise of the new Republican party and the Know-Nothing party.

Pierce strove energetically to restore his crumbling popularity and win renomination. He launched an anti-British drive and demanded the recall of the British Minister Crampton for illegally recruiting troops in the United States for the Crimean War. But the Democratic national convention of 1856, apprehensive of rising Republican strength, looked for a "safer" man; it found him in James Buchanan, who, by having been abroad, had been untouched by the controversies of the Pierce era.

Although humiliated by his rejection for renomination, Pierce labored diligently to reduce and master problems before leaving office. He established a regular (proslavery) government in Kansas and, thanks to the continued presence of troops, he could proclaim that "peace now reigns in Kansas." A treaty was negotiated under which Britain agreed to abandon its interests in Central America except those in Honduras. The Senate, however, withheld its approval. Upon leaving office, Pierce at least had the satisfaction of seeing his party retain control of the Presidency and regain Congress.

After leaving the Presidency, Pierce traveled abroad to aid his wife's health. In the Civil War, having returned to Concord, he was an outspoken critic of Lincoln's, holding that war could have been averted by better leadership. The increasing unpopularity of his views relegated him to obscurity. His death on October 8, 1869, was almost unnoticed.

James Buchanan

James Buchanan, 15th President (1857–1861), was born April 23, 1791, in Cove Gap, Pennsylvania, the second of 11 children and the son of a merchant-farmer. After graduation (1809) from Dickinson College in Carlisle, Pennsylvania, Buchanan studied law in Lancaster and began practice there in 1812. He volunteered for duty in the War of 1812 and helped defend the city of Baltimore.

Originally a Federalist, Buchanan was elected (1814) to the Pennsylvania House of Representatives. In 1816 he ran unsuccessfully for the U.S. Congress but, four years later, he won and began 10 years of service in that body. Joining the Democratic party, he supported the Presidential race of Andrew Jackson in 1824 and again in 1828, when Jackson won. Grateful for Buchanan's continued support, President Jackson appointed him (1831) minister to Russia. After negotiating America's first trade treaty with Russia, Buchanan returned to the United States, and in 1834 he was elected U.S. Senator.

Buchanan was a favorite-son candidate for the Democratic Presidential nomination of 1844, but he withdrew his name before the convention met. James K. Polk, who was elected, made Buchanan his Secretary of State in 1845. In this post,

Buchanan oversaw the negotiations that secured the southern half of the Oregon country and the vast territory in the Southwest from Mexico. His support of the annexation of Texas and the acquisition of Cuba led to the charge that he was a pro-slavery politician.

When the Whigs recaptured the Presidency in 1849, Buchanan retired to Wheatland, his estate near Lancaster. He was an unsuccessful aspirant for the Presidency in 1852. Franklin Pierce, who was nominated and elected, appointed Buchanan minister to Great Britain. By serving abroad, Buchanan avoided the fierce domestic political struggle over the Kansas-Nebraska Act and was, therefore, highly available in 1856 for the Democratic Presidential nomination. As the eventual nominee, Buchanan stressed the necessity of preserving the Union and avoided taking a stand on the slavery question. In a three-cornered race, Buchanan won only a popular plurality, although he secured a large majority of the electoral vote. He was a bachelor and the only Pennsylvanian to have become President.

Buchanan's plan for halting the worsening schism over slavery was revealed in his inaugural address and in the formation of his cabinet. In choosing his department heads, he preserved "the sacred balance," giving equal representation to slaveholding and nonslaveholding states. In his inaugural address, he declared that the question of slavery in the territories was a matter for the courts to determine, a view that he asserted confidently after learning how the pending Dred Scott case would be decided.

Buchanan hoped to deflect national attention from grievous domestic problems by fostering a dynamic foreign policy. He moved to acquire Cuba, but Congress failed to provide the necessary appropriations to begin negotiations. To avoid European intervention, he proposed to bolster the Benito Juarez government in Mexico, but Congress again would not lend financial support to the scheme.

Buchanan's image as a Northern man with Southern sympathies was affirmed by his accepting the Dred Scott decision as final and by his support of the proslavery Kansas constitution. Buchanan stressed that this constitution was republican in form and properly left the question of slavery up to popular determination once Kansas became a state. The President's stand divided the Democratic party into two great factions. It identified the administration with the Southern wing and ignited a revolt by the followers of Stephen A. Douglas.

The growing crisis of disunion was magnified when South Carolina moved toward secession. Buchanan rejected the advice of his military commanders to garrison Southern ports. (In his annual legislative message, however, he had emphatically denied the right of secession.) Simultaneously, he admitted an inability to deal with actual secession, since federal officers in South Carolina, through whom he enforced the law, had resigned. In a close construction of Presidential authority, Buchanan held that except for defending U.S. property in South Carolina and collecting customs, the Chief Executive lacked authority to act. Congress alone could decide whether existing laws were amendable for carrying out the Constitution.

Buchanan dispatched a personal agent, Caleb Cushing, to dissuade the South Carolinians from secession and again rejected military advice to reinforce the forts in Charleston harbor. A South Carolina convention, nevertheless, voted to secede and Major Robert Anderson moved his Federal troops from indefensible Fort Moultrie to Fort Sumter, a step that South Carolina spokesmen said violated a Presidential commitment to keep the status quo.

In the quickening tension, Buchanan's cabinet collapsed, with both Northern and Southern members resigning. The President filled the vacancies with Northern and border-state members, a harbinger of firmer policies. Buchanan sent reinforcements to Fort Sumter and announced his intent to hold it and keep peace until "the question shall have been settled by competent authority." Buchanan proposed new legislation to deal with the crisis, but Congress was unresponsive.

Buchanan retired into obscurity at Wheatland and died on June 1, 1868.

Abraham Lincoln

Abraham Lincoln, 16th President (March 4, 1861–April 14, 1865), was born in a dirt-floor log cabin in Hardin (now Larue) County, Kentucky, on February 12, 1809. His father, Thomas, was a migratory frontier farmer and carpenter, who was nearly always poor and moved from Kentucky to Indiana and, eventually, to Illinois. Of Lincoln's mother, Nancy Hanks of Rockingham County, Virginia, little is known. She died when young Lincoln was nine, and his home seemed empty and lonely after her death, until his father married Sarah (Bush) Johnston, a widow, who brought affection to the family. Lincoln may have spoken of her when he said: "God bless my mother; all that I am or ever hope to be I owe to her."

Lincoln absorbed a scanty frontier education (his formal education probably totaled less than one year). Books were scarce, but Lincoln taught himself to read and was a close student of the family Bible. His boyhood readings in it provided the store of Biblical quotations and references that later abounded, with great effect, in his addresses and writings.

As a strong, large-boned youth of 6 feet, 4 inches, Lincoln was admirably suited for hard work, which he experienced in the full. He split logs for fence rails, plowed fields, cut corn, threshed wheat, and took a flat boat loaded with farm produce to New Orleans. As a boy, he showed talent as a speaker; his knack for telling stories and imitating local personalities made people gather to hear him, often at a store in which he was a clerk. His homely face and black coarse hair added fascination to what he said.

From 1831 to 1837, Lincoln was settled in New Salem, Illinois, a log-cabin community near Springfield. For a time he clerked in a store (which soon failed). As unemployment threatened, the Black Hawk War commenced, and Lincoln volunteered for service. His company elected him captain, but he saw no fighting except, he said, "with the mosquitoes."

Returning (1832) from the war, Lincoln groped for a way to make a livelihood. With a partner, he bought a grocery store in New Salem on credit. When the store failed and the partner died, Lincoln paid off the debts, an accomplishment that won him the nickname "Honest Abe." In 1833, Lincoln was appointed postmaster of New Salem, and eked out a living as a deputy to the county surveyor and from other odd-job fees.

Trying for the state legislature in 1834, Lincoln won as a Whig and served four successive two-year terms. His ready stories and sharp wit enabled him to excel in debate, and his leadership gifts were recognized in his selection as the Whig's floor leader. Simultaneous with his young political career, Lincoln read law and won (1836) his license to practice. In Springfield, he experienced a succession of partnerships, including one with William H. Herndon, who later became his biographer.

Lincoln "traveled the circuit," accompanying judges and fellow lawyers through the counties to try cases. The cases were heard in inns, which permitted Lincoln to indulge his talent for strong, effective argument when he thought his client was right.

Lincoln emerged in national politics when he was elected as a Whig to the U.S. House of Representatives and on December 6, 1847, took his seat in Congress where, to the displeasure of his constituents, he opposed President Polk and his conduct of the Mexican War. When his term ended on March 4, 1849, Lincoln did not dare run again because of the general unpopularity of his war views among his constituency. Convinced that his political career was ended, he returned to Springfield where, through hard work and a fast-growing practice, he became one of the best-known lawyers in Illinois in the 1850s.

In 1855, agitated by the national political issue of slavery, Lincoln again turned to politics. Opposed to slavery, although he was never an abolitionist, Lincoln spoke against the principal author of the Kansas-Nebraska Act, Illinois Senator Stephen A. Douglas, and supported the candidacies of legislators opposed to the act. In that same year, Lincoln ran unsuccessfully for the U.S. Senate. Believing that slavery was the negation of the nation's commitment to freedom and equality, he left the Whigs and joined the antislavery Republican party.

In 1858, Lincoln was nominated to run against Douglas for the U.S. Senate. In his speech at the Illinois Republican convention, Lincoln said that "I believe this government cannot endure permanently half slave and half free." The Senatorial contest included a series of debates between Lincoln and Douglas centered on the extension of slavery into free territory. Holding that he was not an abolitionist, Lincoln condemned slavery "as a moral, social, and political evil." Douglas won the election, but the debates gained Lincoln national attention.

In May 1860, the Republican national convention nominated Lincoln for President on the third ballot, after William H. Seward of New York had led on the first two ballots. Considered a moderate on the slavery question, Lincoln received 180 electoral votes to 72 for Breckinridge, 39 for Bell, and 12 for Douglas. Lincoln, elected President, was pledged not to abolish slavery, but to preserve the Union and to prevent the spread of slavery.

However, Southern secession began as soon as Lincoln's election was assured. On December 20, 1860, South Carolina passed a secession ordinance. By the time Lincoln was inaugurated (March 4, 1861), seven states had seceded and formed the Confederate government. Denying in his inaugural address that the federal government would interfere with slavery in states in which the Constitution protected it, he warned that he would use the full power of the nation to "hold, occupy, and possess" the "property and places belonging to the Federal government."

With the coming of war, Lincoln acted boldly and energetically. He called out the militia to suppress the "insurrection," expanded the regular army and navy, raised a volunteer army, closed the post office to "treasonable correspondence," imposed a blockade on Southern ports, and suspended the writ of habeas corpus in areas where Southern sympathizers were active. He also ordered the spending of unappropriated funds for purposes unauthorized by Congress.

For Lincoln's wartime Presidency, the Civil War was a severe test of the human spirit. A succession of battlefield defeats afflicted the North, and a substantial body of Northern opinion demanded peace. Many were willing to fight to preserve the Union, but not to destroy slavery. Others urged the destruction of slavery as the war's supreme goal. Lincoln had to keep the antislavery extremists in check to prevent the secession of the border states. Jealousies and frictions unsettled his cabinet. He appointed and removed a succession of field commanders in the vain hope of securing a major military victory.

In mid-1862, Lincoln decided to drop his reserve on the slavery question and issue a proclamation of emancipation. On the advice of Secretary of State Seward, he awaited a Northern victory. Seizing upon the dubious success of Union forces at Antietam (September 1862), Lincoln issued the proclamation on September 22. He declared that slaves in states in rebellion on January 1, 1863, would be free. Lincoln's action gave a clear-cut moral purpose to the war, setting the stage for the 13th Amendment to the Constitution (adopted in December 1865) that ended slavery throughout the United States.

The tide of the war ran strongly in the Union's favor in 1863 and 1864. Lincoln was renominated (1864), and easily defeated his Democratic opponent, General George B. McClellan, by an electoral vote of 212 to 21 and a popular majority that exceeded 400,000 votes. When Lincoln again took the oath of office (March 4, 1865), the end of the war was in sight, and his inaugural address outlined a postwar policy. He urged that, instead of vengeance, there be "malice toward none" and "charity for all." Pressed to decide if seceded states were in or out of the Union, Lincoln, in his last public address (April 11, 1865), said that the question was unimportant: the Southern states "finding themselves safely at home, it would be utterly immaterial whether they had ever been abroad."

On April 14, five days after Lee's surrender, Lincoln was mortally shot by John Wilkes Booth—an actor and fanatical supporter of the Confederacy—at Ford's Theater in Washington and died the next morning.

Lincoln as President withstood the trials of war with a granitic self-confidence. Yet he was a man of the purest humility, extraordinary wisdom, and shrewd judgment—a master politician in understanding and shaping public opinion. His lean, beautiful, moving prose brought to his Presidency an eloquence that no other incumbent has matched.

Andrew Johnson

Andrew Johnson, 17th President (April 15, 1865–March 3, 1869), was born on December 29, 1808, at Raleigh, North Carolina. His father, who was a sexton, porter, and constable, died when Johnson was four, and at 10 he was apprenticed to a tailor. Thanks to the tailor's practice of employing someone to read aloud as his workmen stitched, and to the local newspaper and a few books, Johnson became familiar with American history and politics.

In 1826, Johnson moved to Greeneville, Tennessee, where he set up his own tailor shop. His efforts in organizing a workingman's party led to his election as alderman in opposition to the local slave-holding aristocracy's candidate. In 1830, he became mayor of Greeneville, and five years later he was elected to the Tennessee legislature and served continuously until 1843. Although formally unschooled, Johnson continued his political rise when elected (1843) to the U.S. House of Representatives in which he served for 10 years.

In Congress Johnson staunchly represented the interests of the "common people" and, in 1845, he introduced the first homestead bill for providing farms for landless citizens from public lands. Johnson's political beliefs were influenced by his fellow Tennessean, Andrew Jackson. Johnson's powerful voice and quick mind enhanced his popularity while provoking concern among Southern aristocrats who opposed his homestead policy. Johnson was elected (1853) Tennessee governor and U.S. Senator (1857), thus becoming one of the few major Southern officeholders of the time who had supported himself by manual labor. Although a slaveholder and a Democrat, Johnson defended the Union. In fact, he was the only Southern Senator not to resign and secede with his state. When Union armies won back (1862) control of western Tennessee, Lincoln appointed Johnson military governor of the state and, by 1864, he had organized a loyal government. This achievement won Johnson the Vice-Presidential nomination on Lincoln's Republican ticket in 1864.

Upon Lincoln's assassination, Johnson assumed the office of President in an atmosphere of grief and rage. Quickly moving to restore conditions of peace after the Civil War, Johnson disbanded most of the Federal army, revoked the blockade of the South, and restored trade. For the difficult problem of reestablishing local government in the seven states of the former Confederacy, Johnson faced rival Presidential and Congressional plans that had been formulated under Lincoln.

Although claiming to assert Lincoln's plan, Johnson actually altered it in some particulars. Unlike Lincoln, who had offered a general amnesty, Johnson required that 14 classes of persons —particularly the well-to-do—apply for pardon. But in judging the loyalty of a state government, Johnson required neither that there be a stipulated proportion of loyal voters nor that state legislatures or conventions take specific steps.

Under Johnson's stimulation, new state governments were organized, secession ordinances were repealed, and slavery abolished. The 13th Amendment was ratified (1865) by all Southern states, except Mississippi. The new governments, however, failed to extend suffrage to qualified blacks, as Johnson suggested. The President did not curb Southern police regulations that were aimed, presumably, at keeping order among blacks but quickened Northern suspicions of an attempt to restore slavery.

Congress, which had not been in session, met in December 1865. The Radical Republicans, who favored harsh reconstruction terms for the South, realized that they would be outnumbered if Southern legislators were seated. As a result, the Radicals refused to seat the Southerners, arguing that they had been illegally elected. Led by Congressman Thaddeus Stevens of Pennsylvania, the Radicals further contended that the Southern states had to come in as new states or continue to be regarded as conquered territory. However, in his message to Congress, Johnson viewed the states and the Constitution as intertwined: since the act of secession was null and void under the Constitution to begin with, Southern state functions had been in his view simply suspended, not destroyed.

In the conflict that developed, Congress' lawmaking powers were pitted against the President's veto power. Congress passed an act extending the Freedman's Bureau, but Johnson vetoed it. His veto of the Civil Rights Act, however, failed. The act aimed to guarantee the rights of freedmen against violation by state law. Congress also passed (1868) the 14th Amendment, which was designed to incorporate the substance of the act into the Constitution.

With the Congressional elections of 1866 in prospect, Johnson decided to present his case to the people and made his "swing around the circle," as it was known, through the East and Midwest in August and September. Although the venture began well, Johnson was provoked into making some ill-tempered remarks when goaded by Radical hecklers, and a hostile press ran biased accounts of his conduct. The election results imperiled Johnson: Congressional foes increased and, consequently, his veto power deteriorated.

Emboldened by its ability to overwhelm the President's veto power, Congress now began to encroach seriously on his domain. It circumvented the Presidential pardoning power, which Johnson had used on behalf of prominent Confederates, by excluding Confederates from office until Congress granted amnesty. The Tenure of Office Act (1867), which was passed despite Presidential veto, prohibited the Chief Executive from removing, without Senate consent, any officer appointed with the Senate's consent. The Supreme Court declined to review the act.

On August 12, 1867, Johnson suspended Secretary of War Edwin M. Stanton, a Radical informer, and appointed General Ulysses S. Grant as temporary secretary. But Grant was also a Radical sympathizer and, in January 1868, he returned his office to Stanton. On February 21, Johnson, formally removing Stanton, made General Lorenzo Thomas Secretary ad interim. Stanton, however, locked himself in his office to prevent Thomas from taking over, and the Senate refused to confirm Thomas' nomination.

A few days later, the House of Representatives voted 128 to 47 to impeach Johnson on 11 counts. A garish extravaganza of 11½ weeks' duration, the trial was presided over by Chief Justice Salmon P. Chase who, although wanting to be President with an intensity that Lincoln had once likened to insanity, proved to be a model of fairness. If the President was convicted, the new President was to be one of the Senate's own, Ben Wade of Ohio, its president pro tempore, who stood first in the line of succession under a law that dated back to 1792.

As the proceedings moved on, the case against Johnson proved thin and revealed that some Senators were more intent upon punishing him than seeing justice done. Fierce pressure was brought to bear on undecided Senators to build up the two-thirds vote required for conviction.

On May 16, the Senate voted on the eleventh charge, the one that Johnson's opponents believed the most likely to pass. As the vote proceeded, it became clear that the outcome would depend on the vote of Senator Edmund G. Ross of Kansas, who said "not guilty" and saved Johnson by a single vote. Votes were taken on only two other articles with identical results, and the trial ended.

In foreign affairs, Johnson and Secretary of State Seward achieved (1867) the purchase of Alaska from Russia and in 1865, by threat of force, they induced Napoleon III to withdraw his troops from Mexico. Maximilian, who was installed (1864) by Napoleon III as Mexico's emperor while the United States was distracted by the Civil War, was overthrown by Juarez.

For all of his travail, Johnson nonetheless aspired to be the Democratic nominee for President in 1868, but the party chose Governor Horatio Seymour of New York.

After leaving the White House, Johnson ran unsuccessfully for Congress in 1869 and 1872. In 1874, however, he was elected to the U.S. Senate, the only former President to become a Senator. Johnson served only in a special short session in March 1875. After returning to Tennessee, he suffered a paralytic stroke and died on July 31, 1875.

Ulysses Simpson Grant

Ulysses Simpson Grant, 18th President (1869–1877), was born on April 27, 1822, in Point Pleasant, Ohio, the eldest son of a farmer and tanner. An excellent horseman but disinclined toward farm work, Grant applied to West Point.

An average student at West Point, Grant impressed his classmates as academically lazy and careless in dress. Graduating in 1843, he served with distinction in the Mexican War and attained the rank of first lieutenant.

After the war, Grant served in western posts and drank excessively, until his commanding officer ordered him either to reform or to resign. In 1854 he did resign and took up farming near St. Louis. Handicapped by poor land, Grant sold the farm in 1859 and became employed in a real estate office, but performed his main duty—collecting rents—poorly. He next worked, briefly, in the U.S. Customhouse, and in 1860 joined his father's hardware store in Galena, Illinois. As a storekeeper, he was unsuccessful, too.

At the outbreak of the Civil War, Grant, now 40 years old and unsettled, drilled a company of volunteers in Galena and then went to Springfield to work for the Illinois adjutant general. His request to the War Department for a colonelcy was ignored; however, in May 1861 the governor of Illinois appointed him colonel of the 21st Illinois Volunteers. By August, he was a brigadier general of volunteers and was given command of southwestern Missouri. An aggressive field commander, he swept through victories in Missouri, Kentucky, and Tennessee. In 1862, he gave the Union its first major victory when he captured Forts Henry and Donelson. At the latter fort he specified, "No terms other than an unconditional and immediate surrender can be accepted." This earned him the nickname "Unconditional Surrender Grant."

Grant moved on to larger commands and greater victories at Shiloh, Vicksburg, and Chattanooga. In March 1864, Lincoln made him a lieutenant-general, placed him in command of all the Union armies, and said of Grant that "he makes things git." Grant took personal command of the Army of the Potomac to confront the Confederates under General Robert E. Lee. Relentlessly applying superior manpower and force, Grant wore down the enemy and brought Lee to surrender at Appomattox, April 9, 1865. Generous in victory, Grant permitted the vanquished Confederates to keep their horses "for the spring plowing." Lavishly hailed in the victorious Union, Grant was made a full general in 1866, the first such designation since George Washington.

In 1868, Grant the military hero won the Republican nomination for President and triumphed easily over his Democratic opponent, Governor Horatio Seymour of New York. A newcomer to politics, Grant accepted the nomination in a note the brevity of which was unheard of for Presidential candidates, but it did contain the apt sentiment, "Let us have peace." Always a man of opinions, Grant declined to ride in the inaugural with the outgoing President, Andrew Johnson, owing to an estrangement that stemmed from Johnson's imbroglio with the War Department.

Unfamiliar and uneasy with politics, Grant conducted business in the executive mansion in a military style. Military aides did much of the work of the administration and Grant, upon issuing orders, expected battle-command compliance. To his misfortune, he did not readily perceive the subtle resistances and manipulations of civilian administrators.

Cabinet appointments, often used by a President to build support within his party, were devoted by Grant to the indulgence of his personal preferences. As Secretary of State he named his close friend Elihu Washburne. His military aide, John A. Rawlins, became Secretary of War. Grant sought to implant in the Treasury his friend, the merchant Alexander T. Stewart, who proved legally ineligible. Grant also made appointments with little regard to actual job fitness and soon had to redesign his Cabinet to recognize both party considerations and competence.

Aided by a distinguished Secretary of State, Hamilton Fish (Washburne's successor), Grant cleared up the serious controversies with Great Britain over the *Alabama* claims (when the United States claimed damages for British-supported Confederate cruisers) and carefully preserved the neutrality of the United States in Spain's suppression of Cuban insurrection. Grant made a bold, but embarrassingly futile, attempt to annex Santo Domingo, and when Charles Sumner, a powerful Republican leader, denounced Grant, he was removed as chairman of the Foreign Relations Committee; this break with Sumner was perhaps Grant's worst disaster in foreign affairs.

The Civil War left a heritage of bonds and other securities that were easy prey to manipulation by speculators. To foil them, Grant approved legislation establishing the policy of ultimate redemption of legal tender notes in coin. But the speculators and gamblers—especially Jim Fisk and Jay Gould—struck back by cornering gold on the market and by "buying" cronies and administrative associates of the President with favors. Grant, to whom defeat and submission were alien, released a flood of gold from the Treasury to overwhelm the corner. The victory was costly, resulting in the "Black Friday" of 1869, when thousands were ruined.

Never vindictive toward the South, Grant declined to enforce the 14th amendment, which had granted Negro rights. His detachment coincided with the beginnings of intimidation in the old Confederacy of Negro voters.

In 1872, Grant was unanimously renominated and won reelection against Horace Greeley, nominee of the Democrats as well as the Liberal Republicans, who were seeking both a more radical Reconstruction policy and a more competent administration.

Grant's second term was dominated by scandals. His private secretary, Orville Babcock, was implicated in the notorious Whisky Ring and suspected of wrongdoing in the Santo Domingo negotiations. Secretary of War William Belknap was revealed to have accepted bribes from a trader at an Indian post. Through the loyalty of Grant, both escaped punishment. Grant himself was criticized for coarse tastes, excessive appetite for material enjoyment, and low associations. He was seen in public with the "robber baron" Jim Fisk and offered the post of Chief Justice to the notorious political boss Roscoe Conkling.

Although Grant is rated as one of the worst Presidents, he nevertheless piloted the country and the Presidency through the difficult aftermath of Andrew Johnson's confrontation with Congress. He also overcame a severe financial crisis and brought Anglo-American relations into a new era of harmony and mutual respect.

In 1880 Grant was the candidate of Roscoe Conkling and the powerful Stalwart faction for the Republican Presidential nomination, but he was defeated on a late ballot by Garfield.

After leaving office, Grant settled in New York City and lost (1884) his savings in a fraudulent banking firm. A merciful Congress appointed him general at full pay and subsequently added retirement pay. While suffering from throat cancer, Grant wrote his memoirs. Published (2 vols., 1885–86) by Mark Twain, they were a remarkable financial success and rank among the great military narratives of history. Grant soon died, on July 23, 1885, but his courage and indomitable spirit in the face of grave illness had restored his family's security.

Rutherford Birchard Hayes

Rutherford Birchard Hayes, 19th President (1877–1881), was born on October 4, 1822, in Delaware, Ohio. His father, a storekeeper from Vermont, died the year he was born. Raised by an uncle, Hayes graduated from Kenyon College (Ohio) as valedictorian. After study at Harvard Law School, he began the practice of law at Lower Sandusky (now Fremont), Ohio, and in 1849 he moved to Cincinnati.

Upon the outbreak of the Civil War, Hayes volunteered and was commissioned a major. Wounded four times, he advanced to the rank of major general. While on the battlefield, he was nominated for the U.S. House of Representatives and elected. A staunch Republican, he supported the Radical postwar reconstruction program and was reelected. However, he resigned from Congress to become governor of Ohio. Reelected twice, he ran on a platform in 1875 calling for "sound money" in opposition to Democratic monetary policy.

Hayes's hard-money position helped win him the Republican Presidential nomination in 1876 over the better-known James G. Blaine. Hayes defeated the Democratic nominee, Samuel J. Tilden, in a fiercely disputed election that threatened the country with civil war. Although Hayes received only a minority of the popular votes, a partisan election commission awarded him the office.

Hayes became President under a cloud of resentment over the dubious legitimacy of his incumbency. So restive was the country's mood that he took the oath of office privately, and the inaugural parade and ball were omitted. His shadowed Presidency coincided with a critical juncture in the nation's affairs. Wise statesmanship was needed to bring the stormy Reconstruction Period to an end.

Despite his electoral handicap, Hayes bravely faced problems and justified the boast of a forebear that "the name of Hayes began by valor." Days after his inauguration, Hayes removed federal troops from the South, thereby ending the period of Reconstruction. Wade, Blaine, and other leading Republicans angrily protested the step which imperiled the Republican "carpetbag" governments. These had made Hayes's election possible and could not exist without military protection. The wisdom of Hayes's policy was demonstrated by the end of violence and by the emergence of normalcy in the South.

Like other Presidents of his era, Hayes grappled with the problem of civil service reform. He offended the Stalwarts, the spoils-minded faction of his party, by declaring that appointments to office must be made on the basis of ability and tenure must be protected. Beginning with Secretary of the Interior Carl Schurz, Hayes's department heads applied these principles widely.

Hayes won admiration from "sound money" advocates for his devotion to the resumption of specie payments. The farmers of the Midwest and city workingmen, beset by the severe economic depression of 1876–77, widely favored soft money—"an irredeemable paper currency," and the "free coinage of silver." The House of Representatives passed bills for both in 1877. In a vigorous message of opposition to Congress, Hayes insisted upon resumption and payment of the public debt in gold. Hayes's action forestalled the Senate from passing a bill to postpone resumption. His veto, however, could not defeat the Bland-Allison bill calling upon the government to coin each month from $2 million to $4 million in silver dollars to be full legal tender.

Despite the business depression and political opposition, Hayes continued to accumulate a gold reserve, and on January 1, 1879, for the first time since the Civil War, the government declared that it would pay out gold, or "specie," in exchange for paper money.

Just as he showed little sympathy for the economically embattled farmer, Hayes was insensitive to the plight of labor in the economic depression. In 1877, with a railroad strike raging in 10 states, Hayes furnished state authorities with arms from national arsenals and, as commander-in-chief, transferred Federal troops from remote posts to the scenes of trouble.

Assertive toward Congress, Hayes vetoed a Chinese exclusion bill because it violated a treaty with China. He fought Congress successfully on "riders" to two appropriation bills. In an uncommon achievement for a President, he brought Congress to remove the riders.

Convinced that a President performed better if he served for only one term, Hayes in accepting the nomination in 1876 expressed his resolve to be a single-term President. Party leaders, dismayed by his bursts of independence, encouraged him to keep that resolve.

Hayes left office with the satisfaction of seeing the resentment over his flawed Presidential victory evaporate. His hard work, efficiency, and tough moral fiber impressed the public. After leaving office, he devoted his final years to education and philanthropy. He died in Fremont, Ohio, on January 17, 1893.

James Abram Garfield

James Abram Garfield, 20th President (March 4, 1881–September 19, 1881), was born on November 19, 1831, in Orange, Ohio, the son of a frontier farmer. Fatherless at two, Garfield became "a self-made man," who supported his widowed mother by working on farms and as a carpenter.

At 18, Garfield began study at Hiram (Ohio) College and later transferred to Williams College, Williamstown, Massachusetts. Graduating in 1856, Garfield returned to Ohio and rose to a professorship of ancient languages and literature at Hiram College and served as president from 1857 to 1861.

With the outbreak of the Civil War, Garfield was commissioned a lieutenant colonel of an Ohio volunteer regiment. Serving at Chickamauga and as chief of staff to General Rosecrans, he rose to the rank of major general. In 1863 when he was elected to the U.S. House of Representatives, Garfield resigned from the army.

Serving for 17 years in the House, Garfield was a regular Republican of antislavery convictions and a firm advocate of Radical reconstruction. He was an influential member of key House committees on finance and military affairs and in 1876 was minority leader. Garfield was also a member of the Electoral Commission created by Congress to decide state contests in the disputed election of 1876.

In the Republican National Convention of 1880, Garfield, a compromise candidate, was nominated for President on the 36th ballot. A "dark horse," he had defeated ex-President Grant, whom the Stalwarts, a party faction, were promoting for a third term. Because Garfield was a member of a rival Republican faction, Chester A. Arthur, a Stalwart, was nominated for Vice-President.

The Stalwarts, headed by Senator Roscoe Conkling of New York, remained unappeased. Upon becoming President, Garfield became embroiled with Conkling in a war over patronage. Garfield sent to the Senate the nominations of men of his own choice for minor posts in the New York Custom House. Conkling felt the step violated pledges given in return for his acceptance of Gar-

field as Presidential nominee and invoked Senatorial courtesy to defeat the nominations.

Garfield's conflict with leading Republican personalities spread to the Post Office, where the "star route" frauds were uncovered. The Post Office scandalously overpaid certain persons operating these mail routes, including the chairman of the Republican National Committee. Despite intimidation, Garfield had prosecutions launched against offenders. He also withdrew all nominations for New York appointments, except for the Custom House, to stress Presidential independence and integrity in the appointive process.

Since Republican control of the Senate was insecure, the Republican caucus chose not to break with the President and supported his New York Custom House appointments. An outraged Conkling resigned from the Senate and invited the New York legislature to vindicate him.

Garfield approved the proposal of his Secretary of State James G. Blaine to call a conference of Latin-American nations to review the Clayton-Bulwer Treaty with Great Britain, entered into in 1850. Garfield and Blaine were eager to advance a proposed isthmian canal and to shake off the treaty's provision that called for Anglo-American control of the waterway.

Before the conference could take place, Garfield was shot on July 2, 1881, by Charles Guiteau, a Stalwart and an office-seeker disappointed by the deadlock over patronage. Garfield lingered on until September 19, 1881, when he died.

Chester Alan Arthur

Chester Alan Arthur, 21st President (1881–1885), was born on October 5, 1830, at Fairfield, Vermont, the son of a Baptist clergyman. Arthur graduated from Union College, Schenectady, in 1848, where he was elected to Phi Beta Kappa. After teaching school in Vermont and serving as school principal in Cohoes, New York, Arthur moved to New York City to study law, and in 1854 was admitted to the bar.

A brilliant lawyer, Arthur won fame in two civil liberties lawsuits. One, a pre-Civil War case, held that a slave brought into New York became free. The other established that Negroes enjoyed the same rights on New York streetcars as whites.

Arthur, a staunch Republican, was rewarded in 1861 with the post of engineer-in-chief of New York State, and in the Civil War, he held further political positions as inspector general of New York troops and quartermaster of New York State. As such he helped organize the New York militia. After the war, in 1871, President Grant appointed him to the well-paid office of collector of the Port of New York, one of the choicest of political plums.

Competent and honest as the collector, Arthur, in the fashion of the day, ran the Custom House as an adjunct of Roscoe Conkling's New York Republican machine. Patronage was openly distributed, clerks freely attended party caucuses and conventions, got out the vote, and slacked on the job. Eventually, Arthur was removed by his fellow Republican, reform-minded President Rutherford Hayes.

At the Republican national convention of 1880, James Garfield was nominated for the Presidency, after the Conkling clique of New York Republicans, the Stalwarts, failed to nominate Grant for a third term. To sweeten the defeat, the convention chose Arthur, a leading Stalwart, for the Vice-Presidency.

Garfield's assassination soon after his inauguration made Arthur President.

Arthur is a classic instance of a man who became a better President than was generally expected. Forebodings of the day saw Arthur running the Presidency as a machine politician and spoilsman, and opening the hospitality of the White House to the Custom House loafers. Many ridiculed Arthur as a "dude" and "Gentleman Boss," owing to his courtly manners and dandified dress. But Arthur proved otherwise. His bearing as President was dignified, honorable, and constructive. His devotion to principle in the manner of his younger days as a civil liberties attorney quickly transformed his image into that of a man well capable of being President.

In addressing himself to the emerging problems of the day, especially the shabby morality of post-Civil War politics, Arthur suffered imposing handicaps; his cabinet was inherited from the rival Garfield faction, and he lacked a working majority in Congress. Matters worsened after the 1882 elections, when the Democrats won control of the House of Representatives.

Nevertheless, Arthur built a commendable record of effort and achievement. When he recommended the Civil Service Reform Act of 1883—the basis of the present-day personnel system—his former friends and colleagues felt betrayed because it drastically limited patronage.

He demonstrated courage and conscience in vetoing a Chinese exclusion bill that violated a treaty with China. Congress, however, overrode his veto. He also vetoed a river and harbor appropriation bill of 1882, contending that it wastefully committed public funds for improper local purposes. Congress again defeated his veto. His several defeats weakened his standing with professional politicians.

Arthur extracted from Congress laws to build a modern navy to replace the obsolete fleet dating back to the Civil War. He worked for tariff reform, and secured a new protective tariff act, with little reform. The Alaska Territory was organized. A treaty of friendship, commerce, and navigation was signed with Korea; a treaty for the construction of a canal with Nicaragua; and an agreement for a coaling and repair station at Pearl Harbor with Hawaii. Although lacking in drama, Arthur's administration was marked by growing prosperity in the country.

Arthur aspired to renomination for the Presidency in 1884, but his candidacy withered at an early stage. Professional politicians, bitter over his support of the civil service law, widely opposed him and reformers failed to support him.

At the end of his Presidential term, he returned to New York City where he resumed his law practice. He died on November 18, 1886, a little more than a year after leaving office, and was buried in Albany, New York.

Grover Cleveland

Grover Cleveland, 22d (1885–1889) and 24th President (1893–1897), was born in Caldwell, New Jersey, on March 18, 1837. He was the fifth of nine children of a Presbyterian country minister and a relative of Moses Cleaveland, founder of Cleveland, Ohio. While a child, his family moved to Fayetteville and then to Clinton, in upstate New York. His father's death barred Cleveland from a college education. Heading west to seek his fortune, he proceeded no farther than Buffalo, where an uncle secured him a clerkship in a law office. In 1859, at the age of 22, he was admitted to the bar. When the Civil War erupted, Cleveland could not enlist because of the necessity of supporting his mother and sisters, and he borrowed money to hire a conscription substitute.

The industrious Cleveland entered politics as a ward worker for the Democratic party in Buffalo. In 1862, he was elected ward supervisor, and a year later he was appointed assistant district attorney of Erie County. His political career remained uneventful until 1871, when he was elected sheriff of Erie County, and in 1882, he was elected mayor of Buffalo. His efficiency and rigorous honesty ("Public office is public trust," he once said) won him rapid fame. After one year as mayor, he was chosen governor of New York.

In their national convention of 1884, the Democrats nominated Cleveland for President. His Republican opponent was the glamorous James G. Blaine and, in the ensuing campaign, the character of the candidates was viciously assailed. The Democratic party was described by the opposition as the party of "Rum, Romanism, and Rebellion." Offended Catholic voters supported Cleveland, and the "mugwumps," a reform wing of the Republican party, backed him, impressed by his reform record. Winning in a close race, Cleveland became the first Democratic President since the Civil War.

An awaiting question for his Presidency was whether Cleveland could transfer to the larger, more complex arena of national politics the atmosphere of probity and reform he so successfully cultivated in state and local officeholding. He was quickly tested by the new Civil Service Reform Law passed in the twilight of the previous administration. His "mugwump" supporters pressed for civil service reform, but from Cleveland's own party came a long line of Democratic office seekers, hungry for reward after 24 years of exclusion from Presidential patronage.

Pledged to "practical reform," Cleveland gave slow and reserved recognition to partisan demands. Simultaneously, he lent steady support to the new Civil Service Commission and induced Congress to repeal the Tenure of Office Act, a shadow upon the Presidency since 1867. He skillfully preserved Presidential independence in appointments, but his sturdy middle course served to offend both the politicians and the reformers.

Cleveland also championed the cause of tariff reform. Embarrassed by the substantial surplus in the Treasury, and convinced that it was fostered by excessive tariff rates, Cleveland called for tariff revision to diminish what he regarded as improper favoritism to protected industries.

Cleveland was renominated in 1888, and although he won a larger popular vote than his Republican opponent, Benjamin Harrison, the latter mustered a majority of the electoral vote to win the election.

In 1892, Cleveland regained the Presidency, a popular figure in the face of wide disgruntlement over the McKinley Tariff Act of 1890 and its high-rate structure. But the pleasure of victory was quickly displaced by the storms of economic crisis. From the Harrison administration, Cleveland inherited the forces that produced the Panic of 1893; bank failures, bankruptcies, and massive unemployment seized the economy. Cleveland resisted demands for inflation by Western and Southern Democrats and Populists and, instead, chose to combat the crisis through sound money policies and orthodox economic measures. Cleveland won a long, bitter fight only by receiving substantial Republican support, since the Democratic party was characterized by a cleavage between sound money and inflationary factions.

The animosities raised by the fight crippled Cleveland's chances for tariff reform. The Wilson-Gorman bill that finally passed so reflected the views of protectionist Democrats that Cleveland termed the legislation "party perfidy and party dishonor." Unwilling to sign the Wilson bill, Cleveland permitted it to become law without his signature.

Cleveland's sound money policy was beset by sharp declines in Treasury holdings of gold, and he was forced to replenish the reserves through large bond issues arranged with a syndicate of Eastern financiers. His vocal Democratic opponents charged the President with being in alliance with Wall Street.

In the wake of the Panic of 1893, strikes were widespread, and in 1894 striking employees of the Pullman Company and Eugene V. Debs' American Railway Union halted trains across the country. Violence erupted in Chicago, the center of the strike. In a historic intervention, the President declared that the strikers had interfered with the free flow of the mails, and regular army troops were dispatched to Chicago to enforce the laws. Governor J. P. Altgeld of Illinois, who did not want the troops, demanded their recall in vain.

In foreign affairs, Cleveland rejected the imperialist tendencies of recent American policy. He refused to deal with a new government in Hawaii, established by a revolution managed by American residents. Cleveland rejected domestic pressures to intervene in behalf of Cuban insurrectionists and make war with Spain; he ignored a Congressional resolution recognizing Cuba.

Cleveland was assertive in foreign affairs when what he regarded as legitimate American interests were at stake. In Venezuela's boundary dispute with Britain, he gave new precision to the Monroe Doctrine by articulating the hegemony of the United States in the Americas and our specific interest in the boundary dispute.

By the end of Cleveland's term, the "silver" or inflationary Democrats dominated his party and, at the national convention of 1896, they nominated—to Cleveland's great distress—William Jennings Bryan, the silver orator. Cleveland preferred the Republican nominee, William McKinley, and his sound-money policies, but he took no part in the campaign.

After leaving the Presidency, Cleveland lived in Princeton, New Jersey. He lectured at the University, served as a trustee, and in 1904 published *Presidential Problems*, one of the most penetrating books by a former President about the office. He died June 24, 1908, and fittingly, his last words were: "I have tried so hard to do right."

Benjamin Harrison

Benjamin Harrison, 23d President (1889–1893), was born on August 20, 1833, at North Bend, Ohio. Of distinguished ancestry, he was the great-grandson of a signer of the Declaration of Independence, a grandson of President William Henry Harrison, and the son of a congressman. He studied at Miami University (Ohio), graduating in 1852, and was admitted to the bar the following year. In 1854 he moved to Indianapolis, where he practiced law and politics.

During the Civil War Harrison served with distinction on the battlefield and was brevetted brigadier general. A prosperous corporation lawyer in Indianapolis after the war, he was active in Republican politics and held various local and party offices. In 1876 he ran unsuccessfully for governor, but five years later he won a seat in the United States Senate.

His distinguished background, war record, and the importance of Indiana to Republican electoral strategy gained him the Presidential nomination in 1888. He received a majority of the electoral vote, although Grover Cleveland, running for re-election, won a plurality of the popular vote.

In the White House, Harrison and his Secretary of State, James G. Blaine, conducted an assertive foreign policy as the United States moved toward a posture of imperialism. A Pan-American Congress was highly successful. The United States established its claims in Samoa and checked German expansion there. Harrison was less successful, however, in a controversy with Great Britain over the killing of fur seals in the Bering Sea. Aggressive efforts to establish American rights to Mole St. Nicholas in Haiti failed. The Harrison administration also engaged in bitter negotiations with Chile following an attack on American sailors in Valparaiso; the United States demanded an apology and ultimately received it.

One of Harrison's fondest projects was the annexation of Hawaii. In his administration's closing days, he sent a treaty for that purpose to the Senate. His successor, Grover Cleveland, however, withdrew the treaty before the Senate voted.

In domestic affairs, Harrison was torn between the demands of the Civil Service Reform Act of 1883 and the more traditional spoils system. He followed a moderate course that displeased both the reformers and the organization politicians. On balance, his civil service record was statesmanlike. He appointed and retained Theodore Roosevelt as civil service commissioner, and angered the spoilsmen by adding 11,000 civil service positions to the classified list.

In legislation, Harrison was disinclined to oppose policies his party advocated in Congress. Since the party was in the hands of leaders he could not control, his impact upon the laws of the day was minor. Congress passed the McKinley Tariff Act, imposing the highest duties up to that time. Harrison, however, secured the insertion of a reciprocity provision, the act's only popular feature.

Harrison approved the Sherman Silver Purchase Act to help the silver industry. He signed a rivers and harbors act, a giant pork-barrel measure, and an act markedly increasing pension expenditures. He supported a federal elections bill, embodying several reforms, but it failed. Harrison also aided the Sherman Anti-Trust Act, passed to counteract popular feeling that the Republicans were the party of big business. However, this was insufficient to forestall the Democrats from winning control of the House in 1890, which further diminished Harrison's influence on legislation.

Opposed by party leaders and bosses, such as Quay, Platt, and "Czar" Reed, Harrison secured renomination in 1892 only with difficulty. They and other politicians were offended by his limited patronage policy and cold personality. His reserve, a frigid look darting from steel-gray eyes, and his brevity of response wore badly with politicians. Despite his manner, Harrison was a remarkably effective public speaker, bringing one observer to note: "Harrison can make a speech to 10,000 men, and every man of them will go away his friend. Let him meet the same 10,000 men in private, and every one will go away his enemy."

Party apathy, labor hostility to an administration heavily partial to business, and other factors caused Harrison's defeat in his race for reelection in 1892 against Cleveland.

After leaving the Presidency, Harrison continued to gain distinction as a lawyer, and in 1898 he represented Venezuela in her boundary dispute with Great Britain. He died in Indianapolis on March 13, 1901.

William McKinley

William McKinley, 25th President (March 4, 1897–September 14, 1901), was born on January 29, 1843, at Niles, Ohio, the son of an ironfounder. After attending Poland Seminary (Ohio) and Allegheny College (Pennsylvania), McKinley taught school.

Following service in the Union Army in the Civil War, where he rose to the rank of major, McKinley studied at Albany (New York) Law School and was admitted to the bar in 1867; he soon moved to Canton, Ohio, where he began practice.

McKinley began his political career in 1869 by election as prosecuting attorney for Stark County, Ohio. In 1876, he was elected as a Republican to the U.S. House of Representatives, where he remained, except for one term, until 1891. As Congressman, McKinley sponsored the McKinley Tariff Act, which set record-high protective duties, and voted for the Bland-Allison (silver purchase) act.

Defeated for reelection in 1890, McKinley attracted the friendship and support of Mark Hanna, a powerful, wealthy Ohio Republican. Their lasting political partnership helped McKinley win election as governor in 1891 and reelection in 1893.

In 1896, McKinley's popularity and Hanna's shrewd management brought the Republican Presidential nomination to the governor. Pitted against him as the Democratic nominee was the colorful William Jennings Bryan whose free silver doctrines and Populist ties alarmed the business community and alienated many Democratic conservatives. Bryan, a superb orator, made a record number of speaking appearances. McKinley and Hanna, in contrast, perfected the "front porch" campaign; instead of the candidate going to the people, the people came to the candidate. Cooperating railroads gave excursion rates so low that one newspaper said that visiting McKinley was "cheaper than staying home."

McKinley's election was interpreted as a mandate for a high protective tariff and for a gold monetary standard, as opposed to a silver standard. Promptly after his inauguration, McKinley called a special session of Congress to act on the tariff; the Dingley Tariff Act resulted, the high duties of which delighted business. Not until 1900 was a monetary law enacted. It established the gold dollar as the United States standard and strictly limited the coinage of silver.

The monetary law was delayed by the Spanish-American War. When McKinley was inaugurated, Cuba was in revolt against Spain. The United States battleship *Maine* was blown up in Havana harbor, and McKinley was pressed to intervene. He did not want to go to war, nor fight legislators who were demanding war. Ultimately, he referred the problem to Congress, knowing that it favored war; Congress directed the President to intervene in Cuba to establish Cuban independence.

As a war President, McKinley was handicapped by an inadequate war department and army. Disease was more deadly and inefficiency more harassing than the Spanish enemy. Although the navy performed creditably, McKinley was fortunate in facing a weak enemy.

McKinley did not want to annex territory, but as in the coming of the war, his political style prevailed over his political ends. As a politician, he eschewed conflict. His natural kindliness and his background as a tariff negotiator adept at conciliating everyone ruled his approach to foreign affairs. As a public leader, famous for "keeping his ear close to the ground," he was seldom more than a half-step ahead of his constituents. Convinced from a tour of the Midwest that the people favored annexation, he instructed his peace negotiators accordingly. The Philippines, Guam, and Puerto Rico were ceded to the United States. Cuba was placed under American control until it could establish a government of its own. During the war, the Hawaiian Islands were annexed by joint resolution of Congress.

McKinley guided the country through its initial experiences as an imperial nation. A law to govern the new insular possessions was passed. The war department was reorganized. Rebellious Filipinos, seeking independence, were fought, and a commission headed by William Howard Taft was dispatched to the islands to set up the government of the United States there. In 1899 Secretary of State John Hay negotiated the Open Door policy with European nations with interests in China. But the Boxer Rebellion in China soon prompted intervention by many powers, including the United States.

In 1900, McKinley was reelected, upon defeating Bryan, this time to the cry of "a full dinner-pail for four years more." The war had turned the McKinley era into one of booming prosperity, and the election returns showed that the benign McKinley had the support of the people. The electorate also approved the new imperialism.

McKinley was at the crest of popularity and political vindication when he was shot by an anarchist, Leon Czolgosz, on September 6, 1901, at Buffalo, New York. He died on September 14.

McKinley's term, divided between the 19th century and the 20th, aptly symbolizes his contribution as a bridge between the old and the modern Presidency. With him ended the line of Presidents who had fought in the Civil War, and his popularity throughout the country signified that the breach between the North and South had been healed and was no longer a preoccupation of the Chief Executive. Likewise, he presided over the advent of a new era, in which the United States, through war with Spain, first took rank as a world power.

Theodore Roosevelt

Theodore Roosevelt, 26th President (September 14, 1901–March 3, 1909), was born on October 27, 1858, in New York City, the son of a wealthy merchant of Dutch ancestry and of a mother of distinguished Georgian family whose brother served in the Confederate navy. Endowed with great energy, curiosity, and grit, Roosevelt was handicapped by frail health; however, by careful exercise, he built up unusual strength. He traveled widely and was educated by tutors until he entered Harvard (1876). After graduating (1880), he enrolled in Columbia Law School but, legal studies not proving of interest, turned to politics.

In 1881, at the age of 23, Roosevelt, as a Republican, was elected to the New York State Assembly. At first his fellow legislators looked askance at his expensive dress and pronounced sideburns, but his vitality and intelligence won their respect to the point that they elected (1882) him Republican minority leader. His disinclination to follow orders, however, prompted the party bosses to remove him. Roosevelt, nevertheless, remained highly influential in the assembly, working closely with Democratic Governor Grover Cleveland for the advancement of civil service reform.

In 1884, Roosevelt abandoned his political career in remorse over the deaths of his wife and mother, passing the next two years on his ranches in the Dakota Territory. There he developed his skills at riding and hunting and acquired Western flairs. In 1886, he remarried and returned to his home at Sagamore Hill (Oyster Bay) on Long Island. That year he also returned to politics, running unsuccessfully for mayor of New York City against overwhelming Democratic strength.

Roosevelt's speech-making for the Presidential candidacy of Benjamin Harrison was rewarded by Harrison's appointing him (1889) a member of the U.S. Civil Service Commission. Shrewd in cultivating publicity, Roosevelt brought the commission out of the shadows, interested the public in its work, and accomplished remarkable gains against the spoils system. As police commissioner of New York City (1895–97), he again used the power of publicity to restore discipline and stamp out police dishonesty.

In 1897 President William McKinley, for whom Roosevelt had campaigned the year before, appointed him Assistant Secretary of the Navy. Roosevelt worked to strengthen the navy but, when the United States and Spain went to war in 1898, Roosevelt resigned at once and organized the spectacular volunteer cavalry regiment that won fame as the "Rough Riders."

Roosevelt returned from Cuba a military hero and, with the Republican party in New York State besmirched by scandal, his nomination for governor was supported even by Boss Tom Platt, who was personally averse to the reform-minded Roosevelt. Elected, Roosevelt promoted reform

legislation and forced through a law taxing the franchises of public service corporations. Large business interests were angered, and "Boss" Platt and other Republican leaders resolved to rid New York of Roosevelt by moving him into the 1900 national election as McKinley's running mate for the Vice-Presidency, presuming that in that office Roosevelt would be harmless and forgotten. Against his own inclinations, the governor accepted.

Ten months after the Republican victory that ensued, McKinley was assassinated, and Roosevelt became President at the early age of 42. Although he kept all members of McKinley's cabinet and said reassuringly that he would continue the late President's policies "absolutely unbroken," Roosevelt's zest and political skill soon broke the confines of this heritage, and business leaders, recalling his state reform policies, quavered.

In his first message to Congress (December 1901), Roosevelt addressed himself to the growing problem of business trusts, proposing not their prohibition, but regulation. His policy was illustrated by the government's suit (1902) against the Northern Securities Company, which J. P. Morgan interests had formed to control major railroads in the West. The company was charged with reducing competition, and the Supreme Court, upholding the government, ordered its dissolution. In all, the administration filed suits against 43 other corporations and achieved triumphs against the tobacco and oil trusts.

Roosevelt was the first President conspicuously friendly to labor. In 1902, facing a widespread anthracite coal strike and lacking express legal authority, Roosevelt nonetheless intervened, urging the disputants to arbitrate. When the miners agreed, but the mine-owners balked, Roosevelt threatened to have the army seize and operate the pits. Eventually a settlement was reached favorable to the miners, to whom public opinion was sympathetic. At Roosevelt's recommendation, Congress established (1903) a Department of Commerce and Labor.

In the foreign policy of his first term, Roosevelt used "the big stick"—the threat of force to advance his purposes. In 1902, he had applied the Monroe Doctrine when German and British naval forces threatened Venezuelan ports, trying to force payments of debts. Roosevelt warned Germany that the United States might use force if any Venezuelan territory was occupied. As a result, Germany withdrew her vessels, and a settlement was negotiated. In 1904, when Santo Domingo was staggering under European debts, the "Roosevelt Corollary" of the Monroe Doctrine was born. Under it, the United States announced that it was prepared to exercise "an international police power" in instances "of wrongdoing or impotence."

While negotiating (1903) to secure a strip of land across Panama—a prelude to the eventual construction of the canal—Roosevelt supported and recognized a revolutionary Panamanian government that signed the necessary treaty, and American troops protected this new government from Colombian forces.

Roosevelt was reelected (1904) by a record popular majority over the Democratic nominee, Judge Alton B. Parker. At the President's initiative, his often reluctant Congress passed a pure food law, a meat inspection law, and the Hepburn law that conferred on the Interstate Commerce Commission the power of railroad rate-making. Roosevelt promoted an aggressive conservation policy, which added enormous acreage to the national forests, and also promoted the reclamation and irrigation of arid lands.

Foreign affairs continued to be demanding during Roosevelt's second term. His mediation and strong personal influence brought the Russo-Japanese War to an end in 1905, an achievement that brought him the Nobel Peace Prize. Roosevelt, however, retained faith in the efficacy and value of a show of force. When relations with Japan deteriorated and possible attack on the Philippines was feared, he dispatched (1908) the fleet to the Far East and around the world. This step prompted several diplomatic agreements with Japan.

Roosevelt was the first President whose administration was continuously involved in major foreign policy, and his Square Deal program of social justice—he called his office "a bully pulpit" —was also the first of its kind. He was extraordinarily skillful at rallying public opinion; however, a contemporary cartoon that depicted him with large clenched teeth, a thick spiked club, and a belt full of pistols also tells much of his style. Audacious and innovative in legislative relations, he began the practice of supplementing his messages with actual drafts of bills, and he was the first of modern Presidents to appeal to public opinion to advance his measures in Congress.

After his election in 1904, Roosevelt declared that "under no circumstances" would he run again for President. He chose his Secretary of War, William Howard Taft, as his successor, and Taft was both nominated and elected.

After leaving office, Roosevelt went big-game hunting in Africa and, when he returned (1910) to the United States, he was approached by disgruntled progressive Republicans who felt that Taft had betrayed them. Failing to bring Taft around to his own progressive ways, Roosevelt broke with his protégé and, in 1912, he ran for a Presidential third term. After winning in Republican primaries, he was denied the nomination in the Taft-controlled convention. Roosevelt and his supporters bolted and formed the Bull Moose party. In the tumultuous campaign, Roosevelt survived an attempted assassination to run second in the three-way race that was easily won by the Democratic candidate: Woodrow Wilson.

In 1913 and 1914, Roosevelt made pioneering explorations in the Brazilian jungle. After the outbreak of World War I, he was an early advocate of preparedness against Germany and critical of Wilson's caution. When America entered the war, Roosevelt wanted to raise and lead an army division, but Wilson refused. Roosevelt opposed American entry into the League of Nations, which he considered an excessive limitation on national sovereignty. He would probably have been a leading contender for the Republican Presidential nomination in 1920 but for his unexpected death on January 6, 1919. He is buried at Sagamore Hill.

William Howard Taft

William Howard Taft, 27th President (1909–1913), was born on September 15, 1857, in Cincinnati. His father, Alphonso Taft, had served as a judge in Ohio, as a cabinet officer under President Grant, and as U.S. minister to Austria and Russia. A huge, studious youth, William graduated (1878) with honors from Yale and (1880) from the Cincinnati Law School.

Admitted to the bar, he promptly moved into public service. He served (1881–82) as assistant prosecuting attorney for Hamilton County, Ohio. In 1882, President Chester Arthur appointed Taft, a Republican, collector of internal revenue for the first district, with headquarters in Cincinnati. Within a year he resigned, because he could not in good conscience discharge competent employees to open up jobs for Republicans.

After a brief return to private law practice, Taft resumed (1885) his public career as assistant solicitor for Hamilton County. He filled out a vacancy on the Superior Court in 1887, and the following year was elected for a five-year term. Except for the Presidency, this was the only office to which he was ever elected. He moved on to national prominence in 1890 when President Benjamin Harrison appointed him U.S. Solicitor General. Two years later, he became a United States Circuit Court judge, and his rulings occasionally displeased labor unions.

In 1900, Taft was thrust into a totally new endeavor—both for himself and for the nation—when President McKinley appointed him chairman of a commission to govern the Philippine Islands, which had been acquired in the Spanish-American War. Designated governor the following year, Taft was a model administrator, building roads and harbors, establishing civil courts, and installing organs of self-government. In 1904, President Theodore Roosevelt appointed Taft Secretary of War. In addition to presiding with marked competence over a complex department, he also became a kind of trouble-shooter, assisting in Roosevelt's Panamanian policies and in negotiations for concluding the Russo-Japanese War.

When Roosevelt declined (1908) to run, he recommended that Taft become his successor. Preferring appointment to the Supreme Court, Taft acquiesced after some hesitation. He easily defeated the Democratic Presidential nominee, William Jennings Bryan. The ponderous, good-humored Taft, cautious in action and conservative in temperament, illustrates the type of public figure who diminishes his exceptional record as administrator and judge in the Presidency.

At a disadvantage by being the heir to the scintillating Roosevelt, Taft suffered in the inevitable comparison. Almost immediately, he was confronted with a profound struggle in the House of Representatives, in which progressive Republicans, led by George Norris of Nebraska, overthrew "Cannonism"—the almost unlimited power wielded by House Speaker "Uncle Joe" Cannon. Taft declined to support the Norris forces, and they, after their victory, declined to cooperate with the President.

Taft had been elected on a platform pledged to revise the tariff. A believer in protection, he felt that somewhat reduced duties would help control the trusts. Summoning Congress into special session to deal with the tariff, he seemed highly restrained in promoting his views on Capitol Hill. Although the House enacted a bill with big tariff reductions, the Senate, led by the devoted protectionist Nelson W. Aldrich of Rhode Island worked to keep duties high. Although the eventual Payne-Aldrich Tariff Act lowered some rates slightly, the general rate level was undisturbed. Taft disapproved of the bill, but he signed it, deeming it the best that could be then secured.

Taft further damaged his standing with progressive Republicans in the dispute between Chief Forester Gifford Pinchot and Secretary of the Interior Richard Ballinger. Pinchot charged that Roosevelt's conservation policies were being desecrated by the Interior Department, which he accused of selling land concessions too cheaply to water and power companies, as well as of illegal transactions in the sale of Alaskan coal lands. Taft backed Ballinger, whose conduct was investigated and upheld by a Congressional committee. Taft then dismissed Pinchot, and angered progressive Republicans moved back toward Theodore Roosevelt.

Despite its political troubles, the Taft administration made solid accomplishments. The 16th Amendment (income tax) and the 17th (direct election of Senators) were added to the Constitution—the first new amendments since the aftermath of the Civil War. At Taft's initiative, Congress enlarged the powers of the Interstate Commerce Commission and created a commerce court, a children's bureau, the Postal Savings system, and a parcel post. The Department of Labor was also established, and Alaska achieved full territorial government. Taft took the first steps toward establishing a federal budget, by requesting his department heads to submit detailed reports of their financial needs.

Although the Theodore Roosevelt administration tends to be identified with an aggressive antitrust policy, Taft well outdid his predecessor. In four years, the Taft administration launched almost twice as many "trust-busting" prosecutions for violations of the Sherman Anti-Trust Act than Roosevelt had in almost eight years.

In foreign affairs, Secretary of State Philander Knox played a large part in promoting "dollar diplomacy," by which trade, finance, and commerce were used to increase America's diplomatic influence. The U.S. government negotiated loans with China, Honduras, Nicaragua, and other countries, as a step toward encouraging private bankers to make additional loans to these nations.

In 1910, Roosevelt returned from a hunting trip to Africa and hustled into the political arena. His speeches advocating a "new nationalism" attracted Republican progressives, while Republican conservatives moved behind Taft to win him renomination. The conservatives, or "Stand-Patters," proved too strong for the progressives, or insurgents, and the President defeated Roosevelt in 1912 by being renominated on the first ballot. Roosevelt and his followers then left the convention and organized the new Progressive, or "Bull Moose," party, with Roosevelt as its Presidential nominee. With the Republican vote so divided, the Democratic nominee, Woodrow Wilson, was elected. Taft received only 8 electoral votes, Roosevelt 88, and Wilson 435.

Upon leaving the Presidency, Taft became a Yale law professor in 1913, and that year he was also elected president of the American Bar Association. In World War I, he was joint chairman of the National War Labor Board. President Harding appointed him (1921) Chief Justice of the United States, which he deemed his greatest public honor. Taft served with distinction until 1930, when declining health forced his retirement. He died on March 8, 1930, and is buried in Arlington National Cemetery.

Woodrow Wilson

Woodrow Wilson, 28th President (1913–1921), was born on December 28, 1856, at Staunton, Virginia. The son of a Presbyterian minister, Thomas Woodrow Wilson (his full name) was reared in an atmosphere of religious piety and respect for scholarship. Wilson entered Davidson College in North Carolina at the age of 17, transferring after a year to Princeton University, from which he was graduated (1879). He studied law at the University of Virginia, but withdrew (1881) from the school because of poor health.

In 1882, Wilson began to practice law in Atlanta; however, after a year of few clients and a discovered distaste for the commercial world, he returned to academic life and studied political science at Johns Hopkins University, where his thesis, Congressional Government, earned wide acclaim. After taking his Ph.D., he taught at Bryn Mawr College and Wesleyan University. In 1890, he became professor of jurisprudence and political economy at Princeton University. His reputation as a teacher and scholar having grown steadily, Wilson was named (1902) president of Princeton. Highly innovative as an administrator and tenacious in purpose against the most formidable odds, Wilson reorganized the curriculum, but suffered defeats in attempting to reform the eating clubs and revamp the graduate school. Wilson's Princeton controversies resulted in his resignation as president, but the attendant publicity cast him as a fighter for democracy against the snobbery of privilege. New Jersey Democratic boss James Smith, Jr., and Colonel George Harvey, a party leader and publisher of Harper's Weekly, were both impressed with Wilson's political potential and secured (1910) his nomination for governor of New Jersey.

Once elected, Wilson fought Smith and his conservative organization and pushed through a primary election law, a corrupt practices act, an employer's liability law, an improved education law, and other legislation that suddenly placed New Jersey in the vanguard of progressivism. Wilson's gubernatorial achievements also won national attention and established him in the confidence of William Jennings Bryan, who, despite three defeats for the Presidency, was still a dominant force in the Democratic party. At the 1912 national convention in Baltimore, Wilson won the Presidential nomination on the 46th ballot. Bryan's support was invaluable, and Wilson proved acceptable to the party's large progressive wing. With Republicans divided between Taft and Theodore Roosevelt, Wilson won the election easily.

His inaugural address (March 4, 1913) sounded progressive themes: "Here muster not the forces of party, but the forces of humanity." He immediately set a swift pace of initiative and activity, calling Congress into special session and addressing the two houses in person, thus breaking a century-long precedent. Wilson moved through Congress an extraordinary body of legislation that comprised his "New Freedom" program. A new tariff law lowered duties and removed them altogether on such commodities as wool, sugar, and iron ore. The Clayton Anti-Trust Act was passed (1914), and the Federal Trade Commission was established (also 1914) to regulate trusts and interstate trade. The Federal Reserve System was created (1913)—in effect, a central banking system empowered to provide a new currency and to facilitate the flow of capital through 12 reserve banks.

Wilson promoted this extraordinary legislative output with a generous investment of his own energies and skills. He worked closely with Democratic legislative leaders and the powerful committee chairmen. Adroit in using patronage, he was indefatigable in employing his own impressive powers of personal persuasion. He encouraged the revival of the long-dormant Congressional caucus as a forum in which his program might be presented to legislators for the purpose of organizing support. His exceptional gifts of articulation rallied attention to his program.

Wilson's early Presidential years were also preoccupied with foreign policy. He made amends for the recently assertive, if not highhanded, policies of the United States toward its Latin-American neighbors, assuring them (Mobile, Alabama, in 1913) that "the United States would never again seek one additional foot of territory by conquest." When the reform government of Francisco Madero in Mexico was overthrown, Wilson declined to recognize the new master, Victoriano Huerta, who had caused Madero's murder. Against raging turmoil within Mexico and intense pressure at home to intervene because of endangered American interests, Wilson nonetheless held to a policy of "watchful waiting" to permit the Mexican people to choose a government for themselves.

In August 1914, foreign policy compounded its demands on Wilson when World War I exploded. The President echoed the dominant sentiment of the nation when he proclaimed its neutrality. He was continuously buffeted in seeking to hold to this policy by the ravages of German submarines, by Britain's close administration of her blockade that often proved detrimental to American shipping interests, and by the solidifying of different segments of domestic opinion toward the belligerents. In 1915, neutrality was severely tested by the heavy loss of American life suffered when a German submarine sank the British passenger vessel *Lusitania*. Secretary of State William Jennings Bryan resigned, deeming Wilson's protest notes to Germany too strong; other Americans considered Wilson too detached and neutral by stating that there was such a thing as being "too proud to fight."

With Democrats promoting the slogan: "He kept us out of war," Wilson won reelection in 1916. However, he had declined to use neutrality as a campaign promise, and the defeat of Wilson's Republican opponent, Charles Evans Hughes, was a close race. Weeks before Wilson's second inauguration, Germany resumed unrestricted submarine warfare against all shipping, including American vessels. On April 2, 1917, Wilson went before Congress to request a declaration of war, averring that "the world must be made safe for democracy."

Wilson was an impressive war leader. Both for the United States and the world, he more than anyone articulated the purposes and the issues of the war. He infused the conflict with moral aspiration and harmonized its goals with his previous progressive domestic program. In a speech (January 8, 1918), he set forth the Fourteen Points that were his framework for a peace settlement. Among other things, he called for "a general association of nations," "open covenants of peace openly arrived at," freedom of the seas, arms reduction, and independence for various territories and countries. Wilson's guidelines afforded Germany a basis on which to appeal for peace.

Wilson personally headed the American delegation to the peace conference at Paris. Eager to make his Fourteen Points the center of the settlement, he believed that the United States should be represented by its head of government as the other major allies were. In the hard bargaining at the conference table, Wilson, to win acceptance of his plan for the League of Nations, and other of the Fourteen Points, had to make concessions and compromises.

He encountered more difficulty on his return to the United States, where he faced the task of securing Senate approval of the peace treaty and the League of Nations, for not only had Wilson been under criticism for excluding senators in the United States' delegation to the peace conference, but his general political position in the nation had weakened. He had asked for the election of Democrats to Congress in 1918 as a demonstration of popular confidence, but the voters responded by increasing Republican strength.

In the Senate, the peace treaty met fierce resistance from isolationists, such as Senators Hiram W. Johnson, James A. Reed, and William E. Borah as well as from many others, led by Henry Cabot Lodge, who were ready to approve the treaty but with important changes.

Deciding to take his fight for the league to the people, Wilson began (September 4, 1919) an ambitious speaking tour of the Midwest and Far West. Always frail in health, he had been weakened by the recent demands of office, and his doctors had advised against the trip. On September 25, following a speech at Pueblo, Colorado, Wilson collapsed from fatigue and tension aboard his train. The remainder of his tour was abandoned, and he returned to Washington. On October 3, he suffered a paralytic stroke.

The Presidency now sustained its longest and most difficult experience with an invalided Chief Executive. Seldom leaving his bed, Wilson did not call a cabinet meeting for more than six months, until April 13, 1920. The President's second wife, Mrs. Edith Bolling Wilson, not only guided his hand as he signed documents, but selected and digested the matters that were submitted for his personal attention.

From his sickbed, the President waged a losing fight for the peace treaty. The Senate Foreign Relations Committee, led by its chairman Senator Lodge, added 14 reservations, including one that declared the United States undertook no obligation to support the League of Nations. Wilson requested his Senate supporters to vote against the decimated treaty, but his term of office closed without its approval.

Repudiated at home, Wilson nevertheless was honored abroad as the recipient of the Nobel Peace Prize in 1920. He died in Washington on February 3, 1924, and is buried in the National Cathedral.

Warren Gamaliel Harding

Warren Gamaliel Harding, 29th President (1921–1923), was born on November 2, 1865, in Blooming Grove, Ohio; he was the son of a homeopathic doctor and descended from an English family that had landed at Plymouth and migrated (1820) to Ohio. After study at local schools, Harding entered Ohio Central College, when he was only 14 years old and graduated three years later.

Harding moved (1882) with his parents to Marion, Ohio, where he taught briefly in a one-room schoolhouse; he also read law, sold insurance, and eventually turned to journalism. He soon became editor and part owner of the Marion Star. As editor, he was drawn into local political life and gained prominence as an orator. He was elected to the Ohio senate in 1900 and to the lieutenant governorship in 1904. He was the unsuccessful Republican candidate for governor in 1910, but five years later he was elected to the U.S. Senate. In Ohio politics, Harding became the close friend of Harry M. Daugherty, an astute political manager who desired to make Harding President, just as Mark Hanna in an earlier day had charted the course to the White House of his fellow Ohioan, William McKinley.

As Senator, Harding was a member of the Foreign Relations Committee and supported approval of the peace treaty of World War I, with reservations "sufficient to safeguard" American interests. Genial and good-looking, Harding enjoyed the fellowship of the Senate, but introduced no important legislation.

His emergence as a dark-horse, compromise nominee for the Presidency in 1920 was the outcome of deliberations by leading Republican Senators and party bosses in what Harry Daugherty called a "smoke-filled room" in Chicago's Blackstone Hotel. Conducting a "front-porch" campaign, Harding took no clear-cut stand on the leading issue: the League of Nations. He attacked it, but at the same time promised support for an "association of nations." He sidestepped domestic issues by promising a restoration of "normalcy." Harding easily defeated the Democratic nominee, James M. Cox.

Few Presidents have come into office facing more difficult tasks than Harding. The Versailles peace treaty was suspended uncertainly in the political air, having failed to win the Senate's approval under President Wilson. Powerful Republican Senators wanted to scrap the league; other legislators, who were eager to avoid future war, sought to salvage it. Substantial unemployment attended the changeover from a wartime to a peacetime economy. Harding approached these problems with a Presidential theory that looked to Congress and the cabinet for leadership; he rejected Wilson's performance as representing an encroachment on the powers of Congress.

Aided by a strong Secretary of State, Charles Evans Hughes, Harding was assertive in foreign affairs. The President moved quickly and energetically to break the impasse on the League of Nations. He made peace treaties with Germany and other enemy powers that omitted the league covenant. Harding's most conspicuous achievement in foreign policy was the Washington Disarmament Conference (1921), which resulted in treaties among the United States, Britain, France, Japan, and Italy that limited naval armament, restricted submarine use, and banned the use of poison gas in warfare.

The Harding era was marked by a surge of isolation; legislation was passed that for the first time placed quotas on immigration, and the Fordney-McCumber tariff act (1922) raised duties to record highs. Remaining aloof from European politics, the administration declined to take part in conferences at Geneva and The Hague. Unofficial American representatives on the Reparations Commission were withdrawn, and American troops stationed on the Rhine were gradually reduced. Harding himself, however, was a non-isolationist, and he repeatedly urged the promotion of peace through international friendship, as well as advocating American participation in the Permanent Court of International Justice at The Hague.

In domestic affairs, Harding largely acquiesced to what cabinet officers, Congress, and assertive group interests put forward for public policy. The excess profits tax was repealed, to the delight of business. The "farm bloc"—legislators of both parties devoted to agricultural interests—put through measures responsive to their needs.

Harding's cabinet included such strong and highly regarded public personalities as Secretary of State Hughes and Secretary of Commerce Herbert Hoover, as well as appointees who brought the administration into deep discredit. In addition, Harding had about him what became known as "the Ohio gang," whom he enjoyed as social companions and favored with responsible appointments.

Corruption set in and spread widely. Harding suffered a drastic shrinkage of political popularity not only because of betrayal by friends, but also due to deepening agricultural depression that brought heavy losses to Republicans in the 1922 Congressional elections, in which the Republican House majority fell from 165 to 15 and the Senate from 24 to 10.

In June 1923, Harding moved to restore his administration to public approval by embarking on a speaking tour through the West and Alaska. En route he received distressing news concerning the Senate investigation of oil leases, or what soon fanned out as the Teapot Dome scandal. Secretary of the Interior Albert B. Fall was subsequently convicted of accepting a bribe for leasing naval oil reserves to private oil interests. Harding's political manager, Attorney General Harry M. Daugherty, was implicated (but not convicted) in malfeasance in the Alien Property Custodian's Office. A friend and aide of Daugherty, Jesse W. Smith, committed suicide following revelations of settlements that Smith had arranged between the justice department and law violators.

In Seattle, Harding developed an illness that was attributed to food poisoning. His tour was suspended in San Francisco, where doctors said he was suffering from pneumonia. After a brief gair, Harding died there on August 2, 1923. There was no autopsy, and the precise cause of his death remains unknown. He was spared the humiliation of experiencing the trials of his two cabinet officials, Fall and Daugherty.

Historians generally rank Harding as one of the weakest of Presidents. But the qualities that made him weak also made him appealing to the bosses in the "smoke-filled room" and to a nation weary of Wilsonian zeal.

Calvin Coolidge

Calvin Coolidge, 30th President (1923–1929), was born John Calvin Coolidge on July 4, 1872, in Plymouth Notch, Vermont. He was the son of John Calvin Coolidge, a farmer and shrewd, experienced politician who served in the Vermont legislature and held local offices. The son was graduated (1895) from Amherst College. He read law with a firm in Northampton, Massachusetts, was admitted (1897) to the bar, and soon opened his own office in Northampton.

In the tradition of the young smalltown lawyer, Coolidge entered politics as a Republican campaign worker in 1896. Three years later, he was elected a member of the Northampton City Council and, over the next five years, served as city solicitor and clerk of county courts. He was elected (1906) to the Massachusetts House of Representatives and reelected (1907).

Remarkable for his taciturnity—the very opposite of the stereotype extrovert politician—Coolidge moved up a career line of city and state politics with electoral invincibility. He was elected (1909) mayor of Northampton and reelected (1910). From 1912 to 1915, he served in the Massachusetts Senate, of which he was president for two terms. He was elected (1915) lieutenant governor and twice reelected. In 1918, he v as elected governor.

In that office, Coolidge became a national figure by his resolute handling of the 1919 Boston police strike, declaring with cryptic force, "There is no right to strike against the public safety by anybody, anywhere, any time." By his firm action of calling in the militia, Coolidge suppressed the strike and won reelection overwhelmingly. The strike also helped boost him into the 1920 Vice-Presidential nomination. The Harding-Coolidge ticket won easily.

Upon Harding's death in 1923, Coolidge became President and the following year was elected to a full term. He commenced his tenure under extraordinarily difficult political circumstances. Scarcely had he declared his intention to carry out policies begun by Harding, when the Teapot Dome and other scandals of the previous administration were exposed. In this test, too, Coolidge was resolute, acting with fearless probity. He eluded the political temptation to shield the Harding administration against scandalous disclosure by bringing about the resignations of Harding's Attorney General, Harry Daugherty, and other important officials. Only three members of the Harding cabinet continued in office throughout the Coolidge administration.

Coolidge continued Harding's policy of responsiveness to the needs and interests of business. Declaring that "the business of America is business," Coolidge promoted a program of what he called "constructive economy." His principal policies were high tariffs, reduced income taxes, lowering the national debt, and strict governmental economy. So devoted was Coolidge to public thrift that he committed the rare political act of vetoing a (World War I) veterans' bonus bill, although Congress overrode him.

Paradoxically, Coolidge's bent for economy in government was enormously popular at a time when society, thanks to a soaring economy, was spendthrift. It was the era of rampant stock market speculation, freely countenanced Prohibition violations, "flaming youth," and the "jazz age." Champion of a rejected code of thrift and propriety, the President was a beloved figure—a reminder of old values that, although discarded, were still respected. In public addresses, Coolidge's pithy, apt expression of the old philosophy was widely appreciated. For example: "Let men in public office substitute the light that comes from the midnight oil for the limelight."

Distrustful of progressivism and opposed to legislation favoring any interest but business, Coolidge employed the veto in important instances where Congress transgressed his principles. For example, he vetoed legislation authorizing government operation of Muscle Shoals (Tennessee River rapids) for the production of electric power. Agriculture did not share in the booming prosperity, but suffered from falling prices and declining exports. Coolidge nonetheless twice vetoed legislation affording relief for farmers through government purchase of surplus products and sale abroad.

In foreign affairs, Coolidge, aided by Secretary of State Frank B. Kellogg, moved the country away from its isolationist tendencies. The secretary negotiated the Kellogg-Briand Pact, to which many nations subscribed, that sought to outlaw war. Although Coolidge opposed United States membership in the League of Nations, he favored joining the World Court. But when the Senate imposed unacceptable conditions, Coolidge dropped the project. A plan worked out by Vice-President Dawes and an international committee provided a new basis on which Germany might pay her World War I reparations.

Under Coolidge, relations with Mexico improved when Ambassador Dwight Morrow negotiated the settlement of old issues and obtained important concessions for American oil interests. With Japan, however, relations declined following Congress's passage of an immigration law that completely excluded Japanese; the President signed it under protest.

As the expected Republican Presidential nominee in 1928, Coolidge astounded the nation on August 2, 1927, by handing the press a slip of paper on which was written: "I do not choose to run for President in 1928." In his autobiography, he stated his conviction that "the chances of having wise and faithful public service are increased by a change in the Presidential office after a moderate length of time."

After leaving the Presidency, Coolidge returned to Northampton, where he wrote an autobiography and a series of daily newspaper articles that dealt mainly with political and economic topics. He was distressed by the coming of the depression in 1929, and it was reported that he felt he should have used the Presidency more assertively to have prevented it. He died on January 5, 1933.

Herbert Clark Hoover

Herbert Clark Hoover, 31st President (1929–1933) and the first President from west of the Mississippi River, was born in West Branch, Iowa, on August 10, 1874. His father was a farmer and village blacksmith, and the family was strong in the Quaker faith. Orphaned at eight years of age, Hoover was raised by relatives in the West.

After graduation (1895) from Stanford University, Hoover became a successful mining engineer and businessman, with offices in New York, San Francisco, and London. His work took him all over the world and won him a fortune, as well as an international engineering and administrative reputation. In World War I, driven by his Quaker principles, he put aside his business affairs and administered to human suffering as chairman of the American Relief Commission with exceptional success that made him an international public figure.

In 1919, both the Republican and Democratic parties pressed Hoover to become their candidate for President the following year. Hoover clarified the question of his party affiliation by announcing that he was a Republican and that he would not be a candidate. In 1921, President Harding appointed him Secretary of Commerce, a post that Hoover continued in under President Coolidge.

As secretary, Hoover again functioned as a dynamic administrator with wide-ranging concerns. Under his hand, the Department of Commerce dramatically expanded its activities, and he oversaw conferences on foreign trade, industrial production, labor affairs, child welfare, and housing. The new industries of radio communication and aviation also came under his regulation.

When President Coolidge declined to run for reelection in 1928, Hoover easily won the Republican Presidential nomination. In a hard-fought campaign against his Democratic opponent, Governor Alfred E. Smith of New York, Hoover envisaged the day when poverty would be eliminated, and Americans would have "two chickens in every pot and a car in every garage." Impressed with Republican prosperity, voters expected even more of it from Hoover because of his genius for economic success. Elected overwhelmingly, he won 40 of the 48 states, with 444 electoral votes to Smith's 87.

Hoover's inaugural address sounded the notes of optimism. "In no nation," he said, "are the fruits of accomplishment more secure." He moved to help depression-ridden farmers by calling Congress into special session (April 1929) and bringing it to create a Federal Farm Board to encourage the growth of farm cooperatives and to absorb agricultural surpluses. Hoover also proposed an increase of tariff duties on farm imports to protect domestic markets. The resulting Hawley-Smoot Tariff Act not only incorporated Hoover's recommendations, but raised duties on many nonagricultural items. As a result, American foreign trade dropped, a contributing factor to the oncoming depression.

Seven months after Hoover's inaugural, the stock market crashed, and the upheaval of the Great Depression, which had long been building in the Harding-Coolidge era, exploded with devastating fury. Stocks collapsed in value, thousands became unemployed, fortunes evaporated overnight. The depression's root cause, in Hoover's view, was not material or political, but psychological: an erosion of confidence. Consequently, Hoover organized conferences with businessmen and labor leaders to spread reassurance and to secure their help in keeping wages and prices stable and avoiding strikes. The President aimed to improve confidence both by paring back federal expenditure and balancing the budget.

But the depression not only persisted but deepened. Unemployment reached a peak of one-fourth of the labor force. Bank failures rocketed, and mortgage foreclosures became commonplace. Reflecting his political philosophy, Hoover stressed the initiation of public works by states and localities to aid the unemployed. The Federal government, he believed, could help indirectly and, in 1932 at Hoover's request, Congress established the Reconstruction Finance Corporation (RFC), which made loans to banks to save them from bankruptcy and supported state relief programs.

Hoover also promoted conservation and federally administered public works programs to reduce unemployment. Federal flood control and navigation improvement projects were undertaken, and construction of Boulder (now Hoover) Dam on the Colorado River was begun. The Hoover administration substantially increased the acreage of national parks and forests, and it also launched major programs of public buildings and major highway construction.

In June 1932, some 15,000 veterans marched on Washington to pressure Congress into passing a bonus law. Opposing the bonus as financially unsound, Hoover eventually employed troops to drive the veterans out of the capital.

Under Hoover, American foreign policy tended toward forbearance and cooperation. He brought Congress to agree to a moratorium on war debt and reparation payments and also stressed goodwill in relations with Latin America. Following his election, he toured Latin America and as President removed the marines from an extended presence in Nicaragua. Hoover also concluded an agreement with Haiti that looked to the withdrawal of American troops in 1934.

Eager to promote disarmament, Hoover proposed that the principles of the London Naval Treaty of 1930 be extended to reduce land weapons; however, the proposal was declined by other nations. In 1931, when the Japanese invaded Manchuria and the League of Nations condemned Japan as an aggressor, Hoover announced that the United States would not recognize territorial aggrandizement that violated the Kellogg-Briand Pact.

A man whose motto was "Work is life," Hoover put in long hours at his desk and drove his staff hard. "He has the greatest capacity for assimilating and organizing information of any man I ever knew," said his Secretary of State, Henry L. Stimson. Yet a solution to the depression eluded this brilliant administrator. Hoover's critics contended that he overrelied on state, local, and private action, and was handicapped by a philosophical indisposition to exploit federal opportunities and resources.

With the nation still deep in depression, the Republicans dutifully renominated Hoover in 1932; however, his Democratic opponent, Franklin D. Roosevelt, promising a "new deal," defeated him by carrying 42 of the 48 states and by collecting 472 electoral votes to Hoover's 59.

After leaving the Presidency, Hoover was a vigorous critic of Roosevelt's New Deal, and later President Truman named Hoover chairman of the Famine Emergency Commission to report on the needs of many nations suffering from the ravages of World War II. Hoover made a similar study of Germany and Austria. In 1947, Truman appointed Hoover chairman of the Commission on Organization of the Executive Branch of the Government. Better known as "the Hoover Commission," the group proposed important changes in governmental organization and management. A second Hoover Commission was created in 1953. Hoover died on October 20, 1964, at age 90.

Franklin Delano Roosevelt

Franklin Delano Roosevelt, 32d President (March 4, 1933–April 12, 1945), was born on January 30, 1882, at Hyde Park, New York, into a wealthy family which in the 1640s had migrated from Holland to New Amsterdam (later New York City). He was a fifth cousin of Theodore Roosevelt.

After studying at Groton and graduating from Harvard, Franklin extended his studies for another year and entered (1904) Columbia Law School. Admitted to the bar in 1907, Roosevelt evidenced little interest in the practice of law, but he soon discovered a keen taste for politics and won election (1910) as a Democrat to the New York State Senate against great odds. As state senator, he demonstrated extraordinary adroitness as a political leader by thwarting party bosses who were bent on boosting a Tammany nominee into the U.S. Senate.

Following his vigorous campaign for Presidential aspirant Woodrow Wilson in 1912, Roosevelt was appointed Assistant Secretary of the Navy. Tammany secured its revenge two years later by helping defeat his quest in a primary for nomination to the U.S. Senate. Roosevelt's full emergence into national prominence was betokened by his nomination for the Vice-Presidency in 1920, with James M. Cox heading the ticket in an unsuccessful race.

Roosevelt returned to private life as vice-president of the Fidelity and Deposit Company of Maryland. A year later, he succumbed to poliomyelitis, which paralyzed him from the waist down. By great courage and effort, Roosevelt in time managed to walk a little by wearing braces on his legs and using crutches. In 1924, he surged back into national politics by nominating Alfred E. Smith for the Presidency, as a thrilled convention watched him master his crippling illness by walking slowly to the podium.

At Smith's insistence, Roosevelt ran (1928) for governor of New York and was barely elected. Reelected in 1930, Roosevelt won acclaim for his broad attack on the Great Depression with measures that were to find their counterparts in his subsequent program as President.

He received the Democratic Presidential nomination in 1932 and became the first nominee to make an acceptance speech at a national convention. Promising a "new deal" to bring the nation out of the depression, he easily defeated his Republican opponent, President Herbert Hoover.

At the moment of Roosevelt's inaugural, the depression was at its worst: breadlines of unemployed, mounting mortgage foreclosures, closed banks, and the widespread, gray despair that the country's complex paralyzing economic forces might never be fathomed and overcome.

Roosevelt created an immediate impression of action and initiative. He declared a "bank holiday," closing down the banks for federal inspection; those in good financial condition were permitted to reopen. The confidence of depositors, which had been shaken by rampant bank failures, was restored. He summoned Congress into special session, and between March 9 and June 16, 1933, the famous "100 Days," more legislation of major impact was passed than ever before.

The New Deal, as these accumulated economic and social measures became known, included relief for the unemployed, aid for farm mortgages, a civilian conservation corps, a Tennessee Valley Authority, a National Industrial Recovery Act, and an Agricultural Adjustment Act under which a price subsidy was provided to farmers who agreed to limit their output. Roosevelt's measures were directed to the unemployed, the farmer, labor, the young, the aged, and the Negro, all of whom suffered most acutely from the depression.

In advancing his program, Roosevelt gave a bravura performance as Presidential leader and politician. In "fireside chats," as his national radio addresses were called, he explained his purposes, actions, and plans. His press conferences were remarkably newsworthy and conducted with a skill and charm that left many reporters warmly disposed toward his administration. As legislative leader, Roosevelt was adept at attracting bipartisan support, at timing his measures well, and at exploiting his political opportunities. To the country, he appeared a confident leader whose easy humor and ready laughter were marks of self-possession in the face of national crisis.

In 1936, Roosevelt was overwhelmingly reelected, defeating the Republican nominee, Governor Alfred M. Landon of Kansas. Roosevelt's political fortunes now went into something of a tailspin, to the delight of his many foes and detractors, who considered him a "traitor to his class." The Supreme Court held such key measures as the National Industrial Recovery Act, the Agricultural Adjustment Act, and other laws unconstitutional. Roosevelt moved in 1937 to "pack the court." Although rebuffed, he did slow the pace of hostile court decisions.

Foreign policy was largely preoccupied with the war clouds gathering over Europe and the Pacific, culminating in Germany's invasion of Poland on September 1, 1939. Although restricted by neutrality legislation, Roosevelt sought to give "all aid short of war" to nations fighting the Axis. The neutrality laws were modified in the directions that Roosevelt urged. Isolationists, who believed the United States should remain uninvolved, attacked Roosevelt as bent upon bringing the United States into the struggle. When he shattered precedent by running for the Presidency for a third time, he was severely attacked and was driven to promise to try to keep the nation out of war. He prevailed over his Republican opponent, Wendell Willkie, but with reduced majorities.

Following France's surrender to Germany in June 1940, Roosevelt undertook bold initiatives to aid embattled Britain. He exchanged old American destroyers for American assumption of leases on several British bases in the Western Hemisphere. He promoted the Lend-Lease Act that authorized the provision of war supplies to any nation fighting the Axis. In a meeting with Winston Churchill in August 1941 on the high seas, the two leaders adopted the Atlantic Charter that attested to the ideals of freedom of the seas, the territorial integrity of nations, peaceful trade, freedom of choice of governmental form. Earlier in a speech on January 6, 1941, Roosevelt had declared that all men are entitled to at least four freedoms: freedom from want, freedom of worship, freedom of speech, and freedom from fear. The two documents provided a foundation of ideals and aims for the war.

With America's deepening commitment to the Allies, relations with Germany, Italy, and Japan deteriorated rapidly. On December 7, 1941, Japan attacked the United States fleet at Pearl Harbor and the nation found itself quickly at war with the Axis. Decisions of the utmost magnitude faced the President. After conferring with Churchill in Washington, for example, Roosevelt chose to concentrate on the defeat of Germany first, after which the full force of war was to be directed against Japan.

As commander-in-chief, Roosevelt was the chief architect of the North African invasion, which commenced on November 7, 1942. This was followed by invasions of Sicily and Italy, and finally the cross-channel, D-Day invasion of Normandy. In the latter enterprise, Roosevelt was under pressure from Joseph Stalin to create a second front quickly to relieve German pressure on the Russians. Stalin wanted the Normandy venture to begin before the President was convinced the Allies were prepared for it. Churchill preferred a thrust up through the Balkans to check the western surge of the Russians. Roosevelt remained the master of the decision.

The President furthered war diplomacy in a 1943 meeting with Churchill at Casablanca, where they agreed to accept only unconditional surrender by the Axis.

With the war at its peak, Roosevelt reluctantly ran (1944) for a fourth Presidential term, and he easily defeated his Republican opponent, Thomas E. Dewey. Roosevelt began his new term in obviously failing health, yet journeyed to Yalta in the Crimea to confer with Churchill and Stalin. The Crimea Declaration, which emerged from the conference, affirmed the principles of the Atlantic Charter and the objectives of the Casablanca conference. Plans for the defeat and occupation of Germany were drawn, and a future meeting at San Francisco was agreed on at which the United Nations would be organized as an enduring international structure. In return for Far East concessions, Russia agreed to enter the war against Japan.

In the weeks following the Yalta meeting, Roosevelt, whose wartime policies had assumed the continued goodwill and cooperation of the Soviet Union, grew restive with doubts over Soviet attitudes.

On April 12, 1945, about a month before Germany surrendered, Roosevelt suddenly died at Warm Springs, Georgia. He was buried at Hyde Park.

As President, Roosevelt employed the resources of his office with boldness and initiative. He delighted to break precedents and embark on new ways. His cabinet appointees were lively and resourceful, and he was given to employing both "Brain Trusters," who were usually academicians fertile in ideas, and wide-ranging White House assistants. Adroit in political controversy, he impressed fellow politicians with his canny sense of timing. Although given to deviousness, he unfailingly projected an air of rectitude. In the age of radio, he excelled at stirring public opinion, and as party leader he solidified the loyalties of such groups as labor and blacks to the Democratic party. These groups, joined with the South, city party organizations, and farmers constituted "the Roosevelt coalition," which endured for decades after its creator's death.

Harry S Truman

Harry S Truman, 33d President (April 12, 1945–January 20, 1953), was born on May 8, 1884, in Lamar, Missouri. The oldest of three children of a farmer and livestock dealer, Truman was raised on a farm near Independence. A voracious reader of military history, he hoped to attend West Point, but was rejected because of unsatisfactory vision. After finishing high school, he worked as a timekeeper for a railroad construction gang, as a mail clerk for a Kansas City newspaper, and as a bookkeeper in Kansas City banks. In World War I, Truman helped recruit a field artillery regiment. He saw action in France, was discharged (1919) as a major, and later rose to a colonelcy in the reserves.

After the war, Truman invested in a men's clothing store, in Kansas City, but it failed in the farm depression of 1921. At this bleak moment, Truman turned to politics and secured an introduction to "Big Tom" Pendergast, Democratic boss of Kansas City. Impressed with Truman's political promise, Pendergast supported (1922) Truman's successful campaign for administrator of Jackson County; however, after a two-year term, Truman was defeated for reelection because of factional strife within his party. In his free time, Truman studied law at Kansas City Law School, and in 1926, he was elected presiding judge, serving in that capacity until 1934. Overseeing large projects of public works construction, he earned a reputation for probity and efficiency.

With Pendergast's backing, Truman was elected (1934) to the U.S. Senate. During a decade in the Senate, Truman strongly supported the New Deal, and during World War II he achieved national renown as chairman of the Senate's Special Committee to investigate the National Defense Program. The Truman Committee, as it was known, excelled at uncovering waste and inefficiency in war production.

In 1944, Truman won the Democratic Vice-Presidential nomination as a compromise choice in a spirited contest between several contenders. When President Roosevelt suddenly died, Truman became President at a critical moment in the nation's history. Within his first weeks as President, Germany surrendered and the United Nations was launched at the San Francisco conference as a postwar international organization. He met with the British and Soviet leaders at Potsdam, and made the grave decision to employ the atomic bomb against Japan to bring World War II to a quick conclusion.

Truman now had to lead the nation's reconversion from its wartime mobilization to a peacetime footing. In a message to Congress (September 6, 1945), he proposed a sweeping program (the "Fair Deal,") that was an extension of the New Deal. His proposals included an expanded social security system, a higher minimum wage, a permanent fair employment practices commission to protect minority rights, comprehensive housing legislation, government aid for scientific research, and public power projects on the Missouri, Columbia, and Arkansas rivers.

Few of Truman's proposals were enacted. In 1946, the Republicans gained control of both houses of Congress, and the President's program was blocked by a coalition of conservative Republicans and Democrats. His chief success was legislation for public housing that was passed with substantial help from the Senate Republican leader, Robert A. Taft. In 1947, Congress approved Truman's plan to unify the armed forces by creating the U.S. Department of Defense. In that same year, Congress passed the Taft-Hartley Labor Act, a far-ranging measure for regulating labor unions and labor-management relations. In a bitterly worded message, Truman vetoed the act but was overridden by Congress.

In foreign affairs, United States relations with the Soviet Union swiftly deteriorated as the Communists gained control in the nations of Eastern Europe. To check the Communist tide, Truman advanced a doctrine of American aid to nations that resisted either direct or indirect Communist aggression. The Truman Doctrine, as it became known, was prompted by Britain's inability to continue her aid to Greece and Turkey in their struggle against Communist actions, and American aid checked a Communist-supported civil war in Greece and bolstered Turkey's military strength.

In 1947, the Marshall Plan (European Recovery Program) extended the Truman Doctrine to speed the recovery of Western European economies from the devastation resulting from World War II. The Marshall Plan was a combination of European self-help supported by massive American outlays. The Soviet Union was invited to join the plan, but declined.

The continuing decline in American-USSR relations became known as "The Cold War," and the Truman administration's policy of applying counterforce—political, economic, or military—corresponding to the shifts and maneuvers of the Soviet Union was spoken of as the policy of "containment." Congress generously supported the President through appropriations and statutory authority.

While coping with the Cold War, Truman faced sharp political strife at home in the 1948 election. A segment of liberal Democrats formed the Progressive party and nominated Henry A. Wallace for President. Other liberal Democrats sought unsuccessfully to deny Truman the Democratic nomination. Conservative Southern Democrats formed the Dixiecrat party and nominated J. Strom Thurmond. Against mountainous odds and almost miraculously, Truman defeated the Republican nominee, Governor Thomas E. Dewey. Truman relied upon a "whistle-stop" campaign and rousing oratory that was directed at the Republican 80th Congress, which he characterized as "do-nothing" and "the worst in memory."

Foreign affairs dominated Truman's new term. A 1948 Communist coup in Czechoslovakia prompted Western European nations to draw together in their defenses and led to the creation of the North Atlantic Treaty Organization (NATO) under which the United States and other pact nations agreed that an attack on one member would be regarded as an attack on all member nations. An Anglo-American airlift thwarted the Communist blockade of Berlin in 1948.

In his inaugural address, Truman proposed "a bold new program" by which American technical and production skills could help "underdeveloped" areas. Implementation of the proposal began (1950) when Congress established the Point Four Program. In 1951, Truman initiated a foreign-aid program for Southeast Asian countries threatened by Communism. A Mutual Security program was also instituted to improve military defenses in many countries worldwide.

The Cold War became hot (June 25, 1950), when Communist North Korea invaded South Korea. Truman quickly responded by committing United States forces to South Korea's defense under UN auspices. Commanded by General Douglas MacArthur, UN forces overran most of North Korea, only to have Communist China enter the war. MacArthur proposed to bomb Communist bases in Manchuria, but Truman, who did not wish to extend the war, rejected the plan. When MacArthur publicly criticized the administration, Truman removed him from his command, igniting a furor of debate and criticism.

In domestic affairs, Truman fared little better with the new Democratic Congress than he had with the former Republican one. The Truman administration faced charges of Communist infiltration into the U.S. Department of State that were lodged by Senator Joseph McCarthy of Wisconsin. A House investigating committee made similar accusations about other agencies. As a result, Truman set up a federal loyalty board to deal with the problem, and the justice department launched prosecutions of American Communist leaders. The administration was hobbled by exposures of corruption among subordinates, who were generously defended by the President for reasons of friendship or party necessity.

On March 29, 1952, Truman announced that he would not seek reelection. Nevertheless, he campaigned strenuously for the unsuccessful Democratic nominee, Adlai E. Stevenson. After leaving office, Truman wrote his memoirs, which were published in two volumes, commented occasionally on national issues, and remained interested in the Democratic party. He died on December 26, 1972, and is buried at Independence, Missouri.

Winston Churchill credited President Truman with making "great and valiant decisions." Other admirers of his administration cited his courage and his gift of seeing issues divested of complication and of stating them in plain, blunt terms. His critics felt that his candor and affinity for strong language were undignified. Others considered him a man of the people, and Truman acknowledged these differences of opinion by once saying that he expected to be "cussed and discussed" for years to come.

Dwight David Eisenhower

Dwight David Eisenhower, 34th President (1953–1961), was born in Denison, Texas, on October 14, 1890 as David Dwight Eisenhower. Of Swiss and German ancestry, Eisenhower's parents belonged to the River Brethren religious sect, which was opposed to war and violence. While young, Eisenhower moved to Abilene, Kansas; after graduating from high school, he worked in the local creamery where his father was engineer.

To the disappointment of his parents, Eisenhower entered West Point at the age of 21 and graduated in the 1915 class that included Omar Bradley and James Van Fleet. In World War I, he was commander of a tank training center near Gettysburg, Pennsylvania. His postwar career included service in the Canal Zone; study at the General Staff School at Fort Leavenworth, Kansas, and at the U.S. Army War College. Eisenhower became (1933) an aide of General Douglas MacArthur in the Philippines. Brilliance in field maneuvers won him assignment to the war plans division of the war department, and he became (1942) head of the operations division. At mid-year, Eisenhower was named U.S. commander of the European Theater of Operations.

Eisenhower oversaw the North African invasion (November 1942) and directed the invasions of Sicily and Italy. He was named (1943) supreme commander of the Allied Expeditionary Force (AEF) that was organized for the Normandy invasion. He excelled at bringing proud, independent generals of various nations into working harmony and directing the military operations of an unprecedented scale that achieved (1945) the unconditional surrender of Germany. Made a five-star general (1944) and chief of staff of the U.S. Army (1945), Eisenhower played a leading part in the "unification" of the armed services under the newly established U.S. Department of Defense. He retired (1948) from active duty to become president of Columbia University.

After soundings made by both Democratic and Republican sources, Eisenhower announced (1948) his unavailability as a Presidential candidate. After 30 months he left his Columbia post to serve as NATO commander and to organize the forces of that alliance.

The approaching 1952 elections brought new pressures on Eisenhower to run for the Presidency, and he responded. He retired from the army to campaign successfully for the Republican nomination against Senator Robert A. Taft. Promising to "clean up the mess in Washington" and that "I shall go to Korea" to help end the war, the enormously popular "Ike" Eisenhower easily defeated his Democratic opponent, Adlai E. Stevenson. Eisenhower also helped his party win control of both houses of Congress. Soon after the election, he journeyed to Korea to observe the war firsthand.

From long observation of the Presidency during his military career, Eisenhower considered that the office was administered with excessive informality. As a result, he installed a staff system comparable to the military's and designated Sherman Adams, former governor of New Hampshire, as his chief White House aide. For the first time, the cabinet worked regularly according to a prearranged agenda, records of cabinet proceedings were kept, and each cabinet officer was responsible for monitoring problems and taking initiatives in his area of affairs.

Eisenhower was an apostle of what he termed Modern Republicanism, which, in its most ambitious projection, looked for major policy changes in his party. It called for the strengthening of federal social programs, and the President secured an expanded coverage of the social security system—its largest extension since its beginning under FDR. The minimum wage was also increased. Eisenhower was watchful that new measures did not encroach on state jurisdictions.

The President's domestic program included a 13-year highway building program that was urgently needed, because of a construction backlog that had accumulated during World War II. Eisenhower also succeeded in bringing Congress to modify the traditional rigid price supports of certain staple farm products.

In national security, the Eisenhower administration introduced "the new look" that shifted the emphasis of military expenditure from conventional forces and weapons to atomic weapons, which were regarded as more economical. In foreign affairs, an agreement was reached between the United States and Canada for joint development of the St. Lawrence Seaway.

More than most Presidents, Eisenhower faced substantial encroachment (or its threat) on his office and the functioning of the executive branch. Senator John Bricker of Ohio sponsored an amendment to curb the President's power to make treaties and executive agreements. After a strenuous fight, the President and his Secretary of State, John Foster Dulles, defeated the amendment.

Another Republican Senator, Joseph R. McCarthy of Wisconsin, steadily confronted the administration with accusations of subversion and Communist infiltration of the executive branch. Eisenhower, who declined to deal "in terms of personality," refrained from directly attacking McCarthy, a stand that prompted criticism. But when McCarthy charged that the United States Information Agency had Communist books in its European libraries, Eisenhower counseled students in an address at Dartmouth College: "Don't join the bookburners. . . . Don't be afraid to go to the library and read every book."

In foreign affairs, Eisenhower made important gains for peace and guided the Korean war to a close. He advanced (1953) the "Atoms for Peace" program, under which the world nations were to pool atomic energy information and output for peaceful purposes. The proposal led to the creation (1957) of the International Atomic Agency. The President proposed (1955) that the United States and the Soviet Union permit air inspection of each other's military installations, but the USSR declined.

On September 24, 1955, Eisenhower suffered a heart attack, the first of several illnesses with which he was afflicted during his years in office. His good recovery enabled him to run for a second term in 1956, when he again easily defeated Adlai Stevenson.

In his second term, Eisenhower sent (1957) Federal troops to Little Rock, Arkansas, to enforce school desegregation that was being resisted by Governor Orval Faubus. The nation suffered an economic recession in 1957 and 1958, but business improved markedly during the latter half of 1958. Eisenhower lost his chief assistant, Sherman Adams, in 1958, when Congressional investigations revealed that he had accepted gifts from a businessman who was under scrutiny by government agencies. Adams denied any wrongdoing, but resigned his White House post.

Eisenhower's hopes to develop a more peaceful international climate were defeated by repeated difficulties with the Communist world. The Soviet's launching (1957) of Sputnik I—the first manmade satellite—emboldened the Russians. Crisis in the Middle East evoked the "Eisenhower Doctrine," pledging American military aid to any Middle East nation that requested it to repel Communist aggression, and Eisenhower applied (1958) the doctrine to Lebanon. When Chinese Communists shelled Nationalist-held Quemoy island in 1958, the President committed American naval aid to protect Chinese Nationalist convoys.

Eisenhower met (1959) with Soviet Premier Nikita Khrushchev in a summit conference in the United States; however, a further summit conference at Paris (1960) was broken up by Khrushchev, because of an American U-2 reconnaissance aircraft that had been shot down over Russian territory. Following many provocations by Fidel Castro, Eisenhower broke off diplomatic relations with Cuba in 1961.

Eisenhower was the first President to be limited to two terms by the 22d Constitutional Amendment. Retiring to his farm in Gettysburg, Pennsylvania, Eisenhower wrote memoirs of his Presidential years and other books, supported Richard Nixon's Presidential campaigns, and discussed various political questions. He died on March 28, 1969, and is buried at Abilene, Kansas.

John Fitzgerald Kennedy

John Fitzgerald Kennedy, 35th President (January 20, 1961–November 22, 1963) was born into a political family on May 29, 1917, in Brookline, Massachusetts. His paternal grandfather was a state senator and Boston ward boss, and his maternal grandfather was John F. ("Honey Fitz") Fitzgerald–Boston mayor, state senator, and U.S. Representative. Kennedy's father, Joseph P. Kennedy, was a self-made millionaire and ambassador to Great Britain during World War II.

After studies at the London School of Economics and Princeton, Kennedy graduated (1940) from Harvard, where he majored in political science and international relations. His senior thesis, *Why England Slept,* became a best-selling book.

At the outbreak of World War II, Kennedy enlisted in the Navy and served as commander of a PT boat in the South Pacific. In action off the Solomon Islands, a Japanese destroyer sank his boat. Kennedy heroically saved an injured member of his crew. After release from the Navy, Kennedy worked briefly as a reporter for the Hearst newspapers.

The World War II death of his older brother Joe, who had been expected to become the family politician, devolved that function on John Kennedy. He was elected (1946) to the U.S. House of Representatives, defeating eight opponents in the Democratic primary of the Massachusetts 11th district and easily overcoming his Republican opponent. As Congressman, Kennedy voted regularly for Truman's Fair Deal program. Reelected twice, Kennedy became (1952) Senator in an upset defeat of the popular Henry Cabot Lodge. Kennedy underwent (1954–55) operations to correct a spinal injury that he had sustained in the war; while recovering, he wrote *Profiles in Courage,* for which he won the Pulitzer Prize.

In 1956, Kennedy was a strong contender for the Vice-Presidential nomination, losing to Estes Kefauver in a close race. Kennedy was easily reelected (1958) to the Senate. From 1956 onward, however, he was busily preparing to make a Presidential race and eventually won the 1960 Democratic nomination, after scoring several crucial primary victories. In a hard-fought contest with his Republican opponent, Richard M. Nixon, Kennedy—a youthful, handsome, and wealthy figure with an attractive wife and a highly persuasive television style—won the election in the closest race of the century. Vital to his success were his televised debates with Nixon. At the age of 43, Kennedy became the youngest man ever elected President, and he was also the first Roman Catholic to occupy the office.

Kennedy's Presidential campaign had been geared largely to the industrial and urban states.

On attaining office, he promoted legislative measures that he had promised to support if elected. Included in his recommendations to Congress were major educational legislation, medical aid for the aged, the creation of a Department of Urban Affairs, and an increase in the minimum wage.

He suffered severe resistance in the House of Representatives, where a conservative coalition of Republicans and Democrats thwarted much of his program. Because of this opposition, he long held back the promotion of major civil rights legislation. He sustained defeats on his farm bill, the urban department, health care for the aged, and education. His chief legislative triumph was the passage (1962) of the Trade Expansion Act, which gave the President broad powers to reduce tariffs to enable the United States to trade freely with the European Common Market.

In a rare step, President Kennedy sought to break the legislative logjam by seeking, with Speaker Sam Rayburn's help, to enlarge the House Rules Committee, at which point much legislation was stopped. The administration's position in the committee became somewhat improved following the fight, but not sufficiently to push key measures through.

Although blocked on Capitol Hill on civil rights legislation, Kennedy was diligent and ingenious in advancing civil rights policies through executive initiatives and actions. The Kennedy administration, with Robert Kennedy as Attorney General, was aggressive in prosecuting violations of the Supreme Court's school desegregation decisions; it directed U.S. marshals, the regular army, and the federalized National Guard to quell (1961) rioting against black and white "freedom riders" in Montgomery, Alabama; it employed the government contract to improve the civil rights standards of private employers; and it demanded that the civil service improve black recruitment and promotion. In televised appeals, the President promoted understanding of civil rights problems.

More than most modern Presidents, Kennedy was preoccupied with crisis, both foreign and domestic. In 1962, certain steel companies raised their prices, after Kennedy had induced labor to scale down its demands to check inflation. Outraged by management's action, the President moved forcefully against the companies involved and denounced them publicly. The companies withdrew the price rises, but the stock market soon underwent its sharpest drop since 1929. Within weeks, Kennedy faced a civil rights crisis in Mississippi, when the governor refused to obey a federal court order requiring that James Meredith, a black, be enrolled at the University. The President dispatched Federal troops and marshals, and Meredith was enrolled.

In foreign affairs, the President seemed never without crisis. Prepared and outfitted under American auspices, Cuban rebels invaded their homeland to overthrow the Communist-backed leader (1961), Fidel Castro. The assault was savagely repulsed, and Kennedy publicly took responsibility for the disaster. Berlin was a constant concern of the President. Aiming to end the Allied participation in control of the city, the Soviet Union and East Germany engaged in a series of maneuvers that culminated in the erection of the Berlin Wall, which sealed off escape from East to West Berlin. The President called up army reserves and dispatched military units to the border until the tense situation eased.

Kennedy faced (1961–62) spreading Communist penetration in Southeast Asia and made substantial commitments of American troops and matériel to the defense of South Vietnam and Thailand. Military advisers were sent to Laos.

Late in 1962, Kennedy became the first President to engage in a confrontation with another nuclear power. The Soviet Union built missile sites in Cuba from which it would have been possible to launch attacks on American cities. Kennedy imposed a blockade or "quarantine," barring the introduction of any offensive missiles to Cuba. The President also made clear that the United States would respond to any nuclear attack from Cuba on a Western Hemisphere nation by retaliating against the Soviet Union. After 14 days of intense deliberations by the President and his counselors and exchanges of messages with Russia, the crisis was resolved by Premier Khrushchev's ordering that the Cuban bases be dismantled and the missiles returned to Russia. In world eyes, Kennedy emerged from this crisis as a well-poised, rational, and resolute leader who had thoroughly excelled his Soviet opponent.

The Kennedy years were an era when young men were in charge of Presidential institutions. In his inaugural address, the President noted that a new generation was coming into power. Himself the first President born in the 20th century, Kennedy filled his chief posts with men in their 30s and early 40s. His administration he described as the "New Frontier." In foreign affairs, its chief innovations were establishment of the Peace Corps and the Latin-American Alliance for Progress and the nuclear test-ban treaty. In domestic affairs, he demonstrated new "vigor" in attacking urban problems. The Kennedy administration was also marked by new attention to American culture. Not since the days of Theodore Roosevelt did so many musicians, artists, writers, and scientists visit the White House.

For all of the power and majesty of his office, Kennedy displayed a remarkable gift for self-depreciation. A master of irony, both keen and gentle, he directed it at himself as well as at others. A capacity for self-criticism helped Kennedy maintain exceptional composure in crisis, to keep his assessments of problems and people in balance, and to question the well-settled responses of the past.

On November 22, 1963, the Kennedy era was suddenly ended in Dallas, Texas, where Lee Harvey Oswald murdered the President. An appalled nation and world mourned his death. He is buried at a simple site in Arlington National Cemetery.

Lyndon Baines Johnson

Lyndon Baines Johnson, 36th President (November 22, 1963–January 20, 1969), was born on a farm near Stonewall, Texas, on August 27, 1908, the son of a state legislator and school teacher. The family moved (1913) to Johnson City, Texas, where young Johnson was educated in the local public schools. He taught (1928) grade school in Cotulla, Texas, and graduated (1930) from South-west Texas State Teachers College. For the next two years, he taught public school in Houston.

Johnson began his political career in 1932 as secretary to a Texas Congressman and attended Georgetown University Law School in Washington. An enthusiastic supporter of the New Deal, Johnson became (1935) state director of the National Youth Administration in Texas. His first attempt at elective office was successful, when voters chose him to fill a vacancy in 1937 in the U.S. House of Representatives, and he was continuously reelected until 1948.

Immediately after the Japanese attack on Pearl Harbor, Johnson became the first member of Congress to go into uniform, entering active service in the U.S. Navy. He rose to lieutenant commander before being called back to Congress.

Johnson was elected (1948) to the U.S. Senate after winning the Democratic primary election by a hairline margin of 87 votes. Proving himself well-endowed with the gifts for legislative leadership and steeped in knowledge of Congressional procedures, Johnson rose rapidly in the Senate. He became (1951) Democratic whip, and he was elected (1953) Democratic leader, serving until 1960. He was reelected (1954) to the Senate and suffered a serious heart attack a year later. As Senate leader, Johnson was moderate in policy, extraordinarily persuasive, and skillful in effecting compromise. He was a top contender for the Democratic Presidential nomination in 1960, but it was won by John F. Kennedy, who chose him to be his Vice-President.

Kennedy's assassination on November 22, 1963, suddenly brought Johnson into the Presidency. Under these tragic circumstances, he quickly administered the office with a skill and self-possession that reassured the nation and the world. He guided through Congress the Civil Rights Act of 1964, a major education bill, a new tax law, and an economic opportunity act that declared "war on poverty."

In the 1964 Presidential elections, Johnson won an overwhelming victory over his Republican opponent, Barry M. Goldwater. Johnson received the largest percentage of popular votes ever accorded a President and perhaps, more important, he won lop-sided Democratic majorities in Congress.

Against this extraordinarily favorable legislative background, Johnson, with shrewd strategy and relentless drive, pushed legislation through Congress in 1965 and 1966 that instituted more innovations in domestic affairs than any other President in any other single session of Congress in this century. The "Great Society" program, as his platform became known, included medical care for the aged under social security, the first comprehensive aid-to-education law, a voting rights bill, a broad housing program, immigration reform, programs for highway beautification and for combating heart disease and cancer, and water and air pollution measures. After the 1966 Congressional elections that resulted in a loss of Democratic strength, the legislative output fell significantly.

The Presidential Succession Constitutional Amendment (25th) was adopted (1967) with Johnson's strong backing, and Congress passed (1968) a strong civil rights bill that included guarantees of open housing.

Crisis flared (1965) in the Dominican Republic, when the President dispatched U.S. marines to thwart a take-over by what he termed "a band of Communist conspirators."

The dominant preoccupation, however, of the Johnson administration was the Vietnamese war, which was already large in scale by the time that Johnson took office. When U.S. warships were alleged to have been attacked (1964) in the Gulf of Tonkin, Johnson ordered a bombing of North Vietnamese PT-boat bases, and Congress expressed approval in a broadly stated resolution. The President increased (1965) the numbers of American fighting men in Vietnam, although he encouraged the North Vietnamese to begin "unconditional negotiations."

In late 1967, additional U.S. troops were committed to the conflict. In the face of heavy Vietcong offensives in 1968 against South Vietnam cities, the President was criticized by "hawks" for restricting bombing in North Vietnam and by "doves" for not ending the bombing altogether. On March 31, the President announced a partial end to the bombing of North Vietnam and simultaneously appointed representatives to negotiate with the North Vietnamese in Paris. On October 31, Johnson ordered a complete halt to the bombing and shelling of North Vietnam.

Johnson pursued policies aiming toward improved relations with Eastern Europe and the Soviet Union, proposed treaties barring military activity in outer space and the proliferation of nations producing nuclear weapons, conducted a summit conference with Soviet Premier Kosygin at Glassboro, New Jersey, in 1967, and sought to prevent and terminate the Arab-Israeli war of 1967. In 1968, North Korea seized the U.S.S. *Pueblo*, precipitating a potentially major crisis that Johnson contained with diplomacy.

In a televised address (March 31, 1968), announcing a partial halt to the bombing of North Vietnam, Johnson also disclosed that he would "not accept the nomination of my party as your President."

Johnson's forte in the Presidency was clearly in the area of legislative relations, toward which his previous career was so strongly directed. "I am a compromiser and a manipulator," he once described himself. His perceptions of the nature of power moved him more to the backstage than to the frontstage of politics. "In every town," he once said, "there's some guy on top of the hill in a big white house who can get things done. I want to get that man on my side." As a public leader, he was handicapped by the unfriendliness toward him of many academics, the press, and American youth. Johnson did not have the great strength in the national party organization that Franklin D. Roosevelt enjoyed, nor did he have the personal organization for party affairs of John F. Kennedy. These deficiencies undoubtedly added to the troubles involved in his possible renomination in 1968. With roots in Populism and the Southwest, Johnson had difficulty winning national acceptance, particularly in the East. He died Jan. 22, 1973 and is buried near Johnson City, Texas.

Richard Milhous Nixon

Richard Milhous Nixon, 37th President (January 20, 1969–August 9, 1974), was born of Quaker parentage in Yorba Linda, California, on January 9, 1913. When he was nine years old, the Nixon family moved to Whittier, California, where his father ran a combination grocery store and gas station. After graduating from Whittier College (1934) and Duke University Law School (1937), he practiced law in Whittier and worked briefly as an attorney for the Office of Price Administration in Washington, D. C. Following United States entry into World War II, he served (1942–46) as a naval officer.

Nixon's political career began in 1946, when a group of California Republicans urged him to run for Congress. He won a hard-fought contest (during which he accused his opponent, a New Deal Democrat, of being soft on Communism) and was reelected in 1948. In the House of Representatives, he contributed importantly to the development of the Marshall Plan and the Taft-Hartley act. He gained national prominence in 1948–49 by pressing an investigation by the House Un-American Activities Committee into charges that Alger Hiss, a former State Department official, had passed government information to Russian agents in the 1930s. In 1950, a federal district court convicted Hiss of perjury.

On the crest of the prominence attained by the Hiss case, Nixon was elected (1950) to the Senate from California. Two years later, Republicans nominated Nixon as the Vice-Presidential running mate of Dwight D. Eisenhower.

In 1960 Nixon was defeated by John F. Kennedy in a close race for the Presidency. The campaign witnessed the first televised debate between Presidential candidates. Turning to authorship, Nixon published (1962) *Six Crises*, a personal account of major interludes in his career. That year he also ran unsuccessfully against incumbent Edmund (Pat) Brown for governor of California.

He entered a crowded field of contestants for the 1968 Republican Presidential nomination, excelled in the primaries, and by forestalling defection of Southern delegates to his rival, Governor Ronald Reagan of California, won a first-ballot nomination. His selection of Governor Spiro T. Agnew of Maryland as a running mate and the firm adherence of Southern delegates, led by Strom Thurmond of South Carolina, to his nomination, prompted discussion that Nixon was pursuing a "Southern strategy."

Projecting a "New Nixon" image, he appealed to the nation's discontent with the Vietnam War and its concern for preserving law and order. In a close race, he defeated Hubert H. Humphrey, who led a divided Democratic party, and George C. Wallace, nominee of the American Independent party.

Nixon was engrossed, during his first term, in the Indo-China war. He sought a negotiated settlement, but despite both private and public talks in Paris, the war continued to drag on. In August, 1972, the American ground combat role ended in Vietnam as the last combat infantry unit was returned to the U.S. To replace the departing forces, the President depended on a policy of "Vietnamization," and American warplanes based throughout Southeast Asia.

To offset criticism that the United States was absorbed in Vietnam to the neglect of other parts of the world, the President visited several West European capitals in 1969, and he became the first President in nearly 25 years to visit a

Communist nation (Romania). His 1972 visits to Russia and China were hailed as historic moments in American diplomacy.

In domestic affairs Nixon was less successful in combating inflation. In August 1971, he instituted price and wage controls. It was the first time such constraints had been applied to the U.S. economy during peacetime, but by the time he left office in 1974, the economy was in a recession.

The President was reelected in 1972 by one of the greatest margins in U.S. history. He was helped by a disorganized Democratic party that was deeply split when old-line party leaders were routed in their effort to block the nomination of Sen. George McGovern of South Dakota.

Allegations of major scandals broke before the election, but apparently had little effect on the outcome. Not until the following year, when the bugging of Democratic headquarters in the Watergate Hotel was fully understood, did public opinion turn sharply downward.

In 1973 peace negotiations in Paris finally bore fruit, at least for the United States. Peace accords were signed in January which called for the end of all fighting and the withdrawal of American and other foreign troops from Vietnam and the rest of Indochina. What the President called "peace with honor" did not bring a halt in the fighting between North and South Vietnam or between Communist insurgents and government forces in Cambodia. U.S. bombing was halted with the peace treaty in Vietnam but continued in Cambodia until August when Nixon halted the bombing under heavy congressional pressure.

For the first time in years, Vietnam and other foreign crises were completely eclipsed by events in Washington. Although the White House initially wrote off the Watergate incident as of no major significance, the combined forces of the press, a Senate investigating committee, and a special prosecutor, eventually forced Nixon to resign in disgrace and left many of his former top assistants accused of obstruction of justice.

Gerald R. Ford

Gerald Rudolph Ford, 38th President (August 9, 1974-January 20, 1977), is unique in American history. He was neither elected president nor vice president, but rather, was first appointed vice president under a new Constitutional amendment, when Vice President Agnew resigned in disgrace, and then became President when Nixon resigned.

Prior to becoming vice president, Ford had spent his entire political career in the U.S. House of Representatives, where he was the respected Republican House Minority Leader. After assuming the Presidency, Ford's popularity was initially very high, but continuing inflation, the pardon of former President Nixon, and the granting of limited amnesty to Vietnam-era draft evaders and deserters, quickly brought this "honeymoon" to an end.

President Ford was born in Omaha, Neb., on July 14, 1913. His mother and father were divorced shortly after his birth, and when his mother remarried, her second husband adopted the future president, renaming Leslie Lynch King, Jr., Gerald R. Ford, Jr.

Ford was raised in Grand Rapids, Mich.; was graduated from the University of Michigan, where he was captain of the football team; and received his law degree from Yale University.

In 1942 he entered the U.S. Navy, serving 47 months and participating for two years in 3d and 5th Fleet Carrier operations with the U.S.S. Monterey. After discharge, in 1946, Ford resumed his law practice briefly in Grand Rapids before being elected, in 1948, to the U.S. House of Representatives, a seat he retained for 25 years, through the election of 1972. In 1963, Ford was appointed by President Lyndon Johnson as a member of the Warren Commission to investigate the assassination of President Kennedy.

From the time of his entry into Congress, Gerald Ford's views tended toward the conservative. He voted against most social welfare legislation, in favor of weakened minimum wage bills, and he opposed forced school busing. He supported, however, key civil rights bills at the time of their final passage.

By 1959, Ford was gaining increasing party support for leadership of the House Republicans. In 1960, he was endorsed by Michigan Republicans as the state's favorite son for the G.O.P. vice-presidential nomination. By 1964, he had gained sufficient support to challenge successfully Rep. Charles R. Halleck for the post of House Minority Leader. Generally content with Ford's noncombative, middle-of-the-road approach to issues in his years as Minority Leader, his contituency continued to return him to Congress with majorities of over 60 per cent.

When, on October 12, 1973, Ford was nominated to succeed Spiro T. Agnew as Vice President, he willingly offered to make public any personal information or documentation asked for, including a full statement of net worth, as a way of removing any stigma attached to the office by the departed Vice President.

Richard M. Nixon resigned as President of the United States on August 9, 1974, and Gerald R. Ford was sworn in as his successor on the same day. Ford immediately moved to assure a stable transition of power, retaining Henry Kissinger as Secretary of State, meeting with foreign envoys to reaffirm the Nixon Administration's foreign policies, and conferring with members of the Cabinet, the National Security Council, and the government's economic advisors.

In 1975 President Ford twice escaped death at the hands of would-be assassins. In May when a U.S. merchant ship, the "Mayaguez", was fired on, boarded and seized by Cambodians, Ford reminded the world of his enormous power by ordering a swift attack by Marines which resulted in the rescue of the ship and its crew.

The nomination of an incumbent president by his own party is traditionally assured, but Ford had to meet a strong challenge from former Governor of California, Ronald Reagan. In August 1976, Ford was nominated on the first ballot as the Republican presidential candidate at the Republican National Convention in Kansas City, Missouri. In the November election, he was defeated by his Democratic opponent, Jimmy Carter.

Jimmy Carter

Jimmy Carter, 39th President (January. 20, 1977-) was born in the small farming town of Plains, Georgia, on October 1, 1924. His father, James Earl Carter, had managed a dry goods store and brokered in peanuts; his mother, Lillian, was a registered nurse. The Carter family roots in Georgia go back 150 years for eight generations.

The first member of his family to be graduated from high school, Jimmy Carter attended Georgia Southwestern College and Georgia Institute of Technology prior to his entrance into the U.S. Naval Academy at Annapolis. He graduated 59th in a class of 820 and for six years had a series of assignments which took him from battleships to submarines. In 1952 he was selected by Adm. Hyman G. Rickover to be a part of the Navy's nuclear submarine program. When his father died in 1953, Carter left the Navy and returned to Plains, where he took over the family's peanut warehousing business and built it into a thriving operation.

A deacon in the Plains Baptist Church and member of the local school board, Carter entered politics in 1962. He won a seat in the Georgia Senate that year, but it took a court suit to reverse irregularities that at first gave the primary to his opponent. He easily won a second term in 1964. In his bid for the governorship in 1966, he was third in a six-man primary contest. Encouraged by his showing, he campaigned again in 1970, winning the primary nomination and the election by a comfortable margin.

As governor, Carter organized that state's government, consolidating agencies and introducing a system of zero-based budgeting. He extended state hospital services and was a strong advocate of environmental protection. His stand on equal rights for "the poor, rural, black or not influential" brought Carter his first nationwide attention.

Barred by state law from a second term as governor, he announced in December 1974, one month before the end of his term, that he would run for President. For over a year, almost unnoticed by the press, politicians and the public, Jimmy Carter was on the road. A good showing in the Iowa caucus in mid-January brought media attention; and his win in the New Hampshire primary launched the series of victories which ended in June with the Ohio and New Jersey wins that clinched his nomination more than a month before the Democratic convention. Carter won the close election against President Gerald Ford by holding together enough of the basic old Democratic coalition, namely labor, blacks and liberals.

One of Carter's first acts as President was to grant a pardon to almost all Vietnam draft evaders. A reorganization of the complex structure of departments and agencies was begun, and a new, Cabinet-level Department of Energy was created. Late in 1978, Carter's proposals for civil service reform, designed to promote greater efficiency in government, were approved by Congress.

Carter's program on energy, announced in April 1977, called for a reduction of the annual energy-demand growth rate to 2 percent from the mid-1977 rate of 4.6 percent. To reduce gasoline and oil consumption, Carter asked for a tax on "gas guzzlers" and incentives for the purchase of small cars. Increases in coal production, greater use of solar energy and effective insulation were other key elements in the package. After an 18-month legislative stalemate, a substantially modified version of the program was enacted by Congress in October 1978. Missing from the final bill were penalties on heavy energy consumption.

In the area of foreign affairs, the effect of President Carter's policies and methods has been immediate. Carter has set his own course, acting boldly and speaking with fervor, giving a moral content to American foreign policy that has been missing in recent years. He won respect if not total admiration for concluding treaties that would turn the Panama Canal over to Panama by the year 2000 and for the restraint shown in coping with troubles in Iran, Afghanistan and Nicaragua. Carter scored a diplomatic coup in December 1978 when he surprised the world by announcing that, after a lapse of almost 30 years, the U.S. and Mainland China would resume full diplomatic relations.

The President's forthright championing of human rights and his outspoken defense of Soviet dissidents caused an immediate negative reaction in Moscow, which showed its displeasure by cracking down on dissidents and Western correspondents. The strain in relations has been intensified by Western suspicions concerning a Soviet arms build-up and moves by Moscow in Africa. Long, arduous sessions of the Strategic Arms Limitations Talks (Salt II) produced an agreement which now awaits Senate approval, a somewhat chancy matter after the presence of a Russian army brigade on Cuban soil became an issue.

In defense matters, Carter has served notice on the Pentagon that he is in charge. He scrapped the B-1 bomber program, used his veto to block construction of a new nuclear aircraft carrier, and deferred production of the neutron bomb, although Soviet unwillingness to show similar restraint in deploying new weapons led him to keep open the option to produce it later. The President approved the development of the MX mobile intercontinental ballistic missile in June 1979.

In the Middle East, the Carter Administration welcomed and sought to encourage Egyptian President Sadat's peace initiative toward Israel in late 1977. Carter played the role of a mediator, and it was under his auspices that Sadat and Prime Minister Menachem Begin of Israel reached agreement in principle on a Middle East peace plan at Camp David, Maryland in September 1978.

The Carter Administration began to find the promises of 1978 fading into bad breaks and bitter squabbles in 1979. The U.S. economy was hurt by the Iran oil cut-off and subsequent gas crunch. The rate of inflation reached double digits, and each jump in the cost of living, unemployment rate and U.S. trade deficit has cut into Carter's support. A shakeup in the President's cabinet, a move designed to instill a new sense of leadership, backfired and the forced resignation of UN ambassador Andrew Young following contact with the PLO did not help matters. As his popularity declined, the President faced the growing possibility of a challenge by Ted Kennedy for the presidential nomination in 1980.

U.S. PRESIDENTIAL INDEX

(F) = Federal Party; (D-R) = Democratic-Republican Party; (W) = Whig Party; (D) = Democratic Party; (R) = Republican Party.

President and Political Party	Place and Date of Birth	Parents	Ancestry	Religious Affiliation
1. George Washington (F)	Westmoreland Co., Va.; Feb. 22, 1732	Augustine and Mary (Ball) Washington	English	Episcopalian
2. John Adams (F)	Braintree, Mass.; Oct. 19, 1735	John and Susanna (Boylston) Adams	English	Unitarian
3. Thomas Jefferson (D-R)	Goochland Co., Va.; Apr. 13, 1743	Peter and Jane (Randolph) Jefferson	Welsh	No formal affiliation
4. James Madison (D-R)	Port Conway, Va.; Mar. 16, 1751	James and Eleanor (Conway) Madison	English	Episcopalian
5. James Monroe (D-R)	Westmoreland Co., Va.; Apr. 28, 1758	Spence and Elizabeth (Jones) Monroe	Scottish, Welsh	Episcopalian
6. John Quincy Adams (D-R)	Braintree, Mass.; July 11, 1767	John and Abigail (Smith) Adams	English	Unitarian
7. Andrew Jackson (D)	Waxhaw, S.C.; Mar. 15, 1767	Andrew and Elizabeth (Hutchinson) Jackson	Scots-Irish	Presbyterian
8. Martin Van Buren (D)	Kinderhook, N.Y.; Dec. 5, 1782	Abraham and Maria (Hoes) Van Buren	Dutch	Dutch Reformed
9. William H. Harrison (W)	Charles City Co., Va.; Feb. 9, 1773	Benjamin and Elizabeth (Bassett) Harrison	English	Episcopalian
10. John Tyler (W)	Charles City Co., Va.; Mar 29, 1790	John and Mary (Armistead) Tyler	English	Episcopalian
11. James Knox Polk (D)	Mecklenburg Co., N.C.; Nov. 2, 1795	Samuel and Jane (Knox) Polk	Scots-Irish	Presbyterian
12. Zachary Taylor (W)	Orange Co., Va.; Nov. 24, 1784	Richard and Sarah (Strother) Taylor	English	Episcopalian
13. Millard Fillmore (W)	Locke, N.Y.; Jan. 7, 1800	Nathaniel and Phoebe (Millard) Fillmore	English	Unitarian
14. Franklin Pierce (D)	Hillsboro, N.H.; Nov. 23, 1804	Benjamin and Anna (Kendrick) Pierce	English	Episcopalian
15. James Buchanan (D)	Cove Gap, Pa.; Apr. 23, 1791	James and Elizabeth (Speer) Buchanan	Scots-Irish	Presbyterian
16. Abraham Lincoln (R)	Hardin Co., Ky.; Feb. 12, 1809	Thomas and Nancy (Hanks) Lincoln	English	No formal affiliation
17. Andrew Johnson (D)	Raleigh, N.C.; Dec. 29, 1808	Jacob and Mary (McDonough) Johnson	Scottish, Irish, English	No formal affiliation
18. Ulysses Simpson Grant (R)	Point Pleasant, Ohio; Apr. 27, 1822	Jesse and Hannah (Simpson) Grant	Scottish, English	Methodist
19. Rutherford B. Hayes (R)	Delaware, Ohio; Oct. 4, 1822	Rutherford and Sophia (Birchard) Hayes	English, Scottish	No formal affiliation
20. James Abram Garfield (R)	Orange, Ohio; Nov. 19, 1831	Abram and Eliza (Ballou) Garfield	English, Huguenot	Disciples of Christ
21. Chester Alan Arthur (R)	Fairfield, Vt.; Oct. 5, 1830	William and Malvina (Stone) Arthur	Scots-Irish, English	Episcopalian
22., 24. Grover Cleveland (D)	Caldwell, N.J.; Mar. 18, 1837	Richard and Ann (Neal) Cleveland	English, Scots-Irish	Presbyterian
23. Benjamin Harrison (R)	North Bend, Ohio; Aug. 20, 1833	John and Elizabeth (Irwin) Harrison	English	Presbyterian
25. William McKinley (R)	Niles, Ohio; Jan. 29, 1843	William and Nancy (Allison) McKinley	Scots-Irish, English	Methodist
26. Theodore Roosevelt (R)	New York, N.Y.; Oct. 27, 1858	Theodore and Martha (Bulloch) Roosevelt	Dutch, Scottish, English, Huguenot	Dutch Reformed
27. William Howard Taft (R)	Cincinnati, Ohio; Sept. 15, 1857	Alphonso and Louise (Torrey) Taft	English, Scots-Irish	Unitarian
28. Woodrow Wilson (D)	Staunton, Va.; Dec. 28, 1856	Joseph and Jessie (Woodrow) Wilson	Scots-Irish, Scottish	Presbyterian
29. Warren G. Harding (R)	Blooming Grove, Ohio; Nov. 2, 1865	George and Phoebe (Dickerson) Harding	English, Scots-Irish	Baptist
30. Calvin Coolidge (R)	Plymouth Notch, Vt.; July 4, 1872	John and Victoria (Moor) Coolidge	English	Congregationalist
31. Herbert Clark Hoover (R)	West Branch, Iowa; Aug. 10, 1874	Jesse and Huldah (Minthorn) Hoover	German-Swiss, English	Quaker
32. Franklin D. Roosevelt (D)	Hyde Park, N.Y.; Jan. 30, 1882	James and Sara (Delano) Roosevelt	Dutch, Huguenot, English	Episcopalian
33. Harry S Truman (D)	Lamar, Mo.; May 8, 1884	John and Martha (Young) Truman	English, Scots-Irish	Baptist
34. Dwight D. Eisenhower (R)	Denison, Tex.; Oct. 14, 1890	David and Ida (Stover) Eisenhower	German	Presbyterian
35. John F. Kennedy (D)	Brookline, Mass.; May 29, 1917	Joseph and Rose (Fitzgerald) Kennedy	Irish	Roman Catholic
36. Lyndon Baines Johnson (D)	Near Stonewall, Tex.; Aug. 27, 1908	Samuel and Rebekah (Baines) Johnson	English	Disciples of Christ
37. Richard Milhous Nixon (R)	Yorba Linda, Calif.; Jan. 9, 1913	Frank and Hannah (Milhous) Nixon	English, Scots-Irish	Quaker
38. Gerald R. Ford (R)	Omaha, Neb.; July 14, 1913	Gerald R. and Dorothy (Gardner) Ford	English	Episcopalian
39. Jimmy Carter (D)	Plains, Ga.; Oct. 1, 1924	James Earl and Lillian (Gordy) Carter	English	Baptist

Occupation Prior to Politics	Elected From	Age at Inauguration	Date of Death and Place of Burial	Presidential Terms	Vice-President
Surveyor, Soldier, Planter	Virginia	57	Dec. 14, 1799; "Mount Vernon," near Alexandria, Va.	Apr. 30, 1789–Mar. 3, 1793 Mar. 4, 1793–Mar. 3, 1797	John Adams John Adams
Teacher, Lawyer	Massachusetts	61	July 4, 1826; Quincy, Mass.	Mar. 4, 1797–Mar. 3, 1801	Thomas Jefferson
Planter, Lawyer	Virginia	57	July 4, 1826; "Monticello," near Charlottesville, Va.	Mar. 4, 1801–Mar. 3, 1805 Mar. 4, 1805–Mar. 3, 1809	Aaron Burr George Clinton
Planter	Virginia	57	June 28, 1836; "Montpelier," near Orange, Va.	Mar. 4, 1809–Mar. 3, 1813 Mar. 4, 1813–Mar. 3, 1817	George Clinton Elbridge Gerry
Lawyer	Virginia	58	July 4, 1831; Richmond, Va.	Mar. 4, 1817–Mar. 3, 1821 Mar. 4, 1821–Mar. 3, 1825	Daniel Tompkins Daniel Tompkins
Lawyer	Massachusetts	57	Feb. 23, 1848; Quincy, Mass.	Mar. 4, 1825–Mar. 3, 1829	John Calhoun
Planter, Lawyer, Soldier	Tennessee	61	June 8, 1845; "Hermitage," near Nashville, Tenn.	Mar. 4, 1829–Mar. 3, 1833 Mar. 4, 1833–Mar. 3, 1837	John Calhoun Martin Van Buren
Lawyer	New York	54	July 24, 1862; Kinderhook, N.Y.	Mar. 4, 1837–Mar. 3, 1841	Richard Johnson
Soldier, Planter	Ohio	68	Apr. 4, 1841; North Bend, Ohio	Mar. 4, 1841–Apr. 4, 1841	John Tyler
Lawyer	Virginia	51	Jan. 18, 1862; Richmond, Va.	Apr. 6, 1841–Mar. 3, 1845	——
Lawyer	Tennessee	49	June 15, 1849; Nashville, Tenn.	Mar. 4, 1845–Mar. 3, 1849	George Dallas
Soldier, Planter	Louisiana	64	July 9, 1850; near Louisville, Ky.	Mar. 4, 1849–July 9, 1850	Millard Fillmore
Lawyer	New York	50	Mar. 8, 1874; Buffalo, N.Y.	July 10, 1850–Mar. 3, 1853	——
Lawyer	New Hampshire	48	Oct. 8, 1869; Concord, N.H.	Mar. 4, 1853–Mar. 3, 1857	William King
Lawyer	Pennsylvania	65	June 1, 1868; Lancaster, Pa.	Mar. 4, 1857–Mar. 3, 1861	John Breckinridge
Lawyer	Illinois	52	Apr. 15, 1865; Springfield, Ill.	Mar. 4, 1861–Mar. 3, 1865 Mar. 4, 1865–Apr. 15, 1865	Hannibal Hamlin Andrew Johnson
Tailor	Tennessee	56	July 31, 1875; Greeneville, Tenn.	Apr. 15, 1865–Mar. 3, 1869	——
Soldier, Farmer, Clerk	Illinois	46	July 23, 1885; New York, N.Y.	Mar. 4, 1869–Mar. 3, 1873 Mar. 4, 1873–Mar. 3, 1877	Schuyler Colfax Henry Wilson
Lawyer	Ohio	54	Jan. 17, 1893; Fremont, Ohio	Mar. 4, 1877–Mar. 3, 1881	William Wheeler
Laborer, Professor	Ohio	49	Sept. 19, 1881; Cleveland, Ohio	Mar. 4, 1881–Sept. 19, 1881	Chester Arthur
School Teacher, Lawyer	New York	50	Nov. 18, 1886; Albany, N.Y.	Sept. 19, 1881–Mar. 3, 1885	——
Lawyer	New York	47, 55	June 24, 1908; Princeton, N.J.	Mar. 4, 1885–Mar. 3, 1889 Mar. 4, 1893–Mar. 3, 1897	Thomas Hendricks Adlai Stevenson
Lawyer	Indiana	55	Mar. 13, 1901; Indianapolis, Ind.	Mar. 4, 1889–Mar. 3, 1893	Levi Morton
School Teacher, Clerk, Lawyer	Ohio	54	Sept. 14, 1901; Canton, Ohio	Mar. 4, 1897–Mar. 3, 1901 Mar. 4, 1901–Sept. 14, 1901	Garret Hobart Theodore Roosevelt
Historian, Rancher	New York	42	Jan. 6, 1919; Oyster Bay, N.Y.	Sept. 14, 1901–Mar. 3, 1905 Mar. 4, 1905–Mar. 3, 1909	—— Charles Fairbanks
Lawyer	Ohio	51	Mar. 8, 1930; Arlington, Va.	Mar. 4, 1909–Mar. 3, 1913	James Sherman
Lawyer, University President	New Jersey	56	Feb. 3, 1924; Washington, D.C.	Mar. 4, 1913–Mar. 3, 1917 Mar. 4, 1917–Mar. 3, 1921	Thomas Marshall Thomas Marshall
Newspaper Editor and Publisher	Ohio	55	Aug. 2, 1923; Marion, Ohio	Mar. 4, 1921–Aug. 2, 1923	Calvin Coolidge
Lawyer	Massachusetts	51	Jan. 5, 1933; Plymouth, Vt.	Aug. 3, 1923–Mar. 3, 1925 Mar. 4, 1925–Mar. 3, 1929	—— Charles Dawes
Engineer, Relief Administrator	California	54	Oct. 20, 1964; West Branch, Iowa	Mar. 4, 1929–Mar. 3, 1933	Charles Curtis
Lawyer	New York	51	April 12, 1945; Hyde Park, N.Y.	Mar. 4, 1933–Jan. 20, 1937 Jan. 20, 1937–Jan. 20, 1941 Jan. 20, 1941–Jan. 20, 1945 Jan. 20, 1945–Apr. 12, 1945	John Garner John Garner Henry Wallace Harry Truman
Clerk, Haberdasher, Farmer	Missouri	60	Dec. 26, 1972; Independence, Mo.	Apr. 12, 1945–Jan. 20, 1949 Jan. 20, 1949–Jan. 20, 1953	—— Alben Barkley
Soldier	New York	62	Mar. 28, 1969; Abilene, Kan.	Jan. 20, 1953–Jan. 20, 1957 Jan. 20, 1957–Jan. 20, 1961	Richard Nixon Richard Nixon
Author, Reporter	Massachusetts	43	Nov. 22, 1963; Arlington, Va.	Jan. 20, 1961–Nov. 22, 1963	Lyndon Johnson
School Teacher	Texas	55	Jan. 22, 1973; near Johnson City, Texas	Nov. 22, 1963–Jan. 20, 1965 Jan. 20, 1965–Jan. 20, 1969	—— Hubert Humphrey
Lawyer	New York	55	—	Jan. 20, 1969–Jan. 20, 1973 Jan. 20, 1973–Aug. 9, 1974	Spiro Agnew Gerald R. Ford
Lawyer	—	61	—	Aug. 9, 1974–Jan. 20, 1977	Nelson Rockefeller
Businessman, Farmer	Georgia	52	—	Jan. 20, 1977	Walter Mondale

THE VICE-PRESIDENTS

For those Vice-Presidents who became Presidents—John Adams, Thomas Jefferson, Martin Van Buren, John Tyler, Millard Fillmore, Andrew Johnson, Chester A. Arthur, Theodore Roosevelt, Calvin Coolidge, Harry S. Truman, Lyndon B. Johnson, Richard M. Nixon, and Gerald R. Ford—see the Presidential biographies.

Aaron Burr

Vice-President (1801–1805) to Thomas Jefferson *Political Party:* Democratic-Republican *Born:* Newark, New Jersey, February 6, 1756 *Ancestry:* English *Religious Affiliation:* Presbyterian *Education:* College of New Jersey (now Princeton University), 1772; thereafter briefly studied theology *Wives:* Married Mrs. Theodosia Prevost in 1782; she died in 1794. Married Mrs. Stephen Jumel in 1833; she petitioned for divorce a year later *Children:* Two by first wife *Home:* New York *Occupations before Vice-Presidency:* Revolutionary soldier, lawyer, politician, U.S. Senator (1791–1797) *Age at Inauguration:* 44 *Outstanding Facts:* In the Presidential election of 1800, an electoral vote tie between Aaron Burr and Thomas Jefferson threw the election into the House of Representatives, where, mainly through the efforts of Alexander Hamilton, the Presidency was finally won by Jefferson, with the Vice-Presidency going to Burr. In 1804, after Burr had been nominated for the governorship of New York, Hamilton again contributed to his defeat. Burr challenged Hamilton to a duel and killed him. This, as well as President Jefferson's suspicions that Burr had intrigued for the Presidency, effectively ended his political career. As Vice-President, Burr presided over the Senate with impartiality *Occupation after Vice-Presidency:* He became involved in a political conspiracy, the aims of which still remain unclear, and was tried for treason but acquitted. He left the country and schemed abroad but, frustrated in his plans, returned to the United States, where he again took up the practice of law *Died:* Sept. 14, 1836 *Place of Burial:* Princeton, N.J.

George Clinton

Vice-President (1805–1812) to Thomas Jefferson and James Madison *Political Party:* Democratic-Republican *Born:* Little Britain (now Ulster County), New York, July 26, 1739 *Ancestry:* English, Scots-Irish *Religious Affiliation:* Presbyterian *Education:* Private tutoring *Wife:* Married Cornelia Tappen in 1770 *Children:* Six *Home:* New York *Occupations before Vice-Presidency:* Lawyer, Revolutionary soldier, politician, governor of New York (1777–1795, 1801–1804) *Age at Inauguration:* 65 *Outstanding Facts:* An advocate of state sovereignty, Clinton was one of the chief opponents of the Constitution. He hoped to be President but lost out to James Madison, to whom he was openly hostile. He spent much time in New York and was a poor presiding officer of the Senate. Clinton was the first Vice-President to die in office *Died:* April 20, 1812 *Place of Burial:* Washington, D.C.; re-interred (1908) in Kingston, Ulster County, N.Y.

Elbridge Gerry

Vice-President (1813–1814) to James Madison *Political Party:* Democratic-Republican *Born:* Marblehead, Massachusetts, July 17, 1744 *Ancestry:* English *Religious Affiliation:* Episcopalian *Education:* Harvard College, 1762 *Wife:* Married Ann Thompson in 1786 *Children:* Nine *Home:* Massachusetts *Occupations before Vice-Presidency:* Merchant, politician, signer of the Declaration of Independence, governor of Massachusetts (1810–1812) *Age at Inauguration:* 63 *Outstanding Facts:* He socialized a great deal during his brief tenure and is now chiefly remembered for *gerrymander,* the term given to his attempt while governor of Massachusetts to redistrict the state in his party's favor *Died:* November 23, 1814 *Place of Burial:* Washington, D.C.

Daniel D. Tompkins

Vice-President (1817–1825) to James Monroe *Political Party:* Democratic-Republican *Born:* Fox Meadow (now Scarsdale), New York, June 21, 1774 *Ancestry:* Scottish, English *Religious Affiliation:* Presbyterian *Education:* Columbia College, 1795 *Wife:* Married Hannah Minthorne in 1798 *Children:* Eight *Home:* New York *Occupations before Vice-Presidency:* Lawyer, politician, governor of New York (1807–1817) *Age at Inauguration:* 42 *Outstanding Facts:* He spent much time contesting court cases arising out of actions he took over expenditures made while he was governor of New York during the War of 1812 *Occupation after Vice-Presidency:* He continued contesting various court actions *Died:* June 11, 1825 *Place of Burial:* New York City

John Caldwell Calhoun

Vice-President (1825–1832) to John Quincy Adams and Andrew Jackson *Political Party:* Democratic *Born:* Abbeville, South Carolina, March 18, 1782 *Ancestry:* Scots-Irish *Religious Affiliation:* Presbyterian *Education:* Yale College, 1804, studied (1805–1806) at Litchfield (Conn.) Law School *Wife:* Married Floride Calhoun in 1811 *Children:* Nine *Home:* South Carolina *Occupations before Vice-Presidency:* Lawyer, planter, U.S. Congressman (1811–1817), Secretary of War (1817–1825) *Age at Inauguration:* 42 *Outstanding Facts:* A strong supporter of Jackson, he opposed Adams throughout the latter's administration. In 1828 in his *South Carolina Exposition,* he set forth the principles of states' rights and nullification. Originally thought of as Jackson's successor, he broke with the President over a variety of issues, including the very nature of the federal union. Calhoun resigned as Vice-President upon being elected to the Senate in 1832. In the Senate he eloquently defended his states' rights principles and proslavery viewpoint in dramatic debates with Daniel Webster *Occupations after Vice-Presidency:* Senator (1832–1844, 1845–1850), Cabinet officer (Secretary of State, 1844–1845) *Died:* March 31, 1850 *Place of Burial:* Charleston, South Carolina

Richard Mentor Johnson

Vice-President (1837–1841) to Martin Van Buren *Political Party:* Democratic *Born:* Beargrass Creek (a frontier settlement on the present location of Louisville), Kentucky, autumn of 1780 *Ancestry:* English *Religious Affiliation:* Baptist *Education:* Preparatory school and private instruction *Wife:* Johnson was a bachelor *Home:* Kentucky *Occupations before Vice-Presidency:* Lawyer, soldier, educator, politician, U.S. Congressman (1814–1819, 1829–1837), Senator (1819–1829) *Age at Inauguration:* 56 *Outstanding Facts:* A hero of the War of 1812, Johnson was said to be the slayer of Chief Tecumseh at the Battle of the Thames. Johnson has been the only Vice-President ever elected by the Senate; he failed to get enough electoral votes. *Occupations after Vice-Presidency:* Businessman, state legislator (1841-1842, 1850) *Died:* Nov. 19, 1850 *Place of Burial:* Frankfort, Ky.

George Mifflin Dallas

Vice-President (1845–1849) to James K. Polk *Political Party:* Democratic *Born:* Philadelphia, July 10, 1792 *Ancestry:* Scottish, English *Religious Affiliation:* Presbyterian *Education:* Princeton College, 1810 *Wife:* Married Sophia Chew in 1816 *Children:* Eight *Home:* Pennsylvania *Occupations before Vice-Presidency:* Lawyer, politician, diplomat *Age at Inauguration:* 52 *Outstanding Facts:* Although nominated as a protectionist, he cast (1846) the deciding vote for a lower tariff *Occupations after Vice-Presidency:* Lawyer, diplomat, writer *Died:* December 31, 1864 *Place of Burial:* Philadelphia

William Rufus Devane King

Vice-President (1853) to Franklin Pierce *Political Party:* Democratic *Born:* Sampson County, North Carolina, April 7, 1786 *Ancestry:* Scots-Irish, Huguenot *Religious Affiliation:* Presbyterian *Education:* University of North Carolina, 1803 *Wife:* King was a bachelor *Home:* Alabama *Occupations before Vice-Presidency:* Lawyer, politician, U.S. Congressman (1811–1816), Senator (1819–1844; 1848–1852), diplomat *Age at Inauguration:* 66 *Outstanding Facts:* Elected while recovering from tuberculosis in Cuba, he died shortly after his return. *Died:* April 18, 1853 *Place of Burial:* "Kings Bend," Ala.; reinterred in Selma, Ala.

John Cabell Breckinridge

Vice-President (1857–1861) to James Buchanan *Political Party:* Democratic *Born:* "Cabell's Dale" (near Lexington, Kentucky, January 21, 1821 *Ancestry:* English, Scots-Irish *Religious Affiliation:* Presbyterian *Education:* Centre College (Ky.), 1838; thereafter he studied law at Transylvania University *Wife:* Married Mary Cyrene Burch in 1843 *Children:* Five *Home:* Kentucky *Occupations before Vice-Presidency:* Lawyer, soldier, politician, U.S. Congressman (1851–1855) *Age at Inauguration:* 36 *Outstanding Facts:* The youngest man ever to become Vice-President, he was dignified beyond his years and ably presided over the Senate. Breckinridge tried to achieve some kind of compromise during the years prior to the Civil War. *Occupations after Vice-Presidency:* U.S. Senator (1861), Confederate soldier, Confederate Secretary of War (1865), lawyer, businessman *Died:* May 17, 1875 *Place of Burial:* Lexington, Kentucky

Hannibal Hamlin

Vice-President (1861–1865) to Abraham Lincoln *Political Party:* Republican *Born:* Paris, Maine, August 27, 1809 *Ancestry:* English *Religious Affiliation:* Unitarian *Education:* Preparatory studies *Wives:* Married Sarah Jane Emery in 1833; she died in 1855. Married her half-sister Ellen Vesta Emery in 1856 *Children:* Five by first wife, two by second wife *Home:* Maine *Occupations before Vice-Presidency:* Farmer, printer, lawyer, politician, U.S. Senator (1857–1861) *Age at Inauguration:* 51 *Outstanding

Facts: Hamlin was a staunch advocate of emancipation *Occupations after Vice Presidency:* Political appointee, lawyer, businessman, U.S. Senator (1869–1881), diplomat *Died:* July 4, 1891 *Place of Burial:* Bangor, Maine

Schuyler Colfax

Vice-President (1869–1873) to Ulysses S. Grant *Political Party:* Republican *Born:* New York City, March 23, 1823 *Ancestry:* English, Huguenot *Religious Affiliation:* Dutch Reformed *Education:* Grade school *Wives:* Married Evelyn Clark in 1844; she died in 1862. Married Ellen Wade in 1868 *Children:* One by second wife *Home:* Indiana *Occupations before Vice-Presidency:* Political appointee, journalist, U.S. Congressman (1855–1869), speaker of the House (1863–1869) *Age at Inauguration:* 45 *Outstanding Facts:* In 1870, midway through his term, he announced his retirement from political life, hoping that the public would demand that he remain. No such clamor developed, and Colfax rescinded his decision. Colfax failed of renomination. Later it was revealed that Colfax had been involved in the Credit Mobilier railroad scandal, which effectively ended his public career *Occupation after Vice-Presidency:* Lecturer *Died:* January 13, 1885 *Place of Burial:* South Bend, Indiana

Henry Wilson

Vice-President (1873–1875) to Ulysses S. Grant *Political Party:* Republican *Born:* Farmington, New Hampshire, February 16, 1812 *Ancestry:* Scots-Irish *Religious Affiliation:* Congregationalist *Education:* Little formal schooling *Wife:* Married Harriet Malvina Howe in 1840 *Children:* One *Home:* Massachusetts *Occupations before Vice-Presidency:* Indentured worker, school teacher, cobbler, businessman, newspaperman, politician, U.S. Senator (1855–1873) *Age at Inauguration:* 61 *Outstanding Facts:* As Vice-President ill health made his attendance in presiding over the Senate irregular, and he died in office *Died:* November 22, 1875 *Place of Burial:* Natick, Massachusetts

William Almon Wheeler

Vice-President (1877–1881) to Rutherford B. Hayes *Political Party:* Republican *Born:* Malone, New York, June 30, 1819 *Ancestry:* English *Religious Affiliation:* Presbyterian *Education:* Attended (1838–1840) the University of Vermont *Wife:* Married Mary King in 1845 *Children:* None *Home:* New York *Occupations before Vice-Presidency:* Lawyer, banker, businessman, politician, U.S. Congressman (1861–1863, 1869–1877) *Age at Inauguration:* 57 *Outstanding Facts:* Little known nationally when nominated for the office, he performed its major function, presiding over the Senate, with faithfulness *Occupation after Vice-Presidency:* Poor health resulted in general inactivity; unsuccessfully nominated for U.S. Senator in 1881 *Died:* June 4, 1887 *Place of Burial:* Malone, N.Y.

Thomas Andrews Hendricks

Vice-President (1885) to Grover Cleveland *Political Party:* Democratic *Born:* Zanesville, Ohio, September 7, 1819 *Ancestry:* Scottish, English, Huguenot *Religious Affiliation:* Episcopalian *Education:* Hanover College (Indiana), 1841 *Wife:* Married Eliza Morgan in 1845

Children: One *Home:* Indiana *Occupations before Vice-Presidency:* Lawyer, politician, defeated candidate for Vice-President in 1876 *Age at Inauguration:* 65 *Outstanding Fact:* He died 8 months after taking office. *Died:* Nov. 25, 1885 *Place of Burial:* Indianapolis, Ind.

Levi Parsons Morton

Vice-President (1889–1893) to Benjamin Harrison *Political Party:* Republican *Born:* Shoreham, Vermont, May 16, 1824 *Ancestry:* English *Religious Affiliation:* Episcopalian *Education:* Preparatory schools *Wives:* Married Lucy Young Kimball in 1856; she died in 1871 Married Anna Livingston Read Street in 1873 *Children:* One by first wife; six by second wife *Home:* New York *Occupations before Vice-Presidency:* Clerk, school teacher, businessman, U.S. Congressman (1879–1881), diplomat *Age at Inauguration:* 64 *Outstanding Fact:* He was passed over for renomination as Vice-President *Occupations after Vice-Presidency:* Real estate investor, banker, Governor of New York (1895–1897) *Died:* May 16, 1920 *Place of Burial:* Rhinebeck, N.Y.

Adlai Ewing Stevenson

Vice-President (1893–1897) to Grover Cleveland *Political Party:* Democratic *Born:* Christian County, Kentucky, October 23, 1835 *Ancestry:* Scots-Irish *Religious Affiliation:* Presbyterian *Education:* Attended Centre College (Kentucky) two years *Wife:* Married Letitia Green in 1866 *Children:* Four *Home:* Illinois *Occupations before Vice-Presidency:* Lawyer, politician, U.S. Congressman (1875–1877, 1879–1881) *Age at Inauguration:* 57 *Outstanding Facts:* He presided with fairness over a Senate that had recently turned him down for a District of Columbia judicial post. A "soft money" advocate, he was unsympathetic to President Cleveland's monetary views but never embarrassed the administration with open disagreement *Occupations after Vice-Presidency:* Lawyer and politician *Died:* June 14, 1914 *Place of Burial:* Bloomington, Illinois

Garret Augustus Hobart

Vice-President (1897–1899) to William McKinley *Political Party:* Republican *Born:* Long Branch, New Jersey, June 3, 1844 *Ancestry:* English, Dutch, Huguenot *Religious Affiliation:* Presbyterian *Education:* Rutgers College, 1863 *Wife:* Married Jennie Tuttle in 1869 *Children:* Two *Home:* New Jersey *Occupations before Vice-Presidency:* Lawyer, businessman, banker, politician *Age at Inauguration:* 52 *Outstanding Facts:* He presided over the Senate with ability. Hobart cast the deciding vote against granting the Philippine Is. independence *Died:* In office, Nov. 21, 1899 *Place of Burial:* Paterson, N.J.

Charles Warren Fairbanks

Vice-President (1905–1909) to Theodore Roosevelt *Political Party:* Republican *Born:* Near Unionville Center, Ohio, May 11, 1852 *Ancestry:* English *Religious Affiliation:* Methodist *Education:* Ohio Wesleyan, 1872 *Wife:* Married Cornelia Cole in 1874 *Children:* Five *Home:* Indiana *Occupations before Vice-Presidency:* Newspaperman, railroad lawyer, politician, U.S. Senator (1897–1905) *Age at Inauguration:* 52 *Outstanding Facts:* Although Fairbanks and

President Roosevelt represented opposite wings of the Republican Party, they maintained cordial relations *Occupations after Vice-Presidency:* Lawyer, unsuccessful candidate for Vice-Pres. in 1916 *Died:* June 4, 1918 *Place of Burial:* Indianapolis, Ind.

James Schoolcraft Sherman

Vice-President (1909–1912) to William Howard Taft *Political Party:* Republican *Born:* Utica, New York, October 24, 1855 *Ancestry:* English *Religious Affiliation:* Dutch Reformed *Education:* Hamilton College, 1878 *Wife:* Married Carrie Babcock in 1881 *Children:* Three *Home:* New York *Occupations before Vice-Presidency:* Lawyer, banker, politician, U.S. Congressman (1887–1891, 1893–1909) *Age at Inauguration:* 53 *Outstanding Facts:* An affable man known as "Sunny Jim," he presided well over the Senate. Renominated but died before the election *Died:* October 30, 1912 *Place of Burial:* Utica, N.Y.

Thomas Riley Marshall

Vice-President (1913–1921) to Woodrow Wilson *Political Party:* Democratic *Born:* North Manchester, Indiana, March 14, 1854 *Ancestry:* English *Religious Affiliation:* Presbyterian *Education:* Wabash College, 1873 *Wife:* Married Lois Irene Kimsey in 1895 *Children:* None *Home:* Indiana *Occupations before Vice-Presidency:* Lawyer, politician, governor of Indiana (1909–1913) *Age at Inauguration:* 58 *Outstanding Facts:* Marshall was the first Vice-President in nearly a century to succeed himself. While President Wilson was ill, Marshall acted as ceremonial head of state, but he refused to accept any of the President's powers. He was well known for his quip, "What this country needs is a good five-cent cigar" *Occupations after Vice-Presidency:* Lawyer, lecturer, political appointee *Died:* June 1, 1925 *Place of Burial:* Indianapolis, Ind.

Charles Gates Dawes

Vice-President (1925–1929) to Calvin Coolidge *Political Party:* Republican *Born:* Marietta, Ohio, August 27, 1865 *Ancestry:* English *Religious Affiliation:* Congregationalist *Education:* Marietta College, 1884; Cincinnati Law School, 1886 *Wife:* Married Caro D. Blymer in 1889 *Children:* Four (two adopted) *Home:* Illinois *Occupations before Vice-Presidency:* Lawyer, banker, businessman, soldier, politician *Age at Inauguration:* 59 *Outstanding Facts:* Dawes shared the Nobel Peace Prize in 1925 for his work in attempting to settle through the Dawes Plan the problem of German reparations. A short-tempered man, he infuriated the Senate by telling that body it was time to change its antiquated rules *Occupations after Vice-Presidency:* Diplomat, public servant, banker, businessman *Died:* April 23, 1951 *Place of Burial:* Chicago

Charles Curtis

Vice-President (1929–1933) to Herbert Hoover *Political Party:* Republican *Born:* Topeka, Kansas, January 25, 1860 *Ancestry:* American Indian, English, French *Religious Affiliation:* Episcopalian *Education:* High school *Wife:* Married Annie E. Baird in 1884 *Children:* Three *Home:* Kansas *Occupations before Vice-Presidency:* Lawyer, politician, U.S. Congressman (1893–1907), Senator (1907–1913, 1915–1929) *Age at Inauguration:* 69 *Outstanding Facts:*

Lacking a close relationship with President Hoover, Curtis had little to say or do *Occupations after Vice-Presidency:* Lawyer, businessman *Died:* February 8, 1936 *Place of Burial:* Topeka, Kansas

John Nance Garner

Vice-President (1933–1941) to Franklin D. Roosevelt *Political Party:* Democratic *Born:* Blossom Prairie, Texas, November 22, 1868 *Ancestry:* English, Welsh, Scottish *Religious Affiliation:* Methodist *Education:* High school *Wife:* Married Elizabeth Rheiner in 1895 *Children:* One *Home:* Texas *Occupations before Vice-Presidency:* Lawyer, businessman, banker, politician, U.S. Congressman (1903–1933), Speaker of the House of Representatives (1931–1933) *Age at Inauguration:* 63 *Outstanding Facts:* Garner retained much of his influence with Congress while Vice-President and during his first term helped to obtain passage of much New Deal legislation. During his second term, he increasingly found himself out of sympathy with President Roosevelt's programs, and he was not renominated *Occupations after Vice-Presidency:* Businessman, banker, cattle rancher *Died:* November 7, 1967 *Place of Burial:* Uvalde, Texas

Henry Agard Wallace

Vice-President (1941–1945) to Franklin D. Roosevelt *Political Party:* Democratic *Born:* Near Orient, Iowa, October 7, 1888 *Ancestry:* Scots-Irish *Religious Affiliation:* Episcopalian *Education:* Iowa State College, 1910 *Wife:* Married Ilo Browne in 1914 *Children:* Three *Home:* Iowa *Occupations before Vice-Presidency:* Editor, farmer, Secretary of Agriculture (1933–1940) *Age at Inauguration:* 52 *Outstanding Facts:* President Roosevelt cast the Vice-Presidency under Wallace into its most active role up to that time. Wallace served as good-will ambassador to Latin America, the Soviet Union, and the Far East. He also undertook various defense duties. However, his political and social views caused him to be viewed suspiciously by the Democratic Party and he failed of renomination *Occupations after Vice-Presidency:* Secretary of Commerce (1945–1946), author, farmer, defeated candidate for President in 1948 *Died:* November 18, 1965 *Place of Burial:* Des Moines, Iowa

Alben William Barkley

Vice-President (1949–1953) to Harry S Truman *Political Party:* Democratic *Born:* Near Lowes, Kentucky, November 24, 1877 *Ancestry:* Scots-Irish *Religious Affiliation:* Methodist *Education:* Marvin College (Kentucky), 1897; attended University of Virginia Law School *Wives:* Married Dorothy Brower in 1903; she died in 1947. Married Mrs. Carleton S. Hadley in 1949 *Children:* Three by first wife *Home:* Kentucky *Occupations before Vice-Presidency:* Lawyer, politician, U.S. Senator (1927–1949) *Age at Inauguration:* 71 *Outstanding Facts:* Very popular, he was nicknamed "Veep" during his tenure. He was the only Vice-President to marry while in office. After President Truman announced he would not run again, Barkley attempted to win the Presidential nomination but failed *Occupations after Vice-Presidency:* Lawyer, U.S. Senator (1955–1956) *Died:* April 30, 1956 *Place of Burial:* Paducah, Kentucky

Hubert Horatio Humphrey

Vice-President (1965–1969) to Lyndon B. Johnson *Political Party:* Democratic *Born:* Wallace, South Dakota, May 27, 1911 *Ancestry:* Welsh, Norwegian *Religious Affiliation:* Congregationalist *Education:* University of Minnesota, 1939; M.A., Louisiana State, 1940; began work for a Ph.D. *Wife:* Married Muriel Fay Buck in 1936 *Children:* Four *Home:* Minnesota *Occupations before Vice-Presidency:* Pharmacist, teacher, politician, U.S. Senator (1949–1965) *Age at Inauguration:* 53 *Outstanding Facts:* Humphrey was an energetic Vice-President and traveled widely as a spokesman of the United States. He was a vigorous defender of the Johnson administration. Humphrey ran unsuccessfully for the Presidency in 1968. *Occupations after Vice-Presidency:* College teaching, U.S. Senator (1971–1978) *Died:* January 13, 1978 *Place of Burial:* Minneapolis, Minnesota

Spiro Theodore Agnew

Vice-President (1969–1973) to Richard M. Nixon *Political Party:* Republican *Born:* Baltimore, Maryland, November 9, 1918 *Ancestry:* Greek, English *Religious Affiliation:* Episcopalian *Education:* University of Baltimore Law School, 1947 *Wife:* Married Eleanor Isabel Judefind in 1942 *Children:* Four *Home:* Maryland *Occupations before Vice-Presidency:* Lawyer, politician, governor of Maryland (1967–1969) *Age at Inauguration:* 50 *Outstanding Facts:* Agnew resigned his office and pleaded "no contest" to one charge of income tax evasion after being implicated in a kickback scheme. He was the first Vice-President in history to resign under duress.

Nelson Aldrich Rockefeller

Vice-President (1974–1977) to Gerald R. Ford *Political Party:* Republican *Born:* Bar Harbor, Maine, July 8, 1908 *Ancestry:* English, Scottish, German *Religious Affilation:* Baptist *Education:* Dartmouth College, 1930 *Wives:* Mary Todhunter Clark, June 23, 1930 (div. 1962), Margaretta Fitler Murphy, May 1963 *Home:* New York and Bar Harbor, Maine *Occupation before Vice-Presidency:* various government posts, four-term governor of New York *Age at Inauguration:* 66 *Outstanding Facts:* Nominated under the 25th Amendment by President Ford following resignation of Richard M. Nixon as President and Ford's assumption of the presidency *Occupations after Vice Presidency:* Art interests *Died:* January 26, 1979 *Place of Burial:* Pocantico Hills, New York

Walter Frederick Mondale

Vice-President (1977–   ) to Jimmy Carter *Political Party:* Democratic *Born:* Ceylon, Minnesota, January 5, 1928 *Ancestry:* Norwegian *Religious Affiliation:* Methodist *Education:* University of Minnesota Law School, 1956 *Wife:* Married Joan Adams in 1955 *Children:* Three *Home:* Minnesota *Occupation before Vice-Presidency:* Lawyer, state attorney general, U.S. Senator (1965–1977) *Age at Inauguration:* 49 *Outstanding Facts:* His untraditional role as the President's personal international emissary has added new responsibility and power to the previously passive, ceremonial role of the Vice-President.

THE FIRST LADIES

Mrs. George Washington—Born Martha Dandridge, daughter of a planter, in New Kent County, Virginia, on June 21, 1731. At 18, she married Daniel Parke Custis, heir to a large estate, and she bore him four children, two of whom died in infancy. After Custis died on July 8, 1757, leaving her reputedly the richest widow in Virginia, she married Colonel George Washington on January 6, 1759; at 27, she was eight months older than her second husband.

Besides adding substantially to his property (she provided 17,000 acres and 300 slaves, compared with his own estate of 5,000 acres and 49 slaves), she also gave him a happy domestic life. Small, plump, and cheerful, she was amply blessed with common sense, if not brilliance. When Washington became President, many contemporaries thought she humanized her austere husband—"Mrs. Washington is one of those unassuming characters which create love and esteem," Mrs. John Adams wrote to a sister.

In New York, then Philadelphia, where "Lady" Washington held sway in makeshift mansions while the new capital of Washington was being planned, she made an amiable hostess at the formal receptions and dinners her husband instituted as the social side of his official duties.

There were no children of her second marriage, but she was a doting mother to the offspring of her first husband, who were treated as his own by Washington. Although her daughter, Martha (Patsy) Parke Custis, died at 17, her son, John Parke Custis, married and had three daughters and a son. Mrs. Washington survived her husband two years, dying on May 22, 1802, at Mount Vernon, where she was buried.

Mrs. John Adams—Born Abigail Smith on November 11, 1744, in Weymouth, Massachusetts, the daughter of a Congregational minister. Although she had no formal schooling, she read much more widely than most girls, and first attracted the notice of her future husband by the breadth of her intellectual interests. But before they married on October 25, 1764, they were deeply in love, and theirs was a devoted union.

Shrewd, witty, and warm-hearted, Mrs. Adams was of inestimable help in furthering the careers of both her husband and her son, John Quincy Adams, the nation's sixth President: she is the only woman in American history to have been the wife of one President and the mother of another. She also won celebrity in her own right as a gifted letter-writer with a keen political instinct.

Mrs. Adams was the first First Lady to live in the Executive Mansion in Washington, moving there in November 1800 when most of the rooms were still unfinished; she gained lasting fame in American folklore by having her laundry set out to dry before the fire in the East Room, one of the few chambers where some warmth could be obtained. During the brief period before her husband's term expired on March 3, 1801, she had the distinction, too, of holding the first formal gathering in the Mansion—a reception on New Year's Day of 1801, when 135 callers were greeted in the crimson-hung Oval Room. Besides John Quincy, she had two other sons and a daughter; another daughter died in infancy. Mrs. Adams died at the Adams home in Quincy, Massachusetts, on October 28, 1818, and was buried there.

Mrs. Thomas Jefferson—Born Martha Wayles on October 30, 1748, in Charles City County, Virginia, the daughter of a wealthy lawyer and planter. At 18, she married a young Virginian, Bathurst Skelton, who died on September 30, 1768, leaving her with an infant son. No portrait or reliable facts about her have survived, but she was said to be musically inclined and well-off when she married Thomas Jefferson on January 1, 1772. Her firstborn child, and four of the six children she bore her second husband, died in early childhood. After just 10 years as Mrs. Jefferson, she died on September 6, 1782, and was buried at Monticello; so Jefferson had been a widower for 18 years when he became President.

Being opposed to elaborate state entertaining, he held such functions to a minimum, but when he did receive guests, often his hostess was Mrs. James (Dolley) Madison, the wife of his Secretary of State, or one of his two surviving daughters—Mrs. John Wayles Eppes and Mrs. Thomas Mann Randolph, whose eighth child, James Madison Randolph, was the first baby born in the Executive Mansion (on January 17, 1806).

Mrs. James Madison—Born Dolley Paine on May 20, 1768, the daughter of Virginia Quakers temporarily settled in North Carolina. When she was 15, her family moved to Philadelphia, and on January 7, 1790, she married John Todd, a Quaker lawyer who died three years later, leaving her with one son; another had already died. Strikingly handsome despite her plain garb, the young widow quickly attracted new suitors, among them "the great little Madison," as she described him in a letter. They were married on September 15, 1794, when he was 43 and she 26.

She soon blossomed forth in elegant dress, but with a warmth and simplicity of manner that made her one of the best loved figures of her day. As White House hostess during the Jefferson administration, then as First Lady, she reigned socially supreme in Washington from 1801 to 1817. The first Inaugural Ball, on March 4, 1809, marked her husband's assumption of the Presidency, and she appeared there in queenly yellow velvet, set off by a plumed satin headdress.

Dolley Madison put much effort into furnishing the Executive Mansion suitably, but her fine draperies were destroyed when the British burned the building on August 24, 1814. Mrs. Madison is supposed to have saved the famous Gilbert Stuart portrait of Washington from the flames and also her husband's invaluable notes describing the Constitutional Convention of 1787.

While the White House was being rebuilt, the Madisons lived in Octagon House, a private mansion. They had no children, and her one son grew up a ne'er-do-well. Upon leaving Washington, Mrs. Madison continued entertaining on a grand scale at Montpelier, her husband's Virginia plantation. She returned to Washington following his death, and took up residence in 1837 in a small house across Lafayette Square from the White House. Here she received homage till she died on July 12, 1849, and was buried at Montpelier.

Mrs. James Monroe—Born Elizabeth Kortright in New York City on June 30, 1768, the daughter of a former British Army captain. At 17, on February 16, 1786, she married James Monroe, 10 years her senior. Succeeding the popular Dolley Madison as First Lady, Mrs. Monroe precipitated a social storm.

Reserved and regal in manner, she refused to follow Mrs. Madison's custom of paying calls on capital hostesses, and she added to the outrage felt by much of Washington society by declining to make the White House's first wedding into an elaborate official ceremony; only relatives and close friends were invited to the marriage of the younger of the Monroes' two daughters, Maria, to Samuel L. Gouverneur on March 9, 1820. But during her husband's second term, Mrs. Monroe's policy of restricting the social obligations of the Presidential family to the receiving of guests, without any ritual paying of calls, won general approval, and it has been followed ever since. Mrs. Monroe died on September 23, 1830, at Oak Hill, her husband's Virginia plantation, and she was buried in Richmond.

Mrs. John Quincy Adams—Born Louisa Catherine Johnson in London on February 12, 1775, the daughter of a Marylander serving as a financial agent in England. In London, on July 27, 1797, she became the wife of John Quincy Adams, then serving his first diplomatic tour of duty abroad. The mother of three sons—the youngest, Charles Francis Adams, was the highly regarded American Minister to Great Britain during the Civil War—Mrs. Adams was plagued by ill health but made a gracious First Lady.

Much less stiff in manner than her husband, she was noted for her ornate headdresses and fashionable gowns when she received at the fortnightly levees held in the White House during her régime there. Besides her own sons and one daughter, her family during her years in the Executive Mansion also included the three orphaned children of one of her sisters, and many nieces and nephews paid frequent visits. Mrs. Adams died in the family's private residence in Washington on May 15, 1852, and was buried in Quincy, Massachusetts.

Mrs. Andrew Jackson—Born Rachel Donelson in 1767, the daughter of Colonel John Donelson of Virginia. When she was 13, her family moved to Kentucky, where she married Captain Lewis Robards in 1785. He proved a suspicious husband, and five years later he sought permission from the legislature to divorce her.

Mistakenly believing a divorce had been granted, she and Andrew Jackson were married near Natchez in 1791; then on discovering two years afterward that Robards had just obtained the divorce, they were remarried on January 17, 1794. As Jackson's fame spread, gossip about this unfortunate episode hurt his wife increasingly. He fought at least one duel to defend her honor (killing Charles Dickinson in Kentucky in 1806), but when the slander was revived in the scurrilous Presidential campaign of 1828, he could not protect her. Her death of a heart attack on December 22, 1828, just as he was preparing to leave for Washington, was widely blamed on scandalmongers. She was buried at The Hermitage, Jackson's home near Nashville.

A kindly woman fond of smoking a corncob pipe, though by no means illiterate as often charged, Mrs. Jackson had no children, but she and her husband adopted a nephew. During Jackson's administration, Mrs. Andrew Jackson Donelson, wife of his nephew, often served as his hostess.

Mrs. Martin Van Buren—Born Hannah Hoes on March 8, 1783, in Kinderhook, New York, where she knew her future husband from early childhood. Distant relatives on his mother's side, they were married February 21, 1807, and had four sons before she died in Albany on February 5, 1819; she was buried at Kinderhook. A widower for 18 years when he entered the Executive Mansion, Van Buren had as his official hostess Mrs. Abraham Van Buren, the South Carolina-born wife of his oldest son.

Mrs. William Henry Harrison—Born Anna Tuthill Symmes on July 25, 1775, near Morristown, New Jersey, the daughter of Colonel John Cleves Symmes, who later became a judge and large landholder in the Northwest Territory. When Lieutenant William Henry Harrison asked Colonel Symmes for his daughter's hand, the application was rejected on the ground that an Army officer could not support a wife. As a result, the couple ran off to be married by a justice of the peace on November 25, 1795.

While her husband advanced militarily and politically, Mrs. Harrison brought up 10 children. Because she had only recently recovered from an illness, she did not attend her husband's inauguration on March 4, 1841. She remained at the Harrison home in North Bend, Ohio, to complete her convalescence, expecting to be well enough by May to assume her duties as First Lady in Washington. But her husband took cold and died exactly one month after assuming office, and Mrs. Harrison never did move into the Executive Mansion. Surviving until February 25, 1864, when she died and was buried at North Bend, she outlived all but one of her children—John Scott Harrison, whose son Benjamin became President in 1889.

Mrs. John Tyler—The first Mrs. Tyler was born Letitia Christian in New Kent County, Virginia, on November 12, 1790. Married on March 29, 1813, she had eight children, one of whom died in infancy. Partially paralyzed by a stroke in 1839, she was unable to assume any social duties when her husband became President two years later. Her only appearance downstairs at the Executive Mansion came at the wedding of her daughter, Elizabeth, to William Nevison Waller on January 31, 1842. Mrs. Tyler died on September 10, 1842, in the White House and was buried at Cedar Grove, Virginia.

The role of official hostess during most of Tyler's administration was taken by his daughter-in-law, Mrs. Robert Tyler, a former actress born Priscilla Cooper in Bristol, Pennsylvania. But on June 26, 1844, the 54-year-old President married the 24-year-old Julia Gardiner, who in the nine months remaining to his term established herself as one of the nation's most flamboyant First Ladies. Born May 4, 1820, on Gardiner's Island, New York, she belonged to a wealthy society family, and she surrounded herself with a "court" of elegant young ladies when she began entertaining lavishly in Washington. The mother of seven children, she survived her husband 27 years; she died on July 10, 1889, in Richmond and was buried there beside him.

Mrs. James Knox Polk—Born Sarah Childress on September 4, 1803, in Murfreesboro, Tennessee, the daughter of a wealthy merchant. After attending the Female Academy in Salem, North Carolina, considered then to be the South's outstanding school for girls, she married James Polk on January 1, 1824.

A shrewd and ambitious woman, she had no children and devoted herself to advancing her husband's political career. As First Lady, she opened the Executive Mansion to the public two evenings a week, besides holding formal receptions and dinners frequently. Under her direction, the building received its first complete redecorating since Monroe's administration. Though a strict Presbyterian who frowned on dancing and Sunday visiting, she allowed wine to be served and was fond of showy clothes. Mrs. Polk survived her husband 42 years, dying on August 14, 1891, in Nashville, where she was buried.

Mrs. Zachary Taylor—Born Margaret Mackall Smith on September 21, 1788, in Calvert County, Maryland, the daughter of a planter. On June 21, 1810, she married Lieutenant Zachary Taylor and spent most of the next 35 years at frontier Army posts. She had six children, two of whom died in infancy. By the time her husband was elected President, ill health prevented her taking an active role as First Lady, and her youngest daughter, Mrs. William Wallace Bliss, acted as her father's official hostess. Mrs. Taylor died on August 18, 1852, near Pascagoula, Louisiana, and was buried beside her husband in Springfield, Kentucky.

Mrs. Millard Fillmore—The first Mrs. Fillmore was born Abigail Powers on March 13, 1798, in Stillwater, New York. The daughter of a Baptist minister, she met her future husband at a nearby academy when he appeared as a fellow pupil. Two years older than he, and much more cultivated, she helped him with his studies. They were married on February 5, 1826, and had two children.

In poor health when she became First Lady, she assigned her official duties to her daughter, Mary Abigail, her own contribution being her successful effort to secure funds from Congress for setting up a small library in the White House. At the inauguration ceremonies for her husband's successor, she caught a cold which developed into pneumonia, and she died in Washington on March 30, 1853. She was buried in Buffalo.

Five years later, on February 10, 1858, former President Fillmore married Mrs. Caroline C. McIntosh, the 44-year-old widow of a Troy, New York, merchant. The second Mrs. Fillmore, who had no children, survived her husband seven years, dying in Buffalo on August 11, 1881.

Mrs. Franklin Pierce—Born Jane Means Appleton on March 12, 1806, in Hampton, New Hampshire, the daughter of Jesse Appleton, who later became president of Bowdoin College. After the death of her father, she married Franklin Pierce on November 10, 1834. Frail and shy but with strict ideas of propriety, she had a tragic life. Two of her three sons died of infant ailments, and eight weeks before her husband's inauguration as President, their only remaining child—an 11-year-old boy whom she idolized—was killed in a train accident. She never recovered from this blow and spent her years in the White House secluded in her own room, pitifully writing pencil notes to her lost son.

For the limited official entertaining carried on during her husband's administration, her girlhood friend, Mrs. Abby L. Means, who had come to Washington as her companion, served as hostess. Mrs. Pierce died on December 2, 1863, in Andover, Massachusetts, and was buried in Concord, New Hampshire.

Buchanan Administration—James Buchanan, the nation's only bachelor President, had as his official hostess his orphaned niece, Miss Harriet Lane. A charming young woman with a taste for splendor, she entertained elaborately during her uncle's administration. Five years after leaving the White House, in 1866, she married Henry E. Johnson, a Baltimore banker.

Mrs. Abraham Lincoln—Born Mary Ann Todd on December 13, 1818, in Lexington, Kentucky, the daughter of a prosperous merchant. At 22, while visiting a married sister, Mrs. Ninian Edwards, in Springfield, Illinois, she became engaged to one of her brother-in-law's fellow legislators, the backwoods lawyer Abraham Lincoln. Under controversial circumstances—some say Lincoln failed to appear the first time the wedding was scheduled—the engagement was broken; but the marriage finally took place on November 4, 1842.

Lively and intelligent, Mrs. Lincoln was also quick-tempered to the point of emotional instability. In the White House, she aroused widespread criticism for her grasping attitude toward money and her poor judgment in choosing friends. She was so shocked by her husband's assassination that her behavior became increasingly erratic.

After leaving Washington, she brought about a new wave of newspaper abuse by attempting to sell her old clothes and jewelry. On May 19, 1875, a Chicago court adjudged her insane, and she was confined in a private sanitorium at Batavia, Illinois, for four months. Thereafter, she lived quietly abroad and with relatives until she died on July 16, 1882, in Springfield, where she was buried beside her husband. Of their four sons, only the oldest, Robert Todd Lincoln, survived her.

Mrs. Andrew Johnson—Born Eliza McCardle on October 4, 1810, in Leesburg, Tennessee, the daughter of a shoemaker. She was a 16-year-old schoolgirl living with her widowed mother in the Tennessee town of Greeneville when Andrew Johnson arrived to take up tailoring there; a few months later, on May 5, 1827, they were married. Finding he could hardly read and not write at all, she taught him these skills during the next several years. Mrs. Johnson had five children, one of whom died in infancy.

When her husband unexpectedly became President, she was a frail grandmother who told a White House visitor: "We are plain people from Tennessee temporarily in a high place, and you must not expect too much of us in a social way." During her husband's administration, the role of official hostess was shared by their two daughters, Mrs. David Patterson and Mrs. Daniel Stover. Mrs. Johnson died on January 15, 1876, in Greene County, Tennessee and was buried beside her husband in Greeneville.

Mrs. Ulysses S. Grant—Born Julia Boggs Dent on January 26, 1826, in St. Louis, Missouri, the daughter of Colonel Frederick Dent. She met her future husband while he was stationed at the nearby Jefferson Barracks, and they were married on August 22, 1848. The mother of three sons and a daughter, she took the hardships of being an Army wife cheerfully, even living in a tent at times when she joined her husband in the field during the Civil War, but she also enjoyed the glitter of capital society and entertained elaborately as First Lady. Her daughter, Nellie, became Mrs. Algernon Sartoris in a splendid White House wedding on May 21, 1874. Mrs. Grant died on December 14, 1902, in Washington and was buried beside her husband in Grant's Tomb in New York City.

Mrs. Rutherford Birchard Hayes—Born Lucy Ware Webb on August 28, 1831, in Chillicothe, Ohio, the daughter of a physician. A sweet-tempered and devout Methodist, she met her future husband while attending Wesleyan Female College in Cincinnati. He was a lawyer, eight years her senior, who called on her at the urging of his mother, who had already chosen Lucy Webb as the ideal candidate for her son's wife. Rutherford Hayes agreed, the marriage took place on December 30, 1852, and he gained a devoted companion who bore him one daughter and seven sons (three died in infancy). He also gave his country its first First Lady with a college diploma.

But for all her gentle submissiveness, Mrs. Hayes had strong temperance convictions. To please her, President Hayes banished wine from the White House during his administration, thereby inadvertently subjecting her to widespread ridicule as "Lemonade Lucy." Yet Mrs. Hayes was no hard-eyed reformer. She was a warm, friendly woman whose most lasting contribution in the White House was her initiation of annual Easter egg-rolling contests in 1878. She died of a stroke on June 25, 1889, at the Hayes home in Fremont, Ohio, and she was buried there.

Mrs. James Abram Garfield—Born Lucretia Rudolph on April 19, 1832, the daughter of the leading merchant in Hiram, Ohio. She met her future husband while attending a local academy her father had helped to found; after teaching a few years, she married James Garfield on November 11, 1858. They had seven children, two of whom died in infancy. Her tenure as First Lady was brief, but made memorable by tragedy. "The wife of the President is the bravest woman in the Universe," the New York *Herald* said of her. For she had only just recovered from a near-fatal attack of malaria and was convalescing at a seaside cottage in Elberon, New Jersey, when she received word on July 2, 1881, that her husband had been shot.

She immediately returned to Washington and displayed remarkable composure during the 80 days that he lingered on the brink of death. She traveled back to Elberon with him when he was moved there on September 6, and she was at his bedside when he died on September 19, 1881. Mrs. Garfield survived her husband 36 years. She died on March 14, 1918, in Pasadena, California, and was buried beside her husband in Cleveland.

Mrs. Chester Alan Arthur—Born Ellen Lewis Herndon on August 30, 1837, in Fredericksburg, Virginia, the daughter of Captain William Lewis Herndon of the U.S. Navy and explorer of the Amazon. Brought up in gracious Southern style, she was taken on a European tour at 16 and, while visiting New York City a few years later, met Chester Arthur; they were married on October 25, 1859. She had three children, one dying in infancy.

Beautiful and cultivated, she helped her Vermont-born husband develop a taste for elegance but did not live to reign as First Lady. She died of pneumonia in New York on January 12, 1880, ten months before her husband's nomination to the Vice-Presidency, and she was buried in Albany. Arthur's widowed sister, Mrs. John McElroy, served as his hostess while he was in the White House.

Mrs. Grover Cleveland—Born Frances Folsom on July 21, 1864, in Buffalo, New York, the daughter of Oscar Folsom, a lawyer who was killed in a buggy accident in 1875. Her father's partner, Grover Cleveland, then assumed responsibility for her. A tall, attractive young woman, she was attending Wells College when he became President in 1885. He was 48 years old and a bachelor. On June 2, 1886, they were married in the Blue Room of the White House, and this first Presidential wedding in the Executive Mansion was celebrated by the pealing of every church bell in Washington. (John Tyler, the only other President to marry while in office, had been wed at the Church of the Ascension in New York City.)

The 22-year-old Mrs. Cleveland won immediate popularity and was considered the most charming First Lady since Dolley Madison. Her friendliness drew large crowds to her public receptions. She had five children, the second—Esther, who later became Mrs. William Bosanquet—being the only Presidential child to be born in the White House (on September 9, 1893). Mrs. Cleveland survived her husband 39 years and, five years after his death, on February 10, 1913, she became the first Presidential widow to remarry. Her second husband was Thomas J. Preston, a Princeton professor of archaeology. She died on October 29, 1947, in Baltimore and was buried in Princeton.

Mrs. Benjamin Harrison—The first Mrs. Harrison was born Caroline (Carrie) Scott, on October 1, 1832, in Oxford, Ohio. She was the daughter of a Presbyterian minister who also conducted a school for girls. After teaching briefly, she married Benjamin Harrison on October 20, 1853; they had two children. As First Lady, she became the first President General of the National Society of the Daughters of the American Revolution. Prevented by ill health from taking an active social role, she died in the White House on October 25, 1892, and was buried in Indianapolis. The duties of official hostess during much of the Harrison administration were assumed by Mrs. Mary Scott Dimmick, a widowed niece of Mrs. Harrison's.

After leaving office, former President Harrison married Mrs. Dimmick in New York City on April 6, 1896; she was 37, and he was then 62. They had one child. The second Mrs. Harrison, a native of Honesdale, Pennsylvania, survived her husband 46 years, dying in New York on January 5, 1948.

Mrs. William McKinley—Born Ida Saxton on June 8, 1847, the daughter of a leading banker in Canton, Ohio. Charming but high-strung, she was, unconventionally, working as a cashier in her father's bank when she met a handsome newcomer to town, Major William McKinley; they were married on January 25, 1871. A year later, she gave birth to a daughter, then became pregnant again soon afterward. Before the birth of her second baby, her mother died, and Mrs. McKinley became severely depressed. The subsequent death of both her infant daughters left her a nervous invalid subject to frequent epileptic fits. Nevertheless, as her husband rose politically, she insisted on appearing with him at all social functions, and he became adept at shielding her when she suffered a seizure.

The nature of her illness was not generally known when she became First Lady, and her delicate health required many innovations in official entertaining. Despite protocol, she was seated beside the President at state dinners, and Mrs. Garret Hobart, wife of McKinley's Vice-

President during his first term, assisted her in many ceremonial duties. Mrs. McKinley survived her slain husband five years, dying on May 26, 1907, in Canton, where she was buried beside him.

Mrs. Theodore Roosevelt—The first Mrs. Roosevelt was born Alice Hathaway Lee on July 29, 1861, in Chestnut Hill, Massachusetts. As a charming girl of 17, she met her future husband while he was attending Harvard. They were married on October 27, 1880, soon after his graduation, when he was 22 and she 19. But two days after the birth of their first child—a daughter, also named Alice—she died (on February 14, 1884) of a previously unsuspected case of Bright's disease. Roosevelt lost his beloved young wife on the same day his mother died of typhoid fever.

He gradually recovered from the shock of this double tragedy after renewing his childhood friendship with Edith Kermit Carow. They were married in London, where she was temporarily living, on December 2, 1886. The daughter of a New York merchant, she had been born in Connecticut on August 6, 1861. The second Mrs. Roosevelt, who gave her husband four sons and another daughter, made an unusually poised and capable First Lady.

Besides coping with the antics of her high-spirited youngsters, she supervised an extensive remodeling of the White House which changed the mansion, her husband said, from "a shabby likeness of the ground floor of the Astor House into a simple and dignified dwelling for the head of a republic." In addition, she arranged an elegant East Room wedding when "Princess Alice" married Congressman Nicholas Longworth of Ohio on February 17, 1906. Mrs. Roosevelt died on September 30, 1948, at the family's summer home in Oyster Bay, New York, and she was buried there.

Mrs. William Howard Taft—Born Helen Herron on June 2, 1861, in Cincinnati, but always called Nellie. The daughter of Judge John Williamson Herron, she visited the White House at 17 as the guest of her father's former law partner, President Rutherford B. Hayes, and decided then that she would like to be First Lady. Studious as well as ambitious, she taught a few years before marrying William Howard Taft on June 19, 1886.

Two months after she did move into the White House, she suffered a stroke which prevented her from taking part in social activities for more than a year; then after her recovery, she and her husband celebrated their 25th wedding anniversary with an evening garden party for which the grounds of the Executive Mansion were spectacularly illuminated. Mrs. Taft left a lasting physical impression on Washington by sponsoring the planting of the capital's famous Japanese cherry trees, which she admired from the time of a diplomatic trip to Japan with her husband. The eldest of her three children, Robert A. Taft, became the distinguished Senator from Ohio. Mrs. Taft died on May 22, 1943, in Washington and was buried beside her husband in Arlington National Cemetery.

Mrs. Woodrow Wilson—The first Mrs. Wilson was born Ellen Louise Axson in Rome, Georgia, on May 15, 1860. Daughter of a Presbyterian minister, she married Wilson on June 24, 1885. An art student with a fondness for music and literature, she had a great influence on her husband; from their marriage to her death, they were never separated a day. They had three daughters, two

of whom were married in the White House—Jessie, who became Mrs. Francis Bowes Sayre in an elaborate East Room ceremony on November 25, 1913, and Eleanor, who became Mrs. William Gibbs McAdoo at a smaller wedding in the Blue Room on May 7, 1914. The latter occasion was marred by the increasing weakness of Mrs. Wilson, who died in the White House on August 6, 1914.

Her death left the President so depressed by grief and loneliness that his physician, Dr. Cary T. Grayson, became alarmed until he, perhaps inadvertently, provided a cure. Dr. Grayson introduced Mrs. Edith Bolling Galt, an attractive 42-year-old widow, to Wilson's cousin, Miss Helen Woodrow Bones, who was temporarily serving as White House hostess. Miss Bones invited Mrs. Galt to tea in March of 1915. Just two months later, the President proposed marriage to Mrs. Galt, and they were married at her Washington home on December 18, 1915.

Born in Wytheville, Virginia, on October 15, 1872, the second Mrs. Wilson had been married to Norman Galt, a Washington jeweler, in 1896, then widowed twelve years later. As First Lady during World War I, she kept official entertaining to a minimum. After her husband was partly paralyzed by a stroke on October 2, 1919, she shielded him from visitors to the extent that she was called "the nation's first Lady President." She survived him 36 years, dying in Washington on December 28, 1961.

Mrs. Warren Gamaliel Harding—Born Florence Kling on August 15, 1860, the daughter of a banker who was the richest man in the small Ohio city of Marion. At 19, she eloped with Henry De-Wolfe, the black sheep in an old local family. A year later, he abandoned her and an infant son, and she was forced to return to her stern father whose rule she had sought to escape.

After being divorced, she married Warren Harding on July 8, 1891; she was five years his senior. Then she took over the business side of the Marion *Star*, which Harding had recently acquired. Mrs. Harding was sometimes credited with inspiring her husband's political career, and in Ohio political circles she was known as "The Duchess." In the White House, failing health limited her social activities, but she survived her husband by a year, dying on November 21, 1924, in Marion, where she was buried.

Mrs. Calvin Coolidge—Born Grace Goodhue in Burlington, Vermont, on January 3, 1879, the daughter of a mechanical engineer. After graduating from the University of Vermont in 1902, she became a teacher at the Clarke Institute for the Deaf in Northampton, Massachusetts. An exceptionally warm person, she married the silent Calvin Coolidge on October 4, 1905, and was sometimes described as his most important asset.

In the White House, despite her husband's frugal management of menu planning, her charm won her wide popularity. She had two sons, but the younger, Calvin Jr., died at 16 of blood poisoning on July 7, 1924, less than a year after his father succeeded to the Presidency. Mrs. Coolidge died on July 8, 1957, in Northampton, and she was buried in Plymouth, Vermont.

Mrs. Herbert Clark Hoover—Born Lou Henry in Waterloo, Iowa, on March 29, 1874, the daughter of a banker who subsequently moved his family to Monterey, California. She entered Stanford University in 1894, planning to become a geology teacher, but she married Hoover, a fellow student, on February 10, 1899, and went to China with him. After living in many foreign lands, while her husband pursued his career, and raising two sons, Mrs. Hoover enjoyed settling in Washington in 1921, when her husband entered President Harding's Cabinet.

By the time she moved into the White House on March 4, 1929, she had a large circle of friends in the capital, and she entertained extensively as First Lady. But on January 1, 1930, she held what proved to be the last of the annual New Year's Day receptions in the Executive Mansion. When Mrs. John Adams had started the custom in 1801, 135 guests appeared to be greeted by the President and his wife; in 1930, more than 9,000 people sought admission, causing Mr. and Mrs. Hoover to make a point of being out of Washington over New Year's during the rest of his term. (His successor, President Franklin Roosevelt, formally discontinued these gatherings which had grown so unwieldy.) Mrs. Hoover died in New York City on January 7, 1944. The gravesite is located at West Branch, Iowa.

Mrs. Franklin Delano Roosevelt—Born Anna Eleanor Roosevelt on October 11, 1884, in New York City, the daughter of Theodore Roosevelt's younger brother, Elliott. Owing to the early death of both her parents, she was brought up by her maternal grandmother, Mrs. V. G. Hall. A shy and solitary child, she was educated in Europe; then on March 17, 1905, she married her fifth cousin, Franklin Roosevelt. They had six children, one son dying in infancy. After her husband's crippling attack of infantile paralysis in 1921, she took an increasingly active part in politics, serving as his eyes and ears at meetings he could not attend.

In the White House, she continued this role on a much broader scale, traveling thousands of miles to inspect coal mines and prisons and American military installations everywhere. A controversial figure as First Lady because of her outspoken support for humanitarian and civil rights causes, Mrs. Roosevelt broke with tradition by holding regular press conferences, lecturing widely, and writing a syndicated newspaper column, "My Day."

She won worldwide esteem as one of the century's outstanding women. President Truman, after her husband's death, appointed her to the United States delegation to the United Nations. She also served the world organization as chairman of its Commission for Human Rights. She died on November 7, 1962, in New York City, and was buried beside her husband at Hyde Park, New York; President Kennedy and former Presidents Eisenhower and Truman were at her burial.

Mrs. Harry S Truman—Born Elizabeth Virginia Wallace in Independence, Missouri, on February 13, 1885, but always called Bess. Her maternal grandparents owned a flour mill. As a little girl with blond curls, she captivated her future husband at Sunday school in the First Presbyterian Church. Married on June 28, 1919, she had one daughter.

Unassuming and not fond of ceremony, Mrs. Truman tried to avoid personal publicity as First Lady. She was helped in her effort to live quietly by the fact that serious structural weaknesses were discovered in the White House during her residence there; and from November 1948 until March 1952, the Trumans lived diagonally across Pennsylvania Avenue in Blair House. After her husband left office, Mrs. Truman was happy to retire with him to the family home in Independence.

Mrs. Dwight David Eisenhower—Born Mamie Geneva Doud on November 14, 1896, the daughter of a prosperous meat packer in Boone, Iowa. When she was 10, her family moved to Denver, but usually spent the colder months visiting San Antonio. Early in the winter of 1915, while at San Antonio, a young second lieutenant stationed at nearby Fort Sam Houston was introduced to the pretty and popular Miss Doud; on Valentine's Day, they became engaged, and they were married on July 1, 1916. For the next several decades, she lived at Army posts all over the world. She had two sons, but the older died at three.

A warm and friendly woman, Mrs. Eisenhower became accustomed to official entertaining during her Army years. But she described herself as "nonpolitical." After leaving the White House, she enjoyed retirement at the Gettysburg farm that was their first home.

Mrs. John Fitzgerald Kennedy—Born Jacqueline Lee Bouvier on July 28, 1929, in Southampton, New York, the daughter of John Vernon Bouvier 3d, a wealthy stockbroker. With generations of social prominence on both sides of her family, she attended private schools, had her own pony, and made a glittering début at Newport in 1947. (After the divorce of her parents in 1940, her mother married Hugh D. Auchincloss of Washington and Newport.) Then she went on to further study at Vassar, the Sorbonne, and George Washington University, from which she graduated in 1951. As the "Inquiring Camera Girl" for the Washington *Times-Herald*, she interviewed a young senator whom she had recently met at a dinner party; they were married on September 12, 1953, in St. Mary's Roman Catholic Church at Newport.

The nation's third youngest First Lady, she was 31 on moving into the White House. She won admiration everywhere for her tasteful redecoration of the White House and the glamorous receptions she arranged; this "Kennedy style" to which she contributed so much was a major ingredient in her husband's popularity.

With her two children, she lived in New York City after leaving the White House until her marriage on October 20, 1968, to Aristotle Socrates Onassis, the Greek shipping multimillionaire who died on March 15, 1975.

Mrs. Lyndon Baines Johnson—Born Claudia Alta Taylor on December 22, 1912, in Karnack, Texas, the daughter of Thomas Jefferson Taylor, a prosperous landowner and merchant. When she was two, a nursemaid called her Lady Bird—because she was "as purty as a lady bird"—and the nickname stuck. Brought up by an aunt after her mother died when she was five, she grew into a shy and nature-loving girl with an interest in studying.

Shortly after receiving a journalism degree from the University of Texas, she met the tall secretary to a Texas Congressman; and Lyndon Johnson proposed to her the next day. They were married two months later, on November 17, 1934. Mrs.

Johnson helped her husband along every step of his career. She provided the money for his first Congressional campaign (by borrowing against the $67,000 she was due to inherit from her mother), and she ran his Washington office while he took military leave during World War II.

In the White House, Mrs. Johnson's personal warmth was often credited with smoothing over difficulties caused by her husband's more abrasive personality. She showed a broader concern about public questions than any First Lady with the exception of Mrs. Franklin Roosevelt. Mrs. Johnson was particularly interested in promoting efforts to beautify the nation's cities and towns.

Mrs. Richard Milhous Nixon—Born Thelma Ryan on March 16, 1912, in Ely, Nevada, the daughter of a miner who took up farming a year later, and moved his family to Artesia, California. Her father always called her Pat, and the nickname stayed with her.

After graduating with honors from the University of Southern California in 1937, she taught commercial subjects at Whittier High School in Whittier, California, where she met her future husband in a local amateur theater group; they were married on June 21, 1940. Throughout his career, she has tirelessly supported him at every step. She gained valuable experience toward meeting her responsibilities while her husband was Vice-President under President Eisenhower.

Poised and imperturbable, she has brought up two daughters, the younger of whom, Julie, married David Eisenhower, grandson of the former President, in December 1968. Although she fulfilled her role of official hostess with grace, she generally shunned the limelight while in the White House. In 1976 she suffered a partial stroke.

Mrs. Gerald R. Ford—Born Elizabeth Anne Bloomer on April 8, 1918, in Chicago, Illinois, but moved to Grand Rapids, Michigan at the age of three. Mrs. Ford attended the Bennington School of Dance in Vermont and studied modern dance with Martha Graham. She spent two years in New York as a dancer in the Martha Graham Concert Group. On returning to Grand Rapids she organized her own dance group and, in addition, became a model and fashion coordinator for a Grand Rapids department store. On October 15, 1948, Elizabeth Bloomer married Gerald R. Ford. The Fords have four children.

In Washington, Betty Ford was active in the Republican Wives Club, on the Board of Directors of the League of Republican Women in the District of Columbia, and as President of the Senate Red Cross Club. Mrs. Ford is noted for her candor in expressing her opinions and beliefs and is concerned with promoting equal opportunities for women.

Mrs. Jimmy Carter — Born Eleanor Rosalynn Smith on August 18, 1927, on her maternal grandfather's farm in Plains, Georgia, the daughter of town garage mechanic, Edgar Smith. While attending Georgia Southwestern College, Rosalynn studied interior decorating. She lived at home and helped her family from age 15 when she first went to work in a local beauty parlor. When 18-year-old Rosalynn married Jimmy Carter on July 7, 1946, she had known the U.S. Naval Academy midshipman for five years as her best friend's brother. The Carters have four children. Rosalynn enjoyed travelling from base to base until the death of Carter's father caused the couple's return to Plains in 1953 and catalzed their first team effort in the family peanut business. Rosalynn deftly managed bookkeeping, office work, tax returns and helped to create a thriving business. Rosalynn profoundly influenced Carter's key presidential campaign strategy: to run in all possible primaries.

In the White House, Rosalynn has demonstrated extraordinary determination and drive. She has gone along on presidential junkets both at home and abroad. On her own, she has toured the U.S. in support of her favorite causes, campaigning and acting as observer for her husband; abroad she has represented him at a presidential inauguration and a papal funeral. But more importantly, Rosalynn has maintained her position as advisor to the President, a position which has both grown in importance and become increasingly evident.

MINORITY PRESIDENTS

SOURCE: U.S. Library of Congress and other sources

Under the Electoral College System, 15 Presidents have been elected who did not receive a majority of the popular votes cast. Three of them—John Quincy Adams, Rutherford B. Hayes, and Benjamin Harrison—actually trailed their opponents in the popular vote. The table shows the percentage of the popular vote received by the candidates.

Year	Elected	Opponents			Year	Elected	Opponents		
1824	Adams 30.54	Jackson 43.13	Clay 13.24	Crawford 13.09	1888	Harrison 47.86	Cleveland 48.66	Fisk 2.19	Streeter 1.29
1844	Polk 49.56	Clay 48.13	Birney 2.30	————	1892	Cleveland 46.04	Harrison 43.01	Weaver 8.53	Others 2.42
1848	Taylor 47.35	Cass 42.52	Van Buren 10.13	————	1912	Wilson 41.85	Roosevelt 27.42	Taft 23.15	Others 7.58
1856	Buchanan 45.63	Frémont 33.27	Fillmore 21.08	Smith .01	1916	Wilson 49.26	Hughes 46.12	Benson 3.16	Others 1.46
1860	Lincoln 39.79	Douglas 29.40	Breckinridge 18.20	Bell 12.60	1948	Truman 49.51	Dewey 45.13	Thurmond 2.40	H. Wallace 2.38
1876	Hayes 48.04	Tilden 50.99	Cooper .97	————	1960	Kennedy 49.71	Nixon 49.55	Unpledged .92	Others .27
1880	Garfield 48.32	Hancock 48.21	Weaver 3.35	Others .12	1968	Nixon 43.16	Humphrey 42.73	G. Wallace 13.63	Others .48
1884	Cleveland 48.53	Blaine 48.24	Butler 1.74	St. John 1.49					

U.S. PRESIDENTIAL ELECTIONS: 1789—1972

The first four Presidential elections (1789, 1792, 1796, and 1800) were held under Article II, Section 1, of the Constitution, which provided for the College of Electors to vote for two candidates —the one with the majority of votes was elected President, and the next highest became Vice-President. A tie in the Electoral College in 1800 led to the passage of the Twelfth Amendment, which provides for separate ballots for President and Vice-President.

Prior to the election of 1824, records of popular vote are scanty and inaccurate.

ELECTION OF 1789

The Political Scene: The struggle over the ratification of the Constitution had led to the emergence of two political factions, the Federalists, who supported the new Constitution, and the Anti-Federalists, who opposed it.
Nominations and Campaign: George Washington, although identified with the Federalists, was unopposed for the Presidential nomination and received a unanimous vote from the 69 electors.

Results of 1789 Election:

Presidential Candidate	Party	Electoral Votes
George Washington	None	69
John Adams	None	34
Other candidates	None	35
Votes not cast	—	4

Comments: Rhode Island and North Carolina had not yet ratified the Constitution when the electors cast their ballots, and a deadlock between the Federalist Senate and the Anti-Federalist Assembly in New York prevented the choosing of any electors.

ELECTION OF 1792

The Political Scene: Thomas Jefferson and James Madison in Virginia and George Clinton and Aaron Burr in New York provided the leadership of the Democratic-Republican party, which emerged in opposition to Alexander Hamilton's financial policy, to the Federalist emphasis on a strong central government, and to a loose or flexible interpretation of the Constitution.
Nominations: Both parties urged that Washington accept another term, but the Jeffersonians opposed Adams' re-election with Clinton's candidacy.
The Campaign: Adams was accused of being antidemocratic and a secret monarchist, but the real target of the Democratic-Republicans was Hamilton.

Results of 1792 Election:

Presidential Candidate	Party	Electoral Votes
George Washington	Federalist	132
John Adams	Federalist	77
George Clinton	Democratic-Republican	50
Other candidates	—	5
Votes not cast	—	3

ELECTION OF 1796

The Political Scene: Washington, who deplored partisan politics, refused to consider another term, thus insuring the first real contest for the Presidency.
Nominations: Jefferson was the logical candidate for the Democratic-Republicans, but Hamilton was less than

ELECTION OF 1796 (cont.)

happy about the candidacy of John Adams of Massachusetts for the Federalists and hoped that Thomas Pinckney, the ostensible Federalist Vice-Presidential candidate, might win if Federalist electors in the South withheld their votes from Adams.
The Campaign: Adams electors in New England countered Hamilton's scheme by omitting Pinckney from their ballots. The unexpected result of the Federalist bickering was the election of Jefferson to the Vice-Presidency.

Results of 1796 Election

Presidential Candidate	Party	Electoral Votes
John Adams	Federalist	71
Thomas Jefferson	Democratic-Republican	68
Thomas Pinckney	Federalist	59
Aaron Burr	Democratic-Republican	30
Other candidates	—	48

ELECTION OF 1800

The Political Scene: The wars of the French Revolution had created another area of disagreement between the Federalists, who favored Great Britain, and the Democratic-Republicans, who tended to support France. The apparent desire of some Federalist leaders for a war with France alarmed the nation.
Nominations: Congressional caucuses of each party chose the candidates: Adams and Pinckney for the Federalists and Jefferson and Burr for the Democratic-Republicans.
The Campaign: The Federalists gave their opponents a powerful campaign issue in the repressive Alien and Sedition Acts that Jefferson and Madison eloquently denounced in the Virginia and Kentucky Resolutions.

Results of 1800 Election:

Presidential Candidate	Party	Electoral Votes
Thomas Jefferson	Democratic-Republican	73
Aaron Burr	Democratic-Republican	73
John Adams	Federalist	65
Charles C. Pinckney	Federalist	64
John Jay	Federalist	1

Comments: Because the candidates for President and Vice-President were not separately nominated, Jefferson and Burr ended in a tie. The House of Representatives elected Jefferson on the 36th ballot after seven days of balloting. To prevent the situation from arising again, the Twelfth Amendment, ratified in 1804, provided for separate balloting for President and Vice-President. Jefferson's triumph ended the Federalist era and ushered in a quarter century of Democratic-Republican control of the Presidency.

ELECTION OF 1804

The Political Scene: Jefferson's efficient administration and the acquisition of the vast Louisiana Territory gained his party almost universal support and led the more extreme Federalist leaders into the Essex Junto, an abortive scheme to separate the northeastern states from the Union.
Nominations: The Congressional caucuses of each party chose the candidates. A falling-out between Jefferson and Burr led to the latter's replacement as Vice-Presidential candidate by George Clinton of New York. Charles C. Pinckney of South Carolina and Rufus King of New York comprised the Federalist ticket.
The Campaign: The machinations of the Essex Junto all but destroyed the Federalist party; the only question remaining was the size of Jefferson's victory.

Results of 1804 Election:

Presidential Candidate	Party	Electoral Votes	Vice-Presidential Candidate	Party	Electoral Votes
Thomas Jefferson	Democratic-Republican	162	George Clinton	Democratic-Republican	162
Charles C. Pinckney	Federalist	14	Rufus King	Federalist	14

Comments: Jefferson won every electoral vote but those of Connecticut and Delaware and two in Maryland.

ELECTION OF 1808

The Political Scene: The disastrous effects of the Embargo of 1808 on American commerce revived the Federalist party in New England and caused dissension among the Jeffersonians.

Nominations: It took considerable pressure by Jefferson to get the rebellious factions within his party to accept his choice of James Madison of Virginia to succeed him. Clinton of New York was again the Vice-Presidential candidate. Federalist leaders engineered the renomination of the 1804 ticket of Pinckney and King.

The Campaign: Running primarily on the Embargo issue, the Federalists considerably improved their showing over the previous election, but could not overcome the solid Democratic-Republican majority that had been created.

Results of 1808 Election:

Presidential Candidate	Party	Electoral Votes	Vice-Presidential Candidate	Party	Electoral Votes
James Madison	Democratic-Republican	122	George Clinton	Democratic-Republican	113
Charles C. Pinckney	Federalist	47	Rufus King	Federalist	47
George Clinton	Democratic-Republican	6	Other candidates	—	15
Votes not cast	—	1	Votes not cast	—	1

ELECTION OF 1812

The Political Scene: Conflict with Great Britain over maritime rights and alleged incitement of Indian rebellion caused Madison to request a declaration of war in June 1812.

Nominations: The Republican congressional caucus, dominated by young "War Hawk" representatives from the frontier states, renominated Madison, a month before the war message. Elbridge Gerry of Massachusetts received the Vice-Presidential nomination. Insurgent Republicans in New York put up DeWitt Clinton, who thereupon received Federalist support but not an official endorsement. Jared Ingersoll of Pennsylvania ran with him.

The Campaign: Although Clinton tried to avoid running as a Peace-Federalist candidate, his strength clearly lay in the Northeast, the section most unenthusiastic about the war.

Results of 1812 Election:

Presidential Candidate	Party	Electoral Votes	Vice-Presidential Candidate	Party	Electoral Votes
James Madison	Democratic-Republican	128	Elbridge Gerry	Democratic-Republican	131
DeWitt Clinton	Federalist	89	Jared Ingersoll	Federalist	86
Votes not cast	—	1	Votes not cast	—	1

Comments: The vote of Pennsylvania together with the solid backing of the South and West elected Madison.

ELECTION OF 1816

The Political Scene: The end of the War of 1812 and an economic boom assured the continued ascendancy of the Democratic-Republicans.

Nominations: The congressional caucus chose James Monroe of Virginia over William H. Crawford of Georgia in a close contest. The choice of Daniel D. Tompkins for the Vice-Presidency renewed the Virginia-New York alliance. Rufus King of New York, although not selected by any formal process, was considered the Federalist nominee.

The Campaign: King, the last Federalist candidate, received only the votes of Massachusetts, Connecticut, and Delaware in a campaign he hardly contested at all.

Results of 1816 Election:

Presidential Candidate	Party	Electoral Votes	Vice-Presidential Candidate	Party	Electoral Votes
James Monroe	Democratic-Republican	183	Daniel D. Tompkins	Democratic-Republican	183
Rufus King	Federalist	34	John E. Howard	Federalist	22
Votes not cast	—	4	Other candidates	—	12
			Votes not cast	—	4

Comments: Following Washington, Jefferson, and Madison, Monroe was the last of the Virginia dynasty and the last of the men of the revolutionary era to hold the Presidency.

ELECTION OF 1820

The Political Scene: No great national issue disturbed the country enough for anyone to oppose Monroe's reelection.

Nomination and Campaign: Monroe received every electoral vote except that of William Plumer of New Hampshire.

Results of 1820 Election:

Presidential Candidate	Party	Electoral Votes	Vice-Presidential Candidate	Party	Electoral Votes
James Monroe	Democratic-Republican	231	Daniel D. Tompkins	Democratic-Republican	218
John Quincy Adams	Independent	1	Other candidates	—	14
Votes not cast	—	3	Votes not cast	—	3

Comments: The tradition that Plumer voted for John Quincy Adams in order to preserve for Washington alone the honor of a unanimous selection is of dubious validity; Plumer simply disliked Monroe and his policies.

ELECTION OF 1824

The Political Scene: The "Era of Good Feelings" ended as the Democratic-Republican organization dissolved into sectional groupings.

Nominations: A poorly attended congressional caucus selected William H. Crawford of Georgia, while various state ʼislatures nominated Henry Clay of Kentucky, Andrew Jackson of Tennessee, John Quincy Adams of Massachusetts, ɫ John C. Calhoun of South Carolina. Calhoun subsequently withdrew to run for the Vice-Presidency on Jackson's ɫcket.

The Campaign: Clay put forward his celebrated plan calling for a strong protective tariff, domestic improvements, and a national bank—policies that Adams also endorsed. Jackson relied on his popular appeal as a military hero.

Results of 1824 Election:

Presidential Candidate	Party	Electoral Votes	Popular Vote Total	Percentage	Vice-Presidential Candidate and Electoral Votes	Party
John Quincy Adams	None	84	115,696	31.9	John C. Calhoun 182	None
Andrew Jackson	None	99	152,933	42.2	Nathan Sanford 30	None
William H. Crawford	None	41	46,979	12.9	Nathaniel Macon 24	None
Henry Clay	None	37	47,136	13.0	Other candidates 25	—

Comments: Since no candidate had gained a majority of the electoral vote, the House of Representatives, voting by states and with each state having one vote, chose Adams on the first ballot.

ELECTION OF 1828

The Political Scene: More than two-thirds of the electorate had voted against Adams in 1824. This circumstance negated his hopes for a successful administration, and the Jacksonians commenced their plans to unseat him.

Nominations: The Tennessee legislature renominated Jackson in 1825, and the incumbent Vice-President Calhoun once again agreed to be his running mate. This is considered the first ticket of the modern Democratic party. Adams ran for reelection as a National Republican.

The Campaign: Although important differences on national questions divided Adams and Jackson, these issues disappeared in a welter of vituperative personal attacks against each standard-bearer.

Results of 1828 Election:

Presidential Candidate	Party	Electoral Votes	Popular Vote Total	Per-centage	Vice-Presidential Candidate and Electoral Votes		Party
Andrew Jackson	Democratic	178	647,292	56.0	John C. Calhoun	171	Democratic
John Quincy Adams	National Republican	83	507,730	44.0	Richard Rush	83	National Republican
					William Smith	7	Democratic

Comments: The election of Jackson, the frontier hero, represented a triumph for the West and the South. It also symbolized the arrival of the common people to political power.

ELECTION OF 1832

The Political Scene: Internal disputes within Jackson's cabinet and the President's strong stand against nullification caused a break between Jackson and Calhoun. Jackson's veto of a bill rechartering the Bank of the United States, however, created the major issue in the campaign.

Conventions and Nominees: For the first time the national nominating convention was employed by the three parties in the field. All met at Baltimore, with the Anti-Masonic party holding the first convention (September 26, 1831) and choosing William Wirt of Maryland. The National Republicans nominated the legislative champion of the Bank of the United States—Henry Clay of Kentucky, while the Democrats unanimously endorsed Jackson and replaced Calhoun for the Vice-Presidency with Martin Van Buren of New York. The Democratic convention adopted a rule requiring a two-thirds vote of the whole convention for nomination. This remained in effect until 1936.

The Campaign: Clay attacked Jackson's veto of the bank bill and his opposition to internal improvements. He misjudged the popular temper; to the average voter, Jackson's bank policy was a blow against monopoly and privilege.

Results of 1832 Election:

Presidential Candidate	Party	Electoral Votes	Popular Vote Total	Per-centage	Vice-Presidential Candidate and Electoral Votes		Party
Andrew Jackson	Democratic	219	688,242	54.5	Martin Van Buren	189	Democratic
Henry Clay	National Republican	49	473,462	37.5	John Sergeant	49	National Republican
John Floyd	Independent	11	—	—	Henry Lee	11	Independent
William Wirt	Anti-Masonic	7	101,051	8.0	Amos Ellmaker	7	Anti-Masonic
Votes not cast	—	2	—	—	William Wilkins	30	Independent
					Votes not cast	2	—

Comments: The Anti-Masonic party, opposed to the Masons and other secret societies, was the first third party in American history. On December 28, 1832, following the election, Vice-President Calhoun resigned his office.

ELECTION OF 1836

The Political Scene: Opponents of "King Andrew" Jackson formed the Whig party, taking the name of the antimonarchial English political party to emphasize Jackson's alleged autocratic tendencies.

Conventions and Nominees: Jackson desired his Vice-President Martin Van Buren of New York to succeed him, and the Democratic convention at Baltimore (May 20–22, 1835) unanimously ratified his choice. Richard M. Johnson of Kentucky was the Vice-Presidential candidate. The Whigs, lacking a leader with national appeal, nominated three sectional candidates (Daniel Webster of Massachusetts, Hugh L. White of Tennessee, and William Henry Harrison of Ohio) in an effort to throw the election into the House of Representatives.

The Campaign: Jackson's personality and the record of his administration provided the issues for the campaign. The influence of "Old Hickory" was probably decisive, since Van Buren received a bare majority of the popular vote. The Senate, for the only time in history, elected the Vice-President with 33 votes for Johnson, 16 for Granger.

Results of 1836 Election:

Presidential Candidate	Party	Electoral Votes	Popular Vote Total	Per-centage	Vice-Presidential Candidate and Electoral Votes		Party
Martin Van Buren	Democratic	170	764,198	50.9	Richard M. Johnson	147	Democratic
William H. Harrison	Whig	73	549,508	36.6	Francis Granger	77	Whig
Hugh L. White	Whig	26	145,352	9.7	John Tyler	47	Democratic
Daniel Webster	Whig	14	41,287	2.7	William Smith	23	Independent
W. P. Mangum	Independent	11	—	—			

ELECTION OF 1840

The Political Scene: The Panic of 1837, which had been caused mainly by Jackson's erratic financial policies, fell with full force during Van Buren's administration, hurting his prospects for reelection.

Conventions and Nominees: The Whigs in Pennsylvania met at Harrisburg (May 4–5, 1840) to name William Henry Harrison of Ohio and John Tyler of Virginia as their ticket, while the Democrats convening at Baltimore (May 5–7) unanimously renominated Van Buren. The antislavery Liberty party in a convention at Albany, New York, nominated James G. Birney of New York and Thomas Earle of Pennsylvania.

The Campaign: The Whigs avoided any divisive issues and conducted a campaign of parades and ballyhoo, complete with the first memorable political slogan, "Tippecanoe and Tyler too."

Results of 1840 Election:

Presidential Candidate	Party	Electoral Votes	Popular Vote Total	Percentage	Vice-Presidential Candidate and Electoral Votes		Party
William H. Harrison	Whig	234	1,275,612	52.9	John Tyler	234	Whig
Martin Van Buren	Democratic	60	1,130,033	46.8	Richard Johnson	48	Democratic
James G. Birney	Liberty	—	7,053	.3	Thomas Earle	—	Liberty
					L. W. Tazewell	11	Independent
					James K. Polk	1	Democratic

Comments: Barely a month after his inauguration, Harrison became the first President to die in office and was succeeded by Tyler on April 6, 1841.

ELECTION OF 1844

The Political Scene: In his one term Tyler managed to disrupt the Whig party and to secure the annexation of Texas, but he failed to settle the Oregon question.

Conventions and Nominees: The Whigs convened at Baltimore (May 1) to nominate Henry Clay for President and Senator Theodore Frelinghuysen of New Jersey for Vice-President. Later in the month at the same city, the Democrats chose the first "dark horse" nominee for the Presidency. Ex-President Van Buren had a clear majority on the early ballots but could not reach the required two-thirds vote. On the ninth ballot, the convention chose James K. Polk of Tennessee with George M. Dallas of Pennsylvania as the Vice-Presidential candidate. The Liberty party meeting at Buffalo, New York (August 1843), again named James G. Birney with Thomas Morris of Ohio as his running mate.

The Campaign: Polk, an ardent expansionist, favored the Texas annexation and the acquisition of Oregon with the slogan "Fifty-four forty or fight." Clay was hurt in the South by his wavering on Texas, and in the North by the defection of antislavery Whigs to the Liberty party.

Results of 1844 Election:

Presidential Candidate	Party	Electoral Votes	Popular Vote Total	Percentage	Vice-Presidential Candidate
James K. Polk	Democratic	170	1,339,368	49.6	George M. Dallas
Henry Clay	Whig	105	1,300,687	48.1	Theodore Frelinghuysen
James G. Birney	Liberty	—	62,197	2.3	Thomas Morris

Comments: Although far from conclusive, Polk's victory was regarded as a popular endorsement of a vigorous policy of expansion.

ELECTION OF 1848

The Political Scene: Polk settled the Oregon dispute with Great Britain, led the nation through a successful war with Mexico, and secured a vast accretion of territory. Yet he left office immensely unpopular and with the question of the extension of slavery into the new territories threatening to divide the country.

Conventions and Nominees: Polk had renounced a second term and the Democratic convention meeting at Baltimore (May 1848) picked a ticket of Lewis Cass of Michigan and William O. Butler of Kentucky. Although most Whigs had opposed the Mexican War, it provided them with their party's two leading Presidential candidates, Generals Zachary Taylor and Winfield Scott. The convention at Philadelphia named Taylor of Louisiana with Millard Fillmore of New York. Antislavery dissidents from both parties formed the Free Soil party and, meeting at Buffalo (August 1848), nominated ex-President Martin Van Buren with Charles Francis Adams of Massachusetts as his running mate.

The Campaign: On the paramount issue, the Free Soilers opposed extension of slavery into the newly acquired territories, while Cass endorsed the concept of popular sovereignty, or letting the settlers decide. Taylor refused to take any stand at all, correctly counting on his war popularity to carry him to victory.

Results of 1848 Election:

Presidential Candidate	Party	Electoral Votes	Popular Vote Total	Percentage	Vice-Presidential Candidate
Zachary Taylor	Whig	163	1,362,101	47.3	Millard Fillmore
Lewis Cass	Democratic	127	1,222,674	42.4	William O. Butler
Martin Van Buren	Free Soil	—	291,616	10.1	Charles Francis Adams

Comments: Taylor died on July 9, 1850. The succession of Fillmore to the Presidency made possible the Compromise of 1850.

ELECTION OF 1852

The Political Scene: Moderates in both parties had been alarmed by threats of disunion and vainly hoped the Compromise of 1850 would stifle the slavery agitation.

Conventions and Nominees: President Fillmore desired another term, but the Whigs again turned to a military hero, selecting General Winfield Scott of Virginia on the 53d ballot. The convention then named William A. Graham of North Carolina for the Vice-Presidency. The Democrats, who like the Whigs met at Baltimore in June, had a number of potential nominees, but none of the leaders could gain the necessary two-thirds majority. On the 99th ballot, "dark horse" Franklin Pierce of New Hampshire was named with William R. King of Alabama as the party's Vice-Presidential candidate. The remnants of the Free Soil party met in Pittsburgh in August to choose a ticket of John P. Hale of New Hampshire and George W. Julian of Indiana.

The Campaign: Both sides avoided the slavery question, and personalities dominated a rather listless campaign.

Results of 1852 Election:

Presidential Candidate	Party	Electoral Votes	Popular Vote Total	Percentage	Vice-Presidential Candidate
Franklin Pierce	Democratic	254	1,609,038	50.8	William R. King
Winfield Scott	Whig	42	1,386,629	43.8	William A. Graham
John P. Hale	Free Soil	—	156,297	4.9	George Julian

Comments: Scott was the last Presidential candidate of the Whig party.

ELECTION OF 1856

The Political Scene: Despite their overwhelming victory in 1852, the Democrats found it more and more difficult to reconcile their Northern and Southern wings, while the Whigs disintegrated entirely. The passage of the Kansas-Nebraska Act led to the founding of the Republican party.

Conventions and Nominees: In their first national convention at Philadelphia in June, the Republicans nominated John C. Frémont of California and William L. Dayton of New Jersey. Although widely considered to be the ablest leader in the party, Stephen A. Douglas' sponsorship of the Kansas-Nebraska Act prevented his nomination by the Democratic convention at Cincinnati in June. On the 17th ballot a Northerner acceptable to the South, James Buchanan of Pennsylvania, was named with John C. Breckinridge of Kentucky as his running mate. The anti-immigrant, anti-Catholic, American (or Know-Nothing) party had nominated ex-President Fillmore and Andrew J. Donelson at its convention in Philadelphia in February.

The Campaign: The Republicans endorsed a protective tariff and condemned the extension of slavery into the territories. The Democratic platform supported the Kansas-Nebraska Act and the principle of popular sovereignty for the territories.

Results of 1856 Election:

Presidential Candidate	Party	Electoral Votes	Popular Vote Total	Percentage	Vice-Presidential Candidate
James Buchanan	Democratic	174	1,839,237	45.6	John C. Breckinridge
John C. Frémont	Republican	114	1,341,028	33.3	William L. Dayton
Millard Fillmore	American	8	849,872	21.1	Andrew J. Donelson

Comments: Frémont's 114 electoral votes—all from free states—demonstrated the sectional nature of the new Republican party.

ELECTION OF 1860

The Political Scene: The Dred Scott decision, bloody fighting between sectional partisans in Kansas, and John Brown's raid on Harpers Ferry had widened the gulf between the free and slave states. Politicians in the states of the Deep South openly threatened secession if a Republican President was elected.

Conventions and Nominations: The Democrats meeting at Charleston (April 23–May 3, 1860) failed to nominate a candidate after 57 ballots, because the delegations of eight southern states withdrew in protest against the platform statement on slavery in the territories. Reassembling in Baltimore (June 18–23) the party nominated Stephen A. Douglas of Illinois and Benjamin Fitzpatrick of Alabama after further Southern defections. When Fitzpatrick declined to run, the national committee chose Herschel V. Johnson of Georgia. The Southern seceders, calling themselves the National Democratic party, convened in Baltimore on June 28 and nominated John Breckinridge of Kentucky and Joseph Lane of Oregon on a platform that endorsed slavery in the territories. The Constitutional Union party, which was composed mainly of former Whigs and was strongest in the border states, had met in Baltimore (May 9) to choose John Bell of Tennessee and Edward Everett of Massachusetts. Abraham Lincoln of Illinois required only three ballots to defeat preconvention favorite William H. Seward at the Republican convention in Chicago (May 18–20).

The Campaign: The Republicans promised congressional action to preserve freedom in the territories. Slavery and the sectional issues dominated the scene.

Results of 1860 Election:

Presidential Candidate	Party	Electoral Votes	Popular Vote Total	Percentage	Vice-Presidential Candidate
Abraham Lincoln	Republican	180	1,867,198	39.8	Hannibal Hamlin
Stephen A. Douglas	Democratic	12	1,379,434	29.4	Herschel V. Johnson
John C. Breckinridge	National Democratic	72	854,248	18.2	Joseph Lane
John Bell	Constitutional Union	39	591,658	12.6	Edward Everett

Comments: The division among his opponents seemed to insure Lincoln's election. Curiously, however, if all the popular votes cast for his opponents had been given to one man, Lincoln still would have won the electoral vote, because of the heavy distribution of his vote among the more populous states. A little more than a month after the election, South Carolina seceded from the Union.

ELECTION OF 1864

The Political Scene: The apparent inability of the Union armies to end Confederate resistance increased the sentiment for peace, causing many leading Republicans to oppose Lincoln's renomination.

Conventions and Nominees: The Republicans (styling themselves the National Union party) met at Baltimore in June and renominated Lincoln. War-Democrat Andrew Johnson of Tennessee became the Vice-Presidential candidate. The Democrats meeting at Chicago in August nominated a ticket of General George B. McClellan of New Jersey and George H. Pendleton of Ohio.

The Campaign: The Democratic platform pronounced the war a failure and demanded a cessation of hostilities and the restoration of peace on the basis of the Federal Union of States. But spectacular Union victories at Mobile Bay, Atlanta, and in the Shenandoah Valley destroyed this peace platform, and insured Lincoln's victory.

Results of 1864 Election:

Presidential Candidate	Party	Electoral Votes	Popular Vote Total	Percentage	Vice-Presidential Candidate
Abraham Lincoln	Republican	212	2,219,362	55.1	Andrew Johnson
George McClellan	Democratic	21	1,805,063	44.9	George Pendleton
Votes not cast	—	1	—	—	Votes not cast

Comments: John Wilkes Booth assassinated Lincoln, who was succeeded on April 15, 1865, by Andrew Johnson.

ELECTION OF 1868

The Political Scene: President Johnson and the Republican leadership fell out over Reconstruction policies. The Senate failed by one vote of removing the President by impeachment in May 1868.

Conventions and Nominees: The Republicans met (as the Union Republican party) at Chicago in May and selected General Ulysses S. Grant of Illinois with Schuyler Colfax of Indiana as his running mate. The Democrats meeting in Tammany Hall, New York City, in July drafted Horatio Seymour of New York after 21 ballots and complex maneuverings had failed to produce a candidate. The Vice-Presidential nod went to Francis P. Blair of Missouri.

The Campaign: In 1868 and for a generation thereafter, the Republicans used the "bloody shirt" tactic, attempting to label the Democrats as the party of secession and treason.

Results of 1868 Election:

Presidential Candidate	Party	Electoral Votes	Popular Vote Total	Percentage	Vice-Presidential Candidate
Ulysses S. Grant	Republican	214	3,013,313	52.7	Schuyler Colfax
Horatio Seymour	Democratic	80	2,703,933	47.3	Francis P. Blair, Jr.

Comments: Texas, Virginia, and Mississippi were not readmitted to the Union until 1870, therefore they cast no votes in this election. Grant greatly benefited from black votes in the South.

ELECTION OF 1872

The Political Scene: Evidence of corruption within his administration and disagreement with his Southern policy led many Republicans to oppose Grant's renomination.

Conventions and Nominees: When it became apparent, however, that Grant would be renominated, a group of dissenters calling themselves the Liberal Republican party met at Cincinnati in May and nominated a ticket of Horace Greeley of New York and B. Gratz Brown of Missouri. Greeley's nomination provided a dilemma for the Democrats. Greeley had consistently criticized their party, but to nominate someone else would serve only to reelect Grant. Accordingly, the Democrats in convention at Baltimore in July accepted Greeley and Brown. The Republicans at Philadelphia in June had unanimously renominated Grant.

The Campaign: Although tariff and currency questions were debated to some extent, the Republicans relied on Grant's war record to overcome the scandals. Most Democratic voters reacted unenthusiastically to Greeley.

Results of 1872 Election:

Presidential Candidate	Party	Electoral Votes	Popular Vote Total	Percentage	Vice-Presidential Candidate	Electoral Votes
Ulysses S. Grant	Republican	286	3,597,375	55.6	Henry Wilson	286
Horace Greeley	Democratic, Liberal Republican	—	2,833,711	43.8	B. Gratz Brown	47
Thomas A. Hendricks	Democratic	42	—	—	Other candidates	19
B. Gratz Brown	Democratic, Liberal Republican	18	—	—	Votes not cast	14
Other candidates	—	3	—	—		
Votes not cast	—	17	—	—		

Comments: Greeley died after the election and his electoral votes went to other candidates.

ELECTION OF 1876

The Political Scene: Growing national indignation at the scandals of Grant's second administration caused both parties to seek Presidential candidates associated with reform government.

Conventions and Nominees: The Republicans met at Cincinnati in June to select Rutherford B. Hayes of Ohio on the seventh ballot after the reform element had blocked the nomination of James G. Blaine. William A. Wheeler of New York was the Vice-Presidential candidate. Samuel J. Tilden of New York, who was acclaimed for his part in breaking up the notorious Tweed Ring, received a first-ballot nomination from the Democrats at St. Louis in June. Thomas A. Hendricks of Indiana was named for the Vice-Presidency. The inflationary Greenback party named Peter Cooper of New York and Samuel F. Carey of Ohio.

The Campaign: Hayes's good record as governor of Ohio somewhat blunted Democratic efforts to capitalize on the corruption of the Grant regime. Tilden waged a very cautious campaign and probably did not pay enough attention to the "solid South."

Results of 1876 Election:

Presidential Candidate	Party	Electoral Votes	Popular Vote Total	Percentage	Vice-Presidential Candidate
Rutherford B. Hayes	Republican	185	4,035,924	47.9	William A. Wheeler
Samuel J. Tilden	Democratic	184	4,287,670	50.9	Thomas A. Hendricks
Peter Cooper	Greenback	—	82,797	1.0	Samuel F. Carey

Comments: When the returns came in, the 19 electoral votes of South Carolina, Florida, and Louisiana were in dispute. After months of controversy over rival sets of returns, Congress established an electoral commission composed of five senators, five representatives, and five members of the Supreme Court to determine the valid returns. The commissioners—eight Republicans and seven Democrats—voted along strict party lines to award the 19 votes and the Presidency to Hayes.

ELECTION OF 1880

The Political Scene: Throughout the entire period of the "Gilded Age," few significant issues divided the two parties. This was particularly true in 1880 when, appealing to the veteran vote, both Republicans and Democrats nominated former generals.

Conventions and Nominees: The Republicans met in Chicago in June to choose "dark horse" James A. Garfield of Ohio on the 36th ballot, after reform or "Mugwump" delegates had blocked a proposed third term for Grant and a drive for James G. Blaine had collapsed. Chester A. Arthur of New York was named for the Vice-Presidency. Winfield S. Hancock of Pennsylvania and William H. English of Indiana comprised the ticket selected by the Democrats at Cincinnati in June. The Greenback party nominated a third general, James B. Weaver of Iowa, with B. J. Chambers of Texas named for the Vice-Presidency.

The Campaign: Personal attacks on the candidates characterized the campaign. The Democrats emphasized Garfield's involvement in the Crédit Mobilier Scandal, while the Republicans harped on Hancock's inexperience and naiveté.

Results of 1880 Election:

Presidential Candidate	Party	Electoral Votes	Popular Vote Total	Percentage	Vice-Presidential Candidate
James A. Garfield	Republican	214	4,454,433	48.3	Chester A. Arthur
Winfield S. Hancock	Democratic	155	4,444,976	48.2	William English
James B. Weaver	Greenback	—	308,649	3.3	B. J. Chambers

Comments: In July 1881 Charles J. Guiteau, a deranged and disappointed office-seeker, shot Garfield, who died on September 19, 1881. Arthur succeeded to the Presidency the following day.

ELECTION OF 1884

The Political Scene: Although President by accident, Arthur made a respectable record in the office. He failed, however, to build up enough support for a nomination in his own right.

Conventions and Nominees: Despite a challenge from Arthur, James G. Blaine of Maine succeeded in this his third try for the Republican nomination. The Chicago convention meeting in June then picked John A. Logan of Illinois as his running mate. The Democrats convening in Chicago on July 8 nominated Grover Cleveland of New York and Thomas A. Hendricks of Indiana.

The Campaign: In what has been remembered as the dirtiest campaign in American history, Cleveland was charged with fathering an illegitimate child, and Blaine was abused for alleged shady practices while Speaker of the House. Many prominent "Mugwump" Republicans refused to support Blaine and endorsed Cleveland.

Results of 1884 Election:

Presidential Candidate	Party	Electoral Votes	Popular Vote Total	Percentage	Vice-Presidential Candidate
Grover Cleveland	Democratic	219	4,875,971	48.5	Thomas A. Hendricks
James G. Blaine	Republican	182	4,852,234	48.3	John A. Logan
Benjamin F. Butler	Greenback	—	175,066	1.7	A. M. West
John P. St. John	Prohibition	—	150,957	1.5	William Daniel

Comments: Just prior to election day, one of Blaine's supporters referred to the Democrats as the party of "Rum, Romanism and Rebellion," a slur on Irish Catholic voters that probably caused Blaine to lose New York State and, hence, the election.

ELECTION OF 1888

The Political Scene: Cleveland's firm, honest, and conservative administration gained him a great deal of respect, but at the same time offended powerful pressure groups such as the Grand Army of the Republic and the tariff protectionists.

Conventions and Nominees: The Democrats renominated Cleveland by acclamation in St. Louis in June. Allen G. Thurman of Ohio joined him on the ticket. In a convention marked with much intrigues and bargaining, the Republicans named Benjamin Harrison of Indiana and Levi P. Morton of New York at Chicago in June.

The Campaign: The Democrats condemned the inequities of the high protective tariff. The Republicans replied that the system of protection served the interests of America over those of Europe.

Results of 1888 Election:

Presidential Candidate	Party	Electoral Votes	Popular Vote Total	Percentage	Vice-Presidential Candidate
Benjamin Harrison	Republican	233	5,445,269	47.8	Levi P. Morton
Grover Cleveland	Democratic	168	5,540,365	48.6	Allen G. Thurman
Clinton B. Fisk	Prohibition	—	250,122	2.2	John A. Brooks
Aaron J. Streeter	Union Labor	—	147,606	1.3	C. E. Cunningham

Comments: The Republicans managed to turn part of the Irish vote against Cleveland, when, on a pretext, a foolish letter favoring Cleveland over Harrison was obtained from the British Minister in Washington.

ELECTION OF 1892

The Political Scene: Popular anger with veteran and tariff legislation combined with a growing militancy among farmers to hand the Republicans a stunning defeat in the midterm elections of 1890 and brighten Democratic prospects for regaining the Presidency.

Conventions and Nominees: Both parties met in June, the Democrats at Chicago and the Republicans at Minneapolis, to renominate their standard-bearers of 1888—Cleveland and Harrison. For the Vice-Presidency, the Democrats chose Adlai E. Stevenson of Illinois; the Republicans, Whitelaw Reid of New York. The Populist or People's party held its first national nominating convention at Omaha in July, endorsing James B. Weaver of Iowa and James G. Field of Virginia.

Campaign Issues: Debate centered on controversial measures of the Harrison administration together with the demand for the free and unlimited coinage of silver and the general agrarian unrest.

Results of 1892 Election:

Presidential Candidate	Party	Electoral Votes	Popular Vote Total	Percentage	Vice-Presidential Candidate
Grover Cleveland	Democratic	277	5,556,982	46.0	Adlai E. Stevenson
Benjamin Harrison	Republican	145	5,191,466	43.0	Whitelaw Reid
James B. Weaver	Populist	22	1,029,960	8.5	James G. Field
John Bidwell	Prohibition	—	271,111	2.2	James B. Cranfill

Comments: The Populists became the first third party since 1860 to win any electoral votes.

ELECTION OF 1896

The Political Scene: The Panic of 1893 struck with full force after Cleveland's inauguration, and the subsequent "hard times" were blamed on the Democrats. It appeared possible that the Populists could replace the Democrats as the second major party.

Conventions and Nominees: The Republican convention at St. Louis in June nominated William McKinley of Ohio on the first ballot and Garrett Hobart of New Jersey as his running mate. The Democrats meeting at Chicago in July named William Jennings Bryan of Nebraska on the fifth ballot. Arthur Sewall of Maine was selected for the Vice-Presidential nomination. The Populists at their St. Louis convention in July accepted Bryan, but named Thomas E. Watson of Georgia for the Vice-Presidency.

The Campaign: Bryan's stand for the "free and unlimited coinage of silver" brought down on him the fury of the country's conservative interests. McKinley conducted a "front porch" campaign, but a strenuous and expensive effort was carried on in his behalf under the direction of Mark Hanna.

Results of 1896 Election:

Presidential Candidate	Party	Electoral Votes	Popular Vote Total	Percentage	Vice-Presidential Candidate
William McKinley	Republican	271	7,113,734	51.0	Garret Hobart
William J. Bryan	Democratic-Populist	176	6,516,722	46.7	{ Arthur Sewall / Thomas E. Watson
John M. Palmer	National Democratic	—	135,456	.97	Simon Buckner
Joshua Levering	Prohibition	—	131,285	.94	Hale Johnson

Comments: Bryan, whose "Cross of Gold" speech is perhaps the most famous ever made at a convention, failed to win any of the nation's industrial states, indicating the limited appeal of the free-silver issue.

ELECTION OF 1900

The Political Scene: The successful conclusion of the Spanish-American War and returning prosperity buoyed Republican hopes for another Presidential victory.

Conventions and Nominees: At the Republicans' Philadelphia convention in June, McKinley was unanimously renominated and war hero Theodore Roosevelt of New York was selected for the Vice-Presidency. The Democrats met at Kansas City, Missouri, in July to choose Bryan again. Adlai E. Stevenson of Illinois was named for Vice-President. This year Eugene V. Debs of Indiana received the first of his five Presidential nominations by the Socialist party.

The Campaign: Theodore Roosevelt did most of the campaigning for the Republican ticket, stressing the "full dinner pail" of McKinley prosperity and the national pride in territories acquired from Spain. Bryan once more endorsed free silver, but called imperialism the paramount issue. He also criticized the growth of the giant trusts.

Results of 1900 Election:

Presidential Candidate	Party	Electoral Votes	Popular Vote Total	Percentage	Vice-Presidential Candidate
William McKinley	Republican	292	7,219,828	51.7	Theodore Roosevelt
William J. Bryan	Democratic	155	6,358,160	45.5	Adlai E. Stevenson
John C. Wolley	Prohibition	—	210,200	1.5	Henry B. Metcalf
Eugene V. Debs	Socialist	—	95,744	.7	Job Harriman

Comments: McKinley, who was shot by anarchist Leon Czolgosz at the Pan-American Exposition in Buffalo, died on September 14, 1901. At the age of 42, Roosevelt became the youngest President in history.

ELECTION OF 1904

The Political Scene: Roosevelt's moderately progressive policies, his energetic regimen, and his obvious relish of the Presidency made him the most popular President since Lincoln.

Conventions and Nominees: Mark Hanna's death early in 1904 removed the only man capable of challenging Roosevelt for the Presidential nomination. The Republican convention meeting at Chicago in June gave "T.R." its unanimous vote and chose Charles W. Fairbanks of Indiana to run with him. Having lost twice with the progressive Bryan, the Democrats turned to a more conservative candidate, Judge Alton B. Parker of New York. The convention, which met at St. Louis in July, then named Henry G. Davis of West Virginia for Vice-President.

The Campaign: Parker, who endorsed the gold standard, was portrayed by the Democrats as a safe, conservative candidate. A colorless figure, he could not hope to match Roosevelt's popular appeal.

Results of 1904 Election:

Presidential Candidate	Party	Electoral Votes	Popular Vote Total	Percentage	Vice-Presidential Candidate
Theodore Roosevelt	Republican	336	7,628,831	56.4	Charles W. Fairbanks
Alton B. Parker	Democratic	140	5,084,533	37.6	Henry G. Davis
Eugene V. Debs	Socialist	—	402,714	3.0	Benjamin Hanford
Silas C. Swallow	Prohibition	—	259,163	1.9	George W. Carroll

Comments: After his great victory, Roosevelt announced that he would not be a candidate for a third term, a pledge that was to haunt him in 1912.

ELECTION OF 1908

The Political Scene: Roosevelt, the unchallenged leader of his party, determined to pick his successor. Following Parker's decisive defeat, the Democrats were ready to return to Bryan.

Conventions and Nominees: The Republican conclave at Chicago in June ratified Roosevelt's choice of his Secretary of War William Howard Taft of Ohio and named James S. Sherman of New York to run with him. The Democrats meeting at Denver in July picked a ticket of Bryan and John W. Kern of Indiana.

The Campaign: In a dull campaign, Bryan promised to revise the tariff downward; Taft replied that he also intended to work for a downward revision.

Results of 1908 Election:

Presidential Candidate	Party	Electoral Votes	Popular Vote Total	Percentage	Vice-Presidential Candidate
William H. Taft	Republican	321	7,679,114	51.6	James S. Sherman
William J. Bryan	Democratic	162	6,410,665	43.0	John W. Kern
Eugene V. Debs	Socialist	—	420,858	2.8	Benjamin Hanford
Eugene W. Chafin	Prohibition	—	252,704	1.7	Aaron S. Watkins

Comments: Bryan was the only major party candidate in American history to run three unsuccessful races for the Presidency.

ELECTION OF 1912

The Political Scene: The opposition of progressive Republicans to Taft's policies led to an open rupture of the party, with Theodore Roosevelt leading the insurgents.

Conventions and Nominees: When the Republican convention meeting at Chicago in June decided a contest for disputed delegate seats in favor of Taft, Roosevelt ordered his delegates to abstain from voting. Taft and Sherman were renominated on the first ballot, but Roosevelt's delegates became the nucleus of the Progressive or "Bull Moose" party, which met in Chicago in August to nominate Roosevelt and Hiram Johnson of California. The Democrats convening in Baltimore (June 25–July 2) produced a drawn-out but exciting contest. Champ Clark of Missouri obtained a majority on the 10th ballot but could not reach the necessary two thirds. On the 46th ballot, the delegates chose Woodrow Wilson of New Jersey. Thomas R. Marshall of Indiana was selected for the Vice-Presidency.

The Campaign: With Wilson, Roosevelt, and Socialist nominee Eugene V. Debs all campaigning as reform candidates, the voters were asked to decide which man could best implement progressive policies. Wilson's New Freedom program emphasized dissolution of the great trusts and the return to free competition. Roosevelt's New Nationalism stressed regulation of big business by the federal government.

Results of 1912 Election:

Presidential Candidate	Party	Electoral Votes	Popular Vote Total	Percentage	Vice-Presidential Candidate
Woodrow Wilson	Democratic	435	6,301,254	41.8	Thomas R. Marshall
Theodore Roosevelt	Progressive	88	4,127,788	27.4	Hiram Johnson
William H. Taft	Republican	8	3,485,831	23.1	{ James S. Sherman { Nicholas M. Butler
Eugene V. Debs	Socialist	—	901,255	6.0	Emil Seidel
Eugene Chafin	Prohibition	—	209,644	1.4	Aaron S. Watkins

Comments: Three-quarters of the popular vote went to the reform candidates, indicating the strength of the progressive movement in the country. The Republican split insured Wilson's election.

ELECTION OF 1916

The Political Scene: The question of possible American involvement in World War I overshadowed the domestic controversies of the Wilson administration.

Conventions and Nominees: The Republicans nominated Charles Evans Hughes of New York and Charles W. Fairbanks of Indiana at their convention at Chicago in June. The Progressive party disintegrated when Theodore Roosevelt refused to be its candidate again. The Democrats at St. Louis in June renominated Wilson and Marshall.

The Campaign: The Democrats went before the electorate as the party of peace, using the slogan "Wilson and Peace with Honor, or Hughes with Roosevelt and War." Hughes had the difficult task of reconciling the belligerent Theodore Roosevelt with his antiwar supporters among German-Americans and other groups.

Results of 1916 Election:

Presidential Candidate	Party	Electoral Votes	Popular Vote Total	Percentage	Vice-Presidential Candidate
Woodrow Wilson	Democratic	277	9,131,511	49.3	Thomas R. Marshall
Charles E. Hughes	Republican	254	8,548,935	46.1	Charles W. Fairbanks
Allan L. Benson	Socialist	—	585,974	3.2	George R. Kirkpatrick
J. Frank Hanly	Prohibition	—	220,505	1.2	Ira Landrith

Comments: Wilson's carrying of California's electoral vote proved decisive.

ELECTION OF 1920

The Political Scene: An immense reaction against the idealism of the Wilson years and the sacrifices entailed by World War I characterized the mood of the American people, who were anxious to return to normalcy.

Conventions and Nominees: The Republican choice fell upon "dark horse" Warren G. Harding, an Ohio editor, whose selection on the 10th ballot at Chicago on June 12, came after a meeting of party leaders in the famous "smoke-filled room" of the Blackstone Hotel. Calvin Coolidge of Massachusetts, who had won popular acclaim for his opposition to the Boston police strike, received the Vice-Presidential nod.

For the Democrats, Wilson probably desired a third nomination, but his physical incapacity and political unpopularity made this impossible. The San Francisco convention chose a relative unknown in James M. Cox of Ohio on the 44th ballot on July 6th and Franklin D. Roosevelt of New York, the possessor of a magnetic name, as his running mate.

The Campaign: The League of Nations was the most debated campaign topic, with Cox supporting American entry into the world body and Harding straddling the issue.

Results of 1920 Election:

Presidential Candidate	Party	Electoral Votes	Popular Vote Total	Percentage	Vice-Presidential Candidate
Warren G. Harding	Republican	404	16,153,115	60.3	Calvin Coolidge
James M. Cox	Democratic	127	9,133,092	34.1	Franklin D. Roosevelt
Eugene V. Debs	Socialist	—	915,490	3.4	Seymour Stedman
Parley P. Christensen	Farmer-Labor	—	265,229	1.0	Max S. Hayes

Comments: The massive Republican victory represented more of a rejection of Wilson and the Democrats than a personal mandate for Harding, who died in office after a scandal-marred administration and was succeeded by Calvin Coolidge on August 3, 1923.

ELECTION OF 1924

The Political Scene: The cautious conservatism and New England frugality of Calvin Coolidge reduced the political capital the Democrats hoped to make out of the Harding administration's scandals.

Conventions and Nominees: The Republican convention at Cleveland in June chose Coolidge with Charles G. Dawes of Illinois. The Democratic convention in New York City lasted from June 24 until July 29, and the resulting contest between Alfred E. Smith and William Gibbs McAdoo led to the most ballots ever taken in a Presidential nominating convention. Finally after Smith and McAdoo had withdrawn, the delegates nominated John W. Davis of West Virginia on the 103d ballot. Charles W. Bryan of Nebraska was the Vice-Presidential selection. Dissident farm and labor elements in both parties formed the Progressive party, which named a ticket of Robert M. LaFollette of Wisconsin and Burton K. Wheeler of Montana at a convention held in Cleveland in July.

The Campaign: The bitter Democratic convention destroyed what little chance the party had of unseating Coolidge. Both major candidates concentrated their fire on LaFollette rather than each other.

Results of 1924 Election:

Presidential Candidate	Party	Electoral Votes	Popular Vote Total	Percentage	Vice-Presidential Candidate
Calvin Coolidge	Republican	382	15,719,921	54.0	Charles G. Dawes
John W. Davis	Democratic	136	8,386,704	28.8	Charles W. Bryan
Robert M. LaFollette	Progressive	13	4,832,532	16.6	Burton K. Wheeler

Comments: LaFollette won the electoral vote of Wisconsin.

ELECTION OF 1928

The Political Scene: In the summer of 1927, Coolidge announced "I do not choose to run for President . . ." Despite the efforts of a "draft Coolidge" movement, most Republicans were willing to turn to another candidate.

Conventions and Nominees: The Republicans met at Kansas City, Missouri, in June and nominated a ticket of Herbert Hoover of California and Charles Curtis of Kansas. The Democrats meeting at Houston in June needed only one ballot to name Alfred E. Smith of New York for the Presidency and Joseph T. Robinson of Arkansas for the Vice-Presidency.

The Campaign: Smith, who differed with Hoover on the issues of prohibition, public power, and agriculture, found it difficult to make a dent in the public satisfaction with Republican prosperity.

Results of 1928 Election:

Presidential Candidate	Party	Electoral Votes	Popular Vote Total	Percentage	Vice-Presidential Candidate
Herbert C. Hoover	Republican	444	21,437,277	58.22	Charles Curtis
Alfred E. Smith	Democratic	87	15,007,698	40.8	Joseph T. Robinson
Norman M. Thomas	Socialist	—	265,583	.7	James Maurer

Comments: Smith, the first Roman Catholic candidate nominated by a major party, lost many votes particularly in the South because of his religion, but gained many others for the same reason in the Northeast and Midwest.

ELECTION OF 1932

The Political Scene: The Wall Street crash of 1929 and the subsequent economic depression made a Democratic victory almost certain and quickened the race for the party's nomination.

Conventions and Nominees: The Republicans meeting at Chicago in June renominated Hoover and Curtis. The Democrats held their convention during the same month in the same city. Franklin D. Roosevelt of New York, who had outdistanced a large field of contenders in the preconvention maneuvering, was nominated on the fourth ballot with John N. Garner of Texas as his running mate.

The Campaign: Roosevelt promised the country a New Deal and a willingness to experiment with different approaches in an effort to end the economic crisis. Hoover warned of even greater difficulties if the Democrats won.

Results of 1932 Election:

Presidential Candidate	Party	Electoral Votes	Popular Vote Total	Percentage	Vice-Presidential Candidate
Franklin D. Roosevelt	Democratic	472	22,829,501	57.4	John Nance Garner
Herbert C. Hoover	Republican	59	15,760,684	39.6	Charles Curtis
Norman M. Thomas	Socialist	—	884,649	2.2	James Maurer

Comments: Roosevelt's landslide victory carried into office many Democratic Congressmen who were to help implement his program.

ELECTION OF 1936

The Political Scene: New Deal policies enraged political conservatives, but gained the Democrats many new supporters.

Conventions and Nominees: Delegates convening in Cleveland in June named a Republican ticket of Alfred M. Landon of Kansas and Frank Knox of Illinois. The Democrats met later in the month at Philadelphia to renominate Roosevelt and Garner by acclamation. The convention also abolished the two-thirds rule for choosing candidates, making a simple majority sufficient. Father Charles E. Coughlin, Dr. Francis Townsend, and Gerald L. K. Smith, all radical critics of the New Deal, formed the Union party at Cleveland in August and nominated William Lemke of North Dakota and Thomas C. O'Brien of Massachusetts.

The Campaign: The Republicans attacked Roosevelt and the New Deal for allegedly building a giant and wasteful bureaucracy. Roosevelt was content to run on his record.

Results of 1936 Election:

Presidential Candidate	Party	Electoral Votes	Popular Vote Total	Percentage	Vice-Presidential Candidate
Franklin D. Roosevelt	Democratic	523	27,757,333	60.8	John Nance Garner
Alfred M. Landon	Republican	8	16,684,231	36.5	Frank Knox
William Lemke	Union	—	892,267	2.0	Thomas C. O'Brien

Comments: Roosevelt won the most sweeping electoral victory in modern history, carrying every state but Maine and Vermont.

ELECTION OF 1940

The Political Scene: With the outbreak of World War II in 1939, American neutrality once again became the dominant political issue in an election year.

Conventions and Nominees: The Republicans convened in Philadelphia in June. A tremendous groundswell of public opinion for Wendell L. Willkie of New York enabled him to overcome the early lead of Thomas E. Dewey and Robert A. Taft and win the nomination on the sixth ballot. His running mate was Charles L. McNary of Oregon. Roosevelt won his third nomination from the Democratic convention held in Chicago in July. At his insistence, Henry Wallace of Iowa replaced Garner for the Vice-Presidency.

The Campaign: The Democratic platform and Roosevelt were pledged against participation in foreign wars, except in case of attack. Willkie endorsed most New Deal measures and did not differ substantially from Roosevelt on foreign policy, but he stressed that Roosevelt's attempt to win a third term threatened democratic government.

Results of 1940 Election:

Presidential Candidate	Party	Electoral Votes	Popular Vote Total	Percentage	Vice-Presidential Candidate
Franklin D. Roosevelt	Democratic	449	27,313,041	54.7	Henry A. Wallace
Wendell L. Willkie	Republican	82	22,348,480	44.8	Charles L. McNary

Comments: Roosevelt, destined to win a fourth term as well, was the only man to win more than two elections or to serve more than eight years as President.

ELECTION OF 1944

The Political Scene: In the nation's third wartime election, Roosevelt benefited from the general reluctance "to change horses in midstream."

Conventions and Nominees: The Republicans held their convention at Chicago in June. Thomas E. Dewey of New York received all but one vote on the first ballot, and John W. Bricker of Ohio was the unanimous choice as his running mate. The Democrats convening at Chicago in July once again chose Roosevelt, but Wallace had earned the enmity of many party leaders, and the delegates turned to Harry S Truman of Missouri for the Vice-Presidency.

The Campaign: The Republicans called for new political leadership for the work of peace and reconstruction, but agreed with the Democrats in the necessity of American participation in a postwar international organization.

Results of 1944 Election:

Presidential Candidate	Party	Electoral Votes	Popular Vote Total	Percentage	Vice-Presidential Candidate
Franklin D. Roosevelt	Democratic	432	25,612,610	53.3	Harry S Truman
Thomas E. Dewey	Republican	99	22,017,617	45.9	John W. Bricker

Comments: On April 12, 1945, Roosevelt died and was succeeded on the same day by Truman.

ELECTION OF 1948

The Political Scene: Deep splits within the Democratic party and an apparent public desire for a change portended a Republican victory.

Conventions and Nominees: The Republicans meeting at Philadelphia in June again nominated Thomas E. Dewey. Earl Warren of California was the Vice-Presidential choice. The Democrats met in the same city the following month and unenthusiastically nominated a ticket of Truman and Alben W. Barkley of Kentucky. Several Southern delegations that were opposed to the party's civil rights platform bolted the convention and named a States' Rights or "Dixiecrat" ticket of Strom Thurmond of South Carolina for President and Fielding L. Wright of Mississippi for Vice-President. A fourth party, the Progressive, which was composed largely of liberal and left-wing Democrats critical of Truman's foreign policy, ran Henry A. Wallace of Iowa and Glenn Taylor of Idaho.

The Campaign: A distinct underdog because of the Dixiecrat and Progressive tickets, Truman undertook a vigorous campaign in which he castigated the Republican-controlled 80th Congress as a "do nothing" one. Dewey, who was indicated the certain winner in the public opinion polls, conducted a very cool and careful campaign.

Results of 1948 Election:

Presidential Candidate	Party	Electoral Votes	Popular Vote Total	Percentage	Vice-Presidential Candidate
Harry S Truman	Democratic	303	24,179,345	49.6	Alben W. Barkley
Thomas E. Dewey	Republican	189	21,991,291	45.1	Earl Warren
J. Strom Thurmond	States' Rights	39	1,176,125	2.4	Fielding L. Wright
Henry A. Wallace	Progressive	—	1,157,326	2.4	Glenn Taylor

Comments: Truman's upset victory reflected his ability to hold almost the entire labor and Negro vote and to carry the key Midwestern farm states of Ohio, Iowa, and Wisconsin.

ELECTION OF 1952

The Political Scene: Truman announced early in the year that he would not be a candidate for a third term. In any case, the Korean War had dimmed his prospects of reelection.

Conventions and Nominees: General Dwight D. Eisenhower beat off the strong challenge of Robert A. Taft to win the nomination of the Republican convention that was held in Chicago in July. Richard M. Nixon of California received the Vice-Presidential designation. The Democrats convened in Chicago later in the same month and named a ticket of Adlai E. Stevenson of Illinois and John J. Sparkman of Alabama.

The Campaign: The Republicans used the slogan "Communism, Korea, and corruption," and Eisenhower promised a personal visit to Korea. Stevenson, a first-rate campaigner, was nonetheless forced on the defensive.

Results of 1952 Election:

Presidential Candidate	Party	Electoral Votes	Popular Vote Total	Percentage	Vice-Presidential Candidate
Dwight D. Eisenhower	Republican	442	33,936,234	55.1	Richard M. Nixon
Adlai E. Stevenson	Democratic	89	27,314,992	44.4	John J. Sparkman

Comments: Eisenhower carried the Republicans to victory in both houses of Congress, marking the only time since 1931 or after that the party has controlled the executive and legislative branches of government at the same time.

ELECTION OF 1956

The Political Scene: Suffering a serious heart attack in September 1955, Eisenhower waited until the end of February 1956 before announcing that he would run for a second term.

Conventions and Nominees: Senator Estes Kefauver of Tennessee conducted an extensive primary campaign; however, he withdrew in favor of Stevenson a week before the Democrats met in Chicago in August. Kefauver then won a spirited contest with John F. Kennedy for the Vice-Presidency. The Republicans meeting in San Francisco in August renominated Eisenhower and Nixon.

The Campaign: Stevenson proposed the possibility of ending the draft system and an agreement with the Soviet Union on Cold War issues. In addition, the Democrats referred to Eisenhower's health and the possibility of Nixon's succession to the Presidency. The Republicans emphasized the "peace and prosperity" of the Eisenhower years.

Results of 1956 Election:

Presidential Candidate	Party	Electoral Votes	Popular Vote Total	Percentage	Vice-Presidential Candidate
Dwight D. Eisenhower	Republican	457	35,590,472	57.4	Richard M. Nixon
Adlai E. Stevenson	Democratic	73	26,022,752	42.0	Estes Kefauver
Walter B. Jones	No party	1	—	—	—

Comments: Eisenhower became the first winning Presidential candidate since Zachary Taylor in 1848 to fail to carry his party to victory in either the House of Representatives or the Senate.

ELECTION OF 1960

The Political Scene: The mood of the country was somewhat restive, primarily because of economic recessions in 1953, 1957, and 1960, but also because of increasing disquiet over issues relating to civil rights and race relations.

Conventions and Nominations: John F. Kennedy of Massachusetts entered several Presidential primaries to disprove alleged liabilities of his youth and his Roman Catholic religion; victories in key contests in Wisconsin and West Virginia assured his first ballot victory at the Democratic Convention in Los Angeles (July 11–15), where he chose Lyndon B. Johnson of Texas as his running mate. Vice-President Richard Nixon of California easily overcame a challenge from Nelson Rockefeller of New York to win a first ballot endorsement from the Republican National Convention at Chicago (July 25–28).

The Campaign: Nixon emphasized the unity, strength, and stability that he claimed the Republicans had given the country during the previous eight years. Kennedy complained of stagnation and apathy in Washington and decline of American prestige abroad, promising to get the country moving again and, particularly, to revitalize the economy.

Results of 1960 Election:

Presidential Candidate	Party	Electoral Votes	Popular Vote Total	Percentage	Vice-Presidential Candidate
John F. Kennedy	Democratic	303	34,226,731	49.7	Lyndon B. Johnson
Richard M. Nixon	Republican	219	34,108,157	49.5	Henry Cabot Lodge
Harry F. Byrd	No party	15	440,298	.6	—

Comments: Kennedy built his victory on the large industrial states of the Northeast and key states in the South, where Johnson's candidacy helped. Kennedy was assassinated on November 22, 1963, in Dallas by Lee Harvey Oswald.

ELECTION OF 1964

The Political Scene: In less than a year in office, Lyndon Johnson had compiled a record of legislative achievements that put him in excellent position for the campaign.

Conventions and Nominees: The Republican convention meeting at San Francisco in July witnessed the first victory for the conservative wing of the party in over a generation with the nomination of Barry M. Goldwater of Arizona. William Miller of New York was selected as his running mate. The Democrats convened at Atlantic City in August to nominate Johnson and Hubert H. Humphrey of Minnesota, both of whom were named by acclamation.

The Campaign: The Democrats were happy to run on the record of the Kennedy-Johnson administration, while depicting Goldwater as a dangerous reactionary, Goldwater assailed the Johnson administration for permitting a decline in government morality and efficiency and a deterioration of national prestige abroad.

Results of 1964 Election:

Presidential Candidate	Party	Electoral Votes	Popular Vote Total	Percentage	Vice-Presidential Candidate
Lyndon B. Johnson	Democratic	486	43,129,484	61.1	Hubert H. Humphrey
Barry M. Goldwater	Republican	52	27,178,188	38.5	W. E. Miller

Comments: Johnson gained a larger percentage of the popular vote than any candidate in modern times. Only Franklin Roosevelt in 1936 received more electoral votes.

ELECTION OF 1968

The Political Scene: On March 31, Johnson announced he would not seek reelection following repeated attacks on his Vietnam war policy. Sen. Robert F. Kennedy was assassinated in June following his victory in the California primary. Ronald Reagan and Nelson Rockefeller challenged Richard Nixon for the Republican nomination.

Conventions and Nominees: The Republicans met in Miami in August and nominated Richard Nixon on the first ballot. Spiro T. Agnew was chosen for the Vice-Presidency. At a Chicago convention marred by much turbulence, the Democrats chose Hubert H. Humphrey of Minnesota; Edmund S. Muskie of Maine was the Vice-Presidential nominee. George C. Wallace of Alabama ran as Presidential candidate of the American Independent Party among other designations.

The Campaign: Nixon promised an honorable conclusion of the Vietnam war and the restoration of law and order throughout the country. Humphrey pledged to seek a political solution to the struggle in Vietnam and promised to work toward ending divisiveness in American life. Wallace, an extreme conservative, appeared to hope to force the election into the House of Representatives, where his electors might hold the balance of power.

Results of 1968 Election:

Presidential Candidate	Party	Electoral Votes	Popular Vote Total	Percentage	Vice-Presidential Candidate
Richard M. Nixon	Republican	301	31,785,480	43.4	Spiro T. Agnew
Hubert H. Humphrey	Democratic	191	31,275,165	42.7	Edmund S. Muskie
George C. Wallace	American Independent	46	9,906,473	13.5	Curtis E. LeMay

Comments: Nixon received the lowest percentage of the popular vote for a successful candidate since 1912.

ELECTION OF 1972

The Political Scene: The first Nixon administration reveled in its diplomatic gains abroad, while attempting to diminish the domestic problems of unemployment and inflation. The Democrats attacked Nixon's record on domestic affairs, along with hurling charges against the Committee to Reelect the President, accused of masterminding a break-in at the Democratic headquarters in the Watergate complex.

Conventions and Nominees: The Democrats met in Miami, Florida, in July and nominated Sen. George McGovern on the first ballot. His choice for Vice-President, Sen. Thomas F. Eagleton of Missouri, was endorsed by the convention's acclamation. Eagleton resigned from the ticket in late August, however, and was replaced by R. Sargent Shriver of Maryland. The Republicans met in Miami in August, and the incumbents were nominated without opposition.

The Campaign: Nixon did little active campaigning, using his spectacular trips to Moscow and Peking to give him exposure. McGovern had come from behind to win the Democratic nomination, but his campaign never regained its momentum when his first running mate, Sen. Thomas Eagleton, withdrew following disclosures that he had undergone shock treatment for depression. The Democrats were defeated in a near-record landslide.

Results of 1972 Election:

Presidential Candidates	Party	Electoral Votes	Popular Vote Total	Percentage	Vice-Presidential Candidate
Richard M. Nixon	Republican	520	47,167,319	60.7	Spiro T. Agnew
George S. McGovern	Democratic	17	29,169,504	37.5	R. Sargent Shriver
John G. Schmitz	American	—	1,102,963	1.4	Thomas J. Anderson
John Hospers	Libertarian	1	2,691	—	Theodora Nathan

Comments: Division among the Democrats, with many party conservatives turning to Nixon, contributed to the Republican victory, along with apparent voter apathy regarding the Watergate issue.

FINAL 1972 PRESIDENTIAL ELECTION RESULTS

State	Electoral Vote	Popular Vote			Percentages		
		Nixon	McGovern	Schmitz	Nixon	McGovern	Schmitz
Alabama	9	728,701	256,923	11,918	73	26	1
Alaska	3	55,349	32,967	6,903	58	35	7
Arizona	6	402,812	198,540	21,208	65	32	3
Arkansas	6	445,751	199,892	3,016	69	31	—
California	45	4,602,096	3,475,847	232,554	55	42	3
Colorado	7	597,189	329,980	17,546	63	35	2
Connecticut	8	810,763	555,498	17,239	59	40	1
Delaware	3	140,357	92,283	2,638	60	39	1
Dist. Columbia	3	35,226	127,627	—	22	78	—
Florida	17	1,857,759	718,117	—	72	28	—
Georgia	12	881,496	289,529	815	75	25	—
Hawaii	4	168,865	101,409	—	62	38	—
Idaho	4	199,384	80,826	28,869	65	26	9
Illinois	26	2,788,179	1,913,472	2,471	59	41	—
Indiana	13	1,405,154	708,568	—	68	32	—
Iowa	8	706,207	496,206	22,056	58	41	1
Kansas	7	619,812	270,287	21,808	68	30	2
Kentucky	9	676,446	371,159	17,627	64	35	1
Louisiana	10	686,852	298,142	52,099	66	29	5
Maine	4	256,458	160,584	—	61	39	—
Maryland	10	829,305	505,781	18,726	61	37	1
Massachusetts	14	1,112,078	1,332,540	2,877	45	54	—
Michigan	21	1,961,721	1,459,435	63,321	56	42	2
Minnesota	10	898,269	802,346	31,407	51	42	2
Mississippi	7	505,125	126,782	11,598	78	20	2
Missouri	12	1,154,050	698,531	3,110	62	38	—
Montana	4	183,976	120,197	13,427	58	38	4
Nebraska	5	406,298	169,991	—	71	29	—
Nevada	3	115,750	66,016	—	64	36	—
New Hampshire	4	213,724	116,435	3,386	64	35	1
New Jersey	17	1,845,502	1,102,211	34,378	62	37	1
New Mexico	4	235,606	141,084	8,767	61	37	2
New York	41	4,192,778	2,951,084	—	59	41	—
North Carolina	13	1,054,889	438,705	25,018	70	30	—
North Dakota	3	174,109	100,384	5,646	62	36	2
Ohio	25	2,441,827	1,558,889	80,067	60	38	2
Oklahoma	8	759,025	247,147	23,728	72	24	2
Oregon	6	486,686	392,760	46,211	53	42	5
Pennsylvania	27	2,714,521	1,796,951	70,593	59	39	2
Rhode Island	4	220,383	194,645	—	53	47	—
South Carolina	8	477,044	184,559	10,075	71	27	1
South Dakota	4	166,476	139,945	—	54	46	—
Tennessee	10	813,147	357,293	30,373	68	30	2
Texas	26	2,298,896	1,154,291	6,039	67	33	—
Utah	4	323,643	126,284	28,549	68	26	6
Vermont	3	117,149	68,174	—	63	37	—
Virginia	12	988,493	438,887	19,721	68	30	1
Washington	9	837,135	568,334	58,906	57	39	4
West Virginia	6	484,964	277,435	—	64	36	—
Wisconsin	11	989,430	810,174	47,525	54	44	2
Wyoming	3	100,464	44,358	748	69	30	1
Total Popular Votes		47,167,319	29,169,504	1,102,963			
Total Popular Vote, all candidates		77,704,756					

Minor candidates: Dr. Benjamin Spock (People's party), 78,801; Linda Jennis or Evelyn Reed (Socialist Workers), 65,290; Louis Fisher (Socialist Labor), 53,614; Gus Hall (Communist party), 25,229; Earle H. Munn (Prohibition party), 13,444; John Hospers (Libertarian), 2,691; others, 25,901.

UNCOMPLETED TERMS OF PRESIDENTS AND VICE-PRESIDENTS

President	Term	Succeeded by
William H. Harrison	Mar. 4, 1841 —Apr. 4, 1841	John Tyler
Zachary Taylor	Mar. 5, 1849 —July 9, 1850	Millard Fillmore
Abraham Lincoln	Mar. 4, 1865 —Apr. 15, 1865 (2d term)	Andrew Johnson
James A. Garfield	Mar. 4, 1881 —Sept. 19, 1881	Chester A. Arthur
William McKinley	Mar. 4, 1901 —Sept. 14, 1901 (2d term)	Theodore Roosevelt
Warren G. Harding	Mar. 4, 1921 —Aug. 2, 1923	Calvin Coolidge
Franklin D. Roosevelt	Jan. 20, 1945—Apr. 12, 1945 (4th term)	Harry S. Truman
John F. Kennedy	Jan. 20, 1961—Nov. 22, 1963	Lyndon B. Johnson
Richard M. Nixon	Jan. 20, 1973—Aug. 9, 1974 (2d term)	Gerald R. Ford

Vice-President	Term	Vice-President	Term
George Clinton	Mar. 4, 1809—Apr. 20, 1812 (2d term)	Thomas A. Hendricks	Mar. 4, 1885—Nov. 25, 1885
Elbridge Gerry	Mar. 4, 1813—Nov. 23, 1814	Garret A. Hobart	Mar. 4, 1897—Nov. 21, 1899
John C. Calhoun[1]	Mar. 4, 1829—Dec. 28, 1832	James S. Sherman	Mar. 4, 1909—Oct. 30, 1912
William R. King	Mar. 4, 1853—Apr. 18, 1853	Spiro T. Agnew[2]	Jan. 20, 1973—Oct. 10, 1973
Henry Wilson	Mar. 4, 1873—Nov. 22, 1875		

[1] Calhoun resigned to become a U.S. Senator. [2] Agnew resigned after pleading "no contest" to a charge of income tax evasion. He was succeeded by Gerald R. Ford, the first man to succeed to the office.

FINAL 1976 PRESIDENTIAL ELECTION RESULTS

State	Electoral Vote	Popular Vote				Percentages			
		Carter	Ford	McCarthy	Other	Carter	Ford	McCarthy	Other
Alabama	9	659,170	504,070	—	19,610	56	43	—	1
Alaska	3	44,058	71,555	—	7,961	36	58	—	6
Arizona	6	295,602	418,642	19,229	9,246	40	56	3	1
Arkansas	6	498,604	267,903	639	389	65	35	—	—
California	45	3,742,284	3,882,244	—	179,242	48	50	—	2
Colorado	7	460,801	584,278	26,047	10,314	43	54	2	1
Connecticut	8	647,895	719,261	—	19,199	47	52	—	1
Delaware	3	122,461	109,780	2,432	969	52	47	1	—
Dist. Columbia	3	137,818	27,873	—	3,139	82	17	—	1
Florida	17	1,636,000	1,469,531	23,643	21,457	52	47	1	—
Georgia	12	979,409	483,743	—	—	67	33	—	—
Hawaii	4	147,375	140,003	—	3,923	51	48	—	1
Idaho	4	126,549	204,151	—	10,232	37	60	—	3
Illinois	26	2,271,295	2,364,269	55,939	29,779	48	50	1	1
Indiana	13	1,014,714	1,185,958	—	21,690	46	53	—	1
Iowa	8	619,931	632,863	20,051	6,461	48	49	2	1
Kansas	7	430,421	502,752	13,185	11,487	45	53	1	1
Kentucky	9	615,717	531,852	6,837	12,736	53	46	—	1
Louisiana	10	661,365	587,446	6,490	22,082	52	46	—	2
Maine	4	232,279	236,320	10,874	3,495	48	49	2	1
Maryland	10	759,612	672,661	—	—	53	47	—	—
Massachusetts	14	1,429,475	1,030,276	65,637	22,170	56	40	3	1
Michigan	21	1,696,714	1,893,742	47,905	13,229	47	52	1	—
Minnesota	10	1,070,440	819,395	35,490	24,606	55	42	2	1
Mississippi	7	381,329	366,846	4,074	16,141	50	48	—	2
Missouri	12	998,387	927,443	24,029	3,741	51	48	1	—
Montana	4	149,259	173,703	—	5,772	45	53	—	2
Nebraska	5	233,293	359,219	9,383	4,854	38	59	2	1
Nevada	3	92,479	101,273	—	8,124	46	50	—	4
New Hampshire	4	147,645	185,935	4,095	1,952	43	55	1	1
New Jersey	17	1,444,653	1,509,688	32,717	27,414	48	50	1	1
New Mexico	4	201,148	211,419	—	4,023	48	51	—	1
New York	41	3,389,558	3,100,791	—	177,913	51	46	—	3
North Carolina	13	927,365	741,960	—	8,581	55	44	—	1
North Dakota	3	136,078	153,684	2,952	4,594	46	52	—	2
Ohio	25	2,009,959	2,000,626	58,267	41,604	49	49	1	1
Oklahoma	8	532,442	545,708	14,101	—	49	50	1	—
Oregon	6	490,407	492,120	40,207	7,142	48	48	4	—
Pennsylvania	27	2,328,677	2,205,604	50,584	35,922	50	48	1	1
Rhode Island	4	227,636	181,249	—	1,699	55	44	—	1
South Carolina	8	450,807	346,149	—	5,627	56	43	—	1
South Dakota	4	147,068	151,505	—	2,105	49	50	—	1
Tennessee	10	825,879	633,969	5,004	11,494	56	43	—	1
Texas	26	2,082,319	1,953,300	20,118	16,147	51	48	1	—
Utah	4	182,110	337,908	3,907	17,293	34	62	1	3
Vermont	3	77,798	100,387	4,001	1,716	42	55	2	1
Virginia	12	813,896	836,554	—	46,644	48	49	—	3
Washington	9	717,323	777,732	36,986	23,493	46	50	2	2
West Virginia	6	435,864	314,726	—	—	58	42	—	—
Wisconsin	11	1,040,232	1,004,987	34,943	21,174	49	48	2	1
Wyoming	3	62,239	92,717	624	763	40	59	—	1
Total Popular Votes		**40,825,839**	**39,147,770**	**680,390**	**949,348**				
Total Popular Votes, all candidates		**81,603,346**							

Minor candidates: Roger McBride (Libertarian Party), 171,627; Lester G. Maddox (American Independent Party), 168,264; Thomas Anderson (American Party), 152,513; Peter Camejo (Socialist Workers Party), 90,287; Gus Hall (Communist Party), 58,692; Margaret Wright (People's Party), 49,014; Lyndon H. LaRouche (U.S. Labor Party), 40,043; Benjamin C. Bubar (Prohibition Party), 15,902; Jules Levin (Socialist Labor Party), 9,322; Frank P. Zeidler (Socialist Party), 5,991; Others, 187,693.

ELECTION OF 1976

The Political Scene: Following the turmoil of the second Nixon administration, with the resignation of Spiro T. Agnew and then Nixon himself, Gerald R. Ford hoped to retain the Presidency, a position to which he had never been elected. The Democrats saw an opportunity to regain the White House by stressing the need for a return to "moral" government, while Eugene J. McCarthy of Minnesota, an independent, campaigned on a platform which called for the abolition of the two-party system, one which he felt made the government less responsive to the will of the people.

Conventions and Nominees: In July the Democrats met in New York City, with Jimmy Carter of Georgia virtually assured a first-ballot nomination after a string of primary victories. Walter F. Mondale of Minnesota was chosen the Vice-Presidential nominee. Incumbent Gerald R. Ford of Michigan successfully fought off a conservative challenge by Ronald W. Reagan of California in the Republicans' August convention in Kansas City, Missouri. Robert J. Dole of Kansas was selected by Ford to be his running mate. McCarthy picked Willam Clay Ford of Michigan to share his independent ticket.

RESULTS OF 1976 ELECTION

Presidential Candidate	Party	Electoral Votes	Popular Vote		Vice-Presidential Candidates
			Total	Percentage	
Jimmy Carter	Democratic	297	40,825,839	50.0+	Walter F. Mondale
Gerald R. Ford	Republican	240	39,147,770	47.9	Robert J. Dole
Ronald Reagan	No Party	1	—	—	

Comments: Carter was the first President elected from a southern state since Zachary Taylor in 1848.

THE WHITE HOUSE OFFICE

Assistant to the President
and Chief of Staff ...... Hamilton Jordan
Assistant to the President for
National Security Affairs ..... Zbigniew Brzezinski
Counsel to the President .... Lloyd N. Cutler
Chief of Staff to First Lady ..... Edith J. Dobelle
Senior Adviser .... Hedley Donovan
Assistant to the President for
Domestic Affairs and Policy ... Stuart E. Eizenstat
Assistant to the President for
Congressional Liaison .... Frank B. Moore
Assistant to the President for
Reorganization .... (vacant)
Press Secretary to the President .. Joseph L. Powell
Assistant to the President for
Communications .... Gerald M. Rafshoon
Secretary to the Cabinet and
Assistant to the President
for Intergovernmental Affairs .. Jack H. Watson, Jr.
Assistant to the President ...... Sarah C. Weddington
Assistant to the President ...... Ann Wexler
Special Assistant to the President
for Administration .... Hugh A. Carter, Jr.
Special Assistant to the President
for Information Management .. Richard M. Harden
Special Assistant to the
President .... Ray Jenkins
Advisor to the President
on Inflation .... Alfred E. Kahn
Staff Director .... Alonzo L. McDonald, Jr.
Special Assistant to the
President .... Louis E. Martin
Director of the Presidential
Personnel Office .... Arnie Miller
Special Assistant to the President
for Consumer Affairs .... Esther Peterson
Senior Advisor to the President .. Edward Sanders
Special Assistant to the
President .... Esteban E. Torres
Appointments Secretary to the
President .... Phillip J. Wise, Jr.
Counselor to the President
on Aging .... Nelson H. Cruikshank
Deputy Assistant for National
Security Affairs .... David L. Aaron
Deputy Press Secretary .... Patricia Y. Bario
Deputy Assistant to the
President .... Landon Butler
Deputy Assistant for Congressional
Liaison (House) .... William H. Cable
Deputy Assistant to the
President .... Michael H. Chanin
Deputy Assistant to the
President for Intergovernmental
Affairs and Deputy
Secretary to the Cabinet ..... Eugene Eidenberg
Deputy Assistant for
Congressional Liaison .... Leslie C. Francis
Deputy Press Secretary .... Rex L. Granum
Deputy Assistant .... Joel McCleary
Deputy Counsel .... Margaret A. McKenna
Deputy Assistant for Domestic
Affairs and Policy .... David M. Rubenstein
Deputy Assistant for
Communications .... Gregory S. Schneiders
Deputy Assistant for Congressional
Liaison (Senate) .... Danny C. Tate
Deputy Assistant .... Thomas V. Beard

Special Assistant for
Congressional Liaison .... Robert G. Beckel
Senior Associate Counsel ...... Michael H. Cardozo V
Personal Assistant/Secretary
to the President .... Susan S. Clough
Appointments Secretary to
the First Lady .... Jane S. Fenderson
Special Assistant for
Congressional Liaison (House) .. James C. Free
Associate Assistant for
Intergovernmental Affairs .... Lawrence D. Gilson
Deputy Assistant .... Richard Hernandez
Press Secretary to the First Lady
and Staff Coordinator .... Mary Finch Hoyt
Senior Associate Counsel ...... Douglas B. Huron
Staff Secretary .... Richard G. Hutcheson III
Associate Assistant for
Intergovernmental Affairs ..... Bruce Kirschenbaum
Special Assistant for
Congressional Liaison (House) .. Robert Maher
Special Assistant for
Congressional Liaison (House) .. Valerie F. Pinson
Deputy Assistant for Research ... Elizabeth A. Rainwater
Special Assistant for
Congressional Liaison .... Robert K. Russell, Jr.
Deputy Assistant .... S. Stephen Selig III
Special Assistant for
Congressional Liaison (House) .. Terrence D. Straub
Special Assistant for
Congressional Liaison
(Senate) .... Robert Thomson
Deputy Appointments Secretary .. Frances M. Voorde
Deputy Special Assistant —
Military Office .... Marvin L. Beaman, Jr.
Deputy Special Assistant for
Administration .... Valerio L. Giannini
Deputy Special Assistant for
White House Operations ...... Daniel Malachuk, Jr.
Personal Assistant to the
First Lady .... Madeline F. MacBean
Social Secretary .... Gretchen Poston
Deputy Director of the
Presidential Personnel Office .. Harley M. Frankel
Associate Assistant .... Jane D. Hartley
Associate Press Secretary ...... Claudia M. Townsend
Executive Speechwriter .... Bernard Aronson
Associate Director, Presidential
Personnel Office .... Peggy E. Rainwater
Special Assistant to the
Assistant for Domestic
Affairs and Policy .... Joanne K. Hurley
Associate Counsel .... Patrick Apodaca
Director of Projects for the
First Lady .... Kathryn E. Cade
Assistant Press Secretary
to the First Lady .... Paul Costello
Speechwriter .... Achsah P. Nesmith
Associate Press Secretary ...... Jerrold Schecter
Director, Research Office,
Domestic Affairs and Policy ... Stephen M. Travis
Director, Visitors Office .... Nancy A. Willing
Director of Advance .... Ellis A. Woodward
Editor, News Summary .... Patricia E. Bauer
Chief Executive Clerk .... Robert D. Linder
Physician to the President ..... Rear Adm. William M.
Lukash, MC USN
Chief Usher .... Rex W. Scouten

U.S. GOVERNMENT OFFICIALS: ANNUAL SALARIES SOURCE: Office of Personnel Management

Executive Branch		Legislative Branch		Judicial Branch	
President	$200,000	Speaker of the House	$75,000	Chief Justice	$75,000
Vice-President	75,000	President Pro Tem		Associate Justices	72,000
Top Executive		(Senate)	65,000	Judges of U.S. Court of	
Positions[1]		Majority and Minority		Appeals	57,500
I	66,000	Leaders	65,000	Judges of U.S. District	
II	57,500	Members of Congress	57,500	Court	54,500
III	52,500	Comptroller General	57,500	Director of the	
IV	50,000	Heads of Other		Administrative Office of the	
V	47,500	Legislative Agencies	50,000	United States Courts	54,500

[1] Top Executive positions are in levels I–V, ranging from Secretaries of Executive departments at level I to heads of major bureaus at level V; for a listing, see Sections 5312–5316 of Title 5, United States Code.

THE U.S. CABINET: 1979

Secretary of State: Cyrus Roberts Vance, b. March 27, 1917, Clarksburg, W. Va.; ed., Yale University (B.A., 1939; LL.B., 1942). He practiced law from 1949 to 1960 and from 1967 to 1977, served the Government in several special capacities from 1957 to 1962, and from 1967 to 1972, and was Secretary of the Army from 1962 to 1964. He assumed his cabinet post on Jan. 23, 1977.

Secretary of the Treasury: G. William Miller, b. Mar. 9, 1925, Sapulpa, Okla.; ed., U.S. Coast Guard Academy (B.S., 1945), University of California at Berkeley (J.D., 1952). After serving as a line officer in the U.S. Navy (1945-1949), he was in private law practice from 1952 to 1956. He joined a business firm in 1956 and later became. chairman of the board of a large U.S. conglomerate. In March 1978, he became chairman of the Federal Reserve Board. He assumed his cabinet post on August 6, 1979.

Secretary of Defense: Dr. Harold Brown, b. Sept. 19, 1927, New York, N.Y.; ed., Columbia University (A.B., 1945; A.M., 1946; Ph.D., 1949). He taught physics at Columbia University and Stevens Tech (1947-1952), worked in scientific laboratories from 1952 to 1961, and held several special government appointments from 1956 to 1965, when he became Air Force Secretary. He was president of California Institute of Technology from 1969 to 1977, and assumed his cabinet post on January 21, 1977.

Attorney General: Benjamin R. Civiletti, b. July 17, 1935, Peekskill, N.Y.; ed., Johns Hopkins University (B.A., 1950), University of Maryland Law School (LL.B., 1961). He was an assistant U.S. Attorney in Maryland (1962-1964), and practiced law from Oct. 1964 to Feb. 1977. He was appointed assistant attorney general in charge of the Criminal Division in the Justice Department, then promoted to Deputy Attorney General in May 1978. He assumed his position as Attorney General on August 16, 1979.

Secretary of the Interior: Cecil D. Andrus, b. Aug. 25, 1931, Hood River, Oreg.; ed., attended Oregon State University. In the Navy during the Korean conflict, he was an Idaho State Senator between 1960 and 1970, when he became Governor of the state (reelected 1974), and assumed his cabinet post on January 23, 1977.

Secretary of Agriculture: Bob S. Bergland, b. July 22, 1928, Roseau, Minn.; ed., University of Minnesota. A farmer since 1950, he served the state and federal governments from 1961 to 1968. A Congressman from 1970 to 1976, he was sworn in his cabinet post on January 23, 1977.

Secretary of Commerce: Juanita Morris Kreps, b. Jan. 11, 1921, Lynch, Ky.; ed., Berea College (A.B., 1942), Duke University (M.A., 1944). A university professor at Denison and Duke from 1945 on, she served in several executive business capacities, and in special government positions, and assumed.her post on Jan. 23, 1977 ★

Secretary of Labor: F. Ray Marshall, b. Aug. 22, 1928, Oak Grove, La.; ed., Millsaps College (B.A., 1949),

Louisiana State University (M.A., 1950), University of California.(Ph.D., 1954). A university professor at Mississippi, Louisiana State, Kentucky, and Texas from 1953 to 1976, he is the author of several books on labor economics. He was sworn in his post on Jan. 27, 1977.

Secretary of Health, Education, and Welfare: Patricia Roberts Harris, b. 1924, Mattoon, Ill.; ed., Howard University (A.B., 1945), George Washington University (J.D., 1960). Practicing law from 1960 to 1965, and from 1970 to 1976, she was Ambassador to Luxembourg (1965-1967) and a professor at Howard. She has been involved in the civil rights movement for more than 30 years. She became Secretary of Housing and Urban Development on January 23, 1977. She became Secretary of HEW on August 3, 1979.■

Secretary of Housing and Urban Development: Moon Landrieu, b. July 23, 1930, New Orleans, La.; ed., Loyola University - New Orleans (B.B.A., 1952) and (LL.B., 1954). He served in the Judge Advocate General Corps, U.S. Army (1954-1957). After practicing private law (1957-1969), he was elected to the Louisiana House of Representatives (1960-1965); councilman-at-large City of New Orleans (1966-1970); mayor of New Orleans (1970-1978), and served as president of the U.S. Conference of Mayors 1975 to 1976. After two terms as mayor, he became president of a commercial real estate firm. He assumed office on September 24, 1979.

Department of Transportation: Neil E. Goldschmidt, b. June 16, 1940, Eugene, Ore.; ed., University of Oregon (A.B. in Political Science - 1963), University of California Law School at Berkeley (LL.B., 1967). Interned in the Washington office of U.S. Senator Maurine Newberger (1964-1965), and participated in voter registration in Mississippi in 1964. Attorney with Legal Aid Society of Oregon from 1967 until elected to Portland City Council in 1970. Elected Mayor of Portland in 1972 and reelected in 1976. He assumed office on August 15, 1979 on a recess appointment.

Secretary of Energy: Charles W. Duncan, Jr., b. Sept. 9, 1926, Houston, Texas; ed., Rice University (B.S., 1947), and two years of graduate study in management at University of Texas. After service with the U.S. Army Air Corps in World War II, he joined an oil company as a chemical engineer. In 1948, he joined a food business, rising through the ranks to become president of a large soft drink corporation. On January 31, 1977, he became Deputy Secretary of Defense. He became Secretary of Energy on August 24, 1979.

■ **Secretary of Education**

CABINET LEVEL POSTS:

Counsel to the President: Lloyd N. Cutler

Special Representative for Trade Negotiations: Reubin O'D. Askew.

Director of the Office of Management and Budget: James T. McIntyre, Jr.

U.S. Ambassador to the United Nations: Donald F. McHenry

Assistant to the President and Chief of Staff: Hamilton Jordan

FEDERAL EMPLOYMENT†   Source: Office of Personnel Management

	Employees		Employees
Total, All Agencies	**2,869,197***	Interior	78,605
		Agriculture	117,484
		Commerce	43,043
LEGISLATIVE BRANCH	39,059	Labor	23,616
Congress	18,229	Health, Education, and Welfare	165,407
Architect of the Capitol	2,253	Housing and Urban Development	18,197
General Accounting Office	5,354	Transportation	73,283
Government Printing Office	7,298	Energy	20,255
Library of Congress	5,246	ACTION	2,013
JUDICIAL BRANCH	13,294	Environmental Protection Agency	12,967
		Equal Employment Opportunity Commission	2,643
EXECUTIVE BRANCH	2,816,844	Federal Communications Commission	2,127
Executive Office of the President	1,678	Federal Deposit Insurance Corporation	3,583
White House Office	382	Federal Trade Commission	1,912
Office of the Vice-President	26	General Services Administration	37,925
Office of Management and Budget	608	International Communication Agency	8,443
Council of Economic Advisors	35	Interstate Commerce Commission	2,117
		National Aeronautics and Space Administration	23,779
Executive Departments:		National Labor Relations Board	2,966
State (Includes AID)	30,030	Nuclear Regulatory Commission	3,008
Treasury	134,974	Office of Personnel Management	8,569
Defense:		Securities and Exchange Commission	2,057
Military, Total	934,629	Small Business Administration	5,717
Department of the Army	313,925	Smithsonian Institution	4,319
Department of the Navy	309,298	Tennessee Valley Authority	47,350
Department of the Air Force	235,232	U.S. Postal Service	658,221
Civilian, Total	32,955	Veterans Administration	224,942
Justice	54,508		

† List includes selected federal agencies with 1,500 or more employees. The total, however, represents all paid civilian employees of the U.S. government. Employees of the CIA, National Security Agency, and Special Youth Programs are not included. Data as of March 1979.   * Preliminary.   ■ On September 27, 1979 Congress gave final approval to a bill establishing a cabinet-level Department of Education. The Department of Health, Education and Welfare is renamed the Department of Health and Human Services.   ★ Submitted resignation, October 3, 1979.

HEADS OF FEDERAL DEPARTMENTS AND AGENCIES*

Departments and Agencies	Head
ACTION .... 806 Connecticut Avenue N.W. 20525	Samuel W. Brown, Jr. Director
Agency for Int'l Development 320 21st St. N.W. 20523	Douglas J. Bennett Administrator
American Battle Monuments ... Commission 1000 Independence Ave., S.W. 20314	Mark W. Clark Chairman
American National Red Cross ... 17th and D Sts. N.W. 20006	Jerome Holland Chairman
Architect of the Capitol .... The Capitol 20515	George M. White Architect of the Capitol
Central Intelligence Agency .... Washington, D.C. 20505	Adm. Stansfield Turner Director
Civil Aeronautics Board .... 1825 Connecticut Ave. N.W. 20428	Marvin S. Cohen Chairman
Commission of Fine Arts ...... 708 Jackson Pl. N.W. 20006	J. Carter Brown Chairman
Community Services Admin. ... 1200 19 St. N.W. 20506	Dr. Graciela Olivarez Director
Consumer Product Safety Commission 1111 18th St., N.W. 20207	Susan B. King Chairwoman
Council of Economic Advisers .. Executive Office Bldg. 20506	Charles L. Schultze Director
Council on Environmental .... Quality 722 Jackson Place N.W. 20006	Charles Warren Chairman
Council on Wage and Price .... Stability 726 Jackson Pl. N.W. 20506	R. Robert Russel Director
Department of Agriculture ..... 14th St. and Independence Ave. S.W. 20250	Bob S. Bergland Secretary of Agriculture
Deputy Secretary	Jim Williams
Department of Commerce ..... 14th St. between Constitution Ave. and E St. N.W. 20230	Juanita M. Kreps △ Secretary of Commerce
Under Secretary	Luther H. Hodges, Jr.
Patent & Trademark Office. Crystal Plaza, Arlington, Va.	Donald W. Banner Commissioner
Bureau of Economic Analysis 1401 K St. N.W. 20230	George Jaszi Director
Bureau of the Census .... Suitland, Md. 20233	Vincent P. Barabba Director
National Oceanic and Atmospheric Administration 6001 Executive Blvd., Rockville, Md. 20852	Richard A. Frank Administrator
Department of Defense .... The Pentagon 20301	Dr. Harold R. Brown Secretary of Defense
Deputy Secretary of Defense	W. Graham Claytor, Jr.
Joint Chiefs of Staff	Gen. David C. Jones USAF Chairman
Department of the .... Air Force The Pentagon 20330	Dr. Hans M. Mark Secretary of the Air Force
Department of the Army .... The Pentagon 20310	Clifford L. Alexander, Jr. Secretary of the Army
Department of the Navy ... The Pentagon 20350	Edward Hidalgo Secretary of the Navy
Commandant of the ..... Marine Corps	Gen. Robert H. Barrow
† Department of Education	
Department of Energy .... 1110 Independence Ave. S.W. 20314	Charles W. Duncan, Jr. Secretary of Energy
Deputy Secretary	John C. Sawhill
Federal Energy Regulatory ... Commission	Charles B. Curtis Chairman
Office of Energy Research ...	Nelson D. Pewitt (Acting)
Energy Information .... Administration	Lincoln E. Moses Administrator

Departments and Agencies	Head
†Department of Health, ... Education, and Welfare 330 Independence Ave. S.W. 20201	Patricia R. Harris Secretary of Health, Education, and Welfare
Under Secretary	Hale Champion
Office of Education	Dr. Ernest L. Boyer Commissioner
Office of Human Development Services	Arabella Martinez Ass't Sec. for Human Development Services
Public Health Service ... 5600 Fishers Lane, Rockville, Md. 20857	Julius B. Richmond Ass't Sec. for Health
Social Security .... Administration 330 Indiana Ave. S.W. 20201	Stanford G. Ross Commissioner
Department of Housing and ... Urban Development 451 7th St. S.W. 20410	Moon Landrieu Secretary of Housing and Urban Development
Under Secretary	Jay Janis
Department of the Interior .... C St. between 18th and 19th Sts. N.W. 20240	Cecil D. Andrus Secretary of the Interior
Under Secretary	James A. Joseph
Indian Affairs	Forrest J. Gerard Ass't Sec. - Indian Affairs
Bureau of Mines	Roger A. Markle Director
Geological Survey	H. William Menard Director
National Park Service	William J. Whalen Director
Department of Justice .... Constitution Ave. and 10th St. N.W. 20530	Benjamin R. Civiletti Attorney General
Deputy Attorney General ..	Charles F. C. Ruff (Acting)
Solicitor General	Wade Hampton McCree, Jr.
F.B.I. Director	William H. Webster
Immigration and Naturalization Service Commissioner	(vacant)
Department of Labor .... 200 Constitution Ave. N.W. 20210	F. Ray Marshall Secretary of Labor
Under Secretary	Robert J. Brown
Department of State .... 2201 C St. N.W. 20520	Cyrus R. Vance Secretary of State
Deputy Secretary of State .	Warren M. Christopher
Chief of Protocol	Abelardo L. Valdez
Department of Transportation ... 400 7th St. S.W. 20590	Neil E. Goldschmidt Secretary of Transportation
Deputy Secretary	Alan A. Butchman
U.S. Coast Guard, ... Commandant	Adm. John B. Hayes USCG
Federal Aviation .... Administrator	Langhorne M. Bond
Federal Highway .... Administrator	Karl S. Bowers
Federal Railroad .... Administrator	John M. Sullivan
St. Lawrence Seaway ..... Development Corporation	David W. Oberlin Administrator
Department of the Treasury .... 15th St. and Pennsylvania Ave. N.W. 20220	G. William Miller Secretary of the Treasury
Deputy Secretary	Robert Carswell
Commissioner of Customs .	Vernon D. Acrea
Bureau of Engraving ..... and Printing	Harry R. Clements Director
Bureau of the Mint	Stella B. Hackel Director
Commissioner of Public ... Debt	Hubert J. Hintgen
Commissioner, Internal ... Revenue Service	Jerome Kurtz
Comptroller of the .... Currency	John G. Heimann
Treasurer of the U.S.	Azie T. Morton
U.S. Secret Service	H. Stuart Knight Director
Bureau of Alcohol, ... Tobacco & Firearms	George R. Dickerson Director

* All addresses are Washington, D.C., unless otherwise noted.   † On September 27, 1979 Congress gave final approval to a bill establishing a cabinet-level Department of Education. The Department of Health, Education and Welfare is renamed the Department of Health and Human Services.   △ Submitted resignation, October 3, 1979.

District of Columbia .... Marion Barry
District Building, 14 St. & Mayor of the District
E St. N.W. 20004 of Columbia

Domestic Policy Staff .... Stuart Eizenstat
1600 Pennsylvania Ave. N.W. Ass't to the Pres. for
20500 Domestic Affairs and Policy

Environmental Protection ..... Douglas M. Costle
Agency Administrator
401 M St. S.W. 20460

Equal Employment .... Eleanor Holmes Norton
Opportunity Commission Chairperson
2401 E St. N.W. 20506

Farm Credit Administration ... Donald E. Wilkinson
490 L'Enfant Plaza East S.W. Governor
20578

Federal Communications ...... Charles D. Ferris
Commission Chairman
1919 M St. N.W. 20554

Federal Deposit .... Irvine Sprague
Insurance Corporation Chairman
550 17th St. N.W. 20429

Federal Election Commission .. Joan D. Aikens
1325 K St. N.W. 20463 Chairperson

Federal Maritime Commission .. Richard J. Daschbach
1100 L Street 20573 Chairman

Federal Mediation and .... Wayne L. Horvitz
Conciliation Service Director
2100 K St. N.W. 20427

Federal Reserve System, ... Paul A. Volcker
Board of Governors of the Chairman
Constitution Ave. and 20th
St. N.W. 20551

Federal Trade Commission ..... Michael Pertschuk
Pennsylvania Ave. and 6th Chairman
St. N.W. 20580

Foreign Claims Settlement ..... Richard W. Yarborough
Commission of the U.S. Chairman
1111 20th St. N.W. 20579

General Accounting Office ..... Elmer B. Staats
441 G St. N.W. 20548 Comptroller General

General Services Administration Rowland G. Freeman III
18th and F Sts. N.W. 20405 Administrator
Archivist of the U.S. ..... James B. Rhoads

Government Printing Office .... John J. Boyle
North Capitol and H Sts. N.W. Public Printer
20401

International Communication .. John E. Reinhardt
Agency Director
1750 Pennsylvania Ave. N.W.
20547

Interstate Commerce Commission A. Daniel O'Neal
12th St. and Constitution Chairman
Ave. N.W. 20423

Library of Congress .... Daniel J. Boorstin
10 First St. S.E. 20540 Librarian of Congress
Copyright Office .... Barbara A. Ringer
Crystal Mall Annex, Register of Copyrights
Arlington, Va. 20559

National Academy of Sciences .. Philip Handler
2101 Constitution Ave. N.W. President
20418

National Academy of .... Courtland D. Perkins
Engineering President
2101 Constitution Ave. N.W.
20418

National Aeronautics and ...... Robert A. Frosch
Space Administration Administrator
400 Maryland Ave. S.W. 20546

National Credit Union
Administration .... Lawrence Connell, Jr.
2025 M St. N.W. 20456 Administrator

National Foundation on
the Arts and the Humanities
National Endowment ..... Livingston L. Biddle, Jr.
for the Arts Chairman
2401 E St. N.W. 20520
National Endowment ..... Joseph D. Duffey
for the Humanities Chairman
806 15th St. N.W. 20506

National Labor Relations Board John H. Fanning
1717 Pennsylvania Ave. N.W. Chairman
20570

National Mediation Board ..... Robert O. Harris
1425 K St. N.W. 20572 Chairman

National Science Foundation ... Richard C. Atkinson
1800 G St. N.W. 20550 Director

National Security Council ..... Christine Dodson
Executive Off. Bldg. 20506 Staff Secretary

National Transportation Safety James B. King
Board .... Chairman
800 Independence Ave., SW
20594

Occupational Safety and Health Timothy F. Cleary
Review Commission Chairman
1825 K St. 20006

Office of Management and .... James T. McIntyre, Jr.
Budget Director
Executive Office Building 20503

Office of Personnel Management. Alan K. Campbell
1900 E. St. N.W. 20415 Chairman

Office of Technology Assessment Daniel DeSimone
600 Pennsylvania Ave. S.E. Acting Director
20003

Office of the Special Repre- Reubin O'D. Askew
sentative for Trade Negotia- Special Representative for
tions Trade Negotiations
1800 G St. N.W. 20506

Panama Canal Company ...... Thomas M. Constant
425 13th St. N.W. 20004 Secretary

Postal Rate Commission ...... Clyde S. DuPont
2000 L St. N.W. 20268 Chairman

Securities and Exchange ...... Harold M. Williams
Commission Chairman
500 N. Capitol St. N.W.
20549

Selective Service System ...... Robert E. Shuck
600 E St. N.W. 20435 Director

Small Business Administration . A. Vernon Weaver
1441 L St. N.W. 20416 Administrator

Smithsonian Institution ...... S. Dillon Ripley
1000 Jefferson Drive S.W. Secretary
20560

Tennessee Valley Authority .... S. David Freeman
400 Commerce Ave., Chairman
Knoxville, Tenn. 37902

United States Arms Control .... George M. Seignious II
and Disarmament Agency Director
320 21st N.W. 20451

U.S. Commission on Civil ..... Dr. Arthur S. Flemming
Rights Chairman
1121 Vermont Ave. N.W.
20425

United States International Trade Joseph O. Parker
Commission Chairman
701 E St. N.W. 20436

United States Postal Service ... William F. Bolger
475 L'Enfant Plaza West S.W. Postmaster General
20260

Veterans Administration ...... Max Cleland
810 Vermont Ave. N.W. 20420 Administrator

GOVERNORS OF THE STATES AND TERRITORIES
SOURCE: 1979 Congressional Directory

State or territory	Capital	Governor	Politics	Term of service	Expiration of term
STATE				Years	
Alabama	Montgomery	Fob James	D.	4	Jan. 1983
Alaska	Juneau	Jay S. Hammond	R.	4	Jan. 1983
Arizona	Phoenix	Bruce Babbitt	D.	4	Jan. 1983
Arkansas	Little Rock	Bill Clinton	D.	2	Jan. 1981
California	Sacramento	Edmund G. Brown, Jr.	D.	4	Jan. 1983
Colorado	Denver	Richard D. Lamm	D.	4	Jan. 1983
Connecticut	Hartford	Ella T. Grasso	D.	4	Jan. 1983
Delaware	Dover	Pierre S. du Pont IV	R.	4	Jan. 1981
Florida	Tallahassee	Robert Graham	D.	4	Jan. 1983
Georgia	Atlanta	George Busbee	D.	4	Jan. 1983
Hawaii	Honolulu	George R. Ariyoshi	D.	4	Dec. 1982
Idaho	Boise	John V. Evans	D.	4	Jan. 1983
Illinois	Springfield	James R. Thompson	R.	4	Jan. 1983
Indiana	Indianapolis	Otis R. Bowen	R.	4	Jan. 1981
Iowa	Des Moines	Robert D. Ray	R.	4	Jan. 1983
Kansas	Topeka	John Carlin	D.	4	Jan. 1983
Kentucky	Frankfort	Julian Carroll	D.	4	Dec. 1979
Louisiana	Baton Rouge	Edwin W. Edwards	D.	4	Mar. 1980
Maine	Augusta	Joseph E. Brennan	D.	4	Jan. 1983
Maryland	Annapolis	Harry R. Hughes	D.	4	Jan. 1983
Massachusetts	Boston	Edward J. King	D.	4	Jan. 1983
Michigan	Lansing	William G. Milliken	R.	4	Jan. 1983
Minnesota	St. Paul	Al Quie	R.	4	Jan. 1983
Mississippi	Jackson	Charles (Cliff) Finch	D.	4	Jan. 1980
Missouri	Jefferson City	Joseph P. Teasdale	D.	4	Jan. 1981
Montana	Helena	Thomas L. Judge	D.	4	Jan. 1980
Nebraska	Lincoln	Charles Thone	R.	4	Jan. 1983
Nevada	Carson City	Robert List	R.	4	Jan. 1983
New Hampshire	Concord	Hugh J. Gallen	D.	2	Jan. 1981
New Jersey	Trenton	Brendan T. Byrne	D.	4	Jan. 1982
New Mexico	Santa Fe	Bruce King	D.	4	Jan. 1983
New York	Albany	Hugh L. Carey	D.	4	Jan. 1983
North Carolina	Raleigh	James B. Hunt	D.	4	Jan. 1983
North Dakota	Bismarck	Arthur A. Link	D.	4	Jan. 1981
Ohio	Columbus	James A. Rhodes	R.	4	Jan. 1983
Oklahoma	Oklahoma City	George Nigh	D.	4	Jan. 1983
Oregon	Salem	Victor Atiyeh	R.	4	Jan. 1983
Pennsylvania	Harrisburg	Richard L. Thornburgh	R.	4	Jan. 1983
Rhode Island	Providence	J. Joseph Garrahy	D.	2	Jan. 1981
South Carolina	Columbia	Richard W. Riley	D.	4	Jan. 1983
South Dakota	Pierre	William Janklow	R.	4	Jan. 1983
Tennessee	Nashville	Lamar Alexander	R.	4	Jan. 1983
Texas	Austin	Bill Clements	R.	4	Jan. 1983
Utah	Salt Lake City	Scott M. Matheson	D.	4	Jan. 1981
Vermont	Montpelier	Richard A. Snelling	R.	2	Jan. 1981
Virginia	Richmond	John N. Dalton	R.	4	Jan. 1982
Washington	Olympia	Dixy Lee Ray	D.	4	Jan. 1981
West Virginia	Charleston	John D. Rockefeller IV	D.	4	Jan. 1981
Wisconsin	Madison	Lee S. Dreyfus	R.	4	Jan. 1983
Wyoming	Cheyenne	Ed Herschler	D.	4	Jan. 1983
COMMONWEALTH OF PUERTO RICO					
Puerto Rico	San Juan	Carlos Romero Barcelo	N.P.	4	Jan. 1981
TERRITORIES					
Guam	Agana	Paul Calvo	R.	4	Jan. 1983
Virgin Islands	Charlotte Amalie	Juan Luis	I.	4	Jan. 1982
American Samoa	Pago Pago	Peter Tali Coleman		3	Jan. 1981
Trust Territory of the Pacific Islands	Saipan, Marianas	Carlos S. Comacho	D.	4	Jan. 1982

VOTES CAST FOR MEMBERS OF THE U.S. HOUSE OF REPRESENTATIVES IN 1978 BY DISTRICT

Source: 1979 Congressional Directory

State and district	Vote cast in 1978 Democrat	Republican	State and district	Vote cast in 1978 Democrat	Republican	State and district	Vote cast in 1978 Democrat	Republican
Alabama:			**Connecticut:**			**Indiana:**		
1st	40,450	71,711	1st	102,749	67,828	1st	72,367	17,419
2d	49,341	57,924	2d	116,624	50,167	2d	82,402	52,842
3d	74,895	......	3d	96,830	66,663	3d	64,336	50,145
4th	87,380	......	4th	59,918	83,990	4th	42,238	80,527
5th	68,985	......	5th	96,738	88,162	5th	45,479	94,950
6th	40,771	65,700	6th	119,537	66,664	6th	66,421	60,630
7th	77,742	1,841				7th	67,469	86,955
						8th	76,654	83,019
Alaska:			**Delaware:**			9th	99,727	52,218
At large	55,176	68,811	At large	64,863	91,689	10th	73,343	55,999
						11th	61,504	45,809
Arizona:			**Florida:**					
1st	33,178	81,108	1st	85,608	49,715	**Iowa:**		
2d	67,878	58,697	2d	112,649	25,148	1st	45,037	79,940
3d	111,850	......	3d	NA	NA	2d	65,450	72,644
4th	48,661	90,768	4th	113,302	41,647	3d	34,880	103,659
			5th	101,867	106,319	4th	88,526	48,308
Arkansas			6th	40,654	150,694	5th	82,333	57,377
1st	NA	NA	7th	NA	NA	6th	87,139	44,320
2d	62,140	65,285	8th	NA	NA			
3d	35,748	130,086	9th	89,543	56,074	**Kansas:**		
4th	NA	NA	10th	NA	NA	1st	......	131,037
			11th	123,346	99,757	2d	70,460	76,419
California:			12th	107,037	66,610	3d	......	103,265
1st	125,122	85,690	13th	NA	NA	4th	100,139	43,854
2d	99,712	114,451	14th	65,202	38,081	5th	62,402	86,011
3d	105,537	91,966	15th	108,837	37,897			
4th	87,764	70,733				**Kentucky:**		
5th	106,046	52,603	**Georgia:**			1st	44,090	......
6th	81,801	33,515	1st	36,961	......	2d	36,441	......
7th	109,676	58,332	2d	42,234	......	3d	37,346	17,785
8th	94,824	70,481	3d	54,881	......	4th	32,212	62,087
9th	88,179	41,138	4th	60,284	14,221	5th	15,714	59,743
10th	84,488	41,374	5th	52,739	17,132	6th	47,436	52,092
11th	92,882	54,621	6th	39,451	47,078	7th	51,559	15,861
12th	34,472	116,982	7th	47,090	23,698			
13th	100,809	69,306	8th	41,184	......	**Louisiana:**		
14th	76,602	95,962	9th	47,264	14,172	1st	NA	NA
15th	75,212	49,914	10th	50,122	......	2d	NA	NA
16th	104,550	65,808				3d	NA	NA
17th	67,885	81,296				4th	65,583	65,317
18th	58,900	85,663	**Hawaii:**			5th	NA	NA
19th	41,672	123,192	1st	84,552	24,470	6th	NA	NA
20th	65,695	129,714	2d	118,272	15,697	7th	NA	NA
21st	73,869	44,519				8th	NA	NA
22d	54,442	99,502	**Idaho:**					
23rd	117,498	61,496	1st	57,972	86,680	**Maine:**		
24th	85,075	44,243	2d	60,040	80,591	1st	70,348	120,791
25th	45,881	22,205				2d	70,691	87,939
26th	......	113,059	**Illinois:**					
27th	85,880	89,392	1st	47,581	33,540	**Maryland:**		
28th	97,592	......	2d	80,906	11,104	1st	46,093	80,202
29th	65,214	11,512	3d	95,701	51,098	2d	98,601	49,886
30th	66,241	26,511	4th	46,788	94,435	3d	91,189	......
31st	55,667	26,490	5th	98,702	18,802	4th	43,663	71,374
32d	74,004	23,242	6th	44,543	87,193	5th	64,868	19,160
33d	62,540	79,533	7th	64,716	10,273	6th	126,196	14,545
34th	73,608	90,554	8th	81,457	13,302	7th	51,996	6,626
35th	80,388	68,442	9th	87,543	28,637	8th	81,851	77,807
36th	80,448	47,417	10th	89,479	88,829			
37th	60,463	106,581	11th	112,365	40,044	**Massachusetts:**		
38th	75,471	53,298	12th	28,424	110,503	1st	......	131,773
39th	63,891	112,160	13th	40,675	64,060	2d	101,570	37,881
40th	76,358	147,882	14th	39,438	118,741	3d	119,337	39,259
41st	77,540	107,685	15th	48,756	80,856	4th	111,353	......
42d	85,126	30,319	16th	40,471	76,752	5th	90,156	48,685
43d	76,308	167,150	17th	39,260	94,375	6th	97,099	83,511
			18th	44,527	85,973	7th	145,615	......
Colorado:			19th	......	89,770	8th	102,160	28,566
1st	82,742	49,845	20th	48,426	111,054	9th	106,805	......
2d	98,889	88,072	21st	27,054	97,473	10th	64,868	102,080
3d	69,669	69,303	22d	73,331	86,051	11th	133,644	......
4th	65,421	103,121	23d	74,247	25,858	12th	176,704	......
5th	52,194	91,933	24th	110,298	57,763			

NA = Not Available

State and district	Vote cast in 1978 Democrat	Republican
Michigan:		
1st	89,646	6,878
2d	45,631	97,503
3d	83,932	79,572
4th	38,204	95,440
5th	80,622	81,794
6th	97,971	74,718
7th	105,402	29,958
8th	103,346	51,900
9th	53,450	122,363
10th	94,913	89,451
11th	79,081	96,351
12th	82,892	68,063
13th	44,771	11,749
14th	84,032	40,716
15th	95,137	23,177
16th	93,387	26,827
17th	106,303	5,341
18th	113,037	36,913
19th	47,165	117,122
Minnesota:		
1st	83,271	110,090
2d	61,173	145,415
3d	67,120	128,759
4th	95,989	69,396
5th	91,673	55,412
6th	115,880	93,742
7th	93,055	106,573
8th	171,125	
Mississippi:		
1st	57,358	26,734
2d	57,678	35,730
3d	101,685	8,408
4th	34,837	68,225
5th		97,177
Missouri:		
1st	65,950	30,995
2d	102,911	79,495
3d	121,565	26,881
4th	120,748	45,116
5th	82,140	30,360
6th	76,061	96,574
7th	66,351	104,566
8th	96,509	63,109
9th	135,170	45,795
10th	99,148	52,687
Montana:		
1st	86,016	64,093
2d	57,480	75,766
Nebraska:		
1st	71,311	99,013
2d	77,135	70,309
3d	35,371	141,597
Nevada:		
At large	132,513	44,425
New Hampshire:		
1st	82,697	49,131
2d	39,546	84,535
New Jersey:		
1st	106,096	26,853
2d	112,768	56,997
3d	83,349	64,730
4th	69,259	41,833
5th	38,108	100,739
6th	56,874	89,446
7th	78,358	69,543
8th	69,496	23,842
9th	56,888	73,478
10th	55,074	8,066
11th	88,294	35,642
12th	34,423	94,850

State and district	Vote cast in 1978 Democrat	Republican
New Jersey—Continued:		
13th	71,808	77,301
14th	67,008	21,355
15th	55,944	53,108
New Mexico:		
1st	70,761	118,075
2d	95,710	
New York:		
1st	67,180	90,115*
2d	64,807	53,322*
3d	70,526	66,458*
4th	46,508	94,711*
5th	60,519*	84,864*
6th	80,799*	44,304
7th	73,066*	
8th	74,872*	15,165
9th	51,350	42,108*
10th	77,979*	
11th	58,997*	16,206*
12th	25,697*	3,580
13th	68,837*	16,002*
14th	31,339*	7,516
15th	49,272*	20,508
16th	59,703*	9,405*
17th	54,228	33,071*
18th	53,434*	60,867*
19th	59,731*	
20th	64,275*	11,661
21st	23,950*	
22d	58,727*	11,110*
23d	66,354	59,455*
24th	75,397	57,451*
25th	31,213	114,641
26th	41,870*	87,059
27th	83,413	66,177*
28th	139,575	36,017*
29th	84,705*	99,518*
30th	55,785*	85,478*
31st		107,791*
32d	76,251	67,071*
33d	58,286	82,501
34th		122,785*
35th	36,428	96,119
36th	99,497*	31,527*
37th	70,911*	17,585
38th		113,928*
39th	79,385	56,431*
North Carolina:		
1st	67,716	16,814
2d	61,851	15,988
3d	54,452	22,150
4th	74,249	
5th	68,778	58,161
6th	58,193	26,882
7th	53,696	23,146
8th	63,168	43,942
9th	29,761	66,157
10th		67,004
11th	75,460	65,832
North Dakota:		
At large	68,016	147,712
Ohio:		
1st	38,699	73,593
2d	64,522	58,716
3d	62,849	51,833
4th	39,360	85,575
5th	51,071	85,547
6th	46,318	85,592
7th		92,507
8th	32,493	81,156
9th	71,709	34,326
10th	35,309	99,329
11th	37,131	89,327
12th	61,698	81,573
13th	80,875	43,269
14th	82,356	31,311

State and district	Vote cast in 1978 Democrat	Republican
Ohio—Continued:		
15th	37,000	91,023
16th	29,640	105,152
17th	42,117	87,010
18th	71,894	48,931
19th	69,977	71,890
20th	76,973	
21st	58,934	9,533
22d	87,551	30,935
23d	99,975	33,732
Oklahoma:		
1st	73,886	49,404
2d	72,583	59,853
3rd	NA	NA
4th	62,993	41,421
5th	17,978	71,451
6th	103,512	36,031
Oregon:		
1st	158,706	93,640
2d	152,099	67,547
3d	151,895	
4th	124,745	96,953
Pennsylvania:		
1st	104,412	37,913
2d	132,594	25,785
3d	86,015	33,750
4th	87,555	110,445
5th	36,704	110,565
6th	106,431	37,746
7th	79,771	78,403
8th	89,276	56,776
9th	33,882	101,151
10th	35,721	116,003
11th	61,433	45,335
12th	104,216	47,442
13th	47,151	112,711
14th	68,004	49,992
15th	58,077	65,986
16th	27,386	91,910
17th	79,234	53,613
18th	88,299	65,088
19th	28,577	105,424
20th	97,745	37,745
21st	73,712	65,622
22d	99,559	39,518
23d	61,657	73,194
24th	48,894	87,041
25th	68,293	62,160
Rhode Island:		
1st	86,768	54,912
2d	87,397	78,725
South Carolina:		
1st	65,621	42,994
2d	52,598	71,032
3d	80,968	17,924
4th	45,357	51,483
5th	63,013	
6th	69,220	
South Dakota:		
1st	64,683	64,544
2d	55,516	70,780
Tennessee:		
1st	50,694	92,143
2d	27,745	125,082
3d	108,282	
4th	108,695	
5th	68,608	47,288
6th	38,954	114,630
7th	96,863	36,003
8th	80,776	33,679

* Total vote received, as candidate had one or more other party endorsement.   NA = Not Available

State and district	Vote cast in 1978 Democrat	Republican	State and district	Vote cast in 1978 Democrat	Republican	State and district	Vote cast in 1978 Democrat	Republican
Texas:			**Utah:**			**Washington (cont.)**		
1st	73,708	20,700	1st	93,892	85,028	5th	77,201	68,761
2d	66,986	28,584	2d	68,899	121,492	6th	71,057	43,640
3d	......	96,406				7th	67,450	59,052
4th	58,336	36,582	**Vermont:**					
5th	35,524	34,672	At large	23,228	90,688	**West Virginia:**		
6th	66,025	35,393				1st	76,372	44,062
7th	22,415	128,214	**Virginia:**			2d	69,683	56,272
8th	39,429	24,673	1st	34,578	89,158	3d	74,837	51,584
9th	50,792	29,473	2d	......	63,512	4th	70,035	......
10th	94,529	29,328	3d	104,550	14,453			
11th	53,354	49,965	4th	......	77,827	**Wisconsin:**		
12th	46,456	21,364	5th	83,575	......	1st	77,146	64,437
13th	75,271	25,275	6th	......	88,647	2d	99,631	71,412
14th	63,953	24,325	7th	46,950	84,517	3d	96,326	57,060
15th	54,560	27,853	8th	56,137	52,396	4th	101,575	52,125
16th	53,090	22,743	9th	47,367	76,877	5th	85,067	30,185
17th	69,030	32,302	10th	70,892	61,981	6th	48,785	114,742
18th	36,783	......				7th	110,874	65,750
19th	54,729	48,070	**Washington:**			8th	73,925	101,856
20th	51,584	......	1st	52,706	99,942	9th	75,207	118,386
21st	63,501	84,336	2d	70,620	66,793			
22d	53,443	54,643	3d	82,616	58,270	**Wyoming:**		
23d	62,649	......	4th	85,602	54,389	At large	53,522	75,855
24th	39,201	33,314						

An architectural masterpiece reminiscent of an ancient Roman temple, the Capitol sits on the crest of a knoll dominating the Capital City. It is not only a national shrine, but also a worldwide symbol of liberty and a monument to the hopes and aspirations of all mankind. Since 1800, except for a few short periods, it has been the seat of Congress; the flag flies over it day and night. Within its walls, political forces affecting the destiny of our land have recurrently and dramatically clashed. They have been resolved in the enactment of laws influencing the lives of all Americans.

The Capitol is situated on a plateau 88 feet above the level of the Potomac River and covers an area of 175,170 square feet, or approximately 4 acres. Its length, from north to south, is 751 feet 4 inches; its greatest width, including approaches, is 350 feet.

The plans for the original Capitol Building were presented to the Commissioners of Washington, D.C., by Dr. William Thornton in 1792. President Washington approved them in 1793, and in September, 1793, the cornerstone was laid.

Congress met in the new Capitol for the first time in November, 1800.

VOTES CAST FOR SENATORS IN 1974, 1976, AND 1978

SOURCE: 1979 Congressional Directory

(The figures show the vote for the Democratic and Republican nominees, except as otherwise indicated. Compiled from official statistics)

STATE	VOTE 1974 Democrat	1974 Republican	1976 Democrat	1976 Republican	1978 Democrat	1978 Republican	Total vote cast in 1978
Alabama	501,541	....	....	....	{ 401,852[1] { 547,054	316,170[1]	729,842[2] 582,005[2]
Alaska	54,361	38,914	....	....	29,574	92,783	122,741[2]
Arizona	229,523	320,396	400,334	321,236	....	....	....
Arkansas	461,056	82,026	....	....	395,506	84,308	517,138[2]
California	3,639,334	2,176,315	3,502,862	3,748,973	....	....	....
Colorado	471,688	325,526	....	....	330,148	480,801	819,256[2]
Connecticut	690,820	372,055	561,018	785,683	....	....	....
Delaware	....	....	98,042	125,454	93,930	66,479	162,072[2]
Florida	781,031	736,674	1,799,518	1,057,886	....	....	....
Georgia	627,376	246,866	....	....	536,320	108,808	645,128
Hawaii	207,454	....	162,305	122,724	....	....	....
Idaho	145,140	109,072	....	....	89,635	194,412	284,047
Illinois	1,811,496	1,084,884	....	....	1,448,187	1,698,711	3,184,764[2]
Indiana	889,269	814,117	868,522	1,275,833	....	....	....
Iowa	462,947	420,546	....	....	395,066	421,598	824,576[2]
Kansas	390,451	403,983	....	....	317,602	403,354	748,839[2]
Kentucky	398,887	328,260	....	....	290,730	175,766	476,783[2]
Louisiana	434,643	....	....	....	(c)	(c)	(c)
Maine	....	....	292,704	193,489	127,327	212,294	375,114[2]
Maryland	374,563	503,223	772,101	530,439	....	....	....
Massachusetts	....	....	1,726,657	722,641	1,093,283	890,584	2,044,076[2]
Michigan	....	....	1,831,031	1,635,087	1,484,193	1,362,165	2,846,630[2]
Minnesota	....	....	1,290,736	478,602	{ 538,675[5] { 638,375	957,908[5] 894,092	1,557,498[2] 1,580,550[2]
Mississippi	....	....	554,433	....	187,541	267,302	590,236[2]
Missouri	735,433	480,900	813,571	1,090,067	....	....	....
Montana	....	....	206,232	115,213	160,353	127,589	287,942
Nebraska	....	....	313,805	279,284	334,096	159,706	493,802
Nevada	78,981	79,605	127,214	63,471	....	....	....
New Hampshire	(a)	(a)	....	....	127,945	133,745	263,760[2]
New Jersey	....	....	1,681,140	1,054,508	1,082,960	844,200	1,957,515[2]
New Mexico	....	....	176,382	234,681	160,045	183,442	343,487
New York	1,973,781	2,340,188[3]	3,422,594[3]	2,836,633[3]	....	....	....
North Carolina	633,775	377,618	....	....	516,663	619,151	1,135,814
North Dakota	114,675	114,852	175,772	103,466	....	....	....
Ohio	1,930,670	918,133	1,941,113	1,823,774	....	....	....
Oklahoma	387,162	390,997	....	....	493,953	247,857	754,264[2]
Oregon	343,663[4]	420,984	....	....	341,616	550,165	892,518[2]
Pennsylvania	1,596,121	1,843,317	2,126,977	2,381,891	....	....	....
Rhode Island	....	....	167,665	230,329	229,557	76,061	305,618
South Carolina	356,126	146,645	....	....	280,146	351,917	632,063
South Dakota	147,929	130,955	....	....	84,767	170,832	255,599
Tennessee	....	....	751,180	673,231	466,228	642,644	1,157,094[2]
Texas	....	....	2,199,956	1,636,370	1,139,149	1,151,376	2,312,540[2]
Utah	185,377	210,299	223,948	290,221	....	....	....
Vermont	67,125	66,223	85,682	94,481	....	....	....
Virginia	....	....	(b)	(b)	608,511	613,232	1,222,256[2]
Washington	611,811	363,626	1,071,219	361,546	....	....	....
West Virginia	....	....	566,359	....	249,034	244,317	493,351
Wisconsin	740,700	429,327	1,396,970	521,902	....	....	....
Wyoming	....	....	70,558	84,810	50,456	82,908	133,364

(a) John A. Durkin, Democrat, elected by special election Sept. 16, 1975, for unexpired term ending Jan. 3, 1981.

(b) Harry F. Byrd, Jr., Independent, had 890,778 votes; E. R. Zumwalt, Democrat, had 596,009 votes; Martin H. Perper, Independent, had 70,559 votes.

(c) Figures not available.

[1] For unexpired term ending Jan. 3, 1981.

[2] Includes the vote for various other candidates.

[3] Total vote received, as candidate had one or more other party endorsements.

[4] Total votes for both Democratic candidates Betty Roberts (338,591) and Jason Boe (5,072).

[5] For unexpired term ending Jan. 3, 1983.

U.S. CONGRESSIONAL REPRESENTATIVES UNDER EACH APPORTIONMENT: 1790-1970

State	1790	1800	1810	1820	1830	1840	1850	1860	1870	1880	1890	1900	1910[1]	1930	1940	1950	1960	1970
Alabama			[2]1	3	5	7	7	6	8	8	9	9	10	9	9	9	8	7
Alaska																[2]1	1	1
Arizona													[2]1	1	2	2	3	4
Arkansas					[2]1	1	2	3	4	5	6	7	7	7	7	6	4	4
California							[2]2	3	4	6	7	8	11	20	23	30	38	43
Colorado										[2]1	1	2	3	4	4	4	4	5
Connecticut	5	7	7	7	6	6	4	4	4	4	4	4	5	5	6	6	6	6
Delaware	1	1	1	2	1	1	1	1	1	1	1	1	1	1	1	1	1	1
Florida						[2]1	1	1	2	2	2	3	4	5	6	8	12	15
Georgia	3	2	4	6	7	9	8	8	7	9	10	11	11	12	10	10	10	10
Hawaii																[2]1	2	2
Idaho											[2]1	1	1	2	2	2	2	2
Illinois			[2]1	1	3	7	9	14	19	20	22	25	27	27	26	25	24	24
Indiana			[2]1	3	7	10	11	11	13	13	13	13	13	12	11	11	11	11
Iowa						[2]2	2	6	9	11	11	11	11	9	8	8	7	6
Kansas								1	3	7	8	8	8	7	6	6	5	5
Kentucky		2	6	10	12	13	10	10	9	10	11	11	11	9	9	8	7	7
Louisiana			[2]1	3	3	4	4	5	6	6	6	7	8	8	8	8	8	8
Maine				[3]7	8	7	7	6	5	5	4	4	4	3	3	3	2	2
Maryland	6	8	9	9	8	6	6	6	6	6	6	6	6	6	6	7	8	8
Massachusetts	8	14	17	[3]13	13	12	10	11	10	11	12	13	14	16	15	14	14	12
Michigan					[2]1	3	4	6	9	11	12	12	13	17	17	18	19	19
Minnesota							[2]2	2	3	5	7	9	10	9	9	9	8	8
Mississippi			[2]1	1	2	4	5	5	6	7	7	8	8	7	7	6	5	5
Missouri				1	2	5	7	9	13	14	15	16	16	13	13	11	10	10
Montana											[2]1	1	1	2	2	2	2	2
Nebraska								[2]1	1	3	6	6	6	5	4	4	3	3
Nevada								[2]1	1	1	1	1	1	1	1	1	1	1
New Hampshire	3	4	5	6	6	5	4	3	3	3	2	2	2	2	2	2	2	2
New Jersey	4	5	6	6	6	5	5	5	7	7	8	10	12	14	14	14	15	15
New Mexico													[2]1	1	2	2	2	2
New York	6	10	17	27	34	40	34	33	31	33	34	37	43	45	45	43	41	39
North Carolina	5	10	12	13	13	13	9	8	7	9	9	10	10	11	12	11	11	11
North Dakota											[2]1	2	3	2	2	2	2	1
Ohio		[2]1	6	14	19	21	21	19	20	21	21	21	22	24	23	23	24	23
Oklahoma												[2]5	8	9	8	6	6	6
Oregon							[2]1	1	1	1	2	2	3	3	4	4	4	4
Pennsylvania	8	13	18	23	26	28	24	25	24	27	28	30	32	36	34	33	27	25
Rhode Island	1	2	2	2	2	2	2	2	2	2	2	2	3	3	2	2	2	2
South Carolina	5	6	8	9	9	9	7	6	5	5	7	7	7	7	6	6	6	6
South Dakota											[2]2	2	3	2	2	2	2	2
Tennessee	[2]1	3	6	9	13	11	10	8	10	10	10	10	10	9	10	9	9	8
Texas						[2]2	2	4	6	11	13	16	18	21	21	22	23	24
Utah												[2]1	2	2	2	2	2	2
Vermont		2	4	6	5	5	4	3	3	3	2	2	2	1	1	1	1	1
Virginia	10	19	22	23	22	21	15	13	11	9	10	10	10	9	9	10	10	10
Washington											[2]2	3	5	6	6	7	7	7
West Virginia									3	4	4	5	6	6	6	6	5	4
Wisconsin						[2]2	3	6	8	9	10	11	11	10	10	10	10	9
Wyoming											[2]1	1	1	1	1	1	1	1
Total	65	106	142	186	213	242	232	237	243	293	332	357	391	435	435	435	437	435

[1] No apportionment was made in 1920. [2] The following representation was added after the several census apportionments indicated when new States were admitted and is included in the above table: First. Tennessee, 1. Second. Ohio, 1. Third. Alabama, 1; Illinois, 1; Indiana, 1; Louisiana, 1; Mississippi, 1. Fifth. Arkansas, 1; Michigan, 1. Sixth. California, 2; Florida, 1; Iowa, 2; Texas, 2; Wisconsin, 2. Seventh. Minnesota, 2; Oregon, 1. Eighth. Nebraska, 1; Nevada, 1. Ninth. Colorado, 1. Tenth. Idaho, 1; Montana, 1; North Dakota, 1; South Dakota, 2; Washington, 2. Eleventh. Wyoming, 1. Twelfth. Utah, 1. Thirteenth. Arizona, 1; New Mexico, 1. Seventeenth. Alaska, 1; Hawaii, 1. [3] Twenty Members were assigned to Massachusetts, but 7 of these were credited to Maine when that area became a State.

THE HOUSE OF REPRESENTATIVES

Democratic members are in roman, Republicans in *italics*.

Ninety-Sixth Congress, First Session

Democrats (276); *Republicans (159)*; Total: 435

Speaker: Thomas P. O'Neill, Jr., Mass.
Majority Leader: James C. Wright, Jr., Texas
Majority Whip: John Brademas, Ind.
Minority Leader: *John J. Rhodes*, Ariz.
Minority Whip: *Robert H. Michel*, Ill.

Clerk: Edmund L. Henshaw, Jr.
Sergeant at Arms: Kenneth R. Harding
Parliamentarian: William Holmes Brown
Doorkeeper: James T. Molloy
Postmaster: Robert V. Rota
Press Gallery Superintendent: Benjamin C. West
Chaplain: Rev. James David Ford, B.D., A.B.

HOUSE MEMBERS BY STATE AND DISTRICT   Democratic members are in roman, Republicans in *italics*.

Dist.	Representative	Residence
Alabama		
1.	*Jack Edwards*	Mobile
2.	*William L. Dickinson*	Montgomery
3.	Bill Nichols	Sylacauga
4.	Tom Bevill	Jasper
5.	Ronnie G. Flippo	Florence
6.	*John H. Buchanan, Jr.*	Birmingham
7.	Richard C. Shelby	Tuscaloosa
Alaska		
	°*Don Young*	Fort Yukon
Arizona		
1.	*John J. Rhodes*	Mesa
2.	Morris K. Udall	Tucson
3.	Bob Stump	Tolleson
4.	*Eldon Rudd*	Scottsdale
Arkansas		
1.	Bill Alexander	Osceola
2.	*Edwin R. Bethune, Jr.*	Searcy
3.	*John P. Hammerschmidt*	Harrison
4.	Beryl F. Anthony, Jr.	El Dorado
California		
1.	Harold T. Johnson	Roseville
2.	*Don H. Clausen*	Crescent City
3.	Robert T. Matsui	Sacramento
4.	Vic Fazio	Sacramento
5.	John L. Burton	San Francisco
6.	Phillip Burton	San Francisco
7.	George Miller	Martinez
8.	Ronald V. Dellums	Berkeley
9.	Fortney H. Stark, Jr.	Oakland
10.	Don Edwards	San Jose
11.	*Bill Royer*	Redwood City
12.	*Paul N. McCloskey, Jr.*	Menlo Park
13.	Norman Y. Mineta	San Jose
14.	*Norman D. Shumway*	Stockton
15.	Tony Coelho	Merced
16.	Leon E. Panetta	Carmel Valley
17.	*Charles Pashayan, Jr.*	Fresno
18.	*William Thomas*	Bakersfield
19.	*Robert J. Lagomarsino*	Ventura
20.	*Barry M. Goldwater, Jr.*	Woodland Hills
21.	James C. Corman	Van Nuys
22.	*Carlos J. Moorhead*	Glendale
23.	Anthony C. Beilenson	Los Angeles
24.	Henry A. Waxman	Los Angeles
25.	Edward R. Roybal	Los Angeles
26.	*John H. Rousselot*	San Marino
27.	*Robert K. Dornan*	Santa Monica
28.	Julian C. Dixon	Los Angeles
29.	Augustus F. Hawkins	Los Angeles
30.	George E. Danielson	Monterey Park
31.	Charles H. Wilson	Hawthorne
32.	Glenn M. Anderson	Harbor City
33.	*Wayne Grisham*	La Mirada
34.	*Daniel E. Lungren*	Long Beach
35.	James F. "Jim" Lloyd	West Covina
36.	George E. Brown, Jr.	Riverside
37.	*Jerry Lewis*	Highland
38.	Jerry M. Patterson	Santa Ana
39.	*William E. Dannemeyer*	Fullerton
40.	*Robert E. Badham*	Newport Beach
41.	*Bob Wilson*	San Diego
42.	Lionel Van Deerlin	San Diego
43.	*Clair W. Burgener*	La Jolla
Colorado		
1.	Patricia Schroeder	Denver
2.	Timothy E. Wirth	Denver
3.	Ray Kogovsek	Pueblo
4.	*James P. Johnson*	Fort Collins
5.	*Ken Kramer*	Colorado Springs
Connecticut		
1.	William R. Cotter	Hartford
2.	Christopher J. Dodd	Norwich
3.	Robert N. Giaimo	North Haven
4.	*Stewart B. McKinney*	Fairfield
5.	William Ratchford	Danbury
6.	Toby Moffett	Unionville
Delaware		
	°*Thomas B. Evans, Jr.*	Wilmington

* Representative at large.

Dist.	Representative	Residence
Florida		
1.	Earl Hutto	Panama City
2.	Don Fuqua	Altha
3.	Charles E. Bennett	Jacksonville
4.	William V. Chappell, Jr.	Ocala
5.	Richard Kelly	Zephyrhills
6.	*C. W. Young*	St. Petersburg
7.	Sam M. Gibbons	Tampa
8.	Andrew P. Ireland	Winter Haven
9.	Bill Nelson	Melbourne
10.	*L. A. Bafalis*	Fort Myers Beach
11.	Dan Mica	West Palm Beach
12.	Edward J. Stack	Fort Lauderdale
13.	William Lehman	North Miami Beach
14.	Claude D. Pepper	Miami
15.	Dante B. Fascell	Miami
Georgia		
1.	Ronald "Bo" Ginn	Millen
2.	M. Dawson Mathis	Albany
3.	Jack T. Brinkley	Columbus
4.	Elliott H. Levitas	Atlanta
5.	Wyche Fowler, Jr.	Atlanta
6.	*Newt Gingrich*	Carrollton
7.	Larry P. McDonald	Marietta
8.	Billy Lee Evans	Macon
9.	Edgar L. Jenkins	Jasper
10.	D. Douglas Barnard, Jr.	Augusta
Hawaii		
1.	Cecil Heftel	Honolulu
2.	Daniel K. Akaka	Honolulu
Idaho		
1.	*Steven D. Symms*	Caldwell
2.	*George V. Hansen*	Pocatello
Illinois		
1.	Bennett Stewart	Chicago
2.	Morgan F. Murphy	Chicago
3.	Martin A. Russo	South Holland
4.	*Edward J. Derwinski*	Flossmoor
5.	John G. Fary	Chicago
6.	*Henry J. Hyde*	Bensenville
7.	Cardiss Collins	Chicago
8.	Dan Rostenkowski	Chicago
9.	Sidney R. Yates	Chicago
10.		
11.	Frank Annunzio	Chicago
12.	*Philip M. Crane*	Mount Prospect
13.	*Robert McClory*	Lake Bluff
14.	*John N. Erlenborn*	Glen Ellyn
15.	*Tom Corcoran*	Ottawa
16.	*John B. Anderson*	Rockford
17.	*George M. O'Brien*	Joliet
18.	*Robert H. Michel*	Peoria
19.	*Tom Railsback*	Moline
20.	*Paul Findley*	Pittsfield
21.	Edward R. Madigan	Lincoln
22.	*Daniel B. Crane*	Danville
23.	Charles Melvin Price	East St. Louis
24.	Paul Simon	Carbondale
Indiana		
1.	Adam Benjamin, Jr.	Hobart
2.	Floyd J. Fithian	Lafayette
3.	John Brademas	South Bend
4.	*Dan Quayle*	Huntington
5.	*Elwood H. Hillis*	Kokomo
6.	David W. Evans	Indianapolis
7.	*John T. Myers*	Covington
8.	*H. Joel Deckard*	Evansville
9.	Lee H. Hamilton	Columbus
10.	Philip R. Sharp	Muncie
11.	Andrew Jacobs, Jr.	Indianapolis
Iowa		
1.	*Jim Leach*	Davenport
2.	*Thomas J. Tauke*	Dubuque
3.	*Charles E. Grassley*	New Hartford
4.	Neal Smith	Altoona
5.	Tom Harkin	Ames
6.	Berkley W. Bedell	Spirit Lake

Dist. Representative	Residence
Kansas	
1. *Keith G. Sebelius*	Norton
2. *Jim Jeffries*	Atchison
3. *Larry Winn, Jr.*	Overland Park
4. Daniel R. Glickman	Wichita
5. *Robert Whittaker*	Augusta
Kentucky	
1. Carroll Hubbard, Jr.	Mayfield
2. William H. Natcher	Bowling Green
3. Romano L. Mazzoli	Louisville
4. *M. Gene Snyder*	Jefferson Co.
5. *Tim Lee Carter*	Tompkinsville
6. Larry Hopkins	Lexington
7. Carl D. Perkins	Hindman
Louisiana	
1. *Robert L. Livingston, Jr.*	New Orleans
2. Corinne "Lindy" Boggs	New Orleans
3. *David C. Treen*	Metairie
4. Claude Leach	Leesville
5. Thomas J. Huckaby	Ringgold
6. *W. Henson Moore*	Baton Rouge
7. John B. Breaux	Crowley
8. Gillis W. Long	Alexandria
Maine	
1. *David F. Emery*	Rockland
2. *Olympia J. Snowe*	Auburn
Maryland	
1. *Robert E. Bauman*	Easton
2. Clarence D. Long	Ruxton
3. Barbara A. Mikulski	Baltimore
4. *Marjorie S. Holt*	Severna Park
5. Gladys N. Spellman	Laurel
6. Beverly Byron	Frederick
7. Parren J. Mitchell	Baltimore
8. Michael D. Barnes	Kensington
Massachusetts	
1. *Silvio O. Conte*	Pittsfield
2. Edward P. Boland	Springfield
3. Joseph D. Early	Worcester
4. Robert F. Drinan	Newton
5. James M. Shannon	Lawrence
6. Nicholas Mavroules	Peabody
7. Edward J. Markey	Malden
8. Thomas P. O'Neill, Jr.	Cambridge
9. John "Joe" Moakley	Boston
10. *Margaret M. Heckler*	Wellesley
11. Brian J. Donnelly	Dorchester
12. Gerry E. Studds	Cohasset
Michigan	
1. John Conyers, Jr.	Detroit
2. *Carl D. Pursell*	Plymouth
3. Howard Wolpe	Lansing
4. *David A. Stockman*	St. Joseph
5. *Harold S. Sawyer*	Rockford
6. Bob Carr	East Lansing
7. Dale E. Kildee	Flint
8. M. Robert Traxler	Bay City
9. *Guy A. Vander Jagt*	Luther
10. Don Albosta	St. Charles
11. *Robert W. Davis*	Gaylord
12. David E. Bonior	Mount Clemens
13. Charles C. Diggs, Jr.	Detroit
14. Lucien N. Nedzi	Detroit
15. William D. Ford	Taylor
16. John D. Dingell	Trenton
17. William M. Brodhead	Detroit
18. James J. Blanchard	Pleasant Ridge
19. *William S. Broomfield*	Birmingham
Minnesota	
1. *Arlen Erdahl*	West St. Paul
2. *Thomas M. Hagedorn*	Truman
3. *Bill Frenzel*	Golden Valley
4. Bruce F. Vento	St. Paul
5. Martin O. Sabo	Minneapolis
6. Richard M. Nolan	Waite Park
7. Arlan Stangeland	Barnesville
8. James L. Oberstar	Chisholm
Mississippi	
1. Jamie L. Whitten	Charleston
2. David R. Bowen	Cleveland
3. G. V. Montgomery	Meridian
4. *John C. Hinson*	Tylertown
5. *Trent Lott*	Pascagoula

Dist. Representative	Residence
Missouri	
1. William L. Clay	St. Louis
2. Robert A. Young	Maryland Heights
3. Richard A. Gephardt	St. Louis
4. Ike Skelton	Lexington
5. Richard Bolling	Kansas City
6. *E. Thomas Coleman*	Kansas City
7. *Gene Taylor*	Sarcoxie
8. Richard H. Ichord	Houston
9. Harold L. Volkmer	Hannibal
10. Bill D. Burlison	Cape Girardeau
Montana	
1. Pat Williams	Helena
2. *Ronald C. Marlenee*	Scobey
Nebraska	
1. *Douglas K. Bereuter*	Utica
2. John J. Cavanaugh	Omaha
3. *Virginia Smith*	Chappell
Nevada	
*James D. Santini	Las Vegas
New Hampshire	
1. Norman E. D'Amours	Manchester
2. *James C. Cleveland*	New London
New Jersey	
1. James J. Florio	Camden
2. William J. Hughes	Ocean City
3. James J. Howard	Spring Lake Heights
4. Frank Thompson, Jr.	Trenton
5. *Millicent H. Fenwick*	Bernardsville
6. *Edwin B. Forsythe*	Moorestown
7. Andrew Maguire	Ridgewood
8. Robert A. Roe	Wayne
9. *Harold C. Hollenbeck*	E. Rutherford
10. Peter W. Rodino, Jr.	Newark
11. Joseph G. Minish	West Orange
12. *Matthew J. Rinaldo*	Union
13. *James A. Courter*	Hackettstown
14. Frank J. Guarini	Jersey City
15. Edward J. Patten	Perth Amboy
New Mexico	
1. *Manuel Lujan, Jr.*	Albuquerque
2. Harold Runnels	Lovington
New York	
1. *William Carney*	Hauppauge
2. Thomas J. Downey	West Islip
3. Jerome A. Ambro	Huntington Station
4. *Norman F. Lent*	East Rockaway
5. *John W. Wydler*	Garden City
6. Lester L. Wolff	Great Neck
7. Joseph P. Addabbo	Ozone Park
8. Benjamin S. Rosenthal	Elmhurst
9. Geraldine A. Ferraro	Forest Hills
10. Mario Biaggi	Bronx
11. James H. Scheuer	Neponsit
12. Shirley A. Chisholm	Brooklyn
13. Stephen J. Solarz	Brooklyn
14. Frederick W. Richmond	Brooklyn
15. Leo C. Zeferetti	Brooklyn
16. Elizabeth Holtzman	Brooklyn
17. John M. Murphy	Staten Island
18. S. William Green	Manhattan
19. Charles B. Rangel	New York
20. Theodore S. Weiss	New York
21. Robert Garcia	Bronx
22. Jonathan B. Bingham	Bronx
23. Peter A. Peyser	Irvington
24. Richard L. Ottinger	Pleasantville
25. *Hamilton Fish, Jr.*	Millbrook
26. *Benjamin A. Gilman*	Middletown
27. Matthew F. McHugh	Ithaca
28. Samuel S. Stratton	Amsterdam
29. *Gerald B. Solomon*	Glens Falls
30. *Robert C. McEwen*	Ogdensburg
31. *Donald J. Mitchell*	Herkimer
32. James M. Hanley	Syracuse
33. *Gary A. Lee*	Dryden
34. *Frank J. Horton*	Rochester
35. *Barber B. Conable, Jr.*	Alexander
36. John J. LaFalce	Tonawanda
37. Henry J. Nowak	Buffalo
38. *Jack F. Kemp*	Hamburg
39. Stanley N. Lundine	Jamestown

* Representative at large.

Dist.	Representative	Residence

North Carolina

1.	Walter B. Jones	Farmville
2.	L. H. Fountain	Tarboro
3.	Charles O. Whitley, Sr.	Mount Olive
4.	Ike F. Andrews	Siler City
5.	Stephen L. Neal	Winston-Salem
6.	L. Richardson Preyer	Greensboro
7.	Charles G. Rose	Fayetteville
8.	W. G. Hefner	Concord
9.	James G. Martin	Davidson
10.	James T. Broyhill	Lenoir
11.	Lamar Gudger	Asheville

North Dakota

| °Mark Andrews | Mapleton |

Ohio

1.	Willis D. Gradison, Jr.	Cincinnati
2.	Thomas A. Luken	Cincinnati
3.	Tony P. Hall	Dayton
4.	Tennyson Guyer	Findlay
5.	Delbert L. Latta	Bowling Green
6.	William H. Harsha	Portsmouth
7.	Clarence J. Brown	Urbana
8.	Thomas N. Kindness	Hamilton
9.	Thomas L. Ashley	Maumee
10.	Clarence E. Miller	Lancaster
11.	J. William Stanton	Painesville
12.	Samuel L. Devine	Columbus
13.	Donald J. Pease	Oberlin
14.	John F. Seiberling	Akron
15.	Chalmers P. Wylie	Columbus
16.	Ralph S. Regula	Navarre
17.	John M. Ashbrook	Johnstown
18.	Douglas Applegate	Steubenville
19.	Lyle Williams	Warren
20.	Mary Rose Oakar	Cleveland
21.	Louis Stokes	Cleveland
22.	Charles A. Vanik	Euclid
23.	Ronald M. Mottl	Parma

Oklahoma

1.	James R. Jones	Tulsa
2.	Mike Synar	Muskogee
3.	Wesley W. Watkins	Ada
4.	Tom Steed	Shawnee
5.	Marvin H. Edwards	Oklahoma City
6.	Glenn English	Cordell

Oregon

1.	Les AuCoin	Forest Grove
2.	Al Ullman	Baker
3.	Robert B. Duncan	Portland
4.	James Weaver	Eugene

Pennsylvania

1.	Michael O. Myers	Philadelphia
2.	William H. Gray III	Philadelphia
3.	Raymond F. Lederer	Philadelphia
4.	Charles F. Dougherty	Philadelphia
5.	Richard T. Schulze	Malvern
6.	Gus Yatron	Reading
7.	Robert W. Edgar	Broomall
8.	Peter H. Kostmayer	Solebury
9.	E. G. Shuster	Everett
10.	Joseph M. McDade	Scranton
11.	Daniel J. Flood	Wilkes-Barre
12.	John P. Murtha	Johnstown
13.	Lawrence Coughlin	Villanova
14.	William S. Moorhead	Pittsburgh
15.	Donald L. Ritter	Coopersburg
16.	Robert S. Walker	E. Petersburg
17.	Allen E. Ertel	Montoursville
18.	Douglas Walgren	Pittsburgh
19.	William F. Goodling	Jacobus
20.	Joseph M. Gaydos	McKeesport
21.	Don Bailey	Greensburg
22.	Austin J. Murphy	Charleroi
23.	William F. Clinger, Jr.	Warren
24.	Marc L. Marks	Sharon
25.	Eugene V. Atkinson	Aliquippa

Rhode Island

| 1. | Fernand J. St Germain | Woonsocket |
| 2. | Edward P. Beard | Cranston |

Dist.	Representative	Residence

South Carolina

1.	Mendel J. Davis	N. Charleston
2.	Floyd D. Spence	Lexington
3.	Butler C. Derrick, Jr.	Edgefield
4.	Carroll A. Campbell, Jr.	Greenville
5.	Kenneth L. Holland	Gaffney
6.	John W. Jenrette, Jr.	N. Myrtle Beach

South Dakota

| 1. | Thomas A. Daschle | Aberdeen |
| 2. | James Abdnor | Kennebec |

Tennessee

1.	James H. Quillen	Kingsport
2.	John J. Duncan	Knoxville
3.	Marilyn L. Bouquard	Chattanooga
4.	Albert Gore, Jr.	Carthage
5.	Bill Boner	Nashville
6.	Robin L. Beard, Jr.	Franklin
7.	Ed Jones	Yorkville
8.	Harold E. Ford	Memphis

Texas

1.	Sam B. Hall, Jr.	Marshall
2.	Charles Wilson	Lufkin
3.	James M. Collins	Dallas
4.	Ray Roberts	McKinney
5.	James A. Mattox	Dallas
6.	Phil Gramm	College Station
7.	Bill Archer	Houston
8.	Bob Eckhardt	Harris County
9.	Jack Brooks	Beaumont
10.	J. J. Pickle	Austin
11.	J. Marvin Leath	Marlin
12.	James C. Wright, Jr.	Fort Worth
13.	Jack E. Hightower	Vernon
14.	Joe Wyatt	Bloomington
15.	Eligio de la Garza	Mission
16.	Richard C. White	El Paso
17.	Charles Stenholm	Stamford
18.	George T. Leland	Houston
19.	Kent Hance	Lubbock
20.	Henry B. Gonzalez	San Antonio
21.	Tom Loeffler	Hunt
22.	Ron Paul	Lake Jackson
23.	Abraham Kazen, Jr.	Laredo
24.	Martin Frost	Dallas

Utah

| 1. | K. Gunn McKay | Huntsville |
| 2. | David D. Marriott | Salt Lake City |

Vermont

| °James M. Jeffords | Rutland |

Virginia

1.	Paul S. Trible, Jr.	Newport News
2.	G. William Whitehurst	Virginia Beach
3.	David E. Satterfield III	Richmond
4.	Robert W. Daniel, Jr.	Spring Grove
5.	W.C. (Dan) Daniel	Danville
6.	M. Caldwell Butler	Roanoke
7.	J. Kenneth Robinson	Winchester
8.	Herbert E. Harris II	Mount Vernon
9.	William C. Wampler	Bristol
10.	Joseph L. Fisher	Arlington

Washington

1.	Joel Pritchard	Seattle
2.	Al Swift	Bellingham
3.	Don L. Bonker	Olympia
4.	Mike McCormack	Richland
5.	Thomas S. Foley	Spokane
6.	Norman D. Dicks	Port Orchard
7.	Mike Lowry	Mercer Island

West Virginia

1.	Robert H. Mollohan	Fairmount
2.	Harley O. Staggers	Keyser
3.	John M. Slack	Charleston
4.	Nick Joe Rahall II	Beckley

Wisconsin

1.	Les Aspin	Racine
2.	Robert W. Kastenmeier	Sun Prairie
3.	Alvin J. Baldus	Menomonie
4.	Clement J. Zablocki	Milwaukee
5.	Henry S. Reuss	Milwaukee
6.	Thomas E. Petri	Fond du Lac
7.	David R. Obey	Wausau
8.	Tobias Roth	Appleton
9.	F. James Sensenbrenner	Shorewood

Wyoming

| °Richard Cheney | Casper |

° Representative at large.

THE SENATE   Democrats are in roman type, Republicans in *italics*

Ninety-Sixth Congress, First Session
Democrats 58; *Republicans* 41; Independents 1
President: Walter F. Mondale
President Pro Tempore: Warren G. Magnuson, Wash.
Majority Leader: Robert C. Byrd, W.Va.
Majority Whip: Alan Cranston, Calif.
Minority Leader: *Howard H. Baker, Jr., Tenn.*

Assistant Minority Leader: *Theodore F. Stevens,* Alaska
Secretary: Joseph S. Kimmitt
Assistant Secretary: William A. Ridgely
Sergeant at Arms: Frank N. Hoffmann
Secretary for the Majority: Walter J. Stewart
Secretary for the Minority: William F. Hildenbrand
Chaplain: The Rev. Edward L. R. Elson, S.T.D.

State	Senator	Service From	Term Expires	State	Senator	Service From	Term Expires
Alabama	Donald W. Stewart	Nov. 8, 1978	Jan. 3, 1981	Kansas	*Robert J. Dole*	Jan. 3, 1969	Jan. 3, 1981
	Howell T. Heflin	Jan. 3, 1979	Jan. 3, 1985		*Nancy Landon Kassebaum*	Dec. 23, 1978	Jan. 3, 1985
Alaska	*Theodore F. Stevens*	Dec. 24, 1968	Jan. 3, 1985	Kentucky	Walter D. Huddleston	Jan. 3, 1973	Jan. 3, 1985
	Mike Gravel	Jan. 3, 1969	Jan. 3, 1981		Wendell H. Ford	Dec. 28, 1974	Jan. 3, 1981
Arizona	*Barry M. Goldwater*	Jan. 3, 1969	Jan. 3, 1981	Louisiana	Russell B. Long	Dec. 31, 1948	Jan. 3, 1981
	Dennis DeConcini	Jan. 3, 1977	Jan. 3, 1983		J. Bennett Johnston, Jr.	Nov. 14, 1972	Jan. 3, 1985
Arkansas	Dale Bumpers	Jan. 3, 1975	Jan. 3, 1981	Maine	Edmund S. Muskie	Jan. 3, 1959	Jan. 3, 1983
	David H. Pryor	Jan. 3, 1979	Jan. 3, 1985		*William S. Cohen*	Jan. 3, 1979	Jan. 3, 1985
California	Alan Cranston	Jan. 3, 1969	Jan. 3, 1981	Maryland	*Charles McC. Mathias, Jr.*	Jan. 3, 1969	Jan. 3, 1981
	S. I. Hayakawa	Jan. 2, 1977	Jan. 3, 1983		Paul S. Sarbanes	Jan. 3, 1977	Jan. 3, 1983
Colorado	Gary W. Hart	Jan. 3, 1975	Jan. 3, 1981	Massachusetts	Edward M. Kennedy	Nov. 7, 1962	Jan. 3, 1983
	William L. Armstrong	Jan. 3, 1979	Jan. 3, 1985		Paul Tsongas	Jan. 3, 1979	Jan. 3, 1985
Connecticut	Abraham A. Ribicoff	Jan. 3, 1963	Jan. 3, 1981	Michigan	Donald W. Riegle, Jr.	Dec. 30, 1976	Jan. 3, 1983
	Lowell P. Weicker, Jr.	Jan. 3, 1971	Jan. 3, 1983		Carl Levin	Jan. 3, 1979	Jan. 3, 1985
Delaware	*William V. Roth, Jr.*	Jan. 1, 1971	Jan. 3, 1983	Minnesota	*David F. Durenberger*	Nov. 8, 1978	Jan. 3, 1978
	Joseph R. Biden, Jr.	Jan. 3, 1973	Jan. 3, 1985		*Rudy Boschwitz*	Dec. 30, 1978	Jan. 3, 1985
Florida	Lawton M. Chiles, Jr.	Jan. 3, 1971	Jan. 3, 1983	Mississippi	John C. Stennis	Nov. 5, 1947	Jan. 3, 1983
	Richard B. Stone	Jan. 1, 1975	Jan. 3, 1981		*Thad Cochran*	Dec. 27, 1978	Jan. 3, 1985
Georgia	Herman E. Talmadge	Jan. 3, 1957	Jan. 3, 1981	Missouri	Thomas F. Eagleton	Dec. 28, 1968	Jan. 3, 1981
	Sam Nunn	Nov. 8, 1972	Jan. 3, 1985		*John C. Danforth*	Dec. 27, 1976	Jan. 3, 1983
Hawaii	Daniel K. Inouye	Jan. 3, 1963	Jan. 3, 1981	Montana	John Melcher	Jan. 3, 1977	Jan. 3, 1983
	Spark M. Matsunaga	Jan. 3, 1977	Jan. 3, 1983		Max Baucus	Dec. 15, 1978	Jan. 3, 1985
Idaho	Frank Church	Jan. 3, 1957	Jan. 3, 1981	Nebraska	Edward Zorinsky	Dec. 28, 1976	Jan. 3, 1983
	James A. McClure	Jan. 3, 1973	Jan. 3, 1985		John J. Exon, Jr.	Jan. 3, 1979	Jan. 3, 1985
Illinois	*Charles H. Percy*	Jan. 3, 1967	Jan. 3, 1985	Nevada	Howard W. Cannon	Jan. 3, 1959	Jan. 3, 1983
	Adlai E. Stevenson 3d	Nov. 17, 1970	Jan. 3, 1981		*Paul Laxalt*	Dec. 18, 1974	Jan. 3, 1981
Indiana	Birch Bayh	Jan. 3, 1963	Jan. 3, 1981	New Hampshire	John A. Durkin	Sept. 18, 1975	Jan. 3, 1981
	Richard G. Lugar	Jan. 3, 1977	Jan. 3, 1983		*Gordon J. Humphrey*	Jan. 3, 1979	Jan. 3, 1985
Iowa	John C. Culver	Jan. 3, 1975	Jan. 3, 1981	New Jersey	Harrison A. Williams, Jr.	Jan. 3, 1959	Jan. 3, 1983
	Roger W. Jepsen	Jan. 3, 1979	Jan. 3, 1985		Bill Bradley	Jan. 3, 1979	Jan. 3, 1985

State	Senator	Service From	Term Expires
New Mexico	*Pete V. Domenici*	Jan. 3, 1973	Jan. 3, 1985
	Harrison H. Schmitt	Jan. 3, 1977	Jan. 3, 1983
New York	*Jacob K. Javits*	Jan. 9, 1957	Jan. 3, 1981
	Daniel P. Moynihan	Jan. 3, 1977	Jan. 3, 1983
North Carolina	*Jesse A. Helms*	Jan. 3, 1973	Jan. 3, 1985
	Robert B. Morgan	Jan. 3, 1975	Jan. 3, 1981
North Dakota	*Milton R. Young*	Mar. 12, 1945	Jan. 3, 1981
	Quentin N. Burdick	Aug. 8, 1960	Jan. 3, 1983
Ohio	John H. Glenn, Jr.	Dec. 24, 1974	Jan. 3, 1981
	Howard M. Metzenbaum	Jan. 3, 1977	Jan. 3, 1983
Oklahoma	*Henry L. Bellmon*	Jan. 3, 1969	Jan. 3, 1981
	David L. Boren	Jan. 3, 1979	Jan. 3, 1985
Oregon	*Mark O. Hatfield*	Jan. 10, 1967	Jan. 3, 1985
	Robert W. Packwood	Jan. 3, 1969	Jan. 3, 1981
Pennsylvania	*Richard S. Schweiker*	Jan. 3, 1969	Jan. 3, 1981
	H. John Heinz III	Jan. 3, 1977	Jan. 3, 1983
Rhode Island	Claiborne Pell	Jan. 3, 1961	Jan. 3, 1985
	John H. Chafee	Dec. 29, 1976	Jan. 3, 1983
South Carolina	*Strom Thurmond*	Nov. 7, 1956	Jan. 3, 1985
	Ernest F. Hollings	Nov. 9, 1966	Jan. 3, 1981

State	Senator	Service From	Term Expires
South Dakota	George McGovern	Jan. 3, 1963	Jan. 3, 1981
	Larry Pressler	Jan. 3, 1979	Jan. 3, 1985
Tennessee	*Howard H. Baker, Jr.*	Jan. 3, 1967	Jan. 3, 1985
	James R. Sasser	Jan. 3, 1977	Jan. 3, 1983
Texas	*John G. Tower*	June 15, 1961	Jan. 3, 1985
	Lloyd M. Bentsen	Jan. 3, 1971	Jan. 3, 1983
Utah	*Edwin Jacob Garn*	Dec. 21, 1974	Jan. 3, 1981
	Orrin G. Hatch	Jan. 3, 1977	Jan. 3, 1983
Vermont	*Robert T. Stafford*	Sept. 16, 1971	Jan. 3, 1983
	Patrick J. Leahy	Jan. 3, 1975	Jan. 3, 1981
Virginia	Harry F. Byrd, Jr. †	Nov. 12, 1965	Jan. 3, 1983
	John W. Warner	Jan. 2, 1979	Jan. 3, 1985
Washington	Warren G. Magnuson	Dec. 14, 1944	Jan. 3, 1981
	Henry M. Jackson	Jan. 3, 1953	Jan. 3, 1983
West Virginia	Jennings Randolph	Nov. 5, 1958	Jan. 3, 1985
	Robert C. Byrd	Jan. 3, 1959	Jan. 3, 1983
Wisconsin	William Proxmire	Aug. 28, 1957	Jan. 3, 1983
	Gaylord Nelson	Jan. 8, 1963	Jan. 3, 1981
Wyoming	*Malcolm Wallop*	Jan. 3, 1977	Jan. 3, 1983
	Alan K. Simpson	Jan. 1, 1979	Jan. 3, 1985

† Independent

STANDING CONGRESSIONAL COMMITTEES

HOUSE OF REPRESENTATIVES

Agriculture: Agriculture and forestry in general, including price stabilzation, farm credit and security, crop insurance, meat and livestock inspections, sol conservation, and rural electrification.

Appropriations: Appropriation of money for the support of the government, examination of operations of any executive department or agency (including agencies of which the majority stock is government owned).

Armed Services: Matters relating to the national military establishment, including military space activities; conservation of naval petroleum resources; strategic materials; scientific research and development for military purposes; Selective Service.

Banking, Finance and Urban Affairs: Financial matters other than taxes and appropriations, including pree, commodity, rent, or services controls; deposit insurance, the Federal Reserve System; the valuation of the dollar; public and private housing.

Budget: To set ceilings for overall government spending, giving Congress a coordinated approach to the federal budget for the first time; to study effects of legislation on budget outlays and tax expenditures.

District of Columbia: Municpal affairs (except appropriations) of the District.

Education and Labor: Measures relating to education and labor, including child labor and convict labor; wages and hours; arbitration of labor disputes; the school-lunch program.

Foreign Affairs: U.S. relations with other governments; the U.N., and international monetary organizations; the diplomatic service, foreign loans, protection of American citizens abroad; interventions and declarations of war.

Government Operations: Budget and accounting measures other than appropriations; relationships of federal government with states and municipalities; reorganizations of executive branch; studies of all levels of government operations; reports of Comptroller General.

House Administration: General administration of the House, including employment of clerks and reporters; federal elections; corrupt practices; contested elections; and the Library of Congress.

Interior and Insular Affairs: Public lands in general; forest reserves and national parks created from the public domain; the Geological Survey; public mineral resources; irrigation; insular possessions; and American Indian affairs.

Interstate and Foreign Commerce: Commerce, communications, and transportation (except water transportation that is not subject to the Interstate Commerce Commission); interstate power transmission (except installation of connections between government waterpower projects); railroad commerce and labor; civil aeronautics; inland waterways; interstate oil compacts; petroleum and natural gas (except on public lands); securities and exchanges; public health; and the Weather Bureau.

Judiciary: Judicial proceedings in general; federal courts and judges; Constitutional amendments; civil rights; interstate compacts; immigration and naturalization; apportionment of representatives; meetings of Congress and attendance of members; Presidential succession; the Patent Office; claims against the United States;

bankruptcy, mutiny, espionage, and counterfeiting; protection of trade and commerce.

Merchant Marine and Fisheries: The merchant marine in general; navigation and pilotage laws; regulation of common carriers by water (except matters falling under the jurisdiction of the Interstate Commerce Commission); the Coast Guard; the National Ocean Survey; operation and maintenance of the Panama Canal and administration of the Canal Zone; and fisheries and wildlife, including research and conservation.

Post Office and Civil Service: Postal service and federal civil service; the census and collection of statistics; and the National Archives.

Public Works and Transportation: Public buildings and roads; flood control; improvement of rivers and harbors; public works for navigation, including bridges and dams (other than international); water power; and pollution of navigable waters.

Rules: Rules and order of business of the House; recesses and final adjournments of Congress; creation of committees.

Science and Technology: Scientific and astronautical research and development in general; the National Aeronautics and Space Administration; the National Aeronautics and Space Council; the National Science Foundation; the Bureau of Standards; science scholarships.

Small Business: Assistance to and protection of small business; participation of small business enterprises in federal procurement and government contracts.

Standards of Official Conduct: Regulations and standards for members, officers, and employees of the House.

Veterans' Affairs: Veterans' measures in general; pensions, armed forces life insurance, rehabilitation and education; and veterans' hospitals.

Ways and Means: Revenue and tax measures in general, as well as customs, transportation of dutiable goods, federal Social Security, reciprocal trade agreements, U.S. bonded debt, and deposit of public moneys.

SENATE

Agriculture, Nutrition, and Forestry: Agriculture in general, including meat and livestock inspection, farm credit and security, soil conservation, crop insurance, and rural electrification; domestic and foreign matters relating to food, nutrition and hunger; forestry and forest reserves (excluding those created from the public domain) in general.

Appropriations: Appropriation of money for the support of the government.

Armed Services: Matters relating to the national military establishment, including military space activities; maintenance of the Panama Canal and administration of the Canal Zone; conservation of naval petroleum resources; and strategic materials.

Banking, Housing and Urban Affairs: Financial matters other than appropriations and taxes; deposit insurance;

Federal Reserve System; valuation of the dollar; price control; public and private housing; and financial aid to industry on matters assigned to other committees.

Budget: To set ceilings for overall government spending, giving Congress a coordinated approach to the federal budget for the first time; to study effects of legislation on budget outlays and tax expenditures.

Commerce, Science and Transportation: Interstate and foreign commerce; interstate railroads, buses, trucks, and pipelines; communications; civil aeronautics; nonmilitary aeronautical and space sciences; merchant marine and navigation, both inland and oceanic; Coast Guard; oceans, weather, and atmospheric activities; fish and wildlife conservation; consumer product regulation; Bureau of Standards; science, engineering, and technology research and development.

Energy and Natural Resources: Energy policy, regulation, conservation, research and development; nuclear and solar energy; production, distribution and utilization of energy sources; public lands and forests; national parks; territorial possessions.

Environment and Public Works: Environmental policy, research and development; water resources; flood control; public works; pollution control; regional economic development; highway construction and maintenance; public buildings and their grounds.

Finance: Revenue and tax matters in general; deposit of public moneys; U.S. bonded debt; customs; transportation of dutiable goods; reciprocal trade agreements; tariffs; import quotas; Social Security.

Foreign Relations: Relations with foreign nations, as well as treaties; protection of American citizens abroad; interventions and declarations of war; diplomatic service; American business interests abroad; the U.N. and international monetary organizations; foreign loans.

Governmental Affairs: Budget and accounting measures other than appropriations; executive branch reorganizations; Comptroller General reports; studies of all levels of government operations; study of relations between the U.S. and states, municipalities, and international organizations of which the U.S. is a member; postal service; census.

Judiciary: Judicial proceedings; federal courts and judges; Constitutional amendments; the Patent Office; claims against the U.S.; civil liberties; protection of trade and commerce; meetings of Congress and attendance of members; immigration and naturalization; bankruptcy, mutiny, espionage, counterfeiting; apportionment of representatives; interstate compacts.

Labor and Human Resources: Education, health, and public welfare; labor, including foreign laborers; private pension plans; aging; arts and humanities.

Rules and Administration: General administration of the Senate; federal elections; corrupt practices; contested elections; management of Library of Congress; reorganization acts; creation of new standing committees.

Veterans' Affairs: Veterans' hospitals, education, compensation, and welfare.

CONGRESSIONAL JOINT COMMITTEES, COMMISSIONS AND BOARDS

Joint Committees on:
Library
Printing
Taxation
Joint Economic Committee
Commission on Art and Antiquities of U.S. Senate
Commission on Security and Cooperation in Europe
Commission on the West Central Front of the U.S. Capitol
Consumer Product Safety Commission
District of Columbia Law Revision Commission
Franklin Delano Roosevelt Memorial Commission
House Commission on Congressional Mailing Standards
House Office Building Commission
Japan-United States Friendship Commission
Marine Corps Memorial Commission
Migratory Bird Conservation Commission
National Alcohol Fuels Commission
National Commission for Employment Policy
National Commission on Air Quality

National Commission on the International Year of the Child
National Commission on Unemployment Compensation
National Transportation Policy Study Commission
Permanent Committee for the Oliver Wendell Holmes Devise Fund
President's Commission on the Coal Industry
President's Commission on the Holocaust
President's Committee on Mental Retardation
Select Commission on Immigration and Refugee Policy
Temporary Commission on Financial Oversight of the District of Columbia
Environmental Study Conference
Members of Congress for Peace Through Law
North Atlantic Assembly
The Interparliamentary Union
Board for International Broadcasting
Board of Visitors to the Air Force Academy
Board of Visitors to the Coast Guard Academy
Board of Visitors to the Merchant Marine Academy
Board of Visitors to the Military Academy
Board of Visitors to the Naval Academy

MEMBERS OF THE U.S. SUPREME COURT

Source: Supreme Court of the United States and other sources

	Place of Birth	Year of Birth	Education	Appointed by President	Date Oath Taken	Age at Oath	Date Service Ended	Service Ended By	Years of Service	Age at End of Service Term	Date of Death
CHIEF JUSTICES											
Jay, John	New York	1745	King's College (now Columbia University), grad. 1764	Washington	Oct. 1789	44	June 1795	resigned	5	49	May 1829
Rutledge, John*	South Carolina	1739	Studied law at Middle Temple, London	Washington				rejected	0	56	June 1800
Ellsworth, Oliver	Connecticut	1745	Attended Yale College; College of New Jersey (now Princeton University), grad. 1766	Washington	Mar. 1796	50	Dec. 1800	resigned	4	55	Nov. 1807
Marshall, John	Virginia	1755	Attended College of William and Mary	Adams	Feb. 1801	45	July 1835	death	34	79	July 1835
Taney, Roger Brooke	Maryland	1777	Dickinson College, Penn., grad. 1795	Jackson	Mar. 1836	59	Oct. 1864	death	28	87	Oct. 1864
Chase, Salmon Portland	New Hampshire	1808	Attended Cincinnati College; Dartmouth College, grad. 1826	Lincoln	Dec. 1864	56	May 1873	death	8	65	May 1873
Waite, Morrison Remick	Connecticut	1816	Yale College, grad. 1837	Grant	Mar. 1874	57	Mar. 1888	death	14	71	Mar. 1888
Fuller, Melville Weston	Maine	1833	Bowdoin College, grad. 1853; attended Harvard Law School	Cleveland	Oct. 1888	55	July 1910	death	21	77	July 1910
White, Edward Douglass*	Louisiana	1845	Attended Mount St. Mary's College, Md.; Jesuit College in New Orleans, La.; and Georgetown College, Washington, D.C.	Taft	Dec. 1910	65	May 1921	death	10	75	May 1921
Taft, William Howard	Ohio	1857	Yale College, grad. 1878; Cincinnati Law School, LL.B. 1880	Harding	July 1921	63	Feb. 1930	retired	8	72	Mar. 1930
Hughes, Charles Evans*	New York	1862	Attended Colgate University; Brown University, Rhode Island, grad. 1881; M.A. 1884; Columbia Law School, LL.B. 1884	Hoover	Feb. 1930	67	June 1941	retired	11	79	Aug. 1948
Stone, Harlan Fiske*	New Hampshire	1872	Amherst College, Mass., grad. 1894; M.A. 1897; Columbia Law School, LL.B. 1898	Roosevelt, F.	July 1941	68	Apr. 1946	death	4	73	Apr. 1946
Vinson, Frederick Moore	Kentucky	1890	Kentucky Normal College, grad.; Centre College, Ky., grad. 1909; LL.B. 1911	Truman	June 1946	56	Sept. 1953	death	7	63	Sept. 1953
Warren, Earl	California	1891	University of California, LL.B. 1912; J.D. 1914	Eisenhower	Oct. 1953	62	June 1969	retired	16	78	July 1974
Burger, Warren Earl	Minnesota	1907	Attended University of Minnesota; St. Paul College of Law, LL.B. 1931	Nixon	June 1969	61		—			
ASSOCIATE JUSTICES											
Cushing, William	Massachusetts	1732	Harvard College, grad. 1751	Washington	Sept. 1789	57	Sept. 1810	death	20	77	Sept. 1810
Wilson, James	Scotland	1742	Attended University of St. Andrews (Scotland)	Washington	Sept. 1789	47	Aug. 1798	death	8	56	Aug. 1798
Blair, John Jr.	Virginia	1732	College of William and Mary, grad. 1754; studied law at Middle Temple, London	Washington	Feb. 1790	57	Jan. 1796	resigned	6	63	Aug. 1800
Iredell, James	England	1751	Private tutoring	Washington	May 1790	39	Oct. 1799	death	9	48	Oct. 1799
Johnson, Thomas	Maryland	1732	No formal education	Washington	Nov. 1791	59	Jan. 1793	resigned	1	61	Oct. 1819
Paterson, William	Ireland	1745	College of New Jersey (now Princeton University), grad. 1763; M.A. 1766	Washington	Mar. 1793	47	Sept. 1806	death	13	61	Sept. 1806
Chase, Samuel	Maryland	1741	Private tutoring	Washington	Feb. 1796	55	June 1811	death	15	70	June 1811
Washington, Bushrod	Virginia	1762	College of William and Mary, grad. 1778	Adams, J.	Dec. 1798	36	Nov. 1829	death	31	67	Nov. 1829
Moore, Alfred	North Carolina	1755	Attended private schools	Adams, J.	Apr. 1800	44	Jan. 1804	resigned	4	48	Oct. 1810
Johnson, William	South Carolina	1771	College of New Jersey (now Princeton University), grad. 1778	Jefferson	May 1804	32	Aug. 1834	death	30	63	Aug. 1834
Livingston, Brockholst	New York	1757	College of New Jersey (now Princeton University), grad. 1774	Jefferson	Jan. 1807	49	Mar. 1823	death	16	65	Mar. 1823
Todd, Thomas	Virginia	1765	Private tutoring	Jefferson	May 1807	42	Feb. 1826	death	18	60	Feb. 1826
Duvall, Gabriel	Maryland	1752	Dartmouth College, graduation date unknown	Madison	Nov. 1811	59	? 1835	resigned	23	81	Mar. 1844
Story, Joseph	Massachusetts	1779	Harvard College, grad. 1798	Madison	Feb. 1812	32	Sept. 1845	death	33	65	Sept. 1845
Thompson, Smith	New York	1768	College of New Jersey (now Princeton University), grad. 1788	Monroe	Sept. 1823	55	Dec. 1843	death	20	75	Dec. 1843
Trimble, Robert	Virginia	1776	Attended Kentucky Academy (now Transylvania College)	Adams, J. Q.	June 1826	49	Aug. 1828	death	2	51	Aug. 1828
McLean, John	New Jersey	1784	Private tutoring	Jackson	? 1829	44	Apr. 1861	death	32	76	Apr. 1861

* Also served as associate justice: Rutledge (1789–91); White (1894–1910); Hughes (1910–16); Stone (1925–41).

Associate Justices	Place of Birth	Year of Birth	Education	Appointed by President	Date Oath Taken	Age at Oath	Date Service Ended	Service Ended By	Years of Service Term	Age at End of Term	Date of Death
Baldwin, Henry	Connecticut	1780	Yale College, grad. 1797	Jackson	? 1830	50	Apr. 1844	death	14	64	Apr. 1844
Wayne, James M.	Georgia	1790	College of New Jersey (now Princeton University), grad. 1808	Jackson	Jan. 1835	45	July 1867	death	32	77	July 1867
Barbour, Philip P.	Virginia	1783	No record of formal education	Jackson	Mar. 1836	53	Feb. 1841	death	5	58	Feb. 1841
Catron, John	Pennsylvania	1786	No record of formal education	Jackson	Mar. 1837	51	May 1865	death	28	79	May 1865
McKinley, John	Virginia	1780	No record of formal education	Van Buren	? 1837	57	July 1852	death	15	72	July 1852
Daniel, Peter V.	Virginia	1784	Attended College of New Jersey (now Princeton Univ.)	Van Buren	Feb. 1841	57	May 1860	death	19	76	May 1860
Nelson, Samuel	New York	1792	Middlebury College, grad. 1813	Tyler	Mar. 1845	53	Nov. 1872	resigned	27	80	Dec. 1873
Woodbury, Levi	New Hampshire	1789	Dartmouth College, grad. 1809	Polk	May 1845	56	Sept. 1851	death	5	61	Sept. 1851
Grier, Robert C.	Pennsylvania	1794	Dickinson College, grad. 1812	Polk	Aug. 1846	52	Feb. 1870	resigned	23	75	Aug. 1870
Curtis, Benjamin	Massachusetts	1809	Harvard College, grad. 1829	Fillmore	Dec. 1851	42	Sept. 1857	resigned	6	48	Sept. 1874
Campbell, John A.	Georgia	1811	University of Georgia, grad. 1826	Pierce	Mar. 1853	42	Apr. 1861	resigned	8	50	Mar. 1889
Clifford, Nathan	New Hampshire	1803	Attended private schools	Buchanan	Jan. 1858	55	July 1881	death	23	78	July 1881
Swayne, Noah Haynes	Virginia	1804	No record of formal education	Lincoln	Jan. 1862	57	Jan. 1881	retired	18	76	June 1884
Miller, Samuel Freeman	Kentucky	1816	Transylvania University, Ky. grad. 1838	Lincoln	July 1862	46	Oct. 1890	death	28	74	Oct. 1890
Davis, David	Maryland	1815	Kenyon College, Ohio, grad. 1832; Yale Law School, LL.B. 1835	Lincoln	Dec. 1862	47	Mar. 1877	resigned	14	61	June 1886
Field, Stephen Johnson	Connecticut	1816	Williams College, Mass., grad. 1837	Lincoln	May 1863	46	Dec. 1897	retired	34	81	Apr. 1899
Strong, William	Connecticut	1808	Yale College, grad. 1828; M.A. 1831; attended Yale Law School	Grant	Mar. 1870	61	Dec. 1880	retired	10	72	Aug. 1895
Bradley, Joseph P.	New York	1813	Rutgers College, grad. 1836	Grant	Mar. 1870	57	Jan. 1892	death	21	78	Jan. 1892
Hunt, Ward	New York	1810	Union College, N.Y., grad. 1828	Grant	Jan. 1873	62	Jan. 1882	disabled	9	71	Mar. 1886
Harlan, John Marshall	Kentucky	1833	Centre College, Ky., grad. 1850; studied law at Transylvania College, Ky.	Hayes	Dec. 1877	44	Oct. 1911	death	33	78	Oct. 1911
Woods, William Burnham	Ohio	1824	Yale College, grad. 1845	Hayes	Jan. 1881	56	May 1887	death	6	62	May 1887
Matthews, Stanley	Ohio	1824	Kenyon College, Ohio, grad. 1840	Garfield	May 1881	56	Mar. 1889	death	7	64	Mar. 1889
Gray, Horace	Massachusetts	1828	Harvard College, grad. 1845; Harvard Law School, LL.B. 1849	Arthur	Jan. 1882	53	Sept. 1902	death	20	74	Sept. 1902
Blatchford, Samuel	New York	1820	Columbia College, grad. 1837	Arthur	Apr. 1882	62	July 1893	death	11	73	July 1893
Lamar, Lucius Quintus C.	Georgia	1825	Emory College, Ga., grad. 1845	Cleveland	Jan. 1888	62	Jan. 1893	death	5	67	Jan. 1893
Brewer, David Josiah	Asia Minor	1837	Yale College, grad. 1856; M.A. 1859; Albany (N.Y.) Law School, LL.B. 1858	Harrison	Jan. 1890	52	Mar. 1910	death	20	72	Mar. 1910
Brown, Henry Billings	Massachusetts	1836	Yale College, grad. 1856	Harrison	Jan. 1891	54	May 1906	retired	15	70	Sept. 1913
Shiras, George, Jr.	Pennsylvania	1832	Yale College, grad. 1853; Yale Law School, LL.B. 1854	Harrison	Oct. 1892	60	Feb. 1903	retired	10	71	Aug. 1924
Jackson, Howell Edmunds	Tennessee	1832	West Tennessee College, grad. 1849; attended University of Virginia; Cumberland University, Tenn., LL.B. 1856	Harrison	Mar. 1893	60	Aug. 1895	death	2	63	Aug. 1895
Peckham, Rufus Wheeler	New York	1838	Attended Albany (N.Y.) Academy	Cleveland	Jan. 1896	57	Oct. 1909	death	13	70	Oct. 1909
McKenna, Joseph	Pennsylvania	1843	Benicia Collegiate Institute, Calif., grad. 1865	McKinley	Jan. 1898	54	Jan. 1925	retired	26	81	Nov. 1926
Holmes, Oliver Wendell	Massachusetts	1841	Harvard College, grad. 1861; LL.B. 1866	Roosevelt, T.	Dec. 1902	61	Jan. 1932	retired	29	90	Mar. 1935
Day, William Rufus	Ohio	1849	University of Michigan, grad. 1870	Roosevelt, T.	Mar. 1903	53	Nov. 1922	retired	19	73	July 1923
Moody, William Henry	Massachusetts	1853	Harvard College, grad. 1876; att. Harvard Law School	Roosevelt, T.	Dec. 1906	52	Nov. 1910	disabled	3	56	July 1917
Lurton, Horace Harmon	Kentucky	1844	Attended Douglas University, Chicago (now University of Chicago); Cumberland University, Tenn., LL.B. 1867	Taft	Jan. 1910	65	July 1914	death	4	70	July 1914
Van Devanter, Willis	Indiana	1859	Attended Indiana Asbury (now De Pauw University); Cincinnati Law School, LL.B. 1881	Taft	Jan. 1911	51	June 1937	retired	26	78	Feb. 1941
Lamar, Joseph Rucker	Georgia	1857	Bethany College, W. Va., grad. 1877; studied law, Washington and Lee University, Va.	Taft	Jan. 1911	53	Jan. 1916	death	5	58	Jan. 1916
Pitney, Mahlon	New Jersey	1858	College of New Jersey (now Princeton University), grad. 1879	Taft	Mar. 1912	54	Dec. 1922	resigned	10	64	Dec. 1924

Associate Justices (cont.)	Place of Birth	Year of Birth	Education	Appointed by President	Date Oath Taken	Age at Oath	Date Service Ended	Service Ended By	Years of Service	Age at End of Service Term	Date of Death
McReynolds, James Clark	Kentucky	1862	Vanderbilt University, Tenn., grad. 1882; University of Virginia Law School, grad. 1884	Wilson	Oct. 1914	52	Jan. 1941	retired	26	78	Aug. 1946
Brandeis, Louis Dembitz	Kentucky	1856	Harvard Law School, LL.B. 1877	Wilson	June 1916	59	Feb. 1939	retired	22	82	Oct. 1941
Clarke, John Hessin	Ohio	1857	Western Reserve University, Ohio, grad. 1877	Wilson	Oct. 1916	59	Sept. 1922	resigned	5	65	Mar. 1945
Sutherland, George	England	1862	Studied law at the University of Michigan	Harding	Oct. 1922	60	Jan. 1938	retired	15	75	July 1942
Butler, Pierce	Minnesota	1866	Carleton College, Minn., grad. 1887	Harding	Jan. 1923	56	Nov. 1939	death	16	73	Nov. 1939
Sanford, Edward Terry	Tennessee	1865	University of Tennessee, grad. 1883; Harvard University, M.A. 1889; Harvard Law School, LL.B. 1889	Harding	Feb. 1923	57	Mar. 1930	death	7	64	Mar. 1930
Roberts, Owen Josephus	Pennsylvania	1875	University of Pennsylvania, grad. 1895; LL.B. 1898	Hoover	June 1930	55	July 1945	resigned	15	70	May 1955
Cardozo, Benjamin Nathan	New York	1870	Columbia University, grad. 1889; M.A. 1890; attended Columbia Law School	Hoover	Mar. 1932	61	July 1938	death	6	68	July 1938
Black, Hugo Lafayette	Alabama	1886	University of Alabama, Law School, LL.B. 1906	Roosevelt, F.	Aug. 1937	51	Sept. 1971	retired	34	85	Sept. 1971
Reed, Stanley Forman	Kentucky	1884	Kentucky Wesleyan College, grad. 1902; also Yale University, grad. 1906; studied law at Columbia University	Roosevelt, F.	Jan. 1938	53	Feb. 1957	retired	19	72	—
Frankfurter, Felix	Austria	1882	City College of New York, grad. 1902; Harvard Law School, LL.B. 1906	Roosevelt, F.	Jan. 1939	56	Aug. 1962	retired	23	79	Feb. 1965
Douglas, William Orville	Minnesota	1898	Whitman College, Wash., grad. 1920; Columbia Law School, LL.B. 1925	Roosevelt, F.	Apr. 1939	40	Nov. 1975	retired	36	77	—
Murphy, Frank	Michigan	1890	University of Michigan, LL.B. 1914; studied law at Lincoln's Inn, London, and Trinity College, Dublin	Roosevelt, F.	Feb. 1940	49	July 1949	death	9	59	July 1949
Byrnes, James Francis	South Carolina	1879	No record of formal education	Roosevelt, F.	July 1941	62	July 1942	resigned	1	63	Apr. 1972
Jackson, Robert Houghwout	New York	1892	Attended Albany (N.Y.) Law School	Roosevelt, F.	July 1941	49	Oct. 1954	death	13	62	Oct. 1954
Rutledge, Wiley Blount	Kentucky	1894	University of Wisconsin, grad. 1914; University of Colorado, LL.B. 1922	Roosevelt, F.	Feb. 1943	48	Sept. 1949	death	6	55	Sept. 1949
Burton, Harold Hitz	Massachusetts	1888	Bowdoin College, Me., grad. 1909; Harvard Law School, LL.B. 1912	Truman	Oct. 1945	57	Oct. 1958	retired	13	70	Oct. 1964
Clark, Thomas Campbell	Texas	1899	University of Texas, grad. 1921; LL.B. 1922	Truman	Aug. 1949	49	June 1967	retired	18	67	June 1977
Minton, Sherman	Indiana	1890	Indiana University, LL.B. 1915	Truman	Oct. 1949	58	Oct. 1956	retired	7	65	Apr. 1965
Harlan, John Marshall	Illinois	1899	Princeton University, grad. 1920; Rhodes Scholar to Oxford University, 1921–23; New York Law School, grad. 1924	Eisenhower	Mar. 1955	55	Sept. 1971	retired	16	72	Dec. 1971
Brennan, William Joseph, Jr.	New Jersey	1906	University of Pennsylvania, grad. 1928; Harvard Law School, LL.B. 1931	Eisenhower	Oct. 1956	50	—				—
Whittaker, Charles Evans	Kansas	1901	University of Kansas City, LL.B. 1924	Eisenhower	Mar. 1957	56	Apr. 1962	retired	5	61	Nov. 1973
Stewart, Potter	Michigan	1915	Yale University, grad. 1937; attended Cambridge University, England; Yale Law School, LL.B. 1941	Eisenhower	Oct. 1958	43	—				—
White, Byron Raymond	Colorado	1917	University of Colorado, grad. 1938; Rhodes Scholar, Oxford, England, 1939; Yale Law School, LL.B. 1946	Kennedy	Apr. 1962	44	—				—
Goldberg, Arthur Joseph	Illinois	1908	Northwestern University, grad. 1929; J.D. 1930	Kennedy	Oct. 1962	54	July 1965	resigned	3	56	—
Fortas, Abe	Tennessee	1910	Southwestern College, grad. 1930; Yale Law School, LL.B. 1933	Johnson	Oct. 1965	55	May 1969	resigned	4	58	—
Marshall, Thurgood	Maryland	1908	Lincoln University, grad. 1929; Howard University, LL.B. 1933	Johnson	Oct. 1967	59	—				—
Blackmun, Harry Andrew	Minnesota	1908	Harvard College, grad. 1929; Harvard Law School, LL.B. 1932	Nixon	June 1970	61	—				—
Powell, Lewis Franklin, Jr.	Virginia	1907	Washington and Lee University, grad. 1929, LL.B., 1931; Harvard University, LL.M., 1932	Nixon	Jan. 1972	64	—				—
Rehnquist, William Hubbs	Wisconsin	1924	Stanford University, grad. 1948; M.A. Harvard University 1950; LL.B. Stanford 1952	Nixon	Jan. 1972	47	—				—
Stevens, John Paul	Illinois	1920	Univ. of Chicago, grad. 1941; Northwestern Univ. School of Law, J.D. 1947	Ford	Dec. 1975	55	—				—

Members of the Supreme Court (left to right): Front row, Associate Justices Byron R. White, William J. Brennan, Jr., Chief Justice Warren E. Burger, Associate Justices Potter Stewart, Thurgood Marshall; Back row, Associate Justices William H. Rehnquist, Harry A. Blackmun, Lewis F. Powell, Jr., John Paul Stevens.

THE U.S. COURTS
Source: Administrative Office of the U.S. Courts

SUPREME COURT OF THE UNITED STATES
Washington, D.C.

Chief Justice (Salary: $75,000): Warren E. Burger of Virginia.

Associate Justices (Salaries: $72,000): William J. Brennan, Jr., of New Jersey; Potter Stewart of Ohio; Byron R. White of Colorado; Thurgood Marshall of New York; Harry A. Blackmun of Minnesota; Lewis F. Powell, Jr. of Virginia; William H. Rehnquist of Arizona; John P. Stevens of Illinois.

U.S. COURT OF APPEALS
(Salaries: $57,500)

District of Columbia Circuit: J. Skelly Wright, Chief Judge; David L. Bazelon, Carl McGowan, Edward Allen Tamm, Harold Leventhal, Spottswood W. Robinson III, Roger Robb, George E. MacKinnon, Malcolm Richard Wilkey, Patricia M. Wald.

First Circuit (Maine, Massachusetts, New Hampshire, Rhode Island, Puerto Rico): Frank M. Coffin, Chief Judge, Portland, Maine; Levin H. Campbell, Boston, Mass.; Hugh H. Bownes, Concord, N.H.

Second Circuit (Connecticut, New York, Vermont): Irving R. Kaufman, Chief Judge, New York, N.Y.; James L. Oakes, Brattleboro, Vt.; William H. Timbers, Bridgeport, Ct.; Thomas J. Meskill, New Britain, Ct.; Wilfred Feinberg, Walter R. Mansfield, William H. Mulligan, Murray I. Gurfein, Amalya L. Kearse, all of New York, N.Y.; Ellsworth Van Graafeiland, Rochester, N.Y.; Jon O. Newman, Hartford, Ct.

Third Circuit (Delaware, New Jersey, Pennsylvania, Virgin Islands): Collins J. Seitz, Chief Judge, Wilmington, Del.; James Hunter III, Camden, N.J.; A. Leon Higginbotham, Philadelphia, Pa.; Ruggero J. Aldisert, Pittsburgh, Pa.; Arlin M. Adams, Philadelphia, Pa.; John J. Gibbons, Newark, N.J.; Max Rosenn, Wilkes-Barre, Pa.; Joseph F. Weis, Jr., Pittsburgh, Pa.; Leonard I. Garth, Newark, N.J.; Dolores Korman Sloviter, Philadelphia, Pa.

Fourth Circuit (Maryland, North Carolina, South Carolina, Virginia, West Virginia): Clement F. Haynsworth, Jr., Chief Judge, Greenville, S.C.; Harrison L. Winter, Baltimore, Md.; John D. Butzner, Jr., Richmond, Va.; Donald Stuart Russell, Spartanburg, S.C.; H. Emory Widener, Jr., Abingdon, Va.; Kenneth K. Hall, Charleston, W. Va.; James Dickson Phillips, Jr., Durham, N.C., Francis D. Murnaghan, Jr., Baltimore, Md.

Fifth Circuit (Alabama, Florida, Georgia, Louisiana, Mississippi, Texas, Canal Zone): John R. Brown, Chief Judge, Houston, Tex.; Alvin B. Rubin, Baton Rouge, La.; James P. Coleman, Ackerman, Miss.; Irving L. Goldberg, Dallas, Tex.; Robert A. Ainsworth, Jr., New Orleans, La.; John C. Godbold, Frank M. Johnson, Jr., both of Montgomery, Ala.; Gerald B. Tjoflat, Jacksonville, Fla.; Phyllis A. Kravitch, Albert J. Henderson, James C. Hill, all of Atlanta, Ga.; Charles Clark, Jackson, Miss.; Paul H. Roney, St. Petersburg, Fla.; Thomas G. Gee, Thomas M. Reavley, both of Austin, Tex.; Peter T. Fay, Miami, Fla.; Robert S. Vance, Birmingham, Ala.; Henry A. Politz, Shreveport, La.; Joseph W. Hatchett, Tallahassee, Fla.; R. Lanier Anderson III, Macon, Ga.; Carolyn D. Randall, Houston, Tex.; Reynaldo G. Garza, Brownsville, Tex.

Sixth Circuit (Kentucky, Michigan, Ohio, Tennessee): George Clifton Edwards, Jr., Chief Judge, Cincinnati, Ohio; Paul C. Weick, Akron, Ohio; Anthony J. Celebrezze, Cleveland, Ohio; Pierce Lively, Danville, Ky.; Albert J. Engel, Grand Rapids, Mich.; Gilbert S. Merritt, Nashville, Tenn.; Damon J. Keith, Detroit, Mich.

Seventh Circuit (Illinois, Indiana, Wisconsin): Thomas E. Fairchild, Chief Judge, Chicago, Ill.; Luther M. Swygert, Walter J. Cummings, Philip W. Tone, Wilbur F. Pell, Jr., Robert A. Sprecher, William J. Bauer, Harlington Wood, Jr., all of Chicago, Ill.

Eighth Circuit (Arkansas, Iowa, Minnesota, Missouri, Nebraska, North Dakota, South Dakota): Floyd R. Gibson, Chief Judge, Kansas City, Mo.; Donald P. Lay, Omaha, Nebr.; Gerald W. Heaney, Duluth, Minn.; Myron H. Bright, Fargo, N. Dak.; Donald R. Ross, Omaha, Nebr.; Roy L. Stephenson, Des Moines, Iowa; J. Smith Henley, Little Rock, Ark.; Theodore McMillian, St. Louis, Mo.

Ninth Circuit (Arizona, California, Idaho, Montana, Nevada, Oregon, Washington, Alaska, Hawaii, Guam): James R. Browning, Chief Judge, San Francisco, Calif.; Walter Ely, Shirley M. Hufstedler, both of Los Angeles, Calif.; Eugene A. Wright, Seattle, Wash.; Ozell M. Trask, Thomas Tang, both of Phoenix, Ariz.; Herbert Y. C. Choy, Honolulu, Hawaii; Alfred T. Goodwin, Portland, Oregon; J. Clifford Wallace, San Diego, Calif.; Joseph T. Sneed, San Francisco, Calif.; Anthony M. Kennedy, Sacramento, Calif.; J. Blaine Anderson, Boise, Idaho; Procter Hug, Jr., Reno, Nevada.

Tenth Circuit (Colorado, Kansas, New Mexico, Oklahoma, Utah, Wyoming): Oliver Seth, Chief Judge, Santa Fe, N. Mex.; William J. Holloway, Jr., Oklahoma City, Okla.; James E. Barrett, Cheyenne, Wyo.; William E. Doyle and Robert H. McWilliams, both of Denver, Colo.; Monroe McKay, Salt Lake City, Utah; James K. Logan, Olathe, Kansas.

U.S. DISTRICT COURTS
Judges of U.S. District Courts and the Chief Judge of the District of Columbia receive annual salaries of $54,500.

U.S. TERRITORIAL JUDGES
The 4 District Judges earn annual salaries of $54,500.

U.S. COURT OF CLAIMS
717 Madison Place, N.W., Washington, D.C.
(Salaries: $57,500)
Chief Judge: Daniel M. Friedman. **Associate Judges:** Oscar H. Davis, Philip Nichols, Jr., Shiro Kashiwa, Robert L. Kunzig, Marion T. Bennett and Edward S. Smith.

U.S. COURT OF CUSTOMS AND PATENT APPEALS
717 Madison Place, N.W., Washington, D.C.
(Salaries: $57,500)
Chief Judge: Howard T. Markey. **Associate Judges:** Giles S. Rich, Jack R. Miller, Philip B. Baldwin.

U.S. CUSTOMS COURT
1 Federal Plaza, New York, N.Y.
(Salaries: $54,500)
Chief Judge: Edward D. Re. **Judges:** Paul P. Rao, Morgan Ford, Scovel Richardson, Frederick Landis, James L. Watson, Herbert N. Maletz, Bernard Newman, Nils A. Boe.

STATE AND LOCAL GOVERNMENT EXPENDITURES: PER CAPITA
Source: U.S. Bureau of the Census

Year	Total general	Education	Highways	Public welfare	Health and hospitals	Police and fire
1902	$ 12.80	$ 3.22	$ 2.21	$ .47	$ .75	$ 1.14
1913	21.23	5.93	4.31	.53	1.11	1.70
1922	47.41	15.49	11.76	1.08	2.35	3.17
1932	62.15	18.50	13.93	3.55	3.65	4.23
1936	59.63	16.98	11.12	6.45	3.64	4.05
1940	69.85	19.97	11.91	8.75	4.61	4.54
1944	64.04	20.18	8.67	8.19	4.74	4.80
1946	78.00	23.74	11.83	9.97	5.79	5.47
1948	120.60	36.68	20.71	14.31	8.38	7.16
1950	150.22	47.31	25.07	19.38	11.52	8.34
1952	166.29	53.00	29.63	17.76	13.92	9.71
1954	189.06	65.01	34.04	18.84	14.83	10.98
1956	219.42	79.02	41.56	18.76	16.57	12.35
1957	236.98	82.96	45.88	20.45	18.30	13.37
1958	258.76	91.84	49.43	22.03	19.97	14.33
1959	276.96	97.91	54.34	23.43	21.10	14.87
1960	288.21	104.00	52.38	24.47	21.08	15.85
1961	307.01	112.39	53.78	25.78	22.32	16.96
1962	324.00	119.56	55.74	27.36	23.37	17.51
1963	339.19	125.81	59.11	28.74	24.59	17.99
1964	362.20	137.38	60.96	30.13	25.66	18.74
1965	385.30	147.37	63.05	32.58	27.66	19.89
1966	422.97	169.95	65.20	34.50	30.17	21.19
1967	471.79	191.64	70.41	41.53	33.56	22.99
1968	512.41	205.93	72.46	49.32	37.76	25.18
1969	578.14	233.94	76.35	59.97	42.19	28.19
1970	646.20	259.39	80.83	72.23	47.57	32.07
1971	730.52	288.05	87.73	88.36	54.32	36.50
1972	801.38	311.60	91.29	101.18	61.79	41.07
1973	863.60	332.21	88.70	112.37	65.97	45.18
1974	941.19	358.74	94.36	118.67	75.43	48.85
1975	1082.58	412.24	105.71	132.11	88.43	56.54
1976	1195.99	452.89	111.37	151.89	96.37	62.56
1977	1268.37	475.22	106.80	166.14	104.20	67.82

U.S. — BUDGET: 1789-1980
Source: U.S. Office of Management and Budget (in millions of dollars)

Fiscal Year	Receipts	Outlays	Surplus or Deficit (—)	Fiscal Year	Receipts	Outlays	Surplus or Deficit (—)
1789–1849	1,160	1,090	+70	1940	6,361	9,456	—3,095
1850–1900	14,462	15,453	—991	1941	8,621	13,634	—5,013
1901	588	525	+63	1942	14,350	35,114	—20,764
1902	562	485	+77	1943	23,649	78,533	—54,884
1903	562	517	+45	1944	44,276	91,280	—47,004
1904	541	584	—43	1945	45,216	92,690	—47,474
1905	544	567	—23	1946	39,327	55,183	—15,856
1906	595	570	+25	1947	38,394	34,532	+3,862
1907	666	579	+87	1948	41,774	29,773	+12,001
1908	602	659	—57	1949	39,437	38,834	+603
1909	604	694	—89	1950	39,485	42,597	—3,112
1910	676	694	—18	1951	51,646	45,546	+6,100
1911	702	691	+11	1952	66,204	67,721	—1,517
1912	693	690	+3	1953	69,574	76,107	—6,533
1913	714	715	—*	1954	69,719	70,890	—1,170
1914	725	726	—*	1955	65,469	68,509	—3,041
1915	683	746	—63	1956	74,547	70,460	+4,087
1916	761	713	+48	1957	79,990	76,741	+3,249
1917	1,101	1,954	—853	1958	79,636	82,575	—2,939
1918	3,645	12,677	—9,032	1959	79,249	92,104	—12,855
1919	5,130	18,493	—13,363	1960	92,492	92,223	+269
1920	6,649	6,358	+291	1961	94,389	97,795	—3,406
1921	5,571	5,062	+509	1962	99,676	106,813	—7,137
1922	4,026	3,289	+736	1963	106,560	111,311	—4,751
1923	3,853	3,140	+713	1964	112,662	118,584	—5,922
1924	3,871	2,908	+963	1965	116,833	118,430	—1,596
1925	3,641	2,924	+717	1966	130,856	134,652	—3,796
1926	3,795	2,930	+865	1967	149,552	158,254	—8,702
1927	4,013	2,857	+1,155	1968	153,671	178,833	—25,161
1928	3,900	2,961	+939	1969	187,784	184,548	+3,236
1929	3,862	3,127	+734	1970	193,743	196,588	—2,845
1930	4,058	3,320	+738	1971	188,392	211,425	—23,033
1931	3,116	3,577	—462	1972	208,649	232,021	—23,373
1932	1,924	4,659	—2,735	1973	232,225	247,074	—14,849
1933	1,997	4,598	—2,602	1974	264,932	269,620	—4,688
1934	3,015	6,645	—3,630	1975	280,997	326,185	—45,188
1935	3,706	6,497	—2,791	1976	300,005	366,439	—66,434
1936	3,997	8,422	—4,425	TQ	81,773	94,729	—12,956
1937	4,956	7,733	—2,777	1977	357,762	402,725	—44,963
1938	5,588	6,765	—1,177	1978	401,997	450,836	—48,839
1939	4,979	8,841	—3,862	1979 est.	455,989	493,368	—37,379
				1980 est.[1]	502,553	531,566	—29,013

* Less than $500,000. [1] Based on the 1980 budget issued January 22, 1979. [2] Fiscal years through 1976 began on July 1 and ended the following June 30. Beginning with fiscal year 1977, each fiscal year begins on October 1 and ends on the following September 30. The Transition Quarter (TQ) refers to the 3-month period from the end of fiscal year 1976 on June 30, 1976, to the beginning of fiscal year 1977 on October 1, 1976.
Note: Data for 1789–1939 are for the administrative budget; 1940 and thereafter are for the unified budget.

THE BUDGET DOLLAR

SOURCE: Office of Management and Budget
Fiscal Year—1980 Estimate

Where it comes from . . .

Excise Taxes
Other
Borrowing
Corporation Income Taxes
4¢ 5¢ 5¢ 13¢
Individual Income Taxes 43¢
Social Insurance Receipts 30¢

Where it goes . . .

Direct Benefit Payments to Individuals 39¢
National Defense 24¢
Net Interest 9¢
Grants to States and Localities 16¢
12¢
Other Federal Operations

FEDERAL GRANTS TO STATES[1]

SOURCE: Tax Foundation, Inc.

These comparisons of Federal tax burdens for aid payments per $1.00 of assistance do not actually indicate the entire costs which state and local governments incur for obtaining Federal grants. The comparisons, with few exceptions, do not take into account the costs to these governments of administering the programs for which the aid is granted, nor the amounts of matching funds which the state and local governments must make available out of their own revenue in order to qualify as recipients of these grants. In the last few years, it is estimated that state and local governments provided approximately $1.00 of matching funds for each $3.00 of Federal aid.

"PAYING STATES"[1]

Twenty-two states paid more in U.S. taxes to support grant programs than they received in aid in fiscal year 1978.

State	Grants (millions)	Estimated tax burden for grants (millions)	Tax Burden for $1 of Aid All Grants	Rev. Sharing
Ind.	$1,259.0	$1,830.3	$1.45	$1.17
Texas	3,291.3	4,430.0	1.35	1.24
Kansas	613.4	814.3	1.33	1.24
Conn.	1,052.4	1,367.1	1.30	1.54
Ill.	3,466.4	4,519.6	1.30	1.23
Ohio	2,903.8	3,735.2	1.29	1.25
Iowa	796.3	986.1	1.24	1.13
Mo.	1,273.7	1,576.3	1.24	1.12
Fla.	2,360.3	2,801.4	1.19	1.32
N.J.	2,551.3	3,010.6	1.18	1.27
Md.	1,359.7	1,591.2	1.17	1.07
Colo.	797.7	918.9	1.15	1.14
Va.	1,498.0	1,710.7	1.14	1.13
Wash.	1,277.9	1,441.8	1.13	1.28
Neb.	457.3	508.0	1.11	1.11
Calif.	7,944.9	8,546.2	1.08	1.02
Del.	224.9	239.1	1.06	1.06
Mich.	3,277.6	3,436.4	1.05	1.10
Nev.	259.3	268.9	1.04	1.45
Minn.	1,346.4	1,382.0	1.03	.90
Penn.	3,909.9	3,989.2	1.02	1.04
Wy.	160.9	164.3	1.02	1.26

"RECEIVING STATES"[1]

Twenty-eight states and the District of Columbia paid less in taxes to support grant programs than they received in aid.

State	Grants (millions)	Estimated tax burden for grants (millions)	Tax Burden for $1 of Aid All Grants	Rev. Sharing
N.H.	$ 288.1	$ 283.9	$ .99	$1.15
Oregon	871.8	844.2	.97	.99
Wisc.	1,604.3	1,546.4	.96	.86
Ariz.	749.2	702.2	.94	.88
Tenn.	1,279.4	1,187.8	.93	.86
N.C.	1,652.8	1,501.6	.91	.77
Okla.	931.7	851.6	.91	.99
Utah	417.1	358.6	.86	.79
Ky.	1,125.7	941.3	.84	.73
La.	1,354.3	1,135.5	.84	.67
Hawaii	413.2	336.2	.81	.87
R.I.	387.9	313.7	.81	.92
S.C.	900.8	732.1	.81	.69
Ala.	1,219.3	978.6	.80	.76
N.D.	256.7	201.7	.79	1.13
Mass.	2,580.6	2,017.0	.78	.84
N.Y.	8,371.7	6,506.8	.78	.79
Idaho	311.4	239.1	.77	.84
W. Va.	706.0	530.4	.75	.73
Ark.	774.1	545.3	.70	.71
Ga.	2,033.0	1,397.0	.69	.84
S.D.	284.6	194.2	.68	.84
Alaska	399.2	254.0	.64	1.37
Maine	468.2	291.3	.62	.61
Mont.	373.0	231.6	.62	.85
N.M.	542.2	328.7	.61	.61
Miss.	905.8	537.9	.59	.46
Vt.	240.1	127.0	.53	.56
D.C.	1,179.9	321.2	.27	1.07

[1] Excludes shared revenues; includes general revenue sharing and trust fund aids.

EXPENDITURE OF FEDERAL TAX DOLLARS (FISCAL YEAR 1980)

SOURCE: Tax Foundation, Inc.

Item	Federal Tax Burden Per Household
Total	$6,126
Income security	2,018
National defense	1,418
Interest	643
Health	602
Education, training, employment and social services	341
Veterans' benefits	230
Transportation	198
Commerce and housing credit	172
Natural resources & Environment	129
General purpose fiscal assistance	99

Item	Federal Tax Burden Per Household
International affairs	92
Energy	89
Community and regional development	84
General science, space, and technology	61
General government	50
Administration of justice	50
Agriculture	48
Allowances for contingencies and civilian pay raises	16
Undistributed offsetting receipts	—214
Intragovernmental adjustments	—185
Rents and royalties on the Outer Continental Shelf	— 29

THE U.S. BUDGET: RECEIPTS AND OUTLAYS (in billions of dollars)

SOURCE: U.S. Office of Management and Budget

Description	1975 Actual	1976 Actual	TQ[6] Actual	1977 Actual	1978 Actual	1979[1] Est.	1980[1] Est.
Receipts by source: [4]							
Individual income taxes	122.4	131.6	38.8	157.6	181.0	203.6	227.3
Corporation income taxes	40.6	41.4	8.5	54.9	60.0	70.3	71.0
Social insurance taxes and contributions	86.4	92.7	25.8	108.7	123.4	141.8	161.5
Excise taxes	16.6	17.0	4.5	17.5	18.4	18.4	18.5
Estate and gift taxes	4.6	5.2	1.5	7.3	5.3	5.3	6.0
Customs duties	3.7	4.1	1.2	5.2	6.6	6.6	8.4
Miscellaneous receipts	6.7	8.0	1.6	6.5	7.4	7.4	9.9
Total receipts	**281.0**	**300.0**	**81.8**	**357.8**	**402.0**	**456.0**	**502.6**
Outlays by function: [4] [5]							
National defense [2]	85.6	89.4	22.3	97.5	105.2	114.5	125.8
International affairs and finance	6.9	5.6	2.2	4.8	5.9	7.3	8.2
General science, space, and technology	4.0	4.4	1.2	4.7	4.7	5.2	5.5
Energy	2.2	3.1	.8	4.2	5.9	8.6	7.9
Natural resources and environment	7.3	8.1	2.5	10.0	10.9	11.2	11.5
Agriculture	1.7	2.5	.6	5.5	7.7	6.2	4.3
Commerce and housing credit	5.6	3.8	1.4	—*	3.3	3.0	3.4
Transportation	10.4	13.4	3.3	14.6	15.4	17.4	17.6
Community and regional development	3.7	4.7	1.3	6.3	11.0	9.1	7.3
Education, manpower, and social services	15.9	18.7	5.2	21.0	26.5	30.7	30.2
Health	27.6	33.4	8.7	38.8	43.7	49.1	53.4
Income security	108.6	127.4	32.8	137.9	146.2	158.9	179.1
Veterans benefits and services	16.6	18.4	4.0	18.0	19.0	20.3	20.5
Law enforcement and justice	2.9	3.3	.9	3.6	3.8	4.4	4.4
General government	3.2	3.0	.9	3.4	3.8	4.4	4.4
Revenue sharing and general purpose fiscal assistance	7.2	7.2	2.1	9.5	9.6	8.9	8.8
Interest	30.9	34.5	7.2	38.0	44.0	52.8	57.0
Allowances [3]	—	—	—	—	—	—	1.4
Undistributed offsetting receipts	−14.1	−14.7	−2.6	−15.1	−15.8	−18.7	−19.0
Total outlays	**362.2**	**366.4**	**94.7**	**402.7**	**450.8**	**493.4**	**531.6**
Budget deficit	**−45.2**	**−66.4**	**−13.0**	**−45.0**	**−48.8**	**−37.4**	**−29.0**

* $50 million or less. [1] Based on estimates issued in January 1979. [2] Includes civilian and military pay raises for Department of Defense. [3] Includes allowances for civilian agency pay raises and contingencies for relatively uncontrollable programs and other requirements. [4] The amounts of earned income credit in excess of tax liabilities are shown as budget outlays rather than negative budget receipts. The budget totals have thus been ad- justed retroactively. [5] The 1976-78 data have been revised retro- actively to include the exchange stabilization fund in the unified budget instead of with the off-budget Federal entities. Profits on gold sales are now treated as a means of financing rather than an offsetting collection. The budget totals have been ad- justed retroactively, starting with 1975. [6] See footnote 2, page 184.

FEDERAL, STATE & LOCAL GOVERNMENT FINANCES: 1929—1978

SOURCE: U.S. Department of Commerce, Bureau of Economic Analysis   (Billions of dollars)

	1929	1939	1949	1959	1977	1978*
Total Government**						
Receipts	11.3	15.4	55.9	129.4	603.3	682.6
Expenditures	10.3	17.6	59.3	131.0	621.8	684.2
Federal Government						
Receipts	3.8	6.7	38.7	89.8	374.5	431.5
Expenditures	2.6	8.9	41.3	91.0	422.6	461.4
State and Local Government						
Receipts	7.6	9.6	19.5	46.4	296.2	328.1
Expenditures	7.8	9.6	20.2	46.9	266.6	299.7

*Preliminary. **Total government is after subtraction of grants.

STATE PER CAPITA INCOME: 1976 and 1977

SOURCE: U.S. Department of Commerce, Bureau of Economic Analysis

Rank	State	1976 Income	1977 Income	Percent of National Average 1977
	UNITED STATES	$6,396	$7,026	100
	STATES			
1.	Alaska	10,254	10,497	149
—	District of Columbia	8,071	8,984	128
2.	Connecticut	7,312	8,055	115
3.	Nevada	7,202	7,980	114
4.	New Jersey	7,298	7,969	113
5.	Illinois	7,310	7,951	113
6.	California	7,219	7,909	113
7.	Delaware	7,122	7,724	110
8.	Hawaii	7,188	7,704	110
9.	Michigan	6,766	7,606	108
10.	Maryland	6,994	7,569	108
11.	Washington	6,894	7,562	108
12.	New York	6,929	7,519	107
13.	Wyoming	6,766	7,517	107
14.	Massachusetts	6,627	7,262	103
15.	Colorado	6,523	7,166	102
16.	Kansas	6,475	7,141	102
17.	Minnesota	6,227	7,118	101
18.	Ohio	6,395	7,090	101
19.	Oregon	6,374	7,014	100
20.	Pennsylvania	6,399	7,001	100
21.	Indiana	6,256	6,922	99
22.	Iowa	6,105	6,887	98
23.	Wisconsin	6,123	6,864	98
24.	Virginia	$6,315	$6,841	97
25.	Texas	6,158	6,827	97
26.	Rhode Island	6,186	6,775	96
27.	Florida	6,101	6,697	95
28.	Nebraska	6,052	6,679	95
29.	Missouri	5,963	6,661	95
30.	New Hampshire	6,001	6,578	94
31.	Arizona	5,931	6,520	93
32.	Oklahoma	5,700	6,269	89
33.	Montana	5,648	6,093	87
34.	Georgia	5,511	6,002	85
35.	Idaho	5,659	5,998	85
36.	West Virginia	5,476	5,998	85
37.	Kentucky	5,407	5,989	85
38.	South Dakota	5,043	5,953	85
39.	Utah	5,419	5,943	85
40.	North Carolina	5,467	5,916	84
41.	Louisiana	5,347	5,910	84
42.	North Dakota	5,758	5,872	84
43.	New Mexico	5,285	5,846	83
44.	Vermont	5,401	5,822	83
45.	Tennessee	5,293	5,801	83
46.	Maine	5,359	5,751	82
47.	South Carolina	5,191	5,639	80
48.	Alabama	5,128	5,633	80
49.	Arkansas	4,949	5,522	79
50.	Mississippi	4,538	5,027	72

INTERNAL REVENUE TAXES

SOURCE: U.S. Internal Revenue Service

Year	Collections	Cost of Collecting $100	Tax per Capita	Year	Collections	Cost of Collecting $100	Tax per Capita
1866	$310,120,448	$2.47	$8.49	1932	$1,557,729,043	$2.17	$12.47
1868	190,374,926	4.90	4.98	1934	2,672,239,195	1.08	21.13
1870	184,302,828	4.47	4.62	1935	3,299,435,572	1.29	25.91
1873	113,504,013	5.83	2.64	1937	4,653,195,315	1.12	36.08
1875	110,071,515	4.83	2.44	1939	5,181,573,953	1.13	39.55
1876	116,768,096	4.09	2.53	1941	7,370,108,378	0.89	55.04
1878	110,654,163	3.67	2.30	1942	13,047,868,518	0.58	96.39
1880	123,981,916	3.63	2.47	1943	22,371,385,497	0.44	163.00
1881	135,229,912	3.74	2.62	1944	40,121,760,233	0.32	288.82
1883	144,553,345	3.53	2.67	1945	43,800,387,576	0.33	311.82
1885	112,421,121	3.96	1.98	1946	40,672,096,998	0.43	286.55
1886	116,902,896	3.68	2.02	1948	41,864,542,295	0.44	284.39
1888	124,326,475	3.20	2.05	1950	38,957,131,768	0.59	255.84
1890	142,594,697	2.87	2.26	1951	50,445,686,315	0.49	325.71
1891	146,035,416	2.88	2.27	1952	65,009,585,560	0.42	412.62
1893	161,004,990	2.62	2.40	1954	69,919,990,791	0.38	428.89
1895	143,246,078	2.88	2.06	1955	66,288,692,000	0.42	399.50
1896	146,830,616	2.78	2.07	1957	80,171,971,000	0.38	466.16
1898	170,866,819	2.29	2.32	1958	79,978,476,484	0.42	457.33
1900	295,316,108	1.58	3.88	1959	79,797,972,806	0.44	448.73
1901	306,871,669	1.55	3.95	1960	91,774,802,823	0.40	507.96
1903	230,740,925	2.07	2.86	1961	94,401,086,398	0.44	513.91
1905	234,187,976	2.01	2.79	1962	99,440,839,245	0.45	533.09
1906	249,102,738	1.90	2.92	1963	105,925,395,281	0.47	559.74
1908	251,665,950	1.92	2.84	1964	112,260,257,115	0.49	585.03
1910	289,957,220	1.74	3.14	1965	114,434,633,721	0.52	588.95
1911	322,526,300	1.68	3.44	1966	128,879,961,342	0.48	655.68
1913	344,424,454	1.59	3.54	1967	148,374,814,552	0.45	746.68
1915	415,681,024	1.64	4.13	1968	153,636,837,665	0.46	765.48
1916	512,723,288	1.40	5.03	1969	187,919,559,668	0.40	927.19
1917	809,393,640	0.95	7.83	1970	195,722,096,497	0.45	955.31
1918	3,698,955,821	0.33	35.38	1971	191,647,198,138	0.51	925.63
1919	3,850,150,079	0.53	36.65	1972	209,855,736,878	0.54	1,004.83
1921	4,595,357,062	0.72	42.34	1973	237,787,204,058	0.49	1,130.11
1925	2,584,140,268	1.44	22.31	1974	268,952,253,663	0.49	1,269.24
1926	2,835,999,892	1.23	24.16	1975	293,822,725,772	0.54	1,375.96
1928	2,790,535,538	1.17	23.16	1976	302,519,791,922	0.56	1,406.30
1929	2,939,054,375	1.17	24.14	1977	358,139,416,730	0.50	1,647.91
1930	3,040,145,733	1.13	24.68	1978	399,776,389,362	0.49	1,826.61

ADDRESSES OF U.S. INTERNAL REVENUE OFFICES

If you are located in:	Send your return to:	If you are located in:	Send your return to:
Alabama, Florida, Georgia, Mississippi, South Carolina	Internal Revenue Service Center Atlanta, Georgia 31101	Alaska, Arizona, Colorado, Idaho, Minnesota, Montana, Nebraska, Nevada, North Dakota, Oregon, South Dakota, Utah, Washington, Wyoming	Internal Revenue Service Center Ogden, Utah 84201
Delaware, District of Columbia, Maryland, Pennsylvania	Internal Revenue Service Center Philadelphia, Pennsylvania 19255	California, Hawaii	Internal Revenue Service Center Fresno, California 93888
Michigan, Ohio	Internal Revenue Service Center Cincinnati, Ohio 45999	New York City and N.Y. counties of Nassau, Rockland, Suffolk, and Westchester; New Jersey	Internal Revenue Service Center Holtsville, New York 00501
Arkansas, Kansas, Louisiana, New Mexico, Oklahoma, Texas	Internal Revenue Service Center Austin, Texas 73301	Panama Canal Zone, American Samoa	Internal Revenue Service Center Philadelphia, Pennsylvania 19255
Illinois, Iowa, Missouri, Wisconsin	Internal Revenue Service Center Kansas City, Missouri 64999	Guam	Commissioner of Revenue and Taxation Agana, Guam 96910
Connecticut, Maine, Massachusetts, New Hampshire, New York (except N.Y.C., and Nassau, Rockland, Suffolk, and Westchester counties), Rhode Island, Vermont	Internal Revenue Service Center Andover, Massachusetts 05501	Puerto Rico (or if excluding income under section 933), Virgin Islands: Non permanent residents	Internal Revenue Service Center Philadelphia, Pennsylvania 19255
Tennessee, Kentucky, Virginia, Indiana, North Carolina, West Virginia	Internal Revenue Service Center Memphis, Tennessee 37501	Virgin Islands: Permanent residents	Department of Finance, Tax Division Charlotte Amalie, St. Thomas Virgin Islands 00801

U.S. citizens with foreign addresses (except A.P.O. and F.P.O.) and those excluding income under sec. 911 or 931: file with Internal Revenue Service, Philadelphia, Pa. 19255
U.S. citizens with A.P.O. or F.P.O. address; file with center or home state.

TAX TIPS

Prepared by H & R Block, Inc.
America's Largest Tax Service

Early tax planning is helpful in keeping your income tax as low as is possible within the law. The tax tips discussed here are based on current tax law as of July 1, 1979. New tax legislation could result in changes.

KEEP RECORDS AND RECEIPTS!

The federal tax code requires that all deductions be substantiated. Good record-keeping is an important part of minimizing tax liability.

INVESTMENTS, CAPITAL GAINS

U.S. series E bonds may be a worthwhile investment. Interest earned is not taxable until the bonds mature (plus extensions) or are cashed. Or, you may elect to report the interest each year as it accrues. If the latter choice is made, all such interest in all future years is taxable as it accrues. This election may be wise when it is expected that gross income will be greater in the year(s) the bonds will be cashed than in the intervening years (such as bonds purchased for a child which will be used for his or her future). The first year the election is made, a return must be filed with a statement on the option chosen. Thereafter a return is filed or not based on the usual filing requirements.

You may open a savings account or purchase stock to save for your child's college education or future without paying tax on the earnings.

The security or savings must be in the child's name and neither the principal nor earnings can be used for the child's support or in any way used by you. You may be custodian of the investment. The child is not required to file a return for any year that his or her investment income is less than $1000 and gross income is less than $3300. And if the child is required to file, his or her tax on this income would most likely be less than the adult would have paid.

Sales of capital assets should be planned to gain the greatest possible tax advantage without sacrificing economic results. Try to avoid sales at a loss in the same year in which you will have a long-term gain. Only 40% of a net long-term capital gain is taxable, but gains and losses must be combined to determine the net gain or loss. To realize 100% of a long-term loss, sell short-term assets at a gain. (Only 50% of a net long-term loss is deductible against ordinary income.) Generally, property owned over one year is long term. Commodity futures are long term if held over 6 months.

SELLING YOUR PRINCIPAL RESIDENCE

If you sell your home, any gain will not be taxed immediately if, within 18 months, you buy and occupy another home that costs as much or more than the adjusted sales price of the old home. The deferred gain reduces the basis of the new home. Gain on each succeeding sale is deferred as long as a new home of equal or greater value is purchased. A taxpayer age 55 or over on the date of sale may exclude up to $100,000 gain from sale of his or her principal residence. To qualify, you must have owned and lived in the home three of the five years ending on the date of sale. This election may be made only once in a lifetime.

INSTALLMENT METHOD

If you sell your home and cannot defer the gain, you may be able to use the installment method, if payments received the year of sale do not exceed 30% of the selling price. Gain is reported over the years that payments are received instead of all in the year of sale. This method can also be used to report gain from the sale of other real property and certain personal property if qualifications are met.

END-OF-YEAR TAX PLANNING

Before the end of the year, you should estimate whether the total of your itemized deductions will exceed your zero bracket amount. If it will, it may be beneficial to pay any outstanding obligations that are deductible before the end of the year. If the total itemized deductions will not exceed the zero bracket amount, it will be better to postpone (wherever possible) payment of deductible obligations until the beginning of the new tax year. Payment of various items, such as charitable contributions, medical expenses, and the fourth installment of estimated state and local income tax, can be timed to derive the greatest tax benefit.

Special attention should be paid to medical expenses, since they are deductible only in excess of 3 percent of adjusted gross income. If medical expenses approach this level and deductions will be itemized, you may reduce your tax liability by paying outstanding medical bills before the end of the year. Also have necessary optical and dental work done and paid for before the end of the year.

CHARITABLE CONTRIBUTIONS

You may deduct actual transportation expenses incurred in performing volunteer work for a charitable organization. In lieu of actual costs, you may deduct seven cents a mile plus parking fees and tolls. Also deductible are the cost and upkeep of uniforms required to be worn and equipment or supplies purchased to perform volunteer work. All items must be used solely for the charitable work.

You may deduct up to 50 percent of adjusted gross income for cash contributions made to churches, educational organizations, certain medical organizations, public organizations such as libraries and symphony orchestras, and other charities that receive most of their support from the general public or government.

CASUALTY LOSS

Loss or damage to your property resulting from a sudden or unusual event such as severe weather, fire, accident or theft may be deductible. If you sustained such a loss in an area determined by the President to warrant federal disaster assistance, the loss may be claimed on your tax return for the year of the loss or the preceding year, whichever is more advantageous.

AGE 65 BRINGS TAX BENEFITS

You are allowed an additional personal exemption if you are 65 or older on the last day of the year. For tax purposes, you are considered 65 on the day before your 65th birthday.

You may be eligible for a tax credit if you are ge 65 or older or are under age 65 and receive pension or annuity from a public retirement ystem. The maximum credit is $375 for single ndividuals, $562.50 for married individuals ling a joint return, and $281.25 for married ndividuals filing a separate return. Married in-ividuals must file a joint return to claim the redit unless they lived apart during the entire ear. Nonresident aliens are generally not eligible or the credit.

CLAIMING DEPENDENTS

It is not always necessary to provide more than alf of the support for a relative to claim him r her as a dependent. If you and one or more ersons could claim the relative as a dependent, xcept for the support test and together con-ibute more than 50 percent of the support, you an agree to let any one who individually furn-hes more than 10 percent of the support claim e dependent. The other contributors must sign ultiple Support Declarations (Form 2120) hich are to be attached to the return of the dividual who claims the exemption.

Parents who provide over half the total sup-ort of their working child (who is under 19 or a student) may claim a dependent exemption gardless of the amount the child earns. A dou-e benefit — the child claims his or her own per-nal exemption.

DIVORCED TAXPAYERS

Generally, the parent who has custody of the ild for the greater part of the year is entitled claim the exemption. There are two exceptions this rule. The noncustody parent is entitled the exemption if he or she:

) contributed at least $600 toward each child's support during the year and the divorce decree or other agreement specifies that this parent is entitled to the exemption. Any agreement must be in writing. OR

) provided $1,200 or more of support for each child during the year and the parent having custody cannot prove that he or she pro-vided more support.

ese rules do not apply if a third party has stody for more than half the year and/or pro-les more than 50% of the support.

Child support payments are neither deductible the payer nor taxable to the recipient. If the cree does not specify an amount as child sup-rt, the entire payment is alimony. Alimony yments, generally, are deductible by the payer d taxable to the recipient. Deductible alimony claimed as an adjustment, deductible regard-s of whether deductions are itemized.

EARNED INCOME CREDIT

Some individuals will qualify for the earned ome credit. If both your adjusted gross income d your earned income are less than $10,000 d you maintain your home for a qualifying ld you may be eligible for this credit. Maxi-m credit is $500.

OTHER CREDITS

An investment credit is available when quali-d business property is purchased. Employees y be able to claim this credit if required to their own vehicles, tools, etc. in their work.

Residential energy credit is available for in-sulation, storm or thermal windows and certain energy saving devices installed in your home. Also for solar, wind or geothermal equipment. Energy investment credit is available to busi-nesses for energy-conserving expenditures.

You may be able to claim a credit if you pay for the care of your child or disabled dependent that enables you to be gainfully employed.

These credits range from 10% to 30% of the qualified costs.

INDIVIDUAL RETIREMENT ACCOUNTS

An employee who is not covered by a pension, profit-sharing, or other qualified plan may estab-lish an Individual Retirement Account (IRA). If eligible, you may contribute and deduct up to the lesser of 15 percent of your compensation or $1,500 each year. In addition, the amount earned on the contributions is not taxable until it is withdrawn. Generally, no amount may be with-drawn until you reach age 59 1/2.

If you and your spouse are eligible to estab-lish an IRA and your spouse received no earned income during the year, you may con-tribute to a spousal IRA. The maximum de-duction and contribution for a spousal IRA is the lesser of 15% of compensation or $1,750, one-half to each account. You have until the due date of your tax return to establish and contri-bute to an IRA for that year.

DECEASED SPOUSE

A taxpayer whose spouse died during the cur-rent year is considered to be married for the entire year if he or she does not remarry before the end of the year. A joint return, generally, may be filed.

A person meeting the following requirements may file as a qualifying widow or widower for the two tax years immediately succeeding the one in which the spouse died: (1) you must have been entitled to file a joint return with your spouse in the year of death. (2) You must not have remarried before the close of the tax year. (3) You must have a child or stepchild who qualifies as your dependent. (4) You must furnish over half the cost of maintaining a home, which is the principal residence of the depen-dent child for the entire year, except for tem-porary absences. A qualifying widow or widower cannot claim an exemption for the deceased spouse, but can use the zero bracket amount and tax rates for married persons filing a joint return.

After two years the surviving spouse may file as head of household if those qualifications are met.

Life insurance proceeds paid because of the death of the insured, whether received in a lump sum or installments, generally are not taxable. If a surviving spouse elects to receive the pro-ceeds in installments up to $1,000 per year of the interest may be excluded from income. If you elect to receive interest only, it is fully taxable.

The first $5,000 of payments to beneficiaries of deceased employees made by or for an employer because of an employee's death is excludable from the income of the beneficiaries. The ex-cludable amount may not exceed $5,000, regard-less of the number of employers or the number of beneficiaries.

FEDERAL TAX COLLECTIONS

SOURCE: Tax Foundation, Inc. Based on official U.S. Government figures.

SELECTED FISCAL YEARS 1959–1980
(Figures in millions)

SOURCE	1959	1969	1978	1979*	1980*
Total	$77,520	$182,575	$389,164	$441,424	$486,333
Income and profits taxes	54,028	123,927	240,940	273,909	298,309
Individual income	36,719	87,249	180,988	203,602	227,322
Corporate income and profits	17,309	36,678	59,952	70,307	70,987
Excise taxes	10,675	15,222	18,376	18,395	18,455
Alcoholic beverages	2,979	4,482	5,492	5,536	5,580
Tobacco products	1,793	2,136	2,446	2,497	2,551
Manufacturers' excises	3,928	6,243	6,328	6,651	6,766
Gasoline	1,687	3,053	4,296	4,513	4,523
Passenger automobiles[1]	1,031	1,858	—	—	—
Tires and tubes	277	582	803	854	868
Automobile and truck parts and accessories	165	90	183	199	220
Trucks and buses	214	516	834	868	923
Lubricating oils	73	93	104	103	104
Other manufacturers' excises	481	51	108	114	128
Retailers' excises	353	—[2]	526[3]	635[3]	664[3]
Miscellaneous excises	1,624	2,361	3,584	3,076	2,894
Telephone and telegraph	685	1,304	1,642	1,397	1,115
Transportation of persons	225	222	1,107	1,196	1,014
Other miscellaneous excises	714	835	835[4]	483[4]	765[4]
Estate and gift taxes	1,333	3,491	5,285	5,686	6,011
Employment taxes	8,526	34,236	103,893	119,749	139,151
Unemployment taxes[5]	2,024	3,328	13,850	15,870	15,855
Customs	925	2,319	6,573	7,517	8,447
Miscellaneous taxes	9	52	247	298	105

* Data for 1979 and 1980 are estimated.   [1] Repealed as of July 15, 1971.   [2] Repealed as of June 22, 1965.   [3] Includes taxes on noncommercial aviation fuels and diesel fuels used on highways.   [4] Includes Black lung disability fund taxes and undistributed tax deposits and unapplied collections.   [5] Includes state unemployment taxes deposited with the Treasury.

PER CAPITA PROPERTY TAX COLLECTIONS

SOURCE: Bureau of the Census and the Tax Foundation

State	Amount 1967	1977	Percent Increase	State	Amount 1967	1977	Percent Increase	State	Amount 1967	1977	Percent Increase
U.S. Avg.	$133	$289	117.7	La.	53	99	88.8	Ohio	129	249	94.0
Ala.	34	60	74.8	Maine	130	238	82.5	Okla.	88	135	52.8
Alaska	86	1,318	1,441.0	Md.	137	265	93.9	Oreg.	149	353	137.7
Ariz.	143	317	121.1	Mass.	191	491	157.9	Pa.	97	201	108.1
Ark.	51	110	113.8	Mich.	145	332	129.2	R.I.	135	327	142.4
Calif.	216	458	112.3	Minn.	180	271	50.6	S.C.	42	128	203.6
Colo.	161	314	94.7	Miss.	54	116	113.8	S.D.	154	307	98.7
Conn.	171	413	141.2	Mo.	104	193	85.0	Tenn.	63	141	124.6
Del.	67	134	98.8	Mont.	167	362	116.5	Texas	105	233	121.8
Fla.	113	211	86.5	Nebr.	196	357	82.3	Utah	115	191	65.5
Ga.	69	190	175.4	Nev.	152	286	88.3	Vt.	116	331	184.2
Hawaii	83	167	101.4	N.H.	161	382	138.0	Va.	74	194	161.8
Idaho	108	205	89.6	N.J.	179	468	161.0	Wash.	110	255	131.9
Ill.	146	318	118.6	N.M.	65	113	75.0	W. Va.	59	112	88.7
Ind.	156	243	55.2	N.Y.	179	448	149.8	Wis.	143	299	108.5
Iowa	163	291	78.6	N.C.	59	140	138.3	Wyo.	207	402	94.5
Kans.	158	299	89.7	N.D.	131	224	70.2	D.C.	115	240	109.0
Ky.	57	113	96.7								

TAX BURDEN: SELECTED COUNTRIES

SOURCE: Tax Foundation, Inc. based on OECD data

Country	TAXES AS % OF GROSS DOMESTIC PRODUCT 1966	1971	1976	Country	TAXES AS % OF GROSS DOMESTIC PRODUCT 1966	1971	1976
Australia	24.12	26.45	29.98	Luxembourg	32.02	35.21	50.45
Austria	35.54	36.96	38.91	Netherlands	36.99	41.53	46.16
Belgium	32.85	36.14	41.87	New Zealand	26.43	28.15	31.83
Canada	27.56	31.16	32.89	Norway	34.59	42.40	46.18
Denmark	32.56	44.64	44.70	Portugal	19.12	22.92	26.51
Finland	31.77	34.74	42.19	Spain	14.96	17.48	20.27
France	34.77	35.01	39.45	Sweden	36.44	41.49	50.89
Germany, West	32.19	33.20	36.70	Switzerland	21.46	23.51	31.59
Greece	22.20	23.94	27.94	Turkey	16.97	20.85	24.82
Ireland	27.96	32.24	36.81	United Kingdom	32.22	35.64	36.70
Italy	28.98	31.14	35.82	United States	26.85	28.76	29.21
Japan	17.63	19.41	20.91				

STATE INCOME TAX RATES AND EXEMPTIONS: 1980

SOURCE: Reprinted with permission from the *State Tax Guide*, published by Commerce Clearing House, Inc.

Five states have neither personal nor corporate income tax; they are Nevada, South Dakota, Texas, Washington, and Wyoming. Under personal exemptions, additional exemptions for aged and/or blind are not included.

State	Personal Exemptions	Individual Rates		Corporation Rates
ALABAMA	Single ...... $1,500 Married ..... 3,000 Dependent .. 300	1st $1,000 .... 1.5% Next 2,000 3	Next $2,000 ..... 4.5% Over 5,000 5	5%. Financial institutions 6%.
ALASKA	Single ...... $ 750 Married .... 1,500 Dependent .. 750	Single persons and fiduciaries pay at rates ranging from 3% on taxable income not over $2,000 to $25,050 plus 14.5% on taxable income over $200,000.		5.4% plus 4% surtax.
ARIZONA	Single ...... $1,000 Married ..... 2,000 Dependent .. 600	1st $1,000 .... 2% Next 1,000 .... 3 Next 1,000 .... 4 Next 1,000 5	Next $1,000 .... 6% Next 1,000 .... 7 Over 6,000 8	1st $1,000 . 2.5% 2d 1,000 . 4 3d 1,000 . 5 4th 1,000 . 6.5 5th 1,000 . 8 6th 1,000 . 9 Over 6,000 . 10.5
		Joint returns may split their income.		
ARKANSAS	From tax: Single ..... $17.50 Married ..... 35.00 Dependent .. 6.00	1st $2,999 .... 1% Next 3,000 .... 2.5 Next 3,000 .... 3.5	Next $ 6,000 ..... 4.5% Next 10,000 ..... 6 $25,000 and over 7	1st $ 3,000 . 1% 2d 3,000 . 2 Next 5,000 . 3 Next 14,000 . 5 Over 25,000 . 6
CALIFOR- NIA	From tax: Single ..... $25.00 Married ..... 50.00 Dependent .. 8.00	1st $2,000 .... 1% Next 1,500 .... 2 Next 1,500 .... 3 Next 1,500 .... 4 Next 1,500 .... 5 Next 1,500 6	Next $1,500 .... 7% Next 1,500 .... 8 Next 1,500 .... 9 Next 1,500 .... 10 Over 15,500 11	9%. Financial institutions, other than banks, are allowed limited offset for personal property taxes and license fees.
		Tax rates for heads of households range from 1% of taxable income not over $4,000 to 11% of taxable income over $18,000.		
COLORADO	Single ..... $ 850 Married .... 1,700 Dependent . 850	1st $1,000 .... 3% Next 1,000 .... 3.5 Next 1,000 .... 4 Next 1,000 .... 4.5 Next 1,000 5	Next $1,000 .... 5.5% Next 1,000 .... 6 Next 1,000 .... 6.5 Next 1,000 .... 7 Next 1,000 .... 7.5 Over 10,000 8	5%.
		Surtax on intangible income over $5,000 .... 2% Tax reduction credit applies to reduce the effective rate of tax ½ of 1% in each bracket up to $9,000.		
CONNECTI- CUT	Single ...... $ 100 Married, filing jointly 200 Married, filing separately 100	Rates ranging from 1% on net capital gains and dividends of at least $20,000, up to 9% on $100,000 and over.		10%, $50 min., or .31 of 1 mill per dollar of net income, whichever is greatest. $100,000 maximum.
DELAWARE	Single ...... $ 600 Married .... 1,200 Dependent .. 600	1st $ 1,000 .... 1.5% Next 1,000 .... 2.1 Next 1,000 .... 3.15 Next 1,000 .... 4.3 Next 1,000 .... 5.35 Next 1,000 .... 6.4 Next 2,000 .... 7.45 Next 2,000 .... 8.4 Next 5,000 .... 8.5	Next $ 5,000 .... 8.6% Next 5,000 .... 9.05 Next 5,000 .... 9.65 Next 10,000 .... 11.55 Next 10,000 .... 12.8 Next 25,000 .... 14.45 Next 25,000 .... 15 Over 100,000 .... 16.65	7.2%
DIST. OF COLUMBIA	Single ...... $ 750 Married ... 1,500 Dependent ... 750	1st $1,000 .... 2% Next 1,000 .... 3 Next 1,000 .... 4 Next 1,000 .... 5 Next 1,000 6	Next $5,000 .... 7% Next 3,000 .... 8 Next 4,000 .... 9 Next 8,000 .... 10 Over 25,000 11	10%.
FLORIDA	None			5%.
GEORGIA	Single ...... $1,500 Married ..... 3,000 Dependent ... 700	1st $1,000 .... 1% Next 2,000 .... 2 Next 2,000 3	Next $2,000 .... 4% Next 3,000 .... 5 Over 10,000 6	6%.
HAWAII	Single ...... $ 750 Married .... 1,500 Dependent ... 750	1st $ 500 .... 2.25% Next 500 .... 3.25 Next 500 .... 4.5 Next 500 .... 5 Next 1,000 .... 6.5 Next 2,000 .... 7.5	Next $5,000 .... 8.5% Next 4,000 .... 9.5 Next 6,000 .... 10 Next 10,000 .... 10.5 Over 30,000 11	First $25,000 5.85 % Over 25,000 6.435
IDAHO	Single ...... $ 750 Married .... 1,500 Dependent . 750 Credit against tax .... $15 per exemption	1st $1,000 .... 2% Next 1,000 .... 4 Next 1,000 .... 4.5	Next $1,000 ...... 5.5% Next 1,000 ...... 6.5 Over 5,000 ...... 7.5	6.5%. Additional tax $10.
		Additional $10 due from each person (joint returns deemed one person) filing return. Joint returns may split their income.		
ILLINOIS	Single ...... $1,000 Married ..... 2,000 Dependent .. 1,000	2½% of federal adjusted income		4%.
INDIANA	Single ...... $1,000 Married ..... 2,000 Dependent .. 500	1.9% of federal adjusted gross income.		3%+3% supplemental income tax.
IOWA	From tax: Single ..... $15.00 Married .... 30.00 Dependent .. 10.00	1st $1,000 .... .5% 2d 1,000 .... 1.25 3d 1,000 .... 2.75 4th 1,000 .... 3.5	5th, 6th and 7th $1,000 ... 5% 8th and 9th 1,000 .... 6 10th through 15th 1,000 . 7 16th through 20th 1,000 . 8	First $25,000 ... 6% Next $75,000 ... 8 Over $100,000 ... 10

State	Personal Exemptions	Individual Rates	Corporation Rates
IOWA (cont'd)		21st through 25th $1,000 .... 9% 26th through 30th 1,000 ...... 10 31st through 40th 1,000 ...... 11 41st through 75th 1,000 ...... 12 Over 75,000 13	Financial institutions: First $25,000 .. 5% Next 50,000 .. 6 Next 25,000 .. 7 Over 100,000 .. 8
KANSAS	Single ...... $ 750 Married ..... 1,500 Dependent ... 750	1st $2,000 ....2% Next $3,000 ....6.5% Next 1,000 ....3.5 Next 10,000 ....7.5 Next 2,000 ....4 Next 5,000 ....8.5 Next 2,000 ....5 Over 25,000 ....9.0	4.5%+2¼% surtax over $25,000
KEN-TUCKY	From tax: Single ...... $20 Married ..... 40 Dependent .. 20	1st $3,000 .... 2% Next $3,000 .... 5% Next 1,000 ...... 3 Over 8,000 .... 6 Next 1,000 4	1st $25,000 .. 4% Over 25,000 .. 5.8
LOUISI-ANA	Single ...... $2,500 Married ..... 5,000 Dependent .. 400 (Personal exemptions are deductible from 2% tax bracket only.)	1st $10,000 ... 2% Next 40,000 .... 4 Over 50,000 .... 6 Joint returns may split their income.	Up to $25,000 .. 4% Next 25,000 .. 5 Next 50,000 .. 6 Next 100,000 .. 7 Over 200,000 .. 8
MAINE	Single ...... $ 750 Married ..... 1,500 Dependent ... 750	1% on the first $2,000 to 10% of taxable income over $25,000.	1st $25,000 .. 4.95% Over 25,000 .. 6.93
MARYLAND	Single ...... $ 800 Married ..... 1,600 Dependent ... 800	1st $1,000 .... 2% Next $1,000 .... 4% Next 1,000 .... 3 Over 3,000 5	7%.
MASSA-CHUSETTS	From earned income: Single ...... $2,000 Married (joint return) .. 2,000 plus up to $2,000 for spouse with lower income plus $600 if that spouse's income was under $2,000. Dependent .. 600	Interest, dividends, net capital gains .... 10% Earned income, annuities .... 5 (Plus 7.5% surtax)	8.33% of net income plus $2.60 per $1,000 of tangible property, $200 (whichever greater), plus 14% surtax.
MICHIGAN	Single ...... $1,500 Married .... 3,000 Dependent .. 1,500	4.6% of adjusted gross income.	
MINNE-SOTA	From tax: Single .... $30 Married .... 60 Dependent 30	1st $ 500 ...... 1.6% Next $ 2,000 ...... 10.2% Next 500 ...... 2.2 Next 2,000 ...... 11.5 Next 1,000 ...... 3.5 Next 3,500 ...... 12.8 Next 1,000 ...... 5.8 Next 7,500 ...... 14 Next 1,000 ...... 7.3 Next 7,500 ...... 15 Next 1,000 ...... 8.8 Next 7,500 ...... 16 Over 40,000 17	12%. Minimum, $10
MISSIS-SIPPI	Single ..... $4,500 Married .... 6,500 Dependent .. 750	1st $ 5,000 ...... 3% Over 5,000 4	Same as individual.
MISSOURI	Single ...... $1,200 Married .... 2,400 Dependent .. 400	1st $1,000 .... 1.5% 6th $1,000 .... 4% 2d 1,000 .... 2 7th 1,000 .... 4.5 3d 1,000 .... 2.5 8th 1,000 .... 5 4th 1,000 .... 3 9th 1,000 .... 5.5 5th 1,000 .... 3.5 Over 9,000 6	5%.
MONTANA	Single ...... $ 650 Married .... 1,300 Dependent 650	1st $1,000 .... 2% Next $ 4,000 ...... 8% Next 1,000 .... 3 Next 6,000 ...... 9 Next 2,000 .... 4 Next 15,000 ...... 10 Next 2,000 .... 5 Over 35,000 ...... 11 Next 2,000 .... 6 Next 2,000 7	6¾%. Minimum tax corporations, $50.
NEBRASKA	Single ...... $ 750 Married .... 1,500 Dependent ... 750	16% of Adjusted federal income tax liability.	1st $25,000, 4.5 Over $25,000, 4.95%
NEW HAMP-SHIRE	$600 (Interest and dividend tax).	5% on income from interest and dividends.	5%
NEW JERSEY	Single ...... $1,000 Married .... 2,000 Dependent .. 1,000	1st $20,000 .... 2% Over 20,000 .... 2.5 New York and Pennsylvania residents working in New Jersey are taxed at the same respective rate of their state of residence.	7½% or 7¼% on located net income interstate corporation plus additional tax net worth.
NEW MEXICO	Single ...... $ 750 Married .... 1,500 Dependent .. 750	Rates range from 0.8% of net income for 1st $1,000 to 9% of net income over $100,000.	5%. Banks and finan corps., 6%.

State	Personal Exemptions	Individual Rates	Corporation Rates
NEW YORK	Single $700 Married 1,400 Dependent 700	1st $1,000 2% Next 2,000 3 Next 2,000 4 Next 2,000 5 Next 2,000 6 Next 2,000 7 Next 2,000 8 Next $2,000 9% Next 2,000 10 Next 2,000 11 Next 2,000 12 Next 2,000 13 Over 23,000 14	10% of net income, min. $250 or a tax on three alternative bases, whichever produces the greatest tax.
NORTH CAROLINA	Single $1,000 Married 2,000 Dependent 600	1st $2,000 3% Next 2,000 4 Next 2,000 5 Next $1,000 6% Over 10,000 7	6%.
NORTH DAKOTA	Single $750 Married 1,500 (if filing joint return) Dependent 750	1st $3,000 1% Next 2,000 2 Next 3,000 3 Next $4,000 4% Next 18,000 5 Over 30,000 7.5	1st $3,000 3% Next 5,000 4 Next 7,000 5 Next 10,000 6 Over 25,000 8.5
OHIO	Single $650 Married 1,300 Dependent 650	1st $5,000 .5% Next 5,000 1 Next 5,000 2 Next $5,000 2.5% Next 20,000 3 Over 40,000 3.5	4% of first $25,000 of net value; 8% of value over $25,000; or 5 mills per dollar of value, whichever is greater. Min., $50.
OKLAHOMA	Single $750 Married 1,500 Dependent 750	1st $2,000 0.5% Next 3,000 1 Next 2,500 2 Next 2,500 3 Next $2,500 4% Next 2,500 5 Remainder 6%	4%.
OREGON	Single $750 Married 1,500 Dependent 750	1st $500 4% Next 500 5 Next 1,000 6 Next 1,000 7 Next $1,000 8% Next 1,000 9 Over 5,000 10	7½%.
PENNSYLVANIA	None	No personal income tax. 2.2% of specified classes of income.	10.5%
RHODE ISLAND	Single $750 Married 1,500 Dependent 750	19% of modified federal income tax liability.	8% or 40¢ per $100 of corporate excess, whichever is the greater.
SOUTH CAROLINA	Single $800 Married 1,600 Dependent 800	1st $2,000 2% Next 2,000 3 Next 2,000 4 Next $2,000 5% Next 2,000 6 Over 10,000 7	6%; banks 4.5%; associations, 8%.
TENNESSEE	None	6% on dividends and interest.	6%.
UTAH	Single $750 Married 1,500 Dependent 750	Rates for single taxpayers range from 2¼% of taxable income not over $750 to $214 plus 7.75% of taxable income over $4,500. Married couples filing jointly pay rates ranging from 2.75% if taxable income not over $1,500 to $356 plus 7.75% of taxable income over $7,500.	4%. Minimum $25.
VERMONT	Single $750 Married 1,500 Dependent 750	25% of federal income tax liability.	1st $10,000 5% Next 15,000 6 Next 225,000 7 Next 250,000 7.5 Min. $50.
VIRGINIA	Single $600 Married 1,200 Dependent 600	1st $3,000 2% Next 2,000 3 Next 7,000 5 Over $12,000 5¾%	6%.
WEST VIRGINIA	Single $600 Married 1,200 Dependent 600	1st $2,000 2.1% 2d 2,000 2.3 3d 2,000 2.8 4th 2,000 3.2 5th 2,000 3.5 6th 2,000 4.0 7th 2,000 4.6 8th 2,000 4.9 9th 2,000 5.3 10th 2,000 5.4 11th 2,000 6.0 Next 4,000 6.1 Next $6,000 6.5% Next 6,000 6.8 Next 6,000 7.2 Next 6,000 7.5 Next 10,000 7.9 Next 10,000 8.2 Next 10,000 8.6 Next 10,000 8.8 Next 10,000 9.1 Next 50,000 9.3 Next 50,000 9.5 Over 200,000 9.6	6%.
WISCONSIN	From tax: Single $20 Married 40 Dependent 20	1st $3,000 3.4% Next 3,000 5.2 Next 3,000 7.0 Next 3,000 8.2 Next $3,000 8.7% Next 5,000 9.1 Next 20,000 9.5 Over 40,000 10.0	1st $1,000 2.3% Next 1,000 2.8 Next 1,000 3.4 Next 1,000 4.5 Next 1,000 5.6 Next 1,000 6.8 Over 6,000 7.9

STATE SALES AND USE TAX RATES

SOURCE: *State Tax Guide*, Commerce Clearing House, Inc.

State	Sales*	Use*	State	Sales*	Use*	State	Sales*	Use*
Alabama[1]	4%	4%	Kentucky[1]	5%	5%	Ohio[1]	4%	4%
Arizona[1]	4%	4%	Louisiana[1]	3%	3%	Oklahoma[1]	2%	2%
Arkansas[1]	3%	3%	Maine	5%	5%	Pennsylvania[1]	6%	6%
California[1]	4¾%	4¾%	Maryland	5%	5%	Rhode Island	6%	6%
Colorado[1]	3%	3%	Massachusetts	5%	5%	South Carolina	4%	4%
Connecticut	7%[2]	7%[2]	Michigan	4%	4%	South Dakota[1][3]	4%	4%
D.C.	5%	5%	Minnesota[1]	4%	4%	Tennessee[1]	4½%[4]	4½%[4]
Florida	4%	4%	Mississippi	5%	5%	Texas[1]	4%	4%
Georgia[1]	3%	3%	Missouri[1]	3⅛%	3⅛%	Utah[1]	4%	4%
Hawaii	4%	4%	Nebraska[1]	3%	3%	Vermont	3%	3%
Idaho	3%	3%	Nevada[1]	3%	3%	Virginia[1]	3%	3%
Illinois[1]	4%	4%	New Jersey	5%	5%	Washington[1]	4.5%	4.5%
Indiana	4%	4%	New Mexico[1]	3¾%	3¾%	West Virginia[1]	3%	3%
Iowa	3%	3%	New York[1]	4%	4%	Wisconsin[1]	4%	4%
Kansas[1]	3%	3%	North Carolina[1]	3%	3%	Wyoming	3%	3%
			North Dakota[3]	3%	3%			

* As of April, 1978. The list of states imposing sales and use taxes does not include Alaska and Delaware. Alaska imposes a business license (gross receipts) tax, and Delaware imposes a merchants' and manufacturers' license tax and a use tax on leases. Other states impose occupation, admission, license, or gross receipts taxes in addition to sales and use taxes. [1] Local tax rates are additional. [2]Manufacturing production machinery is taxed at 2.5% and enumerated business services are taxed at 3.5%. [3]Tax on farm machinery & agricultural and irrigation equipment is 2%. [4]Sales and use tax rates are decreased to 3%, effective July 1, 1980.

CITY SALES TAX RATES

SOURCE: *All-State Sales Tax Reports*, published by Commerce Clearing House, Inc.

For these selected U.S. cities, the first rate given is the state sales tax applicable in the city. The second is the city or county rate. The third is the additional sales and use tax. The rates added together give total city sales tax rate.

City	Sales Tax Rate	City	Sales Tax Rate	City	Sales Tax Rate	City	Sales Tax Rate
Atlanta	3% + 1%	Houston	4% +1%	New York City	4% + 4%	Salt Lake City	4% + ¾% + ¼%
Birmingham	4% + 1%	Kansas City, Mo.	3⅛% + ½%	Norfolk	3% +1%	San Antonio	4% + 1%
Buffalo	4% + 3%	Los Angeles	4¾% + 1¼% + 1%	Oklahoma City	2% +2%	San Diego	4¾% + 1¼% + 1%
Chicago	4% + 1%	Memphis	3% + 1.5%	Omaha	3% +1½%	San Francisco	4¾% + 1¼% + ½%
Cincinnati	4% + ½%	New Orleans	3% + 2% + 1%	Phoenix	4% + 1%	Seattle	4.5% + ½%
Cleveland	4% + ½%			Richmond	3% +1%		
Dallas	4% +1%			St. Louis	3⅛% + 1%		
Denver	3% +3%						
Greensboro, N.C.	3%+1%						

CITY INCOME TAXES

SOURCE: Commerce Clearing House, Inc.

CITIES (500,000 OR MORE)

	Present rate	Date of introduction
Alabama		
Birmingham	1.0	1970
Maryland		
Baltimore	50% of state income tax[1]	1966
Michigan		
Detroit	2.0	1962
Missouri		
St. Louis	1.0	1948
New York		
New York	0.9 to 4.3	1966
Ohio		
Cleveland	1.5	1967
Columbus	1.5	1947
Pennsylvania		
Philadelphia	4-5/16	1939
Pittsburgh	1.25	1976

CITIES (125,000 TO 499,000)

	Present rate	Date of introduction
Kentucky		
Lexington	2.0	1952
Louisville	2.0	1948
Missouri		
Kansas City	1.0	1964
Michigan		
Flint	1.0	1965
Grand Rapids	1.0	1967
Lansing	2.2	1968
Ohio		
Akron	1.5	1962
Canton	1.5	1954
Cincinnati	2.0	1954
Dayton	1.75	1949
Toledo	1.5	1967
Youngstown	1.5	1948
Pennsylvania		
Erie	1.0	1948

[1] Individual income tax only.

FINANCE/INDUSTRY/LABOR

FACTS ABOUT U.S. MONEY

SOURCE: U.S. Treasury Department

In the early days of our nation, before United States money was issued, there were in circulation English shillings, French louis d'ors, and Spanish doubloons, along with other units of those nations' money. This caused confusion and slowed up trade. The dollar was adopted (1785) by the Congress existing under the Articles of Confederation as the unit of our money, and the decimal system as the method of reckoning. In 1792 the United States monetary system was established, and the U.S. Mint began coining money at Philadelphia in 1793.

Many changes in the laws governing coinage and the denominations themselves have been made since the original 1792 act. Coins no longer in use include the half-cent, two-cent, three-cent, and 20-cent pieces, as well as the silver half dime. The five-cent nickel coin was introduced in 1866. Gold coins were struck from 1795 through 1933, in denominations ranging from $1 to $20. The minting and issuance of gold coins were terminated by Section 5 of the Gold Reserve Act of 1934.

President Johnson signed (July 23, 1965) an historic bill providing for the first major change in U.S. coinage in more than a century. Silver was eliminated altogether from the dime and quarter and substanially reduced in the half dollar.

On Dec. 31, 1970, President Nixon signed the Bank Holding Company Act calling for the removal of all silver from silver dollars and half dollars. This legislation also authorized a silver dollar with a design emblematic of the symbolic eagle of the Apollo 11 landing on the Moon. Once adopted, a coin design may not be changed more often than once in 25 years without specific legislation.

The selection of coin designs is usually made by the Director of the Mint, with the approval of the Secretary of the Treasury. However, Congress has, in a few instances, prescribed them. For example, as a part of the bicentennial celebration of Washington's birth in 1932, Congress declared that the likeness of our first President should appear on the quarter dollar.

The Lincoln penny was the first portrait coin of a regular series minted by the United States. The 100th anniversary of Lincoln's birth aroused sentiment sufficiently strong to overcome a long-prevailing popular prejudice against the use of portraits on coins. A new reverse design was adopted in 1959, when the sesquicentennial of Lincoln's birth was observed. The familiar likeness on the obverse remains unchanged. Others which followed are the 25-cent coin, with Washington's profile, first minted in 1932; the five-cent piece honoring Jefferson, adopted in 1938; the FDR dime, introduced in 1946, and in 1971 the Eisenhower silver dollar, manufacture of which was discontinued in December 1978.

In July 1979, a new, smaller dollar coin was introduced whose size is between the half dollar and the quarter; its smaller size will save in the cost of dollar bill production and help the circulation of the little-used dollar coin. This coin bears the likeness of women's suffrage leader Susan B. Anthony.

Portraits of living persons on American coins are extremely rare and confined to a few commemorative issues of limited minting.

The year 1976 marked the 200th anniversary of American Independence. One of the most far-reaching Government observances was the issuance of specially designed dollars, half dollars, and quarters. Circulation commenced on July 4, 1975, and production ended on December 31, 1976.

The design selection used for American paper currency, including the selection of portraits, is a responsibility of the Secretary of the Treasury, who acts with the advice of the Director of the Bureau of Engraving and Printing, the Treasurer of the United States, and others. By tradition, portraits used on present paper money are those of deceased statesmen of assured historical significance.

The first regular issue of United States currency, the Demand notes that were issued in 1861, carried the portraits of Alexander Hamilton (first Secretary of the Treasury) on the $5 denomination and of Abraham Lincoln on the $10 denomination.

Those design features of U.S. paper currency that have historical or idealistic significance, as distinct from purely ornamental or security implications, include the following:

(1) The New Treasury Seal: Approved on January 29, 1968, the seal of the Department of the Treasury is found on the face of each note. Balance scales, a key, and a chevron with 13 stars appear on the seal, along with the date "1789," the year the Department was created.

(2) The obverse and reverse of the Great Seal of the United States are reproduced on the backs of $1 bills.

(3) Portraits of great Americans used on the face of currency.

(4) Pictures of famous buildings, monuments or events used on the back of currency.

All notes of the same denomination bear the same portrait. Designs on U.S. currency (Federal Reserve Notes) now in circulation are as follows:

Denomination and Class	Portrait	Back
$1 Fed. Reserve Note	Washington	Obverse and reverse of Great Seal of U.S.
$2 Fed. Reserve Note	Jefferson	John Trumbull's "Declaration of Independence"
$5 Fed. Reserve Note	Lincoln	Lincoln Memorial
$10 Fed. Reserve Note	Hamilton	U.S. Treasury Building
$20 Fed. Reserve Note	Jackson	White House
$50 Fed. Reserve Note	Grant	U.S. Capitol
$100 Fed. Reserve Note	Franklin	Independence Hall

Notes of the higher denominations ($500, $1,000, $5,000, and $10,000) have not been printed for many years. As they are returned to Federal Reserve banks, they are removed from circulation and destroyed. The portraits selected for these small-sized notes were McKinley for the $500, Cleveland for the $1,000, Madison for the $5,000, and Chase for the $10,000.

The motto "In God We Trust" owes its presence on U.S. coins largely to the increased religious sentiment existing during the Civil War. Salmon P. Chase, then Secretary of the Treasury, received a number of appeals from devout persons throughout the country urging that the Deity be suitably recognized on our coins as it was on the coins of other nations.

The approved motto first made its appearance on the two-cent coin, authorized by Act of Congress (April 22, 1864), but its use has not been uninterrupted. In 1866 the motto was introduced on the double eagle, eagle, and half eagle gold coins and on the silver dollar, half dollar, and the quarter dollar pieces. It was included in the nickel five-cent design from 1866 to 1883, when it was dropped and not restored until the introduction of the Jefferson nickel in 1938. The motto has been in continuous use on the penny since 1909 and on the dime since 1916.

A law passed by the 84th Congress and approved by the President on July 11, 1955, provides that "In God We Trust" shall appear on all United States paper currency and coins.

By a joint resolution of the 84th Congress, approved by the President on July 30, 1956, "In God We Trust" was declared to be the official motto of the United States.

COMPOUND INTEREST TABLE

What a $1 deposit, compounded monthly, grows to over a thirty-year period.

Interest Rates

Years	5%	5¼%	5½%	5¾%	6%	6¼%	6½%	6¾%	7%	7¼%	7½%	7¾%	8%
1	1.0512	1.0538	1.0564	1.0590	1.0617	1.0643	1.0670	1.0696	1.0723	1.0750	1.0776	1.0803	1.0830
1½	1.0778	1.0812	1.0858	1.0899	1.0939	1.0980	1.1021	1.1062	1.1104	1.1145	1.1187	1.1229	1.1270
2	1.1049	1.1105	1.1160	1.1216	1.1272	1.1328	1.1384	1.1441	1.1498	1.1555	1.1613	1.1671	1.1729
2½	1.1329	1.1399	1.1470	1.1542	1.1614	1.1686	1.1759	1.1833	1.1906	1.1981	1.2055	1.2130	1.2206
3	1.1615	1.1702	1.1789	1.1878	1.1967	1.2056	1.2147	1.2238	1.2329	1.2422	1.2514	1.2608	1.2702
3½	1.1908	1.2012	1.2117	1.2223	1.2330	1.2438	1.2547	1.2657	1.2767	1.2879	1.2991	1.3105	1.3219
4	1.2209	1.2331	1.2455	1.2579	1.2705	1.2832	1.2960	1.3090	1.3221	1.3353	1.3486	1.3621	1.3757
4½	1.2517	1.2658	1.2801	1.2945	1.3091	1.3238	1.3387	1.3538	1.3690	1.3844	1.4000	1.4157	1.4316
5	1.2834	1.2994	1.3157	1.3322	1.3489	1.3657	1.3828	1.4001	1.4176	1.4354	1.4533	1.4715	1.4898
5½	1.3158	1.3339	1.3523	1.3709	1.3898	1.4090	1.4284	1.4480	1.4680	1.4882	1.5087	1.5214	1.5504
6	1.3490	1.3693	1.3899	1.4108	1.4320	1.4536	1.4754	1.4976	1.5201	1.5429	1.5661	1.5896	1.6135
6½	1.3831	1.4057	1.4286	1.4519	1.4755	1.4996	1.5240	1.5489	1.5741	1.5997	1.6258	1.6522	1.6791
7	1.4180	1.4430	1.4683	1.4941	1.5204	1.5471	1.5742	1.6019	1.6300	1.6586	1.6877	1.7173	1.7474
7½	1.4539	1.4813	1.5092	1.5376	1.5666	1.5961	1.6261	1.6567	1.6879	1.7196	1.7520	1.7849	1.8185
8	1.4906	1.5206	1.5511	1.5823	1.6141	1.6466	1.6797	1.7134	1.7478	1.7829	1.8187	1.8552	1.8925
8½	1.5282	1.5609	1.5943	1.6284	1.6631	1.6987	1.7350	1.7721	1.8099	1.8485	1.8880	1.9283	1.9694
9	1.5668	1.6023	1.6386	1.6758	1.7137	1.7525	1.7922	1.8327	1.8742	1.9166	1.9599	2.0042	2.0495
9½	1.6064	1.6449	1.6842	1.7245	1.7658	1.8080	1.8512	1.8954	1.9407	1.9871	2.0346	2.0832	2.1329
10	1.6470	1.6885	1.7311	1.7747	1.8194	1.8652	1.9122	1.9603	2.0097	2.0602	2.1121	2.1652	2.2196
10½	1.6886	1.7333	1.7792	1.8263	1.8747	1.9243	1.9752	2.0274	2.0810	2.1361	2.1925	2.2505	2.3099
11	1.7313	1.7793	1.8287	1.8795	1.9316	1.9852	2.0402	2.0968	2.1549	2.2147	2.2760	2.3391	2.4039
11½	1.7750	1.8266	1.8796	1.9342	1.9903	2.0480	2.1075	2.1686	2.2315	2.2962	2.3627	2.4312	2.5016
12	1.8198	1.8750	1.9319	1.9904	2.0508	2.1129	2.1769	2.2428	2.3107	2.3807	2.4527	2.5269	2.6034
12½	1.8658	1.9248	1.9856	2.0483	2.1130	2.1798	2.2486	2.3196	2.3928	2.4683	2.5462	2.6265	2.7093
13	1.9130	1.9759	2.0408	2.1079	2.1772	2.2488	2.3227	2.3990	2.4778	2.5591	2.6431	2.7299	2.8195
13½	1.9613	2.0283	2.0976	2.1693	2.2434	2.3200	2.3992	2.4811	2.5658	2.6533	2.7438	2.8374	2.9341
14	2.0108	2.0821	2.1560	2.2324	2.3115	2.3934	2.4782	2.5660	2.6569	2.7509	2.8483	2.9491	3.0535
14½	2.0616	2.1374	2.2159	2.2974	2.3817	2.4692	2.5599	2.6538	2.7512	2.8522	2.9568	3.0653	3.1777
15	2.1137	2.1941	2.2776	2.3642	2.4541	2.5474	2.6442	2.7447	2.8489	2.9572	3.0695	3.1860	3.3069
15½	2.1671	2.2524	2.3409	2.4330	2.5286	2.6280	2.7313	2.8386	2.9501	3.0660	3.1864	3.3115	3.4414
16	2.2218	2.3121	2.4061	2.5038	2.6055	2.7112	2.8213	2.9358	3.0549	3.1788	3.3077	3.4419	3.5814
16½	2.2780	2.3735	2.4730	2.5766	2.6846	2.7971	2.9142	3.0363	3.1634	3.2958	3.4337	3.5774	3.7271
17	2.3355	2.4365	2.5418	2.6516	2.7662	2.8856	3.0102	3.1402	3.2757	3.4171	3.5645	3.7183	3.8786
17½	2.3945	2.5011	2.6125	2.7288	2.8502	2.9770	3.1094	3.2477	3.3921	3.5429	3.7003	3.8647	4.0364
18	2.4550	2.5675	2.6852	2.8082	2.9368	3.0712	3.2118	3.3588	3.5125	3.6732	3.8413	4.0169	4.2006
18½	2.5170	2.6357	2.7598	2.8899	3.0260	3.1685	3.3176	3.4738	3.6373	3.8084	3.9876	4.1751	4.3714
19	2.5806	2.7056	2.8366	2.9739	3.1179	3.2688	3.4269	3.5927	3.7665	3.9486	4.1395	4.3395	4.5492
19½	2.6458	2.7774	2.9155	3.0605	3.2126	3.3723	3.5398	3.7157	3.9002	4.0939	4.2971	4.5104	4.7342
20	2.7126	2.8511	2.9966	3.1495	3.3102	3.4790	3.6564	3.8429	4.0387	4.2446	4.4608	4.6880	4.9268
20½	2.7812	2.9268	3.0800	3.2412	3.4108	3.5892	3.7769	3.9744	4.1822	4.4008	4.6037	4.8727	5.1272
21	2.8514	3.0045	3.1657	3.3355	3.5144	3.7028	3.9013	4.1104	4.3307	4.5627	4.8071	5.0646	5.3357
21½	2.9235	3.0842	3.2537	3.4325	3.6211	3.8200	4.0298	4.2511	4.4845	4.7306	4.9902	5.2640	5.5527
22	2.9973	3.1660	3.3442	3.5324	3.7311	3.9410	4.1626	4.3966	4.6438	4.9047	5.1803	5.4173	5.7786
22½	3.0730	3.2501	3.4373	3.6352	3.8445	4.0658	4.2997	4.5471	4.8087	5.0852	5.3776	5.6868	6.0136
23	3.1507	3.3663	3.5329	3.7410	3.9613	4.1945	4.4134	4.7028	4.9795	5.2724	5.5825	5.9017	6.2582
23½	3.2302	3.4249	3.6311	3.8498	4.0816	4.3273	4.5877	4.8637	5.1563	5.4664	5.7951	6.1435	6.5127
24	3.3118	3.5157	3.7321	3.9618	4.2056	4.4643	4.7388	5.0302	5.3394	5.6676	6.0159	6.3854	6.7776
24½	3.3955	3.6090	3.8360	4.0771	4.3333	4.6056	4.8949	5.2024	5.5291	5.8762	6.2450	6.6369	7.0533
25	3.4813	3.7048	3.9427	4.1957	4.4650	4.7514	5.0562	5.3804	5.7254	6.0924	6.4829	6.8983	7.3402
25½	3.5692	3.8031	4.0523	4.3178	4.6006	4.9019	5.2228	5.5646	5.9288	6.3166	6.7928	7.1699	7.6387
26	3.6594	3.9041	4.1651	4.4434	4.7404	5.0570	5.3948	5.7551	6.1393	6.5491	6.9862	7.4523	7.9494
26½	3.7518	4.0077	4.2809	4.5727	4.8844	5.2172	5.5725	5.9521	6.3573	6.7901	7.2523	7.7458	8.2725
27	3.8466	4.1141	4.4000	4.7058	5.0327	5.3823	5.7561	6.1558	6.5831	7.0400	7.5285	8.0508	8.6092
27½	3.9438	4.2232	4.5224	4.8427	5.1856	5.5527	5.9457	6.3665	6.8169	7.2991	7.8153	8.3679	8.9594
28	4.0434	4.3353	4.6482	4.9836	5.3431	5.7285	6.1416	6.5844	7.0590	7.5677	8.1130	8.6974	9.3238
28½	4.1456	4.4504	4.7775	5.1286	5.5055	5.9099	6.3439	6.8098	7.3097	7.8462	8.4220	9.0399	9.7030
29	4.2503	4.5685	4.9104	5.2778	5.6727	6.0970	6.5529	7.0429	7.5693	8.1350	8.7428	9.3959	10.0976
29½	4.3577	4.6897	5.0467	5.4314	5.8450	6.2900	6.7688	7.2839	7.8381	8.4344	9.0758	9.7659	10.5083
30	4.4677	4.8192	5.1874	5.5894	6.0226	6.4872	6.9918	7.5332	8.1165	8.7448	9.4215	10.1505	10.9357

GOLD PRODUCTION

SOURCE: U.S. Bureau of Mines (figures in millions of dollars at $35 per fine ounce through 1971, $38 per fine ounce in 1972 and 1973, and $42.22 per fine ounce beginning in 1974)

	1960	1965	1970	1971	1972	1974	1975	1976	1977	1978[1]
South Africa	784.4	1,069.0	1,128.0	1,098.7	1,109.7	1,029.7	968.4	968.4	950.0	967.0
Canada	162.0	125.6	84.3	77.3	77.2	71.7	69.8	71.2	72.5	72.0
United States	58.8	58.6	63.5	52.3	55.1	47.6	44.4	44.2	46.5	41.0
Other Africa	67.7	55.4	51.1	50.0	53.8	69.1	63.7	63.9	51.3	51.0
Ghana	30.8	26.7	24.6	24.4	27.5	25.9	22.1	22.5	20.3	20.3
Rhodesia	19.7	—	17.5	17.6	19.1	33.8	33.8	33.8	25.3	25.0
Zaire	11.1	2.3	6.2	6.0	5.4	5.5	4.4	4.3	3.4	3.4
Latin America	50.2	39.8	32.4	28.6	34.1	42.4	52.4	61.0	57.3	61.0
Colombia	15.2	11.2	7.1	6.6	7.1	11.2	13.0	12.6	10.9	12.0
Mexico	10.5	7.6	6.9	5.3	5.5	5.7	6.1	6.9	9.0	10.0
Nicaragua	6.9	5.4	4.0	3.7	4.3	3.5	3.0	3.2	2.8	2.8
Peru	4.9	3.7	3.3	2.2	3.0	4.2	3.3	3.4	4.1	4.1
Asia	35.6	41.8	44.2	45.1	47.3	47.3	44.8	45.7	49.4	51.0
Philippines	14.4	15.4	21.1	22.2	23.0	22.7	21.2	21.2	23.6	25.0
Japan	11.8	18.1	24.8	24.9	32.2	5.9	6.1	5.8	7.2	7.5
India	5.6	4.6	3.6	4.1	4.0	4.3	3.8	4.3	3.9	4.0
Europe*	12.2	—	10.4	11.8	13.3	25.2	21.5	28.3	27.2	27.0
Oceania	43.3	36.1	26.7	27.8	47.8	53.0	51.1	76.1	59.7	62.0
Australia	38.0	30.7	21.9	23.9	28.7	21.6	22.2	21.0	26.2	28.0
World Total	1,178	1,440	1,450	1,393	1,442	1,386	1,386	1,359	1,314	1,332

[1] Estimated. * Data exclude U.S.S.R.

COMPANIES WITH THE LARGEST NUMBER OF COMMON STOCKHOLDERS

SOURCE: New York Stock Exchange

(Figures rounded to nearest thousand)

EARLY 1979

Company	Stockholders
American Tel. & Tel.	2,939,000
General Motors	1,249,000
Exxon Corp.	695,000
International Business Machines	605,000
General Electric	552,000
General Tel. & Electronics	456,000
Texaco Inc.	432,000
Gulf Oil	357,000
Southern Company	342,000
Ford Motor	334,000
Sears, Roebuck	326,000
American Electric Power	282,000
Mobil Corp.	268,000
Occidental Petroleum	266,000
Standard Oil of Calif.	264,000
U.S. Steel	261,000
Consolidated Edison	258,000
Philadelphia Electric	257,000
Eastman Kodak	251,000
RCA	246,000
Pacific Gas & Electric	239,000
Tenneco, Inc.	232,000
Commonwealth Edison	229,000
Public Service Electric & Gas	225,000
International Tel. & Tel.	223,000
Detroit Edison	220,000
Chrysler Corp.	209,000
Niagara Mohawk Power	204,000
du Pont de Nemours	204,000
Northeast Utilities	200,000
Westinghouse Electric	195,000
Atlantic Richfield	195,000
General Public Utilities	177,000
Union Carbide	176,000
BankAmerica	175,000
Standard Oil (Indiana)	173,000
Columbia Gas System	165,000
Transamerica Corp.	162,000
Virginia Elec. & Power	162,000
Consumers Power	161,000
Bethlehem Steel	160,000
Union Electric	158,000
Ohio Edison	158,000
Greyhound Corp.	151,000
Pennsylvania Power	150,000
Pan Amer. World Airways	144,000
Long Island Lighting	143,000
Southern California Edison	137,000
Dow Chemical Co.	137,000
Middle South Utilities	133,000

U.S. CORPORATE PROFITS (In billions of dollars)

SOURCE: U.S. Department of Commerce, Bureau of Economic Analysis

Year	Total pre-tax profits	Tax liability	After-tax profits	Dividends	Undistributed profits
1929	10.0	1.4	8.6	5.8	2.8
1930	3.7	.8	2.9	5.5	−2.6
1931	− .4	.5	− .9	4.1	−4.9
1932	−2.3	.4	−2.7	2.5	−5.2
1933	1.0	.5	.4	2.0	−1.6
1935	3.6	1.0	2.6	2.8	− .2
1940	10.0	2.8	7.2	4.0	3.2
1945	19.7	10.7	9.0	4.6	4.4
1950	42.6	17.9	24.7	8.8	15.9
1955	48.4	22.0	26.4	10.3	16.1
1960	48.5	22.7	25.8	12.9	13.0
1965	75.2	30.9	44.3	19.1	25.2
1967	77.3	32.5	44.9	20.1	24.7
1968	85.6	39.4	46.2	21.9	24.2
1969	83.4	39.7	43.8	22.6	21.2
1970	71.5	34.5	37.0	22.9	14.1
1971	82.0	37.7	44.3	23.0	21.3
1972	96.2	41.5	54.6	24.6	30.0
1973	115.8	48.7	67.1	27.8	39.3
1974	126.9	52.4	74.5	31.0	43.6
1975	120.4	49.8	70.6	31.9	38.7
1976	155.9	64.3	91.7	37.9	53.8
1977	173.9	71.8	102.1	43.7	58.4
1978	202.6	84.1	118.5	49.3	59.2

FOREIGN EXCHANGE RATES: 1949-1979   Source: Federal Reserve Bulletin (in U. S. cents)

Year	United Kingdom (pound)	Canada (dollar)	Nether- lands (guilder)	West Germany* (deutsche mark)	Switzer- land (franc)	France† (franc)	Belgium (franc)	Japan‡ (yen)	Italy (lira)
1949	368.72	92.88	34.53	N A	23.31	.3017	2.20	N A	.1699
1950	280.07	91.47	26.25	23.84	23.14	.2858	1.99	N A	.1601
1951	279.96	94.94	26.26	23.84	23.06	.2856	1.99	N A	.1600
1953	281.27	101.65	26.34	23.84	23.32	.2856	2.00	N A	.1600
1956	279.57	101.60	26.11	23.79	23.33	.2855	2.00	.2779	.1600
1958	280.98	103.03	26.42	23.85	23.33	.2858	2.00	.2779	.1601
1960	280.76	103.12	26.51	23.98	23.15	20.39	2.00	.2778	.1610
1962	280.78	93.56	27.76	25.01	23.12	20.41	2.01	.2771	.1611
1964	279.21	92.69	27.72	25.16	23.15	20.40	2.01	.2763	.1601
1966	279.30	92.81	27.63	25.01	23.11	20.35	2.01	.2760	.1601
1968	239.35	92.80	27.63	25.05	23.17	20.19	2.00	.2774	.1604
1970	239.59	95.80	27.65	27.42	23.20	18.09	2.01	.2792	.1595
1972	250.08	100.94	31.15	31.36	26.19	19.83	2.27	.3300	.1713
1973	245.10	99.98	35.98	37.76	31.70	22.54	2.58	.3692	.1719
1974	234.03	102.26	37.27	38.72	33.69	20.81	2.57	.3430	.1537
1975	222.16	98.30	39.63	40.73	38.74	23.35	2.73	.3371	.1533
1976	180.48	101.41	37.85	39.74	40.01	20.94	2.59	.3374	.1204
1977	174.49	94.11	40.75	43.08	41.71	20.34	2.79	.3734	.1133
1978	191.84	87.73	46.28	49.87	56.28	22.22	3.18	.4798	.1178
1979 (April)	207.34	87.24	48.79	52.75	58.22	22.97	3.33	.4624	.1186

* Beginning with June 1950. † Beginning with 1960, 100 old francs = 1 new franc. ‡ Beginning with November 1956. N A = Not available.

MONEY DEPRECIATION: ANNUAL RATES   Source: International Monetary Fund and Citibank

The value of money is here measured by reciprocals of official cost-of-living or consumer price indexes.

	INDEXES: VALUE OF MONEY			RATE OF DEPRECI- ATION		INDEXES: VALUE OF MONEY			RATE OF DEPRECI- ATION		INDEXES: VALUE OF MONEY			RATE OF DEPRECI- ATION
	1966	1971	1978	1971–78		1966	1971	1978	1971–78		1966	1971	1978	1971–78
Switzerland.	100	83	59	4.8	France	100	78	42	8.5	Italy	100	84	34	12.1
West Germany..	100	87	61	4.9	Denmark ..	100	73	37	9.3	Greece	100	90	36	12.3
Panama ...	100	91	58	6.2	South Africa ..	100	83	42	9.3	S. Korea ...	100	58	22	12.9
Malaysia ..	100	93	59	6.3	Japan	100	75	38	9.3	Spain	100	77	27	13.9
Venezuela ..	100	91	57	6.4	China (Taiwan).	100	80	40	9.4	Mexico	100	82	28	14.2
United States ...	100	80	50	6.5	Australia ..	100	79	39	9.6	Jamaica ...	100	74	25	14.4
Austria	100	83	52	6.5	Paraguay ..	100	92	44	10.0	Yugoslavia .	100	65	21	14.9
Honduras .	100	90	56	6.6	Philippines.	100	69	31	10.8	Bolivia	100	77	25	14.9
Luxembourg.	100	85	52	6.8	New Zealand .	100	74	33	10.9	Portugal ...	100	69	22	15.1
Netherlands.	100	78	46	7.3	Finland	100	78	34	11.2	Colombia ..	100	68	17	18.0
Singapore .	100	94	55	7.4	Iran	100	89	42†	11.8†	Turkey	100	61	14	19.0
Canada ...	100	83	48	7.5	Ireland	100	73	30	11.9	Peru	100	64	13	20.4
India	100	78	45	7.6	Kenya	100	92	38	11.9	Indonesia ..	100	11	*	56.0
Belgium ...	100	84	48	7.7	Ecuador ...	100	76	31	12.0	Brazil	100	35	*	60.0
Thailand ..	100	90	50	8.1	U.K.	100	76	31	12.0	Israel	100	79	*	60.8
Norway ...	100	77	42	8.3						Argentina ..	100	40	*	67.6
Sweden ...	100	80	43	8.5						Uruguay ...	100	14	*	70.1
										Chile	100	32	*	82.4

* Less than 1.   † Data for period 1971-77, none available for 1978

CENTRAL BANK DISCOUNT RATES

Source: International Monetary Fund (end of period quotations in percent per annum)

	1959	1961	1963	1965	1967	1969	1971	1973	1975	1977	1978	1979[1]
United States	4.00	3.00	3.50	4.50	4.50	6.00	4.50	7.50	6.00	6.00	6.50	9.50
United Kingdom	4.00	6.00	4.00	6.00	8.00	8.00	5.00	13.00	11.25	7.00	6.50	12.50
Industrial Europe												
Austria	4.50	5.00	4.50	4.50	3.75	4.75	5.00	7.75	6.00	5.50	5.50	3.75
Belgium	4.01	4.50	4.25	4.75	4.00	7.50	5.50	9.00	6.00	9.00	6.50	6.00
France	4.00	3.50	4.00	3.50	3.50	8.00	6.50	11.00	8.00	9.50	9.50	9.50
Germany	4.00	3.00	3.00	4.00	3.00	6.00	4.00	7.00	3.50	3.00	3.00	3.00
Italy	3.50	3.50	3.50	3.50	3.50	3.50	4.50	6.50	6.00	11.50	11.50	10.50
Netherlands	3.50	3.50	3.50	4.50	4.50	6.00	5.00	8.00	4.50	4.50	4.50	6.50
Norway	3.50	3.50	3.50	3.50	3.50	4.50	4.50	4.50	5.00	6.00	6.00	7.00
Sweden	4.50	5.00	4.00	5.50	6.00	7.00	5.00	5.00	6.00	8.00	8.00	6.50
Switzerland	2.00	2.00	2.00	2.50	3.00	3.75	3.75	4.50	3.00	1.50	1.50	1.00
Canada	5.37	3.24	4.00	4.75	6.00	8.00	4.75	7.25	9.00	7.50	7.50	11.25
Japan	7.30	7.30	5.84	5.48	5.84	6.25	4.75	9.00	6.50	4.25	4.25	3.50

[1] January.

MONETARY TERMS

Balance of Payments—A nation's transactions with other nations, for trade, investment, tourism, foreign aid, and the like. A deficit occurs when more is paid out than a nation earns.

Balance of Trade—That part of the balance of payments covering exports and imports of goods.

Devalue or Devaluation—The act of changing a currency's par value downward.

Exchange Control—Government controls on purchase of foreign currencies for various purposes, aimed at protecting a nation's reserves.

Foreign Exchange—The term applied to foreign currencies.

Foreign Exchange Market—The market in which foreign currencies are bought and sold and the daily trading price in terms of dollars is set. It is not a specific place but rather a series of trading "desks," mainly at banks.

Par Value—The international value of a currency, expressed as so many ounces of gold or so many U.S. dollars and cents.

Reserves—A nation's holdings of gold plus certain foreign currencies.

Reserve Currency—A currency in which other nations hold part of their reserves.

"Run" or "Attack"—A mass wave of selling of a particular currency on the foreign exchange markets.

Support—Official intervention in the foreign exchange market by a nation's central bank to hold up the price of the nation's currency.

U.S. GROSS NATIONAL PRODUCT†

SOURCE: U.S. Department of Commerce, Bureau of Economic Analysis

	1929	1933	1938	1945	1955	1965	1975	1978
Gross National Product	103.4	55.8	85.0	212.3	399.3	688.1	1528.8	2106.9
GNP in Constant (1972) Dollars	314.7	222.1	297.1	559.0	654.8	925.9	1202.1	1385.3
Personal Consumption Expenditures	77.3	45.8	64.0	119.5	253.7	430.2	980.4	1340.4
Durable goods	9.2	3.5	5.7	8.0	38.6	62.8	132.9	197.5
Nondurable goods	37.7	22.3	34.0	71.9	122.9	188.6	409.3	526.5
Services	30.3	20.1	24.4	39.6	92.1	178.7	438.2	616.4
Gross Private Domestic Investment	16.2	1.4	6.5	10.6	68.4	112.0	189.1	344.6
Fixed investment	14.5	3.0	7.4	11.7	62.4	102.5	200.6	329.1
Nonresidential	10.5	2.4	5.3	10.1	38.3	71.3	149.1	222.1
Structures	5.0	0.9	1.9	2.8	14.4	26.1	52.9	77.6
Producers' durable equipment	5.5	1.4	3.4	7.3	23.9	45.1	96.3	144.5
Residential	4.0	0.6	2.1	1.6	24.1	31.2	51.5	107.0
Nonfarm structures	3.8	0.5	1.9	1.4	23.0	29.9	49.5	103.8
Farm structures	0.2	*	0.1	0.1	0.6	0.6	0.9	1.4
Producers' durable equipment	*	*	*	*	0.4	0.7	1.1	1.7
Change in business inventories	1.7	−1.6	−0.9	−1.0	6.0	9.5	−11.5	15.5
Net exports of goods and services	1.1	0.4	.1.3	−0.6	2.2	7.6	20.4	−12.0
Government purchases	8.8	8.2	13.2	82.8	75.0	138.4	338.9	434.0
Federal	1.4	2.1	5.5	74.6	44.5	67.3	123.3	153.7
National defense	—	—	—	73.5	38.4	49.4	83.9	99.5
Non-defense	—	—	—	1.1	6.0	17.8	39.4	54.2
State and local	7.4	6.1	7.7	8.2	30.6	71.1	215.6	280.2

† In billions of dollars. * Less than $0.1 billion. ¹ Estimate.

GROSS NATIONAL PRODUCT: SELECTED NATIONS 1978

SOURCE: Department of State

	GNP Total ($ Millions)	GNP Per Capita (Dollars)	Population Mid-1978 (Millions)
Western Europe			
Austria	41,350	5,491	7.5
Belgium	69,720	7,085	9.8
Denmark	38,870	7,607	5.1
Finland	23,760	5,002	4.8
France	411,330	7,719	53.3
Germany, West	513,060	8,372	61.3
Greece	24,160	2,576	9.4
Iceland	1,260	5,706	0.2
Ireland	10,270	3,189	3.2
Italy	210,680	4,211	56.7
Luxembourg	2,480	6,889	0.4
Netherlands	88,090	6,324	13.9
Norway	31,940	7,867	4.1
Portugal	15,400	1,570	9.8
Spain	95,000	2,560	37.1
Sweden	73,730	8,894	8.3
Switzerland	54,590	8,651	6.3
United Kingdom	254,180	4,556	55.8
Africa (Excluding Egypt)			
Algeria	19,530	1,056	18.5
Ethiopia	3,360	114	29.4
Gabon	1,980	3,530	0.6
Ghana	4,370	400	10.9
Ivory Coast	5,770	769	7.5
Kenya	3,750	245	15.3
Libya	18,570	6,750	2.8
Morocco	10,400	534	19.5
Nigeria	40,100	570	70.4
South Africa	37,730	1,372	27.5
Sudan	5,660	334	17.0
Tanzania	2,820	170	16.6
Tunisia	5,780	961	6.0
Uganda	2,120	167	12.8
Zaire	3,730	134	27.8
Zimbabwe-Rhodesia	3,040	452	6.7
South Asia			
Afghanistan	2,510	122	20.7
Bangladesh	8,600	104	82.9
Burma	4,570	142	32.2
India	105,080	159	660.7
Pakistan	16,510	218	75.6
Sri Lanka	3,450	242	14.2
Near East			
Egypt	16,090	394	40.8
Iran	79,080	1,937	35.7
Iraq	21,360	1,737	12.3
Israel	14,830	4,154	3.6
Kuwait	15,160	12,600	1.2
Qatar	4,940	22,000	0.2
Saudi Arabia	54,510	8,400	6.5
Syria	6,370	761	8.4
Turkey	33,360	772	43.2
United Arab Emirates	7,760	9,700	0.8
East Asia			
China, Rep. of (Taiwan)	22,840	1,336	17.1
Hong Kong	13,620	2,971	4.6
Indonesia	46,210	329	140.7
Japan	727,860	6,329	115.0
Korea, South	35,440	958	37.0
Malaysia	13,930	1,077	12.9
Philippines	21,850	475	46.0
Singapore	7,650	3,285	2.3
Thailand	20,610	433	45.2
Oceania			
Australia	96,690	6,800	14.2
New Zealand	15,970	5,119	3.1
Latin America			
Argentina	49,680	1,877	26.4
Bolivia	2,710	444	6.1
Brazil	148,930	1,456	116.4
Chile	16,800	1,572	10.7
Colombia	18,380	715	25.7
Dominican Republic	4,370	833	5.3
Ecuador	5,300	678	7.8
Guatemala	6,620	998	6.6
Jamaica	2,900	1,363	2.1
Mexico	76,200	1,147	66.4
Panama	2,640	1,449	1.8
Peru	16,370	963	17.0
Venezuela	41,210	3,139	13.1
North America			
Canada	196,580	8,323	23.6
UNITED STATES	2,106,900	9,640	218.6
Communist Countries			
Bulgaria	24,750	2,799	8.8
China, People's Rep.	323,940	323	1,003.9
Cuba	11,400	1,163	9.8
Czechoslovakia	70,720	4,673	15.1
Germany, East	81,010	4,834	16.8
Hungary	32,060	3,000	10.7
Korea, North	12,440	684	18.2
Poland	108,340	3,094	35.0
Romania	67,450	3,083	21.9
USSR	1,046,640	4,004	261.4
Vietnam	6,850	132	51.6
Yugoslavia	55,970	2,544	22.0
WORLD	8,173,440	1,889	4,327.5

OIL IMPORTS: 1977-1978   Source: Social and Economic Statistics Administration, U.S. Dept. of Commerce

(Quantity in barrels, value in dollars.)

Country of Origin	General Imports Calendar Year 1978 Net Quantity	F.a.s. Value	Country of Origin	General Imports Calendar Year 1977 Net Quantity	F.a.s. Value
Canada	63,668,088	892,553,098	Canada	110,424,765	1,481,057,571
Mexico	112,152,740	1,490,148,711	Mexico	62,603,440	832,257,895
Trinidad	50,864,009	736,312,271	Trinidad	50,061,303	731,887,030
Venezuela	26,253,303	336,284,017	Venezuela	127,170,947	1,586,835,228
Ecuador	16,721,195	213,566,711	Ecuador	19,779,920	258,296,142
Peru	8,892,552	117,215,881	Bolivia	1,839,821	26,577,563
Bolivia	610,306	9,095,943	Norway	24,532,069	349,564,076
Chile	281,443	4,013,377	United Kingdom	27,901,502	395,612,802
Brazil	127,974	1,597,116	Netherlands	454,342	6,542,525
Norway	48,085,211	670,694,43C	Union of Soviet Socialist		
United Kingdom	52,209,175	719,361,759	Republics	674,931	7,930,440
Union of Soviet Socialist			Syria	868,218	9,582,274
Republics	276,389	3,482,530	Iraq	29,424,606	41,980,698
Syria	1,016,049	11,829,189	Iran	207,020,344	2,638,832,554
Iraq	18,627,040	231,712,015	Kuwait	14,828,921	179,830,825
Iran	211,521,682	2,689,847,062	Saudi Arabia	506,038,224	6,261,285,467
Kuwait	1,718,182	21,075,148	Qatar	22,414,894	291,781,343
Saudi Arabia	406,528,669	5,211,041,303	United Arab Emirates	127,629,671	1,626,700,757
Qatar	24,445,200	317,729,173	Oman	29,983,029	381,165,608
United Arab Emirates	139,006,647	1,851,988,617	Sri Lanka	149,261	1,892,629
Oman	23,699,584	308,699,011	Malaysia	19,225,166	273,144,704
Malaysia	15,684,994	222,658,752	Indonesia	194,642,390	2,587,776,259
Indonesia	196,768,102	2,676,624,618	Brunei	1,576,355	21,542,753
Brunei	2,435,246	34,131,751	Algeria	208,934,428	2,971,043,126
Algeria	232,993,709	3,300,865,263	Tunisia	496,558	6,547,945
Tunisia	1,093,498	15,912,443	Libya	267,489,093	3,712,244,968
Libya	268,731,319	3,706,082,141	Egypt	12,421,879	152,079,528
Egypt	6,002,106	76,408,329	Nigeria	416,717,578	5,958,482,377
Cameroon	2,204,841	28,158,843	Gabon	12,360,485	157,508,542
Nigeria	321,975,860	4,546,457,056	Angola	19,557,830	262,571,364
Gabon	12,676,516	162,735,154	Congo (Brazzaville)	2,312,131	30,944,048
Angola	10,290,837	137,417,434	Zaire	266,880	3,242,592
Congo (Brazzaville)	5,354,671	70,946,776	Other Countries	3,990	49,161
Zaire	263,369	3,529,145	Total	2,519,804,965	33,582,574,518
Other Countries	5	669			
Total	2,283,180,511	30,820,175,736			

LARGEST U.S. COMMERCIAL BANKS   Source: Fortune magazine

Bank	Assets[1] ($000)	Rank '78	'77	Deposits ($000)	Rank	Loans[2] ($000)	Rank
BankAmerica Corp. (San Francisco)	94,902,464	1	1	75,828,044	1	49,312,903	2
Citicorp (New York)	87,190,709	2	2	61,115,062	2	52,299,418	1
Chase Manhattan Corp. (New York)	61,171,529	3	3	48,545,820	3	38,173,305	3
Manufacturers Hanover Corp. (New York)	40,605,849	4	4	32,408,880	4	22,185,226	4
J.P. Morgan & Co. (New York)	38,536,234	5	5	28,602,530	5	18,807,426	5
Chemical New York Corp.	32,769,727	6	6	24,905,496	6	17,852,670	7
Continental Illinois Corp. (Chicago)	31,058,665	7	7	21,160,250	8	18,131,455	6
Western Bancorp. (Los Angeles)	25,956,614	8	10	21,162,178	7	14,842,592	8
Bankers Trust New York Corp.	25,863,346	9	8	18,755,167	9	13,525,523	11
First Chicago Corp.	24,066,073	10	9	17,466,441	10	13,621,525	10
Security Pacific Corp. (Los Angeles)	21,632,621	11	11	16,967,492	11	14,070,346	9
Wells Fargo & Co. (San Francisco)	18,611,436	12	12	14,818,671	12	12,642,908	12
Marine Midland Banks, Inc. (Buffalo)	14,289,371	13	15	11,315,171	13	8,034,314	14
Charter New York Corp.	13,975,444	14	13	11,103,521	15	6,881,780	15
Crocker National Corp. (San Francisco)	13,925,162	15	14	11,212,354	14	8,814,053	13

[1]As of December 31, 1978.   [2] Net of unearned discount and loan loss reserve.

LARGEST DIVERSIFIED FINANCIAL COMPANIES   Source: Fortune Magazine

Company	Assets[1] ($000)	Rank '78	'77	Revenues ($000)	Rank	Net Income ($000)	Rank
Aetna Life & Casualty (Hartford)	24,268,190	1	1	9,453,704	1	501,621	1
Travelers Corp. (Hartford)	17,202,811	2	2	7,316,780	2	366,544	2
American Express (New York)	14,669,800	3	3	4,084,500	4	308,000	3
INA (Philadelphia)	11,933,702	4	5	4,225,132	3	213,695	5
H.F. Ahmanson (Los Angeles)	10,947,631	5	4	1,024,378	18	117,438	17
Merrill Lynch & Co. (New York)	8,648,463	6	6	1,528,742	15	71,325	26
Great Western Financial (Beverly Hills)	8,483,270	7	8	714,561	25	89,680	23
First Charter Financial (Beverly Hills)	8,326,293	8	7	712,762	26	105,347	18
Loews (New York)	7,745,867	9	9	3,455,644	6	168,165	11
Continental (New York)	7,033,248	10	10	3,058,800	7	288,591	4
Lincoln National (Fort Wayne, Ind.)	6,858,605	11	*	2,193,318	8	152,258	13
Transamerica (San Francisco)	6,703,575	12	11	3,526,529	5	209,705	7
American General Insurance (Houston)	5,863,379	13	12	1,740,107	12	170,327	10
Imperial Corp. of America (San Diego)	5,741,647	14	13	490,184	31	68,760	28
C.I.T. Financial (New York)	5,087,043	15	14	555,414	28	86,464	24

[1]As of December 31, 1978.   * Not on last year's list.

LARGEST INDUSTRIAL CORPORATIONS

Source: *Fortune magazine*

Company	Sales ($000)	Rank '78	'77	Assets ($000)	Rank	Net Income ($000)	Rank
General Motors (Detroit)	63,221,100	1	1	30,598,300	2	3,508,000	1
Exxon (New York)	60,334,527*	2	2	41,530,804	1	2,763,000	3
Ford Motor (Dearborn, Mich.)	42,784,100	3	3	22,101,400	4	1,588,900	4
Mobil (New York)	34,736,045*	4	4	22,611,479	3	1,125,638	6
Texaco (Harrison, N.Y.)	28,607,521	5	5	20,249,143	6	852,461	10
Standard Oil of California (San Francisco)	23,232,413	6	6	16,761,021	7	1,105,881	7
International Business Machines (Armonk, N.Y.)	21,076,089	7	7	20,771,374	5	3,110,568	2
General Electric (Fairfield, Conn.)	19,653,800	8	9	15,036,000	8	1,229,700	5
Gulf Oil (Pittsburgh)	18,069,000*	9	8	15,036,000	9	791,000	13
Chrysler (Highland Park, Mich.)	16,340,700	10	10	6,981,200	21	(204,600)	491
International Tel. & Tel. (New York)	15,261,178	11	11	14,034,866	11	661,807	16
Standard Oil (Ind.) (Chicago)	14,961,489*	12	12	14,109,264	10	1,076,412	8
Atlantic Richfield (Los Angeles)	12,298,403	13	13	12,060,210	12	804,325	12
Shell Oil (Houston)	11,062,883*	14	14	10,453,358	14	813,623	11
U. S. Steel (Pittsburgh)	11,049,500	15	15	10,536,300	13	242,000	49

* Does not include excise taxes.

LARGEST UTILITIES

Source: *Fortune Magazine*

Company	Assets[1] ($000)	Rank '78	'77	Operating Revenues ($000)	Rank	Net Income[2] ($000)	Rank
American Telephone & Telegraph (New York)	103,326,945	1	1	40,993,356	1	5,272,606	1
General Telephone & Electronics (Stamford, Conn.)	16,269,462	2	2	8,723,483	2	627,159	2
Southern Company (Atlanta)	9,866,463	3	3	2,906,672	5	201,568	12
Pacific Gas & Electric (San Francisco)	8,502,072	4	4	3,433,232	3	401,584	3
American Electric Power (New York)	8,063,483	5	5	2,389,044	8	236,331	7
Commonwealth Edison (Chicago)	7,924,181	6	6	2,442,788	7	320,958	4
Consolidated Edison (New York)	6,830,638	7	7	3,010,970	4	309,569	5
Southern California Edison (Rosemead, Calif.)	6,057,697	8	8	2,328,798	9	251,683	6
Public Service Electric & Gas (Newark)	5,518,778	9	9	2,219,785	10	228,786	9
Middle South Utilities (New Orleans)	5,501,027	10	11	1,622,177	19	185,438	14
Virginia Electric & Power (Richmond)	5,211,043	11	10	1,464,905	23	203,864	11
Texas Utilities (Dallas)	5,161,808	12	13	1,604,356	20	200,738	13
Duke Power (Charlotte)	4,984,621	13	12	1,396,720	27	230,601	8
Consumers Power (Jackson, Mich.)	4,935,511	14	15	1,866,921	16	185,131	15
Philadelphia Electric	4,850,625	15	14	1,456,758	24	184,861	16

[1]As of December 31, 1978.　　[2]After taxes and extraordinary credits or charges shown on income statement.

LARGEST RETAILING COMPANIES

Source: *Fortune Magazine*

Company	Sales ($000)	Rank '78	'77	Assets ($000)	Rank	Net Income ($000)	Rank
Sears, Roebuck (Chicago)	17,946,336	1	1	15,262,112	1	921,523	1
Safeway Stores (Oakland)	12,550,569	2	2	2,835,767	6	146,118	7
K mart (Troy, Mich.)	11,812,810	3	3	4,836,260	2	343,706	2
J.C. Penney (New York)	10,845,000	4	4	4,833,000	3	276,000	3
Kroger (Cincinnati)	7,828,071	5	6	1,653,029	10	84,596	12
Great Atlantic & Pacific Tea (Montvale, N.J.)	7,288,577	6	5	1,133,231	16	4,791	48
F. W. Woolworth (New York)	6,102,800	7	7	2,707,500	7	130,300	8
Federated Department Stores (Cincinnati)	5,404,621	8	8	2,956,431	5	197,896	5
Montgomery Ward (Chicago)	5,013,514	9	9	3,412,779	4	119,367	9
Lucky Stores (Dublin, Calif.)	4,658,409	10	11	1,042,846	19	80,440	15
Winn-Dixie Stores (Jacksonville)	4,444,255	11	10	765,836	25	84,014	13
American Stores (Wilmington)	3,737,634	12	12	647,473	29	26,596	33
Jewel Companies (Chicago)	3,516,352	13	13	958,138	21	41,142	25
City Products (Des Plaines, Ill.)	3,312,600	14	14	1,062,800	17	64,000	17
Southland (Dallas)	3,076,532	15	15	1,134,476	15	57,097	20

LARGEST LIFE INSURANCE COMPANIES

Source: *Fortune Magazine*

Company	Assets[1] ($000)	Rank '78	'77	Premium & Annuity Income ($000)	Rank	Life Insurance in Force ($000)	Rank
Prudential (Newark)*	50,054,152	1	1	7,683,320	1	330,363,738	1
Metropolitan (New York)*	42,253,040	2	2	5,907,830	2	287,534,251	2
Equitable Life Assurance (New York)*	27,671,541	3	3	4,391,937	3	165,706,260	3
New York Life*	17,118,635	4	4	2,409,581	6	101,342,294	6
John Hancock Mutual (Boston)*	16,227,729	5	5	2,372,648	7	112,816,259	4
Aetna Life (Hartford)	15,744,430	6	6	3,886,529	4	112,264,640	5
Connecticut General Life (Bloomfield)	10,978,951	7	7	2,306,359	8	64,184,217	8
Travelers (Hartford)	10,396,305	8	8	3,308,710	5	87,753,884	7
Northwestern Mutual (Milwaukee)*	9,735,863	9	9	1,123,492	12	45,370,692	10
Massachusetts Mutual (Springfield)*	7,646,843	10	10	1,277,763	10	40,210,569	12
Teachers Insurance & Annuity (New York)	7,060,113	11	11	957,491	14	5,436,612	45
Mutual of New York*	6,608,442	12	12	952,785	15	30,901,073	14
New England Mutual (Boston)*	5,811,425	13	13	889,349	17	25,348,126	19
Bankers Life (Des Moines)*	5,771,025	14	14	1,308,416	9	27,163,421	17
Mutual Benefit (Newark)*	4,685,554	15	16	883,166	18	30,102,101	16

[1]As of December 31, 1978.　　* Mutual company.

LEADING U.S. FARM CROPS
SOURCE: U.S. Department of Agriculture, Crop Reporting Board, ESCS

Crop	Unit	PRODUCTION 1977	PRODUCTION 1978	YIELD PER ACRE[4] 1977	YIELD PER ACRE[4] 1978
Corn, grain	Bushels	6,425,457,000	7,081,849,000	90.7	101.2
Sorghum, grain	Bushels	792,983,000	748,410,000	56.3	55.1
Oats	Bushels	750,901,000	601,477,000	55.8	52.2
Barley	Bushels	420,159,000	447,008,000	43.9	48.4
Wheat, total	Bushels	2,036,318,000	1,798,712,000	30.6	31.6
Winter	Bushels	1,537,113,000	1,248,272,000	31.6	32.1
Durum	Bushels	79,964,000	133,328,000	26.4	33.1
Other spring	Bushels	419,241,000	417,112,000	28.4	30.0
Rice	Cwt.	99,223,000	137,805,000	4,412.0[3]	4,505.0[3]
Rye	Bushels	17,312,000	26,160,000	24.6	26.3
Soybeans for beans	Bushels	1,761,755,000	1,842,647,000	30.6	29.2
Flaxseed	Bushels	15,105,000	10,921,000	11.5	12.7
Peanuts for nuts	Pounds	3,726,015,000	3,977,465,000	2,457.0	2,632.0
Sunflower seeds	Pounds	2,760,470,000	3,748,370,000	1,252.0	1,362.0
Popcorn	Pounds	431,610,000	398,027,000	2,788.0	2,827.0
Cotton, lint	Bales	14,389,200	10,841,000	520.0[3]	421.0[3]
Hay	Tons	131,313,000	142,264,000	2.16	2.31
Beans, dry edible	Cwt.	16,610,000	19,117,000	1,298.0[3]	1,279.0[3]
Peas, dry edible	Cwt.	1,023,000	3,601,000	613.0[3]	1,783.0[3]
Potatoes	Cwt.	354,576,000	360,467,000	261.0	263.0
Sweetpotatoes	Cwt.	12,395,000	13,862,000	110.0	116.0
Tobacco	Pounds	1,912,114,000	2,015,695,000	1,997.0	2,124.0
Sugar beets	Tons	25,007,000	25,868,000	20.6	20.3
Sugarcane	Tons	26,830,000	27,022,000	35.3	35.9
Coffee	Pounds	2,270,000	1,780,000	1,140.0	940.0
Hops	Pounds	54,777,000	55,071,000	1,796.0	1,782.0
Cranberries	Barrels	2,102,200	2,466,500	93.3	106.5
Apples, Com'l	Pounds	6,678,600,000	7,552,600,000		
Peaches	Pounds	2,983,000,000	2,701,000,000		
Pears	Tons	786,600	727,200		
Grapes	Tons	4,297,750	4,428,700		
Oranges	Boxes	242,950,000[1]	219,620,000[2]		
Grapefruit	Boxes	74,600,000[1]	73,700,000[2]		
Lemons	Boxes	26,000,000[1]	26,100,000[2]		
Limes	Boxes	1,000,000[1]	460,000[2]		

[1] 1976-77 production figures.   [2] 1977-78 production figures.   [3] Yield in pounds.   [4] Yield per acre figures not available for fruit.

INCLUSIVE STATE—FARM PAYMENT TOTALS: 1978
SOURCE: U.S. Department of Agriculture, Agricultural Stabilization & Conservation Service

State	Amount	State	Amount	State	Amount
Alabama	$ 31,716,088	Maine	$ 3,739,430	Oregon	$ 29,629,112
Alaska	192,415	Maryland	6,992,587	Pennsylvania	12,468,587
Arizona	9,160,448	Massachusetts	773,392	Rhode Island	61,530
Arkansas	24,445,814	Michigan	42,143,210	South Carolina	20,980,592
California	56,582,635	Minnesota	110,044,040	South Dakota	105,026,338
Colorado	77,712,555	Mississippi	29,544,608	Tennessee	15,414,616
Connecticut	425,010	Missouri	69,191,817	Texas	303,492,666
Delaware	3,435,292	Montana	126,106,097	Utah	20,159,539
Florida	10,310,868	Nebraska	194,180,267	Vermont	4,537,601
Georgia	54,967,886	Nevada	3,352,611	Virginia	26,604,256
Hawaii	798,956	New Hampshire	885,890	Washington	66,068,351
Idaho	62,622,636	New Jersey	1,954,584	West Virginia	3,186,138
Illinois	88,475,260	New Mexico	27,284,456	Wisconsin	37,934,989
Indiana	47,500,445	New York	22,147,359	Wyoming	16,141,574
Iowa	226,919,814	North Carolina	34,672,494	Puerto Rico	738,986
Kansas	273,428,696	North Dakota	250,558,875	Virgin Islands	25,389
Kentucky	12,497,534	Ohio	24,175,067	Undistributed	1,638,674
Louisiana	15,681,520	Oklahoma	95,782,905	Total	$ 2,704,512,499

LIVESTOCK POPULATION ON U.S. FARMS AND RANCHES   (as of January 1)
SOURCE: U.S. Department of Agriculture, Crop Reporting Board, ESCS

Year	CATTLE AND CALVES	SHEEP AND LAMBS	HOGS AND PIGS	CHICKENS[2]
1959	92,322,000	32,606,000	58,045,000	387,002,000
1961[3]	97,700,000	32,725,000	55,560,000	366,082,000
1963	104,488,000	29,176,000	62,726,000[1]	375,575,000
1965	109,000,000	25,127,000	56,106,000	394,118,000
1967	108,783,000	23,953,000	57,125,000	428,746,000
1969	110,015,000	21,350,000	60,829,000	413,287,000
1971	114,578,000	19,731,000	67,285,000	433,280,000[1]
1973	121,539,000	17,641,000	59,017,000	404,191,000
1974	127,788,000	16,310,000	61,614,000	408,769,000
1975	132,028,000	14,515,000	54,693,000	384,101,000
1976	127,980,000	14,311,000	49,267,000	379,754,000
1977	122,810,000	12,766,000	54,934,000	378,238,000
1978	116,375,000	12,348,000	56,539,000	386,429,000
1979	110,864,000	12,224,000	59,860	394,505,000

[1] Begins inventory as of December 1 preceding year   [2] Excludes commercial broilers   [3] Includes Alaska and Hawaii beginning 1961

U.S. PASSENGER CAR PRODUCTION: 1978

SOURCE: Motor Vehicle Manufacturers Association of the United States, Inc.

Company	Automobile Production	Company	Automobile Production	Company	Automobile Production
AMERICAN MOTORS CORP.	163,352	Club Wagon	45,309	Pontiac	184,327
Spirit/AMX (Gremlin)	37,466	Granada	246,407	Grand Prix	206,605
Concord (Hornet)	106,697	Pinto	185,091	LeMans	124,035
Pacer	15,386	Mustang	240,162	Firebird	195,378
Matador	4,803	Fairmont	286,046	Phoenix (Ventura)	67,951
		Total Ford	1,743,445	Sunbird	88,714
CHRYSLER CORP.	1,126,168	Mercury	152,149	Total Pontiac	867,010
Horizon	162,011	Couger	38,460	Oldsmobile	400,714
Voyager	10,673	XR-7	179,648	Toronado	28,251
Volaré	221,761	Monarch	89,974	Cutlass	416,458
Caravelle	4,493	Zephyr	88,254	Omega	47,279
Fury	49,176	Bobcat	38,601	Starfire	17,547
Total Plymouth	468,114	Capri	37,143	Total Oldsmobile	910,249
LeBaron	150,908	Lincoln	98,119	Buick	300,677
Chrysler	85,596	Mark V	75,845	Riviera	25,179
Total Chrysler-Plymouth	684,618	Versailles	15,559	Century	352,212
		Total Lincoln-Mercury	813,752	Skylark	107,276
Omni	126,225	**GENERAL MOTORS CORP.**	5,284,499	Skyhawk	24,980
Sportsman	33,220	Chevrolet	524,094	Total Buick	810,324
Aspen	162,651	Corvette	48,972	Cadillac	244,355
Monaco	28,246	Monte Carlo	325,809	Eldorado	46,612
Diplomat	75,755	Malibu (Chevelle)	373,454	Seville	59,794
St. Regis	15,453	Camaro	281,735	Total Cadillac	350,761
Total Dodge	441,550	Nova	309,941	**CHECKER MOTORS CORP.**	4,225
FORD MOTOR CO.	2,557,197	Monza (Vega)	166,951	**VOLKSWAGEN OF AMERICA**	40,194
Ford	278,949	Chevette	301,614		
LTD II	134,608	Acadian	13,585	**TOTAL PASSENGER CARS**	9,176,635
Thunderbird	326,873	Total Chevrolet	2,346,155		

WORLD MOTOR VEHICLE PRODUCTION: 1978†

SOURCE: *U.N. Monthly Bulletin of Statistics,* © United Nations, July 1979

Country	Passenger Cars	Trucks and Buses	Total	Country	Passenger Cars	Trucks and Buses	Total
United States	9,144,000	3,696,000	12,840,000	Mexico	253,200	105,600	358,800
Japan	5,976,000	3,264,000	9,240,000	Sweden	258,000	—	258,000
Germany, West	3,900,000	300,000	4,200,000	Yugoslavia	193,200	62,400	255,600
France	3,624,000	452,000	4,076,000	Czechoslovakia	175,200	69,400	244,600
U.S.S.R.[1]	1,279,200	781,200	2,060,400	Germany, East	170,400	37,200*	207,600
Canada	1,143,300	675,200	1,818,500	Argentina	135,400	38,300	173,700
Italy	1,510,000	150,900	1,660,900	Romania[1]	77,520	38,760	116,280
United Kingdom	1,224,000	384,000	1,608,000	India	45,600	48,720	94,320
Spain	988,800	150,000	1,138,800	Netherlands	62,400	11,280	73,680
Brazil[1]	463,200	454,800	918,000	Hungary	—	14,880	14,880
Poland	325,000	69,600	394,800	Austria	360	6,240	6,600
Australia	315,600	69,600	385,200				

† Totals for some countries are estimated   * Buses not included   [1] 1977 figures

NEW PASSENGER CARS IMPORTED TO THE UNITED STATES: 1977

SOURCE: Motor Vehicle Manufacturers Association of the United States, Inc.

Japan	1,341,530	United Kingdom	56,889	Belgium	3,510
Canada - APTA*	847,226	Italy	55,437	Netherlands	289
Canada - Duty	2,588	Sweden	39,370	Others	598
West Germany	423,492	France	19,215	**TOTAL**	2,790,144

* Automotive Products Trade Act (APTA) provides for the duty free importation of automobiles manufactured by Canadian subsidiaries of U.S. automobile companies.

LARGEST PASSENGER CAR PRODUCER FOR EACH COUNTRY: 1977†

SOURCE: Motor Vehicle Manufacturers Association of the United States, Inc.

Country	Producer	1977 Production	Country	Producer	1977 Production
Argentina	Fiat Concord S.A.	40,409	Japan	Toyota Motor	1,884,260
Australia	Ford	107,000	Mexico	Volkswagen de Mexico	42,834
Belgium	Ford-Werke A.G. Genk	335,718	Netherlands	Daf & Volvo	44,537
Brazil	Volkswagen	263,701	Peru	Volkswagen	6,075
Canada	General Motors	552,291	Poland	Polski Fiat	243,380
France	Renault	1,398,550	Spain	S.E.A.T.	346,535
West Germany	Volkswagen	1,371,453	Sweden	Volvo	158,885
India	Hindustan Motors	20,256	United Kingdom	British Leyland	651,069
Italy	Fiat	1,057,261	Venezuela	Ford Motors de Venezuela	37,832
			Yugoslavia	Zavodi Crvena Zastava	183,554

† Excluding United States

THE U.S. LABOR FORCE

Source: U.S. Department of Labor, Bureau of Labor Statistics

TOTAL LABOR FORCE*

Year	Number	% of population	Total Civilian Employed
1948	62,080,000	60.4	60,254,000
1950	63,858,000	59.4	58,344,000
1952	65,730,000	59.9	58,920,000
1954	66,993,000	60.0	60,110,000
1955	68,072,000	60.4	62,171,000
1956	69,409,000	61.0	63,802,000
1957	69,729,000	60.6	64,071,000
1958	70,275,000	60.4	63,036,000
1959	70,921,000	60.2	64,630,000
1960	72,142,000	60.2	65,778,000
1961	73,031,000	60.2	65,746,000
1962	73,442,000	59.7	66,702,000
1963	74,571,000	59.6	67,762,000
1964	75,830,000	59.6	69,305,000
1965	77,178,000	59.7	71,088,000
1966	78,893,000	60.1	72,895,000
1967	80,793,000	60.6	74,372,000
1968	82,272,000	60.7	75,920,000
1969	84,239,000	61.1	77,902,000
1970	85,903,000	61.3	78,627,000
1971	86,929,000	61.0	79,120,000
1972	88,991,000	61.0	81,702,000
1973	91,040,000	61.4	84,409,000
1974	93,240,000	61.8	85,936,000
1975	94,793,000	61.8	84,783,000
1976	96,917,000	62.1	87,485,000
1977	99,534,000	62.8	90,546,000
1978	102,537,000	63.7	94,373,000

* Persons 16 years of age and over; includes members of the armed forces.

UNEMPLOYMENT RATES: BY SEX AND RACE

Source: U.S. Department of Labor, Bureau of Labor Statistics

Unemployment Rate

Year	Total	Male	Female	White Total	White Male	White Female	Black and other Total	Black and other Male	Black and other Female
1948	3.8	3.6	4.1	3.5	3.4	3.8	5.9	5.8	6.1
1950	5.3	5.1	5.7	4.9	4.7	5.3	9.0	9.4	8.4
1952	3.0	2.8	3.6	2.8	2.5	3.3	5.4	5.2	5.7
1954	5.5	5.3	6.0	5.0	4.8	5.6	9.9	10.3	9.3
1955	4.4	4.2	4.9	3.9	3.7	4.3	8.7	8.8	8.4
1956	4.1	3.8	4.8	3.6	3.4	4.2	8.3	7.9	8.9
1957	4.3	4.1	4.7	3.8	3.6	4.3	7.9	8.3	7.3
1958	6.8	6.8	6.8	6.1	6.1	6.2	12.6	13.8	10.8
1959	5.5	5.3	5.9	4.8	4.6	5.3	10.7	11.5	9.4
1960	5.5	5.4	5.9	4.9	4.8	5.3	10.2	10.7	9.4
1961	6.7	6.4	7.2	6.0	5.7	6.5	12.4	12.8	11.8
1962	5.5	5.2	6.2	4.9	4.6	5.5	10.9	10.9	11.0
1963	5.7	5.2	6.5	5.0	4.7	5.8	10.8	10.5	11.2
1964	5.2	4.6	6.2	4.6	4.1	5.5	9.6	8.9	10.6
1965	4.5	4.0	5.5	4.1	3.6	5.0	8.1	7.4	9.2
1966	3.8	3.2	4.8	3.3	2.8	4.3	7.3	6.3	8.6
1967	3.8	3.1	5.2	3.4	2.7	4.6	7.4	6.0	9.1
1968	3.6	2.9	4.8	3.2	2.6	4.3	6.7	5.6	8.3
1969	3.5	2.8	4.7	3.1	2.5	4.2	6.4	5.3	7.8
1970	4.9	4.4	5.9	4.5	4.0	5.4	8.2	7.3	9.3
1971	5.9	5.3	6.9	5.4	4.9	6.3	9.9	9.1	10.8
1972	5.6	4.9	6.6	5.0	4.5	5.9	10.0	8.9	11.3
1973	4.9	4.1	6.0	4.3	3.7	5.3	8.9	7.6	10.5
1974	5.6	4.8	6.7	5.0	4.3	6.1	9.9	9.1	10.7
1975	8.5	7.9	9.3	7.8	7.2	8.6	13.9	13.7	14.0
1976	7.7	7.0	8.6	7.0	6.4	7.9	13.1	12.7	13.6
1977	7.0	6.2	8.2	6.2	5.5	7.3	13.1	12.4	14.0
1978	6.0	5.2	7.2	5.2	4.5	6.2	11.9	10.9	13.9

MINORITY GROUP PARTICIPATION IN THE U.S. LABOR MARKET: 1978 Preliminary

Source: Equal Employment Opportunity Commission

% OF MINORITY WORKERS IN PARTICULAR CATEGORY [1]

	Total	WHITE COLLAR Total	Professional	Technical	Clerical	Blue Collar	Service Workers
Black, Total [1]	11.2%	6.8%	4.0%	8.2%	10.1%	14.3%	21.5%
Male	6.1	2.4	1.9	3.5	1.9	9.9	9.8
Female	5.1	4.4	2.1	4.7	8.2	4.4	11.7
Hispanic, Total	5.0	3.1	1.8	3.3	4.1	6.9	7.0
Male	3.1	1.4	1.2	2.1	0.9	4.9	4.1
Female	1.9	1.7	0.6	1.2	3.2	2.0	2.9
Asian or Pacific Islander, Total	1.3	1.6	3.2	2.0	1.5	0.8	1.7
Male	0.7	0.8	2.0	1.2	0.4	0.4	0.8
Female	0.6	0.8	1.2	0.8	1.1	0.3	0.9
American Indian or Alaskan Native, Total	0.4	0.3	0.2	0.4	0.4	0.5	0.4
Male	0.3	0.2	0.2	0.2	0.1	0.4	0.2
Female	0.1	0.2	0.1	0.1	0.3	0.1	0.2
All Minorities, Total	17.9	11.8	9.2	13.8	16.0	22.5	30.6
Male	10.1	4.7	5.2	7.1	3.2	15.6	15.0
Female	7.8	7.0	4.0	6.7	12.8	6.9	15.6

[1] Percent of total employment is given occupational category

MINORITY GROUP EMPLOYEES IN U.S. LABOR MARKET: 1978 Preliminary

Source: Equal Employment Opportunity Commission

Figures are in thousands

	Total	WHITE COLLAR Total	Professional	Technical	Clerical	Blue Collar	Service Workers
All U.S. Employees	36,029	17,952	2,963	1,729	5,659	14,716	3,360
Male	21,634	9,121	1,960	1,081	1,008	10,986	1,526
Female	14,395	8,831	1,003	648	4,651	3,730	1,834
All Black Employees	4,051	1,224	117	142	569	2,105	722
Male	2,209	427	55	61	105	1,452	330
Female	1,842	797	62	81	464	653	392
All Hispanics	1,798	548	53	56	233	1,014	236
Male	1,106	243	35	36	51	724	139
Female	692	305	18	20	182	290	97
All Asian or Pacific Islander	453	278	95	34	84	117	57
Male	236	142	59	21	20	66	28
Female	217	136	36	13	64	51	29
All American Indian or Alaskan Native	146	60	7	6	21	72	14
Male	93	33	5	4	6	54	6
Female	53	27	2	2	15	18	8
All Minority Employees	6,449	2,110	273	239	907	3,308	1,029
Male	3,645	845	155	123	182	2,296	503
Female	2,804	1,265	118	116	725	1,012	526

PRINCIPAL U. S. LABOR UNIONS AND EMPLOYEE ASSOCIATIONS

SOURCE: Bureau of Labor Statistics

The following is a list of selected labor unions with a 1978 membership of more than 100,000.

International Brotherhood of Teamsters, Chauffeurs, Warehousemen, and Helpers of America, * 25 Louisiana Avenue, N. W., Washington, D.C. 20001; **Membership:** 1,888,895

National Education Association, * 1201 16th St., N. W. Washington, D.C. 20036; **Membership** 1,886,532

International Union, United Automobile, Aerospace and Agricultural Implement Workers of America, * 8000 East Jefferson Ave., Detroit, Mich. 48214; **Membership:** 1,500,000

United Steelworkers of America, Five Gateway Center, Pittsburgh, Pa. 15222; **Membership:** 1,400,000

United Food and Commercial Workers Union, 1775 K St., N.W., Washington, D.C. 20006; **Membership:** 1,200,000

International Brotherhood of Electrical Workers, 1125 15th St., N.W., Washington, D.C. 20005; **Membership:** 923,560

International Association of Machinists and Aerospace Workers, 1300 Connecticut Ave., N. W., Washington, D.C. 20036; **Membership:** 917,266

United Brotherhood of Carpenters and Joiners of America, 101 Constitution Ave., N. W., Washington, D.C. 20001; **Membership:** 820,536

American Federation of State, County, and Municipal Employees, 1625 L Street, N. W., Washington, D.C. 20005; **Membership:** 750,000

Laborers' International Union of North America, 905 16th St., N. W., Washington, D.C. 20006; **Membership:** 627,406

Service Employees' International Union, 2020 K St., N. W., Washington, D.C. 20006; **Membership:** 575,000

Communications Workers of America, 1925 K St., N. W., Washington, D.C. 20006; **Membership:** 575,000

Amalgamated Clothing and Textile Workers of America, 15 Union Square, New York, N.Y. 10003; **Membership:** 500,000

American Federation of Teachers, 11 Dupont Circle, Washington, D.C. 20036; **Membership:** 446,045

Hotel and Restaurant Employees and Bartenders International Union, 120 E. Fourth St., Cincinnati, Oh. 45202; **Membership:** 432,171

International Union of Operating Engineers, 1125 17th St., N. W., Washington, D.C. 20036; **Membership:** 420,000

International Ladies' Garment Workers Union, 1710 Broadway, New York, N.Y. 10019; **Membership:** 365,346

American Federation of Musicians, 1500 Broadway, New York, N.Y. 10036; **Membership:** 330,000

United Paperworkers International Union, 163–03 Horace Harding Expressway, Flushing, N.Y. 11365; **Membership:** 300,000

United Mine Workers of America, * 900 15th Street, N. W., Washington, D.C. 20005; **Membership:** 277,000

United Transportation Union, 14600 Detroit Avenue, Cleveland, Ohio 44107; **Membership:** 265,000

American Federation of Government Employees, 1325 Massachusetts Avenue, N. W., Washington, D.C. 20005; **Membership:** 260,000

American Postal Workers Union, 817 Fourteenth Street, N. W., Washington, D.C. 20005; **Membership:** 251,551

International Union of Electrical, Radio, and Machine Workers, 1126 16th St., N. W., Washington, D.C. 20036; **Membership:** 237,693

United Association of Journeymen and Apprentices of the Plumbing and Pipe Fitting Industry of the United States and Canada, 901 Massachusetts Ave., N. W., Washington, D.C. 20001; **Membership:** 228,000

National Association of Letter Carriers, 100 Indiana Ave., N. W., Washington, D.C. 20001; **Membership:** 227,221

Brotherhood of Railway, Airline, and Steamship Clerks, Freight Handlers, Express and Station Employees, 6300 River Rd., Rosemont, Illinois 60018; **Membership:** 211,293

United Rubber, Cork, Linoleum, and Plastic Workers of America, 87 South High St., Akron, Ohio 44308; **Membership:** 211,161

Civil Service Employees Association, Inc. (N.Y.), * 33 Elk St. Albany, N.Y. 12207; **Membership:** 207,000

Retail, Wholesale, and Department Store Union, 101 West 31st St., New York, N.Y. 10001; **Membership:** 200,000

American Nurses Association, * 2420 Pershing Rd., Kansas City, Mo. 64108; **Membership:** 199,691

International Brotherhood of Painters and Allied Trades of the United States and Canada, 1750 New York Avenue, N. W., Washington, D.C. 20006; **Membership:** 195,000

Oil, Chemical, and Atomic Workers International Union, P.O. Box 2812, 1636 Champa St., Denver, Colo. 80201; **Membership:** 180,000

International Association of Bridge and Structural Iron Workers, 1750 New York Ave., N.W., Suite 400, Washington, D.C. 20006; **Membership:** 178,632

International Association of Fire Fighters, 1750 New York Ave., N. W., Washington D.C. 20006; **Membership:** 174,350

Bakery, Confectionary, and Tobacco Workers' International Union of America, 1828 L St., N.W., Washington, D.C. 20036; **Membership:** 174,000

United Electrical, Radio, and Machine Workers of America, * 11 East 51st St., New York, N.Y. 10022; **Membership:** 165,000

Sheet Metal Workers' International Association, United Unions Building, New York Ave., N. W., Washington, D.C. 20006; **Membership:** 153,000

Amalgamated Transit Union, 5025 Wisconsin Ave., N. W., Washington, D.C. 20016; **Membership:** 150,000

National Association of Government Employees, * 285 Dorchester Ave., Boston, Mass. 02127; **Membership:** 150,000

Transport Workers Union of America, 1980 Broadway, New York, New York 10023; **Membership:** 150,000

International Brotherhood of Boilermakers, Iron Ship Builders, Blacksmiths, Forgers, and Helpers, New Brotherhood Bldg., 8th St. at State Ave., Kansas City, Kansas 66101; **Membership:** 145,000

Fraternal Order of Police, * G–3136 Pasadena Ave., Flint, Mich. 48504; **Membership:** 135,000

International Union of Bricklayers and Allied Craftsmen, 815 15th St., N. W., Washington, D.C. 20005; **Membership:** 134,744

Brotherhood of Maintenance of Way Employees, 12050 Woodward Ave., Detroit, Mich. 48203; **Membership:** 119,184

California State Employees Association, * 1108 O St., Sacramento, Calif. 95814; **Membership:** 112,300

International Printing and Graphic Communications Union, 1730 Rhode Island Avenue, N. W., Washington, D.C. 20036; **Membership:** 109,000

International Woodworkers of America, 1622 North Lombard St., Portland, Oregon 97217; **Membership:** 108,717

International Typographical Union, P.O. Box 157, Colorado Springs, Colorado 80901; **Membership:** 100,449

*Independent — not members of AFL-CIO

AVERAGE UNION HOURLY SCALE
SOURCE: U.S. Department of Labor—Bureau of Labor Statistics

Year	Building Journeymen	Building Helpers and laborers	Printing Book and job	Printing Newspapers	Local trucking Drivers	Local trucking Helpers	Local transit workers	Year	Building Journeymen	Building Helpers and laborers	Printing Book and job	Printing Newspapers	Local trucking Drivers	Local trucking Helpers	Local transit workers
1960	$3.86	$2.88	$3.08	$3.48	$2.68	$2.38	$2.37	1973	$8.02	$6.06	$5.91	$6.43	$5.90	$5.30	$5.04
1965	4.64	3.54	3.58	3.94	3.26	2.90	2.88	1974	8.55	6.53	6.34	7.01	6.39	5.84	5.62
1970	6.54	4.86	4.65	5.13	4.41	3.91	4.03	1975	9.32	7.06	6.86	7.57	6.87	6.27	6.25
1971	7.28	5.43	5.11	5.65	4.95	4.41	4.38	1976	9.92	7.54	7.41	8.17	7.42	6.67	6.63
1972	7.69	5.68	5.49	6.09	5.49	4.90	4.68	1977	10.44	8.03	7.91	8.74	8.09	7.28	7.12

UNION CONTRACTS OF 1978
SOURCE: U.S. Department of Labor, Bureau of Labor Statistics

Major collective bargaining settlements reached during 1978 generally provided for a smaller first-year wage and package increase than those of 1977 but higher increases when averaged over the contract term. Wage-rate adjustments achieved during 1978 averaged 7.6 percent for the first year and 6.4 percent annually over the contract life compared with 7.8 percent (first-year) and 5.8 percent (over the life) in 1977.

Wage and benefit gains in major contracts averaged 8.3 percent for the first year and 6.3 percent annually over the contract life. This compares with 9.6 and 6.2 percent, respectively, in 1977. Both wage-rate and package measures exclude cost-of-living gains.

In manufacturing, wage-rate adjustments in new settlements averaged 8.3 percent in the first year and 6.6 percent annually over the contract life, compared with 8.4 percent and 5.5 percent in 1977. In nonmanufacturing, adjustments averaged 7.4 percent in the first year and 6.4 percent annually over the contract life, compared with 7.4 and 6.0 percent in 1977. In construction, wage adjustments averaged 6.5 percent in the first year and 6.2 percent annually over the contract life, compared with 6.3 and 6.3 percent in 1977.

UNEMPLOYMENT INSURANCE BENEFITS (1978 Calendar year)

SOURCE: U.S. Department of Labor

State unemployment insurance benefits for the totally unemployed are listed below. Where two figures are given for legal minimum and maximum benefits, the larger figure includes dependents' allowances.

State	Average Unemployment Benefit	Legal Minimum	Legal Maximum	Actual Average	Legal Range	State	Average Unemployment Benefit	Legal Minimum	Legal Maximum	Actual Average	Legal Range
U.S. Avg.	$83.56†	—	—	13.4†							
ALA.	70.18	$15	$90	10.3	11-26	MONT.	84.14	12	113	12.3	12-26
ALASKA.	85.01	18-28	90-120	19.6	14-28	NEBR.	79.54	12	90	10.5	17-26
ARIZ.	73.82	15	85	12.7	12-26	NEV.	83.54	16	100	12.1	11-26
ARK.	72.00	15	100	10.3	10-26	N.H.	74.35	21	102	6.9	26-26
CALIF.	75.28†	30	104	12.6†	12-26*	N.J.	87.68	20	110	17.8	15-26
COLO.	92.59	25	130	11.2	7-26*	N.M.	68.71	18	90	15.3	18-30
CONN.	89.43	15-20	122-183	10.8	26-26*	N.Y.	83.74	25	115	19.5	26-26
DEL.	93.56	20	150	13.8	17-26	N.C.	71.65	15	112	9.3	13-26
D.C.	106.66	13-14	160*	19.5	17-34	N.D.	87.40	15	121	13.8	18-26
FLA.	63.68	10	82	12.7	10-26	OHIO	100.32	10-16	111-175	13.5	20-26
GA.	73.39	27	90	8.6	9-26	OKLA.	75.91	16	116	11.4	10-26
HAWAII.	93.29	5	126	16.0	26-26*	ORE.	81.18	30	119	13.0	9-26
IDAHO	84.30	17	116	10.0	10-26	PA.	97.83	13-18	143-151	14.2	30-30
ILL.	97.68	15	121-145	17.7	26-26	P.R.	45.53	7	70	14.4	20-20*
IND.	75.75	35	74-124	9.9	4-26	R.I.	76.79	26-31	110-130	9.2	12-26
IOWA	103.96	20	133	13.5	10-39	S.C.	73.31	10	119	11.2	10-26
KANS.	84.47	29	116	12.3	10-26	S.D.	78.35	19	102	10.7	10-26
KY.	79.30	12	111	11.4	15-26	TENN.	65.96†	14	95	11.6†	12-26
LA.	91.62	10	130	14.7	12-28	TEX.	68.18	15	84	12.6	9-26
MAINE	73.33	12-17	90-135	10.5	11-26*	UTAH	88.70	10	128	11.8	10-36*
MD.	76.40	10-13	106*	12.2	26-26	VT.	76.10	18	109	13.7	26-26
MASS.	84.00	12-18	115-173	14.9	9-30*	VA.	83.51	38	115	11.7	12-26
MICH.	92.85	16-18*	97-136	10.8	11-26	WASH.	86.80	17	128	13.8	8-30*
MINN.	96.66	18	133	13.7	13-26	W.VA.	74.75†	18	149	10.6†	26-26
MISS.	60.37	10	80	11.3	12-26	WISC.	94.36	26	139	11.6	1-34*
MO.	75.62	15	85	10.7	8-26*	WYO.	88.03	24	121	10.3	11-26*

† Preliminary   * Provisional.

EMPLOYMENT OUTLOOK TO 1985

Occupation	Average Annual Openings 1979 through 1985
Accountants	51,500
Actors and Actresses	600
Airplane pilots	4,100
All-round mechanics	20,000
Anthropologists	200
Architects	3,100
Commercial artists	3,600
Astronomers	40
Bank clerks	36,000
Bank officers and managers	28,000
Bank tellers	21,000
Barbers	8,100
Blacksmiths	100
Bookkeeping workers	95,000
Bricklayers, stonemasons, etc.	7,500
Local transit busdrivers	5,100
Carpenters	67,000
Chemists	6,300
Chiropractors	1,600
Computer operating personnel	8,500
Construction laborers	40,000
Cooks and chefs	79,000
Cosmetologists	30,000
Dentists	4,800
Dietitians	2,800
Drafters	16,500
Economists	6,400
Electricians (construction)	13,700
Engineers	56,500
Firefighters	8,300
Furniture upholsterers	1,100
Gasoline station attendants	14,800
Geographers	600
Geologists	2,300
Geophysicists	800
Health services administrators	16,000
Historians	900
Home economists	6,100
Hotel managers and assistants	7,000
Industrial designers	500
Insurance agents, brokers, and underwriters	27,500
Interior designers	1,900
Landscape architects	900
Lawyers	23,400
Locomotive engineers	2,400

Occupation	Average Annual Openings 1979 through 1985
Mail carriers	5,300
Mathematicians	1,000
Mechanics and repairers—	
Central office craft occupations	5,000
Line installers and cable splicers	600
Telephone and PBX installers and repairers	4,000
Air-conditioning, refrigeration, and heating	17,400
Appliance repairers	7,000
Automobile body repairers	6,000
Automobile mechanics	32,000
Business machine repairers	3,400
Computer service technicians	5,200
Diesel mechanics	5,000
Farm equipment mechanics	4,000
Industrial machinery repairers	30,000
Jewelers	1,300
Maintenance electricians	15,900
Piano and organ tuners and repairers	650
Shoe repairers	1,800
Television and radio service technicians	6,700
Truck and bus mechanics	6,900
Watch repairers	1,500
Medical laboratory workers	20,000
Meteorologists	200
Newspaper reporters	2,100
Licensed practical nurses	53,000
Registered nurses	83,000
Oceanographers	150
Office machine operators	7,700
Optometrists	1,500
Painters and paperhangers	29,400
Personnel and labor relations workers	23,000
Pharmacists	8,900
Photographers	3,700
Physicians and osteopathic physicians	21,800
Physicists	1,100
Plasterers	900

Occupation	Average Annual Openings 1979 through 1985
Plumbers and pipefitters	30,000
Podiatrists	500
Police officers	32,500
Political scientists	400
Postal clerks	3,700
Printing occupations	
Bookbinders and bindery workers	3,400
Compositors	3,600
Electrotypers and stereotypers	60
Lithographers	1,900
Photoengravers	100
Printing press operators and assistants	5,100
Private household workers	53,000
Programmers	9,700
Psychologists	5,600
Public relations workers	8,300
Purchasing agents	13,800
Radiologic (X-ray) technologists	6,300
Radio & television announcers	1,300
Real estate agents and brokers	45,500
Retail trade sales workers	155,000
Wholesale trade sales workers	41,000
School counselors	1,500
Secretaries and stenographers	295,000
Social workers	25,000
Sociologists	800
Statisticians	1,500
Surveyors	3,500
Systems analysts	7,600
College and university teachers	17,000
Kindergarten and elementary school teachers	70,000
Secondary school teachers	13,000
Telephone operators	11,600
Occupational therapists	1,300
Physical therapists	2,100
Local truck drivers	73,000
Long distance truck drivers	15,400
Typists	63,000
Urban planners	1,100
Veterinarians	1,800
Welders	33,800

U.S. LICENSED COMMERCIAL NUCLEAR POWER PLANTS AS OF JANUARY 1, 1979

Source: Department of Energy

State	Name of Facility	Operating Company	Authorized Power Level (MWe)	Type*
Ala.	Farley 1	Alabama Power Co.	829	PWR
Ala.	Browns Ferry 1	TVA	1,065	BWR
Ala.	Browns Ferry 2	TVA	1,065	BWR
Ala.	Browns Ferry 3	TVA	1,065	BWR
Ark.	Arkansas 1	Arkansas P & L Co.	850	PWR
Ark.	Arkansas 2	Arkansas P & L Co.	912	PWR
Calif.	Humboldt Bay	Pacific Gas & Elec. Co.	63	BWR
Calif.	Rancho Seco	Sacramento Municipal Utility District	918	PWR
Calif.	San Onofre 1	Southern California Edison Co.	430	PWR
Colo.	Ft. St. Vrain	Public Svc Co. of Colo.	330	HTGR
Conn.	Conn. Yankee	Connecticut Yankee Atomic Power Co.	575	PWR
Conn.	Millstone 1	Northeast Nuclear Energy Co.	660	BWR
Conn.	Millstone 2	Northeast Nuclear Energy Co.	830	PWR
Fla.	Crystal River 3	Florida Power Corp.	825	PWR
Fla.	St. Lucie 1	Florida P & L Co.	802	PWR
Fla.	Turkey Point 3	Florida P & L Co.	693	PWR
Fla.	Turkey Point 4	Florida P & L Co.	693	PWR
Ga.	Edwin I. Hatch 1	Georgia Power Co.	786	BWR
Ga.	Edwin I. Hatch 2	Georgia Power Co.	795	BWR
Ill.	Dresden 1	Commonwealth Edison Co.	200	BWR
Ill.	Dresden 2	Commonwealth Edison Co.	794	BWR
Ill.	Dresden 3	Commonwealth Edison Co.	794	BWR
Ill.	Quad-Cities 1	Commonwealth Edison Co.	789	BWR
Ill.	Quad-Cities 2	Commonwealth Edison Co.	789	BWR
Ill.	Zion 1	Commonwealth Edison Co.	1,040	PWR
Ill.	Zion 2	Commonwealth Edison Co.	1,040	PWR
Iowa	Duane Arnold	Iowa Elec L & P Co.	538	BWR
Maine	Maine Yankee	Maine Yankee Atomic Power Co.	790	PWR
Md.	Calvert Cliffs 1	Baltimore G & E Co.	845	PWR
Md.	Calvert Cliffs 2	Baltimore G & E Co.	845	PWR
Mass.	Pilgrim 1	Boston Edison Co.	655	BWR
Mass.	Yankee-Rowe	Yankee Atomic Elec. Co.	175	PWR
Mich.	Big Rock Point	Consumers Power Co.	72	BWR
Mich.	Palisades	Consumers Power Co.	805	PWR
Mich.	D.C. Cook 1	Indiana & Michigan Elec. Co.	1,054	PWR
Mich.	D.C. Cook 2	Indiana & Michigan Elec. Co.	1,060	PWR
Minn.	Monticello	Northern States Power Co.	545	BWR
Minn.	Prairie Island 1	Northern States Power Co.	530	PWR
Minn.	Prairie Island 2	Northern States Power Co.	530	PWR
Neb.	Cooper Station	Nebraska Public Power District	778	BWR
Neb.	Ft. Calhoun	Omaha Public Power District	457	PWR
N.J.	Oyster Creek 1	Jersey Central P & L Co.	650	BWR
N.J.	Salem	Pub. Svc Elec. & Gas Co.	1,090	PWR
N.Y.	Indian Point 2	Consolidated Edison Co. of NY	873	PWR
N.Y.	Nine Mile Point 1	Niagara Mohawk Power Corp.	610	BWR
NY.	Indian Point 3	Power Authority of the State of New York	873	PWR
N.Y.	Fitzpatrick	Power Authority of the State of New York	821	BWR
N.Y.	R.E. Ginna 1	Rochester Gas & Elec. Corp.	490	PWR
N.C.	Brunswck 1	Carolina Power & Light Co.	821	BWR
N.C.	Brunswick 2	Carolina Power & Light Co.	821	BWR
Ohio	Davis-Besse 1	Toledo Edison Co.	906	PWR
Oreg.	Trojan	Portland General Elec. Co.	1,130	PWR
Pa.	Beaver Valley 1	Duquesne Light Co.	852	PWR
Pa.	Three Mile I. 1	Metropolitan Edison Co.	819	PWR
Pa.	Three Mile I. 2	Metropolitan Edison Co.	906	PWR
Pa.	Peach Bottom 2	Philadelphia Elec. Co.	1,065	BWR
Pa.	Peach Bottom 3	Philadelphia Elec. Co.	1,065	BWR
S.C.	H.E. Robinson 2	Carolina Power & Light Co.	700	PWR
S.C.	Oconee 1	Duke Power Co.	887	PWR
S.C.	Oconee 2	Duke Power Co.	887	PWR
S.C.	Oconee 3	Duke Power Co.	887	PWR
Vt.	Vermont Yankee	Vermont Yankee Nuclear Power Corp	514	BWR
Va.	North Anna 1	Virginia Elec. & Pow. Co.	Fuel Loading	PWR
Va.	Surry 1	Virginia Elec. & Pow. Co.	822	PWR
Va.	Surry 2	Virginia Elec. & Pow. Co.	822	PWR
Wisc.	Lacrosse	Dairyland Power Cooperative.	50	BWR
Wisc.	Point Beach 1	Wisc.-Mich. Power Co. & Wisc. Elec Power Co.	497	PWR
Wisc.	Point Beach 2	Wisc.-Mich. Power Co	497	PWR
Wisc.	Kewaunee	Wisc. Pub Svc Corp	535	PWR

*PWR—Pressurized Water Reactor; BWR—Boiling Water Reactor;
HTGR—High Temperature Gas Cooled Reactor

U.S. FUEL PRODUCTION

SOURCE: Energy Information Administration

Fuel	Unit	1977	1978[1]	Percent Change 1977-78	1978[1] Total Value (millions of current dollars)	1978[1] Average Unit Price (in current dollars)
Crude Oil[2]	million barrels	3,009	3,164	+5.2	28,349	8.96
Natural Gas[3]	trillion cubic feet	20.03	19.69	−1.7	18,095	.919*
Anthracite	million short tons	6.20	6.45	+3.9	235.4	36.50
Bituminous & Lignite	million short tons	688.6	653.8	−5.1	14,643	22.40

* Per 1,000 Cu. ft.
[1] Preliminary.   [2] Includes lease condensate.   [3] Marketed production.

NUCLEAR POWER

SOURCE: International Atomic Energy Agency

During the 24 years which have elapsed since the 1955 Geneva Conference, a tremendous development effort has taken place in the nuclear power field. Roughly speaking, the first decade from 1955–1965 was marked by the emergence of several promising nuclear power systems which bridged the gap between prototypes and industrial plants. The second period from 1965 to the present witnessed the rapid introduction of large nuclear stations in the electric systems of industrial coun-

tries and the commissioning of a few nuclear power plants in some developing countries.

In 1956 there were in the world two power reactors with a total capacity of 0.6MWe in two countries. By 1965, these numbers had risen to 44 reactors operating in 9 countries and with a total capacity of 4.9 MWe. By 1979, we find 232 stations with a capacity of over 117,000 MWe operating in 21 countries, and by 1994, 558 plants with close to 422,000 MWe in 33 States.

ESTIMATED WORLD NUCLEAR POWER GROWTH*

Country	1979 No. Reactors	1979 Capacity (1000 MWe)	1994 est. No. Reactors	1994 est. Capacity (1000 MWe)	Country	1979 No. Reactors	1979 Capacity (1000 MWe)	1994 est. No. Reactors	1994 est. Capacity (1000 MWe)
Argentina	1	0.3	4	2.1	Korea, South	1	0.6	5	3.7
Belgium	4	1.7	8	5.5	Mexico	—	—	2	1.3
Brazil	—	—	3	3.1	Netherlands	2	0.5	2	0.5
Bulgaria	2	0.8	4	1.6	Pakistan	1	0.1	2	0.7
Canada	10	5.2	25	15.2	Philippines	—	—	1	0.6
Cuba	—	—	2	0.8	Poland	—	—	2	0.8
Czechoslovakia	2	0.5	4	1.3	Romania	—	—	1	0.4
Finland	2	1.1	5	3.2	South Africa	—	—	2	1.8
France	15	7.3	49	41.7	Spain	3	1.1	18	15.1
Germany, East	4	1.3	9	3.3	Sweden	6	3.7	13	10.3
Germany, West	16	9.0	34	29.1	Switzerland	4	1.9	5	2.9
Hungary	—	—	4	1.6	Turkey	—	—	1	0.6
India	3	0.6	8	1.7	U.S.S.R.	29	9.6	51	28.8
Iran	—	—	4	4.2	U.K.	32	6.9	44	14.4
Israel	—	—	1	0.6	United States	70	50.9	197	191.9
Italy	4	1.4	9	5.3	Yugoslavia	—	—	1	0.6
Japan	21	13.2	38	27.1	Total*	232	117.8	558	422.0

*Does not include People's Republic of China for which no information is available

ENERGY CONSUMPTION PER UNIT OF GROSS DOMESTIC PRODUCT

SOURCE: The National Energy Plan, April 29, 1977

Source of Data: U.N. Statistical Yearbook, 1975

LARGEST FOREIGN INDUSTRIAL COMPANIES: 1978 SOURCE: Fortune magazine, August 13, 1979

Rank '78	'77	Company	Country	Industry	Sales ($000)
1	1	Royal Dutch/Shell Group	Netherlands-Britain	Petroleum	44,044,534
2	3	British Petroleum	Britain	Petroleum	27,407,620
3	2	National Iranian Oil	Iran	Petroleum	22,789,650
4	4	Unilever	Britain-Netherlands	Food products	18,893,176
5	5	Philips' Gloeilampenfabrieken	Netherlands	Electronics, appliances	15,121,166
6	7	Siemens	Germany	Electronics, appliances	13,864,726
7	8	Volkswagenwerk	Germany	Motor vehicles	13,332,059
8	13	Toyota Motor	Japan	Motor vehicles	12,768,821
9	11	Renault	France	Motor vehicles	12,715,866
10	9	ENI	Italy	Petroleum	12,565,727
11	6	Française des Pétroles	France	Petroleum	12,509,942
12	17	Daimler-Benz	Germany	Motor vehicles	12,090,806
13	10	Hoechst	Germany	Chemicals	12,068,207
14	14	Bayer	Germany	Chemicals	11,392,483
15	19	Nestlé	Switzerland	Food products, beverages	11,001,848
16	15	BASF	Germany	Chemicals	10,732,452
17	18	Peugeot-Citroën	France	Motor vehicles	10,620,992
18	27	Matsushita Electric Industrial	Japan	Electronics, appliances	10,020,545
19	26	Nissan Motor	Japan	Motor vehicles	9,751,661
20	16	Nippon Steel	Japan	Metal refining — steel	9,521,847
21	24	Mitsubishi Heavy Industries	Japan	Motor vehicles, industrial equipment	9,200,492
22	20	Thyssen	Cermany	Metal refining — steel	9,182,135
23	22	Hitachi	Japan	Electronics, appliances	9,153,283
24	12	Petróleos de Venezuela	Venezuela	Petroleum	9,137,238
25	21	Petrobrás (Petróleo Brasileiro)	Brazil	Petroleum	9,131,228
26	25	Elf-Aquitaine	France	Petroleum	9,115,703
27	23	Imperial Chemical Industries	Britain	Chemicals	8,701,411
28	28	B.A.T. Industries	Britain	Tobacco	7,750,092
29	29	Saint-Gobain-Pont-à-Mousson	France	Building materials, metal products	7,598,170
30	64	Générale d'Electricité	France	Electronics, appliances	7,004,167

WORLD CRUDE PETROLEUM PRODUCERS

SOURCE: *United Nations Monthly Bulletin of Statistics,* © United Nations, May 1979

The list below is a compilation of the latest available figures on the oil production of selected countries. The figures for Communist countries are generally estimates. All figures are given in thousands of metric tons per average calendar month.

Region and Country	1973	1977	1978
North America:			
Canada	7,336	5,390	N.A.
Mexico	1,938	4,129	N.A.
Trinidad and Tobago	734	986	N.A.
United States	37,849	33,620	35,710
South America:			
Argentina	1,790	1,874	N.A.
Bolivia	183	135	132
Brazil	690*	674*	N.A.
Chile	106	80	70
Colombia	791	592	N.A.
Ecuador	885	765	839
Peru	290	308	643
Venezuela	14,648	9,735	9,420
Europe:			
Austria	215	149	N.A.
France	105	87	93
Germany, West	553	451	422
Hungary	166	183	183
Italy	87	90	N.A.
Netherlands	124	115	117
Norway	132	1,141	1,440
Poland	33	38	N.A.
Romania	1,191	1,221	N.A.
Spain	64	102	N.A.
United Kingdom	31*	3,128*	4,448*
USSR	35,753*	45,823*	47,705*
Yugoslavia	278	329	340

Region and Country	1973	1977	1978
Africa:			
Algeria	4,229	4,287	4,258
Angola	680	720	683
Congo	174	132	132
Egypt	707	1,753	N.A.
Gabon	633	939	949
Libya	8,740	8,345	10,058
Nigeria	8,480	8,692	7,923
Tunisia	324	355	N.A.
Asia:			
Bahrain	284	234	221
Burma	81	108	118
India	600	849	934
Indonesia	5,579	7,829	6,704
Iran	24,403	23,754	21,814
Iraq	8,295	9,269	10,756
Japan	58	49	45
Kuwait	12,702	8,277	8,765
Malaysia	362	728	N.A.
Oman	1,219	1,421	1,309
Pakistan	36	34	41
Qatar	2,292	1,750	1,935
Saudi Arabia	31,482	38,090	34,194
Syria	462	890	834
Turkey	293	226	N.A.
United Arab Emirates	6,183	8,226	7,502
Oceania:			
Australia	1,595*	1,763*	N.A.

* Includes natural gas liquids. N.A.: Data insufficient or not available.

U.S. METALS PRODUCTION

SOURCE: American Iron & Steel Institute; U.S. Bureau of Mines; Zinc Institute Inc. (figures in short tons)

Year	Pig Iron and Ferroalloys	Steel Ingots[1]	Rolled Iron and Steel Products	Aluminum[3]	Copper[3]	Zinc[4]	Lead[3]
1961	66,565,063	98,014,492	73,411,563	1,903,200	1,165,155	896,900	261,921
1965	90,918,000	131,461,601	99,304,221	2,754,500	1,351,734	1,078,300	301,147
1967	89,472,000	127,213,000	93,084,000	3,269,300	954,064	1,010,700	316,931
1970	93,851,000	131,514,000		3,976,148	1,719,657	961,153	571,767
1971	83,468,000	120,443,000	N.A.	3,925,223	1,522,183	840,178	578,550
1972	91,338,000	133,241,000	N.A.	4,122,452	1,664,840	706,898	618,915
1973	103,089,000	150,799,000	N.A.	4,529,116	1,698,337	687,861	603,024
1974	98,332,000	145,720,000	N.A.	4,903,000	1,597,000	590,181	633,870
1975	81,850,000	116,642,000	N.A.	3,879,000	1,413,000	445,916	621,000
1976	88,874,000	128,000,000	N.A.	4,251,000	1,606,000	535,953	610,000
1977	82,968,000	125,330,000	N.A.	4,538,710	1,504,000	434,054	589,000
1978	89,357,000[2]	136,689,000[2]	N.A.	4,803,000	1,490,000	445,870	585,000

[1] Plus castings. [2] Primary. [3] Primary output from domestic ore. [4] Slab smelter output.

WORLD MINERAL-PRODUCTION LEADERS: 1977

SOURCE: *U.N. Monthly Bulletin of Statistics,* June, 1979, © United Nations (data in thousands of metric tons per average calendar month.)

ITEM	COUNTRY AND PRODUCTION			
Bauxite	Australia (2,122)	Jamaica (952)	Guinea (903)	Hungary (246)
Coal	USSR (60,166)	U.S. (48,822)	Poland (15,509)	U.K. (10,179)
Coal, Lignite & brown	E. Germany (21,142)	W. Germany (10,243)	Czechoslovakia (7,770)	Poland (3,398)
Copper Ore	U.S. (115)	Chile (87.3)	Canada (65.2)	Zambia (64.5)
Crude Oil	USSR (45,823)	Saudi Arabia (38,090)	U.S. (33,620)	Iran (23,754)
Iron Ore	USSR (19,976)	Australia (7,967)	Brazil (4,730)	U.S. (4,652)
Lead Ore	U.S. (44.5)	Australia (34.7)	Canada (27.3)	Morocco (13.0)
Natural Gas [1]	U.S. (416,880)	USSR (240,874)	Netherlands (61,050)	Canada (58,620)
Tin Concentrates	Malaysia (5,423)	Thailand (2,590)	Bolivia (2,565)	Indonesia (2,002)
Zinc Ore	Canada (108)	Australia (39.6)	U.S. (34.6)	Japan (23.0)

[1] In teracalories.

U.S. EXPORTS AND IMPORTS: GEOGRAPHIC AREAS

SOURCE: U.S. Dept. of Commerce, Bureau of International Economic Policy and Research

Area	Exports (millions of $)			Imports (millions of $)			Trade Balance
	1976	1977	1978	1976	1977	1978	1978
Total	$114,802	$121,150	$143,575	$120,678	$147,685	$172,026	$ — 28,451
Developed Countries							
Canada	24,106	25,774	28,372	26,238	29,597	33,529	— 5,157
Western Europe	32,396	34,741	39,936	22,783	27,669	36,458	+ 3,411
Japan	10,145	10,534	12,885	15,504	18,548	24,458	— 11,573
Australia, New Zealand & Republic of South Africa	3,948	3,814	4,395	2,466	2,802	4,444	— 50
Developing Countries							
19 American Republics	15,487	16,371	20,183	13,228	16,450	18,560	+ 1,623
Other Western Hemisphere	1,481	1,592	1,835	3,891	4,648	4,391	— 2,556
Near East	10,044	11,021	13,546	9,103	13,020	11,917	+ 1,629
East and South Asia	10,214	10,693	13,505	14,649	17,709	21,702	— 8,197
Developing Africa	3,048	3,509	3,672	11,627	15,690	14,534	— 10,862
Developing Oceania	89	117	147	130	187	166	— 19
Communist Areas	3,640	2,714	4,504	1,059	1,337	1,532	+ 2,672

U.S. EXPORTS AND IMPORTS: PRINCIPAL COMMODITIES

SOURCE: U.S. Dept. of Commerce, Bureau of International Economic Policy and Research

	Exports (millions of $)			Imports (millons of $)			Trade Balance
	1976	1977	1978	1976	1977	1978	1978
Total	$113,318	$117,966	$141,154	$121,795	$147,848	$173,290	$ — 32,136
Excluding military grant-aid	113,133	117,899	141,069	—	—	—	
Crude foods	11,420	9,438	12,723	5,225	7,065	7,241	+ 5,482
Manufactured foods	4,764	5,356	6,687	6,277	6,755	8,128	— 1,441
Crude materials	11,805	13,976	15,604	32,080	40,822	41,141	— 25,537
Agricultural	6,765	8,804	10,436	1,620	1,732	1,957	+ 8,479
Semimanufactures	13,969	14,107	18,905	20,495	24,182	27,575	— 8,670
Finished manufactures	71,365	75,084	87,235	57,716	69,025	89,205	— 1,970
Excluding military grant-aid	71,175	75,022	87,150	—	—	—	

U.S. EXPORTS AND IMPORTS: SELECTED MERCHANDISE

SOURCE: U.S. Dept. of Commerce, Bureau of International Economic Policy and Research

Exports (millions of $)				Imports (millions of $)			
	1976	1977	1978		1976	1977	1978
Food and live animals	$15,710	$14,103	$18,333	Food and live animals	$10,267	$12,490	$13,521
Grains and preparations	10,911	8,755	11,634	Meat	1,447	1,273	1,856
Wheat	4,041	2,883	4,532	Fish	1,618	2,056	2,212
Corn	5,224	4,139	5,301	Coffee	2,632	3,861	3,728
Beverages and Tobacco	1,523	1,847	2,293	Beverages and Tobacco	1,624	1,663	2,221
Crude Inedible Materials (non-fuel)	10,891	12,815	15,553	Crude Inedible Materials (non-fuel)	7,014	7,944	9,334
Mineral Fuels	4,226	4,179	3,878	Mineral Fuels	33,996	44,287	42,105
Animal and Vegetable Oils	978	1,341	1,521	Chemicals	4,772	5,432	6,427
Chemicals	9,958	10,827	12,618	Machinery and Transport Equip.	29,824	35,494	47,626
Machinery and Transport Equip.	49,510	51,037	59,270	Electrical Apparatus	7,424	8,432	6,136
Electronic Computers	2,588	3,264	2,818	Automobiles and Parts	12,269	15,842	20,631
Electrical Apparatus	9,278	10,285	6,967	Other Manufactured Goods	17,615	14,864	19,062
Transport Equipment	18,221	18,520	22,248	Paper	2,103	2,392	2,923
Road Motor Vehicles and Parts	10,949	11,797	13,235	Metals	9,898	12,246	15,714
Aircraft, Parts and Accessories	6,116	5,866	8,204	Textiles & Clothing	5,298	5,926	7,857
				Footwear	1,686	1,848	2,585

LEADING U.S. TRADING PARTNERS: 1978

SOURCE: U.S. Department of Commerce/Bureau of International Economic Policy and Research (figures in millions of dollars)

Export Trade

COUNTRY	VALUE	COUNTRY	VALUE
Canada	$28,372	Mexico	$6,681
Japan	12,885	Netherlands	5,683
United Kingdom	7,119	Saudi Arabia	4,370
West Germany	6,957	France	4,166

Import Trade

COUNTRY	VALUE	COUNTRY	VALUE
Canada	$33,529	Mexico	$6,093
Japan	24,478	Saudi Arabia	5,307
West Germany	9,961	Republic of China	5,171
United Kingdom	6,513	Nigeria	4,714

VALUE OF U.S. EXPORTS AND IMPORTS

SOURCE: U.S. Department of Commerce/Bureau of International Economic Policy and Research (figures in millions of dollars)

Year	Total Exports*	Total Imports	Trade Balance	Year	Total Exports*	Total Imports	Trade Balance	Year	Total Exports*	Total Imports	Trade Balance
1978	143,575	172,026	—28,451	1969	37,332	36,043	1,289	1961	20,226	14,761	5,465
1977	121,150	147,685	—26,535	1968	34,063	33,226	837	1960	19,659	15,073	4,586
1976	115,150	121,009	—5,859	1967	31,030	26,889	4,141	1959	16,426	15,690	736
1975	107,130	96,116	+11,014	1966	29,490	25,618	3,872	1958	16,375	13,392	2,983
1974	97,908	100,997	—13,089	1965	26,742	21,427	5,315	1957	19,516	13,418	6,098
1973	70,823	69,476	+1,347	1964	25,832	18,749	7,083	1956	17,343	12,905	4,438
1972	49,199	55,583	—6,384	1963	22,467	17,207	5,260	1955	14,298	11,566	2,732
1971	43,549	45,563	—2,014	1962	20,986	16,464	4,522	1954	12,857	10,371	2,486
1970	42,659	39,952	+2,707								

* Excluding aid in the form of military grants.

U.S. SHARE OF WORLD TRADE: 1938-1978

SOURCE: United Nations Monthly Bulletin of Statistics, May 1979, © United Nations (figures in millions of dollars)

Year	Total World Exports*	U.S. Exports	Year	Total World Imports*	U.S. Imports
1978	1,169,400	141,154	1978	1,188,200	182,787
1977	1,017,400	119,042	1977	1,042,100	156,758
1976	896,000	113,323	1976	912,400	128,872
1975	788,400	106,157	1975	803,600	102,984
1974	769,300	97,144	1974	774,000	107,112
1973	518,900	70,223	1973	528,900	68,656
1972	372,800	48,968	1972	384,200	55,282
1971	314,300	43,492	1971	328,400	45,516
1970	280,200	42,590	1970	294,100	39,756
1969	243,500	37,462	1969	256,400	35,863
1968	212,500	34,199	1968	224,700	33,066
1967	189,900	31,243	1967	201,500	26,813
1966	180,600	29,998	1966	192,000	25,439
1965	164,800	27,189	1965	174,800	21,348
1964	152,200	26,300	1964	161,000	18,666
1963	135,400	23,104	1963	143,500	17,072
1962	141,400	21,446	1962	149,800	16,317
1960	128,000	20,412	1960	135,500	15,071
1958	108,100	17,755	1958	114,100	13,298
1953	82,700	15,661	1953	84,200	10,915
1948	57,500	12,545	1948	63,600	7,183
1938	23,500	3,064	1938	25,400	2,180

* Excluding trade of the Centrally Planned Economies.

WORLD ECONOMIC SUMMARY: 1970-1978

SOURCE: United Nations Monthly Bulletin of Statistics, May 1979, © United Nations

Item	Unit*	1970	1978	Item	Unit*	1970	1978
Agricultural production:				Sawnwood	1,000 cu.m.	405	434‡
Barley	Mil. tons	139	188	Woodpulp	Mil. tons	104.5	90.8†
Coffee	1,000 tons	3,856	4,623	Newsprint	Mil. tons	21.4	45.9†
Corn	Mil. tons	261	359	Cement[2]	Mil. tons	556	711
Cotton (lint)	1,000 tons	11,722	13,467	Pig iron and ferroalloys[2]	Mil. tons	413	504
Eggs	Mil. tons	21.4	26.2	Crude steel[2]	Mil. tons	574	665
Meat	Mil. tons	84.5	104.3	Tin [2][3][4][5]	1,000 tons	184	177
Potatoes	Mil. tons	312	303	Merchant vessels,			
Rice	Mil. tons	310	377	launched [2][8][4]	Mil. long tons	21.69	15.41
Tobacco	1,000 tons	4,659	5,768	Motor vehicles[2]	Millions	29.33	32.38
Wheat	Mil. tons	319	426	Electric energy[2]	Bil. kw.-hr.	4,836	7,293
Wool, greasy	1,000 tons	2,760	2,587				
Roundwood	Mil.cu.m.	2,400	2,538†	**External trade:** [1][2][4]			
Rubber (natural)	1,000 tons	3,102	3,680	Imports, c.i.f.	Bil. U.S. dol.	293.8	1,186.9
Fish catches	Mil. tons	70.0	73.5†	Exports, f.o.b.	Bil. U.S. dol.	280.0	1,169.4
				Transport:			
Industrial production:				Railway freight	Bil. tons-km	5,019	6,209†
Coal[2]	Mil. tons	1,781	2,007	Merchant shipping,			
Crude petroleum[2]	Mil. tons	2,248	2,903	loaded	Mil. tons	2,605	3,475†
Wheat flour[2]	Mil. tons	118.7	123.5‡	Civil aviation, km flown [4][6]	Millions	6,990	8,360
Sugar	Mil. tons	69.0	130.1†				

* Data are in metric units.   † Latest available figures are from 1977.   ‡ Latest available figures are from 1976.
[1] Excludes Eastern Europe.   [2] Excludes China.   [3] Excludes East Germany.   [4] Excludes USSR
[5] Excludes North Korea.   [6] ICAO members.

WALL STREET GLOSSARY
SOURCE: New York Stock Exchange

Assets: Everything a corporation owns or has outstanding: cash, investments, money due it, materials and inventories (current assets); buildings and machinery (fixed assets); and patents and good will (intangible assets).

Averages: Various ways of measuring the trend of securities prices, the most popular of which is the Dow-Jones average of 30 industrial stocks listed on the New York Stock Exchange. The numbers are not true numerical averages, but take into account such factors as past splits, etc.

Balance Sheet: A condensed statement showing the nature and amount of a company's assets, liabilities, and capital on a given date. In dollar amounts, the balance sheet shows what the company owned, what it owed, and the ownership interest in the company of its stockholders.

Bear: Someone who believes the market will decline.

Bid and Asked: Often referred to as a quotation or quote. The bid is the highest price anyone has declared that he wants to pay for a security at a given time, the asked is the lowest price anyone will take at the same time.

Blue Chip: Common stock in a company known nationally for the quality and wide acceptance of its products or services and its ability to make money and pay dividends. Usually such stocks are relatively high priced and offer relatively low yields.

Blue Sky Laws: A popular name for laws various states have enacted to protect the public against securities frauds. The term is believed to have originated when a judge ruled that a particular stock had about the same value as a patch of blue sky.

Book Value: An accounting term. Book value of a stock is determined from a company's records, by adding all assets (generally excluding such intangibles as good will), then deducting all debts and other liabilities, plus the liquidation price of any preferred issues. The sum arrived at is divided by the number of common shares outstanding and the result is book value per common share. Book value of the assets of a company or a security may have little or no significant relationship to market value.

Bull: One who believes the market will rise.

Capital Gain or Capital Loss: Profit or loss from the sale of a capital asset. Under current federal income tax laws, a capital gain may be either short-term (12 months or less) or long-term (more than 12 months). A short-term capital gain is taxed at the reporting individual's full income tax rate. A long-term capital gain is subject to a lower tax. The capital gains provisions of the tax law are complicated. You should consult your tax advisor for specific information.

Capitalization: Total amount of the various securities issued by a corporation. Capitalization may include bonds, debentures, preferred and common stock. Bonds and debentures are usually carried on the books of the issuing company in terms of their par or face value. Preferred and common shares may be carried in terms of par or stated value. Stated value may be either an arbitrary figure decided upon by the directors, or may represent the amount received by the company from the sale of the securities at the time of issuance.

Common Stock: Securities that represent an ownership interest in a corporation. If the company has also issued preferred stock, both common and preferred have ownership rights, but the preferred normally has prior claim on dividends and, in the event of liquidation, assets. Claims of both common and preferred stockholders are junior to claims of bondholders or other creditors of the company. Common-stock holders assume greater risk than preferred-stock holders, but generally exercise greater control and may gain greater reward.

Convertible: A bond, debenture, or preferred share that may be exchanged by the owner for common stock or another security, usually of the same company, in accordance with the terms of the issue.

Dealer: An individual or firm in the securities business acting as a principal rather than as an agent. Typically, a dealer buys for his own account and sells to a customer from his own inventory. The dealer's profit or loss is the difference between the price he pays and the price he receives for the same security.

Discretionary Account: An account in which the customer gives the broker or someone else discretion, which may be complete or within specific limits, as to the purchase and sales of securities or commodities including selection, timing, amount and price to be paid or received.

Fiscal Year: A corporation's accounting year. Due to the nature of their particular business, some companies do not use the calendar year for their bookkeeping. A typical example is the department store which finds December 31 too early a date to close its books after the Christmas rush. For that reason many stores wind up their accounting year January 31. Their fiscal year, therefore, runs from February 1 of one year through January 31 of the next.

Growth Stock: Stock of a company with prospects for future growth—a company whose earnings are expected to increase at a relatively rapid rate.

Investment Banker: Also known as an underwriter. He is the middleman between the corporation issuing new securities and the public. The usual practice is for one or more investment bankers to buy outright from a corporation a new issue of stocks or bonds. The group forms a syndicate to sell the securities to individuals and institutions. Investment bankers also distribute very large blocks of stocks or bonds.

Legal List: A list of investments selected by various states in which certain institutions and fiduciaries, such as insurance companies and banks, may invest.

Liquidity: The ability of the market in a particular security to absorb a reasonable amount of buying or selling at reasonable price changes. Liquidity is one of the most important characteristics of a good market.

Listed Stock: The stock of a company that is traded on a securities exchange and for which a listing application and a registration statement, giving detailed information about the company and its operations, have been filed with the Securities & Exchange Commission (SEC), unless otherwise exempted, and the exchange itself. The various stock exchanges have different standards for listing. Some of the guides used by the New York Stock Exchange for an original listing are national interest in the company, a minimum of 1 million shares publicly held among not less than 2,000 shareholders. The publicly held common shares should have a minimum aggregate market value of $16 million. The company should have net income in the latest year of more than $2.5 million before federal income tax and $2 million in each of the preceding two years.

Load: The portion of the offering price of shares of open-end investment companies that covers sales commissions and all other costs of distribution. The load is incurred only on purchase, there being, in most cases, no charge when the shares are sold (redeemed).

Margin: The amount paid by the customer when he uses his broker's credit to buy a security. Under Federal Reserve regulations, the initial margin required in the past 20 years has ranged from 50 percent of the purchase price all the way to 100 percent.

NASD: The National Association of Securities Dealers, Inc., an association of brokers and dealers in the over-the-counter securities business. The Association has the power to expel members who have been found guilty of unethical practices.

NYSE Common Stock Index: A composite index covering price movements of all common stocks listed on the "Big Board." It is based on the close of the market December 31, 1965, at 50.00 and is weighted according to the number of shares listed for each issue. The index is computed continuously by the Exchange's Market Data System and printed on the ticker tape each half hour. Point changes in the index are converted to dollars and cents so as to provide a meaningful measure of changes in the average price of listed stocks. The composite index is supplemented by separate indexes for four industry groups: industrials, transportation, utilities, and finances.

Over-the-Counter: A market for securities made up of securities dealers who may or may not be members of a securities exchange. Over-the-counter is mainly a market made over the telephone. Thousands of companies have insufficient shares outstanding, stockholders, or earnings to warrant application for listing on a stock exchange. Securities of these companies are traded in the over-the-counter market between dealers who act either as principals or as brokers for customers. The over-the-counter market is the principal market for U.S. Government bonds and municipals.

Par: In the case of a common share, a dollar amount assigned to the share by the company's charter. Par value may also be used to compute the dollar amount of the common shares on the balance sheet. Par value has little significance so far as market value of common stock is concerned. Many companies today issue no-par stock, but give a stated per share value on the balance sheet.

Par at one time was supposed to represent the value of the original investment behind each share in cash, goods, or services. In the case of preferred shares and bonds, however, par is important. It often signifies the dollar value upon which dividends on preferred stocks and interest on bonds are figured. The issuer of a three percent bond promises to pay that percentage of the bond's par value annually.

Point: In the case of shares of stock, a point means $1. If General Motors shares rise 3 points, each share has risen $3. In the case of bonds, a point means $10, since a bond is quoted as a percentage of $1,000.

Portfolio: Holdings of securites by an individual or institution. A portfolio may contain bonds, preferred stocks and common stocks of various types of enterprises.

Preferred Stock: A class of stock with a claim on the company's earnings before payment may be made on the common stock, usually also entitled to priority over common stock if the company liquidates. It is usually entitled to dividends at a specified rate before payment of a dividend on the common stock.

Price-Earnings Ratio: The current market price of a share of stock divided by earnings per share for a twelve-month period. For example, a stock selling for $100 a share and earning $5 a share is said to be selling at a price-earnings ratio of 20 to 1.

Principal: The person for whom a broker executes an order, or a dealer buying or selling for his own account. The term "principal" may also refer to a person's capital or to the face amount of a bond.

Puts and Calls: Options that give the right to buy or sell a fixed amount of a certain stock at a specified price within a specified time. A put gives the holder the right to sell the stock; a call the right to buy the stock. Puts are purchased by those who think a stock may go down. A put obligates the seller of the contract to take delivery of the stock and pay the specified price to the owner of the option within the time limit of the contract.

The price specified in a put or call is usually close to the market price of the stock at the time the contract is made. Calls are purchased by those who think a stock may rise. A call gives the holder the right to buy the stock from the seller of the contract at the specified price within a fixed period of time.

Quotation: Often shortened to "quote." The highest bid to buy and the lowest offer to sell a security in a given market at a given time. If you ask your broker for a "quote" on a stock, he may come back with something like "45¼ to 45½." This means that $45.25 is the highest price any buyer wanted to pay at the time the quote was given on the floor of the Exchange, and that $45.50 was the lowest price that any seller would take at the same time.

REIT: Real Estate Investment Trust, an organization similar to an investment company in some respects but concentrating its holdings in real estate investments. The yield is generally liberal since REIT's are required to distribute as much as 90% of their income.

Registration: Before a public offering may be made of new securities by a company, or of outstanding securities by controlling stockholders—through the mails or in interstate commerce—the securities must be registered under the Securities Act of 1933. Registration statement is filed with the SEC by the issuer. It must disclose pertinent information relating to the company's operations, securities, management, and purpose of the public offering. Securities of railroads under jurisdiction of the Interstate Commerce Commission (ICC), and certain other types of securities, are exempted. On security offerings involving less than $300,000, less information is required.

Round Lot: A unit of trading or a multiple thereof. On the New York Stock Exchange, the unit of trading is generally 100 shares in stocks and $1,000 par value in the case of bonds. In some inactive stocks, the unit of trading is 10 shares.

Specialist: A member of the New York Stock Exchange who has two functions: First, to maintain an orderly market, insofar as reasonably practicable, in the stocks in which he is registered as a specialist. To maintain an orderly market, the exchange expects the specialist to buy or sell for his own account, to a reasonable degree, when there is a temporary disparity between supply and demand.

Second, the specialist acts as a broker's broker. When a commission broker on the exchange floor receives a limit order, for example, to buy at $50 a stock then selling at $60, he cannot wait at the particular post where the stock is traded until the price reaches the specified level. So he leaves the order with the specialist, who will try to execute it in the market if and when the stock declines to the specified price. The specialist must always put his customers' interests first.

Split: The division of the outstanding shares of a corporation into a larger number of shares. A 3-for-1 split by a company with 1 million shares outstanding would result in 3 million shares outstanding. After the 3-for-1 split, each holder of 100 shares would have 300 shares.

Yield: Also known as return. The dividends or interest paid by a company expressed as a percentage of the current price. A stock with a current market value of $40 a share paying dividends at the rate of $2.00 is said to return 5 per cent ($2.00 − $40.00). The current return on a bond is figured the same way. A 3 per cent yield $1,000 bond selling at $600 offers a current yield return of 5 per cent ($30 − $600).

WALL STREET INDEXES

Dow Jones Industrial Average: The addition of closing prices for 30 stocks divided by the current divisor. The divisor is never the number of stocks listed, but by reflecting splits, mergers, and bankruptcies, it is constantly revised.

NASDAQ Composite Index: The measure of all domestic common issues traded over-the-counter included in the NASDAQ System, exclusive of those listed on an exchange and those with only one market maker. The index is market value-weighted, in that the importance of each stock is proportional to its price times the number of shares outstanding.

New York Stock Exchange Common Stock Index: The current aggregate market value (sum of all shares times the price per share) divided by the adjusted base market value and multiplied by 50. The adjusted value reflects additions or deletions of listings, but remains unaffected by stock splits and dividends.

Standard and Poor's Index: The aggregate market value (price of each share times the number of shares) for 425 industrial stocks, expressed as one-tenth the percentage of the average market value relative to the average market value during the years 1941-43.

THE AMERICAN SHAREHOLDER

The latest NYSE shareownership survey, conducted during 1975, revealed that almost 1 out of 5 shareowners had left the stock market since early 1970. U.S. shareowners numbered 25.3 million and included 1 out of 6 adult Americans in mid-1975. In this five-and-one-half-year period, the median age of shareowners increased by 5 years, from 48 to 53. For the first time since the Exchange began conducting shareownership surveys in 1952, the number of shareowners in the U.S. did not increase.

These 25 million shareowners held shares in some 11,000 publicly owned corporations and investment companies, which had 40.7 billion shares of stock outstanding at a total market value of $800 billion. While the number of shares of stock outstanding increased 12.6% from 36.2 billion in 1970, depressed economic conditions reduced the total market value of stocks outstanding, which declined 21.3% from $1.1 trillion in 1970.

Although the total number of U.S. shareowners declined 18.1%, the number of shareowners of NYSE-listed stocks declined only 1.9% to 18.0 million. Adult female shareowners slightly outnumbered adult males.

The average shareowner's income rose from $13,500 in early 1970 to $19,000 in mid-1975, paralleling changes in purchasing power. The incidence of shareowners with household incomes below $10,000 declined from 28.8% of all U.S. shareowners in 1970 to 14.6% in mid-1975.

Year	Number of Shareowners (millions)	Percent of U.S. Population
1952	6.5	4%
1959	12.5	7
1962	17.0	9
1965	20.1	10
1971	31.9	17
1972	32.5	17
1973	31.7	15
1974	30.9	14
1975	25.3	12

INSTITUTIONAL FAVORITES

SOURCE: Standard & Poor's Corporation

The Standard & Poor's Corporation issues most favored by institutional investors are ranked here by the number of companies owning them.

Issue	Ind. Div. Rate $	% Yld. on Div.	P-E Ratio
Int'l Bus. Mach.	13.76	4.3	15
American Tel. & Tel.	5.00	8.1	8
Exxon Corp.	3.60	6.8	9
General Electric	2.60	5.2	9
General Motors	6.00	10.5	5
Eastman Kodak	2.90	4.4	12
Texaco Inc.	2.00	7.6	8
Xerox Corp.	2.40	4.0	10
Atlantic Richfield	2.80	4.5	9
Sears, Roebuck & Co.	1.28	6.1	7
Mobil Corp.	4.80	6.4	7
Merck & Co.	1.90	2.8	17
Dow Chemical	1.40	4.7	9
Minnesota Mng./Mfg.	2.40	4.1	12
Standard Oil (Ind.)	3.00	5.1	8
Amer. Home Prods.	1.40	5.2	12
Citicorp	1.30	5.6	6
Phillips Petroleum	1.20	3.4	10
Standard Oil of Cal.	2.80	5.9	7
Caterpillar Tractor	2.10	3.4	9
K Mart Corp.	.72	2.9	9
General Tel. & Elect.	2.48	8.8	7
Continental Oil	1.50	4.5	8
Schlumberger, Ltd.	1.10	1.6	18
Philip Morris Inc.	2.50	3.7	10

Issue	Ind. Div. Rate $	% Yld. on Div.	P-E Ratio
Gulf Oil	1.90	7.1	7
Union Carbide	2.80	6.9	7
Ford Motor	3.60	8.2	3
Burroughs Corp.	2.00	2.8	12
Halliburton Co.	1.80	2.6	10
Coca-Cola Co.	1.96	4.8	14
Procter & Gamble	3.00	3.7	12
duPont (E.I.) deNem.	8.25	5.7	9
Pfizer, Inc.	1.32	4.1	11
Texas Utilities	1.64	8.6	8
Avon Products	2.60	5.5	12
Tenneco, Inc.	2.20	6.9	7
Int'l Paper	2.20	4.7	10
Warner-Lambert	1.20	4.8	9
Johnson & Johnson	2.00	2.9	14
Int'l Tel. & Tel.	2.20	7.6	6
Pepsico Inc.	1.00	4.0	10
Bristol-Myers	1.44	4.1	11
Goodyear Tire & Rub.	1.30	7.4	6
Weyerhaeuser Co.	1.00	3.0	10
Penney (J.C.)	1.76	5.9	7
Eli Lilly & Co.	1.80	3.4	14
RCA Corp.	1.60	5.9	7
Monsanto Co.	3.20	6.2	6
Schering-Plough	1.24	4.3	8

Issue	Ind. Div. Rate $	% Yld. on Div.	P-E Ratio
Alcan Aluminium Ltd.	2.00	5.4	5
American Express	1.80	5.7	7
Reynolds (R.J.) Indus.	3.80	6.4	7
BankAmerica Corp.	1.10	4.4	7
INCO Ltd.	.40	1.9	27
Commonwealth Edison	2.60	10.0	8
McDonald's Corp.	.36	.8	11
Morgan (J.P.) & Co.	2.50	5.4	7
Abbott Laboratories	1.00	3.1	13
Georgia-Pacific	1.10	3.6	10
Dresser Industries	.25	.6	8
Emerson Electric	1.44	4.3	11
Central & So. West.	1.42	8.9	7
Beatrice Foods	1.20	5.5	8
Union Pacific	2.30	3.9	11
Southern Co.	1.54	11.4	10
Deere & Co.	1.50	4.1	8
Florida Pwr. & Light	2.08	7.5	6
Houston Industries	2.36	8.0	7
Southern Cal. Edison	2.48	9.1	8
Colgate-Palmolive	1.08	6.4	8
General Foods	1.80	5.5	7
Digital Equipment	—	—	15
American Cyanamid	1.60	6.1	8
Amer. Electric Pwr.	2.18	10.0	10

THE 50 LEADING STOCKS IN MARKET VALUE (AS OF DEC. 31, 1978)

SOURCE: New York Stock Exchange

Issue	Listed Shares (in millions)	Market Value (in millions)
Int'l Business Machines	145.9	$ 43,482
American Tel. & Tel.	669.5	40,591
Exxon Corp.	453.2	22,264
General Motors	287.7	15,608
General Electric	231.5	10,908
Eastman Kodak	161.6	9,492
Standard Oil (Ind.)	152.4	8,628
Schlumberger, N.V.	88.0	8,414
Standard Oil of Cal.	170.8	8,006
Minnesota Mining & Mfg.	117.5	7,391
Mobil Corp.	106.0	7,366
Procter & Gamble	82.7	7,346
Texaco Inc.	274.3	6,549
Sears, Roebuck & Co.	323.8	6,435
Atlantic Richfield	110.6	6,291
duPont deNemours	48.5	6,160
Coca-Cola Company	123.9	5,435
Merck & Co.	75.8	5,129
Caterpillar Tractor	86.4	5,073
Gulf Oil	211.9	5,059
Dow Chemical	199.0	5,000
Shell Oil	151.7	4,891
Phillips Petroleum	154.4	4,884
American Home Products	168.1	4,728
Ford Motor	106.3	4,466

Issue	Listed Shares (in millions)	Market Value (in millions)
Johnson & Johnson	59.9	$ 4,420
Philip Morris Inc.	62.1	4,378
Xerox Corp.	80.2	4,223
General Tel. & Electronics	139.0	3,962
Halliburton Co.	58.8	3,883
BankAmerica Corp.	146.6	3,774
Eli Lilly & Co.	73.3	3,510
Getty Oil	88.5	3,342
Continental Oil	113.0	3,179
Weyerhaeuser Co.	128.6	3,167
Teledyne Inc.	32.3	3,137
Boeing Co.	43.4	3,096
Int'l Tel. & Tel.	112.6	3,055
Citicorp	128.4	3,018
Burroughs Corp.	40.9	2,985
Tenneco Inc.	98.1	2,969
Avon Products	58.2	2,953
Smithkline Corp.	30.2	2,764
K Mart Corp.	122.1	2,763
Reynolds (R.J.) Industries	48.7	2,756
Hewlett-Packard Co.	29.0	2,611
Standard Oil (Ohio)	60.1	2,556
Union Oil of California	44.0	2,503
Georgia-Pacific Corp.	102.9	2,496
Pacific Tel. & Tel.	168.6	2,487
TOTAL	**6,771.0**	**$339,583**

REGULAR DIVIDEND PAYERS

Source: Standard & Poor's Corporation

The following companies have paid quarterly, semi-annual, or annual dividends for 60 years or more. Dividends are for 1978..

Company	Dividends Began	Dividend	Company	Dividend Began	Dividend	Company	Dividends Began	Dividend
Allied Chem.	1887	2.000	ExxonCorp.	1882	3.600	Times Mirror	1892	1.200
Amer. Brands	1905	4.480	Fairmont Fds	1904	.760	Murphy(G.C.)	1913	1.280
Am.Dist.Tele.	1903	1.080	Fidel.Un.Bnk	1893	2.600	Tokheim Corp	1920	.600
Am.Elec.Pwr.	1909	2.180	FstIntBncshr	1875	1.300	Nabisco,Inc.	1899	1.500
Amer.Express	1870	1.800	FstNatBoston	1784	2.000	Trans Union	1914	2.120
Am.HomeProd.	1919	1.400	FstNatStBnCp	1812	2.200	Nat'lFuelGas.	1903	2.380
Am. Nat.Res.	1904	3.200	First Penn.	1828	1.320	TravelerCorp	1864	2.080
Am.Steriliz.	1914	.320	FisherScient.	1907	.440	Nat'l-Stand.	1916	1.240
Am.Tel.&Tel.	1881	5.000	Foxboro Co.	1916	1.200	Tuscon G&E	1918	1.420
Amfac, Inc.	1898	1.200	Gatx Corp	1919	2.000	Nat'l Steel	1907	2.600
Anchor Hock.	1914	1.800	GenBancshrs.	1913	.800	UGI Corp.	1885	1.640
Arz.Pub.Ser.	1920	1.880	Gen.Electric	1899	2.600	N.EnglandT&T	1886	3.160
Atl.Cty.Ele.	1919	1.740	GeneralMills	1898	1.160	UnionBanCorp	1917	.920
AvonProducts	1919	2.600	GeneralMotor	1915	6.000	N.YorkSt.E&G.	1910	1.680
Balt.Gas&El.	1910	2.280	Gillette Co.	1906	1.600	UnionCarbide	1918	2.800
BancalTri-St	1875	.920	GrtLksDrdg&D	1920	2.750	NLIndustries	1906	1.200
Bank,N.Y.Co.	1785	2.530	GrtNrNekoosa	1910	1.400	Union Elec	1906	1.440
Bnkers.Tr.NY	1904	3.000	HackensWater	1886	3.600	NLT Corp.	1920	1.120
BayStateGas.	1853	1.960	Handy&Harman	1905	.600	UnionOilCal	1916	2.600
Bell&Howell	1915	.960	HarrisBnkCrp	1908	1.660	Norf&WestRy	1901	1.840
BellTelofCan	1881	4.560	HawaiianElec	1901	2.240	UnionPacific.	1900	2.300
Borden,Inc.	1899	1.720	Heinz (H.J.)	1911	2.000	NorthnStsPwr	1910	2.160
BostonEdison	1890	2.440	Hercules,Inc.	1913	1.000	United Illum.	1900	2.560
Brist.-Myers	1900	1.440	Hobart,Corp.	1906	1.080	U.S. Gypsum	1919	2.000
Brit.Petrol.	1917	.495	HghtonMifIn	1908	1.400	U.S. Tobacco	1912	1.840
Burrghs.Corp	1895	2.000	HoushldFinan.	1917	1.450	UpJohn Co.	1909	1.520
CampbellSoup	1902	1.760	Huyck Corp.	1907	.720	WashtonGasLt	1852	2.280
Cannon Mills	1890	1.120	Idaho Power	1917	2.280	OklaGas&Elec	1908	1.600
Crpnter.Tech	1907	1.600	IdealBsIndus	1911	1.600	WshtonWtrPwr	1899	2.080
Crter-Wallce	1883	.400	INA Corp.	1874	2.600	Orng&RklUtil	1908	1.520
Castle&Cooke	1896	.800	Ind'l Nat'l.	1791	1.440	WPtPepperall	1888	2.800
CtplerTractr.	1914	2.100	Ingersl-Rand.	1910	3.160	Ownes-Ill.	1907	1.260
Cent.Hud.G&E.	1903	1.960	Interco,Inc.	1913	2.200	WestvacoCorp.	1895	1.320
ChampSpkPlug	1919	.720	IBM	1916	13.760	Pacific G&E	1919	2.320
Charter NY	1865	2.440	Int'lHarvstr	1910	2.300	Wickes Corp	1895	1.040
Chase Manh.	1848	2.400	IowaPwr&Lght	1909	2.400	PacificLight	1909	2.000
Chemical NY	1827	3.160	Jeffrsn-Pilt	1913	2.400	Woolworth	1912	1.400
Chbrgh-Pond	1883	1.080	JohnsonContl	1901	1.100	PennwaltCorp	1863	2.200
Cin. Bell	1879	2.320	J&J	1905	2.000	Wrigley, Jr.	1913	3.900
Cin. G&E.	1853	1.960	K Mart.	1913	.720	Pfizer, Inc.	1901	1.320
Citicorp.	1813	1.300	Kroger Co.	1902	2.320	Phila. Elec.	1902	1.800
ClvldElecIII.	1901	1.920	Liggett Grp.	1912	2.500	PtmacElecPwr	1904	1.340
Coca-Cola,Co	1893	1.960	Lilly & Co.	1885	1.800	PPG Indus.	1899	1.840
ColgtePalmlv	1895	1.080	LincolnNat'l	1920	2.800	Proct&Gamble	1891	3.000
Combust.Engr	1911	2.000	LouisvlleG&E	1913	2.000	PublSrvColo.	1907	1.600
Comwlth Edsn	1890	2.600	Ludlow Corp.	1872	.600	PublSrv E&G	1907	2.200
Cone Mills	1914	1.800	MacAnd&Frbs.	1903	1.050	Pullman Inc.	1867	1.600
Conn.Nat.Gas.	1851	1.600	StandOil Ind.	1894	3.000	Quaker Oats	1906	1.200
Consol.Edsn	1885	2.440	ManhLifeCorp	1851	.300	Raybsto-Manh	1895	1.600
Cnsmers Powr	1913	2.240	StanleyWorks	1877	1.080	Reece Corp.	1882	.600
Cntintl Corp	1854	2.000	ManufHanover	1852	2.280	RepbFin'lSrv	1920	1.840
Conwood Corp	1903	1.500	StaufferChem	1915	2.200	Repb ofTexas	1920	1.000
CorningGlass	1881	1.800	MayDeptStors.	1911	1.400	Rexnord Inc.	1894	.960
CPC Int'l.	1920	3.000	SterlingDrug	1902	.770	Reynolds Ind	1900	3.800
Culbro Corp	1909	1.000	MelvilleCorp.	1916	1.400	Rosario Res.	1896	.650
DytnPwr&Lite.	1919	1.660	Sun Co. Inc.	1904	2.800	SanDiegoG&E.	1909	1.440
DentsplyIntl	1900	.800	Mesta Mach.	1914	.600	Scott Paper.	1915	.840
DetroitEdisn	1909	1.600	Tampa Elect.	1900	1.320	Scovill Mfg.	1856	1.400
Diamond Intl	1882	2.200	MinnMin&Mfg	1916	2.400	SecurtyPacif.	1881	1.800
DomeMinesLTD	1920	1.200	Texaco Inc.	1903	2.000	ShellTpt&Trd	1898	1.396
Donnelley&Sn	1911	1.000	Mirro Alum.	1902	.960	SierraPacPwr	1916	1.220
Dow Chemical	1911	1.400	Texas Comm	1920	1.400	Singer Co.	1863	.800
DowJones&Co.	1906	1.440	Mobil Corp.	1902	4.800	S.EastBankng	1908	.800
DPontDnmours.	1904	8.250	TexasUtility.	1917	1.640	SthrnCalEdsn	1909	2.480
DuquesneLght	1913	1.720	MnrchMchTool	1913	.920	SouthrnNETel	1891	3.600
EastmanKodak	1902	2.900	Thompson(JW)	1917	1.500	SpringsMills	1898	1.050
Emhart Corp.	1902	2.200	Morgan & Co.	1892	2.500	Squibb Corp.	1902	1.080
Equifax Inc.	1913	2.200	Ticor	1894	1.280	Stand Brands	1899	1.360
EquimarkCorp	1872	.960	Mtn.Sts.T&T.	1911	2.080	StandOilCal	1912	2.800

ENERGY: THE NATION'S FUTURE

DWINDLING U.S. PETROLEUM AND NATURAL GAS RESERVES
SOURCE: Geological Survey, Circular 725

Area	Cumulative Production	Reserves		Inferred[4]	Undiscovered Recoverable Resources Range[5] (95%–5%)
		Demonstrated			
		Measured[2]	Indicated[3]		
Crude Oil[1]					
(billions of barrels)					
Lower 48 Onshore	99.892	21.086	4.315	14.3	20–64
Alaska Onshore	0.154	9.944	0.013	6.1	6–19
Total Onshore	100.046	31.030	4.328	20.4	37–81
Lower 48 Offshore	5.634	3.070	0.308	2.6	5–18
Alaska Offshore	0.456	0.150	Negligible	0.1	3–31
Total Offshore	6.090	3.220	0.308	2.7	10–49
Total Onshore and Offshore	106.136	34.250	4.636	23.1	50–127
Natural Gas[1]					
(trillions of cubic feet)					
Lower 48 Onshore	446.366	169.454		119.4	246–453
Alaska Onshore	0.482	31.722		14.7	16–57
Total Onshore	446.848	201.176		134.1	264–506
Lower 48 Offshore	33.553	35.811	Not	67.4	26–111
Alaska Offshore	0.423	0.145	Applicable	0.1	8–80
Total Offshore	33.976	35.956		67.5	42–181
Total Onshore and Offshore	480.824	237.132		201.6	322–655
Natural Gas Liquids					
(billions of barrels)					
Total Onshore and Offshore	15.730	6.350	Not Applicable	6	11–22[6]

[1] Cumulative production and estimates of reserves and resources reflect assumed recovery of about 32% of oil and 80% of gas-in-place. Some portion of remaining oil-in-place is recoverable through application of improved recovery techniques. Estimates based on figures released by the American Petroleum Institute (API) and the American Gas Association (AGA) in April 1975. [2] Identified resources that can be economically extracted with existing technology. Estimates are the "proved reserves" of the API and AGA. [3] Identified resources, economically recoverable by known fluid injection technology. Estimates from the API. [4] Resources estimated recoverable in the future from extensions, revisions of estimates, and new pays in known fields beyond "indicated reserves." [5] Low value of the range is quantity associated with a 95% probability that there is at least this amount. High value is quantity with a 5% probability that there is at least this amount. Totals for the low and high values are derived by statistical methods. [6] Calculated estimates of undiscovered recoverable resources are derived from natural gas estimates by applying historical NGL/Natural Gas ratios. These figures suggest that if added to crude oil estimates, natural gas liquids would increase estimates of petroleum liquids by approximately 20%.

U.S. ENERGY DEMAND AND SUPPLY PROJECTIONS FOR 1985
SOURCE: Congressional Research Service

	Scenario I: Planning base		Scenario II: Possible supply	
	Conventional units	Million barrels per day oil equivalent	Conventional units	Million barrels per day oil equivalent
Total primary energy demand (desired demand):				
CRS, Project Interdependence, base case[1]		44.8		44.8
National energy plan		46.4		46.4
Domestic energy supply:				
Oil and NGL[2]	9.5 million barrels per day	9.5	10.9 million barrels per day[3]	10.9
Natural gas (dry gas to domestic use)[4]	16.9 trillion cubic feet	8.1	17.6 trillion cubic feet[5]	8.5
Coal (domestic use only)[6]	855 million short tons	8.9	965 million short tons[7]	10.0
Nuclear power[8]	113 gigawatts	3.0	126 gigawatts[9]	3.4
Hydro/geo/solar		1.9		1.9
Total domestic supply		31.6		34.8
Oil and natural gas imports:				
Natural gas	2.1 trillion cubic feet	1.0	2.5 trillion cubic feet[10]	1.2
Oil (including 0.3 million barrels per day for storage).	12.7 to 14.3 million barrels per day.	12.7–14.3	9.2 to 10.8 million barrels per day..	9.2–10.8

[1] Assumes 3.5 percent average annual GNP growth rates and 2.9 percent energy growth rates; 50 percent increase of oil price through 1990; doubling of natural gas price through 1990. [2] CRS, Project Interdependence, low supply case. Requires a 50-percent increase of finding rates through 1985 (compared with finding rates of past decade). [3] Assumes that oil reserve additions will almost double between 1977 and 1986 compared with the previous decade. Based on CRS Project Interdependence, base case under optimistic economic and political assumptions. [4] CRS, Project Interdependence, base case (based on mean figure of production estimates under favorable political and economic criteria by 12 of the largest oil and gas producing companies in the U.S.) [5] Assumes slightly higher natural gas finding rates than projected in scenario I. Based on CRS Project Interdependence, high natural gas supply case. [6] CRS, Project Interdependence, base case (700,000,000 tons for utilities, which is comparable to FEA's National Energy Outlook of 1976 for 1985; assumes industrial use by 1985 of only 160,000,000 tons, which would mean virtually no cost conversion in that sector). [7] Assumes considerable exemptions of provisions in the Clean Air Act, and that several other constraints and demand and supply of coal will be removed. [8] July 1977 estimate of probable 1985 capacity by FEA/ERDA/NRC. [9] Assumes speeding up of construction of nuclear powerplants. [10] Assumes approval of additional LNG projects over and above those that have already been approved by the FPC.

MAJOR U.S. VEHICULAR TUNNELS

Source: Federal Highway Administration

UNDERWATER TUNNELS

State or City	Name and Location	Length Portal to Portal (Feet)
Alabama	Bankhead Tunnel at Mobile, Mobile River	3,109
Alabama	George C. Wallace Tunnel, Interstate 10, Mobile River	3,000
California	Posey Tube, Oakland Estuary	3,500
California	Webster St. Tube, Oakland Estuary	3,350
Louisiana	Harvey Tunnel Intracoastal Canal	1,080
Maryland	Baltimore Harbor Tunnel	7,650
Massachusetts	Sumner Tunnel, Boston Harbor	5,650
Massachusetts	Lt. Wm. F. Callahan, Jr. Tunnel, Boston Harbor	5,047
Michigan	Detroit-Windsor Tunnel	5,160
New York City	Holland Tunnel, Hudson River	8,557
New York City	Lincoln Tunnel, Hudson River	8,215
New York City	Lincoln Tunnel (3d Tube), Hudson River	8,013
New York City	Queens Midtown Tunnel, East River	6,414
New York City	Brooklyn-Battery Tunnel, Upper New York Bay	9,117*
Texas	Baytown Tunnel, Houston Ship Channel	3,009
Texas	Washburn Tunnel, Houston Ship Channel	2,936
Virginia	Elizabeth River, near Norfolk	3,920
Virginia	2d Elizabeth River, near Norfolk	4,194
Virginia	Hampton Roads, near Norfolk, I-64	7,479
Virginia	2d Hampton Roads Tunnel near Norfolk, Interstate 64	7,500
Virginia	Chesapeake Bay Crossing (Cape Charles to Cape Henry):	
Virginia	Baltimore Channel Tunnel	5,450
Virginia	Thimble Shoal Tunnel	5,738

LAND TUNNELS

State or City	Name and Location	Length Portal to Portal (Feet)
Arizona	Mule Pass, Benson Douglas Highway	1,400
Arizona	Queen Creek Tunnel, Superior-Miami	1,200
California	Wawona, Yosemite Nat'l Park	4,233
California	Big Oak Flat, Yosemite Nat'l Park	2,083
California	Broadway, Low Level Twin Bore, Oakland	2,944
California	Caldecott (New) Tunnel No. 3, Oakland	3,371
California	Broadway, San Francisco	1,616
California	Park Presidio, San Francisco	1,300
California	Waldo Tunnel, Marin County	1,000
California	Elephant Butte, Plumas	1,187
California	International Airport Underpass, Los Angeles	1,910
Colorado	SN-WPH 81 G(1), near Idaho Springs—U.S. 6	1,036
Colorado	1-F Entrance Road, Mesa Verde Nat'l Park	1,470
Colorado	Eisenhower Memorial Tunnel, I-70	8,950†
Colorado	Interstate 70, near Glenwood Springs	1,045
Connecticut	West Rock Tunnel, near New Haven	1,200
D. C.	9th Street Expressway	1,600
D. C.	Center Leg Mall Tunnel, I-95	3,400
Hawaii	Kalihi Tunnel, Honolulu	2,780
Hawaii	Nuuanu-Pali Tunnel No. 1	1,000

LAND TUNNELS (Cont.)

State or City	Name and Location	Length Portal to Portal (Feet)
Massachusetts	John F. Fitzgerald Expressway, Boston	2,335
Massachusetts	Prudential Passageway, Boston	1,980
Minnesota	Lowry Hill Tunnel at Minneapolis—Interstate 94	1,500
Nevada	Carlin Canyon Tunnel, near Elko on Interstate 80	1,400
New York City	Battery Park	2,300
New York City	First Avenue	1,377
New York City	F.D.R. Drive (42–48 Sts.)	1,600
New York City	F.D.R. Drive (81–89 Sts.)	2,400
New York City	Park Avenue	1,400
New York City	178–179 Sts., Cross-Town	2,414
North Carolina	Beaucatcher Tunnel, Asheville	1,100
North Carolina	Along Pigeon River, Haywood County	1,035
North Carolina	Along Pigeon River, Haywood County	1,122
North Carolina	Blue Ridge Parkway, near Waynesville	820
Ohio	Lytle Park Tunnel in Cincinnati—Interstate 71	850
Oregon	Arch Cape, U.S. 101	1,228
Oregon	Elk Creek Umpqua Highway, State Rt. 58	1,102
Oregon	U.S. Route 26, Vista Ridge, Portland	1,100
Oregon	Sunset Tunnel	779
Oregon	Tooth Park, Route 30	837
Pennsylvania	Squirrel Hill Tunnel, Pittsburgh	4,225
Pennsylvania	Armstrong Hill Tunnel, Pittsburgh	1,325
Pennsylvania	Liberty Tubes, Pittsburgh	6,336
Pennsylvania	Fort Pitt, Pittsburgh	3,550
Pa. Turnpike	Allegheny Tunnel	6,070
—	Tuscarora Tunnel	5,326
—	Kittatinny Tunnel	4,727
—	Blue Mountain	4,339
—	Evans Tunnel, NE Extensions	4,379
Rhode Island	Providence Reconverted Streetcar Tunnel	1,793
Tennessee	Bachman Tunnel, U.S. Route 41, Chattanooga	1,027
Tennessee	Wilcox Tunnel, Chattanooga	1,312
Utah	Copperfield Tunnel, Copperfield	6,989
Utah	Zion Nat'l Park Tunnel, Rt. 1, State Rt. 15	5,766
Virginia	Colonial Parkway, Project 1D3	1,200
Virginia	Route I-77, Big Walker Mountain	4,200
Washington	State Rt. 1-AW-3, Battery Street Tunnel, Seattle	2,140
Washington	State Rt. 2–639, U.S. 10—approach to Lake Washington, Seattle	1,466
Washington	Cayuse Pass Tunnel, Mt. Rainier	510
West Virginia	West Virginia Turnpike	2,669
West Virginia	I-70, Wheeling	1,485
West Virginia	East River Mountain Tunnel, near Bluefield—Interstate 77	5,700
Wyoming	I-80, Green River	1,137

VEHICULAR TUNNELS UNDER CONSTRUCTION

State or City	Name and Location	Length Portal to Portal (Feet)
Colorado	2nd Bore, Eisenhower Memorial Tunnel, I-70	8,950
D. C.	Center Leg Air Rights Tunnel, I-95	1,200
Pennsylvania	Society Hill, Philadelphia, I-95	1,800

* Longest underwater U.S. vehicular tunnel. † Longest U.S. land vehicular tunnel.

RAILROAD PASSENGER SERVICE

Source: Interstate Commerce Commission

Year ended Dec. 31[1]	Average miles of road operated	Passengers carried (Thousands)	Total passenger-miles (Millions)	Revenues per passenger per mile* (Cents)	Revenues per passenger per mile† (Cents)	Passenger train-miles (Thousands)	Train-miles per train-hour	Percent passenger cars unserviceable
1960	94,117	325,872	21,258	3.01	3.03	209,367	40.7	8.7
1965	76,993	298,877	17,389	3.18	3.14	172,344	41.3	7.9
1967	67,827	296,995	10,770	3.90	4.02	92,727	40.1	6.7
1968	59,259	295,618	15,201	3.19	3.13	149,820	41.7	8.2
1969	56,484	295,880	13,120	3.38	3.33	122,591	41.0	8.3
1970	49,533	283,970	12,169	3.60	3.63	107,106	41.0	7.8
1971[2]	40,261	272,401	8,833	4.27	4.64	69,127	37.1	9.6
1972[2]	29,398	261,099	8,560	4.76	5.31	60,993	38.3	15.3
1973[2]	28,286	254,506	9,298	4.76	5.19	60,768	37.6	17.4
1974[2]	31,344	274,298	10,337	5.22	5.85	64,368	38.2	17.1
1975[2]	31,576	269,394	9,735	5.50	6.31	65,766	39.2	17.9
1976[2]	34,474	271,581	10,307	5.72	6.30	66,487	31.2	16.9
1977[2]	31,903	275,322	10,295	5.91	6.64	66,237	33.0	20.4
1978[3]	30,369	281,069	11,223	6.56	6.62	64,190	32.3	19.6

[1] Effective Jan. 1, 1965, the revenue qualification of a Class I railroad was increased from average annual operating revenues of $3 million or more to $5 million or more; effective Jan. 1, 1976, this was again raised to $10 million or more. [2] Includes National Railroad Passenger Corp. (AMTRAK). [3] Preliminary. * Includes commutation. † Excludes commutation.

INTERCITY BUS LINES   SOURCE: American Bus Association

Summary of Operations	1960	1964	1968	1972	1977	1978[5]
Operating companies	1,150	1,100	1,050	1,000	1,050	1,100
Buses	20,974	20,500	21,000	21,400	20,198	20,205
Miles of highway served[1]	265,000	260,000	264,000	270,000	276,000	278,000
Employees[2]	45,000	46,800	47,300	49,100	44,000	43,600
Total bus miles (millions)	1,092	1,183	1,190	1,182	1,102	1,081
Fare-paying passengers (millions)	366	360	398	393	332	335
Fare-paying passenger-miles (millions)	19,300	23,300	24,500	25,600	25,700	25,400
Operating revenue, all services ($ millions)	556.2	686.7	797.6	974.4	1,303.1	1,388.7
Operating expenses ($ millions)	494.8	594.9	708.7	882.1	1,247.6	1,333.6
Net operating revenue before income taxes ($ millions)	61.4	91.8	88.9	92.3	55.5	55.1
Operating ratio[4]	89.0	86.6	88.9	90.5	95.7	96.0
Taxes assigned to operations ($ millions)[3]	53.2	63.5	67.9	84.1	104.3	N/A

[1] Includes duplication between carriers. [2] Operating companies only. [3] Excludes income taxes. [4] Operating expenses divided by operating revenues. [5] Preliminary.

AMTRAK

On May 1, 1971, Amtrak was established as the National Railroad Passenger Corporation. Amtrak had several basic objectives: to reverse the downward trend in passenger ridership, to provide modern, efficient intercity rail passenger service and to develop fully the potential of modern intercity rail service.

The Corporation operates trains through contractual agreements with existing railroads outside of the Northeast. In 1976, Amtrak assumed full ownership and operating control of the Boston-Washington Northeast Corridor.

In Fiscal Year 1978, Amtrak operated an average of 257 trains daily, serving 549 stations, and carried 18.9 million passengers while grossing $313 million. During the fiscal year, the corporation renovated 360 cars and continued work on upgrading the Northeast Corridor, between Washington, D.C., and Boston, for speeds up to 120 miles an hour. The first Superliner, a bi-level long distance car, was delivered in October 1978 with the completion of the order expected in 1980.

CONRAIL

A private, for-profit corporation created by an Act of Congress, the Consolidated Rail Corporation (Conrail) began operations on April 1, 1976. It was conveyed most of the rail properties of the Central of New Jersey, Erie Lackawanna, Lehigh and Hudson River, Lehigh Valley, Penn Central, and Reading lines. Operating over a 17,000-mile system in 16 eastern and midwestern states, the District of Columbia and two provinces of Canada, Conrail is the largest railroad in the United States in traffic carried and freight revenues.

Conrail is primarily a freight railroad, operating more than 1,300 trains a day. In addition, Conrail operates certain rail commuter services under contract with local, regional or state authorities, and some intercity passenger trains under contract with Amtrak.

Conrail's purpose is to create a viable, private-sector rail system in the Northeast quadrant, providing efficient and essential rail service to customers.

LONGEST RAILWAY TUNNELS   SOURCE: Railway Directory and Yearbook

There are considerable discrepancies in figures given by various authorities on precise tunnel lengths.

Tunnel	Date of Opening	Length Miles	Yds.	Operating Railway	Country
Seikan	U.C.	33	810	Japanese National	Japan
Simplon No. II	Oct. 16, 1922	12	559	Swiss Federal & Italian State	Switzerland-Italy
Simplon No. I	June 1, 1906	12	537	Swiss Federal & Italian State	Switzerland-Italy
New Kanmon	March 10, 1975	11	1,059	Japanese National	Japan
Apennine	Apr. 22, 1934	11	892	Italian State	Italy
Rokko	March 15, 1972	10	132	Japanese National	Japan
Gotthard	Jan. 1, 1882(a)	9	562	Swiss Federal	Switzerland
Lötschberg	July 15, 1913	9	140	Bern-Lötschberg-Simplon	Switzerland
Hokuriku	June 10, 1962	8	1,055	Japanese National	Japan
Mont Cenis (Fréjus)	Sept. 17, 1871	8	855	Italian State	France-Italy
New Shimizu	October 1, 1967	8	651	Japanese National	Japan
Aki	March 10, 1975	8	141	Japanese National	Japan
Cascade	Jan. 12, 1929	7	1,397	Great Northern	United States
Kita-Kyushu	March 10, 1975	7	493	Japanese National	Japan
Kubiki	October 1, 1969	7	70	Japanese National	Japan
Flathead	November, 1970	6	5,275	Great Northern	United States
Arlberg	Sept. 20, 1884	6	650	Austrian Federal	Austria
Moffat	Feb. 27, 1928	6	373	Denver & Rio Grande Western	United States
Shimizu	September 1, 1931	6	35	Japanese National	Japan
Kvineshei	Dec. 17, 1943(b)	5	1,112	Norwegian State	Norway
Bingo	March 10, 1975	5	915	Japanese National	Japan
Rimutaka	Nov. 3, 1955	5	821	New Zealand Government	New Zealand
Ricken	Oct. 1, 1910	5	608	Swiss Federal	Switzerland
Grenchenberg	Oct. 1, 1915	5	581	Swiss Federal(c)	Switzerland
Otira	Aug. 4, 1923	5	564	New Zealand Government	New Zealand
Tauern	July 7, 1909	5	551	Austrian Federal	Austria
Haegebostad	Dec. 17, 1943(b)	5	467	Norwegian State	Norway
Fukuoka	March 10, 1975	5	458	Japanese National	Japan
Ronco	Apr. 4, 1889	5	277	Italian State	Italy
Hauenstein (Lower)	Jan. 8, 1916	5	95	Swiss Federal	Switzerland
Connaught	Dec. 6, 1916	5	39	Canadian Pacific	Canada
Karawanken	Oct. 1, 1906	4	1,683	Austrian Federal	Austria-Yugoslavia
New Tanna	Oct. 1, 1964	4	1,663	Japanese National	Japan
Somport	July 18, 1928	4	1,572	French National	France-Spain
Tanna	Dec. 1, 1934	4	1,493	Japanese National	Japan
Ulrikken	Aug. 1, 1964	4	1,338	Norwegian State	Norway
Hoosac	Feb. 9, 1875	4	1,230	Boston & Maine	United States
Monte Orso	Oct. 28, 1927	4	1,230	Italian State	Italy
Lupacino	Sept. 24, 1958	4	1,178	Italian State	Italy
Vivola	Oct. 28, 1927	4	1,004	Italian State	Italy
Monte Adone	Apr. 22, 1934	4	760	Italian State	Italy
Jungfrau	Aug. 1, 1912	4	750	Jungfrau	Switzerland
Borgallo	Aug. 1, 1894	4	700	Italian State	Italy
Severn	Sept. 1, 1886	4	628	Western Region	Great Britain
Lusse (Vosges)	Aug. 9, 1937	4	474	French National	France
Marianopoli	Aug. 1, 1885	4	42	Italian State	Italy

(a) For goods traffic; passengers: June 1, 1882. (b) These were wartime openings under German Occupation. Full traffic began March 1, 1944. (c) The Grenchenberg tunnel is owned but not worked by the Bern-Lötschberg-Simplon Railway.

ESTIMATED AUTOMOBILE REGISTRATIONS: 1978 (In thousands)

SOURCE: U.S. Federal Highway Administration

State	Registrations	State	Registrations	State	Registrations	State	Registrations
Alabama	2,072	Illinois	5,914	Montana	461	Rhode Island	605
Alaska	170	Indiana	2,824	Nebraska	865	South Carolina	1,517
Arizona	1,168	Iowa	1,692	Nevada	431	South Dakota	365
Arkansas	990	Kansas	1,347	New Hampshire	495	Tennessee	2,438
California	11,986	Kentucky	1,813	New Jersey	4,091	Texas	7,355
Colorado	1,718	Louisiana	1,770	New Mexico	606	Utah	641
Connecticut	1,963	Maine	579	New York	6,875	Vermont	265
Delaware	316	Maryland	2,254	North Carolina	3,253	Virginia	2,837
Dist. of Col.	241	Massachusetts	3,218	North Dakota	351	Washington	2,221
Florida	5,194	Michigan	5,152	Ohio	6,532	West Virginia	795
Georgia	2,887	Minnesota	2,149	Oklahoma	1,587	Wisconsin	2,258
Hawaii	459	Mississippi	1,089	Oregon	1,405	Wyoming	224
Idaho	468	Missouri	2,345	Pennsylvania	6,896	Total	117,147

ESTIMATED LICENSED DRIVERS, BY SEX: 1977 (In thousands)

SOURCE: Federal Highway Administration

STATE	MALE DRIVERS	FEMALE DRIVERS	TOTAL DRIVERS	STATE	MALE DRIVERS	FEMALE DRIVERS	TOTAL DRIVERS
Alabama	1,139	984	2,123	Montana	287	229	516
Alaska	133	93	226	Nebraska	538	487	1,025
Arizona	772	647	1,419	Nevada	256	223	479
Arkansas	756	646	1,402	New Hampshire	310	274	584
California	7,749	6,830	14,579	New Jersey	2,241	2,053	4,294
Colorado	982	896	1,878	New Mexico	398	376	774
Connecticut	952	961	1,913	New York	5,026	3,944	8,970
Delaware	199	185	384	North Carolina	1,840	1,650	3,490
Dist. of Col.	194	156	350	North Dakota	211	184	395
Florida	3,562	3,011	6,573	Ohio	5,144	3,361	8,505
Georgia	1,677	1,487	3,164	Oklahoma	983	892	1,875
Hawaii	300	234	534	Oregon	951	803	1,754
Idaho	317	278	595	Pennsylvania	3,931	3,095	7,026
Illinois	3,626	3,115	6,741	Rhode Island	310	290	600
Indiana	1,825	1,649	3,474	South Carolina	931	810	1,741
Iowa	1,073	912	1,985	South Dakota	250	221	471
Kansas	926	843	1,769	Tennessee	1,375	1,222	2,597
Kentucky	1,099	895	1,994	Texas	4,329	3,864	8,193
Louisiana	1,206	1,017	2,223	Utah	400	371	771
Maine	355	312	667	Vermont	177	155	332
Maryland	1,336	1,194	2,530	Virginia	1,691	1,586	3,277
Massachusetts	1,867	1,785	3,652	Washington	1,227	1,112	2,339
Michigan	3,238	2,912	6,150	West Virginia	785	582	1,367
Minnesota	1,396	1,202	2,598	Wisconsin	1,512	1,329	2,841
Mississippi	873	700	1,573	Wyoming	168	141	309
Missouri	1,644	1,456	3,100	**Total**	**74,467**	**63,654**	**138,121**

WORLD TRAFFIC FATALITY RATES

(per 100,000 population)

SOURCE: *U.N. Demographic Yearbook* 1977, ©United Nations

Nation	Rate
Kuwait (1975)	33.4
Venezuela (1975)	33.4
Rhodesia (1976)	30.7
Austria (1976)	28.8
Canada (1974)	28.1
Australia (1975)	27.5
Italy (1972)	25.9
Luxembourg (1976)	25.8
Belgium (1975)	24.2
France (1970)	23.5
West Germany (1975)	23.5
Yugoslavia (1975)	22.2
UNITED STATES (1975)	21.5
Ecuador (1975)	19.9
Czechoslovakia (1975)	18.8
Switzerland (1976)	18.8
Ireland (1974)	18.2
Costa Rica (1976)	18.1
Israel (1976)	17.9
Netherlands (1976)	17.7
Denmark (1976)	17.1
Greece (1976)	16.8
Hungary (1976)	16.0
East Germany (1975)	15.3
Mexico (1974)	15.3
Sweden (1975)	15.1
Bulgaria (1975)	13.5
Norway (1976)	12.7
England & Wales (1976)	12.3
Japan (1976)	11.5

AUTO CASUALTY RATES

SOURCE: International Road Federation

	Vehicles per 1,000 pop.	Rate per 100-million vehicle-kilometers Injuries	Rate per 100-million vehicle-kilometers Deaths
Australia (1976)	473	86[1]	3.5[1]
Belgium (1977)	322	245[1]	7.0[1]
Canada (1975)	479	109[2]	2.9[2]
Denmark (1977)	324	73	3.0
Finland (1977)	257	55[2]	4.0[2]
France (1977)	361	133	5.0
Iceland (1976)	332	48	1.7
Italy (1977)	316	102[2]	4.2[2]
Japan (1976)	266	192[3]	2.9[3]
Netherlands (1976)	299	98	3.8
New Zealand (1977)	471	147[4]	5.0[4]
Norway (1977)	312	71	2.6
United Kingdom (1977)	298	132	2.5
United States (1977)	664	115	1.9
West Germany (1977)	355	167	4.9

[1] 1975.   [2] 1976.   [3] 1977.   [4] 1973.

U.S. DEATHS AND DEATH RATES FROM MOTOR VEHICLE ACCIDENTS

SOURCE: National Center for Health Statistics

Year	Number	Rate per 100,000 population
1977	49,510	22.9
1976	47,038	21.9
1975	45,853	21.5
1974	46,402	22.0
1973	55,511	26.5
1972	56,278	27.0
1970	54,633	26.9

U.S. ROAD MILEAGE

	Atlanta	Baltimore	Birmingham	Boston	Buffalo	Chicago	Cincinnati	Cleveland	Dallas	Denver	Des Moines	Detroit	Houston	Indianapolis	Kansas City, Mo.	Los Angeles	Memphis	Milwaukee	Minneapolis/St. Paul	Montreal	Nashville	New Orleans	New York City	Oklahoma City	Omaha	Philadelphia	Phoenix	Pittsburgh	St. Louis	Salt Lake City	San Francisco	Seattle	Washington, D.C.
Akron	672	331	702	653	207	366	230	33	1173	1385	707	190	1270	295	779	2368	806	455	776	597	519	1048	406	1040	811	532	2003	105	532	1800	2541	2427	331
Albuquerque	1396	1889	1266	2194	1767	1289	1378	1581	639	422	894	1538	829	1272	790	807	1030	1370	1247	2111	1289	1137	2001	454	697	1918	454	1626	1040	611	1127	1482	1838
Atlanta	—	669	152	1068	877	695	461	686	805	1401	894	726	814	508	810	2197	394	784	1105	1247	242	479	855	855	986	762	1810	697	558	1900	2393	2748	630
Baltimore	669	—	787	399	345	687	494	351	1458	1701	1025	511	1449	580	1099	2695	947	776	1097	562	725	1138	187	1365	1138	97	2325	230	817	2118	2716	2748	39
Birmingham	152	787	—	1185	954	636	476	726	647	1282	808	726	662	451	660	2056	247	745	1065	1289	196	351	974	697	841	884	1781	742	500	1781	2393	2575	748
Boston	1068	399	1185	—	461	975	876	632	1819	1989	1311	699	1916	941	1456	3052	1355	1064	1385	324	1105	1536	216	1722	1428	304	2682	598	1178	2405	3163	3036	437
Buffalo	877	345	954	461	—	529	430	186	1373	1543	865	256	1916	495	1010	2606	909	618	939	393	719	1253	445	1257	1018	365	2236	217	802	1958	2716	2590	359
Chicago	695	687	636	975	529	—	295	343	936	1016	338	275	1085	187	499	2095	544	91	412	820	451	929	843	820	459	762	1722	461	291	1431	2189	2063	687
Cincinnati	461	494	476	876	430	295	—	244	943	1169	571	267	1085	108	597	2186	451	386	705	820	274	838	659	705	690	578	2050	284	338	1644	2402	2356	492
Cleveland	686	351	726	632	186	343	244	—	1169	1357	679	167	1284	309	769	2186	723	432	753	578	533	1063	484	1010	769	426	2050	125	546	1772	2530	2404	351
Columbus	549	408	579	769	323	359	107	137	1050	1283	695	182	1147	172	645	2245	586	448	769	713	396	972	557	882	701	476	2005	182	512	1701	2530	2420	392
Dallas	805	1458	647	1819	1373	936	943	1169	—	784	704	1188	242	878	489	1403	464	1015	936	1763	660	498	1526	189	645	1526	1005	1232	645	1241	1806	2112	1372
Denver	1401	1701	1282	1989	1543	1016	1169	1357	784	—	679	1284	1026	1061	604	1134	1035	1040	841	1856	1158	1282	1851	681	538	1770	1430	1482	856	512	1200	1347	1696
Des Moines	894	1025	808	1311	865	338	571	679	704	679	—	606	946	483	193	1801	526	301	252	1152	638	989	1173	542	130	1092	1577	804	336	1094	1852	1773	1018
Detroit	726	511	726	699	256	275	267	167	1188	1284	606	—	1337	277	751	2347	713	364	685	573	519	1085	640	977	1086	586	1977	285	543	1700	2458	2336	511
El Paso	1427	2034	1275	2391	1945	1434	1524	1726	635	654	1139	1686	755	1417	935	798	1086	1513	1339	2280	1308	1114	2254	586	1085	2173	430	1872	1180	869	1200	1740	1983
Hartford	972	303	1090	102	328	903	752	479	1883	1754	1232	731	1752	822	1423	2895	1226	992	1317	317	1197	1445	121	1466	1357	207	2530	477	1059	2326	3076	2955	342
Houston	814	1449	662	1916	1916	1085	1085	1284	242	1026	946	1337	—	997	741	1553	561	1174	1086	2046	783	359	1636	430	881	1546	1153	1319	794	869	1431	1957	1410
Indianapolis	508	580	451	941	495	187	108	309	878	1061	483	277	997	—	484	2080	436	276	597	885	294	825	729	705	572	648	1999	354	237	1536	2294	2245	564
Jacksonville	314	793	426	1191	1067	1009	775	936	994	1708	1208	996	911	792	1123	2397	673	865	1419	1355	570	572	1009	990	1241	735	1943	937	877	2207	2799	3070	754
Kansas City, Mo.	810	1097	660	1456	1010	499	597	769	489	604	193	751	741	484	—	1596	459	570	457	1344	554	840	1198	347	201	1178	1330	821	252	1239	1997	1818	1048
Little Rock	505	1086	384	1543	1048	644	618	920	325	957	573	896	441	595	401	1701	139	735	767	1549	351	416	1282	360	601	1201	1330	937	342	1456	2027	2273	1047
Los Angeles	2197	2695	2056	3052	2606	2095	2186	2186	1403	1134	1801	2347	1553	2080	1596	—	2107	2176	1940	2915	2058	1901	2915	1357	1662	2721	398	2533	1848	734	403	1145	2644
Louisville	394	586	196	1355	909	544	274	723	660	1035	526	713	561	436	459	2107	—	539	831	1085	180	700	821	691	684	684	1807	394	264	1632	2390	2331	596
Memphis	394	947	247	1355	909	544	451	723	464	1040	526	713	561	436	459	2176	210	623	846	1769	210	395	1100	460	688	1073	1466	758	294	2100	2419	2390	908
Mexico City	1800	—	—	—	—	—	—	—	—	—	—	—	—	—	—	—	—	—	—	—	—	—	—	—	—	—	—	—	—	—	—	—	—
Miami	665	1144	776	1542	1418	1360	1126	1287	1332	1982	1559	1347	1216	1173	1474	2712	1024	1216	1769	2622	921	875	1330	1691	1592	1241	2314	1216	1223	2545	3075	3421	1099
Milwaukee	784	776	745	1064	495	91	386	432	1015	1040	301	364	1174	276	570	2176	623	—	326	932	572	1013	932	861	548	851	1806	550	385	1239	1997	1913	776
Minneapolis/St. Paul	1105	1097	1065	1385	939	412	705	753	936	841	252	685	1086	597	457	1940	846	326	—	1258	924	1241	1241	861	380	1172	1630	871	546	1239	1890	1641	1097
Montreal	169	562	1289	324	393	820	820	578	1763	1856	1152	573	2046	885	1344	2915	1085	932	1258	—	1109	1640	388	1503	1381	467	2550	611	1116	2273	3031	2610	600
Montreal*	838	92	—	948	957	748	820	937	—	1862	—	297	—	885	—	—	—	—	—	—	—	—	324	1024	342	935	—	559	—	1670	3025	2512	686
Nashville	230	725	196	1105	719	451	274	533	660	1158	638	519	783	294	554	2058	210	572	924	1109	—	530	949	530	738	868	1655	559	292	1739	2459	2267	686
New Orleans	493	1138	351	1536	1253	929	838	1063	498	1282	989	1085	359	825	840	1901	395	1013	1241	1640	530	—	1325	695	1090	1235	1503	1093	695	2175	2765	2904	1099
New York City	855	187	974	216	445	843	659	484	1526	1851	1173	640	1636	729	1198	2915	1100	932	1241	388	949	1325	—	1462	1312	92	2464	386	966	2273	2944	2823	225
Oklahoma City	1012	1321	697	1684	1308	797	895	1010	215	615	560	975	457	738	347	1357	479	500	865	1503	530	695	1462	—	548	1398	987	1097	506	955	1713	1678	1307
Omaha	1163	1138	884	1386	1253	459	690	769	645	538	139	726	881	572	201	1662	688	548	380	1381	738	1090	1312	548	—	1235	1335	942	459	1113	1667	1556	1156
Philadelphia	766	97	884	304	365	762	578	426	1526	1770	1092	586	1546	648	1178	2721	1073	851	1172	467	868	1235	92	1398	1235	—	2464	305	881	2186	2944	2823	136
Phoenix	1810	2325	1781	2682	2236	1722	2050	2050	1005	1430	1577	1977	1153	1999	1330	398	1466	1806	1630	2550	1655	1503	2464	987	1335	2464	—	2123	1541	653	759	1541	2274
Pittsburgh	697	230	742	598	217	461	284	125	1232	1482	804	285	1319	354	821	2533	758	550	871	611	559	1093	386	1097	942	305	2123	—	599	1890	2648	2522	230
Portland, Ore.	2654	2816	2552	3085	2639	2112	2405	2453	2043	1278	1819	2385	2233	2297	1846	970	2305	2205	1725	2746	2398	2561	2953	1725	1690	2872	1366	2571	2096	802	652	175	2797
Providence	1033	364	1151	45	444	967	820	626	1751	1944	1296	795	1813	883	1367	2956	1088	1056	1381	342	1155	1506	182	1506	1552	342	2591	538	1120	2390	3140	3019	403
Reno	2408	2613	2288	2919	2482	1956	2173	2290	1657	856	1623	2218	1869	1979	1524	477	2041	1979	1773	2803	1944	2175	2765	1367	1108	2685	530	2394	1890	530	225	742	2618
St. Louis	558	817	500	1178	802	291	338	543	645	856	336	543	794	237	252	1848	294	385	546	1116	292	695	966	506	459	885	1478	599	—	1368	2126	2109	801
Salt Lake City	1900	2118	1781	2405	1958	1431	1644	1772	1241	512	1094	1700	1431	1536	1239	734	2100	1239	1239	2273	1739	2175	2273	955	1113	2186	653	1890	1368	—	759	871	2111
San Francisco	2523	2876	2393	3163	2716	2063	2356	2530	1806	1270	1852	2458	1957	2294	1455	403	2303	1997	1890	3031	2456	2765	2944	1678	1667	2944	759	2648	2126	759	—	827	2869
Seattle	2756	2756	2575	3036	2590	2063	2356	2404	2112	1347	1773	2336	1957	2302	1818	1145	2331	1913	1641	2610	2267	2904	2823	1678	1556	2823	1541	2522	2109	871	827	—	2748
Toledo	668	454	683	742	296	241	207	115	1154	1250	572	57	1247	221	517	2313	686	330	651	649	497	1027	610	943	651	529	1943	258	509	1670	2428	2302	454
Topeka	873	1162	664	1519	1073	562	660	835	504	617	276	814	745	554	63	1537	522	643	520	1387	617	884	1387	297	180	1387	1387	884	315	871	1053	1831	1111
Tulsa	783	1219	664	1650	1204	693	740	948	271	693	471	945	513	417	258	1461	417	689	715	1518	351	616	1370	119	386	1289	1091	995	404	1191	1776	2038	1205
Washington, D.C.	630	39	748	437	359	687	492	351	1372	1696	1018	511	1410	564	1048	2644	908	776	1097	600	686	1099	225	136	1099	136	2274	230	801	2111	2869	2748	—

* via Canadian routes.

U.S. AIR DISTANCES

(See also, AIR DISTANCES BETWEEN MAJOR WORLD CITIES, pp. 234–235)

	Atlanta	Birmingham	Boston	Buffalo	Charleston, S.C.	Chicago	Cincinnati	Cleveland	Dallas	Denver	Des Moines	Detroit	Houston	Indianapolis	Jacksonville	Kansas City, Mo.	Los Angeles	Louisville	Miami	Minneapolis	Nashville	New Orleans	New York City	Omaha	Philadelphia	Phoenix	Pittsburgh	Portland, Ore.	St. Louis	Salt Lake City	San Francisco	Seattle	Tulsa	Washington, D.C.
Albuquerque	1272	1138	1972	1580	1539	1129	1251	1261	588	334	670	837	754	669	1169	720	627	578	1698	983	1119	1178	1815	1029	1753	330	1499	1107	942	484	896	1184	604	1653
Amarillo	999	866	1792	1399	1266	894	992	1173	358	287	557	1052	596	776	1049	357	776	613	1521	848	578	915	1560	721	1494	526	1244	1157	598	678	904	930	335	1391
Atlanta	—	140	937	697	267	587	461	554	721	1212	738	594	701	426	285	676	1936	321	595	907	214	424	748	817	666	1583	521	2172	467	1583	2139	2182	678	543
Billings	1519	1425	1861	1473	1761	1003	1304	1336	1092	453	798	1304	1307	1204	1796	846	845	1259	2396	655	1423	1760	1877	702	1877	904	1727	604	1057	552	930	1057	930	1669
Birmingham	140	—	1052	776	402	578	406	618	581	1095	760	609	567	433	352	579	1761	309	661	862	152	316	864	718	783	1456	665	2066	400	1456	2013	2082	552	661
Boston	937	1052	—	400	888	851	639	551	1551	1769	1161	613	1551	807	1017	1251	2596	867	1255	1120	941	1359	188	1282	271	2300	483	2534	1038	2099	2699	2493	1398	393
Buffalo	697	776	400	—	687	454	430	173	1198	1370	716	216	1286	435	882	861	2198	435	1181	731	627	1086	292	883	279	2145	178	2040	662	1848	2299	2117	1023	292
Burlington, Vt.	1049	1182	182	304	699	884	757	506	1474	1769	1161	609	1474	967	1161	1474	2493	1049	1358	819	1049	1474	260	641	357	2385	445	2425	928	2203	2405	2428	1327	432
Charleston, S.C.	267	361	721	687	—	721	506	534	928	1474	819	681	967	506	177	928	2203	455	482	1104	340	649	633	928	562	1783	451	2425	704	1845	2405	2428	853	453
Charlotte	227	361	721	533	177	599	358	435	927	1358	727	528	1049	509	331	826	2119	341	652	1019	343	630	529	918	451	1749	362	2290	568	1727	2301	2285	853	330
Cheyenne	1229	1119	1735	1335	1486	920	1082	1199	726	96	583	1125	879	986	1493	560	882	803	1726	642	1033	1038	1614	463	1556	603	1341	947	679	371	967	973	442	1477
Chicago	587	578	851	454	721	—	252	308	803	920	299	238	940	165	863	414	1745	269	1188	355	397	833	713	416	666	1453	410	1758	262	1260	1858	1737	598	597
Cincinnati	461	406	639	430	506	252	—	222	812	1082	510	229	892	107	630	557	1897	83	1087	692	238	700	567	687	478	1583	257	1985	309	1453	2043	1985	661	404
Cleveland	554	618	551	173	534	308	222	—	1025	1227	617	90	1114	263	700	779	2049	311	1087	622	482	924	405	745	360	1749	115	2055	492	1568	2166	2026	853	306
Dallas	721	581	1551	1198	928	803	812	1025	—	641	674	992	224	766	908	451	1240	726	1111	862	631	443	1374	583	1299	887	1070	1631	547	989	1483	1681	236	1185
Denver	1212	1095	1769	1370	1474	920	1082	1227	641	—	590	1156	780	995	1467	558	831	1017	1726	700	1023	1082	1626	488	1579	586	1317	982	796	371	949	1021	550	1494
Des Moines	738	760	1120	716	819	299	510	617	674	590	—	490	835	406	1023	181	1438	476	1440	232	555	871	1102	123	987	1175	615	1469	273	953	1550	1461	361	896
Detroit	594	609	613	216	681	238	229	90	992	1156	490	—	1105	240	831	645	1983	316	1152	543	447	939	482	651	443	1690	205	1969	455	1492	2091	1938	813	396
El Paso	1291	1152	1963	1479	1552	1045	1254	1300	561	556	983	1479	667	1161	1473	839	701	1173	1716	1073	942	983	1820	707	1836	346	1590	1286	1034	689	995	1396	674	1728
Fargo	1114	1060	1449	919	1317	569	820	835	970	597	232	745	1183	725	1399	549	1427	661	1716	214	902	1222	1210	390	1184	1225	949	1239	660	863	1446	1197	741	1140
Houston	701	567	1551	1286	967	940	892	1114	224	780	835	1105	—	865	821	644	1374	803	968	1056	669	318	1420	794	1341	1017	1131	1836	679	1200	1645	1891	442	1220
Indianapolis	426	433	807	435	506	165	107	263	766	995	406	240	865	—	699	453	1809	107	968	511	240	821	646	525	580	1499	330	1885	231	1356	1949	1872	591	494
Jacksonville	285	352	1017	882	177	863	630	700	908	1467	1023	831	821	699	—	950	2139	594	326	1191	482	504	838	1024	582	1794	712	2565	751	1837	2374	2455	921	647
Kansas City, Mo.	676	579	1251	861	928	414	557	779	451	558	181	645	644	453	950	—	1356	480	1241	413	491	702	1097	166	1096	1045	789	1489	238	1089	1506	1506	231	945
Knoxville	152	235	909	591	397	546	219	421	767	1178	661	513	822	326	397	624	1983	188	736	792	161	547	639	745	552	1593	355	2137	391	1547	2121	2114	676	440
Little Rock	456	325	1259	913	723	561	547	740	293	871	478	723	397	452	759	355	1480	426	1081	563	295	355	1188	492	1085	1137	779	1759	297	1148	1688	1785	231	892
Los Angeles	1936	1802	2596	2198	2203	1745	1897	2049	1240	831	1438	1983	1374	1809	2147	1356	—	1829	2339	1536	1794	1673	2451	1315	2394	357	2136	825	1589	579	347	959	1266	2300
Louisville	321	309	867	435	455	269	83	311	726	1017	476	316	803	107	594	480	1829	—	1024	606	154	623	652	580	582	1508	344	1950	260	1508	2083	1943	582	476
Memphis	307	217	1137	803	640	482	455	485	420	871	485	623	485	436	397	369	1603	320	872	699	197	358	957	529	881	1263	660	1849	240	1250	1802	1867	341	765
Miami	595	665	1255	1181	482	1188	1087	1087	1111	1726	1440	1152	968	968	326	1241	2339	1024	—	1501	815	669	1089	1397	1019	1982	1010	2708	1061	2089	2594	2734	1176	923
Minneapolis	907	862	1123	731	1104	355	692	622	862	700	232	543	1056	511	1191	413	1536	606	1501	—	695	1051	1018	357	985	1276	685	1426	466	987	1584	1395	695	934
Nashville	214	152	941	627	340	397	238	482	631	1023	555	447	669	240	482	491	1794	154	815	695	—	471	760	651	681	1475	464	1969	287	1446	2048	1961	515	569
New Orleans	424	316	1359	1086	649	833	700	924	443	1082	871	939	318	821	504	702	1673	623	669	1051	471	—	1171	847	1089	1434	919	2063	598	1434	1926	2101	548	966
New York City	748	864	188	292	633	713	567	405	1374	1626	1102	482	1420	646	838	1097	2451	652	1089	1018	760	1171	—	1144	83	2145	317	2445	875	1972	2571	2408	1231	205
Omaha	817	718	1282	883	928	416	687	745	583	488	123	651	794	525	1024	166	1315	580	1397	357	651	847	1144	—	1094	1036	847	1369	354	833	1429	1369	352	1014
Philadelphia	666	783	271	279	562	666	478	360	1299	1579	987	443	1341	580	582	1096	2394	582	1019	985	681	1089	83	1094	—	2083	259	2412	811	1925	2523	2380	1163	123
Phoenix	1592	1456	2300	1906	1857	1453	1581	1749	887	586	1175	1690	1017	1499	1794	1045	357	1508	1982	1276	1475	1434	2145	1036	2083	—	1828	1005	1272	504	653	1114	937	1983
Pittsburgh	521	608	483	178	451	410	257	115	1070	1320	715	205	1131	330	712	789	2136	344	1010	685	464	919	317	847	259	1828	—	2165	559	1668	2264	2138	917	192
Portland, Ore.	2172	2066	2534	2040	2425	1758	1985	2055	1631	982	1469	1969	1836	1885	2565	1489	825	1950	2708	1426	1969	2063	2445	1369	2412	1005	2165	—	1723	636	534	145	1531	2354
Raleigh	356	491	609	490	220	642	399	492	1057	1463	832	666	1056	580	751	1008	2237	429	923	1008	485	776	426	1008	345	1923	345	2377	667	1829	2410	2367	972	233
St. Louis	467	400	1038	662	704	262	309	492	547	796	273	455	679	231	751	238	1589	260	1061	466	287	598	875	354	811	1272	559	1723	—	1162	1744	1891	361	712
Salt Lake City	1583	1456	2099	1848	1845	1260	1453	1568	989	371	953	1492	1200	1356	1837	1089	579	1508	2089	987	1446	1434	1972	833	1925	504	1668	636	1162	—	600	701	917	1848
San Antonio	874	744	2699	1186	1122	1051	1254	2428	252	802	882	1238	189	999	1011	702	1204	949	1148	1110	887	527	1584	828	1507	849	1291	1720	792	1087	1490	1787	486	1388
San Francisco	2139	2013	2699	2299	2405	1858	2043	2166	1483	949	1550	2091	1645	1949	2374	1506	347	2083	2594	1584	1926	1926	2571	1429	2523	653	2264	534	1744	600	—	678	1461	2442
Seattle	2182	2082	2493	2117	2428	1737	1985	2026	1681	1021	1467	1938	1709	1872	2455	1506	959	1943	2734	1395	1961	2101	2408	1369	2380	1114	2138	145	1724	701	678	—	1369	2329
Spokane	1961	1865	2266	1888	2204	1508	1752	1798	1489	826	1240	1709	1644	1752	2237	1287	940	1717	2520	1166	1898	2179	2179	1146	2151	1019	2044	290	1500	550	723	229	1353	2190
Syracuse	781	875	264	134	738	593	494	231	1326	1508	881	354	1390	567	928	1009	2336	497	1163	867	739	1187	194	1007	194	2044	198	2281	568	1893	2434	2238	1157	306
Tulsa	678	552	1398	1023	853	598	661	853	236	550	361	813	442	591	921	231	1266	582	1176	695	515	548	1231	352	1163	937	917	1531	361	917	1461	1369	—	1058
Washington, D.C.	543	661	393	292	453	597	404	306	1185	1494	896	396	1220	494	647	945	2300	476	923	934	569	966	205	1014	123	1983	192	2354	712	1848	2442	2329	1058	—
Wichita	776	658	1424	1036	1039	591	702	873	340	437	334	821	559	620	1031	257	1204	879	1297	546	594	677	1266	257	1204	879	950	1411	394	808	1369	1437	130	1106

U.S. RAILROAD DISTANCES

	Albuquerque	Atlanta	Baltimore	Birmingham	Boston	Buffalo	Chicago	Cincinnati	Cleveland	Dallas	Denver	Des Moines	Detroit	El Paso	Houston	Indianapolis	Jacksonville	Kansas City, Mo.	Los Angeles	Memphis	Miami	Mobile	New Orleans	New York City	Oklahoma City	Philadelphia	Pittsburgh	Portland, Ore.	St. Louis	St. Paul	Salt Lake City	San Francisco	Seattle	Washington, D.C.
Albuquerque		1554	2102	1388	2356	1862	1338	1528	1678	723	477	1108	1610	253	925	1430	1819	887	889	1135	2185	1369	1229	2216	648	2124	1776	1849	1190	1363	985	1209	2031	2047
Amarillo	374	1289	1728	1014	2208	1554	1010	1205	1434	370	465	700	1282	444	634	1041	1822	559	1216	761	2038	1047	876	1886	321	1775	1427	2019	816	1130	1039	1537	2019	1690
Atlanta	1554		651	167	1091	934	796	490	741	825	1526	952	748	1471	748	585	350	862	2157	420	611	353	493	862	1047	771	806	2798	612	1130	2051	2718	2824	638
Baltimore	2102	651		799	444	494	734	490	584	1448	1796	1041	465	2095	1517	585	1160	1154	2726	907	1160	1096	1154	187	1454	94	328	3030	920	1153	2310	3059	2810	38
Billings	1133	1921	2085	1788	2296	1802	1278	1559	1618	1491	656	1041	1618	1755	1491	1259	2226	718	1452	1535	2592	1924	1954	1906	1394	2094	1747	961	1310	882	669	1418	903	2043
Birmingham	1388	167	799		1215	925	651	444	718	650	1376	882	739	1304	578	494	415	718	2750	252	718	184	396	990	882	894	797	2665	479	986	1906	2691	2665	454
Boston	2356	1091	444	1215		524	978	938	634	1854	2032	1376	718	2414	1933	938	1550	1550	2750	1418	1576	1550	1550	229	1743	321	658	3217	1202	1414	2532	3281	2691	454
Buffalo	1862	934	494	925	524		494	444	184	1418	1560	882	252	2190	1448	444	1190	1249	2532	882	1550	1118	1280	396	1249	415	260	2787	708	920	2038	2787	2665	434
Butte	2102	2157	2305	2024	2526	2032	1514	1795	1854	1727	892	1259	1854	1780	1691	1495	2462	1112	1216	1771	2828	2160	2194	2169	1631	2330	1983	725	1546	1121	433	1182	667	2273
Cheyenne	583	1532	1591	1399	1856	1259	995	1265	1319	941	106	652	1267	836	1105	845	1877	639	1486	1223	2539	1569	1447	1909	1045	1811	1463	1266	833	855	519	1268	1448	1759
Chicago	1338	734	796	651	978	494		281	340	968	1026	358	272	1396	1099	184	1083	486	2199	527	1449	921	908	908	755	816	468	2199	284	396	1451	2199	2184	764
Cincinnati	1528	490	582	444	938	444	281		260	975	1252	639	258	1561	1205	109	840	593	2370	494	1396	836	836	755	755	664	316	2451	338	677	1778	2527	2422	544
Cleveland	1678	741	584	718	634	184	340	260		1234	1366	688	164	1983	1561	283	1065	1065	2555	673	1466	1096	1258	479	1065	479	131	2539	523	736	1854	2603	2481	477
Columbia, S.C.	1801	254	515	420	930	910	867	586	867	1078	1747	1173	844	1724	836	681	280	1160	2555	607	601	280	641	701	1160	610	772	3019	833	1263	2272	3019	3045	476
Dallas	723	825	1448	650	1854	1418	968	975	1234		835	683	1200	646	246	951	1096	489	1353	470	1724	730	507	1607	206	1543	1291	2130	711	914	1450	1791	2310	1790
Denver	477	1526	1796	1376	2032	1560	1026	1252	1366	835		683	1298	730	881	1099	1721	636	1353	1031	2499	1341	1341	1934	645	1842	1494	1494	886	886	570	1374	1554	1790
Des Moines	1108	952	1041	882	1376	882	358	639	688	683	683		630	1166	730	542	1301	192	1776	547	1668	972	972	1266	565	1174	826	1968	340	249	1266	1920	1944	1112
Detroit	1610	748	465	739	718	252	272	258	164	1200	1298	630		1668	1246	258	1094	648	2499	648	1464	1094	1256	396	1031	611	296	2505	489	722	1840	2588	2413	592
Duluth	253	1471	2095	1304	2414	1920	1396	1561	1736	646	730	411	1668		827	1305	1764	814	2310	1128	2130	1292	1152	2310	718	2190	1834	2002	1223	425	1238	1284	2184	2056
El Paso	1605	1372	1656	1289	2227	1656	1128	1667	1556	646	881	1166	1566	827		1503	1721	822	721	975	2021	975	935	1764	503	1667	1319	1667	1151	1503	975	1175	2578	2208
Fargo	1372	1435	1822	1373	1933	1576	638	822	962	835	683	501	862	1667	1371	793	1760	471	2181	616	2092	1341	1318	2087	819	1824	1454	1107	816	239	1121	2081	1601	1601
Houston	925	856	1517	578	1933	1448	1099	1205	1561	246	881	730	1246	827		1089	845	707	1641	547	1371	490	363	1641	560	1612	1371	2176	782	1107	1607	1966	2325	1115
Indianapolis	1430	585	585	494	938	444	184	109	283	951	1099	542	258	1503	1089		935	485	2310	491	1341	718	827	714	652	719	371	2491	241	589	1703	2489	2184	653
Jacksonville	1819	350	1160	415	1550	1190	1083	840	1065	1096	1721	1301	1094	1721	845	935		1175	2578	691	366	472	612	981	1247	1153	956	3129	917	1459	2486	3129	3049	756
Kansas City, Mo.	887	862	1154	718	1550	1249	486	593	1065	489	636	192	648	822	707	485	1175		1776	452	2130	936	827	1329	248	1237	889	1777	278	547	1329	1777	2131	1160
Knoxville	1556	197	624	254	972	975	572	296	573	903	1353	880	551	1668	1371	491	555	742	2306	422	972	547	569	732	1062	639	542	2907	414	959	1886	2720	2715	607
Los Angeles	889	2285	2726	2750	2750	2532	2199	2370	2555	1353	1353	1776	2499	721	1641	2310	2578	1776		1809	2643	1913	1834	2739	1643	2647	2300	889	2032	2157	783	470	1301	2906
Louisville	1463	420	698	392	938	392	295	114	344	861	1188	547	372	1574	1191	114	690	503	2306	380	1418	747	869	714	679	778	430	2586	274	611	1713	2462	2438	658
Memphis	1135	420	967	253	1382	1119	527	494	758	470	1031	547	648	975	547	491	691	452	1809		1491	305	427	1191	471	1153	867	2491	305	659	1653	2462	2610	929
Miami	2185	611	1160	718	1576	1550	1449	1396	1466	1724	2499	1668	1464	2021	1371	1341	366	2130	2643	1491		758	860	1347	1584	1256	1418	3514	1283	1803	2732	3015	2957	1122
Mobile	1369	353	1096	184	1550	1118	921	836	1096	730	1341	972	1094	975	490	718	472	936	1913	305	758		140	1264	660	1265	1063	2732	658	884	1803	2588	2610	929
Nashville	1135	242	907	184	1256	1118	755	296	658	747	1425	658	747	935	636	371	569	827	1834	427	860	140	560	910	691	835	584	2491	305	659	1573	2732	2610	660
New Orleans	1229	493	1154	396	1550	1280	908	836	1258	507	1341	972	1256	935	363	827	612	827	1834	427	860	140		1356	693	1264	1052	2732	658	1003	1563	2906	2906	1122
New York City	2216	862	187	990	229	396	908	755	479	1607	1934	1266	396	1764	1641	714	981	1329	2739	1191	1347	1264	1356		1426	90	444	3148	1052	1301	2496	3214	2900	225
Oklahoma City	648	1047	1454	882	1743	1249	755	755	1065	206	645	565	1031	503	560	652	1247	248	1643	471	1584	660	693	1426		1390	1152	2045	500	903	1310	1810	2313	1424
Omaha	1374	892	1193	894	1743	1191	488	679	738	712	538	145	760	1178	976	503	1153	202	1809	547	1696	1068	1052	1256	509	1256	908	1664	439	348	1418	1775	1799	1285
Philadelphia	2124	771	94	894	321	415	816	664	479	1543	1842	1174	611	1667	1612	719	1153	1237	2647	1153	1256	1265	1264	90	1390		354	3015	959	1203	2419	3079	2799	133
Portland, Ore.	1849	2798	3030	2665	3217	2787	2199	2451	2539	2130	1494	1968	2505	1667	2176	2491	3148	1777	889	2491	3514	2732	2732	3148	2045	3015	2668		2187	1803	884	718	182	3025
Richmond	2038	579	155	735	570	550	917	705	494	1462	2177	1455	581	2130	2031	640	1390	1390	2845	901	1006	932	1072	341	1390	348	413	3095	919	1258	2359	3095	3003	117
St. Louis	1190	612	920	479	1202	708	284	338	523	711	914	340	489	1283	782	241	917	278	2032	305	1283	658	658	1052	500	959	611	2187		574	1440	2189	2610	882
St. Paul	1363	1130	1193	986	1414	920	396	677	736	914	886	249	722	1047	1107	589	1459	547	2157	659	1803	884	1003	1301	903	1203	865	1803	574		1374	2123	1745	1161
Salt Lake City	985	2051	2310	1906	2532	2038	1451	1778	1854	1450	570	1266	1840	975	1607	1703	2486	1329	783	1653	2732	1803	1563	2496	1310	2419	2071	884	1440	1374		723	1066	2278
San Antonio	1726	2824	2937	2551	3281	2787	2263	2527	2603	236	1182	1380	2588	913	2900	2489	2734	1257	1563	2732	3015	2588	2906	3214	1810	3079	2731	718	2189	2123	723	900	3028	2906
San Francisco	1209	2824	3059	2691	3281	2787	2199	2527	2603	1791	1374	1920	2588	1175	1966	2489	3129	1777	470	2462	3015	2588	2906	3214	1810	3079	2731	718	2189	2123	723		900	3028
Seattle	2031	2824	2810	2665	2691	2665	2184	2422	2481	2310	1554	1944	2413	2578	2325	2184	3049	2131	1301	2610	2957	2610	2906	2900	2313	2799	2610	182	2189	1745	1066	900		2906
Spokane	1363	2596	2596	2381	2849	2355	1887	2112	2171	2113	1112	1403	2179	2189	2189	2325	2348	1435	790	1903	3185	2590	2348	2739	1987	2647	2300	368	1903	1435	790	1086	310	2596
Tucson	638	1783	2407	1616	2726	2232	1708	1873	2048	958	1042	1478	1980	312	1139	1775	2076	1257	502	1572	2363	1464	1464	2586	1257	2494	2131	884	1572	1737	1285	972	972	2368
Washington, D.C.	721	638	38	761	389	454	764	544	427	1410	1790	1122	592	2055	672	653	756	1160	2906	929	1122	929	1003	225	1424	133	296	3025	882	1161	2278	3028	2906	
Wichita	721	986	1401	819	1681	1187	663	819	1003	408	580	433	935	672	672	653	1257	172	1532	481	692	1087	913	1532	172	1440	1092	1971	481	692	1087	1884	2139	1363

TOLL-FREE TELEPHONE NUMBERS

The following lists contain the toll-free telephone numbers for airlines, hotels, motels, and car rental companies. Airline companies often have local telephone numbers for reservations and information. If no local number is listed, dial 800 followed by the number given in the first column. In Atlanta, precede all 800 numbers with "1." EN (Enterprise) numbers require operator assistance.

AIRLINES	800 Toll-Free Number	ATLANTA	CHICAGO	LOS ANGELES	NEW YORK	WASHINGTON, D. C.
Aer Lingus - Irish		800-223-6292	800-223-6292	800-223-6537	212-557-1110	800-223-6270
Aerocondor	327-0743		312-341-9570	213-626-5257	212-765-1700	
Aeroflot					212-661-4050	202-296-8060
Aerolineas Argentinas ..		800-223-5450	312-922-0707	213-683-1633	212-757-6400	202-296-2836
Aeromexico			800-223-9780	213-380-6030	212-391-2900	800-223-9780
AeroPerú	327-4363		800-327-4363		212-765-2200	202-457-0857
Air Canada		800-621-2110	312-527-3900	213-776-7000	212-421-8000	202-638-2132
Air France		800-221-2110	312-782-6181	213-625-7171	212-247-0100	202-337-8711
Air India		800-223-7776	800-223-7776	213-624-7071	212-751-6200	202-347-1827
Air Jamaica		800-523-5585	312-527-3923	800-523-5618	212-421-8750	
Air New Zealand	421-0066			213-629-5454		
Air Panama Internacional			312-341-1640	213-488-1065	800-329-2417	202-347-7298
Alaska Airlines	426-0333					
Alitalia		800-223-9770	312-427-4720	800-223-5730	212-582-8900	202-393-2829
Allegheny (US Air)		800-245-1640	312-726-1201	ZE 9-2400	212-736-3200	202-783-4500
American		404-521-2655	312-372-8000	213-937-6811	212-661-4242	202-393-2345
Avianca	'221-2200				212-586-6040	
Aviateca International ..			312-236-6941			202-656-1370
Bahamasair	327-8080		312-372-9227			
Braniff International ...	327-8080		312-372-9227	213-680-2202	212-687-8200	202-296-2400
British Airways		800-327-9722	312-332-7744	800-252-0045	212-687-1600	202-393-5300
B.W.I.A. International ..		800-327-7401	800-327-7401	800-327-7401	212-581-3200	800-221-6874
CP Air		404-767-1214		800-426-7000	EN 6040	EN 1-4540
Capitol International ...		404-261-5477	312-263-0244	213-986-8445	212-883-0740	202-524-4700
Cathay Pacific			312-782-8191	213-627-3253	212-541-9750	202-833-9393
China Airlines	421-2038	0-WX-6935	800-227-4632	213-624-1161	212-581-6500	202-833-1760
Continental Airlines	621-6104		312-686-6500	213-772-6000		202-628-6666
Czechoslovak Air Lines ..			312-372-1551	800-621-1140	212-682-5833	202-577-4300
Delta Air Lines		404-765-5000	312-346-5300	213-386-5510	212-239-0700	202-920-5500
Eastern Airlines		404-435-1111	312-467-2900	213-380-2070	212-986-5000	202-393-4000
Ecuatoriana Airlines ...	327-1337					
El Al Israel Airlines ...		800-223-6280	800-223-6280	800-223-6700	212-486-2600	800-223-6280
Ethiopian Airlines			312-663-4100	213-462-7291	212-867-0095	202-659-2915
Finnair		800-223-5308	800-223-5308	800-223-5700	212-889-7070	800-223-5260
Gulf Air			312-861-0117	213-879-3645	212-986-4500	202-296-2910
Hawaiian Airlines		404-237-2885	312-236-5196	213-640-1040	212-355-4843	202-659-5770
Iberia Air Lines of Spain	221-9640			800-221-9691	212-796-3300	
Icelandic Airlines-Loftleidir		800-223-5390	800-223-5390	800-223-5500	212-757-8585	800-223-5190
Iran Air	223-9820			213-274-6336	212-949-8200	
Japan Air Lines		800-223-5405	312-263-1384	213-620-9580	212-759-9100	800-223-5450
KLM Royal Dutch Airlines		800-223-5322	312-346-3635	800-231-2164	212-759-3600	800-223-5322
Korean Airlines		404-522-7461	312-726-3622	213-484-1900	800-223-5262	202-785-3644
Kuwait Airways			312-263-3858	213-627-1485	212-581-9412	202-296-4644
Lacsa				213-487-7180	212-245-6370	
Lan-Chile Airlines	327-9676					
Lot Polish Airlines			312-236-3388		212-869-1074	
Lufthansa German Airlines	645-3880				212-357-8400	
Mexicana Airlines......	421-8301	404-237-8661		213-487-6950		800-421-2150
National Airlines		404-688-9534		213-381-5777	212-697-9000	202-549-7633
North Central Airlines[1]..		404-524-0057	312-346-9860		212-581-8851	202-347-0448
Northwest Orient		404-577-3271	312-346-4900	213-380-1511	212-564-2300	202-337-0611
Olympic Airways		800-424-9231	312-329-0200	213-624-6441	212-838-3600	202-659-2525
Ozark Air Lines		404-763-3500	312-686-3821		212-586-3612	202-347-4744

AIRLINES	800 Toll-Free Number	ATLANTA	CHICAGO	LOS ANGELES	NEW YORK	WASHINGTON, D.C.
Pakistan International Airlines			312-263-3082	213-626-0245	212-949-0477	202-296-1755
Pan Am		404-688-9830	312-236-4494	213-629-3292	212-973-4000	202-833-1000
Philippine Airlines	227-4600			800-652-1555		
Piedmont Airlines		404-681-3100	312-263-3656		212-489-1460	202-347-1800
Qantas Airways	227-4500			800-622-0850		
SAHSA Honduras Airlines			312-236-3246	213-485-0261	212-730-0800	
Sabena Belgian World Airlines	645-3790			800-645-1382	212-961-6200	800-645-3933
SAS Scandinavian Airlines	221-2350			800-655-8600	212-657-7700	
Singapore Airlines		404-577-5644	312-263-7330	213-680-2764	212-949-0010	202-466-3747
South African Airways		0-WX-6477	800-223-9870	800-223-9870	212-826-1245	
Southern Airways[1]		404-762-5561	312-726-6273		212-765-4210	202-628-9032
Swissair	221-6030			800-221-4750	212-995-8400	
TAN			312-236-3246	213-485-0261	212-730-0800	
TAP The Airline of Portugal	221-2061			800-221-7370	212-421-8500	
Thai Airways International			312-855-3930		212-489-1634	202-833-1825
Trans Australian Airlines			312-329-1266	213-849-2151	212-687-1600	
Trans International Airlines		404-577-5890	312-332-0411	213-980-2660	212-656-5084	
Trans World Airlines		404-522-5738	312-332-7600	213-483-1100	212-695-6000	202-659-1000
US Air		800-245-1640	312-726-1201	ZE 9-2400	212-736-3200	202-783-4500
UTA French Airlines		0-WX-7250	312-782-6181	213-625-7171	212-421-7250	EN 1-7250
United Airlines		404-394-2234	312-569-3000	213-482-2000	212-867-3000	202-893-3400
Varig	223-5720				212-682-3100	
Vasp Brazilian Airlines	223-0414				212-586-5800	
Viasa Venezuelan International Airways	327-5454				212-421-7722	800-221-2492
Western Airlines	328-4990		312-782-8296	213-776-2311	212-966-1646	202-737-4825
World Airways		404-233-6705	312-663-5433	213-646-7478	212-661-3423	202-298-7155
Yugoslav Airlines			312-782-1322	213-388-0379	212-757-9676	

[1] as of 7/1/79, North Central Airlines and Southern Airways became Republic Airlines

HOTELS and MOTELS	Telephone Number
Americana Hotels	800—228-3278
Best Western Motels	800—528-1234
Club Mediterranee	800—528-3131
Downtowner Motor Inns	800—323-8818
Holiday Inns	800—238-8000
Howard Johnson Motor Lodges	800—654-2000
Hyatt Hotels	800—228-9000
Knott Hotels	800—327-3384
Marriott Hotels	800—228-9290
Omni International Hotels	800—241-5500
Pick Hotels	800—621-4404
Playboy Club-Hotels	800—621-1116
Princess Hotels	800—223-1818
Quality Inns	800—288-5151
Ramada Inns	800—228-2828
Rockresorts	
In Atlanta:	404—939-4896
In Chicago:	312—266-0609
In Los Angeles:	213—657-2667

HOTELS and MOTELS	Telephone Number
In New York:	212—586-4459
In Washington:	202—737-6787
Sheraton Hotels	800—325-3535
Sonesta Hotels	800—225-1372
Stouffer Hotels	800—323-4455
Trust Houses Forte Hotels	800—223-5672
Western International Hotels	800—228-3000

CAR RENTAL COMPANIES

Ajax Rent a Car	800—421-0896
Avis Rent a Car	800—331-1212
Budget Rent a Car	800—228-9650
Dollar Rent-a-Car	800—421-6868
Econo-Car	800—228-1000
Greyhound Rent-a-Car	800—327-2501
Hertz Rent A Car	800—654-3131
National Car Rental	800—328-4567
Sears Rent a Car	800—228-2800
Thrifty Rent A Car	800—331-4200

THE NATIONAL PARK SYSTEM

Source: National Park Service, U.S. Department of the Interior

Park Service Areas	Number	Park Service Areas	Number	Park Service Areas	Number	Park Service Areas	Number
National Parks	37	National Battlefield Parks	3	National Parkways	4	National Scenic Trail	1
National Historical Parks	18	National Battlefield Sites	2	National Capital Parks	1	National Preserves	2
National Monuments	82	National Historic Sites	53	White House	1	"Other" Parks	10
National Military Parks	11	National Memorials	22	National Recreation Areas	16	National Mall	1
National Memorial Park	1	National Seashores	10	National Lakeshores	4	National Visitor Center	1
National Battlefields	8			National Rivers (wile and scenic)	6	**...Total 294**	

OUR NATIONAL PARKS

Acadia National Park, Maine; (gross acreage, 38,523.77). Rugged coastal area on Mount Desert Island, highest elevation on eastern seaboard; picturesque Schoodic peninsula on mainland. Includes Isle au Haut. Sieur de Monts National Monument established July 8, 1916; established as Lafayette National Park, Feb. 26, 1919; changed to Acadia National Park, Jan. 19, 1929. Visits (1978): 3,130,100

Arches National Park, Utah; (gross acreage, 73,378.98). Extraordinary products of erosion in the form of giant arches, windows, pinnacles, and pedestals. Proclaimed as a national monument April 12, 1929; established as a national park November 12, 1971. Visits (1978): 326,900

Badlands National Park, South Dakota; (gross acreage, 243,302.33). Carved by erosion, this scenic landscape contains animal fossils of 40 million years ago. Prairie grasslands support bison, bighorn sheep, deer, and antelope. Authorized Mar. 4, 1929; wilderness designated Oct. 20, 1976. Renamed national park Nov. 10, 1978. Visits (1978): 1,246,900

Big Bend National Park, Texas; (gross acreage, 708,118.40). Spectacular mountain and desert scenery; variety of unusual geological formations; enclosed in the great bend of the Rio Grande. Authorized June 20, 1935; established June 12, 1944. Visits (1978): 362,900

Bryce Canyon National Park, Utah; (gross acreage, 35,835.08). Contains perhaps the most colorful and unique erosional forms in the world. In horseshoeshaped amphitheaters along the edge of the Paunsaugunt Plateau of southern Utah stand innumerable highly colored and grotesque pinnacles, walls, and spires. Bryce Canyon National Monument established June 8, 1923; Utah National Park authorized June 7, 1924; changed to Bryce Canyon National Park Feb. 25, 1928. Established Sept. 15, 1928. Visits (1978): 680,300

Canyonlands National Park, Utah; (gross acreage, 337,570.43). Geological wonderland of rock, spires, and mesas rising more than 7,800 feet. Extensive and sometimes large petroglyphs (stone carvings) chipped by prehistoric Indians about 1,000 years ago. Established Sept. 12, 1964. Visits (1978): 86,300

Capitol Reef National Park, Utah; (gross acreage, 241,904.26). Sixty-mile uplift of sandstone cliffs, with highly colored sedimentary formations dissected by narrow high-walled gorges. Dome-shaped white rock along the Fremont River accounts for the name. Proclaimed as a national monument, August 2, 1937; established as a national park, December 18, 1971. Visits (1978): 427,700

Carlsbad Caverns National Park, New Mexico; (gross acreage, 46,755.33). Largest underground chambers yet discovered; a series of connected caverns with countless magnificent and curious formations. Carlsbad Cave National Monument established Oct. 25, 1923; Carlsbad Caverns National Park established May 14, 1930. Visits (1978): 667,300

Crater Lake National Park, Oregon; (gross acreage, 160,290.33). Lake of deepest blue in heart of once-active volcano, Mt. Mazama; encircled by multicolored lava walls 500 to 2,000 feet high. Established May 22, 1902. Visits (1978): 580,100

Everglades National Park, Florida; (gross acreage, 1,398,800.00). Largest remaining subtropical wilderness in conterminous United States; extensive freshand saltwater areas, open Everglades prairies, mangrove forests; abundant wildlife, including rare birds. Authorized May 30, 1934. Established June 20, 1947. Visits (1978): 1,136,100

Glacier National Park, Montana; (gross acreage, 1,013,594.67). Superb Rocky Mountain scenery, with numerous glaciers and lakes nestling among the highest peaks; forms part of Waterton-Glacier International Peace Park, established May 2, 1932. Established May 11, 1910. Visits (1978): 1,583,000

Grand Canyon National Park, Arizona; (gross acreage, 1,218,375.24). Most spectacular part of the Colorado River's greatest canyon, which is 217 miles long and 4 to 18 miles wide; exposure of rocks representing vast geologic time. First Grand Canyon National Monument established Jan. 11, 1908; national park established Feb. 26, 1919. Marble Canyon and second Grand Canyon National Monuments and other lands absorbed Jan. 3, 1975. Visits (1978): 2,986,200

Grand Teton National Park, Wyoming; (gross acreage, 310,515.93). Series of peaks comprising the most impressive part of the Teton range; once a noted landmark of Indians and "Mountain Men." Includes part of Jackson Hole; winter feding ground of largest American elk herd. Established Feb. 26, 1929. Visits (1978): 4,159,500

Great Smoky Mts. National Park, N.C.-Tenn.; (gross acreage, 517,368.15). Loftiest range east of the Black Hills and one of the oldest uplands on earth. Diversified and luxuriant plant-life, often of extraordinary size. Federal acreage: in N.C., 273,550.70; in Tenn., 241,206.83. Authorized May 22, 1926; established for administration and protection only, Feb. 6, 1930; established for full development June 15, 1934. Visits (1978): 11,555,300

Guadalupe Mts. National Park, Texas; (gross acreage, 76,293.06). Mountain mass rising from desert contains portions of the world's most extensive and significant Permian limestone fossil reef. Also features a tremendous earth fault, lofty peaks, unusual flora and fauna. Authorized Oct. 15, 1966. Visits (1978): 108,800

Haleakala National Park, Hawaii; (gross acreage, 28,655.25). World-famous 10,023-foot Haleakala volcano (dormant), with one of the largest and most colorful craters known, in which grows a species of the rare silversword; native and migratory birdlife. Authorized Sept. 13, 1960; established July 1, 1961. Visits (1978): 739,700

Hawaii Volcanoes National Park, Hawaii; (gross acreage, 229,177.03). Scene of impressive active volcanism on the island of Hawaii; luxuriant vegetation at lower elevations; rare plants and animals. Established as Hawaii National Park Aug. 1, 1916; changed to Hawaii Volcanoes National Park Sept. 22, 1961. Visits (1978): 2,322,000

Hot Springs National Park, Arkansas; (gross acreage, 5,826.48). Mineral hot springs (47), used in the treatment of certain ailments. Set aside as Hot Springs Reservation by federal government, Apr. 20, 1832; national park established Mar. 4, 1921. Visits (1978): 5,421,300

Isle Royale National Park, Michigan; (gross acreage, 571,796.18). Forested island, the largest in Lake Superior, distinguished for its wilderness character; moose and wolves; pre-Columbian copper mines. Authorized Mar. 3, 1931; established Apr. 3, 1940. Visits (1978): 16,400

Kings Canyon National Park, California; (gross acreage, 469,136.20). Mountain wilderness dominated by two enormous canyons of the Kings River and by the summit peaks of the High Sierra. The former General Grant National Park, with its giant sequoias, is a detached section of the park. General Grant National Park established Oct. 1, 1890, abolished Mar. 4, 1940, and its lands made part of Kings Canyon National Park; established Mar. 4, 1940. Visits (1978): 869,900

Lassen Volcanic National Park, California; (gross acreage, 106,372.36). Lassen Peak, only recently active volcano in conterminous United States, erupted between 1914 and 1921, exhibits of volcanic phenomena. Lassen Peak and Cinder Cone National Monuments established May 6, 1907; made part of Lassen Volcanic National Park, Aug. 9, 1916, when it was established. Visits (1978): 442,200

Mammoth Cave National Park, Kentucky; (gross acreage, 52,128.92). Series of underground passages, 146 miles explored; beautiful limestone, gypsum and cave onyx formations; deep pits and high domes; river 360 feet below surface. Authorized May 25, 1926; provided for minimum park area, May 14, 1934; minimum area accepted for administration May 22, 1936; fully established July 1, 1941. Visits (1978): 1,813,800

Mesa Verde National Park, Colorado; (gross acreage, 52,085.14). Best preserved prehistoric cliff dwellings in the United States. Established June 29, 1906. Visits (1978): 654,200

Mount McKinley National Park, Alaska; (gross acreage, 1,939,492.80). Mount McKinley, highest mountain (20,320 feet) in North America; large glaciers of the Alaska Range; caribou, Dall sheep, moose, grizzly bears, wolves, and other spectacular wildlife. Established Feb. 26, 1917. Visits (1978): 460,700

Mount Rainier National Park, Washington; (gross acreage, 235,404.00). Greatest single-peak glacial system in the conterminous United States, radiating from the summit and slopes of an ancient volcano; dense forests, flowered meadows. Established Mar. 2, 1899. Visits (1978): 2,094,400

North Cascades National Park, Wash.; (gross acreage, 504,780.34). Wild alpine region of jagged peaks, mountain lakes, and numerous glaciers. Established Oct. 2, 1968. Visits (1978): 931,400*

Olympic National Park, Wash.; (gross acreage, 908,720.42). Mountain wilderness containing finest remnant of Pacific Northwest rain forest; active glaciers; rare Roosevelt elk. Mount Olympus National Monument established Mar. 2, 1909; transferred from U.S. Department of Agriculture, Aug. 10, 1933; Olympic National Park established June 29, 1938. Visits (1978): 2,996,600

Petrified Forest National Park, Arizona; (gross acreage, 93,492.57). Extensive natural exhibit of petrified wood; Indian ruins and petroglyphs; portion of colorful Painted Desert. Established as a national monument Dec. 8, 1906; changed to national park Dec. 9, 1962. Visits (1978): 957,800

Redwood National Park, California; (gross acreage, 109,026.53). Coastal redwood forests contain virgin groves of ancient trees, including the world's tallest (369.2 feet). Park includes 40 miles of scenic Pacific coastline. Established Oct. 2, 1968. Visits (1978): 513,400

Rocky Mountain National Park, Colorado; (gross acreage, 263,790.69). One of the most diversified sections of the Front Range of the Rocky Mountains with 107 named peaks in excess of 11,000 feet. Established Jan.26, 1915. Visits (1978): 3,037,900

Sequoia National Park, California; (gross acreage, 403,023.00). Great groves of giant sequoias, world's largest and among the oldest living things; magnificent High Sierra scenery, including Mount Whitney, highest mountain (14,494 feet) in conterminous United States. Established Sept. 25, 1890. Visits (1978): 973,400

Shenandoah National Park, Virginia; (gross acreage, 194,327.81). Outstanding portion of Blue Ridge with Skyline Drive traversing crest; magnificent vistas of historic Shenandoah Valley, Piedmont; hardwood forests; wealth of wildflowers. Authorized May 22, 1926; established Dec. 26, 1935. Visits (1978): 2,091,500

Theodore Roosevelt National Park, North Dakota; (gross acreage, 70,394.64). The park includes scenic badlands along the Little Missouri River, some original prairie grasslands, and part of Theodore Roosevelt's Elkhorn Ranch. Established Apr. 25, 1947; renamed as national park Nov. 10, 1978. Visits (1978): 833,300.

Virgin Islands National Park, V.I.; (gross acreage, 14,708.71). St. John, an island of lush green hills and white sandy beaches; rich in tropical plant and animal life; pre-historic Carib Indian relics; remains of Danish colonial sugar plantations. Authorized Aug. 2, 1956; established Dec. 1, 1956. Visits (1978): 643,800

Voyageurs National Park, Minnesota; (gross acreage, 219,128.00). Beautiful northern lakes and forests; interesting geology; historically used as passage between Great Lakes and Northwest Territory by French fur traders. Land area, 144,891.16 acres. Authorized January 8, 1971. Visits (1978): 260.000

Wind Cave National Park, S.D.; (gross acreage, 28,292.08). Limestone caverns in scenic Black Hills, decorated by beautiful boxwork and calcite crystal formations; elk, deer, pronghorn, prairie dog towns and bison herd. Established Jan. 9, 1903. Visits (1978): 1,078,800

Yellowstone National Park, Wyo.-Mont.-Idaho; (gross acreage, 2,219,822.70). World's greatest geyser area, with about 10,000 geyers and hot springs; spectacular falls and canyons of the Yellowstone River; one of the world's greatest wildlife sanctuaries. First and largest national park. By far the greatest portion of the park is situated in Wyoming. Established Mar. 1, 1872. Visits (1978): 2,623,100

Yosemite National Park, California; (gross acreage, 760,917.18). Mountainous region of unusual beauty; Yosemite and other inspiring gorges with sheer granite cliffs; spectacular waterfalls; three groves of giant sequoias. Established Oct. 1, 1890. El Portal administrative site, 991.19 acreas of federal land adjacent to the park, authorized Sept. 2, 1958. Visits (1978): 2,669,200

Zion National Park, Utah; (gross acreage, 146,546.97). Outstanding colorful canyon and mesa scenery; erosion and faulting patterns that create phenomenal shapes and landscapes; former volcanic activity. Zion Canyon, a vertical-walled chasm, readily accessible. Established as Munkuntuweap National Monument, July 31, 1909; changed to Zion National Monument, Mar. 18, 1918; established as a national park (including the National Monument to 1937) Nov. 19, 1919. Visits (1978): 1,307,900

*Acreage and visitor figures include those for Lake Chelan and Ross Lake National Recreation Areas

LARGE FOREIGN PARKS (over 3,000 sq. mi.)

Source: United Nations–I.U.C.N. (1975)

NATIONAL PARKS

Name (Country)	Area (sq. mi.)
Northeast Greenland (Denmark)	270,270
Wood Buffalo (Canada)	17,300
Salonga (Zaire)	14,116
Gemsbok (Botswana)	9,575
Kafue (Zambia)	8,649
Etosha (S.W. Africa)	8,598
Kluane (Canada)	8,500
Baffin Island (Canada)	8,290
Tsavo (Kenya)	8,031
Southern (Sudan)	7,710
Kruger (South Africa)	7,523
Bernardo O'Higgins (Chile)	6,800

Name (Country)	Area (sq. mi.)
Iona (Angola)	6,178
Northeast Svalbard (Norway)	c. 6,000
Manu (Peru)	5,918
Wankie (Rhodesia)	5,645
Namib Desert (S.W. Africa)	5,442
Laguna San Rafael (Chile)	5,213
Serengeti (Tanzania)	5,000
Fiordland (New Zealand)	4,725
Upemba (Zaire)	4,529
Comoé (Ivory Coast)	4,440
Ruah (Tanzania)	4,440
Jasper (Canada)	4,200
Maiko (Zaire)	4,181
Chobe (Botswana)	4,000

Name (Country)	Area (sq. mi.)
Bamingui-Bangoran (Central African Empire)	3,861
Canaima (Venezuela)	3,861
Quiçama (Angola)	3,846
Kalahari Gemsbok (S. Africa)	3,703
South Luangwa (Zambia)	3,494
Gorongosa (Mozambique)	3,359
Niokolo Koba (Senegal)	3,189
Virunga (Zaire)	3,124
Alberto M. de Agostini (Chile)	3,089
Hernando de Magallanes (Chile)	3,089
Skeleton Coast (S.W. Africa)	3,089

THE U.S. PASSPORT

Source: Department of State, Passport Services

A passport is your official identification as a citizen of the United States. Application for a passport should be made, in person, before a passport agent at one of the passport agencies located in Boston; Chicago; Detroit; Honolulu; Houston; Los Angeles; Miami; New Orleans; New York; Philadelphia; San Francisco; Seattle; Stamford, Conn.; and Washington, D.C.; or a clerk of any federal court; or state court of record or a judge or clerk of any probate court accepting applications; or a postal employee designated by the postmaster at a post office which has been selected to accept passport applications.

When you apply for a passport you must present the following items: proof of U.S. citizenship (a previously issued passport, birth certificate, or naturalization papers); two identical photographs taken within six months of the date of your application (have them taken by a professional photographer who knows the requirements concerning pose and size of prints); identification—a document such as a driver's license with your signature and your photograph or physical description on it. The fee for a passport is $10, plus a $4 execution fee. Allow about two to three weeks for processing of your application, longer if you apply during peak travel periods.

A passport is valid for five years from the date of issue unless specifically limited to a shorter period by the Secretary of State. A new passport will be required for travel after expiration of the five-year period.

Application for a new passport must be made in person at the places listed above, or—under certain circumstances—a person who is the bearer of a passport issued within eight years prior to the date of his or her new application may apply for a subsequent passport by mail.

The applicant must submit completed form DSP-82 (Application for Passport by Mail), which is available from travel agents and the places listed above, the previous passport, two new signed passport photographs, and a fee of $10. The applicant should carefully read the instructions on the application to determine his or her eligibility to use this form.

Loss or theft of a valid passport is a serious matter and should be reported in writing immediately to the Passport Office, Department of State, Washington, D.C. 20524 or the nearest Passport Agency. If the passport holder is abroad when the loss occurs, he or she should notify the nearest U.S. consulate. Theft of a passport should also be reported to local police authorities.

Visas

A visa is official permission to visit a country granted by the government of that country. An American who plans to go abroad can check the general visa requirements for each country he or she plans to visit in a booklet entitled "Visa Requirements of Foreign Governments," which is available at any office accepting passport applications. Specific details should be obtained from the nearest embassy or consulate of the country in which you wish to do any traveling.

FOREIGN GOVERNMENT TOURIST OFFICES

Australian Tourist Commission
1270 Ave. of the Americas, Rm. 2908
New York, NY 10020

Austrian National Tourist Office
545 Fifth Avenue
New York, NY 10017

Bahamas Tourist Office
30 Rockefeller Plaza
New York, NY 10020

Belgian National Tourist Office
720 Fifth Avenue
New York, NY 10019

Bermuda Government Official Travel Information Office
630 Fifth Avenue
New York, NY 10020

British Tourist Authority
680 Fifth Avenue
New York, NY 10019

Canadian Government Office of Tourism
1251 Ave. of the Americas
New York, NY 10020

(Cedok) Czechoslovak Travel Bureau
10 East 40th Street
New York, NY 10016

Dominican Republic Tourist Office
64 West 50th Street
New York, NY 10020

Finland National Tourist Office
75 Rockefeller Plaza
New York, NY 10020

French Government Tourist Office
610 Fifth Avenue
New York, NY 10020

German National Tourist Office
630 Fifth Avenue
New York, NY 10020

Greek National Tourist Organization
645 Fifth Avenue
New York, NY 10022

Haiti Government Tourist Bureau
30 Rockefeller Plaza
New York, NY 10020

Indian Government Tourist Office
30 Rockefeller Plaza
New York, NY 10020

Iran Info. & Tourism Center
10 West 49th Street
New York, NY 10020

Irish Tourist Board
590 Fifth Avenue
New York, NY 10036

Israel Government Tourist Office
488 Madison Avenue
New York, NY 10022

Italian Government Travel Office
630 Fifth Avenue
New York, NY 10020

Jamaica Tourist Board
2 Hammarskjold Plaza
New York, NY 10017

Japan National Tourist Organization
45 Rockefeller Plaza
New York, NY 10020

Kenya Tourist Office
60 East 56th Street
New York, NY 10022

Lebanon Tourist Information Office
405 Park Avenue
New York, NY 10022

Malaysian Tourist Center
420 Lexington Ave.
New York, NY 10017

Mexican National Tourist Council
405 Park Avenue
New York, NY 10022

Moroccan National Tourist Office
521 Fifth Avenue
New York, NY 10017

Panama Government Tourist Bureau
630 Fifth Avenue
New York, NY 10020

Polish National Tourist Information Center
500 Fifth Avenue
New York, NY 10036

Romanian National Tourist Office
573 Third Avenue
New York, NY 10016

Scandinavian National Tourist Office
75 Rockefeller Plaza
New York, NY 10020

South African Tourist Corporation
610 Fifth Avenue
New York, NY 10020

Spanish National Tourist Office
665 Fifth Avenue
New York, NY 10022

Sri Lanka Ceylon Tourist Board
609 Fifth Ave.
New York, NY 10017

Surinam Tourist Bureau
1 Rockefeller Plaza
New York, NY 10020

Swiss National Tourist Office
608 Fifth Avenue
New York, NY 10020

Thailand Tourist Organization
5 World Trade Center
New York, NY 10048

Turkish Government Tourism Office
821 United Nations Plaza
New York, NY 10017

Yugoslav State Tourist Office
630 Fifth Avenue
New York, NY 10020

Zambia National Tourist Bureau
150 East 58th Street
New York, NY 10022

FOREIGN CITY WEATHER

Two figures are given for each of the months, thus 88/73. The first figure is the average daily high temperature (°F) and the second is the average daily low temperature (°F) for the month. The boldface figures indicate the average number of days with rain for each month.

	January	February	March	April	May	June	July	August	September	October	November	December
ABIDJAN, Ivory Coast	88/73 3	90/75 4	90/75 6	90/75 9	88/75 16	85/73 18	83/73 8	82/71 7	83/73 8	85/74 13	87/74 13	88/74 6
ACAPULCO, Mexico	85/70 0	88/70 0	88/76 0	87/71 0	89/74 4	89/77 7	89/75 8	89/75 14	88/75 14	88/75 8	88/72 2	87/70 1
ACCRA, Ghana	87/73 1	88/75 2	88/76 4	88/76 6	87/75 9	84/74 10	81/73 4	80/71 3	81/73 14	85/74 6	87/75 3	88/75 2
ADDIS ABABA, Ethiopia	75/43 2	76/47 5	77/49 8	77/50 10	77/50 10	74/49 20	69/50 28	69/50 27	72/49 21	74/63 7	73/43 2	73/43 2
ALGIERS, Algeria	59/49 11	61/49 9	63/52 9	65/55 7	73/59 5	79/65 2	83/70 1	85/71 1	81/69 4	76/63 7	66/56 11	60/51 12
AMSTERDAM, Netherlands	40/34 19	41/34 15	46/37 13	52/43 14	60/50 12	65/55 13	69/59 14	68/59 14	64/56 15	56/48 18	47/41 19	41/35 19
ANKARA, Turkey	39/24 8	42/26 8	51/31 7	63/40 7	73/49 7	78/53 5	86/59 2	87/59 1	78/52 3	69/44 5	57/37 6	43/29 9
APIA, Western Samoa	86/75 22	85/76 19	86/76 19	86/75 14	85/74 12	85/74 11	84/75 9	84/75 9	85/74 11	86/74 16	86/74 13	85/74 19
ATHENS, Greece	54/42 7	55/43 6	60/46 5	67/52 3	77/60 3	85/67 2	90/72 1	90/72 1	83/66 2	74/60 4	64/52 6	57/46 7
BAGHDAD, Iraq	60/39 4	64/42 3	71/48 4	85/57 3	97/67 1	105/73 0	110/76 1	110/76 0	104/70 0	92/61 1	77/51 3	64/42 5
BALI, Indonesia	88/74 19	88/74 14	88/74 13	88/74 7	88/73 5	87/71 3	87/70 1	87/70 1	89/71 2	90/73 2	90/75 5	88/74 14
BANGKOK, Thailand	89/68 1	91/72 1	93/75 3	95/77 3	93/77 8	91/76 10	90/76 13	90/76 13	89/71 15	90/73 14	87/72 5	87/68 1
BARCELONA, Spain	56/42 5	57/44 7	61/47 7	64/51 8	71/57 8	78/64 4	83/69 3	82/69 5	78/65 7	71/58 8	62/50 7	57/44 6
BEIRUT, Lebanon	62/51 15	63/51 12	64/54 9	72/58 3	78/64 2	83/69 1	87/73 0	89/74 0	84/74 1	81/69 4	74/61 7	65/54 15
BELFAST, Northern Ireland	45/34 22	47/34 18	50/35 20	54/38 18	59/43 17	64/49 12	65/52 13	65/52 13	61/50 14	55/47 18	50/37 21	46/35 25
BELGRADE, Yugoslavia	37/27 8	42/31 8	53/35 7	64/45 9	74/53 9	80/61 10	84/61 6	83/60 7	76/55 6	65/47 8	52/39 7	40/30 9
BERLIN, Germany	35/26 10	38/27 8	46/32 7	55/38 9	65/46 9	70/51 9	74/54 10	72/54 10	66/48 8	55/41 8	43/33 8	37/29 11
BIARRITZ, France	54/40 10	52/38 11	63/43 11	55/45 8	69/53 11	72/56 10	80/66 7	87/61 7	77/58 9	64/55 11	58/44 12	53/41 14
BOGOTA, Colombia	67/48 6	67/48 9	67/50 13	67/51 20	66/51 17	65/51 16	64/50 18	65/50 16	66/49 13	66/50 20	66/49 15	66/49 15
BOMBAY, India	83/67 1	83/67 1	86/72 1	89/76 1	91/80 1	89/79 14	85/76 21	85/76 19	85/76 13	89/76 3	89/73 1	87/69 1
BONN, West Germany	39/30 17	43/32 12	51/35 13	58/39 14	67/46 13	72/52 15	73/56 16	72/55 17	67/50 12	57/43 11	47/37 15	44/36 16
BRASILIA, Brazil	80/65 17	81/64 16	86/72 11	82/62 10	79/56 6	81/58 9	78/51 2	82/55 0	87/60 2	82/64 16	82/64 18	78/64 16
BRINDISI, Italy	55/43 10	57/43 8	60/45 5	65/50 5	73/57 5	80/64 4	85/69 1	86/69 3	80/65 4	73/58 6	64/52 10	58/46 8
BUCHAREST, Romania	33/20 6	38/24 5	51/33 6	64/44 8	74/51 8	81/58 9	86/61 7	85/60 5	78/51 5	65/44 5	49/35 6	37/26 6
BUDAPEST, Hungary	35/26 7	40/28 7	51/36 6	62/44 8	72/52 7	78/57 8	82/61 7	81/59 7	74/53 5	61/45 6	47/37 8	38/31 9
BUENOS AIRES, Argentina	85/63 7	83/63 6	79/60 7	72/53 8	64/47 7	57/42 8	57/42 8	60/43 9	64/46 8	69/50 9	76/56 9	82/61 8
CAIRO, Egypt	65/47 1	69/48 1	75/52 1	83/57 1	91/63 1	95/68 0	96/70 0	95/71 0	90/68 0	86/65 1	78/58 1	68/50 1
CALCUTTA, India	80/55 1	84/59 2	93/69 2	97/75 3	96/77 7	92/79 13	89/79 18	89/78 18	90/78 13	89/74 6	84/64 1	79/55 1
CAPE TOWN, South Africa	78/60 3	79/60 2	77/58 3	72/53 6	67/49 9	63/45 10	63/45 10	64/46 9	65/48 6	70/52 5	73/55 3	76/58 3
CARACAS, Venezuela	75/56 6	77/56 2	78/58 2	81/60 4	80/62 9	78/62 14	78/61 15	79/61 15	80/61 13	79/61 12	77/60 13	76/58 8
CHARLOTTE AMALIE, Virgin Islands	82/73 12	81/72 13	82/72 12	83/74 8	85/76 15	86/77 15	87/77 16	88/78 15	90/78 13	89/77 12	85/76 13	83/74 18
COLOMBO, Sri Lanka	86/72 7	87/72 6	88/74 8	88/78 14	87/77 18	85/77 18	87/77 12	85/77 11	85/77 13	85/77 19	85/73 16	85/72 10
COPENHAGEN, Denmark	36/29 9	36/28 7	41/31 6	50/37 9	61/44 8	67/51 7	72/55 9	69/54 12	63/49 9	53/42 9	43/35 9	38/32 11
DARWIN, Australia	90/77 20	90/77 18	91/77 17	92/76 6	91/73 1	89/69 1	87/67 0	89/70 0	91/74 2	93/77 5	94/78 10	92/78 15
DJAKARTA, Indonesia	84/74 18	84/74 17	86/75 15	87/76 11	87/75 9	87/74 7	87/67 4	87/73 4	91/74 2	87/74 5	86/74 12	85/74 14
DUBLIN, Ireland	47/35 13	47/35 11	51/36 10	54/38 11	59/42 11	65/48 11	67/51 13	67/51 12	63/47 12	57/43 12	51/38 12	47/36 13
EDINBURGH, Scotland	43/35 15	43/35 15	47/36 15	50/39 16	56/43 15	62/48 15	65/52 17	64/52 17	60/48 16	53/44 18	47/39 18	44/36 17
FLORENCE, Italy	49/35 9	53/36 9	60/40 7	68/46 7	75/53 9	82/60 6	89/63 4	88/62 4	81/58 6	69/51 9	58/42 10	50/37 9
GENEVA, Switzerland	39/29 10	43/30 9	51/35 9	58/41 9	66/48 12	73/55 11	77/58 9	76/57 10	69/52 10	58/44 11	47/37 11	40/31 10
GUAYAQUIL, Ecuador	88/70 20	87/71 25	89/72 24	89/71 14	88/68 9	88/68 4	84/67 2	86/65 0	87/66 2	86/68 3	88/68 2	88/70 10
HAMBURG, West Germany	35/28 12	37/30 10	42/33 10	52/38 11	63/48 10	67/53 11	70/56 12	69/56 12	63/51 10	53/44 11	44/36 11	38/31 12
HAMILTON, Bermuda	68/58 13	68/57 13	68/57 12	71/59 9	76/64 9	81/69 11	84/72 12	86/73 12	84/72 10	79/68 9	74/63 10	70/60 11
HAVANA, Cuba	79/65 6	79/65 4	81/67 4	84/69 4	86/72 7	88/74 10	89/76 9	89/76 10	88/75 11	84/73 11	81/69 7	79/67 6
HELSINKI, Finland	27/11 11	26/15 8	32/22 7	43/31 6	55/41 5	63/49 7	71/57 8	66/55 12	57/46 11	45/37 12	37/30 11	31/22 11
HONG KONG	64/56 4	63/55 5	67/60 7	75/67 8	82/74 13	85/78 18	87/78 17	87/78 15	85/77 12	81/73 6	74/65 2	68/59 3
JERUSALEM, Israel	55/41 9	56/42 11	65/46 3	73/50 3	81/57 1	85/60 1	87/63 0	87/64 0	85/62 1	81/59 1	70/53 4	59/45 7
JOHANNESBURG, South Africa	78/58 12	77/58 11	75/55 9	72/50 4	66/43 3	62/39 1	63/39 1	68/43 1	73/48 2	77/53 7	77/55 10	78/57 11
KARACHI, Pakistan	77/55 1	79/58 1	85/67 1	90/73 0	93/79 1	93/82 1	91/81 2	88/77 3	88/77 1	91/72 1	87/64 0	80/57 1
KINGSTON, Jamaica	86/67 3	86/67 3	86/67 2	87/70 2	87/72 4	89/74 5	90/73 4	90/73 7	89/73 6	87/73 11	87/71 5	87/69 4
LAGOS, Nigeria	88/74 2	89/77 3	89/78 7	89/77 10	87/76 16	85/74 20	83/74 16	82/73 10	83/74 14	85/74 16	88/75 7	88/75 2
LA PAZ, Bolivia	63/43 21	63/43 18	64/42 16	65/40 9	64/37 3	62/34 2	62/33 2	63/35 4	64/38 9	66/40 9	67/42 11	65/42 18

City	January	February	March	April	May	June	July	August	September	October	November	December
LAS PALMAS, Canary Is.	70/58 8	71/58 5	71/59 5	71/61 3	73/62 1	75/65 1	77/67 1	79/70 1	79/69 1	79/67 5	76/64 7	72/60 8
LENINGRAD, USSR	23/12 17	24/12 15	33/18 13	45/31 11	58/42 12	66/51 12	71/57 13	66/53 15	57/45 14	45/37 15	34/27 17	26/18 18
LIMA, Peru	82/66 2	83/67 1	83/66 1	80/63 1	74/60 6	68/58 2	67/57 1	66/56 2	68/57 1	71/58 1	72/60 1	78/62 1
LISBON, Portugal	56/46 9	58/47 8	61/49 10	64/52 7	69/55 6	75/60 4	79/63 1	80/64 1	76/62 4	69/57 7	62/52 10	57/47 10
LIVERPOOL, England	44/36 13	44/36 13	48/38 13	52/42 12	58/48 14	63/51 13	66/55 13	65/55 16	61/51 15	55/46 17	48/41 17	45/37 18
LONDON, England	44/35 17	45/35 13	51/47 11	56/40 14	63/45 13	69/51 14	73/55 13	72/54 13	67/51 13	58/44 14	49/39 16	45/36 16
MADRID, Spain	47/33 9	51/35 9	57/40 11	64/44 9	71/50 9	80/57 7	87/62 3	86/67 3	77/56 6	66/48 8	54/40 10	48/35 9
MANILA, Philippines	86/69 6	88/69 3	91/74 1	93/75 4	93/75 22	91/75 17	88/74 24	87/75 23	88/75 22	88/74 19	87/72 14	86/70 11
MARACAIBO, Venezuela	90/73 1	90/73 1	91/74 1	92/76 1	92/77 6	93/77 6	94/76 5	94/77 4	94/77 2	92/76 9	91/76 8	91/75 2
MARSEILLE, France	53/38 10	52/37 9	57/40 11	63/45 9	71/52 8	72/52 7	84/64 6	83/61 4	82/63 6	67/50 9	57/41 9	59/43 11
MELBOURNE, Australia	78/57 9	78/57 8	75/55 9	68/51 13	62/47 14	57/44 16	56/42 17	59/44 17	63/46 15	67/48 14	71/51 13	75/54 11
MEXICO CITY, Mexico	66/42 4	69/43 5	75/47 7	78/51 13	78/54 17	76/55 21	73/54 27	73/54 27	74/53 23	70/50 13	68/46 6	66/43 4
MILAN, Italy	40/29 7	47/33 6	56/38 6	65/46 6	74/54 9	80/61 6	84/64 6	82/63 6	76/58 6	64/49 7	51/39 7	42/33 7
MONTEVIDEO, Uruguay	83/62 6	82/61 5	78/59 9	71/53 6	64/48 8	59/43 5	58/43 6	59/43 7	63/46 6	68/49 6	74/54 6	79/59 7
MOSCOW, USSR	33/23 10	23/10 9	32/17 8	47/31 9	65/44 9	73/51 10	76/55 12	72/52 12	61/43 9	46/34 11	31/23 10	23/13 10
MUNICH, West Germany	33/23 11	37/25 9	45/31 10	56/38 10	64/45 11	70/51 12	74/55 14	73/53 12	67/48 11	56/40 11	42/31 10	36/26 11
NAIROBI, Kenya	77/54 5	79/55 6	77/57 11	75/58 16	72/56 12	70/53 9	69/51 6	70/52 7	75/52 6	76/55 8	74/56 15	74/55 11
NAPLES, Italy	54/42 11	55/43 11	60/46 6	66/51 6	73/56 6	81/62 3	87/67 1	86/67 3	81/63 5	72/56 6	63/49 11	57/45 11
NASSAU, Bahamas	77/65 6	77/64 5	79/66 5	81/69 6	84/71 9	87/74 12	88/75 14	89/76 14	88/75 15	85/73 13	81/70 9	79/67 6
NEW DELHI, India	70/44 2	75/49 2	87/58 1	97/68 1	105/79 1	102/83 4	96/81 8	93/79 14	93/75 4	93/65 1	84/52 1	73/46 1
NICE, France	56/41 9	56/41 8	59/45 8	64/49 7	69/56 8	76/62 5	81/66 2	81/66 4	77/62 6	70/55 7	62/48 8	58/43 8
NOUMEA, New Caledonia	89/72 16	85/73 17	85/72 16	83/70 13	79/66 13	77/64 13	75/63 13	76/61 12	77/62 8	80/65 7	83/68 8	86/70 11
ODESSA, USSR	28/22 7	32/20 7	39/32 5	52/41 6	67/55 6	74/62 7	79/65 6	78/65 5	68/56 4	57/47 5	49/38 6	33/27 7
OSLO, Norway	30/20 7	32/20 7	40/25 7	50/34 7	62/43 7	69/51 8	73/56 10	69/53 11	60/45 8	49/37 10	37/29 9	31/24 10
PALERMO, Sicily, Italy	58/47 14	59/43 8	62/49 7	67/53 5	73/59 5	82/66 3	86/71 1	87/72 1	83/69 4	75/62 8	67/55 9	61/50 11
PALMA, Majorca, Spain	59/43 8	59/43 8	62/45 8	66/49 7	73/55 5	80/61 3	86/66 1	86/67 2	81/64 6	75/62 8	65/50 9	59/44 11
PAPEETE, Tahiti	89/72 16	89/72 16	89/72 17	89/72 10	87/70 10	86/69 3	86/66 8	86/68 8	86/69 9	87/70 7	88/71 13	88/72 14
PARIS, France	42/32 15	45/33 13	52/36 15	60/41 14	67/47 13	73/52 11	76/55 12	75/55 12	69/50 11	59/44 14	49/38 15	43/33 17
PEKING, China	35/15 3	41/20 3	53/30 3	68/41 4	80/56 6	88/65 7	89/74 14	87/72 11	80/58 7	69/44 4	50/30 2	37/19 2
PHNOM PENH, Cambodia	87/70 1	90/72 1	93/74 2	94/76 6	92/76 14	91/76 15	89/75 16	89/76 17	88/75 19	87/76 17	86/74 7	87/69 4
PORT-AU-PRINCE, Haiti	88/68 5	88/68 5	89/69 7	90/71 11	92/73 14	94/74 7	94/74 7	93/73 11	91/73 12	90/72 12	89/71 7	87/69 4
PORT OF SPAIN, Trinidad	85/67 14	86/67 8	87/67 8	88/69 7	89/71 11	87/71 17	86/71 20	87/71 21	88/71 18	88/71 16	88/71 17	87/69 16
PRAGUE, Czechoslovakia	34/25 12	38/28 11	45/33 13	55/40 12	65/49 13	72/55 14	74/58 14	73/57 12	65/52 11	54/44 11	41/35 12	34/29 13
RANGOON, Burma	89/65 1	92/67 1	96/71 1	97/76 2	92/77 16	86/76 26	85/76 26	85/76 25	86/76 20	88/76 10	88/73 8	87/67 1
RIO DE JANEIRO, Brazil	84/73 13	85/73 11	83/72 12	80/69 10	77/66 10	76/64 7	75/63 7	76/64 7	75/65 11	77/66 10	79/68 13	82/71 14
ROME, Italy	54/39 8	56/39 11	62/42 5	68/46 6	74/55 5	82/60 3	87/64 2	86/64 2	83/61 6	73/53 8	63/46 8	56/41 9
SAIGON (HO CHI MINH CITY), Vietnam	89/70 2	91/71 1	96/71 1	95/76 4	92/76 16	89/75 21	88/75 23	88/75 21	88/74 21	88/76 20	88/73 8	88/67 1
SAN JUAN, Puerto Rico	80/70 20	80/70 15	82/70 15	84/72 14	85/75 17	85/75 17	85/76 20	85/76 20	86/75 18	85/75 18	84/73 19	82/71 21
SANTIAGO, Chile	85/53 0	84/52 1	80/49 1	74/54 2	64/41 6	58/37 9	59/37 6	62/39 6	66/42 3	73/45 2	78/48 1	83/51 0
SAO PAULO, Brazil	81/63 19	82/64 17	81/62 15	77/58 10	73/54 10	71/51 8	70/49 6	73/51 8	74/59 14	76/57 13	79/59 14	80/61 13
SEOUL, South Korea	32/15 8	37/20 6	47/29 7	62/41 8	73/54 10	80/61 10	84/70 16	85/71 13	78/59 14	67/45 13	51/32 9	37/20 9
SEVILLE, Spain	59/41 8	62/44 9	67/48 9	73/51 8	80/57 5	89/63 2	96/67 1	97/68 1	90/66 3	78/57 5	67/49 9	60/44 9
SHANGHAI, China	46/33 8	47/34 9	55/40 9	66/49 9	77/59 9	82/67 10	91/76 7	90/76 9	82/66 9	74/57 5	63/45 7	53/36 6
SINGAPORE, Singapore	86/73 17	88/73 11	88/75 14	88/75 15	89/75 15	88/75 13	88/75 13	87/75 14	87/75 13	87/74 16	87/74 18	87/74 19
SOFIA, Bulgaria	34/22 6	39/25 9	51/32 8	62/41 8	70/49 11	76/54 11	81/57 7	81/57 5	74/50 6	63/42 7	50/35 7	37/26 8
STOCKHOLM, Sweden	31/23 8	30/22 8	37/26 7	47/34 6	58/43 6	67/53 7	71/57 8	68/56 10	60/49 9	49/41 8	40/34 7	35/29 8
SYDNEY, Australia	78/65 14	78/65 13	76/63 14	71/58 13	66/52 13	61/48 12	60/46 12	63/48 11	67/51 12	71/56 12	74/60 12	77/63 13
TAIPEI, Taiwan, China	66/54 9	65/53 13	70/57 14	77/63 14	83/69 12	89/73 13	92/76 10	91/75 12	88/73 11	81/67 8	75/62 7	69/57 8
TEHRAN, Iran	45/27 4	50/32 4	59/39 5	71/49 4	82/58 2	93/66 0	99/72 1	97/71 0	90/64 1	76/53 1	63/43 3	51/33 4
TEL AVIV, Israel	47/29 5	65/48 5	59/39 5	74/54 3	81/60 1	84/65 0	87/69 0	87/70 0	86/68 1	84/64 2	77/59 7	66/52 11
TOKYO, Japan	47/29 6	48/31 6	54/36 10	63/46 10	71/54 11	76/63 12	83/70 10	86/72 9	79/66 12	69/55 11	60/43 7	52/33 5
VALPARAISO, Chile	72/56 1	72/56 1	70/54 1	65/49 4	63/50 5	60/48 7	60/47 8	61/47 5	62/48 2	65/52 2	71/54 1	71/54 1
VENICE, Italy	43/33 6	46/35 5	54/41 6	63/49 5	71/57 6	78/64 8	82/67 8	82/67 9	78/62 5	65/52 6	54/43 7	46/37 7
VIENNA, Austria	38/28 7	42/30 7	47/34 7	57/41 7	66/50 8	71/56 9	75/58 10	73/58 10	66/52 7	55/44 8	44/36 8	37/30 9
WELLINGTON, New Zealand	69/56 10	69/56 9	67/54 11	63/51 13	58/47 16	55/44 17	53/42 18	54/43 17	57/46 15	60/48 14	63/50 13	67/54 12
ZURICH, Switzerland	48/14 11	52/15 11	62/22 14	70/32 14	77/39 14	83/47 14	86/51 15	84/49 14	78/42 11	68/32 11	57/25 12	49/16 13

CUSTOMS HINTS

SOURCE: U.S. Customs Service

Customs exemptions: These apply only to articles brought back at the time of your return to the United States. You have a $300 exemption, if you are returning from a stay abroad of at least 48 hours (no minimum time limit for Mexico and American Virgin Islands), and you have not used the $300 exemption or any part of it within the preceding 30 days. Articles in excess of the $300 exemption up to $600 in value, based on the fair retail price of each item in the country of purchase, may be entered at a flat rate of 10% (subject to limitations on cigars, cigarettes, and liquor), if accompanying you at the time of your return, if acquired as an incident to your trip, if for personal or household use, and if properly declared to customs.

Cigars and Cigarettes–Not more than 100 cigars and 200 cigarettes (one carton) may be included in your exemption. Your cigarettes, however, may be subject to a tax imposed by state and local authorities.

Liquor–One quart of alcoholic beverages may be included in the exemption if you are 21 years old or older.

Articles imported in excess of your customs exemption: Will be subject to duty unless the items are entitled to free entry or prohibited. After deducting your exemption and the value of any articles duty free, a flat rate of duty will be applied to the next $600 worth (fair retail value) of merchandise. Any dollar amount of an article over $600 will be dutiable at various rates of duty based on wholesale value. The flat rate of duty is 10% of fair retail value in the country of acquisition; 5% for articles purchased in certain U.S. Territories.

Traveling back and forth across border: If you cross the border at one point and then swing back into the United States to enter the foreign country at another point, you might lose your exemption unless certain requirements are met. Ask a customs officer about these.

American Virgin Islands, American Samoa, Guam: If you return either directly or indirectly from these places, you have a $600 customs exemption provided that not more than $300 of it is applied to merchandise obtained elsewhere than these insular possessions. (The American Virgin Islands are exempt from the 48-hour-minimum time requirement.) Articles whole value exceeds $600 and were acquired in the insular possessions will be assessed at a rate of 5%, and they may accompany you or be shipped home. These articles must be for your own use or for gifts.

Customs declarations: All articles acquired abroad and in your possession at the time of your return must be declared to U.S. customs, either orally or in writing. Declaration lists are distributed on planes and ships and should be prepared well in advance. Your declaration must include items that you are bringing back for another person at his request, any article that you intend to use or sell in your business, alterations or repairs of articles taken abroad, and gifts given to you while abroad. Wearing or using an article acquired abroad does not exempt it from duty, and it must be declared at the price you paid for it. The customs officer may make a reduction in value for wear and use.

Necessary written declarations: All articles acquired abroad must be declared in writing when their total value (including alterations and repairs) exceeds $300, when more than one quart of alcoholic beverages or more than 100 cigars are included, when some of the items are intended for other than personal or household use, or when a customs duty or internal revenue tax is collectable on any article in your possession.

Family declarations: A family head may make a joint declaration for all members residing in the same household and returning with him as a group. A family may bring in articles free of duty valued up to $300 for each member (e.g., a family of seven: $2,100), even if the articles acquired by some members exceed their $300 exemptions. Returning infants and children are entitled to the same exemptions as adults (except for alcoholic beverages). Children born abroad who have never resided in the United States are not eligible for the exemption, but may claim Customs exemption as a nonresident.

Value of articles: You must declare the price actually paid for each article. If you do not know the price, say so. If an article was not purchased, state its fair value in the country where it was acquired. If you understate the value of an article or misrepresent an article, you may have to pay a penalty in addition to payment of duty.

Preparation for customs: It is helpful to make a list of items

obtained abroad before reaching the port of entry. Retain sales slips and have these readily available for examination. Pack articles acquired abroad separately.

Foreign-made articles taken abroad: These are dutiable each time they are brought into our country unless you have acceptable proof of prior possession. Documents which fully describe the article, such as a bill of sale or an insurance policy may be considered. Items which may be readily identified by serial number or permanently affixed markings may be taken to the Customs office nearest you and registered before your departure to expedite free entry of these items when you return.

Gifts: These are considered to be for your personal use and may be included in your exemption. This proviso includes both gifts given to you while abroad and those you intend to give to others after your return. Gifts intended for business or pomotional purposes may not be included. While abroad you may send gifts totaling $25 ($40 from U.S. insular possessions) retail value to people in the United States without duty or tax, provided that the addressee does not receive in a single day (at the customs processing station) gift parcels exceeding the $25 limitation. Write "unsolicited gift–Value under $25" in large letters on the outside of package as well as the retail value of the contents. Alcoholic beverages and tobacco products may not be sent, nor alcoholic perfumes valued at more than $5.

Personal belongings sent home: Personal belongings of U.S. origin taken abroad may be sent back by mail duty free if, on the outside wrapper or enclosed in the package, it is stated that the articles were taken out of the U.S. as personal effects and are being returned without having been repaired or altered while abroad.

Automobiles, boats, airplanes: Vehicles taken abroad for non-commercial use may be returned duty free by proving they were taken out of this country. Proof may be the state registration for an automobile, the Federal Aviation Agency certificate of registration for an airplane, a yacht license or motorboat identification, or a customs registration certificate for any vehicle. Dutiable repairs or accessories acquired abroad must be declared. A leaflet entitled "Importing a Car" is available from any customs office for those considering purchase abroad of a foreign car.

Household effects: If you plan to reside overseas for more than one year, household effects may be sometimes duty free. Check with a customs office or U.S. consulate.

$25 exemption: If you are not entitled to the $300 exemption because of the 30-day or 48-hour limitations, you may bring in free of duty or tax articles that were acquired abroad for your personal or household use, if their total retail value does not exceed $25. This is an individual exemption that cannot be grouped on a family declaration. You may include any of the following in this exemption: 50 cigarettes, 10 cigars, four ounces of alcoholic beverages, or four ounces of alcoholic perfume. If the value of any article (or articles) exceeds $25, no article may be exempted from duty or tax.

GSP: Generalized System of Preferences (GSP) is designed to help improve the economy of 101 developing nations and 36 dependent territories by exempting certain items from import duty when brought into the U.S. from these areas. The brochure "GSP & The Traveler" or a customs office can provide further information.

PROHIBITED AND RESTRICTED ARTICLES

Articles considered injurious to the general welfare are prohibited entry. Among these items are obscene publications, lottery tickets, wild birds, their eggs and feathers, endangered wildlife and items made from them, protected marine mammals, liquor-filled candies, switchblade knives.

Narcotics are also prohibited. If your medical condition requires drugs containing narcotics, you should carry a prescription or written statement from your doctor.

Trademarked articles: Foreign-made TM articles may be limited as to the quantity which may be brought into the U.S. if the registered TM has been recorded by an American trademark owner with U.S. Customs. Persons arriving in the U.S. with a TM article are allowed an exemption, usually one article.

Fruits, plants, vegetables: These, with cuttings, seeds, and unprocessed plant products, are either prohibited from entry or require an import license. Address applications to: Quarantines, U.S.D.A., Federal Center Bldg., Hyattsville, Md. 20782.

Meats, livestock, poultry: These items and their by-products (such as sausage, paté), are prohibited or restricted from entering the U.S., depending on the animal disease condition in the country of origin. Fresh meat is generally prohibited; canned meat is permited if the inspector can determine that it is commercially canned, hermetically sealed, and can be kept without refrigeration. Other canned, cured, and dried meat is severely restricted from most countries. Cheese, except cottage cheese, may be brought into the country.

Money or all types of negotiable instruments: Any amount may be brought into or taken out of the United States. Persons importing or exporting an amount of more than $5,000 are required to file a report of the transaction with U.S. Customs. Ask a customs officer for the form at the time you arrive or depart with such amounts.

Pets: If a dog or cat comes from an area with a high incidence of rabies, or arrives under conditions indicating that a special danger of rabies exists, the animal will be subject to exclusion or to such additional requirements as are found necessary.

Dogs–A certificate of vaccination against rabies is required (unless the dog arries directly from certain countries having a low incidence of rabies), except for puppies less than 3 months of age. The vaccination must have taken place at least a month before its arrival here.

Cats–If the animal is in good health on arrival, a vaccination is usually not required.

Birds–All birds are subject to controls and restrictions. For information write: Veterinary Services, APHIS, U.S.D.A., Hyattsville, Md. 20782.

Monkeys–Live monkeys and other non-human primates may not be imported into the United States except by a registered importer for scientific, educational, or exhibition purposes.

Biological materials: Disease organisms and vectors for research and educational purposes require a permit. Write the Foreign Quarantine Program, Center for Disease Control, Atlanta, Ga. 30333.

Prohibited merchandise: The importation (as well as the purchase abroad) of all merchandise originating in Rhodesia is prohibited without a Treasury license. Tourists may import items for their personal use up to a value of $100 from the following countries: Cuba, North Korea, Vietnam, and Cambodia. This allowance may only be used once every six months, and the articles must accompany the visitor upon his return.

Firearms and ammunition: Up to three nonautomatic firearms may be taken out of the country and returned if they are registered with customs or field office of the Bureau of Alcohol, Tobacco and Firearms. Firearms and ammunition are subject to import restrictions. Contact the Bureau of Alcohol, Tobacco and Firearms, Department of the Treasury, Washington, D.C. 20226.

HEALTH HINTS FOR TRAVELERS

SOURCE: U.S. Public Health Service

Under the International Health Regulations adopted by the World Health Organization a country may require International Certificates of Vaccination against Smallpox, Cholera, or Yellow Fever. Some countries require that all travelers be vaccinated against smallpox. Most require Certificates only if a traveler has been in a country reporting smallpox.

Smallpox vaccination is required to return to the U.S. only if, within the preceding 14 days, the traveler has been in a country reporting smallpox. No vaccinations are required to return to the U.S. from any country.

Those immunizations required by governments must be recorded in the International Certificates of Vaccination, form PHS-731–the only acceptable immunization document for international travel. You can obtain this form with your passport application, from your local health department, or from the Superintendent of Documents, Government Printing Office, Washington, D.C. 20402, for 50 cents.

The Certificates must be signed by you and your physician or by a person under his supervision and be validated with an approved stamp. Validation of Smallpox and Cholera Certificates can be obtained at most health departments or from vaccinating physicians who possess a validation stamp. Yellow Fever vaccinations must be given at an officially designated Yellow Fever Vaccination Center and the Certificate validated by the Center that administers the vaccine. Information on the location of Yellow Fever Vaccination Centers is available from state and local health departments.

The Smallpox Certificate is valid for three years, beginning eight days after the date of successful primary vaccination or on the date of revaccination.

The Cholera Certificate is valid for 6 months beginning 6 days after 1 injection of vaccine or on the date of revaccination-if within 6 months of the first injection.

The Yellow Fever Certificate is valid for 10 years beginning 10 days after primary vaccination or on the date of revaccination if within 10 years of the first injection.

Military personnel and their dependents, as well as other persons traveling under the auspices of the Department of Defense, are required to receive the immunizations as set forth by current service regulations.

RECOMMENDED VACCINATIONS

The risk of acquiring illness in international travel depends on the areas visited. In most developed countries such as Canada, Australia, New Zealand, and Europe, the risk to the health of the traveler will be no greater than that incurred while traveling throughout the United States. In the countries of Africa, Asia, South America, and in the countries of southern North America, the South Pacific, Middle East and Far East, living conditions and standards of sanitation and hygiene vary greatly. For travel to primarily tourist areas on itineraries which do not include travel in rural areas and consequently less risk of exposure to food or water of questionable quality, the risk of disease remains quite small. Travelers to smaller cities off the usual tourist routes and those who visit small villages or rural areas for extended periods are at greater risk or acquiring infectious diseases because of exposure to water and food of uncertain quality and closer contact with local residents who may harbor the organisms that cause such diseases. The risk of contacting hepatitis-A varies with living conditions, the prevalence of hepatitis in the areas visited, and particularly the length of stay. Vaccination against plague is not indicated for most travelers to countries reporting cases, particularly if their travel is limited to urban areas with modern lodgings.

There is a risk of acquiring malaria when traveling to parts of the Caribbean, Central and South America, Africa, the Middle East, the Indian subcontinent, and the Far East. You are strongly advised to seek information from your health department or private physician concerning the need for protection against malaria and for instructions on how the prophylactic drugs should be taken.

You are advised to contact your local health department, physician or agency two weeks prior to departure to obtain current information on vaccinations required by and recommended for the countries to be visited.

Unvaccinated Travelers: A traveler who does not have the required vaccinations upon entering a country may be subject to vaccination, medical follow-up, or isolation.

Exemption from Vaccination: If a physician thinks vaccination should not be performed on medical grounds, the traveler should be given a signed, dated statement of the reasons on the physician's letterhead stationery.

HEALTH PROTECTION HINTS

If you wear glasses, take along your lens prescription.
If you need medications regularly, take an adequate supply with you. Because of possible serious consequences to your health, do not buy medications "over the counter" unless you are familiar with the product.

If you have diabetes, are allergic to penicillin, or have any physical condition that may require emergency care, have some identification–a tag or bracelet or card–on your person at all times indicating this. Diabetics should take along an extra supply of medication. Drugs or medicines which must be taken should be accompanied by a letter from the traveler's physician.

Water can be considered safe only if it is obtained from adequately chlorinated sources, if boiled for ten minutes, or if treated with liquid chlorine laundry bleach or tincture of iodine.

Do not swim in unchlorinated pools.

Take it easy in unaccustomed conditions of heat and high altitudes.

It is wise to check with the local American Embassy or consulate for a list of acceptable doctors and dentists, and hospitals, if needed.

WORLD CITIES: COST-OF-LIVING INDEX: 1978

SOURCE: *UN Monthly Bulletin of Statistics* (Special Table H), March 1979, © United Nations

Note: This table shows the relative cost-of-living comparison, based on prices for goods, services and housing for international UN officials stationed in various cities of the world. In the following table, the cost-of-living is based on New York City=100.

City	Index	City	Index	City	Index
Afghanistan, Kabul	91	Greece, Athens	103	Nicaragua, Managua	91
Argentina, Buenos Aires	143	Guatemala, Guatemala	101	Pakistan, Islamabad	84
Australia, Sydney	100	Guinea, Conakry	137	Panama, Panama	89
Austria, Vienna	136	Guyana, Georgetown	92	Paraguay, Asunción	86
Bangladesh, Dacca	89	Haiti, Port-au-Prince	97	Peru, Lima	72
Barbados, Bridgetown	95	Hungary, Budapest	104	Philippines, Manila	94
Belgium, Brussels	150	India, New Delhi	80	Poland, Warsaw	80
Benin, Cotonou	106	Indonesia, Djakarta	93	Romania, Bucharest	88
Brazil, Rio de Janeiro	102	Iran, Tehran	122	Senegal, Dakar	135
Bulgaria, Sofia	100	Iraq, Bagdad	91	Singapore, Singapore	99
Burma, Rangoon	78	Italy, Rome	93	Spain, Madrid	111
Canada, Montréal	80	Jamaica, Kingston	61	Sri Lanka, Colombo	58
Chile, Santiago	97	Japan, Tokyo	199	Sudan, Khartoum	99
Colombia, Bogotá	84	Kenya, Nairobi	87	Swaziland, Mbabane	80
Cuba, Havana	82	Korea, South	109	Switzerland, Geneva	163
Cyprus, Nicosia	80	Kuwait, Kuwait	118	Syria, Damascus	103
Czechoslovakia, Bratislava	76	Liberia, Monrovia	108	Thailand, Bangkok	82
Denmark, Copenhagen	146	Libya, Tripoli	124	Togo, Lomé	103
Dominican Rep, Santo Domingo	89	Madagascar, Antananarivo	101	Tunisia, Tunis	124
Ecuador, Quito	86	Malaysia, Kuala Lumpur	98	Turkey, Ankara	93
Egypt, Cairo	75	Malta, Valletta	73	United Kingdom, London	106
El Salvador, San Salvador	94	Mauritius, Port Louis	91	United States, Washington, DC	93
Ethiopia, Addis Ababa	94	Mexico, Mexico	79	Uruguay, Montevideo	80
Fiji, Suva	88	Morocco, Rabat	115	Venezuela, Caracas	122
France, Paris	136	Nepal, Kathamandu	75	Yemen, San'a	113
Germany, West	148	Netherlands, The Hague	143	Yugoslavia, Belgrade	99

RATES OF CUSTOMS DUTY: 1979   SOURCE: U.S. Customs Service

This abbreviated list of popular items imported by tourists is intended to be used as an advisory guide only. The customs officer examining baggage at the point of entry determines the rates of duty on dutiable articles. Rates are often higher for items imported from Communist-controlled countries. These rates apply to those articles brought in after the $600 maximum has been reached and the 10% flat rate (5% for insular possessions) no longer applies.

Item	Rate
Antiques: produced prior to 100 years before the date of entry	Free
Automobiles, passenger	3%
Beads:	
imitation precious, and semi-precious stones	7 to 13%
ivory	10%
Binoculars, prism	20%
Books, foreign author or foreign language	Free
Cameras:	
motion picture, more than $50 each	6%
still, more than $10 each	7½%
cases, leather	8½ to 10%
lenses	12½%
China:	
bone	17½%
nonbone, other than tableware	22½%
China tableware, nonbone, available in 77-piece sets:	
valued not over $10 per set	10¢ doz. + 48%
valued over $10 but not over $24 per set	10¢ doz. + 55%
valued over $24 but not over $56 per set	10¢ doz. + 36%
valued over $56 per set	5¢ doz. + 18%
Cigarette lighters:	
pocket, valued at over 42 cents each	22½%
table	12%
Clocks, valued over $5 but not over $10	75¢ + 16% + 6¼¢ for each jewel
valued over $10 each	$1.12 + 16% + 6¼¢ for each jewel
Drawings (original works of art)	Free
Earthenware tableware, available in 77-piece sets:	

Item	Rate
valued over $3.30 but not over $12 per set	10¢ doz. + 21%
valued over $12 per set	5¢ doz. + 10½%
Figurines, china	12½ to 22½%
Fur: wearing apparel	8½ to 18½%
other manufactures of	8½ to 18½%
Furniture:	
wood, chairs	8½%
wood, other than chairs	5%
Gloves:	
wool, more than $4 per dozen	37.5¢ lb. + 18½%
horsehide or cowhide	15%
Handkerchiefs, cotton, plain	25%
Ivory, manufactures of	6%
Jade, cut but not set	2½%
other articles of jade	21%
Jewelry, precious metal or stone:	
silver chief value, valued at not more than $18 per doz.	27½%
other	12%
Leather:	
pocketbooks, bags	8½ to 10%
other manufactures of	4 to 14%
Motorcycles	5%
Musical instruments:	
music boxes, wood	8%
woodwind, except bagpipes	7½%
Paintings (works of art), originals	Free
Pearls, loose or temporarily strung and without clasp:	
genuine	Free
cultured	2½%
imitation	20%
permanently or temporarily strung (with clasp attached or separate)	12 to 27½%
Perfume	8¢ lb. + 7½%
Postage stamps	Free

Item	Rate
Radios:	
transistors	10.4%
other	6%
Rattan:	
furniture	16%
other manufacturers of	12½%
Records, phonograph	5%
Shaver, electric	6½%
Shell, manufactures of	8½%
Shoes, leather	2½ to 20%
Sterling flatware and tableware:	
knives and forks	4¢ each + 8½%
spoons and tableware	12½%
Stereo equipment	5 to 10⅝%
Stones, cut but not set:	
diamonds not more than one-half carat	4%
diamonds more than one-half carat	5%
other	Free to 5%
Sweaters, of wool, more than $5 per pound	37.5¢ lb. + 20%
Tape recorders	5½ to 7½%
Toys	17½%
Watches, on $100 watch, duty varies from $6 to $13	
Wearing apparel:	
embroidered or ornamented	21 to 42½%
not embroidered, not ornamented	
cotton, knit	21%
cotton, other	8 to 21%
linen, not knit	7½%
manmade fiber, knit	25¢ lb. + 32½%
manmade fiber, other	25¢ lb. + 27½%
silk, knit	10%
silk, other	16%
wool, knit	37.5¢ lb. + 15½ to 32%
Wood, manufactures of	8%

ALCOHOLIC BEVERAGES IMPORT RESTRICTIONS

State laws: Liquor may not be imported in violation of state law.
Mail importations: United States postal laws prohibit the shipment of alcoholic beverages by mail.
Gift packages: Alcoholic beverages forwarded to persons in the U.S.A. are not entitled to free entry under the $25 gift exemption.

Customs Exemption: A returning resident 21 years old or older may include in his $300 customs exemption one quart of alcoholic beverages free of duty and internal revenue tax. The importation must be for his own use or for a gift and not in violation of the laws of the state of arrival.

MAJOR COMMERCIAL PASSENGER PLANES

Country Company and Type	Maximum Number of Passengers	Maximum Speed (MPH)	Wingspan (Feet)	Length (Feet)	Height (Feet)
International Europe					
Airbus Industrie A300	345	576	147.1	175.1	54.2
France					
Dassault Mercure	134	575	100.3	114.3	37.3
Aerospatiale Caravelle IIR	50	498	112.5	107.3	28.6
Aerospatiale Caravelle III	99	500	112.5	105.0	28.6
Aerospatiale Super Caravelle	118	498	112.5	108.3	28.6
Aerospatiale Concorde	140	1300	84.0	203.9	37.1
United Kingdom					
BAC 111-475	89	541	93.6	93.6	24.6
BAC 111-500	119	541	93.6	107.0	24.6
British Aerospace 1150 Super VC 10	163	600	146.2	171.8	39.5
British Aerospace Trident 1E	139	605	95.0	115.8	27.0
British Aerospace Comet 4	83	530	115.0	111.5	29.5
British Aerospace Avro 748	60	281	98.6	67.0	24.1
British Aerospace Concorde	140	1300	84.0	203.9	37.1
Handley Page HPR 7-200	56	275	94.8	75.5	24.1
Hawker Siddeley Comet 4	81	530	115.0	111.5	29.5
Hawker Siddeley Trident 1E	139	605	95.0	114.8	27.0
Japan					
Nihon YS-11	60	297	105.0	86.3	29.5
Netherlands					
Fokker F27 MK500	60	298	95.2	82.2	28.6
Fokker F27 MK600	48	298	95.2	77.3	27.9
Fokker F28 MK3000	65	524	82.25	89.9	27.8
Fokker F28 MK4000	85	524	82.25	97.1	27.8
Fokker F28 MK6000	85	524	82.25	97.1	27.8
USSR					
Ilyushin IL-18V	110	425	122.7	117.8	—
Ilyushin IL-62	186	560	142.0	174.2	40.5
Tupolev TU-134	72	621	95.2	114.5	29.7
Tupolev TU-144	130	M.2.3	81.0	180.0	—
Tupolev TU-154	164	559	123.3	157.2	37.5
United States					
Boeing 707-120	181	600	130.9	144.5	42.0
Boeing 707-320	219	600 plus	145.7	152.9	42.5
Boeing 707-420	189	593	142.7	152.9	42.5
Boeing 720	167	600	130.9	136.2	41.8
Boeing 727-200	134	600 plus	108.0	153.2	34.0
Boeing 737-100	103	580 plus	93.0	94.0	37.0
Boeing 737-200	130	573	93.0	100.0	37.0
Boeing 747	500	640	195.6	231.3	63.4
Boeing 767	197	NA	155.0	168.6	44.6
Fairchild Hiller F-27	48	275	95.2	77.2	27.5
Fairchild Hiller FH-227	52	300	95.2	83.1	27.5
General Dynamics 240	40	304†	91.8	74.8	26.9
General Dynamics Metropolitan 440	44	310	105.3	81.5	28.2
General Dynamics Convair 580	53	342†	105.3	81.5	29.1
General Dynamics 600	46	317	91.8	74.8	26.9
General Dynamics Convair 880	107	600	120.0	129.0	42.0
General Dynamics Convair 990	130	600	131.0	141.0	42.0
Lockheed TriStar L-1011	400	620	155.4	178.7	55.4
McDonnell Douglas DC-9 Series 10	90	586	89.3	104.3	27.5
McDonnell Douglas DC-9 Series 20	90	586	93.3	104.3	27.5
McDonnell Douglas DC-9 Series 30	139	586	93.3	119.25	27.5
McDonnell Douglas DC-9 Series 40	139	576	93.3	125.5	28.0
McDonnell Douglas DC-9 Series 50	139	576	93.3	133.5	28.0
McDonnell Douglas DC-9 Super 80	172	576	107.8	147.9	29.3
McDonnell Douglas DC-10 Series 10	380	600 plus	155.3	182.25	58.1
McDonnell Douglas DC-10 Series 30	380	600 plus	165.3	181.6	58.1
McDonnell Douglas DC-10 Series 40	380	600 plus	165.3	182.25	58.1

† Best cruising speed. NA = not available.

OPERATIONS AT 30 TOP-RANKING U.S. AIRPORTS: CALENDAR YEAR 1978
SOURCE: Federal Aviation Administration.

Tower	Rank	1978 Operations†	Tower	Rank	1978 Operations†
Chicago O'Hare Int'l, Ill.	1	763,000	San Jose Reid Hillview, Calif.	16	399,000
Santa Ana, Calif.	2	606,000	Denver Arapahoe County, Colo.	17	391,000
Long Beach, Calif.	3	604,000	Honolulu, Hawaii	18	379,000
Van Nuys, Calif.	4	601,000	LaGuardia, N.Y.	19	370,000
Atlanta International, Ga.	5	556,000	Hayward, Calif.	20	367,000
Los Angeles International, Calif.	6	543,000	San Francisco, Calif.	21	355,000
Opa Locka, Fla.	7	497,000	Concord, Calif.	22	354,000
Oakland International, Calif.	8	466,000	Washington National, D.C.	23	352,000
San Jose Municipal, Calif.	9	463,000	San Diego Montgomery, Calif.	24	351,000
Denver Stapleton Int'l, Colo.	10	438,000	Boston Logan, Mass.	25	349,000
Seattle Boeing, Wash.	11	428,000	Ft. Lauderdale, Fla.	26	347,000
Tamiami, Fla.	12	412,000	Memphis International, Tenn.	27	347,000
Phoenix Sky Harbor Int'l, Ariz.	13	411,000	Las Vegas McCarron, Nev.	28	345,000
Torrance Municipal, Calif.	14	408,000	Tulsa Riverside, Okla.	29	344,000
Dallas-Ft. Worth Regional, Tex.	15	406,000	John F. Kennedy Int'l, N.Y.	30	343,000

† Takeoffs and landings.

AIR DISTANCES BETWEEN MAJOR WORLD CITIES (See also, U.S. AIR DISTANCES, p. 221)

SOURCE: USAF Aeronautical Chart and Information Center (in statute miles)

	Bangkok	Berlin	Cairo	Cape Town	Caracas	Chicago	Hong Kong	Honolulu	Istanbul	Lima	London	Madrid	Melbourne
Accra	6,850	3,330	2,672	2,974	4,576	5,837	7,615	10,052	3,039	5,421	3,169	2,412	9,325
Amsterdam	5,707	360	2,015	5,997	4,883	4,118	5,772	7,254	1,372	6,538	222	921	10,286
Anchorage	6,022	4,545	6,116	10,478	5,353	2,858	5,073	2,778	5,388	6,385	4,491	5,181	7,729
Athens	4,930	1,121	671	4,957	5,815	5,447	5,316	8,353	352	7,312	1,488	1,474	9,297
Auckland	4,645	9,995	8,825	6,574	9,620	9,507	4,625	5,346	9,203	7,989	10,570	10,884	1,610
Baghdad	3,756	2,029	798	4,924	7,020	6,430	4,260	8,399	1,006	8,487	2,547	2,675	8,105
Bangkok	—	5,351	4,521	6,301	10,558	8,569	1,076	6,610	4,648	12,241	5,929	6,334	4,579
Beirut	4,272	1,689	341	4,794	6,520	6,097	4,756	8,536	614	7,972	2,151	2,190	8,579
Belgrade	5,073	623	1,147	5,419	5,587	5,000	5,327	7,882	500	7,169	1,053	1,263	9,578
Berlin	5,351	—	1,768	5,958	5,242	4,415	5,443	7,323	1,075	6,893	580	1,162	9,929
Bombay	1,870	3,915	2,717	5,103	9,034	8,066	2,679	8,036	3,000	10,389	4,478	4,689	6,101
Buenos Aires	10,490	7,395	7,360	4,285	3,155	5,582	11,478	7,554	7,608	1,945	6,907	6,236	7,219
Cairo	4,521	1,768	—	4,510	6,337	6,116	5,057	8,818	741	7,725	2,158	2,069	8,700
Cape Town	6,301	5,958	4,510	—	6,361	8,489	7,377	11,534	5,204	6,074	5,988	5,306	6,428
Caracas	10,558	5,242	6,337	6,361	—	2,500	10,171	6,024	6,050	1,699	4,662	4,351	9,703
Chicago	8,569	4,415	6,116	8,489	2,500	—	7,797	4,256	5,485	3,772	3,960	4,192	9,667
Copenhagen	5,361	222	1,964	6,179	5,215	4,263	5,392	7,101	1,252	6,886	595	1,289	9,936
Denver	8,409	5,092	6,846	9,331	3,078	920	7,476	3,346	6,164	3,986	4,701	5,028	8,755
Frankfurt	5,305	50	1,730	5,944	5,290	4,460	5,403	7,341	1,032	6,940	628	1,193	9,882
Helsinki	4,903	689	2,069	6,490	5,658	4,442	4,867	6,818	1,330	7,349	1,135	1,835	9,448
Hong Kong	1,076	5,443	5,057	7,377	10,171	7,797	—	5,557	4,989	11,415	5,986	6,556	4,605
Honolulu	6,610	7,323	8,818	11,534	6,024	4,256	5,557	—	8,118	5,944	7,241	7,874	5,501
Houston	9,261	5,337	7,005	8,608	2,262	942	8,349	3,902	6,400	3,123	4,860	5,014	8,979
Istanbul	4,648	1,075	741	5,204	6,050	5,485	4,989	8,118	—	7,593	1,551	1,701	9,100
Karachi	2,305	3,365	2,222	5,153	8,502	7,564	2,977	8,059	2,457	9,943	3,928	4,152	6,646
Keflavik	6,300	1,505	3,267	7,107	4,269	2,942	6,044	6,085	2,578	5,965	1,188	1,802	10,552
Kinshasa	5,974	3,916	2,618	2,047	5,752	7,085	6,904	11,178	3,241	6,322	3,951	3,305	8,112
Leningrad	4,718	826	2,034	6,500	5,843	4,589	4,687	6,816	1,306	7,534	1,307	1,985	9,263
Lima	12,241	6,893	7,725	6,074	1,699	3,772	11,415	5,944	7,593	—	6,316	5,907	8,052
Lisbon	6,651	1,442	2,352	5,301	4,040	4,001	6,862	7,835	2,015	5,591	989	317	11,049
London	5,929	580	2,158	5,988	4,662	3,960	5,986	7,241	1,551	6,316	—	786	10,508
Madrid	6,334	1,162	2,069	5,306	4,351	4,192	6,556	7,874	1,701	5,907	786	—	10,766
Melbourne	4,579	9,929	8,700	6,428	9,703	9,667	4,605	5,501	9,100	8,052	10,508	10,766	—
Mexico City	9,793	6,054	7,677	8,516	2,234	1,688	8,789	3,791	7,106	2,635	5,558	5,642	8,420
Montreal	8,337	3,740	5,403	7,920	2,443	746	7,736	4,919	4,798	3,967	3,256	3,449	10,390
Moscow	4,394	1,001	1,770	6,277	6,176	4,984	4,443	7,049	1,087	7,855	1,556	2,140	8,965
Nairobi	4,481	3,947	2,217	2,543	7,179	8,012	5,447	10,740	2,957	7,821	4,229	3,840	7,159
New Delhi	1,812	3,598	2,752	5,769	8,837	7,486	2,339	7,413	2,837	10,430	4,178	4,528	6,340
New York City	8,669	3,980	5,598	7,801	2,124	714	8,061	4,969	5,022	3,635	3,473	3,596	10,352
Oslo	5,395	523	2,243	6,477	5,167	4,050	5,342	6,801	1,518	6,857	718	1,485	9,934
Panama City	10,871	5,856	7,118	7,021	867	2,321	10,089	5,254	6,756	1,454	5,285	5,081	9,027
Paris	5,877	549	1,973	5,782	4,735	4,145	5,992	7,452	1,400	6,367	215	652	10,442
Peking	2,027	4,600	4,687	8,034	8,978	6,625	1,195	5,084	4,407	10,365	5,089	5,759	5,632
Rabat	6,652	1,623	2,230	4,954	4,111	4,282	6,954	8,177	2,008	5,590	1,254	474	10,856
Rio de Janeiro	9,987	6,207	6,153	3,773	2,805	5,288	11,002	8,295	6,378	2,351	5,751	5,045	8,218
Rome	5,493	735	1,305	5,231	5,198	4,823	5,773	8,040	853	6,748	892	849	9,940
Saigon (Ho Chi Minh City) ...	467	5,771	4,987	6,534	10,905	8,695	938	6,302	5,102	12,180	6,345	6,779	4,168
San Francisco	7,930	5,673	7,436	10,248	3,908	1,860	6,904	2,397	6,711	4,516	5,369	5,806	7,850
Santiago	10,967	7,772	7,967	4,947	3,033	5,295	11,615	6,861	8,135	1,528	7,241	6,639	7,017
Seattle	7,455	5,060	6,809	10,205	4,096	1,737	6,481	2,681	6,077	4,961	4,799	5,303	8,176
Shanghai	1,797	5,231	5,188	8,062	9,508	7,071	760	4,947	4,975	10,665	5,728	6,386	4,991
Shannon	6,256	940	2,534	6,188	4,320	3,583	6,246	7,006	1,938	5,992	387	884	10,826
Singapore	887	6,167	5,143	6,007	11,408	9,376	1,608	6,728	5,379	11,689	6,747	7,079	3,767
St. Louis	8,763	4,676	6,370	8,549	2,414	265	7,949	4,134	5,744	3,589	4,215	4,426	9,476
Stockholm	5,141	505	2,084	6,422	5,422	4,288	5,115	6,873	1,347	7,109	892	1,613	9,693
Teheran	3,392	2,184	1,220	5,240	7,322	6,502	3,844	8,072	1,274	8,850	2,739	2,974	7,838
Tokyo	2,865	5,557	5,937	9,155	8,813	6,313	1,792	3,860	5,574	9,628	5,956	6,704	5,070
Vienna	5,252	323	1,455	5,656	5,374	4,696	5,432	7,632	791	6,990	767	1,124	9,802
Warsaw	5,032	322	1,588	5,934	5,563	4,679	5,147	7,368	858	7,212	901	1,425	9,609
Washington D.C.	8,807	4,182	5,800	7,892	2,051	2,598	8,157	4,839	5,225	3,504	3,676	3,794	10,174

Mexico City	Montreal	Moscow	Nairobi	New Delhi	New York	Paris	Peking	Rio de Janeiro	Rome	San Francisco	Singapore	Stockholm	Teheran	Tokyo	Vienna	Warsaw
6,677	5,146	4,038	2,603	5,279	5,126	2,988	7,359	3,501	2,624	7,688	7,183	3,835	3,874	8,594	3,100	3,440
5,735	3,426	1,337	4,136	3,958	3,654	271	4,890	5,938	807	5,465	6,526	701	2,533	5,788	581	681
3,776	3,133	4,364	8,287	5,709	3,373	4,697	3,997	8,145	5,263	2,005	6,678	4,102	5,654	3,463	4,856	4,601
7,021	4,737	1,387	2,827	3,120	4,938	1,305	4,757	6,030	654	6,792	5,629	1,498	1,539	5,924	801	996
8,274	10,231	9,018	7,315	6,420	10,194	10,519	5,626	8,259	10,048	7,692	3,848	9,732	7,935	5,017	9,886	9,676
8,082	5,768	1,583	2,431	1,966	6,007	2,405	3,925	6,938	1,836	7,466	4,427	2,164	431	5,199	1,781	1,752
9,793	8,337	4,394	4,481	1,812	8,669	5,877	2,027	9,987	5,493	7,930	887	5,141	3,392	2,865	5,252	5,032
7,707	5,405	1,514	2,420	2,479	5,622	1,987	4,352	6,478	1,368	7,302	4,935	1,931	913	5,598	1,401	1,459
6,610	4,305	1,066	3,328	3,270	4,526	902	4,634	6,145	449	6,296	5,833	1,010	1,741	5,720	309	516
6,054	3,740	1,001	3,947	3,598	3,980	549	4,600	6,207	735	5,673	6,167	505	2,184	5,557	323	322
9,739	7,524	3,132	2,811	722	7,811	4,367	2,953	8,334	3,846	8,406	2,427	3,880	1,743	4,196	3,725	3,601
4,580	5,597	8,369	6,479	9,823	5,279	6,857	11,994	1,231	6,925	6,455	9,870	7,799	8,565	11,411	7,334	7,656
7,677	5,403	1,770	2,217	2,752	5,598	1,973	4,687	6,153	1,305	7,436	5,143	2,084	1,220	5,937	1,455	1,588
8,516	7,920	6,277	2,543	5,769	7,801	5,782	8,034	3,773	5,231	10,248	6,007	6,422	5,240	9,155	5,656	5,934
2,234	2,443	6,176	7,179	8,837	2,124	4,735	8,978	2,805	5,198	3,908	11,408	5,422	7,322	8,813	5,374	5,563
1,688	746	4,984	8,012	7,486	714	4,145	6,625	5,288	4,823	1,860	9,376	4,288	6,502	6,313	4,696	4,679
5,918	3,605	971	4,156	3,640	3,857	642	4,503	6,321	953	5,473	6,195	325	2,287	5,415	540	417
1,438	1,639	5,501	8,867	7,730	1,631	4,900	6,385	5,866	5,887	953	9,079	4,879	7,033	5,815	5,395	5,322
6,127	3,787	961	3,915	3,550	4,028	589	4,567	6,237	729	5,709	6,119	502	2,135	5,533	296	274
6,101	3,845	554	4,282	3,247	4,126	1,192	3,956	6,872	1,370	5,435	5,759	248	2,062	4,872	895	569
8,789	7,736	4,443	5,447	2,339	8,061	5,992	1,195	11,002	5,773	6,904	1,608	5,115	3,844	1,792	5,432	5,147
3,791	4,919	7,049	10,740	7,413	4,969	7,452	5,084	8,295	8,040	2,397	6,728	6,873	8,072	3,860	7,632	7,368
749	1,605	5,925	8,746	8,388	1,419	5,035	7,244	5,015	5,702	1,648	9,954	5,227	7,442	6,685	5,609	5,609
7,106	4,798	1,087	2,957	2,837	5,022	1,400	4,407	6,378	853	6,711	5,379	1,347	1,274	5,574	791	858
9,249	6,997	2,600	2,708	678	7,277	3,817	3,020	8,082	3,306	8,078	2,942	3,340	1,194	4,313	3,175	3,052
4,614	2,317	2,083	5,404	4,749	2,597	1,402	4,951	6,090	2,068	4,196	7,181	1,352	3,568	5,497	1,813	1,745
7,915	6,378	4,328	4,234	4,692	6,378	3,742	7,002	4,105	3,186	8,920	6,132	4,388	3,612	8,307	3,619	3,910
6,276	4,005	396	1,505	3,069	4,291	1,350	3,789	7,028	1,460	5,523	5,575	431	1,926	4,733	986	642
2,635	3,967	7,855	7,821	10,430	3,635	6,367	10,365	2,351	6,748	4,516	11,689	7,109	8,850	9,628	6,990	7,212
5,396	3,255	2,433	4,013	4,844	3,377	904	6,040	4,777	1,163	5,679	7,393	1,862	3,288	6,943	1,432	1,720
5,558	3,256	1,556	4,229	4,178	3,473	215	5,089	5,751	892	5,369	6,747	892	2,739	5,956	767	901
5,642	3,449	2,140	3,840	4,528	3,596	652	5,759	5,045	849	5,806	7,079	1,613	2,974	6,704	1,124	1,425
8,420	10,390	8,965	7,159	6,340	10,352	10,442	5,632	8,218	9,940	7,850	3,767	9,693	7,838	5,070	9,802	9,609
—	2,315	6,671	9,218	9,119	2,086	5,723	7,772	4,769	6,374	1,889	10,331	5,965	8,182	7,036	6,316	6,335
2,315	—	4,397	7,267	7,012	330	3,432	6,541	5,082	4,102	2,544	9,207	3,667	5,879	6,470	4,007	4,021
6,671	4,397	—	3,928	2,703	4,680	1,550	3,627	7,162	1,477	5,884	5,236	764	1,534	4,663	1,039	716
9,218	7,267	3,928	—	3,371	7,365	4,020	5,720	5,556	3,340	9,598	4,636	4,299	2,709	6,996	3,625	3,800
9,119	7,012	2,703	3,317	—	7,319	4,103	2,350	8,747	3,684	7,691	2,574	3,466	1,584	3,638	3,467	3,277
2,086	333	4,680	7,365	7,319	—	3,638	6,867	4,805	4,293	2,574	9,539	3,939	6,141	6,757	4,233	4,271
5,722	3,418	1,024	4,446	3,726	3,686	838	4,395	6,462	1,248	5,196	6,249	260	2,462	5,238	839	661
1,496	2,542	6,720	8,043	9,422	2,213	5,388	8,939	3,296	5,916	3,326	11,692	5,956	8,011	8,441	6,031	6,175
5,723	3,432	1,550	4,020	4,103	3,638	—	5,138	5,681	688	5,579	6,676	964	2,624	6,054	643	853
7,772	6,541	3,627	5,720	2,350	6,867	5,138	—	10,778	5,076	5,934	2,754	4,197	3,496	1,305	4,664	4,340
5,612	3,537	2,579	3,733	4,841	3,636	1,125	6,206	4,589	1,184	5,995	7,348	2,084	3,263	7,174	1,546	1,866
4,769	5,082	7,162	5,556	8,747	4,805	5,681	10,778	—	5,704	6,621	9,776	6,638	7,368	11,535	6,124	6,453
6,374	4,102	1,477	3,340	3,684	4,293	688	5,076	5,704	—	6,259	6,231	1,229	2,126	6,140	476	819
9,718	8,558	4,798	4,874	2,268	8,889	6,303	2,072	10,290	5,943	7,829	682	5,534	3,851	2,689	5,687	5,454
1,889	2,544	5,884	9,598	7,691	2,574	5,579	5,934	6,621	6,259	—	8,449	5,372	7,362	5,148	5,992	5,854
4,094	5,436	8,770	7,180	10,518	5,106	7,224	11,859	1,820	7,391	5,926	10,190	8,120	9,185	10,711	7,760	8,059
2,340	2,289	5,217	9,006	7,046	2,409	5,012	5,432	6,890	5,680	679	8,074	4,731	6,686	4,793	5,381	5,222
8,033	7,067	4,248	5,951	2,646	7,384	5,772	645	11,339	5,679	6,150	2,363	4,837	3,974	1,097	5,281	4,963
5,172	2,873	1,863	4,563	4,529	3,086	563	5,288	5,597	1,247	5,040	7,089	1,135	3,117	6,064	1,153	1,258
10,331	9,207	5,236	4,636	2,574	9,539	6,676	2,754	9,776	6,231	8,449	—	5,993	4,106	3,304	6,039	5,846
1,425	978	5,248	8,231	7,736	878	4,398	6,792	5,218	5,073	1,744	9,544	4,552	6,766	6,407	4,955	4,942
5,965	3,667	764	4,299	3,466	3,939	964	4,197	6,638	1,229	5,372	5,993	—	2,217	5,091	771	504
8,182	5,879	1,534	2,709	1,584	6,141	2,624	3,496	7,386	2,126	7,362	4,106	2,217	—	4,775	1,983	1,878
7,036	6,479	4,663	6,996	3,638	6,757	6,054	1,305	11,535	6,140	5,148	3,304	5,091	4,775	—	5,689	5,346
6,316	4,007	1,039	3,625	3,467	4,233	643	4,664	6,124	476	5,992	6,039	771	1,983	5,689	—	347
6,335	4,021	716	3,800	3,277	4,271	853	4,340	6,453	819	5,854	5,846	504	1,878	5,346	347	—
1,883	490	4,873	7,550	7,500	203	3,841	6,965	4,783	4,496	2,444	9,667	4,135	6,340	6,792	4,436	4,471

WORLD AVIATION RECORDS

SOURCE: National Aeronautic Association

JET AND ROCKET AIRPLANES

Date	Record

1/10-11/62 Distance in a Straight Line
U.S.: 12,532.28 miles
Major Clyde P. Evely, USAF
Boeing B52-H
Kadena, Okinawa, to Madrid, Spain

6/6-7/62 Distance over a Closed Circuit
U.S.: 11,336.92 miles
Captain William Stevenson, USAF
Boeing B52-H
Seymour-Johnson, North Carolina; Kindley, Bermuda; Sondrestrom, Greenland; Anchorage, Alaska; March AFB, California; Key West, Florida; Seymour-Johnson, N.C.

8/31/77 Altitude
USSR: 123,523.58 feet
Alexander Fedotov
E-226M Airplane
Podmoskovnoye, USSR

7/17/62 Altitude (Rocket Powered)
U.S.: 314,750 feet
Major Robert M. White, USAF
North American X-15-1 (NASA Aircraft)
Edwards Air Force Base, California

7/28/76 Altitude in Horizontal Flight
U.S.: 85,068,997 feet
Capt. Robert C. Helt, USAF
Lockheed SR-71

7/28/76 Speed over a Straight Course
U.S.: 2,913.16 miles per hour
Capt. Eldon W. Joersz, USAF
Lockheed SR-71
Beale Air Force Base, California

7/27/76 Speed over a Closed Circuit
U.S.: 2,092.294 miles per hour
Major Adolphus H. Bledsoe, Jr., USAF
Lockheed SR-71
Beale Air Force Base, California

PROPELLER-DRIVEN AIRPLANES

Date	Record

9/29/46 Distance in a Straight Line
U.S.: 11,235.6 miles
Commander T. D. Davies, USN
Lockheed P2V-1 Monoplane
Perth, Australia to Columbus, Ohio

11/7-9/69 Distance in a Closed Circuit
U.S.: 8,974.0 miles
James R. Bede
BD-2 Airplane
Columbus, Ohio, to Kansas City Course

10/22/38 Altitude
ITALY: 56,046 feet
Mario Pezzi
Caproni 161 Biplane
Montecelio, Italy

8/16/69 Speed over a 3-Km. Course
U.S.: 482.462 miles per hour
Darryl Grecnamyer
F8F Bearcat
Edwards AFB, California

4/9/51 Speed over a 15/25-Km. Course
U.S.: 464.374 miles per hour
Jacqueline Cochran
North American P-51
Indio, California

7/20-25/75 Speed around the World
AUSTRALIA: 203.64 miles per hour
Pilot: D. N. Dalton; Copilot: T. Gwynne-Jones
Beechcraft Duke
Brisbane, Tarawa, Honolulu, San Jose, Toronto, Gander, Gatwick, Damascus, Dubai, Madras, Singapore, Darwin, Brisbane
Elapsed Time: 5 days, 2 hours, 19 minutes, 57 seconds

TURBOPROP AIRPLANES

Date	Record

2/20/72 Distance in a Straight Line
U.S.: 8,732.09 miles
Lt. Col. Edgar L. Allison, Jr., USAF
Lockheed HC-130 Hercules
Ching-Chuan Kang, Taiwan to Scott AFB, Ill.

11/4/72 Distance in a Closed Circuit
U.S.: 6,278.05 miles
Cdr. Philip R. Hite, U.S. Navy
Lockheed RP-3D
NAS Patuxent River, Md.

1/27/71 Speed over a 15/25-Km Course
U.S.: 501.44 miles per hour
Commander D. H. Lilienthal, USN
Lockheed P3C Orion
NAS Patuxent River, Md.

3/27/72 Altitude
U.S.: 51,014 feet
Donald R. Wilson
LTV-L450F Airplane
Greenville, Texas

WORLD COMMERCIAL AIRCRAFT SPEEDS

Date	Record

11/2/77 Barbados/London
ENGLAND: 1,134.85 miles per hour
Captain Norman Todd
Concorde
Elapsed time: 3 h, 42 m, 5 s

9/6/62 Chicago/Mexico City
U.S.: 534.15 miles per hour
Captain D. W. Ledbetter
Boeing 720B
Elapsed time: 3 h, 10 m, 06.3 s

4/30/60 London/Athens
GREECE: 506.29 miles per hour
Captain P. Ioanides (Olympic Airways)
Comet DH-106-4B (SXDAK)
Elapsed time: 3 h, 13 m, 42 s

6/5/62 London/Miami
ENGLAND: 321.02 miles per hour
Captain G. N. Henderson (Cunard Eagle Airways); Captain P. Wilson
Boeing 707/465
Elapsed time: 13 h, 46 m, 38 s

12/1/66 Los Angeles/Mexico City
MEXICO: 597.88 miles per hour
Captain Rafael T. Zapata (Mexicana de Aviacion)
Boeing 727-64
Elapsed time 2 h, 36 m

12/8/61 Los Angeles/New York
U.S.: 636.8 miles per hour
Captain William Miller (American Airlines, Inc.)
Boeing 707B-123
Elapsed time: 3 h, 52 m, 43 s

9/6/62 Mexico City/Chicago
U.S.: 558.28 miles per hour
Captain E. Schlanser (American Airlines, Inc.)
Boeing 720B
Elapsed time: 3 h, 1 m, 53.2 s

5/6/62 Miami/London
ENGLAND: 419.94 miles per hour
Captain P. Wilson (Cunard Eagle Airways)
Captain M. Gudmundsson
Boeing 707/465
Elapsed time: 10 h, 31 m, 55 s

5/28/60 Montreal/London
CANADA: 565.29 miles per hour
Captain R. M. Smith (Trans-Canada Air Lines)
Douglas DC 8-40
Elapsed time: 5 h, 44 m, 42 s

6/2/63 New York/Bergen
NORWAY: 533.13 miles per hour
Captain B. Bjornstad (Scandinavian Airlines Systems)
Douglas DC-8
Elapsed time: 6 h, 32 m, 20 s

Date	Record

11/26/54 New York/Madrid
SPAIN: 379.624 miles per hour
Captain C. I. Batida (Iberian Airlines)
Lockheed Super Constellation L-1049E
Elapsed time: 9 h, 29 m

2/19/74 New York/Rio de Janeiro
U.S.: 594.28 miles per hour
Capt. Theodore C. Patecell (Pan American World Airways)
Boeing 707 300 B/A
Elapsed time: 8 h, 5 m, 30 s

6/3/60 New York/San Francisco
AUSTRALIA: 510.092 miles per hour
Captain A. Yates (Quantas Empire Airways)
Boeing 707-138 VH-EBE
Elapsed time: 5 h, 3 m, 48.35 s

8/18/78 Paris/Washington, D.C.
FRANCE: 1,071.86 miles per hour
Captain Pierre Chanoine (Air France)
Concorde
Elapsed time: 3 h, 35 m, 15 s

12/8/61 San Francisco/New York
U.S.: 658 miles per hour
Captain T. E. Jonson (American Airlines, Inc.)
Boeing 707B-123
Elapsed time: 3 h, 55 m, 50 s

NATIONAL COMMERCIAL AIRCRAFT SPEEDS

Date	Record

4/10/63 West to East Transcontinental: 680.90 miles per hour
Captain Wylie H. Drummond (American Airlines, Inc.)
Boeing 707-123
Los Angeles International Airport/Idlewild Airport
Distance: 2,474 statute miles
Elapsed time: 3 h, 38 m

8/15/62 East to West Transcontinental: 575.52 miles per hour
Captain Gene Kruse (American Airlines, Inc.)
Boeing 707-720B
Idlewild Airport/Los Angeles International Airport
Distance: 2,474 statute miles
Elapsed time: 4 h, 19 m, 15 s

8/5/47 Atlanta/Chicago: 290.501 miles per hour
Captain H. T. Merrill (Eastern Air Lines)
Lockheed Constellation
Atlanta Municipal Airport/Chicago Municipal Airport
Distance: 590 miles; 2 hours, 1 minute, 55 seconds

7/19/63 Atlanta/Los Angeles: 566.82 miles per hour
Captain L. L. Caruthers (Delta Air Lines)
Douglas DC-8
Atlanta Municipal Airport/Los Angeles International Airport
Distance: 1,946 miles; 3 hours, 25 minutes, 59 seconds

1/21/63 Atlanta/New York: 589.64 miles per hour
Captain Michael Winicki (Delta Air Lines)
Douglas DC-8-51
Atlanta Municipal Airport/Idlewild Int'l Airport
Distance: 760 miles; 1 hour, 17 minutes, 20 seconds

10/30/62 Baltimore/Los Angeles: 563.46 miles per hour
Captain Howard U. Morton (American Airlines)
Boeing 707
Friendship Int'l Airport/Los Angeles Int'l Airport

Date Record

4/29/65 Boston/Los Angeles: 562.57
miles per hour
Captain George C. Dent (American
Airlines)
Boeing 707
Logan Int'l Airport/Los Angeles Int'l
Airport
Distance: 2,610 miles; 4 hours, 38
minutes, 21 seconds

7/20/63 Boston/New York: 414.61
miles per hour
Captain Peter C. Bals (American Airlines)
Convair 990
Logan Int'l Airport/Idlewild Int'l Airport
Distance: 186 miles; 00 hours, 26
minutes, 55 seconds

8/5/47 Chicago/Atlanta: 326.925
miles per hour
Captain H. T. Merrill (Eastern Air
Lines)
Lockheed Constellation
Chicago Municipal Airport/Atlanta
Municipal Airport
Distance: 590 miles; 1 hour, 48 min-
utes, 20 seconds

2/16/65 Chicago/Boston: 692.28
miles per hour
Captain Alden Young (American Air-
lines)
Convair 990
Chicago O'Hare Airport/Logan Int'l
Airport
Distance: 865 miles; 1 hour, 14 min-
utes, 58 seconds

4/20/65 Chicago/Fort Worth: 548.85
miles per hour
Captain Glen L. Stockwell (American
Airlines)
Boeing 727
O'Hare Int'l Airport/Greater South-
west Int'l Airport
Distance: 809 miles; 1 hour, 28 min-
utes, 26 seconds

4/9/65 Chicago/Indianapolis: 494.93
miles per hour
Captain P. G. Cook (American Air-
lines)
Boeing 707
O'Hare Int'l Airport/WEIR Cook Int'l
Airport
Distance: 179 miles; 00 hours,
21 minutes, 42 seconds

1/2–3/62 Chicago/Miami: 588 miles
per hour
Captain Dean Clifton (Delta Air Lines)
Convair 880
Chicago O'Hare Airport/Miami Int'l
Airport
Distance: 1,184 miles; 3 hours,
5 minutes, 5 seconds

10/28/65 Chicago/New York: 644.36
miles per hour
Captain W. J. Callahan (American
Airlines)
Boeing 727
O'Hare Int'l Airport/LaGuardia Air-
port
Distance: 733 miles; 1 hour, 8 min-
utes, 15 seconds

2/3/65 Chicago/Washington, D.C.
510.58 miles per hour
Captain A. B. Perriello (American Airlines)
Lockheed Electra L-188
O'Hare Int'l Airport/Washington National Airport
Distance: 612 miles; 1 hour, 11 minutes, 5 seconds

3/12/65 Dallas/New York: 686.73
miles per hour
Captain William F. Bonnell (American
Airlines)
Boeing 707/720
Love Field/John F. Kennedy Int'l Air-
port
Distance: 1,384 miles; 2 hours, 6
minutes

Date Record

2/18/65 Dallas/San Francisco:
580.46 miles per hour
Captain W. R. Swain (American Airlines)
Boeing 707/720
Love Field/San Francisco Int'l Airport
Distance: 1,477 miles; 2 hours, 32
minutes, 40 seconds

3/12/65 Dallas/Washington, D.C.:
643.06 miles per hour
Captain W. T. Fleming (American Air-
lines)
Boeing 707/720
Love Field/Dulles Int'l Airport
Distance: 1,162 miles; 1 hour, 48
minutes, 25 seconds

12/7/61 Los Angeles/Baltimore:
657.68 miles per hour
Captain Stan Smith (American Air-
lines)
Boeing 707/123B
Los Angeles Int'l Airport/Friendship
Airport
Distance: 2,329 miles; 3 hours, 32
minutes, 28 seconds

11/26/65 Los Angeles/Boston:
666.61 miles per hour
Captain Simon P. Bittner (American
Airlines)
Boeing 707
Los Angeles Int'l Airport/Logan Int'l
Airport
Distance: 2,610 miles; 3 hours, 54
minutes, 55 seconds

4/9/63 Los Angeles/Chicago: 672.80
miles per hour
Captain George R. Russon (American
Airlines)
Boeing 707/123
Los Angeles Int'l Airport/O'Hare Int'l
Airport
Distance: 1,746 miles; 2 hours, 35
minutes, 42 seconds

3/9/65 Los Angeles/Dallas: 689.00
miles per hour
Captain W. R. Hunt (American Air-
lines)
Boeing 707/123
Los Angeles Int'l Airport/Love Field
Distance: 1,245 miles; 1 hour, 48
minutes, 25 seconds

7/16/47 Miami/Chicago: 300.390
miles per hour
Captain H. T. Merrill (Eastern Air
Lines)
Lockheed Constellation
36th Street Airport/Chicago Municipal Airport
Distance: 1,183 miles; 3 hours, 56
minutes, 22 seconds

5/28/47 Miami/New York: 314.477
miles per hour
Captain E. R. Brown (Eastern Air
Lines)
Lockheed Constellation
36th Street Airport/LaGuardia Airport
Distance: 1,096 miles; 3 hours, 29
minutes, 11.4 seconds

MAN-POWERED AIRCRAFT

Date Record

6/12/79 Duration, Distance
U.S.: 2 hours, 55 minutes; 25 miles
Bryan Allen
Gossamer Albatross
Folkestone, England to Cap Gris-Nez,
France

BALLOONS (LARGE)

Date Record

8/12-17/78 Duration, Distance
U.S.: 137 hrs., 5 min., 50 secs.;
3,107.61 miles
Ben L. Abruzzo, Maxie L. Anderson,
Larry M. Newman; Double Eagle II
Presque Isle, Maine to Miserey,
France

Date Record

5/4/61 Altitude
U.S.: 113,739.9 feet
Commander Malcolm D. Ross, USNR
''Lee Lewis Memorial''
Gulf of Mexico

GLIDERS

Date Record

4/25/72 Distance in a Straight Line
W. GERMANY: 907.7 miles
Hans Werner Grosse
ASK 12 Sailplane
Luebeck, W. Ger. to Biarritz, France.

1/14/78 Distance to a Goal
NEW ZEALAND: Group Flight; David
Wapier Speight, S. H. Georgeson,
Bruce Lindsay Drake
Nimbus 2

5/9/77 Distance to a Goal and
Return
U.S.: 1,015.81 miles
Karl Striedieck
ASW 17 Sailplane
Lock Haven, Pennsylvania

2/25/61 Altitude above Sea Level
U.S.: 46,267 feet
Paul F. Bikle
Schweizer SCG 123 E. Sailplane
Mojave, Lancaster, California

2/25/61 Altitude Gained
U.S.: 42,303 feet
Paul F. Bikle
Schweizer SGA 123 E. Sailplane
Mojave, Lancaster, California

HELICOPTERS

Date Record

4/6–7/66 Distance in a Straight Line
U.S.: 2,213.04 miles
Robert G. Ferry
Hughes YOH 6A helicopter
Culver City, California to Daytona
Beach, Florida

3/26/66 Distance in a Closed Circuit
U.S.: 1,739.96 miles
Jack Schweibold
Hughes YOH-6A helicopter
Edwards AFB, California

6/21/72 Altitude
FRANCE: 40,820 feet
Jean Boulet
Alouette SA 315-001 ''Lama''
Helicopter
Istres, France

11/4/71 Altitude in Horizontal Flight
U.S.: 36,122 feet
CWO James K. Church, USA
Sikorsky CH-54B Helicopter
Stratford, Connecticut

12/14/70 Speed over a 3 Km Course
U.S.: 216.839 miles per hour
Byron Graham
Sikorsky S-67 Helicopter
Windsor Locks, Connecticut

9/21/78 Speed over a 15/25 Km
Course
USSR: 228.91 Miles per hour
Gourguen Karapetyan
Helicopter A-10
Podmoskovnoye Aerodrome

HANG GLIDING

Date Record

7/2/77 Distance
U.S.: 95.44 miles
George D. Worthington
Mitchell Wing
Cerro Gordo Peak, California

7/22/78 Gain in Altitude
U.S.: 11,700 feet
George D. Worthington
Seagull 10 Meter
Cerro Gordo Peak, California

7/21/77 Straight Distance to Goal
U.S.: 95.44 miles
George D. Worthington
ASG-21 Albatross Sails
Cerro Gordo Peak, Calif. to Benton
Station, Calif.

BUSIEST WORLD AIRPORTS Source: International Civil Aviation Organization

Airports are ranked here according to their total passenger traffic (embarked plus disembarked) for 1977. U.S.S.R. airports opened to domestic traffic exclusively are not included.

Airport	Passengers (in millions)	Airport	Passengers (in millions)	Airport	Passengers (in millions)	Airport	Passengers (in millions)
Chicago (O'Hare)	44.0	Frankfurt	14.0	Amsterdam	8.6	Zürich	7.1
Atlanta	30.0	Osaka	13.9	Philadelphia	8.6	Palma de Mallorca	7.0
Los Angeles	28.4	Miami	13.7	Copenhagen	8.5	Seattle	6.8
London (Heathrow)	23.4	Washington (Nat'l)	12.6	Paris (De Gaulle)	8.4	Sydney	6.8
Tokyo (Intl.)	23.2	Paris (Orly)	12.6	Pittsburgh	8.0*	Saint Louis	6.7
New York (J.F.K.)	22.5	Boston (Logan)	12.1	Houston	8.0	London (Gatwick)	6.6
San Francisco	18.7	Honolulu	12.1	Las Vegas	8.0	Cleveland	6.4
Dallas-Fort Worth	17.3	Toronto	11.7	Mexico City	7.8	Montreal (Dorval)	5.8
Denver	15.3	Rome (Fiumicino)	9.8*	Minneapolis	7.8	Dusseldorf	5.7
New York		Madrid	9.4	New York (Newark)	7.3	Tampa	5.6
(La Guardia)	15.1	Detroit	8.6	Athens	7.3	* Estimated data	

MAJOR INTERNATIONAL AIRPORTS Source: International Civil Aviation Organization

Airports on the list are ranked according to the total international passenger traffic for 1977.   * Estimated data.

Airport	City	PASSENGERS (000)			COM'L OPERATIONS (000)		
		International	Domestic	Total	International	Domestic	Total
Heathrow	London	20,568	2,822	23,390	199.1	42.8	241.9
J. F. Kennedy	New York	11,490	11,056	22,546	96.4	176.9	273.3
Frankfurt-Main	Frankfurt	9,634	4,329	13,963	128.1	69.3	197.4
Schiphol	Amsterdam	8,444	147	8,591	129.9	6.4	136.3
De Gaulle	Paris	7,550	853	8,403	86.8	10.2	97.0
Orly	Paris	7,543	5,017	12,560	91.6	70.3	161.9
Kastrup	Copenhagen	6,795	1,680	8,475	115.2	32.0	147.2
Zürich	Zürich	6,741	324	7,065	102.3	6.9	109.2
Tokyo Int'l	Tokyo	6,100*	17,100*	23,200*	55.0*	111.0*	166.0*
Fiumicino	Rome	5,800*	4,000*	9,800*	84.7*	57.4*	142.1*
Gatwick	London	5,786	802	6,588	65.2	19.2	84.4
Toronto Int'l	Toronto	5,516	6,138	11,654	65.8	95.8	161.6
Palma de Mallorca	Palma de Mallorca	5,304	1,706	7,010	50.9	23.2	74.1
Miami Int'l	Miami	5,009	8,727	13,736	NA	NA	255.4
Hong Kong Int'l	Hong Kong	4,899	—	4,899	50.1	.2	50.3
Bruxelles Nat'l	Brussels	4,544	5	4,549	74.9	.3	75.2
Athinai	Athens	4,459	2,816	7,275	65.9	33.8	99.7
Singapore Int'l	Singapore	4,224	—	4,224	60.0	—	60.0
Dusseldorf	Dusseldorf	3,984	1,713	5,697	45.6	32.5	78.1
Barajas	Madrid	3,499	5,880	9,379	48.2	71.8	120.0
Los Angeles Int'l	Los Angeles	3,293	25,070	28,363	29.5	331.0	360.5
Cairo Int'l	Cairo	3,165	189	3,354	45.2	5.3	50.5
Arlanda	Stockholm	3,151	856	4,007	49.6	17.7	67.3
Cointrin	Geneva	3,149	642	3,791	65.4	3.2	68.6
Linate	Milan	2,862	1,936	4,798	49.4	30.0	79.4
München	Munich	2,814	2,143	4,957	40.1	36.8	76.9
Bangkok	Bangkok	2,719	273	2,992	39.0	7.1	46.1
Sheremetievo	Moscow	2,491	914	3,405	42.8	16.3	59.1
O'Hare Int'l	Chicago	2,440	41,590	44,030	29.0	701.3	730.3
Schwechat	Vienna	2,419	3	2,422	47.1	.2	47.3
Benito Juarez	Mexico City	2,385	5,435	7,820	35.4	71.9	107.3

AIRLINE TRAFFIC VOLUME Source: International Civil Aviation Organization

According to estimates released in March 1979 by the International Civil Aviation Organization for its 143 member states,* in 1978 the airlines carried 587 million passengers for a total of 794,000 million kilometers (493,000 million passenger-miles on scheduled services), representing increases of 14.9 percent over 1977.

Year	Miles Flown	Hours Flown	Passengers Carried	Passenger-Miles	Average Number of		
					Passengers per Aircraft	Miles Flown per Passenger	Miles Flown per hr.
	(In Millions)						
1978	5,220	13.8	587	493,000	95	841	377
1977	5,030	13.4	517	429,000	85	830	377
1976	4,870	13.0	475	393,000	81	828	374
1975	4,670	12.6	436	356,000	76	817	371
1974	4,580	12.5	424	340,000	74	802	366
1973	4,660	12.7	405	323,000	69	798	367
1972	4,480	12.2	368	288,500	64	784	367
1971	4,390	12.2	333	253,500	58	771	360
1970	4,355	12.1	311	237,500	55	762	360
1969	4,170	11.8	293	218,000	52	744	354
1968	3,730	11.0	262	192,500	52	736	339
1967	3,290	10.2	233	169,500	52	727	320
1966	2,790	9.3	200	142,000	51	711	301
1965	2,550	8.7	177	123,000	48	696	292
1964	2,300	8.2	155	106,000	46	687	280
1963	2,130	7.9	135	91,500	43	674	270
1962	2,015	7.8	121	80,500	40	668	258
1961	1,940	8.0	111	72,500	38	656	242
1960	1,930	8.6	106	67,500	35	640	224
1959	1,920	9.0	99	61,000	32	615	214
1958	1,820	8.8	88	53,000	29	603	208
1957	1,765	8.7	86	51,000	29	590	202
1956	1,580	8.0	77	44,000	28	570	199
1955	1,425	7.3	68	38,000	27	562	196
1954	1,280	6.7	59	32,500	25	556	193

* Except USSR

SAFETY RECORD: U.S. CERTIFICATED AND SUPPLEMENTAL AIR CARRIERS *

Source: National Transportation Safety Board

Year	Number of Accidents Total	Fatal	Fatalities Passg.	Crew	Others	Total	Aircraft Miles Flown	Accident Rate per Million Aircraft Miles Flown Total Accidents	Fatal Accidents
1960	90	17	429	57	13	499	1,130,069,000	.078	.011
1965	83	9	226	35	0	261	1,536,395,000**	.054	.006
1966	75	8	137	27	108	272	1,768,458,000**	.042	.005
1967	70	12	229	39	18	286	2,179,739,000**	.032	.006
1968	71	15	306	37	6	349	2,498,848,000**	.028	.005
1969	63	10	132	22	4	158	2,736,596,000**	.023	.003
1970	55	8	118	24	4	146	2,684,552,000**	.020	.003
1971	48	8	174	23	6	203	2,660,731,000**	.018	.002
1972	50	8	160	17	13	190	2,619,043,000**	.019	.003
1973	43	9	200	26	1	227	2,646,669,000**	.016	.003
1974	47	9	421	46	0	467	2,464,295,000**	.019	.003
1975	45	3	113	11	0	124	2,477,764,000**	.018	.001
1976	28	4	39	6	0	45	2,568,113,000**	.011	.002
1977	26	5	381	17	257	655	2,684,072,000**	.010	.002
1978[1]	25	6	141	12	10	163	2,797,000,000**	.009	.002

* Beginning in 1975, accidents involving commercial operators of large aircraft are included.
** Nonrevenue miles of the supplemental air carriers are not reported.
[1] Preliminary.

SAFETY RECORD: WORLD SCHEDULED AIRLINES[1]

Source: International Civil Aviation Organization

Year	Number of Accidents: Passenger-carrying Aircraft	Number of Passengers Killed	Fatality Rate (per 100 million Pass.-Mi.)	Fatal Accidents (per 100 million Mi. Flown)	Fatal Accidents†	Year	Number of Accidents: Passenger-carrying Aircraft	Number of Passengers Killed	Fatality Rate (per 100 million Pass.-Mi.)	Fatal Accidents (per 100 million Mi. Flown)	Fatal Accidents†
1950	27	551	3.15	3.02	0.54	1968	35	912	0.47	0.94	0.32
1952	21	386	1.54	1.90	0.34	1969	32	946	0.43	0.77	0.27
1954	28	443	1.36	2.19	0.42	1970	28	687	0.29	0.64	0.23
1956	27	552	1.25	1.71	0.34	1971	31	867	0.34	0.71	0.26
1958	30	609	1.15	1.65	0.34	1972	42	1,210	0.42	0.94	0.34
1960	34	873	1.29	1.71	0.38	1973	36	862	0.27	0.77	0.28
1962	29	778	1.97	1.44	0.37	1974	29	1,299	0.38	0.62	0.23
1964	25	616	0.58	1.09	0.30	1975	20	443	0.13	0.43	0.18
1966	31	1,001	0.70	1.12	0.33	1976	20	734	0.19	0.41	0.15
1967	30	678	0.40	0.91	0.29	1977	24	516	0.11	0.48	0.18
						1978	23	652	0.13	0.43	0.16

† Per 100,000 aircraft hours. [1] Excluding U.S.S.R.

WORLD'S FASTEST TRAINS[1]

Source: Donald M. Steffee

Railroad	Train	From	To	Miles	Time (min.)	Speed (mph)
Passenger						
Japanese National	Hikari Train	Nagoya	Shizouka	108.4	59	110.2
British Rail	High Speed Trains (2 runs)	Stevenage	Peterborough	48.8	27½	106.5
French National	Etendard	St. Pierre des Corps	Poitiers	62.7	37	101.5
German Federal	Two trains	Uelzen	Celle	32.5	21	92.9
Amtrak	Metroliners (2 runs)	Baltimore	Wilmington	68.4	45	91.2
VIA (Canada)	Turbotrain	Kingston	Guildwood	145.1	101	86.2
Italian State	No. 814	Rome	Chiusi	91.9	64	86.2
Swedish State	Two trains*	Hallsberg	Skvode	70.8	55	77.2
Freight						
British Rail	Freightliner	Carlisle	Wigan	105.3	95½	66.2
Atchison, Topeka & Santa Fe	No. 991	Kingman	Seligman	88.1	80	66.1
French National	Freight Express	Orange	St. Rambert de Albon	87.6	81	64.9

* Runs listed in both directions. [1] Fastest run in each country.

FASTEST AMERICAN PASSENGER TRAINS

Source: Donald M. Steffee

Railroad	Train	From	To	Miles	Time (min.)	Speed (mph)
Electrically Operated						
Amtrak	Metroliners (2 runs)	Baltimore	Wilmington	68.4	45	91.2
Amtrak	Metroliners (2 runs)	Baltimore	Wilmington	68.4	46	89.2
Amtrak	Metroliners (2 runs)*	Baltimore	Wilmington	68.4	47	87.3
Amtrak	Metroliner	Trenton	Newark	48.1	35	82.5
Amtrak	Metroliner	Trenton	Metro Park	33.9	25	81.4
Amtrak	Metroliners (3 runs)	Baltimore	Wilmington	68.4	51	80.5
Diesel Operated						
Amtrak	Southwest Limited	Garden City	Lamar	99.9	73	82.1
Amtrak	Lone Star	Marceline	Carrollton	39.1	30	.78.2
Amtrak	Southwest Limited	Lamar	Garden City	99.9	77	77.8
Amtrak	Southwest Limited	Dodge City	Hutchinson	120.1	93	77.5
Amtrak	San Francisco Zephyr	Akron	McCook	142.9	112	76.5

* Runs listed in both directions.

SELECTED MERCHANT FLEETS OF THE WORLD   Source: U.S. Maritime Administration

Country of Registry	Number	Gross Tons	Dead-weight Tons	Country of Registry	Number	Gross Tons	Dead-weight Tons
TOTAL—ALL COUNTRIES	24,096	375,828	641,219	Italy	603	10,679	17,858
United States	840	13,388	19,972	Ivory Coast	19	151	200
Privately Owned	571	11,163	17,321	Japan	1,846	36,471	62,455
Government Owned	269	2,226	2,650	*Korea, North	11	50	75
Reserve Fleet	238	1,919	2,322	Korea, South	241	2,184	3,718
Other	31	306	328	Kuwait	74	1,966	3,408
Algeria	55	945	1,494	Lebanon	53	178	230
Argentina	167	1,593	2,282	Liberia	2,627	81,852	157,788
Australia	79	1,313	2,029	Libya	24	830	1,537
Austria	14	59	92	Malaysia	49	533	796
Bangladesh	24	213	309	Maldives	35	101	125
Belgium	78	1,553	2,501	Mexico	52	548	847
Brazil	277	3,449	5,649	Morocco	39	268	436
British Colonies	140	2,647	4,338	Netherlands	443	4,826	7,687
*Bulgaria	112	956	1,382	New Zealand	24	160	204
Canada	79	576	869	Nigeria	26	307	502
Chile	43	393	599	Norway	978	29,527	52,569
*China (People's Rep.)	462	4,342	6,477	Pakistan	50	448	609
China (Republic of)	146	1,441	2,259	Panama	2,041	18,887	31,251
Colombia	36	234	282	Peru	39	374	571
*Cuba	81	584	791	Philippines	160	1,000	1,522
Cyprus	502	2,508	3,638	Poland	297	3,020	4,539
Czechoslovakia	13	144	217	Portugal	86	1,120	1,805
Denmark	351	4,925	8,316	*Romania	134	1,252	1,874
Ecuador	24	196	283	Saudi Arabia	47	881	1,544
Egypt	69	362	502	Singapore	575	7,083	11,895
Finland	184	2,113	3,353	Somalia	14	64	93
France	416	11,749	20,839	South Africa	42	445	588
Germany, East	157	1,274	1,798	Spain	479	6,910	12,195
Germany, West	590	8,902	14,642	Sweden	286	6,914	11,965
Ghana	22	136	180	Switzerland	25	251	375
Greece	2,379	29,461	49,825	Thailand	44	303	492
Honduras	15	84	88	Tunisia	19	95	144
*Hungary	19	65	92	Turkey	145	1,153	1,742
Iceland	29	54	81	*U.S.S.R.[1]	2,456	15,651	20,481
India	363	5,493	8,891	United Kingdom	1,377	30,495	51,106
Indonesia	209	853	1,145	Venezuela	58	540	761
Iran	59	1,057	1,759	Vietnam	23	107	155
Iraq	35	1,217	2,262	Yugoslavia	244	2,199	3,327
Ireland	21	166	258	Zaire	10	95	141

† Oceangoing ships (1,000 gross tons and more) as of December 31, 1977, Tonnage in thousands.   * Source material limited.
[1] Includes 27 U.S. Government-owned ships transferred to U.S.S.R. under lend-lease agreements.

FOREIGN COMMERCE AT SELECTED U.S. PORTS: 1977

Source: U.S. Corps of Engineers (figures in thousands of short tons of cargo)

Port	Imports	Exports	Port	Imports	Exports
ATLANTIC COAST PORTS			New Orleans, La.	25,214	39,074
New Haven Harbor, Conn.	1,963	209	Pascagoula Harbor, Miss.	8,965	2,228
New Castle and vicinity, Del.	3,407	1	Beaumont, Tex.	23,870	2,934
Wilmington Harbor, Del.	1,248	200	Brownsville, Tex.	848	284
Canaveral Harbor, Fla.	1,328	52	Corpus Christi, Tex.	19,926	4,282
Jacksonville Harbor, Fla.	3,994	1,815	Freeport Harbor, Tex.	10,140	1,277
Miami Harbor, Fla.	957	1,118	Galveston Channel, Tex.	1,653	5,922
Port Everglades Harbor, Fla.	1,705	145	Harbor Island, Tex.	7,392	10
Savannah Harbor, Ga.	4,130	2,074	Houston Ship Channel, Tex.	35,514	15,527
Portland Harbor, Maine	13,288	30	Matagorda Ship Channel, Tex.	2,958	261
Baltimore Harbor and Channels, Md.	14,101	14,040	Port Arthur, Tex.	14,009	2,601
Fall River Harbor, Mass.	5,285	1,947	Texas City Channel, Tex.	12,314	740
Port of Boston, Mass.	7,547	502	**PACIFIC COAST PORTS**		
Salem Harbor, Mass.	1,649	932	Skagway Harbor, Alaska	374	630
Portsmouth Harbor, N.H.	1,977	—	Long Beach Harbor, Calif.	17,545	4,988
Camden-Gloucester, N.J.	1,899	328	Los Angeles Harbor, Calif.	13,661	3,165
Paulsboro and vicinity, N.J.	12,805	66	Oakland Harbor, Calif.	1,737	1,991
Port of Albany, N.Y.	1,765	685	Richmond Harbor, Calif.	10,738	439
Port of New York, N.Y. and N.J.	60,921	5,687	San Francisco Harbor, Calif.	660	745
Port of Wilmington, N.C.	3,405	300	Stockton, Calif.	327	805
Marcus Hook and vicinity, Pa.	15,348	108	Barbers Point Harbor, Hawaii	4,795	—
Penn Manor and vicinity, Pa.	4,613	22	Honolulu Harbor, Hawaii	1,059	89
Philadelphia Harbor, Pa.	26,592	3,477	Coos Bay, Ore.	45	4,816
Providence River and Harbor, R.I.	1,246	408	Port of Astoria, Ore.	32	1,258
Charleston Harbor, S.C.	3,460	1,553	Port of Portland, Ore.	1,736	6,848
Norfolk Harbor, Va.	6,394	26,114	Anacortes Harbor, Wash.	6,161	60
Port of Newport News, Va.	801	5,618	Everett Harbor & Snohomish Riv., Wash.	665	1,305
San Juan Harbor, P.R.	3,312	295	Grays Harbor & Chehalis Riv., Wash.	1	2,138
GULF COAST PORTS			Port Angeles Harbor, Wash.	746	1,539
Mobile Harbor, Ala.	8,167	5,521	Port of Longview, Wash.	684	4,256
Tampa Harbor, Fla.	4,585	16,472	Port of Vancouver, Wash.	1,072	310
Baton Rouge, La.	16,826	8,679	Seattle Harbor, Wash.	4,630	1,990
Lake Charles (Calcasieu Riv. & Pass), La.	8,130	1,530	Tacoma Harbor, Wash.	2,678	4,579

MAJOR WORLD SHIP CANALS

Name	Location	Year Opened	Length (Miles)	Minimum Depth (Feet)	Minimum Width (Feet)
Baltic-White Sea	USSR: Povenets on Lake Onega to Belmorsk on White Sea	1933	140	16	NA
Cape Cod	U.S.: Buzzards Bay to Cape Cod Bay, Mass.	1914	17.4	32	450
Chesapeake and Delaware	U.S.: Delaware River to Chesapeake Bay	1927	19	35	450
Chicago Sanitary and Ship	U.S.: Lake Michigan to Des Plaines River, Ill.	1900	33.8	20	160
Corinth	Greece: Gulf of Athens to Gulf of Corinth	1893	3.5	26.25	69
Houston Ship	U.S.: Houston, Texas, to Gulf of Mexico	1914	50	36	300
Kiel (Nord-Ostsee)	Germany: North Sea to Baltic Sea	1895	53.2	38	144
Manchester Ship	England: Manchester to Mersey River	1894	35.5	28	90
Moscow	USSR: Moscow to Volga River	1937	80	18	280
North Sea	Netherlands: Amsterdam to IJmuiden	1876	17.5	45	443
Panama	Canal Zone: Cristóbal on Atlantic Ocean to Balboa on Pacific Ocean	1914	50.72	41.6	300
St. Lawrence Seaway	U.S.-Canada: Atlantic Ocean to Great Lakes system	1959	2,347*	27	450
Sault Sainte Marie (Canadian)	U.S.-Canada: Lake Huron to Lake Superior	1895	1.38	27	150
Sault Sainte Marie (American)	U.S.-Canada: Lake Huron to Lake Superior	1855	1.8	27	80
Suez	Egypt: Port Said on Mediterranean Sea to Suez on Gulf of Suez	1869	100.76	42	196
Terneuzen-Ghent	Belgium-Netherlands: Ghent to Scheldt Estuary at Terneuzen	1827	11	29	164
Volga-Baltic	USSR: Caspian Sea to Leningrad on Baltic Sea	1964	225	NA	NA
Volga-Don	USSR: Volga River to Don River, as linking waterway for Baltic-Black Sea route	1952	62	NA	NA
Welland	Canada: Lake Erie to Lake Ontario	1932	27.6	27	80

* Distance from Strait of Belle Isle to Duluth, Minnesota. NA = Not Available.

PANAMA CANAL USERS: 1977

SOURCE: *Statistical Abstract of the U.S., 1978*

Commercial Ocean Traffic

Nationality of vessel	Transits	Net tons (1,000)	Cargo (1,000 long tons)
UNITED STATES	1,022	10,900	8,700
Germany, West	582	5,700	3,800
Greece	1,163	14,100	17,500
Japan	893	12,100	9,200
Liberia	1,852	27,700	29,700
Netherlands	229	2,000	1,500
Norway	553	8,800	8,300
Panama	1,118	7,900	7,900
Sweden	260	3,600	2,500
United Kingdom	1,106	12,200	10,000
All Others	3,118	28,400	23,900

PANAMA CANAL TRAFFIC, 1950-1977

SOURCE: *Statistical Abstract of the U.S., 1978*

	Total Transits	Commercial Ocean Traffic	
		Transits	Cargo (long tons)
1950	5,900	5,400	28,900,000
1960	12,100	10,800	59,300,000
1965	12,900	11,800	76,600,000
1970	15,500	13,700	114,300,000
1971	15,300	14,000	118,600,000
1972	15,200	13,800	109,200,000
1973	15,100	13,800	126,100,000
1974	15,300	14,000	147,900,000
1975	14,700	13,600	140,100,000
1976	13,200	12,200	117,200,000
1976, TQ*	3,300	3,000	30,900,000
1977	13,100	11,900	123,000,000

* Transition quarter, July-Sept.

WORLD CITIES: STANDARD TIME DIFFERENCES

When it is 12 noon in New York (Eastern Standard Time), the standard time in other cities is as follows:

City	Time	City	Time	City	Time	City	Time
Alexandria	7:00 p.m.	Delhi	10:30 p.m.	Ketchikan	9:00 a.m.	Rome	6:00 p.m.
Amsterdam	6:00 p.m.	Denver	10:00 a.m.	Kinshasa	6:00 p.m.	Salt Lake City	10:00 a.m.
Anchorage	7:00 a.m.	Djakarta	12:00 Midnight	Lima	12:00 Noon	San Francisco	9:00 a.m.
Athens	7:00 p.m.			Lisbon	6:00 p.m.		
Auckland	5:00 a.m.*	Dublin	5:00 p.m.	London		San Juan	1:00 p.m.
Baghdad	8:00 p.m.	Fairbanks	7:00 a.m.	(Greenwich)	5:00 p.m.	Santiago	1:00 p.m.
Bangkok	12:00 Midnight	Frankfurt	6:00 p.m.	Los Angeles	9:00 a.m.	Seattle	9:00 a.m.
		Frobisher Bay	1:00 p.m.	Madrid	6:00 p.m.	Seoul	2:00 a.m.*
Barcelona	6:00 p.m.			Manila	1:00 a.m.*	Shanghai	1:00 a.m.*
Basra	8:00 p.m.	Gander	1:30 p.m.	Melbourne	3:00 a.m.*	Singapore	12:30 a.m.*
Beirut	7:00 p.m.	Geneva	6:00 p.m.	Miami	12:00 Noon	Stockholm	6:00 p.m.
Berlin	6:00 p.m.	Glasgow	5:00 p.m.	Monrovia	4:15 p.m.	Suva	4:00 a.m.*
Bogotá	12:00 Noon	Halifax	1:00 p.m.	Montevideo	2:00 p.m.	Sydney	3:00 a.m.*
Bombay	10:30 p.m.	Hamilton		Moscow	8:00 p.m.	Tehran	8:30 p.m.
Boston	12:00 Noon	(Bermuda)	1:00 p.m.	New Orleans	11:00 a.m.	Tel Aviv	7:00 p.m.
Brussels	6:00 p.m.	Havana	12:00 Noon	Nome	6:00 a.m.	Tokyo	2:00 a.m.*
Bucharest	7:00 p.m.	Helsinki	7:00 p.m.	Nouméa	4:00 a.m.*	Tucson	10:00 a.m.
Budapest	6:00 p.m.	Ho Chi Minh City		Oslo	6:00 p.m.	Valparaíso	1:00 p.m.
Buenos Aires	2:00 p.m.	(Saigon)	1:00 a.m.*	Papeete	7:00 a.m.	Vancouver	9:00 a.m.
Cairo	7:00 p.m.	Hong Kong	1:00 a.m.*	Paris	6:00 p.m.	Vienna	6:00 p.m.
Calcutta	10:30 p.m.	Honolulu	7:00 a.m.	Peking	1:00 a.m.*	Vladivostok	2:00 a.m.*
Cape Town	7:00 p.m.	Istanbul	7:00 p.m.	Phoenix	10:00 a.m.	Warsaw	6:00 p.m.
Caracas	1:00 p.m.	Jerusalem	7:00 p.m.	Portland	9:00 a.m.	Washington, D.C.	12:00 Noon
Chicago	11:00 a.m.	Johannesburg	7:00 p.m.	Rangoon	11:30 p.m.		
Copenhagen	6:00 p.m.	Juneau	9:00 a.m.	Recife	2:00 p.m.	Whitehorse	9:00 a.m.
Dakar	5:00 p.m.	Karachi	10:00 p.m.	Reykjavík	5:00 p.m.	Yokohama	2:00 a.m.*
Damascus	7:00 p.m.			Rio de Janeiro	2:00 p.m.	Zürich	6:00 p.m.

* = following day.

LARGE PASSENGER LINERS

SOURCE: Cruise Lines International Association

Ship Name	Line	Flag	Length, ft.	Tonnage	Max. No. Passengers
Queen Elizabeth 2	Cunard Line Ltd.	British	963	67,139	1,815
Canberra	P & O	British	820	45,000	1,800
Oriana	P & O	British	804	42,000	1,800
Oceanic	Home Lines Cruises	Panamanian	774	39,241	1,034
Festivale	Carnival Cruise Lines	Panamanian	760	38,175	1,400
Rotterdam	Holland America Cruises	Netherlands Ant.	748	38,000	1,050
Italis	Chandris, Inc.	Panamanian	723	34,449	2,258
Arcadia	P & O	British	721	30,000	1,275
Eugenio C.	Costa Cruises	Italian	713	30,000	1,637
Galileo Galilei	Italian Line Cruises, Int'l	Italian	700	27,905	900
Guglielmo Marconi	Italian Line Cruises, Int'l	Italian	700	27,905	900
Angelina	Costa Cruises	Italian	672	24,400	800
Mardi Gras	Carnival Cruise Lines	Panamanian	650	27,250	1,240
Statendam	Holland America Cruises	Netherlands Ant.	642	24,500	800
Britanis	Chandris, Inc.	Greek	642	24,351	1,600
Ellinis	Chandris, Inc.	Greek	642	24,351	1,642
Carnivale	Carnival Cruise Lines	Panamanian	640	27,250	1,350
Song of Norway	Royal Caribbean Cruise Line	Norwegian	635	23,005	1,040
Doric	Home Lines Cruises	Panamanian	620	25,300	720
Vistafjord	Norwegian America Line	Norwegian	628	25,000	660
Emerald Seas	Eastern Steamship Lines	Panamanian	622	24,458	920
Sagafjord	Norwegian America Line	Norwegian	620	24,000	475
Veendam	Holland America Cruises	Panamanian	617	23,500	666
Volendam	Holland America Cruises	Panamanian	617	23,500	679
Fairsea	Sitmar Cruises	Liberian	608	25,000	830
Fairwind	Sitmar Cruises	Liberian	608	25,000	830
Federico C.	Costa Cruises	Italian	606	20,416	800
Carla C.	Costa Cruises	Italian	600	20,477	748
Royal Viking Sea	Royal Viking Line	Norwegian	583	22,000	500
Royal Viking Sky	Royal Viking Line	Norwegian	583	22,000	500
Royal Viking Star	Royal Viking Line	Norwegian	581	22,000	500
Alexandr Pushkin	Baltic Shipping Company	USSR	580	19,860	700
Mikhail Lermontov	Baltic Shipping Company	USSR	580	19,860	700

WORLD'S LEADING BRIDGES

Bridges listed here are grouped by type of construction and ranked by the length of their spans.

SOURCE: American Society of Civil Engineers

SUSPENSION BRIDGES

Bridge	Span Meters	Feet	Completion Date	Location
Humber	1,410	4,626	*	Hull, England
Verrazano Narrows	1,298	4,260	1964	New York City
Golden Gate	1,280	4,200	1937	San Francisco
Mackinac Straits	1,158	3,800	1957	Mackinaw City, Mich.
Bosporus	1,074	3,524	1973	Bosporus, Turkey
George Washington	1,067	3,500	1931	New York City
Salazar	1,013	3,323	1966	Lisbon
Forth Road	1,006	3,300	1964	Queensferry, Scotland
Severn	988	3,240	1966	Beachley, England
Tacoma Narrows II	853	2,800	1950	Puget Sound, Wash.
Kanmon Straits	712	2,336	1973	Kyushu-Honshu, Japan
Angostura	712	2,336	1967	Ciudad Bolivar, Venezuela
Transbay (2 spans)	704	2,310	1936	San Francisco
Bronx-Whitestone	701	2,300	1939	New York City
Pierre Laporte	668	2,190	1970	Quebec, Canada
Delaware Memorial I & II	655	2,150	1951 & 1968	Wilmington, Del.
Seaway Skyway	655	2,150	1960	St. Lawrence R. at Ogdensburg, New York
Walt Whitman	610	2,000	1957	Philadelphia
Gas Pipe Line Bridge	610	2,000	1951	Atchafalaya R., Louisiana
Tancarville	608	1,995	1959	Tancarville, France
The New Lillebaelt	600	1,969	1970	Lillebaelt Strait, Denmark
Ambassador International	564	1,850	1929	Detroit
Throgs Neck	549	1,800	1961	New York City
Benjamin Franklin	533	1,750	1926	Philadelphia
Skjomen	525	1,722	1971	Narvik, Norway
Kvalsund	525	1,722	1977	Hammerfest, Norway
Emmerich	500	1,640	1965	Emmerich, West Germany
Bear Mountain	497	1,632	1924	Peekskill, N.Y.
Williamsburg	488	1,600	1903	New York City
Wm. Preston Lane Jr. Memorial I & II	488	1,600	1952 & 1973	Sandy Point-Kent Island, Md.
Newport	488	1,600	1969	Newport, R.I.
Brooklyn	486	1,595	1883	New York City
Lions Gate	472	1,550	1939	Vancouver, Canada
Sotra	468	1,535	1971	Knarrevik-Drottningsvik, Norway

CANTILEVER BRIDGES

Bridge	Span Meters	Feet	Completion Date	Location
Quebec (Railway)	549	1,800	1917	Quebec, Canada
Forth (Railway)	2@521	2@1,710	1890	Queensferry, Scotland
Minato Ohashi	510	1,673	1974	Osaka, Japan
Commodore John Barry	501	1,644	1974	Chester, Pa.-Bridgeport, N.J.
Greater New Orleans	480	1,576	1958	New Orleans
Howrah	457	1,500	1943	Calcutta, India
Transbay	427	1,400	1936	San Francisco
Baton Rouge	376	1,235	1968	Baton Rouge, La.
Tappan Zee	369	1,212	1955	Tarrytown, N.Y.
Longview	366	1,200	1930	Longview, Wash.
Patapsco River	366	1,200	1976	Baltimore Outer Harbor Crossing, Md.
Queensboro	360	1,182	1909	New York City

* Under construction.

STEEL ARCH BRIDGES

| | Span | | Comple- | |
Bridge	Meters	Feet	tion Date	Location
New River Gorge	518	1,700	1977	Fayetteville,W. Va.
Bayonne (Kill Van Kull)	504	1,652	1931	New York City
Sydney Harbor	503	1,650	1932	Sydney, Australia
Fremont	383	1,255	1973	Portland, Oregon
Port Mann	366	1,200	1964	Vancouver, British Columbia
Thatcher	344	1,128	1962	Panama Canal
Laviolette	335	1,100	1967	Trois Rivieres, Que., Canada
Zdakov	330	1,083	1967	Vltava River, Czechoslovakia
Runcorn-Widnes	330	1,082	1961	Mersey River, England
Birchenough	329	1,080	1935	Ft. Victoria, Rhodesia
Glen Canyon	313	1,028	1959	Colorado River, Arizona
Lewiston-Queenston	305	1,000	1962	Niagara River, U.S.-Canada
Perrine	303	993	1976	Snake River, Twin Falls, Idaho

CONTINUOUS TRUSS BRIDGES

| | Span | | Comple- | |
Bridge	Meters	Feet	tion Date	Location
Astoria	376	1,232	1966	Astoria, Ore.
Oshima	325	1,066	1976	Oshima Island, Japan
Croton Reservoir	320	1,052	1970	Croton, N.Y.
Tenmon	300	984	1966	Kumamoto, Japan
Kuronoseto	300	984	1974	Nagashima-Kyushu, Japan
Ravenswood	275	902	*	Ohio River, W.Va.
Dubuque	258	845	1943	Mississippi Riv., Iowa
Braga Memorial	256	840	1966	Somerset, Mass.
Graf Spee	256	839	1936	Germany
Earle S. Clements	251	2@826	1956	Shawneetown, Ill.
Lincoln Trail	251	826	1966	Cannelton, Ind.
Cairo	250	821	*	Alexander County, Ill.
Mathews	247	810	1953	Jacksonville, Fla.
St. Louis	245	804	1944	Mississippi Riv., Mo.
Kingston-Rhinecliff	244	800	1957	Hudson River
Sherman Minton	244	800	1961	New Albany, Ind.

CABLE-STAYED BRIDGES

| | Span | | Comple- | |
Bridge	Meters	Feet	tion Date	Location
Second Hooghly	457	1,500	*	Calcutta, India
St. Nazaire	404	1,325	1975	Loire River, France
Mississippi River	376	1,235	*	Luling, La.
Düsseldorf-Flehe	367	1,205	*	Rhine Riv., W. Germany
Duisburg-Neuenkamp	350	1,148	1970	Duisburg, West Germany
Mesopotamia	340	1,116	1972	Corrientes, Argentina
Westgate	336	1,102	1970	Melbourne, Aust.
Zarate	330	1,083	1976	Paraná Riv., Argentina
Brazo Largo	330	1,083	1977	Paraná Riv., Argentina
Kohlbrand	325	1,066	1974	Hamburg, West Germany
"Kniebrucke"	320	1,050	1969	Dusseldorf, West Germany
Brotonne	320	1,050	1976	Seine River, France
Erskine	305	1,000	1971	Glasgow, Scotland
Bratislava	303	994	1972	Danube River, Czechoslovakia
Severinsbrucke Koln	302	991	1959	Cologne, West Germany
Kiev	300	984	1975	Kiev, USSR
Columbia River	299	981	1977	Pasco-Kennewick, Wash.
Deggenau	290	951	1975	Donau Riv., W. Germany
Mannheim-Nord	288	944	1972	Mannheim, West Germany
Wadi Kuf	282	925	1971	Libya, Africa
Leverkusen	280	919	1965	Leverkusen, West Germany
Freidrich Ebert	280	919	1967	Bonn, W. Germany
Bonn-Nord	280	919	1967	Bonn, W. Germany

CONCRETE ARCH BRIDGES

| | Span | | Comple- | |
Bridge	Meters	Feet	tion Date	Location
Gladesville	305	1,000	1964	Sydney, Australia
Amizade	290	951	1964	Parana River, at Foz do Iguassu, Brazil
Arrabida	270	886	1963	Porto, Portugal
Sando	264	866	1943	Kramfors, Sweden
Shibenik	246	808	1966	Krka River, Yugoslavia
Fiumarella	231	758	1961	Catanzaro, Italy
Zaporozhe	228	748	1952	Dnepr R., USSR
Novi Sad	211	692	1961	Danube River, Yugoslavia
Lingenau	210	689	1967	Bregenz, Austria
Van Stadens Gorge	198	650	1970	Port Elizabeth, South Africa
Martin Gil	192	631	1942	Andavias, Spain

LONGEST BRIDGES IN THE WORLD

Measurements that determine the longest bridges in the world include the bridge span or spans, as well as its approach roads.

SOURCE: American Society of Civil Engineers

Name of Bridge	Length in Feet	Completed	Location
Lake Pontchartrain Causeway II	126,055	1969	New Orleans—Lewisburg, La.
Lake Pontchartrain Causeway I	125,827	1956	New Orleans—Lewisburg, La.
Chesapeake Bay Bridge-Tunnel	93,203	1964	Cape Henry—Cape Charles, Va.
Presidente Costa e Silva Bridge	45,866	1974	Rio de Janeiro—Niteroi, Brazil
Marathon Key–Bahia Honda Key Bridge	38,915	1910	Florida Keys
San Mateo—Hayward Bridge I	37,183	1929	San Francisco Bay
San Mateo—Hayward Bridge II	35,708	1967	San Francisco Bay
Lake Maracaibo Bridge	28,473	1962	Punta Piedras—Punta Iguana, Venezuela
Transbay Bridge	27,286	1936	San Francisco-Oakland
Lake Pontchartrain Trestle	24,927	1927	Blind Bayou—Slidell, La.
Mackinac Straits Bridge	23,390	1957	Mackinaw City—St. Ignace, Mich.
James River Bridge	23,177	1928	Chuckatuck Creek—Newport News, Va.
Huey P. Long Bridge	22,996	1935	New Orleans
Sunshine Skyway (Structure C)	22,373	1954	St. Petersburg—Palmetto, Fla.
Richmond—San Rafael Bridge	21,965	1957	San Pablo Bay, Calif.
Astoria Bridge	21,697	1966	Pt. Ellice, Wash.—Astoria, Ore.
Chesapeake Bay Bridge	21,286	1952	Sandy Point—Kent Island, Md.
Öland Island Bridge	19,882	1972	Svinö—Möllstorp, Sweden
Oosterschelde Bridge	16,475	1965	Middelburg—Zierikzee, Netherlands
Tappan Zee Bridge	16,013	1955	South Nyack—Tarrytown, N.Y.

U.S. POPULATION AND AREA: 1790–1978

Source: Bureau of the Census (Series P–25)

POPULATION

Year	Number (1,000)	Percent Increase	Per Square Mile[1]	AREA (1,000 sq. mi.) Land	AREA (1,000 sq. mi.) Water
1790	3,929	(X)	4.5	865	24
1800	5,308	35.1	6.1	865	24
1810	7,240	36.4	4.3	1,682	34
1820	9,638	33.1	5.6	1,749	39
1830	12,866	33.5	7.4	1,749	39
1840	17,069	32.7	9.8	1,749	39
1850	23,192	35.9	7.9	2,940	53
1860	31,443	35.6	10.6	2,970	53
1870	39,818	26.6	13.4	2,970	53
1880	50,156	26.0	16.9	2,970	53
1890	62,948	25.5	21.2	2,970	53
1900	75,995	20.7	25.6	2,970	53
1910	91,972	21.0	31.0	2,970	53
1920	105,711	14.9	35.6	2,969	53
1930	122,775	16.1	41.2	2,977	45
1940	131,669	7.2	44.2	2,977	45
1950	150,697	14.5	50.7	2,975	48
1960	179,323	18.5	50.5	3,541	74
1970	203,235	13.3	57.5	3,537	78
1971*	206,219	1.5	58.3	3,537	78
1972*	208,234	1.0	58.9	3,537	78
1973*	209,860	0.8	59.3	3,537	78
1974*	211,381	0.7	59.8	3,537	78
1975*	213,121	0.8	60.3	3,537	78
1976*	214,659	0.7	60.7	3,537	78
1978*	218,059	0.8	61.7	3,537	78

(X) Not applicable. [1] Land area only. * As of July 1.

U.S. POPULATION BY AGE GROUP

Source: Bureau of the Census (Series P–25)

Age Group	1978	PROJECTIONS (figures in thousands) 1980	1990	2000
All Ages	218,059	222,159	243,513	260,378
Under 5 years	15,361	16,020	19,437	17,852
5 to 9 years	16,885	16,096	19,040	19,000
10 to 14 years	18,577	17,800	16,718	20,153
15 to 19 years	20,996	20,609	16,777	19,727
20 to 24 years	20,243	20,918	17,953	16,898
25 to 29 years	17,944	18,930	20,169	16,649
30 to 34 years	15,833	17,242	20,917	17,981
35 to 39 years	13,020	14,033	19,261	20,435
40 to 44 years	11,300	11,688	17,331	20,909
45 to 49 years	11,353	11,030	13,889	18,990
50 to 54 years	11,824	11,668	11,422	16,885
55 to 59 years	11,236	11,401	10,416	13,106
60 to 64 years	9,432	9,797	10,360	10,151
65 to 69 years	8,575	8,700	10,022	9,192
69 to 74 years	6,359	6,793	7,782	8,244
75 to 79 years	4,168	4,324	5,501	6,394
80 to 84 years	2,746	2,816	3,639	4,236
85 years and over	2,206	2,294	2,881	3,756

RESIDENT U.S. POPULATION BY STATE AND RANK, JULY 1, 1978

Source: U.S. Bureau of the Census (Series P–25)   (Population in thousands)

Rank	State	Population	Rank	State	Population	Rank	State	Population
1	California	22,294	18	Maryland	4,143	35	Nebraska	1,565
2	New York	17,748	19	Minnesota	4,008	36	Utah	1,307
3	Texas	13,014	20	Louisiana	3,966	37	New Mexico	1,212
4	Pennsylvania	11,750	21	Washington	3,744	38	Maine	1,091
5	Illinois	11,243	22	Alabama	3,742	39	Rhode Island	935
6	Ohio	10,749	23	Kentucky	3,498	40	Hawaii	897
7	Michigan	9,189	24	Connecticut	3,099	41	Idaho	878
8	Florida	8,594	25	South Carolina	2,918	42	New Hampshire	871
9	New Jersey	7,327	26	Iowa	2,896	43	Montana	785
10	Massachusetts	5,774	27	Oklahoma	2,880	44	South Dakota	690
11	North Carolina	5,577	28	Colorado	2,670	45	District of Columbia	674
12	Indiana	5,374	29	Oregon	2,444	46	Nevada	660
13	Virginia	5,148	30	Mississippi	2,404	47	North Dakota	652
14	Georgia	5,084	31	Arizona	2,354	48	Delaware	583
15	Missouri	4,860	32	Kansas	2,348	49	Vermont	487
16	Wisconsin	4,679	33	Arkansas	2,186	50	Wyoming	424
17	Tennessee	4,357	34	West Virginia	1,860	51	Alaska	403

LEADING STANDARD METROPOLITAN STATISTICAL AREAS: COUNTY COMPONENTS*

Source: U.S. Bureau of the Census

Anaheim-Sta. Ana-Garden Grove, Calif.: Orange. **Atlanta, Ga.:** Butts, Cherokee, Clayton, Cobb, DeKalb, Douglas, Fayette, Forsyth, Fulton, Gwinnett, Henry, Newton, Paulding, Rockdale & Walton. **Baltimore, Md.:** Anne Arundel, Baltimore, Carroll, Harford, Howard & Baltimore city. †**Boston-Lowell-Brockton-Lawrence-Haverhill, Mass.-N.H.:** Essex, Middlesex, Norfolk, Plymouth & Suffolk, Mass.; Rockingham, N.H. **Buffalo, N.Y.:** Erie & Niagara. **Chicago, Ill.:** Cook, DuPage, Kane, Lake, McHenry & Will. **Cincinnati, Ohio-Ky.-Ind.:** Clermont, Hamilton & Warren, Ohio; Boone, Campbell & Kenton, Ky.; Dearborn, Ind. **Cleveland, Ohio:** Cuyahoga, Geauga, Lake & Medina. **Columbus, Ohio:** Delaware, Fairfield, Franklin, Madison & Pickaway. **Dallas-Ft. Worth, Tex.:** Collin, Dallas, Denton, Ellis, Hood, Johnson, Kaufman, Parker, Rockwall, Tarrant & Wise. **Dayton, Ohio:** Greene, Miami, Montgomery & Preble. **Denver-Boulder, Colo.:** Adams, Arapahoe, Boulder, Denver, Douglas, Gilpin & Jefferson. **Detroit, Mich.:** Lapeer, Livingston, Macomb, Oakland, St. Clair & Wayne. **Houston, Tex.:** Brazoria, Ft. Bend, Harris, Liberty, Montgomery & Waller. **Indianapolis, Ind.:** Boone, Hamilton, Hancock, Hendricks, Johnson, Marion, Morgan & Shelby. **Kansas City, Mo.-Kans.:** Cass, Clay, Jackson, Platte & Ray, Mo.; Johnson & Wyandotte, Kans. **Los Angeles-Long Beach, Calif.:** Los Angeles. **Louisville, Ky.-Ind.:** Bullitt, Jefferson & Oldham, Ky.; Clark & Floyd, Ind. **Memphis, Tenn.-Ark.-Miss.:** Shelby & Tipton, Tenn.; Crittenden, Ark.; De Soto, Miss. **Miami, Fla.:** Dade. **Milwaukee, Wis.:** Milwaukee, Ozaukee, Washington & Waukesha. **Minneapolis-St. Paul, Minn.-Wis.:** Anoka, Carver, Chisago,

Dakota, Hennepin, Ramsey, Scott, Washington & Wright, Minn.; St. Croix, Wis. **Nassau-Suffolk, N.Y.:** Nassau & Suffolk. **Newark, N.J.:** Essex, Morris, Somerset & Union. **New Orleans, La.:** Jefferson, Orleans, St. Bernard & St. Tammany parishes. **New York, N.Y.-N.J.:** Bronx, Kings, New York, Putnam, Queens, Richmond, Rockland & Westchester, N.Y.; Bergen, N.J. **Philadelphia, Pa.-N.J.:** Bucks, Chester, Delaware, Montgomery & Philadelphia, Pa.; Burlington, Camden & Gloucester, N.J. **Phoenix, Ariz.:** Maricopa. **Pittsburgh, Pa.:** Allegheny, Beaver, Washington & Westmorland. **Portland, Oreg.-Wash.:** Clackamas, Multnomah & Washington, Oregon; Clark, Washington. †**Providence-Warwick-Pawtucket, Rhode Island:** Bristol, Kent, Providence & Washington. **Riverside-San Bernardino-Ontario, Calif.:** Riverside & San Bernardino. **Rochester, N.Y.:** Livingston, Monroe, Ontario, Orleans & Wayne. **Sacramento, Calif.:** Placer, Sacramento & Yolo. **St. Louis, Mo.-Ill.:** Franklin, Jefferson, St. Charles, St. Louis & St. Louis city, Mo.; Clinton, Madison, Monroe & St. Clair, Ill. **San Antonio, Tex.:** Bexar, Comal & Guadalupe. **San Diego, Calif.:** San Diego. **San Francisco-Oakland, Calif.:** Alameda, Contra Costa, Marin, San Francisco & San Mateo. **San Jose, Calif.:** Santa Clara. **Seattle-Everett, Wash.:** King & Snohomish. **Tampa-St. Petersburg, Fla.:** Hillsborough, Pasco & Pinellas. **Washington, D.C.-Md.-Va.:** Dist. of Columbia; Charles, Montgomery & Prince Georges, Md.; Arlington, Fairfax, Loudoun, Prince William, & cities of Alexandria, Fairfax, Falls Church, Manassas & Manassas Park, Va.

* Names are counties, unless otherwise specified. †New England County Metropolitan Area.

LARGEST U.S. METROPOLITAN AREAS (Rank by 1977 Estimate)

Source: U.S. Bureau of the Census (Series P-26)

Rank 1977	Standard Metropolitan Statistical Area	1970 Population	1977 Estimate
1	New York, N.Y.-N.J.	9,973,716	9,386,700
2	Los Angeles-Long Beach, Calif.	7,041,980	7,031,000
3	Chicago, Ill.	6,977,611	7,017,400
4	Philadelphia, Pa.-N.J.	4,824,110	4,793,900
5	Detroit, Mich.	4,435,051	4,370,200
6	Boston-Lowell-Brockton-Lawrence-Haverhill, Mass.-N.H.*	3,848,593	3,897,800
7	San Francisco-Oakland, Calif.	3,107,355	3,182,200
8	Washington, D.C.-Md.-Va.	2,910,111	3,020,100
9	Nassau-Suffolk, N.Y.	2,555,868	2,687,900
10	Dallas-Fort Worth, Tex.	2,378,353	2,673,300
11	Houston, Tex.	1,999,316	2,512,200
12	St. Louis, Mo.-Ill.	2,410,602	2,379,800
13	Pittsburgh, Pa.	2,401,362	2,294,500
14	Baltimore, Md.	2,071,016	2,146,900
15	Minneapolis-St. Paul, Minn.-Wis.	1,965,391	2,037,200
16	Newark, N.J.	2,057,468	1,969,200
17	Cleveland, Ohio	2,063,729	1,949,600
18	Atlanta, Ga.	1,595,517	1,831,500
19	Anaheim-Sta. Ana-Garden Grove, Calif.	1,421,233	1,800,800
20	San Diego, Calif.	1,357,854	1,683,000
21	Denver-Boulder, Colo.	1,239,477	1,464,300
22	Miami, Fla.	1,267,792	1,441,200
23	Seattle-Everett, Wash.	1,424,605	1,427,200
24	Milwaukee, Wis.	1,403,884	1,426,500
25	Tampa-St. Petersburg, Fla.	1,088,549	1,380,500
26	Cincinnati, Ohio-Ky.-Ind.	1,387,207	1,375,400
27	Buffalo, N.Y.	1,349,211	1,313,000
28	Riverside-San Bernardino-Ontario, Calif.	1,141,307	1,305,600
29	Kansas City, Mo.-Kans.	1,273,926	1,293,300
30	Phoenix, Ariz.	971,228	1,253,600
31	San Jose, Calif.	1,065,313	1,217,300
32	Indianapolis, Ind.	1,111,352	1,143,800
33	New Orleans, La.	1,046,470	1,133,100
34	Portland, Oreg.-Wash.	1,007,130	1,121,500
35	Columbus, Ohio	1,017,847	1,086,800
36	Hartford-New Britain-Bristol, Conn.*	1,035,195	1,052,000
37	San Antonio, Tex.	888,179	1,024,900
38	Rochester, N.Y.	961,516	970,200
39	Sacramento, Calif.	803,793	929,400
40	Memphis, Tenn.-Ark.-Miss.	834,103	886,500
41	Louisville, Ky.-Ind.	867,330	883,000
42	Fort Lauderdale-Hollywood, Fla.	620,100	864,400
43	Providence-Warwick-Pawtucket, R.I.*	855,495	852,000
44	Dayton, Ohio	852,531	833,100
45	Salt Lake City-Ogden, Utah	705,458	822,200
46	Bridgeport-Stamford-Norwalk-Danbury, Conn.*	792,814	807,000
47	Birmingham, Ala.	767,230	805,300
48	Norfolk-Virginia Beach-Portsmouth, Va.-N.C.	732,600	802,600
49	Albany-Schenectady-Troy, N.Y.	777,977	794,300
50	Toledo, Ohio-Mich.	762,658	777,400
51	Greensboro-Winston-Salem-High Point, N.C.	724,129	774,000
52	Nashville-Davidson, Tenn.	699,271	773,000
53	Oklahoma City, Okla.	699,092	768,500
54	New Haven-West Haven-Waterbury-Meriden, Conn.*	744,948	758,900
55	Honolulu, Hawaii	630,528	723,400
56	Jacksonville, Fla.	621,827	694,200

Rank 1977	Standard Metropolitan Statistical Area	1970 Population	1977 Estimate
57	Akron, Ohio	679,239	660,800
58	Syracuse, N.Y.	636,596	647,500
59	Gary-Hammond-E. Chicago, Ind.	633,367	644,300
60	Worcester-Fitchburg-Leominster, Mass.*	637,037	643,400
61	Northeast Pennsylvania, Pa.	621,882	628,700
62	Allentown-Bethlehem-Easton, Pa.-N.J.	594,382	624,100
63	Tulsa, Okla.	549,153	609,700
64	Richmond, Va.	547,542	603,300
65	Charlotte-Gastonia, N.C.	557,785	597,000
66	New Brunswick-Perth Amboy-Sayreville, N.J.	583,813	593,500
67	Orlando, Fla.	453,270	593,000
68	Springfield-Chicopee-Holyoke, Mass.*	583,031	589,400
69	Omaha, Nebr.-Iowa	542,646	580,900
70	Grand Rapids, Mich.	539,225	575,600
71	Jersey City, N.J.	607,839	564,100
72	Youngstown-Warren, Ohio	537,124	540,600
73	Greenville-Spartanburg, S.C.	473,454	526,400
74	Wilmington, Del.-N.J.-Md.	499,493	516,200
75	Flint, Mich.	508,664	514,400
76	Long Branch-Asbury Park, N.J.	461,849	491,600
77	Raleigh-Durham, N.C.	419,254	487,100
78	West Palm Beach-Boca Raton, Fla.	348,993	476,900
79	Austin, Tex.	323,158	474,300
80	Fresno, Calif.	413,329	471,900
81	New Bedford-Fall River, Mass.*	444,301	467,800
82	Oxnard-Simi Valley-Ventura, Calif.	378,497	467,800
83	Paterson-Clifton-Passaic, N.J.	460,782	461,600
84	Lansing-East Lansing, Mich.	424,271	455,100
85	Tucson, Ariz.	351,667	454,600
86	Knoxville, Tenn.	409,409	449,100
87	Baton Rouge, La.	375,628	435,200
88	El Paso, Tex.	359,291	434,700
89	Harrisburg, Pa.	410,505	428,900
90	Mobile, Ala.	376,690	425,100
91	Tacoma, Wash.	412,344	423,400
92	Johnson City-Kingsport-Bristol, Tenn.-Va.	373,591	408,200
93	Chattanooga, Tenn.-Ga.	370,857	403,200
94	Albuquerque, N. Mex.	333,266	401,900
95	Canton, Ohio	393,789	401,000
96	Wichita, Kans.	389,352	394,900
97	Charleston-N. Charleston, S.C.	336,125	385,400
98	Davenport-Rock I.-Moline, Iowa-Ill.	362,638	375,000
99	Columbia, S.C.	322,880	374,300
100	Fort Wayne, Ind.	361,984	370,400
101	Little Rock-N. Little Rock, Ark.	323,296	369,200
102	Newport News-Hampton, Va.	333,140	364,000
103	Beaumont-Port Arthur-Orange, Tex.	347,568	363,900
104	Bakersfield, Calif.	330,234	363,000
105	Peoria, Ill.	341,979	362,000
106	Las Vegas, Nev.	273,288	359,800
107	Shreveport, La.	333,826	356,500
108	York, Pa.	329,540	351,800
109	Lancaster, Pa.	320,079	347,900
110	Des Moines, Iowa	313,562	333,000
111	Utica-Rome, N.Y.	340,670	326,800
112	Trenton, N.J.	304,116	316,900
113	Madison, Wis.	290,272	313,000
114	Stockton, Calif.	291,073	311,400
115	Spokane, Wash.	287,487	310,200
116	Binghamton, N.Y.-Pa.	302,672	305,700

* New England County Metropolitan Area.

STANDARD CONSOLIDATED STATISTICAL AREAS (SCSA)

Source: U.S. Bureau of the Census

Rank 1977	Standard Consolidated Statistical Area	1970 Population	1977 Estimate
1	New York-Newark-Jersey City, N.Y.-N.J.-Conn.	17,494,149	16,485,000
2	Los Angeles-Long Beach-Anaheim, Calif.	9,983,017	10,605,200
3	Chicago-Gary, Ill.-Ind.	7,610,978	7,661,700
4	Philadelphia-Wilmington-Trenton, Pa.-Del.-Md.-N.J.	5,627,719	5,627,000
5	San Francisco-Oakland-San Jose, Calif.	4,423,797	4,693,400
6	Detroit-Ann Arbor, Mich.	4,669,154	4,620,400
7	Boston-Lawrence-Lowell, Mass.-N.H.	3,848,593	3,525,000 (1976)
8	Cleveland-Akron-Lorain, Ohio	2,999,811	2,874,400
9	Houston-Galveston, Tex.	2,169,128	2,707,600
10	Miami-Fort Lauderdale, Fla.	1,887,892	2,305,600
11	Seattle-Tacoma, Wash.	1,836,949	1,850,600
12	Cincinnati-Hamilton, Ohio-Ky.-Ind.	1,613,414	1,625,900
13	Milwaukee-Racine, Wis.	1,574,722	1,603,300

VOTER PARTICIPATION: PRESIDENTIAL ELECTIONS
PERCENTAGE OF VOTING AGE POPULATION WHO VOTED
Source: U.S. Bureau of the Census

	1976 election	1972 election	1968 election		1976 election	1972 election	1968 election
Sex:				**Residence:**			
Male	59.6	64.1	69.8	Metropolitan	59.2	64.3	68.0
Female	58.8	62.0	66.0	Nonmetropolitan	59.1	59.4	67.3
Race:				**School year completed:**			
White	60.9	64.5	69.1	8 or less	44.1	47.4	54.5
Black	48.7	52.1	57.6	9–11	47.2	52.0	61.3
Spanish origin*	31.8	37.4	N.A.	12	59.4	65.4	72.5
Age:				More than 12	73.5	78.8	81.2
18–20	38.0	48.3	33.3	**Employment:**			
21–24	45.6	50.7	51.1	Employed	62.0	66.0	71.1
25–34	55.4	59.7	62.5	Unemployed	43.7	49.9	52.1
35–44	63.3	66.3	70.8	Not in labor force	56.5	59.3	63.2
45–64	68.7	70.8	74.9				
65 and over	62.2	63.5	65.8	*Persons of Spanish origin can be of any race.			

IMMIGRATION TO THE UNITED STATES
Source: U.S. Immigration and Naturalization Service

Years	Number	Years	Number	Years	Number	Years	Number
1820–1975	47,098,919	1871–1880	2,812,191	1941–1950	1,035,039	1970	373,326
1820	8,385	1881–1890	5,246,613	1951–1960	2,515,479	1971	370,478
1821–1830	143,439	1891–1900	3,687,564	1961–1965	1,450,312	1972	384,685
1831–1840	599,125	1901–1910	8,795,386	1966	323,040	1973	400,063
1841–1850	1,713,251	1911–1920	5,735,811	1967	361,972	1974	394,861
1851–1860	2,598,214	1921–1930	4,107,209	1968	454,448	1975	386,194
1861–1870	2,314,824	1931–1940	528,431	1969	358,579	1976	398,613
						1977	462,315

IMMIGRATION BY COUNTRIES: 1820–1977
Source: U.S. Immigration and Naturalization Service

Countries	1977	Total (1820 to 1977)	Countries	1977	Total (1820 to 1977)
All countries	462,315	48,063,523	Romania	1,506	169,263
Europe	74,048	36,126,807	Spain [2]	5,568	255,285
Albania	51	2,515	Sweden [2]	576	1,271,281
Austria [1]	459	4,314,512	Switzerland	812	348,243
Hungary [1]	475		USSR	5,443	3,368,637
Belgium	531	201,807	Yugoslavia [4]	2,315	111,322
Bulgaria [4]	98	67,692	Other Europe	340	55,198
Czechoslovakia	273	136,591			
Denmark	403	363,761	Asia	150,842	2,610,164
Estonia	1	1,122	China	12,513	513,272
Finland	227	33,128	India	16,849	144,553
France	2,651	747,683	Japan	4,545	401,938
Germany [1]	7,414	6,970,176	Turkey	991	384,533
Great Britain			Other Asia	115,944	1,165,868
England	12,579	3,163,576			
Scotland	884	819,108	America	223,174	8,784,241
Wales	139	94,993	Canada & Newfoundland	18,003	4,081,362
Not specified	438	804,468	Mexico	44,646	2,031,046
Greece	7,792	647,892	West Indies	109,959	1,599,084
Ireland	967	4,722,621	Central America	16,892	292,382
Italy	7,369	5,287,386	South America	33,671	670,944
Latvia	8	2,539	Other America	3	109,423
Lithuania	11	3,822			
Luxembourg	27	2,843			
Netherlands	1,039	358,459	Africa	9,612	121,723
Norway [2]	344	856,046	Australia & New Zealand	2,544	115,843
Poland [3]	3,331	510,001	Pacific Islands	195	24,434
Portugal	9,977	434,837	Not specified	1,900	280,311

[1] Data for Austria-Hungary were not reported until 1861; Austria and Hungary have been recorded separately since 1905. From 1938 to 1945 inclusive, Austria was included with Germany. [2] From 1820 to 1868, the figures for Norway and Sweden were combined. [3] Poland was recorded as a separate country from 1820 to 1898 and again since 1920. [4] Bulgaria, Serbia, and Montenegro were first reported in 1899. Bulgaria has been reported separately since 1920, while the Serb, Croat, and Slovene Kingdom has been recorded as Yugoslavia since 1922.

WORLD POPULATION FACTS

The world's population reached a total of 4.12 billion in mid-1977, according to the UN statistical office. Latest statistical data also indicate that if the present rate of population growth remains at 1.9 percent, as occurred between 1970 and 1977, the world's population will have more than doubled by the year 2013. Other findings reveal that:

In the period from mid-1976 to mid-1977, the world's population increased daily by an average of 219,000 persons.

Two-thirds of the earth's inhabitants live in the developing regions, and more than one-half of the total is found in Asia.

The population of China, including Taiwan, was estimated in mid-1977 at 866 million and increasing annually by 1.7 percent.

The annual rate of population increase between 1965 and 1977 was 2.7 percent in Africa, 2.2 percent in Asia, 0.6 percent in Europe, 2.7 percent in Latin America, 1.0 percent in North America, and 1.0 percent in the Soviet Union. The highest figure — 3.3 percent — was reported from Central America, where the birthrate is 42 per 1,000 but the death rate has been reduced to 9 per 1,000.

MOST POPULOUS URBAN AREAS

City	Population	Year	City	Population	Year
New York	16,485,000	1977 (E)	Peking	7,570,000	1970 (E)
Mexico City	11,943,050	1976 (E)	Seoul	7,500,000	1975
Tokyo	11,683,613	1976	São Paulo	7,198,608	1975 (E)
Shanghai	10,820,000	1970 (E)	Calcutta	7,031,382	1971
Los Angeles	10,605,200	1977 (E)	London	7,028,200	1976
Paris	9,863,000	1975	Bombay	5,970,575	1971
Buenos Aires	8,435,840	1975 (E)	Cairo	5,921,000	1975
Moscow	8,011,000	1979	Philadelphia	5,627,000	1977 (E)
Chicago	7,661,700	1977 (E)	Rio de Janeiro	5,157,000	1974 (E)

(E) Estimated data.

MOST POPULOUS CITIES

City	Population	Year	City	Population	Year
Shanghai	10,000,000	1976 (E)	São Paulo	5,186,752	1970
Tokyo	8,646,520	1975	Jakarta	5,000,000	1973 (E)
Mexico City	8,591,750	1975 (E)	Leningrad	4,588,000	1979
Cairo	8,500,000	1975 (E)	Tehran	4,400,000	1976
Moscow	8,011,000	1979	Tianjin	4,280,000	1970 (E)
Peking	7,570,000	1970 (E)	Rio de Janeiro	4,252,009	1970
Seoul	7,500,000	1977 (E)	Karachi	3,498,634	1972
New York	7,312,200	1977 (E)	Delhi	3,287,883	1971
London	7,028,200	1976 (E)	Calcutta	3,148,746	1971
Bombay	5,970,575	1971	Chicago	3,074,084	1976 (E)

(E) Estimated data.

MOST POPULOUS COUNTRIES

Country	Midyear 1977 Estimate (in Millions)	Annual % Increase 1970–77	Density per Sq. Mi.	Area in Sq. Mi.	Country	Midyear 1977 Estimate (in Millions)	Annual % Increase 1970–77	Density per Sq. Mi.	Area in Sq. Mi.
China (People's Rep.)	865.68	1.7	235	3,691,000	Thailand	44.04	2.8	222	198,455
India	625.02	2.2	492	1,269,339	Turkey	42.13	2.7	140	300,946
Soviet Union	258.93	.9	30	8,649,490	Egypt	38.74	2.2	100	386,659
UNITED STATES	216.81	.8	60	3,615,123	Korea, South	36.44	1.8	955	38,175
Indonesia	143.28	2.6	182	788,430	Spain	36.35	1.1	185	195,988
Japan	113.86	1.3	781	145,730	Poland	34.70	.9	287	120,725
Brazil	112.24	2.8	34	3,286,470	Iran	33.90('76)	—	53	636,293
Nigeria	84.50	—	223	379,628	Burma	31.51	2.2	120	261,789
Bangladesh	80.56	2.4	1,461	55,126	Ethiopia	28.93	2.3	61	471,776
Pakistan	75.28	3.2	243	310,403	Zaire	26.38	2.5	28	918,962
Mexico	64.59	3.5	85	761,600	South Africa	26.13('76)	—	55	472,359
Germany, West	61.40	.2	642	95,704	Argentina	26.07	1.3	24	1,068,296
Italy	56.45	.7	485	116,303	Colombia	25.05	2.9	57	439,735
United Kingdom	55.85	.1	592	94,399	Canada	23.32	1.3	6	3,851,809
France	53.11	.6	253	210,038	Yugoslavia	21.72	.9	220	98,766
Vietnam	47.87	2.9	373	128,405	Romania	21.66	1.0	236	91,699
Philippines	45.03	2.9	389	115,707	Afghanistan	20.34	2.5	81	250,775

LARGEST COUNTRIES, BY GEOGRAPHICAL AREA

Rank	Country	Area in Sq. Mi.	Rank	Country	Area in Sq. Mi.
1	Soviet Union	8,649,490	15	Libya	679,358
2	Canada	3,851,809	16	Iran	636,293
3	China (People's Rep.)	3,691,000	17	Mongolia	606,163
4	UNITED STATES	3,615,123	18	Peru	496,222
5	Brazil	3,286,470	19	Chad	495,752
6	Australia	2,967,909	20	Niger	489,189
7	India	1,269,339	21	Angola	481,351
8	Argentina	1,068,296	22	South Africa	472,359
9	Sudan	967,494	23	Ethiopia	471,776
10	Algeria	919,591	24	Mali	464,873
11	Zaire	918,962	25	Mauritania	452,702
12	Saudi Arabia	829,995	26	Colombia	439,735
13	Indonesia	788,430	27	Bolivia	424,163
14	Mexico	761,600			

NATION'S 50 LEADING COUNTIES* IN MEDIAN FAMILY INCOME: 1969†

SOURCE: U.S. Bureau of the Census, 1970 Census of Population: Characteristics of Population

Rank	County	Income	Rank	County	Income	Rank	County	Income
1.	Montgomery, Md.	$16,710	18.	Fairfield, Conn.	$13,086	35.	Suffolk, N.Y.	$12,084
2.	Fairfax, Va.	15,707	19.	Lake, Ill.	13,009	36.	Baltimore, Md.	12,081
3.	Nassau, N.Y.	14,632	20.	Waukesha, Wis.	12,795	37.	Arapahoe, Colo.	12,063
4.	Du Page, Ill.	14,458	21.	Norfolk, Mass.	12,749	38.	Hartford, Conn.	12,057
5.	Marin, Calif.	13,935	22.	Montgomery, Pa.	12,747	39.	Jefferson, Colo.	12,045
6.	Oakland, Mich.	13,826	23.	Ozaukee, Wis.	12,620	40.	Honolulu, Hawaii	12,035
7.	Westchester, N.Y.	13,784	24.	Union, N.J.	12,593	41.	Putnam, N.Y.	11,996
8.	Rockland, N.Y.	13,753	25.	Santa Clara, Calif.	12,456	42.	Middlesex, N.J.	11,982
9.	Arlington, Va.	13,743	26.	Prince Georges, Md.	12,450	43.	McHenry, Ill.	11,965
10.	Bergen, N.J.	13,597	27.	Monroe, N.Y.	12,423	44.	Lake, Ohio	11,964
11.	Anchorage, Alaska	13,593	28.	Contra Costa, Calif.	12,423	45.	Kane, Ill.	11,947
12.	Howard, Md.	13,472	29.	Geauga, Ohio	12,411	46.	Richmond, N.Y.	11,894
13.	Somerset, N.J.	13,433	30.	St. Louis, Mo.	12,392	47.	King, Wash.	11,886
14.	Morris, N.J.	13,421	31.	Washtenaw, Mich.	12,294	48.	Tolland, Conn.	11,874
15.	Johnson, Kans.	13,384	32.	Orange, Calif.	12,245	49.	Middlesex, Mass.	11,860
16.	San Mateo, Calif.	13,222	33.	De Kalb, Ga.	12,137	50.	Delaware, Pa.	11,822
17.	Macomb, Mich.	13,110	34.	Dakota, Minn.	12,120			

* With 50,000 or more population.   † Figures are for calendar year 1969, as gathered in 1970 census.

NATION'S 50 LARGEST CITIES* RANKED BY MEDIAN FAMILY INCOME: 1970 CENSUS

SOURCE: U.S. Department of Commerce, Bureau of Economic Analysis

Rank	City	SMSA*	City Only	Rank	City	SMSA*	City Only
1.	Honolulu, Hawaii	$12,035	$12,539	26.	Oakland, Calif.	$ 9,626	$ 9,626
2.	San Jose, Calif.	12,456	11,927	27.	Washington, D.C.	12,933	9,583
3.	Seattle, Wash.	11,676	11,037	28.	Nashville-Davidson, Tenn.	9,187	9,473
4.	Indianapolis, Ind.	10,754	10,754	29.	Philadelphia, Pa.	10,783	9,366
5.	St. Paul, Minn.	11,682	10,544	30.	Fort Worth, Texas	10,101	9,271
6.	Los Angeles, Calif.	10,972	10,535	31.	Boston, Mass.	11,449	9,133
7.	San Francisco, Calif.	11,802	10,503	32.	Cleveland, Ohio	11,407	9,107
8.	Toledo, Ohio	10,932	10,474	33.	Oklahoma City, Okla.	9,345	9,106
9.	Long Beach, Calif.	10,282	10,282	34.	Cincinnati, Ohio	10,257	8,894
10.	Milwaukee, Wis.	11,338	10,262	35.	Baltimore, Md.	10,577	8,815
11.	Chicago, Ill.	11,931	10,242	36.	Buffalo, N.Y.	11,430	8,804
12.	Omaha, Nebr.	10,204	10,208	37.	Pittsburgh, Pa.	9,737	8,800
13.	San Diego, Calif.	10,133	10,166	38.	Jacksonville, Fla.	8,671	8,671
14.	Detroit, Mich.	12,117	10,045	39.	Memphis, Tenn.	8,542	8,646
15.	Dallas, Tex.	10,405	10,019	40.	Louisville, Ky.	9,814	8,564
16.	Rochester, N.Y.	11,969	10,002	41.	Atlanta, Ga.	10,695	8,399
17.	Minneapolis, Minn.	9,960	9,960	42.	St. Louis, Mo.	10,504	8,182
18.	Phoenix, Ariz.	9,856	9,956	43.	El Paso, Tex.	7,792	7,963
19.	Kansas City, Mo.	10,588	9,910	44.	Norfolk, Va.	8,705	7,821
20.	Houston, Tex.	10,191	9,876	45.	Birmingham, Ala.	8,295	7,737
21.	Tulsa, Okla.	9,286	9,870	46.	Newark, N.J.	11,847	7,735
22.	Portland, Oreg.	10,463	9,799	47.	San Antonio, Tex.	7,981	7,734
23.	Columbus, Ohio	10,460	9,731	48.	Tampa, Fla.	7,883	7,678
24.	New York, N.Y.	10,870	9,682	49.	New Orleans, La.	8,670	7,445
25.	Denver, Colorado	10,777	9,654	50.	Miami, Fla.	9,245	7,304

* Standard Metropolitan Statistical Areas (city plus outlying areas); for definitions of largest areas, see page 220.

U.S. METROPOLITAN AREA PER CAPITA INCOME: 1977

SOURCE: U.S. Department of Commerce, Bureau of Economic Analysis

SMSA'S WITH HIGHEST INCOMES

Standard Metropolitan Statistical Area[1]	Income
Anchorage, Alaska	$11,430
Bridgeport-Stamford-Norwalk, Connecticut	9,676
Reno, Nevada	9,368
Midland, Texas	9,307
Washington, D.C.-Maryland-Virginia	9,306
San Francisco-Oakland, California	9,260
Newark, N.J.	8,632
San Jose, California	8,632
Nassau-Suffolk, New York	8,614
Detroit, Michigan	8,535
Chicago, Illinois	8,522
Seattle-Everett, Washington	8,457
Los Angeles-Long Beach, California	8,429
Cleveland, Ohio	8,315
Sarasota, Florida	8,249
Houston, Texas	8,247
Anaheim-Santa Ana-Garden Grove, California	8,116
Peoria, Illinois	8,113
New York, New York-New Jersey	8,105
Ann Arbor, Michigan	8,081
Flint, Michigan	8,073
Denver-Boulder, Colorado	8,050
Minneapolis-St. Paul, Minnesota	8,021
New Brunswick-Perth Amboy-Sayreville, N.J.	7,993
Honolulu, Hawaii	7,950

SMAS'S WITH LOWEST INCOMES

Standard Metropolitan Statistical Area[1]	Income
Gadsden, Alabama	$5,674
Lawrence, Kansas	5,626
Charleston-North Charleston, South Carolina	5,619
Wilmington, North Carolina	5,615
Clarksville-Hopkinsville, Tennessee-Kentucky	5,591
Tallahassee, Florida	5,587
Monroe, Louisiana	5,506
Anniston, Alabama	5,486
Pensacola, Florida	5,430
Johnson City-Kingsport-Bristol, Tenn-Va	5,426
Fort Smith, Arkansas-Oklahoma	5,413
Biloxi-Gulfport, Mississippi	5,358
Panama City, Florida	5,311
Fayetteville, North Carolina	5,281
Bryan-College Station, Texas	5,256
Bloomington, Indiana	5,213
Alexandria, Louisiana	5,155
Albany, Georgia	5,147
St. Cloud, Minnesota	5,121
El Paso, Texas	5,071
Lawton, Oklahoma	5,026
Provo-Orem, Utah	4,854
Brownsville-Harlingen-San Benito, Texas	4,253
Laredo, Texas	3,898
McAllen-Pharr-Edinburg, Texas	3,859

[1] For definitions of largest areas see page 244.

URBAN INTERMEDIATE BUDGET FOR A 4-PERSON FAMILY IN SELECTED METROPOLITAN AREAS: 1978 (In dollars)

Source: U.S. Bureau of Labor Statistics, Autumn 1978 Urban Family Budgets and Comparative Indexes for Selected Urban Areas (USDL: 79-305)

Metropolitan area	All Items	Food	Metropolitan area	All items	Food
Anchorage, Alaska	$25,551	$6,944	Houston, Tex.	$18,575	$5,695
Atlanta, Ga.	17,689	5,627	Indianapolis, Ind.	18,935	5,600
Austin, Tex.	17,923	5,375	Kansas City, Mo. - Kans.	19,237	6,069
Bakersfield, Calif.	17,663	5,467	Lancaster, Pa.	18,345	5,897
Baltimore, Md.	18,768	5,720	Los Angeles - Long Beach, Cal.	18,913	5,832
Baton Rouge, La.	18,378	5,776	Milwaukee, Wis.	19,425	5,705
Boston, Mass.	22,767	6,115	Minneapolis - St. Paul, Minn.	18,824	5,835
Buffalo, N.Y.	19,395	5,787	Nashville, Tenn.	18,141	5,310
Cedar Rapids, Iowa	18,616	5,354	New York, N.Y. - N.E. N.J.	22,094	6,520
Champaign-Urbana, Ill.	20,055	5,750	Orlando, Fla.	17,995	5,140
Chicago, Ill. - N.W. Ind.	19,625	5,958	Philadelphia, Pa. - N.J.	19,636	6,349
Cincinnati, Ohio - Ky. - Ind.	18,605	5,925	Pittsburgh, Pa.	18,630	5,978
Cleveland, Ohio	19,663	5,884	Portland, Maine	19,529	5,997
Dallas, Tex.	18,374	5,547	St. Louis, Mo. - Ill.	18,575	6,069
Dayton, Ohio	18,609	5,689	San Diego, Calif.	18,752	5,515
Denver, Colo.	19,083	5,845	San Francisco - Oakland, Calif.	20,161	6,020
Detroit, Mich.	19,746	5,787	Seattle - Everett, Wash.	19,775	5,880
Durham, N.C.	18,093	5,449	Washington, D.C. - Md. - Va.	20,064	5,936
Green Bay, Wis.	18,505	5,231	Wichita, Kans.	18,653	5,567
Hartford, Conn.	20,225	5,956	**URBAN U.S. AVERAGE**	**19,670**	**5,921**
Honolulu, Hawaii	22,907	7,180			

WORLDWIDE COST OF LIVING — 1978

Source: United Nations, Monthly Bulletin of Statistics, May 1979
Consumer Price Index (1970 = 100)

Country	All Items	Food	Country	All Items	Food
Argentina (Buenos Aires)	49,729.0	11,860.0	Malaysia (Peninsular)	160.3	179.3
Australia	224.0	211.6	Martinique (Fort-de-France)	224.1	215.0
Austria	166.8	158.7	Mexico	309.4	311.4
Barbados	292.3	326.9	New Caledonia (Noumea)	188.6	195.6
Belgium	182.6	171.7	New Zealand	243.7	240.8
Brazil (Sao Paulo)	494.3	522.5	Niger (Niamey)	241.8	273.0
Canada	180.2	210.3	Norway	192.5	191.0
Chile (Santiago)	232,773.0	280,924.0	Paraguay (Asuncion)	218.4	251.0
Colombia (Bogota)	428.5	508.0	Peru (Lima)	527.0	589.5
Costa Rica (San Jose)	216.6	221.7	Portugal (Lisbon)	345.1	401.6
Czechoslovakia	104.3	104.0	Puerto Rico	167.8	193.7
Denmark	207.6	221.6	Sierra Leone (Freetown)	211.8	226.9
Finland	244.3	257.5	Singapore	133.1	132.5
France	199.8	211.9	Somalia (Mogadishu)	204.9	236.2
Germany, West	150.1	145.2	Spain	309.8	310.1
Gibraltar	277.2	324.0	Sri Lanka (Colombo)	164.8	174.0
Greece	255.4	280.5	Sudan	294.9	302.2
Guyana	196.5	244.0	Suriname (Paramaribo)	194.6	195.4
Haiti (Port-au-Prince)	205.9	213.8	Sweden	198.1	211.9
Honduras (Tegucigalpa)	163.7	182.1	Switzerland	150.8	146.8
Hong Kong	125.0	122.0	Thailand (Bangkok)	189.7	210.9
Hungary	130.8	132.1	Trinidad and Tobago	252.0	263.6
India	178.8	173.0	Tunisia (Tunis)	153.9	157.7
Indonesia (Djakarta)	351.3	402.6	Turkey (Ankara)	483.3	523.7
Ireland	269.0	290.4	United Kingdom	269.6	315.2
Israel	785.4	833.7	UNITED STATES	167.9	179.5
Italy	265.3	271.6	Uruguay (Montevideo)	4,768.8	5,045.0
Jordan	136.6	135.7	Venezuela (Caracas)	163.7	201.8
Korea, South	295.9	356.7	Yugoslavia	358.5	385.7
Liberia (Monrovia)	203.6	209.6	Zaire (Kinshasa)	1,132.4	1,423.4
Luxembourg	171.1	170.0	Zimbabwe-Rhodesia	175.8	176.0
Madagascar (Antananarivo)	180.0	192.5			

THE AMERICAN CONSUMER: PERSONAL EXPENDITURES (1977)

Source: U.S. Department of Commerce, Bureau of Economic Analysis

	Personal Consumption Expenditures by Type of Product (Millions of Dollars)		Personal Consumption Expenditures by Type of Product (Millions of Dollars)
Food (includes alcohol and tobacco)	$ 261,763	Recreation	$ 81,200
Clothing, accessories, and jewelry	95,561	Private education and research	18,800
Personal care	16,736	Religious and welfare activities	15,384
Housing	184,592	Foreign travel and other, net	5,063
Household operation	176,878	Total personal consumption expenditures	1,206,507
Medical care expenses	117,977	Durable commodities	178,400
Personal business	60,449	Nondurable commodities	479,000
Transportation	172,104	Services	549,200

CONSUMER PRICE INDEX* AND PURCHASING POWER OF THE CONSUMER DOLLAR
(1967=100)   Source: Bureau of Labor Statistics

Year	All items	Food	Housing Total	Rent	Apparel and upkeep	Transportation	Medical care	Personal care	Reading and recreation	Other goods and services	Purchasing power of the consumer dollar
1947	66.9	70.6	65.2	61.1	78.2	55.5	48.1	66.0	68.7	63.8	1.495
1949	71.4	73.5	70.9	68.0	80.1	66.4	52.7	68.3	74.9	68.7	1.401
1951	77.8	82.8	77.2	73.2	86.1	72.5	56.3	74.7	76.6	72.8	1.285
1953	80.1	83.0	80.8	80.3	84.6	79.5	61.4	76.3	77.7	78.5	1.248
1955	80.2	81.6	82.3	84.3	84.1	77.4	64.8	77.9	76.7	79.8	1.247
1957	84.3	84.9	86.2	87.5	87.3	83.3	69.9	84.1	80.7	83.3	1.186
1959	87.3	87.1	88.6	90.4	88.2	89.6	76.4	88.7	85.3	86.1	1.145
1960	88.7	88.0	90.2	91.7	89.6	89.6	79.1	90.1	87.3	87.8	1.127
1962	90.6	89.9	91.7	94.0	90.9	92.5	83.5	92.2	91.3	89.1	1.104
1965	94.5	94.4	94.9	96.9	93.7	95.9	89.5	95.2	95.9	94.2	1.058
1967	100.0	100.0	100.0	100.0	100.0	100.0	100.0	100.0	100.0	100.0	1.000
1968	104.2	103.6	104.2	102.4	105.4	103.2	106.1	104.2	104.7	104.6	.960
1969	109.8	108.9	110.8	105.7	111.5	107.2	113.4	109.3	108.7	109.1	.911
1970	116.3	114.9	118.9	110.1	116.1	112.7	120.6	113.2	113.4	116.0	.860
1971	121.3	118.4	124.3	115.2	119.8	118.6	128.4	116.8	119.3	120.9	.824
1972	125.3	123.5	129.2	119.2	122.3	119.9	132.5	119.8	122.8	125.5	.798
1973	133.1	141.4	135.0	124.3	126.8	123.8	137.7	125.2	125.9	129.0	.752
1974	147.7	161.7	150.6	130.6	136.2	137.7	150.5	137.3	133.8	137.2	.678
1975	161.2	175.4	166.8	137.3	142.3	150.6	168.6	150.7	144.4	147.4	.621
1976	170.5	180.8	177.2	144.7	147.6	165.5	184.7	160.5	151.2	153.3	.587
1977	181.5	192.2	189.6	153.5	154.2	177.2	202.4	170.9	157.9	159.2	.551
1978	195.4	206.3	202.8	164.0	159.6	185.5	219.4	176.6	183.3	182.0	.512

* Consumer Price Index for All Urban Consumers (CPI-U)

AVERAGE U.S. RETAIL FOOD PRICES   Source: Bureau of Labor Statistics (in cents)

Year	Flour, white 10 lbs.	Rice lb.	White bread lb.	Round steak lb.	Rib roast lb.	Chuck roast lb.	Pork chops lb.	Bacon sliced lb.	Milk (delivered) qt.	Butter lb.	Cheese lb.	Potatoes 15 lbs.	Sugar lb.	Eggs doz.	Coffee lb.
1913	33	8.7	5.6	22.3	19.8	16.0	21.0	27.0	8.9	38.3	22.1	25.5	5.5	34.5	29.8
1918	67	12.9	9.8	36.9	30.7	26.6	39.0	52.9	13.9	57.7	35.9	48.0	9.7	56.9	30.5
1919	72	15.1	10.0	38.9	32.5	27.0	42.3	55.4	15.5	67.8	42.6	57.0	11.3	62.8	43.3
1920	81	17.4	11.5	39.5	33.2	26.2	42.3	52.3	16.7	70.1	41.6	94.5	19.4	68.1	47.0
1924	49	10.1	8.9	34.8	31.3	21.6	31.0	38.4	13.4	52.2	36.2	42.0	9.0	51.0	42.6
1927	55	10.7	9.2	38.7	34.1	25.2	37.2	47.8	14.1	56.3	38.6	57.0	7.2	48.7	47.4
1929	51	9.8	8.8	46.0	39.1	31.4	37.5	43.9	14.4	55.5	39.5	48.0	6.4	52.7	47.9
1930	46	9.5	8.6	42.6	36.4	28.6	36.2	42.5	14.1	46.4	36.6	54.0	6.1	44.5	39.5
1932	32	6.6	7.0	29.7	25.6	18.5	21.5	24.2	10.7	27.8	24.4	25.5	5.0	30.2	29.4
1934	49	8.0	8.3	28.1	23.6	17.5	25.5	29.1	11.2	31.5	25.0	34.5	5.5	32.5	26.9
1937	47.9	8.4	8.6	39.1	32.8	25.7	36.7	41.3	12.5	40.7	29.4	41.9	5.6	36.2	25.5
1939	37.9	7.7	7.9	36.0	29.5	23.4	30.4	31.9	12.2	32.5	25.3	37.1	5.4	32.1	22.4
1941	45.2	8.7	8.1	39.1	31.1	25.5	34.3	34.3	13.6	41.1	30.0	35.2	5.7	39.7	23.6
1942	52.8	12.1	8.7	43.5	34.0	29.3	41.4	39.4	15.0	47.3	34.8	51.3	6.8	48.4	28.3
1944	64.7	12.8	8.8	41.4	33.4	28.8	37.3	41.1	15.6	50.0	36.0	69.8	6.7	54.5	30.1
1946	70.8	14.0	10.4	52.1	43.1	36.6	48.5	53.3	17.6	71.0	50.1	70.2	7.7	58.6	34.4
1948	98.0	20.8	13.9	90.5	73.7	64.4	77.2	76.9	21.8	86.7	65.6	83.8	9.4	72.3	51.4
1950	98.2	16.8	14.3	93.6	74.3	61.6	75.4	63.7	20.6	72.9	51.8	69.2	9.7	60.4	79.4
1954	107.2	19.6	17.2	90.7	70.3	51.4	86.3	81.7	23.0	72.4	57.6	78.9	10.5	58.5	110.8
1956	106.6	17.2	17.9	88.2	70.1	48.4	78.2	57.3	24.2	72.1	57.2	101.6	10.6	60.2	103.4
1958	110.4	18.4	19.3	104.2	81.6	63.3	91.8	79.3	25.3	74.2	58.0	93.9	11.3	60.4	90.7
1960	110.8	18.6	20.3	105.5	81.7	61.6	85.8	65.5	26.0	74.9	68.6	107.7	11.6	57.3	75.3
1962	114.0	19.1	21.2	107.8	84.1	62.3	89.8	70.3	26.1	75.2	72.4	94.8	11.7	54.0	70.8
1964	113.4	18.8	20.7	103.9	82.8	56.8	88.0	66.7	26.4	74.4	73.4	113.6	12.8	53.9	81.6
1965	116.2	19.0	20.9	108.4	89.7	59.5	97.3	81.3	26.3	75.4	75.4	140.6	11.8	52.7	83.3
1966	118.8	19.0	22.2	110.7	93.2	62.2	106.3	95.4	27.8	82.2	84.4	112.4	12.0	59.9	82.3
1967	119.2	18.6	22.2	113.9	94.0	60.7	100.4	83.7	28.7	83.0	87.2	112.1	12.1	49.1	76.9
1968	116.8	18.2	22.4	114.3	98.8	63.5	102.9	81.4	30.3	83.6	88.8	114.5	12.2	52.9	76.4
1969	116.2	18.8	23.0	126.7	109.3	70.4	112.2	87.8	31.5	84.6	94.0	122.4	12.4	62.1	76.5
1970	117.9	19.1	24.3	130.2	111.7	72.5	116.2	94.9	33.0	86.6	100.7	134.5	13.0	61.4	91.1
1971	119.9	19.6	25.0	136.1	118.0	75.0	108.1	80.0	33.9	87.6	105.5	129.2	13.6	52.9	93.4
1972	119.2	19.6	24.7	147.7	129.5	82.1	124.6	96.2	34.5	87.1	108.6	138.9	13.9	52.4	92.7
1973	151.2	26.0	27.6	174.6	152.2	102.8	155.9	132.5	37.6	91.6	120.8	205.4	15.1	78.1	104.0
1974	205.0	44.0	34.5	179.8	158.5	102.1	156.5	132.0	[1]	94.6	145.8	249.6	32.3	78.3	122.9
1975	198.8	41.1	36.0	188.5	179.6	102.8	185.6	175.6	[1]	102.5	153.6	201.6	37.2	77.0	133.4
1976	185.2	37.5	35.3	178.3	177.4	96.9	184.8	171.1	[1]	126.1	173.0	219.0	24.0	84.1	187.3
1977	169.2	35.3	35.5	176.1	182.1	92.0	181.2	156.2	[1]	133.1	172.0	224.6	21.6	82.3	347.2

[1] Delivered milk is no longer priced.

THE GROWING AMERICAN FOOD BASKET: 1914-1978   Source: U.S. Department of Agriculture

The table indicates the amount of food that could be purchased through the years with one hour of labor.

Item	Unit	1914	1919	1929	1939	1949	1959	1969	1977	1978[1]
Bread, white	Lb.	3.5	4.7	6.4	7.9	9.8	11.1	13.9	15.9	16.5
Round steak	Lb.	0.9	1.2	1.2	1.7	1.6	2.0	2.5	3.2	2.9
Pork chops	Lb.	1.0	1.1	1.5	2.1	1.9	2.6	2.8	3.1	3.1
Sliced bacon	Lb.	0.8	0.9	1.3	2.0	2.1	3.3	3.6	3.6	3.2
Butter	Lb.	0.6	0.7	1.0	1.9	1.9	2.9	3.8	4.2	4.3
Cheese	Lb.	1.0	1.1	1.4	2.5	2.4	3.8	3.4	3.3	3.3
Milk, fresh	Qt.	—	—	—	5.6	7.0	9.1	11.6	13.5	14.0
Eggs, fresh	Doz.	0.6	0.8	1.1	2.0	2.0	4.1	5.1	6.8	8.1
Oranges	Doz.	—	0.9	1.3	2.2	2.7	3.3	3.8	4.4	4.0
Potatoes	Lb.	12.3	12.4	17.0	25.1	25.1	34.8	38.9	37.6	40.8
Tomatoes* (canned)	....	—	2.9	4.4	7.3	9.1	14.1	16.2	15.0	16.0
Margarine	Lb.	—	1.1	2.1	3.8	4.5	7.8	11.5	9.8	9.8

* #2 can from 1914 to Sept. 1954; #303 can beginning Oct. 1954.   [1] April-June 1978

AMERICAN FAMILY CHARACTERISTICS: 1978

SOURCE: U.S. Bureau of Census

Characteristic	Families	Percent
All families	57,215,000	100.0
White	50,530,000	88.3
Black and Other	6,685,000	11.7
Family Size:		
2 persons	22,033,000	38.5
3 persons	12,629,000	22.1
4 persons	11,774,000	20.6
5 persons	6,269,000	11.0
6 persons	2,649,000	4.6
7 persons or more	1,861,000	3.3
Own Children under 18 Years Old:		
No children	26,846,000	46.9
1 child	11,641,000	20.3
2 children	10,846,000	19.0
3 children	5,013,000	8.8
4 children or more	2,870,000	5.0
Residence:		
Nonfarm	55,042,000	96.2

Characteristic	Families	Percent
Farm	2,172,000	3.8
Headed by Women	8,236,000	14.4
Age of Family Head:		
Under 25 years	3,851,000	6.7
25–34 years	13,432,000	23.5
35–44 years	11,528,000	20.1
45–54 years	10,888,000	19.0
55–64 years	9,304,000	16.3
65 years or older	8,212,000	14.4
Marital Status of Household Heads:		
All Households	76,030,000	100.0
Married	51,090,000	67.2
Separated	2,865,000	3.8
Widowed	9,997,000	13.1
Divorced	6,594,000	8.7
Single	8,350,000	11.0

SEX RATIO OF U.S. POPULATION

SOURCE: U.S. Bureau of the Census (males per 100 females). Figures relate to July 1, and include Armed Forces overseas

Year	All ages	Under 15 years	15 to 24 years	25 to 44 years	45 to 64 years	65 or older	Year	All ages	Under 15 years	15 to 24 years	25 to 44 years	45 to 64 years	65 or older
1978	95.1	104.3	102.3	97.4	92.1	68.5	1968	96.2	103.7	102.2	96.9	92.4	73.8
1977	95.1	104.2	102.3	97.3	92.0	68.7	1966	96.7	103.7	102.1	96.9	93.2	75.7
1976	95.1	104.2	102.3	97.3	91.9	69.0	1964	97.1	103.6	101.8	97.0	94.1	77.9
1975	95.3	104.1	102.2	97.3	91.7	69.4	1962	97.5	103.4	101.5	97.0	94.9	80.2
1974	95.4	104.1	102.2	97.3	91.6	69.7	1960	97.8	103.4	101.4	96.9	95.7	82.6
1972	95.6	104.0	102.1	97.2	91.6	70.8	1956	98.4	103.7	100.6	97.2	97.0	85.8
1970	95.9	103.9	102.2	96.9	91.7	72.0	1950	99.3	103.8	100.0	97.2	100.1	89.5

MARITAL STATUS OF ADULTS (Persons 14 years old and over)

SOURCE: U.S. Bureau of Census

Marital Status and Sex	1955*	1960	1970	1978
Total (millions)	107	114	147	167
Single (millions)	16	17	37	45
Married (millions)	79	84	94	101
Widowed (millions)	10	11	11	12
Divorced (millions)	2	3	5	9
Male, total (millions)	51	55	70	80
Percent distribution	100.0	100.0	100.0	100.0
Single	17.4	17.8	28.2	30.6
Married	76.1	76.0	66.6	62.8
Wife separated	1.5	1.7	1.3	1.8

Marital Status and Sex	1955*	1960	1970	1978
Male, total (cont.)				
Widowed	4.6	4.1	3.0	2.3
Divorced	1.9	2.1	2.2	4.2
Female, total (millions)	56	59	77	87
Percent distribution	100.0	100.0	100.0	100.0
Single	12.0	11.8	22.1	23.9
Married	71.9	71.3	62.0	58.5
Husband separated	2.5	2.2	2.2	2.8
Widowed	13.6	14.0	12.5	11.6
Divorced	2.4	2.9	3.5	6.0

* Excludes Alaska and Hawaii.

U.S. MARRIAGE AND DIVORCE RATES

SOURCE: National Center for Health Statistics

Year	Marriages/Divorces Number (thousands)		Rate (per thousand)		Year	Marriages/Divorces Number (thousands)		Rate (per thousand)	
1910	948	83	10.3	0.9	1963	1,654	428	8.8	2.3
1915	1,008	104	10.0	1.0	1964	1,725	450	9.0	2.4
1920	1,274	171	12.0	1.6	1965	1,800	479	9.3	2.5
1925	1,188	175	10.3	1.5	1966	1,857	499	9.5	2.5
1930	1,127	196	9.2	1.6	1967	1,927	523	9.7	2.6
1935	1,327	218	10.4	1.7	1968	2,069	584	10.4	2.9
1940	1,596	264	12.1	2.0	1969	2,145	639	10.6	3.2
1945	1,613	485	12.2	3.5	1970	2,159	708	10.6	3.5
1950	1,667	385	11.1	2.6	1971	2,190	773	10.6	3.7
1955	1,531	377	9.3	2.3	1972	2,282	845	11.0	4.1
1960	1,523	393	8.5	2.2	1973	2,284	915	10.9	4.4
1961	1,548	414	8.5	2.3	1974	2,230	977	10.5	4.6
1962	1,577	413	8.5	2.2	1975	2,153	1,036	10.1	4.9
					1976	2,155	1,083	10.0	5.0
					1977*	2,178	1,091	10.0	5.0

* Provisional figures.

ILLEGITIMATE BIRTHS IN AMERICA

SOURCE: National Center for Health Statistics (Figures in thousands)

Categories	1940	1950	1960	1965	1970	1974	1975	1976	1977
Total Illegitimate Live Births	89.5	141.6	224.3	291.2	398.7	418.1	447.9	468.1	515.7
By age of mother:									
Under 15 years	2.1	3.2	4.6	6.1	9.5	10.6	11.0	10.3	10.1
15 to 19 years	40.5	56.0	87.1	123.1	190.4	210.8	222.5	225.0	239.7
20 to 24 years	27.2	43.1	68.0	90.7	126.7	122.7	134.0	145.4	168.6
25 to 29 years	10.5	20.9	32.1	36.8	40.6	44.9	50.2	55.4	62.4
30 to 34 years	5.2	10.8	18.9	19.6	19.1	18.6	19.8	21.0	23.7
35 to 39 years	3.0	6.0	10.6	11.4	9.4	8.2	8.1	8.6	8.8
40 and over	1.0	1.7	3.0	3.7	3.0	2.3	2.3	2.3	2.3
By color of mother:									
White	40.3	53.5	82.5	123.7	175.1	168.5	186.4	197.1	220.1
Nonwhite	49.2	88.1	141.8	167.5	215.1	249.6	261.6	271.0	295.5

DIVORCE LAWS 1978

Source: Women's Bureau, U.S. Department of Labor

State or other Jurisdiction	Residence required before filing suit for divorce	"No fault" divorce (a)			Grounds for Absolute Divorce												Period before parties may remarry after final decree	
		Marriage breakdown (b)	Separation	Prior decree of limited divorce	Adultery	Mental and/or physical cruelty	Desertion	Alcoholism and/or drug addiction	Impotency	Non-support by husband	Insanity	Pregnancy at marriage	Bigamy	Unexplained absence	Felony conviction or imprisonment	Other	Plaintiff	Defendant
Alabama	6 mos.(c)	•	2 yrs.(d)		•	•	1 yr.	•	•	•	5 yrs.	*			•	(e)	60 days(f)	60 days(f)
Alaska	90 days	•			•	•	1 yr.				18 mos.	*						
Arizona	90 days	•		2 yrs.														
Arkansas	60 days(g)		3 yrs.		•	•	1 yr.	•	•	*(h)	3 yrs.				•	(i)		
California	90 days	•									(i)							
Colorado	90 days	•																
Connecticut	1 yr.(k)		18 mos.		•	•	1 yr.	•		•	5 yrs.			7 yrs.	•	(l)		
Delaware	3 mos.	•																
Florida	6 mos.	•									3 yrs.(m)					(l, n, o)		
Georgia	6 mos.		2 yrs.(d)	*(q)	•	•	1 yr.	•	•		2 yrs.(m)	*			•		(p)	(p)
Hawaii	3 mos.	•	5 yrs.				•				3 yrs.							
Idaho	6 wks.	•			•	•	1 yr.	2 yrs.			2 yrs.				•	(r, s)	1 yr.(f)	1 yr.(f)
Illinois	90 days				•	•	1 yr.	•	•		3 yrs.				•		30 days	30 days
Indiana	6 mos.	•																
Iowa	1 yr.	•					1 yr.				3 yrs.							
Kansas	60 days	•	2 yrs.		•	•	1 yr.	•	•		3 yrs.				•	(z)		
Kentucky	180 days(t)	•		*(v)														
Louisiana	(u)		2 yrs.		•	•	1 yr.								•		6 mos.(f)	6 mos.(f)
Maine	6 mos.(k)	•	(y)		•	•	3 yrs.	•	•	*(h)	3 yrs.				•			(ab)
Maryland	(x)				•		1 yr.		•				•		•			
Massachusetts	30 days				•	•	1 yr.	•	•	*(h)			•		•	(z)		6 mos.(f)
Michigan	180 days(k)	•																
Minnesota	1 yr.(k)	•					1 yr.				3 yrs.					(n, aa)		
Mississippi	1 yr.				•	•	1 yr.	•	•				•		•			
Missouri	90 days	•																
Montana	90 days	•																
Nebraska	1 yr.	•	1 yr.(p)															
Nevada	6 wks.(k)	•	1 yr.(p)		•	•	2 yrs.				2 yrs.			2 yrs.		(ac, ad)		
New Hampshire	1 yr.(k)	•	18 mos.		•	•	1 yr.	•	•	(ag)	2 yrs.				•	(ae)		
New Jersey	6 mos.				•	•	1 yr.	•	(af)		5 yrs.(af)				•			
New Mexico	6 mos.	•	1 yr.(d)		•	•	1 yr.	•		*(h)	3 yrs.				•	(e)		(p)
New York	1 yr.(k)		1 yr.	1 yr.	•	•	1 yr.			*(h)	5 yrs.				•			
North Carolina	6 mos.		1 yr.		•		1 yr.			*(h)	4 yrs.					(l, ai)	6 mos.	6 mos.
North Dakota	1 yr.		2 yrs.		•	•	1 yr.	•	•	•	5 yrs.				•	(l, ai)	60 days	60 days
Ohio	6 mos.(aj)	*(ah)			•	•	1 yr.	•	•				•		•	(l, n, ak)		(al)
Oklahoma	6 mos.				•	•	1 yr.	•	•		3 yrs.	*	•		•	(an, ao)	6 mos.	6 mos.
Oregon	6 mos.	•																
Pennsylvania	1 yr.		5 yrs.(p)		•	•	2 yrs.		•		3 yrs.		•		•	(s, aq)	6 mos.	6 mos.
Rhode Island	2 yrs.		3 yrs.	2 yrs.(p)	•	•	5 yrs.(am)	•	•	*(h)	5 yrs.				•		30 days(f)	30 days(f)
South Carolina	3 mos.(ap)		3 yrs.		•	•	1 yr.	•										
South Dakota	—				•	•	1 yr.	•	•						•			
Tennessee	6 mos.		3 yrs.(d)		•	•	1 yr.	•	•	(af)	3 yrs.(af)	*	•		•			
Texas	6 mos.		3 yrs.(d)		•	•	1 yr.				5 yrs.				•			
Utah	3 mos.		3 yrs.(d)		•	•	1 yr.		•	*(h)					•			
Vermont	6 mos.(as)		6 mos.		•	•	•			*(h)	5 yrs.				•			

State or other Jurisdiction	"No fault" divorce (a)				Grounds for Absolute Divorce												Period before parties may remarry after final decree	
	Residence required before filing suit for divorce	Marriage break-down (b)	Separation	Prior decree of limited divorce	Adultery	Mental and/or physical cruelty	Desertion	Alcoholism and/or drug addiction	Impotency	Insanity	Non-support by husband	Pregnancy at marriage	Bigamy	Unexplained absence	Felony conviction or imprisonment	Other	Plaintiff	Defendant
Virginia	6 mos.	•	1 yr.	(at)	•	•	1 yr.					•			•		—	—
Washington	1 yr.(k)	•	2 yrs.		•	•	1 yr.	1 yr.		3 yrs.		•			•		—	—
West Virginia	6 mos.		2 yrs.	1 yr.	•	•	1 yr.	1 yr.		2 yrs.		•			•		—	—
Wisconsin	6 mos.		1 yr.		•	•	1 yr.	1 yr.				•			•		6 mos.	6 mos.
Wyoming	60 days(k)		2 yrs.(au)		•	•	1 yr.					•			•		—	—
District of Columbia	6 mos.		6 mos.(au)	* (ay)	•	•											—	—
Puerto Rico	1 yr.(k)		2 yrs.	* (ay)	•	•	1 yr.			7 yrs.				10 yrs.		(av, aw)	(w)	301 days

(a) "No fault" includes all proceedings where it is not necessary to prove one of the traditional grounds for divorce. Not all States shown in this category refer to their proceedings as "no fault." (b) Expressed in statutes as irremediable or irretrievable breakdown of marriage relationship, irreconcilable differences, incompatability, marriage insupportable because of discord, etc. (c) Two years for wife filing on ground of nonsupport. (d) Under decree of separate maintenance and/or written separation agreement. (e) Crime against nature. (f) Except to each other. In Iowa, court can waive restriction. (g) Three-month residency required before final judgment may be entered. (h) Ground available to husband, also. (i) No residency requirement before filing suit, but final decree cannot be entered until party is a resident for 6 months. (j) incurable. (k) In some cases a lesser period of time may be allowed contrary to statute. (l) Fraud, force, or duress. (m) Mental incompetence. (n) Parties related by marriage or blood. (o) Mental incapacity at time of marriage. (p) In the discretion of the court. (q) After expiration of term of separation decree. (r) Loathsome disease. (s) Attempt on life of spouse by poison or other means showing malice. (t) No decree until parties have lived apart for 60 days. (u) Must be domiciled in state and grounds occurred in state: 2 years residence if marriage did not occur in state. (v) Spouse who obtained separation from bed and board may obtain absolute divorce 1 year after the date of the separation decree. (w) Attempt by either parent to corrupt son or prostitute daughter, or proposal by husband to prostitute wife. (x) One year if cause occurred out of state and 2 years if on grounds of insanity. (y) Voluntary living apart for 1 year and no reasonable expectation of reconciliation, or living separate and apart without cohabitation or interruption for 3 years. (z) Any cause which renders marriage null and void from the beginning. (aa) Insanity or idiocy at time of marriage not known to other party. (ab) When divorce is granted on ground of adultery, court may prohibit remarriage. After 1 year, court may remove disability upon satisfactory evidence of reformation. (ac) Membership in religious sect disbelieving in marriage. (ad) Wife's absence out of state for 10 years without husband's consent. (ae) Deviant sexual conduct without consent of spouse. (af) Grounds for annulment. (ag) Grounds for separation. (ah) On petition of both spouses, accompanied by separation agreement executed and confirmed by both spouses in court appearance not less than 90 days after filing of petition. (ai) Five years if on grounds of insanity and insane spouse is in out-of-state institution. (aj) Defendant obtained divorce from plaintiff in another state. (ak) Remarriage after 2 years upon false but well-founded rumor of death of other spouse. (If first spouse reappears, he or she may seek divorce for bigamy within 6 months.) al) If divorce is granted for adultery, the guilty party cannot marry the accomplice in adultery during lifetime of former spouse. (am) Or for shorter period in court's discretion. (an) Void or voidable marriage; in case party is deemed civilly dead from crime or other circumstances, party may be presumed dead. (ao) Gross misbehavior or wickedness. (ap) When both parties residents: 1 year when one is nonresident. insanity. (aq) Refusal by wife to move with husband to this state. (ar) Adjudication of permanent and incurable insanity. (as) Two years if grounds are insanity. (at) Limited divorce granted on the grounds of merged into an absolute divorce after 1 year. (au) Two years separation without material fault by plaintiff. (av) Husband guilty of conduct constituting vagrancy. (aw) Conviction of felony before marriage. (ax) Voluntary; involuntary separation, 1 year. (ay) May be granted for voluntary separation of 6 months, separation for 1 year, adultery, or cruelty.

MEDIAN DURATION OF U.S. MARRIAGES PRIOR TO DIVORCE OR ANNULMENT (in years)

SOURCE: National Center for Health Statistics

State*	1950	1960	1970	1977
Reporting States Average	5.3	7.1	6.7	6.6
Alabama	(NA)	7.3	5.3	4.9
Alaska	5.0	6.2	5.4	5.0
California	(NA)	(NA)	(NA)	7.0
Connecticut	(NA)	(NA)	(NA)	8.3
Georgia	(NA)	6.3	5.4	5.3
Hawaii	(NA)	6.3	7.2	5.7
Idaho	4.2	4.8	4.6	5.0
Illinois	(NA)	(NA)	(NA)	6.2
Iowa	4.5	5.7	5.6	5.8
Kansas	(NA)	5.8	5.1	5.2
Kentucky	(NA)	(NA)	(NA)	5.6
Maryland	(NA)	9.0	8.8	8.4
Michigan	(NA)	(NA)	7.0	7.0
Missouri	(NA)	(NA)	5.4	5.5
Montana	(NA)	5.1	5.1	5.1
Nebraska	5.7	6.3	6.0	6.1
New York	(NA)	(NA)	(NA)	8.1
Ohio	(NA)	(NA)	6.3	6.0
Oregon	4.7	5.9	5.9	5.8
Pennsylvania	(NA)	9.2	8.1	7.7
Rhode Island	(NA)	(NA)	9.2	8.2
South Carolina	(NA)	(NA)	(NA)	6.8
South Dakota	4.8	6.3	5.9	5.8
Tennessee	4.6	6.3	5.6	5.3
Utah	(NA)	4.7	5.3	4.8
Vermont	(NA)	(NA)	(NA)	7.8
Virginia	8.2	8.3	7.7	7.8
Wisconsin	(NA)	8.2	7.9	7.0
Wyoming	4.2	5.4	4.6	4.6

(NA) Not Available. *Based on sample data.

MARRIAGE LAWS: 1978

SOURCE: Women's Bureau, U.S. Department of Labor

State	Age at Which Marriage Can Be Contracted with Parental Consent		Age below Which Parental Consent Is Required		Physical Examination and Blood Test for Male and Female		Waiting Period	
	Male	Female	Male	Female	Period between Examination and Issuance of License	Scope of Medical Examination	Before Issuance of License	After Issuance of License
Alabama	17(a)	14(a)	18	18	30 da.	(b)	—	—
Alaska	16(e)	16(e)	18	18	30 da.	(b)	3 da.	—
Arizona	16(e)	16(e)	18	18	30 da.	(d)	—	—
Arkansas	17(e)	16(e)	18	18	30 da.	(b)	3 da.	—
California	18(a, e)	16(a, e)	18	18	30 da.	(b, f, g, h)	—	—
Colorado	16(e)	16(e)	18	18	30 da.	(b, g, i)	—	—
Connecticut	16(e)	16(e)	18	18	35 da.	(b)	4 da.	—
Delaware	18(e)	16(e)	18	18	30 da.	(b)	—	(j)
Florida	18(a, e)	16(a, e)	18	18	30 da.	(b)	3 da.	—
Georgia	16(e)	16(e)	18(e)	18(e)	30 da.	(b, f)	3 da. (k)	—
Hawaii	16	16	18	18	30 da.	(b)	—	—
Idaho	16(e)	16(e)	18	18	30 da.	(b)	3 da. (l)	—
Illinois	16(e)	16(e)	18	18	15 da.	(b, f)	3 da.	—
Indiana	17(e)	16(e)	18	18	30 da.	(b, f)	3 da.	—
Iowa	16	16	18	18	20 da.	(b)	3 da.	—
Kansas	18(e)	18(e)	18	18	30 da.	(b)	3 da.	—
Kentucky	(a, c)	(a, c)	18	18	15 da.	(b, f)	3 da.	—
Louisiana	18(e)	16(e)	18	18	10 da.	(b)	—	72 hrs.
Maine	16(e)	16(e)	18	18	60 da.	(b)	5 da.	—
Maryland	16(e)	16(e)	18	18	—	(b)	48 hrs.	—
Massachusetts	18(e)	18(e)	18	18	30 da.	(b, g)	3 da.	—
Michigan	(m)	16	18	18	30 da.	(b)	3 da.	—
Minnesota	18	16(n)	18	18	—	(b)	5 da.	—
Mississippi	17(e)	15(e)	21	21	30 da.	(b)	3 da.	—
Missouri	15(e)	15(e)	18	18	15 da.	(b)	3 da.	—
Montana	18(e)	18(e)	18	18	20 da.	(b)	5 da.	3 da.
Nebraska	18	16	19	19	30 da.	(b)	2 da.	—
Nevada	16(a, e)	16(a, e)	18	18	—	(b)	—	—
New Hampshire	14(n)	13(n)	18	18	30 da.	(b)	5 da.	—
New Jersey	18(e)	16(e)	18	18	30 da.	(b)	72 hrs.	—
New Mexico	16(e)	16(e)	18	18	30 da.	(b)	72 hrs.	—
New York	16	14(o)	18	18	30 da.	(b, f)	—	24 hrs.(p)
North Carolina	16	16(e)	18	18	30 da.	(b, g, q, r)	—	—
North Dakota	16	16	18	18	30 da.	(b, s)	—	—
Ohio	18(e)	16(e)	18	18	30 da.	(b)	5 da.	—
Oklahoma	16(e)	16(e)	18	18	30 da.	(b)	(l)	—
Oregon	17	17	18	18	30 da.(u)	(b)	7 da.	—
Pennsylvania	16(e)	16(e)	18	18	30 da.	(b, t)	3 da.	—
Rhode Island	18(e)	16(e)	18	18	40 da.	(b, g, r)	—	(v)
South Carolina	16(e)	14(e)	18	18	—	—	24 hrs.	—
South Dakota	16(e)	16(e)	18	18	20 da.	(b)	—	—
Tennessee	16(e)	16(e)	18	18	30 da.	(b)	3 da. (l)	—
Texas	14(e)	14(e)	18	18	21 da.	(b)	—	—
Utah	16(a)	14(a)	18	18	30 da.	(b)	—	—
Vermont	16(e)	16(e)	18	18	30 da.	(b)	—	5 da.
Virginia	16(a, e)	16(a, e)	18	18	30 da.	(b)	—	—
Washington	17(e)	17(e)	18	18	—	(b, q, r)	3 da.	—
West Virginia	(c)	(c)	18	18	30 da.	(b)	3 da.	—
Wisconsin	16	16	18	18	20 da.	(b)	5 da.	—
Wyoming	17(e)	16(e)	19	19	30 da.	(b)	—	—
District of Columbia	16(a)	16(a)	18	18	30 da.	(b)	3 da.	—

Note: Common law marriage is recognized in Alabama, Colorado, Georgia, Idaho, Iowa, Kansas, Montana, Ohio, Oklahoma, Pennsylvania, Rhode Island, South Carolina, Texas, and the District of Columbia. (a) Parental consent not required if minor was previously married. (b) Venereal diseases. (c) West Virginia and Kentucky no longer have a minimum age for marriage with parental consent. (d) Blood test must be on record for at least 48 hours before issuance of license. (e) Procedure established whereby younger parties may obtain license in special circumstances. (f) Sickle cell anemia. (g) Rubella immunity. (h) Tay-Sachs disease. (i) Rh factor. (j) Residents, 24 hours; nonresidents, 96 hours. (k) Unless parties are 18 years of age or over, or female is pregnant, or applicants are the parents of a living child born out of wedlock. (l) Three days if parties are under 18 years of age. (m) No provision in the law for parental consent for males. (n) Permission of judge also required. (o) If under 16 years of age, consent of family court judge also required. (p) However, marriage may not be solemnized within 3 days of date on which specimen for blood test was taken. (q) Mental competence. (r) Tuberculosis. (s) Marriage prohibited in some cases when one of the parties is institutionalized as severely retarded. (t) No license may be issued without a court order if either applicant is weakminded, insane or of unsound mind. (u) Maximum period between examination and expiration of marriage license. (v) If female is nonresident, must complete and sign license 5 days prior to marriage.

SOCIAL SECURITY AND MEDICARE

SOURCE: U.S. Social Security Administration

The basic idea of social security is a simple one: during working years employees, their employers, and self-employed people pay social security contributions which are pooled in special trust funds. When earnings stop or are reduced because the worker retires, becomes disabled, or dies, monthly cash benefits are paid to replace part of the earnings the family has lost.

Part of the contributions made go into a separate hospital insurance trust fund so that when workers and their dependents reach 65 they will have help in paying their hospital bills. Medicare is available also to people under 65 who have been entitled to social security disability benefits for 2 consecutive years or more and to insured people under 65 and their dependents who need a kidney transplant or dialysis treatment because of permanent kidney failure. Medical insurance, also available, helps pay doctors' bills and other medical expenses. This program is financed out of premiums partially paid for by those who are enrolled with the majority of the cost paid for by the Federal Government. Under present law, the Federal share can never be less than one-half the cost of the program. Starting July 1, 1979, enrollees pay $8.70 a month for this protection.

Nine out of 10 working people in the United States are now building protection for themselves and their families under social security.

FINANCING THE PROGRAMS

Federal retirement, survivors, and disability benefits and hospital insurance benefits are paid for by contributions based on earnings covered under social security.

If you are employed, you and your employer share the contributions. If you are self-employed, you pay contributions for retirement, survivors, and disability insurance at about 1-1/2 times the rate for an employee. However, the hospital insurance contribution rate is the same for the employer, the employee, and the self-employed person.

As long as you have earnings that are covered by the law, you pay contributions regardless of your age and even if you are receiving social security benefits.

How Contributions Are Paid

If you are employed, your contribution is deducted from your wages each payday. Your employer sends it, with an equal amount as his own share of the contribution, to the Internal Revenue Service.

If you are self-employed and your net earnings are $400 or more in a year, you must report your earnings and pay your self-employment contribution each year when you file your individual income tax return. This is true even if you owe no income tax.

Your wages and self-employment income are entered on your individual record by the Social Security Administration. This record of your earnings will be used to determine your eligibility for benefits and the amount of cash benefits you will receive.

The maximum amount of earnings that can count for social security and on which you pay social security contributions is shown in the following table:

Year	Amount	Year	Amount
1937–50	$3,000	1974	13,200
1951–54	3,600	1975	14,100
1955–58	4,200	1976	15,300
1959–65	4,800	1977	16,500
1966–67	6,600	1978	17,700
1968–71	7,800	1979	22,900
1972	9,000	1980	25,900
1973	10,800	1981	29,700

Earnings over the maximums may have been reported to your social security record, but cannot be used to figure your benefit rate.

When you work for more than one employer in a year and pay social security contributions on wages over the social security maximum, you may claim a refund of the excess contributions on your income tax return for that year.

If you work for only one employer and he deducts too much in contrbutions, you should apply to the employer for a refund. A refund is made only when more than the required amount of contributions has been paid. Questions about contributions or refunds should be directed to the Internal Revenue Service. These tables show the schedule of contribution rates now in the law:

SOCIAL SECURITY TAX RATES (in percent)

Year	OASI*[1]	DI*[2]	HI[3]	Total
	Employers & employees, each			
1977	4.375	0.575	0.90	5.85
1978	4.275	.775	1.00	6.05
1979–80	4.330	.750	1.05	6.13
1981	4.525	.825	1.30	6.65
1982–84	4.575	.825	1.30	6.70
1985	4.750	.950	1.35	7.05
1986–89	4.750	.950	1.45	7.15
1990 & later	5.100	1.100	1.45	7.65
	Self-employed			
1977	6.1850	0.8150	0.90	7.90
1978	6.0100	1.0900	1.00	8.10
1979–80	6.0100	1.0400	1.05	8.10
1981	6.7625	1.2375	1.30	9.30
1982–84	6.8125	1.2375	1.30	9.35
1985	7.1250	1.4250	1.35	9.90
1986–89	7.1250	1.4250	1.45	10.00
1990 & later	7.6500	1.6500	1.45	10.75

*By allocation in law. [1]Old Age, Survivors Insurance. [2]Disability Insurance. [3]Hospital Insurance.

Social Security Cash Benefits

To get monthly cash payments for yourself and your family, or for your survivors to get payments in case of your death, you must first have credit for a certain amount of work under social security. This credit may have been earned at any time after 1936.

Starting 1979, all employees and self-employed people receive credit for 1/4 year of work for each $260 of covered annual earnings up to credit for a full year based on annual earnings of $1,040 or more. The $260 measure will increase automatically to keep pace with average earnings.

Before 1978, most employees got credit for 1/4 year of work if they are paid $50 or more in wages in a 3-month calendar quarter. Four quarters are counted for any full year in which a person has $400 or more in self-employment income. A worker who receives farm wages gets credit for 1/4 year of work for each $100 of wages he has in a year up to $400.

You can be either fully or currently insured or both, depending on the total amount of credit you have for work under social security and the amount you have in the last 3 years.

If you stop working under social security before you have earned enough credit to be insured, no cash benefits will be payable to you. The earnings already credited to you will remain on your social security record; if you later return to work, regardless of your age, all your covered earnings will be considered.

Fully Insured

Just how much credit you must have to be fully insured depends upon the year you reach 62 or upon the date of your death or disability.

The amount of credit you will need is measured in quarter-year units of work called quarters of coverage; but for convenience, the table on this page is given in years. The people in your social security office will be glad to give you further details if you have questions.

You are fully insured if you have credit for at least as many years as shown on the appropriate line of the following chart:

When you reach 62 or become disabled	You will be fully insured if you have credit for this much work
1975	6
1977	6½
1979	7
1981	7½
1983	8
1987	9
1991 or later	10

If you become disabled or die before reaching 62 you are fully insured if you have credit for ¼ year of work for each year after 1950 and up to the year of your disability or death. In counting the number of years after 1950, omit years before you were 22.

No one is fully insured with credit for less than 1½ years of work and no one needs more than 10 years of work to be fully insured.

Currently Insured

You will be currently insured if you have social security credit for at least 1½ years of work within the 3 years before you die. If you leave a widow or widower and young children, they are eligible for monthly benefits if you were currently insured.

AMOUNTS OF MONTHLY PAYMENTS

The amount of monthly social security benefits due you or your dependents or survivors is based on your average earnings under social security over a period of years.

The exact amount of your benefit cannot be figured until there is an application for benefits, and all of your earnings up to the time of the application are considered.

A worker who doesn't get any benefits before 65 and who delays his retirement past age 65 will get a special credit that can mean a larger benefit. The credit adds 1 percent for each year (1/12 of 1 percent for each month) from age 65 to age 72 (3 percent for people reaching 65 after 1981).

The law provides a special minimum benefit at retirement for some people who worked under social security more than 20 years. This provision helps people who had low incomes, but above a specified amount, in their working years. The amount of the special minimum depends on the number of years of coverage. For a worker retiring at 65 with 25 years of coverage, the minimum would be $172.50 a month; with 30 or more years of coverage, the minimum would be $230.

DISABILITY PAYMENTS

If you become disabled before 65, you and certain members of your family may be eligible for benefits.

Do not wait too long after you are disabled to apply for benefits; if you wait more than a year, you may lose benefits. Payments may begin with the 6th full month of disability.

If you are found eligible for disability insurance benefits, you will remain eligible as long as you are disabled. When you reach 65, your benefit will be changed to retirement payments at the same rate.

Who Is Considered Disabled?

A person is considered disabled only if he has a severe physical or mental condition which—

Prevents him from working, and
Is expected to last (or has lasted) for at least 12 months or is expected to result in death.

A person with a severe medical condition could be eligible even if he manages to do a little work.

How Much Work Credit Is Required for a Disabled Worker?

If you become disabled before you are 24, you need credit for 1½ years of work in the 3 years before you become disabled.

If you become disabled between 24 and 31, you need social security credits for half the time after you are 21 and before you become disabled.

To get disability benefits if you become disabled at 31 or later, you must be fully insured and have credit for 5 years of work in the 10 years.

People who become disabled because of blindness can get benefits without having to meet the requirement of substantial recent work.

FAMILY PAYMENTS

Monthly payments can be made to certain dependents: *When the worker gets retirement or disability benefits; When the worker dies.*

These dependents are:

Unmarried children under 18, or between 18 and 22 if they are full-time students;

Unmarried children 18 or over who were severely disabled before they reached 22 and who continue to be disabled;

A wife, widow, or widower regardless of age, if caring for a child under 18 or disabled and the child gets payments based on the worker's record;

A wife 62 or widow 60 or older, even if there are no children entitled to payments;

A widow 50 or older (or widower 50 or older) who becomes disabled not later than 7 years after the death of the worker or not later than 7 years after the end of entitlement to benifits as a widow with a chld;

A husband 62 or over or widower 60 or over;

Dependent parents 62 or over after a worker dies.

In addition to monthly benefits, a lump-sum payment of $255 may be made after the worker's death.

Payments may also be made to a divorced wife at 62 or a surviving divorced wife at 60 (or a disabled surviving divorced wife 50 or older) if the marriage lasted at least 10 years.

Benefits also can be paid a dependent surviving divorced wife at any age if she is caring for her deceased former husband's child under 18 or disabled who is entitled to benefits.

For more information about this provision, get in touch with your social security office.

Monthly payments to the wife or dependent husband of a person entitled to retirement or disability payments generally cannot be made until the marriage has been in effect at least 1 year unless the couple are parents of a child.

Payments can generally be made to the widow, stepchild, or dependent widower of a deceased worker if the marriage lasted 9 months or longer.

Examples of monthly social security retirement payments for workers who reach 65 before 1987

Covered yearly earnings after 1950

Benefits can be paid to a:	$923 or less	$3,000	$4,000	$5,000	$6,000	$8,000	$10,000*
Retired worker at 65	121.80	251.80	296.20	343.50	388.20	482.60	534.70
Retired worker at 62	97.50	201.50	237.00	274.80	310.60	386.10	427.80
Wife or husband at 65	60.90	125.90	148.10	171.80	194.10	241.30	267.40
Wife or husband at 62	45.70	94.50	111.10	128.90	145.60	181.00	200.60
Wife under 65 and one child in her care	61.00	133.20	210.00	290.40	324.00	362.00	401.00
Maximum family payment	182.70	384.90	506.20	633.80	712.10	844.50	935.70

*Covered earnings shown in the last column of the chart cannot reach this amount until later because the maximum earnings covered by social security were lower in past years. Because of this, the benefits shown in the last column generally will not be payable until future years. The maximum retirement benefit generally payable to a worker who is 65 in 1979 is $503.40.

Amount of Your Family's Benefits

Cash benefits to your dependents, and to your survivors in case of your death, are figured from the amount of your retirement or disability benefit.

Permanently reduced benefits are received by:

Workers and their wives who choose to start receiving retirement benefits while they are between 62 and 65; Widows and widowers who choose to start receiving benefits between 60 and 65 and

Disabled widows and disabled widowers 50 or older who receive benefits before they reach 65.

The amount of the reduction depends on the number of months they receive benefits before they reach 65. On the average, people who choose to get benefits early will collect about the same value in total benefits over the years, but in smaller installments to take account of the longer period during which they will be paid.

If a person is entitled to monthly benefits based on the social security records of two or more workers, he will receive no more than the largest of the benefits.

The lump-sum payment at a worker's death is $255.

Benefits Not Taxable

Social security benefits you receive are not subject to Federal income tax.

AN APPLICATION IS NECESSARY

Before payments can start, an application must be filed. When you are nearing 65 or if you become disabled, get in touch with your social security office.

It is important for you to inquire at your social security office 2 or 3 months before you reach 65, not only for the possibility of retirement benefits, but also for Medicare benefits, which are available whether or not you retire. If you wait until the month you reach 65 to apply for the medical insurance part of Medicare, you will lose at least one month of protection. It is always to your advantage to apply before you reach 65, even if you do not plan to retire. If you have high earnings which would increase the amount of your benefit in the year you are 65 or later, your benefit amount will be refigured. You will always be sure of receiving benefits at the highest possible rate.

When a person who has worked under the social security law dies, some member of his family should get in touch with the social security office.

If you cannot come to the social security office write or telephone. A representative can arrange to visit you.

Long delay in filing an application can cause loss of some benefits, since back payments for monthly cash benefits can be made for no more than 12 months.

An application for a lump-sum death payment must usually be made within 2 years of the worker's death.

HEALTH INSURANCE (MEDICARE)

Nearly all people 65 and over are eligible for health insurance protection under Medicare, including some people who do not have enough credit for work covered by social security to qualify for monthly cash benefits.

Medicare also covers people who have been getting disability checks for 2 years or more and insured people and their dependents who need a kidney transplant or dialysis treatment because of permanent kidney failure.

There are two parts to Medicare: hospital insurance and, for those who choose, medical insurance.

Eligibility for Hospital Insurance

If you are 65 or over and are entitled to social security or railroad retirement benefits or if you are disabled and have been getting disability benefits for 2 consecutive years or more, you are automatically eligible for hospital insurance; if you are not entitled to either of these benefits, you should ask about hospital insurance and medical insurance at your social security office.

People 65 or older who are not automatically entitled to hospital insurance can buy this protection for a monthly premium of ($69 effective 7/79), although you will also have to purchase medical insurance.

After you establish your eligibility, you receive a health insurance card, which shows that you have hospital insurance, medical insurance, or both.

YOUR HOSPITAL INSURANCE

Hospital insurance will pay the cost of covered services for the following hospital and follow-up care:

Up to 90 days of hospital care in a participating hospital during a "benefit period."[1] For the first 60 days of care in 1979, your hospital insurance will pay all but the first $160 of expenses. For the 61 through the 90th day of care, your hospital insurance will pay all but $40 daily for covered services. (There is a lifetime limit of payment for 190 days of care in mental hospitals.)

You also have 60 reserve days which can be used after you have exhausted your 90 days of hospital care in a "benefit period." Reserve days are not replaced after you use them. Hospital insurance pays all but $80 a day of your covered expenses during the reserve days.

Hospital insurance in many cases also pays for up to 100 days of care in a participating skilled nursing facility after a hospital stay. Hospital insurance pays all the costs for the first 20 days of care and all but $20 per day for up to 80 more days.

Up to 100 home health "visits" from a participating home health agency when prescribed by your physician may also be covered.

WHAT YOUR MEDICAL INSURANCE PAYS

People (except those in Puerto Rico or living in foreign countries) who become entitled to hospital insurance will be covered automatically by the medical insurance part of Medicare unless they say they don't want this protection.

You will have protection at the earliest possible time if you enroll during the 3-month period just before the month you reach 65. You may also enroll the month you reach 65 and during the 3 following months, but your protection will not start until 1 to 3 months after that.

Anyone who declines enrollment in Medicare medical insurance will have other opportunities to enroll during any general enrollment period (January 1 through March 31 of each year). The premium will be 10 percent higher for each full year a person could have had medical insurance but didn't choose to.

Medical insurance is financed with monthly premiums paid by those who are enrolled and by the Federal Government. The basic medical insurance premium is currently $8.70 per month. Once you are enrolled for medical insurance, you do not have to do anything to keep your protection. It continues from year to year without any action.

If you wish to drop your medical insurance, you may give notice to do so at any time.

YOUR MEDICAL INSURANCE

Generally, your medical insurance will pay 80 percent of the reasonable charges for the following services after the first $60 in a calendar year.

Physicians' and surgeons' services, no matter where you receive the services—in the doctor's office, in a clinic, in a hospital, or at home. (You do not have to meet the $60 deductible before your medical insurance will pay for X-ray or laboratory services of physicians when you are a bed patient in a hospital. The full reasonable charge will be paid, instead of 80 percent.) Home health services even if you have not been in a hospital—up to 100 visits during a calendar year. (Medical insurance pays the full cost after you meet the $60 deductible.)

A number of other medical and health services, such as diagnostic tests, surgical dressings and splints, and rental or purchase of medical equipment.

Outpatient physical therapy services—whether or not you are homebound—furnished under supervision of a participating hospital, skilled nursing facility, home health agency, approved clinic, rehabilitation agency, or public health agency. All outpatient services of a participating hospital, including diagnostic tests or treatment.

Certain services by podiatrists (but not routine foot care or treatment of flat feet or partial dislocations). Limited services by chiropractors.

[1] A "benefit period" begins the first time you enter a hospital after your hospital insurance starts. It ends after you have not been an inpatient for 60 days in a row in any hospital or in any facility that mainly provides skilled nursing care.

For More Medicare Information

For more information on the health insurance programs, get in touch with your social security office and ask for a copy of the leaflet, "A brief explanation of Medicare."

MEDICAID

Both Medicare and Medicaid are part of the Social Security Act. They differ, however, in that the former is an insurance program intended to help those 65 (and some disabled people under 65), while Medicaid is designed for certain kinds of needy and low-income people: the aged (65 or older), the blind, the disabled, members of families with dependent children, and other cases involving children.

Medicaid programs, paid for by money from federal, state, and local taxes, were available in all states except Arizona as of April 1974. Under these programs, payment is made for at least the following services: inpatient hospital care; outpatient hospital services; other laboratory and X-ray services; skilled nursing home services; physicians' services; the screening, diagnosis, and treatment of children; and home health care services.

Medicaid can pay what Medicare does not pay for people who are eligible for both programs. For example, Medicaid can pay the $160 coinsurance amount for the first 60 days of hospital care under hospital insurance, and the $40 a day for the next 30 days of care. Medicaid also can pay the $60 deductible and the monthly premium for medical insurance.

OLD-AGE, SURVIVORS, AND DISABILITY INSURANCE PROGRAM

PROJECTED EXPENDITURES, INCOME, AND LEVEL OF THE COMBINED OASI AND DI TRUST FUNDS AFTER THE SOCIAL SECURITY AMENDMENTS OF 1977

(In billions)

Calendar Year	Expenditures	Income	Net increase in funds	Funds at beginning of year	Funds at beginning of year as a percentage of outgo during year
1977	$ 87.6	$ 82.1	$-5.5	$ 41.1	47%
1978	97.2	92.4	-4.8	35.6	37
1979	106.9	106.5	-0.4	30.8	29
1980	117.1	119.1	2.0	30.4	26
1981	127.4	137.1	9.6	32.4	25
1982	138.3	150.2	11.9	42.0	30
1983	149.2	161.3	12.1	53.9	36
1984	161.2	172.9	11.7	66.0	41
1985	174.0	194.2	20.1	77.7	45
1986	187.6	209.0	21.4	97.9	52
1987	202.0	223.7	21.7	119.3	59

SOCIAL SECURITY: 1985–2050 A.D.

Source: Social Security Administration

Note: Social Security is not true insurance because reserves are not built up against all future liabilities. Due to its governmental status the administrators try only to insure that income for a given year is enough to pay all expenses and to add a certain percentage to the Social Security trust fund (they try to keep the fund equal to the sum of all payments the previous year).

In order to keep payments and the trust fund at the proper levels over a long period, the administrators compute probable benefit payments (outgo) and then determine what income will be necessary to make the payments. Because of fluctuations in employment, inflation, and population rates, both figures are very difficult to compute,

but the table below shows the product of all of the administrators' computations. In essence it shows the percentage of taxable payroll required to pay off Social Security obligations in any year. This may sound complicated, but it is not. In order to clarify it, let's look at one year; 1985: in that year it will take a total of 11.16 percent of the taxable payroll (roughly $1,116 for a worker earning $10,000) to keep the system solvent. (This means that for everyone receiving $4,000 in benefits, there will be 4 workers earning $10,000 and paying a tax of $1,000.) NOTE: each worker would not pay entire $1,000; it is divided equally between employee and employer. The table takes into account how many workers there will be, how much they'll be making, the effects of population change on the number of people eligible for benefits, etc.

OLD-AGE, SURVIVORS, AND DISABILITY INSURANCE AND MEDICARE PROGRAMS

PROJECTED EXPENDITURES, TAX INCOME, AND NET DIFFERENCES EXPRESSED AS A PERCENTAGE OF TAXABLE PAYROLL[1]

Year	Old-Age and Survivors Insurance		Disability Insurance		Medicare Hospital Insurance		Total for OASDHI		Medicare Supplementary Medical Ins. Expenditures[2]
	Expend.	Income	Expend.	Income	Expend.	Income	Expend.	Income	
1977	9.39	8.75	1.50	1.15	1.99	1.80	12.88	11.70	0.85
1980	8.63	8.66	1.48	1.50	2.22	2.10	12.33	12.26	0.96
1985	8.79	9.50	1.66	1.90	2.98	2.70	13.43	14.10	1.28
1990	8.71	10.20	1.87	2.20	3.76	2.90	14.34	15.30	1.64
1995	8.68	10.20	2.07	2.20	4.52	2.90	15.27	15.30	1.90
2000	8.63	10.20	2.34	2.20	5.27	2.90	16.24	15.30	2.00
2025	13.49	10.20	2.91	2.20	7.44[3]	2.90	23.84	15.30	2.63
2050	13.35	10.20	2.82	2.20	7.61[3]	2.90	23.78	15.30	2.52

[1]The effective taxable payroll is slightly different for OASDI and HI because of the tax treatment of self-employed persons; however, it does not materially affect the comparisons. In 1977, taxable payroll represented about 85 percent of total earnings in covered employment; in 1981 and later the corresponding percentage will be approximately 91 percent.
[2]Expenditures are approximately equal to total income from premiums and general revenue for the Medicare-SMI program. Although the Medicare-SMI program is not financed by payroll taxes, its cost is shown for comparison as a percentage of payroll which is taxable for HI purposes. Figures after 1977 are based upon unpublished estimates.
[3]Based upon unpublished estimates. For the purpose of this comparison, it was assumed that after the year 2000 medical care unit cost increases would be equal to average wage increases in covered employment.

DISADVANTAGED: A DEFINITION

The level of family income used to determine whether or not a person is poor has been raised an average of $460 by the U.S. Department of Labor to reflect increases in consumer prices over the past year.

The revised poverty-level guidelines for metropolitan area and farm families became effective April 1, 1979, based on the Office of Management and Budget (OMB) recommendations.

Income levels for families of one through six persons are:

Family Size	Income: Non-farm*	Income: Farm*
1	$3,400	$2,910
2	4,500	3,840
3	5,600	4,770
4	6,700	5,700
5	7,800	6,630
6	8,900	7,560

* For Continental U.S.

Income limits for families of more than six persons may be determined by adding for the nonfarm and farm levels these amounts for each additional person: $1,100 and $930 for the Continental U.S.

They will have limited application to Federal, state, and local employment and training programs under the Comprehensive Employment and Training Act (CETA). These levels will be modified by the Bureau of Labor Statistics family income data for use by CETA administrators. The revised Lower Living Standard Income Level will be issued for localities in a few weeks.

The eligibility requirements for CETA titles II B, II D, VII, and most programs funded under title IV, include the definition of "economically disadvantaged" containing provisions incorporating the income poverty levels and the Lower Living Standard income levels.

The income guidelines or the Lower Living Standard Income Level (whichever is higher) is to be used in determining income eligibility for CETA.

The Labor Department's Employment and Training Administration (ETA) defines an economically disadvantaged person as one who is a member of a family that (1) receives cash welfare payments; or (2) has a family income that, in relation to family size and location, represents 70 percent of the lower living income level issued by the department's Bureau of Labor Statistics or poverty levels established by the Office of Management and Budget — whichever is higher.

POVERTY IN THE UNITED STATES:

SOURCE: Bureau of the Census (numbers in millions)

		Number below Poverty Level					Percent below Poverty Level	
Year	Total	White	Black and Other Races	Black Only	Total	White	Black and Other Races	Black Only
1977	24.7	16.4	8.3	7.7	11.6	8.9	29.0	31.3
1976	25.0	16.7	8.3	7.6	11.8	9.1	29.4	31.1
1975	25.9	17.8	8.1	7.5	12.3	9.7	29.3	31.3
1974	23.4	15.7	7.6	7.2	11.2	8.6	28.3	30.3
1973	23.0	15.1	7.8	7.4	11.1	8.4	29.6	31.4
1972	24.5	16.2	8.3	7.7	11.9	9.0	31.9	33.3
1971	25.6	17.8	7.8	7.4	12.5	9.9	30.9	32.5
1970	25.4	17.5	7.9	7.5	12.6	9.9	32.0	33.5
1969	24.1	16.7	7.5	7.1	12.1	9.5	31.0	32.2
1967	27.8	19.0	8.8	8.5	14.2	11.0	37.2	39.3
1965	33.2	22.5	10.7	NA	17.3	13.3	47.1	(NA)

FACTS ABOUT THE POOR

SOURCE: Community Services Administration

Based on 1978 population and 1977 income, there were 24,720,000 poor persons. Despite the fact that there are almost two poor white persons for every poor non-white person, the incidence of poverty among non-whites was 29.0 per cent as compared to 8.9 per cent for whites. Children under 18 years of age made up 31.8 per cent of the poor.

Between 1976 and 1977 the number of poor persons declined by 255,000. At the same time the number of poor persons aged 65 and over decreased by 136,000.

For the 5,311,000 poor families the average income deficit in 1977 was $2,177. For the 5,216,000 poor unrelated individuals the deficit averaged $1,188. (°) In order to bring all the poor to the poverty income threshold it would require a direct payment amounting to $18,758,655,000.

(°) Average income deficit is the amount of income below the income poverty threshold level.

POVERTY IN AMERICA: BY STATES

There were 14,028,000 fewer poor persons in the United States in 1969 than in 1959, according to the Office of Economic Opportunity (OEO). The national incidence of poverty dropped from 22.1 percent to 12.3 percent during this 10-year period.

Significant changes occurred in the numbers of poor within the individual states. Poor farmers moved to urban areas, often

in other states; industry provided employment for increasing numbers of poor persons previously considered unemployable or, for one reason or another, undesirable; and more wives and youths worked to add to their family income. The total for the 1969 census differs from that shown above due to differences in survey methods and family definitions.

State	1959	1969*	State	1959	1969*	State	1959	1969*
Total	38,682	27,125	Kentucky	1,137	718	North Dakota	169	93
Alabama	1,374	857	Louisiana	1,274	933	Ohio	1,508	1,041
Alaska	38	35	Maine	222	131	Oklahoma	680	465
Arizona	314	264	Maryland	523	387	Oregon	262	235
Arkansas	843	523	Massachusetts	608	473	Pennsylvania	1,881	1,228
California	2,199	2,153	Michigan	1,216	819	Rhode Island	135	100
Colorado	312	263	Minnesota	646	398	South Carolina	1,049	595
Connecticut	236	212	Mississippi	1,173	767	South Dakota	202	120
Delaware	73	58	Missouri	1,051	672	Tennessee	1,374	836
District of Columbia	161	123	Montana	129	92	Texas	2,970	2,047
Florida	1,371	1,088	Nebraska	309	188	Utah	135	118
Georgia	1,505	924	Nevada	35	43	Vermont	88	52
Hawaii	102	69	New Hampshire	87	65	Virginia	1,164	691
Idaho	124	92	New Jersey	673	574	Washington	397	336
Illinois	1,446	1,112	New Mexico	278	227	West Virginia	637	380
Indiana	797	493	New York	2,319	1,986	Wisconsin	607	421
Iowa	583	319	North Carolina	1,796	996	Wyoming	51	38
Kansas	419	275						

(Columns headed "Thousands of Poor Persons")

* Source: 1970 Census Fourth Count Summary Tapes

AID TO FAMILIES WITH DEPENDENT CHILDREN

Source: U.S. Department of Health, Education and Welfare (data for December 1978)

State	NUMBER OF RECIPIENTS			PAYMENTS TO RECIPIENTS	Average per —		Percentage change from Dec. 1977	
	Families	Total	Children	Total	Family	Recipient	Recipients	Amount
Total [1]	3,480,872	10,325,333	7,210,565	$891,398,561	$256.08	$86.33	—4.2	.4
Ala.	59,389	174,406	126,858	6,631,893	111.67	38.03	2.1	4.4
Alaska [2]	5,022	12,988	9,173	1,666,721	331.88	128.33	4.0	16.5
Ariz.	17,547	50,116	37,552	2,634,555	150.14	52.57	—6.5	2.7
Ark.	29,280	86,791	64,145	4,197,029	143.34	48.36	—4.2	—2.0
Calif.	469,840	1,375,285	931,485	149,768,211	318.76	108.90	—4.1	—3.1
Colo.	28,019	77,853	54,740	6,228,534	222.30	80.00	—11.5	—5.8
Conn.	45,706	136,441	95,706	15,005,882	328.31	109.98	.5	3.5
Del.	10,867	30,798	21,749	2,323,784	213.84	75.45	—2.3	— .6
D.C.	31,551	90,355	57,131	7,491,397	237.44	82.91	—5.1	—2.3
Fla.	82,028	231,491	168,806	12,271,815	149.61	53.01	—6.0	— .7
Georgia	78,262	208,522	153,972	8,465,351	108.17	40.60	—7.6	— .4
Guam	1,236	4,528	3,402	250,744	202.87	55.38	—8.6	—4.8
Hawaii	18,867	59,444	39,736	7,324,979	388.24	123.22	1.8	7.0
Idaho	6,999	19,529	13,477	1,808,936	258.46	92.63	— .9	5.5
Ill.	211,901	684,097	485,135	58,130,307	274.33	84.97	—6.8	— .9
Ind.	50,625	147,722	106,422	9,526,081	188.17	64.49	—6.0	—5.0
Iowa	32,819	92,204	61,817	9,529,677	290.37	103.35	—2.4	6.1
Kans.	23,674	63,405	46,624	5,600,683	236.58	88.33	—12.2	—12.4
Ky.	60,207	164,424	116,873	10,059,504	167.08	61.18	—4.9	—2.0
La.	63,125	202,408	150,465	8,250,265	130.70	40.76	—3.9	2.8
Maine	20,446	59,677	40,172	4,547,134	222.40	76.20	— .4	6.7
Md.	73,237	205,644	142,631	14,516,430	198.21	70.59	—1.5	4.9
Mass.	124,852	363,376	240,522	39,335,152	315.05	108.25	—1.2	.9
Mich.	202,450	619,862	427,831	71,781,397	354.56	115.80	— .4	7.3
Minn.	46,954	128,649	87,812	14,073,037	299.72	109.39	—2.5	2.2
Miss.	54,033	168,532	126,798	4,324,544	80.04	25.66	.2	76.7
Mo.	64,499	193,206	133,880	12,453,168	193.08	64.46	—11.0	— .8
Mont.	6,268	17,628	12,503	1,309,190	208.87	74.27	—1.1	9.3
Nebr.	12,291	35,482	25,055	3,158,858	257.01	89.03	.6	— .1
Nev.	3,364	9,308	6,664	620,064	184.32	66.62	—14.2	—10.2
N.H.	7,501	21,243	14,340	1,754,647	233.92	82.60	—6.1	—4.8
N.J.	144,775	457,428	318,583	42,552,328	293.92	93.03	—1.5	4.5
N.M.	16,844	50,712	35,763	2,720,340	161.50	53.64	—2.2	5.4
N.Y.	367,146	1,124,614	781,655	132,675,548	361.37	117.97	—5.7	—2.5
N.C.	72,960	191,305	138,286	11,374,370	155.90	59.46	—3.3	— .3
N.D.	4,699	13,347	9,352	1,190,163	253.28	89.17	—2.1	—3.3
Ohio	165,161	478,539	330,735	37,155,120	224.96	77.64	—8.6	.8
Okla.	28,464	85,805	63,232	6,254,920	219.75	72.90	—2.2	6.4
Ore.	43,776	119,236	78,210	11,995,657	274.02	100.60	—2.7	—3.7
Pa. [2]	205,787	619,903	419,247	60,345,604	293.24	97.35	—3.9	— .7
P.R.	41,653	168,535	120,234	1,982,547	47.60	11.76	—8.0	—7.7
R.I. [2]	16,710	49,087	34,082	5,323,070	318.56	108.44	—4.8	—3.7
S.C.	50,868	142,530	102,547	4,557,472	89.59	31.98	.2	7.8
S.D.	7,223	20,557	15,026	1,500,211	207.70	72.98	—7.3	—3.2
Tenn.	58,484	159,638	115,612	6,668,098	114.02 [a]	41.77	—4.9	3.9
Tex.	92,177	287,836	213,453	9,938,685	107.82	34.53	—6.2	—6.6
Utah	12,496	36,861	26,928	3,405,855	272.56	92.40	—3.1	— .1
Vt.	6,515	19,566	12,838	2,047,424	314.26	104.64	1.3	20.8
V.I.	1,000	3,184	2,580	128,394	128.39	40.32	—14.0	—13.3
Va.	57,386	160,774	113,915	11,752,117	204.79	73.10	—3.3	5.1
Wash.	49,022	138,419	89,702	15,591,853	318.06	112.64	—3.2	6.3
W. Va. [2]	23,523	66,939	49,639	4,396,722	186.91	65.68	6.2	.7
Wisc.	69,026	189,155	131,189	22,284,933	322.85	117.81	—3.9	1.7
Wyo.	2,318	5,949	4,281	517,057	223.06	86.91	—4.9	13.6

[1] Incomplete. [2] Estimated data.

DRUG LAW ENFORCEMENT Source: Drug Enforcement Administration

Item	STATE AND LOCAL ARRESTS				DOMESTIC FEDERAL ARRESTS			
	1974	1975	1976	1977	1974	1975	1976	1977
Number of Arrests	454,948	508,189	500,540	569,293	6,782	7,404	9,240	9,369
Arrest Rate per 100,000	339.3	283.6	285.2	298.4				
Estimated % by Drug								
Narcotics (heroin, cocaine)	15.8%	13.1%	9.9%	13.2%	65.2%	66.4%	56.8%	64.8%
Cannabis	69.4%	69.2%	72.4%	71.2%	20.4%	17.5%	29.5%	18.2%
Dangerous Drug	14.8%	17.7%	3.0%	15.6%	13.0%	15.6%	13.3%	16.5%
Other	—	—	14.7%	—	1.4%	0.5%	0.4%	.5%
Estimated % by Race								
White	78.0%	78.7%	77.0%	77.0%	81.0%	84.9%	82.5%	80.6%
Non-White	22.0%	21.3%	22.9%	22.9%	19.0%	15.1%	17.1%	19.4%
Estimated % by Age								
Under 21	56.1%	53.3%	52.4%	50.7%	10.0%	10.1%	9.3%	8.2%
21–24	23.4%	23.7%	76.1%	23.2%	32.3%	30.1%	29.8%	26.5%
25–29	11.9%	13.1%	14.0%	14.5%	26.7%	26.6%	27.3%	28.4%
30–39	6.3%	7.2%	7.2%	8.4%	20.5%	21.7%	22.6%	25.2%
40 or Older	2.3%	2.7%	2.5%	3.2%	10.5%	11.5%	10.9%	12.1%
Estimated % by Sex								
Male	85.8%	86.2%	86.4%	86.1%	86.9%	85.9%	85.6%	85.8%
Female	14.2%	13.8%	13.6%	13.9%	13.1%	14.1%	14.4%	14.2%

DRUGS: USES AND ABUSES

Source: Smith Kline & French

Drugs	Pharmacologic Classification	Federal Controls	Medical Use	Potential for Physical Dependence	How Taken When Abused	Comments
Morphine (an opium derivative)	Central Nervous System Depressant	Narcotic: Schedule II Controlled Substances Act of 1970	To relieve pain	Yes	Orally or by injection	Morphine is the standard against which other narcotic analgesics are compared. Legally available on prescription only.
Heroin (a morphine derivative)	Depressant	Narcotic: Schedule I C. S. A. of 1970	To relieve pain	Yes	Sniffed or by injection	Not legally available in the United States. Used medically in some countries for relief of pain.
Codeine (an opium derivative)	Depressant	Narcotic C. S. A. of 1970	To relieve pain and coughing	Yes	Orally (usually as cough syrup)	Preparations containing specified minimal amounts of codeine are classified as "exempt" narcotics (Schedule V) and can be obtained without prescription in some states.
Paregoric (preparation containing opium)	Depressant	Narcotic: Schedule II C. S. A. of 1970	For sedation and to counteract diarrhea	Yes	Orally or by injection	Paregoric is often boiled to concentrate narcotic content prior to injection. Prescription only.
Meperidine (synthetic morphine-like drug)	Depressant	Narcotic: Schedule II C. S. A. of 1970	To relieve pain	Yes	Orally or by injection	Shorter acting than morphine. Frequent dosing required. Withdrawal symptoms appear quickly. Prescription only.
Methadone (synthetic morphine-like drug)	Depressant	Narcotic: Schedule II C. S. A. of 1970	To relieve pain	Yes	Orally or by injection	Longer acting than morphine. Withdrawal symptoms develop more slowly and are less intense and more prolonged. Prescription only.
Cocaine	Central Nervous System Stimulant	Schedule II C. S. A. of 1970	Local anesthetic	No	Sniffed or by injection	
Marijuana	Hallucinogen	Schedule I	No	No	Smoked or orally	Available legally only for research.
Barbiturates (e.g., amobarbital, pentobarbital, secobarbital)	Depressant	Schedule II and III C. S. A. of 1970	For sedation, sleep-producing, epilepsy, high blood pressure	Yes	Orally or by injection	Written prescription only. No refills for Schedule II barbiturates. For Schedule III barbiturates original prescription expires after 6 months. Only 5 refills permitted within this period. Dependence generally occurs only with the use of high doses for a protracted period of time.
Amphetamine drugs (e.g., amphetamine, dextroamphetamine, methamphetamine—also known as desoxyephedrine)	Stimulant	Schedule II C. S. A. of 1970	For antiappetite, narcolepsy, hyperkinetic behavior disorders	No	Orally or by injection	Written prescription only. No refills permitted.
LSD (also mescaline, peyote, psilocybin, DMT, STP, THC)	Hallucinogen	Schedule I C. S. A. of 1970	Medical research only	No	Orally or by injection	

U.S. INDEX OF CRIME   Source: Federal Bureau of Investigation

TRENDS BY GEOGRAPHIC REGION (Per cent change, 1978 over 1977)

	Total	Violent	Property	Murder	Forcible Rape	Robbery	Aggravated Assault	Burglary	Larceny- theft	Motor Vehicle Theft
Northeastern States	− 3	+ 3	− 3	− 2	+ 1	+ 2	+ 5	− 3	− 3	− 4
North Central States	− 1	+ 2	− 1	− 2	+ 3	− 7	+10	0	− 1	− 2
Southern States	+ 4	+ 6	+ 3	+ 1	+ 9	+ 7	+ 6	+ 3	+ 3	+ 9
Western States	+ 3	+ 8	+ 3	+ 5	+ 8	+ 9	+ 7	+ 3	+ 2	+ 6
TOTAL	+ 1	+ 5	+ 1	0	+ 6	+ 3	+ 7	+ 1	0	+ 1

TRENDS BY YEARS (Per cent change 1968-1978, each year over previous year)

	Total	Violent	Property	Murder	Forcible Rape	Robbery	Aggravated Assault	Burglary	Larceny- theft	Motor Vehicle Theft
1969/1968	+10	+11	+10	+ 7	+17	+14	+ 9	+ 7	+12	+12
1970/1969	+ 9	+12	+ 9	+ 8	+ 2	+17	+ 8	+11	+ 9	+ 6
1971/1970	+ 6	+11	+ 6	+11	+11	+11	+10	+ 9	+ 5	+ 2
1972/1971	− 4	+ 2	− 5	+ 5	+11	− 3	+ 7	− 1	− 6	− 6
1973/1972	+ 6	+ 5	+ 6	+ 5	+10	+ 2	+ 7	+ 8	+ 5	+ 5
1974/1973	+17	+11	+17	+ 5	+ 9	+14	+ 9	+17	+20	+ 4
1975/1974	+ 9	+ 5	+ 9	− 1	+ 1	+ 5	+ 5	+ 7	+12	+ 2
1976/1975	0	− 5	+ 1	−10	0	−10	− 1	− 5	+ 5	− 6
1977/1976	− 3	+ 2	− 4	+ 2	+11	− 4	+ 6	− 1	− 6	+ 1
1978/1977	+ 1	+ 5	+ 1	0	+ 6	+ 3	+ 7	+ 1	0	+ 1

CRIME: U.S. CITIES (Offenses Known to the Police, 1977 and 1978)
Source: Federal Bureau of Investigation

Preliminary figures for cities over 100,000 population reporting more than 9,000 incidents.

City	Crime Index 1977	Crime Index 1978	City	Crime Index 1977	Crime Index 1978
Akron, Ohio	17,689	15,606	Milwaukee, Wis.	34,547	33,822
Albuquerque, N. Mex.	23,955	22,866	Minneapolis, Minn.	32,298	30,542
Anaheim, Calif.	16,043	15,416	Mobile, Ala.	14,272	15,215
Anchorage, Alaska	9,863	10,243	Montgomery, Ala.	12,339	11,988
Atlanta, Ga.	45,597	53,869	Nashville, Tenn.	26,096	26,444
Aurora, Colo.	8,197	9,547	Newark, N.J.	30,313	32,057
Austin, Texas	23,536	24,719	New Haven, Conn.	16,131	17,524
Baltimore, Md.	67,287	69,463	New Orleans, La.	39,897	45,826
Baton Rouge, La.	21,402	21,967	New York, N.Y.	610,077	570,355
Beaumont, Texas	8,796	9,068	Norfolk, Va.	19,443	19,472
Berkeley, Calif.	11,750	11,838	Oakland, Calif.	39,713	38,854
Birmingham, Ala.	24,975	26,659	Oklahoma City, Okla.	27,970	27,638
Boston, Mass.	66,995	65,366	Omaha, Nebr.	22,020	21,459
Bridgeport, Conn.	13,502	12,467	Orlando, Fla.	11,090	12,992
Buffalo, N.Y.	31,781	27,313	Pasadena, Calif.	11,248	10,275
Camden, N.J.	9,530	9,475	Paterson, N.J.	11,229	9,985
Charlotte, N.C.	22,996	23,119	Peoria, Ill.	10,165	10,928
Chattanooga, Tenn.	10,411	12,107	Philadelphia, Pa.	71,827	72,948
Chicago, Ill.	203,839	190,815	Phoenix, Ariz.	68,324	71,575
Cincinnati, Ohio	30,012	30,298	Pittsburgh, Pa.	26,776	26,777
Cleveland, Ohio	54,995	50,952	Portland, Oreg.	36,821	35,615
Colorado Springs, Colo.	13,882	13,259	Providence, R.I.	12,529	12,403
Columbia, S.C.	9,636	11,099	Richmond, Va.	18,014	16,943
Columbus, Ohio	43,229	44,842	Riverside, Calif.	13,537	13,394
Corpus Christi, Texas	16,767	17,326	Rochester, N.Y.	26,510	25,285
Dallas, Texas	85,806	86,569	Rockford, Ill.	8,862	9,684
Dayton, Ohio	24,273	23,826	Sacramento, Calif.	26,998	29,185
Denver, Colo.	53,937	50,993	St. Louis, Mo.	55,450	54,486
Des Moines, Iowa	15,156	16,827	St. Paul, Minn.	21,403	20,162
Detroit, Mich.	123,748	110,511	St. Petersburg, Fla.	15,387	16,272
El Paso, Texas	24,621	23,609	Salt Lake City, Utah	17,622	16,103
Flint, Mich.	20,199	19,167	San Antonio, Texas	55,215	52,526
Fort Lauderdale, Fla.	15,408	16,726	San Bernardino, Calif.	13,689	13,668
Fort Wayne, Ind.	12,505	12,686	San Diego, Calif.	65,436	66,838
Fort Worth, Texas	36,743	36,008	San Francisco, Calif.	71,433	70,386
Fresno, Calif.	20,727	22,997	San Jose, Calif.	39,208	41,831
Gary, Ind.	11,590	10,010	Santa Ana, Calif.	14,606	16,082
Grand Rapids, Mich.	13,807	12,541	Savannah, Ga.	9,241	9,724
Greensboro, N.C.	9,834	9,742	Seattle, Wash.	38,378	44,083
Hartford, Conn.	18,264	18,594	Shreveport, La.	12,539	14,030
Hollywood, Fla.	10,757	10,719	Spokane, Wash.	11,613	12,582
Honolulu, Hawaii	46,984	51,892	Springfield, Mass.	12,265	12,511
Houston, Texas	117,288	132,000	Springfield, Mo.	10,978	11,032
Huntington Beach, Calif.	9,438	9,710	Stockton, Calif.	12,911	12,611
Indianapolis, Ind.	34,274	34,837	Tacoma, Wash.	12,631	13,464
Jacksonville, Fla.	35,999	36,274	Tampa, Fla.	25,606	27,002
Jersey City, N.J.	14,969	15,863	Toledo, Ohio	30,965	29,411
Kansas City, Kans.	15,345	15,459	Topeka, Kans.	8,444	9,111
Kansas City, Mo.	38,960	37,734	Trenton, N.J.	9,103	9,696
Knoxville, Tenn.	10,860	11,031	Tucson, Ariz.	32,025	29,111
Las Vegas, Nev.	27,595	29,371	Tulsa, Okla.	24,449	24,742
Lexington, Ky.	13,774	13,594	Virginia Beach, Va.	11,633	12,812
Little Rock, Ark.	15,238	16,071	Warren, Mich.	9,210	9,568
Long Beach, Calif.	26,669	27,776	Washington, D.C.	49,821	50,950
Los Angeles, Calif.	217,834	233,346	Wichita, Kans.	20,504	19,893
Louisville, Ky.	20,312	19,256	Winston-Salem, N.C.	10,728	19,971
Lubbock, Texas	13,339	14,259	Worcester, Mass.	13,762	12,577
Madison, Wis.	12,136	12,294	Yonkers, N.Y.	11,330	10,344
Memphis, Tenn.	44,992	43,548	Youngstown, Ohio	9,162	9,116
Miami, Fla.	34,099	34,860			

CAPITAL PUNISHMENT SOURCE: National Coalition Against the Death Penalty

ABOLITION COUNTRIES

Argentina*	1921	India (Travencore)	1944
Australia		Northern Ireland	1966
Federal**	1945	Israel***	1954
New South Wales**	1955	Italy***	1944
Queensland**	1922	Liechtenstein	(1798)
Tasmania**	1968	Luxembourg^b	(1821)
Austria	1968	Mexico†	1970
Belgium^a	1867	Monaco	1962
Bolivia	1962	Nepal	1950
Brazil***	1946	Netherlands	1886
Canada	1976	New Zealand	1961
Colombia	1910	Nicaragua*	(1892)
Costa Rica	1870	Norway***	1905
Denmark	1978	Panama	1915
Dominican Republic	1924	Portugal	1867
Ecuador	1897	San Marino	1848
Finland***	1949	Sweden***	1921
West Germany	1949	Switzerland	1942
Great Britain	1965	Uruguay	1907
Honduras	1957	Vatican City State	1969
Iceland	1940	Venezuela	1864

* Capital punishment abolished de jure as of year indicated; if abolished only de facto, date in parentheses indicates year of last execution. ** Death penalty retained for certain exceptional crimes other than murder, rape, burglary, robbery, arson, and kidnapping. *** Death penalty retained for use in wartime or under military law. ^a One murderer executed during World War I in 1918. ^b One multiple murderer executed in 1948. † Death penalty retained in 3 of 32 states.

Death Penalty States	Year of Last Execution	Death Penalty States	Year of Last Execution
Ala.	1965	Mo.	1965
Ariz.	1963	Mont.	1943
Ark.	1964	Neb.	1959
Calif.	1967	Nev.	1961
Conn.	1960	N.H.	1939
Colo.	1967	N.M.	1960
Del.	1946	N.C.	1961
D.C.	1957	Okla.	1966
Fla.	1979	Oregon	NA
Ga.	1964	Penn.	1962
Idaho	1957	S.C.	1962
Ind.	1961	Tenn.	1960
Kan.	1965	Texas	1964
Ky.	1962	Utah	1977
La.	1961	Va.	1962
Mass.	NA	Wash.	1963
Md.	1961	Wyo.	1965
Miss.	1964		

UNITED STATES

In the United States, 15 states and the District of Columbia have no laws authorizing the use of the death penalty: Alaska, Hawaii, Iowa, Kansas, Maine, Michigan, Minnesota, New Jersey, New York, North Dakota, Ohio, South Dakota, West Virginia and Wisconsin.

Except for a few special cases, all states have abolished the mandatory death penalty for murder, rape, and other crimes, leaving the decision between death or life imprisonment to the discretion of the jury or the court. This is the result of a U.S. Supreme Court decision, known as the "Furman" decision, which ruled by a 5 to 4 vote in 1972 that the death penalty for murder and for rape, when imposed mandatorily by the jury, constitutes cruel and unusual punishment and is in violation of the U.S. Constitution's 8th and 14th amendments.

In 1976, the U.S. Supreme Court affirmed that the death penalty did not violate the Constitution's ban on "cruel and unusual" punishment. However, "mandatory" death sentences for crimes such as murder are held not valid. At the same time, the Court upheld state statutes passed in Georgia, Florida, and Texas, while striking down those of Louisiana and North Carolina. Since this 1976 "Gregg" ruling, 35 states have enacted capital punishment laws which have not been successfully challenged in the courts.

Capital punishment continued to cause debate in 1978.

On March 10, Maryland Acting Gov. Blair Lee III signed into law a bill reinstating the death penalty for 10 types of first-degree murder. In July, Ohio's capital punishment law was struck down by the U.S. Supreme Court on grounds that it failed to allow juries to consider mitigating circumstances before imposing a death sentence. California and Oregon voters upheld their respective states' death penalty laws on Nov. 7. Oregon voters reinstated the death penalty by a solid margin, and California voters increased the number of crimes for which death could be imposed. Governors in New York, New Jersey and Pennsylvania vetoed capital punishment bills, but Pennsylvania legislators overrode the veto. Idaho joined Oklahoma and Texas in approving injection of lethal chemicals as an alternative to more traditional methods of execution. As of Dec. 31, 1978, there were 445 persons on death row: 261 white, 181 black and 3 American Indian.

Prisoners on Death Row as of December 31, 1978

State	Total	Law	State	Total	Law
Ala.	41	post-Furman [1]	Mo.	—	post-Gregg
Ariz.	8	post-Furman	Mont.	4	post-Gregg
Ark.	11	post-Furman	Nebr.	8	post-Furman
Calif.	9	post-Gregg	N.H.	—	post-Gregg
Colo.	—	post-Furman	Nev.	6	post-Gregg
Conn.	—	post-Furman	N.C.	7	post-Gregg
Del.	1	post-Gregg	Okla.	16	post-Gregg
Fla.	121	post-Furman	Ore.	—	post-Gregg
Ga.	57	post-Furman	Pa.[2]	—	post-Furman
Idaho	1	post-Gregg	R.I.	2	post-Furman
Ill.	5	post-Furman	S.C.	7	post-Gregg
Ind.	2	post-Furman	Tenn.	7	post-Gregg
Ky.	3	post-Gregg	Tex.	100	post-Furman
La.	1	post-Gregg	Utah	6	post-Gregg
Md.	—	post-Gregg	Vt.	—	pre-Furman [3]
Mass.	—	post-Gregg	Va.	6	post-Gregg
Miss.	10	post-Gregg	Wash.	6	post-Gregg
			Wyo.	—	post-Gregg

[1] Pre-Furman law for homicide by a person serving a life sentence only.
[2] Not including an unknown number held in county facilities.
[3] Violates Furman rule, but unchallenged because unused.

EXECUTIONS IN THE UNITED STATES SOURCE: U.S. Dept. of Justice, Law Enforcement Assistance Administration

Year	Prisoners Executed				Year	Prisoners Executed			
	Total	White	Negro	Other		Total	White	Negro	Other
All years (1930-78)	3,860	1,752	2,066	42	1951	105	57	47	1
Percent	100.0	45.4	53.5	1.1	1950	82	40	42	—
					1949	119	50	67	2
1978	—	—	—	—	1948	119	35	82	2
1977	1	1	—	—	1947	153	42	111	—
1967	2	1	1	—	1946	131	46	84	1
1966	1	1	—	—	1945	117	41	75	1
1965	7	6	1	—	1944	120	47	70	3
1964	15	8	7	—	1943	131	54	74	3
1963	21	13	8	—	1942	147	67	80	—
1962	47	28	19	—	1941	123	59	63	1
1961	42	20	22	—	1940	124	49	75	—
1960	56	21	35	—	1939	160	80	77	3
1959	49	16	33	—	1938	190	96	92	2
1958	49	20	28	1	1937	147	69	74	4
1957	65	34	31	—	1936	195	92	101	2
1956	65	21	43	1	1935	199	119	77	3
1955	76	44	32	—	1934	168	65	102	1
1954	81	38	42	1	1933	160	77	81	2
1953	62	30	31	1	1932	140	62	75	3
1952	83	36	47	—	1930	155	90	65	—

CIVIL RIGHTS/RACE

CIVIL RIGHTS LEGISLATION

Source: Congressional Quarterly Inc.

Six major civil rights bills have been passed by Congress since 1957. Highlights of these bills are:

1957—The Civil Rights Act of 1957 (HR 6127–PL 85-315) was the first civil rights legislation passed by Congress since the Reconstruction period. It prohibited action to prevent persons from voting in federal elections, authorizing the Attorney General to bring suit when a person was deprived of his voting rights. It also created a Civil Rights Commission and set up a Civil Rights Division in the Department of Justice.

1960—The Civil Rights Act of 1960 (HR 8601–PL 86-449) strengthened provisions of the 1957 Act for court enforcement of voting rights and required that voting records be preserved. It also contained limited criminal penalty provisions relating to bombing and to obstruction of federal court orders.

1964—The Civil Rights Act of 1964 (HR 7152–PL 88-352) prohibited discrimination on the basis of race, sex, or national origin in public accommodations and in federally assisted programs. It also prohibited discrimination by employers and unions.

1965—The Voting Rights Act of 1965 (S 1564–PL 89-110) authorized the Attorney General to appoint federal examiners to register voters in certain areas.

1968—A civil rights bill (HR 2516–PL 90-284) prohibited discrimination in the sale or rental of about 80 percent of all housing. It also protected persons exercising specified rights, such as attending school.

1970—A bill (HR 4249–PL 91-285) amended and extended the Voting Rights Act of 1965. It extended its application to Northern cities or counties where literacy tests are required.

1975—The Voting Rights Act was extended for seven years.

COLOR AND RACE OF U.S. POPULATION: 1970

Source: Bureau of the Census

Regions and States	White	Black	Indian	Japanese	Chinese	Filipino	All other
United States, total	177,748,975	22,580,289	792,730	591,290	435,062	343,060	720,520
Northeast Region	44,310,504	4,344,153	49,466	38,978	115,777	31,424	150,401
Maine	985,276	2,800	2,195	348	206	453	770
New Hampshire	733,106	2,505	361	360	420	157	772
Vermont	442,553	761	229	134	173	53	427
Massachusetts	5,477,624	175,817	4,475	4,393	14,012	2,361	10,488
Rhode Island	914,757	25,338	1,390	629	1,093	1,761	1,757
Connecticut	2,835,458	181,177	2,222	1,621	2,209	2,177	6,845
New York	15,834,090	2,168,949	28,355	20,351	81,378	14,279	89,565
New Jersey	6,349,908	770,292	4,706	5,681	9,233	5,623	22,721
Pennsylvania	10,737,732	1,016,514	5,533	5,461	7,053	4,560	17,056
North Central Region	51,641,183	4,571,550	151,287	42,354	39,343	27,824	98,122
Ohio	9,646,997	970,477	6,654	5,555	5,305	3,490	13,539
Indiana	4,820,324	357,464	3,887	2,279	2,115	1,365	6,235
Illinois	9,600,381	1,425,674	11,413	17,299	14,474	12,654	32,081
Michigan	7,833,474	991,066	16,854	5,221	6,407	3,657	18,404
Wisconsin	4,258,959	128,224	18,924	2,648	2,700	1,209	5,067
Minnesota	3,736,038	34,868	23,128	2,603	2,422	1,456	4,456
Iowa	2,782,762	32,596	2,992	1,009	993	614	3,410
Missouri	4,177,495	480,172	5,405	2,382	2,815	2,010	6,222
North Dakota	599,485	2,494	14,369	239	165	204	805
South Dakota	630,333	1,627	32,365	221	163	83	715
Nebraska	1,432,867	39,911	6,624	1,314	551	324	1,902
Kansas	2,122,068	106,977	8,672	1,584	1,233	758	5,286
South Region	50,420,108	11,969,961	201,222	30,917	34,284	31,979	106,896
Delaware	466,459	78,276	656	359	559	392	1,403
Maryland	3,194,888	699,479	4,239	3,733	6,520	5,170	8,370
District of Columbia	209,272	537,712	956	651	2,582	1,662	3,675
Virginia	3,761,514	861,368	4,853	3,500	2,805	7,496	6,958
West Virginia	1,673,480	67,342	751	368	373	722	1,201
North Carolina	3,901,767	1,126,478	44,406	2,104	1,255	905	5,144
South Carolina	1,794,430	789,041	2,241	826	521	1,222	2,235
Georgia	3,391,242	1,187,149	2,347	1,836	1,584	1,253	4,164
Florida	5,719,343	1,041,651	6,677	4,090	3,133	5,092	9,457
Kentucky	2,981,766	230,793	1,531	1,095	558	612	2,351
Tennessee	3,293,930	621,261	2,276	1,160	1,610	846	2,604
Alabama	2,533,831	903,467	2,443	1,079	626	540	2,179
Mississippi	1,393,283	815,770	4,113	461	1,441	475	1,369
Arkansas	1,565,915	352,445	2,014	587	743	289	1,302
Louisiana	2,541,498	1,086,832	5,294	1,123	1,340	1,249	3,970
Oklahoma	2,280,362	171,892	98,468	1,408	999	612	5,488
Texas	9,717,128	1,399,005	17,957	6,537	7,635	3,442	45,026
West Region	31,377,180	1,694,025	390,755	479,041	245,658	251,833	365,101
Montana	663,043	1,995	27,130	574	289	236	1,142
Idaho	698,802	2,130	6,687	2,255	498	206	1,989
Wyoming	323,024	2,568	4,980	566	292	108	878
Colorado	2,112,352	66,411	8,836	7,831	1,489	1,068	9,272
New Mexico	915,815	19,555	72,788	940	563	386	5,953
Arizona	1,604,948	53,344	95,812	2,394	3,878	1,253	9,271
Utah	1,031,926	6,617	11,273	4,713	1,281	392	3,071
Nevada	448,177	27,762	7,933	1,087	955	817	2,409
Washington	3,251,055	71,308	33,386	20,335	9,201	11,462	12,422
Oregon	2,032,079	26,308	13,510	6,843	4,814	1,633	6,198
California	17,761,032	1,400,143	91,018	213,280	170,131	138,859	178,671
Alaska	236,767	8,911	16,276	916	228	1,498	35,786
Hawaii	298,160	7,573	1,126	217,307	52,039	93,915	98,441

AMERICANS OF SPANISH ANCESTRY

SOURCE: Bureau of the Census

The March 1978 Current Population Survey furnished a statistical profile of Americans of Spanish origin. By census definition this group consists of those Americans of Mexican, Puerto Rican, Cuban, Central or South American, or other Spanish origin.

In March 1978 their estimated numbers were:

Mexican	7,151,000
Puerto Rican	1,823,000
Cuban	689,000
Central or South Amer.	863,000
Other Spanish	1,519,000
Total	**12,046,000**

The latest available information, that of the 1970 Census, gave the following breakdown for those states having the largest Spanish origin population: California: 2,368,748; Texas: 1,840,862; New York: 1,352,302; Florida: 405,037; Illinois: 393,347; New Mexico: 308,-340; New Jersey: 288,488; Arizona: 265,006; Colorado: 225,506; Michigan: 151,070.

The population of Spanish origin in March 1978 was a younger population than the overall population of the United States: persons of Spanish origin had a lower median age, 22.1 years old, than the overall population, 29.5 years old. About 12.6 percent of all persons of Spanish origin were under 5 years of age, while the proportion of the total United States population under 5 years of age was 7.2 percent. Only about 4.3 percent of all persons of Spanish origin were 65 years old and over in March 1978 compared to 10.5 percent for the total population.

Since women in general marry at younger ages than men, there was a larger proportion of single Spanish origin men than single Spanish origin women; about 35 percent of Spanish origin men 14 years old and over in 1978 were single, but only about 28 percent of Spanish origin women were single.

Younger persons of Spanish origin have achieved, in recent years, higher levels of educational attainment than their elders. For example, about 56.6 percent of Spanish origin persons 25 to 29 years old had completed 4 years of high school or more, but only 30.3 percent of Spanish persons 45 to 64 years old had done so. Only 5.7 percent of all persons of Spanish origin 25 to 29 years old had completed less than 5 years of school, but about 25 percent of Spanish origin persons 45 to 64 years old had completed less than 5 years of school.

In March 1978 there were about 2.6 million employed men of Spanish origin 16 years old and over in the United States, but only 8 percent of these men were working in professional and technical fields. Among employed men of Spanish origin, those of Mexican origin had the highest proportion, 6.7 percent, employed as farm laborers.

Family income in 1977 was lower for Spanish origin families than for all families in the population. Specifically, median income of families with a family head of Spanish origin was $11,421, as compared with $16,009 for all families. Also, the proportion of Spanish origin families with incomes of under $4,000 was 10.4 percent, but the proportion of all families with incomes under $4,000 was 6.3 percent.

In 1977 there was a marked difference between the individual incomes of men and women of Spanish origin. For example, about 31 percent of Spanish origin men with income earned less than $5,000, but about 63.5 percent of Spanish origin women with income had incomes of less than $5,000. At the higher income range, 2.7 percent of men of Spanish origin had incomes over $25,000, but only 0.2 percent of women of Spanish origin had incomes at this level.

There were about 591,000 families with head of Spanish origin in 1977 below the poverty level, or about one of every 5 families with head of Spanish origin. There was, however, a noticeable difference in the proportions of low-income families between the subcategories of Spanish origin. For example, although only 15 percent of families with head of Cuban origin were below the low-income level, about 39 percent of families with head of Puerto Rican origin were below the low-income level in 1977.

EMPLOYMENT IN URBAN POVERTY AREAS   SOURCE: Bureau of Labor Statistics

U.S. Employment Status	TOTAL 1977	TOTAL 1978	WHITE 1977	WHITE 1978	BLACK AND OTHER 1977	BLACK AND OTHER 1978
Total United States						
Civilian labor force	97,401,000	100,420,000	86,107,000	88,456,000	11,294,000	11,964,000
Unemployed	6,855,000	6,047,000	5,373,000	4,620,000	1,482,000	1,427,000
Unemployment rate (percent)	7.0	6.0	6.2	5.2	13.1	11.9
Poverty Areas						
Civilian labor force	16,049,000	16,285,000	11,545,000	11,694,000	4,504,000	4,591,000
Unemployed	1,474,000	1,412,000	774,000	732,000	700,000	680,000
Unemployment rate (percent)	9.2	8.7	6.7	6.3	15.5	14.8

AMERICAN INDIANS

SOURCE: Bureau of the Census

The Indian population in the United States was determined by the 1970 census to number 792,730, up from the 1960 figure of 523,591. Over fifty percent live in the five states of Arizona, California, New Mexico, North Carolina, and Oklahoma. One-fourth live in the South, one-fifth in the North Central states, and the remaining five percent in the Northeast.

The ten largest Indian tribes and their 1970 populations are:

Navajo	96,743
Cherokee	66,150
Sioux (Dakota)	47,825
Chippewa	41,946
Pueblo	30,971
Lumbee	27,520
Choctaw and Houma	23,562
Apache	22,993
Iroquois	21,473
Creek, Alabama and Coushatta	17,004

Almost one-half of America's Indians live in urban areas, 28 percent on 115 major reservations, and the rest on small reservations and in rural areas. The rural-to-urban migration of Indians has partly resulted in higher educational attainment, better jobs and housing, and higher income levels.

Poverty, however, remains a critical problem among the Indians. Almost forty percent of their population was found to be living below the poverty level in 1969. Their median family income was $5,832 versus the national average of $9,590. Hardest hit financially are the reservation Indians, who must cope with near-subsistence conditions.

Unemployment, nearly three times the national average, affects the reservation Indians most severely, too. This can be attributed in part to a reluctance to establish industrial plants and commercial businesses on the reservation.

Educational advances have taken place. One-third of Indians over 25 years of age have completed high school, while more than one-half of the total population had finished twelve years of school. Twenty-five percent of Indian males between 16 and 21 had dropped out of school. Reservation Indians again fared the worst. The Navajo Reservation Indians completed an average number of only 4.1 school years.

In the area of housing, over twenty-five percent of America's Indians live in overcrowded conditions of more than one person per room. Only seventy-two percent of Indian housing have complete plumbing, in contrast to the national average of ninety-two percent.

WOMEN'S RIGHTS: SOCIAL HISTORY OF AMERICAN WOMEN

1821   Emma Willard founds the Troy Female Seminary, the first endowed school for girls in America.

1848   Seneca Falls Convention held; Elizabeth Cady Stanton, Lucretia Mott and others draft the "Declaration of Sentiments," the first public protest against the inequality of the economic, political, and social positions of women in America.

1849   Elizabeth Blackwell completes her training at Geneva Medical College and becomes the first woman ever to receive an M.D. degree.

1868   New York women form the Working Women's Association to fight for better working conditions.

1868   Susan B. Anthony and Elizabeth Cady Stanton found *The Revolution*, a newspaper with the motto; "Men, their rights and nothing more; women, their rights and nothing less!"

1869   National Woman Suffrage Association founded; American Woman Suffrage Association founded; two organizations merge in 1890 to work for a voting rights amendment to the Constitution.

1873   State of Illinois passes the first women's equal employment legislation.

1890   Wyoming, the first territory to grant political equality to women, joins the Union.

1917   Miss Jeannette Rankin of Montana becomes the first woman to serve in Congress.

1920   Nineteenth Amendment to the Constitution adopted, giving women the right to vote.

1963   Congress passes the Equal Pay Act which stipulates that equal pay must be given for equal work.

1964   Under Title VII of the Civil Rights Act passed by Congress, discrimination based on sex by employers of 15 or more employees is prohibited.

1972   Ms. magazine, written and edited by women, begins publication.

1973   The Supreme Court issues two decisions rendering all state abortion laws unconstitutional.

1973   The Senate July 23 passes a bill to protect consumers against unfair billing practices and to prohibit lenders from discriminating on the basis of sex or marital status in all credit transactions.

1974   Little League Baseball allows girls to play.

1976   The military academies of the Army, Air Force and Navy admit women to their freshman classes.

1977   The National Women's Conference meets in Houston, Texas, in observance of International Women's Year.

1978   Congress passes the Pregnancy Disability Bill, making pregnancy an insurable disability.

1978   Congress passes a bill extending the time by three years three months for ratification of the Equal Rights Amendment.

THE EQUAL RIGHTS AMENDMENT (Pending)

SOURCE: National Organization for Women, 425 13th St. NW, Suite 1001, Washington, D.C. 20004

The Equal Rights Amendment, which would be Amendment XXVII to the U.S. Constitution, was proposed by Congress on March 22, 1972. A total of 38 states must ratify the ERA for its adoption. As of January 18, 1977, 35 states had done so. The text follows:

Section 1.   Equality of rights under the law shall not be denied or abridged by the United States or by any state on account of sex.

Section 2.   The Congress shall have the power to enforce, by appropriate legislation, the provisions of this article.

Section 3.   This amendment shall take effect two years after the date of ratification.

BLACK POPULATION OF LARGE U.S. CITIES

SOURCE: Bureau of the Census

	Black Population				Black Population		
Cities by Rank	1960	1970	% of Total Population	Cities by Rank	1960	1970	% of Total Population
New York City, N.Y.	1,087,931	1,668,115	21.2	Milwaukee, Wis.	62,458	105,088	14.7
Chicago, Ill.	812,637	1,102,620	32.7	Pittsburgh, Pa.	100,692	104,904	20.2
Detroit, Mich.	482,223	660,428	43.7	Richmond, Va.	91,972	104,766	42.0
Philadelphia, Pa.	529,240	653,791	33.6	Boston, Mass.	63,165	104,707	16.3
Washington, D.C.	411,737	537,712	71.1	Columbus, Ohio	77,140	99,627	18.5
Los Angeles, Calif.	334,916	503,606	17.9	San Francisco, Calif.	74,383	96,078	13.4
Baltimore, Md.	325,589	420,210	46.4	Buffalo, N.Y.	70,904	94,329	20.4
Houston, Texas	215,037	316,551	25.7	Gary, Ind.	69,123	92,695	52.8
Cleveland, Ohio	250,818	287,841	38.3	Nashville-Davidson, Tenn.	76,437	87,851	19.6
New Orleans, La.	233,514	267,308	45.0	Norfolk, Va.	78,806	87,261	28.3
Atlanta, Ga.	186,464	255,051	51.3	Louisville, Ky.	70,075	86,040	23.8
St. Louis, Mo.	214,377	254,191	40.9	Ft. Worth, Texas	56,440	78,324	19.9
Memphis, Tenn.	184,320	242,513	38.9	Miami, Fla.	65,213	76,156	22.7
Dallas, Texas	129,242	210,238	24.9	Dayton, Ohio	57,288	74,284	30.5
Newark, N.J.	138,035	207,458	54.2	Charlotte, N.C.	56,248	72,972	30.3
Indianapolis, Ind.	98,049	134,320	18.0	Mobile, Ala.	65,619	67,356	35.4
Birmingham, Ala.	135,113	126,388	42.0	Shreveport, La.	56,607	62,152	34.1
Cincinnati, Ohio	108,754	125,070	27.6	Jackson, Miss.	51,556	61,063	39.7
Oakland, Calif.	83,618	124,710	34.5	Compton, Calif.	28,265	55,781	71.0
Jacksonville, Fla.	105,655	118,158	22.3	Tampa, Fla.	46,244	54,720	19.7
Kansas City, Mo.	83,146	112,005	22.1	Jersey City, N.J.	36,692	54,595	21.0

BLACK-AMERICAN HISTORY

Year	Event

1619 The first Negroes to be brought to the American colonies arrived in Virginia as indentured servants.

1661 Virginia passed the first law making Negroes slaves.

1663 Slavery was legally recognized in Maryland.

1688 Quakers in Germantown, Pa., issued the first formal antislavery protest in the Western Hemisphere.

1770 Crispus Attucks, a runaway slave, was killed in the Boston Massacre.

1775 The Pennsylvania Abolition Society, the first antislavery society in America, was founded.

1776 The Declaration of Independence was signed, the final version omitting an attack on slavery by Thomas Jefferson contained in the draft version.

The Continental Congress approved a proposal by General George Washington to permit the enlistment of free Negroes in the Continental Army. About 5,000 Negroes served in the War of Independence.

1787 Congress barred the extension of slavery into the Northwest Territory.

1791 Eli Whitney invented the cotton gin, spurring the expansion of cotton plantations and the demand for slaves.

1800 Gabriel Prosser, a Virginia slave, led an unsuccessful insurrection and was hanged with 24 conspirators.

1807 British Parliament abolished the slave trade.
Congress barred the importation of new slaves into U.S. territory.

1816 The American Colonization Society was formed to resettle free American Negroes in Africa.

1820 Congress adopted the Missouri Compromise providing for the admission of Missouri into the Union as a slave state, and Maine's entry as a free state. All territory north of 36°30′ was declared free; all territory south of that line was left open to slavery.

1827 The first Negro newspaper, *Freedom's Journal*, began publication in New York City.
Slavery was abolished in New York State.

1830 The U.S. Census Bureau reported that 3,777 Negro heads of families owned slaves.

1831 Federal and state troops crushed a slave rebellion in Southampton County, Va., led by Nat Turner. The rebellion, in which more than 50 whites and more than 100 slaves were killed, ended in the capture and execution of Turner and led to the adoption of more rigid slave codes.

1847 Frederick Douglass, a former slave and a lecturer with the Massachusetts Anti-Slavery Society, began publishing *North Star*, an abolitionist newspaper.

1849 Harriet Tubman escaped from slavery in Maryland. She became one of the most venturesome conductors on the Underground Railroad, leading over 300 slaves to freedom.
Benjamin Roberts filed the first school integration suit on behalf of his daughter. The Massachusetts Supreme Court rejected the suit and established a "separate but equal" precedent.

1850 The Compromise of 1850 admitted California to the Union as a free state but strengthened the Fugitive Slave Law, giving greater inducement for the apprehension of runaway slaves.

1852 Harriet Beecher Stowe's novel *Uncle Tom's Cabin*, a vastly popular antislavery work, was published.

1853 *Clotelle: or the President's Daughter* by historian William Wells Brown was published—the first novel by an American Negro.

1854 James A. Healy was ordained a priest in Notre Dame cathedral, Paris. He later became America's first Negro Roman Catholic bishop.
The first Negro college, Lincoln University, was founded as Ashmun Institute in Oxford, Pa.

1855 The first Negro to win elective office in the United States, John Mercer Langston, was elected clerk of Brownhelm Township, Lorain Co., O.

1863 The Draft Riots took place in New York City. Blacks and abolitionists were attacked and killed.

1865 By the end of the Civil War, some 186,000 Negroes had served with the Union forces.
The Thirteenth Amendment, freeing all slaves, was passed by Congress.
The Freedman's Bureau was organized to aid and protect newly freed blacks in the South.
Dr. John S. Rock, a Boston physician and lawyer, was the first Negro admitted to the bar of the United States Supreme Court.
Southern states passed the "Black Codes" in an attempt to restrict the freedom of emancipated slaves.

1866 Charles L. Mitchell and Edward G. Walker were elected to the Massachusetts House of Representatives, becoming the first Negroes to serve in a U.S. legislature.

1867 Morehouse College, Atlanta, Ga., and Howard University, Washington, D.C., were founded.

1868 Oscar J. Dunn attained the highest elective office held by an American Negro up to that time, becoming lieutenant governor of Louisiana.

1869 Ebenezer Don Carlos Basset was appointed minister to Haiti, the first Negro diplomat to represent the United States.

1870 Hiram Revels was elected to fill the unexpired U.S. Senate term of Jefferson Davis of Mississippi, becoming the first Negro Senator. He served a year.
Joseph H. Rainey of South Carolina became the first Negro in the House of Representatives. He was subsequently reelected four times.

1875 Congress passed a civil rights act prohibiting discrimination in such public accommodations as hotels and theaters.

1877 Henry O. Flipper became the first Negro to graduate from West Point.

1881 Tennessee passed a "Jim Crow" law instituting segregated railroad travel that set a trend among other states in the South.
Booker T. Washington opened Tuskegee Institute in Alabama.

1883 The Supreme Court declared the 1875 Civil Rights Act unconstitutional.

1890 Mississippi instituted restrictions on voting, including a poll tax and literacy tests, which were designed to disenfranchise Negroes. During the decade, other Southern states followed. Louisiana added (1898) the exclusionary device of the "grandfather clause," which set educational and property qualifications for voting but exempted those whose ancestors had been eligible to vote as of Jan. 1, 1867.

1891 The Provident Hospital in Chicago—the first such interracial institution in America—was founded by Negro surgeon Daniel Hale Williams.

1895 Frederick Douglass, the Negro abolitionist whom Lincoln had called "the most meritorious man of the 19th century," died.

1896 The National Association of Colored Women was organized in Washington, D.C.; Mary Church Terrell served as its first president.

1898 Four Negro regiments in the regular army compiled an excellent combat record during the Spanish-American War. Dismounted elements of the black Ninth and Tenth Cavalry rescued the Rough Riders from near annihilation.

1905 Twenty-nine Negro intellectuals from 14 states, headed by Dr. W. E. B. DuBois, organized the Niagara Movement, which demanded the abolition of all racial distinctions. The meeting took place at Fort Erie, N.Y.

1909 Matthew Henson, a Negro member of Admiral Peary's expedition, placed the American flag at the North Pole.

1910 The National Association for the Advancement of Colored People (NAACP) was founded in New York. The "Great Migration" of more than 2 million Southern blacks began.

1911 The National Urban League was founded. It was originally made up of two groups: The Committee for Improving the Industrial Conditions of Negroes and The League for the Protection of Colored Women.

1915 The Association for the Study of Negro Life and History was established by the "father of Negro history," Dr. Carter G. Woodson.

1917 Ten thousand Negroes marched down Fifth Avenue in New York to protest the many lynchings in the South. The parade was led by W. E. B. DuBois. Race riots broke out in East St. Louis, Illinois.

1920 The pioneer black nationalist Marcus Garvey inaugurated the International Convention of the Universal Negro Improvement Association (UNIA) in Harlem. UNIA reached its greatest influence during the following two years.

1928 Oscar De Priest of Illinois was the first black Congressman from a northern state.

1935 Mary McLeod Bethune organized the National Council of Negro Women.

1936 Negro track star Jesse Owen won four gold medals in the Olympics at Berlin.

1937 William H. Hastie became the first Negro to serve as a U.S. Federal judge.

Joe Louis became heavyweight boxing champion of the world, defeating Jim Braddock for the title.

1939 Contralto Marian Anderson, denied the use of Constitution Hall in Washington by the Daughters of the American Revolution, sang on Easter Sunday before 75,000 people at the Lincoln Memorial.

1940 Benjamin O. Davis, Sr., was appointed the first black general in the U.S. armed forces.

Dr. Charles R. Drew did notable research into blood preservation and discovered blood plasma.

1941 A Negro threat to stage a massive protest march on Washington resulted in the issuance of Executive Order 8802 prohibiting racial discrimination in defense industries or the government (but not the armed forces).

1942 The Congress of Racial Equality (CORE), an action-oriented civil rights group, was founded by James Farmer in Chicago.

1947 Statistics amassed by Tuskegee Institute indicated that in the period 1882–1947 3,426 Negroes were lynched in the United States. Of these, 1,217 were lynched in the 1890–1900 decade.

1948 President Truman issued Executive Order 9981 calling for "equality of treatment and opportunity" in the armed forces.

1949 William L. Dawson became the first Negro to head a Congressional committee.

1951 Ralph J. Bunche, who won a Nobel Peace Prize in 1950, was appointed Under-Secretary of the United Nations, the highest ranking American employed by the international body.

Private First Class William Thompson was awarded the Congressional Medal of Honor for bravery in the Korean War, the first Negro to win it since the Spanish-American War.

1952 A Tuskegee Institute report indicated that for the first time in 71 years of compilation, no lynchings were reported in the United States.

1954 In"Brown v. Board of Education of Topeka" the U.S. Supreme Court held that segregation in public education denied equal protection of the laws.

1955 A bus boycott in Montgomery, Ala., was led by Dr. Martin Luther King, Jr., after Rosa Parks was arrested for refusing to give up her seat to a white man.

1957 Central High School in Little Rock, Ark., was integrated by nine Negro children, but not until President Eisenhower had called in troops to keep order.

1960 Four Negro North Carolina A & T College freshmen occupied places at a Woolworth lunch counter, launching a wave of nonviolent sit-ins.

1961 CORE began "Freedom Rides" that rolled through the South, protesting segregation.

1962 The Albany (Ga.) Movement—a citywide attempt, supported by the Southern Christian Leadership Conference, Student Nonviolent Coordinating Committee, NAACP, and CORE, to abolish discrimination in all public facilities—was formed.

James Meredith desegregated the University of Mississippi, after President Kennedy dispatched troops and riots killed two persons.

1963 NAACP leader Medgar Evers was murdered in the doorway of his home in Jackson, Miss.

Birmingham, Ala.: The plight of Negroes in the South and throughout the nation was dramatized here as fire hoses, police dogs, and rough handling by the police, followed by bomb blasts in the black ghetto, became the order of the day. September 15: A bomb blast at the Sixteenth Street Baptist Church killed four girls.

June 11: President Kennedy declared that the black struggle for civil rights is a "moral issue."

August 28: The March on Washington in which more than 200,000 Americans from all walks of life converged on the nation's capital constituted one of the largest single protests in American history. The marchers gathered on the steps of the Lincoln Memorial to dramatize discontent with the Negro's plight.

1964 Three young civil-rights workers—Michael Schwerner, Andrew Goodman, and James E. Chaney—were murdered in Mississippi.

Riots exploded in Harlem and elsewhere.

1965 Malcolm X., former Black Muslim and advocate of black nationalism, was assassinated in New York City.

Thurgood Marshall was named as the first Negro Solicitor General of the United States.

President Johnson signed the Voting Rights Act, under which federal examiners are authorized to register black voters who have been refused by state officials.

Riots erupted in the Watts section of Los Angeles; 35 people were killed, 883 others were injured, and 3,598 were arrested. Damage totaled more than $220 million.

1966 Robert Weaver was appointed head of the Department of Housing and Urban Development (HUD), the first Negro ever to serve at cabinet level.

Constance Baker Motley, former borough president of Manhattan, became the first Negro woman to become a federal judge in American history.

The U.S. Supreme Court outlawed all poll taxes.

The concept of "Black Power" was adopted by CORE.

1967 Solicitor General Thurgood Marshall became the first Negro Supreme Court Justice.

At a four-day Black Power conference—the largest of its kind in American history—more than 400 people representing 45 civil rights groups from 36 cities convened in Newark, N.J., expressing viewpoints that ranged from moderate to militant.

1968 April 4: While standing on the balcony of a Memphis motel, Dr. Martin Luther King, Jr., was shot and killed by a sniper.

The Kerner Commission reported that "our nation is moving toward two societies, one black, one white—separate and unequal."

1969 Educational institutions acceded to demands by black students for more black studies.

James Earl Ray pleaded guilty to the assassination of Martin Luther King; sentenced to 99 years in prison.

1970 The killing in December 1969 of a Black Panther leader, Fred Hampton, led to a federal investigation and the subsequent conclusion that the Chicago police had exercised undue force.

1971 Samuel L. Gravely, Jr., was made the first black admiral in the U.S. Navy.

Thirteen Black Panthers, including two who fled to Algeria during the trial, were acquitted in New York City on charges of conspiring to bomb department stores and police stations and to murder policemen.

The six-month trial in New Haven of Bobby G. Seale, chairman of the Black Panther party, and Mrs. Ericka Huggins, a New Haven Panther, for crimes arising from the death of Alex Rackley, ended in a mistrial as the jury was unable to reach a verdict. Rackley, a Panther, died in May 1969.

1972 Over 8,000 delegates and observers met in Gary, Indiana as the first National Black Political Convention voted to set up a permanent representative body to set the direction for black political and social actions.

Angela Davis, accused of conspiracy to kidnap and murder, was acquitted.

The busing of children, both black and white, from one neighborhood school district to another became an important political issue. The Nixon administration supported and signed into law a bill which prohibited busing solely to achieve racial integration.

1975 Black Muslims agreed to accept white members.

1976 U.S. Supreme Court outlawed discrimination in commercially operated nonsectarian private schools.

1977 The TV dramatization of Alex Haley's book *Roots* was seen by the largest audience ever. The story chronicled the black author's family history from mid-eighteenth century African beginnings.

1978 U.S. Supreme Court ruled that the University of California Medical School at Davis must admit Allan P. Bakke, a 38-year-old white engineer, as the school's minority-admissions plan was inflexible and racially biased. The justices ruled, however, that race could be considered as a university admission factor. Black leaders expressed concern regarding the decision.

PUBLIC HEALTH/MEDICINE

BIOLOGICAL AND MEDICAL SCIENCE REVIEW: 1978/79
Edward R. Brace: Fellow, American Medical Writers Association

Breast Cancer: Nearly 106,000 American women are diagnosed each year as having breast cancer. Despite the best efforts of physicians to treat this disease in its earliest stages, the tragic fact is that mortality from breast cancer has remained basically unchanged for the past three or four decades. And there is growing evidence that a *radical* mastectomy—the most "mutilating" surgical procedure—is not more effective than a *simple* mastectomy followed by radiotherapy.

During the past two years a study has been underway, sponsored by the National Cancer Institute under the chairmanship of Dr. Bernard Fisher, to evaluate the comparative effectiveness of three basic approaches to the treatment of cancer of the breast: (1) total mastectomy; (2) segmental mastectomy; and (3) segmental mastectomy with radiotherapy. The study was designed to determine the extent of surgery needed to control the early stages of the disease. Results of the study remain to be published. But it seems fairly clear, as stated by Dr. Maurice S. Fox (Department of Biology, Massachusetts Institute of Technology), that "Because of our limited understanding of cancer biology, we are without first principles that make it possible to predict the result of different treatments." Continued and extensive clinical trials are thus necessary. However, according to Dr. Fox, "Although various trials have been the subject of criticism, perhaps their most striking feature is that none of the trials provide evidence for any survival benefit when contrasting radical with simple mastectomy."

A so-called *total* mastectomy involves surgical removal of the affected breast as well as the lymph nodes in the armpit (axillary nodes). The *radical* mastectomy goes one step further; in addition to removing the breast and the axillary nodes, the underlying chest muscles are removed as well (the chest muscles are left intact in a *total* mastectomy).

As Dr. Fox states (Feb. 2, 1979), "Radical mastectomy seems to have been generally accepted without convincing evidence of its superiority. On the contrary, there is abundant evidence supporting the proposal that more conservative procedures provide at least equal benefit with substantially less mutilation."

In June 1979 the National Institutes of Health (Bethesda, Maryland) sponsored a conference in which the relative benefits of the various treatments of breast cancer were debated by leading cancer researchers and surgeons. They concluded, after discussing the subject for nine hours, that radical mastectomies "may no longer be the preferred treatment"—except in advanced cases. These experts felt that there is no indisputable evidence to support the claim that *radical* mastectomy can enhance a patient's chance for survival, providing the *total* mastectomy is performed at a relatively early stage in the development of the cancerous growth—even if adjacent lymph nodes are also cancerous.

The panel also suggested another reform in the treatment of women with cancer of the breast. Namely, to change the current practice of many hospitals of requesting the patient to sign a form, on admission to the hospital, that authorizes the surgeon to perform any surgical procedure he considers necessary.

Many of the panel members did not agree that blind trust in the surgeon's judgment was enough, especially when experts themselves disagree on the justification for an extensive and mutilating procedure. At least, they felt, a woman should not wake up from general anesthesia to find that she has undergone removal of one of her breasts (and perhaps her chest muscles as well) when before surgery she was told that only a *biopsy* of the tissues was going to be performed. (A biopsy is removal of a sample of tissue for examination by the pathologist.)

One way to avoid the psychologically traumatic experience of waking up to find a breast removed is to delay, temporarily, the "unannounced" surgery—at least until the patient, her family, and the medical and surgical team have time to reflect on the matter and consider the best treatment in the individual case. The panel considered this "two-step" approach to be most reasonable, providing the necessary surgery was not delayed too long.

Benign Breast Lumps: Dr. John Peter Minton, of the Department of Surgery at the Ohio State University College of Medicine, has suggested that, "Many women with long-standing, clinically benign breast lumps may be able to reassure themselves that they do not have breast cancer by a much simpler means than breast biopsy." As reported in the *Journal of the American Medical Association* (March 23, 1979): "Minton has found that about two thirds of benign breast lumps disappear in women who completely eliminate all forms of methylxanthines—caffeine, theophylline, and theobromine—from their diets."

Dr. Minton discovered, some years ago, that certain chemicals which stimulate the growth of cells and their division ("cyclic nucleotides") are significantly greater in "biopsy tissue from women with fibrocystic disease and fibroadenoma." He was suspicious that the presence of these chemicals might contribute to the growth of the breast lumps.

Methylxanthines are most commonly encountered in drinking coffee and tea and certain other beverages. The report states that, "to test the relationship between methylxanthines and benign breast disease directly, Minton advised a group of 47 women with breast lumps who had come for breast biopsy to eliminate all coffee, tea, chocolate, and cola from their diets." Of the 20 women who did stop methylxanthine consumption, 13 (65%) were shown to have complete resolution of breast disease within two to six months (confirmed by physical examination, echogram, and mammography). Three of the other seven in this group had a resolution of breast symptoms within 1-1/2 years. By contrast, of the 27 women who failed to stop the consumption of methylxanthines, "only one had disappearance of breast disease."

An interesting finding was that each of the women who reported stopping the consumption of methylxanthine "had a headache that started within 24 hours of the restricted diet and continued for up to one week." This fact provided a sort of independent verification that the patients had indeed stopped drinking coffee and the other beverages containing methylxanthine.

It is obvious that only a small fraction of women who drink the proscribed beverages are at risk of developing benign breast disease, or of making the condition worse if they continue to drink beverages containing methylxanthines. But the results of this preliminary study strongly suggest that, at least for some women, there may be a direct causal relationship.

Cancer Risk—"DES Daughters": Diethylstilbestrol (DES) is a synthetic estrogenic substance "capable of producing all the pharmacologic and therapeutic responses attributed to natural estrogens." It was formerly prescribed to prevent miscarriages in women; it is also used in *hormone replacement therapy* (HRT) to relieve the symptoms associated with the menopause. Evidence has been mounting, since the early 1970s, that DES can cause cancer of the vagina or cervix (neck of the womb) in babies whose mothers were given the drug during pregnancy.

Dr. Stanley Robboy, Associate Professor of Pathology at Harvard Medical School, reports (April 1979) that "now there is some good news for the daughters of women who took DES. Early results of a new federal study indicate that the drug may pose less of a risk than previously believed." Dr. Robboy is a principal investigator in a study commissioned by the National Cancer Institute, known as the "DES Adenosis Group (DESAD)." The preliminary results of this study showed that there were no cancers among a group of 1,275 "DES daughters" identified by means of a review of the medical records of their mothers. Another group of 2,064 "DES daughters" were referred to the investigators "specifically because of identified vaginal abnormalities or documented DES exposure." Only four cancers of the genital tract were discovered. It was stated that "the frequency of cancers in this group is not considered significant, however, because of the strong bias that brought these women into the study." The findings are thought to be highly encouraging.

In an interview with a representative of the American Medical Association, Dr. Robboy said: "We found the frequency of clear cell adenocarcinoma and of dysplasia to be very low. Also, the frequency of vaginal epithelial changes was much lower than expected." Despite the good news that the risk of cancer may not be as great in "DES daughters" as once feared, experts continue to caution that all women who took the drug during pregnancy, and their children—both male and female—should be examined regularly.

Heart Disease and Cholesterol: The level of cholesterol in the blood has traditionally been considered a significant index for predicting if an individual patient is at risk of a heart attack. However, a definite causal relationship between the two events—high blood levels of cholesterol and the incidence of heart attack—is far from clear.

It is now known that high blood levels of fats can be good or bad—depending on the lipid. (Lipids are fats or fatlike substances, including cholesterol.) Substances that contain both lipids and protein are known as lipoproteins, to which cholesterol is attached during its journey through the bloodstream. There are two major types of lipoprotein: *high-density* and *low-density* lipoproteins (HDLs and LDLs). An inverse relationship exists between the high-density lipoprotein level and the risk of coronary heart disease. The cholesterol contained in high-density lipoproteins seems to be beneficial.

The current theory is that high-density lipoprotein (HDL) is the "good" cholesterol. That is, experts postulate that HDL somehow removes cholesterol from the smooth muscle cells of arteries and carries it to the liver—where it is catabolized and eventually excreted. HDL may also play a role in limiting or reducing the amount of cholesterol that can *enter* arterial smooth muscle cells. One way it might do this is by inhibiting the action of low-density lipoprotein (LDL)—the "bad" cholesterol.

The American Health Foundation, in May 1979, reported the results of a two-day conference they sponsored in New York. The international panel included heart specialists and experts in nutrition. A major area of discussion was the relationship between coronary heart disease and blood levels of cholesterol. It was generally agreed that, regardless of the "ideal" level of cholesterol, the average adult American has an excessively high level of blood cholesterol.

A difficult task for the panel was to "determine levels of cholesterol and lipoproteins that would be optimal for all cultures." Dr. D. M. Hegsted, of the Human Nutrition Center at the U.S. Department of Agriculture, suggested that, "The only sensible advice to the American public is to reduce their consumption of fat and cholesterol and increase their consumption of fruits and vegetables and grain products." Other panel members thought that this was an oversimplification, and that dramatic dietary changes would be extremely difficult for most Americans to achieve.

Despite the strong implications of the danger of high levels of cholesterol, Dr. Basel Rifkind—Chief of the Lipid Metabolism Branch at the National Heart, Lung,

and Blood Institute—reminded the panel members that the hard facts in the matter are not yet in. He said, "To date, no study has actually shown that lowering cholesterol is of benefit in preventing heart attack."

Venereal Disease: Gonorrhea is the most frequently reported communicable disease in the United States. In 1978 alone, over one million cases were reported (the actual figure is 1,013,559)—an increase of 1.3% over 1977. However, not all cases are reported and it seems obvious that the true incidence of the disease may be much higher.

During 1978 the incidence of syphilis rose in the United States by more than 5% over the previous year. Nearly 22,000 cases were reported, although experts believe that the actual figure may be at least three times higher.

Prenatal Diagnosis of Spina Bifida: One of the most important medical advances of the 1970s has been the development, in the U.K., of a method to detect spina bifida and other "neural tube" defects in an unborn baby. In some parts of the United States the incidence of these congenital defects is as high as 4 per 1,000 births. The defect is basically a failure of a section of the spinal column to close normally around the spinal cord. The severity of the condition varies; in the most severe cases the child may be stillborn or, if he survives, may suffer severe physical and mental handicaps. Many such children die within the first few weeks of birth.

A reliable method of discovering the presence of this defect before birth gives the parents the option of a clinical abortion. Such a test—amniocentesis to estimate the level of *alphafetoprotein* in the fluid surrounding the fetus—is now routine in Britain for mothers who are known to have given birth once before to a baby with spina bifida.

Amniocentesis is a diagnostic technique for withdrawal of a sample of fluid from the amniotic sac—the "bag of water" which surrounds a fetus in the womb. This is done by carefully passing a hollow needle through the mother's abdominal wall and into the amniotic sac. The presence of a specified level of the substance known as alphafetoprotein (AFP) can help establish the diagnosis of spina bifida and other neural tube defects. Although the technique is becoming more prevalent in the United States (prenatal diagnosis of birth defects by amniocentesis has increased by up to nine times during the past two years), it is far from a routine procedure at present.

Report on the Nation's Health: The National Center for Health Statistics and the National Center for Health Services Research issued a report (April 1979) which claims that Americans "are among the healthiest people in the world." The report is for the year 1976, but more recent statistics are even better in some areas. Between 1968 and 1976 the death rate for coronary heart disease fell almost 28%. The cancer death rate for those under the age of 45 fell from 21.8 per 100,000 in 1950 to 14.7 in 1976.

For a person born in 1976, the life expectancy is 72.8 years—compared with 72.5 years in 1975. The estimate for those born in 1977 is a life expectancy of 73.2 years. Infant deaths in 1976 were 15.2 per 1,000 live births, compared with 16.1 the previous year.

HEART ATTACK DEATH RATIOS

Source: American Cancer Society

The following table shows mortality comparisons, by age group and sex, for factors linked with death from heart disease in 1968.

COMPARISONS	CORONARY HEART DISEASE MORTALITY RATIOS							
	Men (Age Groups)				Women (Age Groups)			
	40–49	50–59	60–69	70–79	40–49	50–59	60–69	70–79
Cigarettes: More than 40 vs. 0	5.51*	2.79	1.79	1.47	3.31†	3.73	2.02†	**
Exercise: None vs. heavy	1.80	1.31	2.18	2.85	**	1.00†	1.92	3.53
Relative Weight: 20% over vs. 10% under group average	2.25	1.55	1.27	1.19	2.18	1.79	1.58	1.14
Sleep: 10 hours or more vs. 7 hours	1.33	1.34	1.22	1.76	**	2.29	2.19	1.59
Nervous Tension: Moderate or severe vs. none	1.01	0.88	0.82	1.03	0.96	1.03	0.80	1.19

* Figure indicates mortality rate from coronary heart disease was 5.51 as much for heavy smokers as for nonsmokers. Throughout table, figures under age groups relate to comparison at left. † Indicates rates based on only five to nine deaths. ** Indicates rate was omitted because there were fewer than five deaths. Relative weight figures are not isolated from factors of smoking and exercise.

LONGEVITY IN THE UNITED STATES

Source: 1978 data from Statistical Bureau, Metropolitan Life Insurance Company; earlier years from the National Center for Health Statistics

The expectation of life at birth for the resident population of the United States increased to an all-time high in 1978. Preliminary life tables indicate that the average length of life for the total population rose from 73.2 years in 1977 to 73.3 years in 1978 — a gain of 2.6 years since 1969-71 and of 14.1 years since 1929-31, when the average was only about 59 years.

The expected lifetime rose to 69.5 years for the male newborn and to 77.2 years for the female. The favorable 1978 experience reflected a significant decline in infant mortality.

EXPECTATION OF LIFE IN THE U.S.: 1949-51 to 1978

Age	1949–51	1959–61	1969–71	1975	1976	1977†	1978*
0–1	68.1	69.9	70.7	72.5	72.8	73.2	73.3
1	69.2	70.7	71.2	72.7	72.9	73.2	73.3
15	55.9	57.3	57.7	59.1	59.3	59.6	59.7
25	46.6	47.9	48.4	49.8	49.9	50.3	50.4
35	37.3	38.5	39.1	40.4	40.6	40.9	41.0
45	28.5	29.5	30.1	31.4	31.5	31.8	31.9
55	20.6	21.4	22.0	23.1	23.2	23.5	23.5
65	13.8	14.4	15.0	16.0	16.0	16.3	16.4

†Provisional. *Preliminary.

EXPECTATION OF LIFE — UNITED STATES: 1977

Source: National Center for Health Statistics

AGE	Total (years)	White Male	White Female	All other Male	All other Female	AGE	Total (years)	White Male	White Female	All other Male	All other Female
Birth	73.2	70.0	77.7	64.6	73.1	43	33.6	30.7	37.0	27.9	34.1
1	73.2	70.0	77.6	65.2	73.6	44	32.7	29.8	36.1	27.1	33.2
2	72.3	69.1	76.6	64.3	72.7	45	31.8	29.0	35.2	26.3	32.4
3	71.3	68.1	75.7	63.4	71.7	46	30.9	28.1	34.3	25.6	31.5
4	70.4	67.2	74.7	62.4	70.8	47	30.0	27.2	33.4	24.8	30.7
5	69.4	66.2	73.7	61.5	69.8	48	29.2	26.4	32.5	24.1	29.9
6	68.4	65.2	72.8	60.5	68.9	49	28.3	25.5	31.6	23.4	29.1
7	67.5	64.3	71.8	59.6	67.9	50	27.5	24.7	30.7	22.7	28.3
8	66.5	63.3	70.8	58.6	66.9	51	26.7	23.9	29.8	22.0	27.5
9	65.5	62.3	69.8	57.6	65.9	52	25.9	23.1	29.0	21.3	26.7
10	64.5	61.3	68.8	56.6	65.0	53	25.0	22.3	28.1	20.7	26.0
11	63.5	60.4	67.9	55.7	64.0	54	24.2	21.5	27.2	20.0	25.2
12	62.6	59.4	66.9	54.7	63.0	55	23.5	20.8	26.4	19.4	24.5
13	61.6	58.4	65.9	53.7	62.0	56	22.7	20.0	25.5	18.8	23.7
14	60.6	57.4	64.9	52.8	61.0	57	21.9	19.3	24.7	18.2	23.0
15	59.6	56.5	63.9	51.8	60.0	58	21.2	18.5	23.9	17.6	22.3
16	58.7	55.5	62.9	50.8	59.1	59	20.4	17.8	23.1	17.0	21.6
17	57.7	54.6	62.0	49.9	58.1	60	19.7	17.1	22.3	16.5	21.0
18	56.8	53.7	61.0	49.0	57.1	61	19.0	16.4	21.5	15.9	20.3
19	55.9	52.8	60.1	48.1	56.2	62	18.3	15.8	20.7	15.4	19.7
20	54.9	51.9	59.1	47.2	55.2	63	17.6	15.2	19.9	15.0	19.1
21	54.0	51.0	58.1	46.3	54.3	64	16.9	14.5	19.2	14.5	18.4
22	53.1	50.1	57.2	45.4	53.3	65	16.3	13.9	18.4	14.0	17.8
23	52.1	49.1	56.2	44.5	52.4	66	15.6	13.3	17.7	13.5	17.1
24	51.2	48.2	55.2	43.6	51.4	67	15.0	12.7	16.9	13.0	16.4
25	50.3	47.3	54.3	42.8	50.5	68	14.3	12.2	16.2	12.4	15.8
26	49.3	46.4	53.3	41.9	49.5	69	13.7	11.6	15.5	11.9	15.1
27	48.4	45.5	52.3	41.1	48.6	70	13.1	11.1	14.8	11.4	14.5
28	47.5	44.6	51.4	40.2	47.7	71	12.5	10.5	14.1	11.0	14.0
29	46.5	43.6	50.4	39.4	46.7	72	11.9	10.0	13.4	10.6	13.6
30	45.6	42.7	49.4	38.6	45.8	73	11.4	9.6	12.7	10.3	13.2
31	44.7	41.8	48.5	37.7	44.9	74	10.9	9.1	12.1	10.0	12.8
32	43.7	40.8	47.5	36.9	43.9	75	10.4	8.6	11.5	9.7	12.5
33	42.8	39.9	46.5	36.0	43.0	76	9.9	8.2	10.9	9.5	12.2
34	41.8	39.0	45.6	35.2	42.1	77	9.4	7.8	10.4	9.2	11.9
35	40.9	38.0	44.6	34.3	41.2	78	9.0	7.5	9.8	9.0	11.7
36	40.0	37.1	43.6	33.5	40.3	79	8.6	7.1	9.3	8.9	11.5
37	39.0	36.2	42.7	32.6	39.3	80	8.2	6.8	8.8	8.7	11.3
38	38.1	35.3	41.7	31.8	38.4	81	7.8	6.5	8.4	8.6	11.1
39	37.2	34.3	40.8	31.0	37.5	82	7.4	6.2	7.9	8.4	10.9
40	36.3	33.4	39.8	30.2	36.7	83	7.1	5.9	7.5	8.2	10.7
41	35.4	32.5	38.9	29.4	45.8	84	6.7	5.6	7.1	7.9	10.2
42	34.5	31.6	38.0	28.6	34.9	85 & over.	6.4	5.3	6.8	7.3	9.6

INFANT AND NEONATAL DEATH RATES IN THE UNITED STATES: 1977

Source: National Center for Health Statistics (Deaths per 1,000 live births)

State	Infant Deaths[1]	Neonatal Deaths[2]	State	Infant Deaths[1]	Neonatal Deaths[2]	State	Infant Deaths[1]	Neonatal Deaths[2]	State	Infant Deaths[1]	Neonatal Deaths[2]
Ala.	16.9	11.1	Ill.	16.0	11.3	Mont.	13.7	8.9	R.I.	12.1	8.3
Alaska	15.1	8.5	Ind.	14.2	9.7	Nebr.	12.7	9.3	S.C.	17.6	12.2
Ariz.	13.5	8.7	Iowa	12.4	9.6	Nev.	13.9	8.9	S.D.	16.4	12.4
Ark.	15.4	9.8	Kans.	13.4	10.4	N.H.	10.2	7.9	Tenn.	15.4	10.8
Calif.	12.0	7.9	Ky.	14.4	9.9	N.J.	14.3	10.7	Texas	14.7	10.3
Colo.	12.0	7.4	La.	17.9	13.1	N.M.	13.8	9.6	Utah	10.1	6.8
Conn.	13.5	10.3	Maine	9.5	6.2	N.Y.	14.4	10.5	Vt.	10.0	6.8
Del.	13.6	9.4	Md.	14.3	10.7	N.C.	15.8	11.2	Va.	15.9	11.4
D.C.	27.4	20.5	Mass.	11.9	9.3	N.D.	13.7	10.5	Wash.	12.1	7.4
Fla.	15.5	10.6	Mich.	14.1	9.9	Ohio	13.9	10.1	W.Va.	14.6	10.3
Ga.	15.4	9.6	Minn.	11.1	7.9	Okla.	13.7	8.9	Wis.	11.3	7.5
Haw.	11.5	7.7	Miss.	18.2	12.9	Oreg.	12.2	7.9	Wyo.	13.9	8.3
Idaho	11.3	6.7	Mo.	14.2	10.2	Pa.	14.0	10.6	U.S. avg.	14.1	9.9

[1] Under 1 yr.   [2] Under 28 days.

LEADING CAUSES OF DEATH IN THE UNITED STATES: 1977

Source: National Center for Health Statistics

Rank	Cause of Death	Number of Deaths	Death Rate per 100,000 Population	Rank	Cause of Death	Number of Deaths	Death Rate per 100,000 Population
	ALL CAUSES	1,899,597	878.1	5.	Influenza & Pneumonia	51,193	23.7
1.	Heart Diseases	718,850	332.3	6.	Diabetes Mellitus	32,989	15.2
2.	Cancer	386,686	178.7	7.	Cirrhosis of Liver	30,848	14.3
3.	Stroke	181,934	84.1	8.	Arteriosclerosis	28,754	13.3
4.	Accidents	103,202	47.7	9.	Suicide	28,681	13.3
	Motor Vehicular	49,510	22.9	10.	Diseases of Early Infancy	23,401	10.8
	All Other	53,692	24.8		All Other Causes	209,857	97.0

DEATH RATES FOR SPECIFIED CAUSES, BY COLOR AND SEX: UNITED STATES, 1977

Source: National Center for Health Statistics

(Rate per 100,000 population in specified group)

	Total			White			Nonwhite		
	Both sexes	Male	Female	Both sexes	Male	Female	Both sexes	Male	Female
All causes	878.1	994.1	768.2	882.2	998.2	783.3	813.0	967.1	672.5
Major cardiovascular diseases	444.5	478.8	412.0	460.6	495.5	427.4	340.0	368.3	314.1
Diseases of heart	332.3	376.7	290.2	346.0	392.4	301.8	243.5	273.3	216.4
Hypertension	2.6	2.6	2.7	2.4	2.4	2.5	4.0	4.2	3.8
Cerebrovascular diseases	84.1	73.5	94.1	85.1	73.2	96.5	77.3	75.2	79.2
Arteriosclerosis	13.3	11.1	15.4	14.2	11.7	16.7	7.2	6.9	7.4
Cancer	178.7	200.0	158.6	183.1	202.5	164.5	150.8	183.2	121.2
Accidents	47.7	68.4	28.1	47.1	66.7	28.4	51.6	79.1	26.6
Motor vehicle accidents	22.9	34.0	12.3	23.1	34.1	12.7	21.2	33.8	9.8
All other accidents	24.8	34.3	15.8	24.0	32.7	15.7	30.4	45.4	16.8
Influenza and pneumonia	23.7	26.2	21.2	23.9	25.9	22.0	22.1	28.6	16.2
Cirrhosis of liver	14.3	19.2	9.6	13.6	18.3	9.1	18.6	24.9	12.9
Diabetes mellitus	15.2	13.0	17.4	14.7	12.7	16.5	19.0	14.6	23.1
Suicide	13.3	20.1	6.8	14.2	21.4	7.3	7.3	11.4	3.5
Homicide	9.2	14.6	4.2	5.7	8.7	2.9	31.9	53.6	12.0
Bronchitis, emphysema, and asthma	10.3	15.3	5.6	11.2	16.5	6.1	5.0	7.4	2.8
Tuberculosis, all forms	1.4	1.9	0.8	1.1	1.5	0.7	3.3	5.0	1.7

DEATH RATES IN AMERICA 1977 (per 1,000)

Source: National Center for Health Statistics

	Total			White			Nonwhite		
Age Group	Both sexes	Male	Female	Both sexes	Male	Female	Both sexes	Male	Female
All ages[1]	8.8	9.9	7.7	8.9	10.0	7.8	8.1	9.7	6.7
Under 1	14.9	16.6	13.0	12.7	14.3	10.9	25.5	27.8	23.0
1–4	0.7	0.8	0.6	0.6	0.7	0.6	1.0	1.1	0.9
5–9	0.3	0.4	0.3	0.3	0.4	0.3	0.4	0.5	0.3
10–14	0.4	0.4	0.3	0.3	0.4	0.3	0.4	0.5	0.3
15–19	1.0	1.5	0.6	1.0	1.5	0.6	1.0	1.5	0.6
20–24	1.3	2.0	0.7	1.3	1.9	0.6	1.8	2.8	1.0
25–29	1.3	1.9	0.7	1.1	1.7	0.6	2.5	3.8	1.3
30–34	1.4	1.9	0.9	1.2	1.6	0.8	2.8	4.2	1.7
35–39	2.0	2.6	1.3	1.7	2.2	1.2	3.9	5.6	2.6
40–44	3.0	3.9	2.2	2.6	3.4	1.9	5.8	7.9	4.0
45–49	4.8	6.3	3.5	4.3	5.7	3.1	8.3	11.0	6.0
50–54	7.5	10.0	5.3	7.0	9.3	4.8	12.4	16.2	9.1
55–59	11.4	15.2	7.9	10.7	14.4	7.3	17.8	23.1	13.1
60–64	17.8	24.3	12.2	17.0	23.4	11.4	25.6	33.6	19.0
65–69	24.8	34.7	16.9	24.3	34.4	16.3	28.9	38.0	21.8
70–74	38.5	53.2	27.7	37.3	52.3	26.3	51.6	62.0	43.0
75–79	60.7	81.5	47.4	59.6	81.0	46.0	74.1	86.5	64.5
80–84	88.1	113.6	73.9	89.5	116.0	74.9	73.5	89.9	62.7
85 and over	147.3	173.0	135.4	152.9	180.4	140.4	96.0	112.9	86.7

[1] Figures for age not stated included in "All ages" but not distributed among age groups.

U.S. DEATHS FROM ACCIDENTS

Source: National Center for Health Statistics

Type of Accident	Deaths per 100,000 Population			Type of Accident	Deaths per 100,000 Population		
	1970	1973	1977		1970	1973	1977
All Accidents	56.4	55.2	47.7	Unspecified falls	5.6	5.5	4.4
Railway Accidents	0.4	0.4	0.3	Accidents caused			
Motor vehicle accidents	26.9	26.5	22.9	By fire and flames	3.3	3.1	2.9
Motor vehicle traffic	26.3	25.9	22.4	By firearms	1.2	1.2	0.9
Vehicle-pedestrian	4.4	4.3	3.6	Accidents mainly of industrial type			
Other road vehicle accidents	0.1	0.1	0.1	Cutting or piercing instrument	0.1	0.1	0.1
Water transport accidents	0.8	0.8	0.6	Explosive material	0.3	0.2	0.2
Air and space transport accidents	0.8	0.8	0.8	Hot substances, etc.	0.1	0.1	0.1
Accidental poisoning				Electric current	0.6	0.5	0.5
By solid and liquid substances	0.6	0.6	0.5	Other	1.9	1.8	1.5
By gases and vapors	0.8	0.8	0.7	Inhalation and ingestion of objects	1.4	1.4	1.4
Accidental falls	8.3	7.9	6.4	Accidental drowning	3.1	3.4	2.8
Fall from one level to another	2.4	2.0	1.8	Complications due to medical procedures	1.8	1.7	1.4
Fall on the same level	0.4	0.3	0.2	All other accidents	4.0	3.7	2.5

U.S. HOMICIDES AND SUICIDES
SOURCE: National Center for Health Statistics

	1960		1965		1970		1977	
Item	Male	Female	Male	Female	Male	Female	Male	Female
Homicide	6,269	2,195	8,148	2,564	13,278	3,570	15,355	4,613
Assault by:								
Firearms and explosives	3,460	1,167	4,807	1,351	9,209	2,004	10,520	2,354
Cutting and piercing instruments	1,442	394	1,847	445	2,229	551	2,747	795
Other means	1,069	631	1,216	768	1,512	1,010	1,821	1,462
Intervention of police	242	3	271	—	328	5	266	2
Execution	56	—	7	—	—	—	1	—
Suicide	14,539	4,502	15,490	6,017	16,629	6,851	21,109	7,572
Poisoning	2,631	1,699	3,179	2,816	3,299	3,285	3,340	3,147
Hanging and strangulation	2,576	790	2,453	744	2,422	831	2,982	848
Firearms and explosives	7,879	1,138	8,457	1,441	9,704	2,068	13,342	2,742
Other	1,453	875	1,401	1,016	1,204	667	1,445	835

— Represents zero.

ACCIDENTAL DEATH RATES: BY NATIONS
SOURCE: United Nations Demographic Yearbook, 1977 (Table 21), © United Nations

Nation	Latest Year Available	Accidental Deaths per 100,000 Population*	Nation	Latest Year Available	Accidental Deaths per 100,000 Population*
South Africa			Sweden	1975	48.0
Nonwhite	1971	88.0	Norway	1976	47.3
White	1971	70.9	Switzerland	1976	46.8
France	1970	74.8	Yugoslavia	1975	43.9
Austria	1976	69.8	Scotland	1976	43.1
Portugal	1975	63.3	Greece	1975	42.3
Luxembourg	1976	62.6	Costa Rica	1976	41.9
Belgium	1975	60.1	Bulgaria	1975	41.4
Hungary	1976	58.8	Bahamas	1975	41.2
Canada	1974	57.6	Mauritius	1976	41.0
Czechoslovakia	1975	57.5	Iceland	1976	40.4
Finland	1974	56.8	Chile	1973	40.2
Venezuela	1975	55.7	Netherlands	1976	39.2
West Germany	1975	53.8	Spain	1974	39.1
Ecuador	1975	53.1	Japan	1976	37.8
East Germany	1975	51.9	Denmark	1976	37.0
Northern Ireland	1976	51.0	Uruguay	1974	36.7
Kuwait	1975	50.6	Panama	1975	36.6
Ireland	1974	50.4	Israel	1975	36.4
Mexico	1974	49.6	Trinidad & Tobago	1975	34.0
Australia	1975	49.1	New Zealand	1975	33.8
Italy	1972	48.9	England & Wales	1976	30.6
UNITED STATES	1975	48.3	Barbados	1975	30.1

* Based on population estimates for the designated year.

INTERNATIONAL SUICIDE RATES (per 100,000 population)
SOURCE: United Nations Demographic Yearbook, 1977 (Table 21), © United Nations

Nation	Year	Rate	Nation	Year	Rate
Hungary	1976	40.6	Australia	1975	11.1
Finland	1974	25.1	Norway	1976	10.8
Denmark	1976	23.9	Uruguay	1974	10.4
Austria	1976	22.7	Netherlands	1976	9.4
Switzerland	1976	22.0	New Zealand	1975	9.4
Czechoslovakia	1975	21.9	Iceland	1976	8.6
West Germany	1975	20.9	Portugal	1975	8.5
Sweden	1976	19.4	Trinidad and Tobago	1975	8.4
Japan	1976	17.5	Scotland	1976	8.3
Zimbabwe-Rhodesia	1976	17.3	England and Wales	1976	7.8
Belgium	1975	16.2	Puerto Rico	1975	7.7
France	1970	15.4	Israel	1975	7.5
Cuba	1971	15.0	Mauritius	1976	6.5
Luxembourg	1976	14.6	Italy	1972	5.8
South Africa			Costa Rica	1976	5.7
White	1971	14.5	Chile	1973	5.6
Nonwhite	1971	5.6	Venezuela	1975	5.0
Yugoslavia	1975	13.4	Northern Ireland	1976	4.4
Hong Kong	1976	13.3	Spain	1974	4.0
Bulgaria	1975	12.9	Ireland	1974	3.8
Canada	1974	12.9	Colombia	1969	2.9
UNITED STATES	1975	12.7	Greece	1975	2.8
Poland	1976	12.1	Ecuador	1975	2.7
Singapore	1976	11.3	Mexico	1974	2.1

VENEREAL DISEASE
SOURCE: American Social Health Association

Venereal disease, or more accurately, sexually transmissible disease, encompasses 20 conditions of which gonorrhea, non-gonococcal urethritis/cervicitis, genital herpes, syphilis, cytomegalovirus and group B streptococcal disease are the most dangerous. It is estimated that over ten million persons were affected with some form of VD this year. Complications from prolonged and untreated infection with some forms of VD can lead to serious medical conditions, some of which can be permanently debilitating and even fatal.

Most venereal diseases can be completely cured although at least two are viral and cannot. Genital herpes is spreading at an alarming rate, and is associated with cervical cancer in women and brain damage in newborn babies. With vaccines for any of the venereal diseases still some way off, major attention is given to educating the public. The American Social Health Association produces and distributes films, literature and other material suited for home, classroom or clinic.

REFERENCE CHART: LEADING CANCER SITES, 1979 (Estimated)

SOURCE: American Cancer Society. All figures rounded to nearest 1,000.

Site	Estimated New Cases 1979	Estimated Deaths 1979	Warning Signal If you have one, see your doctor	Safeguards	Comment
BREAST	107,000	35,000	Lump or thickening in the breast or unusual discharge from nipple.	Regular checkup. Monthly breast self-examination	The leading cause of cancer death in women.
COLON AND RECTUM	112,000	52,000	Change in bowel habits; bleeding.	Regular checkup, including digital, occult blood and proctoscopic exams, especially after age 40.	Because of accuracy of available tests, is potentially a highly curable disease.
LUNG	112,000	98,000	Persistent cough, or lingering respiratory ailment.	80% of lung cancer would be prevented if no one smoked cigarettes.	The leading cause of cancer death among men and rising mortality among women.
ORAL (INCLUDING PHARYNX)	24,000	9,000	Sore that does not heal. Difficulty in swallowing.	Regular checkup	Many more lives should be saved because the mouth is easily accessible to visual examination by physicians and dentists.
SKIN	14,000[1]	6,000	Sore that does not heal, or change in wart or mole.	Regular checkup, avoidance of overexposure to sun.	Skin cancer is readily detected by observation, and diagnosed by simple biopsy.
UTERUS	53,000[2]	11,000	Unusual bleeding or discharge.	Regular checkup, including pelvic examination with Pap test.	Uterine cancer mortality has declined 70% during the last 40 years with wider application of the Pap test. Postmenopausal women with abnormal bleeding should be checked.
KIDNEY AND BLADDER	51,000	18,000	Urinary difficulty, bleeding, in which case consult doctor at once.	Regular checkup with urinalysis.	Protective measures for workers in high-risk industries are helping to eliminate one of the important causes of these cancers.
LARYNX	10,000	3,500	Hoarseness—difficulty in swallowing.	Regular checkup, including laryngoscopy.	Readily curable if caught early.
PROSTATE	64,000	21,000	Urinary difficulty	Regular checkup, including palpation.	Occurs mainly in men over 60, the disease can be detected by palpation at regular checkup.
STOMACH	23,000	14,000	Indigestion	Regular checkup	An 80% decline in mortality in 50 years, for reasons yet unknown.
LEUKEMIA	22,000	15,000	Leukemia is a cancer of blood-forming tissues and is characterized by the abnormal production of immature white blood cells. Acute lymphocytic leukemia strikes mainly children and is treated by drugs which have extended life from a few months to as much as ten years. Chronic leukemia strikes usually after age 25 and progresses less rapidly.		
LYMPHOMAS	39,000	20,000	These cancers arise in the lymph system and include Hodgkin's Disease and lymphosarcoma. Some patients with lymphatic cancers can lead normal lives for many years. Five-year survival rate for Hodgkin's Disease increased from 25% to 54% in 20 years.		

[1] Estimate new cases of non-melanoma skin cancer over 300,000.   [2] If carcinoma in situ is included, cases total over 98,000.

PROGRESS AGAINST CANCER

Category	1937	1978
Saved (alive five years after treatment)	Fewer than one in five	One in three
Uterine cancer	Chief cause of cancer death in women	Death rate cut more than 70% since 1930. Could be reduced more
Lung cancer	Mounting: no prospect of control	Still mounting: but upward of 80% could be prevented
Research support	Less than $1,000,000	About $900,000,000
Cancer clinics and registries approved by American College of Surgeons	240 in United States and Canada	Over 800, plus expansion of teaching, research, treatment centers
State control measures	Seven states	All 50 states
Chemotherapy	Almost no research	Major research attack has produced more than 25 useful drugs

One in two patients could be saved today by early diagnosis and prompt treatment

CANCER DEATH RATES AROUND THE WORLD   SOURCE: American Cancer Society

Death Rates per 100,000 Population — 1972–73.

Male Cancer Death Rates		Male Cancer Death Rates		Female Cancer Death Rates		Female Cancer Death Rates	
Scotland	205.0	Hong Kong	170.7	Netherlands	160.2	Northern Ireland	117.1
Czechoslovakia	204.1	Denmark	170.2	Romania	146.5	New Zealand	114.4
Luxembourg	200.7	New Zealand	162.4	Chile	133.3	Sweden	111.7
Uruguay	200.6	Northern Ireland	159.8	Denmark	132.1	Costa Rica	111.2
Austria	191.1	Poland	158.3	Uruguay	131.7	Czechoslovakia	110.9
France	187.0	Australia	158.1	Scotland	128.4	Canada	109.4
Netherlands	186.9	Ireland	158.0	Hungary	125.6	Switzerland	108.7
England & Wales	184.3	Chile	157.8	Austria	124.3	UNITED STATES	106.1
Finland	182.9	UNITED STATES	157.2	Ireland	122.1	Venezuela	104.0
Hungary	182.6	Canada	157.0	Germany, F.R.	121.2	Italy	103.0
Switzerland	178.8	Japan	141.2	Luxembourg	120.8	Poland	102.9
Germany, F.R.	178.0	Spain	137.4	England & Wales	119.6	Norway	101.4
Italy	173.3	Norway	133.2	Israel	118.8	Australia	100.0

ADJUSTED HOSPITAL EXPENSE PER INPATIENT DAY: COMMUNITY HOSPITALS, 1968–1977   SOURCE: American Hospital Association

Expenses per day related to inpatient care adjusted to exclude those expenses incurred for outpatient care.

Hospital Size	1968	1970	1972	1973	1974	1975	1976	1977
All Community Hospitals	$55.80	$73.73	$94.87	$102.44	$113.55	$133.81	$151.79	$173.98
6–24 Beds	41.98	59.68	75.76	77.29	83.44	100.43	117.46	132.19
25–49 Beds	41.10	54.15	68.68	73.86	82.73	98.97	113.42	132.33
50–99 Beds	45.24	58.85	72.98	78.86	86.58	101.96	117.95	134.53
100–199 Beds	51.11	65.87	84.31	91.23	101.06	119.14	135.04	154.64
200–299 Beds	56.22	74.32	92.43	100.97	111.35	129.93	148.37	169.76
300–399 Beds	59.24	77.96	99.34	104.77	116.80	137.82	155.99	177.72
400–499 Beds	60.67	79.68	100.23	109.94	122.11	140.68	160.35	183.55
500 or more Beds	66.27	87.37	115.34	123.95	136.73	161.97	179.80	206.40

HOSPITAL COSTS IN COMMUNITY HOSPITALS   SOURCE: American Hospital Association

Year	Adjusted Expenses per Inpatient Day	Average Length of Stay (Days)	Average Adjusted Expense per Patient Stay	Year	Adjusted Expenses per Inpatient Day	Average Length of Stay (Days)	Average Adjusted Expense per Patient Stay
1963	$35.11	7.7	$270.35	1971	83.43	8.0	$667.44
1965	40.56	7.8	316.37	1972	94.87	7.9	749.47
1966	43.66	7.9	344.91	1973	102.44	7.8	799.03
1967	49.46	8.3	410.52	1974	113.55	7.8	885.69
1968	55.80	8.4	468.72	1975	133.81	7.7	1030.34
1969	64.26	8.3	533.36	1976	151.79	7.7	1168.78
1970	$73.73	8.2	604.59	1977	173.98	7.6	1322.25

ABORTION AND THE LAW   SOURCE: National Abortion Federation

On January 22, 1973, the U.S. Supreme Court issued two landmark abortion rulings in *Roe* vs. *Wade* and *Doe* vs. *Bolton*. They declared the abortion laws of Texas and Georgia, respectively, unconstitutional.

The sweeping terms of these decisions left untouched no state abortion law—not even one so liberal as New York's—and most of them were rendered completely unconstitutional. Since that time, state legislatures have attempted to limit access to abortions primarily by setting up consent requirements or funding regulations.

In 1976 the Supreme Court ruled, in *Planned Parent-hood of Central Missouri* vs. *Danforth*, that the State cannot make a blanket requirement of parental consent to abortions for minors.

The following year in two decisions, *Maher* vs. *Roe* and *Beal* vs. *Doe*, the Court held that the States have the right to decide whether or not to pay for abortions out of public assistance funds. In 1977, the Court ruled that states have no statutory or Constitutional obligation to provide Medicaid funding for elective non-therapeutic abortion for poor women. States may elect to fund elective abortion.

TERMS OF SUPREME COURT ABORTION DECISION: 1973

The Court set three major limitations on state regulations:

A. **For the First Trimester of Pregnancy**—abortion must be left to the judgment of the patient and her doctor.

B. **For the Second Trimester of Pregnancy**—the State may regulate abortion procedures in ways that are reasonably related to maternal health.

C. **For the Third Trimester**—the State may regulate, or even proscribe, abortion (except where it is necessary to preserve the life or health of the mother) because the fetus is potentially capable of life outside the womb.

ABORTION DEBATE: 1979

Since 1973, anti-abortion activists, including Catholic Church leaders, have sought to reverse the Court's decisions through legislative and litigative action. Their major efforts have been in the following areas:

Constitutional Amendments: Two kinds of amendments have been proposed: (1) "right-to-life" amendments, which would accord personhood to the fetus and (2) "states rights" amendments to return abortion regulation to the states. At the state level, anti-abortion activists are pursuing the "alternative" route to amending the Constitution and, by May 1978, 13 state legislatures—of a required 34—had passed resolutions calling for Congress to convene a Constitutional Convention to adopt a "Human Life Amendment."

Funding Restrictions: In 1976, Congress enacted the "Hyde Amendment" to the Labor-HEW Appropriations bill to cut off federal Medicaid funds for most abortions for the poor. The "Hyde Amendment" did not go into effect until August 1977, after the U.S. Supreme Court had ruled that states are not obligated to pay for non-therapeutic abortions and after a federal judge had acted to lift an injunction which had previously prevented the law from going into effect. The Supreme Court's decision, coupled with the federal government's withdrawal of its reimbursements to the states, resulted in two-thirds of the states eliminating most abortion coverage from their Medicaid programs. Consequently, HEW reported a 99% decline in the number of Medicaid abortions for February-December 1978. By May 1978, several state legislatures were debating the issue and only 17 states and the District of Columbia were continuing Medicaid coverage for all or most abortions. Litigation challenging the validity of federal and state restrictions on public funding for medically necessary abortions is still pending. While in New Jersey "medically necessary" was ruled on Jan. 9, 1979, as apparently encompassing more than endangering the life of the mother, Massachusetts Gov. Edward J. King elected to sign into effect on June 12, 1979, the seemingly strictest anti-abortion law in the U.S. The law provides that government funds would be used for abortions *only* if a woman's life were in danger. In addition to public funding restrictions through Medicaid, prohibition of use of monies in the Foreign Assistance Act continues, as does the limitation of Legal Services attorneys' participation in abortion cases. A bill signed on Oct. 13, 1978, provides for the federal funding of abortions for military personnel in the cases of crime or danger to the health of the mother.

Consent Requirements: Various state consent requirements for abortion were ruled unconstitutional by the Supreme Court since the beginning of 1976. Subsequently, states began to consider and enact legislation requiring parental notification or consultation for a minor's abortion. Such laws are being challenged in the courts. Also being considered in the courts is the question of a mandatory 24-hour cooling-off period between the time consent is given for an abortion and the actual procedure.

"Informed Consent" Provisions: Legislatures in several states and Akron City Council have passed laws mandating one-sided counseling procedures for abortion. These include controversial details of fetal development and possible physical and psychological complications resulting from abortion. These are being challenged in the courts.

At the local level, government, public agencies and party structures are being pressured into adopting policies for or against legal abortion.

AIR POLLUTION IN U.S. AIR QUALITY CONTROL AREAS: 1977
Source: Environmental Protection Agency

OZONE/OXIDANT

Note: The new ozone standard is 235 $\mu g/m^3$, daily maximum hour.

Number of Stations

Metropolitan Area	Total Valid	Exceeding 1-hour Average of 160$\mu g/m^3$	Range of Max. 1-Hr. Values ($\mu g/m^3$)*
New York	22	16	217–537
Los Angeles	36	36	195–725
Chicago	19	17	102–674
Philadelphia	13	13	254–399
Detroit	8	6	157–529
San Francisco	7	4	97–293
Boston	5	5	254–333
Washington, D.C.	9	9	244–440
Cleveland	4	4	292–352
St. Louis	8	8	268–409

* $\mu g/m^3$ = micrograms per cubic meter.

CARBON MONOXIDE

Note: The 8-hour standard is 10 milligrams per cubic meter of air ($\mu g/m^3$), arithmetic mean.

Number of Stations

Metropolitan Area	Total Valid	Exceeding 8-Hour Standard	Range of Max. 8-Hour Values ($\mu g/m^3$)*
New York	18	12	6.7–26.0
Los Angeles	34	18	3.1–26.4
Chicago	8	3	4.6–16.7
Philadelphia	16	8	3.6–27.8
Detroit	8	4	8.1–22.0
San Francisco	14	4	6.2–16.3
Boston	6	6	12.7–16.5
Washington, D.C.	11	4	5.7–15.0
Cleveland	3	1	7.5–12.3
St. Louis	8	3	6.3–20.6

* $\mu g/m^3$ = milligrams per cubic meter.

SULFUR DIOXIDE

Note: The primary annual standard is 80 $\mu g/m^3$, arithmetic mean.

Number of Stations

Metropolitan Area	Total Valid	Exceeding Annual Standard	Range of Annual Mean ($\mu g/m^3$)*
New York	33	0	3–86
Los Angeles	29	0	5–69
Chicago	60	0	3–73
Philadelphia	19	1	7–83
San Francisco	6	0	2–13
Detroit	20	0	9–55
Boston	5	0	25–51
Washington, D.C.	22	0	5–40
Cleveland	74	3	19–176
St. Louis	13	1	31–103

* $\mu g/m^3$ = micrograms per cubic meter.

TOTAL SUSPENDED PARTICULATES

Note: The primary annual standard is 75 $\mu g/m^3$, geometric mean.

Number of Stations

Metropolitan Area	Total Valid	Exceeding Annual Standard	Range of Annual Mean ($\mu g/m^3$)*
New York	102	1	20–77
Los Angeles	29	21	50–136
Chicago	98	26	42–170
Philadelphia	36	8	31–95
Detroit	36	5	37–118
San Francisco	18	0	34–71
Boston	15	1	33–76
Washington, D.C.	16	2	36–91
Cleveland	85	14	43–154
St. Louis	23	12	39–184

* $\mu g/m^3$ = micrograms per cubic meter.

MAJOR OIL SPILLS FROM TANKERS AND BARGES IN U.S. WATERS: 1972 to 1977
Covers spills larger than 50,000 gallons, within 200 miles of U.S. coastline. Summer=April through September; winter=October through March.

Source: U.S. Council on Environmental Quality, Major Oil Spills from Tankers, Barges, and Other Vessels in U.S. Waters —Analysis of Recent Trends and Patterns, 1977.

ITEM	1972-73	1973-74	1974-75	1975-76	1976-77
Number of spills, total	12	23	22	16	15
Summer	2	8	7	4	5
Winter	10	15	15	12	10
Oil spilled .... 1,000 gal.	5,294	5,182	7,331	9,251	11,516
Summer	1,998	1,614	1,909	1,259	972
Winter	3,296	3,568	5,422	7,992	10,544

MEDICAL CARE INDEXES
Source: U.S. Bureau of Labor Statistics

Year	All medical care Items*	Physicians' services	Dental services	Optometric examination and eyeglasses	Hospital daily service charges	Prescriptions and drugs	Year	All medical care Items*	Physicians' services	Dental services	Optometric examination and eyeglasses	Hospital daily service charges	Prescriptions and drugs
1935	36.1	39.2	40.8	56.7	11.9	70.7	1969	113.4	112.9	112.9	107.6	127.9	101.3
1945	42.1	46.0	49.6	63.9	16.2	74.8	1970	120.6	121.4	119.4	113.5	143.9	103.6
1955	64.8	65.4	73.0	77.0	41.5	94.7	1971	128.4	129.8	127.0	120.3	160.8	105.4
1960	79.1	77.0	82.1	85.1	56.3	104.5	1972	132.5	133.8	132.3	124.9	102.0†	105.6
1961	81.4	79.0	82.5	87.8	60.6	103.3	1973	137.7	138.2	136.4	129.5	105.6†	105.9
1962	83.5	81.3	84.7	89.2	64.9	101.7	1974	150.5	150.9	146.8	138.6	115.1†	109.6
1963	85.6	83.1	87.1	89.7	69.0	100.8	1975	168.6	169.4	161.9	149.6	132.3†	118.8
1964	87.3	85.2	89.4	90.9	72.4	100.5	1976	184.7	188.5	172.2	158.9	148.7†	126.0
1965	89.5	88.3	92.2	92.8	76.6	100.2	1977	202.4	206.0	185.1	168.2	164.1†	134.1
1966	93.4	93.4	95.2	95.3	84.0	100.5	1978	219.4	223.1	198.1	—	—	143.5
1967	100.0	100.0	100.0	100.0	100.0	100.0							
1968	106.1	105.6	105.5	103.2	113.2	100.2							

* 1967 = 100 † Hospital Service Charges (January 1972 = 100)

MILESTONES OF MEDICINE

Date	Milestone	Discoverer	Nationality
6th cent. B.C.	First recorded dietary and sanitary laws	Book of Leviticus	Hebrew
5th–4th cent. B.C.	Medicine moves from realm of superstition to that of observation; emergence of the idea of nature as healer	Hippocrates	Greek
4th cent. B.C.	Beginning of a systematic study of anatomy	Herophilus	Greek
2d cent. A.D.	Correlation of extant medical knowledge into a single great system that influenced medical thought until the 16th century	Clarissimus Galen	Greco-Roman
9th or 10th cent.	First-known description of smallpox and differentiation between that disease and measles; the approach was used until the 18th century	Rhazes or Rasis	Persian
16th cent.	Reaffirmation of nature as prime healer; also, beginning of chemotherapy	Paracelsus	Swiss
1543	Publication of De humani corporis fabrica, first anatomy textbook based entirely on observation, rather than on Galen's writings	Andreas Vesalius	Flemish
c. 1590	Invention of the microscope	Zacharias Janssen	Dutch
1628	Discovery of blood circulation	William Harvey	English
c. 1648	Founding of biochemistry	Jan Baptista van Helmont	Flemish
1661	Discovery that capillaries are vein-artery junctions, thus completing the explanation of blood circulation	Marcello Malpighi	Italian
1736	First successful appendectomy	Claudius Amyand	French
1757–66	Established physiology as a branch of science	Albrecht von Haller	Swiss
1796	First successful antitoxin vaccination (for smallpox)	Edward Jenner	English
1800	Founding of histology—the study of tissues	Marie F. X. Bichat	French
1816	Invention of the stethoscope	René Laënnec	French
1822	Description of the process of digestion	William Beaumont	American
1838–39	Establishment of cell theory founding of cytology	Matthias Schleiden, Theodor Schwann	German
1842	Use of ether as an anesthetic during surgery	Crawford W. Long	American
1844	Use of nitrous oxide as anesthetic during surgery	Horace Wells	American
1857	Development of the pasteurization process began	Louis Pasteur	French
1860	Experiments that finally destroyed the idea of spontaneous generation	Louis Pasteur	French
1865	Introduction of surgical antisepsis	Joseph Lister	English
1866	Invention of the clinical thermometer	Thomas C. Allbut	English
1870–1909	Founding of neuroanatomy	Camillo Golgi	Italian
c. 1872	Founding of bacteriology	Ferdinand Cohn	German
1877	Publication of postulates for determining the etiology of diseases	Robert Koch	German
1883–84	Discovery of the bacillus that causes diphtheria	Edwin Klebs, Friedrich Löffler	German
1890–95	Founding of serology and immunology	Paul Ehrlich, Emil von Behring	German
1894	Discovery of bubonic plague's causative bacillus	Alexandre Yersin S. Kitasato	French Japanese
1892, 1895	Founding of virology	Dmitri Ivanovski (Independently, M. Beijerinck)	Russian Dutch
1895	Publication of Studies in Hysteria; founding of psychoanalysis	Sigmund Freud	Austrian
1895	Discovery of X rays	Wilhelm Roentgen	German
1897	Development of method for making a differential blood count	Paul Ehrlich	German
1901	Establishment of etiology of yellow fever	Walter Reed and others	American
1906	Development of specific test for syphilis	August Wassermann and others (Independently, Lazlo Detre)	German Hungarian
1906	Passage of U.S. Pure Food Law—the first legislation of its kind	Harvey W. Wiley	American
1912	Discovery of vitamins	Casimir Funk	American, b. Poland
1915	Discovery of pellagra cure	Joseph Goldberger	American, b. Austria-Hungary
1921	Isolation of insulin for use in diabetic therapy	Frederick Banting, Charles Best	Canadian
1926	Discovery of liver extract (vitamin B₁)	George Minot, William Murphy	American
1928	Invention of artificial respirator ("iron lung")	Philip Drinker, Louis Shaw	American
1928	Discovery of penicillin	Alexander Fleming	Scottish
c. 1932	First use of sulfa drugs in therapy	Gerhard Domagk	German
1940	Discovery of the Rh factor	Karl Landsteiner	American, b. Austria
1943	Discovery of streptomycin and its use in treating tuberculosis	Selman Waksman	American, b. Russia
1944	Introduction of corrective heart surgery to enable survival of "blue babies"	Alfred Blalock, Helen Taussig	American
1949	Cortisone introduced into medical therapy	Philip Hench and others	American
1953	Establishment of cryosurgery in which body temperature is lowered to slow circulation, allowing dry-heart surgery	Henry Swan	American
1954	Introduction of open-heart surgery	C. Walton Lillehei	American
1954	Development of hypodermic poliomyelitis vaccine	Jonas Salk	American
1955	Development of oral poliomyelitis vaccine	Albert Sabin	American, b. Russia
1963	First use of artificial heart for circulating blood during heart surgery	Michael De Bakey	American
1967	First surgical transplant of a human heart	Christiaan Barnard	South African
1969	Deciphering of structure of gamma globulin—one of the body's chief defenders against diseases	Gerald Edelman and others	American
1972	Research into the structure of antibodies	Gerald Edelman Rodney R. Porter	American English
1976	Discovery of viral cause of multiple sclerosis	Gertrude Henle and others	American
1978	First "test-tube" baby born	Patrick Steptoe, Robert Edwards	English

MEDICAL GLOSSARY

Abscess: Collection of pus in a tissue cavity resulting from a localized infection associated with cellular disintegration.

Anemia: Decrease in the number of circulating red blood cells or in their hemoglobin (oxygen-carrying pigment) content. Can result from excessive bleeding or blood destruction (either inherited or disease caused) or from decreased blood formation (either nutritional deficiency or disease). In one form, sickle-cell anemia, it is inherited, occurring almost wholly among blacks. Pernicious anemia is caused by inability to absorb vitamin B_{12}.

Angina: Choking pain. Angina pectoris: chest pain resulting from insufficient blood circulation through the vessels supplying blood to the heart, precipitated by exertion or emotion and usually relieved by a vasodilator drug.

Arteriosclerosis: Generalized thickening, loss of elasticity, and hardening of the body's small and medium-size arteries.

Asthma: Disease characterized by repeated attacks of shortness of breath, with wheezing, cough, and choking feeling due to a spasmodic narrowing of the small bronchi (small air tubes opening into the lung respiratory alveoli or cavities).

Biopsy: Removal of a small piece of tissue from the living body for microscopic or chemical examination to assist in disease diagnosis.

Bronchitis: Inflammation of the bronchi (tubular passages leading to lung cavities). It may be acute or chronic and caused by infection or the action of physical or chemical agents.

Cancer (Neoplasm): A cellular tumor (swelling) resulting from uncontrolled tissue growth. Its natural evolution is to spread locally or to other body locations through the blood and lymph stream.

Cataract: Opacity of the normally transparent eye lens; this condition leads to impaired vision and stems from hereditary, nutritional, inflammatory, toxic, traumatic, or degenerative causes.

Catheterization: Introduction of a tubular instrument called a catheter into a body cavity to inject or withdraw liquids (usually via the bladder for urine withdrawal).

Cerebrospinal Fluid Examination: Chemical, miscroscopic, and bacteriological examination of a sample of the usually clear and colorless liquid bathing the brain and spinal cord. The sample is usually removed by needle puncture of the lumbar spine.

Cirrhosis: Chronic liver ailment, characterized by an increase in its fibrous support tissue that results in a progressive destruction of liver cells and impairment of the organ's functions.

Conjunctivitis: Acute or chronic inflammation of the conjunctiva—the delicate transparent membrane lining the eyelids and covering the exposed surface of the eyeball. It results from the action of bacteria, allergens, and physical or chemical irritants.

Cyst: Any normal or abnormal sac in the body, especially one containing a liquid or semiliquid material.

Cystic Fibrosis: An inherited disease of the glands of external secretion, affecting mostly the pancreas, respiratory tract, and sweat glands, and usually appearing in infancy.

Cystitis: Acute or chronic inflammation of the urinary bladder, caused by infection or irritation from foreign bodies (kidney stones) or chemicals. Its symptoms are frequent voiding accompanied by burning sensation.

Diabetes (Mellitus): Hereditary or acquired disorder in which there is a sugar-utilization deficiency in the body, caused by an absolute or relative insufficiency of the normal internal secretion of the pancreas (insulin). Symptoms are thirst, hunger, itching, weakness, and increased frequency of urination. Diabetes can be controlled by diet, drugs, or the administration of insulin. Lack of treatment leads to various complications, including death.

Eczema: Inflammatory skin disease that produces a great variety of lesions, such as vesicles, thickening of skin, watery discharge, and scales and crusts, with itching and burning sensations. Eczema is caused by allergy, infections, and nutritional, physical, and sometimes unknown factors.

Edema: Excessive accumulation of water and salt in the tissue spaces, caused by kidney or heart disease (generalized edema) or by local circulatory impairment stemming from inflammation, trauma, or neoplasm (localized edema).

Electrocardiogram (ECG or EKG): Graphic tracing of the electric current that is produced by the rhythmic contraction of the heart muscle. Visually, a periodic wave pattern is produced. Changes in the wave pattern may appear in the course of various heart diseases; the tracing is obtained by applying electrodes on the skin of the chest and limbs.

Electroencephalogram (EEG): Graphic recording of the electric current created by the activity of the brain. The electrodes are placed on the scalp. It is used in the diagnosis of organic brain disease.

Embolism: Sudden blocking of an artery by a dislodged blood clot (after surgery), a fat globule (after a fracture), gas bubbles (after sudden decompression), bacterial clumps (bacterial endocarditis), or other foreign matter. The arteries most usually affected are those of the brain, heart, lungs, and extremities.

Emphysema (Pulmonary): Lung disease characterized by overdistention of the air sacs of the lungs (alveoli), their loss of elasticity, and destruction of the walls separating them. It results in a reduction of the respiratory surface, chronic shortness of breath, wheezing, and cough.

Epilepsy: Disease characterized by sudden and brief (in some forms momentary) convulsions, which are associated with impairment or loss of consciousness, psychic or sensory disturbances, and autonomic nervous system perturbations. Epilepsy causes the EEG to show characteristic brain wave alterations.

Furuncle (Boil): Acute and painful infection of the skin surrounding a hair root or sebaceous gland. Its center contains pus and dead tissue that has to be discharged either spontaneously or surgically for cure.

Gangrene: A form of necrosis in which localized tissue death is followed by putrefaction.

Gastritis: Acute or chronic inflammation of the lining of the stomach. It may be caused by the ingestion of alcohol, spices, medicines, chemicals, foods, as well as by infections or allergy.

Gastroscopy: Direct visualization of the stomach interior by means of an optical instrument called a gastroscope.

Gastrointestinal Series (G.I. Series): Serial X-ray examination of the stomach and intestines to detect organic or functional alterations, enabling proper diagnosis and treatment of disease.

Glaucoma: Eye disease characterized by an increase in the internal pressure in the eye, caused by alteration of the intraocular fluid flow and resulting in visual impairment, and if untreated, blindness.

Goiter: Enlargement of the thyroid gland that shows as a well-defined swelling at the base of the neck. Goiter is usually associated with iodine deficiency (endemic goiter), or with excessive secretion of thyroid hormones (exophthalmic goiter).

Gout: A disturbance of body chemistry, manifested by elevated uric acid blood levels and excessive deposits in tissues, particularly joints and cartilages. It is characterized by repeated attacks of acute and very painful inflammation of joints, especially those of the big toe but also of ankles, knees, wrists, and elbows.

Hematoma: Swelling produced by a collection of blood escaping from a ruptured blood vessel, resulting from trauma or injury. It is generally located under the skin and subcutaneous tissue, or under the bony structure of the skull.

Hemorrhage (Bleeding): Any copious blood loss from the circulation. If sufficiently severe or unchecked, it may lead to anemia or shock.

Hemorrhoids (Piles): Abnormal dilatation of the veins of the rectum and anus, causing local swelling, pain, itching, bleeding, and induration.

Hepatitis: Liver inflammation, caused by infection or toxic substances. It is characterized by jaundice (yellow coloration of skin and membranes, especially of the eye) and is usually accompanied by fever.

Hernia: Protrusion of a portion of an organ or tissue through an abnormal body opening. Inguinal hernia is one of the most common and consists of an intestinal loop protruding at the groin.

Hypertension: Disease characterized by elevated blood pressure, resulting from the functional or pathological narrowing of the peripheral small arteries. Except in limited instances, its cause is generally unknown.

Immunotherapy: a method of treating certain diseases by stimulating the body's natural immune response, resulting in partial or total immunization.

Intestinal Obstruction: Blocking of the normal flow of the intestinal contents, caused by twisting of a gut loop, benign tumor, cancer, or foreign body.

Kidney Failure (Renal Failure): Severe reduction or impairment of the excretory function of the kidney. The acute form occurs most frequently after crushing injuries, transfusion of mismatched blood, severe burns or shock, generalized infections, obstetric accidents, and certain chemical poisoning.

Laboratory Procedures: Laboratory tests performed to assist in disease diagnosis and treatment. Usually these tests are carried out on samples of blood, urine, or other body fluids. The most common are:

Blood Count: Determination of the number and percentage of red and white blood cells from a blood sample that is obtained by puncturing a vein or the skin. It consists of a red blood cell count (RBC), white blood cell count (WBC), and platelet count.

Blood Grouping: Blood typing for selecting and matching blood transfusion donors and for the diagnosis of various diseases.

Blood Chemistry: Determination of the content of various blood chemicals; the most usual are: sugar, for diabetes; urea nitrogen (BUN), for kidney or liver disease; uric acid, for gout; and cholesterol, for vascular and liver disease.

Blood Culture: Investigation to detect the presence of pathogenic germs by special culturing in artificial media.

Urinalysis (Urine Analysis): Examination of urine constituents, both normal (urea, uric acid, total nitrogen, ammonia, chlorides, phosphate, and others) and abnormal (albumin, glucose, acetone, bile, blood, cells, and bacteria).

Meningitis: Inflammation of the enveloping membranes of the brain or spinal cord, caused by virus, bacteria, yeasts, fungi, or protozoa. It is a serious disease and may be a complication of another bodily infection.

Metabolism: The total of the physical and chemical processes occurring in the living organism by which its substance is produced, maintained, and exchanged with transformation of energy; this energy itself provides fuel for all body functions and heat production.

Metastasis: Transfer of a disease (usually cancer) or the causative agent of a disease (e.g. bacteria or cancer cells) from one organ or part of the body to another, through the blood or lymph vessels.

Multiple Sclerosis: A chronic and slowly progressive disease of unknown cause that is characterized by patches of fibrous tissue degeneration in brain and spinal cord, causing various nervous system symptoms; the disease's course is marked by occasional periods of worsening or improvement.

Muscular Dystrophy: An inherited disease that involves the progressive weakness and degeneration of voluntary skeletal muscle fibers without nerve involvement.

Myocarditis: Inflammation of the heart muscle that is associated with or caused by a number of infectious diseases, toxic chemicals, drugs, and traumatic agents.

Necrosis: Localized death of tissue, following interruption of the blood supply to the area.

Nephritis: Inflammatory, acute or chronic disease of the kidneys, which usually follows some form of infection or toxic chemical poisoning. It impairs renal function, causing headache, dropsy, elevated blood pressure, and appearance of albumin in urine.

Neuralgia: Brief attack of acute and severe shooting pain along the course of one or more peripheral nerves, usually without clear cause.

Neuritis: Inflammation or degeneration of one or more peripheral nerves, causing pain, tenderness, tingling sensations, numbness, paralysis, muscle weakness, and wasting and disappearance of reflexes in the area involved. The cause may be infectious, toxic, nutritional (vitamin B_1 deficiency), or unknown.

Pancreatitis: Inflammation of the pancreas, either mild or acute and fulminating. The chronic form is characterized by recurrent attacks of diverse severity. Symptoms are sudden abdominal pain, tenderness and distention, vomiting and, in severe cases, shock and circulatory collapse.

Pap Smears (Papanicolau Smears): Method of staining smears of various body secretions—especially vaginal but also respiratory, digestive, or genitourinary—to detect cancer by examining the normally shed cells in the smear. The procedure is named for its developer.

Parkinsonism (Paralysis Agitans): A usually chronic condition, marked by muscular rigidity, immobile face, excessive salivation, and tremor. These symptoms characterize Parkinson's disease; however, they are also observed in the course of treatment with psychopharmaceutical drugs or following encephalitis or trauma.

Pellagra: A disease caused by a vitamin (niacin) deficiency and characterized by skin, alimentary tract, and nervous system disturbances.

Pericarditis: Acute or chronic inflammation of the pericardium (fibrous sac surrounding the heart), caused by infection, trauma, myocardial infarction, cancer, or complication from other diseases.

Peritonitis: Acute or chronic inflammation of the serous membrane lining abdominal walls and covering the contained viscera. Its symptoms are abdominal pain and tenderness, nausea, vomiting, moderate fever, and constipation. It is usually caused by infectious agents or foreign matter entering the abdominal cavity from the intestinal tract (perforation), female genital tract, blood dissemination, or the outside (wounds, surgery).

Phlebitis: Condition caused by inflammation of a vein wall, usually resulting in the formation of a blood clot inside its cavity. Phlebitis produces pain, swelling, and stiffness of the affected part, generally a limb.

Pleurisy: Acute or chronic inflammation of the pleura (serous membrane lining the thoracic cavity and lungs). It often accompanies inflammatory lung diseases and may be caused by infection (tuberculous, viral, or other), cancer, or cardiac infarct.

Pneumonia: An acute inflammation of the lungs, usually caused by bacterial or viral infection. Chills, sharp chest pain, shortness of breath, cough, rusty sputum, fever, and headache are primary symptoms.

Pneumothorax: Accumulation of air or gas in the pleural cavity (between the chest wall and the lung), resulting in lung collapse. It may result from a penetrating chest wound or some disease, or may be deliberately induced for treatment of lung ailments (tuberculosis).

Polycythemia: an abnormal increase in the number of circulating red blood cells.

Polyp: A protruding excrescence or growth from a mucous membrane, usually of the nasal passages but also of the uterine cervix, alimentary tract, or vocal cords.

Psoriasis: Chronic, occasionally acute, recurrent skin disease of unknown cause, characterized by thickened red skin patches that are covered with whitish shiny scales. Psoriasis usually affects the scalp, elbows, knees, back, and buttocks.

Pulmonary Edema: Usually an acute condition in which there is a waterlogging of the lung tissue, including its alveolar cavities. Respiration is impaired. If inadequately treated, it may lead to rapid death; it is often a complication of chronic heart disease.

Rheumatic Fever: Disease characterized by initial sore throat, chills, high fever, and painful inflammation of large joints. Frequently cardiac complications follow, leading to permanent organic heart disease.

Rickets: Generally a disease of infants and young children caused by vitamin D deficiency. There is defective bone calcification that causes skeletal deformities, such as bow legs, knock knees, and pigeon chest.

Sciatica: A severe pain along the sciatic nerve, which extends from the buttocks along the back of the thigh and leg to the ankle.

Spinal Curvature: A marked displacement of the normally straight vertical spine, which may be caused by disease or mechanical deviation of the bones or muscles of the spine, hips, or legs.

Septicemia: Presence of bacteria or bacterial toxins in the circulating blood caused by the breakdown of local defenses, permitting a circumscribed infection to spread.

Silicosis: Occupational disease, usually chronic, causing fibrosis of the lungs. It results from inhalation of the dust of stone, flint, or sand that contains silica (quartz). Called "grinders' disease," it is observed in workers who have breathed such dust for a period of years.

Slipped Disk: An acute or chronic condition, caused by the traumatic or degenerative displacement and protrusion of the softened central core of an intervertebral disk (cartilagenous disk between the spine bones), especially of the lower back. Symptoms are low back pain, which frequently extends to the thigh; muscle spasm; and tenderness.

Spastic Paralysis (Cerebral Palsy): A condition probably stemming from various causes present since birth. Associated with nonprogressive brain damage, cerebral palsy is characterized by spastic, jerky voluntary movements, or constant involuntary and irregular writhing.

Stroke (Cerebral Apoplexy): A sudden attack of paralysis, with disturbance of speech and thought. It is caused by the destruction of brain substance, as the result of brain hemorrhage, vascular damage, intravascular clotting, or local circulatory insufficiency.

Thermography: a diagnostic technique for locating the presence of underlying tumors by recording infrared radiations that emanate from the body surface: tumors radiate more heat than the surrounding tissues.

Thrombophlebitis: Condition caused by the inflammation of a vein complicated by the formation of an intravascular blood clot (thrombus). Circulation is obstructed in the affected area, usually the legs.

Thrombosis: Formation, development, or presence of a blood clot inside an artery or vein. This condition can be serious, if it affects the blood vessels of vital organs, such as the brain, heart, or lungs.

Tumor: A swelling or growth of new tissue; it develops independently of surrounding structures and serves no specific function of its own.

Uremia: Toxic clinical condition, caused by renal insufficiency resulting in the retention of urinary waste products in the circulating blood.

Varicose Veins: Abnormally distended and lengthened superficial veins caused by slowing and obstruction of the normal blood backflow. Varicose veins are most commonly observed in the legs, anus and rectum (hemorrhoids), and scrotum (varicocele).

MODERN DRUG ADVANCES

Adrenocorticosteroids—More than 20 synthetic adrenal hormones and their chemical derivatives. They are used primarily in the treatment of "collagen diseases" (e.g., rheumatoid arthritis) and in the suppression of certain inflammatory diseases or immunological processes.

Allopurinol—An oral drug used in suppressing the symptoms of gout.

Ampicillin—A "broad-spectrum" semisynthetic penicillin effective in the treatment of many types of meningitis and severe intestinal, respiratory, and other disorders.

Antithyroid Agents—A group of unrelated compounds, ranging from propylthiouracil to radio-iodide; used for treating hyperthyroidism.

BCG (Bacille Calmette-Guérin): a nonvirulent strain of tubercle bacillus used in vaccines for immunization against tuberculosis and experimentally in controlling some forms of cancer.

Chloramphenicol—An important broad-spectrum antibiotic that is used to treat typhoid fever, certain types of food poisoning, and other infections caused by microorganisms that are resistant to other antibiotics.

Chloroquin Compounds—Antimalarial and certain forms of extraintestinal amebiasis. They are also used in a few unrelated diseases, such as arthritis.

Chlorpromazine and Other Tranquilizers—Over 30 compounds with mild depressant action on the brain, used in certain mental illnesses and anxiety states, and for antinauseant and sedative effects.

Clofibrate—A drug capable of reducing elevated cholesterol and triglyceride concentrations in the blood.

Clomiphene Citrate—A drug that improves fertility, sometimes causing multiple births.

Diphenhydramine and 30 Other Antihistaminics—Employed mainly in treating certain allergic conditions and also for antiemetic and sedative effects.

Estrogen-Progestogen Contraceptives—Oral contraceptive agents.

Ganglionic Blocking Agents, Mostly Quaternary Ammonium Compounds—Used in the treatment of certain types of hypertension.

Griseofulvin—The only drug taken orally that is effective against many fungal infections of the skin and fingernails and toenails.

Halogenated Hydrocarbon Anesthetics—Volatile liquids that are used for inhalation anesthesia.

Hydantoins—Used in the treatment of grand mal (epilepsy) and certain other convulsive states.

Hypnotic Barbiturates—Sedatives and sleeping pills.

Immune Globulins—A protein derived from human blood that, when injected into persons exposed to certain infectious diseases, confers temporary immunity.

Isoniazid—The most important drug in the treatment and prophylaxis of tuberculosis.

Isoproterenol—Used in the treatment of bronchial asthma, particularly to relieve the bronchial-tube spasm.

Lidocaine and Other Local Anesthetics—Injected locally to anesthetize tissues prior to minor surgical operations.

Lithium—A drug found effective in the treatment of manic-depressive psychoses.

Meperidine—A powerful pain-relieving drug.

Methantheline and Other Anticholinergics—Parasympatholytic agents used in cases of peptic ulcer and to decrease hypermotility (or spasm) of the gastrointestinal tract.

Methicillin—The first penicillin effective against staph (staphylococcus) infections that are resistant to ordinary penicillin.

Oral Antidiabetes Agents (e.g., isophane insulin and tolbutamide)—Insulin replacement for some types of diabetes.

Organomercurial Diuretics—Used to remove fluid from the body in certain diseases of the heart, liver, and kidneys.

Pentazocine—A synthetic narcotic analgesic, originally meant to replace morphine because of its lower incidence of addiction.

Propranolol—A drug for heart-rhythm disorders.

Rauwolfia and Veratrum Alkaloids—Principles of plant origin used in treating hypertension or as a tranquilizer.

Streptomycin—An important antibiotic, and one of the primary drugs for treating tuberculosis.

Sulfonamides—Used in the treatment of infections of the respiratory and urinary tracts and in certain types of meningitis.

Surgical Skeletal Muscle Relaxants (About seven surgical, peripherally acting preparations)—These drugs are used to relax muscles during surgery.

Synthetic Anticoagulants—Used to prevent formation or extension of blood clots within arteries and veins.

Ten Basic Penicillins, Plus Salts and Esters—Antibacterial drugs that are used primarily to treat infections of the skin, respiratory tract, and of the genitourinary tract.

Tetracycline Derivatives, Plus Salts and Esters—Used in the treatment of a wide variety of diseases caused by many different types of micro-organisms.

Thiazides—To remove excess fluid from the body in certain types of heart and kidney diseases. Also used in the treatment of hypertension (high blood pressure).

Trihexyphenidyl, Amantadine Hydrochloride, L-Dopa, and Other Anti-Parkinsonism Agents—Used to relieve the muscle symptoms in patients with Parkinson's disease.

Vaccines—For the prevention or modification of infectious diseases, such as poliomyelitis, measles, and mumps.

PSYCHIATRIC TERMS

SOURCE: American Psychiatric Association

Accident Prone: Special susceptibility to accidents due to psychological causes.

Anal Character: In psychoanalysis a pattern of behavior in an adult that originates in the anal eroticism of infancy and is characterized by such traits as excessive orderliness, miserliness, and obstinacy.

Anxiety: Apprehension, the source of which is largely unknown or unrecognized. It is different from fear, which is the emotional response to a consciously recognized and usually external danger.

Autistic Child: In child psychiatry, a child who responds chiefly to inner thoughts, who does not relate to his environment, and whose overall functioning is immature and often appears retarded.

Blocking: Difficulty in recollection, or interruption of a train of thought or speech, caused by unconscious emotional factors.

Castration Anxiety: Anxiety due to danger (fantasied) of loss of the genitals or injuries to them. May be precipitated by everyday events that have symbolic significance and appear to be threatening, such as loss of job, loss of a tooth, or an experience of ridicule or humiliation.

Catalepsy: A condition usually characterized by trance-like states. May occur in organic or psychological disorders or under hypnosis.

Catatonic State (catatonia): A state characterized by immobility with muscular rigidity or inflexibility and at times by excitability, Virtually always a symptom of schizophrenia.

Compensation: (1) A defense mechanism, operating unconsciously, by which the individual attempts to make up for (i.e., to compensate for) real or fancied deficiencies; (2) a conscious process in which the individual strives to make up for real or imagined defects in such areas as physique, performance, skills, or psychological attributes.

Complex: A group of associated ideas that have a common emotional tie. These are largely unconscious and significantly influence attitudes and associations. Examples are:

Inferiority complex: Feelings of inferiority stemming from real or imagined physical or social inadequacies that may cause anxiety or other adverse reactions. The individual may overcompensate by excessive ambition or by the development of special skills, often in the very field in which he was originally handicapped.

Oedipus complex: Attachment of the child for the parent of the opposite sex, accompanied by envious and aggressive feelings toward the parent of the same sex. These feelings are largely repressed (i.e., made unconscious) because of the fear of displeasure or punishment by the parent of the same sex. In its original use, the term applied only to the male child.

Compulsion: An insistent, repetitive, and unwanted urge to perform an act that is contrary to the person's ordinary conscious wishes or standards. Failure to perform the compulsive act results in overt anxiety.

Death Instinct (*Thanatos*): In Freudian theory, the unconscious drive toward dissolution and death. Coexists with and is in opposition to the life instinct (*Eros*).

Defense Mechanism: A specific process, operating unconsciously, that is employed to seek relief from emotional conflict and freedom from anxiety.

Dementia Praecox: Obsolescent term for schizophrenia.

Depression: Psychiatrically, a morbid sadness, dejection, or melancholy; to be differentiated from grief, which is realistic and proportionate to what has been lost. A depression may be a symptom of any psychiatric disorder or may constitute its principal manifestation.

Ego: In psychoanalytic theory, one of the three major divisions of human personality, the others being the *id* and *superego*. The *ego*, commonly identified with consciousness of self, is the mental agent mediating among three contending forces: the external demands of social pressure or reality; the primitive instinctual demands arising from the *id* imbedded as it is in the deepest level of the unconscious; and the claims of the *superego*, born of parental and social prohibitions and functioning as an internal censor or "conscience."

Empathy: An objective awareness of the feelings, emotions, and behavior of another person. To be distinguished from sympathy, which is usually nonobjective and noncritical.

Epilepsy: A disorder characterized by periodic seizures, and sometimes accompanied by a loss of consciousness. May be caused by organic or emotional disturbances.

Major epilepsy (*grand mal*): Characterized by gross convulsive seizures, with loss of consciousness.

Minor epilepsy (*petit mal*): Minor nonconvulsive epileptic seizures; may be limited to only momentary lapses of consciousness.

Euphoria: An exaggerated feeling of physical and emotional well-being inconsonant with reality.

Extroversion: A state in which attention and energies are largely directed outward from the self, as opposed to interest primarily directed toward the self, as in introversion.

Free Association: In psychoanalytic therapy, spontaneous, uncensored verbalization by the patient of whatever comes to mind.

Fugue: A major state of personality dissociation characterized by amnesia and actual physical flight from the immediate environment.

Homosexuality: Sexual attraction or relationship between members of the same sex.

Latent homosexuality: A condition characterized by unconscious homosexual desires.

Overt homosexuality: Homosexuality that is consciously recognized or practiced.

Hypnosis: A state of increased receptivity to suggestion and direction, initially induced by the influence of another person. The degree may vary from mild suggestibility to a trance state so profound as to be used in surgical operations.

Hypochondriasis: Overconcern with the state of physical or emotional health, accompanied by various bodily complaints without demonstrable organic pathology.

Hysterical Personality: A personality type characterized by shifting emotional feelings, susceptibility to suggestion, impulsive behavior, attention seeking, immaturity, and self-absorption; not necessarily disabling.

Inhibition: Interference with or restriction of activities; the result of an unconscious defense against forbidden instinctual drives.

Insight: Self-understanding. A major goal of psychotherapy. The extent of the individual's understanding of the origin, nature, and mechanisms of his attitudes and behavior.

Mania: A suffix denoting a pathological preoccupation with some desire, idea, or activity; a morbid compulsion. Some frequently encountered manias are *dipsomania*, compulsion to drink alcoholic beverages; *egomania*, pathological preoccupation with self; *kleptomania*, compulsion to steal; *megalomania*, pathological preoccupation with delusions of power or wealth; *monomania*, pathological preoccupation with one subject; *necromania*, pathological preoccupation with the dead; *pyromania*, morbid compulsion to set fires.

Manic-Depressive Reaction: A group of psychiatric disorders marked by conspicuous mood swings, ranging from normal to elation or to depression, or alternating. Officially regarded as a psychosis but may also exist in milder form.

Depressed phase: Characterized by depression of mood with retardation and inhibition of thinking and physical activity.

Manic phase: Characterized by heightened excitability, acceleration of thought, speech, and bodily motion, and by elation or grandiosity of mood, and irritability.

Masochism: Pleasure derived from undergoing physical or psychological pain inflicted by oneself or by others. It may be consciously sought or unconsciously arranged or invited. Present to some degree in all human relations and to greater degrees in all psychiatric disorders. It is the converse of sadism, in which pain is inflicted on another, and the two tend to coexist in the same individual.

Narcissism (narcism): Self-love, as opposed to object-love (love of another person). Some degree of narcissism is considered healthy and normal, but an excess interferes with relations with others.

Obsession: Persistent, unwanted idea or impulse that cannot be eliminated by logic or reasoning.

Overcompensation: A conscious or unconscious process in which a real or fancied physical or psychological deficit inspires exaggerated correction.

Paranoid State: Characterized by delusions of persecution. A paranoid state may be of short duration or chronic.

Phobia: An obsessive, unrealistic fear of an external object or situation. Some of the common phobias are *acrophobia*, fear of heights; *agoraphobia*, fear of open places; *claustrophobia*, fear of closed spaces; *mysophobia*, fear of dirt and germs; *xenophobia*, fear of strangers.

Projective Tests: Psychological tests used as a diagnostic tool. Among the most common projective tests is the Rorschach (inkblot) test.

Psychoanalysis: A theory of human development and behavior, a method of research, and a system of psychotherapy, originally described by Sigmund Freud (1856–1939). Through analysis of free associations and interpretation of dreams, emotions and behavior are traced to the influence of repressed instinctual drives in the unconscious. Psychoanalytic treatment seeks to eliminate or diminish the undesirable effects of unconscious conflicts by making the patient aware of their existence, origin, and inappropriate expression.

Psychoneurosis: One of the two major categories of emotional illness, the other being the psychoses. It is usually less severe than a psychosis, with minimal loss of contact with reality.

Psychosis: A major mental disorder of organic and/or emotional origin in which there is a departure from normal patterns of thinking, feeling, and acting. Commonly characterized by loss of contact with reality, distortion of perception, regressive behavior and attitudes, diminished control of elementary impulses and desires, and delusions and hallucinations. Chronic and generalized personality deterioration may occur. A majority of patients in public mental hospitals are psychotic.

Psychosomatic: Adjective to denote the constant and inseparable interdependence of the psyche (mind) and the soma (body). Most commonly used to refer to illnesses in which the manifestations are primarily physical with at least a partial emotional cause.

Psychotherapy: The term for any type of mental treatment that is based primarily upon verbal or nonverbal communication with the patient, in distinction to the use of drugs, surgery, or physical measures such as electric or insulin shock.

Regression: The partial or symbolic return to more infantile patterns of reacting.

Repression: A defense mechanism, operating unconsciously, that banishes unacceptable ideas, emotions, or impulses from consciousness or that keeps out of consciousness what has never been conscious.

Sadism: *See* Masochism.

Schizophrenia: A severe emotional disorder of psychotic depth characteristically marked by a retreat from reality with delusion formation, hallucinations, emotional disharmony, and regressive behavior. Formerly called dementia praecox. Its prognosis has improved in recent years.

Shock Treatment: A form of psychiatric treatment in which electric current, insulin, or carbon dioxide is administered to the patient and results in a convulsive reaction to alter favorably the course of mental illness.

Sublimation: A defense mechanism, operating unconsciously, by which instinctual but consciously unacceptable drives are diverted into personally and socially acceptable channels.

Superego: *See* Ego.

Unconscious: That part of the mind the content of which is only rarely subject to awareness. It is the repository for knowledge that has never been conscious or that may have been conscious briefly and was then repressed.

PATIENT CARE EPISODES IN MENTAL HEALTH FACILITIES

SOURCE: National Institute for Mental Health

Patient care episodes are defined as the number of residents in inpatient facilities at the beginning of the year (or the number of persons on the rolls of noninpatient facilities) plus the total additions to these facilities during the year. Total additions during the year include new admissions, readmissions, and returns from longterm leave. The index, patient care episodes, therefore, is not equal to a true annual prevalence rate nor the annual prevalence of treated mental disorder, since episodes of care are counted rather than cases. This index does present useful measures of the volume of services utilized by persons with mental disorders and as such are useful in describing the distribution of episodes by age, sex, modality and type of facility.

While trend data on day care episodes by type of facility are not available for more than a few years, such data are available for inpatient and outpatient episodes as illustrated below. The number of inpatient and outpatient care episodes in mental health facilities in 1975 — 6.4 million — was almost four times greater than the approximately 1.7 million episodes in 1955.

Number and percent distribution of inpatient and outpatient care episodes[1], in selected mental health facilities, by type of facility: United States, 1955, 1965, 1971 and 1975 (Provisional)

Year	Total All[1] Facilities	Inpatient Services of: State & County Mental Hospitals	Private Mental[2] Hospitals	Gen. Hosp. Psychiatric Service (non-VA)	VA Psychiatric Inpatient Services	Outpatient Psychiatric Services of: Federally Assisted Comm. Men. Health Cen.	Federally Assisted Comm. Men. Health Cen.	Other
				Number of Patient Care Episodes				
1975	6,409,447	598,993	165,327	565,696	214,264	246,891	1,584,968	3,033,308
1971	4,038,143	745,259	126,600	542,642	176,800	130,088	622,906	1,693,848
1965	2,636,525	804,926	125,428	519,328	115,843	—	—	1,071,000
1955	1,675,352	818,832	123,231	265,934	88,355	—	—	379,000
				Percent Distribution				
1975	100.0	9.3	2.6	8.8	3.3	3.9	24.7	47.4
1971	100.0	18.5	3.1	13.4	4.4	3.2	15.4	42.0
1965	100.0	30.5	4.8	19.7	4.4	—	—	40.6
1955	100.0	48.9	7.3	15.9	5.3	—	—	22.6

[1] In order to present trends on the same set of facilities over this interval, it has been necessary to exclude from this table the following: private psychiatric office practice; psychiatric service modes of all types in hospitals or outpatient clinics of Federal agencies other than the VA (e.g., Public Health Service, Indian Health Service, Department of Defense Bureau of Prisons, etc.); inpatient service modes of multiservice facilities not shown in this table; all partial care episodes, and outpatient episodes of VA hospitals. [2] Includes estimates of episodes of care in residential treatment centers for emotionally disturbed children.

Source (All years except 1975): The National Institute of Mental Health, Utilization of Mental Health Facilities, 1971, Series B, No. 5; January 1974, Table 22.

Source (1975): Unpublished provisional data from the National Institute of Mental Health.

RECOMMENDED DAILY DIETARY ALLOWANCES FOR AMERICANS

The schedule is designed for the maintenance of good nutrition of normally active Americans in a temperate climate. The following abbreviations are used: Gm. for gram; Mg. for milligram; I.U. for International Unit.

Family Members	Weight (Pounds)	Height Feet Inches	Calories	Protein (Gms.)	Calcium (Gms.)	Iron (Mg.)	Vitamin A (I.U.)	Thiamine (Mg.)	Riboflavin (Mg.)	Niacin (Mg. Equiv.)	Ascorbic Acid (Mg.)	Vitamin D (I.U.)
MEN												
18–35 years	154	5–9	2,900	70	0.8	10	5,000	1.2	1.7	19	70	—
35–55 years	154	5–9	2,600	70	0.8	10	5,000	1.0	1.6	17	70	—
55–75 years	154	5–9	2,200	70	0.8	10	5,000	0.9	1.3	15	70	—
WOMEN												
18–35 years	128	5–4	2,100	58	0.8	15	5,000	0.8	1.3	14	70	—
35–55 years	128	5–4	1,900	58	0.8	15	5,000	0.8	1.2	13	70	—
55–75 years	128	5–4	1,600	58	0.8	10	5,000	0.8	1.2	13	70	—
CHILDREN												
1–3 years	29	2–10	1,300	32	0.8	8	2,000	0.5	0.8	9	40	400
3–6 years	40	3–6	1,600	40	0.8	10	2,500	0.6	1.0	11	50	400
6–9 years	53	4–1	2,100	52	0.8	12	3,500	0.8	1.3	14	60	400
BOYS												
9–12 years	72	4–7	2,400	60	1.1	15	4,500	1.0	1.4	16	70	400
12–15 years	98	5–1	3,000	75	1.4	15	5,000	1.2	1.8	20	80	400
15–18 years	134	5–8	3,400	85	1.4	15	5,000	1.4	2.0	22	80	400
GIRLS												
9–12 years	72	4–7	2,200	55	1.1	15	4,500	0.9	1.3	15	80	400
12–15 years	103	5–2	2,500	62	1.3	15	5,000	1.0	1.5	17	80	400
15–18 years	117	5–4	2,300	58	1.3	15	5,000	0.9	1.3	15	70	400

DESIRABLE WEIGHTS FOR ADULT MEN AND WOMEN

Height (in shoes, 1-in. heels) FT. IN.	MEN WEIGHT (LB.) IN INDOOR CLOTHING* Small Frame	Medium Frame	Large Frame	Height (in shoes, 2-in. heels) FT. IN.	WOMEN WEIGHT (LB.) IN INDOOR CLOTHING* Small Frame	Medium Frame	Large Frame
5 2	112–120	118–129	126–141	4 10	92– 98	96–107	104–119
5 3	115–123	121–133	129–144	4 11	94–101	98–110	106–122
5 4	118–126	124–136	132–148	5 0	96–104	101–113	109–125
5 5	121–129	127–139	135–152	5 1	99–107	104–116	112–128
5 6	124–133	130–143	138–156	5 2	102–110	107–119	115–131
5 7	128–137	134–147	142–161	5 3	105–113	110–122	118–134
5 8	132–141	138–152	147–166	5 4	108–116	113–126	121–138
5 9	136–145	142–156	151–170	5 5	111–119	116–130	125–142
5 10	140–150	146–160	155–174	5 6	114–123	120–135	129–146
5 11	144–154	150–165	159–179	5 7	118–127	124–139	133–150
6 0	148–158	154–170	164–184	5 8	122–131	128–143	137–154
6 1	152–162	158–175	168–189	5 9	126–135	132–147	141–158
6 2	156–167	162–180	173–194	5 10	130–140	136–151	145–163
6 3	160–171	167–185	178–199	5 11	134–144	140–155	149–168
6 4	164–175	172–190	182–204	6 0	138–148	144–159	153–173

* For nude weight, deduct 5–7 lbs. (male) or 2–4 lbs. (female).

RECOMMENDED FOOD QUANTITIES IN TERMS OF SERVINGS

Source: U.S. Department of Agriculture

Here follows a table of food groups and approximate amounts of foods as served per person per day, according to low-cost and moderate-cost plans. Servings allow for some plate waste. In addition to the food groups mentioned, some fats and oils (available in butter and margarine) and sugar (in its own form or in sweets and preserves) should be included in most diets.

NUMBER OF SERVINGS PER PERSON PER DAY

Food Group	Unit	Plan	Child 1–6 years[1]	Child 6–12 years[1]	Girl 12–20 years	Boy 12–20 years	Woman 20–55 years	Woman 55 years and over	Man 20–55 years	Man 55 years and over
Meat, poultry, fish or alternates	1 oz. cooked lean meat, 1 egg, ½ cup cooked dry beans, or 2 tbsp. peanut butter	Low Cost	3–3½	4–4½	4½–5	4½–6	5½–6	3½–4½	5½–6	4½–5½
		Moderate	3½–4½	5–7	7	7–8	7½	5½–6½	7½–8	7
Milk, cheese, ice cream, ice milk	1 8-oz. cup of milk as beverage or in cooking or cheese or ice cream	Low Cost	2¼	2¼–3	4	4	2	2	2	2
		Moderate	3	3	4	4	2	2	2	2
Vegetables and fruits	½ cup or equivalent vegetable or fruit as served	Low Cost	2–3½	4½–5½	5–6	5½–6½	4½–5½	3½–4½	5–6	4–5
		Moderate	2½–4	4½–6	5½–6½	6–7½	5–6	4–4½	5½–7	5–6
Cereal and bakery products	1 slice of bread or other bakery products with equal flour; 1 oz. ready-to-eat cereal; or ¾ cup cooked cereal or cereal product	Low Cost	5–7	8–9	8–9	14–16	7–8	5–7	12–14	8–9
		Moderate	4–6	8–9	7–8	13–15	7–8	4–5	11–13	7–8

[1] Smaller amount is for younger children.

EARTH: FACTS/FIGURES

EARTH: THIRD PLANET FROM THE SUN

The Earth, our planet, is located at an average distance of 93 million miles from the Sun, which it orbits in 365 days, 6 hours, 8 minutes, and 38 seconds. The Earth completes one rotation on its axis in 23 hours, 56 minutes, and 4 seconds, and its equator is inclined 23 degrees and 27 minutes to the plane of the ecliptic. The equatorial diameter of the Earth is 7,926 miles; its polar diameter is 7,900 miles. The Earth's average density is 5.52 grams/cm³.

The circumference of the Earth around the equator has been estimated at 24,900 miles, while its circumference around the poles is thought to be about 24,820 miles. From these dimensions, it is obvious that the Earth is not a true sphere, but rather a *geoid*—a triaxial ellipsoid that is nearly spherical but flattened at the poles. Small bulges produce four "corners"—at Ireland, off Peru, south of Africa, and near New Guinea. Space-satellite measurements have further indicated two "dimples" in the Northern Hemisphere, giving the Earth a slightly pearlike appearance.

The Earth has an estimated mass of 5.883×10^{21} tons and an estimated volume of 2.6×10^{11} cubic miles. Its total surface area is approximately 197,272,000 square miles, of which the land area makes up only about 57,200,000 square miles. The average land elevation is 2,700 feet; the average ocean depth is 12,500 feet.

It is generally believed that the Earth and the other planets are 4.6 billion years old, although the oldest rocks found on the Earth are only 3.7 billion years old. Scientists have given names to the various geological time periods of Earth's history.

The largest segments of geologic time are called eras and are named according to the type of life that then existed. Eras are divided into periods, which are further divided into epochs. The period names usually refer to locations where rocks of the specific period were first studied (e.g., Devonian signifies Devonshire, England; Cretaceous, the chalk deposits that are found on both sides of the English Channel). Other names, such as Ordovician and Silurian, are actually the names of Celtic tribes that inhabited parts of Wales where rocks from this time interval were first studied.

Era	Period, Epoch	Age (Millions of Years Ago)	Evolution of Life
Cenozoic	Quaternary, Recent & Pleistocene	0 to 2.5	Man
	Tertiary, Pliocene	2.5 to 12	Higher Mammals
	Tertiary, Miocene	12 to 25	
	Tertiary, Oligocene	25 to 36	
	Tertiary, Eocene	36 to 58	
	Tertiary, Paleocene	58 to 63	
Mesozoic	Cretaceous	63 to 135	Modern Vegetation
	Jurassic	135 to 200	Birds
	Triassic	200 to 230	Mammals
Paleozoic	Permian	230 to 280	
	Carboniferous	280 to 345	Reptiles
	Devonian	345 to 405	Amphibians
	Silurian	405 to 425	Land Plants
	Ordovician	425 to 500	Agnathans, Fishes
	Cambrian	500 to 570	Invertebrate Animals
Pre-Cambrian	Late Pre-Cambrian	570 to 700	Algae
	Upper Pre-Cambrian	700 to 1600	
	Middle Pre-Cambrian	1600 to 2700	Unicellular Organisms
	Lower Pre-Cambrian	2700 to 3500	—
	Archaean	3500+	—

THE EARTH'S INTERIOR

The core at the Earth's center is the least-known part of the interior; our knowledge of it stems mostly from study of seismic (earthquake) waves and their propagation. However, it is known that the solid inner core of iron is surrounded by a liquid outer core of iron. The inner core, which has a radius of about 850 miles, is believed to have a very high pressure and high temperature (about 10,000° F) and a density of about 13.5 grams/cm³ (13.5 times the density of water). The outer core has a thickness of about 1,200 miles. Surrounding the outer core is the mantle, which is 1,800 miles thick. The boundary between the mantle and the core is called the Gutenberg-Wiechert Discontinuity.

The mantle has an average density of 5 grams/cm³ and consists of three layers: the plastic inner mantle that surrounds the liquid core, a transition region, and the outer solid mantle. The uppermost region of the Earth's interior is called the crust and is separated from the outer mantle by the Mohorovicic Discontinuity (or M-Discontinuity). The crust consists of continental crust and oceanic crust. The continental crust is composed of relatively light silicon rocks, such as granite, andesite, and various grades of metamorphic rocks known under the general name of *sial* (aluminum silicate, with silicon oxide comprising 60%) which has an average density of 2.7 grams/cm³. The continental crust has an average thickness of 23 miles, reaching 40 to 45 miles under high mountain chains. The oceanic crust is composed of heavier basaltic rocks that contain greater proportions of metallic oxides, such as magnesium and iron, under the general name of *sima* (magnesium silicate, with silicon oxide comprising only 46%) which has an average density of 3.0 grams/cm³. The oceanic crust has an average thickness of 4 miles. As well as being lighter and much thicker, the continental crust is considerably older than the ocean crust.

EARTH'S WATER-COVERED SURFACE

The oceans (hydrosphere) cover some 140 million square miles—70 percent of the Earth's total surface area—to an average depth of 12,500 feet. There are 340 million cubic miles of liquid water on the Earth's surface—making our planet a truly water-covered one. The greatest ocean depth is found in the Marianas Trench in the Western Pacific, being more than 37,500 feet deep.

Chemically, the ocean consists of water (96.5%) and numerous dissolved salts (3.5%), of which common salt (2.8%) is easily the most abundant. The principal elements in seawater are chlorine, sodium, magnesium, sulfur, oxygen, calcium, potassium, bromine, strontium, boron, and smaller amounts of carbon, fluorine, and iodine.

The features of the ocean floor, which result from deformations of the Earth's crust, are either elevations—ridges, rises, seamounts, and sills—or depressions—troughs, trenches, basins, and deeps. For example, the Atlantic Ocean is divided into two troughs by a north-south ridge, the Mid-Atlantic Ridge, which extends into both hemispheres. On either side of the ridge, depths exceeding 16,000 feet exist.

THE EARTH'S ATMOSPHERE

For its first 60 miles, the Earth's atmosphere has a nearly homogeneous composition consisting of the following gases:

Constituent	Percent by Volume
Nitrogen (N_2)	78.084
Oxygen (O_2)	20.946
Argon (A)	0.934
Carbon dioxide (CO_2)	0.033
Neon (Ne)	0.000018
Helium (He)	0.000005
Methane (CH_4) & Krypton (Kr)	0.000001

Water vapor (H_2O) varies within the lower atmosphere (the lowest 7 miles) from 0 to 4 percent, but it generally is present in concentrations of 0.1 to 1 percent. Water vapor is rarely found above the lower atmosphere.

Above 60 miles, the atmosphere is no longer homogeneous, but rather successive layers consisting of atomic oxygen (O), helium (He), and hydrogen (H).

Incoming solar radiation reaching our planet heats up the Earth's surface to about $-18°$ F. At this temperature, the Earth emits infrared radiation into space in all directions; however, the carbon dioxide and water vapor molecules in the Earth's lower atmosphere absorb and then reemit this infrared radiation. Part of the reemitted infrared radiation is directed downward and strikes the Earth's surface, increasing the surface temperature to a value of about 60° F, which is the Earth's actual mean temperature, averaged over the entire year. The absorption and reemission of infrared radiation by CO_2 and H_2O is known as the "Greenhouse Effect" or greenhouse temperature enhancement.

The Earth's neutral atmosphere can be divided into five distinct regions, depending on the region's temperature gradient, which is the variation of temperature with height within a particular atmospheric region. That is, a positive temperature gradient means that temperature increases with height; a negative temperature gradient means that temperature decreases with height; an undefined temperature gradient means that the density of molecules is too low to give a meaningful value to the temperature.

Atmospheric Region	Height	Temperature Gradient
Troposphere	0 to 7 miles	... Negative
Stratosphere	7 to 30 miles	... Positive
Mesosphere	30 to 50 miles	... Negative
Thermosphere ...	50 to 300 miles	... Positive
Exosphere	Above 300 miles	... Undefined

The troposphere contains about two-thirds of the total mass of the atmosphere. Within this layer, the temperature decreases with increasing height at a "lapse rate" of about 3.5° F per 1,000 feet. The decrease of temperature with height results from the atmosphere's being heated by solar radiation mainly from below. Whenever there is warmer below cooler air, vertical motions in the atmosphere result, since warm air is lighter than cool air. Such a condition causes vertical wind motions or convective currents within the troposphere. All of our weather, such as clouds and precipitation, occurs in the troposphere.

At the top of the troposphere, the temperature (about $-75°$ F) stops decreasing with height, and the stratosphere begins. Within the stratosphere, the temperature increases with height from heating that is caused by the absorption of solar ultraviolet radiation by the stratospheric ozone layer. Since ozone absorbs most of the incoming solar ultraviolet radiation, this lethal radiation does not reach the surface, where it would adversely affect life.

At the top of the stratosphere, the temperature reaches its maximum of about 35° F, and the mesosphere begins. Within the mesosphere, the temperature decreases approximately 1.5° F per 1,000 feet. The temperature minimum of the entire atmosphere, about $-130°$ F, is found at the top of the mesosphere.

Above this mesopause, the thermosphere begins. This is a region in which the temperature increases with height because of the absorption and subsequent heating of solar X rays and short wavelength ultraviolet radiation. The temperature of the higher layers of the thermosphere can reach about 2000° F. However, at the extremely low density prevailing in this region temperature is a somewhat meaningless concept. Above the thermosphere is the exosphere, which is the top of the Earth's neutral atmosphere.

In addition to the neutral atmosphere of Earth, there are several regions consisting of large amounts of positive atomic nuclei or ions and negative electrons. The absorption of solar X rays and ultraviolet radiation results in the ionization of the air, which, in turn, results in several ionized layers known as the ionosphere. Another region of charged particles, protons, and electrons comprises the Van Allen Radiation belts, which surround the Earth at distances from about 1250 to 3000 miles and 8000 to 12,000 miles. The protons and electrons are held within the radiation belts by the Earth's magnetic field. Most of the electrons and protons in the belt's outer portion come from the Sun in the form of the solar wind.

There is evidence to suggest that the Earth originally had an atmospheric composition similar to that of Jupiter: mostly hydrogen and helium, some methane and ammonia, and no oxygen. It is possible that life began in this atmosphere. However, at some point in the past, the entire original atmosphere was lost and the present one developed. It is believed that nitrogen came from the Earth's interior via volcanic outgassing, as did the carbon dioxide and water vapor in the present atmosphere. Most of the oxygen in our atmosphere was probably produced by plant photosynthesis. Atmospheric argon was produced by the decay of radioactive potassium in rocks and minerals in the Earth's interior.

ORIGIN OF LIFE ON EARTH

The Earth and the other planets are thought to be about 4.6 billion years old. The earliest known fossil records of living organisms on our planet are about 3 billion years old. It is estimated that life existed on our planet some 3.5 to 4 billion years ago, suggesting that up to 1 billion years elapsed before life evolved on Earth from the material then available. Fundamental to an understanding of the origin of life is knowledge of the chemical makeup of living cells.

Two types of molecules—proteins and nucleic acids—play basic functional roles in living cells. Proteins are large complex molecules consisting of a number of amino acids that are joined together to form a long chain. An amino acid is a carbon compound containing an acid group (—COOH) and a basic amino group (—NH₂). Some 21 different amino acids have been found in proteins. Enzymes are the biochemical catalysts that control many metabolic processes. Enzymes are proteins in which the amino-acid chain has been folded into a very specific shape.

Nucleic acids are formed in the cell nucleus, but some are produced in other cell parts. Like proteins, nucleic acids are complex molecules composed of chains of simpler units. The fundamental unit of nucleic acids is a complex molecule called a nucleotide, which consists of three separate parts: residues of a nitrogenous base, a sugar with five carbon atoms, and phosphoric acid.

In a given nucleic acid, all of the sugar residues are the same. They are either all ribose or all deoxyribose. When the sugar residues are all ribose, the nucleic acids are called ribonucleic acids (RNA) and, when they all are deoxyribose, the nucleic acids are called deoxyribonucleic acids (DNA). Both DNA and RNA are produced in the nuclei of nearly all living cells but, whereas RNA leaves the nucleus and enters the surrounding cytoplasm, essentially all the DNA remains within the nucleus.

Nucleic acids are the key materials for all terrestrial life forms their presence being fundamental to life processes. DNA is the principal component of genes and chromosomes, passed from parents to offspring. The sequence of nucleotides in DNA comprises the genetic code, which determines the type and amount of protein synthesized in a particular living cell. Hence, it appears that the formation of nucleic acids is related to the origin of life. It has been suggested that viruses, which are larger than a single molecule but smaller than a cell nucleus, represent an intermediate stage between nonliving and living systems. However, the modern virus, which needs to inhabit a cell in order to live, is presumed to be a development of a more primitive precursor.

The probable inorganic elements and conditions on Earth during its first billion years, which together combined to form life, were first discussed by the Russian biochemist A. I. Oparin in his 1924 publication The Origin of Life. Oparin described the gradual step-by-step evolution of life from the simple inorganic elements of hydrogen, carbon, nitrogen, and oxygen. A somewhat similar view was expressed (1928) independently by the English biochemist J. B. S. Haldane. The first attempts to simulate early conditions on Earth and produce biological compounds in the laboratory were largely failures. Although oxygen is now the second most abundant gas in the Earth's atmosphere, accounting for some 21% by volume, it was probably not always so abundant.

If oxygen were as abundant in the past as it is today, then carbon would be present mainly as carbon dioxide. Oparin suggested that atmospheric carbon probably existed originally in the reduced form—methane (CH_4)—and not in oxidized form—carbon dioxide (CO_2). Similarly, nitrogen, now present in free state and accounting for some 78% by volume of the atmosphere, would have been in the reduced form of ammonia (NH_3). Like Oparin, but for entirely different reasons, Haldane also concluded that the Earth's primitive atmosphere probably contained little if any free oxygen but consisted mainly of carbon dioxide, ammonia, and water vapor.

In 1952, the American chemist H. C. Urey showed that the Earth's primitive atmosphere should have consisted of methane, ammonia, water vapor, and free hydrogen gas. Urey and S. Miller began a series of lab experiments attempting to synthesize the gases of his theoretical atmosphere into complex organic molecules. After exposing gases to ultraviolet radiation, to simulate the sun's radiation, Urey and Miller reported (1953) that they had successfully produced several amino acids, as well as other organic compounds of biological interest.

From similar laboratory experiments made by P. H. Abelson (1956) and by Pavlovskaya and A. G. Pasinsky (1957) in the USSR, it has been established that amino acids can be produced by passing an electrical discharge (simulating lightning discharges in the Earth's primitive atmosphere) through various gas mixtures other than those used by Urey and Miller. Provided the gaseous system has overall reducing characteristics, amino acids

are always formed. Other experiments have shown that amino acids can even be formed in aqueous solutions.

As life evolved on Earth, it appears certain that later stages took place in a liquid water environment. The presence of large proportions of water in all living organisms reinforces this suggestion. The roughly similar calcium/potassium ratio in seawater and in blood and tissue suggests that life developed, even if it did not originate, in the Earth's oceans. Furthermore, it is improbable that nucleic acids could have survived and flourished if exposed to solar ultraviolet radiation over long periods of time; however, the oceans, which absorb solar ultraviolet radiation within their first several feet, could have protected the nucleic acid from decomposition. Once oxygen and then ozone built up in the atmosphere, the Earth's protection from solar ultraviolet offered by water no longer became essential to the continuation of life. Living organisms then appear to have emerged from the sea, moving onto land.

Laboratory experiments have shown that amino acids and nucleic acids could have been synthesized in a reducing atmosphere of hydrogen, methane, ammonia, and water vapor. It is now believed that the Earth originally had such an atmosphere when life originated.

ANCIENT SUPERCONTINENTS

American scientists of the Environmental Science Services Administration reported in 1969 that they had established that Australia and Antarctica, which are now separated by about 2,000 miles of water, were once part of an ancient supercontinent.

The scientists, Walter Sproll and Dr. Robert S. Dietz, having processed oceanographic data obtained in 1967 by U.S. and Australian scientists during a global cruise of the Coast and Geodetic Survey Ship *Oceanographer*, relate that there was a fit between the two continents.

Sproll and Dietz are supporters of the continental-drift theory: that the continents constantly drift about 1–6 in. each year in the earth's mantle—the part of the earth's interior that rests between the molten central core and the crust. Among the scientists who espouse this theory, some believe that there was once a single supercontinent they call Pangaea; others, including Sproll and Dietz, contend that there were two supercontinents, which they refer to as Gondwana and Laurasia.

Supporters of the two-continent theory believe that Gondwana was composed of Australia, Antarctica, Africa, India, South America, Malagasy, and various submerged fragments, while Laurasia is thought to have consisted of North America and Eurasia.

It was generally believed of the two continents that southern Australia was once linked with another land mass, but opinions differed as to which one. Antarctica was the popular choice, but some thought it was Malagasy; others contended that it was the east coast of Africa, while still others believed it to have been the southwestern coast of South America.

Sproll and Dietz reported that their study shows that the south coast of Australia once joined Antarctica and

identifies the exact position of fit: the SE end of Australia —including Tasmania—fitted into Antarctica's Ross Sea, while the SW end reached to just off Antarctica's Knox Coast; the concave Great Bight of Australia fitted against the convex outline of Wilkes Land.

"Recent geophysical findings on the ocean floor have demonstrated to the satisfaction of most earth scientists that the continents were once together," the ESSA scientists said. "About 200 to 250 million years ago, they commenced to separate and slowly drifted to their present scattered locations around the globe. One of the last units to be sundered—the Australia-Antarctica split—may have occurred as late as 40 million years ago.

The fit of continents is not the only evidence of continental drift. There is a very significant bit of rock formations and other geological structures in landmasses now separated by oceans. Studies of the past positions of the magnetic poles also indicate relative movement between continents. Again the scattered distribution of certain animals and plants in the distant past as well as that of ancient climatic zones can only be satisfactorily explained by continental drift: the discovery in Antarctica of a fossilized bone of an extinct amphibian points to a much milder Antarctic climate in the past.

Continental drift is now explained in terms of plate tectonics. The earth's outer shell is divided into at least 15 rigid rock segments, known as plates, that extend downward through the earth's crust and float on a semimolten layer of the upper mantle. Seven of the plates are of major size and in most cases carry a continental landmass with surrounding ocean floor and island arcs. The plates are slowly moving relative to each other, driven by powerful forces within the earth's mantle. The movements of the plates have produced the present continent locations. At their boundaries plates are either slowly separating with new material added from the mantle, are converging with one plate being ground down and consumed under another, or are gliding past each other. Almost all earthquake, volcanic, and mountain-building activity closely follows these boundaries and is related to movements between them.

THE CONTINENTS

Name	Area (in square miles)	Percent of World's Land	Highest Point (in feet)	Lowest Point (in feet)
Asia	17,129,000	29.7	Mount Everest (29,028), Nepal-China	Dead Sea (1,296 below sea level), Israel-Jordan
Africa	11,707,000	20.0	Kibo (19,340), a peak of Mount Kilimanjaro, Tanzania	Lake Assal, Djibouti (510 below sea level)
North America	9,363,000	16.3	Mount McKinley (20,320), Alaska	Death Valley (282 below sea level), California
South America	6,886,000	12.0	Aconcagua (22,831), Argentina	Salinas Grandes (131 below sea level), Valdés Pen., Argentina
Europe	4,057,000	7.0	El'brus (18,510), USSR	Caspian Sea (92 below sea level), USSR
Australia	2,942,000	5.1	Mount Kosciusko (7,316), New South Wales	Lake Eyre (52 below sea level), South Australia
Antarctica	5,500,000	9.6	Vinson Massif (16,864)	Sea level

PREHISTORIC CREATURES

Allosaurus: This predator of 125 million years ago was the giant of its day: 34-feet long, more than eight feet high, and with a reach of about 15 feet above the ground. It had a massive skull that was nearly a yard long and a lower jaw hinged far back, enabling it to swallow food in unchewed lumps. Allosaurus remains have been found in Utah, Wyoming, and other Rocky Mountain states.

Anatosaurus (*Trachodon*): This 30-foot, duck-billed dinosaur made its home in the swamps of North America about 100 million years ago. Its skull was long, low, and narrow, and it had as many as 2,000 teeth that as they wore out were replaced by Nature. The anatosaurus could swim and wade, as evidenced by its webbed feet and deep oarlike tail.

Archaeopteryx: Appearing about 150 million years ago, the archaeopteryx was the earliest known bird and was about the size of our crow. Although it had feathers, its bony tail, toothed jaws, and handlike wings were reptilian. But its hind limbs were birdlike, thus it could walk and run like a chicken. The archaeopteryx was probably warm-blooded and had an expanded brain case, indicating a comparatively complex nervous system.

Baluchitherium: The largest land mammal ever to have lived. Found in Oligocene (circa 28–30 million years ago) deposits of Western and Central Asia, it was over 16 feet tall, and weighed several tons. Its head alone was over 4 feet long, had small tusks, and was related to the modern rhinoceros. Unlike the rhino it had long, slender limbs and a long neck, which would have suited it for swift running and browsing off leaves on the higher branches of trees.

Brachiosaurus: Ranging from 60 to 80 feet in length and weighing up to 50 tons, the brachiosaurus likely represented a land animal's maximum achievable size, because of muscle, bone, and ligament limitations. The dinosaur's front legs were massive; consequently, its shoulders were high and sloped giraffe-fashion to the hips. Since its nostrils were located on a raised area of the head, the creature could breathe while standing in deep water. The brachiosaurus lived in Colorado, adjacent areas, and eastern Africa more than 125 million years ago.

Brontosaurus (*Apatosaurus*): This quadruped dinosaur probably grew to more than 70 feet in length and 30 tons in weight; thus its name, "thunder lizard," most likely refers to the rumbling it must have caused in moving about. Because of its size, the brontosaurus (as well as the brachiosaurus) had a huge pelvis and long, heavy shoulder blades. It had a short but deep body, a long neck, and massive tail that was controlled by a brain weighing about one pound. The brontosaurus was herbivorous and semiaquatic. It lived about 125 million years ago in Colorado, Wyoming, Texas, and other Western states.

Camptosaurus: Appearing in North America about 125 million years ago, the camptosaurus ranged between four and 15 feet in length. It had strong hind limbs; small, stout forelimbs; and a broad hand with full fingers. Its femur was curved, suggesting that this dinosaur sometimes walked on all fours. The camptosaurus was a nonpredatory planteater, with a flat, beak-like mouth.

Coelacanth: This subgroup of fringe-fishes ranged in weight from 125 to 150 pounds and were strong, armed with sharp teeth, and active. The coelacanths evolved from air-breathing animals by losing one lung; the other one was used as an airbladder that kept the body right side up. They were thought to have become extinct about 65 million years ago; however, in 1938, a commercial fisherman caught a 4½-foot coelacanth off the coast of South Africa.

Compsognathus: This dinosaur was no larger than a big fowl, and two-thirds of its body was neck and tail. Its toes were long and clawed, and its small jaws were lined with sharp teeth. This slender bipedal creature preyed on small reptiles, on the Baltic coast of what is now Germany, about 125 million years ago.

Eohippus (*Hyracotherium*): As its Latin name implies, the "dawn (*eo*) horse (*hippus*)" was the earliest-known horse, appearing about 60 million years ago on the Great Plains of North America. The species varied from 10 to 20 inches high; all of these horses had four toes on each front foot and three on each hind foot. The eohippus was lightly built; its hindquarters were high and its moderately curved back was suited to its running. Some species of the eohippus migrated to Europe about 50 million years ago, becoming ancestors of the Old World

horse. By the time that the Indians reached North America, the New World horse had become extinct.

Hesperornis: This wingless water bird ranged from Europe to North America about 100 million years ago. The hesperornis had an elongated body, with feet that enabled it to paddle. Its legs were turned backward and thus were useful in swimming, but not in walking. Although its ancestors probably had wings, those of the hesperornis were useless evolutionary remnants.

Iguanodon: This species of dinosaur varied in length from 15 to 30 feet and reached a height of 15 feet. All specimens had narrow bodies and compressed tails. They walked on hind feet which had three large toes and one small one. Their small "forefeet" were five-fingered and had a thumb that was shaped into a bony spike. The iguanodon was European, although it may have ranged over other continents; it flourished between 80 and 100 million years ago.

Kronosaurus: Similar to the sperm whale of today, the kronosaurus paddled through Australian seas about 70 million years ago. Its neck was comparatively short, and its elongated skull measured 12 feet. The kronosaurus had large eyes and temporal openings, nostrils in front of the eyes, an almost solid palate, and long sharp teeth.

Lystrosaurus: A member of the dicynodont group of mammal-like reptiles, this animal is dated from the early Triassic Age (circa 220 million years ago) of both South Africa and Asia. It is believed that the dicynodonts may in general have preferred to live in marshy country, but Lystrosaurus is the only one which may have been aquatic to any extent. All dicynodonts were herbivorous and were the most common land animals of their time.

Megatherium: The largest of the extinct giant ground sloths, it flourished in both North and South America during the Pleistocene (circa 3 million to 10,000 years ago). This early mammal was slightly larger than the modern elephant, and possessed extremely massive limbs. Its teeth continually grew throughout life, and were adapted for a leaf-eating diet. It had a short, massive neck and tail, but a relatively long trunk. Its hands possessed powerful claws, which probably served to draw branches down towards its extensible tongue; the animal appears to have walked on the outside of its knuckles.

Pteranodon: This flying reptile lived between 85 and 100 million years ago, ranging from present-day Kansas to Europe and possibly around the world. Its body was small, bulking to about that of a small turkey. Its jaws formed a long toothless beak, and the back of the skull extended into a bony crest that was between about four and six feet long. The pteranodon's large wingspread, about 25 feet, and pelicanlike gular pouch gave it a most unreptilian appearance.

Stegosaurus: This "plated dinosaur" was a quadruped, about 20 feet long and weighing 10 tons. It had short forelegs, two rows of bony plates down its back, and long pointed spikes on its tail. The brain of the stegosaurus weighed only about 2.5 ounces; because of the brain's extreme smallness it is believed that the creature possibly had another brain: a 50-ounce ganglion behind the hips that controlled its hindquarters and tail. This herbivorous dinosaur roamed the American West about 125 million years ago.

Triceratops: This dinosaur was also herbivorous and also lived in the American West, about 100 million years ago. The head of the triceratops was about eight feet long and sheltered a two-pound brain. Its body, which was 20 feet long, was bulky and shaped like a barrel. The dinosaur's four legs were of equal size. The name *triceratops* is derived from the creature's three horns: one on the nose and one over each eye.

Tyrannosaurus: The "tyrant" dinosaur was a flesh-eater and well equipped for predation with six-inch teeth that were housed in a four-foot-long skull. Existing for a short time, about 85 million years ago, this dinosaur was 40 feet long and 19 feet tall. It weighed up to eight tons. Its forelimbs were reduced to such a degree that it is believed that they were not utilitarian; therefore, the creature's predation was probably restricted to its use of its skull and jaws.

Uintatherium: The Uintatheres were primitive ungulates of late Paleocene and Eocene times (circa 50 to 60 million years ago), and are distantly related to the elephants. Their long, low skulls were characterized by a number of large, horn-like bony swellings; they possessed large, saber-like upper canine teeth which were presumably very effective as defensive weapons.

FOSSIL MAN

Remains of what may be man's earliest ancestors were found on two continents in 1934 and in 1961. Fossil bones from sites in India and Africa indicate that these creatures (Ramapithecus and Kenyapithecus), in spite of having lived more than 14 million years ago, were more manlike than apelike.

However, the oldest bones to be placed with certainty in the category "Hominidae," or the family of Man, are about 4 million years old. Hominid remains have been found in several locations. Each archaeologist has given his find a different name (e.g., Zinjanthropus, Paranthropus, Plesianthropus), but today we recognize that all of these individuals who lived between 800,000 and 4 million B.C. have the same general characteristics and can be called by the general genus name, Australopithecus, or "southern ape."

The different genus and species names are given in the chart below to indicate that they probably represent different branches of the same group.

The brain of Australopithecus was about the same size as that of a modern large ape—half that of modern man. In spite of his apelike traits, Australopithecus walked somewhat erect and used stone weapons for hunting.

Some of the specimens found by L. S. B. Leakey in 1960 have been given the classification name Homo, the genus to which modern man belongs. Homo habilis was only 3½ to 4½ feet tall but had a larger brain and more manlike features.

Homo erectus, sometimes called Pithecanthropus or "ape man" (e.g., Java Man, Peking Man), was probably the direct ancestor of modern man, Homo sapiens. He appeared at least 1 million years ago and was structurally similar to us although he lacked a forehead and possessed a bony shelf over his eyes and a small chin. He made tools and knew how to use fire.

The next major evolutionary advance came approximately 100,000 years ago with the appearance of Neanderthal Man; he, too, was short in stature and had low brows, but his brain was equal in size to that of modern man, and he possessed a language. He was not a settler, but instead hunted widely.

At about 35,000 B.C., as the Neanderthals were disappearing, modern man, Homo sapiens (e.g., Cromagnon), appeared. He was taller and more delicate, and he fashioned intricate tools and clothing and drew paintings of his environment. However, it was not until 9,000 years ago that Homo sapiens became a domesticator of animals, a farmer, and a settler.

MAJOR FOSSIL MAN DISCOVERIES

Year	Scientific Name	Period and Estimated Date (B.C.)	Location	Remains	Discoverer
1848	Homo calpicus (Gibraltar Man)	Upper Pleistocene 45,000–70,000	Forbes Quarry, Gibraltar	skull	Lieutenant Flint
1856	Homo neanderthalensis (Neanderthal Man)	Middle Pleistocene 120,000	Neander Valley, nr. Dusseldorf, Germany	skull, bones	Johann C. Fuhlrott
1868	Homo sapiens (Cromagnon)	Upper Pleistocene 35,000	Cromagnon, France	4 skeletons, 1 fetus	Louis Lartet
1891	Pithecanthropus erectus (Java Man)	Lower Pleistocene 700,000	Trinil, Java	skull, femur	Eugene Dubois
1907	Homo heidelbergensis (Heidelberg Man)	Middle Pleistocene 450,000	Mauer, nr. Heidelberg, Germany	lower jaw	Otto Schoetensack
1909–13	Eoanthropus dawsoni* (Piltdown Man)	Holocene (Recent)	Piltdown, Sussex, England	composite skull	Charles Dawson
1924	Australopithecus africanus (Southern Ape)	Pleistocene c. 2,000,000	Taung, South Africa	skull	M. de Bruyn
1921–37	Sinanthropus pekinensis (Peking Man)	Middle Pleistocene 400,000	Choukoutien, nr. Peking, China	skulls, teeth, bones	Davidson Black
1929–34	Mt. Carmel Man	Middle Pleistocene 120,000	Mt. Carmel, Israel	parts of 16 skeletons	Dorothy Garrod
1932	Ramapithecus	Upper Miocene 14,000,000	NW India	parts of jaws	G. E. Lewis
1935–55	Homo sapiens protosapiens (Swanscombe Skull)	Middle Pleistocene 250,000	Swanscombe, Kent, England	parts of skull	A. T. Marston
1938	Paranthropus robustus	Lower Pleistocene c. 1,000,000	Kromdraai, Transvaal	skull part, bones	G. Terblanche
1947	Australopithecus prometheus (Southern Ape)	Lower Pleistocene c. 1,000,000	Makapansgat, Transvaal	skull fragments	J. Kitching
1949	Telanthropus capensis	Lower Pleistocene c. 1,000,000	Swartkrans, Transvaal	jaw	J. T. Robinson
1953–60	Neanderthaloid Man	Upper Pleistocene 50,900	Shanidar, Iraq	skeletons	Ralph Solecki
1959	Zinjanthropus boisei (Nutcracker Man)	Lower Pleistocene c. 1,750,000	Olduvai, Tanzania	skull	Mary D. Leakey
1960	Homo habilis	Lower Pleistocene c. 1,750,000	Olduvai, Tanzania	skull fragments	Louis S. B. Leakey
1961	Kenyapithecus wickeri	Upper Miocene c. 14,000,000	Fort Ternan, Kenya	palate, teeth	Louis S. B. Leakey
1965	Homo erectus palaeohungaricus	Middle Pleistocene 450,000	Vertesszollos, Hungary	occipital bone	Laszlo Vertes
1967	Australopithecus	Upper Pliocene c. 5,000,000	Lothagam Hill, Kenya	1 jaw bone	Arnold Lewis
1969	Australopithecus	Upper Pliocene 4,000,000	Omo Valley, Ethiopia	2 jaw bones, 40 teeth	F. C. Howell
1969	Australopithecus bosei	Upper Pliocene 2,600,000	East Rudolf, Kenya	2 skulls	Richard Leakey
1971	Pithecanthropine? (Arago Man)	Middle Pleistocene 200,000	Arago, France	skull	H. de Lumley
1975	Hominid	Upper Pleistocene c. 3,500,000	Laetolil, Tanzania	jaws, teeth 8 adults, 3 children	Mary D. Leakey

* Exposed as a fraud in 1953 by radioactivity tests.

MAXIMUM LIFE-SPANS OF ANIMALS
The list below reflects the maximum life-span of various animals while in captivity.

Years	Animal	Years	Animal	Years	Animal	Years	Animal
190	Giant Tortoise	37	Chimpanzee	25	Tiger	17	Goat
138	Eastern Box Turtle	36	Toad	25	Zebra	16	Bullfrog
84	Elephant	33	Gorilla	23	Leopard	16	Cheetah
80	Freshwater Oyster	31	Gibbon	23	Domestic Cat	16	Kangaroo
68	Owl	31	Grizzly Bear	22	Domestic Dog	15	Pronghorn
55	Eagle	30	Dolphin	20	Cougar	15	Reindeer
51	Pelican	30	Lion	20	Cow	15	Timber Wolf
50	Domestic Horse	28	Giraffe	20	Moose	14	Chicken
46	Jackass	28	Sea Lion	20	Rattlesnake	14	Coyote
45	Baboon	25	Black Bear	20	Sheep	13	Rabbit
41	Polar Bear	25	Camel	19	Beaver	10	Pig

THE ANIMAL KINGDOM

This classification system of living animals is one of many types available. Subphyla are included only for phylum Chordata, subclasses only for class Mammalia, and orders only for Eutheria in class Mammalia.

SUBKINGDOM PROTOZOA—one-celled animals
  Phylum Protozoa—acellular animals (protozoans)
    Class Mastigophora (Flagellata)—flagellates
    Class Sarcodina (Rhizopoda)—sarcodines
      (Amoeba)
    Class Sporozoa—spore-forming parasites
    Class Ciliophora (Ciliata)—ciliates (Paramecium)
SUBKINGDOM MESOZOA—certain wormlike parasites
  Phylum Mesozoa—mesozoans
SUBKINGDOM PARAZOA—pore-perforated bodies
  Phylum Porifera—sponges
    Class Calcarea—chalky sponges
    Class Hexactinellida—glass sponges
    Class Demospongiae—horny sponges
SUBKINGDOM METAZOA—multi-cellular animals
  Phylum Coelenterata (Cnidaria)—coelenterates
    Class Hydrozoa—hydroids (Portuguese man-of-war)
    Class Scyphozoa—jellyfish
    Class Anthozoa—sea anemones and corals
  Phylum Ctenophora—ctenophores
    Class Tentaculata—with tentacles
    Class Nuda—without tentacles
  Phylum Platyhelminthes—flatworms
    Class Turbellaria—free-living flatworms
    Class Trematoda—flukes
    Class Cestoda—tapeworms
    Class Gnathostomulida—gnathostomulids
  Phylum Nemertea—nemertines (ribbon worms)
    Class Anopla—unarmed proboscis
    Class Enopla—armed proboscis
  Phylum Acanthocephala—thorny-headed worms
  Phylum Aschelminthes—aschelminths
    Class Rotifera (Rotatoria)—rotifers
    Class Gastrotricha—gastrotrichs
    Class Kinorhyncha (Echinodera)—kinorhynchs
    Class Nematoda—nematodes (roundworms)
    Class Nematomorpha—horsehair worms
    Class Priapulida—priapulids
  Phylum Sipunculida—sipunculids
  Phylum Bryozoa (Ectoprocta)—bryozoans
    Class Phylactolaemata—fresh-water
    Class Gymnolaemata—salt-water
  Phylum Entoprocta—entoprocts
  Phylum Phoronida—phoronids
  Phylum Brachiopoda—brachiopods
    Class Inarticulata—without teeth
    Class Articulata—with teeth
  Phylum Mollusca—mollusks
    Class Amphineura—chitons
    Class Monoplacophora—monoplacophs
    Class Gastropoda—gastropods (snails, slugs)
    Class Scaphopoda—tooth shells
    Class Bivalvia (Lamellibranchia)—bivalve mollusks
    Class Cephalopoda—cephalopods (squids, octopi)
  Phylum Echiurida—echiuroid marine worms
  Phylum Annelida—segmented worms
    Class Polychaeta—sand-and bristleworms
    Class Mysostomaria—mysostomarians
    Class Oligochaeta—earthworms
    Class Hirudinea—leeches
    Class Archiannelida—no external segments
  Phylum Onychophora—velvet worms
  Phylum Tardigrada—tardigrades (water bears)

Phylum Pentastomida—tongue worms
Phylum Arthropoda—arthropods
    Class Merostomata—horseshoe & king crabs
    Class Arachnida—spiders, ticks, mites, scorpions
    Class Pycnogonida (Pantopoda)—sea spiders
    Class Crustacea—crustaceans
    Class Chilopoda—centipedes
    Class Diplopoda—millipedes
    Class Pauropoda—pauropods
    Class Symphyla—symphylids (garden centipede)
    Class Insecta—insects
Phylum Chaetognatha—arrowworms
Phylum Pogonophora—beard worms
Phylum Hemichordata—hemichordates
    Class Enteropneusta—acorn worms
    Class Pterobranchia—pterobranchs
    Class Planctosphaeroidea—planctosphaera
Phylum Echinodermata—echinoderms
    Class Echinoidea—sea urchins, sand dollars
    Class Holothuroidea—sea cucumbers
    Class Crinoidea—crinoids (sea lilies, feather stars)
    Class Asteroidea—starfish
    Class Ophiuroidea—brittle & basket stars
Phylum Chordata—chordates
  Subphylum Urochordata (Tunicata)—tunicates
    Class Ascidiacea—sea squirts
    Class Thaliacea—salps
    Class Larvacea—larvaceans
  Subphylum Cephalochordata—lancelets
  Subphylum Vertebrata (Craniata)—vertebrates
    Class Agnatha—jawless vertebrates
    Class Chondrichthyes (Elasmobranchii)—cartilaginous fish (sharks, rays)
    Class Osteichthyes—bony fish
    Class Amphibia—amphibians
    Class Reptilia—reptiles
    Class Aves—birds
    Class Mammalia—mammals
      Subclass Prototheria—egg laying mammals (monotremes)
      Subclass Theria—viviparous (live-bearing) mammals
        Infraclass Metatheria—pouched mammals (marsupials)
        Infraclass Eutheria—placental mammals
          Order Insectivora—moles, shrews, hedgehogs
          Order Dermoptera—flying lemurs (colugos)
          Order Chiroptera—bats
          Order Primates—lemurs, monkeys, apes, man
          Order Edentata—sloths, anteaters, armadillos
          Order Pholidota—pangolins
          Order Lagomorpha—rabbits, hares, pikas
          Order Rodentia—rodents
          Order Cetacea—whales, dolphins, porpoises
          Order Carnivora—carnivores (dogs, cats)
          Order Pinnipedia—seals, sea lions, walruses
          Order Tubulidentata—aardvark
          Order Proboscidea—elephants
          Order Hyracoidea—hyraxes (coneys)
          Order Sirenia—sea cows (manatee, dugong)
          Order Perissodactyla—odd-toe ungulates (horses, zebras, tapirs, rhinoceroses)
          Order Artiodactyla—even-toed ungulates (cattle, deer, sheep, goats, pigs, camels)

ANIMAL GESTATION PERIODS AND LITTERS

SOURCE: Grace Davall, Assistant Curator, Mammals and Birds, New York Zoological Society

Animal	Gestation Period	Litter Size	Animal	Gestation Period	Litter Size
AMERICAN BUFFALO (BISON)	270–285 days	1	HORSE	11 months	1
BABOON	6 months	1–2	KANGAROO	38–39 days	1–2
BLACK BEAR	7 months	1–4	LION	108 days	1–4
CAMEL	12–13 months	1	MACAQUE	160–170 days	1–2
CAT	63 days	1–6	MINK	48–51 days	4–8
CHIMPANZEE	226 days	1–2	MOUSE	19–21 days	1–9
CHINCHILLA	105–111 days	1–4	OPOSSUM	12–13 days	4–13
COW	280 days	1–2	OTTER	9½–12½ months	1–4
DEER (WHITE-TAIL)	7 months	2	PIG	112–115 days	4–6
DOG	61 days	1–12	RABBIT	1 month	1–13
DOLPHIN	9 months	1	RACCOON	63 days	1–6
ELEPHANT	21 months	1	SHEEP	150 days	1–3
FOX	49–55 days	1–8	SKUNK	52 days	4–7
GERBIL	14 days	1–7	SQUIRREL	44 days	2–5
GIRAFFE	14–15 months	1	TIGER	100–108 days	2–4
GORILLA	8½ months	1	WOLF	60–63 days	1–13
HAMSTER	16–19 days	2–12	YAK	just over 9 months	1
			ZEBRA	11–12 months	1

ENDANGERED WILDLIFE   Source: Office of Endangered Species, U.S. Dept. of the Interior

Anyone wishing to know the status of any animal should contact the Office of Endangered Species, Dept. of the Interior, Washington, D.C. 20240. Below is a selection from official List of Endangered Fauna, including the 109 native to the United States.

BONY FISHES (Class *Osteichthyes/Phylum Chordata*) **Sturgeons & Paddlefishes** (Order: *Acipenseriformes):* 1. Sturgeon, Shortnose.

Trout, Salmon & Relatives (Order: *Salmoniformes):* 1. Ala Balik; 2. Cisco, Longjaw; 3. Trout, Arizona (Apache); 4. Trout, Gila; 5. Trout, Greenback cutthroat; 6. Trout, Lahontan cutthroat; 7. Trout, Paiute cutthroat.

Carps, Minnows & Relatives (Order: *Cypriniformes):* 1. Ayumodoki; 2. Bonytail, Pahranagat; 3. \Chub, Humpback; 4. Chub, Mohave; 5. Cicek; 6. Cui-ui; 7. Dace, Kendall Warm Springs; 8. Dace, Moapa; 9. Squawfish, Colorado River; 10. Tanago, Miyako; 11. Woundfin.

Sticklebacks (Order: *Solenichthyiformes):* 1. Stickleback, Unarmored threespine.

Silversides, Topminnows & Relatives (Order: *Atheriniformes):* 1. Gambusia, Big Bend; 2. Gambusia, Clear Creek; 3. Gambusia, Pecos; 4. Killifish, Pahrump; 5. Pupfish, Comanche Springs; 6. Pupfish, Devil's Hole; 7. Pupfish, Owens River; 8. Pupfish, Tecopa; 9. Pupfish, Warm Springs; 10. Topminnow, Gila.

Perches & Relatives (Order: *Perciformes):* 1. Darter, Fountain; 2. Darter, Maryland; 3. Darter, Okaloosa; 4. Darter, Watercress; 5. Pike, Blue.

AMPHIBIANS (Class *Amphibia/Phylum Chordata*) **Salamanders** (Order: *Urodela):* 1. Salamander, Desert slender; 2. Salamander, Santa Cruz long-toed; 3. Salamander, Texas blind. **Frogs** (Order: *Anura):* 1. Frog, Stephen Island; 2. Frog, Israel painted; 3. Toad, Houston.

REPTILES (Class *Reptilia/Phylum Chordata*) **Turtles** (Order: *Testudinata):* 1. Terrapin, River (Tuntong); 2. Tortoise, Galapagos; 3. Tortoise, Madgascar radiated; 4. Tortoise, Short-necked (swamp); 5. Turtle, Aquatic box; 6. Turtle, Atlantic Ridley; 7. Turtle, Hawksbill; 8. Turtle, Leatherback.

Crocodiles (Order: *Crocodilia):* 1. Alligator, American; 2. Crocodile, Cuban; 3. Crocodile, Morelet's.

Lizards & Snakes (Order: *Squamata):* 1. Lizard, Day gecko; 2. Lizard, Round Island day gecko; 3. Lizard, Anegada ground iguana; 4. Lizard, Barrington land iguana; 5. Lizard, Blunt-nosed leopard; 6. Snake, Jamaica boa; 7. Snake, Puerto Rican boa; 8. Snake, San Francisco garter.

BIRDS (Class *Aves/Phylum Chordata*) **Albatrosses, Petrels & Relatives** (Order: *Procellariiformes):* 1. Albatross, Short-tailed; 2. Cahow (Bermuda petrel); 3. Petrel, Hawaiian dark-rumped.

Pelicans (Order: *Pelecaniformes):* 1. Pelican, Brown.

Ducks, Geese, Swans & Relatives (Order: *Anseriformes):* 1. Duck, Hawaiian (koloa); 2. Duck, Laysan; 3. Duck, Mexican; 4. Duck, White-winged wood; 5. Goose, Aleutian Canada; 6. Goose, Hawaiian (nene).

Eagles, Falcons, Vultures & Relatives (Order: *Falconiformes):* 1. Condor, Andean; 2. Condor, California; 3. Eagle, Monkey-eating; 4. Eagle, Southern bald; 5. Eagle, Spanish imperial; 6. Falcon, American peregrine; 7. Falcon, Arctic peregrine; 8. Goshawk, Christmas Island; 9. Hawk, Anjouan Island sparrow; 10. Hawk, Galapagos; 11. Hawk, Hawaiian (io); 12. Kite, Florida Everglade.

Pheasants, Grouse, Curassows & Relatives (Order: *Galliformes):* 1. Curassow, Red-billed; 2. Curassow, Trinidad white-headed; 3. Guan, Horned; 4. Megapode, Maleo; 5. Megapode, LaPerouse's; 6. Pheasant, Bar-tailed; 7. Pheasant, Blyth's tragopan; 8. Pheasant, Brown-eared; 9. Pheasant, Cabot's tragopan; 10. Pheasant, Chinese monal; 11. Pheasant, Edward's; 12. Pheasant, Imperial; 13. Pheasant, Mikado; 14. Pheasant, Palawan peacock; 15. Pheasant, Sclater's monal; 16. Pheasant, Swinhoe's; 17. Pheasant, Western tragopan; 18. Pheasant, White-eared; 19. Prairie Chicken, Attwater's greater; 20. Quail, Masked bobwhite.

Cranes, Rails, Bustards & Relatives (Order: *Gruiformes):* 1. Bustard, Great Indian; 2. Coot, Hawaiian; 3. Crane, Hooded; 4. Crane, Japanese; 5. Crane, Mississippi sandhill; 6. Crane, Siberian white; 7. Crane, Whooping; 8. Gallinule, Hawaiian; 9. Kagu (rail); 10. Rail, Auckland Island; 11. Rail, California clapper; 12. Rail, Light-footed clapper; 13. Rail, Yuma clapper; 14. Wanderer, Plains; 15. Takahe.

Plovers, Snipes, Gulls & Relatives (Order: *Charadriiformes):* 1. Curlew, Eskimo; 2. Gull, Audouin's; 3. Stilt, Hawaiian; 4. Tern, California least.

Pigeons, Doves, Sandgrouse & Relatives (Order: *Columbiformes):* 1. Dove, Cloven-feathered; 2. Dove, Grenada; 3. Dove, Palau ground; 4. Pigeon, Azores wood; 5. Pigeon, Chatham Island; 6. Pigeon, Puerto Rican plain.

Parrots (Order: *Psittaciformes):* 1. Parrot, Puerto Rican; 2. Parakeet, Splendid.

Owls (Order: *Strigiformes):* 1. Owl, Anjouan scops; 2. Owl, Palau; 3. Owl, New Zealand laughing.

Goatsuckers & Relatives (Order: *Caprimulgiformes):* 1. Whip-poor-will, Puerto Rican.

Woodpeckers, Puffbirds, Barbets & Relatives (Order: *Piciformes):* 1. Woodpecker, Imperial; 2. Woodpecker, Ivory-billed; 3. Woodpecker, Red-cockaded.

Perching Birds—Sparrows, Larks, Thrushes & Relatives (Order: *Passeriformes):* 1. Bulbul, Mauritius olivaceous; 2. Crow, Hawaiian (alala); 3. Cuckoo-Shrike, Mauritius; 4. Cuckoo-Shrike, Reunion; 5. Finch, Sao Miguel bullfinch; 6. Flycatcher, Chatham Island robin; 7. Flycatcher, Eyrean grass-wren; 8. Flycatcher, Grey-necked rock-fowl; 9. Flycatcher, Palau fantail; 10. Flycatcher, Seychelles black; 11. Flycatcher, Tahiti; 12. Flycatcher, Western bristlebird; 13. Flycatcher, White-necked rock-fowl; 14. Flycatcher (Tyrant), Euler's; 15. Flycatcher (Tyrant), Scarlet-breasted robin; 16. Flycatcher (Tyrant), Tinian monarch; 17. Grackle, Slender-billed; 18. Honeycreeper, Akiapolaau; 19. Honeycreeper, Crested (akohekohe); 20. Honeycreeper, Hawaii akepa (akepa); 21. Honeycreeper, Kauai akialoa; 22. Honeycreeper, Maui parrotbill; 23. Honeycreeper, Maui akepa (akepuie); 24. Honeycreeper, Molokai creeper (kakawahie); 25. Honeycreeper, Oahu creeper (alauwahio); 26. Honeycreeper, Ou; 27. Honeycreeper, Palila; 28. Honeycreepers, Laysan & Nihoa finches; 29. Honeycreepers, Kauai & Maui nukupuus; 30. Honey-eater, Helmeted; 31. Honey-eater, Kauai Oo (oo aa); 32. Scrub-bird, Noisy; 33. Sparrow, Cape Sable; 34. Sparrow, Dusky seaside; 35. Sparrow, Santa Barbara song; 36. Starling, Ponape Mountain; 37. Starling, Rothschild's (myna); 38. Thrasher, White-breasted; 39. Thrush, Large Kauai; 40. Thrush, Molokai (olomau); 41. Thrush, Seychelles magpie-robin; 42. Thrush, Small Kauai (puaiohi); 43. Thrush, Western whipbird; 44. Warbler, Nihoa millerbird; 45. Warbler, Bachman's; 46. Warbler, Kirtland's.

MAMMALS (Class *Mammalia/Phylum Chordata*) **Bats** (Order: *Chiroptera):* 1. Bat, Indiana; 2. Bat, Hawaiian hoary.

Primates (Order: *Primates):* 1. Avahis; 2. Aye-aye; 3. Colobus, Red; 4. Colobus, Zanzibar red; 5. Gibbon, Kloss; 6. Gibbon, Pileated; 7. Gorilla; 8. Indris; 9. Langur, Douc; 10. Langur, Pagi Island; 11. Lemurs; 12. Lemurs, Gentle; 13. Lemurs, Sportive & Weasel; 14. Lemurs, Dwarf; 15. Lemurs, Mouse; 16. Lemurs, Forkmarked; 17. Macaque, Lion-tailed; 18. Mangabey, Tana River; 19. Marmoset, Goeldi's; 20. Monkey, Spider; 21. Monkey, Spider; 22. Orangutan; 23. Sifakas; 24. Tamarins, Golden-rumped; (Golden Marmosets); 25. Uakari.

Rodents (Order: *Rodentia):* 1. Rat, Morro Bay kangaroo; 2. Mouse, Salt marsh harvest; 3. Prairie dog, Utah; 4. Squirrel, Delmarva fox.

Whales, Dolphins & Porpoises (Order: *Cetacea):* 1. Whale, Blue; 2. Whale, Bowhead; 3. Whale, Finback; 4. Whale, Gray; 5. Whale, Humpback; 6. Whale, Right; 7. Whale, Sei; 8. Whale, Sperm.

Carnivores (Order: *Carnivora):* 1. Bear, Mexican grizzly; 2. Cat, Tiger; 3. Cheetah; 4. Cougar, Eastern; 5. Dog, Asiatic wild; 6. Ferret, Black-footed; 7. Fox, Northern kit; 8. Fox, San Joaquin kit; 9. Hyaena, Barbary; 10. Hyaena, Brown; 11. Jaguar; 12. Leopard; 13. Leopard, Formosan clouded; 14. Leopard, Snow; 15. Lion, Asiatic; 16. Lynx, Spanish; 17. Margay; 18. Marten, Formosan yellow-throated; 19. Ocelot; 20. Otter, Cameroon clawless; 21. Otter, Giant; 22. Otter, La Plata; 23. Panther, Florida; 24. Serval, Barbary; 25. Tiger; 26. Wolf, Eastern timber; 27. Wolf, Northern Rocky Mountain; 28. Wolf, Red; 29. Wolf, Maned.

Sirenians (Order: *Sirenia):* 1. Manatee, Florida.

Even-Toed Ungulates (Order: *Artiodactyla):* 1. Anoa; 2. Banteng; 3. Bison, Wood; 4. Deer, Columbian white-tailed; 5. Deer, Key; 6. Deer, Marsh; 7. Deer, McNeill's; 8. Deer, Swamp; 9. Gazelle, Cuviers; 10. Pronghorn, Sonoran; 11. Hartebeest, Swayne's; 12. Ibex, Pyrenean; 13. Impala, Black-faced.

LONG FOREIGN RIVERS

River	Empties into	Length (in miles)	River	Empties into	Length (in miles)
Amazon	Atlantic Ocean	3,915	Nile-Kagera	Mediterranean Sea	4,145
Amu-Dar'ya	Aral Sea	1,616	Ob'-Irtysh-Black Irtysh	Gulf of Ob' (Kara Sea)	3,362
Amur-Shilka-Onon	Tatar Strait	2,744	Oder	Baltic Sea	538
Angara	Yenisey River	1,135	Oka	Volga River	918
Araguaia	Tocantins River	1,367	Olenek	Laptev Sea	1,411
Athabasca	Lake Athabasca	765	Orange	Atlantic Ocean	1,350
Belaya	Kama River	889	Orinoco	Atlantic Ocean	1,600
Brahmaputra	Bay of Bengal	1,700	Ottawa	St. Lawrence River	790
Churchill	Hudson Bay	1,000	Paraguay	Paraná River	1,584
Congo (Zaire)	Atlantic Ocean	2,718	Paraná-La Plata	Atlantic Ocean	2,450
Cubango-Okovango	Okovango Swamps	994	Peace-Finlay	Slave River	1,195
Danube	Black Sea	1,775	Pechora	Pechora Sea	1,124
Darling	Murray River	1,160	Pilcomayo	Paraguay River	1,000
Dnieper	Black Sea	1,368	Po	Adriatic Sea	420
Dniester	Black Sea	876	Purus	Amazon River	1,995
Don	Sea of Azov	1,222	Rhine	North Sea	820
Dvina, Northern	White Sea	809	Rhone	Gulf of Lions	505
Ebro	Mediterranean Sea	565	Rio Grande	Gulf of Mexico	1,885
Elbe	North Sea	724	St. Lawrence	Gulf of St. Lawrence	1,900
Euphrates	Persian Gulf	1,700	Salween	Gulf of Martaban	1,770
Fraser	Strait of Georgia	850	São Francisco	Atlantic Ocean	1,811
Ganges	Bay of Bengal	1,550	Saskatchewan	Lake Winnipeg	1,205
Hwang Ho (Yellow)	Yellow Sea	2,877	Seine	English Channel	482
Indigirka	East Siberian Sea	1,228	Selenga	Lake Baykal	920
Indus	Arabian Sea	1,800	Si	South China Sea	1,650
Irrawaddy	Bay of Bengal	1,325	Sungari	Amur River	1,130
Japurá	Amazon River	1,500	Syr-Dar'ya-Naryn	Aral Sea	1,859
Kama	Volga River	1,262	Tagus (Tajo, Tejo)	Atlantic Ocean	565
Kasai	Congo River	1,338	Tigris	Euphrates River	1,181
Kolyma	East Siberian Sea	1,562	Tisza	Danube River	800
Lena	Laptev Sea	2,734	Tocantins	Pará River	1,677
Limpopo	Indian Ocean	995	Ural	Caspian Sea	1,509
Loire	Bay of Biscay	628	Uruguay	Rio de La Plata	994
Mackenzie-Peace-Finlay	Beaufort Sea	2,635	Vistula	Gulf of Danzig	664
Madeira	Amazon River	2,013	Volga	Caspian Sea	2,194
Magdalena	Caribbean Sea	1,000	Volta	Atlantic Ocean	710
Mekong	South China Sea	2,610	Yangtze	East China Sea	3,434
Meuse	North Sea	590	Yellow (Hwang Ho)	Yellow Sea	2,877
Murray-Darling	Indian Ocean	2,310	Yenisey	Kara Sea	2,543
Negro	Amazon River	1,400	Yenisey-Angara	Kara Sea	3,100
Nelson-Saskatchewan	Hudson Bay	1,600	Yukon	Bering Sea	1,979
Niger	Gulf of Guinea	2,548	Zambezi	Indian Ocean	1,600

OCEANS AND SEAS

Ocean	Area (in square miles)	Percent of World's Water	Greatest Depth (in feet)	Sea	Area (in square miles)	Greatest Depth (in feet)
Pacific	64,186,000	46	Mariana Trench, off the Mariana Islands, 36,198	Caribbean	970,000	24,720
				Mediterranean Sea	969,000	16,896
				South China Sea	895,000	15,000
Atlantic	31,862,000	22.9	Puerto Rico Trench, (Milwaukee Deep), off Puerto Rico, 28,374	Bering Sea	875,000	15,800
				Gulf of Mexico	600,000	12,300
				Sea of Okhotsk	590,000	11,070
				East China Sea	482,000	9,500
				Sea of Japan	389,000	12,280
Indian	28,350,000	20.3	Java Trench, off Java, 25,344	Hudson Bay	317,500	846
				North Sea	222,000	2,200
Arctic	5,427,000	3.9	Eurasia Basin, north of Svalbard, 17,880	Black Sea	185,000	7,365
				Red Sea	169,000	7,200
				Baltic Sea	163,000	1,506

ELEMENTS IN SEAWATER

Source: U.S. Office of Saline Water

Element	Milligrams per Kilogram*	Element	Milligrams per Kilogram*	Element	Milligrams per Kilogram*
Chlorine	18,980	Aluminum	0.5	Cesium	0.002
Sodium	10,561	Rubidium	0.2	Uranium	0.0015
Magnesium	1,272	Lithium	0.1	Molybdenum	0.0005
Sulfur	884	Phosphorus	0.001–0.10	Thorium	0.0005
Calcium	400	Barium	0.05	Cerium	0.0004
Potassium	380	Iodine	0.05	Silver	0.0003
Bromine	65	Arsenic	0.01–0.02	Vanadium	0.0003
Carbon	28	Iron	0.002–0.02	Lanthanum	0.0003
Strontium	13	Manganese	0.001–0.01	Yttrium	0.0003
Boron	4.6	Copper	0.001–0.01	Nickel	0.0001
Silicon	0.02–4.0	Zinc	0.005	Scandium	0.00004
Fluorine	1.4	Lead	0.004	Mercury	0.00003
Nitrogen (compound)	0.01–0.7	Selenium	0.004	Gold	0.000006

* Parts per million.

MAJOR GLACIERS OF THE WORLD

Based on statistics from "Fluctuation of Glaciers 1965-70," © IAHS/UNESCO, 1973, and other sources.

Name	Locality	*Area (sq. mi.)	*Length (mi.)	Name	Locality	*Area (sq. mi.)	*Length (mi.)
Aletsch	Swiss Alps	45	15	Langjökull†	Iceland	265	40
Amundsén	Antarctica	—	60	Logan	Alaska-Yukon	—	70
Baltoro	Asia (Karakoram)	290	35	Malaspina	Alaska-Yukon	1,350	75
Beardmore	Antarctica	130	100	Muir	Alaska	400	15
Bering	Alaska	—	125	Muldrow	Alaska	735	45
Bivachnyy	Asia (Pamir)	75	15	Mýrdalsjökull†	Iceland	180	30
Chisana	Alaska	135	30	Nabesna	Alaska	775	50
Columbia	Alaska	110	40	Petermann	Greenland	—	90
Denman	Antarctica	—	70	Rennick	Antarctica	185	160
Fedchenko	Asia (Pamir)	350	45	Rider	Greenland	125	—
Gangotri	Asia (Himalaya)	115	20	Rimo	Asia (Karakoram)	200	30
Garmo	Asia (Pamir)	60	15	Robert Scott	Antarctica	—	90
Geographical Society	Asia (Pamir)	50	15	Shackleton	Antarctica	—	90
Grum-Grzhimaylo	Asia (Pamir)	60	25	Shamrock	Alaska	40	15
Hispar	Asia (Karakoram)	240	35	Siachen	Asia (Karakoram)	450	50
Hofsjökull†	Iceland	260	—	Svartisen	Norway	200	20
Hubbard	Alaska-Yukon	—	75	Tasman	New Zealand	50	20
Humboldt	Greenland	—	70	Temir-su	Asia (Tien Shan)	45	25
Inyl'chek, Yuzh.	Asia (Tien Shan)	110	40	Totten	Antarctica	—	45
Jostedalsbreen†	Norway	485	60	Triumvirate	Alaska	170	30
Kahiltna	Alaska	—	45	Vatnajökull†	Iceland	2,200	90
Lambert	Antarctica	—	270	Zemu	Asia (Himalaya)	50	20
				Zeravshan	Asia (Turkestan)	45	15

* Approximate, subject to continuous revision. † Icefield.

LARGE LAKES OF THE WORLD

Lake	Continent	Area (in sq. miles)	Length (in miles)	Max. Depth (in ft.)	Lake	Continent	Area (in sq. miles)	Length (in miles)	Max. Depth (in ft.)
Caspian Sea	Asia-Europe	143,243	746	3,264	Reindeer	N. America	2,568	143	—
Superior	N. America	31,700	383	1,301	Tonlé Sap	Asia	2,500–1,000*	85	40–5
Victoria	Africa	26,724	250	270	Turkana (Rudolf)	Africa	2,463	160	240
Aral Sea	Asia	25,676	266	256	Issyk-Kul'	Asia	2,425	114	2,303
Huron	N. America	23,010	247	748	Urmia	Asia	2,300–1,500*	90	50
Michigan	N. America	22,300	321	923	Torrens	Australia	2,230*	120	—
Tanganyika	Africa	12,650	420	4,700	Vänern	Europe	2,156	85	328
Baykal	Asia	12,162	395	5,316	Winnipegosis	N. America	2,075	125	38
Great Bear	N. America	12,096	190	1,356	Albert	Africa	2,075	100	160
Nyasa (Malawi)	Africa	11,555	360	2,320	Kariba	Africa	2,050	175	295
Great Slave	N. America	11,269	300	2,015	Nettilling	N. America	1,956	65	—
Chad	Africa	10,000–4,000*	175–125	25–15	Chany	Asia	1,931–965*	56	39–23
Erie	N. America	9,910	241	209	Nipigon	N. America	1,872	70	540
Winnipeg	N. America	9,417	265	60	Gairdner	Australia	1,825–0*	100	—
Ontario	N. America	7,340	193	775	Mweru	Africa	1,800	75	60
Ladoga	Europe	7,104	124	738	Manitoba	N. America	1,794	140	12
Balkhash	Asia	7,027	376	87	Taymyr	Asia	1,737	125	85
Maracaibo	S. America	5,120	110	100	Kyoga	Africa	1,700	75	25
Bangweulu	Africa	4,500–1,900*	50	—	Khanka	Asia	1,700	59	33
Tungting	Asia	4,500–1,500*	80	—	Lake of the Woods	N. America	1,679	70	70
Onega	Europe	3,710	154	377	Peipus	Europe	1,400	87	50
Eyre	Australia	3,500–0*	110	—	Koko Nor	Asia	1,625	70	125
Titicaca	S. America	3,200	120	1,000	Nasser-Nubia	Africa	1,550	350	—
Nicaragua	N. America	3,100	100	230	Dubawnt	N. America	1,480	70	—
Athabasca	N. America	3,064	200	400	Van	Asia	1,470	80	—
					Wollaston	N. America	1,035	70	—
					Great Salt	N. America	940	75	27

* Max. and min. of fluctuating water area.

GREAT WORLD DESERTS

Desert	Location	Size	Desert	Location	Size
Arabian (Eastern)	North Africa-Red Sea coast	c. 70,000 sq. mi.	Mojave	Southern California	c. 15,000 sq.mi.
Atacama	Northern Chile	c. 140,000 sq. mi.; c. 600 mi. long	Namib	South-West African coast	c. 800 mi. long; c. 60 mi. wide
Colorado	Southern California	c. 2,500 sq. mi.	Nefud (An Nafud)	Northern Arabia	c. 180 mi. long; c. 140 mi. wide
Dasht-i-Kavir	Iran	c. 450 mi. long; c. 175 mi. wide	Negev	Southern Israel	c. 5,000 sq. mi.
Dasht-i-Lut	Iran	c. 300 mi. long; c. 175 mi. wide	Nubian	Northern Sudan	c.150,000 sq. mi.
			Rub al Khali	Southern Arabia	c. 235,000 sq. mi.
Death Valley	California	c. 140 mi. long; c. 10 mi. wide	Sahara	Northern Africa	c. 3,500,000 sq. mi; c. 3,100 mi. long; c. 1,100 mi. wide
Gibson	Western Australia	c. 250,000 sq. mi.			
Gobi	China and Mongolia	c. 500,000 sq. mi.; c. 1,000 mi. long	Sechura	Peruvian coast	c. 10,000 sq. mi.
Great Salt Lake	Utah	c.125 mi. long; c. 80 mi. wide	Simpson	Central Australia	c. 45,000 sq.mi.
			Syrian (El Hamad)	Northern Arabia, Iraq, Jordan & Syria	c. 450 mi. long; c. 350 mi. wide
Great Sandy	Western Australia	c. 150,000 sq. mi.			
Great Victoria	Western and South Australia	c. 250,000 sq. mi.	Taklamakan	Sinkiang-Uigur Aut. Reg., China	c. 180,000 sq. mi.; c. 500 mi. long; c. 300 mi. wide
Kalahari	Southern Africa	c. 225,000 sq. mi.			
Kara-Kum	Turkmen SSR, USSR	c. 115,000 sq. mi.; c. 650 mi. long	Thar (Great Indian)	India and Pakistan	c. 500 mi. long; c. 275 mi.wide
Kyzyl-Kum	Uzbek & Kazakh SSR, USSR	c. 100,000 sq. mi.	Vizcaino	Baja California Sur, Mexico	c. 6,000 sq. mi.

HIGH MOUNTAIN PEAKS (See page 301 for U. S. peaks over 14,000 feet)

Name	Location	Feet
ASIA		
Everest (Chomolungma)	Nepal-China (Tibet)	29,028
K2 (Godwin-Austen)	India (Kashmir)	28,250
Kanchenjunga I	Nepal-India	28,208
Lhotse	Nepal-China (Tibet)	27,923
Makalu	Nepal-China (Tibet)	27,824
Kanchenjunga II	Nepal-India	27,803
Lhotse Shar	Nepal-China (Tibet)	27,504
Dhaulagiri I	Nepal	26,810
Manaslu I (Kutang)	Nepal	26,760
Cho Oyu I	Nepal-China (Tibet)	26,750
Nanga Parbat I	India (Kashmir)	26,660
Annapurna I	Nepal	26,504
Gasherbrum I	India (Kashmir)	26,470
Broad Peak	India (Kashmir)	26,400
Gasherbrum II	India (Kashmir)	26,362
Gosainthan (Shisha Pangma)	China (Tibet)	26,291
Gasherbrum IV	India (Kashmir)	26,181
Gasherbrum III	India (Kashmir)	26,090
Annapurna II	Nepal	26,041
Gyachung Kang	Nepal-China (Tibet)	25,990
Nanga Parbat II	India (Kashmir)	25,953
Himalchuli	Nepal	25,895
Disteghil Sar	India (Kashmir)	25,868
Nuptse	Nepal	25,850
Khinyang Chhish	India (Kashmir)	25,760
Masherbrum	India (Kashmir)	25,660
Nanda Devi	India	25,645
Cho Oyu II	Nepal-China (Tibet)	25,611
Chomo Lönzo	China (Tibet)	25,558
Rakaposhi	India (Kashmir)	25,550
Batura Muztagh I	India (Kashmir)	25,540
Kanjut Sar	India (Kashmir)	25,460
Kamet	India-China (Tibet)	25,447
Namcha Barwa	China (Tibet)	25,445
Dhaulagiri II	Nepal	25,429
Saltoro Kangri	India (Kashmir)	25,400
Batura Muztagh II	India (Kashmir)	25,361
Gurla Mandhata	China (Tibet)	25,355
Ulugh Muztagh	China (Sinkiang-Tibet)	25,338
Trivor	India (Kashmir)	25,330
Kungur	China (Sinkiang)	25,325
Jannu	Nepal	25,294
Dhaulagiri III	Nepal	25,271
Tirich Mir	Pakistan	25,230
Saser Kangri I	India (Kashmir)	25,170
Chogolisa	India (Kashmir)	25,148
Dhaulagiri IV	Nepal	25,135
Kangchungtse (Makalu II)	Nepal-China (Tibet)	25,128
Dhaulagiri V	Nepal	24,992
Rathong	Nepal-India	24,912
Minya Konka	China	24,900
Annapurna III	Nepal	24,787
Kula Kangri	Bhutan-China (Tibet)	24,784
Changtse	China (Tibet)	24,780
Muztagh Ata	China (Sinkiang)	24,757
Annapurna IV	Nepal	24,688
Communism Peak	USSR	24,590
Noshaq	Pakistan-Afghanistan	24,581
Jongsong Peak	India-China (Tibet)	24,472
Malubiting	Pakistan	24,470
Pobeda Peak	USSR	24,406
Chomo Lhari	Bhutan-China (Tibet)	23,997
Muztagh	China (Sinkiang)	23,891
Amne Machin	China	23,490
Demavend	Iran	18,376
Ararat	Turkey	16,946
Djaja (Carstensz)	Indonesia (New Guinea)	16,503
Klyuchevskaya Sopka	USSR	15,584
Kinabalu	Malaysia (Sabah)	13,455
Kerintji	Indonesia (Sumatra)	12,484
Fuji	Japan	12,389
Semeru	Indonesia (Java)	12,060
AFRICA		
Kilimanjaro (Kibo)	Tanzania	19,340
Kenya (Batian)	Kenya	17,058
Kilimanjaro (Mawenzi)	Tanzania	16,896
Margherita (Ruwenzori)	Uganda-Zaire	16,795
Ras Dashan	Ethiopia	15,157
Meru	Tanzania	14,979
Karisimbi	Rwanda-Zaire	14,787
Elgon (Wagagai)	Kenya-Uganda	14,178
Toubkal	Morocco	13,665
Cameroon (Fako Peak)	Cameroon	13,350
Teide	Canary Is.	12,198
AUSTRALIA and OCEANIA		
Wilhelm	Papua New Guinea	14,793

Name	Location	Feet
Mauna Kea	US (Hawaii)	13,796
Mauna Loa	US (Hawaii)	13,680
Cook (Aorangi)	New Zealand	12,349
Kosciusko	Australia	7,316
ANTARCTICA		
Vinson Massif	16,864	Markham	14,285
Tyree	16,289	Bell	14,117
Gardner	15,374	Mackellar	14,098
Kirkpatrick	14,856	Anderson	13,990
Elizabeth	14,698	Bentley	13,934
EUROPE (including Caucasus)		
El'brus	USSR	18,510
Shkhara	USSR	17,064
Dykh-Tau	USSR	17,054
Koshtan-Tau	USSR	16,877
Dzhangi-Tau	USSR	16,565
Kazbek	USSR	16,558
Mont-Blanc	France	15,771
Dufourspitze (Mte. Rosa)	Switz.-Italy	15,203
Dom (Mischabel)	Switz.	14,911
Lyskamm	Switz.-Italy	14,852
Weisshorn	Switz.	14,780
Täschhorn	Switz.	14,733
Matterhorn	Switz.	14,692
Mont-Maudit	France-Italy	14,649
Dent-Blanche	Switz.	14,293
Nadelhorn	Switz.	14,196
Grand-Combin	Switz.	14,154
Lenzspitze	Switz.	14,098
Finsteraarhorn	Switz.	14,022
Rimpfischhorn	Switz.	13,776
Aletschhorn	Switz.	13,763
Jungfrau	Switz.	13,642
Gran Paradiso	Italy	13,323
Piz Bernina	Switz.-Italy	13,284
Grossglockner	Austria	12,457
Mulhacén	Spain	11,411
Etna	Italy	11,053
Zugspitze	Germany-Austria	9,721
Olympus (Mytikas)	Greece	9,570
Glittertind	Norway	8,110
Ben Nevis	UK (Scotland)	4,406
Vesuvius	Italy	4,190
NORTH AMERICA		
Logan	Canada	19,524
Citlaltépetl (Orizaba)	Mexico	18,855
St. Elias	Canada-US	18,008
Popocatépetl	Mexico	17,887
Iztaccíhuatl	Mexico	17,343
Lucania	Canada	17,147
King Peak	Canada	16,971
Steele	Canada	16,644
Wood	Canada	15,885
Vancouver	Canada-US	15,700
Fairweather	Canada-US	15,300
Toluca (Zinantécatl)	Mexico	15,015
Walsh	Canada	14,780
La Malinche	Mexico	14,635
Nevada de Colima	Mexico	14,205
Cofre de Perote	Mexico	14,050
Tajumulco	Guatemala	13,845
Robson	Canada	12,972
Chirripó Grande	Costa Rica	12,530
Parícutin	Mexico	10,400
SOUTH AMERICA		
Aconcagua	Argentina	22,831
Ojos del Salado	Argentina	22,546
Bonete	Argentina-Chile	22,572
Tupungato	Argentina-Chile	22,310
Pissis	Argentina	22,245
Mercedario	Argentina	22,211
Huascarán	Peru	22,205
Llullaillaco	Argentina-Chile	22,057
Cumbre del Libertador Gen. San Martín	Argentina	22,047
Ancohuma	Bolivia	21,489
Sajama	Bolivia	21,391
Nacimiento	Argentina	21,302
Illampu	Bolivia	21,276
Illimani	Bolivia	21,184
Coropuna	Peru	21,079
Nevados de Huandoy	Peru	20,981
Toro	Argentina-Chile	20,932
Chimborazo	Ecuador	20,561
Cotopaxi	Ecuador	19,347
El Misti	Peru	19,199

DAMS, MAN-MADE LAKES, HYDROELECTRIC PLANTS

SOURCE: Bureau of Reclamation, Dept. of the Interior

HIGHEST DAMS

A = Arch; E = Earth or Rockfill; G = Gravity; M = Multi-Arch; UC = Under Construction.

Name of Dam		Height Meters	Feet	Year Completed	Name of Dam		Height Meters	Feet	Year Completed
1. Rogunsky, U.S.S.R.	E	325	1,066	UC	14. Hoover, U.S.A.	A/G	221	726	1936
2. Nurek, U.S.S.R.	E	317	1,040	UC	15. Contra, Switzerland	A	220	722	1965
3. Grand Dixence, Switzerland	G	285	935	1962	16. Piva (Mratinje), Yugoslavia	A	220	722	1975
4. Inguri, U.S.S.R.	A	272	892	UC	17. Dworshak, U.S.A.	G	219	717	1974
5. Vaiont, Italy	A	262	858	1961	18. Glen Canyon, U.S.A.	A	216	710	1964
6. Chicoasen, Mexico	E	250	820	UC	19. Daniel Johnson, Canada	M	214	703	1968
7. Mica, Canada	E	242	794	1974	20. Toktogul, U.S.S.R.	G	213	699	UC
8. Sayanskaya, U.S.S.R.	A	242	794	UC	21. Auburn, U.S.A.	A	209	685	UC
9. Chivor, Columbia	E	237	778	1975	22. Luzzone, Switzerland	A	208	682	1963
10. Mauvoisin, Switzerland	A	237	777	1957	23. Keban, Turkey	E/G	207	679	1974
11. Oroville, U.S.A.	E	235	770	1968	24. Mohamed Reza Shah				
12. Chirkey, U.S.S.R.	A	233	764	1975	Pahlavi, Iran	A	203	666	1963
13. Bhakra, India	G	226	742	1963	25. Almendra, Spain	A	202	662	1970

LARGEST DAMS

Based on total volume of dam structure.

Name of Dam	Volume (Thousands) Cubic Meters	Cubic Yards	Year Completed
1. New Cornelia Tailings, U.S.A.	209,500	274,026	1973
2. Tarbela, Pakistan	121,000	158,268	1975
3. Fort Peck, U.S.A.	96,034	125,612	1940
4. Guri, Venezuela	70,762	92,557	UC
5. Oahe, U.S.A.	70,343	92,008	1963
6. Oosterschelde, Netherlands	70,000	91,560	UC
7. Yacyreta-Apipe, Argentina–			
Paraguay	70,000	91,560	UC
8. Mangla, Pakistan	65,651	85,872	1967
9. Gardiner, Canada	65,553	85,743	1968
10. Afsluitdijk, Netherlands	63,400	82,927	1932
11. Rogunsky, U.S.S.R.	62,000	81,096	UC
12. Oroville, U.S.A.	59,639	78,008	1968
13. San Luis, U.S.A.	59,378	77,666	1967
14. Nurek, U.S.S.R.	58,000	75,864	UC
15. Garrison, U.S.A.	50,846	66,506	1956
16. Cochiti, U.S.A.	49,417	64,631	1975
17. Tabka, Syria	46,000	60,168	1975
18. Kiev, U.S.S.R.	44,000	57,552	1964
19. W.A.C. Bennett (Portage Mt.),			
Canada	43,733	57,203	1967
20. High Aswan (Sadd-el-Aali),			
Egypt	43,733	57,203	1970
21. Tucurui, Brazil	43,000	56,244	UC
22. Dantiwada Left Earthenbank,			
India	41,040	53,680	1965
23. Saratov, U.S.S.R.	40,400	52,843	1967
24. Mission Tailings #2, U.S.A.	40,088	52,435	1973
25. Fort Randall, U.S.A.	38,383	50,205	1956

GREATEST MAN-MADE LAKES

Name of Dam	Capacity Millions of Cubic Meters	Thousands of Acre-Feet	Year Completed
1. Owen Falls, Uganda	204,800	166,000	1954
2. Bratsk, U.S.S.R.	169,270	137,220	1964
3. High Aswan (Sadd-el-Aali),			
Egypt	169,000	137,000	1970
4. Kariba, Rhodesia-Zambia	160,368	130,000	1959
5. Akosombo, Ghana	148,000	120,000	1965
6. Daniel Johnson, Canada	141,852	115,000	1968
7. Guri, Venezuela	136,000	110,257	UC
8. Krasnoyarsk, U.S.S.R.	73,300	59,425	1972
9. W.A.C. Bennett (Portage Mt.),			
Canada	70,309	57,006	1967
10. Zeya, U.S.S.R.	68,400	55,452	1975
11. Cabora Bassa, Mozambique	64,000	51,900	1974
12. LaGrande, Canada	62,260	50,475	UC
13. Ust-Ilimsk, U.S.S.R.	59,300	48,100	UC
14. Volga-V.I. Lenin, U.S.S.R.	58,000	47,020	1955
15. Bukhtarma, U.S.S.R.	53,000	42,970	1960
16. Irkutsk, U.S.S.R.	46,000	37,290	1956
17. Hoover, U.S.A.	36,703	29,755	1936
18. Vilyui, U.S.S.R.	35,900	29,104	1967
19. Sanmenxia, China	35,400	28,699	1960
20. Sobradinho, Brazil	34,200	27,700	UC
21. Tucurui, Brazil	34,000	27,564	UC
22. Volgograd – 22nd Congress,			
U.S.S.R.	33,500	27,160	1958
23. Glen Canyon, U.S.A.	33,305	27,000	1964
24. Sayanskaya, U.S.S.R.	31,300	25,353	UC
25. Keban, Turkey	31,000	25,110	1974
26. Garrison, U.S.A.	30,000	24,321	1956

LARGEST HYDROELECTRIC PLANTS

MW = Megawatts.

Name of Dam	Rated Capacity MW Present	MW Ultimate	Year of Initial Operation	Name of Dam	Rated Capacity MW Present	MW Ultimate	Year of Initial Operation
1. Italpu, Brazil-Paraguay	—	12,870	UC	25. Foz Do Areia, Brazil	2,250	2,250	UC
2. Grand Coulee, U.S.A.	4,163	10,080	1941	26. High Aswan (Sadd-el-Aali),			
3. Guri, Venezuela	524	6,500	1967	Egypt	2,100	2,100	1967
4. Sayanskaya, U.S.S.R.	—	6,400	UC	27. Bath County, U.S.A.	—	2,100	UC
5. Krasnoyarsk, U.S.S.R.	6,096	6,096	1968	28. Tarbela, Pakistan	700	2,100	1977
6. LaGrande 2, Canada	—	5,328	UC	29. Itumbiara, Brazil	—	2,080	UC
7. Churchill Falls, Canada	5,225	5,225	1971	30. Chief Joseph, U.S.A.	1,024	2,069	1956
8. Bratsk, U.S.S.R.	4,100	4,600	1964	31. Salto Santiago, Brazil	—	1,998	UC
9. Sukhovo, U.S.S.R.	—	4,500	UC	32. Robert Moses-Niagara, U.S.A.	1,950	1,950	1961
10. Ust-Ilimsk, U.S.S.R.	720	4,320	1974	33. Salto Grande, Argentina-			
11. Cabora Bassa, Mozambique	2,000	4,000	1975	Uruguay	—	1,890	UC
12. Tucurui, Brazil	—	3,960	UC	34. Dinorwic, U.K.	—	1,880	UC
13. Rogunsky, U.S.S.R.	—	3,600	UC	35. Ludington, U.S.A.	1,872	1,872	1973
14. Paulo Afonso, Brazil	1,524	3,409	1955	36. St. Lawrence Power Dam,			
15. Solteira, Brazil	3,200	3,200	1973	U.S.A.-Canada	1,824	1,824	1958
16. Inga I, Zaire	360	2,820	1974	37. The Dalles, U.S.A.	1,807	1,807	1957
17. John Day, U.S.A.	2,160	2,700	1968	38. Karakaya, Turkey	—	1,800	UC
18. Nurek, U.S.S.R.	—	2,700	UC	39. Grand Maison, France	1,200	1,800	UC
19. Sao Simao, Brazil	—	2,680	UC	40. Mica, Canada	—	1,740	UC
20. Volgograd-22nd Congress,				41. Itaparica, Brazil	—	1,700	UC
U.S.S.R.	2,560	2,560	1958	42. Kemano, Canada	813	1,670	1954
21. Chicoasen, Mexico	—	2,400	UC	43. Blue Ridge, U.S.A.	—	1,600	UC
22. Volga-V.I. Lenin, U.S.S.R.	2,300	2,300	1955	44. Beauharnois, Canada	1,021	1,574	1950
23. Iron Gates I, Romania-				45. Kariba, Rhodesia-Zambia	1,266	1,566	1959
Yugoslavia	2,300	2,300	1970	46. San Carlos, Colombia	—	1,550	UC
24. W.A.C. Bennett, Canada	1,816	2,270	1969				

VOLCANOES

Key to letters: (E) Last eruption, with year in parentheses; (R) Rumbling; (St) Steaming; (D) Dormant.

Name	Location	Height (in feet)
AFRICA		
Kibo (Kilimanjaro) (D)	Tanzania	19,340
Cameroon Mt. (E-1959)	Cameroon	13,350
El Teide (St)	Canary Is.	12,172
Nyiragongo (E-1977)	Congo	11,385
Nyamulagira (E-1976)	Congo	10,028
Fogo (E-1951)	Cape Verde Is.	9,281
Tristan da Cunha (E-1961)	South Atlantic	6,760
Teneguia (D)	Canary Is.	2,006
ANTARCTICA		
Deception Island (E-1970)		—
Erebus (E-1978)		12,450
Melbourne (St)		8,500
ASIA and AUSTRALASIA		
Klyuchevskaya (E-1962)	USSR	15,584
Kerintji (St)	Indonesia	12,484
Fuji (D)	Japan	12,389
Rindjani (E-1964)	Indonesia	12,224
Tolbachik (E-1941)	USSR	12,080
Semeru (E-1963)	Indonesia	12,060
Ichinskaya (St)	USSR	11,880
Kronotskaya (D)	USSR	11,575
Koryakskaya (E-1957)	USSR	11,339
Slamet (E-1953)	Indonesia	11,247
Raung (St)	Indonesia	10,932
Shiveluch (E-1964)	USSR	10,771
Dempo (St)	Indonesia	10,364
Welirang (D)	Indonesia	10,354
Agung (E-1964)	Indonesia	10,308
Sundoro (D)	Indonesia	10,285
Tjareme (E-1938)	Indonesia	10,098
Gede (E-1949)	Indonesia	9,705
Apo (D)	Philippines	9,369
Merapi (E-1969)	Indonesia	9,551
Bezymyannaya (E-1961)	USSR	9,514
Marapi (D)	Indonesia	9,485
Tambora (D)	Indonesia	9,353
Mayon (E-1978)	Philippines	7,940
Sinila (E-1979)	Indonesia	c. 7,000
Bulosan (E-1978)	Philippines	5,140
Usu (E-1978)	Japan	2,390
Taal (E-1977)	Philippines	990
MID-PACIFIC		
Mauna Kea (D)	Hawaii	13,796
Mauna Loa (E-1975)	Hawaii	13,680
Kilauea (E-1977)	Hawaii	4,077
EUROPE		
Etna (E-1979)	Sicily, Italy	11,053
Askja (E-1961)	Iceland	4,954
Hekla (E-1970)	Iceland	4,892
Vesuvius (St)	Italy	4,190
Stromboli (E-1971)	Lipari Is., Italy	3,038
Surtsey (E-1967)	Iceland	570
Eldfell (E-1973)	Iceland	327

Name	Location	Height (in feet)
NORTH AMERICA		
Popocatépetl (St)	Mexico	17,887
Colima (St)	Mexico	14,205
Wrangell (St)	Alaska	14,163
Torbert (E-1953)	Alaska	11,413
Spurr (E-1953)	Alaska	11,069
Lassen (D)	California	10,457
Paricutín (D)	Mexico	10,400
Redoubt (E-1966)	Alaska	10,197
Iliamna (St)	Alaska	10,016
Shishaldin (St)	Aleutians	9,387
Pavlof (E-1950)	Alaska	8,261
Veniaminof (D)	Alaska	8,225
Griggs (St)	Alaska	7,600
Mageik (St)	Alaska	7,250
Douglas (St)	Alaska	7,064
Chiginagak (D)	Alaska	6,900
Katmai (E-1962)	Alaska	6,715
Kukak (St)	Alaska	6,700
Makushin (D)	Aleutians	6,680
Pogromni (E-1964)	Aleutians	6,568
Martin (E-1960)	Alaska	6,050
Trident (E-1963)	Alaska	6,010
CENTRAL AMERICA and CARIBBEAN		
Tajumulco (R)	Guatemala	13,845
Tacaná (R)	Guatemala	13,428
Acatenango (R)	Guatemala	12,992
Fuego (E-1978)	Guatemala	12,582
Santa Maria (R)	Guatemala	12,362
Atitlan (R)	Guatemala	11,565
Irazú (E-1964)	Costa Rica	11,260
San Pedro (R)	Guatemala	9,921
Poás (St)	Costa Rica	8,930
Pacaya (E-1970)	Guatemala	8,346
Izalco (E-1967)	El Salvador	6,184
Soufrière (E-1979)	St. Vincent	4,048
SOUTH AMERICA		
Guallatiri (E-1959)	Chile	19,882
Lascar (E-1951)	Chile	19,652
Cotopaxi (St)	Ecuador	19,347
Misti (D)	Peru	19,199
Cayambe (D)	Ecuador	18,996
Tupungatito (E-1959)	Chile	18,504
Sangay (E-1946)	Ecuador	17,159
Tungurahua (R)	Ecuador	16,512
Cotacachi (E-1955)	Ecuador	16,204
Pichincha (D)	Ecuador	15,696
Purace (E-1950)	Colombia	15,604
Lautaro (St)	Chile	11,090
Llaima (E-1955)	Chile	10,239
Villarrica (E-1964)	Chile	9,318
Osorno (R)	Chile	8,730
Shoshuenco (E-1960)	Chile	7,743

WORLD WATERFALLS

Location and Name		Height[1] (in feet)
AFRICA		
Aughrabies[a]	S. Africa	482
Baratieri	Ethiopia	460
Chirombo[2]	Zambia	880
Dianzundu (Duque de Braganca)	Angola	344
Finca	Ethiopia	508
Howick	S. Africa	358
Kalambo[2,a]	Tanz.-Zambia	726
Karkloof[2]	S. Africa	350
Livingstone[2]	Zaire	875
Lofoi	Zaire	1,115
Magwa	S. Africa	450
Maletsunyane	Lesotho	630
Murchison[2]	Uganda	400
Ruacana	Angola	406
Stanley[2]	Zaire	200
Tisisat[a]	Ethiopia	140
Tsitsa	S. Africa	375
Tugela[2]	S. Africa	3,110
Verme	Ethiopia	229
Victoria[2,a]	Rhod.-Zambia	355

Location and Name		Height[1] (in feet)
ASIA		
Diyaluma	Sri Lanka	600
Jog (Gersoppa)[2,a]	India	830
Kegon	Japan	330
Kirindi Ela	Sri Lanka	347
Kurundu Oya	Sri Lanka	620
Laksapana	Sri Lanka	377
Nachi	Japan	430
Ramboda	Sri Lanka	329
Ratna Ella	Sri Lanka	305
Sivasamudram (Kaveri)[2]	India	320
Yudaki	Japan	335
OCEANIA		
Akaka	Hawaii (US)	420
Barron	Australia	770
Bowen[2]	New Zealand	540
Helena	New Zealand	860
Leura[2]	Australia	308
Stirling	New Zealand	505
Sutherland[2]	New Zealand	1,904

Location and Name		Height[1] (in feet)
Tully[2]	Australia	972
Wentworth[2]	Australia	518
Wollomombi[2]	Australia	1,580
EUROPE		
Aurstapet[2]	Norway	794
Gastein[2]	Austria	486
Gavarnie	France	1,385
Giessbach[2]	Switz.	1,312
Glomach	UK (Scotland)	370
Golling[2]	Austria	203
Iffigen	Switz.	394
Kile[2]	Norway	1,840
Krimml[2]	Austria	1,246
Låtefoss[2]	Norway	541
Mardalsfoss (E.)[2]	Norway	1,696
Mardalsfoss (W.)	Norway	1,535
Marmore[2]	Italy	525
Mongefossen[2]	Norway	2,539
Reichenbach[2]	Switz.	656
Rjoandefoss[2]	Norway	1,847
Rjukenfoss	Norway	983

[1] Height means total drop whether in one or more leaps. [2] Falls consisting of more than one leap.
[a] Falls that diminish greatly seasonally.

Location and Name		Height[1] (in feet)	Location and Name		Height[1] (in feet)	Location and Name		Height[1] (in feet)
Simme[2]	Switz.	459	Manitou	US (Wis.)	165	Yellowstone[2]		
Skjeggedalsfoss	Norway	525	Minnehaha[3]	US (Minn.)	52	Upper	US (Wyo.)	109
Skykkjedalsfoss	Norway	820	Missouri			Lower		308
Søtefoss	Norway	896	(Great Falls)[2]	US (Mont.)	90	Yosemite[2]	US (Calif.)	2,425
Stalheimsfoss	Norway	413	Montmorency	Canada (Que.)	274	Upper		1,430
Staubbach	Switz.	984	Multnomah[2]	US (Oreg.)	620			
Stäuber	Switz.	590	Narada	US (Wash.)	168	SOUTH AMERICA		
Stigfoss	Norway	590	Necaxa	Mexico	540			
Toce[2]	Italy	470	Nevada	US (Calif.)	594	Angel[2]	Venezuela	3,212
Trümmelbach[2]	Switz.	1,312	Niagara[2]:			Upper		2,648
Tyssefoss[2]	Norway	1,749	American	US (N.Y.)	167	Anta, Cascada da	Brazil	665
Tyssestrengene[2]	Norway	2,795	Canadian			Candelas, Cataratas		
Vermafoss	Norway	1,248	(Horseshoe)	U.S.-Canada	158	de	Colombia	984
Vettisfoss[2]	Norway	1,214	Palouse	US (Wash.)	198	Glass	Brazil	1,325
Vøringfoss	Norway	597	Panther	Canada (Alta.)	600	Grande	Arg.-Uruguay	75
			Passaic			Grande	Brazil	140
NORTH AMERICA			(Great Falls)[3]	US (N.J.)	70	Great	Guyana	500
			Potomac (Great			Iguazú (Iguaçu)[2]	Brazil	237
Basaseachic	Mexico	1,000	Falls)[2]	US (Md.-Va.)	90	Itiquira	Brazil	395
Bridalveil	US (Calif.)	620	Ribbon[3]	US Calif.	1,612	Kaieteur[2]	Guyana	822
Chequaga	US (N.Y.)	156	Saint Anthony	US (Minn.)	60	highest		741
Churchill	Canada (Newf.)	245	Seven	US (Colo.)	266	King Edward		
Comet	US (Wash.)	320	Shawinigan	Canada (Que.)	150	VIII	Guyana	850
Cumberland	US (Ky.)	68	Shoshone[2][3]	US (Idaho)	210	King George		
Della	Canada (B.C.)	1,443	Silver Strand	US (Calif.)	1,170	VI	Guyana	1,600
Fairy	US (Wash.)	700	Sluiskin	US (Wash.)	300	Kukenaam[2]	Venezuela	2,000
Fall Creek	US (Tenn.)	256	Snoqualmie	US (Wash.)	270	Marina[2]	Guyana	500
Feather	US (Calif.)	640	Tahquamenon[2]	US (Mich.)	88	Papagaio	Brazil	350
Grand	Canada (N. Br.)	75	Takakkaw[2]	Canada (B.C.)	1,650	Patos-Maribondo	Brazil	115
Grand	Canada (Ont.)	150	Taughannock	US (N.Y.)	215	Paulo Afonso[2]	Brazil	275
Granite	US (Wash.)	350	Tower	US (Wyo.)	132	Roraima[3]	Guyana	1,500
Illilouette	US (Calif.)	370	Twin[2][3]	US (Idaho)	125	Sete Quedas		
Juanacatlán,			Vernal	US (Calif.)	317	(Guairá)	Brazil-Parag.	360
Salto de[3]	Mexico	70	Virginia	Canada (N.W.T.)	315	Tequendama	Colombia	482
Jumatán	Mexico	394	Xico	Mexico	256	Urubupungá	Brazil	33

[1] Height means total drop whether in one or more leaps. [2] Falls consisting of more than one leap. [3] Falls that diminish greatly seasonally.

OUTSTANDING WORLDWIDE WEATHER EXTREMES

SOURCE: National Oceanic & Atmospheric Administration

TEMPERATURE EXTREMES

Temperature extremes for any place on Earth are determined by a number of factors, including altitude, latitude, and physical characteristics. For an extreme to be recorded, an observation must be made at the precise time and place of occurrence; consequently, more extreme temperatures undoubtedly have occurred.

THE HOTTEST

Area	Max. (°F.)	Place	Elevation (Ft.)	Date
Africa	136	Al'Aziziyah, Libya	380	Sept. 13, 1922
North America	134	Death Valley, California	-178	July 10, 1913
Asia	129	Tirat Tsvi, Israel	-722	June 21, 1942
Australia	128	Cloncurry, Queensland	622	Jan. 16, 1889
Europe	122	Seville, Spain	26	Aug. 4, 1881
South America	120	Rivadavia, Argentina	676	Dec. 11, 1905
Oceania	108	Tuguegarao, Philippines	72	Apr. 29, 1912
Antarctica	58	Esperanza, Palmer Peninsula	26	Oct. 20, 1956

THE COLDEST

Area	Min. (°F.)	Place	Elevation (Ft.)	Date
Antarctica	-127	Vostok Station	11,220	Aug. 24, 1960
Asia	-90	Oymyakon, USSR	2,625	Feb. 6, 1933
Greenland	-87	Northice Station	7,690	Jan. 9, 1954
North America	-81	Snag, Yukon, Canada	1,925	Feb. 3, 1947
Europe	-67	Ust'-Shchugor, USSR	279	date unknown
South America	-27	Sarmiento, Argentina	879	June 1, 1907
Africa	-11	Ifrane, Morocco	5,364	Feb. 11, 1935
Australia	-8	Charlotte Pass, New South Wales	NA	July 22, 1947

RAINFALL EXTREMES

The total annual precipitation recorded at a place may vary greatly from year to year. The rainiest places show the greatest variations from year to year in actual amounts. The drier places show the greatest variation taken as a percentage of the mean value. At Cherrapunji, India, for example, the greatest amount of precipitation in a calendar year was 905.1 inches. The least was 282.6 inches, a difference of over 600 inches. At Arica, Chile, half of the total rainfall recorded from 1931 through 1960 fell in the single year of 1959. No rain at all fell in 19 of the 30 years. Because of such fluctuations, the average annual precipitation may be greatly influenced by the available years of record; the longer the record, the more reliable is the average.

THE WETTEST

Area	Average Annual Rainfall (Inches)	Place	Elevation (Ft.)	Years of Record
Oceania	460.0	Mt. Waialeale, Hawaii	5,075	33
Asia	450.0	Cherrapunji, India	4,309	75
Africa	404.6	Debundscha, Cameroon	30	33
South America	354.0	Quibdó, Colombia	240	11–17
North America	262.1	Henderson Lake, Br. Col.	12	15
Europe	182.8	Crkvice, Yugoslavia	3,337	23
Australia	179.0	Tully, Queensland	220	32

THE DRIEST

Area	Average Annual Rainfall (Inches)	Place	Elevation (Ft.)	Years of Record
South America	0.03	Arica, Chile	95	60
Africa	0.1	Wadi Halfa, Sudan	410	40
Antarctica	0.8	South Pole Station	9,186	11
North America	1.2	Bataques, Mexico	16	15
Asia	1.8	Aden, P.D.R. Yemen	22	51
Australia	4.05	Mulka, South Australia	NA	35
Europe	6.4	Astrakhan, USSR	45	26
Oceania	8.93	Puako, Hawaii	5	14

WORLD'S HIGHEST BUILDINGS *Under construction.

Building	Location	Height (in feet)	Stories	Building	Location	Height (in feet)	Stories
Sears Tower	Chicago	1,454	110	One Astor Plaza	New York City	730	54
World Trade Center	New York City	1,353	110	Peachtree Plaza Hotel	Atlanta	722	60
Empire State Building	New York City	1,250	102	Carlton Centre	Johannesburg	722	50
Standard Oil Building	Chicago	1,136	80	One Shell Plaza	Houston	714	50
John Hancock Center	Chicago	1,107	100	First International	Dallas	710	56
Chrysler Building	New York City	1,046	77	Terminal Tower	Cleveland	708	52
The First Canadian Bank Tower	Toronto	936	70	General Motors Building	New York City	705	50
Citicorp Center	New York City	914	46	Union Carbide Building	New York City	702	52
Water Tower Place	Chicago	859	74	Metropolitan Life Building	New York City	700	50
United California Bank	Los Angeles	858	62	Bank of America	San Francisco	700	52
40 Wall Street	New York City	851	71	Atlantic Richfield Plaza	Los Angeles	699	52
RCA Building	New York City	850	70	500 Fifth Avenue	New York City	697	60
First National Bank	Chicago	850	60	One Shell Square	New Orleans	697	51
Transamerica	San Francisco	843	60	Shinjuku Mitsui Building	Tokyo	696	55
U.S. Steel Building	Pittsburgh	841	64	IBM Building	Chicago	695	52
60 Wall Tower	New York City	826	66	Shinjuku Sumitomo Building	Tokyo	690	52
One Chase Manhattan Plaza	New York City	813	60	1100 Milam	Houston	690	47
Pan Am Building	New York City	808	59	9 West 57 Street	New York City	688	50
Woolworth Building	New York City	792	60	55 Water Street	New York City	687	53
John Hancock Tower	Boston	790	60	Chanin Building	New York City	680	56
M.V. Lomonosov State University	Moscow	787	39	Gulf+Western	New York City	679	43
M.L.C.	Sydney, Australia	786	70	Marine Midland	New York City	677	52
Commerce Court West	Toronto	784	57	McGraw-Hill Building	New York City	674	51
IDS Center	Minneapolis	772	57	Lincoln Building	New York City	673	55
One Liberty Plaza	New York City	772	54	1633 Broadway	New York City	670	48
One Penn Plaza	New York City	766	57	Civic Center (City Hall)	Chicago	662	31
Palace of Science and Culture	Warsaw	758	42	Overseas Chinese Banking Corp.	Singapore	660	52
Chemical Bank	New York City	755	42	Parque Central Torre	Caracas	656	56
Maine Montparnasse	Paris	751	64	Irving Trust Building	New York City	654	49
Prudential Tower	Boston	750	52	Ukraine Hotel (incl. tower)	Moscow	650	34
EXXON	New York City	750	54	American Tobacco Building	New York City	648	44
U.S. Steel	New York City	743	50	Lake Point Towers	Chicago	645	70
Ikebokoru*	Tokyo	741	60	1000 Lakeshore Plaza	Chicago	640	60
20 Exchange Plaza	New York City	741	57	345 Park Avenue	New York City	634	44
Toronto Dominion Bank	Toronto	740	56	Yasuda Kasai Building	Tokyo	633	43
Security Pacific Nat'l Bank	Los Angeles	735	54	1114 Avenue of the Americas	New York City	630	50
				First National Bank	Dallas	628	52
				Waldorf Astoria Hotel	New York City	625	47
				Qantas Building	Sydney, Australia	625	50

SELECTED WORLD STRUCTURES Source: Amer. Society of Civil Engineers

Structure	Location	Height in Feet	Structure	Location	Height In Feet
Polish National TV Service Tower	Plock, Poland	2,120	TV Tower	Munich	951
KTHI-TV	Fargo, N.D.	2,063	Exxon Co. Oil Platform	Santa Barbara, Calif.	945
CN Communication Tower	Toronto	1,815	TV Tower	Hamburg, Germany	856
Ostankino TV tower	Near Moscow, USSR	1,762	Ohio Edison Company Chimney	Stratton, Ohio	853
Moscow TV tower	USSR	1,732	General Post Office Antennae (pair)	Rugby, England	820
B.R.E.N. Tower	Nevada	1,527	TV antenna	Stuttgart, Germany	767
Loran Mast	Snaefellsnes, Iceland	1,378	Radio tower	Transvaal, Rep. of So. Africa	760
Danish Government Navigational Mast	Thule, Greenland	1,345	BBC Antenna, Crystal Palace	London	710
Peking Radio Antenna	China	1,312	TV antenna	West Berlin	696
Tower Zero	N.W. Cape, Western Australia	1,271	National Cathedral Tower	Washington, D.C.	660
TV antenna	Emley Moor, England	1,265	Gateway Arch	St. Louis	630
TV antenna	Belmont, England	1,265	Tour du Maine	Paris	607
Zender Lopik TV Antenna	Near Lopik, Netherlands	1,253	Space Needle	Seattle	606
American Electric Power smokestack	Cresap, W. Va.	1,206	Donauturm	Vienna	597
Utah Copper Div. of Kennecott Copper Corp. Magna Smelter Chimney	Great Salt Lake, Utah	1,200	Radio Luxembourg Antenna	Junglinster	591
East Berlin Antenna	East Germany	1,185	Post Office Tower	London	580
Television Center	Moscow	1,179	San Jacinto Column	Houston	570
TV tower	Vinnitsa, Ukraine, USSR	1,150	Tower of the First Methodist Church	Chicago	568
Loran Tower	Tomil, Yap Island	1,100	Washington Monument	Washington, D.C.	555
CHCHTV Antenna	Hamilton, Canada	1,093	American Smelting and Refining smokestack	Tacoma, Wash.	535
TV tower	Tokyo	1,092	Ulm Cathedral	West Germany	530
Leningrad antenna	USSR	1,065	Vertical Assembly Building	Cape Canaveral, Fla.	525
TV Antenna	Kojál, Czechoslovakia	1,033	Cathedral of Learning	Pittsburgh	523
Weather tower	Obninsk, USSR	1,027	Blackpool Tower	England	519
Lakihegg Antenna	Lakihegg, Hungary	1,006	Cologne Cathedral	West Germany	515
ITA Antenna	Brynychain, Wales	1,000	Mole Antonelliana	Turin, Italy	510
Conemaugh Station Chimney (pair)	Johnstown, Pa.	1,000	Kaknastornet Tower	Stockholm	502
TV antenna	Black Hill, Scotland	1,000	Niagara International Center	Niagara Falls, Canada	500
TV antenna	Durris, Scotland	1,000	Cathedral of Saint John the Divine	New York City	500
TV antenna	Anglia-Mendlesham, England	1,000	Funkturm Radio Antenna	West Berlin	492
ITA Antenna	Strabane, Northern Ireland	1,000	Valley of the Fallen	Near Madrid	492
Factory chimney	Cracow, Poland	985	Rouen Cathedral	France	485
Eiffel Tower (with TV antenna, 1052)	Paris	984			

EARTH'S EXTREMES

SOURCE: National Geographic Society

Wettest spot	Mt. Waialeale, Hawaii; greatest annual average, 460 inches (12-month record, Cherrapunji, India: 1,042 inches between Aug. 1860 and July 1861)
Driest spot	Atacama Desert, Chile; rainfall barely measurable
Coldest spot	Vostok, Antarctica; −127°F. recorded in 1960
Hottest spot	Al'Aziziyah, Libya; 136°F. recorded in 1922
Northernmost town ...	Ny Alesund, Spitsbergen, Norway
Southernmost town ...	Puerto Williams, Chile
Highest town	Aucanquilcha, Chile; 17,500 feet
Lowest town	Villages along the Dead Sea; 1,299 feet below sea level
Largest gorge	Grand Canyon, Colorado River, Arizona; 277 miles long, 1–20 miles wide, 1 mile deep
Deepest gorge	Hells Canyon, Snake River, Idaho; 7,900 feet deep
Strongest surface wind	231 mph; recorded in 1934 at Mount Washington, New Hampshire
Greatest tides	Bay of Fundy, Nova Scotia; 53 feet
Biggest meteor crater ..	New Quebec, Canada; 2 miles wide

PRINCIPAL WORLD ISLANDS

Island	Area (in sq. miles)	Island	Area (in sq. miles)	Island	Area (in sq. miles)
Greenland	840,000	New Caledonia (France)	6,530	Savaii (W. Samoa)	662
New Guinea	305,000	Hawaiian (U.S.)	6,450	Zanzibar (Tanzania)	641
Borneo	290,000	Nordaustlandet (Norway)	6,409	Oahu (Hawaii, U.S.)	608
Madagascar	226,400	Franz Josef Land (USSR)	6,216	Guadeloupe (France)	584
Baffin (Canada)	195,928	Kuriles (USSR)	6,025	Alands (Finland)	581
Sumatra (Indonesia)	164,000	New Hebrides	5,700	Kauai (Hawaii, U.S.)	553
Japan	145,730	Bahamas	5,382	Shetlands (U.K.)	552
Philippines	115,707	Samar (Philippines)	5,050	Rhodes (Greece)	542
New Zealand	103,736	Negros (Philippines)	4,906	Faeroes (Denmark)	540
Great Britain (U.K.)	88,764	Falklands (U.K.)	4,618	Marquesas (France)	492
Honshu (Japan)	88,000	Palawan (Philippines)	4,550	Carolines (Pacific Is.)	463
Victoria (Canada)	83,896	Panay (Philippines)	4,446	Okinawa (Japan)	454
Ellesmere (Canada)	75,767	Jamaica	4,232	Upolu (W. Samoa)	433
Celebes (Indonesia)	72,986	Aleutians (Alaska, U.S.)	4,201	Martinique (France)	425
South (N.Z.)	58,393	Hawaii (U.S.)	4,038	Tahiti (France)	402
Java (Indonesia)	48,842	Viti Levu (Fiji)	4,010	Pemba (Tanzania)	380
North (N.Z.)	44,187	Cape Breton (Canada)	3,981	Orkneys (U.K.)	372
Newfoundland (Canada)	42,031	Mindoro (Philippines)	3,759	Madeiras (Portugal)	307
Cuba	40,533	Kodiak (Alaska, U.S.)	3,670	Dominica	290
Luzon (Philippines)	40,420	Cyprus	3,572	Tonga	270
Iceland	39,768	Puerto Rico (U.S.)	3,435	Molokai (Hawaii, U.S.)	261
Mindanao (Philippines)	36,537	Corsica (France)	3,352	Bahrain	240
Moluccas (Indonesia)	32,307	New Ireland (PNG)	3,340	St. Lucia	238
Novaya Zemlya (USSR)	31,900	Crete (Greece)	3,218	Corfu (Greece)	229
Ireland	31,743	Galápagos (Ecuador)	3,075	Isle of Man (U.K.)	227
Sakhalin (USSR)	29,500	Anticosti (Canada)	3,066	Bornholm (Denmark)	227
Hispaniola (Haiti and		Wrangel (USSR)	2,819	Singapore	226
Dominican Rep.)	29,399	Hebrides (U.K.)	2,812	Guam (U.S.)	212
Hokkaido (Japan)	28,983	Canaries (Spain)	2,808	Isle Royale (Mich., U.S.)	196
Banks (Canada)	27,038	Leyte (Philippines)	2,786	Virgins (U.S.-U.K.)	192
Tasmania (Australia)	26,383	Kerguélen (France)	2,700	Marianas (excluding Guam)	
Ceylon (Sri Lanka)	25,332	Andamans (India)	2,448	(Pacific Is.)	184
Svalbard (Norway)	23,957	Guadalcanal (Solomon Islands)	2,180	Curacao (Neth. Antilles)	182
Devon (Canada)	21,331	Bali (Indonesia)	2,171	Barbados	166
Bismarck Arch. (PNG)	18,976	Prince Edward (Canada)	2,170	Isle of Wight (U.K.)	145
Marajó (Brazil)	17,991	Balearics (Spain)	1,936	Lanai (Hawaii, U.S.)	140
Tierra del Fuego (Chile		Trinidad (Trinidad & Tobago)	1,864	St. Vincent (U.K.)	131
and Argentina)	17,900	Ryukyus (Japan)	1,767	Maltese	122
Axel Heiberg (Canada)	16,671	Madura (Indonesia)	1,752	Grenada	120
Melville (Canada)	16,274	Cape Verde	1,557	Tobago (Trinidad & Tobago)	116
Southampton (Canada)	15,913	South Georgia (U.K.)	1,450	Antigua (U.K.)	108
Solomons	15,600	Euboea (Greece)	1,411	Martha's Vineyard (Mass., U.S.)	93
New Siberian Is. (USSR)	14,672	Long (N.Y., U.S.)	1,401	Elba (Italy)	87
Severnaya Zemlya (USSR)	14,285	Socotra (PDR Yemen)	1,400	Seychelles	85
New Britain (PNG)	14,100	Samoa	1,209	Channel (U.K.)	74
Taiwan (Formosa) (China)	13,836	Gotland (Sweden)	1,153	Marshalls (Pacific Is.)	70
Kyushu (Japan)	13,770	Western Samoa	1,133	Easter (Chile)	63
Hainan (China)	13,127	Manitoulin (Canada)	1,068	Staten (N.Y., U.S.)	58
Prince of Wales (Canada)	12,872	Réunion (France)	969	Tutuila (Amer. Samoa)	53
Spitsbergen (Norway)	12,355	Azores (Portugal)	902	St. Helena (U.K.)	47
Vancouver (Canada)	12,079	Isle of Pines (Cuba)	849	Nantucket (Mass., U.S.)	46
Timor	11,527	Macías Nguema Biyogo		Hong Kong	30
Sicily (Italy)	9,926	(Equat. Guinea)	779	Manhattan (N.Y., U.S.)	22
Somerset (Canada)	9,570	Tenerife (Spain)	745	Bermudas	21
Sardinia (Italy)	9,301	Maui (Hawaii, U.S.)	729	Iwo Jima (Japan)	7.8
Fiji	7,055	Mauritius	720	Nauru	7.7
Shikoku (Japan)	6,860	Skye (U.K.)	670	Governors (N.Y., U.S.)	180 acres

GEOGRAPHIC CENTERS OF THE UNITED STATES

SOURCE: U.S. Geological Survey

Because there is neither a generally accepted definition of a geographic center nor a completely satisfactory method for determining it, there may be as many geographic centers of a state or country as there are definitions of the term.

No marked or monumented point has been established by any government agency as the geographic center of either the 50 states, the conterminous United States, or the North American Continent. However, a monument was erected in Lebanon, Kansas, by a group of citizens who had hired engineers to determine the "geographic center" of the United States.

Sometimes confused with the geographic center of the United States is the reference point for all property lines and city, county, State, and international boundaries on the North American Continent that are tied to the National Triangulation networks of the United States, Canada, Mexico, and Central America. This point

is Meades Ranch Triangulation station located at latitude 39°13'26.686", longitude 98°32'30.506", about 12 miles north of Lucas, Kansas. It is the base point or origin of geodetic positions and directions in the triangulation net of the United States because it is at the junction of the main east-west transcontinental triangulation arc stretching from the Atlantic to the Pacific Coasts and the main north-south arc, which follows approximately the 98th meridian from the Canadian border to the Rio Grande.

In determining the centers of the states, islands adjacent to their coastlines and large bodies of water on their boundaries were excluded.

The geographic centers and positions listed below should be considered as estimates. The center of the United States (without Alaska and Hawaii) is approximately Lebanon, Kansas.

Center	Latitude (N)	Longitude (W)
Conterminous United States (48 States) Near Lebanon, Smith County, Kansas	39°50'	98°35'
Continental United States (49 States) Near Castle Rock, Butte County, South Dakota ...	44°59'	103°38'

Center	Latitude (N)	Longitude (W)
The United States (50 States) West of Castle Rock, Butte County, South Dakota	44°58'	103°46'
North American Continent 6 miles west of Balta, Pierce County, North Dakota	48°10'	100°10'

State	Geographic Center
Alabama	12 miles southwest of Clanton
Alaska	63°50'N., 152°00'W., 60 miles north-west of Mt. McKinley
Arizona	55 miles east-southeast of Prescott
Arkansas	12 miles northwest of Little Rock
California	35 miles east of Madera
Colorado	30 miles northwest of Pikes Peak
Connecticut	at East Berlin
Delaware	11 miles south of Dover
District of Columbia ..	near Fourth and L Streets NW
Florida	12 miles north-northwest of Brooksville
Georgia	18 miles southeast of Macon
Hawaii	20°15'N., 156°20'W., off Maui Island
Idaho	at Custer, southwest of Challis
Illinois	28 miles northeast of Springfield
Indiana	14 miles north-northwest of Indianapolis
Iowa	5 miles northeast of Ames
Kansas	15 miles northeast of Great Bend
Kentucky	3 miles north-northwest of Lebanon
Louisiana	3 miles southeast of Marksville
Maine	18 miles north of Dover-Foxcroft
Maryland	4½ miles northwest of Davidsonville
Massachusetts	north part of city of Worcester
Michigan	5 miles north-northwest of Cadillac
Minnesota	10 miles southwest of Brainerd
Mississippi ......:...	9 miles west-northwest of Carthage

State	Geographic Center
Missouri	20 miles southwest of Jefferson City
Montana	12 miles west of Lewistown
Nebraska	10 miles northwest of Broken Bow
Nevada	26 miles southeast of Austin
New Hampshire	3 miles east of Ashland
New Jersey	5 miles southeast of Trenton
New Mexico	12 miles south-southwest of Willard
New York	12+ miles south of Oneida and 26+ miles southwest of Utica
North Carolina	10 miles northwest of Sanford
North Dakota	5 miles southwest of McClusky
Ohio	25 miles north-northeast of Columbus
Oklahoma	8 miles north of Oklahoma City
Oregon	25 miles south-southeast of Prineville
Pennsylvania	2½ miles southwest of Bellefonte
Rhode Island	1 mile south-southwest of Crompton
South Carolina	13 miles southeast of Columbia
South Dakota	8 miles northeast of Pierre
Tennessee	5 miles northeast of Murfreesboro
Texas	15 miles northeast of Brady
Utah	3 miles north of Manti
Vermont	3 miles east of Roxbury
Virginia	5 miles southwest of Buckingham
Washington	10 miles west-southwest of Wenatchee
West Virginia	4 miles east of Sutton
Wisconsin	9 miles southeast of Marshfield
Wyoming	58 miles east-northeast of Lander

EXTREME POINTS OF THE UNITED STATES

SOURCE: U.S. Geological Survey

The geographic center of an area may be defined as the center of gravity of the surface, or that point on which the surface of the area would balance if it were a cardboardlike plane of uniform thickness. Extreme points are measured from the various

centers of the U.S. Because many factors, such as curvature of the earth, large bodies of water, and irregular surfaces, affect the determination of centers of gravity, the following positions should be considered as approximations only.

Location	Direction from Geographic Center	Coordinates Latitude (N)	Longitude (W)	Distance from Geographic Center (in miles)
From geographic center of United States near Lebanon, Smith County, Kansas, 39°50', 98°35' to—				
Lake of the Woods, Minnesota	Northeast	49°23'	95°09'	680
Key West, Florida	Southeast	24°33'	81°48'	1,436
West Quoddy Head, Maine	East	44°49'	66°57'	1,640
Cape Alava, Washington	West	48°10'	124°44'	1,412
From geographic center of United States (including Alaska) near Castle Rock, Butte County, S.D., 44°59', 103°38' to—				
Point Barrow, Alaska	Northwest	71°23'	156°29'	2,504
Key West, Florida	Southeast	24°33'	81°48'	1,865
West Quoddy Head, Maine	East	44°49'	66°57'	1,779
Cape Wrangell, Attu Island, Alaska	Northwest	52°55'	172°27'(E)	3,623
From geographic center of United States (including Alaska and Hawaii) west of Castle Rock, S.D., 44°58', 103°46' to—				
Point Barrow, Alaska	Northwest	71°23'	156°29'	2,502
Ka Lae (South Cape), Hawaii Island, Hawaii	Southwest	18°56'	155°41'	3,456
West Quoddy Head, Maine	East	44°49'	66°57'	1,785
Cape Wrangell, Attu Island, Alaska	Northwest	52°55'	172°27'(E)	3,620

U.S. COASTLINE & SHORELINE Source: National Ocean Survey, National Oceanic and Atmospheric Administration

General coastline figures represent lengths of the seacoast outline. The coastlines of sounds and of bays are included to a point where they narrow to the width of 30 minutes of latitude, and the distance across at such point is included. Tidal shorelines include the outer coast, offshore islands, sounds, bays, and rivers to the head of tidewater or to a point where tidal waters narrow to a width of 100 feet.

	Coastline	Shoreline
UNITED STATES	12,383	88,633
(without Alaska and Hawaii)	4,993	53,677
Atlantic	2,069	28,673
Maine	228	3,478
New Hampshire	13	131
Massachusetts	192	1,519
Rhode Island	40	384
Connecticut	—	618
New York	127	1,850
New Jersey	130	1,792
Pennsylvania	—	89
Delaware	28	381
Maryland	31	3,190
Virginia	112	3,315
North Carolina	301	3,375
South Carolina	187	2,876
Georgia	100	2,344
Florida (Atlantic only)	580	3,331
Gulf of Mexico	1,631	17,141
Florida (Gulf only)	770	5,095
Alabama	53	607
Mississippi	44	359
Louisiana	397	7,721
Texas	367	3,359

	Coastline	Shoreline
Pacific	7,623	40,298
California	840	3,427
Oregon	296	1,410
Washington	157	3,026
Hawaii	750	1,052
Alaska (Pacific only)	5,580	31,383
Alaska (Arctic only)	1,060	2,521
EXTRATERRITORIAL		
Canal Zone	20	126
Atlantic		
Navassa	5	5
Puerto Rico	311	700
Virgin Islands	117	175
Pacific		
Baker Island	3	3
Guam Islands	78	110
Howland Island	4	4
Jarvis Island	5	5
Johnston Island	5	5
Midway Island	20	33
Palmyra Island	9	16
Samoa Islands	76	126
Wake Island	12	20

AVERAGE AND EXTREME U.S. ELEVATIONS Source: U.S. Geological Survey

State or Territory	Mean Elevation (feet)	HIGH Point	Mean Elevation (feet)	LOW Point	Mean Elevation (feet)
Alabama	500	Cheaha Mountain	2,407	Gulf of Mexico	(1)
Alaska	1,900	Mount McKinley	20,320	Pacific Ocean	(1)
American Samoa	1,300	Lata Mountain (Tau I.)	3,160	Pacific Ocean	(1)
Arizona	4,100	Humphreys Peak	12,633	Colorado River	70
Arkansas	650	Magazine Mountain	2,753	Ouachita River	55
California	2,900	Mount Whitney	14,494	Death Valley	—282
Canal Zone	280	Cerro Galera	1,205	Atlantic Ocean	(1)
Colorado	6,800	Mount Elbert	14,433	Arkansas River	3,350
Connecticut	500	Mount Frissell (So. Slope)	2,380	Long Island Sound	(1)
Delaware	60	On Ebright Road (New Castle County)	442	Atlantic Ocean	(1)
Florida	100	Sec. 30, T. 6N., R. 20W.	345	Atlantic Ocean	(1)
Georgia	600	Brasstown Bald	4,784	Atlantic Ocean	(1)
Guam	330	Mount Lamlam	1,329	Pacific Ocean	(1)
Hawaii	3,030	Mauna Kea	13,796	Pacific Ocean	(1)
Idaho	5,000	Borah Peak	12,662	Snake River	710
Illinois	600	Charles Mound	1,235	Mississippi River	279
Indiana	700	Franklin Township (Wayne County)	1,257	Ohio River	320
Iowa	1,100	Sec. 29, T. 100 N., R. 41 W.	1,670	Mississippi River	480
Kansas	2,000	Mount Sunflower	4,039	Verdigris River	680
Kentucky	750	Black Mountain	4,145	Mississippi River	257
Louisiana	100	Driskill Mountain	535	New Orleans	—5
Maine	600	Mount Katahdin	5,268	Atlantic Ocean	(1)
Maryland	350	Backbone Mountain	3,360	Atlantic Ocean	(1)
Massachusetts	500	Mount Greylock	3,491	Atlantic Ocean	(1)
Michigan	900	Mount Curwood	1,980	Lake Erie	572
Minnesota	1,200	Eagle Mountain	2,301	Lake Superior	602
Mississippi	300	Woodall Mountain	806	Gulf of Mexico	(1)
Missouri	800	Taum Sauk Mountain	1,772	St. Francis River	230
Montana	3,400	Granite Peak	12,799	Kootenai River	1,800
Nebraska	2,600	Johnson Township (Kimball County)	5,426	SE corner of state	840
Nevada	5,500	Boundary Peak	13,143	Colorado River	470
New Hampshire	1,000	Mount Washington	6,288	Atlantic Ocean	(1)
New Jersey	250	High Point	1,803	Atlantic Ocean	(1)
New Mexico	5,700	Wheeler Peak	13,161	Red Bluff Reservoir	2,817
New York	1,000	Mount Marcy	5,344	Atlantic Ocean	(1)
North Carolina	700	Mount Mitchell	6,684	Atlantic Ocean	(1)
North Dakota	1,900	White Butte	3,506	Red River	750
Ohio	850	Campbell Hill	1,550	Ohio River	433
Oklahoma	1,300	Black Mesa	4,973	Little River	287
Oregon	3,300	Mount Hood	11,235	Pacific Ocean	(1)
Pennsylvania	1,100	Mount Davis	3,213	Delaware River	(1)
Puerto Rico	1,800	Cerro de Punta	4,389	Atlantic Ocean	(1)
Rhode Island	200	Jerimoth Hill	812	Atlantic Ocean	(1)
South Carolina	350	Sassafras Mountain	3,560	Atlantic Ocean	(1)
South Dakota	2,200	Harney Peak	7,242	Big Stone Lake	962
Tennessee	900	Clingmans Dome	6,643	Mississippi River	182
Texas	1,700	Guadalupe Peak	8,751	Gulf of Mexico	(1)
Utah	6,100	Kings Peak	13,528	Beaverdam Creek	2,000
Vermont	1,000	Mount Mansfield	4,393	Lake Champlain	95
Virginia	950	Mount Rogers	5,729	Atlantic Ocean	(1)
Virgin Islands	750	Crown Mountain (St. Thomas)	1,556	Atlantic Ocean	(1)
Washington	1,700	Mount Rainier	14,410	Pacific Ocean	(1)
West Virginia	1,500	Spruce Knob	4,862	Potomac River	240
Wisconsin	1,050	Timms Hill	1,952	Lake Michigan	581
Wyoming	6,700	Gannett Peak	13,804	Belle Fourche River	3,100

(1) = Sea level.

PRINCIPAL U.S. RIVERS

Source: U.S. Geological Survey

River	Empties Into:	Length (in miles)	River	Empties Into:	Length (in miles)
Mississippi-Missouri-Red Rock	Gulf of Mexico	3,741	Cumberland	Ohio River	687
Missouri-Red Rock	Mississippi River	2,564	White (Mo.-Ark.)	Mississippi River	685
Mississippi	Gulf of Mexico	2,348	North Platte	Platte River	680
Missouri	Mississippi River	2,315	Yellowstone	Missouri River	671
Yukon (U.S.-Canada)	Bering Sea	1,979	Tennessee	Ohio River	652
St. Lawrence (U.S.-Canada)	Atlantic Ocean	1,900	Mobile-Alabama-Coosa	Gulf of Mexico	639
Rio Grande (U.S.-Mexico)	Gulf of Mexico	1,885	Gila	Colorado River	630
Arkansas	Mississippi River	1,450	Washita	Red River	626
Colorado (U.S.-Mexico)	Gulf of California	1,450	Ouachita	Red River	605
Brazos	Gulf of Mexico	1,309	Little Missouri	Missouri River	560
Ohio-Allegheny	Mississippi River	1,306	Smoky Hill	Kansas River	560
Columbia (U.S.-Canada)	Pacific Ocean	1,243	Porcupine (U.S.-Canada)	Yukon River	555
Red (Okla.-Tex.-Ark.-La.)	Mississippi River	1,222	Koyukuk	Yukon River	554
Mississippi, Upper	to mouth of Missouri River	1,171	Red River of the North (U.S.-Canada)	Lake Winnipeg	545
Snake	Columbia River	1,000	Tombigbee	Mobile River	525
Ohio	Mississippi River	981	Apalachicola-Chattahoochee	Gulf of Mexico	524
Pecos	Rio Grande	926	White (S. Dak.-Nebr.)	Missouri River	507
Canadian	Arkansas River	906	Osage-Marais des Cygnes	Missouri River	496
Tennessee-N. Fk. Holston	Ohio River	900	Pend Oreille-Clark Fork	Columbia River	490
Colorado (Texas)	Gulf of Mexico	894	Pearl	Gulf of Mexico	490
Columbia, Upper (U.S.-Canada)	to mouth of Snake River	890	Powder	Yellowstone River	486
Kuskokwim	Bering Sea	800	Kootenai (U.S.-Canada)	Columbia River	485
Tanana	Yukon River	800	Wabash	Ohio River	475
North Canadian	Canadian River	784	Innoko	Yukon River	463
Kansas-Republican-Arikaree	Missouri River	743	Susquehanna	Chesapeake Bay	458
Green (Wyo.-Colo.-Utah)	Colorado River	730	Neosho	Arkansas River	450
Milk (U.S.-Canada)	Missouri River	729	South Platte	Platte River	442
Trinity	Gulf of Mexico	715	Santee-Wateree-Catawba	Atlantic Ocean	438
James (N. Dak.-S. Dak.)	Missouri River	710	Pee Dee-Yadkin	Atlantic Ocean	435
Cimarron	Arkansas River	698	Niobrara	Missouri River	431
			Wisconsin	Mississippi River	430

LARGE U.S. LAKES

Source: U.S. Geological Survey and Statistics Canada

Natural U.S. lakes with areas of 100 sq. mi. or more are listed

Lake	State	Area (sq. mi.)	Lake	State	Area (sq. mi.)
Superior	Canada, Minnesota, Wisconsin, and Michigan	31,700	Teshekpuk	Alaska	315
Huron	Canada and Michigan	23,010	Naknek	Alaska	242
Michigan	Wisconsin, Illinois, Indiana, and Michigan	22,300	Winnebago	Wisconsin	215
			Mille Lacs	Minnesota	207
			Flathead	Montana	197
Erie	Canada, Michigan, Ohio, Pennsylvania, and New York	9,910	Tahoe	California and Nevada	193
Ontario	Canada and New York	7,340	Leech	Minnesota	176
Great Salt[a]	Utah	1,685[b]	Pyramid[a]	Nevada	172[b]
Lake of the Woods	Minnesota and Canada	1,679	Pend Oreille	Idaho	148
Iliamna	Alaska	1,000	Ugashik (Upper and Lower)	Alaska	147
Okeechobee	Florida	700	Upper Klamath	Oregon	142
Pontchartrain[a]	Louisiana	625	Utah	Utah	140
Becharof	Alaska	458	Bear (including Mud Lake)	Idaho and Utah	136
Red Lake (Upper and Lower)	Minnesota	451	Yellowstone	Wyoming	134
Champlain	New York, Vermont, and Canada	435	Moosehead	Maine	117
St. Clair	Michigan and Canada	432	Tustumena	Alaska	117
Salton Sea[a]	California	374[b]	Clark	Alaska	110
Rainy	Minnesota and Canada	360	Winnibigoshish	Minnesota	109
			Dall	Alaska	100

[a] Salty.   [b] Variable.

HIGHEST U.S. MOUNTAIN PEAKS

Source: U.S. Geological Survey

Peak	State	Elevation	Peak	State	Elevation	Peak	State	Elevation
Mt. McKinley	Alaska	20,320	La Plata Peak	Colorado	14,336	Mt. Shasta	California	14,162
Mt. St. Elias	Alaska	18,008	Uncompahgre			Mt. Sill	California	14,162
Mt. Foraker	Alaska	17,400	Peak	Colorado	14,309	El Diente Peak	Colorado	14,159
Mt. Blackburn	Alaska	16,523	Crestone Peak	Colorado	14,294	Maroon Peak	Colorado	14,156
Mt. Bona	Alaska	16,421	Mt. Lincoln	Colorado	14,286	Tabeguache Mtn.	Colorado	14,155
Mt. Sanford	Alaska	16,237	Grays Peak	Colorado	14,270	Mt. Oxford	Colorado	14,153
South Buttress	Alaska	15,885	Mt. Antero	Colorado	14,269	Mt. Sneffels	Colorado	14,150
Mt. Vancouver	Alaska	15,700	Torreys Peak	Colorado	14,267	Mt. Democrat	Colorado	14,148
Mt. Churchill	Alaska	15,638	Castle Peak	Colorado	14,265	Capitol Peak	Colorado	14,130
Mt. Fairweather	Alaska	15,300	Quandary Peak	Colorado	14,265	Pikes Peak	Colorado	14,110
Mt. Hubbard	Alaska	15,015	Mt. Evans	Colorado	14,264	Snowmass Mtn.	Colorado	14,092
Mt. Bear	Alaska	14,831	Longs Peak	Colorado	14,255	Windom Peak	Colorado	14,087
East Buttress	Alaska	14,730	Mt. Wilson	Colorado	14,246	Mt. Russell	California	14,086
Mt. Hunter	Alaska	14,573	White Mtn.	California	14,246	Mt. Eolus	Colorado	14,084
Mt. Alverstone	Alaska	14,565	North Palisade	California	14,242	Mt. Columbia	Colorado	14,073
Browne Tower	Alaska	14,530	Shavano Peak	Colorado	14,229	Mt. Augusta	Alaska	14,070
Mt. Whitney	California	14,494	Mt. Belford	Colorado	14,197	Missouri Mtn.	Colorado	14,067
Mt. Elbert	Colorado	14,433	Mt. Princeton	Colorado	14,197	Humboldt Peak	Colorado	14,064
Mt. Massive	Colorado	14,421	Crestone Needle	Colorado	14,197	Mt. Bierstadt	Colorado	14,060
Mt. Harvard	Colorado	14,420	Mt. Yale	Colorado	14,196	Sunlight Peak	Colorado	14,059
Mt. Rainier	Washington	14,410	Mt. Bross	Colorado	14,172	Handies Peak	California	14,058
Mt. Williamson	California	14,375	Kit Carson Mtn.	Colorado	14,165	Split Mt.	Colorado	14,048
Blanca Peak	Colorado	14,345	Mt. Wrangell	Alaska	14,163	Culebra Peak	Colorado	14,047

U.S. TEMPERATURE EXTREMES

SOURCE: National Oceanic and Atmospheric Administration

HIGHEST TEMPERATURES

Greenland Ranch, Calif., with 134° on July 10, 1913, holds the record for the highest temperature ever officially recorded in the United States. This station is located in Death Valley, which is about 140 miles long, four to 16 miles wide, and runs north and south in southeastern California and southwestern Nevada. Death Valley is below sea level and flanked by towering mountain ranges with Mt. Whitney, rising to 14,495 feet, less than 100 miles to the west. It has the hottest summers in the Western Hemisphere and is the only known place in the United States where nighttime temperatures sometimes remain above 100°.

In the United States the station normally having the highest annual average is Key West, Fla., 78.2°; the highest summer average, Death Valley, Calif., 98.2°; and the highest winter average, Key West, Fla., 70.2°.

Amazing temperature rises of 40° to 50° in a few minutes occasionally may be brought about by Chinook winds. Some outstanding extreme temperature rises in short periods are:

12 hours: 83°, Granville, N. Dak., Feb. 21, 1918, from —33° to 50° from early morning to late afternoon.

15 minutes: 42°, Fort Assiniboine, Mont., Jan. 19, 1892, from —5° to 37°.

7 minutes: 34°, Kipp, Mont., Dec. 1, 1896; observer also reported that a total rise of 80° occurred in a few hours and that 30 inches of snow disappeared in one-half day.

2 minutes: 49°, Spearfish, S. Dak., Jan. 22, 1943, from —4° at 7:30 a.m., to 45° at 7:32 a.m.

HIGHEST TEMPERATURES IN CONTERMINOUS UNITED STATES BY MONTHS

Month	Temp. (°F.)	Year	Day	State	Place	Elevation Feet	Month	Temp. (°F.)	Year	Day	State	Place	Elevation Feet
Jan.ᵃ	98	1936	17	Texas	Laredo	421	July	134	1913	10	Calif.	Greenland Ranch	—178
Feb.ᵃ	105	1963	3	Ariz.	Montezuma	735	Aug.†	127	1933	12	Calif.	Greenland Ranch	—178
Mar.ᵃ	108	1954	31	Texas	Rio Grande City	168	Sept.	126	1950	2	Calif.	Mecca	—175
Apr.	118	1898	25	Calif.	Volcano Springs	—220	Oct.*	116	1917	5	Ariz.	Sentinel	685
May*	124	1896	27	Calif.	Salton	—263	Nov.*	105	1906	12	Calif.	Craftonville	1,759
June°†	127	1896	15	Ariz.	Ft. Mohave	555	Dec.	100	1938	8	Calif.	La Mesa	539

* Two or more occurrences, most recent given. † Slightly higher temperatures in old records are not used owing to lack of information.

RECORD HIGHEST TEMPERATURES BY STATES

State	Temp. (°F.)	Date	Station	Elevation Feet	State	Temp. (°F.)	Date	Station	Elevation Feet
Ala.	112	Sept. 5, 1925	Centerville	345	Mo.	118	July 14, 1954*	Warsaw & Union	687–560
Alaska	100	June 27, 1915	Fort Yukon	—	Mont.	117	July 5, 1937	Medicine Lake	1,950
Ariz.	127	July 7, 1905*	Parker	345	Nebr.	118	July 24, 1936*	Minden	2,169
Ark.	120	Aug. 10, 1936	Ozark	396	Nev.	122	June 23, 1954*	Overton	1,240
Calif.	134	July 10, 1913	Greenland Ranch	—178	N.H.	106	July 4, 1911	Nashua	125
Colo.	118	July 11, 1888	Bennett		N.J.	110	July 10, 1936	Runyon	18
Conn.	105	July 22, 1926	Waterbury	400	N. Mex.	116	July 14, 1934*	Orogrande	4,171
Del.	110	July 21, 1930	Millsboro	20	N.Y.	108	July 22, 1926	Troy	35
D.C.	106	July 20, 1930*	Washington	112	N.C.	109	Sept. 7, 1954*	Weldon	81
Fla.	109	June 29, 1931	Monticello	207	N. Dak.	121	July 6, 1936	Steele	1,857
Ga.	112	July 24, 1952	Louisville	337	Ohio	113	July 21, 1934*	Gallipolis (near)	673
Hawaii	100	Apr. 27, 1931	Pahala	850	Okla.	120	July 26, 1943*	Tishomingo	670
Idaho	118	July 28, 1934	Orofino	1,027.	Oreg.	119	Aug. 10, 1898*	Pendleton	1,074
Ill.	117	July 14, 1954	E. St. Louis	410	Pa.	111	July 10, 1936*	Phoenixville	100
Ind.	116	July 14, 1936	Collegeville	672	R.I.	102	July 30, 1949	Greenville	420
Iowa	118	July 20, 1934	Keokuk	614	S.C.	111	June 28, 1954*	Camden	170
Kans.	121	July 24, 1936*	Alton (near)	1,651	S. Dak.	120	July 5, 1936	Gannvalley	1,750
Ky.	114	July 28, 1930	Greensburg	581	Tenn.	113	Aug. 9, 1930*	Perryville	377
La.	114	Aug. 10, 1936	Plain Dealing	268	Tex.	120	Aug. 12, 1936	Seymour	1,291
Maine	105	July 10, 1911*	North Bridgton	450	Utah	116	June 28, 1892	Saint George	2,880
Md.	109	July 10, 1936*	Cumberland & Frederick	623–325	Vt.	105	July 4, 1911	Vernon	310
					Va.	110	July 15, 1954	Balcony Falls	725
Mass.	106	July 4, 1911*	Lawrence	51	Wash.	118	Aug. 5, 1961*	Ice Harbor Dam	475
Mich.	112	July 13, 1936	Mio	963	W. Va.	112	July 10, 1936*	Martinsburg	435
Minn.	114	July 6, 1936*	Moorhead	904	Wis.	114	July 13, 1936	Wisconsin Dells	900
Miss.	115	July 29, 1930	Holly Springs	600	Wyo.	114	July 12, 1900	Basin	3,500

* Also on earlier dates at the same or other places.

LOWEST TEMPERATURES

In the United States, the lowest temperature on record, —79.8°, was recorded at Prospect Creek Camp, which is located in the Endicott Mountains of northern Alaska. The lowest temperature in the 48 states, —69.7°, occurred at Rogers Pass (Lewis and Clark County, Montana), which is mountainous and heavily forested terrain, about a half mile east of and 140 feet below the summit of the Continental Divide.

The lowest average annual temperature recorded in the United States is 9.3° at Barrow, Alaska, on the Arctic coast. Barrow also has the coolest summers (June, July, August) with an average of 36.4°. The lowest average winter (December, January, February) temperature is —15.7° at Barter Island on the Arctic coast of northeast Alaska. In Hawaii, average annual temperatures range from 44.0° at Mauna Loa Slope Observatory (elevation 11,146 feet) on the island of Hawaii to 76.6° at Honolulu on the island of Oahu.

In the 48 states, Mt. Washington, N.H. (elevation 6,262 feet) has the lowest mean annual temperature, 26.9° F, and the lowest mean summer (June, July, August) temperature, 46.8°. A few stations in the Northeast and upper Rockies have mean annuals in the high 30's, and at the same stations in the latter

area summers may average in the high 40's. Winter (December, January, February) mean temperatures are lowest in northeastern North Dakota where the average is 5.9° at the Langdon Experiment Farm and northwestern Minnesota where the average is 6.1° at Hallock.

In continental areas of the Temperate Zone, 40° to 50° temperature falls in a few hours caused by advection (horizontal shifting) of cold air masses are not uncommon. Following these large drops, radiation sometimes may cause a further temperature fall resulting in remarkable changes. Some outstanding extreme temperature falls are:

24 hours: 100°, Browning, Mont., Jan. 23–24, 1916, from 44° to —56°.

12 hours: 84°, Fairfield, Mont., Dec. 24, 1924, from 63° at noon to —21° at midnight.

2 hours: 62°, Rapid City, S. Dak., Jan. 12, 1911, from 49° at 6 a.m., to —13° at 8 a.m.

27 minutes: 58°, Spearfish, S. Dak., Jan. 22, 1943, from 54° at 9 a.m., to —4° at 9:27 a.m.

15 minutes: 47°, Rapid City, S. Dak., Jan. 10, 1911, from 55° at 7 a.m. to 8° at 7:15 a.m.

LOWEST TEMPERATURES IN CONTERMINOUS UNITED STATES BY MONTHS

Month	Temp. (°F.)	Year	Day	State	Place	Elevation Feet	Month	Temp. (°F.)	Year	Day	State	Place	Elevation Feet
Jan.	−70	1954	20	Mont.	Rogers Pass	5,470	July*	10	1911	21	Wyo.	Painter	6,800
Feb.	−66	1933	9	Mont.	Riverside	6,700	Aug.*	5	1910	25	Mont.	Bowen	6,080
Mar.	−50	1906	17	Wyo.	Snake River	6,862	Sept.*	−9	1926	24	Mont.	Riverside	6,700
Apr.	−36	1945	5	N. Mex.	Eagle Nest	8,250	Oct.	−33	1917	29	Wyo.	Soda Butte	6,600
May	−15	1964	7	Calif.	White Mtn. 2	12,470	Nov.	−53	1959	16	Mont.	Lincoln 14 NE	5,130
June	2	1907	13	Calif.	Tamarack	8,000	Dec.*	−59	1924	19	Mont.	Riverside	6,700

* Two or more occurrences, most recent given.

RECORD LOWEST TEMPERATURES BY STATES

State	Temp. (°F.)	Date	Station	Elevation Feet	State	Temp. (°F.)	Date	Station	Elevation Feet
Ala.	−24	Jan. 31, 1966	Russellville	880	Nebr.	−47	Feb. 12, 1899	Camp Clarke	3,700
Alaska	−80	Jan. 23, 1971	Prospect Creek Camp	1,100	Nev.	−50	Jan. 8, 1937	San Jacinto	5,200
Ariz.	−40	Jan. 7, 1971	Hawley Lake	8,180	N.H.	−46	Jan. 28, 1925	Pittsburg	1,575
Ark.	−29	Feb. 13, 1905	Pond	1,250	N.J.	−34	Jan. 5, 1904	River Vale	70
Cal.	−45	Jan. 20, 1937	Boca	5,532	N. Mex.	−50	Feb. 1, 1951	Gavilan	7,350
Colo.	−60	Feb. 1, 1951	Taylor Park	9,206	N.Y.	−52	Feb. 9, 1934	Stillwater Reservoir	1,670
Conn.	−32	Feb. 16, 1943	Falls Village	585	N.C.	−29	Jan. 30, 1966	Mt. Mitchell	6,525
Del.	−17	Jan. 17, 1893	Millsboro	20	N. Dak.	−60	Feb. 15, 1936	Parshall	1,929
D.C.	−15	Feb. 11, 1899	Washington	112	Ohio	−39	Feb. 10, 1899	Milligan	800
Fla.	− 2	Feb. 13, 1899	Tallahassee	193	Okla.	−27	Jan. 18, 1930*	Watts	958
Ga.	−17	Jan. 27, 1940	CCC Camp F-16	—	Oreg.	−54	Feb. 10, 1933*	Seneca	4,700
Hawaii	14	Jan. 2, 1961	Haleakala, Maui Island	9,750	Pa.	−42	Jan. 5, 1904	Smethport	—
Idaho	−60	Jan. 18, 1943	Island Park Dam	6,285	R.I.	−23	Jan. 11, 1942	Kingston	100
Ill.	−35	Jan. 22, 1930	Mount Carroll	817	S.C.	−13	Jan. 26, 1940	Longcreek (near)	1,631
Ind.	−35	Feb. 2, 1951	Greensburg	954	S. Dak.	−58	Feb. 17, 1936	McIntosh	2,277
Iowa	−47	Jan. 12, 1912	Washta	1,157	Tenn.	−32	Dec. 30, 1917	Mountain City	2,471
Kans.	−40	Feb. 13, 1905	Lebanon	1,812	Tex.	−23	Feb. 8, 1933*	Seminole	3,275
Ky.	−34	Jan. 28, 1963	Cynthiana	684	Utah	−50	Jan. 5, 1913*	Strawberry Tunnel east portal	7,650
La.	−16	Feb. 13, 1899	Minden	194	Vt.	−50	Dec. 30, 1933	Bloomfield	915
Maine	−48	Jan. 19, 1925	Van Buren	510	Va.	−29	Feb. 10, 1899	Monterey	—
Md.	−40	Jan. 13, 1912	Oakland	2,461	Wash.	−48	Dec. 30, 1968	Mazama	2,120
Mass.	−34	Jan. 18, 1957	Birch Hill Dam	840				Winthrop	1,765
Mich.	−51	Feb. 9, 1934	Vanderbilt	785	W. Va.	−37	Dec. 30, 1917	Lewisburg	2,200
Minn.	−59	Feb. 16, 1903*	Pokegama Dam	1,280	Wis.	−54	Jan. 24, 1922	Danbury	908
Miss.	−19	Jan. 30, 1966	Corinth	420	Wyo.	−63	Feb. 9, 1933	Moran	6,770
Mo.	−40	Feb. 13, 1905	Warsaw	700					
Mont.	−70	Jan. 20, 1954	Rogers Pass	5,470					

* Also on earlier dates at the same or other places.

WIND CHILL

Source: National Oceanic and Atmosphereic Administration

A very strong wind combined with a temperature slightly below freezing can have the same chilling effect as a temperature nearly 50°F lower in a calm atmosphere. Arctic explorers and military experts have developed what is called the "wind-chill factor," which shows the combined effects of wind and temperature as equivalent calm-air temperatures. In effect, the index describes the cooling power of the air on exposed flesh. The wind-chill table here shows this cooling power for various combinations of wind and temperature, and will help you gauge how much protection you really need.

Directions: 1) Find actual (calm) air temperature across top of table. 2) Determine wind speed and follow across to correct calm-air temperature. Number given is equivalent temperature.

For example, a 10° temperature with a 20 mph wind equals the equivalent of −24 degrees.

WIND CHILL

Equivalent Temperatures (°F)

Calm	35	30	25	20	15	10	5	0	−5	−10	−15	−20	−25	−30	−35	−40	−45
5	33	27	21	16	12	7	1	−6	−11	−15	−20	−26	−31	−35	−41	−47	−54
10	21	16	9	2	−2	−9	−15	−22	−27	−31	−38	−45	−52	−58	−64	−70	−77
15	16	11	1	−6	−11	−18	−25	−33	−40	−45	−51	−60	−65	−70	−78	−85	−90
20	12	3	−4	−9	−17	−24	−32	−40	−46	−52	−60	−68	−76	−81	−88	−96	−103
25	7	0	−7	−15	−22	−29	−37	−45	−52	−58	−67	−75	−83	−89	−96	−104	−112
30	5	−2	−11	−18	−26	−33	−41	−49	−56	−63	−70	−78	−87	−94	−101	−109	−117
35	3	−4	−13	−20	−27	−35	−43	−52	−60	−67	−72	−83	−90	−98	−105	−113	−123
40	1	−4	−15	−22	−29	−36	−45	−54	−62	−69	−76	−87	−94	−101	−107	−116	−128
45	1	−6	−17	−24	−31	−38	−46	−54	−63	−70	−78	−87	−94	−101	−108	−118	−128
50	0	−7	−17	−24	−31	−38	−47	−56	−63	−70	−79	−88	−96	−103	−110	−120	−128

Windspeed (Miles per hour)

VERY COLD

BITTER COLD

EXTREME COLD

U.S. CITY WEATHER | Source: National Climatic Center

City	Record Temperature High (F°)	Record Temperature Low (F°)	Precip. (Water equiv.) (in.)	Snow and Sleet (in.)	Wind Speed (mph)	First Freeze Date 32 F° or less Average	First Freeze Date 32 F° or less Earliest on record	Last Freeze Date 32 F° or less Average	Last Freeze Date 32 F° or less Latest on record	Elevation of Station (feet)
Albany	104	—28	36.46	65.7	8.8	Oct. 13	Sept. 23	Apr. 27	May 20	292
Albuquerque	105	—17	8.33	10.7	9.0	Oct. 29	Oct. 11	Apr. 16	May 18	5,314
Atlanta	103	— 9	48.66	1.5	9.1	Nov. 12	Oct. 24	Mar. 24	Apr. 15	1,034
Baltimore	107	— 7	41.62	21.9	9.5	Oct. 26	Oct. 8	Apr. 15	May 11	155
Birmingham	107	—10	53.46	1.2	7.4	Nov. 10	Oct. 17	Mar. 17	Apr. 21	630
Bismarck	114	—45	16.15	38.4	10.6	Sept. 22	Sept. 6	May 11	May 30	1,660
Boise	111	—23	11.97	21.7	9.0	Oct. 12	Sept. 9	May 6	May 31	2,868
Boston	104	—18	41.55	41.9	12.6	Nov. 7	Oct. 5	Apr. 8	May 3	29
Buffalo	99	—21	35.19	88.6	12.3	Oct. 25	Sept. 23	Apr. 30	May 24	706
Burlington, Vt.	101	—30	32.54	78.4	8.8	Oct. 3	Sept. 13	May 10	May 24	340
Charleston, W. Va.	108	—24	43.66	28.8	6.5	Oct. 28	Sept. 29	Apr. 18	May 11	951
Charlotte	104	— 5	45.00	5.6	7.6	Nov. 4	Oct. 15	Apr. 2	Apr. 16	769
Cheyenne	100	—38	14.48	52.0	13.3	Sept. 27	Aug. 25	May 18	June 18	6,141
Chicago	105	—23	33.47	40.7	10.3	Oct. 26	Sept. 25	Apr. 20	May 14	623
Cincinnati	102	—19	40.40	23.2	9.1	Oct. 25	Sept. 28	Apr. 15	May 25	877
Cleveland	103	—19	34.15	51.5	10.8	Nov. 2	Sept. 29	Apr. 21	May 14	805
Columbia, S.C.	107	— 2	45.23	1.8	6.9	Nov. 3	Oct. 4	Mar. 30	Apr. 21	225
Columbus, Ohio	106	—20	36.98	27.7	8.7	Oct. 31	Oct. 7	Apr. 16	May 9	833
Concord, N.H.	102	—37	38.13	64.1	6.7	Sept. 24	Sept. 13	May 17	June 6	346
Dallas-Ft. Worth, Tex.	112	— 8	32.11	2.7	11.1	Nov. 21	Oct. 27	Mar. 16	Apr. 13	596
Denver	105	—30	14.60	60.1	9.0	Oct. 14	Sept. 16	May 2	May 28	5,332
Des Moines	110	—30	31.49	33.2	11.1	Oct. 10	Sept. 28	Apr. 20	May 11	963
Detroit	105	—24	31.49	31.7	10.2	Oct. 21	Sept. 23	Apr. 23	May 12	626
El Paso	109	— 8	8.47	4.4	9.6	Nov. 11	Oct. 31	Mar. 13	Apr. 11	3,916
Great Falls	107	—49	14.83	57.7	13.1	Sept. 26	Sept. 7	May 14	June 8	3,657
Hartford	102	—26	43.00	53.1	9.0	Oct. 15	Sept. 27	Apr. 22	May 10	179
Houston	108	5	47.07	0.4	7.6	Dec. 11	Oct. 25	Feb. 5	Mar. 27	108
Indianapolis	107	—25	39.98	21.3	9.7	Oct. 22	Sept. 27	Apr. 23	May 27	808
Jackson	107	— 5	50.96	0.8	7.7	Nov. 8	Oct. 9	Mar. 18	Apr. 25	331
Jacksonville	105	10	51.75	Trace	8.6	Dec. 16	Nov. 3	Feb. 6	Mar. 31	31
Juneau	90	—22	53.95	109.1	8.5	Oct. 21	Sept. 9	Apr. 22	June 8	24
Kansas City, Mo.	113	—22	36.66	19.7	10.2	Oct. 26	Sept. 30	Apr. 7	May 6	1,025
Little Rock	110	—13	48.17	5.3	8.2	Nov. 15	Oct. 23	Mar. 16	Apr. 13	265
Los Angeles	110	23	11.94	Trace	7.4	—	Dec. 9	—	Jan. 21	104
Louisville	107	—20	42.94	17.3	8.4	Oct. 25	Oct. 15	Apr. 10	Apr. 19	488
Memphis	106	—13	48.74	5.7	9.2	Nov. 5	Oct. 17	Mar. 20	Apr. 15	284
Miami	100	26	59.21	—	9.1	—	—	—	Feb. 6	12
Milwaukee	105	—25	30.18	45.2	11.8	Oct. 23	Sept. 20	Apr. 25	May 27	693
Minneapolis-St. Paul	108	—34	26.62	45.8	10.6	Oct. 13	Sept. 3	Apr. 29	May 24	838
Mobile	104	— 1	63.26	0.4	9.3	Dec. 12	Nov. 15	Feb. 17	Mar. 20	221
Nashville	107	—15	46.61	10.9	7.9	Oct. 31	Oct. 7	Apr. 3	Apr. 24	605
New Orleans	102	7	58.93	0.2	8.4	Dec. 3	Nov. 11	Feb. 15	Apr. 8	30
New York City	106	—15	43.56	29.1	9.4	Nov. 12	Oct. 19	Apr. 7	Apr. 24	87
Norfolk	105	2	45.22	7.2	10.6	Nov. 21	Nov. 7	Mar. 22	Apr. 14	30
Oklahoma City	113	—17	31.71	9.2	12.9	Nov. 7	Oct. 7	Apr. 1	May 3	1,304
Omaha	114	—32	28.48	32.5	10.9	Oct. 20	Sept. 24	Apr. 14	May 11	982
Philadelphia	106	—11	41.18	20.3	9.6	Nov. 17	Oct. 19	Mar. 30	Apr. 20	28
Phoenix	118	16	7.41	Trace	6.1	Dec. 11	Nov. 4	Jan. 27	Mar. 3	1,107
Pittsburgh	103	—20	36.21	45.5	9.4	Oct. 20	Oct. 10	Apr. 21	May 4	1,225
Portland, Me.	103	—39	42.15	74.3	8.8	Sept. 27	Sept. 17	May 12	May 31	63
Portland, Ore.	107	— 3	37.98	7.5	7.8	Dec. 1	Oct. 26	Feb. 25	May 4	39
Providence	104	—17	40.90	37.8	10.8	Oct. 26	Oct. 3	Apr. 14	Apr. 24	62
Reno	106	—19	7.65	26.8	6.4	Oct. 2	Aug. 30	May 14	June 25	4,400
Richmond	107	—12	43.77	14.3	7.6	Nov. 8	Oct. 5	Apr. 2	May 11	177
Sacramento	115	17	17.33	Trace	8.3	Dec. 11	Nov. 4	Jan. 24	Mar. 14	25
St. Louis	115	—23	36.70	17.8	9.5	Oct. 20	Sept. 28	Apr. 15	May 10	564
Salt Lake City	107	—30	15.63	58.1	8.7	Nov. 1	Sept. 25	Apr. 12	Apr. 30	4,227
San Francisco	106	20	18.88	Trace	10.5	—	Dec. 11	—	Jan. 21	18
Seattle	100	0	40.30	15.2	9.3	Dec. 1	Oct. 19	Feb. 23	Apr. 3	450
Spokane	108	—30	16.19	54.0	8.7	Oct. 12	Sept. 13	Apr. 20	May 16	2,365
Washington, D.C.	106	—15	40.00	16.8	9.2	Nov. 10	Oct. 2	Mar. 29	May 12	65
Wichita	114	—22	30.06	16.3	12.6	Nov. 1	Sept. 27	Apr. 5	Apr. 21	1,340
Wilmington, Del.	107	—15	43.63	20.1	9.1	Oct. 26	Sept. 27	Apr. 18	May 9	80

U.S. CITY WEATHER II

Source: National Climatic Center (data based on normals for 1936-1975)

AVERAGE MONTHLY TEMPERATURES (in °F)

City	Jan.	Feb.	Mar.	April	May	June	July	Aug.	Sept.	Oct.	Nov.	Dec.	ANNUAL
Albany	23.0°	23.7°	33.5°	46.5°	58.4°	67.7°	72.5°	70.2°	62.7°	51.4°	39.7°	27.7°	48.1°
Albuquerque	34.5	39.5	46.3	54.8	63.8	73.3	77.1	75.1	68.4	56.8	43.9	35.1	55.7
Atlanta	43.5	45.6	52.6	61.3	69.6	76.4	78.5	77.8	73.1	62.9	52.0	44.7	61.5
Baltimore	33.2	35.0	42.6	53.6	63.1	72.1	76.8	75.3	68.5	57.3	46.0	36.4	55.0
Birmingham	45.6	47.1	55.0	62.9	70.7	77.8	79.9	79.6	75.2	64.6	53.4	46.3	63.2
Bismarck	8.1	12.2	25.3	42.9	54.6	64.1	70.6	68.5	57.9	45.7	28.6	15.4	41.1
Boise	29.9	35.5	42.3	49.6	57.8	65.4	74.5	72.5	62.7	52.3	40.6	32.1	51.3
Boston	28.9	29.1	36.9	46.9	57.7	67.0	72.6	70.7	64.0	54.2	43.5	32.6	50.3
Buffalo	25.1	24.5	32.3	43.3	54.6	64.7	70.3	68.9	62.6	51.8	40.0	29.5	47.3
Burlington, Vt.	18.0	18.4	29.3	42.6	55.2	64.8	69.7	67.3	59.6	48.8	36.6	23.3	44.5
Charleston, W. Va.	36.6	38.0	46.0	56.0	64.8	72.3	76.0	74.8	69.3	58.0	46.7	38.2	56.4
Charlotte	42.0	43.9	51.0	60.0	68.9	76.0	78.7	77.4	72.2	61.6	50.9	43.1	60.5
Cheyenne	26.1	27.7	32.4	41.4	51.0	61.0	67.7	66.4	57.3	46.4	35.2	28.6	45.1
Chicago	24.7	27.1	36.4	47.8	58.2	68.4	73.8	72.5	65.6	54.5	40.4	29.4	49.9
Cincinnati	30.8	33.6	41.7	53.5	63.3	71.9	75.5	74.2	67.3	56.3	43.6	34.4	53.9
Cleveland	27.5	27.8	35.9	47.0	58.3	67.9	72.2	70.6	64.6	53.8	41.6	31.3	49.9
Columbia, S.C.	46.6	48.1	55.1	63.5	71.9	78.5	80.8	79.9	75.1	64.5	54.4	47.2	63.8
Columbus, Ohio	29.4	30.8	40.0	51.1	61.9	70.9	74.8	72.9	66.6	55.0	42.3	32.4	52.3
Concord, N.H.	21.3	22.8	31.9	44.4	56.2	64.9	70.0	67.3	59.7	49.2	37.5	25.6	45.9
Dallas-Ft. Worth, Tex.	45.6	48.8	56.9	65.2	72.7	80.9	84.5	84.6	77.8	67.8	56.1	47.7	65.7
Denver	30.1	32.8	38.7	47.4	56.7	66.6	72.6	71.3	62.6	51.6	39.6	32.3	50.2
Des Moines	20.8	24.7	36.3	50.4	61.5	71.1	76.1	73.7	65.3	54.2	38.5	26.1	49.9
Detroit	25.3	25.8	34.5	46.7	58.1	68.2	73.0	71.1	64.2	53.1	40.1	29.5	49.2
El Paso	44.7	49.3	55.6	63.8	72.2	80.8	81.9	80.2	74.8	64.7	52.5	45.2	63.8
Great Falls	21.2	26.1	31.4	43.3	53.3	60.9	69.7	67.9	57.6	48.3	34.8	27.1	45.1
Hartford	27.1	27.7	36.9	47.9	59.0	67.9	73.1	70.9	63.7	53.3	42.1	30.4	50.0
Houston	53.2	54.6	62.0	67.9	74.3	79.8	82.4	81.3	77.5	70.2	59.6	55.5	68.2
Indianapolis	28.5	30.8	40.1	52.0	62.5	71.8	75.7	73.7	66.9	55.5	42.0	31.9	52.6
Jackson	48.4	50.9	57.3	65.3	72.6	79.6	81.8	81.5	76.9	66.5	55.7	49.5	65.5
Jacksonville	55.0	56.6	61.8	67.5	73.7	78.5	80.4	80.1	77.1	68.9	60.6	54.9	67.9
Juneau	22.2	27.3	31.2	38.4	46.4	52.8	55.5	54.1	49.0	41.5	32.0	26.9	39.8
Kansas City, Mo.	29.7	33.1	43.2	55.5	65.3	74.7	79.5	78.0	70.3	59.1	44.7	33.6	55.6
Little Rock	41.7	44.8	52.9	62.5	70.1	78.2	81.3	80.5	74.1	63.8	51.9	43.8	62.1
Los Angeles	54.6	55.9	56.9	59.3	62.1	64.9	68.3	69.5	68.5	65.2	60.4	56.4	61.8
Louisville	34.7	36.8	45.6	56.3	66.0	74.6	78.3	76.8	70.4	58.9	46.4	37.2	56.9
Memphis	41.3	44.1	52.2	62.1	70.5	78.2	81.2	80.0	74.1	63.5	51.6	43.6	61.9
Miami	67.5	68.0	71.3	74.9	78.0	80.9	82.2	82.7	81.6	77.8	72.3	68.5	75.5
Milwaukee	20.9	23.2	32.6	44.3	54.3	64.5	70.7	69.7	62.5	51.5	37.7	26.1	46.5
Minneapolis-St. Paul	13.2	16.7	29.6	45.7	57.9	67.8	73.1	70.7	61.5	50.0	33.0	19.5	44.9
Mobile	51.9	54.4	60.1	67.1	74.3	80.3	81.8	81.5	78.1	68.9	58.9	53.1	67.6
Nashville	39.1	41.0	49.5	59.5	68.2	76.3	79.4	78.3	72.2	61.1	48.9	41.1	59.6
New Orleans	54.3	56.5	61.7	68.9	75.4	80.8	82.2	82.0	78.8	70.7	60.7	55.6	69.0
New York City	32.3	32.7	40.6	51.1	61.9	70.9	76.1	74.6	68.0	58.0	46.7	35.7	54.1
Norfolk	41.6	42.3	48.8	57.4	66.7	74.7	78.6	77.5	72.4	62.2	52.1	43.6	59.8
Oklahoma City	37.2	40.8	49.8	60.2	68.2	77.0	81.4	81.1	73.7	62.7	49.4	39.9	60.1
Omaha	22.0	26.5	37.5	51.7	62.7	72.3	77.4	75.1	66.3	55.0	39.3	27.5	51.1
Philadelphia	33.1	33.8	41.6	52.2	63.0	71.8	76.6	74.7	68.4	57.5	46.2	36.2	54.6
Phoenix	51.6	55.4	60.5	67.7	76.0	85.2	90.8	89.0	83.6	71.7	59.8	52.4	70.3
Pittsburgh	30.7	31.3	39.9	51.1	62.0	70.6	74.6	72.8	66.6	55.2	43.2	33.6	52.7
Portland, Me.	22.4	23.4	32.3	42.8	53.2	62.4	68.2	66.6	59.6	49.6	38.6	26.9	45.5
Portland, Ore.	38.5	43.0	45.9	50.6	57.0	60.2	65.8	65.3	62.7	54.0	45.7	41.1	52.5
Providence	29.4	29.3	37.6	47.5	57.8	66.9	72.7	71.0	63.9	54.0	43.4	32.6	50.5
Reno	31.8	36.6	41.2	47.4	54.9	62.5	70.2	68.5	60.7	50.9	41.0	33.4	49.9
Richmond	38.0	39.4	46.9	56.9	66.1	74.0	77.6	76.1	69.9	58.9	48.7	39.7	57.7
Sacramento	44.9	49.8	53.1	58.1	64.5	70.8	75.4	74.3	71.6	63.4	52.9	45.7	60.4
St. Louis	31.7	34.8	44.3	56.1	65.9	75.1	79.3	77.5	70.1	59.0	45.3	35.3	56.2
Salt Lake City	28.0	33.2	40.7	49.0	58.3	68.1	77.2	75.4	65.1	53.1	40.5	31.4	51.7
San Francisco	48.0	50.9	52.9	54.6	57.3	60.3	61.5	62.0	62.9	60.0	54.3	49.3	56.2
Seattle	38.2	42.2	43.9	48.1	55.0	59.9	64.4	63.8	59.6	51.8	44.6	40.5	51.0
Spokane	26.8	31.7	39.4	47.6	55.8	62.5	70.2	68.7	59.5	48.7	37.0	30.4	48.2
Washington, D.C.	36.1	37.7	45.7	56.1	65.8	74.3	78.4	76.9	70.3	59.6	48.4	38.4	57.3
Wichita	31.6	35.2	44.7	56.3	65.4	75.3	80.3	79.3	70.9	59.6	45.2	35.0	56.5
Wilmington, Del.	32.6	33.1	41.9	52.2	62.7	71.4	76.0	74.1	67.9	56.8	45.7	35.2	54.2

THE NATIONAL WEATHER SERVICE

Although people are critical of the weather forecaster's failures, they seldom generously acknowledge his successes. Employing a vast network of radar stations, professional and amateur weather observers, orbiting satellites, and other sources of data on a regular basis, the National Weather Service, a division of the National Oceanic and Atmospheric Administration (in the Department of Commerce), has the impressive record of 87% accurate rain predictions for the same day and 80% for the next. The national average of success in forecasting shows that today's and tonight's temperatures are correct within about 3½ degrees and tomorrow's to within about 4½ degrees.

The National Weather Service employs about 5000 full-time people at 400 facilities within the 50 states and at 14 overseas stations. Its physical facilities are valued at approximately $60 million.

The National Meteorological Center receives the following observational reports daily: 14,000 synoptic and 25,000 hourly from surface observation; 2,500 synoptic from ships; 2,500 atmospheric soundings; 3,500 from aircraft; and all available cloud and temperature data from weather satellites.

HURRICANE NAMES: 1980

Atlantic Ocean, Caribbean Sea, Gulf of Mexico
Allen, Bonnie, Charley, Danielle, Earl, Frances, Georges, Hermine, Ivan, Jeanne, Karl, Lisa, Mitch, Nicole, Otto, Paula, Richard, Shary, Tomas, Virginie, Walter.

Eastern North Pacific
Agatha, Blas, Celia, Darby, Estelle, Frank, Georgette, Howard, Isis, Javier, Kay, Lester, Madeline, Newton, Orlene, Paine, Roslyn, Seymour, Tina, Virgil, Winifred.

METEOROLOGICAL GLOSSARY

Anticyclone—An area of high pressure from which air spirals in all directions, usually accompanied by good weather. Anticyclones circulate in a clockwise direction in the northern hemisphere and in a counterclockwise direction in the southern (as seen from above).

Blizzard—A fall of fine, powdery snow accompanied by low temperatures and strong winds, often with low visibility and large accumulations.

Blizzard warning—Considerable amounts of snow will fall, with winds of at least 35 mph and temperatures not higher than 20°F.

Blowing snow—Snow lifted from the ground by the wind enough to restrict visibility.

Cold wave warning—A rapid and dramatic drop in temperature during the following 24 hrs requiring substantially increased protection for agricultural, industrial, commercial and social activities.

Convection—Motion of air produced by thermal or mechanical instability in the atmosphere.

Coriolis force—The force, apparently resulting from the earth's rotation, that causes high-pressure weather systems to circulate in a clockwise direction in the northern hemisphere and in a counterclockwise direction in the southern.

Cyclone—A rotary, usually columnar or funnel-shaped atmospheric system having its lowest pressure at the center of a circulating mass of air and water vapor. Cyclones circulate in a counterclockwise direction in the northern hemisphere and in a clockwise direction in the southern (as seen from above).

Drifting snow—Snow blown into significant drifts by strong winds either during or after a snowfall.

Eddy—(Within a fluid mass) a circulation pattern independent of the surrounding fluid.

Freezing drizzle—A light freezing rain.

Freezing rain—Another name for an ice storm.

Gale warning—Winds of 38–55 mph may be expected, with attendant strong wave action at sea.

Hail—Precipitation in the form of ice (hailstones) formed by the accumulation of sub-freezing water on a growing ice particle either by repeated circulation aloft or by long descent through layers of super-cooled water in clouds.

Hazardous driving (travelers') warning—Falling, blowing, or drifting snow, freezing rain or drizzle, sleet or strong winds will make driving dangerous.

Heavy snow warning—A fall of four inches or more in a 12-hr period or of six inches or more in a 24-hr period.

Hurricane—A well-defined weather system with winds of more than 74 mph and pronounced rotary circulation at the surface.

Hurricane warning—Winds of 74 mph or more may be expected within 24 hrs or high water or high waves may endanger life and property.

Hurricane watch—A hurricane that is nearby may affect the area: prepare for action if a hurricane warning is issued.

Ice storm—A winter storm in which falling rain rapidly freezes on all surfaces, causing hazardous driving conditions.

Inversion—A meteorological system in which temperature increases with an increase in altitude, the reverse of a normal system at lower altitudes.

Lightning—A discharge of electricity between clouds or between clouds and the earth resulting from an equalization between positively and negatively charged masses.

Livestock (stockmen's) warnings—Livestock will require protection from snow or ice accumulations, from a rapid drop in temperature, or from strong winds.

Neutercane—A storm, similar to and formerly identified as a cyclone or tropical storm, observed by weather satellites in areas of the oceans where hurricanes do not usually occur.

Ridge—An elongated high-pressure atmospheric system.

Seeding—The sprinkling of crystals, usually of silver iodide, into clouds and tropical storm formations in order to induce sudden freezing of super-cooled water vapor with a resultant release of latent heat of fusion, raising of cloud temperatures, and attendant reduction in maximum wind speeds. In some experiments, the intention of seeding is to increase the height and volume of storm clouds, thus dissipating the storm's energy over a wider area.

Severe blizzard warning—Considerable amounts of snow will fall, with winds of at least 45 mph and temperature not higher than 10°F.

Sleet storm—A winter storm in which falling rain freezes before striking the surface, usually bouncing on the ground.

Small-craft warning—Wind and water action may threaten the safety of small boats, which are best advised to remain in or return to port.

Snow flurries—Intermittent light snow for short periods with minimal accumulations.

Snow squalls—Brief, heavy snowfalls accompanied by gusty winds.

Storm warning—Winds of 55–74 mph may be expected, with attendant dangerous wave action at sea.

Thunder—A sound produced when lightning suddenly heats the surrounding air and causes it to expand with explosive force.

Thunderstorm—An atmospheric disturbance of varying severity, often accompanied by rain and characteristically by lightning. Thunderstorms are caused by unstable thermal convection currents of air that carry water vapor aloft creating a chimney-like effect. Exchanges of heated and cooled air and water increase and accelerate the effect, with attendant formation of ice and snow at upper altitudes and precipitation as water on the ground.

Tornado—A violently rotating column of air, moving counterclockwise at an estimated 300 mph, descending from a thunderstorm cloud system in a characteristically funnel-shaped form.

Tornado warning—A tornado has been sighted and all are advised to seek shelter.

Tornado watch—Tornadoes are expected to develop.

Tropical depression—A weather system with winds of not more than 39 mph and some circulation at the surface.

Tropical disturbance—Ill-defined weather phenomenon without strong wind and little or no circulation, sometimes better developed at higher altitudes.

Tropical storm—A well-defined weather system with winds of 39–73 mph and strong circulation at the surface.

Trough—An elongated low-pressure atmospheric system.

Waterspout—A tornado over water, in which water vapor is sucked skyward in a funnel-shaped vortex.

Wind-chill factor—The combined effect of temperature and wind velocity as compared with equivalent temperature in calm air.

NATIONAL OCEANIC AND ATMOSPHERIC ADMINISTRATION

The National Oceanic and Atmospheric Administration (NOAA) was formed on October 3, 1970, to explore, map and chart the ocean and its resources; to manage, use, and conserve those resources; and to describe, monitor, and predict conditions in all environments. It also is to issue warnings against impending destructive natural events while developing beneficial methods and assessing the consequences of environmental modification.

Among its principal functions and activities, NOAA reports the weather of the U.S. and provides weather forecasts to the general public, issues warning bulletins against destructive natural events, and provides services for such weather-sensitive activities as aviation, marine activities, and agriculture.

NOAA prepares and issues nautical and aeronautical charts and geodetic surveys. It conducts a broad range of research programs on the environment, including the use of satellites. The agency promotes wise and balanced management of the Nation's coastal zone, including the awarding of grants to states for their own development of their coastal zones. The agency also administers the Marine Mammal Protection Act of 1972.

The National Sea Grant program, which provides grants to institutions for marine research, education, and advisory services, is administered by the NOAA. It is also developing a system of data buoys for obtaining and disseminating marine environment data. Additionally, it tests and evaluates oceanographic instruments and maintains a national reference center for their specifications and characteristics.

DAYLIGHT SAVING TIME

In enacting the Uniform Time Act of 1966 (amended in 1972), the Congress made the observance of advanced (daylight) time automatic throughout the country for the six-month period extending from the last Sunday of April to the last Sunday of October.

That law, however, allows a state which falls in one time zone to exempt itself as a whole, and a state which falls in more than one time zone to exempt itself as a whole, or only that part in the most easterly zone, from the observance of advanced time. In 1977, in addition to the territories, only Arizona, Hawaii and the eastern time zone of Indiana did not observe daylight saving time from April 24 to October 30.

Faced with the energy crisis in 1974, the U.S. government required the use of daylight saving time throughout the year and, as amended later in 1974, it was tem-

porarily observed from January 6 to October 27, 1974, and from February 23 to October 26, 1975.

Time-zone boundaries in the United States have been defined—and from time to time relocated—since 1918 by the Interstate Commerce Commission and by the Department of Transportation beginning in 1967. Prior to 1966, however, a number of communities in the vicinity of the defined boundaries chose not to recognize them. When the Uniform Time Act became effective in 1967 those communities were confronted with a problem. With its automatic advanced (daylight) feature, the 1966 act required a far greater degree of nationwide recognition of the boundaries defined by DOT. The result has been active urging by state, local, and municipal governments, as well as hundreds of requests from private citizens, for the relocation of time zones boundaries.

STANDARD TIME ZONES

Time zone boundaries for the United States are defined by the Secretary of Transportation under the Standard Time Act (1918) as amended by the Uniform Time Act (1966). In the map below, reading from east to west, when it is 1:00 P.M. Atlantic Time (a zone that runs along the Maine-New Brunswick border, and includes Puerto Rico and the Virgin Islands in the Caribbean), it is 12:00 noon Eastern Time; 11:00 A.M. Central Time; 10:00 A.M. Mountain Time; 9:00 A.M. Pacific Time; 8:00 A.M. Yukon Time; 7:00 A.M. Alaska-Hawaii Time; and 6:00 A.M. Bering Time (which includes Nome and Western Alaska). Thus, there is a seven-hour time difference between Nome, Alaska and San Juan, Puerto Rico.

U. S. STANDARD TIME ZONES
Established by the Uniform Time Act
SCALE OF MILES

LATITUDE AND LONGITUDE OF U.S. CITIES

Source: National Ocean Survey

City and State	Lat. ° '	Long. ° '
Akron, Ohio	41 05	81 31
Albany, N.Y.	42 39	73 45
Albuquerque, N. Mex.	35 05	106 39
Allentown, Pa.	40 36	75 28
Amarillo, Tex	35 12	101 50
Anchorage, Alaska	61 12	149 48
Ann Arbor, Mich.	42 17	83 45
Asheville, N.C.	35 35	82 33
Atlanta	33 45	84 24
Augusta, Ga.	33 28	81 58
Austin, Tex.	30 16	97 45
Baltimore	39 17	76 37
Bangor, Me.	44 48	68 46
Baton Rouge, La.	30 27	91 11
Biloxi, Miss.	30 23	88 53
Birmingham, Ala.	33 31	86 49
Bismarck, N. Dak.	46 48	100 47
Boise, Idaho	43 37	116 12
Boston	42 21	71 03
Brattleboro, Vt.	42 51	72 33
Bridgeport, Conn.	41 11	73 11
Buffalo, N.Y.	42 52	78 52
Butte, Mont.	46 01	112 32
Casper, Wyo.	42 51	106 19
Cedar Rapids, Iowa	41 58	91 39
Charleston, S.C.	32 47	79 56
Charlotte, N.C.	35 14	80 51
Chattanooga, Tenn.	35 03	85 19
Cheyenne, Wyo.	41 08	104 49
Chicago	41 52	87 38
Cincinnati	39 06	84 31
Cleveland	41 30	81 42
Columbus, Ohio	39 58	83 00
Concord, N.H.	43 12	71 32
Dallas	32 47	96 48
Dayton, Ohio	39 45	84 11
Daytona Beach, Fla.	29 12	81 01
Denver	39 45	104 59
Des Moines	41 35	93 37
Detroit	42 20	83 03
Dubuque, Iowa	42 30	90 40
Duluth, Minn.	46 47	92 06
Durham, N.C.	36 00	78 54
El Paso, Tex.	31 46	106 29
Eugene, Ore.	44 03	123 05
Fairbanks, Alaska	64 48	147 51
Fargo, N. Dak.	46 53	96 47
Flagstaff, Ariz.	35 11	111 39
Fort Wayne, Ind.	41 04	85 08
Fort Worth, Tex.	32 45	97 20
Gainesville, Fla.	29 39	82 19
Galveston, Tex.	29 18	94 48
Gary, Ind.	41 36	87 20
Grand Rapids, Mich.	42 58	85 40
Green Bay, Wisc.	44 30	88 00
Greenville, S.C.	34 50	82 24
Harrisburg, Pa.	40 15	76 52
Hartford, Conn.	41 46	72 40
Honolulu, Hawaii	21 20	158 00
Houston	29 45	95 22
Indianapolis	39 46	86 10
Iowa City	41 39	91 31
Jacksonville, Fla.	30 19	81 39
Jersey City, N.J.	40 43	74 03
Joplin, Mo.	37 05	94 30
Juneau, Alaska	58 18	134 24
Kalamazoo, Mich.	42 17	85 35
Kansas City, Mo.	39 05	94 35
Knoxville, Tenn.	35 58	83 55
Lancaster, Pa.	40 02	76 18
Las Vegas, Nev.	36 10	115 09
Lincoln, Nebr.	40 49	96 42
Little Rock, Ark.	34 45	92 17
Los Angeles	34 03	118 14
Louisville, Ky.	38 14	85 45
Macon, Ga.	32 50	83 37
Madison, Wis.	43 04	89 23
Memphis, Tenn.	35 09	90 03
Miami	25 47	80 12
Milwaukee	43 02	87 54
Minneapolis	44 59	93 16
Mobile, Ala.	30 42	88 03
Montgomery, Ala.	32 23	86 19
Montpelier, Vt.	44 16	72 35
Nashville	36 10	86 47
Newark, N.J.	40 44	74 10
New Haven, Conn.	41 18	72 55
New Orleans	29 57	90 04
New York City	40 45	74 00
Niagara Falls, N.Y.	43 05	79 03
Nome, Alaska	64 30	165 25
Norfolk, Va.	36 51	76 17
Oakland, Calif.	37 48	122 16
Oklahoma City	35 28	97 31
Omaha	41 16	95 56
Pasadena, Calif.	34 08	118 08
Peoria, Ill.	40 41	89 35
Philadelphia	39 57	75 09
Phoenix	33 27	112 04
Pittsburgh	40 26	80 00
Pocatello, Idaho	42 52	112 27
Portland, Maine	43 39	70 15
Portland, Ore.	45 31	122 41
Providence, R.I.	41 50	71 25
Provo, Utah	40 14	111 39
Reno, Nev.	39 31	119 48
Richmond, Va.	37 32	77 26
Rochester, N.Y.	43 09	77 36
St. Louis	38 38	90 12
Salt Lake City	40 45	111 53
San Francisco	37 47	122 25
Santa Fe, N. Mex.	35 41	105 56
Savannah, Ga.	32 04	81 05
Seattle	47 37	122 20
Shreveport, La.	32 30	93 44
Sioux Falls, S.D.	43 32	96 43
Syracuse, N.Y.	43 03	76 09
Tallahassee, Fla.	30 26	84 16
Texarkana, Texas	33 25	94 02
Topeka, Kans.	39 03	95 40
Tulsa, Okla.	36 09	96 00
Tuscon, Ariz.	32 13	110 58
Utica, N.Y.	43 07	75 13
Washington, D.C.	38 54	77 01
Wichita, Kansas	37 41	97 20
Wilmington, Del.	39 45	75 33

SUNRISE AND SUNSET: 1980

Source: U.S. Naval Observatory

Note: To determine Daylight Saving Time, add one hour to all times; e.g., sunrise at 20° latitude on January 5 is 7:36 D.S.T.

To determine sunrise or sunset for any location, follow these directions:

(1) From the table directly above, determine the latitude and longitude of the city closest to you;

(2) From the tables below, read the sunrise or sunset time for the desired date at the correct latitude (given in degrees at the top of the table).

(3) Determine your time zone:

(a) **Eastern Time Zone:** If longitude is less than 75°, subtract four minutes from the time on the table for each degree. If it is greater than 75°, add four minutes for each degree.

(b) **Central Time Zone:** If longitude is less than 90°, subtract four minutes from the time on the table for each degree. If it is greater, add four minutes for each degree.

(c) **Rocky Mountain Time:** If longitude is less than 105°, subtract four minutes from the time on the table for each degree. If it is greater, add four minutes for each degree.

(d) **Pacific Time:** If longitude is less than 120°, subtract four minutes from the time on the table for each degree. If it is greater, add four minutes for each degree.

Latitude — SUNRISE (UPPER LIMB)

Date	+20° h m	+30° h m	+35° h m	+40° h m	+45° h m	+50° h m
Jan. 0	6 35	6 56	7 08	7 22	7 38	7 59
5	6 36	6 57	7 09	7 22	7 38	7 58
10	6 37	6 57	7 09	7 22	7 37	7 56
15	6 38	6 57	7 08	7 20	7 35	7 53
20	6 38	6 56	7 06	7 18	7 32	7 49
25	6 37	6 54	7 04	7 15	7 28	7 44
30	6 36	6 52	7 01	7 11	7 23	7 38
Feb. 4	6 35	6 49	6 57	7 07	7 17	7 30
9	6 33	6 46	6 53	7 01	7 11	7 23
14	6 30	6 42	6 48	6 55	7 04	7 14
19	6 27	6 37	6 43	6 49	6 56	7 05
24	6 24	6 32	6 37	6 42	6 48	6 55
29	6 21	6 27	6 31	6 35	6 40	6 45
Mar. 5	6 17	6 22	6 24	6 27	6 31	6 35
10	6 13	6 16	6 18	6 19	6 22	6 24

Date	+20° h m	+30° h m	+35° h m	+40° h m	+45° h m	+50° h. m
15	6 08	6 10	6 11	6 12	6 12	6 14
20	6 04	6 04	6 04	6 03	6 03	6 03
25	6 00	5 58	5 57	5 55	5 54	5 52
30	5 55	5 52	5 50	5 47	5 44	5 41
Apr. 4	5 51	5 46	5 43	5 39	5 35	5 30
9	5 47	5 40	5 36	5 31	5 26	5 20
14	5 43	5 34	5 29	5 24	5 17	5 09
19	5 39	5 29	5 23	5 16	5 08	4 59
24	5 35	5 24	5 17	5 09	5 00	4 49
29	5 32	5 19	5 11	5 03	4 52	4 40
May 4	5 29	5 15	5 06	4 56	4 45	4 31
9	5 26	5 11	5 01	4 51	4 38	4 23
14	5 24	5 07	4 57	4 46	4 32	4 15
19	5 22	5 04	4 54	4 41	4 27	4 09
24	5 21	5 02	4 51	4 38	4 22	4 03
29	5 20	5 00	4 48	4 35	4 18	3 58

SUNRISE (UPPER LIMB)

Date		+20°	+30°	+35°	+40°	+45°	+50°	Date		+20°	+30°	+35°	+40°	+45°	+50°
		h m	h m	h m	h m	h m	h m			h m	h m	h m	h m	h m	h m
June	3	5 20	4 59	4 47	4 32	4 15	3 54		21	5 49	5 48	5 47	5 47	5 46	5 45
	8	5 20	4 58	4 46	4 31	4 14	3 52		26	5 50	5 51	5 51	5 51	5 52	5 52
	13	5 20	4 58	4 45	4 30	4 13	3 50								
	18	5 21	4 59	4 46	4 31	4 13	3 50	Oct.	1	5 51	5 53	5 55	5 56	5 58	6 00
	23	5 22	5 00	4 47	4 32	4 14	3 51		6	5 52	5 56	5 59	6 01	6 04	6 08
	28	5 23	5 01	4 48	4 33	4 16	3 53		11	5 54	5 59	6 03	6 06	6 11	6 16
									16	5 55	6 03	6 07	6 12	6 17	6 24
July	3	5 25	5 03	4 50	4 36	4 18	3 56		21	5 57	6 06	6 11	6 17	6 24	6 32
	8	5 26	5 05	4 53	4 39	4 22	4 00		26	5 59	6 09	6 16	6 22	6 30	6 40
	13	5 28	5 08	4 56	4 42	4 26	4 05		31	6 01	6 13	6 20	6 28	6 37	6 48
	18	5 30	5 11	4 59	4 46	4 30	4 11								
	23	5 32	5 14	5 03	4 50	4 35	4 17	Nov.	5	6 03	6 17	6 25	6 34	6 44	6 56
	28	5 34	5 17	5 06	4 55	4 41	4 24		10	6 06	6 21	6 30	6 39	6 51	7 05
									15	6 09	6 25	6 35	6 45	6 58	7 13
Aug.	2	5 36	5 20	5 10	4 59	4 46	4 31		20	6 12	6 29	6 39	6 51	7 04	7 21
	7	5 37	5 23	5 14	5 04	4 52	4 38		25	6 15	6 33	6 44	6 56	7 11	7 28
	12	5 39	5 26	5 18	5 09	4 58	4 45		30	6 18	6 38	6 49	7 02	7 17	7 36
	17	5 41	5 28	5 21	5 13	5 04	4 53								
	22	5 42	5 31	5 25	5 18	5 10	5 00	Dec.	5	6 21	6 41	6 53	7 07	7 22	7 42
	27	5 43	5 34	5 29	5 23	5 16	5 07		10	6 24	6 45	6 57	7 11	7 27	7 48
									15	6 27	6 48	7 01	7 15	7 31	7 52
Sept.	1	5 44	5 37	5 33	5 28	5 22	5 15		20	6 30	6 51	7 04	7 18	7 35	7 56
	6	5 45	5 40	5 36	5 32	5 28	5 22		25	6 32	6 54	7 06	7 20	7 37	7 58
	11	5 47	5 42	5 40	5 37	5 34	5 30		30	6 34	6 55	7 08	7 22	7 38	7 59
	16	5 48	5 45	5 44	5 42	5 40	5 37		35	6 36	6 57	7 09	7 22	7 38	7 58

SUNSET (UPPER LIMB)

Date		+20°	+30°	+35°	+40°	+45°	+50°	Date		+20°	+30°	+35°	+40°	+45°	+50°
		h m	h m	h m	h m	h m	h m			h m	h m	h m	h m	h m	h m
Jan.	0	17 31	17 10	16 58	16 44	16 27	16 07	July	3	18 44	19 05	19 18	19 32	19 50	20 12
	5	17 34	17 14	17 02	16 48	16 32	16 12		8	18 43	19 04	19 17	19 31	19 48	20 09
	10	17 37	17 18	17 06	16 53	16 38	16 18		13	18 43	19 03	19 15	19 29	19 45	20 05
	15	17 41	17 22	17 11	16 58	16 44	16 25		18	18 42	19 01	19 13	19 26	19 41	20 01
	20	17 44	17 26	17 16	17 04	16 50	16 33		23	18 41	18 59	19 10	19 22	19 37	19 55
	25	17 47	17 30	17 21	17 10	16 57	16 41		28	18 39	18 56	19 06	19 18	19 31	19 48
	30	17 50	17 35	17 26	17 16	17 04	16 49								
								Aug.	2	18 36	18 52	19 02	19 13	19 25	19 41
Feb.	4	17 53	17 39	17 31	17 22	17 11	16 58		7	18 34	18 48	18 57	19 07	19 18	19 33
	9	17 56	17 43	17 36	17 28	17 18	17 07		12	18 31	18 44	18 52	19 01	19 11	19 24
	14	17 58	17 47	17 41	17 34	17 25	17 15		17	18 27	18 39	18 46	18 54	19 03	19 14
	19	18 01	17 51	17 46	17 39	17 32	17 24		22	18 23	18 34	18 40	18 47	18 55	19 05
	24	18 03	17 55	17 50	17 45	17 39	17 32		27	18 19	18 28	18 33	18 39	18 46	18 54
	29	18 05	17 58	17 55	17 51	17 46	17 41								
								Sept.	1	18 15	18 22	18 27	18 31	18 37	18 44
Mar.	5	18 07	18 02	17 59	17 56	17 53	17 49		6	18 11	18 16	18 20	18 23	18 28	18 33
	10	18 08	18 05	18 04	18 02	18 00	17 57		11	18 06	18 10	18 13	18 15	18 18	18 22
	15	18 10	18 08	18 08	18 07	18 06	18 05		16	18 02	18 04	18 05	18 07	18 09	18 11
	20	18 11	18 11	18 12	18 12	18 13	18 13		21	17 57	17 58	17 58	17 59	17 59	18 00
	25	18 12	18 15	18 16	18 17	18 19	18 21		26	17 53	17 52	17 51	17 50	17 50	17 49
	30	18 14	18 18	18 20	18 22	18 25	18 29								
								Oct.	1	17 48	17 45	17 44	17 42	17 40	17 38
Apr.	4	18 15	18 21	18 24	18 27	18 32	18 37		6	17 44	17 39	17 37	17 34	17 31	17 28
	9	18 17	18 24	18 28	18 32	18 38	18 45		11	17 40	17 34	17 30	17 26	17 22	17 17
	14	18 18	18 27	18 32	18 37	18 44	18 52		16	17 36	17 28	17 24	17 19	17 13	17 07
	19	18 20	18 30	18 36	18 43	18 51	19 00		21	17 32	17 23	17 18	17 12	17 05	16 57
	24	18 21	18 33	18 40	18 48	18 57	19 08		26	17 29	17 18	17 12	17 05	16 57	16 47
	29	18 23	18 36	18 44	18 53	19 03	19 16		31	17 26	17 14	17 07	16 59	16 50	16 38
May	4	18 25	18 39	18 48	18 58	19 09	19 23	Nov.	5	17 24	17 10	17 02	16 53	16 43	16 30
	9	18 27	18 43	18 52	19 03	19 15	19 31		10	17 22	17 07	16 58	16 48	16 37	16 23
	14	18 29	18 46	18 56	19 07	19 21	19 38		15	17 20	17 04	16 54	16 44	16 31	16 16
	19	18 31	18 49	19 00	19 12	19 27	19 45		20	17 19	17 02	16 52	16 40	16 27	16 10
	24	18 33	18 52	19 03	19 17	19 32	19 51		25	17 19	17 01	16 50	16 37	16 23	16 05
	29	18 35	18 55	19 07	19 21	19 37	19 57		30	17 19	17 00	16 49	16 36	16 20	16 02
June	3	18 37	18 57	19 10	19 24	19 41	20 02	Dec.	5	17 20	17 00	16 48	16 35	16 19	15 59
	8	18 38	19 00	19 13	19 27	19 45	20 07		10	17 21	17 01	16 49	16 35	16 18	15 58
	13	18 40	19 02	19 15	19 30	19 48	20 10		15	17 23	17 02	16 50	16 36	16 19	15 58
	18	18 41	19 03	19 16	19 32	19 50	20 12		20	17 25	17 04	16 52	16 38	16 21	16 00
	23	18 42	19 04	19 18	19 33	19 51	20 13		25	17 28	17 07	16 55	16 40	16 24	16 03
	28	18 43	19 05	19 18	19 33	19 51	20 13		30	17 31	17 10	16 58	16 44	16 27	16 07
									35	17 34	17 14	17 02	16 48	16 32	16 12

CALENDARS: 1801-2000

Select the desired year from the table below. The number shown with each year tells you the calendar to use for that year.

Year	Cal	Year	Cal	Year	Cal	Year	Cal	Year	Cal
1801	5	1841	6	1881	7	1921	7	1961	1
1802	6	1842	7	1882	1	1922	1	1962	2
1803	7	1843	1	1883	2	1923	2	1963	3
1804	8	1844	9	1884	10	1924	10	1964	11
1805	3	1845	4	1885	5	1925	5	1965	6
1806	4	1846	5	1886	6	1926	6	1966	7
1807	5	1847	6	1887	7	1927	7	1967	1
1808	13	1848	14	1888	8	1928	8	1968	9
1801	1	1849	2	1889	3	1929	3	1969	4
1810	2	1850	3	1890	4	1930	4	1970	5
1811	3	1851	4	1891	5	1931	5	1971	6
1812	11	1852	12	1892	13	1932	13	1972	14
1813	6	1853	7	1893	1	1933	1	1973	2
1814	7	1854	1	1894	2	1934	2	1974	3
1815	1	1855	2	1895	3	1935	3	1975	4
1816	9	1856	10	1896	11	1936	11	1976	12
1817	4	1857	5	1897	6	1937	6	1977	7
1818	5	1858	6	1898	7	1938	7	1978	1
1819	6	1859	7	1899	1	1939	1	1979	2
1820	14	1860	8	1900	2	1940	9	1980	10
1821	2	1861	3	1901	3	1941	4	1981	5
1822	3	1862	4	1902	4	1942	5	1982	6
1823	4	1863	5	1903	5	1943	6	1983	7
1824	12	1964	13	1904	13	1944	14	1984	8
1825	7	1865	1	1905	1	1945	2	1985	3
1826	1	1866	2	1906	2	1946	3	1986	4
1827	2	1867	3	1907	3	1947	4	1987	5
1828	10	1868	11	1908	11	1948	12	1988	13
1829	5	1869	6	1909	6	1949	7	1989	1
1830	6	1870	7	1910	7	1950	1	1990	2
1831	7	1871	1	1911	1	1951	2	1991	3
1832	8	1872	9	1912	9	1952	10	1992	11
1833	3	1873	4	1913	4	1953	5	1993	6
1834	4	1874	5	1914	5	1954	6	1994	7
1835	5	1875	6	1915	6	1955	7	1995	1
1836	13	1876	14	1916	14	1956	8	1996	9
1837	1	1877	2	1917	2	1957	3	1997	4
1838	2	1878	3	1918	3	1958	4	1998	5
1839	3	1879	4	1919	4	1959	5	1999	6
1840	11	1880	12	1920	12	1960	13	2000	14

Calendar 1

```
JANUARY              FEBRUARY             MARCH                APRIL
S  M  T  W  T  F  S   S  M  T  W  T  F  S   S  M  T  W  T  F  S   S  M  T  W  T  F  S
   1  2  3  4  5  6  7              1  2  3  4              1  2  3  4                 1
 8  9 10 11 12 13 14   5  6  7  8  9 10 11   5  6  7  8  9 10 11   2  3  4  5  6  7  8
15 16 17 18 19 20 21  12 13 14 15 16 17 18  12 13 14 15 16 17 18   9 10 11 12 13 14 15
22 23 24 25 26 27 28  19 20 21 22 23 24 25  19 20 21 22 23 24 25  16 17 18 19 20 21 22
29 30 31              26 27 28              26 27 28 29 30 31      23 24 25 26 27 28 29
                                                                  30

MAY                  JUNE                 JULY                 AUGUST
S  M  T  W  T  F  S   S  M  T  W  T  F  S   S  M  T  W  T  F  S   S  M  T  W  T  F  S
    1  2  3  4  5  6              1  2  3                    1         1  2  3  4  5
 7  8  9 10 11 12 13   4  5  6  7  8  9 10   2  3  4  5  6  7  8   6  7  8  9 10 11 12
14 15 16 17 18 19 20  11 12 13 14 15 16 17   9 10 11 12 13 14 15  13 14 15 16 17 18 19
21 22 23 24 25 26 27  18 19 20 21 22 23 24  16 17 18 19 20 21 22  20 21 22 23 24 25 26
28 29 30 31          25 26 27 28 29 30      23 24 25 26 27 28 29  27 28 29 30 31
                                            30 31

SEPTEMBER            OCTOBER              NOVEMBER             DECEMBER
S  M  T  W  T  F  S   S  M  T  W  T  F  S   S  M  T  W  T  F  S   S  M  T  W  T  F  S
             1  2     1  2  3  4  5  6  7            1  2  3  4                 1  2
 3  4  5  6  7  8  9   8  9 10 11 12 13 14   5  6  7  8  9 10 11   3  4  5  6  7  8  9
10 11 12 13 14 15 16  15 16 17 18 19 20 21  12 13 14 15 16 17 18  10 11 12 13 14 15 16
17 18 19 20 21 22 23  22 23 24 25 26 27 28  19 20 21 22 23 24 25  17 18 19 20 21 22 23
24 25 26 27 28 29 30  29 30 31              26 27 28 29 30        24 25 26 27 28 29 30
                                                                  31
```

Calendar 2

```
JANUARY              FEBRUARY             MARCH                APRIL
S  M  T  W  T  F  S   S  M  T  W  T  F  S   S  M  T  W  T  F  S   S  M  T  W  T  F  S
    1  2  3  4  5  6              1  2  3              1  2  3   1  2  3  4  5  6  7
 7  8  9 10 11 12 13   4  5  6  7  8  9 10   4  5  6  7  8  9 10   8  9 10 11 12 13 14
14 15 16 17 18 19 20  11 12 13 14 15 16 17  11 12 13 14 15 16 17  15 16 17 18 19 20 21
21 22 23 24 25 26 27  18 19 20 21 22 23 24  18 19 20 21 22 23 24  22 23 24 25 26 27 28
28 29 30 31          25 26 27 28          25 26 27 28 29 30 31  29 30

MAY                  JUNE                 JULY                 AUGUST
S  M  T  W  T  F  S   S  M  T  W  T  F  S   S  M  T  W  T  F  S   S  M  T  W  T  F  S
       1  2  3  4  5                 1  2   1  2  3  4  5  6  7              1  2  3  4
 6  7  8  9 10 11 12   3  4  5  6  7  8  9   8  9 10 11 12 13 14   5  6  7  8  9 10 11
13 14 15 16 17 18 19  10 11 12 13 14 15 16  15 16 17 18 19 20 21  12 13 14 15 16 17 18
20 21 22 23 24 25 26  17 18 19 20 21 22 23  22 23 24 25 26 27 28  19 20 21 22 23 24 25
27 28 29 30 31       24 25 26 27 28 29 30  29 30 31              26 27 28 29 30 31

SEPTEMBER            OCTOBER              NOVLMBER             DECEMBER
S  M  T  W  T  F  S   S  M  T  W  T  F  S   S  M  T  W  T  F  S   S  M  T  W  T  F  S
                1     1  2  3  4  5  6            1  2  3                 1
 2  3  4  5  6  7  8   7  8  9 10 11 12 13   4  5  6  7  8  9 10   2  3  4  5  6  7  8
 9 10 11 12 13 14 15  14 15 16 17 18 19 20  11 12 13 14 15 16 17   9 10 11 12 13 14 15
16 17 18 19 20 21 22  21 22 23 24 25 26 27  18 19 20 21 22 23 24  16 17 18 19 20 21 22
23 24 25 26 27 28 29  28 29 30 31          25 26 27 28 29 30      23 24 25 26 27 28 29
30                                                               30 31
```

Calendar 3

```
JANUARY              FEBRUARY             MARCH                APRIL
S  M  T  W  T  F  S   S  M  T  W  T  F  S   S  M  T  W  T  F  S   S  M  T  W  T  F  S
       1  2  3  4  5                 1  2                 1  2      1  2  3  4  5  6
 6  7  8  9 10 11 12   3  4  5  6  7  8  9   3  4  5  6  7  8  9   7  8  9 10 11 12 13
13 14 15 16 17 18 19  10 11 12 13 14 15 16  10 11 12 13 14 15 16  14 15 16 17 18 19 20
20 21 22 23 24 25 26  17 18 19 20 21 22 23  17 18 19 20 21 22 23  21 22 23 24 25 26 27
27 28 29 30 31       24 25 26 27 28        24 25 26 27 28 29 30  28 29 30
                                           31

MAY                  JUNE                 JULY                 AUGUST
S  M  T  W  T  F  S   S  M  T  W  T  F  S   S  M  T  W  T  F  S   S  M  T  W  T  F  S
          1  2  3  4                    1      1  2  3  4  5  6                 1  2  3
 5  6  7  8  9 10 11   2  3  4  5  6  7  8   7  8  9 10 11 12 13   4  5  6  7  8  9 10
12 13 14 15 16 17 18   9 10 11 12 13 14 15  14 15 16 17 18 19 20  11 12 13 14 15 16 17
19 20 21 22 23 24 25  16 17 18 19 20 21 22  21 22 23 24 25 26 27  18 19 20 21 22 23 24
26 27 28 29 30 31    23 24 25 26 27 28 29  28 29 30 31           25 26 27 28 29 30 31
                     30

SEPTEMBER            OCTOBER              NOVEMBER             DECEMBER
S  M  T  W  T  F  S   S  M  T  W  T  F  S   S  M  T  W  T  F  S   S  M  T  W  T  F  S
 1  2  3  4  5  6  7         1  2  3  4  5                 1  2   1  2  3  4  5  6  7
 8  9 10 11 12 13 14   6  7  8  9 10 11 12   3  4  5  6  7  8  9   8  9 10 11 12 13 14
15 16 17 18 19 20 21  13 14 15 16 17 18 19  10 11 12 13 14 15 16  15 16 17 18 19 20 21
22 23 24 25 26 27 28  20 21 22 23 24 25 26  17 18 19 20 21 22 23  22 23 24 25 26 27 28
29 30                27 28 29 30 31         24 25 26 27 28 29 30  29 30 31
```

Calendar 4

```
JANUARY              FEBRUARY             MARCH                APRIL
S  M  T  W  T  F  S   S  M  T  W  T  F  S   S  M  T  W  T  F  S   S  M  T  W  T  F  S
          1  2  3  4                    1                    1      1  2  3  4  5
 5  6  7  8  9 10 11   2  3  4  5  6  7  8   2  3  4  5  6  7  8   6  7  8  9 10 11 12
12 13 14 15 16 17 18   9 10 11 12 13 14 15   9 10 11 12 13 14 15  13 14 15 16 17 18 19
19 20 21 22 23 24 25  16 17 18 19 20 21 22  16 17 18 19 20 21 22  20 21 22 23 24 25 26
26 27 28 29 30 31    23 24 25 26 27 28     23 24 25 26 27 28 29  27 28 29 30
                                           30 31

MAY                  JUNE                 JULY                 AUGUST
S  M  T  W  T  F  S   S  M  T  W  T  F  S   S  M  T  W  T  F  S   S  M  T  W  T  F  S
             1  2  3   1  2  3  4  5  6  7         1  2  3  4  5                 1  2
 4  5  6  7  8  9 10   8  9 10 11 12 13 14   6  7  8  9 10 11 12   3  4  5  6  7  8  9
11 12 13 14 15 16 17  15 16 17 18 19 20 21  13 14 15 16 17 18 19  10 11 12 13 14 15 16
18 19 20 21 22 23 24  22 23 24 25 26 27 28  20 21 22 23 24 25 26  17 18 19 20 21 22 23
25 26 27 28 29 30 31  29 30                27 28 29 30 31        24 25 26 27 28 29 30
                                                                 31

SEPTEMBER            OCTOBER              NOVEMBER             DECEMBER
S  M  T  W  T  F  S   S  M  T  W  T  F  S   S  M  T  W  T  F  S   S  M  T  W  T  F  S
    1  2  3  4  5  6            1  2  3  4                    1      1  2  3  4  5  6
 7  8  9 10 11 12 13   5  6  7  8  9 10 11   2  3  4  5  6  7  8   7  8  9 10 11 12 13
14 15 16 17 18 19 20  12 13 14 15 16 17 18   9 10 11 12 13 14 15  14 15 16 17 18 19 20
21 22 23 24 25 26 27  19 20 21 22 23 24 25  16 17 18 19 20 21 22  21 22 23 24 25 26 27
28 29 30             26 27 28 29 30 31      23 24 25 26 27 28 29  28 29 30 31
                                           30
```

Calendar 5

```
JANUARY              FEBRUARY             MARCH                APRIL
S  M  T  W  T  F  S   S  M  T  W  T  F  S   S  M  T  W  T  F  S   S  M  T  W  T  F  S
             1  2  3   1  2  3  4  5  6  7   1  2  3  4  5  6  7               1  2  3  4
 4  5  6  7  8  9 10   8  9 10 11 12 13 14   8  9 10 11 12 13 14   5  6  7  8  9 10 11
11 12 13 14 15 16 17  15 16 17 18 19 20 21  15 16 17 18 19 20 21  12 13 14 15 16 17 18
18 19 20 21 22 23 24  22 23 24 25 26 27 28  22 23 24 25 26 27 28  19 20 21 22 23 24 25
25 26 27 28 29 30 31                       29 30 31              26 27 28 29 30

MAY                  JUNE                 JULY                 AUGUST
S  M  T  W  T  F  S   S  M  T  W  T  F  S   S  M  T  W  T  F  S   S  M  T  W  T  F  S
                1  2      1  2  3  4  5  6            1  2  3  4                    1
 3  4  5  6  7  8  9   7  8  9 10 11 12 13   5  6  7  8  9 10 11   2  3  4  5  6  7  8
10 11 12 13 14 15 16  14 15 16 17 18 19 20  12 13 14 15 16 17 18   9 10 11 12 13 14 15
17 18 19 20 21 22 23  21 22 23 24 25 26 27  19 20 21 22 23 24 25  16 17 18 19 20 21 22
24 25 26 27 28 29 30  28 29 30             26 27 28 29 30 31      23 24 25 26 27 28 29
31                                                               30 31

SEPTEMBER            OCTOBER              NOVEMBER             DECEMBER
S  M  T  W  T  F  S   S  M  T  W  T  F  S   S  M  T  W  T  F  S   S  M  T  W  T  F  S
       1  2  3  4  5            1  2  3   1  2  3  4  5  6  7               1  2  3  4
 6  7  8  9 10 11 12   4  5  6  7  8  9 10   8  9 10 11 12 13 14   5  6  7  8  9 10 11
13 14 15 16 17 18 19  11 12 13 14 15 16 17  15 16 17 18 19 20 21  12 13 14 15 16 17 18
20 21 22 23 24 25 26  18 19 20 21 22 23 24  22 23 24 25 26 27 28  19 20 21 22 23 24 25
27 28 29 30          25 26 27 28 29 30 31  29 30                 26 27 28 29 30 31
```

Calendar 6

```
JANUARY              FEBRUARY             MARCH                APRIL
S  M  T  W  T  F  S   S  M  T  W  T  F  S   S  M  T  W  T  F  S   S  M  T  W  T  F  S
                1  2      1  2  3  4  5  6            1  2  3  4  5  6               1  2  3
 3  4  5  6  7  8  9   7  8  9 10 11 12 13   7  8  9 10 11 12 13   4  5  6  7  8  9 10
10 11 12 13 14 15 16  14 15 16 17 18 19 20  14 15 16 17 18 19 20  11 12 13 14 15 16 17
17 18 19 20 21 22 23  21 22 23 24 25 26 27  21 22 23 24 25 26 27  18 19 20 21 22 23 24
24 25 26 27 28 29 30  28                   28 29 30 31           25 26 27 28 29 30
31

MAY                  JUNE                 JULY                 AUGUST
S  M  T  W  T  F  S   S  M  T  W  T  F  S   S  M  T  W  T  F  S   S  M  T  W  T  F  S
                   1            1  2  3  4  5            1  2  3   1  2  3  4  5  6  7
 2  3  4  5  6  7  8   6  7  8  9 10 11 12   4  5  6  7  8  9 10   8  9 10 11 12 13 14
 9 10 11 12 13 14 15  13 14 15 16 17 18 19  11 12 13 14 15 16 17  15 16 17 18 19 20 21
16 17 18 19 20 21 22  20 21 22 23 24 25 26  18 19 20 21 22 23 24  22 23 24 25 26 27 28
23 24 25 26 27 28 29  27 28 29 30          25 26 27 28 29 30 31  29 30 31
30 31

SEPTEMBER            OCTOBER              NOVEMBER             DECEMBER
S  M  T  W  T  F  S   S  M  T  W  T  F  S   S  M  T  W  T  F  S   S  M  T  W  T  F  S
          1  2  3  4               1  2      1  2  3  4  5  6               1  2  3  4
 5  6  7  8  9 10 11   3  4  5  6  7  8  9   7  8  9 10 11 12 13   5  6  7  8  9 10 11
12 13 14 15 16 17 18  10 11 12 13 14 15 16  14 15 16 17 18 19 20  12 13 14 15 16 17 18
19 20 21 22 23 24 25  17 18 19 20 21 22 23  21 22 23 24 25 26 27  19 20 21 22 23 24 25
26 27 28 29 30       24 25 26 27 28 29 30  28 29 30              26 27 28 29 30 31
                     31
```

7

JANUARY
S M T W T F S

FEBRUARY
S M T W T F S

MARCH
S M T W T F S

APRIL
S M T W T F S

MAY **JUNE** **JULY** **AUGUST**

SEPTEMBER **OCTOBER** **NOVEMBER** **DECEMBER**

8

JANUARY **FEBRUARY** **MARCH** **APRIL**

MAY **JUNE** **JULY** **AUGUST**

SEPTEMBER **OCTOBER** **NOVEMBER** **DECEMBER**

9

JANUARY **FEBRUARY** **MARCH** **APRIL**

MAY **JUNE** **JULY** **AUGUST**

SEPTEMBER **OCTOBER** **NOVEMBER** **DECEMBER**

10

JANUARY **FEBRUARY** **MARCH** **APRIL**

MAY **JUNE** **JULY** **AUGUST**

SEPTEMBER **OCTOBER** **NOVEMBER** **DECEMBER**

11

JANUARY **FEBRUARY** **MARCH** **APRIL**

MAY **JUNE** **JULY** **AUGUST**

SEPTEMBER **OCTOBER** **NOVEMBER** **DECEMBER**

12

JANUARY **FEBRUARY** **MARCH** **APRIL**

MAY **JUNE** **JULY** **AUGUST**

SEPTEMBER **OCTOBER** **NOVEMBER** **DECEMBER**

13

JANUARY **FEBRUARY** **MARCH** **APRIL**

MAY **JUNE** **JULY** **AUGUST**

SEPTEMBER **OCTOBER** **NOVEMBER** **DECEMBER**

14

JANUARY **FEBRUARY** **MARCH** **APRIL**

MAY **JUNE** **JULY** **AUGUST**

SEPTEMBER **OCTOBER** **NOVEMBER** **DECEMBER**

HOLIDAYS AND COMMEMORATED DAYS FOR 1980

(Days given in parentheses are not legal holidays)

January

1 / New Year's Day (All states)
2 / Day after New Year's Day (KY)
8 / (Battle of New Orleans Day [LA])
14 / Robert E. Lee's Birthday (AL)
14 / Martin Luther King Day (MI)
15 / Martin Luther King Day (CT, IL, LA, MD, MA, NJ, PA, SC, WDC)
19 / Robert E. Lee's Birthday (AR, GA, LA, NC, SC)
19 / Confederate Hero's Day (TX)
20 / Lee-Jackson Day (VA)
20 / Dr. Martin Luther King, Jr. Day (NY)
21 / Dr. Martin Luther King, Jr. Day (OH)
21 / Robert E. Lee's Birthday (MS)

February

2 / Arbor Day (AZ [part])
2 / (Groundhog Day)
4 / Lincoln's Birthday (DE, OR)
11 / Lincoln's Birthday (AZ)
12 / Abraham Lincoln's Birthday (AK, CA, CO, CT, IL, IN, KS, MD, MO, MT, NJ, NM, NY, PA, UT, VT, WA, WV)
14 / (St. Valentine's Day)
18 / George Washington's Birthday (All states; called "President's Day" in HI, KY, MI, NE, OH, PA, SD, UT, WY; "Washington & Lincoln's Birthday" in MN; "Lincoln-Washington Day" in WI)
19 / Mardi Gras Day (AL, LA)

March

2 / Texas Independence Day (TX)
4 / Town Meeting Day (VT)
10 / Inauguration Day (LA)
17 / (St. Patrick's Day)
17 / Evacuation Day (Suffolk County, MA)
25 / Maryland Day (MD)
26 / Kuhio Day (HI)
31 / Seward's Day (AK)

April

4 / Good Friday (CT, DE, HI, IN, IA, LA, MD, NJ, ND, TN)
4 / Good Friday Afternoon (KY, WI)
6 / Arbor Day (AZ [part])
7 / Easter Monday (NC)
12 / Halifax Resolutions Anniversary (NC)
14 / Thomas Jefferson's Birthday (AL)
21 / Patriot's Day (ME, MA)
21 / San Jacinto Day (TX)
21 / Confederate Memorial Day (AL)
22 / Arbor Day (NE)
22 / Primary Election Day (PA)
25 / Arbor Day (UT)
26 / Confederate Memorial Day (GA)
28 / Fast Day (NH)
28 / Confederate Memorial Day (MS)

May

1 / (May Day)
4 / Rhode Island Independence Day (RI)
6 / Primary Election Day (IN)
8 / Harry S Truman's Birthday (MO)
10 / Confederate Memorial Day (NC, SC)
11 / Mother's Day (AZ, NV, [OK])
17 / (Armed Forces Day)
20 / Mecklenburg Day (NC)
26 / Memorial Day (All states except AL, DE, MD, MS, NH, NM, NY, VA, VT, WV)
26 / Confederate Memorial Day (VA)

27 / Primary Election Day Afternoon (KY)
30 / Memorial Day (DE, MD, NH, NM, NY, VT, WV)

June

2 / Jefferson Davis' Birthday (AL, MS)
3 / Confederate Memorial Day (LA)
3 / Jefferson Davis' Birthday (GA, SC)
8 / Flag Day (NY)
11 / Kamehameha Day (HI)
13 / Flag Day (PA)
14 / (Flag Day)
15 / Father's Day (AZ)
17 / Bunker Hill Day (Suffolk County, MA)
19 / Emancipation Day (TX)
20 / West Virginia (WV)

July

4 / Independence Day (All states)
4 / Indian Rights Day (WI)
13 / Nathan Bedford Forrest Day (TN)
24 / Pioneer Day (UT)

August

3 / American Family Day (AZ)
4 / Colorado Day (CO)
7 / Primary Election Day (TN)
11 / Victory Day (RI)
15 / Admission Day (HI)
16 / Bennington Battle Day (VT)
27 / Lyndon B. Johnson's Birthday (TX)
30 / Huey P. Long Day (LA)

September

1 / Labor Day (All states)
9 / Admission Day (CA)
9 / Primary Election Day (WI)
12 / Defenders' Day (MD)
14 / Grandparents' Day (AZ)
17 / Citizenship Day (VA)
27 / Indian Day (OK)

October

12 / Columbus Day (MD, NM, OR)
13 / Columbus Day (All states except AK, HI, IA, KY, LA, MD, MI, NV, NM, ND, OR, SD, WA)
13 / Discovers' Day (HI)
13 / Pioneers' Day (SD)
15 / Poetry Day (ME)
18 / Alaska Day (AK)
24 / (United Nations Day)
27 / Veteran's Day (PA, NC)
31 / (Halloween)
31 / Nevada Day (NV)

November

1 / All Saints Day (LA)
4 / Election Day Afternoon (KY)
4 / Election Day (CO, DE, HI, IL, IN, LA, ME, MO, NH, NJ, NY, NC, PA, RI, SC, TN, VA, WI, WY)
6 / Return Day Afternoon (Sussex County, DE)
11 / Veteran's Day (All states except KY, MS, NC, PA, RI, WI)
11 / Armistice Day (MS, RI, WI)
27 / Thanksgiving Day (All states)
28 / Thanksgiving Friday (FL, IL, IA, KY, MN, NE, OK, TX, WA)

December

24 / Christmas Eve (AR, TX)
25 / Christmas Day (All states)
26 / Day after Christmas (KY, SC, TX)

NEW WORLD EXPLORERS

NORTH AMERICA

c. 1000 ... Leif Ericsson (Norway) possibly sailed to Labrador and Newfoundland, from Greenland; others theorize that he reached Virginia, Nova Scotia, or New England

c. 1010 ... Thorfinn Karlsefni (Iceland) sailed from Greenland to North America, probably Labrador or New England

1497–98 ... John Cabot (England) sailed to North America, probably Cape Breton Island or Newfoundland

1513 ... Juan Ponce de León (Spain) sailed to near St. Augustine, Florida, and south to Miami Bay

1519 ... Alonso de Pineda (Spain) explored the Gulf of Mexico from Florida to the mouth of the Rio Grande

1524 ... Giovanni da Verrazano (France) explored North American coast, probably from North Carolina to Maine, entering New York Bay

1528 ... Pánfilo de Narváez (Spain) explored Florida from Tampa Bay as far as Tallahassee

1534–36 ... Jacques Cartier (France) sailed to Strait of Belle Isle, Newfoundland, and discovered Prince Edward Island; he also discovered St. Lawrence River as far as Quebec and Montreal (1535–36)

1536 ... Alvar Nuñez Cabeza de Vaca (Spain), shipwrecked on Texas coast, traveled as far as New Mexico, Arizona, and possibly California

1538–39 ... Francisco de Ulloa (Spain) explored Gulf of California to its head, proving that present-day Baja California is a peninsula

1538–41 ... Hernando de Soto (Spain) began (1539) exploring southern coast of United States, as far inland as Mississippi River, Arkansas, and Oklahoma

1539 ... Marcos de Niza (Spain) explored southeastern Arizona and perhaps New Mexico

1540–42 ... Francisco Vásquez de Coronado (Spain) explored New Mexico, Texas Panhandle, Oklahoma, and Kansas

1542 ... Juan Rodríguez Cabrillo (Spain) discovered California mainland, landing at San Diego Bay

1565 ... Pedro Menéndez de Avilés (Spain) founded St. Augustine, Florida, and explored Gulf Coast

1576–78 ... Sir Martin Frobisher (England) explored Frobisher Bay, South Baffin Island, and Hudson Strait in northeastern Canada

1577–79 ... Sir Francis Drake (England) sailed from Chile to Washington, stopping at San Francisco Bay

1585–87 ... John Davis (England) discovered Cumberland Sound off Baffin Island in northeastern Canada

1598–1605 ... Juan de Oñate (Spain) explored New Mexico (1598), Oklahoma, and the plains around Wichita, Kansas (1601), and went down the Colorado River to the Gulf of California (1605)

1602 ... Bartholomew Gosnold (England) explored eastern coast from Maine to Narragansett Bay, naming Cape Cod

1603–9 ... Samuel de Champlain (France) explored St. Lawrence River as far as Lachine (1603), New England south to Martha's Vineyard (1603–6); founded Quebec (1608); and discovered Lake Champlain (1609)

1607–9 ... John Smith (England) helped to found (1607) Jamestown, Virginia, and explored adjacent areas

1609–10 ... Henry Hudson (Netherlands) sailed up Chesapeake, Delaware, and New York Bays; under English flag, he sailed through Greenland, Labrador, Hudson Strait and Bay (1610)

1634 ... Jean Nicolet (France) explored Lake Michigan, Green Bay, and Fox River, Wisconsin

1673 ... Louis Jolliet, Father Jacques Marquette (France) navigated Mississippi, Arkansas, and Illinois Rivers to Chicago; first to establish the existence of a waterway from St. Lawrence River to the Gulf of Mexico

1678–79 ... Frère Louis Hennepin (France) explored Great Plains and the upper Mississippi River region

1678–80 ... Daniel Greysolon Duluth (Du Lhut) (France) claimed Lake Superior and upper Mississippi region for France; his treatment of the Indians gained their lasting friendship

1679–82 ... Robert Cavalier de La Salle (France) crossed Great Lakes and navigated Mississippi River to its mouth

1691–92 ... Henry Kelsey (England) explored the area around Reindeer Lake in western Canada

1692 ... Arnout Viele (France) explored the area from the Great Lakes to the Ohio River

1701 ... Antoine de la Mothe Cadillac (France) explored upper Michigan; founded Detroit

1710–18 ... Jean Baptiste le Moyne, sieur de Bienville (France), founded Mobile (1710) and New Orleans (1718)

1731–43 ... Pierre Gautier de Varennes, sieur de la Vérendrye (Canada), explored central Canada, Red River country, and the Missouri River (1731–34); discovered Lake Manitoba (1739) in central Canada; and traveled probably as far as the Black Hills in north central United States (1742–43)

1769–79 ... Daniel Boone (United States) explored Kentucky territory (1769–71) and blazed the Wilderness Road (1775)

1770–72 ... Samuel Hearne (England) opened areas of north

central Canada, around Great Slave Lake and Coppermine River

1775–76 ... Silvestre Vélez de Escalante (Spain) explored Arizona and Colorado; first white man known to travel in Utah

1792 ... Robert Gray (United States) discovered Columbia River in northwestern United States

1789–93 ... Sir Alexander Mackenzie (Canada) followed Mackenzie River in Canada to Arctic Ocean (1789); explored elsewhere in Canada, making first overland crossing of North America to the Pacific, north of Mexico (1793)

1797–1810 ... David Thompson (Canada) explored Rocky Mountains and all of the Columbia River system

1803–6 ... Meriwether Lewis, William Clark (United States) navigated Missouri River to Bismarck, North Dakota, traveled west through the mountains to the Clearwater, Snake, and Columbia Rivers as far as the Pacific Ocean

1805–7 ... Zebulon Pike (United States) explored Minnesota (1805) and southwestern United States, sighted Pikes Peak (1806)

c. 1807 ... John Colter (United States) crossed Teton Range in the Rocky Mountains, and discovered Yellowstone area

1819–27 ... Sir John Franklin (England) explored northern Canada to the Arctic

1825 ... James Bridger (United States) discovered Great Salt Lake in Utah

1825–27 ... Jedediah Smith (United States) traveled from Great Salt Lake to Colorado River and San Diego, California; on return trip, he crossed Sierra Nevada and Great Salt Desert

1832–35 ... Benjamin Bonneville (United States) helped open Rocky Mountain territory

1842–45 ... John Frémont, Kit Carson (United States) explored Oregon, Nevada, and California

SOUTH AND CENTRAL AMERICA

1492–1502 ... Christopher Columbus (Spain) discovered America: Bahamas, Cuba, and Hispaniola in the Caribbean (1492); Venezuela (1498); and Honduras (1502)

1499 ... Alonso de Ojeda (Spain) explored northeastern coast of South America

1499–1509 ... Vicente Pinzón (Spain) explored coast of Brazil and discovered mouth of the Amazon River in Brazil (1499–1500); skirted along Yucatán, Honduras, and Venezuela (1508–9)

1500 ... Pedro Alvarez Cabral (Portugal) reached coast of Brazil, possibly before Pinzón

1501–2 ... Amerigo Vespucci (Portugal) discovered Río de la Plata, explored about 6,000 miles of South American coast; he was the first to suggest that America was not part of Asia

1513 ... Vasco Núñez de Balboa (Spain) discovered the Pacific Ocean by crossing Isthmus of Panama

1516 ... Juan Díaz de Solís (Spain) sailed up Río de la Plata and explored Uruguay

1517 ... Francisco Fernández de Córdoba (Spain) discovered Yucatán in Mexico

1519 ... Gil González Dávila and Andrés Niño (Spain) explored Pacific coast of Central America from Panama to Nicaragua

1519–21 ... Hernán Cortés (Spain) discovered Aztec capital Tenochtitlán (now Mexico City) and conquered Mexico

1520 ... Ferdinand Magellan (Spain) explored Río de la Plata and Patagonia in Argentina, and discovered the strait at the tip of South America that bears his name

1524–33 ... Francisco Pizarro (Spain) explored the San Juan River between Colombia and Ecuador; conqueror of Peru (1532–33)

1526–30 ... Sebastian Cabot (Spain) explored Río de la Plata country along Paraguay, Plata, and Paraná Rivers

1530–35 ... Nikolaus Federmann (Germany) explored northwestern Venezuela and interior of Colombia through the Andes

1533 ... Sebastián de Belalcázar (Spain) explored and conquered Ecuador and southeastern Colombia

1535–37 ... Diego de Almagro (Spain) explored from Peru south through the Andes as far as Coquimbo and the Atacama Desert in Chile

1535–37 ... Pedro de Mendoza (Spain) explored Río de la Plata and founded Buenos Aires (1536)

1536 ... Gonzalo Jiménez de Quesada (Spain) founded Bogotá, Colombia, and explored the Magdalena River, Colombia

1541 ... Francisco de Orellana (Spain) floated down the Amazon's entire length

1549–52 ... Pedro de Valdivia (Spain) explored Chile, founding Concepción and Valdivia (1552)

1595 ... Sir Walter Raleigh (England) explored Orinoco River, penetrating 300 miles into Guiana's interior

1616 ... Willem C. Schouten (Netherlands) rounded and named Cape Horn at the tip of South America, avoiding the Strait of Magellan

1799–1804 ... Alexander von Humboldt (Germany) explored source of Orinoco and Amazon Rivers, establishing the connecting systems of the two

STARS/PLANETS/SPACE

ORIGIN AND EVOLUTION OF THE UNIVERSE

One of the major and perhaps most fundamental problems in astronomy is to develop a theory of the origin and evolution of the universe, based on actual observations of stars and galaxies and on known physical laws, in the attempt to determine how the universe changes with time. Cosmology deals with the physical structure of the universe, and with the origin of the universe and of its subsystems—that is, galaxies and systems of galaxies. Several different theories of the origin and evolution of the universe have been suggested.

The Einstein-Friedmann relativistic theories of cosmology, which were first formulated (1922) by Albert Friedmann, a Russian physicist, are based on Einstein's theory of general relativity. The relativistic theorists postulate a universe that is in constant motion and originated from one infinitesimal point and subsequently expanded. The expansion of the universe refers to the mutual recession of galaxies from each other, with a recessional velocity proportional to their distance from one another. The observational evidence for the recession of galaxies from one another was first discovered by the American astronomer Edwin Hubble in the late 1920s.

According to the relativistic concept, the geometry of space determines the kind of expansion. At a finite time in the past, the mass and energy density, as well as the temperature of the universe, were extremely high and concentrated in a relatively small location. At this zero point of time, the relativistic equations suggest that the universe "exploded" from its very concentrated original or primordial state. This is referred to as the "big bang" theory. As the universe expanded as a result of this primordial explosion, its constituent particles—initially only hydrogen nuclei, electrons, positrons, and later stars and galaxies, which condensed from hydrogen gas and dust—began dispersing with a certain velocity.

If the curvature of space is positive, which means that space is finite, the relativistic equations predict that the expansion of the universe will come to a halt at some finite time. Thereafter, the universe will begin to contract with increasing velocity until it reaches its initial primordial state of very high density and very high temperature. This concept is sometimes referred to as either a "closed" or an "oscillating" universe. If the curvature of space is negative, the expansion could be permanent; the universe could expand forever. In this "open" universe idea, even after the last star has stopped shining and the entire universe is in total darkness, the universe will still be expanding.

According to the "steady-state" or "continuous creation" theory of cosmology, galaxies recede from one another, but their spatial density remains constant. According to this theory, there is a continuous creation of new matter (hydrogen atoms) throughout space. The newly created matter subsequently condenses to form new stars and galaxies between the older galaxies, and a steady state or constant spatial density with time is maintained. In the steady-state concept, the universe had no beginning and has no end.

However, we can determine an upper limit for the age of the universe, since the rate of expansion of the universe has been continually slowing up since the time of the primordial explosion postulated as first putting the universe in motion. Based on the present rate of the expansion, it appears that the age of the universe is at least 10 billion years, which is also close to the approximate distance of quasars in light-years. Since light travels a distance of one light-year (some 6 trillion miles) in one year, it appears that quasars are about the most distant objects in the universe.

Relativistic cosmology also holds that some 10 billion years ago, just at the time that the universe began to expand, its temperature far exceeded a billion degrees. As the universe began to expand, its temperature fell, and the remnant radiation of that original high temperature should now be about 3 kelvin ($-270°$ C).

In 1965, A. A. Penzias and R. W. Wilson, of the Bell Telephone Laboratories in New Jersey, made an accidental discovery of major cosmological importance. They detected a background radio (microwave) emission of uniform intensity coming from all parts of the sky that corresponded to a temperature of about 3 kelvin. This is believed to be the relic radiation from the original big bang of the universe. Molecules found in interstellar space, such as the hydroxyl radical (OH) and cyanogen (CN), can be used as a cosmic thermometer. Interstellar spectral measurements of CN absorption also confirm the existence of the 3-kelvin universal background radiation.

According to relativistic theory, the number of galaxies per volume of space should have been much greater in the past, before the universe began expanding, than it is today. The steady-state model holds that the number of galaxies per volume of space should be statistically the same everywhere at all times. Martin Ryle, the British Astronomer Royal, has presented very substantial radio astronomical evidence against the steady-state theory, based on counts of the numbers of radio galaxies that are very distant in space (looking farther out into space is really like looking back into time).

At present it appears that the balance of the observational evidence is against the steady-state concept and in favor of the relativistic theory. Unfortunately, some of the observational data are not yet sufficiently accurate or statistically adequate to make the decision conclusive.

STARS AND GALAXIES

Stars are the basic elements in the universe. More than 90 percent of the mass of our own galaxy—the Milky Way—is in the form of stars; the rest of the matter is interstellar hydrogen gas and dust that form stars. The mass of the Sun—the star of our solar system—is 2×10^{30} kg. The range of masses observed for most stars varies from 0.05 of the Sun's mass to 60 times the Sun's mass. The range of luminosity or absolute magnitude (brightness) varies from a tiny fraction of the Sun's luminosity for white dwarf stars to over a million times the Sun's luminosity for the most luminous stars. The range of stellar radii varies from 1/70,000 of the Sun's radius for neutron stars to over 1,000 times the Sun's radius for supergiants. The Sun's density is about 1.4 grams/cm^3 (a little heavier than water). White dwarfs may be over 1 million times as dense as the Sun and neutron stars even more dense; supergiants can be only one-millionth as dense as the Sun.

Multiple star systems consist of more than two stars linked by gravitational forces. Galactic or open clusters are loosely bound stellar systems with up to a few hundred stars. Globular or closed clusters are tightly bound spherical star clusters with maybe over a million stars. Galaxies are the largest stellar systems and are regarded as the basic mass elements of the universe. Galaxies, which occur in clusters, contain from a billion to a thousand billion stars each. It has been estimated that there are at least 10 billion galaxies in the universe. From observations, it appears that there are three distinct types.

In spiral galaxies, spiral arms of gas and dust are distinctly visible. In elliptical galaxies, there are no visible spiral arms or gas, and the exterior shape is either elliptical or spherical. Irregular galaxies have no definite shape.

About 25 years ago, it was discovered that stars in the nucleus of spiral galaxies are different from the stars in the arms of the galaxy. Stars within the spiral arms are called Population I stars and are young and bluish in color. Population II stars are found in the galactic nucleus and are old and reddish in color.

Red giants are cool red stars that have undergone expansion; their luminosity may be well over 1,000 times the Sun's luminosity, and their radius several hundred times the Sun's radius. The red giant has already converted about 50 percent of its hydrogen into helium by thermonuclear processes. As this energy source becomes exhausted, expansion halts and contraction to a white dwarf

may occur. White dwarfs are characterized by low luminosity, relatively high surface temperature and extremely high density. White dwarfs are dying stars and are gradually cooling to become "black dwarfs" or nonluminous chunks of mass. The Sun will become a white dwarf in billions of years time.

The process by which a star dies depends on its mass. When its energy is exhausted, a star with a mass between 1.4 and about 3 times the Sun's mass will, after expansion, contract through the white-dwarf stage and become a tiny immensely dense neutron star. Supernovae are stars that suddenly increase their luminosity by more than 10 million times. The supernova luminosity increase reflects the fact that the star is exploding—literally blowing itself up. It is believed that the remnant of at least one supernova, called the Crab Nebula, is a neutron star, which forms the pulsating radio source or "pulsar" observed in that region of the sky.

QUASARS

Quasars ("quasi-stellar radio sources") were first discovered in 1961; they are starlike objects emitting extremely intense radio and visible radiation. Since then, it has been found that many similar visible radiators are undetectable radio sources ("quasi-stellar objects"), and are sometimes referred to as QSOs. Some quasars emit a million times as much radio radiation as our Milky Way galaxy, which contains some 100 billion stars. It is still a most challenging problem to understand the physical process that leads to the tremendous radio emission in some quasars and the lack of it in QSOs.

In 1963, Maarten Schmidt, of the California Institute of Technology, discovered a large red shift in the location of the emission lines in the spectrum of quasars. It is generally accepted that these large red shifts are caused by the cosmological expansion of the universe. The red shift is used to determine the distance of receding extragalactic objects. The measured red shift of quasars and QSOs would place them at a few billion light years—in fact, the most distant objects in the universe.

This interpretation also implies that they emit between 50–100 times more energy than entire galaxies, each containing about 100 billion stars. The radiative emission from quasars in the visible and in the short radio-wavelength region varies with time. QSOs show similar optical variations. The time scale and amplitude of these brightness variations place a limit on the geometrical size of the emitting object. Thus, quasars and QSOs are in the

order of a few light years or less in diameter, compared to 100,000 light years for a galaxy.

If quasars and QSOs are indeed very distant objects, as the red-shift interpretation suggests, they must have tremendous radiative emission. An alternative suggestion is that quasars and QSOs are the visible manifestations of a gigantic explosion that occurred in the center of a distant galaxy.

It has recently been discovered that some quasars and QSOs are very strong emitters of infrared radiation, while others are very weak, adding to the enigma of these objects. Despite the theories advanced, the actual origin of the tremendous energy output of quasars and QSOs remain unknown. One theory is that the energy released by quasars and QSOs is generated during the evolution of dense, massive star clusters or from supernova chain reactions within star clusters. That is, normal-size stars coalesced to form very massive stars (approximately 30 to 50 times the Sun's mass), which then became exploding stars or supernovae.

Of late, there has been a growing awareness that QSOs show similarities to Seyfert galaxies, which are a rare galaxy class characterized by the small size and high luminosity of their nuclei. Their outer parts, however, are inconspicuous. Since QSOs appear photographically similar and have similar emission spectra to Seyfert galaxies, it appears that these two celestial phenomena may somehow be related.

PULSARS

In 1967 a new class of astronomical object was discovered by a Cambridge University group: a rapidly pulsating radio source, or "pulsar." The radio signals from this object, located in the constellation Vulpecula, were periodic in nature, consisting of brief radio pulses that were separated by about 1.3 seconds. Since then, more than 100 pulsars have been discovered.

The most interesting property of pulsars is the extreme regularity of their radio-emission period, which ranges from 0.033 to over 5 seconds. It was believed that this time period between radio pulses was remarkably constant, varying by not more than a few parts per million annually; however, recently it has been found that the periods of most pulsars are lengthening very slightly due to the transfer of internal rotational energy to the surroundings. Two of these pulsars have been identified with the remnants of exploding stars, the Crab Nebula and one in the constellation of Vela. These two pulsars have the shortest periods of any known—0.033 and 0.089 second, respectively—but their periods are increasing

more rapidly than those of any other pulsars. A pulsar's radio pulses are of very short duration compared to the time periods between those pulses, which typically are some thousandths of a second.

Optical astronomers have gone to considerable lengths to determine if pulsars emit optical pulses as well as radio pulses. At the present time, only the Crab Nebula pulsar and the very faint Vela pulsar have been observed to emit periodic pulses of light. The former also emits X rays, ultraviolet, and infrared radiation.

A pulsar is assumed to be a rapidly rotating neutron star, which is a very dense star with an intense magnetic field. The gravitational collapse of a massive dying star causes it to implode as a supernova and vast quantities of energy are given off. The remaining core is a pulsar. A pulsar has a mass between 1.4 and about 3 times the Sun's mass, but a diameter of only about 10 miles (the Sun's diameter is 865,000 miles). This kind of star rotates so rapidly that it can complete one rotation on its axis in less than a thousandth of a second.

STELLAR AND GALACTIC TERMS

Absolute Magnitude—Apparent magnitude that a star would have at a distance of 10 parsecs.

Albedo—Reflecting power of a nonluminous body.

Apparent Magnitude—A measure of the observed light flux received from a star or other object at Earth.

Astronomical Unit (AU)—The average distance between the Sun and the Earth. It is equal to 92,957,000 miles and is often used as a unit of measurement.

Bands (in spectra)—Emission or absorption lines, usually

in the spectra of chemical compounds or radicals, coalesced into broad emission or absorption bands.

Binary Star—System of two stars revolving about a common center of gravity.

Black Body—A hypothetical perfect radiator that absorbs and reemits all radiation incident upon it.

Clouds of Magellan—Two neighboring galaxies visible to the naked eye from southern latitudes.

Cosmic Rays—Atomic nuclei (mostly protons) that are observed to strike the Earth's atmosphere with exceedingly high energies, probably from supernovae.

Cosmological Red Shift—Red shift of spectral lines in celestial objects arising from the expansion of the universe which, when interpreted with a cosmological model, indicates the distance of those objects.

Cosmology—The study of the organization and evolution of the universe.

Dark Nebula—A cloud of interstellar dust that obscures the light of more distant stars and appears as an opaque curtain.

Diffuse Nebula—A reflection or emission nebula produced by interstellar matter (not a planetary nebula).

Emission Nebula—A gaseous nebula that derives its visible light from the fluorescence of ultraviolet light from a star in or near the nebula.

Extragalactic—Beyond the galaxy.

Gamma Rays—Photons (of electromagnetic radiation) of energy higher than that of X rays—the most energetic form of electromagnetic radiation.

Gravitational Force—Force of attraction between two bodies, directly proportional to product of their masses, inversely proportional to square of distance between them.

"Heavy" Elements—In astronomy, usually those elements of greater atomic number than helium.

Hertzsprung-Russell Diagram—A basic classification of the properties of stars in which luminosity is related to effective surface temperature or star color.

Infrared Radiation—Electromagnetic radiation of wavelength longer than the longest visible (red) wavelengths but shorter than radio wavelengths.

Interstellar Dust—Microscopic solid grains, believed to be mostly dielectric compounds of hydrogen and other common elements, in interstellar space.

Interstellar Gas—Sparse gas in interstellar space.

Kelvin Temperature Scale—An absolute temperature scale, the zero point of which is −273.15° C; temperature in kelvin = temperature in °C − 273.15.

Law of the Red Shifts—The relation between the radial velocity and distance of a remote galaxy: the radial velocity is proportional to the galaxy distance.

Light-year—The distance light travels in a vacuum in one year; $1 \text{ LY} = 9.46 \times 10^{12}$ km, or about 6×10^{12} mi.

Luminosity—The rate of radiation of electromagnetic energy into space by a star or other object.

Magnitude—A measure of the amount of light flux received from a star or other luminous object.

Nebula—Cloud of interstellar gas or dust.

Neutron Stars—A near-final stage in stellar evolution at which nuclear energy sources are exhausted, central densities are nuclear densities, and the stars are supported by degenerate neutron pressure. Rotating neutron stars are of current interest as pulsar models.

Nova—Suddenly exploding or erupting star gradually fading to original brightness.

Nuclear Transformation—Transformation of one atomic nucleus into another.

Occultation—An eclipse of a star or planet by the moon or some other celestial body, as seen from Earth.

Parsec—The distance of an object that would have a stellar parallax of one second of arc; 1 parsec = 3.26 light-years.

Planetary Nebula—A shell of gas ejected from, and enlarging about, a certain kind of extremely hot star.

Population I and II—Two classes of stars (and star systems) classified according to their spectral characteristics, chemical compositions, radial velocities, ages, and galaxy locations.

Proton-Proton Reaction—A chain of thermonuclear reactions by which hydrogen nuclei are built up into nuclei of helium, so producing huge amounts of energy.

Radio Waves—The lowest-energy electromagnetic radiation, lying beyond the infrared region of the spectrum. Narrow bands that can pass through the Earth's atmosphere are used in radio astronomy.

Recurrent Nova—A nova that has been known to erupt more than once.

Red Shift, Redshift—A shift to longer wavelengths of the light from remote galaxies; presumed to be produced by a Doppler shift.

Seyfert Galaxies—Galaxies having very bright nuclei and inconspicuous spiral arms. Their spectra show strong emission lines.

Solar Wind—Flow of high-energy particles (mainly protons and electrons) from the Sun.

Spectral Class (or Type)—A classification of a star according to the characteristics of its spectrum.

Spectrograph—An instrument for photographing a spectrum; usually attached to a telescope to photograph the spectrum of a star.

Spectroscope—An instrument for directly viewing the spectrum of a light source.

Spectrum—The array of colors or wavelengths obtained when light from a source is dispersed, as in passing it through a prism or grating.

Stellar Evolution—The changes that take place in the sizes, luminosities, structures, and the like of stars as they age.

Supergiants—Very bright stars that have undergone considerable expansion.

Ultraviolet Radiation—Electromagnetic radiation of wavelengths shorter than the shortest visible (violet) wavelengths and in the approximate range 10 to 300 nanometers.

X rays—Electromagnetic radiation lying between gamma rays and ultraviolet radiation in energy; totally absorbed by Earth's atmosphere.

THE TWENTY BRIGHTEST STARS*

The 20 brightest stars—stars with smallest apparent magnitude—contain one triple-star system and nine binary systems. The table gives the stars, their distance in parsecs, and the apparent and absolute magnitude of the stars and their components.

Star	Distance (Parsecs)	APPARENT VISUAL MAGNITUDES OF COMPONENTS			ABSOLUTE VISUAL MAGNITUDES OF COMPONENTS		
		1st	2d	3d	1st	2d	3d
Sirius	2.7	−1.47	+ 8.5	—	+1.4	+11.4	—
Canopus	34	−0.73	—	—	−3.3	—	—
Arcturus	11	−0.06	—	—	−0.3	—	—
α Centauri	1.3	−0.00	+ 1.4	+10.7	+4.4	+ 5.8	+15
Vega	8.0	+0.04	—	—	+0.6	—	—
Rigel	261	+0.08	+ 6.6	—	−7.0	− 0.4	—
Capella	14	+0.09	+ 0.5	—	+0.1	+ 0.4	—
Procyon	3.4	+0.34	+10.8	—	+2.6	+13.0	—
Betelgeuse	199	+0.41v	—	—	−5.5	—	—
Achernar	23	+0.47	—	—	−1.6	—	—
β Centauri	101	+0.59	+ 4	—	−4.4	− 0.8	—
Altair	4.9	+0.77	—	—	+1.9	—	—
α Crucis	86	+0.79	+ 1.9	—	−3.9	− 3.5	—
Aldebaran	20	+0.86	+13	—	−0.3	+12	—
Spica	80	+0.96	—	—	−3.5	—	—
Antares	132	+1.08	+ 5.1	—	−4.5	− 0.3	—
Pollux	11	+1.15	—	—	+0.2	—	—
Fomalhaut	7.0	+1.16	+ 6.5	—	+1.7	+ 7.3	—
β Crucis	175	+1.24v	—	—	−5.0	—	—
Deneb	460	+1.26	—	—	−7.0	—	—

* For information about the sun, see page 299.　v = variable magnitude.

THE NEAREST STARS

The following list gives the star, its distance in parsecs (a parsec is equal to 3.26 light-years), and the apparent and absolute magnitudes of the star and its components. The apparent magnitude is the brightness of the star as observed from Earth, while the absolute magnitude is the brightness that the star would have at a distance of 10 parsecs. The larger the magnitude, the fainter the star. A first-magnitude star appears roughly 2.5 times as bright as a second-magnitude star. A zero magnitude star is 2.5 times as bright as a first-magnitude star, and a −1 star is 2.5 times as bright as a zero-magnitude star.

Star	Distance (Parsecs)	APPARENT VISUAL MAGNITUDES OF COMPONENTS			ABSOLUTE VISUAL MAGNITUDES OF COMPONENTS		
		1st	2d	3d	1st	2d	3d
Proxima	1.31	10.7	—	—	15.1	—	—
α Centauri	1.31	0.00	+ 1.4	+10.7	+ 4.4	+ 5.8	+15
Barnard's Star	1.60	+ 9.54	—	—	+13.2	—	—
Wolf 359	2.33	+13.5	—	—	+16.7	—	—
Lalande 21185	2.48	+ 7.48	—	—	+10.5	—	—
Sirius	2.67	− 1.47	+ 8.5	—	+ 1.4	+11.4	—
Luyten 726−8	2.67	+12.5	+12.9	—	+15.4	+15.8	—
UV Cet	2.73	12.5	13.0	—	15.3	+15.8	—
Ross 154	2.91	+10.6	—	—	+13.3	—	—
Ross 248	3.16	+12.24	—	—	+14.7	—	—
ε Eridani	3.28	+ 3.68	—	—	+ 6.1	—	—
Ross 128	3.31	+11.13	—	—	+13.5	—	—
Luyten 789−6	3.31	+12.28	—	—	+14.6	—	—
Procyon	3.37	+ 0.34	+10.7	—	+ 2.6	+13.0	—
61 Cygni	3.43	+ 5.19	+ 6.02	—	+ 7.5	+ 8.4	—
ε Indi	3.43	+ 4.71	—	—	+ 7.0	—	—
Σ 2398	3.53	+ 8.90	+ 9.69	—	+11.1	+11.9	—
BD+43°44	3.56	+ 8.07	+11.04	—	+10.3	+13.2	—
Lac 9352	3.59	+ 7.43	—	—	+ 9.6	—	—
τ Ceti	3.65	+ 3.49	—	—	+ 5.7	—	—
BD+5°1668	3.77	+10.9	—	—	+13.0	—	—
Lac 8760	3.83	+ 6.76	—	—	+ 8.8	—	—
Kapteyn's Star	3.90	+ 8.81	—	—	+10.8	—	—
Kruger 60	3.93	+ 9.85	+11.3	—	+11.9	+13.3	—
Ross 614	4.03	+11.13	+14.8	—	+13.1	+16.8	—
BD−12°4523	4.10	+10.13	—	—	+12.0	—	—
v. Maanen's Star	4.24	+12.36	—	—	+14.3	—	—

THE CONSTELLATIONS

Constellations are configurations of stars supposedly resembling a particular object, person, or animal. Usually, the stars within a given constellation are named with a Greek letter plus the genitive of the constellation, with the brightest star getting the first Greek letter, alpha; the second brightest getting the second Greek letter, beta; and the like. The following table gives the constellation, its genitive, its English name or description, and the abbreviation for it that is usually found on star charts.

Constellation	Genitive	English name or description	Abbreviation
Andromeda	Andromedae	Chained Maiden	And
Antlia	Antliae	Air pump	Ant
Apus	Apodis	Bird of Paradise	Aps
Aquarius	Aquarii	Water bearer	Aqr
Aquila	Aquilae	Eagle	Aql
Ara	Arae	Altar	Ara
Aries	Arietis	Ram	Ari
Auriga	Aurigae	Charioteer	Aur
Boötes	Boötis	Herdsman	Boo
Caelum	Caeli	Chisel	Cae
Camelopardalis	Camelopardalis	Giraffe	Cam
Cancer	Cancri	Crab	Cnc
Canes Venatici	Canum Venaticorum	Hunting dogs	CVn
Canis Major	Canis Majoris	Great dog	CMa
Canis Minor	Canis Minoris	Little dog	CMi
Capricornus	Capricorni	Sea goat	Cap
•Carina	Carinae	Keel of Argonauts' ship	Car
Cassiopeia	Cassiopeiae	Queen of Ethiopia	Cas
Centaurus	Centauri	Centaur	Cen
Cepheus	Cephei	King of Ethiopia	Cep
Cetus	Ceti	Whale	Cet
Chamaeleon	Chamaeleontis	Chameleon	Cha
Circinus	Circini	Compasses	Cir
Columba	Columbae	Dove	Col
Coma Berenices	Comae Berenices	Berenice's hair	Com
Corona Australis	Coronae Australis	Southern crown	CrA
Corona Borealis	Coronae Borealis	Northern crown	CrB
Corvus	Corvi	Crow	Crv
Crater	Crateris	Cup	Crt
Crux	Crucis	Cross (southern)	Cru
Cygnus	Cygni	Swan	Cyg
Delphinus	Delphini	Dolphin	Del
Dorado	Doradûs	Swordfish	Dor
Draco	Draconis	Dragon	Dra
Equuleus	Equulei	Little horse	Equ
Eridanus	Eridani	River	Eri
Fornax	Fornacis	Furnace	For
Gemini	Geminorum	Twins	Gem
Grus	Gruis	Crane	Gru
Hercules	Herculis	Hercules	Her
Horologium	Horologii	Clock	Hor
Hydra	Hydrae	Sea serpent	Hya
Hydrus	Hydri	Water snake	Hyi
Indus	Indi	Indian	Ind
Lacerta	Lacertae	Lizard	Lac
Leo	Leonis	Lion	Leo
Leo Minor	Leonis Minoris	Little lion	LMi
Lepus	Leporis	Hare	Lep
Libra	Librae	Balance	Lib
Lupus	Lupi	Wolf	Lup
Lynx	Lyncis	Lynx	Lyn
Lyra	Lyrae	Lyre	Lyr
Mensa	Mensae	Table Mountain	Men
Microscopium	Microscopii	Microscope	Mic
Monoceros	Monocerotis	Unicorn	Mon
Musca	Muscae	Fly	Mus
Norma	Normae	Rule	Nor
Octans	Octantis	Octant	Oct
Ophiuchus	Ophiuchi	Serpent bearer	Oph
Orion	Orionis	Orion, the hunter	Ori
Pavo	Pavonis	Peacock	Pav
Pegasus	Pegasi	Pegasus, the winged horse	Peg
Perseus	Persei	Perseus, hero who saved Andromeda	Per
Phoenix	Phoenicis	Phoenix	Phe
Pictor	Pictoris	Easel	Pic

Constellation	Genitive	English name or description	Abbreviation	Constellation	Genitive	English name or description	Abbreviation
Pisces	Piscium	Fishes	Psc	Sextans	Sextantis	Sextant	Sex
Piscis Austrinus	Piscis Austrini	Southern fish	PsA	Taurus	Tauri	Bull	Tau
*Puppis	Puppis	Stern of the Argonauts' ship	Pup	Telescopium	Telescopii	Telescope	Tel
				Triangulum	Trianguli	Triangle	Tri
*Pyxis	Pyxidis	Compass on the Argonauts' ship	Pyx	Triangulum Australe	Trianguli Australis	Southern triangle	TrA
				Tucana	Tucanae	Toucan	Tuc
Reticulum	Reticuli	Net	Ret	Ursa Major	Ursae Majoris	Great bear	UMa
Sagitta	Sagittae	Arrow	Sge	Ursa Minor	Ursae Minoris	Little bear	UMi
Sagittarius	Sagittarii	Archer	Sgr	*Vela	Velorum	Sails of the Argonauts' ship	Vel
Scorpius	Scorpii	Scorpion	Sco				
Sculptor	Sculptoris	Sculptor's tools	Scl	Virgo	Virginis	Virgin	Vir
Scutum	Scuti	Shield	Sct	Volans	Volantis	Flying fish	Vol
Serpens	Serpentis	Serpent	Ser	Vulpecula	Vulpeculae	Fox	Vul

* The four constellations Carina, Puppis, Pyxis, and Vela originally formed the single constellation Argo Navis.

SUPERNOVAE, "BLACK HOLES" AND THE GUM NEBULA

Astronomers have recently added two new objects to the growing list of strange and puzzling objects speculated about or found in the universe. A "black hole" is the hypothetical result of a runaway or uncontrolled gravitational collapse of a star or collection of stars. Eventually a collapsing object, such as a star, will reach a limiting size, called the Schwarzschild radius, which depends upon the mass of the object. For the Sun the Schwarzschild radius would be under two miles. If the contracting object continues to contract to less than its Schwarzschild radius it becomes a black hole. The gravitational forces exerted by this object are so strong that no matter or radiation can escape from it. The light emanating from this object is trapped and effectively removed from the "observable universe."

Astrophysicists have speculated that the exploding core of a supernova can become either a neutron star or a black hole. The final mass of the remnant star determines whether gravitational collapse will stop at the stable neutron star stage, instead of running away and becoming a black hole. It is believed that if the star's mass is greater than about 3.0 times the Sun's mass a black hole should readily form. (Neutron stars should form for stars whose mass is above 1.4 times the Sun's mass.) A black hole almost certainly exists in the binary star Cygnus X-1 and maybe in other X-ray binaries. There is also possible evidence of massive black holes at the centers of certain galaxies, notably M87,

that would tear apart and swallow stars in the surrounding galaxy.

Nebulae are extended bright luminosities in the sky. Some nebulae are the glowing remnants of supernovae. Other nebulae are clouds of ionized hydrogen surrounding hot stars, which cause them to glow continuously. Such objects surrounding hot stars are called Stromgren spheres. The Gum Nebula (first discovered by the Australian astronomer, Colin S. Gum, in 1952) appears to be a totally new class of nebula that combines certain characteristics of the other two types of nebulae. The Gum Nebula is about 2,600 light years across in its longest dimension and appears to be somewhat elliptical in shape. It would have required a tremendous supernova to have blown its material up to 1,300 light years into space in all directions, and furthermore, while there are stars within the Gum Nebula, they are not hot enough to ionize such a large volume of space. Hence, the Gum Nebula cannot be either a supernova remnant or an ordinary Stromgren sphere. A group of astronomers from NASA and Kitt Peak National Observatory proposes that the Gum Nebula is a fossil Stromgren sphere produced by a supernova that exploded 11,000 years ago, giving off a tremendous blast of ultraviolet radiation, which ionized interstellar hydrogen clouds for hundreds of light years around. What is now glowing is not the material that was originally ejected from the supernova, but the interstellar hydrogen gas that was there before the supernova explosion. Unlike Stromgren spheres that are continuously being ionized by hot stars, the fossil Gum Nebula is gradually decaying, as the ionized hydrogen gas recombines in the absence of a new ionizing source.

INTERSTELLAR MOLECULES

Within the last 20 years astronomers have found that there is a continuous exchange of material between stars and the interstellar medium. Stars are continually being formed from diffuse interstellar material. This diffuse interstellar material somehow collects into interstellar clouds which may eventually contract under gravitational forces forming stars and, possibly, planetary systems. As stars evolve, material is ejected from them to again become part of the interstellar medium.

The first interstellar molecules ever found—CH, CH+, and CN (cyanogen)—were diatomic (consisting of only two atoms) and were found more than 35 years ago by optical astronomers.

In March 1951 radio astronomers detected interstellar atomic hydrogen (H) and in 1963 they discovered the hydroxyl radical (OH) in the interstellar medium. Up to this time no one had ever detected a polyatomic molecule (consisting of three or more atoms). The formation of molecules more complex than diatomic molecules in interstellar space was believed to be rare, since interstellar densities and temperatures are so low that molecule formation is very difficult.

This idea was upset in 1968 when radio astronomers detected interstellar ammonia (NH_3). In early 1969 radio astronomers detected interstellar water vapor (H_2O). In March 1969 interstellar formaldehyde (H_2CO)—the first polyatomic organic molecule—was discovered by radio

astronomers. On March 13, 1970, a Naval Research Laboratory Aerobee rocket detected molecular hydrogen (H_2) in interstellar space.

Interstellar atomic hydrogen (H) has been observed by radio astronomers since 1951, but molecular hydrogen had previously eluded detection. In 1970 radio astronomers also found interstellar carbon monoxide (CO), hydrogen cyanide (HCN), cyanoacetylene (HC_3N), formic acid (HCOOH), and methanol or wood alcohol (CH_3OH). Another molecule, originally called "X-ogen" has since been identified as HCO†. Since 1970 several more interstellar molecules have been detected, including deuterium (heavy hydrogen), hydrogen sulfide (H_2S), acetaldehyde (CH_3CHO), and silicon monoxide (SiO). Large numbers are found in massive dense interstellar clouds, such as the Great Nebula in Orion and Sagittarius B2.

Additional evidence for the existence of extraterrestrial organic molecules was given in December 1970, when it was announced that a meteorite that fell near Murchison, Victoria, Australia, on September 28, 1969, is believed to contain five of the 20 most common amino acids—glycine, alanine, glutamic acid, valine, and proline. This finding demonstrates that complex amino acids, the basic building blocks of proteins, can be and have been formed outside the Earth by natural chemical processes.

Hence, in recent years, astronomers have found that the interstellar medium is interspersed with molecules, a proportionately high fraction of which are organic compounds. As star and planet formation take place, these organic compounds may play an important role in the chemical evolution and origin of life.

OUR LOCAL GROUP OF GALAXIES

Our local group of galaxies contains over 20 members that cover a region about 3 million light-years in diameter. The largest members are both spiral galaxies—our Milky Way galaxy and the Andromeda galaxy (M-31). All together, there are three spirals, four irregulars, and 11 ellipticals, of which six are dwarf elliptical galaxies. Some of our local galaxies are listed below, with apparent magnitude, distance in thousand parsecs (kiloparsecs), galactic diameter in kiloparsecs, and absolute magnitude.

Galaxy	Visual magnitude	Distance (kilopcs)	Diameter (kilopcs)	Absolute magnitude
The Milky Way	—	—	30	(—21)
Large Magellanic Cloud	0.9	48	10	—17.7
Small Magellanic Cloud	2.5	56	8	—16.5
Ursa Minor system	—	70	1	(—9)
Sculptor system	8.0	83	2.2	—11.8
Draco system	—	100	1.4	(—10)
Fornax system	8.3	190	6.6	—13.3
Leo II system	12.04	230	1	—10.0
Leo I system	12.0	280	1.5	—10.4

Galaxy	Visual magnitude	Distance (kilopcs)	Diameter (kilopcs)	Absolute magnitude
NGC 6822	8.9	460	2.7	—14.8
NGC 147	9.73	570	3	—14.5
NGC 185	9.43	570	2.3	—14.8
NGC 205	8.17	680	5	—16.5
NGC 221 (M32)	8.16	680	2.4	—16.5
IC 1613	9.61	680	5	—14.7
Andromeda galaxy	3.47	680	40	—21.2
NGC 598 (M33)	5.79	720	17	—18.9
Maffei 1	11.0	1000	—	—19.0

ASTRONOMICAL INSTRUMENTATION

The most important property of a telescope is its ability to gather light so that objects that are too remote or too faint to be seen with the naked eye are detectable. The light-gathering power of a telescope varies according to the total surface area of either the objective lens or the mirror in the telescope.

There are two main classes of telescopes that gather visible light: reflectors and refractors. In a reflector, a large curved mirror gathers the light; in a refractor, a large objective lens accomplishes this feat. The largest reflecting telescope now in operation has a 236" mirror; the largest refracting telescope has a 40" objective lens. The Schmidt camera is an optical system that utilizes both a mirror and a lens; it produces excellent star images over a large area of the sky and is in widespread use around the world.

In 1931, K. G. Jansky encountered interference in the form of radio radiation coming from an unknown source, which subsequent investigation showed was the Milky Way. In 1936, Grote Reber built the first antenna that was specifically designed to receive these cosmic radio waves. In 1942, radio radiation was first received from the Sun. After World War II, the technique of making radio astronomical observations was rapidly developed, especially in Australia, England, the Netherlands, and more recently in the United States. The 328-foot radio telescope at Bonn, West Germany is the world's largest fully steerable radio telescope.

In a radio telescope, the radiowave gathering is done by a parabolic metallic reflector, called a "dish," which focuses waves onto an antenna. Sensitivity is increased by using an array of such antennas.

Radio signals have been observed to come from the Sun, the Moon, certain planets, from the center of our galaxy, and from other galaxies. In addition, strong radio signals are given off by quasars while rapidly pulsating radio signals are emitted from pulsars. Radio signals can be used to determine both the surface and lower-atmosphere temperatures of the planets.

Other types of radio emission offer insight into the physical processes within the upper atmosphere of the planets and the Sun, as well as certain physical processes within galaxies. Signals at certain discrete radio wavelengths are caused by the presence of certain interstellar molecules. The amount and distribution of these molecules in space are determinable by using radio telescopes.

Radar astronomy systems consist of a powerful radio transmitter, capable of transmitting high-power radio signals out into space over long distances, and a sensitive antenna, with which the return radar echo is detectable. This returning radar echo can provide information about lunar and planetary surfaces, planetary atmospheres and rotation periods, and the precise values of the distances of different solar system objects. X-ray astronomy gains data from satellites and from rocket and balloon flights, X rays being absorbed by the atmosphere. Since 1962 over 250 X-ray sources have been detected inside and outside our Galaxy and include supernova remnants, quasars, binary systems, and possible black holes.

Only a few bands of infrared wavelengths from space can penetrate the atmosphere. Special detectors of this radiation, on the ground and in rockets, have shown that huge quantities of infrared rays are emitted from dying stars and from stars being born.

MAJOR ASTRONOMICAL FACILITIES

This list includes the world's major astronomical observing facilities: reflecting and refracting optical telescopes, radio telescopes, and radar astronomy systems. UC = Under construction.

REFLECTING TELESCOPES AND SCHMIDT CAMERAS

Mirror Diameter (Inches)	Observatory	In Operation Since
237	Academy of Sciences of the USSR, near Zelenchukskaya, USSR	1976
200	Palomar Observatory, Mount Palomar, California	1948
176*	Smithsonian Astrophysical Observatory, Mount Hopkins, Arizona	1978
158	Kitt Peak National Observatory, Tucson, Arizona	1974
157	Cerro Tololo Observatory, La Serena, Chile	1976
153	Siding Spring Observatory, Siding Spring, NSW, Australia	1975
150	Mount Stromlo Observatory, Canberra, Australia	1972
142	European Southern Observatory, La Silla, Chile	1976
120	Lick Observatory, Mount Hamilton, California	1959
107	McDonald Observatory, Fort Davis, Texas	1968
104	Crimean Astrophysical Observatory, Simeis, Ukrainian SSR	1960
101	Cerro Las Campanas Observatory, La Serena, Chile	1975
100	Hale Observatory, Mount Wilson, California	1917
98	Royal Greenwich Observatory, Herstmonceux, Sussex, England	1967
90	Steward Observatory, University of Arizona, Tucson, Arizona	1969
88	Mauna Kea Observatory, University of Hawaii, Mauna Kea, Hawaii	1970
84	Kitt Peak National Observatory, Tucson, Arizona	1961
82	McDonald Observatory, Fort Davis, Texas	1938
80	Kitt Peak National Observatory, Solar Telescope, Tucson, Arizona	1960
79	Astrophysical Observatory, Ondřejov, Czechoslovakia	1967
77	Observatoire de Haute-Provence, Saint Michel, France	1958
74	David Dunlap Observatory, Richmond Hill, Ontario, Canada	1935
74	Radcliffe Observatory, Pretoria, South Africa	1948
74	Mount Stromlo Observatory, Canberra, Australia	1955

* Light-gathering power of the six 72" mirrors in the Multiple Mirror Telescope.

Mirror Diameter (Inches)	Observatory	In Operation Since
74	Helwan Observatory, Helwan, Egypt	1960
74	Okayama Astrophysical Observatory, Kamogata Machi, Japan	1960
73	Dominion Astrophysical Observatory, Victoria, British Columbia	1918
72	Astrophysical Observatory, University of Padua, Asiago, Italy	1973
72	(Schmidt) Palomar Observatory, Mount Palomar, California	1948
72	(Schmidt) Mount Stromlo Observatory, Canberra, Australia	1973
69	Lowell Observatory, Flagstaff, Arizona	1961
61	Agassiz Station, Harvard College Observatory, Cambridge, Massachusetts	1934
61	National Observatory, Bosque Alegre Station, Argentina	1942
61	U.S. Naval Observatory, Flagstaff, Arizona	1963
61	Lunar and Planetary Laboratory, Tucson, Arizona	1965
60	Hale Observatory, Mount Wilson, California	1908
60	Boyden Observatory, Bloemfontein, South Africa	1930
60	Steward Observatory, Tucson, Arizona	1964
60	Lunar and Planetary Laboratory, Tucson, Arizona	1967
60	Palomar Observatory, Mount Palomar, California	1972
60	University of Mexico, Baja, California	UC
60	Cerro Tololo Observatory, La Serena, Chile	1967
60	Smithsonian Astrophysical Observatory, Mount Hopkins, Arizona	1970

REFRACTING TELESCOPES

Lens Diameter (Inches)	Observatory	In Operation Since
40	Yerkes Observatory, Williams Bay, Wisconsin	1897
36	Lick Observatory, Mount Hamilton, California	1888
33	Observatory of Physical Astronomy, Meudon, France	1893
32	Astrophysical Observatory, Potsdam, Germany	1899
30	Nice Observatory, Nice, France	1880
30	Allegheny Observatory, Pittsburgh, Pennsylvania	1914
28	Royal Greenwich Observatory, Herstmonceux, England	1894
26.5	University Observatory, Vienna, Austria	1878
26.5	Union Observatory, Johannesburg, South Africa	1925
26	U.S. Naval Observatory, Washington, D.C.	1873
26	Leander-McCormick Observatory, Charlottesville, Virginia	1883
26	Royal Greenwich Observatory, Herstmonceux, England	1897
26	Observatory of Acad. of Sciences, Berlin-Babelsberg, Germany	1912
26	Astronomical Observatory, Belgrade, Yugoslavia	1929
26	Tokyo Astronomical Observatory, Mitaka, Tokyo, Japan	1930
26	Mount Stromlo Observatory, Canberra, Australia	1953
26	Astronomical Observatory of the USSR Academy of Sciences, Pulkova	1957
24	Lowell Observatory, Flagstaff, Arizona	1896
24	South African Astronomical Observatory, Cape of Good Hope	1901
24	Hamburg Observatory, Bergedorf, Hamburg, Germany	1908

RADIO TELESCOPES

Antenna Diameter (Feet)	Observatory	In Operation Since
1000	Arecibo Observatory, Arecibo, Puerto Rico	1963
1000 × 115	Observatory of Paris, Nançay, France	1964
600 × 400	University of Illinois, Danville, Illinois	1962
400	University of California, Hat Creek, California	1960
360 × 70	Ohio State-Ohio Wesleyan Radio Observatory, Delaware, Ohio	1962
350	Stanford Radio Astronomy Institute, Stanford, California	1959
328 × 131(2)	Lebedev Physics Institute, Serpukhov, USSR	1963
328	Max Planck Institute, Bonn, West Germany	1971
300	National Radio Astronomy Observatory, Green Bank, West Virginia	1962
250	Nuffield Radio Ast. Lab., Jodrell Bank, England	1957
210	Australian Nat. Radio Astron. Observatory (CSIRO), Parkes, New South Wales	1961
210	Jet Propulsion Laboratory, Goldstone, California	1968
150	Sagamore Hill Radio Observatory, Hamilton, Massachusetts	1963
150	Algonquin Radio Observatory, Lake Traverse, Ontario	1967
140	National Radio Astronomy Observatory, Green Bank, West Virginia	1964
130	California Institute of Technology, Owens Valley, California	1968
120	Haystack Lincoln Laboratory, Massachusetts Institute of Technology, Tyngsboro, Massachusetts	1963
120	Carnegie Institution, Derwood, Maryland	1964
120	University of Illinois, Danville, Illinois	1971
118	Heinrich Hertz Institute, Berlin-Adlershof, Germany	1958
90(2)	California Institute of Technology, Owens Valley, California	1958
85	University of Michigan, Dexter, Michigan	1959
85(2)	Jet Propulsion Laboratory, Goldstone, California	1960
85	Harvard Radio Astronomy Station, Fort Davis, Texas	1961
85	University of California, Hat Creek, California	1962
85(2)	National Radio Astronomy Observatory, Green Bank, West Virginia	1964
interferometer	Westerbork Observatory, Westerbork, Netherlands	1970
interferometer	Mullard Radio Astron. Observatory, Cambridge, England	1972
interferometer	Molonglo Radio Observatory, Sydney University, Hoskinstown, New South Wales	1960

RADAR ASTRONOMY SYSTEMS

Antenna Diameter (Feet)	Observatory	Peak Power (Kilowatts)
1000	Arecibo Observatory, Arecibo, Puerto Rico	2,500
250	Nuffield Radio Ast. Lab., Jodrell Bank, Macclesfield, England	60
120	Haystack Lincoln Laboratory, Massachusetts Institute of Technology, Tyngsboro, Massachusetts	400
85	Jet Propulsion Laboratory, Goldstone, California	100
84	Millstone Lincoln Laboratory, Massachusetts Institute of Technology, Westford, Massachusetts	5,000
50 (8)	Crimean Astrophysical Observatory, Crimea, Ukrainian SSR	60

THE SUN, OUR NEAREST STAR

The Sun is of great importance because of its dominant influence on the Earth and the other planets and its role in the beginning and maintenance of life on our planet. But it is also important because the Sun is the only star near enough to be observed in any detail. Astronomers have inferred that physical processes on other stars are similar to those processes observed on the Sun.

This star is directly responsible for many phenomena on our planet, including the origin and survival of life, clouds, atmospheric motion and weather, and the thermal structure and composition of the Earth's atmosphere and the atmospheres of the other planets. Several billion years ago solar ultraviolet radiation supplied the energy needed to synthesize inorganic elements into the first organic molecules that formed the basis for life on Earth.

The average surface temperature of our planet, which must be within certain limits if life is to flourish and evolve, is determined by the amount of visible solar radiation the Earth's surface receives. Visible solar radiation causes water to evaporate from our oceans, and this atmospheric water vapor eventually condenses to form clouds and precipitation. Solar heating is responsible for the large-scale motions of the atmosphere and ocean, as well as small-scale phenomena, such as cumulus cloud formation. Solar X rays and ultraviolet radiation determine the temperature of the upper atmospheres of the planets, as well as the structure of planetary ionospheres.

Solar electrons and protons reaching the vicinity of the Earth, via solar wind or solar flares, are trapped by the Earth's magnetic field, forming the Van Allen radiation belts. Solar-emitted particles that collide with the atoms in our upper atmosphere cause auroral displays.

Solar particles are also responsible for radio and short-wave communication fadeouts, since clouds of these solar particles imbedded in the Earth's upper atmosphere interfere with the radio reflection characteristics of the ionosphere. Sudden increases in the emission of solar X rays and energetic particles, during periods of high solar activity, may prove dangerous to astronauts orbiting above the protective blanket of atmosphere that shields life at the Earth's surface from the lethal solar radiation and particle flux.

It is believed that the formation of the Sun, the planets, and other stars began with the condensation of an interstellar gas cloud; this cloud consisted almost completely of pure hydrogen with a very small percentage of heavier elements that were produced during the explosion and ejections of exploding stars (supernovae). In fact, the interstellar medium is constantly being supplied with material rich in heavy elements that have been ejected from supernovae.

As the star contracts out of the interstellar cloud under gravitational forces, the temperature and pressure at the star's center (core) increase until the temperature reaches about 10 million degrees. At this temperature, four hydrogen nuclei in the Sun's core fuse together to form a single helium nucleus. However, four hydrogen nuclei weigh a little more than one helium nucleus. This small amount of mass has been converted to energy. Every second the Sun converts some 616 million tons of hydrogen into 612 million tons of helium. This thermonuclear reaction provides the tremendous amount of energy that the Sun radiates out in all directions into space in the form of electromagnetic radiation: X rays; ultraviolet, visible, and infrared rays; and radio waves. Every square meter of the Sun's surface emits 64 million watts into space.

Its high temperature causes the Sun to be a gaseous body or, more precisely, a plasma—the fourth state of matter that is attained when electrically neutral atoms break up into positively charged nuclei and negatively charged electrons. The diameter of the Sun is about 864,900 miles—more than 109 times that of the Earth. The Sun's mass is 2×10^{30} kg—or approximately 333,-000 times the mass of the Earth. The mean density of the Sun is 1.4 grams/cm³—only about one-quarter of the Earth's density—suggesting that the Sun primarily consists of very light elements. The period of the Sun's rotation on its axis depends on the solar latitude, being least (25 days) at the equator; its average rotation period is 27 days.

It is difficult to obtain any evidence that is based on direct observation about the core of the Sun. All of our knowledge of the solar core reflects theoretical considerations; it is a region of very high pressure and temperature, and thermonuclear reactions occur there. The solar energy is transported from the core by radiative processes, in which atoms absorb, reemit, and scatter the radiation. Close to the surface the energy is carried by large looping convection currents in the unstable region known as the convective zone. Shock waves from this zone carry energy into the solar atmosphere.

The solar surface (photosphere or "sphere of light") is what we see when looking up at the Sun. By using high-resolution telescopes, the convection currents' tops can actually be observed on the photosphere. The solar surface is not as smooth as had been thought; it is actually covered with a fine cellular structure (granulation), which is caused by the top of the convection cells breaking across the photosphere. Spectacular gaseous eruptions (prominences) from the surface can extend up to an altitude of 500,000 miles in great arching filaments.

Other photospheric features include sunspots and solar flares, which are discussed below. The convective motions are very important, because they appear to be the source of the mechanical energy that is responsible for heating and the observed temperature increase within the solar atmosphere. The immense temperature—1,000,-000°C—of the outer layer of the atmosphere (the corona) has no dependence on the heat flowing from the photosphere.

The solar atmosphere consists of two regions: the chromosphere and the corona. The chromosphere is 6,000 to 9,000 miles thick, and its lower part is simply an extension of the photosphere at about 6,000° C, the density decreasing very considerably. The upper chromosphere has a temperature that approaches 100,000° C.

The corona, which surrounds the chromosphere, is the region that is observed during a total solar eclipse, when the Moon, which has the same angular size in the sky as the Sun, passes directly in front of it, blocking out the photospheric radiation and permitting the fainter light of the corona to be observed.

The solar atmosphere permeates through the interplanetary medium via a constant stream of solar protons and electrons ("solar wind"). The protons and electrons have enough energy by virtue of the high temperature of the solar atmosphere to escape from the Sun's gravitational field. The solar wind streams radially outward from the Sun, and is a regular feature of the Sun. Study of the X-ray emissions from the corona have revealed large low-density regions, known as coronal holes, usually extending as winding structures from the polar regions. They appear to be the source of the high-speed particles of the solar wind.

Complicated magnetic fields occur in the region extending from the convective zone to the corona and beyond. There is much evidence that magnetic fields are of considerable importance on the Sun. Their most spectacular manifestations are related to photospheric solar activity, particularly prominences, sunspots and solar flares. Sunspots are complicated hydromagnetic phenomena displaying very strong magnetic fields; they appear dark against the bright photosphere because their temperatures are several thousand degrees lower.

Associated with sunspots are solar flares, energetic phenomena that produce both electromagnetic radiation and solar particle emission. These flares occur because their material has gained enough energy—via solar magnetic fields—to be ejected from the Sun and shot into space. One of the remarkable features of both sunspots and solar flares is that they appear to increase numerically in an 11-year cycle of solar activity. Also associated with this cycle are increased emissions of solar X rays and centimeter radio waves.

In recent years, it has been shown from studies of the frictional atmospheric drag on orbiting satellites and from direct in situ measurements with instruments on board rockets and satellites that the temperature, composition, and density of the Earth's upper atmosphere is strongly responsive to changes in solar geometry and the level of solar activity. Some of these responses follow diurnal, 27-day (solar rotation period), and 11-year (sunspot cycle) variations.

THE PLANETS

It is thought that about 4.6 billion years ago, the Earth was formed from the same interstellar gas cloud that gave birth to the other planets of the solar system and the Sun. The gas cloud was mostly hydrogen, with heavier elements making up only a small fraction of its composition. As the gas cloud contracted under gravitational forces, the temperature and pressure of the central core increased tremendously until thermonuclear reactions—the conversion of hydrogen into helium with the accompanying release of huge amounts of light and heat energy—began, and a star, the Sun, formed. Dust grains in the now disk-shaped cloud constantly collided and coalesced into ever larger bodies, which in turn consolidated into planets surrounded by gaseous atmospheres.

During the following 4.6 billion years, the planets and their atmospheres have changed and evolved significantly. The following is a brief survey of the planets in our solar system, with the exception of the Earth, which is discussed in the section *Earth: Facts/Figures.*

MERCURY is the smallest planet in the solar system and the closest to the Sun. This combination provides for a hot and gravitationally "weak" planet that cannot retain a gaseous atmosphere. Mercury rotates within a period of 58.65 days, or exactly two thirds of its period of revolution around the Sun: 88 days.

The U.S. Mariner 10 space probe has relayed to Earth invaluable information and photographs as it flew within 500 miles of Mercury. The surface resembles that of the Moon in being heavily cratered, little eroded, and with smooth areas similar but smaller than the lunar *maria.* The surface material has a low density. Thus the average density, measured accurately by Mariner 10, of 5.5 grams/cc implies a large core of heavy material, possibly iron. The planet could therefore be similar in composition to the Earth. An iron core would mean that Mercury has a magnetic field and in fact a very weak magnetic field was detected by the probe.

No gaseous atmosphere greater than 100-billionths that of the Earth was revealed. Traces of helium were detected but this gas would be rapidly boiled off. Measurements of surface temperature gave a daytime maximum of 350°C (660°F) and a night-time minimum of −170°C (−270°F). Mercury therefore has a greater surface temperature range than any other planet, although its maximum is less than that of Venus.

VENUS, "Earth's twin" in size and mass, is otherwise unlike it. Its surface is hot (about 890°F on dark and light side and from pole to pole), waterless, corrosive and lifeless, with a pressure averaging 90 terrestrial atmospheres (equivalent to an ocean depth of 1/2 mile (molecular light scattering) and a bright Venusian midday would compare to one heavily overcast on Earth. From 21 to about 31 miles there is smog and haze. The cloud layer lies at 31–41 miles and consists of tiny liquid droplets of sulfuric acid, tinged yellow with tiny grains of sulfur.

Sixteen space probes, beginning with Mariner 2 (1962) and culminating with Pioneer Venus 1 and 2 and Venera 11 and 12 (Dec. 1978) have vastly increased our knowledge. Some recently returned data have not yet been interpreted (as of May 1979). For example, the isotropic data for argon are presently contradictory, and reports of lightning and thunder need confirmation, as does the reported incandescent glow of the surface. The 890°F surface temperature is borderline for glowing, depending on the emissivity of the material.

Venera 9 and 10 returned surface photographs. Site 9 was rock-strewn, with 15-20° slopes. The rocks were sharp-edged, indicative of "young" topography. Site 10 was on a plain, with slab-like (layered?) pitted boulders and "rock outcrops." It is a comparatively "mature" topography, suggesting more corrosion and degradation. Gamma ray spectrometers and densitometers measured U, Th and K radioactivities, and densities compatible with basaltic rock.

Venus condensed too close to the Sun ever to have possessed much water. The ambient surface temperature of 890°F is too hot for water-bearing minerals such as micas and amphiboles to be stable. Probably there have never been oceans, or sedimentary rocks such as limestone. It is also doubtful that there has ever been life.

Water and life have greatly altered Earth's primitive atmosphere, locking up most of its CO_2 in the hydrosphere and carbonate rocks. Were this CO_2 released on Earth our atmosphere would be much like that of Venus in bulk, pressure and composition.

The atmosphere of Venus is about 97% CO_2, 3% N_2, with traces of H_2O, O_2, noble gases, CO, SO_2, and others. In its lesser gases it is inhomogeneous in its upper reaches where photochemical reactions occur, but is homogeneous below about 21 miles, where no liquid or solid particles condense. Both Earth and Venus lost their original hydrogen and helium in the "protoplanet" stage. Were all of the atmospheric water of Venus to condense onto a level, cool surface, its depth would be about 1.5 feet.

Like Earth, Venus has an ionosphere. Unlike Earth's it persists at night, and there is an ionopause—i.e., a sharp *upper* boundary where the ionosphere reacts with the solar wind, in the absence of a magnetosphere. The atmosphere of Venus is very dynamic in its upper reaches, driven by the solar energy absorbed. At both poles there is a huge zone of down-flowing air.

The cause of the anomalous 243-day *retrograde* rotation of Venus is unknown. The once suspected spin-orbit resonance control by Earth has been discounted. Venus' spin vector is apparently aligned with the angular momentum vector of the solar system. Since Pluto (in its highly inclined orbit) contributes to this alignment, ultimate determination of Pluto's mass may be possible.

High rock surface temperatures and out-flowing radioactive heat probably caused Venus to "outgas" (liberate gaseous materials from its interior into its atmosphere) early in its history. One might not expect to find current active volcanism, but two large suspected volcanic features have been reported. The hot "crustal" rocks should lack rigidity, eliminating strains that might cause severe "earthquakes."

Venus probably has a molten iron core. Slow rotation precludes the existence of a magnetic field. Earth-based radar mapping, enhanced by probe altimetry and imaging, has found a Tibet-sized plateau and Himalayan-height mountains, a huge valley and (apparently) large impact craters. With no erosional processes known, tectonic activity is suspected. Regional slopes are gentle (less than 5°). Total topographic relief is about 9 miles, comparable to Earth's, but not bi-modally distributed into continental interior plateaus and abysmal ocean basins, as is Earth's relief.

MARS, in direct contrast to Venus, with its hot, heavy, and opaque atmosphere, has one that is cold, thin, and transparent and readily permits observation of the planet's surface features. As observed from Earth, Mars's main surface features include white polar caps and bright and dark regions all of which show seasonal variations.

The bright areas, which constitute almost three-quarters of the total Martian surface area, give the planet its familiar ruddy color. The bright areas are believed to be siliceous, as was found from data sent back in 1971 from the Soviet probe Mars III. The dark areas cover roughly one third of the planet's surface.

Infrared observations have shown that the average temperature of the whole planet is −45° F, with a maximum equatorial noon temperature of 80° F. The daily temperature variation from noon to midnight at the equator is about 180° F, suggesting that the Martian atmosphere is very thin and thus does not retain heat. With an atmosphere much thinner than ours, the atmospheric surface pressure is only 7.7 mbar (Viking readings). Because the Martian atmosphere is so thin, it changes temperature rapidly, thus bringing about the large temperature contrasts that play a major role in driving the high Martian winds.

In 1971 three orbiting Mars probes were launched: two Russian (Mars II and III) and one American (Mariner 9). Mars III deposited a transmitter on the surface of the planet, but this failed almost immediately after arrival. Mariner 9 remained in orbit for almost a year and sent back photographs and scientific information that drastically altered man's ideas about the planet. Only half of the surface, mainly in the southern hemisphere, is substantially cratered. In the northern hemisphere, observed by Mariner 9, four immense volcanic mountains were found as well as a vast system of canyons, tributary gullies, and narrow channels. These features are far greater in scale than anything seen on earth. The largest volcanic mountain, Olympus Mons, the biggest known in the solar system, is more than 300 miles in diameter at the base and about 16 miles high. The sparsely cratered northern regions, strewn with wind-blown debris, are plains of lava that flooded the surface at different times after its earliest history. The heavily cratered southern terrain was also modified by volcanic activity.

Apparently, contrary to earlier ideas, there has been internal activity in the planet, maybe quite recently. This is also suggested by the series of huge canyons, 50 to 75 miles wide and 3 to 4 miles deep stretching along the equator to the east of the volcanic regions.

At the eastern extreme of the canyons lies a large area of chaotic terrain, first observed by Mariner 6 and 7. It is an irregular jumble of topographic forms, possibly the result of some kind of collapse related to that of the canyons. Channels, hundreds of miles long, extend from this terrain in a northwesterly direction. They also appear in other areas on the planet's surface. The channels may have been cut by large amounts of flowing water. The Viking spacecraft have since shown that in Mars' earliest history flowing water was significant in shaping its features. Since then, although surface dust and other debris have been extensively and continuously redistributed by high-speed winds, wind erosion of the surface has been negligible, leaving features sharply defined.

The bright circular region, Hellas, roughly 1000 miles across, is an example of basinlike depressions seen in several regions of the Martian surface. Mariner 7 showed it to be almost devoid of topographical features. It is exceptionally low—over a mile below the mean Martian elevation. Mariner 9 indicated that Hellas probably serves as a collection center for dust and may also be a source of dust.

The lower atmosphere can become filled with dust when the Martian winds become really strong. The dust storms are phenomena whose explanation may be similar to that of the initial stages of a hurricane. When Mariner 9 and the Soviet Mars probes reached Mars, the greatest dust storm in more than a century was raging. The mapping of the Martian surface was consequently delayed for almost three months.

The polar caps appear as a white cover over the north and south poles. This cover grows and recedes with seasonal regularity, alternating from one hemisphere to the other once every Martian year (687 Earth days). The Mariner 7 photographs showed snow-filled craters of the southern polar cap in sharp relief with snow-covered crater rims. The Viking orbiters have indicated that the residual (summer) northern and probably the southern caps are predominantly water ice not frozen carbon dioxide as hitherto suspected. The amount of water vapor in the atmosphere, although very small, was found to increase with latitude, reaching a peak at the edge of the polar caps. In addition infrared measurements showed that the surface temperature (about -70°C) is not cold enough for solid carbon dioxide to form.

The landings of Viking 1 and 2 on Mars on July 20 and September 3, 1976, respectively, have greatly increased our store of Martian information. The mission's purpose was to probe the planet's interior, surface properties, weather, atmosphere and biology. Photographs from the two Viking orbiters and the two landers have shown Mars as a planet that, like Earth, has been shaped by great forces, and have revealed Mars' characteristics to a greater degree than any other unmanned exploration of Mars has been able to accomplish.

Landing site locales were finalized only after the two spacecraft went into orbit around Mars. Viking 1 landed near a region heavily scoured by what are believed to have been ancient floods, while Viking 2 is on a vast flat plain pocked by fewer craters. The color pictures transmitted to earth showed a bright faintly pink sky and a salmon-pink surface. The dry pink dust covering most of the rock-strewn desert-like surface is composed of a mixture of iron-rich clay minerals and carbonate minerals, iron oxide probably giving Mars its red appearance.

The inorganic analysis of Martian soil showed the presence of silicon, iron, calcium, aluminum, titanium, and sulfur (in order of abundance). Analysis of the atmosphere found it to contain 95% carbon dioxide, 2.7% nitrogen, 1.6% argon, and traces of oxygen and water vapor. The presence of argon showed that there was probably a much denser atmosphere and hence a very different climate from today's. The discovery of nitrogen increases the possibility of some form of life having evolved.

Viking landers are the first spacecraft ever sent to another planet with equipment specifically designed to search for alien life forms. Information from biology experiments on Mars are inconclusive but could suggest "the possibility of biological activity in the samples being incubated." Life on Mars has of yet been neither confirmed nor ruled out, but if it does exist, it has made a different adaptation than life forms on Earth.

JUPITER has a dense, cloudy atmosphere of hydrogen and helium, with about 90% hydrogen and 2% CH_4 and NH_3 and traces of ethane and acetylene. It rotates rapidly (in approximately 9 hours 50 minutes), is flattened 1/15, has a low mean density, great mass, a large fraction of the solar system's angular momentum and 13 (possibly 14) satellites. Its interior has a small rock-metal core, a liquid monatomic hydrogen "metallic" mantle 28,000 miles thick, and a liquid diatomic hydrogen mantle overlying that. Parallel clouds characterize its visible surface, divided into white-yellowish zones and reddish-brown belts. They probably consist of H_2O, ammonia, and NH_3SH crystals. Cloud-top temperatures average about −220°F.

Jupiter's central temperature theoretically is about 54,000°F and the planet radiates about two times as much energy as it receives, due possibly to continuing contraction.

The Great Red Spot – 24,000 × 9,000 miles – is an immense hurricane-like atmospheric disturbance, poorly understood. Other smaller, ephemeral spots are known. Since 1954 radio astronomers have detected radio signals, arising in strong magnetic fields and in Jupiter's magnetosphere. This magnetosphere is huge, complex and interacts with the solar wind, Jupiter's atmosphere, and the surface of Io (one of the planet's satellites). A "plasma torus" near Io's orbit surrounds Jupiter, containing ionized sulfur, with a temperature of 180,000°F. A "flux tube" connects Jupiter's magnetic poles and Io, and a powerful electric current flows (possibly as great as 5 million amperes).

The innermost satellite, Amalthea, is dark like an asteroid (166 × 88 miles). Io is fantastic! Seven currently active volcanoes were found spewing umbrella-shaped plumes up to 180 miles. Its surface is orange-red with no impact craters, but over 100 huge caldera-like depressions and lava flows—a "young" surface, renewed about every 10 million years.

Io and Europa are composed of rock; Ganymede and Callisto are composed of mixtures of "water-ice" and rock. Europa has few craters, Ganymede more, and craters are "shoulder-to-shoulder" on Callisto. Europa has a cracked, ice-encrusted surface. Ganymede, larger than Mercury, is also ice-encrusted, with a contorted, involuted and faulted pattern of lines and ridges. Icy Callisto have a huge bull's-eye formation (1,600 miles across), with concentric mountain ridges around a 200-mile central basin.

SATURN, the second largest planet in the solar system, has an internal and atmospheric structure similar to that of Jupiter. But it may have a greater amount of hydrogen and methane, as well as a smaller amount of ammonia in its atmosphere. The density of Saturn is so low—less than the density of water—that, if immersed in a large enough body of water, the planet would float.

First discovered by Galileo, the superb rings of Saturn have the appearance of a large, extremely thin, and flat circular sheet, lying centered on the planet in the equatorial plane. Three distinct rings have been identified; outer ring A is separated from the brightest ring, B, by a narrow gap called Cassini's Division. Interior to ring B is a faint, semitransparent one known as the "Crepe," or ring C. The rings are about ten miles thick, making them too thin to be seen when they are "edge on" to Earth.

The rings of Saturn are very large in extent. Ring A, which has an outer radius of 85,000 miles, is 10,000 miles wide. Cassini's Division is approximately 1,700 miles wide; ring B has a width of 16,500 miles. The Crepe ring is roughly 10,000 miles wide, reaching to within 9,000 miles of Saturn's equator.

In 1969, the discovery of a fourth ring was reported. This new faint ring (D) lies inside the Crepe ring. Probably composed of millions of bits of ice or ice-covered rock fragments, these rings are believed to be the remnants of a satellite of Saturn that broke up under the influence of the planet's gravitational field.

Saturn has a system of 10 satellites. Its largest satellite, Titan, is about the size of Mercury; it is the only satellite in the solar system observed to date that has an appreciable atmosphere, mainly of methane and possibly hydrogen, with a surface pressure which may be similar to that of Earth.

URANUS and **NEPTUNE** are the third and fourth largest planets, respectively, in the solar system. Because of their great distance from the Sun, little is known about either of them. Their mass can be calculated from the orbital period of their satellites. Their diameters have recently been recalculated by balloon measurement (Uranus: 32,200 miles) and by a stellar occultation (Neptune: 30,800).

Uranus was the first planet to be discovered with the aid of a telescope. It was discovered in 1781 by William Herschel. Neptune was telescopically discovered in 1846 by J. G. Galle; this discovery was based on orbital changes of Uranus brought about by the gravitational pull of Neptune. These gravitational perturbations were calculated by J. C. Adams and U. J. Leverrier.

Spectroscopic observations of their atmospheres have established the presence of molecular hydrogen and helium, as in the atmospheres of Jupiter and Saturn, and an increased proportion of methane.

Uranus has a system of five known moons, Neptune has two. Neptune's larger moon, Triton, Jupiter's Ganymede and Callisto, and Saturn's Titan comprise the four largest moons of the solar system.

Observations in 1977 and 1978 indicate that Uranus is surrounded by at least eight rings lying in its equatorial plane, similar to but much narrower than Saturn's rings.

PLUTO, the most distant planet in the solar system, was discovered in 1930 by C. W. Tombaugh. Although little is yet known about Pluto, it appears to resemble a terrestrial planet more than a Jovian one.

Pluto has the most eccentric orbit in the solar system, bringing it at times closer to the Sun than Neptune. Because of its orbit, some theorists have suggested that Pluto may in fact be a runaway moon of Neptune.

For many years it was believed that Pluto's mass was more than 90 percent of the Earth's and that its diameter was only half of the Earth's. These conditions would mean that Pluto is an extremely dense planet—some eight times as dense as the Earth. Recent calculations based on careful observations of Pluto's gravitational-field effect on the motion of Neptune, however, suggest that Pluto's mass is less than 10 percent of the Earth's and that its density is 4.5 g/cc, which is somewhat less than that of Earth. In 1978 a moon was discovered in orbit around Pluto.

THE SPECTRAL SEQUENCE

The spectral class or spectral type of a star is a classification that depends on the star's color or surface temperature. The spectral class and corresponding star color, approximate surface temperature, and principal features of the star's spectrum are:

Spectral Class	Color	Approximate Surface Temperature (° K)	Principal Features of Spectrum
O	blue	>30,000	Relatively few absorption lines in observable spectrum. Lines of ionized helium, nitrogen, silicon, and other atoms. Weak hydrogen lines.
B	blue-white	11,000–30,000	Lines of neutral helium, ionized silicon, oxygen, and magnesium. Hydrogen lines more pronounced.
A	white	7,500–11,000	Strong lines of hydrogen. Weak lines of ionized magnesium, silicon, iron, titanium, calcium, and others. Weak lines of some neutral metals.
F	white to yellowish	6,000–7,500	Hydrogen lines still conspicuous. Lines of ionized calcium, iron, and chromium, and of neutral iron and chromium. Lines of other neutral metals.
G	yellow	5,000–6,000	Very strong lines of ionized calcium. Many lines of ionized and neutral metals. Hydrogen lines weaker.
K	orange to red	3,500–5,000	Lines of neutral metals predominate. Hydrogen lines are quite weak. Bands of molecular titanium oxide.
M	red	<3,500	Strong lines of neutral metals and strong bands of titanium oxide dominate.

IMPORTANT PLANETARY PROBES

Name of probe	Launching Local date	Rocket	Weight, lbs.	Period, min.	Inclination, degrees	Perigee, miles	Apogee, miles	Results of mission—Remarks
				SOVIET UNION				
Venera I	12 Feb. 1961	—	1,417	300 days	0.58	0.7183 A.U.	1.0190 A.U.	In solar orbit; Venus probe; radio contact lost at 4.6 million miles.
Mars I	1 Nov. 1962	—	1,965	519 days	2.683	0.9237 A.U.	1.604 A.U.	In solar orbit; Mars probe; radio contact lost at 66 million miles.
Zond I	2 Apr. 1964		1,700		solar orbit			In solar orbit; probe aimed at Venus; failed to send back information on its target.
Zond II	30 Nov. 1964				solar orbit			In orbit; probe aimed at Mars; failed to send back information on its target.
Venera II	12 Nov. 1965		2,123		solar orbit			In solar orbit; failed to send back data.
Venera III	16 Nov. 1965		2,116		duration of flight: 105 days			First space probe to impact on a planet; entry capsule sent back no data after landing.
Venera IV	12 June 1967	—	2,433		duration of flight: 128 days			Instrumented capsule deployed parachute 18.10.67.

Venera V	5 Jan. 1969	—	2,500	—				Instrumented capsule deployed parachute 16.5.69.
Venera VI	10 Jan. 1969	—	2,500	—				Instrumented capsule deployed parachute 17.5.69.
Venera VII	16 Aug. 1970	—	2,500	—				Instrumented capsule transmitted data for 23 minutes 15.12.70.
Mars II	19 May 1971	—	—	duration of flight: 18 hrs.				Orbited Mars 27.11.72; sent back close-range photos.
Mars III	28 May 1971	—	—	duration of flight: 11 days				Instrumented capsule televised signals from surface.
Venera VIII	26 Mar. 1972	—	—	—				Ceased transmitting on entering atmosphere.
Mars IV	21 July 1973	—	10,250	—				Failed to go into Martian orbit.
Mars V	25 July 1973	—	10,250	—				Went into orbit March 1974.
Mars VI	5 Aug. 1973	—	10,250	—				Released descent module: ceased functioning.
Mars VII	9 Aug. 1973	—	10,250	—				Failed to go into orbit.
Venera IX	6 June 1975	—	—	duration of flight: 139 days				Descent modules landed on Venus at sites of different terrain, relaying data and clear photos of surface.
Venera X	14 June 1975	—	—	duration of flight: 134 days				

UNITED STATES

Pioneer 5	11 Mar. 1960	Thor-Able	'95	312 days	3.55	0.8161 A.U.	0.995 A.U.	In solar orbit; launched toward Venus; studied interplanetary space.
Mariner 2	26 Aug. 1962	Atlas-Agena B	446	348 days	1.66	0.7046 A.U.	1.299 A.U.	In solar orbit; passed within 22,000 miles of Venus.
Mariner 3	5 Nov. 1964	Atlas-Agena D	575	448.7 days	0.524	0.6150 A.U.	0.8155 A.U.	In solar orbit; final speed too low.
Mariner 4	28 Nov. 1964	Atlas-Agena D	575	567.2 days	2.540	1.1089 A.U.	1.5730 A.U.	In solar orbit; highly successful; 22 photographs of Mars sent back in mid-July 1965.
Pioneer 6	16 Dec. 1965	TAID	139	311.3 days	0.1695	0.814 A.U.	0.985 A.U.	In solar orbit; studied Sun and interplanetary space.
Pioneer 7	17 Aug. 1966	TAID	139	402.9 days	0.097	1.010 A.U.	1.125 A.U.	In solar orbit; studied Sun and interplanetary space.
Mariner 5	14 June 1967	Atlas-Agena D	540	duration of flight: 127 days				In solar orbit; Venus probe; fly-by on 19.10.67.
Pioneer 8	13 Dec. 1967	TAID	145	—	—	1.0 A.U.	1.1 A.U.	In solar orbit; studied Sun and interplanetary space.
Mariner 6	24 Feb. 1969	Atlas-Agena D	—	duration of flight: 156 days				Passed within 2,000 miles of Mars on 31.7.69; relayed data and photos.
Mariner 7	27 Mar. 1969	Atlas-Agena D	—	duration of flight: 130 days				Passed within 2,000 miles of Mars on 5.8.69; sent photographs back to Earth.
Mariner 9	30 May 1971	Atlas Centaur	2,200	12 hrs.	65	800	11,000	Entered Mars orbit 14.11.71; sent photographs and instrument readings to Earth.
Pioneer 10	2 Mar. 1972	Atlas Centaur	570	—	—	—	—	Flew past Jupiter 4.12.73 relaying data and photos of planets and satellites.
Pioneer 11	6 Apr. 1973	Atlas Centaur	570	—	—	—	—	Investigated asteroid belt; passed Jupiter 3.12.74; near Saturn Sept. 1979.
Mariner 10	3 Nov. 1973	Atlas Centaur	—	—	—	—	—	Relayed data and photos of Venus, photos of Mercury.
Viking 1	20 Aug. 1975	Titan 3E/Centaur	7,550	entered Mars orbit 6/19/76; landed July 20, 1976				Orbiters studied atmosphere, photographed surface; landers studied surface geology and chemistry, testing soil for signs of life.
Viking 2	9 Sept. 1975	Titan 3E/Centaur	7,550	entered Mars orbit 8/7/76; landed Sept. 3, 1976				
Voyager 1	5 Sept. 1977	Titan 3 E/Centaur	1,820	—	—	—	—	Jupiter (March 1979) and Saturn (1980)
Voyager 2	20 Aug. 1977	Titan 3 E/Centaur	1,820	—	—	—	—	Jupiter (July 1979) and Saturn (1981)
Pioneer Venus 1	20 May 1978	Atlas Centaur	—	—				Orbiters plus multiprobe atmospheric entry craft to study Venusian atmosphere. (see page 322)
Pioneer Venus 2	8 Aug. 1978	Atlas Centaur	—	—				

(see page 322)

THE MOON

The Moon is the closest celestial body to the Earth, at a mean distance of 238,857 miles. Because of its elliptical orbit, the Moon reaches a minimum distance—or perigee —of 221,463 miles and a maximum distance—apogee—of 252,710 miles. The Moon revolves around the Earth in 27 days/7 hours/43 minutes. The Moon's rotation about its axis is equal to its period of revolution, hence the Moon always shows the Earth the same face. However, since its revolution around the Earth is not uniform, speeding up at perigee and slowing down at apogee, and because its equator is inclined 6 degrees to the plane of its orbit, about 59 percent of the Moon's surface is visible at different times from the Earth. The Moon's mass is 1/81 of the Earth's mass, and its radius of 1,080 miles makes it about one-fourth of the Earth's radius. The mean density of the Moon is 3.34 grams/cm³.

The Moon is visible, as are the Earth and the other planets, by virtue of its reflection of solar radiation. However, the Moon is a relatively poor reflector, with an albedo, or reflectivity, of only 7 percent. At full moon, the Earth is between the Sun and the Moon (although usually not in the same plane), and the whole lunar disk facing the Earth is completely illuminated. At new moon, the Moon is between the Sun and the Earth (usually not in the same plane), and the Sun's rays illuminate only the hemisphere facing it, leaving the side facing the Earth in complete darkness, making it invisible from Earth. After new moon, the waxing thin crescent turns into first quarter. Following full moon, the waning gibbous turns into last quarter, then into new moon again.

The origin of the Moon is still a major area of debate. Three different mechanisms have been suggested for its origin: independent formation in Earth orbit, formation via fission of the Earth, and capture by Earth's gravitational field after formation elsewhere.

In the independent-formation theory, the Moon is supposed to have been formed by accretion of small masses from the original interstellar gas cloud that gave birth to the Sun, the Earth, and other planets. The major difficulty with this hypothesis is the disparity in mean density between the Earth and the Moon. This density difference, which is generally believed to represent a difference in the composition—specifically in the proportion of metallic iron and silicates—makes it difficult to explain why objects accumulating in the same part of the gas cloud should have such different compositions.

In 1898, G. H. Darwin, the astronomer son of Sir Charles Darwin, concluded that the Earth and the Moon might have once formed one body that rotated at high speed (about five hours). This rapid rotation might have led to fission into one large and one or more smaller bodies, the latter eventually forming the Moon. However, mathematical objections to this theory have led modern astronomers to abandon it.

According to some hypotheses, the first large solid bodies to form in the solar system were approximately the size of the Moon. These bodies collided, forming the planets. The Moon is considered to be one of these bodies, which escaped destruction by accretion and was later gravitationally captured by the Earth.

The lunar surface is divided into bright highland areas (comprising about two thirds of the total surface) and dark lowland areas, called maria, because they were originally thought to be seas. Craters are the most conspicuous and most plentiful of all lunar surface features. The near side of the Moon has more maria than the far side, which is almost entirely covered by mountainous regions. The major mechanisms believed to be responsible for crater formation are meteoritic impact and lunar volcanism. Impact craters appear to be of two types. Primary craters stem from the actual impact of meteoritic material; secondary craters result in part from the rain of heavy debris ejected from the primary ones. Craters may also be formed by collapse triggered by seismic quakes, which result from the impact of a large meteorite. The frequency with which craters are found on the bright highland areas is more than 15 times that of their incidence on the dark lowland maria. It is known that the Moon, and also possibly Mars, Mercury, and Earth, suffered very intense bombardment by massive bodies (planetesimals) about 4 billion years ago. Shortly after this, volcanic lava flooded gigantic basins on the Moon's surface, covering many craters and creating the maria. Seismic waves indicate activity (moonquakes) still occurring in the Moon's core but its present thick rigid outer layers prevent any surface fracturing.

Lunar rilles,' or deep canyons, some of them more than 100 miles long, were thought to be remnants of long-dried-out rivers on the Moon but are probably collapse features. One of them, the Hadley Rille, was studied at close range by the astronauts of Apollo 15 in 1971.

Mascons—dense lunar mass concentrations—were accidentally discovered in 1968 during analysis of small changes in the motion of Langley Research Center's Lunar Orbiter 5 during 80 consecutive orbits around the Moon. Five conspicuous mascons, ranging from 25 to 100 miles in extent and perhaps 25 miles below the lunar surface, were detected under all five large circular maria on the side of the Moon facing the Earth —Mare Imbrium, Mare Serenitatis, Mare Crisium, Mare Nectaris, and Mare Humorum. A sixth mascon is located in the central part of the lunar disk, between Sinus Aestuum and Sinus Medii. There is also some evidence that a large mascon exists under Mare Orientale. Mascons are absent from the bright lunar highlands and from the irregularly shaped maria. Both the presence of these features under every ringed mare, except Sinus Iridum, and their relative absence elsewhere, suggest a physical relationship.

In 1969, six more mascons were discovered—in Mare Smythii, Mare Humboldtianum, Mare Orientale, the ringed plain Grimaldi, and in two unnamed maria. As with the other mascons, the new mascons were discovered as lunar-orbiting spacecraft speeded up in passing over certain areas, which were revealed as places where the lunar gravitational attraction was stronger than average.

Due to the Moon's smaller mass, its gravitational attraction is only one sixth of the Earth's. Since the Moon is a weak gravitational body, it is believed that it could not retain any atmosphere it may have originally had for any length of time, since the atoms and molecules of the lunar atmosphere could easily drift off the planet. Recent telescopic polarization and photometric observations have established an upper limit for any lunar atmosphere of only one-ten-billionth of the Earth's atmospheric density.

The large day-to-night temperature variation observed on the Moon also suggests that it does not have an appreciable atmosphere. A planetary atmosphere acts as a heat insulator that keeps the planet's surface from experiencing wide temperature extremes from day to night. The day-to-night temperature variations on the Moon range from 300° F in the lunar equatorial region at noon to −220° F before sunrise—a daily change of over 500° F.

The samples of lunar material brought back by the Apollo astronauts consist of basaltic igneous rocks; breccias, which are composed of soil and rock fragments compacted into coherent rock; and lunar soil. The soil is a mixture of crystalline and glassy fragments with a variety of interesting shapes; it also contains fragments of iron meteorites. Most of the breccia rock fragments are similar to the larger igneous rocks and apparently were derived from them; the rocks in turn were probably once part of the underlying lunar bedrock.

The igneous rocks from the Moon contain the minerals pyroxene, plagioclase, ilmenite, olivine, and cristobalite. Three new minerals were found in these igneous rocks: pyroxmanganite, ferropseudobrookite, and a chromium-titanium compound. All of the lunar rocks were found to have unusually high concentrations of chromium, titanium, scandium, zirconium, hafnium, and yttrium, and very low concentrations of sodium. Many elements such as potassium, rubidium, cesium, chlorine, and thallium, which exist in great abundance in Earth rocks, were found to be very deficient in the lunar rocks.

Radioactive isotopic dating of the igneous rocks brought back by the astronauts shows that they were formed 3.3 to 3.7 billion years ago. In May 1970, G. Wasserburg reported that an Apollo 12 rock was found to be 4.6 billion years old, making it the oldest rock yet found on the Moon or Earth. For the soil and breccia such dating gives an age of 4.4 to 4.6 billion years. The existence of complex biological molecules in the lunar samples would be of tremendous significance, but some of the most sophisticated and sensitive analytical techniques ever devised failed to detect any. Lacking an atmosphere and an appreciable magnetic field, the moon is exposed to ultraviolet radiation as well as high-energy cosmic rays and the solar wind.

MODERN PLANETARY DATA

	Distance from Sun in Astronomical Units[1]	Period of Revolution Around Sun	Diameter[2]	Mass[3]	Density[6] (grams/cm³)
MERCURY	0.387	87.97 Days	0.38	0.055	5.5
VENUS	0.723	224.70 Days	0.95	0.815	5.25
EARTH	1.000	365.25 Days	1.00	1.00	5.517
MARS	1.524	1.88 Years	0.53	0.107	3.94
JUPITER	5.203	11.86 Years	11.20	317.9	1.330
SATURN	9.539	29.45 Years	9.36	95.2	0.706
URANUS	19.18	84.01 Years	4.06	14.6	1.21
NEPTUNE	30.06	164.79 Years	3.88	17.2	1.67
PLUTO	39.44	247.7 Years	0.47	0.08	4.5

	Period of Rotation (H = hours; M = minutes)	Amount of Incident Solar Radiation[4]	Albedo[5]	Observed Surface Temp.	Number of Satellites
MERCURY	58.65 Days	6.7	0.06	660°F (Dayside)	0
VENUS	243 Days (retrograde)	1.9	0.76	890°F	0
EARTH	23^H 56^M 4^S	1.0	0.36	70°F	1
MARS	24^H 37^M 23^S	0.43	0.16	— 45°F	2
JUPITER	9^H 50^M*	0.04	0.73	—220°F (Cloud-top)	14
SATURN	10^H 14^M**	0.01	0.76	—290°F (Cloud-top)	10
URANUS	10^H 49^M (retrograde)	0.003	0.93	—350°F (Cloud-top)	5
NEPTUNE	15^H 48^M	0.001	0.84	—360°F (Cloud-top)	2
PLUTO	6.39 Days	0.0006	0.14	—380°F	1

[1] The astronomical unit, defined as the mean distance from the Earth to the Sun, is approximately 93 million miles. [2] Diameter in terms of the Earth's diameter: 7,926 miles. [3] Mass in terms of the Earth's mass: 1.3×10^{25} pounds. [4] Amount of solar radiation falling on the planet in terms of the solar radiation the Earth receives: about 1.4 kilowatts falling on every square meter of the upper atmosphere per second. [5] The albedo is the percentage of the incoming solar radiation that is reflected back to space by the planet and its atmosphere. [6] Density of water is 1.0 gram/cm³. * For the latitudes greater than 12°, the rotation period is 9^H 55^M. ** For temperate latitudes, the rotation period is 10^H 38^M.

SATELLITES OF THE SOLAR SYSTEM

Planet		Satellites	Distance from the Planet (Miles)	Period of Revolution[*] (Days)	Radius (Miles)	Mass (Pounds)
Earth	1	Moon	238,850	27.32	1,080	162 × 10²¹
‡Mars	1	Phobos	5,810	0.32	8.4 × 6.5 × 6	—
	2	Deimos	14,595	1.26	4.7 × 3.7 × 3.4	—
†Jupiter	1	Io	262,075	1.77	1,137	160 × 10²¹
	2	Europa	416,980	3.55	900	104 × 10²¹
	3	Ganymede	665,130	7.15	1,550	339 × 10²¹
	4	Callisto	1,169,820	16.69	1,400	209 × 10²¹
	5	Amalthea	112,470	0.50	60	—
	6	Hestia	7,131,940	250.57	30	—
	7	Hera	7,292,940	259.7	9	—
	8	Poseidon	14,594,300	739	6	—
	9	Hades	14,687,200	758	6	—
	10	Demeter	7,282,700	259	6	—
	11	Pan	14,036,000	692	6	—
	12	Adrastea	13,199,000	631	6	—
	13	—	6,906,700	240	6	—
Saturn	1	Mimas	115,320	0.94	150	0.09 × 10²¹
	2	Enceladus	147,950	1.37	180	0.15 × 10²¹
	3	Tethys	183,150	1.89	310	0.14 × 10²¹
	4	Dione	234,580	2.74	310	2.20 × 10²¹
	5	Rhea	327,590	4.52	400	5.06 × 10²¹
	6	Titan	759,090	15.95	1,500	301 × 10²¹
	7	Hyperion	921,340	21.28	150	0.68 × 10²¹
	8	Iapetus	2,212,200	79.33	340	2.20 × 10²¹
	9	Phoebe	8,047,700	550.34	60	—
	10	Janus	98,500	0.75	90	—
Uranus	1	Ariel	119,200	2.52	250	2.64 × 10²¹
	2	Umbriel	166,020	4.14	190	1.10 × 10²¹
	3	Titania	272,390	8.70	340	8.80 × 10²¹
	4	Oberon	364,270	13.46	310	5.72 × 10²¹
	5	Miranda	81,000	1.41	90	.02 × 10²¹
Neptune	1	Triton	220,700	5.88	1,150	308 × 10²¹
	2	Nereid	3,456,000	360	90	0.07 × 10²¹
Pluto	1	1978-P-1 (Charon)	12,000	6.39	c.400	—

* Around planets. ‡ Satellites are roughly ellipsoidal: principal radii are given. † A 14th satellite of Jupiter was discovered in 1975.

THE ASTEROIDS

Between the orbits of Mars and Jupiter are found several thousand small rocky bodies, density 2-2.5 grams/cm³, orbiting the Sun. Ceres was the first to be discovered in 1801, and is also the largest (620 miles in diameter). Some 2,000 asteroids—minor planets—have now been catalogued and their orbits determined. However, there may be as many as 50,000 asteroids in the asteroid belt, most of which probably have diameters of less than a mile.

Because of their large number and planetary positions, it was originally thought that asteroids were the remnants of an exploded planet; however, since the total mass of the asteroids is less than 1/1000 of the Earth's mass, it is unlikely. Evidence shows that most asteroids have a surface consisting of very primitive material (carbonaceous chondrites) so that they may be the solid primordial remnants of the original dust from which the Sun and Earth and other planets condensed.

Many asteroids are not confined to the zone between Mars and Jupiter but have highly eccentric orbits. Hermes and Icarus pass close to Earth's orbit, Hidalgo close to Saturn's. Chiron, discovered 1977 by C. Kowall, orbits between Saturn and Uranus and has been recognized as an asteroid rather than a comet.

COMETS

Comets are bodies that move around the Sun, most of them in highly elliptical orbits. As a comet approaches the Sun, a somewhat transparent envelope of gas and dust called the *coma* appears around the small compact icy nucleus. The nucleus and coma comprise the comet's head. If the comet comes within two astronomical units of the Sun, it may develop a luminous tail–a long straight gaseous one that always points away from the Sun and a shorter broad dust tail that also curves away from the Sun.

Spectroscopic analysis of the comet's head shows the existence of the following neutral molecules and atoms: H_2O, OH, C, O, CO, CH, CN, NH, NH_2, Fe, and Ni. The following ionized molecules are found in the comet's tail: CH^+, CO^+, CO_2^+, and N_2^+. In addition, large amounts of dust are found in both the head and tail.

The comet's head may be as large as 500,000 miles across, and some comet tails are more than 10 million miles long. Comets circle the Sun in one of three types of orbits: elliptical, parabolic, or hyperbolic. Comets with elliptical orbits are periodic comets: they will continually orbit the Sun, as do the planets. Parabolic or hyperbolic orbits are probably caused by strong planetary perturbation.

The exact origin of comets is unknown. There may be hundreds of millions of comet nuclei in a huge region (Oort cloud) centered on the Sun but way beyond the orbit of Pluto. Occasionally, one may become perturbed and enter into close orbit around the Sun. Comet nuclei, which are only a few miles in diameter, are believed to consist of rocky fragments and frozen gases. As it ap-

proaches the Sun, solar radiation and heat cause the frozen gases in the nucleus to vaporize, forming the coma and later, as it comes still closer to the Sun, the tail.

The coma and head shine as sunlight is scattered by the dust and is also reradiated by fluorescent gas molecules. The gas is ionized by the solar wind streaming out radially from the Sun, carrying the gas ions with it and forming the long gaseous tail.

An enormous cloud of hydrogen, 10 times as large as the Sun, was discovered around comet Bennett in April 1970 by the National Aeronautics and Space Administration's Orbiting Geophysical Observatory (OGO) 5 satellite during a special maneuver to view the comet with a hydrogen-sensing device. Comet Bennett had become visible over portions of the United States and Britain late in March. Its huge hydrogen gas envelope–not visible from Earth–is about 8 million miles across and is probably the largest entity ever observed orbiting the Sun.

The existence of large amounts of hydrogen around comets was first discovered in January 1970 by Orbiting Astronomical Observatory (OAO) 2 when it observed a cloud around the comet Tago-Sato-Kosaka. Hydrogen is the most abundant element in the universe, and the vast amounts of it measured by the OAO and OGO satellites clearly show it to be a major constituent of comets. So it now appears that the newly discovered hydrogen clouds are a fourth feature to be added to the classical three components of a comet: the center, or nucleus; the coma; and the tail, which streams out thousands, sometimes millions of miles, always in a direction away from the Sun.

SOME PERIODIC COMETS

Comet	Period (Years)	Perihelion Distance*	Average Distance from Sun*
Encke	3.3	0.339	2.21
Grigg-Skjellerup	5.12	0.855	2.89
Tempel-2	5.27	1.37	3.0
Giacobini-Zinner	6.3	0.94	3.4
Faye	7.42	1.644	3.8
Whipple	7.44	2.47	3.8
Comas Solá	8.94	1.87	4.3

Comet	Period (Years)	Perihelion Distance*	Average Distance from Sun*
Väisälä	11.28	1.745	4.79
Neujmin-1	17.9	1.54	6.8
Crommelin	27.9	0.744	9.2
Olbers	69.6	1.18	16.9
Pons-Brooks	70.9	0.775	17.2
Halley	76.0	0.587	17.9

* In astronomical units.

METEORS

Meteors are small, usually highly fragile particles that enter the Earth's atmosphere at great speeds. A meteor will burn up or vaporize from frictional heating as it enters the atmosphere. A burning meteor is popularly referred to as a "shooting star" or "falling star." A meteor is called a *meteoroid* before it enters the earth's atmosphere; meteors the size of dust particles are called *micrometeors*. A *fireball* is a bright glowing meteor that is brilliant enough to cast shadows on the ground. A *bolide* is a fireball that explodes in the atmosphere.

In general, an observer at any one location may observe between five and 10 meteors an hour; however, worldwide, there are some 200,000 visible meteors a day that collectively represent a mass influx of about 10 tons. In addition micrometeor influx may account for some 100 tons of extraterrestrial matter that falls to Earth each day.

Meteors usually become visible at about 70 miles above the Earth's surface. Larger bodies may not completely burn up in the Earth's atmosphere and survive the trip through the atmosphere to Earth. These survivors

are called *meteorites*, and may weigh as much as 60 tons; they are fundamentally different from shooting-star meteors.

Meteor showers occur each year as the Earth runs into patches of particle swarms that are scattered about in the Earth's orbit. When the Earth runs into one of these swarms, meteors appear to burst out in all directions from a particular radiant point. The Leonid meteor showers of November 12, 1799, and November 13, 1833, produced some 300,000 meteors per hour. The Leonid shower on the morning of November 17, 1966, may have produced as many as 2,500 meteors per minute.

Analysis of orbits and periods indicates that meteor showers may be associated with the disintegration of comets. Meteorites are probably closely related to asteroids. Meteor showers, which are named after the constellations in which their radiant point appears to lie, usually are visible for several days before and after their date of maximum occurrence. Meteors associated with meteor showers are usually completely disintegrated within the Earth's upper atmosphere.

PRINCIPAL METEOR SHOWERS

Meteor Stream	Date of Maximum Occurrence	Maximum Hourly Rate	Associated Comet
Quadrantids	Jan. 3	110	
Lyrids	Apr. 22	12	1861 I
η Aquarids	May 5	21	Halley?
Arietids	June 8*	40	
ε Perseids	June 9*	30	
β Taurids	June 30*	20	Encke
δ Aquarids	July 28	35	
Perseids	Aug. 12	68	1862 III

Meteor Stream	Date of Maximum Occurrence	Maximum Hourly Rate	Associated Comet
Draconids	Oct. 10	—	1933 III, Giacobini-Zinner
Orionids	Oct. 21	30	Halley?
Taurids	Nov. 8	12	Encke
Andromedids	Nov. 10	—	Biela
Leonids	Nov. 17	10	1866 I
Geminids	Dec. 14	58	
Ursids	Dec. 22	5	Tuttle

* Daytime showers.

ASTRONOMICAL PHENOMENA: 1980 Source: U.S. Naval Observatory

The times in the following tables, dealing with the Moon, with eclipses, and with the seasons, are all given in Greenwich (England) Mean Time (GMT); the new day "begins" at 00 hours 00 minutes (midnight) at the Greenwich meridian and lasts 23 hours and 59 minutes, until one minute before the next day begins. In the United States, there are eight standard time zones, which differ from the Greenwich Mean Time by a fixed number of hours.

To convert any GMT value to that of a particular time zone, subtract from the GMT the number of hours in the table below. If the number of hours to be subtracted is greater than the GMT value, then add 24 hours to the GMT before subtracting. This will then give the time for the preceding day. If the difference is between 00 and 11 hours, the time is A.M.; if the difference is between 12 and 23 hours the time is P.M.

Local Time Zone	To Convert from GMT
Eastern Daylight	Subtract 4 hours
Eastern Standard/Central Daylight	Subtract 5 hours
Central Standard/Mountain Daylight	Subtract 6 hours
Mountain Standard/Pacific Daylight	Subtract 7 hours

Local Time Zone	To Convert from GMT
Pacific Standard/Yukon Daylight	Subtract 8 hours
Yukon Standard/Alaska and Hawaii Daylight	Subtract 9 hours
Alaska and Hawaii Standard	Subtract 10 hours
Bering Standard	Subtract 11 hours

PHASES OF THE MOON: 1980 d = day; h = hour; m = minute (Universal Time or GMT)

New Moon	d	h	m	First Quarter	d	h	m	Full Moon	d	h	m	Last Quarter	d	h	m
Jan.	17	21	19	Jan.	24	13	58	Jan.	2	09	02	Jan.	10	11	49
Feb.	16	08	51	Feb.	23	00	14	Feb.	1	02	21	Feb.	9	07	35
Mar.	16	18	56	Mar.	23	12	31	Mar.	1	21	00	Mar.	9	23	49
Apr.	15	03	46	Apr.	22	02	59	Mar.	31	15	14	Apr.	8	12	06
May	14	12	00	May	21	19	16	Apr.	30	07	35	May	7	20	51
June	12	20	38	June	20	12	32	May	29	21	28	June	6	02	53
July	12	06	46	July	20	05	51	June	28	09	02	July	5	07	27
Aug.	10	19	09	Aug.	18	22	28	July	27	18	54	Aug.	3	12	00
Sept.	9	10	00	Sept.	17	13	54	Aug.	26	03	42	Sept.	1	18	08
Oct.	9	02	50	Oct.	17	03	47	Sept.	24	12	08	Oct.	1	03	18
Nov.	7	20	43	Nov.	15	15	47	Oct.	23	20	52	Oct.	30	16	33
Dec.	7	14	35	Dec.	15	01	47	Nov.	22	06	39	Nov.	29	09	59
								Dec.	21	18	08	Dec.	29	06	32

PERIGEE (Moon closest to Earth)

	d	h			d	h			d	h
Jan.	20	02		June	09	04		Sept.	25	03
Feb.	17	09		July	04	16		Oct.	23	14
Mar.	16	21		July	30	23		Nov.	21	01
Apr.	14	07		Aug.	27	19		Dec.	19	05
May	12	13								

APOGEE (Moon farthest from Earth)

	d	h			d	h			d	h
Jan.	08	08		May	24	11		Oct.	09	15
Feb.	05	02		June	21	06		Nov.	05	17
Mar.	03	11		July	19	00		Dec.	03	04
Mar.	30	12		Aug.	15	18		Dec.	30	23
Apr.	26	20		Sept.	12	09				

SEASONS 1980

Spring begins—Mar. 20: 11 h: 10 m
Summer begins—June 21: 05 h: 47 m

Autumn begins—Sept. 22: 21 h: 09 m
Winter begins—Dec. 21: 16 h: 56 m

SUN DISTANCES 1980

Perihelion (Earth closest to sun)—Jan. 3
Aphelion (Earth farthest from sun)—July 5

ECLIPSES: 1980 h = hour; m = minute

FEBRUARY 16—TOTAL ECLIPSE OF THE SUN
Visible over east, central, and southwest Asia, Africa except the northernmost part and the eastern South Atlantic.

Eclipse begins:	Feb. 16 06 h 15.9 m
Central eclipse at local apparent noon:	Feb. 16 08 h 59.9 m
Eclipse ends:	Feb. 16 11 h 32.0 m

MARCH 1—PENUMBRAL ECLIPSE OF THE MOON
Visible in Asia, Australia, Africa, Europe, extreme northeastern North America and eastern South America.

Moon enters penumbra:	Mar. 1 18 h 44.1 m
Middle of the eclipse:	Mar. 1 20 h 46.0 m
Moon leaves penumbra:	Mar. 1 22 h 48.0 m

JULY 27—PENUMBRAL ECLIPSE OF THE MOON
Visible in the western Pacific, Australasia, Asia, Africa and Europe except the extreme northern and western parts.

Moon enters penumbra:	July 27 17 h 56.8 m
Middle of the eclipse:	July 27 19 h 08.9 m
Moon leaves penumbra:	July 27 20 h 21.4 m

AUGUST 10—ANNULAR ECLIPSE OF THE SUN
Visible in South and Central America, southwestern United States, and the eastern Pacific.

Eclipse begins:	Aug. 10 16 h 14.7 m
Central eclipse at local apparent noon:	Aug. 10 19 h 17.1 m
Eclipse ends:	Aug. 10 22 h 10.0 m

AUGUST 26—PENUMBRAL ECLIPSE OF THE MOON
Visible in Africa, western Asia, Europe, North America except the extreme northwest, South America and the eastern Pacific.

Moon enters penumbra:	Aug. 26 01 h 42.1 m
Middle of the eclipse:	Aug. 26 03 h 31.3 m
Moon leaves penumbra:	Aug. 26 05 h 20.7 m

CONFIGURATIONS OF THE MOON AND BRIGHT PLANETS: 1980

To locate the bright planets, their location in degrees north or south of the Moon is given. For comparison, both the Sun and Moon subtend an area of one-half degree. All times are GMT.

	d	h			d	h			d	h	
Jan.	7	04	Jupiter 0.3° N		24	07	Mars 2° N		12	21	Jupiter 1° S
	7	16	Mars 2° N		24	11	Jupiter 1° N		13	19	Saturn 1° S
	8	14	Saturn 0.2° S		26	05	Saturn 0.3° N		15	21	Mars 5° S
	20	13	Venus 1° S	May	4	06	Mars 0.8° N	Sept.	5	10	Venus 0.04° N
Feb.	3	08	Jupiter 0.5° N		17	04	Venus 8° N		13	18	Mars 5° S
	3	20	Mars 3° N		21	20	Jupiter 0.6° N	Oct.	5	06	Venus 0.8° S
	4	20	Saturn 0.1° S		22	06	Mars 0.4° N		7	09	Jupiter 2° S
	17	14	Mercury 2° N		23	10	Saturn 0.1° N		11	04	Mercury 8° S
	19	05	Venus 4° N	June	14	20	Mercury 4° N		12	18	Mars 6° S
Mar.	1	08	Mars 4° N		18	10	Jupiter 0.01° N	Nov.	4	01	Jupiter 3° S
	1	08	Jupiter 0.9° N		19	14	Mars 2° S		4	10	Saturn 2° S
	3	00	Saturn 0.2° N		19	19	Saturn 0.3° S		4	11	Venus 2° S
	15	13	Mercury 3° N	July	9	19	Venus 0.2° S		10	19	Mars 5° S
	19	20	Venus 7° N		16	03	Jupiter 0.6° S	Dec.	1	17	Jupiter 3° S
	27	23	Mars 4° N		17	07	Saturn 0.7° S		1	21	Saturn 2° S
	28	08	Jupiter 1° N		18	04	Mars 4° S		4	21	Venus 4° S
	30	02	Saturn 0.4° N	Aug.	7	02	Venus 0.3° S		9	21	Mars 4° S
Apr.	18	09	Venus 9° N		9	10	Mercury 2° N		29	07	Jupiter 3° S
									29	08	Saturn 2° S

U.S. SPACE PROGRAM

SOURCE: National Aeronautics and Space Administration

SCIENTIFIC AND APPLICATIONS SATELLITES

Applications Technology Satellites—The Applications Technology Satellites (ATS) are designed to test in space promising techniques and equipment for use in future meteorological, navigation, and communications satellite systems. The satellites also carry scientific experiments such as instruments to measure radiation in space. The approximately 1,600-pound spacecraft was designed to include from 100 to 300 pounds of experimental equipment. A larger model, ATS-6, launched in 1974, weighs 3,000 pounds. It can transmit TV to simple, low-cost ground receivers. Orbits are at synchronous (approximately 22,235-mile) altitude.

Biosatellites—The biosatellites carried into space a wide variety of plants and animals ranging from microorganisms to primates. The experiments were aimed primarily at studying the biological effects of zero gravity—or weightlessness—weightlessness combined with a known source of radiation, and removal of living things from the influence of the Earth's rotation. They have contributed to knowledge in genetics, evolution, and physiology, and have provided new information about the effects of prolonged flight in space.

Discoverer—Discoverer is a U.S. military satellite program that, since its inception (February 28, 1959), has provided valuable data in such areas as radiation, meteoroids, and air density in space near Earth, as well as in aerospace medicine. A major contribution of the program was the development of the technology for midair recovery or sea recovery of packages sent from an orbiting satellite to Earth.

Early Bird—Early Bird (launched April 6, 1965) was the world's first operational commercial communications satellite. Its owner, the International Telecommunications Satellite Organization (INTELSAT), reimbursed NASA for costs involved in launching, tracking, and monitoring the satellite. Early Bird was guided by Earth stations into a nearby stationary position (relative to Earth's surface) over the Atlantic. From that point, it was able to furnish communications service (including telecasts) between Europe and North America.

Earth Resources Technology Satellites (LANDSAT)—LANDSAT is a technology development program designed to provide comprehensive observation of the Earth's surface. The first spacecraft, launched in 1972, carries television cameras and radiometric scanners which will collect global data on the earth's environment: the condition of the atmosphere and oceans, major ecological changes, and variations in weather systems. The 2,100-pound satellite circles the Earth four times a day and has a lifetime of more than a year to cover all four seasons and to account for seasonally-induced variations in the Earth's surface. The satellite's cameras view a 115-mile swath running north to south as the satellite orbits the Earth. This broad synoptic scanning shows more detail and contrast than the mosaiclike maps made from airplane surveys. A second spacecraft was launched in 1975 and a third in 1978. The first Landsat is no longer transmitting.

Echo—Echo 1 (orbited August 12, 1960) proved that it is possible to communicate between distant areas on Earth by reflecting radio microwaves from a manmade satellite. Echo 1 was fabricated of aluminum-vapor-coated polyester film 0.0005 inch thick (about half the thickness of cellophane wrapping on a cigarette package). It was 100 feet in diameter and weighed 123½ pounds. Radio signals were literally bounced off the satellite from one point on the Earth to another.

Echo 2 (launched January 25, 1964) was 135 feet in diameter—as tall as a 13-story building—and weighed 565 pounds. Made up of a laminate of aluminum foil and polymer plastic about 0.00075 inch thick, it was 20 times as rigid as Echo 1.

Explorers—Explorers comprise the largest group of satellites in the United States space program. Explorer 1 (launched February 1, 1958) was the nation's first satellite. It made one of the most significant contributions of the Space Age, confirming existence of the previously theorized Van Allen radiation belts—a zone of intense radiation surrounding the Earth.

Generally, Explorers are small satellites carrying a limited number of experiments. Their orbits vary to serve the particular purposes of the experiments. Their designs also differ.

Explorers have been put into orbit to measure the thin wisps of air in the upper atmosphere; determine air density by latitude and altitude; provide data on the composition of Earth's ionosphere, including the presence of electrons, which enable the ionosphere to bounce back certain radio waves, thus making possible long-range radio communications on Earth; study the composition, density, pressure, and other properties of the upper atmosphere; provide information on micrometeoroids (small particles of matter in space), and measure the small variations in Earth's gravity field and fix more precisely the locations of points on Earth.

High Energy Astronomy Observatory (HEAO)—The HEAO program studies some of the most intriguing mysteries of the universe — pulsars, black holes, neutron stars, quasars and supernovae. HEAO 1, launched Aug. 12, 1977, and HEAO 3, scheduled for launch in 1979, were designed to perform celestial surveys, mapping the sky for sources and background of X-rays. HEAO 2, launched Nov. 13, 1978, a celestial pointing mission, was to spend one year studying individual X-ray objects in detail by using an advanced X-ray telescope.

Interplanetary Explorers—Interplanetary Explorers are a special class of Explorers to provide data on radiation and magnetic fields between the Earth and Moon. The information has been of value to science and contributed to planning for the Apollo program that landed American explorers on the Moon.

Nimbus—Advanced equipment intended for use in future operational weather satellites is tested in Nimbus, a research and development project. Nimbus 1 (launched August 28, 1964) was equipped with advanced television cameras and with a high-resolution infrared observation system. The cameras provided daylight pictures; the infrared equipment, night pictures. Nimbus 1 ceased operation about a month after operation.

The thousands of day and night pictures taken by Nimbus 1 have contributed significantly not only to study and tracking of hurricanes and other weather phenomena but also to geology, geography, oceanography, and other earth sciences.

Nimbus 2 (launched May 15, 1966) contained equipment not only for providing day and night pictures of the Earth and its clouds but also for measuring the Earth's heat balance. Heat balance refers to how much of the Sun's radiation the Earth absorbs and how much it reflects back into the atmosphere. The Nimbus 2 experiment represents the first time such information was obtained on a global basis. Study of heat balance data may increase understanding of how storms are born, develop, and die.

Nimbus 3 (launched April 14, 1969), and Nimbus 4 (launched April, 1970), were both powered by a nuclear system, contained equipment to determine the variation of temperature with height within the atmosphere. Nimbus 5 (launched December 1972) carries instruments to measure temperature in clouds as an indicator of their height. Nimbus 6 was launched on June 12, 1975, and Nimbus 7, an advanced pollution-monitoring satellite, was lofted on October 24, 1978.

Orbiting Astronomical Observatory (OAO)—Man's study of the universe has been narrowly circumscribed because the atmosphere blocks or distorts much electromagnetic radiation (X-rays, infrared rays, ultraviolet rays) from space. These emissions can tell much about the structure, evolution, and composition of celestial bodies. OAO has made it possible to observe the universe in ultraviolet wavelengths for extended periods from a vantage point above the haze of the atmosphere that contains 99 percent of Earth's air.

Orbiting Geophysical Observatory (OGO)—Orbiting Geophysical Observatories are designed to broaden significantly knowledge about the Earth and space and how the Sun influences and affects both. The approximately 1,000-pound OGO furnishes many times the data provided by smaller satellites such as the Explorers.

The principal advantage of OGO is that it makes possible the observation of numerous phenomena simultaneously for prolonged periods of time. This permits study in depth of the relationships between the phenomena. For example, while some OGO experiments report on the erratic behavior of the Sun, others may describe concurrent fluctuations in Earth and interplanetary magnetic fields, space radiation, and properties of the Earth's atmosphere.

Orbiting Solar Observatory (OSO)—OSO is a series of satellites intended for intensive study of the Sun and solar phenomena from a point above the disruptive effects of the atmosphere. The observatory is designed to carry such instruments as X-ray and Lyman Alpha spectrometers, neutron flux sensors, and gamma-ray monitors. OSO scientific equipment is supplied to NASA by leading astronomers as it is to OAO.

Data from OSO have provided deeper insight into the functioning of the Sun, and suggest that techniques could be developed for forecasting the major solar flares that flood space with intensities of radiation lethal to man and detrimental to instruments.

Pegasus—Named for the winged horse of Greek mythology, Pegasus satellites are among the heaviest and largest of U.S. spacecraft. Deployed in space, the great wings of the Pegasus satellites span 96 feet while the center section, resembling the fuselage of an airplane, is 71 feet long. The wings are designed to report punctures by micrometeoroids, tiny particles of matter speeding through space. Data from Pegasus satellites not only have advanced man's understanding of space but are aiding him in design of large craft intended for prolonged missions in space.

Relay—Project Relay demonstrated the feasibility of intercontinental and transoceanic transmission of telephone, television, teleprint, and facsimile radio signals via a medium-altitude (several thousand to 12,000 miles) active-repeater (radio-equipped) satellite.

Syncom—NASA's Project Syncom (for synchronous communication) demonstrated the feasibility of employing synchronous-orbit active-repeater satellites for global communication. Syncom satellites have been used in many experiments and public demonstrations.

Telstar—Telstar—like Relay—was an experiment using active-repeater satellites in medium-altitude orbits. Because the two satellites differed in important structural and other features, they permitted comparison of different designs. This contributed to the acquisition of information needed to develop equipment for an operational communications satellite system.

TIROS—Originally a research and development project, TIROS has evolved into an operational weather observation system. TIROS stands for Television and Infra-Red Observation Satellite. The first TIROS satellite was launched on April 1, 1960. Since then, TIROS 1 and subsequent satellites have proved themselves the most effective storm detection system known. They have provided meteorologists with more than half a million usable cloud-cover pictures, enabling them to track, forecast, and analyze storms. Through TIROS observations, the U.S. Weather Service has issued thousands of storm bulletins to countries throughout the world.

Continued progress has been made in improving the observations made by TIROS and in making these observations available to weather services of other nations. TIROS satellites now provide almost global coverage as compared to the coverage of about 25 percent of the Earth's surface at the program's inception. They can provide high-quality pictures of Earth's cloud cover. Some are equipped with an automatic picture transmission (APT) system that permits receipt of TIROS cloud-cover photographs on the ground with relatively inexpensive ground equipment.

In addition to contributing significantly to the discovery and tracking of hurricanes and other weather phenomena, TIROS satellites are providing valuable data for meteorological research. Such research may lead to long-range weather forecasts and perhaps greater understanding of how hurricanes and other destructive storms breed and how their development can be curbed. TIROS pictures of the Earth are proving useful in geography and geology, in showing the magnitude of river and sea ice, and in furnishing information on snowcover and thus spring flooding. A new advanced TIROS-N satellite was launched on October 13, 1978.

TOS and NOAA—NASA's research and development work with meteorological satellites has led to the world's first operational weather satellite system, called TOS (for TIROS Operational Satellite). The TOS system is furnishing weathermen daily with pictures of the weather over nearly the whole Earth. TOS and an improved version called ITOS are financed, managed, and operated by the Weather Service, a part of the National Oceanic and Atmospheric Administration of the United States Department of Commerce.

Transit and the Navy Navigation Satellite System—Transit was a Department of Defense experimental navigation satellite program designed to lead to a worldwide operational navigation-satellite system for American military ships. The operational system, consisting of four satellites that are properly positioned relative to each other, is intended to provide accurate data for navigational fixes on an average of once every 1¾ hours. The system is designed to allow users to determine their precise position on Earth regardless of weather and time of day.

Vanguard—Project Vanguard was inaugurated as part of the American program for the International Geophysical Year. The first Vanguard satellite went into orbit on March 17, 1958. Among the valuable data acquired from this satellite was information regarding the relatively slight but significant distortion referred to as the "pear shape" of the Earth. Two other Vanguards were successfully launched in 1959 in this now completed program. The Vanguards provided valuable information on Earth and its space environment, including such phenomena as Earth's magnetic field, the Van Allen radiation belts, and micrometeoroids.

UNMANNED INTERPLANETARY MISSIONS

Lunar Orbiter—Lunar Orbiter 1 (launched August 10, 1966) was the first of a series of spacecraft designed to orbit the Moon and return closeup pictures and other information about Earth's only natural satellite. The photographs and other information returned to Earth by Lunar Orbiter spacecraft contributed to manned landings on the Moon and added significantly to knowledge. Analysis of Lunar Orbiter 5's motions around the Moon led to the surprise discovery of lunar mascons.

Mariner—Mariner 9 orbited Mars in 1971–72, sending back via television 7,000 photographs of the Martian surface. Mariner 10, launched in November 1973, flew by Venus and Mercury in February and March 1974, returning the first close-up pictures of those planets. After orbiting around the Sun, Mariner 10 again flew by Mercury on September 21, 1974, and for a third time on March 16, 1975.

Pioneer—Pioneer was the designation of NASA's first series of long-distance spacecraft. Of these, the most notable was Pioneer 5 (launched March 11, 1960), with which radio communication was maintained until June 26, 1960, when the craft was about 22.5 million miles from Earth—a record for the period.

NASA opened a new series of Pioneer experiments with the launch of Pioneer 6 (December 16, 1965). The series is designed to monitor on a continuing basis phenomena of interplanetary space such as radiation, magnetic fields, and the solar wind.

Some Pioneers are investigating space between Earth and Venus; others, between Earth and Mars. The knowledge gained is expected to advance scientific understanding and contribute to planning for manned interplanetary space flights.

Pioneer 10 (launched March 2, 1972) observed Jupiter close up in December, 1973 after passing beyond the orbit of Mars and through the Asteroid belt. Ultimately it should escape the solar system. Pioneer 11, launched March 6, 1973, followed a similar flight path, with a Jupiter encounter Dec. 4, 1974. Pioneer 11 flew past Saturn's rings in Sept. 1979.

Pioneer Venus 1 (launched May 20, 1978) and Pioneer Venus 2 (launched Aug. 8, 1978) began the most extensive study ever made of Venus upon arrival at the planet in December 1978. Swinging into orbit on Dec. 4, Pioneer Venus 1 was to sample upper atmospheric composition, make radar measurements of the surface elevations and roughness, and take daily ultraviolet and infrared pictures of the atmosphere for one Venusian year (225 Earth days) or more. On December 9, the four probes and transporter bus that comprised Pioneer Venus 2 plunged into the Venusian clouds at widely separated points for detailed measurements of the atmosphere from top to bottom.

Ranger—NASA's Project Ranger made possible the greatest single advance in lunar knowledge since Galileo first studied the Moon through a telescope more than three centuries ago. In the program, Ranger spacecraft tele-cast to Earth 17,255 closeups of the Moon. Features as small as 10 inches across on the lunar surface were made visible to man for the first time.

Ranger 7 through Ranger 9, the last of the Ranger series, began telecasting pictures when they were about 20 minutes away from the Moon and continued to telecast until crashing onto the surface. The Rangers with the television packages were about 5 feet in diameter at their hexagonal base and approximately 8¼ feet long. Cruising in space with appendages extended, Ranger spanned 15 feet across its winglike solar panels and measured 10¼ feet to the far edge of its dish-shaped antenna.

Surveyor—Surveyor was designed to decelerate from the lunar approach velocity of 6,000 mph (or 9,000 feet per second) to a touchdown speed of about 3½ mph.

The first Surveyors were designed as engineering test spacecraft intended primarily to test soft-landing techniques. Their legs were instrumented to return data on the Moon's surface hardness, and each carried a single scanning television camera which have transmitted over 90,000 photos of the lunar surface.

Viking—A decade of planning and work came to fruition with the landing of robot spacecraft on Mars to conduct detailed scientific investigation of the planet, including the search for life. After an 11-month journey, Viking 1 touched down on the boulder-strewn Martian plain called Chryse on July 20, 1976. On Sept. 3, its sister ship, Viking 2, landed at Utopia, about 1,600 km (1,000 mi.) nearer to Mars' polar cap.

Specially designed cameras on the craft took closeup pictures of the planet; miniature weather stations monitored the thin Martian air; other instruments noted magnetism, radiation; and Martian soil was analyzed in miniaturized biology laboratories aboard the spacecraft. The "life" experiments data both satisfied and puzzled scientists. The presence of compounds which were conceivably of biological origin was indicated by the data but the organic analysis data did not support that conclusion.

The end of the normal missions of the two spacecraft occurred in mid-November when solar conjunction produced a blackout of Viking-to-Earth communications. By mid-December, there was a return to post-conjunction operations, and the beginning of the "extended missions" which ended in 1978. The landers continued to operate during a "continued mission" phase through February 1979 and mission planners have advocated a plan to keep Viking Lander 1 operating on a reduced schedule through 1989.

Voyager—Two Voyager spacecraft, carrying instruments to conduct 11 science experiments, were launched on Aug. 20 and Sept. 5, 1977, toward Jupiter, Saturn and the outer reaches of the solar system. Voyager 1, launched on the later date, reached Jupiter on March 5, 1979, and almost immediately made two major discoveries — a ring around Jupiter and active volcanoes on Io, the planet's closest satellite. Boosted toward Saturn, Voyager 1 also examined three other satellites — Europa, Ganymede and Callisto. Voyager 2, scheduled to make its closest approach to Jupiter on July 9, 1979, also surveyed Callisto, Ganymede, Europa and Amalthea. Both spacecraft continued to observe Jupiter as they headed for Saturn.

Voyager 1 was scheduled to begin studying Saturn in August 1980 and Voyager 2 in June 1981. On the inbound journey, Voyager 1 was to closely examine the big satellite, Titan, the only satellite known to have a dense atmosphere. Mission planners have left their options open for Voyager 2's course after Saturn and may go on to Uranus.

MANNED SPACE-FLIGHT PROGRAMS

Project Mercury—Project Mercury placed the first Americans into space. The pioneering project was organized (October 5, 1958) to orbit a manned spacecraft, investigate man's reaction to, and abilities in, space flight, and recover both man and spacecraft.

Project Mercury experiments demonstrated that the high-gravity forces of launch and of atmosphere entry as well as weightlessness in orbit for as much as 34 hours do not impair man's ability to control a spacecraft. It proved that man not only augments the reliability of spacecraft controls but also can conduct scientific observations and experiments that expand and clarify information from instruments.

Project Gemini—Project Gemini markedly extended the technology and experience gained through Project Mercury and vastly increased knowledge about space, Earth, and man. The last of the Gemini missions was Gemini 12 (completed November 15, 1966). In achieving all of its major objectives, the Gemini project demonstrated that man can maneuver his craft in space; leave his craft and do useful work in space if he is properly clothed and equipped; rendezvous (find and come near) and dock (link up) his craft with another vehicle in space; function effectively during prolonged space flight of a least two weeks and return to Earth in good physical condition; and control his spacecraft during its descent from orbit and land it within a selected area on Earth.

Project Apollo—Its goals: land American explorers on the Moon and bring them safely back to Earth (which was successfully accomplished by Apollo 11 in July 1969), and establish the technology to meet other national interests in space. The Apollo spacecraft is made up of three sections or modules:

1. COMMMAND MODULE—The command module is designed to accommodate three astronauts in a "shirt-sleeve" environment; i.e., the astronauts are able to work, eat, and sleep in the module without pressure suits. The command module, like the crew compartment of an airliner, has windows, and contains controls and instruments (including a computer) of various kinds to enable the astronauts to pilot their craft. The command module weighs about 5 tons. It stands 11 feet tall and has a base diameter of about 13 feet.

2. SERVICE MODULE—The service module is equipped with rocket engines and fuel supplies to enable the astronauts to propel their craft into and out of lunar orbit and to change their course in space. The service module weighs 24 tons. It is 23 feet long and 13 feet in diameter.

3. LUNAR MODULE—The lunar module (LM) is the space ferry that takes two Apollo astronauts down to the Moon and carries them from the Moon's surface into lunar orbit and rendezvous with the Apollo command and service modules in lunar orbit. At launch from Earth, the LM weighs about 14½ tons. It is some 20 feet high and has a base diameter of 13 feet. After the two-man crew of the LM returns to the command module, the LM is jettisoned in lunar orbit.

Skylab—Skylab was America's first orbiting space laboratory, launched by NASA on May 14, 1973. Eleven days later, the first of three scheduled manned missions made a rendezvous with the space station, activating its extensive facilities to conduct solar astronomy experiments, to relay information on Earth's ecological systems and to study the effects of weightlessness on industrial processes. Most important, however, was the medical and life sciences information obtained from observation of the three-man crews as they lived in space for prolonged periods of time. The Skylab II (actually the first *manned* Skylab) mission lasted 28 days; its success prompted NASA to extend Skylab III's mission (launched July 28, 1973 to 59 days. A fourth (third manned) and final Skylab mission was launched on November 16, 1973, and the crew spent 84 days in space. Skylab descended from orbit and broke up over Australia on July 11, 1979.

Apollo Soyuz Test Project—The first international manned space flight was made by United States and U.S.S.R. spacecraft July 15-24, 1975. Its objective was to accomplish spacecraft rendezvous, docking, undocking, crew transfer, interaction of control centers, and interaction of spacecraft crews. The planned joint activities were carried out successfully and the many ceremonial activities were televised as were many of the other activities.

Space Shuttle—The key element in the United States' future Space Transportation System made its first appearance as the first Space Shuttle orbiter, the Enterprise, was rolled out at the NASA/Rockwell International facility at Palmdale, Calif., in September 1976. The spacecraft successfully completed a series of approach and landing flight tests in 1977. The second Space Shuttle orbiter, Columbia, was transported to the Kennedy Space Center, Florida, in March 1979 for the first orbital flight test in late 1979 or early 1980.

The agency named 15 pilot astronaut candidates and 15 mission specialist astronaut candidates to be crew members on flights of the Space Shuttle which will be operational in the 1980's.

MANNED SPACE FLIGHTS

Spacecraft	Launching Date	Astronauts	Revolutions	Flight Time	Flight Highlights
USSR Vostok I	Apr. 12, 1961	Yuri A. Gagarin	1	1 hr. 48 mins.	First manned flight.
U.S. Mercury-Redstone 3	May 5, 1961	Alan B. Shepard, Jr.	Suborbital	0 hrs. 15 mins.	First American in space.
U.S. Mercury-Redstone 4	July 21, 1961	Virgil I. Grissom	Suborbital	0 hrs. 16 mins.	Evaluated spacecraft functions.
USSR Vostok II	Aug. 6, 1961	Gherman S. Titov	16	25 hrs. 18 mins.	More than 24 hours in space.
U.S. Mercury-Atlas 6	Feb. 20, 1962	John H. Glenn	3	4 hrs. 55 mins.	First American in orbit.
U.S. Mercury-Atlas 7	May 24, 1962	M. Scott Carpenter	3	4 hrs. 56 mins.	Landed 250 miles from target.
USSR Vostok III	Aug. 11, 1962	Andrian G. Nikolayev	60	94 hrs. 22 mins.	First group flight (Vostok III and IV).
USSR Vostok IV	Aug. 12, 1962	Pavel R. Popovich	45	70 hrs. 57 mins.	Came within 3.1 miles of Vostok III on first orbit.
U.S. Mercury-Atlas 8	Oct. 3, 1962	Walter M. Schirra, Jr.	6	9 hrs. 13 mins.	Landed 5 miles from target.
U.S. Mercury-Atlas 9	May 15, 1963	L. Gordon Cooper, Jr.	22	34 hrs. 20 mins.	First long flight by an American.
USSR Vostok V	June 14, 1963	Valery F. Bykovsky	76	119 hrs. 6 mins.	Second group flight (Vostok V and VI).
USSR Vostok VI	June 16, 1963	Valentina V. Tereshkova	45	70 hrs. 50 mins.	Passed within 3 miles of Vostok V; first woman in space.
USSR Voskhod I	Oct. 12, 1964	Komarov; Feoktistov; Yegorov	15	24 hrs. 17 mins.	First 3-man craft.
USSR Voskhod II	Mar. 18, 1965	Leonov; Belyayev	16	26 hrs. 2 mins.	First man outside spacecraft in 10-minute "walk" (Leonov).
U.S. Gemini 3	Mar. 23, 1965	Virgil I. Grissom John W. Young	3	4 hrs. 53 mins.	First manned orbital maneuvers.
U.S. Gemini 4	June 3, 1965	James A. McDivitt Edward H. White, II	62	97 hrs. 48 mins.	21-minute "space walk" (White).
U.S. Gemini 5	Aug. 21, 1965	L. Gordon Cooper, Jr. Charles Conrad, Jr.	120	190 hrs. 56 mins.	First extended manned flight.
U.S. Gemini 7	Dec. 4, 1965	Frank Borman James A. Lovell, Jr.	206	330 hrs. 35 mins.	Longest space flight at the time.
U.S. Gemini 6-A	Dec. 15, 1965	Walter M. Schirra, Jr. Thomas P. Stafford	16	25 hrs. 52 mins.	World's first successful space rendezvous.
U.S. Gemini 8	Mar. 16, 1966	Neil A. Armstrong David R. Scott	6.5	10 hrs. 42 mins.	World's first docking (to Agena target); mission cut short.
U.S. Gemini 9-A	June 3, 1966	Thomas P. Stafford Eugene A. Cernan	44	72 hrs. 21 mins.	Rendezvous, extravehicular activity, precision landing.
U.S. Gemini 10	July 18, 1966	J. W. Young; M. Collins	43	70 hrs. 47 mins.	Rendezvous with 2 targets; Agena package retrieved.
U.S. Gemini 11	Sept. 12, 1966	C. Conrad, Jr.; R. F. Gordon, Jr.	44	71 hrs. 17 mins.	Rendezvous and docking.
U.S. Gemini 12	Nov. 11, 1966	J. A. Lovell, Jr., E. E. Aldrin, Jr.	59	94 hrs. 35 mins.	3 successful extravehicular trips.

MANNED SPACE FLIGHTS (Cont.)

Spacecraft	Launching Date	Astronauts	Revolutions	Flight Time	Flight Highlights
USSR Soyuz I	Apr. 23, 1967	Vladimir M. Komarov	17	26 hrs. 40 mins.	Heaviest manned craft; crashed, killing Komarov.
U.S. Apollo 7	Oct. 11, 1968	W. M. Schirra, Jr.; D. F. Eisele; R. Walter Cunningham	163	260 hrs. 9 mins.	First manned flight of Apollo spacecraft.
USSR Soyuz III	Oct. 26, 1968	Georgi T. Beregovoi	60	94 hrs. 51 mins.	Rendezvous with unmanned Soyuz II.
U.S. Apollo 8	Dec. 21, 1968	F. Borman; Wm. A. Anders; James A. Lovell, Jr.	Moon orbital (10 revolutions)	147 hrs.	First manned voyage around Moon.
USSR Soyuz IV	Jan. 14, 1969	Vladimir A. Shatlow	45	71 hrs. 14 mins.	Rendezvous with Soyuz V.
USSR Soyuz V	Jan. 15, 1969	Volynov; Khrunov; Yeliseyev	46	72 hrs. 46 mins.	Cosmonauts transfer to Soyuz IV.
U.S. Apollo 9	Mar. 3, 1969	J. A. McDivitt; D. R. Scott; Russell L. Schweickart	151	241 hrs. 1 min.	First docking with Lunar Module within Earth's atmosphere.
U.S. Apollo 10	May 18, 1969	Stafford; Cernan; Young	31 (Moon)	192 hrs. 3 mins.	Descent to within 9 miles of Moon.
U.S. Apollo 11	July 16, 1969	Neil A. Armstrong; Edwin E. Aldrin, Jr.; Michael Collins	Moon orbital for Command Module (31 revolutions)	195 hrs. 18 mins.	Armstrong and Aldrin, in Lunar Module, land in Sea of Tranquility. Collins remained in lunar orbit in Command Module. Remained on Moon for 21 hours, 36 minutes.
USSR Soyuz VI	Oct. 11, 1969	G. S. Shonin; V. N. Kubasov	79	118 hrs. 42 mins.	Welding of metals in space.
USSR Soyuz VII	Oct. 12, 1969	Filipchenko; Volkov; Gorbatko	79	118 hrs. 41 mins.	Tests for building an orbiting space laboratory.
USSR Soyuz VIII	Oct. 13, 1969	V. A. Shatalov; A. S. Yeliseyev	79	118 hrs. 50 mins.	Test for building an orbiting space laboratory.
U.S. Apollo 12	Nov. 14, 1969	Charles Conrad, Jr.; A. L. Bean; R. F. Gordon, Jr.	Moon orbital for Command Module (45 revolutions)	244 hrs. 36 mins.	Conrad and Bean, in Lunar Module, land in Sea of Storms. Gordon remained in lunar orbit in Command Module.
U.S. Apollo 13	April 11, 1970	J. A. Lovell, Jr.; F. W. Haise, Jr.; John L. Swigert, Jr.	Swung around Moon; returned to Earth	142 hrs. 52 mins.	Power failure en route to Moon led to the termination of the scheduled lunar landing of Lovell and Haise.
USSR Soyuz IX	June 1, 1970	Nikolayev; Sevastyanov	286	424 hrs. 59 mins.	Studied physical reactions to extended space travel.
U.S. Apollo 14	Jan. 31, 1971	Alan B. Shepard, Jr.; Stuart A. Roosa; Edgar D. Mitchell	Moon orbital for Command Module (34 revolutions)	216 hrs. 0.2 mins.	Shepard and Mitchell, in Lunar Module, land in Fra Mauro area. Roosa remained in lunar orbit in Command Module.
USSR Soyuz X	April 22, 1971	Shatalov; Yeliseyev; Rukavishnikov	32	47 hrs. 46 mins.	Aborted after linking up with unmanned satellite Salyut I.
USSR Soyuz XI	June 6, 1971	Dobrovolsky; Volkov; Patsayev	360	570 hrs. 22 mins.	Docked with Salyut I; dead on return.
U.S. Apollo 15	July 26, 1971	David R. Scott; Alfred M. Worden; James B. Irwin	Moon orbital for Command Module (64 revolutions)	295 hrs. 12 mins.	Scott and Irwin, in Lunar Module, landed in Hadley Rille and explored in Lunar Rover. Worden, from Command Module, performed experiments and first deep space walk.
U.S. Apollo 16	April 16, 1972	Charles M. Duke, Jr.; Thomas K. Mattingly; John W. Young	Moon orbital for Command Module (74 revolutions)	265 hrs. 51 mins.	Young and Duke spent 71 hours, two minutes on the moon's surface. They returned with 214 pounds of lunar rock and soil.

Mission	Date	Crew	Moon orbital for Command Module (75 revolutions)	Duration	Description
U.S. Apollo 17	December 7, 1972	Eugene A. Cernan; Ronald E. Evans; Harrison H. Schmitt	Moon orbital for Command Module (75 revolutions)	301 hrs. 51 mins.	Cernan and Schmitt spent a record 74 hours and 59 minutes on Moon and returned with 250 pounds of lunar material.
U.S. Skylab 2	May 25, 1973	Charles "Pete" Conrad, Jr.; J. P. Kerwin; P. J. Weitz	393	672 hrs. 49 mins.	First manned flight to Skylab space station.
U.S. Skylab 3	July 28, 1973	Alan L. Bean, Owen K. Garriott, Jack R. Lousma	852	1427 hrs. 9 mins.	Second manned flight to space station demonstrating man's ability to function for long periods in space.
USSR Soyuz XII	Sept. 27, 1973	V. G. Lazarev; O. G. Makarov	29	47 hrs. 16 mins.	Testing of modifications in spacecraft.
USSR Soyuz XIII	Dec. 18, 1973	P. I. Klimuk; V. V. Lebedev	119	188 hrs. 55 mins.	Cosmonauts grew nutritive protein samples.
U.S. Skylab 4	Nov. 16, 1973	G. P. Carr; Wm. R. Pogue; Edward G. Gibson	1,214	2017 hrs. 17 mins.	Weightless for 84 days, the astronauts each "grew" an inch.
USSR Soyuz XIV	July 3, 1974	Popovich; Artyukhin	N.A.	377 hrs. 30 mins.	Occupied Salyut III.
USSR Soyuz XV	Aug. 26, 1974	Sarafanov; Demin	N.A.	48 hrs. 12 mins.	Fails to achieve a link-up with Salyut III.
USSR Soyuz XVI	Dec. 2, 1974	Filipchenko; Rukavishnikov	96	142 hrs. 24 mins.	ASTP precursor flight to check out new Soyuz designs.
USSR Soyuz XVII	Jan. 11, 1975	Grechko; Gubarev	N.A.	709 hrs. 20 mins.	Occupied Salyut IV and set Soviet duration record.
USSR Soyuz XVIII	May 24, 1975	Klimuk; Sevastyanov	N.A.	1512 hrs. (est.)	Conducted experiments with Salyut IV.
USSR Soyuz XIX / U.S. Apollo 18	July 15, 1975 / July 15, 1975	Leonov; Kubasov / Stafford; Slayton; Brand	96 Earth orbits / 136 Earth orbits	143 hrs. 31 mins. / 217 hrs. 30 mins.	ASTP joint flight, U.S. and U.S.S.R. link-up in space and hold a joint news conference.
USSR Soyuz XXI	July 6, 1976	Volynov; Zholobov	N.A.	50 days	Conducted experiments with Salyut V
USSR Soyuz XXII	Sept. 15, 1976	Bykovsky; Aksenov	N.A.	8 days	Photographed earth's surface
USSR Soyuz XXIII	Oct. 14, 1976	Zudov; Rozhdestvensky	N.A.	2 days	Fails to achieve linkup with Salyut V
USSR Soyuz XXIV	Feb. 7, 1977	Gorbatko; Glazkov	N.A.	425 hrs. 23 mins.	Conducted experiments with Salyut V
USSR Soyuz XXV	Oct. 9, 1977	Kovalenak; Ryumin	N.A.	48 hrs. 46 mins.	Failed to dock with Salyut VI.
USSR Soyuz XXVI	Dec. 10, 1977	Romanenko; Grechko	1600 (approx.)	96 days, 10 hrs.	Docked with Salyut VI. Returned to Earth in Soyuz XXVII, March 16, 1978.
USSR Soyuz XXVII	Jan. 10, 1978	Dzhanibekov; Makarov	N.A.	6 days	Docked with Salyut VI. Returned to Earth in Soyuz XXVI, Jan. 16, 1978.
USSR Soyuz XXVIII	March 2, 1978	Gubarev; Remek (Czech)	N.A.	7 days	Docked with Salyut VI. Returned to Earth, March 10, 1978.
USSR Soyuz XXIX	June 15, 1978	Kovalenak; Ivanchenkov	N.A.	139 days, 15 hrs.	Docked with Salyut VI. Returned to Earth in Soyuz XXXI. Nov. 2, 1978
USSR Soyuz XXX	June 27, 1978	Klimuk; Hermaszewski (Pole)	N.A.	8 days	Docked with Salyut VI. Returned to Earth, July 5, 1978
USSR Soyuz XXXI	Aug. 26, 1978	Bykovsky; Jaehn (E. Ger.)	N.A.	8 days	Docked with Soyuz VI. Returned to Earth in Soyuz XXIX. Sept. 3, 1978
USSR Soyuz XXXII	Feb. 25, 1979	Lyakhov; Ryumin	N.A.	175 days	Docked with Salyut VI. Returned to Earth on Aug. 19, 1979, in Soyuz XXXIV, a spacecraft sent unmanned to dock with Salyut VI

SCIENCE: PAST/PRESENT

ENGINEERING ACHIEVEMENTS

The following is a list of engineering projects that have received the American Society of Civil Engineers' Outstanding Civil Engineering Achievement Award.

St. Lawrence Seaway and Power Project. A swath for ocean-going vessels from the Atlantic Ocean to the Great Lakes. A combined power generation and navigation project to serve both America and Canada.

John F. Kennedy International Airport, 1961—This airport was designed to handle nearly all of the New York Metropolitan Area's international air traffic, half of its domestic long-haul traffic, and a quarter of its domestic short and medium air traffic.

Intercontinental Ballistic Missile Program, 1962—This program involved ICBM installations in 14 states.

Ohio River Basin Clean Streams Program, 1963—This complex of facilities for pollution control affected the economy of more than 1,500 municipalities in eight states adjacent to 1,000 miles of waterways in the Ohio River Basin.

The Glen Canyon Unit of the Colorado River Project, 1964—Rising 710 feet, the dam is only 16 feet less than Hoover Dam in height; its concrete volume is greater.

Chesapeake Bay Bridge-Tunnel, 1965 — This engineering achievement crosses over and under the open sea and links the Eastern Shore of Virginia with the mainland. Its 12.5 miles of low-level trestle, four man-made islands, two mile-long tunnels, a high and medium-level bridge and several miles of approach roads make up the project.

NASA Complex 39, 1966—This huge complex, the Apollo-Saturn assembly and launch facility at Cape Kennedy (Merritt Island), Florida, is dominated by the world's second largest building: the Vehicle Assembly Building.

St. Louis Gateway Arch, 1967—This 630-foot stainless steel arch commemorates the role of St. Louis as the historic "Gateway to the West."

San Mateo Hayward Bridge, 1968—This bridge spans the San Francisco Bay and is located 17 miles south of San Francisco. Designed to accommodate 50,000 vehicles daily, the bridge is 6.7 miles long.

Oroville Dam and Powerplant, 1969—This dam on Cali-fornia's Feather River is the highest (770 ft.) in the Western Hemisphere and the world's third largest.

Middletown, Ohio, Armco Steelworks, 1970—This steelmaking complex was cited for construction innovations, techniques, materials, and pollution control.

World Trade Center, 1971—When built, these twin towers were the world's two tallest buildings (110 stories, 1,350 feet high).

California State Water Project, 1972—The project to deliver 4.23 million acre-feet of water throughout California. Its major aqueduct extends 444 miles.

Ludington Pumped Storage Project, 1973—During off-peak power hours, water from Lake Michigan is pumped up to a reservoir from which it rushes during peak periods through the turbines of the power plant, which has a generating capacity of over 1.8 million kilowatts of electricity.

Land Reclamation Program of Fulton County, Ill., 1974 — Sludge is barged down the Illinois River to Fulton County, and pumped 11 miles underground until converted into liquid fertilizer.

The Keowee-Toxaway Project, 1975 — of the Duke Power Co., in the Western part of North and South Carolina, a 700-million-dollar power generating complex that includes two hydroelectric projects and a major nuclear generating station, generating over 3.4 million kilowatts of electricity.

Lower Snake River Project, 1976 — a 140-mile development in southeastern Washington, is designed to facilitate navigation and generate power through the construction of four dams and the Lewiston levee and parkway system.

Superior, Wis., Midwest Energy Terminal, 1977 — The nation's largest western coal transshipment terminal, this complex was designed to receive, store, and load Montana coal from rail cars onto Great Lakes carriers for Detroit Edison's fuel needs.

Trans-Alaska Pipeline, 1978 — An 800-mile system of highway, 48-inch steel pipeline from Prudhoe Bay to Valdez, eight pump stations along the route, and storage and tanker facilities at Valdez harbor.

Nation's Capital Metro Transit System, 1979—Some 30 miles of currently operational subway connecting suburban Maryland and Virginia with various sections of Washington, D.C., serving 300,000 weekday travellers.

PERIODIC TABLE OF ELEMENTS

The periodic table, first devised by the Russian chemist Dmitri I. Mendeleev (1834–1907) in 1869, is shown here in its present form. It is an orderly classification of the elements based on physical and chemical similarities. The atomic number of each element denotes the number of protons (positive charge) in the nucleus of its atoms as well as the number of electrons (negative charge) in its orbital shells when the atoms are neutral. In general, the higher the atomic number, the heavier the element. The table is arranged so that elements in the same vertical column possess similar properties (this similarity is related to the number of outer or valence electrons). Elements in the same horizontal row have the same number of electron shells. Numbers in brackets are atomic numbers of undiscovered elements. Elements 104-107 have been detected but are not yet named.

Group																	Inert Gases
I A	II A											III A	IV A	V A	VI A	VII A	
1	H 1																He 2
2	Li 3	Be 4										B 5	C 6	N 7	O 8	F 9	Ne 10
3	Na 11	Mg 12	III B	IV B	V B	VI B	VII B	VIII			I B	II B	Al 13	Si 14	P 15	S 16	Cl 17	Ar 18
4	K 19	Ca 20	Sc 21	Ti 22	V 23	Cr 24	Mn 25	Fe 26	Co 27	Ni 28	Cu 29	Zn 30	Ga 31	Ge 32	As 33	Se 34	Br 35	Kr 36
5	Rb 37	Sr 38	Y 39	Zr 40	Nb 41	Mo 42	Tc 43	Ru 44	Rh 45	Pd 46	Ag 47	Cd 48	In 49	Sn 50	Sb 51	Te 52	I 53	Xe 54
6	Cs 55	Ba 56	La 57	Hf 72	Ta 73	W 74	Re 75	Os 76	Ir 77	Pt 78	Au 79	Hg 80	Tl 81	Pb 82	Bi 83	Po 84	At 85	Rn 86
7	Fr 87	Ra 88	Ac 89	104	105	106	107	(108)	(109)	(110)	(111)	(112)	(113)	(114)	(115)	(116)	(117)	(118)

LANTHANIDE SERIES	Ce 58	Pr 59	Nd 60	Pm 61	Sm 62	Eu 63	Gd 64	Tb 65	Dy 66	Ho 67	Er 68	Tm 69	Yb 70	Lu 71
ACTINIDE SERIES	Th 90	Pa 91	U 92	Np 93	Pu 94	Am 95	Cm 96	Bk 97	Cf 98	Es 99	Fm 100	Md 101	No 102	Lr 103

ELEMENTS AND THEIR DISCOVERERS

Element and Symbol	Atomic Number	Atomic Weight	Discoverer and Date
Actinium (Ac)	89	(227)*	A. Debierne (1899)
Aluminum (Al)	13	27.0	F. Wöhler (1827)
Americium (Am)	95	(243)	G. Seaborg et al. (1944)
Antimony (Sb)	51	121.8	B. Valentine (1604)
Argon (Ar)	18	39.9	W. Ramsay and J. Rayleigh (1894)
Arsenic (As)	33	74.9	A. Magnus (1250) (?)
Astatine (At)	85	(210)	E. Segrè et al. (1940)
Barium (Ba)	56	137.3	H. Davy (1808)
Berkelium (Bk)	97	(247)	S. Thompson et al. (1949)
Beryllium (Be)	4	9.0	N. Vauquelin (1798)
Bismuth (Bi)	83	209.0	C. Geoffroy the Younger (1753)
Boron (B)	5	10.8	H. Davy et al. (1808)
Bromine (Br)	35	79.9	A. Balard (1826)
Cadmium (Cd)	48	112.4	F. Stromeyer (1817)
Calcium (Ca)	20	40.1	H. Davy (1808)
Californium (Cf)	98	(251)	S. Thompson et al. (1950)
Carbon (C)	6	12.0	Prehistoric
Cerium (Ce)	58	140.1	J. Berzelius and W. d'Hisinger (1803)
Cesium (Cs)	55	132.9	R. Bunsen and G. Kirchhoff (1860)
Chlorine (Cl)	17	35.5	K. Scheele (1774)
Chromium (Cr)	24	52.0	N. Vauquelin (1797)
Cobalt (Co)	27	58.9	G. Brandt (c.1735)
Copper (Cu)	29	63.5	Prehistoric
Curium (Cm)	96	(247)	G. Seaborg et al. (1944)
Dysprosium (Dy)	66	162.5	L. de Boisbaudran (1886)
Einsteinium (Es)	99	(254)	A. Ghiorso et al. (1952)
Erbium (Er)	68	167.3	C. Mosander (1843)
Europium (Eu)	63	152.0	E. Demarçay (1896)
Fermium (Fm)	100	(257)	A. Ghiorso et al. (1952)
Fluorine (F)	9	19.0	H. Moissan (1886)
Francium (Fr)	87	(223)	M. Perey (1939)
Gadolinium (Gd)	64	157.3	J. C. de Marignac (1880)
Gallium (Ga)	31	69.7	L. de Boisbaudran (1875)
Germanium (Ge)	32	72.6	C. Winkler (1886)
Gold (Au)	79	197.0	Prehistoric
Hafnium (Hf)	72	178.5	D. Coster and G. von Hevesy (1923)
Helium (He)	2	4.0	J. C. P. Janssen and N. Lockyer (1868)
Holmium (Ho)	67	164.9	J. Soret and M. Delafontaine (1878)
Hydrogen (H)	1	1.0	H. Cavendish (1766)
Indium (In)	49	114.8	F. Reich and T. Richter (1863)
Iodine (I)	53	126.9	B. Courtois (1811)
Iridium (Ir)	77	192.2	S. Tennant (1803)
Iron (Fe)	26	55.8	Prehistoric
Krypton (Kr)	36	83.8	W. Ramsay and M. Travers (1898)
Lanthanum (La)	57	138.9	C. Mosander (1839)
Lawrencium (Lr)	103	(257)	A. Ghiorso et al. (1961)
Lead (Pb)	82	207.2	Prehistoric
Lithium (Li)	3	6.9	A. Arfvedson (1817)
Lutetium (Lu)	71	175.0	G. Urbain (1907)
Magnesium (Mg)	12	24.3	Recognized by J. Black (1755)
Manganese (Mn)	25	54.9	Recognized by K. Scheele et al. (1774)
Mendelevium (Md)	101	(258)	A. Ghiorso et al. (1955)
Mercury (Hg)	80	200.6	Prehistoric
Molybdenum (Mo)	42	95.9	K. Scheele (1778)
Neodymium (Nd)	60	144.2	C. von Welsbach (1885)
Neon (Ne)	10	20.2	W. Ramsay and M. Travers (1898)
Neptunium (Np)	93	(237)	E. McMillan and P. Abelson (1940)
Nickel (Ni)	28	58.7	A. Cronstedt (1751)
Niobium (Columbium) (Nb)	41	92.9	C. Hatchett (1801)
Nitrogen (N)	7	14.0	D. Rutherford (1772)
Nobelium (No)	102	(254)	A. Ghiorso et al. (1958)
Osmium (Os)	76	190.2	S. Tennant (1803)
Oxygen (O)	8	16.0	J. Priestley (1774)
Palladium (Pd)	46	106.4	W. Wollaston (1803)
Phosphorus (P)	15	31.0	H. Brand (1669)
Platinum (Pt)	78	195.1	D. de Ulloa (1735)
Plutonium (Pu)	94	(244)	G. Seaborg et al. (1940)
Polonium (Po)	84	c. 210	P. and M. Curie (1898)
Potassium (K)	19	39.1	H. Davy (1807)
Praseodymium (Pr)	59	140.9	C. von Welsbach (1885)
Promethium (Pm)	61	(145)	J. Marinsky et al. (1947)
Protactinium (Pa)	91	231.0	K. Fajans and A. H. Göhring (1913)
Radium (Ra)	88	226.1	P. and M. Curie (1898)
Radon (Rn)	86	c. 220	E. Rutherford (thoron) (1899)
			E. Dorn (radon) (1900)
Rhenium (Re)	75	186.2	W. Noddack et al. (1925)
Rhodium (Rh)	45	102.9	W. Wollaston (1803)
Rubidium (Rb)	37	85.5	R. Bunsen and G. Kirchhoff (1861)
Ruthenium (Ru)	44	101.1	K. Claus (or Klaus) (1844)
Samarium (Sm)	62	150.4	L. de Boisbaudran (1879)
Scandium (Sc)	21	45.0	L. Nilson (1879)
Selenium (Se)	34	79.0	J. Berzelius (1817)
Silicon (Si)	14	28.1	J. Berzelius (1824)
Silver (Ag)	47	107.9	Prehistoric
Sodium (Na)	11	23.0	H. Davy (1807)
Strontium (Sr)	38	87.6	H. Davy (1808)
Sulfur (S)	16	32.1	Prehistoric
Tantalum (Ta)	73	180.9	A. Ekeberg (1802)
Technetium (Tc)	43	98.9	E. Segrè and C. Perrier (1937)
Tellurium (Te)	52	127.6	M. von Reichenstein (1782)
Terbium (Tb)	65	158.9	C. Mosander (1843)
Thallium (Tl)	81	204.4	W. Crookes (1861)
Thorium (Th)	90	232.0	J. Berzelius (1828)
Thulium (Tm)	69	168.9	P. Cleve (1879)
Tin (Sn)	50	118.7	Prehistoric
Titanium (Ti)	22	47.9	W. Gregor (1791)
Tungsten (Wolfram) (W)	74	183.9	J. and F. d'Elhuyar (1783)
Uranium (U)	92	238.0	E. M. Peligot (1841)
Vanadium (V)	23	51.0	A. del Rio (1801)
Xenon (Xe)	54	131.3	W. Ramsay and M. Travers (1898)
Ytterbium (Yb)	70	173.0	C. Marignac (1878)
Yttrium (Y)	39	88.9	J. Gadolin (1794)
Zinc (Zn)	30	65.4	Prehistoric
Zirconium (Zr)	40	91.2	M. Klaproth (1789)
Unnamed element	104	(257)	A. Ghiorso et al.
Unnamed element	105	(262)	G. Flerov et al.
Unnamed element	106	(262)	
Unnamed element	107	(261)	G. Flerov et al. (1976)

* A number in parentheses under "Atomic Weight" is the mass number of the longest-lived isotope.

SELECTED NATIONAL ACADEMIES OF SCIENCE

Institution	Founded
National Academy of Sciences (Rome)	1603
The Royal Society (London)	1660
Academy of Sciences (Paris)	1666
The Royal Danish Academy of Sciences and Letters (Copenhagen)	1742
Royal Academy of Sciences, Letters, and Fine Arts of Belgium (Brussels)	1772
Royal Society of Edinburgh	1783
Royal Irish Academy (Dublin)	1786
Hungarian Academy of Sciences (Budapest)	1825
Austrian Academy of Science (Vienna)	1847
The Norwegian Academy of Science and Letters in Oslo	1857
National Academy of Sciences (Washington, D. C.)	1863
Yugoslav Academy of Sciences and Arts (Zagreb)	1867
Japan Academy (Tokyo)	1879
Royal Society of Canada (Ottawa)	1882
National Academy of Science (Mexico City)	1884
Brazilian Academy of Sciences (Rio de Janeiro)	1916
Academy of Athens	1926
Academia Sinica (Taipei)	1928
National Academy of Sciences of Buenos Aires	1937
Academy of the Socialist Republic of Rumania (Bucharest)	1948
Academy of Finland (Helsinki)	1947
Chinese Academy of Sciences (Peking)	1949
Czechoslovak Academy of Sciences (Prague)	1952
Polish Academy of Sciences (Warsaw)	1952
Australian Academy of Science (Canberra)	1954
Israel Academy of Sciences and Humanities (Jerusalem)	1961
Academy of Sciences of Cuba (Havana)	1962

LANDMARKS OF SCIENCE

Date	Landmark	Discoverer	Nationality
5th cent. B.C.	The atomic structure of matter postulated	Democritus	Greek
5th cent. B.C.	Postulation of causality in nature: the belief that every natural event has a natural cause	Leucippus	Greek
c. 300 B.C.	Compilation of **Elements**: the first formal statement of geometric principles	Euclid	Greek
3d cent. B.C.	Discovery of the laws of floating bodies, establishing the discipline of hydrostatics	Archimedes	Greek
c. 230 B.C.	First measurement of the Earth's circumference (accomplished without astronomical instruments)	Eratosthenes	Greek
3d cent. B.C.	Observations and calculations leading to the conclusions that the Earth is smaller than the Sun, rotates on an inclined axis, and revolves around the Sun; also, explanation of the seasons	Aristarchus of Samos	Greek
2d cent. B.C.	Measurement of size and distance of the Sun and the Moon	Hipparchus	Greek
2d cent. A.D.	Synthesis of current astronomical knowledge in the **Almagest**, which provided a system of celestial mechanics	Claudius Ptolemaeus (Ptolemy)	Greek
9th cent. A.D.	Establishment of the theory of numbers	Al-Khowarizmi	Arabian
1530	Publication of **De re metallica**, establishing the science of mineralogy	Georg Bauer (Agricola)	German
1543	Publication of **De revolutionibus orbium coelestium**; the solar system described as heliocentric	Mikolaj Kopernik (Copernicus)	Polish
1559	First cylindrical-projection map (commonly known as Mercator's projection), establishing mapmaking	Gerhard Kremer (Mercator)	Flemish
1589–92	Discovery of the laws of motion concerning **falling** bodies, the pendulum, and the inclined plane	Galileo Galilei	Italian
1600	Publication of **De magnete**: the basis for future work on magnetism and electricity	William Gilbert or Gylberde	English
1609/1619	Discovery of the three fundamental laws of planetary motion	Johannes Kepler	German
1614	Invention of logarithms as a powerful method of arithmetical calculation	John Napier	Scottish
1619	Formulation of analytic geometry	René Descartes	French
1620	Publication of **Novum Organum**, elucidating first formal theory of inductive logic	Francis Bacon	English
1643	Proof that air has weight; invention of the barometer	Evangelista Torricelli	Italian
1661	Formulation of the modern concept of the distinction between chemical elements and compounds	Robert Boyle	Anglo-Irish
1662	Discovery of law (Boyle's law) governing relation between pressure and volume of a gas	Robert Boyle	Anglo-Irish
c. 1670	Discovery of the calculus: the most powerful mathematical tool	Isaac Newton [Independently (1675–76) by Gottfried Leibniz, German]	English
1676	First measurement of the velocity of light	Olaus Römer	Danish
1687	Publication of **Philosophiae naturalis principia mathematica**, establishing the laws of gravitation and universal laws of motion	Isaac Newton	English
1690	Propounding of the wave theory of light	Christiaan Huygens	Dutch
1729	Distinction between electrical conductors and nonconductors (insulators)	Stephen Gray	English
1733	Distinction between two kinds of electricity (later called positive and negative); establishment of the fundamental law of electric charges	C. F. Du Fay	French
1735	Publication of **Systema naturae**: the foundation of taxonomy	Karl von Linné (Carolus Linnaeus)	Swedish
c. 1789	Discovery of true nature of combustion	Antoine Lavoisier	French
1795	Publication of **Theory of the Earth**, which paved the way to modern geological science	James Hutton	Scottish
1799	Discovery of the law of definite proportions of elements by weight in chemical compounds	Joseph Proust	French
1801	**Disquisitiones Arithmeticae** advances number theory	Karl F. Gauss	German
1802	Discovery of the dark lines in the solar spectrum	William Wollaston [Independently (1814) by Joseph von Fraunhofer, German]	English
1803	Proposal of an atomic theory of matter to explain the laws of chemical combination	John Dalton	English
1815	Establishment of stratigraphic geology for dating geological formations	William Smith	English
1820	Discovery of electromagnetism	Hans Christian Oersted	Danish
1825–26	Formulation of non-Euclidean geometry	Nikolai I. Lobachevski [Independently (1825–26) by Janos Bolyai, Hungarian]	Russian
1827	Statement of the law (Ohm's law) of electric conduction	Georg S. Ohm	German
1828	First synthesis of an organic compound from inorganic material	Friedrich Wöhler	German
1831	Discovery of electromagnetic induction	Michael Faraday [Independently (c. 1830) by Joseph Henry, American]	English
1840s	Formulation of the law of the conservation of energy (also known as the first law of thermodynamics)	Julius R. von Mayer James P. Joule Hermann L. F. von Helmholtz	German English German
1850	Formulation of the concept of entropy: the second law of thermodynamics	Rudolf J. E. Clausius	German
1850s	Establishment of the science of spectroscopy	Gustav R. Kirchhoff Robert W. Bunsen	German German

LANDMARKS OF SCIENCE (Continued)

Date	Landmark	Discoverer	Nationality
1852	Formulation of the concept of chemical valence	Edward Frankland	English
1854	Invention of Boolean algebra: the mathematization of logic	George Boole	English
1855	Founding of the science of oceanography	Matthew F. Maury	American
1859	Publication of **Origin of Species**, setting forth the idea of natural selection of living things	Charles Darwin [Independently (1858) by A. R. Wallace, English]	English
1861	Establishment of organic chemistry as the chemistry of carbon compounds	Friedrich A. Kekulé	German
1864	Formulation of the mathematical theory of electromagnetic radiation	James C. Maxwell	Scottish
1865	Formulation of the fundamental laws of genetics	Gregor J. Mendel	Austrian
1869	Formulation of the periodic law and periodic table of elements	Dmitri I. Mendeleev	Russian
1884	Formulation of the concepts of transfinite mathematics and the development of set theory, the basis of modern mathematical analysis	Georg Cantor	German
1884	Establishment of the concept of ionic dissociation in solution (ionization)	Svante A. Arrhenius	Swedish
1887	Propagation of electromagnetic waves (radio waves): demonstration that these waves travel at the velocity of light	Heinrich R. Hertz	German
1895	Discovery of X-rays	Wilhelm K. Roentgen	German
1896	Discovery of radioactivity in uranium	Antoine H. Becquerel	French
1897	Discovery of the electron	Joseph J. Thomson	English
1900	Postulation of quantum theory	Max Planck	German
1901	Enunciation of the idea of evolution by mutation	Hugo Marie De Vries	Dutch
	Established nature of radioactive disintegration	Ernest Rutherford	English, b. New Zealand
1905–15	Postulation of the special and general theories of relativity	Albert Einstein	American, b. Germany
1905–16	Completion of first cloud chamber for observing nuclear particles	Charles T. R. Wilson	Scottish
1911	Discovery of superconductivity	Heike Kammerlingh-Onnes	Dutch
1911	Formulation of the concept of the planetary atom	Niels H. D. Bohr	Danish
1913	Establishment of the concept of atomic number and that it is equal to the charge on the nucleus	Henry G. J. Moseley	English
1913	Completion of **Principia Mathematica**, a major contribution to symbolic logic	Bertrand A. W. Russell	English
		Alfred North Whitehead	English
1916	First relativistic theory of ''black holes'' formed by high-density matter	Karl Schwarzschild	German
1924–26	Formulation of wave mechanics	Louis V. de Broglie	French
		Erwin Schroedinger	German
1925	Formulation of matrix mechanics	Werner Heisenberg	German
1926	Publication of **Conditioned Reflexes**	Ivan Petrovich Pavlov	Russian
1931	Postulation of existence of the neutrino	Wolfgang Pauli	German
1932	Discovery of the neutron	James Chadwick	English
1932	Discovery of the positron	Carl D. Anderson	American
1934	Neutron bombardment of uranium leading to the production of transuranium elements	Enrico Fermi	American, b. Italy
1938	First nuclear fission of uranium	Lise Meitner	Austrian-Swedish
		Otto Hahn	German
		Fritz Strassmann	German
1942	Controlled nuclear fission of uranium	Enrico Fermi and others	American, b. Italy
1945	Explosion of first atomic bomb	J. Robert Oppenheimer and others	American
1947	Development of carbon-14 dating	Willard F. Libby	American
1948	Formulation of theory of the transistor and its construction	John Bardeen, Walter H. Brattain, & William Shockley	American
1951	First power-producing, nuclear-fission reactor	Atomic Energy Commission	American
1951	Explosion of first nuclear-fusion (hydrogen) bomb	Atomic Energy Commission	American
1953	Deciphering the double-helix structure of deoxyribonucleic acid (DNA) in the chromosome	Francis Crick, Maurice Wilkins, &	English
		James Watson	American
1954	Construction of first maser	Charles H. Townes	American
1955	Production and detection of the antiproton	Emilio G. Segré	American, b. Italy
		Owen Chamberlain	American
1958	Discovery of belts of high-energy radiation surrounding the Earth	James A. Van Allen	American
1960	First demonstration of laser action	Theodore H. Maiman	American
1967	Deciphering the structure of ribonucleic acid (RNA)	David Harker and others	American
1968	Synthesizing of ribonuclease molecule	R. Bruce Merrifield and others	American
		Ralph F. Hirschman and others	American
1970	Completion of gene synthesis	H. Gobino Khorana	American
1971	Discovery of reverse transcriptase for synthesizing DNA from RNA	H. Temin	American
1974	Detection of psi particle	Sam Ting and others	American
		Burt Richter and others	American
1976	Discovery of a particle with charm, thus confirming the existence of this property	Leon Lederman and others	American
1978	Discovery that some animal genes are interrupted in structure with genetic material of unknown function	P. Chambon and others	French

THE BASIS OF MEASUREMENT

The International System of Units (Système International, SI) is the modernized version of the metric system, established by international agreement to provide a logical and interconnected framework for all measurements in science, industry, and commerce. The seven base units here given are the foundation for the entire system, and all other units are derived from them. (Use of metric weights and measures was legalized in the United States in 1866, and our customary units of weights and measures are defined in terms of the meter and kilogram.)

Length—*Meter*. The meter is defined as 1,650,763.73 wavelengths in vacuum of the orange-red line of the spectrum of krypton-86.

Time—*Second*. The second is defined as the duration of 9,192,631,770 cycles of the radiation associated with a specified transition of the cesium atom.

Mass—*Kilogram*. The standard for the kilogram is a cylinder of platinum-iridium alloy kept by the International Bureau of Weights and Measures at Paris. A duplicate at the National Bureau of Standards serves as the mass standard for the United States. The kilogram is the only base unit still defined by an artifact.

Temperature—*Kelvin*. The Kelvin scale has its base at absolute zero and has a fixed point at the triple point of water defined as 273.16 kelvins. This triple point, at which water forms an interface of solid, liquid, and vapor, is defined as 0. 01° C on the Celsius or centigrade scale, and 32.02° F on the Fahrenheit scale.

Electric Current—*Ampere*. The ampere is defined as the magnitude of the current that, when flowing through each of two long parallel wires separated by one meter in free space, results in a force between the two wires (due to their magnetic fields) of 2×10^{-7} newton for each meter of length. (A newton is the unit of force of such size that a body of one kilogram mass would experience an acceleration of one meter per second per second.)

Luminous Intensity—*Candela*. The candela is defined as the luminous intensity of 1/600,000 of a square meter of a radiating cavity at the temperature of solidifying platinum (2,042 K).

Amount of Substance—*Mole*. The mole is defined as the amount of a substance containing as many elementary units (specified as atoms, molecules, ions, electrons, photons, and so forth) as there are carbon atoms in 0.012 kilogram of carbon-12.

TABLES OF METRIC WEIGHTS AND MEASURES

LINEAR MEASURE

10 millimeters (mm)	= 1 centimeter (cm)	
10 centimeters	= 1 decimeter (dm)	= 100 millimeters
10 decimeters	= 1 meter (m.)	= 1,000 millimeters
10 meters	= 1 dekameter (dam)	
10 dekameters	= 1 hectometer (hm)	= 100 meters
10 hectometers	= 1 kilometer (km)	= 1,000 meters

AREA MEASURE

100 square millimeters	= 1 square centimeter	
10,000 square centimeters	= 1 square meter	= 1,000,000 square millimeters
100 square meters	= 1 are (a)	
100 ares	= 1 hectare (ha)	= 10,000
100 hectares	= 1 square kilometer	= 1,000,000 square meters

VOLUME MEASURE

one liter	= 0.001 cubic meter
10 milliliters (ml)	= 1 centiliter (cl)
10 centiliters	= 1 deciliter (dl) = 100 milliliters
10 deciliters	= 1 liter (l) = 1,000 milliliters

VOLUME MEASURE (Cont.)

10 liters	= 1 dekaliter (dal)
10 dekaliters	= 1 hectoliter (hl) = 100 liters
10 hectoliters	= 1 kiloliter (kl) = 1,000 liters

WEIGHT

10 milligrams (mg)	= 1 centigram (cg)
10 centigrams	= 1 decigram (dg) = 100 milligrams
10 decigrams	= 1 gram (g) = 1,000 milligrams
10 grams	= 1 dekagram (dag)
10 dekagrams	= 1 hectogram (hg) = 100 grams
10 hectograms	= 1 kilogram (kg) = 1,000 grams
1,000 kilograms	= 1 metric ton (t)

CUBIC MEASURE

1,000 cubic millimeters	= 1 cubic centimeter
1,000 cubic centimeters	= 1 cubic decimeter = 1,000,000 cubic millimeters
1,000 cubic decimeters	= 1 cubic meter = 1 stere = 1,000,000 cubic centimeters = 1,000,000,000 cubic millimeters

TABLES OF EQUIVALENTS

The name of a unit enclosed in brackets [1 chain] indicates (1) that the unit is not in current use in the United States, or (2) that the unit is believed to be based on "custom and usage"

rather than on formal definition. Equivalents involving decimals are, in most instances, rounded off to the third decimal place except where exact equivalents are so designated.

1 angstrom[1]	0.1 millimicron (exactly). 0.000 1 micron (exactly). 0.000 000 1 millimeter (exactly). 0.000 000 004 inch.
1 cable's length	120 fathoms. 720 feet. 219.456 meters (exactly).
1 centimeter	0.393 7 inch.
1 chain (Gunter's or surveyor's)	66 feet. 20.1168 meters (exactly).
[1 chain] (engineer's)	100 feet. 30.48 meters (exactly).
1 decimeter	3.937 inches.
1 dekameter	32.808 feet.
1 fathom	6 feet. 1.8288 meters (exactly).
1 foot	0.3048 meter (exactly).
1 furlong	10 chains (surveyor's). 660 feet. 220 yards. 1/8 statute mile. 201.168 meters (exactly).
[1 hand]	4 inches.
1 inch	2.54 centimeters (exactly).
1 kilometer	0.621 mile.
1 league (land)	3 statute miles. 4.828 kilometers.
1 link (Gunter's or surveyor's)	7.92 inches (exactly). 0.201 168 meter (exactly).
[1 link (engineer's)]	1 foot. 0.3048 meter (exactly).
1 meter	39.37 inches. 1.094 yards.
1 micron (μ [the Greek letter mu])	0.001 millimeter (exactly). 0.000 039 37 inch.
1 mil	0.001 inch (exactly). 0.025 4 millimeter (exactly).

1 mile (statute or land)	5,280 feet. 1.609 kilometers.
1 mile (nautical, international)	1.852 kilometers (exactly). 1.151 statute miles. 0.999 U.S. nautical miles.
1 millimeter	0.039 37 inch.
1 millimicron (mμ [the English letter m in combination with the Greek letter mu])	0.001 micron (exactly). 0.000 000 039 37 inch.
1 point (typography)	0.013 837 inch (exactly). 1/72 inch (approximately). 0.351 millimeter.
1 rod, pole, or perch	16½ feet. 5½ yards. 5.0292 meters (exactly).
1 yard	0.9144 meter (exactly).

AREAS OR SURFACES

1 acre	43,560 square feet. 4,840 square yards. 0.405 hectare.
1 are	119.599 square yards. 0.025 acre.
1 hectare	2.471 acres.
[1 square (building)]	100 square feet.
1 square centimeter	0.155 square inch.
1 square decimeter	15.500 square inches.
1 square foot	929.030 square centimeters.
1 square inch	6.4516 square centimeters (exactly).
1 square kilometer	0.386 square mile. 247.105 acres.
1 square meter	1.196 square yards. 10.764 square feet.
1 square mile	258.999 hectares.
1 square millimeter	0.002 square inch.
1 square rod, sq. pole, or sq. perch	25.293 square meters.
1 square yard	0.836 square meter.

CAPACITIES OR VOLUMES

1 barrel, liquid	31 to 42 gallons.[2]
1 barrel, standard for fruits, vegetables, and other dry commodities except cranberries	{ 7,056 cubic inches. / 105 dry quarts. / 3.281 bushels.
1 barrel, standard, cranberry	{ 5,286 cubic inches. / 86 45/64 dry quarts. / 2.709 bushels, struck measure.
1 bushel (U.S.), struck measure	{ 2,150.42 cubic inches. / 35.239 liters.
[1 bushel, heaped (U.S.)]	{ 2,747.715 cubic inches. / 1.278 bushels, struck measure.[3]
[1 bushel (British Imperial) (struck measure)]	{ 1.032 U.S. bushels. / 2,219.36 cubic inches.
1 cord (firewood)	128 cubic feet.
1 cubic centimeter	0.061 cubic inch.
1 cubic decimeter	61.024 cubic inches.
1 cubic foot	{ 7.481 gallons. / 28.316 cubic decimeters.
1 cubic inch	{ 0.554 fluid ounce. / 4.433 fluid drams. / 16.387 cubic centimeters.
1 cubic meter	1.308 cubic yards.
1 cubic yard	0.765 cubic meter.
1 cup, measuring	{ 8 fluid ounces. / ½ liquid pint.
1 dram, fluid or liquid (U.S.)	{ ⅛ fluid ounce. / 0.226 cubic inch. / 3.697 milliliters. / 1.041 British fluid drachms.
1 dekaliter	{ 2.642 gallons. / 1.135 pecks.
1 gallon (U.S.)	{ 231 cubic inches. / 3.785 liters. / 0.833 British gallon. / 128 U.S. fluid ounces.
[1 gallon (British Imperial)]	{ 277.42 cubic inches. / 1.201 U.S. gallons. / 4.546 liters. / 160 British fluid ounces.
1 gill	{ 7.219 cubic inches. / 4 fluid ounces. / 0.118 liter.
1 hectoliter	{ 26.418 gallons. / 2.838 bushels.
1 liter	{ 1.057 liquid quarts. / 0.908 dry quart. / 61.024 cubic inches.
1 milliliter	{ 0.271 fluid dram. / 16.231 minims. / 0.061 cubic inch.
1 ounce, fluid or liquid (U.S.)	{ 1.805 cubic inches. / 29.574 milliliters. / 1.041 British fluid ounces.
[1 ounce, fluid (British)]	{ 0.961 U.S. fluid ounce. / 1.734 cubic inches. / 28.412 milliliters.
1 peck	8.810 liters.
1 pint, dry	{ 33.600 cubic inches. / 0.551 liter.
1 pint, liquid	{ 28.875 cubic inches (exactly). / 0.473 liter.
1 quart, dry (U.S.)	{ 67.201 cubic inches. / 1.101 liters. / 0.969 British quart.
1 quart, liquid (U.S.)	{ 57.75 cubic inches (exactly). / 0.946 liter. / 0.833 British quart.
[1 quart (British)]	{ 69.354 cubic inches. / 1.032 U.S. dry quarts. / 1.201 U.S. liquid quarts.
1 tablespoon	{ 3 teaspoons. / 4 fluid drams. / ½ fluid ounce.
1 teaspoon	{ ⅓ tablespoon. / 1⅓ fluid drams.

WEIGHTS OR MASSES

1 assay ton[4]	29.167 grams.
1 carat	{ 200 milligrams. / 3.086 grains.
1 dram, apothecaries	{ 60 grains. / 3.888 grams.
1 dram, avoirdupois	{ 27 11/32 (= 27.344) grains. / 1.772 grams.
1 grain	64.798 91 milligrams (exactly).
1 gram	{ 15.432 grains. / 0.035 ounce, avoirdupois.
1 hundredweight, gross or long[5]	{ 112 pounds. / 50.802 kilograms.
1 hundredweight, net or short	{ 100 pounds. / 45.359 kilograms.
1 kilogram	2.205 pounds.
1 microgram (μg [the Greek letter mu in combination with the letter g])	0.000 001 gram (exactly).
1 milligram	0.015 grain.
1 ounce, avoirdupois	{ 437.5 grains (exactly). / 0.911 troy or apothecaries ounce. / 28.350 grams.
1 ounce, troy or apothecaries	{ 480 grains. / 1.097 avoirdupois ounces. / 31.103 grams.
1 pennyweight	1.555 grams.
1 point	{ 0.01 carat. / 2 milligrams.
1 pound, avoirdupois	{ 7 000 grains. / 1.215 troy or apothecaries pounds. / 453.592 37 grams (exactly).
1 pound, troy or apothecaries	{ 5 760 grains. / 0.823 avoirdupois pound. / 373.242 grams.
1 ton, gross or long[5]	{ 2,240 pounds. / 1.12 net tons (exactly). / 1.016 metric tons.
1 ton, metric	{ 2,204.623 pounds. / 0.984 gross ton. / 1.102 net tons.
1 ton, net or short	{ 2,000 pounds. / 0.893 gross ton. / 0.907 metric ton.

---

[1] The angstrom is basically defined as 10^{-10} meter. [2] There are a variety of "barrels," established by law or usage. For example, federal laws on fermented liquors are based on a barrel of 31 gallons; many state laws fix the "barrel for liquids" at 31½ gallons; one state fixes a 36-gallon barrel for cistern measurement; federal law recognizes a 40-gallon barrel for "proof spirits"; by custom, 42 gallons comprise a barrel of crude oil or petroleum products for statistical purposes, and this equivalent is recognized "for liquids" by four states. [3] Frequently recognized as 1¼ bushels, struck measure. [4] The assay ton bears the same relation to the milligram that a ton of 2,000 pounds avoirdupois bears to the ounce troy; hence the weight in milligrams of precious metal obtained from one assay ton of ore gives directly the number of troy ounces to the net ton. [5] The gross or long ton and hundredweight are used commercially in the United States to only a limited extent, usually in restricted industrial fields. These units are the same as the British "ton" and "hundredweight."

ROMAN NUMERALS

These are letter symbols used to represent numbers. The seven basic letters and their number equivalents are: I=1, V=5, X=10, L=50, C=100, D=500, M=1,000. All other numbers (there is no zero) are formed using combinations of these letters (reading left to right, highest to lowest) which, when added together, produce the desired total: MCLX=1,160; LXXI=71; XVIII=18, etc.

In most cases a subtraction principle is used to show numbers containing 4's and 9's. Thus, instead of using four consecutive similar letters (IIII, XXXX or CCCC), only one letter is shown, followed by a larger value letter from which the smaller is to be subtracted. Examples of these cases are: IV=4, IX=9, XL=40, XC=90, CD=400, CM=900. 494 is written CDXCIV, 1979 becomes MCMLXXIX.

The addition of a bar line over the Roman numeral increases its value 1,000 times. V̄ represents 5,000, XIX is 19,000, L̄VI is 56,000. A large number such as 145,262 converts to C̄X̄L̄V̄C̄C̄LXII.

BINARY NUMBERS

This number system utilizes only two symbols, 1 and 0. The location of these symbols in the binary number indicates the presence (1) or absence (0) of a certain number of units which, when added together, produce a total numerical value. The number of units to be added is determined by the length of the binary number and the location(s) of the 1 symbol. The extreme right-hand place stands for one unit; each successive place to the left represents double (2 times) the quantity of the place to its right.

Number of Units	32	16	8	4	2	1	Add	Total Value
BINARY						1=	1	1
NUMBERS 10=					1	0	2+0	2
101=				1	0	1	4+0+1	5
1010=			1	0	1	0	8+0+2+0	10
11001=		1	1	0	0	1	16+8+0+0+1	25
101110=1		0	1	1	1	0	32+0+8+4+2+0	46

UNIT CONVERSIONS

To Convert	Into	Multiply By
Acre	hectare	0.4047
Acres	square feet	43,560.0
Acres	square miles	1.562×10^{-3}
Ampere-hours	coulombs	3,600.0
Angstrom unit	inch	3.937×10^{-9}
Angstrom unit	micron	1×10^{-4}
Astronomical unit	kilometers	1.495×10^{8}
Atmospheres	cms of mercury	76.0
Bolt (U.S. cloth)	meters	36.576
BTU	horsepower-hrs	3.931×10^{-4}
BTU	kilowatt-hrs	2.928×10^{-4}
BTU/hr	watts	0.2931
Bushels	cubic inches	2,150.4
Calories, gram (mean)	BTU (mean)	3.9685×10^{-3}
Centares	square meters	1.0
Centimeters	kilometers	1×10^{-5}
Centimeters	meters	1×10^{-2}
Centimeters	millimeters	10.0
Centimeters	feet	3.281×10^{-2}
Centimeters	inches	0.3937
Chain	inches	792.0
Circumference	radians	6.283
Coulombs	faradays	1.036×10^{-5}
Cubic centimeters	cubic inches	0.06102
Cubic centimeters	pints (U.S. liq.)	2.113×10^{-3}
Cubic feet	cubic meters	0.02832
Cubic feet/min	pounds water/min.	62.43
Cubic feet/sec	gallons/min.	448.831
Cubits	inches	18.0
Days	seconds	86,400.0
Degrees (angle)	radians	1.745×10^{-2}
Degrees/sec.	revolutions/min.	0.1667
Dynes	grams	1.020×10^{-3}
Dynes	joules/meter (newtons)	1×10^{-5}
Ell	inches	45.0
Em, pica	inch	0.167
Ergs	BTU	9.480×10^{-11}
Ergs	foot-pounds	7.3670×10^{-8}
Ergs	kilowatt-hours	2.778×10^{-14}
Faradays/sec.	amperes (absolute)	96,500
Fathoms	feet	6.0
Feet	centimeters	30.48
Feet	meters	0.3048
Feet	miles (nautical)	1.645×10^{-4}
Feet	miles (statute)	1.894×10^{-4}
Feet/min.	centimeters/sec.	0.5080
Feet/sec.	knots	0.5921
Feet/sec.	miles/hour	0.6818
Foot-pounds	BTU	1.286×10^{-3}
Foot-pounds	kilowatt-hours	3.766×10^{-7}
Furlongs	miles (U.S.)	0.125
Furlongs	feet	660.0
Gallons	liters	3.785
Gallons of water	pounds of water	8.3453
Gallons/min.	cubic feet/hour	8.0208
Grams	ounces (avoirdupois)	3.527×10^{-2}
Grams	ounces (troy)	3.215×10^{-2}
Grams	pounds	2.205×10^{-3}
Hand	centimeters	10.16
Hectares	acres	2.471
Hectares	square feet	1.076×10^{5}
Horsepower	BTU/min.	42.44
Horsepower	kilowatts	0.7457
Horsepower	watts	745.7
Hours	days	4.167×10^{-2}
Hours	weeks	5.952×10^{-3}
Inches	centimeters	2.540
Inches	miles	1.578×10^{-5}
International ampere	ampere (absolute)	0.9998
International volt	volts (absolute)	1.0003
Joules	BTU	9.480×10^{-4}
Joules	ergs	1×10^{7}
Kilograms	pounds	2.205
Kilometers	feet	3,281.0
Kilometers	meters	1,000.0
Kilometers	miles	0.6214

To Convert	Into	Multiply By
Kilometers/hr.	knots	0.5396
Kilowatts	horsepower	1.341
Kilowatt-hours	BTU	3,413.0
Knots	feet/hour	6,080.0
Knots	nautical miles/hr.	1.0
Knots	statute miles/hr.	1.151
League	miles (approximately)	3.0
Light year	miles	5.9×10^{12}
Links (surveyor's)	inches	7.92
Liters	cubic centimeters	1,000.0
Liters	cubic inches	61.02
Liters	gallons (U.S. liq.)	0.2642
Liters	milliliters	1,000.0
Liters	pints (U.S. liq.)	2.113
Meters	centimeters	100.0
Meters	feet	3.281
Meters	kilometers	1×10^{-3}
Meters	miles (nautical)	5.396×10^{-4}
Meters	miles (statute)	6.214×10^{-4}
Meters	millimeters	1,000.0
Microns	meters	1×10^{-6}
Miles (nautical)	feet	6,080.27
Miles (statute)	feet	5,280.0
Miles (nautical)	kilometers	1.853
Miles (statute)	kilometers	1.609
Miles (nautical)	miles (statute)	1.1516
Miles (statute)	miles (nautical)	0.8684
Miles/hour	feet/min.	88.0
Milligrams/liter	parts/million	1.0
Milliliters	liters	1×10^{-3}
Millimeters	inches	3.937×10^{-2}
Newtons	dynes	1×10^{5}
Ohms (international)	ohms (absolute)	1.0005
Ounces	grams	28.349527
Ounces	pounds	6.25×10^{-2}
Ounces (troy)	ounces (avoirdupois)	1.09714
Parsec	miles	19×10^{12}
Parsec	kilometers	3.084×10^{13}
Pints (liq.)	cubic centimeters	473.2
Pints (liq.)	cubic inches	28.87
Pints (liq.)	gallons	0.125
Pints (liq.)	quarts (liq.)	0.5
Pounds	kilograms	0.4536
Pounds	ounces	16.0
Pounds	ounces (troy)	14.5833
Pounds	pounds (troy)	1.21528
Pounds/sq. inch	grams/sq. cm.	70.31
Quarts (dry)	cubic inches	67.20
Quarts (liq.)	cubic inches	57.75
Quarts (liq.)	gallons	0.25
Quarts (liq.)	liters	0.9463
Quires	sheets	25.0
Radians	degrees	57.30
Radians	minutes	3,438.0
Reams	sheets	500.0
Revolutions	degrees	360.0
Revolutions/min.	degrees/sec.	6.0
Rods	meters	5.029
Rods	feet	16.5
Rods (surveyor's measure)	yards	5.5
Seconds	minutes	1.667×10^{-2}
Slug	pounds	32.17
Tons (long)	kilograms	1,016.0
Tons (short)	kilograms	907.1848
Tons (long)	pounds	2,240.0
Tons (short)	pounds	2,000.0
Tons (long)	tons (short)	1.120
Tons (short)	tons (long)	0.89287
Volt (absolute)	statvolts	3.336×10^{-3}
Watts	BTU/hour	3.4129
Watts	horsepower	1.341×10^{-3}
Watts (international)	watts (absolute)	1.0002
Yards	meters	0.9144
Yards	miles (nautical)	4.934×10^{-4}
Yards	miles (statute)	5.682×10^{-4}

MULTIPLES AND SUBMULTIPLES

Prefix	Symbol	Equivalent	Factor
atto-	a	quintillionth part	$\times 10^{-18}$
femto-	f	quadrillionth part	$\times 10^{-15}$
pico-	p	trillionth part	$\times 10^{-12}$
nano-	n	billionth part	$\times 10^{-9}$
micro-	μ	millionth part	$\times 10^{-6}$
milli-	m	thousandth part	$\times 10^{-3}$
centi-	c	hundredth part	$\times 10^{-2}$
deci-	d	tenth part	$\times 10^{-1}$
deca-	da	tenfold	$\times 10$
hecto-	h	hundredfold	$\times 10^{2}$
kilo-	k	thousandfold	$\times 10^{3}$
mega-	M	millionfold	$\times 10^{6}$
giga-	G	billionfold	$\times 10^{9}$
tera-	T	trillionfold	$\times 10^{12}$

TABLES OF UNITED STATES CUSTOMARY WEIGHTS AND MEASURES

LINEAR MEASURE

12 inches (in.)	= 1 foot (ft.)
3 feet	= 1 yard (yd.)
5½ yards	= 1 rod (rd.), pole, or perch (16½ ft.)
40 rods	= 1 furlong (fur.) = 220 yards = 660 feet
8 furlongs	= 1 statute mile (mi.) = 1,760 yards
	= 5,280 feet
3 land miles	= 1 league
5,280 feet	= 1 statute or land mile
6,076.11549 feet	= 1 international nautical mile

AREA MEASURE

Squares and cubes of units are sometimes abbreviated by using "superior" figures. For example, ft² means square foot, and ft³ means cubic foot.

144 square inches	= 1 square foot
9 square feet	= 1 square yard = 1,296 square inches
30¼ square yards	= 1 square rod = 272¼ square feet
160 square rods	= 1 acre = 4,840 square yards = 43,560 square feet
640 acres	= 1 square mile
1 mile square	= 1 section (of land)
6 miles square	= 1 township = 36 sections = 36 square miles

CUBIC MEASURE

1,728 cubic inches	= 1 cubic foot
27 cubic feet	= 1 cubic yard

LIQUID MEASURE

When necessary to distinguish the liquid pint or quart from the dry pint or quart, the word "liquid" or the abbreviation "liq." should be used in combination with the name or abbreviation of the liquid unit.

4 gills (gi.)	= 1 pint (pt.) (= 28.875 cubic inches)
2 pints	= 1 quart (qt.) (= 57.75 cubic inches)
4 quarts	= 1 gallon (gal.) (= 231 cubic inches) = 8 pints = 32 gills

APOTHECARIES FLUID MEASURE

60 minims (min.)	= 1 fluid dram (fl. dr.) (= 0.2256 cubic inch)
8 fluid drams	= 1 fluid ounce (fl. oz.) (= 1.8047 cubic inches)
16 fluid ounces	= 1 pint (= 28.875 cubic inches) = 128 fluid drams
2 pints	= 1 quart (= 57.75 cubic inches) = 32 fluid ounces = 256 fluid drams
4 quarts	= 1 gallon (= 231 cubic inches) = 128 fluid ounces = 1,024 fluid drams

DRY MEASURE

When necessary to distinguish the dry pint or quart from the liquid pint or quart, the word "dry" should be used in combination with the name or abbreviation of the dry unit.

2 pints	= 1 quart (= 67.2006 cubic inches)
8 quarts	= 1 peck (pk.) (= 537.605 cubic inches) = 16 pints
4 pecks	= 1 bushel (bu.) (= 2,150.42 cubic inches) = 32 quarts

AVOIRDUPOIS WEIGHT

When necessary to distinguish the avoirdupois dram from the apothecaries dram, or to distinguish the avoirdupois dram or ounce from the fluid dram or ounce, or to distinguish the avoirdupois ounce or pound from the troy or apothecaries ounce or pound, the word "avoirdupois" or the abbreviation "avdp." should be used in combination with the name or abbreviation of the avoirdupois unit.

(The "grain" is the same in avoirdupois, troy, and apothecaries weights.)

27 11/32 grains	= 1 dram (dr.)
16 drams	= 1 ounce (oz.) (= 437½ grains
16 ounces	= 1 pound (lb.) = 256 drams = 7,000 grains
100 pounds	= 1 hundredweight (cwt.)*
20 hundredweights	= 1 ton (tn.) = 2,000 pounds*

In "gross" or "long" measure, the following values are recognized:

112 pounds	= 1 gross or long hundredweight*
20 gross or long hundredweights	= 1 gross or long ton = 2,240 pounds*

TROY WEIGHT

24 grains	= 1 pennyweight (dwt.)
20 pennyweights	= 1 ounce troy (oz. t.) = 480 grains
12 ounces troy	= 1 pound troy (lb. t.) = 240 pennyweights = 5,760 grains

APOTHECARIES WEIGHT

20 grains	= 1 scruple (s. ap.)
3 scruples	= 1 dram apothecaries (dr. ap.) = 60 grains
8 drams apothecaries	= 1 ounce apothecaries (oz. ap.) = 24 scruples = 480 grains
12 ounces apothecaries	= 1 pound apothecaries (lb. ap.) = 96 drams apothecaries = 288 scruples = 5,760 grains

GUNTER'S OR SURVEYOR'S CHAIN MEASURE

7.92 inches	= 1 link (li.)
100 links	= 1 chain (ch.) = 4 rods = 66 ft.
80 chains	= 1 statute mile = 320 rods = 5,280 ft.

* When the terms "hundredweight" and "ton" are used unmodified, they are commonly understood to mean the 100-pound hundredweight and the 2,000-pound ton, respectively; these units may be designated "net" or "short" when necessary to distinguish them from the corresponding units in gross or long measure.

TEMPERATURE CONVERSIONS

The table offers temperature conversions that range from the freezing point of water (32° F., 0° C.) to its boiling point (212° F., 100° C.). For conversions below or beyond that range, apply these formulas: to convert Fahrenheit degrees into Celsius, subtract 32, multiply by 5, and divide by 9; to convert Celsius into Fahrenheit, multiply by 9, divide by 5, and add 32. A Fahrenheit degree is smaller than a Celsius degree, one Fahrenheit degree being 5/9 of a Celsius degree.

°F	°C	°F	°C	°F	°C	°F	°C	°F	°C
32	0	53	11·7	72	22·2	89·6	32	103	39·4
33·8	1	54	12·2	73	22·8	90	32·2	104	40
35·6	2	55	12·8	73·4	23	91	32·8	105	40·6
36·5	2·5	56	13·3	74	23·3	91·4	33	105·8	41
37·4	3	57	13·9	75	23·9	92	33·3	106	41·1
38	3·3	57·2	14	75·2	24	93	33·9	107	41·7
39	3·9	58	14·4	76	24·4	94	34·4	107·6	42
39·2	4	59	15	77	25	95	35	108	42·2
40	4·4	60	15·6	78	25·6	96	35·6	109	42·8
41	5	61	16·1	79	26·1	96·8	36	110	43·3
42	5·6	62	16·7	80	26·7	97	36·1	111	43·9
43	6·1	63	17·2	80·6	27	97·3	36·3	112	44·4
44	6·7	64	17·8	81	27·2	98	36·7	113	45
45	7·2	65	18·3	82	27·8	98·6	37	114	45·6
46	7·8	66	18·9	82·4	28	99	37·2	115	46·1
46·4	8	66·2	19	83	28·3	99·5	37·5	116	46·7
47	8·3	67	19·4	84	28·9	100	37·8	117	47·2
48	8·9	68	20	85	29·4	100·4	38	118	47·8
48·2	9	69	20·6	86	30	101	38·3	118·4	48
50	10	69·8	21	87	30·6	101·8	38·8	119	48·3
51	10·6	70	21·1	88	31·1	102	38·9	120	48·9
52	11·1	71	21·7	89	31·7	102·2	39	121	49·4

°F	°C	°F	°C	°F	°C	°F	°C	°F	°C
122	50	140	60	160	71·1	180	82·2	197	91·7
123	50·6	141	60·6	161	71·7	181	82·8	198	92·2
124	51·1	142	61·1	161·6	72	182	83·3	199	92·8
125	51·7	143	61·7	162	72·2	183	83·9	199·4	93
125·6	52	144	62·2	163	72·8	183·2	84	200	93·3
126	52·2	145	62·8	164	73·3	184	84·4	201	93·9
127	52·8	146	63·3	165	73·9	185	85	202	94·4
128	53·3	147	63·9	166	74·4	186	85·6	203	95
129	53·9	148	64·4	167	75	186·8	86	204	95·6
130	54·4	149	65	168	75·6	187	86·1	204·8	96
131	55	150	65·6	168·8	76	188	86·7	205	96·1
132	55·6	151	66·1	169	76·1	188·6	87	206	96·7
133	56·1	152	66·7	170	76·7	189	87·2	207	97·2
134	56·7	152·6	67	171	77·2	190	87·8	208	97·8
134·6	57	153	67·2	172	77·8	190·4	88	208·4	98
135	57·2	154	67·8	173	78·3	191	88·3	209	98·3
136	57·8	155	68·3	174	78·9	192	88·9	210	98·9
136·4	58	156	68·9	175	79·4	193	89·4	210·2	99
137	58·3	156·2	69	176	80	194	90	211	99·4
138	58·9	157	69·4	177	80·6	195	90·6	212	100
138·2	59	158	70	178	81·1	195·8	91		
139	59·4	159	70·6	179	81·7	196	91·1		

SCIENCE GLOSSARY

PHYSICS AND ATOMIC ENERGY

Absolute temperature—Temperature scale on which the zero point is absolute zero ($-273.15°$ C).

Acceleration—Rate of change of velocity; increase or decrease in velocity per unit of time.

Alpha particle—Low-speed, low-penetration helium nucleus emitted during disintegration of radioactive elements.

Anode—The positive electrode in an electric cell or an electron tube.

Angstrom—A unit of length: 1/100,000,000 centimeter.

Atom—Smallest part of a chemical element that takes part in a chemical change.

Atomic number—Number of protons in an atomic nucleus.

Atomic weight—Ratio of the average mass per atom of an element to 1/12 of the mass of an atom of carbon 12.

Beta particle—High-speed, high-penetration electron emitted during radioactive disintegration.

British thermal unit (BTU)—The amount of heat required to raise the temperature of one pound of water through one Fahrenheit degree.

Calorie—The amount of heat required to raise the temperature of one gram of water through 1° C.

Cathode—The negative electrode in an electric cell or an electron tube.

Celsius scale—A temperature scale on which the range between the freezing point of water, 0°, and the boiling point, 100°, is divided into 100 equal degrees. Also called the *Centigrade* scale.

Centrifugal force—The apparent force experienced by a body moving in a curved path that acts outward from the center of the path.

Doppler effect—Apparent change in frequency of sound waves or light waves caused by relative motion of the source toward or away from an observer, and by motion of an observer toward or from a stationary source.

Electron—Negatively charged, stable elementary particle.

Fission—Specifically, the splitting of an atomic nucleus into two parts of approximately the same size, accompanied by the release of great amounts of energy.

Fusion, nuclear—Union of two light atomic nuclei to form a heavier, more complex one, accompanied by the release of great amounts of energy. Also called *thermonuclear fusion.*

Gamma rays—Shortwave, high-frequency electromagnetic radiation emitted during disintegration of radioactive elements.

Gravity—Attraction of the earth or a celestial body for other bodies at or near its surface.

Half life—The time required for half of a radioactive substance to decay.

Hertz—Unit of frequency equal to 1 cycle per second.

Infrared—Electromagnetic radiation with wavelengths longer than visible red.

Ion—Charged atom or group of atoms produced by loss or gain of electrons from the outer orbits.

Ionization—Any process resulting in the formation of ions from atoms or molecules.

Joule—Unit of energy equal to the work done when a force of one newton moves through one meter.

Kinetic energy—Energy due to motion.

Liquid—Fluid phase of matter in which the surface is free, the volume is definite, and the shape is determined by the container.

Magnetic field—Space permeated by magnetic lines of force.

Magnetic pole—One of the two points in a magnet or a celestial body where magnetism seems to concentrate.

Mass Number—Sum of the numbers of protons and neutrons in the nucleus of an atom.

Matter—Anything that has mass and occupies space.

Meson—Any of a group of elementary particles of small mass and very short life.

Neutron—Neutral particle found in the nuclei of atoms with a mass number greater than 1.

Newton—Unit of force equal to the force required to give a mass of 1 kilogram an acceleration of 1 meter per second per second.

Nuclear reactor—Device for starting and regulating nuclear fission for the purpose of producing heat.

Nucleon—Particle found in the structure of an atom's nucleus.

Nucleus—Central, positively charged part of an atom.

Ohm—Unit of electrical resistance.

Photoelectric effect—Emission of electrons by certain substances when struck by light or other radiation.

Photon—A quantum of radiation.

Physical change—An alteration that includes no change in the molecular composition of a substance.

Physics—The study of matter and energy and the interchange of energy among material things.

Positron—Positive electron.

Proton—Positively charged, stable particle found in the nuclei of all atoms.

Quantum mechanics—Modern mathematical form of the quantum theory.

Quantum theory—Theory that all energy is lost or gained in discrete amounts (quanta).

Quark—type of particle with 1/3 electron charge, postulated to be components of other fundamental particles.

Radar—Electronic system for detecting distant objects by means of transmitted high-frequency radio waves and their reflection from the objects.

Radiation—Electromagnetic waves, or particles emitted from nuclei.

Radioactivity—Disintegration of the nuclei of the atoms of certain elements, during which electromagnetic waves and elementary particles are emitted.

Relativity—(1) Einstein's special theory: All motion is relative to observer, and velocity of light in space is constant regardless of motion of light source or observer. Mass may be changed into energy and vice versa according to the law $E = mc^2$ (2) Einstein's general theory: gravitation is a consequence of curved space.

Resistance—Opposition to passage of electric current offered by an electrical conductor.

Specific gravity—Ratio of the mass of a substance to the mass of an equal volume of some standard, such as water or air. Also called *relative density.*

Spectroscope—Optical instrument for the study of spectra.

Spectrum—Band of electromagnetic radiation in which the constituent parts are arranged according to their wavelengths or their frequencies.

Transformer—Device for changing the voltage of alternating current.

Transistor—Device made of semiconductor materials for the control of the flow of electric current.

Ultrasonic—Having a frequency above that audible to human beings: above about 20,000 hertz (cycles per second).

Ultraviolet—Electromagnetic radiation with wavelengths shorter than visible violet but longer than X-rays.

Velocity—Rate of motion in a given direction.

Watt hour—The energy of 1 watt acting for 1 hour.

Wavelength—Distance between two successive points of a wave in the same phase, such as crest to crest.

X-rays—Electromagnetic radiations of short wavelength and high penetration of matter.

MATHEMATICS

Additive inverse of a number—A number with its sign changed to minus if originally plus, or vice versa.

Algorism (Algorithm)—In modern mathematics, any systematic method or procedure for computation.

Analog computer—A calculating device in which magnitudes are determined by measurement along scales rather than by digital counting, e.g., slide rule.

Analytic geometry—The technique of dealing with geometry in terms of algebra.

Antilogarithm—The number corresponding to a given logarithm, e.g., 2 is the logarithm of 100, therefore, 100 is the antilogarithm of 2.

Axiom—In a system of mathematics or logic, a proposition or statement from which secondary propositions or statements are derived.

Binary arithmetic—A system of calculation in which the only numerals used are 0 and 1, and all real numbers are represented as powers of 2.

Bit—Condensation of *binary digit*. In computer and information theory, a single binary digit, either 0 or 1.

Boolean algebra—An algebra obeying special laws that make it suitable for such uses as the study of logic and planning switching circuits.

Calculus—Generally, any system of mathematical calculation, or any system of operations involving symbols, e.g., calculus of finite differences, calculus of probabilities, and the like. Specifically, a method of mathematical analysis (developed independently by Isaac Newton and Gottfried Leibniz) involving the rate of change of a variable function.

Cardinal number—Zero and the counting numbers 1, 2, 3, 4, . . . , as distinguished from the ordinal numbers.

Cartesian coordinates—Two or three lines intersecting at right angles and providing a reference system for locating points in two or three dimensional space; used in analytic geometry.

Compound interest—Interest paid periodically on the sum of a given principle and its accruing interest.

Decimal number system—The ordinary number system (sometimes called the Arabic system) that denotes real numbers according to the place values for multiples of 10 plus the digits 0 through 9.

Derivative—A measure of the rate at which one mathematical variable changes in response to changes in a related variable.

Digital computer—A calculating machine in which mathematical operations are performed by individually tallying every digit.

Duodecimal system—A system of numeration in which the base is 12. The numbers 10 and 11 of the decimal system are rendered in the duodecimal system by arbitrary symbols, two of which in use are t (called dek) and e (called el).

Function—In classical algebra, a variable y so related to another variable x, that for each value given to x there is a value that may be determined for y.

Hardware—The electronic equipment used in a computer system, in contrast to the software.

Infinity—A quantity that is greater than any assignable quantity.

Integral—Mathematical function used in calculus for finding the area under a curve.

Intersection—That portion of two or more sets common to all the sets considered.

Iterative procedure—A means of approximating the solution to an equation by repeating a given procedure several times to get successively closer answers, each based on the preceding approximation.

Logarithm—The exponent of the power to which a number is to be raised to produce a given number. Thus, using the base 10, the logarithm of 100 is 2, because the exponent of the power to which 10 must be raised in order to equal 100 is 2 ($10^2 = 100$).

Machine language—The characters and symbols and the rules for combining them that convey information and instruction to a computer for processing.

Matrix—Usually a rectangular array of numbers, including several columns and rows, that can be manipulated as though it were a single quantity.

Modular arithmetic—A form of arithmetic dealing with the remainders left over when all the numbers considered are divided by a single number, the modulus.

Multiplicative inverse of a number—The reciprocal of that number; for example, 1/5 is the reciprocal of 5.

Non-Euclidean geometry—Any of several geometries that substitute other postulates for Euclid's fifth postulate (in effect, through a point outside a given line, only one line may be drawn parallel to the given line).

Open sentence—An equation containing one or more unknown quantities.

Ordinal number—A number that indicates position or relation; thus, 2d, 3d, 8th.

Postulate—An unproved assumption accepted as basic to a mathematical system, and from which, in combination with other postulates, the propositions of the system are derived, or in terms of which the propositions are proved.

Problem language—The language used by a programmer to state the problem to be solved by a computer.

Program—A sequence of steps to be executed by a computer to solve a given problem.

Reciprocal—The number that results when 1 is divided by a given number. Thus, the reciprocal of 2 is ½; the reciprocal of 4 is ¼; and the reciprocal of a fraction is the fraction inverted, thus the reciprocal of ⅘ is 5/4.

Repeating decimal—A nonterminating decimal in which a pattern of numbers is established and is followed by a continuous repetition of the digit or pattern of digits, thus: .222222222222, .777777777777, .1515151515-15, .234523452345; a repeating decimal is also called a recurring decimal, periodic decimal, or circulating decimal.

Scalar—A quantity indicating magnitude but not direction, in contrast to a vector.

Set—A collection of objects, symbols, or ideas with some common property or attribute.

Slide rule—A computing device usually consisting of a frame and a horizontal slide, on both of which are printed scales graduated logarithmically. Also, usually, a transparent runner, or indicator, containing a hairline that is used to enable accurate reading of the results obtained by manipulation of the slide within the frame.

Software—Programs, procedures, and routines that support and augment a computer system.

Symbolic logic—Logic performed with the use of symbols subject to certain predetermined rules.

Topology—The study of those properties of geometric figures that remain unchanged despite radical distortions of considered figures.

Transformation—A rule for transforming one set of values into another; for example, $y = 2x$ transforms each x into a y twice as large.

Truth set—A set of solutions to an equation or group of equations.

Union—The total of all the members of all the sets of the union being considered.

Vector—A quantity having direction as well as magnitude. Thus, velocity is a vector because it is specified by its direction as well as its magnitude.

CHEMISTRY

Acid—A substance that in aqueous solution turns blue litmus red, furnishes hydronium ions, and contains hydrogen, which can be replaced by a metal.

Alkali—A water-soluble base that ionizes strongly to form hydroxide ions.

Anion—A negative ion.

Base—A substance that in aqueous solution turns red litmus blue, furnishes hydroxyl ions, and reacts with an acid to form a salt and water only.

Buffer—A solution containing either a weak acid and its salt or a weak base and its salt, thereby resisting changes in acidity or basicity.

Carbohydrate—A compound of carbon, hydrogen, and oxygen, usually having hydrogen and oxygen in the proportion of 2 to 1.

Catalyst—A substance that alters the rate at which a chemical reaction takes place, but which itself remains unchanged.

Cation—A positive ion.

Chemical change—Change in a substance involving a change in its identity due to an increase, decrease, or rearrangement of the atoms within its molecules; opposed to physical change, in which the substance keeps its identity.

Colloid—Dispersion in a medium of particles that are very small aggregates of molecules. Also called *colloidal suspension*.

Combustion—Any chemical change that produces heat and, usually, light. Most commonly, the combination of the oxygen of the air with a substance: *burning*.

Compound—A homogeneous chemical substance composed of two or more chemical elements, the proportions of which by weight are fixed and invariable.

Cracking—A method of changing the constituents of petroleum, using pressure, heat, and catalysts, in which the hydrocarbons of high molecular weight are broken down into those of lower molecular weight.

Crystal—A solid in which the component molecules, atoms, or ions are oriented in a definite and repeated geometric pattern.

Deliquescent substance—A substance that absorbs moisture from the air and dissolves in the water so absorbed.

Deuterium—An isotope of hydrogen of mass number 2.

Distillation—Vaporization of a liquid, followed by condensation of the vapor.

Electrolysis—Chemical decomposition of a substance by an electric current passed through the substance in dissolved or molten state.

Element—A substance which cannot be decomposed by ordinary types of chemical change, or made by chemical union.

Emulsion—Dispersion of minute droplets of one liquid (that does not dissolve) in another.

Ester—Organic compounds corresponding to inorganic salts, derived by replacing hydrogen of an acid by an organic group.

Fixation of nitrogen—The combination of atmospheric nitrogen with other elements to form chemical compounds.

Formula—The combination of chemical symbols showing the composition of a chemical element or compound.

Hard water—Water that contains chemicals in solution that react with soap to form a precipitate and which therefore only lathers with difficulty.

Hydrocarbon—A compound containing only carbon and hydrogen.

Hydrolysis—Chemical reaction of a substance with water.

Ion—An atom or group of atoms possessing an electrical charge.

Isomers—Molecules that have the same number and kinds of atoms but different molecular configurations.

Isotopes—Atoms of the same atomic number which differ in the number of protons in the nucleus.

Molecular weight—Relative weight of a molecule compared to the weight of an atom of carbon taken as exactly 12.00; the sum of the atomic weights of the atoms in a molecule.

Molecule—The smallest unit of a substance that can exist free, and retain all the chemical properties of that substance.

Osmosis—Diffusion of a solvent through a semipermeable membrane into a more concentrated solution.

Oxidation—A process in which an atom or group of atoms loses electrons; combination with oxygen.

pH—A symbol for the logarithm of the reciprocal of the hydrogen ion concentration of a solution; thus, an indication of the acidity or basicity of a solution. A neutral solution has a pH of 7; an acid solution has a pH lower than seven, an alkaline, higher.

Photosynthesis—A chemical change that utilizes light energy; e.g., the production in plants of starch from carbon dioxide and water in sunlight.

Polymorphism—The ability of a substance to exist in two or more crystalline forms.

Precipitate—An insoluble solid deposited from a solution.

Protein—Complex organic compounds of very high molecular weight that compose a large part of all living matter; protein molecules invariably contain the elements of carbon, hydrogen, oxygen, and nitrogen.

Radical—A group of atoms that functions as a unit in chemical change.

Reduction—A process in which an atom or group of atoms gains electrons: loss of oxygen or combination with hydrogen.

Salt—A compound made up of the positive ion of a base and the negative ion of an acid.

Solution—A homogeneous mixture of two or more substances of dissimilar molecular structure. In a solution there is a dissolving medium—*solvent*—and a dissolved substance—*solute*.

Standard conditions—0° C and 1 atmosphere (760 mm, or 29.92 in. of mercury) pressure.

Synthesis—The formation of a compound from its elements or from simpler compounds.

Tritium—An isotope of hydrogen of mass number 3.

Valence—A number that represents the combining power of an atom or radical referred to hydrogen as a standard.

MULTIPLICATION AND DIVISION TABLE

A number in the top line (14) multiplied by a number in the extreme left hand column (13) produces the number where the top line and side line meet (182).

A number in the table (208) divided by the number at the top of the same column (13) results in the number (16) in the extreme left hand column. A number in the table (208) divided by the number at the extreme left (16) results in the number (13) at the top of the column.

1	2	3	4	5	6	7	8	9	10	11	12	13	14	15	16	17	18	19	20	21	22	23	24	25
2	4	6	8	10	12	14	16	18	20	22	24	26	28	30	32	34	36	38	40	42	44	46	48	50
3	6	9	12	15	18	21	24	27	30	33	36	39	42	45	48	51	54	57	60	63	66	69	72	75
4	8	12	16	20	24	28	32	36	40	44	48	52	56	60	64	68	72	76	80	84	88	92	96	100
5	10	15	20	25	30	35	40	45	50	55	60	65	70	75	80	85	90	95	100	105	110	115	120	125
6	12	18	24	30	36	42	48	54	60	66	72	78	84	90	96	102	108	114	120	126	132	138	144	150
7	14	21	28	35	42	49	56	63	70	77	84	91	98	105	112	119	126	133	140	147	154	161	168	175
8	16	24	32	40	48	56	64	72	80	88	96	104	112	120	128	136	144	152	160	168	176	184	192	200
9	18	27	36	45	54	63	72	81	90	99	108	117	126	135	144	153	162	171	180	189	198	207	216	225
10	20	30	40	50	60	70	80	90	100	110	120	130	140	150	160	170	180	190	200	210	220	230	240	250
11	22	33	44	55	66	77	88	99	110	121	132	143	154	165	176	187	198	209	220	231	242	253	264	275
12	24	36	48	60	72	84	96	108	120	132	144	156	168	180	192	204	216	228	240	252	264	276	288	300
13	26	39	52	65	78	91	104	117	130	143	156	169	182	195	208	221	234	247	260	273	286	299	312	325
14	28	42	56	70	84	98	112	126	140	154	168	182	196	210	224	238	252	266	280	294	308	322	336	350
15	30	45	60	75	90	105	120	135	150	165	180	195	210	225	240	255	270	285	300	315	330	345	360	375
16	32	48	64	80	96	112	128	144	160	176	192	208	224	240	256	272	288	304	320	336	352	368	384	400
17	34	51	68	85	102	119	136	153	170	187	204	221	238	255	272	289	306	323	340	357	374	391	408	425
18	36	54	72	90	108	126	144	162	180	198	216	234	252	270	288	306	324	342	360	378	396	414	432	450
19	38	57	76	95	114	133	152	171	190	209	228	247	266	285	304	323	342	361	380	399	418	437	456	475
20	40	60	80	100	120	140	160	180	200	220	240	260	280	300	320	340	360	380	400	420	440	460	480	500
21	42	63	84	105	126	147	168	189	210	231	252	273	294	315	336	357	378	399	420	441	462	483	504	525
22	44	66	88	110	132	154	176	198	220	242	264	286	308	330	352	374	396	418	440	462	484	506	528	550
23	46	69	92	115	138	161	184	207	230	253	276	299	322	345	368	391	414	437	460	483	506	529	552	575
24	48	72	96	120	144	168	192	216	240	264	288	312	336	360	384	408	432	456	480	504	528	552	576	600
25	50	75	100	125	150	175	200	225	250	275	300	325	350	375	400	425	450	475	500	525	550	575	600	625

FOREIGN WEIGHTS AND MEASURES

Name of Unit	Country	U.S. Equivalent
Ardeb	Egypt	43.55 gals.
Arroba	Costa Rica	25.35 lbs.
Bak (opium)	Laos	57.9 grains
Barril	Mexico	16.72 gals.
Batman	Iran	6.546 lbs.
Beswa	Afghanistan	116.8 sq. yds.
Bhara	Malaysia	400.0 lbs.
Bocoy	Cuba	18.214 bu.
Botella	Honduras	1.216 pts.
Bu	Japan	.011930 in.
Caballeria	El Salvador	111.11 acres
Cable (nautical)	United Kingdom	200.0 yds.
Cajuela	Costa Rica	3.74 gals.
Cân	South Vietnam	1.333 lbs.
Candy	Burma	18,000.0 lbs.
Caneca	Cuba	4.784 gals.
Cántaro (wine)	Spain	3.572 gals.
Cape inch	South Africa	1.033 ins.
Capicha	Iran	2.32 qts.
Carga	El Salvador	200.0 lbs.
Carga	Mexico	308.6 lbs.
Case (bananas)	Western Samoa	72.0 lbs.
Catty	Indonesia	1.3616 lbs.
Centner	Denmark	110.231 lbs.
Chang	Mongolia	3.50 qts.
Cheung	Hong Kong	4.063 yds.
Chi	South Korea	1.423 sq. ins.
Cho	Japan	119.30 yds.
Chum	Malaysia	1.475 ins.
Chupak	Malaysia	1.0 qt.
Cuadra	Ecuador	91.9 yds.
Cuadra	Peru	2.47 acres
Cuarta	Costa Rica	8.228 ins.
Cuartilla	Ecuador	50.7 lbs.
Cuartillo (oil)	Mexico	.890 pt.
Cubito	Somalia	22.0 ins.
Cuerdo	Puerto Rico	.971 acre
Dariba	Egypt	43.55 bu.
Dawulla	Ethiopia	220.46 lbs.
Dékare	Bulgaria	.247 acre
Dhira	Syria	29.5 ins.
Dira	Saudi Arabia	17.3 ins.
Djuim	Byelorussian SSR	1.0 in.
Dönüm	Cyprus	1,600.0 sq. yds.
Dönüm, metric	Israel	1,196.0 sq. yds.
Doppelzentner	West Germany	220.462 lbs.
Dra (textiles)	Jordan	26.8 ins.
Du	Mongolia	5.72 qts.
El	Surinam	2.26 ft
Fan che	Mainland China	1.19599 sq. ft.
Fanega	Paraguay	63.4 gals.
Farsakh-song	Iran	3.88 mi.
Fatar	Muscat and Oman	Span from first finger to thumb
Fen	Mainland China	.1312 in.
Frasila	Tanzania	36.0 lbs.
Fuder	West Germany	220.0 gals.
Fun	Hong Kong	.14625 in.
Fuss	West Germany	12.36 ins.
Gallon	Haiti	.8326 gal.
Gang	South Vietnam	.4306 sq. ft.
Gantang	Sabah	1.0 gal.
Gaz	Iran	1.14 yds.
Gazi jerib	Afghanistan	29.0 ins.
Gian sheng	Mainland China	27.4961 bu.
Gong qing	Mainland China	2.471054 acres
Grain, colonial	Mauritius	.819 grain
Gun	Hong Kong	1.333 lbs.
Gurraf	Libya	2.03 qts.
Habba (gold)	Sudan	1.543 grains
Hand (height of horses)	United Kingdom	4.0 ins.
Heml	Egypt	550.3 lbs.
Hold (agriculture)	Hungary	1.422 acres
Izenbi	Morocco	2,153.0 sq. yds.
Jemba	Malaysia	144.0 sq. ft.
Jin	Mainland China	1.1023 lbs.
Jutro, katastarsko	Yugoslavia	1.422 acres
Kala	Morocco	19.69 ins.
Kantang	Cambodia	1.650 gals.
Kantar	Lebanon	565.3 lbs.
Kantar	Egypt	99.05 lbs.
Ken	Japan	1.988 yds.
Kettle	Sierra Leone	8.79 qts.
Kilates (troy)	Philippines	3.09 grains
Kin	Japan	1.32 lbs.
Koku	Japan	39.68 gals.
Kosh	Nepal	2.0 mi.
Kung chang	China (Taiwan)	10.9361 yds.
Kwien	Thailand	440.0 gals.
Kwintal	Poland	220.46 lbs.
Legua	Cuba	2.635 mi.
Legua	Uruguay	3.2 mi.
Leaguer	South Africa	127.0 gals.
Lei (Chinese mi.)	Hong Kong	706–745.0 yds.
Lelong	Malaysia	2,400.0 sq. ft.
Li	Mainland China	546.8 yds.
Li	South Korea	2.440 mi.
Libra	Spain	1.014 lbs.
Livre, colonial	Seychelles	1.079 lbs.
Load (cocoa)	Sierra Leone	60.0 lbs.
Ma (Chinese yd.)	Hong Kong	35.10 ins.
Manzana	Guatemala	1.74 acres
Marco	Mexico	1.015 oz.
Marco real	Spain	1.591 acres
Maund (Imperial)	Aden	82.28 lbs.
Mecate	Costa Rica	21.942 yds.
Medida	Honduras	2.527 qts.
Meripeninkulma	Finland	1.15 mi.
Mid (oil)	Jordan	15.8 qts.
Mil	Sweden	6.214 mi.
Mile (geographical)	Indonesia	4.60 mi.
Milla legal	Argentina	1.0 mi.
Misura	Libya	4.36 gals.
Mu	Mainland China	.16474 acre
Mud	Netherlands	2.471 acres
Mudu (rice)	Nigeria	2.5 lbs.
Nim-man	Iran	3.272 lbs.
Oke	Saudi Arabia	2.8 lbs.
Onza	Honduras	1.014 oz.
Ounce, Amsterdam	Indonesia	1.089 oz.
Peninkulma (mil)	Finland	6.21 mi.
Phân	South Vietnam	2.583 sq. ft.
Pié	Argentina	1.0 ft.
Pied anglais	Haiti	1.0 ft.
Pipa	Dominican Republic	15.75 bu.
Pond	Surinam	1.102 lbs.
Poud (grain)	USSR	36.11 lbs.
Pulgada	Philippines	1.0 in.
Quintal	Angola	220.5 lbs.
Quintal	El Salvador	100.0 lbs.
Raummeter	Austria	1.308 cu. yds.
Ri	Japan	2.440 mi.
Roupi (textiles)	Cyprus	3.00 ins.
Rute	West Germany	4.12 yds.
Sâa	Libya	26.13 gals.
Saco (coffee)	Colombia	137.8 lbs.
Saco (coffee)	Peru	152.1 lbs.
Seer	Nepal	2.057 lbs.
Shaku	Japan	.635 fl. oz.
Shō	Japan	1.587 qts.
Sildarmál (herring)	Iceland	4.12 bu.
Solar	Ecuador	.43 acre
Stone	United Kingdom	14.0 lbs.
Stoop (beer)	Netherlands	1.32 gals.
Sun	Japan	1.19303 ins.
Tael	Cambodia	1.323 avoir. oz.
Tanan	Thailand	.880 qt.
Tartous	Syria	1,099.0 sq. yds.
Tercia	El Salvador	1.0 ft.
Thail (opium)	Indonesia	1.241 avoir. oz.
Thôn	South Vietnam	2.870 sq. yds.
To	Japan	3.968 gals.
Tola (standard)	Pakistan	180.0 grains
Tomme	Denmark	1.030 ins.
Tondeland	Denmark	1.363 acres
Tonne	Schleswig-Holstein, W. Ger.	1.35 acres
Tonneau de mer	Belgium	100.0 cu. ft.
Topo (usual)	Peru	.86 acre
Tuuma	Finland	1.0 in.
Ud	Sudan	2.54 yds.
Uyên (rice)	South Vietnam	.880 qt.
Vara	Chile	32.91 ins.
Vara	Paraguay	2.84 ft.
Vara	Spain	2.74 ft.
Voet, Amsterdam	Netherlands	.928 ft.
War	Aden	1.0 yd.
Wari	Kenya	1.0 yd.
Wine gallon	Barbados	.83267 gal.
Wizna	Malta	8.750 lbs.
Yang	South Korea	1.32 oz.
Yarda	Colombia	35.43 ins.
Yen	South Vietnam	13.33 lbs.
Zentner	Austria	220.46 lbs.
Zoll	West Germany	1.03 ins.

SQUARES, CUBES, SQUARE ROOTS, AND CUBE ROOTS

No.	Squares	Cubes	Square roots	Cube roots	No.	Squares	Cubes	Square roots	Cube roots
1	1	1	1.0000000	1.0000000	51	2601	132651	7.1414284	3.7084298
2	4	8	1.4142136	1.2599210	52	2704	140608	7.2111026	3.7325111
3	9	27	1.7320508	1.4422496	53	2809	148877	7.2801099	3.7562858
4	16	64	2.0000000	1.5874011	54	2916	157464	7.3484692	3.7797631
5	25	125	2.2360687	1.7099759	55	3025	166375	7.4161985	3.8029525
6	36	216	2.4494896	1.8171206	56	3136	175616	7.4833148	3.8258624
7	49	343	2.6457513	1.9129312	57	3249	185193	7.5498344	3.8485011
8	64	512	2.8284271	2.0000000	58	3364	195112	7.6157731	3.8708766
9	81	729	3.0000000	2.0800837	59	3481	205379	7.6811457	3.8929965
10	100	1000	3.1622777	2.1544347	60	3600	216000	7.7459667	3.9148676
11	121	1331	3.3166248	2.2239801	61	3721	226981	7.8102497	3.9364972
12	144	1728	3.4641016	2.2894286	62	3844	238328	7.8740079	3.9578915
13	169	2197	3.6055513	2.3513347	63	3969	250047	7.9372539	3.9790571
14	196	2744	3.7416574	2.4101422	64	4096	262144	8.0000000	4.0000000
15	225	3375	3.8729833	2.4662121	65	4225	274625	8.0622577	4.0207256
16	256	4096	4.0000000	2.5198421	66	4356	287496	8.1240384	4.0412401
17	289	4913	4.1231056	2.5712816	67	4489	300763	8.1853528	4.0615480
18	324	5832	4.2426407	2.6207414	68	4624	314432	8.2462113	4.0816551
19	361	6859	4.3588989	2.6684016	69	4761	328509	8.3066239	4.1015661
20	400	8000	4.4721360	2.7144177	70	4900	343000	8.3666003	4.1212853
21	441	9261	4.5825757	2.7589243	71	5041	357911	8.4261498	4.1408178
22	484	10648	4.6904158	2.8020393	72	5184	373248	8.4852814	4.1601676
23	529	12167	4.7958315	2.8438670	73	5329	389017	8.5440037	4.1793390
24	576	13824	4.8989795	2.8844991	74	5476	405224	8.6023253	4.1983364
25	625	15625	5.0000000	2.9240177	75	5625	421875	8.6602540	4.2171633
26	676	17576	5.0990195	2.9624960	76	5776	438976	8.7177979	4.2358236
27	729	19683	5.1961524	3.0000000	77	5929	456533	8.7749644	4.2543210
28	784	21952	5.2915026	3.0365889	78	6084	474552	8.8317609	4.2726586
29	841	24389	5.3851648	3.0723168	79	6241	493039	8.8881944	4.2908404
30	900	27000	5.4772256	3.1072325	80	6400	512000	8.9442719	4.3088695
31	961	29791	5.5677644	3.1413806	81	6561	531441	9.0000000	4.3267487
32	1024	32768	5.6568542	3.1748021	82	6724	551368	9.0553851	4.3444815
33	1089	35937	5.7445626	3.2075343	83	6889	571787	9.1104336	4.3620707
34	1156	39304	5.8309519	3.2396118	84	7056	592704	9.1651514	4.3795191
35	1225	42875	5.9160798	3.2710663	85	7225	614125	9.2195445	4.3968296
36	1296	46656	6.0000000	3.3019272	86	7396	636056	9.2736185	4.4140049
37	1369	50653	6.0827625	3.3322218	87	7569	658503	9.3273791	4.4310476
38	1444	54872	6.1644140	3.3619754	88	7744	681472	9.3808315	4.4479602
39	1521	59319	6.2449980	3.3912114	89	7921	704969	9.4339811	4.4647451
40	1600	64000	6.3245553	3.4199519	90	8100	729000	9.4868330	4.4814047
41	1681	68921	6.4031242	3.4482172	91	8281	753571	9.5393920	4.4979414
42	1764	74088	6.4807407	3.4760266	92	8464	778688	9.5916630	4.5143574
43	1849	79507	6.5574385	3.5033981	93	8649	804357	9.6436508	4.5306549
44	1936	85184	6.6332496	3.5303483	94	8836	830584	9.6953597	4.5468359
45	2025	91125	6.7082039	3.5568933	95	9025	857375	9.7467943	4.5629026
46	2116	97336	6.7823300	3.5830479	96	9216	884736	9.7979590	4.5788570
47	2209	103823	6.8556546	3.6088261	97	9409	912673	9.8488578	4.5947009
48	2304	110592	6.9282032	3.6342411	98	9604	941192	9.8994949	4.6104363
49	2401	117649	7.0000000	3.6593057	99	9801	970299	9.9498744	4.6260650
50	2500	125000	7.0710678	3.6840314	100	10000	1000000	10.0000000	4.6415888

DECIMAL EQUIVALENTS OF COMMON FRACTIONS

8ths	16ths	32ds	64ths	Equivalent
			1	.015625
	1		2	.031250
			3	.046875
1		2	4	.062500
			5	.078125
	3		6	.093750
			7	.109375
1	2	4	8	.125000
			9	.140625
		5	10	.156250
			11	.171875
3	6		12	.187500
			13	.203125
	7		14	.218750
			15	.234375
2	4	8	16	.250000
			17	.265625
	9		18	.281250
			19	.296875
5	10		20	.312500
			21	.328125
	11		22	.343750
			23	.359375
3	6	12	24	.375000
			25	.390625
		13	26	.406250
			27	.421875
	7	14	28	.437500
			29	.453125
		15	30	.468750
			31	.484375
4	8	16	32	.500000
			33	.515625
		17	34	.531250
			35	.546875
	9	18	36	.562500
			37	.578125
		19	38	.593750
			39	.609375
5	10	20	40	.625000
			41	.640625
		21	42	.656250
			43	.671875
	11	22	44	.687500
			45	.703125
		23	46	.718750
			47	.734375
6	12	24	48	.750000
			49	.765625
		25	50	.781250
			51	.796875
	13	26	52	.812500
			53	.828125
		27	54	.843750
			55	.859375
7	14	28	56	.875000
			57	.890625
		29	58	.906250
			59	.921875
	15	30	60	.937500
			61	.953125
		31	62	.968750
			63	.984375
8	16	32	64	1.000000

INVENTORS AND INVENTIONS

Invention	Date	Inventor	Country
abacus	c. 500 B.C.	unknown	China (?)
achromatic lens	1758	John Dolland	England
adding machine	1642	Blaise Pascal	France
adding machine (commercial)	1885	William Burroughs	U.S.
addressing machine	1893	J. S. Duncan	U.S.
aerosol spray	1941	Lyle D. Goodhue	U.S.
air brake	1869	George Westinghouse	U.S.
air conditioning	1911	Willis H. Carrier	U.S.
air-cushion vehicle	1877	J. I. Thornycroft	England
airplane	1903	Orville and Wilbur Wright	U.S.
airplane (multi-motored)	1913	Igor Sikorsky	Russia
airship (nonrigid)	1852	Henri Giffard	France
airship (rigid)	1900	Ferdinand von Zeppelin	Germany
automatic pilot	1929	William Green	U.S.
automobile (electric)	1891	William Morrison	U.S.
automobile (internal combustion)	1887	Gottlieb Daimler	Germany
		Karl Benz (independently)	Germany
Babbitt metal	1839	Isaac Babbitt	U.S.
bakelite	1907	Leo H. Baekeland	U.S.
balloon	1783	J. M. and J. E. Montgolfier	France
barbed wire	1874	Joseph F. Glidden	U.S.
barometer	1643	Evangelista Torricelli	Italy
battery (electric)	1800	Alessandro Volta	Italy
benday process	1879	Benjamin Day	U.S.
Bessemer converter	1856	Henry Bessemer	England
	1857	William Kelly (independently)	U.S.
betatron	1939	Donald W. Kerst	U.S.
bicycle	1816	Karl D. von Sauerbronn	Germany
bifocal lens	1780	Benjamin Franklin	U.S.
blast furnace	1828	J. B. Neilson	Scotland
bottlemaking machine	1903	Michael Owens	U.S.
Braille	1829	Louis Braille	France
breech-loading rifle	1810	John Hall	U.S.
bubble chamber	1952	Donald A. Glaser	U.S.
bulldozer	1923	unknown	U.S.
bullet (rifle)	1849	Claude E. Minié	France
Bunsen burner	1855	Robert W. Bunsen	Germany
calculating machine (digital)	1823	Charles Babbage	England
camera (photographic)	1822	Joseph N. Niepce	France
carburetor	1892	Gottlieb Daimler	Germany
cash register	1879	James Ritty	U.S.
cathode ray tube	1878	William Crookes	England
cellophane	c. 1900	Jacques Brandenberger	Switzerland
celluloid	1855	Alexander Parkes	England
cement (portland)	1824	Joseph Aspdin	England
chronometer	1735	John Harrison	England
clock (pendulum)	1656	Christiaan Huygens	Holland
cloud chamber	1911	Charles T. R. Wilson	Scotland
color photography	1881	Frederic E. Ives	U.S.
combine (harvesting, threshing, cleaning)	1911	Benjamin Holt	U.S.
compressed-air rock drill	1871	Simon Ingersoll	U.S.
computer (differential analyzer)	1928	Vannevar Bush	U.S.
computer (electronic)	1946	J. Presper Eckert, John W. Mauchly	U.S.
condensed milk	1853	Gail Borden	U.S.
cotton gin	1793	Eli Whitney	U.S.
cylinder lock	1865	Linus Yale, Jr.	U.S.
cultivator	1820	Henry Burden	U.S.
daguerrotype	1837	Louis J. M. Daguerre	France
dictating machine	1885	Charles S. Tainter	U.S.
diesel engine	1892	Rudolf C. K. Diesel	Germany
disc brake	1902	Ferdinand W. Lanchester	England
dynamite	1866	Alfred B. Nobel	Sweden
electric flatiron	1882	Henry W. Seely	U.S.
electric generator	1832	Hippolyte Pixii	France
electric motor	1822	Michael Faraday	England
electric shaver	1928	Jacob Schick	U.S.
electric stove	1896	William S. Hadaway, Jr.	U.S.
electric vacuum cleaner	1907	James M. Spangler	U.S.
electromagnet	1824	William Sturgeon	England
electron microscope	1939	Vladimir K. Zworykin	U.S.
electroplating	1805	Luigi Brugnatelli	Italy
electrotype	1839	Moritz-Hermann Jacobi	Russia
elevator (passenger)	1852	Elisha G. Otis	U.S.
evaporated milk	1880	John B. Meyenberg	U.S.
firearm magazine	1854	Horace Smith and Daniel B. Wesson	U.S.
flanged railway rail	1831	Robert L. Stevens	U.S.
flying shuttle	1733	John Kay	England
frequency-modulation (FM) broadcasting	1933	Edwin H. Armstrong	U.S.
galvanometer	1819	Johann S. C. Schweigger	Germany
gas engine (four-cycle)	1876	Nikolaus August Otto	Germany
geiger counter	1913	Hans W. Geiger	England
glider	1853	George Cayley	England
gramophone (disc record)	1887	Emile Berliner	U.S.
gyrocompass	1911	Elmer A. Sperry	U.S.
halftone engraving process	1886	Frederic E. Ives	U.S.
helicopter (man-carrying)	1907	Paul Cornu	France
holography	1949	Denis Gabor	England
hydraulic press	1795	Joseph Brahmah	England
hydrometer	1768	Antoine Baumé	France
hydroplane	1911	Glenn H. Curtis	U.S.
internal combustion engine	1859	Jean J. E. Lenoir	France
internal combustion engine (high speed)	1880	Gottlieb Daimler	Germany
iron lung	1928	Philip Drinker and Louis A. Shaw	U.S.
jet engine	1937	Frank Whittle	England
kaleidoscope	1816	David Brewster	Scotland
knitting machine	c. 1589	William Lee	England
lamp (incandescent)	1879	Thomas A. Edison	U.S.
lamp (mercury vapor)	1901	Peter C. Hewitt	U.S.
lamp (neon)	1910	Georges Claude	France

Invention	Date	Inventor	Country
laser	1960	Theodore H. Naiman	U.S.
lathe (engine-driven)	1800	Henry Maudslay	England
Leyden jar	1746	John Bevis	England
		Pieter van Musschenbroek	Holland
life preserver	1805	John Edwards	England
lightning rod	1752	Benjamin Franklin	American colonies
linoleum	1860	Frederick Walton	England
linotype	1884	Ottmar Mergenthaler	U.S.
lithography	1798	Aloys Senefelder	Germany
long-playing (LP) record	1948	Peter C. Goldmark	U.S.
machine gun	1862	Richard J. Gatling	U.S.
match (friction)	1827	John Walker	England
match (safety)	1855	J. E. Lundstrom	Sweden
metronome	1816	Johann N. Mälzel	Austria
micrometer	1636	William Gascoigne	England
microphone	c. 1877	Thomas A. Edison	U.S.
microscope	1590	Zacharias Janssen	Holland
miner's lamp	1815	Humphry Davy	England
monotype	1887	Tolbert Lanston	U.S.
motion pictures	1872	Eadweard Muybridge and John D. Isaacs	U.S.
motorcycle	1885	Edward Butler	England
mowing machine	1810	Peter Gaillard	U.S.
multiplying machine	1671	Gottfried W. von Leibniz	Germany
nitroglycerine	c. 1846	Ascanio Sobrero	Italy
nylon	1935	Wallace H. Carothers	U.S.
oleomargarine	1868	Hippolyte Mége-Mouriz	France
parachute	1783	Louis S. Lenormand	France
parking meter	1935	Carlton C. Magee	U.S.
percussion cap	1816	Joshua Shaw	U.S.
phonograph (cylindrical record)	1877	Thomas A. Edison	U.S.
photocell	1895	Julius Elster and Hans Geitel	Germany
phototype-setting machine	1945	E. G. Klingberg Fritz Stadelmann H. R. Freund	U.S.
plow, iron	1784	James Small	England
plow (wooden)	c. 2500 B.C.	unknown	Egypt
polarizing glass (Polaroid)	1932	Edwin H. Land	U.S.
printing press (screw type)	c. 1450	Johann Gutenberg	Germany
printing with movable type	11th century	Pi-sheng	China
prism spectroscope	1859–60	Gustave Kirchhoff and Robert Bunsen	Germany
pump (air)	1650	Otto von Guericke	Germany
radar	1935	Robert A. Watson-Watt	England
radio-telegraph	1895	Guglielmo Marconi	Italy
radio-telephone	1902	Reginald A. Fessenden	U.S.
railway (electric)	1881	Werner von Siemens	Germany
railway signal (block)	1863	Ashbel Welch and Robert Stewart	U.S.
railway sleeping car	1859	George M. Pullman	U.S.
reaper	1826	Patrick Bell	Scotland
refrigerator	1858	Ferdinand Carré	France
revolver	1831	Samuel Colt	U.S.
rifle	1520	August Kotter	Germany
roller bearings	c. 1496	Leonardo da Vinci	Italy
rolling mill	c. 1496	Leonardo da Vinci	Italy
safety pin	1849	Walter Hunt	U.S.
sail	c. 3000 B.C.	unknown	Egypt
saw (circular)	1777	Samuel Miller	England
screw propeller	1804	John C. Stevens	U.S.
self-starter (automobile)	1911	Charles F. Kettering	U.S.
sewing machine	1790	Thomas Saint	England
shrapnel shell	1784	Henry Shrapnel	England
silencer (firearm)	1908	Hiram P. Maxim	U.S.
slide rule	c. 1620	William Oughtred	England
spinning machine	1764	James Hargreaves	England
sprinkler (fire)	1723	Ambrose Godfrey	England
steamboat	1783	Marquis de Jouffroy d'Abbans	France
steam engine	1628	Edward Somerset	England
steam engine (condensing)	1765	James Watt	Scotland
steam hammer	1839	James Nasmyth	Scotland
stereoscope	1838	Charles Wheatstone	England
stereotyping	1725	William Ged	Scotland
stock ticker	1870	Thomas A. Edison	U.S.
storage battery	1803	Johann W. Ritter	Germany
street car	1834	Thomas Davenport	U.S.
submarine detector	1917	Max Mason	U.S.
switchboard	1877	Edgar T. Holmes	U.S.
tank, military	1914	Ernest D. Swinton	England
tape recorder (magnetic)	1899	Valdemar Poulsen	Denmark
telegraph (multiwire)	1809	Samuel T. von Soemmering	Germany
telegraph (single wire)	1835	Samuel F. B. Morse	U.S.
telegraph cable (submarine)	1866	Cyrus W. Field	U.S.
telephone	1876	Alexander G. Bell	U.S.
telescope	1608	Hans Lippershey	Holland
telescope (reflecting)	1661	James Gregory	Scotland
television	1926	James Logie Baird	Scotland
television iconoscope scanner	1938	Vladimir K. Zworykin	U.S.
thermometer (air and water)	c. 1592	Cornelius Drebbel	Holland
thermometer (mercury)	1714	Gabriel D. Fahrenheit	Germany
threshing machine	1732	Michael Menzies	Scotland
tire (pneumatic)	1843	Robert W. Thompson	England
toaster (automatic)	1918	Charles Strite	U.S.
tractor	1825	Robert Keeley	England
transformer (electric)	1885	William Stanley	U.S.
transistor	1948	J. Bardeen	U.S.
		W. H. Brattain	U.S.
		W. Shockley	U.S.
typecasting machine	1836	David Bruce	U.S.
typewriter	1714	Henry Mill	England
vacuum bottle	1873	James Dewar	England
vacuum tube (diode)	1904	John A. Flemming	England
vacuum tube (triode)	1906	Lee De Forest	U.S.
vulcanized rubber	1839	Charles Goodyear	U.S.
Wankel engine	1957	Felix Wankel	Germany
warship (steam)	c. 1860	John Ericsson	U.S.
washing machine	1858	Hamilton E. Smith	U.S.
weaving machine	1733	John Kay	England
wirephoto	1881	Shelford Bidwell	England
xerography	1948	Chester Carlson	U.S.
X-ray tube (hot-filament)	1913	William D. Coolidge	U.S.
zipper	1893	Whitcomb L. Judson	U.S.

UNITED STATES
POLYCONIC PROJECTION
SCALE OF MILES

SCALE OF KILOMETRES

Capitals of Countries .... ⊛   State Capitals ....
International Boundaries _____   State Boundaries ....
Copyright by C. S. HAMMOND & Co., N. Y.

ALABAMA

MILES

0   20   40   60

KILOMETERS

0   20   40   60

State Capitals ⊛
County Seats ⊙

© Copyright HAMMOND INCORPORATED, Maplewood, N.J.

THE FIFTY STATES

ALABAMA

Site of the first Confederate capital in the proverbial "Heart of Dixie," Alabama is a traditionally agricultural state in the Southern mold. A continuing concerted drive toward greater economic diversification in the state began in the 1930s, after costly boll weevil infestations and other problems pointed up the perils of an economy overly dependent on any such single factor as cotton. Today, Birmingham has become the South's largest iron and steel producing center, while the Redstone Arsenal and George C. Marshall Space Flight Center in Huntsville have emerged as important research installations; in a single decade (1950-60), Huntsville's population more than quadrupled.

Hydroelectric power provided by the Tennessee Valley Authority has been a key factor in Alabama's growing industrialization. Tourist attractions include the Mound State Monument (Moundsville) and the George Washington Carver Museum at Tuskegee Institute, a school founded by Booker T. Washington, a former slave.

The state's diverse topography ranges from the Appalachian highlands in the northeast to the broad coastal plain comprising about two-thirds of the total area; in the plain's central region is the fertile "Black Belt." Swamps, bayous, and sandy beaches also mark the varied terrain. The state's abbreviated coastline is dominated by Mobile Bay; Dauphin Island lies at the bay's entrance. About 65 percent of the state is forested.

Mound Builders, who lived in the Alabama region in prehistoric times, were followed by a number of Indian tribes, including the Chickasaws, Cherokees, and Creeks. Spaniards Cabeza de Vaca and Hernando De Soto were among the region's early European explorers. The first permanent settlement was made (1702) by Frenchmen at Fort Louis near present-day Mobile; it served as the capital of the Louisiana Territory until 1722. Other French settlements followed, but in 1763 France lost the region to the British.

After the American Revolution, England ceded to the United States all of the Alabama region except the southernmost British West Florida area that included Mobile; this region, together with so-called East Florida, went to Spain.

In 1817, after a short period as part of the Territory of Mississippi, the region was organized as the Alabama Territory. Settlers spurred by the virtual ending of Indian troubles in the area helped the new territory's growth; statehood came in 1819. Slave-supported plantation farming, aided by the recent invention of the cotton gin, soon emerged as the main factor in the state's economy.

After the Mexican War (1846-48), the slavery question became a hotly debated national issue. The first Confederate capital was established (1861) at Montgomery; later it was moved to Richmond. Alabama suffered a great deal from both the Civil War and the harsh, chaotic Reconstruction. The state fell deeply in debt, and extremist groups such as the Ku Klux Klan grew in size and influence.

Race relations continued as a major concern of modern Alabama. The Montgomery bus boycott (1955-56), led by Martin Luther King, is considered a civil rights milestone, as was the enrollment (1956) of Autherine Lucy in the University of Alabama; she was the first Negro to enroll in a previously all-white Alabama public school. In 1965, about 30,000 integrationists took part in a protest march from Selma to Montgomery. A suspect in a 1963 church bombing (considered one of the worst acts of racial terrorism of the '60s) which killed four was tried and convicted in 1978.

George Wallace announced in May 1978 that he was retiring from politics with the expiration of his term of office as governor.

Full name: State of Alabama. **Origin of name:** From the Indian, Alba Amo meaning "I Clear the Thicket." **Inhabitant:** Alabamian. **Capital:** Montgomery. **State motto:** Audemus Jura Nostra Defendere (We Dare Defend Our Rights). **Flag:** Red cross of St. Andrew on white field. **Seal:** A circled map of Alabama with boundaries & rivers. **Flower:** Camellia. **Bird:** Yellowhammer. **Tree:** Southern pine. **Song:** "Alabama." **Nickname:** Yellowhammer State

Governor: Forest James, Jr.. **Annual salary:** $50,000. **Term:** 4 years. **Current term expires:** Jan. 1983. **Voting requirements:** 18 yrs. old & U.S. citizen; resident of state 10 days. **U.S. Congressmen:** 7. **Entered Union:** 1819 (22nd state).

Location & boundaries: Southeastern state: bounded on the north by Tennessee; on the east by the Chattahoochee River & Georgia; on the south by Florida & the Gulf of Mexico; & on the west by Mississippi. **Total area:** 51,609 sq. mi. (ranks 29th). **Extreme length:** 330 mi. **Extreme breadth:** 200 mi. **Coastline:** 53 mi. **Chief rivers:** Mobile, Alabama, Tombigbee, Coosa. **Major lakes:** Wheeler, Guntersville, Wilson, Martin, Mitchell. **No. of counties:** 67.

Population (1978 est.): 3,742,000 (ranks 22nd). **Pop. increase (1970-78):** 8.6%. **Places over 25,000 pop.:** 15. **Places over 100,000:** 4. **Largest cities:** Birmingham, Mobile, Montgomery. **Pop. density:** 72.5 per sq. mi. (ranks 26th). **Pop. projection 1985:** 3,958,000. **Pop. distribution:** 61.8% metropolitan; 38.2% nonmetropolitan. **White:** 73.4%. **Negro:** 26.4%. **Other:** 0.2%. **Marriage rate (1977):** 12.3 per 1,000 people. **Divorce rate:** 6.4 per 1,000 people.

State finances (1977). Revenue: $3,124,417,000. **Expenditures:** $2,966,281,000. **State Taxes:** $380.40 per capita. **State personal income tax:** Yes. **Public debt (1977):** $270.23 per capita. **Federal aid (1977):** $237.20 per capita. **Personal income (1977):** $5,633.

Sectors of the economy (% of labor force employed in 1970): Manufacturing (29%), Wholesale & retail trade (19%), Services (9%), Educational Services (7%), Construction (7%), Government (17%). **Leading products:** primary & fabricated metals, transportation equipment, machinery, food, textiles, apparel, paper, chemicals. **Minerals:** coal, cement, stone, petroleum. **Agricultural products:** broilers, cattle, eggs, corn, soybeans, peanuts. **Fishing:** shrimp, red snappers, blue crabs. **Avg. farm (1978 est.):** 189 acres. **Avg. value of farm:** $452 per acre.

Highway expenditures per capita (1977): $101.14. **Persons per motor vehicle:** 1.38; **Minimum age for driver's license:** 16. **Gasoline tax:** 7¢ per gallon. **Motor vehicle deaths:** 30.7 per 100,000 people.

Birthrate (1977): 16.8 per 1,000 people. **Infant mortality rate per 1,000 births (1977):** 16.9. **Physicians per 100,000 pop. (1976):** 111. **Dentists per 100,000 pop. (1976):** 32. **Acceptable hospital beds:** 6.8 per 1,000 people. **State expenditures per capita for health and hospitals (1977):** $62.43.

Education expenditures (1975-76): $369.88 per capita annually. **No. of pupils in public schools (1976 est.):** 741,000. **No. of institutions of higher learning (1976-77):** 56. **Public school expenditure per pupil in attendance (1974-75):** $1,195. **Avg. salary of public school teachers (1974-75 est.):** $9,503. **No. full-time teachers (1977 est.):** 39,790. **Educational attainment of adult population (1976):** 12.2 median yrs. of school completed; 6.8% with less than 5 years of education; 10.2% with 4 yrs. of college.

Telephones (1976): 59 per 100 people. **State Chamber of Commerce:** Alabama State Chamber of Commerce, 468 South Perry, P.O. Box 76, Montgomery, Alabama 36101.

ALASKA

Alaska is a land of great extremes: first among the states in area, last in population. One of the nation's biggest bargains (Alaska's purchase price was less than 2¢ an acre), it is potentially one of the

ALASKA

MILES

KILOMETERS

State and Provincial Capitals
Court Houses

© Copyright HAMMOND INCORPORATED, Maplewood, N.J.

richest states—particularly in view of the spectacular oil strikes in Prudhoe Bay off the state's frigid Arctic (or North) Slope. Many believe that these strikes will fulfill the century-long promise of "The Last Frontier"; the find has already been called "one of the largest petroleum accumulations known to the world today." In 1969 about $900 million was bid for oil-land leases, even while the U.S. oil tanker *Manhattan*, was forging the Northwest Passage to Point Barrow .

Alaska's awesome terrain has long been a challenge to explorers and settlers. The state, which entered the Union in 1959, is cut into isolated areas by its craggy coast and high mountains, principally the Brooks Range in the north (an extension of the Rocky Mountains) and the Alaska Range in the south, which includes Mount McKinley, the highest peak in North America.

Sticking out into the sea in the northwest is the Seward Peninsula. Off the peninsula, in the Bering Strait, is U.S.-owned Little Diomede Island, separated from the USSR's Big Diomede by about two miles. Alaska is separated from the nearest state, Washington, by about 500 miles.

The Alaskan climate is widely variable. The southeast coast, protected by mountains from the north winds and influenced by the warm Japan Current, is generally temperate and rainy, while interior summers are short and very hot (with exceptionally long days), and the winters very cold.

Captain Vitus Bering, a Dane who explored for Russia, is thought to have been the first white man to visit Alaska (1741), after passing close to it on an earlier voyage. At this time there were about 75,000 Indians, Eskimos, and Aleuts in Alaska; some Arctic Slope campsites date back 8,000 years.

Though several nations tried to get a foothold in the region, mainly for the trade in sea otter pelts it might support, Russia prevailed, establishing Alaska's first white settlement on Kodiak Island in 1784. By the 1850s, Russia, facing increased competition from Americans, British, and Canadians, plus a dwindling supply of fur-bearing animals, wanted to sell. In 1867, U.S. Secretary of State William H. Seward agreed to buy—for $7.2 million—thereby becoming a target of ridicule. Many Americans dubbed Alaska "Seward's Folly" or "Seward's Icebox," considering it a frozen wasteland that was relatively valueless.

But gold was discovered (1896) at Klondike in neighboring Yukon Territory, and in Alaska itself at Nome (1899) and at Fairbanks (1902). Settlement was spurred as prospectors poured in and the economy was strengthened—but the lasting gains were few.

During World War II, the region's importance as a military outpost was dramatized when the Japanese briefly occupied some of the Aleutians—the war's only North American enemy occupation. Today, Alaska contains the Distant Early Warning system (DEW line) and other defense installations, including military bases. Roughly half the state's personal income is from government sources, and 97 percent of the land is federally owned.

With a long coastline punctuated by many bays and fjords, Alaska is a leading state in commercial fishing. Forest products account for a considerable share of the state's revenue, while the value of agricultural products remains far more potential than actual. Only a small fraction of the state's potential cropland of 2 to 3 million acres has so far been developed. Tourism is a major industry.

On Good Friday, March 27, 1964, an exceptionally powerful earthquake struck the south-central part of the state, killing 114 and causing property damage estimated at $750 million.

In one of its last acts of 1971, Congress passed the Alaska Native Land Claims Settlement Act to extinguish the nearly 100-year-old claims of Alaska's 55,000 Eskimos, Indians and Aleuts by providing 40 million acres of land and approximately $925 million in compensation. An enrollment of eligible natives began in 1972.

Construction on the $4.5 billion Trans-Alaska pipeline project, first proposed in 1969 and delayed by legal suits brought by environmentalist interests, was finally begun in 1974. In June 1977 oil began to flow from Prudhoe Bay on the Arctic Ocean through the 799-mile, 48-inch hot-oil pipeline to the Gulf of Alaska port of Valdez.

A proposed trans-Canadian pipeline to deliver natural gas from the Alaskan North Slope to the lower forty-eight states has been approved by the United States and Canada. President Carter promised Canadian Prime Minister Trudeau on March 3, 1979, that he would submit a bill to Congress to establish a U.S. agency corresponding to Canada's Northern Pipeline Agency. Both agencies would then oversee pipeline construction, hopefully act against further delays, and deal with additional proposals for joint development of energy resources. On April 10, Trudeau offered the U.S. a choice of two routes for the pipeline: 1) along the Alaska Highway, running parallel to the Alaskan natural gas pipeline, and 2) from Skagway on the Alaskan panhandle through the Yukon Territory.

On May 16, 1979, the House of Representatives approved a land bill which set aside 126 million acres for 13 national parks, 21 wildlife refuges, 112 wild and scenic rivers and two national forest wildernesses. Of the 76 million acres designated for wildlife refuges, 67 million were classified as wilderness where neither commercial activity nor mechanized vehicles would be permitted. Oil and gas exploration would be allowed in the other nine million wildlife acres not marked as wilderness provided that the wildlife were not disturbed. The approval of this bill was a blow to industry because it prevented much of the development of the economic potential in the area.

Plans begun in 1974 to move the capital of Alaska from Juneau to Willow, a site chosen in 1977, have been recently delayed by the Alaska Legislature. State Senator Bill Ray and his supporters have blocked the move, citing the high cost to the Alaskans. The deadline for the proposal is October 1980.

Full name: State of Alaska. **Origin of name:** From Aleutian word meaning "Great Land." **Inhabitant:** Alaskan. **Capital:** Juneau. **State motto:** North to the Future. **Flag:** Blue field with seven gold stars, representing the Big Dipper; eighth star represents the North Star. **Seal:** Rising sun shines on lake, fishing boat, merchant ship, forests, mining & agricultural activities, symbols of Alaskan resources & occupations. **Flower:** Forget-me-not. **Bird:** Willow ptarmigan. **Tree:** Sitka spruce. **Song:** "Alaska's Flag." **Nickname:** The Great Land.

Governor: Jay S. Hammond. **Annual salary:** $52,992. **Term:** 4 years. **Current term expires:** Dec. 1982. **Voting requirements:** 18 yrs. old & U.S. citizen. **U.S. Congressman:** 1. **Entered Union:** 1959 (49th state).

Location & boundaries: Pacific state: bounded on the north by the Arctic Ocean; on the east by Canada; on the south by the Pacific Ocean; & on the west by the Bering Sea & Arctic Ocean. **Total area:** 586,412 sq. mi. (ranks 1st). **Extreme length:** 2,200 mi. **Extreme breadth:** 1,200 mi. **Coastline:** 6,640 mi. **Chief rivers:** Yukon, Tanana, Kuskokwim. **Major lakes:** Iliamna, Becharof, Tustumena. **No. of boroughs:** 10.

Population (1978 est.): 403,000 (ranks 50th). **Pop. increase (1970-78):** 33.4%. **Places over 25,000 pop.:** 3. **Places over 100,000:** 1. **Largest cities:** Anchorage, Fairbanks. **Pop. density:** 0.7 per sq. mi. (ranks 50th). **Pop. projection 1985:** 455,000. **Pop.**

ARIZONA

distribution: 43.7% metropolitan; 56.3% nonmetropolitan. **White:** 78.8%. **Negro:** 3%. **Other:** 17.2%. **Marriage rate (1977):** 12.5 per 1,000 people. **Divorce rate:** 8.8 per 1,000 people.

State finances (1977). Revenue: $1,391,605,000. **Expenditures:** $1,147,589,000. **State Taxes:** $1,900.43 per capita. **State personal income tax:** Yes. **Public debt (1977):** $2,252.05 per capita. **Federal aid (1977):** $672.71 per capita. **Personal income (1977 est.):** $10,497.

Sectors of the economy (% of labor force employed in 1970): Manufacturing (7%), Wholesale and retail trade (19%), Services (8%), Educational Services (11%), Construction (9%), Government (37%). **Leading products:** seafood, timber, pulp, oil, gas, petrochemicals. **Minerals:** petroleum & natural gas, coal, sand & gravel. **Agricultural products:** dairy items, eggs, cattle, hay, vegetables, wool. **Fishing:** salmon, halibut, crab, shrimp, scallops. **Avg. farm (1978 est.):** 5,452 acres. **Avg. value of farm:** not available.

Highway expenditures per capita (1977): $396.96. **Persons per motor vehicle:** 1.58. **Minimum age for driver's license:** 16. **Gasoline tax:** 8¢ per gallon. **Motor vehicle deaths:** 31.5 per 100,000 people.

Birthrate (1977): 20.6 per 1,000 people. **Infant mortality rate per 1,000 births (1977):** 15.1. **Physicians per 100,000 pop. (1976):** 116. **Dentists per 100,000 pop. (1976):** 52. **Acceptable hospital beds:** 3.9 per 1,000 people. **State expenditures per capita for health and hospitals (1977):** $98.11.

Education expenditures (1975-76): $973.64 per capita annually. **No. of pupils in public schools (1977 est.):** 90,000. **No. of institutions of higher learning (1976-77):** 9. **Public school expenditure per pupil in attendance (1975-76):** $3,710. **Avg. salary of public school teachers (1974-75 est.):** $16,906. **No. full-time teachers (1977 est.):** 4,510. **Educational attainment of adult population (1976):** 12.7 median yrs. of school completed; 2.8% with less than 5 years of education; 17.6% with 4 yrs. of college.

Telephones (1976): 55 per 100 people. **State Chamber of Commerce:** Alaska State Chamber of Commerce, 310 Second Street, Juneau, Alaska 99801.

ARIZONA

Arizona, the last mainland state to join the Union (1912), lies west of the Continental Divide and consists of three general areas: the desert in the southwest, the central highlands, and the Colorado Plateau in the northwest. Almost all of the state is within the Colorado drainage basin. Its principal tourist attraction, the awesome Grand Canyon, is one of the world's natural wonders: a multicolored fissure 217 miles long, four to eight miles wide at the brim, and about a mile deep.

The warm, dry, and reputedly health-restoring climate of the state's southern region—which includes Arizona's two largest cities, Phoenix and Tucson—has made it a popular winter resort area (as well as the site of many senior citizen retirement communities). Tourism is one of the leading industries in Arizona.

In addition to the Grand Canyon, state attractions include Hoover Dam, Lake Mead, 15 national monuments, various Indian villages and reservations (the state has the nation's largest Indian population: about 117,900), the Petrified Forest, and the Painted Desert. A new addition to the list of remarkable sights is legendary London Bridge, which a private group has re-erected at Lake Havasu City.

Bolstered by defense contracts, manufacturing has lately become the state's leading industry, followed by mining and agriculture. Arizona produces a number of metals, including more than half of the country's supply of copper.

Mummies and ancient human relics—such as baskets and cloth—have been found in a strikingly well-preserved condition in Arizona. Several Indian cultures lived there from about 25,000 to

10,000 B.C., and the ancestors of the modern Navajos (or Navahos) and Apaches lived in northern Arizona. One of the oldest continuously inhabited settlements in the country, the community of Oraibi was built sometime in the 1100s by Hopi Indians, over 5,000 of whom presently live on a reservation in northeast Arizona. The first white men were 16th-century Spanish explorers. The United States obtained (1848) most of the land from Mexico following the Mexican War; the rest was included in the Gadsden Purchase (1853).

Arizona was organized as a territory in 1863, with the capital at Prescott (1865-67), then Tucson (1867-77), Prescott again (1877-89), and finally at Phoenix. Over many years, various bloody conflicts raged in Arizona. There was bitter, protracted fighting between the whites and the Apaches, whose leaders included the fabled fighters Cochise and Geronimo. There was conflict between Confederate and Union troops during the Civil War.

In the mining communities, there were strikes and several skirmishes between labor and management. And as sheep grazing became more widespread, hostilities broke out between cattlemen and sheepmen that continued until the turn of the century. Yet another subject of contention through the years has been the water rights along the Colorado River—claimed not only by Arizona but by Nevada and California as well; distribution now follows a 1963 U.S. Supreme Court ruling.

In 1974, Congress began to study several proposals to settle a long-standing land dispute between the Hopi and Navajo Indians of northeastern Arizona. The two tribes have been feuding for years over ownership of 1.8 million acres of desert plateau which acts as a buffer between the much smaller Hopi reservation and the Navajo nation which surrounds it. The U.S. Supreme Court ruled in the early 1960s that the two tribes should share the land equally, but Congress has failed to resolve the matter.

Full name: State of Arizona. **Origin of name:** From the Indian, Alek-zon, meaning "Small Spring." **Inhabitant:** Arizonan. **Capital:** Phoenix. **State motto:** Ditat Deus (God Enriches). **Flag:** A copper-colored star centered on radiating red & yellow stripes & a horizontal blue bar. **Seal:** Miner standing in mountains symbolizes state's mineral industry; irrigated fields & cow represent agriculture. **Flower:** Saguaro cactus. **Bird:** Cactus wren. **Tree:** Paloverde. **Song:** "Arizona." **Nickname:** Grand Canyon State.

Governor: Bruce E. Babbitt. **Annual salary:** $50,000. **Term:** 4 years. **Current term expires:** Jan. 1983. **Voting requirements:** 18 yrs. old & U.S. citizen; resident of state 50 days. **U.S. Congressmen:** 4. **Entered Union:** 1912 (48th state).

Location & boundaries: Southwestern state; bounded on the north by Utah; on the east by New Mexico; on the south by Mexico; & on the west by Baja California (Mexico), the Colorado River, California & Nevada. **Total area:** 113,909 sq. mi. (ranks 6th). **Extreme length:** 395 mi. **Extreme breadth:** 340 mi. **Chief rivers:** Colorado, Little Colorado, Gila. **Major lakes:** Mohave, Theodore Roosevelt, Lake Mead. **No. of counties:** 14.

Population (1978 est.): 2,354,000 (ranks 31st). **Pop. increase (1970-78):** 32.8%. **Places over 25,000 pop.:** 7. **Places over 100,000:** 3. **Largest cities:** Tucson, Phoenix, Mesa. **Pop. density:** 20.7 per sq. mi. (ranks 40th). **Pop. projection 1985:** 2,926,000. **Pop. distribution:** 74.5% metropolitan; 25.5% nonmetropolitan. **White:** 91.1%. **Negro:** 3%. **Indian:** 5.4%. **Other:** 0.5%. **Marriage rate (1977):** 12.3 per 1,000 people. **Divorce rate:** 7.2 per 1,000 people.

State finances (1977). Revenue: $2,107,037,000. **Expenditures:** $1,865,661,000. **State Taxes:** $505.26 per capita. **State personal income tax:** Yes. **Public debt (1977):** $44.95 per capita. **Federal aid (1977):** $158.38 per capita. **Personal income (1977):** $6,520.

Sectors of the economy (% of labor force employed in 1974): Manufacturing (14%), Wholesale and retail trade (21%), Services

ARKANSAS

MILES
10 20 30 40 50 60

KILOMETERS
10 20 30 40 50 60

⊛ State Capital   ⊛ County Seats

© Copyright HAMMOND INCORPORATED, Maplewood, N.J.

(15%), Educational Services (8%), Construction (7%), Government (19%). **Leading products:** electrical & other machinery; transportation equipment; food; primary metals; printing & publishing; stone, clay & glass products. **Minerals:** copper, sand & gravel, molybdenum, silver, cement. **Agricultural products:** cattle, dairy products, cotton lint, hay, lettuce. **Avg. farm: (1978 est.)** 6,167 acres. **Avg. value of farm:** $125 per acre.

Highway expenditures per capita (1977): $104.86. **Persons per motor vehicle:** 1.48. **Minimum age for driver's license:** 16. **Gasoline tax:** 8¢ per gallon. **Motor vehicle deaths:** 43.6 per 100,000 people.

Birthrate (1977): 18.2 per 1,000 people. **Infant mortality rate per 1,000 births (1977):** 13.5. **Physicians per 100,000 pop. (1976):** 183. **Dentists per 100,000 pop. (1976):** 48. **Acceptable hospital beds:** 4.9 per 1,000 people. **State expenditures per capita for health and hospitals (1977):** $41.29.

Education expenditures (1975-76): $524.21 per capita annually. **No. of pupils in public schools (1977 est.):** 495,000. **No. of institutions of higher learning (1976-77):** 22. **Public school expenditure per pupil in attendance (1976-76):** $1,753. **Avg. salary of public school teachers (1974-75 est.):** $11,168. **No. full-time teachers (1977 est.):** 24,810. **Educational attainment of adult population (1976):** 12.6 median yrs. of school completed; 3.3% with less than 5 years of education; 15.7% with 4 yrs. of college.

Telephones (1976): 66 per 100 people. **State Chamber of Commerce:** Arizona State Chamber of Commerce, 3216 N. Third Street, Suite 103, Phoenix, Arizona 85012.

ARKANSAS

Gracing the Arkansas terrain are rugged hills, scenic valleys and streams, and impressive hardwood and pine forests. In the south and east are the generally flat West Gulf Coastal and Mississippi Alluvial Plains, while highlands make up the northwestern region. Magazine Mountain (2,853 feet) is the state's highest point. About three-fifths of the land is wooded, forming the basis for a sizable timber industry. Resources include two large national forests, the Ozark and Ouachita.

Arkansas ranks among the national leaders in cotton, rice, soybean and livestock production; it also contains one of the world's most famous spas (Hot Springs), as well as North America's first diamond mine, near Murfreesboro. No longer commercially operative, the mine is today a state park, popular among tourists; anyone finding a diamond there (up to five carats) is allowed to keep it. Excellent hunting and fishing also contribute to the state's increasingly significant tourism business as do such attractions as the Old Arsenal in Little Rock's MacArthur Park, which marks the birthplace of one of the most famous of Arkansans, General Douglas MacArthur.

The production of oil, the state's major mineral, is another important element in the economy. Arkansas is the nation's chief producer of bauxite ore, from which aluminum is extracted. A further vital asset is an abundant water supply, convertible to hydroelectric power. A modern navigational system on the Arkansas River connects the Gulf of Mexico and Little Rock, now a foreign trade zone, the 14th such zone established in the United States, and the only one on an inland waterway.

The so-called Bluff Dwellers of about A.D. 500 are considered to have been the first inhabitants of the Arkansas region, followed by the culturally superior Mound Builders and, later, by Quapaw, Osage, and Caddo Indians.

The first Europeans to visit (1541) the area were Spanish explorers led by Hernando De Soto. Frenchmen arrived more than a century later: Marquette and Jolliet exploring (1673) the land around the mouth of the Arkansas River, and La Salle claiming (1682) for France the Arkansas region and the rest of the Mississippi Valley. In 1686, Henri de Tonti, established Arkansas Post, the first permanent settlement. The United States obtained all of what is now Arkansas as part of the Louisiana Purchase (1803).

Much of the region's early history is shared with Louisiana, of which it was a part until 1812, when it was attached to the Territory of Missouri. Settlement was spurred by the cotton boom of 1818, and a year later Arkansas Territory, incorporating part of present-day Oklahoma, was created. The 1830s saw the emergence of the slavery-supported plantation system as the state's primary economic force. The virtual absence of Indian troubles encouraged immigration, and between 1830 and 1840 population tripled.

Statehood came (1836) at a time when the slavery issue was more and more seriously dividing the nation. In March 1861, the Arkansas convention voted to remain in the Union, but when President Lincoln asked for troops, the state refused and two months later decided to secede. Many relatively small battles were fought in the state, and from 1864-65 there existed two separate state governments: one at Little Rock controlled by the Union and a Confederate one at Washington, Arkansas. Recovery in the postwar period was slow in coming, and not helped by the violence-engendering struggle (1872-74) for the governorship between Republicans Elisha Baxter and Joseph Brooks, a struggle won by Baxter only after Presidential intervention.

On the cultural scene, the Arkansas Arts Center in Little Rock offers exhibits, plays, and classes in painting, sculpture, dance, photography, music and drama. The Arkansas Symphony Orchestra was established in 1966.

In addition to a fine public school system, there is the Arkansas School for the Deaf, established about 1866 as the Arkansas Deaf-Mute Institute, and the Arkansas School for the Blind. Arkansas Enterprises for the Blind opened in 1947 a rehabilitation center providing personal adjustment, pre-vocational and vocational training for the blind and visually impaired. It has served persons from the fifty states and over twenty-four foreign countries.

In 1966 the state made political history by electing a transplanted New Yorker, Winthrop Rockefeller (now deceased), governor on the Republican ticket, climaxing a six-year effort on his part to build a two-party system in this traditionally Democratic state. Rockefeller served two terms, but lost to a political unknown, Dale Bumpers, in a third term bid in 1970.

In November 1978, Pine Bluff was chosen for the location of a proposed nerve gas plant. According to the plan, production of nerve gas shells and bombs probably would not begin before 1982.

Full name: State of Arkansas. **Origin of name:** From Algonquian name of the Quapaw Indians. **Inhabitant:** Arkansan. **Capital:** Little Rock. **State motto:** Regnat Populus (The People Rule). **Flag:** Star-studded blue & white diamond on a red field; diamond shape represents Arkansas, the only diamond-producing state. **Seal:** Shield design has steamboat, plow, beehive & sheaf of wheat, symbolizing industry & agriculture; angel of mercy & sword of justice guard American eagle; goddess of liberty stands above. **Flower:** Apple blossom. **Bird:** Mockingbird. **Tree:** Pine. **Song:** "Arkansas." **Nickname:** Land of Opportunity.

Governor: William Clinton. **Annual salary:** $35,000. **Term:** 2 years. **Current term expires:** Jan. 1981. **Voting requirements:** 18 yrs. old & U.S. citizen; registered in county of residence 20 days. **U.S. Congressmen:** 4. **Entered Union:** 1836 (25th state).

Location & boundaries: South Central state; bounded on the north by Missouri; on the east by the Mississippi River & the states of

CALIFORNIA

Missouri, Tennessee & Mississippi; on the south by Louisiana; & on the west by Texas & Oklahoma. **Total area:** 53,104 sq. mi. (ranks 27th). **Extreme length:** 275 mi. **Extreme breadth:** 240 mi. **Chief rivers:** Mississippi, Arkansas, Ouachita, White. **Major lakes:** Bull Shoals, Ouachita, Beaver, Norfork. **No. of counties:** 75.

Population (1978 est.): 2,186,000 (ranks 33rd). **Pop. increase (1970-78):** 13.7%. **Places over 25,000 pop:** 8. **Places over 100,000:** 1. **Largest cities:** Little Rock, Fort Smith, N. Little Rock. **Pop. density:** 41.2 per sq. mi. (ranks 34th). **Pop. projection 1985:** 2,353,000. **Pop. distribution:** 38.4% metropolitan; 61.6% non-metropolitan. **White:** 81.4%. **Negro:** 18.3%. **Other:** 0.2%. **Marriage rate (1977):** 11.2 per 1,000 people. **Divorce rate:** 9.0 per 1,000 people.

State finances (1977). Revenue: $1,568,624,000. **Expenditures:** $1,521,155,000. **State Taxes:** $374.49 per capita. **State personal income tax:** Yes. **Public debt (1977):** $65.53 per capita. **Federal aid (1977):** $215.17 per capita. **Personal income (1977):** $5,522.

Sectors of the economy (% of labor force employed in 1970): Manufacturing (26%), Wholesale and retail trade (19%), Services (8%), Educational Services (8%), Construction (7%), Government (15%). **Leading products:** food, lumber & wood, paper products, electrical machinery, chemicals, furniture & fixtures, apparel. **Minerals:** petroleum, natural gas, bauxite, stone, bromine, sand & gravel. **Agricultural products:** broilers, cattle, eggs, soybeans, rice, cotton lint. **Avg. farm (1978 est.):** 254 acres. **Avg. value of farm:** $571 per acre.

Highway expenditures per capita (1977): $115.83. **Persons per motor vehicle:** 1.51. **Minimum age for driver's license:** 16. **Gasoline tax:** 8.5¢ per gallon. **Motor vehicle deaths:** 26.2 per 100,000 people.

Birthrate (1977): 16.7 per 1,000 people. **Infant mortality rate per 1,000 births (1977):** 15.4. **Physicians per 100,000 pop. (1976):** 109. **Dentists per 100,000 pop. (1976):** 32. **Acceptable hospital beds:** 6.3 per 1,000 people. **State expenditures per capita for health and hospitals (1977):** $42.98.

Education expenditures (1975-76): $344.34 per capita annually. **No. of pupils in public schools (1977 est.):** 454,000. **No. of institutions of higher learning (1976-77):** 29. **Public school expenditure per pupil in attendance (1975-76):** $1,161. **Avg. salary of public school teachers (1974-75 est.):** $9,021. **No. full-time teachers (1977 est.):** 22,290. **Educational attainment of adult population (1976):** 12.2 median yrs. of school completed; 6.0% with less than 5 years of education; 9.1% with 4 yrs. of college.

Telephones (1976): 60 per 100 people. **State Chamber of Commerce:** Arkansas State Chamber of Commerce, 911 Wallace Building, Little Rock, Arkansas 72201.

CALIFORNIA

California, the most populous of the states, is the national leader in agriculture, commercial fishing, and motor vehicle ownership. It ranks first in manufacturing and third in land area and oil production.

The heart of the state is the fertile Central Valley, fenced in by two long north-south mountain ranges: the Sierra Nevada (on the east) and the Coast Range. Several small forested ranges of the Klamath Mountains cover the northwestern corner of the state, while below the Coast Range are the Los Angeles Ranges, and below these, the San Diego Ranges. More than 40 percent of the land is forested. Other important land areas are the Cascade Mountains extending northward from the Central Valley and the Basin and Range Region of the southeast and extreme northeast; within the southeastern part of this region are the Mojave and Colorado deserts.

Both the highest mountain peak in the conterminous United States, Mt. Whitney (14,494 feet) and the lowest point in the hemisphere (282 feet below sea level) can be seen from Dante's View, 5,475 feet high and about 3 miles east of that lowest point. The only active volcano in the conterminous

states is 10,457-foot Lassen Peak at Lassen Volcanic National Park, in the northwest corner of the state. Two island groups lie off the coast: the Santa Barbara (or Channel) Islands, consisting of eight major islands 20 to 60 miles from the southern mainland, and the six small rugged Farallon Islands, about 30 miles west of San Francisco, the predominantly large city of the state's northern part (as Los Angeles is of the southern). California's main harbors are San Francisco and San Diego Bays and the man-made Los Angeles harbor, San Pedro Bay. Great extremes mark the climate, with many areas enjoying generally mild and sunny weather, partially befouled in urban areas by palls of smog.

There were about 130,000 Indians living in the California region when Juan Rodriguez Cabrillo, a Portuguese in Spanish employ, discovered it in 1542. English interest in the area began with Sir Francis Drake, who claimed (1579) it for Queen Elizabeth I, but the first permanent settlement was made by Spaniards, who established 21 missions northward along the coast from San Diego (1769) to Sonoma (1823). In 1812, Russian fur-traders from Alaska came down and established Fort Ross on the state's northern coast, but they did not prevail. In 1822, after Mexico won its independence from Spain, California became a Mexican province, and its social, economic, and political life was centered around large cattle ranches. The first organized group of American settlers came to the region by land in 1841; the United States offered to buy the province, but Mexico refused to sell. U.S. forces occupied the area early in the Mexican War, with Mexico formally ceding its claims in 1848.

Less than two weeks before the treaty was signed, an event of massive importance occurred at John A. Sutter's sawmill near Coloma: the discovery of gold, which set off the famous Gold Rush of '49. In the following seven years, the region produced $450 million worth of gold, while the population jumped from about 15,000 to almost 300,000. This influx virtually secured American possession of the territory. San Francisco, for example, grew from an outpost to a great city, in a turbulent, often lawless, atmosphere. Vigilante groups filled the "law-and-order" gap until more stable government was established, beginning with admission of California into the Union as a free state, under terms of the Compromise of 1850. Meanwhile, California's mountain-walled isolation was rapidly ending: the telegraph reached the area in 1861, and eight years later direct rail connection was made with the rest of the country.

The late 19th and early 20th centuries were marked by continued population growth, soaring land values, and economic-rooted social tensions between American-born Californians, Mexican-Americans and Oriental immigrants. Manufacturing, especially the canning and packing of food, increased greatly; and Hollywood became the world motion picture capital.

More recently, defense-contract industries and senior citizen retirement communities have played particularly large roles in the state's economy. Tourist attractions include Disneyland (in Anaheim), San Francisco's Golden Gate Bridge, 17 national forests, five national parks, and many scenic beaches.

With 20 million residents in 1970, California overtook New York as the most populous state, but now the growth rate has dropped somewhat. California has recently experienced a net out-migration to each of its less populated neighbors—Oregon, Nevada and Arizona.

The long struggle of Cesar Chavez' United Farm

Workers to unionize farm workers drew increasingly intense competition from the Teamsters Union. Some growers who had signed contracts with Chavez' union in 1970 following a five-year strike and table grape boycott signed new contracts in 1973 with the Teamsters. In 1975 the United Farm Workers Union was overwhelmingly endorsed by farm workers as a legitimate union in California. Chavez continued in his fight for better wages by announcing a national boycott of iceberg lettuce on April 26, 1979, in support of his union's strike (which began January 19) against West Coast lettuce growers. Two confrontations between growers and workers resulted in one death and about a dozen injuries.

In February 1974 newspaper heiress Patricia Hearst was kidnapped from her Berkeley apartment by a terrorist group calling itself the Symbionese Liberation Army. She was later identified as a participant in a bank robbery committed by the group in April and was sought as a material witness. Six members of the group died in a fire in 1974 as the result of a shootout with police.

Patty and two surviving members of the SLA were arrested in San Francisco in September 1975, having successfully eluded police since the spring of 1974. Patty was tried and convicted on bank robbery charges. She appealed her case and was released on bail in November 1976; she returned to jail to serve the remainder of her term in May 1978 when her appeal was denied. On February 1, 1979, she was released from prison under an executive clemency order signed by President Carter. The order imposed parole conditions upon her and did not restore her civil rights. She had served 22 months of her seven-year sentence.

In the spring of 1978 a taxpayers' revolt against heavy government spending and high tax rates culminated in the adoption of Proposal 13 in the June primary, which passed with 65 percent of the vote. Under the proposal, property taxes would be cut by 57 percent, necessitating a cut in funds for education and the state government. Governor Brown moved to provide funds temporarily from the large budget surplus. After a year in progress, Proposition 13 appears to have had both positive and negative repercussions. While the economy seems healthier, education programs, job prospects, and pay raises have suffered as expected. In addition, citizens are being charged rising fees for services and programs that the local government had previously paid for from the general revenue.

Full name: State of California. **Origin of name:** From an imaginary island in a 16th-century Spanish romance. **Capital:** Sacramento. **State motto:** Eureka (I Have Found It). **Flag:** a bear & a red star on white field with red horizontal bar at the bottom. **Seal:** Grizzly bear stands near seated figure of Minerva; a miner, ships & peaks of Sierra Nevada in background; state motto. **Flower:** Golden poppy. **Bird:** California Valley quail. **Tree:** California redwood. **Song:** "I Love You, California." **Nickname:** Golden State.

Governor: Edmund G. Brown, Jr. **Annual salary:** $49,100. **Term:** 4 years. **Current term expires:** Jan. 1983. **Voting requirements:** 18 yrs. old & U.S. citizen; state resident 29 days. **U.S. Congressmen:** 43. **Entered Union:** 1850 (31st state).

Location & boundaries: Pacific State: bounded on the north by Oregon; on the east by Nevada & Arizona; on the southeast by the Colorado River; on the south by Mexico; & on the west by the Pacific Ocean. **Total area:** 158,693 sq. mi. (ranks 3d). **Extreme length:** 1775 mi. **Extreme breadth:** 1360 mi. **Coastline:** 1,264 mi. **Chief rivers:** Sacramento, San Joaquin, Klamath. **Major lakes:** Salton Sea, Tahoe, Goose. **No. of counties:** 58.

Population (1978 est.): 22,294,000 (ranks 1st). **Pop. increase (1970-78):** 11.7%. **Places over 25,000 pop.:** 150. **Places over 100,000:** 21. **Largest cities:** Los Angeles, San Diego, San Francisco, San Jose. **Pop. density:** 140.5 per sq. mi. (ranks 14th). **Pop. projection 1985:** 23,767,000. **Pop. distribution:** 92.8% metropolitan; 7.2% nonmetropolitan. **White:** 89.1%. **Negro:** 7%. **Other:** 3.9%. **Marriage rate (1977):** 6.9 per 1,000 people. **Divorce rate:** 6.0 per 1,000 people.

State finances (1977). Revenue: $26,108,228,000. **Expenditures:** $22,439,586,000. **State Taxes:** $574.95 per capita. **State personal income tax:** Yes. **Public debt (1977):** $307.94 per capita. **Federal aid (1977):** $263.44 per capita. **Personal income (1977):** $7,909.

Sectors of the economy (% of labor force employed in 1970): Manufacturing (22%), Wholesale and retail trade (21%), Services (9%), Educational Services (8%), Construction (5%), Government (18%). **Leading products:** transportation equipment, food, machinery, ordnance & accessories, fabricated metals, printing & publishing. **Minerals:** petroleum, natural gas, cement, sand & gravel. **Agricultural products:** cattle, dairy items, hay, tomatoes, cotton lint. **Fishing:** tuna, salmon, crabs. **Avg. farm (1978 est.):** 453 acres. **Avg. value of farm:** $761 per acre.

Highway expenditures per capita (1977): $49.19. **Persons per motor vehicle:** 1.46. **Minimum age for driver's license:** 18. **Gasoline tax:** 7¢ per gallon. **Motor vehicle deaths:** 23.8 per 100,000 people.

Birthrate (1977): 15.9 per 1,000 people. **Infant mortality rate per 1,000 births (1977):** 12.0. **Physicians per 100,000 pop. (1976):** 219. **Dentists per 100,000 pop. (1976):** 65. **Acceptable hospital beds:** 5.5 per 1,000 people. **State expenditures per capita for health and hospitals (1977):** $45.89.

Education expenditures (1975-76): $531.69 per capita annually. **No. of pupils in public schools (1977 est.):** 4,316,000. **No. of institutions of higher learning (1976-77):** 252. **Public school expenditure per pupil in attendance (1975-76):** $1,721. **Avg. salary of public school teachers (1974-75 est.):** $14,915. **No. full-time teachers (1977 est.):** 219,190. **Educational attainment of adult population (1976):** 12.7 median yrs. of school completed; 3.3% with less than 5 years of education; 16.8% with 4 yrs. of college.

Telephones (1976): 79 per 100 people. **State Chamber of Commerce:** California State Department of Commerce, P.O. Box 1736, 455 Capitol Mall, Sacramento, California 95808.

COLORADO

Colorado, the Centennial State, is the state with the highest overall elevation; it has more than 1,000 peaks that soar at least 10,000 feet, including legendary Pikes Peak. In the east are the high plains, while the Rockies' peaks and ranges make up the central region; and in the west is the Colorado Plateau. The Continental Divide runs generally north and south through the west-central part of the state. As is typical of mountainous areas, there are great extremes of climate, yet a surprisingly diverse agriculture.

This state is part of the *real* Old West, not the West of romanticized Westerns. Ruthlessly competitive gold mining (starting in 1858) and silver mining (1875) and the decades-long wresting of crops from the arid land shaped Colorado and defined its character: perseverance is both prized and rewarded here.

Many metals are mined in the mountains. Of these, molybdenum, which hardens steel and is used in rocketry, is the state's most valuable: Colorado possesses over half of the world's supply. Oil shale is the state's most important undeveloped resource.

Food and machinery are the state's two main industries. Only California has more irrigated acreage; however, two-thirds of Colorado's farm output consists of livestock and livestock products. It leads in the refining of beet sugar.

Cliff-dwelling Indians are believed to have built (c. A.D. 100) Colorado's first civilization in the Mesa Verde plateau, which lies in the southwest corner

of the state; they carved irrigation ditches and built many-storied pueblos.

In the 1500s, Spanish explorers became the first Europeans to visit the region but, not finding gold, they did not stay. The United States got the eastern and central areas of Colorado as part of the Louisiana Purchase and the western part as a result of the Mexican War.

The gold rush of the late 1850s was followed shortly by the outbreak of the Civil War, which meant fewer Federal troops in the area. During this time, the intense fighting between whites and the Arapaho and Cheyenne Indians posed the very real threat of general lawlessness.

The establishment (1861) of the Colorado Territory was a step toward unity and stability, and the advent of the railroads in the 1870s was another. Statehood came in 1876. This was the era in which the New York journalist Horace Greeley sponsored a Colorado farming colony and advised, "Go West, young man!"

The 1880s brought fiscal health and early growth as a state, but trouble and renewed bloodshed characterized the next decade.

Silver prices dropped badly after the repeal of the Sherman Silver Purchase Act (1893), and many great mines had to close, leaving behind ghost towns with colorful names such as Cripple Creek and Eureka. Range warfare was rife, and bitter hassles took place over railway franchises. Long-simmering labor-management conflict came to a head in 1914 in a battle near Trinidad between striking coal miners and the militia in which innocent women and children were killed. Subsequent reforms included regular government inspection of mines.

The state's economy advanced sharply after both World Wars. There were more years of struggle: the great Wall Street fiasco of 1929 was accompanied, in Colorado, by drought and high winds which created a disastrous dust bowl.

Today, Colorado is prosperous. Denver is an important business center, missile-plant site, and headquarters for Federal agencies. In addition, U.S. coins are minted there, while the National Bureau of Standards laboratory at Boulder has expanded greatly in recent years. Scientists at an observation station near Climax are studying the earth's atmosphere and conducting space research.

Because of the state's magnificent scenery, tourism has developed into a major industry. Tourist attractions include a dozen national forests, hunting and fishing, Balanced Rock in the Garden of the Gods, Buffalo Bill's Grave on Lookout Mountain, and cultural festivals at Aspen and Central City.

The U.S. Air Force Academy, founded in 1958, is located at Colorado Springs. In 1976 the academy admitted the first female cadets.

Full name: State of Colorado. **Origin of name:** From Spanish for "Colored Red." **Inhabitant:** Coloradan. **Capital:** Denver. **State motto:** Nil Sine Numine (Nothing Without the Deity). **Flag:** A red letter C encloses gold ball & rests against blue, white & blue bars. **Seal:** A triangular figure, representing "all seeing" eye of God, bound rods, three mountains & pick & hammer. **Flower:** Rocky Mountain columbine. **Bird:** Lark bunting. **Tree:** Blue spruce. **Song:** "Where the Columbines Grow." **Nickname:** Centennial State.

Governor: Richard D. Lamm. **Annual salary:** $50,000. **Term:** 4 years. **Current term expires:** Jan. 1983. **Voting requirements:** 18 yrs. old & U.S. citizen; resident of state and precinct, 32 days. **U.S. Congressmen:** 7. **Entered Union:** 1876 (38th state).

Location & boundaries: Rocky Mountain state: bounded on the north by Wyoming & Nebraska; on the east by Nebraska & Kansas; on the south by Oklahoma & New Mexico; & on the west by Utah. **Total area:** 104,247 sq. mi. (ranks 8th). **Extreme length:** 387 mi.

Extreme breadth: 276 mi. **Chief rivers:** Colorado, Arkansas, South Platte, Rio Grande. **Major lakes:** Blue Mesa, Dillon, John Martin, Granby. **No. of counties:** 63.

Population (1978 est.): 2,670,000 (ranks 28th). **Pop. increase (1970-78):** 21.0%. **Places over 25,000 pop.:** 18. **Places over 100,000:** 5. **Largest cities:** Denver, Colorado Springs, Lakewood, Aurora, Pueblo. **Pop. density:** 25.6 per sq. mi. (ranks 38th). **Pop. projection 1985:** 3,123,000. **Pop. distribution:** 80.6% metropolitan; 19.4% nonmetropolitan. **White:** 85.5%. **Spanish-surnamed:** 10.2%. **Negro:** 3% **Other:** 1.3%. **Marriage rate (1977):** 11.2 per 1,000 people. **Divorce rate:** 7.8 per 1,000 people.

State finances (1977). Revenue: $2,394,259,000. **Expenditures:** $2,151,503,000. **State Taxes:** $411.33 per capita. **State personal income tax:** Yes. **Public debt (1977):** $75.32 per capita. **Federal aid (1977):** $231.38 per capita. **Personal income (1977):** $7,166.

Sectors of the economy (% of labor force employed in 1970): Manufacturing (15%), Wholesale and retail trade (22%), Services (8%), Educational Services (10%), Construction (7%), Government (20%). **Leading products:** food; machinery; transportation equipment; electrical equipment; printing & publishing; stone, clay & glass items; fabricated metals; chemicals; lumber. **Minerals:** molybdenum, petroleum, coal, sand & gravel. **Agricultural products:** cattle, hay, dairy items, wheat, sugar beets, sheep. **Avg. farm (1978 est.):** 1,345 acres. **Avg. value of farm:** $274 per acre.

Highway expenditures per capita (1977): $94.53. **Persons per motor vehicle:** 1.21. **Minimum age for driver's license:** 21. **Gasoline tax:** 7¢ per gallon. **Motor vehicle deaths:** 26.0 per 100,000 people.

Birthrate (1977): 16.4 per 1,000 people. **Infant mortality rate per 1,000 births (1977):** 12.0. **Physicians per 100,000 pop. (1976):** 198. **Dentists per 100,000 pop. (1976):** 59. **Acceptable hospital beds:** 5.7 per 1,000 people. **State expenditures per capita for health and hospitals (1977):** $55.23.

Education expenditures (1975-76): $552.30 per capita annually. **No. of pupils in public schools (1977 est.):** 562,000. **No. of institutions of higher learning (1976-77):** 39. **Public school expenditure per pupil in attendance (1976-77):** $1,605. **Avg. salary of public school teachers (1974-75 est.):** $11,554. **No. full-time teachers (1977 est.):** 30,280. **Educational attainment of adult population (1976):** 12.8 median yrs. of school completed; 1.3% with less than 5 years of education; 19.4% with 4 yrs. of college.

Telephones (1976): 74 per 100 people. **State Chamber of Commerce:** Colorado Association of Commerce and Industry, 1390 Logan Street, Suite 308, Denver, Colorado 80203.

CONNECTICUT

Connecticut, one of the smallest states in area, is one of the most varied and most prosperous. Generally rectangular in shape, the state is divided by the Connecticut River and its fertile valley into two almost equal regions. Gently rolling hills rise from the southern coastal plain to an average elevation of about 1,000 feet at the northern boundary.

Highly industrialized cities contrast with the scenic, typically New England countryside, 60 percent of which is forested. The southern shore has a number of excellent harbors, and several small islands lie off the coast. The southern section, particularly Fairfield County, is home for many who work in New York City.

Among Connecticut's attractions are Yale University at New Haven, the American Dance Festival at Connecticut College in New London, and this hemisphere's first school for the deaf, at Hartford.

About 7,000 members of the Algonquian Indian family were living in Connecticut before the Europeans came; of these, the Pequot were most powerful. Uncas, chief of the Mohican branch of the Pequots, was immortalized by James Fenimore Cooper in *The Last of the Mohicans*. Relations between the Indians and early settlers were mostly friendly, except for the brief Pequot War (1637) and the more serious King Philip's War (1675-76).

Dutch navigator Adriaen Block was the first European of record to visit the state (1614), sailing up the Connecticut River. In 1633, colonists from Holland set up a trading post (near present-day Hartford), but the Dutch lost control of the area to the English; Puritans from the Massachusetts Bay Colony established the first permanent settlement at the site of modern Windsor that same year, and another at Wethersfield in 1634. English settlements at Hartford and Saybrook began in 1635, and representatives of the three "River Towns" of Windsor, Wethersfield, and Hartford united to form the Connecticut Colony and adopt (1639) the "Fundamental Orders" that gave citizens the right to elect government officials and omitted the religious test for citizenship; the document thus anticipated the U.S. Constitution and is considered the world's first written constitution.

Meanwhile, a wholly new colony came into being with the establishment of New Haven (1638) and other communities in the southern part of Connecticut; called the New Haven Colony, it was more rigidly Puritan than the older colony. In 1662, the Connecticut Colony procured an unusually democratic royal charter resembling the "Fundamental Orders" and providing for the incorporation (1665) of the New Haven Colony, which strongly opposed absorption but reluctantly acquiesced under threat of an alternative take-over by New York. Sir Edmund Andros, who had been named British governor of New England by James II, demanded surrender of the colony's charter; he arrived in Hartford in 1687 to seize the document, but the townspeople are said to have hidden it in the legendary Charter Oak tree.

Connecticut patriots, including Nathan Hale and Governor Jonathan Trumbull, took on a leading role in the Revolutionary War, and the colony served as the Continental Army's major supply area. After the war Connecticut gave up its claims to all western land except the so-called "Western Reserve." Statehood dates from 1788, but boundary disputes with New York, Massachusetts, and Rhode Island persisted until the present borders were established in 1799. Jefferson's Embargo Act of 1807 was highly unpopular in Connecticut, as it was elsewhere in New England. The state's contribution to the Union cause in the Civil War was exceptional; five times the quota of men volunteered.

Most early Connecticut colonists wrested their living from the land and made their own clothes and tools. Enterprising "Yankee peddlers" with horse and rig toured the nation, hawking well-turned wares. During and after the Civil War, better transportation and sharply increased immigration served to shift the economic focus from agriculture to industry. The state, sometimes called "The Arsenal of the Nation," became one of the most industrialized in the country. Its business pioneers included revolver inventor Samuel Colt, rubber magnate Charles Goodyear, and Eli Whitney, who innovated mass production of firearms and helped devise (1793) the cotton gin that proved a boon to the textile industry.

Often called the Insurance Capital of the World, Hartford is the headquarters city for nearly 40 firms in that field.

Connecticut is a leader in the production of such vital items as ball and roller bearings, electronic goods, chemicals and plastics, jet engines, helicopters, and nuclear submarines. United Technologies Corp., the state's largest employer with ten divisions and subsidiaries, and the Electric Boat Division of General Dynamics in Groton are important contributors to the nation's aerospace and submarine production. Electric Boat launched the world's first nuclear submarine in 1954. Shifting emphasis to commercial production has helped the state's numerous defense contractors withstand recent military cutbacks.

In the southeast section the industrial base is shifting from traditional skilled industry and manufacturing. A number of major companies are establishing headquarters facilities in the state, including Xerox, IBM, Pepsico and Union Carbide. The state is the national leader in the utilization of nuclear power for electricity. More than half the power generated in the state comes from its several nuclear generating plants, and more will come on line in the 1980s.

Full name: State of Connecticut. **Origin of name:** From the Indian, Quinnehtukqut, meaning "Beside the Long Tidal River." **Inhabitant:** Nutmegger. **Capital:** Hartford. **State motto:** Qui Transtulit Sustinet (He Who Transplanted Still Sustains). **Flag:** State seal on blue field. **Seal:** Three grapevines symbolize transplanting of culture & traditions of Europe to the colony. **Flower:** Mountain laurel. **Bird:** Robin. **Tree:** White oak. **Song:** None. **Nickname:** Constitution State.

Governor: Ella T. Grasso. **Annual salary:** $42,000. **Term:** 4 years. **Current term expires:** Jan. 1983. **Voting requirements:** 18 yrs. old & U.S. citizen. **U.S. Congressmen:** 6. **Entered Union:** 1788 (5th state).

Location & boundaries: New England state: bounded on the north by Massachusetts; on the east by Rhode Island; on the south by Long Island Sound; & on the west by New York. **Total area:** 5,009 sq. mi. (ranks 48th). **Extreme length:** 100 mi. **Extreme breadth:** 50 mi. **Coastline:** 253 mi. **Chief rivers:** Connecticut, Housatonic, Thames. **Major lake:** Candlewood. **No. of counties:** 8.

Population (1978 est.): 3,099,000 (ranks 24th). **Pop. increase (1970-78):** 2.2%. **Places over 25,000 pop.:** 35. **Places over 100,000:** 5. **Largest cities:** Hartford, Bridgeport, New Haven. **Pop. density:** 618.7 per sq. mi. (ranks 4th). **Pop. projection 1985:** 3,210,000. **Pop. distribution:** 88.3% metropolitan; 11.7% non-metropolitan. **White:** 93.5%. **Negro:** 6%. **Other:** 0.5%. **Marriage rate (1977):** 7.4 per 1,000 people. **Divorce rate:** 3.9 per 1,000 people.

State finances (1977). Revenue: $2,857,967,000. **Expenditures:** $2,656,060,000. **State Taxes:** $468.83 per capita. **State personal income tax:** Yes. **Public debt (1977):** $1,021.05 per capita. **Federal aid (1977):** $174.18 per capita. **Personal income (1977):** $8,055.

Sectors of the economy (% of labor force employed in 1973): Manufacturing (34%), Wholesale & retail trade (22%), Services (14%), Educational Services (8%), Construction (5%), Government (14%). **Leading products:** transportation equipment, electrical and other machinery, primary and fabricated metals, chemicals, instruments. **Agricultural products:** dairy items, eggs, tobacco, forest and nursery truck crops. **Avg. farm (1978 est.):** 118 acres. **Avg. value of a farm:** $1,962 per acre.

Highway expenditures per capita (1977): $55.17. **Persons per motor vehicle:** 1.49. **Minimum age for driver's license:** 18. **Gasoline tax:** 11¢ per gallon. **Motor vehicle deaths:** 14.5 per 100,000 people.

Birthrate (1977): 11.8 per 1,000 people. **Infant mortality rate per 1,000 births (1977):** 13.5. **Physicians per 100,000 pop. (1976):** 224. **Dentists per 100,000 pop. (1976):** 64. **Acceptable hospital beds:** 6.3 per 1,000 people. **State expenditures per capita for health and hospitals (1977):** $60.32.

Education expenditures (1975-76): $400.67 per capita annually. **No. of pupils in public schools (1977 est.):** 626,000. **No. of institutions of higher learning (1976-77):** 46. **Public school expenditure per pupil in attendance (1975-76):** $1,687. **Avg. salary of public school teachers (1974-75 est.):** $12,051. **No. full-time teachers (1977 est.):** 42,180. **Educational attainment of adult population (1976):** 12.6 median yrs. of school completed; 2.1% with less than 5 years of education; 18.3% with 4 yrs. of college.

Telephones (1976): 78 per 100 people. **State Chamber of Commerce:** Connecticut Business & Industry Association, 60 Washington Street, Suite 1202, Hartford, Connecticut 06106.

DELAWARE

Although only Rhode Island is smaller in size and few states are less populous, Delaware has a disproportionate worth because of its natural assets and strategic proximity to New York, Philadelphia, Baltimore, and Washington. This location and the state's convenient incorporation laws have made Delaware the home of about 70,000 chartered firms, including some of the country's largest.

The state is part of the Delmarva Peninsula separating Delaware and Chesapeake Bays, the peninsula being shared with Maryland and Virginia. Almost all of the state consists of a part of the Atlantic Coastal Plain extending from Florida to New Jersey; the exception is that part of the Piedmont Plateau crossing the state's northern tip and having a maximum width of about 10 miles. Rolling hills in the north slope to a nearly sea-level plain. The state has the nation's lowest mean elevation, and along the southern border is a 30,000-acre swamp. The climate is moderate though humid, with few prolonged periods of extreme temperature.

Before the Europeans arrived, the region was inhabited by the Lenni-Lenape (later called Delaware) Indians, of Algonquian linguistic stock. Although others from Europe may have preceded him, explorer Henry Hudson is credited with Delaware's discovery (1609). A year later, Captain Samuel Argall of Virginia named Delaware Bay for his colony's governor, Thomas West, Baron De La Warr. Several countries vied for control of the state; Swedes made the first permanent settlement (1638) at Fort Christina (now Wilmington); but New Sweden, as the colony as a whole was called, gave way (1655) to Dutch forces led by New Netherland Governor Peter Stuyvesant. The English seized the colony in 1664, administering it under the Duke of York until 1682. It was then annexed to Pennsylvania as The Three Lower Counties. In 1704 it became semiautonomous, and fought in the American Revolution as a separate state. It later became (1787) the first state to ratify the U.S. Constitution.

Meanwhile, the Wilmington area developed into the hub of the flour-milling business and, in 1802, Eleuthère Irénée du Pont established a gunpowder mill on nearby Brandywine Creek that was the foundation of the state's enormous chemical industry. British ships shelled Lewes during the War of 1812, but there was little damage. Great tensions were created in Delaware by the advent of the Civil War, for it was a border state, condoning slavery but remaining loyal to the Union. Antiadministration and neutralist views were common; true secessionists were rare throughout the conflict.

Aided by fertile soil and an abundant water supply, agriculture has long been an important part of Delaware's economy, although far superseded over the years by manufacturing, chiefly of chemicals, and food and food products. In the 1950s, there was a new surge of industrial expansion, while the population increased by about 40 percent. Among historical attractions are Fort Christina Monument, Hagley Museum, and Winterthur Museum, in and near Wilmington; central New Castle, a unique survival of a colonial capital, almost unchanged; Dover, with notable public and private buildings; and Lewes, site of the first attempted settlement. Recreation areas include Cape Henlopen, Delaware Seashore, and Trap Pond State Parks. Rehoboth Beach is a popular resort area.

Because the Delaware Bay contains a deep natural channel, a sheltered area, and a convenient route to major east coast oil refineries, the state has frequently been mentioned as a prime site for construction of a deepwater terminal. In 1971, under former Republican Gov. Russell W. Peterson, who later was named chairman of the President's Council on Environmental Quality, the state enacted a broad zoning law which flatly prohibited off-shore ports in state waters and refineries and other heavy industry in its coastal zone.

Supporters argue that the law spells out a policy of moderate growth and is needed to protect Delaware's environment and tourist industry. Environmental supporters have introduced amendments to clarify the language of the 1971 acts which remain intact despite continuing opposition from petroleum companies and industrially related groups.

In November 1978, Dover Air Force Base was the scene of the return of the 913 bodies from Jonestown, Guyana, after the mass murder-suicides there. The base's mortuary staff, plus military pathologists and graves registration experts from the Washington area, began the difficult task of identifying and embalming the corpses. As of April, 546 bodies remained unclaimed, 248 unidentified bodies would be sent to Evergreen Cemetery in Oakland, California, for burial, and an additional 118 bodies would be sent to Los Angeles beginning May 10.

Full name: State of Delaware. **Origin of name:** From Lord De La Warr, English governor of Virginia. **Inhabitant:** Delawarean. **Capital:** Dover. **State motto:** Liberty & Independence. **Flag:** State seal in a buff diamond on a blue field with date Delaware ratified Constitution. **Seal:** A sheaf of wheat, an ear of corn, an ox, a soldier & a farmer under the crest of a ship. **Flower:** Peach blossom. **Bird:** Blue Hen Chicken. **Tree:** American holly. **Song:** "Our Delaware." **Nicknames:** Blue Hen State; Diamond State; First State.

Governor: Pierre S. du Pont IV. **Annual salary:** $35,000. **Term:** 4 years. **Current term expires:** Jan. 1981. **Voting requirements:** 18 yrs. old & U.S. citizen; state resident 1 year; county, 3 mos.; district, 30 da. **U.S. Congressmen:** 1. **Entered Union:** 1787 (1st state).

Location & boundaries: Middle Atlantic state; bounded on the north by Pennsylvania; on the east by New Jersey, Delaware Bay & the Atlantic Ocean; & on the south & west by Maryland. **Total area:** 2,057 sq. mi. (ranks 49th). **Extreme length:** 96 mi. **Extreme breadth:** 35 mi. **Coastline:** 28 mi. **Chief rivers:** Delaware, Nanticoke, Christina. **Major lakes:** None, but many small lakes and ponds. **No. of counties:** 3.

Population (1978 est.): 583,000 (ranks 47th). **Pop. increase (1970-78):** 6.4%. **Places over 25,000 pop.:** 2. **Places over 100,000:** None. **Largest cities:** Wilmington, Newark, Dover. **Pop. density:** 283.4 per sq. mi. (ranks 7th). **Pop. projection 1985:** 626,000. **Pop. distribution:** 68.9% metropolitan; 31.1% non-metropolitan. **White:** 85.1%. **Negro:** 14.3%. **Other:** 0.6%. **Marriage rate (1977):** 6.9 per 1,000 people. **Divorce rate:** 5.2 per 1,000 people.

State finances (1977). Revenue: $712,204,000. **Expenditures:** $696,692,000. **State Taxes:** $671.62 per capita. **State personal income tax:** Yes. **Public debt (1977):** $1,276.13 per capita. **Federal aid (1977):** $234.38 per capita. **Personal income (1977):** $7,724.

Sectors of the economy (% of labor force employed in 1970): Manufacturing (30%), Wholesale and retail trade (19%), Services (8%), Educational Services (8%), Construction (8%), Government (15%). **Leading products:** chemicals & related items, food, apparel, primary & fabricated metals, textile mill items, automobiles, paper. **Agricultural products:** broilers, dairy items, corn, soybeans, potatoes. **Fishing:** clams, crabs. **Avg. farm (1978 est.):** 187 acres. **Avg. value of farm:** $1,500 per acre.

Highway expenditures per capita (1977): $98.75. **Persons per motor vehicle:** 1.56. **Minimum age for driver's license:** 18. **Gasoline tax:** 9¢ per gallon. **Motor vehicle deaths:** 21.6 per 100,000 people.

Longitude West of Greenwich

Birthrate (1977): 14.8 per 1,000 people. **Infant mortality rate per 1,000 births (1977):** 13.6. **Physicians per 100,000 pop. (1976):** 155. **Dentists per 100,000 pop. (1976):** 44. **Acceptable hospital beds:** 7.9 per 1,000 people. **State expenditures per capita for health and hospitals (1977):** $73.85.

Education expenditures (1975-76): $566.38 per capita annually. **No. of pupils in public schools (1977 est.):** 120,000. **No. of institutions of higher learning (1976-77):** 10. **Public school expenditure per pupil in attendance (1975-76):** $1,817. **Avg. salary of public school teachers (1974-75 est.):** $12,110. **No. full-time teachers (1977 est.):** 7,210. **Educational attainment of adult population (1976):** 12.5 median yrs. of school completed; 1.8% with less than 5 years of education; 15.5% with 4 yrs. of college.

Telephones (1976): 81 per 100 people. **State Chamber of Commerce:** Delaware State Chamber of Commerce, Inc., 1102 West Street, Wilmington, Delaware 19801.

FLORIDA

Florida, southernmost of the continental states, is a low-lying peninsula with a coastline second in length only to Alaska's, measuring 1,350 miles—580 on the Atlantic coast and 770 on the Gulf. The state has an average elevation of 100 feet. Curving southwestward for about 200 miles off the southern coast are the Florida Keys, including Elliott Key and Key Largo at the north and Key West at the south.

Indians are thought to have inhabited this region about 10,000 years ago. In 1513 Juan Ponce de León, a Spanish explorer said to be searching for the legendary Fountain of Youth, landed on the east coast and mistakenly thought his find was an island. He named it and claimed it for Spain. That country, France, and England all tried to settle permanently in Florida, and all ultimately failed. Florida became a state in 1845, seceded from the Union in 1861, and was readmitted in 1868.

Florida's early development was severely hampered by two bloody and costly wars with the Seminole Indians, who were not defeated until 1842. Many never succumbed, but fled instead to the Everglades wilderness, became the core of a new tribe, and, eventually, were settled on reservations. In May 1970, the Seminoles were awarded $12,347,500 for land taken from them by U.S. military forces. The Indians estimate there are now 1,500 Seminoles in Florida and 3,500 in Oklahoma.

In 1964, scuba divers found an undersea treasure of old coins and relics worth $2 million off Fort Pierce. Permission is granted by the state for explorers to seek the sunken goods, in return for a quarter of the value of all discoveries.

Among the fastest-growing states in the nation, Florida has risen in population from 2.8 million in 1950 to over 8.5 million today. Land values and industry have grown proportionately, but rapid expansion has created such problems for the state as attempting to keep pace with the spiraling demand for new facilities.

Accounting for more than $5 billion annually, tourism is the state's leading industry, thanks to one of the mildest and most comfortable climates east of the Mississippi and an abundance of swimming, fishing, and other recreational resources. Resort centers along the "Gold Coast" include Miami Beach (a suburb of Miami), Palm Beach, Daytona Beach, and Fort Lauderdale. Formerly a winter industry, tourism is now significant all year round. Disney World, built on a 27,400-acre site near Orlando, is the state's newest attraction; eight times as large as California's Disneyland, it represents the world's largest non-governmental construction project.

Everglades National Park, at Florida's southern tip, draws many visitors. The 5,000-square-mile preserve contains the country's largest remaining tropical wilderness and a multitude of plant and animal types. Other state attractions include Cypress Gardens near Winter Haven, Monkey Jungle near Goulds (a Miami suburb), and the Ringling Museum of Art in Sarasota.

Commercial fishing is a major industry in the state, despite the fact that much of the yieldable water is given over to sport fishermen. There are more kinds of fish in the waters in or off Florida than anywhere else in the country. The state is also important agriculturally; its leading crop—oranges—is worth over $400 million a year. Mining of phosphate is also vital.

An important connection point for North, Central, and South American air traffic, Florida has about 330 airports; Miami International is the 13th busiest in the world in passenger traffic.

Natural dangers the state faces include crop damage by droughts and early frosts, and seasonal (July-October) hurricanes. Destructive hurricanes struck Florida in 1926, 1928, 1935, 1941, and 1964. Today, many federal programs are being implemented to help arm the state against these tropical storms.

In January 1977 Florida was hit by the biggest snow storm in the state's history. Snow fell in several parts of Dade County (Miami area) for the first time in Weather Bureau history. The cold weather accompanying the snow storm caused $2 billion worth of crop damages.

After World War II, Cape Kennedy developed into one of the nation's most important space research centers; it was from here that the world's first moon flight was launched (1969). Employment at Cape Kennedy dropped sharply in 1972 when NASA's budget was cut by Congress. The last manned moon mission was launched December 7, 1972. In May 1973, Skylab, the first orbiting laboratory, was launched. A three-man crew later spent 28 days aboard. Two other teams of astronauts were launched into space during 1973 to carry out experiments aboard Skylab. Skylab fell to earth in July 1979, the bulk of the craft landing in the Indian Ocean, while remnants struck part of the Australian desert. In 1973 the area's historical name of Cape Canaveral was restored, but the space center remains the Kennedy Space Center. In 1975 the U.S. and the U.S.S.R. launched the first joint space flight.

All Florida courts were open in 1977 to news coverage by television and still picture cameras, thus making the state's judicial system the most open to media coverage in the nation.

John A. Spenkelink was put to death in the electric chair on May 25, 1979, at the Florida State Prison. He was the first person to be executed in the U.S. since 1977. His case attracted nationwide attention from those both for and against capital punishment, thereby paving the way for the reconsideration of death penalty sentences.

Full name: State of Florida. **Origin of name:** From Spanish, Pascua Florida, meaning "Feast of Flowers." **Inhabitant:** Floridian. **Capital:** Tallahassee. **State motto:** In God We Trust. **Flag:** State seal lies on white field crossed by diagonal red bars. **Seal:** Sun, steamboat & Indian girl strewing flowers. **Flower:** Orange blossom. **Bird:** Mockingbird. **Tree:** Sabal palm. **Song:** "Old Folks at Home." **Nickname:** Sunshine State.

Governor: Robert Graham. **Annual salary:** $50,000. **Term:** 4 years. **Current term expires:** Jan. 1983. **Voting requirements:** 18 yrs. old & U.S. citizen. **U.S. Congressmen:** 15. **Entered Union:** 1845 (27th state).

FLORIDA

Location & boundaries: South Atlantic state; bounded on the north by Alabama, the Chattahoochee River, Georgia & St. Mary's River; on the east by the Atlantic Ocean; on the south by the Straits of Florida; & on the west by the Gulf of Mexico, the Perdido River & Alabama. **Total area:** 58,560 sq. mi. (ranks 22nd). **Extreme length:** 447 mi. **Extreme breadth:** 361 mi. **Coastline:** 399 mi. on Atlantic; 798 mi. on Gulf Coast. **Chief rivers:** St. Johns, Apalachicola, Suwannee. **Major lakes:** Okeechobee, George, Kissimmee. **No. of counties:** 67.

Population (1978 est.): 8,594,000 (ranks 8th). **Pop. increase (1970-78):** 26.6%. **Places over 25,000 pop.:** 44. **Places over 100,000:** 8. **Largest cities:** Jacksonville, Miami, Tampa, St. Petersburg. **Pop. density:** 146.8 per sq. mi. (ranks 13th). **Pop. projection 1985:** 10,941,000. **Pop. distribution:** 86.0% metropolitan; 14.0% nonmetropolitan. **White:** 84.1%. **Negro:** 15.5%. **Other:** 0.4%. **Marriage rate (1977):** 10.5 per 1,000 people. **Divorce rate:** 7.4 per 1,000 people.

State finances (1977). Revenue: $5,707,077,000. **Expenditures:** $5,391,507,000. **State Taxes:** $387.46 per capita. **State personal income tax:** No. **Public debt (1977):** $237.03 per capita. **Federal aid (1977):** $133.32 per capita. **Personal income (1977):** $6,697.

Sectors of the economy (% of labor force employed in 1970): Manufacturing (14%), Wholesale and retail trade (24%), Services (12%), Educational Services (7%), Construction (9%), Government (16%). **Leading products:** apparel products; transportation equipment; fabricated metal products; chemicals; paper items; food; printing & publishing; electrical machinery; limestone, clay & glass items; fabricated metals. **Minerals:** phosphate rock, stone, clay. **Agricultural products:** dairy items, cattle, citrus, tomatoes, sugarcane for sugar & seed, winter vegetables. **Fishing:** oysters and scallops, crabs, lobsters, shrimp. **Avg. farm (1978 est.):** 364 acres. **Avg. value of farm:** $838 per acre.

Highway expenditures per capita (1977): $69.16. **Persons per motor vehicle:** 1.39. **Minimum age for driver's license:** 18. **Gasoline tax:** 8¢ per gallon. **Motor vehicle deaths:** 26.3 per 100,000 people.

Birthrate (1977): 13.1 per 1,000 people. **Infant mortality rate per 1,000 births (1977):** 15.5. **Physicians per 100,000 pop. (1976):** 175. **Dentists per 100,000 pop. (1976):** 46. **Acceptable hospital beds:** 6.4 per 1,000 people. **State expenditures per capita for health and hospitals (1977):** $49.91.

Education expenditures (1975-76): $375.65 per capita annually. **No. of pupils in public schools (1977 est.):** 1,515,000. **No. of institutions of higher learning (1976-77):** 73. **Public school expenditure per pupil in attendance (1975-76):** $1,576. **Avg. salary of public school teachers (1974-75 est.):** $10,780. **No. full-time teachers (1977 est.):** 78,920. **Educational attainment of adult population (1976):** 12.4 median yrs. of school completed; 3.7% with less than 5 years of education; 13.7% with 4 yrs. of college.

Telephones (1976): 76 per 100 people. **State Chamber of Commerce:** Florida State Chamber of Commerce, P.O. Box 5497, 311 S. Calhoun St., Tallahassee, Florida 32301.

GEORGIA

The largest state east of the Mississippi, and the last of the 13 Colonies to be founded, Georgia consists of three main land regions: in the north is a small section of the Appalachian Mountains; the Piedmont Plateau constitutes the middle; and in the south, coastal flatlands make up about three-fifths of the state's total area. Landmarks include the Okefenokee Swamp, one of the country's largest.

Mound Builders were the first known inhabitants of the Georgia region, followed in modern times by Creek and Cherokee Indians. Spanish explorer De Soto is thought to have been the first European to visit (1540) the area, but British claims soon conflicted with those of Spain; in 1733, English philanthropist James Oglethorpe led a group of his countrymen in launching the first permanent settlement at Savannah as an asylum for debtors. England ended the Spanish threat in 1742, as forces under Oglethorpe defeated their rivals in the battle of Bloody Marsh.

The sale of rum and the introduction of Negro slaves into the region were at first outlawed, but by about 1750 new legislation ended these restrictions. Many foreigners were among the early immigrants, soon followed by settlers mainly from Virginia and the Carolinas.

Statehood dates from 1788. An economic milestone was Eli Whitney's invention (1793) of the cotton gin, near Savannah. The state saw much action during the Civil War; in 1864, Union General William T. Sherman burned Atlanta and led his embittering march to the sea, which left in its wake a vast path of destruction. The Reconstruction period and the subsequent ascendancy of tenant farming and sharecropping did little to foster the state's recovery.

In May 1970, racial disorders in Augusta brought 1,200 National Guard troops into the streets and left six Negroes dead, all shot in the back—five reportedly by the police and one by an unknown assailant. Police said the deaths occurred during the looting of several businesses in the Negro neighborhood.

Changes in social patterns are evident. Public accommodations throughout the state are generally desegregated, in accordance with law, as are most school systems, although residential housing patterns in many areas limit the amount of actual school integration.

As in many other parts of the country, Georgians expressed concern over busing pupils to achieve racial balance in schools. In February, 1972, classroom boycotts to protest busing cut into school attendance at Augusta. There were efforts to promote a statewide boycott, but they failed.

Georgia, the first state (1943) to grant 18-year-olds the right to vote, in 1973 lowered from 21 to 18 the legal age for adults.

Georgia is today involved in the same agriculture-to-industry transformation which the South as a whole is undergoing. Its extensive resources include a wealth of largely untapped hydroelectric power and some of the most valuable marble and gravel deposits in the country. Favorable climate, natural resources and an abundant labor supply have caused many industries to establish plants in the state. Georgia is the nation's largest supplier of peanuts and poultry, and also ranks high in textiles, egg production, lumber, cotton, peaches, and tobacco production, while Atlanta has become one of the South's most important transportation and distributing centers.

Tourism is another significant revenue source, and is aided by such attractions as the Chattahoochee and Oconee National Forests, FDR's "Little White House" at Warm Springs, and Andersonville Prison Park and National Cemetery on the site of the infamous Confederate prison. A major attraction is the enormous Confederate Memorial carving, the world's largest single piece of sculpture, cut into the sheer north face of historic Stone Mountain, near Atlanta; the work, centerpiece of a 3,200-acre park, depicts General Robert E. Lee, Confederate President Jefferson Davis, and General Stonewall Jackson.

Former Gov. Jimmy Carter, often hailed as one of the South's "new breed" of young progressive chief executives, was inaugurated as President of the United States in 1977, the first Southern president since the Civil War.

Full name: State of Georgia. **Origin of name:** In honor of King George II of England. **Inhabitant:** Georgian. **Capital:** Atlanta. **State motto:** Wisdom, Justice & Moderation. **Flag:** State seal on a vertical blue bar; Confederate flag to the right. **Seal:** Arch representing state constitution; three columns with Georgia's motto; date 1776

GEORGIA

MILES

KILOMETERS

Counties indicated by numbers:

1 BALDWIN
2 BARROW
3 CATOOSA
4 CHEROKEE
5 CLAYTON
6 DADE
7 DE KALB
8 DOUGLAS
9 FAYETTE
10 GLASCOCK
11 MONTGOMERY
12 OCONEE
13 ROCKDALE
14 SCHLEY
15 TALIAFERRO
16 TOWNS
17 WALTON
18 WHITFIELD

State Capitals: ⊛ County Seats: ⊙
© Copyright HAMMOND INCORPORATED, Maplewood, N.J.

is year Georgia signed Declaration of Independence. **Flower:** Cherokee rose. **Bird:** Brown thrasher. **Tree:** Live oak. **Song:** "Georgia." **Nickname:** Peach State.

Governor: George Busbee. **Annual salary:** $50,000. **Term:** 4 years. **Current term expires:** Jan. 1983. **Voting requirements:** 18 yrs. old & U.S. citizen. **U.S. Congressmen:** 10. **Entered Union:** 1788 (4th state).

Location & boundaries: South Atlantic state: bounded on the north by Tennessee & North Carolina; on the east by South Carolina, the Atlantic Ocean & the Savannah, Tugaloo & Chattooga Rivers; on the south by St. Mary's River & Florida; & on the west by Florida, Alabama & the Chattahoochee River. **Total area:** 58,876 sq. mi. (ranks 21st). **Extreme length:** 315 mi. **Extreme breadth:** 250 mi. **Coastline:** 100 mi. **Chief Rivers:** Altamaha, Chattahoochee, Savannah. **Major lakes:** Lanier, Allatoona, Seminole. **No. of counties:** 159.

Population (1978 est.): 5,084,000 (ranks 14th). **Pop. increase (1970-78):** 10.0%. **Places over 25,000 pop.:** 12. **Places over 100,000:** 3. **Largest cities:** Atlanta, Columbus, Macon, Savannah. **Pop. density:** 86.4 per sq. mi. (ranks 22nd). **Pop. projection 1985:** 5,721,000. **Pop. distribution:** 56.8% metropolitan; 43.2% nonmetropolitan. **White:** 73.8%. **Negro:** 25.9%. **Other:** 0.3%. **Marriage rate (1977):** 13.3 per 1,000 people. **Divorce rate:** 6.1 per 1,000 people.

State finances (1977). Revenue: $3,579,450,000. **Expenditures:** $3,440,030,000. **State Taxes:** $377.68 per capita. **State personal income tax:** Yes. **Public debt (1977):** $251.28 per capita. **Federal aid (1977):** $194.13 per capita. **Personal income (1977):** $6,002.

Sectors of the economy (% of labor force employed in 1970): Manufacturing (27%), Wholesale and retail trade (20%), Services (9%), Educational Services (7%), Construction (7%), Government (16%). **Leading products:** textile mill items, apparel, food, transportation equipment, lumber, pulp & paper products, chemicals. **Minerals:** clays, stone, cement, sand & gravel. **Agricultural products:** broilers, eggs, cattle, peanuts, tobacco, corn. **Fishing:** shrimp. **Avg. farm (1978 est.):** 246 acres. **Avg. value of farm:** $564 per acre.

Highway expenditures per capita (1977): $69.94. **Persons per motor vehicle:** 1.44. **Minimum age for driver's license:** 16. **Gasoline tax:** 7.5¢ per gallon. **Motor vehicle deaths:** 28.9 per 100,000 people.

Birthrate (1977): 16.8 per 1,000 people. **Infant mortality rate per 1,000 births (1977):** 15.4. **Physicians per 100,000 pop. (1976):** 136. **Dentists per 100,000 pop. (1976):** 39. **Acceptable hospital beds:** 6.2 per 1,000 people. **State expenditures per capita for health and hospitals (1977):** $60.22.

Education expenditures (1975-76): $354.73 per capita annually. **No. of pupils in public schools (1977 est.):** 1,029,000. **No. of institutions of higher learning (1976-77):** 67. **Public school expenditure per pupil in attendance (1975-76):** $1,323. **Avg. salary of public school teachers (1974-75 est.):** $10,641. **No. full-time teachers (1977 est.):** 48,200. **Educational attainment of adult population (1976):** 12.3 median yrs. of school completed; 8.0% with less than 5 years of education; 12.3% with 4 yrs. of college.

Telephones (1976): 71 per 100 people. **State Chamber of Commerce:** Georgia Chamber of Commerce, 1200 Commerce Building, Atlanta, Georgia 30303.

HAWAII

Hawaii, 50th state to join (1959) the Union, is a chain of 132 islands near the center of the North Pacific Ocean, about 2,400 miles from San Francisco. The islands were formed by volcanoes erupting from the ocean floor; there are some still-active volcanoes at the easterly end of the island chain, which extends 1,523 miles, and may be divided into three groups: the sand and coral islands of the northwest, rock islets in the center, and the eight major islands at the southeast end.

The eight major islands make up all except three square miles of the entire area: Hawaii, Oahu, Maui, Kahoolawe, Lanai, Molokai, Kauai, and Niihau. Hawaii is the largest of these islands (4,038 sq. mi.), while Oahu has the highest population (over 80 percent of the state's total). On Oahu are Honolulu and Pearl Harbor. Of these eight islands, only Kahoolawe is uninhabited; it is used as a target island for bombing and artillery training. The coastline of the islands is approximately 750 miles long. Cooling trade winds make for a pleasantly mild climate all year round. Rainfall varies from hundreds of inches in the mountains to less than 10 inches in the lowlands.

A melting pot of nationalities and racial groups, Hawaii was first settled by seagoing Polynesians, most likely from the Marquesas Islands, during the eighth century. The early Hawaiians, who practiced a religion that included human sacrifice and idolatry, developed a feudal form of government. Europe learned of the islands after British explorer Captain James Cook came upon them (1778); he named them the "Sandwich Islands" in honor of the Earl of Sandwich.

Local chieftain King Kamehameha I took control (1795) of the main islands—except Kauai and Niihau—after thirteen years of warfare with other aspirants. The other two islands accepted his rule in 1810.

Missionaries were active on the islands in the 1800s. In 1840, the Kingdom of Hawaii adopted its first constitution. The growth of the vital sugar and pineapple industries increased U.S. business and political involvement, leading to the establishment (1900) of Hawaii as a United States Territory following annexation (1898). The present population includes significant numbers of Polynesians, Chinese, Filipinos, and Japanese, as well as Caucasians.

The "date which will live in infamy"—Dec. 7, 1941—saw the Japanese attack on Pearl Harbor, which drew the nation into World War II.

Hawaii has since consolidated its importance as a strategic U.S. military outpost: Army, Navy, and Air Force units of the Pacific are under a single command located there. The salaries of military personnel and civilians employed at this command constitute one of Hawaii's principal sources of income. Tourism is also a major revenue source. Sugar and pineapple are still exported but are diminishing in the face of foreign competition.

The building boom which critics say created a "concrete jungle" in Waikiki to provide for the tourists is now shifting toward housing for local residents, giving rise to cries of "urban sprawl." There is considerable focus on environmental quality control, with frequent calls for preserving the land. In addition, there is growing concern over the traditional land development pattern. Most of the undeveloped land has been in the hands of a few owners who in the past leased but would not sell to private individuals, who then built homes on their leaseholds. With pressure on landowners to sell rather than lease, and with escalating land values, the future of the real estate market is uncertain.

In addition to such pleasures as swimming, boating and surfing, the islands have much to offer the scientist, historian and general sightseer, including the Bishop Museum in Honolulu—an important center for Polynesian studies; Iolani Palace in Honolulu, the only royal palace in the United States; the world's most active volcano, Kilauea, on Hawaii Island; the extinct Haleakala Crater on Maui Island; and the Waimea Canyon on Kauai Island, often called the "Grand Canyon of the Pacific." The cliff Nuuanu Pali (1,188 feet high) offers a fine view of Oahu's northeast coast.

Full name: State of Hawaii. **Origin of name:** Perhaps from native name of the Polynesians' original home. **Inhabitant:** Hawaiian.

HAWAII

Capital: Honolulu. **State motto:** Ua Mau Ke Ea O Ka Aina I Ka Pono (The Life of the Land Is Perpetuated in Righteousness). **Flag:** Eight alternating white, red & blue bars, representing main islands of state; Union Jack in upper left. **Seal:** Coat of arms of Hawaiian monarchy with King Kamehameha I on right & goddess of liberty on left. **Flower:** Hibiscus. **Bird:** Hawaiian goose. **Tree:** Kukui. **Song:** (unofficial) "Hawaii Ponoi." **Nickname:** Aloha State.

Governor: George R. Ariyoshi. **Annual salary:** $50,000. **Term:** 4 years. **Current term expires:** Dec. 1982. **Voting requirements:** 18 yrs. old & U.S. citizen. **U.S. Congressmen:** 2. **Entered Union:** 1959 (50th state).

Location & boundaries: Pacific state composed of a chain of 132 islands, located about 2,397 miles SW of San Francisco: major islands from east to west are Hawaii, Maui, Kahoolawe, Lanai, Molokai, Oahu, Kauai & Niihau. **Total area:** 6,450 sq. mi. (ranks 47th). **Coastline:** 750 mi. **No. of counties:** 5 (inc. Kalawao County–a leprosy settlement).

Population (1978 est.): 897,000 (ranks 40th). **Pop. increase (1970-78):** 16.5%. **Places over 25,000 pop.:** 4. **Places over 100,000:** 1. **Largest cities:** Honolulu, Kailua. **Pop. density:** 139.1 per sq. mi. (ranks 15th). **Pop. projection 1985:** 1,017,000. **Pop. distribution:** 80.9% metropolitan. **White:** 37.4%. **Negro:** 1%. **Other:** 61.6%. **Marriage rate (1977):** 11.5 per 1,000 people. **Divorce rate:** 5.1 per 1,000 people.

State finances (1977). Revenue: $1,456,564,000. **Expenditures:** $1,502,093,000. **State Taxes:** $766.15 per capita. **State personal income tax:** Yes. **Public debt (1977):** $1,660.64 per capita. **Federal aid (1977):** $385.80 per capita. **Personal income (1977):** $7,704.

Sectors of the economy (% of labor force employed in 1975): Manufacturing (7%), Wholesale and retail trade (24%), Services (21%), Construction (8%), Government (23%). **Leading products:** food, printing & publishing, stone, clay, glass items, fabricated metals, lumber & wood. **Agricultural products:** dairy items, cattle, hogs, sugarcane, pineapples, vegetables. **Fishing:** Aku, Ahi, Akule, tuna, big-eyed scad, marlin. **Avg. farm (1978 est.):** 561 acres. **Avg. value of farm:** not available.

Highway expenditures per capita (1977): $104.77. **Persons per motor vehicle:** 1.71. **Minimum age for driver's license:** 18. **Gasoline tax:** 8.5¢ per gallon. **Motor vehicle deaths:** 21.6 per 100,000 people.

Birthrate (1977): 18.9 per 1,000 people. **Infant mortality rate per 1,000 births (1977):** 11.5. **Physicians per 100,000 pop. (1976):** 174. **Dentists per 100,000 pop. (1976):** 64. **Acceptable hospital beds:** 3.4 per 1,000 people. **State expenditures per capita for health and hospitals (1977):** $112.43.

Education expenditures (1975-76): $481.80 per capita annually. **No. of pupils in public schools (1977 est.):** 172,000. **No. of institutions of higher learning (1976-77):** 11. **Public school expenditure per pupil in attendance (1975-76):** $1,817. **Avg. salary of public school teachers (1974-75 est.):** $13,665. **No. full-time teachers (1977 est.):** 8,930. **Educational attainment of adult population (1976):** 12.7 median yrs. of school completed; 5.5% with less than 5 years of education; 16.8% with 4 yrs. of college.

Telephones (1976): 67 per 100 people. 31. **State Chamber of Commerce:** Chamber of Commerce of Hawaii, Dillingham Building, 735 Bishop Street, Honolulu, Hawaii 96813.

IDAHO

Idaho is a rugged, mountainous state that does not yield its resources easily. It has the nation's deepest canyon (Hells Canyon, on the Oregon border), as well as 50 mountain peaks more than 10,000 feet high. There are three main regions: the southern, dominated by the Snake River plains and desolate volcanic terrain; the central, a primitive area of craggy mountains and canyons, dominated by the Salmon River Mountains; and the northern region, featuring the Cabinet Mountains and the Selkirk Mountains lying on the Canadian border. Forests of fir, pine, spruce, and other varieties cover about 40 percent of the state. Many peaceful, relatively unspoiled lakes set off the rough beauty of these areas and of the snow-capped mountains.

Indians are thought to have been living in the area 10,000 years ago. The region was acquired by the United States in the Louisiana Purchase (1803) and explored two years later by Lewis and Clark, who crossed the Bitterroot Range and camped near the present site of Lewiston (founded 1861). Throughout the 1860s, Idaho experienced a gold rush that drew scores of prospectors but left a legacy of ghost towns. Mining, however, is still important; Idaho ranks first nationally in the production of silver, garnets, and cobalt.

In the 1870s, the growing white occupation of Indian lands—particularly for cattle ranging—led to a series of battles between U.S. forces and the Nez Percé, Bannock, and Sheepeater tribes. Idaho gained statehood in 1890.

During the 1890s, disputes between miners and mineowners often resulted in violence and bloodshed. In 1892, in the Coeur d'Alene area, unionized miners used dynamite and guns to fight nonunion men and mineowners. There was violence again in 1899. Governor Frank Steunenberg declared martial law then and called in federal troops to restore order. Six years later, Steunenberg, no longer in office, was murdered by a member of the Western Federation of Miners; the confessed killer, defended by Clarence Darrow in a famous trial, was sentenced to life imprisonment.

Despite recent ravages by forest fires (including a 78,000-acre blaze in 1967) and troublesome mountain pine beetle infestations, agriculture is still the state's leading industry; crops include potatoes, wheat, apples, corn, barley, and hops.

Irrigation, which has been crucially important, was begun on a large scale under the federal government's Carey Act (1894) and Reclamation Act (1902). By 1950, Idaho had more than 5,000 diversion dams, 360 reservoirs (with 5 million acre-feet of water capacity), and more than 15,000 miles of irrigation canals and ditches. In 1968, the Idaho Power Company completed Hells Canyon Dam in the Snake River Valley, which also includes Oxbow and Brownlee dams. In recent years thousands of acres of new land have been brought into cultivation on high desert plateaus in the Boise area, largely possible through increased water pumping efficiency. With the completion of the Snake River navigation project in 1975, Idaho now has water access to the sea.

Manufacturing has been steadily increasing, particularly the dehydrating and freezing of potatoes of which Idaho produces about one-fourth of the nation's yield. Nearly 75 percent of this crop is now processed before it goes to the consumer.

One of the state's worst tragedies occurred in 1972 when 91 miners died in an underground fire at the Sunshine silver mine near Kellogg. Two other men were trapped alive for a week before they were rescued. The Sunshine is the nation's largest silver producing mine.

Tourism, now the third-ranked industry, is also on the rise, with an estimated 6 million yearly visitors.

Soda Springs, Champagne Springs, Steamboat Spring, and Hooper Spring boast ice-cold, as well as hellishly hot, water discharges. Lava Hot Springs, the site of a state park, has yielded mineral-rich waters since Indian times.

Other attractions of Idaho include the Craters of the Moon National Monument; Sun Valley that offers skating, swimming, skiing and other attractions; and the Sawtooth Mountains in central Idaho, where a new national recreation area was created in 1972. In 1978 federal legislation estab-

IDAHO

lished the large new Gospel-Hump Wilderness Area in north-central Idaho.

In June 1976 the Teton dam burst in the eastern part of the state, causing an estimated one billion dollars damage. Loss of human life was relatively light, but thousands of acres of farmland were destroyed and much of the Idaho cattle industry was temporarily wiped out by floodwaters. Reports indicate the collapse was in part due to poor design.

Full name: State of Idaho. **Origin of name:** Probably from the Indian word meaning "Gem of the Mountains." **Inhabitant:** Idahoan. **Capital:** Boise. **State motto:** Esto Perpetua (It Is Forever). **Flag:** State seal centered on blue field. **Seal:** Woman holding scales & a spear; miner; trees & river; elk's head; horns of plenty & sheaves of grain. **Flower:** Syringa. **Bird:** Mountain bluebird. **Tree:** Western pine. **Song:** "Here We Have Idaho." **Nickname:** Gem State.

Governor: John V. Evans. **Annual salary:** $40,000. **Term:** 4 years. **Current term expires:** Jan. 1983. **Voting requirements:** 18 yrs. old & U.S. citizen; registered 5 days with county clerk or 10 days with registrar. **U.S. Congressmen:** 2. **Entered Union:** 1890 (43rd state).

Location & boundaries: Rocky Mountain state; bounded on the north by Canada; on the east by Montana & Wyoming; on the south by Utah & Nevada; & on the west by Oregon, the Snake River & Washington. **Total area:** 83,557 sq. mi. (ranks 13th). **Extreme length:** 483 mi. **Extreme breadth:** 310 mi. **Chief rivers:** Snake, Salmon, Clearwater. **Major lakes:** Pend Oreille, Coeur d'Alene, Priest. **No. of counties:** 44.

Population (1978 est.): 878,000 (ranks 41st). **Pop. increase (1970-78):** 23.1%. **Places over 25,000 pop.:** 4. **Places over 100,000:** 1. **Largest cities:** Boise, Pocatello, Idaho Falls. **Pop. density:** 10.6 per sq. mi. (ranks 43rd). **Pop. projection 1985:** 979,000. **Pop. distribution:** 16.8% metropolitan; 83.2% non-metropolitan. **White:** 98.1%. **Negro:** 0.3%. **Other:** 1.6%. **Marriage rate (1977):** 15.7 per 1,000 people. **Divorce rate:** 7.0 per 1,000 people.

State finances (1977). Revenue: $785,989,000. **Expenditures:** $772,627,000. **State Taxes:** $429.20 per capita. **State personal income tax:** Yes. **Public debt (1977):** $60.98 per capita. **Federal aid (1977):** $261.95 per capita. **Personal income (1977):** $5,998.

Sectors of the economy (% of labor force employed in 1970): Manufacturing (15%), Wholesale and retail trade (23%), Services (8%), Educational Services (9%), Construction (7%), Government (17%). **Leading products:** food; lumber & chemicals; electronics; printing & publishing; stone, clay & pumice. **Minerals:** silver, phosphate rock, lead, zinc. **Agricultural products:** potatoes, cattle, sheep, dairy items, wheat, hay, sugar beets. **Avg. farm (1978 est.):** 580 acres. **Avg. value of farm:** $445 per acre.

Highway expenditures per capita (1977): $157.49. **Persons per motor vehicle:** 1.64. **Minimum age for driver's license:** 16. **Gasoline tax:** 9.5¢ per gallon. **Motor vehicle deaths:** 37.2 per 100,000 people.

Birthrate (1977): 22.0 per 1,000 people. **Infant mortality rate per 1,000 births (1977):** 11.3. **Physicians per 100,000 pop. (1976):** 105. **Dentists per 100,000 pop. (1976):** 51. **Acceptable hospital beds:** 4.4 per 1,000 people. **State expenditures per capita for health and hospitals (1977):** $41.92.

Education expenditures (1975-76): $412.04 per capita annually. **No. of pupils in public schools (1977 est.):** 197,000. **No. of institutions of higher learning (1976-77):** 9. **Public school expenditure per pupil in attendance (1975-76):** $1,368. **Avg. salary of public school teachers (1974-75 est.):** $9,573. **No. full-time teachers (1977 est.):** 9,510. **Educational attainment of adult population (1976):** 12.6 median yrs. of school completed; 1.5% with less than 5 years of education; 13.5% with 4 yrs. of college.

Telephones (1976): 68 per 100 people. **State Chamber of Commerce:** Idaho Association of Commerce & Industry, 805 Idaho St., Rm. 414, P.O. Box 389, Boise, Idaho 83701.

ILLINOIS

Illinois, the nation's fifth most populous state, consists almost entirely of gently rolling plains that slope gradually from north to south, although there is a range of relatively small hills, known as the Shawnee Hills (or the "Illinois Ozarks"), in the southern part of the state. In the north is Chicago, with 28.8 miles of shoreline along Lake Michigan; it is the state's largest city by far, and the country's second largest after New York. More than 60 percent of the population lives in or around Chicago.

Fertile soil, excellent drainage, and a long growing season have made Illinois one of the nation's major agricultural states, despite a climate that also includes spring and summer tornadoes and wide temperature extremes. The state is usually first or second (to Iowa) in corn production, first in soybeans, and a leading producer of hogs.

Manufacturing and mining are other important revenue sources for the state, which ranks high in oil and coal production and has the nation's largest soft coal reserves. Since 1842, Illinois has been the country's leading producer of fluorspar, or fluorite, which is used in making steel.

Transportation has been a key factor in the state's growth, thanks to its strategic position between the two seaboards and its proximity to important waterways, including Lake Michigan (and the Saint Lawrence Seaway) and the Mississippi River. Canals and an extensive highway system have also helped. Chicago has been the nation's railroad hub for many years, and today is a leading air travel center.

Prehistoric Indians called Mound Builders lived in the Illinois region and left a legacy of more than 10,000 burial and temple mounds. Later inhabitants included a union of Indian tribes known as the "Illinois Confederacy." The Frenchmen Marquette and Jolliet (or Joliet) were the first Europeans of record (1673) to visit the region and, two years later, Marquette founded a mission at the Indian town of Kaskaskia, near the present site of Utica. The first permanent settlement, founded (1699) by French priests of the Seminary of Foreign Missions, was at Cahokia. In 1779 the Commonwealth of Virginia set up the "County of Illinois." The area passed to the Northwest Territory in 1787. The first county, St. Clair, was established in 1790. Illinois became a territory in 1809 and entered the Union as a state in 1818.

Early landmarks in the state's history included the growing migration of eastern settlers following the opening (1825) of the Erie Canal; the Black Hawk War (1832), which virtually ended Indian troubles in the area; and the "Lincoln" years (1831-60), during which Abraham Lincoln rose from New Salem laborer to Springfield lawyer and president-elect. Lincoln's seven 1858 debates on the slavery issue with prominent Democrat Stephen A. Douglas, which were held in seven different Illinois towns, did not win him the Senate seat both men were seeking, but instead won him the national attention that led to his becoming the nation's Civil War President.

Illinois made great economic advances after the Civil War, despite such setbacks as the Chicago fire (October 1871) and a number of serious labor disputes, particularly the Haymarket Square Riot (1886) and the Pullman strike (1894).

Industry boomed during World War II, which also served to put the state into the vanguard of the Atomic Age: in 1942, at the University of Chicago, Enrico Fermi and other scientists set off the world's first controlled atomic reaction.

The state's current problems are many but not unique. There have been racial tensions in the major cities, and critical unemployment in some southern cities. In recent years, Chicago has been plagued by civil unrest and corruption, and there

ILLINOIS

MILES
0 10 20 30 40 50 60

KILOMETERS
0 10 20 30 40 50 60

⊛ State Capital
⊛ County Seats

© Copyright HAMMOND INCORPORATED, Maplewood, N. J.

Longitude West of Greenwich

have been violence, security problems and a number of escapes from Illinois prisons.

The state's tourist attractions include Old Town, the Art Institute, and the Museum of Science and Industry in Chicago; the reconstructed state park in New Salem, where Lincoln lived (1831-37); the Lincoln home and tomb in Springfield; the Dickson Indian Mounds near Havana; and Shawnee National Forest. Chain O'Lakes, a group of lakes in the northeastern part of the state, is a popular summer resort area.

In March 1979, the Illinois River reached a near-record peak causing some of the worst flooding in the state's history. The greatest damage occurred in Peoria and Kampsville.

Full name: State of Illinois. **Origin of name:** From Indian name meaning "The Men." **Inhabitant:** Illinoisan. **Capital:** Springfield. **State motto:** State Sovereignty–National Union. **Flag:** Adaptation of state seal centered on white field. **Seal:** An American eagle holds shield with stars & stripes, representing 13 original states; olive branch stands for peace; prairies & rising sun represent plains of Illinois. **Flower:** Native violet. **Bird:** Cardinal. **Tree:** Oak. **Song:** "Illinois". **Nickname:** Prairie State.

Governor: James R. Thompson. **Annual salary:** $55,000. **Term:** 4 years. **Current term expires:** Jan. 1983. **Voting requirements:** 18 yrs. old & U.S. citizen; resident of state, county, and district 30 da. **U.S. Congressmen:** 24. **Entered Union:** 1818 (21st state).

Location & boundaries: Midwestern state: bounded on the north by Wisconsin; on the east by Lake Michigan, Indiana & the Wabash River; on the southeast by Kentucky; on the southwest by Missouri; & on the west by the Mississippi River, Missouri & Iowa. **Total area:** 56,400 sq. mi. (ranks 24th). **Extreme length:** 381 mi. **Extreme breadth:** 211 mi. **Shoreline:** 63 mi. **Chief rivers:** Mississippi, Illinois, Kaskaskia. **Major lakes:** Michigan, Chain O'Lakes. **No. of counties:** 102.

Population (1978 est.): 11,243,000 (ranks 5th). **Pop. increase (1970-78):** 1.2%. **Places over 25,000 pop.:** 65. **Places over 100,000:** 3. **Largest cities:** Chicago, Rockford, Peoria. **Pop. density:** 199.3 per sq. mi. (ranks 10th). **Pop. projection 1985:** 11,454,000. **Pop. distribution:** 81.3% metropolitan; 18.7% non-metropolitan. **White:** 86.4%. **Negro:** 12.8%. **Other:** 0.8%. **Marriage rate (1977):** 9.6 per 1,000 people. **Divorce rate:** 4.4 per 1,000 people.

State finances (1977). Revenue: $9,852,612,000. **Expenditures:** $9,939,241,000. **State Taxes:** $473.06 per capita. **State personal income tax:** Yes. **Public debt (1977):** $360.50 per capita. **Federal aid (1977):** $184.64 per capita. **Personal income (1977):** $7,951.

Sectors of the economy (% of labor force employed in 1970): Manufacturing (30%), Wholesale and retail trade (20%), Services (7%), Educational Services (7%), Construction (5%), Government (13%). **Leading products:** machinery, food, electrical machinery, primary & fabricated metals, chemicals, printing & publishing. **Minerals:** coal; petroleum; stone, sand & gravel. **Agricultural products:** hogs, cattle, dairy items, corn, soybeans, wheat. **Avg. farm (1978 est.):** 247 acres. **Avg. value of farm:** $1,581 per acre.

Highway expenditures per capita (1977): $100.71. **Persons per motor vehicle:** 1.64. **Minimum age for driver's license:** 18. **Gasoline tax:** 7.5¢ per gallon. **Motor vehicle deaths:** 19.0 per 100,000 people.

Birthrate (1977): 15.8 per 1,000 people. **Infant mortality rate per 1,000 births (1977):** 16.0. **Physicians per 100,000 pop. (1976):** 172. **Dentists per 100,000 pop. (1976):** 51. **Acceptable hospital beds:** 6.9 per 1,000 people. **State expenditures per capita for health and hospitals (1977):** $53.87.

Education expenditures (1975-76): $464.94 per capita annually. **No. of pupils in public schools (1977 est.):** 2,205,000. **No. of institutions of higher learning (1976-77):** 149. **Public school expenditure per pupil in attendance (1975-76):** $1,848. **Avg. salary of public school teachers (1974-75 est.):** $13,469. **No. full-time teachers (1977 est.):** 129,230. **Educational attainment of adult population (1976):** 12.5 median yrs. of school completed; 2.6% with less than 5 years of education; 13.7% with 4 yrs. of college.

Telephones (1976): 80 per 100 people. **State Chamber of Commerce:** Illinois State Chamber of Commerce: Illinois State Chamber of Commerce, 20 North Wacker Drive, Chicago, Illinois 60606.

INDIANA

Although it is the smallest state in the continental United States west of the Alleghenies, Indiana ranks among the national leaders in population, agriculture, and manufacturing. Huge steel mills and oil refineries make the state's 45-mile Lake Michigan waterfront one of the world's great industrial centers, while the fertile plains of the central region produce an abundance of food (especially grain crops) for market and livestock. Mining, especially of coal and oil, is also significant; and the state's vast southern quarries produce two-thirds of the nation's building limestone. The automotive industry maintains a large number of plants in the state.

There are three main land regions: the Great Lakes Plain in the north, the central Till Plains (the largest single area), and, in the south, the Interior Low Plateau, characterized by hills, ridges, knolls, caves, and waterfalls. (The two plains regions are subdivisions of the Central Lowlands.) The generally mild, humid climate is marked by occasional temperature extremes.

The first inhabitants of the Indiana region were the prehistoric Mound Builders, followed by a number of Indian tribes, chiefly the Miamis. Many of the Indians had come into the area from the east after losing their land to the white settlers. The first European of record to visit the region was Robert Cavelier, Sieur de La Salle, who made two explorations (1679, 1681) and paved the way for French fur-trading posts (in the 1720s) and the first permanent settlement at Vincennes (fortified 1732). The English sharply challenged French control, however, and by the 1763 Treaty of Paris they had themselves gained dominance in the area; in 1774 the British government attached the territory to the province of Quebec.

During the American Revolution, George Rogers Clark and a small army financed by Virginia Governor Patrick Henry captured (1778) Vincennes from the British, lost it, and then, in the following year recaptured it. Virginia relinquished (1784) its claim to the Northwest Territory, of which Indiana was the south central part; three years later, the Northwest Ordinance provided for the territory's government, the permanent exclusion of slavery, and basic individual rights. Indiana Territory was created as an entity separate from Ohio in 1800 and initially included the present states of Indiana, Illinois, and Wisconsin, as well as parts of Michigan and Minnesota. After Michigan and Illinois became separate territories (1805, 1809), Indiana had almost the same boundaries as it has today. (The present boundaries were finally established when statehood was attained, in 1816.)

Indian troubles in the area were serious and persistent during the whole early period of white settlement. Anthony Wayne's victory at Fallen Timbers in Ohio (1794) brought peace but it was short-lived. Governor William Henry Harrison, who played a primary role in Indiana's early development, purchased (1809) for the Federal Government nearly 3 million acres of Indian lands in southern Indiana; this outraged the Shawnee chief Tecumseh, who led several tribes on the warpath. Troops led by Harrison won (1811) the Battle of Tippecanoe (near present-day Lafayette) and, during the War of 1812, defeated combined Indian and British forces in the Battle of the Thames, at Moraviantown, Ontario. Thus was British influence in the region ended, and the Indian threat virtually broken.

Indiana's famous "Hoosier" personality was forged in the first half of the 19th century, and its

INDIANA

MILES

0   10   20   30   40   50

KILOMETERS

0   10   20   30   40   50

State Capital ⊛
County Seats ○

Longitude West of Greenwich

© Copyright HAMMOND INCORPORATED, Maplewood, N.J.

hallmarks were rustic simplicity, self-sufficient isolation, and an almost reflexive conservatism. Attempts were made, most notably at New Harmony (1814), to reorganize society fundamentally along idealistic lines; although the experiments failed, they were the basis for the eventual development in the state of enlightened social and legal institutions and practices. The Hoosier spirit has been immortalized by such authors as Edward Eggleston, James Whitcomb Riley, Booth Tarkington, and George Ade, as well as songwriter Paul Dresser ("On the Banks of the Wabash") and artist John T. McCutcheon, whose cartoon "Injun Summer" has become a classic of its kind. And although his themes were more universal, novelist Theodore Dreiser (Sister Carrie, An American Tragedy) was also a Hoosier, and the brother of Paul Dresser.

Internal strife, led by the proslavery Knights of the Golden Circle, marked the Civil War period in Indiana, which, however, largely supported the Union cause. Except for occasional raids, such as that led (1863) by Confederate General John Hunt Morgan, the state saw little action.

Indiana's first public port opened in 1970 on Lake Michigan near Portage after a prolonged battle between proponents of industrial expansion and environmentalists over destruction of the unique dunelands between Gary and Michigan City. A compromise produced the Dunes National Lakeshore. In 1976 the U.S. House of Representatives appropriated funds to enlarge the park.

While the port permits worldwide waterborne trade via the St. Lawrence Seaway, much greater tonnage moves on the Ohio River, where there is a port at Mount Vernon; another port is planned near Jeffersonville.

Railroads and trucks remain the most important transport in Indiana, where Indianapolis is favored by being the crossroads of five interstate highways. Virtually all livestock now moves by truck, and there have been forecasts that Indianapolis will become the largest collecting point in the nation for meat animals.

Hoosiers also brag of the Army Finance Center at Ft. Benjamin Harrison, largest U.S. military building aside from the Pentagon.

Claremont is the site of Raceway Park, home of drag racing.

Full name: State of Indiana. **Origin of name:** Denoted that state was domain of Indians. **Inhabitant:** Hoosier. **Capital:** Indianapolis. **State motto:** The Crossroads of America. **Flag:** Gold torch & 19 gold stars on blue field. **Seal:** Pioneer scene represents westward expansion. **Flower:** Peony. **Bird:** Cardinal. **Tree:** Tulip. **Song:** "On the Banks of the Wabash." **Nickname:** Hoosier State.

Governor: Otis R. Bowen. **Annual salary:** $36,000. **Term:** 4 years. **Current term expires:** Jan. 1981. **Voting requirements:** 18 yrs. old & U.S. citizen; resident of township 60 da.; precinct 30 da. **U.S. Congressmen:** 11. **Entered Union:** 1816 (19th state).

Location & boundaries: Midwestern state; bounded on the north by Lake Michigan & Michigan; on the east by Ohio; on the southeast & south by the Ohio River & Kentucky; & on the west by the Wabash River & Illinois. **Total area:** 36,291 sq. mi. (ranks 38th). **Extreme length:** 280 mi. **Extreme breadth:** 160 mi. **Shoreline:** 45 mi. **Chief rivers:** Wabash, Ohio, White. **Major lakes (other than border-forming):** Monroe Reservoir, Mississinewa Reservoir, Wawasee. **No. of counties:** 92.

Population (1978 est.): 5,374,000. (ranks 12th). **Pop. increase (1970-78):** 3.5%. **Places over 25,000 pop.:** 23. **Places over 100,000:** 6. **Largest cities:** Indianapolis, Fort Wayne, Gary, Evansville. **Pop. density:** 148.1 per sq. mi. (ranks 20th). **Pop. projection 1985:** 5,481,000. **Pop. distribution:** 67.8% metropolitan; 32.2% nonmetropolitan. **White:** 92.8%. **Negro:** 6.9%. **Other:** 0.3%. **Marriage rate (1977):** 10.6 per 1,000 people. **Divorce rate:** 6.3 per 1,000 people.

State finances (1977). Revenue: $3,763,796,000. **Expenditures:** $3,456,564,000. **State Taxes:** $405.80 per capita. **State personal income tax:** Yes. **Public debt (1977):** $110.21 per capita. **Federal aid (1977):** $142.81 per capita. **Personal income (1977):** $6,922.

Sectors of the economy (% of labor force employed in 1970): Manufacturing (36%), Wholesale and retail trade (19%), Services (6%), Educational Services (8%), Construction (5%), Government (13%). **Leading products:** electrical & other machinery, transportation equipment, food, chemicals, primary & fabricated metals. **Minerals:** coal, cement, stone, petroleum. **Agricultural products:** hogs, cattle, dairy items, corn, soybeans, wheat. **Avg. farm (1978 est.):** 180 acres. **Avg. value of farm:** $1,303 per acre.

Highway expenditures per capita (1977): $83.05. **Persons per motor vehicle:** 1.49. **Minimum age for driver's license:** 18. **Gasoline tax:** 8¢ per gallon. **Motor vehicle deaths:** 24.3 per 100,000 people.

Birthrate (1977): 16.0 per 1,000 people. **Infant mortality rate per 1,000 births (1977):** 14.2. **Physicians per 100,000 pop. (1976):** 117. **Dentists per 100,000 pop. (1976):** 39. **Acceptable hospital beds:** 6.6 per 1,000 people. **State expenditures per capita for health and hospitals (1977):** $41.14.

Education expenditures (1975-76): $413.36 per capita annually. **No. of pupils in public schools (1977 est.):** 1,146,000. **No. of institutions of higher learning (1976-77):** 64. **Public school expenditure per pupil in attendance (1976-77):** $1,446. **Avg. salary of public school teachers (1974-75 est.):** $11,358. **No. full-time teachers (1977 est.):** 57,830. **Educational attainment of adult population (1976):** 12.4 median yrs. of school completed; 1.9% with less than 5 years of education; 11.0% with 4 yrs. of college.

Telephones (1976): 70 per 100 people. **State Chamber of Commerce:** Indiana State Chamber of Commerce, 201-212 Board of Trade Building, Indianapolis, Indiana 46204.

IOWA

With about two-thirds of its land mass between 800 and 1,400 feet above sea level, Iowa is a gently rolling plain quilted almost entirely by farms. The border-forming Mississippi and Missouri Rivers provide an abundant water supply and transportation routes.

The soil of Iowa is considered the finest in America and accounts for the fact that Iowa produces a tenth of the nation's food supply. It alternately shares the lead with Illinois in corn production, is second in soybeans and is a major producer of oats. The state's high crop yield supports the country's largest livestock industry; Iowa is the leading hog state and ranks high in cattle.

Because of the soil's economic importance, floods and the quest of greater productivity have made Iowans conservation conscious. In fact, in 1960 it was recognized that only a quarter of the state's water supply was being effectively harnessed.

As impressive as Iowa's agriculture is, manufacturing income is greater. The chief industrial centers are Des Moines; Cedar Rapids, site of its first nuclear power plant (1974); Dubuque and Waterloo. Except for gypsum—Iowa is the nation's third largest producer—mining is not significant.

The state's climate is of the continental, long-summer type, marked by great extremes; there is generally less precipitation in the western regions than in the eastern.

The winter of 1976-77 brought colder than normal temperatures, followed by an early spring and an unusually hot summer. The extreme temperatures and a lighter than normal precipitation had an adverse effect on crops.

A civilization of Mound Builders—sedentary farmers who lived in permanent villages—predated the Indians in Iowa; the Effigy Mounds National Monument contains numerous examples of their building in bird, animal, and serpentine forms. The first Europeans to visit the region were

IOWA

Père Marquette and Louis Jolliet (1673); almost a century later, the Indians allowed Julien Dubuque, a French-Canadian, to mine (1788) lead in the area of the city named for him. The United States obtained control of the state under the Louisiana Purchase (1803). Formation of Iowa Territory dates from 1838.

There was much fighting between white settlers and Indians of the area. A rich strip of land 50 miles wide along the Mississippi was won from the Sauk and Fox in 1832, after Black Hawk and his braves were defeated in battle. Other areas were taken from the Indians in 1836 and 1837. The Sioux ceded their claims in 1851, although an outlaw band of their numbers six years later killed 33 settlers in the Spirit Lake Massacre.

When Iowa became (1846) a state, its capital was at Iowa City; the more centrally located Des Moines became the capital in 1857. It was at this time, too, that the state's present boundaries were drawn up.

From the beginning, the character of Iowa has been a paradoxical amalgam of free-thinking liberalism and close-to-the-vest conservatism. Education has long had a high priority in the state, resulting in the nation's lowest illiteracy rate. Iowa has 3 state-supported universities, over 30 private colleges and approximately 10 private junior colleges. In 1965 a system of 15 area community colleges and vocational-technical schools was established.

The 1976-77 legislative session brought about a revision in the property tax law, limiting increases in taxable value of residential and agricultural buildings for a period of two years and changing the method of taxing farm land from 50 percent on value and 50 percent on productivity to a tax on productivity alone. Land use policy planning committees were set up, and the building code commission was directed to establish energy efficiency standards for new buildings.

Full name: State of Iowa. **Origin of name:** From name of Sioux tribe—the Ioways or Aiouez—meaning "Sleepy Ones." **Inhabitant:** Iowan. **Capital:** Des Moines. **State motto:** Our Liberties We Prize & Our Rights We Will Maintain. **Flag:** Vertical blue, white & red bars; flying eagle carrying state motto. **Seal:** Prairie scene represents Iowa's pioneer days; an eagle flies over scene carrying streamer with state motto. **Flower:** Wild rose. **Bird:** Eastern goldfinch. **Tree:** Oak. **Song:** "The Song of Iowa." **Nickname:** Hawkeye State.

Governor: Robert Ray. **Annual salary:** $55,000. **Term:** 4 years. **Current term expires:** Jan. 1983. **Voting requirements:** 18 yrs. old & U.S. citizen; registration 10 days before election. **U.S. Congressmen:** 6. **Entered Union:** 1846 (29th state).

Location & boundaries: Midwestern state; bounded on the north by Minnesota; on the east by the Mississippi River, Wisconsin & Illinois; on the south by the Des Moines River & Missouri; & on the west by the Missouri River, Nebraska, the Big Sioux River & South Dakota. **Total area:** 56,290 sq. mi. (ranks 25th). **Extreme length:** 324 mi. **Extreme breadth:** 210 mi. **Chief rivers:** Des Moines, Mississippi, Missouri, Big Sioux. **Major lakes:** Clear, Spirit, Storm Red Rock. **No. of counties:** 99.

Population (1978 est.): 2,896,000 (ranks 26th). **Pop. increase (1970-78):** 2.5%. **Places over 25,000 pop.:** 15. **Places over 100,000:** 3. **Largest cities:** Des Moines, Cedar Rapids, Davenport. **Pop. density:** 51.4 per sq. mi. (ranks 29th). **Pop. projection 1985:** 2,957,000. **Pop. distribution:** 37.4% metropolitan; 62.6% nonmetropolitan. **White:** 98.5%. **Negro:** 1.2%. **Other:** 0.3%. **Marriage rate (1977):** 9.2 per 1,000 people. **Divorce rate:** 3.8 per 1,000 people.

State finances (1977). Revenue: $2,542,726,000. **Expenditures:** $2,552,312,000. **State Taxes:** $448.94 per capita. **State personal income tax:** Yes. **Public debt (1977):** $43.05 per capita. **Federal aid (1977):** $194.03 per capita. **Personal income (1977):** $6,887.

Sectors of the economy (% of labor force employed in 1970): Manufacturing (20%), Wholesale and retail trade (22%), Services (7%), Educational Services (9%), Construction (5%), Government (14%). **Leading products:** food; electrical & other machinery; chemicals; printing & publishing; primary & fabricated metals; stone, clay & glass items. **Minerals:** cement; stone, sand & gravel; gypsum. **Agricultural products:** cattle, hogs, dairy items, corn, soybeans, hay. **Avg. farm (1978 est.):** 266 acres. **Avg. value of farm:** $1,268 per acre.

Highway expenditures per capita (1977): $141.31. **Persons per motor vehicle:** 1.30. **Minimum age for driver's license:** 18. **Gasoline tax:** 8.5¢ per gallon. **Motor vehicle deaths:** 22.1 per 100,000 people.

Birthrate (1977): 15.6 per 1,000 people. **Infant mortality rate per 1,000 births (1977):** 12.4. **Physicians per 100,000 pop. (1976):** 115. **Dentists per 100,000 pop. (1976):** 45. **Acceptable hospital beds:** 7.6 per 1,000 people. **State expenditures per capita for health and hospitals (1977):** $54.36.

Education expenditures (1975-76): $476.95 per capita annually. **No. of pupils in public schools (1977 est.):** 596,000. **No. of institutions of higher learning (1976-77):** 61. **Public school expenditure per pupil in attendance (1975-76):** $1,653. **Avg. salary of public school teachers (1974-75 est.):** $10,598. **No. full-time teachers (1977 est.):** 36,790. **Educational attainment of adult population (1976):** 12.5 median yrs. of school completed; 1.0% with less than 5 years of education; 12.8% with 4 yrs. of college.

Telephones (1976): 72 per 100 people.

KANSAS

The popular notion that Kansas consists wholly of flat prairie land is false; the land, in fact, rises from an elevation of about 700 feet in the southeast to more than 4,000 feet in the northwest, where the foothills of the Rockies begin. Three main land regions make up the state: the Great Plains, covering the western two-thirds; the Dissected Till Plains, covering a small area in the northeast corner; and the Southeastern Plains, often subdivided by geographers into the Osage Plains in the east and the Flint Hills in the west. Thousands of rolling hills between 100 and 400 feet high dot the state's terrain, which also features many valleys and picturesque chalk and sandstone formations. The relatively small natural water area is augmented by more than a hundred artificial lakes.

The eastern half of Kansas contains the overwhelmingly larger part of the population: the three largest cities—Wichita, Kansas City, and Topeka—are all in this section. Kansas City, on the eastern border, adjoins Kansas City, Missouri, but the two are separate municipalities.

A number of Indian tribes—including the Kansa, Wichita, Pawnee, and Comanche—were living in the Kansas region before the coming (1541) of the first European, Spanish explorer Francisco Vásquez de Coronado; he and his men were seeking the gold of a land called Quivira and, finding none, departed without establishing settlements. La Salle's far-reaching land claims (1682) on behalf of France included the Kansas region but, although French fur traders dealt with area Indians in the years immediately following, the Indians retained actual possession of the land. France yielded its claim to West Louisiana (including Kansas) to Spain in 1763, and Spain retroceded it to France (1800), which three years later sold it in the Louisiana Purchase to the United States.

Lewis and Clark, Zebulon M. Pike, and Major Stephen H. Long made (1803-19) the first serious explorations of the area, but their reports were incomplete and such as to discourage immediate American settlement. Erroneously considered a part of the "Great American Desert," the Kansas

region was primarily used (1825-42) as a resettlement area for uprooted Indian tribes.

With the establishment of the Santa Fe Trail (1821), which cut across the region diagonally from northeast to southwest, and the Oregon Trail (c. 1830), which traversed part of the northeastern region, the first permanent settlements (Fort Leavenworth-1827, Fort Scott-1842, and Fort Riley-1853) were founded as outposts to protect travelers against Indian raids.

The passage of the Kansas-Nebraska Act (1854), repealing the slavery-prohibiting Missouri Compromise of 1821 in favor of "squatter sovereignty," thrust Kansas into a bloody tug-of-war between proslavery and antislavery forces who rushed into the territory and fought savagely for political control. This was the era of "Bleeding Kansas," which saw the free-state "Jayhawkers" (including famed abolitionist John Brown) pitted against the advocates of slavery; the Jayhawkers ultimately won out and, in 1861 Kansas entered the Union as a free state.

Often called the Nation's Breadbasket, Kansas is the leading wheat producer and flour miller as well as one of the most important mining states. Today, Kansas is moving toward economic diversification, and manufacturing has now surpassed agriculture as the primary revenue source. The massive wheat and cattle raising operations have spawned an impressive manufacturing segment producing farm and heavy equipment. Hesston Corporation is now a world leader in farm machinery and exemplifies Kansas' growth in this area.

The production of transportation equipment is the major industrial activity. Wichita produces more than half of the nation's aircraft, while Topeka is a center for the manufacture and repair of railroad cars, and is also a major tire production center. Kansas' strategic location in the center of America makes it attractive to industries with nationwide distribution.

Occasional periods of drought or flood have prompted a massive program of flood control, water conservation and utilization. More than 30 federal reservoirs have been constructed or authorized along with dozens of watershed districts.

The reservoirs and lesser impoundments assure cities and industries of a stable water supply and provide facilities for camping, fishing, swimming, boating and water skiing. There are state park facilities at many of the reservoirs and an outstanding system of roadside parks.

Among the top tourist attractions is the Dwight D. Eisenhower Center at Abilene, featuring the boyhood home, Museum, Presidential Library, and Chapel where the former President and World War II commander is buried. Reconstruction of Early Day Front Street at Dodge City and Old Ft. Larned are other tourist attractions.

As a result of the food shortage of recent years, thousands of acres of Kansas farmland were pressed back into production. Bumper crops of wheat and corn were harvested in 1976 and 1977, both here and abroad, with the result that U.S. stockpiles were at their highest level in many years and prices dropped sharply in the face of a lessening demand for American grains abroad. The farmers here and in other states launched a protest in November, 1977, calling for a strike and demanding Federal price supports at 100 percent of parity. A nationwide strike of farmers belonging to the American Agriculture movement heavily supported by Kansas farmers began in December. Legislation was passed in Congress in May, 1978, providing for increased price supports for cotton and wheat.

Full name: State of Kansas. **Origin of name:** From name of Sioux tribe, meaning "People of the South Wind." **Inhabitant:** Kansan. **Capital:** Topeka. **State motto:** Ad Astra per Aspera (To the Stars through Difficulties). **Flag:** Blue field with wreath & yellow sunflower over state seal. **Seal:** Rising sun represents east; buffalo, log cabin, riverboat, wagon & plowing farmer suggest early history of region. **Flower:** Sunflower. **Bird:** Western meadowlark. **Tree:** Cottonwood. **Song:** "Home on the Range." **Nickname:** Sunflower State.

Governor: John Carlin. **Annual salary:** $45,000. **Term:** 4 years. **Current term expires:** Jan. 1983. **Voting requirements:** 18 yrs. old & U.S. citizen; registration 20 days before election. **U.S. Congressmen:** 5. **Entered Union:** 1861 (34th state).

Location & boundaries: Midwestern state; bounded on the north by Nebraska; on the east by the Missouri River & Missouri; on the south by Oklahoma; & on the west by Colorado. **Total Area:** 82,264 sq. mi. (ranks 14th). **Extreme length:** 411 mi. **Extreme breadth:** 208 mi. **Chief rivers:** Arkansas, Missouri, Kansas. **Major lakes:** Tuttle Creek, Cedar Bluff, Cheney, Perry. **No. of counties:** 105.

Population (1978 est.): 2,348,000 (ranks 32nd). **Pop. increase (1970-78):** 4.4%. **Places over 25,000 pop.:** 10. **Places over 100,000:** 3. **Largest cities:** Wichita, Kansas City, Topeka. **Pop. density:** 28.5 per sq. mi. (ranks 37th). **Pop. projection 1985:** 2,380,000. **Pop. distribution:** 45.9% metropolitan; 54.1% non-metropolitan. **White:** 94.4%. **Negro:** 4.8%. **Other:** 0.8%. **Marriage rate (1977):** 10.1 per 1,000 people. **Divorce rate:** 5.4 per 1,000 people.

State finances (1977). Revenue: $1,766,107,000. **Expenditures:** $1,718,799,000. **State Taxes:** $416.60 per capita. **State personal income tax:** Yes. **Public debt (1977):** $173.18 per capita. **Federal aid (1977):** $182.49 per capita. **Personal income (1977):** $7,141.

Sectors of the economy (% of labor force employed in 1975): Manufacturing (15.8%), Wholesale and retail trade (18.7%), Services (13.1%), Government (16.9%). **Leading products:** aerospace equipment, food, chemicals, crude oil & natural gas items, machinery, printing & publishing. **Minerals:** petroleum, helium, natural gas & gas liquids. **Agricultural products:** cattle, hogs, dairy items, wheat, sorghum grain, hay. **Avg. farm (1978 est.):** 638 acres. **Avg. value of farm:** $380 per acre.

Highway expenditures per capita (1977): $101.60. **Persons per motor vehicle:** 1.23. **Minimum age for driver's license:** 16. **Gasoline tax:** 8¢ per gallon. **Motor vehicle deaths:** 24.4 per 100,000 people.

Birthrate (1977): 15.9 per 1,000 people. **Infant mortality rate per 1,000 births (1977):** 13.4. **Physicians per 100,000 pop. (1976):** 144. **Dentists per 100,000 pop. (1976):** 44. **Acceptable hospital beds:** 7.9 per 1,000 people. **State expenditures per capita for health and hospitals (1977):** $56.93.

Education expenditures (1975-76): $432.04 per capita annually. **No. of pupils in public schools (1977 est.):** 430,000. **No. of institutions of higher learning (1976-77):** 52. **Public school expenditure per pupil in attendance (1975-76):** $1,538. **Avg. salary of public school teachers (1974-75 est.):** $9,770. **No. full-time teachers (1977 est.):** 27,230. **Educational attainment of adult population (1976):** 12.6 median yrs. of school completed; 1.0% with less than 5 years of education; 14.6% with 4 yrs. of college.

Telephones (1976): 73 per 100 people. **State Chamber of Commerce:** Kansas Assn. of Commerce and Industry, 500 First National Tower, One Townsite Plaza, Topeka, Kansas 66603.

KENTUCKY

Kentucky, renowned for the quality of its tobacco, whiskey, and racehorses, was the first state west of the Alleghenies to be settled by pioneers. A state of sometimes bizarre contrasts, Kentucky has the nation's gold reserves (at Fort Knox) and many fine farms and estates, yet much of its land has been devastated by reckless lumbering and strip-mining practices, and in some eastern areas chronic unemployment prevails. Two Kentuckians, Abraham Lincoln and Jefferson Davis, were the opposing presidents in the Civil War.

Roughly triangular in shape, the state consists of the Appalachian Plateau (known locally as the Cumberland Plateau and constituting the largest single area—more than a fourth of the total), the northcentral Bluegrass Region, the Pennyroyal Region (or Southwestern Mississippian Embayment), the Western Coal Field, and the East Gulf Coastal Plain (or Jackson Purchase Region), which makes up the state's western tip. A double hairpin turn in the Mississippi River separates a small bit of extreme southwestern Kentucky from the rest of the state; this area can be reached only by going through (or passing over, if by air) Missouri or Tennessee. Most of the state's surface is a much-furrowed plain sloping gently to the west.

About half the land is farmed, and agriculture (especially tobacco) is still important, although it has been surpassed in recent years by manufacturing. Commercial fishing is limited, while mining continues as a major activity; Kentucky ranks as the country's leading coal producer. Spurred by the building of new roads, tourism is also a significant revenue source; attractions include Mammoth Cave National Park, Abraham Lincoln Birthplace National Historical Site, Daniel Boone National Forest, Natural Bridge, and the annual Kentucky Derby.

Indians are thought to have lived in the forests of what is now western Kentucky as long as 15,000 years ago. Although other Europeans visited the region during the latter part of the 17th century, the first serious exploration of record was conducted (1750) by Dr. Thomas Walker, who passed through, and named, Cumberland Gap. About this time, a number of Indian tribes—including the Cherokee, Iroquois, and Shawnee—who were using the region as hunting grounds strongly resisted the advance of the white man. Daniel Boone explored eastern Kentucky (1767) and later spent two years in the Bluegrass Region. In 1773 he led a group of settlers into Kentucky, but Indians forced him out. James Harrod established (1774) the first permanent settlement at Harrodsburg; in the following year Daniel Boone, acting at this time as an agent for the Transylvania Company, returned to hack out the Wilderness Road and establish Boonesboro.

Indian raids were a continuing menace and such troubles persisted until General Anthony Wayne's victory in the Battle of Fallen Timbers in Ohio (1794) virtually ended them. Politically, the Kentucky region was originally a county of Virginia known as Fincastle, but independent statehood was gained relatively early, in 1792. The 1795 Pinckney's Treaty with Spain and the 1803 Louisiana Purchase made travel on the Mississippi more secure and aided development.

Kentucky's growth has been marked by an unusual degree of conflict and violence that has continued to the present day. Kentuckians fought hard against the Alien and Sedition Acts (1798), vigorously supported the War of 1812 and the Mexican War (1846-48), and, despite an official stance of neutrality in the Civil War, became caught in the middle of that conflict, supplying each side with thousands of troops. The slavery issue, a particularly contentious one for a slaveholding state containing many abolitionists, was officially resolved in 1865 with the adoption of the 13th Constitutional Amendment. There have also been bitter battles on a smaller scale, including the Hatfield-McCoy wrangle (1882-96), troubles surrounding the assassination (1900) of Democratic gubernatorial candidate William Goebel, the so-called Black Patch War (1904-09) between tobacco farmers and buyers, and frequent strife between mine owners and the United Mine Workers.

In response to the energy crisis forced in the early 1970s by the oil shortage and rising prices, coal mines were reopened, resulting in a drop in the state's unemployment. After two methane gas explosions which claimed 26 lives in 1976, a mine safety bill was passed, calling for more stringent measures.

The Beverly Hills Supper Club in Southgate burned to the ground in the spring of 1977, killing 164 people in what many term the worst disaster in the state's history.

Full name: Commonwealth of Kentucky. **Origin of name:** From Wyandot name, Ken-tah-teh, meaning "Land of Tomorrow." **Inhabitant:** Kentuckian. **Capital:** Frankfort. **State motto:** United We Stand, Divided We Fall. **Flag:** State seal on a blue field. **Seal:** Two men greeting each other; state motto. **Flower:** Goldenrod. **Bird:** Cardinal. **Tree:** Tulip poplar. **Song:** "My Old Kentucky Home." **Nickname:** Bluegrass State.

Governor: Julian M. Carroll. **Annual salary:** $35,000. **Term:** 4 years. **Current term expires:** Dec. 1979. **Voting requirements:** 18 yrs. old & U.S. citizen; resident of state 30 days; county 30 days; precinct 30 days. **U.S. Congressmen:** 7. **Entered Union:** 1792 (15th state).

Location & boundaries: Southeastern state: bounded on the north by the Ohio River, Illinois, Indiana & Ohio; on the east by the Big Sandy & Tug Fork Rivers, West Virginia & Virginia; on the south by Tennessee; & on the west by the Mississippi River & Missouri. **Total area:** 40,395 sq. mi. (ranks 37th). **Extreme length:** 350 mi. **Extreme breadth:** 175 mi. **Chief rivers:** Ohio, Kentucky, Tennessee. **Major lakes:** Kentucky, Barkley & Cumberland Reservoirs. **No. of counties:** 120.

Population (1978 est.): 3,498,000 (ranks 23rd). **Pop. increase (1970-78):** 8.7%. **Places over 25,000 pop.:** 8. **Places over 100,000:** 2. **Largest cities:** Louisville, Lexington, Owensboro, Covington. **Pop. density:** 86.6 per sq. mi. (ranks 21st). **Pop. projection 1985:** 3,751,000. **Pop. distribution:** 45.5% metropolitan; 54.4% nonmetropolitan. **White:** 92.6%. **Negro:** 7.2%. **Other:** 0.2%. **Marriage rate (1977):** 9.8 per 1,000 people. **Divorce rate:** 4.5 per 1,000 people.

State finances (1977). Revenue: $2,980,435,000. **Expenditures:** $2,848,694,000. **State Taxes:** $451.24 per capita. **State personal income tax:** Yes. **Public debt (1977):** $590.11 per capita. **Federal aid (1977):** $221.95 per capita. **Personal income (1977):** $5,989.

Sectors of the economy (% of labor force employed in 1970): Manufacturing (26%), Wholesale and retail trade (19%), Services (7%), Educational Services (8%), Construction (7%), Government (16%). **Leading products:** food, chemicals, tobacco items, machinery, primary & fabricated metals, transportation equipment. **Minerals:** coal, petroleum, stone, natural gas. **Agricultural products:** cattle, hogs, tobacco, dairy items, corn, hay. **Avg. farm (1978 est.):** 132 acres. **Avg. value of farm per acre:** $671.

Highway expenditures per capita (1977): $120.49. **Persons per motor vehicle:** 1.41. **Minimum age for driver's license:** 16. **Gasoline tax:** 9¢ per gallon. **Motor vehicle deaths:** 25.1 per 100,000 people.

Birthrate (1977): 17.0 per 1,000 people. **Infant mortality rate per 1,000 births (1977):** 14.4. **Physicians per 100,000 pop. (1976):** 128. **Dentists per 100,000 pop. (1976):** 38. **Acceptable hospital beds:** 5.6 per 1,000 people. **State expenditures per capita for health and hospitals (1977):** $39.32.

Education expenditures (1975-76): $369.85 per capita annually. **No. of pupils in public schools (1977 est.):** 684,000. **No. of institutions of higher learning (1976-77):** 38. **Public school expenditure per pupil in attendance (1975-76):** $1,122. **Avg. salary of public school teachers (1974-75 est.):** $9,240. **No. full-time teachers (1977 est.):** 35,290. **Educational attainment of adult population (1976):** 12.1 median yrs. of school completed; 5.7% with less than 5 years of education; 10.0% with 4 yrs. of college.

Telephones (1976): 59 per 100 people. **State Chamber of Commerce:** Kentucky Chamber of Commerce, P.O. Box 817, Versailles Rd., Frankfort, Kentucky 40602.

LOUISIANA

With its French and Spanish background, Louisiana is rich in history and among the nation's leaders in oil and natural gas, salt, sulphur, commercial fishing, fur trapping and rice, sugar cane and sweet potato production. The Michoud plant at New Orleans was a vital rocket-assembly installation during NASA's earth orbit and Apollo moon shots, contributing to the emergence of manufacturing as a major industry in the state.

New Orleans lies 100 miles up the Mississippi River from the Gulf of Mexico. It has been the nation's second busiest seaport since 1840 but is perhaps better known as the site of the annual Mardi Gras. The world's longest bridge, the 24-mile Lake Pontchartrain Causeway, connects New Orleans to Mandeville. A sizeable timber industry is fed by extensive forest lands.

In the north are low rolling hills, and in the east many bluffs dot the river plain. Coastal marshes and sluggish streams (bayous) are features of the southern terrain. The Mississippi Delta, a fertile sedimentary deposit, comprises a third of the state's total area.

Indians are thought to have lived in the northern part of the Louisiana region nearly 3,000 years ago. Spanish explorer Cabeza de Vaca may have visited the area about 1530, and Hernando De Soto did so (1540-42). Approximately 12,000 Indians were then living in the region.

In 1682 Robert Cavelier, Sieur de La Salle, reached the mouth of the Mississippi and claimed all the land drained by it and its tributaries for King Louis XIV of France.

Permanent French settlement of the Louisiana region began (1699) with its founding as a royal colony and the establishment of a community near present-day Biloxi, Mississippi. In 1717 the area was granted to a company headed by John Law, who initially centered his development in the region that is now Arkansas, but then moved south. New Orleans was founded in 1718 and four years later became the capital. Law's venture spurred immigration, but eventually failed.

French control of the region gave way (1762) to Spanish; France regained possession in 1800. Three years later, Napoleon Bonaparte, seeking funds to support his European military activities, sold the land to the United States, as part of the vast Louisiana Purchase. In 1804 the territory was divided at the state's present northern border: the northern portion, now made up of other states, was at first called the District of Louisiana, then the Territory of Louisiana, and later Missouri Territory; the southern portion, originally the Territory of Orleans, became the present state of Louisiana. The period between 1760 and 1790 was marked by an influx of Acadians, or Cajuns, from Canada, who settled mainly in the southern region.

In the early 19th century, the natives of Louisiana were a heterogeneous mixture of French, Spanish, Isleños from the Canary Islands, and Germans. Although the Louisianians generally did not welcome the coming of the Americans, they did unite behind Andrew Jackson to defeat (1815) the British in the Battle of New Orleans at the end of the War of 1812. The state, which entered the Union in 1812, was enlarged by the settlement of the West Florida Controversy, which had stemmed from conflicting Spanish and American land claims involving portions of Florida, Alabama, Mississippi, and Louisiana; the Transcontinental Treaty of 1819 gave control of the disputed regions to the United States.

Early statehood was marked by the advent of the Mississippi steamboat trade and its attendant prosperity, and by the rise of plantation agriculture. The Civil War and the Reconstruction period brought considerable hardship and chaos. White rule was ultimately reestablished and farm tenancy and sharecropping replaced the plantation system. The discovery of oil (1901) and natural gas (1916) greatly aided the state's economic recovery.

The 1927 Mississippi flood, which forced 300,000 people from their homes, remains the worst on record. But the 1973 high water flooded nearly four million acres of Louisiana for months before the crisis ebbed away into the Gulf. Enormous damage was averted by the levee system.

Huey P. Long, elected governor in 1927 and assassinated in 1935, remains the state's most renowned political figure. His first term launched a political dynasty that continued even after he was killed. As governor and later (1930) as U.S. senator, Long was an advocate of a "Share the Wealth" program that challenged powerful Louisiana oil interests. He was responsible for much material progress but also was blamed for considerable political corruption.

Louisiana today is becoming increasingly industrialized, often to the detriment of its tradition-ripe picturesqueness. One reason for the spurt is that the state grants 10-year tax exemptions to new industries. Tourism also has grown, and today accounts for over $1 billion annually. Those seeking to preserve the traces of the past were heartened by the federal government's refusal (July 1969) to grant funds for part of a highway system that would have "seriously impaired the historic quality of New Orleans' famed French Quarter." An alternate route was not acceptable because of its disruptive effects on the city, excessive costs, and construction hazards to the city's river levee. The ruling was believed to be the first denial of federal funds for a highway on the basis of preserving a historic area.

The Louisiana Offshore Oil Port (Loop) is being constructed 18 miles off Grand Isle. Tankers too large to dock at any existing U.S. ports will unload their cargo at the superport, and the oil will be sent to the mainland by pipeline. The port is scheduled to be operational by 1980.

Between September 21-26, 1978, a fire raged in a cavern at Hackberry which stores oil for the nation's strategic petroleum reserve. One man was killed and another injured during the explosion which initiated the blaze. Between 50,000 and 70,000 barrels of crude oil were lost in the fire according to a federal official. The monetary loss of oil was valued between $750,000 and $1,050,000.

Full name: State of Louisiana. **Origin of name:** In honor of King Louis XIV of France. **Inhabitant:** Louisianian. **Capital:** Baton Rouge. **State motto:** Union, Justice & Confidence. **Flag:** State seal & motto on a blue field. **Seal:** Mother pelican feeding brood. **Flower:** Magnolia. **Bird:** (unofficial) Brown pelican. **Tree:** Bald cypress. **Song:** "Give Me Louisiana." **Nickname:** Pelican State.

Governor: Edwin W. Edwards. **Annual salary:** $50,000. **Term:** 4 years. **Current term expires:** Mar. 1980. **Voting requirements:** 18 yrs. old & U.S. citizen; resident of state 1 yr.; county, 6 mos.; district, 3 mos. **U.S. Congressmen:** 8. **Entered Union:** 1812 (18th state).

Location & boundaries: Gulf state; bounded on the north by Arkansas; on the east by the Mississippi & Pearl Rivers & Mississippi; on the southeast & south by the Gulf of Mexico; & on the west by Texas & the Sabine River. **Total area:** 48,523 sq. mi. (ranks 31st). **Extreme length:** 237 mi. **Extreme breadth:** 236.5 mi. **Coastline:** 397 mi. **Chief rivers:** Mississippi, Atchafalaya, Red, Ouachita. **Major lakes:** Pontchartrain, Grand, White. **No. of parishes (counties):** 64.

LOUISIANA

Population (1978 est.): 3,966,000 (ranks 20th). **Pop. increase (1970-78):** 8.9%. **Places over 25,000 pop.:** 11. **Places over 100,000:** 3. **Largest cities:** New Orleans, Baton Rouge, Shreveport. **Pop. density:** 81.7 per sq. mi. (ranks 24th). **Pop. projection 1985:** 4,096,000. **Pop. distribution:** 63.4% metropolitan; 36.6% nonmetropolitan. **White:** 69.7%. **Negro:** 29.9%. **Other:** 0.4%. **Marriage rate (1977):** 9.8 per 1,000 people. **Divorce rate:** Not Available.

State finances (1977). Revenue: $3,685,114,000. **Expenditures:** $3,646,738,000. **State Taxes:** $438.32 per capita. **State personal income tax:** Yes. **Public debt (1977):** $451.22 per capita. **Federal aid (1977):** $246.55 per capita. **Personal income (1977):** $5,910.

Sectors of the economy (% of labor force employed in 1970): Manufacturing (16%), Wholesale & retail trade (21%), Services (10%), Educational Services (9%), Construction (8%), Government (17%). **Leading products:** chemicals, food, petroleum and paper items, transportation equipment, lumber, primary metals. **Minerals:** petroleum, natural gas, sulfur. **Agricultural products:** cattle, dairy items, rice, sugar cane, soybeans. **Fishing:** shrimp, menhaden, oysters. **Avg. farm (1978 est.):** 258 acres. **Avg. value of farm per acre:** $669.

Highway expenditures per capita (1977): $135.37. **Persons per motor vehicle:** 1.62. **Minimum age for driver's license:** 17. **Gasoline tax:** 8¢ per gallon. **Motor vehicle deaths:** 27.2 per 100,000 people.

Birthrate (1977): 19.1 per 1,000 people. **Infant mortality rate per 1,000 births (1977):** 17.9. **Physicians per 100,000 pop. (1976):** 141. **Dentists per 100,000 pop. (1976):** 38. **Acceptable hospital beds:** 6.4 per 1,000 people. **State expenditures per capita for health and hospitals (1977):** $79.16.

Education expenditures (1975-76): $385.08 per capita annually. **No. of pupils in public schools (1977 est.):** 827,000. **No. of institutions of higher learning (1976-77):** 31. **Public school expenditure per pupil in attendance (1975-76):** $1,391. **Avg. salary of public school teachers (1974-75 est.):** $9,800. **No. full-time teachers (1977 est.):** 46,620. **Educational attainment of adult population (1976):** 12.3 median yrs. of school completed; 8.7% with less than 5 years of education; 11.5% with 4 yrs. of college.

Telephones (1976): 63 per 100 people. **State Chamber of Commerce:** Louisiana Association of Business & Industry, P.O. Box 3988, Baton Rouge, Louisiana 70821.

MAINE

Four-fifths of Maine is covered by forests that feed an enormous wood-processing industry. There are three general land areas: the White Mountains region in the northwest, the New England Uplands extending through the heart of the state, and the coastal lowlands of the southeast. Many bays and harbors dot the craggy, convoluted coastline. Southwest of Portland, the rockbound coast is supplanted by sandy beaches. Sailors coasting downwind from Boston gave the shore its nickname, "Down East." Fishermen are attracted by the state's 2,500 lakes and ponds and 5,000 rivers and streams. Waterpower availability is correspondingly excellent. Ten mountains rise more than 4,000 feet; undersea peaks form 400 offshore islands.

The climate is marked by generally severe winters, and summer evenings occasionally so cool that people heat their homes. Yet this very ruggedness of terrain and climate has proved an asset in drawing tourists. Skiing, camping, and other outdoor activities are especially popular, and many city-worn visitors seek out the unspoiled Allagash wilderness, the 92-mile-long Allagash Wilderness Waterway, and Mount Katahdin (5,268 ft.), which is the first place in the nation to catch the rays of the rising sun. Other attractions include Bar Harbor on Mount Desert Island, most of which is part of Acadia National Park.

Maine may have been sighted by Norse explorer Leif Ericsson as early as A.D. 1000, and English-employed Italian sea captain John Cabot is considered to have been the first European to reach the area, in 1498. Thousands of Abnaki and Etchemin Indians were living there at the time. They peaceably coexisted with the earliest settlers but occasionally joined together to fight off raiding Iroquois. The legendary city of Norumbega, thought to have contained vast riches, drew adventurers up the Penobscot River, upon which the city was said to have been located.

Maine lands were granted (1622) by the Council for New England (successor to the Plymouth Company) to two wealthy Englishmen, Sir Ferdinando Gorges and Captain John Mason. Gorgeana (now York) became (1641) the first chartered English city in the New World. After Gorges' death (1647), Maine was largely neglected. Its settlers came under the jurisdiction of Massachusetts, which later bought (1677) the proprietary rights of Gorges' heirs for about $6,000. French efforts to control the region ended with the Treaty of Paris (1763), terminating the French and Indian Wars that had begun in 1689.

Revolt against England was in the air in the 1760s because of taxes and restrictions. In 1774, Maine men followed Boston's example of a year earlier and burned a supply of British tea (York Tea Party). The first naval encounter of the American Revolution took place (June 1775) off Machias, as patriots captured the British ship *Margaretta*. The eastern part of the state passed under British control during the War of 1812.

Maine stayed a part of Massachusetts until 1820, when it was admitted to the Union as a free state under the terms of the Missouri Compromise, thus balancing Missouri's admission as a slave state. A long-simmering boundary dispute with New Brunswick was settled by the Webster-Ashburton Treaty (1842), which ended the bloodless Aroostook War.

Maine was the first state to outlaw (1851) alcohol, which remained illegal until 1934. From 1909 to 1955, to keep the state's hydroelectric power within its borders and thus attract new industries, the sale of such power outside the state was prohibited. The state's textile business has declined since the 1920s, while the food-processing industry has grown significantly. Lobsters, canned sardines, potatoes, and blueberries are among the state's most famous products, as well as shoes, beet sugar and wood pulp and paper. Mining is limited, despite large deposits of granite, limestone, and slate. The communications satellite station near Andover (completed 1962) is part of a worldwide satellite communications system that includes Telstar and Early Bird.

The New York Mercantile Exchange, the only market for the round, white Maine potatoes, suspended trading March 9, 1979, on contracts for delivery in March, April, and May. While the NYME said it acted to prevent a collapse of the market which could have resulted from the shortage of high-quality Maine potatoes, the Maine farmers, who lost millions of dollars because of the halt, contended that the supply problems were caused by the manipulation of the market by a few big traders. May 9, Gov. Joseph Brennan (D) asked the Commodity Futures Trading Commission to prohibit all futures trading in Maine potatoes.

In July 1979 the Passamaquoddy and Penobscot Indians received hope regarding their land claims to more than half the state's territory. If jurisdiction in the case is settled and it goes to the Supreme Court, there is a chance that the Court may rule in the Indians' favor and thereby bolster their negotiation stand.

MAINE
MILES
0 10 20 30 40 50
KILOMETERS
0 10 20 30 40 50

State and Provincial Capitals ⊛
County Seats ◉
© Copyright HAMMOND INCORPORATED, Maplewood, N.J.

Full name: State of Maine. **Origin of name:** From name of ancient province in France. **Inhabitant:** Mainer. **Capital:** Augusta. **State motto:** Dirigo (I Guide). **Flag:** State seal on a blue field. **Seal:** Farmer & seaman represent two chief occupations; pine tree symbolizes forests; moose, wildlife; northern star stands for northern location. **Flower:** White pine cone & tassel. **Bird:** Chickadee. **Tree:** White pine. **Stone:** Tourmaline. **Song:** "State of Maine Song." **Nickname:** Pine Tree State.

Governor: Joseph E. Brennan. **Annual salary:** $35,000. **Term:** 4 years. **Current term expires:** Jan. 1983. **Voting requirements:** 18 yrs. old & U.S. citizen, resident of state and municipality of registration. **U.S. Congressmen:** 2. **Entered Union:** 1820 (23d state).

Location & boundaries: New England state: bounded on the north & east by Canada; on the south by New Hampshire & the Atlantic Ocean; & on the west by New Hampshire & Canada. **Total area:** 33,215 sq. mi. (ranks 39th). **Extreme length:** 332 mi. **Extreme breadth:** 207 mi. **Coastline:** 228 mi. **Chief rivers:** Androscoggin, Kennebec, Penobscot, St. Croix. **Major lakes:** Moosehead, Chesuncook, Sebago, Rangeley. **No. of counties:** 16.

Population (1978 est.): 1,091,000 (ranks 38th). **Pop. increase (1970-78):** 9.8%. **Places over 25,000 pop.:** 3. **Places over 100,000:** none. **Largest cities:** Portland, Lewiston, Bangor. **Pop. density:** 32.8 per sq. mi. (ranks 36th). **Pop. projection 1985:** 1,196,000. **Pop. distribution:** 23.3% metropolitan; 76.7% nonmetropolitan. **White:** 99.3%. **Negro:** 0.3%. **Other:** 0.4%. **Marriage rate (1977):** 10.6 per 1,000 people. **Divorce rate:** 5.2 per 1,000 people.

State finances (1977). Revenue: $1,024,998,000. **Expenditures:** $981,474,000. **State Taxes:** $431.76 per capita. **State personal income tax:** Yes. **Public debt (1977):** $519.88 per capita. **Federal aid (1977):** $252.50 per capita. **Personal income (1977):** $5,751.

Sectors of the economy (% of labor force employed in 1970): Manufacturing (32%), Wholesale and retail trade (20%), Services (7%), Educational Services (8 2%) Construction (6%), Government (15%). **Leading products:** paper items, leather items, food, textile items, lumber & wood, transportation equipment, printing & publishing. **Minerals:** sand & gravel, cement, stone, peat. **Agricultural products:** broilers, dairy items, potatoes, hay, apples. **Fishing:** lobster, ocean perch, clams. **Avg. farm (1978 est.):** 222 acres. **Avg. value of farm per acre:** $441.

Highway expenditures per capita (1977): $102.81. **Persons per motor vehicle:** 1.51. **Minimum age for driver's license:** 17. **Gasoline tax:** 9¢ per gallon. **Motor vehicle deaths:** 21.8 per 100,000 people.

Birthrate (1977): 14.9 per 1,000 people. **Infant mortality rate per 1,000 births (1977):** 9.5. **Physicians per 100,000 pop. (1976):** 136. **Dentists per 100,000 pop. (1976):** 43. **Acceptable hospital beds:** 6.8 per 1,000 people. **State expenditures per capita for health and hospitals (1977):** $38.25.

Education expenditures (1975-76): $378.56 per capita annually. **No. of pupils in public schools (1977 est.):** 245,000. **No. of institutions of higher learning (1976-77):** 25. **Public school expenditure per pupil in attendance (1975-76):** $1,406. **Avg. salary of public school teachers (1974-75 est.):** $13,202. **No. full-time teachers (1977 est.):** 14,390. **Educational attainment of adult population (1976):** 12.5 median yrs. of school completed; 1.2% with less than 5 years of education; 13.6% with 4 yrs. of college.

Telephones (1976): 65 per 100 people. **State Chamber of Commerce:** Maine State Chamber of Commerce, 477 Congress Street, Portland, Maine 04111.

MARYLAND

Maryland has been called "America in Miniature" because, although small in area, it is uncommonly diverse and rich in history. Hills, valleys, rolling plains, swamps, and plateaus are all found there, and contrasting life-styles abound: from tobacco farmers in the southern part of the state to the missile makers of the highly industrialized Baltimore area, where more than half of the state's population lives. It was from Maryland that Washington, D.C. received (1791) part of its land (the rest was ceded by Virginia); when the capital was

threatened by Confederate forces, Maryland became the scene of much fighting, including one of the bloodiest Civil War battles of all: Antietam (1862). Earlier, during the War of 1812, Marylander Francis Scott Key, watching the British bombardment of Baltimore's Fort McHenry, was inspired to write "The Star-Spangled Banner."

Maryland's coastline along the Atlantic Ocean is short, but Chesapeake Bay, which divides the state into an Eastern and Western Shore, provides many fine harbors, and a number of important islands dot the bay. A section of the Atlantic Coastal Plain, sometimes called "Tidewater Maryland," makes up all of the low-lying Eastern Shore. Fishing is a significant industry, and wild fowl abound.

Indians, mainly of the Algonquian family, were living in what is now Maryland before John Cabot, probably the region's first European explorer, sailed along the eastern coast in 1498. Virginian William Claiborne established the first settlement, a fur-trading post, on Kent Island.

The Maryland region was named for Henrietta Maria, queen consort of Charles I, who granted it (1632) to George Calvert, first Baron Baltimore. But Calvert died the same year, and his son Cecilius, second Baron Baltimore, was given the grant. He soon began developing the colony as both an income source and a religious haven for persecuted fellow Catholics. The Act of Toleration (1649) was passed in behalf of the Catholics, but when the Puritans gained control of the area they repealed (1654) this instrument. A short civil war followed (1655), from which the Puritans emerged victors. In 1657 a compromise briefly restored the proprietorship to Lord Baltimore.

The English government eventually (1691) made Maryland a royal province. Commercial development proceeded rapidly in the next century, particularly in the Baltimore area. Indian troubles were infrequent and comparatively mild. Boundary quarrels with Pennsylvania were settled by the drawing of the Mason-Dixon Line (1767). Marylanders staged (1774) a Boston-style "tea party" in Annapolis, protesting British rule, and fought so well in the American Revolution that George Washington nicknamed Maryland "The Old Line State," in honor of its dependable "troops of the line." The state, which entered the Union in 1788, prospered early, thanks largely to the famous Baltimore clipper ships and the opening (1830) of the Baltimore and Ohio Railroad, first in the hemisphere to carry both passengers and freight.

During the Civil War, Maryland was a sharply divided slave state that remained loyal to the Union under great pressure; the state's inherited racial problems are compounded by such factors as inadequate urban housing and public apathy.

Maryland becomes increasingly less part of the Old South and seems to grow smaller every year. Expressways now link all areas of the state; two of them serve the rapidly developing Baltimore-Washington corridor, while Interstate 70 reaches into Western Maryland and the dual-lane U.S. 50 and U.S. 13 funnel traffic through the Eastern Shore. The Francis Scott Key Bridge was opened in February 1977. It is Baltimore's second harbor crossing and teams with the Harbor Tunnel. A second span of the Chesapeake Bay Bridge opened in June 1973.

Maryland's tourist attractions include a wide variety of parks and forests stretching from Appalachia to the Atlantic Ocean. Annapolis is the site of the U.S. Naval Academy, with the nation's oldest statehouse in use and more original colonial buildings than any other U.S. city. Columbia, the planned city built by James Rouse halfway be-

MARYLAND

MILES
5 10 20 30

KILOMETERS
0 5 10 20 30

● National Capital ⊕ County Seats
◉ State Capitals

WESTERN PART OF MARYLAND
Same scale as main map

tween Baltimore and Washington, celebrated its 10th anniversary in 1977.

In November 1975, Maryland's Governor Mandel and five associates were indicted by a Federal grand jury on charges of mail fraud and "racketeering" activity. The trial began in September 1976 and ended abruptly in December 1976 with two separate cases of tampering. A second trial held in 1977 resulted in conviction, and Mandel was sentenced to four years in prison. The sentence was voided when the 4th U.S. Circuit Court of Appeals set aside his conviction on technical grounds on January 11, 1979. January 15, Mandel briefly resumed his office for 45 hours until the newly elected governor, Harry R. Hughes, was sworn in on January 17.

Full name: State of Maryland. **Origin of name:** From Queen Henrietta-Maria of England, wife of Charles I. **Inhabitant:** Marylander. **Capital:** Annapolis. **State motto:** "Fatti maschi, parole femine" ("Manly deeds, womanly words"). **Flag:** Geometric black & gold pattern in opposite quarters; red & white crosses in the others. **Seal:** Shield with coats of arms of Calvert & Crossland families; farmer represents Maryland; fisherman, Lord Baltimore's Avalon colony in Newfoundland. **Flower:** Blackeyed Susan. **Bird:** Baltimore oriole. **Tree:** White oak. **Song:** "Maryland, My Maryland." **Nickname:** Old Line State.

Governor: Harry R. Hughes **Annual salary:** $60,000. **Term:** 4 years. **Current term expires:** Jan. 1983. **Voting requirements:** 18 yrs. old & U.S. citizen; resident of state 30 days. **U.S. Congressmen:** 8. **Entered Union:** 1788 (7th state).

Location & boundaries: Middle Atlantic seaboard state: bounded on the north by Pennsylvania; on the east by Delaware & the Atlantic Ocean; on the south by the Potomac River, Virginia & West Virginia; & on the west by West Virginia. **Total area:** 10,577 sq. mi. (ranks 42d). **Extreme length:** 198.6 mi. **Extreme breadth:** 125.5 mi. **Coastline:** 31 mi. (coastline including Chesapeake Bay, 3,190 mi.). **Chief rivers:** Potomac, Susquehanna, Patuxent. **Major lakes:** Deep Creek Lake (man-made). **No. of counties:** 23, plus 1 independent city.

Population (1978 est.): 4,143,000 (ranks 18th). **Pop. increase (1970-78):** 5.6%. **Places over 25,000 pop.:** 7. **Places over 100,000:** 1. **Largest cities:** Baltimore, Rockville, Hagerstown, Bowie **Pop. density:** 391.7 per sq. mi. (ranks 5th). **Pop. projection 1985:** 4,637,000. **Pop. distribution:** 85.6% metropolitan; 14.4% nonmetropolitan. **White:** 81.5%. **Negro:** 17.9%. **Other:** 0.7%. **Marriage rate (1977):** 10.9 per 1,000 people. **Divorce rate:** 4.0 per 1,000 people.

State finances (1977). Revenue: $3,933,699,000. **Expenditures:** $3,918,843,000. **State Taxes:** $514.06 per capita. **State personal income tax:** Yes. **Public debt (1977):** $737.15 per capita. **Federal aid (1977):** $194.53 per capita. **Personal income (1977):** $7,569.

Sectors of the economy (% of labor force employed in 1970): Manufacturing (20%), Wholesale and retail trade (19%), Services (7%), Educational Services (8%), Construction (7%), Government (26%). **Leading products:** food and kindred products, primary metals, electrical equipment and supplies, transportation equipment, chemical and allied products, apparel, printing. **Agricultural products:** dairy items, broilers, cattle, corn, hay, tobacco. **Fishing:** oysters, crabs, clams. **Avg. farm (1978 est.):** 167 acres. **Avg. value of farm per acre:** $1,578.

Highway expenditures per capita (1977): $97.07 **Persons per motor vehicle:** 1.60. **Minimum age for driver's license:** 18. **Gasoline tax:** 9¢ per gallon. **Motor vehicle deaths:** 17.1 per 100,000 people.

Birthrate (1977): 13.5 per 1,000 people. **Infant mortality rate per 1,000 births (1977):** 14.3. **Physicians per 100,000 pop. (1976):** 271. **Dentists per 100,000 pop. (1976):** 56. **Acceptable hospital beds:** 6.1 per 1,000 people. **State expenditures per capita for health and hospitals (1977):** $76.27.

Education expenditures (1975-76): $516.83 per capita annually. **No. of pupils in public schools (1977 est.):** 848,000. **No. of institutions of higher learning (1976-77):** 52. **Public school expenditure per pupil in attendance (1975-76):** $2,054. **Avg. salary of public school teachers (1974-75 est.):** $13,282. **No. full-time**

teachers (1977 est.): 48,400. **Educational attainment of adult population (1976):** 12.6 median yrs. of school completed; 2.1% with less than 5 years of education; 18.6% with 4 yrs. of college.

Telephones (1976): 75 per 100 people. **State Chamber of Commerce:** Maryland State Chamber of Commerce, 60 West Street, Annapolis, Maryland 21401.

MASSACHUSETTS

Today a key New England state, Massachusetts was also one of the most important of the 13 Colonies. It was at Plymouth in 1620 that the Pilgrims landed. And the Boston Massacre (1770) and Tea Party (1773) were major, irreversible steps on the road to the American War of Independence, which began at Lexington and Concord in 1775. Statehood dates from 1788.

The topography of the state is unusually varied. The eastern third is a low coastal plain that includes the Cape Cod peninsula and the islands due south: the Elizabeth Islands, Martha's Vineyard, and Nantucket. The New England Uplands, part of a high plateau stretching from Maine to New Jersey, extend westward for roughly 50 miles. Due west of this area is the Connecticut Valley, which extends from Massachusetts to southern Connecticut; the Connecticut River flows through it, providing fine soil for farming. Farther west lies the Berkshire Valley, surrounded by the Berkshire Hills and, near the northwestern border, the Taconic Mountains.

Besides its historic sites, the state's attractions include the Museum of Fine Arts and Symphony Hall in Boston, the summer Tanglewood music festival in the Berkshires, and literary landmarks, such as the homes of Emerson, Hawthorne and Thoreau in Concord. Cape Code is a leading Eastern summer resort area, with long, sandy beaches and picturesque towns.

Norsemen including Leif Ericsson may have visited the region about A.D. 1000, but this remains more conjecture than fact. In 1602 English explorer Bartholomew Gosnold landed on Cuttyhunk Island in the Elizabeth chain and gave Cape Cod its name, and Captain John Smith explored the coast in 1614. Oddly enough, the arrival of the Pilgrims at Plymouth six years later, after a brief stop at what is now Provincetown, was purely accidental; the *Mayflower's* destination was a point south of the Hudson River, but a severe storm diverted the ship north. Because this area was beyond the bounds of the sponsoring company in London, a provisional instrument of government called the "Mayflower Compact" was drawn up. Designed to serve until more permanent institutions could be established, this covenant of the Massachusetts Bay Colony, as the settlement was called, formed the foundation of American democracy. But it was not originally a very democratic democracy, because while the Puritans insisted on religious freedom for themselves, they denied it to others, and some they banished from the colony. Roger Williams and the Reverend Thomas Hooker were exiled in 1636, and settled in Rhode Island and Connecticut respectively; they played an enormous part in the history of those states. Puritan oppression climaxed with the Salem witch trials at the end of the seventeenth century; about 20 persons accused of witchcraft were put to death.

Indian troubles began with an engagement with the Pequot Indians in 1637. In 1675-76, settlers and Wampanoag Indians, led by Metacom, who was known as King Philip, battled in "King Philip's War," which the colonists won at great expense in men and money. At various times from 1689 to

1763, the colonists fought against the French and their Indian allies, and ultimately prevailed. Soon after, they began resisting the royal tax laws, setting the stage for general revolt. In 1775 General George Washington arrived in Cambridge to assume command of the Continental Army. A year later, he routed the redcoats from Boston in the war's first major American victory. Then the scene of battle shifted to New York, New Jersey, and Pennsylvania.

The American Revolution was followed in Massachusetts by hard times. There came a business depression, and friction between the legislature and farmers, many of whom suffered foreclosures for debts and taxes; an insurrection (1786-87) led by former army captain Daniel Shays became known as Shays' Rebellion. But prosperity gradually returned, only to fade away again as Jefferson's 1807 Embargo Act, intended to keep the country from involvement in European wars, seriously hurt the state's sea-oriented economy. As it happened, the precaution was a failure: war came anyway in 1812, and Massachusetts turned to manufacturing for its principal livelihood.

Over the years, steady influxes of immigrants provided a plentiful source of labor, and workers were often exploited. Labor unions fought hard for recognition, and there were strikes, occasionally marked by violence as in the 1912 textile strike at Lawrence. Governor Calvin Coolidge gained national prominence when he broke a policemen's strike in Boston in 1919.

Today Massachusetts still ranks among the national leaders in manufacturing, as well as commercial fishing. With the passing of the once-important textile industry, electronics have become particularly important to the state's economy, as well as tourism and its many private colleges and universities.

Full name: Commonwealth of Massachusetts. **Origin of name:** From Algonquian name, Massa-dchu-es-at, meaning "Great-Hill-Small-Place." **Inhabitant:** Bay Stater. **Capital:** Boston. **State motto:** Ense Petit Placidam Sub Libertate Quietem (By the Sword We Seek Peace, but Peace Only under Liberty). **Flag:** State seal on white field is on one side; other side has green pine tree on blue field. **Seal:** Coat of arms of Commonwealth of Massachusetts; Indian points arrow downward, symbolizing peace; star over his right shoulder represents Massachusetts as a state. **Flower:** Mayflower. **Bird:** Chickadee. **Tree:** American elm. **Song:** "Hail Massachusetts." **Nickname:** Bay State.

Governor: Edward J. King. **Annual salary:** $40,000. **Term:** 4 years. **Current term expires:** Jan. 1983. **Voting requirements:** 18 yrs. old & U.S. citizen; resident of state, no durational requirement. **U.S. Congressmen:** 12. **Entered Union:** 1788 (6th state).

Location & boundaries: New England state: bounded on the north by Vermont & New Hampshire; on the east by the Atlantic Ocean; on the south by the Atlantic Ocean, Rhode Island & Connecticut; on the west by New York. **Total area:** 8,257 sq. mi. (ranks 45th). **Extreme length:** 190 mi. **Extreme breadth:** 110 mi. **Coastline:** 192 mi. **Chief rivers:** Connecticut, Merrimack, Charles, Housatonic. **Major lakes:** Assawompset Pond; Quabbin, Wachusett Reservoirs. **No. of counties:** 14.

Population (1978 est.): 5,774,000 (ranks 10th). **Pop. increase (1970-78):** 1.5%. **Places over 25,000 pop.:** 59. **Places over 100,000:** 4. **Largest cities:** Boston, Worcester, Springfield, Cambridge. **Pop. density:** 699.3 per sq. mi. (ranks 3rd). **Pop. projection 1985:** 6,209,000. **Pop. distribution:** 86.2% metropolitan; 13.8% nonmetropolitan. **White:** 96.3%. **Negro:** 3.1%. **Other:** 0.6%. **Marriage rate (1977):** 6.9 per 1,000 people. **Divorce rate:** 2.9 per 1,000 people.

State finances (1977). Revenue: $5,669,948,000. **Expenditures:** $5,520,145,000. **State Taxes:** $507.48 per capita. **State personal income tax:** Yes. **Public debt (1977):** $893.75 per capita. **Federal aid (1977):** $228.97 per capita. **Personal income (1977):** $7,262.

Sectors of the economy (% of labor force employed in 1970): Manufacturing (29%), Wholesale and retail trade (20%), Services (6%), Educational Services (9%), Construction (5%), Government (15%). **Leading products:** electrical machinery, apparel, leather items, fabricated metals, printing, food. **Agricultural products:** dairy items, poultry, greenhouse & nursery items, vegetables, tobacco. **Fishing:** haddock, flounder, scallops. **Avg. farm (1978 est.):** 126 acres. **Avg. value of farm per acre:** $1, 242.

Highway expenditures per capita (1977): $60.54. **Persons per motor vehicle:** 1.64. **Minimum age for driver's license:** 18. **Gasoline tax:** 8.5¢ per gallon. **Motor vehicle deaths:** 15.0 per 100,000 people.

Birthrate (1977): 11.8 per 1,000 people. **Infant mortality rate per 1,000 births (1977):** 11.9. **Physicians per 100,000 pop. (1976):** 245 **Dentists per 100,000 pop. (1976):** 67. **Acceptable hospital beds:** 8.3 per 1,000 people. **State expenditures per capita for health and hospitals (1977):** $66.05.

Education expenditures (1975-76): $434.26 per capita annually. **No. of pupils in public schools (1977 est.):** 1,152,000. **No. of institutions of higher learning (1976-77):** 119. **Public school expenditure per pupil in attendance (1975-76):** $2,059. **Avg. salary of public school teachers (1974-75 est.):** $12,468. **No. full-time teachers:** not available. **Educational attainment of adult population (1976):** 12.6 median yrs. of school completed; 2.4% with less than 5 years of education; 16.8% with 4 yrs. of college.

Telephones (1976): 71 per 100 people. **State Chamber of Commerce:** Massachusetts Commonwealth Chamber of Commerce, % Tri-Community Chamber of Commerce; 348 Main St., Southbridge, Massachusetts 07550

MICHIGAN

Michigan, world's largest producer of automobiles and among the most populous of the states, extends across two peninsulas and consists of two land regions: the Great Lakes Plain that makes up all of the mitten-shaped Lower Peninsula (where 90 percent of the people live) and the eastern portion of the irregularly shaped Upper Peninsula and the Superior Upland that comprise the rest. The state is touched by four of the five Great Lakes (all but Ontario) and has a longer shoreline than any other inland state.

Dividing the peninsulas and linking Lakes Michigan and Huron are the Straits of Mackinac, crossed by one of the world's longest suspension bridges. Largest among the state's approximately 500 islands is the 209-square-mile Isle Royale (a national park) in Lake Superior. Many mountains, forests, rivers, and waterfalls make the state a sportsman's paradise. The somewhat moist climate is marked by well-defined seasons.

Several Indian tribes were living in the Michigan region when the first European, Étienne Brulé of France, arrived (1618). Other Frenchmen, including Marquette, Jolliet, and La Salle, followed, and the first permanent settlement was established (1668) at Sault Sainte Marie. By 1700 there were French missions, fur-trading posts, and forts on both peninsulas; Fort Pontchartrain (founded 1701) was to become the city of Detroit. But the French were more interested in the lucrative pelt trade than in extensive development of the territory; while Mackinac Island became a busy trading center, most of the rest of the region remained sparsely settled and vulnerable to attack by the British, who gained possession in 1763. The Indians in the area, who had lived in peace with the French, detested the British and tried to drive them out, but eventually they joined with them to fight the Americans in the American Revolution and in the War of 1812.

Michigan was initially part of the old Northwest Territory and then of Indiana Territory; it was made a separate territory in 1805, with Detroit as

MICHIGAN

MILES
0 10 20 40 60 80

KILOMETERS

State Capital
County Seats

© Copyright HAMMOND INCORPORATED, Maplewood, N. J.

Longitude West of Greenwich

its capital (succeeded by Lansing in 1847). State-hood was delayed by a boundary dispute with Ohio and Southern opposition to forming another free state. Compromises broke the impasse, as Michigan's admission (1837) was offset by that of slave state Arkansas, while Ohio was given the disputed land in return for awarding to Michigan the Upper Peninsula, which had been a part of the Territory of Wisconsin.

Michigan's development as a state was rapid, and a number of important roads, rail lines, and canals were soon built—including the vital Soo Ship Canal at Sault Sainte Marie (completed 1855), which allows ships to travel between Lakes Huron and Superior; these new routes spurred the state's mining industry. In the political sphere, the Republican Party was founded in 1854 at Jackson, and abolitionist sentiment was strong throughout the state which contributed 100,000 troops to the Union cause during the Civil War.

Today Michigan is both a center of tourism and industry. Greenfield Village in Detroit's suburban Dearborn, to which Ford moved some of early America's famous landmarks, including the court-house where Abraham Lincoln practiced, attracts more than 1.6 million sightseers annually. The spectacular, colorful turning of the Upper Peninsula's forests in fall attract thousands there, and the state has many annual events aimed at attracting others. Summer resorts abound along both the inland and Great Lakes.

The United Automobile, Aerospace and Agricultural Implement Workers of America (UAW), now the nation's third largest union with over 1.5 million members, got its start in the famed "Sit-Down Strikes" of the 1930s with workers refusing to leave auto plants until their fledgling union was recognized as bargaining agent. UAW international headquarters are in Detroit.

Social reforms, including open housing, have occurred in a number of Michigan communities in recent years and the new constitution created an independent Civil Rights Commission with police powers. A state referendum in 1976 banned the use of throwaway containers for beer and soft drinks.

The state's dairy industry was hard-hit by widespread 1973 contamination of milk and dairy products by the fire retardant chemical PBB (Polybrominated Biphenyl), forcing the destruction of thousands of animals and causing extensive human illness since then.

Full name: State of Michigan. **Origin of name:** From Michigama, meaning "Great Water." **Inhabitant:** Michiganian. **Capital:** Lansing. **State motto:** Si Quaeris Peninsulam Amoenam, Circumspice (If You Seek a Pleasant Peninsula, Look Around You). **Flag:** State seal on a blue field. **Seal:** Sun rising over water & man in field appear on shield supported by an elk & a moose. **Flower:** Apple blossom. **Bird:** Robin. **Tree:** White pine. **Song:** (unofficial) "Michigan, My Michigan." **Nickname:** Wolverine State.

Governor: William G. Milliken. **Annual salary:** $61,500. **Term:** 4 years. **Current term expires:** Jan. 1983. **Voting requirements:** 18 yrs. old & U.S. citizen; registered resident of state 30 days. **U.S. Congressmen:** 19. **Entered Union:** 1837 (26th state).

Location & boundaries: Midwestern state: bounded on the north by Lake Superior, the Straits of Mackinac & Lake Huron; on the east by Lakes Huron & St. Clair, Canada & Lake Erie; on the south by Ohio & Indiana; & on the west by Wisconsin & Lake Michigan. **Total area:** 58,218 sq. mi. (ranks 23d). **Extreme length:** Upper peninsula 334 mi.; lower peninsula 286 mi. **Extreme breadth:** Upper peninsula 215 mi.; lower peninsula 200 mi. **Shoreline:** 2,232 mi. **Chief rivers:** Grand, Kalamazoo, Escanaba, Saginaw. **Major lakes (other than border-forming):** Houghton, Torch, Charlevoix, Burt. **No. of counties:** 83.

Population (1978 est.): 9,189,000 (ranks 7th). **Pop. increase (1970-78):** 3.5%. **Places over 25,000 pop.:** 45. **Places over 100,000:** 6. **Largest cities:** Detroit, Grand Rapids, Warren, Lansing. **Pop. density:** 157.8 per sq. mi. (ranks 11th). **Pop. projection 1985:** 9,546,000. **Pop. distribution:** 81.4% metropolitan; 18.6% nonmetropolitan. **White:** 88.2%. **Negro:** 11.2%. **Other:** 0.6%. **Marriage rate (1977):** 9.4 per 1,000 people. **Divorce rate:** 4.7 per 1,000 people.

State finances (1977). Revenue: $9,689,212,000. **Expenditures:** $9,070,835,000. **State Taxes:** $530.59 per capita. **State personal income tax:** Yes. **Public debt (1977):** $213.71 per capita. **Federal aid (1977):** $223.71 per capita. **Personal income (1977):** $7,606.

Sectors of the economy (% of labor force employed in 1970): Manufacturing (36%), Wholesale and retail trade (19%), Services (6%), Educational Services (8%), Construction (5%), Government (14%). **Leading products:** primary & fabricated metals, food, electrical machinery, paper. **Minerals:** iron ore, cement, sand & gravel, copper. **Agricultural products:** cattle, poultry, dairy items, corn, hay, wheat. **Fishing:** whitefish, chubs, lake herring. **Avg. farm (1978 est.):** 158 acres. **Avg. value of farm per acre:** $860.

Highway expenditures per capita (1977): $81.04. **Persons per motor vehicle:** 1.53. **Minimum age for driver's license:** 18. **Gasoline tax:** 9¢ per gallon. **Motor vehicle deaths:** 22.2 per 100,000 people.

Birthrate (1977): 15.2 per 1,000 people. **Infant mortality rate per 1,000 births (1977):** 14.1. **Physicians per 100,000 pop. (1976):** 145. **Dentists per 100,000 pop. (1976):** 50. **Acceptable hospital beds:** 5.8 per 1,000 people. **State expenditures per capita for health and hospitals (1977):** $59.59.

Education expenditures (1975-76): $526.25 per capita annually. **No. of pupils in public schools (1977 est.):** 2,006,000. **No. of institutions of higher learning (1976-77):** 94. **Public school expenditure per pupil in attendance (1975-76):** $1,902. **Avg. salary of public school teachers (1974-75 est.):** $14,224. **No. full-time teachers (1977 est.):** 99,360. **Educational attainment of adult population (1976):** 12.5 median yrs. of school completed; 1.8% with less than 5 years of education; 12.6% with 4 yrs. of college.

Telephones (1976): 72 per 100 people. **State Chamber of Commerce:** Michigan State Chamber of Commerce, 501 South Capitol Avenue, Lansing, Michigan 48933.

MINNESOTA

Home of the headwaters of the Mississippi, Minnesota is one of the most scenic states in the nation, rich in natural resources and boasting more than 15,000 lakes. Manufacturing, mainly of farm products, has in recent years become the leading industry, while improved techniques and new copper, nickel, and taconite finds signal a resurgence in mining. Tourism is today a major revenue producer for the state, which also ranks high agriculturally, with livestock and corn recently surpassing wheat—the traditional staple—in importance. Politically, Minnesota has gained a reputation for voter independence, experimentation in local government, and the institution of Scandinavian-type cooperatives.

Duluth has the nation's largest inland harbor and, since the completion of the St. Lawrence Seaway and Power Project (1959), the port has handled an increasingly significant amount of foreign trade. In Minneapolis are the central offices of the University of Minnesota, one of the largest universities in the country, while in Rochester is the famous Mayo Clinic, an international center of medical practice and research. About half of the population is centered in the "Twin Cities" of Minneapolis and St. Paul.

Minnesota's topography is marked by rolling prairies, fertile valleys, high bluffs, deep pine woods, and wilderness areas. The two main land regions are the Superior Upland (or, locally, the "arrowhead country"), consisting of a roughly triangular northeastern land segment, and the Central Lowlands, comprising the rest except, in the

MINNESOTA

MILES
KILOMETERS

State Capital ● County Seats

NORTHEASTERN MINNESOTA

Longitude West of Greenwich

south, a small projection of the Wisconsin Driftless Area and two small projections of the Dissected Till Plains. The state's continental climate has a relatively low mean temperature, and is subject to wide and often sudden fluctuation.

The timber industry, which flourished from about 1870 to the early 1900s, was vital to the state's early development, while incidentally fostering the well-known legend of Paul Bunyan and his giant ox Babe.

The first inhabitants of the Minnesota region are thought to date from about 20,000 years ago. Norsemen may have visited in the 14th century, but the first Europeans of record to do so were the French fur traders and missionaries of the 17th century, beginning with Radisson and Groseilliers (1659-61) and including La Salle, Marquette and Jolliet, and Daniel Greysolon—Sieur Du Lhut, or Duluth—who claimed (1679) the region for King Louis XIV.

Principal Indian tribes in the region at the time were the Sioux in the west and south and the Ojibwa in the heavily wooded northern section; the two groups, often at war with one another, were generally friendly to the French, who built up a vast pelt-marketing empire but ultimately lost it (1763) to the British.

Serious American development began after the War of 1812, with the powerful American Fur Company leading the way. Eastern Minnesota at this time was still part of the Northwest Territory, while the western region had been acquired (1803) as part of the Louisiana Purchase. A short-lived Spanish claim to the region (dating from 1762) was never effectively enforced. The year 1819 saw the building of Fort St. Anthony (later called Fort Snelling), and in 1832 Henry R. Schoolcraft discovered the source of the Mississippi at Lake Itasca. Six years later, Pierre Parrant settled on the site of present-day St. Paul.

In 1849 the Minnesota region—which in whole or part had been successively a portion of the French, English, and Spanish empires, the Northwest Territory, and seven U.S. territories—was made a territory in its own right. A comprehensive Indian treaty (1851) and statehood (1858) both spurred settlement, which was not deterred by a brief, ill-fated Sioux uprising in 1862.

Although not without its problems, modern Minnesota is enjoying a period of economic expansion with the building of a number of giant taconite plants.

Minneapolis boasts of the Tyrone Guthrie Theater, critically acclaimed as one of the best off-Broadway theaters in the nation. A facility for the Minnesota Orchestra was recently completed and is now in use.

The ongoing dispute between the state and Reserve Mining came closer to being resolved in 1975, when as a result of the Federal Appeals Court ruling that over a reasonable time Reserve would have to cease dumping tailings into Lake Superior and go to an on-land disposal system, the state and Reserve began work on an acceptable plan. In 1976 the Federal court ordered Reserve to shift to on-land disposal within one year. A court ruling early in 1977 gave the company the right to dump waste on its preferred site near Silver Bay.

David Durenberger (I-R), a Minneapolis lawyer, convincingly won the Senate seat opened by Hubert Humphrey's death by defeating Robert Short.

Violence broke out in mid-May 1979 on the Chippewa Indian Reservation at Red Lake because of discontent with the leadership of tribal chairman Roger Jourdain. Two youths were killed and seven buildings and 45 vehicles were destroyed by fire. Five Indians were convicted of conspiracy and assault charges in the incident.

Full name: State of Minnesota. **Origin of name:** From the Sioux meaning "Sky-Tinted Water." **Inhabitant:** Minnesotan. **Capital:** St. Paul. **State motto:** L'Etoile du Nord (The Star of the North). **Flag:** State seal & 19 gold stars on blue field. **Seal:** Indian riding into sunset, farmer plowing field, waterfall, forest. **Flower:** Pink & white lady's-slipper. **Bird:** Common loon. **Tree:** Norway pine. **Song:** "Hail Minnesota." **Nickname:** North Star State.

Governor: Albert H. Ovie. **Annual salary:** $62,000. **Term:** 4 yrs. **Current term expires:** Jan. 1983. **Voting requirements:** 18 yrs. old & U.S. citizen; state resident 20 days. **U.S. Congressmen:** 8. **Entered Union:** 1858 (32nd state).

Location & boundaries: Northern Midwestern state; bounded on the north by Canada; on the east by Lake Superior, Wisconsin & the Mississippi River; on the south by Iowa; & on the west by South Dakota, North Dakota & Red River of the North. **Total area:** 84,068 sq. mi. (ranks 12th). **Extreme length:** 406 mi. **Extreme breadth:** 358 mi. **Coastline:** 180 mi. **Chief rivers:** Mississippi, Red River of the North, Minnesota. **Major lakes:** Superior, Red, Lake of the Woods. **No. of counties:** 87.

Population (1978 est.): 4,008,000 (ranks 19th). **Pop. increase (1970-78):** 5.3%. **Places over 25,000 pop.:** 21. **Places over 100,000:** 2. **Largest cities:** Minneapolis, St. Paul, Duluth, Rochester. **Pop. density:** 47.7 per sq. mi. (ranks 33rd). **Pop. projection 1985:** 4,179,000. **Pop. distribution:** 64.4% metropolitan; 35.6% nonmetropolitan. **White:** 98.2%. **Negro:** 0.9%. **Other:** 0.9%. **Marriage rate (1977):** 7.9 per 1,000 people. **Divorce rate:** 3.5 per 1,000 people.

State finances (1977). Revenue: $4,385,035,000. **Expenditures:** $4,157,681,000. **State Taxes:** $625.30 per capita. **State personal income tax:** Yes. **Public debt (1977):** $311.11 per capita. **Federal aid (1977):** $229.49 per capita. **Personal income (1977):** $7,118.

Sectors of the economy (% of labor force employed in 1970): Manufacturing (21%), Wholesale and retail trade (22%), Services (7%), Educational Services (9%), Construction (6%), Government (15%). **Leading products:** food; electrical & other machinery; printing & publishing; paper items; chemicals; stone, clay & glass items. **Minerals:** iron ore, taconite, sand & gravel, cement, stone. **Agricultural products:** cattle, hogs, dairy items, corn, soybeans. **Fishing:** yellow pike, lake herring, tullibee. **Avg. farm (1978 est.):** 268 acres. **Avg. value of farm per acre:** $730.

Highway expenditures per capita (1977): $96.28. **Persons per motor vehicle:** 1.41. **Minimum age for driver's license:** 18. **Gasoline tax:** 9¢ per gallon. **Motor vehicle deaths:** 24.0 per 100,000 people.

Birthrate (1977): 15.2 per 1,000 people. **Infant mortality rate per 1,000 births (1977):** 11.1. **Physicians per 100,000 pop. (1976):** 177. **Dentists per 100,000 pop. (1976):** 59. **Acceptable hospital beds:** 7.9 per 1,000 people. **State expenditures per capita for health and hospitals (1977):** $56.60.

Education expenditures (1975-76): $549.00 per capita annually. **No. of pupils in public schools (1977 est.):** 850,000. **No. of institutions of higher learning (1976-77):** 65. **Public school expenditure per pupil in attendance (1975-76):** $1,911. **Avg. salary of public school teachers (1974-75 est.):** $12,852. **No. full-time teachers (1977 est.):** 50,950. **Educational attainment of adult population (1970):** 12.5 median yrs. of school completed; 1.1% with less than 5 years of education; 13.2% with 4 yrs. of college.

Telephones (1976): 72 per 100 people. **State Chamber of Commerce:** Minnesota Association of Commerce and Industry, 200 Hanover Bldg., 480 Cedar Street, St. Paul, Minnesota 55101.

MISSISSIPPI

Without renouncing the history that has been both its pride and its handicap, this Deep South state has begun to rework its economic and social structures after a period of transition that began during the Great Depression.

In 1936, wealthy lumberman Hugh White became governor and instituted a "Balance Agriculture with Industry" (BAWI) program which al-

MISSISSIPPI

MILES

State Capitals ⊛

County Seats ⊙

© Copyright HAMMOND INCORPORATED, Maplewood, N.J.

lowed cities to issue bonds and build plants for private industry. By 1965, industrial employment had inched ahead of agricultural employment.

Tourists from outside the state enrich Mississippi's economy by over $400 million yearly as they flock to the beaches of the Gulf Coast winter resort area and other attractions.

The petroleum industry has become a major factor since the discovery of oil in the Tinsley field in 1939. Mississippi is a leading producer of oil and natural gas in the U.S.

Topographically, the state is made up of two main land regions: the flat and fertile Delta area along the Mississippi River in northwest Mississippi and the rolling hills which cover most other areas, though broken by occasional river valleys. The Bay of St. Louis and Biloxi or Back Bay break the coastline and a chain of small islands lie offshore.

Mississippi was inhabited by the Choctaw, Chickasaw, Natchez and Yazoo Indians before Hernando DeSoto explored it for Spain in 1540. French explorers La Salle, Iberville and Bienville came later.

The French ceded Mississippi to the British under the treaty of Paris in 1763 but the Spanish claimed it along with West Florida in 1781. Spanish influence virtually ended in 1798 when Mississippi flew the United States flag as a territory of the new republic.

The early settlement of the state was handicapped by conflicting land claims, Indian troubles and the Yazoo Land Fraud in which Georgia, claiming the region, sold lots to speculators. Georgia finally ceded its claim to the Federal Government in 1802 and the Louisiana Purchase in 1803 insured free access to the Mississippi River. The state was cut out of the territory and admitted to the union in 1817.

By the time the Civil War began, Mississippi was among the wealthiest states in the nation. Property assessments totaled $509 million in 1860. By 1880 property assessments had fallen to 110 million. Not until 1920 did assessments reach the pre-Civil War level.

Blacks did not vote in numbers until the civil rights movement of the 1960s cleared registration of literacy requirements and the segregated social structures which had grown up in the interim.

The attacks on segregation brought turbulence. Two persons were killed in rioting at the University of Mississippi; NAACP leader Medgar Evers was shot to death in ambush at his Jackson home in 1963; and three civil rights workers were killed in 1964 near Philadelphia, Miss. However, the state joined the FBI in a massive crackdown on the Ku Klux Klan group behind much of the trouble, and tensions then eased.

Massive public school desegregation came later and Mississippi experienced less trouble than Northern and Eastern states under similar orders. Mississippi experienced some campus unrest as the 1960s closed and two persons were shot to death in a riot at Jackson State College in 1970.

In recent years blacks have made important gains, with an improvement in job opportunities and an increase in numbers elected to public office.

Mississippi's recent bid for trade with Middle Eastern and South American countries has paid off in millions of dollars of sales of such products as farm machinery, food products, soybeans and cotton.

The Tennessee-Tombigbee Waterway project, one of a number of such measures cancelled by President Carter as an economy move, was reinstated after Congressional pressure was brought to bear.

The project, estimated to cost $1.8 billion, is expected to be a shot in the arm for Mississippi's economy.

In April 1979, the Pearl River at Jackson crested at 43.2 feet, leaving more than 17,000 homeless, eight dead, and damage estimated around $500 million. Much of the state was declared a disaster area.

Full name: State of Mississippi. **Origin of name:** From the Indian, Maesi, meaning "Large," & Sipu, meaning "River." **Inhabitant:** Mississippian. **Capital:** Jackson. **State motto:** Virtute et Armis (By Valor & Arms). **Flag:** Horizontal red, white & blue bars with Confederate battle flag in upper left. **Seal:** American eagle holds olive branch, representing peace, & three arrows, symbolizing war. **Flower:** Magnolia. **Bird:** Mockingbird. **Tree:** Magnolia. **Song:** "Go Mis-sis-sip-pi." **Nickname:** Magnolia State.

Governor: Cliff Finch. **Annual salary:** $43,000. **Term:** 4 years. **Current term expires:** Jan. 1980. **Voting requirements:** 18 yrs. old & U.S. citizen; resident of state 1 yr.; county, 1 yr.; precinct 6 mos. **U.S. Congressmen:** 5. **Entered Union:** 1817 (20th state).

Location & boundaries: Southeastern state bounded on the north by Tennessee; on the east by Alabama; on the south by the Gulf of Mexico & Louisiana; & on the west by the Mississippi River, Louisiana & Arkansas. **Total area:** 47,716 sq. mi. (ranks 32nd). **Extreme length:** 352 mi. **Extreme breadth:** 188 mi. **Coastline:** 44 mi. **Chief rivers:** Mississippi, Yazoo, Pearl, Big Black. **Major lakes:** Grenada, Barnett, Sardis, Enid, Okatibbee Reservoirs. **No. of counties:** 82.

Population (1978 est.): 2,404,000 (ranks 30th). **Pop. increase (1970-78):** 8.4%. **Places over 25,000 pop.:** 8. **Places over 100,000:** 1. **Largest cities:** Jackson, Biloxi, Meridian. **Pop. density:** 50.4 per sq. mi. (ranks 31st). **Pop. projection 1985:** 2,521,000. **Pop. distribution:** 26.5% metropolitan; 73.5% nonmetropolitan. **White:** 62.8%. **Negro:** 36.8%. **Other:** 0.4%. **Marriage rate (1977):** 11.1 per 1,000 people. **Divorce rate:** 5.3 per 1,000 people.

State finances (1977). Revenue: $2,030,629,000. **Expenditures:** $1,922,027,000. **State Taxes:** $405.71 per capita. **State personal income tax:** Yes. **Public debt (1977):** $339.93 per capita. **Federal aid (1977):** $242.29 per capita. **Personal income (1977):** $5,027.

Sectors of the economy (% of labor force employed in 1970): Manufacturing (26%), Wholesale and retail trade (18%), Services (7%), Educational Services (9%), Construction (8%), Government (18%). **Leading products:** food, lumber & wood, apparel, chemicals, transportation equipment. **Minerals:** petroleum, natural gas, sand & gravel. **Agricultural products:** cattle, broilers, eggs, cotton lint, soybeans, cottonseed. **Fishing:** menhaden, shrimp, oysters. **Avg. farm (1978 est.):** 208 acres. **Avg. value of farm per acre:** $464.

Highway expenditures per capita (1977): $119.38. **Persons per motor vehicle:** 1.60. **Minimum age for driver's license:** 15. **Gasoline tax:** 9¢ per gallon. **Motor vehicle deaths:** 32.6 per 100,000 people.

Birthrate (1977): 19.0 per 1,000 people. **Infant mortality rate per 1,000 births (1977):** 18.2. **Physicians per 100,000 pop. (1976):** 102. **Dentists per 100,000 pop. (1976):** 30. **Acceptable hospital beds:** 7.3 per 1,000 people. **State expenditures per capita for health and hospitals (1977):** $45.56.

Education expenditures (1975-76): $363.00 per capita annually. **No. of pupils in public schools (1977 est.):** 503,000. **No. of institutions of higher learning (1976-77):** 45. **Public expenditure per pupil in attendance (1975-76):** $1,072. **Avg. salary of public school teachers (1974-75 est.):** $8,338. **No. full-time teachers (1977 est.):** 27,510. **Educational attainment of adult population (1976):** 12.1 median yrs. of school completed; 7.9% with less than 5 years of education; 11.5% with 4 yrs. of college.

Telephones (1976): 56 per 100 people. **State Chamber of Commerce:** Mississippi Economic Council, Standard Life Building, P.O. Box 1849, Jackson, Mississippi 39205.

MISSOURI

Traditional "Gateway to the West," centrally located Missouri owes much of its industrial and

MISSOURI

agricultural importance to the nation's two largest rivers—the Mississippi and Missouri—which form part of the state's borders while facilitating transportation and enriching its soil. Lead mining, in which the state ranks first nationally, has been important in the region for 200 years, being conducted chiefly in the Viburnum and Bixby areas. Most of the state's manufacturing activity is concentrated in and around St. Louis and Kansas City.

The state is made up of four principal land regions: the Dissected Till Plains, lying north of the Missouri; the Osage Plains in the west; the West Gulf Coastal Plain (known locally as the Mississippi Alluvial Plain), covering the southeastern corner; and the Ozark Plateau, making up most of the southern section and constituting the largest single region. The Dissected Till and Osage Plains are considered subdivisions of the Central Lowlands. Ten major artificial lakes formed by dams in the Ozark region have helped make that area a popular vacationland, contributing greatly to the state's nearly $1 billion annual tourism business. Although two-thirds of the state was once covered by forests, today only about half that amount remains, including Mark Twain and Clark National forests.

The Mound Builders, the earliest known inhabitants of the Missouri region, predated the Osage and Missouri Indians, who were living there when the first European explorers—Frenchmen Marquette and Joliet—visited (1673). France's claim to the entire Mississippi Valley, including what is now Missouri, was based on La Salle's travels in 1682. In the following years, French fur trading posts were established along the river, and the working of the lead mines was begun. Established about 1735, Ste. Genevieve was the first permanent white settlement.

Having met defeat in the French and Indian Wars, France secretly yielded (1762) to Spain all its territory west of the Mississippi; even so, Frenchmen Laclede and Chouteau founded St. Louis two years later. Napoleon regained (1800) possession of the region for France, then sold it three years later as part of the Louisiana Purchase. A year later, in 1804, President Thomas Jefferson sent Meriwether Lewis and William Clark westward up the Missouri River on the famous expedition that tied the United States together as a continental nation. The area was briefly a district of the Territory of Indiana, but was made a separate territory in 1805, comprising at that time all U.S. land west of the Mississippi and north of 33° north latitude and therefore including the future state of Missouri.

The question of admitting Missouri to the Union became bound up, in Congress, with the volatile slavery issue. Bitter controversy was arduously resolved by the Missouri Compromise (1820), which provided for the admission of Missouri (1821) as a slave state and Maine as a free one, while banning slavery in all future states north of Missouri's southern border. Missouri was at this time the nation's western frontier, and fur trading was still its foremost economic pursuit. The state's six northwestern counties were added by the Platte Purchase (1837). An unusual boundary dispute between Missouri and Illinois, involving the latter's first capital, was settled early in 1970, giving Illinois the site of Old Kaskaskia, the state's original capital, now an island as a result of shifts by the Mississippi River. Illinois would receive Kaskaskia and Beaver islands, and Missouri, Cottonwoods and Roth islands.

The years preceding the Civil War were marked by growing prosperity in an increasingly tense political climate. The settlement of Independence became the starting point of the much-traveled Santa Fe and Oregon Trails, while St. Louis continued its growth as a thriving inland port. St. Joseph was the eastern starting point of the briefly active (1860-61) Pony Express. But bitter Missouri-Kansas border wars over the slavery issue had begun, and although Missouri voted (February 1861) not to secede from the Union, Missourians were sharply divided in their allegiances, supplying both sides with troops.

Missouri today seeks to attract new industry by stressing its central location, good transportation facilities, availability of labor, and relatively low taxes. The state's biggest private employer is the General Dynamics Corporation, followed by McDonnell-Douglas. Missouri is also second in the nation in automobile assembly. Tourism has emerged in recent years as one of Missouri's leading businesses.

Full name: State of Missouri. **Origin of name:** From name of Sioux tribe. **Inhabitant:** Missourian. **Capital:** Jefferson City. **State motto:** Salus Populi Suprema Lex Esto (Let the Welfare of the People Be the Supreme Law). **Flag:** State seal centered on horizontal red, white & blue bars. **Seal:** Two grizzly bears hold shields of United States & Missouri; 24 stars represent Missouri's entrance into Union. **Flower:** Hawthorn. **Bird:** Bluebird. **Tree:** Flowering dogwood. **Song:** "Missouri Waltz." **Nickname:** Show-Me State.

Governor: Joseph P. Teasdale. **Annual salary:** $37,500. **Term:** 4 years. **Current term expires:** Jan. 1981. **Voting requirements:** 18 yrs. old & U.S. citizen. **U.S. Congressmen:** 10. **Entered Union:** 1821 (24th state).

Location & boundaries: Southern Midwestern state: bounded on the north by Iowa; on the east by Illinois, Kentucky, Tennessee & the Mississippi River; on the south by Arkansas; & on the west by Oklahoma, Kansas, Nebraska & the Missouri River. **Total area:** 69,686 sq. mi. (ranks 19th). **Extreme length:** 284 mi. **Extreme breadth:** 308 mi. **Chief rivers:** Missouri, Mississippi, Osage. **Major lakes:** Lake of the Ozarks; Stockton, Taneycomo, Clearwater, and Wappapello lakes; Table Rock & Pomme de Terre Reservoirs. **No.of counties:** 114 & the city of St. Louis.

Population (1978 est.): 4,860,000 (ranks 15th). **Pop. increase (1970-78):** 3.9%. **Places over 25,000 pop.:** 16. **Places over 100,000:** 3. **Largest cities:** St. Louis, Kansas City, Springfield, Independence. **Pop. density:** 69.7 per sq. mi. (ranks 27th). **Pop. projection 1985:** 4,985,000. **Pop. distribution:** 63.5% metropolitan; 36.5% nonmetropolitan. **White:** 89.3%. **Negro:** 10.3%. **Other:** 0.4%. **Marriage rate (1977):** 10.9 per 1,000. people. **Divorce rate:** 5.3 per 1,000 people.

State finances (1977). Revenue: $3,099,660,000. **Expenditures:** $2,790,077,000. **State Taxes:** $332.87 per capita. **State personal income tax:** Yes. **Public debt (1977):** $91.73 per capita. **Federal aid (1977):** $164.35 per capita. **Personal income (1977):** $6,661.

Sectors of the economy (% of labor force employed in 1970): Manufacturing (24%), Wholesale and retail trade (22%), Services (7%), Educational Services (8%), Construction (6%), Government (15%). **Leading products:** transportation equipment, food, chemicals, printing & publishing, machinery, fabricated metals. **Minerals:** stone, cement, lead, iron ore. **Agricultural products:** cattle, hogs, dairy items, corn, soybeans, hay. **Avg. farm (1978 est.):** 245 acres. **Avg. value of farm per acre:** $602.

Highway expenditures per capita (1977): $82.82. **Persons per motor vehicle:** 1.57. **Minimum age for driver's license:** 16. **Gasoline tax:** 7¢ per gallon. **Motor vehicle deaths:** 24.5 per 100,000 people.

Birthrate (1977): 15.2 per 1,000 people. **Infant mortality rate per 1,000 births (1977):** 14.2. **Physicians per 100,000 pop. (1976):** 155. **Dentists per 100,000 pop. (1976):** 45. **Acceptable hospital beds:** 7.3 per 1,000 people. **State expenditures per capita for health and hospitals (1976):** $43.44.

Education expenditures (1975-76): $368.55 per capita annually. **No. of pupils in public schools (1977 est.):** 936,000. **No. of institutions of higher learning (1976-77):** 83. **Public school expenditure per pupil in attendance (1975-76):** $1,389. **Avg. salary of public school teachers (1974-75 est.):** $10,257. **No. full-time**

teachers (1977 est.): 53,210. Educational attainment of adult population (1976): 12.4 median yrs. of school completed; 2.5% with less than 5 years of education; 11.8% with 4 yrs. of college.

Telephones (1976): 71 per 100 people. State Chamber of Commerce: Missouri Chamber of Commerce, P.O. Box 149, Jefferson City, Missouri 65101.

MONTANA

As its Spanish name suggests, Montana is a mountainous region: the Rocky Mountains cover the western two-fifths of the state and the high, gently rolling Great Plains make up the rest. The state is large, ranking fourth nationally in area, but it is sparsely populated. The Rockies' Bitterroot Range, marking the Montana-Idaho boundary, is one of the most rugged and remote areas in the country. Many of the state's mountains are thick with forests below the timber line; fir, pine, and spruce abound. The state produces about three million Christmas trees a year.

Montana's climate is generally cool to cold, and dry. Tourists—mainly hunters, fishermen, and dude ranch patrons—have been coming to the state in growing numbers, attracted by plentiful fish and game and the varied scenery. As an industry, tourism has become increasingly vital in recent years. Attractions include Glacier National Park, 11 national forests, the Lewis and Clark Cavern (one of the country's largest), and a number of annual rodeos and Indian ceremonials. Yellowstone National Park, most of which is in Wyoming, has three entrances in Montana.

Arapaho, Blackfoot, Cheyenne, Crow, Atsina, Bannock, Kalispel, Kutenai, and Shoshoni Indians were living in the region before the arrival of the first Europeans, who were probably fur trappers of the Hudson Bay Company or the Northwest Company. In 1805, Lewis and Clark explored the area on their journeys to and from the Pacific Coast. The American Fur Company, in 1829 and 1846, built two of Montana's earliest settlements, Forts Union and Benton.

The major Indian wars (1867-77) included the famous 1876 Battle of Little Bighorn, popularly known as "Custer's Last Stand," in which Cheyennes and Sioux killed General Custer and more than 200 of his men. But the Indians' moment of glory was something of a brief one, for in 1877, when Chief Joseph and his Nez Percé warriors surrendered to federal troops near the Canadian border, Indian resistance in Montana virtually ended. Today, the state has some 30,000 Indians, almost all of whom live on seven reservations.

The United States obtained most of Montana as part of the Louisiana Purchase (1803). The remaining northwestern section passed into U.S. hands following the 1846 treaty with England. Montana was originally part of the Territory of Idaho, created in 1863; Montana Territory came into being in 1864. Statehood came in 1889.

Much of Montana's early history was bound up with mining, which is still a leading industry: oil, coal, copper, and sand and gravel are important products. The capital of Helena was originally a mining camp called Last Chance Gulch. The Anaconda Company branched out from Butte ("the richest hill on earth") to become a giant conglomerate of its day, with interests in railroading, journalism, banking, and other fields.

Another of Montana's major occupations, ranching, came into its own in 1866 when a cattleman by the name of Nelson Story drove his herd of a thousand longhorn from Texas to Montana, setting an example that many others soon followed. The com-

ing of the railroad in 1883 was another impetus. But the severe winter of 1886-87 spelled disaster; thousands of cattle perished in subzero blizzards. Although the industry eventually recovered, for a long time profit margins were narrow. Ranching is economically important: the state has over three times as many cattle (including calves) and about as many sheep as it has people.

Montana today is attempting to attract new industry while preserving clean air and water. The aims have touched off a clash between environmentalists and the energy companies which are developing reserves of strippable coal. Early in 1977, coal leases on the Crow Indian Reservation were revoked by the Federal Government in a dispute over recompense for the strip mining venture, which had never become an actuality.

Full name: State of Montana. Origin of name: From Spanish word meaning "Mountainous." Inhabitant: Montanan. Capital: Helena. State motto: Oro y Plata (Gold & Silver). Flag: State seal on blue field. Seal: A plow, pick & shovel rest on soil, symbolizing Montana's agricultural & mineral industries; Great Falls of Missouri River & mountain scenery. Flower: Bitterroot. Bird: Western meadowlark. Tree: Ponderosa pine. Song: "Montana." Nicknames: Treasure State; the Big Sky Country; Land of the Shining Mountains.

Governor: Thomas L. Judge. Annual salary: $35,000. Term: 4 years. Current term expires: Jan. 1981. Voting requirements: 18 yrs. old & U.S. citizen; resident of state & county 30 days. U.S. Congressmen: 2. Entered Union: 1889 (41st state).

Location & boundaries: Rocky Mountain state: bounded on the north by Canada; on the east by North Dakota & South Dakota; on the south by Wyoming & Idaho; & on the west by Idaho. Total area: 147,138 sq. mi. (ranks 4th). Extreme length: 570 mi. Extreme breadth: 315 mi. Chief rivers: Missouri, Yellowstone, Kootenai. Major lakes: Flathead; Fort Peck & Canyon Ferry Reservoirs. No. of counties: 56.

Population (1978 est.): 785,000 (ranks 43rd). Pop. increase (1970-78): 13.1%. Places over 25,000 pop.: 4. Places over 100,000: None. Largest cities: Billings, Great Falls, Missoula. Pop. density: 5.3 per sq. mi. (ranks 48th). Pop. projection 1985: 843,000. Pop. distribution: 24.4% metropolitan; 75.6% nonmetropolitan. White: 95.5%. Negro: 0.3%. Other: 4.2%. Marriage rate (1977): 9.9 per 1,000 people. Divorce rate: 6.2 per 1,000 people.

State finances (1977). Revenue: $850,823,000. Expenditures: $783,421,000. State Taxes: $410.51 per capita. State personal income tax: Yes. Public debt (1977): $133.24 per capita. Federal aid (1977): $349.12 per capita. Personal income (1977): $6,093.

Sectors of the economy (% of labor force employed in 1970): Manufacturing (10%), Wholesale and retail trade (22%), Services (7%), Educational Services (10%), Construction (6%), Government (21%). Leading products: lumber & wood; primary metals; food; petroleum & coal items; printing & publishing; stone, clay & glass items; chemicals. Minerals: copper, petroleum, lead & zinc, sand & gravel, phosphate rock, silver, gold. Agricultural products: cattle, dairy items, sheep, wheat, hay, barley, flax seed, sugar beets. Avg. farm (1978 est.): 2,712 acres. Avg. value of farm per acre: $168.

Highway expenditures per capita (1977): $212.08. Persons per motor vehicle: 1.05. Minimum age for driver's license: 16. Gasoline tax: 8¢ per gallon. Motor vehicle deaths: 34.5 per 100,000 people.

Birthrate (1977): 17.5 per 1,000 people. Infant mortality rate per 1,000 births (1977): 13.7. Physicians per 100,000 pop. (1976): 126. Dentists per 100,000 pop. (1976): 55. Acceptable hospital beds: 5.8 per 1,000 people. State expenditures per capita for health and hospitals (1977): $48.99.

Education expenditures (1975-76): $540.40 per capita annually. No. of pupils in public schools (1977 est.): 168,000. No. of institutions of higher learning (1976-77): 12. Public school expenditure per pupil in attendance (1975-76): $1,745. Avg. salary of public school teachers (1974-75 est.): $10,160. No. full-time teachers (1977 est.): 10,110. Educational attainment of adult

MONTANA

population (1976): 12.6 median yrs. of school completed; 1.2% with less than 5 years of education; 14.2% with 4 yrs. of college.

Telephones (1976): 67 per 100 people. **State Chamber of Commerce:** Montana Chamber of Commerce, Box 1730, 110 Neill Ave., Helena, Montana 59601.

NEBRASKA

Nebraska is rich with grass (more forage varieties grow here than anywhere else in the United States) and grain; agriculture is its mainstay. The grassy Sand Hills make up the state's central region, and rolling farmland, found in the east, rises gradually from 840 feet above sea level to 5,300 feet in the western High Plains region. A portion of the South Dakota Badlands takes up about 1,000 square miles of the northwest corner of the state. The climate of Nebraska is one of extremes: severe winters and sweltering summers.

Nebraska annually harvests large crops of corn, sorghum, oats, wheat, rye, soybeans, alfalfa and dry edible beans. Omaha, with its surrounding area, forms the nation's largest meat-packing center, and it is the second-largest cattle market of both the United States and the world.

The state's numerous rivers and lakes are vitally important to its agricultural and allied processing industries. Many conservation practices, such as dam construction, systematic tree-planting, and irrigation, are widely employed to keep the land productive. Larger farms, more modern equipment, and improved farming techniques have resulted in vastly increased production even with a smaller farm population.

Judging by stone tool and weapon remnants that have been unearthed, the first inhabitants of Nebraska existed between 10,000 and 25,000 years ago. In the early 1700s, Spanish and French explorers found, among others, the Omaha and Oto Indians living peacefully along the region's rivers. The buffalo-hunting Pawnee, however, battled other tribes—especially the Sioux—but were generally friendly to whites. The Sioux, Arapaho, and Cheyenne Indians constituted the white settlers' principal resistance, waging a losing battle to keep their hunting grounds.

The United States gained possession of the area with the Louisiana Purchase (1803). Pioneers going west along the Oregon Trail, which followed the Platte Valley, stimulated trading and settlement; many early Nebraskans earned a living supplying food, lodging, and fresh mounts. Statehood came in 1867.

Early times were very hard for settlers. There was bitter, protracted conflict between them and the cattlemen, who wanted the land for their herds. (This struggle was not fully resolved until the 1904 Kinkaid Act gave over the last of the state's open range land to the homesteaders.) And there were harsh blows from nature: blizzards, locust infestations, and droughts.

World War I brought prosperity, but hard times returned: depression and drought hit the state simultaneously. Overextended farmers faced foreclosure. Widespread violence was averted by the enactment of a series of farm mortgage moratorium acts; New Deal legislation also helped. In 1937, the Nebraska legislature was reorganized into a "one house" (unicameral) system, under which state senators are elected on a nonpartisan basis. No party designations appear on the ballot.

Border disputes with Iowa have plagued Nebraska ever since the Missouri River was made the dividing line (1867). Through the years, the river's shifting has transferred parcels of land from one state to the other, giving rise to a number of conflicts among those in the areas affected.

Full name: State of Nebraska. **Origin of name:** From Omaha Indian name for the Platte River. **Inhabitant:** Nebraskan. **Capital:** Lincoln. **State motto:** Equality before the Law. **Flag:** State seal on blue field. **Seal:** Blacksmith represents mechanical arts; settler's cabin, growing corn & shocks of grain stand for agriculture; steamboat & train symbolize transportation. **Flower:** Goldenrod. **Bird:** Western meadowlark. **Tree:** American elm. **Song:** "Beautiful Nebraska." **Nickname:** Cornhusker State.

Governor: Charles Thone. **Annual salary:** $40,000. **Term:** 4 years. **Current term expires:** Jan. 1983. **Voting requirements:** 18 yrs. old & U.S. citizen; no residency requirements. **U.S. Congressmen:** 3. **Entered Union:** 1867 (37th state).

Location & boundaries: Midwestern state: bounded on the north by South Dakota; on the east by Iowa, the Missouri River & Missouri; on the south by Kansas; on the southwest by Colorado; & on the west by Wyoming. **Total area:** 77,227 sq. mi. (ranks 15th). **Extreme length:** 415 mi. **Extreme breadth:** 205 mi. **Chief rivers:** Missouri, North Platte, South Platte. **Major lakes:** Lewis & Clark, McConaughy. **No. of counties:** 93.

Population (1978 est.): 1,565,000 (ranks 35th). **Pop. increase (1970-78):** 5.5%. **Places over 25,000 pop.:** 3. **Places over 100,000:** 2. **Largest cities:** Omaha, Lincoln, Grand Island. **Pop. density:** 20.3 per sq. mi. (ranks 41st). **Pop. projection 1985:** 1,665,000. **Pop. distribution:** 44.7% metropolitan; 55.3% nonmetropolitan. **White:** 96.6%. **Negro:** 2.7%. **Other:** 0.7%. **Marriage rate (1977):** 8.3 per 1,000 people. **Divorce rate:** 3.9 per 1,000 people.

State finances (1977). Revenue: $1,119,368,000. **Expenditures:** $1,042,162,000. **State Taxes:** $392.64 per capita. **State personal income tax:** Yes. **Public debt (1977):** $37.99 per capita. **Federal aid (1977):** $175.13 per capita. **Personal income (1977):** $6,679.

Sectors of the economy (% of labor force employed in 1970): Manufacturing (14%), Wholesale and retail trade (22%), Services (7%), Educational Services (9%), Construction (6%), Government (16%). **Leading products:** food, electrical & other machinery, chemicals, fabricated metal items, printing & publishing, primary metals, transportation equipment. **Agricultural products:**cattle, hogs, dairy items, corn, hay, wheat, sorghums. **Avg. farm (1978 est.):** 706 acres. **Avg. value of farm per acre:** $385.

Highway expenditures per capita (1977): $125.10. **Persons per motor vehicle:** 1.29. **Minimum age for driver's license:** 16. **Gasoline tax:** 9.5¢ per gallon. **Motor vehicle deaths:** 22.3 per 100,000 people.

Birthrate (1977): 16.1 per 1,000 people. **Infant mortality rate per 1,000 births (1977):** 12.7. **Physicians per 100,000 pop. (1976):** 138. **Dentists per 100,000 pop. (1976):** 55. **Acceptable hospital beds:** 7.3 per 1,000 people. **State expenditures per capita for health and hospitals (1977):** $57.02.

Education expenditures (1975-76): $435.53 per capita annually. **No. of pupils in public schools (1977 est.):** 307,000. **No. of institutions of higher learning (1976-77):** 29. **Public school expenditure per pupil in attendance (1975-76):** $1,477. **Avg. salary of public school teachers (1974-75 est.):** $9,715. **No. full-time teachers (1977 est.):** 20,040. **Educational attainment of adult population (1976):** 12.5 median yrs. of school completed; 1.0% with less than 5 years of education; 12.8% with 4 yrs. of college.

Telephones (1976): 74 per 100 people. **State Chamber of Commerce:** Nebraska Association of Commerce & Industry, P.O. Box 81556, 424 Terminal Bldg., Lincoln, Nebraska 68501.

NEVADA

Except for its northeast and southeast corners, Nevada lies entirely within the Great Basin, a broad plateau averaging 5,500 feet in elevation and broken by mountain ranges. The Sierra Nevadas on the California border interrupt moisture-carrying clouds from the Pacific, making Nevada the driest state in the country; its average annual rainfall is only 3.73 inches. Much of the state is uninhabited, sagebrush-covered desert dotted by alkali sinks in

NEBRASKA

which rivers have dried up. Only three states have fewer inhabitants than Nevada, which in 1970 had but 4.5 persons per square mile.

Nevada's minimal agriculture depends largely on irrigation. Most crops go for livestock feed. Leading income sources have been, first, tourism, then mining—followed by a modest mineral and metals processing industry. In the Reno area, warehousing, aided by a free port law, is growing substantially. Thanks mainly to legalized gambling and lenient divorce laws, tourism today accounts for billions of dollars in revenue. The Las Vegas and Reno metropolitan areas, where nearly four of every five Nevadans live, are the principal tourist attractions. Others include Lake Tahoe on the California-Nevada border and Death Valley National Monument.

Indians are thought to have inhabited the Nevada region between 10,000 and 20,000 years ago. In more recent times, the Shoshoni, Washoe, Northern Paiute, and other tribes lived there.

In 1775 a Spanish missionary named Francisco Garcés passed through what is now Nevada on his way to the West Coast. In the early 1800s, trappers searched the area for new fur sources. John C. Frémont and Kit Carson explored (1843-45) the Great Basin and Sierra Nevada.

The United States obtained (1848) the region, following the Mexican War, and the first permanent settlement (1851) was a Mormon trading post called Mormon Station (now Genoa). Amid the conflicting pressures of the Civil War, Nevada was made a state (1864), although the territory did not meet the population requirement. But her loyalty to the Union—and her mineral wealth—were of vital importance, and so an exception was made.

In 1859 the discovery of the Comstock (silver and gold) Lode, near what became Virginia City, brought an influx of both settlers and adventurers. During the next 20 years, the lode yielded more than $300 million of mineral wealth, which had great impact on the country. Besides helping the North in the war, it was the basis of many American fortunes, built railroads and newspapers, laid ocean cables, and lifted California from a depression. Recently, the U.S. Interior Department's Geological Survey detected remnants of treasure in the lode, and indicated that modern mining techniques might be used to extract lower-grade ore deposits of mercury, tin, and platinum, as well as gold and silver. Today copper is the major ore mined with plants at McGill (Kennecott) and Yerington (Anaconda).

The Federal Government, which owns 87 percent of the land in Nevada, has sponsored many projects there. The Newlands Irrigation Project (completed 1907) along the Carson and Truckee Rivers was the country's first federal irrigation project; it supplies a region in west-central Nevada. The Southern Nevada Project, completed in 1971, transports water from Colorado Basin reservoirs to the southwestern cities.

Since the early 1950s, some of the state, including Yucca Flats near Las Vegas, has been used by the AEC to test nuclear devices; in the process, some questions have been raised about the damaging side effects of the tests.

Recently an admission was made that a neutron bomb had been exploded at the Nevada Test Site.

In the 1970s, Nevada has become increasingly image-conscious and has tried to promote its tourism industry outside the state. Gaming, scenic and recreational offerings have been the subject of numerous promotional efforts. Skiing, concentrated in the Sierra near Reno and Lake Tahoe, attracted hundreds of thousands. The state's desert areas,

dotted with century-old ghost towns, are attracting renewed interest.

Full name: State of Nevada. **Origin of name:** From Spanish for "Snow-Clad." **Inhabitant:** Nevadan. **Capital:** Carson City. **State motto:** All for Our Country. **Flag:** Blue field with gold & green insignia in upper left; words "Battle Born" recall that Nevada gained statehood during Civil War. **Seal:** Plow & sheaf of wheat represent Nevada's agricultural resources; quartz mill, mine tunnel & carload of ore symbolize mineral wealth of state; 36 stars. **Flower:** Sagebrush. **Animal:** Nelson bighorn sheep. **Bird:** Mountain bluebird. **Tree:** Single-leaf piñon. **Song:** "Home Means Nevada." **Nickname:** Silver State.

Governor: Robert F. List. **Annual salary:** $50,000. **Term:** 4 years. **Current term expires:** Jan. 1983. **Voting requirements:** 18 yrs. old, & U.S. citizen; state resident 30 days. **U.S. Congressmen:** 1. **Entered Union:** 1864 (36th state).

Location & boundaries: Rocky Mountain state: bounded on the north by Oregon & Idaho; on the east by Utah & Arizona; & on the south & west by California. **Total area:** 110,540 sq. mi. (ranks 7th). **Extreme length:** 483 mi. **Extreme breadth:** 320 mi. **Chief rivers:** Humboldt, Colorado, Truckee. **Major lakes:** Pyramid, Walker, Tahoe, Mead. **No. of counties:** 17.

Population (1978 est.): 660,000 (ranks 45th). **Pop. increase (1970-78):** 35.0%. **Places over 25,000 pop.:** 5. **Places over 100,000:** 1. **Largest cities:** Las Vegas, Reno, North Las Vegas. **Pop. density:** 6.0 per sq. mi. (ranks 47th). **Pop. projection 1985:** 734,000. **Pop. distribution:** 80.9% metropolitan; 19.1% nonmetropolitan. **White:** 91.7%. **Negro:** 5.7%. **Other:** 2.6%. **Marriage rate (1977):** 170.6 per 1,000 people. **Divorce rate:** 16.2 per 1,000 people.

State finances (1977). Revenue: $762,457,000. **Expenditures:** $632,780,000. **State Taxes:** $519.86 per capita. **State general income tax:** No. **Public debt (1977):** $86.26 per capita. **Federal aid (1977):** $224.83 per capita. **Personal income (1977):** $7,980.

Sectors of the economy (% of labor force employed in 1970): Manufacturing (5%), Wholesale and retail trade (19%), Services (22%), Educational Services (6%), Construction (8%), Government (18%). **Leading products:** stone, clay & glass items; chemicals; printing & publishing; food items; lumber; electrical machinery; fabricated metals. **Minerals:** copper, gold, sand & gravel, diatomite. **Agricultural products:** sheep, cattle, hay, alfalfa seed, wheat, dairy items. **Avg. farm (1978 est.):** 4,286 acres. **Avg. value of farm per acre:** $97.

Highway expenditures per capita (1977): $137.19. **Persons per motor vehicle:** 1.15. **Minimum age for driver's license:** 16. **Gasoline tax:** 6¢ per gallon. **Motor vehicle deaths:** 46.4 per 100,000 people.

Birthrate (1977): 16.1 per 1,000 people. **Infant mortality rate per 1,000 births (1977):** 13.9. **Physicians per 100,000 pop. (1976):** 128. **Dentists per 100,000 pop. (1976):** 51. **Acceptable hospital beds:** 5.2 per 1,000 people. **State expenditures per capita for health and hospitals (1977):** $47.87.

Education expenditures (1975-76): $459.82 per capita annually. **No. of pupils in public schools (1977 est.):** 140,000. **No. of institutions of higher learning (1976-77):** 6. **Public school expenditure per pupil in attendance (1975-76):** $1,617. **Avg. salary of public school teachers (1974-75 est.):** $12,854. **No. full-time teachers (1977 est.):** 6,050. **Educational attainment of adult population (1976):** 12.4 median yrs. of school completed; 1.2% with less than 5 years of education; 13.1% with 4 yrs. of college.

Telephones (1976): 91 per 100 people. **State Chamber of Commerce:** Nevada Chamber of Commerce Association, P.O. Box 3499, Reno, Nevada 89505.

NEW HAMPSHIRE

New Hampshire is a relatively small but well wooded and scenic state of mountains, lakes, and rapid rivers that provide a good water supply and large hydroelectric-power potential. There are three main land areas: the coastal lowlands covering the southeast corner; the New England Uplands, covering most of the southwest, west central, and south central area; and the White

NEVADA

MILES
0 10 20   40   60   80

KILOMETERS
0   20   40   60   80

State Capital ⊛   County Seats ⊙

© Copyright HAMMOND INCORPORATED, Maplewood, N.J.

Longitude West of Greenwich

Mountains region in the north, which includes Mount Washington, the Northeast's highest peak (6,288 feet). Near the coast are the rough-hewn Isles of Shoals, three of which belong to New Hampshire. The state's largest harbor is at Portsmouth, near the mouth of the Piscataqua. The climate features cool summers with low humidity and winters marked by heavy snowfall. The ocean tempers the weather along the 17.8 mile Atlantic coastline, shortest of any state bordering an ocean.

About 5,000 Indians were living in the New Hampshire region before the Europeans came. The various tribes coexisted peacefully but often banded together to fight the Iroquois. The first explorers in the area are thought to have been Captain Martin Pring (1603), Samuel de Champlain (1605), and Captain John Smith (1614). Permanent settlement began in 1623, when David Thomson established Little Harbour, now in the town of Rye. Captain John Mason, who had a hand in the founding (1630) of Portsmouth, gave New Hampshire its name. Though the state was once part of Massachusetts, it became a separate royal colony in 1679; the two states had the same governor from 1699 to 1741. New Hampshire established an independent government (1776), one designed to be only temporary but which in fact operated until 1784, when the present constitution was adopted. New Hampshire was the ninth state to ratify the U.S. Constitution (1788), and the one that made that document legal.

Complicated boundary disputes with all its neighbors have marked New Hampshire's history. Royal orders eventually defined the Massachusetts (1741) and New York (1764) boundaries, while the state's northern border was set by the Webster-Ashburton Treaty (1842), which established the international line between the United States and Canada. But not until a 1934 U.S. Supreme Court ruling was the Vermont boundary decided. A border dispute with Maine over 2,400 acres of coastal waters that began in 1974 was resolved in 1976, when the U.S. Supreme Court awarded the bulk of the disputed territory to Maine.

The state is one of the most industrialized in the nation, based on the percentage of its population working in manufacturing. The electronic, chemical, and machinery industries are major employers.

New Hampshire, with its beneficial tax climate, is experiencing an influx of new industrial development, especially in the southern sections along the Massachusetts border. In the absence of a general sales or income tax, New Hampshire finances the cost of state government through the state-operated liquor monopoly, pari-mutuel betting on racing, state taxes on business profits and rooms and meals. Education is funded by the local property tax.

Tourism, meanwhile, has mushroomed into an annual $500-million business. One fifth of the land is in public parklands, including 724,000 acres of the White Mountain National Forest, which extends into Maine. Hiking, boating, and camping are popular, and the state has more than 60 ski lifts. Attractions include Strawbery Banke, a preservation project that has restored about 30 buildings and homes of the original settlement at Portsmouth, N.H., the Kancamagus Highway between Lincoln and Conway, Daniel Webster's birthplace near Franklin, the Mount Washington Cog Railway, the first (1869) in North America, and the famous "Old Man of the Mountain" granite head profile at Franconia, the state's official emblem.

New Hampshire today functions as an exceptionally democratic entity, with the state's 222 towns (nicknamed "little republics") using the traditional town meeting to provide a forum for all voters. The state, which for decades had a sometimes disputed reputation as a political bellwether, has been relieved of its position as the first to hold a presidential primary by Puerto Rico, which in 1980 will hold its first such election.

During 1976, nuclear power remained a controversial topic in New Hampshire, in particular the application by the Public Service Company of N.H. to build twin nuclear reactors to generate power in the environmentally sensitive seacoast area at Seabrook. Construction began in 1976 but was slowed by a regional Environmental Protection Agency order. In mid-1977 EPA Administrator Douglas Costle overruled his regional office and approved a company plan to discharge heated water through cooling tunnels into the Atlantic Ocean. Anti-nuclear power forces from all over New England focused on the Seabrook issue in early 1977, and in May, a mass occupation of the construction site resulted in the arrest of 1,414 demonstrators by authorities. Since then the project has not moved much closer to completion. A final approval was given, and hearings and demonstrations continued. The Federal Nuclear Regulatory Commission ruled in July 1978 that construction must be suspended before the end of the month, not to be resumed until EPA decides whether seawater-cooling is permissible. Though the construction resumed in August 1978 amid protest, another shutdown of up to one year may occur because of financial difficulties.

Full name: State of New Hampshire. **Origin of name:** From the English county of Hampshire. **Inhabitant:** New Hampshirite. **Capital:** Concord. **State motto:** Live Free or Die. **Flag:** State seal on a blue field. **Seal:** A reproduction of Revolutionary War frigate "Raleigh" is surrounded by nine stars in a laurel wreath to symbolize victory. **Flower:** Purple lilac. **Bird:** Purple finch. **Tree:** White birch. **Songs:** "Old New Hampshire" & "New Hampshire, My New Hampshire." **Nickname:** Granite State.

Governor: Hugh J. Gallen. **Annual salary:** $44,520. **Term:** 2 years. **Current term expires:** Jan. 1981. **Voting requirements:** 18 yrs. old & U.S. citizen; registered. **U.S. Congressmen:** 2. **Entered Union:** 1788 (9th state).

Location & boundaries: New England state: bounded on the north by Canada; on the east by Maine & the Atlantic Ocean; on the south by Massachusetts; & on the west by Vermont, Canada & the Connecticut River. **Total area:** 9,304 sq. mi. (ranks 44th). **Extreme length:** 180 mi. **Extreme breadth:** 93 mi. **Coastline:** 17.8 mi. **Chief rivers:** Connecticut, Merrimack, Androscoggin. **Major lake:** Winnipesaukee. **No. of counties:** 10.

Population (1978 est.): 871,000 (ranks 42nd). **Pop. increase (1970-78):** 18.0%. **Places over 25,000 pop.:** 3. **Places over 100,000:** None. **Largest cities:** Manchester, Nashua, Concord. **Pop. density:** 87.2 per sq. mi. (ranks 20th). **Pop. projection 1985:** 935,000. **Pop. distribution:** 36.3% metropolitan; 63.7% non-metropolitan. **White:** 99.4%. **Negro:** 0.3%. **Other:** 0.3%. **Marriage rate (1977):** 10.4 per 1,000 people. **Divorce rate:** 5.2 per 1,000 people.

State finances (1977). Revenue: $636,339,000. **Expenditures:** $677,139,000. **State Taxes:** $235.84 per capita. **State personal income tax:** Yes. **Public debt (1977):** $427.77 per capita. **Federal aid (1977):** $186.78 per capita. **Personal income (1977):** $6,578.

Sectors of the economy (% of labor force employed in 1970): Manufacturing (36%), Wholesale and retail trade (19%), Services (6%), Educational Services (8%), Construction (7%), Government (14%). **Leading products:** leather items, electrical & other machinery, textile mill items, paper items, food items, printing & publishing. **Agricultural products:** dairy items, eggs, cattle, hay, apples, potatoes. **Avg. farm (1978 est.):** 193 acres. **Avg. value of farm per acre:** $729.

Highway expenditures per capita (1977): $129.90. **Persons per motor vehicle:** 1.51. **Minimum age for driver's license:** 18. **Gas-**

NEW HAMPSHIRE

MILES

KILOMETERS

State Capitals ⊛   County Seats ⊙

© Copyright HAMMOND INCORPORATED, Maplewood, N.J.

Longitude West of Greenwich

oline tax: 10¢ per gallon. Motor vehicle deaths: 19.6 per 100,000 people.

Birthrate (1977): 14.2 per 1,000 people. Infant mortality rate per 1,000 births (1977): 10.2. Physicians per 100,000 pop. (1976): 159. Dentists per 100,000 pop. (1976): 52. Acceptable hospital beds: 6.2 per 1,000 people. State expenditures per capita for health and hospitals (1977): $67.63.

Education expenditures (1975-76): $389.87 per capita annually. No. of pupils in public schools (1977 est.): 173,000. No. of institutions of higher learning (1976-77): 24. Public school expenditure per pupil in attendance (1975-76): $1,493. Avg. salary of public school teachers (1974-75 est.): $10,016. No. full-time teachers (1977 est.): 11,180. Educational attainment of adult population (1976): 12.6 median yrs. of school completed; 1.1% with less than 5 years of education; 15.3% with 4 yrs. of college.

Telephones (1976): 72 per 100 people. State Chamber of Commerce: Business and Industry Association of New Hampshire, 23 School Street, Concord, New Hampshire 03301.

NEW JERSEY

New Jersey's importance is disproportionate to its modest size. Strategically located, amid many rich markets, the state has extraordinary transportation facilities and a correspondingly large volume of interstate traffic: railway trackage, highways, tunnels, and bridges abound. The nation's most densely populated state, it is a manufacturing giant with limited but valuable farming and fishing industries.

Many sandy beaches, coupled with a generally mild climate marked by ocean breezes, have made New Jersey popular with vacationers, and tourism is today a major industry, accounting for over $2 billion a year. Attractions include such resort areas as Atlantic City and Wildwood, as well as the Thomas A. Edison National Historic Site in West Orange, the Walt Whitman House in Camden, the Garden State Arts Center in Telegraph Hill Park, and several ski areas.

Before the coming of the Europeans, the region was inhabited by Lenni-Lenape (later called Delaware) Indians of the Algonquian group. The area's early colonial history is bound up with that of New York (then New Netherland), of which it was a part. With the passing of power from Dutch to English hands (1664), New Jersey began to emerge as a more distinct entity. Proprietorship of lands between the Hudson and Delaware Rivers was granted by James II to Lord John Berkeley and Sir George Carteret, who then offered territory to settlers in return for sworn allegiance to the king and payment of quitrent (fixed rent). Berkeley eventually sold (1676) his land share to a group of Quakers, who then agreed with Carteret to divide the region into East and West Jersey, the line running southeastward from the Delaware River near the Water Gap to the Atlantic Ocean near Little Egg Harbor. Carteret owned East Jersey—about three-eighths of the total area—until his death (1680), while West Jersey became the nation's first Quaker settlement. Control of both Jerseys eventually reverted to England which governed it jointly with New York from 1702 to 1738, when Lewis Morris was made governor of New Jersey alone.

The region remained turbulent for many years. A decade of virtual lawlessness began in 1745, ended only by the advent of the French and Indian War of the mid-1750s, which served to unify New Jerseyans against a common enemy. Because of its location between New York City and Philadelphia, New Jersey was the scene of many important battles of the American Revolution. In 1783 Princeton served briefly as the nation's capital. Statehood dates from 1787.

After the Revolution, many scientific breakthroughs took place in the state, and the country's first model factory town was founded in 1791 at the site of the present Paterson, under the auspices of Alexander Hamilton's Society for the Establishment of Useful Manufactures. (A few years later, Hamilton was killed in Weehawken in a notorious duel with Aaron Burr.)

The state was sharply divided by the Civil War. Most New Jerseyans accepted the ending of slavery, but many businessmen were against the war because of the profitable Southern market. When peace came, the state's population and economy continued their rapid growth, interrupted by the Panic of 1873. Powerful special-interest groups grasped undue political control, bringing a counterwave of reform under Governor Woodrow Wilson, who was elected in 1910. But after Wilson left in 1913 to become president, much of the impetus toward reform in the state withered away.

The institution (1966) of a general sales tax has helped lighten the state's severe financial problems, as has the March 1970 hike in that tax, from three to five percent. One side effect of these measures has been to detract somewhat from the state's traditionally favorable tax climate which, together with streamlined corporation laws, has been a vital weapon in the continuing battle with other states for new industry. New Jersey enacted an income tax in 1976 as a replacement for portions of local property tax burdens, and in December 1977 the tax was made permanent.

Large-scale urban-renewal projects that would eliminate blight while creating jobs are seen as a means of alleviating a major part of the problem. A vast $300-million Hackensack Meadowlands project built on land from ten different north Jersey towns opened in 1976, with the National Football League Giants and the Cosmos professional soccer team as the major long-term tenants and including a racetrack. In 1977 the New York Nets announced plans to move to a permanent home to be constructed in the complex. Port Jersey, a 707-acre, $160-million industrial center with a 17-berth terminal for containerships has been planned for the New Jersey side of Upper New York Bay, adjoining the U.S. Military Ocean Terminal in Bayonne.

In mid-1977 the courts lifted the ban on drilling East Coast offshore oil leases, and exploration commenced by the end of the year. After six months there had been no announcement of any profitable strikes in the Baltimore Canyon off the New Jersey Coast. Since that time, however, both Texaco Inc. and the U.S. Geological Survey have announced offshore gas finds.

In 1976 New Jersey passed a constitutional amendment authorizing the establishment of gambling casinos in Atlantic City as a means of rejuvenating the ailing resort and rebuilding the tourist industry in general. The first casino opened in May 1978 and has proved successful. It was granted a permanent license by the New Jersey Casino Control Commisssion on February 26, 1979.

Full name: State of New Jersey. Origin of name: From Channel Island of Jersey. Inhabitant: New Jerseyite. Capital: Trenton. State motto: Liberty & Prosperity. Flag: State seal on yellow field. Seal: Three plows & goddess Ceres holding a cornucopia represent agriculture; a horse's head lies above sovereign's helmet. Flower: Purple violet. Bird: Eastern goldfinch. Tree: Red oak. Song: (unofficial) "New Jersey Loyalty Song." Nickname: Garden State.

Governor: Brendan T. Byrne. Annual salary: $65,000. Term: 4 years. Current term expires: Jan. 1982. Voting requirements: 18

NEW JERSEY

MILES

KILOMETERS

State Capitals   County Seats

© Copyright HAMMOND INCORPORATED, Maplewood, N.J.

Longitude West of Greenwich

yrs. old & U.S. citizen; resident of state & county 30 days. **U.S. Congressmen:** 15. **Entered Union:** 1787 (3rd state).

Location & boundaries: Middle Atlantic state: bounded on the north by New York; on the east by New York, the Hudson River & the Atlantic Ocean; on the south by Delaware Bay; on the southwest by Delaware & the Delaware River; & on the west by Pennsylvania & the Delaware River. **Total area:** 7,836 sq. mi. (ranks 46th). **Extreme length:** 166 mi. **Extreme breadth:** 57 mi. **Coastline:** 130 mi. **Chief rivers:** Raritan, Delaware, Hudson, Passaic. **Major lakes:** Hopatcong, Budd, Culvers. **No. of counties:** 21.

Population (1978 est.): 7,327,000 (ranks 9th). **Pop. increase (1970-78):** 2.2%. **Places over 25,000 pop.:** 64. **Places over 100,000:** 4. **Largest cities:** Newark, Jersey City, Paterson, Elizabeth. **Pop. density:** 935.0 per sq. mi. (ranks 1st). **Pop. projection 1985:** 7,741,000. **Pop. distribution:** 92.2% metropolitan; 7.8% nonmetropolitan. **White:** 88.6%. **Negro:** 10.7%. **Other:** 0.7%. **Marriage rate (1977):** 6.8 per 1,000 people. **Divorce rate:** 2.8 per 1,000 people.

State finances (1977). Revenue: $7,038,175,000. **Expenditures:** $6,827,632,000. **State Taxes:** $423.49 per capita. **State personal income tax:** Yes. **Public debt (1977):** $552.84 per capita. **Federal aid (1977):** $195.15 per capita. **Personal income (1977):** $7,969.

Sectors of the economy (% of labor force employed in 1970): Manufacturing (32%), Wholesale and retail trade (19%), Services (7%), Educational Services (7%), Construction (5%), Government (14%). **Leading products:** chemicals, machinery, food items, primary & fabricated metals, transportation equipment, apparel. **Agricultural products:** dairy items, cattle, tomatoes, potatoes, corn, hay, asparagus. **Fishing:** clams, flounder, oysters. **Avg. farm (1978 est.):** 122 acres. **Avg. value of farm per acre:** $2,057.

Highway expenditures per capita (1977): $41.10. **Persons per motor vehicle:** 1.66. **Minimum age for driver's license:** 17. **Gasoline tax:** 8¢ per gallon. **Motor vehicle deaths:** 15.3 per 100,000 people.

Birthrate (1977): 12.8 per 1,000 people. **Infant mortality rate per 1,000 births (1977):** 14.3. **Physicians per 100,000 pop. (1976):** 177. **Dentists per 100,000 pop. (1976):** 61. **Acceptable hospital beds:** 6.5 per 1,000 people. **State expenditures per capita for health and hospitals (1977):** $52.57.

Education expenditures (1975-76): $440.96 per capita annually. **No. of pupils in public schools (1977 est.):** 1,406,000. **No. of institutions of higher learning (1976-77):** 65. **Public school expenditure per pupil in attendance (1975-76):** $2,122. **Avg. salary of public school teachers:** Not available. **No. full-time teachers (1977 est.):** 91,320. **Educational attainment of adult population (1976):** 12.4 median yrs. of school completed; 2.7% with less than 5 years of education; 14.9% with 4 yrs. of college.

Telephones (1976): 80 per 100 people. **State Chamber of Commerce:** New Jersey State Chamber of Commerce, 5 Commerce Street, Newark, New Jersey 07102.

NEW MEXICO

New Mexico is a land of great contrast. It is rich in history yet in the forefront of the Atomic Era—the world's first A-bomb, produced at Los Alamos, was exploded (1945) at Trinity Site near Alamogordo. Three major cultures intermingle within the state—Spanish, Indian, and Anglo-American—and within each is a variety of types and subcultures.

Indians are thought to have lived in this region between 20,000 and 25,000 years ago. In 1975, a total of 100,280 Indians—mainly Navajo, Apache, and Pueblo—were to be found in New Mexico, living much as their ancestors had, despite a few modern trappings. Within the state is the country's largest Indian reservation (more than 16 million acres), which is inhabited by Navajos. At Gallup each August is held the colorful Inter-tribal Indian Ceremonial.

Sharp contrasts also mark the face of the land. The often spectacular landscape is a complex blending of deserts, rugged blue-rimmed mesas, and forested mountain regions, with an average mean elevation of 5,700 feet. The generally thin, dry air cools rapidly at night, making for wide daily temperature variations. Because of the great ranges in altitude and rainfall, the state supports six distinct life zones and a correspondingly large variety of plants and animals.

Water is generally scarce in New Mexico, and irrigation difficult. Much of the land, however, is devoted to grazing, sustaining a sizable ranching industry. Cotton lint is the main crop in the irrigated areas. In the dry-farming regions (about two-thirds of the state's farmland), hay and wheat are among the significant outputs. Dry-farmers are gradually shifting to irrigation, as more dams and wells are built. In the river valleys, especially along the Rio Grande, fruits and vegetables are grown.

At the northwest corner, four states—New Mexico, Arizona, Utah, and Colorado—meet at right angles, the only such point in the nation.

Francisco Vásquez de Coronado, in search of the fabled "Seven Cities of Cibola," explored (1540-42) the region that became New Mexico, but found no treasure. In 1598 the first Spanish colony was established at the Pueblo of San Juan de Los Caballeros. Santa Fe was founded in 1610 and made provincial capital. Roman Catholic missionaries set up schools in the region. Subjected to harsh treatment and forbidden to worship their gods, the Pueblo Indians revolted in 1680; Spain regained control in 1692. Mexico governed from 1821 until the United States took possession via the 1848 Mexican treaty and the 1853 Gadsden Purchase. Vital to early-day commerce, the Santa Fe Trail between New Mexico and Missouri was opened in 1821; today, east of Santa Fe, the Trail is still in use as U.S. 85.

During the Civil War there were Confederate forces in Santa Fe and Albuquerque, but they were soon dispatched by Union troops. The surrender (1886) of Geronimo terminated the Apache Wars and marked the virtual end of area Indian troubles. During the 1880s, the mining and ranching industries boomed. New Mexico entered the Union in 1912.

New Mexico is one of the largest energy-producing states in the nation. The state is the leading producer of potash and uranium. It has almost half of the nation's uranium reserves and large deposits of low-sulphur coal and natural gas. Historically, it has been a massive exporter of energy, sending out of the state more than half the electricity it has produced, about three-quarters of the gas generated and almost all of the petroleum pumped in the state.

Since 1945, the state has been a leader in the field of energy research and development. It helps the nation solve its energy needs through research conducted by Los Alamos Scientific Laboratory and Sandia Laboratories in the nuclear, solar and geothermal fields. Northwest New Mexico is presently undergoing a massive coal gasification project that will provide additional energy for the Western United States.

The increased demand for domestic energy and the pattern of growth it shares with other states of the sunbelt have brought problems as well as prosperity to New Mexico. School systems are overcrowded and there is a housing shortage in some places. Urban sprawl is spreading around Grants, Albuquerque and Santa Fe, intensifying the contrast between the relatively low economic level of the rural areas and the prosperity of some cities and mining communities. As a result, political power, which has been in the hands of agricultural

NEW MEXICO

interests (ranching is still the state's chief industry), is beginning to shift a little to represent newcomers from out of state and the growing Mexican-American population.

Tourist attractions in New Mexico include the Carlsbad Caverns National Park, Inscription Rock at El Morro National Monument, and the ruins of Fort Union, which in its day was one of the largest U.S. military outposts on the southwest frontier. At Lincoln are mementos of Billy the Kid, the outlaw who was involved (1878) in the Lincoln County cattle war. And near Aztec are Indian ruins, including a 500-room, E-shaped pueblo dating from A.D. 800-1200.

Full name: State of New Mexico. **Origin of name:** From the Aztec, Mexitli, meaning "War God." **Inhabitant:** New Mexican. **Capital:** Santa Fe. **State motto:** Crescit Eundo (It Grows As It Goes). **Flag:** Stylized red sun, symbol of Zia pueblo of Indians, on a yellow field. **Seal:** Two eagles represent annexation of New Mexico by the United States; scroll under eagles bears state's motto. **Flower:** Yucca. **Bird:** Road runner. **Tree:** Piñon or nut pine. **Gem:** Turquoise. **Vegetable:** Chile and Pinto Beans. **Song:** "O, Fair New Mexico." **Nickname:** Land of Enchantment.

Governor: Bruce King. **Annual salary:** $40,000. **Term:** 4 years. **Current term expires:** Dec. 1982. **Voting requirements:** 18 yrs. old & U.S. citizen; state resident 42 days (30 da for Pres. election). **U.S. Congressmen:** 2. **Entered Union:** 1912 (47th state).

Location & boundaries: Southwestern state: bounded on the north by Colorado; on the east by Oklahoma & Texas; on the south by Texas & Mexico; & on the west by Arizona. **Total area:** 121,666 sq. mi. (ranks 5th). **Extreme length:** 391 mi. **Extreme breadth:** 352 mi. **Chief rivers:** Rio Grande, San Juan, Pecos, Canadian. **Major lakes:** Navajo, Conchas, Cochiti, Elephant Butte Reservoir. **No. of counties:** 32.

Population (1978 est.): 1,212,000 (ranks 37th). **Pop. increase (1970-78):** 19.3%. **Places over 25,000 pop.:** 7. **Places over 100,000:** 1. **Largest cities:** Albuquerque, Santa Fe, Las Cruces. **Pop. density:** 10.0 per sq. mi. (ranks 44th). **Pop. projection 1985:** 1,361,000. **Pop. distribution:** 33.6% metropolitan; 66.4% nonmetropolitan. **White:** 90.1%. **Indian:** 7.2%. **Negro:** 1.9%. **Other:** 0.8%. **Marriage rate (1977):** 10.5 per 1,000 people. **Divorce rate:** 7.7 per 1,000 people.

State finances (1977). Revenue: $1,349,306,000. **Expenditures:** $1,137,043,000. **State Taxes:** $502.19 per capita. **State personal income tax:** Yes. **Public debt (1977):** $178.21 per capita. **Federal aid (1977):** $273.92 per capita. **Personal income (1977):** $5,846.

Sectors of the economy (% of labor force employed in 1970): Manufacturing (7%), Wholesale and retail trade (21%), Services (11%), Educational Services (12%), Construction (7%), Government (27%). **Leading products:** food items, petroleum & coal items, electronics, apparel. **Minerals:** coal, lead, zinc, gold, petroleum, silver, natural gas, potassium salts, copper, uranium, molybdenum. **Agricultural products:** cattle, sheep, dairy items, cotton lint, hay, sorghum, grain, poultry. **Avg. farm (1978 est.):** 3,695 acres. **Avg. value of farm per acre:** $93.

Highway expenditures per capita (1977): $105.49. **Persons per motor vehicle:** 1.31. **Minimum age for driver's license:** 16. **Gasoline tax:** 7¢ per gallon. **Motor vehicle deaths:** 54.5 per 100,000 people.

Birthrate (1977): 19.4 per 1,000 people. **Infant mortality rate per 1,000 births (1977):** 13.8. **Physicians per 100,000 pop. (1976):** 146. **Dentists per 100,000 pop. (1976):** 42. **Acceptable hospital beds:** 5.6 per 1,000 people. **State expenditures per capita for health and hospitals (1976):** $63.96.

Education expenditures (1975-76): $495.82 per capita annually. **No. of pupils in public schools (1977 est.):** 281,000. **No. of institutions of higher learning (1976-77):** 17. **Public school expenditure per pupil in attendance (1975-76):** $1,509. **Avg. salary of public school teachers (1974-75 est.):** $10,200. **No. full-time teachers (1977 est.):** 13,600. **Educational attainment of adult population (1976):** 12.5 median yrs. of school completed; 5.7% with less than 5 years of education; 15.3% with 4 yrs. of college.

Telephones (1976): 60 per 100 people. **State Chamber of Commerce:** Association of Commerce and Industry of New Mexico, 117 Quincy, N.E., Albuquerque, New Mexico 87108.

NEW YORK

New York is a state of superlatives, ideally located and richly endowed. In many respects, it is a nerve center of the nation, a major marketplace, and a national leader in manufacturing, finance, fashion, art, and communications. Second to California in population, New York is the region that George Washington foresaw as a "seat of empire"—hence its nickname, the Empire State. New York City, the nation's largest city, was the first U.S. capital (1789-90), and Washington was first inaugurated (1789) there.

Roughly triangular in shape, the state has a highly diversified terrain, with many lakes, wooded hills, and fertile valleys. Most of the area south of the Mohawk Valley falls within the province of the Appalachian Plateau, which covers more than half the state and slopes upward from northwest to southeast. New York's land features include the scenic Adirondack Mountains in the north and the Catskill range in the south, as well as imposing Niagara Falls. New York is the only state to border both the Atlantic Ocean and the Great Lakes.

Florentine explorer Giovanni da Verrazano is thought to have discovered New York by entering New York Bay in 1524. In 1609 Henry Hudson, an Englishman in the employ of the Dutch, sailed up the river bearing his name and the same year Samuel de Champlain discovered what is now Lake Champlain. The Dutch West India Company began (1624) settlement of the region, then called New Netherland, at Fort Orange (now Albany). Soon after, Governor Peter Minuit is said to have bought Manhattan Island from the Indians for trinkets worth about $24.

Indian troubles, misgovernment, and other woes hindered the colony's development. As a countermeasure, the Dutch began (1629) the "patroon" (landholder's) system that tended to concentrate economic and governmental power in the hands of a few. Squabbling broke out among the patroons, other settlers, and the home company, and Minuit was rescinded (1631) for granting the patroons undue privileges. He then entered the service of Sweden; its colony (New Sweden), along the Delaware River south of Dutch interests, was viewed by the Dutch as a territorial threat. Minuit's successors—Wouter Van Twiller and Willem Kieft—were failures, but Peter Stuyvesant for a time did better. In 1655 he captured New Sweden for the Dutch and reorganized New Amsterdam (now New York City). Stuyvesant was a strict Calvinist whose tactics often provoked resentment.

Meanwhile, English penetration of Long Island and the southeastern part of what is now the mainland state was steadily progressing. In the north and west of the state, Canadian French allied themselves with the Huron Indians, but met with hostility from the Iroquois. Comprised of five tribes confederated about 1570, the Iroquois greatly influenced the struggle for control of the region between France and England that ensued after the Dutch surrender (1664) of the land to the British. New Netherland thus became the colonies New York and New Jersey, granted by King Charles II to his brother, the Duke of York (later James II). The Dutch recaptured New York in 1673, but had to yield it again a year later.

The period was marked by the development of English governmental institutions, amid a welter of conflicts and confrontations. A popular legislative assembly was formed in 1683, after years of struggle by townspeople wanting a meaningful voice in their government; but two years later the

NEW YORK

State Capital ⊛ County Seats

NORTHERN PART OF NEW YORK

© Copyright HAMMOND INCORPORATED, Maplewood, N.J.

assembly was dissolved by James II. In 1686 the king sought to combine New York, New Jersey, and the New England colonies under the vice-regal authority of governor general Edmund Andros, but Andros was very unpopular, and when the king was dethroned in England in 1688, Andros was forced out of power by irate citizens. New York City merchant Jacob Leisler, hoping to foster more democratic government, then seized control, but was soon replaced by a royal governor and executed. Leisler's ill-fated rebellion served to sharpen class differences while preserving New York as a separate entity.

New York played a major role in the French and Indian Wars (1689-1763) in which France was helped by Algonquian Indians, while the Iroquois aided the English. The region also saw much action in the American Revolution and the War of 1812. (Statehood dates from 1788.) With the opening of the Erie Canal (1825), which linked the Hudson River and the Great Lakes, the state entered an era of great prosperity, reinforced a few years later by the massive industrial demands of the Civil War. Despite the Draft Riots (1863) in New York City, the state contributed more men (nearly 500,000), supplies, and money to the Union cause than any other.

The postwar period was marked by continued industrialization, large-scale immigration, and a corrupt political climate that often led to ineffective reform pressures: it was the notorious era of Boss Tweed and Tammany Hall. The most successful reform efforts were those made between World Wars I and II.

Recent important state developments include a $1 billion state office building complex called the Empire State Plaza in Albany; the Artpark near Niagara Falls, an area devoted to the visual and performing arts, with summer artists-in-residence; and the expansion of the higher education system. The State University of New York is the largest higher education system in the country, with 21 campuses throughout the state and an enrollment of over 225,000.

New York today faces a wide range of pressing problems, including rising governmental costs, expensive education and welfare programs and incursions by housing developers into forest lands. Despite this upward trend of costs, the state has enacted legislation designed to appease unhappy taxpayers by lowering income tax rates, increasing personal exemptions and deductions beginning in 1979.

Full name: State of New York. **Origin of name:** In honor of the Duke of York. **Inhabitant:** New Yorker. **Capital:** Albany. **State motto:** Excelsior (Ever Upward). **Flag:** State coat of arms on blue field. **Seal:** Coat of arms surrounded with legend "The Great Seal of State of New York." Coat of arms has figures representing Liberty & Justice, a typical New York river scene & an eagle perched on globe. **Flower:** Rose. **Bird:** Bluebird. **Tree:** Sugar maple. **Gem:** Garnet. **Song:** None. **Nickname:** Empire State.

Governor: Hugh L. Carey. **Annual salary:** $85,000. **Term:** 4 years. **Current term expires:** Dec. 1982. **Voting requirements:** 18 yrs. old & U.S. citizen; resident of city or village 30 days. **U.S. Congressmen:** 39. **Entered Union:** 1788 (11th state).

Location & boundaries: Middle Atlantic state; bounded on the north by the St. Lawrence River & Canada; on the east by Vermont, Massachusetts & Connecticut; on the south by the Atlantic Ocean, New Jersey, the Delaware River & Pennsylvania; & on the west by Pennsylvania, Lake Erie, Niagara River, Lake Ontario & Canada. **Total area:** 49,576 sq. mi. (ranks 30th). **Extreme length** (exclusive of Long Island): 320 mi. **Extreme breadth:** 310 mi. **Coastline:** 127 mi. on Atlantic; 371 mi. on Lakes Ontario & Erie. **Chief rivers:** St. Lawrence, Hudson, Mohawk. **Major lakes:** Finger Lakes, Champlain, Erie, Ontario. **No. of counties:** 62.

Population (1978 est.): 17,748,000 (ranks 2nd) **Pop. increase (1970-78):** -2.7%. **Places over 25,000 pop.:** 36. **Places over 100,000:** 6. **Largest cities:** New York, Buffalo, Rochester, Syracuse, Cheektowaga. **Pop. density:** 358.0 per sq. mi. (ranks 6th). **Pop. projection 1985:** 17,927,000. **Pop. distribution:** 88.5% metropolitan; 11.5% nonmetropolitan. **White:** 86.8%. **Negro:** 11.9%. **Other:** 1.3%. **Marriage rate (1977):** 7.3 per 1,000 people. **Divorce rate:** 3.1 per 1,000 people.

State finances (1977). Revenue: $22,667,068,000. **Expenditures:** $21,252,546,000. **State Taxes:** $599.38 per capita. **State personal income tax:** Yes. **Public debt (1977):** $1,116.49 per capita. **Federal aid (1977):** $270.20 per capita. **Personal income (1977):** $7,519.

Sectors of the economy (% of labor force employed in 1970): Manufacturing (24%), Wholesale and retail trade (20%), Services (8%), Educational Services (8%), Construction (5%), Government (17%). **Leading products:** printing & publishing, apparel, machinery, instruments, transportation equipment, food items. **Minerals:** cement, stone, sand & gravel, salt. **Agricultural products:** dairy items, poultry, fruit, vegetables. **Fishing:** clams, scallops, flounder. **Avg. farm (1978 est.):** 195 acres. **Avg. value of farm per acre:** $589.

Highway expenditures per capita (1977): $38.46. **Persons per motor vehicle:** 2.32. **Minium age for driver's license:** 18. **Gasoline Tax:** 8¢ per gallon. **Motor vehicle deaths:** 13.8 per 100,000 people.

Birthrate (1977): 13.4 per 1,000 people. **Infant mortality rate per 1,000 births (1977):** 14.4. **Physicians per 100,000 pop. (1976):** 126. **Dentists per 100,000 pop. (1976):** 70. **Acceptable hospital beds:** 8.4 per 1,000 people. **State expenditures per capita for health and hospitals (1977):** $86.40.

Education expenditures (1975-76): $516.47 per capita annually. **No. of pupils in public schools (1977 est.):** 3,330,000. **No. of institutions of higher learning (1976-77):** 287. **Public school expenditures per pupil in attendance (1975-76):** $2,580. **Avg. salary of public school teachers (1974-75 est.):** $15,000. **No, full-time teachers (1977 est.):** 211,540. **Educational attainment of adult population (1976):** 12.5 median yrs. of school completed; 3.0% with less than 5 years of education; 16.0% with 4 yrs. of college.

Telephones (1976): 73 per 100 people. **State Chamber of Commerce:** Empire State Chamber of Commerce, Inc., 150 State Street, Albany, New York 12207.

NORTH CAROLINA

One of the 13 Colonies and the Southeast's foremost industrial state, North Carolina presents an unusual amalgam of tradition and progress. It is a leader in both small-farm agriculture and business-applied research, and the nation's major producer of tobacco and tobacco products. The state also ranks high as a producer of textiles, bricks, wood products, and seafood. The first sustained airplane flight, by Orville and Wilbur Wright, took place (1903) near Kitty Hawk. Today, the state boasts of its famous "Research Triangle" at the University of North Carolina, Duke University, and North Carolina State University; the schools use their pooled resources to assist industry.

The state is topographically similar to its sister state South Carolina, sharing the same three principal land regions: (from east to west) the Atlantic Coastal Plain, the Piedmont Plateau, and the Blue Ridge Mountains. Mount Mitchell is the highest peak east of the Mississippi. Beyond the state's coastline are the islands, reefs, sheltered sounds, dunes, and capes of the Outer Banks, including Capes Fear and Hatteras—the latter so treacherous to ships that it is often called the graveyard of the Atlantic. About 60 percent of the state is forested.

Much of North Carolina's early history is shared with South Carolina, of which it was a part until 1712. Highlights of this period include Sir Walter

NORTH CAROLINA

WESTERN PART OF NORTH CAROLINA
Same scale as main map.

State Capital ⊛   County Seats ⊙

© Copyright HAMMOND INCORPORATED, Maplewood, N.J.

Raleigh's unsuccessful attempts (1585, 1587) to establish a colony on Roanoke Island. Although it lasted only about a year, Raleigh's initial settlement was the first English colony in the New World; when all members of his second settlement (1587-?) disappeared, it came to be called the "Lost Colony"; among the missing was Virginia Dare, first child of English parentage born in America.

Among the region's problems were Culpeper's Rebellion (1677), involving colonists angered by the English Navigation Acts; and the Cary Rebellion (1708), brought about by Quakers and other dissenters who refused to support the established Anglican church. In 1705, French Huguenots from Virginia established North Carolina's first permanent settlement, at Bath.

Growth in the Carolinas was slow. Swamps and dense forests made land communication difficult, and there were serious Indian troubles, especially during the Tuscarora War (1711-13). Pirates, too, were a hindrance, often menacing the colony's seabound trade; the slaying (1718) of the infamous "Blackbeard" (Edward Teach) in a battle near Ocracoke Island eased the problem. From 1712 to 1729, the proprietors appointed separate governors to administer North and South Carolina. A bitter North Carolina-Virginia boundary dispute was settled in 1728. Dissatisfied with the proprietary system, England eventually made (1729) the region a royal colony, a move that marked a period of progress in which farming and industry expanded as the population rose.

North Carolina contributed troops and materials to help England in its various colonial wars, while a persistent east-west sectionalism began to develop; this rift was caused by sharp differences in geography, politics, economics, and religion. Indian troubles were virtually ended in 1761 by a treaty with the Cherokees, but their final removal from the area did not begin until 1835. In 1768 irate back-country farmers, protesting taxes they considered excessive, organized the short-lived Regulator Movement for reform. The insurgents were eventually suppressed (1771) at Alamance by the provincial militia.

During the American Revolution, there was relatively little fighting on the state's soil, but many North Carolinians saw action elsewhere. In 1779 North Carolina annexed an area of present-day Tennessee settled by the Watauga Association, which lay immediately beyond North Carolina's present border. North Carolina administered the region until 1784, when it ceded its claim to the United States. The "Watauga" settlers then established the independent state of Franklin. Failing to gain official recognition, the new state's territory was again absorbed in 1789 by North Carolina, which later that same year ceded it once more to the Federal government; North Carolina's statehood dates from that year. The North Carolina-Georgia boundary was not definitively surveyed until 1819.

From 1815 to 1835, North Carolina languished in backwardness and apathy, and came to be called the "Rip Van Winkle State"; this period was followed until 1860 by one of progress, which saw a resurgence of political democracy and a lessening of unproductive sectionalism.

Despite the presence of considerable pro-Union and antislavery sentiment, North Carolina joined the Confederacy after the Civil War began. During the conflict, the port of Wilmington became a haven for Confederate blockade-runners. In the postwar period, Reconstruction was followed by the return of white supremacy and a suffrage amendment (1900) that again disenfranchised the Negro.

Among modern North Carolina's most pressing preoccupations is the continued strengthening and diversification of its economy, to curb reliance upon any single factor, such as tobacco. Another task is the peaceable achievement of racial integration. A majority of the rural and small-city school districts in the state are headed toward complete desegregation, but in the larger cities, such as Charlotte, Raleigh, Winston-Salem, and Durham, breaking down the dual systems has been difficult because there are more all-black schools and more rigid residential patterns. The desegregation issue is continuing to have its effect on institutions of higher learning. The H.E.W.'s nine-year attempt to enforce desegregation at the University of North Carolina has led to the university's July 1979 request for a preliminary hearing into what it considers to be intrusion into academic affairs on H.E.W.'s part.

The U.S. Supreme Court, in an historic ruling in the spring of 1971, upheld U.S. District Judge James B. McMillan's ruling that busing was a legitimate tool to use in ending racial segregation. The decision was applied to several school districts and by the fall, few racially identifiable schools remained in the state.

The headwaters of the scenic New River in North Carolina were saved from inundation by power company dams in legislation enacted in Congress in 1976 and backed by every major environmental group in the country. The river is considered one of the oldest in the Western Hemisphere.

Full name: State of North Carolina. **Origin of name:** In honor of Charles I of England. **Inhabitant:** North Carolinian. **Capital:** Raleigh. **State motto:** Esse Quam Videri (To Be Rather Than to Seem). **Flag:** Gold scrolls & NC (separated by white star) on blue bar; a red & white horizontal bar to right. **Seal:** Liberty holds scroll inscribed "Constitution"; seated figure of plenty; date "May 20, 1775." **Flower:** Dogwood. **Bird:** Cardinal. **Tree:** Pine. **Song:** "The Old North State." **Nickname:** Tar Heel State.

Governor: James B. Hunt, Jr. **Annual salary:** $47,700. **Term:** 4 years. **Current term expires:** Jan. 1981. **Voting requirements:** 18 yrs. old & U.S. citizen; resident of state 1 yr.; district, 30 da. **U.S. Congressmen:** 11. **Entered Union:** 1789 (12th state).

Location & boundaries: South Atlantic state: bounded on the north by Virginia; on the east by the Atlantic Ocean; on the south by South Carolina & Georgia; & on the west by Tennessee. **Total area:** 52,586 sq. mi. (ranks 28th). **Extreme length:** 503 mi. **Extreme breadth:** 187 mi. **Coastline:** 301 mi. **Chief rivers:** Yadkin, Cape Fear, Neuse, Roanoke. **Major lakes:** Fontana, Mattamuskeet, Norman. **No. of counties:** 100.

Population (1978 est.): 5,577,000 (ranks 11th). **Pop. increase (1970-78):** 9.7%. **Places over 25,000 pop.:** 18. **Places over 100,000:** 5. **Largest cities:** Charlotte, Greensboro, Winston-Salem, Raleigh. **Pop. density:** 106.1 per sq. mi. (ranks 17th). **Pop. projection 1985:** 6,185,000. **Pop. distribution:** 45.3% metropolitan; 54.7% nonmetropolitan. **White:** 76.6%. **Negro:** 22.4%. **Other:** 1%. **Marriage rate (1977):** 7.9 per 1,000 people. **Divorce rate:** 4.5 per 1,000 people.

State finances (1977). Revenue: $4,574,592,000. **Expenditures:** $4,357,782,000. **State Taxes:** $431.63 per capita. **State personal income tax:** Yes. **Public debt (1977):** $146.15 per capita. **Federal aid (1977):** $219.59 per capita. **Personal income (1977):** $5,916. **Sectors of the economy (% of labor force employed in 1970):** Manufacturing (36%), Wholesale and retail trade (18%), Services (8%), Educational Services (7%), Construction (7%), Government (13%). **Leading products:** textile items, tobacco items, furniture & fixtures, food items, electrical machinery, chemicals, apparel. **Agricultural products:** broilers, dairy items, tobacco, corn, soybeans. **Fishing:** shrimp, menhaden, crabs. **Avg. farm (1978 est.):** 114 acres. **Avg. value of farm per acre:** $694.

Highway expenditures per capita (1977): $82.05. **Persons per motor vehicle:** 1.35. **Minimum age for driver's license:** 18. **Gasoline tax:** 9¢ per gallon. **Motor vehicle deaths:** 23.9 per 100,000 people.

Birthrate (1977): 15.3 per 1,000 people. **Infant mortality rate per 1,000 births (1977):** 15.8. **Physicians per 100,000 pop. (1976):** 139. **Dentists per 100,000 pop. (1976):** 35. **Acceptable hospital beds:** 6.2 per 1,000 people. **State expenditures per capita for health and hospitals (1977):** $70.29.

Education expenditures (1975-76): $410.23 per capita annually. **No. of pupils in public schools (1977 est.):** 1,174,000. **No. of institutions of higher learning (1976-77):** 116. **Public school expenditure per pupil in attendance (1975-76):** $1,394. **Avg. salary of public school teachers (1974-75 est.):** $11,275. **No. full-time teachers (1977 est.):** 54,280. **Educational attainment of adult population (1976):** 12.2 median yrs. of school completed; 6.4% with less than 5 years of education; 11.8% with 4 yrs. of college.

Telephones (1976): 63 per 100 people. **State Chamber of Commerce:** North Carolina Citizens Association, P.O. Box 2508, Insurance Building, Raleigh, North Carolina 27602.

NORTH DAKOTA

North Dakota is the most rural of the states, with more than 90 percent of the land in farms. Agriculture and mining are two of its economic mainstays. Only Kansas produces more wheat, and the state's coal and oil reserves are among the nation's largest. Manufacturing is limited but growing, with food processing leading the way. Tourism is aided by excellent hunting and fishing and such attractions as the Theodore Roosevelt National Park in the Badlands and numerous historic sites including Fort Abercrombie (established 1857), the first U.S. military post in the region. A number of rodeos and fairs take place in the state in the summer and early fall.

Three main regions make up the state: the Red River Valley, comprising a ten-to-40-mile-wide strip along the eastern border; the Young Drift Plains, just west of this strip; and, covering the state's southwestern half, the Great Plains (also known locally as the Missouri Plateau). The state's continental climate is marked by wide temperature variation, light-to-moderate precipitation, and considerable windiness.

North Dakota's prestatehood history is shared in large part with that of South Dakota. The first Europeans to explore the area were the Sieur de la Vérendrye and sons who visited in 1738, four years before their travels in South Dakota. First settlement attempts were made (1812) at Pembina by Scottish and Irish families. After statehood (1889) separated it from its sister state, North Dakota experienced a spurt in population, growing from about 191,000 in 1890 to more than 577,000 in only 20 years.

In the early years of statehood, there was widespread farmer resentment of the powerful out-of-state grain monopolies. The Nonpartisan League (founded 1915) supported the farmers, thousands of whom became members; the league called for state ownership of storage and processing facilities, and it urged banks to extend easier credit to farmers. Among league-inspired legislation passed in a brief period beginning in 1919 were bills giving more funds to rural schools and lowering taxes on farm improvements. Dissension, however, soon eroded the league's power, and a conservative reaction set in.

Hard times did serve to spur the enactment of important soil conservation measures, including the establishment of shelter belts. Work was begun in 1968 on the first stage of an irrigation system that eventually will carry water through nearly 2,000 miles of canals to irrigate a million acres of North Dakota soil. The entire project is expected to cost over $500 million. The Lonetree Reservoir and Dam project has come under fire from the Federal

Government, the State of Minnesota, and the Canadian government, so work has been halted on the partially completed construction.

The $9 million Omega all-weather navigation system permitting any ship or aircraft with a proper receiver to determine its exact position was completed near Lamoure in 1973. Unique in North America, it is one of eight in the world.

In 1975, legislature was 34th in the nation to ratify the ERA constitutional amendment. Legislature also passed an education reciprocity plan whereby resident students of North Dakota and Minnesota may attend school in either state without paying "out of state" tuition.

The recent energy crisis resulted in the exploitation, chiefly by strip mining, of the coal reserves in the western part of the state, a development protested by environmentalists.

Full name: State of North Dakota. **Origin of name:** From the Sioux meaning "Alliance with Friends." **Inhabitant:** North Dakotan. **Capital:** Bismarck. **State motto:** Liberty & Union, Now & Forever, One & Inseparable. **Flag:** Eagle with American shield on breast, holding sheaf of arrows in left claw & olive branch in right & carrying in beak a banner inscribed "E Pluribus Unum"; above eagle is sunburst enclosing 13 stars, beneath is scroll inscribed "North Dakota"–all on blue field with yellow fringe. **Seal:** Elm tree & setting sun; plow, sheaves of wheat & anvil symbolize agriculture; bow & arrows & Indian hunting a buffalo represent North Dakota's history. **Flower:** Wild prairie rose. **Bird:** Western meadowlark. **Tree:** American elm. **Song:** "North Dakota Hymn." **Nickname:** Flickertail State.

Governor: Arthur A. Link. **Annual salary:** $27,500. **Term:** 4 years. **Current term expires:** Jan. 1981. **Voting requirements:** 18 yrs. old & U.S. citizen; resident 30 days. **U.S. Congressmen:** 1. **Entered Union:** 1889 (39th state).

Location & boundaries: Northern Midwestern state: bounded on the north by Canada; on the east by Minnesota at the Red River of the North; on the south by South Dakota; & on the west by Montana. **Total area:** 70,664 sq. mi. (ranks 17th). **Extreme length:** 360 mi. **Extreme breadth:** 210 mi. **Chief rivers:** Red River of the North, Missouri, Sheyenne. **Major lakes:** Devils, Sakakawea Reservoir. **No. of counties:** 53.

Population (1978 est.): 652,000 (ranks 46th). **Pop. increase (1970-78):** 5.5%. **Places over 25,000 pop.:** 4. **Places over 100,000:** None. **Largest cities:** Fargo, Grand Forks, Bismarck, Minot. **Pop. density:** 9.2 per sq. mi., ranks 45th). **Pop. projection 1985:** 675,000. **Pop. distribution:** 22.7% metropolitan; 77.3% nonmetropolitan. **White:** 97%. **Negro:** 0.4%. **Other:** 2.6%. **Marriage rate (1977):** 8.7 per 1,000 people. **Divorce rate:** 3.0 per 1,000 people.

State finances (1977). Revenue: $736,073,000. **Expenditures:** $678,657,000. **State Taxes:** $453.80 per capita. **State personal income tax:** Yes. **Public debt (1977):** $103.10 per capita. **Federal aid (1977):** $328.07 per capita. **Personal income (1977):** $5,872.

Sectors of the economy (% of labor force employed in 1970): Manufacturing (5%), Wholesale and retail trade (23%), Services (7%), Educational Services (11%), Construction (6%), Government (19%). **Leading products:** food items, printing & publishing, machinery. **Minerals:** petroleum, sand & gravel, natural gas, lignite coal. **Agricultural products:** cattle, dairy items, poultry, potatoes, sugar beets, wheat, barley, hay. **Avg. farm (1978 est.):** 1,005 acres. **Avg. value of farm per acre:** $273.

Highway expenditures per capita (1977): $170.12. **Persons per motor vehicle:** 1.13. **Minimum age for driver's license:** 16. **Gasoline tax:** 8¢ per gallon. **Motor vehicle deaths:** 27.9 per 100,000 people.

Birthrate (1977): 17.5 per 1,000 people. **Infant mortality rate per 1,000 births (1977):** 13.7. **Physicians per 100,000 pop. (1976):** 118. **Dentists per 100,000 pop. (1976):** 44. **Acceptable hospital beds:** 8.8 per 1,000 people. **State expenditures per capita for health and hospitals (1977):** $46.22.

Education expenditures (1975-76): $474.78 per capita annually. **No. of pupils in public schools (1977 est.):** 127,000. **No. of institutions of higher learning (1976-77):** 15. **Public school ex-**

NORTH DAKOTA

penditure per pupil in attendance (1975-76): $1,408. **Avg. salary of public school teachers (1974-75 est.):** $9,176. **No. full-time teachers (1977 est.):** 8,120. **Educational attainment of adult population (1976):** 12.5 median yrs. of school completed; 1.7% with less than 5 years of education; 12.2% with 4 yrs. of college.

Telephones (1976): 71 per 100 people. **State Chamber of Commerce:** Greater North Dakota Association—State Chamber of Commerce, P.O. Box 2467, 107 Roberts Street, Fargo, North Dakota 58108.

OHIO

A leading industrial state and the first to be carved out of the Northwest Territory, Ohio enjoys a variety of important natural resources and a strategic location near many rich markets. Predominantly a producer of iron and steel and their products, the state also ranks high in mining and agriculture (especially livestock). It is among the most populous of states, and only Virginia has produced more U.S. Presidents than Ohio, which claims eight.

Four land regions make up the state: the Appalachian Plateau, making up almost all of the eastern half; the fertile Till Plains, constituting the bulk of the western half; a five-to-50-mile-wide strip of the Great Lakes Plain bordering Lake Erie; and, in the south, an extension of Kentucky's Bluegrass Region forming a small wedge between the plateau and the lowlands. The climate is generally temperate but marked somewhat by extremes and sudden changes. Many dams and reservoirs have been built as a bulwark against disasters such as the floods of 1913 that killed about 500 persons and caused some $150 million in property loss.

Early Amerindian peoples are thought to have lived in the Ohio region between 5,000 and 7,000 years ago, followed by the Adena and Hopewell Mound Builders (c. 800 B.C.—A.D. 1300).

Algonquian and Iroquois Indians were living in the region when the first Europeans arrived. Robert Cavelier, Sieur de La Salle, passed through about 1670, providing a basis for French claims to the region that were sharply contested by the British, who claimed all the territory extending westward from their colonies. Victory in the French and Indian Wars (1689-1763) gave England the upper hand until the American Revolution. Massachusetts, Connecticut, and Virginia land claims in the area were resolved by the Northwest Ordinance (1787). A band of New Englanders led by General Rufus Putnam established (1788) the first permanent white settlement at Marietta. Early settlers were beset by serious Indian troubles that were largely ended after troops under General Anthony Wayne won (1794) the Battle of Fallen Timbers, near present-day Toledo. The Division Act of 1800 created the Indiana Territory out of the western part of the region, then still called the Northwest Territory. In 1803, Ohio entered the Union. A border dispute with the Territory of Michigan gave rise (1835) to the "Toledo War" but, before any actual fighting broke out, Congress awarded the area—about 520 square miles along Lake Erie—to Ohio. At present another land controversy between the two states—over a 200-square-mile area beneath Lake Erie that is rich in oil and natural gas—remains to be resolved.

Ohio was in the forefront of events leading to the Civil War. The abolition movement began at St. Clairsville, and many Ohioans helped slaves escape to Canada via the Underground Railroad. Although there was relatively little actual fighting on its soil, Ohio contributed heavily to the Union cause. In the postwar period the state rapidly emerged as an industrial power while retaining its agricultural status. In the years just prior to the turn of the century, big business became inordinately involved in Ohio politics, causing discontent among the less well-off. Labor troubles developed that culminated in Jacob S. Coxey's march on Washington, D.C. (1894) and a voting shift toward reform candidates. More recent troubles of this nature include major strikes during the mid-1930s, 1949, and 1959.

Tourism, aided by a surge in new highway construction, has developed into a valuable revenue-producer, now bringing in over $3 billion a year. Attractions include numerous state park and recreation areas, prehistoric Indian mounds, and historic sites such as Commodore Perry's Victory and International Peace Memorial at Put-in-Bay on Lake Erie, which commemorates his vital victory there during the War of 1812. Annual events include the All-American Soap Box Derby, held in Akron each summer.

Honda Motor Company Ltd., the Japanese motor-cycle manufacturer, announced plans to build a motorcycle assembly plant (its first in this country) in Allen Township, Ohio. The plant would employ about 500 persons.

Full name: State of Ohio. **Origin of name:** From Iroquois name meaning "Great." **Inhabitant:** Ohioan. **Capital:** Columbus. **State motto:** With God, All Things Are Possible. **Flag:** Pennant-shaped flag; white-bordered red circle & white stars on a blue triangle, with red & white bars. **Seal:** Sheaf of wheat; bundle of arrows; sun rising behind mountains, indicating Ohio was first state west of Allegheny Mountains. **Flower:** Scarlet carnation. **Bird:** Cardinal. **Tree:** Buckeye. **Song:** "Beautiful Ohio." **Nickname:** Buckeye State.

Governor: James A. Rhodes. **Annual salary:** $50,000. **Term:** 4 years. **Current term expires:** Jan. 1983. **Voting requirements:** 18 yrs. & U.S. citizen; resident of county and precinct 30 days. **U.S. Congressmen:** 23. **Entered Union:** 1803 (17th state).

Location & boundaries: Midwestern state; bounded on the north by Michigan & Lake Erie; on the east by Pennsylvania & West Virginia; on the south by West Virginia, Kentucky & the Ohio River & on the west by Indiana. **Total area:** 41,222 sq. mi. (ranks 35th). **Extreme length:** 230 mi. **Extreme breadth:** 210 mi. **Shoreline:** 312 mi. **Chief rivers:** Ohio, Miami, Muskingum. **Major lakes:** Erie, Grand. **No. of counties:** 88.

Population (1978 est.): 10,749,000 (ranks 6th). **Pop. increase (1970-78):** 0.9%. **Places over 25,000 pop.:** 46. **Places over 100,000:** 7. **Largest cities:** Cleveland, Columbus, Cincinnati, Toledo. **Pop. density:** 260.8 per sq. mi. (ranks 8th). **Pop. projection 1985:** 10,861,000. **Pop. distribution:** 79.9% metropolitan; 20.1% nonmetropolitan. **White:** 90.6%. **Negro:** 9.1%. **Other:** 0.3%. **Marriage rate (1977):** 9.1 per 1,000 people. **Divorce rate:** 5.4 per 1,000 people.

State finances (1977). Revenue: $8,975,675,000. **Expenditures:** $8,168,648,000. **State Taxes:** $333.69 per capita. **State personal income tax:** Yes. **Public debt (1977):** $299.53 per capita. **Federal aid (1977):** $154.79 per capita. **Personal income (1977):** $7,090.

Sectors of the economy (% of labor force employed in 1970): Manufacturing (36%), Wholesale and retail trade (19%), Services (6%), Educational Services (7%), Construction (5%), Government (13%). **Leading products:** transportation equipment, primary & fabricated metals, machinery, rubber & plastic items. **Minerals:** bituminous coal, limestone, sand & gravel, salt, oil. **Agricultural products:** milk, hogs, cattle & calves, corn, soybeans. **Fishing:** yellow perch, catfish, white bass, yellow pike. **Avg. farm (1978 est.):** 156 acres. **Avg. value of farm per acre:** $1,263.

Highway expenditures per capita (1977): $73.69. **Persons per motor vehicle:** 1.43. **Minimum age for driver's license:** 18. **Gasoline tax:** 7¢ per gallon. **Motor vehicle deaths:** 19.1 per 100,000 people.

Birthrate (1977): 15.1 per 1,000 people. **Infant mortality rate per 1,000 births (1977):** 13.9. **Physicians per 100,000 pop. (1976):** 150. **Dentists per 100,000 pop. (1976):** 45. **Acceptable hospital beds:** 6.6 per 1,000 people. **State expenditures per capita for health and hospitals (1977):** $51.88.

OHIO

MILES
0 10 20 30 40 50

KILOMETERS
0 10 20 30 40 50

⊛ State Capital
⦿ County Seats

Education expenditures (1975-76): $415.77 per capita annually. **No. of pupils in public schools (1977 est.):** 2,217,000. **No. of institutions of higher learning (1976-77):** 131. **Public school expenditure per pupil in attendance (1975-76):** $1,481. **Avg. salary of public school teachers (1974-75 est.):** $9,176. **No. full-time teachers (1977 est.):** 118,810. **Educational attainment of adult population (1976):** 12.4 median yrs. of school completed; 1.7% with less than 5 years of education; 11.5% with 4 yrs. of college.

Telephones (1976): 70 per 100 people. **State Chamber of Commerce:** Ohio Chamber of Commerce, Huntington Bank Building, 17 S. High Street, 8th Floor, Columbus, Ohio 43215.

OKLAHOMA

Oil-rich Oklahoma, the nation's Indian Territory in the early 19th century has the largest Indian population of any state. Generally considered an agricultural state, even though the value of its manufacturing and mining output exceeds cash farm revenue, the state earns more from livestock and livestock products (especially cattle) than it does from crops. Manufacturing, although gradually becoming more diverse, is still based for the most part on the processing of the state's own farm and mineral products. Most industry is located in and around Oklahoma City and Tulsa, which also rank among the world's foremost gas and oil centers.

Topographically, the state is largely a rolling plain sloping generally from northwest to southeast, with a mean altitude of 1,300 feet. About three-fourths of the state, especially the central area, consists of the Osage Plains section of the Central Lowlands. The Great Plains region, making up the northwestern panhandle, slopes from 4,973 feet at Black Mesa in the west (the state's highest point) to about 287 feet in the extreme Southeast. Vast wheat fields and broad grazing lands characterize much of the terrain, punctuated by such features as the Wichita, Arbuckle, Ouachita, and Ozark Mountains in the southwest, southcenter, southeast and northeast, respectively. A segment of the West Gulf Coastal Plains covers the extreme southeastern corner of the state. A quarter of the land is forested, but only pine and hardwood in the southeast are commercially significant.

Various bands of buffalo-hunting Indians roamed the Oklahoma region before the coming of the first European, Spanish explorer Coronado, who crossed (1541) what is today the Oklahoma panhandle. All the area except it came under U.S. sovereignty via the Louisiana Purchase (1803), and a year later that part of the purchase north of present-day Louisiana was made the District of Louisiana and was governed as part of Indiana Territory. The district became in turn the Territory of Louisiana (1805) and the Missouri Territory (1812).

In 1819, Arkansas Territory, including the present state of Oklahoma, was formed from a part of Missouri Territory. A few years later, the U.S. Government designated part of the region Indian Territory and used it for the forcible resettlement of the Five Civilized Tribes (Cherokee, Choctaw, Chickasaw, Creek, and Seminole), who had been living in relatively close contact with white men of the southeastern states for more than 100 years. Some of these Indians pursued farming in the traditional Southern mold, even maintaining slaves. When the Civil War erupted, the Indians were caught up in it, fighting on both sides and suffering invasions from both Confederate and Union forces.

After the war, the five tribes were punished collectively for those Indians who had supported the Confederacy; the western part of the Indian Territory was taken from them, and much of it was assigned to other tribes in the country that the government wanted resettled. White encroachments, led by Kansas-bound Texas cattlemen, soon followed despite laws and Indian treaties; a number of cattle trails, including the famed Chisholm Trail, were forged across the state. The first railroad across the region (built 1870-72) brought still more white settlers. The influx was legalized when a large strip of land was opened for settlement on April 22, 1889. Some of the settlers who entered before the proper time were called "sooners," giving rise to Oklahoma's nickname, the Sooner State.

The western section of present-day Oklahoma was made Oklahoma Territory in 1890, and for a time Oklahoma and Indian (the "twin") Territories existed side by side. The Indians wanted separate admission to the Union, as the state of Sequoyah, but in 1907 the territories were merged and admitted as a single state.

Oklahoma's advances in the economic sphere include expanding aerospace facilities in Tulsa, several tire manufacturing plants, one of the world's largest paper mills at Valliant in the southeastern section, and Western Electric, General Motors and Honeywell plants, the FAA center and Wilson & Co., all in Oklahoma City. The Arkansas River navigation project, the largest single domestic project ever undertaken by the Army Corps of Engineers, has made Tulsa a port city via a new channel and system of locks dredged from Tulsa across Arkansas to the Mississippi River. In agriculture, conservation methods have been inaugurated since the Dust Bowl days of the 1930s and, in some areas, irrigation is used to offset frequent droughts. Wheat is the principal crop.

Tourism in recent years has boomed with an increased advertising program, with much of the emphasis put on the state parks, lodges and recreation areas located on the system of large manmade lakes. Other tourist attractions include the Will Rogers Memorial (at Claremore, near his birthplace at Oologah), the Philbrook Art Center (Tulsa), Indian City U.S.A. (near Anadarko) with authentic copies of Indian villages of the early 1800s, Tsa-La-Gi Cherokee Indian village (Tahlequah) where "The Trail of Tears," pageant depicting the Cherokee removal to Oklahoma, is performed during the summer, and the National Cowboy Hall of Fame and Western Heritage Center (Oklahoma City). Rodeos, Indian pow-wows and rattlesnake hunts also are among the state's annual events.

Full name: State of Oklahoma. **Origin of name:** From Choctaw meaning "Red People." **Inhabitant:** Oklahoman. **Capital:** Oklahoma City. **State motto:** Labor Omnia Vincit (Labor Conquers All Things). **Flag:** Symbols of war & peace on a blue field. **Seal:** Indian & white man shaking hands before justice, representing cooperation of all people of state; large star has symbols of the Five Civilized Tribes from the southeastern states, forced by the government to resettle in this region. **Flower:** Mistletoe. **Bird:** Scissortailed flycatcher. **Tree:** Redbud. **Song:** "Oklahoma!" **Nickname:** Sooner State.

Governor: George Nigh. **Annual salary:** $48,000. **Term:** 4 years. **Current term expires:** Jan. 1983. **Voting requirements:** 18 yrs. old & U.S. citizen; resident of state; registered with County Election Board. **U.S. Congressmen:** 6. **Entered Union:** 1907 (46th state).

Location & boundaries: South Central state: bounded on the north by Colorado & Kansas; on the east by Missouri & Arkansas; on the south by Texas & the Red River; & on the west by Texas & New Mexico. **Total area:** 69,919 sq. mi. (ranks 18th). **Extreme length:** 464 mi. **Extreme breadth:** 230 mi. **Chief rivers:** Red, Arkansas, Cimarron, Canadian. **Major lakes:** Texoma, Eufaula, Oologah Reservoir. **No. of counties:** 77.

OKLAHOMA

Population (1978 est.): 2,880,000 (ranks 27th). **Pop. increase (1970-78):** 12.5%. **Places over 25,000 pop.:** 13. **Places over 100,000:** 2. **Largest cities:** Oklahoma City, Tulsa, Lawton, Norman. **Pop. density:** 41.2 per sq. mi. (ranks 34th). **Pop. projection 1985:** 3,016,000. **Pop. distribution:** 55.6% metropolitan; 44.4% nonmetropolitan. **White:** 88.9%. **Negro:** 7%. **Other:** 4.1%. **Marriage rate (1977):** 14.7 per 1,000 people. **Divorce rate:** 7.8 per 1,000 people.

State finances (1977). Revenue: $2,283,116,000. **Expenditures:** $2,138,132,000. **State Taxes:** $405.19 per capita. **State personal income tax:** Yes. **Public debt (1977):** $333.42 per capita. **Federal aid (1977):** $207.95 per capita. **Personal income (1977):** $6,269.

Sectors of the economy (% of labor force employed in 1974): Manufacturing (14.4%), Wholesale & retail trade (14.8%), Services (12.7%), Educational Services (9%), Construction (4.2%), Government (20%). **Leading products:** food items; machinery; petroleum and coal items; stone, clay & glass items; transportation equipment; fabricated metals; apparel. **Minerals:** petroleum and coal, natural gas & natural gas liquids, cement. **Agricultural products:** cattle, dairy items, hogs, wheat, hay, sorghum grain. **Avg. farm (1978 est.):** 432 acres. **Avg. value of farm per acre:** $402.

Highway expenditures per capita (1977): $94.50. **Persons per motor vehicle:** 1.22. **Minimum age for driver's license:** 16. **Gasoline tax:** 6.58¢ per gallon. **Motor vehicle deaths:** 31.3 per 100,000 people.

Birthrate (1977): 16.2 per 1,000 people. **Infant mortality rate per 1,000 births (1977):** 13.7. **Physicians per 100,000 pop. (1976):** 121. **Dentists per 100,000 pop. (1976):** 38. **Acceptable hospital beds:** 6.2 per 1,000 people. **State expenditures per capita for health and hospitals (1977):** $45.23.

Education expenditures (1975-76): $381.21 per capita annually. **No. of pupils in public schools (1977 est.):** 589,000. **No. of institutions of higher learning (1976-77):** 44. **Public school expenditure per pupil in attendance (1975-76):** $1,278. **Avg. salary of public school teachers (1974-75 est.):** $9,208. **No. full-time teachers (1977 est.):** 31,050. **Educational attainment of adult population (1976):** 12.4 median yrs. of school completed; 2.8% with less than 5 years of education; 11.7% with 4 yrs. of college.

Telephones (1976): 72 per 100 people. **State Chamber of Commerce:** Oklahoma State Chamber of Commerce, 4020 N. Lincoln Blvd., Oklahoma City, Oklahoma 73105.

OREGON

With more than 30 million acres of trees (nearly half the state's total area), Oregon is the nation's leading lumber state. Its awesome scenery includes mountains, plains, lush valleys, and immense forests. The 400-mile Pacific coast is marked by the thickly forested Coast Range and the Klamath Mountains that parallel it.

There are four other general land areas: the Cascade Mountains, the Willamette Valley between the coastal elevations and the Cascades, the Columbia Plateau, and the Basin and Range Region.

The Cascade Range is a climatic dividing line: there is mild, moist weather in the west, and in the east dry weather that is warmer in summer and colder in winter than the west's.

Except for the section in the southeast known as the Basin and Range Region, the entire area east of the Cascades is called the Columbia Plateau; this plateau, comprising two-thirds of the state, was formed thousands of years ago when lava gushed forth from the Earth's crust, which has since been covered by rolling plains, and, along the desolate southern edge, the Harney Desert. It was across these plains that settlers from the East came, along the Oregon Trail.

Portland, 100 miles inland, is reached from the Pacific via the Columbia River, and is one of the West Coast's major ports; the Portland area contains about half of Oregon's total population.

Oregon produces about a fourth of the nation's lumber and about 70 percent of our plywood. Centered in the Willamette Valley, wood processing is the state's leading manufacturing industry.

There is some mining in the state, principally of nickel, gemstones, and construction materials. Agriculture, shipping, fishing (mainly for Chinook and silver salmon), metal and food processing, and tourism are also economically significant. Attractions include Hells Canyon, Mount Hood, and Crater Lake, a brilliantly blue, clear body of water that is the principal feature of the national park bearing its name; the nation's deepest lake (1,932 feet), it is six miles wide and was formed 6,600 years ago when the peak of Mount Mazama, in which the lake is set, collapsed after violent volcanic activity. Another tourist attraction is Kah-Nee-Ta Vacation Resort in the Warm Springs Indian Reservation, which was developed by 2,000 Northwest tribesmen; it offers hot mineral baths, swimming, fishing, and riding.

Chinook, Tillamook, Clackama, and Multnomah Indians were among the Oregon Country's earliest known inhabitants. Spanish seamen, sailing from Mexico to the Philippines, are thought to have been the first Europeans to sight the Oregon coast, in the 1500s and 1600s. Captain Cook, seeking the Northwest Passage to the Atlantic, charted some of the coastline in 1778. The Columbia River was discovered in 1792, and the Lewis and Clark expedition passed through the region in 1805.

The nineteenth century was marked by the conflict of British and American claims to the area that were eventually resolved by treaty in 1846. Two years later, Oregon became a territory, which until 1853 also included present-day Washington. Statehood came in 1859. In 1860 the discovery of gold in what is now Idaho turned Portland into a vital trade center for the entire Pacific Northwest. Transcontinental rail service came to Oregon in 1883.

In the early part of the 20th century, a series of reform measures were enacted in what came to be known as the Oregon System; this system, designed to make government more responsive to those governed, featured a referendum amendment, a direct primary, and a recall provision. Oregon women were given the vote in 1912.

The state also has developed a broad program for improving the environment and given its Department of Environmental Quality the power to enforce the regulations. Noise, pollution and solid waste also fall under the jurisdiction of the Department of Environmental Quality. In addition, Oregon has adopted a Scenic Waterways plan for state ownership of land along many rivers in the state as well as a law for public ownership of the ocean beaches. It was the first state to prohibit throwaway beverage bottles and cans. It also has eliminated criminal penalties for possession of marijuana. In 1975, Gov. Robert Straub signed a bill making Oregon the first state to ban aerosol cans using fluorocarbons, effective Feb. 1977.

Full name: State of Oregon. **Origin of name:** Probably from Spanish, Orejon, meaning "Big-eared men." **Inhabitant:** Oregonian. **Capital:** Salem. **State motto:** The Union. **Flag:** State seal & lettering in yellow on a blue field. **Seal:** Departing British man-of-war & arriving American merchant ship symbolize end of British influence & rise of American power; sheaf of grain, pickax & plow represent mining & agriculture. **Flower:** Oregon grape. **Bird:** Western meadowlark. **Fish:** Chinook salmon; **Rock:** Thunderegg. **Tree:** Douglas fir. **Song:** "Oregon, My Oregon." **Nickname:** Beaver State.

Governor: Victor Atiyeh. **Annual salary:** $50,372. **Term:** 4 years. **Current term expires:** Jan. 1983. **Voting requirements:** 18 yrs. old

& U.S. citizen; must be registered 20 days before election. **U.S. Congressmen:** 4 **Entered Union:** 1859 (33rd state).

Location & boundaries: Pacific state: bounded on the north by the Columbia River & Washington; on the east by Idaho & the Snake River; on the south by Nevada & California; & on the west by the Pacific Ocean. **Total area:** 96,981 sq. mi. (ranks 10th). **Extreme length:** 295 mi. **Extreme breadth:** 395 mi. **Coastline:** 360 mi. **Chief rivers:** Columbia, Snake, Willamette. **Major lakes:** Upper Klamath, Malheur, Crater. **No. of counties:** 36.

Population (1978 est.): 2,444,000 (ranks 29th). **Pop. increase (1970-78):** 16.9%. **Places over 25,000 pop.:** 7. **Places over 100,000:** 1. **Largest cities:** Portland, Eugene, Salem. **Pop. density:** 25.2 per sq. mi. (ranks 39th). **Pop projection 1985:** 2,610,000. **Pop. distribution:** 59.9% metropolitan; 40.1% non-metropolitan. **White:** 97.2%. **Negro:** 1.2%. **Other:** 1.6%. **Marriage rate (1977):** 8.8 per 1,000 people. **Divorce rate:** 6.9 per 1,000 people.

State finances (1977). Revenue: $2,638,018,000. **Expenditures:** $2,272,393,000. **State Taxes:** $409.57 per capita. **State personal income tax:** Yes. **Public debt (1977):** $1,023.25 per capita. **Federal aid (1977):** $258.89 per capita. **Personal income (1977):** $7,014.

Sectors of the economy (% of labor force employed in 1970): Manufacturing (21%), Wholesale and retail trade (22%), Services (7%), Educational Services (10%), Construction (6%), Government (17%). **Leading products:** lumber & wood items, food items, paper items, machinery, fabricated metals, printing & publishing. **Agricultural products:** wheat, livestock, barley, oats, hops, legumes, potatoes, berries, fruits, nuts, truck crops, dairy and poultry products, sugar beets, corn, green beans and peppermint. **Fishing:** salmon, tuna, bottom fish (sole, rockfish, halibut, cod, etc.) and shellfish. **Avg. farm (1978 est.):** 565 acres. **Avg. value of farm per acre:** $303.

Highway expenditures per capita (1977): $99.74. **Persons per motor vehicle:** 1.34. **Minimum age for driver's license:** 16. **Gasoline tax:** 7¢ per gallon. **Motor vehicle deaths:** 28.9 per 100,000 people.

Birthrate (1977): 15.8 per 1,000 people. **Infant mortality rate per 1,000 births (1977):** 12.2. **Physicians per 100,000 pop. (1976):** 173. **Dentists per 100,000 pop. (1976):** 67. **Acceptable hospital beds:** 5.2 per 1,000 people. **State expenditures per capita for health and hospitals (1977):** $58.31.

Education expenditures (1975-76): $548.98 per capita annually. **No. of pupils in public schools (1977 est.):** 468,000. **No. of institutions of higher learning (1976-77):** 43. **Public school expenditure per pupil in attendance (1975-76):** $1,995. **Avg. salary of public school teachers (1974-75 est.):** $10,958. **No. full-time teachers (1977 est.):** 25,150. **Educational attainment of adult population (1976):** 12.7 median yrs. of school completed; 1.1% with less than 5 years of education; 15.4% with 4 yrs. of college.

Telephones (1976): 70 per 100 people. **State Chamber of Commerce:** Associated Oregon Industries, Inc., P.O. Box 12519, 1149 Court Street, N.E., Salem, Oregon 97309.

PENNSYLVANIA

Called the "Keystone State" because of its central location among the 13 Colonies, Pennsylvania is today an important economic center and a rich repository of Americana. The state, which enjoys an abundant water supply, is the nation's fourth most populous, and manufacturing, mining, farming, and tourism are all important to its economy.

Pennsylvania produces nearly all the country's hard coal and a fourth of its steel. Oil is also important, although not so much so as in the 1890s; the first oil well in the world was drilled (1859) near Titusville. Dairy farming flourishes today in the northeast, as does cattle raising in the southwest; throughout the fertile, well-farmed southeast countryside can be seen the highly decorated barns of the Pennsylvania Dutch.

Pittsburgh was the home (1920) of the first radio broadcasting station, and the first electric computer was built (1945) in Philadelphia; these cities, along with Erie, provide the state with three fine ports. Philadelphia is the dominantly large city of the eastern region (as Pittsburgh is of the western).

Roughly rectangular, the state is crossed from west to east by the Erie Lowland, Appalachian Plateau (by far the largest single region), Great Appalachian Valley, Blue Ridge, Piedmont Plateau, New England Uplands, and Atlantic Coastal Plain. Among the many attractions are 495 state park and recreation areas, as well as Valley Forge and Gettysburg Battlefield national shrines, scenes of decisive events in the American Revolution and the Civil War.

The state's early history is shared in large part with neighboring Delaware, which it once contained. Swedes made the first permanent settlement (1643) in the Pennsylvania region at Tinicum Island in the Schuylkill River, but Swedish rule soon gave way (1655) to Dutch. The English supplanted the Dutch in 1664, as King Charles II put the region under the control of his brother James, Duke of York. In 1681, the king granted the region to Quaker William Penn, naming it after Penn's father, an admiral in the Royal Navy to whom the king was indebted. Penn's era, which except for a brief interruption (1692-94) lasted until his death in 1718, was an enlightened and fruitful one.

The so-called Charter of Privileges (1701) gave Pennsylvania the most liberal of colonial governments, and there shortly followed a cultural flowering as well. Benjamin Franklin of Philadelphia published *The Pennsylvania Gazette* (1729-1766) and the *Poor Richard's Almanack* (1732-1757), in addition to pursuing his interest in politics and science. The nation's first magazine, *The American Magazine, or A Monthly View of the Political State of the British Colonies*, was established (1741) in Philadelphia. Penn's notably fair-minded dealings with the Indians, including his famous treaty, kept the region free of the usual frontier bloodshed. But Penn's successors—especially his son Thomas, who took over in 1746—lacked his vision and conciliatory gifts, and troubles with the French and Indians lasted from 1754 until the suppression of Pontiac's Rebellion in 1763. Pennsylvania was involved at various times in boundary disputes with four other colonies: Maryland, Virginia, Connecticut, and New York. The bitterest wrangle was the one with Connecticut over the Wyoming Valley, which gave rise to the Pennamite Wars (1769-71 and 1784). The northwestern "Erie triangle" was bought first from the Indians, and later from the federal government, following a 1789 agreement with New York setting the northern border at the 42nd parallel; the parcel was purchased to secure an Erie port for the colony. The establishment of the Mason-Dixon line (1767) settled Pennsylvania's differences with Maryland and Virginia.

After the American Revolution, in which Pennsylvania played a central role, settlement increased in the western region and in the upper Susquehanna Valley. The country's first paved road, the Philadelphia-Lancaster Turnpike, was completed in 1794. In 1811, a Robert Fulton steamboat was launched at Pittsburgh and became the first to traverse the Ohio and Mississippi rivers. The Schuylkill Canal, one of the nations first long canals (completed 1825), connected Philadelphia and Reading.

The state strongly supported the Union cause in the Civil War, and only New York contributed more troops.

The most widespread flood in the state's history struck in June 1972, when Hurricane Agnes, di-

PENNSYLVANIA

minished to a tropical storm remained stationary over the central part of the state for 24 hours. Officials termed it the worst natural disaster in the state's history. In September 1975 the Susquehanna again overflowed its banks in the wake of Hurricane Eloise, with damage estimated at over $200 million.

The Three Mile Island nuclear power plant, located ten miles south of Harrisburg, became a hotbed of tension and controversy beginning March 28, 1979, as a series of breakdowns in the cooling system of its No. 2 reactor led to a major accident. The significant threats facing the area were two-fold: the possibility of a core meltdown which would have spelled disaster in terms of human lives and the chance of an explosion of the hydrogen gas bubble that had formed in the overheated reactor vessel. Neither threat became a reality, however. On March 31 the first situation seemed to stabilize as federal officials observed a cooling and slowdown in abnormal activity within the reactor core. Five days later after the accident there was some sign that the hydrogen bubble had been reduced and by day seven it had been announced that the bubble had been eliminated.

Amid debate and protest after the incident, it was reported that a combination of human, mechanical and design errors had contributed to the accident. Among the significant errors detailed, Metropolitan Edison Co., the plant operator, was cited for a major violation of federal regulations.

The incident resulted in President Carter's announcing April 5 the formation of a panel to investigate the accident, and in a number of states moving to either curtail or reassess their commitment to nuclear power. On July 16, the utility company announced that it would take four years and about $400 million to repair the reactor.

Full name: Commonwealth of Pennsylvania. **Origin of name:** In honor of William Penn, father of the founder. **Inhabitant:** Pennsylvanian. **Capital:** Harrisburg. **State motto:** Virtue, Liberty & Independence. **Flag:** State seal & motto supported by two horses on gold-bordered blue field. **Seal:** Eagle, ship, plow & sheaves of wheat stand for strength, commerce & agricultural abundance; stalk of corn & olive branch represent peace & plenty. **Flower:** Mountain laurel. **Bird:** Ruffed grouse. **Tree:** Hemlock. **Song:** None. **Nickname:** Keystone State.

Governor: Richard L. Thornburgh. **Annual salary:** $66,000. **Term:** 4 years. **Current term expires:** Jan. 1983. **Voting requirements:** 18 yrs. old & U.S. citizen; resident of state (or district) for 30 days. **U.S. Congressmen:** 25. **Entered Union:** 1787 (2nd state).

Location & boundries: Middle Atlantic state: bounded on the north by New York; on the east by the Delaware River, New York & New Jersey; on the southeast by Delaware & the Delaware River; on the south by Maryland & West Virginia; on the west by West Virginia & Ohio; & on the northwest by Lake Erie. **Total area:** 45,333 sq. mi. (ranks 33rd). **Extreme length:** 307 mi. **Extreme breadth:** 169 mi. **Shoreline:** 51 mi. **Chief rivers:** Delaware, Allegheny, Susquehanna. **Major lakes:** Erie, Wallenpaupack; Pymatuning & Bear Creek Reservoirs. **No. of counties:** 67.

Population (1978 est.): 11,750,000 (ranks 4th). **Pop. increase (1970-78):** 80.4%. **Places over 25,000 pop.:** 23. **Places over 100,000:** 4. **Largest cities:** Philadelphia, Pittsburgh, Erie, Allentown. **Pop. density:** 259.2 per sq. mi. (ranks 9th). **Pop. projection 1985:** 12,032,000. **Pop. distribution:** 80.5% metropolitan, 19.5% nonmetropolitan. **White:** 91.1%. **Negro:** 8.6%. **Other:** 0.3%. **Marriage rate (1977):** 7.8 per 1,000 people. **Divorce rate:** 3.2 per 1,000 people.

State finances (1977). Revenue: $11,091,470,000. **Expenditures:** $11,207,936,000. **State Taxes:** $474.40 per capita. **State personal income tax:** No. **Public debt (1977):** $541.70 per capita. **Federal aid (1977):** $190.01 per capita. **Personal income (1977):** $7,001.

Sectors of the economy (% of labor force employed in 1970): Manufacturing (34%), Wholesale and retail trade (19%), Services (6%), Educational Services (7%), Construction (5%), Government (13%). **Leading products:** primary and fabricated metals, food items, machinery, chemicals, apparel. **Minerals:** coal, cement, stone, sand & gravel. **Agricultural Products:** dairy items, cattle, hogs, hay, corn, oats, wheat. **Avg. farm (1978 est.):** 139 acres. **Avg. value of farm per acre:** $1,092.

Highway expenditures per capita (1977): $80.32. **Persons per motor vehicle:** 1.45. **Minimum age for driver's license:** 18. **Gasoline tax:** 9¢ per gallon. **Motor vehicle deaths:** 17.8 per 100,000 people.

Birthrate (1977): 13.0 per 1,000 people. **Infant mortality rate per 1,000 births (1977):** 14.0. **Physicians per 100,000 pop. (1976):** 173. **Dentists per 100,000 pop. (1976):** 51. **Acceptable hospital beds:** 7.8 per 1,000 people. **State expenditures per capita for health and hospitals (1977):** $68.34.

Education expenditures (1975-76): $407.55 per capita annually. **No. of pupils in public schools (1977 est.):** 2,162,000. **No. of institutions of higher learning (1976-77):** 179. **Public school expenditure per pupil in attendance (1975-76):** $1,914. **Avg. salary of public school teachers (1974-75 est.):** $12,200. **No. full-time teachers (1977 est.):** 135,270. **Educational attainment of adult population (1976):** 12.4 median yrs. of school completed; 2.3% with less than 5 years of education; 11.9% with 4 yrs. of college.

Telephones (1976): 76 per 100 people. **State Chamber of Commerce:** Pennsylvania Chamber of Commerce, 222 North Third Street, Harrisburg, Pennsylvania 17101.

RHODE ISLAND

Rhode Island, the nation's smallest state, is not an island, although many small islands are contained within it, including one in Narragansett Bay, Aquidneck Island.

The Bay, which extends inland 28 miles from the Atlantic Ocean, is the predominant feature of the state's eastern section, which comprises about two-thirds of the total area and includes Providence, Pawtucket, and most of Rhode Island's other major cities. The remaining northeastern third of the state is rough, hilly terrain rising east to northwest from 200 to 800 feet above sea level—this section being a part of the New England Uplands, which extend from Maine to Connecticut. Offshore, ten miles south of the mainland, is Block Island, an important navigation landmark. Sixty-seven percent of the state's area is forested, but mostly with "restocked" trees not yet suitable for lumber. Damaging hurricanes occasionally plague the coast.

Once dominated economically by the textile industry, Rhode Island has added many new industries, in a continuing drive toward greater diversification. Small commercial fishing fleets operate out of several ports.

Explorer Giovanni da Verrazano is thought to have been the first European to visit (1524) the region. Adriaen Block explored there in 1614. In 1636, Roger Williams, looking for a place where "persons distressed for conscience" could go, left Puritan-controlled Massachusetts and founded Providence, the state's first settlement. Two years later Williams organized the country's first Baptist congregation.

Despite harsh, costly combat with the Indians in King Philip's War (1675-76), the region prospered, thanks in large measure to the "triangular trade"—vessels carried rum from Newport to Africa, slaves from there to the West Indies, and molasses from there to Newport, where it was made into rum. Later, Rhode Island renounced slavery, prohibiting (1774) the importation of slaves; it also strongly backed the Union in the Civil War. The economic gap that the passing of the triangular trade left was soon filled by the rapid growth of manufacturing, spurred by Samuel Sla-

RHODE ISLAND

MILES
0   2   4   6   8   10

KILOMETERS
0   2   4   6   8   10

State Capital ⊛   Courthouses ◉

© Copyright HAMMOND INCORPORATED, Maplewood, N.J.

Longitude West of Greenwich

ter's pioneering in mechanized textile production and by a heavy influx of European immigrants who provided an ample labor pool.

From its beginnings, Rhode Island has been famous for its insistence on political and religious freedom, attracting oppressed and refuge-seeking settlers, and the state's rebellious, iconoclastic character streak soon became evident. In 1769, Newport rebels scuttled the British revenue ship *Liberty* and, three years later, in protest to British trade and navigation laws, a group of Providence men burned the English ship *Gaspee* to the water's edge in Narragansett Bay where it had run aground. Rhode Island was the last of the original 13 states to ratify (1790) the Constitution.

Rhode Island also balked at Jefferson's Embargo Act of 1807, and in the War of 1812 it refused to allow its militia to serve outside its borders. Thomas Wilson Dorr and other Rhode Islanders made an abortive revolution in 1842 ("Dorr's Rebellion"), which nonetheless effected a small measure of legislative reform.

In the late 1800s Newport became a fashionable summer home for the very rich, and many palatial mansions were built, some of which are now open for tourists to visit. Today Newport is the country's yachting capital, host to the America's Cup, Newport-Bermuda, and transatlantic races. In 1976, Newport was the first port of welcome for the spectacular fleet of Tall Ships, which sailed from throughout the world to commemorate the bicentennial of the United States. The flotilla assembled was one of the largest ever.

Rhode Island is presently trying to broaden its economic base by expanding its tourist industry. Music festivals and dramas highlight the summer's entertainment possibilities, along with fishing tournaments and regattas.

In February 1979, the Supreme Court of the state overturned the state's death penalty on the grounds that it was cruel and unusual punishment. The court ruled that the 1973 law did not allow a judge to consider mitigating circumstances.

Full name: State of Rhode Island & Providence Plantations. **Origin of name:** In honor of the Isle of Rhodes: name chosen by General Court of Colony. **Inhabitant:** Rhode Islander. **Capital:** Providence. **State motto:** Hope. **Flag:** Golden anchor & 12 gold stars on white field. **Seal:** State motto printed above anchor, symbolizing hope; date 1636 was year Roger Williams founded Providence. **Flower:** (unofficial) Violet. **Bird:** Rhode Island red. **Tree:** Red maple. **Song:** "Rhode Island." **Nickname:** Little Rhody.

Governor: John J. Garrahy. **Annual salary:** $42,500. **Term:** 2 years. **Current term expires:** Jan. 1981. **Voting requirements:** 18 yrs. old & U.S. citizen; resident of city or town 30 days. **U.S. Congressmen:** 2. **Entered Union:** 1790 (13th state).

Location & boundaries: New England state; bounded on the north & east by Massachusetts; on the west by Connecticut; & on the south by New York where Block Island Sound meets Long Island Sound in the Atlantic Ocean. **Total area:** 1,214 sq. mi. (ranks 50th). **Extreme length:** 48 mi. **Extreme breadth:** 37 mi. **Coastline:** 40 mi. **Chief rivers:** Sakonnet, Blackstone, Woonasquatuket, Pawtuxet. **Major lakes:** Worden Pond, Scituate Reservoir. **No. of counties:** 5.

Population (1978 est.): 935,000 (ranks 39th). **Pop. increase (1970-78):** -1.6%. **Places over 25,000 pop.:** 11. **Places over 100,000:** 1. **Largest cities:** Providence, Warwick, Cranston. **Pop. density:** 770.2 per sq. mi. (ranks 2nd). **Pop. projection 1985:** 1,003,000. **Pop. distribution:** 92.3% metropolitan, 7.7% non-metropolitan. **White:** 96.6%. **Negro:** 2.7%. **Other:** 0.7%. **Marriage rate (1977):** 7.6 per 1,000 people. **Divorce rate:** 3.7 per 1,000 people.

State finances (1977). Revenue: $1,037,637,000. **Expenditures:** $972,252,000. **State Taxes:** $469.35 per capita. **State personal income tax:** Yes. **Public debt (1977):** $684.84 per capita. **Federal aid (1977):** $277.93 per capita. **Personal income (1977):** $6,775.

Sectors of the economy (% of labor force employed in 1970): Manufacturing (35%), Wholesale and retail trade (19%), Services (6%), Educational Services (8%), Construction (5%), Government (16%). **Leading products:** jewelry & silverware, textile items, primary metals, machinery, fabricated metals, electrical equipment, rubber and plastic items. **Avg. farm (1978 est.):** 92 acres. **Avg. value per farm per acre:** $1,939.

Highway expenditures per capita (1977): $40.21. **Persons per motor vehicle:** 1.40. **Minimum age for driver's license:** 18. **Gasoline tax:** 10¢ per gallon. **Motor vehicle deaths:** 11.6 per 100,000 people.

Birthrate (1977): 12.4 per 1,000 people. **Infant mortality rate per 1,000 births (1977):** 12.1. **Physicians per 100,000 pop. (1976):** 195. **Dentists per 100,000 pop. (1976):** 50. **Acceptable hospital beds:** 7.8 per 1,000 people. **State expenditures per capita for health and hospitals (1977):** $101.08.

Education expenditures (1975-76): $433.78 per capita annually. **No. of pupils in public schools (1977 est.):** 170,000. **No. of institutions of higher learning (1976-77):** 12. **Public school expenditure per pupil in attendance (1975-76):** $1,722. **Average salary of public school teachers (1974-75 est.):** $12,885. **No. full-time teachers (1977 est.):** 10,960. **Educational attainment of adult population (1976):** 12.4 median yrs. of school completed; 3.4% with less than 5 years of education; 14.9% with 4 yrs. of college.

Telephones (1976): 72 per 100 people. **State Chamber of Commerce:** Rhode Island Chamber of Commerce Federation, 206 Smith Street, Providence, Rhode Island 02908.

SOUTH CAROLINA

South Carolina, where the Civil War began, was the first state to secede from the Union. One of the 13 Colonies, it is particularly rich in historic sites, which help draw a growing number of tourists annually. Vivid contrasts often confront the visitor: inlet-dotted swampland gives way to hill country, and estates graced by handsome Georgian homes are set off by poor areas in which shacks are not uncommon. A major U.S. Marine Corps training center is located at Parris Island, near Beaufort.

Vast projects such as the Atomic Energy Commission's $1.2-billion Savannah River Plant (near Aiken) underscore South Carolina's transition from a basically agrarian economy to one in which industry plays the leading part. Livestock raising and commercial fishing are also significant.

Two main land regions make up the roughly triangular-shaped state: the "low country," making up two-thirds of the total area and consisting of a part of the Atlantic Coastal Plain rising northwest from the ocean to a fall line running parallel to the coast and bisecting Columbia; and the "up country," consisting of a portion of the Piedmont Plateau and, in the extreme northwest, a small segment of the Blue Ridge Mountains of the Appalachian range. South of the Santee River's mouth are the Sea Islands, a long chain of offshore isles reaching down the rest of the state's length. Water is abundant, and the sharp drops in the land surface make the state rich in hydroelectric-power potential. About two-thirds of the land is forested, contributing to a sizable timber industry.

Giovanni da Verrazano is thought to have been the first to explore (1524) the coast of the region that later became North and South Carolina; an initial Spanish settlement (1526) at Winyah Bay suffered a malaria outbreak and did not endure.

The first English settlement in present-day South Carolina was made (1670) at Albemarle Point on the Ashley River, but poor conditions drove the settlers to the site of Charleston (originally Charles Town). There grew the core of a prosperous though ultimately unstable economy based on the slave-supported cultivation of rice and

SOUTH CAROLINA

indigo. Although North and South Carolina were officially a single province, they had separate governors until 1691; from that year until 1712, a sole governor was based at Charleston while his deputy governed North Carolina. After 1712, North and South Carolina were governed independently again, and in 1729 they officially became separate royal provinces; the definition of the boundary between them was not completed, however, until 1815.

South Carolina, in the years before the American Revolution, progressed economically despite wars with the Spanish and French, and with pirates and Indians; there was a revolt against proprietary rule in 1719, and a slave uprising in 1739. An influx of Germans, Swiss, and Scots-Irish—from abroad and from neighboring states—helped settle the uplands and the lower middle country. Social and economic differences between the small-scale farmers of the up country and the plantation lords of the low country gave rise to regional disputes, culminating in the Regulator Movement for up country reforms. Statehood dates from 1788.

The early part of the 19th century in South Carolina was marked by a decline in agriculture and an increasingly contentious dialogue between the state and the Federal government on the issue of states' rights. South Carolina's Nullification Act (1832) declared a new, higher U.S. tariff act null and void; the immediate issue was resolved (1833) by compromise, but the larger question of the division of power between nation and state remained. A leading national figure of the period was South Carolina's Senator John C. Calhoun, who defended not only the values and rights of his own state, but of the South as a whole. After South Carolina led the way to secession (1860), Confederate artillery fire on Federal troops at Fort Sumter in Charleston Harbor started (April 12, 1861) the Civil War.

During the conflict, there was much fighting along the state's coast, and a Union blockade of Charleston Harbor crippled the economy. In 1865, troops led by General William T. Sherman marched across the state, destroying many plantations and burning Columbia. Reconstruction brought a measure of material recovery, but there was also much waste and political corruption. White supremacy and Negro disenfranchisement soon returned.

The South Carolina legislature in 1977 reinstated the death penalty along the lines of a Georgia measure that has been declared constitutional by the U.S. Supreme Court. An earlier death penalty statute in the state was declared unconstitutional following a ruling by the Supreme Court. The state legislature also passed a constitutional amendment that will do much to equalize property taxes in South Carolina. Among other things, it will enable farm property to be taxed at lower rates and standardize rate structures in all areas of the state.

Full name: State of South Carolina. **Origin of name:** In honor of Charles I of England. **Inhabitant:** South Carolinian. **Captial:** Columbia. **State mottoes:** Animis Opibusque Parati (Prepared in Mind & Resources); Dum Spiro, Spero (While I Breathe, I Hope). **Flag:** White palmetto & crescent on blue field. **Seal:** Palmetto tree, symbolizing successful defense (1776) of fort on Sullivan's Island against British; figure of hope carrying laurel branch across sword-covered beach. **Flower:** Yellow jessamine. **Bird:** Carolina wren. **Tree:** Palmetto. **Song:** "Carolina." **Nickname:** Palmetto State.

Governor: Richard W. Riley. **Annual salary:** $60,000. **Term:** 4 years. **Current term expires:** Jan. 1983. **Voting requirements:** 18 yrs. old & U.S. citizen; registration 30 days before election. **U.S. Congressmen:** 6. **Entered Union:** 1788 (8th state).

Location & boundaries: South Atlantic state: bounded on the north & northeast by North Carolina; on the east by the Atlantic Ocean; & on the south & west by Georgia & the Savannah River. **Total area:** 31,055 sq. mi. (ranks 40th). **Extreme length:** 273 mi. **Extreme breadth:** 210 mi. **Coastline:** 281 mi. **Chief rivers:** Pee Dee, Santee, Edisto, Savannah. **Major lakes:** Marion, Moultrie, Murray. **No. of counties:** 46.

Population (1978 est.): 2,918,000 (ranks 25th). **Pop. increase (1970-78):** 12.6%. **Places over 25,000 pop.:** 10. **Places over 100,000:** 1. **Largest cities:** Columbia, Charleston, Greenville, North Charleston. **Pop. density:** 94.0 per sq. mi. (ranks 19th). **Pop. projection 1985:** 3,261,000. **Pop. distribution:** 48.3% metropolitan; 51.7% nonmetropolitan. **White:** 69.3%. **Negro:** 30.4%. **Other:** 0.3%. **Marriage rate (1977):** 17.8 per 1,000 people. **Divorce rate:** 3.7 per 1,000 people.

State finances (1977). Revenue: $2,414,949,000. **Expenditures:** $2,334,336,000. **State Taxes:** $412.93 per capita. **State personal income tax:** Yes. **Public debt (1977):** $455.98 per capita. **Federal aid (1977):** $212.42 per capita. **Personal income (1977):** $5,639.

Sectors of the economy (% of labor force employed in 1970): Manufacturing (36%), Wholesale and retail trade (17%), Services (9%), Educational Services (7%), Construction (7%), Government (15%). **Leading products:** textile items, chemicals, paper items, food items, machinery, lumber & wood items. **Agricultural products:** dairy items, cattle, tobacco, soybeans, cotton, peaches, corn. **Fishing:** shrimp, oysters, crabs. **Avg. farm (1978 est.):** 171 acres. **Avg. value of farm per acre:** $543.

Highway expenditures per capita (1977): $63.20. **Persons per motor vehicle:** 1.55. **Minimum age for driver's license:** 16. **Gasoline tax:** 9¢ per gallon. **Motor vehicle deaths:** 30.3 per 100,000 people.

Birthrate (1977): 17.4 per 1,000 people. **Infant mortality rate per 1,000 births (1977):** 17.6. **Physicians per 100,000 pop. (1976):** 123. **Dentists per 100,000 pop. (1976):** 34. **Acceptable hospital beds:** 6.2 per 1,000 people. **State expenditures per capita for health and hospitals (1977):** $73.53.

Education expenditures (1975-76): $398.40 per capita annually. **No. of pupils in public schools (1977 est.):** 612,000. **No. of institutions of higher learning (1976-77):** 56. **Public school expenditure per pupil in attendance (1975-76):** $1,278. **Avg. salary of public school teachers (1974-75 est.):** $9,770. **No. full-time teachers (1977 est.):** 32,570. **Educational attainment of adult population (1976):** 12.2 median yrs. of school completed; 6.9% with less than 5 years of education; 10.4% with 4 yrs. of college.

Telephones (1976): 62 per 100 people. **State Chamber of Commerce:** South Carolina Chamber of Commerce, 1002 Calhoun St., Columbia, South Carolina 29201.

SOUTH DAKOTA

Since the admission of Alaska and Hawaii, South Dakota has contained (near Castle Rock) the geographical center of the United States, as well as the largest gold mine in the world, Homestake, at the town of Lead. Rich in Old West lore, with such place names as Belle Fourche, Deadwood, and Wounded Knee, the state is home for nearly 30,000 Indians (mostly Sioux), living on 8,400 square miles of reservations. Also within the state's borders is one of the country's most famous landmarks and tourist attractions, Mount Rushmore, in the Black Hills; carved into its granite face, at an altitude of more than a mile, are 60-foot-high busts of Presidents Washington, Jefferson, Lincoln, and Theodore Roosevelt. Badlands National Park contains fantastic pinnacles and canyons in a desert setting.

The state, which has less than five percent forested land, is cut by the Missouri into broadly contrasting, irregularly shaped halves. In the west are the Badlands, the spectacular Black Hills, and the rolling grasslands of the Great Plains, while in the east are the rich farmlands that continue to make agriculture South Dakota's main industry. There is a heavy emphasis on livestock, including

SOUTH DAKOTA

large numbers of cattle, hogs and sheep. Manufacturing consists mainly of meat processing.

The first inhabitants were the Mound Builders, dating from about 1200. Living there after 1600 were the Arikara Indians, an advanced agricultural people, eventually forced out by the more warlike Sioux, or Dakota, Indians. South Dakota and southwestern North Dakota were part of the vast territory claimed (1682) for France by Robert Cavelier, Sieur de La Salle, but Frenchmen did not actually visit the region until 1742-43, when the brothers François and Louis Joseph Vérendyre made explorations and planted a lead plate at the site of what is now Pierre. The area was ceded to Spain in 1762, and toward the end of the century it became part of the St. Louis fur-trading empire. Napolean Bonaparte soon reclaimed (1800) the territory for France, but three years later sold it to the United States, as part of the Louisiana Purchase.

Although Lewis and Clark, in their explorations, visited (1804, 1806) the region now comprising the two Dakotas, actual control remained in the hands of the Sioux until shortly after Custer's famous "last stand" (1876) at Little Bighorn, in what is now Montana. The passing of the buffalo from the American scene was another factor leading to the end of Indian troubles in the area. Fort Pierre, the first settlement (1817), became a major fur-trading center, and in 1831 the first steamboat on the upper Missouri began operations.

Dakota Territory—comprising both Dakotas and parts of Montana and Wyoming—was created in 1861, but settlement did not begin in earnest until the coming of the railroad and the discovery of gold in the 1870s. Rough mining towns grew up, and population soared from about 98,000 (1880) to nearly 350,000 (1890). North and South Dakota were admitted to the Union on November 2, 1889.

The Pine Ridge Indian Reservation was the focus of recurring violence in the early part of the decade. Wounded Knee, the site of a massacre of Indians in 1890, was the scene of a 71-day takeover by members of the militant American Indian Movement (AIM) in 1973. There were also numerous incidents on the reservation, including the shooting deaths of two FBI agents in 1975, for each of which a member of AIM was sentenced to life imprisonment in 1977. On June 13, 1979, the U.S. Court of Claims awarded the Sioux nation $17.5 million (with interest on that figure amounting to a total settlement of perhaps over $100 million) for the Black Hills area which was confiscated from them late in the last century, thereby violating their constitutional rights. It was the largest court settlement ever awarded to American Indians.

Full name: State of South Dakota. **Origin of name:** From the Sioux meaning "Alliance with Friends." **Inhabitant:** South Dakotan. **Capital:** Pierre. **State motto:** Under God the People Rule. **Flag:** State seal surrounded by gold circle, stylized sun & lettering in yellow on a blue field. **Seal:** Smelter chimney, represents mining; plowman stands for farming; riverboat symbolizes transportation. **Flower:** Pasqueflower. **Bird:** Ringnecked pheasant. **Tree:** Black Hills spruce. **Song:** "Hail, South Dakota." **Nickname:** Coyote State; Sunshine State.

Governor: William J. Janklow. **Annual salary:** $37,000. **Term:** 4 yrs. **Current term expires:** Jan. 1983. **Voting requirements:** 18 yrs. old & U.S. citizen; no durational residency requirements. **U.S. Congressmen:** 2. **Entered Union:** 1889 (40th state).

Location & boundaries: Northern Midwestern state: bounded on the north by North Dakota; on the east by Minnesota, Iowa & Big Sioux & Red Rivers; on the south by Nebraska & the Missouri River; & on the west by Wyoming & Montana. **Total area:** 77,047 sq. mi. (ranks 16th). **Extreme length:** 380 mi. **Extreme breadth:** 245 mi. **Chief rivers:** Missouri, James, Cheyenne. **Major lakes:** Lewis & Clark, Big Stone. **No. of counties:** 67.

Population (1978 est.): 690,000 (ranks 44th). **Pop. increase (1970-78):** 3.6%. **Places over 25,000 pop.:** 2. **Places over 100,000:** None. **Largest cities:** Sioux Falls, Aberdeen, Rapid City. **Pop. density:** 9.0 per sq. mi. (ranks 46th). **Pop. projection 1985:** 707,000. **Pop. distribution:** 14.7% metropolitan; 85.3% nonmetropolitan. **White:** 94.7%. **Negro:** 0.3%. **Other:** 5%. **Marriage rate (1977):** 14.9 per 1,000 people. **Divorce rate:** 3.5 per 1,000 people.

State finances (1977). Revenue: $543,702,000. **Expenditures:** $528,910,000. **State Taxes:** $290.44 per capita. **State personal income tax:** No. **Public debt (1977):** $336.04 per capita. **Federal aid (1977):** $268.78 per capita. **Personal income (1977):** $5,953.

Sectors of the economy (% of labor force employed in 1970): Manufacturing (4%), Wholesale and retail trade (22%), Services (7%), Educational Services (10%), Construction (5%), Government (19%). **Leading products:** food items; printing & publishing; machinery; stone, clay & glass items; lumber; fabricated metals. **Agricultural products:** cattle, hogs, dairy items, wheat, corn, hay. **Avg. farm (1978 est.):** 1,058 acres. **Avg. value of farm per acre:** $227.

Highway expenditures per capita (1977): $137.80. **Persons per motor vehicle:** 1.23. **Minimum age for driver's license:** 16. **Gasoline tax:** 8¢ per gallon. **Motor vehicle deaths:** 27.7 per 100,000 people.

Birthrate (1977): 17.5 per 1,000 people. **Infant mortality rate per 1,000 births (1977):** 16.4. **Physicians per 100,000 pop. (1976):** 98. **Dentists per 100,000 pop. (1976):** 44. **Acceptable hospital beds:** 8.5 per 1,000 people. **State expenditures per capita for health and hospitals (1977):** $71.76.

Education expenditures (1975-76): $451.94 per capita annually. **No. of pupils in public schools (1977 est.):** 146,000. **No. of institutions of higher learning (1976-77):** 17. **Public school expenditure per pupil in attendance (1975-76):** $1,445. **Avg. salary of public school teachers (1974-75):** $8,860. **No. full-time teachers (1977 est):** 8,830. **Educational attainment of adult population (1976):** 12.5 median yrs. of school completed; 1.1% with less than 5 years of education; 11.4% with 4 yrs. of college.

Telephones (1976): 66 per 100 people. **State Chamber of Commerce:** Greater South Dakota Chamber of Commerce, P.O. Box 190, Pierre, South Dakota 57501.

TENNESSEE

Traces of Tennessee's traditionally hardy frontier spirit remain today in its museums and restored buildings, as well as in the character and life-style of many Tennesseans themselves. The first state to be created out of national territory, Tennessee came to be called the Volunteer State because of its readiness to furnish troops in the War of 1812 and the Mexican War. Its history and culture have been deeply influenced by its three main land regions— East, Middle, and West Tennessee.

In East Tennessee, with the heaviest population outside of the major urban areas in the state, are the Great Smoky Mountains and the eastern slope of the Cumberland Mountains, both in the Appalachian range. Middle Tennessee consists of the fertile Nashville Basin and an elevated plain (the Highland Rim) and the western slope of the Cumberlands, which divide the two sections of the state, the features being part of the Interior Low Plateaus. Middle Tennesseans of this gently rolling bluegrass region tend to identify with the Old South. West Tennessee lies between the western bend of the Tennessee River and the Mississippi River and includes a portion of the East Gulf Coastal Plain and a thin strip of the Mississippi Alluvial Plain flanking the Mississippi. Here farming predominates. About half of the state is forested.

Tennessee, once a basically rural region, has become a largely industrial state. Chemicals, textiles, and food and metal products are among the major manufactures. Massive hydroelectric in-

TENNESSEE

stallations, developed (beginning 1933) by the Tennessee Valley Authority (TVA), provide power for Tennessee and six other states as well. Mining, lumbering, and the production of cotton and tobacco are also vital elements of the state's economy, as is livestock.

Indians similar to the Mound Builders are thought to have been the first inhabitants of the Tennessee region. The Chickasaw, Cherokee, and Shawnee were among the tribes living there when the first Europeans, led by De Soto, arrived in 1540. De Soto was soon followed by countryman Juan Pardo, but the Spaniards were seeking gold and did not settle. A long period of French-British contention over the land was foreshadowed by the arrival in the same year (1673) of Marquette and Jolliet, and Englishmen James Needham and Gabriel Arthur. In 1682, La Salle and his party paused in their exploration of the Mississippi Valley and built Fort Prudhomme at the mouth of the Hatchie River.

Spurred by reports of scouts such as Daniel Boone, a steady stream of settlers from Virginia and the Carolinas soon began to enter the region. French influence waned, and by 1763 the British were in control, despite strong resistance from the Cherokees. Between 1772 and 1790 several abortive attempts were made by settlers to establish self-government and achieve statehood.

In 1790 Congress organized the region into the "Territory of the United States South of the River Ohio," commonly called the Southwest Territory. Tennessee entered the Union in 1796.

Tennessee began life as a state with what Jefferson called the nation's "least imperfect and most republican" constitution. By 1800, immigration had swelled the population to 100,000, and the coming of steam and rail transportation did much to develop the state's economy. When the Cherokees and the Chickasaws were forced to move west in the late 1830s, another, smaller wave of immigration ensued. Politically, the new state's dominant figure was Andrew Jackson, who served as a U.S. representative and senator from Tennessee before becoming (1829) president.

Although a slaveholding state, Tennessee was at first pro-Union in the years before the Civil War, but after Fort Sumter a referendum was held and two-thirds of the people backed secession (1861). Tennessee was the last Confederate state to secede, and the first to be readmitted.

The Reconstruction Era triggered a strong reaction that included the founding (1866) of the Ku Klux Klan in Pulaski and the adoption (1870) of a new constitution limiting Negro suffrage via a poll tax. On the farms, a tenancy system replaced the plantations, and the state's crippled economy turned toward increased industrialization for new life. In 1878, the worst yellow-fever epidemic in U.S. history hit Memphis, killing thousands.

Among the state's attractions is Great Smoky Mountains National Park, which it shares with North Carolina. Parts of five states can be seen from Lookout Mountain on the Tennessee River near Chattanooga. The Historic State Capital and a reproduction of the Parthenon are in Nashville, the home of the famed "Grand Ole Opry." The new Opry House and Opryland, U.S.A., a 300-acre theme park are popular tourist attractions. Libertyland, a theme park at Memphis, was opened during the nation's bicentennial.

In 1973, six years after the repeal of the ban on the teaching of the theory of evolution, a new version was enacted. It requires that equal emphasis be given to Genesis in the classroom as well as other theories of man's origin.

The original law resulted in the 1925 trial of biology teacher John Scopes in the little town of Dayton, Tenn. The trial pitted Clarence Darrow for the defense against special prosecutor William Jennings Bryan.

The Clinch River nuclear energy project was the subject of contention in 1977-79. President Carter opposed the project as unnecessary, too expensive and as a producer of plutonium as a by-product, a substance likely to cause proliferation of atomic weapons technology. It was reported in March 1978 that a new study would be undertaken to plan an alternative project which would provide more energy without producing the controversial plutonium. After much controversy, a House committee approved going ahead with the reactor early in 1979, despite Carter's strenuous objections.

Lamar Alexander replaced Governor Ray Blanton on January 17, 1979 (three days before the appointed inauguration day) to stop further convicted criminals from being granted executive clemency. Blanton's clemency grants were in question because of their possible link to a federal probe of his administration's alleged clemency-for-sale scandal. On April 10, the Tennessee Court of Criminal Appeals upheld 52 grants of clemency allowed by Blanton the day before he left office. Six persons (Blanton not among them) were indicted in connection with the pardon sales.

Full name: State of Tennessee. **Origin of name:** From Tennese, name of leading Cherokee town. **Inhabitant:** Tennessean. **Capital:** Nashville. **State motto:** Agriculture & Commerce. **Flag:** Three white stars in a white-bordered blue circle on a red field; narrow white & blue stripe at right. **Seal:** Plow, sheaf of wheat & cotton plant represent agriculture; riverboat symbolizes commerce; Roman numerals indicate Tennessee was 16th state to be admitted to Union. **Flower:** Iris. **Bird:** Mockingbird. **Tree:** Tulip poplar. **Song:** "The Tennessee Waltz." **Nickname:** Volunteer State.

Governor: Andrew L. Alexander. **Annual salary:** $68,227. **Term:** 4 years. **Current term expires:** Jan. 1983. **Voting requirements:** 18 yrs. old & U.S. citizen; resident of state for 20 days. **U.S. Congressmen:** 8. **Entered Union:** 1796 (16th state).

Location & boundaries: Southeastern state: bounded on the north by Kentucky & Virginia; on the east by North Carolina; on the south by Georgia, Alabama & Mississippi; & on the west by Arkansas, Missouri & the Mississippi River. **Total area:** 42,244 sq. mi. (ranks 34th). **Extreme length:** 432 mi. **Extreme breadth:** 110 mi. **Chief rivers:** Mississippi, Tennessee, Cumberland. **Major lakes:** Watts, Chickamauga, Douglas, Cherokee. **No. of counties:** 95.

Population (1978 est.): 4,357,000 (ranks 17th). **Pop. increase (1970-78):** 11.0%. **Places over 25,000 pop.:** 11. **Places over 100,000:** 4. **Largest cities:** Memphis, Nashville, Knoxville, Chattanooga. **Pop. density:** 103.1 per sq. mi. (ranks 18th). **Pop. projection 1985:** 4,592,000. **Pop. distribution:** 63.1% metropolitan; 36.9% nonmetropolitan. **White:** 83.7%. **Negro:** 16.1%. **Other:** 0.2%. **Marriage rate (1977):** 12.9 per 1,000 people. **Divorce rate:** 6.4 per 1,000 people.

State finances (1977). Revenue: $2,933,213,000. **Expenditures:** $2,854,020,000. **State Taxes:** $355.79 per capita. **State personal income tax:** No. **Public debt (1977):** $279.87 per capita. **Federal aid (1977):** $190.13 per capita. **Personal income (1977):** $5,801.

Sectors of the economy (% of labor force employed in 1973): Manufacturing (13.8%), Wholesale and retail trade (16.9%), Services (13.9%), Educational Services (7%), Construction (6.1%), Government (15.8%). **Leading products:** chemicals, food items, electrical equipment, apparel, textile items, primary metals. **Minerals:** stone, coal, zinc, cement, copper. **Agricultural products:** cattle, soybeans, dairy items, cotton, tobacco. **Avg. farm (1978 est.):** 133 acres. **Avg. value of farmper acre:** $608.

Highway expenditures per capita (1977): $103.49. **Persons per motor vehicle:** 1.43. **Minimum age for driver's license:** 16. **Gasoline tax:** 7¢ per gallon. **Motor vehicle deaths:** 28.4 per 100,000 people.

Birthrate (1977): 15.5 per 1,000 people. Infant mortality rate per 1,000 births (1977): 15.4. Physicians per 100,000 pop. (1976): 147. Dentists per 100,000 pop. (1976): 45. Acceptable hospital beds: 7.2 per 1,000 people. State expenditures per capita for health and hospitals (1977): $45.01.

Education expenditures (1975-76): $352.65 per capita annually. No. of pupils in public schools (1977 est.): 830,000. No. of institutions of higher learning (1976-77): 67. Public school expenditure per pupil in attendance (1975-76): $1,214. Avg. salary of public school teachers (1974-75 est.): $9,878. No. full-time teachers (1976 est.): 42,130. Educational attainment of adult population (1977): 12.2 median yrs. of school completed; 6.4% with less than 5 years of education; 10.5% with 4 yrs. of college.

Telephones (1976): 65 per 100 people. State Chamber of Commerce: State Chamber Division of the Tennessee Taxpayers Assoc., 1070 Capitol Hill Bldg., Nashville, Tennessee 37219.

TEXAS

Second largest of the states and among the most populous, Texas is a fiercely independent land of awesome expanses and great natural resources. It leads the nation in the production of oil, natural gas, cattle, and cotton, and ranks high in commercial fishing and electric power. Texas is also a major agricultural state, as well as a growing industrial region. It contains the facilities of 19 of the top 20 U.S. chemical companies, and is the home of the Manned Spacecraft Center (Houston) and other space age projects. And while keeping pace technologically, it can also claim a richly varied heritage, having flown the flags of six nations: Spain, France, Mexico, the Republic of Texas, the Confederate States of America, and the United States.

The state consists of four main land regions: the West Gulf Coastal Plain, the largest single area, making up more than two-fifths of the total area and consisting of a 150 to 350-mile-wide strip of land in the east and southeast extending from the Gulf of Mexico to the Balcones Escarpment; the Central Lowland, known locally as the Osage Plains and extending southward to a line running roughly from Fort Worth, through Abilene, to Big Springs and including the southern fringe of the Texas panhandle; the Great Plains, reaching mostly westward (but also north and southward) from the Central Lowland into New Mexico and including the bulk of the panhandle; and the Basin and Range (or Trans-Pecos) Region, making up the westernmost part of the state below New Mexico and including high, rugged, partly arid plains crossed by spurs of the Rocky Mountains; in this region are the Guadalupe Mountains and the state's highest point, Guadalupe Peak (8,751 feet).

Texas has more farmed area than any other state, and about half the land consists of forest, woodland, or brush land. The state's widely varied climate ranges from the warm, damp, subtropical Gulf Coast and lower Rio Grande Valley to the continental weather of the northern panhandle. Hot, dry weather is typical of the far south as are frequent droughts. Narrow sand bars, enclosing shallow lagoons, lie along the coast and afford some protection against ocean storms and tidal waves. The U.S.-Mexican border, where it follows the Rio Grande has been a continuing problem for the state, because the riverbed shifts occasionally, cutting off land from one or the other country. These shifts have given rise to nearly a century of minor but annoying border disputes. In August 1970, however, Presidents Nixon and Ordaz met in Mexico and announced agreement on current disputes and ways to prevent future ones. New, major

reservoirs, built in cooperation with Mexico, will prevent any substantial change in the Rio Grande.

Indians inhabited what is now Texas about 20,000 years before the coming of the Europeans. Spaniards (including Cabeza de Vaca and Francisco Vásquez Coronado) visited the region in the 16th and 17th centuries, settling (1682) at Ysleta (near present-day El Paso). Spain increased its settlement efforts after French explorer Robert Cavelier, Sieur de La Salle, established (1685) a short-lived colony near Matagorda Bay. The first Spanish mission, San Francisco de los Tejas, was founded in 1690 and others soon followed, but generally Spain's efforts to exploit the region's wealth and convert the Indians were not very successful. After the Louisiana Purchase (1803) gave the United States a common border with Texas, Americans began challenging Spanish rule there.

Moses Austin secured (1821) a grant from local authorities permitting him, as an *empresario*, to bring in American settlers; when he died that same year, his son, Stephen F. Austin, established the first permanent Anglo-American settlement at San Felipe de Austin. Often called the "Father of Texas," Austin brought approximately 8,000 colonists to the region. Other *empresarios* brought hundreds more, and during the next 15 years the total approached 30,000. Preoccupied with its birth as an independent republic (1824), Mexico was not effective in curbing what it saw as a growing encroachment on its territory, despite an 1830 law restricting immigration, and the establishment of customs stations and a military force in Texas.

The Anglo-Americans were moved to action when Antonio López de Santa Anna set up (1835) a Mexican dictatorship in Texas; the Texans then proclaimed (1836) a provisional government at Washington-on-the-Brazos and turned command of the revolutionary army over to Sam Houston, who was to rival Austin as a shaper of Texas history. Santa Anna and his men quickly gained the upper hand in the battle, recapturing San Antonio, which had initially fallen to the Texans; the Mexican victory came despite the famous heroic defense of the Alamo by greatly outnumbered Texans (including Davy Crockett and Jim Bowie) who fought to the last man. After more than 300 Texas prisoners were shot at Goliad, Houston rallied his still relatively small army and, with a surprise attack, won (April 21, 1836) the Battle of San Jacinto, ending the war and bringing to birth the Independent Republic of Texas.

Under its famed Lone Star flag, Texas remained independent for nearly a decade, with Houston twice serving as president. The country was beset by many grave problems, including Indian and Mexican raids and a chronic money shortage. The issue of annexation by the United States, which most Texans favored, arose early. Slavery, condoned in Texas, made the issue highly controversial: the Southern states favored annexation, while the Northern ones opposed it. Annexation, which came in 1845, precipitated the Mexican War (1846-48).

Settlers, drawn by inexpensive land, came to Texas in great numbers in the pre-Civil War period. Partly because of its slave-holding status but more importantly because of states' rights views, the state sided with the Confederacy, seceding in 1861. Texas saw little action during the war, but contributed 50,000 troops and much matériel to the Southern cause. The state suffered much during the excesses of Reconstruction.

The development of modern Texas was spurred by the growth of the cattle industry, the coming of

TEXAS

KEY TO NUMBERS ON MAP

County	County Seat
1 DELTA	Cooper
2 FRANKLIN	Mt. Vernon
3 CAMP	Pittsburg
4 MORRIS	Daingerfield
5 ROCKWALL	Rockwall
6 RAINS	Emory
7 GREGG	Longview
8 SOMERVELL	Glen Rose
9 SAN JACINTO	Coldspring

State Capital ⊛   County Seats ⊚

WESTERN PART OF TEXAS
Same scale as map

HOUSTON

© Copyright HAMMOND INCORPORATED, Maplewood, N. J.

the railroad, and the discovery, among others before it, of the spectacular Spindletop oil field (1901) near Beaumont. Texas today, while enjoying great growth, faces serious challenges, such as ways to irrigate with surface water its dry western areas where shrinking underground supplies now help to grow vast crops.

The planned Seadock superport, a project similar to the Loop superport being constructed off Louisiana, remained a possibility through the establishment in July 1977 of a state authority which could fund the project. In July 1979 the U.S. Justice Department endorsed the proposal as not violating antitrust laws.

A tornado termed the most deadly to strike Texas in 25 years hit Wichita Falls on April 10, 1979, killing 44 and injuring 700. The city was declared a disaster area two days later with damages estimated at $200 million by insurance adjusters. Besides Wichita Falls, the twisters hit the communities of Vernon, killing 11 and causing $6 million in damage and Harrold, killing one.

Full name: State of Texas. **Origin of name:** From the Indian meaning "Friends" or "Allies." **Inhabitant:** Texan. **Capital:** Austin. **State motto:** Friendship. **Flag:** Single star on vertical blue bar with a red & a white bar to the right. **Seal:** Single star with branch of oak, representing strength, on left; olive branch, symbolizing peace, to the right. **Flower:** Bluebonnet. **Bird:** Mockingbird. **Tree:** Pecan. **Song:** "Texas, Our Texas." **Nickname:** Lone Star State.

Governor: William P. Clements, Jr. **Annual salary:** $71,400. **Term:** 4 years. **Current term expires:** Jan. 1983. **Voting requirements:** 18 yrs. old & U.S. citizen; resident of state 30 days. **U.S. Congressmen:** 24. **Entered Union:** 1845 (28th state).

Location & boundaries: Southwestern state: bounded on the north by Oklahoma & the Red River; on the northeast by Arkansas; on the east by Louisiana & the Sabine River; on the south by the Gulf of Mexico, the Rio Grande River & Mexico, & on the west by New Mexico. **Total area:** 267,338 sq. mi. (ranks 2d). **Extreme length:** 801 mi. **Extreme breadth:** 773 mi. **Coastline:** 367 mi. **Chief rivers:** Rio Grande, Red, Pecos, Brazos, Colorado. **Major lakes:** Texoma, Toledo Bend, Amistad, Falcon. **No. of counties:** 254.

Population (1978 est.): 13,014,000 (ranks 3rd). **Pop. increase (1970-78):** 16.2%. **Places over 25,000 pop.:** 46. **Places over 100,000:** 9. **Largest cities:** Houston, Dallas, San Antonio, El Paso. **Pop. density:** 48.7 per sq. mi. (ranks 32rd). **Pop. projection 1985:** 14,277,000. **Pop. distribution:** 79.1% metropolitan; 20.9% nonmetropolitan. **White:** 86.6%. **Negro:** 12.7%. **Other:** 0.7%. **Marriage rate (1977):** 12.6 per 1,000 people. **Divorce rate:** 6.4 per 1,000 people.

State finances (1977). Revenue: $8,847,332,000. **Expenditures:** $7,829,437,000. **State Taxes:** $370.23 per capita. **State personal income tax:** No. **Public debt (1977):** $165.63 per capita. **Federal aid (1977):** $161.03 per capita. **Personal income (1977):** $6,827.

Sectors of the economy (% of labor force employed in 1970): Manufacturing (19%), Wholesale and retail trade (22%), Services (9%), Educational Services (8%), Construction (8%), Government (16%). **Leading products:** chemicals, petroleum & coal items, food items, transportation equipment, machinery, primary & fabricated metals. **Minerals:** petroleum, natural gas & natural gas liquids, cement. **Agricultural products:** cattle, sheep, swine, dairy items, mohair, sorghum grain, cotton lint, rice, wheat, oats, barley, pecans. **Fishing:** shrimp, oysters, menhaden. **Avg. farm (1978 est.):** 710 acres. **Avg. value of farm per acre:** $316.

Highway expenditures per capita (1977): $54.63. **Persons per motor vehicle:** 1.35. **Minimum age for driver's license:** 18. **Gasoline tax:** 5¢ per gallon. **Motor vehicle deaths:** 30.3 per 100,000 people.

Birthrate (1977): 17.9 per 1,000 people. **Infant mortality rate per 1,000 births (1977):** 14.7. **Physicians per 100,000 pop. (1976):** 146. **Dentists per 100,000 pop. (1976):** 41. **Acceptable hospital beds:** 6.2 per 1,000 people. **State expenditures per capita for health and hospitals (1977):** $53.56.

Education expenditures (1975-76): $427.48 per capita annually. **No. of pupils in public schools (1977 est.):** 2,781,000. **No. of institutions of higher learning (1976-77):** 146. **Public school expenditure per pupil in attendance (1975-76):** $1,487. **Avg. salary of public school teachers (1974-75 est.):** $10,136. **No. full-time teachers (1977 est.):** 49,180. **Educational attainment of adult population (1976):** 12.4 median yrs. of school completed; 6.0% with less than 5 years of education; 13.7% with 4 yrs. of college.

Telephones (1976): 71 per 100 people. **State Chamber of Commerce:** Texas State Chamber of Commerce, 7701 N. Lamar, Suite 302, Austin, Texas 78752

UTAH

Utah is a rough-hewn, scenically spectacular state consisting of two relatively arid regions (eastern and western), divided by the rain-catching Wasatch Range of the Rocky Mountains. In the west is the Great Basin, which includes the Great Salt Lake (about 75 miles long and 30 miles wide) and the 4,000-square-mile Great Salt Lake Desert. East of the Wasatch Range are the Uinta Mountains (with 11 peaks that rise more than 13,000 feet) and the awesome, many-hued Colorado Plateau. Most of the towns and cities, situated at the base of the mountains, enjoy a pleasant climate with few temperature extremes.

A number of factors—mainly scarcity of water—have limited the state's agricultural growth. Nearly three-quarters of the annual farm revenue comes from livestock and livestock products.

The struggle for better irrigation in Utah began with the early Mormon settlers and still goes on. In 1967 the $325-million Central Utah Project was begun; if completed, it will consist of a vast complex of dams, canals, and aqueducts.

Stimulated by the demands of World War II, manufacturing has become increasingly vital. Leading manufactures include food products; fabricated steel; stone, clay and glass products; missiles; chemicals; and in recent years, electronics equipment. In rural communities, the fabric and apparel industries are active.

In the last ten years, distribution services have become an important part of the Utah economy. Since the state legislature eliminated all taxes on inventories, the state has become an important shipping and receiving point for the entire Western market.

Tourism is important, attracting visitors to the Great Salt Lake; Arches, Bryce Canyon, Canyonlands, Capitol Reef and Zion National Parks; Natural Bridges National Monument, Glen Canyon National Recreation Area, and Golden Spike National Historic Site.

Disfavored by the agrarian Mormons, mining got off to a slow start, but in 1863 huge deposits of copper, silver, and lead were unearthed in Bingham Canyon, which contains the largest open-pit copper mine in the country. The industry came into its own with the coming of the railroad in 1869. Since 1948, significant quantities of oil, natural gas and uranium have been found. Recent discoveries of large oil-shale and tar-sands deposits have raised hopes of further energy development, but uncertainties in the economy and a lagging technology have slowed the exploitation of these resources.

Archaeological findings (1968) in the Great Basin at Hogup Cave, 75 miles northwest of Salt Lake City, show that there was continuous Indian habitation in the area from 6400 B.C. to A.D. 1600. An even older human habitation, Danger Cave near Wendover, was excavated a decade ago and dates to 9000 B.C. Some doubt exists as to whether or not Spanish explorers visited the region in 1540 when they discovered the Grand Canyon, but it has

UTAH

MILES
0 10 20 30 40 50 60

KILOMETERS
0 10 20 30 40 50 60

State Capitals ⊛
County Seats ◎

© Copyright HAMMOND INCORPORATED, Maplewood, N.J.

been established that in 1776 two Spanish Franciscan friars—Silvestre Velez de Escalante and Francisco Atanasio Dominguez—did explore the area. They recommended colonization, but Spain was apparently not interested. Between 1811 and 1840 British and American fur trappers hunted their prey there.

Permanent occupation of the territory was begun in 1847 by the persecuted Mormons—members of the Church of Jesus Christ of Latter-day Saints—who had emigrated from New York via Missouri, Ohio, and Illinois to Utah in search of "a [secluded] gathering place for Zion." They were led by the church's first president, Joseph Smith, who was killed on the way, and by Brigham Young, the second president. From the time of its founding (1847) Salt Lake City has been the world headquarters of the L.D.S. church.

The Utah region at that time belonged to Mexico, but after the Mexican War (1846-48), it became the property of the United States. At least 70 percent of the state's area is still federally owned and administered, and about ten percent of the people work for Federal agencies.

Two Indian wars were fought: the Walker War (1853-54) and the Black Hawk War (1865-68), involving a number of tribes but principally the Utes, who were eventually placed on a reservation in the Uinta basin.

As early as 1849 Utah asked to be admitted to the Union, but Congress refused—mainly because the Mormon practice of polygamy was frowned upon.

President James Buchanan wanted to take territorial control away from Young and the Mormons, which gave rise to the "Utah" or "Mormon" War (1857-58). Federal troops were dispatched to the area, but there was more bad feeling than actual fighting. When the Civil War broke out in 1861, the troops were recalled and peace reigned, although there remained a residue of bitterness between the Mormon stronghold and the "outside" world which time has gradually erased. Utah finally entered the Union in 1896.

The controversial Kaiparowits power project planned for southern Utah was dropped in 1976, but other projects in that area are in the planning stage, and the possibility remains that other power plants may be built to take advantage of Utah's coal deposits.

Some residents of St. George have filed claims against the Energy Department charging that nuclear blasts which occurred some 25 years ago at the Nevada Testing Site caused cancer deaths among members of their families who lived in the area.

Full name: State of Utah. **Origin of name:** From the Indian tribe of Utes. **Inhabitant:** Utahn. **Capital:** Salt Lake City. **State motto:** Industry. **Flag:** State seal in a gold circle on blue field. **Seal:** Beehive on shield represents industry; sego lilies surrounding beehive symbolize time when Mormon pioneers ate lily bulbs to avoid starvation. **Flower:** Sego lily. **Bird:** Seagull. **Tree:** Blue spruce. **Song:** "Utah, We Love Thee." **Nickname:** Beehive State.

Governor: Scott M. Matheson. **Annual salary:** $40,000. **Term:** 4 years. **Current term expires:** Dec. 1980. **Voting requirements:** 18 yrs. old & U.S. citizen; state residence 30 days. **U.S. Congressmen:** 2. **Entered Union:** 1896 (45th state).

Location & boundaries: Rocky Mountain state: bounded on the north by Idaho; on the northeast by Wyoming; on the east by Colorado; on the south by Arizona; & on the west by Nevada. **Total area:** 84,916 sq. mi. (ranks 11th). **Extreme length:** 345 mi. **Extreme breadth:** 275 mi. **Chief rivers:** Colorado, Green, Sevier. **Major lakes:** Great Salt Lake, Utah, Sevier, Bear Lake. **No. of counties:** 29.

Population (1978 est.): 1,307,000 (ranks 36th). **Pop. increase (1970-78):** 23.4%. **Places over 25,000 pop.:** 7. **Places over 100,000:** 1. **Largest cities:** Salt Lake City, Ogden, Provo. **Pop. density:** 15.4 per sq. mi. (ranks 42nd). **Pop. projection 1985:** 1,449,000. **Pop. distribution:** 78.8% metropolitan; 21.2% nonmetropolitan. **White:** 97.4%. **Negro:** 0.6%. **Other:** 2%. **Marriage rate (1977):** 12.0 per 1,000 people. **Divorce rate:** 5.5 per 1,000 people.

State finances (1977). Revenue: $1,237,698,000. **Expenditures:** $1,177,333,000. **State Taxes:** $418.99 per capita. **State personal income tax:** Yes. **Public debt (1977):** $114.78 per capita. **Federal aid (1977):** $271.28 per capita. **Personal income (1977):** $5,943.

Sectors of the economy (% of labor force employed in 1970): Manufacturing (15%), Wholesale and retail trade (22%), Services (7%), Educational Services (12%), Construction (6%), Government (25%). **Leading products:** food items; stone, clay, & glass items; machinery; printing & publishing; fabricated metals; petroleum & coal items. **Minerals:** copper, petroleum, coal, molybdenum. **Agricultural products:** cattle, dairy items, turkeys, hay, wheat, barley. **Avg. farm (1978 est.):** 963 acres. **Avg. value of farm per acre:** $248.

Highway expenditures per capita (1977): $102.22. **Persons per motor vehicle:** 1.40. **Minimum age for driver's license:** 16. **Gasoline tax:** 9¢ per gallon. **Motor vehicle deaths:** 28.3 per 100,000 people.

Birthrate (1977): 29.9 per 1,000 people. **Infant mortality rate per 1,000 births (1977):** 10.1. **Physicians per 100,000 pop. (1976):** 163. **Dentists per 100,000 pop. (1976):** 63. **Acceptable hospital beds:** 4.1 per 1,000 people. **State expenditures per capita for health and hospitals (1977):** $53.43.

Education expenditures (1975-76): $570.03 per capita annually. **No. of pupils in public schools (1977 est.):** 310,000. **No. of institutions of higher learning (1976-77):** 14. **Public school expenditure per pupil in attendance (1975-76):** $1,471. **Avg. salary of public school teachers (1974-75 est.):** $10,150. **No. full-time teachers (1977 est.):** 13,110. **Educational attainment of adult population (1976):** 12.8 median yrs. of school completed; 1.0% with less than 5 years of education; 17.5% with 4 yrs. of college.

Telephones (1976): 71 per 100 people.

VERMONT

Vermont, the only New England state lacking an ocean coastline, is noted for the independence of thought and action that stem, in part, from this relative insularity; there is much truth to the saying, "Vermonters will do nothing that you tell them to; most anything that you ask them to."

Four main land areas make up the state: the extensively forested Green Mountains, forming a north-south backbone through the center (and inspiring the state's French-rooted name); the White Mountains in the northeast, Lake Champlain and the Champlain Valley in the northwest, and the Taconic Hills in the southwest. Many lakes, ponds, streams, and rivers—including the eastern-border-forming Connecticut River—provide an abundant water supply. Forests cover about 60 percent of the area.

Called a "state in a very natural state" by poet Robert Frost (who lived the latter part of his life near Ripton), Vermont is famous for the rustic charm of its towns and villages, winding roads, covered bridges, and largely unspoiled scenery. In the early 1900s, manufacturing began to replace agriculture in importance through small-scale industralization: only a quarter of the state's land is now devoted to agriculture. Maple sugar and syrup and the finest marble in the United States are among Vermont's better-known products, while about nine-tenths of the nation's asbestos comes from the Hyde Park region. Machine tools, computer components and armaments are the state's leading industrial products.

VERMONT

State Capitals
County Seats

MILES
0 5 10 15 20 25 30

KILOMETERS
0 5 10 15 20 25 30

© Copyright HAMMOND INCORPORATED, Maplewood, N. J.

Longitude West of Greenwich

Four-season tourism has grown enormously in recent years (Vermont's skiing industry alone accounts for over $50 million annual revenue), and attractions include the Green Mountain National Forest, Shelburne and Bennington museums, and many state parks.

French explorer Samuel de Champlain was most likely the first European to visit the region, discovering (1609) the lake now bearing his name. The British established (1724) the first permanent settlement at Fort Dummer (near present-day Brattleboro), and the English assumed control at the end of the French and Indian War (1763). Beginning in the mid-1700s New Hampshire and New York made conflicting claims on the region, and violence erupted when Ethan Allen and his "Green Mountain Boys" resisted New York officers who sought to take possession of the territory.

These differences were soon overshadowed by the American Revolution, in which the Vermonters played an important part, including the capture of Fort Ticonderoga and Crown Point. In 1777, Vermont proclaimed its independence, drawing up the first state constitution that outlawed slavery and established universal manhood suffrage without property qualifications. Land disputes continued, but were finally ended (1791) when Vermont paid New York a $30,000 claims settlement and was admitted to the Union, the first state to be added to the original 13.

The Embargo Act of 1807 and the War of 1812 were unpopular with Vermonters, who relied heavily on trade with Canada. But involvement in the war was unavoidable. Invasion by the British from Canada was averted when Americans, led by Captain Thomas Macdonough, gained a vital naval victory on Lake Champlain in 1814. Two years later, disastrous frosts ruined the state's crops, and thousands of farmers went west; immigration, which had been significant, fell sharply and never regained its former level.

Abolition was popular in the state, which strongly supported Abraham Lincoln in the 1860 presidential election. Vermont's casualties, as a proportion of the male population, in the Civil War were among the heaviest of any Northern state.

Historically a Republican state, Vermont has increasingly become a state in which the two parties are in close balance. The first Democratic governor was elected in 1962 and served until 1968. A second Democrat was elected for two terms beginning in 1972. The Republicans recaptured the governor's chair in 1976 and 1978, although in 1976 they lost control of the House of Representatives for the first time since the early 19th century. The House seat was regained by the GOP with the 1978 elections. The first Democratic U.S. Senator in the state's history is currently serving in Washington.

Full name: State of Vermont. **Origin of name:** From the French words meaning "Green Mountain." **Inhabitant:** Vermonter. **Capital:** Montpelier. **State motto:** Freedom & Unity. **Flag:** State seal on a blue field. **Seal:** Pine tree with 14 branches represents 13 original states & Vermont; cow & sheaves of wheat stand for dairying & agriculture; wavy lines at top & bottom symbolize sky & sea. **Flower:** Red clover. **Bird:** Hermit thrush. **Tree:** Sugar maple. **Song:** "Hail, Vermont." **Nickname:** Green Mountain State.

Governor: Richard A. Snelling. **Annual salary:** $41,340. **Term:** 2 years. **Current term expires:** Jan. 1981. **Voting requirements:** 18 yrs. old & U.S. citizen; state resident. **U.S. Congressmen:** 1. **Entered Union:** 1791 (14th state).

Location & boundaries: New England state; bounded on the north by Canada; on the east by New Hampshire & the Connecticut River; on the south by Massachusetts; & on the west by New York & Lake Champlain. **Total area:** 9,609 sq. mi. (ranks 43rd) **Extreme length:** 159 mi. **Extreme breadth:** 86 mi. **Chief rivers:** Connecti-

cut, Winooski, Lamoille. **Major lake:** Champlain. **No. of counties:** 14.

Population (1978 est.): 487,000 (ranks 48th). **Pop. increase (1970-78):** 9.4%. **Places over 25,000 pop.:** 1. **Places over 100,000:** None. **Largest cities:** Burlington, Rutland. **Pop. density:** 50.7 per sq. mi. (ranks 30th). **Pop. projection 1985:** 517,000. **Pop. distribution:** 100% nonmetropolitan; 0.0% nonmetropolitan. **White:** 99.6%. **Negro:** 0.2%. **Other:** 0.2%. **Marriage rate (1977):** 10.0 per 1,000 people. **Divorce rate:** 4.4 per 1,000 people.

State finances (1977). Revenue: $572,997,000. **Expenditures:** $535,769,000. **State Taxes:** $475.78 per capita. **State personal income tax:** Yes. **Public debt (1977):** $941.09 per capita. **Federal aid (1977):** $375.50 per capita. **Personal income (1977):** $5,882.

Sectors of the economy (% of labor force employed in 1970): Manufacturing (24%), Wholesale and retail trade (18%), Services (8%), Educational Services (11%), Construction (8%), Government (15%). **Leading products:** machinery, food items, computer components, printing, stone items, lumber, wood & paper items, rubber & plastic items. **Agricultural products:** dairy items, cattle, apples, hay, maple items. **Avg. farm (1978 est.):** 269 acres. **Avg. value of farm per acre:** $597.

Highway expenditures per capita (1977): $124.22. **Persons per motor vehicle:** 1.51. **Minimum age for driver's license:** 18. **Gasoline tax:** 9¢ per gallon. **Motor vehicle deaths:** 25.9 per 100,000 people.

Birthrate (1977): 14.5 per 1,000 people. **Infant mortality rate per 1,000 births (1977):** 10.1. **Physicians per 100,000 pop. (1976):** 203. **Dentists per 100,000 pop. (1976):** 55. **Acceptable hospital beds:** 7.5 per 1,000 people. **State expenditures per capita for health and hospitals (1977):** $68.33.

Education expenditures (1975-76): $497.47 per capita annually. **No. of pupils in public schools (1977 est.):** 103,000. **No. of institutions of higher learning (1976-77):** 23. **Public school expenditure per pupil in attendance (1975-76):** $1,504. **Avg. salary of public school teachers (1974-75 est.):** $9,206. **No. full-time teachers (1977 est.):** 7,170. **Educational attainment of adult population (1976):** 12.5 median yrs. of school completed; 1.0% with less than 5 years of education; 15.6% with 4 yrs. of college.

Telephones (1976): 66 per 100 people. **State Chamber of Commerce:** Vermont State Chamber of Commerce, P.O. Box 37, Montpelier, Vermont 05602.

VIRGINIA

Virginia, home of the first English settlement in North America (Jamestown, 1607), is a state particularly rich in American history. A Virginian, Richard Henry Lee, introduced (June 7, 1776) the motion for separation of the 13 Colonies from England; Virginian Thomas Jefferson was the main author of the Declaration of Independence; and Virginian George Washington led the way to victory in the American Revolution. Eight U.S. Presidents were Virginians, including four of the first five: Washington (1st), Jefferson (3rd), James Madison (4th), and James Monroe (5th); the latter three, in office 24 consecutive years, made up the so-called "Virginia Dynasty." Famed Chief Justice John Marshall was also a Virginian.

The state, which is named for Elizabeth I ("The Virgin Queen"), has acquired several nicknames including "The Mother of States," because all or part of eight other states were formed from western territory it once claimed: West Virginia, Kentucky, Illinois, Indiana, Michigan, Minnesota, Ohio, and Wisconsin. In the American Revolution, General Charles Cornwallis' surrender (1781) to Washington at Yorktown virtually ended hostilities. During the Civil War, Virginia was the central battleground. Among the major battles fought within it were First and Second Bull Run (Manassas), Fredericksburg, Chancellorsville, the Wilderness, and Richmond; Confederate General

VIRGINIA

MILES
0 10 20 30 40 50 60
KILOMETERS
0 10 20 30 40 50 60

National Capital
State Capitals
County Seats
Independent Cities *Bristol

© Copyright HAMMOND INCORPORATED, Maplewood, N.J.

WESTERN PART OF
VIRGINIA
Same scale as main map

Robert E. Lee, another Virginian, surrendered at Appomattox (April 9, 1865).

Roughly triangular in shape, the state has four principal land regions (west to east): the Appalachian Plateau, the Great Appalachian Valley (known also locally as the Valley of Virginia, a series of ridges and valleys including the historic Shenandoah Valley), the Piedmont Plateau (the largest single area), and the Atlantic Coastal Plain, also called the Tidewater Region. Prominent local features of the Appalachian range include the Allegheny Mountains along the western border and the Blue Ridge range rising between the Valley and Piedmont sections. Across Chesapeake Bay, making up the lower part of the Delmarva Peninsula, is the state's Eastern Shore. About two-thirds of the land is forested.

Significant agriculture includes fruit, hay, corn, peanuts, and tobacco, the largest crop and a crucial factor n the state's development. Leading manufactures include chemical and tobacco products. Fishing and, to a lesser degree, mining (especially of coal) are considerable, as is tourism. Attractions include the reconstructed colonial town of Williamsburg, Washington's birthplace (Wakefield) and residence (Mount Vernon), and Jefferson's Monticello, as well as Virginia Beach, Shenandoah National Park, Arlington National Cemetery, and the various Civil War battlegrounds.

Indians of three major language groups (Algonquian, Siouan, and Iroquoian) were living in the region when the first British arrived, about 25 years after an unsuccessful settlement by Spanish Jesuits. English settlement proceeded despite great hardship, mainly through the efforts of such men as Captain John Smith and Thomas West, Baron De La Warr, Virginia's first governor. The House of Burgesses, first legislative body in the New World, was convened (1619) at Jamestown, and five years later Virginia became England's first royal colony. The importation of Negroes, first as indentured servants and later as slaves, was begun. The production and exportation of tobacco, which was first cultivated (1612) by John Rolfe, spurred the colony's growth, and the plantation became the earliest social unit. Rolfe's famous marriage (1614) to Pocahontas helped induce a brief period of peace with the Indians, but there were massacres in 1622 and 1644, and not until Lord Dunmore's War (1774) did Indian troubles decrease.

At the time of Sir William Berkeley's governorship (1641-52, 1660-77), the colony was thriving, with freeholders and merchants controlling the government. Hard times came (1660) with the Restoration's Navigation Acts, which stipulated the exclusive use of English ships and ports for the tobacco trade, causing initial transport bottlenecks, price drops, and widespread discontent. This unrest was aggravated by Berkeley's increasingly unpopular practices (including a slacking of vigilance against the Indians) and an abortive revolt (Bacon's Rebellion, 1676) was mounted; when Berkeley harshly overreacted, England recalled him.

Inflamed by such orators as Patrick Henry ("Give me liberty or give me death!"), Virginians in the 18th century traveled a path of inevitable revolt and, after Washington's final military victory had decided the issue, they provided the first federal leadership. In 1788 Virginia ratified the Constitution and relinquished all its western land claims except Kentucky and West Virginia (Kentucky became an independent state in 1792, as did West Virginia in 1863; two counties were added to the latter state in 1866). Virginia seceded from the Union in 1861 and was readmitted in 1870.

A new constitution was drafted (1902) that imposed a poll tax, virtually disenfranchising Blacks, but state and Federal court decisions in the 1960s held the poll tax unconstitutional as a requisite for voting and a new state constitution approved by voters in 1970 eliminated the tax.

Virginia adopted a stance of "massive resistance" to public school desegregation after the Supreme Court's 1954 desegregation ruling, and a few schools were temporarily closed to avoid integration. During the 1960s and 1970s racial tensions have sharply declined. Tension was renewed, however, when Federal courts issued orders for massive busing of pupils, climaxed by the decision of a U.S. District Judge ordering the consolidation of the school systems of Richmond and two adjacent, mostly white counties. That order later was overturned by a Federal Appeals Court, and this has been upheld by the U.S. Supreme Court.

Full name: Commonwealth of Virginia. **Origin of name:** In honor of Queen Elizabeth of England, the "Virgin Queen." **Inhabitant:** Virginian. **Capital:** Richmond. **State motto:** Sic Semper Tyrannis (Thus Ever to Tyrants). **Flag:** State seal on blue field. **Seal:** State motto; standing figure representing virtue, dressed as woman warrior, standing triumphant over figure of tyranny. **Flower:** American Dogwood. **Bird:** Cardinal. **Tree:** American Dogwood. **Song:** "Carry Me Back to Old Virginia." **Nickname:** Old Dominion State.

Governor: John N. Dalton. **Annual salary:** $60,000. **Term:** 4 years. **Current term expires:** Jan. 1982. **Voting requirements:** 18 yrs. old & U.S. citizen; registered in precinct of residence. **U.S. Congressmen:** 10. **Entered Union:** 1788 (10th state).

Location & boundaries: South Atlantic state; bounded on the north by Maryland; on the west by West Virginia & Kentucky; on the south by Tennessee & North Carolina; & on the east by the Atlantic Ocean. **Total area:** 40,817 sq. mi. (ranks 36th). **Extreme length:** 440 mi. **Extreme breadth:** 200 mi. **Coastline:** 342 mi.; 112 mi. along the Atlantic Ocean & 230 mi. along Chesapeake Bay. **Chief rivers:** James, Potomac, Rappahannock. **Major lakes:** Smith Mountain, John H. Kerr Reservoir. **No. of counties:** 95.

Population (1978 est.): 5,148,000 (ranks 13th). **Pop. increase (1970-78):** 10.8%. **Places over 25,000 pop.:** 15. **Places over 100,000:** 9. **Largest cities:** Norfolk, Richmond, Virginia Beach. **Pop. density:** 126.1 per sq. mi. (ranks 16th). **Pop. projection 1985:** 5,730,000. **Pop. distribution:** 65.6% metropolitan; 34.4% nonmetropolitan. **White:** 80.9%. **Negro:** 18.5%. **Other:** 0.6%. **Marriage rate (1977 est.):** 11.3 per 1,000 people. **Divorce rate:** 4.2 per 1,000 people.

State finances (1977). Revenue: $4,098,080,000. **Expenditures:** $3,926,729,000. **State Taxes:** $399.97 per capita. **State personal income tax:** Yes. **Public debt (1977):** $169.92 per capita. **Federal aid (1977):** $180.58 per capita. **Personal income (1977):** $6,841.

Sectors of the economy (% of labor force employed in 1970): Manufacturing (22%), Wholesale and retail trade (18%), Services (8%), Educational Services (8%), Construction (7%), Government (24%). **Leading products:** chemicals, textile items, apparel, food items, transportation equipment, furniture & fixtures, electrical equipment & supplies. **Minerals:** coal, stone, sand & gravel, lime. **Fishing:** crabs, oysters, menhaden. **Agricultural products:** livestock & livestock items, dairy items, poultry & poultry items, tobacco, corn, hay. **Avg. farm (1978 est.):** 162 acres. **Avg. value of farm per acre:** $732.

Highway expenditures per capita (1977): $126.90. **Persons per motor vehicle:** 1.58. **Minimum age for driver's license:** 18. **Gasoline tax:** 9¢ per gallon. **Motor vehicle deaths:** 20.6 per 100,000 people.

Birthrate (1977): 14.5 per 1,000 people. **Infant mortality rate per 1,000 births (1977):** 15.9. **Physicians per 100,000 pop. (1976):** 162. **Dentists per 100,000 pop. (1976):** 46. **Acceptable hospital beds:** 6.4 per 1,000 people. **State expenditures per capita for health and hospitals (1977):** $72.06.

Education expenditures (1975-76): $417.42 per capita annually. **No. of pupils in public schools (1977 est.):** 1,085,000. **No. of**

WASHINGTON

State and Provincial Capitals
County Seats

institutions of higher learning (1976-77): 72. **Public school expenditure per pupil in attendance (1975-76):** $1,488. **Avg. salary of public school teachers (1974-75 est.):** $11,279. **No. full-time teachers (1977 est.):** 63,560. **Educational attainment of adult population (1976):** 12.4 median yrs. of school completed; 4.6% with less than 5 years of education; 16.4% with 4 yrs. of college.

Telephones (1976): 67 per 100 people. **State Chamber of Commerce:** Virginia State Chamber of Commerce, 611 East Franklin Street, Richmond, Virginia 23219.

WASHINGTON

Washington, traditional gateway to Alaska and the Far East, is a leader in the vital areas of aircraft production, nuclear research, lumbering, and actual and potential waterpower production. It is also a land of rugged beauty that particularly appeals to lovers of the great outdoors.

The Cascade Mountains, running north and south, divide the state in two, the eastern part comprising about three-fifths of the total area. The Olympic Mountains make up the northwest corner of the state, while the Puget Sound Lowland lies between the Olympic Mountains on the west and the Cascades on the east. In the southwest corner is the Coast Range, which extends south into Oregon. East of the Cascades are the Rocky Mountains in the north and the Columbia Plateau in the south.

Most of the state's larger cities, including Seattle and Tacoma, are in the western region along Puget Sound, an unusual 200-mile-long arm of the Pacific Ocean; it varies in width up to 40 miles and harbors more than 300 islands. This area has a milder climate than any other in the country that is as far north. Generally, the weather is drier in the east than in the west, which receives moist Pacific winds and considerable rainfall. Principal irrigated regions are in the Columbia Basin and the valleys of the Walla Walla, Snake, and Yakima rivers. The Lower Granite Dam and Lock System extends navigation on the Columbia and Snake rivers as far inland as Lewiston, Idaho.

Washington is a leading producer of apples, wheat, and hops. Livestock and livestock products make up a third of the total farm revenue, while commercial fishing is significant. Mineral production, including gold, silver, and uranium, accounted for about $187 million in 1976. Aircraft, lumber and food industries dominate the manufacturing sector of the economy.

Today, the state is trying to diversify and stabilize its industry, with less dependency on federal defense contracts. One area of concentration is the brisk tourist trade, which has gained greatly in recent years as more facilities are built to augment the exceptional hunting, fishing, and skiing available. Mount Rainier and Olympic National Parks, and the Grand Coulee Dam National Recreation Area, are among the major attractions. Seattle Center, consisting of structures from the 1962 Century 21 Exposition, includes a monorail and 606-foot "Space Needle." Whitman Mission National Historic Site denotes the place Marcus Whitman founded an Indian mission in 1836; it is also the site of the 1847 Indian massacre in which Whitman and others were killed. The state's Indian troubles persisted until about 1859.

Originally, Washington itself had been but the northern portion of the massive Oregon Country. Conflicting British and American claims to the area threatened briefly to trigger a war during the 1844 U.S. Presidential campaign. Candidate James K. Polk claimed that all the region south of latitude 54°44′ belonged to the United States, and the cry of "Fifty-four Forty or Fight!" was frequently voiced. But diplomacy ultimately prevailed; and in 1846 Polk, as President, made a treaty with England setting the boundary at the present 49th parallel. Statehood came in 1889.

Washington has had its share of hard times and controversy. The period after World War I was one of discontent and strife in the labor field. There were many disputes, especially between businessmen and the Industrial Workers of the World (IWW); violence erupted at Centralia. During World War II, the state's sizable Japanese-American population suffered discrimination and disruption; over 15,000 people were displaced eastward.

In May 1978 salmon fishing by Canadian boats off the Washington coast was prohibited by court injunction in a controversy over fishing rights, pending adoption of a treaty fixing U.S. and Canadian fishing boundaries. The establishment of the 200-mile fishing limit in 1976 had left the two countries without legal guidelines. In July 1978 President Carter signed legislation authorizing him to lift the ban on Canadian fishing in U.S. waters, providing that Canada agrees to allow American fishing in Canadian waters.

It was reported on November 10, 1978, that three electrical generators of the Grand Coulee Dam had been sabotaged thereby causing some $500,000 worth of damage and indefinite delay of the completion of the dam's hydroelectric project.

Full name: State of Washington. **Origin of name:** In honor of George Washington. **Inhabitant:** Washingtonian. **Capital:** Olympia. **State motto:** Alki (By & By). **Flag:** State seal on green field. **Seal:** Portrait of George Washington & date 1889, the year state was admitted to Union. **Flower:** Western rhododendron. **Bird:** Willow goldfinch. **Tree:** Western hemlock. **Song:** "Washington, My Home." **Nickname:** Evergreen State.

Governor: Dixy Lee Ray. **Annual salary:** $55,000. **Term:** 4 years. **Current term expires:** Jan. 1981. **Voting requirements:** 18 yrs. old & U.S. citizen; state resident 30 days. **U.S. Congressmen:** 7. **Entered Union:** 1889 (42d state).

Location & boundaries: Pacific state: bounded on the north by Canada; on the east by Idaho; on the south by Oregon & the Columbia River; & on the west by the Pacific Ocean. **Total area:** 68,192 sq. mi. (ranks 20th). **Extreme length:** 358 mi. **Extreme breadth:** 240 mi. **Coastline:** 157 mi. **Chief rivers:** Columbia, Snake, Yakima. **Major lakes:** Chelan, Franklin D. Roosevelt. **No. of counties:** 39.

Population (1978 est.): 3,774,000 (ranks 21st). **Pop. increase (1970-78):** 10.7%. **Places over 25,000 pop.:** 14. **Places over 100,000:** 3. **Largest cities:** Seattle, Spokane, Tacoma. **Pop. density:** 55.3 per sq. mi. (ranks 28th). **Pop. projection 1985:** 3,792,000. **Pop. distribution:** 71.4% metropolitan; 28.6% nonmetropolitan. **White:** 95.4%. **Negro:** 2.1%. **Other:** 2.5%. **Marriage rate (1977):** 11.3 per 1,000 people. **Divorce rate:** 7.3 per 1,000 people.

State finances (1977). Revenue: $4,478,273,000. **Expenditures:** $4,092,803,000. **State Taxes:** $574.09 per capita. **State personal income tax:** No. **Public debt (1977):** $385.94 per capita. **Federal aid (1977):** $245.76 per capita. **Personal income (1977):** $7,562.

Sectors of the economy (% of labor force employed in 1970): Manufacturing (22%), Wholesale and retail trade (22%), Services (7%), Educational Services (9%), Construction (6%), Government (19%)..**Leading products:** transportation equipment, machinery, food items, lumber & wood, paper items, chemicals, primary metals, printing & publishing. **Agricultural products:** dairy items, cattle, poultry, wheat, apples, hay. **Fishing:** salmon, oysters, crabs. **Avg. farm (1978 est.):** 444 acres. **Avg. value of farm per acre:** $528.

Highway expenditures per capita (1977): $102.70. **Persons per motor vehicle:** 1.26. **Minimum age for driver's license:** 18. **Gasoline tax:** 11¢ per gallon. **Motor vehicle deaths:** 26.1 per 100,000 people.

NORTHERN PART OF
WEST VIRGINIA
Same scale as main map

WEST
VIRGINIA

⊛ State Capital   ⊙ County Seats ◉ N.J.
© Copyright HAMMOND INCORPORATED, Maplewood, N.J.

Birthrate (1977): 15.6 per 1,000 people. Infant mortality rate per 1,000 births (1977): 12.1. Physicians per 100,000 pop. (1976): 178. Dentists per 100,000 pop. (1976): 69. Acceptable hospital beds: 4.5 per 1,000 people. State expenditures per capita for health and hospitals (1977): $50.17.

Education expenditures (1975-76): $515.16 per capita annually. No. of pupils in public schools (1977 est.): 769,000. No. of institutions of higher learning (1976-77): 48. Public school expenditure per pupil in attendance (1975-76): $1,684. Avg. salary of public school teachers (1974-75 est.): $12,538. No. full-time teachers (1977 est.): 36,000. Educational attainment of adult population (1976): 12.7 median yrs. of school completed; 1.0% with less than 5 years of education; 16.1% with 4 yrs. of college.

Telephones (1976): 72 per 100 people. State Chamber of Commerce: Association of Washington Business, P.O. Box 658, Olympia, Washington 98507.

WEST VIRGINIA

West Virginia, second leading coal producer in the U.S., has rugged, ravine-slashed terrain and highly irregular boundaries. There are two main land regions: the Appalachian Plateau constitutes more than 80 percent of its area, and the Great Appalachian Valley consists of a wide strip along the eastern border and includes an expanse of the Allegheny Mountains and a small section of the Blue Ridge. Most of the state's coal, oil, gas, and salt deposits are in the plateau region. Moderately cold winters, warm summers, and adequate rainfall are features of the climate, but the craggy land is not conducive to large-scale farming.

Manufacturing and commerce buttress the state's mineral-oriented economy. The Ohio and Kanawha Valleys are vital chemical centers. Fine scenery, mineral springs, and varied wildlife make for a sizable tourism business. Attractions include the Harpers Ferry National Historical Park and the Monongahela National Forest.

West Virginia's early history is largely shared with Virginia, of which it was a part until antiabolitionist Virginia joined the Confederacy in 1861; the western counties then adopted their own government and sided with the Union; statehood dates from 1863. Two counties were added to the state in 1866.

Indians known as Mound Builders were the region's earliest inhabitants, but they were gone long before the advent of the Europeans in the 1670s. Several Indian tribes continued, however, to use the area as hunting grounds. Welsh, Scots-Irish, and Germans may have lived in the region before him, but credit is often given to Morgan Morgan for having established (1731) the first known permanent settlement on Mill Creek in the eastern panhandle. In 1742 coal was discovered on the Coal River, an event that was a major determinant of West Virginia's destiny. The Indians' hold on the region virtually ended in 1774 but fighting erupted three years later and continued until 1794.

When the state broke away from Virginia, many West Virginians, including General Thomas J. (Stonewall) Jackson, remained loyal to the mother state. A famous long-running (1882-96) feud between the Hatfields of West Virginia and the McCoys of Kentucky resulted in many killings and involved the governors of those states in an acrimonious rift.

Industrial expansion marked the late 19th and early 20th centuries, despite serious labor disputes, especially in the coal mining industry. Not until the 1930s were the mines unionized and working conditions appreciably improved.

A public employee strike for union recognition in 1968 resulted in mass dismissals of state highway workers. The coal mines were shut down 45 days in late 1971 as the United Mine Workers negotiated a new contract. Wildcat strikes have erupted in the mines over such issues as safety and health benefits. Some 25,000 coal miners stayed off the job for three weeks in early 1974 in a protest over gas rationing measures at the height of the fuel crisis.

Recently the coal industry has come under attack by labor activists charging that priority is given to production and profits over the health of miners, and by environmentalists who charge the state's land is being destroyed for the benefit of out-of-state interests.

In the spring of 1975 there was a major resurgence in the state's coal industry, in both deep and strip mining. In 1976 progress was slowed by a wildcat strike which began in Logan, spreading to eight other states before it ended. With the announcement of President Carter's energy program in 1977, increased importance was placed on West Virginia's industry, but again production was hampered by a series of wildcat strikes by the miners. In December 1977 a national strike was begun by the United Mine Workers, the longest strike in the nation's history. A new agreement was not reached until March 1978, ending what threatened to become an energy emergency in nearly a dozen states.

Full name: State of West Virginia. Origin of name: In honor of the "Virgin Queen," Elizabeth I of England. Inhabitant: West Virginian. Capital: Charleston. State motto: Montani Semper Liberi (Mountaineers Are Always Free). Flag: State seal on blue-bordered white field. Seal: Rock (with date June 20, 1863, when state entered Union) stands between farmer & miner, symbolizing state's industries. Flower: Big rhododendron. Bird: Cardinal. Tree: Sugar maple. Songs: "The West Virginia Hills," "This Is My West Virginia." Nickname: Mountain State.

Governor: John D. Rockefeller IV. Annual salary: $50,000. Term: 4 years. Current term expires: Jan. 1981. Voting requirements: 18 yrs. old & U.S. citizen; resident of state. U.S. Congressmen: 4. Entered Union: 1863 (35th state).

Location & boundaries: Southeastern state: bounded on the north by the Ohio River, Pennsylvania, Maryland & the Potomac River; on the east by Maryland & Virginia; on the south by Virginia; & on the west by Kentucky, Ohio & the Ohio River. Total area: 24,181 sq. mi. (ranks 41st). Extreme length: 265 mi. Extreme breadth: 237 mi. Chief rivers: Ohio, Potomac, Kanawha. Major lake: East Lynn Reservoir. No. of counties: 55.

Population (1978 est.): 1,860,000 (ranks 34th). Pop. increase (1970-78): 6.7%. Places over 25,000 pop.: 7. Places over 100,000: None. Largest cities: Huntington, Charleston, Wheeling. Pop. density: 76.9 per sq. mi. (ranks 25th). Pop. projection 1985: 1,907,000. Pop. distribution: 36.4% metropolitan; 63.6% non-metropolitan. White: 95.6%. Negro: 4.2%. Others: 0.2%. Marriage rate (1977): 9.4 per 1,000 people. Divorce rate: 5.2 per 1,000 people.

State finances (1977). Revenue: $1,875,742,000. Expenditures: $1,832,035,000. State Taxes: $485.97 per capita. State personal income tax: Yes. Public debt (1977): $718.03 per capita. Federal aid (1977): $270.49 per capita. Personal income (1977): $5,998.

Sectors of the economy (% of labor force employed in 1970): Manufacturing (23%), Wholesale and retail trade (19%), Services (7%), Educational Services (8%), Construction (7%), Government (17%). Leading products: chemicals; stone, clay & glass items; primary & fabricated metals; food items; machinery; printing & publishing. Minerals: coal, natural gas & natural gas liquids, stone. Agricultural products: cattle, dairy items, hay, apples, corn. Avg. farm (1978 est.): 177 acres. Avg. value of farm per acre: $403.

Highway expenditures per capita (1977): $183.79. Persons per motor vehicle: 1.64. Minimum age for driver's license: 18. Gasoline tax: 10.5¢ per gallon. Motor vehicle deaths: 25.1 per 100,000 people.

Birthrate (1977): 16.2 per 1,000 people. Infant mortality rate per 1,000 births (1977): 14.6. Physicians per 100,000 pop. (1976): 131. Dentists per 100,000 pop. (1976): 34. Acceptable hospital beds: 8.6 per 1,000 people. State expenditures per capita for health and hospitals (1977): $51.07.

WISCONSIN

MILES

0   10   20   40   60

KILOMETERS

0   20   40   60

State Capitals ⊛   County Seats ●

© Copyright HAMMOND INCORPORATED, Maplewood, N.J.

Education expenditures (1975-76): $377.18 per capita annually. No. of pupils in public schools (1977 est.): 399,000. No. of institutions of higher learning (1976-77): 28. Public school expenditure per pupil in attendance (1975-76): $1,382. Avg. salary of public school teachers (1974-75 est.): $9,124. No. full-time teachers (1977 est.): 20,670. Educational attainment of adult population (1976): 12.1 median yrs. of school completed; 5.0% with less than 5 years of education; 9.2% with 4 yrs. of college.

Telephones (1976): 54 per 100 people. State Chamber of Commerce: West Virginia Chamber of Commerce, P.O. Box 2789, 1101 Kanawha Valley Bldg., Charleston, West Virginia 25330.

WISCONSIN

Although Wisconsin is best known as the leading U.S. dairy state, manufacturing today represents its major economic activity; top products include nonelectrical machinery and the many pulp and paper items that the state's extensive forests make possible. Wisconsin is also the country's largest supplier of beer, with brewers concentrated most heavily in the Milwaukee area. Politically, the state has gained a reputation for progress and reform.

The land itself, rich and diverse, consists of two principal regions: the Superior Upland in the north and the Central Lowlands, covering the lower two-thirds of the state and consisting of the Wisconsin Driftless Area in the west and the Great Lakes Plain in the east. Rolling hills, ridges, and fertile valleys and plains, punctuated by many clear lakes, have made Wisconsin famous for its scenic beauty, and, despite past exploitation, forests still cover almost half the state. By far the largest part of the population lives in the southeastern region. The state's climate is marked by sharply defined seasons that are tempered somewhat by the bordering Lakes Superior and Michigan.

Frenchman Jean Nicolet was the first European to explore the Wisconsin region, landing (1634) at Green Bay in search of a fur-trading fortune and the legendary "Northwest Passage" to the Orient. At the time, Ottawa, Huron, and other Indians from the east were forcing indigenous Indians (including the Winnebago) westward, and only the Menominees were relatively settled there. The arrival of Nicolet and other Frenchmen soon after established France's claim to the region that was valid until 1763, when the British gained possession.

After the American Revolution, England theoretically ceded (1783) the region to the United States, but the British retained actual control until after the War of 1812. A part of the Northwest Territory until 1800, the Wisconsin region became, successively, a part of the territories of Indiana (1800-09), Illinois (1809-18), and Michigan (1818-36). When it was made a separate territory in 1836, Wisconsin included its present area in addition to parts of Iowa, Minnesota, and those sections of North and South Dakota east of the Missouri and White Earth Rivers. In 1838, the territory west of the Mississippi was organized as the Territory of Iowa, Wisconsin retaining its present area and a northward extension to Lake of the Woods in what is now Minnesota. A decade later, Wisconsin entered the Union.

Wisconsin's Indian troubles reached a climax in the Black Hawk War (1832), which virtually ended the Indian threat in the area and caused a settlement boom. There followed a substantial influx of immigrants—especially Germans, Irish, English, and Welsh. Liberal leaders, like Carl Schurz, settled in Wisconsin and added to the intellectual development of the state. In 1871, Wisconsin was hit by the great Peshtigo forest fire, the worst natural disaster in its history, which killed more than 1,000 persons and destroyed more than $5 million worth of property. An extensive reforestation program is part of Wisconsin's current far-reaching conservation efforts.

Wisconsin is the home of the three major league sports teams. The Green Bay Packers have won the NFL championship eleven times and the Milwaukee Bucks became the NBA champions in 1971. Major league baseball returned to the state in 1970 when the Seattle club of the American League became the Milwaukee Brewers.

In 1976 Wisconsin became the first of the 1976 primary states to hold an open presidential primary election. The Democratic National Committee decided on June 9, 1978 to bar open primaries in this state as well as in Michigan and Montana.

Full name: State of Wisconsin. Origin of name: From an Indian name, Wisconsinite. Capital: Madison. State motto: Forward. Flag: State seal on a blue field. Seal: A sailor & a miner hold shield with symbols representing Wisconsin's industries; badger is state's nickname; horn of plenty; pyramid of lead. Flower: Wood violet. Bird: Robin. Tree: Sugar maple. Rock: Granite. Mineral: Galena. Domestic Animal: Dairy Cow. Song: "On, Wisconsin!" Nickname: Badger State.

Governor: Lee S. Dreyfus. Annual salary: $65,801. Term: 4 years. Current term expires: Jan. 1983. Voting requirements: 18 yrs. old & U.S. citizen; resident of voting district 10 days. U.S. Congressmen: 9. Entered Union: 1848 (30th state).

Location & boundaries: Midwestern state; bounded on the north by Lake Superior & the state of Michigan; on the east by Lake Michigan; on the south by Illinois; & on the west by Iowa, Minnesota, the Mississippi River & the St. Croix River. Total area: 56,154 sq. mi. (ranks 26th). Extreme length: 315 mi. Extreme breadth: 289 mi. Shoreline: 785 mi. Chief rivers: Mississippi, Wisconsin, St. Croix, Black, Fox. Major lakes: Winnebago, Poygan, Mendota, Pentenwell, Castle Rock. No. of counties: 72.

Population (1978 est.): 4,679,000 (ranks 16th). Pop. increase (1970-78): 5.9%. Places over 25,000 pop.: 23. Places over 100,000: 2. Largest cities: Milwaukee, Madison, Racine, Green Bay. Pop. density: 83.3 per sq. mi. (ranks 23rd). Pop. projection 1985: 4,972,000. Pop. distribution: 60.2% metropolitan; 39.8% nonmetropolitan. White: 96.4%. Negro: 2.9%. Other: 0.7%. Marriage rate (1977): 8.0 per 1,000 people. Divorce rate: 3.1 per 1,000 people.

State finances (1977). Revenue: $4,931,994,000. Expenditures: $4,455,535,000. State Taxes: $587.68 per capita. State personal income tax: Yes. Public debt (1977): $362.22 per capita. Federal aid (1977): $218.78 per capita. Personal income (1977): $6,864.

Sectors of the economy (% of labor force employed in 1970): Manufacturing (31%), Wholesale and retail trade (20%), Services (6%), Educational Services (8%), Construction (5%), Government (14%). Leading products: machinery, food items, transportation equipment, paper items, primary & fabricated metals. Agricultural products: dairy items, cattle, hogs, hay, corn, oats. Fishing: whitefish, lake herring, chubs, carp, buffalo. Avg. farm (1978 est.): 192 acres. Avg. value of farm per acre: $690.

Highway expenditures per capita (1977): $69.56. Persons per motor vehicle: 1.74. Minimum age for driver's license: 18. Gasoline tax: 7¢ per gallon. Motor vehicle deaths: 20.9 per 100,000 people.

Birthrate (1977): 14.8 per 1,000 people. Infant mortality rate per 1,000 births (1977): 11.3. Physicians per 100,000 pop. (1976): 141. Dentists per 100,000 pop. (1976): 55. Acceptable hospital beds: 6.7 per 1,000 people. State expenditures per capita for health and hospitals (1977): $53.55.

Education expenditures (1975-76): $525.51 per capita annually. No. of pupils in public schools (1977 est.): 932,000. No. of institutions of higher learning (1976-77): 58. Public school expenditure per pupil in attendance (1975-76): $1,792. Avg. salary of public school teachers (1974-75 est.): $13,046. No. full-time teachers (1977 est.): 57,970. Educational attainment of adult population (1976): 12.1 median yrs. of school completed; 1.4% with less than 5 years of education; 12.7% with 4 yrs. of college.

Telephones (1976): 68 per 100 people. **State Chamber of Commerce:** Wisconsin Association of Manufacturers & Commerce, 111 E. Wisconsin Ave., Room 1600, Milwaukee, Wisconsin 53202.

WYOMING

Wyoming, an awesome, sparsely settled state of alternating plains and mountains, is crossed by the Continental Divide—the junction of the Great Plains and the Rocky Mountains, which slash across the state's rectangle from the northwest corner to the center of the southern boundary.

The plains-mountains dividing line is less marked in the central and northern "intermontane" areas. The horizons are distant, and the land generally high—its average altitude of 6,700 feet is second only to Colorado's. The spectacular Devil's Tower—the country's first national monument—is a volcanic plug in the northeastern plains that stands 865 feet above its 415-foot base and can be seen for many miles.

The face of the land provides a clue to its economy. Short, tough grass covers much of the terrain, 80 percent of which is used for cattle and sheep grazing (Wyoming is second only to Texas in wool production). Recent consolidations have increased the size but decreased the number of farms and ranches within the state. About 20 percent of the farms produce commercial crops; the others are devoted to livestock production.

The growth of agriculture, however, is limited by the state's water supply. Although Wyoming theoretically has sufficient precipitation and underground springs to foster crop growth, as late as 1966 only ten percent of these resources were being utilized effectively. The perennial problem is distribution: in some places, where the soil is suitable for farming, the streamflow and precipitation are too light, while many large rivers like the Yellowstone and Tongue run through steep, rocky canyons.

More important to the state than agriculture is mining. In 1975, the assessed valuation on minerals was 48 percent of the entire state valuation. Oil and oil products constitute one of Wyoming's leading industries. Other minerals include bentonite, trona, coal, uranium, and iron ore. Wyoming is the second largest uranium producing state. Devastated by the conversion of railroad locomotives to diesel power, coal is making a comeback following formulation of emission standards which make Wyoming's low sulphur coal very much in demand. The state's coal reserves are estimated at 36 billion tons, of which two-thirds is recoverable through strip mining and underground mining methods.

John Colter, a fur-trapper and a member of the Lewis and Clark expedition (1804-06), is the first European known to have entered the state; in 1807 he explored the Yellowstone area and brought back news of its geysers and hot springs.

By 1850, pioneers were "going west" via three famous trails, all of which passed through Wyoming: the California, Mormon (to Utah), and Oregon (to the Pacific Northwest). Meanwhile the Plains Indians, their homeland challenged, grew increasingly hostile, raiding wagon trains and defying accompanying troops. These troubles climaxed in 1865-66, then tapered off.

The Union Pacific Railroad was built (1867-68) across the southern part of Wyoming, following the coal deposits and bringing in laborers to work the mines. The scant farmland caused many homesteaders to bypass Wyoming, leaving it open for cattlemen, who enjoyed bonanza days from 1865 to 1887.

Rustlers, declining market prices, and the severe winter of 1886-87 in which one-sixth of the herds starved all helped to curtail the cattle industry's dominance. About this time, sheep raising began to increase, leading to an era of conflict between sheepmen and cattlemen over grazing rights.

Today tourism is increasingly vital to Wyoming's economy: over nine million persons—including many sportsmen—visit the state annually. Yellowstone and Grand Teton National Parks are prime attractions. Wyoming has been decisively thrust into the missile age by Warren AFB (Cheyenne), one of the largest in the nation's ICBM complex.

Full name: State of Wyoming. **Origin of name:** Named after Wyoming Valley, Pennsylvania; Indian word means "Alternating Mountains & Valleys." **Inhabitant:** Wyomingite. **Capital:** Cheyenne. **State motto:** Equal Rights. **Flag:** State seal & buffalo on a red-&-white-bordered blue field. **Seal:** Woman & motto, "Equal Rights," symbolize equal treatment women have had in state; two men represent Wyoming's livestock & mining industries; dates Wyoming became territory & state. **Flower:** Indian paintbrush. **Bird:** Meadowlark. **Tree:** Cottonwood. **Song:** "Wyoming." **Nickname:** Equality State.

Governor: Ed Herschler. **Annual salary:** $55,000. **Term:** 4 years. **Current term expires:** Jan. 1983. **Voting requirements:** 18 yrs. old & U.S. citizen; resident of state & registered to vote. **U.S. Congressmen:** 1. **Entered Union:** 1890 (44th state).

Location & boundaries: Rocky Mountain state: bounded on the north by Montana; on the east by South Dakota & Nebraska; on the south by Colorado & Utah; & on the west by Utah, Idaho & Montana. **Total area:** 97,914 sq. mi. (ranks 9th). **Extreme length:** 365 mi. **Extreme breadth:** 265 mi. **Chief rivers:** North Platte, Bighorn, Green, Snake. **Major lakes:** Yellowstone, Jackson, Flaming Gorge Reservoir. **No. of counties:** 23.

Population (1978 est.): 424,000 (ranks 49th). **Pop. increase (1970-78):** 27.7%. **Places over 25,000 pop.:** 2. **Places over 100,000:** None. **Largest cities:** Cheyenne, Casper, Laramie. **Pop. density:** 4.3 per sq. mi. (ranks 49th). **Pop. projection 1985:** 442,000. **Pop. distribution:** 100% nonmetropolitan; 0.0% non-metropolitan. **White:** 97.2%. **Negro:** 0.8%. **Other:** 2%. **Marriage rate (1977):** 14.3 per 1,000 people. **Divorce rate:** 7.6 per 1,000 people.

State finances (1977). Revenue: $563,376,000. **Expenditures:** $535,769,000. **State Taxes:** $574.72 per capita. **State personal income tax:** No. **Public debt (1977):** $180.49 per capita. **Federal aid (1977):** $448.58 per capita. **Personal income (1977):** $7,517.

Sectors of the economy (% of labor force employed in 1970): Manufacturing (6%), Wholesale and retail trade (20%), Services (9%), Educational Services (11%), Construction (7%), Government (22%). **Leading products:** petroleum & coal items; food items; stone, clay & glass items; lumber & wood; printing & publishing. **Minerals:** petroleum, natural gas, sodium salts, iron ore, uranium. **Agricultural products:** cattle, sheep, wool, hay, sugarbeets, wheat. **Avg. farm (1978 est.):** 4,412 acres. **Avg. value of farm per acre:** $105.

Highway expenditures per capita (1977): $255.66. **Persons per motor vehicle:** 1.08. **Minimum age for driver's license:** 16. **Gasoline tax:** 8¢ per gallon. **Motor vehicle deaths:** 56.8 per 100,000 people.

Birthrate (1977): 20.4 per 1,000 people. **Infant mortality rate per 1,000 births (1977):** 13.9. **Physicians per 100,000 pop. (1976):** 113. **Dentists per 100,000 pop. (1976):** 46. **Acceptable hospital beds:** 6.9 per 1,000 people. **State expenditures per capita for health and hospitals (1977):** $48.49.

Education expenditures (1975-76): $624.03 per capita annually. **No. of pupils in public schools (1977 est.):** 89,000. **No. of institutions of higher learning (1976-77):** 8. **Public school expenditure per pupil in attendance (1975-76):** $2,142. **Avg. salary of public school teachers (1974-75 est.):** $10,350. **No. full-time teachers (1977 est.):** 5,080. **Educational attainment of adult population (1976):** 12.6 median yrs. of school completed; 1.2% with less than 5 years of education; 14.5% with 4 yrs. of college.

Telephones (1976): 74 per 100 people.

REPRESENTATIVE AMERICAN CITIES

ALBUQUERQUE

Location: North-central New Mexico, on upper Rio Grande **County:** Bernalillo **City area:** 88.12 sq. miles (289.99 sq. kilometers) **Altitude:** 4,958 feet (1506.6 meters)
Mayor: David Rusk **Chief Administrative Officer:** Jim Jaramillo
City population: 243,751 (1970 census), 284,617 (1976 est.)
Metro area population: 333,266 (1970 census), 401,900 (1977 est.)
Daily newspapers: 2 **No. of commercial radio stations (AM):** 15 (1979) **No. of commercial TV stations:** 4 (1979)
City Chamber of Commerce: Greater Albuquerque Chamber of Commerce, 401 2nd Street, NW, Albuquerque, New Mexico 87102

Albuquerque, seat of Bernalillo County, is the largest city in New Mexico; a fast-growing center of trade, clean industry, and Federal agencies; and a famous health resort.

The old town of Albuquerque was founded in 1706 and named for the Duke of Alburquerque. After the Mexican War (1846-48), New Mexico was organized as a U.S. territory. Albuquerque was occupied by Confederate forces briefly in 1862. The new Albuquerque was mapped out in 1880 in connection with railroad construction.

After World War II, the city began to grow rapidly, primarily because of Sandia Laboratory (a nuclear weapons laboratory) and Kirtland Air Force Base, which functions as a nuclear effects research laboratory and satellite tracking station. Lovelace Foundation for medical research is also located here. Albuquerque now has railroad shops, lumber mills, and food-processing plants. Manufactures include brick and tile, wood products, Indian jewelry, clothing, business machines, and metal and plastic components.

Of historic interest is the Old Town Plaza, laid out by Spanish settlers in 1706. Some of the buildings are two centuries old and have recently been restored. The Church of San Felipe de Neri (1706), once used as a fortress against the Indians, is in the Old Town. Other attractions are the University of New Mexico, founded in 1889, with pueblo-style buildings; the Ernie Pyle Memorial Branch Library, former home of the war correspondent; the annual state fair; and the magnificent vistas from the Sandia Peak Aerial Tramway.

ATLANTA

Location: Northwest Georgia, at foot of Blue Ridge Mountains, about 75 miles from northern border **County:** mostly in Fulton, part in DeKalb **City area:** 131 sq. miles (339.3 sq. kilometers) **Altitude:** 1,050 feet (319.1 meters)
Mayor: Maynard H. Jackson
City population: 495,039 (1970 census), 425,666 (1976 est.)
Metro area population: 1,595,517 (1970 census), 1,831,500 (1977 est.)
Daily newspapers: 3 **No. of commercial radio stations (AM):** 23 (1979) **No. of commercial TV stations:** 8 (1979)
City Chamber of Commerce: Atlanta Chamber of Commerce, P.O. Box 1740, Atlanta, Georgia 30301

Atlanta, seat of Fulton County and capital and largest city of Georgia, is the leading commercial, industrial, and distribution center of the southeastern United States. It is also a port of entry and cultural center.

The first settler, Hardy Ivy, built a cabin on former Creek Indian land in 1833. The town, founded as Terminus in 1837, was later called Marthasville and in 1845 assumed the name Atlanta. It is said that the name was given it by railroad builder J. E. Thomson for its location at the end of the Western and Atlantic Railroad. It was incorporated as a city in 1847.

An important Confederate communications center during the Civil War, Atlanta fell to General W. T. Sherman on September 2, 1864, and on November 15 was put to the torch and almost completely destroyed. After the war, a new city was constructed and industrialization proceeded rapidly. In 1868 Atlanta became the state capital.

Today there are more than 1,500 manufacturing plants in the area. Products include automobiles, airplanes, chemicals, furniture, steel, paper, fertilizers, soft drinks, and processed foods. Atlanta is also a financial center and home of a Federal Reserve district bank. The Na-

tional Center for Disease Control of the U.S. Public Health Service has its national headquarters here.

The image of the city itself was marred in 1966 when riots broke out in the Negro section of Summerhill. Earlier, Atlanta had been the first city of the Deep South to experience peaceful school integration.

In 1973 Andrew J. Young was elected from the racially mixed metro area Fourth District, the first black Georgia Congressman since Reconstruction days, and in 1977 was appointed as U.S. Ambassador to the UN. Maynard H. Jackson, the first black mayor in modern times, was elected to a second term in 1977.

A billion-dollar building boom has included major privately financed projects plus several public facilities: a stadium and coliseum are in operation; the $70-million Georgia World Congress convention complex opened in September 1976. The Atlanta Memorial Arts Center, in memory of the 100 members of the Atlanta Art Association killed in a plane crash, opened in 1968. The Metropolitan Atlanta Rapid Transit Authority's $2.1 billion Federally financed subway system started services July 1, 1979.

In recent years Atlanta has developed its international trade, with a dozen foreign banks, 11 consulates and 10 foreign trade bureaus opening, earning the nickname "Paris of the South."

Of historic interest are the capitol and state library; the state archives building; the Cyclorama of the Battle of Atlanta; Oakland Cemetery of Civil War dead; Fort McPherson; and Wren's Nest, the home of the late Joel Chandler Harris, noted fabulist.

BALTIMORE

Location: In Maryland, 40 miles northeast of Washington, D.C., on the Patapsco River **County:** Baltimore is an independent city **City area:** 78 sq. miles (202 sq. kilometers) **Altitude:** 20 feet (6.1 meters)
Mayor: William Donald Schaefer **Chief Administrative Officer:** Walter S. Orlinsky
City population: 905,787 (1970 census), 804,900 (1977 est.)
Metro area population: 2,071,016 (1970 census), 2,146,900 (1977 est.)
Daily newspapers: 3 **No. of commercial radio stations (AM):** 24 (1979) **No. of commercial TV stations:** 5 (1979)
City Chamber of Commerce: Greater Baltimore Committee, Inc., Suite 900, Two Hopkins Plaza, Charles Center, Baltimore, Maryland 21201

Baltimore, largest city in Maryland, is an industrial and commercial center and major seaport. Named for Lord Baltimore, first proprietor of Maryland, it was settled in the early 1600s but not officially founded until 1729.

The shipbuilding industry grew highly profitable during the Revolution and War of 1812. The famous Baltimore clippers were built in the early 1800s. During the First and Second World Wars, the city was a major shipbuilder and supply port.

Baltimore was the site of the Continental Congress after the British occupation of Philadelphia (1777-78). The city's location, near the eastern terminus of the National Road that eventually ran from Cumberland to St. Louis, helped it develop into a major center of commerce. The opening in 1825 of the Erie Canal, in New York State, diverting trade, led to the chartering of the Baltimore & Ohio Railroad to bolster Baltimore's position.

During the Civil War, Maryland remained in the Union, but many Baltimore residents were pro-Southern and in 1861 some of them attacked Union troops. The city suffered a disastrous fire in 1904 but emerged as a better-planned metropolis.

Of historic interest are the Maryland Historical Society; the Baltimore Cathedral, the 175-year-old U.S. Frigate *Constellation;* Edgar Allan Poe's grave in Westminster Churchyard, and Ft. McHenry.

Today Baltimore handles the fourth largest volume of foreign trade of any American port. It has attracted diverse industries, including sugar and food processing. Petroleum and chemicals, aircraft, guided missiles, and steel and gypsum products are important industries.

Bethlehem Steel Company's Sparrows Point complex, the largest tidewater steel plant in the world, is located here.

Baltimore, which suffers from the deterioration and shrinking population common to all Eastern cities, has attacked these problems vigorously. Through careful planning, long-term renewal efforts have begun to reverse the trend without adding to the city's debt load. A major program of urban redevelopment has reshaped the downtown area. Charles Center, begun twenty years ago, is virtually complete, as is the Civic Center. In the Inner Harbor area, now under renewal, an Academy of Science has been completed, the Convention Center opened in August, 1979, and an aquarium is due to open soon.

Baltimore celebrated its 250th anniversary in April 1979, and festivities, which ran from April to October, emphasized its maritime, historical and ethnic elements.

BIRMINGHAM

Location: North-central Alabama, in the Jones Valley at the foot of Red Mt. **County:** Jefferson **City area:** 89.7 sq. miles (232.4 sq. kilometers) **Altitude:** 600 feet (182.3 meters)
Mayor: David Vann
City population: 305,893 (1970 census), 280,544 (1976 est.)
Metro area population: 767,230 (1970 census), 805,300 (1977 est.)
Daily newspapers: 5 **No. of commercial radio stations (AM):** 11 (1979) **No. of commercial TV stations:** 3 (1979)
City Chamber of Commerce: Birmingham Area Chamber of Commerce, 1914 6th Avenue North, Birmingham, Alabama 35203

Birmingham, seat of Jefferson County, is Alabama's principal industrial city and the South's leading iron-and-steel center.

Named after Birmingham, England, the city was founded and incorporated in 1871. A decade earlier the iron ore, coal, and limestone deposits in the region were used by Confederate forces to produce cannonballs and rifles. As railroads expanded and the steel industry developed, Birmingham prospered. A financial panic briefly interrupted its growth in 1900.

Since World War II, the city's economy has undergone diversification. Birmingham, "the Pittsburgh of the South," is now a leader in transportation equipment, construction materials, chemicals, and food processing.

Birmingham experienced a building boom during the 1960s; a $37.5-million civic center includes a coliseum, music hall, theater, and exhibit hall. Development of the University of Alabama in Birmingham is entering its final phase of completion on a 236-acre site adjacent to downtown. Within five years, the $100-million complex of 40 buildings is expected to outstrip U.S. Steel as the area's biggest employer. By 1990, an estimated 50,000 people—about one resident in 15—will be either an employee, a student, or both.

Of interest is the Arlington Historical Shrine, one of Alabama's few remaining antebellum homes. Overlooking the city on nearby Red Mountain is a giant statue of Vulcan, the largest iron figure ever cast. The city is also the home of the Southern Research Institute, which has a technical staff of 360.

BOSTON

Location: In Massachusetts, on Massachusetts Bay, between Neponset River and the mouths of the Charles and Mystic rivers **County:** Suffolk **City area:** 49.9 sq. miles (129.2 sq. kilometers) **Altitude:** 27 feet (8.2 meters)
Mayor: Kevin H. White
City population: 641,071 (1970 census), 618,250 (1976 est.)
Metro area population: 3,848,593 (1970 census), 3,897,800 (1977 est.)
Daily newspapers: 8 **No. of commercial radio stations (AM):** 14 (1979) **No. of commercial TV stations:** 8 (1979)
City Chamber of Commerce: Greater Boston Chamber of Commerce, 125 High Street, Boston, Massachusetts 02110

Boston, seat of Suffolk County and capital of Massachusetts, is New England's largest city. It was settled in 1630 by Puritan colonists. It became the center of American Puritanism and a fount of culture and intellect. The Boston Public Latin School, founded in 1635,

and Harvard College, founded the following year in nearby Cambridge, were the first American schools.

An important commercial center because of its busy harbor, Boston became a leader in opposing British rule. Among pre-Revolutionary War actions were the Boston Massacre (1770) and the Boston Tea Party (1773). The Battle of Bunker Hill, one of the first of the Revolution, was fought close by in June 1775.

Shortly after the war, Boston experienced a long period of prosperity and became a city in 1822. Prominent families such as the Cabots, Lowells, and Lodges ("the Boston Brahmins") made fortunes in shipping, textiles, and shoes. Because of the cultivated tastes of wealthy Bostonians, the city became known as "the Athens of America." Despite the conservative and wealthy atmosphere, however, it was noted as a center of abolitionism before the Civil War.

A 19th-century flood of immigrants, largely Irish at first, converted Boston into a thriving industrial metropolis. Although the area declined during the first half of the 20th century, primarily because of industries moving to the South, Boston remained a national cultural center and is still the financial and trading center of New England, a leading U.S. port, and an important market for fish, seafood, and wool. The electronics industry has been a significant factor in reviving Boston's economic life.

Boston is also noted for its hospitals and its universities, among them Northeastern, Boston University and Boston College, as well as Harvard and MIT across the Charles River in Cambridge.

History-steeped Boston has many points of interest from colonial and Revolutionary War times, including the Old North Church, Old South Meeting House, Old State House, Paul Revere House, King's Chapel, Boston Common and Faneuil Hall.

The downtown area has undergone a major redevelopment in recent years, with the building of a number of high-rise commercial and residential buildings, the new Government Center and the renovation of the Faneuil Hall Marketplace, including Quincy Market, South Market and North Market, the Downtown Crossing Pedestrian shopping mall, and the Boston Waterfront Park, all important links in the city's plans to revitalize the waterfront.

BUFFALO

Location: Western New York, at mouth of Niagara River on Lake Erie **County:** Erie **City area:** 42.6 sq. miles (110.3 sq. kilometers) **Altitude:** 585 feet (177.8 meters)
Mayor: James D. Griffin
City population: 462,768 (1970 census), 400,234 (1976 est.)
Metro area population: 1,349,211 (1970 census), 1,313,000 (1977 est.)
Daily newspapers: 2 **No. of commercial radio stations (AM):** 8 (1979) **No. of commercial TV stations:** 4 (1979)
City Chamber of Commerce: Buffalo Area Chamber of Commerce, 107 Delaware Ave., Buffalo, New York 14202

Buffalo, seat of Erie County and second largest city in New York State, was named after a local creek, which in turn derived its name from that of an Indian who once lived in the area.

A village was laid out on the site of the present city by Joseph Ellicott for the Holland Land Company in 1803. Almost completely destroyed by fire during the War of 1812, Buffalo grew slowly until the opening of the Erie Canal in 1825 after which it mushroomed. Buffalo was chartered as a city in 1832, became an important transportation center, a major Great Lakes port, and since the opening of the St. Lawrence Seaway, a world port.

The city has had a long association with the Presidency. Millard Fillmore, a resident of Buffalo, was elected Vice-President in 1848 and two years later became President after the death of Zachary Taylor. Grover Cleveland, mayor of Buffalo in 1881, was elected to the Presidency in 1884 and 1892. During the 1901 Pan-American Exposition, President McKinley was assassinated in Buffalo.

Industry in the Buffalo area has flourished, largely because of hydroelectric power from Niagara Falls augmented by the Niagara Power Project, one of the largest hydroelectric power projects in the world. Buffalo is the largest grain-milling center in the world. Bethlehem

Steel and General Motors are the two largest industrial employers in the area, while the State University at Buffalo is the single largest employer.

Downtown Buffalo has undergone a tremendous facelift in the past ten years. In Oct. 1978, the Buffalo Convention Center was completed, strengthening the Niagara Frontier as a prime locale for conventions. The rapid transit rail system is underway and will be completed by 1984.

Of interest in the area are nearby Niagara Falls; the Buffalo Museum of Science, Historical Museum, and Zoological Gardens; the Albright-Knox Art Gallery; Roswell Park and Children's Hospitals; the Eye Bank; and Niagrara Square.

Buffalo's professional sports teams include the Bills, Braves, Sabres and Blazers in soccer and the Breskis in women's baseball.

CHARLESTON

Location: In southeastern part of South Carolina, along coast, on peninsula between Ashley and Cooper Rivers **County:** Charleston **City area:** 20.6 sq. miles (53.5 sq. kilometers) **Altitude:** sea level **Mayor:** Joseph P. Riley, Jr.
City population: 66,945 (1970 census), 60,772 (1976 est.) **Metro area population:** 336,125 (1970 census), 385,400 (1977 est.)
Daily newspapers: 2 **No. of commercial radio stations (AM):** 10 (1979) **No. of commercial TV stations:** 3 (1979)
City Chamber of Commerce: Charleston Trident Chamber of Commerce, P.O. Box 975, Charleston, South Carolina 29401

Charleston is a major Atlantic seaport and, as one of America's oldest cities, a leading tourist center. It was originally called Charles Towne in honor of Charles II by the English settlers who first landed in 1670 at Albemarle Point, about 7 miles from modern Charleston. Ten years later they moved to Oyster Point, where the city had been laid out according to the *Grande Modell* sent from England by the Lords Proprietor. It was incorporated in 1783 as Charleston and became the economic and social center of the region.

By the time of the Revolution, Charleston was the most important city and port south of Philadelphia. It was a wealthy cultural center to which French Huguenots and other non-English immigrants gave a cosmopolitan touch.

Charleston's role in the Civil War began when the South Carolina ordinance of secession was passed there in December 1860. The city's harbor was also the site of the first hostile act of the war: the firing on Fort Sumter on April 12, 1861. Although under continuous siege from 1863 to 1865, Charleston did not fall to Union forces until February 1865.

Despite the ravages of two wars, disastrous fires, a violent earthquake in 1886, and periodic hurricanes, Charleston has retained many historic buildings and colonial mansions. Of interest are: Fort Sumter, a national monument since 1948; Patriot's Point, a naval museum; the Dock Street Theater, opened in 1735; the original Catfish Row, made famous in Gershwin's *Porgy and Bess;* the Charleston Museum, founded in 1773; the Huguenot Church built in 1680 and rebuilt in 1844; and numerous ante-bellum homes in the peninsula city. Nearby are notable plantation homes and three world famous gardens: Cypress, Magnolia and Middleton. Charles Towne Landing (a park, pavilion, and natural zoo), was established at the time of the city's tricentennial anniversary in 1970.

The city's growing economy is linked to port and transportation expansion and commerce; diversified business, industrial, and education centers; and military installations and facilities maintained by the Army, Navy, Air Force, and the Coast Guard. New construction projects, such as the proposed Charleston Convention Center and a $13-million hotel, will bring in more tourists and more tax revenue, revitalizing the downtown area. However, controversy over the location of the convention center site, on land surrounded by areas under restoration, has held up construction.

Spoleto Festival USA, "the world's most comprehensive art festival," has become an annual event, featuring music, drama, ballet, films, opera, dance and visual arts.

CHICAGO

Location: Northeastern corner of Illinois on shore of Lake Michigan **County:** Cook **City area:** 228.1 sq. miles (590.8 sq. kilometers) **Altitude:** 578.5 feet (175.8 meters)
Mayor: Jane Byrne
City population: 3,369,357 (1970 census), 3,074,084 (1976 est.)
Metro area population: 6,977,611 (1970 census), 7,017,400 (1977 est.)
Daily newspapers: 2 **No. of commercial radio stations (AM):** 14 (1979) **No. of commercial TV stations:** 7 (1979)
City Chamber of Commerce: Chicago Association of Commerce and Industry, 130 S. Michigan Ave., Chicago, Illinois 60603

Chicago, seat of Cook County, Illinois, is the nation's second largest city, the most important Great Lakes port, and the world's largest railroad terminal. Its O'Hare International Airport is considered the world's busiest.

Father Marquette and Louis Jolliet visited the site of Chicago in 1673, but more than a century elapsed before a trading post was established, by Jean Baptiste Point du Sable. He was succeeded in 1804 by the first permanant settler, John Kinzie, who is usually regarded as the "father of Chicago."

The Erie Canal, which was opened in 1825, stimulated growth and helped convert Chicago into a prosperous commercial town. Incorporated as a city in 1837, it developed into a major rail hub and the nation's mid-continent shipping center soon after the arrival of the railroads in the 1840s. By the time of the Civil War, meatpacking had become a leading industry.

In 1871 the city was almost completely destroyed by a great fire. It was quickly rebuilt, and its booming industry attracted immigrants from all over the world. Labor problems led to violent eruptions, such as the Haymarket Riot of 1886 and Pullman strikes in 1894.

Chicago is a leading producer of steel, telephone equipment, appliances, electrical machinery, plastic products, and diesel engines. It boasts a Federal Reserve district bank, the Midwest Stock Exchange, the Chicago Mercantile Exchange, and the Chicago Board of Trade—the world's largest commodity futures market.

The skyscraper was Chicago's contribution to American architecture. The first skyscraper, designed by William Le Baron Jenney, was built here in 1883, and of the world's ten tallest buildings, four are in Chicago. Two of the nation's greatest architects, Louis H. Sullivan and Frank Lloyd Wright, worked in Chicago.

Landmarks of interest in the Chicago area include the Merchandise Mart, the largest commercial building in the world; the Art Institute; the Museum of Science and Industry; and the Water Tower, one of the few structures to survive the 1871 fire. In 1974 the Chagall mosaic was unveiled at the First National Bank Plaza; it consists of a colorful wall of glass and stone from all over the world.

Chicago was one of the hardest hit cities in one of the worst snow storms the Midwest has ever had on Jan. 12, 1979 and again on Jan. 24, 1979. Temperatures hovered at −20°F and below, and the snowfall measured 20 inches in some places.

Chicago's first female mayor was elected by a landslide margin of 82% on April 3 after previously defeating incumbent Michael A. Bilandic in the Democratic primary of Feb. 27. Bilandic's defeat was an upset for the old-line Daley political machine.

On May 25, 1979, the worst disaster in U.S. aviation history occurred when an American Airlines' DC-10 crashed shortly after takeoff at Chicago's O'Hare International Airport, killing all 272 persons aboard. The plane suffered difficulties with an engine on the left wing (the engine then fell off), rolled to the left, stalled and plunged into a nearby field. This led to the grounding and inspection of all DC-10s; officials found "grave deficiencies" in the engine mountings.

CINCINNATI

Location: Southwestern Ohio, on Ohio River **County:** Hamilton **City area:** 78 sq. miles (202 sq. kilometers) **Altitude:** 550 feet (167.1 meters)
Mayor: Bobbie Sterne
City population: 453,514 (1970 census), 410,441 (1976 est.)
Metro area population: 1,387,207 (1970 census), 1,375,400 (1977 est.)

Daily newspapers: 2 **No. of commercial radio stations (AM):** 9 (1979) **No. of commercial TV stations:** 4 (1979)
City Chamber of Commerce: Greater Cincinnati Chamber of Commerce, 120 West Fifth Street, Cincinnati, Ohio 45202

Cincinnati, seat of Ohio's Hamilton County, is an industrial, commercial, and cultural center. The first settlers arrived in 1788 and named their village Losantiville.

In 1790 General Arthur St. Clair, first governor of the Northwest Territory, renamed it Cincinnati for the Society of the Cincinnati, which was formed by Continental Army officers at the end of the American Revolution. Cincinnati was the first seat of the legislature of the Northwest Territory; it was incorporated in 1802 and chartered as a city in 1819.

Completion of the Miami Canal (1827) and the Ohio and Erie Canal in the 1830s increased the growth of Cincinnati and its importance as a shipping center. The city was also a major station on the Underground Railroad.

Cincinnati suffered disastrous floods in 1884 and 1937. The Cincinnati riot (March 28-31, 1884) was the result of a crime wave and corrupt politics. Later the notorious political boss G. B. Cox took control, but a reform movement in the 1920s led to the establishment (1924) of the city-manager type of government.

Located on the Ohio River, Cincinnati is a major manufacturing center and a leading producer of machine tools, soap products, and playing cards. Cosmetics, radar equipment, automobiles, leather goods, jet engines, and metal goods also are important to the economy. In January 1976 the Environmental Protection Agency Laboratory opened here.

Recent additions to the refurbished downtown area are the new Cincinnati Plaza Hotel and the First National Bank Center being constructed across from Fountain Square.

Riverfront Stadium, built in 1970, houses the Cincinnati Bengals Football Team and the Cincinnati Reds Baseball Team.

CLEVELAND

Location: Northeastern Ohio, on Lake Erie at mouth of the Cuyahoga River **County:** Cuyahoga **City area:** 76 sq. miles (196.8 sq. kilometers) **Altitude:** 680 feet (206.6 meters)
Mayor: Dennis J. Kucinich
City population: 750,879 (1970 census), 625,643 (1976 est.)
Metro area population: 2,063,729 (1970 census), 1,949,600 (1977 est.)
Daily newspapers: 2 **No. of commercial radio stations (AM):** 9 (1979) **No. of commercial TV stations:** 4 (1979)
City Chamber of Commerce: Greater Cleveland Growth Association, 690 Union Commerce Building, Cleveland, Ohio 44115

Cleveland, seat of Cuyahoga County and largest city in Ohio, is a port of entry on Lake Erie. It was laid out in 1796 by General Moses Cleaveland, an ancestor of President Grover Cleveland. Three years later a permanent settlement was established by Lorenzo Carter, and in 1836 Cleveland was chartered as a city.

After the completion of the Ohio and Erie Canal in the 1830s and the arrival of the railroad in 1851, Cleveland became a significant link between the interior of Ohio and eastern markets. Coal from Pennsylvania and iron ore shipped from Minnesota by way of the Great Lakes made the city an important iron and steel producer. It also developed into the main refining area for Pennsylvania oil, and in 1870 John D. Rockefeller began his oil dynasty in Cleveland. Immigrants from all over the world settled in the city to work in the industries. Many of their descendants still live in pleasant suburbs.

Besides iron and steel production, mainstays of the economy today are the manufacture of electrical equipment, machine tools, automobile parts, and chemicals.

Cleveland has experienced a decline common to many large cities, its own accelerated by riots in the 1960s. However, cooperative efforts have produced an almost new downtown skyline, with new commercial and federal and local government buildings. The old flats area along the river has been restored, providing evening entertainment in the many restaurants and pubs.

The Cuyahoga River, Lake Erie, and the air itself have had a notorious reputation for pollution, but extensive efforts to clean up the environment have met with some success.

Of special interest is the Emerald Necklace—a system of parks, trails, and bridle paths looping the city—along with the downtown Convention Center and Municipal Stadium. The East Side's University Circle area is a cultural center housing the Art Museum, Museum of Natural History and Severance Hall.

In December 1978, the city defaulted and was doomed to bankruptcy unless alternative money-seeking methods could be sought. In February, 1979, Mayor Kucinich suggested a 50% increase in city income taxes. Opponents opted for additional financial protection for the city through the sale of the Municipal Light Plant. On February 27, 1979, in a special referendum, Cleveland voters chose the tax increase. The increase, plus a 20% lay-off of city employees, which cut the city's services to a minimum, and an extension on credit payments until the end of the year have kept Cleveland from bankruptcy.

COLUMBUS

Location: Central Ohio, on Scioto River **County:** Franklin **City area:** 174.5 sq. miles (451.9 sq. kilometers) **Altitude:** 780 feet (237.0 meters)
Mayor: Tom Moody
City population: 540,025 (1970 census), 533,075 (1976 est.)
Metro area population: 1,017,847 (1970 census), 1,086,800 (1977 est.)
Daily newspapers: 2 **No. of commercial radio stations (AM):** 6 (1979) **No. of commercial TV stations:** 3 (1979)
City Chamber of Commerce: Columbus Area Chamber of Commerce, 50 West Broad Street, P.O. Box 1527, Columbus, Ohio 43216

Columbus, capital of Ohio and seat of Franklin County, is the state's largest city in area. It was laid out to be the capital in 1812, a position it assumed four years later, and chartered as a city in 1834. A feeder canal (1831) to the Ohio and Erie Canal, along with the National Road (1833), spurred development. By the middle of the 19th century the railroad had arrived, making Columbus a commercial and transportation center.

During the Civil War Columbus was an assembly point for recruits and the site of a Union arsenal. A cemetery at Camp Chase, a former Civil War prison, contains the graves of 2,260 Confederate soldiers. By the end of the century the city was a leader in the manufacture of buggies, producing about 20,000 a year. In 1913 the Scioto River flooded, causing the death of more than 100 people and destroying much property.

Today about 20 percent of the working population is employed by the federal, state, or municipal government. Industry is also a large employer, and among the city's products are coal-mining machinery, concrete mixers, aircraft assemblies, auto parts, paints, shoes, glassware, and refrigerators. Columbus is the headquarters of the Battelle Memorial Institute, an organization engaged in scientific, technological, and economic research.

The city began an urban renewal program on the near north and south sides in the mid 1960s. Several construction projects in the downtown area have generated new excitement and new confidence about Columbus as a place to work, to shop, and to live. Residential development on the west edge and the completion of the Ohio Center (convention center) and the Capitol South recreation center insure continued growth of the downtown area.

DALLAS

Location: Northeastern Texas on Trinity River, about 75 miles south of Oklahoma border **County:** Dallas **City area:** 350 sq. miles (906.5 sq. kilometers) **Altitude:** 481 feet (146.2 meters)
Mayor: Robert Folsom **City Manager:** George Schrader
City population: 844,303 (1970 census) 848,829 (1976 est.)
Metro area population: 2,378,353 (1970 census) 2,673,300 (1977 est.)
Daily newspapers: 3 **No. of commercial radio stations (AM):** 8 (1979) **No. of commercial TV stations:** 5 (1979)
City Chamber of Commerce: Dallas Chamber of Commerce, 1507 Pacific Avenue, Dallas, Texas 75201

Dallas, seat of Dallas County and second largest city in Texas, is the financial and commercial center of the Southwest.

John Neely Bryan settled here in 1841 and later founded Dallas, probably naming it after George M. Dallas, then Vice President under James K. Polk.

In 1858 followers of the French social philosopher Charles Fourier abandoned their nearby socialist community, La Réunion, and moved to Dallas. Two years later a fire destroyed most of the town, but residents quickly rebuilt it. During the Civil War the Confederate Army had quartermaster, commissary, and administrative headquarters here.

Oil was discovered in eastern Texas in the 1930s, increasing the growth of Dallas, which was the site of the Texas Centennial Exposition in 1936. During and after World War II, population boomed following introduction of first the aircraft and then the electronics industries. Today the city's economy is highly diversified, with a strong manufacturing base and many corporate headquarters of the electronics, oil, gas, finance and insurance industries.

President Kennedy was assassinated in Dallas in 1963.

Dallas is the home of the annual Texas state fair, the Cotton Bowl football stadium, the NFL Dallas Cowboys, and shares with Fort Worth the American Baseball League's Texas Rangers. Dallas hosts annually final matches of the $100,000 World Championship of Tennis, the Byron Nelson Golf Classic, the U.S. Karate National Championships, and the Avon Futures Tennis Finals.

Another advantage which Dallas has created for itself is its role as a tourist/convention center. Its role as a merchandise distribution center helped make it a major buyers' market. Dallas/Fort Worth Airport is one of the world's largest airports. The city's latest landmark, the 560-feet Reunion Tower and adjoining hotel, opened in the spring of 1978.

Dallas is also the cultural center of Texas. Each year the city is host to the Metropolitan Opera and has its own Civic Opera and Symphony as well. There are other community enterprises in the cultural field including the Summer Musicals, the Civic Ballet, the Civic Chorus, the Dallas Theatre Center, and the Bob Hope Theatre.

DENVER

Location: North-central Colorado, on South Platte River **County:** Denver; city and county are coextensive **City area:** 117 sq. miles (303 sq. kilometers) **Altitude:** 5,280 feet (1604.5 meters) **Mayor:** William H. McNichols, Jr. **City population:** 514,678 (1970 census) 476,200 (1977 est.) **Metro area population:** 1,239,477 (1970 census) 1,464,300 (1977 est.) **Daily newspapers:** 2 **No. of commercial radio stations (AM):** 17 (1979) **No. of commercial TV stations:** 5 (1979) **City Chamber of Commerce:** Denver Chamber of Commerce, 1301 Welton, Denver, Colorado 80204

Denver, capital and largest city of Colorado, is a major commercial and financial center. It was settled in 1858 after the discovery of placer gold at the junction of the South Platte River and Cherry Creek, and named for James W. Denver, governor of the Kansas Territory, which then included eastern Colorado.

Denver was incorporated in 1861 and became the capital of the Colorado Territory six years later. During the 1870s and 1880s rich lodes of silver, gold, and copper were found in the Rocky Mountains, bringing fortune seekers to the area. The city boasted plush opera houses with singers imported from the East, makeshift boarding houses, and noisy saloons, such as the famous Silver Dollar.

By the end of the 19th century, Denver was beginning to develop into a large processing, shipping, and distributing point for an extensive agricultural area, making mining and metalworking less important. Today the aerospace industry makes a significant contribution to Denver's economy, and food processing is also a major occupation. In addition, the city is the regional center for many federal agencies. The Atomic Energy Commission's Rocky Flats plant is nearby, and the federal Solar Energy Research Institute opened in 1978. in nearby Golden, Colo. A federal mint has been in operation for more than a century.

Military establishments in the area include Lowry Air Force Base; the Air Force Accounting and Finance Center; the army's Rocky Mountain Arsenal, where the army stores nerve-gas weapons; and Fitzsimmons General Hospital. The Air Force Academy is in Colorado Springs, less than 100 miles south of Denver.

In March of 1979, the Environmental Protection Agency began searching within the Denver city limits for radioactive dump sites, used by local radium refineries over 50 to 60 years ago. EPA officials confirmed 15 sites of excessive radiation emission.

Denver, which maintains the largest system of public parks and recreational facilities in the world, is a tourist mecca. Of interest are the Colorado State Historical Museum, the tomb of Buffalo Bill, the Cody Museum, and the $6.1-million Denver Art Museum, a block-square, fortresslike structure set against a distant backdrop of Rocky Mountains, and the Denver Botanic Gardens.

DETROIT

Location: Southeastern Michigan, on Detroit River, between Lakes St. Clair and Erie, 18 miles north of Lake Erie **County:** Wayne **City area:** 139.6 sq. miles (361.6 sq. kilometers) **Altitude:** 581 feet (176.6 meters) **Mayor:** Coleman A. Young **City Clerk:** James H. Bradley **City population:** 1,514,063 (1970 census), 1,314,206 (1976 est.) **Metro area population:** 4,435,051 (1970 census), 4,370,200 (1977 est.) **Daily newspapers:** 2 **No. of commercial radio stations (AM):** 7 (1979) **No. of commercial TV stations:** 9 (1979) **City Chamber of Commerce:** Greater Detroit Chamber of Commerce, 150 Michigan Ave., Detroit, Michigan 48226

Detroit, seat of Wayne County, is the largest city in Michigan and the sixth largest in the United States. Antoine de la Mothe Cadillac established a French fort (Pontchartrain) and settlement on the site in 1701.

The settlement took the name Detroit from the French word for "strait," because it was on the water link between Lake Erie and Lake St. Clair. Detroit was ceded to the British in 1763, turned over to the United States in 1796, destroyed by fire in 1805, rebuilt, and occupied by the British for a year during the War of 1812. It became an important commercial center after the opening of the Erie Canal in 1825.

From 1837, when Michigan became a state, until 1847, Detroit was the capital. It was connected by rail to Chicago in 1852 and to New York two years later. The city was also an important terminus of the Underground Railroad, which was a secret network of refuge "stations" via which abolitionists helped escaped slaves fleeing the South make their way to Canada and freedom.

Detroit assumed great importance after the middle of the 19th century because of its shipping, shipbuilding, and manufacturing.

Today Detroit is known as the "Motor City," and General Motors, American Motors, Ford and Chrysler all have their world headquarters there or in adjoining suburbs. The Detroit-Pontiac-Flint corridor produces some 25 percent of all the cars and trucks built in the United States. Detroit is linked to Windsor, Ont., by a bridge over and a tunnel under the Detroit River.

The city also is international headquarters for the United Automobile, Aerospace and Agricultural Implement Workers of America (UAW), which has been embroiled in many of the labor disputes that have erupted here, some in the 1930s resulting in bloodshed.

Detroit has had two major racial riots. One in 1943 and the other in 1967.

Renaissance Center, recently completed along Detroit's downtown riverfront, the new $30-million Riverfront Arena, and the Senator Philip A. Hart Plaza are three of the new construction projects completed or underway. The Horace E. Dodge & Son Memorial Fountain, designed by Isamu Noguchi, has become the center of community activity and the permanent home of Detroit's famous international ethnic festivals.

The Detroit Symphony Orchestra, Detroit Institute of Arts, and the Detroit Zoo are rated among the nation's best. Henry Ford Museum and Greenfield Village, which contains Thomas A. Edison's original laboratories and many early American landmarks, attract more than 1.6 million visitors annually to suburban Dearborn. Belle

Isle, a 1,000-acre park in the Detroit River, is a major recreation center, with gardens, a conservatory, children's zoo and aquarium among attractions.

FORT WORTH

Location: Northern Texas, at the junction of the Clear and West forks of the Trinity River about 30 miles west of Dallas **Counties:** Tarrant, Hood, Wise, Parker and Johnson **City area:** 242 sq. miles (541.1 sq. kilometers) **Altitude:** 670 feet (203.6 meters)
Mayor: Woodie Woods **City Manager:** Robert Herchert
City population: 393,455 (1970 census), 367,909 (1976 est.)
Metro area population: 2,378,353 (1970 census), 2,673,300 (1977 est.)
Daily newspapers: 3 **No. of commercial radio stations (AM):** 12 (1979) **No. of commercial TV stations:** 6 (1979)
City Chamber of Commerce: Fort Worth Area Chamber of Commerce, 700 Throckmorton, Fort Worth, Texas 76102

Fort Worth, often considered in conjunction with nearby Dallas, is the seat of Tarrant County and a prime cog in the massive North Texas industrial complex, serving as a transportation center, oil-pipeline hub and a major grain and livestock market. It is also one of the nation's largest producers of aircraft, an outgrowth of the days of World War II, when aircraft assembly first flourished there.

Settlement of the area began in 1843. Four years later Camp Worth (later Fort Worth) was established by Major Ripley A. Arnold as a frontier outpost to protect settlers against Comanche Indian raids; it was named in honor of Major General William J. Worth, then commander of U.S. troops in Texas, and proved of great use to the Army during the Mexican War.

After the Army departed (1853), the town suffered a brief decline, but soon began to boom. Cowboys driving Longhorn cattle up the Chisholm Trail to the railheads of Kansas would bed their herds outside of Fort Worth and go into town for supplies and relaxation. This brought a heavy influx of merchants and contributed much to the city's growth, which was further spurred by the coming of the railroad in 1876, three years after the city's incorporation. Meat-packing and the milling and shipping of grain were the mainstays of the fledgling town's economy. With the 20th century, came widespread industrialization and a continuing trend toward greater diversification. Besides those mentioned, other of the city's chief industries include brewing, food processing, and the manufacture of automobiles, containers, furniture, leather goods and machinery.

Despite the bustle of its industry, Fort Worth today retains a distinctive, easy-going Western flavor. It is known all over the world as "Cowtown" or "Where the West Begins," and is committed to retaining its Western heritage. Fort Worth has become increasingly involved in the arts, rivaling Dallas as the state's cultural leader. Its attractions include Casa Mañana, a theater-in-the-round that presents Broadway productions; the Fort Worth Art Center and the Amon Carter Museum of Western Art, the latter housing an exceptional collection of works by Frederic Remington and Charles Russell; the Fort Worth Opera; Heritage Hall and Trinity Park. In addition, the area boasts the Fort Worth Water Garden Park, the Museum of Science and Industry, and the Tarrant County Convention Center. Fort Worth is host annually to the Van Cliburn Piano Competition and the Colonial Invitational Golf Tournament and is the home of Six Flags Over Texas. Popular annual events include the Southwestern Exposition, Fat Stock Show and Rodeo.

HONOLULU

Location: In Hawaii, in Pacific Ocean, 2,397 miles southwest of San Francisco **County:** Honolulu **City area:** 608 sq. miles 574.7 sq. kilometers) **Altitude:** 21 feet (6.4 meters)
Mayor: Frank F. Fasi **Managing Director:** Edward Y. Hirata
City population: 324,871 (1970 census), 723,400 (1977 est.)
Metro area population: 630,528 (1970 census), 723,400 (1977 est.)
Daily newspapers: 2 **No. of commercial radio stations (AM):** 17 (1979) **No. of commercial TV stations:** 4 (1979)

City Chamber of Commerce: The Chamber of Commerce of Hawaii, Dillingham Building, 735 Bishop Street, Honolulu, Hawaii 96813

Honolulu, capital and principal city of Hawaii, is on the island of Oahu at the crossroads of the Pacific. (The name "Honolulu" is Hawaiian for "sheltered harbor.") Although Honolulu city and county are usually thought of as consisting of Oahu only, Honolulu is technically the largest city in the nation, with boundaries extending officially 1,381 miles northwest to Kure Island. (Oklahoma City, with 647 square miles of contiguous territory, thus ranks second in extent but first in landmass.)

Honolulu became the seat of the Kamehameha dynasty, which had succeeded in unifying the Hawaiian Islands in 1810, and in 1845 it was named the permanent capital of the Kingdom of Hawaii. During the 19th century, American and European whalers and sandalwood traders came to Honolulu, and it was occupied successively by Russian, British, and French forces. It developed into an important commercial city after U.S. annexation of Hawaii in 1898.

In the early 20th century, the U.S. Navy established its famous base at Pearl Harbor, now the headquarters of the U.S. Pacific Fleet. Honolulu was bombed during Japan's surprise attack on Pearl Harbor on Dec. 7, 1941, and during World War II became a major staging area for U.S. forces in the Pacific.

The postwar years saw a tourist boom coupled with a diversification of industry. The military, with all branches represented in Hawaii, continues to maintain its position as the state's biggest industry, but tourism continues to increase; 3.7 million visitors came to the islands in 1978. Sugar and pineapple are the third major industry; farm revenues for diversified agriculture registered a 13% increase over last year.

Numerous new high-rise office buildings have changed the skyline and helped revitalize downtown Honolulu. Harbor facilities have been expanded and the Honolulu International Airport has been enlarged.

Structures of interest in the city are Iolani Palace, former home of Hawaii's monarchs and the only royal palace in the U.S.; the state capitol; the Bishop Museum (of Polynesian Ethnology and Natural History); Washington Place, former private home of Queen Lilioukalani; and the Neal Blaisdell Center, a 22-acre complex of public buildings.

HOUSTON

Location: Southeastern Texas, on Houston Ship Channel, 50 miles from Gulf of Mexico **Counties:** Brazoria, Harris, Fort Bend Liberty, Montgomery and Walles. **City area:** 556.4 sq. miles (1441.0 sq. kilometers) **Altitude:** 49 feet (15 meters)
Mayor: Jim McConn
City population: 1,253,479 (1970 census), 1,699,000 (1978 est.)
Metro area population: 1,999,316 (1970 census), 2,512,200 (1977 est.)
Daily newspapers: 2 **No. of commercial radio stations (AM):** 14 (1979) **No. of commercial TV stations:** 5 (1979)
City Chamber of Commerce: Houston Chamber of Commerce, 1100 Milam, 25th Floor, Houston, Texas 77002

Houston, seat of Harris County, is the leading industrial metropolis not only of Texas but also of the surrounding region. It is the largest city in the Southwest and South, the fifth largest in the nation, and the country's third-largest seaport.

Founded in 1836 by J. K. and A. C. Allen, the city was named for General Sam Houston, hero of the Battle of San Jacinto (1836), by which Texas gained independence from Mexico. The city served as capital of the Republic of Texas from 1837 until 1840.

The discovery of oil in Southeast Texas at Spindletop in 1901 and the opening of the man-made Houston Ship Channel in 1914 stimulated the rapid development of the Houston area.

Strategically situated in an area rich in oil, gas, sulfur, salt, lime, timber, industrial soil, seawater and freshwater, the Houston metropolitan area ranks first in the nation in petroleum refining, petrochemical manufacturing, manufacturing and distribution of petroleum equipment and pipeline transmission.

Houston, which became the U.S. center of manned spacecraft activities in the early 1960s, has experienced increasing economic diversification over the past two decades. The city emerged as a corporate center in the 1960s, and since 1970 over 200 major companies have moved their headquarters, subsidiaries or divisions to Houston, capitalizing on the growing nucleus of energy, space and medical technology available in the area.

The Texas Medical Center is a $632-million complex of 35 buildings on 235 acres in central Houston, and 84 research firms maintain research facilities there. The number of life, earth, and physical scientists in metropolitan Houston has risen to 10,300, up 78 percent since 1970, while technical engineers have increased 50 percent in the same period, to stand at 27,100.

In addition, the city is growing in prominence in international business. More than 40 foreign banks maintain representative offices in Houston, and 50 nations maintain consular offices there.

Bordering the City of Houston on the southeast is the Lyndon B. Johnson Space Center, a $202-million complex for astronaut training, equipment testing, and flight control for the Skylab and Space Shuttle programs.

Houston's Alley Theatre is nationally known, performing repertory works as well as new plays. Elegant Jones Hall for the Performing Arts features the Houston Symphony Society and Houston Grand Opera, both of which tour nationally. The Astrodome, a huge, enclosed and air-conditioned arena, has convertible seating arrangements which allow the presentation of widely varied sports events. The Summit, another sports and entertainment arena, is located in Houston's Greenway Plaza.

Houston is home of the Houston Astros of the National Baseball League, the Houston Oilers of the American Conference of the National Football League, the Houston Aeros of the World Hockey Association, and the Houston Hurricanes of the North American Soccer League.

Prominent tourist attractions in the area include the Harris County Domed Stadium and Astrohall; Astroworld, a 65-acre family amusement park; Johnson Space Center; and San Jacinto Battleground, plus the battleship Texas, a veteran of two World Wars.

The worst fire in the city's recent history occured on August 1, 1979. Approximately 700 apartments of the 1,100 unit Woodway Square complex were destroyed or damaged, leaving 1,500 people homeless. Damage was estimated at $20 million. No one was killed, and only one resident was hospitalized.

INDIANAPOLIS

Location: In central Indiana, on White River County: Marion City area: 379.4 sq. miles (982.6 sq. kilometers) Altitude: 710 feet (215.8 meters)
Mayor: William H. Hudnut, III
City population: 729,768 (1970 census), 708,867 (1976 est.)
Metro area population: 1,111,352 (1970 census), 1,143,800 (1977 est.)
Daily newspapers: 2 **No. of commercial radio stations (AM):** 8 (1979) **No. of commercial TV stations:** 5 (1979)
City Chamber of Commerce: Indianapolis Chamber of Commerce, 320 North Meridian Street, Indianapolis, Indiana 46204

Indianapolis, seat of Marion County and capital of Indiana, is the largest city in the state. Its name combines "Indiana" with "polis," the Greek term for "city." It was settled in 1820.

Indianapolis grew slowly until the arrival of the first railroad in 1847. Toward the end of the 19th century the discovery of nearby natural gas, plus the beginning of the automobile industry, helped the city's expansion. On Jan. 1, 1970, the City of Indianapolis merged with surrounding Marion County in the nation's first major city-county consolidation to occur without a popular referendum since modern New York City was formed in 1898.

Leading products are processed foods, electronics equipment, heavy machinery, and pharmaceuticals. Indianapolis is also an insurance center, with offices of more than 70 firms.

Indianapolis might be called the educational hub of Indiana. It includes the Indiana University Medical School and Center, Butler University, Indiana Central University, Indiana University/Purdue University at Indianapolis (IUPUI), and Marian College.

Urban renewal has made enormous changes in the city's skyline in the last ten years. Indianapolis has kept its famous Soldiers' and Sailors' Monument on Monument Circle, but the city is now dominated by such structures as the Indiana National Bank Tower, Indiana Bell Telephone Building, the Market Square Arena, a new Hyatt Hotel, the new Federal Building, and the Indiana Convention and Exposition Center.

Three of Indianapolis' newest points of interest are: the Museum of Art, the Indiana State Museum, and the Children's Museum, the largest of its kind in the nation. Indianapolis is national headquarters for the American Legion and home of the Army Finance Center at Fort Harrison. Tourist attractions include the homes of President Benjamin Harrison, James Whitcomb Riley and Booth Tarkington. Eagle Creek Park is the country's largest municipal park.

The city has professional baseball and basketball teams and is the home of the Indianapolis 500 motor speedway track. Indianapolis is also the home of the Amateur Athletic Union and the U.S. Automobile Club.

KANSAS CITY

Location: Western Missouri, on Kansas-Missouri border, on Kansas and Missouri rivers **Counties:** Jackson, Clay, Platte **City area:** 316 sq. miles (818 sq. kilometers) **Altitude:** 750 feet (227.9 meters)
Mayor: Richard L. Berkley **City Manager:** Robert A Kipp
City population: 507,330 (1970 census), 458,251 (1976 est.)
Metro area population: 1,273,926 (1970 census), 1,293,300 (1977 est.)
Daily newspapers: 2 **No. of commercial radio stations (AM):** 14 (1979) **No. of commercial TV stations:** 4 (1979)
City Chamber of Commerce: Chamber of Commerce of Greater Kansas City, 600 Ten Main Center, 920 Main Street, Kansas City, Missouri 64105

Kansas City, Missouri's second largest metropolis, is an important industrial, commercial, and banking center. It is separated from Kansas City, Kansas, by the state line, but both are served by the same railroad terminals and transit and telephone systems.

The area was explored by the French early in the 18th century and toward the end of the century by Daniel Morgan Boone (son of the famous frontiersman), who was probably the first American to set foot in the vicinity. François Chouteau established a trading post in 1826, and a settlement later developed known as Westport Landing. The city was incorporated in 1850 as the Town of Kansas, and under a new charter (1889) it became Kansas City. Its name reflects its location on the Kansas (Kaw) River, in turn named for an Indian tribe.

Kansas City grew into an important trade and transportation hub for pioneers migrating westward over the Oregon and Santa Fe Trails; it was an early center of the nation's cattle business. In 1865 the railroad arrived, and four years later Hannibal Bridge, the first structure to span the Missouri River, was opened.

Today Kansas City is a major market for winter wheat and cattle. Its stockyards are among the nation's busiest. It leads the nation in the manufacture of vending machines, is the country's second largest assembly center for cars and trucks, and is an important warehousing center.

In June, 1979, Crosby Kemper Memorial Arena's roof collasped after a heavy rainstom. The arena had made dramatic use of exterior supporting structures and had won an honor award from the American Institute of Architects in 1976.

LOS ANGELES

Location: Southwestern California, between Santa Monica and San Pedro bays, near the Pacific coast **County:** Los Angeles **City area:** 464 sq. miles (1201.8 sq. kilometers) **Altitude:** 275 feet (83.6 meters)
Mayor: Thomas Bradley **City Administrative Officer:** Dr. C. Erwin Piper
City population: 2,811,801 (1970 census), 2,743,994 (1976 est.)
Metro area population: 7,041,980 (1970 census), 7,031,000 (1977 est.)

Daily newspapers: 2 No. of commercial radio stations (AM): 35 (1979) **No. of commercial TV stations:** 8 (1979)
City Chamber of Commerce: Los Angeles Chamber of Commerce, 400 South Bixel Street, Los Angeles, California 90017

Los Angeles, seat of California's Los Angeles County, is the nation's second most populous city.

Gaspar de Portolá led an expedition to the site in 1769, and in 1781 El Pueblo de Nuestra Señora la Reina de los Angeles de Porciuncula (The Town of Our Lady the Queen of the Angels of Porciuncula) was founded. The name was later shortened to Los Angeles.

In 1846 during the Mexican War, U.S. military forces took the town. Four years later, Los Angeles was incorporated as a city; that same year California entered the Union. It was soon linked with the Eastern seaboard as railroads arrived: the Southern Pacific in 1876 and the Santa Fe nine years later. Discovery of oil in the 1890s stimulated commercial growth, and the opening of the Panama Canal in 1914 brought further expansion. The motion-picture industry grew up in the early 20th century and more recent years have seen the establishment of television studios.

The Los Angeles area is rich in agricultural resources and well known for its citrus fruit. It ranks third nationally in manufacturing, finance, and trade, and leads the U.S. in production of aircraft and aircraft parts. In addition, Greater Los Angeles is the nation's sportswear center and the world's second largest garment manufacturer. Other important industries are food processing and the production of machinery, chemicals, and electronics equipment. As a port Los Angeles handles the largest cargo tonnage of deep-sea vessels on the Pacific Coast and is a major fishing complex.

Los Angeles County has the heaviest per-capita concentration of automobiles in the world, and the city is famous for its vast system of freeways radiating from the center of town to outlying areas. Dozens of independent municipalities are incorporated in the county, some completely surrounded by the city. Shore areas include Santa Monica, Manhattan Beach, Hermosa Beach, Redondo Beach, and Long Beach. The industrial section includes Lynwood, Downey, Norwalk, and Torrance.

Los Angeles is the home of a $33.5 million Music Center, the Los Angeles County Museum of Art and the recently constructed Los Angeles Convention Center.

Of interest to the thousands of tourists who flock to the Los Angeles area are Disneyland, at nearby Anaheim, considered the biggest attraction in the West; Mount Wilson Observatory; Mission San Gabriel Arcángel, dedicated in 1771; Santa Catalina Island; the Hollywood Bowl; Griffith Park with its zoo, golf course, and observatory; and Laguna Beach.

California began gasoline rationing on an odd-even license plate plan May 9, 1979 in Los Angeles, San Diego and four other counties, in an attempt to stem panic buying. During the first seven days of May, as the shortage of gas became apparent, lines had grown longer at gas stations throughout the state. Panic buying had aggravated the shortage. The Energy Department had predicted on the 7th that gasoline supplies for May and for the Spring and Summer would be tight.

Los Angeles will host the 1984 Summer Olympics. The decision by the city to ratify a contract with the International Olympic Committee came after 15 months of conflict between the two over who would bear financial responsibility. Under a compromise incorporated into the agreement, Los Angeles would have no financial liability. The burden would be shared by the U.S. Olympic Committee and a private group.

LOUISVILLE

Location: Northwest Kentucky, at the falls of the Ohio River
County: Jefferson **City area:** 65.2 sq. miles (168.9 sq. kilometers)
Altitude: 477 feet (144.9 meters)
Mayor: William B. Stansbury
City population: 361,706 (1970 census) 330,011 (1976 est.) **Metro area population:** 867,330 (1970 census), 883,000 (1977 est.)
Daily newspapers: 2 No. of commercial radio stations (AM): 12 (1979) **No. of commercial TV stations:** 4 (1979)
City Chamber of Commerce: Louisville Area Chamber of Commerce, 300 West Liberty, Louisville, Kentucky 40202

Louisville, seat of Jefferson County, is the largest city in Kentucky and a major Southern industrial center. The city lies over a mammoth glacial deposit called an "aquifer," which is drawn upon for water.

Laid out in 1773 by General George Rogers Clark and settled six years later, it was named Louisville in 1780 by the Virginia legislature in honor of King Louis XVI of France. Two years later at Louisville, General Clark built Fort Nelson, which served as headquarters for his expeditions to the Northwest. It was then widely known as the "Settlement at the Falls."

Louisville was incorporated as a city in 1828 and grew into an important river port after the opening of the Louisville and Portland Canal in 1830. Arrival of the railroad in 1851 enhanced its position as a transportation center. During the Civil War it was a major Union base, despite the divided loyalties of its citizens.

Today the city has the world's largest electrical and neoprene plants. Other important industries are the manufacture of bourbon whiskey, tobacco processing, auto and truck manufacturing, and meat packing. The American Printing House for the Blind, the world's largest publisher of Braille books and magazines and talking books, is located in Louisville. More than $300-million in private and public funds have been committed to the redevelopment of the downtown area.

Of historic interest are the grave of George Rogers Clark, in Cave Hill Cemetery, and the site of Fort Nelson. The state's tourist attractions include Churchill Downs, scene of the annual Kentucky Derby; the State Fair Grounds; the Louisville Zoological Garden featuring a children's zoo, and the Filson Club, which houses a Kentucky history museum.

MEMPHIS

Location: Southwestern corner of Tennessee, on Mississippi River
County: Shelby **City area:** 290 sq. miles (651.1 sq. kilometers)
Altitude: 275 feet (83.6 meters)
Mayor: Wyeth Chandler **Chief Administrative Officer:** Henry Evans
City population: 657,007 (1970 census), 667,880 (1976 est.)
Metro area population: 834,103 (1970 census), 886,500 (1977 est.)
Daily newspapers: 2 No. of commercial radio stations (AM): 12 (1979) **No. of commercial TV stations:** 4 (1979)
City Chamber of Commerce: Memphis Area Chamber of Commerce, 555 Beale Street, P.O. Box 224, Memphis, Tennessee 38101

Memphis, seat of Shelby County, is the largest city in Tennessee and a port of entry. It is the commercial center for much of Tennessee, Arkansas, and Mississippi, as well as parts of Missouri and Alabama. It was named after the ancient Egyptian city.

According to tradition, De Soto crossed the Mississippi River in 1540 at the site of this Tennessee city. In 1682 La Salle built Fort Prudhomme overlooking the river, and for almost a century the area was involved in the imperial rivalries of Great Britain, France, and Spain. The United States built Fort Adams in 1797, and in 1819 Memphis was laid out. Thirty years later it was incorporated as a city, having become an important port noted for its gambling casinos and glittering wealth.

The fall of Memphis to Union forces on June 6, 1862, ended the city's early prosperity. After the Civil War, yellow-fever epidemics caused about 25,000 people to flee.

Today Memphis is a major hardwood-lumber center and manufacturer of furniture and flooring. It is also a leading cotton and livestock market and home of the Memphis Cotton Exchange. The city's products include rubber goods, cottonseed oil, textiles, farm machinery, drugs, and livestock feeds. It is headquarters for Plough, Inc., Holiday Inns of America, Inc. and Cook Industries, grain exporters. Sharp Electronics Corporation, a Japanese microwave and television production plant, will open in late 1979.

The Tennessee Chute Project has provided Memphis with a dam connecting the mainland to Presidents Island in the Mississippi and has given the city a stillwater harbor with two barge terminals. A 963-acre industrial park is now on the island; across the harbor is the 6,800-acre Frank C. Pidgeon Industrial Park.

Of interest in Memphis is Confederate Park, which contains ramparts used in defense against Union gunboats in 1862; and Beale Street, which was immortalized by jazz composer W.C. Handy. Memphis is the only four-time winner of the Ernest T. Trigg (Cleanest City in the Nation) Award.

MIAMI

Location: Southeastern Florida, on Biscayne Bay **County:** Dade City area: 34 sq. miles (88.1 sq. kilometers) **Altitude:** 25 feet (7.6 meters)
Mayor: Maurice A. Ferre **City Manager:** Joseph R. Grassie
City population: 334,859 (1970 census), 352,424 (1976 est.)
Metro area population: 1,267,792 (1970 census), 1,441,200 (1977 est.)
Daily newspapers: 4 **No. of commercial radio stations (AM):** 13 (1979) **No. of commercial TV stations:** 6 (1979)
City Chamber of Commerce: Greater Miami Chamber of Commerce, 1200 Biscayne Boulevard, Miami, Florida 33132

Miami, seat of Florida's Dade County, is a world-famous resort. The city was founded in 1870 at the site of Fort Dallas, which the United States had built in the 1830s during the war against the Seminoles. "Miami" is an Indian word meaning "big water."
In 1896 the financier Henry M. Flagler extended the Florida East Coast Railroad to Miami, built the Royal Palm Hotel, and dredged the city's harbor. The city was incorporated the same year. By 1910 it was booming.
During the 1920s the Miami region was the scene of wild land speculation in which many fortunes were lost. However, the city continued to grow, despite disastrous hurricanes in 1926 and 1935.
Miami has the largest population of Cuban refugees in the United States—in excess of 400,000. In 1978-79, former Cuban political prisoners and their families were flown from Havana to Miami as a gesture to improve U.S.-Cuban relations.
A major rail, air and shipping point, Miami is considered the principal gateway to Latin America; the Dodge Island passenger terminal is home base for the many cruise ships serving South America and the Caribbean.
Although tourism is the leading industry in the area, the city is the nation's third largest garment manufacturing center. Concrete, metal, meat products, and commercial fishing also make substantial contributions to Miami's economy. The U.S. Environmental Science Services Administration's Oceanographic and Meteorological Laboratories have made Miami a world leader in undersea studies.
Greater Miami, which consists of over two dozen independent municipalities, is renowned for its luxurious resort hotels and fine beaches. Tourist attractions include Bay-front Park, the Museum of Science, the Miami Seaquarium, and Vizcaya, formerly the estate of James Deering and now the Dade County Art Museum. Everglades National Park, a preserve for tropical birds and flora, is nearby. The area has year-round horse racing at Hialeah, Gulfstream and Calder racetracks. Miami is home to the annual Orange Bowl Festival and January 1 football classic, and to the National Football League's Miami Dolphins.
Construction of the $900-million, 20.5-mile elevated rail system, linking downtown Miami with its suburbs, began in June, 1979.
The Florida Review Commission of the National Register has declared a one-square-mile area of Miami Beach a historical landmark for its vintage Art Deco buildings of the 1920s and 30s.

MILWAUKEE

Location: Southeastern Wisconsin, on Lake Michigan **County:** Milwaukee **City area:** 96.5 sq. miles (249.9 sq. kilometers) **Altitude:** 581 feet (176.6 meters)
Mayor: Henry W. Maier **Common Council President:** Ben E. Johnson
City population: 717,372 (1970 census) 661,082 (1976 est.) **Metro area population:** 1,403,884 (1970 census) 1,426,500 (1977 est.)
Daily newspapers: 2 **No. of commercial radio stations (AM):** 9 (1979) **No. of commercial TV stations:** 5 (1979)

City Chamber of Commerce: Metropolitan Milwaukee Association of Commerce, 828 North Broadway, Milwaukee, Wisconsin 53202

Milwaukee, seat of Milwaukee County and largest city in Wisconsin, is a leading Great Lakes port and major industrial metropolis.
French missionaries and the French explorer La Salle visited the site in the late 17th century. French Canadian fur traders came to barter with the Indians, and in 1795 the North West Company established a trading post. The first permanent settler, Solomon Juneau, an agent of the American Fur Company, arrived in 1818. His settlement and several neighboring villages merged after 1835 to form Milwaukee, which was incorporated as a city in 1846. Its name is derived from an Indian term interpreted to mean either "gathering place by the waters" or "beautiful land."
The city's excellent harbor, accessible raw materials, and growing population made it a shipping and industrial center, and German immigrants, arriving after 1848, stimulated its political, economic, and social development.
Milwaukee produces more beer than any other city and is the home of three of the four largest breweries. However, machinery manufacturing is the area's largest industry. Milwaukee is also a leading grain market and a major meat packer.
Of interest in the city are the Greek Orthodox Annunciation Church, designed by Frank Lloyd Wright; the War Memorial Center, on the lakeshore, designed by Eero Saarinen and housing the Milwaukee Art Center; the Milwaukee County Zoo, one of the most modern in the nation; the Mitchell Park Botanical Conservatory, three domed buildings for display of plants under arid, moist and temperate conditions; and the world-famous breweries, which offer tours to the public. A $12-million Performing Arts Center with a large park and fountains is served by a giant parking structure connected to the center by an all-weather bridge. MECCA, the Milwaukee Exposition and Convention Center and Arena, one of Milwaukee's newest buildings, has won national attention because of its artistic design and colors.
The harbor freeway bridge, spanning the entrance to the port, has changed the city's downtown skyline. The bridge is designed to connect to the Interstate system, but court actions have held up work on approaches to the bridge through a lakefront park.

MINNEAPOLIS

Location: East-central Minnesota, on both sides of Mississippi River at Falls of St. Anthony **County:** Hennepin **City area:** 58.8 sq. miles (152.2 sq. kilometers) **Altitude:** 815 feet (247.7 meters)
Mayor: Albert S. Hofstede **Chief Administrative Officer:** David C. Niklaus
City population: 434,400 (1970 census) 371,896 (1976 est.)
Metro area population: 1,965,391 (1970 census), 2,037,200 (1977 est.)
Daily newspapers: 2 **No. of commercial radio stations (AM):** 7 (1979) **No. of commercial TV stations:** 4 (1979)
City Chamber of Commerce: Greater Minneapolis Chamber of Commerce, 15 South Fifth Street, Minneapolis, Minnesota 55402

Minneapolis, seat of Hennepin County, is the largest city in Minnesota and an important industrial and railroad center. It is contiguous to St. Paul, its twin city and the state capital.
Father Louis Hennepin visited the site in 1680 and gave the Falls of Saint Anthony their name. In 1819 the U.S. government established Fort Snelling, and two years later a sawmill was built at the falls. The village of St. Anthony was soon settled on the east bank of the Mississippi River, while Minneapolis grew up (c. 1847) on the west bank. Minneapolis, from the local Indian "minnea," or water, combined with "polis," Greek for city, was incorporated as a town in 1856 and as a city the following year. In 1872 St. Anthony was annexed.
During the 1890s the lumber business thrived as logs were floated downstream to the sawmills of Minneapolis from the great forests of the north. Minneapolis was also known as the "Flour City of the World" until a change in freight rates after World War I shifted the center of the flour-milling industry to Buffalo.

Today the city is the home of the Minneapolis Grain Exchange, the world's largest cash grain market, and headquarters for a Federal Reserve district bank. A leading industry is the manufacture of linseed oil, paint, and industrial finishes. Other important products are precision instruments and farm machinery; printing and publishing are also important.

Minneapolis and St. Paul constitute the financial and industrial center of a large area rich in natural resources, power, and transportation facilities. The two cities are connected by a massive freeway system that runs through the suburban areas, plus a $300-million Minneapolis Gateway Center in the Loop. Minneapolis has 25 industrial parks and a 12-acre river terminal to handle shipping and storage of grain, fertilizer, petroleum products, sand gravel, salt and coal.

The major landmarks in Minneapolis are the 57-story IDS skyscraper and Nicollet Mall. Within the city are 153 parks with 22 lakes; Minnehaha Park with its Stevens House, dating from 1849; the Tyrone Guthrie Theater; the $5.5-million Walker Art Center; and the Minnesota Orchestra's new concert hall.

NEWARK

Location: Northeastern New Jersey, on Passaic River and Newark Bay **County:** Essex **City area:** 24 sq. miles (62.2 sq. kilometers) **Altitude:** 55 feet (16.7 meters)
Mayor: Kenneth A. Gibson
City population: 381,930 (1970 census), 331,495 (1976 est.)
Metro area population: 2,057,468 (1970 census), 1,969,200 (1977 est.)
Daily newspapers: 1 **No. of commercial radio stations (AM):** 2 (1979) **No. of commercial TV stations:** 3 (1979)
City Chamber of Commerce: Greater Newark Chamber of Commerce, 50 Park Place, Newark, New Jersey 07102

Newark, seat of Essex County and largest city in New Jersey, is an important industrial and commercial center.

It was settled in 1666 by Puritans from Connecticut led by Robert Treat and is said to have been named after the town of Newark, England, although some contend its name was New Ark and had a religious connotation.

During the Revolutionary War, the city was the scene of several skirmishes; General George Washington passed through in 1776 leading his troops south to the Delaware River.

Newark's industrial growth began in the early 19th century. The arrival of railroads and canals in the 1830s stimulated the expansion of shoemaking and tanning and the development of the jewelry, insurance, and shipbuilding industries. After 1880 swarms of immigrants arrived, living in hastily built tenements. In 1915 Port Newark opened; during World War I Newark was the nation's leading shipbuilding city.

Today Newark is the country's third leading insurance center. A significant factor in its economic life is the Port of New York Authority, which operates Port Newark and Newark International Airport. Among the city's products are leather goods, jewelry, malt liquors, plastics, electrical equipment, auto parts, and chemicals.

Of interest in the city are Trinity Cathedral, the Sacred Heart Cathedral (begun in 1898), the First Presbyterian Church (1791); and the old County courthouse (1906), designed by Cass Gilbert.

Newark began to deteriorate economically and politically in the 1930s, a process which continued for 30 years or more. The city suffered the same ills which plagued many of the country's major cities—an exodus of population and business from the central city, with the concommitant drop in revenues, and a high unemployment rate among the remaining population, which is now over 75 percent Black and Hispanic. Newark is fighting hard to lure business back to the downtown area and to improve the lot of its underprivileged citizens. Local efforts aided by the receipt of large federal health-care funds have dramatically reduced the death rate over a ten-year period since the mid 60s.

The Prudential and Mutual Benefit life insurance companies have since built new headquarters here, Blue Cross-Blue Shield of New Jersey is also headquartered here, and Public Service Electric and Gas Company, a major utility, plans to replace its downtown headquarters with a new $60-million, 27-story corporate complex on an adjacent site. Since then millions of dollars have been spent to rebuild the city. The New Jersey Institute of Technology expanded its facilities. In 1974 New Jersey College of Medicine and Dentistry, Essex County College, Seton Hall and Rutgers University began construction of university facilities. In 1976 construction was completed at Seton Hall Law School, the School of Dentistry, Rutgers University and Essex County College.

The Federal Communications Commission ordered 7 New York City and 3 Philadelphia TV stations to establish offices and studios in New Jersey if they wished to have their licenses renewed. New Jersey and Delaware are the only states in the nation without their own VHF television stations.

NEW ORLEANS

Location: Southeastern Louisiana, on Mississippi River, near Lake Pontchartrain, about 100 miles from Gulf of Mexico **Parish:** Orleans **City area:** 366 sq. miles (947.9 sq. kilometers) **Altitude:** 5 feet (1.5 meters)
Mayor: Ernest N. Morial **Chief Administrative Officer:** Reynaud Rochon
City population: 593,471 (1970 census), 561,200 (1977 est.)
Metro area population: 1,046,470 (1970 census), 1,133,100 (1977 est.)
Daily newspapers: 2 **No. of commercial radio stations (AM):** 11 (1979) **No. of commercial TV stations:** 5 (1979)
City Chamber of Commerce: Chamber of Commerce of the New Orleans Area, 201 Camp Street, P.O. Box 30240, New Orleans, Louisiana 70190

New Orleans, coextensive with Louisiana's New Orleans Parish (county), is one of the largest cities in the South, the nation's second largest port, and the third largest port in the world. It was founded in 1718 by the Sieur de Bienville and named for Philippe II, duke of Orleans. Four years later it became the capital of the French colony of Louisiana. In 1762 the city passed to Spain, but remained culturally French.

New Orleans was returned to France in 1800 and in 1803 came under U.S. jurisdiction with the Louisiana Purchase. It developed into a flourishing cotton and slave-trade center, and was an important stopover on the southern routes to the West. After Andrew Jackson's victory over the British at New Orleans (January 8, 1815), the city's prosperity reached great heights, and New Orleans became famous for gaiety and elegance. (Today its colorful Mardi Gras, which is held every February, is one of the country's best-known festivals.) 1979's Mardi Gras was cancelled due to striking policemen.

In 1862 the city fell to Admiral David G. Farragut and did not fully recover from occupation by Union troops under General Benjamin Butler and the subsequent Reconstruction era until the end of World War I. Discovery of oil and the renewed commercial importance of sugar and cotton helped the city regain prosperity.

Today New Orleans is the banking and business center of the New South. It has the world's largest sugar refinery and is surrounded, offshore and on, by some of the most productive sources of oil in the nation. Other important industries are aerospace and shipbuilding.

The city's Vieux Carré, the French quarter, which comprised the original settlement, is a popular tourist attraction. Among the points of interest are Royal Street (Rue Royale) and the French Market on Decatur Street. Dixieland jazz was born on Bourbon Street.

The Lake Pontchartrain Causeway, completed in 1956, is the world's longest overwater highway bridge (126,055 feet). A second causeway was opened to traffic in 1969.

Other landmarks include the Hibernia Tower, 33-story International Trade Mart, and the 52-story One Shell Square. The $178-million air-conditioned Superdome, the largest in the world was dedicated August 3, 1975. The downtown area is being developed with five large-scale multi-use projects, provided for by some $1-billion in investments by private and public sectors. These projects are the Poydras Plaza, the International Rivercenter, the Pan-American Life Insurance Company Headquarters, the Canal Place, and the Piazza D'Italia.

NEW YORK CITY

Location: Southeastern New York, at mouth of Hudson River **Counties:** New York, Bronx, Kings, Queens, and Richmond **City area:** 320 sq. miles (828.8 sq. kilometers) **Altitude:** 55 feet (16.7 meters)
Mayor: Edward I. Koch
City population: 7,895,563 (1970 census), 7,312,200 (1977 est.)
Metro area population: 9,973,716 (1970 census), 9,386,700 (1977 est.)
Daily newspapers: 7 **No. of commercial radio stations (AM):** 16 (1979) **No. of commercial TV stations:** 6 (1979)
City Chamber of Commerce: New York Chamber of Commerce and Industry, 65 Liberty Street, New York, New York 10005

New York, the nation's largest city and richest port, is a national leader in business, finance, manufacturing, communications, service industries, fashion, and the arts. It is also one of the world's largest cities, one of the world's leading ports, and headquarters of the United Nations.

As the financial headquarters of the world, New York is the home of some of the world's largest corporations and the New York and American Stock Exchanges.

As a cultural capital and influential arbiter of taste, the city has its renowned theater district and the cultural complex of Lincoln Center for the Performing Arts. It also has innumerable museums, art galleries, and related attractions, as well as scientific collections, libraries, and educational institutions.

Giovanni da Verrazano, a Florentine, was probably the first European to visit (1524) the site of New York. Henry Hudson's explorations (1609) up the river named after him led to the first permanent European settlements. In 1625 the colony of New Netherland was established, with its capital, New Amsterdam, located at the southern tip of Manhattan Island. The following year Peter Minuit of the Dutch West India Company bought the entire island from the Indians for the equivalent of about $24 in trinkets and beads. In 1664 the English seized the city for the Duke of York, for whom it was renamed. Later the Dutch regained control for a brief period (1673-74).

New York was active in the colonial opposition to British rule, and during the first year of the Revolution several battles were fought in the area. In 1776 the British captured the city and controlled it for the rest of the war.

New York, the first capital (1789-90) of the United States under the Constitution, was the site of George Washington's first inauguration. Until 1797 the city was also the capital of New York State.

The opening of the Erie Canal (1825) accelerated the growth of the city, already the nation's largest, and established its dominance over Boston and Philadelphia. The New York and Harlem Railroad was completed in 1832. By 1840 New York was the country's leading port.

During the 19th century, the city expanded northward from the tip of Manhattan, until by 1874 it covered the entire island. That same year saw annexation of parts of Westchester County that later formed the Bronx. New York assumed its present boundaries in 1898, after annexing Brooklyn, Queens County and Staten Island.

New York's best known attractions include Central Park, the Bronx Zoo and Botanical Gardens, the Aquarium at Coney Island, Hayden Planetarium, the Fifth Avenue shops, the Broadway theatrical district, the United Nations Headquarters, Radio City Music Hall, the Statue of Liberty and the Staten Island ferry, Rockefeller and Lincoln Centers, Madison Square Garden, Yankee and Shea Stadiums, Greenwich Village, Chinatown and the Financial District, the Metropolitan Museum of Art, St. Patrick's Cathedral and the World Trade Center.

A strike by the pressmen's union closed down publication of New York City's three major general newspapers for 88 days, and ended in November 1978. Newspapers shut down were the New York *Daily News*, the New York *Times* and the New York *Post*, which settled earlier in October after a 56-day strike. The effects of the strike on the city's business community did not appear to be as drastic as predicted

1979 has seen a further easing of New York City's fiscal problems. A group of out-of-state and foreign banks agreed to join city banks in acting as "backup" lenders for up to $600 million in short-term notes. This is the first time this has happened since the crisis began in 1975.

New York City has been chosen as the site of the 1980 Democratic National Convention because of its large hotelroom capacity.

OKLAHOMA CITY

Location: Central Oklahoma, on North Canadian River **Counties:** Oklahoma, Canadian, Cleveland and McClain **City area:** 647 miles (1,675.7 sq. kilometers) **Altitude:** 1,207 feet (366.8 meters)
Mayor: Patience Latting **City Manager:** James J. Cook
City population: 368,164 (1970 census), 369,438 (1976 est.)
Metro area population: 699,092 (1970 census), 768,500 (1977 est.)
Daily newspapers: 3 **No. of commercial radio stations (AM):** 10 (1979) **No. of commercial TV stations:** 4 (1979)
City Chamber of Commerce: Oklahoma City Chamber of Commerce, One Santa Fe Plaza, Oklahoma City, Oklahoma 73102

Oklahoma City, seat of Oklahoma County and state capital, is the largest municipality in Oklahoma. It is also the state's financial, commercial, and industrial center.

The city's origin is one of the most colorful in American history. When the first land run into Indian Territory took place on April 22, 1889, a small Santa Fe Railroad water and coaling station blossomed into a city of 10,000 people between noon and sundown. The name of the city and territory means "red people" and had been proposed by a Choctaw chief in 1866 to designate the area set off for Indians. Oklahoma City was incorporated in 1890 and became the state capital in 1910.

Oil was struck in 1928, and it soon became apparent that rich oil and gas lands lay beneath the city itself. An extensive system of oil wells in the metropolitan area, reaching almost to the governor's mansion, is a large factor in the city's economy.

Oklahoma City is a rapidly growing regional, national and international marketing center. The U.S. Customs Bureau opened an office in 1967 to expedite exports and imports. Industry includes meat packing, including the headquarters of Wilson & Co., automobile assembling, electronics components and the production of transportation equipment and oil field supplies. The city also is noted as a convention site.

Oklahoma City has grown into an aeronautical complex with such Federal Aviation Administration facilities as the Aeronautical Center and Civil Aeromedical Institute. Nearby is Tinker Air Force Base with equipment and inventory of over $2 billion.

Of interest are the National Cowboy Hall of Fame and Western Heritage Center, with western art and a recreation of a western scene; the State Historical Society Building and Museum; the zoo; Kirkpatrick Center; and the State Capitol.

OMAHA

Location: East-central Nebraska, on Missouri River **County:** Douglas **City area:** 87.8 sq. miles (226.5 sq. kilometers) **Altitude:** 985 feet (299.3 meters)
Mayor: Al Veys
City population: 358,452 (1970 census), 371,012 (1976 est.)
Metro area population: 542,646 (1970 census) 580,900 (1977 est.)
Daily newspapers: 1 **No. of commercial radio stations (AM):** 8 (1979) **No. of commercial TV stations:** 3 (1979)
City Chamber of Commerce: Greater Omaha Chamber of Commerce, Suite 2100, 1620 Dodge, Omaha, Nebraska 68102

Omaha, seat of Douglas County, is the largest city in Nebraska. It is an important cattle market and the nation's largest meat packing center. It took its name from the Omaha Indians living nearby, who were known as "those who go upstream or against the current."

Omaha's history is associated with the opening of the West beginning with Lewis and Clark's conference with the Indians in 1804. A trading post was set up by Jean Pierre Cabanne in 1825, and the first settlement came in 1846-47, when the Mormons spent the winter there on their way to Utah. The city was officially founded in 1854 after Indians ceded the present Douglas County to the United States. Three years later Omaha was incorporated as a city and was capital of the Nebraska Territory from 1855 to 1867.

As a supply point for westward migration, Omaha grew quickly. The Union Pacific Railroad arrived in 1865, augmenting river traffic and making Omaha, on the west bank of the Missouri, a major transportation and shipping center.

Despite floods, droughts, and a plague of grasshoppers later in the 19th century, the city continued to expand. Today it is an important market for livestock and farm produce and has large meat-packing and food-processing plants, grain elevators, and stockyards. It also has oil refineries, a large lead smelter, and factories manufacturing farm implements and appliances.

The headquarters of the Strategic Air Command are located here as are the regional headquarters of the Farm Credit Administration and the Reconstruction Finance Corporation. Boys Town, the youth community founded by Father Edward J. Flanagan in 1917, is 11 miles west of the city.

Of interest are Fort Omaha, built in 1868, and the Mormon Cemetery with the Winter Quarters Monument. Riverview Park contains a monument to Friedrich von Schiller and Levi Carter Park has a lake and picnic grounds. The Joslyn Art Museum contains paintings by many of the world's greatest artists.

PHILADELPHIA

Location: Southeastern Pennsylvania, at the junction of the Delaware and Schuylkill rivers, 88 miles from Atlantic Ocean **County:** Philadelphia **City area:** 129 sq. miles (334.1 sq. kilometers) **Altitude:** 100 feet (30.4 meters)
Mayor: Frank L. Rizzo Managing Director: Hillel S. Levinson
City population: 1,949,996 (1970 census), 1,784,500 (1977 est.)
Metro area population: 4,824,110 (1970 census), 4,793,900 (1977 est.)
Daily newspapers: 7 **No. of commercial radio stations (AM):** 9 (1979) **No. of commercial TV stations:** 6 (1979)
City Chamber of Commerce: The Greater Philadelphia Chamber of Commerce, Suburban Station Building, 1617 John F. Kennedy Blvd., Philadelphia, Pennsylvania 19103

Philadelphia, coextensive with Philadelphia County, is the largest city in Pennsylvania and the fourth largest in the nation. The site was originally settled by Swedes early in the 17th century. In 1682 William Penn founded a Quaker settlement, naming it Philadelphia from the Greek phrase for "brotherly love."

The city was the largest and wealthiest in the 13 Colonies and served, except during a brief British occupation, as the capital from 1777 to 1788—the period of the adoption of the Articles of Confederation (1778) and the drafting of the United States Constitution (1787). From 1790 to 1800 it was the capital of the United States.

Philadelphia was the site of both Banks of the United States—the first from 1791 to 1811, and the second from 1816 to 1836. It was also an important center of the abolition movement and a major station on the Underground Railroad.

Philadelphia was host to the 1876 Centennial Exposition, commemorating the 100th anniversary of American independence, and the 1926 Sesquicentennial Exposition.

Today its diversified economy includes such industries as printing and publishing, shipbuilding, and the manufacture of machinery, chemicals, and textiles. It is the largest petroleum refining center on the East Coast and the second largest in the nation. It has the largest freshwater port in the world, with 50 miles of waterfront, and is also a major financial center.

A major renovation of the waterfront, referred to as Penn's Landing, is nearing completion, and a University City Science Center is being developed. Ground was broken in April 1972 for the first unit of a $300-million complex called Market Street East, which will transform Philadelphia's main shopping street from City Hall to Independence Mall into a mall and transportation center. In November 1975 the Chestnut Street Transitway opened to transform the 10 blocks between 8th and 18th streets into a buses-only transitway and a modern shrublined pedestrian promenade and shopping mall.

Voters rejected a city charter amendment to permit Mayor Rizzo to run for a third term by a 3-1 margin. The city's Democratic primary ballot was the longest in its history, involving 356 candidates. Former Rep. William J. Green won the Democratic primary, and David W. Marston won the Republican primary.

The U.S. Civil Rights Commission has been investigating reports of police brutality and lawlessness in Philadelphia. A federal prosecutor and an official of the

Philadelphia District Attorney's office charged the Mayor and top police administrators with shielding the Police Department from public scrutiny.

There are numerous historic monuments in the city. Independence Hall, where the Declaration of Independence was signed, is in Independence National Park. Nearby is Congress Hall, seat of Congress from 1790 to 1800; and Carpenters' Hall, meeting place for the First Continental Congress. Other points of interest are Elfreth's Alley, one of the nation's oldest streets; Christ Church; and the Betsy Ross House. Fairmount Park, one of the largest in the world, contains many historic monuments and a famous zoo.

PHOENIX

Location: South-central Arizona on Salt River **County:** Maricopa
City area: 324 sq. miles (521.3 sq. kilometers) **Altitude:** 1,117 feet (340.4 meters)
Mayor: Margaret Hance **City Manager:** Marvin Andrews
City population: 589,016 (1970 census), 680,000 (1976 est.)
Metro area population: 971,228 (1970 census), 1,253,600 (1977 est.)
Daily newspapers: 2 **No. of commercial radio stations (AM):** 19 (1979) **No. of commercial TV stations:** 5 (1979)
City Chamber of Commerce: Phoenix Metropolitan Chamber of Commerce, 34 W. Monroe Street, Phoenix, Arizona 85003

Phoenix, seat of Maricopa County and state capital, is the largest city in Arizona and one of the fastest growing in the nation. Because Phoenix grew up on a site that showed traces of an ancient Indian settlement, it was named after the mythological bird that rose from its own ashes.

The area was probably visited by the Spanish explorers Cabeza de Vaca in 1536, Marcos de Niza in 1539, and Coronado in 1540. John Y. T. Smith established a hay camp on the Salt River in 1866, and the following year Phoenix was officially founded. It was incorporated as a city in 1881 and became territorial capital in 1889, two years after the first railroad arrived. In 1912 Arizona was admitted to the Union, and Phoenix became the state capital.

The completion in 1911 of Roosevelt Dam, part of the first successful large-scale irrigation project in the country, made it possible to grow citrus fruits, dates and other crops in the desert climate. The city has also prospered from rich mineral deposits in the region. Since 1945 electronics, aircraft, furniture, steel, aluminum and chemical manufacturing have become important.

In 1972 the Phoenix Civic Plaza, a $19-million commercial and cultural complex, and the 40-story Valley National Bank Building, Arizona's tallest, were completed.

Abundant sunshine has made Phoenix a health resort and winter vacationland. Of interest in the area are the city's museums; nearby South Mountain Park; and Taliesin West, home of the late Frank Lloyd Wright and now an architectural school directed by Mrs. Wright. An annual rodeo simulates the atmosphere of the Old West each spring.

Phoenix has a mushrooming population—Americans are moving into this city at a rate of more than 400 a day. Newcomers are discovering that the reasons they moved away—air pollution, traffic congestion, inflation, overburdened utilities and suburban sprawl—are problems that already exist in Phoenix. Major long-range plans for the city are in the beginning stages, with redevelopment and "in-filling" of areas within the inner city being the new direction taken.

As Phoenix has mushroomed in population and development, so it has in athletic stature. Professional sports teams such as the National Basketball Association Phoenix Suns and the World Tennis Team Phoenix Racquets have found a home in the Valley of the Sun and are popular drawing cards.

PITTSBURGH

Location: Southwestern Pennsylvania, at junction where the Allegheny and Monongahela rivers form the Ohio River **County:** Allegheny **City area:** 55.5 sq. miles (143.8 sq. kilometers) **Altitude:** 745 feet (226.4 meters)

Mayor: Richard Caliguiri Executive Secretary: Dave Matter
City population: 520,089 (1970 census), 449,092 (1976 est.)
Metro area population: 2,401,362 (1970 census), 2,294,500 (1977 est.)
Daily newspapers: 2 **No. of commercial radio stations (AM):** 11 (1979) **No. of commercial TV stations:** 6 (1979)
City Chamber of Commerce: The Greater Pittsburgh Chamber of Commerce, 411 Seventh Avenue, Pittsburgh, Pennsylvania 15219

Pittsburgh, seat of Allegheny County, is the second largest city in Pennsylvania, an important inland port, and one of the world's great steel centers.

It was founded on the site of Shannopin, an Indian settlement that was a fur-trading post in the late 17th century. In the 18th century the French built Fort Duquesne on the site, and after it fell to the British it was renamed Fort Pitt in honor of William Pitt. The fort withstood attack in 1763 during Pontiac's Rebellion, and in the ensuing years a village grew up around it.

When the Northwest Territory opened up, the village became an important trading and shipping center. Anthony Wayne negotiated (1795) with Indian tribes in the area, allowing Pittsburgh to develop in peace. It was incorporated as a city in 1816. Completion of the Pennsylvania Canal in 1837 and rail lines in 1851 further stimulated industrial and commercial development. One of the world's first cable suspension bridges was constructed here in 1847.

In 1936 Pittsburgh suffered the most disastrous flood of its history when the Allegheny and the Monongahela rivers rose 46 feet, inundating much of the business and industrial district, paralyzing the city, and taking 45 lives. Damages amounted to $25 million.

The city is headquarters for some of the country's biggest corporations. Among them are U.S. Steel, Gulf Oil, Rockwell International, Heinz foods, Westinghouse, Alcoa, Consolidation Coal, PPG Industries, and Koppers Co. The reactors for the *Nautilus* and *Skate*, the first nuclear submarines, were built here.

Pittsburgh's revolutionary urban-renewal program began when public-spirited citizens formed the Allegheny Conference on Community Development in 1943. Demolition work began in 1950 for the famous Gateway Center and $22-million Civic Auditorium with a retractable dome. The program has been eminently successful in rebuilding the Golden Triangle—the triangular-shaped business district bounded by the Allegheny, Monongahela, and Ohio rivers. It has also been so successful in controlling smoke emitted by the steelmaking and other industrial complexes that Pittsburgh is no longer "Smoky City," a nickname it bore for more than a century. Other redevelopment highlights are the Market Square Redevelopment Project, a downtown block filled with night spots and restaurants, and a $25-million Convention Center and Exhibition Hall, to be completed in 1979.

Pittsburgh has a fine park system. City landmarks include the Carnegie-Mellon University, established by Andrew Carnegie in 1895; the University of Pittsburgh and its Cathedral of Learning, noted for its medical and law schools; the Buhl Planetarium and Institute of Popular Science; and Highland Park, site of the Pittsburgh Zoo and a memorial to Stephen Foster, who was born there. Heinz Hall for the Performing Arts opened in September 1971. It is home for the Pittsburgh Symphony, Pittsburgh Opera, Civic Light Opera, Pittsburgh Ballet and Pittsburgh Youth Symphony.

The bold skyline of Pittsburgh is clearly visible from the top of Mount Washington reached from the south bank of the Monongahela by the "incline," one of two in the city, which acts as a near-verticle tramway up the steep slope.

PORTLAND

Location: Northwestern Oregon, near the junction of the Willamette and Columbia rivers **Counties:** Multnomah and Washington **City area:** 100 sq. miles (259 sq. kilometers) **Altitude:** 77 feet (23.4 meters)
Mayor: Connie McCready
City population: 382,352 (1970 census), 379,826 (1976 est.)
Metro area population: 1,007,131 (1970 census) 1,121,500 (1977 est.)

Daily newspapers: 3 **No. of commercial radio stations (AM):** 18 (1979) **No. of commercial TV stations:** 4 (1979)
City Chamber of Commerce: Portland Chamber of Commerce, 824 S.W. 5th, Portland, Oregon 97204

Portland, seat of Multnomah County and largest city in Oregon, is a trading, transportation, and manufacturing center, an important deepwater port with shipyards and a port of entry.

When it was founded in 1845, a coin was flipped to decide whether it should be named after Boston, Massachusetts or Portland, Maine. Incorporated in 1851, it expanded with the establishment of the salmon industry after the Civil War, the arrival of the railroad (1883), the Alaska gold rush (1897-1900), and the Lewis and Clark Centennial Exposition (1905). A disastrous fire in 1873 destroyed part of the city, but it was rapidly rebuilt. The city made history in 1889 with the first long-distance transmission of electricity; power from a plant on the Willamette Falls at Oregon City was sent over wires to light the streets of Portland. During World War II, Portland emerged as a major shipbuilding port.

Today the city is a major export point for wheat, wool, bauxite and lumber, and the leading manufacturer of specialized lumbering equipment. Also important to the city's economy are the numerous chemical industries. The $84-million Port of Portland Swan Island Project, when completed in 1979, will be the largest floating dry dock on the U.S. Pacific Coast.

Portland instituted a popularly elected regional government that embraces parts of three counties. The reorganization is the first of its kind in the nation, and calls for a two-tiered government of municipal, county and other local jurisdictions and a regional government

In late July, 1979, President Carter appointed former mayor Neil Goldschmidt as his Secretary of Transportation. While as mayor, Goldschmidt's successful efforts at killing an inter-city freeway (which would have displaced 600 families), and at pushing for a 22-block-long downtown pedestrian mall (open only to buses), have brought additional prosperity to downtown Portland. His recent recommendation for the construction of a $60-million, 10-mile light-rail system between Portland and a suburb would result in one of the country's most effective urban transportation systems.

Of interest in Portland are the annual rose festival, the Pacific International Livestock Exposition, the Portland Zoo, the Portland Art Museum, and the fine views of various mountains, occasionally including distant Mount Rainier and Mount Jefferson. Mount Tabor, an extinct volcanic crater, is located in Portland.

PROVIDENCE

Location: Northeastern Rhode Island, at the head of the Narragansett Bay, on Providence River **County:** Providence **City area:** 20 sq. miles (51.8 sq. kilometers) **Altitude:** 80 feet (24.3 meters)
Mayor: Vincent A. Cianci, Jr.
City population: 179,116 (1970 census), 164,989 (1976 est.)
Metro area population: 855,495 (1970 census), 852,000 (1977 est.)
Daily newspapers: 2 **No. of commercial radio stations (AM):** 10 (1979) **No. of commercial TV stations:** 2 (1979)
City Chamber of Commerce: Greater Providence Chamber of Commerce, 10 Dorrance Street, Providence, Rhode Island 02903

Providence, seat of Providence County and state capital, is the largest city in Rhode Island and a port of entry. It was founded by Roger Williams in 1636 after he was exiled from Massachusetts. The Narragansett Indians granted him title to the site, which he named in gratitude for "God's merciful providence." Early settlers formed (1638) a "Proprietors Company" cooperative.

The settlement developed slowly during the 17th century and suffered much destruction during King Philip's War (1675-76) when Indians raided it and burned more than a third of its homes. Later, however, Providence developed into an important commercial center, and many families amassed fortunes as ships engaged in the West Indian trade.

Providence served the patriotic cause during the Revolutionary War and signed the Rhode Island Independence Act two months before the signing of the Declaration of Independence. After the War of 1812, Providence became a jewelry and textile manufacturing center. In 1832 the city charter became effective.

In 1842 Thomas Wilson Dorr, a Providence man, led a rebellion that collapsed; however, it was influential in the formation of a more democratic state constitution. In 1900 Providence became Rhode Island's sole capital, having been joint capital with other communities since colonial days.

Today Providence is still noted as a jewelry manufacturing center. Silverware, textiles, machinery, metal products, and rubber goods are also important products.

Among the city's historic structures are the old market building (1773), the Stephen Hopkins House (c. 1755), the John Brown House (1786), and the First Baptist Meetinghouse (1775). Roger Williams Park contains a museum of natural history and a natural amphitheater where concerts are given.

Westminster Hall and downtown Providence are under reconstruction.

Providence is the home of Brown University, Providence College, Rhode Island College, and Rhode Island School of Design, one of the country's leading art schools.

ROCHESTER

Location: Western New York State, at the mouth of the Genesee River on Lake Ontario, 65 miles east of Buffalo **County:** Monroe City area: 36 sq. miles (93.2 sq. kilometers) **Altitude:** 510 feet (154.9 meters)
Mayor: Thomas P. Ryan, Jr. **City Manager:** L. Joe Miller
City population: 295,011 (1970 census), 262,766 (1976 est.)
Metro area population: 961,516 (1970 census), 970,200 (1977 est.)
Daily newspapers: 3 **No. of commercial radio stations (AM):** 16 (1979) **No. of commercial TV stations:** 4 (1979)
City Chamber of Commerce: Rochester Area Chamber of Commerce, Ind., 55 St. Paul Street, Rochester, New York 14604

Rochester, seat of Monroe County, is situated on the falls of the Genesee River, the New York State Barge Canal and Lake Ontario. Known as the home of Eastman Kodak, Bausch & Lomb, R. T. French, and Xerox, the city enjoys an unusually diverse economy; major industries include machinery, optical goods, foundry products, nurseries, food packing and processing, leather goods, printing and publishing. It also has great natural beauty, its many parks and gardens earning for it the nickname, "The Flower City."

The Rochester region was originally the home of the Seneca Indians. In 1789 Ebenezer Allen built a mill at the falls of the Genesee, on land he had been granted on condition he serve the Senecas' needs. But the mill failed, and Allen's land was sold to Colonel Nathaniel Rochester and two friends. In 1811 Colonel Rochester laid out the village and a year later the first white settlement was made; its original name, Rochesterville, was shortened in 1812. The village was incorporated in 1817, the city in 1834.

Blessed with abundant waterpower, and the rich yields of the Genesee Valley, a significant milling industry developed and played a large part in Rochester's early growth. The industry's success was assured by the opening of the Erie Canal to the city in 1823.

Before the Civil War, the city was in the forefront of the anti-slavery movement and a station on the Underground Railroad; it was in Rochester that black abolitionist Frederick Douglass published a newspaper, The North Star. The period 1850-1900 saw the decline of milling as the city's chief economic pursuit, and the rise of the nursery trade and a number of technical industries to take its place. In 1916 the city was extended northward, in a strip along the banks of the Genesee, to Lake Ontario.

Among the city's attractions are the Eastman Kodak Company, whose plants are open to tours; the George Eastman House of Photography; the Rochester Museum of Arts and Sciences; the Strassenburgh Planetarium; Eastman Theatre, home of the Rochester Philharmonic and the Susan B. Anthony House, commemorating the women's rights pioneer and former Rochester resident.

SACRAMENTO

Location: North-central California, at the confluence of the Sacramento and American rivers, 90 miles northeast of San Francisco **County:** Sacramento **City area:** 93.8 sq. miles (242.9 sq. kilometers) **Altitude:** 17 feet (5.2 meters)
Mayor: Phillip Isenberg **City Manager:** Walter Slipe
City population: 257,105 (1970 census), 262,305 (1976 est.)
Metro area population: 803,793 (1970 census), 929,400 (1977 est.)
Daily newspapers: 3 **No. of commercial radio stations (AM):** 9 (1979) **No. of commercial TV stations:** 6 (1979)
City Chamber of Commerce: Sacramento Metropolitan Chamber of Commerce, P.O. Box 1017, Sacramento, California 95805

Sacramento, capital of California and seat of Sacramento County, is a rare amalgam of industrial strength and natural beauty, and the focal point of the profusely fertile Sacramento Valley. Fruits, vegetables, cattle and dairy products abound, supporting a large food packing and processing industry. Other important resources include oil, natural gas, timber, lead, pottery clay and a plentiful supply of waterpower for generating electricity. In 1963 the city opened deep-water port facilities, with direct access to the Pacific Ocean. The city is also an important missile development center.

The history of Sacramento is rich in drama and color, dating from its founding in 1839 by John Augustus Sutter, a German-born Swiss citizen who received permission from the Mexican governor to establish a colony for fellow Swiss immigrants. Originally called New Helvetia, it received its present name (from the river which ran beside it) in 1848, when it was laid out as a town.

The following year brought the new community immediate and widespread renown, when gold was discovered (by James W. Marshall) on Sutter's property, triggering the legend-engendering Gold Rush of 1849. Fortune followed fame in swift abundance, as Sacramento became the supply center for prospectors, in an often ruthless seller's market. (Ironically, the Gold Rush brought only impoverishment to Sutter himself, as hordes of prospectors pillaged his property and put him heavily in debt.)

Sacramento was incorporated as a town in 1850 and selected as the state capital four years later. City incorporation came in 1863.

From 1849 to 1862, Sacramento was plagued by a series of disasters, including a serious fire and three devastating floods; yet always the town came back to flourish anew. (Over the years, the development of flood control techniques has greatly aided the city's growth.) A hub of river transport since its inception, Sacramento also became (in 1856) the terminus of California's first railroad and (in 1860) the western terminus of the Pony Express. In 1863 the Central Pacific Railroad began laying track east from Sacramento to meet the westward-reaching Union Pacific, and six years later the link was made, giving the country its first transcontinental rail route.

In 1978, a comprehensive plan was issued to guide public and private efforts in developing and revitalizing the center city. A $30-million redevelopment project is planned in an effort by retailers to move back into the downtown area. Also scheduled for redevelopment are transportation facilities and residential areas.

Among Sacramento's many attractions are old Fort Sutter, built by Sutter and now maintained as a museum; the 1860 State Capitol; the Crocker Art Gallery, Old Sacramento, a re-creation of the original city, including restaurants, theaters, shops and such museums as the Pony Express Museum and the Railroad Museum.

ST. LOUIS

Location: East-central Missouri, near junction of Mississippi and Missouri rivers **County:** St. Louis is an independent city **City area:** 61 sq. miles (158 sq. kilometers) **Altitude:** 455 feet (138.3 meters)
Mayor: James F. Conway
City population: 622,236 (1970 census), 514,100 (1977 est.)
Metro area population: 2,410,602 (1970 census), 2,379,800 (1977 est.)
Daily newspapers: 2 **No. of commercial radio stations (AM):** 11 (1979) **No. of commercial TV stations:** 5 (1979)
City Chamber of Commerce: St. Louis Regional Commerce and Growth Association, 10 Broadway, St. Louis, Missouri 63102

St. Louis, the largest city in Missouri and the Mississippi River Valley, is surrounded by, but independent of, St. Louis County.

In 1763 the French fur trader Pierre Laclede chose the site for a trading post and a year later dispatched René Auguste Chouteau to build it. It was named St. Louis after Louis IX, the patron saint of France.

The settlement, which became part of the United States in 1803 with the Louisiana Purchase, was an important point of embarkation for expeditions to the West, such as that of Lewis and Clark in 1804. Incorporated in 1808, it did not expand rapidly until after the War of 1812, when immigrants coming by flatboat began to settle the West. Great Americans associated with the city include Charles Lindbergh, Thomas Hart Benton and Joseph Pulitzer.

Today manufacturing is the most important aspect of the economy. The St. Louis industrial area is the only one in the nation producing six basic metals: iron, lead, zinc, copper, aluminum, and magnesium. The city is also a major center for chemical industries and research. St. Louis is second only to Detroit in automobile assembly; it has one of the pioneer aerospace manufacturers; and it claims the world's largest brewery, Anheuser-Busch, Inc.

In 1966 St. Louis completed its 50,000-seat Busch Memorial Stadium. The following year the Jefferson National Expansion Memorial, a project of the National Park Service, was dedicated. The city erected the 630-foot stainless steel Gateway Arch, tallest monument in the country, as part of the memorial. The Arch attracts between 4 and 6-million visitors a year.

St. Louis, like many other cities, is seeking to rejuvenate its downtown area. In the Laclede's Landing section on the riverfront, old warehouses are being restored, and new restaurants and nightspots have revived night life in the area. A new $25-million Convention Center and new hotels are bringing more visitors to the city.

Points of interest in St. Louis include the Old Courthouse, scene of the Dred Scott case; Forest Park; the Missouri Botanical Garden; the Municipal Opera; the McDonnell Planetarium; and the Powell Symphony Hall.

ST. PAUL

Location: Eastern Minnesota, adjacent to Minneapolis at the junction of the Minnesota River with the Mississippi **County:** Ramsey **City area:** 52.2 sq. miles (135.2 sq. kilometers) **Altitude:** 780 feet (237.0 meters)
Mayor: George Latimer
City population: 309,866 (1970 census), 272,465 (1976 est.)
Metro area population: 1,965,391 (1970 census), 2,037,200 (1977 est.)
Daily newspapers: 2 No. of commercial radio stations (AM): 2 (1979) **No. of commercial TV stations:** 2 (1979)
City Chamber of Commerce: St. Paul Area Chamber of Commerce, Suite 300, Osborn Bldg., St. Paul, Minnesota 55102

St. Paul, capital of Minnesota and seat of Ramsey County, is contiguous with Minneapolis, with which it forms the Twin Cities metropolitan area, home for about half the state's population. A port of entry and a major transportation and industrial center, the city is situated on bluffs overlooking the Mississippi, close to the head of navigation. Its diverse economy includes meat packing, printing, publishing, steel fabrication, and the manufacture of automobiles, machinery, petroleum products, aerospace equipment, food products, abrasives and cosmetics.

Permanent white settlement in the area began in 1819 with the establishment of an army post on the Minnesota River, on the site of Mendota, now a St. Paul suburb. The following year, the post was moved across the river, where Josiah Snelling built Fort St. Anthony, later named Fort Snelling. Thanks to its strategic location and a large supply of game, fur-trading flourished at Mendota, as did the trading of food and dry goods. After treaties with the Indians paved the way for settlement, many traders, lumbermen and others came from the East to make the area home.

In 1838 a community was begun on the site of present-day St. Paul, which was originally named Pig's Eye, after one of the settlers, a French-Canadian trader named Pierre "Pig's Eye" Parrant. But it soon came to be called St. Paul, in honor of the church built there in 1841 by Father Lucian Galtier. St. Paul was made the capital of Minnesota Territory in 1849, and was incorporated five years later. It was made the state capital in 1858, when Minnesota was admitted to the Union. With the advent of the railroad and the ready availability of immigrant labor (expecially German and Irish), St. Paul's early prosperity was assured. The city limits were extended to the Minneapolis line in 1884.

Among the city's attractions are the Capitol Building (completed in 1904), which has the world's largest supported marble dome; the Cathedral of St. Paul; the St. Paul Arts and Science Center; the St. Paul Civic Opera, which specializes in light opera and operettas; Indian Mounds Park; and, on the outskirts of the city, Fort Snelling State Park. A major annual event is the St. Paul Winter Carnival, for which an ice palace is sculptured and a pageant enacted.

SALT LAKE CITY

Location: North-central Utah, southeast of the Great Salt Lake, at the foot of the Wasatch range **County:** Salt Lake **City area:** 56 sq. miles (145 sq. kilometers) **Altitude:** 4,260 feet (1294.5 meters)
Mayor: Ted Wilson
City population: 175,885 (1970 census), 168,667 (1976 est.)
Metro area population: 705,458 (1970 census), 822,200 (1977 est.)
Daily newspapers: 2 No. of commercial radio stations (AM): 13 (1979) **No. of commercial TV stations:** 4 (1979)
City Chamber of Commerce: Salt Lake Area Chamber of Commerce, 19 East 2nd South, Salt Lake City, Utah 84111

Salt Lake City, seat of Salt Lake County, is Utah's capital, its largest city, and headquarters of the 3.5 million members of the Mormon faith—the Church of Jesus Christ of Latter-day Saints. It was founded in 1847 by the Mormon leader Brigham Young. Mormon settlers soon transformed the arid region into irrigated farmland.

After 1849 Salt Lake City (called Great Salt Lake City until 1868) was a supply point for California-bound pioneers. A link to the transcontinental railroad in 1870 brought non-Mormons to the city and contributed to its growth. When Utah entered the Union in 1896, Salt Lake City became its capital.

Today the metropolis is an important distribution point for a rich agricultural and mining area, as well as an important air and rail hub. Its industries include printing and publishing, oil refining, copper refining, and the smelting of copper and iron. Electronics manufacturing is increasingly becoming an important industry. Major employers are Hill Air Force Base, 30 miles to the north, local defense industries, and the Kennecott Copper Corp.

The city lies at the foot of the beautiful Wasatch Mountains. The magnificent Utah State Capitol with its copper dome houses noted works of art and many interesting exhibits. The Salt Palace, a $17-million civic auditorium complex, was completed in 1969.

Centrally located Temple Square contains the most important buildings of the Mormon Church—the Mormon Temple, a mammoth granite structure designed under Brigham Young's direction and built between 1853 and 1893; and the Tabernacle, housing one of the world's largest organs.

Now completed is the tallest building in Salt Lake City, a 28-story office building for the Mormon church. A multimillion dollar arts project is the latest phase of the city's building boom. When completed, the center will include a concert hall for the Utah Symphony and a performing arts center. Also under construction is a $65-million downtown shopping mall.

SAN ANTONIO

Location: South-central Texas, on the San Antonio River about 190 miles west of Houston **County:** Bexar **City area:** 263 sq. miles (681.1 sq. kilometers) **Altitude:** 701 feet (231.3 meters)
Mayor: Lila Cockrell **City Manager:** Tom Huebner
City population: 708,582 (1970 census), 783,765 (1976 est.)
Metro area population: 888,179 (1970 census), 1,024,900 (1977 est.)

Daily newspapers: 4 **No. of commercial radio stations (AM):** 13 (1979) **No. of commercial TV stations:** 5 (1979)
City Chamber of Commerce: Greater San Antonio Chamber of Commerce, 602 East Commerce Street, P.O. Box 1628, San Antonio, Texas 78296

San Antonio, port of entry and seat of Bexar County, has developed into the banking and commerce hub of south central Texas, while retaining its history-rich Spanish-Mexican character, redolent of the days when Indian, Spanish, Mexican, Texan and United States forces all sought dominion there. Only 154 miles from the U.S.-Mexico border at Laredo, it is a bilingual city whose old missions and historic landmarks offer charming contrast to its modern factories, refineries and military installations.

Although the federal government is San Antonio's largest employer, farming, stock-raising, food processing and diversified manufacture are also important to its economy. The city's mild climate and natural beauty have made it a popular winter resort.

The site of San Antonio had been known to the Spanish, and to the Coahuiltecan Indians, long before 1718, when a military expedition led by Martín de Alarcón, Spanish governor of Coahuila and Texas, founded a town and fort there, the Villa (and Presidio) de Béjar. At the same time, missionaries founded the Mission San Antonio de Valero nearby; in 1724 the mission was moved from its original site to where the Alamo stands today.

In 1731 Spanish colonists from the Canary Islands founded San Fernando de Béjar, just west of Alarcón's settlement. By 1791 the three settlements—Villa de Béjar, Mission San Antonio de Valero and San Fernando de Béjar—came to be known as one, San Antonio de Béjar (later, simply, San Antonio).

The settlement grew in prominence and was the principal objective of the Mexican and Texas Revolutions (1821, 1836). In the latter conflict, on March 6, 1836, the famous battle of the Alamo took place, in which all of the nearly 200 defenders (including Davy Crockett) were killed by Mexican forces numbering over 2,400. However, the following month, spurred by the battlecry "Remember the Alamo!," the Texans gained ultimate victory at San Jacinto, and the Texas republic was born; a year later, San Antonio was incorporated.

During the later part of the 19th century, the town became a major cattle center, where herds were assembled and started on overland drives up the Chisholm Trail to the Kansas railheads. San Antonio's prosperity was aided by the advent of the railroad and, later, by the increased military presence there.

Among the city's attractions are the Alamo; La Villita, a reconstructed old Spanish settlement; the historic Governor's Palace and San Fernando Cathedral, both restored, the Arneson River Theater, and the Tower of the Americas, built during Hemisphere 1968. San Antonio is the home of five major universities and has one of the largest medical centers in the country at the University of Texas (San Antonio campus).

SAN DIEGO

Location: Southern California, on east side of San Diego Bay **County:** San Diego **City area:** 319.5 sq. miles (810.7 sq. kilometers) **Altitude:** sea level
Mayor: Pete Wilson **City Manager:** Ray Blair
City population: 697,027 (1970 census), 789,059 (1976 est.)
Metro area population: 1,357,854 (1970 census), 1,683,000 (1977 est.)
Daily newspapers: 2 **No. of commercial radio stations (AM):** 11 (1979) **No. of commercial TV stations:** 3 (1979)
City Chamber of Commerce: San Diego Chamber of Commerce, 110 W. "C" Street, Suite 3600, San Diego, California 92101

San Diego, seat of San Diego County, is a port of entry and the oldest permanent European settlement in California. The city has risen rapidly in size, from fifteenth largest in the country in 1970, and now ranks as the ninth largest in the United States.

Since Juan Rodriguez Cabrillo sailed into its bay in 1542, the area has been under four flags—that of Spain, Mexico, California, and the United States. In 1769 San Diego de Alcalá Mission was established by Junipero Serra, a Franciscan missionary. A settlement grew up and was incorporated (1850) as a city after California became part of the Union.

San Diego's excellent natural harbor has made it an important commercial center and the site of several large U.S. Navy installations. It is the distribution and processing hub for the surrounding farm and dairy region and has a wide variety of manufactures. It is the home of the Atlas missile, an aircraft producer, and it is an important oceanographic and health sciences center. San Diego has a large electronics industry. In the last 12 months 30 new companies have relocated to San Diego because of the availability of land and workers. Its magnificent climate and proximity to Mexico have made tourism a significant part of the economy.

San Diego's Balboa Park contains an art gallery, museums, gardens, a zoo, and some buildings from the Panama-California International Exposition (1915-16) and the California Pacific International Exposition (1935-36). In the Old Town area is a state park containing adobes from the Spanish and Mexican era. The Mission Bay park includes boat landings, water ski, fishing and swimming areas, hotels and Sea World, a huge marine animal amusement park.

In September, 1978, one of the country's worst airplane disasters occurred over San Diego. 151 persons were killed as a result of a mid-air collision of a Pacific Southwest Airlines jetliner and a single-engine training plane.

SAN FRANCISCO

Location: West-central California, on a peninsula between Pacific Ocean and San Francisco Bay **County:** San Francisco **City area:** 46.3 sq. miles (119.9 sq. kilometers) **Altitude:** 65 feet (19.6 meters)
Mayor: Dianne Feinstein **Chief Administrative Officer:** Roger Boas
City population: 715,674 (1970 census), 654,400 (1977 est.)
Metro area population: 3,107,355 (1970 census), 3,182,200 (1977 est.)
Daily newspapers: 4 **No. of commercial radio stations (AM):** 16 (1979) **No. of commercial TV stations:** 8 (1979)
City Chamber of Commerce: Greater San Francisco Chamber of Commerce, 465 California Street, San Francisco, California 94104

San Francisco, coextensive with California's San Francisco County, is the financial center of the West and, together with the San Francisco Bay area, the largest port on the Pacific Coast.

In 1579 Sir Francis Drake stopped in the vicinity on his voyage around the world. In 1776 a mission, later known as Mission Dolores, and fort were founded at a site chosen by Juan Bautista de Anza. In 1846, during the Mexican War, a U.S. naval force under John Montgomery took Yerba Buena, the settlement that had grown up. The following year the community assumed the name of its bay, which, according to tradition, had been named after St. Francis of Assisi by Spanish voyagers in 1595.

In 1848 the California gold rush began and a flood of fortune seekers, adventurers, and settlers brought a period of lawlessness, during which San Francisco's waterfront section became notorious as the Barbary Coast, and vigilantes were organized to restore order. Newcomers from all over the world, including China, gave the city a cosmopolitan air. It was incorporated in 1850 and linked with the East by railroads in 1869.

On April 18, 1906, a disastrous earthquake and fire almost completely destroyed the city; an estimated 700 persons perished.

The opening of the Panama Canal, which stimulated trade, was celebrated by the Panama-Pacific Exposition of 1915. By 1939, the year of the Golden Gate International Exposition, San Francisco had become the leading industrial and commercial center of the Pacific Coast. During the Second World War, the city was the major mainland supply point and port of embarkation for the struggle in the Pacific.

San Francisco is the home of the Pacific Coast Stock Exchange and a Federal Reserve district bank. More than 65 industrial parks lie within a 50-mile radius of the city. Major industries include food processing, shipbuilding, petroleum refining, and the manufacture of metal products and chemicals. The city is also a noted cultural center.

Situated among steep hills, San Francisco is a colorful city of lovely vistas, graceful bridges, ornate mansions, imposing public buildings, and unusual districts. The Golden Gate Bridge (1937) links the city with Marin County to the north. San Francisco's scenic hills now hold apartment complexes and shopping centers, but despite the changes the city maintains its warm personality.

Rejuvenation of the inner city has come from the creation of block and merchant associations and the arrival of new department stores in the downtown area.

San Francisco is famous for its fine restaurants; its cable car system, preserved as a historic landmark; Chinatown—the country's largest—with its Oriental architecture, tearooms, and temples; Telegraph Hill, where in earlier times a signal tower sent word to the city of the arrival of ships; and Nob Hill, once the home of millionaires. Also of interest are Fisherman's Wharf and Golden Gate Park, with its planetarium, museum of natural history, aquarium, and flower gardens. The Cow Palace is the home of political conventions, sports events, and livestock exhibitions.

The nation was stunned when it learned that San Francisco Mayor George Moscone and Supervisor Harvey Milk were shot to death in their City Hall offices by former Supervisor Dan White, who was sentenced to 7 years and 8 months in prison on a manslaughter conviction. The verdict lead to violent protests from the city's gay community.

SAN JOSE

Location: Western California, about 40 miles southeast of San Francisco in the Santa Clara Valley **County:** Santa Clara **City area:** 136.2 sq. miles (352.8 sq. kilometers) **Altitude:** 90 feet (27.3 meters)
Mayor: Janet Gray Hayes **City Manager:** James Alloway
City population: 461,212 (1970 census), 573,806 (1976 est.)
Metro area population: 1,065,313 (1970 census), 1,217,300 (1977 est.)
Daily newspapers: 2 **No. of commercial radio stations (AM):** 13 (1979) **No. of commercial TV stations:** 3 (1979)
City Chamber of Commerce: San Jose Chamber of Commerce, One Paseo De San Antonio, San Jose, California 95113

San Jose, seat of Santa Clara County, is virtually contiguous with the city of Santa Clara, the two communities together forming the focal point of the fertile Santa Clara Valley, the world's largest dried fruit packing and canning region. In addition to its agricultural importance, San Jose has recently developed into a significant center for electronics research and diversified manufacturing. The area is the nation's leading producer of semi-conductors.

San Jose (originally the Pueblo de San José de Guadalupe) was founded in 1777 by José Joaquin Moraga, as a Spanish military supply base, and soon also became an ecclesiastical center. After the territory came under U.S. control, San Jose was made (in 1849) California's first capital, although statehood was not officially achieved until 1850, the year San Jose also became the state's first incorporated city. It remained the capital until 1851, when the seat of state government shifted to Vallejo.

In its early years, San Jose served as a supply base for gold prospectors and as a bustling fruit trade depot. The coming of the railroad (in 1864), connecting the community to San Francisco, consolidated its importance as a distribution point for the increasingly bountiful produce of the Santa Clara Valley. This in turn gave rise to the growth of industries to equip the region's farms and service the needs of a growing populace.

Between 1940 and 1960, San Jose's population increased three-fold; from 1960 to 1970, it more than doubled, making San Jose-Santa Clara one of the nation's largest urban areas. This rapid growth was seen as a plus by developers, politicians and retailers. However, the growth has led to the decay of the downtown area, air pollution and traffic congestion. A rethinking of San Jose's growth future has come with Mayor Hayes' reelection. Initial efforts at "in-filling" and redevelopment of areas within the city, instead of continued urban sprawl, appears to be successful.

Places of interest in San Jose include the Municipal Rose Garden; Mission San José de Guadalupe, dating from 1779; the home of poet Edwin Markham; Winches-

ter Mystery House; Rosicrucian Park; and, nearby the Lick Observatory (atop Mount Hamilton) and Alum Rock Park, a popular 687-acre spa well known for its mineral springs and scenic allure.

SEATTLE

Location: West-central Washington, on Puget Sound and west shore of Lake Washington **County:** King **City area:** 91.5 sq. miles (237 sq. kilometers) **Altitude:** 10 feet (3.0 meters)
Mayor: Charles Royer
City population: 530,831 (1970 census), 490,586 (1976 est.)
Metro area population: 1,424,605 (1970 census), 1,427,200 (1977 est.)
Daily newspapers: 2 **No. of commercial radio stations (AM):** 18 (1979) **No. of commercial TV stations:** 4 (1979)
City Chamber of Commerce: Seattle Chamber of Commerce, 215 Columbia Street, Seattle, Washington 98104

Seattle, seat of King County, is Washington's largest city and the largest in the Pacific Northwest. It is a manufacturing, trade, and transportation center, and a major port of entry. The city is situated on seven hills and is flanked by the majestically beautiful Cascade and Olympic Mountains. Within its limits are four lakes, 48 parks and more than 22 miniparks.

Seattle began as a small lumber settlement in 1851. It was platted two years later and named for a chief of the Duwamish and Suquamish Indians. Incorporated in 1869, it remained a small lumber town until the arrival of the railroad in 1884. Subsequent strikes, anti-Chinese riots, and a great fire in 1889 did not prevent the city from growing rapidly. With the 1897-98 Alaska gold rush, Seattle became a boom town and was the nation's chief link with Alaska. Further growth came with the Alaska-Yukon-Pacific Exposition (1909), the opening of the Panama Canal (1914), and the completion (1917) of a canal and locks making the city both a saltwater and freshwater port. In 1919 the International Workers of the World led a general strike in Seattle, long a center of the radical labor movement. A series of various municipal scandals led to the election in 1926 of a reform candidate, Bertha K. Landis, the first woman mayor of a large American city.

World War II made the city a center of aircraft manufacturing and shipbuilding. The Boeing Company is the largest employer in the area. Although the region underwent a severe recession in the early 1970s due to a slackening of the aerospace industry, the area's economy has now stabilized. The construction of the trans-Alaska crude oil pipeline did much to bolster Seattle's economy. Other important industries today are food processing, lumber, chemical products, metal goods and machinery production.

The Seattle downtown area has taken on a new look. Since 1970 almost half of the downtown has been rebuilt. Seattle has become an important cultural center on the West Coast. It boasts a first-rate Opera House, the Seattle Symphony Orchestra, several active theater companies, and a fine arts museum. Of interest in the city is the Seattle Center, site of the Century 21 Exposition. It contains the opera house, arena, coliseum, and International Fountain, the world-famous 606-foot Space Needle, and the Pacific Science Center.

Seattle is the home of the Mariner Baseball Team, the Seahawks Football Team, and the Sounders Soccer Team. In June, 1979, the Seattle Supersonics won the National Basketball Association championship against the Washington Bullets for their first NBA title.

TAMPA

Location: On the west coast of Florida at the mouth of the Hillsboro River on Tampa Bay. **County:** Hillsborough **City area:** 84.5 sq. miles (218.9 sq. kilometers) **Altitude:** 15 feet (4.6 meters)
Mayor: William F. Poe
City population: 277,714 (1970 census), 271,365 (1976 est.)
Metro area population: 1,088,549 (1970 census), 1,380,500 (1977 est.)
Daily newspapers: 2 **No. of commercial radio stations (AM):** 9 (1979) **No. of commercial TV stations:** 4 (1979)

City Chamber of Commerce: Greater Tampa Chamber of Commerce, P.O. Box 420, 801 East Kennedy Boulevard, Tampa, Florida 33601

Tampa, a port of entry and the closest port to the Panama Canal, is located on Tampa Bay, an inlet of the Gulf of Mexico. Once known almost exclusively as a vacation spot and a source of fine cigars, Tampa, which is the seat of Hillsborough County, today has also emerged as one of Florida's most industrialized cities and the trade center of the state's west coast. Its economy ranges from food processing and phosphate shipping to the manufacture of a wide variety of goods, including fertilizer, paint, cement, cigars, fabricated steel, and electronic equipment. Nearby is MacDill Air Force Base, headquarters for the U.S. Readiness Command. Tampa International Airport serves Disney World, Florida's chief tourist attraction, 60 miles to the west.

At least two Spanish explorers, and probably more, visited the site of Tampa in the 16th century: Panfilo de Narváez (1528) and Hernando de Soto (1539). Seminole Indians successfully resisted white men's efforts to settle in the area until 1823, when a contingent of U.S. troops established Fort Brooke there. By 1831 the settlement that had grown up around the fort had come to be known by its former Indian name of Tampa; it was incorporated in 1849. During the Civil War, Tampa was bombarded by gunboats.

Development of Tampa began in earnest in 1885 with the coming of Henry B. Plant's narrow-gauge South Florida Railroad—and his port improvements and tourism promotions. The economy got another boost when the manufacture of cigars was begun (in 1886) at Ybor City, which soon became a part of Tampa proper. Tourism was spurred in 1891 by the completion of the lavish, Moorish-style Tampa Bay Hotel, which today houses the University of Tampa. In 1898, during the Spanish-American War, Tampa served as the embarkation point for Colonel "Teddy" Roosevelt and his "Rough Riders." In the mid-1920s the man-made Davis Islands in Tampa Bay were completed, providing choice sites for hotels, residences and various resort facilities.

Among Tampa's attractions are the De Soto Oak (near the University of Tampa), site of the legendary meeting between Hernando de Soto and Seminole Indian leaders, and the Busch Gardens, Florida's second largest attraction. Tampa Museum, opened in July, 1979, is the city's first major public effort at a permanent art museum. Under construction is the Center for Science and Industry, expected to be completed in 1980. It has already won the Owen Corning Energy Conservation Award for its energy conservation design and for its use of solar panels. The Gasparilla Festival, a one-day event in honor of the alleged pirate José Gaspar, is celebrated in February with a mock invasion of the city.

WASHINGTON, D.C.

Location: Between Virginia and Maryland, on Potomac River **City area:** 68.2 sq. miles (176.7 sq. kilometers) **Altitude:** 72 feet (21.9 meters)
Mayor: Marion S. Barry, Jr. **City Administrator:** Elijah B. Rogers
City population: 756,668 (1970 census), 685,000 (1977 est.)
Metro area population: 2,910,111 (1970 census), 3,020,100 (1977 est.)
Daily newspapers: 2 **No. of commercial radio stations (AM):** 18 (1979) **No. of commercial TV stations:** 5 (1979)
City Chamber of Commerce: District of Columbia Chamber of Commerce, 1319 F Street, N.W., Suite 904, Washington, D.C. 20004

Washington, D.C., is not only the capital of the United States but an important business and financial center, with over 1,800 professional and trade associations head-quartered there. Since 1895, when Georgetown became part of Washington, it has been coextensive with the District of Columbia. Washington's large government work force insures a more recession-proof climate than in other major markets.

The District was established by Congress in 1790-91, and George Washington selected the exact site for the "Federal City," which was designed by Pierre L'Enfant and laid out by Andrew Ellicott. Maryland and Virginia ceded land for the District, and the capital moved there from Philadelphia in 1800. Thomas Jefferson was the first President to be inaugurated in Washington.

During the War of 1812, the city fell to the British, who burned the Capitol, White House, and other public buildings. During the Civil War, the city was threatened by Confederate forces.

1878 marked the end of home rule for the district, with city officials thereafter being appointed by the President. Since 1961, however, when residents were given the right to vote in Presidential elections, Washingtonians have sought to increase local self-government and national political representation. Residents were allowed to elect their own school board in 1968, and full home rule followed in 1975. Under the Nixon Administration, the District of Columbia was granted non-voting representation in Congress, with Walter E. Fauntroy sworn in on April 19, 1971, as Washington's first Representative in nearly 100 years. And in an historic move, Congress voted in 1978 to approve a constitutional amendment giving the District full elected representation in both the House and the Senate. The amendment gives Washington two Senators—expanding the Senate from 100 to 102—and either one or two Representatives, based on the District's 1980 census. The amendment must now be ratified by at least 38 state legislatures by the summer of 1985 for it to become law. So far, five states have ratified and eight have rejected the amendment.

Washington, with its broad tree-shaded thoroughfares and open vistas, has many imposing buildings. The Capitol and White House are the most historic. Other leading tourist attractions are the Washington Monument and Lincoln and Jefferson Memorials. The many additional points of interest in or near the city include the Library of Congress; the National Archives, which houses the Declaration of Independence, the Constitution, and the Bill of Rights; the Supreme Court Building; Constitution Hall; the Smithsonian Institution; the numerous embassies; the Pentagon; the U.S. Naval Observatory; and Mount Vernon. The fashionable Georgetown area was designated a national monument in 1967.

The Arlington Memorial Bridge across the Potomac River connects Washington with Arlington National Cemetery. Among the city's beautiful parks are West Potomac Park, which includes the Tidal Basin with the famous Japanese cherry trees; East Potomac Park; Rock Creek Park and the adjoining National Zoological Park; and Anacostia Park.

Washington's Metro, the computerized subway system which opened in 1976, is having mixed results. While linking the downtown area with the airport, Capitol Hill and Washington's suburbs, the Metro must accomodate the multitude of passengers with a shortage of cars due to malfunctions.

Public and private redevelopment has given downtown Washington a new face. Currently underway is the joint $500-million public-private Pennsylvania Avenue Development Plan for combined residential-commercial use, and the $60-million expansion of the Sheraton Park Hotel in northwest Washington, But plans for a $110-million Civic Center are stalled, pending city compliance with Congressional funding guidelines.

Following the reactor accident at the Three Mile Island Nuclear Plant in March, on May 6, 1979, the largest anti-nuclear power demonstration in the U.S. occurred in Washington D.C. At least 65,000 people marched peacefully from the White House to the Capitol.

U.S. OUTLYING AREAS

The areas under United States sovereignty or otherwise associated with some type of American jurisdiction extend through the Caribbean and almost across the Pacific. From east to west, the Virgin Islands of the United States, in the Caribbean, lie 160° from the Palau Islands in the American-administered Trust Territory of the Pacific Islands, nearly halfway around the world. The distance between Point Barrow in northern Alaska, 71.5° north of the equator, and American Samoa in the southwest Pacific, 14° south of the equator, is nearly half of that from pole to pole.

American Samoa—*Status:* Unorganized unincorporated territory. *Population:* 31,500 (1977 est.). *Area:* 83 sq. mi. *Seat of government:* Pago Pago (2,451).

American Samoa consists of six small Pacific islands in that part of the Samoan islands lying east of 171°W., plus Swains Island, 250 miles north of Tutuila. It is roughly 2,200 miles southwest of Hawaii and 1,600 miles northeast of the northern tip of New Zealand.

In 1978 American Samoa held its first popular election for governor. The victor, Peter Tali Coleman, a native of the islands, was inaugurated on January 3, 1978. There is a legislature, the *Fono*, with limited authority, the House of Representatives being elected by universal suffrage, the Senate by the native chiefs. Samoan society is rigidly stratified, and the chiefs, of whom there are some 600 of varying ranks, have firm, paternalistic control over their followers.

The six islands in the Samoan group came under American hegemony in 1899, when Great Britain and Germany renounced their claims in favor of the United States, and Swains was added in 1925. American Samoa's native inhabitants are U.S. nationals; they are not American citizens but may migrate freely to the United States. In October 1978, President Carter signed into law an act of Congress giving the islands a nonvoting delegate to the U.S. House of Representatives.

Guam—*Status:* Organized unincorporated territory. *Population:* 115,000 (1977 est.). *Area:* 212 sq. mi. *Capital* Agana (2,110).

This island in the western Pacific is the most southerly of the Marianas, 1,300 miles east of the Philippines and 1,475 miles south of Japan, at 13°27'N. and 144°47'E. Of volcanic origin, it is mountainous in the south, a plateau in the north. The climate is tropical, with moderately heavy rainfall. The indigenes—the Chamorros—make up about half the population. Most of the rest are military or other government transients. English is the official language. About 95 percent of the native Guamanians are Roman Catholics.

U.S. military installations and tourism are the most significant factors in the economy. Guam is the only American territory without excise duties (except for tobacco, liquid fuel, and liquor).

Guam's administration is under the U.S. Department of the Interior. Its people are U.S. citizens (however, they do not vote in national elections but do have a nonvoting delegate in the House of Representatives). The governor and lieutenant governor are elected by the people. There is an elected unicameral legislature. On August 4, 1979, Guam residents rejected a proposed constitution drafted in December 1977 which allowed the island more self-government. Most islanders felt that it did not provide residents with the same rights as other Americans.

Howland, Baker, and Jarvis Islands—*Status:* Unincorporated possession. *Population:* Uninhabited. *Area:* 2.77 sq. mi.

These three small islands are situated in the South Pacific: Howland and Baker a few miles north of the equator, Jarvis a few miles south. Howland and Baker are coral atolls about 35 miles apart and some 2,000 miles southwest of Honolulu. Jarvis lies some 1,500 miles south of Hawaii. They had rich guano deposits that were worked by American interests in the 1850s; however, when that industry faded, the islands had no value until the trans-Pacific aviation era began in the 1930s. In 1934 the United States reasserted its claim to them, based on the fact that they had been mentioned in the Guano Act of 1856.

Johnston Atoll—*Status:* Unincorporated possession. *Population:* 1,007 (1970 census). *Area:* .91 sq. mi.

This Pacific atoll lies 715 miles southwest of Honolulu, at 16°45'N. and 169°30'W. It consists of a reef around four islets. Johnston was annexed in 1858 by both the United States and the Kingdom of Hawaii. A quantity of guano was removed during the next 50 years, and for a long time the area was also a bird reservation. It was taken over by the U.S. Navy in 1934.

In 1958 and 1962 it was the site of high-altitude nuclear tests. In 1971 the Defense Department started to move 13,000 tons of nerve and mustard gas stored on Okinawa to igloo-shaped structures on Johnston.

Kingman Reef—*Status:* Unincorporated possession. *Population:* Uninhabited. *Area:* .01 sq. mi.

This bare reef in the Pacific lies 35 miles northwest of Palmyra Island and 1,000 miles south of Honolulu. It was annexed by the United States in 1922 and placed under the U.S. Navy in 1934.

Midway Islands—*Status:* Unincorporated possession. *Population:* 2,000 (1977 est.). *Area:* 1.9 sq. mi.

Midway is near the western end of the Hawaiian chain, 1,200 miles northwest of Honolulu, at 28°12'-17'N. and 177°19'-26'W. It consists of an atoll with two islets.

Made a possession in 1867 and placed under the U.S. Navy in 1903, Midway was the scene of one of the great air/sea battles of World War II. Today it is a naval installation; its chief executive is a naval officer. Midway is noted as a nesting site for seabirds.

Navassa Island—*Status:* Unincorporated possession. *Population:* Uninhabited. *Area:* 2 sq. mi.

Navassa lies in the Caribbean between Jamaica and Haiti, 30 miles west of the latter. It was certified in 1865 as appertaining to the United States under the Guano Act of 1856. A presidential proclamation of 1916 declared it to be under the sole jurisdiction of the United States and reserved it for lighthouse purposes. It is administered by the Coast Guard.

Palmyra Island—*Status:* Unincorporated possession. *Population:* Uninhabited. *Area:* 3.85 sq. mi.

An atoll of more than 50 islets, Palmyra is located in the Pacific 1,000 miles south of Honolulu, at 5°52'N. and 162°06'W. It is covered with dense foliage, coconut trees, and pisonis grandis, a 100-foot-tall balsaline tree.

Claimed by the Kingdom of Hawaii in 1862, the atoll was annexed by the United States with Hawaii in 1898. Excluded from Hawaii's boundaries when the latter became a state in 1959, it was placed under the administration of the U.S. Secretary of the Interior in 1961. In 1979 the U.S. government proposed purchasing the privately-owned island for use as a nuclear waste storage site.

Panama Canal Zone—*Status:* Under U.S. jurisdiction. *Population:* 45,000 (1977 est.). *Area:* 647 sq. mi. *Capital:* Balboa Heights (232)

On October 1, 1979, jurisdiction over the Canal Zone is scheduled to be transferred to Panama. The following article describes the Zone as it existed under U.S. control.

The Canal Zone in Central America extends five miles on either side of the axis of the canal that crosses the Isthmus of Panama from the Atlantic to the Pacific. It stretches southeast from Colón and Cristobal at the Atlantic entrance, to Balboa on the Pacific side, the latter entrance being 27 miles east of the Atlantic one.

Most of the residents are U.S. citizens, the rest being Panamanian and other Caribbean peoples.

The zone is completely dependent on the operation of the canal. There are some market gardens but most food and all other material are imported.

There are two operating agencies involved in the zone: the Canal Zone Government, which is responsible for police and fire protection, education, social services, and the like, while the Panama Canal Company operates the canal. The zone governor is usually a U.S. Army officer, who is also president of the U.S. government-owned company.

The treaty between the United States and the Republic of Panama that made it possible for the United States to build and operate the canal dates from 1903. It granted the United States full sovereign rights to the zone in exchange for $10 million, an annuity of $250,000, and a

U.S. guarantee of Panamanian independence. A 1936 treaty increased the annuity to $430,000 and, at Panama's request, withdrew the guarantee of independence. In 1955 the annuity was increased to $1.93 million, and after 1974 to $2.33 million.

In 1964, there was rioting in the zone over the raising of the American and Panamanian flags. By 1967, U.S. and Panamanian negotiators had produced draft treaties that would provide for Panamanian participation in canal management and profits and terminate exclusive U.S. sovereignty in the zone. The treaties ran into political difficulties—both in the United States and Panama—and their ratification was further obstructed by the internal upheavals in Panama when, in 1968, newly elected president Arnulfo Arias was overthrown by a military junta. In the U.S. Senate and House of Representatives there was strong opposition to a transfer to Panama of sovereignty over the Canal Zone, but a compromise resolution requiring that any new agreement protect the interest of the U.S. was reached.

In August 1977, after six months of discussion, U.S. and Panamanian representatives completed an agreement regarding the future of the Canal Zone. Under its terms, Panama will obtain full control of the canal in the year 2000, but roughly 65 percent of the land area of the Zone will be transferred to Panama when the treaty takes effect. Until the year 2000, the United States will pay Panama $10 million annually in toll revenues plus additional amounts dependent on canal traffic. On September 7, 1977, President Carter and Panamanian leader Torrijos signed the treaty in Washington. Following ratification by the U.S. Senate and Panamanian approval in a popular referendum, Carter visited Panama City, where the final treaty ceremonies were held.

Puerto Rico—*Status:* Commonwealth *(Estado Libre Asociado). Population:* 3,214,000 (1977 est.). *Area:* 3,435 sq. mi. *Capital:* San Juan (452,749).

Puerto Rico, 885 miles southeast of the southern coast of Florida, is the easternmost island of the Greater Antilles in the Caribbean. It is separated from the Dominican Republic to the west by the 61 miles of Mona Passage. To the east, St. Thomas of the U.S. Virgin Islands is 34 miles away. Among the offshore islands are Vieques and Culebra to the east, Mona to the west.

The island is crossed by mountain ranges and ringed by a coastal plain that is 15 miles wide at its broadest. The climate is mildly tropical. Rainfall is moderate in the coastal areas, but heavier in the interior mountains.

Many of the people are of mixed African-Spanish descent. (The original Arawak Indians were destroyed in the 16th century.) English and Spanish are the official languages, but Spanish is commonly spoken. Roman Catholicism predominates.

Before World War II, the Puerto Rican economy was based on sugar and such related products as rum. Needlework, mostly piecework produced by women at home, was the second most important activity, and tobacco growing the third. Unemployment was high, poverty widespread; however, after the war a determined drive was begun to foster industrialization on the island.

Under then Governor Rexford Guy Tugwell and the Puerto Rican legislative leader Luis Muñoz Marin, the framework for economic expansion was established. In 1948, "Operation Bootstrap" commenced, giving tax exemptions to new or expanded industry. By 1971 the program had attracted $2 billion in industrial investments and 2,000 plants. The successor program will continue or expand incentives and hopes to attract $4 billion more by 1980.

Today, income from manufacturing is more than three times that from agriculture, although sugar, coffee, tobacco, and rum are still produced and exported. Among the industries attracted by the tax abatement and lower wage scales in Puerto Rico are textiles and apparel, leather and shoes, electronic components, pharmaceuticals, tuna canning, and—increasingly—such heavy industries as metal products and petrochemicals.

In addition, tourist facilities and tourism have greatly expanded. Despite the general economic advance, unemployment continues to be much higher than in the United States. The per capita income, while far below that of the United States, exceeds that of any Latin American country.

Puerto Ricans are U.S. citizens and, if they migrate to this country, vote subject only to local electoral requirements. Puerto Rico does not send members to Congress (although it has a Resident Commissioner in the House of Representatives who may introduce legislation but does not have a vote) and Puerto Rico is not liable to federal taxation.

Beginning in 1948 (as the first elected governor), Luis Muñoz Marin—leader of the Popular Democratic Party and the force behind "Operation Bootstrap"—served four terms, retiring in 1964. During this period the main minority faction was the Statehood Republican Party, which advocated U.S. statehood for Puerto Rico as opposed to the commonwealth status championed by the Popular Democrats. In a plebiscite held in 1967, the vote was 60.5 percent for continuation of commonwealth status, and 38.9 percent for statehood.

In the 1968 gubernatorial election, however, Luis A. Ferré, long a prominent Statehood Republican, who ran as the candidate of the New Progressive Party (which he had helped form during the plebiscite campaign), won with more than 44 percent of the vote. Although Ferré's platform advocated statehood for Puerto Rico, he had made it clear that such a step would depend on a plebiscite "separate from the general elections." In 1972 Ferré was defeated by Rafael Hernández-Colón of the Popular Democratic Party, but in 1976 the New Progressives returned to power under Carlos Romero Barcelo.

Although advocates of Puerto Rican independence have had little impact at the polls, there has long been such a movement on the island. Perhaps its leading figure was the Harvard-educated Pedro Albizu Campos, who died in 1965, aged 73. A leader of the Nationalist Party in Puerto Rico, in 1950 he staged an abortive armed revolt, which included an attempt by some of his followers to assassinate President Truman.

The island was ceded to the United States by Spain in 1898. Congress provided for its civil government by the Foraker Act of 1900 and granted Puerto Ricans U.S. citizenship in 1917 by an "Organic Act," known as the Jones Act. Operating under a constitution much like that of the United States, Puerto Rico has an elected legislature consisting of a Senate and a House of Representatives. In 1977, the Puerto Rican legislature provided for the selection of delegates to the Democratic and Republican conventions by presidential primary, with the first to be held in February 1980.

Migration from Puerto Rico to the mainland has varied with the economic conditions here and on the island. It was very heavy during much of the 1950s, and the 1970 census counted more than 1.8 million persons of Puerto Rican birth in the United States. Substantial numbers of Puerto Ricans have also returned to the island from the United States.

In September 1978, the United Nations Decolonization Committee passed a Cuban-sponsored resolution calling for self-determination for Puerto Rico, recommending that it be included on the UN's list of nongoverning territories as a U.S. colony. In response, committees in both houses of Congress approved resolution in 1979 reaffirming American support of self-determination for the island's people; Gov. Romero-Barceló has pledged to call a referendum on the island's status after the 1980 gubernatorial elections.

Trust Territory of the Pacific Islands—*Status:* UN Trust Territory. *Population:* Trust Terr. 130,000 (1977 est.), Northern Mariana Is. 15,700 (1976 est.). *Area:* 8,511 sq. mi. including lagoons (707 sq. mi. of land). *Administrative Center:* Kolonia, on Ponape.

These islands and atolls, generally known as Micronesia, are scattered over an area of more than three million sq. mi. There are more than 3,000 of them, about 100 inhabited. They stretch 2,300 miles from some 500 miles east of the Philippines almost as far east as the international date line, from about 1° to 22°N. and from 130° to 172°E. The islands fall into three major groups—the Carolines (including the Palau Islands), the Marshalls, and the Marianas (excluding Guam). A number of the islands were the scene of bitter fighting during World War II—Peleliu in the Carolines, Saipan in the Marianas, Kwajalein in the Marshalls. Bikini and Enewetak in the Marshalls have been used as nuclear-test sites.

Subsistence agriculture and fishing are the main economic activities; copra-is the chief export.

The area is under the jurisdiction of the U.S. Secretary of the Interior; administrative authority is vested in a high commissioner who is appointed by the President. The Congress of Micronesia is an elected bicameral legislature with a Senate and a House of Representatives, and has limited powers.

Before World War I, the islands constituted Germany's Pacific possessions north of the equator; after the war, they were placed under Japanese mandate. In 1947, they entered the UN Trusteeship system under American administration as a "strategic" trust: one in which military bases are permissible.

For many years after assuming its trusteeship, the United States neglected the area, permitting the Japanese-built road system and sanitary facilities to deteriorate. In 1966, the World Health Organization reported that health conditions were bad; the United States pledged improvements in this field.

In 1969, Secretary of the Interior Hickel visited the islands and promised immediate steps would be taken to increase the territory's self-government and assure that equal wages would be paid to Micronesians and Americans for doing comparable work. At the same time, it was reported that a political status commission, appointed by the Congress of Micronesia in 1967, had recommended that the territory be made a self-governing nation in free association with the United States or, failing that, seek complete independence. An offer by the United States of "Commonwealth status" like that of Puerto Rico was rejected by the Congress of Micronesia in 1970.

In a July 12, 1979 referendum, four of the six island districts of the Trust Territory—Ponape, Yap, Kosrae and Truk—voted to accept "free association" with the U.S. as the Federated States of Micronesia. Such status entails continued American financial support for 15 years, with Washington to retain responsibility for defense; otherwise the islands will become fully self-governing when the United States terminates its UN Trusteeship in 1981. The Palau (eastern Carolines) and Marshall Islands districts rejected free association, and are seeking to negotiate their independence from Washington. But progress has been hampered by U.S. insistence that any new status must abide by the terms of the UN Trusteeship. Palau and the Marshalls have opposed this as a violation of their sovereign right to draft their own constitutions. For Palau, this means declaring its territorial waters a "nuclear-free zone" and barring permanent military bases—provisions that Washington cannot accept. A July 9, 1979, constitutional referendum is scheduled to deal with these and other substantive issues.

In 1975 the Northern Marianas voted in favor of future commonwealth status and in 1976 the U.S. Congress approved a plan making the islands a commonwealth associated with the United States. Following a March 1977 referendum approving a new constitution—providing for an elected bicameral legislature and an elected governor—Carlos S. Camacho became the islands' first democratically elected chief executive, and the first native islander to administer the Northern Marianas in over 400 years of foreign domination.

Virgin Islands—*Status:* Organized unincorporated territory. *Population:* 110,000 (1977 est.). *Area:* 133 sq. mi. *Capital:* Charlotte Amalie (12,220), on St. Thomas.

The Virgin Islands of the United States form the western end of the Lesser Antilles between the Caribbean and the Atlantic, about 34 miles east of Puerto Rico. They comprise nearly 100 islands and cays, but only three islands are significant—St. Thomas (27 sq. mi.), St. Croix (82 sq. mi.), and St. John (19 sq. mi.). The United States bought the Virgin Islands from Denmark for $25 million in 1917.

St. Thomas is mountainous, with many harbors, of which Charlotte Amalie is one of the finest in the Caribbean. The climate is subtropical, moderated by the trade winds. Rainfall is variable and sometimes so light as to cause drought. Seventy percent of the population is black. Of the rest, considerably more than half are from the United States. English is the official language.

Since the recent phasing out of the peasant-based sugarcane agriculture, there has been little farming on the islands. Tourism is the major industry, and the area has the greatest number of cruise-ship calls in the world. Oil refining and bauxite processing are important. More than half the island of St. John is occupied by the Virgin Islands National Park.

The U.S. Department of the Interior has jurisdiction over the islands. The governor has been elected since 1970. Virgin Islanders are U.S. citizens, but cannot vote in national elections and have no Congressional representation, except for a non-voting delegate in the House since April 1972.

Wake Island—*Status:* Possession. *Population:* 150 (1974 est.). *Area:* 2.5 sq. mi. *Administrative Center:* Wake Islet.

Wake lies in the Pacific some 2,000 miles west of Honolulu and 1,500 miles northeast of Guam, at 19°17′N. and 166°35′E. It is an atoll comprising three islets—Wake, Wilkes, and Peale. They are formed of coral built up on the rim of an underwater volcano; the land averages only 12 feet above sea level.

The island has an aviation base with a 9,800-foot runway. Responsibility for its civil administration was vested in the U.S. Secretary of the Interior in 1962, but since 1974 has been under the Air Force Department.

Wake Island was annexed in 1899. It was attacked by the Japanese on December 7, 1941, and later that month fell after an heroic defense by the small Marine garrison.

U.S. TERRITORIAL ACQUISITIONS, POSSESSIONS, AND LEASEHOLDS

Year	Acquisition
——	**Gross Area (888,685 sq. mi.)** Original territory of the first 13 states and their claims, including part of drainage basin of Red River of the North, south of the 49th parallel, sometimes considered part of Louisiana Purchase; completely acquired by independence treaty (1783; ratified, 1784) with Great Britain.
1803	**Gross Area (827,192 sq. mi.)** Louisiana Purchase acquired from France for about $15 million (60 million francs); total payment, including interest: $23,-213,567.73.
1819	**Gross Area (72,003 sq. mi.)** Florida and adjacent areas purchased from Spain for amount not exceeding $5 million; treaty ratified 1821.
1845	**Gross Area (390,144 sq. mi.)** Independent Republic of Texas annexed and admitted as a state.
1846	**Gross Area (285,580 sq. mi.)** Oregon Territory acquired by treaty with Great Britain, terminating joint occupation.
1848	**Gross Area (529,017 sq. mi.)** Mexican Cession acquired out of the Mexican War; the United States paid $15 million.
1853	**Gross Area (29,640 sq. mi.)** Gadsden Purchase negotiated with Mexico for $10 million; treaty ratified 1854.
1858	**Gross Area (.91 sq. mi.)** By terms of the Guano Island Act (1856), stipulating that the United States could take possession of any uninhabited guano island, Johnston and Sand Islands in the Pacific were claimed; they constitute a possession.
1862	**Gross Area (3.85 sq. mi.)** Palmyra Island, 1,000 miles south of Honolulu, annexed by Hawaii but not included in the state; it constitutes a possession.
1863	**Gross Area (1 sq. mi.)** Under the Guano Island Act (1856), the Swan Islands in the Caribbean were claimed by the United States. The U.S. recognized Honduran sovereignty over the islands on September 1, 1972.
1865	**Gross Area (2 sq. mi.)** Under the Guano Island Act (1856), Navassa in the Caribbean was claimed; it constitutes a possession.
1867	**Gross Area (586,412 sq. mi.)** Alaska purchased from Russia for $7.2 million.
	Gross Area (1.9 sq. mi) Midway Islands, 1,200 miles NW of Honolulu, annexed; they are a possession.
1898	**Gross Area (6,450 sq. mi.)** Independent Republic of Hawaii annexed.
	Gross Area (212 sq. mi.) Guam, in the Marianas, conquered from Spain and formally annexed by peace treaty (ratified, 1899); it constitutes an organized unincorporated territory.
	Gross Area (115,707 sq. mi.) Philippines conquered from Spain; peace treaty (ratified, 1899) stipulated payment of $20 million for the islands; the Philippines became independent on July 4, 1946.
	Gross Area (3,435 sq. mi.) Puerto Rico conquered from Spain and formally annexed by peace treaty (ratified, 1899); granted commonwealth status by Act of Congress on July 25, 1952.
1899	**Gross Area (2.5 sq. mi.)** Wake Island in Central Pacific claimed; it constitutes a possession.

Year	Acquisition
1899	**Gross Area (83 sq. mi.)** American Samoa acquired by partition treaty (ratified, 1900) with Great Britain and Germany; it constitutes an unorganized, unincorporated territory.
1903	**Gross Area (647 sq mi.)** Canal Zone leased from Panama (treaty ratified, 1904); United States paid $10 million supplemented by annual amounts of $250,000 (1913-33); $430,000 (1934-55); $1.93 million (1956-1971); $2.095 million (1972); and $2.33 million (1974 to date). Under the terms of the new treaty of 1977, the Canal Zone will revert to Panama in 1979.
	Gross Area (30 sq. mi.) Guantanamo leased from Cuba for coaling and naval station.
1914	**Gross Area (4.6 sq. mi.)** Corn Islands leased for 99 years from Nicaragua for payment of $3 million; treaty (ratified, 1916) included perpetual right to construct and maintain a ship canal through Lake Nicaragua. The canal rights and the lease of the islands were terminated on April 25, 1971.
1916	**Gross Area (133 sq. mi.)** Virgin Islands purchased from Denmark for $25 million by treaty (ratified in 1917); they constitute an organized unincorporated territory.
1919	**Gross Area (each less than 0.5 sq. mi.)** By terms of the Guano Island Act (1856), Quita Sueño Bank, Roncador Cay, and Serrana Bank in the Caribbean were claimed; 1928 treaty provided Colombia with fishing rights in adjacent waters. On September 8, 1972, the United States renounced all claims.
1922	**Gross Area (.01 sq. mi.)** Kingman Reef in the South Pacific annexed by Act of Congress; it constitutes a possession.
1925	**Gross Area (1.33 sq. mi.)** Swains Island in the Pacific annexed by Resolution of Congress and incorporated in American Samoa.
1934	**Gross Area (2.77 sq. mi. combined)** U.S. control of Howland, Baker, and Jarvis islands in the South Pacific was reasserted under terms of the Guano Island Act (1856); they are possessions.
1939	**Gross Area (27 sq. mi.)** Canton and Enderbury Islands, 1,660 miles SW of Honolulu, controlled jointly by Britain and the United States. They are to be ceded to Kiribati, when the 1979 draft treaty comes into force.
1947	**Gross Land Area (707 sq. mi)** Trust Territory of the Pacific Islands, about 3,000 Micronesian islands and atolls including the Caroline, Marshall, and Mariana groups (except Guam) placed under U.S. jurisdiction by UN Trusteeship System.
1952	**Gross Area (848 sq. mi.)** Ryukyu Islands, including Okinawa, under U.S. jurisdiction by peace treaty with Japan; other islands included in treaty but returned to Japan by an agreement, June 26, 1968, are: Volcano Islands, including Iwo Jima (11 sq. mi.), Bonin Islands (40 sq. mi.), Marcus Island (1 sq. mi.), Rosario Island (less than 0.5 sq. mi.), and Parece Vela. All of the remaining territory was formally returned to Japan on May 15, 1972.
1968	**Gross Area (193 acres)** Mexico ceded to the United States the northern half of Cordova Island in the Rio Grande in return for the Chamizal (630 acres) on December 13, 1968, readjusting the border near El Paso, Texas.

ADMISSION DATES OF STATES TO THE UNION

Delaware	Dec. 7, 1787	Louisiana	April 30, 1812	West Virginia	June 20, 1863
Pennsylvania	Dec. 12, 1787	Indiana	Dec. 11, 1816	Nevada	Oct. 31, 1864
New Jersey	Dec. 18, 1787	Mississippi	Dec. 10, 1817	Nebraska	March 1, 1867
Georgia	Jan. 2, 1788	Illinois	Dec. 3, 1818	Colorado	Aug. 1, 1876
Connecticut	Jan. 9, 1788	Alabama	Dec. 14, 1819	North Dakota	Nov. 2, 1889
Massachusetts	Feb. 6, 1788	Maine	March 15, 1820	South Dakota	Nov. 2, 1889
Maryland	April 28, 1788	Missouri	Aug. 10, 1821	Montana	Nov. 8, 1889
South Carolina	May 23, 1788	Arkansas	June 15, 1836	Washington	Nov. 11, 1889
New Hampshire	June 21, 1788	Michigan	Jan. 26, 1837	Idaho	July 3, 1890
Virginia	June 26, 1788	Florida	March 3, 1845	Wyoming	July 10, 1890
New York	July 26, 1788	Texas	Dec. 29, 1845	Utah	Jan. 4, 1896
North Carolina	Nov. 21, 1789	Iowa	Dec. 28, 1846	Oklahoma	Nov. 16, 1907
Rhode Island	May 29, 1790	Wisconsin	May 29, 1848	New Mexico	Jan. 6, 1912
Vermont	March 4, 1791	California	Sept. 9, 1850	Arizona	Feb. 14, 1912
Kentucky	June 1, 1792	Minnesota	May 11, 1858	Alaska	Jan. 3, 1959
Tennessee	June 1, 1796	Oregon	Feb. 14, 1859	Hawaii	Aug. 21, 1959
Ohio	March 1, 1803	Kansas	Jan. 29, 1861		

CANADA

Area: 3,851,809 sq. mi. **Population:** 23,597,600 (Jan. 1, 1979 est.)

Official Name: Canada **Capital:** Ottawa **Nationality:** Canadian **Language:** English and French are both official languages. About 13% of the population is bilingual; 67% speaks English only, 18% French only, and 2% other languages, such as Italian, German and Ukrainian **Religion:** Roman Catholic 46%, United Church 18% and Anglican 12%. The rest is made up of Presbyterian, Lutheran, Baptist, Jewish, etc. **Flag:** A single red maple leaf with eleven points, centered on a white square; flanked by vertical red bars one half the width of the square. **Anthem:** O Canada; God Save the Queen (royal anthem) **Currency:** Canadian Dollar (1.14 per U.S. $1 as of April, 1979)

Location: North America, occupying all of the continent north of the United States except for Alaska and the French islands of St. Pierre and Miquelon, in the Gulf of St. Lawrence. The second largest country in the world, Canada is bordered on the north by the Arctic Ocean; on the east by Baffin Bay, Davis Strait and the Atlantic Ocean; on the south by the United States; and on the west by the Pacific Ocean and Alaska **Features:** The Shield, a rugged area of pre-Cambrian rock, covers most of eastern and central Canada, or roughly half the entire country. To the north is the Arctic Archipelago and to the west of the Shield is a vast prairie region stretching to the Canadian Rockies. Westernmost Canada, which comprises most of British Columbia, is laced with towering mountain ranges **Chief Rivers:** Mackenzie, Yukon, St. Lawrence, Nelson, Columbia, Churchill

Head of State: Queen Elizabeth II, represented by a governor-general, Edward R. Schreyer, born 1936, assumed office 1978 **Head of Government:** Prime Minister Joseph ("Joe") Clark, born 1939, elected May 22, 1979 **Effective Date of Present Constitution:** The British North America Act of 1867 provides Canada with a form of written constitution; however, as in Britain, many of the country's legal and parliamentary practices are based on unwritten conventions **Legislative Body:** Parliament (bicameral), consisting of a Senate and a House of Commons. The Senate is composed of a maximum of 104 members, appointed until age 75 by the Governor-General on the advice of the Prime Minister. The House of Commons has 282 members, elected for 5 years **Local Government:** 10 provinces, governed by a premier and an elected legislature. There are also 2 large northern territories, Yukon and the Northwest Territories. Yukon is governed by a federal government commissioner and a council of 7 elected members. The Northwest Territories are governed by a commissioner and a council of 9, of whom 5 are appointed and 4 elected

Ethnic Composition (1971): 44.6% of the population is of British Isles descent; 28.7% of French origin; German 6.1%; Italian, 3.4%; Ukrainian 2.7%; Netherlands 2.0% and others 12.5% **Population Distribution:** 75.5% urban **Density:** 6.5 inhabitants per square mile

Largest Cities (M.A. = Metropolitan Area 1977) 1976: Toronto, 633,318 (M.A. 2,849,200); Montreal, 1,080,546 (M.A. 2,809,900); Vancouver, 410,188 (M.A. 1,172,200); Ottawa, 304,462 (M.A. 702,200); Winnipeg, 560,874 (M.A. 581,800); Edmonton, 461,361 (M.A. 573,700); Quebec, 177,082 (M.A. 545,100); Hamilton, 312,003 (M.A. 533,100); Calgary, 469,917 (M.A. 495,100); Kitchener, 131,870 (M.A. 275,400); London, 240,392 (M.A. 273,100); Halifax, 117,882 (M.A. 269,900); Windsor, 196,526 (M.A. 248,600); Victoria, 62,551 (M.A. 218,300); Sudbury, 97,604 (M.A. 157,800); Regina, 149,593 (M.A. 154,600)

Per Capita Income: $7,411 (1977) **Gross National Product (GNP):** $231.8 billion (1978) **Economic Statistics:** Manufacturing accounts for 20% of Gross Domestic Product (chief industries: motor vehicles manufacturers, pulp and paper mills, meat slaughtering and processors, petroleum refining, iron and steel mills, motor vehicles parts and accessories manufacturers, dairy products industry, sawmills and planing mills, miscellaneous machinery and equipment manufacturers, and smelting and refining); about 29% is derived from public administration and services; 24% from trade and finance; 8% from primary industries (agriculture, forestry, fishing, trapping, and mining) **Minerals and Mining:** Crude petroleum, copper, nickel, iron ore, zinc, natural gas, natural gas by-products, sand and gravel, and coal, are exploited in large quantities. Value of mineral production: $19.7 billion (1978) **Labor Force:** 10,004,000 employed (April 1979) with 20% employed in manufacturing, 35% in services and public admin-

istration, 7% in primary industries and 23% in trade and finance **Average industrial earnings (Feb. 1979):** $278.19 per week. The average monthly wage for agricultural workers is $617.00 with board **Foreign Trade:** Exports, chiefly motor vehicles and parts, crude petroleum, fabricated metals, other machinery and equipment, other fabricated inedible materials, metal ores and concentrates, wheat, totaled $51.7 billion in 1978. Imports, chiefly machinery and equipment, motor vehicles and parts, crude petroleum, food, fabricated metals and other fabricated inedible materials, totaled $49.6 billion **Principal Trade Partners:** United States, Britain, Japan, West Germany, Venezuela, Italy, France, Australia, Netherlands, Iran

Vital Statistics: Birthrate, 15.7 per 1,000 of population; death rate, 7.3 **Life Expectancy:** males 69.34 females 76.36 **Health Statistics:** 7.9 hospital beds per 1,000 inhabitants **Infant Mortality:** 13.5 per 1,000 births **Education Statistics:** 15,204 primary and secondary schools, with combined enrollment of 5,368,981 **Enrollment in Higher Education:** 617,110 **GNP Expended on all forms of Education:** 8.0%

Transportation: Surfaced roads total 442,999 miles; earth roads 106,463; total roads 549,462 **Passenger Cars:** 9,554,290 **Railway Mileage:** 43,476 of first main track; total 59,022 **Principal Ports:** Vancouver, Sept Iles, Port Cartier, Montreal, Halifax, Quebec City, Saint John, Hamilton, Baie Comeau, Sarnia **Major Airlines:** Air Canada, the government line, and Canadian Pacific Airlines, a private carrier, operate domestic and international services

Communications: There are both government and privately owned radio and TV stations **No. of Radio Stations:** 436 AM; 323 FM; 8 short wave: 98.5% of homes have radios (excludes car radios) **No. of TV Stations:** 933: 97.3% of homes have TV's; 72.3% have color TV's **No. of Telephones:** 14,488,000: 96.5% of homes have telephones **No. of Newspapers:** 120 dailies; daily circulation 5,193,852 **Weights and Measures:** Old British standards with gradual implementation of the metric system **Travel Requirements:** for entry into Canada proper identification and valid passport

1979 saw the curtain fall on eleven years of Liberal government headed by Prime Minister Pierre Elliott Trudeau. Since assuming office in 1968, Trudeau had waged a continuing battle to maintain a viable, unified Canada. Yet despite Trudeau's best efforts, the many deep-seated problems that have plagued the heterogeneous Canadian nation remain.

Provincial sentiment for greater autonomy and less federal interference, bred of long hostility to Ottawa and the peculiarities of Canada's federal system, was accelerated when, in November 1976, the separatist *Parti Québécois* won a legislative majority in Quebec's provincial elections. René Lévesque, Quebec's new premier, promptly announced his government in favor of independence and for an end to bilingualism in the province, calling the very nature of the Canadian federation into question. However, the PQ has since somewhat modified its stance on separation; in 1979 Premier Lévesque called for acceptance of "sovereignty" for Quebec within an economic association with Canada, as perhaps the best the province could expect to be agreed to by the rest of the nation. And a Canadian Broadcasting Corporation poll conducted in March 1979 revealed fully half of the province's residents would support such a plan. Yet Canadian unity remains fragile. An official report issued in January 1979 by the Task Force on Canadian Unity explicitly recognized Quebec's right to self-determination—even to the point of secession—and urged the federal government to accommodate Quebec (as well as other dissatisfied provinces) or risk breaking up the Canadian federation.

Unfortunately, no national consensus on Québécois separation—or provincial autonomy in

general–has emerged. Trudeau, a federalist Prime Minister whose base of political support remained in French Canada, could not resolve traditional English-versus-French divisions, despite his policies designed to foster bilingualism and to integrate Quebec politically into the mainstream of Canadian life. The Official Languages Act of 1968, making French equal to English in all branches of the federal service, came too late to satisfy the Québécois, and was seen as an affront to non-Francophone Canadians, who do not understand why the language spoken in Quebec must be "official." This animosity became apparent in 1978, when four western provinces joined Ontario in opposition to any future economic association with an independent Quebec.

In addition, suspicion towards the federal government and the economically dominant "eastern establishment" of southern Ontario have contributed to the centrifugal tendencies that could conceivably spell the end to confederation. Alberta, riding the crest of prosperity with an unprecedented oil boom, wants greater control over its mineral wealth. The Maritimes, faced with the highest rates of unemployment in the nation despite federal attempts to help diversify their resource-dependent industries, continue to decry their backward economic situation. And the sparsely-settled Yukon and Northwest Territories, long under the direct tutelage of Ottawa, are pressing their demands for provincial status.

Many of the problems to be faced in uniting a far-flung nation of quarreling provinces can be traced to Canada's form of constitutional government. The British North American Act of 1867 makes the Canadian charter an act of British Parliament, giving greater power to the federal government than to the provinces. Despite revisions such as the Citizenship Act of 1977, ending Canadians' status as "British subjects," all constitutional changes must be approved in London, after the unanimous approval of Ottawa and the provinces. But subsequent attempts to delineate the scope of federal authority and preserve provincial prerogatives have been hampered by a lack of consensus on just what powers can be delegated to the provinces. Although a conference held in Ottawa by Prime Minister Trudeau with the ten provincial premiers in February 1979 did agree on the transfer of federal authority over divorce laws and family matters to the provinces, it failed to achieve unanimity on such issues as provincial authority over fiscal matters. Trudeau subsequently proposed further major revisions in the charter, such as codification of a Canadian bill of rights and the removal of the amendment procedure from the jurisdiction of the British parliament.

Early in his administration, Trudeau had sought to reduce Canada's various international commitments to concentrate on his "just society" domestic policy. Canada has nonetheless increased her world influence–especially among the developing nations–through the foreign assistance programs of the Canadian International Development Agency and by increasing exports of the nation's abundant raw materials; consequently, Canada's balance of payments surplus soared to $3.52 billion in 1978, the largest ever recorded.

But Trudeau's long-range plans to give Canada firmer control over its own economy have been eclipsed by persistent unemployment and continually rising inflation–reaching an annual rate as of May, 1978 of 7.9 and 9.8 percent, respectively–this despite three years of mandatory wage and price controls, imposed by the federal government in 1975.

The twin problems of Quebec separatism and severe economic woes contributed to Prime Minis-

ter Trudeau's defeat in the May 22, 1979, general elections. Opposition leader Joe Clark, side-stepping Trudeau's charges of "treason" for declining to stress the unity issue, instead campaigned on the economy, calling for less government intervention and proposing tax incentives for both business and consumers to spur spending and production. His Progressive Conservatives won 136 seats in the House of Commons–six short of a majority–but only 36 percent of the popular vote. The Liberals won 40 percent of the popular vote, but only 114 parliamentary seats, mostly in Quebec and Ontario. The leftist New Democratic Party increased its standing from 17 to 26 seats, with 18 percent of the vote. And the Quebec-based Social Credit Party won six seats and five percent of the total vote.

HISTORY: Although the Vikings are believed to have visited Canada about A.D. 1000, the first recorded landing was made by John Cabot in 1497. Cabot, an Italian-born explorer in the service of Henry VII of England, landed near Newfoundland and claimed the area for the English king. In 1534, Jacques Cartier planted a cross on the Gaspé Peninsula and claimed the region for France. The intense rivalry that followed as each country tried to extend its claims was to dominate the history of Canada for more than two centuries

1689-1763: French and Indian Wars, a series of colonial wars in North America that reflect Anglo-French rivalry in Europe, culminate in the loss of French control of Canada and the establishment of British rule

1774: Quebec Act is passed, reversing favored treatment accorded British in Quebec and providing for preservation of French culture; the act is to prove instrumental in maintaining loyalty of Canada to Britain following outbreak of the American Revolution

1791: Constitutional Act divides Lower Canada, now southern Quebec, from Upper Canada, now southern Ontario, and establishes limited self-government

1837-41: Rebellions in the two Canadas and growing movement for responsible government cause British government to reunite the two Canadas

1867: British North America Act establishes Dominion of Canada, a confederation of Nova Scotia, New Brunswick, and Lower and Upper Canada, the latter two becoming the provinces of Quebec and Ontario, respectively. (The other components of present-day Canada are added in subsequent years, the last, Newfoundland, not until 1949.)

1914-18: Canada fights on Allied side in World War I; issue of conscription arouses strong opposition from French Canadians, deepening split between the French and English-speaking

1931: Statute of Westminster establishes equality of Canadian Parliament with that of Britain

1939-45: Canada plays vital role in World War II and emerges as one of the major nations of the world

1957: Conservatives, led by John Diefenbaker, take office after 22 years of Liberal Party rule

1963: Liberals, led by Lester Pearson, return to power

1967: French President Charles de Gaulle, on a visit to Canada, calls for a "free Quebec" during speech in Montreal; his speech prompts a sharp rebuke from the Canadian government, causing the French leader to cut short his Canadian visit

1968: Pearson retires and is succeeded by Pierre Elliott Trudeau, a French Canadian lawyer and former justice minister; new elections are held in which decisive Liberal victory gives Canada its first majority government in six years

1969: Canada opens negotiations with Communist China for the establishment of diplomatic relations between the two countries; Commons passes government-sponsored language bill requiring bilingual federal facilities wherever 10 percent of the people of any district speak French

1970: Government invokes wartime powers after separatist terrorists kidnap British diplomat and Quebec labor minister, who is subsequently slain

1971: Trudeau and Kosygin sign a protocol agreement in Moscow calling for regular, high-level consultations; Communist China and Canada exchange ambassadors

1974: Trudeau re-elected with Parliamentary majority

1975: Wage and price controls are imposed for three years

1976: The death penalty is abolished throughout Canada. Parti Québécois takes the Quebec provincial elections

1977: Bill establishing French as primary language in government and education introduced into Quebec's National Assembly. Berger Commission calls for 10-year halt to construction of natural gas pipeline in Northwest until native land claims settled. Citizenship Act becomes law

1978: Soviet nuclear-powered satellite crashes in northern Canada; radiation threat minimal. Trudeau introduces new federal constitution to supercede 1867 Dominion Act. Government halts all development in northern Yukon, considers measures to protect caribou migration. Brief nationwide postal strike halted by act of Parliament which threatens heavy fines and jail sentences for union leaders

1979: Progressive Conservatives elected to power under Joe Clark, ending 11-year term of Prime Minister Trudeau. Official Task Force on Canadian Unity report calls for recognition of Quebec's right to self-determination and secession, proposes granting province powers to "protect and develop its distinctive character" within the Canadian federation. U.S. and Canada sign treaty on disputed Atlantic and Pacific fishing grounds, agreeing to international arbitration on boundary issue and setting up of a joint Fisheries Commission to manage equitably the annual marine harvest

---

ALBERTA

Area: 255,219 square miles **Population:** 1,838,037 (1976 Census); 1,950,300 (June 1, 1978 est.) ranks fourth; population density 3.03; urban, 75.0%; rural 25.0%

Capital: Edmonton **Major Cities, (1976 Census metropolitan area populations):** Edmonton 554,228; Calgary, 469,917**Ethnic Composition:** British Isles, 47%; German, 14%; Ukrainian, 8%; Scandinavian, 6%; French, 6%; Netherlands, 4%; and Native Indian, 3%; other, 12% **Religion:** United Church, 28%; Roman Catholic, 24%; Anglican, 10%; Lutheran, 8%; Presbyterian, 4%; other, 26% **Vital Statistics (per 1,000 population, 1978):** birth rate, 16.9; death rate, 6.0; marriage rate, 9.3; divorce rate (1976), 3.1; infant mortality (per 1,000 live births, 1975), 14.9

Location and Geography: Except for the northeast corner and the mountainous fringe on its western border, Alberta is underlain with arable soil, and irrigation has made the semi-arid far south and east productive for agricultural purposes. Most of the province is now very fertile agricultural land

Government: Alberta became a province in 1905 and is represented in the Federal Government by 21 members in the House of Commons and 5 Senators. The provincial government is unicameral with a Legislative Assembly of 79 members. In March 1979, 74 Progressive Conservatives, four members of the Social Credit Party and one New Democrat were elected to the Legislature **Premier:** Honourable Peter Lougheed **Salary and allowance:** $46,195

Education (1977-78): In Alberta, there are 1,389 primary and secondary schools; 18,725 schoolrooms; 23,876 teachers; and 443,408 grades 1-12 students enrolled. Total full-time winter session students enrolled at 3 universities, 31,827, and 8,190 full-time students enrolled at 6 Alberta public colleges

Net value of production in goods-producing industries (1978 est.): $16,922,000,000. Mining represented 53.3% of this total, construction 20.1%, agriculture 8.9% and manufacturing 15.5%. Oil and natural gas revenue is increasing annually and has made the province Canada's leading producer of mineral products with a value of $9,271 million in 1978. In 1978 Alberta produced 85% of the crude petroleum, 87% of the natural gas and 33% of the coal in the nation **Leading manufacturing industries (1978):** slaughtering and meat processing, petroleum refining, metal fabricating industries, chemical & chemical products industries, primary metals industries. **Average industrial earnings (Jan. 1979):** $292.22 per week **Cash receipts from farming operations (1978):** $2,326,127,000; 42.3% derived from cattle and calves, 13.6% from wheat, 9.1% from barley, 10.9% from rapeseed, and 4.6% from dairy products **Families with incomes over $10,000 (1977):** 65.7% **Per capita personal income (1977):** $7,730

Provincial Finances: Gross budgetary revenue (est., fiscal year 1979-80): $5.26 billion (excl. funds allocated to the Alberta Heritage Savings Trust Fund). Gross budgetary expenditures (est., fiscal year 1979-80): $4.52 billion

Daily newspapers: 9 **Telephones in service: (February 1979):** 1,439,765 **Radio stations:** 109 **Homes with radios (1978):** 98% **Homes with TV's (1978):** 96%**Hospital beds (March 31, 1977):** 14,076 (7.5 beds per 1,000 population) **Residents per physician (Dec. 1978):** 707

Motor vehicles (1977-78): 1,467,280 **Residents per motor vehicle:** 1.3 **Motor vehicle deaths (1978):** 503

The first European to explore Alberta was Pierre Boucher, Sieur de Boucherville, in 1751. Boucher was an agent of the English Hudson's Bay Company, but it was not until over forty years later, in 1795, that the Company and its rival, the French Northwest Company, established the first European settlements in the province. Both of the companies set up their trading posts near Edmonton, although trapping activities were concentrated further north.

In 1869 the government of the region was transferred from the Hudson's Bay Company to the newly formed Dominion of Canada, but widespread settlement was delayed until the Canadian Pacific Railroad reached the province in the mid-1880's. After the railroad made eastern markets accessible, settlers—mostly ranchers and farmers—began trickling into the region. They found that although it is far north in latitude, most of the land in Alberta is fertile.

With the development and introduction of early-ripening Marquis wheat in the early part of the 20th century, settlers poured into the west, coming in almost equal numbers from the U.S., the U.K., eastern Canada, and northern Europe. Alberta's population rose from 73,000 in 1901 to 374,000 in 1911. Since then its population has risen steadily, although less spectacularly.

Following World War II, the agricultural nature of the province began to change with the discovery of new oil fields near Leduc in 1947. In 1970, for the first time since those finds, Alberta suffered a decline in oil revenue due to increased demand, lack of major discoveries, and a drop in exploration as the oil industry shifted its attention to the far north. In early 1975, however, the federal government along with Ontario and Alberta agreed to invest $600 million to keep alive the Athabasca tar sands development. Alberta also has reserves of more than 100 billion tons of high quality coking coal. In an effort to make northern Alberta more attractive to developers, the federal and provincial governments have reached agreement on a program to build and improve transportation facilities in the north.

Alberta has had only four changes of government since it became a province. The Liberal Party held office from 1905 to 1921, the United Farmers Association from 1921 to 1935, and the Social Credit Party until 1971, when the Conservatives, led by Peter Lougheed, unseated them. In early 1973 Lougheed made good on a campaign pledge by authorizing rebates on property-tax payments. He was subsequently rewarded with landslide election victories in 1975 and 1979.

BRITISH COLUMBIA

Area: 366,255 square miles **Population:** 2,466,608 (1976 Census); 2,555,800 (Jan. 1, 1979 estimate); ranks third; population density (1978): 6.9; urban, 75.7%; rural 24.3% **Capital:** Victoria **Major Cities (1976 Census Metropolitan Areas):** Vancouver, 1,166,348; Victoria, 218,250

Ethnic Composition: British Isles, 58%; German, 9%; Scandinavian, 5%; French, 4%; Netherlands, 3%; Ukrainian, 3%; Italian, 2%; and Native Indians, 2% **Religion:** United Church, 25%; Roman Catholic, 19%; Anglican, 18%; Lutheran, 6%; Presbyterian, 5%; Baptist, 3%; no religion, 13% **Vital Statistics (per 1,000 population, 1978):** birth rate, 14.7; death rate, 7.5; marriage rate, 8.5; divorce rate, 3.3; infant mortality (per 1,000 live births), 12.0

Location and Geography: Parallel ranges of mountains and fertile valleys cover all but the northeast corner of the province. There is also a deeply indented Pacific shoreline. Because it is warmed by the Japanese Current, the climate of the coastal region is moderate

Government: British Columbia became a province in 1871 and is represented in the Federal Government by 23 members in the House of Commons and 6 Senators. The provincial government is unicameral with a Legislative Assembly of 57 members. In May 1979, 31 members of the Social Credit Party and 26 members of the New Democratic Party were elected to the Legislature **Premier:** Honourable William R. Bennett **Salary and allowance:** $52,000

BRITISH COLUMBIA

Provincial and State Capitals

Education: Of the population five years of age and over, 18% have less than Grade 9 education, 63% have a secondary school education and 19% have a university degree (1976 Census). **Total expenditures on education (1977-78):** $948,000,000 **Schools:** 1,615 primary and secondary schools (Sept. 1978) with a combined enrollment of 517,786 **Colleges:** Three degree-granting universities, 18 vocational schools and community colleges and one technical institute with a combined enrollment of 112,711 (1977-78)

Value added in goods-producing industries (1976): $8,889,789,000; manufacturing represents 46% and construction 26%. Slightly more than half of the manufacturing total comes from wood industries and pulp paper. Mining which accounted for 20% of the province's industry in the 1940's now accounts for only 11% **Leading manufacturing industries (1975):** Pulp and paper mills, sawmills and planing mills, and veneer and plywood mills **Average industrial earnings (1978):** $301.28 per week **Value of fishery products (1977):** $372 million **Cash receipts from farming operations:** $558 million (1978), of which 23% is derived from dairy products, and 17% from poultry and eggs **Families with incomes of $10,000 and over (1976):** 62% **Per capita personal income (1978):** $8,718 **Unemployment (1978):** 8.3%

Provincial Finances: Gross general revenue (fiscal year 1977-78): $4.52 billion; gross general expenditure, $4.37 billion

Daily Newspapers: 19 **Combined circulation (1978):** 571,227 **Telephones (1978):** 1,692,238 **Homes with radios (1978):** 99% **Homes with TV's (1978):** 96%

Hospital beds (1978): 18,039 (7.1 beds per 1,000 population) **Physicians (1977):** 3,892 (1.6 per 1,000 population)

Motor vehicles (1978): 1,452,700 **Residents per motor vehicle (1978):** 1.7 **Motor vehicle deaths (1978):** 640

The first European to visit what is now the province of British Columbia was a Spaniard, Juan Perez, who came while on a voyage in search of the Northwest Passage. Two years later Capt. James Cook explored and established the general outline of the northwest coast. Cook stopped only briefly on the coast of Vancouver Island, but while there he obtained several sea-otter pelts from the Indians. When he arrived in Macao, on the south China coast, and traded the pelts, the potential profits of the sea-otter became clear. Soon after Cook published an account of his voyage, a legion of trading ships descended on the coast, setting the stage for a decades-long controversy between Spain and England over which was the rightful claimant to the area.

With the coming of trappers and traders after the 1790's, English control was established, and the merged Northwest and Hudson Bay Companies controlled the region until the middle of the nineteenth century. In 1849 and 1858 Vancouver Island and mainland British Columbia, respectively, were made English colonies. In 1866 the two were united and agreed to become part of the Dominion of Canada in 1871 on condition that a transcontinental railroad be built.

The completion of the railroad in 1885 spurred the development of agriculture, forestry and mining. The economy received a second boost in 1914 when the Panama Canal opened, giving Vancouver direct sea-borne access to European markets.

During the twentieth century the province has continued to grow. The demands of World War II sparked spectacular growth in the forest industries, hydroelectric power, and manufacturing. These additional jobs contributed to a trebling of the population since 1941.

In December 1975, the New Democratic Party was unseated by the Social Credit Party headed by William Bennett. The "Socreds" pledged to repeal the Mineral Royalties Act of the previous administration, legislation which had been strongly opposed by the mining industry. But the May 1979 elections saw the Social Credit majority reduced to 31 seats in the Assembly, with the NDP winning the remaining 26 seats.

MANITOBA

Area: 251,000 square miles **Population:** 1,021,506 (1976 Census); 1,029,900 (Jan. 1, 1979 estimate): ranks fifth; population density 4.8; urban, 69.9%; rural, 30.1% **Capital:** Winnipeg **Largest Cities (1976 Census):** Winnipeg, 578,217; Brandon, 34,901

Ethnic Composition: British Isles, 42%; German, 12%; Ukrainian, 12%; French, 9%; Native Indian, 4%; Polish, 4% and Scandinavian, 4% **Religion:** United Church, 26%; Roman Catholic, 25%; Anglican, 12%; Lutheran, 7%; Mennonite, 6%; Ukrainian Catholic, 6% **Vital Statistics (per 1,000 population):** birth rate, 16.4; death rate, 8.1; marriage rate, 8.1; divorce rate, 1.90; infant mortality (per 1,000 live births), 15.6

Location and Geography: Located between Ontario and Saskatchewan, Manitoba is a vast plain which rises gradually to the west and south. On the southern prairie the fertility of the land varies greatly, from the black gumbo of the Red River valley to sandy soil in the southwest and stonier soil between Lakes Winnipeg and Manitoba

Government: Manitoba became a province in 1870 **No. of representatives in Parliament:** 14 members in the House of Commons and 6 Senators **Type of legislature:** Unicameral with a Lieutenant-Governor, Executive Council and a Legislative Assembly of 57 members **Current government:** In October 1977, 33 Progressive Conservatives, 23 New Democrats and one Liberal were elected to the Legislature **Premier:** Honourable Sterling Lyon **Salary and allowance:** $38,799

Education (April 1979): 25.1% of the population 15 years of age and over had Grade 8 or less; 49.5% attended high school; 8.1% had some post-secondary education, 10.1% had a post-secondary certificate or diploma and 7.2% had a university degree **Total education expenditures (1977-78):** $677,942,000 **Schools:** 811 primary and secondary schools (1977-78) with a combined enrollment of 237,153 **Colleges:** Seven degree-granting universities and eight post-secondary non-university institutions with a combined enrollment of 20,880

Value added in goods-producing industries (1976): $2,760,935,000; manufacturing represented 42.3% of this total, construction 22.2%, agriculture 19.9%, and mining 8.6% **Value of manufacturing shipment (1976):** $2,772,543,000 **Leading manufacturing industries:** slaughtering and meat processing, agricultural implements, dairy products, feed, miscellaneous food processing, fabricated structural metal industry **Average industrial earnings (Feb. 1979):** $250.17 per week **Cash receipts from farming operations (1978):** $1,129,649,000 with 21.0% derived from wheat, 25.2% from cattle and calves, 8.7% from barley, 8.8% from hogs, 5.0% from flaxseed, 7.8% from rapeseed and 5.1% from dairy products **Per capita personal income (1977):** $6,899 **Unemployment (1977):** 6.5%

Provincial Finances: Estimated gross general revenue, fiscal year 1978-79, $1,744.7 million; estimated gross general expenditure, $1,863.3 million

Daily newspapers: 8 **Total circulation:** 254,929 **Number of telephones per 100 population (1977):** 60.9 **Homes with radios:** 98% **Homes with TV's:** 96%

Hospital beds (1978): 7,900 (7.7 beds per 1,000 population) **Physicians (1976):** 1,769 (population per physician, 581)

Motor Vehicles (1977): 603,318 **Residents per motor vehicle:** 1.7 **Motor vehicle deaths (1976):** 220

Despite the fact that it is known as a "prairie province," only a small southern portion of Manitoba's 251,000 square miles is actually treeless grassland. The remainder ranges from forest land, to lakes, subarctic tundra, and—most surprisingly of all for a "prairie" province—nearly 400 miles of salt-water coast on Hudson Bay. Its name and reputation derives from the fact that only the prairie area south of the infertile Pre-Cambrian shield is suitable for large-scale settlement.

Manitoba is bounded on the south by the U.S., on the west by Saskatchewan, on the north by the Keewatin District, and on the east by Ontario, but it was through its Hudson Bay sea coast that early European explorers, trappers, and settlers first came to the province. The first European to enter the territory was probably Sir Thomas Button in 1612. Nearly 60 years later, in 1670, the Hudson's Bay Company began building forts in the area, principally at the mouths of the Nelson and

MANITOBA

MILES

KILOMETERS

⊕ Provincial Capital

MANITOBA
NORTHERN PART

HUDSON BAY

N.W. TERRITORIES

SASKATCHEWAN

ONTARIO

MINNESOTA

N. DAKOTA

SASKATCHEWAN

Longitude West of Greenwich

© C.S. HAMMOND & Co.—Maplewood, N.J.

NEW BRUNSWICK

Provincial Capitals ⊛

© C. S. HAMMOND & Co., Maplewood, N. J.

Churchill rivers. Throughout the 18th century the area was affected by the feud between the English Hudson's Bay Company and the French North-west Company. The feud between the two fur-trading companies continued until 1821 when the rivals amalgamated.

Until the advent of the steamship and railroad in the mid-19th century, white men came to the provinces mostly as trappers and traders. An exception was the historic Red River Settlement (now Winnipeg), which was established in 1812, but it was not until the late 1860's that steam navigation from the north and railroads from the south and east made the area accessible to large numbers of settlers.

In 1870 the province of Manitoba was organized. It was linked by rail to the U.S. in 1878 and with eastern Canada in 1881, and the population, which was a mere 25,000 in 1871, grew to 250,000 in 1901 and 700,000 in 1931.

Like their prairie neighbors in both Canada and the U.S., Manitobans suffered during the 1920s and '30s, but since the hard years of the Great Depression, the growth of mineral, forest, and manufacturing industries, and the return of markets for its agricultural products have helped the province become one of Canada's richest. While it was once solely dependent on agriculture, its economy is now substantially diversified. Manufacturing accounts for over 40 percent of the province's net produced value; agriculture less than 25 percent.

In 1969 the New Democratic Party won control after eleven years of Conservative rule. The NDP introduced public automobile insurance, medicare, and other wide-ranging social programs. In 1974, the province agreed to fund 25 percent of a pilot project which would give a guaranteed minimum income to 2,500 residents, the federal government paying the balance.

An upset victory in the October 1977 elections returned the Progressive Conservatives to office after eight years.

NEW BRUNSWICK

Area: 27,633 square miles **Population:** 677,250 (1976 Census); 699,200 (Apr. 1, 1979 estimate); ranks eighth; population density 24.5 per square mile; urban, 52%; rural, 48% **Capital:** Fredericton **Major cities (1976 census agglomeration) populations:** Fredericton, 45,885; Moncton, 77,571; Saint John, 112,974

Ethnic Composition: British Isles, 58%; French, 37% **Religion:** Roman Catholic, 52%; Baptist, 14%; United Church, 13%; Anglican, 11% **Vital Statistics (per 1,000 population 1976):** birth rate, 17.4; death rate, 7.7; marriage rate, 8.5; divorce rate, 1.38; infant mortality (per 1,000 live births), 13.2

Location and Geography: Nearly rectangular in shape, New Brunswick has an extensive sea coast: on the Bay of Chaleur on the north, the Gulf of St. Lawrence and Northumberland Strait on the east, and the Bay of Fundy on the south. Much of the soil is rocky and unfit for agriculture, but generous rainfall produces prolific forest growth. The Bay of Fundy, which separates New Brunswick and Nova Scotia, has the world's highest tides, and there are proposals to harness these to produce electric power

Government: New Brunswick became a province in 1867 and is represented in the Federal Government by 10 members in the House of Commons and 10 Senators. The provincial government is unicameral with a Legislative Assembly of 58 members. In October 1978, 30 Progressive Conservatives and 27 Liberals, plus the speaker were elected to the Legislature **Premier:** Honourable Richard Hatfield **Salary and allowance:** $44,357

Education (1972): In the Atlantic Provinces (New Brunswick, Newfoundland, Nova Scotia, and Prince Edward Island) 95% of the population had over Grade IV education; 28.8%, secondary school; and 4.5%, university **Total expenditures on education** (school year ended June 30, 1978): $197,800,000 **Schools:** 469 primary and secondary schools (1978-79) with a combined enrollment of 158,906 (Sept. 30, 1978) **Colleges:** Four degree-granting universities with a total enrollment of 10,817. There are 8 campuses known as New Brunswick Community Colleges which com-

prise what used to be trade schools and institutes of technology with a full-time enrollment of 3,982 (Sept. 30, 1979)

Value added in goods-producing industries (1977 est.): $1,506,000. Manufacturing represented 46% of this total, construction 29%, electric power 8%, agriculture 4%, forestry 5%, mining 6% **Leading manufacturing industries (1975):** pulp and paper mills, sawmills and planing mills, and fishery products **Average industrial earnings (Mar. 1979):** $255.00 per week **Cash receipts from farming operations (1978):** $118,185,000 **Families with incomes over $10,0u0 (1977 est.):** 59.1% **Per capita personal income (1978):** $5,996 **Unemployment (1978):** 12.6%

Provincial Finances: Estimated gross general revenue, fiscal year 1978-79, $1,267.1 million; estimated gross general expenditure, $1,208.9 million

Daily newspapers (1978): 6 **Circulation:** 145,690 **Telephones per 100 population (1978):** 51 **Homes with radios:** 98.4% **Homes with TV's:** 97.4%

Hospital beds (excluding provincial hospitals, 1978): 4,293 (6.2 per 1,000 population) **Physicians (1977):** 670 (population per physician, 975)

Motor vehicles (1977): 322,049 **Residents per motor vehicle:** 2.1

Motor vehicle deaths (1975): 190

There was little settlement of New Brunswick during the French period, and for 20 years following the beginning of British rule (1763), the sea coasts and river valleys were largely left to the fur traders. Then "Tories"– "Loyalists" as they are called in New Brunswick–escaping from the rebelling American Colonies southward, settled the area in 1783. At that time the County of Sunbury was split from Nova Scotia and made a separate province named New Brunswick, after the family name of the reigning monarch, George III.

Other immigrations brought Scottish farmers and laborers and immigrants from Great Britain after the Napoleonic wars of the next century. By 1842 the population had swelled to 74,000.

The 600 mile long New Brunswick coast and the softwood forests of the interior encouraged the development of lumbering, shipbuilding, and fisheries and, helped by preferential tariffs and trade agreements with England, the colony was initially prosperous. Its resources were a mixed blessing, however, for they hindered the development of a well balanced economy and political system.

By 1866 declining economic fortunes forced the colony into a not wholly welcome union with the nascent Dominion of Canada. A major railroad link with Montreal was established as a result of a pre-unification agreement, but its promise of economic salvation was dimmed as the coming of the steamship, and the depletion of its forest reserves brought economic ruin to many provincial industries.

Since World War II some success has occurred in developing a more balanced economy. Although still heavily oriented towards extractive industries and their exportation, the province has attempted to develop manufacturing industries for processing the raw materials.

The service sector accounts for 70 percent of provincial employment; nearly one-quarter of the labor force works in the public sector, including military establishments at Oromocto and Chatham.

NEWFOUNDLAND

Area: 156,185 square miles **Population:** 557,725 (1976 Census); 572,900 (Jan. 1, 1979 estimate); ranks ninth; population density 3.9; urban 58.9%; rural 41.1% **Capital:** St. John's **Major cities (1976 metropolitan area populations):** St. John's, 143,390; Corner Brook, 25,198

Ethnic Composition: British Isles, 94%; French, 3%; **Religion:** Roman Catholic, 37%; Anglican, 28%; United Church, 19% **Vital**

Statistics (per 1,000 population): birth rate, 20.0; death rate, 6.0; marriage rate, 7.5; divorce rate, 0.76; infant mortality (per 1,000 live births), 14.6

Location and Geography: Newfoundland includes the island of Newfoundland (43,359 square miles) and the coast of Labrador (112,828 square miles) on the mainland. They are separated by the Strait of Belle Isle which is nine and a half miles wide at its narrowest point. The island's surface is low, rolling, and rocky. Its highest point is Lewis Hill (2,672 feet) in the Northern peninsula. The west coast and river valleys are thickly forested

Government: Newfoundland became a province in 1949 and is represented in the Federal Government by 7 members in the House of Commons and 6 Senators. The provincial government is unicameral with a House of Assembly of 52 members. In June 1979, 33 Progressive Conservatives and 19 Liberals were elected to the House **Premier:** Honourable Brian Peckford **Salary and allowance:** $43,690

Education (April 1979): 36.4% of the population 15 years of age and over had Grade 8 or less; 43.1% attended high school; 6.2% had some post-secondary education; 9.2% had a post-secondary certificate or diploma; 5.4% had a university degree **Total expenditures on education (1977-78):** $344,657,000 **Schools:** 710 primary and secondary schools (1977-78) with a combined enrollment of 156,550 **Colleges:** One degree-granting university and six non-university post-secondary institutions with enrollment of 8,820

Value added in goods-producing industries (1976): $1,295,826,000; Construction represented 31.1% of this total; mining 29.5%, manufacturing 20.1%, electric power 10.6% and fisheries 5%. (The development of the huge iron ore deposits in Labrador has boosted Newfoundland to 6th position in the nation's production of minerals. In 1978 production was valued at $611,357,000. Iron ore contributed 82.6% of the total and represented 43.9% of the total Canadian production.) **Value of manufacturing shipments (1976):** $599,084,000 **Leading manufacturing industries:** pulp and paper mills and fishery products **Average industrial earnings (Feb. 1979):** $265.77 per week **Families with incomes over $12,000 (1977):** 57.8% **Per capita personal income (1977):** $5,039 **Unemployment (1978):** 16.4%

Provincial Finances: Estimated gross general revenue, fiscal year 1978-79: $1,179.1 million; estimated gross general expenditure, $1,242.1 million

Daily newspapers (1976): 3 **Circulation:** 50,302 **Telephones per 100 population (1977):** 39.1 **Homes with radios:** 97.1% **Homes with TV's:** 97.0%

Hospital beds (1978): 3,646 (6.4 per 1,000 population) **Physicians (1976):** 779 (population per physician, 720)

Motor Vehicles (1977): 178,425 **Residents per motor vehicle:** 3.2 **Motor vehicle deaths:** 78

Newfoundland, which consists of the island of Newfoundland itself and the coast of Labrador, is a land of great natural resources. Huge forests of spruce and pine cover much of the area; the inland wilderness has an abundance of wildlife; great mineral wealth lies hidden beneath the surface; hydroelectric power is abundant; and the Grand Banks, in which it is located, is a fishing ground of legendary richness.

Despite these resources, the history of Newfoundland is largely one of great promise only partially fulfilled. It was discovered by John Cabot in 1497, and Sir Humphrey Gilbert made a formal claim for Britain in 1583, but the island remained a distant outpost visited only by fishing boats until the end of the 18th century. By then a court system and land-based commerce had been established, but by 1850 the population had only increased to 30,000.

Fishing and forestry gave the island limited prosperity through the 1860s and '70s, and fueled by this the small province chose not to join the Canadian nation when it was granted dominion status in 1867. The question of union was taken up again in the 1890s, but by then the province's precarious economic condition made it impossible. It remained independent until February 16, 1934 when, after surveying the province's debts, Britain reestablished direct rule, which was then

maintained until Newfoundland was united with Canada in 1949.

Many economists today believe that Newfoundland's continuing economic problems can be solved only by developing resource industries and increasing the volume of local processing and refining, as opposed to the continuing export of raw natural resources.

Provincial elections on June 18, 1979 saw the Progressive Conservatives increase their majority in the 52-member Assembly to 33, with the Liberals winning the remaining 19 seats.

NOVA SCOTIA

Area: 21,425 square miles **Population:** 828,571 (1976 Census); 839,600 (Jan. 1, 1978 estimate); ranks seventh; population density 40.6 **Capital:** Halifax **Major city populations (1976 metropolitan populations):** Halifax, 235,440; Dartmouth, 65,341

Ethnic Composition: British Isles, 77%; French, 10%; German, 5% **Religion:** Roman Catholic, 36%; United Church, 21%; Anglican, 17%; Baptist, 13%; Presbyterian, 5% **Vital Statistics (per 1,000 population, 1975):** birth rate, 15.5; death rate, 8.4; marriage rate, 8.4; divorce rate, 2.1; infant mortality (per 1,000 live births), 13.8

Location and Geography: The province is a 380-mile long peninsula. The Atlantic coast is generally rocky; the slopes facing the Bay of Fundy and Gulf of St. Lawrence, sheltered from the Atlantic storms by a series of low ridges that run through the center of the province, consist of fertile plains and river valleys. Cape Breton Island, the northeast portion of the province, is mostly rugged upland and is divided almost in two by the saltwater Bras d'Or Lake, in reality a land-enclosed extension of the sea

Government: Nova Scotia became a province in 1867 and is represented in the Federal Government by 11 members in the House of Commons and 10 Senators. The provincial government is unicameral with a House of Assembly of 52 members. In October 1978, 31 Progressive Conservatives, 17 Liberals and four New Democrats were elected to the House **Premier:** Honourable John M. Buchanan, Q. C. **Salary and allowance:** $53,000 (aprox.)

Education (1971): In Nova Scotia 91% of the population had completed Grade IV education; 46.5% secondary school; and 8.3% have at least some university training **Total expenditures on education (1977-78):** $350 million **Schools:** 632 primary and secondary schools (1977-78) with a combined enrollment of 202,000 **Colleges:** 10 degree-granting universities and colleges with a full-time enrollment of 19,800 in 1977-78

Value added in goods-producing industries (1976): $1,541,015,000; manufacturing represents 46.7% of this total; construction, 30.2%; mining, 5.9%; and fisheries, 6.9%. The province vies with British Columbia each year as the nation's leading producer of fish products. These in 1977 had a total value of $294,208,000 **Leading manufacturing industries (1978):** Petroleum and coal products, food and beverage, paper and allied industries, and transportation equipment industries **Average industrial earnings (1978):** $223.72 per week

Cash Receipts from farming operations (1978): $143,891,000, with 32.0% derived from dairy products, 24.8% from livestock, 20.6% from poultry and eggs, 24.8% from crops **Families with incomes over $10,000 (1976):** 76% **Per capita personal income (1978 est.):** $6,563 **Unemployment (1978):** 10.6%

Provincial Finances: Revenue plus recoveries, forecast fiscal year 1978-79, $1,380,740,400; estimated 1978-79, $1,506,661,700. Expenditure, forecast 1978-79, $1,426,242,100; estimated 1979-80, $1,493,629,200

Daily newspapers (1978): 6 **Circulation:** 183,417 **Telephones per 100 population (1978):** 53.7 **Homes with radios:** 94.2% **Homes with TV's:** 96.7%

Hospital beds (1978): 6,385 (7.2 per 1,000 population) **Physicians:** 1,304 (population per physician approx. 645)

Motor vehicles (1978): 456,045 **Motor vehicle deaths (1977):** 183

John Cabot is regarded, on the basis of his 1497 visit to Cape Breton Island, as the "discoverer" of Nova Scotia, despite the belief that Norsemen and European fishermen probably visited the island long before Columbus arrived in the New World. Britain's claim to Nova Scotia began with Cabot's

Labrador

LABRADOR
(PART OF NEWFOUNDLAND)

0   50   100   150 mi.
0   50 100 150 km.

Labrador
Sea

SAGUENAY
PROVINCIAL
PARK
Havre-
St-Pierre

QUEBEC

NEWFOUNDLAND

L A B R A D O R

MEALY MTS.

QUEBEC

Gulf

of

St. Lawrence

LONG RANGE MTS.

N E W F O U N D L A N D

ATLANTIC

OCEAN

St. John's

Avalon

Pen.

ST. PIERRE & MIQUELON
(France)

NEWFOUNDLAND

MILES
0 20 40   60   80   100

KILOMETERS
0 10 20 40   60   80 100

Provincial Capital

© C.S. HAMMOND & Co., Maplewood, N.J.

NOVA SCOTIA

MILES

KILOMETERS

⊕ Provincial Capitals

© C.S. HAMMOND & Co., Maplewood, N.J.

ONTARIO

visit, but its sovereignty was contested by France until Halifax was firmly established as a naval and military base in 1749, and the Acadians were expelled in 1755. Following the American Revolution, nearly 30,000 "Loyalists" emigrated to Nova Scotia, becoming its first citizens. The province was a founding member of the Canadian confederation.

Population growth, increased trade, and wealth marked the first half of the 19th century. In 1846 the colony had one-third as much shipping tonnage as France, but today Nova Scotia shares many of the problems of its neighboring provinces. Its economy is largely dependent on low-technology industries such as fishing and mining, and though the federal government is attempting to diversify the economy, unemployment and economic disparity between the Maritime Provinces and the rest of Canada remains.

A growing vacationland, Nova Scotia has two national parks and nine designated historic parks.

ONTARIO

Area: 412,582 square miles **Population:** 8,264,465 (1976 Census); 8,479,900 (Jan. 1, 1979 estimate); ranks first; population density, 23.3; urban, 61.2% rural, 18.8% **Capital:** Toronto **Major cities (1977 metropolitan area population estimates):** Toronto, 2,849,000; Ottawa, 702,200; Hamilton, 533,100; St. Catharines-Niagara Falls, 304,600; London, 273,100; Kitchener, 275,400; Sudbury, 157,800; Thunder Bay, 119,900; Oshawa, 138,600

Ethnic Composition: British Isles, 59%; French, 10%; German, 6%; Italian, 6% **Religion:** Roman Catholic, 33%; United Church, 22%; Anglican, 16%; Presbyterian, 7%; Lutheran, 3%; Baptist, 4% **Vital Statistics (per 1,000 population):** birth rate, 14.8; death rate, 7.3; marriage rate, 8.4; divorce rate, 2.25; infant mortality (per 1,000 live births), 12.3

Location and Geography: Located in the center of Canada, Ontario is a geographic and cultural transition between eastern Quebec and the midwestern prairie provinces. It has a freshwater shoreline of 1,700 miles on the Great Lakes and St. Lawrence River and 750 miles of salt-water shorelines on Hudson and James Bays. The northern part is within the Canadian Shield, but nearly 17.5 million acres are arable

Government: Ontario became a province in 1867 and is represented in the Federal Government by 95 members in the House of Commons and 24 Senators. The provincial government is unicameral with a Legislative Assembly of 125 members. In June 1977, 58 Progressive Conservatives, 34 Liberals, and 33 New Democrats were elected to the Legislature **Premier:** Honourable William G. Davis **Salary and allowance:** $52,000

Education (April 1979): 21.9% of the population 15 years of age and over had Grade 8 or less; 53.5% attended high school; 7.7% had some post-secondary education; 8.4% had a post-secondary certificate or diploma; 8.5% had a university degree **Total expenditures on education (1977-78):** $6,157,725,000 **Schools:** 5,232 primary and secondary schools (1977-78), with a combined enrollment of 2,012,985 **Colleges:** 22 degree-granting universities and 30 non-university post-secondary institutions with enrollment of 222,850

Value added in goods-producing industries (1976): $31,421,357,000, 38.3% of Canada's total; manufacturing contributed 70.3%; construction, 16.9%; mining, 4.6%; and agriculture, 4.4%. The province is the second largest producer of mineral products with a total value of $2,595 million in 1978 **Value of manufacturing shipments (1976):** $49,644,516,000, 50.6% of the national total **Leading manufacturing industries:** motor vehicles and their parts and accessories, iron and steel mills, slaughtering and meat processing, miscellaneous machinery and equipment, pulp and paper mills and petroleum refining **Average industrial earnings (Feb. 1979):** $273.84 per week **Cash receipts from farming operations (1978):** $3,357,154,000, with 27.1% derived from cattle and calves, dairy products 15.7%, hogs 11.7%, tobacco 7.4%, poultry 5.8% and vegetables 4.8% **Families with incomes over $12,000 (1977):** 77.1% **Per capita personal income (1977):** $8,109 **Unemployment (1978):** 7.2%

Provincial finances: Estimated gross general revenue, fiscal year 1978-79 was $14.0 billion; estimated gross general expenditure, $15.0 billion

Daily newspapers: 48 English and 1 French **Combined circulation:**

2,247,821 **Telephones per 100 population (1977):** 66.0 **Homes with radios:** 99.0% **Homes with TV's:** 97.4%
Hospital beds (1978): 59,777 (7.0 beds per 1,000 population) **Physicians (1977):** 15,251 (population per physician, 546)
Motor vehicles (1977): 4,352,290 **Residents per motor vehicle:** 1.9 **Motor vehicle deaths (1976):** 1,496

Ontario was the site of the first European settlement in the interior of North America. In 1639 a combined Jesuit mission, French fort, and Norman town, called Sainte-Marie Among the Hurons, was established on the River Wye, nearly 800 miles from Quebec. The colony lasted for ten years, when it was burned by its founders in the face of attacking Iroquois, who with the Huron Indians were the settlers' chief rivals in the fur trade. Archaeologists and historians have recently restored the outpost on its site 90 miles north of Toronto.

At the time of the founding of Sainte-Marie, Huronia was the most densely populated area of what is now Canada. It was the home of 30,000 Hurons, who controlled the best trade routes and acted as middlemen, trading for furs with more distant tribes and with white settlements on the St. Lawrence River.

In 1774, eleven years after cession to England, the Quebec Act made the area a western extension of Quebec. Loyalist refugees from the American Revolution settled the area around the St. Lawrence, and in 1791 a division was effected, Upper Canada being the future Ontario.

During the War of 1812 the Loyalists defended their lands against the U.S., the town of York suffering invasion and burning by U.S. forces. After the war emigration by U.S. and British citizens seeking land brought rapid population expansion. The fur trade was slowly replaced with lumbering and wheat production, and by the mid-19th century the economy began to boom as development of railroads and canal systems started a major transportation network. The establishment of the Dominion of Canada in 1867 and of the capital of Ottawa added to the importance of the province.

Today Ontario is the largest province in terms of wealth and population. Its industrial production accounts for nearly 40 percent of the national income and it is the major industrial center of Canada, producing 97 percent of the motor vehicle parts, and over 90 percent of all office and store machinery, motor vehicles and household radios and televisions manufactured domestically. Yet the province's farming, lumber and fishing are still vitally important to the Canadian economy. And its famous lake regions have made Ontario a favorite summer and winter vacationland for Canadians and Americans alike.

For all its wealth, Ontario still suffers from unemployment. Resentment over the extent of American control of Canadian business is growing, as are accusations of the exertion of undue U.S. influence on the affairs of the Canadian nation. With growing sentiment toward independence in Quebec, Ontario's position as the center of commerce and industry for Canada may be enhanced by the exodus of businesses from its eastern neighbor.

PRINCE EDWARD ISLAND

Area: 2,184 square miles **Population:** 118,229 (1976 Census); 122,300 (Jan. 1, 1979 estimate); ranks tenth; population density, 54.1; urban, 37.1%; rural, 62.9% **Capital:** Charlottetown (1976 population), 17,063

Ethnic Composition: British Isles, 83%; French 14% **Religion:** Roman Catholic, 46%; United Church, 25%; Presbyterian, 12%; Anglican, 6%; Baptist, 6% **Vital Statistics (per 1,000 population):**

PRINCE EDWARD ISLAND

MILES

KILOMETERS

⊛ Provincial Capital

GULF OF ST. LAWRENCE

PRINCE EDWARD ISLAND NATIONAL PARK

Charlottetown

Summerside

Kensington

Georgetown

Montague

NORTHUMBERLAND STRAIT

NEW BRUNSWICK

NOVA SCOTIA

North Pt.
Nail Pond
Tignish
St. Louis
St. Edward
C. Kildare
Elmsdale
Piusville
C. Gage
Ebbsfleet
Campbellton
Keolsford
Glenwood
Howlan
O'Leary
Trout R.
Alberton
Alberton South
Poplar Grove
Ellerslie
Tyne Valley
Northam
W. Devon
Mt. Carmel
St. Chrysostom
Wellington
Miscouche
St. Eleanors
Lennox I.
Malpeque
Margate
Sherbrooke
Central Bedeque
Dunk R.
Emerald
Kinkora
Albany
Carleton
Borden
C. Traverse
Cape Tormentine
Bayfield
Melrose
Port Elgin
Tidnish
Northport
Oulegurrig Hd.
Baie Verte
Brooklyn
Sackville
Gaspereau
Cornier Village
C. Bald
Rojechaud
Hampton
Crapaud
Victoria
Hunters River
New Wiltshire
Milton Sta.
New Haven
New Glasgow
Mayfield
Rustico
Cavendish (Green Gables)
Covehead
Oyster Bed Br.
Canoe Cove
Bonshaw
Eliot
Clyde R.
Cross Roads
Bunbury
Southport
I. Verde
Cherry Valley
Vernon
Millview
New Perth
Belfast
Orwell
Pinette
Prim Pt.
Pinette Bay
St. Peter
Bay
Hillsborough Bay
Point Prim
Wood Islands
Wood Is.
Belle River
C. Bear
Murray Hbr.
Gladstone
Abney
Murray River
Murray Hbr. N.
Beach Pt.
Peters Road
Valleyfield
Iona
Montague
Sturgeon
Panmure I.
Cardigan Bay
Boughton I.
Cardigan
Newport
Lower Montague
Brudenell
Georgetown
Cardigan R.
Brudenell R.
Montague R.
L. St. Peters
L. Peake
Peakes (Peakes Rd.)
Lorne Valley
Ft. Augustus
Mt. Stewart
St. Andrews
Tracadie
Savage Har.
Bangor
Morell
Strathcona
St. Peters
St. Peters Bay
Boughton
Little Pond
Souris
New Zealand
Bear River
Hermanville
Monticello
Elmira
Kingsborough
East Pt.
Fortune Br.
St. Charles
Bothwell
Baltic
Sorry Pt.
Boughton Bay
Rollo Bay
Poplar Point
Wilmot Valley
Kelvin Grove
Sevogle Har.
Séven Mile Bay
Bedeque Bay
Malpeque Bay
Hog I.
Conway Inlet
Cavendish Inlet
Grand R.
Egmont Bay
Cape Egmont
West Pt.
Baccumpeque Bay
Grand Tracadie

Longitude West of Greenwich

© C.S. HAMMOND & Co., Maplewood, N.J.

birth rate, 16.4; death rate, 9.3; marriage rate, 8.2; divorce rate, 0.98; infant mortality (per 1,000 live births), 14.4

Location and Geography: Separated from the mainland by Northumberland Strait, nine to 25 miles wide, the island is about 120 miles in length and has an average width of 20 miles. The irregular coastline has many large bays and deep inlets and all inland waters are tidal except for one river and one lake. The rich soil is of a distinctive red color; more than half of the area is farmed. There is no mining and forestland is limited to small farm woodlots

Government: Prince Edward Island became a province in 1873 and is represented in the Federal Government by four members in the House of Commons and four Senators. The provincial government is unicameral with a Legislative Assembly of 32 members. In April 1979, 21 Progressive Conservatives and 11 Liberals were elected to the Legislature **Premier:** Honourable Angus MacLean **Salary and allowance:** $39,500

Education (April 1979): 27.3% of the population 15 years of age and over had grade 8 or less; 51.1% attended high school; 8.0% had some post-secondary education; 8.0% had a post-secondary certificate or diploma; 5.7% had a university degree **Total expenditures on education (1977-78):** $77,004,000 **Schools (1977-78):** 74 primary and secondary schools with a combined enrollment of 27,699. In the same year full-time enrollment in one degree-granting university and two post-secondary non-university institutions was 2,300

Value added in goods-producing industries (1976): $180,330,000. Agriculture represented 38.8% of the total; construction 25.4%; manufacturing 23.0%; and fisheries 7.1% **Leading manufacturing industries:** fish products, dairy products, fruit and vegetable processing **Average industrial earnings (Feb. 1979):** $206.02 per week **Cash receipts from farming operations (1978):** $96,922,000, with 24.7% derived from potatoes, 18.9% from cattle and calves, 17.8% from hogs, and 15.3% from dairy products **Families with incomes over $12,000:** 58.4% **Per capita personal income (1977):** $4,975 **Unemployment (1978):** 9.9%

Provincial Finances: Estimated gross general revenue, fiscal year 1978-79, $268.4 million; estimated gross general expenditure, $268.6 million

Daily Newspapers: 3 **Combined circulation:** 31,922 **Number of telephones:** 45.4 per 100 population **Homes with radios:** 98% **Homes with TV's:** 98%

Hospital beds (1978): 988 (8.1 beds per 1,000 population) **Physicians:** 140 (population per physician, 857)

Motor Vehicles (1977): 61,138 **Residents per motor vehicle:** 2.0 **Motor vehicle deaths (1976):** 29

The great explorer Jacques Cartier, in 1534, was the first European to visit Prince Edward Island. The French called it Ile St. Jean and used the island as a fishery. When the British took over in 1758 most of the nearly 5,000 Acadians living there were deported. The British divided their newly won territory into lots which were granted to persons in Britain, largely Scots, who had a claim on the patronage of the Crown. Few of the new owners fulfilled their obligation to develop their holdings, however, and a century of struggle followed between tenant farmers and nonresident proprietors. It was resolved only after Confederation in 1873 when the Dominion government advanced $800,000 to the provincial government to buy out the landlords and resell the land to tenants. The development of Prince Edward Island was further delayed by its separation from Nova Scotia in 1769 by the British government, leaving a political unit simply too small to function effectively. Despite the fact that an 1864 meeting in Charlottetown eventually led to the Canadian Confederation, ironically Prince Edward Island itself did not enter the Dominion until 1873.

The province has abundant good soil, and today agriculture remains the principal industry. Silver fox farming originated on the island. From 1910 to 1940 the island was world-famous for the breed, which is now virtually extinct there. Tourism is a growing industry on the Island. A replica of the house from Anne of Green Gables, found in the National Park, is a favorite of travelers. Fort

Amherst National Historic Park, at Rocky Point, contains earthworks of the fort built by the British after its capture from the French in 1758.

Premier Bennett Campbell's Liberal government, in power since 1966, was defeated in the April 23, 1979 provincial elections. The Progressive Conservatives, led by Angus MacLean, won a comfortable 21-seat majority in the Legislature, with the Liberals being returned in only 11 ridings (districts).

QUEBEC

Area: 594,860 square miles **Population:** 6,234,445 (1976 Census); 6,289,600 (Jan. 1, 1979 estimate); ranks second; population density, 11.9; urban, 79.1%; rural, 20.9% **Capital:** Québec **Major cities (1977 metropolitan estimates):** Montréal, 2,809,900; Québec, 545,100; Chicoutimi-Jonquière, 129,200 **(1976 metropolitan area population):** Laval, 246,243; Longueuil, 122,429; Montréal-Nord, 97,250; Sherbrooke, 76,804; Verdun, 68,013; La Salle, 76,713; Ste-Foy, 71,237; Hull, 61,039; St-Laurent, 64,404; Trois Rivières, 52,518; St-Léonard, 78,452

Ethnic Composition: French, 79%; British Isles, 11% **Religion:** Roman Catholic, 87%; United Church, 3%; Anglican, 3% **Vital Statistics (per 1,000 population):** birth rate, 15.5; death rate, 6.9; marriage rate, 8.1; divorce rate, 2.44; infant mortality (per 1,000 live births), 13.5

Location and Geography: The province's northern four-fifths lies in the Canadian Shield, a lake-dotted, partly wooded, rolling plateau. The St. Lawrence Lowlands have climate and soil well suited for general farming. The Appalachian region, south of the St. Lawrence River and including the Gaspé peninsula, is a succession of plateaus and plains, much of it arable and the remainder wooded

Government: Québec became a province in 1867 and is represented in the Federal Government by 75 members in the House of Commons and 24 Senators. The provincial government is unicameral with a National Assembly of 110 members. In November 1976, party standings were: Parti Québécois 71, Liberals 26, Union Nationale 11, Social Credit one, Independent one **Prime Minister:** Honourable René Lévesque **Salary and allowance:** $76,500

Education (April 1979): 31.3% of the population 15 years-of age and over had Grade 8 or less; 47.0% attended high school; 5.2% had some post-secondary education; 10.2% had a post-secondary certificate or diploma; 6.3% had a university degree **Expenditures on Education (1977-78):** $4,986,155,000 **Schools (1977-78):** 2,858 primary and secondary, with a combined enrollment of 1,318,955 **Colleges:** Seven degree-granting universities and 76 post-secondary non-university institutions with a total enrollment of 213,640

Value added in goods-producing industries (1976): $17,885,888,000; manufacturing represented 62.7% of this total and construction, 22.1% **Value of manufactured shipments (1976):** $25,809,621,000, 26.3% of the national total **Leading manufacturing industries (1975):** pulp and paper, petroleum refining, dairy products, smelting and refining, slaughtering and meat processing, women's clothing **Average industrial earnings (Feb. 1979):** $273.84 per week **Cash receipts from farming operations (1978):** $1,647,753,000; dairy products contributed 34.7%; cattle and calves, 10.1%; hogs, 22.6%; and poultry, 9.7% **Families with incomes over $12,000:** 70.2% **Per capita personal income (1977):** $6,903 **Unemployment (1978):** 10.9%

Provincial Finances: Estimated gross general revenue (fiscal year 1978-79) $14.0 billion; estimated gross general expenditure, $14.8 billion

Daily newspapers: 10 French language, three English **Combined Circulation:** 1,173,154 **Telephones per 100 population (1977):** 59.5 **Homes with radios:** 98.3% **Homes with TV's:** 98.2%

Hospital beds (1978): 53,283 (8.5 beds per 1,000 population) **Physicians (1976):** 11,262 (population per physician, 556)

Motor vehicles (1977): 3,135,593 **Residents per motor vehicle:** 2.0 **Motor vehicle deaths (1976):** 1,458

It was at Quebec that Cartier landed in 1534, proclaiming French sovereignty. In 1608 Champlain established a settlement at the site of Quebec City, and by 1750 65,000 French-Canadian descendants of the original settlers inhabited the

QUEBEC

National Capital ⊛
Provincial Capitals ✪

MILES
0 20 40 60
0 20 40 60
KILOMETERS

C.S. HAMMOND & CO., Maplewood, N.J.

land around the St. Lawrence River. When New France, subject of the crown of France, was ceded to Britain in 1763, and the colony officially became the "province of Quebec," it was a land where French law, religion and custom were firmly entrenched. The confusion created by the co-existence of French-Canadian and British rule was somewhat resolved in 1774 by an act guaranteeing maintenance of French civil law and customs, freedom of worship and education, but the problem remains a source of great controversy to this day.

The French nationalist sentiment has become increasingly strident since the late 1950s. French-speaking Canadians have insisted on greater control of their province's industry and commerce, with demands that Quebec become a separate nation. In 1974, the legislature gave voice to the separatists' demands and established French as the province's official language.

The November 1976 elections in Quebec gave the majority of legislative seats to the separatist *Parti Québécois.* Provincial Prime Minister René Lévesque announced his government's intention to seek independence from the federal government and create a sovereign Quebec. A white paper declaring an end to bilingualism in this "French society" was issued and promptly attacked by Ottawa. Canada's Prime Minister Trudeau called for a referendum on the question of Quebec's secession, with the resignation of Lévesque if the results did not indicate support for his proposal.

In 1977, the *Parti Québécois* exhibited moderation in its drive for independence, reversing it's previous stand on abolition of English language schools and easing language demands on large, English-using corporations. But Lévesque and the PQ remain adamant on demanding greater autonomy and self-rule for the French province. In 1978 French was established as the primary language of government, education and legal record, despite charges by the federal government and the other provinces that this would "sabotage" national unity. In 1979, the Lévesque government proposed a 1980 referendum on a "sovereign-association" plan that would give Quebec greater self-government while maintaining economic ties to the rest of the Canadian federation.

SASKATCHEWAN

Area: 251,700 square miles **Population:** 921,325 (1976 Census); 952,500 (Jan. 1, 1979 estimate); ranks sixth; population density, 4.33; urban, 55.5%; rural, 44.5% **Capital:** Regina **Major cities (1977 population):** Regina, 154,600; Saskatoon, 136,800
Ethnic Composition: British Isles, 42%; German, 19%; Ukrainian, 9%; Scandinavian, 6%; French, 6%; and Native Indian, 4% **Religion:** United Church, 30%; Roman Catholic, 28%; Anglican, 9%; Lutheran, 10%; Ukrainian Catholic, 4%; Mennonite, 3% **Vital Statistics (per 1,000 population 1976):** birth rate, 15.7; death rate, 7.3, marriage rate, 8.4; divorce rate, 1.3; infant mortality (per 1,000 live births), 14.3

Location and Geography: Situated between Manitoba and Alberta, the southern portion of the province consists of a rolling plain. The northern third begins the Canadian shield
Government: Saskatchewan became a province in 1905 and is represented in the Federal Government by 14 members in the House of Commons and six Senators. The provincial government is unicameral with a Legislative Assembly of 61 members. In October 1978, 44 New Democrats and 17 Conservatives were elected to the Legislature **Premier:** Honourable A. E. Blakeney **Salary and allowance:** $49,750
Education (1973): In the Western Provinces (Alberta, British Columbia, Manitoba and Saskatchewan) 95.7% of the population had completed Grade IV; 39.4%, secondary schools and 6.5%, university **Total expenditures on education (1977-78):** $349,223,248
Schools and students: 1,060 primary and secondary schools with a combined enrollment of 225,407 **Colleges:** Two degree-granting universities and 15 community colleges, and technical and vocational institutes with an enrollment of 117,546
Value added in goods-producing industries (1978): $4,930,000; agriculture represented 41% of this total, mining 26%, construction 17%, and manufacturing 13% **Value of Mineral Shipments (1978):** $1,220,000,000 **Leading manufacturing industries:** slaughtering and meat processing, petroleum refining, dairy products, metal fabricating and potash mining **Average industrial earnings (1978):** $250.44 per week **Cash receipts from farming operations (1978):** $2,509,898,000; with 49% derived from wheat, 19% from cattle and calves, and 7% from barley **Families with incomes over $10,000 (1977):** 67% **Per capita personal Income (1978):** $7,643 **Unemployment (1978):** 4.9%
Provincial Finances: Estimated gross general revenue, fiscal year 1977-78, $1,460 million; estimated gross general expenditure, $1,503 million

Daily newspapers: 4 **Combined circulation:** 134,564 **Telephones per 100 population:** 59 **Homes with radios:** 99% **Homes with TV's:** 97%
Hospital beds (1977): 7,859 (8.2 per 1,000 population) **Physicians (1978):** 947 (1,006 population per physician)
Motor Vehicles (1977): 654,446 **Residents per motor vehicle:** 1.5 **Motor vehicle deaths (1976):** 278

The first European to reach what is now Saskatchewan and to see the vast buffalo herds that roamed the central plains was Henry Kelsey, an agent of the Hudson's Bay Company. In 1690 he was sent into the Northwest to explore the vast territory and ensure the Company's fur supply by pacifying the Indians. For two centuries fur trading continued; and settlement only began in 1870 with the building of the railroad and the practice of homesteading.

Today the province has Canada's largest area of occupied agricultural land. Yet, after the disasters of the dust bowl of the 1930s, diversification has been a priority and now 65 percent of the province's gross product is from industry, only 35 percent from farming. Petroleum, mining and manufacturing are the major industries; farms are large and highly mechanized.

The 1978 elections affirmed support for the NDP and Premier Blakeney's policy of taking over one-half of the potash mining industry, much of which is owned by United States interests.

SASKATCHEWAN

SASKATCHEWAN
NORTHERN PART
N. W. TERRITORIES

MANITOBA

Provincial Capital ⊛

MILES

KILOMETERS

PRINCIPAL CANADIAN AGRICULTURAL CROPS Source: Statistics Canada

	Area in Acres		Yield per Acre		Total Production	
	1977	**1978**	**1977**	**1978***	**1977**	**1978***
			Bushels		Bushels	
Winter wheat	590,000	335,000	52.5	41.0	30,973,000	13,737,000
Spring wheat	22,612,100	22,207,100	28.8	29.7	651,916,000	659,922,000
Durum wheat	1,800,000	3,600,000	26.1	28.7	46,900,000	103,300,000
All wheat	25,002,100	26,142,100	29.2	29.7	729,789,000	776,959,000
Oats for grain	5,268,000	4,518,000	53.0	52.0	279,015,000	234,777,000
Barley for grain	11,738,900	10,533,400	46.2	45.3	541,906,000	477,083,000
Fall rye	565,000	736,000	26.4	30.6	14,899,000	22,528,000
Spring rye	52,000	52,000	21.2	25.1	1,100,000	1,305,000
All rye	617,000	788,000	25.9	30.2	15,999,000	23,833,000
Mixed grains	1,542,600	1,497,000	51.0	53.6	78,737,000	80,298,000
Flaxseed	1,470,000	1,280,000	17.4	17.2	25,600,000	22,000,000
Rapeseed	3,590,000	6,930,000	24.2	22.1	87,000,000	153,200,000
Corn for grain	1,789,000	1,933,000	92.3	85.8	165,209,000	165,931,000
Buckwheat	107,000	149,000	18.8	22.5	2,016,000	3,346,000
Peas, dry	85,000	97,000	23.8	30.2	2,020,000	2,930,000
Soybeans	500,000	650,000	38.8	26.9	19,377,000	17,458,000
			Cwt		Cwt	
Beans, dry	173,000	165,000	6.4	11.5	1,107,000	1,891,000
Potatoes	275,600	274,000	199.0	196.6	54,841,000	53,864,000
			Pounds		Pounds	
Mustard seed	182,000	242,000	962	942	175,000,000	228,000,000
Sunflower seed	168,000	214,000	1,062	1,173	178,500,000	251,000,000
			Tons		Tons	
Tame hay	13,840,000	13,847,000	1.97	2.14	27,266,000	29,670,000
Fodder corn	1,215,000	1,200,500	13.18	12.68	16,010,000	15,222,000
Sugar beets	63,674	61,002	17.50	17.10	1,114,268	1,043,400

* As indicated on or about November 15, 1978

CANADA: PRINCIPAL TRADE PARTNERS Source: Statistics Canada

EXPORTS $000,000				IMPORTS $000,000			
Country	1978*	1977	1976	Country	1978*	1977	1976
United States	36,455	30,319	25,233	United States	35,246	29,630	25,752
Japan	3,052	2,513	2,392	Japan	2,268	1,803	1,524
United Kingdom	1,985	1,929	1,856	United Kingdom	1,600	1,281	1,150
Germany, West	782	768	701	Venezuela	1,283	1,360	1,299
Venezuela	686	568	374	Germany, West	1,244	964	781
U S S R	567	358	549	Saudi Arabia	749	712	482
Netherlands	563	512	451	France	684	522	437
People's Repub. China	503	369	196	Iran	594	537	695
Italy	481	498	552	Italy	525	399	365
Belgium/Luxembourg	475	510	478	Taiwan	397	321	293
France	460	360	416	South Korea	363	323	304
Brazil	417	276	332	Australia	350	353	339
Australia	412	410	366	Hong Kong	332	280	284
India	254	136	155	Sweden	325	260	263
Saudi Arabia	235	109	110	Switzerland	285	220	163
Mexico	229	218	213	Brazil	248	214	163
Poland	224	148	126	Netherlands	227	191	181
Cuba	218	184	261	Belgium/Luxembourg	202	160	125
South Korea	216	144	117	Mexico	185	195	145
Algeria	161	186	113	South Africa	149	150	146
Other Countries	3,306	2,991	2,585	Other Countries	2,350	2,281	2,553
All Countries	51,681	43,506	37,576	All Countries	49,606	42,156	37,444

* Preliminary, by order of rank.

SALARIES OF SENIOR MEMBERS OF HOUSE OF COMMONS

Position	Sessional Allowance	Expense Allowance	Salary	Motor Vehicle Allowance	Total
Prime Minister	$28,600	$12,700	$35,400	$2,000	$78,700
Cabinet Ministers and Leaders of Opposition in the House of Commons	28,600	12,700	21,200	2,000	64,500
Members of Parliament	28,600	12,700*	—	—	41,300*

* Certain members for larger northern constituencies have larger expense allowances.

YUKON TERRITORY

MILES
0 25 50 75 100 125

KILOMETERS
0 25 50 75 100 125

Territorial and State Capitals ✪

BEAUFORT SEA

Demarcation Pt.
Herschel I.
Herschel
Mackenzie Bay
Kugmallit Bay
Richards I.
Tuktoyaktuk
Eskimo (Husky) Lakes
Liverpool Bay
BRITISH MTS.
Old Crow R.
Reindeer Sta.
Sitidgi L.
Aklavik
Inuvik
Porcupine
Old Crow
McDougall Pass
Travaillant Lake
Arctic Red River
Ft. McPherson
N. W. TERRS.
L. Belot
L. des Bois
Arctic Circle
Ft. Good Hope
RICHARDSON MOUNTAINS
Eagle R.
Firth R.
Mt. Burgess 5,580
Peel R.
Smith Arm
Great Bear Lake
ALASKA
Yukon R.
OGILVIE MOUNTAINS
Ogilvie
Chapman Lake
Hart R.
Bonnet Plume R.
Snake R.
FRANKLIN
Norman Wells
Ft. Franklin
Canol
Ft. Norman
Eagle
Forty Mile
Mt. Campbell 7,750
Beaver
ROCKY
MACKENZIE
SELWYN MOUNTAINS
Keele R.
Redstone R.
Wrigley
Glacier Creek (Sixtymile)
Dawson
Bear Cr.
Klondike
Sulphur
Granville
Clear Creek
Barlow
McQuesten
Wernecke
Elsa
Keno Hill
Mayo
KLONDIKE
Stewart River
Stewart R.
Hess R.
Keele Pk. 9,750
Macmillan Pass
Christie Pass
Coffee Creek
Donjek
River
Pelly Crossing
Ft. Selkirk
Macmillan R.
Mt. Selous 7,140
MOUNTAINS
Snag
Beaver Creek
Koidern
White R.
Minto
McCabe Crossing
Pelly R.
Faro
Mt. Sir James MacBrien 9,000
NAHANNI NAT'L PARK
Yukon Crossing
Nisling R.
Carmacks
Ross River
South Nahanni R.
Aishihik
Aishihik L.
Big Salmon
N. W. TERRS
Burwash Landing
Kluane
Kluane Lake
Little Salmon R.
Frances Lake
Highland R.
Destruction Bay
Mt. Lucania 17,147
KLUANE
Kluane
Lower Laberge
L. Laberge
Frances Lake
Coal R.
Mt. Logan 19,850
NAT'L PARK
Canyon
Champagne
Takhini
Upper Laberge
Johnsons Crossing
Mt. St. Elias 18,008
ST. ELIAS MOUNTAINS
Haines Jct.
MacRae
Whitehorse
Robinson
Kusawa L.
Tagish
Watson Lake
Yakutat Bay
Yakutat
Carcross
Tagish Lake
Teslin
Teslin Lake
Swift River
Upper Liard
Smith River
Kluksku
Johnsons Crossing
Lower Post
Liard River
GULF OF ALASKA
BRITISH COLUMBIA
Chilkat Pass
Skagway
Atlin
Atlin Lake
CASSIAR MTS.
Cassiar
McDame
MUNCHO LAKE PROV. PK.
GLACIER BAY NAT'L MON.
Glacier Bay
Haines
Chilkoot Pass
ALASKA
Juneau
Tulsequah
Dease Lake
STONE MTN. PROV. PK.

© C.S. Hammond & Co., Maplewood, N. J.

Longitude West of Greenwich

NORTHWEST TERRITORIES

MILES
0 50 100 200 300 400

KILOMETERS
0 50 100 200 300 400

● State and Territorial Capitals

CANADIAN IMPORTS BY SELECTED COMMODITY GROUPS

SOURCE: Statistics Canada

	($000)		
	1976	1977	1978
1. Motor Vehicles and Parts	9,399,782	11,396,230	13,022,563
Motor vehicle parts, except engines	4,455,345	5,458,067	6,128,393
Passenger automobiles and chassis	2,800,317	3,349,788	3,784,474
Motor vehicle engines	508,046	545,322	808,022
Trucks, truck tractors and chassis	838,649	1,009,550	1,218,954
Motor vehicle engine parts	460,877	691,095	707,615
Other motor vehicles	336,548	342,408	375,105
2. Non-farm machinery	3,212,173	3,492,763	4,262,983
3. Crude petroleum	3,280,086	3,209,497	3,446,508
4. Iron and Steel and Alloys	721,932	869,438	1,090,034
5. Communications equipment	1,092,191	1,251,889	1,509,698
6. Electronic computers	428,323	558,805	842,567
7. Aircraft and parts	405,959	439,262	766,915
8. Wearing apparel and accessories	955,518	902,541	987,167
9. Agricultural machinery and tractors	1,317,810	1,334,944	1,502,613
10. Fruits and vegetables	860,808	1,038,745	1,250,849

CANADIAN EXPORTS BY SELECTED COMMODITY GROUPS

SOURCE: Statistics Canada

	($000)		
	1976	1977	1978
1. Motor Vehicles and Parts	8,227,789	10,339,043	12,234,297
Passenger automobiles and chassis	3,686,051	4,412,761	4,887,816
Trucks, truck tractors and chassis	1,410,486	2,113,423	2,667,922
Other motor vehicles	160,032	194,220	256,500
Motor vehicle engines and parts	776,710	944,934	1,061,787
Motor vehicle parts, except engines	2,189,510	2,673,705	3,360,272
2. Crude Petroleum	2,286,675	1,750,637	1,577,848
3. Wheat and Wheat Flour	1,849,427	1,941,532	2,063,135
4. Wood and Similar Pulp	2,181,135	2,156,026	2,176,197
5. Newsprint Paper	2,001,093	2,381,265	2,866,687
6. Copper, Ores and Alloys	865,290	832,734	825,254
7. Lumber	1,648,707	2,387,101	3,219,433
8. Nickel, Ores and Alloys	968,812	974,379	859,250
9. Machinery (except farm)	891,016	1,164,318	1,526,413
10. Aircraft and Parts	453,480	485,647	691,023

CANADA: POPULATION, 1851-1978

SOURCE: Statistics Canada

	1851	1871	1891	1931	1951	1971	1978[3]
Newfoundland	—	—	—	—	361,416	522,104	568,900
Prince Edward Island	62,678[1]	94,021	109,078	88,038	98,429	111,641	122,000
Nova Scotia	276,854	387,800	450,396	512,846	642,584	788,960	841,200
New Brunswick	193,800	285,594	321,263	408,219	515,697	634,557	695,000
Quebec	890,261	1,191,516	1,488,535	2,874,662	4,055,681	6,027,764	6,285,000
Ontario	952,004	1,620,851	2,114,321	3,431,683	4,597,542	7,703,106	8,443,800
Manitoba	—	25,228	152,560	700,139	776,541	988,247	1,032,400
Saskatchewan	—	—[2]	—[2]	921,785	831,728	926,242	947,100
Alberta	—	—[2]	—[2]	731,605	939,501	1,627,874	1,950,300
British Columbia	55,000	36,247	98,173	694,263	1,165,210	2,184,621	2,530,200
Yukon	—	—	—	4,230	9,096	18,388	21,700
Northwest Territory	5,700	48,000	98,967	9,316	16,004	34,807	43,500
Total Canada	**2,436,297**	**3,689,257**	**4,833,239**	**10,376,786**	**14,009,429**	**21,568,311**	**23,481,100**

[1] 1848 figure. [2] Included with the Northwest Territories. [3] Postcensal estimate.

LARGEST CANADIAN CITIES

SOURCE: Statistics Canada

	1851	1901	1951	1961	1971	1976
Calgary, Alberta	—	4,091	129,060	249,641	403,343*	469,917
Edmonton, Alberta	—	—	159,631	281,027	438,152	461,361
Halifax, Nova Scotia	20,749	40,832	85,589	92,511	122,035	117,882
Hamilton, Ontario	14,112	52,634	208,321	273,991	309,173	312,003
London, Ontario	—	37,981	95,343	169,569	223,222	240,392
Montreal, Quebec	57,715	267,730	1,021,520	1,191,062	1,214,352	1,080,546
Ottawa, Ontario	—	59,928	202,045	268,206	302,341	304,462
Quebec, Quebec	42,052	68,840	164,016	171,979	187,833*	177,082
Regina, Saskatchewan	—	—	71,319	112,141	139,479*	149,593
Saint John, N.B.	22,745	40,711	50,779	55,153	89,039	85,956
St. John's Newfoundland	—	—	52,873	63,633	88,414*	86,576
Toronto, Ontario	30,775	208,040	675,754	672,407	712,786	633,318
Vancouver, British Columbia	—	26,133	344,833	384,522	426,298*	410,188
Windsor, Ontario	—	12,153	120,049	114,367	203,300	196,526
Winnipeg, Manitoba	—	42,340	235,710	265,429	504,150*	560,874

Revised, based on 1976 areas.

WORLD NATIONS

AFGHANISTAN

Area: 250,775 sq. mi. **Population:** 19,900,000 (1978 est.)

Official Name: Democratic Republic of Afghanistan **Capital:** Kabul **Nationality:** Afghan **Languages:** Pushtu, spoken by the Pathans, and Dari, a Persian dialect spoken by the Tajiks, are official languages **Religion:** About 99% of the population are Moslems, most of whom belong to the Sunni sect. Islam is the state religion **Flag:** Red field with the state coat-of-arms represented in upper left corner **Anthem:** N.A. **Currency:** Afghani (45 per U.S. $1)

Location: Central Asia. Landlocked Afghanistan is bordered by the U.S.S.R. on the north, China on the extreme northeast, Pakistan on the east and south, and Iran on the west **Features:** The towering Hindu Kush range and its parallel extensions run through the center of the country from northeast to southwest. Mountains and desert country are interspersed by small, fertile valleys irrigated by snow-fed mountain streams **Chief Rivers:** Helmand, Farah Rud, Hari Rud, Khulm, Amu Darya

Head of State: President Nur Mohammad Taraki, born 1917, elected by the Revolutionary Council following the coup of April 1978. He also serves as Chairman of the Council **Head of Government:** Prime Minister Hafizullah Amin **Effective Date of Present Constitution:** Rule by decree since annulment of 1977 constitution in 1978 **Legislative Body:** Revolutionary Council of 35 members **Local Government:** 28 provinces, each headed by a governor

Ethnic Composition: The Pathans (Pushtus) make up about half the total population; the rest is made up largely of Tajiks, Uzbeks, Hazara, and Turkmen **Population Distribution:** 15% urban **Density:** 79 inhabitants per sq. mi.

Largest Cities: (1976 estimates) Kabul 603,969, Kandahar 160,684, Herat 115,165; (1973 est.) Baghlan 110,874, Tagab 106,777, Charikar 100,443

Per Capita Income: $122 (1978 est.) **Gross National Product (GNP):** $2.5 billion (1978 est.) **Economic Statistics:** about 53% of GNP comes from agriculture (wheat, corn, barley, rice, cotton, sugar beets and cane) and animal husbandry (sheep, cattle, goats); 16% from trade and services; 11% from industry and handicrafts (textiles, cement, flour, sugar, fruit processing, handwoven carpets); 20% from other activities **Minerals and Mining:** Fields of natural gas in northern Afghanistan are being developed with Soviet assistance. There are large coal deposits; known deposits of iron ore, chromite and beryl are unexploited; lapis lazuli of world-renowned quality is produced. Hydroelectricity is an important source of energy **Labor Force:** 4,600,000 (1970), with 67% in agriculture, and 8% in industry **Foreign Trade:** Exports, chiefly fruit, karakul skins, natural gas, wool and carpets, totaled $223 million in 1975. Imports , mainly foodstuffs, textiles, petroleum products, chemicals and drugs, machinery and vehicles, and rubber manufactures, totaled $350 million **Principal Trade Partners:** U.S.S.R., United States, Britain, Japan, West Germany, India, Pakistan, Iran

Vital Statistics: Birthrate, 49.2 per 1,000 of pop. (1975); death rate, 23.8 **Life Expectancy:** 40.3 years **Health Statistics:** 6,592 inhabitants per hospital bed; 28,313 per physician (1974) **Illiteracy:** 88% **Infant Mortality:** 182 per 1,000 births **Education Statistics:** 3,355 primary schools, with enrollment of 748,359 (1976) **Enrollment in Higher Education:** 12,256 (1975) **GNP Expended on Education:** 1.3% (1974)

Transportation: Paved roads total 1,900 mi. (1975) **Motor Vehicles:** 64,500 (1971) **Passenger Cars:** 38,400 **Railway Mileage:** None **Ports:** None **Major Airlines:** Ariana Afghan Airlines operates both international and domestic flights **Communications:** Government owned **Radio Transmitters:** 6 **Receivers:** 115,000 (1976) **Television Stations:** None **Telephones:** 28,000 (1976) **Newspapers:** 17 dailies, 27 per 1,000 inhabitants (1975)

Weights and Measures: Metric system and local units are used **Travel Requirements:** Passport, tourist visa, $7 fee, valid for 3 months, for 30-day stay

---

Divided by tribal loyalties and the country's mountainous terrain, many in Afghanistan live now as their forefathers did: as herdsmen, nomads, and farmers. The cities, especially the capital, Kabul, show tentative signs of modernity, but the gap between the way urban and rural Afghans live and think is a major problem in the attempt to consolidate the national mosaic.

Afghanistan's modern history has seen foreign

* Taraki resigned in September 1979, and was succeeded by Hafizullah Amin.

interference—but never total conquest—tribal rebellions, bloody royal successions and two military coups. King Mohammed Zahir Shah, who succeeded his assassinated father in 1933 at the age of 19, was a near-prisoner of relatives for years. He did not assume full governmental powers until 1963. Zahir attempted to introduce reforms and presented his people with the first democratic constitution in 1964. Lasting political changes did not take place, however, and a two-year drought in 1971-72 brought an already poor economy to a crisis condition, sealing the fate of the monarchy.

In July 1973 a group of young military officers deposed the king and proclaimed a republic. The leader of the coup, Lt. Gen. Mohammad Daud Khan, a cousin of the king and a former prime minister (1953-1963), became both president and prime minister of the new republic. The constitution of 1964 was put aside and rule by decree instituted. In April 1978 President Daud, members of his family and some 100 police officers and other officials were among an undetermined number who were killed as leftist military elements overthrew the government in two days of fierce fighting in Kabul. The rebels set up a Revolutionary Council to run the country by decree and installed a civilian, Nur Mohammad Taraki, general secretary of the Marxist Khalq Party, as president and prime minister of what became "the Democratic Republic of Afghanistan." On Dec. 5, Taraki signed a 20-year Afghan-U.S.S.R. friendship treaty in Moscow.

Protesting the Taraki government's atheistic policies, village tribesmen began sporadic attacks on government forces in 1978. By early 1979, groups of Moslem conservatives had organized into guerrilla units that were active in at least 10—some sources said 15—of Afghanistan's 28 provinces. One group, reports said, captured an army post. Some 40,000 Afghans fled to Pakistan, where a network of military camps was set up in the remote Baluchistan province to command operations within Afghanistan. In July 1979 most U.S. government employees and their dependents were withdrawn from Afghanistan because of the spreading civil war.

On Feb. 14, 1979, Moslem extremists kidnapped U.S. Ambassador Adolph Dubs on a street in the capital and took him to the Kabul Hotel, where he died in a shootout as government security officers stormed in. The U.S. protested the role of Soviet advisers in the gunfire. Soon the U.S. dropped all aid to Afghanistan except for two humanitarian projects.

In March the Revolutionary Council appointed Hafizulla Amin as prime minister; however Taraki retained the office of president.*

HISTORY: Afghanistan has suffered invasions from east and west—by Persians, Greeks, Mongols, and Turks. Among the foreign conquerors was Alexander the Great, in the 4th century B.C. After him came the independent kingdom of Bactria, which lasted until the middle of the 2nd century B.C. Buddhism spread from the east but was superseded by Islam in the 7th century A.D., after which several Moslem kingdoms were set up

11th cent.: Mahmud of Ghazni, an Afghan Moslem, forms kingdom stretching from Caspian Sea to the Ganges River

13th cent.: Genghis Khan and his hordes overrun the country

18th cent.: Persians under Nadir Shah conquer Afghanistan; after Nadir's death in 1747, Ahmad Shah unifies the country for the first time and sets up the Durrani dynasty

1838-42: Attempts by Emir Dost Mohammed to exploit Anglo-Russian rivalry in central Asia and to seize control of British possessions in India lead to first Afghan War, which ends with British withdrawal from Afghanistan

1878-80: Dost Mohammed's son, Shere Ali, turns to Russia for aid, setting off second Afghan War with Britain; Shere Ali is ousted and replaced by Anglophile Abd ur-Rahman

1907: Anglo-Russian agreement guarantees independence of Afghanistan under British influence

1926-29: Afghanistan becomes kingdom, with Amanullah as first king; he attempts to modernize the country but ultra-conservative elements force him to abdicate

1930-33: His successor, Mohammed Nadir Shah, continues reforms until killed; Mohammed Zahir Shah becomes king

1964-65: A new, liberal constitution goes into effect and parliamentary elections are held for the first time

1973: King Mohammed Zahir Shah is overthrown by brother-in-law, General Mohammad Daud Khan; Daud proclaims Afghanistan a republic, declares himself president and prime minister

1974: Daud and Brezhnev sign a joint statement of interest in a collective Asian security system and establishment of a commission to expand Soviet-Afghan cooperation

1975: Daud nationalizes all banks and land reform laws are announced. Increased foreign aid is received

1978: Daud killed as leftist military coup succeeds; Nur Mohammad Taraki becomes president and prime minister. Rural Moslem conservatives begin guerrilla warfare

1979: U.S. Ambassador Adolph Dubs dies in government-rebel shootout. Hafizullah Amin becomes prime minister

ALBANIA

Area: 11,100 sq. mi. **Population:** 2,650,000 (1978 est.)

Official Name: People's Socialist Republic of Albania **Capital:** Tirana **Nationality:** Albanian **Languages:** Albanians are divided into two main language groups: Gheg, north of the river Shkumbi , and Tosk in the south. The official language is based on Tosk. Greek is spoken by the Greek minority in the south **Religion:** 50% Moslem, 20% Orthodox, 10% Roman Catholic. In 1967, however, all religious institutions were closed by the government **Flag:** A red field, with a double-headed black eagle and a gold-edged, five-pointed star above it **Anthem:** Anthem of the Flag **Currency:** Lek (4.1 per U.S. $1)

Location: Southeast Europe, on the west coast of the Balkan peninsula. Albania is bordered on the north and east by Yugoslavia, on the south by Greece, and on the west by the Adriatic Sea **Features:** About 20% of the country consists of a flat-to-rolling coastal plain. Most of the country, however, consists of hills and mountains, frequently covered with scrub forest **Chief Rivers:** Drin, Mat, Shkumbi, Semun, Vijosë

Political Leader: First Secretary of the Albanian (Communist) Party of Labor: Enver Hoxha, born 1908; in power since 1945 as First Secretary of the Central Committee **Head of State:** Chairman of the Presidium of the People's Assembly: Haxhi Lleshi, born 1913, elected by People's Assembly 1953 **Head of Government:** Chairman of the Council of Ministers (premier): Mehmet Shehu, born 1913, reappointed by the People's Assembly in 1976 **Effective Date of Present Constitution:** 1976 **Legislative Body:** People's Assembly (unicameral), consisting of 250 members, elected for 4 years. The People's Assembly is nominally the supreme organ of government, but in practice meets only a few days each year. Real power is vested in the Politburo and Central Committee of the Communist party **Local Government:** 26 districts and one independent city, more than 200 localities, and 2,500 villages, with locally elected people's councils in each of these subdivisions

Ethnic Composition: The population is homogeneous, with a small Greek minority **Population Distribution:** 34% urban (1971) **Density:** 239 inhabitants per sq. mi.

Largest Cities: (1975 estimates) Tirana 170,000, Durrës 80,000, Vlorë 57,000, Korcë 53,000, Shkodër 49,000

Per Capita Income: $647 (1978 est.) **Gross National Product (GNP):** $1.7 billion (1978 est.) **Economic Statistics:** GNP components are not available. In 1968, however, industrial production accounted for 61.5% of total production in the country; the principal industries are oil refining, chemicals, fertilizers, construction materials, textiles, pig iron, processed minerals, and agricultural products. Agricultural production is chiefly devoted to corn, sugar beets, wheat, cotton, tobacco, and livestock **Minerals and Mining:** Oil, coal, copper, iron, and nickel are exploited and are among Albania's chief exports. Hydroelectric and thermoelectric plants provide the country with full electrification **Labor Force:** In 1972, 343,228 workers were employed in the socialist sector of the economy, with about 30% in industry and 60% in agriculture **Foreign Trade:** Exports, chiefly metal ores, crude petroleum, bitumen and tobacco, amounted to $91 million in 1970. Imports, chiefly machinery and equipment, rolled steel and wheat, totaled about $159 million **Principal Trade Partners:** China, Czechoslo-

vakia, East Germany, Romania, Yugoslavia, West Germany, Italy, Hungary, Canada, Greece

Vital Statistics: Birthrate, 33.3 per 1,000 of pop.; death rate, 8.1 (1971) **Life Expectancy:** 69 years **Health Statistics:** 164 inhabitants per hospital bed; 159 per physician (1972) **Infant Mortality:** 86.8 per 1,000 births (1965) **Illiteracy:** 25% **Education Statistics:** 1,429 schools with a combined enrollment of 750,000 pupils (1975) **Enrollment in Higher Education:** 28,668 (1971) **GNP Expended on Education:** N.A.

Transportation: There were 4,200 mi. of paved roads in 1969 **Motor Vehicles:** 10,100 (1967) **Passenger Cars:** 2,600 (1967) **Railway Mileage:** 188 **Ports:** Durrës, Vlorë **Major Airlines:** The airport at Ranas is served by Alitalia, Interflug, Malev, Yugoslav, and Pakistan International **Communications:** Government owned **Radio Transmitters:** 19 **Receivers:** 180,000 (1976) **Television Transmitters:** 1 **Receivers:** 4,500 (1976) **Telephones:** 10,150 (1963) **Newspapers:** 2 dailies, 46 copies per 1,000 inhabitants (1975)

Weights and Measures: Metric system **Travel Requirements:** (1971) Passport, visa obtainable in Paris or Rome

Albania's present, like its past, is influenced by its forbidding hills and poor soil. In a land unattractive to migrants, the Albanians have preserved their ancient culture. But the land cannot feed the people; Albania is a food-importing nation. Fearful of strangers, Albania must depend on strangers for its survival.

Since 1946, Albania has been dominated by the Albanian Party of Labor—a party fanatically devoted to Marxist-Leninist ideology. The Party's leaders have rejected calls for de-Stalinization and for détente with the West and have maintained a rigid police state. The government has fallen out, successively, with Yugoslavia, the Soviet Union and China, as these states have moved away from ideological rigidity.

At the beginning of the 20th century, Albania was part of the Ottoman Empire. Serbia took from that Empire much territory inhabited by ethnic Albanians before an alarmed Austria, in 1912, helped the rest of the country to win independence. After World War I, Albania was caught up in the rivalry between Yugoslavia and Italy; the latter annexed Albania in 1939.

Nominally independent under Communist rule in 1946, Albania was virtually a Yugoslav satellite. The two countries joined in aiding Communist guerrillas in Greece. But Albania broke with Yugoslavia in 1947 and ended the Greek adventure, after Yugoslavia broke with the Soviet Union. Territorial claims against Yugoslavia and loyalty to Joseph Stalin led Albania to remain in the Soviet camp, and the Soviet Union took over the task of supplying most of Albania's food.

In 1961, however, Albania's relations with the Soviet Union soured because of Soviet policies of de-Stalinization. Albania turned to Communist China for friendship and food. Food, however, proved not to be China's most available asset; for practical reasons Albania resumed relations with Yugoslavia in 1970 and with Greece in 1971. Later, China's course became increasingly pragmatic, and Albania criticized the lack of devotion to the Communist cause. After Mao's death in 1976, Albania was lukewarm to his successors and eventually became hostile. China ended assistance to Albania in 1978.

HISTORY: Around 300 B.C., the Illyrian kingdom covered much of what is now Albania. Greek colonies were established along the coast, but the hinterland remained independent. In the 6th century A.D., while nominally under Byzantine rule, Albania was invaded by the Slavs and in the 9th century was annexed to Bulgaria. The Turks conquered the country in the 15th century

1912-20: Albania proclaims its independence with the support of Austria-Hungary. During World War I, Albania is occupied by Allied troops but reasserts its independence

1925-28: Ahmed Zogu, chief of the Mat district, seizes power with Yugoslav support. He rules as president until 1928, when he establishes a monarchy and becomes King Zog I

1939: Italy occupies Albania and unites it with Italian crown

1946: Albania becomes a people's republic under the leadership of Enver Hoxha, head of the Communist resistance group during the Italian occupation

1955-60: Backed by the U.S.S.R., Albania joins the Warsaw Pact and the United Nations. Relations with the Soviet Union soon cool, however, as Moscow attempts to improve relations with Yugoslavia, behind whose frontiers live more than 750,000 ethnic Albanians; estrangement is sharpened by Albania's support for Peking in Sino-Soviet ideological split

1961: U.S.S.R. breaks diplomatic relations with Albania

1968: Albania withdraws from Warsaw Pact

1970: Albania signs trade pact with Yugoslavia

1971: Greece and Albania resume full diplomatic relations

1973: Purge of eight officials for anti-party activity

1976: A new constitution is approved by People's Assembly

1978: Chinese aid ended. New agreement with Greece increases trade and opens air route

---

ALGERIA

Area: 919,591 sq. mi. **Population:** 18,000,000 (1978 est.)

Official Name: Democratic and Popular Republic of Algeria **Capital:** Algiers **Nationality:** Algerian **Languages:** Arabic is the official and principal language. French is also widely spoken and serves as a quasi-official language. Berber dialects are spoken by one-fourth the population **Religion:** 99% Moslem; Islam was declared the state religion in 1976 **Flag:** A red star in a red crescent in center of background of green (left hand of flag) and white (right hand) **Anthem:** We Pledge **Currency:** Algerian dinar (3.9 per U.S. $1)

Location: North Africa. Algeria is bordered on the north by the Mediterranean Sea, on the east by Tunisia and Libya, on the south by Niger and Mali, and on the west by Mauritania, Western Sahara, and Morocco **Features:** Two mountain chains, the Tell Atlas and the Saharan Atlas. The mountains of the Tell Atlas rise from a narrow coastal plain along the Mediterranean and are separated from the Saharan Atlas by a corridor of semiarid plateaus dotted with salt marshes and shallow salt lakes. To the south lies the Sahara itself, broken only by a few oases **Chief River:** Chéliff

Head of State and of Government: President: Chadli Bendjedid, born 1929, elected 1979. He is assisted by Premier Mohamed Ben Ahmed Abdelghani, appointed 1979 **Effective Date of Present Constitution:** 1976 **Legislative Body:** A new National Popular Assembly of 261 members was elected in February 1977 for 5-year terms. **Local Government:** 31 departments, each administered by a governor who is responsible to the Minister of the Interior

Ethnic Composition: The population is of Arabo-Berber stock **Population Distribution:** 43% urban (1977) **Density:** 19.6 inhabitants per sq. mi.

Largest Cities: (1977 est.) Algiers 2,000,000, Oran 600,000, Constantine 500,000, Annaba 250,000

Per Capita Income: $1,056 (1978) **Gross National Product (GNP):** $19.5 billion (1978 est.) **Economic Statistics:** In 1976, 7% of the GNP came from agriculture (wheat, vineyard, orchards), livestock raising (sheep, cattle, donkeys, mules, horses, pigs, goats) and fishing; 35% from trade and services; and 44% from mining and industry (food processing and beverages, textiles, leather, chemicals, building materials, steel, and engineering) **Minerals and Mining:** Vast deposits of oil and gas, iron ore, phosphates, and coal; small amounts of lead, zinc and copper **Labor Force:** 2.6 million (1975 est.), of which 60% is engaged in agriculture, 12% in industry, and the rest in services **Foreign Trade:** Exports, chiefly petroleum, natural gas, fruit and wine, totaled $4.9 billion in 1976. Imports, mainly textiles , cereals, chemicals, motor vehicles, iron and steel products, sugar, machinery, and electrical apparatus, totaled $5.5 billion (1976) **Principal Trade Partners:** France, West Germany, Italy, United States, USSR, Japan, Spain, Canada

Vital Statistics: Birthrate, 47.8 per 1,000 of pop. (1975); death rate, 15.4 **Life Expectancy:** 53.3 years (1975) **Health Statistics:** 356 inhabitants per hospital bed, 8,192 per physician (1976) **Infant Mortality:** 70 per 1,000 births **Illiteracy:** 70% **Education Statistics:** 7,798 primary and secondary schools (1975), with a combined enrollment of 3,300,000 (1977) **Enrollment in Higher Education:** 59,100 (1977) **GNP Expended on Education:** 9% (1977)

Transportation: Paved roads total 22,125 mi. (1977) **Motor Vehicles:** 440,800 (1975) **Passenger Cars:** 286,100 **Railway Mileage:** 2,423 **Ports:** Algiers, Oran, Annaba, Bejaia, Arzew **Major Airlines:** Air Algérie operates international and domestic flights **Communications:** Government owned **Radio Transmitters:** 27 **Receivers:** 3,220,000 (1974) **Television Transmitters:** 75 **Receivers:** 525,000 (1976) **Telephones:** 273,000 (1976) **Newspapers:** 4 dailies, 17 copies per 1,000 inhabitants (1975)

Weights and Measures: Metric system **Travel Requirements:** Passport, tourist visa, no charge, valid for 3 months, 4 photos

---

Algeria won independence from France in a long struggle organized by a disciplined party—the National Liberation Front (NLF). Independence brought one-party rule, economic dislocation, and a period of military control. The NLF is a party of Islam, socialism, and concern for the aspirations of the Third World in general and of the Arab states in particular. It is strident in its support of those it considers oppressed, and has made Algeria a haven for many kinds of self-proclaimed revolutionaries—including airplane hijackers. Israel is a favorite target of Algerian rhetoric, although not of Algerian military action. Ironically, Algeria's only actual military adventure is that against Morocco and Mauritania—in support of the Polisario movement for Western Saharan independence.

Despite its ideology, Algeria must trade with the capitalist West. Its economy was ruined by the departure of its European inhabitants after independence, and recovery is incomplete. Fortunately, Algeria has oil and gas which the West needs.

France agreed to independence in 1962, after a plebiscite showed a majority to favor "independece in cooperation with France." Benyoussef Ben Khedda, who had headed the NLF's exile government, became Premier. But his power was broken by Ahmed Ben Bella, a firebrand NLF official who had spent most of the struggle in a French jail. Ben Bella established a one-party system that tended toward personal dictatorship. He was deposed in 1965 by Colonel Houari Boumédienne, who established military rule within the NLF framework.

Boumédienne created most of the salient features of the new Algeria. Finding that cooperation with France was working to France's advantage, he ended it in 1971. Then, he increased trade with the United States, although he had broken diplomatic relations with the U.S. in 1967 because of U.S. support for Israel. Discontent of NLF leaders with military rule led him to convene a constitutional conference in 1976. The conference drafted a one-party constitution after lively, but not entirely free, discussion. The voters approved it and ratified the NLF's choice of Boumédienne as President. The constitution did not bring democracy, but it broadened the limits within which divergent views were tolerated.

The system of semi-democratic one-party rule was tried and found workable in 1978, when Boumédienne died after weeks in a coma. As the constitution provided, Rabah Bitat, the President of the National Popular Assembly, became interim President. In 1979, the Congress of the NLF nominated Colonel Chadli Bendjedid, the Minister of Defense, for a six-year term as President. Given the option of voting for or against the choice, a majority of the voters voted for it. Although not democratic, the succession was constitutional, orderly, and peaceful.

HISTORY: In prehistoric times, Algeria was inhabited by a mixture of peoples from whom the Berbers of today are probably descended. About 1200 B.C. the Phoenicians made settlements in the area, and it eventually fell under the control of Carthage. After the destruction of Carthage in 146 B.C., the Romans gradually gained control of the entire North African coast. With the weakening of the Roman Empire, Algeria fell prey to Vandals from Europe and eventually to the Arabs

7th cent.: Algeria, along with the rest of North Africa, falls to Moslem conquerors from Arabia. Islam takes root

11th cent.: Saharan nomads sweep into the country and destroy farms and pastures, forcing the coastal Berbers into seafaring and piracy. The Berbers spread through North Africa and, in the Moorish Conquest, move to the Iberian peninsula to occupy much of Spain

16th cent.: Spain gains a foothold in Algeria and Algerians turn to Turkish corsairs for help in 1518. Turkish rule is established

1830: France sends an expedition to pacify turbulent tribes along the coast and in the interior. French naval forces seize Algiers, depose the bey, and establish French rule

1942: Allies invade North Africa during World War II

1954-61: Discontent with French rule erupts in a widespread rebellion. Rebel leaders form a "provisional government of Algeria" in Cairo, but the fighting continues until the opening of peace talks with the French

1962-63: Algeria becomes an independent republic. Benyoussef Ben Khedda, premier of the provisional government in exile, takes control but is ousted by Vice-Premier Ahmed Ben Bella who later becomes President under one-party constitution

1965: A military revolt led by Colonel Houari Boumédienne overthrows Ben Bella. A revolutionary council assumes power; Ben Bella placed in "comfortable" confinement

1967-68: Algeria declares war on Israel, but no Algerian troops take part in Middle East fighting. Boumédienne fosters closer economic and military ties with U.S.S.R.

1969: Algeria accuses U.S. State Department and C.I.A. of involvement in a conspiracy to overthrow the government

1971: French oil companies in Algeria partly nationalized; France ends "special relations" with Algeria

1973: The United States arranges to import 1 billion cubic feet of Algerian liquefied natural gas daily for 25 years

1974: Algeria resumes diplomatic relations with U.S. after severance in 1967

1976: Algerian troops clash with Moroccan and Mauritanian forces in Western Sahara. New constitution approved and elections held. Boumédienne elected President

1978: Boumédienne dies

1979: Chadli Bendjedid elected President. Confinement of Ben Bella lifted

ANDORRA

Area: 188 sq. mi. **Population:** 28,000 (1978 est.)

Official Name: Principality of Andorra **Capital:** Andorra la Vella **Nationality:** Andorran **Languages:** Catalan is the official language. French and Spanish are also spoken **Religion:** Roman Catholic **Flag:** Vertical blue, yellow, and red stripes, with the national coat of arms in the center **Anthem:** The Great Charlemagne **Currency:** French franc (4.37 per U.S. $1) and Spanish peseta (66.0 per U.S. $1)

Location: Eastern Pyrenees, between France and Spain Features: Drained by the Valira River, Andorra consists of narrow valleys and gorges, bounded by high peaks **Chief Rivers:** Valira

Head of State: Andorra is a co-principality under the joint sovereignty of the president of France and the Spanish bishop of Urgel, each of whom is represented by a *viguier*, or agent **Head of Government:** Syndic-General Estanislau Sangrá Font, elected 1978 **Legislative Body:** Parliament (unicameral General Council) **Effective Date of Present Constitution:** 1866 Plan of Reform **Local Government:** 7 parishes, each with an elected council

Ethnic Composition: Native Andorrans, who constitute one third of the population, are of Catalan stock. The rest of the population is primarily Spanish and French **Population Distribution:** 81% urban **Density:** 149 inhabitants per sq. mi. **Largest Towns:** (1977 est.) Andorra la Vella 19,764, Sant Juliá 3,510, Encamp 2,268

Per Capita Income: N.A. **Gross National Product (GNP):** N.A. **Economic Statistics:** Tourism is the chief source of income. Rye, wheat, potatoes, livestock raising and tobacco are dominant, while tobacco processing is the chief industry. Timber production and building are also important activities. There is considerable smuggling of merchandise shipped between France and Spain **Minerals and Mining:** Small amounts of iron ore and lead are mined **Labor Force:** 9,500, with about 80% in local industries and 20% in agriculture **Foreign Trade:** Principal exports are timber, cattle and derivatives, and furniture; the chief imports are fuel, perfumes, clothing, radio and television sets. Imports in 1969 totaled $38.9 million **Principal Trade Partners:** France, Spain, West Germany, Japan

Vital Statistics: Birthrate, 16.5 per 1,000 of pop. (1976); death rate, 5.0 **Life Expectancy:** 70 years **Health Statistics:** N.A. **Infant Mortality:** 16 per 1,000 births **Illiteracy:** negligible **Education Statistics:** 22 primary and secondary schools, with combined enrollment of 2,185 pupils (1974) **Enrollment in Higher Education:** N.A. **GNP Expended on Education:** The French government pays part of the costs of the French-language schools. Schools in the southern areas, near Spain, are supported by the Roman Catholic Church

Transportation: Surfaced roads total 77 mi. **Motor Vehicles:** 9,346 (1970) **Passenger Cars:** 8,200 (1969) **Railway Mileage:** None **Ports:** None **Major Airlines:** No air service **Communications:** Privately owned **Radio Stations:** 4 **Licenses:** 6,600 (1976) **Television Stations:** None **Receivers:** 3,000 (1976) **Telephones:** 4,000 (1977) **Newspapers:** One daily established in 1974; French and Spanish periodicals are imported and sold locally

Weights and Measures: Metric system **Travel Requirements:** See *France*

Modern tourism, bringing about a million visitors a year, has altered the formerly leisurely pace of life in Andorra. And the pace is destined to quicken even more with easier access to the tiny state in the fastness of the Pyrenees, for France is building a modern highway to Andorra from Toulouse, by way of Foix, on the Ariége River.

Motoring tourists—and automobile traffic in general—are especially important to Andorra, which obtains more than a third of its revenue from gasoline taxes and automobile fines. Tourism as an industry supplements Andorran wool-combing, spinning, tobacco processing, and the manufacture of sandals. Smuggling of goods from France into Spain is also a substantial industry.

What draws tourists is the attraction of towering passes; peaks topped with snow as late as June; a countryside dotted with sheep, goats, and mules; and bargains. Despite the state's need of revenue, there are no sales taxes or customs duties.

HISTORY: According to tradition, Charlemagne granted the people of Andorra a charter because of their help in battling the Moors. In 843 Charles the Bald made the Spanish count of Urgel overlord of Andorra. In 1278 the bishop of Urgel was made joint suzerain after contending that Andorra was part of the endowment of his cathedral. The rights of the count eventually passed by inheritance to Henry IV of France and eventually to the presidents of France

1793: French revolutionary government renounces its claims to Andorra

1806: Napoleon restores co-principality at Andorrans' request

1933: Suffrage is granted to all men over the age of 25

1941: Suffrage is restricted to heads of families

1970: Limited women's suffrage granted

1971: New bishop of Urgel installed as the 80th co-prince

1977: Personal income tax voted by the General Council

ANGOLA

Area: 481,351 sq. mi. **Population:** 7,000,000 (1978 est.)

Official Name: People's Republic of Angola **Capital:** Luanda **Nationality:** Angolan **Languages:** Portuguese is the official language. A number of African languages, chiefly of Bantu origin, are commonly spoken **Religion:** About 45% adhere to traditional tribal religions; over half profess Christianity, chiefly Roman Catholicism **Flag:** Two equal horizontal stripes of red over black, with yellow five-pointed star, machete, and half a cogwheel in the center **Anthem:** N.A. **Currency:** Kwanza (46.0 per U.S. $1)

Location: West-central Africa. Bounded by the Atlantic Ocean on the west, Namibia on the south, and Zaire and Zambia on the north and east. The exclave of Cabinda lies on the Atlantic coast north of the Congo River mouth **Features:** A narrow coastal strip rises sharply toward an interior plateau, which ranges from 3,000 to 5,000 feet in elevation. A highland area of 6,000 to 7,000 feet lies in the west-central region. Cabinda consists of a low-lying rain forest **Chief Rivers:** Cubango, Cuanza, Cunene, Cuango, Cassai, Cuando, Congo, Cuito

Head of State and of Government: President: Dr. Agostinho Neto,[*] born 1922, succeeded at independence on November 11, 1975. He is chairman of the cabinet **Effective Date of Present Constitution:** 1975 **Legislative Body:** A 36-member Council of the Revolution governs, directed by the MPLA-Labor Party's Central Committee and Political Bureau **Local Government:** 16 provinces, under appointed commissars

Ethnic Composition: Predominantly indigenous Bantus, with minorities of Europeans (mostly Portuguese), and mixed peoples **Population Distribution:** N.A. **Density:** 14.5 inhabitants per sq. mi.

Largest Cities: (1972 est.) Luanda 540,000; (1970 census) Huambo 61,885; Lobito 59,528; Benguela 40,996; Lubango 31,674; Malanje 31,599; Cabinda 21,124

Per Capita Income: $527 (1978 est.) **Gross National Product (GNP):** $3.2 billion (1978 est.) **Economic Statistics:** The economy remains heavily dependent upon agriculture (subsistence and cash crops such as coffee, sisal, cotton, wheat, and tobacco, with fish and timber of importance). Industry (cement, oil refining, paper, agricultural processing, and metal products) is becoming more important **Minerals and Mining:** Iron ore and diamonds are exploited, and petroleum is being produced in the Cabinda exclave **Labor Force:** Total currently unknown, with an estimated 80% in agriculture, and 10% in industry **Foreign Trade:** Exports, chiefly petroleum, coffee, iron ore, diamonds, cotton, and fish meal, totaled $945 million in 1975. Imports, mainly machinery, textiles, transportation and construction equipment, iron and steel prod-

[*]Died September 1979

ucts, rice, and electrical products, totaled $480 million **Principal Trade Partners:** Portugal, West Germany, United States, Britain, Spain, Japan, France

Vital Statistics: Birthrate, 47.2 per 1,000 of pop. (1975); death rate, 27 (1974) **Life Expectancy:** 38.5 years **Health Statistics:** 322 inhabitants per hospital bed; 15,404 per physician (1972) **Infant Mortality:** 20.8 per 1,000 births **Illiteracy:** 85% **Education Statistics:** 5,208 primary and secondary schools, with combined enrollment of 595,186 (1972) **Higher Education:** 2,660 (1971) **GNP Expended on Education:** 2.2% (1972)

Transportation: Surfaced roads total 8,371 mi. (1974) **Motor Vehicles:** 183,031 (1973) **Passenger Cars:** 127,271 **Railway Mileage:** 1,895 **Ports:** Lobito, Luanda, Moçamades, Cabinda **Major Airlines:** Domestic flights are by TAAG (Angolan Airlines) **Communications:** Government owned **Radio Transmitters:** 19 (1972) **Receivers:** 116,000 (1976) **Television:** None **Telephones:** 31,000 (1976) **Newspapers:** 1 daily, 2 copies per 1,000 inhabitants (1975)

Weights and Measures: Metric system **Travel Requirements:** Passport; at present travel is inadvisable; telegraph Foreign Ministry at Luanda, Angola, giving name, passport no., travel date and reason for travel

---

Fifteen years of rebellion against colonial rule culminated in the granting of Angolan independence by Portugal on November 11, 1975. However, independence did not bring peace to Angola, the largest and most important territory of the former Portuguese overseas empire. Three factions contended for power in this resource-rich country: the Marxist-oriented Popular Movement for the Liberation of Angola (MPLA), the pro-Western National Front for the Liberation of Angola (FNLA), and the pro-Western National Union for the Total Independence of Angola (UNITA). The MPLA, backed by the Soviet Union and Cuba, held the Angolan capital, Luanda, while the pro-Western forces occupied most of the country north and south of the capital. The civil war raged throughout 1975.

Initially, following independence, the pro-Western FNLA and UNITA forces scored military successes against the Marxist MPLA in the central area around Luanda. Both sides employed foreign troops in their fight for full control of the nation. Particularly important was the contribution to the MPLA of trained manpower by Cuba and of arms by the U.S.S.R. South African armed forces crossed into Angola from Namibia (South-West Africa) to aid the FNLA and UNITA.

In late November and early December the military tide turned in favor of the MPLA as a result of the massive Soviet and Cuban assistance. The situation grew increasingly grim for the pro-Western factions on December 19 when the U.S. Senate voted to cut off covert financial aid to the combatants. By mid-February 1976 the MPLA forces had smashed the two pro-Western factions and had overrun most of Angola. South African troops withdrew into Namibia in late March. But elements of both the defeated FNLA and UNITA continue to wage guerrilla warfare today.

The violent conditions of this period resulted in the flight of most of the Portuguese population. The departure of the educationally and technically advanced segment of Angolan society resulted in a drastic decline in the economic life of the country.

As the MPLA (renamed the MPLA-Labor Party in 1977) gained victory in early 1976, diplomatic recognition was extended by many nations to the Luanda group under President Cuito Agostinho Neto. The continued presence of Cuban troops after the cessation of hostilities denied American recognition to the new nation. The Neto government faces massive economic problems. While declaring that the Cuban presence is vital as long as South African forces continue raids in his country, Neto edged closer to the West. In December 1978, he cordially greeted U.S. Sen. George McGovern (D-S.D.) and expressed the desire to establish diplomatic relations with the U.S.

HISTORY: Prior to the coming of the Portuguese in 1483, present-day Angola was part of the African Kingdom of the Kongo. During the 16th century Portugal established trading posts along the coast and exploited Angola as a prime source of the lucrative slave trade. The Dutch captured and held the Angolan port cities for seven years until the Portuguese recaptured them in 1648.

1884-5: At Berlin Conference the Portuguese receive "right of occupation" to Angola while losing all claim to central African territory

1910-20: Portugal begins serious colonizing effort in Angola

1926: Portuguese Republic overthrown. Subsequent authoritarian regime of Salazar tightens Portuguese rule over colony

1961: Rebellion against Portugal breaks out, beginning 15-year violent struggle for independence

1962: UN General Assembly votes condemnation of Portuguese administration of colonies

1975: Portugal grants Angolan independence. Rival factions battle for supremacy

1976: Marxist MPLA group wins control of Angola. Angola admitted to the UN

1978: In April 5,000 Cuban troops lead government offensive against pro-Western guerrillas. In May South African forces enter Angola from South-West Africa in "limited military operation" against guerrillas of SWAPO (South-West African People's Organization) South Africa's action is unanimously condemned by UN Security Council. In December Pres. Neto makes overtures to U.S.

1979: In March, South African forces attack SWAPO bases in Angola. President Neto dies in September

---

ARGENTINA

Area: 1,068,296 sq. mi. **Population:** 26,500,000 (1978 est.)

Official Name: Argentine Republic **Capital:** Buenos Aires **Nationality:** Argentine **Languages:** Spanish is the official and principal language. Italian, French, and German are also frequently heard **Religion:** About 95% of the population belongs to the Roman Catholic Church, which is officially recognized in the Constitution. There are small minorities of Protestants and Jews **Flag:** Horizontal stripes of blue, white, and blue, with the sun on the white stripe **Anthem:** Argentine National Anthem, beginning "Hear, mortals, the sacred cry of Liberty" **Currency:** New Argentine peso (1,204 per U.S. $1)

Location: Southern South America. Argentina is bordered on the north by Bolivia and Paraguay, on the northeast by Brazil and Uruguay, on the east and south by the Atlantic Ocean, and on the west by Chile **Features:** The heartland of Argentina is the rich, temperate plains area known as the Pampas, which fans out from the east-central sector of the country. The north consists of subtropical lowlands, while the west is dominated by the Andean Mountains and the south by the Patagonian steppe and the rainy Tierra del Fuego **Chief Rivers:** Paraná, Negro, Salado, Colorado, Chubut

Head of State and Government: President: Lt. Gen. Jorge Rafael Videla, born 1925, took office following the coup of March 1976, confirmed for three-year term in May 1978 by the 3-man junta. The junta, which reserves final executive power, will serve a 3-year term, and is advised by a military Legislative Advisory Commission **Effective Date of Present Constitution:** Although the constitution of 1853 is still in effect, its provisions have been made subject to the Statutes of the Revolution, issued after a military coup in 1966 **Legislative Body:** The National Congress was dissolved in 1976 **Local Government:** 22 provinces, 1 national territory, and 1 federal district, each administered by an appointed military governor

Ethnic Composition: 97% of the population is of European origin; persons of Arab descent, Indians and mestizos constitute about 3% **Population Distribution:** 81.1% urban (1975) **Density:** 24.8 inhabitants per sq. mi.

Largest Cities: (M.A. = Metropolitan Area): Buenos Aires (1974 est.) 2,976,000 (M.A. 8,925,000); others (1970 census) Córdoba 781,565 (M.A. 790,508), Rosario 750,455 (M.A. 806,942), Lanús 449,824, Lomas de Zamora 410,806, La Plata 391,247 (M.A. 478,666)

Per Capita Income: $1,877 (1978) **Gross National Product (GNP):** $49.7 billion (1978 est.) **Economic Statistics:** In 1975, 48% of the GNP came from trade and services; 36% from industry (iron and steel, automobiles, machinery, chemicals, cement); 11% from agriculture (meat, hides, grain, fruits); and 8% from mining and construction **Minerals and Mining:** Oil and natural gas supply domestic needs; low-grade iron ore and small amounts of coal, lead, zinc, silver, bismuth, vanadium, beryllium, tantalite, and tungsten are mined **Labor Force:** 9,928,234 in 1975, of which 29% is employed in manufacturing and 15% in agriculture; approximately 2.5 million are organized in unions **Foreign Trade:** Exports, chiefly grains, meat, wool, hides, linseed oil and other agricultural products totaled $5.5 billion in 1977. Imports, mainly machinery and equipment, iron and steel products, chemicals, textiles and fuels, totaled $4 billion **Principal Trade Partners:** United States, Brazil, West Germany, Netherlands, Italy, Britain, Japan

Vital Statistics: Birthrate, 21.8 per 1,000 of pop. (1975); death rate, 8.8 **Life Expectancy:** 68 years **Health Statistics:** 176 inhabitants per hospital bed; 479 per physician (1972) **Infant Mortality:** 59 per 1,000 births (1970) **Illiteracy:** 7% **Education Statistics:** 20,837 primary and secondary schools, with combined enrollment of 4,822,812 (1975) **Enrollment in Higher Education:** 596,736 **GNP Expended on Education:** 4% (1974)

Transportation: Paved roads total 23,000 mi. (1975) **Motor Vehicles:** 3,500,000 (1976) **Passenger Cars:** 2,160,000 (1974) **Railway Mileage:** 25,794 **Ports:** Buenos Aires, Bahía Blanca, La Plata, Rosario **Major Airlines:** Aerolíneas Argentinas is the major international and domestic carrier **Communications:** Partly government owned **Radio Transmitters:** 163 (1974) **Receivers:** 26,000,000 (1973) **Television Transmitters:** 82 **Receivers:** 4,500,000 (1974) **Telephones:** 2,400,000 (1976) **Newspapers:** 167 dailies, 179 copies per 1,000 inhabitants (1974)

Weights and Measures: Metric system **Travel Requirements:** Passport, no visa for 90 days

---

Extending 2,300 miles from north to south and with an Atlantic coastline 1,600 miles long, Argentina is the second-largest country on the South American continent, after Brazil. Its topography and climate are as varied as those of the United States, the terrain ranging from the subtropical lowlands of the north to the towering Andean Mountains in the west and the bleak Patagonian steppe and rainy Tierra del Fuego in the south. More than 60 percent of the country's area is suitable for agriculture, of which about 8 percent is under cultivation and the remainder is pastureland upon which a massive livestock population thrives (there are currently more than two animals for every Argentine man, woman and child). The heartland of Argentina is the rich, temperate plains area known as the Pampas, which fans out for almost 500 miles from Buenos Aires in the east-central sector; here is found some of the richest topsoil in the world.

Politically, the dominant factor of life in Argentina has been turmoil. In the early months of 1976, Argentina was a country on the edge of anarchy, racked by daily kidnappings and bombings. Its treasury, down to its last foreign reserves, was about to default on its overseas debt. Then, on March 24, in a bloodless coup led by the Commander in Chief of the army, Jorge Rafael Videla, the military deposed Isabel Perón, the first woman chief of state in the Americas, from the presidency, her inept government falling along with her.

Mrs. Perón had come into power on the death of her husband, Juan Perón, in July 1974. He had returned to Argentina in June 1973, after 18 years of exile, which had been preceded by an 11-year rule as Argentina's president. He was re-elected to the presidency in September of that year, with his wife as vice-president.

After the ouster of Mrs. Perón, Videla was sworn in as president on March 29, 1976. The final executive power was entrusted to a military junta that set two goals: crushing terrorism and reviving the economy. By 1979, President Videla was able to say, "The war [against terrorism] is over, and now we must win the peace," and there were numerous signs that the iron rule was being relaxed. On the other front, the government's economic program scored some successes, notably in boosting agricultural production and in lifting foreign reserves to $7 billion—up from virtually nothing at the end of the Perón regime. But inflation persisted: prices rose 160 percent in 1977 and 170 percent the next year. Stores were marking up prices twice a month; the larger companies were raising wages once a month.

The armed forces are believed to have killed more than 5,000 Peronist and Marxist guerrillas or guerrilla suspects since taking power in the spring of 1976. The terrorists initially had inflicted heavy losses, numbering into the hundreds as they assassinated officers and businessmen and attacked military bases. The government conceded that 3,000 persons were held in the jails in 1979, but it said they were common criminals or terrorists rather than political prisoners. Students, journalists, nuns, and others "disappeared" in 1978 even after the apparent suppression of the left-wing terrorists. The leftists, however, did kill the 15-year-old daughter of Admiral Armando Lambruschini, the naval commander-in-chief, with a bomb intended for him in his Buenos Aires apartment.

The battle against inflation was made more difficult by increased military purchases in 1978. They arose out of heated negotiations with Chile over ownership of three Beagle Channel islands. Late in the year, 500,000 reservists were called up, and some cities staged blackouts and air raid drills.

President Videla retired from the army on July 31, 1978, and turned over his command there to General Roberto Viola. Videla's term as president was extended to March 1981—a date when, the military pledged, it will bring civilian leaders into a broader government. During a visit to Rome in September, Videla told the world press that his "national reorganization" program will eventually lead to democracy.

Ex-President Isabel Perón, after being held in preventive detention for 22 months on the naval base at Azul, was transferred to house arrest at her family estate in August 1978. In one case, she was convicted of embezzling $200,000 from a public charity that she headed while in office. Other charges of conspiracy and misfeasance in office were still in the courts.

HISTORY: The treeless plains of the Pampas were inhabited by fierce nomadic Indian tribes of unknown origin for centuries before 1516, when a band of eight conquistadors led by Juan Díaz de Solís landed on the shores of Río de la Plata. Magellan and Sebastian Cabot soon followed on other voyages of exploration and in 1580 Juan de Garay reached what is now Buenos Aires by way of Paraguay. By the 18th century Buenos Aires had become the capital of a vast Spanish viceroyalty that included Argentina

1810: Argentine revolutionists depose Spanish viceroy and form their own government

1817-19: General José de San Martín crosses the Andes with 5,000 men, defeats Spanish crown forces at Battle of Maipú (1818), and goes on to liberate Chile and Peru. New Argentine constitution sets off civil war between "federalists" and "unitarians," with the latter favoring a central government dominated by Buenos Aires

1829: Juan Manuel de Rosas, the federalist leader, establishes one-man rule

1845-52: Rosas interferes in neighboring countries; aided by Brazil, Uruguay, France and Britain, Justo José de Urquiza overthrows Rosas, who flees to England

1880-81: Long struggle between Buenos Aires and federalist forces ends, with the city becoming a federal district; settlers end Indians' resistance by virtually wiping them out

1916-30: Period of vast immigration and prosperity begins; Hipólito Irigoyen, leader of the Radicals, a bourgeois reform party, is elected president and enacts wide social-reform legislation. He is succeeded in 1922 by another Radical, but returns to power in 1928. Two years later he is overthrown by the military

1943-45: The latest in a string of military coups places Colonel Juan Domingo Perón in a relatively unimportant post as labor secretary. Perón, effecting sweeping social and economic reforms, wins popularity among masses; he is thrown in jail by frightened military men. Released after nine days, Perón asks for election

1946: Perón wins election. A widower, he takes as his second wife Eva Duarte, a radio star, who helps Perón establish trade unions along militant, Fascist lines

1952-55: Eva Perón dies (1952); Perón, unsettled, faces charges of immorality and corruption. After thwarting several coups, he is overthrown and makes his way to Spain

1972-73: Following a long succession of civilian and military presidents, Peronist puppet Héctor J. Cámpora is elected president, pledged to returning Perón to full power; Perón returns from exile on June 20, 1973; Cámpora resigns, Raúl A. Lastiri becoming interim president; presidential election set for September 1973; Perón runs on coalition ticket and is returned to power

1974: Perón dies; is succeeded by his wife, Isabel Perón

1976: Coup topples Mrs. Perón's government. Argentina is governed by junta led by General Jorge Rafael Videla

1978: Argentina wins World Cup soccer championship

AUSTRALIA

Area: 2,967,909 sq. mi. **Population:** 14,248,500 (1978)

Official Name: Commonwealth of Australia **Capital:** Canberra **Nationality:** Australian **Languages:** English **Religion:** 36% Anglican, 31% Roman Catholic, 10% Methodist, 9% Presbyterian, 2% Baptist, 12% others **Flag:** A blue field, with the Union Jack in the upper left corner, a large, 7-pointed white star directly beneath, and five smaller white stars in the right half **Anthem:** God Save the Queen (National Song: Advance Australia Fair) **Currency:** Australian dollar (0.91 per U.S. $1)

Location: An island continent between the Indian and Pacific oceans, lying southeast of Asia. It is bounded on the north by the Torres Strait and the Timor Sea, on the east by the Coral and Tasman seas, and on the south and west by the Indian Ocean. The continent and the island of Tasmania, off the eastern part of the south coast, make up the Commonwealth of Australia **Features:** The continent is roughly a low, irregular plateau, with a flat, arid center. The southeastern quarter of the continent is a huge fertile plain covering some 500,000 sq. mi. Relatively low mountains lie close to the east coast **Chief Rivers:** Murray, Darling, Murrumbidgee, Burdekin, Fitzroy, Ord

Head of State: Queen Elizabeth II, represented by a governor-general, Sir Zelman Cowen, born 1919, appointed 1977 **Head of Government:** Prime Minister John Malcolm Fraser, born 1930, reelected 1977 **Effective Date of Present Constitution:** 1900, revised 1977 **Legislative Body:** Federal Parliament (bicameral), consisting of a Senate and House of Representatives. There are 64 Senators, elected for 6-year terms. The House consists of 124 members, elected every 3 years **Local Government:** 6 states, each headed by a governor appointed by the sovereign and with an elected legislature, premier, and a cabinet. There is also one internal territory, one capital territory, and six external territories

Ethnic Composition: The population is mainly of British origin; Aborigines (excluding mixed-bloods) number 40,000 **Population Distribution:** 86% urban **Density:** 4.8 inhabitants per sq. mi.

Largest Cities (Metropolitan Area): (1976 census) Sydney 3,021,300, Melbourne 2,603,000, Brisbane 957,000, Adelaide 900,000, Perth 805,000, Canberra 215,400, Hobart 162,000

Per Capita Income: $6,324 (1978) **Gross National Product (GNP):** $88 billion (1978 est.) **Economic Statistics:** About 30% of GNP comes from industry (steel, automobiles, ships, textiles, chemicals, petroleum refining, electrical equipment). Agriculture and mining, however, are the mainstays of the economy. Australia is the world's foremost wool-growing country, producing almost one-third of the world's wool, and is a leading producer of meats and dairy products. Mining, which accounts for 3% of GNP, plays an important role in the country's export trade **Minerals and Mining:** Coal, iron ore, bauxite, copper, lead, zinc, uranium, nickel, crude oil, and other minerals are mined. Australian wells provide 50% of the nation's crude oil requirements. About 90% of indigenous oil production is from offshore wells in the Bass Strait, discovered in 1964 and estimated to have reserves of 1,500 million barrels. There have been several natural gas finds; reserves are estimated at 20 trillion cu. ft. of gas **Labor Force:** 6.2 million (1978), of which 22% is employed in manufacturing, 6% in agriculture, and 51% in services **Foreign Trade:** Exports, chiefly wool, wheat, meat, dairy products, and iron ore, totaled $14.2 billion in 1978. Imports, mainly machinery and transportation equipment, manufactured goods, chemicals, mineral fuels, crude materials, food and beverages, totaled $14 billion **Principal Trade Partners:** Japan, United States, Britain, West Germany, New Zealand, Canada, Singapore, France

Vital Statistics: Birthrate, 16.1 per 1,000 of pop. (1977); death rate, 7.7 **Life Expectancy:** 71 years **Health Statistics:** 80 inhabitants per hospital bed; 600 per physician (1975) **Infant Mortality:** 14 per 1,000 births **Illiteracy:** Negligible **Education Statistics:** 9,452 primary and secondary schools, with combined enrollment of 2,957,494 (1974) **Enrollment in Higher Education:** 274,738 (1975) **GNP Expended on Education:** 6.3% (1975)

Transportation: Paved roads total 261,170 mi. (1973) **Motor Vehicles:** 6,328,600 **Passenger Cars:** 5,124,000 (1976) **Railway Mileage:** 25,166 **Ports:** Sydney, Melbourne, Newcastle, Port Kembla, Fremantle, Port Hedland, Port Adelaide, Dampier, Brisbane **Major Airlines:** Qantas Airways is the major international carrier; domestic flights are operated by Trans-Australia Airlines and the privately-owned Ansett Airlines of Australia **Communications:** Both government and privately owned **Radio Transmitters:** 219 **Receivers:** 10,500,000 (1976) **Television Transmitters:** 198 Li-

censes: 4,785,000 (1976) **Telephones:** 5,502,000 (1976) **Newspapers:** 70 dailies, 394 copies per 1,000 inhabitants (1975)

Weights and Measures: British standards are being replaced by the metric system **Travel Requirements:** Passport, visa valid for 48 months or life of passport, no fee

Political and economic pressures of the postwar era, enhanced by the communications revolution of the times, have propelled Australia out of easygoing isolation into an increasing involvement in world and regional affairs.

Australia is one of the foremost donors of foreign aid in terms of the assistance given compared with the national income. Much of this aid goes to Papua New Guinea, which became independent on September 16, 1975. The emergence of new independent island states in the South Pacific has thrust demands for leadership on Australia as the most advanced and affluent power in its geopolitical sphere.

Ties between Australians and the "mother country," Britain, loosened significantly in World War II when it became clear that the hard-pressed British forces were unable to defend Australia against the Japanese onslaught. Americans filled the breach, and from that time on the Australians have looked toward the United States as the guarantor of national security. The new relationship was cemented after the war in the ANZUS (Australia, New Zealand, United States) Treaty of Mutual Security.

Recently, Australia had adopted a more independent stance in international affairs. The government recognized the People's Republic of China in late 1972 and opened diplomatic relations with Peking in 1973.

Assistance to the country's 50,000 full-blood aborigines and 150,000 part-aborigines has been stepped up, but advancement programs have foundered due to administrative problems. Aborigines have been demanding a greater say in their own affairs. There is one aborigine in Parliament. In November 1978, the government agreed to grant Northern Territory aborigines a 4.25 percent royalty (estimated $11 million per year) on uranium oxide extracted from a ranger site.

The application of postwar technology to the exploitation of vast mineral resources revolutionized the Australian economy. By the 1970s, Australia had become the leading supplier of lead and zinc, the chief iron ore exporter and furnished 90 percent of the world's rutile and zircon.

Development of underground wealth required massive importation of capital, principally from Japan, Britain and the United States. A major consequence has been the emergence of Japan as Australia's major customer overseas, taking 27 percent of the country's total exports. The relationship has shown signs of broadening into a political partnership, with the two countries examining possible avenues of cooperation in southeast Asian and Pacific affairs.

There has been a nationalist backlash against the extent of foreign ownership of business, particularly in the mining industry. Foreign takeover bids for major Australian companies are subject to government approval. To protect local firms from exploitation by foreign mineral buyers, the government announced in October 1978 its intention to supervise all mineral exportation negotiations.

HISTORY: Long before it was first sighted by European explorers in the 17th century, Australia was inhabited by primitive native groups with various languages and customs. In 1770, Captain James Cook explored the east coast of the continent and claimed it for Britain. Within 50 years, the whole of Australia became a British dependency, serving as a penal colony and dumping ground for British criminals and undesirables

1851-59: Gold strikes in Victoria and New South Wales in 1851 attract thousands of new settlers; within two decades the rising population is settled in six self-governing colonies

AUSTRALIA

BONNE PROJECTION

SCALE OF MILES

SCALE OF KILOMETRES

National Capitals ─────⦿

State and Territorial Capitals ─────⦿

1901: Constitution providing for federation of colonies is approved by British Parliament; Commonwealth of Australia comes into being

1914-18: Australia fights on Allied side during World War I

1939-45: Australia fights alongside Allies in World War II

1946-48: Immigrants, numbering 2 million by 1965, begin to pour into Australia

1952-54: Australia signs Pacific defense pact (ANZUS) with New Zealand and United States and joins SEATO

1972: The first Labor Party government in 23 years is elected, recognizes the People's Republic of China

1975: The Labor Party government is dismissed. Liberal-Country Party coalition government is elected by a large majority vote. Papua New Guinea is granted independence

1977: Liberal-Country Party government decisively reelected

1978: In November worsening economy prompts division of Ministry of Employment and Industsrial Relations into two separate cabinet departments

1979: In January Cyclone Peter causes extensive damage in north Queensland. In February, Prime Minister Fraser streamlines cabinet, delegating more authority to ministers

AUSTRIA

Area: 32,375 sq. mi. **Population:** 7,620,000 (1978 est.)

Official Name: Republic of Austria **Capital:** Vienna **Nationality:** Austrian **Languages:** German is the official and principal language. Slovenian, Croatian, and Hungarian are spoken by small minorities **Religion:** 90% Roman Catholic **Flag:** Red, white, and red horizontal stripes, with the national emblem centered on the white stripe **Anthem:** Land of Mountains, Land on the River **Currency:** Schilling (14.0 per U.S. $1)

Location: Central Europe. Landlocked Austria is bordered by West Germany and Czechoslovakia on the north, Hungary on the east, Yugoslavia and Italy on the south, and Switzerland and Liechtenstein on the west **Features:** The country is 70% mountainous, with the Alps and their outliers dominating the west and south. The east and Vienna are located in the Danube basin **Chief Rivers:** Danube, Inn, Mur, Drau, Enns

Head of State: President Rudolf Kirchschlaeger, born 1915, elected 1974 **Head of Government:** Chancellor Bruno Kreisky, born 1911, took office April 1970, reappointed May 1979 **Effective Date of Present Constitution:** 1920, amended 1929, reinstated 1945 **Legislative Body:** Federal Assembly (bicameral parliament), consisting of the Federal Council (upper house), or Bundesrat, with 58 members, and the National Council (lower house), or Nationalrat, with 183 members. Members of the Upper House are appointed by provincial diets for 4 to 6-year terms; members of the Lower House are elected for 4 years **Local Government:** 9 provinces, each administered by an elected governor and provincial legislature

Ethnic Composition: Austrians are generally of South Germanic stock, with Slavic admixtures. The only sizeable minority group consists of some 70,000 Slovenes in Carinthia **Population Distribution:** 54% urban **Density:** 235.4 inhabitants per sq. mi.

Largest Cities: (1973 est.) Vienna 1,700,000, Graz 251,900, Linz 205,700, Salzburg 122,100, Innsbruck 115,800

Per Capita Income: $5,491 (1978) **Gross National Product (GNP):** $41.4 billion (1978 est.) **Economic Statistics:** About 61% of GNP comes from industry (machinery, iron and steel, food and beverages, chemicals, textiles, ceramics, stone and glass, and metal goods); 5% from agriculture and forestry **Minerals and Mining:** Iron ore, petroleum, magnesite, lignite, and natural gas **Labor Force:** 2,700,000 (1978), of which 60% is employed in commerce and industry, 14% in agriculture, and 26% in services **Foreign Trade:** Exports, mainly machinery, iron and steel, textiles, chemicals, wood and paper, totaled $10 billion in 1977. Imports, chiefly machinery, transportation equipment, textiles, mineral fuels and chemicals, totaled $14 billion **Principal Trade Partners:** West Germany, Switzerland, Italy, Britain, United States, Sweden, Netherlands, France, U.S.S.R., Poland, Yugoslavia

Vital Statistics: Birthrate, 11 per 1,000 of pop. (1976); death rate, 13.5 **Life Expectancy:** 73 years **Health Statistics:** 88 inhabitants per hospital bed; 479 per physician (1975) **Infant Mortality:** 16.9 per 1,000 births (1977) **Illiteracy:** Negligible **Education Statistics:** 3,711 primary and secondary schools, with combined enrollment of 1,247,343 (1974) **Enrollment in Higher Education:** 96,376 (1975) **GNP Expended on Education:** 5.7% (1975)

Transportation: Surfaced roads total 20,357 mi. **Motor Vehicles:** 2,287,200 (1976) **Passenger Cars:** 1,828,100 **Railway Mileage:** 4,081 **Ports:** None **Major Airlines:** Austrian Airlines operates international and domestic flights **Communications:** Government owned **Radio Transmitters:** 399 **Licenses:** 2,185,000 (1976) **Television Transmitters:** 461 **Licenses:** 1,772,000 (1976) **Telephones:** 2,281,000 (1976) **Newspapers:** 30 dailies, 320 copies per 1,000 inhabitants (1975)

Weights and Measures: Metric system **Travel Requirements:** Passport, no visa for 3 months

Once the core of the Hapsburg Empire that covered much of Central and Southern Europe, Austria has been reduced by wars to a relatively small state and, by its geographical position, to a land that is officially neutral between East and West. But its actual sympathies and economic ties lie with the West.

Because Austria was forced by Hitler's 1938 *Anschluss* to become part of the Nazi war machine, the victors of World War II granted it a special state treaty in 1955, which specified the country's official neutrality.

But most of Austria's trade is with Western Europe. After the European Economic Community was organized in 1958, Austria sought association with it, despite the objections of the Soviet Union, which argued that association was incompatible with neutrality. Austria joined the European Free Trade Association in 1960, and, over token Soviet opposition, negotiated a special agreement with the EEC in 1973

Internal politics have been influenced by an almost equal division of voting strength between the People's party—which professes Christian values and respect for property—and the Socialist party. From 1945 to 1966, the People's party had a plurality, but not a majority, in the *Nationalrat* and governed in coalition with the Socialists. The two parties made this arrangement because neither trusted the small Freedom party, which held the rest of the seats, and because memories of the chaos of the 1930s caused a desire for stability. This "grand coalition" ended in 1966, when a special election gave the People's party a one-seat majority; the Socialists were offered a coalition, but imposed conditions which the winners thought unreasonable. In 1970 the Socialists won a plurality, but not a majority, and formed a minority government with Bruno Kreisky as Chancellor after attempts to reorganize the grand coalition broke down. This government remained in office after winning majorities in the elections of 1971, 1975 and 1979. There is little real difference between the parties, and the economy has remained basically capitalist, but with much state intervention.

Aside from the basic industries, an important source of income in Austria is tourism, as visitors are attracted to Alpine ski slopes and lakes and tocity attractions such as the summer festival in Mozart's native city, Salzburg, and the spring festival week in Vienna.

HISTORY: Austria was settled by various tribes in prehistoric times and was subject to numerous invasions long before the Roman conquest around 15 B.C. About A.D. 800 it became a province of Charlemagne's empire and was joined to the Holy Roman Empire two centuries later. German-speaking rulers sponsored migrations, and the German language became predominant. By the end of the 13th century most of Austria was firmly under the rule of the Hapsburgs, who were to build a huge empire in central and southern Europe. By 1815, Austria had also become the leading power in the German Confederation, only to lose that position half a century later

1848: Nationalistic minorities in the Austrian Empire revolt against the monarchy but are subdued by Austrian forces

1866: Austro-Prussian War ends in Austrian defeat and terminates Austrian influence in German Confederation

1867: Hungary gains equal rights with Austria under a dual monarchy

1914-18: On June 28, 1914, a Serbian nationalist assassinates Archduke Francis Ferdinand, triggering World War I; Austria is allied with Germany and other Central Powers and shares in their defeat; Hapsburg monarchy collapses and Austria is proclaimed a republic

1932-34: Engelbert Dollfuss becomes chancellor and opposes Anschluss (union) with Germany; the outlawed Nazi party carries out his assassination (1934)

1938: Hitler annexes Austria to Germany

WORLD FLAGS and MAPS

AFGHANISTAN	ALBANIA	ALGERIA	ANDORRA *
ARGENTINA	AUSTRALIA	AUSTRIA	BAHAMAS
BAHRAIN	BANGLADESH	BARBADOS	BELGIUM
BELIZE	BHUTAN	BOLIVIA	BOTSWANA
BRAZIL	BULGARIA	BURMA	BURUNDI
CAMBODIA	CAMEROON	CANADA *	CENTRAL AFRICAN EMP.
CHAD	CHILE	CHINA (MAINLAND)	CHINA (TAIWAN)
COLOMBIA *	CONGO	COSTA RICA	CUBA
CYPRUS	CZECHOSLOVAKIA	BENIN (DAHOMEY)	DENMARK *

* For flags of ANGOLA, CAPE VERDE, COMOROS, DJIBOUTI and DOMINICA see page 517

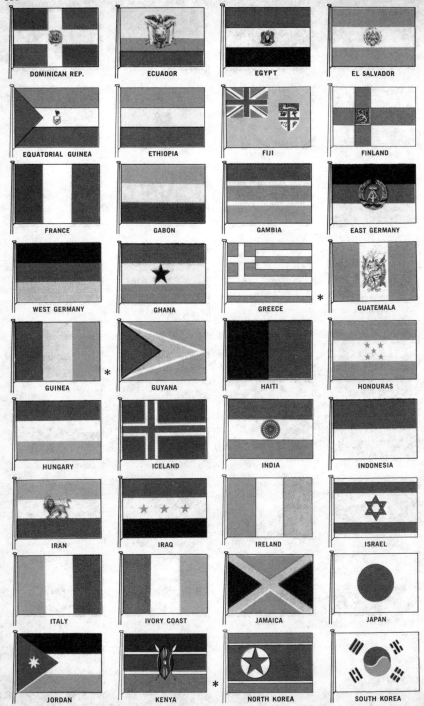

DOMINICAN REP. ECUADOR EGYPT EL SALVADOR

EQUATORIAL GUINEA ETHIOPIA FIJI FINLAND

FRANCE GABON GAMBIA EAST GERMANY

WEST GERMANY GHANA GREECE * GUATEMALA

GUINEA * GUYANA HAITI HONDURAS

HUNGARY ICELAND INDIA INDONESIA

IRAN IRAQ IRELAND ISRAEL

ITALY IVORY COAST JAMAICA JAPAN

JORDAN KENYA * NORTH KOREA SOUTH KOREA

* For flags of GRENADA, GUINEA-BISSAU and KIRIBATI see page 517

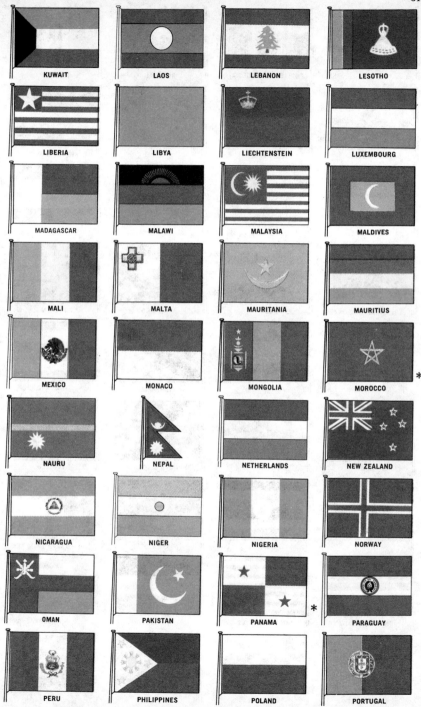

515

KUWAIT

LAOS

LEBANON

LESOTHO

LIBERIA

LIBYA

LIECHTENSTEIN

LUXEMBOURG

MADAGASCAR

MALAWI

MALAYSIA

MALDIVES

MALI

MALTA

MAURITANIA

MAURITIUS

MEXICO

MONACO

MONGOLIA

MOROCCO *

NAURU

NEPAL

NETHERLANDS

NEW ZEALAND

NICARAGUA

NIGER

NIGERIA

NORWAY

OMAN

PAKISTAN

PANAMA *

PARAGUAY

PERU

PHILIPPINES

POLAND

PORTUGAL

* For flags of MOZAMBIQUE and PAPUA NEW GUINEA see page 517

516

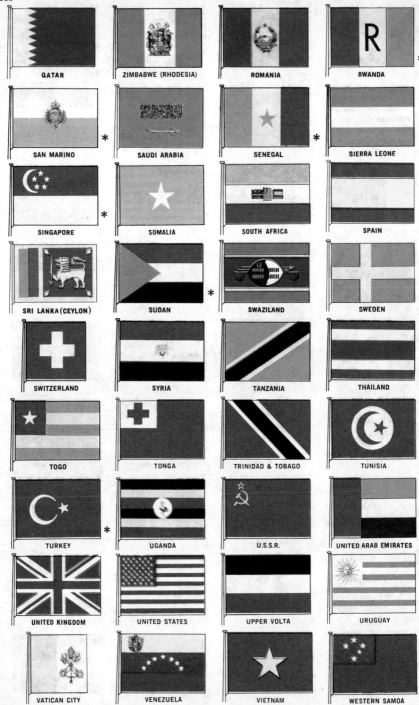

QATAR ZIMBABWE (RHODESIA) ROMANIA RWANDA *

SAN MARINO * SAUDI ARABIA SENEGAL * SIERRA LEONE

SINGAPORE * SOMALIA SOUTH AFRICA SPAIN

SRI LANKA (CEYLON) SUDAN * SWAZILAND SWEDEN

SWITZERLAND SYRIA TANZANIA THAILAND

TOGO TONGA TRINIDAD & TOBAGO TUNISIA

TURKEY * UGANDA U.S.S.R. UNITED ARAB EMIRATES

UNITED KINGDOM UNITED STATES UPPER VOLTA URUGUAY

VATICAN CITY VENEZUELA VIETNAM WESTERN SAMOA

* For flags of ST. LUCIA, SÃO TOMÉ E PRÍNCIPE, SEYCHELLES, SOLOMON IS., SURINAME and TUVALU see next page

517

YEMEN (PEOPLES REP.)

YEMEN ARAB REP.

YUGOSLAVIA

ZAIRE

ZAMBIA

INDEPENDENT
NATIONS
1974-1979

GRENADA (1974)

GUINEA-BISSAU (1974)

MOZAMBIQUE (1975)

CAPE VERDE (1975)

COMOROS (1975)

SÃO TOMÉ E
PRÍNCIPE (1975)

PAPUA NEW GUINEA (1975)

ANGOLA (1975)

SURINAME (1975)

SEYCHELLES (1976)

DJIBOUTI (1977)

SOLOMON ISLANDS (1978)

TUVALU (1978)

DOMINICA (1978)

ST. LUCIA (1979)

KIRIBATI (1979)

TIME ZONES OF THE WORLD

STANDARD TIME ZONES

Areas using half hour deviations.

Areas not using zone system.

NOTE: Standard time zones in the U.S.S.R. are always advanced one hour.

THE WORLD

MERCATOR PROJECTION

Capitals of Countries..............☆

Longitude West of Greenwich

Longitude East of Greenwich

EUROPE

LAMBERT AZIMUTHAL EQUAL-AREA PROJECTION

SCALE OF MILES

0   100   200   300   400   500   600

SCALE OF KILOMETRES

0   100   200   300   400   500   600

Capitals of Countries .... ⊛   International Boundaries ....
Internal Boundaries ....

Copyright by C.S. HAMMOND & CO., N.Y.

AFRICA

LAMBERT AZIMUTHAL EQUAL-AREA PROJECTION

SCALE OF MILES
0   100   200   400   600   800

SCALE OF KILOMETERS
0   200   400   600   800

Capitals of Countries........⋆
Other Capitals..............●
Canals.....................
International Boundaries........
Mountain Peaks..............▲
Elevations in Feet..........8,534

CAPE VERDE

Ribeira Grande
Santo Antão
Mindelo
São Vicente
Santa Luzia
São Nicolau
Sal
Sal Reis
Boa Vista
Sta. Maria
Maio
Fogo
Brava
São Tiago
⋆Praia

MILES
0   20   40   60

AFRICA 1939

British
French
Italian
Portuguese
Spanish
Belgian
Mandates

MOROCCO
TUNISIA
ALGERIA
LIBYA
EGYPT
RIO DE ORO
FRENCH WEST AFRICA
GAMBIA
PORT. GUINEA
SIERRA LEONE
LIBERIA
GOLD COAST
TOGO
NIGERIA
CAMEROONS
RIO MUNI
ANGLO-EGYPTIAN SUDAN
FR. SOM. COAST
ITALIAN EAST AFRICA
EQUATORIAL AFRICA
UGANDA
KENYA
R. U.
BELGIAN CONGO
TANGANYIKA
ANGOLA
NO. RHODESIA
SO. RHODESIA
NYASALAND
MOZAMBIQUE
SOUTH WEST AFRICA
BECH. PROT.
UNION OF SOUTH AFRICA
SWAZILAND
BASUTOLAND
MADAGASCAR

Longitude West of Greenwich 20°   Longitude East of Greenwich

ASIA

LAMBERT AZIMUTHAL EQUAL-AREA PROJECTION

SCALE OF MILES

SCALE OF KILOMETERS

Capitals of Countries...... ☆
International Boundaries..... — — —
Canals.......... — — —

© Copyright HAMMOND INCORPORATED, Maplewood, N.J.

THE NEAR and MIDDLE EAST

CONIC PROJECTION

SCALE OF MILES

0 100 200 300 400

KILOMETERS

0 100 200 300 400

Capitals of Countries .... ☆

Other Capitals .... ◉

International Boundaries ....

Other Boundaries ....

Copyright by C. S. HAMMOND & Co., N.Y.

527

NORTH AMERICA
LAMBERT AZIMUTHAL EQUAL-AREA PROJECTION

SCALE OF MILES

SCALE OF KILOMETRES

Capitals of Countries
International Boundaries
Other Boundaries
Canals

Copyright by C. S. HAMMOND & Co., N.Y.

PACIFIC OCEAN
LAMBERT AZIMUTHAL EQUAL-AREA PROJECTION

Capitals of Countries
Other Capitals

Copyright by C. S. HAMMOND & Co., N.Y.

1945: United States, U.S.S.R., Britain, and France divide Austria into occupation zones following World War II People's party wins elections; forms coalition with Socialist party

1955: Occupation forces leave and Austria proclaims permanent neutrality

1966: The conservative People's Party gains absolute majority in parliamentary election, ending 20-year rule of Socialist-conservative coalition

1969: Parliament, by overwhelming majority, ratifies treaty to prevent spread of nuclear weapons. Austria and Italy agree to give major autonomy to the 230,000 German-speaking inhabitants of the Italian province of Alto Adige. Socialists win, but without majority; their leader, Bruno Kreisky, becomes Chancellor of minority government

1975: Socialist government wins second majority

1976: 12th Winter Olympics are held in Innsbruck.

BAHAMAS

Area: 5,382 sq. mi. **Population:** 235,000 (1978 est.)
Official Name: Commonwealth of the Bahamas **Capital:** Nassau **Nationality:** Bahamian **Language:** English **Religion:** There are Baptist, Methodist, Anglican, and Roman Catholic congregations **Flag:** Three horizontal stripes, the upper and lower aquamarine, the middle gold, with a black equilateral triangle on the hoist **Anthem:** March on, Bahamaland **Currency:** Bahamian dollar (1.00 per U.S. $1)

Location: An archipelago located in the northern portion of the West Indies in the Atlantic **Features:** The Bahamas include 700 islands and 2,000 rocks and cays, but less than 30 of the islands are inhabited. The islands are generally low and flat, with many splendid beaches. The climate is pleasantly warm throughout the year

Head of State: Queen Elizabeth II, represented by acting governor-general Gerald C. Cash **Head of Government:** Prime Minister Lynden O. Pindling, reelected 1977 **Effective Date of Present Constitution:** July 1973 **Legislative Body:** A General Assembly consists of a Senate with 16 members and a House of Assembly with 38 elected members **Local Government:** 18 districts, administered by appointed commissioners

Ethnic Composition: 85% Negro; the rest are of British, Canadian, and U.S. descent **Population Distribution:** 57.9% urban **Density:** 44 inhabitants per sq. mi.

Largest Cities: (1970 census) Nassau 105,352, Freeport 15,546

Per Capita Income: $3,310 (1975) **Gross National Product (GNP):** $698 million (1973 est.) **Economic Statistics:** Tourism is the main source of income, about $412 million per year. About 7% of the work force is engaged in agriculture, and about 54% in industry. **Minerals and Mining:** Salt is extracted from brine by solar radiation; cement and petroleum products are produced **Labor Force:** 69,791 (1970), with 20% in industry, 7% in agriculture, and the rest in trade and services **Foreign Trade:** Exports, mainly cement, petroleum products, alcoholic beverages, pulp-wood, used motor cars, crawfish, and salt extracted from brine by solar radiation totaled about $3.4 billion in 1975. Imports of food, drink, tobacco, crude oil, manufactured articles, and animals totaled $3.6 billion **Principal Trade Partners:** Britain, Canada, United States, Saudi Arabia, Nigeria, Libya

Vital Statistics: Birthrate, 18.1 per 1,000; death rate, 3.9 per 1,000 **Life Expectancy:** 68.8 years **Infant Mortality:** 29.2 per 1,000 (1975) **Illiteracy:** 7% **Health Statistics:** 229 inhabitants per hospital bed; 1,242 per physician (1975) **Education Statistics:** 228 primary and secondary schools with a combined enrollment of 55,761 pupils (1974) **Enrollment in Higher Education:** 2,160 (1975) **GNP Expended on Education:** 5.4% (1973)

Transportation: Surfaced roads total about 1,000 mi. **Motor Vehicles:** 41,800 (1976) **Passenger Cars:** 36,500 **Railway Mileage:** None **Ports:** Nassau, Freeport **Major Airlines:** Nassau is served by numerous international carriers, and Bahamasair services the Family Islands **Communications:** Government-owned **Radio Transmitters:** 6 **Receivers:** 96,000 (1976) **Television:** None **Telephones:** 58,000 (1976) **Newspapers:** 2 dailies, 152 copies per 1,000 inhabitants (1975)

Weights and Measures: British and metric systems **Travel Requirements:** Passport and visa not required of tourist with onward/return ticket and citizenship identification

After three centuries as a British colony, The Bahamas became an independent nation on July 10, 1973. The new country at the same time became an independent member of the British Commonwealth—the 33rd British possession to gain its freedom since World War II. Bahamian Prime Minister Lynden O. Pindling and his ruling Progressive Liberal Party had received a mandate for independence in elections held in September 1972. The party was formed in 1953 by blacks discontented with the policies of the white-dominated government.

In opposition to Pindling's ruling party is the Free National Movement, made up of whites and black PLP dissidents.

Because of the warm climate and beautiful beaches, tourism is the major industry, accounting for over $412 million a year.

Citrus fruit, bananas, and vegetables are grown, but most food must still be imported. Pulpwood, cement, rum, and salt are exported. Nassau, the capital, is a major center for banking and insurance and for corporate operations. There is one bank for every 600 Bahamians. The Bahamas is also an oil transshipment point to the United States and has large refineries.

Despite these economic efforts, unemployment has persisted. With the jobless rate at 23 percent in 1978, the government ordered illegal aliens to leave the country. This action was directed mainly at an estimated 40,000 Haitians, several hundred of whom fled to Florida on crowded boats in the summer of 1978.

HISTORY: On Oct. 12, 1492, Christopher Columbus made his first landfall in the Western Hemisphere at San Salvador (now known as Watling Island) in the Bahamas. At the time the islands were inhabited by the Arawak Indians

1647: First permanent European settlement in the Bahamas

1860: Royal Victoria Hotel first attracts winter tourists

1964: Bahamas granted complete internal self-government

1973: Britain grants independence July 10

1975: A five-year treaty is signed with the European Community

BAHRAIN

Area: 255 sq. mi. **Population:** 305,000 (1978 est.)
Official Name: State of Bahrain **Capital:** Manama **Nationality:** Bahraini **Languages:** Predominantly Arabic; English used widely **Religion:** Moslem, the Sunni sect predominating in urban centers and the Shi'a sect in rural areas **Flag:** Red, with vertical serrated white band on the hoist **Anthem:** "National Anthem" **Currency:** Bahraini dinar (0.39 per U.S. $1)

Location: Southwest Asia. Eleven islands in the Persian Gulf. The main island, Bahrain, and those nearby lie 15 miles east of the coast of Saudi Arabia and about the same distance west of the coast of Qatar

Head of State: Emir Isa ibn Salman al Khalifa, born 1933 **Head of Government:** Prime Minister: Sheikh Khalifa ibn Salman al Khalifa, assisted by a cabinet **Effective Date of Present Constitution:** 1973 **Legislative Body:** Rule is by the emir's decree **Local Government:** 6 municipalities—4 urban, each administered by a partly-elected municipal council; and 2 rural

Ethnic Composition: 80% Arab, with about 12% Indians, Pakistanis, and Iranians and about 3,000 Europeans **Population Distribution:** 78.1% urban **Density:** 1,196 inhabitants per sq. mi.

Largest Cities: (1977 est.) Manama 100,000; (1972 est.) Muharraq 50,000

Per Capita Income: $5,167 (1978) **Gross National Product (GNP):** $1.6 billion (1978 est.) **Economic Statistics:** Petroleum refining and the production of crude oil are the most important economic resources. About 50% of the oil refined is piped from Saudi Arabia. There is in addition an aluminum smelter and smaller industrial plants. The islands produce dates, rice, and vegetables; fishing and shrimping are important regionally **Minerals and Mining:** Considerable deposits of natural gas exist, in addition to oil deposits **Labor Force:** 110,000 (1977 est.), with 5% in agriculture and 90% in industry (chiefly petroleum and aluminum refining) **Foreign Trade:** Exports, chiefly crude oil, totaled $1.4 billion in 1976. Imports, including machinery, foods, chemicals, industrial equipment, and vehicles, totaled $976 million in 1976 **Principal Trade Partners:** Britain, Saudi Arabia, United States, Japan, Iran, Kuwait, U.A.E.

Vital Statistics: Birthrate, 46 per 1,000 of pop. (1974); death rate, 9 **Infant Mortality:** 23 per 1,000 births (1974) **Health Statistics:** 257 inhabitants per hospital bed; 1,469 per physician (1975) **Illiteracy:** 48% **Education Statistics:** 107 primary and secondary schools, with a combined enrollment of 62,039 (1974) **Enrollment in Higher Education:** 703 (1975) **GNP Expended on Education:** -3.4% (1974)

Transportation: Roads total about 20 mi. **Motor Vehicles:** 32,800 (1975) **Passenger Cars:** 23,300 **Ports:** Sitra, Mina Salman **Major Airlines:** Gulf Air and several international companies service the country **Radio Transmitters:** 5 **Receivers:** 150,000 (1976) **Television Transmitters:** 1 **Receivers:** 31,000 (1976) **Telephones:** 31,000 (1976) **Newspapers:** 1 daily, 11 weeklies, 29 copies per 1,000 inhabitants
Weights and Measures: Metric system, plus local measures
Travel Requirements: Passport and visa required, $14 fee

Bahrain consists of a number of desert islands in the west central Persian Gulf, chief among these being Bahrain, Muharraq, Sitra, Umm Na'san, and the Hawar group. Bahrainis, who are Moslem Arabs, constitute about 80 percent of the population. There are also Arabs from elsewhere, Iranians, Indians, and Europeans.

The oil industry and transit trade are the mainstays of the economy. There is a large refinery on Sitra, and trade passes through Manama and Mina Salman, a duty-free transit center. "Offshore" service banking has become a new source of revenue for Bahrain.

Internally, the ruler, or emir, wields almost absolute power. In 1970 a Council of State was established, responsible to the ruler and serving at his pleasure. In 1971 Bahrain declared independence, ending its special relationship with Britain. Iran informally became Bahrain's protector—a position called into doubt by the revolution of 1979.

HISTORY: Bahrain may have been "Dilmun," a trade center mentioned in Sumerian records, but little is known of its history before it was occupied by Portugal (1501-1602). The present dynasty was founded in 1783 by an adventurer from Arabia

1820: British protectorate status begins

1971: Bahrain declares independence on August 15, and is admitted to the UN and the Arab League

1973: New constitution is in effect

1975: National Assembly is dissolved by Emir Khalifa

BANGLADESH

Area: 55,126 sq. mi. **Population:** 84,700,000 (1978 est.)
Official Name: People's Republic of Bangladesh **Capital:** Dacca **Nationality:** Bangladeshi **Languages:** Bengali is official; English is also widely used **Religion:** About 85% Moslem and 14% Hindu, with some Buddhists and Christians **Flag:** Rectangular, in bottle green, with a red circle, slightly left of center, on the green body **Anthem:** Amar Sonar Bangla (My Golden Bengal) by Rabindranath Tagore **Currency:** Taka (15.48 per U.S. $1)
Location: Bangladesh is bordered on the north, east, and west by India, on the southeast by Burma, and on the south by the Bay of Bengal **Features:** a subtropical alluvial plain, with many river valleys and deltas. Average annual temperature 49°F-80°F. Jute fields, rice paddies, tea plantations, tropical jungles, and swamps are prominent features of its landscape **Chief Rivers:** Ganges and Brahmaputra
Head of State: President: Maj. Gen. Ziaur Rahman, born 1936, assumed office in April 1977, elected June 1978 for a 5-year term **Head of Government:** Shah Azizur Rahman, appointed 1979 **Effective Date of Present Constitution:** Nov. 1972 **Legislative Body:** Unicameral 330-member Parliament; 30 seats are reserved for women **Local Government:** 19 districts grouped into 4 divisions
Ethnic Composition: The population is overwhelmingly Bengali, with a few tribal peoples in the hills near the Burma border **Population Distribution:** 8.8% urban (1974) **Density:** 1,537 inhabitants per sq. mi.
Largest Cities: (1974 census), Dacca 1,310,976, Khulna 436,000, Chittagong 416,733
Per Capita Income: $104 (1978) **Gross National Product (GNP):** $8.6 billion (1978) **Economic Statistics:** In 1976 about 60% of GNP was from agriculture (jute, rice, tea, sugarcane, chillies, wheat, and tobacco); 10% from industry and 22% from trade and services **Minerals and Mining:** There are large reserves of natural gas and some deep-lying coal **Labor Force:** 28,000,000 (1976), with 78% engaged in agriculture; some 8% are employed in industry **Foreign Trade:** Exports are chiefly raw jute and jute products, hides and skins and tea, and totaled about $497 million in 1978. Imports, chiefly fuels, machinery, clothing, foodstuffs, and chemicals, totaled $1.3 billion **Principal Trade Partners:** United States, Britain, Canada, India, Japan, U.S.S.R., Italy, United Arab Emirates, Mozambique, Pakistan

Vital Statistics: Birthrate, 49.5 per 1,000 of pop. (1975); death rate, 28.1 **Life Expectancy:** 47 years **Health Statistics:** 5,644 inhabitants per hospital bed; 15,054 per physician (1975) **Infant Mortality:** 140 per 1,000 births **Illiteracy:** 78% **Education Statistics:** 36,165 primary and secondary schools, with a total enrollment of 10,634,864 (1975) **Enrollment in Higher Education:** 183,833 **GNP Expended on Education:** 1.2% (1975)
Transportation: Surfaced and nonsurfaced roads total 3,607 mi. **Motor Vehicles:** 56,500 (1972) **Passenger Cars:** 31,700 **Railway Mileage:** 1,776 **Ports:** Chittagong, Chalna **Major Airlines:** The Bangladesh Biman (Air Bangladesh) operates both international and domestic services **Communications:** Government owned **Radio Transmitters:** 16 **Receivers:** 350,000 (1973) **Television Stations:** 1 **Telephones:** 80,000 (1975) **Newspapers:** 30 dailies (1975)
Weights and Measures: Metric system and British standards
Travel Requirements: Passport and visa required

In December 1970 the Awami League, a Bengali nationalist party concentrated in East Pakistan and led by the enormously popular Sheik Mujibur Rahman, won a majority of the seats in the Pakistan National Assembly. This unexpectedly strong showing in the first national elections held in Pakistan since independence emphasized the fissure between the Bengalis in East Pakistan and their rulers in Islamabad.

The old state of Bengal, now Bangladesh, has been a perennial disaster zone. It has virtually no industry, and the market for jute—its main export crop—has declined steadily with the introduction of synthetic fibers. Its population density is among the highest in the world, and most of its people live at the subsistence level. Bengalis long resented the relative prosperity of West Pakistan, contending it was the result of exploitative economic policies.

Demands for Bengali autonomy came to a head in the campaign of the Awami League. Sheik Mujib's six-point program called for a loose federation amounting to internal self-government for the Bengalis.

On March 1, 1971, Pakistan's President Yahya Khan announced that the convening of the National Assembly would be postponed. Leaders of the Awami League claimed they were being cheated of the fruits of the election, which had made them the majority party of Pakistan.

Widespread rioting and strikes in the Bengali province ensued, and on March 25, President Yahya Khan ordered the national army into the province to crush the separatist movement by force and arrest Sheik Mujib as a traitor. The next day, before his arrest, Sheik Mujib in a radio broadcast declared the independence of Bangladesh. The East Bengal Regiment of the army promptly defected to form the Bangladesh armed forces. For a few days the national army was pinned down. On April 10 a constituent assembly of the Awami League candidates elected to the National Assembly convened and confirmed the declaration of Bengali independence, naming Sheik Mujib president of the republic. But a military campaign of great ferocity, resulting in a death toll in the hundreds of thousands, quickly subdued the Bangladesh forces and cowed the population. In addition, several million Bengalis fled to neighboring India, and an occupation army remained.

Reports of clashes between Indian and Pakistani forces began to be heard. On December 3, Pakistani planes attacked western Indian military airfields, and Indian troops launched an attack in Bangladesh. Three days later India recognized the Bangladesh provisional government. After a whirlwind Indian campaign, the Pakistani forces in Bangladesh surrendered on December 16.

Sheik Mujib, freed from jail in Pakistan, returned to Bangladesh early in 1972, and on January 12 was named prime minister. The Sheik rapidly lost his charismatic hold as Bangladesh suffered from a disintegrating economy, corruption and famine.

Following the assassination of Sheik Mujib during a military coup in August 1975, Bangladesh experienced the turmoil of two new leaders within a period of two and a half months. Khandakar Mushtaque Ahmed was sworn in as president, but was forced to resign in November. Mohammad Sayem, chief justice of the Supreme Court, succeeded to the presidency. On assuming office, Sayem dissolved Parliament.

Public opinion in Bangladesh, and especially in the armed forces, on which the Sayem regime largely depended for support, was divided in the first part of 1976 among four main forces: the supporters of Gen. Ziaur Rahman, the army chief of staff; the supporters of the late Sheik Mujib and the Awami League; the Islamic right; and the left-wing National Socialist Party. Unrest was widespread inside the army.

Taking advantage of these divisive conditions, General Rahman assumed full power as chief martial law administrator on November 30, 1976, and arrested at least 11 prominent political leaders, including former Pres. Khandakar Mushtaque Ahmed. National elections that had been promised for early 1977 were postponed. On April 21, 1977, General Rahman was sworn in as president following the resignation of Sayem. On October 2, 1977, at Dacca Airport, dissident junior officers attempted unsuccessfully to overthrow the government. Some reports put the death toll as high as 230.

In a field of 10 candidates, General Rahman won a five-year presidential term on June 3, 1978, by garnering about 75 percent of the votes cast. In February 1979, his Bangladesh Nationalist Party swept 207 of the 300 contested parliament seats in national elections. The Awami League was left far behind, winning only 40 seats. Martial law was lifted and Parliament restored with Shah Azizur Rahman as Prime Minister.

HISTORY: In the 12th century, Moslem invaders brought Islam to Bengal, part of which is now Bangladesh. Moslem power and culture in the Indian subcontinent reached their zenith under the Mogul empire (1526-1857). Despite cultural interchange with the Hindus, the Moslem community continued to maintain its distinct identity under British rule

1970: In November a massive cyclone kills 200,000

1971: The Awami League, a Bengali nationalist party, leads a movement and civil war for Bengali independence

1972: Awami leader Sheik Mujibur Rahman is named prime minister. New constitution is effected

1973: First parliamentary elections held; Awami League controls the National Assembly

1975: Sheik Mujib is assassinated in a military coup and Khandakar Mushtaque Ahmed is named president. He is forced to resign during a power struggle within the army, and Mohammad Sayem assumes the presidency. Sayem dissolves Parliament

1977: A martial law court in Dacca convicts and sentences former president Khandakar Mushtaque Ahmed to 5 years in prison on charges of corruption and abuse of official power. Gen. Ziaur Rahman is sworn in as president. Coup attempt by dissident officers fails; government, charging involvement, bans Democratic League, National Socialist Party and Soviet Bangladesh Communist Party

1978: Gen. Ziaur Rahman is elected to presidency for five-year term

1979: President Rahman's Bangladesh Nationalist Party wins parliamentary elections. Martial law lifted

BARBADOS

Area: 166 sq. mi. **Population:** 265,000 (1978 est.)

Official Name: Barbados **Capital:** Bridgetown **Nationality:** Barbadian **Languages:** English is the official and universal language **Religion:** About 70% of the population belongs to the Anglican Church. The rest are mainly Methodists, Moravians, and Roman Catholics **Flag:** Vertical bands of blue, gold, and blue, with a black trident centered on the gold band **Anthem:** National Anthem of Barbados, beginning "In plenty and in time of need" **Currency:** Barbadian dollar (2.01 per U.S. $1)

Location: West Indies. The most easterly of the Caribbean islands, Barbados lies immediately east of the Windward Islands and about 270 miles northeast of the mainland of South America **Features:** The island, which is of coral origin, is relatively flat, rising gently from the west coast in a series of terraces to a ridge in the center **Chief Rivers:** None

Head of State: Queen Elizabeth II, represented by a governor-general, Sir Deighton Harcourt Lisle Ward **Head of Government:** Prime Minister John Michael Geoffrey ("Tom") Adams. born 1932, elected 1976 **Effective Date of Present Constitution:** 1966 **Legislative Body:** Parliament (bicameral), consisting of a House of Assembly and a Senate. The House of Assembly is composed of 24 members, elected for 5 years. The Senate consists of 21 members, 12 of whom are appointed by the governor-general on the advice of the prime minister, 2 on the advice of the leader of the opposition, and 7 appointed by the governor-general to represent various social and economic groups **Local Government:** 11 parishes and the city of Bridgetown

Ethnic Composition: About 80% of the population is of African descent; 5% is white, mainly of British origin **Population Distribution:** 37% urban **Density:** 1,596 inhabitants per sq. mi.

Largest City: (1970 census) Bridgetown 8,868 (Metropolitan Area 97,565)

Per Capita Income: $1,450 (1976 est.) **Gross National Product (GNP):** $376 million (1976) **Economic Statistics:** In 1973 about 42% of GNP was derived from trade and services; 16% from agriculture (sugar cane), fishing and animal husbandry; 11% from industry (sugar, rum, molasses, electronic parts) **Minerals and Mining:** Limestone and coral are quarried for domestic needs; there are small quantities of natural gas **Labor Force:** 90,000 (1970), of which 16% is employed in agriculture and 28% in industry **Foreign Trade:** Exports, chiefly sugar, rum, and molasses, totaled $66 million in 1976. Imports, mainly food, machinery, transportation equipment, chemicals and petroleum products, totaled $211 million **Principal Trade Partners:** Britain, United States, Canada, West Indies, Japan

Vital Statistics: Birthrate, 18.6 per 1,000 of pop. (1976); death rate, 9.2 **Life Expectancy:** 70 years **Health Statistics:** 111 inhabitants per hospital bed; 1,446 per physician (1975) **Infant Mortality:** 28.3 per 1,000 births **Illiteracy:** 2% **Education Statistics:** 159 primary and secondary schools, with combined enrollment of 63,800 (1974) **Enrollment in Higher Education:** 1,417 (1973) **GNP Expended on Education:** 8% (1973)

Transportation: Improved roads total 720 mi. **Motor Vehicles:** 25,800 (1975) **Passenger Cars:** 24,000 **Railway Mileage:** None **Ports:** Bridgetown **Major Airlines:** British West Indies Airways, British Airways, Air France, and Pan American Airways operate international flights **Communications:** Both government and privately owned **Radio Transmitters:** 3 **Receivers:** 130,000 (1976) **Television Transmitters:** 2 **Receivers:** 48,000 (1976) **Telephones:** 44,000 (1976) **Newspapers:** 1 daily, 98 copies per 1,000 inhabitants (1975)

Weights and Measures: Metric system **Travel Requirements:** Passport and visa not required up to 6 months; must have return ticket and citizenship proof

Four centuries ago, the Portuguese sailors who sighted the 21-mile-long strip of coral first noticed its trees, their long branches drooping to the ground, and gave their name, Barbados—the bearded fig tree—to the island. The name is the only sign that Barbados has not always been British, perhaps even more British than Britain.

Nevertheless, since it won independence in 1966, the West Indian country has moved to expand its regional and hemispheric ties. It was admitted to the United Nations immediately after gaining independence and has also joined the Organization of American States and the Inter-American Development Bank.

In recent years the Barbadian economy, once totally dependent on the sugar crop, has been diversified by the development of tourism and light manufacturing industries.

After a year of unsuccessful negotiations for a new agreement, the United States announced in 1978 that it would close its naval facility in Barbados. Operated for 22 years, the facility dealt with underwater research and communications.

HISTORY: Although both Arawak and Carib Indians had at one time inhabited Barbados, the island was uninhabited when the first white settlers arrived from England in 1627. In less than a decade slaves were brought from Africa to work the sugar plantations, which continue to serve as the mainstay of the island's economy. Slavery was abolished in 1834, but the island's political life continued to be dominated by a small white upper class until well into the 20th century

1954: Sir Grantley Adams, a Negro Barbadian and founder of the Barbados Labour Party, becomes the first prime minister of the island

1966: Barbados achieves full independence

1968-69: Barbados joins Caribbean Free Trade Area and Inter-American Development Bank

1973: Prime ministers of Barbados, Trinidad and Tobago, Guyana, and Jamaica establish CARICOM, a Caribbean common market and community

1975: A five-year treaty is signed with the EEC

1976: J. M. G. Adams is elected prime minister

BELGIUM

Area: 11,781 sq. mi. **Population:** 9,890,000 (1978 est.)
Official Name: Kingdom of Belgium **Capital:** Brussels **Nationality:** Belgian **Languages:** French, Flemish (Dutch), and German are the official and principal spoken languages. Flemish is spoken by the Flemings (Dutch) in the north and west, and French by the Walloons in the south and east; Brussels is bilingual **Religion:** The population is predominantly Roman Catholic, but there are several Protestant denominations and a Jewish community **Flag:** Vertical stripes of black, yellow, and red **Anthem:** La Brabançonne ("Song of Brabant") **Currency:** Belgian franc (30.2 per U.S. $1)

Location: Northwest Europe. Belgium is bordered by the Netherlands and the North Sea on the north, by Germany and Luxembourg on the east, and by France on the southwest and west **Features:** Although generally flat, Belgium has increasingly hilly and forested terrain toward the Ardennes region in the southeast **Chief Rivers:** Scheldt, Meuse

Head of State: King Baudouin I, born 1930, ascended the throne 1951 **Head of Government:** Premier Wilfried Martens, born 1936, appointed 1979 **Effective Date of Present Constitution:** 1831, amended December 1970 **Legislative Body:** Parliament (bicameral), consisting of a Senate and Chamber of Representatives. The Senate, consisting of 182 members elected for 4 years, is partly elected directly and in part chosen by provincial councils and fellow senators. The Chamber, with 212 members, is elected by direct universal suffrage for 4 years **Local Government:** 9 provinces and 589 (1976) communes, with considerable autonomy in local matters

Ethnic Composition: Flemings 58%, French (Walloons) 41%, Germans 1% **Population Distribution:** 87.1% urban **Density:** 839 inhabitants per sq. mi.

Largest Cities: (1971 est.) Brussels 1,071,194, Antwerp 226,570, Ghent 149,265, Liège 147,277, Bruges 117,220

Per Capita Income: $7,085 (1978) **Gross National Product (GNP):** $69.7 billion (1978) **Economic Statistics:** 30% of the GNP comes from industry (steel, metal manufacturing, nonferrous metal, textile, diamond cutting, chemical, glass); 25% from commerce; 24% from services; 7% from construction; 8% from transport and communications; 4% from agriculture (livestock, sugar beets, hay, potatoes, grain) **Minerals and Mining:** Coal is the only mineral resource of major importance. Iron, lead, zinc, copper, manganese, and phosphates are mined in small quantities **Labor Force:** 4 million (1977), with 47% in services, 30% in industry, 8% in construction, 3% in agriculture and 12% in civil service **Foreign Trade:** Exports, chiefly chemicals, textiles, diamonds, iron and steel products, machinery, automotive vehicles, textiles, glass, and nonferrous metals, totaled $37.5 billion in 1977. Imports, mainly grains, ores, petroleum, chemicals, textiles, diamonds, metals and products, machinery, electrical equipment and automotive vehicles, totaled $40.2 billion **Principal Trade Partners:** West Germany, Netherlands, France, Italy, United States, Britain

Vital Statistics: Birthrate, 12.3 per 1,000 of pop. (1977); death rate, 11.4 **Life Expectancy:** 71 years **Health Statistics:** 112 inhabitants per hospital bed; 530 per physician (1975) **Infant Mortality:** 14 per 1,000 births **Illiteracy:** 3% **Education Statistics:** 13,118 primary and secondary schools, with combined enrollment of 1,763,425 (1974) **Enrollment in Higher Education:** 150,131 **GNP Expended on Education:** 5.1% (1973)

Transportation: Surfaced roads total 7,664 mi. **Motor Vehicles:** 3,031,600 (1976) **Passenger Cars:** 2,738,000 **Railway Mileage:** 2,575 **Ports:** Antwerp, Zeebrugge, Ghent, Ostend **Major Airlines:** Sabena airline operates both domestic and international services **Communications:** Government controlled **Radio Transmitters:** 48 **Licenses:** 4,044,000 (1976) **Television Transmitters:** 28 **Licenses:** 2,646,000 (1976) **Telephones:** 2,949,000 (1976) **Newspapers:** 30 dailies, 239 copies per 1,000 inhabitants (1975)

Weights and Measures: Metric system **Travel Requirements:** Passport, no visa for 3 months

The geography of Belgium has brought it misfortune and fortune: the misfortune of having a largely low-lying countryside that served as a route for foreign armies, and the fortune of a location in Western Europe that helps to make the country a key trading and manufacturing center.

In its military misadventures, Belgium was the scene of Caesar's conquest of the Gallic tribes; the site of Napoleon's ultimate defeat, at Waterloo; and the stage for invasion by German armies in both world wars. But conflict also brought Belgium independence; the Belgians revolted against Dutch domination in 1830.

The northern part of the country, in which Belgian basic industry is largely situated, is inhabited by Dutch-speaking Flemings. Most of the rest of Belgium is Walloon country, where French is spoken. Currently the Flemings are dominant, with a majority in both the Senate and Chamber. The bilingual nature of the land has led to much friction.

In 1970, in order to reduce linguistic tensions, the unitary constitution of 1831 was revised to recognize "three cultural communities: French, Dutch, and German." Four linguistic regions—the Flemish and Walloon areas, a small German area along the border of West Germany, and bilingual Brussels—were created. Each has a council with limited authority over education, culture, and the economy. But proposals to increase their authority have been the most divisive issue of the 1970's.

Dependent on trade, Belgium has been a leader in the movement for European integration. It merged its customs with those of Luxembourg in 1921. The Netherlands joined this union to form *Benelux* by an agreement which took full effect in 1950. The Benelux countries joined the European Economic Community in 1958, and their earlier experience has helped to guide the Community. European integration helped to make Belgium prosperous in the 1960's; the country received more than $1 billion in foreign investment. The Walloon region gained new industries—to the chagrin of the Flemings, who were accustomed to industrial leadership.

In addition to industry, Belgium has gained as the headquarters of major international organizations—NATO, which had run out of its welcome in France, and the European Community, which is headquartered in Brussels.

HISTORY: Belgium, named after ancient Celtic settlers, the Belgae, was conquered by Julius Caesar about 50 B.C. and later formed part of Charlemagne's empire. Ruled by Burgundy in the 15th century, it passed to the Hapsburgs of Austria and then of Spain. In the 16th century, the Low Countries (including modern Belgium, Luxembourg, and the Netherlands) revolted against Spanish rule. But while the northern and predominantly Protestant Netherland provinces won their independence, Belgium remained under Spanish rule until the 18th century

1713: Belgium is ceded to Austria by the Treaty of Utrecht, which ends the War of the Spanish Succession

1792-97: French armies invade Belgium; country is ceded to France by Treaty of Campo Formio

1815: Belgium is united with the Netherlands by Treaty of Paris

1830-39: Belgians revolt against affiliation with Protestant Netherlands, a provisional government declares Belgium independent; Dutch invade Belgium but are forced by Britain and France to recognize the country's independence. Belgian Parliament chooses Prince Leopold of Saxe-Coburg-Gotha as ruler of the new kingdom

1885-1908: Leopold II becomes absolute monarch of Congo Free State. Belgium reluctantly annexed the area in 1908

1914-18: Germans invade and occupy neutral Belgium

1940-44: Germany again invades Belgium; King Leopold III surrenders unconditionally. Belgian cabinet sets up government-in-exile in London and declares surrender illegal; Belgian underground continues to fight German invaders

1950-51: Belgian electorate votes for return of king, but uprisings against Leopold by Socialists and Liberals force him to abdicate in favor of his son, Baudouin

1960: Belgium grants Congo independence

1968: Cultural-language conflict between Flemish and French-speaking population (Walloons) leads to fall of center-right coalition government; new coalition of Christian Socialists and Socialists is formed

1969: Cultural conflict continues to simmer as Senate studies constitutional reform proposals for regional autonomy

1970: Belgium amends constitution giving autonomous cultural and economic powers to each of the two communities, Flemings and Walloons

1973: Heretofore provisional double presidency (one Fleming, one Walloon) is made permanent part of Socialist party structure

1974: Iran's withdrawal from joint oil refining project adds to Belgium's economic woes and topples Leburton government. Leo Tindemans forms three-party coalition government

1975: Severe inflation and 6 percent unemployment force wage-price measures

1977: Tindemans' coalition government wins April election after cabinet crisis brought on by withdrawal of leftist Walloons

1978: Linguistic tensions trouble coalition. Crisis is resolved in June, but Tindemans resigns in October. Paul Vanden Boeynants becomes caretaker Premier pending elections. Elections produce no major changes, and caretaker government remains in office as coalition negotiations falter. Belgian Army enters Zaire to rescue victims of violence

1979: Wilfried Martens becomes Premier in five-party coalition

---

BENIN

Area: 43,483 sq. mi. **Population:** 3,270,000 (1978 est.)
Official Name: People's Republic of Benin **Capital:** Porto Novo **Nationality:** Beninese or Beninois **Languages:** French is the official language; the most common African dialects are Fon, Mina, Yoruba, and Dendi **Religion:** Animists 65%, Moslems 15%, Roman Catholics 14% **Flag:** A green flag with a red five-pointed star in the upper left **Anthem:** The New Dawn **Currency:** CFA Franc (219.0 per U.S. $1)

Location: West Africa. Benin is bordered on the north by Upper Volta and Niger, on the east by Nigeria, on the south by the Bight of Benin, and on the west by Togo **Features:** A 75-mile coastline of sandy beaches and lagoons is unbroken by natural harbors; north of it is a flat area that is the main oil palm region; further inland, a swampy depression is succeeded by hills, plateaus, and the Atakora Mountains, which stretch into Togo **Chief Rivers:** Ouémé, Mono, Couffo

Head of State and of Government: President and Prime Minister: Lt. Col. Mathieu Kérékou, assumed power in 1972; he also is defense minister **Effective Date of Present Constitution:** March 31, 1968 **Legislative Body:** None. Control is by the Central Committee's Political Bureau of the People's Revolutionary Party **Local Government:** 6 departments

Ethnic Composition: Of some 45 distinctive African groups the main ones are the Fon, Yoruba, Adja, Bariba, Peul, and Somba. There are also about 5,000 Europeans **Population Distribution:** 13.5% urban (1975) **Density:** 75 inhabitants per sq. mi.

Largest Cities: (1975 est.) Cotonou 178,000, Porto Novo 104,000; (1973 est.) Natatingou 49,000, Abomey 38,000

Per Capita Income: $133 (1978) **Gross National Product (GNP):** $500 million (1978 est.) **Economic Statistics:** In 1973, 39% of GNP came from agriculture (coffee, cotton, peanuts, cassava, fish, yams, corn, oil palm products); 35% from trade and services; 7% from industry (palm oil products, textiles, kenaf, beverages, furniture, nails, compressed air, and acetylene) and mining **Minerals and Mining:** Some low-grade iron ore and limestone deposits are located in the north **Labor Force:** 1.1 million, 80% in agriculture and some 29,000 salaried workers **Foreign Trade:** Exports, chiefly palm kernel oil, cotton, peanuts, and coffee, totaled $50.9 million in 1976. Imports, chiefly food products, textiles, machinery, vehicles, and iron and steel products, totaled $222.7 million **Principal Trade Partners:** France and the rest of the Franc Zone, United States, West Germany, Netherlands, Nigeria

Vital Statistics: Birthrate, 49.9 per 1,000 of pop. (1975); death rate, 23 **Life Expectancy:** 41 years **Health Statistics:** 781 inhabitants per hospital bed; 32,737 per physician (1975) **Infant Mortality:** 109.6 per 1,000 births **Illiteracy:** 80% **Education Statistics:** 1,325 primary and secondary schools, with combined enrollment of 301,852 (1974) **Enrollment in Higher Education:** 2,118 (1975) **GNP Expended on Education:** 7.4% (1976)

Transportation: Paved roads total 500 mi. **Motor Vehicles:** 26,500 (1976) **Passenger Cars:** 17,000 **Railway Mileage:** 395 **Ports:** Cotonou **Major Airlines:** Air Afrique, UTA, and Nigeria Airways provide intercontinental and regional services; small planes operated by the Benin government service the interior **Communications:** State-controlled **Radio Transmitters:** 4 (1972) **Receivers:** 150,000 (1976) **Television Stations:** None **Receivers:** 100 (1972) **Telephones:** 8,000 (1974) **Newspapers:** 1 daily, 0.3 copies per 1,000 inhabitants (1975)

Weights and Measures: Metric system **Travel Requirements:** Passport, visa valid for 15 days, $3.00; 1 month, $5.00; 3 months, $8.00; 2 photos

In addition to being one of the smallest, poorest, and most densely populated countries in West Africa, Benin has the unenviable distinction of having had more changes of government than any other newly independent African nation.

Counting the government that was in office when the former French territory won independence in 1960 under the name Dahomey, there have been 11 governments in the last two decades. Six of these were installed by military coups—a record for coup-prone Africa that has been equaled only by the Sudan.

In 1970 the government sought to bring a measure of stability to the country by creating a civilian presidential commission which consisted of three former leaders who had served as president or premier in the past. Starting with Hubert Maga, as first president, the chairmanship of the commission was to rotate every two years.

According to schedule Mr. Maga stepped down in May 1972 and was replaced by Justin Ahomadegbe. Five months later, however, the transfer of power by military coup was again the case. On October 26 junior and middle-grade army officers seized power, replacing Ahomadegbe's regime with an 11-man military government headed by then Maj. Mathieu Kérékou.

The Kérékou government represented a clear break from earlier regimes. Persons long in positions of power were swept aside and replaced by a younger generation. A guiding principle of "Marxist Leninist Scientific Socialism" was proclaimed by President Kérékou and some changes in the political and economic system began to appear. Reports of corruption, incompetence in government and attempted coups followed by wholesale arrests continue to come from Benin, however.

Much of Benin's political instability has been caused by the country's weak economy and dependence on French aid. Producing only a small quantity of palm products, coffee, cotton, and peanuts for export, Benin has been unable to earn enough revenue to meet development requirements.

In many cases, Beninese governments resigned or were ousted simply because they could not meet a payroll and a new leader had to be found who might succeed in a mission to Paris to persuade the French government to increase its subsidy.

Benin's imports climbed to an annual level of $222 million in 1976 while exports lagged at $51 million. Membership in the French franc pool is the only thing that makes such a deficit possible.

HISTORY: In the 17th century, the powerful Kingdom of Abomey gained dominance over neighboring kingdoms; it maintained its pre-eminent position until the late 19th century, when it was occupied by the French. Abomey armies, which included an elite corps of women soldiers, warred constantly with Yorubas in the east and raided Ashanti territory to the west. Until well into the 19th century, much of the fighting was stimulated by the slave trade, since prisoners were readily sold to European slavers

1851: French make treaty with King Gezo of Cotonou, where they establish trading post

1892-1904: French crush Abomey rebellion, push inland, and make country part of French West Africa

1958-59: Territory of Dahomey becomes autonomous state within French community; constitution is adopted and in National Assembly elections Hubert Maga becomes premier

1960: Dahomey becomes fully independent, with Maga as president

1963: Maga government is forced to resign in coup led by Col. (later General) Christophe Soglo, army chief of staff, who forms provisional government

1964: In national elections, Sourou Migan Apithy is chosen as president, Justin Ahomadegbe as vice-president

1965: Dissension among government leaders prompts second coup by General Soglo; provisional civilian government is formed and elections are announced, but Soglo again intervenes, proclaims himself president and premier of military regime, bans political activity

1967: Soglo government is overthrown by military junta

1968: Military regime returns government to civilian administration headed by Emile-Derlin Zinsou

1972: Dahomey's first peaceful transition of power is aborted by the country's fifth coup since independence. Maj. Mathieu Kérékou assumes power

1974: President Kérékou declares that a "socialist society" will be established with Marxism-Leninism as its "revolutionary philosophy and basis"

1975: Rebellion led by Minister of Labor quashed. Dahomey is renamed the People's Republic of Benin by President Kérékou

1977: In January, foreign airborne assault fails to overthrow Kérékou, who claims invasion was French inspired

---

BHUTAN

Area: 18,147 sq. mi. **Population:** 1,220,000 (1978 est.)
Official Name: Kingdom of Bhutan **Capital:** Thimphu **Nationality:** Bhutanese **Languages:** Dzongka, a Tibetan dialect, is the official and principal language; Nepali and tribal dialects are also spoken **Religion:** About 75% are Mahayana Buddhists and many live in Buddhist monasteries; the Nepalese of southern Bhutan are predominantly Hindu **Flag:** Divided diagonally with saffron to the left and red to the right, with a white dragon outlined in black in the center **Anthem:** National Anthem, beginning "In the sandal-wood ornamented Kingdom of Dragonland" **Currencies:** Ngultrum (9.1 per U.S. $1) and Indian rupee (8.3 per U.S. $1)

Location: Eastern Himalayas of Central Asia. Bhutan is bordered by China (Tibet) on the north and northwest, and by India on the east, west and south **Features:** The undemarcated northern boundary with Tibet stretches along 300 miles of snow-capped peaks that are almost inaccessible. The inner Himalayan region in central Bhutan contains densely populated, fertile valleys; the Duar Plain of southern Bhutan contains dense forests **Chief Rivers:** Manas, Sankosh, Tongsa, Torsa, Raidak

Head of State and of Government: King Jigme Singye Wangchuk, born 1955, ascended the throne 1972. The king governs with the aid of a 4-man council of ministers; he is subject to a vote of confidence every 3 years **Effective Date of Present Constitution:** No formal written constitution; pronouncements, meanwhile, serve as an uncodified constitution. In May 1958, the king declared that Bhutan was henceforth to be a constitutional monarchy **Legislative Body:** Tsongdu (unicameral national assembly), consisting of not more than 150 members, 25% appointed by the king and the rest nominated by villages for 3-year terms. Parliamentary government is still rudimentary **Local Government:** 4 regions under appointed governors

Ethnic Composition: Bhutanese, or Bhotias, who are ethnically related to the Tibetans, make up 60% of the population. Nepalese constitute about 25% and the rest consist of various tribal groups, including the Lepcha, an indigenous people, and the Santal, descendants of migrants from India **Population Distribution:** The population is chiefly rural **Density:** 67 inhabitants per sq. mi.

Largest Cities: (1970 est.) Thimphu 50,000, Paro Dzong 35,000, Taga Dzong 18,000, Punakha 12,000, Bumthang 10,000

Per Capita Income: $90 (1978) **Gross National Product (GNP):** $110 million (1978 est.) **Economic Statistics:** The economy is still at a primitive level and many transactions are on a barter basis. The country is self-sufficient in food; the main crops are rice, wheat, and barley, and together with butter from yaks provide a sufficient diet. Large forests provide the potential for lumber and paper-processing plants, and several turbulent rivers furnish a potential source of hydroelectric power. Bhutan's first 5-year development plan was begun in 1961 with the aid of India, the third plan covered the years 1971-1976 **Minerals and Mining:** Copper, dolomite, graphite, and coal deposits have been discovered; limestone and some 30,000 tons of coal are produced per annum **Labor Force:** Virtually the entire working population is engaged in agriculture and pastoral activities **Foreign Trade:** All external trade is with India, chiefly exports ($1 million) of timber and fruit and imports ($51.4 million) of textiles and light equipment

Vital Statistics: Birthrate, 43.6 per 1,000 of pop. (1975); death rate, 28.1 **Life Expectancy:** 43.6 years **Health Statistics:** N.A. **Infant Mortality:** N.A. **Illiteracy:** 95% **Education Statistics:** 105 primary and middle schools, with combined enrollment of 14,598 (1974) **Enrollment in Higher Education:** About 50 Bhutanese are studying in foreign institutions **GNP Expended on Education:** 3.6% (1974)

Transportation: Three all-weather highways, covering the western, central, and eastern sectors, link India with Bhutan **Motor Vehicles:** N.A. **Passenger Cars:** N.A. **Railway Mileage:** None **Ports:** None **Major Airlines:** Jamair, an Indian airline, operates flights from Hashimara, West Bengal, to Paro Dzong, where Bhutan's first airport was opened in 1968 **Communications:** A small radio transmitter in Paro Dzong maintains contact with the Bhutanese mission in India. Telephone connections exist from Paro Dzong and Thimphu to India. Most internal communication is by letter or by messenger **Radio Licenses:** 10,000 (1976) **Telephones:** N.A. **Newspapers:** A fortnightly government newspaper is published in 3 languages

Weights and Measures: Traditional and British standards are used **Travel Requirements:** Passport, visa (applications can be made at any Indian consulate), $2 visa fee; smallpox and cholera immunization certificates are required

---

Well into the 20th century, the Buddhist kingdom of Bhutan was still living in the 19th, content to be isolated politically from the rest of the world. In 1959 the Chinese take-over of Tibet, Bhutan's northern neighbor, jolted the country into closing its trade routes to Tibet and into building a road to the south.

It took six days then, on the back of a mule, to travel from Bhutan to India. The same trip now, by bus, takes five hours. With the help of foreign, mainly Indian, aid and advisers, similar advances have been made in other sectors in the agrarian kingdom. Where only 2,600 of Bhutan's people had gone even to primary school a decade ago, now 14,000 are studying in schools of all levels. A country where slavery and witchcraft are still strong memories, Bhutan has become a constitutional monarchy—and probably the first feudal society in which the ruler has given his subjects the right to dismiss him.

Bhutan's king from 1952 to 1972 was Jigme Dorji Wangchuk, whose name means "fearless thunderbolt master of the cosmic powers." Despite his awesome appellation, the king was surprisingly informal and genuinely loved by his people. To give his rule a popular base, he persuaded the National Assembly to pass a bill empowering it by a two-thirds vote to replace the king with the next in the royal line of succession if the monarch loses the assembly's confidence. After his death, he was succeeded by his son, Jigme Singye Wangchuk.

Bhutan is largely independent and insists that it is not an Indian protectorate, though by a treaty of 1949 it "agrees to be guided by the government of India in regard to external relations." Bhutan has no troops guarding its border with Tibet, to avoid antagonizing the Chinese.

Bhutan's people are thinly spread over a beautiful, mountainous country. Most Bhutanese live as farmers on their own land, bartering for what they need. Most foreign assistance which Bhutan has received beyond that provided by India has come through the Colombo Plan, of which Bhutan is a member.

HISTORY: Bhutan's early history is obscure. In the 16th century it was conquered by Tibet and nominally came under a dual spiritual and temporal rule. In the 19th century the southern part of the country was occupied by the British and annexed to India, and Britain began paying Bhutan an annual subsidy. In 1907 Sir Ugyen Wangchuk, a former local governor, established a hereditary monarchy, and in a 1910 treaty Bhutan agreed to British direction of its external affairs

1949: India signs treaty with Bhutan assuming Britain's role in subsidizing kingdom and directing its foreign relations; India returns areas annexed by Britain in 1865

1959: Communist China publishes maps showing parts of Bhutan as Chinese territory; Communist spokesmen claim Bhutan belongs to greater Tibet. Indian government warns that any attack on Bhutan will be regarded as an act of aggression against India

1969: National Assembly adopts bill under which king is required to abdicate in the event of a no-confidence motion approved by two thirds of the legislature

1971: Bhutan is admitted to the United Nations

1973: Bhutan signs agreement with U.N. under which Bhutan will receive $2.5 million in aid to carry out projects under third five-year plan

1974: King Jigme Singye Wangchuk formally crowned

BOLIVIA

Area: 424,163 sq. mi. **Population:** 4,810,000 (1978 est.)
Official Name: Republic of Bolivia **Capital:** La Paz is the administrative capital, Sucre the legal and judicial capital **Nationality:** Bolivian **Languages:** Spanish, the official language, is spoken by about 55% of the population (but only 36% as a mother tongue). The rest speak a variety of Indian dialects, chiefly Quechua and Aymara **Religion:** The population is about 95% Roman Catholic **Flag:** Red, yellow, and green horizontal stripes, with the national coat of arms on the yellow stripe **Anthem:** National Anthem, beginning "Bolivians, provident destiny" **Currency:** Bolivian peso (20 per U.S. $1)
Location: South America. Landlocked Bolivia is bordered on the north and east by Brazil, on the south by Paraguay and Argentina, and on the west by Chile and Peru **Features:** The country is divided into three distinct regions: the Altiplano, a bleak plateau lying between two ranges of the Andes Mountains and one of the world's highest inhabited regions; an intermediate region (yungas) containing the eastern mountain slopes and valleys, and the Amazon-Chaco lowlands (llanos) **Chief Rivers:** Beni, Guaporé-Iténez, Mamoré-Río Grande, Pilcomayo, Paraguay
Head of State and of Government: President Walter Guevara Arze, born 1911, elected by the National Congress August 1979 **Effective Date of Present Constitution:** 1967; many provisions suspended after 1969 coup **Legislative Body:** Bicameral National Congress with 27 Senators and 117 Deputies **Local Government:** 9 departments, each headed by an appointed prefect. The departments are subdivided into 94 provinces
Ethnic Composition: 65% Amerindian (mainly Quechua and Aymará), 10% of European origin, 25% of mixed origin (Cholo) **Population Distribution:** 38.6% urban (1975) **Density:** 11.3 inhabitants per sq. mi.
Largest Cities: (1975 est.) La Paz 660,700, Cochabamba 184,340, Santa Cruz 149,230, Oruro 110,490, Sucre 106,590
Per Capita Income: $444 (1978) **Gross National Product (GNP):** $2.71 billion (1978 est.) **Economic Statistics:** In 1973 about 21% of GNP came from agriculture (sugar, corn, potatoes, wheat, and rice); 12% from manufacturing (food processing, textiles, leather goods, cement, and glass ceramics); 15% from mining; 28% from trade and services; 4% from construction; 9% from transportation **Minerals and Mining:** Mining is the most important element of the nation's economy and accounts for the major share of the country's exports. Tin still dominates these exports, which also include lead, zinc, silver, copper, tungsten, bismuth, antimony, gold, natural gas, and sulphur. Oil accounts for about 11% of the export total **Labor Force:** 2.4 million (1975); 58% in agriculture, 19% in government, 18% in industry, 5% in commerce **Foreign Trade:** Exports, chiefly tin, petroleum, tungsten, silver, antimony, copper, lead, zinc, and coffee, totaled $660 million in 1977. Imports, mainly machinery, vehicles, iron and steel, and food staples, totaled $670 million **Principal Trade Partners:** United States, Argentina, Brazil, Japan, Switzerland
Vital Statistics: Birthrate, 48 per 1,000 of pop. (1976); death rate, 18 **Life Expectancy:** 47 years **Health Statistics:** 522 inhabitants per hospital bed; 2,117 per physician (1974) **Infant Mortality:** 77.3 per 1,000 births **Illiteracy:** 37% **Education Statistics:** About 8,755 primary and secondary schools, with combined enrollment of 942,779 (1974) **Enrollment in Higher Education:** 51,585 (1976) **GNP Expended on Education:** 3.3% (1974)
Transportation: Paved roads total 1,050 mi. **Motor Vehicles:** 84,745 (1975) **Passenger Cars:** 23,576 **Railway Mileage:** 2,661 **Ports:** None, but under a 1904 treaty Arica and Antofagasta in Chile are free ports for Bolivian commerce **Major Airlines:** Lloyd Aéreo Boliviano operates domestic and international services **Communications:** Government controlled **Radio Transmitters:** 106 (1976) **Receivers:** 476,000 (1975) **Television Transmitters:** 2 **Receivers:** 100,000 (1976) **Telephones:** 49,000 (1974) **Newspapers:** 14 dailies, 35 copies per 1,000 inhabitants (1975)
Weights and Measures: Metric system; old Spanish units are still used **Travel Requirements:** Passport, 90-day extendable tourist card, no fee

---

Often called the "Tibet of South America," landlocked Bolivia is made up of three distinct topographical regions: a mineral-rich high plateau region, an extensively farmed middle region of semitropical rain forests and somewhat drier valleys, and the sparsely populated Amazon-Chaco lowlands.

Bolivia is among the poorest countries in Latin America, with its Andean Indian peasants and its miners widely separated from the urban minorities of European origin.

Signs of economic and social advance, however, include skyscraper office buildings, modern jet airliner service between La Paz and the tropical lowlands, and the large growth in primary school enrollment.

Bolivia's economy is based on natural gas and petroleum, which make the country self-sufficient in energy, and iron ore and nonferrous minerals, including tin, of which Bolivia is the world's second-largest producer. The prevailing economic philosophy is nationalist capitalism.

The country had three presidents—all military men—in 1978. The first was Hugo Banzer Suárez, who had gained the office in a bloody coup in 1971 and had subsequently put down at least seven attempted coups. Banzer announced a presidential election for July 9, 1978 (moving it up from a scheduled 1980 date), and declared himself a candidate. However, because of opposition within the military, he withdrew his name. Gen. Juan Pereda Asbún, an air force officer, ran as the official candidate and claimed victory in a field of nine. On July 19, Bolivia's electoral court declared the election void on the grounds of fraud. Two days later, Pereda launched a bloodless coup from Santa Cruz, and Banzer went into self-imposed exile in Argentina.

In turn, the Pereda regime was toppled on November 24 without bloodshed, and the army's Gen. David Padilla Arancibia became the interim president. His government promised a presidential election by "universal democratic vote" on July 1, 1979.

The popular election resulted in a victory for Hernán Siles Zuazo, candidate of the left-wing Popular Democratic Union. However, the electoral court annulled 50,000 votes cast for Siles Zuazo, thus forcing the National Congress to make the final choice. In the Congress a deadlock developed between those congressmen supporting Siles Zuazo and those backing former President Paz Estenssoro. Finally on August 7, the Congress selected Walter Guevara Arze to serve as president. A new presidential election is scheduled for May 1980.

HISTORY: The Bolivian Altiplano was a center of Indian life long before the days of the Incas, who conquered the region in the 13th century. The Spanish conquest began in the 1530s, and the Indians were soon virtually enslaved to work the rich silver mines of Upper Peru, as Bolivia was then called. Following the occupation of Spain by Napoleon in 1809, Upper Peru became one of the first Spanish colonies to revolt against Spain

1824-26: Revolutionary army under Antonio José de Sucre, chief lieutenant of Simón Bolívar, defeats Spanish forces at Ayacucho. Bolivian independence is proclaimed in 1825

1879-84: Bolivia and Peru fight Chile in War of the Pacific. Chile is victorious and Bolivia is forced to cede province of Atacama, nation's only coastal territory

1903: After bitter conflict, Bolivia cedes large rubber-tree area on Acre River to Brazil

1932-35: Discovery of oil at the foot of the Bolivian Andes precipitates Chaco War with Paraguay, which lays claim to region. More than 100,000 lives are lost on both sides; a defeated Bolivia loses three-quarters of disputed Chaco Boreal area to Paraguay

1943: Economic unrest culminates in widespread strikes by miners; pro-miner Movement of the National Revolution (MNR) stages revolt and takes power

1951-56: Victor Paz Estenssoro, the MNR candidate, wins presidential elections but is prevented from taking office by military junta; he is finally swept into power by a party-led uprising

1964-66: Second administration headed by Paz is overthrown and a military junta installed. Air Force General René Barrientos Ortuño is elected president in 1966

1967: Cuban guerrilla leader Ernesto "Che" Guevara, who had been waging a "liberation" movement in Bolivia, is executed

1969: Barrientos is killed in helicopter crash and is succeeded by Vice-President Luis Adolfo Siles Salinas; Siles is ousted, however, in coup led by General Alfredo Ovando Candia

1970: Ovando regime is overthrown in leftist coup led by General Juan José Torres

1971: Torres is overthrown in rebel uprising; Col. Hugo Banzer Suárez is appointed president

1974: Banzer's government orders price rises to cope with a food shortage; labor strikes and a peasant revolt result

1976: Negotiations are entered into with Chile and Peru concerning their granting Bolivia an outlet to the Pacific Ocean. Juan José Torres is slain in Argentina, resulting in massive strikes and unrest. State takes over all iron ore and manganese deposits

1977: Civilian-military coup attempt fails

1978: Gen. Juan Pereda Asbún seizes presidency in coup following elections but is toppled four months later by Gen. David Padilla Arancibia

1979: July elections result in victory for left-wing Hernán Siles Zuazo, but electoral court rejects 50,000 ballots cast for him. Walter Guevara Arze is then chosen by Congress as interim president until May 1980 elections

BOTSWANA

Area: 224,764 sq. mi. **Population:** 710,000 (1978 est.)
Official Name: Botswana **Capital:** Gaborone **Nationality:** Batswana **Languages:** English is the official language; Setswana is the main African language. Various dialects of the *Khoisan* "click" language are spoken by the Bushmen; Afrikaans is also used **Religion:** About 15% Christian; the rest practice tribal religions **Flag:** A blue field divided by a black horizontal band edged in white **Anthem:** Our Land **Currency:** Pula (0.83 per U.S. $1)

Location: Southern Africa. Landlocked Botswana is bordered by Namibia (South-West Africa) on the north and west, by Zambia and Zimbabwe Rhodesia on the east, and by South Africa on the southeast and south **Features:** Most of the country is a tableland, with a mean altitude of 3,300 feet. The Kalahari Desert covers much of the southwest; in the northwest the waters of the Okavango River form a great inland delta, known as the Okavango Swamps, which extend over 6,500 sq. mi. **Chief Rivers:** Okavango, Molopo, Shashi, Limpopo

Head of State and of Government: President: Sir Seretse M. Khama, born 1921, elected 1965 **Effective Date of Present Constitution:** September 30, 1966 **Legislative Body:** Parliament (unicameral), consisting of a 36-member National Assembly. Of the total membership, 32 are directly elected and 3 chosen by the elected members. The remaining seat is held by the attorney general, who may speak but not vote. The Constitution also provides for a House of Chiefs, which plays an advisory role in government affairs **Local Government:** 10 districts and 3 independent towns, governed by local councils

Ethnic Composition: The majority in Botswana are Bantu, grouped into 8 main tribes; in addition, there are some 30,000 Bushmen, a non-Negroid people with Mongoloid characteristics; 5,000 Europeans, and smaller groups of Asians, Hottentots, and those of mixed origin **Population Distribution:** 12.3% urban **Density:** 3.2 inhabitants per sq. mi.

Largest Cities: (1974 est.) Selebi-Pikwe 40,000, Francistown 22,000, Gaborone 21,000

Per Capita Income: $337 (1978) **Gross National Product (GNP):** $250 million (1978) **Economic Statistics:** In 1973, 36% of GNP came from animal husbandry (cattle, goats, sheep) and agriculture (corn, sorghum, cotton); 17.3% from trade and services; and 16% from industry (meat processing) and mining **Minerals and Mining:** Manganese, copper and copper/nickel, coal, and diamonds are mined **Labor Force:** About 280,000, with 70% in agriculture **Foreign Trade:** Exports, chiefly livestock, hides and skins, canned meats, beans, sorghum, and diamonds, totaled $170 million in 1976. Imports, chiefly cereals, petroleum products, textiles, sugar, and motor vehicles, totaled $207 million **Principal Trade Partners:** South Africa, Britain, Zambia, United States

Vital Statistics: Birthrate, 45.6 per 1,000 of pop. (1975); estimated death rate, 23 **Life Expectancy:** 45 years **Health Statistics:** 332 inhabitants per hospital bed; 10,476 per physician (1974) **Infant Mortality:** 24.1 **Illiteracy:** 67% **Education Statistics:** 323 primary and secondary schools, with combined enrollment of 130,579 (1975) **Enrollment in Higher Education:** 469 (1975) **GNP Expended on Education:** 7.7% (1973)

Transportation: Paved roads total 2,655 mi. **Motor Vehicles:** 13,300 (1976) **Passenger Cars:** 4,100 **Railway Mileage:** 394 **Ports:** None **Major Airlines:** Air Botswana operates domestic flights and maintains services to South Africa and Zambia **Communications:** Government owned **Radio Transmitters:** 4 (1974) **Receivers:** 6,000 (1976) **Television:** None **Telephones:** 8,000 (1975) **Newspapers:** 1 daily, 20 per 1,000 inhabitants (1975)

Weights and Measures: British standards **Travel Requirements:** Passport, no visa

Since gaining independence in 1966, the former British protectorate of Bechuanaland has seen its previously bleak economic prospects brightened by the discovery of substantial mineral wealth—diamonds, copper, and nickel.

The mineral wealth found in the country's arid northeastern area includes a diamond "pipe" (the core of an ancient volcano) at Orapa, which is one of the largest ever discovered anywhere. Development of the diamonds and other minerals by American and South African companies involves an investment of some $130 million.

With mineral development and new industry, this impoverished African country hopes to gain economic independence that will significantly add to its political independence.

Nearly surrounded by white-ruled areas, Botswana previously had seemed destined to be no more than a cattle ranch for South Africa. As head of a newly independent Black African state, Botswana's president, Sir Seretse Khama, had asserted opposition to South Africa's racist policies, but acknowledged his country's economic dependence on its southern neighbor. Still, Botswana is devoted to strengthening its commercial and psychological ties with Zambia and other independent states of Black Africa, while refusing to have diplomatic relations with either Pretoria or Salisbury. Relations between Botswana and Zimbabwe Rhodesia became strained as a result of incidents arising out of the guerrilla war between Zimbabwe Rhodesian Black nationalists and Zimbabwe Rhodesian security forces.

The Botswana deeply resent the infiltration of Zimbabwe Rhodesian security forces into their country. In a series of clashes with police in 1978, residents registered their protest over the arrest of Ompatile Tswaipe, a member of the Botswana Defense Force, who was charged with the murder of a British student and two South African game wardens. Tswaipe, whom many Botswana believed was quite properly defending his country from foreign infiltration when the incident occurred, was later acquitted.

Sir Seretse, an Oxford-educated lawyer, had himself experienced the effects of racial prejudice following his marriage to an Englishwoman in 1948. The marriage caused a controversy in South Africa as well as in Sir Seretse's homeland. Victorious in the preindependence elections of 1965, Sir Seretse proclaimed a policy of non-racial democracy for Botswana.

HISTORY: Little is known of the origins of Botswana's peoples. The early inhabitants, the Bushmen, who now are dying out, have no recorded history. The ancestors of most of the present-day population, the Batswana, probably arrived centuries ago in Bantu migrations from Central or East Africa. In the 19th century, the great chief Khama III loosely united the Batswana against incursions of the neighboring Matabele people and Boer trekkers from the Transvaal. Under British protection, the southern area was made part of the South African Cape Colony, while the northern part, known as Bechuanaland, remained under direct British administration until it became independent Botswana

1909: Constitution of Union (now Republic) of South Africa is drafted, with a provision that Bechuanaland and other British protectorates in southern Africa, Basutoland (now Lesotho) and Swaziland, will some day be included in the union

1920-61: Advisory councils, one representing Africans, the other, Europeans, are established by British Central Authority. Central Authority establishes a Joint Advisory Council with African and European membership, which resolves to form legislative council to assist in government of the territory. A constitution for this purpose is promulgated

1965: New constitution is made effective and general elections are held for new National Assembly; seat of government is moved from Mafeking in South Africa to Gaborone

1966: Bechuanaland becomes independent member of the British Commonwealth and adopts name of Botswana

1968: Botswana joins IMF, Int'l Bank for Reconstruction and Development (World Bank), and Int'l Development Assn.

1973: Botswana severs diplomatic relations with Israel as a result of Middle East war

1974: Botswana establishes relations with Communist China and asks Nationalist Chinese representatives to leave the country

1975: A five-year treaty is signed with EEC

1977: UN Security Council adopts a resolution demanding the cessation of all hostile acts against Botswana by Rhodesia

BRAZIL

Area: 3,286,470 sq. mi. **Population:** 113,100,000 (1978 est.)
Official Name: Federative Republic of Brazil **Capital:** Brasília **Nationality:** Brazilian **Languages:** Portuguese is the official and principal language. In central and southern Brazil, Italian, German, and Japanese immigrants still use their native languages **Religion:** About 93% of the population is Roman Catholic. There are about 8 million Protestants and 150,000 Jews **Flag:** Green, with a yellow diamond enclosing a blue globe containing 23 white stars and a white band inscribed with the words "Ordem e Progresso" (Order and Progress) **Anthem:** Brazilian National Hymn, beginning "From peaceful Ypiranga's banks" **Currency:** Cruzeiro (22.7 per U.S. $1)

Location: South America. The fifth largest nation in the world, Brazil is bordered by every country in South America except Chile and Ecuador. It is bounded by French Guiana, Suriname, Guyana, Venezuela, and Colombia on the north, by Peru, Bolivia, and Paraguay on the west, and by Uruguay and Argentina on the south **Features:** The country is divided into four distinct major regions: the northern tropical basin of the Amazon, which flows more than 1,500 miles within the country, bordered on the north by the Guiana Highlands; the semiarid scrub land of the northeast; the agricultural and mineral heartland of the south-central plains, plateaus and highlands; and the narrow coastal belt, fringed by interior mountain ranges, extending from Natal to Porto Alegre **Chief Rivers:** Amazon, São Francisco, Paraná, Uruguay, Paraguay

Head of State and of Government: President João Baptista de Oliveira Figueiredo, born 1921, inaugurated on Mar. 15, 1979, following selection by Electoral College in 1978 for six-year term **Effective Date of Present Constitution:** January 24, 1967 **Legislative Body:** National Congress (bicameral), composed of the Chamber of Deputies and the Senate **Local Government:** 22 states, each with an indirectly elected governor and legislature, 4 federal territories, and 1 federal district

Ethnic Composition: The primary elements are 60% European, 12% African and a complex mixture (28%) of both **Population Distribution:** 59.1% urban **Density:** 34.4 inhabitants per sq. mi.

Largest Cities: (1974 est.—Metropolitan Areas) São Paulo 7,195,100, Rio de Janeiro 5,157,000, Belo Horizonte 1,468,000, Recife 1,317,000, Salvador 1,200,000, Porto Alegre 1,007,600

Per Capita Income: $1,456 (1978) **Gross National Product (GNP):** $148.9 billion (1978 est.) **Economic Statistics:** 38% of GNP comes from industry (food processing, chemicals, textiles, metallurgical products, vehicles and accessories, electrical and communications equipment), mining and construction; 32% from services; 8% from agriculture (rice, corn, coffee, sugarcane, soybeans, manioc, cotton); 16% from trade, and 6% from transportation and communications **Minerals and Mining:** Large deposits of iron, manganese, and bauxite; nickel, lead, tin, asbestos, chrome ore, gold, tungsten, and copper are also mined but supplies must be augmented by imports. Coal and petroleum production are also supplemented by imports **Labor Force:** Approximately 38,000,000 (1978); of which 38% is employed in agriculture, 24% in industry **Foreign Trade:** Exports, chiefly coffee, soybeans, cotton, iron ore, cane sugar, pine wood, corn, and cocoa beans, totaled $12.6 billion in 1978. Imports, mainly wheat, crude petroleum, machinery, chemicals, metals and heavy equipment, totaled $13.6 billion **Principal Trade Partners:** United States, West Germany, Argentina, Italy, The Netherlands, United Kingdom, France, Japan, Saudi Arabia, Iraq

Vital Statistics: Birthrate, 37.1 per 1,000 of pop. (1975); death rate, 8.8 **Life Expectancy:** 61 years **Health Statistics:** 266 inhabitants per hospital bed; 2,025 per physician (1973) **Infant Mortality:** about 88 per 1,000 births **Illiteracy:** 32% **Education Statistics:** 191,133 primary and secondary schools, with combined enrollment of 15,558,386 (1973) **Enrollment in Higher Education:** About 1,000,000 (1976) **GNP Expended on Education:** 3.5% (1974)

Transportation: Paved roads total 45,000 mi. (1976) **Motor Vehicles:** 5,983,800 (1975) **Passenger Cars:** 4,907,800 **Railway Mileage:** 20,447 **Ports:** Santos, Rio de Janeiro, Vitória, Salvador, Rio Grande, Recife, Paranagua, Macapá **Major Airlines:** VARIG and Cruzeiro do Sul operate domestic and international services **Communications:** Government controlled **Radio Transmitters:** 999 **Receivers:** 16,980,000 (1975) **Television Transmitters:** 66 (1973) **Receivers:** 10,680,000 (1975) **Telephones:** 4,036,000 (1976) **Newspapers:** 280 dailies, 39 per 1,000 inhabitants (1973)

Weights and Measures: Metric system **Travel Requirements:** Passport; obtain visa by applying to Brazilian consulate nearest one's home; one passport-size photo required

Long considered the country of the future, Brazil has begun to grow visibly through industrialization within its vast geographical outline. Since 1930 the activist governments of the country, the largest in Latin America and the fifth largest in the world in area, have—despite wide ideological differences—followed roughly similar policies of industrial development and national integration of the huge hinterland and the urban coast. As a result, Brazil is the industrial leader of South America, with by far the largest gross national product.

For all its economic progress, Brazil has had more than its share of political upheaval. It has been by turns a Portuguese colony, an independent empire, a republic, a dictatorship, and, up to 1964, a representative democracy. Since the ousting of a civilian president, João Goulart, in that year, Brazil has had a succession of five army generals as presidents.

Leaving the economy largely under civilian management, the first three military administrations reformed the tax structure, began the reorganization of the state's inefficient bureaucracy, shifted some resources to the country's backward regions, attracted large amounts of U.S. and other foreign investment capital, and whipped up the pace of industrial expansion. The result is often described as Brazil's "economic miracle."

Brazil's economy fared less well under the fourth military administration, in which Ernesto Geisel, a career artillery general, served a five-year term that ended March 15, 1979. The cost of living rose about 41 percent in 1978, and strikes became common even though the military had long discouraged them. The nation's industrial and farm exports were still growing, but these advantages were offset by increased imports.

Despite U.S. opposition, Geisel's government moved ahead in 1978 with plans to buy eight nuclear power plants and a uranium reprocessing facility from West Germany. The U.S. complained that the deal would give Brazil the technology for making nuclear weapons; Geisel flew to West Germany and received Chancellor Helmut Schmidt's assurance that the equipment would be delivered. U.S. President Jimmy Carter, though on record as against both the nuclear deal and against the Geisel government's repression of human rights, visited Brazil later in 1978 and reaffirmed his nation's friendship. He got a chilly reception, but a thaw began during the visit. But government officials turned chilly again when Carter pointedly held conversations with Brazilians who opposed their government's repression of political opponents, Church liberals, and press freedom.

Gen. João Baptista de Oliveira Figueiredo, a four-star officer who had been chief of the intelligence service, was sworn in as president on March 15, 1979. He had been elected five months earlier in Brazil's first contested presidential election since the coup that ousted Goulart. The print media—but not television and radio—received full freedom during the campaign. Figueiredo, the nominee of the National Renovating Alliance, the government party, won the election in the electoral college, 355 to 226, over the candidate of the only legal opposition party, the Brazilian Democratic Movement.

In his inauguration speech, Figueiredo praised Geisel and said he would follow his "true path," but the new president also announced his "unswerving purpose" of restoring democracy to the political system in the future.

The world's largest petrochemical complex, built at a cost of more than $3 billion in state and private funds, went into operation in 1979 near Salvador in Brazil's impoverished Northeast. This project capped a 20-year industrialization effort in that region, which has salt deposits, plenty of hydroelectric power, and a deepwater port. Some foreign investors have been attracted there, and a federal agency is actively seeking more through special tax incentives.

HISTORY: In 1500 Pedro Alvares Cabral landed on the Brazilian coast and claimed the land for Portugal. The first Portuguese governor-general of Brazil was appointed in 1549. In 1727 coffee was introduced in Brazil. In 1808 King John VI, fleeing the Napoleonic invasion of Portugal, arrived in Rio de Janeiro, and in 1815 all Portuguese dominions were designated the United Kingdom of Portugal, Brazil, and the Algarves. The King returned to Portugal in 1821, leaving behind Dom Pedro, his son, as regent

1822: Dom Pedro, later Pedro I, declares Brazil independent of Portugal and assumes title of Emperor

1840: Dom Pedro II begins his 40-year rule as Emperor

1888: Slavery is abolished and 700,000 slaves are emancipated

1889: The monarchy is toppled by a bloodless revolution and Brazil becomes a republic

1930: Getúlio Vargas comes to power through a revolution and establishes dictatorial rule

1942: Brazil enters WW II and declares war against Axis powers

1945-54: Military coup topples the Vargas dictatorship and restores democracy. In 1951 Vargas again becomes president. Faced with army opposition and threatened with impeachment, he commits suicide in 1954

1956-61: Presidency of Juscelino Kubitschek; capital moved from Rio de Janeiro to Brasília

1961: President Janio Quadros resigns after seven months in office under pressure from traditional political forces, and is succeeded by Vice President João Goulart

1964: The elected government of João Goulart is ousted in a military coup led by General Humberto de Alencar Castelo Branco

1974: General Ernesto Geisel "elected" as the fourth successive president from the military

1975: Geisel rejects any return to democratic system of 1954-64

1979: General João Baptista de Oliveira Figueiredo sworn in as president after winning a two-party contest in late 1978

BULGARIA

Area: 42,823 sq. mi. **Population:** 8,900,000 (1978 est.)

Official Name: People's Republic of Bulgaria **Capital:** Sofia **Nationality:** Bulgarian **Languages:** Bulgarian is the official and principal language; Turkish, Greek, and Armenian are spoken by minority groups **Religion:** Bulgarian Orthodox 70%, Moslem 9%; other denominations are Roman Catholicism, Protestantism, and Judaism. The government is officially atheist **Flag:** Horizontal stripes of white, green, and red, with the state emblem, a lion framed by wheatstalks, located on the white stripe near the hoist **Anthem:** Mila Rodino (Dear Fatherland) national anthem (1964) **Currency:** Lev (.88 per U.S. $1)

Location: Southeast Europe, on the eastern part of the Balkan peninsula. Bulgaria is bordered on the north by Romania, on the east by the Black Sea, on the south by Turkey and Greece, and on the west by Yugoslavia **Features:** The country is divided into several roughly parallel east/west zones: the Danubian tableland in the north; the Stara Planina (Balkan) Mountains through the central part; and the Thracian Plain and Rhodope Mountains in the south and southwest **Chief Rivers:** Danube, Maritsa, Iskur, Tundzha

Political Leader and Head of State: Todor Zhivkov, born 1911; First Secretary of the Central Committee of the Communist party since 1954, reelected 1976. In 1971 he was elected chairman of the State Council **Head of Government:** Stanko Todorov, born 1920, Chairman of the Council of Ministers (premier). The Chairman of the National Assembly is Vladimir Bonev **Effective Date of Present Constitution:** May 1971 **Legislative Body:** Parliament (unicameral National Assembly), consisting of 400 members elected for 5 years. Although the National Assembly is nominally the supreme organ of state power, real power is, in fact, wielded by the Politburo and Secretariat of the Communist party **Local Government:** 27 provinces and one city commune, each governed by an elective people's council

Ethnic Composition: 85% of the population consists of ethnic Bulgarians; the only sizable minority is the Turks, who make up about 9%. Macedonians, Armenians, Gypsies, and Greeks constitute smaller ethnic groups **Population Distribution:** 58.7% urban (1975) **Density:** 208 inhabitants per sq. mi.

Largest Cities: (1975 census) Sofia 965,000; (1974 est.) Plovdiv 305,091, Varna 269,980, Ruse 171,264, Burgas 148,236

Per Capita Income: $2,799 (1978 est.) **Gross National Product (GNP):** $25 billion (1978) **Economic Statistics:** About 43% of GNP comes from industry (food processing, engineering and metallurgy, textiles, chemicals, rubber); 20% from agriculture (wheat, corn, barley, sugar beets); 7% from commerce; and the rest from other activities **Minerals and Mining:** Lead, zinc, and copper are produced in substantial quantities; iron ore production has quadrupled in recent years. Large coal reserves exist but the coal is of low caloric value **Labor Force:** 4.3 million (1975), of which 57% is employed in industry and construction, and 38% in agriculture

(1974) **Foreign Trade:** Exports, mainly foodstuffs, machines and equipment and dairy products, fuels, raw materials and minerals, totaled $6.3 billion in 1977. Imports, chiefly machines and equipment, fuels, minerals, raw materials, metals, animal and vegetable products, totaled $6.3 billion **Principal Trade Partners:** U.S.S.R., East Germany, France, Japan, Yugoslavia, West Germany, Italy, Poland, Czechoslovakia, Romania, Libya, Iraq

Vital Statistics: Birthrate 16.1 per 1,000 of pop. (1977); death rate 10.7 **Life Expectancy:** 71 years **Health Statistics:** 116 inhabitants per hospital bed: 465 per physician (1975) **Infant Mortality:** 23.7 per 1,000 births (1977) **Illiteracy:** 5% **Education Statistics:** 3,444 primary and secondary schools, with combined enrollment of 1,348,809 (1974) **Enrollment in Higher Education:** 128,593 (1975) **GNP Expended on Education:** 5.5% (1975)

Transportation: Surfaced roads total 18,808 mi. (1970) **Motor Vehicles:** 39,000 (1967) **Passenger Cars:** 11,400 (1967) **Railway Mileage:** 3,780 **Ports:** Burgas, Varna **Major Airlines:** Bulgarian Civil Aviation-Balkan operates domestic and international services **Communications:** Government controlled **Radio Transmitters:** 32 **Licenses:** 2,750,000 (1976) **Television Transmitters:** 154 **Licenses:** 1,546,000 (1976) **Telephones:** 853,000 (1976) **Newspapers:** 13 dailies, 232 per 1,000 inhabitants (1975)

Weights and Measures: Metric system **Travel Requirements:** Passport; visa not required for tourists staying 48 hours to 2 months

---

Long one of the more backward countries of Eastern Europe, Bulgaria has sought to modernize itself under Communist rule along several directions. The country has expanded its industry, often in close coordination with the Soviet Union.

Also, Bulgaria has been developed as a producer of early fruits and vegetables for the rest of the Soviet bloc as Florida and southern California farms produce winter crops for the rest of the United States. And there has been extensive development of Bulgaria's Black Sea coast as a summer resort.

At the 10th congress of the Bulgarian Communist Party, held in April 1971 and attended by Soviet leader Leonid Brezhnev, a new constitution and a new party program were adopted. The congress reaffirmed the dominance of Todor Zhivkov, the country's veteran Communist Party boss, while the new party program hailed the "indissoluble Bulgar-Soviet friendship."

This show of solidarity was at least partially cosmetic, a public closing of ranks amid undercurrents of domestic unrest, principally among workers seeking higher pay and better living conditions. In June 1973, the government responded to repeated pressures from the trade unions by authorizing a 23 percent raise in minimum wages.

HISTORY: Bulgaria, part of ancient Thrace and Moesia, was settled by Slavic tribes in the 6th century. In the 7th century the Slavs were conquered by Turkic-speaking Bulgars, who in time fully merged with the Slavs and whose domain continued to expand until the early part of the 11th century, when the Bulgarian state was annexed by the Byzantine Empire. Bulgaria again became a major Balkan power in the 12th and 13th centuries. In the 14th century, however, it was overrun by the Ottoman Turks and remained under their rule for 5 centuries

1876: Bulgarians revolt against Turkish rule but rebellion is crushed by brutal Turkish reprisals

1878: A large Bulgaria is created under Treaty of San Stefano ending Russo-Turkish Wars. However, treaty is revised by Congress of Berlin, making northern Bulgaria a principality under Turkish suzerainty and leaving southern Bulgaria, known as Eastern Rumelia, under direct Turkish rule

1885-1908: Alexander of Battenberg, first prince of Bulgaria, annexes Eastern Rumelia. His successor, Prince Ferdinand of Saxe-Coburg-Gotha, profiting from revolution of Young Turks in 1908, proclaims Bulgaria's independence

1912-13: Bulgaria, allied with Serbia, Greece, and Montenegro, enters first Balkan War against Turkey, which is expelled from all of Europe except the Constantinople area. Bulgarian claims to Macedonia result in second Balkan War, with Bulgaria fighting the armies of Serbia, Romania, Greece, and Turkey; Bulgaria is defeated and loses territory to all its enemies

1915-1918: Bulgaria enters World War I on side of Germany and Austria-Hungary, is defeated and loses territory

1941-44: Bulgaria joins Axis powers in World War II, declaring war on Britain and United States but not on U.S.S.R.; in 1944

U.S.S.R. declares war on Bulgaria and occupies country; Communists seize power with Soviet help

1946-48: Monarchy is abolished and a people's republic established. Industry is nationalized and resistance to collectivization of agriculture is broken

1955: Bulgaria joins Warsaw Pact

1969: Zhivkov regime launches campaign against Western influences in arts and culture and warns against anti-Soviet "revisionist" nationalism

1971: New constitution and new Bulgarian Communist Party program adopted

1976: Bulgaria meets with other Balkan nations for first conference on Balkan cooperation since WW II

1978: Bulgaria extradites suspected West German terrorists. Diplomatic problems arise over steel dumping and assassinations of Bulgarian exiles

BURMA

Area: 261,789 sq. mi. **Population:** 32,000,000 (1978 est.)

Official Name: Socialist Republic of the Union of Burma **Capital:** Rangoon **Nationality:** Burmese **Languages:** Burmese, the official language, is spoken by 80%; the rest speak a variety, including Tamil, Hindi, Chinese, Shan, Karen, Kachin, Chin and Kayah; English is used in business **Religion:** 85% of the people are Buddhists; minority religions are Hinduism, Islam, Christianity, and animism **Flag:** A red field with a blue rectangle in the upper left corner containing a cog wheel and ear of paddy surrounded by 14 white stars **Anthem:** Our Free Homeland **Currency:** Kyat (6.75 per U.S. $1)

Location: Southeast Asia. Burma is bordered on the north and northeast by China, on the east by Laos and Thailand, on the south by the Andaman Sea and the Bay of Bengal, and on the west by Bangladesh and India **Features:** The country is rimmed on the north, east, and west by mountain ranges forming a giant horseshoe. Enclosed within this mountain barrier is a central basin containing most of the country's agricultural land and population. The Salween River, cutting deep gorges through the Shan Plateau and Karenni hills in the east separates the narrow Tenasserim coast from the central basin. A similar narrow coastal strip lies in the west between the Bay of Bengal and the Arakan Yoma mountain range **Chief Rivers:** Irrawaddy, Salween, Sittang, Mekong

Head of State and Government: President: General U Ne Win, born 1911, chairman of the Council of State, elected president in 1974, reelected 1978 for four years. He is assisted by a Cabinet headed by Prime Minister U Maung Maung Kha, elected 1977 **Effective Date of Present Constitution:** January 1974 **Legislative Body:** Parliament (unicameral People's Assembly) with 451 members elected for 4-year terms **Local Government:** 7 states and 7 divisions. Since March 1974, Peoples Councils have been elected at various local levels

Ethnic Composition: Burmans, ethnically related to the Tibetans, make up about 72% of the population; the Karens (7%), the Shans (6%), the Kachins (2%), and the Chins (2%) are the next largest ethnic groups. Chinese (3%) and Hindus and Pakistanis (6%) constitute the other major ethnic groups **Population Distribution:** 19% urban **Density:** 122 inhabitants per sq. mi.

Largest Cities: (1973 est.) Rangoon 2,055,000; Mandalay 417,000; Moulmein 202,000

Per Capita Income: $142 (1978 est.) **Gross National Product (GNP):** $4.6 billion (1978 est.) **Economic Statistics:** In 1973, 37% of GNP came from agriculture, fishing, and forestry; 11% from industry and mining; and 43% from trade and services **Minerals and Mining:** Burma is rich in minerals, but production is low; petroleum and tin are exploited; small quantities of tungsten, lead, copper, zinc, nickel, cobalt, and precious stones are produced **Labor Force:** 11 million, of which 65% is employed in agriculture, and 20% in industry and commerce **Foreign Trade:** Exports, chiefly rice and teak, totaled $173 million in 1976. Imports, mainly textiles, machinery, transport equipment, and foodstuffs, totaled $237 million **Principal Trade Partners:** Japan, Britain, India, Sri Lanka, China, Indonesia, Mauritius, EEC countries

Vital Statistics: Birthrate 39.5 per 1,000 pop. (1975); death rate 15.8 **Life Expectancy:** 53 years **Health Statistics:** 1,180 inhabitants per hospital bed; 5,436 per physician (1975) **Infant Mortality:** 60 per 1,000 births **Illiteracy:** 30% **Education Statistics:** 18,670 primary and secondary schools with a total enrollment of 4,370,987 (1976) **Enrollment in Higher Education:** 56,083 (1975) **GNP Expended on Education:** 2.4% (1973)

Transportation: Surfaced roads total 13,512 mi. **Motor Vehicles:** 78,200 (1976) **Passenger Cars:** 37,700 **Railway Mileage:** 2,690 **Ports:** Rangoon, Sittwe, Bassein, Moulmein, Tavoy, Mergui **Major Airlines:** Union of Burma Airways operates both domestic and international services **Communications:** Government owned **Radio Transmitters:** 5 **Licenses:** 665,000 (1976) **Television:** None **Telephones:** 32,000 (1976) **Newspapers:** 7 dailies, 10 copies per 1,000 inhabitants (1975)

Weights and Measures: British weights and measures as well as local units are used **Travel Requirements:** (1974) 7-day tourist visa available at Burmese missions abroad

A neglected adjunct of imperial India until 1937, Burma started its modern nationhood doubly colonialized: by the British and by the Indians, who ran the lower levels of government and, with the Chinese, dominated commerce.

The Japanese occupation of Burma during World War II turned the lush, rich land into a battlefield on which Burmese nationalists first fought the British and then the Japanese, whom they found to be worse oppressors.

The inability of the government to mollify the rebellious hill peoples, the demise of the coalition which had ruled since 1948, and the prevalence of corruption led to the unopposed military takeover of General Ne Win in 1958. He gave Burma two years of comparatively able government and then returned authority to civilians. While U Nu's faction won a convincing victory, the country's troubles proved too powerful for his new government.

In 1962 Ne Win again took over, jailing many politicians and banning all parties but his own. The 15-man Revolutionary Council began broad nationalization, driving out Indians and generally sealing off Burma. The replacement of Indians and Chinese with Burmese proved politically popular but economically disastrous.

Under a new constitution adopted in 1974, Ne Win was elected president, and in 1978 he was reelected for another four-year term. The 1978 national elections gave the appearance of unity, since all candidates were members of Burma's single party, the Socialist Program Party. Burma was beset, however, by internal disunity, underscored by the exodus of Moslems and in stepped-up guerrilla strife.

In the Arakan division in western Burma, about 200,000 Moslems fled into Bangladesh in the first half of 1978, voicing fear of the Burmese army. And on Burma's eastern border, Communists were increasingly active. For the first time in years of guerrilla activity, they were joined by minorities who have been traditionally anti-Communist. The nation's economy suffered as the sporadic fighting limited mining and lumbering.

HISTORY: A Mongoloid race from Tibet, the Burmese moved southward before the 9th century and settled along the Irrawaddy. In the 11th century, King Anawratha established supremacy over the Irrawaddy delta and introduced Hinayana Buddhism. His kingdom fell to Kublai Khan in 1287, after which it passed to the Shans, who ruled until 1546 as tributaries of China. Following the rise of new Burmese dynasties, Burma was once again unified, only to be annexed piecemeal by Britain in the 19th century

1937: Burma obtains dominionlike status

1942-45: Japan invades Burma during World War II and expels the British from most of the country. U.S., British, and Chinese forces mount a counterattack and expel the Japanese

1948: The Union of Burma is set up as an independent republic. U Nu becomes the first premier

1962: General Ne Win takes over from U Nu

1970: Government troops clash with rebels in northern Burma

1971: Large Karen minority plans new drive against government; Chinese-backed Burmese Communists launch widespread attacks on troop positions in northeast Burma

1974: New constitution adopted by referendum. Ne Win installed as president

1975: Army claims defeat of insurgents. Students riot

1976: Karen rebels and Communist Shan insurgents renew fighting with government forces. Military plot to overthrow Ne Win aborted

1978 Ne Win reelected for second four-year term. About 200,000 Moslems flee into Bangladesh, telling of beatings, rapes and executions

BURUNDI

Area: 10,747 sq. mi. **Population:** 4,200,000 (1978 est.)

Official Name: Republic of Burundi **Capital:** Bujumbura **Nationality:** Barundi **Languages:** Kirundi (Rundi), a Bantu tongue, and French are the official languages; Swahili is the trade language **Religion:** 60% are Christians, chiefly Roman Catholic; there are some 25,000 Moslems and the rest are animists **Flag:** A white saltire (diagonal cross) with green and red quarters, and a white circle in the center bearing 3 red six-pointed stars outlined in green **Anthem:** Dear Burundi, O Sweet Land **Currency:** Burundi franc (90 per U.S. $1)

Location: East-central Africa. Burundi is bordered by Rwanda on the north, Tanzania on the east and south, Lake Tanganyika on the southwest, and Zaire on the northwest **Features:** Most of the country consists of grassy uplands and high plateaus. The Ruzizi River Valley and Lake Tanganyika, both along the western boundary with the Congo, constitute part of the Great Rift Valley **Chief Rivers:** Kagera, Ruvubu, Malagarazi, Ruzizi

Head of State and Government: President: Col. Jean-Baptiste Bagaza, born 1946, seized power in 1976 and appointed president **Effective Date of Present Constitution:** 1974, suspended 1976 **Legislative Body:** None. Rule is by the Supreme Revolutionary Council **Local Government:** 8 provinces, each headed by a military governor

Ethnic Composition: 85% are Bahutu (Hutu), farmers of Bantu origin; 14% are Tutsi (Watusi, Batutsi), a tall warrior people of Hamitic origin; and 1% Twa (Batwa), aboriginal pygmies **Population Distribution:** 5% urban **Density:** 391 inhabitants per sq. mi.

Largest Cities: (1976 est.) Bujumbura 160,000, Gitega 25,000; (1970 est.) Ngozi 5,000

Per Capita Income: $122 (1978) **Gross National Product (GNP):** $490 million (1978) **Economic Statistics:** In 1973, 65% of GNP was derived from agriculture (coffee, cotton, tea, bananas, sweet potatoes, cassava, millet and sorghum); and 8% from industry (chiefly food processing) **Minerals and Mining:** Bastnaesite, used for the manufacture of color TV tubes, and small amounts of cassiterite, tungsten, and gold are mined **Labor Force:** 800,000 (1978), with 95% in agriculture **Foreign Trade:** Exports, chiefly coffee, cotton, hides, and minerals, totaled $57 million in 1976. Imports, mainly textiles and leather, vehicles, machinery, food products, petroleum, consumer goods, totaled $58 million **Principal Trade Partners:** United States, Belgium, Luxembourg, West Germany, France, Kenya, Tanzania, Britain, Iran

Vital Statistics: Estimated birth rate, 46.8 per 1,000 of pop. (1975); death rate, 20.4 **Life Expectancy:** 41.5 years **Health Statistics:** 806 inhabitants per hospital bed; 45,432 per physician (1974) **Infant Mortality:** 150 per 1,000 births **Illiteracy:** 86% **Education Statistics:** 970 primary and secondary schools, with a total enrollment of 147,757 (1974) **Enrollment in Higher Education:** 1,002 (1975) **GNP Expended on Education:** 2.4% (1975)

Transportation: Of some 3,700 miles of road only about 75 miles are paved **Motor Vehicles:** 7,300 (1976) **Passenger Cars:** 5,100 **Railway Mileage:** None **Ports:** None **Major Airlines:** Air Burundi provides service to neighboring countries **Communications:** Government owned **Radio Transmitters:** 6 **Receivers:** 105,000 (1976) **Television:** None **Telephones:** 4,000 (1976) **Newspapers:** 2 dailies, 0.3 per 1,000 inhabitants (1974)

Weights and Measures: Metric system **Travel Requirements:** Passport, visa, $11 fee, 3 pictures

One of Africa's least-known and poorest countries, Burundi was until independence in 1962 the southern half of the former Belgian trust territory of Ruanda-Urundi. The landlocked country—Bujumbura, the capital, is nearly 1,000 miles by lake-rail routes from the nearest seaport, Dar es Salaam, in Tanzania—remains a geophysical, ethnic and economic twin of neighboring Rwanda.

Like Rwanda, Burundi is small, densely populated, heavily eroded, and the home of diverse peoples—the tall Tutsi (better known as Watusi), the traditional ruling minority; the medium-height Hutu, the majority peasant folk; and the dwindling pygmy Twa. However, in contrast to Rwanda where the majority Hutu rule, in Burundi the minority Tutsi caste has control and is reluctant to better the lives of the Hutu masses. As a result, foreign assistance to Burundi is less than half that provided to Rwanda, since donors assume their aid would end up serving the Tutsi elite.

The overthrow of the monarchy and proclamation of a republic in 1966 by a young Tutsi prime minister, Capt. Michel Micombero, opened the way to relative stability and concentration on needed economic development. While there have been gains in fiscal stability, Burundi continues to depend primarily on a small and fluctuating production of coffee.

Discontent among the Hutu has been an obstacle to more rapid development. In 1970 an alleged Hutu plot to massacre the Tutsi and seize power led to executions. In 1972-73 hostilities between the ruling Tutsis and the more numerous Hutus escalated, as Hutu tribesmen entered the country from Tanzania and Rwanda, precipitating fighting in which more than 100,000 were killed.

In November 1976 Burundi's armed forces deposed the president without violence, and the Uprona, the only political party, was dissolved. A Belgian-trained political scientist, Col. Jean-Baptiste Bagaza, is now in control.

HISTORY: Burundi's earliest inhabitants, the pygmy Twa, were supplanted by the Hutu, a Bantu people, who, in turn, were subjugated in the 15th or 16th century by the Tutsi, a tall, warrior people, coming probably from Ethiopia. Although Burundi was visited briefly by European explorers, it was not until the late 19th century that serious efforts at colonization were attempted

1899: Burundi, along with neighboring Rwanda, is made part of German East Africa

1916: Belgian forces from the Congo defeat Germans, occupy Burundi and Rwanda

1923-61: Burundi and Rwanda become Belgian mandated territory known as Ruanda-Urundi which in 1946 is made United Nations trusteeship. Louis Rwagasore, son of the Tutsi Mwami (king), becomes premier; he is assassinated

1962: Kingdom of Burundi attains full independence under Mwami Mwambutsa IV

1965: Premier Pierre Ngendandumwe assassinated; Dr. Pie Masumbuko becomes acting premier

1966: Premier Michel Micombero deposed King Ntare V, declares himself President of Republic

1972-73: Tutsi-Hutu war results in more than 100,000 deaths

1974: New Republican constitution put into effect

1977: Col. Jean-Baptiste Bagaza deposes Micombero

1978: In Oct., outbreak of cholera draws foreign medical teams

CAMBODIA

Area: 69,898 sq. mi. **Population:** 7,735,279 (1976 est.)

Official Name: Democratic Kampuchea **Capital:** Phnom Penh **Nationality:** Cambodian **Languages:** Cambodian, or Khmer, is the official and predominant language; French is the second language **Religion:** The vast majority practice Theravada Buddhism **Flag:** Red, with a stylized yellow five-towered temple in the middle **Currency:** None known to exist at present

Location: Southeast Asia. Cambodia is bounded by Thailand and Laos on the north, by South Vietnam on the southeast, by the Gulf of Thailand on the southwest, and by Thailand on the west **Features:** The country largely consists of a saucer-shaped alluvial plain drained by the Mekong River and shut off by mountains **Chief Rivers:** Mekong, Stung Sen

Head of State: President Heng Samrin, born 1934, is head of the People's Revolutionary Council **Effective Date of Present Constitution:** None **Legislative Body:** Legislative and executive power is in the hands of the 8-man People's Revolutionary Council **Local Government:** 5 regions and a special capital region

Ethnic Composition: Cambodians, or Khmer, make up about 87% of the population; Chinese 5%, and Chams (Moslems descended from the people of the ancient kingdom of Champa) make up the rest **Density:** 111 inhabitants per sq. mi.

Largest Cities: Phnom Penh 600,000 (1970 est.); reported to be c. 150,000 in late 1976; (1972 est.) Battambang 80,000, Kompong Cham 50,000, Pursat 20,000

Per Capita Income: $76 (1978 est.) **Gross National Product (GNP):** $610 million (1978 est.) **Economic Statistics:** Overwhelmingly agricultural (rice, rubber, beans, corn), with a little industry (textiles, cement, rubber products) **Mineral and Mining:** Phosphates, gemstones and gold are produced, and there are known quantities of unexploited iron ore, manganese, and phosphates **Foreign Trade:** Rubber and dried fish are known exports, and oil and machinery are imported **Principal Trade Partners:** Vietnam, Laos, Soviet Bloc

Transportation: Roads totaled 3,225 mi. in 1970 **Railway Mileage:** 400 (1970) **Port:** Kompong Som **Communications:** Government owned

Weights and Measures: Metric system **Travel Requirements:** No U.S. relations exist, and tourists are not accepted at present

During 22 years of existence as an independent nation, caught in the middle of the East-West political and military struggle in Southeast Asia, Cambodia managed to walk the tightrope of neutrality. Its success was credited to the diplomatic skill of Prince Norodom Sihanouk, who started as a youthful king under the French, abdicated to fill a more active political role as premier, and then became the country's first chief of state.

Sihanouk managed to maintain Cambodia's neutrality even as the Vietnam War intruded increasingly on—and over—the eastern border. Then, in March 1970, while he was out of the country, his government was overthrown in a coup led by Lt. Gen. Lon Nol.

Within a month, Cambodia's small and ill-equipped army was fighting the Vietnamese Communists and Prince Sihanouk was forming a government in exile based in Peking. The war went badly for the Cambodians, who appealed to the world for help against the enemy's sudden consolidation of its enclaves in the east. Late in April there was a response: South Vietnamese and American troops drove across the border to smash the sanctuaries. Many Vietnamese Communists moved west and assumed control of large sections of the country, including the temples at Angkor. Phnom Penh itself was often isolated from the only seaport.

In mid-1973, the United States was hoping to nudge Cambodia's exiled Prince Sihanouk and Khmer insurgent leaders into serious peace talks with members of General Lon Nol's regime. The diplomatic pressure was being brought to bear against a backdrop of urgency caused by the steady advance of Communist troops toward Phnom Penh and the imminent end of U.S. bombing raids in the country. It was at this time that the Pentagon admitted having secretly bombed Communist forces in Cambodia as early as 1969 and supplying false statistics to the U.S. Senate.

The war, with U.S. help, continued through 1974 and into 1975, with Khmer Rouge forces moving ever closer to the capital city of Phnom Penh. The end came swiftly in April 1975, with the departure of President Lon Nol and the evacuation of U.S. civilians and embassy personnel. According to Cambodian estimates, nearly 800,000 people had been killed in the war and 200,000 wounded.

In the first months after the war, refugees who escaped to Thailand reported that hundreds of thousands of people had been forcibly moved from the cities to rural areas. Almost the entire population of Phnom Penh—a city swollen by 2 million refugees—was evacuated and put to work in the rice fields. Refugees spoke of long forced marches, starvation and wholesale killings by the Khmer Rouge.

In January 1976 a new constitution went into effect and the state took a new name: Democratic Kampuchea. Elections were held on March 20 and a People's Representative Assembly of 250 was selected. Prince Sihanouk, who had returned to Phnom Penh in late 1975, announced his resignation as Head of State on April 5 and Khieu Samphan became President of the State Presidium. In September 1977, Pol Pot ended his country's virtual isolation by making a trip to Peking, where he was identified as the Secretary of the Central Committee of the Cambodian Communist Party, Prime Minister and the prime force in making sweeping changes.

Under Pol Pot—he had been Saloth Sar, a schoolteacher, according to Prince Sihanouk—the country's economy and manpower were reshaped drastically. All lands and means of production belonged to the state. Private plots, permitted even in China and the U.S.S.R., were forbidden. Wages were paid as food rations, but they were meager,

and no money was circulated. The foremost economic activity was the rebuilding of irrigation canals and dikes that had been destroyed in the civil war.

The outside world was ignored, except for China, which sent technical advisers and delivered supplies through Kompong Som, Cambodia's only port. Reports carried to neighboring countries said that the harsh treatment had produced a high death toll—possibly somewhere between 500,000 and 2 million. U.S. President Carter accused Cambodia of being the world's worst violator of human rights.

Enemies for centuries, Cambodia and Vietnam fought frequent border clashes in 1977 and 1978. In December 1978, Vietnamese troops moved steadily across Cambodia with, Hanoi said, the aid of Cambodian insurgents. On Jan. 9, 1979, Phnom Penh fell, and Pol Pot's government was replaced with the Hanoi-backed People's Revolutionary Council of Cambodia. A Cambodian, Heng Samrin took over as president, and he declared that "during the last three years, they [the Khmer Rouge under Pol Pot] killed millions." Entire villages and communes had been slaughtered, he said. On Feb. 18, he signed a treaty of peace and friendship with Vietnam.

Despite the change in governments, the fighting continued. Khmer Rouge loyalists fled into the jungles or mixed with the population, and Pol Pot reportedly was with them. The Khmer Rouge recaptured the port of Kompong Som in January for their first major victory. Soon they were cutting roads and thus denying supplies to Vietnam troops, but they pursued a policy of avoiding big-scale confrontations. Estimates were that Vietnam had 100,000 soldiers in Cambodia, and they were joined by 1,000 Laotians, whose homeland was being used as a staging ground for incursions. Prince Sihanouk, in Geneva, estimated that the Pol Pot forces had 40,000 to 50,000 men and said they were getting aid through Thailand. In July the pro-Vietnam government of Heng Samrin reported that total victory had been achieved over the Pol Pot forces. The continued fighting raised the specter of mass starvation for 2.25 million Cambodians as a result of war-caused crop losses, according to United Nations and Red Cross observers.

HISTORY: Modern Cambodia is what remains of the great Khmer Empire, which by the 1200s stretched across Southeast Asia from the South China Sea westward into Burma. By the 1800s the Khmer holdings had been steadily reduced to the present size of Cambodia by the invasions of the Vietnamese and Siamese

1863: French protectorate is established over Cambodia

1887: Cambodia is incorporated in the Union of Indo-China

1945: Japanese invade Cambodia, driving out the Vichy French

1946: French return and grant Cambodia autonomy within the French Union

1953-54: Cambodia achieves full independence; leaves French Union

1970: Prince Sihanouk is ousted in pro-Western coup; U.S. and South Vietnamese troops enter Cambodia in drive against North Vietnamese forces; Cambodians and South Vietnamese continue fighting after withdrawal of U.S. ground troops. Cambodia is declared a republic

1971: United States expands bombing strikes and troop-ferrying missions; South Vietnamese driven from Seoul

1973: Pentagon admits it conducted 14 months (1969/70) of secret bombings in Cambodia. Bombing halted Aug. 15

1974: Government troops and insurgents continue military operations. Long Boret forms 15-member wartime cabinet to replace the coalition government, which resigned June 13. The U.S. airlifts supplies

1975: U.S. triples its airlift to overcome effect of insurgents' blockade of roads into Phnom Penh and of Mekong River. April 1: Lon Nol leaves country. Government resistance begins to crumble. April 12: U.S. closes Phnom Penh embassy and evacuates staff. April 16: Government surrenders and insurgents enter Phnom Penh. War ends. May 14: U.S. air, sea and ground forces battle Cambodians after seizure of the American merchant ship

Mayaguez in the Gulf of Siam. The ship and crew of 39 were freed. American casualties in the rescue operations were 15 killed, 3 missing and 50 wounded

1976: New constitution adopted in December goes into effect. Elections held on March 20. April 5: Prince Sihanouk resigns as Head of State

1977: Pol Pot identified as nation's leader

1978: Border clashes with Vietnam and Thailand intensify

1979: Phnom Penh falls, Pol Pot's government collapses, and the People's Revolutionary Council takes over, with Heng Samrin as president

CAMEROON

Area: 183,568 sq. mi. **Population:** 6,800,000 (1978 est.)
Official Name: United Republic of Cameroon **Capital:** Yaoundé **Nationality:** Cameroonian **Languages:** French (spoken by 75%) and English (25%) are both official languages; 24 African languages are spoken **Religion:** 33% Christian (mainly in the south); 15% Moslem (mainly in the north); the rest are animists **Flag:** Vertical green, red, and yellow stripes, with a yellow star in the center of the red stripe **Anthem:** O, Cameroon, Cradle of Our Ancestors **Currency:** CFA Franc (219.0 per U.S. $1)

Location: West-central Africa. Cameroon is bordered by Lake Chad on the north, by Chad and the Central African Empire on the east, by the Congo, Gabon, and Equatorial Guinea on the south, by the Gulf of Guinea on the west, and by Nigeria on the west and northwest **Features:** Of the country's four distinct regions, the south consists of a low coastal plain with equatorial rain forests, the center forms a transitional plateau, the west is an area of mountainous forests, and the north is low rolling savanna **Chief Rivers:** Sanaga, Nyong

Head of State and of Government: President Ahmadou Ahidjo, born 1924, reelected to fourth 5-year term in May 1975, assisted by a cabinet headed by the premier, Paul Biya **Effective Date of Present Constitution:** May 1972 **Legislative Body:** National Assembly (unicameral), consisting of 120 members elected by universal suffrage for 5 years **Local Goverment:** 7 provinces with appointed governors

Ethnic Composition: Estimates of the number of tribal groups run as high as 200. The main divisions are the Bantus and semi-Bantus, which include the Beti and Bamiléké; the Sudnese, mainly Kirdis; and the Arab Foulbé. Pygmies inhabit the equatorial forest **Population Distribution:** 25% urban **Density:** 37 inhabitants per sq.mi.

Largest Cities: (1975 estimates) Douala 435,000, Yaoundé 274,000, N'Kongsamba 67,000

Per Capita Income: $409 (1978 est.) **Gross National Product (GNP):** $2.8 billion (1978) **Economic Statistics:** In 1976, 33% of GNP came from agriculture (coffee, bananas, cotton, peanuts, livestock, rubber, palm oil); 25% from commerce; and 12% from industry (aluminum, chemicals) **Minerals and Mining:** Large deposits of bauxite ore, iron ore, and limestone; traces of mica and phosphates; small deposits of tin and gold. Petroleum and natural gas exploitation has begun **Labor Force:** Over 3 million; 80% in agriculture **Foreign Trade:** Exports, chiefly coffee, cocoa beans, aluminum, wood, cotton, and rubber, totaled $508 million in 1976. Imports, mainly vehicles and transportation equipment, industrial machinery and other capital goods, consumer goods, food, beverages, and tobacco, totaled $608 million **Principal Trade Partners:** EC countries (mainly France), United States, Japan, Chad, adjacent African nations

Vital Statistics: Birthrate, 40.4 per 1,000 of pop. (1975); death rate, 22 **Life Expectancy:** 41 years **Health Statistics:** 390 inhabitants per hospital bed;17,790 per physician (1974) **Infant Mortality:** 137 per 1,000 births **Illiteracy:** 35% **Education Statistics:** 4,319 primary and secondary schools, with combined enrollment of 1,122,560 (1973) **Enrollment in Higher Education:** 7,191 (1975) **GNP Expended on Education:** 4.2% (1973)

Transportation: Paved roads total about 900 miles **Motor Vehicles:** 110,700 (1976) **Passenger cars:** 59,500 **Railway Mileage:** 700 **Ports:** Douala, Tiko, Victoria, Kribi **Major Airlines:** Air Cameroun and Cameroons Air Transport operate internal services; Air Afrique operates international services **Communications:** Government owned **Radio Transmitters:** 4 **Receivers:** 603,000 (1974) **Television:** None **Telephones:** 22,000 (1973) **Newspapers:** 2 dailies, 4 copies per 1,000 inhabitants (1975)

Weights and Measures: Metric system **Travel Requirements:** Passport, visa required beyond 1 month stay, $5 fee, 2 pictures

avan trade to the north. Extending nearly 800 miles in length from the Gulf of Guinea to Lake Chad, the country is a cross section of Africa from desert north through central plateau and grasslands to southern rain forest.

Formerly a German colony, Cameroon was divided between France and Britain after World War I, with the French getting about four-fifths of the area. The country was reunited as a federal republic in 1961, after a UN plebiscite had resulted in the addition of the northern part of former British Cameroons to Nigeria.

The two areas, West Cameroon (formerly British) and the larger East Cameroon (formerly French) were governed as constituent states, each with its own legislature. The new constitution which went into effect in May 1972 calls for a unitary state with a strong executive authority and an elected national assembly.

Cameroon is the only African country in which both French and English are official languages. The Federal University of Cameroon, established in Yaoundé in 1962, is the first in Africa to teach courses in French and English, as well as one of the first to establish a medical school.

Cameroon has been one of Africa's "quiet" countries, in which the single-party government of President Ahmadou Ahidjo has maintained a measure of political and economic stability.

Before Cameroon became an independent republic in 1960, the formerly French eastern area was torn by a terrorist revolt. Protracted rebel activities in the central part of the country were suppressed in 1970. Despite the diversity of its peoples, cultures, and religions, however, Cameroon has escaped the coups and civil wars that have plagued neighboring countries.

Cameroon's great diversity of tropical produce—timber, cocoa, coffee, rubber, palm oil, cotton, and a wide range of food crops—has been the basis for an economic growth that has been averaging nine percent a year. Although France remains the country's chief partner in trade and investment, British, American, West German, and Japanese interests have been attracted by the favorable economic and investment climate. Petroleum production began in 1978.

Education and health services also are increasing and Cameroonians take pride in the fact that 70 percent of the country's children attend school, a high rate for developing Africa.

HISTORY: The country was given its name by 15th century Portuguese explorers. Impressed with the number of shrimp in one of the rivers, they called it Rio dos Camarões (River of Shrimp) and extended the name to the entire region. After being made a German colony in the late 19th century, the country was occupied during World War I by the French and British, who divided it under League of Nations mandates

1946: French and British mandates are converted into United Nations Trusteeships

1959: UN General Assembly votes end of French trusteeship

1960: On Jan. 1, French Cameroon becomes independent Cameroon Republic; draft constitution is approved by referendum; National Assembly names Premier Ahmadou Ahidjo president

1961: In U.N.-supervised plebiscites, southern part of British Cameroons votes for reunification with Cameroon Republic, northern part for union with Nigeria; federation of East and West Cameroon is established

1966: After unification of major political parties in East and West Cameroon, all opposition parties are dissolved or join in single new party, the Cameroon National Union

1970: President Ahidjo is reelected for third successive term

1971: Political trials and executions end 10-year guerrilla insurrection

1972: Cameroon Labor Minister Ekangaki is elected Secy.-Gen. of the Organization of African Unity

1974: Cameroon becomes 100th member of the Int'l Finance Corporation

1975: President Ahidjo is reelected for his fourth five-year term. Paul Biya is named as Cameroon's first premier

Cameroon has been one of the main racial crossroads of Africa as a result of Bantu migrations from the east and links to the Sahara car-

CANADA
(See separate Canada section)

CAPE VERDE

Area: 1,557 sq. mi. **Population:** 312,000 (1978 est.)

Official Name: Republic of Cape Verde **Capital:** Praia **Nationality:** Cape Verdean **Languages:** Officially Portuguese, with most speaking a dialect, Crioulo **Religion:** 65% Roman Catholic, and 30% animist **Flag:** Two horizontal stripes, yellow over green, with a red vertical stripe at the hoist, the latter having an emblem of a black star over a yellow seashell, framed by two cornstalks **Anthem:** N.A. **Currency:** Cape Verdean escudo (47 per U.S. $1)

Location: In the Atlantic Ocean, 390 miles west of Dakar, Senegal, off the coast of Africa. Ten islands and 5 islets comprise the nation **Features:** Summer climate is extremely hot and there is a lack of potable water. Three of the main islands are flat; the other seven are mountainous, volcanic in origin **Chief Rivers:** No large rivers

Head of State: President Aristides Pereira, named 1975 **Head of Government:** Premier Pedro Pires, appointed 1975 **Effective Date of Constitution:** Not yet formulated **Legislative Body:** National Assembly (unicameral), with 56 members. The only political party permitted to operate in the Republic is the PAIGC **Local Government:** 24 Electoral Districts

Ethnic Composition: 71% are Creoles (mulattoes) of mixed African and Portuguese descent, 28% are Africans, and 1% Europeans **Population Distribution:** N.A. **Density:** 200 inhabitants per sq. mi. **Largest Cities:** (1970 census) Mindelo 28,797, Praia 21,494, Espargos 3,978

Per Capita Income: $180 (1978) **Gross National Product (GNP):** $57 million (1978 est.) **Economic Statistics:** The main economic function of the country is ship and aircraft refueling. The soil is poor and dry, and although some food (corn, beans, coffee, sugar) is grown, much must be imported. Fishing is important **Minerals and Mining:** Salt, pozzolana (used in making cements) **Labor Force:** 84,869 in 1970, with 67% in agriculture, and 5% in industry **Foreign Trade:** Exports, chiefly fish products, bananas, salt, coffee, pozzolana, totaled $1.4 million in 1976. Imports, chiefly corn, wheat, cement, vehicles, totaled $26.8 million **Principal Trade Partners:** Portugal, EEC, United States

Vital Statistics: Birthrate, 27.6 per 1,000 of pop. (1975); death rate, 9.4 **Life Expectancy:** 45 years **Health Statistics:** 665 per hospital bed; 19,230 per physician (1969) **Infant Mortality:** 78.9 per 1,000 births **Illiteracy:** 63% **Education Statistics:** 431 primary and secondary schools, with a total enrollment of 75,000 (1972) **Enrollment in Higher Education:** N.A. **GNP Expended on Education:** 1.5% (1972)

Transportation: Paved roads total 380 mi. **Motor Vehicles:** 3,700 (1976) **Passenger Cars:** 2,900 **Railway Mileage:** None **Ports:** Mindelo, Praia **Major Airlines:** T.A.P. provides international service, and Cape Verde Air Transport domestic service **Communications:** Government owned **Radio Transmitters:** 4 **Receivers:** 36,000 (1976) **Television:** None **Telephones:** 2,000 (1976) **Newspapers:** Three, several times a week

Weights and Measures: Metric system **Travel Requirements:** Passport, visa

Cape Verde became independent on July 5, 1975, ending 515 years of Portuguese rule. In 1460 the Portuguese navigators Diego Gomes and Antonio da Noli discovered Maio and São Tiago Islands, and in 1462 the first settlers landed on São Tiago.

Cape Verde, one of five territories relinquished by Portugal (the others being Guinea-Bissau, Mozambique, São Tomé and Príncipe, and Angola), has strong ties with Guinea-Bissau. Aristedes Pereira and Pedro Pires, heroes of the guerrilla war waged against Portugal in Guinea-Bissau, were named President and Premier, respectively in 1975.

The islands have been afflicted with disastrous drought and famine in recent years. Since the mid-1900s, an estimated 300,000 Cape Verdeans have emigrated because of the difficulty in earning a living. Workers' remittances sent home from abroad are estimated at $8 million annually.

HISTORY: The islands were discovered in 1460 by Portuguese navigators in the service of Prince Henry the Navigator. Settlement began two years later. The archipelago was a center for the slave trade with the West African coast

1975: On June 30, the Party for the Independence of Guinea-Bissau and Cape Verde (PAIGC) is the only political group to run candidates for the 56-member Assembly at the first general election. The Assembly is to write a constitution and decide whether Cape Verde should form a nation with Guinea-Bissau. Officials of the U.S. Agency for International Development sign a $5-million assistance agreement with Cape Verde's new government. Admitted to the UN

1976: Cape Verde and U.S.S.R. sign pact granting reciprocal use of each other's ports.

1978: Union with Guinea-Bissau being considered

CENTRAL AFRICAN EMPIRE

On September 21, 1979 it was announced that the Emperor and the Empire had been overthrown.

Area: 236,293 sq. mi. **Population:** 2,100,000 (1978 est.)

Official Name: Central African Empire **Capital:** Bangui **Nationality:** Central African **Languages:** French is the official language; Sangho is the national language **Religion:** 40% Protestant, 28% Roman Catholic, 24% animist, 8% Moslem **Flag:** Horizontal bars of blue, white, green, and yellow, bisected by a vertical red bar. A yellow star appears on the blue band at the upper left **Anthem:** La Renaissance **Currency:** CFA Franc (219 per U.S. $1)

Location: At almost the exact center of the African continent. The landlocked country is bordered by Chad on the north, Sudan on the east, Zaire and Congo on the south, and Cameroon on the west **Features:** The country is a huge, well-watered plateau drained by 2 major river systems **Chief Rivers:** Ouham, Ubangi, Kotto, Lobaye, Sangha

Head of State and of Government: Emperor Bokassa I (Jean-Bedel Bokassa), born 1921, seized power in a coup in 1966; appointed president for life 1972; crowned emperor in 1977. He is assisted by a premier, Henri Maidou **Effective Date of Present Constitution:** December 1976 **Legislative Body:** Rule is by the 31-man Council of the Revolution, created in 1976 **Local Government:** 14 prefectures; prefects are assisted by councils

Ethnic Composition: Of some 80 different ethnic groups, the main ones (66%) are the Banda in the east-central area; the Baya and the Mandjia in the west and in the west-central area; 7% are M'baka **Population Distribution:** 20% urban **Density:** 9 inhabitants per sq. mi.

Largest Cities: (1974 est.) Bangui 301,000, Bouar 48,000, Bangassou 46,000, Bambari 35,000

Per Capita Income: $194 (1978 est.) **Gross National Product:** $370 million (1978 est.) **Economic Statistics:** Agriculture (cotton, coffee, rice, tobacco, rubber, peanuts, palm oil) and livestock (cattle, sheep, goats, pigs, poultry) make up 34% of the GNP; diamond and uranium mining, and small-scale manufacturing (textiles, beer, shoes, bicycles and motor bikes, plastics) 16%; and trade and services 29% **Minerals and Mining:** Diamonds, uranium and gold are exploited. Deposits of iron ore, zinc, copper, and tin exist **Labor Force:** 80% of the population is engaged in farming **Foreign Trade:** Exports, chiefly diamonds, wool, cotton, and coffee, totaled $81 million in 1976. Imports, mainly machinery and equipment, textiles, and petroleum products, totaled $50 million **Principal Trade Partners:** France, other EC countries, United States, Israel, Cameroon

Vital Statistics: Birthrate, 43.4 per 1,000 of pop. (1975); death rate, 22.5 **Life Expectancy:** 40 years **Health Statistics:** 522 inhabitants per hospital bed; 20,833 per physician (1975) **Infant Mortality:** 190 per 1,000 births **Illiteracy:** 93% **Education Statistics:** 717 primary and secondary schools, with combined enrollment of 236,936 (1974) **Enrollment in Higher Education:** 318 (1974) **GNP Expended on Education:** 3.3% (1973)

Transportation: Paved roads total 113 mi. **Motor Vehicles:** 13,000 (1974) **Passenger Cars:** 9,100 **Railway Mileage:** None **Ports:** None **Major Airlines:** Air Banguie and Air Centrafrique operate domestic services; Air Afrique, Aeroflot, and UTA operate international services **Communications:** Government owned **Radio Transmitters:** 6 (1972) **Receivers:** 75,000 (1976) **Television:** None **Telephones:** 5,000 (1973) **Newspapers:** One, several times a week

Weights and Measures: Metric system **Travel Requirements:** Passport, visa

Isolation in the heart of Africa constitutes the main problem of the Central African Empire (Central African Republic until December 4, 1976), a problem that is compounded by a paucity of resources and a small population.

A burning ambition of the country's ruler, Emperor Bokassa I, is to have a railroad that will link his capital, Bangui, to a port in either neighboring Cameroon or Congo.

Most of the former French colony of Ubangi-Shari is a plateau of 2,000-foot elevation, a condition that makes for a relatively temperate climate during the dry season. Stretches of grassy savanna and woodland, in which there is an abundance of wildlife, give the land a magnificent beauty.

At Bangui, a rambling African town with only a few modernistic structures, the broad Oubangui River provides a water-skiing playground for the small number of French residents who still dominate the country's commerce.

With modern techniques, cotton production has increased more than three times to 60,000 metric tons a year and provides a major export. Diamond production and small quantities of coffee and peanuts have also added to exports and income.

While the diamonds may be shipped by air, the other products must be transported at considerable cost by road or river to the nearest ports. Aid from France, the World Bank, and other sources has helped improve roads and create small industry, but clearly a rail link is needed for further crop expansion and development of timber resources.

The recent discovery of uranium at Bakouma, 540 miles east of Bangui, has brightened economic prospects and, with new exploration indicating deposits of iron ore, manganese, and copper, has heightened the need for a railroad.

Bokassa, who seized power in a bloodless coup in 1966, is a former French Army sergeant with 23 years of service. He was made president for life in 1972 and in 1976 proclaimed himself emperor. (He crowned himself in a $22-million ceremony in December 1977.) He rules his subjects by imperial decree and sometimes with brutal barracks-like discipline.

One government decree, that students wear state uniforms, prompted protest demonstrations in the capital in January 1979, resulting in 12 deaths. Amnesty International reported the killing of 100 schoolchildren in prison following their arrest for further rioting in April. A later report by judges from five African nations stated that Emperor Bokassa was present at the prison during the massacre of the 8 to 16-year-old children.

HISTORY: For centuries, what is now the Central African Empire was a crossroads for numerous migrations by various groups, mainly of Bantu origin. In the 19th century, French expeditions penetrated the country, which was named Ubangi-Shari after its two main rivers. Early in the 20th century, the country was joined with Chad and became one of the territories of French Equatorial Africa

1946: French constitutional reform confers French citizenship on people of Ubangi-Shari

1958: In a referendum, Ubangi-Shari votes to become an autonomous republic within the French Community. The Central African Republic is proclaimed, with Barthélémy Boganda as president

1959: Boganda, founder of the republic and its mass political party, Social Evolution Movement of Black Africa, is killed in plane crash and succeeded by his cousin, David Dacko

1960-65: Republic becomes a fully independent nation under President Dacko, who dissolves all political parties. He is reelected in an election in which he is the only candidate

1966: Colonel Jean-Bedel Bokassa, chief of staff of the armed forces, overthrows Dacko government, ousts Communist Chinese mission, and establishes rule by revolutionary council

1969: Central African Republic suspends relations with Congo (Kinshasa) after latter's accusation that Bokassa regime had murdered a number of Congolese

1970: C.A.R. resumes relations with Zaire and Chad

1972: Congress of the sole political party appoints Bokassa president for life

1974: Bokassa promotes himself to Marshal of the Republic. French consulate ordered closed; French journals prohibited

1975: Bokassa names Elizabeth Domitien as Africa's first woman premier

1976: Bokassa escapes assassination attempt in February. He dismisses Domitien and declares his country a parliamentary monarchy with himself as emperor

1979: Amnesty International claims that 100 schoolchildren were killed in prison following riots against the forced wearing of uniforms

CHAD

Area: 495,752 sq. mi. **Population:** 4,400,000 (1978 est.)
Official Name: Republic of Chad **Capital:** N'Djamena **Nationality:** Chadian **Languages:** French is the official language. An Arabic dialect is spoken in northern and central Chad; in the south the main tribal languages are Sara, Massa, and Moudang **Religion:** More than 50% of the population is Moslem, 40% animist, and 5% Christian **Flag:** Vertical stripes of blue, yellow, and red **Anthem:** La Tchadienne, beginning "Chadians, Stand up and Set to Work!" **Currency:** CFA Franc (219 per U.S. $1)
Location: North-Central Africa. Landlocked Chad is bordered by Libya on the north, Sudan on the east, the Central African Empire on the south, and by Niger, Nigeria, and Cameroon on the west **Features:** The country is shaped like a shallow basin, rimmed by mountain ranges on the north and east. The northern part of the country is desert, the central part a savanna, and the south tropical, with wooded savanna. Lake Chad on the western border is believed to be the remnant of an inland sea **Chief Rivers:** Shari, Logone

Head of State and Government: President Lol Mohamed Shawa (Choua), appointed April 1979 **Effective Date of Present Constitution:** 1962; suspended 1975 **Legislative Body:** None **Local Government:** 14 prefectures, under appointed governors

Ethnic Composition: The population is about evenly divided between the northern and eastern people, of predominantly Sudanic origin, and the Nilotic southerners. There are some 3,000 Europeans, mainly French **Population Distribution:** 13.9% urban **Density:** 9 inhabitants per sq. mi.
Largest Cities: (1972 est.) N'Djamena 179,000, Sarh 43,700, Moundou 39,600, Abécher 28,100

Per Capita Income: $86 (1978 est.) **Gross National Product (GNP):** $370 million (1978 est.) **Economic Statistics:** In 1973 about 50% of GNP came from agriculture (cotton, sorghum, rice, peanuts, gum arabic, livestock) and fishing, 8% from industry and mining, and 23% from trade and services **Minerals and Mining:** Natron, a low-grade salt, is the only exploited mineral. Traces of shale oil, uranium, kaolin, and tungsten have been found in the north. Petroleum has been discovered **Labor Force:** 1.3 million (1970), with about 88% in agriculture **Foreign Trade:** Exports, chiefly cotton and cattle, totaled $81 million in 1976. Imports, mainly mineral products (including petroleum products), foodstuffs and beverages, electrical machinery and parts, textiles, and transportation equipment, totaled $97 million **Principal Trade Partners:** France, Japan, West Germany, Cameroon, United States, Nigeria

Vital Statistics: Estimated birthrate, 47.7 per 1,000 of pop.; estimated death rate, 25 **Life Expectancy:** 43 years **Health Statistics:** 1,140 inhabitants per hospital bed; 44,382 per physician (1974) **Infant Mortality:** 160 per 1,000 births **Illiteracy:** 95% **Education Statistics:** 806 primary and secondary schools, with combined enrollment of 221,672 (1974) **Enrollment in Higher Education:** 547 (1975) **GNP Expended on Education:** 2.2% (1975)

Transportation: Paved roads total 180 mi. **Motor Vehicles:** 12,100 (1973) **Passenger Cars:** 5,800 **Railway Mileage:** None **Ports:** None **Major Airlines:** Air Chad is the domestic carrier; Air Afrique, Air Cameroun, UTA, and Sudan Airways operate services to Chad **Communications:** Government owned **Radio Transmitters:** 6 **Receivers:** 76,000 (1976) **Television:** None **Telephones:** 5,000 (1975) **Newspapers:** 4 dailies, 0.4 copies per 1,000 inhabitants (1975)

Weights and Measures: Metric system **Travel Requirements:** (1971) Passport; visa, $6.25, 3 photos, round-trip ticket

---

The remote outpost of former French Equatorial Africa, landlocked Chad suffers from isolation, internal strife, and a loss of arable land.

With its productive area more than 1,000 miles from any seaport, Chad is difficult to reach except by air. There is no railroad and a good part of the network of dirt roads and tracks is impassable during the rainy season.

Since 1968 Arab guerrillas in the northern and eastern part of the country have waged a rebellion against the Bantu-dominated government. Some 3,500 French troops were sent to help the Chadian government quell the revolt, an action that has raised controversy both in France and in Africa. French forces actively fighting the rebels were withdrawn in 1971.

The chief cause of the nomadic northerners' enmity toward the Chadian government was the fact that it had been dominated by southerners— Negroid river peoples whom the Arabs tradi-

tionally scorned as slaves. In addition, the northerners, mainly the Toubous, resented the government's tax on their cattle.

The regime of François Tombalbaye, which had
been in power since 1962, was toppled by a military coup in 1975. General Félix Malloum, the
new Bantu ruler, called for national unity but already has had attempts on his life by Arab
nationalists.

In February 1979, Premier Hissene Habré
staged a coup attempt against Malloum, resulting
in streetfighting in the capital that killed hundreds. A cease-fire agreement was arranged by
neighboring Nigeria at a conference in Kano attended by Malloum, Habré and the leaders of two
other contending factions. A provisional government was set up representing the four groups, and
Nigerian troops were sent to N'Djamena to maintain order as the faction armies were withdrawn.
Unfortunately, only Malloum's forces withdrew,
and the remaining guerrilla groups looted the
city. Malloum then fled to Nigeria and attempts to
hold a second government-organizing conference
in Kano failed when five new guerrilla factions
demanded representation.

Habré and Ouaddeimi Goukouni, leader of the
Frolinat faction, dissolved the provisional govern-
ment in April. The two leaders then created a new
government on April 29 with Lol Mohamed
Shawa as the figure-head President of Chad.
Power remains with Habré and Goukouni.

In addition to the ravages of political strife the
economy of Chad was damaged by six years of
severe drought from 1967. Thousands of persons
died, cattle perished and valuable grazing land
became sandy desert.

The main export crop, cotton, has declined recently. Because of the high cost of transportation,
Chad's exports of cotton require a high subsidy by
France, which also provides about half of Chad's
national budget. Chad developed little during
colonialism and seems to rely more on France,
economically, since independence.

HISTORY: Chad is believed to have been a center of ancient cultures before the southward encroachment of the Sahara. The varied ethnic make-up of present-day Chadians is evidence also of a
succession of migrations and invasions in past centuries by Bantu
southerners, Sudanese Moslems, and Nilotic peoples. Throughout
the ages, Chad was the domain of conquerors and warrior slave
traders, some of whom held sway until the late 19th century.
Among the last of these was Rabah Amoney, a Sudanese ex-slave
turned slave merchant and chieftain, whose conquest of the Bornu
Kingdom was to lead to French intervention

1897-1900: Traditional rulers, threatened by Rabah's army, seek
protection of French, whose forces march across the Sahara
from Algeria, defeat Sudanese, and impose own rule

1910: Chad is made one of the four territories of French Equatorial
Africa, along with Gabon, the present Congo (Brazzaville), and
Ubangi-Shari (now the Central African Empire)

1940: Chad becomes first territory to rally to Free French

1959-60: Chad becomes autonomous member of French Community. On Aug. 11, 1960, complete independence and the Republic of Chad are proclaimed

1962: All opposition parties are banned under new constitution and
single-party rule is set up by Chadian Progressive party, led by
President François Tombalbaye

1963: State of emergency is declared after abortive coup d'état and
arrest of Moslem leaders; constitutional amendments are
adopted and new elections are held in an effort to heal the rift
between Moslem north and Bantu south

1969: Moslem guerrillas step up attacks on government installations as Arab-Bantu split widens; President Tombalbaye calls in
French troops to help quell growing revolt

1973: U.N. reports Chad is most severely affected of the Sub-
Saharan countries suffering from drought

1975: President Tombalbaye assassinated (April 13). Military junta
headed by Gen. Félix Malloum takes control

1977: Attempted coup against Malloum fails

1979: Fighting continues between Chadian troops and Libyan-
backed Moslem guerrillas; more than 1,000 die in riots in south.
Malloum flees Chad. Lol Mohamed Shawa is installed as President by faction leaders

CHILE

Area: 292,256 sq. mi. **Population:** 10,850,000 (1978 est.)

Official Name: Republic of Chile **Capital:** Santiago **Nationality:**
Chilean **Languages:** The official and virtually universal language is
Spanish **Religion:** 90% Roman Catholic **Flag:** A white horizontal
stripe over a longer red stripe, with a blue square in the upper left
corner containing a 5-pointed white star **Anthem:** National Anthem; refrain "Sweet Country, receive the pledge" **Currency:**
Chilean peso (36 per U.S. $1)

Location: Southwest coast of South America. Chile is bordered on
the north by Peru, on the east by Argentina and Bolivia, on the
south by Drake Passage, and on the west by the Pacific Ocean
Features: The country stretches some 2,650 miles along the Pacific coast and is at no point wider than 250 miles. The north is
desert, the central region agricultural, and the south is forest land.
The towering Andes dominate most of the eastern frontier **Chief
Rivers:** Loa, Maule, Bio-Bio, Valdivia

Head of State and of Government: President: Maj. Gen. Augusto
Pinochet Ugarte, assumed power September 1973 as head of a 4-
man military junta, advised by a cabinet **Effective Date of Present
Constitution:** 1925; a new one is being drafted **Legislative Body:**
Congress (dissolved) **Local Government:** 12 regions, subdivided
into 40 provinces, and the metropolitan region of Santiago

Ethnic Composition: About 68% of the population is of Spanish-
Indian descent, 30% of European (mainly Spanish) descent, and
less than 1% Indian **Population Distribution:** 82% urban **Density:**
37 inhabitants per sq. mi.

Largest Cities: (1975 est.) Santiago 3,262,990, Valparaíso
248,972 Concepción 169,570, Viña del Mar 229,020, Antofagasta
149,720, Temuco 138,430

Per Capita Income: $1,572 (1978 est.) **Gross National Product
(GNP):** $16.8 billion (1978 est.) **Economic Statistics:** In 1977,
29% of GNP was derived from trade and services; 20% from
industry (paper and paper products, iron and steel, petrochemicals, chemicals, and metal products); 7% from mining; and 10%
from agriculture (wheat, wine grapes, potatoes, sugar beets, tobacco, fruit), forestry and fishing **Minerals and Mining:** Chile is
one of the world's leading copper producers; iron ore is second in
importance; natural nitrates, iodine, molybdenum and coal are
also exploited **Labor Force:** 3,323,301 (1975), about 27% in services, 28% in agriculture, 25% in manufacturing, and 14% in
commerce **Foreign Trade:** Exports, mainly copper and copper
manufactures, iron ore, pulp and paper, fishmeal, wine, seafood,
wool, and fruit, totaled $2.2 billion in 1977. Imports, mainly ma-
chinery and equipment, agricultural products, and transport
equipment, totaled $2.2 billion **Principal Trade Partners:** United
States, Latin American Free Trade Association, EEC, Iran

Vital Statistics: Birthrate, 23.9 per 1,000 of pop. (1976); death
rate, 7.8 per 1,000 (1976) **Health Statistics:** 279 inhabitants per hospital bed; 1,836 per physician (1973) **Infant Mortality:**
54.7 per 1,000 births (1976) **Illiteracy:** 8% **Education Statistics:**
8,461 primary and secondary schools, with combined enrollment
of 2,709,209 (1976) **Enrollment in Higher Education:** 149,647
(1975) **GNP Expended on Education:** 3.8% (1974)

Transportation: Paved roads total 5,197 mi. (1971) **Motor Vehicles:** 424,400 (1975) **Passenger Cars:** 255,700 **Railway Mileage:**
5,511 **Ports:** Valparaíso, Arica, Antofagasta, Coquimbo, Iquique,
Talcahuano **Major Airlines:** LAN-Chile, the government-owned airline, operates domestic and international services **Communications:** Government controlled **Radio Transmitters:** 229 (1971)
Receivers: 3,100,000 (1974) **Television Transmitters:** 27 **Receivers:** 1,000,000 (1976) **Telephones:** 451,000 (1976) **Newspapers:** 47 dailies (1975); 94 copies per 1,000 inhabitants (1972)

Weights and Measures: Metric system **Travel Requirements:**
Passport, no visa

Chile has long had an outstanding potential—immense natural resources and a relatively sophisticated population—but efforts to match living
standards to promise have fallen short. Inflation,
once chronic and at runaway rates—it rose 340
percent in 1975, for instance—has been brought
down to a manageable 20-25 percent a year, but at
the expense of large-scale unemployment and
other social problems.

Nature is largely responsible for the economic
and social status of Chile, a land dominated by the
geological immaturity of the Andes, a mountain
range that runs the entire length of the long and
narrow country. Relatively "new" and earth-
quake-prone, the Andes yield the copper and
other metals that account for more than half of
Chile's foreign-exchange earnings.

Politically, Chile has also been a victim of
abrupt change and contrasts. The pride of South

American democracies from 1932 until the 1970's, the country since 1973 has seen its military employ coercion at the expense of human rights to remove all vestiges of the Marxist experiment of Salvador Allende Gossens. Allende in 1970 became the first Marxist to be elected president in South America, but on September 11, 1973, one week after the third anniversary of Allende's election, a military junta staged the first successful coup against a civilian government in Chile since 1927. President Allende was reported to have committed suicide. A year later it was learned that the United States had funneled more than $8 million through the CIA to anti-Allende groups.

The current military regime, headed by Chile's president, Gen. Augusto Pinochet Ugarte, is facing world criticism for political repression, torture and news censorship. The regime continues to hold political prisoners, but, under pressure from the U.S. and other democratic nations, the number has been reduced. The junta's aim has been to entrench political power by dictatorial rule, and Pinochet has succeeded in establishing an "authoritarian democracy."

After the UN General Assembly reported that Chile was violating human rights, President Pinochet ordered a national referendum on Jan. 4, 1978, that upheld his government. "In the face of the international aggression against the government of the homeland," the referendum read in part, "I [the voter] support President Pinochet in his defense of the dignity of Chile." The "yes" vote was announced as 75 percent. Despite this ringing support, the government eased up by restoring some autonomy to civil judges and by limiting the president's punitive powers. Also, an amnesty program was set in motion, leading to pardons or voluntary exile for some prisoners.

In July 1978, the junta removed one of its members, Air Force Gen. Gustavo Leigh, who had advocated a swifter return to civilian rule. His replacement, Gen. Fernando Matthei, supports the retention of Pinochet as president through 1985.

On Feb. 12, 1979, the U.S. District Court in Washington, D.C., found three Cuban exiles guilty in the murder of Orlando Letelier, who had been Allende's ambassador to the United States. Letelier, Chile's most prominent political exile, was killed when a bomb blew up his car in Washington in 1976. An American, Michael V. Townley, said he made and planted the bomb on orders of DINA, the old Chilean secret police force. On May 14, Chile's chief justice refused to extradite three Chilean army officers to the United States for trial, and the U.S. State Department recalled its ambassador to Chile.

On the economic front, Chile brought the inflation rate down to an acceptable 20-25 percent rate, was running in the black on the balance of payments, and was receiving more foreign investment, notably in mining and banking but also in diversified small industries.

HISTORY: Prior to the Spanish conquest of Chile in the 16th century, the northern portion of the country was under the rule of the Inca Empire and the south was mainly controlled by the Araucanian Indians, who were to prove fiercely hostile to the Spanish colonists until almost the end of the 19th century. During most of its colonial history, Chile was a captaincy general dependent on the viceroyalty of Peru

1817-18: Argentine revolutionist José de San Martín brings an army over the Andes from Argentina to Chile and, in 1818, defeats Spanish army at Battle of Maipú. Bernardo O'Higgins, who had been chosen supreme director, formally proclaims Chile's independence (Feb. 12)

1879-83: Chile defeats Peru and Bolivia in the War of the Pacific, acquiring the mineral-bearing northern desert region

1891-1925: Internal struggle between executive and legislative branches culminates in overthrow of President José Balmaceda (1891); congressional dictatorship lasts until 1925

1932-38: President Arturo Alessandri, elected for second term, institutes a kind of state capitalism in efforts to wipe out aftermath of 1929 depression; however, he turns to repressive measures and alienates working class

1946-48: Economic dislocations lead to riots and strikes encouraged by aggressive Communist activity

1964-68: Eduardo Frei Montalva is elected president and his Christian Democratic Party wins control of Chamber of Deputies after defeating coalition of Marxist parties. Frei launches reform program

1969: National discontent becomes manifest in congressional elections, when Frei's party retains majority in lower house but loses more than a third of its former seats; right-wing National party scores heavy gains

1970: Salvador Allende Gossens becomes the first Marxist to be elected president of a Latin American country

1971: Government nationalizes all U.S. copper investments

1972: Chile furthers relations with Communist countries

1973: Allende coalition gains 14 Chamber and 3 Senate seats. On September 11, Allende government is overthrown by a military junta. Allende dies in coup. State of siege declared

1974: Military junta returns to private ownership 150 companies nationalized by left-wing Allende government. CIA bankrolling of anti-Allende groups is revealed

1975: Government accelerates expulsion of political prisoners and grants safe conduct to Chilean refugees in foreign embassies, allowing them to leave the country

1978: Referendum shows wide support for Pinochet; opposition charges fraud. Government declares amnesty for political prisoners and exiles and lifts state of siege. Border disputes with neighbors continue; Bolivia breaks diplomatic relations, alleging Chile has hindered negotiations to grant it a corridor to Pacific

1979: Three anti-Castro Cuban exiles are found guilty in Washington, D.C., in the 1976 murder of Orlando Letelier, former Chilean ambassador (under Allende) to the U.S., in Washington. But Chile's Chief Justice refuses to extradite three Chilean army officers to the United States for trial in connection with the murder plot

CHINA (PEOPLE'S REPUBLIC)

Area: 3,691,000 sq. mi. **Population:** 958,000,000 (1979 est.)

Official Name: People's Republic of China **Capital:** Peking (Beijing) **Nationality:** Chinese **Languages:** Chinese, spoken with many regional phonetical differences but written with a uniform script, is the principal language. Mandarin, based on the Peking dialect, forms the basis of the new national language being promoted by the government; Shanghai, Cantonese, Fukienese, and Hakka dialects are spoken in the south. Among the national minorities, the Tibetans have their own highly distinctive language and script, while the Uigurs of Xinjiang (Sinkiang) speak a Turkic language **Religion:** Freedom of religion is guaranteed under the constitution, but during the Cultural Revolution places of worship were converted to secular use. The 3 long-established religions are Confucianism, Buddhism, and Taoism; the average Chinese practiced a mixture of all 3 faiths. About 5% of the people are Moslems, and there is a small minority of Christians **Flag:** A red field with a gold star and an arc of 4 smaller stars to the right in the upper left corner **Anthem:** Anthem beginning, "March on, brave people of our nation," set to the music of The March of the Volunteers **Currency:** Yuan (renminbi) (1.60 per U.S.$1)

Location: East Asia. China, the third largest country in the world after the U.S.S.R. and Canada, is bounded on the north by Mongolia and the U.S.S.R.; on the east by the U.S.S.R., North Korea, the Yellow Sea, and the East China Sea; on the south by the South China Sea, Vietnam, Laos, Burma, India, Bhutan, and Nepal; and on the west by Afghanistan, Pakistan, and the U.S.S.R. **Features:** Two-thirds of the country is mountainous or semidesert. The eastern part consists of fertile plains and deltas **Chief Rivers:** Chang Jiang (Yangtze), Huang (Yellow), Amur, Xi (Si)

Head of State: Executive responsibility is vested in a State Council, headed by the premier. Control is exercised by the Standing Committee of the Central Committee's Politburo, within the National People's Congress **Head of Government:** Premier Hua Guofeng, born c. 1920, appointed by the party's Central Committee in 1976 and reappointed in 1978, Chairman of the Politburo of the Communist Party **Effective Date of Present State Constitution:** March 15, 1978 **Legislative Body:** National People's Congress (unicameral), consisting of 3,497 members elected for 5-year terms. The provinces elect 1 deputy for every 800,000 inhabitants; municipalities directly under central authority elect 1 deputy for every 100,000 inhabitants. Ethnic minorities are represented by 381 deputies, the armed forces by 505 deputies, and overseas Chinese by 35 deputies **Local Government:** 21 provinces, 5 autonomous regions, and 3 municipalities directly under central authority. Revolutionary committees and people's congresses are the principal local organs of power.

Ethnic Composition: 94% Han Chinese; 6% Uigur, Hui, Yi, Tibetan, Miao, Manchu, Mongol, Chuang, Korean, and numerous lesser minorities **Population Distribution:** 20% urban **Density:** 260 inhabitants per sq. mi.

Largest Cities: (1976 est.) Shanghai 10,000,000; (1970 est.) Peking (Beijing) 7,570,000, Tianjin 4,280,000, Shenyang 2,800,000, Wuhan 2,560,000, Canton 2,500,000, Chongqing 2,400,000, Nanjing 1,750,000, Harbin 1,670,000, Luda 1,650,000

Per Capita Income: $323 (1978 est.) **Gross National Product (GNP):** $324 billion (1978 est.) **Economic Statistics:** Agriculture is still the foundation of the economy. GNP components are not available but official figures disclosed in 1971 indicate that industrial capacity is still comparatively small. The State Statistical Bureau had estimated $356 billion for the gross value of industrial, transport and agricultural production in 1978. Grain output for 1978 was 305 million metric tons; chemical fertilizer, 14 million metric tons; cotton cloth, 11 billion meters; petroleum output, more than 104 million metric tons **Minerals and Mining:** Coal, petroleum, iron ore, tin, molybdenum, tungsten, mercury, manganese, antimony **Labor Force:** The working age population is about 476 million, with 75% in agriculture **Foreign Trade:** Exports are estimated at about $10.5 billion for 1978, with imports of about $22.2 billion. Exports are chiefly agricultural and food products, metals, and textiles. Imports are mainly wheat, chemical fertilizers, iron and steel, transport equipment, machinery, and raw materials such as rubber **Principal Trade Partners:** Japan, Hong Kong, West Germany, Romania, Singapore, Britain, United States, Malaysia, Canada, France, Australia **Vital Statistics:** Birthrate, 26.9 per 1,000 pop. (1975); death rate, 10.3 **Life Expectancy:** 62 years **Illiteracy:** 45%. Recent statistics on health, infant mortality and education: N.A.

Transportation: Surfaced roads total 300,000 mi. **Motor Vehicles:** 499,000 (1969) **Passenger Cars:** 60,000 (1969) **Railway Mileage:** 27,000 **Ports:** Shanghai, Tianjin, Luda, Canton **Major Airlines:** The Civil Aviation Administration of China operates domestic flights and international flights abroad; 8 foreign airlines fly to Peking or Shanghai **Communications:** Government owned **Radio Transmitters:** 122 **Receivers:** 15,000,000 (1972) **Television Transmitters:** 109 **Receivers:** 500,000 (1973) **Telephones:** N.A. **Newspapers:** N.A.

Weights and Measures: Metric System and local standards **Travel Requirements:** Passport, visa; contact Chinese Embassy, Washington, D.C.

Developments of the early 1970s made the world dramatically aware that domestic conditions in the world's most populous country had stabilized; that China had come out of the disorders of the Cultural Revolution and that a new posture had been taken to break out of the diplomatic isolation of the 1950s and 60s.

The resulting circumstances have brought about a pronounced change for the better in a country the economy of which had been dislocated by factional strife and nationalistic excesses during the Cultural Revolution in 1966-69.

The Peking regime initiated a fresh approach in foreign affairs in April 1971 by inviting an American table tennis team, with accompanying journalists, to tour China. This gesture was a surprise even in the context of the new moderation that had become increasingly evident during the year before.

Relations had been established with Canada, Italy, and a number of smaller countries; more Chinese delegations had been sent abroad; more foreign trade agreements had been signed; and Chinese diplomatic missions in foreign countries, which operated without ambassadors during the Cultural Revolution, had been restaffed. But almost no one foresaw the trend going as far as the April invitation and what followed. The United States, after all, was still regularly the target of hate attacks from Peking.

After April there came a small but steady flow of Americans and other Western nationals. These visitors made possible illuminating new appraisals of internal conditions, and Peking climaxed their visits in July by arranging to receive President Nixon.

Impressed by Washington's new policy of military pullback in Asia, the Chinese moved to ease relations with the United States. Simultaneously

Peking acted to strengthen the home front by slowing the pace of the Cultural Revolution and stabilizing conditions under a reshuffled, pragmatic leadership built with the assent of Communist party Chairman Mao Zedong, around Premier Zhou Enlai.

Thus a situation was created of far-ranging significance for today and the future. Peking's move has shaken loose accustomed world-power alignments and brought about a "big three" constellation susceptible to shifting and jockeying of unpredictable ramifications.

The new Peking policy also led to formal diplomatic relations with Japan in 1972 and culminated in the signing of a 10-year treaty of peace and friendship in 1978.

Trade with the United States began in 1972 following the lifting of the American trade embargo, and by 1978 had reached more than $1.4 billion. In 1978, initial steps were taken for the exchange of American technology and turnkey industrial facilities for Chinese exports and those products to be derived from future industrial developments, particularly oil. In May 1979, China concluded an agreement on establishing formal commercial relations with the United States. The agreement, which provides for the lowering of United States tariff restrictions on Chinese imports and the granting of a most-favored nation trade status to China, must still be ratified by both governments.

Americans who have seen the stable new China attest to the effective functioning of the new Maoist power structure evolved during the Cultural Revolution, the seeming general acceptance of conditions by the population, striking accomplishments in eliminating poverty and inequality, and willing energy and industriousness being put into efforts for economic progress. New high levels of agricultural and industrial output are making China a major economic power.

In February 1974, the late Lin Biao was condemned, along with the Chinese philosopher Confucius, as China launched a new Cultural Revolution campaign, aimed at "consolidating and carrying to a higher stage" the earlier revolution in 1966-69.

Following the death of Premier Zhou Enlai on January 8, 1976, the succession of crises intensified. A mounting debate between moderates and radicals culminated in April in the most serious riots since the Cultural Revolution of 1966-69. The Politburo, acting quickly to defuse the potentially explosive situation, dismissed the "moderate" Deng Xiaoping from all his posts, and elevated Hua Guo-feng to the premiership.

With the death of Mao Zedong and his chief lieutenants the main task facing Hua Guo-feng, Mao's successor, was to resolve the conflict between radical and moderate factions in the party. Late in 1976, he moved decisively against the radicals, known as the "Gang of Four," led by Mao's widow, Jiang Jing. After their arrest in October, the Peking regime seemed to embark on a moderate course. In July 1977, in an apparent effort to liberalize Maoist doctrine along pragmatic lines, Deng Xiaoping was brought back into the government as first deputy premier. Together with Chairman Hua and the honorary head of state, Ye Jianying, he is part of China's ruling triumvirate.

Slowly through the suceeding months, Deng's power grew with the implementation of the slogan "four modernizations"—rapid development of agriculture, industry, defense, and science and technology. Organizational changes were planned in the agricultural sector which included more state aid to poorer areas, state planning becoming more centralized, and the return of private plots to the farmers. In the industrial sphere, workers were granted a 60 percent wage increase as part of an effort to spur the economy and to achieve "com-

PINYIN: THE NEW CHINESE SPELLING SYSTEM

Since January 1, 1979, all proper names appearing in press dispatches from the People's Republic of China have been spelled according to the Pinyin system of transcribing Chinese speech sounds. The new system has been adopted by the United States government, the United Nations, wire services, newspapers and newsmagazines.

In the accompanying article on the People's Republic of China, names have been rendered according to the new Pinyin system. There are three exceptions: Peking, Canton and Tibet are spelled the old, conventional way. The following lists compare the old and new forms and provide a pronunciation guide. The lists were adapted from the *Beijing Review*.

PERSONAL NAMES Pinyin spelling in boldface; old form in parentheses

Deng Xiaoping (Teng Hsiao-ping)
Hua Guofeng (Hua Kuo-feng)

Mao Zedong (Mao Tse-tung)
Ye Jianying (Yeh Chien-ying)

Zhou Enlai (Chou En-lai)
Zhu De (Chu Teh)

PLACE NAMES Pinyin spellings in boldface; old form in parentheses

MUNICIPALITIES UNDER CENTRAL GOVERNMENT

Beijing (Peking)
Shanghai (Shanghai)
Tianjin (Tsientsin)

PROVINCES AND AUTONOMOUS REGIONS FOLLOWED BY MAJOR CITIES OF EACH

Anhui (Anhwei)
  Hefei (Hofei)
  Bengbu (Pengpu)
Fujian (Fukien)
  Fuzhou (Foochow)
  Xiamen (Amoy)
Gansu (Kansu)
  Lanzhou (Lanchow)
Guangdong (Kwangtung)
  Guangzhou (Kwangchow)
  Shantou (Swatow)
Guangxi Zhuang (Kwangsi Chuang)
  Nanning (Nanning)
  Guilin (Kweilin)
Guizhou (Kweichow)
  Guiyang (Kweiyang)
  Zunyi (Tsunyi)
Hebei (Hopei)
  Shijiazhuang (Shihchiachuang)
  Tangshan (Tangshan)
Heilongjiang (Heilungkiang)
  Harbin (Harbin)
  Daqing Oilfield
  (Taching Oilfield)
  Qiqihar (Chichihar)

Henan (Honan)
  Zhengzhou (Chengchow)
  Luoyang (Loyang)
  Kaifeng (Kaifeng)
Hubei (Hupeh)
  Wuhan (Wuhan)
Hunan (Hunan)
  Changsha (Changsha)
Jiangsu (Kiangsu)
  Nanjing (Nanking)
  Suzhou (Soochow)
  Wuxi (Wuhsi)
Jiangxi (Kiangsi)
  Nanchang (Nanchang)
  Jiujiang (Chiuchiang)
Jilin (Kirin)
  Changchun (Changchun)
Liaoning (Liaoning)
  Shenyang (Shenyang)
  Anshan (Anshan)
  Luda (Luta)
Nei Monggol (Inner Mongolia)
  Hohhot (Huhehot)
  Baotou (Paotou)
Ningxia Hui (Ningsia Hui)

Yinchuan (Yinchuan)
Qinghai (Chinghai)
  Xining (Sining)
Shaanxi (Shensi)
  Xian (Sian)
  Yanan (Yenan)
Shandong (Shantung)
  Jinan (Tsinan)
  Qingdao (Tsingtao)
  Yantai (Yentai)
Shanxi (Shansi)
  Taiyuan (Taiyuan)
  Dazhai (Tachai)
Sichuan (Szechuan)
  Chengdu (Chengtu)
  Chongqing (Chungking)
Xinjiang Uygur (Sinkiang Uighur)
  Urumqi (Urumchi)
Xizang (Tibet)
  Lhasa (Lhasa)
Yunnan (Yunnan)
  Kunming (Kunming)
  Dali (Tali)
Zhejiang (Chekiang)
  Hangzhou (Hangchow)

PRONUNCIATION GUIDE Pinyin letters in boldface; old letters (Wade Giles system) in parentheses

a (a) as in *far*
b (p) as in *be*
c (ts) as in *its*
ch (ch) as in *church,* strongly aspirated
d (t) as in *do*
e (e) as in *her*
f (f) as in *foot*
g (k) as in *go*
h (h) as in *her,* strongly aspirated
i (i) two pronunciations:
  1) as in *eat*
  2) as in *sir* in syllables
  beginning with c, ch, r, s, sh, z and zh
j (ch) as in *jeep*
k (k) as in *kind,* strongly aspirated
l (l) as in *land*

m (m) as in *me*
n (n) as in *no*
o (o) as "aw" in *law*
p (p) as in *par,* strongly aspirated
q (ch) as in *cheek*
r (j) pronounced as "r" but not rolled, or like "z" in *azure*
s (s, ss, sz) as in *sister*
sh (sh) as in *shore*
t (t) as in *top,* strongly aspirated
u (u) as in *too,* also as in the French "u" in *tu* or the German "ü" in *München*

v (v) is used only to produce foreign and national minority words, and local dialects
w (w), used as a semi-vowel in syllables beginning with "u" when not preceded by consonants, pronounced as in *want*
x (hs) as in *she*
y, used as a semi-vowel in syllables beginning with "i" or "u" when not preceded by consonants, pronounced as in *yet*
z (ts, tz) as in *zero*
zh (ch) as in *jump*

prehensive modernization" by the year 2000. Change was evident in the science technology and education areas, with the emergence of new journals, new institutes and academies, new exchanges with foreign scientists and the reduction of time spent by scientists in political activity. Also, universities began to abolish the revolutionary committees set up by Mao during the Cultural Revolution. Admission to the universities was increasingly determined by entrance exam rather than recommendation on the basis of political attitude and membership in the worker and peasant social status.

China's chief defense goal is to achieve parity with the United States and the Soviet Union. To do this, the Peking regime has called for the introduction of foreign technology and the purchase of foreign weapons as part of the modernization effort for China's military, considered by Westerners as 20 years behind the Russians.

Relations with the United States improved in 1978 with the announcement of the formal establishment of official diplomatic relations between the two countries, effective on March 1, 1979. At the same time, the announcement included the abrogation of the mutual security treaty between the United States and the offshore Republic of China and the termination of formal diplomatic relations with Taiwan.

On February 17, 1979, China invaded Vietnam with about 200,000—300,000 troops backed by planes and artillery. According to Deng Xiaoping, this was to "punish" Vietnam for its invasion of Cambodia and for claimed Vietnamese incursions along their common border. The four-week war resulted in no territorial gains but caused heavy casualties on both sides. It also strained the new American-Chinese relations and provoked the Soviet Union, supporter of Vietnam.

HISTORY: The home of the oldest continuing civilization on earth, China has a recorded history dating back more than 2,000 years before the birth of Christ. By the advent of the Christian era, the Chinese had lived under a succession of dynasties that succeeded in unifying the country and protecting it from the outside world by building the Great Wall. In the end, however, the wall was to prove useless against invaders

1644: Manchu (Ching) dynasty is established, completing the gradual conquest of China by the Manchu peoples of the north

1839-42: Britain provokes Opium War and defeats Chinese; China opens ports and grants extraterritorial rights to British traders, cedes Hong Kong to Britain

1894-95: China and Japan war for control over their co-protectorate of Korea; a defeated China is forced to cede Formosa (Taiwan), Liaotung peninsula, and Pescadores to Japan; Korea becomes independent but falls under Japanese domination

1898-1900: Resentment against foreign influence erupts in Boxer Rebellion; revolt is quelled after intervention by European, U.S., and Japanese forces. U.S. Open Door policy, calling for equal treatment for all nations in Chinese ports and respect for China's territorial integrity, wins lip service from European powers

1911-12: Manchu dynasty is overthrown in revolution led by Sun Yat-sen; a republic is established with Sun as president

1917-30: Civil war breaks out between supporters of Sun's Kuomintang Party in the south and the national government and its warlords in the north; Kuomintang army, led by Chiang Kai-shek, sweeps north and defeats warlords. A new civil war breaks out, however, after Chiang breaks alliance formed by Sun with Chinese Communists

1931-39: Japan, taking advantage of turmoil in China, invades Manchuria and sets up puppet government. In 1934, some 100,000 Communist troops led by Mao Zedong, Lin Biao, and Zhou Enlai, begin 6,000-mile march to the north to avoid encirclement by Kuomintang army. More than three-quarters of the troops are lost during the 12-month "Long-March." Kuomintang and Communists later agree to truce to repel Japanese, but agreement collapses and sporadic fighting resumes

1945-49: U.S. attempts to mediate civil war fail; Communists launch offensive and drive Chiang's forces from mainland to Taiwan; People's Republic of China is proclaimed Oct. 1, 1949

1950: China overruns Tibet; Chinese Communist forces intervene on side of North Korea in Korean War

1960-64: Growing rift between U.S.S.R. and "hard-line" Chinese

Communist leaders breaks into open. China explodes its first nuclear bomb

1966-67: Mao Zedong launches "Cultural Revolution" in attempt to reverse trend toward "revisionist" Communism. New policy is marked by widespread purge of leading officials and wave of terrorism by Mao's youthful followers, known as Red Guards. China explodes its first hydrogen bomb

1969: Chinese and Soviet troops exchange fire along borders

1971: Mainland China replaces Nationalist China in UN General Assembly and Security Council. Lin Biao, Mao's designated successor, dies following an abortive coup

1972: Nixon visits China, meets Zhou Enlai and Mao Zedong

1973: Mainland China's first envoy to U.S. warmly received

1974: Mao Zedong announces the launching of a new Cultural Revolution

1975: China adopts a revised constitution of 30 articles endorsing the doctrines that emerged from the "Great Proletarian Cultural Revolution" of the late 1960s. Kissinger and Ford visit China

1976: Zhou Enlai and Zhu De die. Hua Guofeng confirmed as premier following riots in cities. Nixon revisits China. Mao Zedong dies in September. Hua named chairman of Communist Party. Tangshan earthquake estimated to have killed 700,000

1977: Deng Xiaoping returns to Politburo

1978: Maoist doctrine continues undergoing pragmatic liberalization. Chairman Hua reappointed, travels to North Korea, Eastern Europe and Iran. Deng Xiaoping signs friendship treaty in Tokyo. Joint American-Chinese communique issued in December for the establishment of formal diplomatic relations

1979: Deng Xiaoping visits the United States and signs scientific and cultural exchange agreements. China invades Vietnam in February. China and the United States establish formal diplomatic relations on March 1. The 5th National People's Congress (the highest legislative power) convenes in Peking

NATIONALIST CHINA (TAIWAN)

Area: 13,971 sq. mi. **Population:** 17,149,000 (1979 est.)

Official Name: Republic of China **Capital:** Taipei **Nationality:** Chinese **Languages:** Mandarin Chinese is the official language; native Taiwanese speak a variant of the Amoy dialect, although the Hakka dialect is used in northwestern Taiwan; Japanese and English are also widely used by the inhabitants **Religion:** The predominant religion is a blend of Buddhism and Taoism; there are about 400,000 Christians, and some 40,000 Moslems **Flag:** A red field with a blue rectangle in the upper left corner containing a 12-pointed white sun **Anthem:** National Anthem of the Republic of China, beginning "Our aim shall be to found a free land" **Currency:** New Taiwan yuan (dollar) (34 per U.S.$1)

Location: The seat of the Republic of China is the island of Taiwan, 90 miles off the southeast coast of the Chinese mainland. In addition to the island proper, Taiwan comprises 14 islands in the Taiwan group and 63 in the Penghu group, known as the Pescadores. The islands of Quemoy and Matsu, just off Fukien province on the China mainland, are also under the control of the Republic of China. Taiwan, also known as Formosa, is bordered on the north by the East China Sea, on the east by the Pacific Ocean, on the south and southwest by the South China Sea, and on the west by the Taiwan (Formosa) Strait **Features:** About two-thirds of the island of Taiwan is composed of rugged foothills and mountain chains. The mountains, towering along the eastern coast, run from northeast to southwest. A flat coastal plain, running from north to south, occupies the western third and supports most of the population **Chief Rivers:** Cho-shui, Tan-shui, Hsia-tan-shui

Head of State: President Chiang Ching-kuo, born 1910, elected 1978 **Head of Government:** Premier Sun Yun-suan, appointed 1978 **Effective Date of Present Constitution:** 1947 **Legislative Body:** The National Assembly (unicameral); its members (elected 1947) are serving indefinitely. Of the original 3,045 there are now about 1,300. The 5 branches of government are the Legislative, Executive, Control, Examination, and Judicial yuans. The Legislative Yuan is the highest body and now has 410 members; both it and the National Assembly have some parliamentary function, and are dominated by the Nationalist Party (the Kuomintang) under its chairman, the premier **Local Government:** The Provincial Government is under a governor appointed by the national government. There is an elective Provincial Assembly with limited powers

Ethnic Composition: With the exception of about 250,000 aborigines of Indonesian origin, the Taiwanese are descendants of Chinese who migrated from the provinces of Fukien and Kwangtung of mainland China during the past 3 centuries; post-World War II refugees from the mainland constitute about 18% of the population **Population Distribution:** 77% urban (1975) **Density:** 1,227 inhabitants per sq. mi.

Largest Cities: (1977 est.) Taipei 2,165,519; (1979 est.) Kaohsiung 1,002,000, Taichung 549,000, Tainan 525,000, Keelung 343,000

Per Capita Income: $1,336 (1978) **Gross National Product (GNP):** $22.8 billion (1978 est.) **Economic Statistics:** 24% of GNP comes from industry (textiles, electronics, plastics, furniture, other goods), and 12% from agriculture (rice, sweet potatoes, bananas, sugarcane, pineapple, peanuts, and soybeans are the major crops) **Minerals and Mining:** Taiwan is deficient in minerals with the exception of coal. There are reserves of volcanic sulphur and deposits of natural gas and petroleum **Labor Force:** 6.7 million (1975), 37% employed in agriculture, 23% in industry, 40% in services **Foreign Trade:** Exports, chiefly textiles, chemicals, metals and machinery, plywood, sugar, bananas, and canned mushrooms, totaled $9.3 billion in 1977. Imports, chiefly machinery, chemicals, transportation equipment, soybeans, raw cotton, timber, crude oil, and wheat, totaled $8.5 billion **Principal Trade Partners:** United States, Japan, Hong Kong, West Germany, Australia, Britain, Singapore, Canada, Thailand, Saudi Arabia, South Korea, Kuwait

Vital Statistics: Birthrate, 26 per 1,000 of pop (1976); death rate, 5 **Life Expectancy:** 70 years **Health Statistics:** 580 inhabitants per hospital bed; 1,377 per physician **Infant Mortality:** 14 per 1,000 births **Illiteracy:** 11% **Education Statistics:** 3,269 primary and secondary schools, with combined enrollment of 3,932,000 (1975) **Enrollment in Higher Education:** 282,300 **GNP Expended on Education:** 4.8%

Transportation: Surfaced roads total 5,496 mi. (1974) **Motor Vehicles:** 2,600,000 (1976) **Passenger Cars:** 122,517 (1974) **Railway Mileage:** 2,672 (1974) **Ports:** Kaohsiung Keelung, Hualien, Taichung, Suao **Major Airlines:** China Airlines operates domestic and international services **Communications:** Both government and privately owned **Radio Stations:** 111 **Receivers:** 3,000,000 **Television Stations:** 3 **Receivers:** 747,444 **Telephones:** 598,504 **Newspapers:** 31 dailies, 80 copies per 1,000 inhabitants

Weights and Measures: Metric system and local units are used **Travel Requirements:** Passport, visa

The government of the Republic of China, defeated on mainland China by the Communists in 1949, established itself on Taiwan, with the goal of regaining power over all of China. That goal, with time, has become more and more remote. In the meantime, with the help of massive American aid, the government has built Taiwan into a prosperous, industrializing island state.

In 1971 a steady stream of countries switched diplomatic recognition from Taiwan to Communist China. With the shift in U.S. policy on China and American support for the seating of Peking in the United Nations, the Nationalist diplomatic position underwent further erosion. Nationalist China was eventually expelled from the UN and replaced by the Communist-led People's Republic of China.

Because of its insistence that it was not only the government of Taiwan, 90 miles off the China mainland, but also the only legal government of all China, the Nationalist regime would not sanction elections that would change the central leadership. But it has held local elections.

The government has been dominated by the Kuomintang, or Nationalist Party, and the party in turn was dominated by President Chiang Kai-shek until his death in April 1975. Criticism of government policies and officials is permitted in the press, though the president and his relatives are an exception. Editors practice a form of self-censorship.

Nationalist officials, who like to refer to Taiwan as "Free China," readily concede that the province is still under martial law and freedom is in some respects limited. But they point out that freedom and democracy have to be understood in an Asian context, and declare that, whatever Taiwan's shortcomings, it is infinitely more free and democratic than the People's Republic.

Taiwan, which was devastated when China regained control from Japan after World War II, is flourishing, if overpopulated. The 17.1 million people, the vast majority of whom are native-born Taiwanese, enjoy one of the highest standards of living in Asia. But critics, especially those who advocate an independent Taiwan, say that the current huge military expenditures impede more rapid economic growth. The island developed its economy partly because it has enjoyed U.S. military protection and received U.S. military aid.

In a November 1977 election for local offices, independent candidates scored their largest, if still limited, victory since 1949. Moreover, the unusual fairness of the election was seen as reflecting a decision by the government to allow native Taiwanese a greater share in the political process than did Chiang Kai-shek.

When President Yen Chia-kan (C.K. Yen) retired in March 1978 the National Assembly named Premier Chiang Ching-kuo to succeed him, in an election in which he was the only candidate. The former Economics Minister, Sun Yun-suan, was named premier in May.

In December 1978, the United States announced the termination of formal diplomatic relations with Taiwan, and the eventual abrogation of the mutual security treaty, but stated that it would maintain cultural, commercial and unofficial relations with the people of Taiwan. Although the Taiwan leaders were momentarily disturbed by this announcement, the commerical relations remained good, showing a U.S.-Taiwan 1978 trade amounting to $7.3 billion.

HISTORY: Chinese emigration to Taiwan began in the 7th century. In the 16th century the Portuguese arrived, naming the island Formosa, meaning "beautiful." The Dutch assumed control in 1641 but were driven out in 1662 by Ming dynasty forces fleeing the Manchu takeover in mainland China. In 1683 Taiwan, too, fell to the Manchus. At the end of the Sino-Japanese War of 1894-95 it was ceded to Japan, which held it until the conclusion of World War II, when it was restored to China

1949: The Nationalist government of Chiang Kai-shek and remnants of his army flee to Taiwan, as the Communist forces of Mao Tse-tung gain control of the Chinese mainland

1950: President Truman orders U.S. Seventh Fleet to patrol the Taiwan Strait, thwarting a planned invasion of Taiwan by Communist China

1955: Following shelling of Nationalist-held offshore islands, the United States pledges to defend Taiwan and the Pescadores

1965: Because of Taiwan's impressive economic growth, U.S. aid is terminated except for surplus-food shipments

1966: Chiang Kai-shek is reelected president for fourth term

1969: Chiang Ching-kuo, elder son of Chiang Kai-shek, is named deputy premier

1970: Chiang Ching-kuo escapes assassination attempt by Taiwanese while visiting New York City

1971: Nationalist China replaced in UN by Mainland China

1972: Chiang Kai-shek is re-elected president for fifth term; Chiang Ching-kuo is named premier

1973: U.S. announces gradual withdrawal of its forces on Taiwan as relations with Communist China improve

1974: U.S. pledges to continue to "safeguard the security of Taiwan"

1975: Generalissimo Chiang Kai-shek, 87, dies of a heart attack in Taipei, April 5, and Yen Chia-kan (C. K. Yen) succeeds him

1976: U.S. troop withdrawal increased

1978: Yen Chia-kan retires; Chiang Ching-kuo succeeds him in presidency. Taiwan terminates treaty with Japan following the signing of a treaty of friendship between Japan and the People's Republic of China

1979: American and Taiwan embassies are closed on March 1, quasi-official offices are established in each country

COLOMBIA

Area: 439,735 sq. mi. **Population:** 25,600,000 (1978 est.)

Official Name: Republic of Colombia **Capital:** Bogotá **Nationality:** Colombian **Languages:** Spanish is the official language and is spoken by all but a few Indian tribes **Religion:** Roman Catholicism is the state religion and that of 95% of the population **Flag:** The top half of the flag is yellow; the bottom half consists of a blue stripe and red stripe of equal widths **Anthem:** National Anthem, beginning "O unwithering glory, immortal joy" **Currency:** Colombian peso (42.4 per U.S. $1)

Location: Northwest South America. Colombia is bordered on the north by the Caribbean Sea, on the east by Venezuela and Brazil, on the south by Peru and Ecuador, and on the west by the Pacific Ocean and Panama **Features:** Colombia is divided by the Andes Mountains into flat coastal areas, a highland or plateau area, and an eastern plains area **Chief Rivers:** Magdalena, Cauca, Amazon

Head of State and of Government: President Julio César Turbay Ayala, born 1916, elected June 1978 **Effective Date of Present Constitution:** August 1886 **Legislative Body:** Congress (bicameral), consisting of a Senate and a Chamber of Representatives. The Senate has 112 members; the Chamber has 199 members **Local Government:** 22 departments, the Special District of Bogotá, 4 intendencies, and 4 commissaries, under appointed governors and administrators

Ethnic Composition: 58% Mixed European, Indian and African descent, 20% European stock, 14% European and African descent, 4% African stock, and 1% Indian **Population Distribution:** 64% urban **Density:** 58 inhabitants per sq. mi.

Largest Cities: (1973 census) Bogotá 2,855,065, Medellín 1,070,924, Cali 898,253, Barranquilla 661,009, Cartagena 292,512, Bucaramanga 291,661, Manizales 199,904

Per Capita Income: $715 (1978) **Gross National Product (GNP):** $18.4 billion (1978 est.) **Economic Statistics:** 23% of GNP comes from agriculture (coffee, rice, cotton, potatoes, bananas, sugar); 17% from trade; 20% from industry (food, beverages, tobacco, textiles, chemicals, metal products and machinery) **Minerals and Mining:** Petroleum, gold, salt, limestone, sand and gravel, platinum and emeralds are exploited **Labor Force:** Wage-earners totaled 7,841,742 (1975), with 41% in agriculture, 23% in industry, and 14% in services **Foreign Trade:** Exports, chiefly coffee, crude petroleum, agricultural products, textiles, cattle, and emeralds, totaled $2.3 billion in 1977. Imports, chiefly machinery and electronic equipment, chemicals, transport vehicles, metals and metal products, totaled $2.7 billion **Principal Trade Partners:** United States, West Germany, Japan, Italy, Britain, Sweden, the Andean Group

Vital Statistics: Birthrate, 30 per 1,000 of pop. (1976); death rate, 8.8 **Life Expectancy:** 61 years **Health Statistics:** 530 inhabitants per hospital bed; 2,184 per physician (1973) **Infant Mortality:** 62.8 per 1,000 births **Illiteracy:** 19% **Education Statistics:** 32,230 primary and secondary schools, with combined enrollment of 5,128,604 (1974) **Enrollment in Higher Education:** 148,613 **GNP Expended on Education:** 3.3% (1973)

Transportation: Paved roads total 3,728 mi. (1971) **Motor Vehicles:** 494,700 (1976) **Passenger Cars:** 401,300 **Railway Mileage:** 2,121 **Ports:** Buenaventura, Sta. Marta, Barranquilla, Cartagena, Tumaco **Major Airlines:** Avianca and Aerocondor operate domestic and international services **Communications:** Government and privately owned **Radio Transmitters:** 340 **Receivers:** 2,850,000 (1976) **Television Transmitters:** 3 **Receivers:** 1,700,000 (1976) **Telephones:** 1,769,000 (1976) **Newspapers:** 36 dailies, 69 copies per 1,000 inhabitants (1974)

Weights and Measures: Metric system **Travel Requirements:** Passport, tourist card valid for visits up to 90 days

Colombia, in effect, is a federation of city-states that are reflections of the isolation imposed by the Andes. Traditionally, the economy has been based on coffee on the rocks: Small farmers strive to raise quality coffee beans on the steep and rocky slopes of the Andes. Their crop accounts for the largest part of the nation's legal exports. In recent years, however, the illicit growing and exporting of marijuana and cocaine has risen fast as a major economic activity, estimated at from $1 billion to $2 billion a year even in the face of a government crackdown.

Colombia's social problems are staggering; its population is growing by 2.4 percent a year, despite efforts to expand family-planning programs, and its cities are swelling because of migration from rural areas. (Bogotá's population has doubled in the past 10 years.)

With illiteracy widespread, Colombia has a high unemployment rate and the income distribution of her population is highly skewed in favor of the upper fifth of the population. Access to health services and the quality of health care are even more unequally distributed.

Colombia's people are as varied as its geography. The top hundred or so families are basically European, and American-educated. The bulk of the people are of part-Indian stock, and some are descendants of African slaves. About 18 percent of the population is black or mulatto. There are small groups of nomads who wander the deserts of the northern fringe of the land as well as primitive Amazon Indians in the forests of the south. Indians make up 1 percent of the population.

Politically, Colombia is the largest working democracy in Latin America. Its 25 million people are still awed by *La Violencia*, the bloody period of anarchy from 1948 to 1958, which cost about 200,000 lives. Its cause is still debated. *La Violencia* gave the Spanish language a new word, *bogotazo*, referring to the sudden eruption of violence in the capital on April 9, 1948, an uprising not clearly linked to a specific cause.

In any event, the civil war led first to the military dictatorship (1953-57) of General Gustavo Rojas Pinilla, then to a return to democracy on the basis of cooperation between the two traditional parties, the Liberals and the Conservatives, who began to rotate the presidency. Colombia permits its notably ineffectual Communist Party to operate openly and legally.

With the advent to power of President Misael Pastrana Borrero in August 1970, following an election bitterly contested by General Rojas, Colombia began to achieve substantial progress for the people as a whole. In 1973, however, there were renewed indications that the violence that had marked so much of her history was not yet dead.

In January, after a number of bloody guerrilla actions, the government adopted several emergency security measures, including the establishment of special groups within the armed forces to pursue guerrilla bands operating in rural areas. By spring of 1974, however, Colombia's three main guerrilla bands were disorganized and decaying.

In February 1973, President Borrero's government passed an agrarian reform bill, after a year of negotiations between the ruling Liberal and Conservative parties. The bill was designed to bail the Agrarian Reform Institute out of bankruptcy and spur expropriation of poorly farmed estates. It reduced by 70 percent the amount of land that could be retained by an individual and gave him three years to make the land productive.

Inflation, rather than land reform, however, was the major issue of the 1974 presidential election campaign. Alfonso López Michelsen, the Liberal Party candidate, won a landslide victory with a margin of one million votes by his promise to solve this and other socioeconomic problems.

The April 1974 elections represented the first open-polls elections, after 16 years of the National Front Liberal-Conservative alternate rule. López won a constitutional mandate for a four-year term in coalition with the Conservatives. A member of the Liberal Party, López announced that his Administration would be left-of-center.

The April 1976 election results were moderately encouraging for the ruling Liberal Party, although 76 percent of eligible voters did not go to the polls. Throughout 1976 and 1977 there were widespread protests and strikes by workers and students, and attacks by left-wing guerrillas continued, as did periodic rumors of an impending military coup attempt.

The Liberals were the big winners in the 1978 congressional elections in February, and their candidate, Julio César Turbay Ayala, won the presidency in a close race in June. He was sworn into office on Aug. 7 and became quickly involved in the twin problems of increased terrorism and rising drug traffic.

On the first day of 1979, the M-19 guerrilla group attacked the main military arsenal in Bogotá and took 4,300 guns. Within the next two months, soldiers searched Bogotá and other cities and arrested 200 alleged left-wing guerrillas by government count—or 1,000 by another estimate. Nicolas Escobar Soto, the head of Texaco's Colombia subsidiary, held by guerrillas for seven months, was killed by them on Jan. 4 when soldiers surrounded a hideout.

Inflation receded somewhat, dropping to a 20 percent rate in 1978. Colombia's coffee crop was high, but worldwide prices dropped sharply and cut coffee-export revenue by 24 percent.

The government, meanwhile, was trying to stop another kind of export—illicit drugs. Soldiers swarmed over the Guajira Peninsula, a major point for shipping marijuana to the United States, in late 1978 and in 1979, and the government reported the seizure and burning of more than 100,000 tons of marijuana. Scores of small planes, most of them from the United States, were seized by troops or crashed.

HISTORY: Colombia was inhabited perhaps as early as 5000 B.C. by Indian tribes of whom little is known. Prominent among pre-Colombian cultures was that of the highland Chibchas, a sedentary agricultural people located in the eastern chain of the Andes, in the center of the country. European colonization began about five years after Spanish explorers came to Colombia in 1499. With the founding of Bogotá in 1538, Colombia became the nucleus of New Granada, a vast territory that included parts of Panama, Venezuela, and Ecuador. The struggle for Colombian independence was, as elsewhere in Latin America, precipitated by Napoleon's invasion of Spain in the early 19th century

1810: Revolutionary leaders stage uprising in Bogotá

1819: By defeating Spanish royalist forces, Simón Bolívar secures independence of the new republic of Greater Colombia, which includes the former territory of New Granada

1830: Greater Colombia breaks up and New Granada (now Colombia and Panama) becomes a separate state

1863: New Granada becomes a federal republic, the United States of Colombia

1899: Civil war breaks out between liberal and conservative elements and results in more than 100,000 deaths and virtual economic ruin for the country

1903: Panama proclaims its independence from Colombia and achieves it with U.S. support

1948-53: Assassination of left-wing liberal leader Jorge Gaitán in 1948 sets off a major revolt, ultimately costing 200,000 lives and leading to the declaration of a state of siege. President Laureano Gómez, an archconservative, takes power in 1950 but is ousted in a coup d'état led by the chief of the armed forces, General Gustavo Rojas Pinilla

1957: Rojas, in turn, is ousted by a military junta, which promises and provides presidential and congressional elections within the year. An amendment to the constitution is approved by plebiscite, providing for 12 years of parity (equal representation) between Liberal and Conservative parties in the 3 branches of government

1968: President Lleras forces resignation of his cabinet after accusing opposition Conservatives of sabotaging social and economic reforms

1969: Colombia joins Andean common market

1970: Departmental and municipal elections result in overwhelming defeat for Rojas' ANAPO and victory for Conservative party

1974: Alfonso López Michelsen elected in landslide Liberal victory in the first open-polls elections in 16 years

1975: President López declares a state of siege because of unrest

1976: Ruling Liberal and Conservative parties receive 90 percent of vote in local elections following period of student and labor unrest

1977: Protests against high prices and continued martial law rule erupt in violence; 13 die, 4,000 arrested

1978: Following Liberal Party election victory, Turbay Ayala wins presidency

COMOROS

Area: 719 sq. mi. **Population:** 290,000 (1978 est.)

Official Name: Comoros Federal Islamic Republic **Capital:** Moroni **Nationality:** Comorian **Languages:** Arabic, French, Swahili **Religion:** Moslem, some Christians **Flag:** A green field with a white crescent in the center, set at an angle and encompassing four five-pointed stars in a line **Anthem:** N.A. **Currency:** CFA Franc (219 per U.S. $1)

Location: The Comoros lie in the Mozambique Channel of the Indian Ocean 300 miles northwest of Madagascar. There are three main islands: Anjouan, Mohéli and Grand Comoro, and a number of minor ones **Features:** The islands are of volcanic origin and Karthala (elevation 8,399 ft.) on Grand Comoro is still active. The climate is tropical with a hot rainy season from November to April, becoming more temperate the rest of the year **Chief Rivers:** There are no large rivers

Head of State: President Ahmed Abdallah, born 1919, head of state since coup of May 1978 **Head of Government:** Prime Minister Salim Ben Ali, appointed 1978 **Effective Date of Constitution:** 1978

Legislative Body: Federal Assembly (unicameral) of 39 members **Local Government:** The island group is divided into 3 prefectures, corresponding to the 3 major islands

Ethnic Composition: The people are largely descendants of Moslem settlers with strains from Africa and Madagascar; there is a small European colony **Population Distribution:** N.A. **Density:** 403 inhabitants per sq. mi.

Largest Cities: (1975 est.) Moroni 12,000

Per Capita Income: $153 (1976 est.) **Gross Domestic Product (GDP):** $51 million (1976) **Economic Statistics:** A wide variety of crops flourish in the rich volcanic soil: rice, cassava, ambrevade (a pea-family plant), sweet potatoes, citrus fruits, and some European vegetables. The chief commercial crops are vanilla, perfume plants, and copra. Fishing and stock raising are important. In 1976, 40% of GDP came from agriculture, 34% from industry **Minerals and Mining:** There are practically no mineral resources **Labor Force:** 184,000 (1976) with 87% in agriculture **Foreign Trade:** Exports chiefly vanilla, ilang-ilang essence for perfumes, copra and sisal totaled $9 million in 1976. Imports, primarily rice, vegetables, mineral products, textiles, metals and automobiles, totaled $13 million **Principal Trade Partners:** France, United States, West Germany, Madagascar, Kenya

Vital Statistics: Birthrate, 46.6 per 1,000 of pop. (1975); death rate, 21.7 **Life Expectancy:** 49 years **Health Statistics:** 458 inhabitants per hospital bed; 13,810 per physician (1973) **Infant Mortality:** 51.7 per 1,000 births **Illiteracy:** 85% **Education Statistics:** 130 primary and secondary schools, with a total enrollment of 26,391 (1973) **Enrollment in Higher Education:** N.A. **GNP Expended on Education:** 7.2% (1971)

Transportation: Roads total 435 mi. **Motor Vehicles:** N.A. **Passenger Cars:** N.A. **Railway Mileage:** None **Ports:** Mutsamudu, Moroni, Fomboni, Bambao **Major Airlines:** Air France **Communications:** Government controlled **Radio Transmitters:** 3 (1973) **Receivers:** 36,000 (1976) **Television:** None **Telephones:** 2,000 (1976) **Newspapers:** None; imported from Madagascar

Weights and Measures: Metric system **Travel Requirements:** N.A.

After 133 years as, successively, a French colony attached to Madagascar and a French Overseas Territory, three of the four Comoro Islands unilaterally declared independence on July 6, 1975. Still French territory but claimed by the Republic of the Comoros is the fourth island, Mayotte. Ahmed Abdallah was elected president of the new nation. These actions followed a vote in favor of independence in a referendum of December 1974.

In 1975, Ahmed Abdallah was overthrown in a bloodless coup led by Ali Soilih who was selected as president on January 2, 1976. The new nation has been vexed with the problem of the status of the largely Christian island of Mayotte. In 1976, the inhabitants of Mayotte voted to remain within the French Republic and not to join with the other largely Moslem Comoro Islands in independence. An April 12 referendum showed a preference for departmental status within France.

President Ali Soilih was overthrown on May 13, 1978, in a coup led by Said Atthoumani, Interior Minister in the former Ahmed Abdallah government of 1975. The new government, headed by Ahmed Abdallah and Mohammed Ahmed, announced the release of political detainees and the restoration of rights and religious freedom. Mohammed Ahmed resigned in October 1978, leaving Ahmed Abdallah in sole command.

HISTORY: The original settlers of the Comoros came from mainland Africa. The first detailed knowledge of the area is undoubtedly due to Arab sailors, although the Phoenicians probably visited the islands much earlier. Two Arab invasions swept over the Comoros, the last coming from the Persian Gulf in the 15th century. In the 16th century the islands were visited by Portuguese, Dutch, French and Malagasy navigators

1843: French seize Mayotte

1886: Anjouan, Grand Comoro and Mohéli come under French protection

1912: The islands join administratively with Madagascar

1946: The Comoros become partially autonomous and receive the status of an Overseas Territory

1961: The islands receive complete internal autonomy

1975: Independence is declared. Admitted to UN. Government of Ahmed Abdallah overthrown by Ali Soilih

1976: Mayotte votes to remain French

1978: Ali Soilih overthrown in coup. Political-Military Directory under Ahmed Abdallah emerges; voters approve new constitution in Oct. 1 referendum

CONGO

Area: 132,046 sq. mi. **Population:** 1,420,000 (1978 est.)

Official Name: People's Republic of the Congo **Capital:** Brazzaville **Nationality:** Congolese **Languages:** French is the official language; Lingala and Kikongo are the principal spoken languages **Religion:** 48% animist, 47% Christian (mainly Roman Catholic), and 5% Moslem **Flag:** A red field; in the upper left corner is a yellow 5-pointed star above crossed yellow hammer and hoe, surrounded by green palm branches **Anthem:** The Internationale **Currency:** CFA Franc (219 per U.S. $1)

Location: West-central Africa. The Congo is bordered on the north by Cameroon and the Central African Empire, on the east and south by Zaire, on the southwest by the Angolan exclave of Cabinda and the Atlantic Ocean, and on the west by Gabon and Cameroon **Features:** The country consists of a coastal plain, savanna, highlands, and a plateau. Roughly half the land area is covered by dense equatorial forest, and a quarter of the country covered by marshes **Chief Rivers:** Congo, Ubangi, Sangha, Kouilou-Niari

Head of State and Government: President and Premier: Col. Denis Sassou-Ngouesso, born 1941, appointed by the Congolese Workers' Party in 1979 **Effective Date of Present Constitution:** 1973, suspended 1977 **Legislative Body:** Power is in the hands of the sole political party, the Congolese Workers' Party (PCT) **Local Government:** 9 regions and a capital district, under appointed commissioners

Ethnic Composition: The 15 groups and 75 tribes are predominantly Bantu; major ones include the Bakongo, Bateke, M'Boshi, and Sangha. Pygmies number about 5,000; of some 9,000 Europeans most are French **Population Distribution:** 40% urban (1976) **Density:** 11 inhabitants per sq. mi.

Largest Cities: (1974 census) Brazzaville 298,967, Pointe-Noire 141,700

Per Capita Income: $500 (1978 est.) **Gross National Product (GNP):** $710 million (1978 est.) **Economic Statistics:** In 1973 about 17% of GNP was from agriculture (peanuts, palm kernels, coffee, cocoa, bananas, sugarcane, rice, corn, manioc, and sweet potatoes), forestry, and fishing; 14% from industry (forest products, sugar refining, palm and peanut oil, brewing, flour milling) and mining; and 38% from trade and services **Minerals and Mining:** Crude petroleum and high-grade potash are the major exploited mineral resources. There are high-grade iron-ore reserves, and some zinc, gold, lead, and natural gas are produced **Labor Force:** 600,000 (1970), with 80% engaged in subsistence agriculture, and 20% in industry and mining **Foreign Trade:** Exports, chiefly petroleum, potash, wood, sugar, tobacco, and industrial diamonds, totaled $270 million in 1975. Imports, mainly machinery, electrical equipment, vehicles, textiles, clothing, mineral products, foods, and chemicals, totaled $488 million **Principal Trade Partners:** France, West Germany, United States, Italy

Vital Statistics: Birthrate, 45.1 per 1,000 of pop. (1975); death rate, 20.8 **Life Expectancy:** 43.5 years **Health Statistics:** 195 inhabitants per hospital bed; 6,338 per physician (1975) **Infant Mortality:** 180 per 1,000 births **Illiteracy:** 80% **Education Statistics:** 1,033 primary and secondary schools, with combined enrollment of 395,162 (1974) **Enrollment in Higher Education:** 3,249 **GNP Expended on Education:** 5.4% (1974)

Transportation: Paved roads total 186 miles **Motor Vehicles:** 29,500 (1974) **Passenger Cars:** 19,000 **Railway Mileage:** 500 **Ports:** Pointe-Noire **Major Airlines:** Air Congo and Lina Congo operate internal services; Air Afrique, Aeroflot, Air France, KLM, Sabena, and UTA operate international services **Communications:** Government owned **Radio Transmitters:** 10 (1973) **Receivers:** 83,000 (1976) **Television Transmitters:** 1 **Receivers:** 3,300 (1976) **Telephones:** 11,000 (1976) **Newspapers:** 3 dailies, 1 copy per 1,000 inhabitants (1974)

Weights and Measures: Metric system **Travel Requirements:** Apply to nearest consulate outside U.S. for requirements

Since gaining independence from France in 1960, Congo has swung sharply from right to left politically while moving forward very slowly economically.

Despite much leftist rhetoric, Congo's Marxist-Leninist "orientation" remains confusing—perhaps more expedient than orthodox. China and the Soviet Union appear to wield considerable influence over the government and speculation about which of them is in the ascendancy is a popular pastime in Brazzaville.

Among other things, the Chinese have built a textile mill and the Russians a hotel. Now the Russians are to build a power-irrigation dam in the less-developed northern region.

But it is capitalistic France that continues to be Congo's chief trading partner and source of economic and financial aid. Private French companies control most of the country's commerce and small industry.

It is also the French who recently opened the potash-mines, the country's largest enterprise. Potash production, currently about 430,000 metric tons a year, has become a major new export. Other exports are diamonds smuggled from Zaire, timber, and tropical produce. Meanwhile, offshore oil exploration has boosted sagging production of crude oil.

President Marien Ngouabi, who came to power in 1968, was assassinated in March 1977. The nine-member Council of State which he created named Brig. General Joachim Opango to succeed him. Opango resigned in favor of Col. Denis Sassou-Ngouesso in February 1979.

HISTORY: When the Portuguese explorer Diego Cão arrived off the mouth of the Congo River in 1482, he found two long-established Bantu empires. To the north lay the Kingdom of Loango and its vassal states, and to the south, the great Mani-Congo stretching into Angola. Four centuries later, Count Pierre Savorgnan de Brazza (for whom Brazzaville is named) established French control over the area north of the river. In 1885, the Congress of Berlin recognized French claims to the region, later renamed Middle Congo

1910: Middle Congo becomes part of French Equatorial Africa, which also includes Gabon, Ubangi-Shari (now the Central African Empire), and Chad

1958-60: President de Gaulle announces formation of French Community as step toward independence for French possessions; new Republic of the Congo becomes autonomous member of the community. In 1960 full independence is proclaimed

1964: Relations are established with Soviet Union and Communist China; Chinese mission takes over direction of economy

1965: Following arrests of American diplomats, United States closes Brazzaville embassy

1966: Cuban Communists arrive to serve as Massemba-Débat's private militia

1968: Captain Marien Ngouabi, popular northern army officer, leads coup that ousts Massemba-Débat and establishes new revolutionary regime

1969-70: Government resigns; a council of state takes over and sets up the first people's republic in Africa

1974: Ngouabi is reelected president

1977: Ngouabi assassinated March 18. Emile Cardinal Biayenda, archbishop of Brazzaville, is murdered a few days later. U.S. reopens Brazzaville embassy after 12-year break in relations

1978: President Joachim Opango reports defeating Western-backed coup attempt

1979: Opango resigns in favor of Col. Denis Sassou-Ngouesso

COSTA RICA

Area: 19,652 sq. mi. **Population:** 2,200,000 (1978 est.)

Official Name: Republic of Costa Rica **Capital:** San José **Nationality:** Costa Rican **Languages:** Spanish is the official and predominant language; a Jamaican dialect of English is spoken by many of the country's Negroes, descendants of Jamaican workers who emigrated to Costa Rica in the 19th century **Religion:** Overwhelmingly Roman Catholic **Flag:** A blue stripe at top and bottom, separated by two white stripes from a broad center red stripe bearing the national coat of arms on the lefthand side **Anthem:** National Anthem, beginning "Noble country, thy beautiful banner" **Currency:** Colón (8.57 per U.S. $1)

Location: Central America. Costa Rica is bordered on the north by Nicaragua, on the east by the Caribbean Sea, on the southeast by Panama, and on the west by the Pacific Ocean **Features:** About two-thirds of the country is covered by forests. There is a fairly wide coastal plain on the eastern side and a narrower plain on the Pacific coast. A volcanic mountain system composed of 3 ranges crosses the country lengthwise **Chief Rivers:** Río Grande, San Carlos

Head of State and of Government: President: Rodrigo Carazo Odio, born 1926, elected 1978 **Effective Date of Present Constitution:** November 1949 **Legislative Body:** Legislative Assembly (unicameral), consisting of 57 members elected by popular vote for 4 years **Local Government:** 7 provinces, each with a governor appointed by the president

Ethnic Composition: The population is predominantly of European (mainly Spanish) descent, with a large mestizo (mixed European and Indian) minority. Negroes of Jamaican origin number about 1% of the population **Population Distribution:** 43% urban **Density:** 112 inhabitants per sq. mi.

Largest Cities: (1973 census) San José 215,441, Alajuela 33,122, Limón 29,621, Puntarenas 26,331, Heredia 22,700, Cartago 21,753

Per Capita Income: $1,276 (1978) **Gross National Product (GNP):** $2.7 billion (1978) **Economic Statistics:** In 1973 about 23% of GNP came from agriculture (coffee, bananas, cocoa, sugarcane, rice, beans, and livestock), forestry, and fishing; 20% from industry (food and beverages, textiles, fertilizers, shoes, furniture); and 37% from trade and services **Minerals and Mining:** Gold, bauxite, copper, sulphur, manganese, and iron ore are mined **Labor Force:** 646,456 (1975); 35% in agriculture, 21% in manufacturing, 37% in services **Foreign Trade:** Exports, chiefly coffee, bananas, meat, sugar, cocoa, and fertilizers, totaled $742 million in 1977. Imports, mainly manufactures, machinery and transport equipment, chemicals, foodstuffs, and fuel and mineral oils, totaled $885 million **Principal Trade Partners:** United States, West Germany, Nicaragua, El Salvador, Guatemala, Japan

Vital Statistics: Birthrate, 29.7 per 1,000 of pop. (1976); death rate, 4.6 **Life Expectancy:** 70 years **Health Statistics:** 261 inhabitants per hospital bed; 1,524 per physician (1975) **Infant Mortality:** 37.6 per 1,000 births **Illiteracy:** 10% **Education Statistics:** 2,790 primary and secondary schools, with combined enrollment of 484,667 (1976) **Enrollment in Higher Education:** 32,928 (1975) **GNP Expended on Education:** 5.2% (1974)

Transportation: Paved roads total 948 mi. **Motor Vehicles:** 102,500 (1975) **Passenger Cars:** 59,800 **Railway Mileage:** 661 **Ports:** Limón, Puntarenas, Golfito **Major Airlines:** LACSA (Costa Rican Airlines) operates domestic and international flights **Communications:** Government controlled **Radio Transmitters:** 51 **Receivers:** 150,000 (1976) **Television Transmitters:** 8 **Receivers:** 155,000 (1976) **Telephones:** 127,000 (1976) **Newspapers:** 6 dailies, 88 copies per 1,000 inhabitants (1975)

Weights and Measures: Metric system and old Spanish weights and measures are used **Travel Requirements:** Passport and visa not required if tourist card obtained prior to departure (valid 30 days)

Born in the bloodshed of civil war in 1948, the stable and progressive political institutions of Costa Rica have since provided relative peace and democracy despite severe pressures.

The country's republican form of government, in which presidential power is held in check by a strong Assembly, has been able to renew itself every four years through peaceful and honest elections held under the exclusive authority of a jealously independent electoral board.

The sophistication of Costa Rica's politics goes hand in hand with economic and social levels much higher than the rest of Central America has been able to achieve. For example, per capita income is considerably higher than in most of the rest of Central America. Although there are extremes of wealth and poverty here as elsewhere, distribution is generally more equitable.

Even with its orderly process of government, Costa Rica has experienced political problems. In 1966 the country retained the reformist National Liberation party in control of the Assembly while electing as President the candidate of a conservative anti-Liberation coalition, José Joaquín Tréjos Fernández. Legislative and executive branches were at constant loggerheads in a period of financial difficulty requiring decisive action. The voters remedied this in 1970 when they elected the Liberation candidate for president, José Figuéres Ferrer, and his party kept control in the Assembly. In 1974, the National Liberation party retained the presidency with the election of its candidate, Daniel Oduber Quirós.

In the 1978 elections, political power passed peacefully to a new president, Rodrigo Carazo Odio, an economist and businessman, and his Unity party, a coalition of four parties. For years, the biggest issue in the nation's political life had been the presence in Costa Rica of Robert Vesco, a fugitive from U.S. charges of embezzling $224 million from a mutual fund he controlled. Carazo

had vowed, as his first order of business, to expel Vesco "for the nation's health." When Vesco left on a business trip to the Bahamas, Carazo acted on his pledge by ordering all ports of entry to bar Vesco's return. Further, the civil registry at San José rejected Vesco's application for citizenship, apparently closing the door completely. Costa Rica has no army, and its lightly armed guardsmen could not stop Nicaraguan leftist guerrillas from crossing the border at will in 1978. The government, as a consequence, borrowed 1,000 rifles from Venezuela, but it denied any effort in "militarizing the country."

The first electricity from the vast Arenal Project in Guanacaste province was generated in 1978. Construction on the project in the next five years will double the country's electrical capacity and will increase irrigation considerably.

HISTORY: Prior to Costa Rica's discovery in 1502 by the Spanish, the country was inhabited by the Guaymi Indians. During the Spanish colonial period, Costa Rica was largely ignored by the mother country because of the paucity of minerals, and administered as part of the captaincy general of Guatemala

1821: Costa Rica obtains independence from Spain, and along with the rest of Central America is annexed to Mexico

1823: Costa Rica and the other Central American countries secede from Mexico and establish the Central American Federation

1838: Costa Rica becomes an independent republic

1856-57: William Walker, an American adventurer, attempts to conquer Costa Rica but is defeated by Central American alliance

1917-19: Revolution breaks out; dictatorship is set up by Frederico Granados

1948-49: President Teodoro Picado annuls elections won by presidential candidate Otilio Ulate. José Figueres leads civilian uprising, installs his own junta, and then turns presidency over to Ulate

1962: Costa Rica joins Central American Common Market

1963: The volcano Irazú erupts, destroying productive land

1968: The volcano Arenal erupts, bringing new devastation

1970: José Figuéres, leader of National Liberation Party and a conciliator between labor and management, wins presidential election

1974: Daniel Oduber Quirós is elected president

1976: Trade relations restored with Cuba

1978: Rodrigo Carazo Odio is elected president, vows to expel fugitive millionaire Robert Vesco

CUBA

Area: 42,827 sq. mi. **Population:** 9,600,000 (1978 est.)

Official Name: Republic of Cuba **Capital:** Havana **Nationality:** Cuban **Languages:** Spanish is the official and universal language **Religion:** Predominantly Roman Catholic **Flag:** Three horizontal blue stripes separated by two white stripes, with an equilateral red triangle at the left containing a 5-pointed white star **Anthem:** Hymn of Bayamo **Currency:** Cuban peso (0.72 per U.S. $1)

Location: Northern rim of the Caribbean Sea. The largest and most westerly island of the West Indies, Cuba lies at the entrance of the Gulf of Mexico and some 90 miles south of Florida. **Features:** About three fifths of the country consists of flat to gently rolling terrain with many wide and fertile valleys and plains. The rest is mountainous or hilly **Chief Rivers:** Cauto, Sagua la Grande, Zaza, Caonao, San Pedro, Toa

Political Leader, Head of State and of Government: President Fidel Castro Ruz, born 1926, First Secretary of the Central Committee of the Cuban Communist party, and president of the councils of state and of ministers, seized power in 1959 **Effective Date of Present Constitution:** December 1976 **Legislative Body:** National Assembly of People's Power (unicameral), with 481 deputies elected for 5-year terms. Power lies in the Communist party Politburo **Local Government:** 14 provinces (including Havana city and the special municipality of the Isle of Pines), with locally elected assemblies

Ethnic Composition: About 73% of the population is of European (mainly Spanish) ancestry, 15% mulatto (mixed European and Negro), 12% Negro **Population Distribution:** 60.5% urban (1971) **Density:** 224 inhabitants per sq. mi.

Largest Cities: (1976 est.) Havana 1,949,000, Santiago de Cuba 322,000, Camagüey 228,000, Guantánamo 158,000, Holguín 153,000, Santa Clara 150,000

Per Capita Income: $1,163 (1978 est.) **Gross National Product (GNP):** $11 billion (1978 est.) **Economic Statistics:** 10% of GNP is derived from agriculture (sugar, tobacco, cattle, coffee); 41% from industry (mainly sugar refining, cigarettes and cigars, rum, and textiles); and 33% from trade and finance (1974) **Minerals and Mining:** Cuba has the world's largest deposit of nickel; reserves of iron ore, manganese, cobalt, copper, chromite, salt, petroleum, gold, silver

Labor Force: 2,848,030 (1975), with 30% in agriculture, 28% in industry and construction, and 31% in trade and services (1973) **Foreign Trade:** Exports, chiefly sugar (86% of total), nickel (10%), tobacco, shrimps, lobster, and beef (5%), were $3.2 billion (1976). Imports, mainly petroleum, equipment and machinery, and food, totaled $4 billion **Principal Trade Partners:** Soviet bloc, Japan, Spain, Canada, Britain

Vital Statistics: Birthrate, 19.6 per 1,000 of pop. (1976); death rate, 5.5 **Life Expectancy:** 72 years **Health Statistics:** 234 inhabitants per hospital bed; 1,121 per physician (1974) **Infant Mortality:** 22.9 per 1,000 births (1976) **Illiteracy:** 3.1% **Education Statistics:** 16,878 primary and secondary schools, with combined enrollment of 2,451,988 (1975) **Enrollment in Higher Education:** 68,890 **GNP Expended on Education:** 9.3% (1974)

Transportation: Paved roads total 8,135 mi. (1976) **Motor Vehicles:** 120,000 (1976) **Passenger Cars:** 80,000 **Railway Mileage:** 9,236 **Ports:** Havana, Matanzas, Nuevitas, Cienfuegos, Santiago de Cuba **Major Airlines:** Cubana de Aviación, the government-owned airline, operates domestic and international flights **Communications:** Government controlled **Radio Transmitters:** 115 (1975) **Receivers:** 2,100,000 (1976) **Television Transmitters:** 19 **Receivers:** 650,000 (1976) **Telephones:** 289,000 (1974) **Newspapers:** 15 dailies (1975), 107 per 1,000 inhabitants

Weights and Measures: Metric system **Travel Requirements:** Passport, visa; apply to Czechoslovak Embassy, Washington, D.C. 20009

Cuba, largest of the West Indies and the only Communist-controlled country in the Western Hemisphere, lies only 90 miles south of Key West, Florida. Cuba's capital, Havana, is less than an hour's flight southwest from Miami. The country's largest city and principal port, Havana, was originally important as a well-situated way station between Spain and her colonies in the Western Hemisphere. Eventually, settlers moved inland, devoting themselves mainly to growing sugarcane and tobacco.

Despite the physical proximity of Cuba to the U.S. and the potential trade and other ties, the relationship between the two countries has never developed quite as one might expect. Cuba was the last Latin American nation to gain independence from Spain. The United States actually opposed the first attempt to free Cuba begun by Simón Bolívar. A native-based liberation movement starting in 1868 sputtered out after 10 years of fighting. It was not until 1895 that a revolution led by José Martí successfully challenged Spain. The revolutionaries also won strong sentiments of support in the U.S. After the mysterious sinking of the *Maine*, the U.S. declared war on Spain.

When a freely elected Cuban government took office in 1902, it found it had little to sell except land. Many foreign investors, chiefly Americans, stepped forward and purchased enormous areas and began to rebuild the sugar industry. For years after, Cuba was locked into a one-crop agricultural economy with American ownership of the land, mines and other resources. Income was, and still is, almost totally dependent on the world price of sugar. American interests were protected by the Platt Amendment that allowed U.S. to intervene in Cuban affairs, which it did in 1906-1909 and again in 1912.

Fulgencio Batista, a former army sergeant, dominated the political scene either directly or indirectly from 1934 to 1944 and from 1952 to 1959. Cuba's basic problems went unresolved during the Batista era and various groups sought his downfall.

President Batista's regime became repressive and increasingly unpopular, and on July 26, 1953, an armed opposition group led by a young lawyer, Fidel Castro, attacked the Moncada army barracks at Santiago de Cuba. The attack failed and many of those not killed were imprisoned, including Castro. He was released by President Batista under an amnesty in May 1955 and went into exile in Mexico, where he formed his "26th of July Movement." While a number of other groups in Cuba also actively opposed Batista, it was Castro's forces, eventually numbering several thousands, who finally succeeded in forcing Batista to flee the country, on January 1, 1959.

The Castro regime's early promises of agrarian reform to benefit the peasants resulted in state ownership of most of the land and in the organization of state farms. Cuba's business and industrial sectors were nationalized and placed under the direction of the state, which has also effectively abolished all opposition political activity. Thousands of politically troublesome Cubans are in prisons or in forced-labor camps, and about 600,000—including many professionals and skilled technicians—have gone into exile, most of them to the United States.

A major element of Cuba's foreign policy under Castro has been the "exporting" of revolutionary techniques. To this end, Cuba has supported guerrilla movements in various countries in the Western Hemisphere and elsewhere—notably Africa—by providing weapons, financing, propaganda and, in some cases, advisory personnel.

Cuba's home economy was in bad straits even as it pursued costly African adventures. The plunge in world sugar prices from a peak of 50¢ a pound in 1974 to a subsequent low of 7¢ had a devastating effect on Cuban life. The Soviet Union had been spending heavily—estimates range from $3 million to $6 million a day—to keep Cuba's economy going. With little hard cash to buy badly needed food staples and with oil prices rising ever higher, Cuba found herself totally dependent upon Moscow. Imports were costly, on account of worldwide inflation and the extra cost of long shipments because of the U.S. trade embargo in effect since 1961. Scarce items had to be strictly rationed.

A nod toward normalizing U.S.-Cuban relations was made in 1975 by U.S. Secretary of State Henry Kissinger. But the nod became a "no" when Cuba dispatched troops to help Russian-backed forces in Angola's civil war. After Jimmy Carter became President, he first tested the water with some qualified public overtures toward Cuba, and then on March 9, 1977, announced an end to travel restrictions in Cuba. The two countries soon negotiated fishing and maritime rights agreements. The thaw progressed no further, however, as the Cubans moved on to military activity in Ethiopia and Yemen. Other obstacles, so far as the U.S. was concerned, were the holding of political prisoners and inability to arrange compensation for U.S. property confiscated in 1960.

On Jan. 1, 1979, Castro used the 20th anniversary of his revolution as an occasion to make sharp verbal jabs against his northern neighbor. The 20-year trade embargo, he asserted, was "a criminal attempt at the strangulation and economic genocide of our people." He added that the United States is "a rotten pseudo-democracy." When he visited Mexico in May—his first Latin American trip since going to Chile in 1973—Castro again blasted away at the U.S. embargo, saying that it is "miserable and grotesque...to deny a country the right to buy medicines abroad." He characterized Cuban-U.S. relations as "perfectly bad."

For its part, the United States kept a wary eye on military gifts to the Cubans from the Soviets. The gifts include MiG-23 jet planes in 1978, described as fitted out for defense only, and Cuba's first submarine (diesel-powered, not nuclear-powered) in 1979.

HISTORY: Following the discovery of Cuba by Columbus in 1492, the island remained under Spanish rule until almost the end of the

19th century. A revolt against Spain broke out in 1895 and evoked strong sympathy in the United States. After the brief Spanish-American War of 1898, Cuba became an independent republic, though under U.S. protection. With the abrogation of the Platt Amendment in 1934, the U.S. gave up the right to intervene in Cuban affairs, but retained its right to the naval base at Guantánamo

1934-59: Fulgencio Batista y Zaldívar, an army sergeant, overthrows regime and becomes dominant figure in Cuban politics. After ruling through puppet presidents, Batista proclaims new constitution in 1940 and is elected president for four-year term. In 1952 he returns to power through an army coup but his regime is increasingly threatened by rebel uprisings led by Fidel Castro, who finally forces Batista to flee

1960: Castro begins to transform Cuba into socialist state modeled on Soviet pattern and installs Communists in leading government posts. Most U.S.-owned property is nationalized without compensation; United States rescinds Cuban sugar quota

1961: United States severs diplomatic relations with Havana. Castro turns increasingly to Soviet Union for aid and protection, receiving supplies of arms and oil. Cuban exiles in United States, trained and equipped by Central Intelligence Agency, land invasion force at Bay of Pigs in abortive attempt to overthrow Castro

1962: Organization of American States excludes Cuba from membership. Installation of Soviet missiles in Cuba leads to U.S. demand for their removal and to imposition of naval blockade of island to bar further Soviet shipments. Strong U.S. reaction results in Soviet backdown and missiles are withdrawn

1967: Soviet Premier Aleksei N. Kosygin visits Cuba in effort to improve relations between two countries

1970: Castro concedes that sugar harvest fell far below 10-million-ton goal

1971: Cuba signs economic pact with the Soviet Union

1972: Premier Castro makes his third official visit to Moscow at the end of a two-month world tour of socialist countries

1975: An abortive CIA plot to assassinate Castro and other Cuban officials in 1960 is revealed. OAS passes resolution to lift the 11 years of formal diplomatic and economic isolation of Cuba

1976: A new constitution, drafted in 1975, is approved by referendum, replacing Castro's more informal type of government with a hierarchy of strictly structured institutions

1977: U.S. lifts restrictions on travel to Cuba

1978: U.S.-Cuba thaw is stalled, principally on issues of U.S. economic blockade against Cuba, $1.8 billion in claims against Cuba by American companies and individuals, and continued Cuban presence in Africa (estimated at 26,000 men, mostly military, in Angola, Ethiopia and 14 other nations). U.S. accuses Cuba of having role in rebel invasion of Zaire from Angolan bases. Castro denies charge

1979: Castro visits Mexico's President José Lopez Portillo, notes that Mexico was the only Latin land that kept up diplomatic relations with Cuba throughout 20 years of U.S. blockade. Havana opens "dialogue" with Cuban exiles in U.S., leading to pledges to release nearly 3,000 political prisoners

---

CYPRUS

Area: 3,572 sq. mi. (including the 99 sq. mi. British-leased Sovereign Base Area) **Population:** 685,000 (1978 est.)

Official Name: Republic of Cyprus **Capital:** Nicosia **Nationality:** Cypriot **Languages:** Greek and Turkish are the official languages. English is widely understood **Religion:** 78% of the population belongs to the Eastern Orthodox Church; the rest are almost all Moslems **Flag:** An outline map of Cyprus in gold above crossed green olive branches on a white field **Anthem:** None established **Currency:** Cypriot pound (0.36 per U.S. $1)

Location: Middle East. The third largest island in the Mediterranean, Cyprus lies 44 miles south of Turkey, 60 miles west of Syria, and 260 miles east of Rhodes, the nearest part of Greece **Features:** The Troodos Mountains in the southwest and the Kyrenia range along the northern coast dominate the island. The central plain, or Mesaoria, lies between the two mountain ranges **Chief River:** Pedieos (Pedias)

Head of State and of Government: President: Spyros Achilles Kyprianou, born 1932, succeeded August 1977, reelected for full 5-year term 1978 **Effective Date of Present Constitution:** 1960 **Legislative Body:** House of Representatives (unicameral), consisting of 35 Greek Cypriot members, elected for 5 years. Turkish Cypriots declared their independence and established in February 1975 the Turkish Federated State of Cyprus, with a president (Rauf R. Denktash elected in 1976), premier (Mustafa Cagatay, appointed 1978), and a 40-member unicameral Constituent Assembly; a referendum in 1976 approved a constitution **Local Government:** 6 districts

Ethnic Composition: About 78% of the population is of Greek descent, 18% of Turkish origin, and the rest composed of Armenians, Maronites, and other minorities **Population Distribution:** 42.2% urban (1974) **Density:** 192 inhabitants per sq. mi.

Largest Cities: (1973 census) Nicosia 116,125; (1972 estimates) Limassol 61,400, Famagusta 44,200, Larnaca 21,800, Paphos 12,100, Kyrenia 5,200

Per Capita Income: $1,954 (1978) **Gross National Product (GNP):** $1.4 billion (1978) **Economic Statistics:** In 1976 about 18% of GNP was derived from agriculture, 15% from manufacturing and mining, 16% from transportation and communication, and 51% from trade and services **Minerals and Mining:** Copper is the most important mineral, but the mines are becoming depleted; asbestos is becoming increasingly important. Other minerals are iron pyrites, chromite, umber, and yellow ocher **Labor Force:** 250,000 (1976, Greek area only), with 36% in agriculture, 26% in manufacturing, 10% in construction, 9% in commerce, 8% in government **Foreign Trade:** Exports, chiefly fruits and vegetables, copper and concentrates, iron pyrites, wine, and asbestos, totaled $258 million in 1976. Imports, mainly machinery and transportation equipment, manufactures, and food, totaled $434 million **Principal Trade Partners:** Britain, West Germany, United States, U.S.S.R., Greece, Libya, Italy, Japan, Saudi Arabia, France, Lebanon, Iraq

Vital Statistics: Birthrate, 19.6 per 1,000 of pop. (1976); death rate, 9.8 **Life Expectancy:** 71.5 years **Health Statistics:** 195 inhabitants per hospital bed; 1,168 per physician (1975) **Infant Mortality:** 27.2 per 1,000 births **Illiteracy:** 11% **Education Statistics:** (Greek only): 393 primary and secondary schools, with total enrollment of 105,975 (1975) **Enrollment in Higher Education:** 602 (1975) **GNP Expended on Education:** 4.3% (1975)

Transportation: Paved roads total 2,700 mi. **Motor Vehicles:** 86,300 (1976) **Passenger Cars:** 69,190 **Railway Mileage:** None **Ports:** Famagusta, Limassol, Larnaca, Karavostassi **Major Airlines:** Cyprus Airways (government owned) operates domestic and international flights; there is also a Turkish-Cypriot airline **Communications:** State controlled **Radio Transmitters:** 4 **Licenses:** 200,000 (1976) **Television Transmitters:** 5 (1972) **Licenses:** 57,000 (1976) **Telephones:** 77,000 (1976) **Newspapers:** 12 dailies (1975), 107 copies per 1,000 inhabitants (1970)

Weights and Measures: Both British standards and the metric system are used along with local units **Travel Requirements:** Passport, no visa

---

The picturesque island of Aphrodite, Cyprus has been an independent but strife-torn nation since 1960. Previously, its strategic location had attracted many foreign conquerors, including the Egyptians, Phoenicians, Assyrians, Persians, Romans, Greeks, Turks and British. Today Cyprus is divided into two separate states and its future as a single nation is in doubt.

The island is the homeland of two antagonistic peoples—some half million ethnic Greeks and slightly more than 120,000 ethnic Turks. The Greek Cypriots have traditionally favored *enosis* (union) with Greece, while the Turkish Cypriots want partition or cantonization of the country. In any case, virtually all Cypriots regard themselves as Greeks or Turks, Christians or Moslems first and as Cypriots second.

More than half the total area of Cyprus is cultivated, a noteworthy accomplishment in the largely arid Middle East, and about 40 percent of the population is engaged in agriculture. Mineral resources maintain a modest industrial complex.

The constitution, in effect after independence in 1960, required that the president be a Greek Cypriot and the vice-president a Turkish Cypriot. Archbishop Makarios III, head of the Greek Orthodox Church on Cyprus became president. The Greek and Turkish communities lived under a form of de facto segregation.

Civil war between the two communities erupted in 1963 and terroristic campaigns became a part of Cypriot life. In 1964, the United Nations sent a peace-keeping force to minimize clashes. Turkish Cypriot leaders withdrew from active participation in the government of Cyprus. In 1967 war between Greece and Turkey over Cyprus was narrowly averted, mainly through the mediation of the United States. Turkey had threatened to invade the island but Greece finally agreed to remove nearly all of the 8,000 troops it had there.

The Cypriot national guard which was dominated by officers from Greece continued to press for union with Greece. In 1971 the EOKA B, a guerrilla movement favoring ties to Greece and led by Gen. George Grivas, stepped up its terrorist activities, which tended to undermine the government of President Makarios, who began his third five-year term in February 1973. (His second term had been extended.)

On July 15, 1974, Greek officers of the Cypriot national guard led a coup which overthrew President Makarios and replaced him with an EOKA B terrorist, Nikos Sampson. Turkey responded by invading Cyprus on July 20, and quickly conquered the northern two-fifths of the island. Most of the Greek Cypriots in the conquered territory fled south, and most of the Turkish Cypriots elsewhere moved north. Sampson's government collapsed.

Amid fears of a wider conflict, the UN ordered a cease-fire. Fighting continued sporadically but order was restored with Glafkos Clerides, president of the Cyprus House of Representatives, as interim president. By the time international pressure effected a real cease-fire on August 16, 200,000 Greek Cypriots were refugees. Makarios returned to power in December 1974.

In February 1975 a Turkish-Cypriot Federated State of Cyprus was created in the occupied area without the approval of Makarios, and in June a Turkish Cypriot referendum established a constitution for the state. Talks to establish a unified form of government continue, but accord at times seems distant. In April 1978 the Cypriot government rejected Turkish proposals for a settlement of the dispute between the island's Greeks and Turks, charging they were aimed at permanently dividing the island into two states. The Turkish Cypriots said the rejection of the proposals by Spyros Kyprianou, the new Greek Cypriot president, was an effort to block moves in the U.S. Congress to lift the arms embargo against Turkey. However, both houses of Congress eventually voted to lift the embargo.

HISTORY: Cyprus, which derives its name from "kypros," the Greek word for copper, was settled first by the Greeks c. 1500 B.C. and passed to the Romans in 58 B.C. Later a part of the Byzantine Empire, the island slumbered until 1191, when Richard I of England conquered Cyprus and it became a base for the Crusaders. In the 16th century, the island was conquered by Turkey. Administration was transferred to Britain in 1878 and in 1928 the island became a Crown Colony.

1946: Greece demands union (enosis) with Cyprus

1956: Archbishop Makarios, spiritual and political leader of the Greek Cypriots, is deported by British

1959: Greek-Turkish conferences in Zurich and London reach agreement on independence for Cyprus. Archbishop Makarios returns and is elected president

1960: Independence is officially proclaimed

1963: Violence between Greeks and Turks erupts in Nicosia

1964: Turks withdraw from active participation in government. Threat of war between Greece and Turkey over Cyprus brings United Nations peace-keeping force to island

1968: Makarios announces restoration of freedom of movement for Turkish Cypriots, ending blockade of Turkish sectors

1973: Struggle for enosis erupts into widespread violence

1974: Cypriot National Guard ousts President Makarios. Turkish forces invade Cyprus and gain control of 40 percent of the island. Two-way migration makes occupied territory predominantly Turkish, rest of island predominantly Greek. Makarios returns and resumes the presidency

1975: Turkish Cypriots proclaim their own state in northern Cyprus

1976: Turkish Cypriots elect Rauf Denktash to serve as president of the Turkish Cypriot Zone

1977: Turkish and Greek Cypriot leaders begin talks. Makarios dies. Spyros Kyprianou succeeds him

1978: Cypriot-Egyptian diplomatic relations severed after Cypriot troops in Larnaca kill 15 Egyptian commandos who were storming a Cyprus Airways jet in which two Palestinians held hostages. Continued deadlock in talks between Greek and Turkish Cypriots

CZECHOSLOVAKIA

Area: 49,373 sq. mi. **Population:** 15,100,000 (1978 est.)
Official Name: Czechoslovak Socialist Republic **Capital:** Prague **Nationality:** Czechoslovak **Languages:** Czech and Slovak are the official and principal languages; Hungarian and German are minority languages **Religion:** About 77% of the population is Roman Catholic; 8% are members of the Czechoslovak Church; and 8% are Protestants. All churches are under close government control **Flag:** A blue triangle on the hoist with its apex toward the center; the rest of the flag consists of a white band on top and a red band on the bottom **Anthem:** Where Is My Home? **Currency:** Koruna (10.5 per U.S. $1)

Location: Central Europe. Landlocked Czechoslovakia is bordered on the north by Poland, on the east by the USSR, on the south by Hungary and Austria, on the west by West Germany, on the northwest by East Germany **Features:** Bohemia, Moravia, and Slovakia are the country's principal regions. Bohemia, in the west, is a plateau surrounded by mountains; Moravia, in the central region, is somewhat hillier; and Slovakia, in the east, is partly mountainous and partly lowland **Chief Rivers:** Labe, Vltava, Danube, Morava, Váh, Nitra, Hron, Ohre, Horná

Political Leader and Head of State: President Gustav Husák, born 1913, reelected 1975; general secretary of the Central Committee of the Communist Party **Head of Government:** Premier Lubomir Strougal, born 1935, appointed January 1, 1970

Effective Date of Present Constitution: 1960; the constitution was amended in 1969 to provide for Czech and Slovak local autonomy within a federal state, and again in 1971 and 1975 **Legislative Body:** Federal Assembly (bicameral), consisting of 2 equal chambers, the Chamber of the People and the Chamber of the Nations. The Chamber of the People has 200 members. The Chamber of the Nations consists of 75 representatives from the Czech Republic and 75 from the Slovak Republic. Both houses are elected for 5 years. The Federal Assembly is subordinate to the Central Committee of the Presidium of the Communist Party **Local Government:** The two republics have separate premiers and national councils, subordinate to the Federal Assembly. They are divided into 10 regions and 2 independent cities

Ethnic Composition: Czechs make up about 65% of the population and Slovaks 30%; Hungarians, Germans, Poles, Ukrainians, and Gypsies make up the rest **Population Distribution:** 66.7% urban (1974) **Density:** 306 inhabitants per sq. mi.

Largest Cities: (1975 est.) Prague 1,161,266, Brno 335,661, Bratislava 333,012, Ostrava 293,454, Kosice 169,083, Plzen 155,006

Per Capita Income: $4,673 (1978 est.) **Gross National Product (GNP):** $70.7 billion (1978 est.) **Economic Statistics:** About 45% of GNP comes from industry (iron and steel, glass, leather products, brewing, and textiles); 12% from agriculture (grains, sugar beets, hops, fruits and vegetables); 8% from construction; 9% from transport and communications; 9% from trade; 5% from housing; 11% from government and other services **Minerals and Mining:** Coal, antimony, magnesite, lignite and uranium **Labor Force:** 8.3 million (1976), with about 37% in industry and construction, and 18% in agriculture **Foreign Trade:** Exports, chiefly machinery, motor vehicles, iron and steel, and chemicals, totaled $10 billion in 1977. Imports, mainly machinery, industrial raw materials, food, fuel, and manufactured goods, totaled $10.9 billion **Principal Trade Partners:** USSR, East Germany, Poland, Hungary, Romania, West Germany, Britain, Bulgaria, Switzerland, China, Austria, Yugoslavia

Vital Statistics: Birthrate, 18.7 per 1,000 of pop. (1977); death rate, 11.5 **Life Expectancy:** 71 years **Health Statistics:** 99 inhabitants per hospital bed; 418 per physician (1975) **Infant Mortality:** 19.6 per 1,000 births (1977) **Illiteracy:** Negligible **Education Statistics:** 10,804 primary and secondary schools, with combined enrollment of 2,296,703 (1975) **Enrollment in Higher Education:** 155,059 (1975) **GNP Expended on Education:** 4.7% (1975)

Transportation: Roads 45,671 mi. (1974) **Motor Vehicles:** 1,952,900 (1976) **Passenger Cars:** 1,677,500 **Railway Mileage:** 8,228 **Ports:** None **Major Airlines:** Czechoslovak Airlines operates domestic and international services **Communications:** State owned **Radio Transmitters:** 123 **Licenses:** 3,928,000 (1976) **Television Transmitters:** 788 **Licenses:** 3,793,000 (1976) **Telephones:** 2,743,000 (1976) **Newspapers:** 29 dailies, 300 copies per 1,000 inhabitants (1975)

Weights and Measures: Metric system **Travel Requirements:** Passport; visa; 2 pictures; $8 fee

The problem of Czechoslovakia today is trying to mold a socialist state of Marxist-Leninist traditions as determined by its Russian guardians while satisfying a native desire for the freedom and openness of a Western democracy.

The Communist Party seized power in 1948, and established one of the world's least free societies.

In the 1960s, with a new constitution, a cautious liberalizing movement emerged. A flowering of Czechoslovak artistry in films, the theater and other arts began. When the economy stagnated, Slovak Communists found a chance to replace hard-liner Antonin Novotny with Alexander Dubcek as first secretary of the Communist Party in January 1968.

Under Dubcek the trend toward freedom accelerated. Press censorship was reduced and grievances were aired, thus adding to the pressure for reforms while at the same time arousing the fears of Soviet leaders. The radical experiment to establish "socialism with a human face" ended abruptly on August 20, 1968, when armored units of the Warsaw Pact countries, led by Soviet tanks, entered Czechoslovakia at night to ensure the restoration of a more orthodox brand of Communism.

The dramatic incursion was characterized by its initiators as necessary to thwart a "threatened counterrevolution" by "imperialist forces." It was seen by Western observers—and most Czechs—as a final desperate move by Leonid I. Brezhnev, the Soviet Communist party chief, to curtail Dubcek's essay in Socialist democracy.

Dubcek was forced in succeeding days to sign a protocol in Moscow accepting the military "assistance." He was formally replaced in April 1969 by Gustav Husák, who has since moved resolutely to restore the former system of state control in Czechoslovakia.

The aftermath of Dubcek's "Prague Spring" has been characterized by a reversal of his reforms; a broad purge of liberal economists, writers, educators and artists; and a "cleansing" of party ranks as well as the removal of the former leader himself from public life.

Dubcek's error had been to move too quickly, too prominently, and certainly too radically to shed the restrictions and repressions of the earlier Stalinist period of postwar Communist rule.

The new Czech party chief, Husák, has spent the intervening years walking a line between hard-liners in the party, who want to carry the anti-Dubcek purges beyond the stages of ousters and restrictions to arrests and trials, and the many Czechs—revisionists, in party terminology—who watch now with sullen hostility to the withering of a brief, bright flowering of intellectual freedom.

As politically adroit as Dubcek was unsophisticated, Husák removed 400,000 members from the Czech Communist Party—one-fifth of the national membership—but only a few have been tried for "anti-State" activities. Many leading educators, commentators, economists, and other leaders who supported Dubcek left the country.

In recent years a slight easing can be detected. Husák has given a second chance to lesser participants in the reform movement and hard-liners were unable to dominate the Communist Party congress in April 1975. Dissidents continue to voice their loyalty to the ideas of the 1968 "Prague Spring." The voice is muted somewhat, because the Helsinki agreements are interpreted by Czech authorities according to Marxist-Leninist goals. Dissident attacks on Husák's "normalization" manage to circulate and are leaked to the West where they hinder Czech officials seeking better trade contacts with the non-Communist world.

HISTORY: In the 6th and 7th centuries, Slavic migrants absorbed Celtic, Germanic, and other cultures. The Czechs, in Bohemia and Moravia, and the Slovaks, in Slovakia, were united in the Great Moravian Empire in the ninth century, a period that also saw the introduction of Christianity. After the empire's collapse in the 10th century, the Slovaks were incorporated into the Kingdom of Hungary and the Czechs established the Kingdom of Bohemia. The 14th century, with its Hussite Revolution, marked the beginning of religious wars in the Czech lands that were to continue through the Reformation and Counter-Reformation. During the decline of the Kingdom of Bohemia, the Czechs came under foreign dynasties, ending up, along with the Slovaks, in the Austro-Hungarian Empire

- **1918:** Following the defeat of Austria-Hungary in World War I, Czechoslovakia, incorporating the Czech lands and Slovakia, is proclaimed an independent republic with nationalist leader Thomas Masaryk its first president
- **1935:** Masaryk dies. Eduard Benes elected President
- **1938:** Britain, France, Germany, and Italy, without having invited Czechoslovakia to the negotiating table, sign the Munich Pact, a capitulation to German demands for the Sudetenland, the border region of Bohemia inhabited by a large German minority. President Eduard Benes resigns and goes into exile
- **1939-46:** German troops occupy Czechoslovakia during World War II. The country is liberated by Soviet and U.S. forces. Benes returns and resumes presidency
- **1948:** Communists seize power; Benes resigns; Foreign Minister Jan Masaryk, son of Thomas Masaryk, plunges to death from a window. Though officially termed a suicide, he is believed to have been murdered by the Communists
- **1955:** Czechoslovakia joins the Warsaw Pact, the Soviet-bloc military organization
- **1968:** Alexander Dubcek, a progressive, becomes first secretary of the Czechoslovak Communist Party, replacing Antonín Novotny. The Soviet Union, alarmed by liberalization measures in Czechoslovakia, invades the country
- **1969:** Gustav Husák replaces Dubcek as leader of the Czechoslovak Communist Party and rescinds liberalization; Dubcek is ousted from ruling Presidium in purge of party progressives
- **1970:** Dubcek is expelled from the Communist Party and removed from his post as ambassador to Turkey
- **1973:** First direct consular agreement between Communist Czechoslovakia and the United States is signed
- **1974:** U.S. and Czechoslovakia reach preliminary agreement on settlement of postwar financial counterclaims
- **1975:** Husák is elected President by Federal Assembly
- **1977:** Czech dissidents publish manifesto (Charter 77) protesting the suppression of human rights; detention of signers follows
- **1978:** Subdued public protests and destruction of statue mark 10th anniversary of invasion
- **1979:** Charter 77 group falters, elects new leaders

DENMARK

Area: 16,629 sq. mi. **Population:** 5,120,000 (1978 est.)

Official Name: Kingdom of Denmark **Capital:** Copenhagen **Nationality:** Danish **Languages:** Danish is the official and universal language **Religion:** About 97% of the people belong to the established Lutheran Church **Flag:** A white cross on a red field **Anthem:** There is a Lovely Land **Currency:** Danish krone (5.3 per U.S. $1)

Location: Northwest Europe. Denmark is bordered on the north by the Skagerrak; on the east by the Kattegat, Öresund, and the Baltic Sea; on the south by West Germany; and on the west by the North Sea **Features:** Low-lying elevation, with flat or rolling landscape **Chief Rivers:** Stora, Skjern, Varde, Gudena

Head of State: Queen Margrethe II, born 1940, ascended the throne 1972 **Head of Government:** Premier Anker Joergensen, born 1922, appointed 1972 and 1975, reappointed 1978 **Effective Date of Present Constitution:** 1953 **Legislative Body:** Parliament (unicameral *Folketing*), with 179 members, including 2 each from Greenland and the Faeroe Islands, elected on the basis of proportional representation for 4 years **Local Government:** 14 counties and two urban communes, with elected chief administrative officers and councils

Ethnic Composition: Except for foreign "guest workers" the population is almost entirely Scandinavian **Population Distribution:** 80% urban **Density:** 308 inhabitants per sq. mi.

Largest Cities (M.A. = **Metropolitan Area)** (1973 est.): Copenhagen 603,368 (M.A. 1,362,158), Aarhus 243,496, Odense 167,324, Aalborg 155,424

Per Capita Income: $7,607 (1978) **Gross National Product (GNP):** $38.9 billion (1978 est.) **Economic Statistics:** About 35% of GNP (1976) comes from manufacturing (food processing, machinery, chemicals), crafts, building and construction; 6% from agriculture (dairy and poultry farming, cattle raising, hog breeding, grain and root crops), forestry and fisheries **Minerals and Mining:** Oil and gas produced from North Sea wells **Labor Force:** 2,500,000 (1977); 24% in manufacturing, 16% in trade, 8.0% in building and construction, 9% in agriculture **Foreign Trade:** Exports, chiefly machinery and equipment, textiles and agricultural commodities, totaled $11.1 billion in 1978. Imports, mainly machinery and fittings, fuels, chemicals, iron and steel, totaled $13 billion **Principal Trade Partners:** Sweden, West Germany, Britain, United States, Norway, Netherlands

Vital Statistics: Birthrate, 12.2 per 1,000 of pop. (1977); death rate, 9.9 **Life Expectancy:** 73 years **Health Statistics:** 103 inhabitants per hospital bed; 624 per physician (1972) **Infant Mortality:** 8.9 per 1,000 (1977) **Illiteracy:** Negligible **Education Statistics:** 2,215 primary and secondary schools, with combined enrollment of 933,932 (1974) **Enrollment in Higher Education:** 110,271 (1975) **GNP Share Expended on Education:** 8.3% (1975).

Transportation: Roads total 40,000 mi. **Motor Vehicles:** 1,606,200 (1976) **Passenger Cars:** 1,344,200 (1976) **Railway Mileage:** 1,580 **Ports:** Copenhagen, Aalborg, Aarhus, Esbjerg **Major Airlines:** Scandinavian Airlines System (SAS) operates domestic and international services. Danair operates domestic routes **Communications:** Government owned **Radio Transmitters:** 19 **Licenses:** 1,851,000 (1976) **Television Transmitters:** 30 (1974) **Licenses:** 1,637,000 (1976) **Telephones:** 2,505,000 (1976) **Newspapers:** 49 dailies, 341 copies per 1,000 inhabitants (1974)

Weights and Measures: Metric system **Travel Requirements:** Passport, no visa for 3 months

Denmark, located strategically at the mouth of the Baltic Sea, consists of the Jutland Peninsula (projecting north from West Germany) and about 500 islands, of which 100 are inhabited. It is one of the smallest countries in the world if only its low-lying islands and the Jutland Peninsula are considered. However, the kingdom also embraces the Faeroe Islands and the island of Greenland, both of which now enjoy great autonomy.

Occupied during World War II by the Nazis, Denmark did not return in the postwar era to the policy of neutrality that it had followed through World War I. Instead it became a charter member of the North Atlantic Treaty Organization in 1949 and joined with the West Germans in forming a joint Baltic command within the alliance in 1961. But the Danes, like the Norwegians, have limited their NATO membership by declaring that neither foreign troops nor nuclear weapons may be stationed on their territory in peace-time.

Small-scale production of oil from wells on the Danish share of the North Sea continental shelf began in 1972, and surface mining of iron ore began in Greenland on a limited scale in 1973. But so far Denmark's natural resources remain largely limited to its rich farmland, and the nation relies heavily upon imports.

Through membership in the British-led European Free Trade Association (EFTA), Denmark and its neighbors—Norway, Sweden and Finland—created what amounted to a Nordic common market in 1960. Most of this was retained when Denmark, along with Britain and Ireland, opted out of EFTA to join the European Communities (European Economic Community, European Coal and Steel Community and European Atomic Energy Community) on January 1, 1973.

The political process is firmly democratic. But no election since 1945 has given any party a majority in the *Folketing*. The Social Democratic party is the largest and usually leads the governing coalition, but decision-making is slow and marked by compromise. Efforts to reduce unemployment and to promote needed exports also require the help of unions and businesses, which are reluctant to help unstable coalitions and which resent the country's high taxes. A two-year austerity program, involving strict wage controls, took effect in 1977 after strikes thwarted it for eight months.

HISTORY: During the Viking age the Danes figured importantly in the Norse raids on Western Europe. Denmark became at once an Atlantic and a Baltic power and warred with the English, with German princes, and with Norwegian and Swedish kings. Denmark's period of expansion lasted until about 1600 and was followed by a losing struggle against Swedish and German rivals.

1643-60: Wars with Sweden determine eastern borders

1815: Denmark, having sided with France in the Napoleonic Wars, is among the losers and is forced by Sweden to cede Norway

1864: War with Prussia and Austria ends with the loss of Schleswig-Holstein, a third of Denmark's territory, to Prussia

1914-18: Denmark remains neutral in World War I

1920: Denmark's present southern border is established as northern Schleswig is recovered in a plebiscite

1940-45: Nazi troops invade Denmark and occupy country until its liberation by British forces in May 1945

1949: Denmark joins in forming NATO

1960: Denmark joins European Free Trade Association

1968: Social Democrats, Denmark's largest party, are ousted in general elections after 15 years in office

1972: King Frederik IX dies; is succeeded on the throne by Queen Margrethe II, Denmark's first reigning queen in six centuries

1973: Denmark joins the EEC

1974-75: Economic recession results in high unemployment

1976: Denmark negotiates largest foreign loan in its history

1978: Social Democratic prime Minister Anker Joergensen forms minority coalition with Liberals and others

1979: Greenland is granted autonomy

DJIBOUTI

Area: 8,880 sq. mi. **Population:** 250,000 (1978 est.)

Official Name: Republic of Djibouti **Capital:** Djibouti **Nationality:** Djibouti **Languages:** French is the official language; Somali (Issa) and Afar are spoken by their communities; Arabic **Religion:** Predominantly Sunni Moslem, with Christian minorities **Flag:** Horizontal stripes of light blue over green, with a red star on a white triangle at the hoist **Anthem:** N.A. **Currency:** Djibouti franc (178 per U.S. $1)

Location: Northeastern Africa, around the Gulf of Tadjoura at the western end of the Gulf of Aden, near the southern entrance to the Red Sea. Bordered on the north, west and southwest by Ethiopia, and on the southeast by Somalia **Features:** An arid rocky coastal plain (with salt and freshwater pans) fringed by foothills of the Ethiopian ranges, and an interior plateau in the north and west **Chief Rivers:** None

Head of State: President Hassan Gouled Aptidon, born 1916, assumed office June 1977 **Head of Government:** Premier Barkat Gourad Hamadou, appointed October 1978 **Effective Date of Present Constitution:** Not yet drafted **Legislative Body:** Parliament (unicameral Assembly), with 65 members (33 Issas, 30 Afars, 2 Arabs) elected for 5 years **Local Government:** 5 districts

Ethnic Composition: Somalis (chiefly Issas), Afars (including seasonal nomads), French, Arabs, Italians, Greeks, Sudanese and Indians **Population Distribution:** c. 65% urban **Density:** 28 inhabitants per sq. mi.

Largest City: (1977 est.) Djibouti 130,000

Per Capita Income: $1,727 (1978 est.) **Gross National Product (GNP):** $190 million (1978 est.) **Economic Statistics:** Derivation from GNP not available. An underdeveloped area, nomadic herding (goats, cattle, sheep, camels, donkeys) is the chief occupation in the hinterland. In the capital, shipbuilding, repair and servicing, construction, and the production of liquid gas and foodstuffs (bottling) are the chief activities **Minerals and Mining:** No production other than salt panning **Labor Force:** N.A. **Foreign Trade:** Exports (transit from Ethiopia), chiefly hides and skins, sugar, and Ethiopian coffee, totaled $20 million in 1973. Imports, chiefly machinery, fuels, steel products, chemicals, foods, and grain, totaled $74 million **Principal Trade Partners:** France, Ethiopia, Japan

Vital Statistics: Birthrate, 42 per 1,000 of pop. (1970); death rate, 7.6 **Life Expectancy:** N.A. **Health Statistics:** 107 inhabitants per hospital bed; 2,115 per physician (1975) **Infant Mortality:** N.A. **Illiteracy:** 90% **Education Statistics:** 34 primary and secondary schools, with a total enrollment of 11,464 (1974) **Enrollment in Higher Education:** N.A. **GNP Expended on Education:** 4.9% (1971)

Transportation: Surfaced roads total 118 mi. **Motor Vehicles:** 14,000 (1975) **Passenger Cars:** 11,000 **Railway Mileage:** 56 **Port:** Djibouti **Major Airlines:** Air France and five other lines provide international service; Air Djibouti, which also flies to Ethiopia, Yemen, Southern Yemen and Somalia, provides domestic service **Communications:** Government controlled **Radio Transmitters:** 4 (1974) **Receivers:** 15,000 (1976) **Television Transmitters:** 1 **Receivers:** 3,500 (1974) **Telephones:** 3,000 (1976) **Newspapers:** 1 several times a week, 34 copies per 1,000 inhabitants (1975)

Weights and Measures: Metric system **Travel Requirements:** Passport, visa

On June 27, 1977, the last remnant of France's once vast empire on the African continent achieved independence as the Republic of Djibouti.

During its first 83 years of existence, the dependency was known as French Somaliland, but in 1967 this small coastal area was renamed the French Territory of Afars and Issas, in recognition of the two major ethnic groups comprising the population. The Republic of Djibouti takes its name from its capital city, a Red Sea port with a majority of the nation's population.

Economic prospects for the Republic of Djibouti are not auspicious, as the barren tract, smaller in area than New Hampshire, lacks resources. The sole economic reason for the existence of the Republic is the commercial activity at the port of Djibouti, which is the terminus of the 486-mile railway from Addis Ababa, Ethiopia. The line carries half of Ethiopia's exports along its single track, and Djibouti is the transshipment point to the outer world for this trade. Out beyond the urban environment of the capital, the meager population subsists through nomadic herding.

The indigenous population is divided between the Afars, or Danakils, and the Issas, a branch of the Somali ethnic family. Though the two groups had disagreed in the past about the timing of independence, a majority of voters approved an independence proposal on May 8, 1977. France, by agreement, continues to maintain a military force in Djibouti.

In March Ethiopian forces, aided by 1,000 Soviet advisers, and 11,000 Cuban troops, ended the eight-month Ogaden war by driving the Somalis from the region—however, Ethiopia said there would be no cease-fire until Somalia formally renounced its territorial claims on the Ogaden, as well as on Djibouti and northern Kenya. Meanwhile, thousands of refugees have flooded Djibouti, thus placing greater strains on the fledgling nation. Further complicating matters in 1979 was the fighting between North and South Yemen. Showing its concern, Djibouti welcomed U.S. warships to its port in March.

HISTORY: French interest in the area began in the 1840s, culminating in the signing of friendship treaties with the local sultans. The purchase of the anchorage at Obock signalled the beginning of French occupation. The opening of the Suez Canal in 1869 and growing Anglo-French competition for territorial spoils in Africa caused France to expand its toehold to include all of the shores of the Gulf of Tadjoura

1884-85: The protectorate of French Somaliland is established

1896: The administrative capital is moved from Obock to Djibouti

1897-1917: The Franco-Ethiopian railway is built from Djibouti to Addis Ababa

1958: French Somaliland becomes an Overseas Territory of the French community

1967: In a referendum on independence, 60 percent of the voters choose to continue the ties with France. The area is renamed the French Territory of Afars and Issas

1977: Following a majority vote for independence, the independent Republic of Djibouti is proclaimed. Premier Ahmed Dini resigns after renewal of tensions between Afars and Issas

1978: Abdallay Mohamed Kamil appointed premier in February. In October, he is followed in office by Barkat Gourad Hamadou

DOMINICA

Area: 291 sq. mi. **Population:** 80,000 (1976 est.)

Official Name: Commonwealth of Dominica **Capital:** Roseau **Nationality:** Dominican **Languages:** English is the official language and is everywhere understood, but a patois, based on French and containing many African elements is widely spoken **Religion:** Mainly Roman Catholic; some Anglicans and Methodists **Flag:** A dark green field quartered by three equal vertical and horizontal stripes of yellow, white and black. In the center a large red disk bears a parrot surrounded by a circle of ten five-pointed stars **Anthem:** N.S. **Currency:** Dominican dollar (2.7 per U.S. $1)

Location: The island, located in the Windward Islands of the West Indies, lies between the French islands of Guadeloupe to the north and Martinique to the south. It is 20 miles long and 16 miles wide with a thickly forested mountainous terrain

Head of State: President L. A. Pinnard, assumed office June 1979 **Head of Government:** James Oliver Seraphine, appointed June 1979 **Effective Date of Present Constitution:** November 3, 1978 **Legislative Body:** House of Assembly (unicameral) with 21 elected representatives and 9 appointed senators **Local Government:** 2 town councils and 25 village councils

Ethnic Composition: Nearly all of the population is of African or mixed African-European origin. There is a small Carib Indian community **Density:** 275 inhabitants per sq. mi.

Largest Cities: (1976 est.) Roseau 16,800, Portsmouth 3,500

Per Capita Income: $460 (1976) **Gross National Product (GNP):** N.A. **Economic Statistics:** The economy is primarily agricultural, with bananas dominant. Citrus fruit and coconut production are also important. Industry and tourism are to be developed **Minerals and Mining:** None **Labor Force:** 25,150 (1976), primarily employed in agriculture **Foreign Trade:** Exports are chiefly bananas, grapefruit, lime juice, essential oils and coconuts; imports, chiefly foods, machinery and consumer goods **Principal Trade Partners:** Britain, United States, Canada, Caribbean nations

Vital Statistics: Birthrate, 21.8 per 1,000 of pop. (1977); death rate, 6.7 **Life Expectancy:** N.A. **Health Statistics:** 234 inhabitants per hospital bed (1973); 5,385 per physician (1971) **Infant Mortality:** 24.1 per 1,000 births (1977) **Illiteracy:** 41% **Education Statistics:** 60 primary and secondary schools (1975) **Enrollment in Higher Education:** N.A. **GNP Expended on Education:** N.A.

Transportation: Surfaced (paved) roads total 400 mi. **Motor Vehicles:** 4,000 (1975) **Passenger Cars:** N.A. **Railway Mileage:** None **Port:** Roseau **Major Airlines:** LIAT, Air Martinique and Air Guadeloupe provide service to neighboring islands **Communications:** Government and privately owned **Radio Transmitters:** 2 **Receivers:** N.A. **Television Transmitters:** 1 **Receivers:** N.A. **Telephones:** 4,000 (1976) **Newspapers:** 2 weeklies

Weights and Measures: British and metric systems

The northernmost of the Windward Islands, Dominica's pleasant climate and great natural beauty make it a haven for the sightseer, but its sparse, rocky soil makes life difficult for its predominantly black population, one of the poorest in the Caribbean.

Like many of its neighbors, one of the country's most urgent priorities since gaining independence in 1978 is the balanced development of the island's economy. Unemployment is chronic, over 20 percent, and agriculture is the mainstay of most islanders, with one crop—bananas—representing almost 80 percent of exports. Yet barely one-third of the arable land is cultivated, mainly due to the mountainous and heavily wooded terrain. Foreign aid has become increasingly important, with Britain being Dominica's chief benefactor since independence.

Since achieving nationhood, Dominica has tottered on the brink of civil turmoil, with islanders divided betweeen two political factions; the social-democratic Dominica Labor Party (DLP), headed since 1975 by Prime Minister Patrick R. John, which had pressed for independence by termination of the association with the United Kingdom, and the more conservative Dominica Freedom Party (DFP), led by Eugenia Charles, which had opposed independence except by referendum.

On May 29, 1979, amid charges of governmental corruption, anti-democratic moves and secret ties to South Africa, police fired on a demonstration of 15,000 in Roseau called to protest legislation curtailing press freedoms and banning the right to strike; two bystanders were killed. This sparked an island-wide general strike by all labor unions, which was joined by businessmen and opposition political figures demanding Prime Minister John's ouster. By June 20 John had resigned, succeeded by one of his Cabinet members, James Oliver Seraphine, who has promised reforms and pledged to bring John "to justice."

HISTORY: The warlike Carib Indians are thought to have migrated north from South America to the West Indies in the 1300s, capturing the islands from the more peaceful Arawaks. Columbus first sighted the island on a Sunday in 1493 (by tradition) and named it Dominica after the Latin for that day of the week. Permanent European occupation did not occur until the mid-eighteenth century, when the French established settlements along the coast. Since that time the island has changed hands three times: captured by the British in 1759, retaken by the French in 1778, and restored to Britain by the Treaty of Paris in 1783. With the abolition of the slave trade in 1834, restricted local government developed under British colonial administration

1871: Dominica and other British islands to the north are formed into a federation of the Leeward Islands

1940: Dominica transferred to jurisdiction of Windward Islands group, under same government as Grenada, St. Vincent and St. Lucia

1958: Dominica joins Federation of the West Indies; remains member until its dissolution in 1962

1960: Windward Islands Group dissolved; direct rule by Britain reestablished

1967: Dominica becomes self-governing member of the West Indies Associated States within British Commonwealth

1970: DLP led by Premier Edward O. LeBlanc wins first general election under Associated status

1974: Legislature approves emergency powers to combat "Dread" Black Power terrorist movement; Dominica joins Caribbean Community and Common Market (CARICOM)

1975: DLP under Patrick R. John, who succeeds LeBlanc, retains power in March 24 elections against opposition DFP

1978: Dominica becomes fully independent November 3, the second Associated State (following Grenada in 1974) to achieve nationhood; Dominica admitted as 151st member of United Nations

1979: Antigovernment demonstrations in Roseau May 29 fired on by police, sparking general strike that forces Prime Minister John to resign a month later. James Oliver Seraphine takes over as prime minister

DOMINICAN REPUBLIC

Area: 18,816 sq. mi. **Population:** 5,200,000 (1978 est.)

Official Name: Dominican Republic **Capital:** Santo Domingo **Nationality:** Dominican **Languages:** Spanish is the official and universal language **Religion:** About 95% of the people are Roman Catholic, the state religion **Flag:** Four rectangular sections divided by a white cross bearing the national coat of arms in the center; the upper left and lower right sections are dark blue and the other two sections are red **Anthem:** National Anthem, beginning "Brave men of Quisqueya" **Currency:** Dominican peso (1 per U.S. $1)

Location: West Indies, occupying the eastern two-thirds of the Island of Hispaniola. The Dominican Republic is bounded on the north by the Atlantic Ocean; on the east by the Mona Passage, which separates the country from Puerto Rico; on the south by the Caribbean Sea; and on the west by Haiti **Features:** The country is crossed by four east-west mountain ranges, the principal one being the Cordillera Central, which runs across the middle of the country. In the upper central part of the country lies the Cibao valley, often known as the nation's "food basket" **Chief Rivers:** Yaque del Norte, Jaina, Ozama, Yaque del Sur

Head of State and of Government: President Antonio Guzmán Fernández, born 1911, elected May 1978 to a 4-year term **Effective Date of Present Constitution:** November 28, 1966 **Legislative Body:** National Congress (bicameral), consisting of a 27-member Senate and a 91-member Chamber of Deputies, with members of both houses elected every 4 years by popular vote **Local Government:** 26 provinces and 1 national district, each headed by a governor appointed by the president

Ethnic Composition: 73% mulatto, 16% of European (chiefly Spanish) origin, 11% Negro **Population Distribution:** 43.5% urban (1973) **Density:** 276 inhabitants per sq. mi.

Largest Cities: (1970 census—Metropolitan Areas) Santo Domingo 802,619, Santiago 173,975, San Cristóbal 69,875, La Vega 64,370

Per Capita Income: $833 (1978 est.) **Gross National Product (GNP):** $4.4 billion (1978 est.) **Economic Statistics:** In 1973 about 23% of GNP came from agriculture (sugar, coffee, cocoa, tobacco, bananas); 35% from trade and services; 19% from manufacturing (sugar refining, processing of other food products, beverages, tobacco, chemicals) and mining; and 5% from construction **Minerals and Mining:** Bauxite, nickel, gold, silver and some iron ore are exploited **Labor Force:** 1.4 million (1977), with 55% in agriculture **Foreign Trade:** Exports, chiefly sugar, coffee, chocolate, tobacco, bauxite, and nickel, totaled $780 million in 1977. Imports, mainly wheat, vegetable oils, automobiles, tractors, and pharmaceutical products, totaled $848 million **Principal Trade Partners:** United States, Netherlands, West Germany, Venezuela, Japan, Morocco

Vital Statistics: Birthrate, 45.8 per 1,000 of pop. (1975); death rate, 11 **Life Expectancy:** 61 years **Health Statistics:** 351 inhabitants per hospital bed; 1,866 per physician (1973) **Infant Mortality:** 43.4 per 1,000 births (1974) **Illiteracy:** 33% **Education Statistics:** 5,245 primary and secondary schools, with combined enrollment of 984,039 (1973) **Enrollment in Higher Education:** 41,352 (1974) **GNP Expended on Education:** 2.6% (1973)

Transportation: Paved roads total 3,246 mi. **Motor Vehicles:** 116,700 (1976) **Passenger Cars:** 77,300 **Railway Mileage:** 1,062 **Ports:** Santo Domingo, Haina, Barahona, Puerto Plata, La Romana, San Pedro de Macorís **Major Airlines:** CDA, the national airline, provides internal and limited international services **Communications:** Partly government controlled **Radio Transmitters:** 146 **Receivers:** 200,000 (1976) **Television Transmitters:** 7 **Receivers:** 160,000 (1976) **Telephones:** 127,000 (1976) **Newspapers:** 10 dailies, 42 copies per 1,000 inhabitants (1975)

Weights and Measures: Metric system **Travel Requirements:** Passport, visa, tourist card valid for 15 days

With the possible exception of Cuba, the Dominican Republic has been the most disrupted Latin American country of this century. Its proximity—physically, historically, and economically—to the United States has produced two armed interventions ordered by Washington since 1916. In the years between 1930 and 1961, the country, which occupies the eastern two-thirds of the island of Hispaniola, lived under the oppression of Generalissimo Rafael Leonidas Trujillo Molina.

Since 1966 the Dominican Republic has enjoyed a measure of stability, thanks to improved economic planning and agrarian reform. With massive assistance from the United States and from international lending agencies, the country continues to be one of the most dynamic and stable nations in Latin America.

In May 1978, after 12 years in office, President Joaquín Balaguer was defeated in his bid for a fourth straight four-year term by Antonio Guzmán of the opposition Dominican Revolutionary Party (a centrist movement despite its misleadingly radical name). The election was marked by an armed intervention by Dominican troops who seized the electoral commission headquarters in Santo Domingo and stopped the ballot-count after a tally of a fourth of the votes showed Guzmán ahead by about a 3-to-2 margin. Several Latin American leaders spoke out against the action, as did President Carter, who threatened to cut off U.S. aid that includes a $38 million-a-year sugar-import program. At that point, Balaguer met with his generals, who may have acted without his consent, and (after some 30 hours) the counting resumed.

In his first state-of-the-nation speech, made in 1979, President Guzmán announced that agricultural development would be stressed in an effort to overcome a stagnant economy. And in its first venture into the Eurodollar market, the Dominican Republic signed a $185-million loan agreement with a group of international banks.

Memories of romantic earlier days were revived with the announcement that the Spanish galleon *Concepcion*, which sank in 1641, had been found in the waters off the Dominican Republic by Burt Webber, Jr., of Annville, Pa., a treasure hunter, in November 1978. The government is to get half the artifacts recovered, and it plans to build a museum to house them.

HISTORY: The eastern part of the island of Hispaniola was known in pre-Columbian times as Quisqueya and was first settled by Carib and Arawak Indians. The island was discovered by Columbus in 1492 and soon became the springboard for Spanish conquest of the Caribbean. The western third of Hispaniola (Haiti) was ceded to France in 1697, and in 1795 France acquired the eastern part, known as Santo Domingo. The French were expelled from the eastern region in 1809 and in 1814 it reverted to Spain

1821: Dominicans proclaim their independence and attempt to unite with the Republic of Gran Colombia, founded by Bolívar

1822: Dominicans are conquered by Haiti and the whole island of Hispaniola falls under oppressive Haitian rule

1844: Dominicans revolt against Haiti and regain independence; a republic is established under Pedro Santana

1861-69: Widespread revolts and continued attacks from Haiti lead Santana to place country under Spanish rule, but popular opposition forces Spain to withdraw (1865). Opposition leader Buenaventura Báez, who succeeds Santan, negotiates treaty calling for annexation of country to the United States; U.S. Senate, however, refuses to ratify it

1905-24: United States takes over administration of Dominican customs to forestall intervention by foreign powers seeking to collect their debts; following mounting disorders, the republic is occupied by U.S. forces in 1916 and remains under U.S. military rule until mid-1924

1930-61: Republic is ruled by dictator Rafael Leonidas Trujillo Molina, who is assassinated in 1961

1962-63: Juan Bosch, a leader of the democratic left, is elected president in republic's first free elections since 1924; after only seven months in office Bosch is overthrown by the military

1965: Civilian triumvirate installed by leaders of the 1963 coup is overthrown, precipitating civil war between left-wing forces seeking to restore Bosch and right-wing and military elements; U.S. troops intervene against pro-Bosch forces but fail to halt civil war, which ends after mediation by the OAS

1966: Joaquin Balaguer defeats Bosch for the presidency

1970: Balaguer is reelected president in a disputed election

1971: An attempted coup fails

1974-75: Balaguer is reelected to his third consecutive term as president. Antigovernment violence and general political uncertainty plague the country

1976: King Juan Carlos and Queen Sofia of Spain visit, the first ruling Spanish monarchs ever to set foot in Latin America

1978: Antonio Guzmán is elected president; ballot count is halted by troops, but is resumed after President Carter and several Latin American leaders publicly condemn action

1979: Hurricane David devastates republic

ECUADOR

Area: 109,483 sq. mi. **Population:** 7,300,000 (1978 est.)

Official Name: Republic of Ecuador **Capital:** Quito **Nationality:** Ecuadorean **Languages:** Spanish, the official language, is spoken by about 93% of the population, and Quechua by 7% **Religion:** Overwhelmingly Roman Catholic **Flag:** Half the width of the flag is yellow and the remaining half consists of blue and red bands; in the center is the national coat of arms **Anthem:** Hail, O Fatherland **Currency:** Sucre (25 per U.S. $1)

Location: South America. Crossed by the Equator, from which the country gets its name, Ecuador is bordered on the north by Colombia, on the east and south by Peru, and on the west by the Pacific Ocean. The Galápagos Islands, some 600 miles west of the mainland, are part of the national territory **Features:** About a fourth of the country consists of a coastal plain, and another fourth of the Sierra, or highlands, lying between two chains of the Andes Mountains. The Oriente, or eastern jungle, covers the remaining half of the country **Chief Rivers:** Guayas, Esmeraldas

Head of State and of Government: President Jaime Roldós Aguilera, born 1940, inaugurated August 10, 1979, for seven-year term **Effective Date of Present Constitution:** August 10, 1979 **Legislative Body:** Congress (unicameral) with 12 national and 57 provincial deputies **Local Government:** 20 provinces, each headed by an appointed governor

Ethnic Composition: 40% Indian, 40% mestizo, 10% of European (chiefly Spanish) origin, 10% African **Population Distribution:** 50% urban (1975) **Density:** 67 inhabitants per sq. mi.

Largest Cities: (1974 census) Guayaquil 814,064, Quito 597,133, Cuenca 104,667, Ambato 77,052, Machala 68,379

Per Capita Income: $678 (1978) **Gross National Product (GNP):** $5.3 billion (1978) **Economic Statistics:** In 1976 about 22% of GNP was derived from agriculture (bananas, coffee, cocoa, rice, sugar, cotton, grains, fruits and vegetables), forestry, and fishing; 16% from manufacturing (textiles, food processing, petroleum refining, cement) and mining; and 22% from trade and services **Minerals and Mining:** Petroleum is the primary mineral product. There are large deposits of calcium carbonate and copper; small quantities of gold are mined **Labor Force:** 2,400,000 (1978), of which 55% is employed in agriculture **Foreign Trade:** Exports, chiefly bananas, petroleum, coffee, and cocoa, totaled $1.2 billion in 1977. Imports, mainly machinery, transportation equipment, chemicals, and paper products, totaled $1.3 billion **Principal Trade Partners:** United States, West Germany, Japan, Britain, Italy, Colombia

Vital Statistics: Birthrate, 41.8 per 1,000 of pop. (1975); death rate, 9.5 **Life Expectancy:** 57 years **Health Statistics:** 495 inhabitants per hospital bed; 2,165 per physician (1973) **Infant Mortality:** 65.8 per 1,000 births **Illiteracy:** 23% **Education Statistics:** 9,777 primary and secondary schools, with combined enrollment of 1,646,624 (1975) **Enrollment in Higher Education:** 57,677 (1972) **GNP Expended on Education:** 3.2% (1971)

Transportation: Paved roads total 1,895 mi. **Motor Vehicles:** 112,000 (1974) **Passenger Cars:** 43,600 **Railway Mileage:** 726 **Ports:** Guayaquil, Puerto Bolívar, Manta, Bahía de Caráquez, Salinas, Esmeraldas **Major Airlines:** AREA and Ecuatoriana de Aviación operate internal and international flights **Communications:** Government and privately owned **Radio Transmitters:** 232 (1972) **Receivers:** 1,700,000 (1970) **Television Transmitters:** 19 **Receivers:** 300,000 (1976) **Telephones:** 202,000 (1976) **Newspapers:** 29 dailies, 49 copies per 1,000 inhabitants (1975)

Weights and Measures: Metric system; Spanish measures are also used **Travel Requirements:** Passport, migratory control card, onward ticket

Despite incredibly rich mineral and agricultural resources, Ecuador remains one of the least developed countries in South America—the result of sharp racial, geographic, and political differences.

Two-fifths of Ecuador's population is Indian—people held in low esteem by those of mixed blood, African heritage, and the small ruling élite of European background. Although many of the Indians retain their languages and customs, they have been stripped of the rest of their culture by four centuries of European domination.

Aside from the Indians in the Andean highlands and the Amazonian tribes in the east, most of the rest of Ecuador's people live along the western littoral that borders the Pacific Ocean. Mainly of mixed African/Indian/European background, the coastal people have a tropical culture that differs markedly from the highlanders.

In a further division, Ecuador is dominated by the mutual dislike of two "city-states"—Quito, the capital, and Guayaquil, the industrial port.

Some 9,300 feet above sea level in the Andes, long considered the most beautiful city in South America and certainly the cleanest, Quito is a conservative, gracious administrative center. Its residents look with distaste on the boisterous, tropical people of Guayaquil, who, for their part, resent their tax payments to the capital. Despite their industry and commercial aggressiveness, they say, the appalling slums of their city reflect the indifference of Quito.

Since petroleum exports started in 1972, there has been a spurt in overall economic development. The oil, which is pumped out of the Amazon jungles by Texaco and by the government oil company, CEPE, is Ecuador's No. 1 export. The banana trade, in which a long-term contract is held with the Del Monte company, is another large source of export revenue. The country is now accustomed to trade and balance-of-payments surpluses, and its inflation rate—just under 11% in 1978—is below the South American average.

In 1978 and 1979 the country held its first free national elections since the military seized power in 1972. First, in a referendum on Jan. 15, 1978, the voters chose a new constitution over a revision of the 1945 constitution. Then, on July 16, Jaime Roldós Aguilera, a law professor and a member of the Concentration of Popular Forces (CFP), led the first-round balloting for president. The military, wary because Roldós is a protégé of populist leader Assad Bucaram, delayed the final election for six months, but Roldós won handily in a two-party contest on April 29, 1979. There were fears that the military still would prevent his inauguration on August 10, but Admiral Alfred Poveda Burbano, the head of a three-man junta, declared on the day after the election: "August 10 will establish constitutional order and lead the way to stable institutions." Roldós was inaugurated with Rosalynn Carter in attendance.

HISTORY: Ecuador was ruled by the Incas until their empire fell to the Spanish conquistadors in 1533. Spanish rule, which lasted until the early 19th century, was marked by ruthless exploitation of the native Indians and bloody rivalry among the Spaniards

1822: Ecuador is freed from Spanish rule after Spanish forces are defeated at Battle of Pichincha; country becomes part of Greater Colombia, a confederation consisting of the present territories of Ecuador, Colombia, Panama, and Venezuela, constituted under the leadership of Simón Bolívar

1830-45: Federation is dissolved in 1830; Republic of Ecuador is proclaimed, with Juan José Flores as first president; his conservative dictatorial rule arouses liberal opposition

1861-75: Gabriel García Moreno rules as virtual dictator; he consolidates country after years of domestic strife and carries out major economic and social reforms, but his strong conservatism results in bitter strife that culminates in his assassination

1895-1912: Liberals dominate Ecuador's politics; separation of church and state is clearly defined, and basic personal freedoms are established

1913-44: Liberals continue to dominate political scene, but rival factions, supported by military juntas, bring about rapid changes in government

1948-52: Galo Plaza Lasso becomes president; his regime is marked by unprecedented political freedom

1961: President José María Velasco Ibarra is forced into exile; Vice-President Julio Arosemena Monroy succeeds as president

1963: Arosemena is ousted in military coup; a four-man military junta, headed by Rear Admiral Ramon Castro Jijon, takes over. Junta dissolves Congress, decrees martial law, suspends the constitution, and bans Communist Party

1968-69: In the first election held in seven years, Velasco Ibarra is elected president for fifth time as Ecuador experiences widespread economic and social unrest. Within eight months after taking office, president loses support of Liberal Party

1970: President Velasco assumes dictatorial powers

1971: U.S. imposes financial sanctions on Ecuador following seizure of U.S. tuna boats

1972: Brig. Gen. Guillermo Rodriguez Lara replaces Velasco Ibarra in bloodless military coup. Lara declares a "nationalist, military, and revolutionary government"

1974: President Lara suspends elections and other political activities for five years

1975: Seizure of American fishing boats continues. Gen. Raúl González Alvear leads unsuccessful revolt against Lara

1976: President Lara is overthrown in a bloodless coup led by armed forces commanders, who form a military junta

1977: Ecuadorean government buys the local assets of Gulf Oil Corp. of the U.S., giving the government a 62.5 percent share in Ecuador's petroleum operations

1978: Elections held to choose new president; Jaime Roldós Aguilera is leader in first round

1979: In a run-off that had been delayed by the military for six months, Roldós wins the presidency and is inaugurated on Aug. 10

EGYPT

Area: 386,659 sq. mi. **Population:** 38,900,000 (1978 est.)

Official Name: Arab Republic of Egypt **Capital:** Cairo **Nationality:** Egyptian **Languages:** Arabic is the official and national language **Religion:** About 90% of the population is Sunni Moslem and Islam is the state religion; about 7% belongs to the Coptic Church (perhaps as high as 18%) **Flag:** Red, white, and black horizontal stripes with a golden hawk and Arabic inscription on the white stripe **Anthem:** National Anthem, beginning "The Time Has Come to Reach for Our Arms" **Currency:** Egyptian pound (0.70 per U.S. $1)

Location: Northeast Africa. Egypt is bordered on the north by the Mediterranean Sea; on the east by Israel and the Red Sea; on the south by the Sudan; and on the west by Libya **Features:** About 95% of the country is desert, with only the Nile Valley and delta, and a few oases, under cultivation **Chief River:** Nile

Head of State: President Anwar Sadat, born 1918, reelected for 6 years in 1976 **Head of Government:** Prime Minister Mustafa Khalil, appointed in 1978 **Effective Date of Present Constitution:** 1971 **Legislative Body:** People's Assembly (unicameral), consisting of 392 members **Local Government:** 25 governorates headed by governors appointed by the president

Ethnic Composition: The homogeneous population is mainly Hamitic **Population Distribution:** 44.6% urban (1975) **Density:** 101 inhabitants per sq. mi.; inhabitable areas 2,630.7

Largest Cities: (1975 est.) Cairo 8,500,000; (1974 est.) Alexandria 2,259,000, Giza 853,700, Suez 368,000

Per Capita Income: $394 (1978 est.) **Gross National Product (GNP):** $16 billion (1978) **Economic Statistics:** 30% of GNP comes from agriculture (cotton, wheat, corn, rice); 22% from industry (food processing, textiles, petroleum and petroleum products, iron and steel manufactures, chemicals) and mining; 25% from services; 19% from trade and finance **Minerals and Mining:** Petroleum is the chief mineral resource; others are phosphate, iron ore, salt, manganese, and limestone **Labor Force:** 12,700,000 (1977), of which 44% is in agriculture, 13% in industry, 24% in services **Foreign Trade:** Exports, chiefly cotton and cotton goods, rice, crude oil, and oil products, totaled $2.1 billion in 1977. Imports, mainly wheat, petroleum, industrial machinery, vehicle parts, and edible oils, totaled $5.3 billion **Principal Trade Partners:** USSR, EC countries, United States, East Germany, Japan, Czechoslovakia, Greece

Vital Statistics: Birthrate, 37.7 per 1,000 of pop. (1977); death rate, 11.8 **Life Expectancy:** 54 years **Health Statistics:** 464 inhabitants per hospital bed; 1,516 per physician (1973) **Infant Mortality:** 101.3 per 1,000 births **Illiteracy:** 57% **Education Statistics:** 10,005 primary and secondary schools, with combined enrollment of 6,128,206 (1974) **Enrollment in Higher Education:** 408,235 **GNP Expended on Education:** 5.8% (1975)

Transportation: Paved roads total 8,078 mi. **Motor Vehicles:** 303,000 (1976) **Passenger Cars:** 245,600 **Railway Mileage:** 4,200 **Ports:** Alexandria, Port Said, Suez, Mersa Matruh, Safaga **Major Airlines:** Egypt Air operates internal and international services **Communications:** Government owned **Radio Transmitters:** 43 (1973) **Receivers:** 5,250,000 (1976) **Television Transmitters:** 28 (1977) **Receivers:** 1,300,000 (1977) **Telephones:** 503,000 (1974) **Newspapers:** 14 dailies, 21 copies per 1,000 inhabitants (1974)

Weights and Measures: Metric system is official but various local units are also used **Travel Requirements:** (1971) Passport, visa good for stay up to 1 month, $3.00 contribution to save Nubian monuments

For Egypt, recent years have brought one pressing challenge after another: adjustments to the death of President Gamal Abdel Nasser, fateful decisions on war or peace with Israel, conspiracies against President Anwar el-Sadat, friendship with the United States at the expense of Soviet-Egyptian amity, and relentless economic problems.

Added to these challenges are the realities of Egypt's difficulties as the most populous country in the Arab world and the second most populous on the African continent, with 99 percent of its people compressed into 3.5 percent of its area.

President Sadat, who had been a leading figure in the 1952 revolution led by Nasser against King Farouk, quickly emerged as an unexpectedly strong president in the "collective leadership" that succeeded Nasser. He won support by curbing arbitrary police procedures and surveillance, calling for a society based on "the sovereignty of law," and outlining a program for accelerated economic development.

Egypt's economic problems are extensive and resistant to ready solutions. There are few natural resources, limited cultivable land and investment funds; in addition, bureaucracies are swollen with unproductive workers. Unemployment and inflation are rising, and illiteracy is 57%. The increasing number of university-trained graduates have little prospect for professional advancement.

To present a more progressive image while dealing with these economic difficulties, Sadat has implemented limited political reforms, including an upgrading of the People's Assembly. In late 1976, he announced that he would allow the formation of independent political parties, which had been banned since 1953, when the Arab Socialist Union was made the only legal political organization. Three parties were subsequently formed, but in 1978, new restrictions on them were enacted.

The peace treaty with Israel, signed in 1979, calls for Israel's phased withdrawal from Sinai within three years; withdrawal from the Sinai oil fields is to occur within 1979. The treaty binds Egypt to sell oil to Israel, and other exports to Israel are likely. Such trade, renewed control over oil, increases in United States aid (previously $900 million a year), and reduced military needs should help Egypt economically. But peace has provoked a movement among Arab states to isolate Egypt—long a leader among them. Most of the Arab foreign ministers met at Baghdad and called for an end to all diplomatic and economic relations and mapped the strategy which led to the suspension of Egypt from several Arab organizations. Despite these actions, Sadat was confident of domestic support. He submitted the treaty to a referendum, which approved it overwhelmingly, then dissolved Parliament and authorized parties other than the dissolved Arab Socialist Union to contest seats in the new Parliament.

The treaty was the result of 14 months of difficult negotiations, which began in 1977, when President Sadat visited Israel and Israeli Prime Minister Menachem Begin returned the visit. After this dramatic opening, Palestinian raids on

Israel, Israeli strikes at Palestinians in southern Lebanon, and arguments about the future of Palestinian territory slowed the negotiations. United States officials, including President Jimmy Carter, helped at crucial times to prevent a rupture, and promised U.S. aid.

HISTORY: The history of Egypt dates back about 5,000 years. The country was united into a single kingdom about 3200 B.C. and was ruled by a succession of dynasties down to the time of Alexander the Great, who conquered Egypt in 332 B.C. Less than three centuries later, the country was under Roman rule. In 616, Egypt was conquered by the Persians before being invaded by the Arabs, who introduced Islam

1517: Egypt becomes part of the Ottoman Empire

1798: Napoleon conquers Egypt

1801-5: British and Turkish troops drive out the French; Mohammed Ali, an Albanian soldier, is appointed Egyptian pasha

1869: The Suez Canal is completed

1914: Egypt becomes a British protectorate

1936: Britain agrees to withdraw eventually from all of Egypt, except the Suez Canal Zone

1940-42: British forces use Egypt as a base to fight Italy and Germany in World War II

1948-49: Egypt plays major role in war between Arab states and the newly established state of Israel, but suffers humiliating defeats; war ends with an armistice

1952: King Farouk is deposed in army coup

1953-54: A republic is proclaimed, with Gen. Mohammed Naguib as president; Naguib is forced out of office and replaced by Col. Gamal Abdel Nasser

1956: Nasser nationalizes Suez Canal. Israel, barred from the canal, invades the Gaza Strip and the Sinai peninsula; England and France attack Egypt. Forces of all three invading countries are forced to withdraw under pressure from the United States, the USSR and the United Nations

1958: Egypt and Syria form the United Arab Republic (U.A.R.)

1961: Syrian army revolts and proclaims Syria's withdrawal from U.A.R.

1962: Egypt sends troops to Yemen to aid a republican revolution

1967: In the Six-Day War with Israel, Egypt loses the entire Sinai peninsula and the Gaza Strip, which are occupied by Israeli armies; Egypt withdraws its troops from Yemen

1968: Widespread student riots break out in protest against Nasser regime, which is accused of police-state rule. Egyptian and Israeli troops engage in repeated artillery duels along Suez Canal

1970: Egypt agrees to U.S.-sponsored truce with Israel as step toward peace talks; talks are stalled after Israel charges truce is being violated by the installation of Soviet-built missiles in the Suez Canal zone. Nasser dies of heart attack and is succeeded by Vice President Anwar el-Sadat

1971: Sadat allows cease-fire with Israel to lapse but defers warfare. Conspiracy against Sadat erupts; six cabinet members, Vice President Aly Sabry, and dozens of others are arrested. New constitution approved by national referendum

1972: Dr. Aziz Sidky replaces Dr. Mahmoud Fawzi as premier. President Sadat orders the departure of all Soviet military advisers (about 10,000) and their replacement by Egyptian personnel

1973: Sadat forces Sidky to resign, assumes premiership himself; Egypt launches an attack across the Suez Canal, beginning the fourth Arab-Israeli War. The Arabs attack on Yom Kippur, the holiest day of the year for Jews. It takes several days for the Israelis to mobilize, but they soon outmaneuver the Arab armies. Iraq, Tunisia, Morocco, and other Arab countries send troops to aid Egypt and Syria. Egypt and Israel negotiate ceasefire

1974: President Sadat changes the date of Egypt's national holiday from July 23 to October 6 to commemorate the onset of the Yom Kippur War; Sadat relinquishes the office of premier and appoints Abdul Aziz Hegazy in his place

1975: Premier Hegazy resigns and is replaced by Mamdouh Salem. The Suez Canal, closed since 1967, reopens. With the assistance of U.S. Secretary of State Kissinger, Egypt and Israel agree on removal of troops in the Sinai Peninsula. American Congress approves of U.S. civilian presence in Sinai to supervise electronic early warning stations

1976: Egyptian Parliament approves of President Sadat's proposal to end 15-year Treaty of Friendship and Cooperation with the USSR; Saudi Arabia, Kuwait, Qatar and the United Arab Emirates establish the Gulf Authority for Egyptian Development with a capital of $2 billion. Sadat is elected to a second six-year term

1977: Egyptian and Libyan forces clash along desert border. President Sadat launches peace initiative; he and Israeli Premier Begin trade historic visits

1978: Peace talks bog down as Israeli troops enter southern Lebanon following Palestinian terror raid in Israel. Diplomatic relations with Cyprus severed after Cypriot troops kill 15 Egyptian commandos who were storming jet at Larnaca Airport in which Palestinian terrorists held 16 hostages. Egypt to get 50 F-5E fighter-bombers from the U.S. National referendum gives Sadat mandate to carry out proposals for curtailing political dissent, "to protect the home front and social peace"

1979: Egypt and Israel sign peace treaty, calling for phased Israeli withdrawal from Sinai within three years, withdrawal from oil fields in 1979. Representatives of most Arab states meet in Baghdad and agree to isolate Egypt. Egypt is suspended from several Arab organizations. Referendum in Egypt approves treaty. Sadat dissolves Parliament, authorizes new parties to seek seats in new Parliament. Sadat's National Democratic Party wins overwhelming victory in June election

---

EL SALVADOR

Area: 8,260 sq. mi. **Population:** 4,400,000 (1978 est.)

Official Name: Republic of El Salvador **Capital:** San Salvador **Nationality:** Salvadorean **Languages:** Spanish is the official and predominant language; a small number of Indians still speak Nahuatl **Religion:** Overwhelmingly Roman Catholic **Flag:** Blue, white, and blue horizontal stripes, with the national coat of arms centered on the white stripe **Anthem:** National Anthem, beginning "We proudly hail thee, motherland" **Currency:** Salvadorean colón (2.5 per U.S. $1)

Location: Central America. El Salvador is bordered on the north, northeast, and east by Honduras, on the south and southwest by the Pacific Ocean, and on the west and northwest by Guatemala **Features:** Mountain ranges running east to west divide the country into a narrow Pacific coastal belt on the south; a subtropical central region of valleys and plateaus, where most of the population lives; and a mountainous northern region **Chief Rivers:** Lempa, Grande de San Miguel

Head of State and of Government: President: Gen. Carlos Humberto Romero Mena, born 1924, assumed office July 1977 **Effective Date of Present Constitution:** 1962 **Legislative Body:** National Assembly (unicameral), consisting of 54 members elected by popular vote every 2 years **Local Government:** 14 departments, each headed by a governor appointed by the president

Ethnic Composition: 89% mestizo (of mixed European—mainly Spanish—and Indian descent); the rest consists of small minorities of European and of Indian ancestry **Population Distribution:** 41.9% urban (1975) **Density:** 533 inhabitants per sq. mi.

Largest Cities: (1973 est.) San Salvador 368,000; (1971 census) Santa Ana 96,306, San Miguel 59,304

Per Capita Income: $705 (1978 est.) **Gross National Product (GNP):** $3.1 billion (1978 est.) **Economic Statistics:** In 1973 about 27% of GNP was from agriculture (coffee, cotton, sugar, rice, livestock); and 19% from industry (food processing, textiles, shoes, chemicals) **Minerals and Mining:** Substantial deposits of quartz, diatomaceous earth, kaolin, gypsum, limestone, and pumice **Labor Force:** 1,538,200 (1975), with 47% in agriculture and 8% in industry (1970) **Foreign Trade:** Exports, chiefly coffee, cotton, shrimp, sugar, cottonseed cakes, and cotton fabric, totaled $721 million in 1976. Imports, mainly transport equipment, chemical products, fuels and lubricants, raw materials, industrial machinery, and consumer goods, totaled $691 million **Principal Trade Partners:** United States, Latin America, Japan

Vital Statistics: Birthrate, 41.7 per 1,000 of pop. (1977); death rate, 7.5 **Life Expectancy:** 64 years **Health Statistics:** 563 inhabitants per hospital bed (1975); 3,592 per physician (1974) **Infant Mortality:** 55.2 per 1,000 births (1976) **Illiteracy:** 38% **Education Statistics:** 3,346 primary and secondary schools, with combined enrollment of 763,325 (1975) **Enrollment in Higher Education:** 26,069 **GNP Expended on Education:** 3.6% (1973)

Transportation: Paved roads total 773 mi. **Motor Vehicles:** 61,000 (1974) **Passenger Cars:** 41,000 **Railway Mileage:** 432 **Ports:** La Unión (Cutuco), Acajutla, La Libertad **Major Airlines:** TACA operates internal and international flights **Communications:** Partly government controlled **Radio Transmitters:** 65 **Receivers:** 1,400,000 (1976) **Television Transmitters:** 3 **Receivers:** 136,000 (1976) **Telephones:** 60,000 (1976) **Newspapers:** 12 dailies, 51 copies per 1,000 inhabitants (1974)

Weights and Measures: Metric system is official but various local units are also used **Travel Requirements:** Proof of citizenship for issuance of tourist card on arrival

---

As the most densely populated country on the entire American mainland, El Salvador has long aroused suspicions of expansionism among its neighbors, particularly Honduras, which has had up to 600,000 immigrant Salvadoreans among its populace. The constant pressure of too many people for El Salvador's diminutive land area has led to frequent border clashes with Honduras and, in July 1969, to a four-day war. In late 1976, an agreement was signed between the two countries providing for mediation by a third country in this recurrent, and often violent, dispute.

Much of the populace of this agriculturally-based economy is poverty-stricken, living on small plots of land owned by a few controlling families. Social reform is seen by the oligarchy as a communist concept to give political power to peasants.

Violence erupted immediately after the disputed 1977 election won by Gen. Carlos Humberto Romero. Three leftist guerrilla groups emerged, and they have bombed, killed police, and kidnapped foreign business executives, raising about $30 million through ransoms in two years. The virulently anti-leftist government responded with its own repressive tactics; in 1979 the Inter-American Commission on Human Rights accused it of murdering political opponents, torturing citizens in secret jails, and persecuting the Roman Catholic Church.

On May 9, 1979, the violence reached a new peak with the slaying of at least 24 persons at the Metropolitan Cathedral in downtown San Salvador. The deaths occurred as columns of national police opened fire upon members of the Popular Revolutionary Bloc (BPR) demonstrating on the cathedral steps. The 30,000-member BPR—a seven-group peasant-labor coalition but not a gurerrilla group—organized a funeral procession of 20,000 marchers the next day. To call attention to the holding of political prisoners, the BPR also occupied six other churches and the French and Venezuelan embassies in San Salvador in May. Fourteen protesters were killed by troops in front of the Venezuelan embassy on May 22.

HISTORY: El Salvador was the home of the Pipil Indians before the arrival of Pedro de Alvarado, who conquered the country for Spain in the 1520s. Until its independence in the 19th century, El Salvador was administered as part of the captaincy general of Guatemala

1821: El Salvador and the other Central American countries gain independence from Spain and are annexed to Mexico

1824-39: Central American countries withdraw from Mexico and establish the Central American Federation; the union is dissolved in 1839

1841-56: El Salvador's independence is decreed in January 1841; a republic is formally proclaimed in 1856

1931-44: General Maximiliano Hernández Martínez seizes power

1945-61: Nation is wracked by political instability as governments rise and fall in numerous coups d'état; in 1961 a civilian-military directorate is formed

1962-67: A new constitution is promulgated and Lt. Col. Adalberto Rivera is elected president; during his term nation's currency is stabilized, an income tax is introduced, and pro-labor laws are passed. In 1967 Col. Fidel Sánchez Hernández is elected president

1968: Government's National Conciliation party suffers setback as reform-minded Christian Democrats score gains in legislative and municipal elections

1969: El Salvador wages brief war with Honduras, the underlying cause of which is immigration of Salvadoreans into Honduras. OAS mediation helps end fighting

1970: El Salvador and Honduras agree to set up demilitarized zone along border

1973: Peace talks break down and border disputes resume

1977: Violent unrest grips the country after Gen. Carlos Humberto Romero wins the presidency amid charges of fraud

1978: Scores die as widespread unrest continues

1979: Twenty-four persons are killed on the steps of the Metropolitan Cathedral in San Salvador as national police fire into a Popular Revolutionary Bloc protest

EQUATORIAL GUINEA

Area: 10,831 sq. mi. **Population:** 330,000 (1978 est.)
Official Name: Republic of Equatorial Guinea **Capital:** Malabo **Nationality:** Equatorial Guinean **Languages:** Spanish is the official language. On the mainland Fang is spoken, while the principal local language on Macías Nguema Biyogo island is Bubi **Religion:** About 60 percent of the population is Roman Catholic, the rest chiefly animists, with a small number of Moslems **Flag:** Green, white, and red horizontal stripes, with a blue triangle joining them at the staff side; in the center is the national coat of arms **Anthem:** National Anthem, beginning "Let's walk through the jungle of our immense happiness" **Currency:** ekuele (68.2 U.S. $1)

Location: West Africa. Equatorial Guinea consists of 2 areas: the mainland—Río Muni (Mbini), bordered by Cameroon on the north, Gabon on the east and south, and the Atlantic Ocean on the west; and Macías Nguema Biyogo (Fernando Po), consisting of the main island of that name, Pagalu, and other small islands **Features:** There are 2 large volcanic formations on the main island, separated by a valley which crosses the island from east to west at its narrowest point. Río Muni consists of a coastal plain, and a series of valleys separated by low hills and spurs of the Crystal Mountains **Chief Rivers:** Benito, Muni, Campo

Head of State and of Government: President (Francisco) Masie Nguema Biyogo Negue Ndong, born 1924, elected October 1968, and made president for life in 1972. In early Aug. 1979, it was reported that President Masie had been overthrown in a coup, and had been replaced by a military junta, the Revolutionary Military Council, led by Masie's nephew, Lt. Col. Teodoro Obiang Nguema Mbazago **Effective Date of Present Constitution:** July 1973 **Legislative Body:** National Assembly (unicameral), consisting of 60 deputies elected for 5-year terms **Local Government:** 2 provinces

Ethnic Composition: On Macías Nguema Biyogo the aboriginal Bubis are the major ethnic group; others include the descendants of liberated slaves. In Río Muni the main tribes are the Fang, Kombe, and Bujeba **Population Distribution:** 15% urban **Density:** 30 inhabitants per sq. mi.

Largest Cities: (1973 est.) Malabo 60,000, Bata 30,000

Per Capita Income: $312 (1978) **Gross National Product (GNP):** $100 million (1978) **Economic Statistics:** Production is predominantly agricultural, although forestry and fishing are also important. High-grade cocoa, coffee, bananas, and palm oil are the main crops. There is little industry **Minerals and Mining:** Geological surveys have raised hopes for the eventual discovery of petroleum; uranium deposits have been found and there are indications of iron ore **Labor Force:** More than 95% of the working population is engaged in agriculture **Foreign Trade:** Exports, chiefly cocoa, wood, and coffee, totaled $42.7 million in 1974. Imports, principally foodstuffs, building materials, petroleum products, textiles, motor vehicles, and pharmaceutical products, totaled $21.6 million **Principal Trade Partners:** Spain, United States, Britain, West Germany, France

Vital Statistics: Birthrate, 36.8 per 1,000 of pop. (1975); death rate 19.7 **Life Expectancy:** 43.5 years **Health Statistics:** 171 inhabitants per hospital bed (1967); 62,000 per physician (1975) **Infant Mortality:** 53.2 per 1,000 births **Illiteracy:** 60% **Education Statistics:** 559 primary and secondary schools, with combined enrollment of 41,477 (1973) **Enrollment in Higher Education:** N.A. **GNP Expended on Education:** N.A.

Transportation: Surfaced roads total 94 mi. **Motor Vehicles:** about 1,000 **Passenger Cars:** N.A. **Railway Mileage:** None **Ports:** Malabo, Bata **Major Airlines:** Iberia Airlines provides an international service **Communications:** State controlled **Radio Transmitters:** 2 **Receivers:** 80,000 (1976) **Television:** None **Telephones:** 1,451 (1969) **Newspapers:** 1 daily, 3 copies per 1,000 inhabitants

Weights and Measures: Metric system **Travel Requirements:** Passport, visa

One of the smallest of Africa's nations, Equatorial Guinea gained independence from Spain in 1968. Since then, the country has experienced repressive rule by President Masie Nguema Biyogo Negue Ndong, along with economic deterioration.

While severing all ties with Spain and taking a sharply anti-Western stance, President Masie has welcomed new links with Communist China and North Korea. He has also maintained relations with the Soviet Union.

Equatorial Guinea consists chiefly of the island of Macías Nguema Biyogo (Fernando Po), site of the capital, Malabo, and, 100 miles to the southeast, the larger area of Río Muni, a square of land between Cameroon and Gabon.

The island people of Macías Nguema Biyogo, until recently more prosperous, include the native

Bubis; Fernandinos, descendants of freed African slaves; Nigerians, who have been contract laborers on cocoa plantations; and a number of Europeans.

The poorer, majority mainland people, the Fangs, have looked to independence and the leadership of President Masie, a Fang, to improve their lot, a hope as yet unmaterialized.

Europeans, mainly Spanish and Portuguese, who ran the high-quality cocoa plantations, coffee and lumber production, and other businesses, numbered 7,000 in 1968. But with increasing physical terrorism by government and a youth movement, the Juventud, only a few hundred Europeans now remain in the country. In January 1978 there were reports that thousands of people have been executed by the Masie regime.

A broadcast from Equatorial Guinea reported that President Masie had been overthrown in a coup on August 3, 1979. The report stated that Masie had been replaced by a Revolutionary Military Council, led by his nephew, Lieut. Col. Teodoro Obiang Nguema Mbazago.

HISTORY: Equatorial Guinea's island province of Fernando Po was discovered in the late 15th century by the Portuguese explorer Fernão do Po. It was ceded to Spain, along with mainland trading rights, in 1778. In the early 19th century, the island port of Santa Isabel was leased for a time to the British, who made it a naval base and refuge for freed slaves. Not until the 20th century did Spain actively begin administering and developing the colony, known as Spanish Guinea

1958-60: Spain makes colony a Spanish province, grants inhabitants Spanish citizenship and representation in Cortés

1963-64: Colony is renamed Equatorial Guinea; limited self-government is instituted

1968: After numerous appeals to United Nations and long negotiations, Equatorial Guinea becomes an independent republic

1969: Rivalry between the continental and island portions results in serious riots. President Masie assumes dictatorial powers, purges opposition leaders

1973: Equatorial Guinea becomes a unitary state under a new constitution, ending the autonomy of the provinces

1979: President Masie is reportedly deposed in coup

ETHIOPIA

Area: 471,776 sq. mi. **Population:** 29,400,000 (1978 est.)

Official Name: Ethiopia **Capital:** Addis Ababa **Nationality:** Ethiopian **Languages:** Amharic is the official and predominant language; English is frequently used. Arabic is spoken by about one-third of the population; other spoken languages are Gallinya, Tigrinya, Ge'ez, and Italian **Religion:** About 40% of the population belongs to the established Ethiopian Orthodox (Coptic Christian) Church; 40% is Moslem and the rest animist **Flag:** Green, yellow, and red horizontal stripes **Anthem:** National Anthem, beginning "Let Ethiopia be joyous!" **Currency:** Birr (2.07 per U.S. $1)

Location: Eastern Africa. Ethiopia is bordered on the north by the Sudan and the Red Sea, on the east by Djibouti and Somalia, on the south by Kenya, and on the west by the Sudan **Features:** The center of the country consists of a high, partly mountainous plateau cut by numerous rivers and split diagonally by the Rift Valley. The terrain gradually slopes to lowlands in the west and to a plains region in the southeast **Chief Rivers:** Shibeli, Abbai (Blue Nile), Ganale Dorya, Awash, Omo

Head of State and of Government: Lt. Col. Mengistu Haile-Mariam, named chairman of the Provisional Military Administrative Council (Dergue) in 1977 **Effective Date of Present Constitution:** 1955 (suspended) **Legislative Body:** The bicameral National Assembly was dissolved in 1974. All decisions are made by the Dergue **Local Government:** 14 provinces

Ethnic Composition: The Amharas and the Tigreans are of Semitic origin and make up 37% of the population; the Gallas, a Hamitic people, account for 40%. There are also numerous mixed, Negroid, and other groups, including the Falashas, or so-called "Black Jews," Sidamas, Somalis, and Yemenite Arabs, as well as some 30,000 Europeans, chiefly Italians **Population Distribution:** 11.7% urban (1975) **Density:** 62 inhabitants per sq. mi.

Largest Cities: (1975 est.) Addis Ababa 1,161,267, Asmara 317,950; (1972 est.) Dire Dawa 63,700, Dessye 49,750, Harar 48,440

Per Capita Income: $114 (1978 est.) **Gross National Product (GNP):** $3.4 billion (1978) **Economic Statistics:** About 48% of GNP comes from agriculture (coffee, cotton, corn, sugar, wheat, sorghum, oilseeds, pulses) and livestock raising; 5% from indus-

try (textiles, food processing, building materials, printing, leather, chemicals); and 8% from trade **Minerals and Mining:** Limited output of gold, platinum, salt, iron, and manganese ore. Deposits of potash, copper, nickel, and asbestos have been discovered **Labor Force:** 11,300,000 (1971), with some 86% engaged in subsistence agriculture **Foreign Trade:** Exports, chiefly coffee, hides and skins, oilseeds, and pulses, totaled $241 million in 1975. Imports, mainly machinery and transport equipment, textiles, yarns and fabrics, foodstuffs, building materials, and petroleum products, totaled $378 million **Principal Trade Partners:** United States, West Germany, Saudi Arabia, Italy, Japan, Britain, Djibouti

Vital Statistics: Birthrate, 49.4 per 1,000 of pop. (1975); death rate, 25.8 **Life Expectancy:** 38 years **Health Statistics:** 3,081 inhabitants per hospital bed; 73,314 per physician (1972) **Infant Mortality:** 84.2 per 1,000 births **Illiteracy:** 94% **Education Statistics:** 2,759 primary and secondary schools, with combined enrollment of 1,150,194 (1973) **Enrollment in Higher Education:** 6,474 **GNP Expended on Education:** 2.5% (1974)

Transportation: Paved roads total about 1,000 mi. **Motor Vehicles:** 66,600 (1976) **Passenger Cars:** 52,500 **Railway Mileage:** 680 **Ports:** Massawa, Assab; a substantial portion of Ethiopia's trade moves through Djibouti **Major Airlines:** Ethiopian Airlines, the government line, operates domestic and international services **Communications:** State controlled **Radio Transmitters:** 8 (1975) **Receivers:** 210,000 (1976) **Television Transmitters:** 8 (1975) **Receivers:** 21,000 (1976) **Telephones:** 73,000 (1976) **Newspapers:** 8 dailies, 2.5 copies per 1,000 inhabitants (1975)

Weights and Measures: Metric system is official but traditional units are also used **Travel Requirements:** Passport; visa, $4.85, valid 30 days, 3 photos

The 44-year reign of Emperor Haile Selassie ended September 12, 1974, when a group of army officers completed a process which months before had begun to strip the emperor of most of his powers. This Provisional Military Administrative Council (PMAC) or *Dergue* removed him and installed his son, Asfa Wossen, 57, as a figurehead king. And in March 1975 a proclamation ended the monarchy, annulling the Crown Prince's appointment.

Since he became emperor in 1930, the Lion of Judah had promoted economic innovation and political reform, but progress was slow. Strong resistance came from farmers, aristocratic landowners and the Coptic Church, which owns about a third of all land in a country where agriculture is a livelihood for 86 percent of the population.

Civilian rioting and strikes protesting soaring prices, unemployment, and the government's mismanagement of relief efforts dealing with the country's drought and famine undermined Selassie's power. What finally led to his downfall was the cover-up of the 1973 famine, which caused the deaths of over 100,000 peasants.

In February 1974 an army mutiny forced Selassie's cabinet to resign. Selassie sought to maintain control of the country by naming a new premier, Endalkachew Makonnen, installing a new cabinet, and raising army wages. Meanwhile, Ethiopia remained under military control.

In March, Selassie agreed to call a constitutional convention that could lead to a replacement of his absolute monarchy by a more democratic form of government. Finally, in September, came the coup which ousted him. He died in 1975.

A turning point for the ruling PMAC came in November 1974 when its members voted to execute 60 Ethiopians, including their chairman, Lt. Gen. Aman Michael Andom. These executions solidified the powers of Maj. Mengistu Haile-Mariam, the First Deputy Chairman, and Lt. Col. Atnafu Abate, the Second Deputy Chairman, while the chairman of the Military Council, Brig. Gen. Teferi Bante, remained a figurehead. In February 1977 Bante and six other members of the *Dergue* were killed in a shootout.

With Lt. Col. Mengistu now in control of one of the most brutal and arbitrary regimes in power today, Ethiopia's secretive council has turned into a one-man dictatorship. Among the problems Mengistu faces are the implementation of the land reform program ending 2,000 years of feudalism, domestic dissidence (especially that of the Ethiopian People's Revolutionary Party) and the consolidation of the "Socialist revolution."

Under his rule the government is taking a harder and more violent path in dealing with its enemies, both in and outside the country. Among the regime's enemies in arms are three different forces of Eritrean guerrillas fighting for the past 17 years for independence of the northernmost province, containing Ethiopia's entire 540-mile Red Sea coastline; a right-wing army of exiles loyal to the era of Haile Selassie that has made gains in the provinces of Gojjam and Gondar; Somali irrendentists along the Somali frontier; and guerrillas who control one-third of Tigre province.

In March 1978 Ethiopian forces, aided by some 16,000 Cuban troops and 1,500 Soviet military advisers, ended the eight-month Ogaden War by driving the Somalis from the region—however Ethiopia has said there can be no lasting peace in the region until Somalia renounces its territorial claims on the Ogaden, Djibouti and northern Kenya, and pays compensation for damages caused in the war. In May, again with Cuban and Soviet help, Ethiopia launched its long-expected, full-scale offensive against the Eritrean rebels. Although insurgents claimed to have captured 90% of the coastal province, the government regained the offensive. In November government forces broke a 16-month guerrilla siege of Asmara, the provincial capital, and drove rebels from Keren, their last urban stronghold. Still, much of the countryside remains in rebel hands.

The Ethiopian Orthodox Christian church, a dominant force under Haile Selassie, is struggling against government attempts to control or crush it. In March 1979, Mengistu launched a full-scale crackdown on the country's 11 million Christians, forcing some to register with the government and others to renounce their faith. Some reportedly were executed for refusing to cooperate.

HISTORY: Long isolated from outside influences, Ethiopia developed a culture still suggestive of biblical times. Among its proudest traditions is that of the descent of Ethiopian emperors from King Solomon and the Queen of Sheba, who according to legend was the Ethiopian Queen Makeda of Aksum. Christianity was introduced by Coptic missionaries in the 4th century A.D. Over the centuries, repeated incursions by Arabs and constant feuding by feudal lords disrupted the empire, and it was not until the reign of Menelik II (1889-1913) that it was consolidated. In 1896, Menelik defeated an invading Italian army, but the invaders later took over Eritrea

1916: Menelik's grandson, Lij Yasu, suspected of Moslem leanings, is deposed; Menelik's daughter, Judith, is installed as empress, with her cousin, Ras Tafari Makonnen, as regent and heir

1930-31: Following death of the empress in 1930, Ras Tafari becomes emperor, taking the name Haile Selassie, meaning "Power of the Trinity"; he proclaims the first constitution

1935-36: Italians occupy Ethiopia; emperor flees the country and appeals vainly to the League of Nations for protection

1941: Following Italian defeat in World War II East African campaign, Haile Selassie, with Ethiopian and British forces, returns in triumph to Addis Ababa

1942: Emperor begins modernization and reforms

1952: United Nations approves federation of Eritrea, former Italian colony, with Ethiopia

1955: Revised constitution provides for popularly elected Chamber of Deputies and first elections are held

1960: Attempted coup by military involving crown prince is crushed

1974: Army mutiny and general strikes cause Selassie to appoint new cabinet and premier and promise reforms; Haile Selassie's rule ended. Lt. Gen. Aman Michael Andom is appointed premier and chairman of the military government (Sept.). Andom shot to death. Brig. Gen. Teferi Bante emerges as figurehead controlled by Maj. Mengistu Haile-Mariam and Lt. Col. Atnafu Abate

1975: Fighting erupts between Eritrean rebels and government troops in Asmara, provincial capital of Eritrea. Selassie dies

1977: Bante is killed. Mengistu becomes chief of state and commander in chief of armed forces

1978 Eight-month Ogaden War ends as Cubanand Soviet-aided Ethiopian forces drive Somalis from region. Ethiopia launches major offensive against Eritrean rebels, again with Cuban and Soviet help. A million-and-a-half Ethiopians are reportedly starving in nation's worst famine since 1973. In November Ethiopia and the Soviet Union sign a 20-year friendship pact, in which Moscow promises increased economic and technical assistance

1979: Government persecutes Christians

FIJI

Area: 7,055 sq. mi. **Population:** 610,000 (1978 est.)

Official Name: Fiji **Capital:** Suva **Languages:** English is the official language; Fijian, Hindi **Religion:** Almost all indigenous Fijians are Christians, mainly Methodist. The Indian population is mostly Hindu **Flag:** A light blue field with the Union Jack in the upper left and the shield of the Fiji coat of arms in the fly **Anthem:** God Bless Fiji **Currency:** Fijian dollar (0.85 per U.S. $1)

Location: Southwest Pacific. Fiji consists of about 320 islands, grouped around the Koro Sea, about 1,100 miles north of New Zealand. The largest of the islands, Viti Levu, constitutes more than half the land area and is the seat of the capital. The island of Rotuma, about 240 miles north of Vanua Levu, is part of the Fijian group **Features:** The larger islands are of volcanic origin, mountainous, and surrounded by coral reefs. The windward sides of the islands are covered with dense tropical forests; the leeward sides contain grassy plains **Chief Rivers:** Rewa, Dreketi, Sigatoka, Navua, Mba

Head of State: Queen Elizabeth II, represented by a governor-general, Ratu Sir George Cakobau, appointed 1972 **Head of Government:** Prime Minister: Ratu Sir Kamisese Mara, born 1920, appointed Chief Minister in 1967, assumed the office of prime minister in 1970, and reappointed in 1977 **Effective Date of Present Constitution:** October 1970 **Legislative Body:** Parliament (bicameral), consisting of the Senate and the House of Representatives. The Senate has 22 members, half of whom are appointed for 6 years and the other half for 3 years. The House of Representatives has 52 members elected on a communal basis for 5 years **Local Government:** 4 administrative divisions, each headed by a government-appointed commissioner; 8 urban areas have elected councils

Ethnic Composition: 51% of the population is descended from Indian laborers who came to Fiji in the late 19th century; the indigenous Fijians, who number 44%, are Melanesians, but with a considerable admixture of Polynesian blood. 2% are Europeans and part Europeans, 2% Rotumans and other Pacific islanders, and 1% Chinese **Population Distribution:** 33% urban **Density:** 86 inhabitants per sq. mi.

Largest Cities: (1976 census) Suva 66,622, Lautoka 22,672, Nandi 6,938, Ba 5,917, Nausori 5,262, Labasa 4,328

Per Capita Income: $1,313 (1978) **Gross National Product (GNP):** $790 million (1978) **Economic Statistics:** In 1973 about 27% of GNP was from agriculture (sugar, coconuts, rice, bananas, ginger); 16% from industry (sugar milling, coconut oil) and mining; and 41% from trade and services **Minerals and Mining:** Gold is mined and exported, and there has been some mining of copper and bauxite; iron ore and phosphate are known to exist in some of the islands but it is not yet known whether they are commercially valuable. Manganese ore is also mined **Labor Force:** 149,000 (1970), with about 52% in agriculture, 11% in manufacturing, 22% in construction and engineering, and 13% in services **Foreign Trade:** Exports, chiefly sugar, coconut oil, unrefined gold, molasses, and lumber, totaled $134 million in 1976. Imports, mainly machinery, fuels, clothing, cotton fabrics, and food, totaled $261 million **Principal Trade Partners:** Australia, Japan, Britain, New Zealand, United States, Canada, Malaysia, Singapore

Vital Statistics: Birthrate, 28.6 per 1,000 of pop. (1976); death rate, 4.4 **Life Expectancy:** 70 years **Health Statistics:** 320 inhabitants per hospital bed; 1,763 per physician (1976) **Infant Mortality:** 17.2 per 1,000 births (1976) **Illiteracy:** 15% **Education Statistics:** 726 primary and secondary schools, with combined enrollment of 167,260 (1976) **Enrollment in Higher Education:** 1,810 (1975) **GNP Expended on Education:** 5.1% (1974)

Transportation: All-weather roads total 1,200 mi. **Motor Vehicles:** 32,300 (1975) **Passenger Cars:** 21,500 **Railway Mileage:** 362 miles of narrow-gauge track **Ports:** Suva, Lautoka, Levuka **Major Airlines:** Fiji and Polynesian Airlines operate domestic or regional services; long-haul services are provided by 8 major international carriers **Communications:** State owned **Radio Transmitters:** 11 **Receivers:** 300,000 (1976) **Television:** None **Telephones:** 31,000 (1976) **Newspapers:** 1 daily, 35 copies per 1,000 inhabitants (1975)

Weights and Measures: British standards are used **Travel Requirements:** Passport and onward/return ticket required. Visa issued on arrival for 4 months stay

In 1874, when Fiji was the haunt of cannibals, its chiefs ceded the islands to Queen Victoria. Ninety-six years to the day later, on October 10, 1970, Britain granted Fiji independence. With independence, domestic problems have risen to the surface, such as differences between mainly urban-dwelling Indians, who make up more than half of the population, and the indigenous Melanesians, who number about a sixth less than the Indians, but who own over 80 percent of the land.

Political equanimity is kept by an arrangement in which each group elects an equal number of members of government, the balance of power being held by representatives of the minority of voters who are neither Indian nor Melanesian.

Since 1975, political harmony has been threatened because of the formation of splinter groups from both major parties. This imbalance was exemplified in the 1976 elections in which Prime Minister Sir Kamisese Mara resigned after his ruling Alliance Party suffered defeat in the general election. The defeat meant political turmoil for Fijians, with no party able to gain an overall majority in the House of Representatives. As a result of this impasse, the governor-general reappointed Mara prime minister. A measure of stability was regained in September 1977 when the Alliance Party, led by Mara, won by a landslide in the general elections. The victory was seen as vindicating Mara's determination to preserve Fiji's multiracial society.

Today, Fiji is more than a tourist haven. In education, Fiji draws islanders to its University of the South Pacific, its medical school, and even its Protestant theological school. It is a leading voice of the South Pacific in the United Nations. In commerce, Fiji is a transshipment point for trade to the Pacific islands. Exports include sugar, coconut products, and gold.

HISTORY: Vanua Levu, Taveuni and some smaller islands in the northeast of the Fiji archipelago were discovered by the Dutch navigator Tasman in 1643. Other islands in the group were discovered in the following century by Captain James Cook and other British explorers, but it was not until 1804 that the first European settlement was established, at Levuka. Missionaries soon followed and succeeded in abolishing cannibalism and in converting Cakobau, the most influential of the native chiefs, to Christianity

1874: Britain annexes the islands at the request of the tribal chiefs

1879: Importation begins of indentured Indian laborers for work on the sugar plantations

1900: Plan by European settlers for federation with New Zealand is rejected

1904: Europeans win elective representation in a 10-man Legislative Council, whose one Indian member and two Fijian members are nominated by governor

1929: Indians win right to elective representation in council

1963: Legislative Council is reconstituted, giving Fijians elective representation

1965: New constitution is introduced, providing for greater self-government

1970: Fiji wins independence and joins the U.N.

1972: First general elections since independence are held

1975: Treaty is signed with EEC

1976: Prime Minister Sir Kamisese Mara resigns, but is reappointed by the governor-general

1977: Alliance Party wins by landslide in general elections

1978: Fiji contributes 500-man contingent to the United Nations Interim Force in Lebanon (UNIFIL) peacekeeping force

1979: Two Fijian soldiers of the UNIFIL peacekeeping force are killed Feb. 3 in clashes with Palestinian guerrilias. Cyclone Meli devastates part of Fiji archipelago (March 27); 52 are killed, thousands left homeless

---

FINLAND

Area: 130,128 sq. mi. **Population:** 4,760,000 (1978 est.)
Official Name: Republic of Finland **Capital:** Helsinki **Nationality:** Finnish **Languages:** Finnish, the dominant tongue, and Swedish, spoken by 6.5% of the population, are both official languages. Lappish is spoken by a small minority **Religion:** More than 92% of the population belongs to the established Evangelical Lutheran Church; less than 8% belongs to the Orthodox Church of Finland and the so-called free churches **Flag:** An extended blue cross on a white field with the national coat of arms centered on the cross **Anthem:** Our Land **Currency:** Markka (4.02 per U.S. $1)

Location: Northern Europe. Finland is bordered by Norway on the north, by the USSR on the east, by the Gulf of Finland and the Baltic Sea on the south, and by the Gulf of Bothnia and Sweden on the west. A third of Finland's total length lies north of the Arctic Circle **Features:** Finland is a land of 60,000 lakes, nearly all of them in the southern half of the country. About 70% of the land area is covered with forests; swamps, many of them wooded, cover about 30%. The generally low-lying coastal belt rises slightly to a forested plateau. The far north is marked by low, mountainous terrain **Chief Rivers:** Kemijoki, Oulujoki, Muoniojoki-Torniojoki

Head of State: President Urho Kaleva Kekkonen, born 1900, in office since 1956, reelected (to fifth term) in 1978 **Head of Government:** Premier Mauno Koivisto, appointed May 1979 **Effective Date of Present Constitution:** 1919 **Legislative Body:** Parliament (unicameral Edhuskunta), consisting of 200 members elected by direct universal suffrage for 4-year terms **Local Government:** 12 provinces, (including autonomous Ahvenanmaa—the Aland Islands), each headed by a governor. Urban and rural communes have elected councils

Ethnic Composition: Finnish-speaking Finns make up 93.2% of the population and Swedish-speaking Finns 6.6%. Lapps number about 3,000 and "Kazan Turks" 1,000 **Population Distribution:** 59% urban **Density:** 37 inhabitants per sq. mi.

Largest Cities: (1976 est.) Helsinki 493,324, Tampere 166,179, Turku 164,520, Espoo 123,954, Vantaa 122,301

Per Capita Income: $5,002 (1978) **Gross National Product (GNP):** $23.8 billion (1978 est.) **Economic Statistics:** 30% of GNP comes from industry (metals, engineering, foodstuffs, paper and paper products, furniture, textiles, chemicals); 13% from agriculture (oats, barley, wheat, rye), fishing and forestry; 14% from commerce and finance **Minerals and Mining:** Copper, nickel, iron, zinc, vanadium, silver and lead are mined in substantial quantities **Labor Force:** 2.2 million (1977), with 14% in agriculture and forestry, 34% in industry and construction, and 38% in trade and services **Foreign Trade:** Exports, chiefly paper products, machinery, transport equipment, chemicals, textiles, dairy products totaled $7.68 billion in 1977. Imports, mainly raw materials for industry, fuels and lubricants, machinery, automobiles, aircraft, foodstuffs, and textiles, totaled $7.62 billion **Principal Trade Partners:** Britain, Sweden, USSR, West Germany, United States

Vital Statistics: Birthrate, 13.9 per 1,000 of pop. (1977); death rate, 9.4 **Life Expectancy:** 72 years **Health Statistics:** 66 inhabitants per hospital bed; 703 per physician (1975) **Infant Mortality:** 12 per 1,000 births (1977) **Illiteracy:** Negligible **Education Statistics:** 5,899 primary and secondary schools, with combined enrollment of 977,200 (1975) **Enrollment in Higher Education:** 80,400 (1975) **GNP Expended on Education:** 6.7%

Transportation: Paved roads total 19,261 mi. (1976) **Motor Vehicles:** 1,228,400 (1976) **Passenger Cars:** 1,032,884 (1976) **Railway Mileage:** 3,705 **Ports:** Helsinki, Turku, Naantali, Hamina, Hanko, Kemi, Oulu, Pori, Kotka, Sköldvik **Major Airlines:** Finnair operates domestic and international flights **Communications:** Government owned **Radio Transmitters:** 101 **Licenses:** 2,199,575 (1976) **Television Transmitters:** 83 **Licenses:** 1,779,469 (1976) **Telephones:** 1,936,000 (1976) **Newspapers:** 57 dailies, 537 copies per 1,000 inhabitants (1976)

Weights and Measures: Metric system **Travel Requirements:** Passport; no visa for 3 months

---

With a self-assurance that has grown over the last decade, neutral Finland, which borders the Soviet Union, has been playing a role in international affairs unthinkable a decade ago.

It has served a two-year term (1969-70) on the UN Security Council, where small powers, in taking their turn in the chair, find themselves presiding at times over big-power disputes. Ministers of 35 nations, including the United States and Canada, met in Helsinki in June 1973 to lay groundwork for a European détente. The Conference on Security and Cooperation in Europe (CSCE), held in August 1975 in Helsinki, dealt with the inviolability of frontiers, economic cooperation, and freer movement of people and ideas. The conference was regarded by Finland as an assurance of its independence from the Soviet Union.

To the Finns, these actions are among a series of initiatives that would have been out of the question at the beginning of the 1960s, a period of uneasy relations with the neighboring Soviets.

At the time, a major Finnish political organization, the Social Democratic Party, was being kept out of government to avoid repercussions in Moscow. But the Social Democrats returned to Cabinet posts in 1966 and were part of the coalition government that achieved the signing of the Free Trade Agreement with the European Economic Community (EEC). President Kekkonen's third six-year term was lengthened by parliamentary decision after the major parties failed to find a candidate who could run Finland's sensitive foreign policy—especially Finland's relations to the Soviet Union—as well as Kekkonen, at the helm since 1956.

The Free Trade Agreement with the EEC came after 13 months of hesitation and often bitter political debate in which Finland's relations with the Soviet Union played a significant part.

In January 1978, in the first presidential election in a decade, President Kekkonen was reelected by a large margin to his fifth consecutive term in office. Concern is growing in Finland over the question of who will succeed the aging president when his term expires in 1984.

HISTORY: The earliest known inhabitants of Finland were the Lapps. By the 8th century A.D., however, they had been pushed northward by the Finns, coming from the south and southeast. In the 12th century Finland was Christianized by the Swedes and in the 16th century became a grand duchy under the Swedish crown. Russia acquired the province of Vyborg in 1721 and was ceded the rest of the duchy in 1809. Although Finland enjoyed considerable autonomy under Russian rule, Finnish nationalism developed into a powerful movement

1899-1906: Tsar Nicholas II begins strong Russification program, evoking stiff Finnish resistance. Russian governor-general is assassinated and a general strike breaks out. Finns win concessions, set up a unicameral diet and introduce universal suffrage

1917-20: Following the Bolshevik seizure of power in the Russian Revolution, Finnish diet proclaims Finland's independence. Civil war breaks out between Russian sympathizers (Reds) and Finnish nationalists (Whites), led by Marshal Carl Gustav Mannerheim and aided by German troops. Whites are victorious and after a brief regency under Mannerheim, a republic is set up. The Soviet Union recognizes Finland

1939-40: Soviet Union, which has been given a free hand in Finland under Moscow's nonaggression pact with Nazi Germany, demands demilitarization of Finnish fortifications on Karelian Isthmus north of Leningrad, use of a naval base in Finland, and the cession of islands in Gulf of Finland. Finns refuse to bow to demands and Soviet troops attack. Despite strong resistance by Finnish troops, led by Mannerheim, Finland is defeated and is forced to cede one-tenth of its territory to USSR

1941-45: Finland is caught up in war between the Soviet Union and Nazi Germany, the Finns fighting what they regard as the Continuation War against the Russians and not as allies of Germany. Full-scale Soviet offensive results in Finnish defeat in 1944. Armistice terms oblige Finns to expel German troops; resulting warfare leads to further devastation of Finland

1947: Under peace treaty signed in Paris, Finland cedes more territory to USSRand agrees to pay heavy indemnity

1955-61: Finland joins Nordic Council, and becomes associate member of European Free Trade Association; continues policy of neutrality and cooperation with Soviet Union

1973: Finland signs Free Trade Agreement with the EEC. President Kekkonen's term extended by four years

1975: Finland hosts concluding session of the Conference on Security and Cooperation in Europe (CSCE)

1976: Finland hit by first police strike in postwar Europe

1977: Kalevi Sorsa succeeds Martti Miettunen as premier

1978: President Kekkonen reelected to fifth straight term

1979: Mauno Koivisto succeeds Sorsa as premier

FRANCE

Area: 210,038 sq. mi. **Population:** 53,800,000 (1978 est.)
Official Name: French Republic **Capital:** Paris **Nationality:** French **Languages:** French is the official and predominant language. Other languages spoken include Breton (akin to Welsh) in Brittany; a German dialect in Alsace and Lorraine; Flemish in northeastern France; Spanish, Catalan, and Basque in the southwest; and Italian in the southeast and on the island of Corsica **Religion:** Chiefly Roman Catholic, 4% Moslem (mostly immigrants from North Af-

rica), 2% Protestant, 1% Jewish **Flag:** A tricolor of blue, white, and red vertical stripes **Anthem:** La Marseillaise **Currency:** Franc (4.4 per U.S. $1)

Location: Western Europe. France is bounded on the north by the English Channel and the Strait of Dover; on the northeast by the North Sea, Belgium and Luxembourg; on the east by Germany, Switzerland, and Italy; on the southeast by the Mediterranean Sea; on the south by Andorra and Spain; and on the west by the Atlantic Ocean **Features:** About two-thirds of the country consists of flat or gently rolling terrain, and the remaining third is mountainous. A broad plain covers most of northern and western France, from the Belgian border in the northeast to Bayonne in the southwest. The lowland plains area is bounded on the south by the Pyrenees; on the southeast by the mountainous Massif Central; and on the east by the Alps, Jura, and Vosges mountains **Chief Rivers:** Seine, Loire, Garonne, Rhône, Rhine

Head of State: President Valéry Giscard d'Estaing, born 1926, elected 1974 for 7 years **Head of Government:** Premier Raymond Barre, born 1924, reappointed 1978 **Effective Date of Present Constitution:** 1958 **Legislative Body:** Parliament (bicameral), with a National Assembly and the Senate. The National Assembly, elected by direct universal suffrage for 5 years, is composed of 491 deputies. The Senate is composed of 295 members, elected indirectly for 9 years by an electoral college made up of National Assembly members, the General Departmental Councils, and the delegates of the Municipal Councils. The National Assembly can be dissolved by the president with the advice of the premier **Local Government:** Metropolitan France is divided into 96 departments, each headed by a prefect appointed by the central government and each under the authority of a popularly elected General Council. The departments are divided into cantons and communes, with each commune electing its own municipal council and designated mayor

Ethnic Composition: The French are a mixture of the 3 basic European stocks: Nordic, Alpine, and Mediterranean. The largest foreign-born groups are North Africans, Italians, Portuguese, Spaniards, Czechoslovaks, Poles, and Yugoslavs **Population Distribution:** 71% urban **Density:** 256 inhabitants per sq. mi.

Largest Cities: (1975 census) Paris 2,291,554 (Metropolitan Area 9,878,524), Marseille 901,421, Lyon 454,265, Toulouse 371,143, Nice 331,002, Nantes 252,537, Strasbourg 251,520, Bordeaux 220,830, Saint-Étienne 218,289, LeHavre 216,917, Rennes 194,094, Toulon 180,508, Reims 177,320, Lille 171,010, Grenoble 165,431, Brest 163,940

Per Capita Income: $7,719 (1978) **Gross National Product (GNP):** $411 billion (1978 est.) **Economic Statistics:** About 38% of GNP comes from industry (metalworking, machinery, chemicals, transport equipment, food and beverages, textiles, clothing) and construction; 57% from trade and services; 5% from agriculture and fishing (wheat, barley, potatoes, beet sugar, apples, wine, fish, beef cattle, and pigs) **Minerals and Mining:** The country is an important producer of iron ore, potash, bauxite, coal, natural gas, sulphur, and building raw materials. It also has deposits of zinc, lead, pyrites, phosphates, and uranium **Labor Force:** 22.5 million (1976), with 38% in manufacturing and construction, 54% in trade and services, 10% in agriculture, fishing, and forestry **Foreign Trade:** Exports, chiefly machinery, chemicals, textiles, automobiles, steel, grain, and aircraft, totaled $65.2 billion in 1977. Imports, mainly machinery, foodstuffs, petroleum, chemicals, steel, nonferrous metals, and transportation equipment, totaled $67.5 billion **Principal Trade Partners:** West Germany, Belgium, Luxembourg, Italy, United States, Switzerland, Britain, Netherlands, Algeria, Japan

Vital Statistics: Birthrate, 14.0 per 1,000 of pop. (1977); death rate, 10.1 **Life Expectancy:** 72 years **Health Statistics:** 98 inhabitants per hospital bed, 681 per physician (1974) **Infant Mortality:** 11.4 per 1,000 births **Illiteracy:** Negligible **Education Statistics:** 89,953 primary and secondary schools, with combined enrollment of 9,656,549 (1975) **Enrollment in Higher Education:** 989,439 (1974) **GNP Expended on Education:** 5% (1975)

Transportation: Surfaced roads total 490,658 mi. **Motor Vehicles:** 18,310,000 (1976) **Passenger Cars:** 15,900,000 **Railway Mileage:** 22,940 **Ports:** Marseille, Le Havre, Dunkirk, Nantes, St-Nazaire, Rouen, Bordeaux, Brest, Nice **Major Airlines:** Air France and UTA operate international flights; Air-Inter operates domestic flights **Communications:** Government owned **Radio Transmitters:** 290 **Licenses:** 26,000,000 (1976) **Television Transmitters:** 3,001 (1974) **Licenses:** 14,197,000 (1975) **Telephones:** 15,554,000 (1976) **Newspapers:** 98 dailies, 214 copies per 1,000 inhabitants (1975)

Weights and Measures: Metric system **Travel Requirements:** Passport; no visa for 3 months

---

For a country with a reputation for being ungovernable, France has moved and is continuing to move through a difficult period of transition, politically, economically, and socially, with an uncharacteristic amount of smoothness.

FRANCE
CONIC PROJECTION

SCALE OF MILES
0   20   40   60   80   100

KILOMETRES
0   20   40   60   80   100

Capitals of Countries ✪

Copyright by C.S. HAMMOND & Co., N.Y.

PARIS and ENVIRONS

CORSICA

That there is some unrest and dissatisfaction is attested to by strikes, demonstrations, manifestations of violence, and angry meetings. But these fits of temper surge up and die down quickly, and the appearance of crisis they create is quickly dissipated.

Despite some dire predictions, France has moved out of the Gaullist era into more prosaic leadership with the institutions that General de Gaulle had bequeathed intact. A people that history books describe as undisciplined and individualistic appear to accept strong executive power as a fact of political life, particularly when it concentrates as it now does on domestic problems and eschews to a large extent the kind of global diplomacy practiced by de Gaulle.

The main goal of de Gaulle's successor, Georges Pompidou, was to eliminate France's industrial backwardness and move her into the forefront of advanced technical nations. The rich, varied soil of France that produces the food and wines that have also contributed to the French art of living have also produced a powerful, conservative rural society that over the centuries has dominated the country.

The shift to an urban, industrialized society is one of the great central facts of contemporary France. As people move from farm to city and enter into radically different ways of life and work, tensions are created. They are aggravated by the failure of the cities to accommodate ever increasing populations with adequate housing and transport. More and more, once sleepy provincial centers are starting to take on the bustle, noise, and discomfort of Paris.

More than just the rural population is in transition. Shopkeepers and artisans who flourished in a slow-moving, small-scale economy are finding themselves squeezed out of the market by the demand for more efficient and cheaper ways of making and distributing goods and services. Workers in small inefficient plants or in traditional industries that are dying out are finding themselves having to adjust to new lines of work in new places. Students and educational authorities are trying to make their schools relevant to a new kind of society that places a premium on technical proficiency and accords declining prestige to the contemplative man of letters.

All these are long-range problems that are more or less painful to resolve and create tensions that sometimes may cause explosions. In May 1968, students and workers exploded together, bringing the government of General de Gaulle and the whole regime into peril. Although de Gaulle weathered the storm, it was the beginning of the end for him; the following year he was defeated in a referendum and was forced into lonely and somewhat bitter retirement. When he died in November 1970, there was a great national and international outpouring of sentiment for him.

The events of May 1968 left a decided impact. The franc was no longer sacrosanct and monetary policies henceforth were more closely coordinated with those of France's European partners. The upheaval has led to a style of government that places great importance on discussion and participation in decisions. At the same time, the memory of the 1968 disorders made most Frenchmen very law-and-order conscious. How to protect civil liberties while putting down the disorders that continue to crop up has become a major subject of debate.

Another great theme of debate is how to loosen the power of one of the most highly centralized countries in the world without destroying national unity. The move is on to satisfy municipal and regional desires for more of a say over personal futures, but the habit of deciding everything in Paris is deep-rooted and hard to change.

Abroad, France, no longer a colonial power, has paid the greatest attention to the movement toward western European unity. Under Pompidou, European unity, long blocked by his predecessor's refusal to accept Britain as a European partner, began again to show movement. The successful negotiation with Britain for entry into the Common Market was due largely to Pompidou.

In April 1974 Pompidou died at the age of 62. On May 19, Finance Minister Valéry Giscard d'Estaing was elected president by a narrow margin. In his years in office, Giscard d'Estaing displayed an informal style and a willingness to attack France's problems. He received a resounding vote of confidence in the legislative elections of March 1978 when candidates of his center-right coalition won a formidable 291-200 majority in the new National Assembly. It was a surprising and humiliating defeat for the alliance of Socialists and Communists, which the public opinion polls had projected as winning. Giscard, magnanimous in victory and seeking to substitute a political consensus for the left-right polarization so characteristic of French politics, vowed to bring the leftists "on the sidelines" into active participation in the government. With the strengthening of Giscard's hand, Paris Mayor Jacques Chirac—a Gaullist leader with presidential ambitions—has ceased to be the dominant influence in the government coalition. Following the elections, Giscard reappointed Premier Raymond Barre, who has been given much of the credit for keeping the annual inflation rate under 10 percent, substantially reducing unemployment and cutting the international payments deficit.

In 1978, with its army already involved in the civil war in Chad and the United Nations peacekeeping force in Lebanon, France sent units of its air force to rescue victims of violence in Zaire and became briefly involved in helping Mauritania against the Polisario Front. In 1979, France notified the UN that it was taking French soldiers out of Lebanon, but involvement in Chad only grew worse.

HISTORY: The land of France was inhabited in ancient times by the Gauls, who, by 51 B.C., had been subdued by the Romans. The Latin language predominated by the 5th century A.D., when Roman power collapsed, and the Franks from Germany made the land part of a large domain. Charlemagne ruled from 768 to 814 and extended the domain, but it was divided in 838—"Francia," with its Latin-based language, going to Charles the Bald. The kings lost power to local nobles in the 10th century, but recovered it slowly in later centuries.

1337: The Hundred Years War breaks out, actually a series of short wars and truces between France and England, whose kings lay claim to the French throne

1429-53: Joan of Arc successfully leads French armies in lifting the siege of Orléans but is burned at the stake in 1431 after falling into English hands; English are finally driven out

1643-1715: Louis XIV gains military and political primacy for France in continental Europe, creates a great overseas empire, and establishes an absolute monarchy with a highly centralized government; his reign marks the golden age of French culture

1789-94: The French Revolution sweeps away Old Regime. A National Convention is formed, the monarchy abolished, Louis XVI executed, and a republic proclaimed. The Reign of Terror sets in, leading to arrest and execution of a huge number of royalists and members of minority political blocs. France's neighbors form an alliance to suppress the Revolution

1799-1804: Napoleon Bonaparte becomes first consul under the Consulate, a tripartite executive body; he restores domestic stability and defeats Austrian-British coalition

1804-14: Napoleon proclaims himself emperor, leads French armies in a series of unequaled victories against the other powers of Europe. His attempt to conquer Russia, however, results in a decisive defeat for France and the formation of an armed European coalition which forces his abdication

1815: Napoleon escapes from exile on Elba, rallies a French army, and is decisively defeated at Waterloo

1848: Revolution overthrows Bourbon monarchy, restored after Napoleon; the Second Republic is formed

1852: Louis Napoleon, Bonaparte's nephew, engineers coup d'état and overthrows republic; as Napoleon III, he establishes the Second Empire

1870-71: France defeated in Franco-Prussian War; Second Empire collapses and the Third Republic is formed

1914-18: France plays a major role in World War I against the Austro-German coalition. Nation shares in Allied victory but its economy is devastated by the war

1939: France joins Britain in declaring war on Germany following Nazi invasion of Poland

1940: France suffers ignominious defeat by Germany. Marshal Henri Pétain forms government at Vichy and sues for peace; Germans occupy half of France. General Charles de Gaulle escapes to London, forms a wartime government and the Free French army

1944: Paris is liberated by Allied armies. De Gaulle's provisional exile government is officially recognized by the Allies

1945-46: De Gaulle is unanimously elected provisional president of the Fourth Republic but resigns after leftists withdraw support

1958-61: De Gaulle is recalled to power as the Fourth Republic is threatened with collapse because of the Algerian conflict. He engineers a new constitution vesting strong powers in the executive and establishing the Fifth Republic; despite considerable opposition, he negotiates Algerian independence

1966: De Gaulle withdraws French forces from NATO

1968: Student-worker uprisings paralyze France and threaten to topple Gaullist regime, but de Gaulle weathers the storm; his Gaullist party wins smashing victory in parliamentary election

1969: President de Gaulle resigns after the defeat of a referendum for constitutional reform; Gaullist candidate Georges Pompidou is elected president; he devalues the franc

1970: President Pompidou initiates broad reforms designed to benefit blue-collar workers

1974: Pompidou dies; Giscard d'Estaing is elected president. Laws on voting age of 18 and legalized abortion are passed

1975: Giscard d'Estaing visits Algeria; first such trip by French head of state since Algerian independence

1976: Political parties of the Left win a majority in nationwide local elections in March. French Communist Party drops some of the rigid Soviet Marxist doctrine. Premier Jacques Chirac resigns, reconstitutes Gaullist party into the Assembly for the Republic. Raymond Barre, nonpartisan technocrat, becomes Premier

1977: Socialists and Communists gain in municipal elections, Chirac elected mayor of Paris. Territory of Afars and Issas (Djibouti), last French colony in Africa, gains independence

1978: Center-right candidates win large majority in legislative elections, repulsing strong leftist challenge. Socialist-Communist alliance collapses. France reportedly explodes neutron bomb at South Pacific test base. Brief military actions in Mauritania and Zaire; long-term involvement in Chad

GABON

Area: 103,346 sq. mi. **Population:** 560,000 (1978 est.)
Official Name: Gabonese Republic **Capital:** Libreville **Nationality:** Gabonese **Languages:** French is the official language; Fang is spoken in the north and a variety of Bantu tongues in the rest of the country **Religion:** About 46% of the population is Christian, mainly Roman Catholic; there are about 3,000 Moslems and the rest are animists **Flag:** Green, yellow, and blue horizontal stripes **Anthem:** Harmony **Currency:** CFA Franc (219.0 per U.S. $1)

Location: West-central Africa. Gabon is bordered on the north by Equatorial Guinea and by Cameroon, on the east and south by the Congo, and on the west by the Atlantic Ocean **Features:** About 85% of the entire country is covered by dense equatorial rain forest. The coastal plain is deeply indented in the north, while inland there are plateaus and mountains through which rivers have carved deep valleys and channels **Chief Rivers:** Ogooué, Ngounié, Abanga

Head of State and of Government: President: El Hadj Omar (Albert-Bernard) Bongo, born 1935; succeeded 1967; reelected 1973. He is assisted by the appointed prime minister, Léon Mébiame **Effective Date of Present Constitution:** 1961 **Legislative Body:** National Assembly (unicameral), consisting of 47 members elected for 7-year terms **Local Government:** 9 regions divided into 36 prefectures, and 8 urban communes, with appointed officials

Ethnic Composition: Almost all Gabonese are of Bantu origin. The Fang are the largest of the country's tribes, followed by the Eshira, Bapounou, Bateke, and Okandé **Population Distribution:** 32% urban **Density:** 5.4 inhabitants per sq. mi.

Largest Cities: (1973 est.) Libreville 57,000, Port-Gentil 35,000, Franceville 5,000

Per Capita Income: $3,530 (1978) **Gross National Product (GNP):** $2.0 billion (1978) **Economic Statistics:** In 1973 about 18% of GNP was from agriculture (cocoa, coffee, palm oil, rice, cassava, bananas, yams, corn, and peanuts) and forestry; 14% from manufacturing and construction; (largely timber and mineral processing); 30% from mining; 22% from trade and services **Minerals and Mining:** Very rich deposits of manganese and iron ore; uranium and gold are also produced; there are known deposits of lead, zinc, phosphate, and diamonds. Rich offshore oil and natural gas deposits are being developed **Labor Force:** About 274,000 (1970), of which 58% are engaged in agriculture **Foreign Trade:** Exports, wood, petroleum, uranium, manganese and coffee, totaled $942 million in 1975. Imports, chiefly machinery, foods, transportation equipment, metal products, tobacco, refined petroleum products, and industrial chemicals, totaled $470 million **Principal Trade Partners:** France, United States, West Germany, Netherlands, Britain

Vital Statistics: Birthrate, 32.5 per 1,000 of pop.; death rate, 22 **Life Expectancy:** 39 years **Health Statistics:** 98 inhabitants per hospital bed; 5,208 per physician (1971) **Infant Mortality:** 83 per 1,000 births **Illiteracy:** 70% **Education Statistics:** 734 primary and secondary schools, with combined enrollment of 142,406 (1974) **Enrollment in Higher Education:** 986 **GNP Expended on Education:** 3.4% (1975)

Transportation: Improved roads total 2,957 mi. **Motor Vehicles:** 17,400 (1974) **Passenger Cars:** 10,100 **Railway Mileage:** 184 miles; the 400-mile Transgabon line is under construction **Ports:** Libreville, Port-Gentil **Major Airlines:** Air Service and Air Affaires are domestic carriers; Air Gabon provides international services **Communications:** Government owned **Radio Transmitters:** 10 **Receivers:** 93,000 (1976) **Television Transmitters:** 3 **Receivers:** 8,500 (1976) **Telephones:** 11,000 (1976) **Newspapers:** 1 daily, 1 copy per 1,000 inhabitants (1975)

Weights and Measures: Metric system **Travel Requirements:** Passport; visa; $10 fee

As the smallest territory of French Equatorial Africa, jungle-matted Gabon was noted chiefly as a source of tropical hardwoods and as the unhealthy land where for 53 years the famous medical missionary, the late Dr. Albert Schweitzer, operated a hospital at Lambaréné.

Most of Gabon is still a humid tangle of trees and creepers, but the increasing number of roads slicing through the jungle attest to the dramatic change that has made the country potentially one of the richest in Africa.

Not long after gaining independence from France in 1960, Gabon was found to possess some of the world's largest deposits of manganese, iron ore, and uranium.

Development of these resources is proceeding impressively, and the airline passenger approaching Libreville, the capital and chief port, may see evidence of new wealth also in the offshore oil rigs glinting above the gray Atlantic.

While tropical woods, particularly those from which the best plywood is made, are still a major export, the rising production of minerals has given Gabon a continuing trade surplus and the highest per capita annual income in Black Africa.

Meanwhile, on the economic scene, because of the attractions of newfound mineral wealth, French participation in Gabon's development has grown even greater than it was in the colonial period. In February 1974 the two nations agreed that a detachment of French troops, would remain in Gabon, which was to stay within the French zone.

Frenchmen run the new enterprises, the schools, banks, shops, and most businesses, and six French advisers serve in the President's office. President Bongo is actively seeking trade ties and investment from the United States, Britain, and West Germany in an effort to reduce French domination.

By 1976, relations with France had grown increasingly cool, with verbal attacks by President Bongo against "savage capitalism" and "exploitation" of Gabon's natural resources, becoming more frequent. However, Gabon still participates in the annual French-African summit, and severing of ties between the two nations does not appear to be imminent.

HISTORY: In the 15th century, Portuguese voyagers became the first Europeans to explore the coastal area of Gabon. However, because of dense jungles and impenetrable highlands the country remained relatively undisturbed by Europeans until the mid-19th century, when the French began making treaties with coastal chieftains and penetrating the interior. In 1890 Gabon formally became part of the French Congo and in 1910 was made a separate colony as part of French Equatorial Africa

1913: Dr. Albert Schweitzer, Alsatian-born physician, theologian, and musicologist, establishes medical mission at Lambaréné

1958-59: Republic of Gabon is established as autonomous member of the French Community; Léon M'Ba, leader of Gabonese Democratic party, becomes premier of provisional government

1960: Republic proclaims full independence

1961-63: Two main parties agree on joint list of candidates for election, in which M'Ba becomes president; factional disputes disrupt coalition and new elections are called

1964: When election decrees bar opposition candidates, Gabonese Army overthrows M'Ba government, but it is promptly restored by French military intervention; in subsequent elections in which opposition participates, M'Ba forces win 31 seats, compared with 16 for the opposition

1967: President M'Ba dies and is succeeded by Vice-President Albert-Bernard Bongo

1968: President Bongo declares Gabon a one-party state and forms new Gabonese Democratic Party open to all citizens

1971: A new $500-million four-year plan is begun to further develop timber and mineral resources that include large deposits of manganese, iron ore, and uranium

1973: Bongo is elected to a seven-year term as president

1975: Léon Mébiame is named premier. Treaty is signed with EEC. Gabon is admitted to full membership in OPEC

1976: Gabon becomes world's largest exporter of manganese

1978: Gabon takes its seat as a nonpermanent member of the UN Security Council

THE GAMBIA

Area: 4,127 sq. mi. **Population:** 546,000 (1978 est.)
Official Name: Republic of The Gambia **Capital:** Banjul **Nationality:** Gambian **Languages:** English is the official language; Malinke and Wolof are the main spoken languages **Religion:** Approximately 85% of the population is Moslem; about 5% Christian; and the rest animist **Flag:** Red, blue, and green horizontal stripes, with the center blue stripe edged in white **Anthem:** For the Gambia, Our Homeland **Currency:** Dalasi (1.94 per U.S. $1)
Location: West Africa. The Gambia is a narrow strip 7-20 miles wide on either side of the Gambia River, extending eastward 200 miles from the Atlantic, and surrounded by Senegal on the land sides **Features:** Coastal mangrove swamps and salt water flats graduate to sand hills and inland plateaus **Chief River:** Gambia

Head of State and of Government: President: Alhaji Sir Dawda Kairaba Jawara, born 1924; prime minister since 1962, he became president in April 1970, and was reelected in 1977 **Effective Date of Present Constitution:** 1970 **Legislative Body:** House of Representatives (unicameral); 34 members elected by universal suffrage for a 5-year term, and 6 special members **Local Government:** Banjul, and 6 administrative divisions

Ethnic Composition: The principal groups are the Mandingo (40%), Fula (13%), Wolof (12%), Jola (7%), and Serahuli (7%) **Population Distribution:** 10% urban **Density:** 132 inhabitants per sq. mi.

Largest Cities: (1975 est.) Banjul 42,689; (1973 census) Sarrekunda 16,637

Per Capita Income: $196 (1978) **Gross National Product (GNP):** $110 million (1978) **Economic Statistics:** In 1973 about 55% of GNP was from agriculture (chiefly peanuts), 26% from trade and services, and 5% from manufacturing and mining **Minerals and Mining:** No known resources of value apart from laterite and stone **Labor Force:** 165,000, about 85% being engaged in agriculture **Foreign Trade:** Exports, mainly peanuts and palm kernels, totaled $35 million (1976). Imports, chiefly food, textiles and clothing, machine and transport equipment, totaled $74 million **Principal Trade Partners:** Britain, Netherlands, France, United States, Japan

Vital Statistics: Birthrate, 43.3 per 1,000 of pop. (1975); death rate, 24.1 **Life Expectancy:** 43 years **Health Statistics:** 697 inhabitants per hospital bed; 18,947 per physician (1970) **Infant Mortality:** 82.6 per 1,000 births **Illiteracy:** 90% **Education Statistics:** 103 primary and secondary schools, with combined enrollment of 31,235 pupils (1975) **Enrollment in Higher Education:** 947 (1971) **GNP Expended on Education:** 3.5% (1974)

Transportation: Paved roads total 180 mi. **Motor Vehicles:** 6,092 (1973) **Passenger Cars:** 3,000 **Railway Mileage:** None **Ports:** Banjul **Major Airlines:** Gambia Airways, Air Senegal, British United Airways, and Nigeria Airways operate international and regional flights **Communications:** Partly government owned **Radio Stations:** 4 **Receivers:** 61,000 (1976) **Television:** None **Telephones:** 3,000 (1976) **Newspapers:** 1 newspaper published 3 times a week

Weights and Measures: British Imperial system is used; transfer to metric system started in 1976 **Travel Requirements:** Passport; visa; $5 fee

The Gambia, Africa's smallest country, has been gaining increasing self-reliance through the unlikely combination of peanut production, Scandinavian tourists, and careful fiscal management. Recently, attention has been focused on The Gambia because of the 1976 bestseller by Alex Haley, *Roots*, which chronicles the story of Haley's ancestors from tribal life in The Gambia to slavery in America.

Formerly Britain's oldest African colony, The Gambia became independent in 1965 and proclaimed itself a republic in 1970. It added "The" to its official name to avoid confusion with Zambia, another African country.

Except for a short Atlantic coast, the country is enclosed within Senegal. A sandy strip of land, it stretches some 200 miles in length along either side of the Gambia River and varies in width from seven to 30 miles.

The broad mouth of the Gambia River is one of West Africa's finest harbors and the site of the capital, Banjul. Mandingoes, a handsome, friendly people, form the main element of the population.

Peanuts, planted on most of the available land, account for 95 percent of exports, but, in recent years, tourism has become a welcome and fast-growing addition to the economy, luring 25,000 Scandinavians a year.

Old hotels have been enlarged and new ones built to meet growing demand. With tourist organizations in other countries now showing interest in The Gambia, prospects are bright for a continuance of the boom and creation of more jobs and revenue. With Soviet, Chinese and British aid, The Gambia is beginning fishery development and irrigation projects.

HISTORY: Along with neighboring Senegal, The Gambia was inhabited in past ages by peoples associated with the great empires of Ghana, Mali, and Songhay. Reached by Portuguese navigators in the 15th century, in 1588 the territory became, through purchase, the first British colony in Africa. After prolonged struggle, the British and French fixed the borders of Senegal and Gambia; in 1888 the latter became a crown colony

1965: The Gambia becomes a fully independent member of the British Commonwealth; a referendum to make the country a republic fails to receive necessary two-thirds majority

1966: Elections give Prime Minister Sir Dawda Jawara's People's Progressive Party an increased majority

1967-69: Britain loans The Gambia over $10 million

1970: The Gambia becomes a republic

1975: Treaty is signed with EEC

1976: The Gambia, along with 14 other African nations, signs agreement creating the Economic Community of West African States (ECOWAS)

EAST GERMANY

Area: 41,768 sq. mi. **Population:** 16,750,000 (1978 est.)
Official Name: German Democratic Republic **Capital:** East Berlin **Nationality:** German **Languages:** German is the official and universal language **Religion:** 59% Protestant, 8% Roman Catholic, 32% no affiliation. Although the constitution provides for religious freedom, all churches are closely regulated by the state **Flag:** Black, red, and gold horizontal stripes, with the national emblem in the center **Anthem:** Arisen from the Ruins **Currency:** GDR mark (1.90 per U.S. $1)
Location: North-central Europe. East Germany is bordered on the north by the Baltic Sea, on the east by Poland, on the southeast by Czechoslovakia, and on the southwest and west by the Federal Republic of Germany **Features:** In the north are the lakes and low hills typical of the Baltic Sea country; the center is partly mountainous and in addition consists of a sandy arid section and a fertile plain. The heavily forested southern region consists of the Mittelgebirge, and the extension of the North German lowlands **Chief Rivers:** Elbe, Oder, Saale, Havel, Spree, Neisse

Political Leader and Head of State: Erich Honecker, born 1912, secretary general of the Central Committee of the Socialist Unity Party and chairman of the State Council **Head of Government:** Willi Stoph, born 1914, appointed October 1976 chairman of the Council of Ministers (premier) **Effective Date of Present Constitution:** 1968, amended 1974 **Legislative Body:** *Volkskammer* (unicameral) consisting of 500 members, elected by universal suffrage for 5-year terms; final decisions are made by the party's Politburo **Local Government:** 15 administrative districts named after their respective chief towns. All urban and rural divisions have locally elected bodies

Ethnic Composition: The population is ethnically homogeneous. The only minority is a Slavic group called the Sorbs which makes up about 0.2% of the population **Population Distribution:** 75.4% urban **Density:** 401 inhabitants per sq. mi.

Largest Cities: (1975 estimates) East Berlin 1,094,000, Leipzig 567,000, Dresden 508,000, Karl-Marx-Stadt (Chemnitz) 305,000, Magdeburg 276,000, Halle 241,000, Rostock 210,000, Erfurt 203,000

Per Capita Income: $4,834 (1978) **Gross National Product (GNP):** $81 billion (1978) **Economic Statistics:** About 54% of GNP comes from industry, and 20% from agriculture. The chief industries are iron and steel, chemicals, fertilizers, machinery, transport equipment, synthetic rubber and fibers, drugs, plastics, and vehicles. The chief crops are barley, oats, potatoes, rye, sugar beets, and wheat **Minerals and Mining:** The arbitrary division of Germany left the East with few natural resources. Its only major resources are lignite, potash and uranium **Labor Force:** 8,214,000 (1975), with 42% in industry, 11% in agriculture, 18% in trade and commerce, 21% in services. The average wage for industrial workers is $185 a month **Foreign Trade:** Exports, chiefly machinery, railway rolling stock, chemicals, fertilizers and pesticides, fuel oil, construction materials, ships, motor vehicles, clothing and textiles, were estimated at $12.7 billion in 1977. Imports, mainly mineral ores, coal, rolled steel, fertilizer, tires, crude oil, wood, cotton and wool, paper pulp, foodstuffs, forage and feeds, and raw skins, were estimated at $14.3 billion **Principal Trade Partners:** USSR, Czechoslovakia, Poland, Hungary, France, Britain, West Germany, Japan, Netherlands, Sweden

Vital Statistics: Birthrate, 13.3 per 1,000 of pop. (1977); death rate, 13.4 **Life Expectancy:** 72 years **Health Statistics:** 92 inhabitants per hospital bed; 538 per physician (1975) **Infant Mortality:** 13.1 per 1,000 births (1977) **Illiteracy:** Negligible **Education Statistics:** 19,578 primary and secondary schools, with combined enrollment of 3,039,421 (1975) **Enrollment in Higher Education:** 306,783 (1974) **GNP Expended on Education:** 5.6% (1974)

Transportation: Surfaced roads total 8,032 mi., with 951 mi. of superhighways **Motor Vehicles:** 2,600,300 (1976) **Passenger Cars:** 2,052,200 **Railway Mileage:** 8,856 (1974) **Ports:** Rostock, Wismar, Stralsund **Major Airlines:** Interflug operates domestic and international services **Communications:** State controlled **Radio Transmitters:** 66 **Licenses:** 6,167,000 (1976) **Television Transmitters:** 461 **Licenses:** 5,180,000 (1976) **Telephones:** 2,751,000 (1976) **Newspapers:** 40 dailies, 472 copies per 1,000 inhabitants (1975)

Weights and Measures: Metric system **Travel Requirements:** Passport; visa obtainable at border or at East German Embassy; visa entitlement certificate

---

The German Democratic Republic is mainly the work of one man, Walter Ulbricht, a ruthless and fanatical leader. Without his dedication and his seemingly tireless efforts from 1945 to 1971, his ruling Communist Party and state apparatus, East Germany would undoubtedly have remained in a kind of Central European limbo.

Throughout the 1960s his prestige and power increased dramatically. In this period East Germany grew to be the 10th industrial power in the world and the country with the best living standard in the Communist world. Working to his advantage was the desire for security and comfort of the East Germans and their willingness to persevere under adverse conditions.

A major threat to Ulbricht's rule was posed by the reform program of the new Czechoslovak Communist leadership in 1968. The reform aims proclaimed in Prague by Alexander Dubcek were viewed in East Berlin as an elemental danger to the more or less orthodox, militant Marxism/Leninism practiced by the Ulbricht team. The East German leader recommended suppression; his advice was followed by the Soviet leaders who ordered the August 21, 1968, invasion of Czechoslovakia. Ulbricht was at his zenith in the wake of

this move, and it seemed, for a while, that he was setting the tone of Russian foreign policy in Central Europe until his dismissal in 1971 as First Party Secretary for bypassing the Central Committee, overemphasizing large-scale development projects and obstructing Soviet aims for an accommodation with West Germany.

Ulbricht's successor, Erich Honecker, had less of a base for an independent position. Under Soviet guidance, he negotiated agreements with West Germany. The two states recognized each other in 1974, and other Western governments recognized East Germany. Negotiations between the Germanys have continued—though not without long interruptions. In 1978, agreement was reached on construction of a new highway to West Berlin, and Honecker showed a degree of independence by criticizing the policy of COMECON.

HISTORY: The Germans made their first major appearance in recorded history when they came into contact with the Romans in the 1st century B.C. By the 5th century A.D. various Germanic tribes had overrun the Roman Empire. After the division of Charlemagne's possessions in 843, the kingdom of the Eastern Franks emerged as the nucleus of Germany, but for most of Germany's history political unification was to prove beyond reach. In 1517 Martin Luther precipitated the Protestant Reformation and Germany was torn by religious strife until the end of the Thirty Years' War (1618-48). In the 18th century Prussia began to emerge as an important power and in the next century successfully challenged Austria for domination of Germany

1815: Congress of Vienna perpetuates the political divisions of Germany and provides for a German Confederation

1862: Bismarck becomes chancellor of Prussia; his goal is to create a unified Germany dominated by Prussia and excluding Austria

1866: Prussia is victorious in the Austro-Prussian War

1870-71: Prussia defeats France in the Franco-Prussian War, enabling Bismarck to achieve his goal of a unified Germany under Prussia; in 1871 William I of Prussia is proclaimed German Emperor

1914-19: Germany is ranged against Allied Powers in World War I and suffers crushing defeat; German Empire collapses and newly formed Weimar Republic is forced to accept harsh terms of Versailles Treaty

1933-36: Hitler is appointed chancellor in 1933 and assumes dictatorial powers; Germany is transformed into a brutal police state; anti-Semitism becomes official policy, culminating eventually in the extermination of six million European Jews; intensive rearmament begins

1938: Hitler annexes Austria and later takes over the Sudetenland from Czechoslovakia

1939-45: Hitler seizes the rest of Czechoslovakia in March 1939; six months later Nazi forces invade Poland, triggering World War II; Nazi forces overrun Western Europe and in 1941 invade the Soviet Union; by 1945, however, Germany is totally defeated, its cities in ruins, and its territory under U.S., Soviet, British, and French occupation; Hitler commits suicide

1945-48: East Germany and part of Berlin come under Soviet occupation and are brought under the control of the Communist-dominated Socialist Unity Party. A separate East German state is established under Soviet auspices as a result of the failure of the USSR and the Western occupying powers to agree on a uniform policy for all of Germany

1948-49: Soviet opposition to the plans of the three other Allies for Germany's future results in breakdown of joint Four Power rule; Russians attempt to blockade Berlin, whereupon Western Allies mount gigantic airlift to bring food to West Berliners; in October 1949, following the creation of the Federal Republic of Germany, Russians set up the German Democratic Republic

1953: Anti-Communist revolt in East Germany is crushed by Soviet forces

1955: Soviet Union signs treaty declaring East Germany a sovereign state

1961: Wall is erected around non-Soviet sectors of Berlin to prevent flight of East Germans to the west via West Berlin

1968: East German leader Walter Ulbricht meets with other East European leaders and calls for concerted action to halt liberalization in Czechoslovakia; within months, East German troops join in Soviet-led invasion of Czechoslovakia

1971: Ulbricht resigns as head of Socialist Unity Party, is succeeded by Erich Honecker of the party's Central Committee

1972: Traffic Treaty is signed with West Germany, providing for access to West Berlin

GERMANY

CONIC PROJECTION

SCALE OF MILES
0 10 20 30 40 60

SCALE OF KILOMETRES
0 10 20 30 40 60

Capitals of Countries ★
State and District Capitals ▲
Canals

Copyright by C. S. HAMMOND & Co., N.Y.

1973: East and West Germany ratify a treaty calling for closer relations. Later in the year, both join the UN. Ulbricht dies

1974: U.S. establishes diplomatic relations with East Germany in September. The two Germanys exchange representatives

1975: The Government begins extensive housing projects

1978: Agreement reached with West Germany on construction of new highway to West Berlin and other transit matters. Diplomatic problems arise over status of East Berlin

WEST GERMANY

Area: 95,704 sq. mi. **Population:** 62,200,000 (1978 est.)

Official Name: Federal Republic of Germany **Capital:** Bonn **Nationality:** German is the official and universal language **Religion:** 49% Protestant, 45% Roman Catholic **Flag:** Black, red, and gold horizontal stripes **Anthem:** The official national anthem consists of the third verse of the old Deutschlandlied, beginning "Unity and Justice and Freedom" **Currency:** Deutsche Mark (1.90 per U.S. $1)

Location: North-central Europe. West Germany is bordered by Denmark and the North Sea on the north, by East Germany and Czechoslovakia on the east, by Austria and Switzerland on the south, and by France, Luxembourg, Belgium, and the Netherlands on the west **Features:** The country is generally flat in the north and hilly in the central and western areas, rising to more than 4,000 feet in the Black Forest and to more than twice that height in the Bavarian Alps **Chief Rivers:** Rhine, Danube, Ems, Weser, Elbe, Main, Mosel, Neckar, Isar

Head of State: President Karl Carstens, born 1914, elected 1979 for 5 years **Head of Government:** Chancellor Helmut Schmidt, born 1918, appointed 1974, Elected 1976 **Effective Date of Present Constitution:** May 23, 1949 **Legislative Body:** Parliament (bicameral), consisting of the *Bundestag* and *Bundesrat*. The *Bundestag* has 496 elected members and 22 nonvoting members representing West Berlin, chosen for a term of 4 years. The *Bundesrat* has 41 members appointed by the state governments and 4 consultative members appointed by the West Berlin Senate **Local Government:** 10 states (*Laender*), each with its own legislative and ministerial government. West Berlin, though not legally a component state of West Germany, is closely integrated into the government's political and administrative system

Ethnic Composition: With the exception of a small Danish population in Schleswig-Holstein, the population is German **Population Distribution:** 86% urban **Density:** 650 inhabitants per sq. mi.

Largest Cities: (1976 est.) Berlin (West) 1,984,837, Hamburg 1,717,383, Munich 1,314,865, Cologne 1,013,771, Essen 677,568, Düsseldorf 664,336, Frankfurt-am-Main 636,157, Dortmund 630,609, Stuttgart 600,421

Per Capita Income: $8,372 (1978) **Gross National Product (GNP):** $513 billion (1978) **Economic Statistics:** About 54.6% of GNP is derived from manufacturing (food industry, chemicals, iron and steel, electrical engineering, machinery); 18.5% is from trade, transportation and communications; 13.5% is from agriculture (rye, wheat, oats, barley, potatoes), forestry and fishing **Minerals and Mining:** Coal is the most important mineral resource. There are also substantial deposits of iron ore (mostly low grade), lead and zinc, potash, salt, fluorspar, barites, pyrites, graphites, and basalt. Petroleum and natural gas production meets about 20% of the nation's requirements **Labor Force:** 25.6 million (1976), with 46% in industry, 29% in services, 18% in trade, and 7% in agriculture **Foreign Trade:** Exports, chiefly mechanical engineering products, motor vehicles, chemicals, electrical engineering products, and iron and steel, totaled $118 billion in 1977. Imports, mainly foodstuffs, nonferrous metals and semifinished products, chemical products, iron and steel, textiles, totaled $101 billion **Principal Trade Partners:** United States, Canada, France, Netherlands, Great Britain, Belgium, Italy, Japan, Switzerland, Austria, Sweden

Vital Statistics: Birthrate, 9.6 per 1,000 of pop. (1977); death rate, 11.8 **Life Expectancy:** 71 years **Health Statistics:** 87 inhabitants per hospital bed, 516 per physician (1974) **Infant Mortality:** 17.4 per 1,000 births **Illiteracy:** Negligible **Education Statistics:** 38,076 primary and secondary schools, with combined enrollment of 11,889,493 (1975) **Enrollment in Higher Education:** 840,757 **GNP Expended on Education:** 4.5% (1974)

Transportation: Surfaced roads total 104,487 mi., with 4,000 mi. of superhighways **Motor Vehicles:** 20,273,600 (1976) **Passenger Cars:** 18,919,700 **Railway Mileage:** 19,876 **Ports:** Hamburg, Wilhelmshaven, Bremen, Kiel, Emden, Lübeck **Major Airlines:** Lufthansa operates domestic and international services **Communications:** Partly government controlled **Radio Transmitters:** 346 **Licenses:** 20,909,000 (1975) **Television Transmitters:** 1,153 **Licenses:** 19,226,000 (1975) **Telephones:** 21,162,000 (1976) **Newspapers:** 320 dailies, 289 copies per 1,000 inhabitants (1974)

Weights and Measures: Metric system **Travel Requirements:** Passport; no visa for 90 days

The Federal Republic of Germany was created in 1949 in the British, French, and U.S. occupation zones of Germany, as a vehicle for solving the German problem. Located in the center of Europe and in the center of big-power politics, Germany was divided for centuries; in eight decades as a unified nation, it twice frightened the world. At first resentful of their division into two after 1949, the Germans gradually became accustomed to it.

The Christian Democratic Union/Christian Social Union (CDU/CSU) has been the largest party in every West German *Bundestag*, but has had a majority in only one. Konrad Adenauer, CDU/CSU Chancellor from 1949 to 1963, aligned West Germany with NATO, and presided over an "economic miracle" in which the country recovered from the ravages of war and absorbed millions of ethnic German immigrants from East Germany and Eastern Europe. The free-enterprise policies of Adenauer's Minister of Economics, Ludwig Erhard, were credited with the country's surprising growth, but West Germany was aided by having inherited most of prewar Germany's iron ore, coal, and hydropower, and—after 1958—by membership in the European Economic Community.

The Social Democratic Party of Germany (SPD) has been the second-largest in every *Bundestag*; the Free Democratic Party (FDP) has held the balance of power between the CDU/CSU and the SPD since 1961. The FDP went into coalition with the CDU/CSU in 1961, forced the aging Adenauer to retire in favor of Ludwig Erhard in 1963, and brought down Erhard by withdrawing from the coalition in 1966. Kurt Kiesinger then became leader of the CDU/CSU, formed a "grand coalition" with the SPD, and served as chancellor until 1969.

Originally a socialist party, the SPD has become a party of moderate reform within capitalism. Willy Brandt, former Mayor of West Berlin, was its leader in 1969, when it took power in coalition with the FDP. He concentrated on foreign policy, and shocked many Germans by abandoning talk of reunification and by recognizing the East German regime. He also improved relations with other Communist countries and worked to strengthen and expand the EEC. Forced to resign because of an espionage scandal in 1974, he was succeeded by Helmut Schmidt, also a Social Democrat. Two successive SPD chancellors have done little to modify their predecessors' free-enterprise policies, and West Germany has remained an economic giant. Growth is slower than in the heady years of the economic miracle, but inflation and unemployment are lower than elsewhere, and the balance of payments is actually too favorable. Schmidt especially has been criticized by other Western governments for not curbing West German exports.

Prosperity has not eliminated discontent. Terrorist activity has been severe, especially in 1977. In 1978, a controversial new law increased the authority of the police.

In 1979, the broadcast on West German television of the U.S. series "Holocaust" indicated a new willingness to face the Nazi past.

HISTORY: The history of West Germany is bound up with that of Germany as a whole until the years immediately following World War II (See East Germany for pre-WW II chronology)

1948-49: Western Allies mount massive airlift to Berlin, thwarting Soviet attempt to blockade city; West German constituent assembly adopts provisional constitution for the Federal Republic of Germany; Konrad Adenauer is elected chancellor; East Germany, under Soviet occupation, is set up as a Communist state named the German Democratic Republic

1961: East German government erects Berlin Wall in effort to halt flight of East Germans to the west via West Berlin

1963: Adenauer retires and is succeeded by Ludwig Erhard

1966: Country is rocked by student demonstrations following attempted slaying of left-wing student leader in West Berlin

1968: Kurt Kiesinger becomes chancellor

1969: Willy Brandt becomes chancellor

1970: A nonaggression treaty, recognizing present European borders, is signed with Soviet Union

1972: Nonaggression pact with Soviet Union and Poland ratified. U.S., USSR, Britain, and France sign Final Quadripartite Protocol in Berlin, putting into effect earlier agreements on civilian travel in and around Berlin

1974: Chancellor Willy Brandt resigns over a spy scandal involving a member of his staff. Helmut Schmidt succeeds him. Legal age of majority is lowered from 21 to 18. Two German states recognize each other

1975: Economy is slowed by inflation and high unemployment

1976: Treaty with Poland to allow ethnic Germans to emigrate is ratified. Ruling coalition of Social Democrats and Free Democrats wins close victory in nationwide parliamentary elections

1978: Controversial anti-terrorist laws enacted. Bonn promises East Germany to increase efforts to stem East-to-West refugee flow

1979: Karl Carstens is elected President by the Federal Convention (the *Bundestag* plus members of the *laender* parliaments)

GHANA

Area: 92,099 sq. mi. **Population:** 10,400,000 (1978 est.)

Official Name: Republic of Ghana **Capital:** Accra **Nationality:** Ghanaian **Languages:** English is the official and commercial language; of some 50 tribal languages and dialects spoken, the chief ones are Twi, Fanti, Ga, Ewe, Hausa, Dagbani, and Akan **Religion:** About 42% Christian, 12% Moslem, and the rest animist **Flag:** Red, gold, and green horizontal stripes, with a 5-pointed black star centered on the gold stripe **Anthem:** National Anthem, beginning "Lift high the flag of Ghana" **Currency:** Cedi (2.75 per U.S. $1)

Location: West Africa. Ghana is bordered on the north by Upper Volta, on the east by Togo, on the south by the Gulf of Guinea, and on the west by the Ivory Coast **Features:** Half of Ghana is less than 500 feet above sea level. The coastline is largely a low sandy shore, backed by plains and intersected by rivers. Northward is a belt of tropical rain forest, broken by densely forested hills and rivers. The far north is a region covered by savanna and grassland plains **Chief Rivers:** Volta, Pra, Tano

Head of State and of Government: Rule is by Armed Forces Revolutionary Council, headed by Flight Lieut. Jerry Rawlings, following the coup of June 4, 1979. Hilla Limann, elected July 10, is scheduled to become President on Oct. 1, 1979 **Effective Date of Present Constitution:** August 1969; suspended 1972; a new constitution is being formulated **Legislative Body:** None **Local Government:** 9 regions divided into districts; each region is administered by a regional commissioner

Ethnic Composition: Ghanaians are chiefly of black Sudanese stock, the principal groups being the Akan, living mostly along the coast, and the Ashanti, in the forest areas immediately to the north; the Guans, living on the plains of the Volta River; the Gaand Ewe-speaking peoples of the south and southeast; and the Moshi-Dagomba-speaking tribes of the north **Population Distribution:** 29% urban **Density:** 113 inhabitants per sq. mi.

Largest Cities (M.A. = Metropolitan Area): (1970 census) Accra 564,194 (M.A. 738,498); Kumasi 260,286 (M.A. 345,117); Sekondi-Takoradi 91,874 (M.A. 160,868); Tema 60,767

Per Capita Income: $400 (1978) **Gross National Product (GNP):** $4.4 billion (1978 est.) **Economic Statistics:** In 1975 about 45% of GNP was from agriculture (cocoa, of which Ghana is the world's leading producer, livestock, fish); 15% from manufacturing and mining; and 40% from trade and services. Industry consists of aluminum smelting and the processing of cocoa, kola nuts, coffee, coconuts, oil palms, and rubber **Minerals and Mining:** Gold is the most important mineral exploited, followed by diamonds (the world's second largest producer). There are large reserves of manganese and bauxite; other minerals include low-grade deposits of iron ore, and deposits of beryl, ilmenite, nickel, graphite, and chromite **Labor Force:** 3.4 million, of which 57% is employed in agriculture, forestry, and fishing, 15.5% in industry and mining, and 27.5% in trade and services **Foreign Trade:** Exports, chiefly cocoa, cocoa butter, manganese, gold, diamonds, timber and aluminum, totaled $804 million in 1976. Imports, mainly machinery and transport equipment, cereals, alumina, petroleum, and textiles, totaled $842 million **Principal Trade Partners:** Britain, United States, Netherlands, West Germany, China, Switzerland

Vital Statistics: Birthrate, 47 per 1,000 of pop. (1976); death rate, 22 per 1,000 of pop. (1976) **Life Expectancy:** 52 years **Health Statistics:** 599 inhabitants per hospital bed; 10,511 per physician (1975) **Infant Mortality:** 59 per 1,000 births **Illiteracy:** 70% **Education Statistics:** 10,554 primary and secondary schools, with combined enrollment of 1,582,978 (1974) **Enrollment in Higher Education:** 9,079 (1975) **GNP Expended on Education:** 3.9% (1973)

Transportation: Paved roads total 2,870 mi. **Motor Vehicles:** 110,000 (1976) **Passenger Cars:** 64,000 **Railway Mileage:** 790 **Ports:** Tema, Takoradi **Major Airlines:** Ghana Airways operates internal and international services **Communications:** Government controlled **Radio Transmitters:** 10 **Receivers:** 10,080,000 (1976) **Television Transmitters:** 4 **Receivers:** 35,000 (1976) **Telephones:** 62,000 (1976) **Newspapers:** 4 dailies, 51 copies per 1,000 inhabitants (1975)

Weights and Measures: British standards are being replaced by the metric system **Travel Requirements:** Passport; visa, valid up to 14 days; $2.25 fee; 3 photos

The first of Britain's African possessions to gain freedom in the postwar decolonization era, Ghana has gone from a democratic parliamentary system, through dictatorship, rule by a military junta, a return to democracy, and, at present, control by the military.

During this time, the country also experienced overly ambitious industrialization and near bankruptcy as a result of the extravagances of Kwame Nkrumah, its first leader. Nkrumah was deposed in 1966, and died in exile in 1972.

Ghana, however, possesses a potentially strong economy; major resources range through cocoa, timber, manganese, gold, and electric power. Her people are capable and progressive.

As the Gold Coast, the country had moved steadily toward self-government prior to independence in 1957 and with its new name of Ghana—that of an ancient African empire—was otherwise well prepared for complete sovereignty.

Ghana has many educators, lawyers, doctors, economists, and a well-trained civil service. Development programs are concentrating on diversification of agriculture, an increase of arable land, and the improvement of rural communities. The prime objective is to reduce Ghana's dependency on cocoa exports by increasing exports and self-sufficiency in other products.

Ghana is still the world's leading supplier of cocoa, but with lagging production and increases by other countries, her share of the market has declined.

In April 1978 the Ghana government banned three political organizations (and arrested 17 leading civilian politicians) after a nationwide referendum showed a majority of voters favor single-party rule. In 1977 those outlawed had spearheaded an "intellectual's revolt" that posed the gravest crisis to the government since its seizure of power in 1972. Students, doctors, lawyers, engineers and other professionals had joined in accusing the nation's military rulers of repression, corruption and fiscal mismanagement, and had demanded they resign.

Gen. Ignatius Kutu Acheampong, head of state since 1972, resigned on July 5, 1978, and was succeeded by Lt. Gen. Fred W.K. Akuffo. His first act was to release the civilians who had been arrested earlier in 1978. Strikes by civil servants and energy industry workers prompted the government to declare a state of emergency, which lasted from November to the end of 1978. While lifting the state of emergency on January 1, 1979, officials also legalized political activity for the first time in seven years.

On June 4 the government of General Akuffo was overthrown in a coup staged by junior army officers, and an Armed Forces Revolutionary Council, headed by Flight Lieut. Jerry Rawlings, took control. Former heads-of-state Akwasi Afrifa, Ignatius Acheampong and Fred Akuffo were executed shortly thereafter, in spite of an appeal for mercy from UN Secretary-General Waldheim. Nigeria halted oil deliveries to Ghana to register its displeasure.

An election for a new President held on July 10 ended in inconclusive results. The runoff on July 28 was won by Hilla Limann, who is scheduled to take office on October 1.

HISTORY: Ghana was dominated by independent black kingdoms in precolonial times. Following the arrival of the Portuguese in the 15th century, the coastal region soon became known as the Gold Coast because of the rich trade in gold. The gold trade later gave way to the slave trade, which was eventually abolished by the British in the 19th century. In 1874, Britain established the colony of the Gold Coast and in 1901 annexed the neighboring Ashanti kingdom. In the same year a region to the north, known as the Northern Territories, became a British protectorate

1922: Part of neighboring Togoland, a former German colony, is mandated to Britain by League of Nations and administered as part of the Gold Coast

1942-48: Africans are admitted into the government of the Gold Coast, but native agitation for independence mounts under the leadership of United Gold Coast Convention Party; party leaders Joseph B. Danquah and Kwame Nkrumah are imprisoned

1949: Nkrumah, following his release, breaks with Danquah and forms his own party, the Convention People's Party, and leads campaign of civil disobedience against the British

1951-52: Britain grants new constitution and elections are held; Nkrumah becomes prime minister

1957: The state of Ghana, comprising the Gold Coast and British Togoland, obtains independence, becoming the first black African colony to do so. Joins the UN

1960: Ghana becomes a republic within the British Commonwealth; Nkrumah becomes both chief of state and head of government, and is given the power to rule without parliament whenever he deems it necessary

1962-64: Nkrumah establishes one-party rule; several attempts on his life lead to arrests of numerous leaders in his own Convention People's Party and of opposition leader Joseph Danquah, who dies in prison

1966: Nkrumah is deposed by a military coup; a National Liberation Council, headed by Lieutenant General Joseph A. Ankrah, is set up to rule the country

1969: Ankrah resigns after admitting he received money for political purposes and is succeeded by General Akwasi Afrifa. Civilian government is restored under new constitution

1970: Three-man presidential commission headed by Afrifa is dissolved; former Chief Justice Edward Akufo-Addo is elected president by electoral college

1972: Colonel Ignatius Kutu Acheampong leads military coup against the Busia Government and assumes power as head of state; offices of president and prime minister abolished and constitution withdrawn. Kwame Nkrumah dies and his body is returned from Guinea for burial in Ghana

1975: Treaty is signed with EEC

1978: July 1, 1979, set as beginning date of new government made up of military officers, police and civilians. Acheampong is replaced as head of state by Lt. Gen. Fred W.K. Akuffo

1979: Akuffo is overthrown on June 4, and is replaced by an Armed Forces Revolutionary Council, headed by Flight Lieut. Jerry Rawlings. Afrifa, Acheampong and Akuffo are executed. Hilla Limann is elected President on July 18

GREECE

Area: 50,944 sq. mi. **Population:** 9,175,000 (1978 est.)

Official Name: Hellenic Republic **Capital:** Athens **Nationality:** Greek **Languages:** Modern Greek; Turkish and Albanian are minority languages **Religion:** 97% of the population belongs to the Greek Orthodox Church; 2% are Moslems **Flag:** Nine equal horizontal stripes of blue and white with a white cross on a blue field in the upper left corner **Anthem:** Hymn of Liberty **Currency:** Drachma (37.1 per U.S. $1)

Location: Southeast Europe, occupying the southern part of the Balkan peninsula and more than 3,000 offshore islands. The Greek mainland is bordered on the north by Bulgaria, Yugoslavia, and Albania; on the east by Turkey and the Aegean Sea; on the south by the Mediterranean Sea; and on the west by the Ionian Sea **Features:** The country is predominantly mountainous, with much of the land dry and rocky **Chief Rivers:** Aliakmon, Peneus, Vardar, Achelous, Nestos, Alpheus, Struma

Head of State: President Konstantinos Tsatsos, born 1899, elected June 1975 **Head of Government:** Premier Constantine Karamanlis, born 1907, installed 1974 **Effective Date of Present Constitution:** June 1975 **Legislative Body:** Parliament (unicameral), consisting of 300 deputies **Local Government:** 51 prefectures, each headed by an appointed prefect and the autonomous Mt. Athos district

Ethnic Composition: About 96% of the population is Greek. Minorities include Turks (1%), Slavs, Vlachs, Albanians and Bulgarians **Population Distribution:** 64.8% urban **Density:** 180 inhabitants per sq. mi.

Largest Cities (M.A. = Metropolitan Area): (1971 census) Athens 867,023 (M.A. 2,566,775), Salonika 345,799 (M.A. 482,361), Piraeus 187,362, Patras 111,607 (M.A. 112,228)

Per Capita Income: $2,576 (1978) **Gross National Product (GNP):** $24.1 billion (1978) **Economic Statistics:** Agriculture accounted for about 17% of the GNP in 1975 (the principal crops are wheat, tobacco, currants, grapes, olives, citrus fruits, and cotton); the industrial sector contributed about 31% (major industries include textiles; aluminum, nickel and chemical refineries; food processing; mining); services accounted for 50% **Minerals and Mining:** Lignite, bauxite, iron ore, chromite, barite and magnesite are exploited **Labor Force:** 3,388,000 (1975), with 39% in agriculture, 35% in trade and services, and 26% in industry **Foreign Trade:** Exports, mainly tobacco, currants, cotton, unprocessed aluminum, iron, nickel, and citrus fruits, totaled $2.7 billion (1977). Imports, chiefly machinery, iron and steel, crude oil, meat, passenger cars and trucks, totaled $6.8 billion **Principal Trade Partners:** West Germany, Italy, United States, France, Japan, Saudi Arabia, Britain, Libya

Vital Statistics: Birthrate, 15.4 per 1,000 of pop. (1977); death rate, 8.2 **Life Expectancy:** 71 years **Health Statistics:** 155 inhabitants per hospital bed; 491 per physician (1975) **Infant Mortality:** 23 per 1,000 births (1976) **Illiteracy:** 10% **Education Statistics:** 12,120 primary and secondary schools, with combined enrollment of 1,552,690 (1972) **Enrollment in Higher Education:** 111,435 (1975) **GNP Expended on Education:** 1.7% (1974)

Transportation: Paved roads total 9,875 mi. **Motor Vehicles:** 747,400 (1976) **Passenger Cars:** 510,000 **Railway Mileage:** 1,580 mi. **Ports:** Piraeus, Salonika, Iraklion, Patras, Eleusis, Volos **Major Airlines:** Olympic Airways operates domestic and international services **Communications:** Government controlled **Radio Transmitters:** 51 **Receivers:** 2,750,000 (1976) **Television Transmitters:** 54 **Receivers:** 1,165,000 (1976) **Telephones:** 2,180,000 (1975) **Newspapers:** 106 dailies, 107 copies per 1,000 inhabitants (1975)

Weights and Measures: Metric system **Travel Requirements:** Passport; no visa for 2 months

The Hellenes (Greeks) inhabit a mountainous peninsula and its neighboring rocky islands. Agriculture is difficult—and so is administration. Trade and navigation—fostered by excellent harbors—have been vital for thousands of years. Individualism and loyalty to locality are strong.

The ancient Greeks had no national unity, but they were leaders in art, literature, and philosophy; and some of their city-states were the world's first democracies.

Conquered by Macedonia, then by Rome, then by the Ottoman Empire, Greece achieved independence and unity in struggles against the last in the 19th and 20th centuries. Disputes with Turkey concerning land and—more recently—territorial waters are still troublesome. Political stability within Greece has been rare.

Greece was occupied by Germany in World War II and needed considerable assistance from the United States to quell a Communist guerrilla movement in the war's aftermath. Greece entered NATO, despite the misgivings of many Greeks about U.S. influence, and Turkish membership, in the alliance. Later, the troubles in Cyprus aggravated ill-feelings toward Turkey.

Governed by short-lived coalition governments from 1946 until 1952, Greece achieved stability under Premier Alexander Papagos in 1952. He died in 1955, and Constantine Karamanlis succeeded him, serving until 1963, when he went into exile after a squabble with King Paul. George Papandreou formed a stable government in 1964, but anti-NATO elements in his past worried many. King Constantine II fired him in 1965, and political unrest followed until the army seized power in 1967.

Colonel George Papadopoulous emerged as strong man and premier. He abolished the monarchy and made himself president in 1973, only to be deposed by military colleagues. General Demetrios Ioannides ran the government from behind the scenes until 1974, when he sponsored the ill-fated coup against President Makarios of Cyprus. His fellow-officers deposed him and invited Constantine Karamanlis to resume the premiership.

Karamanlis held an election, which his own New Democracy party won handily. He loosened Greece's connection with NATO and objected to the decision of the United States to end the arms embargo against Turkey. In a special election in 1977, his party won, but by a reduced margin, and the Panhellenic Socialist Movement (PASOK), with a policy favoring neutrality, emerged as the second-largest party.

Despite his reduced mandate, Karamanlis took bold initiatives in foreign affairs. A trade treaty with Albania, negotiated in 1978, represented a new opening to the outside world for the strict Albanian Communist regime. For Greece, an opening of an even greater importance came in 1979, when a treaty was negotiated to make Greece a full member of the European Community in 1981. An associate member for years, Greece will be the first full member outside the heavily industrial region of Western Europe. Membership is opposed by PASOK, which fears that Greece will become an agricultural colony of other members.

HISTORY: Ancient Greece, a small land fragmented into frequently warring city-states, attained its golden age in the Athens of the 5th century B.C. In the following century it fell to the forces of Philip of Macedon, whose son, Alexander the Great, spread Hellenistic civilization widely. In the 2nd century B.C., Greece became a territory of the Roman Empire and eventually was incorporated into the Byzantine Empire. Turkish conquests, completed in the 15th century, made Greece part of the Ottoman Empire

1821-30: Greeks wage war of independence against Tucks, who gain help of Egypt; following intervention by Britain, France, and Russia, Greece wins autonomy and finally independence

1832-63: European powers choose Prince Otto of Bavaria to be king of a fully independent Greece; he is deposed in 1862. The following year a Danish prince is chosen as monarch, becoming King George I of the Hellenes

1912-22: Greece takes part in the Balkan Wars of 1912-13 and increases its territory. Outbreak of World War I leads to split between pro-Allied government and neutralist King Constantine I; king abdicates in 1917; Greece joins Allied side and gains additional territory in the postwar settlements; Greece invades Asia Minor and is defeated by Turks

1923: Hostility to dynasty forces George II to leave Greece

1924-35: Greece is proclaimed a republic; after more than a decade of political strife, a plebiscite restores the monarchy

1936-41: John Metaxas becomes premier and institutes a dictatorship that lasts through Italy's World War II invasion of Greece, begun in 1940, and continues up to his death in 1941

1941-50: Germany invades in 1941 and Greece is occupied by Axis forces. With the expulsion of the last of the German troops in 1944, rivalry between Greek Communist and royalist guerrillas erupts into civil war. Under the Truman Doctrine, announced in 1947, the United States sends advisers to the Greek Army and provides $300 million in economic and military aid; Communist forces are finally defeated in 1950

1967: Military junta seizes power. King Constantine II and the royal family flee to Rome after an abortive countercoup; Col. George Papadopoulos becomes premier

1973: Papadopoulos decrees end to monarchy, appoints himself head of new "Hellenic Republic." He is toppled by a bloodless coup. Gen. Phaedon Gizikis becomes president with Dimitrios Ioannides as military dictator; elections are postponed indefinitely

1974: Ioannides sponsors coup in Cyprus. Turkish army invades Cyprus. Military junta leaders turn government over to civilians, ending seven years of military rule. Former Premier Constantine Karamanlis returns from self-imposed exile in Paris and is sworn in as premier by President Gizikis. Britain, Turkey, and Greece, meeting in Geneva, impose new cease-fire on Cyprus. Soon after, when Geneva peace talks break down, Turkish forces resume their advance on Cyprus. Greece withdraws its armed forces from NATO. First free elections in more than a decade result in decisive victory for Premier Karamanlis. In national referendum voters reject monarchy in favor of republican form of government

1975: Parliament adopts a new constitution and elects Konstantinos Tsatsos as president. Trial of the principal organizers of the 1967 coup results in their death sentences being commuted by Cabinet to life imprisonment

1977: Karamanlis's New Democracy Party loses 41 seats in parliamentary election, Panhellenic Socialist Movement gains 77; five other groups share remaining seats

1978: Greek leaders deplore Carter Administration plan to end U.S. arms embargo against Turkey. Controversial new law makes terrorism a capital offense

1979: Agreement reached on membership in European Community, effective 1981

GRENADA

Area: 133 sq. mi. **Population:** 100,000 (1978 est.)

Official Name: Grenada **Capital:** St. George's **Nationality:** Grenadine **Languages:** English, with a rarely used Franco-African patois **Religion:** Roman Catholicism, Protestantism **Flag:** A diagonally divided field, yellow at top and bottom and green at sides, with red border on all sides, bearing along top and bottom three yellow stars each; in center a yellow star on a red disk; in hoist a green triangle with a nutmeg with yellow shell and brown fruit **Anthem:** N.A. **Currency:** East Caribbean dollar (2.70 per U.S. $1)

Location: The southernmost of the Windward Islands in the West Indies. Includes the southern Grenadines, the largest of which is Carriacou **Features:** Volcanic in origin, the islands are chiefly mountainous **Chief Rivers:** There are no large rivers

Head of State: Queen Elizabeth II, represented by a governorgeneral, Sir Paul Scoon **Head of Government:** Prime Minister Maurice Bishop, born 1945, seized power in 1979 **Effective Date of Present Constitution:** 1967, suspended 1979 **Legislative Body:** Rule is by a 14-member People's Revolutionary Government (PRG) **Local Government:** 7 parishes

Ethnic Composition: Largely of mixed descent, with strains of white settlers, Africans brought in as slaves, and Carib Indians **Population Distribution:** N.A. **Density:** 752 inhabitants per sq. mi.

Largest Cities: (1970 census) St. George's 6,313, Gouyave 2,498, Grenville 1,723, Victoria 1,673

Per Capita Income: $380 (1974 est.) **Gross National Product (GNP):** $38 million (1977 est.) **Economic Statistics:** The economy is agricultural, with sugar, coconuts, nutmeg, cocoa, and bananas the chief exports. Yams, rice, breadfruit, and corn are grown for food. Tourism is increasingly important **Minerals and Mining:** Offshore exploration for gas and oil in progress **Labor Force:** 30,196, of which 40% are employed in agriculture, forestry and fishing **Foreign Trade:** Exports, chiefly cocoa, nutmeg and bananas, totaled $12 million (1975 est.). Imports totaled $24 million **Principal Trade Partners:** Britain, United States, Canada, Caribbean countries

Vital Statistics: Birthrate, 27.4 per 1,000 of pop. (1975); death rate, 5.9 **Life Expectancy:** 63 years **Health Statistics:** 144 inhabitants per hospital bed; 4,000 per physician (1974) **Infant Mortality:** 23.5 per 1,000 births **Illiteracy:** 24% **Education Statistics:** 71 primary and secondary schools with a combined enrollment of 34,863 (1971) **Enrollment in Higher Education:** c. 100 (1974) **GNP Expended on Education:** 5.7% (1972)

Transportation: Surfaced roads total 480 mi. **Motor Vehicles:** 3,900 (1971) **Passenger Cars:** 3,800 **Railway Mileage:** None **Ports:** St. George's, Grenville, Hillsborough **Major Airlines:** LIAT **Communications:** Government owned **Radio Transmitters:** 5 **Receivers:** 22,000 (1976) **Television:** None **Telephones:** 5,000 (1976) **Newspapers:** 1 daily (1975), 13 copies per 1,000 inhabitants (1965)

Weights and Measures: British and metric systems **Travel Requirements:** Passport and visa not required for first 6 months

Formerly a dependency of the United Kingdom and later a member of the British-controlled Federation of the West Indies, Grenada became an internally self-governing state on March 3, 1967. The United Kingdom retained responsibility for defense and external affairs. On February 7, 1974, Grenada became independent within the British Commonwealth of Nations, with a parliamentary system of government based on Great Britain's.

Grenada, known as the "Isle of Spice," is famous for its nutmeg, cocoa and cinnamon. Tourism is another mainstay of the island's economy, contributing an estimated $9 million to the Grenadine livelihood.

Politically, Grenada has been the scene of widespread unrest since independence. The controversy centered on Prime Minister Eric Gairy's rule, considered by many Grenadians to be dictatorial. Rioting broke out in 1973 and 1974, and a secret police squad retaliated by employing strong-arm tactics. Subsequently, tourism declined and many Grenadians fled. In late 1976 Gairy was narrowly reelected with rural support.

In a coup marked by one death, Maurice Bishop and the socialist New Jewel Movement seized the government on March 13, 1979, while Gairy was in New York. The coup was accomplished by seizing the radio station and police barracks, along with government officials in their homes.

Bishop became prime minister, and a 14-member People's Revolutionary Government took office. The constitution was suspended March 25, but Grenada remained within the British Commonwealth.

HISTORY: The original inhabitants of the islands were Arawak Indians who were expelled by the warlike Caribs shortly before the visit of Columbus in 1498. An abortive English settlement in 1609 was followed by French settlement and control from 1650 to 1762. Britain controlled the islands for over 200 years, except for five years of French rule (1779-83) during the American Revolution

1833: Slavery is abolished

1967: Grenada assumes Associated State status

1974: Independence is attained. Grenada is admitted to UN

1975: Treaty is signed with EEC

1979: The New Jewel Movement seizes the government in an almost bloodless coup, and Maurice Bishop becomes prime minister

GUATEMALA

Area: 42,042 sq. mi. **Population:** 6,450,000 (1978 est.)

Official Name: Republic of Guatemala **Capital:** Guatemala **Nationality:** Guatemalan **Languages:** Spanish is the official and predominant language; 20 varieties of the Maya-Quiché Indian dialects are spoken in the countryside **Religion:** Overwhelmingly Roman Catholic **Flag:** Blue, white, and blue vertical bands, with the national coat of arms in the center **Anthem:** National Anthem, beginning "Blessed Guatemala" **Currency:** Quetzal (1 per U.S. $1)

Location: Central America. Guatemala is bordered on the north by Mexico, on the east by Belize and the Caribbean, on the southeast by Honduras and El Salvador, on the southwest by the Pacific Ocean, and on the west by Mexico **Features:** The central highland region constitutes about one-fifth of the country's land surface. The Pacific plain is a narrow belt between mountains and ocean, while the Caribbean lowlands consist of fertile river valleys. The northern part of the country is dominated by the lowland forest of Petén **Chief Rivers:** Motagua, Usumacinta, Polochic, Samalá

Head of State and of Government: President: Gen. Fernando Romeo Lucas García, born 1924, elected 1978 **Effective Date of Present Constitution:** September 15, 1965 **Legislative Body:** National Congress (unicameral), consisting of 61 deputies elected by universal suffrage for 4 years **Local Government:** 22 departments, administered by governors appointed by the president and a central district, the capital city

Ethnic Composition: Pure-blooded descendants of the Maya Indians make up almost 50% of the population; the rest is largely of mixed Spanish and Indian descent **Population Distribution:** 36% urban **Density:** 153 inhabitants per sq. mi.

Largest Cities: (1973 census) Guatemala 700,538, Tiquisate 67,555, Quezaltenango 65,526, Escuintla 64,851

Per Capita Income: $998 (1978) **Gross National Product (GNP):** $6.6 billion (1978 est.) **Economic Statistics:** In 1973 about 28% of GNP came from agriculture (coffee, cotton, sugar cane, bananas, corn, beans, rice, wheat); 16% is derived from industry (foodstuffs, tobacco, textiles, furniture, paper and paper products), leather goods, chemical products, machinery and metal products); and 44% from trade and services **Minerals and Mining:** Zinc, silver, lead, nickel, and limestone are exploited **Labor Force:** 1,895,168 (1975), of which 58% is employed in agriculture, 24% in trade and services and 18% in industry **Foreign Trade:** Exports, chiefly coffee, bananas, cotton, sugar and meat, totaled $1.2 billion in 1977. Imports, mainly industrial machinery, textiles, chemicals and pharmaceutical products, and construction materials, totaled $1.1 billion **Principal Trade Partners:** United States, Central American countries, West Germany, Japan, Venezuela

Vital Statistics: Birthrate, 40 per 1,000 of pop. (1976); death rate, 14 (1976) **Life Expectancy:** 52 years **Health Statistics:** 457 inhabitants per hospital bed; 4,338 per physician (1971) **Infant Mortality:** 77 per 1,000 births (1976) **Illiteracy:** 54% **Education Statistics:** 5,912 primary and secondary schools, with combined enrollment of 675,802 (1973) **Enrollment in Higher Education:** 22,881 (1975) **GNP Expended on Education:** 1.7% (1973)

Transportation: Paved roads total 1,450 mi. **Motor Vehicles:** 132,800 (1976) **Passenger Cars:** 82,700 **Railway Mileage:** 514 **Ports:** Pto. Barrios, Sto. Tomás de Castilla, San José, Champerico **Major Airlines:** AVIATECA operates domestic and international services **Communications:** Partly government controlled **Radio Transmitters:** 95 **Receivers:** 265,000 (1976) **Television Transmitters:** 12 **Receivers:** 120,000 **Telephones:** 53,000 (1974) **Newspapers:** 11 dailies, 39 copies per 1,000 inhabitants (1972)

Weights and Measures: Metric system and local units **Travel Requirements:** Proof of citizenship; tourist card good for stay up to 6 months but usable only within 30 days of issue; $1 fee

Assassinations and kidnappings by extremists of both the left and right continue to plague Guatemala, the largest and potentially the wealthiest of the Central American republics.

In effect, there are two Guatemalas—one Spanish and one Indian. The Indians, concentrated in the picturesque central highlands, speak little Spanish and cling to peasant ways that originated with their Mayan ancestors well before the Spanish conquest. Constituting almost half the population, they account for the low economic and social standards of the country as a whole.

The educational deficit alone is staggering. Illiteracy still hovers at over 50 percent, and about half the children of school age get little or no schooling despite some progress in school construction. The problem is complicated by the necessity of teaching in the Indian languages before transferring to Spanish. Those who hold economic power in Guatemala have been reluctant to provide funds for education and other improvements.

Guatemala's wealth has traditionally been land-based. Coffee and cotton, the major products, are picked by the Indian population at low wages. In recent years, wider industrial opportunities have been provided by the Central American Common Market. Tires, clothing, foodstuffs, and pharmaceuticals have helped to diversify the economy although many of the industries are little more than assembly operations employing few workers. Oil reserves were discovered in 1976.

Murders in 1979 pointed up Guatemala's peasant discontent and political turbulence. Sen. Alberto Fuentes Mohr, leader of the Authentic Revolutionary Party, was slain by an unidentified gunman on Jan. 25, and Manuel Colom Argueta, leader of the Revolutionary United Front, was killed, also by an unidentified gunman, on March 22. "Death squads" from the right continued in action, and in January they reportedly killed 18 "petty criminals" in Guatemala City.

HISTORY: The Mayas, one of the most advanced of the Indian tribes, flourished in Guatemala for centuries before the arrival of the Spanish conquistadors. In the 12th century, however, Mayan civilization began to decline and its downfall was completed by the Spanish conquest in the 16th century. Under Spanish rule Guatemala was the seat of a captaincy general that administered most of Central America

1821: Guatemala is granted independence from Spain and with the other Central American countries is annexed to Mexico

1823-1825: Central American nations secede from Mexico and establish United Provinces of Central America

1839-1944: Guatemala becomes an independent republic and for more than a century is governed by the military

1951-57: Col. Jacobo Arbenz Guzmán, a leftist-leaning president, institutes social and agrarian reforms and expropriates holdings of foreign plantation owners, including United Fruit Co. Communist influence in Arbenz regime leads to strained relations with United States. With U.S. support, Col. Carlos Castillo Armas overthrows Arbenz in 1954 and returns expropriated land; Castillo Armas is assassinated in 1957

1958-63: Country is thrown into political turmoil and ruled by military juntas. State of siege is declared in 1963 to deal with growing terrorism and sabotage by extremists of right and left

1965-68: A new constitution takes effect in 1965; free elections are held the following year and Julio César Méndez Montenegro, candidate of moderately leftist Revolutionary Party, becomes president. He suspends constitutional guarantees in January 1968 following terrorist slayings of two U.S. military officials. In August, U.S. Ambassador John Mein is killed

1970: Carlos Arana Osorio, leading a right-wing coalition, wins presidential election. Terrorists kidnap several foreign diplomats, including the West German Ambassador, Count Karl von Spreti, who is slain. State of siege imposed

1974: Alleged vote fraud installs Gen. Kjell Laugerud García as president; violence ensues

1975: Britain agrees to resume talks with Guatemala on future of Belize (British Honduras). Guatemala has claimed sovereignty over the British dependency for more than 100 years

1976: Severe damage and 22,500 deaths are caused by a series of earthquakes

1977: Amnesty International reports that since 1966 over 20,000 Guatemalans, mainly political dissidents, have been killed or have disappeared as a result of government action, or action by semi-official forces

1978: Gen. Romeo Lucas García, government-backed moderate conservative, is elected president in runoff vote in Congress

---

GUINEA

Area: 94,925 sq. mi. **Population:** 4,850,000 (1978 est.)

Official Name: Popular and Revolutionary Republic of Guinea **Capital:** Conakry **Nationality:** Guinean **Languages:** French is the official language; the languages of 8 ethnic groups are recognized as national languages. The two main languages are Peul (Fulani) and Mandé **Religion:** About 75% Moslem, 24% animist, less than 1% Christian **Flag:** Red, yellow, and green vertical stripes **Anthem:** Liberty **Currency:** Syli (19.4 per U.S. $1)

Location: West Africa. Guinea is bordered by Senegal and Mali on the north, the Ivory Coast on the east, Liberia and Sierra Leone on the south, the Atlantic Ocean on the west, and Guinea-Bissau on the northwest **Features:** The country consists of a low-lying coastal area, a pastoral plateau, a forest region along the Liberian border, and a dry area in the north **Chief Rivers:** Niger, Bafing, Konkouré, Koliba, Milo

Head of State: President Ahmed Sékou Touré born 1922; in power since 1958, reelected 1975 for 7 years; he is secretary-general of the country's only party **Head of Government:** Premier: Dr. Lansana Béavogui took office April 1972 **Effective Date of Present Constitution:** November 12, 1958 **Legislative Body:** National Assembly (unicameral), consisting of 150 members elected for 5 years. All members belong to the Democratic Party of Guinea **Local Government:** 33 administrative regions, headed by appointed governors

Ethnic Composition: Of about 18 tribes in the country the most important are the Peuls (Fulani), Malinké (Mandingo), and Soussou **Population Distribution:** 9% urban **Density:** 51 inhabitants per sq. mi.

Largest City: (1973 est.) Conakry 198,000

Per Capita Income: $178 (1978) **Gross National Product (GNP):** $850 million (1978) **Economic Statistics:** In 1973 about 49% of GNP was from agriculture (coffee, palm products, corn, millet, pineapples, bananas, rice, cassava), forestry, and fishing; 13% from manufacturing (alumina, textiles, truck assembly, sawmilling, canning, paints, soap, cigarettes, plastics, furniture) and mining **Minerals and Mining:** Bauxite and iron ore deposits are among the richest in the world; other minerals are diamonds and gold **Labor Force:** About 85% of the working population is engaged in plantation and subsistence agriculture. About 136,000 are wage earners (1976), mostly in public service **Foreign Trade:** Exports, chiefly alumina, bananas, and iron ore, totaled $272 million in 1976. Imports, cotton textiles, rice, vehicles, cement, machinery, petroleum products, and sugar, totaled $206 million **Principal Trade Partners:** United States, France, West Germany, Spain, Italy, Romania, Canada, USSR, Britain

Vital Statistics: Birthrate, 47 per 1,000 of pop. (1974); death rate, 24 **Life Expectancy:** 41 years **Health Statistics:** 599 inhabitants per hospital bed; 22,394 per physician (1973) **Infant Mortality:** 172 per 1,000 births **Illiteracy:** 90% **Education Statistics:** 2,287 primary and secondary schools, with combined enrollment of 241,033 (1971) **Enrollment in Higher Education:** 2,874 (1972) **GNP Expended on Education:** 5.9% (1972)

Transportation: Improved roads total 4,700 mi. **Motor Vehicles:** 21,000 (1972) **Passenger Cars:** 10,200 **Railway Mileage:** 410 **Ports:** Conakry, Kassa, Benty, Kamsar **Major Airlines:** Air Guinée is the local carrier; 7 other lines provide international service **Communications:** State owned **Radio Transmitters:** 5 **Receivers:** 120,000 (1976) **Television:** None **Telephones:** 10,000 (1974) **Newspapers:** 1 daily, 1 copy per 1,000 inhabitants (1975)

Weights and Measures: Metric system **Travel Requirements:** Passport; visa, valid 3 months; $5 fee, 3 pictures

---

Committed by its militant leader, Ahmed Sékou Touré, in 1958 to "poverty in freedom rather than riches in slavery," Guinea has followed a tortuous course that has assured poverty but little freedom.

In 1958 Guinea was the only French colony to vote non to General de Gaulle's proposed community of semiautonomous nations still closely linked to France. Although, for France's former colonies, the community was to be a step toward eventual sovereignty, accompanied by aid and trade, Guinea opted for independence.

Hostility between France and Guinea persisted for the next two decades and ended officially only

with a state visit by French President Valéry Giscard d'Estaing in December 1978.

Until recently, Guinea's huge mineral resources and great hydroelectric potential had been neglected. In addition to iron ore, gold, and diamonds, Guinea possesses bauxite deposits estimated to be a third of the world's total. An international consortium of aluminum companies, in which the Guinean government holds 49 percent interest, is now operating a big bauxite mining complex at Boké in northern Guinea. Production at more than nine million tons a year is expected to earn Guinea $500 million over a 20-year period.

In late 1970, Touré's long rule was shaken by the landing at Conakry of a small, seaborne guerrilla force, which Touré charged was an invasion by Portuguese mercenaries and Guinean renegades, backed by Portugal and launched from neighboring Portuguese Guinea. Denied by Portugal, the charge was supported by a UN commission.

HISTORY: Guinea possesses a rich ethnic and cultural heritage derived from the empires of Ghana, Mali, and Songhai, which ranged from the western Sudan to the West African coast between the 10th and 15th centuries. In the 15th century, the Portuguese, followed by the Dutch, English, and French, opened the country to European contacts and trade. Following the establishment of a protectorate by France in 1849, French penetration inland met with strong resistance from Fulani and Malinké chieftains. Resistance was finally crushed with the defeat in 1898 of the popular hero and chieftain Samory Touré, from whom President Sékou Touré is said to be descended

1958: Guinea, the only French West African territory to vote against membership in the French Community, becomes an independent republic; Sékou Touré, an acknowledged Marxist although rejecting Marxism as inapplicable to Africa, becomes president and his Democratic Party of Guinea becomes the only political party; France abruptly withdraws all aid

1959-61: Guinea turns to the Soviet bloc and Communist China for assistance, and promotes African unity by forming short-lived union with Ghana and Mali

1965: Guinea suspends relations with France after charging that France encouraged a plot to overthrow Touré government

1966: Touré grants asylum to deposed Ghanaian President Nkrumah and names him honorary co-president of Guinea; new Ghanaian government breaks relations with Guinea

1970: Dispute with Portugal develops over charges of rebel infiltration from Guinea to Portuguese Guinea. Post of prime minister is created and the government is reorganized. Dr. Louis Lansana Béavogui becomes prime minister

1975: Relations restored with France. Touré elected for third seven-year term

1976: Discovery of a series of assassination plots on the life of President Touré announced by his administration. Government and military officials are implicated and arrested

1977: Apparently to improve relations with U.S., Guinea withdraws permission for Soviet Union to stage reconnaissance flights from its territory

1978: Guinea and Senegal restore diplomatic relations; French President Giscard d'Estaing visits

---

GUINEA-BISSAU

Area: 13,948 sq. mi. **Population:** 580,000 (1978 est.)

Official Name: Republic of Guinea-Bissau **Capital:** Bissau **Nationality:** Guinean **Languages:** Portuguese and Crioulo, a creole lingua franca **Religion:** 69% animist, 30% Moslem, 1% Christian **Flag:** A black star on a red vertical stripe at the hoist and equal horizontal stripes in the fly of gold over light green **Anthem:** N.A. **Currency:** Guinea-Bissau escudo (34.6 per U.S. $1)

Location: On the west coast of Africa, bounded by the Atlantic Ocean on the west, Senegal on the north, and Guinea on the east and south **Features:** A low-lying coastal plain with savanna, swamps, and rain forest. Large sections are frequently covered by tidal waters. There are 18 main offshore islands, including the Bijagós Archipelago **Chief Rivers:** Cacheu, Mansoa, Geba, Grande de Buba, Corubal

Head of State: President Luiz de Almeida Cabral, head of the State Council **Head of Goverment:** Premier (Chief Commissioner) Maj. João Bernardo Vieira, appointed 1978 **Effective Date of Constitution:** 1973 **Legislative Body:** National Assembly, 150 members of the PAIGC party elected for periods up to three years. It is the supreme organ of government, meets at least once a year and elects the president. The 15-member State Council serves for 3-

year terms **Local Government:** 12 administrative regions, with elected regional councils

Ethnic Composition: Except for small groups of Portuguese and mulattos the people are mostly indigenous (Balanta, Fulani, Mandyako, Malinké, and Pepel) **Population Distribution:** N.A. **Density:** 42 inhabitants per sq. mi.

Largest Cities: (1970 census) Bissau 71,169, Bafata 7,717

Per Capita Income: $187 (1976 est.) **Gross National Product (GNP):** $100 million (1976 est.) **Economic Statistics:** Agriculture probably accounts for well over 50% of the GNP. About 70% of the agricultural production is consumed locally **Minerals and Mining:** No commercial mining exists. There are potentially large deposits of bauxite **Labor Force:** N.A. **Foreign Trade:** Exports, chiefly cashew nuts, rice, groundnuts, palm kernels, timber, totaled $5.3 million in 1976. Imports, chiefly textiles, vehicles, consumer goods, fuel totaled approximately $38 million **Principal Trade Partners:** Portugal, Sweden, Senegal, China, Nigeria, Cape Verde

Vital Statistics: Birthrate, 40.1 per 1,000 of pop. (1975); death rate 25.1 **Life Expectancy:** 34 years **Health Statistics:** 596 inhabitants per hospital bed; 17,667 per physician (1969) **Infant Mortality:** 47.1 per 1,000 births **Illiteracy:** 95% **Education Statistics:** There are 343 primary and secondary schools, with a total enrollment of 58,577 (1975) **Enrollment in Higher Education:** N.A. **GNP Expended on Education:** 1.2% (1972)

Transportation: Paved roads total 265 mi. **Motor Vehicles:** 5,124 **Passenger Cars:** 3,268 **Railway Mileage:** None **Ports:** Bissau, Bolama **Major Airlines:** TAP **Communications:** Government owned **Radio Transmitters:** 2 **Licenses:** 11,000 (1976) **Television:** None **Telephones:** 3,000 (1973) **Newspapers:** 1 daily, 11 copies per 1,000 inhabitants (1975)

Weights and Measures: Metric system **Travel Requirements:** Passport, visa

Poor, diseased and subject to forced labor, Africans of Portuguese Guinea developed a national liberation movement in the early 1960s. By 1970 rebels claimed control of two-thirds of the country. The movement was led by the African Party for the Independence of Guinea and Cape Verde (PAIGC), whose basic tenet of doctrine was the "unity" of Guinea-Bissau and Cape Verde Islands, and was headed by Amilcar and Luis Cabral. The PAIGC proclaimed independence in 1973, but Portugal rejected the claim. However, the 1974 coup in Portugal ultimately resulted in an agreement granting independence for Guinea-Bissau on September 24 of that year, making Guinea-Bissau the first Portuguese African territory to achieve independence. Luis de Almeida Cabral became president, Amilcar Cabral having been killed in 1973.

Guinea-Bissau is currently struggling with all the problems that face developing nations, especially in the areas of education, health care, road development and electrification.

HISTORY: The Portuguese, sailing for Prince Henry the Navigator, reached the area in 1446. Slave trading was important in the 17th and 18th centuries

1879: Portuguese Guinea is separated from the administrative control of the Cape Verde Islands

1962: Revolt against Portuguese rule begins

1974: Portuguese Guinea attains independence as Guinea-Bissau

1975: Treaty signed with EEC

1978: Premier Francisco Mendes dies in auto crash. He is succeeded by Maj. João Bernardo Vieira

GUYANA

Area: 83,000 sq. mi. **Population:** 820,000 (1978 est.)

Official Name: Cooperative Republic of Guyana **Capital:** Georgetown **Nationality:** Guyanese **Languages:** English is the official language; other spoken languages include various East Indian dialects, Chinese, Portuguese, and a patois used by those of African origin **Religion:** About 57% Christian (chiefly Anglican), 33% Hindu, 9% Moslem **Flag:** A green field with a black-edged red triangular pennant superimposed on a white-edged yellow triangular pennant **Anthem:** Dear land of Guayana **Currency:** Guyana dollar (2.55 per U.S. $1)

Location: Northeast coast of South America. Guyana is bordered on the north by the Atlantic Ocean, on the east by Suriname, on the south and southwest by Brazil, and on the northwest by Venezuela **Features:** The country is divided into a low-lying coastal region, a heavily forested interior, and a region of mountains and

savannas in the south and west **Chief Rivers:** Essequibo, Courantyne, Berbice, Mazaruni, Cuyuni, Demerara

Head of State: President Raymond Arthur Chung, born 1918, elected the republic's first president in 1970, and reelected in 1976 for 6 years **Head of Government:** Prime Minister Linden Forbes Sampson Burnham, born 1923, reappointed 1973 to 3rd 5-year term **Effective Date of Present Constitution:** 1966; a new one is in preparation **Legislative Body:** National Assembly (unicameral), consisting of 53 members elected by proportional representation for 5 years. The life of the present Assembly was extended 15 months beyond its normal July 10, 1978, closing, so that it might act as a Constituent Assembly to draft a new Constitution **Local Government:** 10 regions, with regional ministers

Ethnic Composition: About 51% of the population is of East Indian descent; 31% African and African mixed; 6% indigenous Amerindians, and small groups of Portuguese and Chinese **Population Distribution:** 40% urban **Density:** 9.9 inhabitants per sq. mi.

Largest Cities (M.A. = **Metropolitan Area):** (1971 estimates) Georgetown 100,855 (M.A. 195,250); Linden 23,956; New Amsterdam 17,782; Corriverton 10,502; Rosehall 5,018

Per Capita Income: $624 (1978) **Gross National Product (GNP):** $520 million (1978) **Economic Statistics:** In 1973 about 20% of GNP came from agriculture (sugar, rice, corn, coconuts, coffee); 12% from manufacturing (cigarettes, matches, margarine, edible oils, beverages, sugar milling, aluminum smelting, wood and pulp); 18% from mining; and 22% from trade and services **Minerals and Mining:** Bauxite is the principal mineral. Diamonds and gold are also mined **Labor Force:** 210,000 (1970), with 32% in agriculture and 24% in industry **Foreign Trade:** Exports, chiefly bauxite and aluminum, sugar, rice, timber, shrimp, gold, and diamonds, totaled $362 million in 1975. Imports, mainly foodstuffs, manufactured goods, machinery, petroleum products, beverages, and tobacco, totaled $350 million **Principal Trade Partners:** Britain, United States, Commonwealth Caribbean countries, Canada, Japan, USSR, China

Vital Statistics: Birthrate 26.6 per 1,000 of pop. (1976); death rate, 7.1 **Life Expectancy:** 67 years **Health Statistics:** 199 inhabitants per hospital bed; 3,249 per physician (1974) **Infant Mortality:** 40 per 1,000 births **Illiteracy:** 13% **Education Statistics:** 608 primary and secondary schools, with combined enrollment of 199,876 (1973) **Enrollment in Higher Education:** 2,307 (1973) **GNP Expended on Education:** 6.3% (1974)

Transportation: Paved roads total 480 mi. **Motor Vehicles:** 41,400 (1976) **Passenger Cars:** 27,500 **Railway Mileage:** 80 **Port:** Georgetown **Major Airlines:** Guyana Airways Corp. operates domestic passenger and international cargo flights **Communications:** Government and privately owned **Radio Transmitters:** 7 **Receivers:** 275,000 (1976) **Television:** None **Telephones:** 23,000 (1976) **Newspapers:** 3 dailies, 155 copies per 1,000 inhabitants (1974)

Weights and Measures: British standards **Travel Requirements:** Passport; no visa for 30 days; onward ticket

Aptly termed the "land of the waters" by the indigenous Amerindians, Guyana, about most of its coastline, is below sea level. The land along the Atlantic, where most people of the South American country live, is made habitable by the 300-year-old seawalls and drainage system built by the Dutch.

Until the early 19th century, under the British, various colonization plans failed before the lucrative sugar industry was introduced. The British imported African slaves, indentured Portuguese and East Indians, and Chinese. These waves of immigration have determined Guyana's racial composition and the experience of slavery and indentured servitude has molded the country's political and social life.

Guyana has unresolved boundary disputes with two of its neighbors, Venezuela and Suriname. Venezuela claims the area west of the Essequibo River, more than half the size of Guyana as now constituted, while the dispute with Suriname relates to which interior river—the Courantyne or the New River—is the Guyana/Suriname border.

Independent from Britain since 1966, Guyana insists on traveling the autonomous line of a "cooperative republic." As Prime Minister Forbes Burnham puts it, his government will "pursue relentlessly the policy of owning and controlling our natural resources." Burnham has established the only Marxist government in South America.

The most far-reaching initiatives taken by the

government in furtherance of its socialist aims have been in the assertion of local control of the country's national economy. On January 1, 1975, the government nationalized the local mining operations of Reynolds Metal Co., completely bringing the country's bauxite mining industry under state control. By June 1976, when the British-owned Booker-McConnell Sugar Co. was nationalized, 80 percent of the nation's goods and services was in government hands.

A mass-murder suicide on an appalling scale at Jonestown, a community set up in the jungle by the San Francisco-based People's Temple, turned world attention to Guyana in November 1978. The bizarre tragedy began with the murders of U.S. Representative Leo J. Ryan of California, who had flown to Guyana to investigate reports that cult members were being held against their will, and four members of his party. The five were killed at the Port Kaituma airport on November 18, just after visiting Jonestown and getting word that 20 Temple members wanted to defect. After news of the murders was radioed to Jonestown, the Rev. Jim Jones, self-proclaimed messiah, led the whole community in a previously rehearsed suicide plan. It was carried out mainly by mixing a flavored drink with cyanide, but there was also some gunfire. The U.S. military removed 913 bodies of Temple members by air to Dover (Del.) Air Force Base. Guyana officials declared that none of their citizens were involved; further, they cited glowing recommendations sent by high-ranking U.S. leaders when the cult moved into Guyana. However, in May 1979, a staff report to the U.S. House Foreign Affairs Committee said that Guyana had granted the community special privileges in immigration and customs. Guns and cash, it said, had been smuggled in.

HISTORY: Little is known of the history of Guyana before the arrival of Europeans. When European explorers came to Guyana in the late 1500s and early 1600s, they found Arawak, Carib, and Warrau Indians living in the area. In the late 17th century the country was settled by the Dutch and in the following century alternated between Dutch and British rule. By 1815, British rule was firmly established

1831: Three colonies of Berbice, Essequibo, and Demerara are united into the colony of British Guiana

1837: Slaves are emancipated

1928: British Guiana gains limited representative government

1953-57: A new constitution is adopted providing for a bicameral legislature and ministerial responsibility. Elections are held, People's Progressive Party (PPP), led by Cheddi Jagan and generally supported by East Indians, captures 18 of the 24 elective seats. Six months after the election, the British suspend the constitution, charging Communist subversion of the British Guiana government; interim regime takes over

1961: Colony is granted full internal self-government, a new constitution is introduced; the PPP wins 20 of the 35 seats in the Legislative Assembly, Jagan is named prime minister

1962-64: Rivalry between PPP and People's National Congress (PNC), supported by the Negroes, leads to violence

1964: Two parties, PNC and the United Force, form a coalition government, with PNC leader Forbes Burnham as prime minister. Communal rioting re-erupts, a state of emergency is declared, and British troops are brought in to restore order

1966: Guyana becomes an independent state within the British Commonwealth and joins the UN

1968: Burnham's PNC wins general election

1970: Guyana is proclaimed a republic

1973: Guyana joins with Barbados, Jamaica, and Trinidad-Tobago to establish the Caribbean Community and Common Market (CARICOM)

1976: People's Progressive Party (PPP), led by Dr. Cheddi Jagan, ends its three-year boycott of the National Assembly

1978: More than 900 die in murder-suicide tragedy of the People's Temple cult in Jonestown

HAITI

Area: 10,683 sq. mi. **Population:** 4,900,000 (1978 est.)

Official Name: Republic of Haiti **Capital:** Port-au-Prince **Nationality:** Haitian **Languages:** French is the official language but is spoken by only about 10% of the population; Creole, a mixture of 17th century French, African dialects, and English, Spanish, and Indian words, is spoken by 90% **Religion:** Most of the population professes Roman Catholicism, the state religion; voodoo is widely practiced, especially in the rural areas **Flag:** Black and red vertical halves **Anthem:** Song of Dessalines **Currency:** Gourde (5 per U.S. $1)

Location: West Indies, occupying the western third of the island of Hispaniola in the Caribbean Sea. Haiti's only land border is with the Dominican Republic, on the east **Features:** About two-thirds of the country is mountainous terrain unsuitable for cultivation **Chief Rivers:** Artibonite, Guayamouc

Head of State and of Government: President Jean-Claude Duvalier, born 1951; elected president in February 1971, he assumed the title "President for Life" on the death of his father, François Duvalier, in April 1971 **Effective Date of Present Constitution:** June 1964, amended in 1971 **Legislative Body:** Legislative Chamber (unicameral), consisting of 58 deputies, elected for 6 years but with little power **Local Government:** 5 departments, each headed by an appointed prefect

Ethnic Composition: About 95% of the population is of African descent, the remaining 5% is chiefly mulatto **Population Distribution:** 20.8% urban **Density:** 459 inhabitants per sq. mi.

Largest Cities: (1971 census) Port-au-Prince 306,053, Cap-Haïtien 46,217, Pétionville 35,257, Gonaives 29,261

Per Capita Income: $219 (1978 est.) **Gross National Product (GNP):** $1.1 billion (1978) **Economic Statistics:** 44.7% of GNP comes from agriculture (coffee, sugar, sisal, cotton); 37% from services, of which 21.8% is derived from tourism; 14.4% from manufacturing (processing of coffee, sugarcane, sisal, and edible oils; textiles, soap, cement); 3.9% from mining **Minerals and Mining:** Bauxite and copper are mined; deposits of gold, silver, antimony, tin, sulphur, coal, nickel, and gypsum are undeveloped **Labor Force:** 3,004,544 (1975), with 80% self-employed in agriculture **Foreign Trade:** Exports, mainly coffee, sugar, bauxite, essential oils, baseballs and softballs, sisal, shellfish, and fruits, totaled $100 million in 1976. Imports, mainly wheat, fish, fats and oils, paper, cotton fabrics, vehicles, petroleum, machinery, electrical equipment, and raw materials, totaled $190 million **Principal Trade Partners:** United States, European Common Market, Japan, Curaçao

Vital Statistics: Birthrate, 35.8 per 1,000 of pop. (1975); death rate, 16.3 **Life Expectancy:** 50 years **Health Statistics:** 1,344 inhabitants per hospital bed; 8,505 per physician (1973) **Infant Mortality:** 200 per 1,000 births **Illiteracy:** 85% **Education Statistics:** 2,083 primary and secondary schools, with combined enrollment of 368,414 (1971) **Enrollment in Higher Education:** 1,494 (1967) **GNP Expended on Education:** 0.7%

Transportation: Paved roads total 400 mi. **Motor Vehicles:** 17,200 (1974) **Passenger Cars:** 15,700 **Railway Mileage:** 150 **Ports:** Port-au-Prince, Miragoâne, Les Cayes **Major Airlines:** Cohata, the state-owned airline, operates internal services **Communications:** Partly government controlled **Radio Transmitters:** 72 **Receivers:** 95,000 (1976) **Television Transmitters:** 1 **Receivers:** 14,000 (1976) **Telephones:** 18,000 (1976) **Newspapers:** 7 dailies, 20 copies per 1,000 inhabitants (1975)

Weights and Measures: Metric system **Travel Requirements:** Passport; tourist card valid for 30 days; $2 fee

Fourteen years of implacable dictatorship, with little economic or social progress for compensation, ended for Haiti in 1971 with the death of Dr. François Duvalier at the age of 64. Under the harsh rule of his police state, the country had become an anachronism in the Western Hemisphere after having been in the vanguard to win freedom from foreign rule.

Haiti's politics and economy are primitive. The country is nominally a republic with a president, but Dr. Duvalier—"Papa Doc"—was all-powerful. For most of Haiti's independent life, the country was dominated by a cultured and literate, generally mulatto, minority.

Illiteracy persists at nearly 85 percent, and most people lead subsistence lives on little plots of land amid luxuriant and colorful vegetation set against stark, eroded mountains. Roman Catholicism is the dominant religion, but it is mixed with voodoo, a religion of fetish and incantation rooted in the Haitians' African past. Manifestations of Duvalier rule include a force called the *Tontons Macoute*, or Bogeymen, a bulwark of the regime feared for its arbitrary dealings with ordinary people.

All in all, Papa Doc left a staggering legacy to his successor as "President for Life," his son Jean-Claude. When "Baby Doc" assumed power in April 1971, at the age of 19, there were few who assumed he could last long. But so far he has been successful in walking a political tightrope between the "old dinosaurs" of his father's era, who seek to hold the status quo, and the younger technocrats and businessmen who, while not desiring a dramatic change in the form of government, do seek a modernization of Haitian life. Recently the young Duvalier has acted to ease repression somewhat, in an apparent attempt to gain favor with the Carter Administration, which has been critical of Haiti's bleak human rights record. The government said that it released the last political prisoners in 1977, and it invited the Red Cross and the Inter-American Commission on Human Rights to inspect its jails. On the other hand, there are reliable reports that conditions are improved solely for such visits and that inhumane conditions prevail again soon afterward. In 1978, the American Convention on Human Rights—ratified by Haiti and other members of the Organization of American States—came into force. The convention provides for an international court to rule on human rights cases.

The country has few resources with which to solve its staggering economic and social problems and has been characterized as an "environmental disaster." The destruction of the forests for charcoal has triggered massive soil erosion, reducing the amount of arable land. Exports remain largely confined to primary products such as sugar, coffee, essential oils, sisal, and some minerals. Over 150 U.S. companies now have plants in Haiti, and Haitian-controlled companies assemble imported U.S. components. Another major resource is tourism.

HISTORY: Haiti was largely ignored by Spain following the discovery of the island of Hispaniola by Columbus in 1492. While most Spanish colonists settled on the eastern part of the island, Haiti became a base for English and French pirates and was eventually ceded to France in the late 17th century. French colonists began to settle in the area, developing a plantation economy based on sugar and worked by black slaves. Following the outbreak of the French Revolution, the slaves rebelled and murdered most of their former masters

1793: A French army sent to crush the rebellion is defeated by guerrilla bands led by Toussaint L'Ouverture, a former slave

1801-3: Toussaint occupies the entire island of Hispaniola, abolishes slavery, and introduces a constitution; his rule ends when he is captured by an army sent by Napoleon to restore French power

1804-11: Jean Jacques Dessalines, another black general, continues the struggle against the French and defeats their army; he assumes title of emperor but is soon assassinated; nation becomes split into a northern kingdom ruled by Henri Christophe, a black, and a southern republic governed by a mulatto, Alexandre Pétion

1820-44: Haiti is reunited by Jean Pierre Boyer, who also brings Santo Domingo, in the eastern part of the island, under Haitian control; Boyer overthrown; nation regains independence

1849-59: Haiti is ruled by a former president and self-declared emperor, Faustin Élie Soulouque, a black; he is dethroned in a revolution led by a mulatto, Nicholas Fabre Geffrard

1905-34: United States takes Haiti's customs into receivership in 1905; in 1915, United States takes full control of country; occupation, which lasts for 19 years, results in many material improvements but arouses hostility throughout Latin America

1957-64: François Duvalier, a black middle-class physician, is elected president; with the help of a secret police force known as Tontons Macoute, he establishes dictatorship; in 1964 Duvalier has himself declared president for life

1968: Haitian exiles attempt to invade the country but fail

1969: The Organization of American States charges Duvalier government with terrorism

1970: Haitian Coast Guard vessels shell presidential palace in abortive coup

1971: François Duvalier dies after 14-year rule; his son, Jean-Claude, succeeds him

1977: Severe drought brings hundreds of thousands to brink of starvation and causes major shortages of electricity

1978: Repression eased. The press is allowed to criticize the government, and a sugar workers' union is permitted to elect new representatives

HONDURAS

Area: 43,277 sq. mi. **Population:** 3,250,000 (1978 est.)

Official Name: Republic of Honduras **Capital:** Tegucigalpa **Nationality:** Honduran **Languages:** Spanish is the official and predominant language; English is spoken along the north coast and on the Bay Islands **Religion:** Overwhelmingly Roman Catholic **Flag:** Two blue horizontal stripes separated by a white stripe bearing a cluster of five blue stars **Anthem:** National Anthem, beginning "Thy flag is a heavenly light" **Currency:** Lempira (2 per U.S. $1)

Location: Central America. Honduras is bordered on the north by the Caribbean Sea; on the southeast by Nicaragua; on the southwest by El Salvador and the Pacific Ocean; and on the west by Guatemala **Features:** Except for the Caribbean and Pacific coastal plains, the country is generally mountainous **Chief Rivers:** Guayape, Patuca, Aguán, Ulúa

Head of State and of Government: President: Gen. Policarpo Paz García heads three-man military junta that seized power in August 1978 **Effective Date of Present Constitution:** June 6, 1965, except where altered by decree **Legislative Body:** Congress (unicameral) suspended **Local Government:** 18 departments, each with a governor appointed by the president

Ethnic Composition: About 90% of the population is mestizo (of mixed European and Indian origin); Indians, Negroes, and Caucasians constitute small minorities **Population Distribution:** 31% urban **Density:** 75 inhabitants per sq. mi.

Largest Cities: (1976 est.) Tegucigalpa 316,500, San Pedro Sula 213,600, Choluteca 51,700, La Ceiba 49,900

Per Capita Income: $583 (1978 est.) **Gross National Product (GNP):** $1.8 billion (1978 est.) **Economic Statistics:** About 35% of GNP comes from agriculture (bananas, coffee, lumber, corn, meat, cotton, forestry and fishing; about 15% from industry (light consumer goods; processing of sugar, fruit juices, vegetable oils; meat packing); and 14% from trade **Minerals and Mining:** Gold, silver, lead, zinc, cadmium, mercury, and lime are extracted; other minerals are antimony, iron, copper, tin, coal, limestone, marble, and pitchblende. Petroleum exploration is under way **Labor Force:** 938,159 (1975), with some 62% in agriculture, 24% in trade and services, 12% in manufacturing and mining **Foreign Trade:** Exports, chiefly bananas, coffee, lumber, silver, meat, shellfish, cotton and tobacco, totaled $437 million in 1976. Imports, mainly transportation equipment, machinery, chemicals, fertilizer, petroleum products, and consumer durables, totaled $562 million **Principal Trade Partners:** United States, West Germany, Japan, Britain, Venezuela, Nicaragua, Guatemala

Vital Statistics: Birthrate, 47 per 1,000 of pop. (1976); death rate, 12 **Life Expectancy:** 56 years **Health Statistics:** 598 inhabitants per hospital bed; 2,992 per physician (1975) **Infant Mortality:** 31 per 1,000 births (1976) **Illiteracy:** 43% **Education Statistics:** 4,602 primary and secondary schools, with combined enrollment of 529,614 (1975) **Enrollment in Higher Education:** 11,907 (1975) **GNP Expended on Education:** 3.3% (1974)

Transportation: Paved roads total 775 mi. **Motor Vehicles:** 50,700 (1976) **Passenger Cars:** 20,500 **Railway Mileage:** 750 **Ports:** Puerto Cortés, Tela, La Ceiba, Amapala, Trujillo **Major Airlines:** SAHSA and TAN operate domestic and international services **Communications:** Partly government controlled **Radio Transmitters:** 151 **Receivers:** 161,000 (1976) **Television Transmitters:** 5 **Receivers:** 48,000 (1976) **Telephones:** 19,000 (1976) **Newspapers:** 8 dailies (1975), 44 copies per 1,000 inhabitants

Weights and Measures: Metric system, but local units are also used **Travel Requirements:** Passport; visa

The weak link in the Central American Common Market, Honduras is the archetype of a Central American banana republic, with a slow economic growth rate and 62 percent of the population involved in agriculture. It is a small country, constantly struggling to keep up with its neighbors and always falling further behind; its politics are frequently subject to military intervention; its economy did bow for many years to the wishes of United Brands and Standard Fruit—the leading businesses—and, of course, the leading export is bananas. However, in 1975 the government cancelled the special privileges and concessions of these foreign companies after United Brands was involved in a bribery scandal attempting to bring about a reduction in the banana export tax.

In foreign affairs, Honduras' two principal problems have been its border dispute with El Salvador (600,000 Salvadoreans have left their overcrowded country for Honduras' limited opportunities) and a struggle to regain the Swan Islands, two specks in the Caribbean, from the United States, where Honduran sovereignty was attained in 1971.

Economically, Honduras seems to have little hope of catching up to its neighbors. Its few resources have been squandered by administrative incompetence and inexperience. Hopes for new growth are in part pinned on development of timbering in a 3-million-acre forest in northern Honduras.

The military has ruled Honduras since 1972. In January 1978 President Juan Melgar announced he would convene a constituent assembly in 1979 to "reform" the constitution, which could eventually lead to the election of a civilian president and to the constitutional ratification of Melgar's rule by decree.

However, in August 1978, Melgar was overthrown by a three-member military junta headed by Gen. Policarpo Paz García. The junta promised free elections by 1980.

HISTORY: Honduras was a center of Mayan civilization centuries before the arrival of Columbus in 1502. Following attempts by rival Spanish factions in Central America to gain control of it, Honduras was made part of the captaincy general of Guatemala

1821: Honduras declares independence from Spain and, along with the other Central American countries, is annexed to Mexico

1825: Honduras secedes from Mexico and becomes part of the Central American Federation

1838: Honduras becomes an independent republic in 1838

1933-49: Tiburcio Carias Andino rules as dictator

1957-63: Ramón Villeda Morales is elected first Liberal president in 25 years; he is overthrown by a military coup led by Oswaldo López Arellano, who takes over government

1965: Honduras returns to democratic rule when a Constituent Assembly elects López president and adopts a new constitution

1969: Honduras invaded by El Salvador. The two nations wage a short war

1970: Honduras and El Salvador agree to set up demilitarized zone along disputed border

1971: Honduras holds first direct election of a president since 1932; National Party candidate Ramón Ernesto Cruz wins. U.S. recognizes Honduran sovereignty over long-disputed Swan Islands

1972: Bloodless coup puts Gen. Oswaldo López Arellano back in power

1973: State of emergency declared due to severe drought

1974: Hurricane Fifi strikes, killing about 9,000

1975: Pres. López Arellano overthrown in bloodless coup after reports that he accepted $1.25 million bribe from United Brands. Juan Alberto Melgar Castro, Commander in Chief of armed forces, becomes president

1978: Melgar overthrown by three-member military junta

HUNGARY

Area: 35,919 sq. mi. **Population:** 10,700,000(1978 est.)
Official Name: Hungarian People's Republic **Capital:** Budapest **Nationality:** Hungarian **Languages:** Hungarian is the official and universal language **Religion:** 68% Roman Catholic, 20% Calvinist, 5% Lutheran, 7% other (Unitarian, Jewish, etc.) **Flag:** Red, white, and green horizontal stripes **Anthem:** God bless the Hungarians **Currency:** Forint (20.3 per U.S. $1)

Location: East-central Europe. Landlocked Hungary is bordered on the north by Czechoslovakia, on the northeast by the USSR, on the east by Romania, on the south by Yugoslavia, and on the west by Austria **Features:** Most of the country is a flat plain, with the exception of low mountain ranges in the north-central and north-eastern portions and to the north and south of Lake Balaton in the west **Chief Rivers:** Danube, Tisza, Drava, Rába

Political Leader: First Secretary of the Hungarian Socialist Workers' (Communist) party: János Kádár, born 1912, reappointed 1970 **Head of State:** The Presidential Council is collectively the head of state, usually represented by its president, Pál Losonczi, born 1919, reappointed 1975 **Head of Government:** Premier György Lázár, appointed 1975 **Effective Date of Present Constitution:**

1949, amended 1972 **Legislative Body:** National Assembly (unicameral) consisting of 352 members elected for 4 years **Local Government:** 19 counties (each divided into districts with locally elected councils); 4 autonomous cities and the capital, all with county status

Ethnic Composition: Hungarians (Magyars) make up 97% of the population; minority groups include Germans, Slovaks, Gypsies, Serbs, Croats, and Romanians **Population Distribution:** 49.8% urban **Density:** 298 inhabitants per sq. mi.

Largest Cities: (1974 est.) Budapest 2,051,354, Miskolc 194,648, Debrecen 179,755, Szeged 166,040, Pécs 160,488, Gyor 114,709

Per Capita Income: $3,000 (1978) **Gross National Product (GNP):** $32 billion (1978 est.) **Economic Statistics:** About 38.5% of GNP is derived from industry (mining, chemical refining, metallurgy, food processing); 18.6% from agriculture (corn, wheat, sugar beets, vegetables, wine grapes); 12% from trade; 11% from services **Minerals and Mining:** Coal, bauxite, iron ore, and lignite are mined **Labor Force:** 4,988,676 (1970), of which 44% is employed in industry and construction, and 24% in agriculture. **Foreign Trade:** Exports, chiefly transport equipment, medicine, machinery and shoes, totaled $6.3 billion in 1976. Imports, mainly crude oil, raw cotton, passenger cars, trucks, and rolled steel, totaled $7 billion **Principal Trade Partners:** USSR, E. Germany, Czechoslovakia, Poland, Italy, W. Germany, Austria

Vital Statistics: Birthrate, 16.7 per 1,000 of pop. (1977); death rate, 12.4 **Life Expectancy:** 70 years **Health Statistics:** 121 inhabitants per hospital bed; 471 per physician (1973) **Infant Mortality:** 26.1 per 1,000 births **Illiteracy:** 2% **Education Statistics:** 5,895 primary and secondary schools, with combined enrollment of 1,424,134 (1974) **Enrollment in Higher Education:** 107,555 (1975) **GNP Expended on Education:** 4.8% (1975)

Transportation: Surfaced roads total 18,414 mi. **Motor Vehicles:** 866,200 (1976) **Passenger Cars:** 654,800 **Railway Mileage:** 5,420 **Ports:** None **Major Airlines:** Malev, the state-owned airline, operates domestic and international services **Communications:** Government owned **Radio Transmitters:** 37 **Licenses:** 2,538,000 (1975) **Television Transmitters:** 22 **Licenses:** 2,495,000 (1976) **Telephones:** 1,076,000 (1976) **Newspapers:** 27 dailies, 233 copies per 1,000 inhabitants (1975)

Weights and Measures: Metric system **Travel Requirements:** Passport; visa valid for 30 days; fee $6; 2 photos

"Socialism with gaiety" is the way a top Hungarian has described his country's political formula to an American audience. The slogan is not far from the Czechoslovakian idea of "Socialism with a human face"—a concept that brought the violent downfall of Alexander Dubcek and his reformist government in 1968. However, the implementation of the formula in Hungary is so cautious, moderate, and delicate that no analogy with Czechoslovakia is appropriate.

In the midst of ideological regimentation, the breakdown of which brought Warsaw Pact troops into Prague, there is gaiety in Hungary. Political cabarets in Budapest pull few punches in criticizing bureaucratic ineptness and stuffiness. A television forum in which listeners quiz political leaders on their performance and promises brings sharp questions out into public discussion. Music, dancing, and plentiful good food add esthetic grace notes to the sense of gradual political progress.

The country is no longer traumatized by the uprising that Russian tanks crushed in 1956 and that caused some 200,000 Hungarians to flee to the West. The regime of János Kádár, imposed to fight the liberal ideas of the 1956 revolt, has proved far more progressive than was first thought possible. A surprising degree of dissent is allowed, though there are definite if generally unexpressed limits. Hungary remains, after all, a Communist state, basically faithful to the party line.

Thus, when it was necessary for someone to attack Romania for flirting with Communist China, a Hungarian editor was detailed to fire the first critical salvo. Similarly, the economic liberalization has been only partially mirrored in an effort to develop local political autonomy in small towns and not reflected at all in the repressive policies toward the Catholic Church.

What has emerged in Hungary, however, is a consumer-oriented economy that is the envy of all its neighbors. Without serious inflation, such as Yugoslavia has experienced, Hungarians have refined their New Economic Model since its introduction in 1968 to boost exports and imports.

The economy, however, is not without its problems. The high degree of centralization in Budapest sometimes results in mismanagement and inefficiencies, and in return for supplying oil needs in excess of rigid, outdated quotas, the Soviet Union requires agricultural surpluses that might otherwise earn valuable hard currency in the West. In April 1978, the regime adopted a two-year program of phasing out most price controls, most subsidies to consumer goods (subsidies having accounted for more than a third of the 1977 budget), and the heavy producer taxes that pay for the subsidies. Prices increased considerably in 1979, but so did some wages.

HISTORY: The Magyars migrated from beyond the Urals about the end of the 9th century A.D., conquered most of present-day Hungary, and established a dynasty that lasted more than four centuries. Pre-Magyar inhabitants had included Celts, Germans, Huns, Slavs, and Avars. In the last years of the 10th century, the Magyars embraced Christianity and made alliances with the Holy Roman Empire. Following a disastrous defeat by the Turks in 1526, a faction of Hungarian nobles elected Ferdinand I of Austria as king of Hungary, laying the foundations of Hapsburg rule

1686: Budapest is liberated from the Turks, who cede most of Hungary proper and Transylvania to Austria

1713: Hungarian Diet accepts Pragmatic Sanction aimed at guaranteeing the integrity of the Hapsburg possessions, thereby binding Hungary to Austria

1848-49: Hungarian revolt against Austrian rule is suppressed by Austrian and Russian armies

1867: Austro-Hungarian monarchy is established, giving Hungary nearly equal status with Austria

1918-19: Monarchy collapses in the aftermath of World War I defeat. A Hungarian republic is proclaimed but is soon supplanted by a Communist regime headed by Bela Kun; Romanian troops invade Hungary and help to suppress leftist government

1920: Under Treaty of Trianon, Hungary is deprived of three-fourths of its territory and over one-third of its population; country becomes a kingdom without a king, under the regency of Admiral Nicholas Horthy

1938-40: Aided by Italy and Germany, Hungary recovers lands lost to Czechoslovakia and Romania. In 1940 Hungary joins Axis powers and enters World War II

1944: Soviet troops occupy Hungary; a provisional government is set up and declares war against Germany

1947: Communists win 22 percent of vote in general elections

1948-49: Hungarian Communists seize power with Soviet support; in 1949 Hungary is proclaimed a People's Republic

1955: Hungary joins the UN

1956: Popular anti-Communist uprising breaks out in Budapest and spreads to rest of the country; a new coalition government under Imre Nagy declares Hungary neutral and withdraws country from Warsaw Pact; János Kádár sets up counter-government and calls for Soviet support; Soviet troops and tanks suppress revolution, causing nearly 200,000 Hungarians to flee the country

1958: Imre Nagy and some of his ministers are executed. János Kádár resigns as premier and is succeeded by Ferenc Münnich

1961: Kádár resumes premiership

1965: Gyula Kallai becomes premier; Kádár remains First Secretary of ruling Hungarian Socialist Workers' Party

1967: Hungary signs a new 20-year friendship and mutual assistance pact with Soviet Union, replacing one signed in 1948. Jeno Fock succeeds Gyula Kallai as premier

1968: Hungarian troops march with Soviet troops when Soviets invade Czechoslovakia

1971: Government holds first general elections in which voters could choose between nonofficial and official candidates. Newcomers unseat eight incumbents in parliament

1975: György Lázár becomes premier

1978: Crown of St. Stephen, 1,000-year-old traditional symbol of Hungary's nationhood, is returned by U.S. after having been held in protective custody since the end of World War II. Government announces measures to phase out most subsidies for consumer goods and end heavy taxes producers pay on larger profits; selective wage hikes are promised

1979: Major price increases, especially of oil

ICELAND

Area: 39,768 sq. mi. **Population:** 222,000 (1978 est.)

Official Name: Republic of Iceland **Capital:** Reykjavík **Nationality:** Icelandic **Languages:** Icelandic is the official and universal language **Religion:** 98% of the population belongs to the state church, the Evangelical Lutheran Church **Flag:** A red cross edged in white on a field of blue **Anthem:** Our Country's God **Currency:** Króna (330.2 per U.S. $1)

Location: North Atlantic. A large island extending about 300 miles from east to west and about 190 miles from north to south, Iceland is the westernmost state of Europe, lying 600 miles west of Norway. The Arctic Circle runs through the small island of Grímsey off Iceland's northern coast **Features:** Almost three-fourths of the country's land area, which is of recent volcanic origin, consists of glaciers, lakes, a mountainous lava desert, and other wasteland, with the remainder used for cultivation or grazing. Most of the inhabited areas are on the coast, particularly, in the southwest **Chief Rivers:** Thjórsá, Jökulsa, Ölfusá-Hvítá, Skjálfandafljót

Head of State: President Kristján Eldjárn, born 1916, elected 1968, reelected 1976 for 4 years **Head of Government:** Premier Olafur Jóhannesson, born 1913, appointed August 1978 **Effective Date of Present Constitution:** 1874, amended 1903 and 1944 **Legislative Body:** Parliament (Althing), composed of 60 members elected for 4 years. After elections it becomes bicameral, dividing itself into 2 chambers with equal powers, one of 20 members and the other of 40 members. The 2 houses often meet together **Local Government:** 16 counties, each with a council, and 14 urban municipalities

Ethnic Composition: The population is homogeneous **Population Distribution:** 86.4% urban **Density:** 5.6 inhabitants per sq. mi.

Largest Cities: (1975 est.) Reykjavík 84,855; (1973 est.) Kópavogur 11,639, Akureyri 11,484, Hafnarfjördhur 10,926

Per Capita Income: $5,706 (1978) **Gross National Product (GNP):** $1.3 billion (1978) **Economic Statistics:** About 14% of GNP comes from fishing and fish processing; 18% from industry other than fish processing (manufacture of electric motors, fertilizer, chemicals, cement, clothing, furniture, books); 7% from agriculture (sheep raising, dairy products, hay, potatoes); 32% from services; 15% from construction **Minerals and Mining:** Diatomite, peat, lignite, perlite; hydroelectric power **Labor Force:** 100,000 (1977), of which 42% is employed in fishing, fish processing, and other industries; 11% in agriculture; 46% in trade and services **Foreign Trade:** Exports, chiefly fish and fish products (about 75% of the total), aluminum ingots, and agricultural products, totaled $478 million in 1977. Imports, mainly machinery, textiles, petroleum products, metals and metal products, ships, and food grains, totaled $568 million **Principal Trade Partners:** United States, West Germany, Britain, USSR, Norway, Denmark, Portugal, Poland

Vital Statistics: Birthrate, 17.8 per 1,000 of pop. (1977); death rate, 6.6 **Life Expectancy:** 75 years **Health Statistics:** 69 inhabitants per hospital bed; 612 per physician (1973) **Infant Mortality:** 11.1 per 1,000 births **Illiteracy:** Negligible **Education Statistics:** 332 primary and secondary schools with combined enrollment of 51,950 (1974) **Enrollment in Higher Education:** 2,970 (1975) **GNP Expended on Education:** 4.2% (1975)

Transportation: Paved roads total 120 miles; there are over 6,000 miles of gravel road **Motor Vehicles:** 73,400 (1976) **Passenger Cars:** 65,700 **Railway Mileage:** None **Ports:** Reykjavík, Akureyri **Major Airlines:** Icelandair operates domestic and international services. Icelandic Airlines operates international services **Communications:** Government owned **Radio Transmitters:** 29 **Licenses:** 64,000 (1976) **Television Transmitters:** 80 **Licenses:** 53,000 (1976) **Telephones:** 91,000 (1976) **Newspapers:** 5 dailies, 431 copies per 1,000 inhabitants (1975)

Weights and Measures: Metric system **Travel Requirements:** Passport; no visa for 3 months

Out in the North Atlantic, closer to Greenland than to Western Europe, lies the rugged, largely desolate island of volcanic origin called Iceland, with 222,000-plus fiercely individualistic inhabitants who have a tradition of preserving their heritage. Their language, for example, has remained virtually unchanged since the 12th century.

Although Iceland has no armed forces, it joined in the cold-war days of 1949 in forming the North Atlantic Treaty Organization. As its contribution, it granted NATO the right to establish a base, manned by Americans, at Keflavík, 30 miles outside of Reykjavík, the capital. A leftist coalition formed in 1971 announced plans to phase out the installation, but in 1974 a coalition of the former governing and opposition parties agreed to allow the base to remain.

The government extended the fishing limits in 1972 from 12 miles offshore to 50, and in 1975 from 50 to 200 miles. With fish and fish products accounting for 14 percent of the country's gross national product and 75 percent of its total exports, the moves were a logical progression of a conservation drive begun in 1958 when Iceland extended its fishing limits from four miles to 12.

Foreign reaction to these extensions has been far more serious than in 1958. In 1973 and 1975-76, Britain, which gets 45 percent of its fish from the waters off Iceland, sent heavily armed frigates into the disputed waters, touching off a "cod war" between the two countries, with shots being fired, boats rammed and nets cut.

In 1976 the two countries reached a diplomatic settlement and British ships were removed. In conjunction with this agreement, important tariff concessions by the European Economic Community (EEC) for fish products became effective for Iceland. The EEC's adoption of a common 200-mile fishing limit imposed new problems, as it excludes Icelandic vessels from rich waters to which they had previously had access.

In parliamentary elections in June 1978, Premier Geir Hallgrimsson's center-right coalition lost heavily, and a left-center cabinet headed by Olafur Jóhannesson was formed in August. The People's Alliance, a Communist group, became part of the new governing coalition.

Troubled by an unfavorable balance of trade, Iceland devalued the króna in 1978 after its central bank suspended currency trading.

HISTORY: The first permanent settler of Iceland was Ingolfur Arnason of Norway, who arrived with his family around 870. Others of Norwegian origin followed, some bringing with them Irish and Scottish wives and slaves. In 930 a commonwealth was established and a general assembly, the Althing, instituted. Christianity was introduced in the year 1000. Iceland came under the Norwegian crown in the 13th century, but in 1380 both Iceland and Norway passed under the Danish crown. The former was destined to remain linked to Denmark until the 20th century

1918: Iceland is declared a sovereign state in union with Denmark

1940-41: British troops occupy Iceland following Germany's World War II occupation of Denmark; U.S. forces take over Iceland's defense in 1941

1944: Icelanders vote to terminate union with Denmark; Iceland is proclaimed a republic

1949: Iceland joins in forming NATO

1958-61: Fishing limits are extended from four miles to 12; so-called "cod war" begins, with Britain challenging the Icelandic pronouncement by sending in trawlers backed by warships; in 1961 Britain finally agrees to the 12-mile limit

1970: Iceland becomes member of European Free Trade Association. Premier Bjarni Benediktsson perishes in fire; Justice Minister Johann Hafstein is designated his successor

1971: Government defeated in elections. Hafstein resigns. New left-wing coalition government announces it will close the American-manned NATO base at Keflavik

1972-73: Fishing limits are extended from 12 miles to 50, touching off new "cod war" with Britain; West Germany joins Britain in protesting extension

1973: Iceland signs agreement with Britain giving limited fishing rights within the new zone

1974: Iceland signs agreement with U.S. allowing U.S. to maintain NATO base at Keflavik

1975: Fishing limits extended from 50 to 200 miles

1976: British and Icelandic foreign ministers sign an interim pact to end the "cod war" between the two countries and restore diplomatic relations which had been severed. British frigates, sent into fishing zone in November '75 to protect British trawlers from harassment by Icelandic patrol boats, withdraw. Dr. Kristján Eldjárn is returned unopposed for third four-year term as president

1978: Strike by government workers virtually isolates nation from world for two weeks by cutting international flights, mail and telephone links; center-left cabinet is formed in August

INDIA

Area: 1,269,339 sq. mi. **Population:** 635,000,000 (1978 est.)
Official Name: Republic of India **Capital:** New Delhi **Nationality:**

Indian **Languages:** Hindi is the official language; English is an associate language. In addition to Hindi, the constitution recognizes 14 national languages, although as many as 1,652 languages and dialects are spoken in the country. Hindi, however, is spoken by 38% of the population. Telugu 9%, Bengali 8%, Marathi 8%, Tamil 7%, Urdu 6%, Gujarati 5%, Kanarese 4%, Punjabi 3%, Oriya 3%, Malayalam 3% **Religion:** 84% Hindu, 10% Moslem, 3% Christian, 2% Sikh, 1% Buddhist, Jain and others **Flag:** Saffron, white, and green horizontal stripes, with the 24-spoke Wheel of Asoka (chakra) in blue on the white stripe **Anthem:** Morning Song of India **Currency:** Rupee (8.3 per U.S. $1)

Location: Southern Asia, occupying most of the Indian sub-continent. India is bordered on the north by Afghanistan, China, Nepal, and Bhutan; on the east by Bangladesh, Burma, and the Bay of Bengal; on the south by the Indian Ocean's Gulf of Mannar and Palk Strait, which separate India from Sri Lanka; on the west by the Arabian Sea; and on the northwest by Pakistan **Features:** The country consists of three major topographical areas: the Himalaya mountains extending along the whole of the northern border; the Indo-Gangetic Plain, a fertile and heavily populated region; and the southern peninsula, including the Deccan Plateau, which is of moderate elevation and less densely populated **Chief Rivers:** Ganges, Brahmaputra, Godavari, Kistna (Krishna), Narbada, Mahanadi

Head of State: President Neelam Sanjiva Reddy, born 1913, elected July 1977 **Head of Government:** Prime Minister Chaudhury Charan Singh, born 1902, appointed July 28, 1979, resigned on Aug. 20. Remains as caretaker prime minister until new elections **Effective Date of Present Constitution:** 1950 **Legislative Body:** Parliament (bicameral), consisting of the Lok Sabha (House of the People) and the Rajya Sabha (Council of States). The Lok Sabha has 542 members, elected by universal suffrage for 6 years. The Rajya Sabha has 244 members, 13 of whom are appointed by the president and the rest elected for 6 year terms by the state and territorial legislatures **Local Government:** 122 states and 9 union territories, each with an appointed governor and with its own elected legislature

Ethnic Composition: Two major strains predominate: the Indo-Aryan (72%) in the north and the Dravidian (25%) in the south. There is also an aboriginal population in the central part, and some Mongoloid peoples in the north **Population Distribution:** 21% urban **Density:** 500 inhabitants per sq. mi.

Largest Cities: (1971 census) Bombay 5,970,575, Delhi 3,287,883, Calcutta 3,148,746 (with suburbs 7,031,382), Madras 2,469,449, Hyderabad 1,607,396, Ahmadabad 1,585,544, Bangalore 1,540,741, Kanpur 1,154,388

Per Capita Income: $159 (1978) **Gross National Product (GNP):** $105 billion (1978) **Economic Statistics:** About 43% of GNP comes from agriculture (rice, wheat, tea, jute, pulses, cotton, sugar, peanuts); 23% from mining and manufacturing (iron and steel, textiles, chemicals, cement, industrial machinery and equipment); 16% from commerce, transportation, and communications **Minerals and Mining:** Coal and iron are the country's main mineral assets; mica, manganese, and bauxite are also abundant. Iron ore reserves are estimated at about one-fourth of the world's total; oil supplies about 60% of the nation's refinery requirements **Labor Force:** 240 million (1976), of which 72% is engaged in agriculture, 11% in industry, and 17% in trade and services **Foreign Trade:** Exports, chiefly cotton and jute textiles, tea, sugar, coffee, metallic ores, and iron and steel manufactures, totaled $6.4 billion in 1977. Imports, mainly petroleum, food grains, nonelectrical machinery and fertilizer, totaled $6.5 billion **Principal Trade Partners:** United States, Japan, Britain, USSR, Iran, West Germany

Vital Statistics: Birthrate, 35.2 per 1,000 of pop. (1975); death rate, 15.9 **Life Expectancy:** 51 years **Health Statistics:** 1,571 inhabitants per hospital bed; 4,162 per physician (1973) **Infant Mortality:** 130 per 1,000 births (1974) **Illiteracy:** 66% **Education Statistics:** 787,580 primary and secondary schools, with combined enrollment of 91,144,460 (1975) **Enrollment in Higher Education:** 3,000,000 **GNP Expended on Education:** 2.5% (1973)

Transportation: Surfaced roads totaled about 320,000 mi. **Motor Vehicles:** 1,397,300 (1976) **Passenger Cars:** 769,200 **Railway Mileage:** 60,137 **Ports:** Calcutta, Bombay, Madras, Mormugao, Cochin, Kandla, Visakhapatnam, Paradeep, Mangalore, Tuticorin **Major Airlines:** Indian Airlines Corporation is the domestic carrier and Air India the international line **Communications:** Government controlled **Radio Transmitters:** 153 **Licenses:** 14,848,000 (1976) **Television Transmitters:** 5 **Licenses:** 280,000 (1976) **Telephones:** 2,096,000 (1976) **Newspapers:** 835 dailies, 16 copies per 1,000 inhabitants (1975)

Weights and Measures: Metric system and local units are used **Travel Requirements:** Passport; tourist visa, valid 3 months; $1.80 fee; 2 photos

Successive invasions and a long period of subjugation under alien rule have made India what it is today—a land of diverse, often conflicting cultures, religions, and people that is held in unity by a complicated yet resilient political system. The British, who were the masters of the subcontinent for a century and a half, brought its disparate regions under one administration. To overcome the myriad languages and dialects, they made English the communication medium of the elite, the tiny minority that still dominates the government, industry, education, and art.

Indian leaders, as fruit of their long fight for freedom, inherited a truncated land after the carving out of Pakistan as a homeland for Moslems; they have been struggling with the overwhelming problems of the subcontinent ever since.

The country's successive five-year plans, while laying the foundation for a prosperous industrial nation at some future date, have not so far produced any substantial improvement in the average Indian's quality of life. All the benefits of the large development expenses over the last 25 years have been neutralized by a runaway population increase—now about two percent a year—that has pushed more and more people below the poverty line. Unemployment has risen sharply. Pressure is increasing on living space, schools, and hospitals. Despite recent record food crops and a rise in industrial output, the population increase, on which only a marginal dent has been made by a costly birth-control program, has resulted in deteriorating living conditions for most Indians.

The social structure, ever in conflict, throws up many obstacles to progress. The Hindus, who make up 84 percent of the population, are divided into countless subcastes. The downtrodden untouchables, who constitute one seventh of the population, have begun asserting their rights. Clashes with upper-caste Hindus have become frequent and often violent.

The Moslem minority, 10 percent of the population, has remained suspect in the eyes of the majority ever since the creation of Pakistan. They live in constant insecurity and threat from militant Hindus. Bloody riots between Hindus and Moslems erupt periodically. The smaller minorities, the Sikhs, Buddhists, Jains, Parsis, and Christians, live in relative security, but the chances of their assimilation into the Hindu-dominated national life are remote.

In 1975 India went through the most important political crisis in its years as a republic when in April the government declared a state of emergency, arrested political leaders opposed to Prime Minister Indira Gandhi, began press censorship and suspended protection of fundamental rights. This repressive action was precipitated by Gandhi's conviction on charges of corrupt practices in the 1971 general election.

In July 1975 Mrs. Gandhi's power was restored when new laws approved by Parliament permitted her to rule by proclamation, barred the courts from reviewing her actions and changed the election law retroactively to remove any criminal offenses. In December Gandhi's Congress Party delayed general elections, due in March 1976, for at least a year and extended the state of emergency for six months.

In January 1977 Mrs. Gandhi announced the elections that had been postponed would be held in March; press censorship was subsequently lifted. In what was hailed as a victory for Indian democracy, Morarji R. Desai, 81, and his Janata Party defeated Mrs. Gandhi and her 30-year-old son, Sanjay, in the election. It was the first defeat suffered by the ruling Congress Party in the 30 years of India's independence. The new government immediately revoked the emergency rule legislation and released the political prisoners who had been jailed without charges. And since Desai himself was one of the thousands of political

prisoners detained during Mrs. Gandhi's 19-month "emergency rule" period, it came as no surprise when the new government launched a series of civil and crimial investigations into her alleged abuses of power.

What was surprising, though, was a swift—even though relatively short-lived—upturn in Mrs. Gandhi's fortunes. In February 1978, a month after leaving the Congress Party to form a splinter group, she reemerged as a major force in Indian politics when her Congress-I (for Indira) Party entered a series of state elections and won decisively in two important states and did better than expected in a third. Her comeback surge possibly contributed to the split, two months later, in the ruling Janata Party, resulting in the creation of a separate West Bengal Janata Party. Moreover, Mrs. Gandhi was elected to Parliament in November 1978, defeating 27 candidates in a by-election in Chickmagalur in the state of Karnataka.

However, Mrs. Gandhi found herself fighting for political survival a month later when the *Lok Sabha*, the lower house of Parliament, expelled her on charges of contempt of the house and breach of privilege for her actions while as prime minister. In addition, the government set up special courts that would keep her tied up in litigation. In February 1979 her son, Sanjay, was convicted of the theft and burning of a film (during the "emergency rule" period) that ridiculed his mother's conduct in office. Sentenced to prison, he was freed on bail pending appeal.

Desai meanwhile grappled with a host of other problems, including an increase in crime, caste violence, and an unfavorable balance of payments. Food grain production was a bright spot, rising almost high enough to meet all of the country's needs. In March 1979, Desai and Soviet Premier Kosygin, meeting in New Delhi, signed trade and scientific and technological agreements. India will exchange rice for Soviet oil of equal value, and the Soviet Union will join in oil exploration in India. The Soviets will build one new steel mill in India and expand two others.

In general, however, India was turning away from emphasis on large-scale industrialism and toward a "cottage industry" system. For instance, foreign companies engaged in large-scale manufacturing of matches, soaps, and cosmetics in India were directed to curtail or end their activities so that these fields could be opened up to home industry.

On July 15, 1979 Prime Minister Desai resigned from his office following growing defections from and splits within his Janata Party. President Reddy appointed Chaudhury Charan Singh to serve as prime minister on July 28, but Singh resigned on August 20.

HISTORY: The Indus Valley was the site of a flourishing civilization from the 3rd millennium to about 1500 B.C., when the region was conquered by the Aryans who, over the next 2,000 years, developed a Brahmanic civilization and introduced a caste system. In 327-325 B.C., Alexander the Great invaded northwest India, only to be driven out, and in the following century most of the subcontinent was united under Asoka the Great, who established Buddhism as the state religion. After his death, however, Buddhism declined in India as Hinduism experienced a resurgence

4th cent.: Hindu kingdoms are established

8th cent.: Islam is introduced into Sind by Arab invaders

1498-1510: European contact with India, begun with the arrival of Portuguese explorer Vasco da Gama, is followed by Portuguese conquest of Goa and spurs rivalry among European powers for trade with subcontinent

1526-1707: India is ruled by Mogul dynasty; a large Moslem population grows up and a new culture evolves, developing a characteristic Indo-Islamic style in art and architecture, as evidenced by the Taj Mahal

1746-63: India is turned into a battleground for the forces of France and Britain as each tries to carve out colonial domains; with the 1763 Treaty of Paris, British supremacy is assured

1857-58: Sepoy Rebellion by native soldiers in the employ of British East India Company is brutally suppressed; company is dissolved and India is placed under the direct rule of the British crown

1919: Mohandas K. Gandhi, later known as the Mahatma or "great-souled," organizes the first of many passive resistance campaigns against British rule; he is imprisoned

1942-45: Indian National Congress, largely Hindu-supported, splits with Moslem League, which favors creation of Pakistan as a separate Moslem state, over support for Britain during World War II; Congress is outlawed, while League, which supports Britain, gains strength

1947: Subcontinent is partitioned into the independent nations of India and Pakistan; Jawaharlal Nehru becomes India's first prime minister; bloody riots break out between Hindus and Moslems and millions flee in crisscross migration to new states; India and Pakistan fight over Kashmir

1948: Gandhi is assassinated by Hindu fanatic who blames him for partition; Kashmir fighting ends with UN cease-fire

1950: India becomes republic within Commonwealth of Nations

1954: India signs nonaggression pact with Communist China

1956: Constitutional amendment redrawing state boundaries along linguistic lines put into effect

1962: Chinese Communist troops occupy Ladakh region of Kashmir

1964: Nehru dies and is succeeded by Lal Bahadur Shastri

1965-66: India and Pakistan fight three-week war in 1965 over Kashmir; hostilities end in a truce, followed by accord signed in 1966 at Tashkent, in the Soviet Union. Indian Prime Minister Lal Bahadur Shastri dies at Tashkent and is succeeded by Mrs. Indira Gandhi, daughter of the former prime minister, Jawaharlal Nehru

1969: Death of President Zakir Husain touches off power struggle in governing Congress Party as Mrs. Gandhi and old guard party bosses clash over choice of successor; party splits following election of V.V. Giri, the candidate backed by Mrs. Gandhi, as President; bulk of party members remain with her New Congress Party but she loses majority strength in Parliament, forcing her to rely on Communists and independents for crucial votes

1970: Supreme Court rules bank nationalization law unconstitutional; prime minister counters court's action by issuing new ordinance nationalizing the banks. Mrs. Gandhi dissolves lower house of Parliament and orders new elections

1971: Mrs. Gandhi's party is landslide victor in the elections held in March, winning two-thirds of the parliamentary seats. Civil war breaks out in Pakistan. Millions of East Pakistani refugees flee to India. India supports East Pakistan in fight against West Pakistan, and latter is soon defeated. East Pakistan becomes Bangladesh

1972: At Simla Conference India and Pakistan agree to observe "lines of control" in Kashmir

1973: At Delhi Conference India and Pakistan agree to repatriation of 93,000 Pakistani POWs held since their 1971 war. Soviet Union lends India two million tons of wheat and rice

1974: World Health Organization estimates 30,000 have died in northern India in worst smallpox epidemic of the century. Sikkim becomes an associated state of India. Worst famine since 1943 in West Bengal, Assam, and Bihar

1975: India is first non-Arab country to give full diplomatic status to Palestine Liberation Organization. Prime Minister Gandhi is convicted on charges of illegal activities in connection with her election. Gandhi suspends civil liberties and orders arrest of hundreds of political opponents. Gandhi's powers are restored by Parliament and the Supreme Court

1976: Suspension of civil liberties continues throughout the year. India and Pakistan formally establish diplomatic ties

1977: Morarji R. Desai elected prime minister. President Fakhruddin Ali Ahmed dies; he is succeeded by Neelam Sanjiva Reddy. Government launches probes into alleged abuses of power by Mrs. Gandhi during her "emergency rule" period. India acts to improve relations with neighbors and U.S. while stressing friendship with Soviet Union, along with policy of "genuine nonalignment" less subject to Soviet influence than was the case in Mrs. Gandhi's administration

1978: High-level talks between India and Pakistan begin; disputed state of Kashmir tops agenda. Mrs. Gandhi's newly formed Congress-I party wins two important state elections and does better than expected in a third. Elected to Parliament, she is expelled; special courts are set up to try her for actions taken when prime minister

1979: The Soviet Union and India sign agreements covering trade and technological and scientific cooperation for 10 to 15 years. Indian rice will be traded for Soviet oil. Simultaneously, the government curtails some large-scale industry and encourages "cottage industry" such as production of matches, candy, and cookies. Desai resigns and is succeeded by Chaudhury Charan Singh on July 28. Singh resigns on Aug 20

INDONESIA

Area: 788,430 sq. mi. **Population:** 142,000,000 (1978 est.)

Official Name: Republic of Indonesia **Capital:** Jakarta **Nationality:** Indonesian **Languages:** Bahasa Indonesia, a form of Malay developed as a product of Indonesia's nationalist movement, is the official language; English is the second language and is compulsory in secondary schools **Religion:** 90% Moslem, 5% Christian, 3% Hindu (Bali has retained its Buddhist/Hindu heritage) **Flag:** A red horizontal stripe above a white stripe **Anthem:** Great Indonesia **Currency:** Rupiah (625 per U.S. $1)

Location: Southeast Asia, in the Malay archipelago. Indonesia consists of six large and 13,662 lesser islands, which form an arc between Asia and Australia. The principal group of islands is the Greater Sunda Islands, which include Java, Bali, Sumatra, Borneo (Kalimantan), and Celebes (Sulawesi). The country shares land borders with Malaysia, Brunei, and Papua New Guinea **Features:** The large islands have a central mountain range rising from fairly extensive lowlands and coastal plains. Many islands throughout the archipelago are dotted with volcanoes, both active and dormant **Chief Rivers:** Kapuas, Digul, Barito, Mahakam, Kajan, Hari, Mamberamo, Idenburg

Head of State and of Government: President: Gen. Suharto, born 1921, reelected 1978 **Effective Date of Present Constitution:** 1945 **Legislative Body:** Peoples' Consultative Assembly, consisting of 920 members, within it a 460-member (360 elected and 100 nominated by the president) House of Representatives (Parliament) **Local Government:** 23 provinces, each with an appointed governor and an elected legislature, 2 autonomous regions, 1 capital region, and the special territory of East Timor

Ethnic Composition: Malayans and Papuans constitute the main ethnic groups, each with numerous subdivisions. Chinese make up the largest nonindigenous group **Population Distribution:** 18.2% urban **Density:** 180 inhabitants per sq. mi.

Largest Cities: (1973 est.) Jakarta 5,000,000, Surabaya 2,000,000, Bandung 2,000,000, Medan 1,000,000, Yogyakarta 500,000; (1971 census) Semarang 646,590, Palembang 582,961

Per Capita Income: $329 (1978 est.) **Gross National Product (GNP):** $46 billion (1978) **Economic Statistics:** About 36% of GNP comes from agriculture (rubber, copra, tea, coffee, tobacco, sugar, palm oil, rice), 16% from manufacturing (chiefly processing of agricultural and mineral products and light manufactures), 12% from mining **Minerals and Mining:** The country is one of the world's leading producers of tin and rubber and is the leading oil producer in the Far East. Other minerals are bauxite, nickel, copper, natural gas, and coal **Labor Force:** 48,000,000 (1977, of which some 61% is in agriculture and 6% in industry **Foreign Trade:** Exports, chiefly petroleum and petroleum products (67%), tin ore, nickel, copra, coffee, and tobacco, totaled $10.8 billion in 1977. Imports, mainly textiles, machinery, transportation equipment, rice, fertilizer, and chemicals, toaled $6.2 billion **Principal Trade Partners:** Japan, United States, West Germany, Netherlands, Singapore, Britain, Trinidad & Tobago

Vital Statistics: Birthrate, 42.9 per 1,000 of pop. (1975); death rate, 19.4 **Life Expectancy:** 48 years **Health Statistics:** 1,415 inhabitants per hospital bed; 18,863 per physician (1974) **Infant Mortality:** 126 per 1,000 births **Illiteracy:** 40% **Education Statistics:** 72,760 primary and secondary schools, with combined enrollment of 16,939,466 (1975) **Enrollment in Higher Education:** 278,200 (1975) **GNP Expended on Education:** 3.1% (1975)

Transportation: Paved roads total c.12,500 mi. **Motor Vehicles:** 684,000 (1976) **Passenger Cars:** 420,900 **Railway Mileage:** 4,200 **Ports:** Jakarta, Surabaya, Semarang, Palembang, Belawan, Dumai, Balikpapan, Samarinda **Major Airlines:** Garuda Airways and Merapti Nusantara operate domestic and international services **Communications:** Government controlled **Radio Transmitters:** 588 **Licenses:** 5,100,000 (1976) **Television Transmitters:** 29 **Licenses:** 325,000 (1976) **Telephones:** 314,000 (1976) **Newspapers:** 172 dailies (1975), 10 copies per 1,000 inhabitants

Weights and Measures: Metric system and traditional units are used **Travel Requirements:** Passport; tourist visa (to 30 days, $2.80 fee); 2 photos

Indonesia, with 13,662 tropical islands (992 of them inhabited), strung like a necklace along the Equator, is one of the world's most beautiful nations. It is green and fertile, but until recently political upheavals guaranteed its backward, impoverished status among nations.

Ruled by Dutch colonialists for about 300 years, Indonesia declared its independence on August 17, 1945, following Japanese occupation during

World War II. Four years of fighting and negotiation followed and its sovereignty was recognized in 1949.

The colonial economic and administrative machinery decayed under President Sukarno, who concentrated on building a national identity and pride among a conglomeration of races and religions scattered throughout the islands. He also sought to cast Indonesia in the role of leader of the "third world" while slowly moving closer to Communist China for support.

It was the gradual growth of the ideology of Communism that eventually led to Sukarno's downfall and plunged Indonesia into not only political and economic chaos but also resulted in one of the worst bloodbaths in history.

On the night of September 30, 1965, the Communists and other leftists attempted a coup that was put down by anti-Communist military units under General Suharto. In an ensuing purge of Communists, more than 300,000 Indonesians were slaughtered. Political prisoners were held for years, but the government, pressured by Amnesty International and others, released 10,000 in 1977 and 10,000 more the following year, it said.

President Sukarno was gradually eased out of power and General Suharto became president, running the country under the tight rein of the military. The Communist Party was banned.

President Suharto found Indonesia in financial ruin and deeply in debt to other nations for money Sukarno had borrowed to spend on military equipment and prestige projects such as public buildings and monuments. Under the new regime capital was lured into the country with tempting interest rates and guarantees.

Indonesia faces enormous problems, and overpopulation tops the list. Java, where an estimated 80 million people live, is one of the most densely populated islands in the world. Efforts to move people to underpopulated outer island regions have largely failed. Despite development of roads, electrification, hospitals and schools, much of the outer island area still remains a wilderness.

However, a vast natural treasure of oil, minerals and forests is beginning to be harvested, to the benefit of both Indonesia and the foreign investors who have poured in the money and technical skills to exploit it. Currently, Indonesia is East Asia's main oil exporter and the world's eighth-largest exporter. Its 1978 oil shipments amounted to about $6.5 billion. Indonesia raised oil prices again in 1979, but less than the full increase by OPEC, thus indicating an intent to gain a larger share of the market. Caltex Pacific Indonesia, a joint venture of Texaco and Standard Oil Co. of California, produces about half of Indonesia's oil.

In March 1978 President Suharto was unanimously reelected to a third five-year term by Indonesia's Congress. Adam Malik, chairman of the Congress, was elected vice president. A new Cabinet was also installed; its makeup—including 10 generals, double the number in the last Cabinet—underscored the fact that the president's power base remains the military. The losers were the two elements most vocal in criticizing the government in the often tense months since Indonesia's last parliamentary election in May 1977. These were the activist university and high school students, who demanded that Suharto step down, and the Moslem Unitary Development Party, which opposes Suharto's insistence on giving formal recognition in this predominantly Moslem nation to widespread mystical practices that take place mainly in Java and Bali.

HISTORY: The complex racial mixture found in Indonesia today is the result of two waves of invasions from Asia and the Pacific. Early in the Christian era the country came under the influence of Indian civilization and of Hinduism and Buddhism. In the 16th century, however, both of these were replaced by Islam as the dominant religion. In the 17th century, the Dutch emerged as the dominant power in Indonesia, maintaining their rule almost uninterruptedly until World War II, when the islands were occupied by Japan

1945-49: Nationalist leaders Sukarno and Mohammad Hatta proclaim Indonesia an independent republic following Japanese defeat in World War II. Attempts to reestablish Dutch rule evoke nationalist resistance; agreement is finally reached for creation of the United States of Indonesia, linked to Netherlands

1950-54: United States of Indonesia is dissolved; Republic of Indonesia is proclaimed, with Sukarno as president. Netherlands-Indonesian Union is dissolved

1959-60: Sukarno combines premiership with office of president and adopts authoritarian system of "guided democracy"; following disagreement with Hatta, who resigns as vice-president, Sukarno dissolves parliament and bans political parties

1962: Dutch withdraw from West Irian, on island of New Guinea, under agreement with United Nations, on condition that territory's people be permitted to decide their own political future

1965-66: Indonesia withdraws from UN; Sukarno adopts policy of collaboration with Communist China, which the Indonesian Communist Party (PKI) supports in Sino-Soviet split. An attempted Communist coup is suppressed by army and is followed by anti-Communist riots in which more than 300,000 Indonesians are killed; General Suharto emerges as new strong man

1967-68: Sukarno is stripped of power and Suharto named acting president. Abandonment of pro-Peking stance is followed by riots directed against Indonesia's economically important Chinese minority; Suharto is formally elected president by People's Consultative Congress

1969: Government quells uprising by Papuan natives in West Irian; despite widespread native opposition, Indonesia annexes territory with the approval of tribal leaders

1971: July parliamentary elections are first to be held since 1955. The government party wins a majority of House seats

1973: Suharto reelected to second five-year term

1974: Japanese Premier Tanaka visits Jakarta. Students demonstrate against alleged policy of economic exploitation of the region

1975-76: Portuguese Timor is incorporated into Indonesia, becoming its 27th province

1977: Ruling Golkar Party wins elections. Government releases 10,000 political prisoners

1978: Weeks of student protests precede presidential election; hundreds arrested, some campuses occupied; Suharto is reelected to third five-year term by Indonesian Congress. Government says it freed another 10,000 political prisoners

1979: A volcanic eruption on Mount Sinila, in central Java, kills 175 persons and injures 1,000

IRAN

Area: 636,293 sq. mi. **Population:** 34,500,000 (1978 est.)

Official Name: Islamic Republic of Iran **Capital:** Tehran **Nationality:** Iranian **Languages:** Persian, or Farsi, an Aryan language of the Indo-European group and written Arabic characters, is the official and dominant language. Kurdish, various forms of Turkic, and Arabic are among the other languages spoken **Religion:** About 98% of the population is Moslem, with 90% belonging to the Shi'a sect of Islam and the rest to the Sunni sect. Minofity religious groups include Jews, Baha'is, Zoroastrians, and Christian Armenians and Assyrians **Flag:** Green, white, and red horizontal stripes, with a golden lion brandishing a sword, and a rising sun behind him, centered on the white stripe **Anthem:** N.A. **Currency:** Iranian rial (70.5 per U.S. $1)

Location: Southwest Asia. Iran is bordered on the north by the USSR and the Caspian Sea, on the east by Afghanistan and Pakistan, on the south by the Persian Gulf, and on the west by Iraq and Turkey **Features:** The country is largely a semiarid plateau, with high mountain ranges and much barren desert. The Caspian coastal region is semitropical and fertile; the area around the Persian Gulf is extremely hot and dry **Chief Rivers:** Karun, Safid, Karkheh, Zayandeh, Dez

Head of Government: Premier Mehdi Bazargan, born 1905, is head of the provisional government, established during the February 1979 revolution. The religious leader, Ayatollah Ruhollah Khomeini, born 1900, exercises great power and influence in the provisional government through his control of the Council of the Islamic Revolution **Effective Date of Present Constitution:** A new constitution is being prepared (Aug. 1979) **Legislative Body:** The new constitution is purported to provide for a unicameral legislature elected by universal suffrage every four years **Local Government:** 20 provinces and 2 governorates

Ethnic Composition: Iranians (Persians) make up 63% of the population; about 25% consists of Turkic elements **Population Dis-**

tribution: 44% urban **Density:** 54 inhabitants per sq. mi.

Largest Cities: (1976 est.) Tehran 4,400,000, Isfahan 800,000, Meshed 600,000, Tabriz 550,000, Shiraz 380,000, Ahwaz 350,000, Abadan 340,000, Kermanshah 250,000

Per Capita Income: $1,937 (1978 est.) **Gross National Product (GNP):** $79 billion (1978 est.) **Economic Statistics:** About 25% of GNP comes from agriculture (wheat, cotton, barley, rice, fresh and dried fruits and vegetables, pulses, oilseeds, sugar beets), forestry, and fishing; 27% from oil; 17% from industry (textiles, food processing, building materials, rubber tires and mining); 5% from construction; and 21% from trade and services **Minerals and Mining:** Oil (Iran has 10% of the world's known oil resources), iron ore, chromite, natural gas, copper, lead, zinc, coal, gypsum, gold, manganese, and salt **Labor Force:** 10,000,000 (1976) of which 37% is engaged in agriculture and 30% in industry **Foreign Trade:** Exports, mainly oil, carpets, cotton, and fruits, totaled $18.4 billion in 1977. Imports, chiefly machinery, iron and steel, chemicals and drugs, totaled $14.6 billion **Principal Trade Partners:** West Germany, United States, Britain, USSR, Japan, France, Italy, India, Eastern European countries

Vital Statistics: Birthrate, 41.7 per 1,000 of pop (1976); death rate, 13 **Life Expectancy:** 54 years **Health Statistics:** 650 inhabitants per hospital bed; 2,696 per physician (1975) **Infant Mortality:** 100 per 1,000 births (1977) **Illiteracy:** 56% **Education Statistics:** 40,961 primary and secondary schools, with combined enrollment of 7,287,997 (1976) **Enrollment in Higher Education:** 151,905 **GNP Expended on Education:** 3.8% (1974)

Transportation: Paved roads total 11,620 mi. (1976) **Motor Vehicles:** 2,134,000 (1976) **Passenger Cars:** 1,892,000 **Railway Mileage:** 3,700 **Ports:** Khorramshahr, Bandar Shahpur, Bushire, Bandar Abbas, Kharg, Abadan, Pahlavi **Major Airlines:** Iran National Airlines operates internal and international services **Communications:** Largely government controlled **Radio Transmitters:** 64 **Receivers:** 6,500,000 (1976) **Television Transmitters:** 157 **Receivers:** 1,720,000 (1976) **Telephones:** 1,000,000 (1977) **Newspapers:** 20 dailies, 15 copies per 1,000 inhabitants (1974)

Weights and Measures: Metric system **Travel Requirements:** Passport; visa (no fee), valid 3 months; 1 photo

Iran's Islamic revolution of 1979, which sent shock waves throughout the world, was a violent uprising of civilians—one of the most important such uprisings since the aftermath of World War II, occurring as it did, in a country rich in oil, with a population of almost 35 million, and with a well-equipped standing army, units of which were stationed abroad. The prerevolutionary government of Shah Mohammed Reza Pahlavi was favorable to the United States and an exporter of oil—the major supplier to Israel and South Africa. The new Islamic regime tends toward isolation, conservation of oil, and identity with the Third World; it has forbidden exports to Israel and South Africa.

The revolution was carried out in the name of the Shi'a school of Islam. Shi'a mullahs (teachers) advocate strict adherence to Moslem tradition. Although less than a complete success, the revolution encouraged advocates of strict tradition in other Moslem countries and raised the morale of Shi'ite Moslems in countries where they are in the minority.

Iran is a large country, prone to earthquakes, its arable portions divided from each other by mountain ranges and deserts. Its most important ethnic group are the Farsi (Persians, whence the traditional name of the country—Persia), but a third of the population are of other ethnic groups, most of them Indo-European, as are the Farsi. Its oil industry, founded in 1908, is the oldest in the Middle East and the backbone of the national economy. The wells, although they are beginning to run out, still have enormous potential.

Seat of ancient empires, Iran was conquered by Moslem Arabs in the 7th century A.D. Over centuries, most Iranians became Moslems, but kept their Indo-European languages. In the 15th century, Iran adhered to the Shi'a movement, turning away from Arab leadership.

Shah Reza Pahlavi, who seized power in a military coup in 1921, was favorable to the army and to the promotion of Western ways. Britain and the USSR ousted him in 1941 because he looked to Nazi Germany as a counterweight to British and Soviet influence.

His son and successor, Mohammed Reza Pahlavi, ruled mostly as a figurehead until 1953, when, with the help of the army and Western governments, he ousted Prime Minister Mohammed Mossadegh. The Shah was identified with foreign influence, and he became more and more dictatorial.

The Shah launched a "revolution from the throne" in 1961. He announced plans to modernize the country, to improve public health, and to raise the status of women and poor people. He accomplished many of his ambitions, but did not become popular because he trusted no one but himself and his close advisors to know the meaning of modernization. He did not consult the people, and offended the mullahs by disregarding their interpretations of the Koran and by seizing mosque property..SAVAK, his secret police, dealt harshly with those he considered to be enemies of progress. Increasing wealth concentrated in the cities, and city ways became strange and offensive to country people.

When Britain withdrew its soldiers from the Persian Gulf region in 1970, the Shah began to give military assistance to neighboring countries. U.S. strategists considered his army crucial to the stability of the region. The army, from which his father had sprung, supported him, and the United States gave him aid.

The mosques became the centers of opposition to the Shah—even the opposition of Moslems who favored loose construction of the Koran and of socialists and others with little or no attachment to Islam. In 1978, riots broke out in the name of Ruhollah Khomeini, an exiled mullah who bore the holy title *Ayatollah*.

In 1979, the Shah left Iran, after appointing Shahpur Bakhtiar, a Mossadegh partisan, prime minister. Khomeini, still in exile, mocked the government and appointed a Council of the Islamic Revolution. He returned to Iran and designated Mehdi Bazargan, another Mossadegh partisan, prime minister. There were violent demonstrations on behalf of Bazargan. The armed forces at first supported Bakhtiar, but the defection of a few air force cadets and the strength of the revolution led the chiefs of staff to call for neutrality. Bakhtiar's government collapsed.

Khomeini, Bazargan, and the Council of the Islamic Revolution became power centers—not always in cooperation with each other. Mullahs and *ad hoc* militia units took most of the local authority. But the new order was less than totally effective. With the last vestiges of the Shah's authority gone, armed bands of revolutionaries began to pursue their own special ends. Non-Farsi areas were especially rife with bands demanding regional autonomy. More peaceful demonstrations were effective as well—notably the demonstration launched by educated women against Khomeini's suggestion that all women should wear *chador*—a kind of traditional Iranian costume considered by more rigid Moslems to be the only suitable modest dress. The turmoil disrupted transportation, manufacturing, and oil drilling, causing widespread hunger and unemployment in Iran and gasoline shortages in other countries.

Where the revolution could enforce its authority, there was little tolerance for dissent, and there were trials of former officials of the Shah, the usual sentence being death. On March 30 and 31, a referendum was held among Iranians 16 years old and older on a proposal to abolish the monarchy and proclaim an Islamic republic—which, according to Khomeini, would not necessarily be a democratic republic. The proposal passed overwhelmingly—but there were wide-

IRAN and IRAQ
CONIC PROJECTION
MILES
0 25 50 100 150 200
KILOMETRES
0 25 50 100 150 200
Capitals of Countries ⊛
International Boundaries ----
Ruins ∴ Elevations in Feet

spread charges of intimidation and fraudulent counting.

HISTORY: An agricultural civilization existed in Iran as far back as 4000 B.C. The Aryans arrived about 2000 B.C. and split into two main groups, the Medes and the Persians. About 550 B.C., Cyrus the Great founded the Persian Empire, which later fell to successive invaders. The Arabs conquered the country and introduced Islam in the 7th century A.D.; they were in turn replaced by the Turks and Mongols. Internal order was restored by the Safavid dynasty, which ruled from 1499 to 1736

1736-47: Nadir Shah establishes Afshar dynasty; he invades India in 1738 and brings back great riches; a despotic ruler, he is assassinated in 1747

1794: Aga Mohammad Khan established Kajar dynasty

19th cent.: Iran loses vast territories to Afghanistan and Russia

1901: Discovery of oil intensifies the rivalry between Britain and Russia over Iran

1907: Anglo-Russian agreement divides Iran into spheres of influence

1921-25: Reza Khan, an army officer, stages coup d'état, overthrows Kajar dynasty, and establishes military dictatorship; he is elected shah and founds Pahlavi dynasty

1941: British and Soviet forces occupy Iran to counter German threat; Reza Shah abdicates and is succeeded by his son, Mohammad Reza Pahlavi

1946: Soviet troops are withdrawn from Iran

1951-53: Premier Mohammad Mossadegh, a militant nationalist, forces parliament to nationalize oil industry, which virtually collapses after Britain imposes a blockade. Shah, who opposes Mossadegh, flees the country but returns a few days later after Mossadegh is ousted

1961-62: Shah launches "revolution from the throne," calling for the end of serfdom, for land distribution, and electoral reform; he personally distributes crown land to peasants

1963: Women gain vote

1971: U.S. and Britain underwrite a $1-billion defense program for Iran as prelude to British withdrawal from the Persian Gulf

1972: Earthquake leaves over 5,000 dead

1974: Seven persons sentenced to death for plotting to assassinate the Shah

1975: Shah dissolves two-party system, declaring a one-party state. U.S. and Iran sign $15 billion economic pact for non-oil trade

1978: Ultraconservative Moslems, leftist extremists and others join in widespread riots. Theater fire kills about 380 in port city of Abadan; government blames extremists

1979: Shah appoints Shahpur Bakhtiar, former Mossadegh partisan, Prime Minister, and leaves country on Bakhtiar's insistance. Exiled Ayatollah Ruhollah Khomeini condemns government and returns to Iran, designating Mehdi Bazargan as prime minister. Mass uprising sweeps out Bakhtiar government. Ethnic minorities revolt against government for local autonomy. Bazargan government holds referendum which results in 98% majority for "Islamic republic"

IRAQ

Area: 172,476 sq. mi. **Population:** 12,029,000 (1978 est.)

Official Name: Republic of Iraq **Capital:** Baghdad **Nationality:** Iraqi **Languages:** Arabic is the official and dominant language; Kurdish is spoken in the northeast **Religion:** About 95% of the population is Moslem, almost evenly divided between the Shi'a sect and the Sunni sect; about 3% is Christian **Flag:** Red, white, and black horizontal stripes, with three five-pointed green stars on the white stripe **Anthem:** Anthem of the Republic, no words **Currency:** Iraqi dinar (.29 per U.S. $1)

Location: Southwest Asia. Iraq is bordered on the north by Turkey, on the east by Iran, on the southeast by Kuwait and the Persian Gulf, on the southwest by Saudi Arabia, and on the west by Jordan and Syria **Features:** The country consists of a mountain region in the northeast, a rugged and sparsely wooded area with some good pastures; the vast Syrian Desert, contiguous with the Arabian desert; and a fertile lowland region between the mountains and the desert, watered by the Euphrates and Tigris rivers **Chief Rivers:** Tigris, Euphrates

Head of State and of Government: President: General Saddam Hussein, born 1935, elevated to Presidency on retirement of Ahmad Hassan al-Bakr on July 16, 1979. He is chairman of the Revolutionary Command Council and the Arab Socialist (Ba'ath) Party **Effective Date of Present Constitution:** A provisional constitution was issued in 1970; a National Charter was drafted in 1971 as a basis for a permanent Constitution **Legislative Body:** Plans for a National Assembly have not materialized; rule is by decree **Local Government:** 16 provinces, each headed by a governor

Ethnic Composition: Arabs constitute about 75% of the popula-

tion; Kurds constitute an estimated 20% **Population Distribution:** 63.7% urban **Density:** 70 inhabitants per sq. mi.

Largest Cities: (1970 estimates) Baghdad 1,028,083, Mosul 333,177, Basra 286,955

Per Capita Income: $1,737 (1978) **Gross National Product (GNP):** $21.4 billion (1978) **Economic Statistics:** In 1976, 8% of GNP was from agriculture (dates, wheat, barley, rice, cotton, wool, hides, and skins); 16% from industry, excluding the petroleum industry (foodstuffs, water and power services, bricks and cement, beverages, cigarettes and textiles); 26% from trade and services; and 50% from oil industry **Minerals and Mining:** Petroleum, sulphur, phosphate, natural gas, and salt are exploited **Labor Force:** 3,200,000, of which 53% is employed in agriculture, 17% in industry, 11% in services **Foreign Trade:** Exports, chiefly petroleum (98% of total), agricultural products, livestock, and cement, totaled $9.6 billion in 1977. Imports, mainly industrial machinery, iron and steel, automobiles, tea, sugar, clothing, and pharmaceutical products, totaled $5 billion (1977) **Principal Trade Partners:** EC countries, USSR, Japan, UAE, China, United States, Lebanon, Kuwait, Yugoslavia

Vital Statistics: Birthrate, 48.1 per 1,000 of pop. (1975); death rate, 15.5 **Life Expectancy:** 62 years **Health Statistics:** 485 inhabitants per hospital bed; 2,471 per physician (1975) **Infant Mortality:** 27.5 per 1,000 births **Illiteracy:** 49% **Education Statistics:** 7,664 primary and secondary schools, with combined enrollment of 2,291,155 (1974) **Enrollment in Higher Education:** 78,784 (1974) **GNP Expended on Education:** 4.3% (1974)

Transportation: Surfaced roads total 4,550 mi. **Motor Vehicles:** 160,400 (1975) **Passenger Cars:** 98,600 **Railway Mileage:** 1,462 **Ports:** Basra, Umm Qasr, Fao, Az Zubair **Major Airlines:** Iraqi Airways operates domestic and international services **Communications:** Government controlled **Radio Transmitters:** 12 **Receivers:** 1,252,000 (1975) **Television Transmitters:** 6 **Receivers:** 425,000 (1976) **Telephones:** 320,000 (1976) **Newspapers:** 7 dailies (1975), 22 copies per 1,000 inhabitants (1974)

Weights and Measures: Metric system and native units are used **Travel Requirements:** Passport; visa, valid 3 months; 1 photo

Iraq, known to archaeologists as Mesopotamia—the site of the ancient Sumerian, Babylonian, and other civilizations, was among the first Arab countries to free itself from Western European domination, joining the League of Nations in 1932, at the termination of British-mandate rule.

In 1958, after the monarchy was overthrown in a bloody military coup, Iraq became a republic. Ten years later, in the fourth coup in a decade, Major General Ahmed Hassan al-Bakr came to power as the head of a military junta. Thirteen days later, he deposed his two partners in the junta and proclaimed himself president. But his ill health resulted in the rise to prominence of Saddam Hussein, Deputy Chairman of the Revolutionary Command Council. On July 16, 1979, Bakr resigned and Saddam Hussein became president.

It is generally accepted that the country is ruled today by the inner core of the Ba'ath Party, an ultranationalistic, left-wing, Pan-Arab group, a rival faction of which controls Syria. The Iraqi inner core consists of young intellectual zealots, who rarely appear in public, leaving such functions to the president.

Although the Iraqi authorities have tended to isolate themselves even from the rest of the Arab world, there have been some recent indications that they are beginning to make an effort to enhance their reputation abroad.

The mainstay of Iraq's economy is oil. The revenue it receives through its petroleum exports pays for the bulk of the national expenditure. The oil revenues have been handled sensibly by Iraqi officials and not squandered on prestige projects as in other oil-producing Middle Eastern lands. There has been a gradual improvement in general living standards.

The militant Kurdish minority in the north has long been a problem to Iraqi officials. The Kurds, a nomadic non-Arab people, have traditionally been hostile to rule from Baghdad, and in recent years they engaged the Iraqi army in sporadic guerrilla warfare. Early in 1974, Iraq announced its plan for the autonomy of the Kurdish minority; the Kurds, however, rejected the government's terms for self-rule, and Kurdish leaders declared all-out war in April.

Closely related to the issue of the Kurds, who have ethnic ties to the Persians, is Iraq's conflict with Iran over navigation rights in the Shatt al Arab, the estuary formed by the confluence of the Tigris and Euphrates that forms part of a mutual border. In 1975 Iran and Iraq signed a reconciliation agreement, with Iraq abandoning its claim to the estuary and with Iran ending its support of the Kurdish rebellion. Shortly thereafter, the Kurdish rebellion collapsed.

In September 1977 there was a major government reshuffle which expanded the power base of President Ahmed Hassan al-Bakr. The nation's highest authority, the Revolutionary Command Council, was increased by presidential decree from 5 members to 22. All of the new members are also leaders of the ruling Ba'ath Party.

In 1978, Iraq clashed with the Palestine Liberation Organization. A series of terrorist attacks and counterattacks took place, directed at Iraqi and PLO offices and officials in various European and Middle Eastern cities. Relations with the Soviet Union grew strained.

HISTORY: About 3000 B.C. the Sumerians, already long established in the region. founded city-states in southern Mesopotamia. Among the civilizations that flourished there later were the Akkadian, Babylonian. and Assyrian. After about 500 B.C., Persia, and later Macedonia. dominated the area. In the 7th century A.D., Mesopotamia was overrun by the Arabs, who established their capital at Baghdad Mongol invasions followed in the 12th and 15th centuries, and in the 16th century the region fell to the Ottoman Turks, under whose rule it remained until World War I

1920: Iraq is made a British mandate under the League of Nations

1932: An independent Iraq is admitted to the League

1941: A pro-Axis government, briefly in power, collapses under British military attack

1948-49: Iraq and the other Arab League member-states send their forces into Palestine during Arab/Israeli War. The war ends with an armistice

1958: Army coup led by Brigadier General Abdul Karim Kassem overthrows monarchy and proclaims a republic; King Faisal and Crown Prince Abdul Illah, the king's uncle, are slain

1961: Civil war flares as Kurdish tribesmen rebel

1963: A Ba'athist military coup, headed by Colonel Abdul Salem Aref, ousts regime of Kassem, who is executed

1964: Cease-fire is arranged between army and Kurdish rebels, but fighting soon resumes

1966: Abdul Salem Aref is killed in helicopter crash; he is succeeded by his brother Abdul Rahman Aref

1967: Following Arab defeat in Six-Day War with Israel, Aref forms a new government under Lt. Gen. Tahir Yahya

1968: Bloodless coup overthrows Aref and Yahya; Revolutionary Command Council takes control under Gen. Ahmed Hassan al-Bakr

1969: Iraq executes about 40 Iraqis. many of them Jews, convicted of spying for Israel. the United States, and Iran

1970: Periodic war with Kurds is ended by granting of a degree of autonomy. Dispute with Iran over Persian Gulf area grows

1971: Iraq, in support of Palestinian militants, closes its border with Jordan. U.S. Embassy properties in Iraq are seized

1973: Coup attempt led by Col. Nazem Kazzar, Iraqi security chief, fails; Kazzar and 35 followers are executed

1974: Kurds declare war on Iraq

1975: Agreement with Iran, which had supported Kurds. Iraqi troops complete the takeover of former Kurdish strongholds in the northeast. encountering no resistance

1977: President Bakr's power base is widened as Revolutionary Command Council is increased from 5 to 22 members

1978: Amid signs of growing strain in Iraq's relations with the Soviet bloc, the government reportedly executes 14 Communists. Iraq feuds with Palestine Liberation Organization

1979: Iraq helps to settle dispute between North Yemen and South Yemen, and hosts conference of Arab ministers protesting Israel-Egypt peace treaty. Bakr resigns on July 16, turning the presidency over to Saddam Hussein

IRELAND

Area: 27,136 sq. mi. **Population:** 3,200,000 (1978 est.)
Official Name: Ireland **Capital:** Dublin **Nationality:** Irish **Languages:** Irish (Gaelic) and English are the official languages; English, however, is the language in common use **Religion:** About 94% of the population is Roman Catholic, about 5% Protestant Episcopal **Flag:** Green, white, and orange vertical stripes **Anthem:** The Soldier's Song **Currency:** Irish Pound (.50 per U.S. $1)

Location: The republic of Ireland is situated on the second largest of the British Isles, occupying all of the island of Ireland with the exception of Northern Ireland (part of the United Kingdom) with which the republic has its only land border. It is bounded on the east by the Irish Sea, on the southeast by St. George's Channel, and on the west by the Atlantic Ocean **Features:** The country is shaped like a basin, with high coasts sloping inland to low-lying plains **Chief Rivers:** Shannon, Liffey, Suir, Boyne, Blackwater, Erne, Barrow

Head of State: President: Dr. Patrick John Hillery, born 1923, inaugurated 1976 **Head of Government:** Prime Minister John M. Lynch, born 1917, elected June 1977 for 4 years **Effective Date of Present Constitution:** December 29, 1937 **Legislative Body:** Parliament (bicameral *Oireachtas*) consisting of the Senate (*Seaned*) and the House of Representatives (*Dáil*). The Senate is composed of 60 members, of whom 11 are nominated by the prime minister, 6 elected by the National University of Ireland and the University of Dublin, and 43 from 5 panels of candidates established on a vocational basis. The *Dáil* as 148 elected members. The maximum term of office is 5 years in both houses **Local Government:** 26 administrative counties and 4 county boroughs, each with popularly elected councils

Ethnic Composition: The population is mainly Irish, with an Anglo-Irish minority **Population Distribution:** 52.2% urban **Density:** 118 inhabitants per sq. mi.

Largest Cities: (1971 census) Dublin 567,866, Cork 128,645, Limerick 57,161, Dùn Laoghaire 53,171, Waterford 31,968

Per Capita Income: $3,189 (1978) **Gross National Product (GNP):** $10 billion (1978) **Economic Statistics:** In 1973 about 17% of GNP came from agriculture (cattle, dairy products, barley, wheat, oats, potatoes, sugar beets); 34% from industry (food processing, metal and engineering products, beverages, tobacco, textiles, chemicals, clothing, and footwear); and 41% from trade and services **Minerals and Mining:** Rich deposits of lead, zinc, copper, iron ore, natural gas, and silver **Labor Force:** 1,100,000 (1974), of which 30% is employed in industry, 23% in agriculture and fishing, and 40% in services **Foreign Trade:** Exports, chiefly meat, livestock, textiles, machinery and transportation equipment, dairy products, and metal ores, totaled $4.6 billion in 1977. Imports, mainly machinery and transportation equipment, chemicals, grains and other foodstuffs, textiles, metals and metal products, and petroleum, totaled $5.7 billion **Principal Trade Partners:** Britain, United States, West Germany, France, Netherlands

Vital Statistics: Birthrate, 21.4 per 1,000 of pop. (1977); death rate, 10.5 **Life Expectancy:** 71 years **Health Statistics:** 93 inhabitants per hospital bed; 830 per physician (1975) **Infant Mortality:** 14.6 per 1,000 births **Illiteracy:** Negligible **Education Statistics:** 3,659 primary and secondary schools, with combined enrollment of 675,461 (1974) **Enrollment in Higher Education:** 39,928 **GNP Expended on Education:** 6.5% (1975)

Transportation: Surfaced roads total 52,067 mi. **Motor Vehicles:** 615,300 (1976) **Passenger Cars:** 556,400 **Railway Mileage:** 1,334 **Ports:** Dublin, Cork, Limerick, Waterford, Rosslare, New Ross **Major Airlines:** Aer Lingus-Irish International Airlines operates domestic and international services **Communications:** Government controlled **Radio Transmitters:** 18 **Licenses:** 949,000 (1976) **Television Transmitters:** 28 **Receivers:** 655,000 (1976) **Telephones:** 480,000 (1976) **Newspapers:** 7 dailies, 222 copies per 1,000 inhabitants (1975)

Weights and Measures: Both British standards and the metric system are used **Travel Requirements:** Passport; no visa

After 30 years of something of an economic miracle in which Ireland turned from an agrarian to an industrial society, a little of the power has gone out of Ireland's boom. A period of relatively slow growth, high inflation and unemployment, and problems with its balance of payments has confronted the government with warnings of trouble. Even so, Ireland has come a long way.

Over a half a century ago, when the 26 counties constituting the republic became an independent state, the economy was unbalanced and in indifferent shape. More than 90 percent of exports were agricultural and went to one market—Britain. Beyond a few established businesses—breweries, distilleries, and bakeries—there was no industry. As a result, the drain upon the nation's young through emigration—first to the United States, and later to Britain—was excessive.

Ireland has been greatly aided by foreigners—both as tourists and as developers. Canadians were given mining rights and their exploration and development have shown that Ireland has rich deposits of zinc, lead, copper, and silver. Additionally, Germans helped harness the Shannon River and gave Ireland its first big hydroelectric generators. Beet sugar production was begun, and for many years Ireland has been self-sufficient in sugar supplies. And promising reserves of oil and gas have recently been discovered off the Irish coast in the Irish Sea. In 1977 foreign investment in Ireland amounted to $1 billion.

Ireland, although committed to upholding the rights of private property and private enterprise, has governmental industries. The national transport company, the airline, the sugar company, the tourist board, the peat board, the radio and television service, and the electricity supply board are all owned by the state and administered by semigovernmental bodies. In January 1973, Ireland's economic prospects were brightened somewhat by its entry into the European Common Market.

Economic progress, however, has not erased the age-old "Irish Question," which again came to the fore with the 1969 outbreak of violence between Catholics and Protestants in Northern Ireland. Sporadic street violence has continued since that time. A series of bombings and bank and post-office raids, coupled with the 1976 assassination of British ambassador Christopher Ewart-Biggs by I.R.A. members, unleashed a chain of events which disrupted the government. An Emergency Powers Bill and a Criminal Law Bill, giving police broad powers in dealing with extremist groups was passed; President Cearbhall O'Dálaigh resigned after a dispute with the Minister of Defense over the constitutionality of the laws, and Dr. Patrick J. Hillery subsequently became president.

In May 1978 Prime Minister Lynch appealed to the United States and Britain to help solve the problems of Northern Ireland. He urged Irish-Americans to stop sending money to aid violent Irish militants, while pressing the British to indicate their support for the island's eventual reunification. In 1979, Ireland joined the continental members of the European Community in the European Monetary System, and cut the link between the British and Irish currencies.

HISTORY: Celtic tribes from Gaul or Iberian Galicia conquered Ireland about the 4th century B.C. and established a Gaelic civilization. By the 3rd century A.D., five Gaelic kingdoms had been established and gradually became Christianized. Until the 8th century arrival of the Vikings, Ireland remained free from foreign invasion, escaping even the Roman conquest that befell neighboring Britain. In the end, however, beginning with the 12th-century Anglo-Norman conquest, that neighbor was to prove the most troublesome shaper of all

1542: Henry VIII of England assumes the title of King of Ireland

1649: Oliver Cromwell confiscates nine-tenths of Irish land and distributes it among English Protestant settlers

1801: United Kingdom of Great Britain and Ireland is formed

1846-54: About one million Irish die of starvation as a result of famine, brought on by recurring potato blight; more than 1.5 million Irish emigrate, mostly to the United States

1916-20: Easter Rebellion against British rule breaks out in 1916 under leadership of Sinn Fein, a nationalist movement; rebellion is crushed and its leaders executed

1921-22: Irish Free State is set up as a British dominion; six northern counties of Ulster remain in United Kingdom. Sinn Fein splits into conservative and republican groups, the latter headed by Eamon de Valera and opposed to division of Ireland; civil war breaks out but conservative elements prevail

1931: Equality with Britain is affirmed by Statute of Westminster

1932: De Valera becomes prime minister

1937: New Constitution makes British monarch ceremonial head of Ireland for external purposes only

1939-45: Ireland remains neutral during World War II, but many Irish volunteer for service with British forces

1949: Ireland declares itself a republic, withdraws from British Commonwealth, and maintains jurisdictional claims over Northern Ireland

1951-59: De Valera becomes prime minister, following victory by Fianna Fáil in parliamentary elections; De Valera resigns his post as prime minister to take over presidency

1966: De Valera is reelected president for seven-year term; Jack Lynch becomes prime minister

1969: Lynch's Fianna Fáil party wins overall majority in parliament in general elections; government sends troops to northern border as Catholics battle Protestants in Ulster

1973: Erskine Childers succeeds De Valera as president. Liam Cosgrave is elected prime minister

1974: Cearbhall O'Dálaigh becomes fifth president on death of Childers

1975: Severe drought conditions imperil crops

1976: British ambassador to Ireland, Christopher Ewart-Biggs, is killed in Dublin by a land mine explosion. O'Dálaigh resigns presidency; Dr. Patrick J. Hillery becomes president

1977: Jack Lynch's Fianna Fáil Party wins election, making him new prime minister

1978: Prime Minister Lynch appeals to U.S. and Britain to help solve problems of Northern Ireland

ISRAEL

Area: 7,847 sq. mi. **Population:** 3,760,000 (1978 est.)

Official Name: State of Israel **Capital:** Jerusalem; Tel Aviv is the diplomatic capital **Nationality:** Israeli **Languages:** Hebrew is the official and dominant language; Arabic is spoken by about 15% of the population; English and German are often used in business **Religion:** Judaism is the predominant religion; the Arab minority is largely Moslem and the Christian Arabs chiefly Greek Catholic and Greek Orthodox **Flag:** A white field with a blue six-pointed Star of David bordered above and below by blue horizontal stripes **Anthem:** The Hope **Currency:** Israeli pound (21.4 per U.S. $1)

Location: Middle East, at the eastern end of the Mediterranean. Israel is bordered on the north by Lebanon, on the east by Syria and Jordan, on the south by Egypt, and on the west by the Mediterranean Sea **Features:** The Negev Desert in the south constitutes about 50% of the country. The rest of the country consists of a narrow coastal plain in the center and a hilly region to the north **Chief Rivers:** Jordan, Kishon

Head of State: President Yitzhak Navon, born in 1921, elected by Parliament in 1978 for a 5-year term **Head of Government:** Prime Minister Menachem Begin, born 1913, assumed office June 1977 **Effective Date of Present Constitution:** There is no written constitution; the structure of government is defined by fundamental laws **Legislative Body:** Parliament (unicameral Knesset) consisting of 120 members elected by universal suffrage for 4 years **Local Government:** 6 administrative districts, headed by appointed commissioners

Ethnic Composition: Jews constitute about 85% of the population, with the rest mainly Arabs **Population Distribution:** 82% urban **Density:** 472 inhabitants per sq. mi.

Largest Cities: (1975 est.) Tel Aviv 357,600, Jerusalem 344,200, Haifa 225,000, Ramat Gan 120,200, Bat Yam 114,000

Per Capita Income: $4,154 (1978) **Gross National Product (GNP):** $14.8 billion (1978) **Economic Statistics:** 7% of GNP comes from agriculture (citrus fruits, eggs, vegetables); 29% from manufacturing (food processing, metals and machinery, textiles, chemicals, and petroleum products), mining, and quarrying; 20% from commerce and finance; 19% from services **Minerals and Mining:** Potash, phosphate, bromine, phosphate rock, copper, iron, ceramic clays and glass sand, and gypsum are exploited **Labor Force:** 1,200,000 (1977), of which 25.3% is employed in industry, 32.8% in services, 12.2% in commerce, 6.5% in agriculture **Foreign Trade:** Exports, chiefly polished diamonds, citrus fruits, textiles, clothes, food products, chemicals, fertilizers, and mining products, totaled $3.4 billion in 1977. Imports, chiefly rough diamonds, machinery, transport equipment, nonmetallic mineral manufactures, food and live animals, raw materials, and chemicals, totaled $4.6 billion **Principal Trade Partners:** United States, Britain, West Germany, Netherlands, Belgium, France, Switzerland

Vital Statistics: Birthrate, 26.1 per 1,000 of pop. (1977); death rate, 6.8 **Life Expectancy:** 72 years **Health Statistics:** 171 inhabitants per hospital bed; 351 per physician (1973) **Infant Mortality:** 23 per 1,000 births **Illiteracy:** 10% **Education Statistics:** 6,445 primary and secondary schools, with combined enrollment of 693,335 (1974) **Enrollment in Higher Education:** 75,338 (1974) **GNP Expended on Education:** 7.3% (1974)

Transportation: Paved roads total 3,350 mi. **Motor Vehicles:** 406,700 (1975) **Passenger Cars:** 284,000 **Railway Mileage:** 562 **Ports:** Haifa, Ashdod, Eilat **Major Airlines:** El Al Israel Airlines, the government airline, handles foreign travel, while Arkia, its subsidiary, handles domestic travel **Communications:** State controlled

Radio Transmitters: 39 **Receivers:** 655,000 (1976) **Television Transmitters:** 28 **Receivers:** 475,000 (1976) **Telephones:** 888,000 (1976) **Newspapers:** 23 dailies, 208 copies per 1,000 inhabitants (1975)

Weights and Measures: Metric system **Travel Requirements:** Passport; no visa for 3 months

The proclamation of Israel as a nation in 1947 again established after an absence of many centuries a Hebrew state in a land regarded by Jews as their homeland. The ancient kingdoms of Israel and Judah had been conquered repeatedly through several centuries, and the Jews had scattered through many lands. Following the Moslem conquest of the 7th century A.D., Arab culture had become predominant. The 19th-century Zionist movement for restoration of the Jewish homeland promoted Jewish migration to the land—then the Ottoman province of Palestine. Palestine was occupied during World War I by Britain, which governed it as a mandate of the League of Nations from 1919 to 1946, and of the United Nations from 1946 to 1948. Jewish immigration continued, especially after the Nazi persecutions; by 1947, the Jews were in the majority in many areas of Palestine.

The UN moved to divide Palestine into an Arab and a Jewish state, over the objections of the Palestine Arabs, who rejected the UN proposal to organize a state. Israel declared its independence on May 14, 1948, and was attacked by five Arab nations. An uneasy cease-fire in 1949 gave Israel almost 50 percent more territory than originally granted; Jordan (then Transjordan) annexed the rest.

Arab-Israeli hostilities continued to seethe under the surface until they erupted in war on October 29, 1956, when Israel staged a "pre-emptive attack" on Egypt's Sinai during the Suez Canal crisis. A UN cease-fire ended the fighting on November 6, 1956, and Israel withdrew its forces under pressure.

During the Six Day War of 1967, Israel made large-scale territorial gains in the Gaza Strip, Sinai Peninsula, Old Jerusalem, the Golan Heights, and Jordan's West Bank. The memory of these gains set the stage for the war of 1973-74, when Egyptian, Syrian, and Iraqi forces attacked on October 6. The Arab forces first made large gains, but these were considerably reduced by the time a truce ended the fighting on November 7.

Despite the truce, sporadic fighting continued between Israel and Syrian troops, until U.S. Secretary of State Henry Kissinger arranged a cease-fire on May 31, 1974.

Border agreements with Syria and Egypt which included UN buffer zones were a stabilizing factor in those areas, but in November 1974 there was increased Israeli concern for the future of the West Bank of the Jordan River when the UN General Assembly voted that Palestinians should be entitled to return to their land and property, and granted the Palestine Liberation Organization (PLO) permanent observer status.

In September 1975 Kissinger completed negotiations for a second Egyptian-Israeli disengagement agreement setting out details of the new military position in the Sinai Peninsula and the extent of Israeli withdrawal to the eastern entrances of the Giddi and Mitla passes and from the Abu Rudays and Ras Sudar oil fields, which had been supplying 55 percent of Israel's oil needs. By February 1976 the final phase of the troop disengagement agreement was implemented.

Meanwhile, many Israelis had settled in the occupied territory, claiming that all of the historic homeland was as their land.

In 1977, the Labor Alignment, which had been the largest bloc in every previous legislature, suffered scandal and internal discord. The Likud

Party won the ensuing election and with two religious groups formed a coalition government.more favorable to private enterprise and to Jewish religious tradition. Menachem Begin became prime minister.

Despite Begin's reputation as a hard-liner, President Anwar el-Sadat of Egypt visited Israel in 1977 as an initiative to peace. Begin returned the visit, and negotiations for peace opened. Problems arose, however, over the Jewish settlements in the occupied lands. Sadat could not ignore the fate of the Palestinians, and Begin could not retreat from his position supporting the Israeli settlements.

In March 1978 the climate for dialogue was dampened considerably when a PLO terror raid—the worst in Israel's history—began yet another violent cycle of strike and counterstrike, the Israelis in this case taking revenge by invading southern Lebanon and smashing Palestinian strongholds there. After a three-month occupation, the Israelis withdrew, handing over most of a six-mile deep border zone to Lebanese Christian militia units and the rest to UN peacekeeping forces.

Substantial migration and a booming economy helped Israel to prosper following independence, but the high amounts expended on defense (set at a third of the national product) placed a heavy burden on the Israeli taxpayer, already beset by rampant inflation.

Despite these problems, Israel and Egypt finally agreed to a treaty in March 1979. Israel agreed to withdraw from occupied Sinai within three years, and from the oil fields it still occupied within a year, and agreed to take steps toward Palestinian self-government. Promises of assistance from the United States—and the diplomacy of U.S. President Jimmy Carter—were helpful. Moreover, Israel's position had been weakened by the decision of the new Islamic regime in Iran to embargo oil to Israel. The peace treaty obligates Egypt to sell oil to Israel.

Poor in soil and minerals, beset by inflation, high taxes, and an enormous military budget, Israel nevertheless attracts many Jewish immigrants by promising a new life. Tourists are also attracted by sites of historic importance and places sacred to Islam and Christianity, as well as to Judaism.

HISTORY: In biblical times Israel (then Canaan and later Palestine) was the home of scattered Hebrew tribes. By about 1000 B.C. a Hebrew kingdom was firmly established at Jerusalem, under King David. After the reign of Solomon, the kingdom split into two states, Israel and Judah, which were respectively destroyed by Assyria and Babylonia. Palestine later fell to the Greeks and finally to the Romans. In the 7th century, the region was conquered by the Moslems. Later, it was an Ottoman province. During World War I, it came under British control. Modern Israel marks the culmination of the Zionist movement for the reconstitution of a Jewish state

1947: United Nations adopts Palestine partition plan to divide Palestine into two states, one Jewish and one Arab

1948: Israel is proclaimed a nation and British withdraw from Palestine. Armies of surrounding Arab states attack Israel

1949: Fighting ends with Israel in possession of almost 50 percent more territory than originally granted. Armistice agreements, but no peace treaties, are signed with Arab countries

1956: Israeli forces invade Egypt and occupy Sinai Peninsula and Gaza Strip

1957: Under American and Soviet pressure, Israel completes withdrawal to old borders. United States guarantees Israeli passage into Red Sea through previously blockaded Strait of Tiran

1964: Palestine Liberation Organization is formed

1967: Egyptians reimpose blockade. Israel attacks in Sinai and then into Jordan and Syria. At end of Six-Day War, Israelis occupy all of Sinai Peninsula, Gaza, and east bank of Suez Canal, the Gaza Strip, all of west bank of Jordan, and Golan Heights of Syria

1969: Prime Minister Levi Eshkol dies and is succeeded by Mrs. Golda Meir of the Israel Labor Party. Arab guerrilla activity continues; Labor Alignment is returned to power

1972: Terrorist activity by PLO guerrillas and sympathizers increases, extending to a random massacre at Lod Airport and the kidnapping and death of Israeli athletes at the Olympic games in Munich. Israel carries out retaliatory raids on guerrilla settlements in Lebanon

1973: David Ben-Gurion, first prime minister and principal founder of the state of Israel, dies

1973-74: Fourth Arab-Israeli war breaks out when Egyptian, Syrian, and Iraqi forces launch surprise attack on October 6, 1973, Yom Kippur, the holiest day of the year for Jews. In January, Israel and Egypt agree on disengagement of forces. Fighting with Syria continues through May 1974

1975: Sporadic raids and bombing incidents, are carried out chiefly by the PLO, followed by Israeli reprisals on PLO camps in Syria; tension makes settlement of Arab-Israeli differences difficult

1976: Israeli airborne commandos rescue 103 hostages held at Uganda's Entebbe Airport by pro-Palestinian hijackers of an Air France airliner

1977: Israeli troops cross into Southern Lebanon and fight with Palestinians in the first direct clash between the two sides in more than two years. Likud Party is victorious in general elections; Menachem Begin becomes prime minister. Begin confers with Pres. Carter in Washington. Austerity moves, defense spending cuts, and Israeli pound devaluation are announced. President Sadat's Mideast "peace initiative" spurs round of talks

1978: PLO terror attack, worst in Israel's history, leaves 37 dead and 82 wounded; Israeli forces retaliate by invading southern Lebanon in biggest antiterrorist raid ever mounted by Israel; they occupy area for three months; events contribute to stalling of peace talks

1979: Peace treaty with Egypt signed. Treaty requires Israel to withdraw from Egypt within three years, from remaining oil fields within one year; and requires Egypt to sell oil to Israel. Palestinians continue terrorist activity; Israel continues raids on Palestinian bases in Lebanon

---

ITALY

Area: 116,303 sq. mi. **Population:** 56,450,000 (1978 est.)

Official Name: Italian Republic **Capital:** Rome **Nationality:** Italian **Languages:** Italian is the official and predominant language; German, French, Friulian, Slovene, Ladin, Albanian, and Greek are spoken by minorities **Religion:** Roman Catholicism is the religion of about 99% of the population. **Flag:** Green, white, and red vertical stripes **Anthem:** Hymn of Mameli **Currency:** Italian lira (847 per U.S. $1)

Location: Southern Europe. Italy has common land frontiers in the west with France, and in the north with Switzerland, Austria, and Yugoslavia. Its boot-shaped peninsular coastline is bordered by three branches of the Mediterranean: the Tyrrhenian Sea on the west, the Ionian Sea on the south, and the Adriatic Sea on the east. Major offshore islands are Sicily and Sardinia **Features:** The country is rugged and mountainous, except for the Po Valley area in the north, the heel of "the boot" in the south, and small coastal areas **Chief Rivers:** Po, Tiber, Arno, Adige

Head of State: President Alessandro Pertini, born 1896, elected in 1978 by Electoral Assembly (Parliament plus 58 regional representatives) **Head of Government:** Premier Francesco Cossiga, born 1928, appointed 1979 **Effective date of Present Constitution:** January 1, 1948 **Legislative Body:** Parliament (bicameral), consisting of the Senate and the Chamber of Deputies. The Senate is composed of 322 members elected for 5 years. The Chamber of Deputies has 630 members elected for 5 years **Local Government:** 94 provinces, each headed by a prefect appointed by the central government. These are grouped into 20 regions, with limited governing powers

Ethnic Composition: The population is virtually homogeneous, with small minority groups of Germans, Friulians, Slovenes, Albanians, Ladins and French **Population Distribution:** 48% urban **Density:** 485 inhabitants per sq. mi.

Largest Cities: (1975 est.) Rome 2,868,248, Milan 1,731,281, Naples 1,223,785, Turin 1,202,215, Genoa 805,855, Palermo 662,567, Bologna 493,120, Florence 465,823

Per Capita Income: $4,211 (1978) **Gross National Product (GNP):** $211 billion (1978) **Economic Statistics:** Over 40% of GNP comes from industry (automobiles, oil refining, textiles, machinery, chemicals, food processing); 7% from agriculture (wheat, rice, grapes, olives, fruit and vegetables); 24% from services, 14% from commerce **Minerals and Mining:** Italy is a leading producer of mercury, but is poor in most other minerals. Iron ore, petroleum, natural gas, lignite, pyrites, and sulphur are produced in small quantities **Labor Force:** 20.5 million, with some 38% in industry and 15% in agriculture **Foreign Trade:** Exports, chiefly industrial machinery, office machines, motor vehicles, textiles, and footwear, totalled $45 billion in 1977. Imports, mainly crude oil, minerals, machinery iron and steel, totaled $48 billion **Princi-**

pal Trade Partners: EC and EFTA countries, Latin America, United States, Canada, Libya

Vital Statistics: Birthrate, 13.2 per 1,000 of pop. (1977); death rate, 9.6 **Life Expectancy:** 70 years **Health Statistics:** 95 inhabitants per hospital bed; 502 per physician (1973) **Infant Mortality:** 17.6 per 1,000 births **Illiteracy:** 5% **Education Statistics:** 51,538 primary and secondary schools, with combined enrollment of 9,675,168 (1975) **Enrollment in Higher Education:** 976,712 **GNP Expended on Education:** 5.0% (1975)

Transportation: Surfaced roads total 179,241 mi., including 3,216 mi. of superhighways **Motor Vehicles:** 17,607,300 (1976) **Passenger Cars:** 15,925,300 **Railway Mileage:** 12,624 **Ports:** Genoa, Augusta, Venice, Naples, Trieste, Taranto, La Spezia **Major Airlines:** Alitalia, a government airline, conducts international flights while Elivie and Ati, also government owned, are domestic **Communications:** Partly government controlled **Radio Transmitters:** 1,964 **Licenses:** 13,024,000 (1976) **Television Transmitters:** 1,199 **Licenses:** 12,377,000 (1976) **Telephones:** 15,246,000 (1976) **Newspapers:** 78 dailies, 113 copies per 1,000 inhabitants (1974)

Weights and Measures: Metric system **Travel Requirements:** Passport; no visa for 3 months

Italy—one of the younger of Europe's nation-states, home of one of its oldest civilizations—is a society undergoing profound political, economic, and cultural transformations.

Unified politically only a century ago, Italians still seek a common sense of nationhood that will bridge their vast regional differences and rivalries. The Brenner Pass, in the Alps, and Cape Correnti, on the southern tip of Sicily, lie 750 miles apart, but the distance between them is far greater in terms of the environment, culture, traditions, and temperaments of their peoples.

The northerner is the heir to the Renaissance and *risorgimento*: vigorous, forward-looking, in the mainstream of European life, living in a temperate climate on land endowed with the lion's share of Italy's slender resources.

The southerner, on the other hand, has been less favored both by nature and by history. His land is poor, his climate marked by extremes, his political and cultural tradition still rooted in the aftermath of a feudalism that long resisted the liberating winds of the Renaissance, the French Revolution, and 19th-century liberalism.

The task of molding and governing a postwar republican Italy that will reconcile these vastly divergent interests and enlist equally the loyalties of the Milan industrialist, Roman aristocrat or shopkeeper, and Calabrian peasant has fallen on shifting coalitions of the democratic parties of the center and moderate left.

As of 1979, the Christian Democratic party has been the largest in every Parliament—and has supplied every premier—since 1946. But it has never had a majority, and has had to negotiate agreements for coalition or support with other parties. Some coalitions included parties suspected of lacking dedication to democracy. The Christian Democrats lost much support in the 1970s because of corruption of their leadership.

The Communist Party of Italy (PCI) became the second-largest in Parliament by professing dedication to democracy and to national independence and by governing a number of cities with scrupulous honesty. But participation in the Cabinet eluded it because the Christian Democrats and others feared both the PCI's motives and the difficulties that a government with Communist ministers would face with the United States.

In 1978, for the first time, a coalition including the Communists was formed—to support a Cabinet consisting entirely of Christian Democrats. The Communists withdrew in 1979 after being rebuffed in their demand for seats in the Cabinet. In 1979 Giulio Andreotti resigned the premiership and was eventually succeeded by Francesco Cossiga.

Italy has been troubled by acts of political terrorism, the most spectacular being the kidnap and murder of former Premier Aldo Moro in 1978.

HISTORY: About 500 B.C. Rome began its rise to power, supplanting the earlier Etruscan civilization. The Roman Empire fell in the 5th century A.D. and thereafter the Italian peninsula was largely politically fragmented until modern times. After the great cultural and intellectual flowering of the Renaissance, which reached its height in the late 15th century, much of Italy, divided into kingdoms, principalities, duchies, city-republics, and the Papal States, fell increasingly under foreign sway

1815: Following collapse of Napoleonic Empire, former states of Italian peninsula are reconstituted—some under Austrian rule

1848-49: Movement for the unification of Italy, known as the *risorgimento*, leads to revolts, but these are suppressed after initial successes

1859: Kingdom of Sardinia, aided by France, defeats Austrians at Solferino

1860-70: The Italian unification movement, whose most notable figures were Giuseppe Garibaldi, Giuseppe Mazzini, and Camillo di Cavour, moves ahead as various Italian states vote for union with Sardinia; following conquest of Kingdom of Two Sicilies by Garibaldi, that kingdom also votes for union with Sardinia, and in 1861 the Kingdom of Italy is proclaimed under Victor Emmanuel II. With the seizure of the papal possessions, Italian unification is completed by 1870

1915-18: Italy engages in World War I on side of Allies after initially declaring neutrality; country suffers heavy losses

1922: Benito Mussolini comes to power in wake of severe depression and establishes a fascist dictatorship

1935-36: Italy conquers Ethiopia

1940-43: Italy enters World War II as ally of Nazi Germany; Italian defeats in Greece and North Africa, and the Allied invasion of Sicily, help topple Mussolini's regime. New government is set up and an armistice signed with the Allies

1945: Mussolini is executed by Italian partisans

1946: Italy becomes a republic after voters decide by plebiscite to abolish the monarchy

1947: Peace treaty is ratified; Italy loses Fiume, Zara, Pula, and Istria to Yugoslavia and the Dodecanese Islands to Greece; its African colonies are placed under UN supervision

1949: Italy becomes a founding member of NATO

1966: Floods in northern and central Italy destroy or damage many art treasures, especially in Florence

1974: Premier Aldo Moro forms Christian-Democratic/Republican minority government

1975: Voting age is lowered to 18. The 1954 partition of Trieste territory becomes official

1976: Death toll from earthquake in Friuli reaches 1,200. Aldo Moro's government falls and new elections held. Italian Communist Party makes major gains but Christian Democrats retain slight edge. Giulio Andreotti is sworn in as premier

1977: Italy and Yugoslavia ratify agreement ending World War II border dispute over area south of Trieste, with Italy ceding territory to Yugoslavia. Public protest and extremist violence erupts over Italy's economic crisis

1978: Government resigns as wave of violence continues; Communists withdraw tacit support and demand cabinet seats in emergency coalition. President Giovanni Leone reappoints Premier Andreotti to form new government, nation's 40th since World War II. Red Brigades kidnap former Permier Aldo Moro on same day Andreotti presents new government to parliament; Communists given direct role (short of cabinet-level) for first time since 1947. Red Brigades demand release of 13 leftist prisoners for Moro's life; government refuses to negotiate, as huge manhunt is mounted; government decree enhances power of police; Moro found dead; public reaction against Red Brigades noted. Abortion is legalized. President Leone resigns in face of corruption charges and is replaced by Alessandro Pertini. Trial of Red Brigades members ends (29 are sentenced up to 15 years in prison; 16 are acquitted)

1979: Communists withdraw from coalition after their demand for cabinet seats is rebuffed. Andreotti resigns, forms coalition Cabinet, which loses confidence vote in Senate but remains in office as Parliament is dissolved. Communists lose seats in elections for new Parliament. Francesco Cossiga replaces Andreotti as premier

IVORY COAST

Area: 127,520 sq. mi. **Population:** 7,000,000 (1978 est.)
Official Name: Republic of Ivory Coast **Capital:** Abidjan **Nationality:** Ivorian **Languages:** French is the official and commercial language, but the most common African language is Dioula **Religion:** 63% animist, 25% Moslem, 12% Roman Catholic **Flag:** Orange, white, and green vertical stripes **Anthem:** L'Abidjanaise, beginning "Greetings, O land of hope" **Currency:** CFA Franc (219 per U.S. $1)

Location: West Africa. Ivory Coast is bordered on the north by Mali and Upper Volta, on the east by Ghana, on the south by the Gulf of Guinea, and on the west by Liberia and Guinea **Features:** From the coast, a rain forest extends over about 40% of the country. The remainder is wooded and grassy savanna, with a mountainous area in the northwest **Chief Rivers:** Bandama, Sassandra, Komoé, Nzi, Cavally

Head of State and of Government: President Félix Houphouët-Boigny, born 1905, reelected November 1975 for fourth 5-year term **Effective Date of Present Constitution:** 1960, amended 1975 **Legislative Body:** National Assembly (unicameral), consisting of 120 members elected for 5 years. All members belong to the Democratic Party of the Ivory Coast, the nation's only party **Local Government:** 24 administrative departments, each headed by an appointed prefect and elected council, and 2 autonomous municipalities

Ethnic Composition: About 60 groups, the largest being the Mande (26%), Akan (25%), Krou (18%), Sénoufo (13%), Lagoon people (7%) **Population Distribution:** 28% urban **Density:** 55 inhabitants per sq. mi.

Largest Cities: (1977 est.—Metropolitan Area) Abidjan 950,000; (1974 est.) Bouaké 140,000

Per Capita Income: $769 (1978) **Gross National Product (GNP):** $5.8 billion (1978) **Economic Statistics:** In 1976 about 31% of GNP came from agriculture (coffee, palm oil, cocoa, cotton, bananas, pineapples, rice, coconuts, sugar, rubber, yams, cassava, corn, millet, sorghum, livestock, tropical woods), 15% from industry (tuna-packing, sawmilling, agricultural processing, textiles, clothing, auto, truck and bus assembly, oil refining); and 26% from trade and services **Minerals and Mining:** Small quantities of diamonds and manganese have been produced and exploitation of iron ore, oil, nickel and gold is under way **Labor Force:** 2,600,000 (1970), with 78% in agriculture and 14% in industry and trade. Only 356,000 are wage earners **Foreign Trade:** Exports, chiefly coffee, wood, cocoa, palm oil, cotton, bananas, and pineapples, totaled $2.3 billion in 1977. Imports, mainly machinery, transport equipment, electrical equipment, and petroleum products, total $1.87 billion **Principal Trade Partners:** France, Netherlands, West Germany, Italy, Japan, United States

Vital Statistics: Birthrate, 45.6 per 1,000 of pop. (1975); death rate, 20.6 **Life Expectancy:** 43 years **Health Statistics:** 496 inhabitants per hospital bed; 13,839 per physician (1973) **Infant Mortality:** 138 per 1,000 births **Illiteracy:** 75% **Education Statistics:** 2,700 primary and secondary schools, with combined enrollment of 745,011 (1974) **Enrollment in Higher Education:** 8,701 (1976) **GNP Expended on Education:** 5.9% (1974)

Transportation: Surfaced roads total 745 mi. **Motor Vehicles:** 147,900 (1972) **Passenger Cars:** 90,500 **Railway Mileage:** 398 **Ports:** Abidjan, Sassandra, San Pedro **Major Airlines:** State-owned Air Ivoire is the domestic carrier; Air Afrique, a multinational airline, provides the main regional service **Communications:** Government owned **Radio Transmitters:** 17 **Receivers:** 600,000 (1976) **Television Transmitters:** 12 **Receivers:** 257,000 (1976) **Telephones:** 58,000 (1976) **Newspapers:** 3 dailies, 7 copies per 1,000 inhabitants (1975)

Weights and Measures: Metric system **Travel Requirements:** Passport; visa (4 copies) valid for 3 months from date of issue; no fee; 4 pictures; visa for next country; onward ticket

The Ivory Coast, the richest and most economically self-sufficient state in former French West Africa (now Senegal, Guinea, Mali, Upper Volta, Mauritania, Benin, Niger, and Ivory Coast), is located on the south side of the African bulge and is slightly larger than New Mexico. The southern boundary is a 340-mile coastline on the Gulf of Guinea, characterized by heavy surf and a lack of natural harbors. Early European voyagers were discouraged by this coastline and the dense tropical forest, as well as by the scant gold to be found there. As a result, they established their forts farther to the east on the Gold Coast, now Ghana.

Shortly after the former French colony became independent in 1960, officials of the International Monetary Fund advised Ivorian leaders to coordinate fiscal and development planning, encourage competitive private enterprise, and create a favorable investment climate—advice Ivorians followed with huge success.

Ivorian Prsident Félix Houphouët-Boigny, who continues to head the government, set up incentives for foreign investors. Himself an experienced administrator in French government service, he brought in top French economic planners to minutely map development.

Helped by high earnings from coffee and cocoa, the Ivory Coast concentrated initially on diversifying agriculture. Systematically, large new plantations of rubber, palm oil, pineapples, sugarcane, rice, and cotton were established. These products now supply new industries and add to exports.

Since 1960 the Ivorian gross national product has grown by more than 11 percent a year, and the per capita income is the highest in Black Africa. Projects are under way to spread the prosperity of Abidjan, the capital, to other parts of the country. The new port of San Pedro, designed to open up the little-developed southwestern area, was completed recently and iron-ore deposits in the northwest are being readied for development.

Although the French still maintain a strong economic position, they have had to share it with increasing numbers of German, Dutch, British, American, Italian, and Israeli enterprises.

Despite the impressive progress, along with increases of public housing, education, and health facilities, there remains an urgent need for raising rural living standards and creating employment.

HISTORY: Although evidence of a neolithic culture has been found in the Ivory Coast, little is known of the country's past before the first contacts by Portuguese and French in the 16th century. The Baoulés and the Agnis, both related to the Ashantis of Ghana, did not arrive until the 18th century, and most of the other tribal groups have their main centers in neighboring countries. The French began to establish control over the area in the 19th century and succeeded in colonizing it after much local resistance

1893: Ivory Coast is organized as a French protectorate

1898: Anti-French resistance collapses with the defeat of Almamy Samory, the Malinké warrior chief

1946-57: Félix Houphouët-Boigny founds African Democratic Rally, the first all-African political party; he is elected to the French National Assembly and wins far-reaching freedoms for France's African territories

1947: Upper Volta is detached from the Ivory Coast and made a separate territory

1958: Ivory Coast becomes an autonomous republic within the French Community

1959: Houphouët-Boigny becomes premier

1960: Ivory Coast achieves full independence; Houphouët-Boigny is elected president

1963: More than 80 persons, including government ministers and Guinean nationals, are convicted of plotting to stage a coup and assassinate the president

1967: Ivory Coast and Guinea exchange prisoners in effort to smooth relations

1968: Ivory Coast becomes first Black African country to float a loan on the Eurodollar market, obtaining a credit of $10 million

1970: President Houphouët-Boigny, unopposed, is elected to his third term as president

1974: Proposals for dialogue between Black African nations and South Africa lead to talks between South African Premier John Vorster and President Houphouët-Boigny

1975: President Houphouët-Boigny reelected without opposition for another five-year term. Constitution is amended so that in event of his death or incapacity the automatic successor would be the president of the National Assembly

JAMAICA

Area: 4,244 sq. mi. **Population:** 2,200,000 (1978 est.)

Official Name: Jamaica **Capital:** Kingston **Nationality:** Jamaican **Languages:** English is the official and dominant language; a Jamaican Creole, a mixture of archaic English and African, is also used **Religion:** 75% Protestant, 5% Roman Catholic, 20% other religions or no affiliation **Flag:** A gold diagonal cross, or saltire, divides the flag into four triangles; the top and bottom triangles are green and the remaining two are black **Anthem:** National Anthem, beginning "Eternal Father bless our land" **Currency:** Jamaican dollar (1.76 per U.S. $1)

Location: West Indies. The island of Jamaica lies in the Caribbean Sea, about 90 miles south of Cuba and 100 miles west of Haiti **Features:** Mountains cover about 80% of the island; lowlands stretch across the western end and a narrow plain covers the south **Chief Rivers:** Black, Minho, Cobre

Head of State: Queen Elizabeth II, represented by a governor-general, Florizel Glasspole, appointed June 1973 **Head of Govern-**

ment: Prime Minister Michael N. Manley, appointed 1972 and again in 1976 **Effective Date of Present Constitution:** 1962 **Legislative Body:** Parliament (bicameral), consisting of the Senate and the House of Representatives. The Senate is composed of 21 members, 13 of whom are appointed by the governor-general on the advice of the prime minister and the rest on the advice of the leader of the opposition. The 60-member House of Representatives is elected; terms in both houses cannot exceed 5 years **Local Government:** 14 parishes, 12 of which are administered by elected councils. Kingston and St. Andrew are jointly governed by a corporation

Ethnic Composition: About 95% of the population is of African and mixed descent; other racial and nationality groups are Chinese, East Indian, Syrian, and European **Population Distribution:** 41% urban **Density:** 518 inhabitants per sq. mi.

Largest Cities: (1975 est.) Kingston 600,000 (metro area), Montego Bay 50,000, Spanish Town 50,000, May Pen 26,074 (1970)

Per Capita Income: $1,363 (1978) **Gross National Product (GNP):** $2.9 billion (1978) **Economic Statistics:** About 15% of GNP comes from manufacturing (sugar processing, rum, beer, clothing, furniture); 14% from wholesale and retail trade; 11% from agriculture (sugar, bananas, cocoa, coffee, citrus fruits, copra), forestry and fishing; 11% from construction; and 10% from mining and refining **Minerals and Mining:** Jamaica is the world's largest producer of bauxite; other minerals of commercial significance are gypsum, silica, marble, and limestone **Labor Force:** 859,500 (1975), with 31% in agriculture, forestry, fishing and mining; 26% in public administration and commerce; 19% in manufacturing and construction; 4% in transport and communication; and 20% in ether services **Foreign Trade:** Exports, chiefly bauxite, alumina, sugar, rum, molasses, and bananas, totaled $630 million in 1976. Imports, mainly foodstuffs, manufactured goods, machinery and transportation equipment, totaled $800 million **Principal Trade Partners:** United States, Britain, Canada, Venezuela, Caribbean countries

Vital Statistics: Birthrate, 29 per 1,000 of pop. (1976); death rate, 7 **Life Expectancy:** 69 years **Health Statistics:** 257 inhabitants per hospital bed; 3,509 per physician (1974) **Infant Mortality:** 22 per 1,000 births (1976) **Illiteracy:** 18% **Education Statistics:** 981 primary and secondary schools, with combined enrollment of 564,143 (1974) **Enrollment in Higher Education:** 9,039 **GNP Expended on Education:** 7.1% (1974)

Transportation: Paved roads total about 2,100 mi. **Motor Vehicles:** 151,591 (1974) **Passenger Cars:** 109,628 **Railway Mileage:** 205 **Ports:** Kingston, Portland Bight **Major Airlines:** Air Jamaica operates flights to Miami and New York; Air Caribbean Transport Ltd. operates services to Central America; Jamaica Air Services operates domestic services. **Communications:** Partly government controlled **Radio Transmitters:** 21 **Receivers:** 555,000 (1976) **Television Transmitters:** 13 **Receivers:** 111,000 (1976) **Telephones:** 109,000 (1976) **Newspapers:** 3 dailies, 91 copies per 1,000 inhabitants (1976)

Weights and Measures: Metric and British standards are used **Travel Requirements:** Proof of U.S. citizenship; return ticket

Like other Caribbean countries, Jamaica is trying to deal with an economy and a society in difficult transition. From slave days, Jamaica's mountains and lush fields, under British ownership, produced sugar, coffee, bananas, and spices. While these are still the economic mainstays, the island is striving now for more balance.

Industry and tourism are the watchwords, and investment in both in the last decade has been considerable. Although tourism slumped in 1976 and 1977, following a rise in violence, it has begun to revive. The sugar industry remains the island's single biggest employer, but, agriculture overall has fallen behind industry in its contribution to the gross national product.

Disaffection with agriculture—particularly with the sugar industry, an activity associated with slave exploitation—has caused an influx into Kingston in search of industrial and service jobs. Industry and tourism have not kept pace with the demand, and the result has been a jobless rate currently of about 25 percent and heavy emigration to the U.S. and Britain.

Although the government keeps an eye out for potential trouble through the police and the Jamaica Defense Force, it also seeks permanent relief of Jamaica's social stresses through wider opportunities.

Jamaica's current unrest is largely due to Prime Minister Manley's efforts to turn the island nation into a socialist state. The Jamaican dollar has been devalued five times since Manley began his second term in 1976. On the fifth cut—10 percent in 1978—it stood at only 48 percent of its original value. However, the fifth devaluation paved the way for a $250 million loan from the International Monetary Fund.

HISTORY: Jamaica was inhabited by Arawak Indians when Columbus discovered the island in 1494. It was settled by the Spaniards early in the 16th century and remained under Spanish rule until 1655, when it was captured by the English. By the 18th century most of the Arawaks had died off, but a huge population of black slaves grew up around the island's sugar plantations. With the abolition of slavery in 1833, the plantation economy suffered a severe blow, resulting in long-lasting poverty and social unrest

1865-66: Uprising by blacks leads to imposition of martial law; British parliament establishes a crown colony government

1944: Britain grants the island a new constitution based on adult suffrage and a wide measure of self-government

1953: Island is granted full internal autonomy

1958-62: Jamaica joins West Indies Federation in 1958 along with nine other British possessions in the Caribbean; three years later, however, the island withdraws; in August 1962, Jamaica wins full independence, with Sir Alexander Bustamente, the island's labor leader, as prime minister

1967: Hugh Shearer becomes prime minister following sudden death of Sir Donald Sangster, leader of Jamaica Labor Party

1968: Jamaica joins Caribbean Free Trade Association

1972: Jamaica Labor Party is defeated in general election by People's National Party; Michael Manley becomes prime minister

1974: The Suppression of Crime Act passed unanimously by the legislature. Its purpose is to reduce the rash of murders and other violent crimes on Jamaica. It provides for secret trials, no bail, and, for convicted offenders, indeterminate prison sentences

1975: Jamaica signs treaty with EEC and reaches agreements with foreign companies mining bauxite on the island whereby the government would purchase controlling shares of stock

1976: Martial law is declared in Kingston because of violence among warring extremist factions of Prime Minister Manley's People's National Party (PNP) and the opposition Jamaica Labor Party (JLP). PNP wins overwhelming victory

1977: U.S. announces $63.3-million aid package to help Jamaica with its economic problems

1978: Government launches five-year economic program based on land reform

1979: Seven die Jan. 8-10 in riots that follow a government order increasing the price of gasoline 13 cents a gallon to $1.99. Manley says that the violence led many tourists to cancel hotel reservations

JAPAN

Area: 145,730 sq. mi. **Population:** 114,150,000 (1978 est.)
Official Name: Japan **Capital:** Tokyo **Nationality:** Japanese **Languages:** Japanese is the official and universal language **Religion:** Buddhism and Shintoism are the chief religions; virtually all Japanese practice one or the other and most subscribe to both **Flag:** A red sun on a white field **Anthem:** The Reign of Our Emperor **Currency:** Yen (222 per U.S. $1)

Location: Japan is an archipelago forming a 2,360-mile-long arc off the east coast of Asia, between the Sea of Japan and the Pacific Ocean proper. It consists of four main islands: Hokkaido, Honshu, Shikoku, and Kyushu, and more than 3,000 smaller islands **Features:** 72% of the country is covered by hills and mountains, many of them active or dormant volcanoes. Because of the country's unstable geological position beside the Pacific deeps, numerous earthquakes are felt throughout the islands **Chief Rivers:** Tone, Shinano, Ishikari, Kitakami

Head of State: Emperor Hirohito, born 1901, ascended the throne 1926 **Head of Government:** Prime Minister Masayoshi Ohira, born 1910, elected 1978 **Effective Date of Present Constitution:** May 3, 1947 **Legislative Body:** Parliament, or Diet (bicameral), consisting of the House of Representatives and the House of Councillors. The House of Representatives has 511 members elected for 4 years. The House of Councillors has 252 members elected for 6 years **Local Government:** 43 prefectures, each with an elected governor and local assembly, 2 urban prefectures, 1 metropolitan prefecture, and 1 territory

Ethnic Composition: The Japanese are a Mongoloid people, closely related to the other groups of east Asia, although there is evidence of admixture with Malayan and Caucasoid strains. Some 650,000 Koreans constitute the only important minority group; about 15,000 Ainu in Hokkaido, physically similar to Caucasians, are rapidly being assimilated **Population Distribution:** 76% urban **Density:** 783 inhabitants per sq. mi.

Largest Cities: (1975 census) Tokyo 8,646,520, Osaka 2,778,987, Yokohama 2,621,771, Nagoya 2,079,740, Kyoto 1,461,059, Kobe 1,360,605, Sapporo 1,240,613, Kitakyushu 1,058,058, Kawasaki 1,014,951

Per Capita Income: $6,329 (1978) **Gross National Product (GNP):** $727.9 billion (1978) **Economic Statistics:** 36.8% of GNP comes from industry (transportation equipment, electrical machinery, iron and steel, ships, chemicals), 8.1% from agriculture (rice, vegetables, fruit, wheat, barley, fish, and potatoes), 23.1% from trade, 11.1% from services **Minerals and Mining:** Coal is plentiful, but only about 25% can be used for industrial purposes. There are small amounts of zinc, limestone, lead, and sulphur **Labor Force:** 54,500,000 (1977) with 36% employed in industry, 12% in agriculture, and 52% in trade and services **Foreign Trade:** Exports, chiefly iron and steel, textiles, electronic equipment, motor vehicles, ships, totaled $80.5 billion in 1977. Imports, chiefly mineral fuels, metal ores and scrap, machinery and equipment, and foodstuffs, totaled $70.8 billion **Principal Trade Partners:** United States, Australia, Canada, Iran, South Korea, West Germany, Kuwait, Britain, Saudi Arabia, Indonesia, Liberia

Vital Statistics: Birthrate, 15.4 per 1,000 of pop. (1977); death rate, 6.3 per 1,000 **Life Expectancy:** 74 years **Health Statistics:** 78 inhabitants per hospital bed; 868 per physician (1973) **Infant Mortality:** 9.3 per 1,000 births **Illiteracy:** Negligible **Education Statistics:** 51,399 primary and secondary schools, with combined enrollment of 21,752,000 pupils (1975) **Enrollment in Higher Education:** 2,248,000 (1975) **GNP Expended on Education:** 5.5% (1975)

Transportation: Surfaced roads total 17,495 mi. **Motor Vehicles:** 30,100,000 (1976) **Passenger Cars:** 18,500,000 **Railway Mileage:** 31,000 mi. **Ports:** Yokohama, Kobe, Tokyo, Nagoya, Osaka, Chiba, Kawasaki, Hakodate **Major Airlines:** Japan Air Lines, partly government owned and partly privately financed, operates international and domestic flights **Communications:** Government and privately owned **Radio Transmitters:** 944 **Receivers:** 59,650,000 (1976) **Television Transmitters:** 6,117 **Receivers:** 26,545,000 (1975) **Telephones:** 48,431,000 **Newspapers:** 180 dailies, 526 copies per 1,000 inhabitants (1974)

Weights and Measures: Metric system **Travel Requirements:** Passport; visa, valid 60 days

---

Japan, having soared from crushing defeat in World War II to a position among the world's leading industrial nations, is today building for itself an international role commensurate with its economic power, while attempting at the same time to resolve the great social problems caused by swift industrialization.

Crowded into a small island territory off the Asian mainland and isolated from the world by their own choice for centuries prior to 1854, the Japanese created a distinctive society and culture. There has been a large measure of modernization and Westernization, but traditional customs, social practices, and business procedures still are deep-rooted.

Close government/business ties and encouragement for export industries enabled Japan to build a huge international trade throughout the 1970s, while curbs on imports and foreign investments continued to afford protection for domestic industry. Eventually, the trade gap between Japan and the U.S. widened so greatly that relations between the two countries became acrimonious. In 1978, for example, Japan's surplus in the two-way trade was $11.6 billion. As protectionist sentiment rose in the U.S., the Japanese voluntarily cut down on their shipments of TV sets and automobiles, removed some restraints on importing foreign goods, and sent buying missions to the U.S. The Tokyo Round of trade agreements, completed in 1979, saw Japan pledging a 46 percent reduction in tariffs on U.S.-made goods, in contrast to a 32 percent American cut on Japanese products. In June 1979 a "buy Japanese" policy on telecommunications equipment was relaxed in a pact that will let foreign companies seek business from the Nippon Telegraph and Telephone Public Corporation and other government-run operations.

With only one brief interruption, Japan has been ruled by conservatives during the postwar years under the "no-war" 1946 constitution, which was imposed by American occupation authorities.

JAPAN

CONIC PROJECTION

Copyright by C. S. HAMMOND & CO., N.Y.

SCALE OF MILES

SCALE OF KILOMETERS

Capitals of Countries
International Boundaries

Longitude East of Greenwich

The constitution provided the framework for democratic development and made the emperor, who had served as the nationalist symbol for prewar militarism, a largely ceremonial chief of state.

Support for the ruling Liberal Democratic Party (LDP), which derived much of its strength in rural areas, has gradually declined as a result of the migration, within two decades, of more than one-third of Japan's population from the countryside to the cities. The 1976 Lockheed scandal, involving LDP members accused of accepting bribes from the U.S.-based Lockheed Aircraft Corporation in exchange for lucrative sales contracts, also damaged the party's standing. The 1979 McDonnell Douglas and Grumman scandal, also arising from aircraft sales, again turned the spotlight on the activities of the trading companies and Japanese politicians. The U.S. Securities and Exchange Commission opened up the matter by publishing reports of bribes, and a Japanese trading company executive committed suicide. After a four-month investigation, Tokyo investigators placed charges against four businessmen, but they found no criminal links to three politicians mentioned in the case.

Pollution of air and water have reached near-crisis proportions. Despite depletion of the rural population, farmland remains fragmented and an outdated subsidy system has caused huge overproduction of rice. A critical housing shortage persists, transport systems are overburdened, the educational structure is in need of broad reform, and social welfare systems are still on a modest scale.

In recent years American troops and bases in Japan have been substantially reduced and, though still sheltered under the American nuclear umbrella, Japan has assumed responsibility for its own defense against any conventional attack. The security treaty with the United States, which provoked a major crisis in 1960, was quietly allowed to remain in effect indefinitely.

Although in 1972 Japan restored diplomatic ties with China, its giant neighbor and source of much of its cultural tradition, the peace treaty was not ratified until October 1978, because special care had to be exercised to avoid offending another giant neighbor and traditional enemy, the Soviet Union.

In May 1978 the $2.9-billion New Tokyo International Airport (at nearby Narita) opened for business—five years behind schedule, and with 14,000 police standing guard against protesters who tried to disrupt flights. Farmers and young leftist radicals had protested against the airport for 12 years. The protests resulted in five deaths, 8,100 injuries, and 1,900 arrests. Now, however, the airport is running full force and has the capability of handling 10 million travelers a year.

HISTORY: Legend attributes the founding of the Japanese empire to Jimmu, a lineal descendant of the sun goddess and ancestor of the present imperial dynasty, in 660 B.C. Reliable records of Japanese history, however, date back only to about 400 A.D. From the 6th to 8th century, Japan came under the strong cultural influence of China and Buddhism was introduced. The development of a feudal system weakened the already diminished power of the emperors, who were to remain in obscurity for 700 years

1192: Yoritomo, leader of the feudal family of Minamoto, takes the title of shogun (military governor) and sets up dictatorship

1542: First European contact is established with the arrival of Portuguese sailors

1637: Tokugawa shogunate bans all intercourse with the outside world, with the exception of Dutch traders in Nagasaki

1854: Commodore Matthew C. Perry, a U.S. naval officer, forces the opening of Japanese trade with the West

1867-68: Shogunate collapses and power is restored to Emperor Mutsuhito; Meiji Restoration, so called after emperor's reign name, is followed by formation of a pro-Western government which proceeds to modernize Japan

1894-95: Japan defeats China in Sino-Japanese War and annexes Formosa, the Pescadores, and Liaotung peninsula

1904-05: Russian power is smashed by Japanese in Russo-Japanese War

1910: Japan annexes Korea

1931: Japan seizes Manchuria from China and sets up puppet state of Manchukuo

1937: Japan invades China's northern provinces; Chinese resistance leads to full-scale though undeclared war

1940: Japan signs military alliance with Germany and Italy

1941-45: Surprise Japanese attack on Pearl Harbor in December 1941 triggers U.S. entry into World War II; successive Japanese victories give Japan control over vast territories stretching from India to the Aleutians; in late 1942, however, tide begins to turn and Japan loses ground to Allies; with the dropping of U.S. atomic bombs on Hiroshima and Nagasaki, Japan is forced to surrender and is occupied by U.S. forces

1946-47: The occupation, under direction of General Douglas MacArthur, initiates series of reforms aimed at democratization and demilitarization of Japan; a new constitution is adopted and emperor publicly disclaims his divinity

1954: Japan and United States sign military assistance pact

1960: Antigovernment riots and protests against military pacts force cancellation of visit by U.S. President Eisenhower

1964: Eisaku Sato becomes prime minister

1969: Japan steps up demand for the return of Okinawa, occupied by U.S. forces since World War II

1970: Japan renews security pact with United States

1971: Agreement is reached on reversion of Okinawa from U.S. to Japanese rule; Emperor Hirohito becomes first reigning monarch to leave Japan, visiting seven countries in Europe

1972: Okinawa is returned to Japan; Japan opens diplomatic relations with China. Eisaku Sato resigns as prime minister and is succeeded by Kakuei Tanaka

1974: Tanaka resigns as a result of accusations that he used his political office to amass a personal fortune. Takeo Miki becomes prime minister

1975: Emperor Hirohito makes first visit to U.S. by a reigning Japanese monarch

1976: Revelations emerge concerning $12.6 million in alleged payoffs by Lockheed Aircraft Corp. (U.S.) to secure Japanese aircraft contracts. Tanaka is arrested. Miki resigns after his party (LDP) suffers setback in elections. LDP leader, Takeo Fukuda, is elected prime minister by House of Representatives

1977: Prime Minister Fukuda shuffles cabinet in effort to better deal with Japan's mounting trade surplus and strained economic relations with industrial nations; he calls it the "gravest situation" since World War II

1978: New Tokyo International Airport opens under heavy guard as protesters try to disrupt flights (the facility has long been opposed by displaced farmers and leftist radicals, who delayed its opening five years). Earthquake near Tokyo is worst in 14 years; 21 persons are killed, 350 injured. On October 23, four decades after Japan invaded China, the two countries exchange ratifications of a peace treaty. Masayoshi Ohira defeats Fukuda in a party election and as a result becomes Japan's prime minister on Dec. 7

1979: Ohira visits U.S. President Carter and they jointly pledge to seek "over the next several years a more harmonious pattern of international trade and payments." Leaders of 7 major Western powers meet in Tokyo in June and set oil import limits for their countries

JORDAN

Area: 37,737 sq. mi. **Population:** 2,800,000 (1978 est.)

Official Name: Hashemite Kingdom of Jordan **Capital:** Amman **Nationality:** Jordanian **Languages:** Arabic is the official and universal language **Religion:** 95% Sunni Moslem, 5% Christian **Flag:** Horizontal black, white, and green stripes, with a seven-pointed white star on a red triangle at the staff **Anthem:** The Royal Salute **Currency:** Jordanian dinar (.31 per U.S. $1)

Location: Southwest Asia. Jordan is bordered by Syria on the north, Iraq on the northeast, Saudi Arabia on the east and south, and Israel on the west **Features:** About four-fifths of the country consists of desert. The Jordan River valley divides the land into the small, rocky West Bank and the large East Bank, the latter forming a dry plateau that slopes to flat terrain in the northeast **Chief Rivers:** Jordan, Yarmuk

Head of State: King Hussein Ibn Talal, born 1935, ascended the throne 1953. He has veto power over the National Assembly **Head of Government:** Prime Minister Mudar Badran, born 1934, appointed 1976 and again in 1977 **Effective Date of Present Constitution:** 1952, amended 1974 and 1976 **Legislative Body:** National Assembly (bicameral), at present dissolved, subject to recall if required. A National Consultative Council, with advisory functions, was established in 1978 **Local Government:** 8 governorates, each headed by an appointed governor

Ethnic Composition: Virtually 100% Arab **Population Distribution:** 44% urban **Density:** 74 inhabitants per sq. mi.

Largest Cities: (1974 est.—Metropolitan Areas) Amman 615,000, Zarqa 226,000, Irbid 125,000

Per Capita Income: $704 (1978) **Gross National Product (GNP):** $2.1 billion (1978) **Economic Statistics:** About 10% of GNP comes from agriculture (wheat, citrus fruits, olives, grapes, melons, vegetables, barley), 25% from industry (phosphate mining, cement, beverages, tobacco, soap, oil refining, tanning, vegetable oils), and 65% from trade and services **Minerals and Mining:** Exploited minerals include phosphates, potash, copper, and marble; manganese, iron, sulphur and oil deposits also exist **Labor Force:** 400,000 (1977), with 20% in agriculture, 20% in industry, and 60% in trade and services **Foreign Trade:** Exports, chiefly fruits and vegetables, phosphates, cement, petroleum products, and marble, totaled $188 million in 1977. Imports, mainly foodstuffs, machinery, vehicles, crude petroleum, and textiles, totaled $1.4 billion **Principal Trade Partners:** EC countries, United States, Lebanon, Iraq, Kuwait, Saudi Arabia, Japan, Iran, Syria, Romania

Vital Statistics: Birthrate, 41.0 per 1,000 of pop. (1977); death rate, 14.7 **Life Expectancy:** 52 years **Health Statistics:** 937 inhabitants per hospital bed; 2,438 per physician (1974) **Infant Mortality:** 21.6 per 1,000 births **Illiteracy:** 38% **Education Statistics:** 1,866 primary and secondary schools, with combined enrollment of 514,957 (1974) **Enrollment in Higher Education:** 9,302 **GNP Expended on Education:** 4.4% (1975)

Transportation: Paved roads total 3,440 mi. **Motor Vehicles:** 54,700 (1976) **Passenger Cars:** 41,500 **Railway Mileage:** 255 **Port:** Aqaba **Major Airlines:** Royal Jordanian Airlines (ALIA) operates international services **Communications:** Government owned **Radio Transmitters:** 7 **Receivers:** 531,000 (1976) **Television Transmitters:** 2 **Receivers:** 125,000 (1976) **Telephones:** 44,000 (1976) **Newspapers:** 4 dailies, 18 copies per 1,000 inhabitants (1975)

Weights and Measures: Metric system **Travel Requirements:** Passport; visa valid for 1 year for multiple entry; no fee

---

The Hashemite Kingdom of Jordan is a largely uninhabited desert, about the size of Indiana. In 1921, after centuries of Turkish rule, the area now comprising Jordan and Israel was awarded to the United Kingdom by the League of Nations as the Mandates for Palestine and Transjordan. In 1922, Britain divided the administration of the Mandate and established Abdullah, grandfather of the present King Hussein, as ruler of a semi-autonomous Amirate of Transjordan in the area east of the Jordan River. The western portion (Palestine) remained under the administration of a British High Commissioner.

Britain granted the eastern territory full independence in 1946, with Abdullah as king. When Arab Palestinians and Jews fought each other and the British for the control of Palestine, Britain asked the UN to help settle the conflict. The UN suggested that Palestine be divided into two states, one Jewish and one Arab.

In the fighting which broke out upon the proclamation of Israeli statehood in 1948, the Transjordan Arab Legion occupied most of the West Bank territories allotted to the Arab Palestinians in the United Nations partition plan, including East Jerusalem, and the Jews established the state of Israel, in large measure on the land given to them in the UN plan. Transjordan became the Hashemite Kingdom of Jordan in 1949.

The present ruler, Hussein Ibn Talal, became king in 1953. In 1967, during the Six-Day War, Israel occupied the West Bank territories.

The problems of the Middle East—particularly, resolution of Arab-Israeli issues—dominate Jordan's foreign policy. The current Mideast peace negotiations, with respect to Jordan, revolve around the ultimate disposition of the Israeli-occupied West Bank and Arab Jerusalem and the issue of the roles for Jordan and the Palestinian Liberation Organization (PLO) in the negotiations. Within Jordan, there is friction between the Palestinian refugees and the Bedouins—the principal ethnic group of unoccupied Jordan.

Following the decision of the Rabat summit conference of Arab heads of state in October 1974 to recognize the PLO's right to represent all Palestinians, King Hussein gave the PLO and its leader, Yassir Arafat, the responsibility for the West Bank. The king dissolved parliament and reorganized his cabinet, reducing its Palestinian membership. He summoned a new parliament in 1976.

Hussein's foreign policy—long pro-Western—has become increasingly favorable to Arab aspirations—largely because of increasing foreign aid from Arab oil states to his resource-poor kingdom. The oil states have encouraged him to strengthen ties to Syria. In 1979, he denounced the peace treaty between Israel and Egypt, which carried vague promises of autonomy for the West Bank, and sent diplomats to mediate the dispute between Yemen and Southern Yemen.

HISTORY: The present territory of Jordan was the biblical home of the Moabites, the Ammonites, the Edomites, and some Hebrew tribes. It was conquered in 64 B.C. by Rome, in the 7th century A.D. by Moslem Arabs (from whom it derived its now-prevailing language and religion), in the 16th century by the Ottoman Empire, and in 1916 by Britain

1916: Sykes-Picot Agreement between France and Britain divides Ottoman holdings, with Transjordan (the present East Bank) in British sphere of influence

1921: British recognize Abdullah as ruler of Transjordan and Hashemite dynasty is founded

1928: Britain recognizes Transjordan as independent but retains suzerainty in the form of military and financial control

1946: Kingdom of Transjordan is proclaimed

1948: British mandate ends, fighting breaks out with new state of Israel

1949: Transjordan and Israel sign armistice, with Transjordan in control of West Bank and part of Jerusalem. Transjordan adopts name of Hashemite Kingdom of Jordan

1950: Arab Palestine (West Bank) is formally annexed by Jordan

1951: King Abdullah is assassinated in Jerusalem. His son, Talal, becomes king

1952: Talal is declared insane and ousted; his son, Hussein, becomes king

1967: King Hussein and President Nasser of Egypt sign mutual defense pact. Jordan is drawn into Six-Day War with Israel, which occupies all of Jerusalem and all of West Bank

1968-69: Israel attacks Arab guerrilla bases on East Bank

1970: Guerrillas hijack four Western airliners to Jordan and hold crews and passengers hostage; all are later released. Civil war breaks out between guerrillas and Jordanian forces

1971: Jordanian army's July offensive virtually eliminates all guerrilla bases. Syria severs relations with Jordan. Prime Minister Wasfi Al Tal is assassinated in Cairo

1973: Jordan joins in war against Israel

1974: Arab leaders at a summit conference recognize the Palestine Liberation Organization as the sole representative of the Palestinian people; King Hussein concurs

1975: Syria and Jordan establish a joint military command

1976: Syria and Jordan co-ordinate their foreign diplomatic representation in countries where either one maintains a mission. King Hussein reconvenes parliament, with representatives of the West Bank in attendance, after having dissolved it in 1974 to decrease Palestinian participation in Jordanian politics. Prime Minister Zaid al-Rifai resigns and King Hussein asks Mudar Badran, chief of the Cabinet, to form a new government

1977: Queen Alia is killed in helicopter crash

1978: King Hussein marries Elizabeth Halaby, 26-year-old American and proclaims her Jordan's new queen

1979: Jordan helps to mediate dispute between Yemen and Southern Yemen

---

KENYA

Area: 224,960 sq. mi. **Population:** 14,200,000 (1978 est.)

Official Name: Republic of Kenya **Capital:** Nairobi **Nationality:** Kenyan **Languages:** Swahili and English are used officially; of more than 30 languages, Kikuyu and Luo are the most used **Religion:** 38% of the people are animists, 59% Christian, and 3% Moslem or Hindu **Flag:** Horizontal stripes of black, red, and green, with the center red stripe bordered in white; a shield with black and white markings, and crossed spears behind, appears in the center of the flag **Anthem:** National Anthem, beginning "O, God of all Creation" **Currency:** Kenya shilling (7.6 per U.S. $1)

Location: East Africa. Kenya is bordered on the north by Sudan and Ethiopia, on the east by Somalia and the Indian Ocean, on the south by Tanzania, and on the west by Uganda **Features:** The Great

Rift Valley in the center and west is girded by rugged plateaus and mountains. To the east are dry bush land and a marshy coastal plain. In the north the land turns to scrub and desert. Kenya has numerous lakes, including a portion of Lake Victoria **Chief Rivers:** Tana, Athi-Galana, Suam-Turkwel, Keiro

Head of State and of Government: President Daniel arap Moi, born 1924, took office in 1978 **Effective Date of Present Constitution:** 1964, revised 1969 **Legislative Body:** National Assembly (unicameral), consisting of 158 members elected for up to 5 years and 12 members nominated by the president **Local Government:** 7 provinces and the Nairobi area

Ethnic Composition: 30-40 groups fall into four main linguistic divisions: the Bantu, who constitute the majority, Nilo-Hamitics, Nilotics, and Hamitics. The largest tribes are the Kikuyu, Luhya, Luo, Kamba, Kisii and Meru. There are some 200,000 non-Africans, including Arabs, Europeans, and Hindu and Moslem Indians **Population Distribution:** 10% urban **Density:** 63 inhabitants per sq. mi.

Largest Cities: (1976 est.—Metropolitan Areas) Nairobi 800,000, Mombasa 351,000, Nakuru 66,000, Kisumu 46,000

Per Capita Income: $245 (1978) **Gross National Product (GNP):** $3.8 billion (1978) **Economic Statistics:** About 20% of GNP comes from manufacturing (chiefly agricultural processing, oil refining, and small-scale consumer goods), mining and quarrying; 18% from trade, transportation and communications; 27% from services and about 31% from agriculture (coffee, tea, pyrethrum, sisal, livestock, meat and dairy products, wool, hides, corn, wheat, millet, and cassava), forestry, and fishing **Minerals and Mining:** Small quantities of soda ash, fluorspar, limestone, salt, copper, gold, and silver are produced **Labor Force:** 5,400,000 (1971), 86% in agriculture and 13% in industry. 826,300 were salaried in 1975 **Foreign Trade:** Exports, chiefly coffee, tea, sisal, pyrethrum extract and flowers, meat and meat preparations, totaled $668 million in 1976. Imports, mainly machinery, transport equipment, manufactured goods, lubricants, and chemicals, totaled $945 million **Principal Trade Partners:** EC countries, United States, Japan, Saudi Arabia, Iran, Zambia, India, Sweden, Australia, China

Vital Statistics: Birthrate, 48 per 1,000 of pop.; (1976) death rate, 14 **Life Expectancy:** 51 years **Health Statistics:** 759 inhabitants per hospital bed; 16,292 per physician (1973) **Infant Mortality:** 51.4 per 1,000 births **Illiteracy:** 70% **Education Statistics:** 9,304 primary and secondary schools, with combined enrollment of 3,116,156 (1975) **Enrollment in Higher Education:** 11,351 (1974) **GNP Expended on Education:** 5.9% (1974)

Transportation: Paved roads total 1,493 mi. **Motor Vehicles:** 167,500 (1975) **Passenger Cars:** 98,300 **Railway Mileage:** 3,670 **Port:** Mombasa **Major Airlines:** Kenya Airways operates domestic and international services **Communications:** Government controlled **Radio Transmitters:** 18 **Receivers:** 514,000 (1976) **Television Transmitters:** 4 **Receivers:** 50,000 (1976) **Telephones:** 132,000 (1976) **Newspapers:** 3 dailies, 10 copies per 1,000 inhabitants (1975)

Weights and Measures: Metric system, with some English measures still used **Travel Requirements:** Passport; visa, valid 6 months; $3.15 fee

Kenya is one of Africa's best-known countries; the land of the safari, gameparks, and the lure of the green hills Ernest Hemingway made famous. Tourism has grown spectacularly, with annual earnings of over $70 million rivaling those from coffee, the major export.

The Asian population is being rapidly reduced under a phased program of canceling government permits for Asians to carry on businesses. The influence of the European community is also declining.

Kenya has made considerable progress in industry and in agriculture, particularly in the success of African farmers settled on the former large British holdings in the old "White Highlands." But these gains have been offset by high population growth, unemployment, and drought. A slump in world demand for coffee and tea produced a severe trade deficit for the first half of 1978, prompting the government to impose restrictions on imports and foreign travel in 1979.

In leading the former British colony to independence in 1963, President Jomo Kenyatta stressed the need for unity with the slogan of *Harambee!* (Swahili for "Let us all pull together"). Kenyatta, affectionately known as *Mzee* ("the Old One"), was able to hold Kenya together, but not without strain. The Kenyatta government's strength was

tested in 1975 when a wave of political unrest was touched off by the murder of Josiah Kariuki, a popular member of parliament and critic of Kenyatta. An investigation committee implicated police officials and top aides of Kenyatta, and the Assembly voted to accept the committee's report on the murder.

Although all Assembly members belong to Kenya's only party, the Kenya African National Union (KANU), dissident members formed an opposition group, which resulted in a KANU leadership decree that any Assembly member not following the party position would be expelled.

In August 1978, Kenyatta died peacefully in his sleep. Daniel arap Moi, 54, became president.

HISTORY: Kenya's coast was a familiar area to mariners of past eras, including Phoenicians, Egyptians, and Greeks. Arab coastal colonies were established as early as the 8th century and in the 15th century Portuguese joined in the thriving spice and slave trade. Britain gained a foothold in the 19th century and in 1895 established a protectorate over the area, then known as British East Africa. With the influx of British and South African settlers, Kenya continued to be dominated by the white population until well after World War II

1944: Africans win token political representation with the appointment by the governor of the first black member of the Legislative Council

1952-59: Mau Mau rebellion, led by secret terrorist organization comprising mainly Kikuyu tribesmen, results in brutal slayings of whites and Africans serving whites, and equally brutal retaliation by white community; Africans are granted larger, but still minority, representation in Legislative Council

1960-61: Britain agrees to new elections for Legislative Council, in which Africans win majority

1961-62: Jomo Kenyatta, imprisoned as alleged Mau Mau leader, is released; he enters Legislative Council as leader of the Kenya African National Union (KANU), backed largely by the Kikuyu and Luo tribes, and forces cooperation with the governing Kenya African Democratic Union (KADU), which is chiefly supported by the smaller tribal units

1963: Kenyatta leads KANU to overwhelming election victory; Kenya gains independence, with Kenyatta as prime minister

1964: Kenya becomes a republic within the British Commonwealth, under the presidency of Kenyatta; KADU voluntarily dissolves itself and Kenya becomes a one-party state

1966: Vice-President Oginga Odinga, an early Kenyatta follower and Luo tribal leader, resigns, charging KANU government with being "capitalistic"; he forms new opposition party, the Kenya People's Union.

1968: Thousands of Asians leave Kenya amid controversy over "Kenyanization" of trade and business

1969: Economics Minister Tom Mboya, a Luo, is slain by a Kikuyu; slaying sparks antigovernment demonstrations and arrest of Oginga Odinga. KPU party is dissolved

1970: Government orders 1,000 Asian businessmen to close down

1971: Opposition leader Oginga Odinga is released from detention. Severe drought and famine plague Kenyans

1974: Kenyatta orders all unauthorized noncitizen traders to leave. Swahili declared official language. Severe drought affects 70 percent of country

1975: Josiah Kariuki, one of Kenya's most popular politicians, who championed Kenya's poor, is murdered, allegedly by political enemies

1977: Tanzania closes 500-mile border with Kenya indefinitely. This action follows Kenya's withdrawal from participation in East African Airways, which forced the airline to close. Government bans all game hunting in an effort to save wildlife from extinction. Kenya claims Somali troops cross border. The two nations set up border commission to prevent recurrence

1978: Kenyatta dies. Daniel arap Moi becomes president

KIRIBATI

Area: 264 sq. mi. **Population:** 56,000 (1979 est.)

Official Name: Republic of Kiribati **Capital:** Bairiki, on Tarawa **Nationality:** Kiribati (Gilbertese) **Languages:** Gilbertese and English **Religion:** Evenly divided between Protestant and Roman Catholic **Flag:** Bottom half consists of six wavy, horizontal white stripes over navy blue; top half is red with a flying yellow frigate bird over a yellow sun, displaying nine straight and eight wavy yellow rays **Anthem:** N.A. **Currency:** Australian dollar (0.91 per U.S. $1)

Location: The island nation extends widely over the western Pacific, from 5° N to 11° S and 169°E. to 150° W., and is scattered over two million sq. mi. of ocean. It includes 33 islands and atolls in the Gilbert, Phoenix and Line groups, plus Banaba (Ocean Island). All but Banaba have coral-ringed lagoons circling the tops of submerged mountains

Head of State and Government: Ieremia Tabai, born 1950, assumed office, July 12, 1979 **Effective Date of Present Constitution:** July 12, 1979 **Legislative Body:** a unicameral House of Assembly (Maneaba ni Maungatabu) of 35 elected members **Local Government:** 35 election districts **Ethnic Composition:** Predominantly Micronesian with some Polynesians, mixed Micronesian-Polynesian, and Europeans **Population Distribution:** 30 % urban **Density:** 212 inhabitants per sq. mi.

Largest City: Bairiki 1,300

Per Capita Income: $730 (1974) **Gross National Product (GNP):** $40 million (1974) **Economic Statistics:** The economy is based largely on the export of copra. The brine shrimp industry on Christmas Island grows shrimps and shrimp eggs for fish farms throughout the world. There is a soft drink factory, a biscuit factory and a boatbuilding concern **Minerals and Mining:** Phosphate mining on Banaba (Ocean Island) is due to end in 1979 **Labor Force:** N.A. **Foreign trade:** Exports, chiefly phosphate rock and copra, totaled $15.7 million in 1977. Imports totaled $10.3 million **Principal Trade Partners:** Britain, Australia

Vital Statistics: Birthrate, 22.3 per 1,000 of pop. (1971); death rate, 6.5 **Life Expectancy:** 58 years **Health Statistics:** 201 inhabitants per hospital bed (1977); 2,692 per physician (1975) **Infant Mortality:** 48.9 per 1,000 births (1971) **Illiteracy:** under 50% **Education Statistics:** 86 primary and secondary schools (1977), with combined enrollment of 14,511 (1977) **Enrollment in Higher Education:** N.A. **GNP Expended on Education:** N.A.

Transportation: Motorable roads total 300 mi. **Motor Vehicles:** N.A. **Passenger Cars:** N.A. **Railway Mileage:** None **Ports:** Tarawa, Canton Island **Major Airlines:** Domestic island-to-island service is provided by International Air Service; Fiji Airways, Air Pacific and Air Nauru connect Tarawa with Fiji **Communications:** Government owned **Radio Transmitters:** 1 **Receivers:** 8,200 (1975) **Television Transmitters:** None **Telephones:** 250 **Newspapers:** 3 non-dailies, 89 copies per 1,000 inhabitants (1974)

Weights and Measures: British and metric

In November 1943, U.S. Marines landed on Tarawa, the central island in the far-flung Gilbert chain, and fought one of the bloodiest battles of the Second World War, defeating an entrenched Japanese garrison of 5,000. Although time seemed to have forgotten these peaceful islands since, the realities of the modern world have caught up to this newly independent nation—one of the world's poorest—of 33 coral atolls stretched across two million square miles of the South Pacific, at the crossroads of the equator and the international date line.

Independence came to the former Gilbert Islands on July 12, 1979, after 87 years of British rule. One of the most pressing problems facing Kiribati (pronounced "Kiribass") is economic; 99 percent of its $18-million annual income derives from phosphate mining, located only on Banaba (Ocean Island). But the joint Australian-New Zealand authority that controls mining there states the phosphate will run out by the end of 1979. Diversification is thus the main priority facing the new government on Tarawa. Agriculture is limited by poor soil, although the export of copra—derived from the native coconut palms—has been a source of revenue. There are plans to develop local industries—mainly fruit canning and handicrafts—as well as to exploit the potentially rich fishing grounds within Kiribati's 200-mile offshore boundaries. British pledges of $35 million in continued aid over the next four years, coupled with the approximately $60 million in royalties due from the British Phosphate Commission, also hold promise for future economic development.

Although fourteen of the islands in the Phoenix and Line groups have long been claimed by both Britain and the United States—including Canton, Enderbury and Christmas Islands—the U.S. has agreed to relinquish Canton and Enderbury by 1980, and will cede the rest to Kiribati by treaty in the near future.

But the birth pangs of the new nation have caused other political problems the new government must face. The former residents of Banaba (Ocean Island), who were relocated after World War II after mining had despoiled their island, have fought for 10 years to reassert their claims to their traditional homes, and continue to oppose being part of an independent Kiribati. Kiribati, while assuring the islanders of their continued rights on Banaba, has refused so far to agree to Banaban demands for separation.

HISTORY: The main wave of Micronesian settlement of the area is thought to have originated from Samoa around the thirteenth century. Although Spanish navigators are credited with sighting some of the islands in 1537 and 1606, true European discovery of the area came only much later, with the first white settlement dating from the 1830s. Missionaries visited the islands in 1857, and by the 1860s, a flourishing trade in coconut oil and copra had been established. Between 1850 and 1875 the islands were raided by "blackbirders" for slave labor in South America. Fiji. Tahiti, Hawaii and Austrlia. To stamp out this activity, the British established the High Commmision for the Western Pacific over the area in 1877

1888-89: Britain annexes Christmas, Fanning and Washington Islands

1892: Britain establishes protectorate over Gilberts and neighboring Ellice Islands

1915: Protectorate reorganized as Gilbert and Ellice Islands Colony, extended to include Ocean Island (Banaba) and the Northern Line Islands by 1919

1937: Phoenix Islands incorporated into Gilbert and Ellice Islands Colony

1939: Britain and U.S. sign treaty providing for joint control of Canton and Enderbury

1941-45: Japanese seize Tarawa and Ocean Island (Banaba) from British at outset of World War II. U.S. forces land on Tarawa November 1943, defeating Japanese occupation force. Australian forces liberate Ocean Island (Banaba) in 1945

1945-47: Banabans, dispersed during conflict, are resettled on Rabi, in Fiji Islands

1972: Gilbert and Ellice Islands, removed from jurisdiction of Western Pacific Commission, are placed under a British governor

1975: Ellice Islands separate from Gilberts, becoming Tuvalu (independent in 1978)

1978: London conference, Nov.21-Dec. 7, sets constitutional framework for independence; Banaba representatives bolt meeting after Gilbertese officials reject demands for separation

1979: Gilbert Islands become independent nation of Kiribati, July 12

NORTH KOREA

Area: 46,540 sq. mi. **Population:** 16,700,000 (1978 est.)

Official Name: Democratic People's Republic of Korea **Capital:** Pyongyang **Nationality:** Korean **Languages:** Korean is the official and universal language **Religion:** The traditional religions are Buddhism, Confucianism, Shamanism, and Ch'ondokyo, which combines elements of Buddhism and Christianity; the practice of religion has been discouraged by the government **Flag:** A broad center red stripe bordered on top and bottom by a thin white stripe and a broader blue stripe; left of center is a white disc containing a five-pointed red star **Anthem:** National Anthem, beginning "Morning sun, shine over the rivers and mountains" **Currency:** Won (2.57 per U.S. $1)

Location: North Korea occupies the northern portion of a peninsula in northeast Asia projecting southeast from Manchuria. It is bordered on the north by China, on the extreme northeast by the USSR, on the east by the Sea of Japan, on the south by South Korea, and on the west by the Yellow Sea and Korea Bay **Features:** A land of mountains, North Korea contains thousands of peaks, leaving less than one-fifth of the total area as cultivable **Chief Rivers:** Tumen, Yalu, Ch'ongch'on, Taedong, Yesong

Political Leader: President: Marshal Kim Il Sung, born 1912 **Head of State:** Premier Li Jong Ok **Head of Government:** Chairman of the Presidium of the Assembly: Cho Yong Kun, born 1903, elected by the Assembly in 1957 **Effective Date of Present Constitution:** 1972 **Legislative Body:** Supreme People's Assembly (unicameral), consisting of 579 members elected by universal suffrage for 4 years. It actually does little more than ratify decisions taken by the Central People's Committee of the Korean Workers' (Communist) Party **Local Government:** 9 provinces, 4 municipalities, and two urban special districts, each with a locally elected people's assembly

Ethnic Composition: North Koreans, like the South Koreans, are believed to be of Tungusic stock, ethnically related to the Mongols with some Chinese mixture. There are no ethnic minorities **Popu-**

lation Distribution: 38.1% urban **Density:** 359 inhabitants per sq. mi.

Largest Cities: (1972 est.) Pyongyang 1,500,000, Hamhung 484,000, Chongjin 306,000, Sinuiju 300,000, Wonsan 275,000

Per Capita Income: $684 (1978) **Gross National Product (GNP):** $12.4 billion (1978 est.) **Economic Statistics:** About 70% of GNP comes from industry and mining (coal, iron ore, steel, machinery, textiles); 15% from agriculture (rice, corn, barley, wheat, cotton); and the rest from other activities **Minerals and Mining:** Large deposits of coal, iron ore, lead, zinc, molybdenum, gold, graphite, and tungsten **Labor Force:** 7,500,000, with 55% in industry and services, and 45% in agriculture **Foreign Trade:** Exports, mainly ferrous and nonferrous metals, minerals, chemicals, fuel and oil, machinery and equipment, totaled $482.4 million in 1973. Imports, chiefly machinery and equipment, fuels, chemicals, and textiles, totaled $778.6 million **Principal Trade Partners:** USSR, China and other Communist countries, Japan, West Germany, France

Vital Statistics: Birthrate, 35.7 per 1,000 of pop. (1975); death rate, 9.4 **Life Expectancy:** 61 years **Health Statistics:** 333 inhabitants per hospital bed; 909 per physician **Infant Mortality:** N.A. **Illiteracy:** Negligible **Education Statistics:** 8,691 primary and secondary schools, with combined enrollment of 3,840,000 (1974) **Enrollment in Higher Education:** 214,000 (1973) **GNP Expended on Education:** N.A.

Transportation: Total road mileage is c. 12,350 **Motor Vehicles:** 60,000 (1971) **Railway Mileage:** 2,690 **Ports:** Chongjin, Hamhung, Nampo, Wonsan, Unggi **Major Airlines:** Civil Aviation Administration operates both international and domestic flights **Communications:** State controlled **Radio Transmitters:** 19 **Receivers:** 800,000 (1971) **Television Transmitters:** 1 **Receivers:** 50,000 (1973) **Telephones:** N.A. **Newspapers:** 11 dailies

Weights and Measures: Metric system and old Korean units are used

---

To the West, North Korea is one of the most isolated and least known Communist countries. Personal contacts even between North and South Koreans are almost nonexistent since North and South are still in a technical state of war; the demilitarized zone across the peninsula, set up by the armistice in 1953, is probably the world's most tightly closed border.

The division of Korea along the 38th parallel at the end of World War II left the North with almost all the country's mineral resources and a major share of the industries developed by the Japanese in the former colony. The three-year Korean War devastated much of the industry, but planning, regimentation, and utilization of a trained labor force brought great strides in production by the early 1960s.

The highly authoritarian, military-dominated government of Marshal Kim Il Sung has sought to steer an independent course between the Soviet Union and China, while remaining antagonistic toward United States "imperialism" and what it calls the "puppet" South Korean regime.

Premier Kim, previously a guerrilla against the Japanese, arrived in Pyongyang with Soviet troops in October 1945 as a leader in the émigré forces trained by the Russians to take over in Korea. He established his dominance as premier when the Democratic People's Republic of Korea was set up in September 1948.

North Korea's military forces were strengthened rapidly as Soviet troops were withdrawn, and in June 1950 a North Korean military attack came close to seizing the entire peninsula before United Nations forces, led by American troops, gained the initiative.

The end of the war was followed by collectivization of agriculture; industry in the North had already been nationalized. Economic progress has been notable, educational facilities have been expanded, and extreme poverty has been sharply reduced.

However, life in the North is highly regimented. Consumer goods are scarce, the vast housing projects are drab, travel is tightly controlled and freedom of expression is restricted.

In a June 1973 dispatch, Premier Kim was quoted as saying: "We hold that the North and the South should not enter the United Nations separately but as one state under a confederation." Since that time, he has reiterated his wish for a unified Korea under Communist rule.

In 1972 spokesmen for Seoul and Pyongyang, in a rare display of agreement, had argued that the emotional desire of all Koreans for unity was too strong, and that Koreans must unite to survive in the shifting balance of power in East Asia.

Yet although the general rhetoric of the two Koreas seemed to be in tune, the details of translating words into deeds still appeared difficult. Reunification talks held in 1974 proved fruitless.

In 1975 tension between the two countries increased after the finding in November 1974 of tunnels under the demilitarized zone emerging into South Korea. The victories of the Communists in South Vietnam and Cambodia and a visit to China by Premier Kim, allegedly to seek Chinese support for military pressure on South Korea, had a negative effect on relations between the two Koreas. A new era was in prospect after the 1977 announcement by the U.S. that it plans the gradual withdrawal of all American ground forces from the demilitarized zone over the next five years.

When South Korea proposed, on Jan. 19, 1979, that fresh talks be held in an effort to prevent war and to unify the two countries, North Korea answered, only six days later, that a "new start" would be a good idea. Delegations began talks almost immediately—one day in February and another in March—but quickly got bogged down with procedures.

HISTORY: Korean history goes back into a legendary past, with one of the earliest legends centering around Kitze, or Kija, a scholar credited with the introduction of Chinese culture into the Korean peninsula in the 12th century B.C. Chinese influence remained strong until well after the emergence of separate Korean kingdoms in the early centuries of the Christian era, and it was with Chinese help that one of these, the kingdom of Silla, conquered its rivals in the 7th century A.D. and unified the peninsula. In the 10th century Silla fell to the Koryo dynasty of Kaesong, under whose rule Confucianism gradually replaced Buddhism as the dominant religion

1231-60: Mongols occupy Korea

1392: Yi Sung-ke, a Korean general, seizes Korean throne

1592: Yi dynasty, aided by China, repels invasion by Japanese

1637: Korea is made a vassal of Manchu China, beginning a period of isolation from the rest of the world and giving Korea the name of "hermit kingdom"

1876-82: Korean ports are opened to Japanese, U.S. and European trade after Japan compels Korea to agree to commercial treaty

1894-1905: Japanese victories in Sino-Japanese and Russo-Japanese wars end in complete control of Korea by Japan

1910: Japan formally annexes Korea

1919: Nationalist leader Syngman Rhee sets up Korean government-in-exile in Shanghai

1945: Soviet and U.S. forces occupy Korea after Japan's defeat in World War II; they establish the 38th parallel as the dividing line between their occupation zones, with the Russians in the north and the Americans in the south

1948: Division of the peninsula is formalized with the establishment of the two separate regimes of North Korea and South Korea; Democratic People's Republic of North Korea is set up in 1948 under Premier Kim Il Sung, a Moscow-trained military man; Soviet forces evacuate North Korea

1950-53: North Korea invades South Korea in 1950; in response to UN request, the U.S. and 15 other member nations send troops to aid South Korea; after initial retreats, UN forces stage counteroffensive and drive North Koreans deep into North Korea; in October 1950 Chinese Communists join North Koreans in successful counterattack; fighting continues until a cease-fire is reached in 1953, leaving Korea divided as before

1954-61: Kim Il Sung pushes ambitious program of industrialization; North Korea is economically integrated with Soviet Union and Communist China; military aid treaties are signed with both

1968: North Korea seizes U.S. intelligence ship *Pueblo*, charging vessel violated North Korean territorial waters; crew is released after 11 months when U.S. signs a statement, which it labels false, admitting the *Pueblo's* intrusion

1970: Kim government proposes a federated Korea, conditional upon U.S. withdrawal from the south

1975: North Korea becomes first Communist country to not meet payment of Western debts

1976: Premier Kim resigns and is replaced by Pak Sung Chul. North Korean soldiers kill two U.S. Army officers at Panmunjom

1977: Travel restrictions for U.S. citizens to North Korea are lifted

1978: Working-level talks between North and South Korea break down. Communist Chinese Premier Hua visits, describes North Korea as "sole legitimate sovereign Korean state" and calls for complete withdrawal of U.S. forces from Korea. North Korea denounces "slow" pace of U.S. troop pullout, calls for direct talks with U.S. on reunification of Korea

1979: In response to a South Koean suggestion, North Korea enters into unification talks. Foreigners get a rare glimpse of Pyongyang in April and May as 900 table-tennis players from 70 countries participated in a world tournament. Press dispatches emphasize the physical splendor of Pyongyang which, virtually leveled during the Korean War, has been rebuilt with broad avenues and vistas extending toward many monuments

SOUTH KOREA

Area: 38,175 sq. mi. **Population:** 36,400,000 (1978 est.)

Official Name: Republic of Korea **Capital:** Seoul **Nationality:** Korean **Languages:** Korean is the official and universal language **Religion:** The traditional religions are Buddhism, Confucianism, Shamanism, and Ch'ondokyo, which combines elements of Buddhism and Christianity. However, accurate figures of the numbers of their adherents are not available. There are at least 2 million Christians, chiefly Protestant **Flag:** A divided circle of red (top) and blue (bottom) centered on a white field. A black bar design appears in each corner of the flag **Anthem:** National Anthem, beginning "Until the Eastern Sea is drained" **Currency:** Won (484 per U.S. $1)

Location: South Korea occupies the southern portion of a peninsula in northeast Asia projecting southeast from Manchuria. It is bounded on the north by North Korea, on the east by the Sea of Japan, on the south by the Korea Strait, and on the west by the Yellow Sea **Features:** The country is largely mountainous, with the limited arable land in the lowlands and river valleys of the south and southwest **Chief Rivers:** Somjin, Kum, Naktong, Han, Pukhan

Head of State and of Government: President Park Chung Hee, born 1917, elected to fifth consecutive term in 1978. A state council is under an appointed premier, Choi Kyu Hah, born 1919, approved March 1976 **Effective Date of Present Constitution:** 1948, amended in 1972 **Legislative Body:** National Assembly (unicameral), consisting of 219 members partly elected for 6 years **Local Government:** 9 provinces administered by appointed governors, and 2 specially administered cities

Ethnic Composition: The Korean population is one of the most homogeneous in the world. The primary stock is believed to be Tungusic, related to the Mongols with some Chinese mixture **Population Distribution:** 60% urban **Density:** 954 inhabitants per sq. mi.

Largest Cities: (1977 est.) Seoul 7,500,000; (1975 census) Pusan 2,454,051; Taegu 1,311,078, Inchon 799,982, Kwangju 607,058

Per Capita Income: $958 (1978) **Gross National Product (GNP):** $35 billion (1978 est.) **Economic Statistics:** 22% of GNP comes from agriculture (rice, barley, soybeans, potatoes, wheat, millet, livestock raising); 34% from manufacturing (textiles, chemicals, food processing, clay, glass and stone products, transportation equipment) and mining **Minerals and Mining:** South Korea has less than 30% of the peninsula's estimated reserves of gold, silver, tungsten, molybdenum, and graphite, and about 10% of its coal and iron ore. It nevertheless produces anthracite coal, tungsten, iron ore, lead, amorphous graphite, fluorite, kaolite, and talc **Labor Force:** 14.1 million (1976), with 53.5% in agriculture and forestry, 18% in manufacturing, 28% in commerce and services **Foreign Trade:** Exports, chiefly clothing and textiles, plywood, ships, iron and steel products, wigs, marine products, raw silk, and electronic products, totaled $10 billion in 1977. Imports, mainly nonelectric machinery, transportation equipment, food grains, electric machinery, textiles yarns and fabrics, totaled $10.8 billion **Principal Trade Partners:** United States, Japan, Saudi Arabia, Kuwait, West Germany

Vital Statistics: Birthrate, 28.8 per 1,000 of pop. (1975); death rate 8.9 **Life Expectancy:** 65 years **Health Statistics:** 1,310 inhabitants per hospital bed; 2,128 per physician (1976) **Infant Mortality:** 38 per 1,000 births **Illiteracy:** 6.8% **Education Statistics:** 9,339 primary and secondary schools, with combined enrollment of 8,651,387 (1976) **Enrollment in Higher Education:** 297,219 (1975) **GNP Expended on Education:** 4.1% (1974)

Transportation: Paved roads total 5,369 mi. **Motor Vehicles:** 213,600 (1976) **Passenger Cars:** 96,100 **Railway Mileage:** 3,500 **Ports:** Pusan, Inchon, Pohang, Masan, Mokpo **Major Airlines:** Korean Airlines operates domestic and international services **Communications:** Government and privately owned **Radio Transmitters:** 94 **Receivers:** 12,000,000 (1976) **Television Transmitters:** 59 **Licenses:** 3,046,338 (1976) **Telephones:** 1,643,000 (1976) **Newspapers:** 36 dailies, 173 copies per 1,000 inhabitants (1975)

Weights and Measures: Metric system and old Korean units are used **Travel Requirements:** Passport; tourist visa valid for initial period of 2 months; no fee

The Korean peninsula has often been described as a dagger pointed from the Asian heartland toward Japan, and its strategic position made it several times a battleground for more powerful neighbors. Long a "hermit kingdom" with a strong indigenous culture, Korea was annexed by the Japanese in 1910. Until the end of World War II it was ruled by a repressive colonial regime and exploited for its mineral resources, living space, and markets.

Considerable dislocation occurred when the primarily agricultural and densely populated South was separated from the industrial North in 1945 and put under United States occupation. After unsuccessful attempts to arrange nationwide elections under United Nations supervision, voting was held in 1948 in the South only and the government of the Republic of Korea was established under the presidency of Syngman Rhee.

The Korean War caused more than 800,000 military and civilian casualties in South Korea and approximately $3 billion worth of property damage. For a decade thereafter the huge U.S. aid effort, coupled with international assistance, was directed toward providing food and shelter, repairing war damage, and laying the groundwork for eventual economic development. During the 1970s, the South Korean economy flourished, and the nation became an important industrial power.

President Rhee won reelection in 1952 and 1956, but as he grew more despotic and ruthless, police repression and official corruption aroused wide protests. Finally, rigging of elections in 1960 set off student demonstrations that overthrew Dr. Rhee. The subsequent government of Dr. John M. Chang proved ineffective and a military coup in May 1961 brought to power a junta led by the current president, Park Chung Hee, then a major general. General Park retired from the army, won the presidency in a national election in 1963, and was reelected in 1967 and 1972. In 1978 his presidency was extended for six years; no other name was on the ballot as the electoral college, the National Conference for Unification, elected him, 2,577 to 0. At the time of voting, all opposition leaders were under house arrest in Seoul.

At his inauguration in 1972 President Park touched on a recurrent theme of Korean politics, North and South, when he pledged to pursue the peaceful unification of the divided country.

Since 1971, the most significant contacts between North and South have been through Red Cross teams. But in June 1973, in a dramatic reversal of policy, Park announced a large forward step: "We shall not object to our admittance into the United Nations with North Korea"—an action he had previously sworn never to take.

In 1975 Park's government attempted to solidify its position at home with numerous arrests to control the opposition to the current methods of running the country, and with further efforts to secure more military support from the U.S. His government's constitutional changes, drawn up after imposing martial law in 1972, were approved in a national referendum which was boycotted by the opposition New Democratic Party. Since 1975 all political dissent has been banned in South Korea and the U.S. has expressed concern over human rights violations in the country.

In May 1978 the U.S. began the gradual pullout of its 33,000 ground troops from South Korea; the move, to be completed by about 1982, will not affect some 7,000 Air Force personnel, who will remain. The U.S. plans to give Seoul $800 million in arms as compensation for the withdrawal, to offset North Korea's advantage in tanks, artillery and fighter aircraft.

In 1979 the U.S. Department of Defense issued its first estimates in five years on relative troop strengths; 430,000 men in 41 combat-ready North Korean divisions, 530,000 men in the South Korean forces, organized into fewer divisions. The report prompted renewed questions in the U.S. Congress about the wisdom of an American withdrawal.

HISTORY: The history of South Korea is bound up with that of Korea as a whole up until 1948 when the government of the Republic of Korea was established under the presidency of Syngman Rhee

1953-53: Korean War, brought on by North Korea's invasion of South Korea, rages for three years as U.S. troops and forces of 15 other nations, responding to a request for help by the United Nations, try to repel the invaders; the conflict, broadened in 1951 with the entry of Communist China on the side of North Korea, ends with the establishment of a cease-fire and the continued division of the peninsula at the 38th parallel

1960: Rhee is elected for fourth term as president but is accused of rigging the elections; after widespread rioting he is forced from office and goes into exile

1961: South Korean armed forces overthrow government; General Park Chung Hee takes power

1963-67: Park is elected president in 1963 and is reelected in 1967 amid charges by his opponents that elections were rigged

1969: South Korean voters approve a constitutional amendment that allows president to seek a third consecutive term

1970: United States agrees to bolster South Korean army after announcing U.S. troop cuts in South Korea

1972: Following secret talks, governments of North and South Korea announce agreement in principle on unification. Park institutes constitutional changes that increase his power

1973: Opposition leader Kim Dae-Jung is kidnapped in Japan, resulting in widespread demonstrations. Brought back to Korea, he is placed under house arrest and later released

1975: Assassination attempt on President Park fails but wife is victim. North Korea rejects a South Korean proposal to renew talks on unification

1978: Economy continues on uptrend. Strained relations between South Korea and U.S. worsen over planned pullout of American ground forces (as withdrawal begins); U.S. bugging of South Korean executive mansion is alleged, and influence-buying scandal comes to light, in which South Korean businessman Tongsun Park and former ambassador Kim Dong Jo allegedly paid U.S. Congressmen for continued American economic and military aid; Kim Dong Jo resigns post as national security adviser. Park, unopposed, is reelected for another six-year presidential term. On Dec. 27, Park's inauguration day, Kim Daejung is released from jail again after serving 31 months for criticizing the government

1979: Park asks North Korea for talks "any time, any place" to reunify the countries; delegations meet but bog down on procedural questions. U.S. President Carter visits Seoul in June, prompting government's release of many political dissidents

---

KUWAIT

Area: 7,780 sq. mi. **Population:** 1,100,000 (1978 est.)

Official Name: State of Kuwait **Capital:** Kuwait **Nationality:** Kuwaiti **Languages:** Arabic is the official and universal language; English is widely spoken **Religion:** About 99% Moslem, chiefly of the Sunni sect; and 1% of other or no affiliation **Flag:** Green, white, and red horizontal stripes with a black trapezoid at the staff **Anthem:** National Anthem (no words) **Currency:** Kuwaiti dinar (.28 per U.S. $1)

Location: Northeast corner of the Arabian Peninsula. Kuwait is bordered on the north and west by Iraq, on the east by the Persian Gulf, and on the south by Saudi Arabia **Features:** The country is mainly flat desert, with a few oases **Chief Rivers:** There are no rivers

Head of State and of Government: Emir: Sheikh Jabir al-Ahmad al-Jabir as-Sabah, born 1928, acceded 1977. The emir is assisted by a council of ministers headed by a prime minister, Sheikh Saad al-Abdullah al-Salim as-Sabah, appointed 1978 **Effective Date of Present Constitution:** 1962, partly suspended in August 1976; a revision is planned **Legislative Body:** National Assembly (unicameral), dissolved in August 1976, with rule by royal decree **Local Government:** 3 governorates

Ethnic Composition: The population is about 85% Arab but only 47% are native-born. Non-Kuwaitis include Palestinians, Iraqis, Iranians, Egyptians, Indians, Syrians, Lebanese, and others **Population Distribution:** 99% urban **Density:** 141 inhabitants per sq. mi.

Largest Cities: (1975 census) Hawalli 130,302, Salimiya 113,874, Kuwait 108,211

Per Capita Income: $12,600 (1978 est.) **Gross National Product (GNP):** $15.2 billion (1978 est.) **Economic Statistics:** The economy is based almost entirely on oil, which accounts for about 70% of GNP. About 15% comes from trade and services; the remainder from nonoil industries (chemical fertilizers, building materials, fishing) **Minerals and Mining:** Kuwait possesses nearly one-fifth of the world's oil reserves. Oil concessions are held by the Kuwait National Petroleum Company (60% government owned) and British, American, and Japanese firms. Large amounts of natural gas are produced from the oil fields **Labor Force:** 300,000, with 70% held by non-Kuwaitis. 40% of the labor force is employed by the government, 34% are in industry (less than 5% in the heavily automated oil industry), and 1% in agriculture **Foreign Trade:** Exports, 96% crude oil and petroleum products, totaled $9.8 billion in 1976. Imports, chiefly foodstuffs, building materials, automobiles, industrial equipment and electrical products, totaled $4.8 billion (1977) **Principal Trade Partners:** Japan, United States, Britain, West Germany, Italy, Korea

Vital Statistics: Birthrate, 43.3 per 1,000 of pop. (1976); death rate, 4.4 **Life Expectancy:** 69 years **Health Statistics:** 235 inhabitants per hospital bed; 918 per physician (1975) **Infant Mortality:** 34.3 per 1,000 births **Illiteracy:** 20% **Educational Statistics:** 392 primary and secondary schools, with combined enrollment of 121,285 (1975) **Enrollment in Higher Education:** 8,104 (1975) **GNP Expended on Education:** 2.6% (1974)

Transportation: Paved roads total 1,000 mi. **Motor Vehicles:** 320,800 (1976) **Passenger Cars:** 237,100 **Railway Mileage:** None **Ports:** Mina al-Ahmadi, Shuwaikh, Shuaibah, Mina Abdullah **Major Airlines:** Kuwait Airways, government owned, operates international flights, as does Gulf Air **Communications:** Government owned **Radio Transmitters:** 8 **Television Transmitters:** 7 **Receivers:** 375,000 (1978) **Telephones:** 140,000 (1976) **Newspapers:** 8 dailies, 86 copies per 1,000 inhabitants (1976)

Weights and Measures: Metric system **Travel Requirements:** Passport; visa, valid 60 days; 1 photo

---

Tiny, torrid Kuwait, an opulent strip of desert at the northwestern end of the Persian Gulf, enjoys one of the world's highest standards of living.

Since 1967 Kuwait has helped to subsidize the national economies of Egypt, the leading Arab power, and of Jordan, both of which were defeated in the war with Israel. It is a garish, nouveau-riche country that must import all of its food but is able to export enough oil to pay for the basic needs of all of its people.

As a capitalistic welfare state, where poverty is virtually unknown, it provides lavish public services that include: free universal medical service, free education through the university level (including free food and clothing for students), free telephone service, subsidized housing for which only token rentals are paid, and subsidies for those wishing to start business enterprises.

Kuwait has a higher proportion of the latest American cars than any country outside the United States, and the cars are driven over wide, well-surfaced roads. It has more than twice as many air-conditioning units as people, and there is said to be a millionaire for every 230 citizens.

As late as the 1940s, before large-scale oil exports began, Kuwait was little more than a feudal wilderness. It was a primitive, forbidding land, where the temperature would often reach 125 degrees in the shade.

Abd Allah al-Salim as-Sabah, who was emir when the oil boom began, developed the growth program. Following his death in 1965, his policies were continued by his successor, Sheikh Sabah al-Salim as-Sabah. On December 31, 1977, Sheikh Sabah died and his cousin, Sheikh Jabir al-Ahmad al-Jabir as-Sabah, became emir.

The Kuwaitis themselves are a minority of the population of their own country, and they make up only 30 percent of the work force. Of those Kuwaitis who are employed, 70 percent are on the government payroll. Non-Kuwaitis (mainly Palestinians, Saudis, Egyptians, Iraqis, Pakistanis, Indians, and Americans), share in the welfare services, but are not permitted to own property or to vote.

Kuwaiti society generally consists of five layers, with the members of the ruling family at the top, followed by the old Kuwaiti merchant families. Then come the former Bedouins now living in luxurious urban surroundings, the Arabs from other countries who have been granted Kuwaiti citizenship, and, last, the foreigners.

Many foreigners feel unappreciated by the Kuwaitis, and members of a large Palestinian underground have tried to force the government to take a stronger position that it has against Israel. The actvities of this underground were cited by the government in explaining its decision to dissolve the National Assembly and restrict the press in 1976.

A British protectorate from 1897 to 1961, Kuwait received informal military protection from the Iranian Shah after 1970. After the Shah fell in 1979, Britain's Queen Elizabeth and Foreign Secretary David Owen visited Kuwait to indicate continuing commitment.

Despite the connection with Britain, Kuwait is very much involved in he Arab bloc. It sent soldiers to fight in the Yom Kippur War against Israel in 1973. In 1979, The presidents of Yemen and Southern Yemen met in Kuwait to negotiate an agreement to merge their two countries, and the Kuwaiti government joined other Arab states in breaking relations with Cairo after Egypt made peace with Israel.

HISTORY: Kuwait was settled by Arab tribes in the early 18th century. The present dynasty was established in 1756 by Sheikh Sabah Abdul Rahim. Nominally an Ottoman province, Kuwait asked for British protection in 1897, when the ruling sheikh feared that the Turks wanted to make their authority effective

1899: In return for British protection, Kuwait undertakes not to cede or lease any of its territory without Britain's approval

1914-22: Britain declares Kuwait independent of Turkey and under British protection. British troops help repel invasion by Saudi Arabia; Saudis and Kuwait set up neutral zone in which they share sovereignty

1934: Kuwait's ruler grants a concession to Kuwait Oil Company, a joint American-British enterprise, to drill for oil

1961: Britain recognizes Kuwait as an independent state and pledges protection against foreign aggression; Iraq claims Kuwait as a province; British troops prevent Iraqi invasion

1967: During Arab-Israeli war, Kuwait declares support for the Arab cause and contributes large subsidies to Egypt and Jordan

1969: Government shows increasing alarm over growing Soviet inroads in Persian Gulf area; proposal for the formation of a federation of nine neighboring sheikhdoms raises fear that many will succumb to revolutionary movements

1973: Kuwait's forces fight along Suez Canal during Yom Kippur war. Along with other oil-producing nations, Kuwait announces huge increase in oil prices. Oil embargo is imposed on pro-Israel nations, but is later lifted

1975: Government announces it intends to acquire 100 percent ownership of domestic oil operations

1977: An arms buildup begun in 1976 continues with the purchase of sophisticated Soviet weaponry

---

LAOS

Area: 91,428 sq. mi. **Population:** 3,600,000 (1978 est.)

Official Name: Lao People's Democratic Republic **Capital:** Vientiane (a new capital on the Plain of Jars is planned) **Nationality:** Laotian **Languages:** Lao, a tonal language of the Thai group, is the official and dominant language; French serves as the second language but has recently declined **Religion:** Theravada Buddhism is the official and predominant religion (90%); the country's mountain tribes are principally animist **Flag:** Two narrow red bands either side of a wide blue band, with a white disc in the middle **Anthem:** N.A. **Currency:** Kip (200 per U.S. $1)

Location: Southeast Asia. Landlocked Laos is bordered on the north by China, on the east by Vietnam, on the south by Cambodia, on the west by Thailand, and on the northwest by Burma **Features:** Northern Laos is laced with jungle-covered mountains and plateaus cut by narrow valleys. Lower Laos is marked by arid limestone terraces, sparsely forested and descending westward to the Mekong River Valley **Chief Rivers:** Mekong, Nam Hou

Head of State: President: Prince Souphanouvong, named in 1975 **Head of Government: Premier:** Kaysone Phoumvihan, born 1920, appointed 1975; he is also secretary general of the party **Effective Date of Present Constitution:** 1947, revised 1957 **Legislative Body:** An appointed 45-member People's Supreme Assembly. The government is actually controlled by the Central Committee of the Lao People's Revolutionary (Communist) Party under its secretary general **Local Government:** 20 provinces

Ethnic Composition: More than half of the people are ethnic Lao, descendants of the Thai, a people who migrated from southwestern China in the 13th century. Mountain tribes of Sino-Tibetan and Thai strains are found in the north; many of these tribes, as well as others of Malay background, inhabit central and south Laos. Vietnamese, Cambodians, Chinese, Indians, and Pakistanis constitute influential minorities **Population Distribution:** 15% urban **Density:** 39% inhabitants per sq. mi.

Largest Cities: (1970 est.) Vientiane 150,000, Savannakhet 39,000, Pakse 37,200, Luang Prabang 25,000, Khammouane 13,000

Per Capita Income: $79 (1978 est.) **Gross National Product (GNP):** $280 million (1978 est.) **Economic Statistics:** Components of GNP are not available. The economy of the country, the least developed of the nations of the Indochinese peninsula, is 85% agricultural. Major crops are rice, corn, coffee, cotton, tea, and tobacco. Industry is limited to light consumer goods, with some cottage and family-type production. Lumber, cigarettes, soft drinks, alcohol, and cement are produced in small plants **Minerals and Mining:** Tin is the major mineral resource; surveys indicate deposits of iron ore, gold, copper, and manganese **Labor Force:** About 90% of the population is engaged in agriculture **Foreign Trade:** Exports, chiefly wood, tin, coffee, and resins, totaled $11 million in 1974. Imports, mainly foods, petroleum products, and transportation equipment, totaled $153 million (1975) **Principal Trade Partners:** Thailand, Japan, Malaysia, Singapore, Vietnam

Vital Statistics: Birthrate, 44.6 per 1,000 of pop. (1975); death rate, 22.8 **Life Expectancy:** 48 years **Health Statistics:** 401 inhabitants per hospital bed (1975); 21,667 per physician (1976) **Infant Mortality:** N.A. **Illiteracy:** 72% **Education Statistics:** 3,413 primary and secondary schools, with combined enrollment of 346,649 (1976) **Enrollment in Higher Education:** 828 (1974) **GNP Expended on Education:** 2.9% (1972)

Transportation: Improved roads total about 2,175 mi. **Motor Vehicles:** 16,600 (1974) **Passenger Cars:** 14,100 **Railway Mileage:** None **Ports:** None **Major Airlines:** Thai Airways and Aeroflot Soviet Airlines operate international flights; Lao Airways flies domestically **Communications:** Government owned **Radio Transmitters:** 9 **Licenses:** 200,000 (1976) **Television:** None **Telephones:** 5,000 (1973) **Newspapers:** 8 dailies (1975)

Weights and Measures: Metric system and local units are used **Travel Requirements:** Passport; visa

---

The old Kingdom of Laos, which formed part of French Indochina, was little known to the outside world until the Vietnam War made its strategic location significant. The largest segment of French Indochina, it was also the most remote and the least developed. French rule did little to turn the local and ethnic groups into a united Laotian nation.

Most of the people live in the western quarter of the nation, where they practice subsistence agriculture. Widely scattered hill tribes inhabit the rest of the country, which is mountainous and jungle-covered. Laos lacks modern industrial facilities and technological resources. The country has few significant exports.

The development of Laos has been impeded both by warfare and by the country's physical features. The absence of a network of roads makes communication between the Mekong Valley towns and the rest of the country difficult. The North Vietnamese supply trails into South Vietnam ran through Laos, and these had been the target of intense bombing by U.S. planes. The land war itself spilled over from Vietnam into Laos in 1971, when the South Vietnamese launched a drive into eastern Laos with the stated intention of cutting off the Ho Chi Minh Trail.

The fighting was not confined to the southeast. A civil war was waged, with varying intensity, elsewhere in the country, with the United States supporting the Laotian government forces and the North Vietnamese helping the pro-Communist Pathet Lao.

On February 21, 1973, the war in Laos officially ended, as the Pathet Lao and the government signed a cease-fire agreement. By the end of July, a political settlement was reached, whereby the two Laotian parties agreed on the sharing of ministries, the creation of two deputy premierships, and the formation of a political consultative council. On the military side, the parties agreed to the neutralization of the two capitals, Vientiane and Luang Prabang, and the division of the country into two zones.

In April 1974, a third coalition government of neutralists, rightists and pro-Communist Pathet Lao was established and in May and June Thai and U.S. forces withdrew, ending their 10 years of military involvement.

By December of 1975, as an indirect result of the South Vietnamese collapse, a relatively low-key Pathet Lao takeover of Laos was completed with the abolition of both the 600-year-old monarchy and the coalition government and the establishment of a People's Democratic Republic. Prince Souphanouvong, titular leader of the Pathet Lao, was named president and Kaysone Phoumvihan, head of the Marxist-Leninist Laos People's Party, was appointed premier.

The tide of refugees flowing out of Vietnamese-dominated Laos has drained the country of most of its professional and commercial elite. The refugees are estimated variously at 130,000 to 250,000, imposing a heavy burden on neighboring Thailand and other Southeast Asian countries. Other Laotians, possibly 40,000, many of whom had been civilian officials and military officers in the previous government, are being detained in "political re-education" centers. On the economic front, a shortage of locally grown food caused sharp price increases.

HISTORY: The Lao began moving south from China in the 13th century, gradually settling in the territory of the Khmer Empire. After centuries of warfare among the small feudal states of the region, the ruler of Luang Prabang state united most of what is now Laos and Northeast Thailand in the Kingdom of Lan Xang (Kingdom of the Million Elephants). The kingdom split into 2 states in 1707; after constant quarreling they were overrun by neighboring armies. By the early 1800s the Thai had won ascendancy and retained this hold until the French moved in and established a protectorate in 1893

1945-46: Japanese invade Lao region of French Indochina. French return and reestablish control

1949: Laos becomes independent state within French Union

1950: Pathet Lao, a Communist nationalist movement, is founded by Prince Souphanouvong

1953: Government battles Pathet Lao and Viet Minh, Vietnamese Communist forces

1954: Under terms of Geneva Conference agreement ending Indochina war, Laos becomes fully independent and Pathet Lao is permitted to occupy country's two northern provinces

1960: Neutralist-Pathet Lao coalition breaks down. Tug-of-war between Moscow-backed neutralists, American-backed rightists, and Pathet Lao erupts. Rightist General Phoumi Nosavan drives neutralists from Vientiane; Premier Souvanna Phouma, the neutralist leader, flees to Cambodia

1962: U.S. troops move into northeast Thailand to discourage Pathet Lao drive on Vientiane. Three factions reach accord on coalition, and second Geneva Conference agrees on Laotian neutrality. Prince Souvanna Phouma returns as premier

1963: Pathet Lao abandons its role in the government as neutralist and leftist forces renew fighting

1965: Right-wing faction seizes government, banishing General Phoumi Nosavan and reinstating Souvanna Phouma as premier. Neutralist-led government agrees to U.S. flights over Laos and to bombing of Ho Chi Minh Trail

1967: The premier, Prince Souvanna Phouma, states that Laos has been invaded by more than 40,000 North Vietnamese troops

1969: U.S. planes bomb Ho Chi Minh Trail and other North Vietnamese infiltration routes through Laos

1971: South Vietnamese troops supported by U.S. planes and artillery invade Laos in a drive against North Vietnamese supply lines; invasion ends after the retreat of South Vietnamese

1973: War in Laos ends as government, Pathet Lao sign cease-fire in February and agree on political settlement in July

1974: King Savang Vatthana dissolves Vientiane government and installs new coalition cabinet under Prince Souvanna Phouma, who remains premier

1975: National Assembly is dissolved by Pathet Lao. Prince Souphanouvong becomes president

1977: Rebels mount attacks against government throughout Laos. Vietnam and Laos sign a 25-year agreement for military and economic cooperation

1978: Laos faces flood and drought-caused food shortages and likelihood of famine in many areas. Rebel attacks continue; government is helped by Vietnamese troops. U.S. promises Laos $5 million worth of rice to help ease food shortages, the first U.S. aid to an Indochinese country since the Communist victories in 1975

1979: The 1977 Vietnam-Laos pact is alluded to indirectly in the 1979 Vietnam-Cambodia pact, which says that the three countries "must unite with one another in political, military, diplomatic, and other affairs." Soon Laos contributes 1,000 soldiers to the Vietnamese operations in Cambodia. Laos becomes involved in China's brief invasion of Vietnam in that Chinese troops, by Laotian accounts, invade Laotian territory on three occasions while maneuvering against the Vietnamese

---

LEBANON

Area: 4,015 sq. mi. **Population:** 3,300,000 (1978 est.)
Official Name: Republic of Lebanon **Capital:** Beirut **Nationality:** Lebanese **Languages:** Arabic is the official and dominant language; French and English are also widely used **Religion:** 62% Moslem (Sunni and Shi'ite) and 37% Christian (Maronite, Greek Orthodox, Armenian, Greek and Roman Catholic). There are also about 90,000 Druzes and 7,000 Jews **Flag:** A broad white horizontal stripe between narrower red stripes; in the center is a green cedar tree with a brown trunk **Anthem:** National Anthem, beginning "All of us" **Currency:** Lebanese pound (3.2 per U.S. $1)

Location: Southwest Asia. Lebanon is bordered on the north and east by Syria, on the south by Israel, and on the west by the Mediterranean Sea **Features:** The country consists of a narrow costal plain behind which are the high Lebanese Mountains. Farther east are the fertile Beqaa Valley and finally the Anti-Lebanon Mountains extending to the Syrian frontier **Chief Rivers:** Litani, Hasbani

Head of State: President Elias Sarkis, born 1924, assumed office in September 1976. By convention, the president is a Maronite **Head of Government:** Premier Dr. Selim Ahmad al-Hoss, appointed December 1976. By convention, the premier is a Sunni Moslem **Effective Date of Present Constitution:** 1926, amended 1976 **Legislative Body:** Parliament (Unicameral National Assembly), consisting of 99 members elected for 4 years. By convention, the speaker is a Shi'ite Moslem **Local Government:** 5 provinces, under appointed governors and provincial councils

Ethnic Composition: 93% Arab, 6% Armenian, and 1% others **Population Distribution:** 60% urban **Density:** 822 inhabitants per sq. mi.

Largest Cities: (1972 est.) Beirut 1,000,000, Tripoli 200,000

Per Capita Income: $1,030 (1978 est.) **Gross National Product (GNP):** $3.2 billion (1978 est.) **Economic Statistics:** In 1973 about 55% of GNP came from trade and services; 9% from agriculture (citrus fruits, vegetables, tobacco, livestock production); 21% from industry (food processing, textiles, cement, oil refining) **Minerals and Mining:** Small amounts of bitumen, iron ore, lime, and salt **Labor Force:** 570,000 (1970), with about 20% in agriculture; and 20% in industry **Foreign Trade:** Exports, chiefly fruits, vegetables, and textiles, totaled $1.2 billion in 1974. Imports, mainly aircraft, motor vehicles, cigarettes, household appliances, wheat and corn, totaled $1.7 billion **Principal Trade Partners:** Saudi Arabia, Kuwait, Jordan, United States, West Germany, France, Britain.

Vital Statistics: Birthrate 39.8 per 1,000 of pop. (1975); death rate, 9.9 **Life Expectancy:** 63 years **Health Statistics:** 260 inhabitants per hospital bed; 1,330 per physician (1973) **Infant Mortality:** 82 per 1,000 births **Illiteracy:** 14% **Education Statistics:** 2,774 primary and secondary schools, with combined enrollment of 672,434 (1972) **Enrollment of Higher Education:** 44,296 (1971) **GNP Expended on Education:** 3.0% (1973)

Transportation: Paved roads total 3,775 mi. **Motor Vehicles:** 243,600 (1974) **Passenger Cars:** 220,200 **Railway Mileage:** 250 **Ports:** Beirut, Tripoli, Sidon **Major Airlines:** Middle East Airlines operates international services **Communications:** Government and privately owned **Radio Transmitters:** 6 **Receivers:** 1,600,000 (1976) **Television Transmitters:** 8 **Receivers:** 425,000 (1976) **Telephones:** 222,000 (1975) **Newspapers:** 33 dailies (1975), 92 copies per 1,000 inhabitants

Weights and Measures: Metric system **Travel Requirements:** Passport; 6-month visa valid for 2 entries; $5 fee

Lebanon is situated on the eastern shore of the Mediterranean and has an area slightly smaller than that of Connecticut. Bounded on the north and east by Syria and on the south by Israel, its chief topographic features are a narrow coastal plain behind which are the Lebanese Mountains, then the fertile Beqaa Valley, and finally the Anti-Lebanon Mountains extending to the Syrian border. An estimated 64 percent of the land is desert, waste, or urban; 27 percent farmland; and nine percent forest. The Litani River, flowing into the sea north of Tyre, is the main river.

Traditionally a part of Greater Syria, which in turn was a sector of the Ottoman Empire, Lebanon became a separate entity after World War I to satisfy its Christian inhabitants. It was administered by France from 1920 to 1941, when it was declared independent by the Free French. With few natural resources besides a good location, Lebanon became a center of commerce and banking. For a time, general prosperity and a desire to keep peace discouraged challenges to the privileged position of the Christians. Uneasy political stability prevailed. So did laissez-faire capitalism and personal freedom; the government governed as little as possible to avoid offending anybody.

In the 1970s, however, Palestinian guerrillas established bases in Lebanon and began raids on Israel, prompting Israeli retaliation. Bitter disputes resulted between the Moslems, who tended to sympathize with the Palestinian cause, and the Christians, who had less sympathy for it. Open war broke out in the spring of 1975, with armed Christian bands on one side, Palestinians and Lebanese Moslem and Druse bands on the other. Israel armed the Christians, but their opponents came close to winning, and Syria sent in army units to protect the Christians and deny Israel a pretext for intervening. Later, under the nominal command of the Arab League, the Syrians actually became a disturbing element, clashing with the Christians, whom they were supposed to protect.

The worst fighting ended in 1976, but Lebanon remained functionally divided along communal lines and unable to repair the damage of the war or to return to its former commercial and banking activities. Most of the soldiers in its army had joined warring bands, but the government retained its ability to collect taxes—and paid soldiers for fighting each other. The legislature elected Elias Sarkis, a Christian respected by Moslems, as president, and he appointed a Moslem, Selim al-Hoss, premier; their conciliatory efforts were of little avail.

Israel occupied much of southern Lebanon in 1978, in order to create a buffer zone there. The United Nations sent soldiers from many countries to police the area, and Israel withdrew, but turned some of the area over to Lebanese Christian warriors, instead of the UN. Meanwhile, Christian factions in northern Lebanon clashed with each other. Warriors of all factions sometimes attacked UN soldiers. Low-level fighting continued into 1979, pitting Christians against Syrian soldiers, Moslems, Druzes, and other Christians. Palestinian raids into Israel and Israeli raids on Palestinian bases also continued. Saad Haddad, Christian commander in the area near the Israeli border, proclaimed the independence of a Free Lebanese State in the border area.

HISTORY: In ancient times, Hittite and Aramaean kingdoms occupied the area that is now Lebanon. The Lebanese coast later became the base for the sea-trading Phoenicians, but their cities soon fell prey to the Assyrians, Persians, and Greeks. Along with neighboring Syria, Lebanon was then brought under Roman rule and afterwards became part of the Byzantine Empire. Maronite Christians established themselves in the area, and even after the spread of Islam by the Arabs, who invaded Lebanon in the 7th century, the country long remained largely Christian

1516-17: Lebanon and Syria are absorbed into the Ottoman Empire, but Lebanon retains considerable autonomy

1841-64: Massacres of Maronite Christians by Druzes cause European governments to force Ottoman sultans to agree to a pro-Christian government for the area and to the establishment of autonomous province of Mount Lebanon

1918: Anglo-French force occupies Lebanon following collapse of Ottoman Empire in World War I

1920: Lebanon, along with Syria, becomes a French mandate

1941-45: Lebanon, under Free French occupation, is declared independent in 1941; however, French retain actual control of country until 1945

1958: Opposition to pro-Western policies of President Camille Chamoun erupts in rebellion; at Chamoun's request, U.S. troops are ordered to Lebanon by President Eisenhower; troops are withdrawn after formation of new Lebanese government

1968: Israeli commandos raid Beirut airport, destroying 13 civil aircraft; Israel claims raid was in retaliation for an earlier attack on Israeli airliner in Athens, carried out by two Arab terrorists from Beirut; Lebanon disclaims responsibility for commandos operating against Israel from Lebanese territory

1970: Suleiman Franjieh is elected president by legislature; Saeb Salaam succeeds Rashid Karami as premier

1972: Israel raids guerrilla bases in Lebanon in retaliation for the killing of Israeli athletes at the Munich Olympics

1973: Israeli commando raid on Beirut in which three guerrilla leaders are slain forces resignation of Premier Saeb Salaam and sparks two weeks of fighting in Beirut between guerrillas and Lebanese army; new Premier Takieddin Solh negotiates uneasy truce, but guerrilla activity and Israeli reprisals continue before and after Arab-Israeli war in October

1974: Border clashes between Israeli forces and Palestinian guerrillas based in Lebanon continue

1975-76: Some 60,000 die in 19-month civil war between Christians and Moslems; army disintegrates; economy nears collapse. Syria invades; Arab summit arranges cease-fire and establishes Arab League peacekeeping forces—consisting mostly of Syrians who are already there. Elias Sarkis becomes president; he appoints Selim al-Hoss premier

1977: Moslem leader Kamal Jumblat is assassinated

1978: Israelis, avenging a PLO terror raid, invade southern Lebanon, attacking PLO bases there; about 200,000 Lebanese and 65,000 Palestinian refugees flee to the north; most return as Israelis pull out three months later. UN peacekeeping forces form buffer zone between Israelis and PLO guerrillas. Tony Franjieh, son of former Lebanese President Suleiman Franjieh, is killed in Phalangist attack north of Beirut, as rival Christian factions battle; Syrian peacekeepers clash with Phalangists. Conflict develops in southern border zone between central government, attempting to reassert its authority, and Israeli-backed Christian militia units. Israeli planes raid Palestinian camps in retaliation for terrorist attack on airline bus in London

1979: Continued fighting on all fronts. Saad Haddad, Christian militia officer, proclaims independent "Free Lebanese State" in Christian region along Israeli border

LESOTHO

Area: 11,720 sq. mi. **Population:** 1,200,000 (1978 est.)

Official Name: Kingdom of Lesotho **Capital:** Maseru **Nationality:** Basotho **Languages:** Sesotho, the language of the Sotho people, and English are the official languages **Religion:** About 70% Christian, chiefly Roman Catholic, the rest being mostly animist **Flag:** Green and red vertical stripes to the left of a blue field bearing a white conical Sotho hat **Anthem:** National Anthem, beginning "Lesotho, the country of our fathers" **Currency:** South African rand (.85 per U.S. $1)

Location: An enclave within the east-central part of the Republic of South Africa, Lesotho is bordered on the west and north by the Orange Free State Province, on the east by the Province of Natal, and on the south by Cape Province and Transkei **Features:** About a fourth of the western sector is lowland terrain; the rest of the country is mountainous **Chief Rivers:** Orange, Caledon

Head of State: King Moshoeshoe II, born 1938; formerly Paramount Chief, he became king in 1966 **Head of Government:** Prime Minister, Dr. Leabua Jonathan, born 1914, appointed 1965; he seized power in 1970, acts also as defense and internal security minister, and rules by decree **Effective Date of Present Constitution:** 1966, suspended 1970 **Legislative Body:** Parliament (bicameral), suspended 1970. An interim National Assembly with limited powers was formed in 1973, the members being nominated by the government **Local Government:** 10 districts, with appointed administrators

Ethnic Composition: The population is almost entirely Bantu, with 85% Sotho and 15% Nguni. There are less than 1% South Africans, Asians and mixed **Population Distribution:** 1% urban **Density:** 94 inhabitants per sq. mi.

Largest City: (1972 est.) Maseru 20,000

Per Capita Income: $117 (1978) **Gross National Product (GNP):** $350 million (1978) **Economic Statistics:** In 1976 about 40% of GNP came from agriculture (corn, sorghum, wheat, beans, peas, livestock), 10% from industry (printing, carpet weaving, brewing, candlemaking, tire retreading) and mining **Minerals and Mining:** Few known mineral deposits except for diamonds **Labor Force:** 430,000 (1970), with 57% in agriculture, and only 22,500 wage earners. About 200,000 work in South Africa **Foreign Trade:** Exports, mainly diamonds, wool, mohair, and livestock, totaled $16.8 million in 1976. Imports, chiefly foodstuffs, textiles, clothing, transportation equipment, and chemicals, totaled $206.9 million **Principal Trade Partners:** South Africa, Britain, United States

Vital Statistics: Birthrate, 39 per 1,000 of pop. (1975); death rate, 19.7 per 1,000 **Life Expectancy:** 46 years **Health Statistics:** 482 inhabitants per hospital bed; 20,400 per physician (1974) **Infant Mortality:** 114.4 per 1,000 births **Illiteracy:** 60% **Education Statistics:** 1,171 primary and secondary schools, with combined enrollment of 238,384 (1975) **Enrollment in Higher Education:** 577 (1974) **GNP Expended on Education:** 4.4% (1971)

Transportation: Improved roads total 625 mi. **Motor Vehicles:** 7,800 (1975) **Passenger Cars:** 4,600 **Railway Mileage:** One mile of track links Maseru with South Africa **Ports:** None **Major Airlines:** Government-owned Lesotho Airways operates domestic services **Communications:** Government owned **Radio Transmitters:** 2 **Licenses:** 23,000 (1976) **Television:** None **Telephones:** 4,000 (1974) **Newspapers:** 1 daily

Weights and Measures: Metric and British standards **Travel Requirements:** Passport; visa valid for 20 days; 2 photos

---

An enclave in the southeastern area of South Africa, Lesotho, the former British protectorate of Basutoland, is an island of Black African nationalism in a sea of apartheid. The small mountainous kingdom is the remnant of a larger realm, the refuge to which the Basotho were driven by tribal wars and Boer incursions.

In 1818, Moshesh I, a tribal chief from the north, succeeded in uniting the Basotho people. He ruled from about 1820 to 1870 and consolidated various tribes that had been scattered earlier by Zulu and Matabele warriors. During his reign, a series of wars with the Orange Free State (1856-68) resulted in the loss of a large area to the Free State, now known as the "Conquered Territory." Moshesh appealed to the British for help, and in 1868 the country was annexed by Britain.

For a considerable time thereafter the energies of the British administrators were absorbed largely in the task of settling intertribal disputes and in maintaining the position of the Paramount Chief as a symbol of national unity. From 1884 to 1959 legislative and executive authority was vested in a British High Commissioner. In 1910, the Basutoland Council, which had come into existence on an informal basis in 1903, was formally established as a consultative body.

Badly eroded and subject to droughts, the country produces mohair, wool, and hides from livestock. There are only about 1,000 square miles of cultivable land and many food supplies must be imported.

Although there has been an increase of revenue under a revised customs union with South Africa, much of Lesotho's income is derived from the wages of Basotho men who work as contract laborers in South African gold and coal mines.

There has been some development of light industry, tourism, and an increase of diamond mining, but Lesotho has little prospect of ending its economic dependence on South Africa. To a large extent, Lesotho is little more than one of the bantustans, or separate African homelands, that have been created in South Africa itself.

With the attainment of political independence in 1966, the traditional ruler, King Moshoeshoe II,

tried to reassert royal authority, but after being forced into exile by the prime minister, Chief Leabua Jonathan, agreed to accept a titular, symbolic position.

Although professing to abhor apartheid, Chief Jonathan has advocated what he calls a realistic "bread-and-butter good-neighbor policy." But despite extreme poverty, Lesotho has achieved considerable progress in education—it has one of the highest literacy rates in Africa—and many Basotho, who are well educated and highly politicized, resent South Africa's racist regime.

When in early 1970, Jonathan appeared to have lost the country's first national elections, he declared the results invalid, jailed his leading opponents, and seized control. Although threatened with withdrawal of British aid, the plump, disarmingly jolly Jonathan has since ruled by decree.

Chief Jonathan has welcomed back the king from exile, talked of political reconciliation, and successfully suppressed several outbreaks of rebellion, including one in 1974 in which 20 rebels were killed in a plot allegedly hatched by the opposition Congress Party.

HISTORY: Decimated by Zulu and Matabele raids in the early 19th century, the Basotho were later fused into a new nation in the mountains of Basutoland (Lesotho) by Moshesh (Moshoeshoe) I. The king soon had to contend with Boers in the neighboring Orange Free State and sought the protection of the British Cape Colony. Annexation by the colony in 1868, however, led to more fighting, and in 1884 Basutoland again was made a British protectorate. In 1909 an Act of Parliament, establishing the Union of South Africa, stipulated that Basutoland, as well as Bechuanaland (Botswana) and Swaziland, would not be transferred to their more powerful neighbor without prior consent of the inhabitants

1910: A consultative Basutoland Council, made up of Basotho chiefs and leaders, is established by the British

1959-60: A constitution is promulgated and a more representative legislative body, the Basutoland National Council, is set up

1961: South Africa's apartheid policies cause Britain to reaffirm that Basutoland and other protectorates will not be handed over to South African rule

1966: Basutoland gains independence as Lesotho

1967: Held under house arrest after attempting to assert absolute authority, King Moshoeshoe II accedes to Prime Minister Leabua Jonathan's demands that he reign as constitutional monarch

1970: Prime Minister Jonathan seizes control, suspends constitution, declares a state of emergency, and imprisons his opponent, Ntsu Mokhehle, following disputed election

1973: Prime Minister Jonathan announces end of three-year state of emergency

1974: 20 rebels killed in attempt to overthrow government

1975: Miners recruited from Lesotho strike gold mine in South Africa to protest a Lesotho law requiring miners to remit 60 percent of their pay and deposit it in Lesotho banks

---

LIBERIA

Area: 43,000 sq. mi. **Population:** 1,800,000 (1978 est.)

Official Name: Republic of Liberia **Capital:** Monrovia **Nationality:** Liberian **Languages:** English, the official and commerical language, is spoken by about 20% of the population; some 28 African dialects are also spoken **Religion:** 75% animist, 10% Christian, 15% Moslem **Flag:** Eleven red and white horizontal stripes, with a five-pointed white star on a blue field in the upper left corner **Anthem:** National Anthem, beginning "All hail, Liberia, hail!" **Currency:** U.S. (Liberian) dollar

Location: West Africa. Liberia is bordered on the northeast by Guinea, on the east by the Ivory Coast, on the south and west by the Atlantic Ocean, and on the north by Sierra Leone **Features:** The country is flat, with the exception of some hills in the region of Monrovia, the Bomi Hills, and the Guinea Highlands. About 40% of the country is covered by tropical woodlands **Chief Rivers:** Mano, Lofa, St. Paul, St. John, Cestos

Head of State and of Government: President William R. Tolbert, Jr., born 1913; he took office in July 1971 and was elected for 8 years in January 1976 **Effective Date of Present Constitution:** 1847 **Legislative Body:** Congress (bicameral), consisting of a Senate and a House of Representatives. The Senate has 18 members elected for 6 years. The House of Representatives has 70 members elected for 4 years. All members of Congress belong to the True Whig Party, the only legal party **Local Government:** 9 counties, headed by appointed superintendents

Ethnic Composition: More than 97% of the population is made up of indigenous Africans belonging to about 16 tribal groups. About 2.5% of the population are Americo-Liberian descendants of 19th century emancipated black American slaves **Population Distribution:** 28% urban **Density:** 42 inhabitants per sq. mi.

Largest Cities: (1976 est.) Monrovia 204,000, Harbel 60,000, Buchanan 25,000, Yekepa 16,000, Harper 14,000

Per Capita Income: $660 (1978) **Gross National Product (GNP):** $1 billion (1978 est.) **Economic Statistics:** About 33% of GNP comes from mining; 17% from agriculture (rubber, casava, rice, bananas, plantains), forestry, and fishing; and 11% from wholesale and retail trade **Minerals and Mining:** Liberia is the world's 10th largest producer of high-grade iron ore. Diamonds are of importance, and there are unexploited reserves of manganese, gold, columbite, tantalite, and bauxite **Labor Force:** 425,000, with 72% in agriculture, and only 25% in the monetary economy, chiefly on rubber plantations, in government, construction, and mining **Foreign Trade:** Exports, chiefly iron ore, rubber, and diamonds, totaled $447 million in 1977. Imports, mainly manufactured goods, machinery, transportation equipment, and food, totaled $464 million **Principal Trade Partners:** United States, West Germany, Japan, Britain, Italy, Sweden

Vital Statistics: Birthrate, 49.8 per 1,000 of pop. (1971); death rate, 20.9 **Life Expectancy:** 46 years **Health Statistics:** 509 inhabitants per hospital bed; 12,576 per physician (1973) **Infant Mortality:** 159.2 per 1,000 births **Illiteracy:** 76% **Education Statistics:** 1,155 primary and secondary schools, with combined enrollment of 191,972 (1975) **Enrollment in Higher Education:** 2,404 (1975) **GNP Expended on Education:** 2.2% (1975)

Transportation: Paved roads total 325 mi. **Motor Vehicles:** 22,100 (1974) **Passenger Cars:** 12,100 **Railway Mileage:** 304 **Ports:** Monrovia, Buchanan, Greenville, Harper **Major Airlines:** Air Liberia, Air Taxi Company, and Ducor Air Transport Company operate internal services **Communications:** Partly government owned **Radio Transmitters:** 15 **Receivers:** 265,000 (1976) **Television Transmitters:** 4 **Receivers:** 18,800 (1974) **Telephones:** 7,500 (1974) **Newspapers:** 3 dailies, 8 copies per 1,000 inhabitants

Weights and Measures: U.S. standards are used **Travel Requirements:** Passport; visa valid for 90 days; $2 fee; 3 pictures

A green, rainy land settled in the early 1820s by freed black slaves from the United States, Liberia is Africa's oldest independent republic. Originally a neglected stepchild of the United States, the first Liberian commonwealth managed to survive, and in 1847 established itself as a sovereign state. The United States refused to recognize the country until 1862, long after the European powers had done so. Its constitution, institutions and flag are closely modeled on those of the United States; through American investment, aid, and other ties, the West African nation has maintained close relations with the U.S.

The making of Liberia into a modern country, with a viable economy and position of leadership in African affairs, has been almost entirely the work of the late William V.S. Tubman, Liberia's president from 1944 until his death in 1971.

A forceful and sometimes autocratic leader, Mr. Tubman spurred economic development through industry and iron-ore mining at a time when Liberia seemed to be lagging behind newer African nations. He established an "open door" policy on foreign investment and programs to improve agriculture and the living standards of the indigenous tribal peoples, who benefited from his National Unification Policy.

Liberia's colonization by American blacks was the outgrowth of manumission, a system by which slaves could be freed by their owners. As more and more slaves were freed, however, many Americans became uneasy about their numbers and legal status. In 1816 the American Colonization Society was chartered by Congress to promote a "back-to-Africa" movement.

Lacking money and technology, as well as outside interest, the early Liberians were unable to progress beyond a simple rural economy. Contemporary Liberians often comment, "We missed out on the benefits of colonialism."

During World War II, however, American money and manpower poured in to give the country the big Robertsfield Airport; a new seaport at the cap-

ital, Monrovia; and the first network of modern roads. There followed the iron-ore boom of the 1950s with huge investments by American and European mining companies, which resulted in Liberia ranking as Africa's most important iron ore-producing nation. There are large foreign investments in rubber plantations, and half of the country's wage earners are in the rubber industry.

William Tolbert succeeded Tubman as president. In 1973, Tolbert was the target of an assassination attempt by two army colonels and a former deputy defense minister, who were later sentenced to death for their plot.

HISTORY: Before being colonized early in the 19th century by freed black slaves from the United States, Liberia was known as the Grain Coast for its production of grains of melegueta pepper. The indigenous peoples, among them Kru, Gola, Mandingo, and Vai, are believed to derive from ancient black nations of sub-Saharan regions farther north. During the several centuries of the slave trade, the country was steadily drained of population

1816: American Colonization Society is founded to send freed slaves to Western Africa

1822: First group of settlers arrives from United States and establishes colony on Providence Island, at present site of Monrovia, purchased by American Colonization Society

1824: Name "Liberia" is adopted and chief settlement is named Monrovia in honor of U.S. President James Monroe

1847: Joseph Jenkins Roberts, governor of the Liberian Commonwealth, a Virginia-born freeman of part-black ancestry, proclaims independent Republic of Liberia and becomes first president

1850-1920: Territory is lost to neighboring British, French colonies; economy and finances deteriorate, but government rejects proposal for international receivership

1923-26: Firestone Tire and Rubber Company assists government financially and begins development of rubber

1943: True Whig Party candidate William V.S. Tubman becomes president; begins programs of social unification to speed assimilation of indigenous population into the rest of the community, and policy of "open door" for foreign investment

1955: Opposition Reformation and Independent True Whig parties are charged with plot to overthrow government by force and are banned; True Whig Party becomes dominant

1967: President Tubman is reelected to sixth successive term

1971: Tubman dies and is succeeded by Vice-President Tolbert

1975: Treaty is signed with EEC. Tolbert is elected for an eight-year term as president

1979: 41 rioters, protesting rise in prices of rice, are killed by police and army in Monrovia. Organization for African Unity holds conference in capital

LIBYA

Area: 679,358 sq. mi. **Population:** 2,600,000 (1978 est.)

Official Name: Socialist People's Libyan Arab Jamahiriya **Capital:** Tripoli **Nationality:** Libyan **Languages:** Arabic is the official and dominant language; English and Italian are also used **Religion:** 97% Sunni Moslem **Flag:** A plain green field **Anthem:** Almighty God **Currency:** Libyan dinar (30 per U.S. $1)

Location: North Africa. Libya is bordered on the north by the Mediterranean Sea, on the east by Egypt, on the southeast by the Sudan, on the south by Chad and Niger, on the west by Algeria, and on the northwest by Tunisia **Features:** About 90% of the terrain consists of barren, rock-strewn plains and deserts, with three elevated regions in the northwest, northeast and extreme south **Chief Rivers:** There are no permanent rivers

Head of State: Colonel Muammar Qaddafi, born 1943; seized power in 1969; re-elected July 1972. He also is defense minister **Head of Government:** Jadallah Azzuz al Talhi, chairman of the General People's Committee (prime minister), appointed 1979 **Effective Date of Present Constitution:** 1969, amended 1977 **Legislative Body:** Parliament (bicameral), dissolved 1969; a general People's Congress, headed by a General Secretary, Abd al Ati Ubaydi, born 1939 **Local Government:** 10 governorates, each under an appointed governor

Ethnic Composition: The population is chiefly a racial mixture of Arabs and Berbers **Population Distribution:** 30% urban **Density:** 4 inhabitants per sq. mi.

Largest Cities: (1973 census) Tripoli 281,497, Benghazi 131,970, Zawia 52,327, Misurata 45,146, Sabratha 30,817, Tarhuna 23,338

Per Capita Income: $6,750 (1978) **Gross National Product (GNP):** $18.6 billion (1978) **Economic Statistics:** In 1975 about 52% of GNP came from oil, 3% from agriculture (wheat, barley, tomatoes, dates, citrus fruits, olives, livestock); and 13% from manufacturing (food processing, textiles, soaps, detergents, paper bags and wrapping paper) **Minerals and Mining:** Libya is one of the world's largest oil producers. Other minerals are gypsum, natural gas, marble, iron ore, and potassium **Labor Force:** 745,000 (1976) with 20% in agriculture, 5% in industry; and 20% in services **Foreign Trade:** Exports, consisting almost exclusively of crude oil, totaled $9.7 billion in 1977. Imports, mainly oil drilling equipment and machinery, iron and steel pipes, tubes, and fittings, manufactured goods, and food products, totaled $3.2 billion (1976) **Principal Trade Partners:** West Germany, Britain, Italy, United States, France, Japan

Vital Statistics: Birthrate, 45 per 1,000 of pop. (1975); death rate, 14.7 **Life Expectancy:** 53 years **Health Statistics:** 242 inhabitants per hospital bed; 944 per physician (1975) **Infant Mortality:** N.A. **Illiteracy:** 64% **Education Statistics:** 1,940 primary and secondary schools, with combined enrollment of 662,541 (1974) **Enrollment in Higher Education:** 11,997 **GNP Expended on Education:** 2.8% (1975)

Transportation: Paved roads total 3,790 mi. **Motor Vehicles:** 394,400 (1975) **Passenger Cars:** 263,100 **Railway Mileage:** none (790 mi. planned in 1976) **Ports:** Tripoli, Benghazi, El Brega, Ras Lanuf, Zueitina, Syrte, El Hariga, Derna, Tobruk **Major Airlines:** Libyan Arab Airways operates domestic and international services **Communications:** Government-owned **Radio Transmitters:** 12 **Licenses:** 110,000 (1976) **Television Transmitters:** 2 **Licenses:** 10,000 (1975) **Telephones:** 45,000 (1975) **Newspapers:** 2 dailies, 17 copies per 1,000 inhabitants (1975)

Weights and Measures: Metric system and local units are used **Travel Requirements:** Passport (with Arabic translation); visa valid for 3 months for 30-day stay; $7 fee; 2 pictures

HISTORY: In ancient times, Libya was successively ruled by Carthage, Rome, and the Vandals. The Arabs conquered the country in the 7th century A.D. In the Middle Ages, Egypt and Tunisia vied for control of the country, and in the early 16th century Spain and the Knights of Malta replaced the African rivals in dominating Libya. The Ottoman Empire seized control in 1551, although Libya's local pashas continued to enjoy autonomy

1830: Turks reassert control over Libya

1911-33: Italy occupies Libya following Turco-Italian War (1911-12) and engages in long series of wars of pacification against the Sanusi, a Moslem religious brotherhood

1943-49: Libya is conquered by Allied forces in World War II; Tripolitania and Cyrenaica are placed under British administration and the Fezzan under French administration

1951: Kingdom of Libya gains formal independence, with Idris I, leader of the Sanusi brotherhood, as the country's first king

1954: United States is granted military air base in Libya

1959-61: Oil is discovered in Tripolitania and Cyrenaica in 1959

1967: Libya charges United States with helping Israel in Six-Day Middle Eastern War, calls on United States to liquidate Wheelus Air Force Base

1969: Monarchy is overthrown by a military junta composed of young nationalist army officers. Colonel Qaddafi, their leader, becomes prime minister in 1970

1970: Junta takes over Wheelus Air Force Base, buys Mirage jets from France, and renegotiates contracts with Western oil companies to gain greater share of oil revenues

1973: Qaddafi introduces the "cultural revolution," an attempt to govern Libya according to the tenets of Islam. Establishes "people's committees" to carry out the revolution

1974: Qaddafi relinquishes political and administrative functions; announces he will concentrate on ideology and organization. Premier Abdul Salam Jalloud assumes Qaddafi's former duties. When President Sadat of Egypt rejects a merger between their countries, Qaddafi's relations with Egypt cool

1975: Creation of 618-member General National Congress is decreed to implement theories of Colonel Qaddafi

1976: Relations with Egypt deteriorate when Libyan soldiers are arrested in Cairo in connection with a plot to kidnap Major Omar Meheishi, a dissident member of the Revolutionary Command Council who fled Libya in 1975 after an attempted coup against Colonel Qaddafi. In retaliation Egyptians are expelled from Libya and their property confiscated. Libya purchases 10 percent interest in Fiat, the Italian auto manufacturer

1977: Libyan and Egyptian troops and aircraft battle along border

1979: Libya secretly sends soldiers to Uganda to defend government of President Idi Amin Dada against Tanzanian attack. Libyan airplane bombs Tanzania. Libya invades Chad in attempt to annex Chadian territory; invasion fails

Consisting mostly of arid desert, the land that is now Libya was a bone of contention among empires for thousands of years. Its most influential conquerors were the Moslem Arabs of the seventh century A.D.; they gave Libya the language and the religion that now prevail. Its most recent conqueror was Italy. After losing World War II, Italy was forced to grant independence to Libya in 1951. Idris, a Moslem chieftain, became king. But, with no natural resources except a location that was strategic in the Cold War, Libya was heavily dependent on the United States, which gave considerable assistance in return for the use of Wheelus Air Force Base.

With the discovery of oil in 1959, Libya, with less than 3 million people, became potentially a power in its own right. King Idris used the oil revenue to build schools, hospitals, highways, and low-cost housing.

But Libya did not achieve its real international potential until after the overthrow of King Idris by the army in 1969. A Revolutionary Command Council of military officers, headed by Colonel Muammar Qaddafi, took control of the nation. Desert-born, with little understanding of the non-Moslem world, Qaddafi made Libya a bastion of strict Moslem traditionalism; he was in the vanguard of the Islamic revival. He outlawed liquor, imposed a strict dress code for women, and made amputation the standard penalty for theft. A bitter enemy of big powers, he closed Wheelus Air Force Base, published manifestos condemning U.S. action in Vietnam and Soviet action in Czechoslovakia, and helped Malta to force the closing of British bases. A strident foe of Israel, he used foreign aid to move Jordan toward a militant stance. He continued King Idris' policy of aiding Moslem rebels in Chad, and quarreled with Egypt over boundaries and over Egypt's more moderate approach to Israel.

The first half of 1979 was a good time for Libyan diplomacy and a bad time for Libyan arms. Libya was leader in the successful movement to isolate Egypt from the Arab world after Egypt's peace treaty with Israel; and the Islamic revolution in Iran created a regime similar to Libya's. But Libya failed in its surreptitious intervention in Uganda on behalf of President Idi Amin Dada; despite Libyan aid, Amin, an unpopular Moslem dictator of a non-Moslem country, was overthrown. Libya's attempt to annex a strip of Chad also failed.

LIECHTENSTEIN

Area: 61 sq. mi. **Population:** 25,000 (1978 est.)

Official Name: Principality of Liechtenstein **Capital:** Vaduz **Nationality:** Liechtensteiner **Languages:** German is the official language; Alemannic, a dialect, is spoken by most **Religion:** Roman Catholicism is the official religion and claims about 92% of the population **Flag:** Blue and red horizontal stripes, with a golden crown near the staff end of the blue stripe **Anthem:** National Anthem, beginning "Above on the German Rhine" **Currency:** Swiss franc (1.72 per U.S. $1)

Location: Western Europe. Liechtenstein, situated in the Rhine River Valley, is bordered by Austria on the east and by Switzerland on the south and west **Features:** One-third of the area is level land bordering the right bank of the Rhine, and an upland and mountainous area occupies the remainder **Chief Rivers:** Rhine, Samina

Head of State: Prince Franz Josef II, born 1906, ascended the throne 1938 **Head of Government:** Prime Minister: Hans Brunhart, chairman of the 5-man Collegial Board, appointed April 1978 **Effective Date of Present Constitution:** 1921 **Legislative Body:** Parliament (unicameral *Landtag*), consisting of 15 members, elected for 4 years by male suffrage **Local Government:** 11 communes, with limited powers of self-government

Ethnic Composition: The population is of Germanic descent; one-third is alien, mostly Swiss, Austrian and German **Population Distribution:** Predominantly rural **Density:** 410 inhabitants per sq. mi.

Largest Cities: (1974 est.) Vaduz 7,500; (1970 census) Schaan 3,890, Balzers 2,704, Triesen 2,637, Mauren 2,055

Per Capita Income: $16,864 (1978) **Economic Statistics:** Some 40% of the land is used for raising crops (corn and other cereals, potatoes, garden produce, fruits), but the main source of income from land use is raising beef and dairy cattle. Industry is mainly devoted to the small-scale production of precision manufactures (calculating machines, optical lenses, high vacuum pumps), false teeth and textiles. About 10,000 foreign firms maintain nominal headquarters in Vaduz, because of liberal tax incentives. Tourism and the sale of stamps are also important sources of income **Minerals and Mining:** Except for some quarrying, there is no mining **Labor Force:** About 10,500, of which 59% is in industry, 20% in trade and commerce, 13% in the professions, and 7% in agriculture **Foreign Trade:** Exports are chiefly special machinery and tools, artificial teeth, textiles, chemicals, and food. Liechtenstein has a customs union with Switzerland and there are no records of foreign trade totals **Principal Trade Partners:** EFTA and Common Market countries

Vital Statistics: Birthrate, 12.6 per 1,000 of pop. (1975); death rate, 7.3 **Life Expectancy:** 65 years **Health Statistics:** Hospital facilities exist in nearby Switzerland; 1,633 inhabitants per physician (1971) **Infant Mortality:** 7.4 per 1,000 births **Illiteracy:** Negligible **Education Statistics:** 17 primary and secondary schools, with combined enrollment of 4,445 pupils (1972) **Enrollment in Higher Education:** 243 **GNP Expended on Education:** N.A.

Transportation: Good paved roads serve the principality **Motor Vehicles:** 11,000 (1976) **Passenger Cars:** 10,000 **Railway Mileage:** 11.5 **Ports:** None **Major Airlines:** None **Communications:** Served by Switzerland **Radio Stations:** None **Licenses:** 5,000 (1976) **Television Stations:** None **Licenses:** 4,500 (1976) **Telephones:** 16,000 (1976) **Newspapers:** 1 daily, 286 copies per 1,000 inhabitants

Weights and Measures: Metric system **Travel Requirements:** Passport; no visa for 3 months

---

Since 1923 the tiny principality of Liechtenstein, wedged between Austria and Switzerland, has had a customs union with Switzerland, and that country also provides Liechtenstein's currency, administers its postal, telegraph, and telephone services; and handles Liechtenstein's international affairs. In World War II, Liechtenstein, like Switzerland, was a neutral.

Though bucolic, with lush green valleys and houses with red-tile roofs, the state has mainly an industrial economy. Only seven percent of the population is engaged in agricultural pursuits.

Liechtenstein has become industrialized in the last quarter of a century: it contains Europe's biggest producer of false teeth and dental supplies, and is noted for such precision products as thin optic coatings and electronic microscopy. The industrialization has brought an influx of Swiss, Austrian, and German workers.

The principality is a tax haven for corporations and holding companies. Additional sources of income are tourism and the sale of postage stamps. Though Liechtenstein has neither a broadcasting station nor an airport, it is the repository of art valued at somewhere near $150 million, the holdings of Liechtenstein's monarch, Prince Franz Josef II.

In 1978, Liechtenstein joined the Council of Europe, although other nations represented in the Council objected to the principality's voting laws; alone in Europe, Liechtenstein does not allow women to vote for members of its national legislature. Women may vote in local elections in Vaduz.

HISTORY: The principality of Liechtenstein was created in 1719 as a fief of the Holy Roman Empire by uniting the barony of Schellenberg and the county of Vaduz, both of which had been purchased from the counts of Hohenem by the Austrian family of Liechtenstein. During the Napoleonic Wars, the principality was invaded by the French. In 1815, after Napoleon's downfall, Liechtenstein joined the newly formed Germanic Confederation

1866: Germanic Confederation is dissolved after Prussia's victory over Austria in the Seven Weeks' War, thus ending Liechtenstein's ties to other German states

1868: Liechtenstein, which had furnished Austria with 80 soldiers during the war with Prussia, disbands its military force and adopts policy of permanent neutrality

1919-24: Switzerland assumes control of Liechtenstein's external affairs and forms customs union with principality

1938: Prince Franz I is succeeded by his great-nephew, who, as Franz Josef II, becomes the first ruler to make Liechtenstein his permanent home

1945-65: Having avoided involvement in World War II, Liechtenstein enjoys rapid economic growth, developing into a center of tourism, trade, and small-scale manufacturing

1970: Traditional minority Patriotic Union wins one-vote majority in

Landtag, ending 42-year leadership of coalition government by Progressive Citizens Party

1973: Electorate again denies women the franchise

1974: Progressive Citizens Party regains majority in parliament

1978: Hans Brunhart of Fatherland Union Party is appointed prime minister; government is virtually paralyzed for two months as outgoing prime minister balks at relinquishing post of foreign minister, in addition to prime ministership; president rules former prime minister and his successor may share foreign ministership

---

LUXEMBOURG

Area: 999 sq. mi. **Population:** 360,000 (1978 est.)

Official Name: Grand Duchy of Luxembourg **Capital:** Luxembourg **Nationality:** Luxembourgian **Languages:** French is the official language. German is used in local newspapers. Luxembourgeois (Letzeburgisch) is the everyday language **Religion:** 97% Roman Catholic; 3% Protestant and Jewish **Flag:** A tricolor of red, white, and blue horizontal stripes **Anthem:** Our Homeland **Currency:** Luxembourg franc (30.2 per U.S. $1)

Location: Western Europe. Landlocked Luxembourg is bordered on the north and west by Belgium, on the east by the Federal Republic of Germany, and on the south by France **Features:** The northern part of the country contains the rugged uplands of the Ardennes plateau, while the south consists of undulating terrain with broad valleys **Chief Rivers:** Alzette, Sûre, Moselle, Our

Head of State: Grand Duke Jean, born 1921, ascended the throne 1964 **Head of Government:** Premier Pierre Werner, appointed 1979 **Effective Date of Present Constitution:** 1868 **Legislative Body:** Parliament (bicameral), consisting of a Chamber of Deputies of 59 members, elected for 5 years, and a Council of State appointed by the Grand Duke **Local Government:** 12 cantons grouped into 3 districts; the 126 communes are the administrative units of local government, administered by elected councils

Ethnic Composition: Luxembourgers are ethnically a mixture of French and German. Throughout the 20th century, a considerable number of immigrants from Italy and other Mediterranean countries have settled in Luxembourg **Population Distribution:** 69% urban **Density:** 360 inhabitants per sq. mi.

Largest Cities: (1974 est.) Luxembourg 78,403; (1970 census) Esch/Alzette 27,574, Differdange 17,964, Dudelange 14,615

Per Capita Income: $6,889 (1978) **Gross National Product (GNP):** $2.5 billion (1978) **Economic Statistics:** About 5.3% of GNP comes from agriculture (livestock, dairy products, wine), 52% from industry (steel, rubber, synthetic fibers), 15.4% from trade and finance, 27.3% from services **Minerals and Mining:** Vast deposits of iron ore are mined; slate is also quarried in commercial quantities **Labor Force:** 147,700 (1976) of which 46% is in industry, 6% in agriculture (grapes, livestock), 48% in services **Foreign Trade:** Exports, chiefly steel, chemical products, plastic fibers, rubber and textiles, totaled $1.8 billion in 1977. Imports, mainly coal and iron ore, machinery, transportation equipment, and food, totaled $2 billion **Principal Trade Partners:** EEC countries

Vital Statistics: Birthrate, 11.4 per 1,000 of pop. (1977); death rate, 12.6 **Life Expectancy:** 73 years **Health Statistics:** 88 inhabitants per hospital bed; 978 per physician (1974) **Infant Mortality:** 14.8 per 1,000 births (1975) **Illiteracy:** 2% **Education Statistics:** 1,667 primary and secondary schools with combined enrollment of 55,928 (1973) **Enrollment in Higher Education:** 483 (1975) **GNP Expended on Education:** 5.2% (1973)

Transportation: Surfaced roads total 3,085 mi. **Motor Vehicles:** 141,000 (1976) **Passenger Cars:** 130,700 **Railway Mileage:** 215 **Ports:** None **Major Airlines:** LUXAIR operates regular services to Western Europe; Icelandic Airlines maintains a regular service to the United States **Communications:** Privately owned **Radio Transmitters:** 7 **Licenses:** 205,000 (1976) **Television Transmitters:** 4 **Licenses:** 105,000 (1976) **Telephones:** 158,000 (1976) **Newspapers:** 7 dailies, 560 copies per 1,000 inhabitants (1975)

Weights and Measures: Metric system **Travel Requirements:** Passport; no visa for less than 3 months

---

The Grand Duchy of Luxembourg, covering an area of 999 square miles, and with a population of over 350,000, is the equal of Sweden in the production of iron and steel. Centered at Esch-sur-Alzette, Luxembourg's iron and steel industry draws on iron ore deposits in the Luxembourg/Lorraine basin for half its needs, importing the remainder, as well as coal for its mills. The duchy, however, has avoided dependence on a single industry and has achieved considerable economic diversification with the construction of chemical plants, factories making automotive parts and tires, and other industries. American capital was the source of much of this diversification, with investments coming also from Luxembourg's Common Market partners.

Agriculture is of the small-scale, mixed-farming type, and livestock breeding is important. Among Luxembourg's exports are dairy products, pigs, and roses, and its vineyards in the Moselle Valley produce fine white wines. Trilingual Luxembourgers, speaking their own patois plus French and German, call the southern part of the grand duchy *Bon Pays* or *Gutland*—in English, the "Good Land"—because of its agricultural qualities.

Most industry is concentrated in the extreme south, and all in all Luxembourg offers the tourist picturesque scenery, good food and drink, an excellent road system, and, for the hiker, extensive paths between old villages.

On the darker side is the fact that the duchy has twice been overrun in this century by German troops, with liberation coming both times with the arrival of American forces. At Hamm, outside Luxembourg City, more than 5,000 American soldiers, including General George S. Patton, Jr., lie buried.

Since the war Luxembourg has officially abandoned neutrality. In 1949 it became a charter member of the North Atlantic Treaty Organization and has since been one of the leading promoters of closer European cooperation. It was a pioneer in the kind of economic cooperation now exemplified by the European Community, having formed, in 1921, a customs union with Belgium; the union became *Benelux* when the Netherlands joined in 1948.

HISTORY: The county of Luxembourg, including the present Belgian province of Luxembourg, emerged in the 10th century and rose to prominence in 1308, when its ruler was elected Holy Roman Emperor. Raised to a duchy in 1354, Luxembourg passed to the Hapsburgs in 1482. During the next three centuries, the duchy's history was bound up with the southern Netherlands, which passed from Spanish to Austrian rule in 1714. France occupied the duchy during the French Revolutionary Wars and formally annexed it in 1797

1815: Congress of Vienna makes Luxembourg a grand duchy, in personal union with the Kingdom of the Netherlands

1839: Belgium, having won its independence from the Netherlands, annexes the present Belgian province of Luxembourg; it constituted the major part of the grand duchy

1867: Luxembourg is declared an independent, neutral state in personal union with the Netherlands by the Treaty of London

1890: William III of the Netherlands dies and is succeeded on the Dutch throne by his daughter Wilhelmina; however, Luxembourg passes to Duke Adolf of Nassau, who becomes grand duke

1914-18: Luxembourg, its neutrality violated by Germany, is occupied by German forces during World War I

1940: German forces invade grand duchy in World War II; ducal family and cabinet flee to London

1944: Luxembourg is liberated by Allied forces

1949: Grand duchy formally abandons its perpetual neutrality and joins North Atlantic Treaty Organization

1964: Grand Duchess Charlotte abdicates in favor of son Jean

1968-69: Christian Socialist/Socialist coalition government of Premier Pierre Werner falls in October 1968 after government refuses to agree to demands by Socialist trade union leaders for higher wages and greater welfare benefits; following new elections, Werner forms a new government of Christian Socialists and Socialists and is reappointed premier in 1969

1972: Voting age is lowered from 21 to 18

1974: Premier Werner's government falls, ending 55 years of unbroken control by Christian Socialists. Democrat Gaston Thorn becomes premier, leading a coalition of socialists and liberals

1977: Government studies problem of low birthrate of native Luxembourgers. Southern European immigrants, with higher birth rate, now constitute 24 percent of population

MADAGASCAR

Area: 226,657 sq. mi. Population: 8,520,000 (1978 est.)
Official Name: Democratic Republic of Madagascar Capital: Antananarivo Nationality: Malagasy Languages: Malagasy and French are the official languages; Hova and other dialects are also widely spoken Religion: About 55% animist; 40% Christian, and 5% Moslem Flag: A white vertical band at the staff and 2 horizontal bands, the upper red, the lower green Anthem: O, Our Beloved Fatherland Currency: Malagasy franc (219 per U.S. $1)

Location: Indian Ocean. The 4th largest island in the world—after Greenland, New Guinea, and Borneo—Madagascar is situated some 250 miles off the east coast of Africa, from which it is separated by the Mozambique Channel Features: The terrain consists of a central belt of eroded highlands extending from the northeast to the southwest, sloping steeply eastward to a narrow, swampy coast and passing gradually to more extensive lowlands in the west. An inland plateau rises to 9,450 feet Chief Rivers: Mangoro, Ikopa, Onilahy, Tsiribihina, Mangoky, Sofia

Head of State and of Government: President: Commander Didier Ratsiraka, born 1936, assumed power in a coup in June 1975 as head of Supreme Revolutionary Council, and elected president in December 1975; he is aided by an elected People's National Development Council, and by a cabinet headed by the premier, Desire Rakotoarijaona, appointed August 1977 Effective Date of Present Constitution: 1975 Legislative Body: A National Popular Assembly of 137 members was elected in 1977 Local Government: 6 provinces, each headed by an administrator

Ethnic Composition: The population is of Malayan-Indonesian origin, with an admixture of Arab and African strains; of 18 major groups, the most numerous are the Merina (Hova), Betsileo, Betsimisaraka, Sakalava and Tsimihety. There are about 10,000 French, 17,000 Indians, 9,000 Chinese, and 34,000 immigrants from the Comoro Islands Population Distribution: 14% urban Density: 38 inhabitants per sq. mi.

Largest Cities: (1971 est.) Antananarivo 400,000, Antsirabe 70,000, Tamatave 59,000, Fianarantsoa 59,000, Majunga 55,000, Diego-Suarez 45,000, Tulear 39,000

Per Capita Income: $227 (1978) Gross National Product (GNP): $2.2 billion (1978) Economic Statistics: In 1973 about 30% of the GNP came from agriculture (rice, coffee, tobacco, cloves, cocoa, vanilla, livestock), 13% from industry (including oil refining) and mining, and 31% from trade and services Minerals and Mining: Graphite, mica, gold, and industrial beryl are mined, but are not extensive Labor Force: 3.6 million, of which 84% is in agriculture; and 5% in industry Foreign Trade: Exports, chiefly coffee, vanilla, sugar, rice, cloves, and raffia, totaled $292 million in 1976. Imports, mainly transportation machinery, textiles, chemicals, pharmaceuticals, machinery, and electrical appliances, totaled $214 million Principal Trade Partners: France, United States, West Germany, Japan, Italy

Vital Statistics: Birthrate, 46.0 per 1,000 of pop. (1966); death rate 25.0 Life Expectancy: 38 years Health Statistics: 405 inhabitants per hospital bed; 10,665 per physician (1975) Infant Mortality: 53.2 per 1,000 births (1972) Illiteracy: 60% Education Statistics: 6,072 primary and secondary schools, with combined enrollment of 1,161,368 (1973) Enrollment in Higher Education: 8,385 (1975) GNP Expended on Education: 4% (1973)

Transportation: Paved roads total 2,500 mi. Motor Vehicles: 106,000 (1974) Passenger Cars: 55,000 Railway Mileage: 532 Ports: Tamatave, Majunga, Nossi-Be, Diego-Suarez, Tulear Major Airlines: Air Madagascar operates domestic and international services Communications: Government controlled Radio Transmitters: 16 Receivers: 609,000 (1975) Television Transmitters: 5 Receivers: 8,000 (1976) Telephones: 32,000 (1976) Newspapers: 9 dailies, 9 copies per 1,000 inhabitants (1974)

Weights and Measures: Metric system Travel Requirements: Passport; visa valid for stay up to 1 month; $6.10 fee; 4 photos

Madagascar, known as the Malagasy Republic until 1976, is "the land at the end of the earth," a blend of Shangri-la and Lost World. Although near Africa—250 miles off the continent's southeast coast—Madagascar and its people, the Malagasy, appear to be more a part of southeast Asia. The island was settled, according to Malagasy folklore, more than 2,000 years ago by people who drifted or sailed across the Indian Ocean from the Malay-Indonesia area. Their descendants speak a language considered to be of Malayan-Polynesian origin and, while some show admixtures of African and Arab settlers, most have an Indochinese physique.

While unknown to much of the world, Madagascar was prized as a naval base in the contest of the British and French imperialisms. Triumph by the French brought an overthrow of the Malagasy monarchy, but not submission.

Despite their placid appearance, the Malagasy rose in a bloody and unsuccessful revolt against

French rule in 1947. When, in 1960, the island became a fully sovereign republic under President Philibert Tsiranana, the Malagasy regarded the event as a return to self-rule rather than a granting of independence by a colonial power.

With self-rule, Madagascar has faced problems of resolving internal conflicts, mainly between the traditionally dominant Merina, or plateau people and the *côtiers*, or coastal peoples. President Tsiranana was a *côtier* and former professor who sought to promote both national unity and the development of a sluggish agricultural economy.

Tsiranana favored continued close ties with France and, despite Madagascar's membership in the Organization of African Unity and his own condemnation of apartheid, he welcomed investment and economic aid from South Africa. That policy changed in 1972.

The economy is overwhelmingly agricultural, largely of a subsistence type. Rice is the main crop. New development efforts have been concentrated in mining, with occasional investments made in light manufacturing.

A major change in Madagascar's political life came in 1972 when President Tsiranana was removed from office. Student riots had begun to plague his administration, and a formal referendum was held which transferred power to a new military government headed by Premier Gabriel Ramanantsoa, a moderate leftist.

In February 1975, Ramanantsoa turned over full power to Col. Richard Ratsimandrava after 12 days of political crisis. After six days, Ratsimandrava was assassinated by paramilitary policemen.

The National Military Guidance Committee governed the country until June 15 when it invested Cmdr. Didier Ratsiraka as head of state and dissolved itself. In a referendum, Ratsiraka's presidency and a new constitution were approved by 95 percent of the voters. The nation was to be known henceforth as the Democratic Republic of Madagascar. The military, in control since 1972, has sought to nationalize important segments of the economy.

HISTORY: Despite Madagascar's proximity to Africa, Malagasy tradition and language support the belief that the first waves of migration came from the Sunda Islands (present-day Indonesia), starting a century or two before the Christian era. About A.D. 900, Arab settlers and Africans, brought by slave traders, were added to the population. Beginning in the 16th century, Portuguese, French, and English contested with rival Malagasy kingdoms for dominance of the island, which finally became a French protectorate in the 19th century

1885-1905: France invades Madagascar and establishes a limited protectorate. French consolidate control, but local resistance continues for many years

1942-43: British occupy Vichy-ruled Madagascar to prevent seizure by Japanese; Free French take over

1947: Armed revolt by Malagasy nationalists breaks out in opposition to "French Union" self-rule, lasts nearly a year before French suppress it; death toll is put as high as 80,000

1958: After reforms in 1956 paving way for independence, Madagascar votes "yes" in referendum creating Malagasy Republic within the French Community

1959: Philibert Tsiranana, a former teacher and founder of the Social Democratic Party, is elected first president of the republic

1960: Madagascar is proclaimed a sovereign, independent nation

1965: President Tsiranana is reelected by smashing majority

1972: Following a series of strikes and demands for President Tsiranana's resignation, executive powers are transferred to Gen. Ramanantsoa as premier of a military government

1975: Ramanantsoa turns over power to Col. Richard Ratsimandrava, who is assassinated after six days. A military committee invests Cmdr. Didier Ratsiraka as head of state. Nation renamed Democratic Republic of Madagascar

1978: Rioting in the capital by students and the unemployed leaves three dead. Madagascar lays claim to four Indian Ocean islands administered by French Réunion

MALAWI

Area: 45,747 sq. mi. **Population:** 5,530,000 (1978 est.)

Official Name: Republic of Malawi **Capital:** Lilongwe **Nationality:** Malawian **Languages:** English is the official language. Among the various Bantu languages are Chichewa, Nyanja, Tumbuka, Yao, Tonga, and Ngoni **Religion:** About 50% of the people are Christians, a third Moslems, and the rest animists **Flag:** 3 horizontal stripes of black, red, and green with a red rising sun on the black stripe **Anthem:** National Anthem, beginning "O God, bless our land of Malawi" **Currency:** Malawian kwacha (.83 per U.S. $1)

Location: East Africa. Landlocked Malawi is bordered on the north and northeast by Tanzania, on the southeast and southwest by Mozambique, and on the northwest by Zambia **Features:** The Great Rift Valley traverses the country from north to south, its deep trough containing the 360-mile-long Lake Nyasa (Malawi). West of the valley, the land rises to form high plateaus between 3,000 and 4,000 feet above sea level, while in the north the Nyika uplands rise to 8,500 feet. South of Lake Nyasa are the Shire Highlands, which rise to steep mountains ranging up to 10,000 feet **Chief Rivers:** Shire, Bua, Rukuru

Head of State and of Government: President: Dr. Hastings Kamuzu Banda, born 1906, elected by National Assembly in 1966, made president for life by constitutional amendment in November 1970; he also holds 5 cabinet posts **Effective Date of Present Constitution:** July 1966 **Legislative Body:** National Assembly (unicameral); 87 members for 5-year terms **Local Government:** 3 regions, divided into 24 districts. Each region has an appointed regional minister, and each district an appointed commissioner

Ethnic Composition: The people are almost all descended from Bantu tribes that arrived between the 16th and 19th centuries. They include the Chewa and the Nyanja, descendants of the Maravi, who emigrated from the southern Congo; the Yao; the Tumbuka; the Lonwe; and the Sena **Population Distribution:** 10% urban **Density:** 121 inhabitants per sq. mi.

Largest Cities: (1974 est.) Lilongwe 75,000; (1971 est.) Blantyre 170,000, Zomba 20,000

Per Capita Income: $159 (1978) **Gross National Product (GNP):** $910 million (1978) **Economic Statistics:** In 1973 over 50% of the GNP was derived from agriculture (tea, tung nuts and oil, tobacco), 13% from industry, and 19% from trade and services **Minerals and Mining:** Production is limited to quarrying constructional stone and limestone; however there are unexploited deposits of bauxite and coal **Labor Force:** 1,500,000, with 85% in subsistence agriculture **Foreign Trade:** Exports, chiefly tobacco, tea, peanuts, corn, and cotton, totaled $160 million in 1976. Imports, mainly textiles, motor vehicles, petroleum products, medical and pharmaceutical goods, and food products, totaled $205 million **Principal Trade Partners:** Britain, South Africa, Netherlands, United States, Japan, West Germany

Vital Statistics: Birthrate, 50.5 per 1,000 of pop. (1974); death rate, 26 **Life Expectancy:** 42 years **Health Statistics:** 639 inhabitants per hospital bed; 37,982 per physician (1970) **Infant Mortality:** 142.1 per 1,000 births **Illiteracy:** 78% **Education Statistics:** 2,929 primary and secondary schools with combined enrollment of 628,745 (1974) **Enrollment in Higher Education:** 1,148 (1975) **GNP Expended on Education:** 2.4% (1974)

Transportation: Improved roads total 1,071 mi. **Motor Vehicles:** 20,800 (1976) **Passenger Cars:** 10,200 **Railway Mileage:** 305 (1970) **Ports:** None **Major Airlines:** Air Malawi, Ltd., the national airline, operates domestic and international services **Communications:** Government controlled **Radio Transmitters:** 15 **Receivers:** 130,000 (1976) **Television:** None **Telephones:** 21,000 (1976) **Newspapers:** 2 dailies, 1.8 copies per 1,000 inhabitants (1975)

Weights and Measures: Metric and British standards **Travel Requirements:** Passport; no visa required for stay up to 1 year

---

Malawi is among Africa's most picturesque yet poorest countries. It is distinguished also in being one of the few independent black African countries to establish official relations with South Africa and in having a despotic president, Dr. H. Kamuzu Banda, who banned the miniskirt, set rules on the length of men's shorts, and, in 1978, banned foreign journalists from the country indefinitely for what he considered unfair, false reporting of recent elections.

Soaring mountains and the long inland sea of Lake Nyasa have won the country the title of "Switzerland of Africa." But the resemblance ends with the scenery. Malawi's economy has been gaining with increased production of tea and tobacco and industrial investment from South Africa and Rhodesia, but with a dense population and per capita income of $159 a year, the country is still far from economic takeoff.

Dr. Banda, an associate and admirer of Ghana's erstwhile ruler, Kwame Nkrumah, has been president of Malawi since the former British protectorate became independent in 1964. In 1970 he had himself made president for life.

While maintaining that he is as much opposed to South Africa's racial policies as any black African leader, Dr. Banda has cited Malawi's need and landlocked position in southern Africa as necessitating close economic ties with her white-ruled neighbors. "I would do business with the Devil himself to help Malawian development," he has said. Nevertheless, Malawi joined 14 other African nations in 1973 in calling for diplomatic and economic sanctions against nations which cooperate with South Africa.

Tourism has become an important business for Malawi. Many hotels, however, have recently reported a drop in bookings as a result of Dr. Banda's rulings about dress, which were aimed at tourists.

Pressures for "Africanization" of property and jobs have been aimed at European landowners and Asian traders. As many as 200,000 Asians have had their businesses "Africanized."

The building of a new capital at Lilongwe, a pet project of Dr. Banda's, was aided by South African loans. Most of the $60-million cost of the new capital is being underwritten by South Africa.

In addition to increasing industry, plans are progressing for bauxite mining and construction of a large aluminum plant. Dr. Banda has said that Malawi either will become economically viable in the next 5 to 10 years or will cease to exist as a truly independent state.

HISTORY: Little is known about the history of Malawi, formerly Nyasaland, prior to the arrival of the Scottish missionary and explorer David Livingstone in 1859. His revulsion at the Arab slave trade moved him to promote establishment of Scottish missions and business groups to develop legitimate commerce as a substitute for the trade in human beings. Britain, in fighting the slave trade and also seeking to prevent encroachment by the Portuguese and Germans, gradually gained control of Nyasaland and set up a protectorate in 1891

1953: Nyasaland, despite strong Nyasa opposition, is joined to new Central African Federation, including also Northern and Southern Rhodesia

1959: Dr. Hastings Kamuzu Banda, leader of Nyasaland African Congress, and more than 1,000 of his followers, are imprisoned, charged with plotting massacre of white officials; after they were absolved they set up Malawi Congress Party

1960-61: Britain grants Nyasaland constitution assuring African majority in Legislative Council; Malawi party wins overwhelming victory in council election

1963: Nyasaland secedes from Central African Federation, which is dissolved; Banda becomes prime minister under new constitution

1964-65: Nyasaland becomes independent Malawi

1966: Malawi becomes a republic within British Commonwealth, with Banda as president

1969: Malawi, at meeting of East and Central African States, refuses to join in manifesto criticizing white-dominated governments of Rhodesia and South Africa

1970: Prime Minister John Vorster of South Africa makes official visit to Malawi, the first such visit by a South African leader to a black African state

1971: President Banda visits South Africa, continuing close relations between Malawi and South Africa

1973: President Banda takes over control of press and radio

1975: Official transfer to new capital at Lilongwe takes place on January 1. Jehovah's Witnesses movement protests alleged persecution of 30,000 members by government

1977: President Banda dismisses his entire cabinet

MALAYSIA

Area: 128,308 sq. mi. **Population:** 12,600,000 (1978 est.)
Official Name: Malaysia **Capital:** Kuala Lumpur **Nationality:** Malaysian **Languages:** Malay (Bahasa Malaysia) is the official language; English, Tamil, and a variety of native, Chinese, and Indian dialects are also spoken **Religion:** Chiefly Moslem, and Islam is the state religion; in Sabah and Sarawak there are many animists. Most of the Chinese follow Buddhism, Confucianism, and Taoism.

Of the Indian community, about 70% are Hindu, 20% Moslem, 5% Christian, and 2% Sikh **Flag:** Fourteen red and white stripes with blue field in upper left corner containing crescent and star in yellow **Anthem:** Our Country **Currency:** ringgit (2.23 per U.S. $1)

Location: Southeast Asia. Malaysia consists of West Malaysia (Malaya), and East Malaysia (Sabah and Sarawak). West Malaysia, on the Malay Peninsula, is bordered on the east by the South China Sea, on the south by the Strait of Johore, on the west by the Strait of Malacca and the Andaman Sea, and on the north by Thailand. Sarawak and Sabah, on the northwestern coast of the island of Borneo, are bordered by Brunei, and by the Indonesian province of Kalimantan on the southeast; on the west, north, and east are the South China, Sulu, and Celebes seas **Features:** Some 80% of the total land area of the country is forested. The Malay Peninsula consists of a spinal mountain range running roughly north and south and flanked by coastal plains. In Sabah and Sarawak, coastal plains rise to mountainous interiors **Chief Rivers:** Perak and Pahang in Malaya; Rajang in Sarawak, Kinabatangan in Sabah

Head of State: Paramount Ruler: Tuanka Haji Ahmad Shah Al-Mustain Billah Ibni Al-Marhum Sultan Abu Bakar Ri'ayatuddin Al-Mu'adzam Shah, shah of Pahang, elected April 1979 by the Conference of Rulers for a 5-year term **Head of Government:** Prime Minister Datuk Hussein bin Onn, born 1922, appointed 1976 **Effective Date of Present Constitution:** September 1963 **Legislative Body:** Parliament (bicameral), consisting of a Senate (Dewan Negara) and a House of Representatives (Dewan Rakyat). The Senate is composed of 58 members, 32 appointed by the Paramount Ruler and 26 elected by state assemblies, for 4-year terms. The House of Representatives consists of 154 members, 114 from West Malaysia, 24 from Sarawak, and 16 from Sabah, all elected for a 5-year term **Local Government:** 13 states, headed by titular rulers and governors. Effective power is in the hands of the chief ministers, selected from the state assemblies

Ethnic Composition: Malayans constitute about 45% of the population, Chinese 36%, non-Malay indigenous peoples 8%, and Indians and Pakistanis 9.1% **Population Distribution:** 29% urban **Density:** 98 inhabitants per sq. mi.

Largest Cities: (1970 census) Kuala Lumpur 451,810, Pinang (Penang, George Town) 269,247, Ipoh 247,969

Per Capita Income: $1,077 (1978) **Gross National Product (GNP):** $13.9 billion (1978 est.) **Economic Statistics:** In 1978, 30% of GNP was derived from agriculture (rubber, timber, rice, palm oil, coconut oil, fruits, sago, tea, and pepper); 16% from manufacturing (oil and sugar refining, steel plants, fertilizers, and many smaller import-substitute industries); and 6% from mining (tin, oil, iron) **Minerals and Mining:** Tin, oil and iron ore are the chief minerals **Labor Force:** About 4,800,000 (1978 est.), with approximately 50% engaged in agriculture and fishing, and 14% in industry **Foreign Trade:** Exports, chiefly rubber, oil, tin, and forest products, totaled $6.8 billion in 1977. Imports, mainly foodstuffs, industrial machinery, transportation equipment, metals, electrical equipment, and petroleum products, totaled $4.6 billion **Principal Trade Partners:** Britain, Singapore, Japan, United States, Australia, China

Vital Statistics: Birthrate, 32.4 per 1,000 of pop. (1974); death rate, 5.4 **Life Expectancy:** 67 years **Health Statistics:** 347 inhabitants per hospital bed; 8,319 per physician (1974) **Infant Mortality:** 32.5 per 1,000 births **Illiteracy:** 39% **Education Statistics:** 6,374 primary and secondary schools, with combined enrollment of 2,690,083 (1974) **Enrollment in Higher Education:** 35,246 **GNP Expended on Education:** 5.1% (1971)

Transportation: Paved roads total 10,480 mi. **Motor Vehicles:** 631,900 (1975) **Passenger Cars:** 474,700 **Railway Mileage:** 1,416 **Ports:** Pinang, Port Dickson, Klang, Malacca, Kuching, Miri, Sandakan, Tawau, Kota Kinabalu **Major Airlines:** Malaysia Airline System operates international and domestic flights **Communications:** Government owned **Radio Transmitters:** 92 **Receivers:** 1,450,000 (1976) **Television Transmitters:** 38 **Receivers:** 555,000 (1976) **Telephones:** 320,000 (1976) **Newspapers:** 31 dailies, 87 copies per 1,000 inhabitants (1975)

Weights and Measures: British standards are used; metric conversion scheduled for 1976-1982 **Travel Requirements:** Passport; no visa for 3 months

For more than a century Malaya, with its rich deposits of tin and its ideal climate for growing rubber trees, has been prosperous and sought after. With the addition in 1963 of Sarawak and Sabah, the former British colonies on the island of Borneo, the new Federation of Malaysia now contains one of the largest undeveloped areas in Asia.

The long center spine of Malaya and vast sections of Sarawak and Sabah are covered solidly with towering rain forests and low mountain ranges. Only the coastal areas and the occasional valleys are open and settled. Malaya, economically balanced and commercially progressive, continues to clear new tracts of jungle land for planting for rubber and coconut palm oil. But the efforts to enlarge the slender bands of modern development in Sarawak and Sabah have barely crept along since British colonial rule over these remote territories ended.

Although Malaysia enjoys a healthy balance of trade, and its people enjoy the highest per capita income in Southeast Asia after Singapore's, the economy suffers from overspecialization. Two commodities, rubber and tin, account for about half of the export trade. Both are vulnerable to price swings in world markets. In addition, synthetic rubber has been gaining favor while readily exploitable tin reserves are dwindling. On the plus side the new oil fields in Sabah are now producing; they now account for almost half of Malaysia's exports.

Malaysia, which was actively anti-Communist, has since 1970 modified her foreign policy in favor of peaceful coexistence. In 1974, Prime Minister Abdul Razak visited Peking and established full diplomatic relations with Communist China.

The level of living in Malaysia's cities and small towns is the highest in Southeast Asia and there are no pressures on the land from the population. Malaya has been notably successful in completing a series of five-year development plans. Similar, though less ambitious, plans have been prepared for East Malaysia. The British, whose business firms reaped impressive profits from Malaya, left behind in that region an excellent civil service, comparatively good medical facilities, and a soundly administered school system that has been markedly successful in the cities and towns where most of the ethnic Chinese and Indians are concentrated.

But amid the prosperity of Malaysia there runs a continuing struggle between the Moslem Malays, who consider themselves the indigenous owners of Malaya, and the ethnic Chinese. The Chinese own 90 percent of the federation's commercial outlets, occupy the majority of the positions in medical, legal, and engineering circles, and possess an energy and drive that the graceful, deliberate, and highly religious Malays do not admire. Since Malaya first became independent in 1957 there has been a subsurface fear among the Malays that the ethnic Chinese may take control by winning a majority in the elected parliament.

The Malays, who now dominate the government, are also in conflict with the native groups in Sarawak and Sabah, with whom they are neither religiously nor culturally allied.

The bloody race riots of 1969 led to a 21-month suspension of parliament and rule by decree. Though parliament reconvened in February 1971, full democracy did not return. A constitutional amendment to outlaw discussion of sensitive issues likely to inflame race hatred was adopted. The 48-member National Unity Council became the sole body permitted to question the government's racial and linguistic policies.

A heavy tide of refugees from Vietnam, known as the "boat people" because of their arrival from across the South China Sea, caused political turbulence in Malaysia in 1978 and 1979. They were mostly Chinese and therefore were viewed by the Malays as a threat to the country's delicate political and social balance. The government had about 53,000 refugees in makeshift camps at the start of 1979, and it tried to persuade other nations—especially those that had been involved in the war in Indochina—to accept them.

HISTORY: By the beginning of the 13th century the coasts of Malaya, Sarawak, and Sabah, which now are joined in the Federation of Malaysia, were dotted with small trading ports where the natives, most of them of ethnic Malay stock, fished and produced spices. The lure of this spice trade brought the Portuguese, Dutch, and British merchant adventurers. As their trade grew, they found it profitable to take control of the ports to protect their enterprises from the natives and from the other European merchants. In 1511 the Portuguese occupied Malacca, on the west coast of Malaya, and in 1592 the British East India Company appeared at Penang

1867: British establish the Straits Settlements—Penang, Malacca, Singapore—as a crown colony

1888: British declare North Borneo (Sabah), Sarawak, and Brunei British protectorates

1941: Japanese invade Malaya in World War II, eventually driving the British and Dutch from the East Indies

1946: After Japanese surrender, British form Union of Malaya by uniting Penang and Malacca with the nine Malay states; Singapore, Sabah, and Sarawak become crown colonies

1948: Union of Malaya is succeeded by Federation of Malaya; Communist insurrection by ethnic Chinese breaks out, and government declares state of emergency

1957: Malaya becomes independent and member of British Commonwealth

1960: Emergency is ended with defeat of Communist guerrillas

1962-63: Britain and Malaya agree on formation of new Federation of Malaysia that is to include Malaya, Sarawak, Sabah, the tiny Sultanate of Brunei, and Singapore. Brunei decides at last minute to remain outside federation; Malaysia is officially created and joins Commonwealth

1965: After months of dispute over status of ethnic Chinese and Malays, stimulated by Malay fear of Chinese dominance, Singapore secedes from federation

1966: After three years of sporadic guerrilla war and threats of invasion from Indonesia, which had opposed the creation of the federation, Malaysia and Indonesia agree to peace

1969: Tension and rioting between Chinese and Malays in capital leads to suspension of the constitution and formation of a state-of-emergency ruling council

1970: Prime Minister Abdul Rahman, the founder and leader of Malaysia, resigns and is succeeded by Abdul Razak

1971: State of emergency, in effect for 21 months, is ended on February 19 and parliamentary government restored

1974: Prime Minister Razak's National Front Coalition wins an overwhelming election victory

1975: Prosperity of early 1970s ends and government faces an ailing economy, student unrest and guerrilla war by the Communists

1976: Razak dies on January 14, Deputy Prime Minister Datuk Hussein bin Onn takes office. Government tightens security measures in drive on Communist insurgents. Ethnic Chinese professionals flee to avoid racial discrimination

1978: Hoping to gain by the relative political and economic stability, Prime Minister Hussein bin Onn calls parliamentary elections a year earlier than required and wins large majority. Number of refugee "Boat People" who crossed the South China Sea from Vietnam to Malaysia rises to a total of about 53,000 "illegal immigrants" by year-end. After a freighter bearing 2,500 is denied permission to land in November, 197 of those aboard set out in a small boat but drown when it upsets in rough water

1979: On Jan. 5, Prime Minister Hussein announces that the government will accept no more refugees. On March 3, a Vietnamese boat is turned back by naval gunfire; eventually it capsizes and 104 persons drown. Meanwhile, Malaysia gets 100,000 more refugees—Moslems from the southern Philippines who flee to the state of Sabah (formerly northeast Borneo)

MALDIVES

Area: 115 sq. mi. **Population:** 140,000 (1978 est.)

Official Name: Republic of Maldives **Capital:** Male **Nationality:** Maldivian **Languages:** Divehi, a dialect of Sinhalese, is the official and universal language; Arabic is also spoken **Religion:** Virtually all Maldivians are Sunni Moslems and Islam is the state religion **Flag:** A green rectangle with a white crescent superimposed on a red field **Anthem:** National Anthem **Currency:** Maldivian rupee (8.9 per U.S. $1)

Location: Indian Ocean. The Maldive Islands are a 500-mile-long archipelago of some 2,000 coral islands, 400 miles southwest of Sri Lanka **Features:** The Maldives rest on a submarine ridge, believed to be of volcanic origin. They are grouped into 19 atolls, or rings of coral islands, each ring encircling a lagoon. Most of the islands are covered with coconut palms **Chief Rivers:** None

Head of State and of Government: President: Maumoon Abdul Gayoom, named president by legislature in 1978 **Effective Date of Present Constitution:** 1964, amended 1968, 1970, 1972, 1975 **Legislative Body:** Majlis (unicameral), 54 members, of whom 8 are appointed by the president and 46 are popularly elected for a 5-year term **Local Government:** Each of the 19 atolls has an elected committee with a head man (Verin) appointed by the government

Ethnic Composition: The people are of mixed Indian, Sinhalese, and Arabic descent **Population Distribution:** 12% urban **Density:** 1,217 inhabitants per sq. mi. (215 islands are inhabited) **Largest City:** (1977 est.) Male 25,000

Per Capita Income: $85 (1978 est.) **Gross National Product (GNP):** $10 million (1978) **Economic Statistics:** The economy has a narrow base, being almost totally dependent on fisheries for its export earnings. Fishing is the basic industry, the catch consisting mainly of bonito and tuna. Cooked and smoked, they are known as Maldive fish and are used as a condiment. The second largest commercial industry is copra and coconut oil production. A cottage industry based on coir yarn weaving provides work for many of the women in the islands. Tourism is growing **Minerals and Mining:** There are no mineral resources **Labor Force:** 50% of the population is engaged in fishing **Foreign Trade:** Exports, chiefly fish, coconuts, copra, coir, cowrie shell, tortoise shell, and local handicraft products, totaled $2.9 million in 1972. Imports, mainly rice, flour, kerosene, oil, sugar, textiles, and drugs, totaled $2.4 million **Principal Trade Partners:** Sri Lanka, India, Pakistan, Burma, Japan, Britain, Czechoslovakia, the Netherlands

Vital Statistics: Birthrate, 45.3 per 1,000 of pop. (1976); death rate, 11.6 **Health Statistics:** 2,556 inhabitants per hospital bed; 24,000 per physician (1973) **Infant Mortality:** N.A. **Illiteracy:** 42% **Education Statistics:** 25 primary and secondary schools, with a combined enrollment of 1,262 (1971) **GNP Expended on Education:** 3% (1970)

Transportation: N.A. **Motor Vehicles:** 97 (1969) **Passenger Cars:** 20 (1969) **Railway Mileage:** None **Port:** Male **Major Airlines:** Air Maldives, established in 1974, connects Male with India and Sri Lanka **Communications:** Government and privately controlled **Radio Transmitters:** 5 **Licenses:** 3,500 (1976) **Television:** None **Telephones:** 227 (1969) **Newspapers:** 1 daily (1975), 182 copies per 1,000 inhabitants

Weights and Measures: Local units are used **Travel Requirements:** Passport, no visa required

---

The 2,000 islands that comprise the Maldives in the Indian Ocean consist of atolls, none of which are more than 20 feet in elevation. The islands are mostly protected by reefs, which have been the scene of numerous shipwrecks. The total land area is a third that of New York City. The 135,000 Maldivians inhabit only 215 of the islands.

Coconut palms cover the larger islands, on which breadfruit, figs, millet, and edible nuts are grown. Widespread in the hot and humid Maldive climate, malaria has been fought by the World Health Organization.

The Maldivian people live at a more or less subsistence level, and their basic economy is of the one-crop type—what is known as "Maldive fish." This is bonito, caught in local waters, cut up, boiled, smoked, and dried until it resembles hardwood. It is considered a delicacy in Sri Lanka and India, where it is whittled into fragments, cooked with onions and spices, and served as a condiment.

The staple foods of the Maldives are fish and rice. The rice has to be imported along with a host of other necessities, such as salt, sugar, kerosene, oil, and textiles.

There is no income tax, and the bulk of internal revenue is derived from customs duties, the rental of uninhabited islands, the licensing of boats and vehicles, and sale of postage stamps. Tourism is booming, reaching a total of 30,000 visitors annually, most of them West Germans traveling in tour groups that promise sun-and-swim vacations at soft, white beaches.

According to native legend, it was a Sinhalese prince who was the first sultan, having stayed on to rule after becoming becalmed in the Maldives with his royal bride. The country, with one brief exception in 1953, was a sultanate for eight centuries before adopting a republican form of government in 1968.

The role of the Maldives in international affairs has thus far been a limited one, but in 1974 the Maldives and India issued a joint communiqué expressing "full support for the concept of the Indian Ocean as a zone of peace free from great power rivalries, tensions and military escalations." To stay clear of big-power involvement, the Maldives

declined, in 1977, a Soviet offer to move into the Gan Island air base that the British had abandoned two years earlier. Peaceful international ventures, however, include Indian and Japanese aid to the fishing industry through canneries and boat-building in the Maldives.

HISTORY: Sighted and described by Ibn Batuta in the 14th century, the Maldive Islands were occupied by the Portuguese from 1518 until the 17th century, when they came under the protection of the Dutch, then in control of Ceylon. The Maldives retained a similar status under the British, who expelled the Dutch from Ceylon during the occupation of the Netherlands by French Revolutionary forces

1887: British protection of the Maldives is formally recorded in an exchange of letters between the sultan and the governor of Ceylon

1948: After Ceylon achieves full independence, new agreement provides that British will control Maldivian foreign affairs but not interfere internally

1953: Sultanate is abolished and Maldives become a republic; efforts at reform by the new president arouse opposition from conservative elements; National Assembly votes to restore the sultanate

1957: An agreement allowing Britain to reactivate an air base on Gan Island stirs wide opposition

1960: Government makes "free gift" to Britain of Gan Island until 1986 in return for British help in quelling a rebellion in the three southernmost atolls

1965: Maldives achieve full independence

1968: Republican form of government is adopted; Ibrahim Nasir is elected president

1975: Premier Ahmed Zaki deposed for attempted coup and exiled in March. British withdraw from base on Gan

1977: USSR proposal to use the old air base is declined

1978: President Nasir goes into exile under unclear circumstances. He is succeeded by Maumoon Abdul Gayoom

1979: About 20 officials of the Nasir government are tried and sentenced. The usual punishment is banishment to a remote island for three or four years

---

MALI

Area: 464,873 sq. mi. **Population:** 6,100,000 (1978 est.)

Official Name: Republic of Mali **Capital:** Bamako **Nationality:** Malian **Languages:** French is the official language and is the language of instruction in the nation's schools. The chief native languages are Bambara, Malinké, and Dyula **Religion:** About 90% Moslem, 9% animist, 1% Christian **Flag:** 3 vertical stripes of green, yellow, and red **Anthem:** National Anthem, beginning "At thy call, O Mali" **Currency:** Mali franc (437 per U.S. $1)

Location: West Africa. Landlocked Mali is bordered on the north by Algeria, on the east by Niger, on the south by Upper Volta, Ivory Coast, and Guinea, and on the west by Senegal and Mauritania **Features:** The country is mainly flat and dry, varying from the desolate Sahara in the north to pasture and croplands in the center and savanna scrub land in the south. The flatness of the landscape is broken in places by striking sandstone mountains and plateaus **Chief Rivers:** Niger, Senegal

Head of State and of Government: President: Head of the Military Committee of National Liberation: Gen. Moussa Traoré, born 1936; seized power in 1968 **Effective Date of Present Constitution:** June 2, 1974 **Legislative Body:** National Assembly abolished in 1968; legislative functions are exercised by the Military Committee **Local Government:** 6 regions, each headed by an appointed governor

Ethnic Composition: Of some 23 ethnic groups, about 50% are Mandé, 17% Peul (Fulani), 12% Voltaic, 6% Songhai, and 5% Tuareg and Moor **Population Distribution:** 11% urban **Density:** 13 inhabitants per sq. mi.

Largest Cities: (1972 est.) Bamako 200,000, Mopti 32,400, Kayes 28,500, Ségou 28,100, Sikasso 21,800, Gao 15,400

Per Capita Income: $87 (1978) **Gross National Product (GNP):** $540 million (1978 est.) **Economic Statistics:** In 1977 about 45% of GNP was from agriculture (millet, sorghum, rice, cotton), livestock-raising, and fishing; 19% was derived from industry (textiles, cement, fruit processing) **Minerals and Mining:** Unexploited deposits of bauxite, uranium, oil, copper, manganese, phosphates, and iron. Salt and a small amount of gold are mined **Labor Force:** 2,400,000 with about 90% engaged in agriculture and livestock-raising **Foreign Trade:** Exports, mainly cotton, livestock, peanuts, and fish, totaled $84 million in 1977. Imports, chiefly vehicles and parts, cotton cloth, iron and steel, and petroleum products, totaled $146 million **Principal Trade Partners:** France, West Germany, Ivory Coast, Senegal, Britain, China, Cuba, USSR, United States

Vital Statistics: Birthrate, 50.1 per 1,000 of pop. (1975); death rate, 25.9 **Life Expectancy:** 38 years **Health Statistics:** 1,347 inhabitants per hospital bed; 42,769 per physician (1974) **Infant Mortality:** 200 per 1,000 births **Illiteracy:** 95% **Education Statistics:** About 1,500 primary and secondary schools, with combined enrollment of 287,636 (1974) **Enrollment in Higher Education:** 2,445 (1974) **GNP Expended on Education:** 4.7% (1975)

Transportation: Paved roads total 1,050 mi. **Motor Vehicles:** 24,200 (1976) **Passenger Cars:** 15,000 **Railway Mileage:** 401 **Ports:** None **Major Airlines:** Air Mali operates both domestic and international services **Communications:** Government owned **Radio Transmitters:** 14 **Receivers:** 82,000 (1976) **Television:** None **Telephones:** 5,000 (1971) **Newspapers:** 1 daily, 0.5 copies per 1,000 inhabitants (1972)

Weights and Measures: Metric system **Travel Requirements:** Passport; visa valid 1 week; $8 fee; 2 photos

---

Once the center of a succession of mighty African empires, present-day Mali lives in the shadow of past glories. The old empires gained power and wealth from conquest and the caravan trade in slaves, gold, and salt. But with the decay of this trade and the imposition of French colonial rule, the country reverted to a meager agricultural and pastoral economy.

Now independent, modern Mali, while hoping for the discovery of oil or other minerals, struggles to improve a limited production of cotton, livestock, and food crops.

Mali's most famous city—the fabled Timbuktu—is a symbol of lost prosperity and also of the efforts to regain some of that prosperity. This golden city of the 14th-century Songhai empire, built at the edge of the Sahara on the northern bend of the Niger River, is today a dusty town of 9,000 inhabitants. Malian officials have discovered that the old lure of Timbuktu has lost none of its appeal for tourists.

The majority of Malians, on the other hand, are more concerned with regaining a healthy economy and restoration of traditional freedom of enterprise.

Under former President Modibo Keita, Mali was set "irreversibly" on a path of socialism mainly of the Maoist variety. Large numbers of Communist Chinese were brought in to manage the economy, state enterprises were created and a program of farm collectivization started.

Keita acquired all power and even began wearing Mao tunics in place of the traditional boubou. The people were increasingly terrorized by the president's private militia, which also became a threat to the regular army.

The "irreversible" Keita Socialism was reversed in 1968 with a bloodless coup by a group of young army officers. Although aware of growing opposition, the former president took no measures to prevent the military revolt and seemed to accept his ouster fatalistically.

Under the new government, the Military Committee of National Liberation, headed by Lieutenant Moussa Traoré, farm collectivization has been abolished and a start made, with French help, on converting state enterprises into mixed-economy enterprises.

While ties have been retained with Communist China and also Soviet Russia, the military government has actively restored private business and adopted incentives to encourage private foreign investment.

The ending of farm collectives has brought a marked increase in crop production, and in Bamako and other cities, private business and availability of goods have increased substantially. An American company is exploring for oil and a West German company for uranium. Financial aid has come also from France, the United States, and West Germany, as well as from the Soviet Union and East European countries.

The economy of Mali was seriously hurt by the drought of 1969-74. The famine took a heavy toll

in human life and livestock, and forced a large, dependent mass of refugees into the cities.

HISTORY: Modern Mali was a major part of past Sudanic empires—Ghana, Malinké (Mali), and Songhai—that flourished from the 8th through the 16th century. Ancient Mali reached its zenith about 1325 with the conquest of Gao and Timbuktu, the fabulous Saharan center of trade and learning. Following destruction of the Songhai empire by Moroccan invaders, the country came under the shifting rule of local chieftains. Two of these, Al-Haji Umar, a Tukulor, and Samory Touré, the Mandingo warrior hero and slave trader, waged fierce resistance against the incursions of French forces during the 19th century. With the defeat of Samory in 1898, French control was effectively extended over the country, which became known as French Sudan.

1946: Sudanese Territorial Assembly is established with limited internal authority

1957: Territorial Assembly is given increased powers

1958: Sudan votes in constitutional referendum to become autonomous republic within the French Community

1959: Sudan and Senegal form union as the Federation of Mali

1960: Federation collapses as result of political and economic differences; Sudan proclaims itself the independent Republic of Mali with Modibo Keita as president, and cuts diplomatic and trade ties with Senegal

1963: Relations with Senegal are resumed

1964: Under single-party socialist rule, President Keita and his Sudanese Union are reelected

1968: Army officers overthrow Keita government in bloodless coup

1969-74: Drought and famine hamper new government

1974: Referendum approves the new constitution, which provides that the president be elected by universal suffrage for not more than two five-year terms and that the National Assembly be elected for a four-year term

1975: Fighting occurs along frontier with Upper Volta

1978: Malian defense minister, foreign minister and two others are accused of treason. They are convicted in 1979

MALTA

Area: 122 sq. mi. **Population:** 330,000 (1978 est.)

Official Name: Republic of Malta **Capital:** Valletta **Nationality:** Maltese **Languages:** Maltese, a Semitic dialect, and English are the official languages. Maltese is the principal spoken language but Italian is also widely spoken **Religion:** Roman Catholicism is the official religion and about 98% of the population is Catholic **Flag:** Two vertical stripes of white and red with a George Cross edged in red in the upper left corner **Anthem:** To This Sweet Land **Currency:** Maltese pound (0.37 per U.S. $1)

Location: Mediterranean Sea, about 58 miles south of Sicily and 180 miles from the coast of North Africa. Malta is comprised of 2 main islands, Malta and Gozo, and several smaller ones **Features:** The country consists of a series of low hills, with terraced fields on the slopes **Chief Rivers:** The country has no rivers

Head of State: President: Dr. Anton Buttigieg, elected December 1976 **Head of Government:** Prime Minister Dominic Mintoff, born 1916, appointed June 1971; he is also foreign affairs and interior minister **Effective Date of Present Constitution:** 1964, revised 1974 **Legislative Body:** House of Representatives (unicameral), consisting of 65 members elected for 5-year terms **Local Government:** There is no formally organized local government

Ethnic Composition: Chiefly of Carthaginian and Phoenician stock, later mixed with Arabs, Italians, and British **Population Distribution:** 94% urban **Density:** 2,705 inhabitants per sq. mi.

Largest Cities: (1973 est) Sliema 21,768, Valletta 15,525, Rabat (Victoria) 5,505

Per Capita Income: $2,225 (1978) **Gross National Product (GNP):** $750 million (1978) **Economic Statistics:** 29% of GNP comes from public (nonmilitary) and private services; 26% from manufacturing (food, beverages, and tobacco, textiles and clothing, chemical and allied industries, rubber and transport equipment, and metals); 18% from wholesale and retail trade; 9% from military services; 6% from agriculture and fishing; 5% from construction and quarrying; and 4% from transport and communications **Minerals and Mining:** There are no mineral resources except for salt and stone **Labor Force:** 110,000 (1970) of which 38% is employed in industry, 6% in agriculture and fishing, and most of the rest in trade and services **Foreign Trade:** Exports, chiefly textiles, potatoes, flowers and seed, totaled $289 million in 1977. Imports, mainly machinery, chemicals, meat, mineral fuels and lubricants, and motor vehicles, totaled $516 million (1977) **Principal Trade Partners:** Britain, EC countries, Libya

Vital Statistics: Birthrate, 18.0 per 1,000 of pop. (1977); death rate, 8.9 **Life Expectancy:** 70 years **Health Statistics:** 96 inhabitants per hospital bed; 988 per physician (1971) **Infant Mortality:** 15 per 1,000 births **Illiteracy:** 17% **Education Statistics:** 229 primary and secondary schools, with combined enrollment of 62,799 (1974) **Enrollment in Higher Education:** 2,158 **GNP Expended on Education:** 4.5% (1973)

Transportation: Surfaced roads total 760 mi. **Motor Vehicles:** 69,600 (1976) **Passenger Cars:** 56,400 **Railway Mileage:** None **Ports:** Valletta **Major Airlines:** Air Malta operates flights to Europe and Africa **Communications:** Both government and privately owned **Radio Transmitters:** 2 **Licenses:** 63,000 (1976) **Television Transmitters:** 1 **Licenses:** 63,000 (1976) **Telephones:** 55,000 (1976) **Newspapers:** 6 dailies (1975)

Weights and Measures: English and local standards are used **Travel Requirements:** Passport; visa for stay exceeding 3 months

Over the centuries, the islands of Malta have been occupied by powers that sought control of the Mediterranean. And while under such occupations, the strategically placed islands have suffered much from attackers: in 1565, held by the Knights Hospitalers, a Turkish siege was defied; in World War II, Malta, as the "unsinkable aircraft carrier," withstood merciless Axis aerial bombardment, earning Britain's George Cross for heroism.

Independent from Britain since 1964, a republic since 1974, Malta has asserted some control over its own destiny. In 1971, Dominic Mintoff, returned to power as Labor party prime minister following the defeat of the coalition of Giorgio Borg Olivier, the pro-Catholic prime minister, set a course to what was said to be a neutral position between the Soviet and Western blocs. He forced Britain to renegotiate its lease on Maltese military facilities. The new lease called for increased rent to be paid to Malta and fixed an expiration date of April 1, 1979. Britain withdrew on schedule, and Malta was free of foreign soldiers for the first time in centuries.

Mintoff promoted light industry, notably textiles and plastics, and cultivated relations with the Arab states. Libya especially has been a good customer for the new industries—and a good provider of foreign aid. But loss of the revenue from the bases is expected to cause problems.

HISTORY: The strategic importance of Malta was recognized as far back as the time of the Phoenicians, whose occupation of the island was followed by invasions by the Greeks, Carthaginians, Romans, Byzantines, and Arabs. Malta was seized by the Normans in 1091. In 1530 it was given by Holy Roman Emperor Charles V to the Knights Hospitalers, who became known as the Knights of Malta and who in 1565 successfully withstood a siege by the Turks. The Knights continued to hold the island until 1798, when it was surrendered to Napolean

1800: The French are ousted from the island by Britain, with the aid of a revolt by the Maltese

1814: Treaty of Paris confirms British possession

1921: Malta is granted limited self-government

1939-45: Malta sustains heavy bombing by Germans and Italians during World War II; entire population is awarded the George Cross in 1942

1964: Malta becomes independent

1969: Last British warships leave Malta

1972: Malta signs new financial and defense agreements with Britain and NATO, replacing the 1964 agreements

1974: Malta becomes a republic. Sir Anthony Mamo sworn in as first president

1976: Dr. Anton Buttigieg is elected president

1977: China promises continued economic and technical aid

1979: British lease of military bases ends

MAURITANIA

Area: 397,954 sq. mi. **Population:** 1,500,000 (1978 est.)

Official Name: Islamic Republic of Mauritania **Capital:** Nouakchott **Nationality:** Mauritanian **Languages:** Arabic, known in Mauritania as Hassaniyah, is the language most spoken, though French is the official one; Wolof and Tukolor are also spoken in the South **Religion:** The population is almost entirely Moslem, and Islam is the state religion **Flag:** A gold star and crescent centered on a green field **Anthem:** National Anthem (no words) **Currency:** Ouguiya (45.9 per U.S.$1)

Location: West Africa. Mauritania is bordered on the north by

Morocco, Algeria and the contested Western Sahara area, on the east and southeast by Mali, on the southwest by Senegal, and on the west by the Atlantic Ocean **Features:** The country on the whole is fairly flat. The Sahara zone in the north consists of shifting dunes and gravel plains, while the south is more fertile and suitable for cultivation **Chief River:** Senegal

Head of State: President: Lt. Col. Mohamed Mahmoud Ould Ahmed Louly, took office June 4, 1979 **Head of Government:** Premier: Lt. Col. Mohamed Khouna Ould Haidalla, appointed May 31, 1979 **Effective Date of Present Constitution:** 1961, suspended 1978 **Legislative Body:** Mauritania is now governed by a Military Committee of National Recovery (MCNR) comprised of 18 senior military officers **Local Government:** 13 regions and one district (Nouakchott)

Ethnic Composition: Divided equally into three groups: Arab-Berber (Moors), Arab-Berber-Negroid, Negroid **Population Distribution:** 22% urban, **Density:** 3.8 inhabitants per sq. mi.

Largest Cities: (1976 est.) Nouakchott 125,000; (1972 est.) Nouadhibou 24,000, Zouérate 16,000, Kaédi 15,700, Rosso 11,400, Boghé 10,600, F'Derick 10,000

Per Capita Income: $213 (1978) **Gross National Product (GNP):** $330 million (1978) **Economic Statistics:** In 1977 about 22% of the GNP was derived from agriculture (livestock, millet, corn, rice, sweet potatoes, peanuts, beans, gum arabic); 21% from industry, mining, and fish processing **Minerals and Mining:** Mauritania is second only to Liberia in West African iron-ore production. There are large deposits of gypsum **Labor Force:** 420,00 (1975), of which 90% is in agriculture **Foreign Trade:** Exports, chiefly iron ore, livestock, fish, dates, and gum arabic, totaled $161 million in 1977. Imports, mainly machinery, vehicles, electrical equipment, petroleum products, cement, tires, and tea, totaled $283 million **Principal Trade Partners:** United States, France, Italy, Britain, West Germany, Senegal, Japan, Spain

Vital Statistics: Birthrate, 44.8 per 1,000 of pop. (1975); death rate, 24.9 **Life Expectancy:** 39 years **Health Statistics:** 2,328 inhabitants per hospital bed; 15,172 per physician (1975) **Infant Mortality:** 187 per 1,000 births **Illiteracy:** 88% **Education Statistics:** 603 primary and secondary schools, with combined enrollment of 61,275 (1976) **Enrollment in Higher Education:** c. 1,000 study abroad **GNP Expended on Education:** 4.1% (1972)

Transportation: Improved roads total 700 mi. **Motor Vehicles:** 11,800 (1974) **Passenger Cars:** 4,400 (1972) **Railway Mileage:** 450 **Ports:** Nouadhibou, Nouakchott **Major Airlines:** Air-Mauritanie operates domestic and regional services; Air Afrique is the major international carrier **Communications:** Government controlled **Radio Transmitters:** 4 **Receivers:** 95,000 (1976) **Television:** None **Telephones:** 1,300 est. (1969) **Newspapers:** 1 daily, 0.2 per 1,000 inhabitants (1972)

Weights and Measures: Metric system **Travel Requirements:** Passport; visa valid for 3 months; $10 fee; 3 photos

Mauritania is a borderland between Moorish/Arab North Africa and black West Africa. Although cast in the mold of a modern state and with membership in the Organization of African Unity, the former West African territory continues to be divided by racial distinctions dating from the medieval migrations of light-skinned Arabs and Berbers, who forced the darker-skinned natives into the southern region and enslaved many of them. French rule, established by 1920, favored the blacks, who were more inclined than the Arabs to take advantage of European education.

President Moktar Ould Daddah, the country's leader from 1960 to 1978, steered an enlightened and adroit course racially and politically. While promoting more education for the Moorish/Arab majority, President Moktar sought to gain foreign aid from both Western and Eastern sources. In July 1978 the president was overthrown in a bloodless coup led by military officers. Colonel Mustapha Ould Salek was named president. In June 1979 Salek resigned and was succeeded by Colonel Ahmed Louly.

Although France continues to provide most of the country's aid and development funds, Communist China recently has played a major role in such projects as rice-growing, irrigation, and cement manufacture and in drilling numerous wells to tap ground water.

Mauritania's main source of wealth has been rich deposits of iron ore and copper, which have been developed since independence by French interests. These have provided substantial earnings that have made it possible for the government to embark on the improvement of social services and of agriculture, on which more than 80 percent of Mauritanians depend. Copper production ceased in 1978.

Meanwhile, in addition to French and Chinese aid, Mauritanian development is being aided by countries such as the United States, Yugoslavia, and Spain.

Mauritanian gains in territory from the southern part of former Spanish Sahara were offset by the disruption to the nation's economy caused by raids of the *Polisario Front*, a Saharan liberation guerrilla group based in Algeria. But, after the seizure of power by the army in 1978, the *Polisario* proclaimed a unilateral cease-fire. The military government informally decided to respect the truce, and fighting fell to a sporadic level. On August 5, 1979, Mauritania signed a peace agreement with the *Polisario* under which it renounced all claim to its portion of the contested Western Sahara area. Morocco promptly occupied the region.

HISTORY: Mauritania's original inhabitants, a Sudanic black people, were enslaved or driven southward by the 11th-century Berber invasion that destroyed the empire of Ghana to the east. The Berbers in turn were conquered in the 16th century by Arab invaders, the Beni Hassan. Trade with Europeans, opened by the Portuguese in the 15th century, attracted the Dutch, English, and French. Throughout the 19th century, the French gradually extended control over the country, and established a protectorate in 1903. Mauritania was made a French colony in 1920

1946-56: Internal self-rule gradually increases along with Mauritanian representation in French parliament and Assembly of the French Union

1958: In referendum, Mauritania votes to become autonomous republic within new French Community

1960: Mauritania wins full independence, with Moktar Ould Daddah continuing as prime minister

1961: With adoption of presidential system, Daddah, the only candidate, is elected president; new People's Party becomes the sole political organization

1963-66: Completion of iron-ore mining project by French-led consortium and development of extensive copper deposits give strong boost to nation's economy

1973-74: Drought causes widespread famine

1975: Agreement is signed among Spain, Morocco and Mauritania providing for the transfer of power and withdrawal of the Spanish presence from Western Sahara. Daddah is reelected president

1976: Morocco and Mauritania partition Western Sahara, giving Mauritania the southern third. The proclamation of an independent republic by the *Polisario Front*, the Saharan liberation movement, is ignored. *Polisario* guerrillas raid capital city of Nouakchott

1977: *Polisario* units raid iron-mining center at Zouérate

1978: Group of Western and Arab banks lends Mauritania $360 million for exploitation of iron ore mines. French military planes help government forces stop *Polisario* rebels advancing on Zouérate. President Moktar Ould Daddah is overthrown in a bloodless coup by military officers, led by Col. Mustapha Ould Salek who becomes Chairman of Military Committee for National Recovery and president. *Polisario* proclaims cease-fire

1979: Premier Ahmed Oul Bouicf and 10 other Mauritanian delegates to the Economic Community of West African States die in air crash. He is succeeded by Lt. Col. Mohamed Khouna Ould Haidalla. President Salek resigns. Lt. Col. Mohamed Mahmoud Ould Ahmed Louly is chosen by the MCNR to replace him

MAURITIUS

Area: 790 sq. mi. **Population:** 910,000 (1978 est.)
Official Name: Mauritius **Capital:** Port Louis **Nationality:** Mauritian **Languages:** English is the official language, but a Creole patois, basically French, is spoken by 52% of the people; Chinese, Hindi, Urdu, and French are also spoken **Religion:** About 51% Hindu, 17% Moslem, and 31% Christian (chiefly Roman Catholic) **Flag:** Four horizontal stripes of red, blue, yellow, and green **Anthem:** Motherland **Currency:** Mauritian rupee (6.1 per U.S. $1)

Location: Indian Ocean. Mauritius lies about 500 miles east of Madagascar. Dependencies include Rodrigues and distant smaller islands **Features:** The island is volcanic in origin and almost entirely surrounded by coral reefs. The land rises to a central plateau, surrounded by mountains believed to be the rim of an ancient volcano **Chief Rivers:** Grand (S.E. and N.W.), Rempart, Poste

Head of State: Queen Elizabeth II, represented by an acting governor-general, Dayendranath Burrenchobay **Head of Government:** Prime Minister: Sir Seewoosagur Ramgoolam, born 1900; reappointed 1976 **Effective Date of Present Constitution:** 1968 **Legislative Body:** Parliament (unicameral Legislative Assembly), 70 members with 5-year terms, 62 of whom are elected **Local Government:** 9 administrative districts, with local councils

Ethnic Composition: Indo-Mauritians (69%), Creoles (29%), Sino-Mauritians, and Franco-Mauritians **Population Distribution:** 44% urban **Density:** 1,152 inhabitants per sq. mi.

Largest Cities: (1975 est.) Port Louis 138,161, Beau Bassin/Rose Hill 81,353, Curepipe 53,068, Quatre Bornes 52,134

Per Capita Income: $817 (1978 est.) **Gross National Product (GNP):** $730 million (1978 est.) **Economic Statistics:** 29% of the GNP comes from agriculture (sugar [90%], tea, ginger, tobacco, vegetables, bananas, peanuts), 23% from industry (sugar processing, rum, beer) and construction, and 16% from services **Minerals and Mining:** There are no known mineral deposits **Labor Force:** 260,000 in 1975, with 28% in agriculture and 12% in industry, and 34% in services **Foreign Trade:** Exports, 90% sugar and sugar products, and molasses, totaled $213 million in 1976. Imports, chiefly foodstuffs, manufactured goods, machinery and transportation equipment, chemicals and fertilizers, totaled $336 million **Principal Trade Partners:** Britain, South Africa, Réunion, Indonesia, Iran, Hong Kong, Iraq, Australia, United States, Canada, Japan, West Germany

Vital Statistics: Birthrate, 25.1 per 1,000 of pop. (1976); death rate, 7.5 **Life Expectancy:** 67 years **Health Statistics:** 271 inhabitants per hospital bed; 4,438 per physician (1973) **Infant Mortality:** 40 per 1,000 births **Illiteracy:** 20% **Education Statistics:** 521 primary and secondary schools, with combined enrollment of 217,973 (1975) **Enrollment in Higher Education:** 1,096 (1975) **GNP Expended on Education:** 3.3% (1974)

Transportation: Paved roads total 650 mi. **Motor Vehicles:** 31,900 (1976) **Passenger Cars:** 20,700 **Railway Mileage:** None **Ports:** Port Louis **Major Airlines:** Air Mauritius and several foreign airlines link Mauritius with Europe, Africa, and Asia **Communications:** Government controlled **Radio Transmitters:** 3 **Licenses:** 200,000 (1976) **Television Transmitters:** 4 **Licenses:** 41,000 (1976) **Telephones:** 27,000 (1976) **Newspapers:** 12 dailies, 91 copies per 1,000 inhabitants (1975)

Weights and Measures: Metric system **Travel Requirements:** Passport; visa; no charge except postage

Encircled by coral reefs and the blue-green Indian Ocean, Mauritius looks like the perfect model of a placid tropical island. The former British crown colony, lying nearly 1,500 miles east of southern Africa—its closest proximity to any continent—is renowned as the source of rare postage stamps and as the last refuge of the extinct dodo bird.

The remote volcanic island is also a microcosm of the present-day problems of less-developed countries: overpopulation, racial conflict, and dependence on a single crop, sugar. With no solutions in sight, it seems only a matter of time before the combined pressures of these problems bring an eruption. Indeed, a ban on 12 unions was imposed by the government in 1971 and only lifted in 1974, following lengthy negotiations between dockworkers and government officials.

Within the island's 790 square miles, there are, in addition to a large Indian-Hindu majority, major groups of Africans, Europeans (mainly French), and Creoles (an Afro-French mixture), and a small element of Chinese. Despite efforts of a coalition government headed by Prime Minister Sir Seewoosagur Ramgoolam to promote harmony, racial rivalries are intense. Violent racial rioting and also labor unrest preceded and accompanied Mauritius' independence in 1968.

Since elimination of malaria recently, the island's population is growing by 1.5 percent a year and birth control is opposed equally by Hindu, Catholic, and Moslem groups.

Some 90 percent of cultivated land is planted with sugarcane, but production is often drastically reduced by cyclones. In addition to depressed sugar prices, Mauritius has been faced with the loss of a preferential market through

Britain's entry into the European Common Market.

At the same time, the Mauritian government has found itself in a dilemma in being opposed to white minority rule in South Africa even though South Africa is one of Mauritius' main trading partners. South Africa itself has shown interest in aiding Mauritius in return for a less anti-Pretoria stand and, in view of the island's problems, Mauritian officials appear inclined to accept.

It has been a rule of thumb on Mauritius that one ton of sugar exports was needed for each inhabitant. But sugar production is unlikely to exceed 700,000 tons a year, although population is now climbing toward the one million mark.

HISTORY: Originally uninhabited, Mauritius was first settled and named by the Dutch in the 17th century. The island was abandoned early in the 18th century, after which it was claimed by the French, who renamed it Ile-de-France and laid the foundations of a slave-owning plantation economy based on sugar. In 1814, the island was ceded to Britain and reverted to its original name. Slavery was abolished in 1834, and the planters began importing indentured Indians. Although they soon came to form a majority, the Indians long remained politically powerless because of a restricted franchise based on property qualifications

1948: Franchise is broadened by new constitution; in new elections, Indians win majority in legislative council, overthrowing dominance of Franco-Mauritians but causing other minority groups to fear Indian domination

1957: Ministerial government is introduced

1961: Constitutional conference in London paves way toward full self-government, but talks are marred by disputes between Hindu-dominated majority Labour Party, which favors eventual independence, and minority parties that oppose it for fear of Hindu domination

1967: Mauritius becomes self-governing; Labour Party leader Seewoosagur Ramgoolam is appointed prime minister; island is wracked by racial and labor unrest

1968: Mauritius wins independence amid Creole-Moslem rioting

1970: Government begins drafting plans for crop diversification, light industry, and tourism

1971: Plagued by strikes that severely injure the economy, the government declares a state of emergency

1975: Cyclone Gervaise leaves 90,000 homeless and destroys 30 percent of sugar harvest

MEXICO

Area: 761,600 sq. mi. **Population:** 65,000,000 (1978 est.)

Official Name: United Mexican States **Capital:** Mexico City **Nationality:** Mexican **Languages:** Spanish is the official and predominant language; 7% speak only Indian dialects **Religion:** 97% Roman Catholic; there are some 600,000 Protestants and 100,000 Jews **Flag:** Green, white, and red vertical stripes with the national emblem in the center **Anthem:** National-Anthem, beginning "Mexicans, to the call of war" **Currency:** Mexican peso (22.8 per U.S. $1)

Location: North America. Mexico is bordered on the north by the United States, on the east by the Gulf of Mexico, on the south by Belize and Guatemala, and on the west by the Pacific Ocean **Features:** The country consists of a large central plateau, flanked by the eastern and western coastal ranges of the Sierra Madre. From a low desert plain in the north, the plateau rises to 8,000 feet near Mexico City **Chief Rivers:** Rio Bravo (Rio Grande), Lerma, Santiago, Usumacinta, Grijalva, Balsas, Pánuco

Head of State and of Government: President José López Portillo y Pacheco, born 1920, elected 1976 for 6-year term **Effective Date of Present Constitution:** 1917 **Legislative Body:** Congress (bicameral), consisting of the Senate and the Chamber of Deputies. The Senate is composed of 64 members elected for 6-year terms. The Chamber of Deputies has 400 members elected for 3 years **Local Government:** 31 states, 1 federal district. Each state has its own governor and popularly elected legislature

Ethnic Composition: About 60% of the population are mestizos of mixed Indian and Spanish descent. 30% are pure Indian, while 9% are of Spanish or other European ancestry **Population Distribution:** 66% urban **Density:** 85 inhabitants per sq. mi.

Largest Cities: (1975 est.) Mexico City 8,591,750; Guadalajara 1,560,805; Monterey 1,049,957; Ciudad Juárez 520,539; León 496,598; Puebla 482,155; Tijuana 386,852; Acapulco 352,673

Per Capita Income: $1,147 (1978) **Gross National Product (GNP):** $76.2 billion (1978) **Economic Statistics:** In 1977 about 12% of GNP came from agriculture (farming, livestock), forestry, and fishing, 37% from industry (cars, machinery, construction, pe-

trochemicals, steel, cement) and mining (including oil) **Minerals and Mining:** Mexico is the world's largest producer of silver and a major producer of oil, gas, gold, sulfur, lead, and zinc. Coal, tin, antimony, mercury, copper, and iron are also mined **Labor Force:** 16.6 million (1975), 41% in agriculture, 34% in industry and mining, and 25% in services **Foreign Trade:** Exports, chiefly cotton, sugar, fruits, vegetables, coffee, sulfur, petroleum, and shrimp, totaled $4.6 billion in 1977. Imports, mainly industrial machinery, motor vehicles and parts, chemicals, communications and transportation equipment, and electric power equipment, totaled $5.5 billion **Principal Trade Partners:** United States, West Germany, Britain, Japan, France, Sweden

Vital Statistics: Birthrate, 34.6 per 1,000 of pop. (1976); death rate, 6.8 **Life Expectancy:** 65 years **Health Statistics:** 530 inhabitants per hospital bed; 1,385 per physician (1972) **Infant Mortality:** 52 per 1,000 births (1973) **Illiteracy:** 25% **Education Statistics:** 52,792 primary and secondary schools, with combined enrollment of 14,187,600 (1975) **Enrollment in Higher Education:** 700,000 (1976) **GNP Expended on Education:** 3.2% (1974)

Transportation: Paved roads total 42,727 mi. **Motor Vehicles:** 3,568,400 (1976) **Passenger Cars:** 2,580,400 **Railway Mileage:** 20,000 **Ports:** Veracruz, Tampico, Coatzacoalcos, Guaymas, Salina Cruz, Mazatlán, Manzanillo **Major Airlines:** Aeronaves de México, the government-owned line and Mexicana de Aviación, a privately owned line, operate both international and domestic flights **Communications:** Partly government controlled **Radio Transmitters:** 668 **Receivers:** 17,514,000 (1974) **Television Transmitters:** 150 **Receivers:** 4,885,000 **Telephones:** 3,309,000 (1976) **Newspapers:** 256 dailies (1975), 116 copies per 1,000 inhabitants (1975)

Weights and Measures: Metric system **Travel Requirements:** Tourist card good for 90 days from date of issue, valid for stay up to 6 months; 4 photos 2″ × 2″; no charge

Mexico experienced the world's first social and political revolution of the 20th century, but to this day it still suffers seriously from economic underdevelopment. The bloody struggle that began in 1910 and cost over a million lives gave Mexico stable institutions and a strong constitution, yet most of the revolution's high-sounding principles have yet to be implemented. Glittering long-term hopes for economic advancement were raised, however, with major oil discoveries in the late 1970s.

Today this third-largest of Latin American republics enjoys a large measure of political solidity, under a system of government that falls somewhere between dictatorship and democracy. But the benefits of an economic "miracle" have reached only a small part of Mexico's 65 million inhabitants, and the country's large peasant population is only marginally better off now than in 1910. The unemployed and underemployed exceed 50 percent of the work force.

In politics, as in other fields, the contrasts between theory and practice in Mexico are vast. Under the republican form of government, contending parties are permitted, and six of them participated in the 1979 elections. In reality, however, Mexican politics is dominated by one amorphous party—the Revolutionary Institutional Party (PRI)—which has provided every president since its creation in 1929.

During his six-year term, the president is an immensely powerful figure, but it is the party that reflects a wide spectrum of national opinion and eventually dictates the limits within which he can move. All significant support for and opposition to a president's policies come from within the ruling party. However, because the constitution forbids immediate reelection for members of the Senate and Chamber of Deputies, many talented politicians are attracted to the bureaucracy instead. Congress traditionally has been regarded as little more than a rubber stamp that ratifies executive decisions.

Although the PRI is technically structured around the three pillars of the peasant, worker, and popular movements, business interests have gained increasing control over the party and government in the past 20 years, giving weight to the

MEXICO
CONIC PROJECTION

National Capitals......⊛   State Capitals......⊛

© Copyright HAMMOND INCORPORATED, Maplewood, N.J.

States Indicated by Numbers:

1 Tlaxcala
2 Morelos
3 Distrito Federal
4 México
5 Hidalgo

6 Querétaro
7 Guanajuato
8 Aguascalientes
9 Nayarit
10 Colima

saying that "in Mexico business is government and government is business." The economic boom that gave political strength to the business sector also spawned a host of conservative politicians to represent its interests.

The Roman Catholic Church has carried little political weight in Mexico, unlike most Latin American countries, since the revolution, although most people are nominally Catholic. The constitution defends religious freedom, and in practice there is considerable tolerance of different creeds.

Mexico's economy, which had been growing at a remarkable average of 6.5 percent annually for the past 20 years, reversed that trend beginning in 1973 with an accelerating inflation rate. In an effort to stimulate exports, investments, and job creation, the government devalued the peso in 1976 for the first time in 22 years. The extremely high unemployment rate also increased the number of Mexicans crossing the border to the U.S. illegally to search for work.

Despite a fundamental agrarian reform following the revolution, which gave most peasants their own small plots of land and established a system of farm cooperatives, the absence of irrigation, credit, and marketing facilities has kept most peasants living at subsistence level.

Mexico's considerable social and economic problems are made more acute by the country's population growth rate, at present about 3.5 percent per year. Improved health facilities have brought down the death rate dramatically since World War II, but successive governments have strongly opposed an official family planning program.

In foreign policy, Mexico has long followed a policy of nonintervention, which led it to maintain diplomatic relations with Cuba when all other members of the Organization of American States broke their ties in 1964.

Because of proximity and close economic ties, the United States has considerable influence in Mexican politics. This reality sometimes leads Mexico to take strongly nationalist stands, although differences between the countries are usually settled amicably.

Mexico's oil boom picked up speed with the announcement on November 13, 1978, that a new petroleum basin had been discovered. It was the Chicontepe Field, a 75-by-17-mile area along the Gulf of Mexico between Tampico and Poza Rica. Since the field lacks porosity and permeability, it will require the drilling of many small wells—a years-long undertaking. Government-owned Petroleos Mexicano, or PEMEX, doubled its proven oil reserves during the year, up to 40.1 billion barrels. Its potential reserves rose to 300 billion barrels, or double Saudi Arabia's proved reserves. By the start of 1979, Mexico was producing about 1.4 billion barrels of crude per day, but it was expecting a 50 percent step-up in production by 1981. Meanwhile, a pipeline was being built northward toward Monterrey.

By reason of its oil wealth and large labor pool, Mexico was being acclaimed by economists at the outset of the 1980s as one of a handful of less-developed countries likely to gain rapidly in economic power and worldwide political influence.

HISTORY: Before the Spanish conquest of Mexico in 1519, Indian civilizations had flourished there for centuries, with that of the Mayas dating as far back as about 1500 B.C. With the conquest of the Aztecs by Hernán Cortéz, Indian culture was modified and the Indians themselves reduced to peonage on the land and in the mines. Corruption in the Spanish administration helped fan growing discontent among the Creoles, Mexican-born descendants of the Spaniards, leaving the country ripe for the revolutionary ideals spread by the French Revolution.

1810: Miguel Hidalgo y Costilla, a Creole priest, begins the fight for independence; revolutionary armies spring up under various leaders

1821: Mexico is granted independence; anarchy, corruption, and political rivalry are rife

1836-45: Texas, under domination of U.S. settlers, secedes from Mexico and declares its independence; it is ultimately annexed by the United States

1846-48: Annexation brings on Mexican War with the United States; Mexico is defeated, signs Treaty of Guadalupe Hidalgo ceding vast block of territory to the United States

1857-61: Benito Juárez, reform-minded minister of justice and later president, introduces liberal constitution transferring power from Creoles to mestizos and secularizing church lands; conservative opposition leads to War of the Reform (1858-61), which ends in victory for liberals

1864-67: France establishes puppet empire under Austrian-born Emperor Maximilian; Juárez leads popular resistance; empire collapses

1876-1909: Porfirio Díaz leads successful revolt and establishes ruthless dictatorship; he reforms Mexico's finances, but despite nation's growing prosperity vast numbers of people are reduced to virtual slavery when their communal lands are apportioned to large estate owners; almost three quarters of Mexico's mineral resources become by purchase the property of foreign interests

1910-17: Francisco I. Madero organizes rebellion and forces Díaz to resign; Mexico is thrown into ferment of revolt culminating in rise of leaders such as Venustiano Carranza, Francisco (Pancho) Villa, and Emiliano Zapata. Villa breaks with Carranza, who has U.S. support, and Villa's irregulars raid New Mexico (1916); U.S. General John J. Pershing leads punitive expedition into Mexico in pursuit of Villa. Carranza frames liberal constitution of 1917 nationalizing mineral resources and restoring communal lands to Indians

1934-40: President Lázaro Cárdenas undertakes extensive land reform and expropriates foreign-owned companies

1967: Land reform continues as government distributes 2.5 million acres of land to peasants

1968: Scores are killed and more than 100 wounded in series of riots during which army and police clash with students protesting alleged government repression and violation of constitutional rights

1969: Protest by Díaz government causes United States to relax drug smuggling drive along Mexican border

1970: Luis Echeverría Alvarez, the governing party's candidate, is elected president

1973: Echeverría tours the world hoping to make strong trade agreements with the European Community, China and the Soviet Union. Mexican terrorists kidnap diplomatically and politically prominent people and ransom them for the release of political prisoners and for money to support their cause

1974: The state petroleum organization, PEMEX, finds new oil in Veracruz. Echeverría signs an agreement for commercial co-operation with the European Community as the first Latin American nation to do so

1976: José López Portillo is elected president. Outgoing President Echeverría orders expropriation with compensation of 200,000 acres for use of landless peasants, but court cases tie up action

1977: President López Portillo visits the U.S., stressing Mexico's independent stance, yet seeking cooperation with the U.S. U.S. and Mexico sign first formal trade agreement since 1942. Oil revenues for year reach $700 million. On the basis of price, the U.S. government blocks the sale of Mexican natural gas to U.S. companies

1978: Carter Administration couples promise of "no massive deportations" of Mexicans working illegally in the U.S. with offers of U.S. support for job-producing loans. Government legalizes Communist Party for first time in 40 years, enabling it to compete openly in July 1979 congressional elections. Dismissing complaints about the dangers of marijuana treated with herbicide as pro-legalization "propaganda," government continues campaign of spraying marijuana fields with toxic chemical known as "paraquat." The government confirms the finding of a vast oil basin near Tampico. President López Portillo, visiting Japan, makes arrangements to sell oil there and concludes agreements by which Japanese banks will finance oil-related projects

1979: The year opens with Mexico's proven oil reserves at 40.1 billion barrels—a 100 percent increase in 12 months. Pope John Paul II draws throngs when he visits Mexico City, Oaxaca, Guadalajara, and Monterrey. U.S. President Carter visits President López Portillo, receives a cool reception, and expresses a hope that the U.S. can buy natural gas from Mexico. No progress is made in talks on immigration and trade. On June 3, a flaming gusher of oil erupts at Ixtoc One, a well 50 miles out in the Gulf of Mexico, off Ciudad del Carmen. The July elections expand Chamber of Deputies to 400 members, up from 300. The additional 100 seats are granted, through proportional representation, to parties opposing the ruling PRI

MONACO

Area: 0.708 sq. mi. (453 acres) **Population:** 25,000 (1978 est.)
Official Name: Principality of Monaco **Capital:** Monaco **Nationality:** Monacan or Monégasque **Languages:** French is the official language; the principal spoken languages are French, Monégasque, English and Italian **Religion:** 95% Roman Catholic, the official religion **Flag:** Red over white horizontal stripes **Anthem:** Monacan Hymn, beginning "Principality of Monaco, my fatherland" **Currency:** French franc (4.4 per U.S. $1)
Location: A coastal enclave within the Alpes-Maritimes department of southeastern France, bordering the Mediterranean Sea **Features:** The principality consists of 3 main areas: La Condamine, the business district around the port; Monte Carlo, the site of the famous casino, which is at a higher elevation; and Monaco, the capital, known also as the Rock because of its situation on a high promontory extending into the sea **Chief Rivers:** There are no rivers
Head of State: Prince Rainier III, born 1923, succeeded to the throne in 1949 **Head of Government:** Minister of State André Saint-Mleux (by law a French citizen), appointed 1972. He is assisted by a 3-man Council of Government **Effective Date of Present Constitution:** 1911, revised December 1962 **Legislative Body:** National Council (unicameral), consisting of 18 members elected for 5 years **Local Government:** 1 commune (with 4 quarters), under a mayor and a 15-member elected council
Ethnic Composition: The native Monacans are a minority (19%); 58% are French, and 17% Italian **Population Distribution:** 100% urban
Largest Cities: (1968 census) La Condamine 11,438, Monte Carlo 9,948; (1972 est.) Monaco 1,685
Per Capita Income: N.A. **Gross National Product (GNP):** N.A. **Economic Statistics:** About 55% of the income is derived from tourism, 30% from local industry, and 4% from the casino. The substantial part of the tourist revenue is derived from the government controlled Société Anonyme des Bains de Mer, which operates the gambling casino at Monte Carlo as well as hotels and motion picture theaters. Many foreign companies have established their headquarters in Monaco because of the low taxation **Minerals and Mining:** There are no minerals **Labor Force:** Most of the working population is employed by SBM; and some are employed by the small handicraft industry and by service establishments **Foreign Trade:** Statistical information is not available **Principal Trade Partners:** France
Vital Statistics: Birthrate 8.2 per 1,000 of pop. (1974); death rate, 12.3 **Life Expectancy:** 75 years **Health Statistics:** 75 inhabitants per hospital bed; 351 per physician (1974) **Infant Mortality:** 9.3 per 1,000 births (1970) **Illiteracy:** Negligible **Education Statistics:** 11 primary and secondary schools, with combined enrollment of 4,227 (1973) **Enrollment in Higher Education:** N.A. **GNP Expended on Education:** N.A.
Transportation: Surfaced roads total about 30 mi. **Motor Vehicles:** 11,450 (1969) **Passenger Cars:** 2,685 (1969) **Railway Mileage:** 0.6 **Port:** La Condamine **Major Airlines:** None **Communications:** Both government and privately owned **Radio Transmitters:** 6 **Receivers:** 7,500 (1976) **Television Transmitters:** 3 **Receivers:** 16,000 (1976) **Telephones:** 24,000 (1976) **Newspapers:** French and other newspapers are on sale; the Journal de Monaco, an official weekly, is the only local newspaper
Weights and Measures: Metric system **Travel Requirements:** Passport; no visa for 3 months

Monaco has been a principality of three towns covering an area about half the size of New York's Central Park, but Monaco is growing and expanding into the sea. A land-filling program added more than 20 percent to Monaco's area, to a total of 453 acres, or about 0.7 square miles.

Still, the microscopic principality is a state, the second smallest independent state in the world, after the Vatican City. Crammed into its small size are Riviera weather, scenery to match, the gambling paradise of Monte Carlo's casino, a reigning Prince Rainier with a movie-queen wife (Grace Kelly), the world-famous Oceanographic Museum (under the direction of France's Jacques Cousteau), and the daily changing of the Caribinier Guard at Palace Square.

Of course, as a long-time vacation resort, Monaco is filled with noted hotels. To keep pace with modernization of the principality, existing hotels are being modernized and new ones built, all with government help.

Monaco has a customs union and interchangeable currency with France, whose consent, by a treaty of 1918, is required for accession to the throne of the principality. The birth of Princess Grace's son in 1958 assured a male ruler to follow Prince Rainier.

Without this royal line, Monaco would come under French protection, making the Monégasques, now free of income taxes, subject to French levies. Tax freedom for Monaco-based companies was curtailed by a 1963 fiscal convention with France, under which concerns in Monaco doing more than 25 percent of their business elsewhere must pay taxes. The convention also applies French income taxes to French citizens who moved to Monaco after mid-October 1957.

HISTORY: Monaco was occupied by the Phoenicians from the 10th to the 5th century B.C. and then by the Greeks. During the early Christian era it was dominated by Rome until occupied by the barbarians and Saracens. In 1191, the Genoese took possession of Monaco; the Grimaldi family took control in 1297. The male line died out in 1731, but the French Goyon-Matignon family, which succeeded by marriage, assumed the name Grimaldi, still used by the ruling prince

1793: Monaco is annexed to France

1815: Monaco is placed under the protection of the Kingdom of Sardinia

1861: Monaco becomes a French protectorate

1918: Principality signs treaty with France, stipulating that succession to the throne of Monaco must be approved by the French government

1949: Prince Rainier III succeeds his father, Prince Louis II, as ruler

1956: Prince Rainier marries American movie star, Grace Kelly

1963: "Tax war" with France ends in signing of new fiscal convention under which Monégasques and others remain free of direct taxation, but French citizens who had taken up residence in Monaco after October 13, 1957, have to pay income taxes, and companies doing more than a quarter of their business outside Monaco are made subject to a levy

1967: Prince Rainier wrests control of Société des Bains de Mer (SBM) from Greek shipping magnate Aristotle Onassis, principal stockholder and director of the company, which through its control of the Monte Carlo casino and the principality's hotels, was accused of impeding Monaco's tourist development

1978: Princess Caroline, daughter of Prince Rainier and Princess Grace, marries Philippe Junot, French investment banker

MONGOLIA

Area: 606,163 sq. mi. **Population:** 1,530,000 (1978 est.)
Official Name: Mongolian People's Republic **Capital:** Ulan Bator **Nationality:** Mongol **Languages:** Khalkha Mongolian, one of the large dialect groups of the Mongolian branch of the Altaic language family, is the official and dominant spoken language (90%). About 7% of the population speak Turkic languages **Religion:** Lamaistic Buddhism is the predominant religion (95%), but religious activity is discouraged by the Communist regime; Moslem 4% **Flag:** Vertical stripes of red, blue, and red with a yellow star and traditional symbols on the left **Anthem:** Our Free Revolutionary Land **Currency:** Tughrik (3.0 per U.S. $1)
Location: North Central Asia. Landlocked Mongolia is bordered on the north by the USSR, and on the east, south, and west by China **Features:** The country is essentially a huge steppe plateau with an average elevation of 4,000 feet. It is fringed by forested mountains in the north, while the south includes much of the Gobi Desert **Chief Rivers:** Selenga, Kerulen, Orkhon, Dzabkhan
Political Leader, Head of State and of Government: Yumjaagiyn Tsedenbal, born 1916; first secretary of the Mongolian People's Revolutionary (Communist) party since 1958; chairman of the presidium of the Hural since June 1974. He is assisted by Jambyn Batmonh, chairman of the Council of Ministers **Effective Date of Present Constitution:** July 1960 **Legislative Body:** People's Great Hural (unicameral), 354 members elected for a 4-year term by universal suffrage; actual power lies with the Politburo of the Party's Central Committee **Local Government:** 18 provinces and 1 independent city
Ethnic Composition: Khalkha Mongols make up about 76% of the population, Oirat Mongols and Buryat Mongols 13%, and Kazakhs, a Turkic-speaking people about 2%. Russians, Chinese, Khotan Turks, and Tuvinians form smaller minorities **Population Distribution:** 46% urban **Density:** 2.5 inhabitants per sq. mi.
Largest Cities: (1973 est.) Ulan Bator 310,000; (1969 census) Darkhan 23,300, Choibalsan 20,500, Nalaikha 14,100, Ulangom 14,000, Uliassutai 13,000, Kobdo 12,400
Per Capita Income: $720 (1978 est.) **Gross National Product (GNP):** $1.1 billion (1978 est.) **Economic Statistics:** Statistics on

GNP components are not available. The mainstay of the economy, however, is animal husbandry (sheep, goats, camels, cattle, and horses) and some field crops. Most industry is related to the processing of livestock products. Coal, copper, and molybdenum are the chief mining industries **Minerals and Mining:** Coal, copper and molybdenum **Labor Force:** Most work in state farms and collectives. Agriculture employs 55%, industry 11%, and services 10% **Foreign Trade:** Exports are chiefly cattle, coal, copper, molybdenum, wool, raw hides, and butter and meat products. Imports are mainly consumer goods, machinery, equipment, and industrial raw materials **Principal Trade Partners:** USSR (80%), Czechoslovakia, East Germany, Hungary, Poland, Romania

Vital Statistics: Birthrate, 38.8 per 1,000 of pop. (1975); death rate, 9.3 **Life Expectancy:** 64 years **Health Statistics:** 103 inhabitants per hospital bed; 538 per physician (1974) **Infant Mortality:** N.A. **Illiteracy:** 20% **Education Statistics:** 614 primary and secondary schools, with combined enrollment of 321,955 (1975) **Enrollment in Higher Education:** 9,861 (1975) **GNP Expended on Education:** N.A.

Transportation: Surfaced roads total 992 mi. **Motor Vehicles:** 24,000 **Passenger Cars:** N.A. **Railway Mileage:** 1,282 **Ports:** None **Major Airlines:** Air Mongol flies internally and to the Soviet Union **Communications:** Government owned **Radio Transmitters:** 2 **Receivers:** 115,000 (1976) **Television Stations:** 1 **Receivers:** 3,600 (1976) **Telephones:** 38,000 (1976) **Newspapers:** 1 daily, 78 copies per 1,000 inhabitants (1975)

Weights and Measures: Metric system and traditional units are used **Travel Requirements:** Passport; visa (obtainable in London, Paris, or Moscow)

One of the most thinly populated countries in the world, Mongolia is three times as large as France, but most of its territory is desert and semiarid rangeland. Mongolia's importance in international politics is less a matter of its size than of its position: wedged directly between Communist China and the Soviet Union, and long a cause for friction between them.

All of Mongolia was considered part of China for centuries. A Mongol movement to gain independence at the turn of the century, supported by the tsarist Russian government, resulted in "autonomy" for Outer Mongolia. However, in 1919, after the tsarist government itself was overthrown by the 1917 revolution, the Chinese sent troops into Mongolia and canceled its autonomy. The Chinese troops were expelled in the early 1920s by White Russian forces, which in turn were defeated by the Soviet Red Army. Outer Mongolia was then established as the second Socialist state in the world and the first Soviet satellite.

Lavish Soviet aid has enabled Mongolia to make impressive economic advances. The economy still relies heavily on its livestock base—the country's most important resource—but collective farms for stockbreeding have been established and there are a few nomadic herdsmen left. Industrial production has increased sharply.

The help given by the Soviet Union has not gone unnoticed in China. In a 1973 speech before the UN General Assembly, Chinese Deputy Foreign Minister Chiao Kuan-hua challenged the Soviet Union to remove its troops from Mongolia. China's problem is that there are more Mongols in China—in Inner Mongolia—than there are in the Mongolian Republic, and fears that Mongol nationalism might result in efforts to detach further segments of Chinese territory are apparently real. Possibly to guard against a Mongol nationalist movement in China, Peking in 1970 assigned large segments of Inner Mongolia to neighboring provinces.

In 1968 and 1969 there were small flare-ups along the 2,500-mile Chinese/Mongolian border, and the Mongols charged that the Chinese had sought to subvert their government and install a pro-Peking regime.

A nation of pivotal importance, Mongolia seems to have no alternative but to try to maneuver between Moscow and Peking while striving to maintain its independence.

HISTORY: The Mongols, loosely organized nomadic tribes living in Mongolia, China, and Siberia, were united in the 13th century under the leadership of Genghis Khan, who established a far-flung Eurasian empire. After his death, the empire was divided and eventually disintegrated, and a cleavage developed between the southern, or inner, Mongols, ruled by the Chinese, and the northern, or outer, Mongols. In 1691 the northern Mongols accepted Chinese authority and remained under their rule until the 20th century

1911: Mongol princes proclaim Outer Mongolia an independent monarchy following the overthrow of China's Manchu dynasty; the throne is given to Bogdo Gegen, the Living Buddha of Urga

1915: Outer Mongolia signs treaty with republican China and tsarist Russia accepting autonomous status under Chinese authority; Russia gains control over Mongolia's foreign affairs

1919-21: Attempts by China to reassert sovereignty over Outer Mongolia following the Russian Revolution are defeated; Russian forces expel Chinese, and Outer Mongolia again proclaims its independence

1924: Mongolian People's Republic is proclaimed following the death of the Living Buddha; Communist rule is inaugurated with Soviet help

1950: Communist China and USSR sign treaty guaranteeing Mongolia's independence

1962: Mongolia and Communist China sign treaty fixing their 2,500-mile border. Premier Tsedenbal backs Soviet policy on peaceful coexistence, challenged by Peking

1963: Mongolia establishes diplomatic relations with Britain in the first such pact with a Western power. Mongolia asks Communist China to withdraw laborers sent by Peking to work on Mongolian construction projects

1964: Pro-Peking sympathizers are purged from Mongolian Communist party

1966-67: Relations between Mongolia and Communist China become strained. Soviet troops are stationed on Mongolia border

1969: Soviet and Communist Chinese troops clash at the Ussuri River, and tension rises on the Chinese-Mongolian frontier. Yumjagiyn Tsedenbal reelected premier

1970: Soviet-Mongolian five-year economic plan drafted. Border troubles with Communist China continue

1976: Tsendenbal reelected first secretary for the fifth time

1978: The government introduces restrictions to stop the flow of rural people to the cities

---

MOROCCO

Area: 172,413 sq. mi. **Population:** 18,240,000 (1978 est.)

Official Name: Kingdom of Morocco **Capital:** Rabat **Nationality:** Moroccan **Languages:** Arabic, the official language, is spoken by about 65%; Berber dialects are spoken by about 35%. French is also widely used **Religion:** The majority of Moroccans are Sunni Moslems and Islam is the state religion; there are small minorities of Christians and Jews **Flag:** A red field with a green 5-pointed star in the center **Anthem:** National Anthem (no words) **Currency:** Moroccan dirham (4.0 per U.S. $1)

Location: Northwest Africa. Morocco is bordered on the north by the Mediterranean Sea, on the east by Algeria, on the south, with the contested Western Sahara area interposed, by Mauritania, and on the west by the Atlantic Ocean **Features:** The center is occupied by the dry, rocky Atlas Mountains, which slope downward to narrow fertile coastal plains along the Mediterranean and the Atlantic. The south is occupied by the Sahara **Chief Rivers:** Oum-er-Rbia, Dra, Moulouya, Sous, Sebou

Head of State: King Hassan II, born 1929, ascended the throne 1961. Under the 1972 constitution, the king has limited authority to circumvent parliament by proclaiming a state of emergency or putting major issues to a referendum, which cannot be appealed **Head of Government:** Prime Minister Maati Bouabid, appointed March 1979 **Effective Date of Present Constitution:** March 1972 **Legislative Body:** Parliament (unicameral Chamber of Representatives), with 264 members elected for 4 years **Local Government:** 30 provinces and 2 urban prefectures, each headed by an appointed governor

Ethnic Composition: The majority of Moroccans are of Arab descent; about 35% are of Berber origin **Population Distribution:** 38% urban **Density:** 76 inhabitants per sq. mi.

Largest Cities: (1973 est.—Metropolitan Areas) Casablanca 1,753,400, Rabat 596,600, Marrakech 436,300, Fez 426,000, Meknès 403,000, Oujda 394,400, Kénitra 341,600, Tetuan 308,700, Safi 214,600, Tangier 208,000, Agadir 189,000

Per Capita Income: $534 (1978) **Gross National Product (GNP):** $10.4 billion (1978 est.) **Economic Statistics:** 22% of the GNP is derived from agriculture (wheat, barley, fruits, corn, sugar, livestock), forestry and fishing; 21% from commerce; 16% from transportation and services; 12% from industry (food processing and canning, sugar refining, milling, tobacco production); and 4%

from mining **Minerals and Mining:** Leading minerals are phosphates (45% of all minerals produced by the state), iron ore, coal, manganese, fluorite, cobalt, lead, zinc, copper **Labor Force:** 4.1 million in 1977, with 51% in agriculture, 20% in industry, and 29% in services **Foreign Trade:** Exports, chiefly vegetables, citrus fruit, phosphates, wine, and canned fish, totaled $1.3 billion in 1977. Imports, mainly wheat, sugar, industrial machinery and equipment, cotton and synthetic textile yarn, iron and steel products, are estimated at $3.2 billion **Principal Trade Partners:** EC countries, Poland, United States, USSR, Spain

Vital Statistics: Birthrate, 46.2 per 1,000 of pop. (1975); death rate, 15.7 **Life Expectancy:** 54 years **Health Statistics:** 748 inhabitants per hospital bed; 13,982 per physician (1975) **Infant Mortality:** 117 per 1,000 births **Illiteracy:** 79% **Education Statistics:** 5,248 primary and secondary schools have a combined enrollment of 2,030,038 (1975) **Enrollment in Higher Education:** 45,322 (1975) **GNP Expended on Education:** 15.3% (1973)

Transportation: Paved roads total 10,727 mi. **Motor Vehicles:** 493,200 (1976) **Passenger Cars:** 347,400 **Railway Mileage:** 1,156 **Ports:** Casablanca, Safi, Kénitra, Mohammedia, Agadir, Essaouira **Major Airlines:** Royal Air Maroc operates both domestically and internationally **Communications:** Government controlled **Radio Transmitters:** 33 **Receivers:** 1,500,000 (1976) **Television Transmitters:** 23 **Receivers:** 522,000 (1976) **Telephones:** 204,000 (1976) **Newspapers:** 9 dailies; 21 copies per 1,000 inhabitants (1975)

Weights and Measures: Metric system **Travel Requirements:** Passport; no visa for 3 months

---

Geographically, Morocco is the westernmost Arab country, the only one with a border on the Atlantic coast of North Africa. It stands almost as close to the United States as to the eastern end of the Arab world, and at one point—the Strait of Gibraltar—it is literally within sight of Europe.

Politically, too, Morocco shows Western tendencies. Although nominally a member of the Arab League, it remains outside the main thrust of Arab politics, commerce, and culture. In recent years, it has made great efforts to cultivate the friendship of the United States and Western Europe, with which it seems to have closer interests than with the militant Arab countries to its east.

Since independence from France in 1956, Morocco has been a monarchy with a liberal-sounding constitution, but King Hassan II has been as absolute as any in the world.

Dissolving the National Assembly in 1965, the king instituted a "state of exception" that gave him virtually unlimited power. In 1970, by national referendum, a new constitution provided a modified form of parliamentary government; the 1972 constitution further limited the king's powers to challenge legislative decisions. He retains the power to declare a state of emergency.

The nation's chief problems are its rapidly expanding population—the growth rate is three percent a year—and the inability of its economy to keep pace. Since independence, investment has been mostly in agriculture, dams, and irrigation projects.

Although there has been some economic progress, considerably more is still needed. It is estimated that 40 percent of the youth between 20 and 30 are unemployed. Unemployment has forced workers to emigrate to western Europe to find jobs. The money they have returned to their families in Morocco has provided a valuable addition to the Moroccan balance of payments. Tourism has increased greatly in recent years.

A Communist party exists in the country, but most Moroccan intellectuals, like their Algerian neighbors, have their own ideas about socialism and are not particularly attracted by either the Soviet or Chinese brand. The main support for the king—who is also the country's religious leader—comes from the rural areas.

By Arab-world standards, Morocco has a large middle class, imbued with both Arab and French culture, whose high standard of living coexists with the feudal rural society. In addition, it has the largest remaining French community—numbering some 100,000—in North Africa. The coexistence of the Arab and French cultures, however, adds to the frustration of many young intellectuals, who are increasingly demanding the Arabization of their country.

In March 1973 King Hassan reacted to steadily mounting pressures for an economic shake-up by decreeing the nationalization of farmlands in foreign hands and the elimination of foreign ownership of businesses.

In 1974 opposition to Spain's plans to grant self-rule to the Spanish Sahara, which Morocco claimed, united all Moroccan political elements behind the monarchy for the first time since the early 1960s. By November 1975 Spain agreed to partition Spanish Sahara. Despite Algeria's opposition to the partition, the northern two thirds, including rich phosphate deposits at Bu Craa, went to Morocco and the southern third to Mauritania, and in December Moroccan officials proclaimed the annexation of Western Sahara as Moroccan troops marched into its capital.

When Mauritania and Morocco divided Western Sahara and the Saharan assembly ratified its annexation in 1976, they did not recognize the proclamation of the *Polisario Front*, the Saharan liberation movement, of the Saharan Arab Democratic Republic (SADR). Algeria's recognition of the SADR caused Morocco to sever diplomatic relations. After the Mauritanian army deposed President Moktar Ould Daddah in 1978, the *Polisario* made a tacit cease-fire with the new Mauritanian government and concentrated its energies on Morocco. In 1979 Mauritania gave up its claim to the southern portion of Western Sahara, which Morocco promptly occupied. The conflict has placed a burden on the Moroccan economy.

In 1979, Ahmed Osman resigned as premier, and King Hassan appointed Maati Bouabid, a former labor leader, to succeed him.

HISTORY: In ancient times, Morocco was part of the empire of Carthage. Under the Romans it was formed into the province of Mauritania and later experienced successive invasions until conquered by the Arabs c. A.D. 683. Morocco became an independent kingdom in 788, but by the 10th century had broken up into several tribal states. The country was ultimately united under the Almoravids, a Berber Moslem dynasty that established a kingdom stretching from Senegal to Spain

15th cent.: Portugal and Spain capture all Moroccan ports

17th cent.: Morocco recaptures many European strongholds

1906: Algeciras Conference grants France special privileges in Morocco

1912: Morocco becomes a protectorate; under a French-Spanish agreement the country is divided administratively into French Morocco, Spanish Morocco, and a Southern Protectorate of Morocco, administered as part of the Spanish Sahara, and the international zone of Tangier

1953: Faced with growing movement for independence, French depose Sultan Sidi Mohammed ben Youssef and exile him to Madagascar

1955: French permit Sultan to return

1956-57: Morocco gains independence in 1956; Tangier is restored. In 1957 Sidi Mohammed ben Youssef becomes King Mohammed V

1961-62: King Mohammed dies and is succeeded by his son, Hassan II. In 1962 a draft constitution presented by Hassan is approved by referendum

1965: Hassan declares state of emergency and assumes executive and legislative power

1970: New constitution is adopted ending king's absolutist rule

1971: Hassan survives attempted coup by rebellious army officers and cadets; king charges Libya with inciting the rebellion

1972: Hassan survives second attempted coup within 13 months. Defense Minister Oufkir, who had exercised wide civil and military powers after the 1971 attempt, found dead after leading counterattack on rebels. He is charged by Hassan with organizing the attempted takeover

1974: Massive deposit of oil shale discovered in Middle Atlas Mountains. King Hassan presses Spain to return Spanish Sahara territory to Morocco

1975: Some 200,000 unarmed Moroccans who moved over the

border in the "Green March" into Spanish Sahara "to regain the Sahara peacefully," are called back by Hassan

1976: Morocco and Mauritania divide the disputed Western Sahara. Relations are severed with Algeria because of Algeria's support of *Polisario* guerrillas

1977: Moroccan troops are sent to Zaire to help repel invaders of Shaba province

1978: Moroccan government sends troops to Shaba Province in Zaire following invasion there by Katangan rebels. Railway workers and civil servants strike for higher pay

1979: Maati Bouabid succeeds Ahmed Osman as premier. Morocco occupies southern third of Western Sahara, after Mauritania renounces claim to area

MOZAMBIQUE

Area: 303,769 sq. mi. **Population:** 9,680,000 (1978 est.)
Official Name: People's Republic of Mozambique **Capital:** Maputo **Nationality:** Mozambican **Languages:** Bantu languages; Portuguese is the official language **Religion:** Chiefly traditional African religions, though there are some Moslems and Roman Catholics. The present Marxist regime has discouraged religious practices **Flag:** Four diagonal wedges of green, red, black and yellow separated by narrow white wedges, the national emblem of a white cogwheel with red star, white book, black silhouettes of hoe and rifle is at the upper left **Anthem:** N.A. **Currency:** Mozambique escudo (32.8 per U.S. $1)
Location: On the east coast of Africa, bounded by the Mozambique Channel on the east, Swaziland on the south, South Africa on the south and west, Zimbabwe Rhodesia on the west, Zambia and Malawi on the northwest, and Tanzania on the north **Features:** Lowlands along the 1,700-mile-long coast rise to an 8,000-ft. plateau, with mountains to the north. The northern coastal plain is hot and humid, but is cooler to the south and inland **Chief Rivers:** Ruvuma, Lurio, Zambezi, Save, Limpopo
Head of State and of Government: President Samora Moisés Machel, born 1934, installed June 1975. He is head of the Marxist-Leninist Party **Effective Date of Present Constitution:** 1975 **Legislative Body:** National People's Assembly of 220 members **Local Government:** 10 provinces
Ethnic Composition: The people are mostly of Bantu stock, with a minority (perhaps 10,000) Europeans (mostly Portuguese) **Population Distribution:** 8% urban **Density:** 32 inhabitants per sq. mi.
Largest Cities: (1970 census) Maputo 101,754, Beira 46,293, Nampula 23,072, Quelimane 10,522, Xai-Xai 5,234
Per Capita Income: $153 (1978 est.) **Gross National Product (GNP):** $1.5 billion (1978 est.) **Economic Statistics:** In 1975 the service sector (including transportation and tourism) accounted for 30% of the GNP; agriculture, 40%; and industry 20% **Minerals and Mining:** Copper, coal, beryl, columbite, fluorite, bauxite and tantalite **Labor Force:** 600,000 wage earners, with 80% of the population in subsistence agriculture **Foreign Trade:** Exports, chiefly cashew nuts, cotton and cotton products, sugar, copra, sisal fiber, tea and vegetable oils, amounted to $303 million in 1976. Imports, chiefly machinery, transportation equipment, metals and metal products, petroleum and wheat, reached $334 million **Principal Trade Partners:** France, Britain, Portugal, Iran, United States, Japan
Vital Statistics: Birthrate, 43 per 1,000 of pop. (1975); death rate, 23 per 1,000 **Life Expectancy:** 43.5 years **Health Statistics:** 549 inhabitants per hospital bed; 16,392 per physician (1971) **Infant Mortality:** 92.5 per 1,000 births **Illiteracy:** 88% **Educational Statistics:** 4,274 primary and secondary schools, with a total enrollment of 632,647 (1974) **Enrollment in Higher Education:** 2,621 (1972) **GNP Expended on Education:** 1.1% (1972)
Transportation: Paved roads total 2,100 mi. **Motor Vehicles:** 110,800 (1972) **Passenger Cars:** 89,300 **Railway Mileage:** 2,350 miles **Ports:** Maputo, Beira, Nacala, Pemba, Quelimane **Major Airlines:** The domestic airline is DETA; international services are provided by several African airlines **Communications:** Government controlled **Radio Transmitters:** 49 **Licenses:** 225,000 (1976) **Television Transmitters:** None **Telephones:** 52,000 (1976) **Newspapers:** 5 dailies, 9 copies per 1,000 inhabitants (1975)
Weights and Measures: Metric system **Travel Requirements:** Apply to Permanent Mission of the People's Republic of Mozambique, New York 10017

Portuguese rule left an inheritance of poverty and disease for much of Mozambique's population. Forced labor was widespread, political rights and education limited. Ten years of pre-independence guerrilla war, the flight of skilled whites and the imposition of doctrinaire socialism have also taken their toll.

Nationalist forces aiming at independence be-

gan guerrilla warfare in 1964, starting in the north. The chief rebel movement was the Front for the Liberation of Mozambique (FRELIMO) which had been working for independence since 1962.

Clashes between the Portuguese army and insurgents increased in early 1974. In September after the military overthrew the home government in Portugal, FRELIMO and the Portuguese High Commissioner signed an agreement under which Mozambique would be ruled by a joint transitional government until full independence.

On June 25, 1975, Mozambique achieved full independence after 500 years of colonial rule, becoming the 45th African state to do so. Samora Moisés Machel, the first president, pledged to transform the country into the "first truly Marxist state in Africa." FRELIMO became the country's sole political party in the new state and the nucleus for the new People's Republic of Mozambique government. Since then the government has been establishing its authority and Marxist-oriented philosophy at all levels of society and planning a post-colonial economy. Among the goals of the FRELIMO program is the eradication of tribalism, regionalism, and racism.

At first Mozambique's future looked relatively bright in comparison to Portugal's other African territories, but most of the 220,000 whites fled, leaving the country almost without skilled and professional workers. All land was nationalized and food production declined by 75 percent in some areas while production of major cash crops was off by half. Many factories have been abandoned and the government now offers incentives for Portuguese managers to stay on. The major income remaining is foreign exchange earned by Mozambique miners in South Africa.

In March 1976 Machel closed the border with Rhodesia, imposed sanctions and proclaimed a state of war. As Mozambique increased its efforts to train Rhodesian guerrillas and help them infiltrate the white-ruled nation because of its commitment to black nationalism, it was itself having greater economic and political problems. The border closing shut off Mozambique's major source of food and cost the country $165 million a year.

HISTORY: Bantu peoples entered Mozambique after 1000 A.D. from Central Africa. Arab traders touched on the coast prior to the coming of the Portuguese under Vasco da Gama in 1498. The Portuguese developed trading posts and a thriving slave trade during the following centuries. Mozambique's colonial boundaries were fixed by the end of the 19th century

1951: Portugal establishes Mozambique as an Overseas Province

1964: Independence forces begin guerrilla warfare

1974: FRELIMO (Mozambique Liberation Front) and Portugal agree to joint rule prior to independence

1975: Mozambique achieves independence

1976: Mozambique closes border with Rhodesia and declares a state of war. Intermittent border clashes occur

1977: Border clashes continue. Black refugees from Rhodesia fill camps in Mozambique. Mozambicans vote in first election since independence. Rhodesia reports its troops killed at least 1,200 "armed terrorists" 132 miles inside Mozambique

1978: Virtually all foreign and local banks are nationalized. Government denounces Rhodesian settlement reached between Rhodesian Prime Minister Ian Smith and three nationalist leaders. Flooding of Zambezi leaves more than 200,000 homeless. Rhodesian troops with air support strike at two points in Mozambique, but reportedly kill refugees and UN technicians rather than guerrillas

NAMIBIA
(*see* Territories and Dependencies *section*)

NAURU

Area: 7.7 sq. mi. **Population:** 7,100 (1978 est.)
Official Name: Republic of Nauru **Capital:** Yaren (district) **Nationality:** Nauruan **Languages:** Nauruan and English **Religion:** Christian, mainly Protestant **Flag:** A blue field halved by a horizon-

tal gold bar, with a white star at the lower left. **Anthem:** N.A.
Currency: Australian dollar (0.91 per U.S. $1)

Location: Central Pacific. The island of Nauru lies just south of the equator, about 1,300 miles northeast of Australia **Features:** The island is completely surrounded by a coral reef. A narrow, fertile coastal strip lying between a sandy beach and coral cliffs is the most populated part of the island. The interior consists of a barren plateau containing extensive phosphate deposits, Nauru's major economic resource **Chief Rivers:** There are no rivers

Head of State and of Government: President Hammer De Roburt, born 1922, took office in 1978 **Effective Date of Present Constitution:** 1968 **Legislative Body:** Parliament (unicameral Legislative Assembly), consisting of 18 members elected by universal suffrage for 3 years **Local Government:** The island is divided into 14 districts, grouped into 8 electoral units

Ethnic Composition: The Nauruans are believed to be a mixture of Polynesian, Micronesian, and Melanesian, with Polynesian predominating. Other Pacific Islanders number about 1,800, Chinese 1,100, and Europeans 500 **Population Distribution:** Virtually the entire population is concentrated in settlements along the coast **Density:** 922 inhabitants per sq. mile

Per Capita Income: $17,000 (1975) **Gross National Product (GNP):** $120 million (1975) **Economic Statistics:** Nauru's economy is built around the phosphate industry, which produces a revenue of more than $100 million annually and enables the islanders to enjoy one of the highest per capita incomes in the world. Although some food products are grown on the island, the inhabitants are largely dependent on imports of food supplies and all manufactured goods **Labor Force:** Nauruans, as a rule, do not engage in manual labor, and the phosphate industry is largely dependent on outside labor, employing 1,389 Chinese, Gilbertese, Australians, and Nauruans in 1975. About 60% of Nauruans are employed in the civil service **Foreign Trade:** Exports, consisting entirely of phosphates, totaled $123 million in 1975. Imports, chiefly hardware, food, vehicles, machinery, timber, furniture, medicines, and fuels, amounted to $15 million **Principal Trade Partners:** Australia, New Zealand, Britain, Hong Kong, Japan, South Korea, China (Taiwan), Mexico

Vital Statistics: Birthrate, 19.8 per 1,000 of pop. (1976); death rate, 8.3 **Life Expectancy:** 53 years **Health Statistics:** 34 inhabitants per hospital bed; 700 per physician (1971) **Infant Mortality:** 19 per 1,000 births **Illiteracy:** Negligible **Educational Statistics:** 10 primary and secondary schools with combined enrollment of 1,973 (1975) **Enrollment in Higher Education:** 92 studying abroad (1975) **GNP Expended on Education:** 2.8% (1970)

Transportation: A road 18-22 feet wide circles the island; another, 16 feet wide, runs to the Buada district **Motor Vehicles:** There are more than 1,000 vehicles of all kinds on the island **Railway Mileage:** A three-and-one-quarter-mile stretch of railway links the phospate workings with the coast **Ports:** None. Nauru's shores go nearly straight down into deep waters, requiring the construction of special moorings for ships **Major Airlines:** Air Nauru operates flights to Pacific and Asian cities **Communications:** Government owned **Radio Transmitters:** 1 **Receivers:** 3,600 (1976) **Television:** None **Telephones:** 700 **Newspapers:** 1 weekly (Pinnacle Press is produced by the British Phosphate Commission and distributed free)

Weights and Measures: British standards are used **Travel Requirements:** Applications for permission to enter Nauru must be made in writing to the Secretary of Justice in Nauru or to the Nauruan representative in Melbourne, Australia

---

The barren central plateau of Nauru, the tiny Pacific island, which is the smallest independent republic in the world, consists of large phosphate deposits, the result of centuries of bird droppings, that provide Nauru with a good source of income: the phosphate, much prized as fertilizer, is the island's main natural resource and only export.

This unique export helps to give the people of Nauru one of the highest per capita incomes in the world, as well as shops filled with luxury goods, free medical care, good housing, good schools, no taxes, and jobs for all.

Only 12 miles in circumference and three-and-a-half-miles wide, Nauru was named Pleasant Island by the captain of a British whaling ship who discovered it in 1798. Early contacts with Europeans brought guns and disease, and a consequent ravaging of the population. The people of Nauru now are more concerned with depletion of the phosphate deposits. Estimated to total 45 million tons, the deposits are expected to be exhausted in the 1990s.

Intense debate over the nation's course once the phosphate has been depleted has led to a rare period of political instability. In April 1978 President Dowiyogo, reelected the preceding November, resigned; his plan to raise a $22-million development loan overseas had been opposed by parliament. He was succeeded by Lagumot Harris, who himself resigned a month later after a money bill of his met a similar fate. Harris was succeeded by Hammer de Roburt, the man who led Nauru to independence in 1968.

HISTORY: Nauru, discovered by a British whaling team in 1798, was long known as Pleasant Island. In 1888 it was annexed by Germany and henceforth known by its native name. Phosphate was discovered on the island in the late 1890s and exploitation begun in 1901. With the outbreak of World War I, Australian forces occupied the island. After the war, Nauru was administered by Australia under a League of Nations mandate, which also named Britain and New Zealand as cotrustees

1942-45: Nauru is occupied by Japanese forces; 1,200 islanders are deported to Truk as forced labor

1947: Island is placed under United Nations Trusteeship, with Australia acting as administrator on behalf of the Australian, New Zealand, and British governments

1964: In anticipation of the exhaustion of Nauru's phosphate deposits, expected in about 30 years, Australia proposes that inhabitants be resettled on Curtis Island, off the Queensland coast; islanders reject proposal, choosing to remain on Nauru

1968: Nauru becomes independent republic; islanders reject proposals that Australia handle their defense and external affairs. Hammer De Roburt is elected president

1970: Nauru assumes management of its phosphate industry

1976: Bernard Dowiyogo is elected president

1977-78: Debate over nation's "post-phosphate" future leads to period of instability. President Dowiyogo resigns; Lagumot Harris succeeds him. Harris resigns; Hammer de Roburt succeeds Harris

---

NEPAL

Area: 54,663 sq. mi. **Population:** 13,136,000 (1978 est.)

Official Name: Kingdom of Nepal **Capital:** Kathmandu **Nationality:** Nepalese **Languages:** Nepali, the official language, is the first language of roughly 50% of the population and is spoken by another 30%; Tibeto-Burman languages (chiefly Newari), Indo-Aryan dialects, and English are also spoken **Religion:** Hinduism, the official religion, is the dominant faith (90%); Mahayana Buddhism is the dominant religion in the sparsely inhabited north, and both faiths are followed by many people of the central region **Flag:** Two red right-angled triangles bordered in blue at the hoist; the upper with a white moon crescent, the lower with a white sun **Anthem:** National Anthem, beginning "May glory crown our illustrious sovereign" **Currency:** Nepalese rupee (12 per U.S. $1)

Location: Central Asia. Landlocked Nepal is bordered on the north by China (Tibet), and on the east, south and west by India **Features:** The country is mountainous, with dense swampy jungles. Across the south lies the 20-mile-wide Terai, a region of plain and swamp. Most of the country, a band across the center, is broken by sharp mountain ranges and traversed by high, fertile valleys. Along the northern border lies the high Himalaya, with 8 of the world's 12 highest peaks, including Mount Everest, whose 29,028-ft. elevation is the highest in the world **Chief Rivers:** Kali, Karnali, Gandak, Kosi

Head of State: King Birendra Bir Bikram Shah Dev, born 1946, acceded to the throne January 1972 **Head of Government:** Prime Minister: Surya Bahadur Thapa, appointed June 1979 **Effective Date of Present Constitution:** December 1962, amended December 1975 **Legislative Body:** Parliament (unicameral National Panchayat), with 135 representatives from zonal assemblies and class groups, and 23 nominees of the king. A third of the members are elected for 6 years; the others serve for 2 or 4 years **Local Government:** 14 zones, each headed by an appointed commissioner, and 75 districts, each with a district assembly and 11-member executive committee known as the district panchayat. The latter, in turn, form a zonal assembly

Ethnic Composition: The Nepalese are descendants of 3 major migrations from India and Tibet. In addition to the Brahmans and Chetris whose ancestors came from India, the numerous tribes, called castes, include the Gurungs and Magars in the west; Tamangs and Newars in the center; Bhotias in the north; Rais, Limbus, and Sherpas in the east; and Tharus in the south **Population Distribution:** 5% urban **Density:** 240 inhabitants per sq. mi.

Largest Cities: (1971 census) Kathmandu 150,402, Lalitpur 59,049, Biratnagar 45,100, Bhaktapur 40,112

Per Capita Income: $116 (1978) **Gross National Product (GNP):** $1.5 billion (1978) **Economic Statistics:** In 1973 about 65% of GNP was from agriculture (paddy rice, maize, wheat, millet, jute) and forestry; 12% from mining and manufacturing (jute, textiles, yarns, cigarettes, vegetable oil-crushing); and 17.3% from trade and services **Minerals and Mining:** Coal is mined. There are unexploited deposits of iron ore, copper, mica, lead, zinc, cobalt, nickel, and talc **Labor Force:** 4,852,524 (1971), 94% of which is in agriculture and 2% in industry **Foreign Trade:** Exports, chiefly rice, jute and jute products, ghee, oilseeds, timber, and herbs, totaled $98 million in 1977. Imports, mainly textiles, foodstuffs, petroleum products, machinery and equipment, vehicles and parts, totaled $169 million **Principal Trade Partner:** India

Vital Statistics: Birthrate, 42.9 per 1,000 of pop. (1975); death rate, 20.3 **Life Expectancy:** 40 years **Health Statistics:** 6,630 inhabitants per hospital bed; 36,450 per physician (1974) **Infant Mortality:** 152 per 1,000 births **Illiteracy:** 80% **Education Statistics:** 8,314 primary and secondary schools, with combined enrollment of 714,830 (1975) **Enrollment in Higher Education:** 23,504 **GNP Expended on Education:** 1% (1973)

Transportation: All-weather roads total 1,906 (1973) **Motor Vehicles:** 12,646 (1970) **Passenger Cars:** 7,281 **Railway Mileage:** 63 **Ports:** None **Major Airlines:** Royal Nepal Airlines operates domestic and international services **Communications:** Government-owned **Radio Transmitters:** 5 **Receivers:** 150,000 (1976) **Television:** None **Telephones:** 9,162 (1974) **Newspapers:** 29 dailies (1975), 3 copies per 1,000 inhabitants (1974)

Weights and Measures: Metric system and local standards used **Travel Requirements:** Passport; visa valid for 30-day stay; $5 fee; 1 photo

Beguiled by the slightly touristic, but not untrue, face that Nepal presents to the outside world, mountaineers, tourists, and hippies have flocked there and found what they sought: a peaceful Himalayan kingdom, backward but pleasant, a land of green valleys and towering mountains (including the world's highest, 29,028-ft. Mt. Everest, shared with Tibet), all presided over by the world's only Hindu king, thought by his people to be an incarnation of the god Vishnu.

The other side of Nepal's character is harsher, but no less true. Nepal is a primitive, divided, stratified society caught between two powerful and jealous neighbors, China and India, and unsettled by the pressures of modernization. With its history marked by bitter political feuding, Nepal is in a difficult position to shape the modernity its leaders want.

In recent years Nepal has halted Indian interference in its internal affairs and has established close relations with China.

Rising taxes, high prices, and shortages have contributed to recent unrest. The antigovernment Nepali Congress Party is seeking to restore parliamentary democracy while retaining the king as a constitutional monarch. In 1979, what began as student demands for academic changes turned into broad political protests joined by peasants, laborers, and the middle class. Five or more persons died in riots in several towns. As a result of the demonstrations Prime Minister Bista resigned, and was replaced by Surya Bahadur Thapa.

HISTORY: Nepal, the world's only Hindu kingdom, has a long historical continuity, although little is known about the country before the 15th century. The modern kingdom of Nepal was established in the 18th century by the ruler of Gurkha, a small principality west of Kathmandu. His descendants introduced Hinduism as the state religion and established most of the present boundaries

1790-93: Gurkhas invade Tibet. A large Chinese army counterattacks and forces the Gurkhas to come to terms. Seeking assistance against the Chinese, the Gurkhas sign treaty with the British in India

1814-16: Series of frontier incidents leads to war between the British and Nepal. Nepal surrenders much of its territory and permits a British residency to be set up at Kathmandu

1846: Jung Bahadur Rana seizes the government and reduces the king to a figurehead

1951: An end is made to more than a century of rule by a succession of hereditary prime ministers from a noble family, the Ranas, during which the royal family played little part in governing. King Tribhuvana assumes power with Indian help, promises elections to a constituent assembly to formulate new constitution

1955: King Tribhuvana dies and is succeeded by Crown Prince Mahendra. Nepal joins UN

1959: King Mahendra declares Nepal a constitutional monarchy. In the country's first election, the Nepali Congress Party wins an absolute majority

1960: King Mahendra dismisses the cabinet, dissolves parliament, bans political parties, and assumes powers of government; many political leaders are arrested

1962: New constitution is promulgated, introducing *panchayat* system of government from the village to the national level

1963: King Mahendra forms a state council with the right to advise the monarch

1972: King Mahendra dies and is succeeded by his son, Crown Prince Birendra Bir Bikram Shah Dev

1974: Nepal and China sign trade pact

1975: King Birendra, who received part of his education at Harvard, is formally crowned. Prime Minister Nagendra Prasad Rijal is replaced by Dr. Tulsi Giri. Heavily armed Khampa refugees from Tibet are driven from the Himalayan passes by Nepalese troops.

1977: Prime Minister Tulsi Giri resigns; Kirti Nidhi Bista, who has held the post three times in eight years, succeeds him

1978: King Birendra slightly eases his stern control of Nepalese life

1979: Students, joined by other dissidents, stage violent demonstrations to demand that the monarchy be liberalized. B.P. Koirala, former prime minister who leads efforts for constitutional reform, is charged with sedition and incitement to armed rebellion. Prime Minister Bista resigns; Surya Bahadur Thapa is appointed in his place

THE NETHERLANDS

Area: 15,892 sq. mi. **Population:** 13,871,000 (1978 est.)

Official Name: Kingdom of the Netherlands **Capital:** Amsterdam, but the seat of government is at The Hague **Nationality:** Netherlands or Dutch **Languages:** Hollands, or Dutch, is the official and predominant language; Frisian is spoken in the northern province of Friesland **Religion:** About 32.9% Protestant, 40.4% Roman Catholic, and 23.6% no religion **Flag:** Red, white, and blue horizontal stripes **Anthem:** Wilhelmus van Nassouwen (William of Nassau) **Currency:** Guilder (florin) (2.1 per U.S. $1)

Location: Northwest Europe. The Netherlands is bounded on the west and north by the North Sea, on the east by West Germany, and on the south by Belgium **Features:** The country is low and flat except for some hills in the southeast. About one-third of the land area is below sea level, and more than one-fifth reclaimed from the sea and protected by dikes **Chief Rivers:** Maas, IJssel, Waal, Lek

Head of State: Queen Juliana, born 1909, acceded to the throne in 1948 **Head of Government:** Premier Andries A.M. van Agt, born 1931, appointed 1977 **Effective Date of Present Constitution:** 1814; frequently revised **Legislative Body:** The States General (bicameral), consisting of the First Chamber, or upper house, and the Second Chamber, or lower house. The First Chamber consists of 75 members chosen by the 11 provincial legislatures for 6 years. The Second Chamber has 150 members elected directly for 4 years **Local Government:** 11 provinces, with elected provincial executive councils and appointed commissioners, and the IJsselmeer polders

Ethnic Composition: The population is largely of Germanic stock, with some Gallo-Celtic mixture **Population Distribution:** 78% urban **Density:** 873 inhabitants per sq. mi.

Largest Cities: (1976 est.) Amsterdam 751,156, Rotterdam 614,767, The Hague 479,369, Utrecht 250,887, Eindhoven 192,562, Haarlem 164,672, Groningen 163,357, Tilburg 151,513

Per Capita Income: $6,324 (1978) **Gross National Product (GNP):** $88.1 billion (1978) **Economic Statistics:** About 42.3% of GNP comes from industry (capital and consumer goods, food processing, chemicals, textiles), mining, construction, and utilities; 17.8% from commerce, banking, and finance; 6.5% from agriculture; and the rest from other activities **Minerals and Mining:** Large reserves of natural gas are exploited along with some salt, and crude oil **Labor Force:** 4,800,000 (1977), of which 35% is employed in industry, 7% in agriculture, 58% in services **Foreign Trade:** Exports, mainly meats, flower bulbs, petroleum products, chemicals, textiles, machinery, and electrical equipment, totaled $44 billion in 1977. Imports, chiefly grains, petroleum, chemicals, textiles, iron and steel products, machinery and electrical equipment, and motor vehicles, totaled $46 billion **Principal Trade Partners:** Common Market countries, United States, Saudi Arabia

Vital Statistics: Birthrate, 12.5 per 1,000 of pop. (1977); death rate, 8.3 **Life Expectancy:** 77 years **Health Statistics:** 99 inhabitants per hospital bed; 670 per physician (1974) **Infant Mortality:** 9.5 per 1,000 births **Illiteracy:** Negligible **Education Statistics:** 11,525 primary and secondary schools, with combined enrollment of 3,629,828 (1975) **Enrollment in Higher Education:** 288,026 (1975) **GNP Expended on Education:** 7.9% (1973)

Transportation: Surfaced roads total 53,470 mi. **Motor Vehicles:** 4,118,000 (1976) **Passenger Cars:** 3,768,000 **Railway Mileage:** 1,760 **Ports:** Rotterdam, Amsterdam, IJmuiden, Terneuzen, Vlissingen, Delfzijl **Major Airlines:** K.L.M. (Royal Dutch Airlines) operates domestic and international flights **Communications:** Government owned **Radio Transmitters:** 30 **Licenses:** 3,997,000 (1976) **Television Transmitters:** 21 **Licenses:** 3,774,000 (1976) **Telephones:** 5,412,000 (1976) **Newspapers:** 93 dailies, 311 copies per 1,000 inhabitants (1973)

Weights and Measures: Metric System **Travel Requirements:** Passport; no visa up to 90 days

---

The Netherlands is just that, as much of the country lies below sea level. To a large extent it is manmade and is still being made. In 1932 a barrier dam closed the North Sea mouth of the Zuyder Zee, creating a vast freshwater lake, the IJsselmeer, out of which the hard-working Dutch have been carving habitable tracts, which by 1980 will have increased the Netherlands' arable land by a tenth. Spurred by a destructive storm in 1953, the country began to erect dams to create lakes and keep the sea out of southern estuaries.

This age-old battle against the depredations of the sea and the Rhine, Maas, and Scheldt rivers mirrors the centuries-old struggle of the Dutch against encroachment by man, from the conquest by Julius Caesar's legions in 55 B.C. to German occupation in World War II.

Aside from enlarging the country and bringing it freedom, the unity of purpose in the Netherlands' struggles has produced a people able to get along harmoniously and tolerant of other cultures, as shown in the integration of more than 300,000 nonwhite colonials from the former far-flung overseas empire. However the recent seizures of hostages by South Moluccan terrorists has led to a deterioration in relations between the Moluccans and the Dutch. The South Moluccans had emigrated to the Netherlands in the late 1940s when their islands became part of Indonesia.

Binding the loyalty of its citizens to the state is the four-centuries-old House of Orange, now headed by Queen Juliana. The modern Dutch governments reflect the tenor of the people. Though political parties are organized on religious and ideological principles, recent cabinets have been coalitions. A constitutional democracy, the Netherlands reflects rule by Burgundian kings five centuries ago, Dutch republicanism of the 16th to 18th centuries, and modern liberalism.

Ultimate power lies with parliament, which presides over jammed cities that blend charming old architecture with the new, and a countryside filled with canals, broad rivers, and tidy farms, few of which are larger than 50 acres. In fact, though the Netherlands is popularly believed to be an agricultural land, national income depends more on commerce and industry than on farming.

HISTORY: At the time of the conquest of the Lowland areas by Julius Caesar in 55 B.C., the region was settled by Celtic and Germanic tribes. The dominant tribes were the Saxons and Frisians. In the 3rd century A.D. the West Franks (Salic Franks) invaded the Low Countries and gradually conquered the region. Following the breakup of Charlemagne's empire in the 9th century, the Lowlands were parceled up into numerous duchies and counties. In the 16th century, the area passed to Charles V of the House of Hapsburg and then to his son, Philip II of Spain

1568-81: Dutch wage war of independence against Spain under leadership of William the Silent, Prince of Orange, who unites the seven northern provinces; Spanish garrisons are expelled and United Provinces declare their independence

17th cent.: Treaty of Westphalia (1648), ending the Thirty Years War, recognizes independence of United Provinces. Meanwhile, Dutch build vast overseas empire and by 1700 the Netherlands is the world's leading maritime and commercial power

18th cent.: Dutch power begins to decline after 1715. In 1794, French revolutionary forces invade Netherlands; the following year French set up the Batavian Republic

1815: Congress of Vienna establishes Kingdom of Netherlands composed of Belgium and Holland

1830: Belgium revolts and gains independence

1914-39: Netherlands pursues policy of neutrality

1940-45: During World War II German forces overrun the Netherlands and subject country to ruthless occupation

1948: Queen Wilhelmina abdicates and is succeeded by her daughter, Juliana

1949: Netherlands grants Indonesia independence after four years of bitter strife

1954: The colonies of Surinam and Netherlands Antilles are incorporated into the Kingdom of the Netherlands

1957: Netherlands joins Common Market

1962-63: Netherlands turns western New Guinea (West Irian) over to the United Nations, which places it under Indonesian jurisdiction pending a referendum

1975: Independence is granted to Surinam (now Suriname) after 300 years of Dutch rule

1976: South Moluccan terrorists, who in support of the independence of South Molucca from Indonesia had in December 1975 hijacked a train and laid siege to the Indonesian consulate, are convicted and sentenced

1977: Prime Minister den Uyl's Labor Party captures a plurality in parliament in May elections. South Moluccan terrorists hold 100 children hostage in a school and 50 others hostage in a train in an effort to force the Dutch government to help them in their independence struggle. The siege is ended by a Dutch military team staging a raid in which six terrorists and two hostages are killed. Mr. den Uyl's coalition soon collapses as Laborites and Christian Democrats clash over division of power; den Uyl presides over caretaker government until appointment in December of Christian Democrat Andries van Agt as prime minister; van Agt heads center-right coalition of Christian Democrats and Liberals (who, despite their name, are conservative)

1978: In Assen, South Moluccan terrorists seize hostages for fourth time since 1975, in attempt to force granting of various demands; the three captors kill one of the 72 hostages, though one is killed in crossfire; terrorists arrested. Christian Democrats gain in provincial elections, strengthening their position as senior partner in van Agt's coalition

---

NEW ZEALAND

Area: 103,736 sq. mi. **Population:** 3,150,000 (1978 est.)

Official Name: New Zealand **Capital:** Wellington **Nationality:** New Zealander **Languages:** English is the official and predominant language; Maori, a Malayo-Polynesian language, is also spoken, but for the Maoris English is the first language **Religion:** 34% Anglican, 22% Presbyterian, 15% Roman Catholic, 7% Methodist, 22% other denominations or non-affiliated **Flag:** A blue field, with the British Union Jack in the upper left and the four stars of the Southern Cross in red edged in white on the right **Anthem:** God Save the Queen; National Song: God Defend New Zealand **Currency:** New Zealand dollar (1.0 per U.S. $1)

Location: South Pacific, about 1,200 miles southeast of Australia. New Zealand consists of two principal islands, North Island and South Island, separated by Cook Strait; Stewart Island lies off the southern tip of South Island; the Chatham Islands are about 400 miles east of South Island **Features:** North Island contains 72% of the country's population. The northern part of the island has rolling hills and low mountains; the southern half rises from fertile coastal plains to volcanic mountain peaks in the center. South Island is narrow and contains 28% of the population. The Southern Alps extend the entire length of the island and include New Zealand's highest peak, Mount Cook, with an elevation of 12,349 feet. Stewart Island is covered with rugged, forested peaks that rise more than 3,000 feet **Chief Rivers:** Waikato, Clutha, Taieri, Clarence, Oreti, Rangitikei, Wanganui, Waitaki, Mataura

Head of State: Queen Elizabeth II, represented by a governor-general, Sir Keith Jacka Holyoake, appointed March 1977 **Head of Government:** Prime Minister Robert D. Muldoon, born 1922, re-elected November 1978 **Effective Date of Present Constitution:** No written constitution **Legislative Body:** Parliament (unicameral House of Representatives), with 87 members elected by universal suffrage for 3 years **Local Government:** In 1976 there were 362 local authority areas

Ethnic Composition: About 92% of the population is of European descent; Maoris number 8% **Population Distribution:** 77.4% urban **Density:** 30 inhabitants per sq. mi.

Largest Cities (Urban Areas): (1976 census) Auckland 742,786, Wellington 327,414, Christchurch 295,296, Dunedin 113,222, Lower Hutt Valley 97,194, Hamilton 94,777, Palmerston North 63,873

Per Capita Income: $5,119 (1978) **Gross National Product (GNP):** $16 billion (1978) **Economic Statistics:** In 1972, agriculture, forestry and fishing accounted for 14.2% of the GNP, industry and mining 34.8%, and services 51.2%. The chief industries are food processing (meat and dairy products), transport equipment, textiles, cement, oil refining, and fertilizers. Wool, meat, and dairy products form the bulk of agricultural output **Minerals and Mining:** Iron sands, natural gas, coal, gold, and industrial minerals such as aggregate, limestone, pumice, serpentine, clays, and bentonite **Labor Force:** 1,255,000 (1976) of which 36% is engaged in industry, 12% in agriculture, 52% in services. The average monthly wage in industry is $310 **Foreign Trade:** Exports, chiefly meat, dairy products, and wool, amounted to $2.8 billion in 1976. Imports, mainly machinery and related equipment, and industrial raw materials, totaled $3.3 billion **Principal Trade Partners:** Britain, Australia, United States, Japan, Canada, West Germany, France

Vital Statistics: Birthrate, 17.7 per 1,000 of pop. (1976); death rate, 7.6 **Life Expectancy:** 72 years **Health Statistics:** 93 inhabitants per hospital bed; 844 per physician (1975) **Infant Mortality:** 14.7 per 1,000 births (1975) **Illiteracy:** Negligible **Education Statistics:** 2,917 primary and secondary schools, with combined enrollment of 758,037 (1975) **Enrollment in Higher Education:** 66,739 (1974) **GNP Expended on Education:** 5.6% (1974)

Transportation: Surfaced roads total 27,927 mi. **Motor Vehicles:** 1,427,100 (1976) **Passenger Cars:** 1,205,400 **Railway Mileage:** 2,987 **Ports:** Auckland, Wellington, Lyttelton, Whangarei, Tauranga, Dunedin, Napier, Nelson **Major Airlines:** Air New Zealand operates domestic and international services **Communications:** Both government and privately owned **Radio Transmitters:** 61 **Receivers:** 2,715,000 (1976) **Television Transmitters:** 144 **Receivers:** 813,000 (1976) **Telephones:** 1,610,000 (1976) **Newspapers:** 39 dailies. 376 copies per 1,000 inhabitants (1975)

Weights and Measures: Metric system **Travel Requirements:** Passport; no visa for 30 days; onward ticket

---

Blessed with an equable climate that lets grass grow green the year around, New Zealand is renowned for butter, race horses, and lush scenery. The New Zealand dairy industry is said to be the most efficient anywhere, and the export of dairy products is the largest in the world despite the country's small size and population.

The reorganization of overseas markets for pastoral products resulting from the formation of the European Economic Community (Common Market), particularly the prospective phasing out of special trading advantages in Britain for New Zealand butter and cheese, accelerated the postwar trend toward economic diversification. Many dairy farmers have turned successfully to raising meat animals, especially sheep, with government encouragement. The opening of the country's first steel mill near Auckland, and an aluminum smelter at the port of Bluff at the southern tip of South Island, converting Australian bauxite, were among the important industrial developments. Exploration for minerals in various parts of the country has shown promising indications of a variety of metals in commercial quantities. In the early 1960s, enough natural gas and oil was discovered in the Taranaki district of the North Island to supply, when developed, almost half of New Zealand's petroleum requirements and all of the North Island's needs for natural gas.

With the appearance of new independent states in the South Pacific, New Zealand began providing needed guidance and assistance to the fledgling nations. The first conference of new heads of government, attended also by high-ranking representatives of Australia and New Zealand, was held in Wellington in August 1971 at the joint request of all the new states—Fiji, Western Samoa, Tonga, Nauru, and the Cook Islands, a self-governing dependency of New Zealand.

The island peoples are attracted to New Zealand by a variety of factors, including the high quality of education available to islanders and the easy interracial relationships. (8 percent of the New Zealand population are Maoris, a branch of the Polynesian race; Auckland is said to be the biggest Polynesian city in the world, with more than 70,000 Maoris, Cook Islanders, Samoans, Tongans and others in the population.)

Like their Australian neighbors, the New Zealanders are overwhelmingly of British stock. Many of the hardworking pioneer white settlers came from Scotland, some to escape religious conflicts.

With a small population heavily endowed with skills, New Zealand enjoys one of the highest standards of living in the world. Government welfare programs provide "womb-to-tomb" security.

The New Zealanders have shared with the Australians a growing consciousness since World War II of belonging to the Pacific and Asian region. New Zealand has joined with Australia and Britain in a five-power pact for the defense of Singapore and Malaysia, and is a partner in the ANZUS (Australia, New Zealand, United States) Treaty of Mutual Security, the keystone of national defense. New Zealand also assisted in the defense of South Vietnam with a token contingent of 500 men and with economic aid.

The year 1975 saw the replacement of Wallace Rowling's Labour government by Robert Muldoon and the National Party after a period of economic uncertainty and acrimonious political debate. Prime Minister Muldoon launched a campaign against abortion and came into conflict with the nation's intellectuals and the media. His party won reelection in November 1978, but their 22-seat majority in the legislature dwindled to seven.

HISTORY: The first European to discover New Zealand was the Dutch explorer Abel Tasman, who sighted the islands in 1642 but was prevented from landing by hostile Maori natives. The British explorer Captain James Cook visited the islands in 1769, and by the end of the century British whaling settlements were established along the coast. It was not until the 19th century, however, that large-scale British immigration began

1840: By the Treaty of Waitangi, Maoris surrender sovereignty to Britain in exchange for guarantees that they would be allowed to remain in possession of their lands; British New Zealand Company begins first organized attempt to colonize islands with British settlers

1845-48: Maoris, angered by Britain's failure to honor land guarantees, rebel against British rule until uprisings are suppressed by military force

1860-70: Maori Wars against Britain are resumed; Maoris are again defeated by superior British force after 10 years of fighting; immigrant population continues to rise, spurred by discovery of gold in 1861

1907: New Zealand wins dominion status

1914-18: New Zealand fights on Allied side in World War I

1939-45: New Zealand fights on Allied side again in World War II

1945: New Zealand becomes a founding member of the UN

1951: United States, New Zealand, and Australia sign ANZUS treaty binding three nations in mutual defense alliance

1960: National Party defeats ruling Labour Party in general election; Keith J. Holyoake becomes prime minister

1972: Norman E. Kirk becomes prime minister when Labour Party wins

1973: New Zealand and Australia unsuccessfully attempt to block French nuclear testing in the Pacific

1974: Wallace Rowling succeeds after Kirk's death

1975: The EEC, in renegotiating Britain's membership terms, agrees that duty-free butter imports from New Zealand after 1977 will remain at the current level until 1980. Rowling is defeated by Robert Muldoon of National Party

1978: Muldoon reelected with reduced majority

NICARAGUA

Area: 50,193 sq. mi. **Population:** 2,312,000 (1978 est.)

Official Name: Republic of Nicaragua **Capital:** Managua **Nationality:** Nicaraguan **Languages:** Spanish is the official and universal language; some English is spoken on the east coast **Religion:** 95% Roman Catholic **Flag:** Horizontal stripes of blue, white, blue with the national coat of arms in the center **Anthem:** Hail Nicaragua **Currency:** Córdoba (10.0 per U.S. $1)

Location: Central America. Nicaragua, the largest of the Central American republics, is bounded on the north by Honduras, on the east by the Caribbean Sea, on the south by Costa Rica, and on the west by the Pacific Ocean **Features:** The western part of the country consists of a coastal plain, gradually rising toward rugged mountains. Beyond these mountains lies the interior, a sparsely populated wilderness of timbered plains and rolling hills cut by rivers. The eastern coastal plain extends about 50 miles inland and is partly swampland **Chief Rivers:** Grande de Matagalpa, Escondido, Coco, San Juan

Head of State and Government: As of August 1979 the country is being governed by a 5-member junta: Sergio Ramírez Mercado (recognized leader), Violeta de Chamorro, Alfonso Robela Callejas, Moisés Hassan Morales and Daniel Ortega Saavedra **Effective Date of Present Constitution:** April 1974 **Legislative Body:** Congress (bicameral), consisting of a Senate of 30 members, and a Chamber of Deputies of 70 members, both elected for 6 years **Local Government:** 16 departments, each headed by a civil governor **Ethnic Composition:** 70% of the population is mestizo (of mixed European and Indian ancestry), 17% of European ancestry, 9% Negro, and 4% Indian **Population Distribution:** 50% urban **Density:** 46 inhabitants per sq. mi.

Largest Cities: (1976 est.) Managua 437,666, León 73,757, Granada 50,094, Masaya 40,907, Chinandega 38,646

Per Capita Income: $866 (1978) **Gross National Product (GNP):** $2.2 billion (1978 est.) **Economic Statistics:** In 1973 about 26% of GNP came from agriculture (cotton, coffee, cattle), forestry and fishing; 10% from industry (chemicals, insecticides, food processing, textiles), and mining; and 40% from trade and services **Minerals and Mining:** Copper, gold, silver, tungsten, gypsum, and precious stones **Labor Force:** 641,497 (1975), of which 48% is in agriculture, 14% in manufacturing and construction, and 30% in trade and services **Foreign Trade:** Exports, mainly cotton, cottonseed, coffee, meat, gold, sesame, and wood, totaled $526 million in 1976. Imports, mainly machinery, transportation equipment, manufacturing products, chemical products, and raw materials for industry, totaled $525 million. **Principal Trade Partners:** Central American Common Market countries, United States, Venezuela, Japan, West Germany

Vital Statistics: Birthrate, 42.6 per 1,000 of pop. (1975); death rate, 6.7 **Life Expectancy:** 54 years **Health Statistics:** 450 inhabitants per hospital bed; 1,600 per physician (1975) **Infant Mortality:** 46.4 per 1,000 births **Illiteracy:** 43% **Education Statistics:** 2,555 primary and secondary schools, with combined enrollment of 430,721 (1975) **Enrollment in Higher Education:** 17,184 **GNP Expended on Education:** 2.2% (1973)

Transportation: Paved roads total 935 mi. **Motor Vehicles:** 52,000 (1973) **Passenger Cars:** 32,000 **Railway Mileage:** 235 **Ports:** Corinto, San Juan del Sur **Major Airlines:** Líneas Aéreas de Nicaragua (LANICA) operates domestic and international flights **Communications:** Partly government controlled **Radio Transmitters:** 7 **Receivers:** 126,000 (1974) **Television Transmitters:** 2 **Receivers:** 90,000 (1976) **Telephones:** 55,000 (1976) **Newspapers:** 7 dailies, 26 copies per 1,000 inhabitants (1975)

Weights and Measures: Metric system **Travel Requirements:** Passport; visa valid for 30 days, no fee; 2 pictures, or proof of citizenship; tourist card (obtainable from airline for U.S.-born), no fee

A civil war that cost an estimated 15,000 lives brought an end in 1979 to the Somoza family's political and economic rule of Nicaragua after more than four decades. President Gen. Anastasio ("Tacho") Somoza Debayle, who had made a Managua bunker his home and command post for almost two years, fled by helicopter and airplane to exile in the United States on July 17. The Sandinist National Liberation Front (FSLN in its Spanish initials), winner over the National Guard that the Somozas had headed since 1933, named a five-member junta as the provisional government during the war. At war's end, the junta appointed a 15-member Cabinet made up of all shades of the country's political opinion.

On the victory day, July 19, cheering Managua crowds toppled the statue of Tacho Somoza's father, Gen. Anastasio Somoza García, founder of the family dynasty. The elder Somoza had taken command of the National Guard in 1933, just after the U.S. Marines ended intermittent intervention that had begun in 1912. It was allegedly Somoza's guardsmen who, in 1934, assassinated Gen. Augusto César Sandino, the revolutionary hero from whom the Sandinists took their name. The elder Somoza seized the presidency on Jan. 1, 1937, and held virtually complete control of Nicaragua—the largest country in Central America—until his assassination in 1956. A son, Luis, president of the Senate, was named president immediately; Luis' brother, Anastasio, a West Point graduate, became president in a 1967 election in which charges of fraud and intimidation arose.

The assassination of Pedro Joaquín Chamorro, publisher of *La Prensa* and a longtime critic of Somoza, in downtown Managua in January 1978 was widely attributed to the Somoza regime. Massive unrest and violence followed, culminating in the seizure of the National Palace by the FSLN seven months later. That action won release of 58 political prisoners and safe conduct out of the country. But the National Guard largely succeeded in putting the lid back on the violence until the Sandinists launched a successful revolution from the Costa Rican border on May 29, 1979.

In the closing weeks of warfare, central American neighbor nations, and through them the United States, conducted complex negotiations on the makeup of the new government, which ranges from avowed leftists to conservative businessmen.

A large segment of the population is impoverished, and the war's displacement of 600,000 persons aggravated this. Most of the jobs are in agriculture, where cotton and coffee lead the farm exports, which make up 80 percent of Nicaragua's foreign exchange. Industry accounts for only 10 percent of the gross national product. What is more, the war set back industry as dozens of Managua factories were ruined by bombs, rockets, or arson in the wake of looting. The country's trade and services long were dominated by the Somoza family, whose prewar wealth was estimated at $500 million. The ex-president said, however, that his net worth was about $100 million, and that 80 percent of it had been left behind in Nicaragua. The family holdings included land, cattle, lumber interests, a bank, automobile dealerships, an airline, a shipping line, a newspaper and the country's TV station, a slaughterhouse, a construction company and a cement company, a sugar-refining complex, and numerous other companies.

HISTORY: Various Indian tribes inhabited Nicaragua before the arrival of the Spanish conquistador Gil González de Avila in 1552. During the Spanish colonial period, Nicaragua was administered as part of the captaincy general of Guatemala.

1821: Nicaragua wins independence from Spain and along with the other countries of Central America becomes annexed to Mexico

1825-38: Nicaragua secedes from Mexico and joins Central American Federation. In 1838 the federation is dissolved, and Nicaragua becomes an independent republic

1856-57: U.S. soldier of fortune William Walker seizes presidency but is ousted by alliance of Central American states

1912-33: Prolonged political turmoil between Liberals and Conservatives leads Provisional President Adolfo Díaz to ask for intervention of U.S. Marines to maintain order. In 1916 the Bryan-Chamorro Treaty is ratified, giving United States an option on route for a canal, but Liberals continue guerrilla warfare in protest against American intervention. U.S. Marines, withdrawn in 1925, again occupy country from 1926 to 1933

1934: Gen. Augusto César Sandino, who had defied efforts of U.S. Marines to catch him and who later had won concessions from the government, is assassinated, apparently by members of Gen. Anastasio Somoza's National Guard

1936-57: General Somoza seizes power; until his death by an assassin's bullet in 1956 he rules country as virtual private estate. His son Luis finishes his father's term and is elected to presidency in 1957

1967: Anastasio Somoza Debayle, brother of Luis and head of armed forces, is elected president

1972: On December 23, earthquakes destroy much of Managua, killing an estimated 10,000, injuring about 15,000 and leaving half the city's population homeless

1974: Somoza is reelected for second presidential term, after resigning in 1972 because of election provisions but retaining full power in the interim as commander of the armed forces

1975: Somoza reimposes martial law as part of increasing repression of civil liberties following the kidnapping of prominent officials by left-wing Sandinist Liberation Front in 1974

1977: Leftist guerrillas make series of attacks on National Guard barracks

1978: Widespread civil unrest follows assassination of publisher Pedro Joaquín Chamorro, longtime Somoza foe. National Palace seized by leftist guerrillas, who hold members of Congress hostage until they win release of 58 political prisoners and safe conduct out of country. Guerrillas gain broad support in efforts to oust Somoza, who vows to serve out term. Even the National Federation of the Chambers of Commerce joins a general strike in August, and the guerrillas capture several towns. However, in heavy fighting, the National Guard recaptures the places

1979: On May 29, the Sandinist rebels launch a five-pronged attack from the Costa Rican border. León, the second largest city, is taken quickly, and many towns soon fall. Rebels control the *barrios* of Managua, but loss of life is high there as National Guard planes drop 500-lb. bombs and oil drums filled with explosives. World television audiences see a National Guardsman execute U.S. television reporter Bill Stewart at a roadblock. President Somoza flees the country on July 17; Sandinist rebels take control of the capital July 19. A five-member junta appoints a 15-member Cabinet dominated by moderates

NIGER

Area: 489,189 sq. mi. **Population:** 4,800,000 (1978 est.)

Official Name: Republic of Niger **Capital:** Niamey **Nationality:** Nigerien **Languages:** French is the official language; the principal African languages are Fulani, Tamashek, Djerma, Songhai, and Hausa, used primarily in trade **Religion:** The population is predominantly Moslem **Flag:** Horizontal stripes of orange, white, and green with an orange disc in the center **Anthem:** La Nigérienne **Currency:** CFA Franc (219 per U.S. $1)

Location: West-central Africa. Landlocked Niger is bordered on the north by Algeria and Libya, on the east by Chad, on the south by Nigeria and Benin, on the southwest by Upper Volta, and on the west by Mali **Features:** Four-fifths of the country (north) is arid desert, and the remainder (south) is mostly savanna **Chief River:** Niger

Head of State and of Government: President of the Supreme Military Council: Lt. Col. Seyni Kountché, born 1931, assumed power in 1974 **Effective Date of Present Constitution:** 1960, suspended 1974 **Legislative Body:** All powers in the hands of the Council **Local Government:** 7 departments under appointed prefects, divided into 32 districts

Ethnic Composition: Hausa make up almost 50% of the population and Djerma-Songhai 23%, the rest are nomadic and seminomadic Peuls, or Fulani (15%), Tuaregs (12%), Toubous, and others **Population Distribution:** 8% urban **Density:** 10 inhabitants per sq. mi. **Largest Cities:** (1975 est.) Niamey 130,299; (1972 est.) Zinder 39,000, Maradi 37,000, Tahoua 31,000

Per Capita Income: $127 (1978) **Gross National Product (GNP):** $640 million (1978) **Economic Statistics:** In 1973 over 50% of GNP was derived from agriculture (peanuts, cotton, tobacco, millet, sorghum, beans, rice, livestock), 12% from manufacturing (textiles, peanut oil, oxygen-acetylene) and mining, and 27% from trade and services **Minerals and Mining:** Work has begun at a French-backed plant for processing uranium deposits—the fifth-largest in the world—in the Arlit region; tin has been the only other mineral mined, but there are large unexploited coal and iron-ore deposits **Labor Force:** 1,900,000 (1970), with about 95% in agriculture and stockraising **Foreign Trade:** Exports, mainly peanuts, uranium and livestock, totaled $86 million in 1976. Imports, chiefly fuels, machinery, motor vehicles and parts, food and clothing, totaled $173 million **Principal Trade Partners:** France, Japan, Nigeria, Ivory Coast, United States

Vital Statistics: Birthrate, 52.2 per 1,000 of pop. (1975); death rate, 25.5 **Life Expectancy:** 39 years **Health Statistics:** 1,526 inhabitants per hospital bed; 41,101 per physician (1974) **Infant Mortality:** 200 per 1,000 births **Illiteracy:** 94% **Education Statistics:** 990 primary and secondary schools, with combined enrollment of 133,317 (1975) **Enrollment in Higher Education:** 541 (1975) **GNP Expended on Education:** 2% (1972)

Transportation: Improved roads total 2,200 mi. **Motor Vehicles:** 21,700 (1976) **Passenger Cars:** 9,900 **Railway Mileage:** None **Ports:** None **Major Airlines:** Air-Niger, a government-owned company operates domestic flights; Air-Afrique, UTA and Sabena operate international services **Communications:** Government-owned **Radio Transmitters:** 13 **Receivers:** 150,000 (1971) **Television Transmitters:** 1 **Receivers:** Used exclusively in schools **Telephones:** 8,000 (1976) **Newspapers:** 2 dailies, 0.5 copy per 1,000 inhabitants (1974)

Weights and Measures: Metric system **Travel Requirements:** Passport; visa valid for 7 days, no fee; for stay up to 3 months, $6.25 fee; 2 pictures; onward ticket or guarantee from a bank

Niger has been called "a land where the harvest is won with the soul's scythe." For most of this neglected hinterland of former French West Africa is rocky desert, broken by bleak mountains. The productive southern area, watered in part by the Niger River, is semi-arid and subject to droughts and floods.

While rich uranium deposits are being developed in the northern desert area and there is

hope for discovery of oil and exploitation of other minerals, Niger still must depend on cattle and on limited export and food crops, chiefly peanuts, cotton, and grains. A hostile climate and need for irrigation are obstacles to increased production.

Lack of transportation is Niger's most serious problem. The landlocked country has no railroad and the rapids-strewn Niger River, a potentially low-cost route to the seacoast, has yet to be made navigable. The nearest seaport, Cotonou, in Benin, is 600 miles from Niamey, Niger's capital, and it is often noted that it takes more than two gallons of gasoline to import a single gallon.

Internal roads and links to neighboring countries, however, are gradually being built with French, American, World Bank, and United Nations aid. Canada, through new ties with French-speaking African countries, has recently become a major aid source for Niger.

A $60-million uranium project at Arlit, which began production in 1971, is a joint Nigerien/French/German/Italian undertaking. A second uranium project, organized in 1974 under a company started by the Nigerien government, the French Atomic Energy Commission, and a Japanese company, will develop uranium deposits in the Akouta district. Meanwhile, several American companies are prospecting for oil.

Like the other nations of the West African Sahel, Niger suffered greatly during the drought and famine of 1968-74. In 1973 cattle were dying; in 1974 people were dying. An estimated two million were starving in the Tuareg tribe alone. By October 1974, the drought was ended though massive international relief efforts, largely from the U.S. and the UN, were required to prevent starvation and malnutrition. Appeals for emergency food supplies continue as the problems of marginally productive land and overgrazing remain.

Hamani Diori, Niger's president from the time the country gained independence from France in 1960 until 1974, sought to promote national development and to unify Niger's traditionally hostile nomadic and settled farming peoples. He emphasized government stability; gradual improvement of agriculture, health, and education; and economic aid from numerous sources.

However, in 1974 when Diori was unable to stop his people's starvation in the famine resulting from the drought in the Sahel, he was overthrown by Lt. Col. Seyni Kountché who formed a 12-member military government with himself as president. Kountché dissolved the National Assembly, suspended the constitution and banned all political groups.

HISTORY: The region around Niger was probably known to Egyptians before the beginning of recorded history. Through the next 1,000 years it was a battleground for Arabs; Berbers; Toubous; the Ghana, Mali, Songhai, and Bornu empires; the Hausa states; and the Djermas, Fulanis, and Tuaregs. The first European explorers arrived in the late 18th century and were soon followed by French forces pushing forward still another empire

1901-22: French build chain of forts, crush Tuareg resistance, and establish colony of Niger

1946: French set up local advisory assembly, grant people of Niger French citizenship

1958: Niger becomes an autonomous republic within the French Community

1960: Complete independence is declared and Niger joins the UN

1964-65: Terrorist attacks and attempts to assassinate President Hamani Diori, directed from Ghana by exiled opposition leader Djibo Bakary, are quelled by government forces

1968-74: Drought and famine strike the Sahel

1974: Army Chief of Staff Lt. Col. Seyni Kountché ousts Diori, and declares himself head of state. Drought ends

NIGERIA

Area: 379,628 sq. mi. **Population:** 84,500,000 (1978 est.)

Official Name: Federal Republic of Nigeria **Capital:** Lagos **Nationality:** Nigerian **Languages:** English is the official and business language. Among the 250 African languages and dialects of the country, the most widely spoken are Hausa, Yoruba, Ibo, and Edo. Sizable minorities speak Fulani, Kanuri, Ijaw, Ibibio, and Tiv **Religion:** Northern Nigeria is largely Moslem, while the south and west have been strongly influenced by Christianity. Overall, about 19% of the population are animist; 47% Moslem, and 34% Christian **Flag:** Vertical stripes of green, white, green **Anthem:** National Anthem, beginning "Nigeria, we hail thee". **Currency:** Naira (219 per U.S. $1)

Location: West Africa. Nigeria is bounded on the northwest and north by Niger, on the northeast by Lake Chad, on the east by Cameroon, on the south by the Gulf of Guinea, and on the west by Benin **Features:** The coastal area consists of a belt of mangrove swamps intersected by delta branches of the Niger and innumerable smaller rivers and creeks. Inland, a belt of tropical rain forest extends up to 100 miles over gradually rising country. The country then rises to a plateau, which reaches an elevation of over 6,000 feet in the east. In the north, the savanna approaches the southern part of the Sahara **Chief Rivers:** Niger, Benue, Sokoto, Yobe, Gana, Kaduna, Cross, Gongola, Ogun

Head of State and of Government: President Alhaji Shehu Shagari, elected Aug. 1979, takes office Oct. 1 **Effective Date of Present Constitution:** 1979 **Legislative Body:** Legislative power is divided between a 95-member Senate and a 430 member House of Representatives **Local Government:** 19 states

Ethnic Composition: Of the country's 250 tribal groups, the dominant ones are the Yoruba (15%) in the west, the Ibo (16%) in the east, and the Hausa (19%) and Fulani (10%) in the north. Other large groups are the Edo (900,000) in the west, the Ibibio (about 1 million) and the Ijaw (900,000) in the east, and the Kanuri (2.9 million), Nupe (500,000), and Tiv (1.5 million) in the north **Population Distribution:** 23% urban **Density:** 223 inhabitants per sq. mi.

Largest Cities: (1975 est.) Lagos 1,060,848, Ibadan 847,000, Ogbomosho 432,000, Kano 399,000, Oshogbo 282,000, Ilorin 282,000, Abeokuta 253,000, Port Harcourt 242,000

Per Capita Income: $570 (1978) **Gross Domestic Product (GDP):** $40 billion (1978) **Economic Statistics:** More than 33% of GDP comes from oil and mining, an estimated 23% from agriculture (cocoa, peanuts, African oil palm products, rubber and cotton), and 7% from manufacturing (mainly food processing, oil refining, cotton textiles and cement) **Minerals and Mining:** Nigeria is the world's sixth largest oil producer; other minerals are tin, coal, and limestone. **Labor Force:** 30 million of which 70% are in agriculture, forestry and fishing, and 10% in industry **Foreign Trade:** Exports, crude petroleum (94%), cocoa, peanuts, palm nuts, rubber, tin and raw cotton, totaled $9.3 billion in 1976. Imports, chiefly machinery, transport equipment, industrial raw materials, manufactured goods, chemicals and food, amounted to $7.9 billion (1976) **Principal Trade Partners:** Britain, United States, West Germany, Japan, Netherlands, France

Vital Statistics: Birthrate, 49.3 per 1,000 of pop. (1975); death rate, 22.7 **Life Expectancy:** 50 years **Health Statistics:** 1,378 inhabitants per hospital bed; 19,000 per physician (1976) **Infant Mortality:** 150 per 1,000 births **Illiteracy:** 65% **Education Statistics:** 16,330 primary and secondary schools, with combined enrollment of 4,913,298 (1974) **Enrollment in Higher Education:** 32,971 (1975) **GNP Expended on Education:** 2.6% (1975)

Transportation: Paved roads total 11,000 mi. **Motor Vehicles:** 255,000 (1975) **Passenger Cars:** 150,000 **Railway Mileage:** 2,680 **Ports:** Lagos, Port Harcourt, Bonny, Burutu **Major Airlines:** Nigeria Airways operates international and domestic services **Communications:** Government controlled **Radio Transmitters:** 46 **Licenses:** 5,100,000 (1976) **Television Transmitters:** 10 **Licenses:** 121,000 (1976) **Telephones:** 121,000 (1976) **Newspapers:** 12 dailies, 9 copies per 1,000 inhabitants (1974)

Weights and Measures: Metric system is used **Travel Requirements:** Passport; visa valid 3 months from date of issue; $2.30 fee; onward ticket

---

Nigeria, a country of extraordinary potential—oil, agricultural diversity, talented political leaders, a population that embraces fully a fifth of the black people in Africa—is also a country with extraordinary problems of instability. One of the underlying reasons for that instability is the nation's great ethnic diversity.

Nigeria's major tribal divisions consist of the semi-nomadic Hausa-Fulani of the north, the urbanized Yorubas in the west, and in the east, the industrious Ibos. Under British rule, the three regions, together with Lagos, the administrative center, were amalgamated into one vast colonial possession.

As Britain prepared Nigeria for self-government after World War II, it was recognized that the country could achieve its great economic potential only if it remained intact. Nigerian leaders and British authorities were confident, however, that old animosities could be submerged. In 1960 Britain granted full independence and in 1963 Nigeria became a republic.

The largely Moslem north dominated the new government. Distrust soon fanned tribal rivalries into open conflict after incidents of corruption, nepotism, and rigged elections. Ibos grew increasingly resentful as they saw excessive shares of the oil revenues from their region go to northern projects.

Early in 1966, a coup led by young Ibo army officers was accompanied by the murder of many Northern and Western officials, including Prime Minister Sir Abubakar Tafawa Balewa. Gen. Johnson Aguiyi-Ironsi, an Ibo who promised a government free of corruption and tribalism, was installed as president.

However, in a counter-coup led by northern officers in July 1966, Ironsi was murdered. He was replaced by Lt. Col. (later Maj. Gen.) Yakubu Gowon, who as a Christian and member of a minor tribe was regarded as a neutralist in the tribal conflicts.

Late in 1966 thousands of Ibos working in the north were massacred. Thousands more fled back to their homeland and Gowon's efforts for new political cooperation were frustrated by Ibo fear and distrust. Ibo leader Lt. Col. Odumegwu Ojukwu unsuccessfully sought autonomy for the Eastern Region, then, in May 1967, proclaimed a Republic of Biafra.

In the ensuing conflict Biafran forces were at first victorious, but with growing federal strength, the rebel state was gradually reduced to a small area. As the war dragged on, starvation ravaged the East—a densely populated, food-deficient region. Despite relief efforts by many groups, Biafran resistance collapsed in January 1970, and Ojukwu fled to the Ivory Coast. The struggle took an estimated one million lives. In the years since there has been a gradual reintegration of Ibos into the national economy, if not the political arena.

The Biafra trouble was scarcely over when prolonged drought desiccated the Sahel region in northern Nigeria. Cattle died by the thousands, farm lands suffered and fishing industry on Lake Chad collapsed as the lake shrank in size. The area is now recovering, but many problems remain.

In October 1974 General Gowon announced that a previously scheduled return to civilian government (1976) had been cancelled because of dispute over the 1973 census and the violent sectional political ambitions that were emerging. This announcement led to student demonstrations. Labor unrest increased over pay demands.

On July 29, 1975, Gowon was deposed in a bloodless coup; Brig. Gen. Murtala Rufai Mohammed was named head of state. In February 1976 Brig. Gen. Mohammed was assassinated by a group of "young revolutionaries" who later failed to gain control of the government. The nation's ruling Supreme Military Council named Lt. Gen. Olusegun Obasanjo as head of state.

A total of 37 persons were executed for their alleged involvement in the abortive coup and assassination. Nigeria's request that Great Britain extradite former head of state Gowon, so that he could defend himself against accusations of involvement in the attempted coup, was denied.

Political activity, banned since 1966, was restored in September 1978. Four parties sprang up to compete for the right to form the long-promised civilian government. In August 1979 Alhaji Shehu Shagari was declared the winner of the election balloting for president, held under Nigeria's new constitution.

Oil, first discovered in 1958, has made Nigeria the wealthiest black African nation. Oil exports account for more than 90 percent of the nation's foreign-exchange earnings and provide most of its government revenues. The country supplies about 6 percent of the oil consumed in the U.S. and is its second-largest source. Within OPEC Nigeria has joined those advocating the steepest hikes in oil export prices.

Backed by its oil revenues, Nigeria has increasingly pushed its image as a leading power in Africa. The country is still plagued, however, by deep-rooted corruption in public office, widespread poverty, backward living conditions, and acute shortages of trained manpower. Earnings from oil exports could support more imports but port facilities at Lagos cannot handle the increased amount of goods.

Nigeria has pushed for closer trading ties with its West African neighbors. The government is also seeking greater "Nigerianization" of foreign-owned-and-run enterprises to give Nigerians a greater share of the wealth. Although militant on anti-colonial issues involving the white-ruled nations of Africa, Nigeria maintains a moderate foreign policy.

HISTORY: Nigeria's earliest known culture, Nok, flourished around 700-200 B.C. During the 12th century, Nigeria's next great culture grew up around Ife, a sacred Yoruba city. In medieval times, northern Nigeria had contact with the large kingdoms of the western Sudan and by the end of the 14th century A.D. Islam was firmly established in the north. Between the 15th and 17th centuries, the Portuguese and British engaged in commerce and slave trading on the coast

1861-1914: British annex Lagos (1861); gradually establish administrative control over Nigeria

1947-54: Successive steps are taken to allow participation in the government by Africans in preparation for self-government

1960: Nigeria becomes an independent federal state within the British Commonwealth

1963: Nigeria becomes a federal republic within the Commonwealth

1966: Government is ousted by a military coup and a military government is established under Gen. Johnson Aguiyi-Ironsi (an Ibo from the Eastern Region); Ironsi is murdered when another military coup is staged by anti-Ibo elements in the army; a federal military government is set up under Lt. Col. (later Maj. Gen.) Yakubu Gowon. Thousands of Ibos are massacred and more than a million are driven from the north

1967: Military government announces the creation of 12 ethnically based states to replace the previous four regions. The Eastern Region, under the leadership of Lt. Col. Odumegwu Ojukwu, secedes from the Federation of Nigeria and proclaims itself the independent Republic of Biafra. Federal troops invade Biafra, marking the start of civil war

1968-69: Mass starvation threatens millions in Biafra as a result of the federal government's blockade of the region

1970: Surrender of Biafran forces brings end to 30-month civil war; federal government chief, Gen. Yakubu Gowon, pledges protection and political rights to former Biafrans

1972: Nigeria issues Nigerian Enterprises Promotion Decree requiring that many small foreign-owned businesses be "Nigerianized"

1975: General Gowon is deposed in a bloodless coup. Brig. Gen. Murtala Rufai Mohammed is named head of state

1976: Mohammed assassinated in unsuccessful coup. Lt. Gen. Olusegun Obasanjo is named head of state. Nigeria discards British Parliament as a model for its upcoming 1979 civilian government and looks instead to presidential system of the U.S.

1978: Oil production down; yearly inflation rate is put at 25-40 percent. Nigeria warns Soviets and Cubans "not to overstay their welcome" in Africa. Twelve-year-old ban on political activity lifted

1979: Nigeria leads bid for steeper hikes in OPEC oil. Alhaji Shehu Shagari is elected president under the new constitution

NORWAY

Area: 125,053 sq. mi. **Population:** 4,042,000 (1978 est.)
Official Name: Kingdom of Norway **Capital:** Oslo **Nationality:** Norwegian **Languages:** Norwegian is the official and predominant language; Lappish and Finnish are spoken in the north **Religion:** The state church, the Evangelical Lutheran Church, includes 94% of the population **Flag:** An extended white bordered blue cross on a red field **Anthem:** Yes, We Love This Land of Ours **Currency:** Norwegian krone (5.2 per U.S. $1)

Location: Northern Europe, occupying the smaller, western part of the Scandinavian peninsula. Norway has common land frontiers in the east with Sweden, Finland, and the Soviet Union. It is bounded on the north by the Arctic Ocean, on the west by the Norwegian Sea, and on the south by the Skagerrak, an arm of the North Sea **Features:** The country has a 2,125-mile coastline, deeply indented by numerous fjords. From the coast, the land rises to high plateaus and mountain ranges, the highest of which, Glittertind, reaches 8,110 feet. The highlands are cut by fertile valleys and rapid rivers and are dotted with lakes. Forests cover roughly one fourth of the country, which also has numerous glaciers. Jostedalsbreen, in the southwest, is the largest ice field in Europe **Chief Rivers:** Glomma, Lagen

Head of State: King Olav V, born 1903, acceded to the throne in 1957 **Head of Government:** Premier Odvar Nordli, born 1928, reappointed 1977 **Effective Date of Present Constitution:** 1814 **Legislative Body:** Storting (bicameral parliament) consisting of 155 members elected by universal suffrage for a 4-year term. When assembled, Parliament divides itself by election into 2 chambers, one of 39 members, the other of 116. Bills are introduced in the larger chamber and, when passed, are sent to the smaller one. If the chambers disagree, a joint session is held in which the fate of the bill is decided by a two-thirds majority **Local Government:** 19 counties and the city county of Oslo, each with a council and a governor

Ethnic Composition: Norwegians are mainly of Nordic origin; there has been some mixture with the Finns and Lapps, especially in the north, where some 20,000 Lapps still live **Population Distribution:** 57% urban **Density:** 32 inhabitants per sq. mi.

Largest Cities: (1976 est.) Oslo 462,732, Bergen 213,434, Trondheim 134,910, Stavanger 86,639, Kristiansand 59,488

Per Capita Income: $7,867 (1978) **Gross National Product (GNP):** $32 billion (1978) **Economic Statistics:** 6% of GNP comes from agriculture (dairy farming, beef, pork, eggs and poultry), including animal husbandry, forestry, fishing and whaling; 21% from industry (transport equipment, shipbuilding, metal products, food manufactures, chemicals and chemical products, printing and publishing, paper and paper products, electrical and other machinery, nonmetallic mineral products); 20% from trade and finance **Minerals and Mining:** Limestone, pyrites, ilmenite, iron ore, coal, molybdenite, copper, zinc, lead, offshore oil **Labor Force:** 1,771,000 (1976), of which 25% is employed in industry, 10% in agriculture, and 31% in services **Foreign Trade:** Exports, chiefly fish, petroleum, nonferrous metals, paper and paperboard, paper pulp, iron and steel, totaled $8.7 billion in 1976. Imports, mainly industrial machinery, petroleum and petroleum products, iron and steel, and textiles, amounted to $12.9 billion **Principal Trade Partners:** Britain, West Germany, Sweden, Denmark, United States, Japan, Netherlands, Liberia, France

Vital Statistics: Birthrate, 13.7 per 1,000 of pop. (1976); death rate, 7.6 **Life Expectancy:** 75 years **Health Statistics:** 71 inhabitants per hospital bed; 582 per physician (1975) **Infant Mortality:** 10.5 per 1,000 births **Illiteracy:** Negligible **Education Statistics:** 4,444 primary and secondary schools, with combined enrollment of 732,972 (1975) **Enrollment in Higher Education:** 65,410 **GNP Expended on Education:** 7.1% (1975)

Transportation: Paved roads total 22,976 mi. **Motor Vehicles:** 1,169,600 (1976) **Passenger Cars:** 1,022,000 (1976) **Railway Mileage:** 2,635 **Ports:** Oslo, Narvik, Bergen, Stavanger, Tonsberg, Porsgrunn, Trondheim, Tromso **Major Airlines:** Scandinavian Airlines System (SAS), a consortium owned by the governments of Norway, Denmark, and Sweden, operates domestic and international services **Communications:** Government owned **Radio Transmitters:** 347 **Radio Licenses:** 1,288,000 (1976) **Television Transmitters:** 665 **Licenses:** 1,087,000 (1976) **Telephones:** 1,476,000 (1976) **Newspapers:** 80 dailies, 412 copies per 1,000 inhabitants (1975)

Weights and Measures: Metric system **Travel Requirements:** Passport; no visa for 3 months

Lying atop Western Europe with nearly half its 1,100-mile length north of the Arctic Circle, Norway—a rugged land of mountains, forests, glaciers, and a coastline deeply cut by fjords—is the most sparsely populated country on the Continent. It has, however, one of the highest living standards in Europe and, like the other Nordic lands, a far-reaching social welfare system.

Norway helped to form NATO in 1949, following its experience during World War II as a country invaded and occupied by the Germans. In doing so, it departed from the strict neutrality that it had observed since 1814, when it was forced during brief hostilities to enter with Sweden into a dual monarchy. Like Denmark, Norway, which, with Denmark, Sweden, and Finland, is a member of the Nordic Council, limits its membership in NATO by stipulating that neither foreign troops nor nuclear weapons may be stationed on its soil. The only Western European country that shares a frontier with the Soviet Union, Norway has a small garrison guarding that border, which is 122 miles long, in the far northeast.

The Norwegians were charter members of the British-led European Free Trade Association, organized in 1960, and for a time sought entry to the European Economic Community (Common Market). But in a national referendum held September 24-25, 1972, the Norwegian electorate decisively rejected such entry. However, the government negotiated a free trade agreement with the EEC to gain advantages for Norway's major exports, particularly fish, aluminum, paper, and steel.

Rich in hydroelectric power, Norway has developed into an industrial nation that produces more than a third of its gross national product through manufacturing. All but about nine percent of Norwegian enterprises are privately owned. Small and medium-size plants predominate, with about 70 percent employing fewer than 10 persons.

Along with its promise of considerable riches, the 1968 discovery of huge oil and gas deposits on the continental shelf of the North Sea has brought Norway some major economic problems as well. After borrowing heavily to finance development, the government has found reserves to be smaller than first thought, and production costs higher. In April 1977 a spectacular oil well blowout cost $111 million in lost revenues and has delayed development of the Statfjord fields, where the nation expects to get most of its future oil. Overall, production of oil and natural gas, expected to total the equivalent of 25 million tons in 1977, came to only about two-thirds of that, while the nation's balance of payments showed a record $5.3-billion deficit. As a result, the government devalued the krone by eight percent, froze prices and tightened up credit. Further austerity measures are likely, including a cut in workers' benefits and a reduction of the enormous government subsidies to industry.

HISTORY: The history of Norway before the age of the Vikings is indistinct from that of the rest of Scandinavia. Norse Vikings emerge as an identifiable group in the 8th century, when the Anglo-Saxon Chronicle records their arrival in Britain. Norway itself, split into kingdoms and earldoms, was united in the 11th century and reached its peak in the 13th century, holding sway over Iceland and Greenland. Briefly united with Sweden in 1319, Norway formally joined with Denmark and Sweden in the Union of Kalmar in 1397, which lasted until the end of the Napoleonic Wars, although Sweden seceded in the 16th century

1814: Denmark, having sided with France in the Napoleonic Wars, is among the losers and is forced to cede Norway to Sweden. The Norwegians react by adopting a constitution of their own and choose a Danish prince to be king of Norway, but a Swedish army forces Norway to agree to a dual monarchy with Sweden

1905: Union with Sweden is dissolved and Norway becomes independent. Prince Charles of Denmark is elected king of Norway and ascends throne as Haakon VII

1914-18: Norway remains neutral during World War I, but its merchant fleet suffers heavy losses

1940-45: Nazi Germany attacks Norway and quickly occupies most of country despite strong Norwegian resistance. King Haakon and his cabinet leave the country and set up a government in exile in London. In occupied Norway, meanwhile, a puppet government is established under Norwegian Nazi leader Vidkun Quisling; despite his attempts to promote collaboration with Germans, the Norwegians continue to defy invaders. Norway is liberated in May 1945

1945: Norway becomes founding member of the UN. Trygve Lie elected first UN Secretary-General

1957: King Haakon dies and is succeeded by son, Olav V

1965: Labor Party, which has been dominant for 30 years, is swept

out of office in general elections; Per Borten, leader of Center Party, forms non-socialist coalition government, which remains in power till 1971

1968: Huge oil and gas deposits are discovered in Norwegian sector of North Sea

1972: Voting in a national referendum, the Norwegian electorate rejects entry to the European Economic Community (Common Market), toppling Labor government of Premier Bratteli, in power since 1971 and a strong advocate of EEC entry; Lars Korvald of the Christian People's Party forms a minority coalition government

1973: In general elections the Labor Party obtains 35.29 percent of popular vote as the largest single group and returns to power with a minority government headed by Premier Trygve Bratteli

1974: Norway and the Soviet Union open negotiations to define the disputed boundary of the potentially oil-rich continental shelf of the Barents Sea

1975: The Storting (parliament) passes a tax law providing for a large surtax on North Sea oil production by oil companies, which will bring the government $1 billion a year

1976: Odvar Nordli becomes premier

1977: Oil well blowout in the Ekofisk Field is capped after a spill lasting eight days; the cost to Norway is put at $111 million

1978: Further austerity measures proposed as Norway's foreign debt nears $19 billion. Work proceeds on nation's third major oil find, the Statfjord field (discovered in 1974), which is expected to begin producing in late 1979. Survey indicates 1978 oil and gas production could reach 30 million tons

---

OMAN

Area: 120,000 sq. mi. **Population:** 820,000 (1978 est.)

Official Name: Sultanate of Oman **Capital:** Muscat **Nationality:** Omani **Languages:** Arabic is the official and predominant language; Hindi, Baluchi, English, Farsi, and Urdu are spoken by the minorities **Religion:** 50% are Ibadi Moslems and about 25% Sunni Moslems. Islam is the official religion **Flag:** Horizontal white, red, and green bands, with a vertical red band at the hoist, a white symbol of crossed swords in the upper left **Anthem:** National Anthem, beginning "God save our sultan" **Currency:** Omani rial (0.35 per U.S. $1)

Location: Southeast Arabia. Bounded on the north and northwest by the Gulf of Oman and the United Arab Emirates, on the east and south by the Arabian Sea, and on the west by Southern Yemen and Saudi Arabia **Features:** The coastline extends for about 1,000 miles, with fertile coastal plain (the Batina), a range of barren hills, and a plateau and desert area with an average height of 1,000 feet. Also included are the detached tip of the Musandam Peninsula, and offshore the Kuria Muria and Masira islands **Chief Rivers:** There are no permanent rivers

Head of State and of Government: Sultan Qabus ibn Said al Bu Said, born 1939, seized power in July 1970. The sultan is an absolute monarch **Constitution and Legislative Body:** None **Local Government:** 37 regions, one province and the capital area, ruled by appointed governors

Ethnic Composition: The population is almost evenly divided between those of South and North Arabian stock. Significant minorities (60,000) of Iranians, Pakistanis, Indians, and East Africans live in the coastal districts **Population Distribution:** 10% urban **Density:** 6.8 inhabitants per sq. mi.

Largest Cities: (1974 estimate) Matrah 20,000, Salala 10,000, Nizwa 10,000, Muscat 7,000

Per Capita Income: $2,788 (1978) **Gross National Product (GNP):** $2.4 billion (1978) **Economic Statistics:** About 2% of GNP is derived from agriculture (dates, bananas, onions, limes, tobacco, oranges, coconuts, melons, grapes, wheat, livestock), and 74% from industry (oil providing 70% of the total GNP, fishing, date-drying) **Minerals and Mining:** Oil is the country's chief mineral resource, and there are deposits of asbestos, marble, chrome and copper **Labor Force:** About 150,000 (1970), with 73% in agriculture, and 13% in industry **Foreign Trade:** Exports, oil (99%), dates, fish, and limes, totaled $1.6 billion in 1977. Imports, chiefly foods, machinery, manufactured goods, materials, and clothing, totaled $1.2 billion **Principal Trade Partners:** India, Pakistan, Australia, UAE, Britain, Japan, United States, West Germany

Vital Statistics: Birthrate, 50 per 1,000 of pop. (1974); death rate, 19 **Life Expectancy:** 45 years **Health Statistics:** 860 inhabitants per hospital bed; 7,500 per physician (1976) **Infant Mortality:** N.A. **Illiteracy:** 75% **Education Statistics:** 201 primary and secondary schools, with a combined enrollment of 65,000 (1976) **GNP Expended on Education:** 7.4% (1975)

Transportation: Paved roads total 800 mi. **Motor Vehicles:** 8,168 **Railway Mileage:** None **Ports:** Muscat (Port Qabus), Matrah, Mina al Fahal, Rasyut **Major Airlines:** Gulf Air, an independently run line, and several major international airlines **Communications:** Government controlled **Radio Transmitters:** 4 **Receivers:** 1,000

Television Transmitters: 2 **Receivers:** 55,000 **Telephones:** 9,000 (1976) **Newspapers:** 6 weeklies

Weights and Measures: Metric system **Travel Requirements:** Passport; visa; $4.50 fee; valid 90 days; 2 photos

---

In 1970, Sultan Qabus ibn Said al Bu Said changed the name of Muscat and Oman to simply Oman, but he has not been able to change the fact that Oman is, in a sense, several countries. He belongs to the dynasty of the ancient port city of Muscat, the dynasty which survived the long-standing rivalry among port cities and foreign conquerors for control of the coast. And whoever has controlled the coast has also tried to control the nomads of the desert interior—part of which is traditionally known as Oman. Despite Sultan Qabus's attempt to give a single name to his dominion, Oman is more a dynastic conglomeration than a nation-state. It has no definite boundaries; control of the interior is weak; and the port cities have little loyalty to the dynasty, and less to an entity called "Oman."

For more than a century, the dynasty has relied on British assistance, and many of the high-ranking officers in the army are on loan from the British army. During most of the 1970s, Sultan Qabus could also borrow entire army units from Shah Mohammed Reza Pahlavi of Iran; the Shah's overthrow in 1979 increased Britain's importance to Oman. Britain's Queen Elizabeth and Foreign Secretary David Owen visited Oman to symbolize continuing commitment.

Sultan Qabus, who had been educated in Britain, came to power in 1970 by overthrowing his father, Said ibn Taimur, who had been sultan since 1932. The older man had tried to keep his domain together by fear and by preventing change; he had forbidden nomads to enter the cities and city people to enter the interior, outlawed the cultivation of new land, and required his personal approval to build a new house or to repair an old one. Long an exporter of dates and camels, Muscat and Oman began to export oil in 1967, but the common people received no benefits from the enormous revenues. In 1969, the country had only six primary schools and no secondary schools at all. That year, open revolt broke out in Dhofar, a region in the south with a proud past; Southern Yemen aided the rebels.

With assistance from Iraq and Jordan, as well as Iran and Britain, Sultan Qabus put down the rebellion in Dhofar. He built schools, hospitals, clinics, and highways, and took an interest in external Arab affairs. In 1979, however, he risked isolation from the Arab world by endorsing the peace treaty between Egypt and Israel. He has expressed a desire to become a constitutional monarch of a democratic country, but seems to believe that Oman—with its lack of national feeling—is not yet ready for democracy.

HISTORY: Muscat and Oman was converted to Islam in the 7th century, during the lifetime of Mohammed. In 1508, the Portuguese conquered the the coastal region. In the 17th century, they were driven out by the Turks, who were themselves expelled in 1741 by Ahmed Ibn Said of Yemen, founder of the present ruling family. In the early 19th century, Muscat and Oman was the most powerful state in Arabia, controlling Zanzibar, much of the Persian coast, and part of present-day West Pakistan, but during this period Muscat lost control of Oman—the interior region

1856-61: Rival heirs dispute succession to throne on death of Said ibn Sultan in 1856; dispute is settled through British mediation under an arrangement in 1861 calling for separation of Zanzibar from Muscat

1913-20: Tribes in interior of Oman rebel against sultan of Muscat, who controls only the cities of Muscat and Matrah, and elect Imam spiritual head of country; Imam is murdered in 1920, and sultan signs treaty with his successor calling for internal tribal autonomy and mutual nonaggression

1951: Traditional association with Britain is confirmed by new treaty of friendship, commerce, and navigation

1954-57: Imam dies in 1954; his successor breaks 1920 treaty and

is driven from his capital; Muscat regains control of Oman; pro-Imam uprising breaks out, but is suppressed with British help

1958: Port of Gwadar and its hinterland in Baluchistan is sold to Pakistan

1965-66: United Nations General Assembly adopts resolution in 1965 calling for elimination of British presence in Muscat and Oman; question is raised again in 1966 but no decision is reached

1969: Leftist rebels in Dhofar province engage in guerrilla warfare in effort to overthrow sultan

1970: Sultan Said ibn Taimur is overthrown by son, Qabus bin Said, who promises to establish modern government, end country's isolation, and use oil revenues for the good of the people

1971: Oman joins the UN

1975: Victory over rebels in Dhofar province is declared by sultan

1977: Britain closes its military base on the Omani island of Masira

PAKISTAN

Area: 310,403 sq. mi. **Population:** 74,500,000 (1978 est.)

Official Name: Islamic Republic of Pakistan **Capital:** Islamabad **Nationality:** Pakistani **Languages:** Urdu (spoken by only 9%) is the official language, but English is also widely used in government and commerce; Punjabi (65%), Sindhi (11%), Pushtu, Brahui, and Baluchi are regional languages **Religion:** Islam is the state religion and is practiced by 97% of the population; the rest are Hindus, Christians, Buddhists, or of no religious affiliation **Flag:** Green with a white vertical stripe at the hoist and a white crescent and a 5-pointed star in the center **Anthem:** National Anthem, beginning "Blessed be the sacred land" **Currency:** Pakistani rupee (9.9 per U.S. $1)

Location: South Asia, partly on the Indian subcontinent. It extends c. 1,000 miles from the sea north to the mountain wall of the Hindu Kush and the towering peaks of the Karakoram. It adjoins Iran and Afghanistan on the west and northwest, India on the east, and the Arabian Sea on the south. A barren plain stretches along the foothills of the mountains; in the center is the fertile Indus plain **Chief Rivers:** Indus, Sutlej, Chenab, Ravi

Head of State and Government: President: Gen. Mohammad Zia-ul-Haq, born 1924, assumed office in 1978. He is also Chief Martial Law Administrator, an office he has occupied since the coup of July 1977 **Effective Date of Present Constitution:** 1973, amended 1976, Party suspended 1977 **Legislative Body:** Parliament (bicameral), with a National Assembly and a Senate, dissolved 1977; rule is by President Zia and a council of military chiefs **Local Government:** 4 provinces, presently governed by the provincial chief justices, and a federal capital territory

Ethnic Composition: The population of Pakistan is made up chiefly of Punjabi, Sindhi, Pathan, and Baluchi. Several small tribes live in the mountainous areas **Population Distribution:** 26% urban **Density:** 240 inhabitants per sq. mi.

Largest Cities: (1972 census) Karachi 3,498,634, Lahore 2,165,372, Lyallpur 822,263, Hyderabad 628,310, Rawalpindi 615,392, Multan 542,195, Gujranwala 360,419; (1974 est.) Islamabad 250,000

Per Capita Income: $218 (1978) **Gross National Product (GNP):** $16.5 billion (1978) **Economic Statistics:** In 1977 about 33% of GNP came from agriculture (wheat, cotton, rice, jute); 16% from manufacturing (textiles, food processing, chemicals, cement, paper, metal manufacturing) and mining; 6% from construction; and 15% from trade **Minerals and Mining:** There are large reserves of natural gas, copper, and some crude oil **Labor Force:** 21 million (1977), with 55% in agriculture **Foreign Trade:** Exports, chiefly raw jute, cotton, jute and cotton products, leather goods, rugs, tea, fish, and rice, amounted to $1.3 billion in 1977. Imports, mainly machinery, transportation equipment, iron and steel, animal and vegetable oils and fats, petroleum and products, chemicals, and food grains, amounted to $2.7 billion **Principal Trade Partners:** United States, Japan, Saudi Arabia, Britain, Hong Kong, Sri Lanka, West Germany, Australia

Vital Statistics: Birthrate, 40.5 per 1,000 of pop. (1976); death rate, 12 **Life Expectancy:** 51 years **Health Statistics:** 1,871 inhabitants per hospital bed; 4,049 per physician (1973) **Infant Mortality:** 115 per 1,000 births (1970) **Illiteracy:** 80% **Education Statistics:** 51,568 primary and secondary schools, with combined enrollment of 7,165,414 (1975) **Enrollment in Higher Education:** 238,037 (1974) **GNP Expended on Education:** 2.3% (1975)

Transportation: Surfaced roads total 16,000 mi. **Motor Vehicles:** 287,800 (1975) **Passenger Cars:** 196,100 **Railway Mileage:** 5,475 **Ports:** Karachi, Port Qasim **Major Airlines:** Pakistan International Airlines, operates domestic and international services **Communications:** Partly government owned **Radio Transmitters:** 22 **Licenses:** 1,200,000 (1976) **Television Transmitters:** 7 **Receivers:** 350,000 (1976) **Telephones:** 240,000 (1975) **Newspapers:** 102 dailies (1975), 18 copies per 1,000 inhabitants

Weights and Measures: Metric system **Travel Requirements:** Passport; visa not required for stay up to 30 days

Throughout its relatively short history, Pakistan has been shot through with powerfully divisive forces. When the Indian subcontinent was granted independence from Britain in 1947, it was decided that a national homeland for Moslems should be created as a nation separate from predominantly Hindu India. For centuries there had been periodic bloodbaths resulting from communal rioting between Hindus and Moslems, and an independent Pakistan was seen as the solution.

Unfortunately, Indian Moslems were concentrated in two widely separated parts. The first consisted of all or part of four provinces now known as Pakistan, which borders Afghanistan, Iran, India, and China. The second and more populous part was carved from the old state of Bengal and is now Bangladesh, bordering India and Burma.

The gulf between the two wings of Pakistan was reflected in and intensified by the 1970 election, the first since independence. Of the 313 seats that were to be filled in the new National Assembly, 167 were won by the Awami League—a Bengali nationalist party, all the strength of which was in Bangladesh. The runner-up was the Pakistan People's Party with 88 seats, all for West Pakistan. There was no major national party to bridge the two wings, and virtually the only cement holding them together was a common religion.

On March 1, 1971, at the urging of the Pakistan People's Party, Gen. Yahya Khan announced that the convening of the National Assembly would be postponed pending further discussions of major constitutional issues. Leaders of the Awami League claimed they were being cheated of the fruits of the election, which had made them the majority party of Pakistan.

Widespread rioting in Bangladesh ensued, and strikes crippled the cities. Bengali extremists murdered substantial numbers of non-Bengalis.

On March 25, President Yahya Khan ordered the national army into Bangladesh to crush the separatist movement. The East Bengal Regiment of the army promptly defected to join Bangladesh armed forces, and key bridges, railroads, and communications were blown up or damaged.

An occupation army remained in Bangladesh and had to contend with hostility from the province, sniping and sabotage from Bangladesh guerrillas, and a vast economic drain on the nation as a whole. Millions of refugees fled and hundreds of civilians were killed in the conflict. Complicating matters even more was a deterioration of relations with India.

In the ensuing months tension between India and Pakistan increased, and on December 4 Indian troops entered the Bengali province. On December 16 the Pakistani armed forces there surrendered to the Indian and Bangladesh command.

This defeat, and the secession of Bangladesh, for which the Pakistani public had been unprepared, led to the resignation of President Yahya Khan and the succession of Zulfikar Ali Bhutto, leader of the People's Party, as the first civilian president. Bhutto negotiated the release of 90,000 prisoners and, as a spellbinding orator, set out to restore national pride. He put in train a series of reforms in education, politics, and social life and announced that the state would assume control, but not ownership, of ten basic industries.

In July 1977, following four months of political violence in which at least 350 people were killed, the Pakistani army seized power in a bloodless coup. The Army Chief of Staff, Gen. Mohammad Zia ul-Haq, then became chief martial law administrator. The initial violence was touched off by alleged election fraud on the part of the ruling People's Party.

In March 1978, Bhutto, the most popular civil-ian politician in Pakistan's history, was convicted of a 1974 political murder and sentenced to hang. Denying his guilt, he appealed to the nation's Supreme Court but lost, 4-3. Hundreds of leaders of his Pakistan Party were jailed in what Bhutto supporters said was a campaign to eliminate a political opposition; Zia, however, called the actions a continuing "process of accountability." Despite pleas for clemency from Pope John Paul II, U.S. President Carter, Soviet Union's Leonid Brezhnev, and China's Hua Guofeng, Bhutto was hanged secretly at 2 A.M. on April 4, 1979, in a Rawalpindi jail. Extensive rioting followed.

In 1979, the U.S. accused Pakistan of secret efforts to build nuclear weapons by importing various pieces and materials from Europe and the U.S. There were other reports that Libya had provided the purchase money in an effort to obtain an atomic bomb for the Moslem world.

HISTORY: In the 8th century Moslems from Arabia introduced Islam to the lower reaches of what is now West Pakistan. Two centuries later, Moslem warriors swept from the northwest down through the Khyber Pass and conquered the upper reaches of West Pakistan, converting millions of the inhabitants to Islam. In the 13th century, Moslem invaders brought Islam to Bengal, part of which is now Bangladesh. Moslem power and culture on the Indian subcontinent reached their zenith under the Mogul empire (1526-1857). Despite cultural interchange with the Hindus, the Moslem cummunity continued to maintain its distinct identity under British rule, which lasted until the middle of the 20th century

1906-40: The Moslem League is founded as a separate political organization. Led by Mohammad Ali Jinnah, it demands the establishment of a Moslem state in India

1947: Pakistan is set up as a separate British dominion, with Jinnah as governor-general and Liaqat Ali Khan as prime minister. Establishment of the new state is followed by widespread communal strife between Moslems and Hindus, costing more than a million lives and uprooting millions of Hindus and Moslems

1948-49: Pakistan and India are involved in an undeclared war over the state of Jammu and Kashmir (a state whose predominantly Moslem population is ruled by a Hindu prince who signs Kashmir over to India). A cease-fire is arranged, and the state partitioned by a temporary demarcation line

1951-56: Liaqat Ali Khan is assassinated (1951), ushering in a period of political instability and tension between East and West Pakistan. A new constitution is adopted, and Pakistan becomes a republic within the British Commonwealth with Gen. Iskander Mirza as president

1958-62: Following continued turmoil in both parts of the country, Mirza abrogates the constitution, dismisses the cabinet, and hands over power to the army under Gen. Ayub Khan. Ayub takes over the presidency, dismisses the prime minister, and rules by decree. The new president proclaims new constitution

1965: Ayub Khan is elected president. Pakistan and India fight a brief war over the Rann of Kutch and Kashmir

1969: Ayub resigns in the face of widespread political unrest. Martial law is proclaimed under Gen. Agha Mohammad Yahya Khan, who takes over as president

1970: Yahya Khan proclaims Pakistan an Islamic federal state

1971: Civil war breaks out between Bengali armed forces and Bengalis are defeated; in December brief war between India and Pakistan results in defeat of Pakistan and the secession of the Bengali province, now Bangladesh. Yahya Khan resigns and Zulfikar Ali Bhutto becomes president

1972: Pakistan and India sign Simla agreement to stabilize relations

1973: New constitution is adopted. Fazal Elahi Chaudhry is elected president by the National Assembly. Former President Bhutto becomes prime minister with no loss of power

1974: Civil rights restored. Earthquake kills more than 5,000. Pakistan recognizes Bangladesh

1975: Assassination of Provincial Minister Sherpao leads to opposition Awami Party being declared illegal. U.S. lifts 10-year ban on sale of arms to Pakistan

1976: India and Pakistan agree to resume diplomatic relations

1977: Pakistani army under Gen. Mohammad Zia ul-Haq seizes power in a bloodless coup, ending the Bhutto regime. Elections, promised for October, are cancelled; political activity is banned; martial-law rule is extended indefinitely; General Zia calls measures needed because of nation's "political turmoil"

1978: Bhutto is convicted of a 1974 murder and sentenced to die; denying charge, he appeals to Supreme Court; worldwide reaction includes appeals for clemency from the U.S. and several of

Pakistan's Moslem neighbors. General Zia assumes the office of president following the resignation of Chaudhry

1979: On April 4, Bhutto, still declaring his innocence, is hanged secretly in the Rawalpindi District Jail. Days of rioting follow; 30,000 march in protest in Larkana, his hometown. The U.S. cuts off economic aid, contending that Pakistan is secretly trying to build nuclear weapons with equipment and materials purchased—often through dummy organizations—in Europe and the U.S. Zia declares Islamic law to be the country's law; two bank robbers are sentenced to have their right hands and left feet amputated. Afghanistan charges that Pakistan trains Moslem Afghan rebels and even sends disguised troops along on some cross-border raids

PANAMA

Area: 29,208 sq. mi. (excluding Canal Zone with an area of 647 sq. mi.) **Population:** 1,800,000 (1978 est.)

Official Name: Republic of Panama **Capital:** Panama **Nationality:** Panamanian **Languages:** Spanish is the official and predominant language; English is widely used in the capital and Colón; and small minorities of Italians, French, Greeks, East Indians, and indigenous Cuna Indians retain their national languages **Religion:** 95% Roman Catholic, 5% Protestant **Flag:** Divided into 4 rectangles: the lower left is blue; the upper right red; the upper left white with a blue star in the center; the lower right white with a red star in the middle **Anthem:** Istmeño Hymn **Currency:** Balboa (1 per U.S. $1)

Location: Latin America, occupying the southern end of the Isthmus of Panama, which forms the land connection between the North and South American continents. Panama is bounded on the north by the Caribbean Sea, on the east by Colombia, on the south by the Gulf of Panama and the Pacific Ocean, and on the west by Costa Rica **Features:** The country is largely mountainous and hilly, with 2 mountain ranges forming the backbone of the isthmus. Lowlands lie along both coastlines; the Atlantic side and eastern Panama are covered almost entirely by tropical rain forests. The Panama Canal bisects the country **Chief Rivers:** Tuira, Bayano, Santa María, Chepo, Indio

Head of State and Government: President Aristides Royo, born 1940, elected 1978 for 6 years **Effective Date of Present Constitution:** 1946, revised October 1972 **Legislative Body:** A National Assembly of Community Representatives, with 505 members elected for 6 years, a National Legislative Council performs legislative functions when the Assembly is not in session **Local Government:** 9 provinces, each headed by an appointed governor, and one intendency (territory)

Ethnic Composition: The population is 70% mestizo, 14% Antilleans (immigrants from the West Indies and their descendants), 10% white and 6% Indian **Population Distribution:** 53.7% urban **Density:** 62 inhabitants per sq. mi.

Largest Cities: (1978 est.) Panama 438,000, San Miguelito 139,000, Colón 85,600, David 70,700

Per Capita Income: $1,449 (1978) **Gross National Product (GNP):** $2.6 billion (1978) **Economic Statistics:** About 31% of the GNP is derived from the operations of the Panama Canal. In 1973 about 18% came from agriculture (rice, sugar, and bananas); 16% from industry (food processing, textiles, clothing, shoes, cement, pharmaceuticals, oil refining, sugar refining); and 18% from trade **Minerals and Mining:** There are many minerals that remain unexploited because of poor quality; however, major copper and molybdenum deposits are to be exploited **Labor Force:** 525,039 (1975), of which 40% was engaged in agriculture, 19% in services, 10% in commerce, 18% in manufacturing, and 6% in activities in the Canal Zone **Foreign Trade:** Exports, chiefly bananas, shrimp, sugar and petroleum derivatives, totaled $227 million in 1976. Imports, mainly machinery, vehicles and parts, petroleum and food totaled $838 million **Principal Trade Partners:** United States, Saudi Arabia, Ecuador, Venezuela

Vital Statistics: Birthrate, 29.5 per 1,000 of pop. (1977); death rate, 7.1 (1975) **Life Expectancy:** 59 years **Health Statistics:** 284 inhabitants per hospital bed; 1,335 per physician (1977) **Infant Mortality:** 28.5 per 1,000 births **Illiteracy:** 18% **Education Statistics:** 2,190 primary and secondary schools, with combined enrollment of 471,007 (1976) **Enrollment in Higher Education:** 26,289 (1975) **GNP Expended on Education:** 5.9% (1974)

Transportation: Paved roads total 1,187 mi. **Motor Vehicles:** 85,800 (1975) **Passenger Cars:** 66,200 **Railway Mileage:** 215 **Ports:** Colón, Bocas del Toro, Puerto Armuelles **Major Airlines:** Compañia Panameña de Aviación, Panameña de Aviación Internacional, and Aerovias Internacional operate international services. Aerovias Panama Airways operates domestic flights **Communications:** Partly government controlled **Radio Transmitters:** 117 **Receivers:** 270,000 (1976) **Television Transmitters:** 10 **Receivers:** 186,000 (1976) **Telephones:** 155,000 (1976) **Newspapers:** 6 dailies, 79 copies per 1,000 inhabitants (1975)

Weights and Measures: British standards and the metric system are used **Travel Requirements:** Passport; visa or 30-day tourist card obtainable from airline; $2 fee

Panama, the narrow serpentine isthmus connecting North and South America, is a largely mountainous country, bisected by a 51-mile-long Panama Canal. Since Nov. 1, 1979, Panama has been building up its financial and commercial status through possession of the land, dry docks, ports, and railroads of the former Canal Zone. (The waterway itself is scheduled to be controlled until Dec. 31, 1999, by the U.S.-operated Canal Commission, in which Panama is a junior partner.) As the home of 85 international banks, and well situtated for the distribution or transshipment of goods, Panama is rapidly becoming the business center of Central America—and it has hopes of becoming the Hong Kong of the West.

Within the country, access roads are sparse, a handicap that the government, with outside help, has been trying to remedy. The eastern half of the country, down to the Colombian border, consists largely of impenetrable jungle inhabited by a few primitive Indian tribes.

The Panama Canal dominates life in the central populated areas, and it has played an overriding role in Panamanian politics, at the same time emerging as a symbol of North American domination.

On June 16, 1978, in Panama City, President Carter and Panamanian head of state Brig. Gen. Omar Torrijos Herrera took part in ceremonies formally concluding the two new Panama Canal treaties, thus bringing to fruition 13 years of often difficult negotiations. Basically, one treaty covers control of the canal while the other establishes its future neutrality. Under the accords, Panama will obtain full control of the canal in the year 2000, the U.S. will pay Panama $10 million annually in toll revenues (plus added amounts dependent on traffic), and the U.S. has the right to intervene unilaterally in Panama if the canal's operation is ever threatened after the year 2000.

In the final phase of the canal talks, both leaders absorbed considerable criticism from countrymen who felt too much was being given to the other nation. Carter narrowly averted a serious political setback in April 1978 when the U.S. Senate ratified, with but one vote to spare, the second of the two treaties. In order to gain ratification, the Administration accepted reservations favorable to the U.S. but politically embarrassing for Torrijos, who nonetheless accepted them.

A new oil transshipment port was opened on the Pacific Coast in 1979. It will transfer Alaskan oil from supertankers to smaller craft that can go through the canal. In addition, a new $20-million convention hall was announced for Panama City.

HISTORY: Little is known about the Indians inhabiting Panama before the arrival of the Spanish explorer Rodrigo de Bastidas in 1502. The region soon fell under the control of Balboa, who in 1513 made his famous crossing of the isthmus and discovered the Pacific. Under Spanish occupation the isthmus became the route by which Inca treasures were shipped to Spain. But Panama was to lose most of its importance in the carrying trade with the collapse of the Spanish Empire

1821: Panama breaks away from Spain and becomes part of Colombia

1848-49: California gold rush enhances importance of Panama as westward-bound U.S. settlers use isthmus as bridge between Atlantic and Pacific; crossings stimulate interest in construction of a canal across isthmus

1881-89: French company headed by Ferdinand de Lesseps begins work on a canal in 1881; disease among workers and financial problems drive company into bankruptcy within the decade

1903: Panamanians revolt when Colombian senate refuses to ratify Hay-Herrán Treaty granting United States right to build a canal across Panamanian isthmus; United States prevents Colombia from quelling rebellion and Panamanians declare their independence; new republic grants United States exclusive control of a canal zone in perpetuity and permits United States to intervene to protect Panamanian independence

1914: Panama Canal is opened

1939: Canal treaty is amended, eliminating U.S. right to intervene in Panamanian affairs

1959: Mobs of Panamanian youths invade Canal Zone in protest against U.S. sovereignty and demand revision of canal treaty

1964: Riots break out in Canal Zone as Panamanians protest U.S. failure to abide by agreement calling for simultaneous display of Panamanian and American flags

1967: United States and Panama negotiate new treaties under which United States would give up sovereignty over canal to U.S.-Panamanian authority and provide military defense for canal, and under which construction of a new canal might be undertaken; treaties, however, remain unratified

1968: National Assembly impeaches President Marco Aurelio Robles for having violated constitution by backing government candidate in presidential election; Assembly's decision is voided by Supreme Court. Following a dispute over the outcome of the election, opposition candidate Arnulfo Arias is declared president but is overthrown on October 1, 11 days after taking office, in coup led by National Guard; National Assembly is dissolved and constitutional guarantees suspended; Colonel José M. Pinilla is sworn in as provisional president

1969: Brigadier General Omar Torrijos Herrera, one of the principal leaders of the 1968 coup, emerges as nation's strong man after banishing other leaders

1972: Torrijos acquires full civil and military powers by vote of National Assembly

1975: Government moves toward nationalization of banana industry. U.S. and Panama sign a preliminary agreement to end U.S. jurisdiction over the Panama Canal and Zone

1977: President Carter and General Torrijos sign two new Panama Canal treaties in Washington, providing for transfer of canal to Panama by the year 2000 and establishing its future neutrality. Panamanians approve treaties in referendum

1978: U.S. Senate barely ratifies second of two treaties; last-minute reservations favorable to U.S. prove a political embarrassment to Torrijos but he finally accepts them; Carter visits Panama for formal conclusion of pacts. Aristides Royo, a lawyer and former education minister who helped negotiate the canal treaties, is elected president by the congress, or National Assembly of Community Representatives. However, Torrijos continues as commander of National Guard

1979: Panamanian possession of the Canal Zone, exclusive of the waterway itself, begins

---

PAPUA NEW GUINEA

Area: 183,540 sq. mi. **Population:** 2,910,000 (1978 est.)

Official Name: Papua New Guinea **Capital:** Port Moresby **Nationality:** Papua New Guinean **Languages:** Melanesian Pidgin and Hiri (Police) Motu serve as linguas franca, but are not universal; English is the official language; about 750 localized Papuan languages are spoken **Religion:** About 1,400,000 (52%) profess Christianity, with half a million Roman Catholics and the rest Protestants; the rest practice animistic forms of worship **Flag:** Divided diagonally from upper left to lower right; the upper section is red with a gold bird of paradise, and the lower section is black with the five principal stars of the Southern Cross in white **Anthem:** N.A. **Currency:** Kina (.72 per U.S. $1)

Location: Southwest Pacific. About 100 miles northeast of Australia, it occupies the eastern half of the island of New Guinea and is bordered on the west by Indonesia. 15% of the area is on islands to the north and east: the Bismarck Archipelago, the northwestern Solomons, and the smaller Trobriand, Woodlark, D'Entrecasteaux and Louisiade groups **Features:** A high mountain ridge bisecting the New Guinea portion rises to about 15,000 feet, graduating north and south to broad upland valleys, plains, and along much of the coast vast swamps. The larger islands are mountainous, some with active volcanoes **Chief Rivers:** Fly, Sepik, Markham, Ramu

Head of State: Queen Elizabeth II, represented by a governor-general, Sir Tore Lokoloko, born 1929, appointed March 1977 **Head of Government:** Prime Minister Michael Thomas Somare, born 1936, took office 1975 and was reappointed in 1977; he is assisted by a National Executive Council **Effective Date of Present Constitution:** 1975 **Legislative Body:** Parliament (unicameral), with 109 members elected for 5 years **Local Government:** 19 provinces (5 with internal autonomy), with appointed administrators and elected assemblies, and a national capital province

Ethnic Composition: The indigenous population is composed of two major groups, Papuans in the interior and on the south coast of New Guinea, and Melanesians on the north and east coastal areas, and on the islands; minorities include Chinese, Europeans, and Polynesians **Population Distribution:** 13% urban **Density:** 16 inhabitants per sq. mi.

Largest Cities: (1977 est.) Port Moresby 117,000; (1973 est.) Rabaul 62,329, Lae 50,834; (1971 census) Madang 16,866, Wewak 15,015, Goroka 12,066, Mt. Hagen 10,621

Per Capita Income: $448 (1976) **Gross National Product (GNP):** $1.3 billion (1976) **Economic Statistics:** In 1973 about 62% of GNP was derived from agriculture (coffee, cocoa, rubber, copra, tea, palm products, timber, livestock) and fishing; 5% from manufacturing (meat packing, lumbering, fish and tobacco processing, light industries) and mining; and 17% from trade and services **Minerals and Mining:** Copper, gold, and silver are exploited, and a search for oil and gas has been started **Labor Force:** 521,109 (1971), with 80% engaged in subsistence agriculture and 9.5% in industry **Foreign Trade:** Exports, chiefly copra, palm oil, coffee, cocoa, rubber, tea, plywood, tuna, gold, silver and copper, totaled $636 million in 1977. Imports, mainly foods, machinery, and manufactured goods, chemicals, and petroleum products, totaled $484 million **Principal Trade Partners:** Australia, Japan, United States, West Germany, Singapore, Britain, Spain

Vital Statistics: Birthrate, 40.6 per 1,000 of pop. (1975); death rate, 17.1 **Life Expectancy:** 49 years **Health Statistics:** 169 inhabitants per hospital bed; 11,327 per physician (1973) **Infant Mortality:** 10.2 per 1,000 births **Illiteracy:** 67% **Education Statistics:** 1,897 primary and secondary schools (1975), with combined enrollment of 285,202 (1976) **Enrollment in Higher Education:** 9,667 **GNP Expended on Education:** 6.8% (1971)

Transportation: Paved roads total 2,703 mi. **Motor Vehicles:** 41,430 (1975) **Passenger Cars:** 17,923 **Railway Mileage:** None **Ports:** Kieta, Rabaul, Lae, Port Moresby, Madang **Major Airlines:** Qantas Airways and Air Niugini maintain international services; domestic flights are handled by Ansett Airlines of Australia, Talair and Trans-Australia Airlines **Communications:** Government owned **Radio Transmitters:** 20 **Receivers:** 100,000 (1974) **Television:** None **Telephones:** 38,000 (1976) **Newspapers:** 1 daily, 7 copies per 1,000 inhabitants (1974)

Weights and Measures: British Standards are being replaced by the metric system **Travel Requirements:** Passport, visa

Papua New Guinea is one of the more recent additions to the world family of nations. The people of this Pacific island country until recent years lived in a near-Stone Age culture. For many of the dark-skinned Melanesian and Papuan indigenous population, the modern world of the 20th century did not exist until the area became the battleground for opposing Japanese and Allied forces.

The native population, one of the most heterogeneous in the Pacific, includes, besides Melanesians and Papuans, a number of Chinese, Australian and Polynesian peoples. These ethnic groups are divided by language, custom and tradition. The land itself is divisive, with physical isolation, difficult terrain and heavy vegetation reinforcing the pattern of diversity. Contact with the outside world was a hit-or-miss proposition for the long colonial period. Today for many of its people the main way of life is still subsistence farming based on taro, yams and bananas.

Commercial agriculture is largely in the hands of foreign investors who have developed plantations for coffee, copra, rubber and tea. Timber is a more recent cash crop that is being developed and has a great potential. The plantation economy has traditionally exploited native workers with low wages while nourishing enclaves of white colonialism. Agricultural products are the dominant exports of Papua New Guinea. However, copper is an increasingly important source of export income.

Despite the great potential for self-sufficiency, Papua New Guinea is dependent on food imports. With a growing urban population and a poor, almost nonexistent road network, rice and other staples have to be imported. It also continues to rely heavily on Australia and New Zealand for financial aid.

Since independence, continuing border problems with the neighboring Indonesian province of Irian Jaya (West New Guinea) due to an off-and-on guerrilla war waged by separatists of the Free West Papua Movement has strained relations between the two nations. And refugees that crossed the border to flee the fighting—and reported Indonesian reprisals—have added to the economic burden on Port Moresby. In 1978, the government cracked down on the guerrilla's highland sanctuaries, and in October captured West Papuan leader Jacob Prai. Indonesia and Papua New

Guinea began talks in March 1979 to set permanent boundaries in the western highlands area—one of the most rugged and inaccessible in the world.

HISTORY: Little is known about the prehistory of Papua New Guinea but it is now established that man was in the New Guinea highlands at least by 8000 B.C. and perhaps as early as 50,000 B.C. The area was settled by Asian peoples by way of Indonesia. The first Europeans to sight New Guinea were probably Portuguese and Spanish navigators in the early 16th century

1828: Dutch take possession of West New Guinea; occasional contact is made with eastern regions

1870s: German firm began to develop copra trade to meet European demand for coconut oil

1884: The British establish protectorate over southern littoral (Papua) after concern in Australia over German encroachment

1906: British New Guinea turned over to Australia

1914: Australian troops occupy German New Guinea

1920: Australia assumes League of Nations mandate over Territory of New Guinea

1941: Japanese invade New Guinea

1942-43: American and Australian forces halt Japanese advance on Port Moresby and regain control of New Guinea and adjacent islands in a series of hard fought campaigns

1947: Australian rule is reconfirmed by United Nations

1949: Australian territory of Papua and UN trust territory of New Guinea joined under single international trusteeship

1950-60: Native local government councils are established

1951: Legislative Council is established but with limited indigenous participation

1964: House of Assembly replaces Legislative Council

1968-72: Self-government movement gains strength

1973: Self-government established in December with Michael Somare as Chief Minister. Australia retains control of defense and foreign relations

1975: Full independence is achieved on September 16

1976: Agreement is reached with Bougainville secessionist leaders after eruption of violence

1977: Prime Minister Michael Somare's Pangu Pati coalition is returned to power in general elections for Parliament

1978: Government, proclaiming 200-mile offshore economic zone, takes control of coastal fishing and seabed resources. Papua New Guinea and Australia sign (Dec. 18) treaty settling 6-year boundary dispute with Queensland over Torres Strait

PARAGUAY

Area: 157,047 sq. mi. **Population:** 2,805,000 (1978 est.)

Official Name: Republic of Paraguay **Capital:** Asunción **Nationality:** Paraguayan **Languages:** Spanish, the official language spoken by 75%, and Guaraní, spoken by 90%, are the national languages **Religion:** Roman Catholicism is the state religion and embraces about 97% of the population; there are Mennonite colonies in the Chaco **Flag:** Horizontal stripes of red, white, and blue; the national coat of arms in the center of the obverse and the treasury seal in the center of the reverse **Anthem:** National Anthem, beginning "Once the land of America" **Currency:** Guaraní (126 per U.S. $1)

Location: Southern South America. Landlocked Paraguay is bordered on the northeast and east by Brazil, on the south by Argentina, and on the west and north by Bolivia **Features:** The country is divided by the Paraguay River into 2 disparate regions. The eastern part consists of rolling terrain, with wooded hills, tropical forests, and fertile grasslands. To the west is the Chaco, a low plain covered with marshes and dense scrub forests **Chief Rivers:** Paraguay, Pilcomayo, Paraná, Verde

Head of State and of Government: President: Gen. Alfredo Stroessner, born 1912, originally elected in 1954; in 1978 reelected to sixth term of office **Effective Date of Present Constitution:** 1967, amended 1977 **Legislative Body:** Congress (bicameral), consisting of the Senate and the Chamber of Deputies. The Senate is composed of 30 members and the Chamber of Deputies has 60 members, with members of both houses elected for 5 years. Two-thirds of the seats in each house are allocated to the majority party and the remaining third proportionately divided among the minority parties **Local Government:** 19 departments, each headed by a government delegate appointed by the president, and a federal district

Ethnic Composition: About 95% of the population is of mixed Spanish and Indian (Guaraní) descent. Italians, Germans, and Japanese constitute small minorities **Population Distribution:** 40% urban **Density:** 18 inhabitants per sq. mi.

Largest Cities: (1972 census) Asunción 392,753, Fernando de la Mora 36,834, Lambaré 31,656, Encarnación 23,343, Pedro Juan Caballero 21,033

Per Capita Income: $680 (1978) **Gross National Product (GNP):** $1.9 billion (1978) **Economic Statistics:** 33.4% of the GNP comes from agriculture (livestock, lumber, bananas, rice, coconuts, cocoa); 23.1% from commerce and finance; and 15.9% from manufacturing (meat packing, refining of quebracho and cotton, sugar, wood, vegetable oils) **Minerals and Mining:** No important deposits of minerals exist **Labor Force:** 853,900 (1975), with 53% in agriculture; 15.2% in manufacturing; 6.8% in commerce; 3% in transportation and communications; 3% in construction; and 16.7% in services **Foreign Trade:** Exports, chiefly cotton, soybeans, meat products, quebracho extract, vegetable oils, and essential oils, totaled $179 million in 1976. Imports, mainly foodstuffs, machinery and motors, transportation equipment, nonferrous metals and manufactures, and iron and its products, totaled $200 million **Principal Trade Partners:** United States, Argentina, EC countries, Brazil

Vital Statistics: Birthrate, 39.8 per 1,000 of pop. (1975); death rate, 8.9 **Life Expectancy:** 62 years **Health Statistics:** 694 inhabitants per hospital bed; 1,189 per physician (1975) **Infant Mortality:** 38.6 per 1,000 births (1971) **Illiteracy:** 18% **Education Statistics:** 3,673 primary and secondary schools, with combined enrollment of 526,500 (1974) **Enrollment in Higher Education:** 12,212 (1973) **GNP Expended on Education:** 1.4% (1974)

Transportation: Paved roads total 374 mi. **Motor Vehicles:** 30,000 (1971) **Passenger Cars:** 16,000 **Railway Mileage:** 296 **Ports:** Asunción and Concepción on the Paraguay River **Major Airlines:** Lineas Aéreas Paraguayas, Lineas Aéreas de Transporte Nacional (LATN), Lloyd Aéreo Paraguayo, S.A., and Transporte Aéreo Militar (military and civilian flights) all operate international and domestic services **Communications:** Government and privately owned **Radio Transmitters:** 28 **Receivers:** 180,000 (1976) **Television Transmitters:** 1 **Receivers:** 55,000 (1976) **Telephones:** 40,000 (1976) **Newspapers:** 8 dailies (1975), 40 copies per 1,000 inhabitants (1973)

Weights and Measures: Metric system **Travel Requirements:** Passport no visa for 3 months

Wars have shaped Paraguay's progress to an uncommon degree; the most disastrous was the War against the Triple Alliance—Uruguay, Argentina, and Brazil—in which hundreds of thousands of Paraguayans were killed. The six-year conflict ended in 1870. In the Chaco War, which was fought from 1932 to 1935 in the desert lands with Bolivia, Paraguay lost additional men.

World War II brought a period of prosperity, as the prices of beef, hides, and quebracho wood extract (used in tanning leather) rose sharply. But the war had a more lasting effect on Paraguay's economy. The universal shortages of imported goods and the introduction of cargo aircraft in South America combined to produce a still-flourishing, highly lucrative contraband trade.

The last major civil war was in 1947, in which Gen. Alfredo Stroessner rose to power. He assumed command in 1954 and has been president since then, making Paraguay Latin America's most durable dictatorship. Until recently, political dissidents suffered repression in anonymity because Paraguay is a small country out of the spotlight of world attention. However, U.S. President Carter's emphasis on human rights has brought increased attention to these violations.

By late 1978, Paraguay had only an estimated 15 political prisoners—a sharp drop from a reported 2,000 in 1976. Relations with the U.S. were strained that year when Domingo Laino, a leader of the Authentic Radical Liberal Party, was arrested upon his return home after denouncing Paraguayan human rights' practices before the Organization of American States. The U.S. ambassador pointedly expressed "condolences" in a visit to Mrs. Laino. Carlos Pastore of the Liberal Party was expelled for trying to organize an opposition front.

The employment picture has been brightened as work progresses on a gigantic Brazilian-Paraguayan hydroelectric project on the Paraná River. In addition, Brazil is lending Paraguay money to build its first steel mill, to be located 9 miles from Asunción.

HISTORY: The several Indian tribes that inhabited eastern Paraguay before the advent of Europeans were known collectively as Guaraní because of their common language. While not as advanced as the Incas or the Mayas, the Guaraní were farmers and lived in large thatched houses, thus presenting a strong contrast to the nomadic tribes of the Chaco and the Amazon Valley. With the coming of the Spaniards in the 16th century, Paraguay at first dominated the La Plata region but by the 18th century was reduced to an outpost of the viceroyalty, which had become centered on Buenos Aires

1811-13: Paraguay gains its independence from Spain and rejects the leadership of Buenos Aires

1865-70: Paraguay is disastrously defeated in a war against Argentina, Brazil, and Uruguay, losing 55,000 square miles of territory and more than half its population

1932-35: Unsettled boundary dispute leads to Chaco War between Paraguay and Bolivia; Paraguay wins but is economically ruined

1940-48: President Higinio Morínigo, leader of the Colorado party, establishes a period of dictatorial stability, but civil war breaks out when rival forces rise against him. Rebels are defeated, but the Colorados split into two rival groups; the group opposing Morínigo forces him to leave the country

1954: Gen. Alfredo Stroessner engineers a successful coup and is elected president without opposition

1958: Stroessner, unopposed, is reelected to the presidency for five years; all 60 congressmen elected are members of Stroessner's Colorado Party

1959-60: Government troops crush rebel uprisings

1964: A "colonels' plot," allegedly organized by exiled officers in Argentina to overthrow Stroessner's government, is crushed

1967: A new constitution is adopted providing for redistribution of congressional seats

1968: Stroessner is reelected for his fourth term of office; for the first time since 1954, opposition parties are permitted to take part in elections, but Stroessner's Colorado party wins majority in both chambers

1969-70: Catholic Church throws down sharp challenge to Stroessner regime, calling on president to undertake widespread reforms

1973: General Stroessner is reelected with 84 percent of the popular vote. Paraguay and Brazil agree to construct a huge hydroelectric complex on the Paraná River

1974: Reports of new antigovernment plots lead to stricter controls and political imprisonments

1975: U.S. oil companies continue explorations in the Chaco region under pacts strongly criticized as unfavorable to Paraguayan interests

1977: Three Communist Party leaders and 11 other political prisoners, jailed since General Stroessner's takeover in 1954, are released, in apparent response to U.S. pressure. Constitutional amendment is approved allowing General Stroessner to run for the presidency in 1978 for another five-year term

1978: Stroessner is reelected to sixth term

PERU

Area: 496,222 sq. mi. **Population:** 16,580,000 (1978 est.)

Official Name: Republic of Peru **Capital:** Lima **Nationality:** Peruvian **Languages:** Spanish and Quechua are official languages, many Indians speaking only the latter or Aymara **Religion:** More than 90% of the population is Roman Catholic **Flag:** Vertical bands of red, white, and red with the national coat of arms in the center **Anthem:** National Anthem, beginning "We are free, let us always be so" **Currency:** Sol (211 per U.S. $1)

Location: West coast of South America. Peru is bordered on the north by Ecuador and Colombia, on the east by Brazil and Bolivia, on the south by Chile, and on the west by the Pacific Ocean **Features:** The country is divided into a narrow coastal desert; the high sierra, the zone of the great Andean cordilleras; and the eastern lowlands (montaña), with uncharted hills, forests, and tropical jungles **Chief Rivers:** Amazon, Ucayali-Apurímac, Marañón-Huallaga

Head of State and of Government: President: Gen. Francisco Morales Bermúdez Cerrutti, born 1922, installed in military coup in 1975. He is assisted by a cabinet headed by prime minister (and war minister) Gen. Pedro Richter Prada, appointed Feb. 1979 **Effective Date of Present Constitution:** 1933; it is to be replaced by a new one to take effect in 1980 **Legislative Body:** Congress (bicameral), suspended in 1968 **Local Government:** 23 departments and the constitutional province of Callao, each headed by an appointed prefect

Ethnic Composition: 46% Indian, 38% mestizo, 15% white **Population Distribution:** 55% urban **Density:** 33 inhabitants per sq. mi.

Largest Cities: (1972 census) (M.A. = Metropolitan Area) Lima 2,981,292 (M.A. 4,000,000), Arequipa 304,653, Callao 296,220, Chimbote 159,045, Chiclayo 148,932

Per Capita Income: $963 (1978) **Gross National Product (GNP):** $16.4 billion (1978 est.) **Economic Statistics:** 26% of the GNP is derived from manufacturing (textiles, foodstuffs, iron and steel, ships, metal products and chemicals, automobile assembly); 13% from agriculture (cotton, sugar, rice, coffee), fisheries, and forestry and 8% from mining **Minerals and Mining:** Copper, silver, lead, zinc, iron, bismuth, molybdenum, gold, and tungsten **Labor Force:** 5 million (1975), with 42% engaged in agriculture, 14% in industry, and 17% in services **Foreign Trade:** Exports, mainly copper, fishmeal, silver, iron, sugar, cotton, and coffee, totaled $1.8 billion in 1977. Imports, chiefly capital goods, industrial raw materials, and intermediate goods, totaled $2.1 billion **Principal Trade Partners:** United States, West Germany, Argentina, Britain, Japan, Belgium

Vital Statistics: Birthrate, 41 per 1,000 of pop. (1975); death rate, 11.9 **Life Expectancy:** 58 years **Health Statistics:** 497 inhabitants per hospital bed; 1,802 per physician (1972) **Infant Mortality:** 65.1 per 1,000 births (1970) **Illiteracy:** 28% **Education Statistics:** 19,701 primary and secondary schools with combined enrollment of 3,855,800 (1976) **Enrollment in Higher Education:** 190,635 (1976) **GNP Expended on Education:** 4.2% (1974)

Transportation: Paved roads total 3,159 mi. **Motor Vehicles:** 406,800 (1974) **Passenger Cars:** 266,900 **Railway Mileage:** 1,798 **Ports:** Callao, Talara, Chimbote, Matarani, Ilo, Paita, Pisco **Major Airlines:** Compañía de Aviación Faucett and Aeroperú fly internationally and domestically **Communications:** Government controlled **Radio Transmitters:** 279 **Receivers:** 2,068,000 (1976) **Television Transmitters:** 52 **Receivers:** 600,000 (1976) **Telephones:** 389,000 (1976) **Newspapers:** 35 dailies (1975), 118 copies per 1,000 inhabitants (1974)

Weights and Measures: Metric system **Travel Requirements:** Passport; 90-day tourist card obtainable at port of entry; $2 fee; smallpox and yellow fever certificates required

Peru's economy and social structure were long controlled by a few rich families and foreign mining interests. The aristocrats, however, have always been reluctant to see to the business of government themselves, and consequently the army and, occasionally, popular governments have filled the gap. Racial strains between the three major groups—Indian, mestizo, and white—have further complicated politics.

Inflation and crippling political infighting led, on October 3, 1968, to a coup by a military junta, which named Gen. Juan Velasco Alvarado as president. Despite broad social and economic reforms—including land reform and redistributions, a half share in business profits for the workers in Peruvian companies, and nationalization of large industries and public utilities—no protest was heard when Velasco was deposed by Gen. Francisco Morales Bermúdez in August 1975. By that time a faltering economy with rampant unemployment and a rise in the cost of living had offset any benefits gained from the socioeconomic changes. Morales at once consolidated his position with his reaffirmation of the social and economic policies of the 1968 revolution.

Morales' government suffered from internal unrest, however, when it imposed an unpopular austerity program in its efforts to cope with an immense foreign debt. Its rule was marked by repression of extremist political publications and expulsions of leftist military officers and labor leaders. Meantime, a 100-member Constituent Assembly, elected in 1978, was drawing up a constitution in anticipation of a return to civilian rule in 1980.

HISTORY: At the time of the Spanish Conquest, Peru was the heartland of the great Inca Empire extending from northern Ecuador to central Chile. In 1532 the empire, which had recently undergone a civil war, fell to Spaniards led by Francisco Pizarro. In the colonial era the Indians of Peru were reduced to a serfdom from which the majority still have not fully emerged. In 1824 Spain's colonial rule came to an end with the defeat of Spanish forces by the revolutionary armies led by José de San Martín and Simón Bolívar

1863-79: Futile attempts by Spain to regain its former colonies lead to an intermittent war of small naval engagements; in a peace treaty signed in 1879 Spain finally recognizes the independence of Peru

1879-84: Peru and Bolivia fight unsuccessful War of the Pacific with Chile; Peru is forced to cede the nitrate province of Tarapacá to Chile and to allow Chilean occupation of the provinces of Tacna and Arica

1924: Victor Raúl Haya de la Torre founds APRA (Alianza Popular Revolucionaria Americana), dedicated to radical economic and social reforms to improve the lot of the lower classes, especially the Indians, and nationalization of foreign enterprises

1929: A controversy over Tacna and Arica dating back to the War of the Pacific is resolved through U.S. mediation; Arica is awarded to Chile and Tacna is returned to Peru

1945-48: APRA, though barred from putting up candidates, helps elect José Luis Bustamante to the presidency; he is deposed by a military junta led by General Manuel Odría

1956: Ex-President Manuel Prado is elected president with APRA support and legalizes the party

1962: Haya de la Torre wins slim plurality in disputed presidential elections; attempts to form a coalition government fail and army seizes power

1963-68: Military junta permits new elections and Fernando Belaúnde Terry, a moderate, becomes president; his government confronts rising opposition from legislature and a deteriorating economy; in 1968 Belaúnde is overthrown by a military junta headed by Gen. Juan Velasco Alvarado, which nationalizes U.S.-owned oil property

1969: Junta seizes American tuna boats

1970: An earthquake hits northern Peru, killing 50,000

1971: Government takes over U.S. copper concession

1972: Government seizes U.S. potash and phosphate concessions

1974: Major newspapers are expropriated and transferred to community guilds by the military regime

1975: Government action against striking civil employees results in widespread rioting in Lima, where hundreds are arrested as army quells demonstrations. Velasco overthrown by Morales

1976: Government declares a state of emergency after students and workers riot to protest a new set of austerity measures and call for a return to elected civilian government. Entire cabinet resigns after Prime Minister Fernandez Maldonado quits following an army crisis. Morales replaces resigning leftists with moderates. Huge foreign debt is accumulated

1977: Trans-Andean oil pipeline begins operation. Peru, in grave cash squeeze, is told by international banking community to enact austerity measures as condition for further credit

1978: Peru's foreign debt is put at $5.5 billion; annual inflation rate reaches 80 percent; unemployment and recession deepen. Government launches austerity program; its announcement of steep price hikes on consumer staples triggers two-day nationwide general strike and sets off wave of violence in which 31 persons are killed. Government, blaming "leftist agitators" for violence, declares brief period of martial law. APRA wins largest bloc of Constituent Assembly seats in Peru's first nationwide election since 1963; the Assembly has the task of rewriting the constitution and leading the nation to civilian government by 1980

1979: The government arranges to postpone payment of almost $800 million interest and amortization due to 283 foreign banks in 1980. Angered by a 40 percent drop in real wages in three years, the General Confederation of Peruvian Workers declares a general strike, but it collapses on the second day as the government arrests hundreds. Later, the copper miners strike briefly. In February, General Pedro Richter Prada is sworn in as prime minister, war minister, and army commander, succeeding General Oscar Molina Pallocchia. New constitution gains limited approval by President Morales

---

PHILIPPINES

Area: 115,707 sq. mi. **Population:** 45,030,000 (1978 est.)
Official Name: Republic of the Philippines **Capital:** Manila **Nationality:** Filipino **Languages:** Pilipino (the national language based on Tagalog), English and Spanish are the official languages; almost 90 Philippine languages and dialects are spoken **Religion:** 74% Roman Catholic, 9% Protestant, 7% Moslem, and the rest of other or no affiliation **Flag:** Top half blue, bottom, red, with a white triangle at the hoist containing a gold star in each corner and a golden sun in the center **Anthem:** National Anthem *(Pambansang Awit),* beginning "Land of the morning, child of the sun returning" **Currency:** Philippine peso (piso) (7.39 per U.S. $1)
Location: Southeast Asia. The Philippines is an archipelago of 7,107 islands stretching about 1,100 miles along the southeastern rim of Asia, with the northern islands about 330 miles from China and the southwestern tip about 30 miles from Malaysia **Features:** 11 islands account for 94% of the total land area and population. Most of the larger islands are mountainous, and are also characterized by extensive coastal plains, wide valleys, volcanoes, mineral and hot springs **Chief Rivers:** Cagayan, Agno, Pampanga, Agusan, Cotabato

Head of State and of Government: President and Prime Minister Ferdinand E. Marcos, born 1917, elected 1965, reelected 1969 assuming full powers under martial law in 1972. In 1978, he became prime minister **Effective Date of Present Constitution:** 1973 (not yet fully implemented), amended 1976 **Legislative Body:** Interim National Assembly of 187 members, subject to override by president **Local Government:** 73 provinces, each headed by a governor appointed by the president, and 61 chartered cities

Ethnic Composition: The dominant racial stock of the Philippines is Malay, with an admixture of Indonesian and Chinese strains. Chinese, Americans, and Spaniards constitute the largest alien minorities **Population Distribution:** 32% urban **Density:** 389 inhabitants per sq. mi.

Largest Cities: (1975 est.) Manila 1,438,252 (Metropolitan Area 4,500,000), Davao 515,520, Cebu 418,517, Iloilo 247,956, Bacolod 196,492

Per Capita Income: $475 (1978) **Gross National Product (GNP):** $22 billion (1978) **Economic Statistics:** 29% of the GNP is derived from agriculture (including rice cultivation, sugar, copra, abaca, logs, coconuts); 39% from services; 24% from industry (mining, textiles, and other durable items manufacture) **Minerals and Mining:** There are deposits of iron ore, copper, gold, manganese, chromite, nickel, zinc, coal, and molybdenum. Oil production is beginning **Labor Force:** 15,400,000 (1976), with 57% in agriculture, forestry, and fishing; about 16% are in industry (1970) **Foreign Trade:** Exports, mainly copra, logs and lumber, sugar, coconut oil, copper concentrates, abaca, and canned pineapple, totaled $3.5 billion in 1978. Imports, chiefly nonelectrical machinery, transportation equipment, mineral fuel and lubricants, base metals, cereals, electric machinery, and textiles, totaled $4.7 billion **Principal Trade Partners:** United States, Japan, EEC, Australia, Indonesia, Saudi Arabia

Vital Statistics: Birthrate, 43.8 per 1,000 of pop. (1975); death rate, 10.5 **Life Expectancy:** 58 years **Health Statistics:** 639 inhabitants per hospital bed (1973); 3,154 per physician (1975) **Infant Mortality:** 58.9 per 1,000 births (1974) **Illiteracy:** 17% **Education Statistics:** 42,080 primary and secondary schools, with combined enrollment of 9,894,073 (1975) **Enrollment in Higher Education:** 764,725 **GNP Expended on Education:** 1.6% (1975)

Transportation: Paved roads total c. 10,000 mi. **Motor Vehicles:** 667,200 (1976) **Passenger Cars:** 386,200 **Railway Mileage:** 1,268 **Ports:** Cebu, Manila, Zamboanga, Iloilo, Davao, Batangas **Major Airlines:** Philippine Air Lines, privately owned, operates domestic and international flights; Air Manila International, privately owned, operates domestically **Communications:** Partly government controlled **Radio Transmitters:** 333 **Receivers:** 1,875,000 (1976) **Television Transmitters:** 22 **Receivers:** 800,000 (1976) **Telephones:** 542,000 (1976) **Newspapers:** 15 dailies, 18 copies per 1,000 inhabitants (1975)

Weights and Measures: Metric and local standards are used
Travel Requirements: Passport; no visa for 21 days; onward ticket

---

The Philippines, an island nation of plentiful resources, has been unable thus far to realize its rich potential for development. Independence, gained in 1946, has failed to produce effective democratic government. A high rate of population growth has eaten up much of the slow increase in gross national product, while the gap between the ruling rich and the restless poor remains wide.

Among the bright spots have been the dramatic advance in food production and the modest growth of industry. Aided by new agricultural technology, the Philippines progressed from being a major rice importer to self-sufficiency in the staple. An effort to reduce the 2.9 percent rate of population growth is apparent in an incipient family-planning program.

Three hundred years of Spanish rule made the Filipinos, a people of basic Malayan stock, the only Roman Catholic nation in Asia, and left a deep Latin imprint. The subsequent 48-year administration of the extensive archipelago by the United States helped impose a Western educational and political structure, but surging nationalism has recently led the people to try to cast off their long dependence on the United States.

Philippine elections have never been free of violence and corruption, and Mr. Marcos' decisive victory in the November 1969 race was accompanied by widespread charges of fraud, vote-buying, and intimidation, as well as by huge spending.

Marcos, assaulted by a mob in January 1970 as

he was leaving the national Congress building, blamed Communism for the climate of violence that has plagued the Philippines in recent years, while acknowledging that the discontent could be resolved only by creating more jobs, removing social inequities, reforming the machinery of government and developing a constructive nationalism.

In September 1972, Marcos tightened his grip on the reins of power by imposing martial law. In January 1973, he proclaimed the ratification of a new constitution changing the Philippines from a presidential to a parliamentary form of government. Yet he also extended martial law.

Miffed by U.S. criticism of reported human rights violations and eager to show his countrymen—and the world—that his nation was indeed back on the road to "normalcy," Marcos called a national election for April 1978 (the first in six years) to choose members of an interim parliament that is to legislate until martial law is lifted and a regular parliament is formed. (Before permitting the vote, Marcos guaranteed himself a seat in the new assembly, along with the offices of president and prime minister.)

Marcos' strategy, however, backfired badly, as his brief cautious relaxation of restrictions on political activity just prior to the election led to an outburst of antigovernment sentiment, punctuated by public demonstrations against his authoritarian rule. (His main rival, former Senator Benigno Aquino, had to campaign from prison, where he faced a death sentence on a questionable murder conviction.) Though the election results—widely considered fraudulent—showed Aquino to have done poorly, the episode is thought to have gained him considerable new support. At one rally, 30,000 persons cheered as youthful protestors burned Marcos in effigy. An attempted march on Manila, protesting the disputed election, led to the arrest of about 600 workers, students and nuns. Marcos, who said it was the opposition that had cheated, blamed the disturbances on subversives, drug users and foreign journalists.

HISTORY: For centuries after the birth of Christ the Philippine archipelago was an area of trade and settlement for Southeast Asian people of Malay stock. The area came into the sphere of European influence when it was discovered in 1521 by Magellan. By 1571 the Spanish had assumed control over the Philippines (named for Philip II of Spain) and for next 300 years ruled the islands as a colony

1898: Control of Philippines is ceded to the United States following Spanish-American War

1899: Guerrilla war breaks out against the Americans, ending with complete pacification of islands by 1905

1934: United States passes Philippine independence law providing for a 10-year period for final transfer of sovereignty

1941: Japanese attack Philippines without warning

1945: All of Philippines are freed of Japanese troops

1946: On July 4 the Republic of the Philippines is proclaimed. Independence is followed by widespread unrest and violence by Communist-led Huk guerrillas

1947: Under a 99-year treaty (amended, 1959), Philippines grants U.S. use of 23 strategically vital military bases

1954: Huk rebellion is largely put down

1970: Leftist students stage antigovernment demonstrations; Manila is crippled by general strike

1971: Urban disturbances and guerrilla violence continue. President Marcos accuses Communists of inciting rebellion

1972: Marcos imposes martial law

1973: New constitution goes into effect. Marcos assumes indefinite rule; extends martial law; receives endorsement by electorate, voting in national referendum. Conflict triggered by Moslem insurgency grows

1976: Manila absorbs the national capital area of Quezon City

1977: Voters reject a plan calling for a provisional government in the southwestern portion of the Philippines. Talks are deadlocked over the demands of the Moro National Liberation Front for control of the proposed autonomous region

1978: With an eye on U.S. and world opinion, Marcos briefly lifts ban (imposed in 1972) on political activity, prior to election of

"interim" national assembly. Election results, allegedly fraudulent, show big win for Marcos' New Society Movement. Propaganda value is mitigated by antigovernment demonstrations and mass arrests. Two Moslem countries, Malaysia and Indonesia, fail in attempts to settle conflict between Marcos' government and the Mindanao-Sulu Moslems. The warfare is costing the government more than $27 million a month

1979: The total of Moslems fleeing the southern Philippines for Sabah, a nearby Malaysian state, passes the 100,000 mark. Some 2,300 Vietnamese refugees on a cargo ship are unloaded at Manila Bay and sent to other countries

POLAND

Area: 120,725 sq. mi. **Population:** 35,000,000 (1978 est.)

Official Name: Polish People's Republic **Capital:** Warsaw **Nationality:** Polish **Languages:** Polish is the official and universal language **Religion:** About 95% of the population is Roman Catholic; the rest are Eastern Orthodox, Protestant, Jewish, and of other or no affiliation **Flag:** Horizontal bands of white over red **Anthem:** National Anthem, beginning "Poland still is ours forever" **Currency:** Zloty (33 per U.S. $1)

Location: Eastern Europe. Poland is bounded on the north by the Baltic Sea, on the east by the Soviet Union, on the south by Czechoslovakia, and on the west by East Germany **Features:** The country consists mainly of lowlands, except the mountains on its southern border **Chief Rivers:** Vistula, Oder, Bug, Warta, Narew, San

Political Leader: First Secretary of the Central Committee of the United Workers' Party: Edward Gierek, born 1913, reelected 1976 **Head of State:** Chairman of the Council of State: Henryk Jablonski, reelected 1976 **Head of Government:** Chairman of the Council of Ministers (Premier): Piotr Jaroszewicz, born 1909, reelected 1972 and 1976 **Effective Date of Present Constitution:** July 1952, amended 1976 **Legislative Body:** Parliament (unicameral Sejm), with 460 members elected for 4 years. The Sejm is virtually a rubber stamp for the endorsement of party programs **Local Government:** 49 provinces and 3 city provinces, each with a local people's council and a presidium

Ethnic Composition: The population is virtually homogeneous (98% Polish), with Ukrainians, Byelorussians, and Germans constituting tiny minorities **Population Distribution:** 56.4% urban **Density:** 290 inhabitants per sq. mi.

Largest Cities: (1974 est.) Warsaw 1,400,000, Lodz 784,000, Cracow 662,900, Wroclaw 565,000, Poznan 502,800

Per Capita Income: $3,094 (1978) **Gross National Product (GNP):** $108 billion (1978) **Economic Statistics:** 65.9% of the GNP is derived from industry (mining, steel, machine manufacture, chemicals, power production, and foodstuffs. Poland is the ninth-greatest producer of ships); 8.9% is derived from agriculture (wheat, rye, potatoes, oats, barley, sugar beets); and 9.1% from commerce **Minerals and Mining:** There are large deposits of coal, lignite, sulphur, copper ore, salt, vanadium, titanium, natural gas and zinc **Labor Force:** 17,033,000 (1976), with 26% in industry, 33% in agriculture and forestry, and 14% in trade and transportation **Foreign Trade:** Exports, chiefly copper, sulphur, coal, ships, textiles, steel, cement, chemicals, and foodstuffs, totaled $12.3 billion (1977). Imports, mainly oil, iron ore, fertilizers, wheat, and leather footwear, totaled $14.6 billion **Principal Trade Partners:** USSR, East Germany, Czechoslovakia, West Germany, Britain, United States, Iran, Italy, France, Romania, Austria

Vital Statistics: Birthrate, 19 per 1,000 of pop. (1977); death rate, 9.6 **Life Expectancy:** 71 years **Health Statistics:** 129 inhabitants per hospital bed; 584 per physician (1975) **Infant Mortality:** 24 per 1,000 births (1977) **Illiteracy:** negligible **Education Statistics:** 27,465 primary and secondary schools, with combined enrollment of 6,975,820 (1976) **Enrollment in Higher Education:** 575,499 (1975) **GNP Expended on Education:** 6% (1976)

Transportation: Paved roads total 88,911 mi. **Motor Vehicles:** 1,757,200 (1976) **Passenger Cars:** 1,290,100 **Railway Mileage:** 16,588 **Ports:** Gdansk, Gdynia, Szczecin **Major Airlines:** Polish Airlines LOT operates both domestically and internationally **Communications:** Government controlled **Radio Transmitters:** 51 **Licenses:** 8,230,000 (1976) **Television Transmitters:** 69 **Licenses:** 6,822,000 (1976) **Telephones:** 2,753,000 (1976) **Newspapers:** 44 dailies, 248 copies per 1,000 inhabitants (1975)

Weights and Measures: Metric system **Travel Requirements:** Passport; visa (2 photos, $10 fee) for 90 days

Twice in Poland's postwar history workers' revolts have set the nation on new economic and political courses. The first was in 1956, when factory employees in Poznan took to the streets to demand food. A political convulsion followed, bringing Wladyslaw Gomulka to power as first secretary of the Polish United Workers (Communist) Party and ending much of the repression of the Stalinist period. Fourteen years later, in December 1970, port workers in Gdansk marched in protest and set in motion the riots that led to Mr. Gomulka's downfall. His replacement, Edward Gierek, has charted new policies in an effort to repair the errors of Gomulka's autocratic rule and improve the living conditions of the average Polish citizen. The June 1976 riots over food-price increases were a warning to Gierek's regime of what had happened twice before.

The new Polish leader with his premier, Piotr Jaroszewicz, a trained economist, recharted Poland's five-year economic plan for 1971-75. Investment emphasis was transferred from heavy industries to light, consumer-oriented ones. By the mid-1970s wages had been raised significantly along with the standard of living. Since the 1976 riots the planning has been even more consumer-oriented.

In an effort to encourage greater production among the private farmers, who account for 80 percent of the country's agriculture, laws were changed abolishing many "disincentives." A system of compulsory deliveries was replaced by long-term contract deliveries. Land sale and inheritance procedures were simplified and consolidation of small private holdings encouraged.

Gierek opened the state-controlled press to a limited measure of meaningful debate and ended the anti-Semitic campaign of Gomulka. He also sought to resume normal relations with the nation's powerful Roman Catholic Church. Poland has expanded business and political relations with the West, especially West Germany, Britain and the U.S.

In 1979, the Polish-born Pope, John Paul II, visited Poland—according to the government as Sovereign of the Vatican City-State on the occasion of the 35th anniversary of the Communist regime. But the Pope ostensibly paid tribute to the 900th anniversary of the murder of Saint Stanislaw—whose festival the government had refused to allow him to attend—and praised the saint as an opponent of oppresive government. The large crowds attracted by the Pope strengthened the hand of the Church against the government. About 70% of the population are practicing Catholics.

HISTORY: The recorded history of Poland dates from the 10th century, when Slavic tribes in the region united and their conversion to Christianity began. The medieval era was one of incessant wars, culminating in the defeat of the Teutonic Knights by Poland and Lithuania, united under the Jagiello dynasty. After the last Jagiello king died in 1572, Polish power began a gradual decline as a result of internal weaknesses and external conflicts. Beginning in 1772, and despite the national uprising of 1794 led by Thaddeus Kosciusko, successive partitions eliminated Poland as a sovereign state, a condition that persisted until the close of World War I

1918-21: Independent Polish republic is proclaimed; Versailles Treaty gives Poland access to Baltic Sea through Polish Corridor, free city of Danzig is set up; attempts by Allies to award Poland's eastern provinces to Russia lead to war between the 2 countries in 1920; Poles, aided by French, defeat Russians and win most of territorial claims in 1921 Treaty of Riga

1926-35: General Joseph Pilsudski, former chief of state, governs as virtual dictator after overthrowing democratic government; at his death in 1935, he is succeeded by Edward Smigly-Rydz

1939-45: Germany and Soviet Union, allied in nonaggression pact, invade Poland in September 1939, and the country is once again partitioned; all Poland comes under Nazi rule after Germany attacks USSR in 1941; about six million Poles, half of them Jews, are exterminated by Nazis; and 2.5 million more are deported to Germany as slave labor; Soviet troops reenter Poland in 1944; in August, Poles stage Warsaw uprising, which is crushed by Germans while Soviet forces remain inactive outside city; Germans are expelled in 1945

1947: Soviet-dominated government claims huge majority in the officially controlled elections of 1947; Communist regime proceeds to Sovietize country

1956: Workers and students in Poznan stage mass demonstration against Communist rule and Soviet control; Wladyslaw Gomulka becomes leader of the Polish United Workers (Communist) Party; Stefan Cardinal Wyszynski, under arrest since 1953, is released

1968: Poland joins Soviet Union and other Warsaw Pact members in invasion of Czechoslovakia. At home a campaign against "Zionists" and "revisionists" is waged

1970: Agreement is reached with West Germany on diplomatic relations, including acceptance of Oder-Neisse line as border between Germany and Poland. Economic unrest leads to ouster of Gomulka, who is succeeded by Edward Gierek

1973: Rapprochement with the Vatican

1974: Land reform law reorganizes small farms into larger units in exchange for increased social benefits

1975: Administrative reform changes the three-level system of local government into a two-level system, increasing Gierek's power. Gierek is named first secretary for a second five-year term

1976: Workers stage violent demonstrations and strikes to protest proposed drastic increases in food prices

1978: World's first Polish astronaut accompanies Russian on eight-day mission in Soviet spacecraft during which they rendezvous with two Russian astronauts aboard Salyut 6 space lab

1979: Polish-born Pope John Paul II draws huge crowds during visit to Poland. It is revealed that Poland owes $15 billion to Western creditors

PORTUGAL

Area: 35,549 sq. mi. **Population:** 9,800,000 (1978 est.)

Official Name: Portuguese Republic **Capital:** Lisbon **Nationality:** Portuguese **Languages:** Portuguese is the official and universal language **Religion:** 95% Roman Catholic **Flag:** Green and red vertical stripes, the red covering two-thirds of the flag; at the dividing line is the national coat of arms encircled in gold **Anthem:** The Portuguese **Currency:** Escudo (49.1 per U.S. $1)

Location: Western Europe, occupying the western portion of the Iberian peninsula. Portugal is bounded on the north and east by Spain and on the south and west by the Atlantic Ocean **Features:** The Tagus River divides the country into 2 distinct regions, the north being mountainous and the south consisting of rolling plains **Chief Rivers:** Tagus, Douro, Guadiana, Sado, Mondego

Head of State: President: Gen. António dos Santos Ramalho Eanes, born 1935, elected 1976 **Head of Government:** Premier Maria de Lurdes Ruivo da Silva Matos Pintassilgo, born 1930, appointed Aug. 1, 1979, to serve until October election **Effective Date of Present Constitution:** April 1976 **Legislative Body:** Parliament (unicameral Assembly), with 246 members elected for 4 years **Local Government:** 22 districts (including locally autonomous Madeira and the Azores), each with an appointed governor and district assembly

Ethnic Composition: The people are a homogeneous mixture of ethnic strains, including Celtic, Arab, Berber, Roman, Germanic, and Iberian **Population Distribution:** 37% urban **Density:** 276 inhabitants per sq. mi.

Largest Cities: (1975 est.) Lisbon 829,900, Oporto 335,700; (1973 est.) Amadora 65,870, Coimbra 55,985, Barreiro 53,690

Per Capita Income: $1,570 (1978) **Gross National Product (GNP):** $15.4 billion (1978) **Economic Statistics:** 18% of the GNP is derived from agriculture (grains, fruits, vegetables, wines); 43% from mining, manufacturing, and construction (electronics, textiles, wines, cork, food processing, ship-building, and ship repair); 14% from commerce and finance; and 25% from services **Minerals and Mining:** Wolfram, cassiterite, beryl, copper pyrites, and iron ore **Labor Force:** The labor force, 3.5 million in 1976, earned the lowest wages in Western Europe. 28% are engaged in agriculture, and 34% in industry **Foreign Trade:** Exports, chiefly cork, sardines, wines, textiles, minerals, machinery, and diamonds, totaled $2 billion in 1977. Imports, mainly machinery and industrial equipment, petroleum products, optical instruments, cotton, steel, wheat, and corn, amounted to $4.9 billion **Principal Trade Partners:** West Germany, United States, Britain, France, Italy, Spain, Sweden

Vital Statistics: Birthrate, 19.2 per 1,000 of pop. (1976); death rate, 12.1 (1975) **Life Expectancy:** 69 years **Health Statistics:** 181 inhabitants per hospital bed; 851 per physician (1975) **Infant Mortality:** 39 per 1,000 births (1975) **Illiteracy:** 29% **Education Statistics:** 18,992 primary and secondary schools, with combined enrollment of 1,668,567 (1974) **Enrollment in Higher Education:** 59,845 (1973) **GNP Expended on Education:** 2.4% (1974)

Transportation: Roads total 19,790 mi. (1975) **Motor Vehicles:** 1,322,000 (1976) **Passenger Cars:** 1,034,000 **Railway Mileage:** 2,214 **Ports:** Lisbon, Leixões, Setúbal, Funchal, Douro **Major Airlines:** Transportes Aéreos Portugueses (TAP) flies internationally **Communications:** Government owned **Radio Transmitters:** 180 **Licenses:** 1,525,000 (1976) **Television Transmitters:** 41 **Licenses:** 723,000 (1976) **Telephones:** 1,119,000 (1976) **Newspapers:** 30 dailies, 70 copies per 1,000 inhabitants (1975)

Weights and Measures: Metric system **Travel Requirements:** Passport; no visa for 60 days

Portugal is the poorest country in Western Europe. Most of its people still make their living from the soil, but there is a bitter division between the hilly north, with its small independent farmers, and the more level south, where landless peasants lived for centuries in fear of the owners of huge estates. Portugal's experiment in democratic socialism, which began in 1976, has been complicated by misunderstanding between the individualistic northerners and the southern peasants, who tend to favor collectivism.

Another complicating factor is Portugal's relative lack of experience with democracy. António de Oliveira Salazar, who was premier from 1932 to 1968, governed as a harsh dictator, and his successor, Marcello Caetano, made few meaningful changes.

Salazar and Caetano hoped that Portugal would become a developed capitalist state, and favored the tiny class of entrepreneurial families. But these families drew most of their surplus capital from Portugal's African territories, which revolted against Portuguese rule in the 1960s. Linked to the entrepreneurial class and caught up in romantic nationalism, Salazar and Caetano drained Portugal of manpower and resources to suppress the revolts in Africa.

Caetano was overthrown in 1974 by the Armed Forces Movement (MFA), a coalition of soldiers who were tired of the struggle in Africa and sympathetic to socialism. The MFA government granted independence to the African territories—destroying the entrepreneurial class and all chance of development along completely capitalistic lines.

A National Assembly was elected in April 1975. "Rightist" parties had been outlawed, but the Social Democratic Center became the voices of those favoring a role for private enterprise. The Socialist Party won a plurality, but not a majority, in the Assembly. But the MFA remained in control of the government, and its leadership became increasingly sympathetic to the Communist Party. Although the Communists had fared badly in the Assembly elections, they boasted that they would soon dominate the country in any case. The Communist scheme was checkmated by uprisings in the north and by the vigilance of the anti-Communist elements in the MFA. In August, the pro-Communist premier, Col. Vasco dos Santos Gonçalves, was replaced by Adm. José Pinheiro de Azevedo.

Despite continued unrest, a new constitution was adopted in 1976; it is distinctly socialist, and is democratic in all its essentials, although it reserves some power for the military-dominated Revolutionary Council. Gen. António dos Santos Ramalho Eanes was elected president; the National Assembly became an effective legislature; most restrictions on freedom of expression ended; and peace returned to the country.

The weak economy and continued arguments over the return to private ownership of farms illegally seized in 1974 have troubled the fledgling democracy. Mário Soares was premier in a minority socialist government from July 1976 to December 1977. In January 1978, he formed a majority coalition with the Social Democratic Center—actually the most non-socialist of the major parties. President Eanes dismissed him in July after the coalition broke down, and appointed a government of technocrats who were not members of the Assembly. Soares complained that a government drawn from outside the Assembly was unconstitutional, and the Assembly rejected the technocratic government. But Soares did not object at first when a second government of technocrats, with

Carlos Alberto Mota Pinto as premier, took office in October with the Assembly's approval. However, in June 1979, Soares and the socialists joined the Communists in forcing Mota Pinto to submit to his government's resignation. Maria de Lurdes Ruivo da Silva Matos Pintassilgo was appointed to head a caretaker government until the October parliamentary elections.

HISTORY: Lusitania, the western part of the Iberian peninsula, was conquered by Julius Caesar and Augustus. The Visigoths gained control over most of the region in the 5th century A.D. and maintained their rule until the coming of the Moors three centuries later. Portugal was established as an independent state by 1185 and was consolidated after the final expulsion of the Moors in 1249. Its independence, however, remained threatened by Castile until 1385, when the Castilians were defeated in battle

15th cent.: Prince Henry the Navigator captures Ceuta, on northwest African coast, in 1415; under his aegis, Portuguese navigators undertake series of voyages that result in rediscovery of Madeira Islands and penetration of Africa; Vasco da Gama becomes first European to sail to India (1497-99)

1500-20: Pedro Cabral reaches coast of Brazil in 1500 and claims land for Portugal

1580-1640: Philip II of Spain seizes Portuguese throne, beginning Portugal's 60-year period of "Spanish Captivity"; Portuguese revolt against Spanish rule and regain independence under John of Braganza, who becomes king

1807: Napoleon's forces march on Portugal

1822: Brazil declares its independence

1910: Manuel II is deposed by revolution; Portugal is declared a republic

1932: António de Oliveira Salazar, former finance minister, becomes premier after a long period of civil unrest and political instability; he institutes dictatorial rule

1961: India annexes Portuguese enclave of Goa; Portuguese crush insurrection in Angola, in southwest Africa

1968: Marcello Caetano becomes premier

1974: Liberal reforms initiated following bloodless coup which toppled Caetano and installed António de Spínola as president. He is succeeded later the same year by Francisco da Costa Gomes. Violent clashes occur between revolutionary and rightist forces

1975: In April, the first free elections in almost half a century give an Assembly majority to moderates and centrists. Azevedo replaces Gonçalves as premier

1976: New constitution is enacted. António dos Santos Ramalho Eanes is elected president and appoints Mário Soares premier

1977-78: International Monetary Fund issues stringent conditions as price to Portugal for $750-million loan; ensuing austerity measures lead to collapse of government. Soares forms new government of Socialists and conservatives, which also collapses; President Eanes dismisses him. Carlos Alberto Mota Pinto becomes premier in government of technocrats

1979: Mota Pinto submits government's resignation after Socialists and Communists introduce resolutions of no confidence. Senhorita Pintassilgo is appointed caretaker premier until October election

---

QATAR

Area: 4,247 sq. mi. **Population:** 180,000 (1978 est.)

Official Name: State of Qatar **Capital:** Doha **Nationality:** Qatari **Language:** Arabic is the official and dominant language; English and Farsi are spoken by some **Religion:** 98% of Qataris are Sunni Moslems of the Wahabi sect. **Flag:** Maroon with white serrated border near the hoist **Anthem:** N.A. **Currency:** Qatari riyal (3.84 per U.S. $1)

Location: Southwest Asia. Qatar forms a 100-mile long peninsula stretching north into the Persian Gulf. It borders Saudi Arabia and the United Arab Emirates on the south **Features:** A low, hot, dry plain, consisting of nearly flat limestone with loose sand and gravel on top **Rivers:** None

Head of State and of Government: Emir: Khalifa ibn Hamad al-Thani, born 1937, assumed power in 1972. He is advised by an appointed Council of Ministers which he heads as prime minister **Effective Date of Present Constitution:** 1970; not fully implemented **Legislative Body:** A 23-member advisory council **Local Government:** 6 municipal councils

Ethnic Composition: Arabs (56%), Iranians (23%), Pakistanis (7%), others (14%). The population is almost 50% non-native **Population Distribution:** 71% urban **Density:** 42 inhabitants per sq. mi.

Largest Cities: Doha 150,000, (1976 est.); Umm Said 5,500 (1972 est.)

Per Capita Income: $22,000 (1978 est.) **Gross National Product**

(GNP): $4.9 billion (1978 est.) **Economic Statistics:** Qatar's national income derives almost wholly from oil recovery; revenues total $2 billion in 1977 **Minerals and Mining:** Oil is the chief resource; natural gas deposits are being developed; limestone and clay are also mined **Labor Force:** 85,000 with about 30% engaged in subsistence agriculture and fishing, and 70% in industry (chiefly oil) **Foreign Trade:** Exports totaled $2 billion in 1977, 96% from oil. Imports, chiefly consumer goods and industrial equipment, totaled $1.2 billion **Principal Trade Partners:** EC countries, United States, Japan, India

Vital Statistics: Birthrate, 50 per 1,000 of pop. (1974); death rate, 19 **Life Expectancy:** 47 years **Health Statistics:** 96 inhabitants per hospital bed; 938 per physician (1974) **Infant Mortality:** 42 per 1,000 births (1972) **Illiteracy:** 75% **Education Statistics:** 97 primary and secondary schools, with combined enrollment of 30,098 (1974) **Enrollment in Higher Education:** 779 (1975) **GNP Expended on Education:** 2.0% (1975)

Transportation: Surfaced roads total over 200 mi. (1976) **Motor Vehicles:** 17,000 (1969) **Railway Mileage:** None **Ports:** Doha, Umm Said **Major Airlines:** Gulf Air and several major foreign airlines serve Doha **Communications:** Government owned **Radio Transmitters: 6 Receivers:** 40,000 (1976) **Television Transmitters: 3 Receivers:** 30,000 (1976) **Telephones:** 29,400 (1978) **Newspapers:** 1 daily, 4 weeklies (1976)

Weights and Measures: Metric system **Travel Requirements:** Passport; visa, valid 6 months; 2 photos

Oil production, begun shortly after World War II and now valued at roughly $2 billion a year, is the country's economic base. With oil proceeds, roads have been built, a sea-distilled water supply established, an educational program instituted, and free medical services introduced. Steps toward diversification have included the exploitation of the Gulf's fishery potential, the production of cement from local raw materials, encouragement of investment in domestic projects, investigation of the mechanics of natural gas recovery, transportation, marketing and usage, and the introduction of domestic refining. Qatar has developed a steel industry.

Following an announcement by Britain that she would withdraw her forces from the Persian Gulf area by the end of 1971, Qatar considered joining a projected federation with the neighboring British protectorates, Bahrain and the United Arab Emirates. In August 1971, however, Bahrain proclaimed its independence and decided against joining the federation, and Qatar also decided not to join. Qatar declared its independence on September 1, 1971.

The ruler of Qatar, Emir Ahmad ibn Ali ben Abdullah al-Thani, was deposed in a bloodless coup by his cousin, Emir Khalifa ibn Hamad al-Thani, on February 22, 1972.

Qatar relied for emergency defense on the army of Shah Mohammed Reza Pahlavi of Iran; his overthrow in 1979 was a shock to Qatar's leaders. **HISTORY:** For a long time Qatar was under Persian rule, and paid a bounty to the governor of Bushire for the right to fish for pearls. In the 19th century it became independent of Persia under Thani, the founder of the al-Thani dynasty

1871-1913: Qatar is occupied by Ottoman Turks

1916: Qatar comes under British protection

1971: Qatar declares its independence

1973: Qatar announces embargo on oil to U.S.

1977: Government completes nationalization of all oil operations

ROMANIA

Area: 91,699 sq. mi. **Population:** 21,700,000 (1978 est.)

Official Name: Socialist Republic of Romania **Capital:** Bucharest **Nationality:** Romanian **Languages:** Romanian is the official and dominant language. Hungarian, German, Ukrainian, and Yiddish are minority languages **Religion:** About 80% of the population nominally belongs to the Romanian Orthodox Church, and about 9% to the Roman Catholic Church. The rest are mainly Protestant, Jewish, and Moslem **Flag:** Blue, yellow, and red vertical stripes with the national coat of arms in the center **Anthem:** The Tricolored Song **Currency:** Leu (4.47 per U.S. $1)

Location: Southeastern Europe. Romania is bounded on the northeast by the Soviet Union, on the east by the Black Sea, on the

south by Bulgaria, on the southwest by Yugoslavia, and on the west by Hungary **Features:** The Carpathian Mountains and Transylvanian Alps form a semi-circle through the center of the country, separating the plains in the east and south from the Transylvanian plateau in the northwest **Chief Rivers:** Danube, Prut, Siret, Olt, Ialomita, Jiu, Mures

Political Leader and Head of State: President Nicolae Ceausescu, born 1918, elected 1974, reelected 1975; since 1965, Secretary-General of the Central Committee of the Romanian Communist Party, and since 1967 president of the State Council, the primary legislative body **Head of Government:** Prime Minister Ilie Verdet, born 1924, appointed 1979 **Effective Date of Present Constitution:** August 1965 **Legislative Body:** Grand National Assembly (unicameral), consisting of 349 members elected for 5 years; it actually performs little legislative work **Local Government:** 39 counties with people's councils elected for 5 years, and Bucharest municipality

Ethnic Composition: 88% of the population is of Romanian stock, tracing its ancestry back to the Latin settlers of the Roman Empire. Hungarians (8%) are the leading ethnic minority, with smaller numbers of Germans, Ukrainians, Serbo-Croats, Jews, and Turks **Population Distribution:** 48% urban **Density:** 237 inhabitants per sq. mi.

Largest Cities: (1977 est.—Metropolitan Areas) Bucharest 1,934,025, Constanta 290,226, Iasi 284,308, Timisoara 282,691, Cluj 262,421, Brasov 262,041

Per Capita Income: $3,083 (1978) **Gross National Product (GNP):** $67 billion (1978) **Economic Statistics:** In 1975 industry and construction accounted for 70% of the national income, while agriculture accounted for 16% **Minerals and Mining:** Large deposits of petroleum, copper, lead, zinc, bauxite, manganese, bismuth, mercury, silver, iron ore, and coal **Labor Force:** 10,362,000 in 1975. In 1975 about 38% of the labor force was engaged in agriculture, 31% in industry, and 10% in commerce **Foreign Trade:** Exports, mainly fuel oil, gas, cereals, cement, and wood products, totaled $7 billion in 1977. Imports, chiefly machinery and equipment, iron ores, coke, motor vehicles, and electric motors, totaled $7 billion **Principal Trade Partners:** West Germany, USSR, Czechoslovakia, Italy, Britain, France, East Germany, Poland, China, United States, Iran, Switzerland

Vital Statistics: Birthrate, 19.5 per 1,000 of pop. (1976); death rate, 9.1 **Life Expectancy:** 70 years **Health Statistics:** 110 inhabitants per hospital bed; 805 per physician (1973) **Infant Mortality:** 31.4 per 1,000 births (1976) **Illiteracy:** 2% **Education Statistics:** 28,051 primary and secondary schools, with combined enrollment of 4,320,613 (1975) **Enrollment in Higher Education:** 381,321 (1976) **GNP Expended on Education:** N.A.

Transportation: Surfaced roads total 7,891 mi. **Motor Vehicles:** 45,100 (commercial—1970) **Railway Mileage:** 6,855 **Ports:** Constanta, Galati, Braila **Major Airlines:** Tarom and Lar fly internationally and domestically **Communications:** Government owned **Radio Transmitters:** 62 **Licenses:** 3,104,000 (1976) **Television Transmitters:** 194 **Licenses:** 2,963,000 (1976) **Telephones:** 1,076,000 (1974) **Newspapers:** 20 dailies, 129 copies per 1,000 inhabitants (1974)

Weights and Measures: Metric system **Travel Requirements:** Passport; visa, valid 60 days

For centuries a rural, backward country, Romania has the largest oil fields of any country in Eastern Europe. Building on oil wealth, the Romanians have invested in modern chemical, steel, machinery, and related industries. Close economic ties have been fostered with Western Europe as well as with the Soviet bloc.

Although it remains a member of the Warsaw Pact military alliance and of the Communist Council for Mutual Economic Assistance, Romania has successfully asserted its right to conduct its own foreign affairs, most notably when it condemned the Soviet-led invasion of Czechoslovakia in August 1968.

Not wanting to be merely a supplier of raw materials and agricultural products to the more developed Communist countries, Romania has persistently refused to subordinate its desire for rapid economic development to Soviet plans for complete integration of Eastern European and Soviet economies.

The heart of Romanian tactics aimed at resisting Moscow's pressure is a balancing act. Its essence is the matching of moves that irritate Moscow with moves that are pleasing. For instance, President Nicolae Ceausescu was the first East European leader to establish (1967) diplomatic relations with West Germany and the first leader of an Iron Curtain country in a quarter century to be visited by a U.S. president (Nixon in 1969).

More recently, this balancing act has become noticeable in Ceausescu's handling of political dissidents. Early in 1977, a group of dissidents issued an open letter charging human rights violations in Romania. Subsequently, its author was jailed, then later freed, along with 19,000 other prisoners, as part of an amnesty program in celebration of Romania's 100th anniversary of independence from Turkey. The amnesty has been seen by experts as a public relations gesture to the West; however, Ceausescu continues to keep a tight rein on the dissidents.

Ceausescu in 1974 strengthened his position as undisputed leader by naming himself president, installing a colorless loyalist, Manea Manescu, as premier, and abolishing the nine-member presidium, the top ruling body of the Communist Party. He replaced the presidium with a twenty-three-member Executive Committee which is packed with loyalists. In 1979 President Ceaucescu appointed Ilie Verdet as Premier on the retirement of Manescu.

HISTORY: Ancient Dacia, comprising most of present-day Romania, was part of the Roman Empire until the 3rd century A.D. After the Romans legions withdrew, the region was overrun by Goths, Huns, Avars, Slavs, and Mongols. The withdrawal of the Mongols in the 13th century was followed by the establishment of the principalities of Walachia and Moldavia, which soon fell under Turkish rule. Both were to remain in the Ottoman Empire until well into the 19th century

1828-29: Walachia and Moldavia are occupied by Russia in Russo-Turkish War; although technically remaining part of the Ottoman Empire, they actually become Russian protectorates

1859-66: Alexander John Cuza is elected prince of Walachia and Moldavia, which are officially united as Romania in 1861; 5 years later, Cuza is deposed and is succeeded by Carol I of the house of Hohenzollern-Sigmaringen

1878: Congress of Berlin grants Romania full independence

1916-19: Romania fights on Allied side in World War I; overrun by Austro-German forces, it is forced to accept a harsh peace treaty, which is later annulled by the Allied victory; Romania seizes Bessarabia from Russia, Bukovina from Austria, and Transylvania from Hungary

1938: King Carol II establishes Fascist dictatorship

1940-45: Under German pressure, Romania returns territories taken from Russia and Hungary; King Carol is overthrown by Marshal Ion Antonescu, aided by Iron Guard, a militaristic Fascist group; in 1941, Romania enters World War II on Axis side; following the invasion of Soviet troops in 1944, Antonescu is overthrown and Romania switches to Allied side; a Communist-led government is set up in 1945

1964: Showing increasing independence of the Soviet Union, Romanian Communist Party asserts the right of each Communist Party to form its own political program without interference

1968: Romania supports liberalization program in Czechoslovakia and refuses to join in invasion of Czechoslovakia by Soviet and other Warsaw Pact forces

1971: After declining to do so a year earlier, Romania joins the Soviet bloc's new international investment bank

1974: Communist Party Central Committee approves constitutional change establishing the office of President, which is assumed by Ceausescu. Manea Manescu becomes premier

1975: U.S. Congress passes resolution granting Romania most-favored-nation trade status

1977: Earthquake kills at least 1,500. Ceausescu asks for eight more years of austerity and sacrifice to raise Romania to ranks of developed nations

1979: Government established regional councils to supervise agriculture. Ilie Verdet becomes premier.

RWANDA

Area: 10,169 sq. mi. **Population:** 4,460,000 (1978 est.)

Official Name: Republic of Rwanda **Capital:** Kigali **Nationality:** Rwandan **Languages:** Kinyarwanda (the national language) and French are the official languages; Kiswahili is spoken in the commercial centers **Religion:** More than 60% of the population is Christian, chiefly Roman Catholic; the rest are animist and Moslem **Flag:** Vertical stripes of red, yellow, and green with a black "R" in the center **Anthem:** Our Rwanda **Currency:** Rwanda franc (92.8 per U.S. $1)

Location: Central Africa. Landlocked Rwanda is bordered on the north by Uganda, on the east by Tanzania, on the south by Burundi, and on the west by Zaire **Features:** Known as the "Land of a Thousand Hills," the country consists largely of grassy uplands and hills, which roll down southeastward from the chain of volcanoes in the northwest **Chief Rivers:** Kagera, Nyabarongo, Akanyaru

Head of State and Government: President: Maj. Gen. Juvénal Habyarimana seized power in a bloodless coup July 1973 **Effective Date of Present Constitution:** November 1962 **Legislative Body:** National Assembly (unicameral) suspended. Members of the former Committee for National Peace and Unity and the present Council of Government are consulted by the president **Local Government:** 10 prefectures, administered by appointed prefects

Ethnic Composition: 89% Hutu, a Bantu farming people; 10% Tutsi, a pastoral people of Hamitic origin; 1% Twa pygmies **Population Distribution:** 5% urban **Density:** 439 inhabitants per sq. mi.

Largest Cities: (1975 est.) Kigali 60,000, Butare 20,000

Per Capita Income: $174 (1978) **Gross National Product (GNP):** $760 million (1978) **Economic Statistics:** 18% of the GNP is derived from mining (cassiterite, columbo-tantalite, wolfram, amblygonite, beryl); 60% from agriculture (bananas, coffee, pyrethrum, tea, cotton, manioc, corn, spices, sweet potatoes); 16% from commerce; and 6% from construction and manufacturing **Minerals and Mining:** Cassiterite is the most abundant mineral, although columbo-tantalite, wolfram, amblygonite, and beryl are also mined. There are unexploited deposits of bismuth, phosphates, monazite, magnatite, and natural gas **Labor Force:** 1,940,000 (1970), with 95% engaged in small handicrafts or agriculture, and less than 5% in industry. Wage earners numbered 70,000 in 1973 **Foreign Trade:** Exports, mainly Arabica coffee (25,000 metric tons in 1976), cassiterite, tea, and wolfram, totaled $81 million in 1976. Imports, chiefly textiles, iron, petroleum, and vehicles, totaled $105 million **Principal Trade Partners:** Belgium, France, United States, Britain, Japan, Kenya, Iran, West Germany

Vital Statistics: Birthrate, 50 per 1,000 of pop. (1975); death rate, 23.6 **Life Expectancy:** 44 years **Health Statistics:** 583 inhabitants per hospital bed; 40,385 per physician (1975) **Infant Mortality:** 132.9 per 1,000 births **Illiteracy:** 75% **Education Statistics:** 3,200 primary and secondary schools, with combined enrollment of 425,226 (1974) **Enrollment in Higher Education:** 1,023 (1974) **GNP Expended on Education:** 3.2% (1975)

Transportation: Main roads total 1,300 mi. **Motor Vehicles:** 11,300 (1975) **Passenger Cars:** 6,500 **Railway Mileage:** None **Ports:** None **Major Airlines:** Transport Airline of Rwanda operates international and domestic flights **Communications:** Government controlled **Radio Transmitters:** 4 **Receivers:** 70,000 (1976) **Television:** None **Telephones:** 3,000 (1975) **Newspapers:** 1 daily, .04 copies per 1,000 inhabitants (1975)

Weights and Measures: Metric system **Travel Requirements:** Passport; visa for stay up to 1 month; $7 fee, 3 photos

Rwanda, formerly part of the Belgian UN trust territory of Ruanda-Urundi, is Africa's most densely populated country. Nearly four and a half million people live in an area slightly smaller than the state of Maryland. Small and landlocked, it lies atop the mountainous western slope of the Great Rift Valley known as "the Roof of Africa." Through centuries of migratory settlement and population increase, the clearing of land for food production, together with overgrazing of cattle, has made Rwanda one of tropical Africa's most eroded areas. Its people contend with drought as well as poor soil in raising their crops of beans, bananas, sorghum, cassava, corn, and potatoes.

Despite erosion, Rwanda possesses scenic grandeur and great touristic potential, especially around Lake Kivu, considered by many the most beautiful of African lakes. However, the serene-looking highlands have known dark tragedy. In 1959-60, the Hutu people, the short stocky peasants who made up 85 percent of the population, rose up in bloody revolt against the Tutsi (or Watusi), the tall aristocratic people who kept the Hutu in feudal bondage for centuries. Thousands of Tutsi were killed or fled into neighboring countries. Neither willing nor able to stem the tide of Hutu unrest, the Belgian administration gave support to the Hutu on the eve of independence. In 1961 the Tutsi king, Mwami Kigeri V, was deposed and a republic declared, causing more than

160,000 Tutsi to flee to Burundi. Many returned later but in 1963-64 an armed invasion by Tutsi refugees set off another massacre of the tall people and put an apparent end to their minority caste domination.

Since independence, the government has concentrated on food production and the building of internal roads and road links into neighboring coastal countries. More than a fourth of national expenditures are for education and there has been some progress in light industry, but the major problems—population pressures, malnutrition, and poverty—remain largely unsolved.

In July 1973 Rwanda's manifold problems were compounded further as the government of President Grégoire Kayibanda was overthrown in a bloodless military coup, after months of tribal unrest between the governing Hutu majority and the Tutsi minority. The leader of the coup, Maj. Gen. Juvénal Habyarimana emerged as the apparent leader of the country.

HISTORY: Rwanda, along with neighboring Burundi, originally was inhabited by the pygmy Twa people, and later occupied by Bantu Hutus from the Congo basin. By the 15th century, the Tutsi, or Watusi, a tall, cattle-keeping people believed to have originated in Ethiopia, had arrived in both countries and imposed a feudal overlordship on the more numerous Hutus. European explorers reached the area in the 19th century, and in 1885 the region was taken over by Germany. It was made a Belgian League of Nations mandate after World War I and remained under Belgian control after World War II. With the growth of African nationalism, Hutu leaders in Rwanda began seeking independence and emancipation from Tutsi domination.

1955-58: Tutsi extremists, viewing Belgian political reforms as threat, repress Hutu movement and murder several Hutu leaders

1959: Bloody Hutu revolt overthrows Tutsi monarchy; Tutsis suffer heavy casualties and 120,000 of them flee to Burundi and other neighboring countries

1960: Leaders of Hutu Emancipation Movement (PARMEHUTU) establish provisional government

1961: Belgium recognizes PARMEHUTU regime, but United Nations, hoping to preserve ethnic-economic union of Rwanda and Burundi, rules it unlawful and orders elections; PARMEHUTU scores overwhelming victory

1962: UN resolution ends Belgian trusteeship and grants Rwanda full independence

1963: Abortive Tutsi invasion from Burundi results in massacre of 12,000 Tutsi in Rwanda and renewed Tutsi exodus from the country

1970: Rwanda signs friendship pact with Belgium; work is begun on road link to Kampala, Uganda

1973: President Grégoire Kayibanda overthrown in bloodless military coup; Maj. Gen. Juvénal Habyarimana takes over as president

1974: Death sentences of ex-President Kayibanda and seven other government officials commuted to life imprisonment

1976: Ugandan oil blockade brings economic hardship

SAINT LUCIA

Area: 238 sq. mi. **Population:** 111,800 (1975 est.)

Official Name: State of Saint Lucia **Capital:** Castries **Nationality:** Saint Lucian **Languages:** English is the official language; a French patois containing many African elements is widely spoken **Religion:** Chiefly Roman Catholic (90%) with several Protestant churches represented **Flag:** A blue field containing a white-bordered black triangle covered at the bottom by a yellow triangle **Anthem:** N.A. **Currency:** East Caribbean dollar ($2.70 per U.S. $1)

Location: St. Lucia, the second largest of the Windward Islands, lies south of Martinique and northeast of St. Vincent in the Eastern Caribbean **Features:** The island is of volcanic origin and mountainous, with magnificent scenery; there is a good harbor at Castries. The climate is tropical and humid, with heavy rainfall in the summer

Head of State: Queen Elizabeth II through Governor-General Sir Allen Montgomery Lewis **Head of Government:** Prime Minister Allan Louisy, born 1914, elected July 2, 1979 **Effective Date of Present Constitution:** Feb. 22, 1979 **Legislative Body:** Parliament (bicameral) consisting of a House of Assembly with 17 elected members and a Senate of 11 members, of whom 6 are appointed on the advice of the prime minister, 3 by the Opposition, and two by the Governor-General. The Parliament has a five-year term unless dissolved before that time **Local Government:** 16 parishes

Ethnic Composition: Chiefly African or of mixed origin **Population Distribution:** N.A. **Density:** 470 inhabitants per sq. mi.

Largest Cities: (1970 est.) Castries 40,451, Micoud 10,145, Vieux Fort 8,108, Soufrière 7,250

Per Capita Income: $530 (1974) **Gross Domestic Product (GDP):** $60 million (1974) **Economic Statistics:** The economy is primarily agricultural, with tourism and industry gaining in importance. The chief crops are bananas, coconuts, cocoa, citrus fruits, sugar, spices; there is a limited amount of timber production and commercial fishing. Industrial development is increasing rapidly. An oil refining and transshipment facility and an industrial free port zone are under construction **Labor Force:** 26,339 (1970), with 40% engaged in agriculture, 33% in industry, and 21% in services **Foreign Trade:** Exports, including bananas and a growing amount of manufactured goods, totaled $12.7 million in 1978, and imports, including manufactured goods, machinery, food, fuel and clothing, totaled $37.2 million **Principal Trade Partners:** Britain, Commonwealth and CARICOM countries, United States

Vital Statistics: Birthrate, 35.0 per 1,000 of pop. (1971); death rate, 7.3 per 1,000 **Life Expectancy:** 57 years **Health Statistics:** 202 inhabitants per hospital bed; 4,231 per physician (1975) **Infant Mortality:** 19.2 per 1,000 births (1977) **Illiteracy:** 20% **Education Statistics:** 88 primary and secondary schools (1975), with combined enrollment of 35,400 (1975) **Enrollment in Higher Education:** N.A. **GDP Expended on Education:** N.A.

Transportation: Surfaced roads total 280 mi. **Motor Vehicles:** 5,500 (1975) **Passenger Cars:** 3,700 **Railway Mileage:** None **Port:** Castries **Major Airlines:** BWIA, Eastern Airlines, British Airways, LIAT **Communications:** Government and privately owned **Radio Transmitters:** 2 **Receivers:** 82,000 (1975) **Television Transmitters:** 1 **Receivers:** 1,700 (1974) **Telephones:** 7,000 (1976) **Newspapers:** 3: 1 twice weekly, 1 weekly, 1 fortnightly; 78 copies per 1,000 inhabitants;

Weights and Measures: Metric and British systems are used **Travel Requirements:** Passport or birth certificate; return ticket

---

A former British possession in the Windward Islands, Saint Lucia is an island nation characterized by its African heritage, French accent, British political system and all the social and economic burdens attendant on many newly independent mini-states. Independence was attained on February 22, 1979.

Traditionally tied to agriculture for its livelihood, the island had embarked on the path of new industrial and commercial development under the leadership of Prime Minister John Compton. The largest single project is a combined oil transshipment terminal and free trade zone being developed by American oil interests. The manufacturing sector has been expanded, accounting for nearly half of the island's exports. The island's even climate and great beauty has made tourism a major industry, especially since the construction of a modern jetport outside Castries in 1975. In addition, traditional cash crops such as bananas, cocoa and coconuts have been bolstered under a development plan supported by the World Bank and the International Monetary Fund.

Yet, although St. Lucia's future appears bright in comparison with some of its neighbors, it shares many of their problems. Dependence on imports of finished goods was responsible for a balance of payment deficit of $24 million in 1978. And unemployment remains endemic, at a staggering 30 percent annually. These economic woes, plus continued political strife over the process towards independence, has sometimes marred the tranquility of this tropical paradise.

A landslide victory for the opposition Labor Party in the July 2, 1979, general elections turned Prime Minister Compton and his United Workers Party out of power after 15 years. A moderate, Compton had sought close cooperation with the Caribbean Economic Community (CARICOM) and closer ties with oil-rich Venezuela, as well as opting for termination of the island's colonial status by mutual agreement with Britain. The new prime minister is Allan Louisy, a retired judge.

HISTORY: Little is known of the island's early history, but successive waves of Amerindian migration are thought to have populated the island in the 1300s. By the time of the first European landing, in the 16th century, the island was inhabited by the war-like Caribs. Initially a Spanish possession, the first attempts at settlement were made by the English, in 1605 and 1638-40; both succumbed to the Caribs. Subsequent French settlement proved more successful. Britain and France fought for control of the island over the next 150 years, with the last British occupation—in June, 1803—finally accepted by France in the Treaty of Paris in 1814. A plantation economy flourished, based on slavery; by 1834, when slavery was abolished in all British possessions, the island's African population numbered over 13,000.

1838: St. Lucia, administered as a separate colony, is merged with the government of the Windward Islands

1958: St. Lucia joins Federation of the West Indies; remains member until its dissolution is 1962

1959: St. Lucia separated from Windward group, becomes dependency under direct British administration

1962-65: Discussions ensue between St. Lucia and other smaller British territories on federation with Barbados, without success

1967: St. Lucia becomes self-governing member of the West Indies Associated States May 3

1974: Elections return United Workers Party government to power; Prime Minister John G.N. Compton promises full independence

1977: July 24-27 constitutional conference in London agrees on framework for independence

1979: Independence attained Feb. 22; Labor Party boycotts ceremony, as striking teachers and civil servants threaten the new nation's stability. Government studies possible common diplomatic service with St. Vincent, Antigua and St. Kitts. Labor Party scores upset victory over Compton's UWP, winning 12 of 18 Assembly seats in first post-independence election. Allan Louisy becomes prime minister

SAINT VINCENT

(See Territories and Dependencies section)

SAN MARINO

Area: 23.4 sq. mi. **Population:** 21,000 (1978 est.)

Official Name: Most Serene Republic of San Marino **Capital:** San Marino **Nationality:** Sanmarinese **Language:** Italian is the official and universal language **Religion:** Roman Catholicism **Flag:** Horizontal bands of white and blue with the national coat of arms in the center **Anthem:** National Anthem, beginning "Honor to you, O ancient Republic" **Currency:** Italian lira (847 per U.S. $1)

Location: Landlocked San Marino is situated in the Apennines, southwest of Rimini, Italy **Features:** The town of San Marino is situated on the slopes of Mount Titano, and much of the republic is coextensive with the mountain, which has three pinnacles **Chief Rivers:** San Marino, Fumicello

Head of State and of Government: 2 Captains Regent, elected by the Council for six-month terms, assisted by a Congress of State (cabinet) **Effective Date of Present Constitution:** October 1600 **Legislative Body:** Great and General Council (unicameral), with 60 members elected every 5 years **Local Government:** 9 parishes (castelli), headed by Captains of the Castle and elected committees

Ethnic Composition: The Sanmarinese are of Italian origin. A small number of aliens reside in the republic **Population Distribution:** 92% urban **Density:** 897 inhabitants per sq. mi. **Largest City:** San Marino (1974 est.) San Marino 4,423

Per Capita Income: N.A. **Gross National Product (GNP):** N.A. **Economic Statistics:** The principal occupations are farming, manufacturing, and animal husbandry. Main agricultural products are wheat, cheese and wine, while chief industrial goods are textiles, cement, paper, leather, and furs. Tourism (2.5 million a year) and the sale of postage stamps are major sources of income **Minerals and Mining:** Building stones are quarried for export **Labor Force:** 5,381 mostly employed in the agricultural sector. The rest work for manufacturing and service industries. Average monthly wage is $750 **Foreign Trade:** Exports consist of wine, woolens, furniture, ceramics, and postage stamps. Manufactured goods of all kinds make up the main imports. Because of a customs union with Italy, exports and imports are not subject to customs duties, and no record is kept of foreign payment transactions **Principal Trade Partner:** Italy

Vital Statistics: Birthrate, 14.8 per 1,000 of pop.; death rate, 7.7 **Life Expectancy:** 72 years **Health Statistics:** Public health institutions include a hospital, a dispensary, and a laboratory of hygiene; 750 inhabitants per physician **Infant Mortality:** 14.8 per 1,000 births **Illiteracy:** Negligible **Education Statistics:** 18 primary and secondary schools **Enrollment in Higher Education:** 579 students are studying abroad **GNP Expended on Education:** 4.5% (1971)

Transportation: Streets and roads total more than 60 miles **Motor Vehicles:** 9,584 **Passenger Cars:** 4,724 **Railway Mileage:** 20

miles of electric funicular railway **Ports:** None **Radio Transmitters:** There are no local radio or television transmitters; broadcasts are received from Italy **Radio Licenses:** 6,000 (1976) **Television Licenses:** 4,000 (1976) **Telephones:** 6,000 (1976) **Newspapers:** No dailies, but an edition of Il Resto Del Carlino of Bologna gives special attention to San Marino news; there are 3 fortnightlies

Weights and Measures: Metric system **Travel Requirements:** Passport, no visa

The Apennine slopes shelter a tiny country with a legendary beginning and an existence almost as fabled. Its founder is said to be Marinus, a Christian stonecutter from Dalmatia seeking refuge from persecution in the fourth century. The republic, named San Marino after the canonized Saint Marinus, is the world's smallest and oldest, having remained independent for some 1,600 years. It lived on after the collapse of the Roman Empire and survived such upheavals as an interdiction by the pope in the Middle Ages, occupation by troops of Giulio Cardinal Alberoni in 1739-40, the conquests of Napoleon, and the unification of Italy in the late 19th century.

San Marino's knack for survival carried it through the Mussolini era and World War II. In 1943 it rid itself of the Fascistlike regime of the Mussolini period, and from 1945 to the autumn of 1957 was ruled by a coalition of Communists and left-wing Socialists. After the defection of six members of the ruling group, an anti-Communist coalition gained control and went on to win subsequent elections. In 1973 that coalition resigned over economic policy disputes. The Christian Democrats formed a new coalition cabinet with Socialists and a splinter party. A coalition of Christian Democrats and Socialists governed from 1976 to 1977; in 1978, a coalition of Communists and Socialists formed a government. No major changes in government policy were made.

San Marino, situated on three-peaked Mount Titano, derives approximately 80 percent of its gross national product from tourism and the sale of postage stamps to collectors. The tourists, numbering about 2.5 million annually, are afforded a magnificent view of Rimini and the Adriatic Sea from three old fortresses and may visit stately buildings, churches, and museums.

HISTORY: According to tradition, San Marino was founded in the 4th century A.D. by Marinus, a Christian stonecutter from Dalmatia who was later canonized. Reputedly the world's oldest republic, it is the last of the Italian peninsula's once-numerous city-states

1631: Pope Urban VIII recognizes the independent status of San Marino

1739-40: San Marino is occupied by a military force under a papal legate, Giulio Cardinal Alberoni, who attempts to establish sovereignty over republic; occupation is terminated by Pope Clement II

1862: San Marino and Italy form a customs union

1939-44: San Marino, although officially neutral in World War II, is occupied by the German army and is the scene of heavy fighting during Allied advance into northern Italy

1945: Communist and left-wing Socialist coalition wins majority of seats in elections for the Grand Council

1957: Defection of six Council members leads to fall of coalition; anti-Communist councillors form new government

1973: Coalition government resigns; new cabinet is formed with Socialists and Christian Democrats; women are given expanded legal rights

1974: General elections are held and coalition of Christian Democrats and Socialists remains in power. New cabinet is formed. Three women win seats in the Council

1975: Socialists withdraw from the two-party coalition, leaving the Christian Democrats without an absolute parliamentary majority

1976: New coalition of Socialists and Christian Democrats is formed

1977: Socialist-Christian Democrat coalition collapses; Communists fail to form new government

1978: Communists form new government after Christian Democrats, winners of a plurality in May elections, fail to do so

SÃO TOMÉ and PRÍNCIPE

Area: 272 sq. mi. **Population:** 85,000 (1978 est.)
Official Name: Democratic Republic of São Tomé and Príncipe **Capital:** São Tomé **Nationality:** Sao Tomean **Languages:** Portuguese is the main language, and a local creole is also spoken **Religion:** Roman Catholicism is the predominant religion: **Flag:** Three equal horizontal stripes of green, yellow and green with a red triangle at the hoist and two black stars on the yellow stripe **Anthem:** N.A. **Currency:** Dobra (35.6 per U.S. $1)

Location: These two islands are in the Gulf of Guinea, about 125 miles off the west coast of Africa **Features:** Hilly, wooded interiors and flat coastal plains **Chief Rivers:** Grande, Abade

Head of State and of Government: President Manuel Pinto da Costa, elected 1975, assisted by a cabinet under Prime Minister Miguel Trovoada **Effective Date of Constitution:** 1975 **Legislative Body:** Popular Assembly (unicameral), with members elected for 4 years. Control is in the hands of the MLSTP party, headed by the president **Local Government:** 2 island provinces

Ethnic Composition: The native population is mostly African, with some Portuguese admixture **Population Distribution:** N.A. **Density:** 228 inhabitants per sq. mi.

Largest Cities: (1970 census) São Tomé 7,681; Santo António 1,618

Per Capita Income: $160 (1974) **Gross Domestic Product (GDP):** $19.4 million (1974) **Economic Statistics:** Most of the population is engaged in the growing of plantation agricultural products and fishing **Minerals and Mining:** None **Labor Force:** 40,000, with 62% in agriculture (coffee, cocoa, coconuts, bananas), 7% in industry (beverages, copra, palm oil and fish processing) and commerce **Foreign Trade:** Exports, mostly palm products, coffee, cocoa and fruit, totaled $6.5 million (1976). Imports totaled $6.9 million **Principal Trade Partners:** Portugal, Netherlands

Vital Statistics: Birthrate, 45 per 1,000 of pop.; death rate, 11.2 **Life Expectancy:** N.A. **Health Statistics:** 33 inhabitants per hospital bed; 6,666 per physician (1973) **Infant Mortality:** 64.3 per 1,000 births (1973) **Illiteracy:** 90% **Education Statistics:** 50 primary and secondary schools, with a total enrollment of 12,409 **Enrollment in Higher Education:** N.A. **GDP Expended on Education:** 2.2% (1972)

Transportation: All roads total 179 mi. **Motor Vehicles:** 2,000 (1973) **Passenger Cars:** 1,600 **Railway Mileage:** None **Ports:** São Tomé (on São Tomé) and Santo António (on Príncipe) **Major Airlines:** Air Gabon and TAG have mainland links **Communications:** Government owned **Radio Transmitters:** 4 **Licenses:** 20,000 (1976) **Television:** None **Telephones:** 677 **Newspapers:** 2 weeklies (1972)

Weights and Measures: Metric system **Travel Requirements:** Passport, visa

---

One of Africa's smallest countries, São Tomé and Príncipe is part of an extinct volcanic mountain range.

The islands' economy is based on cocoa, with copra and coffee also important. A steep drop in the world price of cocoa has greatly affected the new country's financial outlook. The crops are grown on company-owned plantations worked by labor imported from Mozambique and Angola. This temporary labor force outnumbers the permanent population, which largely refuses to work on the plantations, where conditions have been much criticized. Most of the 1,000 white settlers, who ran the plantations, and the Cape Verdeans, who served as foremen, left the islands after independence was declared. Malnutrition is a major health problem.

São Tomé and Príncipe, which lie 150 miles west of Gabon in the Gulf of Guinea, became independent on July 12, 1975, after 500 years of Portuguese rule, the fourth and smallest of Portugal's African territories to emerge from colonial status. Manuel Pinto da Costa was proclaimed first president by the political bureau of the Gabon-based Movement for the Liberation of São Tomé and Príncipe.

HISTORY: São Tomé and Príncipe were discovered in 1471 by the Portuguese, who began to settle convicts and exiled Jews on the islands and to establish sugar plantations using slaves from the African mainland

1951: The islands are designated a Portuguese Overseas Province

1967: São Tomé becomes the principal staging area for European troops heading toward Africa to help subdue uprisings in Portuguese colonies there

1975: São Tomé and Príncipe becomes independent

SAUDI ARABIA

Area: 829,995 sq. mi. **Population:** 7,900,000 (1978 est.)
Official Name: Kingdom of Saudi Arabia **Capital:** Riyadh (Jidda serves as the administrative center, and Taif is the summer capital) **Nationality:** Saudi Arabian **Languages:** Arabic is the official and universal language **Religion:** The overwhelming majority of the population is Sunni Moslem, and Islam is the state religion **Flag:** Green, with a white sword below the Arabic inscription "There is no god but God, and Mohammed is His Prophet" **Anthem:** Royal Anthem of Saudi Arabia, a short instrumental selection **Currency:** Saudi riyal (3.38 per U.S. $1)

Location: Arabian peninsula in Southwest Asia, Saudi Arabia is bounded on the north by Jordan, Iraq, and Kuwait; on the east by the Persian Gulf, Qatar, the United Arab Emirates, and Oman; on the south by Yemen and Southern Yemen, and on the west by the Red Sea **Features:** Nine-tenths of the country is covered by a barren plateau, including the Rub al-Khali and Al-Nafud desert regions. In the west, the Hejaz mountains border the narrow coastal plain along the Red Sea; to the east of the central plateau is the low-lying coastal region along the Persian Gulf **Chief Rivers:** There are no permanent rivers

Head of State and of Government: King Khalid ibn Abdul-Aziz Al Saud, born 1913, succeeded to the throne in March 1975. He named himself premier and his brother, Crown Prince Fahd ibn Abdel Aziz Al Saud, first deputy premier **Effective Date of Present Constitution:** None. A set of "Organic Instructions" established in Hejaz in 1926 and a decree of October 1953, amplified by later regulations, contain elements of constitutional law **Legislative Body:** None. The appointed Council of Ministers performs some legislative functions **Local Government:** 18 provinces, 6 major and 12 minor, each with an appointed governor

Ethnic Composition: The population is largely homogeneous, descended from indigenous Arab tribes, with some admixture of Africans, Turks, Iranians, Indians, and Indonesians. At present almost one-quarter are expatriates **Population Distribution:** 28% urban **Density:** 10 inhabitants per sq. mi.

Largest Cities: (1974 census) Riyadh 666,840, Jidda 561,104, Mecca 366,801, Taif 204,857, Medina 198,186, Dammam 127,844

Per Capita Income: $8,400 (1978) **Gross National Product (GNP):** $55 billion (1978) **Economic Statistics:** 62% of GNP is derived from industry, (oil refining, electrical goods, fertilizers, cement, iron and steel) and mining (80% in oil); 15% from trade and services; and 4% from agriculture **Minerals and Mining:** Saudi Arabia is the world's second-largest producer of oil. Other abundant minerals are natural gas, gypsum, copper, salt, manganese, silver, gold, sulphur, and lead **Labor Force:** 1,900,000, with 75% in agriculture (grains, vegetables, dates, livestock) and 10% in industry (chiefly related to petroleum) **Foreign Trade:** Exports, 99% petroleum and petroleum products, totaled $40 billion in 1977. Imports, principally motor vehicles, cereals, and power generating machinery, totaled $15 billion **Principal Trade Partners:** United States, West Germany, Japan, Italy, Netherlands, Britain, France

Vital Statistics: Birthrate, 49.5 per 1,000 of pop. (1975); death rate, 20.2 **Life Expectancy:** 45 years **Health Statistics:** 968 inhabitants per hospital bed; 2,485 per physician (1975) **Infant Mortality:** over 110 per 1,000 births (1976) **Illiteracy:** 70% **Education Statistics:** 3,597 primary and secondary schools, with combined enrollment of 805,000 (1976) **Enrollment in Higher Education:** 26,437 (1975) **GNP Expended on Education:** 10% (1977)

Transportation: Paved roads total 15,000 mi. **Motor Vehicles:** 112,000 (1974) **Passenger Cars:** 59,400 **Railway Mileage:** 357 **Ports:** Jidda, Dammam, Yenbo, Ras Tanura, Jubail **Major Airlines:** Saudi Arabian Airlines, government owned, operates both domestic and international flights **Communications:** Government controlled **Radio Transmitters:** 20 **Receivers:** 260,000 (1976) **Television Transmitters:** 10 **Receivers:** 130,000 (1976) **Telephones:** 160,000 (1976) **Newspapers:** 11 dailies, 11 copies per 1,000 inhabitants (1974)

Weights and Measures: Metric system **Travel Requirements:** Passport; visa, valid 3 months; $5.64 fee; 1 photo; religious certificate. Fine imposed for overstaying

---

The world's 500 million adherents of Islam regard Saudi Arabia with a special reverence because it contains Mecca, the holiest of holy sites. The birthplace of the Prophet Mohammed, Mecca s the direction to which these Moslems turn as they bow in prayer five times each day. It is the destination of some half million people a year from all parts of the world who follow the Koranic exhortation of making the pilgrimage, or Haj, during one's lifetime. Closed to non-Moslems, the city contains the Great Mosque, or Haram, and the Kaaba, with its sacred Black Stone.

The ruler of Saudi Arabia is considered the custodian of the holy sites and the chief defender of Islam. In addition, the present ruler, King Khalid, is the secular head of one of the world's leading oil-exporting countries and, consequently, one of its richest men, although his realm consists mostly of vast expanses of trackless desert. The combination of these functions has long given the Saudi king a strong voice in the Arab world.

Saudi Arabia has been also a country in which the deep Arab tradition of hospitality conflicts with an equally strong xenophobic tendency. It is a country where distrust of Western "imperialism" and American support for Zionism is often overshadowed by dependence on American technology and a fear of Communism.

The assassination of King Faisal by a nephew in 1975 caused reverberations throughout the Middle East. Faisal's brother, Crown Prince Khalid, succeeded him as king and named himself premier and Crown Prince Fahd first deputy premier. The new leaders are less concerned with fierce anti-Communism and are slightly more moderate on the Arab-Israel dispute.

Saudi Arabia has used its tremendous financial power to exert diplomatic pressure and has assumed a major role as a mediator in Middle Eastern affairs. In 1975 Saudi Arabia made efforts to mediate between Syria and Iraq in their dispute over the Euphrates waters and in 1976 the political breach between Egypt and Syria was repaired. Saudi Arabia negotiated an end to the Lebanese civil war after 18 months of fighting and was also involved in mediating the dispute among Algeria, Morocco and Mauritania over Western Sahara.

The Saudi position in regard to the United States is ambivalent. On the one hand, the government maintains close ties with Washington as the leader of the non-Communist world and admires American know-how; but Saudi Arabia does not hesitate to pressure the United States to stop supporting Israel.

In practice, the chief link between Saudi Arabia and the United States is their oil relationship. Saudi Arabia has the largest known oil reserves in the world (180 billion barrels), and the United States has been the world's leading consumer, by far, of Saudi Arabian oil, now being produced at the rate of about 9.5 million barrels a day. (Experts say that by 1985 the country's oil output could reach 14 million barrels a day.) Soon after oil was discovered in the Saudi deserts in the 1930s, King Ibn Saud, Khalid's father, granted primary exploitation rights to the Standard Oil Company of California. The concession was subsequently transferred to the Arabian American Oil Company, known as Aramco, a conglomerate of several oil companies. Still 40 percent owned by four American oil companies, (full nationalization is being worked out), Aramco is the world's largest oil-producing company.

Aside from Islam, Aramco is perhaps the dominant force in Saudi Arabia. The Saudis have made some attempts to diversify the economy by encouraging agricultural and industrial development, but even the new projects involve Aramco for the company is often the final contractor. It has become almost an administrative arm of the Saudi government; it builds and runs schools and housing, constructs and maintains roads, and manages other important projects.

In 1979, the fall of Shah Mohammed Reza Pahlavi of Iran and the war between Yemen and Southern Yemen worried Saudi Arabia's leaders. The United States sent a battalion of jet fighters to Saudi Arabia as a gesture of friendship, and Saudi Arabia cooperated with the U.S. in supplying arms to Yemen for defense against its Marxist neighbor. Saudi Arabia disapproved of the peace treaty between Egypt and Israel, and ended foreign aid to Egypt, but did not withdraw funds from Egyptian banks.

Before his assassination, King Faisal drafted a far-reaching and comprehensive plan calling for $142 billion in investment and affecting all areas of development. Experts have given the plan little chance of fulfillment by 1980. But the work goes on; cities are being transformed with modern buildings; new highway systems are complete, even with rush-hour traffic jams. Two major new industrial centers (each to cost $40 billion, and to comprise petrochemical, steel, aluminum, fertilizer, oil-refining and other plants) will be built; one at Jubail in the midst of Saudi Arabia's Gulf Coast oil fields and the other at Yanbu, the Red Sea port for Medina. A $15-20 billion gas-gathering system—a project larger than the trans-Alaska pipeline—is being built by an Arabian-American company. Other projects are giant desalination plants and a new airport the size of Manhattan Island to serve Jidda.

Although much of Saudi Arabia's oil revenue goes either to these projects or to the armed forces, some of it is now being spent for social welfare. Free medical service has been made available to all citizens, and elementary, secondary, and higher education is also free. Education is not, however, compulsory. By contrast, the religious tenets of Islam, which form the common law of the land, are enforced with fundamentalist zeal.

HISTORY: Arabia has been inhabited for thousands of years by nomadic Semitic tribes. Followers of Mohammed, who was born in Mecca in the 6th century A.D., conquered most of the area between Persia on the east and Spain on the west, but Arabia itself declined in importance. As a political unit, Saudi Arabia is of relatively recent origin, dating from the 18th century, when the Saud family, adherents of the puritanical Wahabi movement, gained control over most of the Arabian peninsula

19th cent.: Wahabi movement is crushed (1811) by Egyptian expedition led by Mohammed Ali; movement revives temporarily, only to be defeated by Rashid dynasty, which gains control of central Arabia and expels Saud family

1902-32: Ibn Saud, the exiled Wahabi leader, conquers the Nejd, Hasa, and Hejaz regions and forms the kingdom of Saudi Arabia

1936: Oil is discovered near the Persian Gulf

1953: Ibn Saud dies and is succeeded by his eldest son, Saud

1962: Saud dispatches aid to royalist troops in Yemen after pro-Nasser revolutionaries depose Imam. Relations with Egypt are severed

1964: Saud is deposed and succeeded by Crown Prince Faisal, who introduces sweeping government reorganization and abolishes slavery. Relations with Egypt are restored

1967-68: Saudi Arabian troops are sent to Jordan during six-day Arab-Israeli war but take no part in fighting. King Faisal halts aid to Yemeni royalists in return for withdrawal of Egyptian troops; however, aid is temporarily resumed to counteract support for republicans by Soviet Union, Syria, and Southern Yemen

1969: Hundreds are arrested as government acts to head off attempt at coup d'état

1970: Resumption of ties to Yemen is marked by financial aid from Saudi Arabia

1973: The Yom Kippur War prompts King Faisal to cut exports of oil to the U.S. by 10 percent in order to compel the U.S. to demand a cease-fire and Israeli withdrawal from Arab territory

1975: King Faisal is assassinated by his nephew, Prince Faisal ibn Musad Abdel Aziz, 31, and his brother, Crown Prince Khalid ibn Abdul-Aziz al Saud, 62 succeeds him

1976: Saudis hold down OPEC price increases to 5 percent

1978: U.S. Senate upholds President Carter's controversial decision to sell advanced jet warplanes in a package deal to Saudi Arabia, Egypt and Israel; Saudi Arabia to buy 60 F-15 fighters

SENEGAL

Area: 76,124 sq. mi. **Population:** 5,300,000 (1978 est.)

Official Name: Republic of Senegal **Capital:** Dakar **Nationality:** Senegalese **Languages:** French is the official language; among the spoken African languages, Wolof is used by nearly 50%, and Peul (Fulani), Mende, Diola and Mandingo are other main languages **Religion:** More than 80% of the population are Moslems organized into brotherhoods; about 10% are Christians, and the rest animists

Flag: Vertical stripes of green, yellow, and red with a green star in the center **Anthem:** National Anthem, beginning "Pluck your koras, strike the balafons" **Currency:** CFA Franc (219 per U.S. $1)
Location: West Africa. Senegal is bounded on the north by Mauritania, on the east by Mali, on the south by Guinea and Guinea-Bissau, and on the west by the Atlantic Ocean. The nation of The Gambia is an enclave within Senegal **Features:** The country is a transitional zone between the Sahara and the equatorial jungle with semidesert in the north, and open savanna in the center and south **Chief Rivers:** Senegal, Saloum, Gambia, Casamance
Head of State: President Léopold Sédar Senghor, born 1906, re-elected 1978 **Head of Government:** Premier Abdou Diouf, born 1935, reappointed 1978 **Effective Date of Present Constitution:** March 3, 1963, amended 1976 **Legislative Body:** National Assembly (unicameral), consisting of 100 members elected for 5 years **Local Government:** 8 regions, each headed by an appointed governor
Ethnic Composition: The largest ethnic group, the Wolof, makes up about 36% of population. Other important groups are the Peul (Fulani), with 17.5%; the Serere, with 16.5%; the Diola, with 9%; Mandingo, with 9%; and the Tukulor, with 6.5%. A small non-African population, largely French, is concentrated in Dakar **Population Distribution:** 35% urban **Density:** 70 inhabitants per sq. mi.
Largest Cities: (1976 census) Dakar 798,792, Thiès 117,353, Kaolack 106,899, St-Louis 88,404, Ziguinchor 72,726, Rufisque 66,995, Diourbel 50,618, Mbour 37,663, Louga 35,063
Per Capita Income: $360 (1978) **Gross National Product (GNP):** $2 billion (1978) **Economic Statistics:** In 1976 about 38% of GNP was derived from trade and services; 30% from agriculture and fishing (peanuts, accounting for about half of total production; fish; millet; sorghum; rice; cassava; potatoes; livestock); 16% from government activities; 16% from manufacturing (peanut oil mills, cement, food processing, textiles, leather, shoes, chemicals, and phosphate mining) **Minerals and Mining:** Calcium and aluminum phosphates, limestone, titanium, salt, and ilmenite are being worked **Labor Force:** Of 1,648,000, 80% are engaged in agriculture, and 8% in industry **Foreign Trade:** Exports, chiefly peanuts, phosphates, and canned fish, totaled $426 million in 1976. Imports, mainly food, textiles, machinery, chemical and petroleum products, totaled $731 million **Principal Trade Partners:** France, United States, Britain, Netherlands
Vital Statistics: Birthrate, 47.6 per 1,000 of pop. (1975); death rate, 23.9 **Life Expectancy:** 44 years **Health Statistics:** 754 inhabitants per hospital bed; 14,092 per physician (1974) **Infant Mortality:** 62.7 per 1,000 births (1972) **Illiteracy:** 90% **Education Statistics:** 6,104 primary and secondary schools, with combined enrollment of 371,640 (1974) **Enrollment in Higher Education:** 8,213 (1975) **GNP Expended on Education:** 3.3% (1975)
Transportation: Paved roads total 2,500 mi. **Motor Vehicles:** 69,800 (1974) **Passenger Cars:** 44,800 **Railway Mileage:** 715 **Ports:** Dakar, Kaolack, Ziguinchor, Saint-Louis **Major Airlines:** Air Senegal flies internationally **Communications:** Government controlled **Radio Transmitters:** 14 **Receivers:** 290,000 (1976) **Television Transmitters:** 2 **Receivers:** 35,000 (1974) **Telephones:** 39,000 (1976) **Newspapers:** 2 dailies (1975), 7 copies per 1,000 inhabitants (1974)
Weights and Measures: Metric system **Travel Requirements:** Passport; visa, 2 photographs, valid 3 months; $4.75 fee

---

Ever since it gained independence, discouraging economic reverses have beset Senegal, the former administrative and commercial center of the defunct French West African empire. In colonial times, the French federation, with a population of 20 million, was the market for industry and business based on the great port of Dakar, the Senegalese capital.

With the grant of independence also to other French African possessions, the federation was divided into nine separate and sovereign states. Although still closely tied to France economically, all were eager for their own commercial and industrial development as well as new trade outlets through other countries.

Forced to rely on its own meager resources and limited aid from France and other sources, Senegal has experienced increasing economic difficulty. Peanuts, introduced by the French more than a century ago, are the main cash crop. In the past, they have accounted for nearly 80 percent of exports and provided the main income for more than 90 percent of Senegalese. But with the end of French subsidies, lower prices and droughts, production has fallen sharply and, despite urgent

government appeals, growing numbers of farmers have stopped planting peanuts.

American and other foreign assistance is gradually increasing production of rice, millet, sorghum, sugar, and livestock, but the effort is offset by the rapid fall in export earnings, rising debt, and tightened budgets.

Compounding these problems have been the continuing severe drought and famine plaguing not just Senegal but other countries of the sub-Sahara. An estimated 100,000 people died in 1973 and millions more were starving in the sub-Sahara region. Relief efforts were hampered by poor transportation and communications facilities.

President Léopold Senghor, Senegal's leader before and since independence, has shown considerable skill in maintaining stability despite his many problems. A longtime Francophile and also a poet of note, Senghor has appeared confident that economic problems would be solved by France. In March 1974 Senegal and France signed 44 agreements constituting a total renegotiation of the accords reached upon Senegal's independence in 1960. Terms of the accords included partial withdrawal of French troops and the transfer of a military base at Dakar to Senegal. Relations with Arab countries, however, have become closer. Senegal broke off diplomatic relations with Israel in October 1973, and in 1976 sponsored a UN Commission on Human Rights resolution accusing Israel of war crimes in the occupied Arab territories. Relations with Israel grew more hostile in 1979 as Jerusalem refused to permit Senegalese troops to cross its borders with the rest of the UN Interim Force in Lebanon after Israeli authorities had arrested a Senegalese officer on charges of aiding Arab guerrillas.

In the 1970s the aging Senghor brought younger men and union leaders into his government. His choice as new premier was Abdou Diouf, an industrious and capable administrator. A 1976 constitutional amendment providing for the succession of the head of state makes Diouf the successor-designate to Senghor.

HISTORY: Senegal was largely dominated by the Moslem Tukuler tribe until 1893, when the Tukuler dynasty was overthrown by the French. European settlement, however, had begun as early as the 15th century, when the Portuguese settled along the Senegalese coastline. The French established a foothold in the area in the 17th century and by the 19th century Senegal was the center of French West Africa. In 1946, along with other parts of French West Africa, Senegal became part of the French Union

1958: Senegal becomes an autonomous republic within the newly formed French Community. Léopold-Sédar Senghor elected president

1959-60: Senegal is joined with the Sudanese Republic in the short-lived Mali Federation, which is dissolved after strong political differences develop between the two states

1962-63: Premier Mamadou Dia is ousted after bitter conflict with National Assembly; Senghor takes control of government and new constitution is adopted incorporating the office of premier with the presidency; new elections are held and Senghor, the only presidential candidate, is reelected

1964: All opposition parties are banned, except for small African Reunion Party

1968: Senghor is reelected for five-year term and an unopposed list of 80 candidates of his party, the Senegalese Progressive Union, is elected to National Assembly. Widespread strikes by students and workers break out in protest against government austerity measures

1969: Senghor declares state of emergency to deal with domestic upheaval

1970: Senegal denies use of its roads as supply route for Portuguese Guinea rebels. Constitution revised; post of premier is reinstated and Abdou Diouf is chosen to fill it

1973: Severe drought affects crop production

1974: New political party, Senegalese Democratic Party, formed

1976: At a conference of the Organization of African Unity and the Arab League in Dakar, President Senghor calls for a union of the two groups and for the establishment of an Arab-African arbitration and conciliation court. A third party, the National Democratic Assembly (RND) is formed

1978: Senghor is reelected in first multiparty election in 12 years. Senegal secures $26-million loan from International Monetary Fund to offset economic effects of drought

1979: Work begins on $550-million three-nation Senegal River irrigation and hydroelectric project

SEYCHELLES

Area: 171 sq. mi. **Population:** 60,000 (1978 est.)
Official Name: Republic of Seychelles **Capital:** Victoria **Nationality:** Seychellois **Languages:** Creole is spoken by 94% of the population; English and French are official **Religion:** 91% Roman Catholic, 8% Anglican **Flag:** A field of red over green separated by a wavy white band **Anthem:** National Anthem, beginning "Seychellois both staunch and true" **Currency:** Seychellois rupee (6.48 per U.S. $1)

Location: Indian Ocean. The republic lies about 1,000 miles east of Kenya, just south of the Equator **Features:** An archipelago of about 90 islands, it is divided almost equally between a Granitic Group and a Coralline Group. Mahé, the mountainous m island, comprises just over half of the total area, and contains about 88% of the population **Chief Rivers:** There are no large rivers

Head of State and of Government: President France Albert René, born 1934, assumed office in a coup in June 1977 **Effective Date of Present Constitution:** March 26, 1979 **Legislative Body:** National Assembly (unicameral) consists of 25 members. The Seychelles People's Progressive Front is the only political party **Local Government:** 8 districts, one including all outlying island groups

Ethnic Composition: Most are descendants of 18th century French settlers and their African slaves, with a later mixture of other Europeans and Asians; there is a small minority of Indians and Chinese **Population Distribution:** 26% urban **Density:** 351 inhabitants per sq. mi.

Largest City: (1971 census) Victoria 13,736

Per Capita Income: $600 (1977 est.) **Gross National Product (GNP):** $31 million (1974 est.) **Economic Statistics:** Percentages of GNP not available. Plantation agriculture (coconuts, vanilla, cinnamon, patchouli, fibers) and fishing at a subsistence level engage most of the population. Tourism is the chief income-making industry, and there is processing of coconuts and vanilla **Minerals and Mining:** None **Labor Force:** 19,827 in 1971. 27% of the wage earners are engaged in plantation agriculture, and about 55% in tourism and agricultural processing **Foreign Trade:** Exports, chiefly copra, coconut oil, cinnamon bark, dried fish, vanilla oil, and patchouli, totaled $1.75 million (1975). Imports, mainly foods, manufactured goods, textiles, machinery, and petroleum products, totaled $25 million **Principal Trade Partners:** India, United States, Britain, Kenya

Vital Statistics: Birthrate, 27.7 per 1,000 of pop. (1976); death rate, 7.9 **Life Expectancy:** 65 years **Health Statistics:** 147 inhabitants per hospital bed; 3,125 per physician (1972) **Infant Mortality:** 39.3 per 1,000 births (1974) **Illiteracy:** 20% **Education Statistics:** 48 primary and secondary schools, with a total enrollment of 14,046 (1975) **Enrollment in Higher Education:** 142% (1976) **GNP Expended on Education:** 6.2% (1972)

Transportation: Surfaced roads (entirely on Mahé and Praslin islands) total 80 mi. **Motor Vehicles:** 3,600 (1976) **Passenger Cars:** 2,800 **Railway Mileage:** None **Port:** Victoria **Major Airlines:** British Airways operates international services; Air Mahé operates domestic flights **Communications:** Partly government owned **Radio Transmitters:** 2 **Receivers:** 17,000 (1976) **Television:** None **Telephones:** 4,000 (1976) **Newspapers:** 2 dailies, 60 copies per 1,000 inhabitants (1975)

Weights and Measures: British system is used; metric system is anticipated **Travel Requirements:** Passport; no visa

This 90-island archipelago is a beautiful tropical paradise largely isolated from the rest of the world. The climate is equable and healthful, although quite humid, since the islands are small and subject to marine influences. Temperatures on the main island of Mahé vary from 75° to 85°F, and high winds are rarely encountered, as this "lotus land" lies outside the cyclone belt. The fortunate natural environment once caused an early visitor to declare seriously that the Seychelles archipelago was the home of the original Garden of Eden.

Although the new republic is promoting agriculture, its principal hopes lie in tourism. The opening of the islands' first commercial airport in 1971 has increased the number of tourists attracted by the beautiful beaches, impressive scenery and fine climate. The government has made considerable effort to assure that the expansion of tourism neither disrupts the islands' cultural life nor spoils the natural beauty on which tourism is based. Beaches are not "walled off" by hotels and condominiums but are well-spaced and secluded.

Under the stimulus of development and tourism, the Seychelles has virtually obtained full employment for its work force. But even paradise must pay a price, and in the Seychelles, like elsewhere, progress has brought inflation.

Under the nation's first president, James Mancham, the Seychelles remained neutral in foreign affairs, with a pro-Western outlook. The only intrusion of big-power presence is the hosting of an American satellite tracking station on the island of Mahé.

In 1977 Mancham was overthrown by leftist rebels thought to have been supplied with Chinese and Soviet weapons from Tanzania. Mancham's ouster was attributed to his playboy lifestyle, his frequent absences from the country, and his proposal to postpone the 1979 elections. Former Prime Minister France Albert René subsequently became president and vowed some form of socialism for the country, as well as an emphasis on housing, agriculture, fishing and tourism.

HISTORY: Although the islands appeared on Portuguese charts as early as 1505 and may have been visited by Arabs much earlier, the Seychelles remained unclaimed and uninhabited until 1742. In that year the French governor of Mauritius, Mahé de Labourdonnais, sent an expedition to the islands. However, the full settlement of the archipelago did not take place until 1794. As a result of French defeat in the Napoleonic Wars, the Seychelles passed to the British in 1814 and became a dependency of Mauritius

1903: The Seychelles become a separate crown colony

1970: Limited internal self-government is granted

1976: Independence is proclaimed on June 29

1977: President Mancham overthrown in leftist coup. Former Prime Minister France Albert René assumes presidency

1978: State of emergency imposed May-August following alleged coup attempt

1979: New constitution proclaimed

SIERRA LEONE

Area: 27,925 sq. mi. **Population:** 3,470,000 (1978 est.)
Official Name: Republic of Sierra Leone **Capital:** Freetown **Nationality:** Sierra Leonean **Languages:** English is the official language. Mende and Temne are widely spoken, but the most commonly spoken language is Krio, a form of pidgin English **Religion:** 70% are animists, 25% Moslems, and 5% Christians **Flag:** Horizontal stripes of green, white, and blue **Anthem:** National Anthem, beginning "High we exalt thee, realm of the free" **Currency:** Leone (1.06 per U.S. $1)

Location: West Africa. Sierra Leone is bounded on the north and east by Guinea, on the southeast by Liberia, and on the west by the Atlantic Ocean **Features:** The country consists of a coastal plain of mangrove swamps that gradually gives way to wooded hills and upland plateaus in the interior, with mountains near the eastern border **Chief Rivers:** Rokel, Sewa, Moa, Jong, Little and Great Scarcies, Sherbro

Head of State and of Government: President Siaka P. Stevens, born 1905, elected April 1971, reelected 1976 for 5 years, sworn in for 7-year term in 1978 under new constitution **Effective Date of Present Constitution:** 1978 **Legislative Body:** Parliament (unicameral House of Representatives), with 85 members elected by universal suffrage, 12 indirectly elected paramount chiefs, and 1 appointed by the president, all for 5 years. The All-People's Congress is the sole officially recognized party **Local Government:** 3 provinces governed by a minister with cabinet rank, and the Western (Freetown) area, under a council

Ethnic Composition: 18 tribal groups, with the Mende and Temne each making up about 30% of the population; others include the Limba, Loko, Kono, Sherbro, Vai, Gallina, Susu, Kissi, Mandingo, and Peul (Fulani). Less than 2% are Creoles, descendants of freed slaves, mostly from the Americas **Population Distribution:** 18% urban **Density:** 124 inhabitants per sq. mi.

Largest Cities: (1974 est.) Freetown 214,443, Bo 45,000, Kenema 30,000

Per Capita Income: $222 (1978) **Gross National Product (GNP):** $710 million (1978) **Economic Statistics:** 31% of the GNP is derived from agriculture (palm kernels, cocoa, coffee, piassava, ginger, cola nuts); 19% from extractive industries (diamonds, rutile, palm produce, rice, wheat); 6% from manufacturing (soap, min eral water, furniture); and 26% from trade and services **Minerals and Mining:** Chiefly diamonds, iron ore, bauxite and the world's largest deposits of rutile **Labor Force:** 938,000, with 75% in agriculture, and 15% in industry **Foreign Trade:** Exports, diamonds, palm kernels, rutile, coffee, and cocoa, totaled $151 million in 1977. Imports, chiefly manufactured goods, machinery and transportation equipment, and food (principally grains), totaled $173 million **Principal Trade Partners:** Britain, Japan, United States, EC countries, China

Vital Statistics: Birthrate, 44.7 per 1,000 of pop. (1975); death rate, 20.7 **Life Expectancy:** 44 years **Health Statistics:** 927 inhabitants per hospital bed; 17,114 per physician (1970) **Infant Mortality:** 136.3 per 1,000 births **Illiteracy:** 90% **Education Statistics:** 1,132 primary and secondary schools, with combined enrollment of 237,271 (1974) **Enrollment in Higher Education:** 1,646 **GNP Expended on Education:** 3.3% (1974)

Transportation: Paved roads total 643 mi. **Motor Vehicles:** 25,200 (1976) **Passenger Cars:** 18,900 **Railway Mileage:** 56 **Ports:** Freetown, Bonthe, Pepel **Major Airlines:** Sierra Leone Airways, government owned, operates both international and domestic flights **Communications:** Government owned **Radio Transmitters:** 3 **Receivers:** 62,000 (1975) **Television Transmitters:** 2 **Receivers:** 8,500 **Telephones:** 15,000 (1976) **Newspapers:** 2 dailies, 10 copies per 1,000 inhabitants (1975)

Weights and Measures: British standards are used **Travel Requirements:** Passport; visa valid for 1 month; $6.50 fee; 3 photos

---

One of the oldest and most progressive of Britain's former West African colonies, Sierra Leone got off to a favorable start on independence in 1961 with stable government and promising economic development. But since then the small nation, which depends mainly on the production of diamonds and iron ore, has experienced increasingly violent political upheaval.

In addition to the tendency of some officials to seek personal fortunes at public expense, Sierra Leone has been plagued by coups, states of emergency and, in March 1971, an attempted assassination of the country's present leader, President Siaka Stevens. In the process, economic improvements—particularly in agriculture—have been repeatedly disrupted and new development programs delayed.

Serious trouble began with elections in 1967. Then opposition leader, Stevens appeared to have won by a narrow margin over the bumptious Sir Albert Margai, whose government had been marked by corruption. But almost as soon as Stevens had been sworn in as prime minister, a group of army officers ousted him in a coup. The junta said it had acted to prevent a civil war between the Mende, the country's largest tribal group, and the rival Temne, a main source of Stevens' strength.

Rule by the military group proved unpopular, and in 1968 it was ousted by a counter-coup led by noncommissioned officers and police. This group promptly restored Stevens to the premiership and the country settled down to legally elected government. Two years later, however, opposition to Stevens' party resumed, with clashes that led to the declaration of a state of emergency.

Then in March 1971 Brig. Gen. John Bangura, the army commander, led an attempted coup and assassination plot. The coup fizzled when other army officers arrested Bangura and proclaimed their loyalty to the Stevens government. Another state of emergency was declared and, under a new mutual defense pact by Stevens and Guinean President Sékou Touré, 200 Guinean troops were flown into Freetown to bolster local troops. Bangura and three followers were executed.

On April 19, 1971, Stevens proclaimed Sierra Leone a republic and two days later he was sworn in as president. His power was reconfirmed by elections in 1973 and 1976. In 1978 Stevens pushed through legislation introducing a new constitution which extended the presidential term of office to seven years, abolished the office of prime minister and made the All-People's Congress the only legal party.

On the economic scene, Sierra Leone has taken strides towards the development of the production of bauxite, which amounted to 700,000 tons in 1974, in addition to the ongoing exploitation of major iron ore deposits. Another resource, rutile, a mineral used in paint manufacture, is being developed under a U.S. investment agreement. Sierra Leone's deposits are among the world's largest.

HISTORY: Sierra Leone was originally divided into numerous kingdoms or chiefdoms. The Portuguese explorer Pedro da Cintra visited the coastal area in 1460 and named the mountainous peninsula at the mouth of the Rokel River Serra Lyoa (Lion Mountain), later corrupted to Sierra Leone. Until the 18th century, the region was an important source of slaves. In 1787, a group of abolitionists founded Freetown to resettle freed slaves from Britain, and in 1808 the settlement became a crown colony. In 1896, the interior was made a British protectorate

1924: New constitution is introduced permitting nomination of protectorate chiefs to legislative council but fails to satisfy nationalist aspirations

1943: Africans are admitted to the executive council

1951: New constitution is introduced, providing a framework for decolonization

1957-58: Elected House of Representatives replaces legislative council; Dr. Milton Margai, whose Sierra Leone People's Party wins a majority of seats, becomes prime minister

1961: Sierra Leone becomes an independent Commonwealth state

1964: Prime Minister Milton Margai dies; his brother, Finance Minister Albert Margai, is asked by governor-general to form new government

1967: Siaka Stevens, leader of the opposition All People's Congress, is appointed prime minister after hotly contested election but is ousted by army chief; group of young army officers stage bloodless coup and a National Reformation Council composed of army and police officers is set up under chairmanship of Col. Andrew Juxon-Smith; House of Representatives is dissolved and constitution is suspended

1968: Military coup is staged by noncommissioned officers and police; House of Representatives is reconvened and asks Stevens to resume premiership

1969: Sierra Leone People's Party loses strength in House of Representatives following by-elections; party leaders charge that losses were due to government intimidation of voters

1971: An attempted coup led by Brig. Gen. John Bangura, the army commander, is crushed; Prime Minister Stevens calls in troops from Guinea to help suppress dissident elements. Sierra Leone is declared a republic

1973: A plot to overthrow the government is uncovered. Sierra Leone increases its military capacity. The All People's Congress wins election, taking 84 of 97 parliamentary seats

1976: President Stevens is elected for second five-year term

1977: State of emergency is declared after students and government supporters clash over student demands, including the resignation of President Stevens and the holding of free elections. National elections in May give ruling APC party a decisive victory, amidst charges of vote fraud

1978: New constitution increases presidential term to seven years and makes APC sole recognized party

---

SINGAPORE

Area: 226 sq. mi. **Population:** 2,310,000 (1978 est.)

Official Name: Republic of Singapore **Capital:** Singapore **Nationality:** Singaporean **Languages:** Malay, the national language, and English, Chinese, and Tamil are all official languages; Hindi is also spoken **Religion:** The majority of the ethnic Chinese are Buddhists, Taoists, or Confucianists; the Malays and Pakistanis are Moslems; and the Indians mainly Hindus. The Europeans and Eurasians are almost all Christians **Flag:** Horizontal stripes of red and white with a white crescent and 5 white stars in the upper left-hand corner **Anthem:** Forward Singapore **Currency:** Singapore dollar (2.21 per U.S. $1)

Location: Southeast Asia. The island of Singapore lies south of the Malay peninsula, separated by the Strait of Johore. A three-quarter-mile-long causeway connects the island with Malaysia; 54 small islets lie offshore **Features:** Except for a central plateau, most of the island is low lying and originally consisted of swamp and jungle. The city of Singapore occupies land that for the most part was reclaimed from the sea **Chief Rivers:** Sungei Seletar, Singapore

Head of State: President: Dr. Benjamin Henry Sheares, born 1908, in office since 1971 **Head of Government:** Prime Minister Lee Kuan Yew, born 1923, appointed 1965, reelected 1976 **Effective Date of**

Present Constitution: 1963, amended 1965 **Legislative Body:** Parliament (unicameral), consisting of 69 members elected by adult suffrage for 5 years

Ethnic Composition: About 76% of the population is ethnically Chinese, 15% Malays, and 7% Indians and Pakistanis. The rest are largely Europeans and Eurasians **Population Distribution:** 100% urban **Density:** 10,221 inhabitants per sq. mi.

Largest City: (1972 est.) Singapore 2,147,400

Per Capita Income: $3,285 (1978) **Gross National Product (GNP):** $7.6 billion (1978) **Economic Statistics:** In 1973 about 56% of GNP came from trade and services (including banks, financial institutions, transportation and communications); 21% from quarrying and manufacturing; and 3% from agriculture and fishing **Minerals and Mining:** None **Labor Force:** 995,000 wage earners, with 35% in industry and 3% in agriculture **Foreign Trade:** Exports, mainly crude rubber, petroleum products, electrical machinery, electronics, textiles, timber and coffee, totaled $8.3 billion in 1977. Imports, chiefly rubber, petroleum products, machinery, vehicles, and woven fabrics other than cotton, totaled $10.5 billion **Principal Trade Partners:** Malaysia, United States, Japan, Saudi Arabia, Britain, China, Hong Kong, Australia, West Germany

Vital Statistics: Birthrate, 16.6 per 1,000 of pop. (1977); death rate, 5.3 **Life Expectancy:** 69 years **Health Statistics:** 252 inhabitants per hospital bed; 1,380 per physician (1976) **Infant Mortality:** 13.9 per 1,000 births **Illiteracy:** 25% **Education Statistics:** 558 primary and secondary schools, with combined enrollment of 518,243 (1974) **Enrollment in Higher Education:** 22,607 (1975) **GNP Expended on Education:** 2.9% (1975)

Transportation: Paved roads total 1,286 mi. **Motor Vehicles:** 218,300 (1976) **Passenger Cars:** 142,100 **Railway Mileage:** 23 **Port:** Singapore **Major Airlines:** Singapore Airlines, which operates international flights, is owned by the government of Singapore **Communications:** Government controlled **Radio Transmitters:** 16 **Licenses:** 356,000 (1976) **Television Transmitters:** 1 **Licenses:** 294,000 **Telephones:** 329,000 (1976) **Newspapers:** 10 dailies, 201 copies per 1,000 inhabitants (1974)

Weights and Measures: Metric system; British, Chinese, and local standards are used **Travel Requirements:** Passport; no visa

Since 1819, when Singapore was created out of a mangrove swamp by Sir Stamford Raffles, the visionary agent of the British East India Company, it has served as East Asia's major transshipping point, as the wholesaler for other countries' products, as the bastion of the British Empire, and, more recently, as the area's leading processor of other countries' raw materials.

Blessed with one of the few natural harbors in the region, Singapore grew to become the largest port in Southeast Asia and the fourth largest in the world. Through this port have flowed rubber and tin from Malaysia and Indonesia to the markets of Europe and the United States.

The expanding rubber and tin industries early this century spurred immigration, mainly from southern China. In fact, up to 1957, Singapore's population consisted predominantly of noncitizen aliens. Today, Singapore is the only nation in the world with a population made up primarily of overseas Chinese, although immigration has now been slowed to a minimum. Malays, Indians, and Pakistanis are the other dominant ethnic groups.

Economically, Singapore has continued to thrive and maintains the highest per capita income in Southeast Asia, as well as virtually full employment. The Jurong area, a sprawling section of the island devoted to industrial development, today pulses with the processing of many types of raw materials and the manufacturing of finished goods. In 1977 it was announced that a consortium of Japanese companies plans to build an $800-million petrochemical complex which will be half owned by the Singapore government, on one of Singapore's offshore islands.

Business travel and tourism have increased sharply, raising the number of Singapore's visitors from less than one million in 1973 to more than two million in 1978. In the latter year Singapore Airlines placed the largest single order ever made for commericial aircraft—$900 million to the Boeing Company for 10 long-range 747 jumbo jets and four medium-range 727 trijets.

Since 1959, when Singapore was granted internal self-government, the People's Action Party, headed by Lee Kuan Yew, has controlled the island's affairs. In recent years the government has been accused of authoritarianism and repression. In 1974 drastic penalties were decreed for armed robbers, gun runners, and traffickers in illegal immigrants.

The Internal Security Act provides for detention without trial for those accused of pro-Communist activities. In 1977 a new campaign was begun to repress dissent—a series of arrests of prominent critics of government policies, who subsequently have been pressured into signing confessions and appearing on television to recant.

In 1975 Foreign Minister S. Rajaratnam responded to Peking's more moderate attitude by leading Singapore's first goodwill mission to China where he met with the late Premier Zhou Enlai. In 1976 Prime Minister Lee was one of the last foreign officials to be allowed to meet with Chairman Mao Zedong. With a population that is overwhelmingly of Chinese ancestry, many of whom retain warm feelings for their ancestral land, Singapore cannot afford to antagonize Peking, but neither does it want to be a Chinese satellite.

HISTORY: For centuries the island of Singapore was little more than a mangrove swamp occupied by Malay fishermen who owed allegiance to the Sultan of Johore. In 1819, Sir Stamford Raffles of the British East India Company, who saw in Singapore potential for a great trading post, founded a trading post on the island

1824: Sultan of Johore cedes Singapore to the British East India Company

1826: Singapore becomes part of the British Straits Settlements

1942: Supposedly impregnable fortress of Singapore is captured by the Japanese in World War II

1946: Singapore becomes a separate British crown colony

1959: Singapore becomes a self-governing colony

1963: Federation of Malaysia is formed and Singapore joins Malaya, Sarawak, and Sabah in new nation

1965: Singapore withdraws from Malaysia federation

1971: Singapore, Malaysia, Britain, Australia, and New Zealand sign accord on joint defense arrangements for Singapore and Malaysia

1972-73: Australia announces that it will withdraw all but about 150 support troops by July 1973

1976: Prime Minister Lee's ruling People's Action Party, in its fifth straight election victory, wins all 69 seats in Parliament

1978: Amnesty International alleges serious human rights violations in Singapore, including detention without trial of at least 70 political dissenters

1979: As one of five countries making up the Association of South east Asian Nations (ASEAN), Singapore joins in a decision June 30 to accept no more Vietnamese refugees

SOLOMON ISLANDS

Area: 11,500 sq. mi. **Population:** 200,000 (1978 est.)

Official Name: Solomon Islands **Capital:** Honiara **Nationality:** Solomon Islander **Language:** English is the official language; Melanesian Pidgin is the universal lingua franca. A variety of Melanesian tongues are spoken throughout most of the islands. On Vella Lavella, Savo and the Russell Islands the dominant languages are of the Papuan family. Polynesian languages, closely related to Maori, are spoken on the outlying islands of Ontong Java, Rennell and Tikopia **Religion:** 33% Anglican, 17% Roman Catholic, 17% South Sea Evangelical Church. The remainder of the inhabitants are members of the United Church and the Christian Fellowship Church, except for 5%, who are animists **Flag:** A blue triangle with five white stars in the upper left and a plain green triangle in the lower right separated by a diagonal yellow stripe **Anthem:** God Save Our Solomons **Currency:** Solomon Islands dollar (.91 per U.S. $1)

Location: Southwest Pacific Ocean. About 1000 miles northeast of Australia, the islands form a scattered archipelago stretching 900 miles in a southeasterly direction from Papua New Guinea. The six major islands are Choiseul, New Georgia, Santa Isabel, Guadalcanal, Malaita and San Cristobal **Features:** The large islands have a mountainous spine which on one side drops steeply to sea level and on the other drops through a series of foothills to the coast. The highest peaks are found on Guadalcanal, which possesses the only extensive coastal plains in the Solomons. The weather varies from warm to hot and is humid, with annual rainfall exceeding 100 inches **Chief Rivers:** There is an abundance of short rivers on the larger islands

Head of State: Queen Elizabeth II, represented by a governor-general, Baddeley Devesi, born 1941, sworn in July 1978 **Head of Government:** Prime Minister Peter Kenilorea, born 1943, sworn in July 1978 **Effective Date of Present Constitution:** July 1978 **Legislative Body:** National Parliament (unicameral) consisting of 38 members elected for 4 years **Local Government:** At present 4 districts; provinces are to be established

Ethnic Composition: Melanesians 93%, Polynesians 4%, Gilbertese 1%, European stock 1% **Population Distribution:** 9% urban **Density:** 17 inhabitants per sq. mi.

Largest City: (1976 census) Honiara 14,942

Per Capita Income: $310 (1974) **Gross National Product (GNP):** $60 million (1974) **Economic Statistics:** Copra and rice are the only important cash crops. Fisheries contribute to the economy, and the timber industry is being developed **Minerals and Mining:** Copper, bauxite and nickel deposits are being developed **Labor Force:** 14,184 (1974) **Foreign Trade:** Exports, chiefly fish, timber, and copra, amounted to $23.8 million in 1976. Imports, mainly machinery, transport equipment, food and fuels totaled $26.8 million **Principal Trade Partners:** Japan, Australia, Britain, American Samoa, EEC, Malaysia, Singapore

Vital Statistics: Birthrate, 41 per 1,000 of pop. (1970); death rate, 11 **Life Expectancy:** 51 years **Health Statistics:** 120 inhabitants per hospital bed; 5,135 per physician (1975) **Infant Mortality:** 68 per 1,000 births **Illiteracy:** 90% **Education Statistics:** 354 primary and secondary schools, with combined enrollment of 29,243 (1976) **Enrollment in Higher Education:** 160 (1976) **GNP Expended on Education:** 3.7% (1972)

Transportation: All weather roads total 283 miles **Motor Vehicles:** 1,796 (1972) **Passenger Cars:** 727 **Railway Mileage:** None **Ports:** Honiara, Gizo, Yandina **Major Airlines:** Solomon Islands Airways operates domestic flights **Communications:** Government owned **Radio Transmitters:** 3 **Radio Receivers:** 11,000 (1976) **Television Transmitters:** None **Television Receivers:** None **Telephones:** 800 (1972) **Newspapers:** 1 weekly

Weights and Measures: Imperial weights and measures are still in use, but the metric system has been adopted as the future standard **Travel Requirements:** Passport; no visa

For a short period during World II the Solomon Islands were a focus of world attention as Japan and the United States engaged in land, air and sea battles for the control of the South Pacific. Guadalcanal, New Georgia, "the Slot," and Iron Bottom Sound—scenes of major clashes in 1942 and 1943—are all within the confines of the newly independent Solomon Islands.

Following hostilities, the islands returned to the peaceful obscurity of being a remote British protectorate unbothered by the tides of history. However, the worldwide retreat of colonialism during the 1960s resulted in a growing interest in eventual independence for the Solomons on the part of both the British and the islanders. Finally, on July 7, 1978, the Duke of Gloucester, representing Queen Elizabeth II, handed over power to the government of the new nation.

The most pressing problem facing the Solomon Islands is the maintenance of unity among the diverse and geographically separated peoples of the island chain. The commercially developed western islands have demanded more autonomy, and the non-Melanesian minority fears the neglect of its needs by the central government.

One of the main objectives of the government is to diversify the economy. In the past, production has been limited to copra planting, timber cutting and fishing. It is hoped that plans for the introduction of beef cattle and the growing of rice and oil palm will be implemented. Another source of future economic growth would be the successful exploitation of the islands' copper, bauxite and nickel ores.

HISTORY: Ancestors of the present Melanesian inhabitants entered the area from the Malay Archipelago some time between 1000 and 500 B.C. Polynesians came to the islands much later, from Uvea in the Wallis group, northeast of Fiji. The Spaniards reached Santa Isabel in the Solomons in 1568. During the 19th century missionaries and coconut traders made contact with the Solomon Islanders, and many of the inhabitants were recruited, sometimes forcibly, for labor in Fiji, Australia and New Caledonia

1893-98: Britain establishes a protectorate over the Solomons

1899: Germany transfers Santa Isabel, Choiseul, the Shortlands and Ontong Java to Britain

1942-43: Japanese invade the Solomons. American counteroffensive recaptures Guadalcanal; fighting continues on the islands until Allied forces move on to Bougainville

1946-52: Opposition to British rule is carried on by "Marching Rule" movement, a nativist cargo-cult

1960: Legislative Council established

1976: The protectorate is abolished, and the Solomons become a self-governing dependency

1977: Constitutional conference is held in London to plan for independence

1978: Full independence is achieved on July 7

1979: Government opens talks with Papua New Guinea on boundary dispute in North Solomons island group

SOMALIA

Area: 246,200 **Population:** 3,400,000 (1978 est.)

Official Name: Somali Democratic Republic **Capital:** Mogadishu **Nationality:** Somali **Languages:** Somali is the official language; Arabic, English, and Italian are still used extensively **Religion:** 99% are Sunni Moslems and Islam is the state religion **Flag:** Blue field with a 5-pointed white star in the center **Anthem:** Long Live Somalia **Currency:** Somali shilling (Somalo) (6.30 per U.S. $1)

Location: East Africa. Somalia is bounded on the north by the Gulf of Aden and Djibouti, on the southeast by the Indian Ocean, and on the west by Kenya and Ethiopia **Features:** Much of the country is arid or semiarid. The northern region is mountainous; the southern part is mostly desert, but with a large fertile area crossed by two large rivers flowing from Ethiopia **Chief Rivers:** Juba, Shebelli

Head of State and Government: President: Maj. Gen. Mohamed Siad Barré, born 1919, secretary general of the Somali Socialist Revolutionary Party (SRSP), assumed power in 1969 **Effective Date of Present Constitution:** 1979 **Legislative Body:** The new constitution provides for a unicameral People's Parliament and makes the SRSP the sole political party and the supreme ruling body **Local Government:** 15 regions divided into 78 districts

Ethnic Composition: The Hamitic population is mainly Somali. Other sizable ethnic groups include some 35,000 Arabs, 1,000 Indians and Pakistanis, and about 2,000 Italians **Population Distribution:** 9% urban **Density:** 14 inhabitants per sq. mi.

Largest City: (1973 est.) Mogadishu 400,000

Per Capita Income: $70 (1978) **Gross National Product (GNP):** $260 million (1978) **Economic Statistics:** Industry accounts for only about 8% of the GNP with the rest from livestock (cattle, camels, sheep, goats), the mainstay of the Somali economy; banana growing; wild animal hides such as Somali leopard skins; spices, fishing, and some minerals **Minerals and Mining:** Commercial production is confined to salt, charcoal, limestone, and meerschaum; uranium, iron ore and certain rare earths are currently being explored **Labor Force:** 1,100,000 (1970). Livestock production employs about 60% of the total; and agriculture 20% **Foreign Trade:** Exports, chiefly livestock, bananas, hides, meat and tuna, totaled $115 million in 1976. Imports, mainly manufactured goods, cereals, food preparations, transportation equipment, and chemicals, totaled $165 million **Principal Trade Partners:** Italy, Britain, United States, Saudi Arabia, USSR, Kuwait, Guatemala, Yugoslavia

Vital Statistics: Birthrate, 47.2 per 1,000 of pop. (1975); death rate, 21.7 **Life Expectancy:** 41 years **Health Statistics:** 569 inhabitants per hospital bed; 15,544 per physician (1973) **Infant Mortality:** 177 per 1,000 births **Illiteracy:** 80% **Education Statistics:** 730 primary and secondary schools with combined enrollment of 229,900 (1975) **Enrollment in Higher Education:** 2,100 (1976) **GNP Expended on Education:** 2.7% (1973)

Transportation: Paved roads total 398 mi. **Motor Vehicles:** 16,000 (1972) **Passenger Cars:** 8,000 **Railway Mileage:** None **Ports:** Mogadishu, Berbera, Merka, Kismayu **Major Airlines:** Somali Airlines, 51% owned by the government and 49% by Alitalia, operates domestically and internationally **Communications:** Government owned **Radio Transmitters:** 5 **Receivers:** 69,000 (1976) **Television:** None **Telephones:** 5,000 (1971) **Newspapers:** 2 dailies, 1 copy per 1,000 inhabitants (1973)

Weights and Measures: Metric system **Travel Requirements:** Passport; visa; $4 fee, 3 pictures

Major power changes in the strategically located Horn of Africa have spotlighted Somalia, an arid East African country at the juncture of the Indian Ocean and the Gulf of Aden, as a link important to both the Middle East and Africa. A union of the former Italian and British Somalilands, Somalia became independent in 1960, but efforts at transforming its seminomadic society into a modern state have made scarcely any headway.

Somalis, a lean, handsome, fiercely proud people, have an oral history going back 2,000 years. Because of disputes among scholars, the Somali language had no written form until, in 1972, President Siad announced a system would be developed using the Roman alphabet.

Western and Communist aid has added some modern facilities—an American-built seaport and a Russian-built slaughterhouse—but the Somali economy remains largely a low-yield herding/farming system.

The current regime of Major General Mohamed Siad Barré, who overthrew the government of Premier Mohammed Ibrahim Egal in 1969, until recently had been marked by close ties with the Soviet Union and vociferous anti-Westernism. In exchange for military aid, Somalia provided the Soviets with a missile storage base. Angered by the Soviet buildup in Ethiopia, Somalia's arch-foe, Siad Barré began to seek arms from the U.S., as well as the anti-Soviet Arab bloc. Meanwhile, Siad Barré stepped up aid to the Somali rebels in Ogaden, an area of Ethiopia claimed by Somalia.

In mid-July 1977 contention over Ogaden erupted in all-out war as Somali forces invaded the area. In November Somalia expelled all Soviet advisers, ended Soviet use of strategic naval facilities on the Indian Ocean and renounced a 1974 treaty of friendship and cooperation—the moves prompted by anger over Soviet support for Ethiopia in the war. But in January 1979 Siad Barré held out the prospect of rapprochement with the Soviets.

In March 1978 the eight-month Ogaden War ended ignominiously for the Somalis as Ethiopian forces, aided by some 11,000 Cuban troops and 1,000 Soviet military advisers, drove them from the region. Ethiopia has said there can be no lasting peace in the area until Somalia renounces its territorial claims on Ogaden, Djibouti and northern Kenya, and pays for damages caused in the war. Meanwhile, two "western Somali" liberation groups continue to fight on, guerrilla-style.

HISTORY: Although arid and desolate in many areas, Somalia was known as the Land of Punt (God's Land) in ancient Egyptian writings. It was reputedly the source of the biblical frankincense and myrrh, and was probably also the breeding ground of the locusts that invaded Egypt in the time of Joseph. Over the centuries the Somalis, a blend of Asian and African peoples, formed a confederation of closely knit clans in which Arab trading enclaves and sultanates evolved. Later, the nation was divided into British and Italian possessions, and, with union of these in 1960, it began a new era as the Somali Republic.

19th cent.: British and Italians, through treaties with sultans and mutual agreements, divide country, with British occupying northwestern portion, Italians, the east and south

1901-20: Mohammed bin Abdallah Hasan, the "Mad Mullah," wages holy war against British

1936: Italian Somaliland is merged with Eritrea and Ethiopia as "Italian East Africa," following Ethiopian defeat in Italo-Ethiopian War of 1935-36

1940-41: Italians occupy British Somaliland during World War II; they are ousted by British, who take over Italian Somaliland

1947-50: Italy renounces colonial rights and is given 10-year UN trusteeship to prepare former possession for independence

1960: British and Italian Somaliland are united as Somali Republic

1961-64: Droughts and floods deplete crops, livestock; food shipments by United States and other countries avert famine

1969: President Abdirashid Ali Shermarke is slain by an assassin; army, with police backing, seizes power

1975: 120,000 Somali nomads are airlifted by Soviet planes from drought-stricken areas of north to southern regions

1977: Kenya and Somalia pledge maintenance of peace along border, following Kenya's charge of a Somali invasion

1978: Eight-month Ogaden war ends in March as Cuban and Soviet-aided Ethiopian forces drive Somalis from region. Somalia reports that army officers "influenced by foreign powers" attempted coup which failed; thwarted rebels are said to have

killed 20 people and injured 34. Ethiopian jets bomb Somali towns and villages while Somali guerrillas recapture major military base in southern part of Ogaden region. Siad Barré raps Western "paralysis" in not helping Somalia and indicates arms requested from U.S. are vital

1979: Somalia criticizes U.S. for failure to deliver $15 million in weapons as promised. New constitution adopted

---

SOUTH AFRICA

Area: 472,359 sq. mi. (inc. Bophuthatswana, Transkei and Venda) **Population:** 26,130,000 (1978 est.) (inc. Bophuthatswana, Transkei and Venda)

Official Name: Republic of South Africa **Capitals:** Cape Town (legislative), Pretoria (administrative), and Bloemfontein (judicial) **Nationality:** South African **Languages:** English and Afrikaans are the official languages. Of the white population, 63% speak Afrikaans and 37% speak English. In the *Bantustans*, the individual African languages are official. Indians, who constitute the bulk of the Asian minority, speak Tamil, Hindi, Gujarati, and Telugu **Religion:** Most of the population is Christian, chiefly Protestant. About 50% of the Africans in the *Bantustans* are animists. Most of the Asians are Hindus and Moslems **Flag:** Horizontal stripes of orange, white, and blue with small replicas of the Union Jack, the Boer flag of the Orange Free State, and old Transvaal Vierkleur banner in the center **Anthem:** Die Stem (The Voice of South Africa) **Currency:** Rand (0.84 per U.S. $1)

Location: Southern tip of the African continent, between the South Atlantic Ocean on the west and the Indian Ocean on the east. South Africa is landbound on the north and northeast by Namibia, Botswana, Zimbabwe, Swaziland, and Mozambique. Independent Lesotho lies entirely within the borders of South Africa. Walvis Bay, on the Namibian coast, is an exclave of the Cape Province **Features:** On the west, south, and east is a narrow coastal belt of lowlands extending into an extensive interior plateau **Chief Rivers:** Orange, Limpopo

Head of State: President Marais Viljoen, elected 1979 **Head of Government:** Prime Minister Pieter W. Botha, born 1916, appointed 1978 **Effective Date of Present Constitution:** May 1961, a new constitution is being considered **Legislative Body:** Parliament (bicameral), consisting of the Senate and the House of Assembly. The Senate is composed of 51 members, of whom 42 are elected by provincial electoral colleges and 9 by the state president. The House of Assembly consists of 165 members directly elected by voters. Only white candidates and voters take part in parliamentary elections **Local Government:** 4 provinces, each with an appointed administrator and an elected provincial council. Ten self-governing *Bantustans* have been created since 1963, three of which, Transkei, Bophuthatswana and Venda have been granted independence

Ethnic Composition: Africans (Bantus) constitute 70.2% of the population, whites (largely of Dutch and British descent) 17.5%, Coloreds (mixed white and African) 9.4%, and Asians 2.9% **Population Distribution:** 48% urban **Density:** 55 inhabitants per sq. mi.

Largest Cities: (1970 census) (M.A. = Metropolitan Area) Johannesburg 654,232 (M.A. 1,417,818), Cape Town 697,514 (M.A. 833,731), Durban 736,852 (M.A. 975,494), Soweto 602,043, Pretoria 545,450 (M.A. 573,283), Port Elizabeth 392,231 (M.A. 413,961), Germiston 221,972 (M.A. 293;257)

Per Capita Income: $1,372 (1978) **Gross National Product (GNP):** $37.7 billion (1978) **Economic Statistics:** About 28% of GNP is derived from manufacturing (textiles, iron and steel, chemicals, fertilizer, automobile assembly, metalworking, electrical and nonelectrical machinery and equipment, mining machinery); 8% from agriculture (sugar, tobacco, wool, corn, fruit, dairy products, wheat, fish); 12% from mining (gold, platinum, coal, diamonds, antimony, iron ore, copper, uranium, manganese, chrome, asbestos); and 32% from trade and services **Minerals and Mining:** Extensive mineral deposits, including gold, platinum, coal, diamonds, vanadium, antimony, iron ore, copper, uranium, manganese, chrome, asbestos **Labor Force:** 9,532,000 (1976), with 22.8% in industry, 9.6% in agriculture, and 23.4% in services **Foreign Trade:** Exports, chiefly diamonds, wool, fruit, copper, iron and steel, and gold, amounted to $5.2 billion in 1976 (excluding gold bullion). Imports, mainly industrial machinery and equipment, transportation equipment, and precision instruments, totaled $6.8 billion (excluding petroleum and munitions) **Principal Trade Partners:** Britain, West Germany, Japan, United States

Vital Statistics: Birthrate, 42.9 per 1,000 of pop. (1975); death rate, 15.5 **Life Expectancy:** 52 years **Health Statistics:** 152 inhabitants per hospital bed; 2,016 per physician (1973) **Infant Mortality:** 59 per 1,000 births (1974) **Illiteracy:** Negligible (white); 30% (others) **Education Statistics:** 15,688 primary and secondary schools, with combined enrollment of 5,216,646 (1972) **Enrollment in Higher Education:** 261,475 **GNP Expended on Education:** N.A.

Transportation: Paved roads total 20,000 mi. **Motor Vehicles:** 2,990,000 (1976) **Passenger Cars:** 2,169,000 **Railway Mileage:** 20,114 **Ports:** Durban, East London, Port Elizabeth, Cape Town, Richards Bay, Saldanha Bay **Major Airlines:** South African Airways, the government-owned airline, operates international and domestic flights **Communications:** Government controlled **Radio Transmitters:** 177 **Radio Receivers:** 2,500,000 (1976) **Television Transmitters:** 34 **Licenses:** 719,000 (1977) **Telephones:** 1,940,000 (1975) **Newspapers:** 24 dailies, 70 copies per 1,000 inhabitants (1975)

Weights and Measures: Metric system **Travel Requirements:** Passport; visa valid for 1 year

BOPHUTHATSWANA

Area: 15,570 sq. mi. **Population:** 1,200,000 **Density:** 77 inhabitants per sq. mi. **Official Name:** Republic of Bophuthatswana **Capital:** Mmabatho **Flag:** An orange diagonal stripe across a blue field with a white disk bearing a black leopard head in the upper hoist **Head of State and of Government:** President and Prime Minister: Chief Lucas Mangope, born 1923, elected December 1977 **Legislative Body:** Legislative Assembly (unicameral), with 99 members of which 48 are elected, 48 appointed by the 12 regional authorities, and 3 appointed by the president **Largest Cities:** (1970 census) Garankuwa 45,631, Mabopane 22,559

TRANSKEI

Area: 16,910 sq. mi. **Population:** 2,000,000 **Density:** 118 inhabitants per sq. mi. **Official Name:** Republic of Transkei **Capital:** Umtata **Flag:** Ochre, white, and green horizontal stripes **Head of State and Government:** President: Dr. Kaiser Daliwonga Matanzima, born 1915, took office October 1976 as prime minister, December 1978 as president **Legislative Body:** National Assembly (unicameral), with 150 members, composed of 75 elected, 70 nominated chiefs, and 5 paramount chiefs, all serving 5-year terms **Largest Cities:** (1974 est.) Umtata 28,100, Butterworth (Gcuma) 24,000

VENDA

Area: 2,510 sq. mi. **Population:** 449,000 **Density:** 179 inhabitants per sq. mi. **Official Name:** Republic of Venda **Capital:** Sibasa **Flag:** Three equal horizontal stripes of green, yellow and brown with a vertical blue stripe at the hoist. A brown "V" is centered on the yellow stripe **Head of State and Government:** Chief Patrick R. Mphephu **Legislative Body:** N.A. **Largest Centers:** Sibasa, Makwarela, Thohoyandou

---

South Africa is a land of great physical beauty and harsh social contrasts. Its rugged coastlines, steep escarpments, sweeping plateaus, and magnificent mountains afford unparalleled vistas. The setting of Cape Town, the country's oldest city, is among the most beautiful in the world. The modern skyscrapers of Johannesburg tower above the rolling countryside of the plateau *highveld*. The 19th century buildings that dominate the center of the administrative capital, Pretoria, form reminders of the period of conflict between Boer and Briton and the emergence of the Union of South Africa, predecessor of the present Republic.

Contrasted against the wealthy suburbs, modern highways, beach resorts and golf courses lie the bleak, much poorer African townships that house the urban labor reservoirs, the crowded workers' quarters near the mines, the traditional but often deteriorated African villages in the Bantu homelands. Rich South Africa is white South Africa; poorer South Africa tends to be the domain of the black, colored, and to a lesser extent the Asian communities. All nationwide statistics relating to the Republic should be considered in this context.

Although racial segregation as a way of life had characterized South Africa for many decades, a turning point came in 1948 when D. F. Malan's National Party defeated the United Party led by J. C. Smuts. Apartheid now became official state policy, and even the slightest trend toward racial integration was reversed. Public facilities became rigorously segregated, the major universities were restricted to whites, and numerous other steps were taken to eliminate racial contact in daily life. More significantly, however, the Nationalist government also embarked on a program of racial-territorial separation for the country as a whole, with the ultimate aim of the creation of a set of autonomous African states within South Africa's borders. Initially these areas were called *Bantustans*, and the first such territory to be awarded a degree of self-government was the Transkei in 1963. The independence of Transkei,

granted by South Africa in 1976, is not recognized by most other nations. The implications of the African Homeland program are far-reaching, and involve land exchanges, population movements, and numerous hardships for many of the people affected by this reorganization. When, in December 1977, independence was granted to a second black homeland, Bophuthatswana, most of its 1.2 million people viewed the move with hostility. A third homeland, Venda, was created in September 1979.

South Africa's policies of separate development have been the target of increasingly sharp criticism throughout the world, and especially in black Africa. Demands have been voiced for boycotts on trade, business, and sports contests with the Republic. In South Africa itself, leaders of the African Homelands also have begun to put pressure on the government for greater sovereignty than the *Bantustan* plan had first envisaged, and for better conditions for Africans still residing and working in "white" South Africa. The response has been comparatively slight. Some concessions have been made in areas of job opportunity for blacks, equalization of salaries, acceptance of some interracial sports events and in ending discrimination in the use of restrooms and elevators. However, the legacy of apartheid and the straightjacket of separate development continue to dominate life in the Republic.

In 1979 a major political scandal rocked Pretoria, forcing John Vorster to resign the ceremonial post of president. An official investigation alleged that Vorster, while prime minister, had approved, and later tried to cover up, a propaganda program under which some $90 million in secret funds were funneled to friendly politicians and other leaders in Europe and the U.S. Part of the slush fund allegedly was used to purchase new organs around the world to assure more favorable coverage of South Africa. Marais Viljoen, former president of the Senate, became South Africa's president in June.

HISTORY: When European settlers first arrived, there were several distinct native groups occupying different parts of the territory, including the Bushmen, nomadic hunters of the western desert upland country, and the Hottentots, a pastoral people who occupied the southern and eastern coastal areas. At the same time, Bantu people were moving toward the Cape of Good Hope, having already occupied territories in the north and east

1488: Portuguese led by Bartholomew Diaz arrive at Cape of Good Hope

1652: First Dutch settlers arrive in South Africa and establish Cape Colony

1814: Britain gains formal possession of the Cape Colony as a result of the Napoleonic Wars. Dutch begin eastward movement to Cape frontier

1835-36: In a migration known as the Great Trek, the Boers (descendants of the Dutch settlers) leave Cape Colony for the north in protest against British rule

1899-1902: Boer War breaks out with Britain. After three years of fighting, peace is declared by the Treaty of Vereeniging, in which the Boers acknowledge British sovereignty over Transvaal and the Orange Free State

1910: Union of South Africa is constituted under the terms of the South Africa Act passed by the British Parliament

1926-47: Ruling whites initiate separatist policies

1948: Afrikaner National Party, led by D. F. Malan, defeats J. C. Smuts' governing United Party and apartheid is introduced as official state policy

1959: Promotion of Bantu Self-Government Act is passed, providing for eight self-governing African states

1960: Seventy-two blacks are killed in protest demonstration against forced carrying of identity passes in Sharpeville

1961: South Africa becomes a republic and formally withdraws from British Commonwealth

1963: The first partially self-governing *Bantustan* (Bantu "homeland"), the Transkei, is established

1966: Prime Minister Hendrik Verwoerd is assassinated and is succeeded by Balthazar J. Vorster

1969: UN Security Council condemns South Africa for its refusal to permit the UN to take control of South-West Africa following the termination of a League of Nations mandate

WORLD NATIONS

1971: World Court rules that South Africa's administration of South-West Africa is illegal

1975: Vorster, with the help of Zambia's Kaunda, unsuccessfully attempts a negotiated peace in Rhodesia

1976: South African troops intervene unsuccessfully in Angolan civil war. Forced use of Afrikaans language in black schools precipitates rioting in Soweto, leaving 380 dead. Transkei homeland granted independence in October

1977: Black political activist Stephen Biko dies under suspicious circumstances while in police custody; "Stephen Biko affair" triggers international protest against South African government. UN Security Council unanimously orders worldwide mandatory embargo on arms supplies to South Africa because of its racial policies. Government scores overwhelming victory in general elections. Bophuthatswana granted independence

1978: Transkei breaks diplomatic relations with South Africa, the only nation that recognizes its existence. South African forces enter Angola from South-West Africa in "limited military operation" against guerrillas of SWAPO (South-West African People's Organization); action is condemned by UN Security Council. Prime Minister Vorster resigns and is named president. Pieter W. Botha is appointed prime minister

1979: South Africa continues to reject UN proposals for black majority rule in South-West Africa (Namibia). Government program to provide more skilled jobs to blacks prompts wildcat strike by white mineworkers. Prime Minister Botha expels U.S. embassy personnel after revealing U.S. ambassador's airplane had been conducting reconnaissance over South Africa. President Vorster resigns amid scandal. His successor is Marais Viljoen. Third black homeland, Venda, is granted indepedence

SPAIN

Area: 195,988 sq. mi. **Population:** 36,400,000 (1978 est.)

Official Name: Spanish State **Capital:** Madrid **Nationality:** Spanish **Languages:** Spanish is the official and predominant language; Catalan, Galician, Valencian, and Basque are regional languages officially recognized for legal purposes since 1976 **Religion:** The population is overwhelmingly Roman Catholic **Flag:** Horizontal stripes of red **Anthem:** Royal March **Currency:** Peseta (66 per U.S. $1)

Location: Southwest Europe, occupying most of the Iberian peninsula. Spain is bounded on the north by the Bay of Biscay, on the northeast by France and Andorra, on the east and south by the Mediterranean Sea, and on the west by Portugal and the Atlantic Ocean **Features:** Most of the country consists of a high plateau divided by mountains and broad depressions. The landmass rises sharply from the sea, leaving a narrow coastal plain except in the Andalusian lowlands in the south **Chief Rivers:** Ebro, Guadalquivir, Duero, Tajo, Guadiana, Miño

Head of State: King Juan Carlos I (de Borbón), born 1938, proclaimed king in 1975 **Head of Government:** Premier Adolfo Suárez González, born 1932, reappointed March 1979 **Effective Date of Present Constitution:** December 29, 1978 **Legislative Body:** Cortes (bicameral), with an elected 350-member Chamber of Deputies, and a Senate with 207 elected and 41 appointed members, all for 4 years **Local Government:** 50 provinces, each headed by an appointed governor and a provincial council, and the 2 African presidios of Ceuta and Melilla. The regions of Spain are being granted autonomy under the new constitution

Ethnic Composition: The Castilians of central Spain, the Basques in the north, the Catalans in the northeast, the Galicians in the northwest, the Valencians in the east, and the Andalusians in the south represent separate cultural groups **Population Distribution:** 49% urban **Density:** 186 inhabitants per sq. mi.

Largest Cities: (1975 est.) Madrid 3,520,320, Barcelona 1,809,722, Valencia 713,026, Seville 588,784, Saragossa 542,317, Bilbao 457,655, Málaga 402,978

Per Capita Income: $2,560 (1978) **Gross National Product (GNP):** $95 billion (1978) **Economic Statistics:** About 9% of GNP is derived from agriculture (cereals, fruits, vegetables, olive oil); 38% from mining, manufacturing, construction, energy; and 53% from trade and services. Tourism is of great importance **Minerals and Mining:** Coal, iron, mercury, pyrites, zinc, copper and potash are produced **Labor Force:** 13,300,000 (1978), with 36% in industry and construction, 40% in services and 20% in agriculture **Foreign Trade:** Exports, mainly footwear, textiles and clothing, steel products, transportation equipment, machinery, chemicals, and furniture, totaled $13 billion in 1978. Imports, chiefly feed grains, machinery, transportation and electrical equipment, fuels, metals, chemicals, and tobacco, totaled $18.7 billion **Principal Trade Partners:** United States, West Germany, France, Britain, Saudi Arabia, Iran, Netherlands

Vital Statistics: Birthrate, 18 per 1,000 of pop. (1977); death rate, 7.7 **Life Expectancy:** 72 years **Health Statistics:** 190 inhabitants per hospital bed; 647 per physician (1975) **Infant Mortality:** 10.7 per 1,000 births (1976) **Illiteracy:** 3% **Education Statistics:** 142,426 primary and secondary schools, with combined enroll-

ment of 6,571,446 (1975) **Enrollment in Higher Education:** 453,389 (1974) **GNP Expended on Education:** 1.7% (1974)

Transportation: Surfaced roads total 86,665 mi. **Motor Vehicles:** 6,443,000 (1976) **Passenger Cars:** 5,351,400 **Railway Mileage:** 10,824 **Ports:** Barcelona, Bilbao, Valencia, Cartagena, Sta. Cruz de Tenerife, Gijón, Huelva, Algeciras, Cádiz, Vigo **Major Airlines:** Iberia operates domestic and international flights, Aviaco operates domestic flights **Communications:** Government controlled **Radio Transmitters:** 406 **Receivers:** 9,300,000 (1976) **Television Transmitters:** 741 **Receivers:** 6,640,000 (1976) **Telephones:** 8,605,000 (1976) **Newspapers:** 115 dailies, 48 copies per 1,000 inhabitants (1975)

Weights and Measures: Metric system is official **Travel Requirements:** Passport; no visa for 6 months

Since the death of the dictatorial head of state, Francisco Franco, on November 20, 1975, Spain has moved steadily toward democracy. Two days after the passing of *El Caudillo*, the 500-year-old monarchy was restored with the proclamation of Juan Carlos de Borbón as king of Spain. King Juan Carlos I is the grandson of Alfonso XIII, who lost his throne in 1931.

In 1977, in the first free election in 41 years, Premier Adolfo Suárez González and his Democratic Center Union, a center-right grouping, captured 34 percent of the popular vote, with the Socialists coming in a close second with 28 percent. Suárez, a former Franco supporter, has held the premiership since his appointment by the King in 1976. The pardoning of more than half of the country's 1,600 political prisoners, the granting of the right of assembly, a loosening of press controls and legalization of the Communist Party have all occurred since the new monarch promised "profound improvements" at his swearing-in ceremony on November 22, 1975. A new bicameral parliament was instituted in place of the appointed parliament left by Franco.

However, the problem of the "nations within the Spanish nation" still remains; Basque and Catalan separatism and Galician and Valencian regionalism present difficulties. Some concessions have been made to the aspirations to cultural freedom of the non-Castilian peoples, but many more will be required before the ethnic sensibilities of these ethnic groups will be satisfied.

In its economic life, Spain has progressed far from the devastation left by the 1936-1939 civil war. A good part of the prosperity results from the popularity of Spain as a tourist haven for other Europeans and for North Americans. The beauty of the Iberian seaside, plus its easy accessibility from Western Europe and relative inexpensiveness, have turned sleepy fishing villages into thriving vacation resorts.

Burgeoning industry, flourishing foreign trade and an ever-increasing middle class are all signs pointing to the fact that Spain has become a prosperous, 20th-century nation. Though there are still wide areas of poverty, the better life is noticeable in the cities—such as Madrid, Barcelona and Seville—and the wealthier provinces—such as Castile and Catalonia. However, the rising curve of economic growth has not been without its dips, and in 1978 a definite downturn began.

A new constitution was adopted in December 1978. It limited the king to an essentially ceremonial role, contained firm guarantees of human rights, and protected the electoral system which favored the rural areas. It also provided for the establishment of autonomous regions.

The Democratic Center Union won a plurality in the elections of 1979, and Suárez was reappointed premier.

HISTORY: About 1000 B.C. the Iberian peninsula was invaded by Celtic tribes from the north, and two centuries later Phoenicians and Greeks began to establish colonies along the Spanish coast. The Carthaginians conquered most of the peninsula in the 3rd century B.C., but were forced out by the Romans, during whose rule political unity was established and Christianity introduced.

Early in the 5th century, Spain was overrun by the Germanic Vandals and Visigoths. After forcing the Vandals to emigrate to Africa, the Visigoths were themselves conquered by the Moors

711-18: Roderick, the last of the Visigothic kings, is defeated in battle by the Moors, who gain control over virtually the entire peninsula. Asturias, the only remnant of Visigothic Spain, becomes the focus of the Christian reconquest

1492: King Ferdinand of Aragon and his wife, Queen Isabella of Castile, complete the reconquest of Spain by capturing Granada, the last remaining Moorish stronghold. The Catholic rulers order the expulsion of the Jews. Columbus wins the monarchs' support for his voyages and discovers America, where a vast Spanish empire is soon to be established

1588: Defeat of the Spanish Armada by England hastens the demise of Spanish power

1808-14: Napoleon's armies invade Spain and his brother Joseph is placed on the Spanish throne. The French are finally driven out by Spanish resistance fighters and British troops led by Wellington. Wars of independence break out in Spanish America, leading to the disruption of the empire

1898: Spanish-American War destroys remaining empire

1931-36: Alfonso XIII is deposed and a republic established. Economic and political unrest culminate in an army revolt against the republic, under the leadership of General Francisco Franco. The revolt precipitates the Spanish Civil War

1936-39: The war rages for two and a half years, with the Loyalists (Republicans), aided by the Soviet Union and foreign volunteers, gradually defeated by Franco's forces, aided by Nazi Germany and Fascist Italy. The Loyalist government flees to France, and Franco sets up a dictatorship, with the Fascist Falange as the only legal party

1942-47: Franco reestablishes the *Cortes* but on Fascist lines without genuine popular representation. The Law of Succession is promulgated, declaring Spain a kingdom and setting up a regency council, with Franco as head of state

1966-68: A new constitution curbing the political power of the National Movement and its political organ, the Falange, is approved by referendum. The position of president of government (premier) is created. However, dissatisfaction with the regime makes itself felt in strikes and university unrest, which lead to severe police repression

1969: Franco designates Prince Juan Carlos de Borbón y Borbón to be chief of state and king upon Franco's death or incapacitation

1970-71: Military court sentences six Basque separatists to death; Franco commutes sentences following world outcry

1973: Spain establishes full diplomatic relations with East Germany and Communist China; Premier Carrero Blanco is assassinated; Carlos Arias Navarro becomes premier

1975: Right of U.S. military to use Spanish bases is renewed. Franco dies. Prince Juan Carlos becomes head of state as King Juan Carlos I

1976: Spain withdraws from Western Sahara, last remnant of this once-vast colonial empire. Carlos Arias Navarro resigns premiership. He is replaced by Adolfo Suárez González

1977: Communist Party is legalized and declared eligible for participation in national elections. Premier Suárez' Democratic Center Union emerges victorious in first free elections in 41 years. Government devalues peseta by 22 percent as economy continues slump. Catalanians and Basques granted provisional self-rule. Socialists and Communists, achieving regional power for the first time since civil war, obtain half the ministries in Catalonia's government

1978: Basques legally celebrate their national day for first time since civil war. Communist Party, holding its ninth congress (first since 1932), drops "Leninist" label despite strong Soviet advice against doing so. Suárez government suffers setback as Senate by-elections show victory for opposition Socialists and big surge by Communists. Government grants provisional autonomy to Balearic Islands and two other regions. Annual running-of-the-bulls festival in Pamplona is cancelled by violence sparked by police reaction to clash of Basques and Navarrese nationalists; disorders, which spread to San Sebastián and elsewhere (leaving two dead), underscore urgency of Basque separatism issue (and related question of future of Navarre). New constitution limits king's role and contains detailed bill of rights

1979: Democratic Center Union wins plurality in new elections; Suárez is reappointed premier

SRI LANKA

Area: 25,332 sq. mi. **Population:** 14,100,000 (1978 est.)

Official Name: Democratic Socialist Republic of Sri Lanka **Capital:** Colombo **Nationality:** Sri Lankan **Languages:** Sinhala is the official language; both Sinhala and Tamil are national languages. English is used widely **Religion:** 67% Hinayana Buddhist, 17% Hindu, 8%

Christian (mainly Roman Catholic), 7% Moslem, 1% other **Flag:** Narrow green and orange vertical stripes on the left side, with a yellow lion carrying a sword in one upraised paw against a red background occupying the rest of the flag. The entire flag is bordered in yellow, with a vertical yellow band separating the orange and green stripes from the red background of the rest of the flag **Anthem:** Hail, Hail, Motherland **Currency:** Sri Lanka rupee (15.6 per U.S. $1)

Location: Island in the Indian Ocean, off the southeastern tip of India. Sri Lanka is bounded on the north by the Palk Strait, on the east by the Bay of Bengal, on the south by the Indian Ocean, and on the west by the Gulf of Mannar **Features:** A low-lying plain makes up the northern half of the island and continues around the southern coast. The south-central part is mountainous **Chief Rivers:** Mahaweli, Ganga, Kelani, Walawe, Kalu, Gal

Head of State and of Government: President Junius Richard Jayewardene, born 1906, sworn in 1978 for a 6-year term. He is assisted by a prime minister, Ranasinghe Premadasa, born 1924, appointed 1978 **Effective Date of Present Constitution:** September 7, 1978 **Legislative Body:** Parliament (unicameral), with 196 members for 6-year terms **Local Government:** 22 districts, each headed by a governor

Ethnic Composition: 72% Sinhalese and 20% Tamil. (11% of the Tamil population are "Sri Lanka Tamils," citizens whose ancestors have lived in Sri Lanka for many generations and who have full voting rights. The 9% "Indian Tamils" came from south India in the 19th century) **Population Distribution:** 22.4% urban **Density:** 557 inhabitants per sq. mi.

Largest Cities: (1973 est.) Colombo 618,000, Dehiwala-Mount Lavinia 136,000, Jaffna 112,000; (1971 census) Moratuwa 96,489, Kandy 93,602, Kotte 93,042, Galle 72,720

Per Capita Income: $242 (1978) **Gross National Product (GNP):** $3.5 billion (1978) **Economic Statistics:** In 1973 about 34% of GNP was from agriculture (tea, rice, rubber, pineapples, coconuts), forestry, and fishing; 33% from trade and services; and 13% from industry (foodstuffs, tobacco products, chemicals, garments, leather and footwear, cement, paper and paperboard, tires and tubes, metal products) and mining **Minerals and Mining:** Graphite mining is the principal mineral industry; there are also gemstones, mineral sands and limestone **Labor Force:** 5.2 million (1977), with 45% in agriculture, and 13% in industry **Foreign Trade:** Exports, chiefly tea, rubber, gems, graphite, and coconut products, totaled $800 million in 1977. Imports, mainly rice and other food products, textiles, machinery and transport equipment and petroleum, totaled $900 million **Principal Trade Partners:** Britain, China, United States, Japan, India, West Germany, Pakistan, Saudi Arabia

Vital Statistics: Birthrate, 26.5 per 1,000 of pop. (1976); death rate, 9 (1976) **Life Expectancy:** 67 years **Health Statistics:** 333 inhabitants per hospital bed; 4,007 per physician (1972) **Infant Mortality:** 47 per 1,000 births (1973) **Illiteracy:** 22% **Education Statistics:** 8,649 primary and secondary schools, with combined enrollment of 2,863,873 (1976) **Enrollment in Higher Education:** 19,752 (1974) **GNP Expended on Education:** 2.7% (1974)

Transportation: Surfaced roads total 13,392 miles **Motor Vehicles:** 143,000 (1976) **Passenger Cars:** 93,800 **Railway Mileage:** 954 **Ports:** Colombo, Trincomalee, Galle **Major Airlines:** Air Lanka operates domestic and international services **Communications:** Government controlled **Radio Transmitters:** 24 **Receivers:** 800,000 (1976) **Television:** None **Telephones:** 72,000 (1975) **Newspapers:** 18 dailies (1975), 42 copies per 1,000 inhabitants (1971)

Weights and Measures: The metric system is being introduced **Travel Requirements:** Passport; no visa for 30 days

Isolated from global and regional rivalries at independence in 1948, Sri Lanka, formerly known as Ceylon, was without an enemy and appeared to be assured of peace and prosperity. But parliamentary democracy has been a forum for radical communal nationalism that has divided the Sinhalese Buddhist majority and the large Tamil minority and often brought the country near civil war. A positive action was the program to settle the "Indian Tamils" question through the naturalization of some and the repatriation to India of others. However, the Tamils have continued to press for a separate state.

In April 1971 ultraleftist students plunged the country into a full-scale guerrilla war before they faded into the jungled countryside. The movement was believed to have been born in 1964 when youth wings of the various Communist Party factions split from adult leaders, accusing them of being both corrupt and irrelevant to the needs of Sri Lanka's peasantry.

The revolutionary movement had an obvious attraction to the many students who were the sons of peasants and who had taken advantage of free college education only to find no jobs available upon graduation. The 1971 uprising led to the declaration of a state of emergency that did not end until February 1977.

Mrs. Sirimavo Bandaranaike, the prime minister from 1960-65 and again from 1970-77, was defeated in the general elections of 1977 by Junius Jayewardene's United National Party. Nepotism, abuses of power, and corruption, in addition to the poor economic situation, were the major issues in the campaign. In 1976 there had been severe student and labor unrest.

Under the Jayewardene government, Sri Lanka made a dramatically swift turn away from socialism and toward capitalism. The tea plantations, for instance, had been allowed to run down after being seized by the government in the early 1970s; under Jayewardene, private managers were put in charge of money-losing state corporations, particularly in efforts to boost the major exports—tea, rubber, and coconut. Foreign investment increased sharply, and the government set out to increase electricity generation and farm irrigation by drafting plans for five major dams and reservoirs to be built within six years. To bring hope to the rural poor, Prime Minister Ranasinghe Premadasa, who is also Minister of Housing, built the first of what he said would be 25,000 model villages.

HISTORY: The earliest inhabitants of Sri Lanka (formerly Ceylon) have left few traces. The Sinhalese, who form the bulk of the present population, came to the island from northern India in the 6th century B.C. They founded their capital at Anuradhapura, which became a major religious center following the conversion of Sri Lanka to Buddhism in the 3rd century B.C. Invasions from south India, notably by the Tamils, forced the Sinhalese into the southwest of the island. In the 12th century A.D., Arab traders appeared in Ceylon. The island's coastal areas were occupied by the Portuguese in the 16th century. By the middle of the 17th century, their possessions had been taken over by the Dutch

1795: The Dutch possessions are taken over by Britain

1802: The Crown Colony of Ceylon is established

1815: All of the island of Ceylon is brought under British rule

1948: Sri Lanka becomes independent, with dominion status in the British Commonwealth

1956-59: S.W.R.D. Bandaranaike becomes prime minister, heading a leftist coalition. His term is marked by bloody riots between Sinhalese and Tamils, and ends with his assassination

1960-65: New elections bring another leftist coalition to power, with Mrs. Sirimavo Bandaranaike, wife of the slain leader, as the world's first woman prime minister. Her government adopts a neutralist policy and nationalizes a number of Western oil companies. A dispute with the United States and Britain results

1965-66: Elections result in the victory of the pro-Western United National Party, led by Dudley Senanayake. His government agrees to compensation for the expropriated oil companies, and the United States agrees to resume economic aid to Sri Lanka, cut off at the time the companies were nationalized

1968: Sri Lanka becomes first of the developing nations to achieve the goal of a 5 percent rise in per capita income

1970: Mrs. Bandaranaike returns to power; new leftist government recognizes North Korea, North Vietnam, the Vietcong's provisional government of South Vietnam, and East Germany

1971: Revolutionary students, seeking to replace the government with one more militantly socialist, lead an uprising that results in the death of thousands of rebels and civilians

1972: Ceylon becomes a republic within the Commonwealth and is renamed Sri Lanka under a new constitution; William Gopallawa is appointed the republic's first president by Mrs. Bandaranaike; National Assembly approves land reform plan

1977: Sirimavo Bandaranaike's Freedom Party is defeated in general elections; Junius Richard Jayewardene becomes prime minister following his United National Party's victory. Sri Lanka amends constitution to give nation French-style presidential governing system which dilutes power of elected assembly, reduces prime minister and cabinet to figureheads and concentrates power in hands of popularly elected, all-powerful president, to be chosen every six years (after initial term by Prime Minister Jayewardene). Opposition attempts to stir anti-government feeling over the changes prove futile

1978: At ceremony combining presidential inauguration with celebration of Sri Lanka's 30th year of independence, Prime Minister Jayewardene is sworn in as first president under new system. Tamil is granted the status of a national language. A jet crash in Colombo takes the lives of 183 Indonesians, Moslems returning from a pilgrimage to Mecca. New constitution becomes effective

1979: Foreign investment, encouraged by President Jayewardene's politics, rises to an annual rate of $40 million, 13 times greater than in the last year of the previous government. The Liberation Tigers, young Tamil extremists, stage a wave of killings, with more conservative Tamils as the main victims

SUDAN

Area: 967,494 sq. mi. **Population:** 16,800,000 (1978 est.)

Official Name: Democratic Republic of the Sudan **Capital:** Khartoum **Nationality:** Sudanese **Languages:** Arabic, the official language is the native tongue of about 51% of the population; the Negroes of southern Sudan speak about 32 different languages, with English the chief commercial language **Religion:** The religion of the 12 northern provinces is Islam, whose adherents include about 70% of the population; most of the southern tribes are animist (25%). There are also some small Christian communities (5%) **Flag:** Horizontal stripes of red, white, and black, with a green triangle at the hoist **Anthem:** Soldiers of God **Currency:** Sudanese pound (.40 per U.S. $1)

Location: Northeast Africa. Sudan, the largest country in Africa is bounded on the north by Egypt, on the east by the Red Sea and Ethiopia, on the south by Kenya, Uganda, and Zaire, and on the west by the Central African Empire, Chad, and Libya **Features:** An immense plateau sprawls over 3 distinct natural regions, ranging from the Libyan and Sahara deserts and plateaus in the north to grassy plains in the center to a great swamp and tropical savanna in the south **Chief Rivers:** Nile (the Blue Nile and White Nile join at Khartoum)

Head of State and of Government: President: Gen. Jaafar Muhammad al-Nimeiry, born 1929, seized power in 1969, became the first elected president in 1971 and was reelected in 1977. He is also prime minister (since 1977) **Effective Date of Present Constitution:** 1973 **Legislative Body:** People's Assembly (unicameral), with 304 members (274 popularly elected) belonging to the Sudanese Socialist Union party **Local Government:** 18 provinces, headed by appointed commissioners and councils; the 6 provinces of the Southern Region have a joint semiautonomous government

Ethnic Composition: The population of the 12 northern provinces is comprised mainly of Moslem Arabs and Nubians, who together constitute more than two-thirds of the population; in the south are Nilotic, Sudanic and black tribes **Population Distribution:** 13.2% urban **Density:** 17 inhabitants per sq. mi.

Largest Cities: (1975 est.) Khartoum 321,666, Omdurman 305,308, Khartoum North 161,278, Port Sudan 123,000

Per Capita Income: $334 (1978) **Gross National Product (GNP):** $5.7 billion (1978) **Economic Statistics:** In 1973, 39% of GNP was from agriculture (long-staple cotton, sugarcane, gum arabic, livestock), 11% from industry (food, and vegetable oil processing), and 27% from trade and services **Minerals and Mining:** Small-scale production of iron ore, chromite, manganese ore, slate, gold, and gypsum; deposits of asbestos, slate and tin exist **Labor Force:** 8,000,000 (1976), with 77% in agriculture **Foreign Trade:** Exports, mainly cotton, gum arabic, sesame, peanuts, oil cake and meal, and sheep and goats, totaled $483 million in 1976. Imports, chiefly cotton textiles, motor vehicles and parts, electrical and nonelectrical machinery, base metals and manufactures, chemicals and petroleum products, totaled $853 million **Principal Trade Partners:** Britain, India, Japan, France, Iran, China, West Germany, Italy, United States, Egypt, Saudi Arabia, Iran

Vital Statistics: Birthrate, 47.8 per 1,000 of pop. (1975); death rate, 17.5 **Life Expectancy:** 50 years **Health Statistics:** 982 inhabitants per hospital bed; 11,236 per physician (1975) **Infant Mortality:** 93.6 per 1,000 births **Illiteracy:** 80% **Education Statistics:** 4,530 primary and secondary schools, with combined enrollment of 1,386,517 (1974) **Enrollment in Higher Education:** 21,342 (1975) **GNP Expended on Education:** 8% (1974)

Transportation: Paved roads total 335 mi. (1976) **Motor Vehicles:** 50,400 (1972) **Passenger Cars:** 29,200 **Railway Mileage:** 2,895 **Ports:** Port Sudan, Suakin **Major Airlines:** Sudan Airways, government owned, operates domestically and internationally **Communications:** Government owned **Radio Transmitters:** 7 **Licenses:** 1,300,000 (1973) **Television Transmitters:** 3 **Receivers:** 100,000 (1975) **Telephones:** 60,000 (1976) **Newspapers:** 4 dailies, 8 copies per 1,000 inhabitants (1975)

Weights and Measures: Metric system is the legal standard, but British and Egyptian standards are also used **Travel Requirements:** Passport; visa, valid 3 months; $14.65 fee; 4 photos

The Sudan is Africa's largest country, almost one-third the size of the continental United States, but only a small part of its area, ranging from barren desert to tropical rain forest, is productive. Forty percent of the potentially arable land in the Arab world lies within its boundaries, but only 10 percent of this is under cultivation. Long-staple cotton, the chief export, is grown mainly in the irrigated triangle of land known as the Gezira Plain. This fertile area, just below the confluence of the White and Blue Niles at Khartoum, the capital, and other irrigated areas are a major source also of food and fodder crops.

Crops are raised also in the central rainlands, but production is uncertain because of droughts. Waters of the White Nile backing up into northern Sudan behind Egypt's Aswan Dam will eventually fill the need for additional irrigation.

Of all the African nations only Benin has had a greater number of coups and countercoups. Only Nigeria and Zaire have fought civil wars as cruel as the 17-year conflict, during which 500,000 died, between the Sudan's majority-status Arabs in the north and the minority Christian and pagan blacks in the south. Major General Jaafar al-Nimeiry, who himself had seized power in a coup in May 1969, negotiated an end to the war in 1972 by granting regional autonomy to the south.

Nimeiry has survived numerous assassination attempts and two coups that were uncovered before they were begun. Three that were attempted did not succeed, including the revolt led by dissident army elements in July 1976. In this most recent attempt the rebels were defeated by loyal soldiers after having managed to travel 1,000 miles across the desert undetected. Accusing Libya of being behind the uprising, the Sudanese government severed diplomatic relations with the Libyans.

In foreign affairs, the Sudan is a member of the UN, the Arab League, and the Organization of African Unity. The nation participated on the Arab side in the Yom Kippur War. Relations with the U.S. had been troubled by the Arab-Israeli War, by the commutation in 1974 of the sentences of eight Black September terrorists found guilty of the murders of three diplomats 15 months earlier, and by their subsequent release to the Palestinians. But more recently, Nimeiry, following Egypt's lead, brought the Sudan closer to the West.

In 1979, the Sudan was one of only three Arab states to endorse Egypt's peace treaty with Israel.

HISTORY: Nubia, the northern half of Sudan, was colonized by Egypt centuries before the Christian era. In the 6th century A.D., the Nubians embraced Coptic Christianity, but in the 15th century were converted to Islam by conquering Arabs. Although the Arabs extended their conquests to the south, it was not until 1821 that all of Sudan was unified by Egypt

1881-85: Sudanese, led by the Mahdi, a Moslem religious fanatic, revolt against Egyptian rule and win control over most of Sudan

1898-99: Anglo-Egyptian army defeats Mahdi's followers; Sudan is proclaimed an Anglo-Egyptian condominium under a governor-general; however, Britain dominates the administration of the Sudan

1924: Egyptian troops mutiny in the Sudan; the British governor-general is murdered; the British expel the Egyptians from the Sudan and assume its rule

1936: Status of Sudan is affirmed by Anglo-Egyptian treaty

1948: In Sudan's first elections, Independence Front, favoring an independent republic, wins large majority over National Front, which favors union with Egypt

1953: Britain and Egypt conclude an agreement providing for Sudanese self-government

1956: Sudan is proclaimed an independent republic

1958: Gen. Ibrahim Abboud seizes power in military coup, dissolves parliament, nullifies constitution, and promises reforms

1964-65: Abboud resigns following popular rioting against his regime and a civilian government is set up; elections are held for a constituent assembly to draft new constitution; Mohammed Ahmed Mahgoub becomes prime minister of a coalition government; black Sudanese rebels in southern provinces launch widespread attacks against government forces

1968: Constituent assembly is dissolved and new elections are held; new assembly elects a supreme council, with Ismail al-Azhari as president

1969: A military coup led by Colonel (now Major General) Jaafar al-Nimeiry overthrows supreme council, annuls provisional constitution, and establishes revolutionary council

1971: Nimeiry is briefly toppled by Communist-backed rebel officers but regains power in countercoup and is elected president

1973: Sudan adopts a new constitution. Oil discovered in Red Sea

1976: Diplomatic relations with Libya are severed following Libyan support of an abortive coup against Nimeiry

1977: U.S. agrees to sell 12 F-5 jet fighters to Sudan

1978: Government and opposition announce reconciliation, formally ending nine years of intermittent conflict

SURINAME

Area: 60,239 sq. mi. **Population:** 450,000 (1978 est.)

Official Name: Republic of Suriname **Capital:** Paramaribo **Nationality:** Surinamese **Languages:** Dutch is the official language; English is also widely used. The majority speak a Creole lingua franca called Sranang Tongo, or Taki Taki **Religion:** 26% Hindu, 26% Moslem, 24% Protestant, and 23% Roman Catholic **Flag:** A wide horizontal red band with a centered golden yellow star, separated by narrow white stripes from green stripes top and bottom **Anthem:** N.A. **Currency:** Suriname guilder (florin) (1.785 per U.S. $1)

Location: Northeast coast of South America. It is bordered on the north by the Atlantic Ocean, on the east by French Guiana, on the south by Brazil, and on the west by Guyana **Features:** The three chief zones are the coastal belt (partly protected by dikes), the central zones of forests and savannas, and the southern hill zone, comprising 75% of the area, and rising to over 4,000 feet **Chief Rivers:** Suriname, Saramacca, Coppename, Nickerie, Tapanahoni, Marowijne (Maroni), Corantijn (Courantyne)

Head of State: President: Dr. Johan Henri Eliza Ferrier, elected 1975 **Head of Government:** Minister-President (premier) Henck A.E. Arron, born 1937, reappointed 1977 **Effective Date of Present Constitution:** November 1975 **Legislative Body:** Parliament (unicameral), called the *Staten*, with 39 members elected for 4 years **Local Government:** 9 districts, under appointed commissioners

Ethnic Composition: 37% Hindustanis (descendants of Indian laborers), 31% Creoles (of African descent), 17% Javanese, 11% Bush Negroes (descendants of escaped African slaves), 3% Amerindians (of Carib and Arawak stock), and minorities of 7,000 Chinese and 7,000 Europeans (chiefly Dutch) and Lebanese. More than 100,000 Surinamese Hindustani are currently living in the Netherlands **Population Distribution:** N.A. **Density:** 7.5 inhabitants per sq. mi.

Largest Cities: (1974 est.) Paramaribo 150,000; (1964 census) Nieuw-Nickerie 7,400, Meerzorg 5,000, Marienburg 3,500, Moengo 2,100

Per Capita Income: $1,519 (1978) **Gross National Product (GNP):** $680 million (1978) **Economic Statistics:** About 36% of the GNP is derived from the bauxite industry. Most of the balance comes from agriculture (rice, coffee, sugar, citrus fruits, coconuts, corn, cocoa, tobacco), fishing and shrimping, and lumbering. Industry, other than the processing of alumina and aluminum from bauxite, is confined to sawmilling, rice and sugar milling, and the production of rum and cement **Minerals and Mining:** Suriname is the third-ranking source of bauxite, producing more than 10% of the world supply; gold is also mined commercially **Labor Force:** In 1974, 29% of the workers were engaged in agriculture and 15% in industry **Foreign Trade:** Exports, more than 90% of which was bauxite ore, alumina and aluminum, the rest being citrus fruits, bananas, shrimp, rice, and plywood, totaled $277 million in 1975. Imports, mainly machinery, manufactured goods, textiles, vehicles, petroleum products, iron and steel, and foods, totaled $262 million **Principal Trade Partners:** United States, Netherlands, Britain, Norway, Venezuela, Japan

Vital Statistics: Birthrate, 40.9 per 1,000 of pop.; death rate, 7.2 **Life Expectancy:** 66 years **Health Statistics:** 180 inhabitants per hospital bed; 2,030 per physician (1974) **Infant Mortality:** 30.4 per 1,000 births **Illiteracy:** 16% **Education Statistics:** About 550 primary and secondary schools, with a total enrollment of 141,043 (1975) **Enrollment in Higher Education:** 2,138 GNP Expended on Education: 4.7%

Transportation: Paved roads total about 300 mi. **Motor Vehicles:** 39,000 (1976) **Passenger Cars:** 28,800 **Railway Mileage:** 100 **Ports:** Paramaribo, Nieuw-Nickerie, Albina **Major Airlines:** Suriname Airways handles domestic and international flights **Communications:** Government and privately owned **Radio Transmitters:** 5 **Receivers:** 112,000 (1976) **Television Transmitters:** 3 **Receivers:** 38,000 (1976) **Telephones:** 19,000 (1976) **Newspapers:** 7 dailies (1975), 52 copies per 1,000 inhabitants (1974)

Weights and Measures: Metric system **Travel Requirements:** Passport; no visa; onward ticket

On attaining independence in 1975, Suriname immediately faced a major problem stemming from its multiracial composition—37 percent Hindustani, 31 percent Creole of African descent, 17 percent Javanese, 11 percent Bush Negro. Owing to Hindustani fears of the Creole-dominated government, over 100,000 Surinamers emigrated to the Netherlands prior to independence, thus stripping the emerging nation of between a quarter and a third of its human resources. The emigrants were predominantly well-educated middle and upper-class entrepreneurs, managers and technicians. The Surinamese government has appealed for the émigrés to return home to help in the development of the resource-rich former colony. To assist in this development the Netherlands has promised to grant Suriname $1.5 billion in aid over the next decade. It has been suggested that the Dutch generosity is based on a desire to improve economic conditions in Suriname enough so that the Surinamese refugees will return to their tropical homeland and leave poor-paying jobs and welfare rolls in Amsterdam. Another problem is the migration from the countryside to the city, with the result that Suriname may have to import food rather than export it.

Suriname is rich in minerals, forests and potential water power. The country's bauxite deposits are believed to be among the richest in the world. The mining, processing, and exporting of this resource (and since 1965 of alumina and aluminum) constitute the backbone of the economy. Sites of the two major bauxite deposits—Moengo and Paranam—are accessible to navigable rivers emptying into the Atlantic. Food processing and lumbering account for other important industries. Alcoa Aluminum, at a cost of $150 million, has built a dam for the production of hydroelectric energy on the Suriname River.

The present government, headed by Premier Henck Arron, took power in the 1973 elections, when the National Party Coalition, composed mostly of Creoles, unseated the United Reformed Party, led by Jaggernath Lachmon and composed mainly of Hindustanis and Javanese.

HISTORY: Christopher Columbus sighted the coast of the area in 1498, but the first successful settlement was not established until 1651 by the British. The colony prospered on a plantation economy based on slave labor imported from Africa. Notable among the emigrants from other New World colonies were Jews from Brazil, who in 1665 erected the first synagogue in the Western Hemisphere. The Netherlands acquired Suriname from Britain in exchange for Dutch rights in Nieuw Amsterdam (Manhattan Island, New York). In the 18th and early 19th centuries the colony, as a result of wars and treaties, was shuffled among England, France and the Netherlands

1815: Netherlands finally regains Suriname at Vienna Congress

1863: Slavery is abolished. Importation of Hindustani, Javanese and Chinese contract laborers follows

1954: Suriname is granted internal autonomy

1973: Creole-dominated National Party Coalition (NPK) wins elections. NPK leader Henck Arron becomes premier

1975: Suriname gains independence

1978: National Party Coalition reelected by landslide in nation's first elections since independence

1979: A 200-mile zone is announced to regulate fishing and other economic activities in the Atlantic Ocean

SWAZILAND

Area: 6,705 sq. mi. **Population:** 500,000 (1978 est.)
Official Name: Kingdom of Swaziland **Capital:** Mbabane **Nationality:** Swazi **Languages:** The official languages are English and si-Swati; Zulu is used by a minority **Religion:** About 43% are animists, with about 500 Moslems; the rest of the population is Christian **Flag:** Horizontal stripes of blue, yellow, red, yellow, and blue with a traditional Swazi shield, spears and staff in black and white in the center **Anthem:** National Anthem, beginning "O God, Bestower of the blessings of the Swazi" **Currency:** Lilangeni (0.84 per U.S. $1)

Location: Southern Africa. Swaziland is almost entirely surrounded by South Africa, except for a 70-mile-long border with Mozambique on the east **Features:** The country consists of three well-defined regions known locally as the high, middle, and low velds, all roughly of equal breadth. The humid highveld in the west is mountainous; a plateau lies in the center, and to the east is a subtropical low plain **Chief Rivers:** Komati, Umbuluzi, Great Usutu, Mkonda

Head of State: King Sobhuza II, born 1899; Ngwenyama (the Lion), head of the Swazi nation since 1921, made head of state in 1968 **Head of Government:** Prime Minister: Gen. Maphevu Dlamini, reappointed Jan. 1979 **Effective Date of Present Constitution:** October 13, 1978 **Legislative Body:** Parliament, or Liblandla, (bicameral) consists of a 20-member Senate, and a 50-member House of Assembly; 10 of each are appointed by the king, the rest are elected by the populace. There are no political parties, and the function of parliament is restricted to advising the king and debating proposals **Local Government:** 4 districts, under appointed commissioners, and the 2 municipalities of Mbabane and Manzini

Ethnic Composition: The African population is predominantly Swazi, with a Zulu minority; both belong to the Bantu group. About 3% are non-Africans **Population Distribution:** 15% urban **Density:** 75 inhabitants per sq. mi.

Largest Cities: (1976 est.) Manzini 26,000, Mbabane 22,000

Per Capita Income: $634 (1978) **Gross National Product (GNP):** $340 million (1978) **Economic Statistics:** 75% are engaged in subsistence agriculture (maize, the subsistence crop, and such commercial crops as sugar, timber, citrus fruits, cotton, rice, and pineapples), which accounts for about 29% of GNP. Mining and manufacturing (machinery, beverages, chemicals, apparel, metal products, processed agricultural products) contribute about 37% of GNP **Minerals and Mining:** Deposits of iron ore, asbestos, and coal are exploited; kaolin, barites, gold, and pyrophyllite are exploited on a smaller scale **Labor Force:** 180,000 (1970), with 75% engaged in agriculture, and 5% in industry; many work in South Africa **Foreign Trade:** Exports, chiefly iron ore, sugar, wood pulp and other forest products, and asbestos, totaled $152 million in 1975. Imports, mainly manufactured goods, machinery and transport equipment, food and beverages, and tobacco, totaled $151 million **Principal Trade Partners:** South Africa, Britain, Japan

Vital Statistics: Birthrate, 49 per 1,000 of pop. (1975); death rate, 21.8 **Life Expectancy:** 44 years **Health Statistics:** 285 inhabitants per hospital bed; 7,538 per physician (1975) **Infant Mortality:** N.A. **Illiteracy:** 64% **Education Statistics:** 412 primary and secondary schools, with combined enrollment of 106,347 (1975) **Enrollment in Higher Education:** 1,150 (1976) **GNP Expended on Education:** 5% (1975)

Transportation: Paved roads total 241 mi. **Motor Vehicles:** 15,000 (1976) **Passenger Cars:** 7,900 **Railway Mileage:** 200 **Ports:** None **Major Airlines:** Royal Swazi National Airways operates international flights **Communications:** Government owned **Radio Transmitters:** 7 **Receivers:** 60,000 (1976) **Television:** None **Telephones:** 8,000 (1976) **Newspapers:** 1 several times a week, 111 copies per 1,000 inhabitants (1974)

Weights and Measures: Metric system **Travel Requirements:** Passport; no visa

The smallest of three former British protectorates in southern Africa to attain independence, Swaziland is the home of a gentle Bantu people. For the Swazis, British protection was not merely a colonialist device. It saved them from Zulu and Boer invasions and was also the shield against absorption into South Africa's apartheid system when the black African nation of Swaziland became independent in 1968.

Along with the other former protectorates, Botswana and Lesotho, Swaziland is geographically and economically linked to South Africa, but all three nations have asserted a determination to preserve political independence. Although all are members of the South African Customs and Monetary Area, in 1974 Swaziland issued its own currency, and political and economic tensions with South Africa have increased.

Despite its small size and landlocked situation between South Africa's highveld and the Mozambique border, Swaziland possesses exceptional potential for economic independence. In addition to major resources of iron ore, asbestos, and coal, the country produces sugar, rice, tobacco, cotton, citrus fruits, and other crops. It also has a wood-pulp industry based on a rapidly growing forest of pine and eucalyptus. Japan has become a major customer for iron ore, and rice production has been increased with the help of Nationalist China.

Most of the country's industries are still owned by British and South African interests, but, particularly in farmland, there is a program in operation under which Swazis are buying back foreign-owned property.

One of the major revenue producers for the government is the gambling casino of the Royal Swazi Hotel, near Mbabane, the capital. Since gambling is illegal in South Africa, a large part of the clientele is made up of white South Africans. But those around the gaming tables also include whites from Europe and black Africans.

In 1973 King Sobhuza discarded Swaziland's five-year-old constitution and, in 1977, replaced the nation's parliamentary system with an assembly of tribal leaders. The electoral process was restored in October 1978, under a new constitution, as Swazis voted for members of an electoral college, which in turn, was to name 40 members of the 50-man National Assembly and 10 of the nation's 20 senators. The remaining legislators were to be appointed by King Sobhuza.

HISTORY: The Swazis settled in present-day Swaziland in 1820 after being expelled by the Zulus from the land north of the Pongola River. Continued harassment by the Zulus led them to seek aid from the British, who succeeded in establishing friendly relations between the two tribes. The country's independence was guaranteed by the British and Transvaal governments in 1881 and 1884, and was followed by the establishment in 1890 of a provisional government representative of the Swazi and the two guarantors

1902-7: The Transvaal's rights in Swaziland pass to Britain following the Boer War; after a period of administration by the British governor of the Transvaal, Swaziland becomes a high commission territory ruled by a British commissioner

1921: Sobhuza II becomes Ngwenyama, head of the Swazi nation, after 20-year regency of his mother

1949: Opposition to South Africa's apartheid policy causes Britain to reject request that Swaziland, along with Basutoland (now Lesotho) and Bechuanaland (now Botswana), be transferred to South African control

1967: Swaziland wins self-government under a new constitution with Sobhuza as king

1968: Swaziland becomes independent state and a UN member

1969: Swaziland, disappointed by aid offered by Britain, moves to expand trade with African neighbors to boost national revenue; joins in customs union with South Africa

1973: In April, King Sobhuza repeals the constitution and assumes supreme power

1976: Colonel Maphevu Dlamini becomes prime minister

1977: King Sobhuza abolishes the parliamentary system and replaces it with an assembly based on tribal leadership

1978: Voters create electoral college under new constitution

1979: King Subhuza celebrates 80th birthday with big party

SWEDEN

Area: 173,665 sq. mi. **Population:** 8,268,086 (1978 est.)
Official Name: Kingdom of Sweden **Capital:** Stockholm **Nationality:** Swedish **Languages:** Swedish, the official language, is spoken by the vast majority; in the north there are Lappand Finnish-speaking minorities **Religion:** About 95% of the population is Lutheran, the state religion **Flag:** An extended yellow cross on a field of blue **Anthem:** Thou Ancient, Thou Freeborn **Currency:** Swedish Krona (4.4 per U.S. $1)

Location: Northern Europe, occupying the eastern part of the Scandinavian Peninsula. It is bordered on the northeast by Finland, on the east and south by the Gulf of Bothnia and the Baltic Sea, on the southwest by the Öresund, Kattegat, and Skagerrak, and on the west by Norway **Features:** The land is gently rolling in the south and mountainous in the north. About half the country is wooded, and lakes cover some 9% of the area **Chief Rivers:** Göta-Klar, Lule, Ume, Angerman, Dal

Head of State: King Carl XVI Gustaf, born 1946, succeeded 1973
Head of Government: Premier Ola Ullsten, born 1931, assumed office 1978 **Effective Date of Present Constitution:** January 1975
Legislative Body: Parliament (unicameral). The *Riksdag* consists of 349 members elected for 3-year terms **Local Government:** 24 counties, with appointed governors and elected councils

Ethnic Composition: The population is largely homogeneous, with a Lapp minority of 17,000. There are 425,000 immigrants, mainly from other Nordic countries, Greece and Turkey **Population Distribution:** 81.4% urban (1970) **Density:** 48 inhabitants per sq. mi.

Largest Cities: (M.A. = Metropolitan Area) (1977 est.) Stockholm 658,743 (M.A. 1,374,897), Göteborg 440,211 (M.A. 693,562), Malmö 238,567 (M.A. 453,914), Uppsala 141,234, Norrköping 120,669, Västeras 118,131

Per Capita Income: $8,894 (1978) **Gross National Product (GNP):** $74 billion (1978) **Economic Statistics:** About 5% of the GNP is derived from agriculture (chiefly oats, wheat, rye, barley, potatoes, and dairy produce), 59% from trade and services, and 36% from manufacturing (a major ship producer due to the wealth of timber and minerals), construction and mining **Minerals and Mining:** High grade iron ore is the primary mineral but there are also smaller deposits of gold, silver, lead, copper, zinc, pyrites, tungsten, manganese, granite, quartz, and marble **Labor Force:** 4,100,000 (1976), with 37% in mining, manufacturing and construction; 22% in trade and transportation; 6% in agriculture; 31% in public service **Foreign Trade:** Exports, chiefly lumber, pulp and paper, ships, iron ore, machinery, and base metals totaled $21.7 billion in 1978. Imports, mainly machinery, chemicals and fuel products, and base metals, totaled $20.4 billion **Principal Trade Partners:** EC countries, United States, Canada, Norway, Finland, USSR, Saudi Arabia

Vital Statistics: Birthrate, 11.6 per 1,000 of pop. (1977); death rate, 10.7 **Life Expectancy:** 74 years **Health Statistics:** 66 inhabitants per hospital bed; 615 per physician (1974) **Infant Mortality:** 8.0 per 1,000 births (1977) **Illiteracy:** Negligible **Education Statistics:** 4,819 primary, secondary, and vocational schools, with an enrollment of 1,289,500 (1974) **Enrollment in Higher Education:** 162,640, (1975) **GNP Expended on Education:** 7.5% (1974)

Transportation: Surfaced roads total 17,514 mi. (1973) **Motor Vehicles:** 3,043,400 (1976) **Passenger Cars:** 2,881,000 **Railway Mileage:** 7,538 **Ports:** Göteborg, Stockholm, Malmö, Helsingborg, Trelleborg, Gävle, Luleå, Sundsvall, Norrköping **Major Airlines:** Scandinavian Airlines System (SAS), owned jointly by Sweden, Norway and Denmark, operates internationally; AB Linjeflyg, the Swedish affiliate of SAS, operates domestically **Communications:** Government controlled **Radio Transmitters:** 282 **Licenses:** 3,203,000 (1976) **Television Transmitters:** 358 **Licenses:** 2,988,000 (1976) **Telephones:** 5,673,000 (1976) **Newspapers:** 135 dailies, 572 copies per 1,000 inhabitants (1975)

Weights and Measures: Metric system **Travel Requirements:** Passport; no visa for 3 months

---

Once upon a time Sweden was world-renowned for its idyllic stability; for life without hunger, war, or other material distress; for an overall reasonableness in settling its affairs. Intruding on the Swedish idyll in the last few years, however, have been such extraordinary developments as strikes by workers in defiance of union leaders now considered part of the Establishment, a new militance among organized salaried employees in the face of heavy taxes and an increasingly steep cost of living. However, Swedish unemployment is still among the world's lowest, and Swedish per capita gross national product is among the world's highest.

Although Sweden is often described abroad as a socialist state, it is not so in the Marxist sense. According to Swedish authorities, theirs is a pragmatic socialism dedicated to assuring material security for all and establishing state-owned enterprises only in areas that private enterprise cannot or will not enter. Roughly 90 percent of Swedish industry is privately owned. A little more than 5 percent is in public hands, and the remaining enterprises are cooperatives.

The high cost of social welfare, for which roughly one-third of the budget is earmarked, is met from the high taxes and from contributions to compulsory insurance plans. Among the principal features of the social welfare state are a national health insurance, a pension system, free prenatal care and child delivery, annual allowances to the mother until a child reaches the age of 16, free tuition at Swedish universities, home-furnishing loans for newlyweds, and rent rebates for large families.

Under a national policy of full employment, the state operates a job service, moves unemployed persons to areas where work is available and offers retraining to those who lose jobs through automation or disability. Despite recent labor troubles, Sweden's union-management relations, compared with those of most other highly industrialized countries, have on the whole been placid since the 1930s. In general, labor's demands have been tempered by the need to compete in world markets; exports account for roughly one-fourth of the GNP.

Figuring largely in Sweden's economic and social achievements is its policy of neutrality, under which it has managed to avoid war for close to 160 years. But Sweden's neutrality, the Swedes insist, is an avoidance of alliances, not a neutrality of opinion. This policy, they say, is not abridged by strong stands taken on conflicts far from their shores, notably denunciations by government ministers of U.S. involvement in Vietnam and the military takeover in Chile.

The welfare programs were developed by the Social Democratic party, which dominated Swedish politics from 1936 until 1976, when amid complaints that high taxes and the power of an unimaginative bureaucracy were stifling initiative and threatening freedom, a coalition of three nonsocialist parties won control of the *Riksdag*. Thorbjörn Fälldin became prime minister in the coalition government. But the coalition broke down in 1978, when the Liberal party and the Moderate Unity (formerly Conservative) party rejected the proposal of Fälldin's Center party to end the construction of nuclear power plants. Henry Allard, Speaker of the *Riksdag*, installed a minority Liberal government, with Ola Ullsten as prime minister. In 1979, after the Three Mile Island accident in the United States, Fälldin promised a strong anti-nuclear campaign for the fall elections. Despite the *Riksdag's* fragmentation, it managed to come together on a family issue to pass overwhelmingly a controversial law against spanking and "verbally abusing" children.

HISTORY: The earliest known reference to the Swedes is by the Roman historian Tacitus, who wrote in A.D. 98 that the Suiones (of the Lake Mälaren area) had a mighty fleet and a host of warriors, and were ruled by an absolute king. By the 6th century they had conquered their southern neighbors, the Götar, and merged with them. During the Viking period (9th—12th centuries), Swedes extended their influence across Russia to the Black Sea and joined with Danes and Norwegians in raids and voyages to Western Europe and the British Isles

829: Christianity is introduced by a Frankish monk, St. Anskar

1150-60: Erik IX stamps out paganism among the Swedes and undertakes a crusade against the Finnish heathens, adding Finland to the Kingdom of Sweden

1319: Sweden and Norway are united under Norway's Magnus VII

1397: Denmark, Sweden, and Norway are united under Denmark's Queen Margrethe to combat the superiority of the German mercantile organization, the Hanse

1523-60: Gustav Eriksson, elected king as Gustavus I, establishes Vasa dynasty, ends the union with Denmark and Norway, cuts ties to the Roman Catholic Church, and establishes a Lutheran state church

1611-32: Gustavus II establishes Sweden as a great European power, expanding the kingdom in wars with Russia and Poland and in the Thirty Years War against the Hapsburgs

1648: Peace of Westphalia gives Sweden German territory and makes Swedish kings princes of the Holy Roman Empire

1700-21: Charles XII launches a brilliant defensive campaign against Russia, Poland, and Denmark in the Northern War, but a series of victories is followed by a disastrous invasion of Russia, capped by the capitulation of the Swedish Army at Poltava (1709). After further defeats, Sweden declines as a major European power, having been forced to give up most of its continental conquests and possessions

1805-09: Sweden joins the Allies against Napoleon, loses its German Territories to France and Finland to Russia. Gustavus IV is overthrown; constitutional monarchy is established

1813-14: Entering its last major war, Sweden again joins the Allies against Napoleon, with Swedish forces led by the former French Marshal Jean Bernadotte, the chosen successor to the Swedish throne. He and his forces compel Denmark to cede Norway to Sweden

1818: Bernadotte ascends throne as Charles XIV; he steers Sweden toward a policy of neutrality

1905: Union with Norway is terminated peacefully

1917: Parliamentary form of government is established

1920: Sweden's first Social Democratic government is formed

1959: Sweden joins European Free Trade Association

1973: Carl XVI Gustaf succeeds to the throne upon the death of his grandfather, Gustaf VI Adolf

1975: A new constitution comes into effect which restricts the function of the king to a ceremonial role and approves the unicameral parliament in effect since 1971

1976: King Carl XVI Gustaf marries Sylvia Sommerlath. Swedish parliament adopts a law giving employees of certain companies the right to place two worker-delegates on the board of directors. Nonsocialist bloc (Center, Liberal and Moderate Unity parties) wins election; Thorbjörn Fälldin becomes prime minister

1977: Swedish cradle-to-grave "welfare state" palls as economy continues slumping badly, with many once-profitable exports reaching uncompetitive price levels due to high labor costs and sated world markets. Three of nation's largest shipbuilders are nationalized and merged; similar moves are made in other industries. Three devaluations of krona improve its position against major world currencies. Investments, GNP decline

1978: Economy reaches crisis stage as prices and unemployment continue rising; recession is considered nation's worst in 40 years. *Riksdag* abrogates Salic Law, thus allowing female succession to the throne; second parliamentary vote needed to make this part of constitution. Liberal and Moderate Unity parties reject plans of Fälldin's Center party to stop building nuclear power plants. Fälldin resigns. Ola Ullsten becomes minister in minority Liberal government

1979: Second parliamentary vote regarding Salic Law is pending

SWITZERLAND

Area: 15,943 sq. mi. **Population:** 6,550,000 (1978 est.)
Official Name: Swiss Confederation **Capital:** Bern **Nationality:** Swiss **Languages:** German (65%), French (18%), Italian (12%), and Romansch, a Romance language spoken in eastern Switzerland (1%) are official languages. Many Swiss speak more than one language **Religion:** About 48% Protestant, 49% Roman Catholic, 0.3% Jewish **Flag:** A square red field with a white cross in the center **Anthem:** Swiss Psalm **Currency:** Swiss franc (1.72 per U.S. $1)

Location: Central Europe. Switzerland is bounded on the north by Germany, on the east by Austria and Liechtenstein, on the south by Italy, and on the west by France **Features:** About 60% of the country is covered by the great Alpine mountain chain running through the south. The Jura Mountains in the west make up about 10% of the land. The rest is a plateau between the two mountain ranges **Chief Rivers:** Rhine, Rhône, Aare, Inn

Head of State and of Government: Executive authority is vested in the Federal Council, composed of 7 councilors elected for 4 years by the Federal Assembly; each year a president and vice-president are elected. The council, whose members head the 7 federal departments, is the directing power in the nation. President (for 1979): Hans Hürlimann **Effective Date of Present Constitution:** 1848, amended 1874 **Legislative Body:** Federal Assembly (bicameral), consisting of the Council of State, with 46 members and either 3 or 4 year terms, and the National Council, with 200 members elected directly for 4 years **Local Government:** 26 cantons, with elected unicameral legislatures, divided into communes

Ethnic Composition: Traditionally 4 ethnic groups: German, French, Italian, and Romansch, with 932,743 resident foreigners (1978) **Population Distribution:** 58% urban **Density:** 411 inhabitants per sq. mi.

Largest Cities: (1975 est.) Zürich 396,300, Basel 195,700, Geneva 159,200, Bern 152,800, Lausanne 135,200

Per Capita Income: $8,651 (1978) **Gross National Product (GNP):** $54.6 billion (1978) **Economic Statistics:** 7% of GNP is derived from agriculture (dairy products, grains, fruit and vegetables, and wine-growing); 47% from industry (machinery, chemicals, watches); and 46% from commerce and services **Minerals and Mining:** None; rich in forests and waterpower **Labor Force:** 2,700,000 (1976), about one-tenth of whom are self-employed. About 20% are foreigners. Of the total, some 44% are in industry, 8% in agriculture and forestry, and 48% in trade and services **Foreign Trade:** Exports, chiefly machinery, watches, chemicals, and textiles, totaled $17.6 billion in 1977. Imports, mainly chemicals, crude oil, clothing, machines, and motor vehicles, totaled $17.9 billion **Principal Trade Partners:** West Germany, France, United States, Italy, Britain, Austria

Vital Statistics: Birthrate, 11.5 per 1,000 of pop. (1977); death rate, 8.8 **Life Expectancy:** 75 years **Health Statistics:** 88 inhabitants per hospital bed; 559 per physician (1975) **Infant Mortality:** 10.7 per 1,000 births (1977) **Illiteracy:** Negligible **Educational Statistics:** Number of schools N.A.; total enrollment is 1,061,102 (1974) **Enrollment in Higher Education:** 64,720 (1975) **GNP Expended on Education:** 5.3% (1975)

Transportation: Surfaced roads total 37,000 mi. **Motor Vehicles:** 2,011,000 (1974) **Passenger Cars:** 1,723,000 **Railway Mileage:** 3,110 (1972) **Ports:** None **Major Airlines:** Swissair operates domestic and international flights **Communications:** Government controlled **Radio Transmitters:** 211 **Licenses:** 2,108,000 (1976) **Television Transmitters:** 583 **Licenses:** 1,809,000 (1976) **Telephones:** 4,016,000 (1976) **Newspapers:** 95 dailies, 402 copies per 1,000 inhabitants (1975)

Weights and Measures: Metric system **Travel Requirements:** Passport; no visa for 3 months

---

If pacifists want proof of their contentions, they can point to Switzerland, the country that has not sent its troops into foreign wars since 1815. Switzerland has low unemployment amid growing joblessness in much of the rest of the world, and it ranks among the world's wealthiest countries. But, like other countries, it has been plagued by growing inflation rates during the past few years, and federal budgets recently ceased to be balanced.

The Swiss guard their neutrality with a modern army. Switzerland's neutrality was guaranteed by the Congress of Vienna in 1815; dedication to neutrality has even kept Switzerland out of the United Nations. However, Switzerland is a member of several special agencies of the UN and has a permanent observer at the UN.

A member of the Council of Europe, Switzerland in 1972 was one of five members of the European Free Trade Association that signed a free-trade agreement with the EEC.

In part, the Swiss have been able to remain neutral because of the rugged Alps, which cover half the country and are uninviting as a battleground. At the same time, the country, which lacks actual mineral resources, has in its terrain and geographical location features that act as natural resources, and which are in fact the bases of the country's prosperity.

Snow-clad Alpine peaks from whose rushing streams hydroelectric power has been widely developed also constitute a winter vacation mecca, and the central European location of their country has enabled the hardworking Swiss to make it a center for trade, shipping, freight-forwarding, banking, and insurance. And more than a third of Swiss exports consists of machinery, precision instruments, and watches.

The Swiss spirit of tolerance is more recent than the policy of neutrality; religious disputes produced a civil war as late as 1847—a revolt of Catholic rural cantons against the increasing influence of the Protestant cities over the federal government. But division along ethnic lines of French-, German-, and Italian-speaking peoples has been avoided by giving the cantons much power and keeping the federal government tightly reined. Taxes, for example, cannot be increased without a constitutional amendment, which requires a national referendum.

Hard-fought issues are usually absent, because Switzerland has been governed for decades by a coalition of major parties. One of the hardest-fought issues was resolved when the male electorate voted in 1971 to enfranchise Swiss women in federal elections, ending Swiss political backwardness and reversing a decision of 12 years before. The national trend of reaching decisions by consensus has produced a well-ordered country where even strikes are almost unknown, and there are no drastic extremes of wealth and poverty.

In 1979, after long discussion, the French-speaking communes of the Canton of Bern were organized into a new canton—Jura. Nuclear power, on which Switzerland become heavily dependent, became an issue in 1979; a referendum in February rejected a constitutional amendment to restrict it, but, after the Three Mile Island acci-

dent in the United States, the Swiss voted to forbid the construction of any new plant without the approval of the Federal Assembly.

HISTORY: The Helvetii, a Celtic tribe, were the first known inhabitants of Switzerland. The land was conquered by the Romans in 58 B.C. and remained a Roman province for approximately 300 years. In the 5th century, it was overrun by the Alemanni and the Burgundii, and then passed to the Franks. After being split between Swabia and Transjurane Burgundy in the 9th century, it was united under the Holy Roman Empire in 1033

1291: Forest cantons of Schwyz, Uri, and Unterwalden form defensive league in face of growing encroachments by House of Hapsburg

1315: League defeats Austrian armies at Morgarten Pass

1386-88: Joined by five other cantons, the league decisively defeats Austrians, insuring existence of the confederation

1499: Swiss gain virtual independence from Holy Roman Emperor Maximilian I

1519: Ulrich Zwingli, vicar of Zurich Cathedral, attacks practices of Roman Catholic Church; his lectures on New Testament mark beginning of Protestant Reformation in Switzerland

1541: John Calvin introduces Protestantism into Geneva and establishes a theocratic state

1648: Switzerland's formal independence is recognized in the Peace of Westphalia, which ended the Thirty Years War

1798-1803: French Revolution results in creation of Helvetic Republic, which is governed as a French appendage

1815: Perpetual Swiss neutrality is guaranteed by Congress of Vienna

1914-18: Swiss remain neutral in World War I

1939-45: Swiss maintain neutrality during World War II

1959: Women's suffrage, in federal elections, although advocated by federal council and federal assembly, is rejected in referendum

1971: Constitutional amendment gives Swiss women the vote in federal elections and the right to hold federal office

1974: A plebiscite in the French-speaking Jura region of the largely German-speaking canton of Bern results in a narrow majority favoring a separate Jura canton

1978: Acting to stem rise of Swiss franc and protect its export industry and tourism business, government decides to ban further foreign capital investment

1979: Canton of Jura established

SYRIA

Area: 71,722 sq. mi. **Population:** 7,840,000 (1978 est.)

Official Name: Syrian Arab Republic **Capital:** Damascus **Nationality:** Syrian **Languages:** Arabic is the official and predominant language; French and English are also used, and Armenian and Kurdish are spoken by minorities **Religion:** 70% Sunni Moslem, 16% other Moslem, and 13% Christian **Flag:** Horizontal stripes of red, white, black with a centered golden hawk and inscription **Anthem:** National Anthem, beginning "Defenders of the homeland, salute" **Currency:** Syrian pound (3.95 per U.S. $1)

Location: Southwest Asia. Syria is bounded on the north by Turkey, on the east by Iraq, on the south by Jordan and Israel, and on the west by Lebanon and the Mediterranean Sea **Features:** The country consists of a narrow coastal plain, east of which is a highland region that is continued to the south by the Lebanon and Anti-Lebanon Mountains. Fertile plains form the central region, with the Syrian Desert to the southeast. North of the desert region lies the fertile Euphrates River Valley **Chief Rivers:** Euphrates, Orontes

Head of State: President: Lt. Gen. Hafez al-Assad, born 1928, reelected in 1978 for 7 years **Head of Government:** Premier: Mohammed Ali al-Halabi, appointed March 1978 **Effective Date of Present Constitution:** 1973 **Legislative Body:** People's Council (unicameral), consisting of 195 elected members **Local Government:** 13 provinces, each headed by an appointed governor and a partly elected council, and the municipality of Damascus

Ethnic Composition: 90% are Arabs; minorities include Circassians, Armenians, Turks, and Kurds **Population Distribution:** 50% urban **Density:** 109 inhabitants per sq. mi.

Largest Cities: (1976 est.) Damascus 936,567, Aleppo 710,636, Homs 314,744; (1970 census) Hama 137,421, Latakia 125,716

Per Capita Income: $761 (1978) **Gross National Product (GNP):** $6.4 billion (1978) **Economic Statistics:** 18% of the GNP is derived from agriculture (wheat, barley, cotton); 19% from commerce; 26% from industry (petroleum refining, textiles, cement, glass, apparel, soap, food processing); and 36% from services **Minerals and Mining:** Oil, natural gas, phosphates, asphalt, gypsum and rock salt **Labor Force:** 1,715,000 in 1972; 50% engaged in agriculture and 20% in industry **Foreign Trade:** Exports, chiefly petroleum (62% of total) and raw cotton, totaled $1 billion in 1976. Imports, mainly textiles, machinery, petroleum products, vehicles, and foodstuffs, totaled $2.6 billion **Principal Trade Partners:** EC countries, USSR, Arab countries, United States

Vital Statistics: Birthrate, 45.4 per 1,000 of pop. (1975); death rate, 14.8 **Life Expectancy:** 57 years **Health Statistics:** 1,071 inhabitants per hospital bed; 3,063 per physician (1975) **Infant Mortality:** 21.7 per 1,000 births (1972) **Illiteracy:** 47% **Education Statistics:** 6,760 primary and secondary schools, with combined enrollment of 1,672,975 (1974) **Enrollment in Higher Education:** 64,094 **GNP Expended on Education:** 4% (1973)

Transportation: Paved roads total 6,820 mi. **Motor Vehicles:** 118,,700 (1976) **Passenger Cars:** 62,800 **Railway Mileage:** 940 **Ports:** Latakia, Baniyas, Tartus **Major Airlines:** Syrian Arab Airlines, government owned, operates domestically and internationally **Communications:** Government owned **Radio Transmitters:** 13 **Receivers:** 2,500,000 (1972) **Television Transmitters:** 7 **Receivers:** 230,000 (1976) **Telephones:** 177,000 (1976) **Newspapers:** 6 dailies (1975), 9 copies per 1,000 inhabitants

Weights and Measures: Metric system and local units are used

Once the center of one of the most ancient civilizations on earth, Syria today seeks a leadership role in the Arab world. As an ardent champion of the Palestinian Liberation Organization, Syria has trained and armed guerrillas at bases within the country.

Syria merged with Egypt in 1958, but seceded in 1961. In the 1970s, it established a joint command and diplomatic coordination with Jordan. In 1979, President Hafez al-Assad of Syria and President Ahmed Hassan al-Bakr of Iraq formed a joint political command. They also agreed to merge their two Ba'ath socialist countries, but took no immediate steps to implement the agreement. Relations between Syria and Iraq have been marred by squabbles about ideological points and national goals; a merger of the two countries, if it occurs, will require dedication and tact on both sides.

President Assad is a military man who took power in a coup in 1970 and has brought stability to Syria.

Before World War I, Syria was part of the Ottoman Empire and loosely included all of what is now Lebanon, Israel, and Jordan, as well as Syria itself. Even today some people speak wistfully of a "Greater Syria." Between the two world wars, the country was under French mandate; it became independent in 1946.

The Syrian people are considered among the most sophisticated in the Arab world, largely because for centuries the country has been a passageway between the Mediterranean world and the Far East.

In recent years Syria has aligned itself closely with the Soviet Union. Its armed forces are equipped by Moscow, and there are believed to be upward of 1,000 Soviet military and civilian advisers in the country. However, Syrian intervention in Lebanon has placed a strain on Soviet relations because Russia has been a supporter of the Palestinians in Lebanon and the use of Soviet weapons by Syria against them has embarrassed Moscow. President Assad tried to patch up the differences in his spring 1977 trip to Moscow.

In spite of the Soviet presence, the left-wing military rulers have outlawed the Syrian Communist Party. President Assad's Ba'ath (Socialist) party is predominant. The press and radio are directly controlled by the state.

Israeli soldiers have occupied part of southwestern Syria since 1967. A demilitarized zone, patrolled by a multinational force under United Nations command, has been established between the Israeli and Syrian forces. The Israeli-occupied area is of strategic importance, and many Israelis want their government to annex it. Syria has little to gain from negotiations with Israel and opposes Egypt's negotiations.

Most recently Syria has been concerned with the civil war in Lebanon, having historically regarded Lebanon as part of "Greater Syria" and not wanting a radical state on its western frontier. In the final phase of the 19-month conflict, Syrian troops and tanks intervened against Palestinian-led forces when it appeared they might win, install a radical state and incite war with Israel. In February 1978 Syrian-dominated peacekeeping forces and Lebanese (both regular troops and right-wing Christian militias) began battling in and around Beirut. In 1979, Syria often sent air force planes into Lebanese air space as a warning to Israel. On one occasion there was a clash between Syrian and Israeli airplanes.

The use of Syrian forces to "stabilize" Lebanon—at first by moving against radical Palestinians and more recently by attacking pro-Israeli Christians—has created a dilemma for President Assad. If he withdraws his forces, he risks renewed civil war and possibly the installation of a pro-Israeli government in Beirut; but if he keeps Syrian troops in Lebanon indefinitely, he continues putting a severe strain on Syrian manpower, morale and material resources.

HISTORY: Ancient Syria was the home of Amorites, Aramaeans, Phoenicians, and Hebrews. After a succession of invaders that included Assyrians, Babylonians, Egyptians, Hittites, and Persians, the country was unified under Alexander the Great in 331 B.C. It later fell under Roman rule, becoming part of the Byzantine Empire when the Roman Empire was divided between East and West. In the 7th century, the country was conquered by the Arabs and became the center of a vast Islamic domain

11th cent: Seljuk Turks invade Syria from Asia Minor

12th cent: Crusaders gain control over Syrian coastal areas (1189-92) and fight the Moslems led by Saladin

1516-1918: Syria is conquered by the Ottoman Empire, remains largely stagnant during four centuries of Turkish rule

1920: Syria is made a French mandate

1941-46: Free French and British forces occupy Syria during World War II; French proclaim an independent Syrian republic but complete independence is not achieved until 1944. All foreign troops are withdrawn in 1946

1958-61: Egypt and Syria form United Arab Republic under presidency of Egypt's President Nasser; attempts to integrate the two economies, nationalization of Syrian industry, and domination of Syrian army posts by Egyptian officers cause widespread discontent, culminating in military coup and restoration of Syrian independence

1963-66: Series of military coups results in succession of governments, although left-wing Ba'ath party continues to dominate political scene. In 1966, a new coup leads to installation of Nureddin al-Attassi as president

1967: Syria shares in Arab defeat in Six-Day War with Israel, whose forces occupy Golan Heights in southwestern Syria

1968-71: Power struggle between factions of Ba'ath party led by President Attassi and those led by Gen. Hafez al-Assad ends with Assad's seizing power in 1970 and being elected president in 1971

1971: Syria breaks off relations with Jordan after border clash

1973: Syria settles her differences with Jordan, joins other Arab nations in a full-scale war against Israel and adopts a new constitution

1975: King Hussein of Jordan and President Assad announce that their countries will establish a Permanent Joint High Commission to coordinate political, economic, and cultural policies

1976: Syria sends troops into Lebanon during the civil war there

1977: Syria rejects Egyptian proposals for preliminary meeting to prepare for Geneva Middle-East peace talks involving Israel; it takes part in so-called "refusal summit" with Iraq, Algeria, Libya, Southern Yemen and the PLO; events constitute virtual rupture between Syria and Egypt

1978: Syrians and Lebanese Christians battle in Beirut area in heaviest fighting there since Lebanese civil war. Assad, first Syrian president to serve full seven-year term since nation gained independence in 1946, runs unopposed and is reelected in "yes-or-no" referendum; overwhelming "yes" vote seen as indicating broad support for his opposition to peace initiatives of Egyptian President Sadat. Mohammad Ali al-Halabi appointed prime minister. Cost of Syria's 30,000-man presence in Lebanon is put at $3 million a day; death toll includes estimated 600-700 Syrian troops. Israeli jets buzz Beirut, apparently to warn Syrians to stop shelling city's Christian quarter. Syria and PLO denounce planned U.S.-Egyptian-Israeli summit meeting as prelude to a Middle East War.

1979: Syrian and Israeli warplanes clash in Lebanese air space. President Assad and President Ahmed Hassan al-Bakr of Iraq establish joint political command and discuss eventual merger of the two countries

TANZANIA

Area: 363,708 sq. mi. **Population:** 16,070,000 (1978 est.)

Official Name: United Republic of Tanzania **Capital:** Dar es Salaam (future capital by 1990—Dodoma) **Nationality:** Tanzanian **Languages:** English and Swahili, the national language, are official languages. Some 120 dialects, mostly Bantu, are also spoken **Religion:** 35% Moslem, 35% Christian, and the rest animist **Flag:** A green triangle in the upper left and a blue one in the lower right, separated by a diagonal black band edged in yellow **Anthem:** National Anthem, set to new words of hymn "God Bless Africa" **Currency:** Tanzanian shilling (8.27 per U.S. $1)

Location: East Africa, comprising the former republics of Tanganyika and Zanzibar. Mainland Tanzania (Tanganyika) is bounded on the north by Lake Victoria, Kenya and Uganda, on the east by the Indian Ocean, on the south by Mozambique, Malawi, and Zambia, and on the west by Rwanda, Burundi, and Zaire. The island of Zanzibar lies some 20 miles to the east of Tanganyika's coastline, in the Indian Ocean **Features:** Tanganyika consists of a low-lying eastern coastal area, a high plateau in the west-central region, and scattered mountainous zones. Zanzibar is a low-lying island of coral limestone **Chief Rivers:** Pangani, Wami, Rufiji, Malagarasi, Ruvuma

Head of State and of Government: President Julius Kambarage Nyerere, born 1922, reelected 1975, head of the Revolutionary Party. He is assisted by the first vice-president (chairman of the Zanzibar Revolutionary Council), Sheikh Mwinyi Aboud Jumbe, born 1920, and by a prime minister, Edward M. Sokoine, born 1938, appointed February 1977 **Effective Date of Present Constitution:** April 1977 **Legislative Body:** National Assembly (unicameral), with 230 members, of whom 106 were elected for 5 years by universal suffrage and the rest appointed **Local Government:** 25 regions, including 20 on the mainland and 5 in Zanzibar, each administered by an appointed regional commissioner

Ethnic Composition: About 99% of the population are Africans who belong to some 130 different tribes, mostly Bantu. Only the Sukuma numbers over a million members. European, Arab, and Indo-Pakistani minorities total about 150,000 **Population Distribution:** 7% urban **Density:** 44 inhabitants per sq. mi. (658 per sq. mi. on Zanzibar island)

Largest Cities: (1975 est.) Dar es Salaam 517,000, Zanzibar 80,000; (1967 census) Tanga 61,058, Dodoma 35,000, Mwanza 34,861, Arusha 32,452

Per Capita Income: $170 (1978) **Gross National Product (GNP):** $2.8 billion (1978) **Economic Statistics:** In 1976, 39% of GNP was from agriculture (sisal, cotton, coffee, oilseeds, nuts, tea, tobacco, sugar, livestock; Zanzibar is the world's largest producer of cloves); 25% from trade and services; and 12% from manufacturing and mining **Minerals and Mining:** Diamonds and gold are the most important minerals being exploited, in addition to salt, mica sheets, gem stones and tin concentrates. Coal and iron deposits are to be exploited **Labor Force:** 5,600,000 (1970), with 90% engaged in subsistence agriculture, and 15% in industry. The monetary-sector employment in 1976: 457,000 workers **Foreign Trade:** Exports, chiefly cotton, coffee, diamonds, sisal, petroleum products, cloves, and cashew nuts, totaled $574 million in 1977. Imports, mainly machinery and transportation equipment, manufactured goods, and textiles, totaled $784 million **Principal Trade Partners:** Britain, China, United States, West Germany, Zambia, India

Vital Statistics: Birthrate, 47 per 1,000 of pop. (1967); death rate, 22 **Life Expectancy:** 45 years **Health Statistics:** 587 inhabitants per hospital bed; 17,856 per physician (1973) **Infant Mortality:** 160 per 1,000 births **Illiteracy:** 55% **Education Statistics:** 8,825 primary and secondary schools, with combined enrollment of 1,655,021 (1975) **Enrollment in Higher Education:** 3,064 **GNP Expended on Education:** 3.8% (1971)

Transportation: Paved roads total 1,992 mi. **Motor Vehicles:** 83,800 (1976) **Passenger Cars:** 42,000 **Railway Mileage:** 2,788 **Ports:** Dar es Salaam, Tanga, Mtwara, Lindi **Major Airlines:** Air Tanzania and Zanair fly domestically and internationally **Communications:** Government owned **Radio Transmitters:** 10 **Receivers:** 300,000 (1976) **Television Transmitters:** 1 **Receivers:** 4,000 (1970) **Telephones:** 66,000 (1976) **Newspapers:** 3 dailies, 5 copies per 1,000 inhabitants (1974)

Weights and Measures: Metric system **Travel Requirements:** Passport; visa, $3.15 fee; 2 photos; onward ticket

Tanzania, a union of Tanganyika and Zanzibar, is the site of some of the oldest and newest forms of human society. Its link to man's past was established in 1959 at Olduvai Gorge in the northern part of what was then Tanganyika. There Dr. Louis S. B. Leakey, the British-born anthropologist, unearthed one of the oldest human fossils ever found, the skull of *Homo zinjanthropus*. Its age was estimated to be more than 1.5 million years.

Now, over a decade after independence from Britain, Tanzania is the testing ground for a form of African Socialism—*ujamaa*—as conceived by President Julius K. Nyerere. *Ujamaa*, which means familyhood in Swahili, refers to kibbutzlike rural developments whose members join in communal farming and general improvement on a basis of "love, sharing, and work." On a broader scale, it means a joint effort by which all Tanzanians may gain an equal share of the nation's resources. In 1973 the ruling party, the Tanganyika African National Union (TANU), decided that all peasants had to join *ujamaa* villages, making the movement no longer voluntary.

The Nyerere government has progressively nationalized private business, banks, and privately owned buildings and homes. The economy depends largely on agriculture—coffee, tea, cotton, sisal and other crops—and between rising population and the vagaries of African weather, there has been little gain on a per-capita share basis.

The government, while striving for self-reliance, has not scorned foreign aid. U.S. funds are providing new highways, but the main new project is the Tanzam Railway, which was built with money, equipment, and labor provided by Communist China, and was handed over to Tanzania and Zambia by China in July 1976 after six years of construction. Although Tanzania had seemed to favor the Chinese, Soviet President Podgorny's 1977 visit to Tanzania was warmly received because of the Zimbabwe (Rhodesia) nationalist cause, which is actively supported by both countries.

In November 1978 Tanzanian forces invaded neighboring Uganda after Idi Amin had occupied more than 700 square miles of Tanzanian soil. Within five months Tanzanians and Ugandan rebels captured Kampala and drove the Ugandan dictator into exile. The war cost Tanzania more than $500 million.

HISTORY: Archaeological discoveries indicate that man inhabited Tanzania more than one million years ago. However, little is known about the early history of the area. Zanzibar, colonized by the Arabs in the 8th century, controlled the East African coastal region until the early 16th century, when both the island and the coast came under Portuguese rule. Arab rule was reestablished in the 17th century by the sultans of Muscat, under whom a large trade in ivory and slaves was established

1861: Zanzibar, under British pressure, is separated from control of Sultan of Muscat and becomes an independent sultanate

1885: Germany establishes a protectorate over the mainland region, which becomes known as German East Africa

1920: As a result of Germany's defeat in World War I, German East Africa is mandated to Britain; territory's name is changed to Tanganyika and German settlers are expelled

1946: Tanganyika becomes a trust territory under British administration

1961: Tanganyika wins independence; Julius K. Nyerere, head of Tanganyika African National Union (TANU) party, becomes prime minister

1962: Tanganyika becomes independent republic within Commonwealth; Nyerere is named as republic's first president

1963: Zanzibar achieves independence within the Commonwealth

1964: Afro-Shirazi Party, representing the African majority in Zanzibar, overthrows Arab minority government and forces sultan to flee; Zanzibar becomes a republic, with Sheik Abeid Amani Karume as president. Tanganyika and Zanzibar agree to form United Republic of Tanzania, with Nyerere as president and Karume as first vice-president

1965-69: Tanzania becomes one-party state, with TANU constituting the one party in Tanganyika and the Afro-Shirazi Party in Zanzibar, and both sharing power on national level. In 1967 government announces plans for socialist development and embarks on widespread nationalization in industry and agriculture; in 1969 it accepts offer of loan by Communist China to finance railroad linking Dar es Salaam with Zambian capital of Lusaka

1971: Refusal of Tanzania to recognize Uganda government of General Idi Amin leads to bitter dispute and border clashes

1972: Sheik Abeid Amani Karume, Chairman of the Revolutionary Council which governed Zanzibar, assassinated. General Amin charges Tanzania with invading Uganda and threatens retaliation

1975: Kenya reopens Tanzanian border saying that outbreak of cholera was under control. Tanzania agrees to meet with Kenya and Zambia to settle road and border disputes. Zaire rebels kidnap one Dutch and three American students from the Gombe Stream Research Center in Western Tanzania. All are released. Nyerere is elected to a fourth term as president

1976: Tanzania is a training ground for Zimbabwe (Rhodesia) guerrillas. Tanzam Railway is completed

1977: Tanzania closes its border with Kenya after Kenya withdraws from jointly-operated East African Airways in order to form separate Kenya Airlines. The Tanganyika African National Union and the Afro-Shirazi Party of Zanzibar merge into one party called the Revolutionary Party, headed by President Nyerere

1978: Government takes steps to combat cholera epidemic, which it reports has killed more than 400 persons. President Nyerere says he is worried that people in Carter administration seek to make Africa the site of a confrontation between superpowers. War with Uganda breaks out

1979: Tanzanian forces liberate Uganda

THAILAND

Area: 198,455 sq. mi. **Population:** 44,160,000 (1978 est.)

Official Name: Kingdom of Thailand **Capital:** Bangkok **Nationality:** Thai **Languages:** Thai is the official language and is spoken by most of the population; minority languages are Chinese, Malay, Khmer, and Lao **Religion:** Hinayana Buddhism is the religion of 95.5% of the population; Islam (4%), Confucianism and Christianity are minority religions **Flag:** Horizontal stripes of red, white, blue (double width), white, red **Anthem:** National Anthem, beginning "Thailand is the place for all Thais" **Currency:** Baht (20.4 per U.S. $1)

Location: Southeast Asia. Thailand is bounded on the north and east by Laos, on the east by Cambodia, on the south by Malaysia, and on the west and north by Burma. It extends down the Malay Peninsula between the Andaman Sea and the Gulf of Thailand **Features:** The core of the country is the central plain, with flat alluvial lands watered by a network of canals and irrigation projects. The north consists of parallel north-south mountain ranges and narrow, fertile valleys, while the region east of the central plain, the Khorat Plateau, is relatively barren. North-south mountain ranges also dominate peninsular Thailand **Chief Rivers:** Chao Phraya, Mekong, Nan, Ping, Mun, Pa Sak, Mae Klong

Head of State: King Bhumibol Adulyadej (Phumiphol Aduldet), born 1927, succeeded 1946 **Head of Government:** Prime Minister: Kriangsak Chamanan, reelected 1979 **Effective Date of Present Constitution:** December 1978 **Legislative Body:** Parliament (bicameral), consisting of 225-member Senate, appointed by the prime minister, and a popularly elected 301-member House of Representatives **Local Government:** 72 provinces, under appointed governors

Ethnic Composition: 75% Thai, 14% Chinese, 11% minorities (Malays, northern hill tribes, Khmer, Lao) **Population Distribution:** 25% urban **Density:** 223 inhabitants per sq. mi.

Largest Cities: (1970 census) Bangkok 1,867,297, Thonburi 628,015, Chiengmai 83,729, Nakhon Ratchasima 66,071

Per Capita Income: $433 (1978) **Gross National Product (GNP):** $20.6 billion (1978) **Economic Statistics:** 28% of 1974 GNP was derived from agriculture; 25% from commerce and finance (wholesale and retail trade, banking, insurance, real estate, ownership of dwellings); 33% from industry (mining and quarrying, manufacturing, construction, transportation and communications); 10% from services **Minerals and Mining:** Major natural gas fields are being exploited. Sizeable tin, tungsten and lignite deposits. Other minerals are manganese, molybdenum, antimony and gem stones **Labor Force:** 16,243,000 (1975); 67% agriculture and forestry, 10% industry **Foreign Trade:** Exports, chiefly tapioca, rubber, rice, maize, tin, sugar, brought in $3.6 billion in 1977. Imports, mainly machinery, spare parts, fuel, iron, steel, automobiles, electrical equipment, totaled $4.5 billion **Principal Trade Partners:** United States, Japan, Malaysia, Hong Kong, Singapore, West Germany, Britain, Netherlands

Vital Statistics: Birthrate, 35 per 1,000 of pop. (1976); death rate, 10, **Life Expectancy:** 61 years **Health Statistics:** 796 inhabitants per hospital bed (1974); 8,374 per physician (1975) **Infant Mortality:** 25 per 1,000 births (1976) **Illiteracy:** 18% **Education Statistics:** 29,713 primary and secondary schools with a combined enrollment of 7,853,616 (1976) **Enrollment in Higher Education:** 78,229 (1975) **GNP Expended on Education:** 2.6% (1974)

Transportation: Paved roads total 12,150 mi. (1975) **Motor Vehicles:** 532,800 (1975) **Passenger Cars:** 266,100 **Railway Mileage:** 2,339 **Ports:** Bangkok, Sattahip **Major Airlines:** Thai Airways, domestic and international (gov't owned) **Communications:** Government controlled **Radio Transmitters:** 217 **Receivers:** 5,500,000 (1976) **Television Transmitters:** 48 **Receivers:** 761,000 (1976) **Telephones:** 334,000 (1976) **Newspapers:** 56 dailies, 24 copies per 1,000 inhabitants (1975)

Weights and Measures: Metric system and local units are used **Travel Requirements:** Passport; no visa for 15 days

One of the largest countries in Southeast Asia, Thailand is favored with superb rice land, vast stands of teak, and a guaranteed rainfall that insures agricultural abundance. Thailand is the only Southeast Asian nation that has never been colonized: the word *thai* itself means free, and the Thai people are proud of this heritage.

For generations they have successfully resisted pressure not only of China to the north but also of Cambodia to the east. The Thais, the vast majority of whom are Buddhists, have lived for centuries under the cohesive influence of their line of kings.

A constitutional monarchy replaced the absolute rule of the kings in 1932, but parliamentary democracy was placed in abeyance in 1958, when a military junta seized control of the government in a bloodless coup. Since that time, a series of coups has occurred—the most recent being a bloodless coup in October 1977 led by Defense Minister Sangad Chaloryu, a former admiral who said he was deposing Premier Thanin Kraivchien's civilian government because it was taking too long to restore democracy.

Thailand's military commander, Gen. Kriangsak Chamanan, was named to replace Thanin as premier, while a 23-member Revolutionary Council was established as the nation's new governing body; the Council is almost identical to the National Administration Reform Council, which came to power in the previous military takeover in October 1976. Premier Kriangsak stayed in power as a result of the elections of April 1979. None of the 36 political groupings won a majority in the 301-seat lower house; he appointed all 225 senators as called for by the constitution, and then the members of the two houses, meeting jointly, reelected him premier.

Thailand continues to be beset by insurgent activities in the south, north and northeastern provinces, involving groups as diverse as the Thai Communists, the Thai-Muslim separatists and a group of Meo mountain tribesmen. Thai troops have been kept active; in one action they smashed concentrations of guerrillas by capturing 30 jungle camps in four provinces in April 1979.

With an economy that is based on agriculture and is rising 7 percent annually even when inflation is taken into account, Thailand is prospering. The tapioca root, exported to Europe as an animal feed, became the nation's top agricultural moneyearner in 1978, surpassing rice. Rubber and tin remain important, but light industry is adding further economic strength. The discovery of gas in the Gulf of Siam, to be piped ashore by Union Oil Co., will ease the shock of higher fuel prices.

An influx of Indochinese refugees threatened, however, to overwhelm Thailand in 1979. Some 80,000 Cambodians also crossed the border to escape hunger and death in their embattled country. A Thai official predicted that as many as one million refugees from all Southeast Asia might pour into Thailand's "rice bowl," and Thai troops forcibly returned 45,000 Cambodians. One older camp, at Nong Khai in northern Thailand, contained 46,000 Laotians and was the largest "city" in the province.

HISTORY: In the 11th century the Thai people, living in Yunnan Province of what is now China, began moving southward under pressure from the expanding Chinese. They settled in the valleys of the Chao Phraya and Mekong Rivers and formed political states, many of which were under the rule of King Rama Kamhaeng. In the

15th century they were united with other Thais around Chiang Mai, in the northeast, and with the northern Malays in the south. By the 18th century trade had been established with Europe and Thailand began to consolidate as a nation

1833: Trade agreement is signed with the United States

1917: Siam (as Thailand was then called) declares war on Germany and sends expeditionary force to Europe

1932: Coup d'état by army officers establishes constitutional government to replace absolute monarchy

1941: Japanese troops enter Thailand, which is forced to sign alliance

1946: King Ananda Mahidol is found shot to death and is succeeded on throne by his younger brother, Bhumibol Adulyadej

1947: Coup by military officers forces change in government

1957-58: In another bloodless coup, government is replaced by a short-lived military junta. This is followed by another shift of power when Field Marshal Sarit Thanarat seizes control

1962: U.S. military unit is sent to northeast Thailand as Lao Communists threaten to sweep to Mekong River

1963: Sarit dies and is replaced by Marshal Thanom Kittikachorn

1970: United States discloses it has been paying $50 million annually for support of Thai combat division in South Vietnam

1971: On November 17, Thanom's government takes absolute power in bloodless coup

1973: U.S. congressional order ends U.S. bombing flights from Thai bases. Antigovernment protests organized by students result in violence. Thanom's government resigns and university rector Sanya Thammasak is named premier

1974: Exiled former premier Thanom Kittikachorn returns and is expelled. Agreement reached for U.S. to withdraw two of its six remaining air bases by the end of 1974. Air America, funded by CIA, ceases operations in Thailand

1975: Kukrit Pramoj becomes premier. Government accepts U.S. apology for unauthorized use of territory by airlifting 1,100 U.S. Marines to Thailand in military operations to free ship *Mayaguez* and her crew from Cambodian gunboats

1976: Seni Pramoj becomes premier. All operations are ended at U.S. installations and military personnel are withdrawn

1977: Thai and Cambodian troops fight along the border. Thai military leadership takes power under Gen. Kriangsak Chamanan; 23-member Revolutionary Council is established; new government proclaims interim constitution promising elections by 1979; parliament is dissolved; King appoints 360-member national legislature, made up mostly of active or retired members of the military

1978: Amnesty International, estimating there are possibly up to 1,000 political prisoners in Thailand, calls for their release. Thailand and Cambodia agree to try to end bloody border fighting and to exchange ambassadors

1979: Premier Kriangsak visits President Carter, who declares that the U.S. "is deeply committed to the integrity of Thailand's borders." A tide of 80,000 Cambodian refugees into Thailand, whose military eventually forces 45,000 back across the border. By midyear, Thailand relents to the extent of letting 1,000 Cambodians come back a second time to enter UN transit camps, pending resettlement elsewhere

TOGO

Area: 21,853 sq. mi. **Population:** 2,350,000 (1978 est.)

Official Name: Togolese Republic **Capital:** Lomé **Nationality:** Togolese **Languages:** French is the official language; the dominant indigenous languages are Ewe, Twi, and Hausa. In all, more than 44 different languages are spoken **Religion:** 60% animist, 20% Christian (mostly Roman Catholics), 20% Moslem **Flag:** Five alternating horizontal stripes of green (3) and yellow (2), with a white star on a red square in the upper left **Anthem:** National Anthem, beginning "Hail to thee, land of our forefathers" **Currency:** CFA Franc (219 per U.S. $1)

Location: West Africa. Togo is bounded on the north by Upper Volta, on the east by Benin, on the south by the Gulf of Guinea, and on the west by Ghana **Features:** The country is cut in two from the northeast to the southwest by the Chaine du Togo hills. To the north is a large savanna, with a plain in the east and south **Chief Rivers:** Oti, Mono, Haho, Anié

Head of State and of Government: President: General Gnassingbé Eyadéma, born 1937, seized power in 1967 **Effective Date of Present Constitution:** 1963, suspended 1967 **Legislative Body:** National Assembly (unicameral), dissolved 1967. All powers are in the hands of the Assembly of the Togolese People party (RPT) **Local Government:** 4 regions, headed by appointed inspectors

Ethnic Composition: Of the nation's 18 major ethnic groups, the dominant ones are the Ewe and Mina in the south and the Kabyé in the north **Population Distribution:** 15% urban **Density:** 108 inhabitants per sq. mi.

Largest Cities: (1970 census) Lomé 148,443, Sokodé 30,271

Per Capita Income: $328 (1978) **Gross National Product (GNP):** $790 million (1978) **Economic Statistics:** In 1973, 44% of GNP was from agriculture (coffee, cocoa, yams, cassava, corn, millet, sorghum, rice); 20% from trade and services; 18% from mining (phosphates) and manufacturing (food processing, cement, a brewery, textile mills) **Minerals and Mining:** Phosphates are abundant; there are also unexploited amounts of iron ore and limestone **Labor Force:** 730,000, with 78% in agriculture and 22% in industry. There were 44,000 wage earners **Foreign Trade:** Exports, mainly phosphates, cocoa, coffee, palm nuts, and cotton, totaled $143 million in 1976. Imports, chiefly cotton textiles, machinery, motor vehicles, tobacco, and petroleum products, totaled $267 million **Principal Trade Partners:** France, Japan, Britain, West Germany, United States, China, Netherlands, Belgium

Vital Statistics: Birthrate, 50.6 per 1,000 of pop. (1975); death rate, 23.3 **Life Expectancy:** 40 years **Health Statistics:** 680 inhabitants per hospital bed; 21,200 per physician (1973) **Infant Mortality:** 127 per 1,000 births **Illiteracy:** 84% **Education Statistics:** 1,362 primary and secondary schools, with combined enrollment of 427,485 (1975) **Enrollment in Higher Education:** 2,353 (1975) **GNP Expended on Education:** 5.3% (1975)

Transportation: All-weather roads total 1,210 mi. **Motor Vehicles:** 20,000 (1974) **Passenger Cars:** 13,000 **Railway Mileage:** 305 **Ports:** Lomé, Kpémé **Major Airlines:** Air Afrique and UTA maintain international services **Communications:** Government owned **Radio Transmitters:** 5 **Receivers:** 52,000 (1976) **Television Transmitters:** 3 **Telephones:** 10,000 (1976) **Newspapers:** 1 daily, 6 copies per 1,000 inhabitants (1975)

Weights and Measures: Metric system **Travel Requirements:** Passport; visa for a 3 months maximum; $2.39 fee for stay up to 15 days; $3.58 fee for stay up to 30 days; 3 photos

One of West Africa's smallest countries, Togo has had a disproportionate amount of trouble since it attained independence from France in 1960. The country's first president, Sylvanus Olympio, was assassinated. He was succeeded by his brother-in-law, the late Nicolas Grunitzky, the son of a Polish father and a Togolese mother.

The Grunitzky government became increasingly insecure, and on January 13, 1967 Grunitzky was ousted by then Lt. Col. Étienne Eyadéma (now Gen. Gnassingbé Eyadéma). Eyadéma admitted that he was responsible for the killing of President Olympio in the 1963 coup.

General Eyadéma has maintained firm control over the country. He has forecast a return to civilian rule, but as yet has set no date. With political stability, the nation's economy—based on phosphates, cocoa, and coffee—has shown steady progress. The government also hopes to exploit the country's large limestone deposits. Largely because of improving economic conditions, an attempted coup in August 1970 was taken with relative calm by the Togolese. Nevertheless, President Eyadéma charged that a French mining company had plotted to kill him by causing the crash of an airplane in which he was a passenger in January 1974. Two weeks earlier, Eyadéma had announced a 15 percent increase in the government's controlling interest in the mining company. Shortly after making the charges, the Eyadéma government took over the mining facilities.

Liberal trade policies have strengthened an otherwise feeble Togolese economy. Following independence, Togo was the only former French African colony not to give preferential tariff treatment to French goods. As a result, imports from all countries enter Togo at the same relatively low rates. Togo's famous marketing women have consequently benefited from the lower prices generated by the competition in imports.

Although officially nonaligned, Togo has sought closer identification with the Third World, but maintains close ties with Western nations. France remains Togo's principal trading partner.

HISTORY: The Ewes, who now constitute the population of southern Togo, moved into the region from the Niger River Valley between the 12th and 14th centuries. Portuguese explorers and traders visited the coast of Togo in the 15th and 16th centuries.

During the next two centuries, the coastal region was a major raiding ground for European traders in search of slaves, gaining Togo the name "Coast of Slaves." In 1884, Germany set up a small protectorate on the coast and later expanded inland

1914: Togoland is occupied by the French in the east and by the British in the west after the outbreak of World War I

1922: League of Nations confirms a French mandate in eastern Togoland and a British mandate in western Togoland

1946: United Nations changes the British and French mandates to trusteeships

1956: British Togoland votes to join the Gold Coast; as the result of a plebiscite among the French-ruled Togolese, French Togoland is made an autonomous republic within the French Union, but the UN Trusteeship Council rejects this method of ending France's trusteeship

1958: In a UN-supervised election, the Committee for Togolese Unity party (CTU), wins control of Togo's legislature; its leader, Sylvanus Olympio, becomes premier

1960: French Togoland becomes the independent Republic of Togo, with Sylvanus Olympio as president

1963: Olympio, a southerner, is assassinated by a group of northern noncommissioned army officers; Nicolas Grunitzky, leader of the Togolese Party for Progress, is named president

1967: Army chief of staff Lt. Col. Étienne Eyadéma overthrows the Grunitzky government, names himself president, and institutes direct military rule; the constitution is suspended, the National Assembly dissolved, and all political activity prohibited

1968: Eyadéma announces indefinite postponement of a referendum for a new constitution and return to civilian government, which he promised upon taking over the government

1969: After carefully staged demonstrations demanding that he remain as president, Eyadéma announces he has "acceded to the popular will"

1970: Government announces the thwarting of a plot to overthrow Eyadéma

1974: Eyadéma survives alleged assassination plot

1977: Attempted assassination of President Eyadéma fails

TONGA

Area: 270 sq. mi. **Population:** 92,000 (1978 est.)

Official Name: Kingdom of Tonga **Capital:** Nuku'alofa **Nationality:** Tongan **Languages:** Tongan and English **Religion:** Christian, with 60% belonging to sects of the Wesleyan (Methodist) faith, and 20% to the Latter Day Saints (Mormons) **Flag:** A red field with a white rectangle in the upper left containing a red cross **Anthem:** National Anthem, beginning "O Almighty God above" **Currency:** Pa'anga (.91 per U.S. $1)

Location: Southwest Pacific Ocean. An archipelago of 150 islands (45 inhabited), covering 100,000 sq. mi. of sea, about 400 miles east of Fiji **Features:** There are 3 principal groups. Divided by a north-south line, the eastern chain (including the main island of Tongatapu) is low-lying coralline. The western chain (Ha'apai and Vava'u groups) is volcanic

Head of State and of Government: King Taufa'ahau Tupou IV, born 1918, ascended the throne in 1965. He is also president of the appointed Privy Council (cabinet) which includes the prime minister, Prince Fatafehi Tu'ipelehake, born 1922, appointed 1965 **Effective Date of Present Constitution:** 1875, revised 1970 **Legislative Body:** Parliament (unicameral Legislative Assembly), with 23 members, with the 7 cabinet ministers, 7 nobles elected by the 33 hereditary nobles, 7 elected by adult suffrage for 3 years, and the ex-officio governors of Ha'apai and Vava'u **Local Government:** 3 island districts, under appointed governors

Ethnic Composition: The Tongans are Polynesians, and make up 98% of the population, which also includes small groups of other Pacific islanders, Europeans and mixed **Population Distribution:** 60% is on Tongatapu **Density:** 341 inhabitants per sq. mi.

Largest Cities: (1976 census) Nuku'alofa 18,396; (1966 census) Neiafu 3,593, Mu'a 3,502

Per Capita Income: $400 (1975 est.) **Gross National Product (GNP):** $39 million (1975) **Economic Statistics:** The economy is based on agriculture, (sweet potatoes, yams, taro, tapioca, cassava, corn, coconuts, bananas, pineapples, melons, fish, citrus fruits, livestock) and manufacturing (coconut and agricultural processing and canning, coir, tobacco, handicrafts, plastic products) **Minerals and Mining:** None **Labor Force:** 14,493 (1966), chiefly in government, services, and the few small industries, with 75% of the total population in agriculture **Foreign Trade:** Exports, chiefly copra and bananas, totaled $7.2 million in 1975. Imports, mainly food, fuels and textiles, totaled $19.8 million **Principal Trade Partners:** Australia, New Zealand, Britain, Japan, Fiji, Netherlands

Vital Statistics: Birthrate 13.0 per 1,000 of pop.; death rate, 1.9 **Life Expectancy:** 37 years **Health Statistics:** 303 inhabitants per hospital bed; 3,333 per physician (1975) **Infant Mortality:** 20.5 per

1,000 births (1976) **Illiteracy:** Negligible **Education Statistics:** 220 primary and secondary schools, with a combined enrollment of 40,834 (1975) **Enrollment in Higher Education:** 15 (1976), with 116 studying abroad (1974) **GNP Expended on Education:** 4.4% (1973)

Transportation: Surfaced roads total 121 mi. **Motor Vehicles:** 1,400 (1974) **Passenger Cars:** 1,000 **Railway Mileage:** None **Ports:** Nuku'alofa, Neiafu, Pangai **Major Airlines:** Air Pacific and Polynesian Airlines operate international services; South Pacific Islands Airways operates domestically **Communications:** Government owned **Radio Transmitters:** 2 **Receivers:** 15,000 (1976) **Television:** None **Telephones:** 1,090 (1974) **Newspapers:** 1 several times a week, 49 copies per 1,000 inhabitants (1974)

Weights and Measures: British standards are used, but the metric system is being introduced **Travel Requirements:** Passport; no visa for 30 days; onward ticket

Though comprising 150 coral and volcanic islands, the Pacific kingdom of Tonga is considered to be one of the world's tiniest countries. For 70 years, it was a British protectorate, becoming an independent nation in the British Commonwealth in 1970. With independence, Tonga has moved to broaden the base of its economy, which has been based on the export of copra, bananas and coconuts.

There are two long-range hopes for broadening the economy. One is oil, the existence of which was discovered through seepage into water wells. An agreement with an international consortium provides that the country will get half the profits from possible oil production.

The other hope is to make Tonga a vacation paradise, with the kingdom looking for further economic development stemming from earnings from planned tourist hotels. Present air service to Tonga is only by small regional airlines that fly from Samoa and Fiji. The drive to independence from Britain was spurred by reported British reluctance to encourage the building of a jetport. In 1976 the Soviets agreed to upgrade the airport and Tonga's dockyard in return for the establishment of fisheries. Japan also expressed interest in Tonga through the signing of an agreement on hotel and fisheries development.

However, King Taufa'ahau Tupou IV has cautioned his countrymen, who wear ta'ovalas, or woven mats, around their waists, against basing their future on income from tourism, warning that "if too much tourism happens, we will become like Hawaii, where there are no more Hawaiians."

HISTORY: Tonga was at one time ruled by a line of sacred kings, one of whom eventually divested himself on his executive powers and delegated them to a temporal king. The system of dual kingship had become firmly established by the 17th century, when the first European contact was made by Dutch navigators. The peaceful conditions on the islands so impressed the 18th-century explorer Captain James Cook that he christened one of them the Friendly Island, a name later applied to the whole group. Within a few years of his departure, however, the islands were rent by civil war

1845-93: Taufa'ahau, a leading chief, rules over a united Tonga as King George Tupou I after suppressing civil war. He makes treaties with France, Germany, the United States and Britain, all of which recognize his sovereignty, and introduces parliamentary government and a land system under which every male Tongan taxpayer is entitled to eight and one-quarter acres of land suitable for planting

1900: Tonga becomes a British protectorate

1918-65: Reign of Queen Salote, granddaughter of George Tupou I, sees the elimination of illiteracy and of Tonga's national debt

1970: Tonga gains independence from Britain

1978: Tonga's Bank of the South Pacific declared bankrupt after American bank president Jack Meier flees, defaulting on $600,000 contract to develop Fua'a'motu airport to handle jumbo jets

1979: King Taufa'ahau Tupou IV negotiates with Libyan strong man Col. Muammar Qaddafi for a $3-million loan to finish airport

TRINIDAD AND TOBAGO

Area: 1,980 sq. mi. **Population:** 1,175,000 (1978 est.)

Official Name: Republic of Trinidad and Tobago **Capital:** Port-of-Spain **Nationality:** Trinidadian, Tobagonian **Languages:** English is the official and predominant language; Hindi and other Indian languages are also spoken **Religion:** About 71% Christian, chiefly Roman Catholic and Anglican; 23% Hindu; 6% Moslem **Flag:** Red with a black diagonal stripe bordered in white running from upper left to lower right **Anthem:** National Anthem, beginning ''Forged from the love of liberty'' **Currency:** Trinidad/Tobago dollar (2.4 per U.S. $1)

Location: West Indies. Trinidad and Tobago are the most southerly of the Lesser Antilles. They lie 7 miles northeast of the Venezuelan coast and are separated from each other by a 19-mile channel **Features:** Three relatively low mountain ranges cross Trinidad from east to west. The land between the northern and central ranges is flat and well watered; south of the central range it is undulating. On Tobago, a main ridge of volcanic origin runs down the center of the island **Chief Rivers:** Ortoire, Caroni, Oropuche

Head of State: President: Sir Ellis Emmanuel Innocent Clarke, born 1917, elected by Parliament 1976 **Head of Government:** Prime Minister: Dr. Eric Eustace Williams, born 1911, reelected 1976 **Effective Date of Present Constitution:** August 1976 **Legislative Body:** Parliament (bicameral), consisting of a Senate with 31 appointed members, and a House of Representatives with 36 members elected for 5 years **Local Government:** 8 counties, 3 municipalities, and 1 ward (Tobago), governed by elected councils

Ethnic Composition: 43% of Trinidad's population is black, 40% East Indian, 12% of mixed ancestry, 3% European, and 2% Chinese. Tobago's population is largely black **Population Distribution:** 18% urban **Density:** 593 inhabitants per sq. mi.

Largest Cities: (1970 census) Port-of-Spain 62,680 (Metropolitan Area 250,000), San Fernando 36,879, Arima 11,636

Per Capita Income: $1,588 (1978 est.) **Gross National Product (GNP):** $2.1 billion (1978) **Economic Statistics:** Trinidad is a major producer of crude oil and is also a major supplier of natural asphalt. Chief crops are sugar, fruits, bananas, coconuts, cocoa, and rice. Industries (12%) are oil refining and the manufacture of sugar, chemicals, fertilizers, molasses, rum, fruit juices, and cotton textiles. Tourism is important **Minerals and Mining:** Petroleum, lignite, asphalt, coal, gypsum, iron, clay, and natural gas **Labor Force:** 395,800 (1978), with 13% in agriculture; 50% in manufacturing and construction; and 19% in commerce and transportation **Foreign Trade:** Exports, mainly mineral fuels, lubricants and related products, sugar, chemicals, fertilizers, fruits and vegetables, and coffee, totaled $2.21 billion in 1976. Imports, chiefly petroleum for refining, machinery and transportation equipment, foodstuffs, manufactured goods by material, and chemicals, totaled $1.97 billion **Principal Trade Partners:** United States, Britain, Venezuela, Netherlands, Caribbean countries, Canada, Japan

Vital Statistics: Birthrate, 23 per 1,000 of pop. (1975); death rate, 6.5 **Life Expectancy:** 66 years **Health Statistics:** 224 inhabitants per hospital bed; 1,964 per physician (1975) **Infant Mortality:** 27.2 per 1,000 births (1977) **Illiteracy:** 8% **Education Statistics:** 713 primary and secondary schools, with combined enrollment of 283,693 (1972) **Enrollment in Higher Education:** 2,962 (1974) **GNP Expended on Education:** 4.3% (1973)

Transportation: Paved roads total 2,480 mi. **Motor Vehicles:** 127,000 (1975) **Passenger Cars:** 101,300 **Railway Mileage:** None **Ports:** Port-of-Spain, Pte-à-Pierre, Point Lisas **Major Airlines:** British West Indian Airways operates domestically and internationally **Communications:** Partly government controlled **Radio Transmitters:** 9 **Receivers:** 270,000 (1976) **Television Transmitters:** 3 **Receivers:** 110,000 (1976) **Telephones:** 70,000 (1976) **Newspapers:** 3 dailies, 92 copies per 1,000 inhabitants (1975)

Weights and Measures: British standards are used; the metric system is being introduced **Travel Requirements:** Passport; no visa to 6 months; onward ticket

Trinidad's petroleum-fed industry has long been the most advanced in the former British West Indies. Offshore oil and gas finds have also contributed to the economy of Trinidad and its smaller sister island of Tobago, and have helped to make Trinidad a major oil exporter in the Western Hemisphere.

The economic problems are those of any developing country—lack of investment capital, shortage of jobs and lack of skilled personnel to fill those that are available, a small market for the products of light industry, and lack of administrative and technical capability below the top echelons of business and government. However, the democratic legislative and judicial structure inherited from the British makes meaningful political action in these areas possible without bringing down the government.

Trinidad's main problem is the lack of jobs, with the unemployment rate hovering around 15 per

cent and mainly affecting the islands' blacks—43 percent of the population. In an attempt to bolster the economy, the government of Prime Minister Eric Eustace Williams has emphasized a development program with large investment incentives for foreign capital and has imposed high import duties to give local products a competitive advantage. The government has also introduced a family-planning program—which has substantially reduced the rate of population growth—and is encouraging emigration to England and North America to relieve the labor-market pressure.

Domestically, race is the pivot of Trinidad's politics. Williams'.People's National Movement claims the loyalties of most of Trinidad's blacks, while the principal opposition is the Democratic Labor Party, the party of the less numerous East Indians. Complaints of discrimination in government jobs still come from the East Indians, but many of the highest officials are drawn from that bloc.

HISTORY: Trinidad and Tobago were discovered by Columbus in 1498 but were long ignored by the Spaniards because of the lack of precious metals in the islands. Spanish colonists began to establish plantations on Trinidad in the 17th century, importing African slaves to work them. The British captured the island in 1797 and in 1802 it was formally ceded to Britain. Tobago changed hands repeatedly during the 17th and 18th centuries, and in 1814 passed under the British crown

1834: Slavery is abolished in Trinidad

1845: Trinidad begins to import contract workers from India to replace the former slaves

1889: Trinidad and Tobago are amalgamated into a single colony

1958: Trinidad and Tobago joins the West Indies Federation

1962: Federation is dissolved; Trinidad and Tobago becomes independent

1970: Government restores order after island is rocked by black power demonstrations and mutiny in armed forces

1971: Elections result in complete victory for the People's National Movement under Prime Minister Dr. Eric Williams

1975: Strikes paralyze oil and sugar industries, causing worst government crisis since black power unrest in 1970

1976: Trinidad and Tobago becomes a republic, ending a 179-year link with the British monarchy. Governor General Sir Ellis Clarke becomes the first president. People's National Movement retains majority in Parliament following the general elections

1978: The nation's reserves of dry natural gas are put at 12 trillion cu. ft., and drilling continues. The government announces plans to build an aluminum smelter of 150,000-ton capacity. A government shipping company is set up jointly with Seatrain Lines

---

TUNISIA

Area: 63,170 sq. mi. **Population:** 6,070,000 (1978 est.)

Official Name: Republic of Tunisia **Capital:** Tunis **Nationality:** Tunisian **Languages:** Arabic is the official language, but French is widely used **Religion:** 98% are Moslems; and Islam is the official religion **Flag:** A red field with a white disc containing a red crescent and star in the center **Anthem:** National Anthem, beginning "Immortal and precious the blood we have shed" **Currency:** Tunisian dinar (0.41 per U.S. $1)

Location: North Africa. Tunisia is bounded on the north and east by the Mediterranean Sea, on the south by Libya, and on the west by Algeria **Features:** The country consists of a wooded and fertile region in the north, a central region comprising the coastal plains, and a southern region bordering the Sahara **Chief River:** Medjerda

Head of State and of Government: President Habib Bourguiba, born 1903, named president for life in 1975. He is assisted by a premier, Hédi Nouira, appointed 1970 **Effective Date of Present Constitution:** 1959, amended April 1976 **Legislative Body:** National Assembly (unicameral), consisting of 112 members elected by universal suffrage for 5 years **Local Government:** 18 governorates, under appointed governors

Ethnic Composition: The population is largely Arab, with a Berber minority in the mountains; Europeans number about 50,000 **Population Distribution:** 49% urban **Density:** 96 inhabitants per sq. mi.

Largest Cities: (1975 census—Metropolitan Areas) Tunis 873,515, Sfax 256,739, Bizerte 109,879, Sousse 102,097, Kairouan 67,589

Per Capita Income: $961 (1978) **Gross National Product (GNP):** $5.8 billion (1978) **Economic Statistics:** 23% of the GNP is derived from commerce and finance; 30% from services; 28% from industry including mining; 19% from agriculture **Minerals and Mining:**

There are large phosphate deposits and smaller amounts of oil, natural gas, lead, zinc **Labor Force:** 1,400,000, with 58% in agriculture, 19% in industry, and 23% in services **Foreign Trade:** Exports, chiefly phosphates, petroleum, olive oil, wine, and cork, totaled $976 million in 1977. Imports, mainly foodstuffs, industrial raw materials, machinery and equipment, and transportation equipment, totaled $1.9 billion **Principal Trade Partners:** EC countries, United States, Greece

Vital Statistics: Birthrate, 36.4 per 1,000 of pop. (1976); death rate, 13.8 **Life Expectancy:** 55 years **Health Statistics:** 427 inhabitants per hospital bed; 4,636 per physician (1975) **Infant Mortality:** 52.1 per 1,000 births (1974) **Illiteracy:** 45% **Education Statistics:** 2,342 primary and secondary schools with combined enrollment of 1,134,632 (1975) **Enrollment in Higher Education:** 23,137 (1976) **GNP Expended on Education:** 8% (1974)

Transportation: Paved roads total 6,663 mi. **Motor Vehicles:** 169,800 (1975) **Passenger Cars:** 102,600 **Railway Mileage:** 1,256 **Ports:** Tunis, Sousse, Sfax, Bizerte, Skhirra **Major Airlines:** Tunis Air, a government-owned line, operates domestically and internationally **Communications:** Government owned **Radio Transmitters:** 8 **Receivers:** 280,000 (1975) **Television Transmitters:** 10 **Receivers:** 208,000 (1976) **Telephones:** 135,000 (1976) **Newspapers:** 4 dailies, 33 copies per 1,000 inhabitants (1975)

Weights and Measures: Metric system and local units are used **Travel Requirements:** Passport; no visa for 4 months

Wedged in between Algeria and Libya—two larger and more militant neighbors—Tunisia has traditionally been one of the most stable and moderate Arab countries.

No Arab country has been more closely identified with one individual than Tunisia with Habib Bourguiba, its only president since the establishment of the republic in 1957. Bourguiba has long been one of the most magnetic and controversial figures in the Arab world. A professed "pragmatic idealist," he has befriended both the West and the Soviet Union and has not hesitated to quarrel publicly over the Arab struggle against Israel. His dovish views on that subject have infuriated many Arab leaders. However, Tunisia gained some prestige in the Arab world after the 1970 Jordanian civil war, which was mediated by an inter-Arab conciliation mission headed by Bourguiba's personal envoy. Moreover, Tunisia has condemned the peace treaty between Egypt and Israel.

The only Arab President outside of Lebanon without a military background, Bourguiba is a French-educated lawyer. He brought to Tunisia a benevolent despotism that has been comparatively free of corruption, and he has permitted relative individual freedom.

As part of a program to modernize the country, special attention was placed on the status of women, who enjoy few rights in much of the Arab world. Polygamy was outlawed; the marriageable age for girls was raised from 15 to 17; and divorce was made a matter of court discretion, rather than that of the husband.

The increase in Tunisia's literacy rate in the last decade was among the most rapid in the world, although some 45 percent of the population has had no schooling. In fact, Tunisia is turning out more educated people than the economy can absorb and they have much trouble in finding suitable jobs.

Economically, Tunisia is a significant producer of phosphates, oil, textiles and olives. The government has actively promoted foreign investment in all of these areas, although France remains Tunisia's principal trade partner. Since a 1976 trade agreement with the European Community, the first such pact signed with an Arab country, it is expected that large-scale investment will increase greatly.

Relations have deteriorated between Tunisia and neighboring Libya since a failed merger attempt in 1974, attributed to Tunisia's more moderate Arab-Israeli stance. A further erosion of relations occurred after a 1976 assassination plot against Bourguiba by Libyan commandos was uncovered. Subsequently, Tunisian workers were expelled from Libya, and diplomats were withdrawn from both countries. Relations have been restored.

Tunisia today is a nation poised, not always peacefully, on the brink of change. Many Tunisians contend that although a single party system was tolerable during the early years of nationhood, the time has come for full freedom of political expression. They are also concerned that a struggle for power could destroy Tunisian stability, following the aged Bourguiba's death. In fact, the struggle may already have begun. In January 1978 Tunisia was rocked by an outbreak of antigovernment violence, the nation's worst since gaining independence in 1956. The street fighting in Tunis and other cities left at least 100 dead and about 450 hurt. Although it began in peace—and legality—a general strike led by the nation's powerful labor unions (demanding more pay and attention to grievances) resulted in widespread vandalism, looting and arson, as the initial protests escalated into a direct challenge to Bourguiba's leadership. The government, meanwhile, has blamed the disorders on "extremist" labor leaders and "outside agitators." But though it has hinted that it suspects Libyan involvement, the government has stopped short of openly making such a charge.

HISTORY: Tunisia was settled by seafaring Phoenicians as far back as the 12th century B.C. In the 6th century B.C. the city of Carthage was founded near modern Tunis and became the center of a powerful city-state that lasted until 146 B.C., when it was destroyed by Rome. A new city of Carthage, built by Julius Caesar, was conquered by the Vandals in the 5th century A.D. and was later recovered for the Byzantine Empire. The Arabs conquered the region in the 7th century and during the Middle Ages transformed it into a major center of Arab power

1574: Turks add Tunisia to Ottoman Empire, but under its Turkish governors (beys) country enjoys virtual independence

1705: Hussein dynasty of hereditary beys is established

1881: Tunisia becomes a French protectorate

1934: Habib Bourguiba founds Neo-Destour (New Constitution) Party, which becomes spearhead of independence movement

1942-43: Tunisia becomes the site of World War II campaigns

1956: Tunisia wins independence

1957: Bey Sidi Lamine is deposed; Tunisia is proclaimed a republic; Bourguiba is elected as president

1963: France evacuates naval base at Bizerte

1968: Tunisia, at meeting of Arab League in Cairo, accuses Egypt of having provoked Six-Day War with Israel in 1967 and calls for Arab recognition of Israel; charges provoke uproar and Tunisian delegation walks out of meeting

1973: Tunisia sends token force to aid Arabs in Yom Kippur War

1974: Merger is proposed between Libya and Tunisia to form single nation, but the plan fails to materialize

1975: Bourguiba is named president for life

1976: Relations with Libya are strained by Libyan plot against Tunisian leaders

1977: Tunisian police arrest alleged Libyan agents suspected of plotting to assassinate Premier Hédi Nouira

1978: At least 100 die as general strike leads to worst antigovernment violence since nation gained independence; government blames disorders on "extremist" labor leaders and "outside agitators"

TURKEY

Area: 300,946 sq. mi. **Population:** 42,000,000 (1978 est.)

Official Name: Republic of Turkey **Capital:** Ankara **Nationality:** Turkish **Languages:** Turkish is the official language and is spoken by 90% of the population; Kurdish (7%) and Arabic are spoken by the leading minorities **Religion:** 98% Sunni Moslem; the rest are Christians and Jews **Flag:** A white star and crescent on a red field **Anthem:** March of Independence **Currency:** Turkish lira (26.7 per U.S. $1)

Location: Asia Minor and Southeast Europe. Asiatic Turkey (Asia Minor) occupies 97% of the total area. Turkey is bounded on the north by the Black Sea, on the northeast by the USSR, on the east by Iran, on the south by Iraq, Syria, and the Mediterranean Sea, on the west by the Aegean Sea, and on the northwest by Greece and Bulgaria **Features:** European Turkey (Eastern Thrace) is separated from Asia Minor by the Dardanelles, the Sea of Marmara, and the Bosporus. The European part consists of rolling agricultural land. Asiatic Turkey has fertile coastal strips and is occupied in the center by the semiarid Anatolian plateau, surrounded by hills and mountains **Chief Rivers:** Kizilirmak, Yesilirmak, Seyhan, Menderes, Tigris (Dicle), Euphrates (Firat), Sakarya

Head of State: President Fahri Korutürk, born 1903, elected April 1973 for 7 years **Head of Government:** Premier Bulent Ecevit, born 1925, appointed January 1978 **Effective Date of Present Constitution:** October 1961 **Legislative Body:** Parliament (bicameral Grand National Assembly), with a National Assembly and a Senate of the Republic. The National Assembly has 450 members elected by popular vote for 4 years. The Senate consists of 150 elected members for 6 year terms, 19 lifetime members, 15 members appointed by the president, and former presidents **Local Government:** 67 provinces, under governors

Ethnic Composition: Turks constitute 90% of the population; ethnic minorities include 7% Kurds and small groups of Greeks, Armenians, and Jews **Population Distribution:** 43% urban **Density:** 140 inhabitants per sq. mi.

Largest Cities (M.A. = Metropolitan Area): (1973 est.) Istanbul 2,376,296 (M.A. 3,135,354), Ankara 1,461,345 (M.A. 1,553,897), Izmir 590,997 (M.A. 819,276), Adana 383,046 (M.A. 454,188), Bursa 318,209 (M.A. 426,567)

Per Capita Income: $772 (1978) **Gross National Product (GNP):** $33.4 billion (1978) **Economic Statistics:** About 22% of the GNP is derived from agriculture (cereals, tobacco, grapes, fruits, and cotton) and animal husbandry, 25% from industry (steel, iron, sugar and cotton refining, tires, textiles, fertilizers) and construction, 12% from commerce and finance, and 23% from transportation and services **Minerals and Mining:** Partly exploited minerals include copper, chrome (about 10% of the world's production), boracite, mercury, iron, manganese, coal, oil **Labor Force:** 16,400,000 (1977), with 61% in agriculture, and 13% in industry **Foreign Trade:** Exports, mainly tobacco, cotton, hazelnuts, raisins, chrome, and citrus fruits, totaled $1.8 billion in 1976. Imports, chiefly machinery and transportation equipment, petroleum products, iron, steel and related products, fertilizers, and plastics, totaled $5.8 billion **Principal Trade Partners:** West Germany, France, Iraq, United States, Britain, Switzerland, Italy

Vital Statistics: Birthrate, 27.1 per 1,000 of pop (1966); death rate, 14.6 **Life Expectancy:** 54 years **Health Statistics:** 456 inhabitants per hospital bed; 1,804 per physician (1975) **Infant Mortality:** 145 per 1,000 births (1970) **Illiteracy:** 38% **Education Statistics:** 45,416 primary and secondary schools (1976), with combined enrollment of 6,871,473 (1974) **Enrollment in Higher Education:** 218,934 **GNP Expended on Education:** 4.6% (1976)

Transportation: Surfaced roads total 8,700 mi. Motor Vehicles: 664,341 (1975) **Passenger Cars:** 393,815 **Railway Mileage:** 5,700 **Ports:** Istanbul, Izmir, Mersin, Samsun, Iskenderun, Izmit, Trabzon **Major Airlines:** Turkish Airlines, government owned, operates domestically and internationally **Communications:** Government owned **Radio Transmitters:** 21 **Licenses:** 4,228,000 (1976) **Television Transmitters:** 38 **Receivers:** 1,769,000 (1976) **Telephones:** 1,131,000 (1976) **Newspapers:** 450 dailies

Weights and Measures: Metric system **Travel Requirements:** Passport; no visa for 3 months

In many ways, modern Turkey is the product of its first president, Mustafa Kemal, later surnamed Kemal Atatürk, or Father of the Turks. He was a dictator who believed that he had to be ruthless in bringing his country into the 20th century. Before his death in 1938, Atatürk cut as many ties with the past as possible. He had the Turkish alphabet transcribed from Arabic to Latin characters, outlawed the wearing in public of the traditional fez for men and the veil for women, and secularized the theocratic Moslem state of the former sultans. Islam is still a strong force among Turks, however; more people from Turkey make the holy pilgrimage to Mecca than from any other Moslem country.

Turkey is still plagued by a wide disparity between life in its more affluent cities and its backward rural areas in Asia Minor. There has been a rapid migration to the cities, causing crowding and a demand for goods and services on the part of the peasant who will wait no longer for the benefits of modernization to reach him.

The country's economy is still largely based on agriculture, but the government has been pushing industrial expansion at a rapid pace, causing a strain resulting in high inflation, a foreign exchange crisis marked by declining foreign reserves, and a huge balance-of-payments deficit. After India, Turkey is the world's largest producer

of opium. Under international accords, Turkey is one of seven countries permitted to export opium for legitimate medical requirements. U.S.-Turkish cooperation, with UN help, has led to an effort to control opium production in order to prevent illegal trafficking of the drug.

Turkey, which under the sultans ruled virtually the entire Arab world, is the only Moslem country to maintain formal diplomatic relations with Israel. Its chief concern in foreign policy—other than the presence of the Soviet Union as a neighbor—is a recurring conflict with Greece over the nearby island republic of Cyprus. Enmity between the ethnic Turkish minority and the ethnic Greek majority on the island has been a constant source of friction. In 1974 Turkey sent troops there to protect the Turkish Cypriot community following the overthrow of the Cyprus government. Despite strong U.S. pressure Turkey's occupation of the northern part of the island continues. In addition to the Cyprus question, Greece and Turkey are at odds over control of oil and air rights in the Aegean Sea.

In January 1978, Bulent Ecevit became premier in a cabinet supported by a fragile coalition of his Republican People's party, two small parties, and defectors from the Justice party. He faced an economy that was in shambles and poor relations with the United States, where there was more sympathy for Greece than for Turkey. Moreover, riots broke out—notably among the underprivileged Alevis, a community of Shia Moslems in a country where Sunni Moslems were in the majority. In December 1978, the legislature imposed martial law in the areas most affected by the violence. The United States ended its embargo on arms to Turkey in August 1978, and Turkey allowed the U.S. to reopen military bases. In 1979, the Shia revolution in Iran encouraged the Alevis and complicated Turkey's economic plight. A major importer of oil from Iran before the Revolution, Turkey turned to the Soviet Union and Iraq for substitute supplies.

HISTORY: Asiatic Turkey is one of the oldest inhabited regions on Earth and for centuries served as a battleground for foreign conquerors. It was the site of the ancient states of Hatti, Urartu, Phrygia, Troy, Lydia, and Armenia. In the 7th century B.C., the Greeks founded the city of Byzantium on the site of present-day Istanbul. It was captured by the Romans in A.D. 196 and later rebuilt as Constantinople by the Christian Emperor Constantine. The Ottoman Empire was founded in 1299 by Turkish tribes from Central Asia on the remnants of the Byzantine and the Seljuk Turkish empires in Asia Minor. With its collapse in 1918, modern Turkey was born. The Turks had absorbed most of the major ethnic groups; the major exception were the Armenians, who were virtually exterminated by Ottoman attacks in the early 20th century.

1920-23: Allied powers strip Ottoman Empire of its vast possessions, reducing it to a small state; Sultan Mohammed VI accepts Allied terms, but Turkish nationalists rally under Mustafa Kemal, later known as Kemal Atatürk, and organize resistance. Sultan is deposed and Turkey is declared a republic, with Atatürk as president

1924-38: A constitution is promulgated, providing for parliamentary government, but Atatürk rules as virtual dictator. He introduces sweeping reforms to westernize Turkey, which undergoes an unparalleled revolutionary transformation

1950-59: Celal Bayar, leader of the Democratic Party, becomes president, with Adnan Menderes as premier. Turkey joins NATO in 1952. In 1955, Turkey and Iraq sign a mutual defense agreement, the Baghdad Pact. Marshall Plan aid leads to expansion of Turkish economy, but rapid industrialization results in economic crisis, forcing government to adopt restrictive measures to deal with discontent. Menderes is returned to office in 1957 elections; political controls tightened

1960: Army junta, led by General Cemal Gursel, stages coup, bans Democratic Party, and puts Menderes, Bayar, and hundreds of other Democratic Party members on trial for having violated the constitution. Most receive long prison sentences, but Menderes and several others are hanged

1961-62: A new constitution providing for a bicameral legislature and a strong executive is approved by referendum. Gursel is elected president and Ismet Inonu becomes premier. An attempted coup by army elements is crushed and many officers purged. Government amnesties most of imprisoned supporters of Menderes but keeps Bayar and a number of others in jail

1964: Relations between Turkey and Greece, long embroiled in dispute over Cyprus, become further strained as heavy fighting breaks out between Greek and Turkish Cypriots

1965: Suleyman Demirel, leader of Justice Party, becomes premier following general elections

1966: Gursel falls ill; national assembly chooses General Cevdet Sunay, army chief of staff, to succeed him

1971: Following prolonged political and economic unrest, armed forces commanders demand resignation of Demirel government; Nihat Erim is named premier

1973: Bulent Ecevit elected premier. Retired Admiral Fahri Korutürk elected president

1974: Cypriot National Guard, under Greek officers, overthrows Cyprus President Archbishop Makarios. Turkish troops invade Cyprus and fight Greek Cypriots. Cease-fire arranged by UN representatives. Ecevit's coalition government collapses; interim government formed

1975: Citing "lack of progress" in Cyprus peace negotiations, U.S. Congress votes to cut off all military aid to Turkey. Turkey responds by seizing all American installations except the NATO base at Adana. Former Prime Minister Suleyman Demirel forms new coalition government

1976: Turkish exploration for oil in Aegean produces new tension with Greece. Earthquake in eastern Turkey kills thousands

1977: Ecevit's Republican People's Party wins close to a majority of parliamentary seats in the general elections. Ecevit resigns the premiership 10 days later after his center-left government loses its first vote of confidence in parliament; subsequently former Prime Minister Suleyman Demirel is asked to form new government. Economy continues serious decline. Total of 262 people die in recurrent political violence. Ecevit's party gains, Demirel's loses in local elections; latter's governing coalition dissolves

1978: Ecevit named premier. Turkey and Soviet Union sign nonaggression, trade and cultural pacts. U.S. Congress votes to allow President Carter to end embargo on arms sales to Turkey and provide substantial military aid. U.S. military bases reopen. Legislature proclaims martial law in 13 provinces

1979: Martial law imposed in 6 additional provinces

TUVALU

Area: 9.78 sq. mi. **Population:** 10,000 (1978 est.)

Official Name: Tuvalu **Capital:** Fongafale, on Funafuti **Nationality:** Tuvaluan **Languages:** Tuvaluan and English **Religion:** Christian, mostly Protestant **Flag:** A light blue field with the Union Jack in the upper left corner and nine yellow five-pointed stars in the right half **Anthem:** N.A. **Currency:** Australian dollar (0.91 per U.S. $1)

Location: Tuvalu is comprised of nine low-lying coral atolls, eight of which are inhabited; the islands form a chain approximately 360-miles long in the southwest Pacific Ocean. Tuvalu's nearest neighbors are Fiji and Kiribati **Features:** The islands have a tropical climate and are mostly covered with coconut palms

Head of State: Queen Elizabeth II through a governor-general, Penitala Fiatau Teo, born 1912 **Head of Government:** Prime Minister Toalipi Lauti, born 1932, took office October 1, 1978 **Effective Date of Present Constitution:** October 1, 1978 **Legislative Body:** Unicameral Parliament, consisting of 12 members elected by universal suffrage **Local Government:** Island councils for the eight inhabited islands

Ethnic Composition: Almost entirely Polynesian **Population Distribution:** N.A. **Density:** 1,022.5 inhabitants per sq. mi.

Largest center: (1973 census) Fongafale 871

Per Capita Income: less than $50 annually **Gross National Product (GNP):** N.A. **Economic Statistics:** A large part of personal income in Tuvalu is derived from cash remittances from Tuvaluan men working as seamen and in the phosphate industries of Nauru and Banaba (Ocean Island) in Kiribati. Other income is derived from copra, the chief cash crop, the sale of postage stamps and coins, and handicrafts. Fishing is on a subsistence basis. Other agricultural crops are pulaka (taro), pandanus fruit, bananas and pawpaws **Minerals and Mining:** None **Labor Force:** N.A. **Foreign Trade:** Exports of copra (59 tons) totaled $4,277 in 1976. Copra exports usually average 120 tons per year. Imports include food and fuel **Principal Trade Partners:** N.A.

Vital Statistics: Birthrate, N.A; death rate, N.A. **Life Expectancy:** N.A. **Health Statistics:** 42 inhabitants per hospital bed (1978) **Infant Mortality:** N.A. **Illiteracy:** Over 50% **Education Statistics:** 8 primary schools with an enrollment of 1,540 (1976) **Enrollment in the one secondary school:** 248 **GNP Expended on Education:** N.A.

Transportation: There are no paved roads **Motor Vehicles** N.A. **Railway Mileage:** None **Port:** Funafuti **Major Airlines:** Air Pacific provides service to Fiji and Kiribati; there is no inter-island service

Communications: Government owned **Radio Transmitters:** 1 **Receivers:** 1,200 **Television:** None **Telephones:** N.A. **Newspapers:** 1 fortnightly

Weights and Measures: N.A.

On October 1, 1978, the nine atolls of the Ellice Islands (Tuvalu's name before 1975) became the independent nation of Tuvalu (Polynesian for "cluster of eight islands," after the eight inhabited atolls). The main post-independence aim of Tuvalu's people is for greater economic self-sufficiency. This goal, however, is not readily forthcoming. The climate makes these "paradise islands" beautiful to see; but the thin, alkaline soil makes them ill-suited for agriculture. The islands are dotted with coconut palms, and copra is the main export. Handicrafts and subsistence fishing are the chief occupations. The chief source of revenue is from remittances from overseas Tuvaluans, working as seamen or as phosphate workers on nearby Nauru and Banaba (Ocean Island). With phosphate production on Banaba scheduled to end in 1979, the economic impact of returning workers will exacerbate the present situation; per capita income is now less than 50 U.S. dollars annually.

Future development will probably center on the potentially rich fishing grounds to be found in Tuvalu's lagoons and ocean waters. The South Pacific Commission plans to open a tuna canning plant, and fisheries and other industrial projects may be forthcoming. Foreign aid will also be important in further development. Great Britain has been the islands' chief benefactor and has built up the new nation's administrative infrastructure, but independence is expected to attract aid and possible investment from Australia, New Zealand, the United States and Japan.

HISTORY: Tuvaluans consider Samoa as their ancestral home, with which they share a common Polynesian language and culture. Fishermen are thought to have drifted westward from the central Pacific and populated the islands, which were periodically raided by Micronesians from Tonga and the Gilberts. The Spaniard Mendaña is thought to have sighted Nui in 1568 and Niulakita in 1595. Permanent contact with Westerners came in the late 18th and early 19th centuries; the first European settlers were from the London Missionary Society, who arrived in 1865 and soon converted the islanders to Protestantism. During the "blackbirders" slave trade from 1850 to 1875, the islands' population was reduced from 20,000 to about 3,000

1856: Guano Act of U.S. Congress establishes American claims to Funafuti, Nukefetau, Nukulaelae and Niulakita atolls

1877: Britain establishes the High Commission for the Western Pacific to stamp out "blackbird" raiders

1892: Britain proclaims a protectorate over Ellice Islands and neighboring Gilberts

1915: Protectorate reorganized as Gilbert and Ellice Islands Colony

1973: Britain appoints commissioner to study growing Polynesian demands for autonomy of the Ellice Islands

1974: August-September referendum, observed by UN, shows overwhelming support for separation from Gilbert Islands

1975: The islands are established as a separate dependency under British administration under the name Tuvalu

1977: U.S. announces its willingness to negotiate claims to four disputed islands

1978: Independence is declared October 1. Tuvalu becomes 38th member of the Commonwealth

1979: Prime Minister Toalipi Lauti signs Friendship Treaty with the United States; pact recognizes U.S. renunciation of claims over disputed islands and provides for continued consultations on security and marine reserves

UGANDA

Area: 91,076 sq. mi. **Population:** 12,350,000 (1978 est.)

Official Name: Republic of Uganda **Capital:** Kampala **Nationality:** Ugandan **Languages:** English is the official language and Swahili the national language; of the many local languages the most important is Luganda **Religion:** About half the population is Christian, 10% Moslem, and the rest animists **Flag:** 6 alternate horizontal stripes of black, yellow, and red, with the national emblem, a crested crane, in a white circle in the center **Anthem:**

National Anthem, beginning "O Uganda! May God uphold thee".
Currency: Ugandan shilling (7.5 per U.S. $1)

Location: East Africa. Landlocked Uganda is bordered on the north by Sudan, on the east by Kenya, on the south by Tanzania, Lake Victoria, and Rwanda, and on the west by Zaire **Features:** Most of the country consists of a plateau about 4,000 feet above sea level. About 18% of the total area consists of swamps and open water, including Lakes Victoria, George, Albert (Mobutu Sese Seko), Edward, and Kyoga. Thick forest covers parts of the south; the north is largely savanna with some semidesert areas in the northeast **Chief Rivers:** Victoria Nile, Albert Nile, Katonga

Head of State and of Government: President Godfrey L. Binaisa, born 1920, appointed June 20, 1979 **Effective Date of Present Constitution:** 1967, suspended 1971; a new constitution is being drafted **Legislative Body:** 30-member National Consultative Council **Local Government:** 10 provinces, divided into 26 districts

Ethnic Composition: About 98% of the population is African. The largest tribes include the Baganda, Iteso, Banyankore, and Basoga. Asians, mainly of Indian extraction, now number fewer than 500, and Europeans less than 3,500 **Population Distribution:** 7% urban **Density:** 136 inhabitants per sq. mi.

Largest Cities: (1973 est.) Kampala 380,000; (1969 census) Jinja 52,509, Mbale 23,544, Entebbe 21,096

Per Capita Income: $167 (1978) **Gross National Product (GNP):** $2.1 billion (1978) **Economic Statistics:** 52.7% of the GNP is derived from agriculture (coffee, cotton, tea, tobacco); 18.7% from commerce and finance; 15.7% from services; and 12.9% from industry (the manufacture of food products and textiles, cigarettes, brewing, enamel hollow ware, cement, wooden boxes, and soap) **Minerals and Mining:** There are substantial deposits of copper and smaller amounts of wolfram, beryl, and cassiterite **Labor Force:** 308,000 salaried workers (1970). 90% of the population is in agriculture, 4% in industry **Foreign Trade:** Exports, mainly coffee, copper, cotton, tea and feeds, totaled $361 million in 1976. Imports, chiefly machinery and transportation equipment, cotton and synthetic fabrics and petroleum products, totaled $160 million **Principal Trade Partners:** Britain, Kenya, United States, West Germany, Japan, Italy

Vital Statistics: Birthrate, 43.2 per 1,000 of pop.; death rate, 17.6 **Life Expectancy:** 49 years **Health Statistics:** 636 inhabitants per hospital bed; 27,113 per physician (1975) **Infant Mortality:** 160 per 1,000 births **Illiteracy:** 65% **Education Statistics:** 3,417 primary schools, with combined enrollment of 1,032,418 (1975) **Enrollment in Higher Education:** 5,474 (1975) **GNP Expended on Education:** 3.4% (1973)

Transportation: Paved roads total 1,200 mi. **Motor Vehicles:** 35,900 (1975) **Passenger Cars:** 27,000 **Railway Mileage:** 756 **Ports:** None **Major Airlines:** Uganda Airlines operates both domestically and internationally **Communications:** Government owned **Radio Transmitters:** 7 **Receivers:** 250,000 (1976) **Television Transmitters:** 6 **Licenses:** 71,000 (1976) **Telephones:** 46,000 (1976) **Newspapers:** 4 dailies, 5 copies per 1,000 inhabitants (1974)

Weights and Measures: Metric system **Travel Requirements:** Passport; visa; $3.15 fee; 1 photo

From the lushly green shores of Lake Victoria to the snow-capped Mountains of the Moon on its western border, Uganda's natural beauty is the fulfillment of a tourist's dream. Until recently elephant herds, great flocks of birds and other wildlife, vivid flowers, neat tea plantations, and farmlands rich in coffee and cotton delighted the visitor and gave support to the country's claim to being "the pearl of East Africa."

But Uganda changed drastically under the harsh regime of Field Marshal Idi Amin Dada. The eight-year reign of terror claimed the lives of possibly as many as 300,000 Ugandans. An estimated 250,000 fled to neighboring Kenya, and many more lived in exile in Britain.

Though bright at the outset of independence from British rule in 1962, Ugandan hopes soon faded. Bent on forming a strong unity state, Uganda's leader, President Milton Obote, moved to eliminate the country's old kingdoms. In 1966 government forces attacked the palace of the revered *Kabaka*, or traditional king, of Buganda—the largest of four Ugandan kingdoms. Obote then proclaimed a move to the left modeled on the African Socialism of President Nyerere in neighboring Tanzania.

But in January 1971, Obote was ousted in a coup led by the Ugandan army commander, Maj. Gen.

Idi Amin. Amin then declared himself president for life, abolished parliament and purged the judiciary and the civil service.

Amin, a Moslem, waged war against the predominantly Christian Acholi and Lango tribesmen. At least 3,000 of the tribesmen were killed when Amin came to power, and another 2,000 were killed in early 1977 after Amin uncovered an attempted coup which he linked to the two tribes.

From 1972 General Amin expelled 50,000 Ugandan Asians holding British passports and nationalized 41 chiefly British-owned businesses and tea estates. These actions spurred inflation and depressed exports. Overall, the economy deteriorated badly under the regime's inefficiency and lavish military spending.

Amin committed a fatal mistake in October 1978 when he sent troops to Tanzania and occupied more than 700 square miles of foreign soil. Tanzania quickly counteracted, carried the war into Uganda the next month, and in April 1979 captured Kampala, whose residents greeted the invaders as liberators. Amid eluded capture and reportedly is living in exile in Libya.

Virtually the entire world welcomed Amin's ouster. The U.S. quickly lifted the trade embargo it had imposed against Uganda in 1978.

Yet problems remain. Yussufu Lule, the man chosen to succeed Amin, survived barely two months before political wrangling forced his resignation. He was replaced in June 1979 by Godfrey Binaisa, a former attorney general and longtime defender of human rights. His government was soon threatened by a general strike and random acts of violence from Lule supporters.

HISTORY: Until the latter part of the 19th century, Uganda experienced a series of migrations extending over hundreds of years. As a result, a number of major chiefdoms grew up, the most powerful of which were the chiefdom of Bunyoro-Kitara and the rival state of Buganda. Britain established a protectorate over Buganda in 1894 and subsequently extended the protectorate to the rest of Uganda. However, the stubborn independence of Buganda's rulers, which continued well into the 20th century, hampered the development of national unity

1953: Kabaka (king) Mutesa II of Buganda is deposed and exiled to London when he refuses to help put down riots by local chiefs

1955: British restore Mutesa but stipulate he is to reign as constitutional monarch and that Buganda will participate in the central government of Uganda

1962: Uganda gains independence with a federal constitution that gives Buganda large measure of autonomy; Milton Obote becomes prime minister

1963: Post of-governor-general is abolished; Mutesa is elected president by parliament

1966: Obote removes Mutesa, suspends constitution, abolishes federal system, and assumes full powers of government

1967: Uganda adopts republican constitution with a presidential form of government headed by Obote; traditional kingdoms are abolished

1971: Obote is ousted in coup led by Maj. Gen. Idi Amin, who assumes presidency; refusal of Tanzania to recognize his government results in minor warfare between the two countries

1972: Amin orders the expulsion of the estimated 50,000 Asians in Uganda holding British passports

1973: Lakes Albert and Edward, along Zaire border, renamed "Mobutu Sese Seko" and "Idi Amin Dada" (after Zairese and Ugandan presidents) in what is described as "another step in the decolonization of the minds of the people." U.S. severs ties with Uganda after repeated threats against U.S. Embassy officials and the detention of 100 American Peace Corps volunteers

1974: Amin suppresses military coup

1976: Israeli commandos rescue skyjacked hostages being held at Entebbe airport, crippling Amin's Soviet-equipped air force

1977: Anglican Archbishop Janani Luwum and two of Amin's cabinet ministers are arrested and murdered; the government claims the three were killed in an automobile accident after attempting to escape. Two hundred Americans are barred from leaving Uganda, following a remark by President Carter that the murders had "disgusted the entire civilized world." The order is rescinded after protest is lodged. Britain severs diplomatic ties with Uganda after it is revealed that a British subject had been murdered during the 1976 Entebbe raid. Thirty-three Commonwealth nations, including 13 African nations, condemn Amin's regime for its repression. Twelve Ugandans are convicted of plotting a coup and are shot. Thirteen die in new anti-Christian purge; many arrested. Amin curtails travel, tightens security

1978: U.S. passes Britain as largest buyer of Ugandan coffee. U.S. imposes trade embargo against Uganda. Ugandan forces invade Tanzania; general war ensues

1979: Kampala falls to Tanzanian forces and Ugandan rebels; Amin driven into exile. U.S. lifts trade embargo. Yussufu Lule is sworn in as president in April; replaced in June by Godfrey Binaisa

.UNION OF SOVIET SOCIALIST REPUBLICS

Area: 8,649,490 sq. mi. **Population:** 262,400,000 (1979 census)
Official Name: Union of Soviet Socialist Republics **Capital:** Moscow **Nationality:** Soviet **Languages:** Russian, the official language, is the native tongue of about 60% of the population and is spoken as a second language by less than half of the rest; other languages are Ukrainian, Byelorussian, Lithuanian, Latvian, Estonian, Moldavian, Yiddish, Georgian, Armenian, Uzbek, Tatar, Kazakh, Azerbaijani, and over 100 other languages and dialects **Religion:** Atheism, officially propagated by the government, is followed by about 70% of the population; there are also 18% Russian Orthodox, 9% Moslems, and small groups of Roman Catholics, Protestants, Jews, and Buddhists **Flag:** Red field with a golden hammer and sickle (representing the industrial and farm workers) under a golden star in the upper left corner **Anthem:** Hymn of the Soviet Union **Currency:** Ruble (0.66 per U.S. $1)

Location: Northern Eurasia, from the Baltic Sea to the Pacific, with the Arctic Ocean on the north. The largest country in the world, the USSR is bordered on the northwest by Norway and Finland; on the west by Poland, Czechoslovakia, Hungary, and Romania; on the south by Turkey, Iran, and Afghanistan, and on the southeast by China, Mongolia, and North Korea **Features:** In the west, from the Pripet Marshes near the Polish frontier to the Ural Mountains, the land consists of a broad plain broken by occasional low hills and crossed by numerous rivers. Between the Black and Caspian seas lie the Caucasus Mountains. East of the Ural Mountains, which mark the traditional division between European and Asiatic Russia, are the Aral Sea, vast Siberian lowlands, steppes, and deserts of Central Asia. Beyond are the vast Siberian highlands and mountain ranges of the Soviet Far East. The highest ranges lie along the Chinese and Mongolian borders **Chief Rivers:** In Europe, the Dnieper, Dniester, Don, Volga; in Asia, the Ob, Yenisey, Lena, Amur, Kolyma, Amu Darya, Syr Darya

Political Leader and Head of State: Chairman of the Presidium of the Supreme Soviet (President) and General Secretary of the Central Committee of the Communist Party: Marshal Leonid Ilyich Brezhnev, born 1906, appointed general secretary in 1964 and president in 1977 **Head of Government:** Chairman of the Council of Ministers (Premier): Aleksey Nikolayevich Kosygin, born 1904, appointed 1964 **Effective Date of Present Constitution:** 1977 **Legislative Body:** Supreme Soviet (bicameral), consisting of the Soviet (Council) of the Union and the Soviet of Nationalities. The Soviet of the Union has 767 members elected on the basis of population; the Soviet of Nationalities has 750 elected on the basis of territorial units. Elections are called for every 5 years. Formal power is vested in the Presidium of the Supreme Soviet, which also appoints the Council of Ministers. Under Communist party direction, the council supervises all of the work of the government **Local Government:** 15 republics, each with its own Supreme Soviet and Council of Ministers, the latter headed by a premier. Ethnic divisions within the republics include 20 autonomous republics, 8 autonomous regions, and 10 national districts

Ethnic Composition: Russians constitute 53% of the population, Ukrainians 17%, Byelorussians 4%, Uzbeks 4%, and more than 150 other nationalities **Population Distribution:** 61% urban **Density:** 30 inhabitants per sq. mi.

Largest Cities: (1979 census) Moscow 8,011,000, Leningrad 4,588,000, Kiev 2,144,000; Tashkent 1,779,000, Baku 1,550,000, Khar'kov 1,444,000, Gor'kiy 1,344,000, Novosibirsk 1,312,000, Minsk 1,276,000, Kuybyshev 1,216,000, Sverdlovsk 1,211,000, Dnepropetrovsk 1,066,000, Tbilisi 1,066,000, Odessa 1,046,000

Per Capita Income: $4,004 (1978) **Gross National Product (GNP):** $1,047 billion (1978) **Economic Statistics:** 77.5% of the GNP is derived from industry (in 1969 more than 30,000 of 45,000 enterprises accounted for 75% of total production; main industries include oil, steel, electricity, cement, pig iron, foodstuffs, textiles, and other heavy industry); 16.5% from agriculture (2 million square-miles of arable land provide wheat, rye, corn, oats, potatoes, sugarbeets, linseed, sunflower seed, cotton, and flax; main livestock are cattle, sheep, and pigs); and the rest from other sources **Minerals and Mining:** Vast deposits of coal, iron, petroleum, copper, nickel, bauxite, zinc, lead, gold, manganese, platinum, and tin **Labor Force:** Of 99,600,000 workers in 1974, there were 10,000,000 engaged in agricultural labor, 40,000,000 in industry and construction, 11,000,000 in transportation and

communications, 13,000,000 in education, social security, and public health, and 25,000,000 in other sectors of the economy **Foreign Trade:** Exports, mainly machinery, iron and steel, crude oil, foodstuffs, lumber and paper products, and textiles, amounted to $43 billion in 1977. Imports, chiefly machinery, foodstuffs, and consumer goods, totaled $40 billion **Principal Trade Partners:** East Germany, Czechoslovakia, Poland, Hungary, Bulgaria, Romania, Cuba, Japan, West Germany, Finland, United States, Italy, France, Yugoslavia

Vital Statistics: Birthrate, 18.5 per 1,000 of pop. (1976); death rate, 9.5 **Life Expectancy:** 70 years **Health Statistics:** 85 inhabitants per hospital bed; 347 per physician (1975) **Infant Mortality:** 27.7 per 1,000 births (1974) **Illiteracy:** Negligible **Education Statistics:** 187,680 primary and secondary schools, with combined enrollment of 56,400,000 (1975) **Enrollment in Higher Education:** 4,853,958 **GNP Expended on Education:** 7.6% (1974)

Transportation: Surfaced roads total 372,823 mi. (1973) **Motor Vehicles:** 4,950,000 (1967) **Passenger Cars:** 1,100,000 **Railway Mileage:** 85,489 (1975) **Ports:** Main terminal ports on the Volga-Don system are Astrakhan, Rostov, Moscow, Perm; main transfer ports: Volgograd, Saratov, Kuybyshev, Kazan, Gorky, Yaroslavl; seaports: Leningrad, Odessa, Kaliningrad, Murmansk, Archangel, Riga, Vladivostok **Major Airlines:** Aeroflot operates all international and domestic flights **Communications:** Government controlled **Radio Transmitters:** 3,034 **Receivers:** 122,477,000 (1975) **Television Transmitters:** 1,749 **Receivers:** 55,181,000 (1975) **Telephones:** 18,000,000 (1976) **Newspapers:** 691 dailies, 347 copies per 1,000 inhabitants (1975)

Weights and Measures: Metric system **Travel Requirements:** Passport; visa, valid 3 months; 3 photos. Make arrangements through travel agency that has a contract with Intourist.

The Soviet Union, the world's largest country and one of the leading superpowers, has in recent years been experiencing alternating success and setbacks. Its policy of détente, the peaceful co-existence with non-Communist nations, has raised more ideological dilemmas than its original supporters could have imagined.

Leonid Brezhnev, General Secretary of the Communist Party, the only political body in the Soviet Union, has now been in power longer than any of his predecessors since Stalin. Brezhnev's active role in the 25th Congress of the Communist Party of the Soviet Union dispelled rumors of possible illness or lack of support in the Soviet power structure. The Congress, which met in February–March 1976, endorsed the leadership of Secretary Brezhnev. In June 1977 Brezhnev was elected Chairman of the Presidium of the USSR and thus became the first leader in Soviet history to hold both the chief party and state post.

In the present five-year plan the party leaders have had to lower their targets for economic growth. In effect this was an admission of failure in the previous five-year plan to reach anticipated goals. For 1976-80 heavy industry receives strong emphasis at the expense of consumer goods. There is to be a retrenchment in the expansion of agriculture. The harvest failures before 1976 plagued Soviet planners hoping to achieve self-sufficiency in food needs.

Foreign trade, once a small part of the Russian economy, is now of great importance. Commerce with the West has reached an unprecedented level. Trade with the United States was over $2.8 billion in 1978 compared to $200 million in 1971. Purchases of much needed wheat in the United States and Canada have had substantial impact on world prices. Other Western nations, Japan, Britain, West Germany, have become involved with the USSR in trade pacts and long-range projects that require large investments in plant technology and resource development. The Soviets have been funding their trade deficits with the Western nations by selling gold or taking long-term loans.

Traditionally a land power, the USSR built up its navy in the 1960s and 70s, and sought influence in the Middle East and Africa, sometimes shipping Cuban soldiers to the assistance of pro-Soviet governments. The combination of Soviet

UNION OF SOVIET SOCIALIST REPUBLICS
(European Part)
CONIC PROJECTION

MILES
0   50   100   200   300

KILOMETRES
0   100   200   300

National Capitals ⊛
Capitals of Union Republics ⊚
International boundaries
Union Republic boundaries
Canals

transport and Cuban men has helped Angola defeat domestic enemies, Ethiopia drive Somalia out of the disputed Ogaden, and Southern Yemen invade Yemen.

Enmity between China and the USSR continues to divide the Communist world. The passing of Mao Zedong has not lessened the hostility. In East Europe the Soviets still can count on the solidarity of Communist nations with the exception of Yugoslavia and Albania (Romanian disenchantment is a sometime thing). Overtures to Belgrade and Tirana for a return to the ideological fold have proved unsuccessful. In Western Europe the Communist parties of several nations have declared their freedom to depart from the standard Soviet line. In Italy and France the question of national Communism has become especially critical with the strong showing of local Communists in recent elections. In Spain the local Communist Party leadership has been disavowed by Moscow. At this time of change the Kremlin has been unable to assert leadership in its own camp.

Nor has the Kremlin achieved unity within its own national boundaries. A minority voice, the dissident movement, still draws attention to ills in Soviet society. For every proclamation of the need for détente and the free exchange of people and ideas, the Soviet leadership by its actions works against the spirit of détente. Dissidents are imprisoned or lose their jobs. Emigration, immigration and internal movement are rigidly controlled. Brezhnev has denounced the human rights appeals of U.S. President Carter as interference in internal affairs of the Soviet Union and has tightened the pressure against all artistic and political expression that deviates from the party view.

HISTORY: About the 5th century A.D. the Russian steppes began to be peopled by the Slavs. By the 9th century, despite repeated invasions by other tribes, the Slavs constituted the majority of Russia's inhabitants

862-79: Rurik, a Scandinavian chieftain, establishes the first Russian city-state, at Novgorod. His successor, Oleg, expands his territory in 879 and makes Kiev his capital

1237-40: Mongol (Tatar) hordes overrun Russia, initiating two centuries of the "Tatar Yoke"

1547: Ivan IV (the Terrible), Prince of Moscow, is crowned tsar

1712: Peter the Great transfers capital from Moscow to St. Petersburg (now Leningrad)

1812: Napoleon invades Russia and occupies Moscow. Returning westward, he loses almost his entire army in the Russian snows

1861: Alexander II liberates the serfs

1914: Russia enters World War I

1917: Military setbacks lead to overthrow of Tsar Nicholas II. Succeeding Provisional Government is ousted by Bolsheviks, led by Lenin, who ends war by surrendering much territory

1922: Four Communist-ruled states—all formerly parts of Tsar's domain—form Union of Soviet Socialist Republics

1924-38: Lenin dies (1924). After a power struggle with Leon Trotsky, Stalin emerges as dictator. He institutes the forcible collectivization of agriculture, liquidating more than five million peasant families. In a great purge of his opponents, thousands of leading officials are executed

1941-45: Germany invades the USSR. After years of bitter warfare on Soviet soil, the Nazi armies are crushed. USSR regains most land surrendered in 1917 and becomes dominant in Eastern Europe

1953-56: Stalin dies (1953), causing another Kremlin power struggle. Nikita Khrushchev assumes leadership, denounces Stalin's "personality cult," and begins "de-Stalinization." Soviet forces invade Hungary and suppress anti-Communist revolution

1957: USSR launches world's first artificial satellite (Sputnik)

1961: Sino-Soviet split emerges over Khrushchev's policies of de-Stalinization and "peaceful coexistence" with the West

1962: USSR secretly installs missiles in Cuba; withdraws them after U.S. Navy quarantines island

1968: Soviet troops invade Czechoslovakia in move to halt liberalization of country's Communist regime

1969: Soviet and Chinese troops trade heavy fire in repeated border incidents; Moscow and Peking agree to talks

1974: Novelist Alexander Solzhenitsyn is arrested and deported for his criticisms of Soviet political repression

1975: Serious failure in grain crop; Soviet grain purchases abroad affect world food prices. In July, the joint U.S.-USSR Apollo/Soyuz space flight is successfully completed

1976: Egypt breaks off Soviet pact of 1971. Leadership of Brezhnev is reaffirmed at 25th Communist Party Congress. New five-year plan calls for lowered economic goals

1977: Brezhnev chosen Chairman of the Presidium. Economic growth targets are significantly reduced, indicating leveling off of economy after period of rapid expansion

1979: Brezhnev and U.S. President Jimmy Carter sign treaty to limit strategic arms (SALT II). Brezhnev expresses annoyance at U.S. Senate's delay in ratifying treaty

UNITED ARAB EMIRATES

Area: 32,278 sq. mi. **Population:** 760,000 (1978 est.)
Official Name: United Arab Emirates **Capital:** Abu Dhabi **Nationality:** Arab **Languages:** Arabic is the official language; Farsi and English are widely used, and Hindu and Urdu are also spoken **Religion:** 90% Sunni Moslem **Flag:** Equal green, white, and black horizontal stripes, with a red vertical stripe at the hoist **Anthem:** The National Anthem **Currency:** UAE Dirham (3.84 per U.S. $1)
Location: Southwest Asia on the Persian Gulf. The federation of seven emirates is bounded by Oman, Saudi Arabia, Qatar, and the Persian Gulf **Features:** A flat, barren island-dotted coastal plain gives way to extensive sand dunes in the interior. At the eastern end are the western Hajar Mountains
Head of State: President: Sheikh Zaid ibn Sultan al-Nahayan of Abu Dhabi, born 1918, reelected 1976, assisted by a Vice President, Sheikh Rashid ibn Said al-Maktum of Dubai, elected 1971, and a Supreme Council of the 7 rulers **Head of Government:** Premier: Sheikh Rashid ibn al-Maktum of Dubai, appointed 1979 **Effective Date of Present Constitution:** 1971 interim constitution amended 1976, and extended to 1981 **Legislative Body:** National Assembly (unicameral), of 40 members in proportion to emirate population, appointed by the seven rulers **Local Government:** Each of the seven emirates (Abu Dhabi, Ajman, Dubai, Fujairah, Ras al-Khaimah, Sharjah, Umm al-Qaiwain) is self-governing, under a sheikh
Ethnic Composition: Arabs (72%), Iranians, Pakistanis, and Indians; only about 25% are native-born **Population Distribution:** 90% urban **Density:** 24 inhabitants per sq. mi.
Largest Cities: (1977 est.) Abu Dhabi 210,000; (1972 est.) Dubai 60,000, Sharjah 25,000, Ras al-Khaimah 10,000, Ajman 4,000
Per Capita Income: $9,700 (1978) **Gross National Product (GNP):** $7.8 billion (1978) **Economic Statistics:** National income from oil revenues in 1976 were $7 billion from Abu Dhabi alone (70% of the country's total). Aside from the area's rich oil deposits, the economy includes herding, date growing, fishing, and trading **Minerals and Mining:** There are rich oil and natural gas deposits, notably in Abu Dhabi, and copper, gypsum, and limestone exist **Labor Force:** 420,000 (1976), with 65% in the oil industry, and 10% in agriculture and fishing **Foreign Trade:** Exports, 94% oil, totaled $9.5 billion in 1977. Imports, chiefly machinery, foods, and consumer goods, totaled $4.6 billion **Principal Trade Partners:** EC countries, United States, Japan
Vital Statistics: Birthrate, 50 per 1,000 of pop. (1974); death rate, 18 **Life Expectancy:** N.A. **Health Statistics:** 995 inhabitants per physician (1973) **Illiteracy:** 75% **Education Statistics:** 190 schools. Primary and secondary enrollment totaled 90,000 (1977) **Enrollment in Higher Education:** 2,100 (1976) **GNP Expended on Education:** 9.1% (1976)
Transportation: N.A. **Motor Vehicles:** 15,000 (1978) **Railway Mileage:** None **Ports:** Dubai, Abu Dhabi **Major Airlines:** Gulf Air **Communications:** Government controlled **Radio Transmitters:** 12 **Receivers:** 55,000 (1976) **Television Transmitters:** 2 **Receivers:** 26,065 **Telephones:** 75,000 (1976) **Newspapers:** 3 dailies
Weights and Measures: Metric system; British and local standards are also used **Travel Requirements:** Passport; visa, valid 1 month; $2.50 fee; 2 photos; copy of round-trip ticket

The United Arab Emirates consists of seven emirates on the eastern Arabian Peninsula, extending from the southern base of the Qatar Peninsula to Fujairah on the Gulf of Oman. From west to east, they are Abu Dhabi, Dubai, Sharjah, Ajman, Umm al-Qaiwain, Ras al-Khaimah, and Fujairah. Before independence, the area was sometimes referred to as Trucial Oman, the Trucial Coast, or the Trucial Sheikdoms. Boundaries are vague and in many places disputed. The sheikdoms are largely desert, hot and dry.

The main economic link among the emirates is the desire to share in the vast oil wealth of one of them, Abu Dhabi, at least until reserves are found in their own areas, as has happened in Dubai.

British influence in the area was formalized by treaty with the principal sheiks of the coast as early as 1820. The Exclusive Agreement of 1892 provided for British control of foreign agreements and affairs. The agreement terminated, however, following the withdrawal of British troops. Independence was declared on December 2, 1971. The pending withdrawal, coupled with the possibility of border claims by Iran and Saudi Arabia, had led to a proposal for federation with Qatar and Bahrain. But in August 1971, Bahrain announced it would go it alone and Qatar followed suit.

The UAE supported the Arab states in their war against Israel in 1973, and ended economic aid to Egypt after Egypt made peace with Israel in 1979.

HISTORY: European and Arab pirates roamed the Trucial Coast area from the 17th to the 19th centuries, hence the former label "Pirate Coast." Successful British expeditions against the pirates led to further campaigns against their headquarters at Ras al-Khaimah and other harbors along the southwest coast in 1819. In 1820 the sheiks signed a General Treaty of Peace with Britain

1853: Coastal sheiks sign treaty with the United Kingdom agreeing to a "perpetual maritime truce"

1892: UK and the Trucial States establish closer bonds in another treaty, similar to those entered into by the British and other Persian Gulf principalities

1955: UK effectively intervenes on the side of Abu Dhabi in the latter's dispute with Saudi Arabia over the Buraimi Oasis, resulting in control of the Oasis being shared between Abu Dhabi and the Sultanate of Oman

1958-60: Vast oil reserves are discovered in Abu Dhabi

1971: British protective treaty with the Trucial Sheikdoms ends. They become fully independent as the United Arab Emirates. Oil is discovered in Dubai

1975: UAE joins OPEC as its third largest contributor

1976: Supreme Defense Council unites the UAE's armed forces. Dubai officials announce plans for a $765-million port, a new airport and an oil refinery at Jebel Ali

1978: Dubai pulls forces from federal army and puts them on alert in dispute with Abu Dhabi over appointment of UAE armed forces commander

UNITED KINGDOM

Area: 94,399 sq. mi. **Population:** 56,100,000 (1978 est.)
Official Name: United Kingdom of Great Britain and Northern Ireland **Capital:** London **Nationality:** British **Languages:** English is the official and predominant language; Gaelic is spoken in parts of Scotland and Northern Ireland, while Welsh is the first language in western Wales and enjoys equal validity with English as an official language in Wales **Religion:** Although the Church of England and the Church of Scotland are established churches, there is complete religious freedom. About half the population belongs to the Church of England (Protestant Episcopal) and to its nonestablished branches in Scotland, Wales, and Northern Ireland. The Church of Scotland (Presbyterian) has about 1.3 million members. The other major Christian denominations are Roman Catholic (6 million); Methodist (900,000); Baptist (300,000); and Congregationalist (200,000). There are several hundred thousand Moslems, 450,000 Jews, and several thousand Buddhists **Flag:** Known as the Union Jack, the flag is a superimposition of the red cross of St. George of England, the white cross of St. Andrew of Scotland, and the red cross of St. Patrick of Ireland, all on a blue background **Anthem:** God Save the Queen **Currency:** Pound sterling (.49 per U.S. $1)
Location: Off the northwest coast of Europe. The island of Great Britain, containing England, Scotland, and Wales, is bordered by the Atlantic Ocean on the north and west, and is separated from the European continent by the North Sea, the Strait of Dover, and the English Channel on the east and south. The Irish Sea and the North Channel separate Great Britain from Ireland, the northern area of which constitutes Northern Ireland, bordered on the south by the Republic of Ireland **Features:** England is divided into hill districts in the north, west, and southwest, and the undulating downs and low-lying plains in the east and southeast. In the extreme north, the Cheviot Hills, running from east to west, separate England from Scotland. The Pennine Chain extends southward from the Cheviots into the Midlands, a plains region with low, rolling hills and valleys. Scotland has three natural topographic

divisions: the Southern Uplands; the Central Lowlands; and the Northern Highlands, which contain the highest point in the British Isles. Wales is generally mountainous. Northern Ireland contains many plateaus and hills **Chief Rivers:** Severn, Thames, Trent, Aire, Great Ouse, Wye, Tay, Nene, Clyde, Spey, Tweed, Tyne, Forth, Dee

Head of State: Queen Elizabeth II, born 1926, ascended the throne 1952 **Head of Government:** Prime Minister Margaret Thatcher, born 1925, appointed May 4, 1979 **Effective Date of Present Constitution:** The British Constitution is formed partly by statute, partly by common law, and partly by "traditional rights" known as conventions. The rules of the constitution have never been codified, and can be adaptedto changing conditions at any time by Act of Parliament or by the general acceptance of a new convention **Legislative Body:** Parliament (bicameral), consisting of the House of Lords and the House of Commons. The House of Commons, which is the ultimate authority for lawmaking, consists of 635 members elected by universal suffrage for a maximum term of 5 years. The House of Lords, which also functions as the highest court in the land, consists of some 1,200 members, including hereditary and life peers and peeresses, law lords appointed for life to carry out the judicial duties of the house, and the 2 archbishops and 24 senior bishops of the Church of England. The House of Lords has the power to delay, but not prevent, legislation **Local Government:** England is divided into 39 counties, 6 metropolitan counties, Greater London, and the Isles of Scilly; Wales is divided into 8 counties. Scotland is divided into 9 regions and 3 island areas. Northern Ireland is divided into 26 districts. Each local authority division throughout the United Kingdom is administered by its own elected council. In Northern Ireland the shape of the new institutions which will replace the former parliament had not been completely decided, although a 78-seat assembly and an executive or provincial cabinet which shares power between Roman Catholics and Protestants had been formed. A Constitutional Convention begun in 1975 was dissolved in 1976, having failed to agree on a system of government. Direct rule, first initiated in 1974, was therefore renewed. Northern Ireland continues to be represented in the U.K. House of Commons

Ethnic Composition: The contemporary Briton is descended from varied racial stocks that settled in the British Isles before the 12th century. Under the Normans, descendants of Scandinavian Vikings, pre-Celtic, Celtic, Roman, Anglo-Saxon, and Norse influences were blended into the Briton. The population includes some 1.9 million immigrant Pakistanis, Indians, West Indians and their British-born children **Population Distribution:** 78% urban **Density:** 594 inhabitants per sq. mi.

Largest Cities: (1976 est.) London 7,028,200, Birmingham 1,058,800, Glasgow 816,265, Leeds 744,500, Sheffield 558,000, Liverpool 539,700, Manchester 490,000, Bradford 458,900, Edinburgh 445,000, Bristol 416,300, Belfast 350,000

Capita Income: $4,556 (1978) **Gross National Product (GNP):** $254 billion (1978) **Economic Statistics:** About 32% of the GNP comes from manufacturing (iron and steel, engineering [vehicles and aircraft], textiles, chemicals, food products, and consumer goods); 12% from mining and quarrying (coal, iron ore, limestone, tin, gravel, oilshale, natural gas), construction, and public utilities; 9% from transportation and communications; 42% from trade and services; and 3% from agriculture **Minerals and Mining:** There are significant amounts of coal, small deposits of iron, limestone, tin, gravel and oilshale. There are large quantities of natural gas and oil in the North Sea **Labor Force:** 26.1 million (1977), with 28% in manufacturing and 2% in agriculture **Foreign Trade:** Exports, mainly manufactured goods including engineering products, motor vehicles, nonelectric and electric machinery, and nonmetallic mineral manufactures, totaled $63 billion in 1977. Imports, chiefly petroleum and petroleum products, machinery, nonferrous metals, meat and meat preparations, fruit and vegetables, amounted to $70 billion **Principal Trade Partners:** United States, West Germany, South Africa, Ireland, Canada, France, Netherlands, Switzerland

Vital Statistics: Birthrate, 11.8 per 1,000 of pop. (1977); death rate, 11.7 **Life Expectancy:** 72 years **Health Statistics:** 96 inhabitants per hospital bed; 703 per physician (1974) **Infant Mortality:** 14 per 1,000 births (1977) **Illiteracy:** Negligible **Education Statistics:** 33,070 primary and secondary schools, with combined enrollment of 11,000,000 (1975) **Enrollment in Higher Education:** 656,800 **GNP Expended on Education:** 6.3% (1973)

Transportation: Surfaced roads total 209,305 mi. **Motor Vehicles:** 16,460,000 (1976) **Passenger Cars:** 14,562,400 **Railway Mileage:** 11,643 (1976) **Ports:** London, Liverpool, Glasgow, Southampton, Belfast, Cardiff, Milford Haven, Manchester, Bristol, Hull, Swansea, Edinburgh, Newcastle **Major Airlines:** British Airways flies both domestically and internationally. There are some 30 independent air transport operations **Communications:** Government and privately owned **Radio Transmitters:** 364 **Receivers:** 39,500,000 (1976) **Television Transmitters:** 596 **Licenses:** 17,729,000 (1976) **Telephones:** 22,012,000 (1976) **Newspapers:** 111 dailies, 388 copies per 1,000 inhabitants (1975)

Weights and Measures: Metric system **Travel Requirements:** Passport; no visa

UNITED KINGDOM

BONNE PROJECTION

Copyright by C. S. HAMMOND & Co., N.Y.

SCALE OF MILES

KILOMETERS

Capitals of Countries ☆

Canals

The basic problem for Great Britain has been that ever since losing an empire it has been unable to find a new role. When Britain dismantled the Empire, beginning in 1947, it also lost its captive markets and sources of supply. Britain was forced to compete in a changed world market with the disadvantages of aging industrial plants, war-depleted natural resources and an agricultural base that produced only half of the nation's food needs. In the postwar rebuilding, it did not do as well as its competitors, especially West Germany, France and Japan. Even the traditional British luxury goods—autos, liquor, and clothing, faced strong competition.

In economic terms Britain has suffered from slow growth, poor foreign trade results, low investment, weak currency, high inflation—in sum, a sluggish economy. No government has been able to arrest this decline. Entry into the Common Market in January 1973 was supposed to revitalize the British economy. It has not. Europe sells more to Britain than it buys. Trade balances improved only slightly.

But the economic picture is not all grim. The trickle of North Sea oil which began to flow from the British sector in 1974 has now grown to half a million barrels a day. By 1980 Britain will not only be self-sufficient in oil but also able to earn enough in exports to put the country in the black for the first time since before World War II.

Although Britain has lost most of its 19th and early 20th century empire, troubles from former colonies as well as parts of the United Kingdom persist, most notably in Northern Ireland, Zimbabwe (Rhodesia), Belize, Scotland, and Wales. The violent troubles in Northern Ireland, where some 14,000 troops are stationed, have resisted solution ever since the rioting between Protestant and Catholic communities broke out in Belfast and Londonderry in 1969. A definitive solution to the Ulster impasse has proved elusive, with violence continuing through 1979.

The Labour party, originally an outgrowth of the trade-union movement, has promoted social programs and nationalization of industry. It won a plurality, but not a majority, in the House of Commons in 1974 by promising a deal with the trade unions to end crippling strikes. Harold Wilson became prime minister in a Labour government and made the promised "social compact" with the unions. He retired in 1976 and was succeeded by a close ally, James Callaghan.

Improvements in the economy occurred in 1977 and 1978, but patience wore thin during the miserable winter of 1978-1979. Prices increased rapidly. Unions violated the social compact by striking for wage increases to keep up with prices. Inconveniences caused by the strikes led to resentment of the labor movement—and of the Labour party.

As winter turned to spring, referendums were held in Wales and Scotland on laws passed in 1978 to grant autonomy to those regions. Wales decisively rejected autonomy, but the vote in Scotland was annoyingly ambiguous; 33 percent of the electorate voted yes, 31 percent no, and 36 percent did not bother to vote. The Scottish Nationalist party, which was part of Callaghan's tacit majority in Commons, demanded implementation of the Scottish autonomy law, even though the law forbade its own implementation without the approval of 40 percent of the electorate. When Callaghan tried to delay the issue, the Scottish Nationalists joined the conservative party in a resolution of no confidence, which passed by one vote.

Callaghan dissolved Commons and faced an election in which the Conservative party promised a less onerous tax structure, denationalization of some industries, austerity to promote hard work, and repeal of the autonomy laws. Traditionally skeptical of nationalization and of welfare programs, the Conservatives were led by one of their most outspoken free enterprisers—Margaret Roberts Thatcher. The Conservatives won a majority in Commons, and Thatcher became the first woman prime minister.

HISTORY: The first known settlers of Britain were the Celts, who invaded the island from northern Europe before the 6th century B.C. A brief invasion by Julius Caesar in 55 B.C. paved the way for a long Roman occupation that began in the 1st century A.D. and lasted until the early 5th century. As the Roman army withdrew, waves of Anglo-Saxons and Jutes invaded Britain, forcing the Celts to retreat westward and into Brittany. The newcomers gradually established kingdoms of their own but were in turn invaded by the Danes, one of whom, Canute, became king of a united England in 1016

1066: William the Conqueror leads Norman army in the last successful invasion of England

1215: King John signs Magna Carta; the most important document of the British constitution, it establishes supremacy of law over the king and lays the foundation for parliamentary government

1337-1453: Hundred Years War rages as English kings seek to enforce claims to French territory; England is ultimately defeated and ceases to be a continental power

1455-85: Houses of York and Lancaster contend for English throne in Wars of the Roses, which end in victory for Henry Tudor, the Lancastrian claimant, and establishment of Tudor dynasty

1534: Breach with Rome, precipitated by pope's refusal to grant Henry VIII a divorce, is completed by Act of Supremacy declaring king head of the Church of England

1558-1603: Reign of Elizabeth I sees the rise of England as a leading European power, strengthened by the defeat of the Spanish Armada in 1588, and the flowering of the Renaissance in English literature; queen is succeeded by James VI of Scotland who, as James I of England, rules over both kingdoms

1642-49: Civil war rends England as Charles I and parliament struggle for power; war ends in defeat and execution of the king and establishment of a commonwealth dominated by Oliver Cromwell

1660: Monarchy is restored under Charles II

18th cent.: Britain undergoes marked transformation with development of parliamentary government and beginning of the Industrial Revolution; overseas, a huge empire is gained in Canada and India and another lost with the American Revolution, followed by war with Napoleonic France

1815: Duke of Wellington's army defeats Napoleon at Waterloo

1832: Enactment of Reform Bill extends franchise to middle class

1837-1901: Reign of Queen Victoria witnesses Britain's rise to world leadership in commerce and industry; reign closes with Britain industrially outstripped by United States and Germany, and fighting Boer War in South Africa

1902: Boers are defeated and accept British sovereignty

1914-18: Britain plays leading role in World War I, sharing in Allied victory over Germany but drained of wealth

1921: Southern Ireland is separated from United Kingdom

1924: Ramsay MacDonald forms Britain's first Labour Cabinet

1939-45: Britain again fights Germany in World War II; standing virtually alone after fall of France in 1940, British, under leadership of Winston Churchill, withstand intensive German bombing and defeat Luftwaffe in Battle of Britain; war ends with Britain again victorious but economically weakened; Labour Party, under Clement Attlee, is swept into power

1956: Britain, under Conservative government of Anthony Eden, joins France and Israel in invasion of Egypt following nationalization of Suez Canal

1964: Labour Party, led by Harold Wilson, is returned to power

1969: Troops are rushed to Northern Ireland after bloody riots break out between Protestants and Roman Catholics

1970: Wilson is defeated by Conservative leader Edward Heath

1971: Common Market approves Britain's bid for admission. New violence flares in Ulster

1972: Intensification of IRA terrorism in Ulster; Westminster assumes direct rule over the province

1973: Participation in Common Market (EEC) begins

1974: National strike by coal miners threatens to halt industry. Conservative Prime Minister Edward Heath calls election for renewed mandate and loses. Harold Wilson becomes prime minister in minority Labour government, negotiates "social compact" with unions for labor peace

1975: Voters in referendum approve the government's recommendation to remain in EEC under new terms. Naval forces protect fishing boats during "Cod War" with Iceland

1976: Wilson resigns. He is succeeded by James Callaghan

1979: Unions call winter-time strikes despite social compact. Electorate in Wales rejects autonomy. Ambiguous results of autonomy referendum in Scotland lead to dispute between Callaghan and Scottish Nationalists. House of Commons votes no confidence in Callaghan and is dissolved. Conservatives win majority in new House; their leader, Margaret Thatcher, becomes Britain's first woman prime minister. Thatcher and 6 other leaders of industrial nations agree to restrict oil imports

UNITED STATES

Area: 3,615,123 sq. mi. **Population:** 219,250,000 (1979 est.)

Official Name: United States of America **Capital:** Washington, D.C. **Nationality:** American or United States **Languages:** English is the official and predominant language. Spanish is the preferred language of about 4 million, Italian of 400,000, French and Chinese of 300,000 each, and German, Greek, Japanese, Filipino, and Korean of 100,000 each. Other minority languages include Polish, Yiddish, Russian, and American Indian tongues **Religion:** About two-thirds of the population is Protestant, one-fourth Roman Catholic, 3% Jewish, and the rest of other or no affiliation **Flag:** Popularly known as the "Stars and Stripes" or "Old Glory," the flag consists of 13 horizontal, alternate red and white stripes, and a union of 50 five-pointed white stars arranged in alternate rows of 6 and of 5 on a blue field in the upper left corner **Anthem:** The Star-Spangled Banner

Location: The United States proper (excluding Hawaii and Alaska) stretches across North America from the Atlantic Ocean on the east to the Pacific Ocean on the west, from Canada on the north to Mexico and the Gulf of Mexico on the south **Features:** The United States proper (excluding Hawaii and Alaska) consists of the Atlantic coastal plain, the Appalachian highlands, a vast interior plains region, the Rocky Mountains belt, the intermontane basin and plateaus west of the Rockies, and the mountains and valleys of the Pacific borderland. Another division, part of the Laurentian Plain of Canada, dips into the United States in the Great Lakes region. Alaska's main physical divisions are the Pacific mountain system, the Central Plateau, the Arctic mountain system, and the Arctic Slope. Hawaii consists of a 1,610-mile-long chain of 122 islands, which represent mountain peaks of volcanic origin largely submerged in the Pacific **Chief Rivers:** Mississippi, Missouri, Rio Grande, Yukon, Arkansas, Colorado, Ohio-Allegheny, Red, Columbia, Snake, Pecos, Canadian

Head of State and of Government: President Jimmy Carter, born 1924, took office 1977 **Effective Date of Constitution:** March 4, 1789 **Legislative Body:** Congress (bicameral), consisting of the Senate and the House of Representatives. The Senate consists of 100 members—2 from each state—chosen by popular vote for a 6-year term; a third of its membership is renewed every 2 years. The House of Representatives has 435 members elected by popular vote every 2 years; each state is entitled to at least one Representative, with the total number determined periodically according to population **Local Government:** 50 states, each with a popularly elected governor and legislature. Below the state level, local self-government is usually conducted through municipalities, townships, and counties

Ethnic Composition: The nation's ethnic diversity is chiefly due to large-scale immigration, most of which took place before 1920. Whites comprise about 87% of the population, Blacks 11.5%, and other races the remaining 1.5% **Population Distribution:** 74% urban **Density:** 60.6 inhabitants per sq. mi.

Largest Cities: (1976 est.; M.A. = Metropolitan Area—1977 est.) New York (1977) 7,312,200 (M.A. 9,386,700), Chicago 3,074,084 (M.A. 7,017,400), Los Angeles 2,743,994 (M.A. 7,031,000), Philadelphia (1977) 1,784,500 (M.A. 4,793,900), Houston (1978) 1,699,000 (M.A. 2,512,200), Detroit 1,314,206 (M.A. 4,370,200), Dallas 848,829 (M.A. 2,673,300), Baltimore (1977) 804,900 (M.A. 2,146,900), San Diego 789,059 (M.A. 1,683,000), San Antonio 783,765 (M.A. 1,024,900), Honolulu 723,400, Indianapolis 708,867 (M.A. 1,143,800), Washington (1977) 685,000 (M.A. 3,020,100)

Per Capita Income: $9,640 (1978) **Gross National Product (GNP):** $2,106.9 billion (1978) **Economic Statistics:** About 26% of the GNP is derived from manufacturing; 17% from wholesale and retail trade; 14% from finance, insurance, and real estate; 14% from services; 15% from government and government enterprises; 3% from agriculture, forestry, and fisheries; 5% from construction; 6% from transportation and communications; 2% from electric, gas, and sanitary services; and 2% from mining **Minerals and Mining:** The United States produces a great variety of minerals and consumes more than any other nation in the world. It is the world's leading producer of coal, copper, lead, natural gas, and molybdenum. Though no longer the leading producer, the United States ranks among the top group in petroleum and iron ore. Zinc, sulfur, vanadium, cadmium, uranium, phosphate-rock, bauxite, gypsum, aluminum, nitrates, magnesium, potash, titanium, tungsten, feldspar and barite are among the other major minerals produced, and the nation is also rich in waterpower **Labor Force:**

102,537,000 (1978), of which 96% is engaged in nonagricultural industries. The average hourly wage was $5.14 in 1977 **Foreign Trade:** Exports, chiefly machinery and transport equipment, food and live animals, crude materials (soybeans, textile fibers, ores and metal scrap), chemicals, other manufactured goods (metals and manufactures, scientific instruments, textiles, rubber, and paper), and mineral fuels, totaled $143.6 billion in 1978. Imports, mainly machinery and transport equipment, other manufactured goods (metals and manufactures, textiles, iron and steel-mill products, and nonferrous base metals), food and live animals, crude materials, and mineral fuels, totaled $172 billion in 1978 **Principal Trade Partners:** Canada, Japan, Britain, West Germany, Saudi Arabia, Netherlands, Mexico, Nigeria, Italy, France, Venezuela, Iran, Brazil, Belgium and Luxembourg, China (Taiwan), South Korea

Vital Statistics: Birthrate, 15.3 per 1,000 of pop. (1977); death rate, 8.8 **Life Expectancy:** 73 years **Health Statistics:** 130 inhabitants per hospital bed; 621 per physician (1976) **Infant Mortality:** 14.1 per 1,000 births (1977) **Illiteracy:** Negligible **Education Statistics:** 106,022 primary and secondary schools, with combined enrollment of 49,800,000 (1977) **Enrollment in Higher Education:** 10,200,000 **GNP Expended on Education:** 7.5% (1976)

Transportation: Surfaced roads total 3,857,000 mi. (1976) **Motor Vehicles:** 143,800,000 (1976) **Passenger Cars:** 114,100,000 **Railway Mileage:** 199,000 (1975) **Ports:** New York, Philadelphia, Portland, Baltimore, Boston, Houston, Norfolk, Tampa, San Francisco, New Orleans, Los Angeles, Corpus Christi, Baton Rouge **Major Airlines:** Major international and domestic carriers are American Airlines, Braniff Airways, Eastern Airlines, Trans World Airlines, Pan American World Airways, Continental Air Lines, Delta Airlines, Northwest Orient Airlines, and United Air Lines **Communications:** Privately owned **Radio Transmitters:** 7,307 (1976) **Receivers:** 402,000,000 (1975) **Television Transmitters:** 3,853 (1974) **Receivers:** 121,100,000 (1974) **Telephones:** 155,173,000 (1976) **Newspapers:** 1,893 dailies (1978)

Weights and Measures: Avoirdupois units of weight and linear measures. Metric system gradually being introduced

For articles and statistics on the separate states, see **The Fifty States**; for important national events, see **'78/'79 Month-By-Month Chronology**

UPPER VOLTA

Area: 105,869 sq. mi. **Population:** 6,400,000 (1978 est.)

Official Name: Republic of Upper Volta **Capital:** Ouagadougou **Nationality:** Upper Voltan **Languages:** The official language is French. Mossi is the main African language, others being Samo, Gourounsi, and Lobi, which belong to the Niger-Congo family of languages **Religion:** The majority of the population are animists. There are over 1 million Moslems, 130,000 Roman Catholics, and 9,000 Protestants **Flag:** Horizontal stripes of black, white, and red **Anthem:** The Volta **Currency:** CFA Franc (219 per U.S. $1)

Location: West Africa. Landlocked Upper Volta is bordered on the west and north by Mali, on the east by Niger, and on the south by Benin, Togo, Ghana, and Ivory Coast **Features:** The country consists for the most part of a vast plateau, slightly inclined toward the south and notched by valleys and formed by the three main rivers, with some savanna and semidesert **Chief Rivers:** Black, White, and Red Voltas, and their main tributaries

Head of State: President: Maj. Gen. Aboubacar Sangoulé Lamizana, born 1916, seized power in 1966, elected 1978 for 7-year term **Head of Government:** Premier: Joseph Conombo, appointed 1978 **Effective Date of Present Constitution:** 1977 **Legislative Body:** National Assembly (unicameral) with 57 members, serving 5-year terms **Local Government:** 10 departments

Ethnic Composition: The two main ethnic groups are the Voltaic people and the Mande (Mandingos). Among the Voltaic, 65% are Mossi and 15% Bobo; the Samo are the most numerous of the Mande group **Population Distribution:** 11% urban **Density:** 60 inhabitants per sq. mi.

Largest Cities: (1973 est.) Ouagadougou 105,000, Bobo-Dioulasso 90,000, Koudougou 40,000, Ouahigouya 20,000, Kaya 18,000, Fada N'Gourma 12,000, Banfora 7,000

Per Capita Income: $114 (1978) **Gross National Product (GNP):** $740 million (1978) **Economic Statistics:** In 1976 about 67% of GNP was from agriculture (sorghum, millet, cotton, sesame, maize, rice, livestock products, peanuts); 6% from industry (textiles, bicycle assembly, maintenance and repairing of vehicles) **Minerals and Mining:** Manganese deposits are being exploited; deposits of copper, gold, bauxite, and limestone exist **Labor Force:** 2,700,000 in 1976, with 87% engaged in subsistence agriculture **Foreign Trade:** Exports, chiefly livestock, cotton, and peanuts, totaled $89 million in 1977. Imports, mainly textiles, petroleum products, motor vehicles and parts, fruits and vegetables, and machinery, totaled $237 million **Principal Trade Partners:** EEC countries, Ivory Coast, Ghana, Senegal, Mali

Vital Statistics: Birthrate, 48.5 per 1,000 of pop. (1975); death rate, 25.8 **Life Expectancy:** 38 years **Health Statistics:** 1,174 inhabitants per hospital bed; 59,595 per physician (1974) **Infant Mortality:** 260 per 1,000 births **Illiteracy:** 90% **Education Statistics:** 974 primary and secondary schools, with combined enrollment of 149,423 (1974) **Enrollment in Higher Education:** 1,067 (1975) **GNP Expended on Education:** 2.9% (1973)

Transportation: Improved roads total 3,000 mi. **Motor Vehicles:** 19,600 (1975) **Passenger Cars:** 9,500 **Railway Mileage:** 341 **Ports:** None **Major Airlines:** Air Afrique provides international services; Air Volta flies domestically **Communications:** Government owned **Radio Transmitters:** 4 **Receivers:** 105,000 (1976) **Television Transmitters:** 1 **Receivers:** 6,000 (1974) **Telephones:** 6,000 (1975) **Newspapers:** 1 daily, 0.3 copies per 1,000 inhabitants (1975)

Weights and Measures: Metric system **Travel Requirements:** Passport; visa valid for 3 months; $2 fee; 2 photos

---

Upper Volta's name derives simply from the fact that its central region is watered by the upper tributaries of the Volta River, which flows southward through Ghana. Most of the country is a plateau where woodland and pasture contrast with a dry northern area seared by the desert wind.

Once the center of the ancient Mossi empire that provided a shield against Moslem conquest of the coastal regions, Upper Volta today is a land of hardworking farmers and cattle-raisers. Poor soil and variable rains, however, make the task of raising food and export crops, chiefly peanuts and cotton, a recurrent struggle. The nation's landlocked situation adds a further handicap.

Since independence from France in 1960, the country has faced the familiar trials of new African nations. Its first president, Maurice Yaméogo, proved an inept financial administrator. In 1966, with the country in virtual bankruptcy, his government was ousted by a military regime headed by army chief Lt. Col. Sangoulé Lamizana.

Elections were held in 1970, establishing a civilian parliament, but in 1974 Lamizana created a new cabinet composed largely of military officers. In 1976 another change occurred, when after two months of strife between the government and the unions, President Lamizana dismissed the military government and formed a new, largely civilian government. In May 1978, in an election marking the end of military rule, Lamizana was elected to the office he had assumed.

Meanwhile Upper Volta has received new aid from France, the Common Market, and the World Bank for further improvement of agriculture and transportation. At the same time, an even greater boost for the country's development is expected from the manganese deposits at Tambao, where tests indicate proven reserves of more than 10 million tons.

Offsetting these pluses in the early 1970s was the long siege of severe drought and famine that plagued Upper Volta and five other nations of the sub-Sahara (Chad, Mali, Mauritania, Niger, and Senegal); at least 150,000 persons were estimated to have died of starvation. Steps were taken in 1977 to deal with this problem through the adoption of an agricultural development program. The program, approved by Upper Volta and 8 other African nations of the drought-ridden Sahel region, would create food self-sufficiency within 20 years.

HISTORY: Upper Volta occupies the site of the former Mossi empire and its early history is mostly that of the Mossi people. According to legend, they entered the region as a warrior group between the 11th and 13th centuries and established three independent kingdoms, the most powerful of which was Ouagadougou. Between the 14th and 19th centuries, the Mossi engaged in recurrent wars with the neighboring empires of Mali and Songhai, and after severe defeats their power declined

1896: French subjugate territory and establish a protectorate

1904: Present-day Upper Volta is incorporated into a French colony called Upper Senegal and Niger

1919: Upper Volta is established as a separate French colony

1932: Upper Volta is divided among the colonies of French Sudan, Niger, and the Ivory Coast

1947: France reestablishes Upper Volta as a territorial unit

1958: Upper Volta becomes a self-governing state, called the Voltaic Republic, within the French Community

1959: Republic's name is changed to Upper Volta; in a general election, the pro-French African Democratic Rally wins a majority of seats in the national assembly and party's leader Maurice Yaméogo is elected premier

1960: Upper Volta becomes an independent republic; with Maurice Yaméogo as president

1966: Army chief of staff Lt. Col. Sangoulé Lamizana seizes control of the government, dismisses President Yaméogo and declares himself chief of state

1970-71: Elections and adoption of a new constitution mark return to constitutional rule the following year

1974: Lamizana suspends constitution, abolishes office of prime minister, and dissolves legislature

1975: Foreign firms are warned of intention to require 51 percent state participation by October 1977

1976: President Lamizana dismisses military government and forms a new, largely civilian cabinet

1977: Government lifts three-and-one-half-year ban on political parties. Upper Voltans vote in favor of draft constitution aimed at restoring civilian rule after twelve years of military rule

1978: Military rule ends as Lamizana is elected president

URUGUAY

Area: 68,536 sq. mi. **Population:** 2,814,000 (1978 est.)

Official Name: Oriental Republic of Uruguay **Capital:** Montevideo **Nationality:** Uruguayan **Languages:** Spanish is the official and universal language **Religion:** 66% Roman Catholic, 2% Protestant, 2% Jewish, 30% other **Flag:** Four blue stripes and 5 white stripes, with a golden sun on a white field in the upper left corner **Anthem:** National Anthem, beginning "Easterners our country or death" **Currency:** New Uruguayan peso (7.5 per U.S. $1)

Location: Southeast coast of South America. Uruguay is bounded on the north and northeast by Brazil, on the east by the Atlantic Ocean, on the south by the Río de la Plata estuary, and on the west by Argentina **Features:** The country consists of rolling, grassy plains and low hills. There are scattered forest areas along the banks of the numerous streams, which provide natural irrigation for the soil **Chief Rivers:** Uruguay, Negro, Río de la Plata, Cuareim, Yaguarón

Head of State and of Government: President Aparicio Méndez Manfredini, born 1904, took office in 1976 **Effective Date of Present Constitution:** 1967, nullified June 1973; a new one is planned **Legislative Body:** Congress dissolved 1973; a National Council of 45 members govern at present, while a new bicameral legislature is planned **Local Government:** 19 departments

Ethnic Composition: About 85% of the population is of European origin, mainly Spanish and Italian, with 10% mestizo, and 5% mulatto or black **Population Distribution:** 82% urban **Density:** 41 inhabitants per sq. mi.

Largest Cities: (1975 census) Montevideo 1,229,748; (1970 est.) Las Piedras 90,000, Salto 80,000

Per Capita Income: $1,543 (1978) **Gross National Product (GNP):** $4.4 billion (1978) **Economic Statistics:** In 1973 about 15% of GNP was from agriculture (livestock products, beef, wool, wheat, corn, rice); 9% from transportation and communications; 24% from manufacturing (meat packing, textiles, construction and building materials, beverages, chemicals); 13% from government activities; and 34% from trade and services **Minerals and Mining:** Marble, building stone, gravel, and small deposits of iron ore **Labor Force:** 1,174,376 (1975), with 34% in industry; 8% in agriculture; 40% in trade and services; 5% in construction; and 6% in transportation and communications **Foreign Trade:** Exports, chiefly wool, meat, and hides, totaled $536 million in 1976. Imports, mainly raw materials, fuels and lubricants, machinery and parts, automotive vehicles and parts, construction materials, and foodstuffs, totaled $599 million **Principal Trade Partners:** Brazil, Britain, West Germany, Argentina, Kuwait, United States, Iraq

Vital Statistics: Birthrate, 21.1 per 1,000 of pop. (1975); death rate, 9.9 per 1,000 **Life Expectancy:** 71 years **Health Statistics:** 193 inhabitants per hospital bed; 911 per physician (1972) **Infant Mortality:** 48.8 per 1,000 births (1975) **Illiteracy:** 6% **Education Statistics:** 2,338 primary and secondary schools, with combined enrollment of 550,472 (1973) **Enrollment in Higher Education:** 32,627 (1975) **GNP Expended on Education:** 3.6% (1970)

Transportation: Paved roads total 3,728 mi. **Motor Vehicles:** 237,300 (1974) **Passenger Cars:** 151,600 **Railway Mileage:** 1,849 **Ports:** Montevideo **Major Airlines:** Primeras Líneas Uruguayas de Navegación Aérea (PLUNA) operates domestically and internationally **Communications:** Government and privately controlled

Radio Transmitters: 101 **Receivers:** 1,600,000 (1976) **Television Transmitters:** 17 **Receivers:** 355,000 (1976) **Telephones:** 258,000 (1976) **Newspapers:** 30 dailies, 140 copies per 1,000 inhabitants (1974)

Weights and Measures: Metric system **Travel Requirements:** Passport; no visa for 3 months

The Oriental Republic of Uruguay takes its name from the fact that it is situated on the east bank of the Uruguay River. Uruguay, the second smallest country in South America, is characterized by a high literacy rate and a large urban middle class.

Economic reverses and political repression have seriously affected Uruguayans in the last decade. Although politically stable since 1903, Uruguay began to experience problems in the late 1960s with a series of student riots, general strikes, and the rise of urban terrorism. A series of repressive government measures followed, then a 1973 coup against the presidency of Juan Bordaberry. The military group responsible for the coup retained Bordaberry as president and began tightening its already firm grip on the country. Political stability was not enhanced by Bordaberry's government, and dissidents were eliminated through a campaign of arrests, torture and murder. By June 1976 the military had ousted Bordaberry in a peaceful putsch because he planned to set up a corporate state structure with the participation of the armed forces written into law. The military preferred a gradual return to representative democracy. Bordaberry was replaced by Aparicio Méndez, who was named president by the conservative Council of the Nation.

Things were not always so sorrowful for Uruguay. Not long ago it could boast one of the highest per capita incomes in the hemisphere and a widely desired currency. The country was envied for its advanced laws, six-hour work day, retirement of workers at age 50 or 55, and incredibly rich soil. But the utopian social system, based on a growing population, became overburdened and began to fall behind in its payments. A 1963 census showed that the population had not grown, that, in fact, well-educated Uruguayans had been leaving for other lands in large numbers.

The economy has been marked by high inflation and, until recently, a high balance of payments deficit. In an effort to deal with the situation, the government has issued a series of mini-devaluations of the peso.

The political situation looks no brighter under Méndez. Upon taking office he immediately issued a decree suspending the political rights of the leaders of existing parties for 15 years. It has been reported that Uruguay, with a population of less than three million, has the highest proportion of political prisoners to total population. In 1978, The Military Supreme Court conceded that 2,511 persons accused of "crimes against state security" had served jail sentences and been released in the preceding six years, and that 1,909 were still held.

HISTORY: The eastern side of the Uruguay and La Plata rivers was occupied by warlike and seminomadic Indians, the Charrúa, until late in the colonial period when Europeans began to settle the area. The first settlers were the Spanish, who established a colony at Soriano in 1624. They were followed by the Portuguese, who were driven out in the 18th century by the Spanish, under whom Uruguay became part of a viceroyalty centered in Argentina. During the Napoleonic Wars, Uruguay was briefly occupied by the British, and the spread of revolutionary ideas during this period soon swept the country into the general Latin American fight for independence

1810-14: A war of independence, led by José Gervasio Artigas, begins; Uruguay, with aid from Argentina, ends Spanish rule

1820-28: Uruguay is occupied by Brazil. In 1825, a group of patriots known as the Thirty-Three Immortals declare Uruguay an independent republic; country throws off Brazilian rule and, in 1828, Uruguay is established as an independent buffer state between Brazil and Argentina

1830: New constitution is promulgated, but civil strife soon breaks out between rival political factions

1865-70: Argentina, Brazil, and Uruguay unite in a victorious war against Paraguay

1911-15: President José Batlle y Ordóñez introduces wide range of social and economic reforms

1919-51: Fearful of the development of a dictatorship, nation adopts new constitution restricting president's power and vesting broad powers in Council of Administration; resulting conflict leads to restoration of strong executive powers to president in 1934. In 1951, office of president is abolished and executive power vested in nine-member national council

1958: The conservative Blancos (National Party) win general elections, displacing liberal Colorado Party which had governed for more than 90 years

1965: General strike paralyzes economic life of country

1966: Presidential form of government is restored in referendum held in conjunction with general elections which give Colorados new majority

1967-68: President Oscar D. Gestido dies and is succeeded by Vice-President Jorge Pacheco Areco; general strikes and student riots become widespread

1969: Pacheco decrees a limited state of siege in June following a new wave of disabling strikes; government closure of left-wing newspaper results in virtual shutdown of nation's press; move is made in Congress to impeach Pacheco

1973: President Bordaberry's military-dominated civilian government suspends constitutional rule, replaces congress with a council of state, and curbs opposition press

1976: Bordaberry is ousted. Aparicio Méndez is named president

1977: U.S. moves to reduce aid to Uruguay because of human rights violations; Uruguay then rejects aid linked to human rights, claiming it is an internal matter

1978: OAS panel charges Uruguay with wholesale violations of human rights. Lt. Gen. Gregorio Alvarez becomes commander-in-chief of the army, and the responsible foreign press pictures him as the real ruler, with Méndez as the figurehead

VATICAN CITY

Area: 0.17 sq. mi. (108.7 acres) **Population:** 726 (1976 est.)

Official Name: State of the Vatican City **Nationality:** The Papacy has a citizenship of its own, which is granted to those residing in the Vatican because of their work or rank **Languages:** Italian is the official language of the state; Latin is the official language of the Holy See, the administrative and legislative body for the Roman Catholic Church, and is used for most papal encyclicals and other formal pronouncements **Flag:** Yellow and white vertical bands, with the crossed keys of St. Peter under the triple papal tiara on the white band **Anthem:** Pontifical March (no words) **Currency:** Italian lira (848 per U.S. $1)

Location: Located in Rome, Vatican City is roughly a triangular area lying near the west bank of the Tiber River and to the west of Castel Sant' Angelo. On the west and south it is bounded by the Leonine Wall. The Vatican area comprises St. Peter's Square; St. Peter's Basilica, the largest Christian church in the world; a quadrangular area north of the square, containing the museums, library, and administrative buildings, and Belvedere Park; the Vatican Palace; and the Papal Gardens. Outside the Vatican City itself, extraterritoriality (but not sovereignty) is exercised over 12 churches and palaces in and near Rome, including St. John Lateran, St. Mary Major, and St. Paul Without the Walls Basilicas, and the papal villa at Castel Gandolfo

Government: Vatican City is the center of the worldwide organization of the Roman Catholic Church and the seat of the pope, who is the absolute sovereign of the tiny state. The Supreme Pontiff is John Paul II (Karol Wojtyla), born 1920, elected pope on October 16, 1978. He is assisted as temporal ruler by the Pontifical Commission, consisting of the cardinals, and the Administration of the Patrimony of the Apostolic See. Both of these organizations are presided over by a secretary of state (premier), at present held by Archbishop Agostino Casaroli, appointed 1979. Religious affairs are governed under the pope's direction by a number of ecclesiastical bodies collectively known as the Roman Curia. The pope rules from his election until death, at which time a successor is chosen by the College of Cardinals

Ethnic Composition: While the citizenry of the Vatican includes cardinals and other clergymen from all over the world, most of the inhabitants are Italian. The 75 members of the Swiss Guard are a notable exception

Economic Statistics: Vatican City does not engage in the economically productive activity common to other states. It is almost entirely dependent for income on the receipt of charitable contributions, the sale of Vatican stamps and tourist mementos, fees for admission to Vatican museums, and the sale of Vatican publications

Illiteracy: None **Enrollment in Higher Education:** 7,910 (1973)
Transportation: Vatican City is easily reached by the public transportation system of Rome. It has its own railroad station **Communications:** State controlled Radio Vatican, with 17 transmitters. There is no television **Newspapers:** 1 daily, the semiofficial *l'Osservatore Romano*
Weights and Measures: Metric system

For a long time after the unification of Italy in 1870, which stripped the popes of most of their temporal possessions, the status of the Vatican, the chief papal residence, was uncertain. Then, by the 1929 Lateran Treaty with Italy, the independent enclave of Vatican City came into being. In the treaty, the pontificate formally renounced all claims to the former Papal States.

Vatican City stands on the spot where Caligula constructed a circus and Nero had gardens. The ruler of Vatican City, the pope, bears the title of Bishop of Rome, Vicar of Jesus Christ, Successor of the Prince of Apostles, Supreme Pontiff of the Universal Church, Patriarch of the West, Archbishop and Metropolitan of the Roman Province, and Sovereign of the State of the Vatican City. Currently he is Pope John Paul II. His .17-square-mile realm includes St. Peter's basilica, the largest church in Christendom; St. Peter's square, a roughly circular plaza set off by Giovanni Lorenzo Bernini's colonnade; and the pontifical palaces, or the Vatican proper, with magnificent chapels, museums, archives, a library, and a new hall for mass papal audiences.

Among the chapels are the Sistine, the ceiling and one wall of which are decorated with paintings by Michelangelo. The museums, galleries, and various interiors contain works by such masters as Raphael, Leonardo da Vinci, Fra Angelico, Titian, and Correggio, priceless sculpture that includes the Apollo Belvedere and Laocoön, and Egyptian, Etruscan, and other collections. The library, with its enormous wealth of books and manuscripts, is one of the world's great research institutions, and the archives house original material on such matters as the trial of Galileo and the request for annulment of the marriage of Henry VIII to Catherine of Aragon. Among other things, Vatican City also has gardens, courts, and quiet streets; its own daily newspaper and postal, telegraph, and broadcasting facilities; its own "armed forces," the colorfully garbed Swiss Guards; and its own railroad station, used almost exclusively as a freight terminal. Outside its confines but nonetheless enjoying extraterritoriality are a number of churches, palaces, and other structures in Rome and the papal villa at nearby Castel Gandolfo.

Vatican City is administered by a commission of cardinals, and a papal decree of 1968 established a body of 21 lay experts to advise them. A simultaneous decree reorganized the papal court, renaming it the papal household, abolishing hereditary offices, and putting an end to various picturesque anachronisms.

HISTORY: The State of the Vatican City and other places over which the Vatican retains control are the remnants of the old Papal States. For almost 1,000 years the papacy held vast temporal possessions, including large areas of Italy, and, until the French Revolution, parts of southern France. During the unification of the Italian peninsula in the 19th century, virtually all these possessions were absorbed by the House of Savoy, leaving only Rome and surrounding territory, protected by a French garrison, still under papal control

1870: French garrison withdraws and Rome is annexed by the Kingdom of Italy; Pope Pius IX refuses to recognize the loss of temporal power and initiates what becomes more than a half-century of self-imposed "imprisonment" of popes

1929: Lateran Treaty is signed, by which Italy recognizes the sovereignty and independence of the new Vatican City state

1947: Italian Republic reaffirms Italy's adherence to Lateran Treaty

1962: Pope John XXIII convenes Second Vatican Council to promote Christian unity

1963: Archbishop Giovanni Montini of Milan is elected pope on death of John XXIII and reigns as Paul VI

1965: Pope Paul VI makes a historic journey to speak before the UN in New York "for the cause of peace in the world"

1978: Pope Paul VI dies on August 6 at age 80; during reign he sought to mediate between progressive and conservative forces within the Church. Conclave of cardinals convenes to elect Albino Cardinal Luciani, Patriarch of Venice, as the new pope. The new pontiff, John Paul I, dies on September 28. Karol Cardinal Wojtyla, Archbishop of Krakow, Poland, succeeds as Pope John Paul II on October 16

1979: Pope John Paul II visits Mexico and Poland

VENEZUELA

Area: 352,143 sq. mi. **Population:** 12,740,000 (1978 est.)

Official Name: Republic of Venezuela **Capital:** Caracas **Nationality:** Venezuelan **Languages:** Spanish is the official and universal language **Religion:** 96% Roman Catholic **Flag:** Horizontal stripes of yellow, blue, and red with an arc of 7 white stars in the center and the national coat of arms in the upper left **Anthem:** National Anthem, beginning "Glory to the brave people" **Currency:** Bolívar (4.3 per U.S. $1)

Location: North coast of South America. Venezuela is bounded on the north by the Caribbean Sea, on the east by Guyana, on the south by Brazil, and on the west by Colombia **Features:** The main regions are the Andes Mountains and outliers in the northwest; the northern coastal zone, the plains, or llanos, stretching from the mountains south and east to the Orinoco River; and the Guayana Highlands south and east of the Orinoco, consisting of high plateaus and rolling plains **Chief Rivers:** Orinoco, Caroní, Caura, Apure

Head of State and of Government: President Luis Herrera Campins, born 1925, inaugurated, March 1979 for 5 years **Effective Date of Present Constitution:** January 1961 **Legislative Body:** Congress (bicameral), consisting of the Senate, with 47 members and the 199-man Chamber of Deputies, both elected by adult suffrage for 5-year terms **Local Government:** 20 states, 2 federal territories, a federal district, and the 72 islands of the federal dependencies. The governors of each are appointed by the president, and each, except the dependencies, has its own elected legislature

Ethnic Composition: About 70% of the population is mestizo (of mixed Indian and European ancestry), 17% of European (mainly Spanish) origin, 7% black, 1% Indian, and the rest mulattos of mixed Indian and black ancestry **Population Distribution:** 82% urban **Density:** 36 inhabitants per sq. mi.

Largest Cities: (Metropolitan Areas) (1976 est.) Caracas 3,000,000; (1974 est.) Maracaibo 685,578, Valencia 405,177, Barquisimeto 386,023, Maracay 330,441

Per Capita Income: $3,139 (1978) **Gross National Product (GNP):** $41.2 billion (1978) **Economic Statistics:** 27% is derived from services; 16% from industry (including oil refining, textiles, building materials, clothing, shoes, food, steel, and chemicals), 16% from commerce and finance; and 7% from agriculture **Minerals and Mining:** There are large deposits of oil, natural gas, bauxite, iron ore, salt, and smaller amounts of coal, gold, and diamonds **Labor Force:** 3,596,063 (1975); 19% were in agriculture, 23.5% in industry, and 26% in services **Foreign Trade:** Exports, chiefly petroleum (97%) and products, and iron ore, totaled about $9.3 billion in 1976. Imports, mainly vehicles, iron and steel, wheat, mining and construction equipment, machinery and chemicals, totaled $6.4 billion **Principal Trade Partners:** United States, West Germany, Japan, Britain, Netherlands Antilles, France, Canada, Italy

Vital Statistics: Birthrate, 33.5 per 1,000 of pop.; death rate, 6.0 **Life Expectancy:** 67 years **Health Statistics:** 334 inhabitants per hospital bed; 915 per physician (1975) **Infant Mortality:** 46 per 1,000 births (1976) **Illiteracy:** 13% **Education Statistics:** 12,204 primary and secondary schools, with combined enrollment of 3,016,304 (1974) **Enrollment in Higher Education:** 225,000 (1976) **GNP Expended on Education:** 7% (1976)

Transportation: Paved roads total 12,400 mi. **Motor Vehicles:** 1,324,515 (1975) **Passenger Cars:** 955,151 **Railway Mileage:** 446 **Ports:** La Guaira, Maracaibo, Puerto Cabello, Puerto La Cruz **Major Airlines:** VIASA, a government-owned airline, flies internationally; Avensa, privately owned, and LAVA, government owned, fly domestically **Communications:** Government and privately controlled **Radio Transmitters:** 235 **Receivers:** 5,034,000 (1976) **Television Transmitters:** 39 **Receivers:** 1,431,000 (1976) **Telephones:** 742,000 (1976) **Newspapers:** 49 dailies, 93 copies per 1,000 inhabitants (1975)

Weights and Measures: Metric system **Travel Requirements:** Passport; tourist card or visa, valid 45 days

Venezuela's prosperity has been based for years on petroleum, and this richest, most dynamic and most "American" country in Latin America is one of the world's largest petroleum exporters. In 1975-76 Venezuela nationalized the huge holdings of foreign petroleum and iron-ore mining companies, but did so peacefully, and the firms have been compensated. A government holding company, PETROVEN, controls and regulates the industry. Estimated production ran about 2.3 million barrels per day in 1979, and total oil revenue appeared on the way to surpassing 1978's $5.8 billion.

After the quadrupling of the price of oil in 1974, the government of President Carlos Andrés Pérez, with the largest and most sophisticated oil industry in Latin America, began pumping billions into development to promote the lagging agriculture industry, steel and petrochemicals production and construction. Rapid industrialization created an urban people, alleviating the problem of land hunger, but decreasing agricultural production. Government subsidies did little to stimulate agriculture and there were charges of government corruption and mismanagement, particularly following the severe food shortages in early 1977.

Venezuela's political stability—its last dictatorship was overthrown in 1958—was further demonstrated in 1978 when a new president was elected in what was basically a two-party race. Luis Herrera Campins, the candidate of the Social Christians, the "out" party, defeated Luis Piñerúa Ordaz, of the Action Democratic Party. In a six-party contest, the two top parties polled 85 percent of the vote. In his inaugural speech in 1979, Herrera declared he had inherited "a mortgaged country." He promised to halt runaway public spending, and corruption, and give private business more flexibility in its operations.

Basic industries, such as steel and power, are owned and subsidized by the state. Venezuela's best hope for an industrial base to take the place of oil's proved reserves, which will last only through the year 2000, lies in Guayana, a region containing natural reserves of iron ore, sufficient for 75 years of production at current levels, and the hydroelectric potential of the Caroní River. Enough bauxite has been found to make the aluminum industry self-sufficient. The nation's oil riches are being used in a $12-billion industrialization program, in which the U.S. accounts for slightly more than half the foreign participation. However, a Spanish-Canadian group received the contracts for a national railroad grid, and the French are building the $250-million Caracas subway.

HISTORY: Prior to the Spanish conquest in the 16th century, Venezuela was inhabited by 2 dominant Indian tribes—the Arawaks, who lived in agricultural communities, and the warlike Caribs. Charles I of Spain granted the Welsers, a German banking firm, the right to explore and colonize Venezuela but rescinded the right in 1546, after which the colony reverted to the Spanish crown

1811: Venezuela, under the leadership of Francisco de Miranda, declares its independence from Spain, but royalist forces maintain control

1812-21: Simón Bolívar leads a bloody war of independence against Spain, sets up Greater Colombia, encompassing the present territories of Venezuela, Colombia, Panama, and Ecuador, and is named president

1830-1900: Venezuela breaks away from Greater Colombia and becomes an independent republic; during the remainder of the century the nation is wracked by internal strife as dictator succeeds dictator. In 1895, Venezuela loses territory to British Guiana after a heated boundary dispute with Britain

1908-35: General Juan Vicente Gómez becomes dictator; a tyrannical ruler, he succeeds in lifting the country to solvency by allotting oil concessions to foreign companies

1937-38: General Eleázar López Contreras, Gómez' successor as president, exiles opposition political and labor leaders, declaring a moratorium on political and labor activities; he inaugurates a broad program of social and economic development

1945: A revolution breaks out and a liberal government headed by President Rómulo Betancourt takes power; he declares universal suffrage, and institutes social reforms

1947-48: A new constitution is adopted, providing for election of the president by direct popular vote for the first time in the country's history. Rómulo Gallegos, of the Democratic Action Party, is elected president but is ousted in 1948 by a military junta led by Colonels Marcos Pérez Jiménez and Carlos Delgado Chalbaud

1953-59: Pérez Jiménez takes power; he is overthrown in 1958 during a revolt supported by liberal elements of the armed forces. After brief interim government by a civilian-military junta, Betancourt is elected president

1962: Venezuela adopts new constitution limiting president to five-year term. Communists launch terrorist campaign aimed at ousting Betancourt because of his support for U.S. blockade of Cuba

1963-67: Raúl Leoni, leader of the liberal Democratic Action Party, is elected president on a platform pledging economic and social reform; he suspends constitutional guarantees in drive against Castro-supported terrorists

1968: Rafael Caldera, the Social Christian candidate, is elected president; Democratic Action Party retains control of Congress

1970: Venezuela and Guyana declare 12-year moratorium on border dispute

1973: Caldera government quadruples petroleum reference prices. Venezuela joins the Andean Pact, formed by Bolivia, Chile, Colombia, Ecuador and Peru. Carlos Andrés Pérez of Democratic Action Party is elected president and party retains control of Congress

1976: Oil industry is nationalized

1977: President Pérez announces a series of austerity measures aimed at controlling inflation and cutting government spending. Pérez visits President Carter; commonality of aims voiced

978: In Caracas, Presidents Pérez and Carter sign agreements establishing maritime boundaries between Venezuela and U.S. and providing for more cooperation in curbing flow of illicit drugs into U.S. Luis Herrera Campins of the Social Christian Party wins the presidential election on Dec. 6

1979: Herrera is inaugurated on March 12. He is visited by U.S. Vice President Mondale, who reports that Venezuela has agreed to increase oil production to meet U.S. needs. A U.S. businessman, William F. Niehous, formerly operations manager in Venezuela for the Owens-Illinois Glass Co., is freed by police after being held prisoner 41 months by an obscure extremist political group

VIETNAM

Area: 128,405 sq. mi. **Population:** 47,870,000 (1978 est.)

Official Name: Socialist Republic of Vietnam **Capital:** Hanoi **Nationality:** Vietnamese **Languages:** Vietnamese, spoken by the majority of the people, is the official language; minorities speak Chinese, French, Khmer, Cham, and Montagnard (mountain tribal) languages **Religion:** The majority of the people nominally practice Buddhism and animism, although many combine these with elements of Taoism, Confucianism, and Christianity. However, organized religious activities have been discouraged in the North **Flag:** A yellow five-pointed star centered on a red field **Anthem:** Tien Quan Ca (Hymn of the Marching Army) **Currency:** Dong (2.17 per U.S. $1)

Location: Southeast Asia, occupying the eastern part of the Indochinese peninsula. It is bordered by China on the north, by the South China Sea on the east and south, and by Laos and Cambodia on the west **Features:** The jungle-covered hills in the north and northwest rise southeastward into the Annamese Cordillera and its outlying plateaus. East of the mountains are fertile coastal lowlands, with the deltas of the Mekong and Red rivers being the largest and most densely populated **Chief Rivers:** Red, Black, Lo, Ca, Mekong, Ba, Dong Nai

Political Leader: Le Duan, Secretary General of the Communist Party, born 1908, appointed 1960 **Head of State:** President Ton Duc Thang, born 1888, elected July 1976 **Head of Government:** Premier Pham Van Dong, born 1906, elected 1976 **Effective Date of Present Constitution:** 1960 (North), currently being revised **Legislative Body:** National Assembly (unicameral), with 492 members. Its 36-member Presidium, or Standing Committee, under chairman Truong Chinh, born 1917, represents the ruling Communist Party in the Assembly. The chief executive and legislative organ of government is the party's 17-man Politburo, the core of the 133-member Central Committee headed by Le Duan **Local Government:** 38 provinces, including 3 city provinces

Ethnic Composition: Vietnamese constitute about 85% of the population; Montagnards of both Malayo-Polynesian and Mon-Khmer ethnic groups make up about 8%, and the rest include Chinese, Khmer, and Cham minorities **Population Distribution:** North—14% urban; South—30% urban **Density:** 373 inhabitants per sq. mi.

Largest Cities: (1977 est.) Ho Chi Minh City (Saigon) 1,000,000; (1972 est.) Hanoi 643,000, Da Nang 438,000, Hue 200,000, Nha

...

Trang 195,000, Quí Nhon 189,000, Can Tho 154,000; (1970 est.) Haiphong 276,000, Nam Dinh 105,360

Per Capita Income: $132 (1978) **Gross National Product (GNP):** $6.9 billion (1978) **Economic Statistics:** Basically agricultural (rice, sugarcane, tea, maize, manioc, coffee, fish, rubber), rice, the staple food, still has to be imported. Light industry is confined to food processing, textiles, glass, paper, machinery, cement and, in the North, steel **Minerals and Mining:** Coal, iron ore, apatite, phosphates, chromite, tin, salt, granite, and limestone **Labor Force:** North—About 10,000,000, with 75% in agriculture and 10% in industry; South—About 8,000,000, with 67% in agriculture and 17% in industry **Foreign Trade:** Exports ($170 million, 1976) consist mainly of coal, rubber, wood, tea, spices, and coffee. Imports ($1 billion, 1976) include rice, heavy machinery, transportation equipment, vehicles, chemicals, and fuels **Principal Trade Partners:** USSR, Eastern Europe, Japan

Vital Statistics: Birthrate, 42.1 per 1,000 of pop. (1975); death rate, 13 **Life Expectancy:** 44 years **Health Statistics:** About 750 per hospital bed; 11,000 per physician **Infant Mortality:** North—N.A.; South—36.7 per 1,000 births **Illiteracy:** About 25% **Education Statistics:** North—6,282 primary and secondary schools, with a total enrollment of about 4,700,000 (1970); South—9,492 primary and secondary schools, with a total enrollment of 4,117,412 (1973) **Enrollment in Higher Education:** North—75,000 (1973); South—88,104 (1972) **GNP Expended on Education:** North—N.A.; South—1.9% (1973)

Transportation: North—Improved roads total 5,823 mi., South—Surfaced roads total 5,673 mi. **Motor Vehicles:** North—N.A.; South—253,492 (1972) **Railway Mileage:** 1,718 Ports: Saigon, Haiphong, Da Nang, Qui Nhon, Cam Ranh, Ben Thuy, Hong Gai, Nha Trang **Major Airlines:** Air Vietnam **Communications:** Government controlled **Radio Transmitters:** North—3; South—27 **Receivers:** North—1,000,000 (1974); South—1,550,000 (1973) **Television Transmitters:** North—1; South—6 **Receivers:** North—N.A.; South—500,000 (1974) **Telephones:** North—N.A.; South—46,509 **Newspapers:** North—4 dailies, 8 copies per 1,000 inhabitants (1974); South—N.A.

Weights and Measures: Metric system **Travel Requirements:** Traveler should consult U.S. Department of State

---

A unified Vietnam, from the China border to the Gulf of Siam, came into being on July 2, 1976. The formal reunification after 22 years of division came 16 months after the collapse and surrender of the South Vietnamese government in Saigon to its North Vietnamese conquerors. After 30 years of struggle against foreign powers and the regimes they fostered, revolutionary forces of Vietnam realized the goal of the late Ho Chi Minh. The Communists, with more than a little help from their friends, had all of Vietnam under one flag and one government. In the years since the fall of the Saigon Government the problems of peace have proved as hard to solve as those of war.

The split into North Vietnam and South Vietnam that marked the end of French presence and the beginnings of American involvement occurred in 1954. As a colonial war ended, a period of insurgency and war began. It was to last over two decades and leave a legacy of bomb craters, street rubble, bullet-pocked buildings, abandoned rice fields and patches of defoliated forest—in addition to the thousands of lost, maimed and dislocated Vietnamese people.

The long war that could not be won came to a close for U.S. troops in 1973. A peace accord that could not be enforced lasted only 20 months after the American withdrawal. The end to the tragic war came with unbelievable swiftness in April of 1975 as the Communist forces swept the coastal cities and took Saigon almost unopposed. The cost to the United States for its misadventure in Indochina was 57,000 lives and $150 billion.

For Vietnam, the process of rebuilding a shattered economy and restructuring society in the South left little time for looks backward. In the South a provisional government took over from the military and began the task of dealing with three million unemployed urban residents and reshaping the economy to fit a different ideology.

To achieve self-sufficiency in food the new unified government resettled millions of refugees from the cities into rural areas so they could resume food production. It is said that nearly 700,000 were moved from Saigon to work abandoned rice fields or develop new agricultural areas, and the population of Da Nang was reduced by half. For many, life in the "new economic zones" is tough, with former clerks, unaccustomed to manual labor, trying to coax crops from marginal lands.

The transfer of people also involves Northerners. Tens of thousands of civil servants, teachers and tax collectors have been moved to the South to provide a dependable cadre at lower echelons. Plans call for the eventual movement of millions from densely populated rural places in the North to the more agriculturally productive South.

To restore trade and industry the unified government has shown surprising flexibility and respect for private business. Factories that had not been abandoned by their owners were allowed to continue operating. However, inflation in Saigon (now called Ho Chi Minh City) has pushed up food prices while salaries have been cut.

Vietnam found itself involved in two wars in 1979, piling up further troubles for its wrecked economy and internal tumult—the latter attested to by an outflow of hundreds of thousands of refugees. The fighting in Cambodia seemingly ended on Jan. 7, when Vietnamese troops captured the enemy capital, Phnom Penh, but it turned into a guerrilla war, with Pol Pot's rebels controlling the countryside and the Vietnamese troops dominant around Phnom Penh. Then on Feb. 17, the Chinese, saying they wanted to "teach a lesson" to Vietnamese who allegedly crossed their border in hundreds of incidents, invaded northern Vietnam. The Chinese fought for four weeks, advanced no more than 20 miles, and then departed, calling their punitive invasion a victory. Vietnam's defenders obviously put up a strong fight, because months later China conceded that its own army suffered 20,000 killed and wounded. (China placed Vietnam's casulaties at 50,000.) The fighting did cause Vietnam to remove some veteran troops from Cambodia, China's ally, but Vietnam quickly sent great numbers of less-experienced troops to Cambodia.

The warfare and economic distress have made the Soviet Union a closer ally of the Vietnamese, who have a 2,000-year history of animosity toward the Chinese. Soviet planes are flying Hanoi's troops to forward bases along the China border and in Cambodia, and Soviet warships have used the old U.S. naval base at Cam Ranh Bay. Vietnam and the Soviet Union signed a 25-year treaty of friendship and cooperation in November 1978. But in 1979 a Vietnamese diplomat said that "the door is very widely open" to resumption of diplomatic relations with the U.S. The forced exodus of ethnic Chinese from Vietnam, however, was among the factors hindering that.

HISTORY: The Vietnamese are believed to have originated in North China, from where they were slowly driven southward by the Han Chinese. By the 3rd century B.C., the Vietnamese had become settled in the Red River Delta in northern Vietnam. China annexed the region in the 2nd century B.C. and ruled it until 938 A.D., when independence was reestablished by Ngo Quyen. The new state gradually expanded, occupying much of Cambodia and southern Vietnam

1858: French and Spanish forces intervene in Vietnam's southern region of Cochin China to halt persecution of native Catholics

1862-67: Vietnam is gradually forced to yield Cochin China to the French

1884: France establishes a protectorate over Annam, in central Vietnam, and over Tonkin, in the north

1887: Cambodia, Cochin China, Annam, and Tonkin are incorporated into the Indo-Chinese Union

1940-45: Vietnam is occupied by Japanese forces during World War II; with defeat impending, Japan grants Vietnam independence under a puppet government headed by Bao Dai, emperor of Annam; following Japan's surrender to the Allies, Communist Viet Minh guerrillas, under leadership of Ho Chi Minh, set up Democratic Republic of Vietnam

1946-54: Viet Minh wages war against the French for eight years, culminating in the defeat of French forces at Dien Bien Phu; armistice is signed under a series of agreements concluded at Geneva, providing for the partition of Vietnam along the 17th parallel, with the north going to the government of Ho Chi Minh and the south placed under the control of Saigon. The agreements provided for the joining of North and South Vietnam into one country by holding elections in 1956. These were never held

NORTH VIETNAM

1955: Ho Chi Minh visits Communist China and USSR and signs aid agreements with both

1956: Peasant revolts break out in opposition to government's land collectivization program, but are crushed by troops

1959: North Vietnam, working through Viet Cong guerrillas, instigates campaign of terror and subversion in South Vietnam in attempt to annex state and unify Vietnam under Communist rule

1964-65: U.S. planes bomb North Vietnamese military targets following attacks on U.S. warships in Gulf of Tonkin in 1964; sustained U.S. air attacks are begun in 1965 to stem flow of equipment and North Vietnamese troops into the south

1968: United States orders halt to all bombing north of 20th parallel; move leads to an agreement between Hanoi and Washington to open peace talks in Paris

1969: Ho Chi Minh dies

1971: North Vietnamese troops drive South Vietnamese forces from Laos after the latter fail to cut Ho Chi Minh Trail

1973: Peace agreement signed in Paris officially ends Vietnam War, though fighting continues on a diminished scale

1974-75: Fighting escalates as both North and South repeatedly violate the cease-fire agreement. A stepped-up Communist offensive in early 1975 results in the abandonment by Saigon forces of the Central Highlands. The last resistance from the Saigon government ends on April 30 as Viet Cong and North Vietnamese troops enter Saigon

SOUTH VIETNAM

1955: Bao Dai is deposed and a republic established under the presidency of former Prime Minister Ngo Dinh Diem; a U.S. military advisory group is set up in South Vietnam

1959-63: South Vietnamese Communist guerrillas, known as Viet Cong, wage war against Diem government; harsh security measures introduced by regime incur wide popular resentment; Buddhist monks immolate themselves to protest what they charge is persecution by Diem regime. After violent demonstrations the government is overthrown and Diem is murdered

1965: New military regime is formed, with General Nguyen Van Thieu as chief of state and Air Vice Marshal Nguyen Cao Ky as premier; U.S. planes begin systematic bombing of North Vietnam, while in the south U.S. troop strength mounts to 200,000 men by year's end

1967: In South Vietnam's first national elections, Nguyen Van Thieu becomes president and Nguyen Cao Ky is chosen vice-president

1968: President Johnson announces a halt of U.S. bombings over most of North Vietnam; peace talks between United States and North Vietnam open in Paris

1970: South Vietnamese and U.S. troops invade Cambodia in drive against Viet Cong and North Vietnamese forces; Saigon troops continue operations after U.S. withdrawal

1971: South Vietnamese forces attempting to cut Ho Chi Minh Trail in Laos are driven out by North Vietnamese. Enemy steps up attacks in South Vietnam on eve of elections. Thieu runs unopposed for president and is reelected

1973: Paris peace agreement formally ends Vietnam War in January, but fighting continues on reduced level. The first prisoner exchanges worked out at the conference table begin

1974: Fighting intensifies in the central highlands near the Cambodian border; the Saigon government suspends its participation with the Viet Cong in Paris reconciliation talks

1975: North Vietnamese and Viet Cong forces step up their offensive in the South, seizing major cities. President Ford orders U.S. naval ships to help evacuate refugees. President Thieu resigns but the Viet Cong refuse to negotiate with the new South Vietnamese leadership. Communist troops enter and occupy Saigon. War ends as the South Vietnamese government unconditionally surrenders to the Viet Cong on April 29, 1975. Provisional Revolutionary Government takes control on June 6

UNIFIED VIETNAM

1976: First countrywide assembly elections are held April 25. North and South are officially reunited July 2. Rail link between Hanoi and Saigon reopened

1977: Security Council approves Vietnam membership in the UN. Border fighting flares up between Vietnam and Cambodia. Vietnamese face serious food problem, with rice shortage estimated at 18 percent of need. Talks with U.S. on establishing relations

recess after making little progress; behind impasse is Hanoi's insistence that promise of U.S. aid be made before ties are established, while U.S. rejects any preconditions

1978: Government introduces new national currency, cracks down on black-marketeers. Vietnamese-Cambodian border war intensifies. Refugees reportedly leaving Vietnam at highest rate since end of war in 1975. President Carter approves interim refugee policy permitting admission of Vietnamese "boat people" refused asylum elsewhere. In July, Vietnam is admitted to Soviet bloc's economic and trade group; in November, Vietnam and the Soviet Union sign a 25-year friendship treaty. China blames Vietnam in first shooting incident along their mutual border, ends aid to Vietnam and closes Vietnamese consulates in southern China. Government inducts over 350,000 into armed forces "to defend country's territorial integrity against foreign aggressors" and to work at construction sites. Vietnamese and Chinese clash at border pass. Vietnamese Premier Pham Van Dong declares he seeks normalization of relations and "indeed friendship" with U.S. The worst floods in 35 years destroy 500,000 homes and almost three million tons of rice. In December, Vietnamese troops advance steadily across Cambodia

1979: Vietnamese troops, together with Cambodian rebels, capture Phnom Penh on Jan. 7. But the deposed Cambodian premier, Pol Pot, escapes, and some 130,000 Vietnamese are tied down in Cambodia fighting guerrillas. On Feb. 7, China invades Vietnam with 100,000 troops that penetrate 15 or 20 miles in four weeks. The main fighting is at Lang Son, which is evacuated. The Chinese depart, with both sides claiming victory. By midyear, the number of ethnic Chinese fleeing Vietnam is estimated at 300,000 in a 12-month span. Vietnamese police are collecting more than $3,000 in gold from each adult leaving southern Vietnam; departure is on unsafe and overcrowded boats that have no specific destination

---

WESTERN SAMOA

Area: 1,133 sq. mi. **Population:** 151,800 (1978 est.)

Official Name: Independent State of Western Samoa **Capital:** Apia **Nationality:** Western Samoan **Languages:** Samoan, the predominant Polynesian language, and English are official **Religion:** The population is almost entirely Christian, with 50% Congregationalist, 20% Methodist, and 20% Roman Catholic **Flag:** A red field with a blue rectangle in the upper left corner bearing 5 white stars representing the Southern Cross **Anthem:** The Flag of Freedom **Currency:** Tala (0.76 per U.S. $1)

Location: South Pacific, forming part of an island group lying midway between Honolulu and Sydney, Australia. Western Samoa consists of the islands of Savai'i and Upolu and seven smaller islands of which only Manono and Apolima are inhabited **Features:** The islands are formed mainly of volcanic rock, with coral reefs surrounding much of the coasts. Rugged mountain ranges form the core of the two main islands, and there are many dormant volcanoes and lava fields

Chief Rivers: There are no large rivers

Head of State: Chief Malietoa Tanumafili II, born 1913, appointed in 1962; future holders of the office will be elected by the Legislative Assembly for 5-year terms **Head of Government:** Prime Minister Taisi Tupuola Efi, born 1948, appointed March 1976; he is also external affairs and immigration minister **Effective Date of Present Constitution:** January 1962 **Legislative Body:** Legislative Assembly (unicameral), consisting of 47 members, 45 of whom are Samoans elected by family chiefs (matai), and 2 are elected by universal suffrage, all for 3-year terms **Local Government:** 24 legislative districts (faipule), grouped into 12 political districts. Local government is carried out by the village councils (fono)

Ethnic Composition: Samoans, who form the second-largest branch of the Polynesian race, constitute 88% of the population. Euronesians (of mixed Polynesian and European ancestry) make up 10%, and the rest consists of Europeans (1,900) and other Pacific Islanders **Population Distribution:** 21% urban **Density:** 134 inhabitants per sq. mi.

Largest City: (1974 est.) Apia 32,616

Per Capita Income: $290 (1974) **Gross National Product (GNP):** $46 million (1974) **Economic Statistics:** There are no GNP statistics available; however, industries include handicrafts, foods, fruit processing, clothing, soap, and furniture; and agricultural products include taro, timber, fish, coconuts, cocoa, bananas, and pineapples **Minerals and Mining:** None **Labor Force:** There are 35,985 workers, with 90% in agriculture and fishing, and 10% in industry **Foreign Trade:** Exports, mainly copra, cocoa, bananas, timber, and taro, totaled $13 million in 1977. Imports, chiefly clothing and textiles, flour, canned fish and meat, motor vehicles, tobacco, sugar, and timber totaled $29 million (1975) **Principal Trade Partners:** New Zealand, Australia, Britain, West Germany, United States, Japan, Tonga

Vital Statistics: Birthrate, 35.0 per 1,000 of pop. (1977); death rate, 6.6 **Life Expectancy:** 67 years **Health Statistics:** 229 inhabitants per hospital bed; 2,727 per physician (1975) **Infant Mor-**

tality: 39.9 per 1,000 births (1974) **Illiteracy:** 10% **Education Statistics:** 208 primary and secondary schools, with combined enrollment of 48,585 (1975) **Enrollment in Higher Education:** 180 **GNP Expended on Education:** 3% (1977)

Transportation: Surfaced roads total 80 mi. **Motor Vehicles:** 3,100 (1976) **Passenger Cars:** 1,300 **Railway Mileage:** None **Ports:** Apia, Asau **Major Airlines:** Polynesian Airlines, owned jointly by the government and private business, operates international and domestic flights **Communications:** Government controlled **Radio Transmitters:** 1 **Receivers:** 50,000 (1973) **Television Transmitters:** None; received from American Samoa **Receivers:** 1,800 **Telephones:** 3,000 (1976) **Newspapers:** 2 several times a week, 103 copies per 1,000 inhabitants

Weights and Measures: British standards are used **Travel Requirements:** Passport; no visa for stay up to 7 days

---

Western Samoa became, on January 1, 1962, the first fully independent Polynesian state. Until then, the country, along with Eastern Samoa, had been under foreign control or tutelage since the turn of the century. In 1899 the Samoan islands were apportioned between Germany, which got Western Samoa as a protectorate, and the United States, which obtained, and still holds, the eastern part as American Samoa. Western Samoa was held from 1914 to 1962 by New Zealand, which, after ousting the Germans in World War I, obtained a League of Nations mandate and then a UN trusteeship. Although independent, Western Samoa still has New Zealand handling its foreign relations.

Western Samoa is a nation in transition, struggling to preserve its traditional ways while grappling with a backward economy. The most striking of those ways, perhaps, is the social system, based on *aigas*, or extended family groups, which are headed by *matais*, or chiefs. The *matais* direct the use of *aiga* assets. Supported by most Western Samoans, the system is a conservative force that many observers feel hampers the country, but the government, now headed by younger men, points to the possiblity of change.

Western Samoa's economy is predominantly agricultural but efforts are underway to develop its fishing industry and increase tourism.

HISTORY: Archaeological evidence indicates that Samoa may have been settled as far back as 1000 B.C., but little is known with certainty of its early history. The first Europeans to visit Samoa were the Dutch in 1722. Throughout the 19th century, the islands became pawns in a struggle for control by the United States, Germany, and Britain. After a brief attempt at tripartite control of Samoa, a treaty was signed in 1899 assigning Eastern Samoa to the United States and Western Samoa to Germany

1914-20: New Zealand occupies Western Samoa following outbreak of World War I and is later awarded mandate over islands by League of Nations

1927-36: Samoans and European settlers wage campaign of civil disobedience in opposition to the administration; campaign develops into movement for independence

1946: Western Samoa becomes United Nations trusteeship under continued supervision of New Zealand

1962: Western Samoa becomes independent, with Chief Tupua Tamasese Meaole and Chief Malietoa Tanumafili II as joint heads of state; New Zealand agrees to act as official channel with foreign governments and international organizations

1963: Tupua Tamasese Meaole dies, leaving Western Samoa with a single head of state

1970: Tamasese Lealofi IV is named prime minister as head of reform-minded government of younger men

1973: Fiame Mata'afa Mulinuu is elected prime minister

1975: Treaty is signed with EEC. Mata'afa dies and is replaced by Tamasese Lealofi IV

1976: Taisi Tupuola Efi becomes prime minister. Western Samoa becomes a UN member

1979: Prime Minister Tupuola Efi barely retains post in 24-23 vote of the parliament following February 28 *matai* elections; criticized for seeking too rapid a rate of economic growth, Tupuola reshuffles Cabinet, reflecting a shift toward a policy of consolidating past economic progress

---

YEMEN

Area: 77,220 sq. mi. **Population:** 7,080,000 (1978 est.)
Official Name: Yemen Arab Republic **Capital:** San'a **Nationality:**

Yemeni **Languages:** Arabic is the official and universal language **Religion:** Islam is the state religion, with the population almost equally divided between the Zaidi Shi'ite and Shafai Sunnite sects **Flag:** Horizontal stripes of red, white, and black with a green star in the center **Anthem:** National Anthem, beginning "Peace to the land" **Currency:** Yemeni rial (4.56 per U.S. $1)

Location: Southwest Arabia. Yemen is bounded on the north and east by Saudi Arabia, on the south by Southern Yemen, and on the west by the Red Sea **Features:** The country consists of a semi-desert coastal plain (the Tihama) along the Red Sea and a mountainous area in the interior which receives abundant rainfall **Chief Rivers:** There are no permanent rivers

Head of State: President: Col. Ali Abdullah Saleh, born 1942, elected July 1978 **Head of Government:** Premier Abd al-Aziz Abd al-Ghani, appointed in January 1975 **Effective Date of Present Constitution:** 1971 **Legislative Body:** Constituent People's Assembly of 99 members appointed by the Command Council **Local Government:** 10 governorates under appointed emirs, divided into 40 districts

Ethnic Composition: The population is predominantly Arab, with black slaves present in the Tihama **Population Distribution:** 11% urban **Density:** 92 inhabitants per sq. mi.

Largest Cities: (1975 census) San'a 134,588, Hodeida 80,314, Ta'izz 78,642, Dhamar 19,467, Ibb 19,066, Al Beida 5,975

Per Capita Income: $322 (1978) **Gross National Product (GNP):** $1.8 billion (1978) **Economic Statistics:** About 50% of GNP comes from agriculture (cotton, Mocha coffee, livestock, cereals, vegetables, fruit). There is some light industry (textiles, food products) **Minerals and Mining:** The only industrial mining enterprise is the extraction of salt. There are traces of copper, coal, sulfur, gypsum and quartz **Labor Force:** 800,000; 70% of the population is engaged in agriculture and animal husbandry, and 13% in trade **Foreign Trade:** Exports, mainly cotton, coffee, hides and skins, salt, and qat, totaled $11 million in 1977. Imports, chiefly textiles, machinery, fuels, foods, totaled $948 million **Principal Trade Partners:** Southern Yemen, USSR, Saudi Arabia, Australia, China, EC countries, India, Japan, United States

Vital Statistics: Birthrate, 49.6 per 1,000 of pop.; death rate 20.6 **Life Expectancy:** 38 years **Health Statistics:** 1,443 inhabitants per hospital bed; 26,449 per physician (1974) **Infant Mortality:** N.A. **Illiteracy:** 90% **Education Statistics:** 2,075 primary and secondary schools, with combined enrollment of 276,155 (1975) **Enrollment in Higher Education:** 2,408 **GNP Expended on Education:** 0.7% (1974)

Transportation: Paved roads total 600 mi. **Motor Vehicles:** 44,500 (1975) **Passenger Cars:** 14,000 **Railway Mileage:** None **Ports:** Hodeida, Mocha **Major Airlines:** Yemen Airways, government owned, operates domestic and international flights **Communications:** Government controlled **Radio Transmitters:** 4 **Receivers:** 90,000 (1976) **Television Transmitters:** 1 **Receivers:** N.A. **Telephones:** 5,000 (1975) **Newspapers:** 6 dailies, 10 copies per 1,000 inhabitants (1970)

Weights and Measures: Local units are used **Travel Requirements:** Passport; visa, valid 3 months; $2 fee; 3 photos

---

Yemen is a land whose interior contains gauntly beautiful mountains and green, cultivated fields—a rarity in the Arabian peninsula—and whose crucially important location between the Gulf of Aden and the Red Sea, athwart the Arabian oil route to the West, has brought it a disproportionate degree of world attention.

Yemen remains a country that is difficult to govern, where tribal loyalties are stronger than national considerations. Those tendencies have been aggravated by a civil war (1962-1969), and by memories of ancient times when Yemen and Southern Yemen had common ties. The civil war began in 1962 as a revolt against Mohammed al-Badr, heir to a dynasty of Imams (religious rulers) who had become arbitrary and capricious. The rebels established a republic with Egyptian backing; the Imam continued resistance from the hills, with an army of tribesmen and mercenaries supported by Saudi Arabia. Egypt sent almost a third of its army to help the republic. Egypt and Saudi Arabia agreed to end their intervention in 1967, and the Imam's forces were defeated by those of the republic in 1969. But the republic was, and remained, unstable, plagued by a series of coups and counter-coups.

In a 48-hour period in June 1978, the Presidents of both Yemen and Southern Yemen were killed. The violence began in Sa'na just as Yemen's President Ahmed Hussein al-Ghashmi, a close ally of Saudi Arabia, was about to consider Southern Yemen's proposals for a merger of the Yemens. Yemen, blaming Soviet-backed Southern Yemen for the killing, severed their relations. Two days later, Southern Yemen President Salem Rubaye Ali, a moderate Marxist, lost a power struggle with the ultraleftist General Secretary of the country's National Liberation Front party, Abdul Fattah Ismail, whom Western and Arab observers suspect may have been behind Ghashmi's murder. Ghashmi was succeed by Ali Abdullah Saleh, and tensions with Southern Yemen continued to build. Southern Yemeni soldiers—with Soviet, Cuban, and East German help—invaded Yemen in February 1979. Saudi Arabia and the United States rushed arms to Yemen, and U.S. ships showed the flag in nearby waters. In March, the League of Arab States arranged a cease-fire; and a special force, under the League's command, was established to patrol the border. President Saleh and President Ismail met in Kuwait and drew up a plan to merge their two countries, but, as of August 1979, had done nothing to implement the plan.

HISTORY: Yemen formed part of what was known as Arabia Felix in classical times and was the site of a series of rich mercantile kingdoms. One of these was Sheba, or Saba, which flourished from about 750 to 115 B.C. The Sabaeans were superseded by the Himyarites, under whom Judaism and Christianity took root. Himyarite rule was ended in 525 by an invading force of Christian Ethiopians, who in turn were driven out by the Persians in 575

7th cent.: Islam is introduced

9th cent.: Yemen comes under the control of the Rassite dynasty, religious leaders, called imams, of the Zaydi sect, who lay the foundations of a theocratic political structure lasting to 1962

1517-1918: Ottoman Empire exercises nominal sovereignty

1948: Imam Yahya is assassinated; his son, Crown Prince Ahmad, defeats forces of new government and succeeds as imam

1958: Yemen and United Arab Republic (union of Egypt and Syria) form confederation called United Arab States

1961: Following Syria's withdrawal from UAR, President Nasser dissolves the association with Yemen, denouncing Imam Ahmad as a reactionary

1962: Ahmad dies and is succeeded by Crown Prince Mohammad al-Badr, who favors a neutralist foreign policy; he is overthrown by pro-Nasser army officers who proclaim a republic under the leadership of Col. Abdullah al-Salal; civil war breaks out between republican and royalist forces, who win the respective backing of Egypt and Saudi Arabia

1963: Egypt sends 40,000 troops to Yemen to assist republicans

1967: Egypt withdraws troops from Yemen; riots in San'a force al-Salal to form new government free of Egyptian influence; he is deposed, however, while on a visit to Moscow and a new republican government is set up; royalist forces move on San'a

1968: Republicans, aided by Soviet-built aircraft, regain initiative; royalists retreat, reorganize their forces and in an effort to widen their political base fill top posts with officials not related to the Imam, who is deprived of all political power

1969: Republican government asserts that civil war has ended; Lt. Gen. Hassan al-Amri resigns as prime minister; a new cabinet is formed and Abdullah al-Karshumi becomes prime minister

1970: Amicable settlement is reached between republicans and royalists; Moshen al-Aini is named premier

1972: Yemen and Southern Yemen end hostilities after series of border clashes; they agree to future merger. Aini is replaced by Abdullah al-Hagri

1973: Border clashes resume between the two Yemens

1974: Hagri is replaced by Hassan Makki. Army ousts government in bloodless coup and establishes military junta headed by Col. Ibrahim al-Hamdi. Aini forms new government

1975: Premier Aini is replaced by Abd al-Aziz Ad al-Ghani

1977: Col. Ibrahim al-Hamdi is assassinated; new military rulers impose martial law, as Maj. Ahmed Hussein al-Ghashmi assumes leadership of government

1978: Constituent assembly formally elects Ghashmi president. Ghashmi is assassinated; Yemen blames Southern Yemen, severs relations. Ghashmi's murder is factor in overthrow two days later of Southern Yemen's President Rubaye Ali by colleagues in pro-Soviet National Front. Constituent People's Assembly elects Col. Ali Abdullah Saleh president

1979: Southern Yemen invades Yemen, which gets aid from United States and Saudi Arabia. Cease-fire agreement places Yemen-Southern Yemen border under patrol commanded by League of Arab States. Presidents Saleh and Ismail agree to merger plan

SOUTHERN YEMEN

Area: 111,101 sq. mi. **Population:** 1,800,000 (1978 est.)

Official Name: People's Democratic Republic of Yemen **Capital:** Aden **Nationality:** Southern Yemenite or Yemeni **Languages:** Arabic is the official language; Mahri is spoken in the east, and English is also widely understood **Religion:** 98% of the population are Sunni Moslems of the Shafai sect **Flag:** Horizontal stripes of red, white, and black with a red star on a blue triangle at the hoist **Anthem:** National Anthem (no words) **Currency:** Yemeni dinar (0.35 per U.S. $1)

Location: Southern part of the Arabian peninsula. Southern Yemen is bounded on the north by Saudi Arabia, on the east by Oman, on the south by the Gulf of Aden, and on the northwest by Yemen **Features:** A narrow, sandy plain along the coast gives way to mountainous terrain, interspersed with deep valleys. The land retains its mountainous character until it reaches the interior sands. Offshore islands include Socotra, Perim, and Kamaran **Chief Rivers:** There are no permanent rivers

Head of State: Chairman of the Presidium of the Supreme People's Council (President): Abdul Fatah Ismail, born 1937, elected 1978 **Head of Government:** Prime Minister Ali Nasir Mohammed al-Hassani, appointed 1971 **Effective Date of Present Constitution:** December 1, 1970 **Legislative Body:** People's Supreme Assembly (unicameral) of 111 elected members **Local Government:** 7 governorates under appointed governors, divided into 24 districts

Ethnic Composition: The population is mainly Arab; Indians, Pakistanis, and Somalis constitute small minorities **Population Distribution:** 33% urban **Density:** 16 inhabitants per sq. mi.

Largest Cities: (1973 est.) Aden 264,326; (1972 est.) Mukalla 45,000, Seiyun 20,000

Per Capita Income: $344 (1978) **Gross National Product (GNP):** $640 million (1978) **Economic Statistics:** The subsistence economy is based on agriculture (sorghum, millet, wheat) and fishing, though some cotton is grown for export. Aden, a leading oil bunkering port, is slowly recovering with the reopening of the Suez Canal. There is an oil refinery, and some light industry **Minerals and Mining:** Salt **Labor Force:** 395,568 (1977), with 62% in subsistence agriculture, and 18% in industry, with 72% of the latter in oil refining **Foreign Trade:** Exports, mainly petroleum products, raw cotton, hides and skins, and fuel oil, totaled $187 million in 1975. Imports, chiefly rice, wheat flour, tea, cotton and rayon piece goods, and petroleum products, totaled $312 million **Principal Trade Partners:** Kuwait, Britain, Iran, Japan, Yemen, India, Iraq

Vital Statistics: Birthrate, 49.6 per 1,000 of pop. (1975); death rate, 20.6 **Life Expectancy:** 45 years **Health Statistics:** 665 inhabitants per hospital bed (1973); 13,000 per physician (1970) **Infant Mortality:** 79.9 per 1,000 births **Illiteracy:** 73% **Education Statistics:** 963 primary and secondary schools, with combined enrollment of 236,162 (1974) **Enrollment in Higher Education:** 934 **GNP Expended on Education:** 3.5% (1971)

Transportation: Surfaced roads total 1,150 mi. **Motor Vehicles:** 22,400 (1976) **Passenger Cars:** 11,900 **Railway Mileage:** None **Port:** Aden **Major Airlines:** Democratic Yemen Airlines, government owned, operates services **Communications:** Government controlled **Radio Transmitters:** 4 **Receivers:** 100,000 (1976) **Television Transmitters:** 5 **Receivers:** 32,000 (1976) **Telephones:** 10,000 (1973) **Newspapers:** 3 dailies, 1 copy per 1,000 inhabitants (1973)

Weights and Measures: British standards are generally used in Aden; local measures are used in the rest of the country **Travel Requirements:** Traveler should consult U.S. Department of State for travel information

One of the poorest member of the Arab League, Southern Yemen comprises the former colony of Aden, at the southwestern corner of the Arabian peninsula, and a forbidding hinterland with poorly defined borders. Under British rule, the country was known as "Aden," and later as the "Federation of South Arabia." It declared independence in 1967 as "People's Republic of Southern Yemen." In 1970, the official name was changed to the "People's Democratic Republic of Yemen." Hopes for union with the neighboring "Yemen Arab Republic" exist in both states, but each wants union on its own terms.

With its oppressively hot climate and barren terrain, Southern Yemen has few natural resources and little industry, and must rely heavily on foreign aid for its 1974-79 five-year development plan. About 62 percent of the population is engaged in primitive agriculture.

The departure of the British in 1967 and the closing of their naval base at Aden has further scarred the country's economy. Aden, once a flourishing port, now gripped by poverty, has not experienced the revitalization which was expected after the reopening of the Suez Canal in 1975.

In a two-day period in June 1978, as Yemen and Southern Yemen were about to work out details of a proposed merger, both Yemeni presidents were killed—the first in an unsolved assassination plot and the latter before a firing squad following a military coup led by Abdul Fattah Ismail, staunchly pro-Soviet General Secretary of the country's National Liberation Front party. Assisted by the Soviet Union, East Germany, and Cuba, Southern Yemen invaded the Yemen Arab Republic in February 1979. Saudi Arabia and the United States supplied arms to the YAR In March, both countries agreed to a resolution of the League of Arab States, under which their armies withdrew from the border, and soldiers under the League's command were stationed between them. The governments of the two Yemens agreed on a plan to merge their countries, but, as of August, had taken no steps to implement the plan.

HISTORY: Southern Yemen formed part of the Minaean, Sabaean, and Himyarite kingdoms that flourished between 1200 B.C. and the 6th century A.D. The Himyarites were conquered in 525 by Christian Ethiopians, who were driven out by the Persians in 575. Islam was introduced in the 7th century and by the 9th century the highland regions of Southern Yemen had fallen under the rule of the Islamic religious leaders, or imams, of Yemen. The coastal area recognized the primacy of the Baghdad Caliphate and later fell under Egyptian and Turkish rule

19th cent.: Britain gains control of Aden and concludes treaties with southern Yemeni sheikhs to protect them from overland attack from Turkey

1914: Anglo-Turkish convention establishes demarcation line separating British-controlled Southern Yemen from Turkish-occupied Yemen

1959: Six of the states of Southern Yemen form Federation of Arab Emirates of the South, later renamed Federation of South Arabia

1963-66: Aden joins federation; revolt, led by National Liberation Front (NLF), breaks out against British rule; Britain promises to grant southern Yemen independence by 1968 but NLF refuses to negotiate; joined by other groups, it forms Front for the Liberation of Occupied South Yemen (FLOSY) but soon breaks away from new group

1967: NLF defeats FLOSY. Britain withdraws from all of Southern Yemen

1969: Qahtan al-Shaabi, Southern Yemen's first president, resigns and is replaced by a five-man Presidential Council

1970: Al-Shaabi is ousted from NLF

1971: Ali Nasir Mohammed al-Hassani is appointed prime minister, succeeding Mohammed Ali Haithem

1972: Southern Yemen and Yemen sign truce after brief border fighting; agreement provides for future merger

1973: Border clashes resume between the two Yemens

1974: U.S. charges Soviet military buildup in Red Sea-Indian Ocean area involves use of Aden as submarine base

1975: Perim Island, which controls southern entrance to Red Sea, is leased to Egypt, as agent for the Arab League, in return for financial aid. Discussion on unity with Yemen is revived

1976: A cease-fire between Southern Yemen and Oman, where Southern Yemen had supported left-wing rebel forces, comes into force

1978: Yemen blames Southern Yemen for assassination of Yemen president; two days later ultraleftist Abdul Fattah Ismail ousts President Salem Rubaye Ali, who is immediately tried and shot; five-man council headed by Prime Minister al-Hassani takes over government. NLF and two smaller parties form Yemen Socialist Party. Ismail is elected president

1979: Southern Yemen invades Yemen, withdraws after both sides agree to station between them a multinational patrol under command of League of Arab States. President Ismail and President Ali Abdullah Saleh of Yemen agree on merger plan

YUGOSLAVIA

Area: 98,766 sq. mi. **Population:** 21,720,000 (1978 est.)

Official Name: Socialist Federal Republic of Yugoslavia **Capital:** Belgrade **Nationality:** Yugoslavia is officially made up of 6 "nations": Serbs, Croats, Slovenes, Macedonians, Montenegrins and Moslems. "Moslem" does not mean religion but nationality. Officially there exists no Yugoslav nation **Languages:** All "national" languages are official, with Serbo-Croatian serving as a lingua franca **Religion:** About 34% of the population belong to the Orthodox Church; 24% are Roman Catholics and 8% Moslems; 34% are of other or no affiliation **Flag:** Horizontal stripes of blue, white, and red with a red star edged in gold in the center **Anthem:** Fellow Slavs **Currency:** Yugoslav dinar (18.7 per U.S. $1)

Location: Southeast Europe. Yugoslavia, on the Balkan Peninsula, is bounded on the north by Austria and Hungary, on the east by Romania and Bulgaria, on the south by Greece and Albania, and on the west by the Adriatic Sea and Italy **Features:** The northern and eastern part consists of lowland hills and plains, with a few mountain ranges. The remaining two-thirds of the country is mountainous, culminating in the Dinaric Alps **Chief Rivers:** Danube, including its tributaries (Drava, Sava, Morava, Tisza), and Vardar

Political Leader and Head of State: President Josip Broz Tito, born 1892, in office since 1945, as head of the Communist party, elected president in 1953 and president for life in 1974; he is head of a 9-member Presidency **Head of Government:** Premier Veselin Djuranović, born 1926, appointed president of the 29-member Federal Executive Council in 1977 **Effective Date of Present Constitution:** February 1974 **Legislative Body:** Federal Assembly (bicameral), with a Federal Council of 220 proportionately elected delegates, and a Council of Republics and Provinces with 58 delegates **Local Government:** 6 republics and 2 autonomous provinces (within Serbia), each with its own locally elected executive council and assembly

Ethnic Composition: Serbs (40%), Croats (22%), Slovenes (8%), Bosnian Moslems (8%), Macedonians (6%), Albanians (6%), Montenegrins (2%), Hungarians (2%), Turks (1%) **Population Distribution:** 39% urban **Density:** 220 inhabitants per sq. mi.

Largest Cities: (Metropolitan Areas) (1976 est.) Belgrade 1,319,000; (1974 est.) Zagreb 700,000; Skopje 440,000, Sarajevo 400,000, Ljubljana 300,000; (1971 census) Novi Sad 216,358

Per Capita Income: $2,544 (1978) **Gross National Product (GNP):** $56 billion (1978) **Economic Statistics:** About 17% of the GNP is derived from agriculture (corn, wheat, fruits including wine grapes, sugar beets, tobacco, livestock, timber); 37% from mining and manufacturing (metals, woodworking, chemicals, textiles, food processing). Tourism is also an important source of revenue **Minerals and Mining:** Coal, copper, iron ore, lead, zinc, petroleum, bauxite, natural gas **Labor Force:** 10,700,000 (1977), with 35% in agriculture and 52% in industry **Foreign Trade:** Exports, chiefly fresh meat, ships, machinery, clothing, and hardwood, totaled $5.3 billion in 1977. Imports, mainly machinery and transport equipment, iron and steel, wheat, raw materials, and chemicals, totaled $9.6 billion **Principal Trade Partners:** USSR, West Germany, Italy, United States, France, Poland, Iraq

Vital Statistics: Birthrate, 17.7 per 1,000 of pop. (1977); death rate, 6 **Life Expectancy:** 68 years **Health Statistics:** 169 inhabitants per hospital bed; 849 per physician (1974) **Infant Mortality:** 35.2 per 1,000 births (1977) **Illiteracy:** 15% **Education Statistics:** 13,540 primary and secondary schools, with combined enrollment of 3,694,635 (1973) **Enrollment in Higher Education:** 394,992 (1975) **GNP Expended on Education:** 6% (1974)

Transportation: Surfaced roads total 42,644 mi. **Motor Vehicles:** 1,922,800 (1976) **Passenger Cars:** 1,732,100 **Railway Mileage:** 7,493 **Ports:** Rijeka, Split, Dubrovnik, Kotor; on the Danube River: Novi Sad, Belgrade **Major Airlines:** Yugoslav Airlines operates domestically and internationally **Communications:** Government owned **Radio Transmitters:** 487 **Licenses:** 4,526,000 (1976) **Television Transmitters:** 430 **Licenses:** 3,463,000 (1976) **Telephones:** 1,431,000 (1976) **Newspapers:** 26 dailies (1975), 80 copies per 1,000 inhabitants (1976)

Weights and Measures: Metric system **Travel Requirements:** Passport; visa valid up to 1 year; no fee

A perennial subject of debate among orthodox Communists has been whether Yugoslavia is really Communist. The Yugoslavs insist they are. Others insist that they are not and that Yugoslavia's brand of political ideology is more Titoism than Communism. The question now being asked as President Josip Broz Tito approaches his 88th birthday is, can there be Titoism in Yugoslavia without Tito?

The Communist party of Yugoslavia was renamed the League of Communists of Yugoslavia in 1952. It has remained the dominant political force. But some scope for political activity is provided by the less disciplined Socialist Alliance of Working People of Yugoslavia, to which all League members and about half of the other adults belong. There are few state or collective farms; agriculture is dominated by private small holdings. Most businesses are managed by councils elected by the workers, and workers have been known to strike against their own councils. The worker-managed businesses compete vigorously against each other, and they are allowed to advertise. Individuals may own businesses with no more than five employees, and occupational licensure is almost unknown. More than half of Yugoslavia's trade is with non-Communist countries, and many Yugoslavs work in Western Europe, entering and leaving Yugoslavia across an open frontier. The press is not strictly controlled, and foreign publications are available to those who can read them.

The political system features a parliament with genuine independent power and a decentralization of authority among the nationality sub-republics. Yugoslavia is made up of many different peoples—notably the Serbs, Croats, Slovenes, and Macedonians—and their rivalry has not been diminished by the attempt to give each group a sense of political and cultural independence.

In February 1974, the Yugoslav government underwent several major changes. A new constitution was enacted that strengthened the powers of the central government and the League of Communists while enlarging the political power of workers' councils. A collective presidency was also instituted, to consist of nine members to take power after Tito's death. Yet the danger of domestic disarray and possible Soviet intervention remains a real concern to many Yugoslavs.

After 1948, when Yugoslavia was expelled from the world Communist movement, Marshal Tito moved closer to and received much aid from the United States, Britain, and France. After the reconciliation with the Soviet Union in 1955, Yugoslavia tended to follow the Soviet line on many world issues. Nevertheless, it sought a measure of independence in foreign policy by rallying African and Asian countries into a bloc of nonaligned nations over which it tried to exert leadership.

Relations with the Soviet Union once again grew tense following the 1968 Russian invasion of Czechoslovakia and the subsequent Soviet enunciation of the doctrine of limited sovereignty for socialist countries. Fearing a similar invasion, the Belgrade government tightened its own security. In recent years exchanges of visits between Soviet and Yugoslav officials have signaled something of a thaw between the two countries.

HISTORY: In ancient times, what is now Yugoslavia was inhabited chiefly by Illyrian peoples who came under Roman rule in the 1st century B.C. In the 6th century A.D., Slavic immigrants settled in the country; their languages and cultures gradually became dominant. Most of the Yugoslav (Southern Slav) peoples were conquered by the Ottoman Empire in the 14th and 15th centuries. The House of Hapsburg pushed back the Turkish tide, and, by 1878, ruled Croatia, Slovenia, and Bosnia-Hercegovina. Montenegro had maintained a precarius independence, and Serbia had become independent in the 19th century, and had assumed the leadership of the movement for a Pan-Slav state

1914-15: Serbia and Montenegro are overrun by Central Powers in World War I, precipitated by assassination of Archduke Francis Ferdinand at Sarajevo, in Bosnia, by a Serbian nationalist

1918: Kingdom of Serbs, Croats, and Slovenes is proclaimed under the rule of King Peter I of Serbia

1929: Alexander I, Peter's successor, establishes dictatorship following moves toward separatism by Croatia; country's name is changed to Yugoslavia

1934: Alexander is assassinated in Marseilles by Croat terrorist; his son succeeds him as Peter II under the regency of Prince Paul, Alexander's cousin

1941: Yugoslavia signs Berlin-Rome-Tokyo Pact; Prince Paul and his pro-German government are ousted in bloodless coup; new government signs nonaggression pact with USSR; Germany and Italy, joined by Hungary and Bulgaria, invade Yugoslavia, which collapses a week later

1943: Civil war breaks out between Chetniks, a Serbian resistance force headed by Draja Mikhailovich, and Communist partisans led by Josip Broz Tito

1944: Tito's forces expel Germans

1945: Monarchy is abolished and the People's Republic of Yugoslavia is proclaimed under Tito's leadership

1946: Tito launches vigorous program of socialization; political opposition is crushed and Mikhailovich executed; Roman Catholic Church comes under government attack, culminating in arrest and imprisonment of Archbishop Aloysius Stepinac

1948: Yugoslavia is expelled from Cominform after Tito resists Soviet attempts to control his regime; Tito begins to develop "national communism" and turns to West for aid

1955-60: Yugoslavia attempts to resume more cordial relations with USSR but new rift develops following the crushing of the 1956 Hungarian revolt by the Russians; in 1960 Yugoslavia again moves toward closer relations with Moscow

1968: Soviet-led invasion of Czechoslovakia draws warning from Yugoslav Communists that Yugoslavia stands ready to defend its independence

1972: Tito introduces presidency of Yugoslavia, a collective body designed to rule the country after he leaves

1972-73: Croatian nationalist Communist leadership sides with separatist movement, but Tito clamps down in December 1972, purging some top Communist leaders

1973: Tito purges Serbian and Slovenian Communist party leaders accused of "liberalism;" new constitution calls for collective presidency of Yugoslavia

1976: Tito attends European Communist party meeting, ending Yugoslav boycott of such Communist conferences since 1957

1977: U.S. agrees to expand military ties with Yugoslavia. Government frees dissident author Mihajlo Mihajlov in amnesty affecting 723 prisoners

1978: Tito visits U.S. China's Hua Guofeng visits Yugoslavia

1979: Tito visits USSR

ZAIRE

Area: 918,962 sq. mi. **Population:** 26,380,000 (1978 est.)

Official Name: Republic of Zaire **Capital:** Kinshasa **Nationality:** Zairean **Languages:** French is the official and only common language; about 700 languages and dialects are spoken, the four serving as linguas franca being Lingala, Kingwana, Kikongo, and Tshiluba **Religion:** About 50% Christian (75% Roman Catholic); most of the remaining population practices traditional religions, especially animism **Flag:** A green field with yellow disc, in which a brown hand holds a red and brown torch **Anthem:** Song of Independence **Currency:** Zaire (1.55 per U.S. $1)

Location: South-central Africa. The Republic of Zaire is bordered on the west and north by the Congo, the Central African Empire, and Sudan; on the east by Uganda, Rwanda, Burundi, and Tanzania; and on the south by Angola and Zambia. Its only outlet to the ocean is a narrow strip of land on the north bank of the Congo (Zaire) estuary on the Atlantic **Features:** The huge Congo Basin, a low-lying, basin-shaped plateau sloping toward the west, is covered by tropical rain forest. Surrounding it are mountainous terraces on the west, plateaus merging into savannas to the south and southeast, and dense grasslands toward the northwest. High mountains lie to the east **Chief Rivers:** The Congo (Zaire) and its many tributaries, including the Ubangi, Aruwimi, Lindi, Lualaba, Lomami, Lomela, Momboyo, Kasai, Kwango, and Kwilu

Head of State and of Government: President: Lt. Gen. Mobutu Sese Seko, born 1930; seized power in a coup in 1965, reelected 1977 for a second seven-year term. Also the commissioner for defense, he is assisted by the first state commissioner (premier), Bo-Boliko Lokongo, appointed 1979 **Effective Date of Present Constitution:** 1967, amended 1974, 1978 **Legislative Body:** Legislative Council (unicameral), with 268 members, elected for 5 years. Actual power resides with the president, as head of the Political Bureau of the Popular Revolutionary Movement (MPR) **Local Government:** 8 regions, each with an appointed commissioner

Ethnic Composition: There are some 200 tribal groups, which can be divided into 3 main categories: the Negroes (Bantu [80%], Sudanese, and Nilotics); the Hamites; and the Pygmies **Population Distribution:** 30% urban **Density:** 29 inhabitants per sq. mi.

Largest Cities: (1974 est.) Kinshasa 2,008,352, Kananga 601,239, Lubumbashi 403,623, Mbuji-Mayi 336,654, Kisangani 310,705, Bukavu 181,774, Kikwit 150,253, Matadi 143,598

Per Capita Income: $134 (1978) **Gross National Product (GNP):** $3.7 billion (1978) **Economic Statistics:** About 17% of GNP comes from industry (food processing, consumer durables, and construction materials); 15% from public administration; 15% from commerce and transportation; 15% from subsistence production; 13% from agriculture (coffee, rubber, and palm oil); 7% from mining **Minerals and Mining:** The country is the world's largest producer of industrial diamonds; copper provides one-half of export earnings. Other important minerals include cobalt, bauxite, gold, cassiterite, manganese, oil, gas, and zinc **Labor Force:** 8.3 million, with about 75% in agriculture **Foreign Trade:** Exports, chiefly copper, cobalt, zinc, diamonds, coffee, palm oil and rubber totaled $1 billion in 1976. Imports, mainly machinery, transportation equipment, textiles, and foodstuffs, totaled $800 million **Principal Trade Partners:** Belgium, United States, Italy, France, West Germany, Britain, Japan

Vital Statistics: Birthrate, 45.2 per 1,000 of pop. (1975); death rate, 20.5 **Life Expectancy:** 44 years **Health Statistics:** 327 inhabitants per hospital bed; 28,802 per physician (1973) **Infant Mortality:** 104 per 1,000 births **Illiteracy:** 70% **Education Statistics:** About 11,000 primary and secondary schools, with combined enrollment of 3,627,223 (1973) **Enrollment in Higher Education:** 21,021 (1974) **GNP Expended on Education:** 4.2% (1970)

Transportation: Improved roads total about 1,200 mi. **Motor Vehicles:** 161,200 (1974) **Passenger Cars:** 84,800 **Railway Mileage:** 3,593 (1970) **Ports:** Matadi, Banana, Boma **Major Airlines:** Air Zaire provides domestic and international services **Communications:** Partly government owned **Radio Transmitters:** 22 **Receivers:** 2,448,000 (1974) **Television Transmitters:** 3 **Receivers:** 7,000 (1976) **Telephones:** 48,000 (1976) **Newspapers:** 11 dailies, 9 copies per 1,000 inhabitants (1974)

Weights and Measures: Metric system **Travel Requirements:** Passport; visa, valid 1 to 3 months; $4 fee; 1 photo

Torn by bloody strife through more than half of its first decade of independence, Zaire's early name of Congo had been almost a synonym for disorder. For 85 years the big African country—its area equal to that of the United States east of the Mississippi—was the possession of Belgium. While Belgian administration checked tribal enmities, colonial monopolies reaped the wealth of ivory, gold, copper, and other minerals. Plantations used labor under conditions little different from slavery.

Although the colonial regime grew less harsh in the 20th century, with missionary schools and better economic treatment for Zaireans (Congolese), Belgium administrators did little to prepare for self-government.

In 1960, spurred by rebellion in Zaire and the wave of decolonization elsewhere in Africa, the Belgian government reluctantly acceded to the independence demands of Zaire leaders headed by Joseph Kasavubu and Patrice Lumumba. The calm, conservative Kasavubu, who became the first president, and other leaders favored a loose federation, while the passionate, radical Lumumba, who became premier, wanted a strong central government. And with the formal grant of independence on June 30, 1960, the issue remained basically unresolved.

Peaceful independence lasted only five days. On July 5 the army mutinied, public authority broke down and on July 10 Belgian troops intervened to protect Belgian nationals caught in a wave of terror. On July 11 Moise Tshombe, governor of Katanga, declared his mineral-rich province an independent country.

With a UN force backing up the national army, there began the long struggle to quell the Katangan secession. The Katangan forces, with a hard core of white mercenaries—*les affreux* ("the frightful ones")—put up a stiff resistance and it was not until mid-1963 that Tshombe was defeated and forced into exile.

Meanwhile, breakaway governments arose in South Kasai and in Kivu Province. Following a quarrel between Kasavubu and Lumumba, the national army commander, Col. Joseph D. Mobutu, a tough, Israeli-trained paratrooper, took over the government on September 5, 1960 and expelled Soviet and Communist-bloc diplomats and technicians.

The following November, the deposed Lumumba was captured while trying to flee to Kivu Province. Lumumba was taken to Katanga and assassinated in February 1961, becoming a martyr for third-world radicals. That same month Mobutu returned the reins of government to Kasavubu and four groups then contended for power. The country was not unified until 1963.

In 1964 when Zaire seemed to be pulling itself together, Kasavubu, in a gesture of national reconciliation, recalled Tshombe from exile and made him premier. There followed renewed rebellion by former Lumumba followers. The rebels, however, were soon defeated in an attack by Belgian paratroopers brought in by U.S. planes.

But neither Tshombe nor his successor could end the country's malaise of disunity (Tshombe went into exile and died in Algeria in 1969.) Mobutu, now a general, seized power in November 1965. He reduced provincial authority and began building a strong central government to unify the country's 100 tribes into a true nation. By offering attractive incentives to foreign investment, he set out to make the Zaire a leading industrial country.

Elected president in 1970, Mobutu has proved an effective salesman in promoting investment through state visits to the United States, West Germany, Japan, and other countries. Early in 1974 the government created a state-owned company to take over all petroleum product distribution. Mobutu, in a campaign of "African authenticity," renamed the country Zaire and dropped his Christian names and called himself Mobutu Sese Seko.

Twice in a 14-month period, Zaire was invaded by Katangan soldiers who had fled the southern province of Shaba (formerly Katanga) after losing the secessionist war of the mid-1960s. In March 1977 President Mobutu's rule was threatened by the first invasion of Shaba, which contains copper mines that provide the bulk of the nation's annual revenues of $1.3 billion. Some 2,000 rebels, armed with Soviet-bloc weapons, had entered from bases in Angola; Zaire defeatd them with the help of Moroccan troops and military aid from France and Belgium. (The U.S. supplied $13 million in "nonlethal" equipment.) In May 1978 the Katangans mounted another invasion of Shaba from Angola, this time with a force twice as large as before. Attacking after passing through a sliver of Zambian territory, the rebels quickly seized control of Kolwezi and Mutshatsha. Once again outside help—this time in the form of French and Belgian paratroopers, and more U.S. shipments of nonlethal matériel—repulsed the attack.

HISTORY: Pygmy tribes are believed to be among the earliest inhabitants of Zaire. Bantus from eastern Africa and Nilotes from the Nile region later entered the area. The Bantus established several kingdoms, including Bahuba, Baluba, and the Cóngo. When Portuguese explorers arrived at the mouth of the Zaire (Congo) River in the 15th century, the kingdom of the Congo included what is now Zaire and Angola.

1879-84: Henry Stanley explores Zaire on behalf of Belgian King Leopold II

1885: Leopold II sets up the Congo Free State and becomes its absolute monarch

1908: Congo Free State becomes Belgian Congo

1960: Colony is granted independence; within a week Congolese Army mutinies and Belgian troops intervene to protect Belgian nationals. Premier Moise Tshombe of Katanga, the Congo's richest region, proclaims his province an independent country; Albert Kalonji proclaims the independence of part of Kasai Province. At the request of the central government, UN troops are sent to the Congo to maintain order. Intense rivalry breaks out between Joseph Kasavubu, the head of state, and his premier, Patrice Lumumba; Col. Joseph Mobutu, commander of the Congo Army, seizes control of the government

1961: Mobutu returns reins of government to Kasavubu. Lumumba is killed under mysterious circumstances and his death plunges the Congo into further strife

1962-63: Heavy fighting takes place between UN troops and Katanga forces; secession of Katanga is ended

1964: Tshombe, who had gone into exile, is invited to return and is sworn in as Congo's new premier

1965: Tshombe is dismissed and goes into exile. Mobutu again stages military coup and overthrows Kasavubu government

1967: Mobutu announces new constitution providing for a federal system of government, with strong president and unicameral legislature. Central government takes over assets of Union Minière, the rich Belgian-controlled copper mining company in Katanga

1969: Kasavubu dies in March. In June, Tshombe dies, a captive in Algeria

1971-73: In Africanization campaign, Democratic Republic of the Congo becomes Republic of Zaire, and Congo River becomes Zaire River. Many foreign-owned firms are nationalized

1974-75: World price of copper falls, earnings are cut

1976: Angolan war disrupts export of Zaire copper. Mobutu establishes relations with Agostinho Neto's victorious Marxist government in Angola after backing losing pro-Western faction

1977: Shaba Province invaded by former Katangan soldiers; Moroccan troops, and French, Belgian and U.S. aid end threat. Mobutu wins new seven-year term as president

1978: Zairean troops brutally supress revolt in Bandundu Province. About 4,000 Angolan-based Katangan rebels capture towns in Shaba; France and Belgium drop in paratroopers to rout rebels and evacuate some 2,500 Europeans; about 150 foreigners are found dead as rebels retreat. Cuba, in UN, denies President Carter's charges that Cuba played role in latest rebel invasion of Zaire. Moroccan soldiers and token forces from Senegal and Gabon replace departing French and Belgians. U.S. and four Western allies chart joint economic and military plan to aid Zaire. Zaire and Angola agree to establish full ties and reopen rail line from Kolwezi to Angolan coast. Mobutu offers amnesty to political exiles, refugees and persons convicted of crimes against state authority—a policy responsible for the return of some 140,00 Zairese to Shaba Province

ZAMBIA

Area: 290,586 sq. mi. **Population:** 5,350,000 (1978 est.)
Official Name: Republic of Zambia **Capital:** Lusaka **Nationality:** Zambian **Languages:** The official language is English. Some 70 different Bantu languages and dialects are spoken, but 5 main languages are recognized for educational and administrative purposes: Nyanja, Bemba, Lozi, Luvale, and Tonga. Afrikaans is also widely spoken **Religion:** Most of the African population follow traditional religions. Christians number about 700,000, and the small Asian community practices Islam and Hinduism **Flag:** A green field with a swatch in the lower right corner of red, black, and orange vertical stripes topped by an orange flying eagle **Anthem:** National Anthem, beginning "Stand and sing of Zambia, proud and free" **Currency:** Zambian kwacha (.79 per U.S. $1)

Location: South-central Africa. Landlocked Zambia is bordered on the north by Zaire, on the east by Tanzania and Malawi, on the southeast by Mozambique, on the south by Zimbabwe, Botswana, and Namibia, and on the west by Angola **Features:** Most of the land mass is a high plateau lying between 3,500 and 4,000 feet above sea level. In the northeast the Muchinga Mountains exceed 7,000 feet in height. Elevations below 2,000 feet are encountered in the valleys of the major river systems. There are 3 large natural lakes: Bangweulu, Mweru, and Tanganyika, all in the northeast **Chief Rivers:** Zambezi, Luangwa, Chambeshi, Kafue, Luapula

Political Leader and Head of State: President: Dr. Kenneth David Kaunda, born 1924, head of the United National Independence party, reelected 1978 **Head of Government:** Prime Minister Daniel Lisulo **Effective Date of Present Constitution:** August 1973 **Legislative Body:** National Assembly (unicameral), consisting of 125 members elected for 5 years, and 10 appointed members **Local Government:** 9 provinces, each administered by a cabinet member, divided into districts

Ethnic Composition: Over 95% of the population are Africans belonging chiefly to various Bantu-speaking tribes. There are approximately 70,000 Europeans and Asians **Population Distribution:** 40% urban **Density:** 18 inhabitants per sq. mi.

Largest Cities: (1974 est.—Metropolitan Areas) Lusaka 415,000, Kitwe 314,000, Ndola 222,000; (1972 est.) Chingola 181,500, Mufulira 124,100, Luanshya 110,500

Per Capita Income: $470 (1978) **Gross National Product (GNP):** $2.5 billion (1978) **Economic Statistics:** Quarrying and mining account for 50% of the GNP. Agriculture (tobacco, corn, peanuts, cotton) accounts for 11%; indigenous manufacturing (food processing, textile, furniture and construction materials) for 8%; other activities for the remainder **Minerals and Mining:** Zambia is a ranking producer of copper with an output of 715,000 metric tons in 1976, cobalt, lead, zinc, and unexploited deposits of iron are also abundant **Labor Force:** 1,210,000 (1970), with 365,000

(1975) in the money economy; 21% in construction; 16% in mining and quarrying; 11% in commercial agriculture; 8% each in commerce and manufacturing; and 6% each in transportation and communications **Foreign Trade:** Exports, mainly refined copper, lead, zinc, cobalt, and unmanufactured tobacco, totaled $987 million in 1976. Imports chiefly machinery and transportation equipment, petroleum products, manufactured articles, chemicals, and food totaled $686 million **Principal Trade Partners:** Britain, Japan, West Germany, United States, Italy, South Africa

Vital Statistics: Birthrate, 51.5 per 1,000 of pop. (1975); death rate, 20.3 **Life Expectancy:** 45 years **Health Statistics:** 313 inhabitants per hospital bed; 8,159 per physician (1971) **Infant Mortality:** 259 per 1,000 births **Illiteracy:** 53% **Education Statistics:** 2,669 primary and secondary schools, with combined enrollment of 929,165 (1975) **Enrollment in Higher Education:** 8,403 (1975) **GNP Expended on Education:** 5.3% (1974)

Transportation: Paved roads total 2,400 mi. **Motor Vehicles:** 147,800 (1974) **Passenger Cars:** 85,800 **Railway Mileage:** 1,360 **Ports:** None **Major Airlines:** Zambia Airways operates domestically and internationally **Communications:** Government owned **Radio Transmitters:** 22 **Receivers:** 110,000 (1976) **Television Transmitters:** 4 **Receivers:** 25,000 (1976) **Telephones:** 55,000 (1976) **Newspaper:** 2 dailies, 22 copies per 1,000 inhabitants (1975)

Weights and Measures: British standards are used **Travel Requirements:** Passport; visa; $3.51 fee; 2 pictures

The land above the Zambezi River, Zambia was called a "rich pauper" when, as the former British protectorate of Northern Rhodesia, it adopted a new name and became independent in 1964. The designation was based on the fact that while the country produced great wealth in copper, most Zambians gained barely enough to eat from their meager agricultural economy. Since then Zambian President Kenneth D. Kaunda has taken forceful measures to end the paradox. By 1975 Zambia assumed full control of its copper industry.

The government has faced a costly adjustment in trade and transportation in line with black Africa's boycott of Rhodesia (now "Zimbabwe"). Zambian copper, which formerly had gone out through Rhodesia, was rerouted northward through Tanzania. The Tanzam railroad, constructed to link Zambian copper mines with Indian Ocean ports, was completed in 1976, but has proved inadequate by itself in getting the product to market. Zambia has also been hard hit by a drop in the world price of copper.

Kaunda has played an important role in the Rhodesian situation, by encouraging African Rhodesian leaders to reach agreement among themselves and by allowing guerrillas to establish bases in Zambia. The bases have drawn air strikes from Zimbabwe. Claiming many innocent Zambians have been killed in these raids, Kaunda obtained weapons from Britain and China and in 1978 vowed to increase the defense budget at the expense of sorely-needed domestic programs in an effort to counter the threat.

Kaunda has committed Zambia to a form of socialism which he calls "humanism," designed to satisfy all Zambians' requirements through even distribution of the nation's wealth.

In December 1972 a bill went into effect making the governing United National Independence Party (UNIP) Zambia's only legal political party. At the same time, President Kaunda ordered UNIP officials owning businesses to convert them into producers' cooperatives or relinquish their managing directorships.

HISTORY: The history of the territory constituting present-day Zambia before the coming of the white man is sparse. The first European to penetrate into the region was the Scottish missionary David Livingstone, who made extensive explorations of the area between 1851 and 1873. In 1891, the British South Africa Co., which was developing the local copper resources, took over administration of the territory, naming it Northern Rhodesia

1924: British South Africa Co. is relieved of the administration of Northern Rhodesia, which becomes a British protectorate

1930-44: Discovery of large copper deposits brings rush of Europeans to Northern Rhodesia; as influx grows Europeans step up demands on Britain for more control of local government

1964: Northern Rhodesia becomes independent republic of Zambia; Kenneth Kaunda, leader of the ruling United National Independence party, becomes the nation's first president

1967: Zambia accepts offer by Communist China to finance 1,000-mile railroad linking Lusaka with Dar es Salaam

1968: Kaunda is reelected president in Zambia's first general election since independence

1969: Kaunda announces measures for government takeover of country's $1.2-billion copper industry from foreign owners

1971: Vice-President Simon Kapwepwe resigns and forms new opposition party after accusing the government of corruption

1973: New constitution is enacted to coincide with new one-party system of government. Kaunda is reelected for third term. Border with Rhodesia is closed

1975: All privately held land and two major newspapers are nationalized

1976: Angolan MPLA government recognized and Rhodesian guerrillas aided

1978: Zambia undertakes austerity measures to meet International Monetary Fund terms for $390-million loan needed to bolster ailing economy. Rhodesia raids guerrilla camps in Zambia. Kaunda visits Zaire as two nations try to mend relations strained in May by use of Zambian territory by Katangan rebels. Kaunda is reelected president without opposition

1979: Kaunda reportedly prevails upon Zimbabwe (Rhodesian) guerrillas to suspend border attacks during the visit of Queen Elizabeth II to Lusaka in late July and early August

ZIMBABWE

Area: 150,803 sq. mi. **Population:** 6,740,000 (1978 est.)

Official Name: State of Zimbabwe **Capital:** Salisbury **Nationality:** Zimbabwean **Languages:** English, the official language, is spoken by the white population and a great number of Africans; the chief Bantu languages are Shona and Ndebele **Religion:** Over 50% practice a combination of animism and Christianity. There are also 24% Moslems and 24% Christians (mainly Anglicans) **Flags:** 3 equal vertical stripes of green, white, and green, with the coat of arms in the center **Anthem:** Rise, O Voices of Zimbabwe **Currency:** Rhodesian dollar (0.61 per U.S. $1)

Location: South-Central Africa. Landlocked Zimbabwe is bordered on the north by Zambia, on the east by Mozambique, on the south by the Republic of South Africa, and on the west by Botswana **Features:** Most of the country is a high, rolling plateau between 3,000 and 5,000 feet above sea level. The land is largely South African veld, or grassland, with scattered shrubs or trees **Chief Rivers:** Zambezi, Limpopo, Sabi, Gwai, Shangani

Head of State: President Josiah Zion Gumede, born 1920, elected May 1979 **Head of Government:** Prime Minister: Bishop Abel Tendekai Muzorewa, born 1925, appointed May 1979 **Effective Date of Present Constitution:** January 1979 **Legislative Body (1977):** Parliament (bicameral), consists of (1) a House of Assembly with 72 black members, elected by the black populace, and 28 white members, elected by white voters, (2) a 30-member Senate with 10 black and 10 white members, elected by the Assembly, and 10 black tribal chiefs **Local Government:** 7 provinces under appointed commissioners

Ethnic Composition: 95.2% are indigenous Bantus, principally Mashona and Matabele; 4.3% are of European descent, chiefly British **Population Distribution:** 20% urban **Density:** 45 inhabitants per sq. mi.

Largest Cities: (1975 est.—Metropolitan Areas) Salisbury 569,000, Bulawayo 340,000, Gwelo 64,000, Umtali 62,000, Que Que 41,000, Gatooma 32,000, Wankie 26,000

Per Capita Income: $452 (1978) **Gross National Product (GNP):** $3 billion (1978) **Economic Statistics:** In 1973 about 6% of GNP was derived from mineral wealth; 25% from manufacturing (metals and metal products, food processing, textiles, clothing and footwear, beverages, tobacco, chemicals); 17% from agriculture (Oriental tobacco, stock-raising, maize, groundnuts, cotton); and 36% from trade and services **Minerals and Mining:** There are deposits of asbestos, chrome ore, coal, copper, gold, iron ore, limestone, lithium, nickel, phosphate rock, and tin **Labor Force:** 1,063,800 (1975) **Foreign Trade:** Exports, mainly tobacco, asbestos, copper, apparel, meats, chrome, and sugar, totaled $652 million in 1973. Imports, chiefly machinery and transportation equipment, textiles, petroleum products, iron and steel products, fertilizers, and foodstuffs, totaled $541 million **Principal Trade Partner:** South Africa

Vital Statistics: Birthrate, 47.9 per 1,000 of pop. (1976); death rate, 14.4 **Life Expectancy:** 52 years **Health Statistics:** 316 inhabitants per hospital bed; 5,700 per physician (1973) **Infant Mortality:** 17 per 1,000 births **Illiteracy:** 61% **Education Statistics:**

4,141 primary and secondary schools with a total of 932,688 (1975) **Enrollment in Higher Education:** 1,076 (1972) **GNP Expended on Education:** 3.6% (1973)

Transportation: Improved roads total 4,194 mi. (1974) **Motor Vehicles:** 250,000 (1974) **Passenger Cars:** 180,000 **Railway Mileage:** 1,568 **Ports:** None **Major Airlines:** Air Rhodesia, government-owned airline, operates domestic flights **Communications:** Government and privately controlled **Radio Transmitters:** 22 **Receivers:** 255,000 (1976) **Television Transmitters:** 3 **Receivers:** 72,000 (1976) **Telephones:** 190,000 (1976) **Newspapers:** 3 dailies, 18 copies per 1,000 inhabitants (1975)

Weights and Measures: British Standards are being replaced by the metric system **Travel Requirements:** Inquire British Embassy or nearest British consulate

At midnight May 31, 1979, nine decades of white rule ended in this landlocked bastion of white supremacy. The nation changed its name from Rhodesia to Zimbabwe Rhodesia, thus reflecting its status as a black majority government with much power still retained by the 4% white minority (on August 26 the name was shortened to "Zimbabwe"). Methodist Bishop Abel Muzorewa became the nation's first black prime minister. Muzorewa, the son of peasants of the Shona tribe, studied at Methodist colleges in Missouri and Tennessee before returning to his homeland to preach. As prime minister he faces seemingly insurmountable problems, most notably the guerrilla war that for seven years has drained the country of blood and treasure.

Leading the estimated 12,000 guerrillas of the Patriotic Front and more than ever seeming to hold the key to a solution of the Rhodesian dilemma are Joshua Nkomo, patriarchial figure of Zimbabwe nationalism and Soviet-backed leader of the Zambian-based wing of the Front, and Robert Mugabe, whose Chinese-trained forces, operating from bases in Mozambique and Tanzania, have so far largely borne the brunt of the war.

The guerrillas do not recognize the elections of April 1979 that brought Muzorewa to power. Although blacks were permitted to vote for the first time, no provision was made for Patriotic Front participation and, according to the Constitution adopted in a virtually all-white referendum, whites are assured of representation far in excess of their numbers for the next 10 years. Among the 100 seats in Parliament, 28 are reserved for whites, a number sufficient to block any black attempts to amend the Constitution. Thus, although Muzorewa's United African National Council party netted more than two-thirds of the popular vote, it won just 51 seats, a bare majority. A faction of the Zimbabwe African National Union led by Rev. Ndabaningi Sithole picked up 12 seats but refused to fill them in protest against what Sithole charged had been "gross irregularities" in voting procedures. Nine seats went to the followers of Chief Kayisa Ndweni, who later accepted appointment to Muzorewa's cabinet.

That whites will continue at least temporarily to play a major role in this country of 96% blacks is made clear by the presence of former Prime Minister Ian D. Smith as minister without portfolio in the Muzorewa government. It was Smith who put forth the "unilateral declaration of independence" from Britain in 1965.

With Smith's proclamation of a State of Rhodesia in March 1970, following a referendum the previous year in which white Rhodesians formally renounced their last British tie, loyalty to the Crown, there was an eventual withdrawal of all diplomatic missions except that of South Africa.

Despite diplomatic isolation, a total British trade blockade, UN economic sanctions, and its landlocked position in southern Africa, Rhodesia has managed to survive the years as an economic outcast.

Smith steadfastly refused to support equal voting rights as a step toward black rule. He relented only when escalating guerrilla warfare left him no alternative and not before safeguards had been built into the agreement to protect white interests.

The surprisingly large turnout (64%) at the polls in the face of guerrilla threats to disrupt the election encouraged the government to expect international recognition and an end to economic sanctions. The election of a Conservative government in Britain favorably disposed to Salisbury further enhanced Muzorewa's chances. And the U.S. Senate urged an end to sanctions in light of the Rhodesian elections.

But many governments vowed to continue sanctions until some accomodation is reached with the Patriotic Front. Every black African state has refused to recognize the Muzorewa government. In June 1979 President Jimmy Carter announced his intention to retain sanctions until Salisbury achieves "more genuine black majority rule." Meanwhile, as the guerrilla war continues, many whites are fleeing (or making contingency plans to flee) the country.

HISTORY: The remains of Stone Age culture dating back 500,000 years have been found in Zimbabwe and it is thought that the Bushmen, who still survive, mostly in the Kalahari Desert of Botswana, are the last descendants of these original inhabitants. The first Bantu are thought to have reached Zimbabwe between the 5th and 10th centuries A.D. though southward migrations continued long after. The first Europeans to visit the region were 16th-century Portuguese explorers

1889-97: Cecil Rhodes forms the British South Africa Company; assisted by British troops, the company conquers the Mashona and Matabele; European colonists follow

1923: Southern Rhodesia becomes a self-governing colony within the British Commonwealth

1953: Britain establishes the Federation of Rhodesia and Nyasaland, linking Northern Rhodesia (now Zambia), Southern Rhodesia, and Nyasaland (now Malawi); the Federation remains dominated by the European settlers

1964: Federation of Rhodesia and Nyasaland is dissolved. Britain grants the two northern territories independence under African majority rule, but refuses independence to Southern Rhodesia unless representative government is assured.

1965: Prime Minister Ian Smith unilaterally declares Rhodesia's independence from Britain and promulgates a new constitution. Britain declares the Smith government an illegal, rebel regime

1966: UN Security Council calls on all member states to break off economic relations with Rhodesia; only Portugal and South Africa refuse to impose an embargo

1968: Smith government executes five black Africans convicted of murder, despite commutation of death sentences by Queen Elizabeth; act is viewed as most serious act of defiance against Britain by break-away Rhodesian regime

1969: Government publishes proposed constitution designed to perpetuate white minority rule. In a referendum in which 81,583 whites as against 6,634 blacks are eligible to vote, the Smith regime wins a mandate to place the proposed constitution before the Legislative Assembly and to proclaim Rhodesia a republic and cut formal remaining ties to British crown

1970: Rhodesia proclaims a republic, severing last ties with Britain; neither Britain nor the United Nations recognizes the new republic

1974: Government suppression of black nationalists resumed as terrorism against white minority continues

1975: New 90-mile railway link with South Africa is opened

1976: John Wrathall is sworn in as Rhodesia's second president. Mozambique closes its 800-mile border with Rhodesia and imposes sanctions

1978: On March 3, Prime Minister Smith and three moderate nationalist leaders (Bishop Abel Muzorewa, Rev. Ndabaningi Sithole and Senator Chirau) agree on plan for black majority rule; while containing many guarantees for whites. Guerrilla leaders Joshua Nkomo and Robert Mugabe denounce pact as "sellout." Bush war turns bloodier as some 2,500 are killed in first four and a half months since March 3 accord. Rhodesian forces stage major "preemptive" strike against guerrilla bases in Mozambique

1979: During April 17-21 blacks vote in national elections for the first time; Bishop Abel Muzorewa is elected the first black prime minister; Josiah Gumede is elected president, a largely ceremonial position. Whites retain much power. Zimbabwe Rhodesia born May 31. Muzorewa forms racially mixed "unity government," offers amnesty to guerrillas, calls for international recognition and end to economic sanctions. Guerrilla war continues. On August 26, Muzorewa announces that national name is shortened to Zimbabwe.

TERRITORIES AND DEPENDENCIES

Anguilla—*Status:* British Colony. *Population:* 6,600 (1977 est.). *Area:* 35 sq. mi. *Capital:* The Valley (760).

The island of Anguilla lies in the northern part of the Leeward group of the Lesser Antilles, in the eastern Caribbean. Anguilla is approximately 65 miles N.N.W. of St. Christopher and 9 miles from its nearest neighbor, St. Martin.

Anguilla is a flat, coralline island with its highest point at 213 feet above sea level. The island is covered with low scrub and fringed with white coral-sand beaches. Apart from sheep and goats, Anguilla's main product is salt. The majority of the population are African or of mixed descent, with a small white minority.

Anguilla unilaterally seceded from the associated state of St. Christopher-Nevis-Anguilla when it was formed in 1967. Britain took control of the island in 1969 after landing an "invasion" force, and in 1971 began direct administration of the island. On February 10, 1976, Anguilla was established as a self-governing British Colony with a new constitution (but it remains a legal part of the associated state). The charter created a seven-member House of Assembly and a chief minister, and gave the British Commissioner authority over defense, police and civil service, and foreign affairs.

Antigua—*Status:* British Associated State. *Population:* 73,000 (1978 est.). *Area:* 171 sq. mi. *Capital:* St. John's (25,000).

Antigua, with its dependency of Barbuda and the small uninhabited island of Redonda, is in the Leeward Islands of the West Indies at the eastern edge of the Caribbean, 250 miles southeast of Puerto Rico. Its topography is rolling; its climate tropical and subject to drought. Most of the people are of Negro-white descent. English is the formal language and everywhere understood, but a patois is commonly spoken.

Primarily agricultural, Antigua produces cotton and sugar. Bananas, citrus fruits, yams, and rice are also grown. Tourism is increasingly important.

There is a Crown-appointed governor, a premier, and a parliament consisting of an elected House of Representatives and an appointed Senate. In 1978, proposals were made to obtain independence in 1979, but the Labour party of Antigua requested a general election before proceeding.

Ashmore and Cartier Islands—*Status:* Australian External Territory. *Population:* Uninhabited. *Area:* 1.9 sq. mi.

These islands lie in the Indian Ocean, about 300 miles north of Broome in northwestern Australia. They are administered by the Northern Territory of Australia.

Australian Antarctic Territory—*Status:* External Territory of Australia. *Population:* Uninhabited. *Area:* 2,362,875 sq. mi. (of which 29,251 sq. mi. are ice shelf).

Australia claims all Antarctic islands and territories south of 60°S. and between 45° and 160°E., except for French-claimed Adélie Land. (The United States does not recognize any Antarctic claims south of 60°S.)

Belize (formerly British Honduras)—*Status:* British Colony. *Population:* 145,000 (1978 est.). *Area:* 8,867 sq. mi. *Capital:* Belmopan (3,000).

The colony is on the east coast of Central America, bounded on the east by the Bay of Honduras of the Caribbean Sea, on the south and west by Guatemala, and on the northwest and north by Mexico. It has a swampy coast that rises gradually toward the interior, which is dominated by tropical jungle growth. The climate is subtropical and humid, with annual rainfall from 50 inches in the north to 175 inches in the far south. Forty percent of the people are of African descent, others are of Latin-Indian descent, with a few Europeans and East Indians. English is the official language.

Sugar, citrus, and clothing are the main exports. Fishing and cattle farming are being developed, as are the cultivation of bananas, cocoa, and vegetables. The discovery of large oil deposits in northern Belize was reported in 1978.

The government consists of a bicameral national assembly, with an elected House of Representatives and an appointed senate, and a cabinet headed by a premier. The Crown-appointed governor is responsible for foreign affairs, defense, internal security, and civil service employment. The colony was renamed Belize in 1973.

Belize is claimed by Guatemala on the grounds that it inherited Spanish sovereignty over the area and that British claims are void. Under the leadership of Premier George Price, Belize aims for eventual independence.

In November 1975 Britain reinforced its army garrison in Belize because of an alleged threat of a Guatemalan invasion. In December the UN General Assembly passed a resolution supporting "the inalienable right of the people of Belize to self-determination and independence," and stated that the territorial integrity of the British colony "must be preserved." The resolution asked Britain and Guatemala to renew their negotiations on the future of Belize. Britain rushed troops to the colony in 1977 to counter the deployment of Guatemalan forces along the border. However, talks are continuing between the two nations.

Bermuda—*Status:* British Colony. *Population:* 56,000 (1977 est.). *Area:* 21 sq. mi. *Capital:* Hamilton (3,000).

The colony is in the western Atlantic, less than 600 miles east of Cape Hatteras, North Carolina. There are some 150 small islands, about 20 of which are inhabited. The main islands are close together, connected by bridges, and collectively called Bermuda. The islands are rocky, with lush vegetation. The climate, moderated by the Gulf Stream, is warm and pleasant. About two-thirds of the people are African or of mixed descent, the rest mostly British in origin. They are predominantly Protestant.

Tourism, largely from the United States, is the major factor in the economy. Also important is the provision of goods to British and American servicemen stationed on the islands. Almost all food is imported.

In 1968 a new constitution put most executive powers in the hands of the premier, who is the head of the majority party in the elected House of Assembly of the bicameral legislature (the oldest among British possessions). The Crown-appointed governor retains direct responsibility for external affairs, defense, internal security, and the police; otherwise, he acts only on the advice of the governor's (legislative) Council.

On March 10, 1973, the islands' governor, Sir Richard Sharples, and his aide-de-camp were assassinated. The execution of the killer on December 2, 1977, resulted in a week of protest rioting, the declaration of a state of emergency, and the rushing of British troops to the colony. Property damage was great and tourism suffered. A Royal Commission, meeting in London in 1978, recommended independence for the islands.

Bouvet Island—*Status:* Norwegian Dependency. *Population:* Uninhabited. *Area:* 23 sq. mi.

Situated between the extreme tip of South Africa and the Antarctic coast, Bouvet is in the South Atlantic Ocean at 54°26′S. and 3°24′E. It is volcanic in origin and almost completely ice-covered. There are fur seals and seals of other varieties, penguins, and petrels.

British Antarctic Territory—*Status:* British Colony. *Population:* Uninhabited, except for personnel at scientific stations (76 in 1973). *Area:* 600,000 sq. mi. *Administrative Center:* Stanley, Falkland Islands.

The territory, created in 1962, extends below 60°S. from 20° to 80°W. and includes the South Orkney Islands, the South Shetland Islands, and the Antarctic Peninsula. Argentina claims the area and occupied one of the South Shetlands in 1976, resulting in a British protest.

British Indian Ocean Territory—*Status:* British Colony. *Population:* 1,400 (1977 est.) *Area:* 29 sq. mi. (land). *Administration Center:* London (U.K.).

The territory, made a separate colony in 1965, includes only the Chagos Archipelago at 7°20′S. and 72°25′E., formerly a dependency of Mauritius; Diego Garcia (11 sq. mi.) is the largest island. The climate is tropical, with heavy rainfall.

The territory is administered from London by a commissioner, with a local islands magistrate. The U.S. naval base on Diego Garcia is to be completed in 1979.

British Virgin Islands—*Status:* British Crown Colony. *Population:* 11,000 (1978 est.). *Area:* 59 sq. mi. *Capital:* Road Town (3,500) on Tortola.

These are in the eastern Caribbean to the east of the U.S. Virgin Islands. They include 36 islands, 16 of which are inhabited, plus numerous rocks and *cays*. Tortola, Virgin Gorda, Anegada, and Jost Van Dyke are the largest islands. The climate is subtropical and pleasant; rainfall is light. Almost all of the people are of African descent.

Cattle raising, farming, and fishing are the main activities. The shortage of water is a major problem. Tourism is an increasing factor in the economy.

The colony is governed by a Crown-appointed governor assisted by an appointed executive council and a chief minister. There is a partly elected legislative council.

Brunei—*Status:* British Protected State. *Population:* 177,000 (1978 est.). *Area:* 2,226 sq. mi. *Capital:* Bandar Seri Begawan, formerly Brunei Town (41,000).

This sultanate is on the north coast of Borneo, being two enclaves within the Malaysian state of Sarawak, washed by the South China Sea. The climate is tropical and humid, the rainfall heavy. The population is more than half Malay and is largely Moslem. Chinese are the second-largest element, and there are Dayak groups.

Oil and natural gas are the major factors in Brunei's economy, making it the richest state in Southeast Asia. Rice, cassava and bananas are grown.

Britain is responsible for Brunei's defense and foreign relations. A Crown-appointed high commissioner conducts relations between the two states. There is a council of ministers, presided over by the sultan. In 1967, after 17 years of rule, the Sultan, unwilling to bow to British demands for more representative government, abdicated and was succeeded by his son. In 1970, the new ruler dissolved the partly elected legislative council in favor of an entirely appointive body. Under a 1971 agreement with Britain, Brunei is fully self-governing in internal affairs. In 1978 it was announced in London that Brunei is to become independent in 1983.

Cayman Islands—*Status:* British Crown Colony. *Population:* 14,000 (1978 est.). *Area:* 100 sq. mi. *Capital:* George Town (3,975) on Grand Cayman.

Consisting mainly of three islands—Grand Cayman, Little Cayman, and Cayman Brac—this colony is in the Caribbean about 175 miles west of Jamaica. Grand Cayman is flat and rockbound, protected by coral reefs. The climate is tropical, hot and humid. About one-half of the people are of mixed Negro-white descent, about a third of European, and the rest of African ancestry. Ceuta, Seafaring, commerce, and banking are the principal occupations. Tourism is important.

There is a Crown-appointed governor, a partly elected legislative assembly and an executive council.

Ceuta and Melilla—*Status:* Under Spanish sovereignty. *Population:* Ceuta, 67,187; Melilla, 65,271 (1970 census). *Area:* Ceuta, 7.5 sq. mi.; Melilla, 4.8 sq. mi.

These two enclaves are on the Mediterranean coast of Morocco. Ceuta is opposite Gibraltar; Melilla, some 200 miles farther east, is on a rocky promontory. A good deal of fish are caught and exported from both towns. Ceuta, with a splendid climate, is increasingly visited by tourists. In 1975 Morocco laid formal claim.

Channel Islands—*Status:* British Crown Bailiwicks. *Population:* 129,000 (1977 est.). *Area:* 74 sq. mi.

These islands lie 80 miles south of the English coast, off the northwest coast of France. They consist of Jersey, Guernsey, and the latter's dependencies of Alderney, Brechou, Sark, Herm, Jethou, and Lihou. Ecrehou Rocks and Les Minquiers are dependencies of Jersey. The land is low and undulating and the climate mild with about 40 inches of annual rainfall. The people are mainly of Norman descent, with some of Breton ancestry. French is the official language of Jersey, English of Guernsey; in some country districts of Jersey and Guernsey and throughout Sark, a Norman-French dialect is spoken. English, however, is commonly used throughout the islands.

The main occupations are agriculture, dairying, and tourism. Agriculture is highly specialized, with

Guernsey being noted for its hothouse tomatoes and cut flowers, Jersey for new potatoes and open-grown tomatoes. The farms of Jersey and Guernsey are, typically, tiny fields, the result of centuries of subdivision among heirs.

The Crown appoints the chief executives of Jersey and Guernsey, both of whom have the titles of lieutenant-governor and commander-in-chief. Jersey's partly elected legislature is called the States of Jersey, and St. Helier is the administrative center. The legislative body of Guernsey, partially elected, is the States of Deliberation. St. Peter Port is Guernsey's administrative center. Alderney and Sark have local legislative bodies subordinate to that of Guernsey. The Anne is the administrative center of Alderney, Creux that of Sark. The head of Sark is *Le Seigneur de Sercq.*

Chilean Antarctica—*Status:* Chilean Dependency. *Population:* No permanent inhabitants. *Area:* 482,502 sq. mi.

Chile claims the Antarctic (or O'Higgins) Peninsula in the Antarctic, lying between 59° and 67°W. Parts of the area are also claimed by Great Britain and Argentina.

Christmas Island—*Status:* Australian External Territory. *Population:* 3,094 (1978). *Area:* 52 sq. mi. *Administrative Center:* Flying Fish Cove (1,300).

The island is in the Indian Ocean some 1,630 miles northwest of Perth, Australia, and 225 miles south of the island of Java. It is hilly and rather barren. The climate is warm and dry. About two-thirds of the people are Chinese, with some Malayans and fewer Europeans.

Phosphate extraction, undertaken by the governments of Australia and New Zealand, is the island's only economic activity. Most of the deposits are expected to be exhausted at the end of this century.

Cocos (Keeling) Islands—*Status:* Australian External Territory. *Population:* 435. *Area:* 5.4 sq. mi. *Administrative Center:* West Island (92).

The territory, two separate atolls with 27 small coral islands, is in the Indian Ocean about 1,725 miles southwest of Perth, Australia, at 12°05′S. and 96°53′E. The principal islands are West, Home, Direction, South, and Horsburgh. The climate is pleasant, with moderate rainfall. Three-quarters of the people are Cocos Islanders living on Home Island; the rest are of European descent, most of whom live on West Island, and Asians. Coconuts are the principal product.

Though the islands were placed under Australian authority in 1955, it was not until July 1978 that the Australian government purchased the Cocos from their owner, John Clunies Ross. His family had been granted title to the islands in 1886.

Cook Islands—*Status:* New Zealand Dependency. *Population:* 18,112 (1976 census). *Area:* 91 sq. mi. *Administrative Center:* Avarua (4,429) on Rarotonga.

Situated in the South Pacific some 2,000 miles northeast of New Zealand, between 8° and 23°S. and 156° and 167°W., the islands are in two groups—the Northern, with seven islands or atolls, and the Lower or Southern Group, with eight. (The United States claims four islands of the Northern Group.) The Northern islands are low and barren; the Lower ones, which are more elevated and fertile, support the greater part of the population. The climate is warm and humid, and the islands sometimes experience hurricanes. The people are Polynesian Christians, similar in language and traditions to the New Zealand Maori. Since 1971 the population has generally declined due to emigration, chiefly to New Zealand.

The economy is basically agricultural, with citrus fruits and juices, copra, and tomatoes, among other produce, being exported. Manufactured wearing apparel is also exported. The sale of postage stamps to collectors throughout the world is an important source of revenue.

The Cooks attained internal self-government in 1965, with New Zealand responsible for external affairs and defense. There is a prime minister and cabinet, and an elected legislative assembly. In 1978 Prime Minister Albert Henry was removed from office by the High Court for engaging in election practices.

Coral Sea Islands Territory—*Status:* Australian External Territory. *Population:* 3 (1971 census). *Area:* 8.5 sq. mi.

These islands, spread over 400,000 square miles, are situated east of Queensland, Australia, between the Great Barrier Reef and the 157°10′E. meridian. One of

the islands in the Willis Group has a meteorological station. The land consists mainly of scattered reefs and sand cays, many little more than sandbanks.

The Coral Sea Islands became an Australian External Territory on August 14, 1969, after having been acquired by acts of sovereignty over a number of years. The governor-general of Australia is empowered to make ordinances for the Territory. The Supreme Court and the Court of Petty Sessions of Norfolk Island have jurisdiction in the Territory.

Easter Island—*Status:* Chilean Dependency. *Population:* 1,598 (1970 census). *Area:* 63 sq. mi. *Settlement:* Hanga Roa (900).

Easter Island (*Rapa Nui* in Polynesian) lies in the Pacific Ocean some 2,300 miles west of Chile. It is volcanic in origin, rising sharply from the sea. The climate is subtropical: warm, somewhat humid, and there is moderate rainfall. The island has no streams or lakes, and rainwater collects in the extinct volcanoes. The people, who are believed to be Polynesian in origin, speak Spanish.

Sheep raising is the most important activity. Despite the scarcity of fresh water, certain crops, including corn, wheat, taro, and tropical fruits, are grown. The island is administered as part of Valparaíso Province.

Easter Island is noted for its monolithic, stylized heads carved of volcanic rock, probably religious in significance.

Faeroe Islands—*Status:* Integral part of the Danish Kingdom. *Population:* 42,000 (1977 est.). *Area:* 540 sq. mi. *Capital:* Tórshavn (10,726) on Streymoy.

These islands are in the Atlantic Ocean, north of Scotland, between 61°26′ and 62°24′N. and 6°15′ and 7°41′W. Among the larger of the 18 islands (17 are inhabited) are Streymoy, Eysturoy and Váagar. They contain many lakes and peat bogs. The climate is mild, rainy, and foggy. Norse-descended, the inhabitants speak an old Norse dialect; Danish, however, is the official language. Most of the people are Lutherans.

The economy is based on fishing and sheep raising. Root vegetables, potatoes, and barley are grown.

A self-governing community within the Danish kingdom with a Crown commissioner, the Faeroes have their own elected parliament (*Lögting*) which chooses an administrative body (*Landsstyri*). The Faeroes send two representatives to the Danish parliament.

Falkland Islands—*Status:* British Crown Colony. *Population:* 1,950 (1977 est.). *Area:* 6,198 sq. mi. *Capital:* Stanley (1,079) on East Falkland.

Located in the South Atlantic some 500 miles northeast of Cape Horn, this group's major islands are East Falkland and West Falkland (4,618 sq. mi.), South Georgia (1,450 sq. mi.), and Sandwich Islands (130 sq. mi.). East and West Falkland, which contain most of the population, consist largely of hilly moorland. The climate is cool and rainy, with persistently strong winds. The people are mostly of British origin.

Sheep farming is the main occupation, wool the main export. There is whaling and sealing. Large offshore oil and gas deposits are believed to exist.

The colony is administered by a Crown-appointed governor, assisted by partly elected councils. Argentina claims sovereignty over the islands, and refers to them as *Las Malvinas.* British and Argentine diplomats held discussions over the future sovereignty of the islands during 1977 and 1978.

French Guiana—*Status:* French Overseas Department. *Population:* 62,000 (1977 est.). *Area:* 35,135 sq. mi. *Capital:* Cayenne (29,405).

Situated on the northeast coast of South America, French Guiana is bounded by the Atlantic Ocean on the north, by Brazil on the east and south, and by Suriname on the west. Its coastline is 200 miles long, and Devil's Island (no longer used as a prison) is among its offshore islands. Extending almost 250 miles into the continent, French Guiana is divided into a low, swampy coastal area that ranges from 10 to 30 miles in width, and a plateau forming a series of low, steep hills inland. Most of the country is covered by rain forest. The climate is tropical, tempered by trade winds, and there is heavy rainfall from December to July. Ninety percent of the people live in the coastal areas; these are mostly a Negro-white mixture. In the interior are small groups of Indians (Carib,

Arawak, Tupi-Guaraní) and descendants of escaped African slaves.

Forestry, including wood-veneer production, is a major element in the economy. Gold is mined, and bauxite and tantalite deposits are to be exploited. Arable land is scarce and limited to the coastal areas, where manioc, yams, sugarcane, and bananas are grown. The main source of income is French investment and contributions toward operating expenses and welfare.

Guiana is administered by a Paris-appointed prefect, assisted by an elected general council. It elects a deputy and a senator to the French Parliament.

A border dispute with Suriname, in which France claims 780 square miles of jungle presumed to contain gold, is not yet resolved.

French Polynesia—*Status:* French Overseas Territory. *Population:* 137,382 (1977 census). *Area:* 1,544 sq. mi. *Capital:* Papeete (62,700) on Tahiti.

These widely scattered islands in the south central Pacific lie mainly between 7° and 27°S. and 134° and 155°W. The territory includes a number of island groups totaling 118 islands and atolls. The Society Islands (named after the Royal Society by their British discoverers) are the most important group and include Tahiti and Moorea; they contain about 70 percent of the Territory's population. Other groups are the Marquesas Islands, the Tuamotu Archipelago, the Gambier Islands, and the Tubuai or Austral Islands. All of these except the Tuamotus are volcanic in origin and mountainous, with fast-flowing streams, and are often circled by coral reefs and lagoons. The climate is hot and humid, tempered by steady winds. The people are predominantly Polynesians, with some Asians and a smaller number of Europeans, principally French. More than 60 percent of the people are Protestants.

The economy is based on agriculture. The main crops are copra, vanilla, and coffee. All common tropical plants and most European vegetables are grown. There has been extensive building in the islands to provide facilities for French nuclear tests, the first of which was held in 1966 on Mururoa Atoll, 800 miles southeast of Tahiti. In August 1968 the French exploded their first H-bomb nearby, at Fangataufa Atoll. In 1971 and 1973, French nuclear test activity in the Mururoa Atoll area met with worldwide protest. French nuclear testing has since continued. Vocal adherents of autonomy increased their representation in the assembly in 1976, and again in 1977.

The Territory is administered by a Paris-appointed governor, aided by a government council, with an elected territorial assembly, and elects two deputies and a senator to the French Parliament. In 1979, Clipperton Island was placed under the direct control of the French government in Paris.

French Southern and Antarctic Territories—*Status:* French Overseas Territory. *Population:* 183 (1975). Area: 202,916 sq. mi. *Administrative Center:* Port-aux-Français (94) on Kerguélen.

These territories comprise a number of islands in the far southern Indian Ocean and Adélie Land on the Antarctic continent. The latter, with an area of 200,000 sq. mi., lies between 136° and 142°E. The Kerguélen Islands are between 48° and 50°S. and 68° and 70°E. The principal island, Kerguélen, has an area of 2,510 sq. mi. and is mostly mountainous. The Crozet Islands at 46°S. and between 50° and 52°E. are also mountainous, cold, windy, and inhospitable. Saint Paul Island is at 38°S. and 77°E. and its center is occupied by a large crater with volcanic hot springs. Amsterdam Island is at 37°S. and 70°E., and maintains a hospital.

The Territory, on which various research stations have been established, is under the authority of a high administrator assisted by a consultative council in Paris.

Gibraltar—*Status:* British Colony. *Population:* 30,000 (1978 est.). *Area:* 2.28 sq. mi. *Administrative Center:* Gibraltar.

Gibraltar is a tiny peninsula jutting into the western Mediterranean from Spain. It rises from a sandy plain to the 1,400-foot Rock, a cave-riddled, fortified limestone mass. The climate is temperate. The people are mostly of Genoese, Portuguese and Maltese descent. The language of the home is generally Spanish, with English the language of instruction in school. Most of the civilian population are Roman Catholics.

The colony has no natural resources other than its strategic position at the mouth of the Mediterranean, and is dependent on its naval and military bases, transshipments, dockyards, and tourist traffic.

Gibraltar is administered by a governor (also the commander of the fortress) appointed by the Crown, with the advice of the Gibraltar Council, the elected members of which compose a council of ministers presided over by a chief minister. There is also a partly elected House of Assembly.

Gibraltar was ceded in 1713 to Great Britain by Spain in the Treaty of Utrecht. Since 1964, Spain has been seeking its return, applying such pressures as the restriction of transit to and from the mainland. In a 1967 referendum, the people of Gibraltar voted overwhelmingly to retain the British connection. Nevertheless, at the end of 1968, the UN General Assembly's Trusteeship Committee called on Great Britain to surrender control of Gibraltar to Spain. Talks have been held between Great Britain and Spain on the Gibraltar question since 1972.

Greenland (Kalâtdlit-Nunât)—*Status:* Semiautonomous state of the Danish Kingdom. *Population:* 49,000 (1978 est.). *Area:* 840,000 sq. mi. *Capital:* Nûk (Godthab) (8,995).

Greenland, the largest island in the world, lies northeast of Canada between the Arctic Ocean on the north and the Atlantic Ocean on the south. Its ice-free areas—the coastal strips plus the coastal islands—cover 132,000 sq. mi. The rest of Greenland is sheathed in ice at places 11,000 feet thick. The climate is arctic, with considerable variation in temperature between localities. The population, predominantly Eskimo, with some Europeans, lives mostly on the west coast. Danish and Greenlandic are the official languages. The principal occupations are fishing and hunting. In 1975 the Danish government granted the first concessions for oil and natural gas exploration off the west coast.

Home rule was established on May 1, 1979, with Denmark retaining control of defense and foreign affairs, and retaining mineral rights. A prime minister, the leader of the majority party in the 21-member parliament *(Landsting)* and four secretaries preside over the government *(Landsstyre)*. Greenland sends two elected members to the Danish Parliament.

Guadeloupe—*Status:* French Overseas Department. *Population:* 355,000 (1977 est.). *Area:* 687 sq. mi. *Capital:* Basse-Terre (16,000) on the island of that name.

Guadeloupe lies in the Leeward Islands of the West Indies.

In addition to Guadeloupe proper (584 sq. mi.), which a narrow channel divides into two islands, Basse-Terre and Grande-Terre, there are the nearby dependencies of Marie-Galante, La Désirade, Îles des Saintes, and Îles de la Petite Terre. About 135 miles to the northwest are the dependencies of Saint Barthélemy and Saint Martin (which shares its island with St. Maarten of the Netherlands Antilles).

Basse-Terre has a 4,000-foot active volcano, La Soufrière. Grande-Terre is low and encircled by coral reefs; it has the largest town in the department, Point-à-Pitre, twice the size of the capital. The climate is tropical, moderated by trade winds. Basse-Terre's mountains receive heavy rainfall, which feeds numerous streams. The people are blacks and, especially on the dependencies, descendants of Normans and Bretons who settled there in the 17th century, or a racial mixture.

The main crops are sugar and bananas, with cotton, sisal, coffee, vegetables and tropical fruits also grown. Fishing and rum production are significant activities.

Guadeloupe is administered by a Paris-appointed prefect and an elected general council; the department elects three deputies and two senators to the French Parliament.

There were serious riots in Guadeloupe in 1967, reportedly sparked by an organization advocating independence. Sporadic unrest has continued since that time.

Heard and McDonald Islands—*Status:* Australian External Territory. *Population:* Uninhabited. *Area:* 113 sq. mi.

These islands lie in the south Indian Ocean, 2,575 miles southwest of Perth, Australia. Heard Island is mountainous, the McDonald Islands, small and rocky.

Hong Kong—*Status:* British Colony. *Population:* 4,500,000 (1977 est.). *Area:* 403 sq. mi. *Capital:* Victoria (658,042) on the island of Hong Kong.

The colony is on the southern coast of China about 80 miles southeast of Canton, and surrounded by the Chinese province of Kwangtung. It includes Hong Kong proper, an island of about 30 sq. mi., many other islands, and Kowloon and the New Territories on the mainland. The New Territories (370 sq. mi., including a number of small islands) are held under a 99-year lease from China, which expires in 1997. Most of the area is either swampy or rocky and hilly. The climate is subtropical, with hot, humid summers and heavy rainfall, but can be chilly January to April.

The population density of Hong Kong is very high, as more than 80 percent of the people live in the urban area. An overwhelming number of them are Chinese, including more than a million refugees. (English and Chinese are both official languages.)

Hong Kong is a major center for shipping, banking, commerce and industry, situated as it is at a crossroad of world trade. Light industries, particularly machinery, textiles and clothing, are important. Tourism is important and growing. Agriculture and fishing are intensively practiced, but much food must be imported, mostly from China. A large part of the water supply must also be brought in from China. A tunnel now links Hong Kong Island with the mainland.

Hong Kong is administered by a Crown-appointd governor, advised by executive and legislative councils. Communist China officially claims Hong Kong.

Isle of Man—*Status:* British Crown Fiefdom. *Population:* 62,000 (1977 est.). *Area:* 227 sq. mi. *Capital:* Douglas (20,262).

Situated in the Irish Sea, the Isle of Man is about 35 miles from Northern Ireland and the northwest coast of England. The central mass consists of treeless hills, extending in the north and south to low-lying agricultural land. The climate is pleasant, with mild winters and cool summers. The people are mainly of Scandian-Celtic origin. Wesleyan Methodists predominate, but there are Roman Catholics and members of the Church of England.

By far the most important factor in the economy is the tourist trade; more than half a million British a year holiday on the island. The major export is kippered herring, processed from fish landed by a Scottish fleet. Oats are the main crop, and there is sheep raising and dairying.

The Isle is administered under its own laws (Acts of Parliament do not apply unless they specifically so note). The ruling body is the Court of Tynwald, composed of the Crown-appointed governor, a legislative council, and the elected House of Keys.

Jan Mayen—*Status:* Norwegian Dependency. *Population:* 36. *Area:* 143 sq. mi.

This island 300 miles north-northeast of Iceland is bleak and desolate. The Norwegian government operates radio, meteorological, and navigational stations at the South Lagoon, and since 1963 an airstrip has been maintained. In 1979 Norway and Iceland debated the legal right of Norway to lay claim to the 200-mile limit offshore area around Jan Mayen. The area is rich in sea life and might contain oil, gas and minerals.

Juan Fernández—*Status:* Chilean Dependency. *Population:* 540. *Area:* 70 sq. mi. (the two main islands). *Administrative Center:* Juan Bautista, on Robinson Crusoe Island.

This island group is in the Pacific Ocean some 360 miles west of Valparaíso, Chile. Volcanic in origin, rugged and wooded, it was discovered in 1572 by Juan Fernández, a Spanish explorer. The two main islands, about 100 miles apart from east to west, are Robinson Crusoe and Alejandro Selkirk. Lobster fishing is the main occupation.

The islands are administered by Valparaíso Province.

Daniel Defoe's *Robinson Crusoe* is generally acknowledged to have been inspired by Alexander Selkirk's stay on Robinson Crusoe Island (1704-09).

Macao—*Status:* Portuguese Overseas Province. *Population:* 280,000 (1978 est.). *Area:* 6.2 sq. mi. *Capital:* Macao (226,880).

Macao or Macau (*Ao-men* in Chinese) is situated on a small peninsula of the south coast of China. It lies at the mouth of the Pearl (Canton) River and 40 miles west of Hong Kong; the province also includes two small islands. Macao proper is almost entirely urban, the islands forested. The climate is quite hot and humid, but southwest sea breezes make the temperatures tolerable. Only about 10 percent of the population is Portuguese, the rest is Chinese.

Macao is almost completely dependent on imported food, mostly from China. Fishing, commerce, and, in recent years, light industry—textiles, cameras, and optical instruments—are important. Macao is one of the few entirely free gold markets in the world, and trade in coin and bullion is a notable activity. There is a brisk tourist trade, some attracted by Macao's gambling houses—which accounted for one-third of total government income in 1977.

The province is administered by a Lisbon-appointed governor, a council, which serves as a cabinet, and a partially elected 18-member provincial council, the *Leal Senado*. Macao sends a representative to the Portuguese National Assembly. China still officially claims dominion over Macao.

Martinique—*Status:* French Overseas Department. *Population:* 365,000 (1977 est.). *Area:* 425 sq. mi. *Capital:* Fort-de-France (98,561).

This island is in the West Indies some 130 miles south of Guadeloupe. It is largely mountainous, and its two highest peaks are active volcanoes. In 1902, Mount Pelée erupted and destroyed the city of St-Pierre. The climate is tropical, tempered by the trade winds. The people are descendants of blacks, Europeans, and Carib Indians.

Martinique's economy is agricultural, with sugarcane and bananas being the principal crops. Rum is distilled, and there is livestock raising and fishing. Tourism is increasing. The economy is heavily dependent on direct and indirect French subsidies, and substantial emigration to France has not solved the island's stubborn unemployment problem. Efforts have been made for some time to broaden and diversify Martinique's economic base. Yet demand for Martinique's major export crops is leveling off at a time when the number of young persons coming into the labor market is increasing as a result of a higher birthrate since the 1940s. Half the population of the island is less than 20 years of age.

Martinique's international airport is its primary link with principal cities in France, the United States, and elsewhere. The island also is visited by numerous oceangoing vessels and cruise ships. Martinique has good road and telecommunications systems.

Administration is in the hands of a Paris-appointed prefect with the aid of an elected general council of 36 members. Martinique elects three deputies and two senators to the French Parliament.

Mayotte—*Status:* French Territorial Collectivity. *Population:* 47,300 (1978 census). *Area:* 144 sq. mi. *Capital:* Mamoutzou (1,090).

The easternmost of the Comoro Islands in the Indian Ocean, Mayotte is a volcanic island surrounded by coral reefs and islets, with a tropical climate. The population is of African, Arab, and Malagasy origin, and the majority are Moslems. French, Arabic, and Swahili are spoken. Most of the people are engaged in the production of such agricultural products as vanilla, sisal, sugarcane, essential oils, and rum.

An Arab dynasty from Shiraz reigned from the 16th century to 1843, when a French colony was established. It was attached first to Réunion and later to Madagascar as a part of the Comoro Islands territory. When a future Comoro Islands referendum was first announced in 1974, Mayotte was the only island to vote against it, and after the unilateral declaration of independence in 1975, Mayotte refused to be considered a part of the new republic. In 1976 an island referendum resulted in 99.41 percent voting to remain French, and two months later the status as a French Territorial Collectivity was approved. The island sends one deputy to the French Parliament. A referendum may be held in the future to decide between departmental status or independence for the island.

Montserrat—*Status:* British Crown Colony. *Population:* 13,000 (1977 est.). *Area:* 40 sq. mi. *Capital:* Plymouth (1,300).

Situated in the Leeward Islands of the West Indies, Montserrat is 260 miles southeast of Puerto Rico and north of Guadeloupe. In 1493, on his second voyage, Christopher Columbus reached the island and gave it its present name, after a mountain in Spain. It has elevations of more than 3,000 feet, and the climate is tropical and humid. The people are mostly of Negro-white descent. English is the formal language and everywhere understood, but a patois is commonly spoken. As a result of an Irish settlement in the 1630s, many people on the island speak with a brogue.

The island is agricultural, sugar being the main export crop, and cotton and bananas also being grown. Yams, rice, breadfruit, and corn are raised for food. Tourism is of increasing economic importance.

There is a Crown-appointed governor, who presides over an executive council and a partly elected legislative council. In 1967, Montserrat elected to remain a British colony.

Namibia—*Status:* In dispute; administered by South Africa. *Population:* 960,000 (1978 est.). *Area:* 317,827 sq. mi. *Capital:* Windhoek (61,369).

Namibia (formerly South-West Africa) is bounded by Angola on the north, by Zambia on the northeast, by South Africa on the east and south, and by the Atlantic Ocean on the west. The Namib Desert, stretching for 1,000 miles along the coast, is uninhabited except for three towns, including the South African enclave of Walvis Bay (434 sq. mi.), and the diamond workings at the mouth of the Orange River in the south. The Kalahari Desert of sand and limestone is on the east. The Caprivi Strip, 20 to 60 miles wide and some 300 miles long, extends from the northeast corner of the country and separates Botswana from Angola. The greater part of the country consists of a plateau, averaging 3,600 feet, with scattered mountains. The climate is generally hot and dry. There are only a few rivers and water must generally be obtained from boreholes. The people are largely African of various tribal groups, including Ovambo, Damara, Herero, Nama, and Bushmen. Whites are a minority of about 15 percent, mostly of South African and German descent. There is a smaller number of mixed descent, including the Rehoboth Bastards, of Nama-white ancestry. In general, the whites live in the Police Zone in the south, the native population in homelands in the north. Official languages are Afrikaans and English, but German is widely used, as are tribal languages.

Parts of the nonwhite population follow the traditional animist religions, although many Africans have been converted to Christianity. Missionary activity, which began in the 1800s, encompasses several denominations, including Lutheran, Roman Catholic, Methodist, Anglican, and Dutch Reformed.

Diamonds are Namibia's most valuable economic product, and copper, zinc, lead, uranium, cadmium, and manganese are also mined. Sheep, cattle, and goats are raised, and the production of karakul sheep pelts is increasingly important. The annual haul of fish has reached over three-quarters of a million tons.

South-West Africa had been mandated to South African administration by the League of Nations. When the UN Trusteeship System was established in 1945, South Africa refused to place South-West Africa under it (it was the only such case), claiming that the UN was not the legal successor to the League. In 1966 the UN General Assembly declared that the mandate was terminated; in 1967 it established a council to administer the area until independence; and in 1968 it proclaimed that the area be renamed Namibia. South Africa, however, declaring that the removal of the mandate was an "illegal act" because the UN charter makes no provision for such a move, announced its intention to continue administration, and has done so even after a 1971 ruling against its position by the International Court of Justice.

In June 1975, the all-white legislative assembly in Windhoek passed laws permitting people of all races to enter hotels, restaurants, and cafes at their owners' discretion, banning discriminatory signs, and ending "petty apartheid."

In January 1976, the UN Security Council voted to invoke mandatory sanctions against South Africa if it failed to accept a UN-supervised election leading to independence. In August the South African government announced plans for a multiracial Namibian government to bring about independence by December 31, 1978. Inasmuch as the South African proposal did not mention a specific date for elections, both the UN and the powerful guerrilla group, the South-West Africa People's Organization (SWAPO) rejected the plan. At a conference in the Turnhalle in Windhoek in August 1976, South Africa announced that it intended to set up an interim government. Sanctions against South Africa for not withdrawing were vetoed in the UN. In 1977 the United States, Britain, France, Canada and West Germany began diplomatic efforts to arrive at an independence plan acceptable to both South Africa and SWAPO. South Africa agreed to the Western plan in April, but SWAPO withheld its consent after a South African raid on its bases in Angola. Further efforts were made by the Western powers, and SWAPO's agreement was secured in July with the help of five black-ruled "front-line" states. Under the plan, all South African troops would be withdrawn except for 1,500 men who would be restricted to camps near the Angolan border. A United Nations force of 5,000 men would be sent into the territory to insure a free election, after which the territory would become independent. In the period leading up to the election, the territory would be administered jointly by a South African administrator and a UN representative. A dispute has arisen between South Africa and SWAPO over the Walvis Bay enclave, the future status of which was not determined in the Western powers' plan.

Negotiations between the UN and South Africa continued throughout 1978 and into 1979 without resolution of their differences regarding Namibian independence, originally scheduled for Dec. 31, 1978. A South African-sponsored election in Namibia in early Dec. 1978 elected a 50-member constituent assembly, with the Democratic Turnhalle Alliance winning 41 seats. SWAPO did not vote, and the UN Security Council declared the election null and void. The assembly, later known as the South-West African-Namibian National Assembly, met on May 21, with limited legislative powers, while South Africa retained ultimate powers over the territory. On May 31, the UN General Assembly voted to demand the Security Council to embargo trade with South Africa until it consented to free UN-supervised elections in Namibia.

Netherlands Antilles—*Status:* Autonomous Part of the Kingdom of the Netherlands. *Population:* 242,000 (1977 est.). *Area:* 390 sq. mi. *Capital:* Willemstad (95,000) on Curaçao.

The Netherlands Antilles, in the Caribbean, consists of two groups of three islands each: Curaçao, Aruba, and Bonaire, 15 to 38 miles off the northern coast of Venezuela; and Saba, St. Eustatius, and St. Maarten, which shares an island with the French St. Martin, more than 500 miles to the northeast. Curaçao and Aruba are by far the most populous and important. On these two islands, Dutch, English, Spanish, and Papiamento (a mixture of the three) are spoken.

The Leewards are semiarid and flat, the Windwards are mountainous, with enough rainfall for flourishing vegetation. The climate is warm and humid. The people are largely blacks, or Carib Indians, or either of these mixed with white strains. Dutch is the official language, and English is current in the Windwards. Papiamento, a lingua franca derived from Dutch and English as well as French, Spanish, Portuguese, and African elements, is common. Catholicism predominates on the Leeward Islands, Protestantism on the Windward.

Curaçao and Aruba, with a higher per capita income than the Netherlands, owe their prosperity to oil refineries, which process crude oil from Venezuela. The refineries also stimulate other industries and commerce on the two islands. After oil refining, tourism is their most important economic factor. On Curaçao and Aruba little farming is possible because the land is so rocky. Most food is imported. On the other islands, small-scale agriculture and fishing are pursued.

In an effort to lessen dependence on the petroleum industry, the government has been attempting to attract new industries by offering tax holidays and custom exceptions to firms locating there and by creating free zones on Curaçao and Aruba.

Fully autonomous in internal affairs, the Netherlands Antilles are constitutionally equal with the Netherlands. There is a governor, who represents the sovereign, and a council of ministers—headed by a prime minister—which is responsible to an elected legislature

(Staten). Aruba, Curaçao, Bonaire, and the Windward group each have autonomy in local affairs.

In the spring of 1974, Juancho Evertsz, premier of the Netherlands Antilles, met with the Dutch premier at The Hague to discuss the future status of the islands. It was decided that they would wait at least until 1980 to achieve independent status. In March 1977, Aruba held its own referendum, with 57 percent voting for separate independence. As a result, the future date and form of independence for Aruba and the rest of the Netherlands Antilles is being deliberated by the Netherlands government and the islands' representatives.

New Caledonia—*Status:* French Overseas Territory. *Population:* 134,000 (1977 est.). *Area:* 7,335 sq. mi. *Capital:* Nouméa (74,335).

This group of about 25 islands in the South Pacific is situated about 750 miles east of Australia. The territory takes its name from the main island (New Caledonia or Grande-Terre), which is 6,530 square miles in area and mountainous. The territory includes the dependencies of Île des Pins, Loyalty Islands, Île Huon, Îles Belep, Îles Chesterfield, and Île Walpole. The British explorer, James Cook, was the first European to visit New Caledonia (1774). Other Europeans followed. In 1853, France took over control and, eleven years later, turned it into a prison colony. The climate is mildly tropical, tempered by the trade winds. About half the people are Australo-Melanesian indigenes. Most of the rest are of French descent, with a fluctuating labor force of temporary migrant workers, mostly Javanese and Vietnamese.

Agriculture and mining are the basic economic activities. Coffee and copra are the commercial crops, while root plants, wheat, corn, fruits, and vegetables are also grown, but food must be imported. Nickel is mined on a large scale, and iron and chrome are also exploited.

Administration is in the hands of a Paris-appointed governor (who is also French High Commissioner for the Pacific). An elected council, formerly assisting in governing the island, was dissolved in 1979. Two deputies and a senator are elected to the French Parliament.

New Hebrides—*Status:* Anglo-French Condominium. *Population:* 101,606 (1978 est.). *Area:* 5,700 sq. mi. *Capital:* Vila (17,367) on Efate.

These islands, which form part of the region known as Melanesia, lie in the southwestern Pacific about 500 miles west of Fiji and 250 miles northeast of New Caledonia. Among the larger ones are Espiritu Santo (the largest), Malekula, Epi, Pentecost, and Efate. The condominium includes the Banks and Torres Islands. Most of the islands are mountainous. The climate is hot and wet, and the islands suffer from earthquakes and hurricanes. The people are Melanesian and Polynesian, with British, French, and Chinese settlers.

Copra is the principal product, and cocoa and coffee are also grown. Yams, taro, manioc, and bananas are produced for local consumption, and there are a large number of cattle. Manganese, copra and frozen fish are exported.

The condominium was established in 1906. France is represented by a high commissioner who is also governor of New Caledonia, Great Britain by its high commissioner, resident in London. Both commissioners delegate authority to resident commissioners for the affairs of their respective national groups, and, jointly, for native affairs.

Since 1976 a new Representative Assembly has met and new elections are scheduled for 1979. Complete independence may come in 1980.

Niue—*Status:* New Zealand Territory. *Population:* 3,843 (1976 census). *Area:* 100 sq. mi. *Administrative Center:* Alofi (957).

Niue is in the South Pacific some 1,340 miles northeast of New Zealand; although geographically associated with the Cook Islands, its distance and cultural differences have led to separate administration. Niue is a coral island with fertile but sparse soil. The climate is hot and the islands suffer from hurricanes. The people are of Polynesian stock, speaking Samoan.

There is an appointed resident commissioner, a prime minister and cabinet, and an elected island assembly. Niue became self-governing on September 3, 1974.

Norfolk Island—*Status:* Australian External Territory. *Population:* 1,913 (1978). *Area:* 13.3 sq. mi. *Administrative Center:* Kingston.

The island lies in the South Pacific 930 miles northeast of Sydney, Australia. Many of its inhabitants are descendants of H.M.S. *Bounty* mutineers, who were moved here in 1856 when they became too numerous for Pitcairn Island. Fruits and bean seed are grown and tourism is important. In 1976 an official commission in Australia proposed that the island be incorporated directly into the Commonwealth, but the islanders announced their preference for self-government in association with Australia.

Peter I Island—*Status:* Norwegian Dependency. *Population:* Uninhabited. *Area:* 96 sq. mi.

An Antarctic island, it is southwest of the South Shetland Islands, at 68°47'S. and 90°35'W. It is of volcanic origin and almost entirely ice-covered.

Pitcairn Islands—*Status:* British Colony. *Population:* 74 (1976 census). *Area:* 18 sq. mi. *Administrative Center:* Adamstown.

The colony is in the South Pacific, 4,000 miles southwest of the Panama Canal and 3,200 miles northeast of New Zealand. There are four islands: Pitcairn (1.75 sq. mi.), Henderson, Ducie, and Oeno, of which only Pitcairn is inhabited. The climate is warm throughout the year. The people are descendants of H.M.S. *Bounty* mutineers and Polynesian women from Tahiti. The inhabitants were resettled on Norfolk Island in 1856 when their numbers grew too large for Pitcairn, but several families of them returned soon after.

Subsistence agriculture and fishing are the main occupations. Some fruits, vegetables, and handicrafts are sold to passing ships.

The colony is administered by the British High Commissioner in New Zealand with the assistance of a partly elected island council, presided over by an island magistrate.

Queen Maud Land—*Status:* Norwegian Dependency. *Population:* Uninhabited.

The portion of Antarctica between 20° W. and 45° E., it is claimed by Norway.

Réunion—*Status:* French Overseas Department. *Population:* 480,000 (1978 est.). *Area:* 969 sq. mi. *Capital:* Saint-Denis (103,513).

An island in the Indian Ocean, it is about 400 miles east of Madagascar. Réunion is of volcanic origin and mountainous, the highest peak—Piton des Neiges—rising to more than 10,000 feet. One of its volcanoes is still active. There are many torrential rivers. The climate is essentially tropical, but varies greatly with altitude and exposure to the trade winds. Rainfall is heavy, and there are severe tropical storms. The people are of Malabar Indian, black, Malay, Vietnamese, Chinese, and French descent; the last make up about 20 percent of the population. Eighty percent of the population is Roman Catholic.

The cultivation of sugarcane is the main economic activity. Essential oils from geranium and vetiver plants are also important. Corn, potatoes and beans are grown for consumption, but food must be imported.

Réunion is administered by a Paris-appointed prefect and an elected general council; the island elects three deputies and two senators to the French Parliament.

Ross Dependency—*Status:* New Zealand Territory. *Population:* No permanent inhabitants. *Area:* 290,000 sq. mi. (of which 130,000 sq. mi. are ice shelf).

New Zealand claims that portion of Antarctica south of 60°S. between 160°E. and 150°W.

There are research and exploration activities in the area, and whaling in its territorial waters.

Saint Christopher-Nevis—*Status:* British Associated State. *Population:* 64,900 (1977 est.). *Area:* 120 sq. mi. *Capital:* Basseterre (12,771) on St. Christopher.

In the Leeward Islands of the West Indies, it includes St. Christopher (commonly called St. Kitts; 68 sq. mi.), Nevis (50 sq. mi.), and Sombrero (2 sq. mi.). The climate of the islands is tropical and humid. The people are largely of mixed black-white descent. English is the formal language, but a patois is commonly spoken.

Sugar, molasses, and cotton are the chief exports. Yams, rice, breadfruit, and corn are grown for food. Tourism is increasingly important.

There is a Crown-appointed governor, a prime minister, and a partially elected house of assembly. Robert Bradshaw, prime minister since 1967, died in May 1978. In 1975 separatist delegates from Nevis won their assembly seats. Although Anguilla became a self-governing British colony in 1976, it legally remains a part of the associated state of St. Christopher-Nevis-Anguilla. In 1979, the government continued to seek a formula for St. Kitts-Nevis's early attainment of full independence, which would take into account both the de facto separation of Anguilla and the separatist aspirations of the people of Nevis.

Saint Helena—*Status:* British Colony. *Population:* 6,400 (1977 est.). *Area:* 162 sq. mi. *Capital:* Jamestown (1,601).

The island of Saint Helena (47 sq. mi.) is in the southeastern Atlantic about 1,200 miles from Africa, at 16°S. and 5°21'W. Its dependencies—Tristan da Cunha (38 sq. mi.) and Ascension (34 sq. mi.)—are about 1,500 miles south-southwest and 750 miles northwest, respectively. Near Tristan da Cunha are the uninhabited islands of Gough, Nightingale, and Inaccessible. St. Helena is rocky, with a pleasant climate due to the trade winds. Tristan da Cunha suffered a volcanic eruption in 1961, and the tiny population of 248 was resettled in England. They suffered from respiratory diseases in that climate, however, and returned to their island in 1963. The people of the colony are of mixed origin, and their language is English.

St. Helena grows flax, fodder, and vegetables. Potatoes are the staple subsistence crop on Tristan da Cunha. Ascension is an important cable station.

The colony is administered by a Crown-appointed governor, assisted by an executive council and a partly elected legislative council.

St. Helena was the place of Napoleon's exile from 1815 until his death in 1821.

Saint Kitts-Nevis: See Saint Christopher-Nevis.

Saint Pierre and Miquelon—*Status:* French Overseas Department. *Population:* 5,900 (1977 est.). *Area:* 93.5 sq. mi. *Capital:* Saint Pierre (5,232) on St. Pierre.

This archipelago lies some 15 miles south of Newfoundland in the North Atlantic. There are three main islands, Saint Pierre, Miquelon, and Langlade, the latter two connected by a low isthmus. Although volcanic in origin, the islands are low-lying. The climate is cool to cold, with seasons of strong winds and heavy fogs; there is a good deal of rain and snow. The people are mostly descendants of Breton, Norman, and Basque settlers.

The chief occupation is cod fishing, together with fish freezing and fish meal production.

The department is administered by a Paris-appointed prefect, aided by a privy council. There is an elected general council, and a deputy and a senator are elected to the French Parliament.

Saint Vincent—*Status:* British Associated State. *Population:* 100,000 (1977 est.). *Area:* 150 sq. mi. *Capital:* Kingstown (23,645).

In the Windward Islands of the West Indies, Saint Vincent is south of Saint Lucia and north of Grenada. The northern Grenadines are administered as part of this colony. It is volcanic in origin, with a hot and humid climate and heavy summer rains. The people are largely of mixed descent from white settlers, black slaves, and Carib Indians. English is the formal language and universally understood, but a patois based on French, containing many African elements, is widely spoken.

The economy is agricultural; exports include bananas, arrowroot, and Sea Island cotton, which is thought to be the best in the world. Rice, breadfruit, and corn are grown for food. Tourism is increasingly important.

There is a Crown-appointed governor, a prime minister, and a partly elected house of representatives. Full independence is scheduled for October 27, 1979, with a Crown-appointed governor-general, and with the current

prime minister, Robert Milton Cato, becoming the first prime minister of the independent state.

Sala y Gómez Island—*Status:* Chilean Dependency. *Population:* Uninhabited. *Area:* .05 sq. mi.

In the Pacific Ocean, some 2,100 miles west of Chile and 250 miles east of Easter Island, Sala y Gómez, an arid island of volcanic origin, is administered by Valparaíso Province.

San Ambrosio Island and San Felix Island—*Status:* Chilean Dependencies. *Population:* Uninhabited. *Area:* 1.29 sq. mi.

These two small islands—some 12 miles apart—are in the Pacific Ocean, about 600 miles west of Chile. They were discovered by the Spanish navigator, Juan Fernández, in 1574, and are administered by Atacama Province.

Svalbard—*Status:* Norwegian Dependency. *Population:* 3,431 (1975 est.). *Area:* 23,957 sq. mi. *Administrative Center:* Longyearbyen.

Svalbard is the name of an island territory in the Arctic Ocean between 74° and 81°N. and 10° and 35°E. By far the most important of these islands is the Spitsbergen group, the largest of which are Spitsbergen, North East Land, Edge Island, and Barents Island. The islands are bleak and rugged, largely covered with ice running to the sea in glaciers. The climate is moderated, however, by winds from the Atlantic, and the Gulf Stream keeps open water for six months of the year. About two-thirds of the people are Russians who live in mining camps, the rest are Norwegians. Coal is the principal product.

Tokelau—*Status:* New Zealand Territory. *Population:* 1,625 (1977 est.). *Area:* 3.95 sq. mi. *Administrative Center:* Fenuafala (649) on Fakaofo.

These islands are in the South Pacific 2,100 miles northeast of New Zealand, 300 miles north of Samoa. Geographically the group consists of four atolls—Atafu, Nukunono, Fakaofo, and Swains—but the last belongs to American Samoa (and the United States claims the other three). The people are of Polynesian origin. Their language, now dying, resembles Samoan, the official language.

Subsistence farming and copra production for export are the main occupations. Revenue is also derived from the sale of postage stamps.

The islands are administrated by the New Zealand Minister for Foreign Affairs. An islands' administrator exercises all executive and administrative functions.

Turks and Caicos Islands—*Status:* British Colony. *Population:* 6,000 (1977 est.). *Area:* 166 sq. mi. *Capital:* Cockburn Town (2,287), on Grand Turk.

Geographically part of the Bahamas, of which they form the southeastern groups, the Turks and Caicos lie in the Atlantic Ocean some 575 miles southeast of Florida. Of the 30 or so small islands, only six are inhabited, among them Grand Turk, Grand Caicos, and Salt Cay. The climate is hot, dry, and subject to hurricanes. The people are almost all of African descent.

Fishing and salt production are economic staples.

The administration of the islands is under a Crown-appointed governor and a state council, which consists of nominated and elected members.

Wallis and Futuna—*Status:* French Overseas Territory. *Population:* 9,162 (1976 census). *Area:* 106 sq. mi. *Capital:* Mata Utu (566) on Wallis.

These two small island groups are in the South Pacific, Wallis and its surrounding uninhabited islands being about 250 miles west of Samoa, while Futuna and the uninhabited Alofi island are some 120 miles to the southwest. The islands are of volcanic origin. The climate is tropical, somewhat mitigated by sea breezes, with seasons of hurricanes and torrential rain. The people are mostly Polynesians. The principal export crop is copra.

The territory is administered by a Paris-appointed high administrator, advised by a territorial council which includes the three traditional chiefs of the islands. A territorial assembly is elected, as are a deputy and a senator to the French Parliament.

DISPUTED ISLANDS IN THE PACIFIC

In the south-central part of the Pacific Ocean lie 25 islands over which the U.S. claim to sovereignty is disputed. Tuvalu claims four of them, Kiribati, fourteen, and New Zealand, seven.

Only one island (Christmas) lies north of the equator. In more general terms, the cluster of these disputed islands as a whole is northeast of the Fiji Islands, north of the Samoa Islands, and northwest of Tahiti. The 25 islands comprise the Line Islands, Tuvalu, Phoenix Islands, Tokelau Islands, and so-called Northern Cook Islands.

Those islands formerly in dispute with the United Kingdom have come under the sovereignty of Tuvalu and Kiribati since their recent independence from the United Kingdom. The United States signed a treaty in February 1979 with Tuvalu indicating that the United States was prepared to release four disputed islands to Tuvalu—this treaty has yet to be ratified by the U.S. Senate (August

1979). The fourteen islands transferred by the United Kingdom to Kiribati are subject to a separate treaty with Kiribati, yet to be signed or ratified by the U.S. Senate (August 1979).

ISLANDS CLAIMED BY THE UNITED STATES AND TUVALU: **A. Tuvalu**—1. Funafuti Atoll; 2. Nukufetau Atoll; 3. Nukulaelae Atoll; 4. Niulakita.

ISLANDS CLAIMED BY THE UNITED STATES AND KIRIBATI: **B. Line Islands**—5. Caroline Atoll; 6. Christmas Island; 7. Flint Island; 8. Malden Island; 9. Starbuck Island; 10. Vostock Island. **C. Phoenix Islands**—11. Birnie Atoll; 12. Gardner Atoll; 13. Hull Atoll; 14. McKean Atoll; 15. Sydney Atoll; 16. Phoenix Atoll; 17. Canton; 18. Enderbury.

ISLANDS CLAIMED BY THE UNITED STATES AND NEW ZEALAND: **D. Tokelau**—19. Atafu Atoll; 20. Fakaofo Atoll; 21. Nukunono Atoll. **E. Northern Cook Islands**—(the Manihiki group) 22. Pukapuka Atoll; 23. Manihiki; 24. Rakahanga Atoll; 25. Penrhyn Atoll.

DIPLOMATIC AFFAIRS

HEADS OF MISSIONS TO THE UNITED NATIONS (as of August 1, 1979)

Country	Permanent Representative
Afghanistan	Dr. Bismellah Sahak
Albania	Abdi Baleta
Algeria	vacant
Angola	Elisio de Figueiredo
Argentina	Enrique Jorge Ros
Australia	H.D. Anderson
Austria	Thomas Klestil
Bahamas	Davidson L. Hepburn
Bahrain	Salman Mohamed Al Saffar
Bangladesh	Khwaja Mohammed Kaiser
Barbados	vacant
Belgium	André Ernemann
Benin	Thomas Setondji Boya
Bhutan	Dago Tshering
Bolivia	Sergio Palacios de Vizzio
Botswana	Thomas Tlou
Brazil	Sérgio Corrêa da Costa
Bulgaria	Alexander Yankov
Burma	U Maung Maung Gyee
Burundi	Artémon Simbananiye
Byelorussian SSR	Leonid Aleksandrovich Dolguchits
Cambodia (Kampuchea)	Thiounn Prasith
Cameroon	Ferdinand Léopold Oyono
Canada	William H. Barton
Cape Verde	Amaro Alexandre Da Luz
Central African Empire	Simon Pierre Kibanda
Chad	Beadengar Dessandé
Chile	Sergio Diez
China	Chen Chu
Colombia	Indalecio Lievano Aguirre
Comoros	vacant
Congo	Nicolas Mondjo
Costa Rica	Rodolfo Piza Escalante
Cuba	Raúl Roa Kouri
Cyprus	Andreas V. Mavrommatis
Czechoslovakia	Ilja Hulínský
Denmark	Wilhelm Ulrichsen
Djibouti	Saleh Haji Farah Dirir
Dominica	vacant
Dominican Republic	Emmanuel T. Esquea Guerrero
Ecuador	Migual A. Albornoz
Egypt	Ahmen Esmat Abdel Meguid
El Salvador	Miguel Rafael Urquia
Equatorial Guinea	Owono Asangono
Ethiopia	Mohamed Hamid Ibrahim
Fiji	Berenado Vunibobo
Finland	Ilkka Olavi Pastinen
France	Jacques Leprette
Gabon	Léon N'Dong
Gambia	Ousman Ahmadou Sallah
Germany (Democratic Rep.)	Peter Florin
Germany (Federal Rep.)	Rüdiger von Wechmar
Ghana	Henry V.H. Sekyi
Greece	Nicolas Katapodis
Grenada	Kendrick Bernard Radix
Guatemala	Eduardo Castillo Arriola
Guinea	vacant
Guinea-Bissau	Gil Vicente Vaz Fernandes
Guyana	Noel G. Sinclair
Haiti	Serge Elie Charles
Honduras	Mario Carías
Hungary	Imre Hollai
Iceland	Tómas A. Tómasson
India	Brajesh Chandra Mishra
Indonesia	Abdullah Kamil
Iran	vacant
Iraq	Salah Omar Al-Ali
Ireland	Paul J.G. Keating
Israel	Yehuda Z. Blum
Italy	Umberto La Rocca
Ivory Coast	Amoakon Thiemele
Jamaica	Donald O. Mills
Japan	Masahiro Nisibori
Jordan	Hazem Nuseibeh
Kenya	Charles Gatere Maina
Kuwait	Abdalla Yaccoub Bishara

Country	Permanent Representative
Laos	Vithaya Sourinho
Lebanon	Ghassan Tuéni
Lesotho	Thabo Makeka
Liberia	Winston A. Tubman
Libya	Mansur Rashid Kikhia
Luxembourg	Paul Peters
Madagascar	Blaise Rabetafika
Malawi	T. Jacob X. Muwamba
Malaysia	Ibrahim Tasn Sri Zaiton
Maldives	Ahmed Zaki
Mali	vacant
Malta	Victor J. Gauci
Mauritania	Sid'Ahmed Ould Taya
Mauritius	Radha Krishna Ramphul
Mexico	Francisco Cuevas Cancino
Mongolia	Buyzntyn Dashtseren
Morocco	Abdellatif Filali
Mozambique	José Carolos Lobo
Nepal	vacant
Netherlands	Hugo Scheltema
New Zealand	Harold Huyton Francis
Nicaragua	vacant
Niger	Idé Oumarou
Nigeria	B. Akporode Clark
Norway	Ole Aalgaard
Oman	Mahmoud Aboul-Nasr
Pakistan	Niaz A. Naik
Panama	Jorge Enrique Illueca
Papua New Guinea	Paulias Nguna Matane
Paraguay	Luis Gonzales Arias
Peru	Carlos T. Alzamora
Philippines	Alejandro D. Yango
Poland	Henryk Jaroszek
Qatar	Jasim Yousif Jamal
Romania	Teodor Marinescu
Rwanda	Ignace Karuhije
São Tomé and Príncipe	vacant
Saudi Arabia	vacant
Senegal	Médoune Fall
Seychelles	vacant
Sierra Leone	George Gelaga-King
Singapore	T.T.B. Koh
Solomon Islands	vacant
Somalia	Abdirizaq Haji Hussen
South Africa	vacant
Spain	Don Jaime de Piniés
Sri Lanka	Biyagamage Jayasena Fernando
Sudan	Sayed Ali Ahmed Sahloul
Suriname	Henricus A.F. Heidweiller
Swaziland	Norman M. Malinga
Sweden	Anders I. Thunborg
Syria	Hammoud El-Choufi
Tanzania	Salim Ahmed Salim
Thailand	Pracha Guna-Kasem
Togo	Akanyi-Awunyo Kodjovi
Trinidad and Tobago	Frank Owen Abdulah
Tunisia	Mahoud Mestiri
Turkey	Orhan Eralp
Uganda	Louis Kayanda Mwangaguhunga
Ukrainian SSR	Vladimir Alekseyevich Kravets
USSR	Oleg Aleksandrovich Troyanovsky
United Arab Emirates	Ali Humaidan
United Kingdom	Ivor Richard, Q.C.
United States	Andrew J. Young, Jr.*
Upper Volta	Aïssé Mensah
Uruguay	Edmundo Narancio
Venezuela	Dr. Germán Nava-Carrillo
Vietnam	Ha Van Lau
Western Samoa	Maiava Iulai Toma
Yemen	Ahmed Ali Al-Haddad
Yemen (Southern)	Abdalla Saleh Ashtal
Yugoslavia	Miljan Komatina
Zaire	Kabeya wa Mukeba
Zambia	Paul J.F. Lusaka

*Resigned August 15, 1979. Resignation becomes effective when successor takes office.

PRINCIPAL ORGANS OF THE UNITED NATIONS

There are six principal organs of the UN: the General Assembly, the Security Council, the Economic and Social Council, the Trusteeship Council, the International Court of Justice, and the Secretariat. The official languages in all these organs, other than the International Court of Justice, are Chinese, English, French, Russian, and Spanish. Working languages are English and French, with the addition of Russian, Spanish and Chinese in the General Assembly and the Security Council and Spanish in the Economic and Social Council. Arabic is an official and working language in the General Assembly. The official languages in the International Court of Justice are English and French.

General Assembly

The UN's main deliberative body, the General Assembly, consists of all member states, each of which has one vote. Any question may be discussed that is within the scope of the UN Charter or relates to the functions of any organ provided for in the Charter, as well as any questions on international peace and security that are brought up by a member, by the Security Council, or by a nonmember, if that state accepts in advance obligations of pacific settlement. The General Assembly may make recommendations to member states or to the Security Council with one exception: it may not make recommendations on any dispute under consideration by the Security Council unless the Council so requests.

Regular sessions of the Assembly convene once a year, commencing on the third Tuesday in September. There is provision for special and emergency special sessions. Voting is by simple majority of those present and voting, except on questions adjudged important, when a two-thirds majority is required. The Assembly controls the finances of the UN; it also elects the 10 nonpermanent members of the Security Council, all the members of the Economic and Social Council, and—with, but independently of, the Security Council—the International Court of Justice. On Security Council recommendations, the Secretary-General is appointed by the General Assembly.

The assembly elects its president and 17 vice-presidents for each session and adopts its own rules of procedure. It distributes most agenda items among its seven main committees. These are: *First Committee*—political and security, including armaments regulations; *Special Political Committee*—shares the work of the First Committee; *Second Committee*—economic and financial; *Third Committee*—social, humanitarian, cultural; *Fourth Committee*—decolonization; *Fifth Committee*—administrative and budgetary; *Sixth Committee*—legal.

Recommendations of these committees go to the full Assembly for approval. There is also a General Committee that organizes the work of each session, a Credentials Committee, an Advisory Committee on Administrative and Budgetary Questions, and a Committee on Contributions, which recommends the scale of members' payments to the UN. They may establish *ad hoc* and subsidiary bodies such as the Conference on Trade and Development (UNCTAD).

General Assembly Committee Chairmen, 33rd Session:

First Committee (Political and Security) — Ilkka Olavi Pastinen, Finland

Special Political Committee — Rodolfo E. Piza Escalante, Costa Rica

Second Committee (Economic and Financial) — Louis Kayanda Mwangaguhunga, Uganda

Third Committee (Social, Humanitarian and Cultural) — Leticia R. Shahani, Philippines

Fourth Committee (Decolonization) — Leonid A. Dolguchits, Byelorussia SSR

Fifth Committee (Administrative and Budgetary) — Clarus Kobina Sekyi, Ghana

Sixth Committee (Legal) — Luigi Ferrari-Bravo, Italy

Assembly Actions of the 33rd Session:

The opening session of the UN General Assembly took place on September 19, 1978. During this session the membership of the world body was raised to 151. The Solomon Islands were admitted in September and Dominica in December. Both were formerly British possessions. Indalecio Liévano Aguirre of Colombia was elected president of the Assembly.

The Assembly adopted in December 1978 resolutions on disarmament with special urging for all states to accede to the prohibition of chemical and biological weapons and for the nuclear powers to expedite their negotiations on arms limitations.

SOUTHERN AFRICA — As in previous years the Assembly passed a number of resolutions condemning racist and colonial regimes in southern Africa. A Charter of Rights for Migrant Workers was adopted to work for the abolition of the apartheid migratory labor system practiced in South Africa. South African policies in Namibia also were subjects of the Assembly's deliberations. On the policies of apartheid of the South African government, the Assembly passed on Dec. 24, 1978 a total of 15 resolutions, among them one requesting the Security Council "to consider urgently a mandatory embargo on the supply of petroleum and petroleum products to South Africa."

MIDDLE EAST — As in previous years, the Assembly adopted numerous resolutions, mainly reaffirming earlier decisions, on matters arising out of the Arab-Israeli conflict. One resolution passed called for an embargo on armaments and nuclear materials for Israel. In regard to the situation in Lebanon with the loss of life and immense damage to the economic structure and to property resulting from four years of hostilities, the Assembly on Dec. 20, 1978 endorsed an appeal by the UN Secretary-General for assistance to Lebanon and requested the UN Secretary-General to establish in Beirut a joint co-ordinating committee of the UN specialized agencies.

*HUMAN RIGHTS — The Assembly adopted a number of resolutions on human rights questions, including the establishment of a voluntary UN Trust Fund for Chile to receive and distribute contributions for humanitarian, legal and financial aid "to persons whose human rights have been violated by detention or imprisonment in Chile." It voted to convene in Copenhagen in 1980 a world conference of the UN Decade for Women and to organize a World Assembly on the Elderly in 1982 "as a forum to launch an international action program aimed at guaranteeing economic and social security to older persons." The year 1979, by General Assembly Resolution, has been proclaimed "The International Year of the Child." It has involved the

UN in conferences and special programs aimed at helping children in all parts of the world.

OTHER MATTERS — An Assembly condemnation of airplane hijacking was adopted without formal vote on November 33, 1978. It called for all nations to increase airport security; as a result, the International Federation of Airline Pilots' Associations dropped a threat to stage a world-wide strike to dramatize requests for greater protection of flight crews and passengers. The Assembly adopted the recommendations of the Committee on the Peaceful Uses of Outer Space relating to the convening of a second UN conference on the exploration and peaceful uses of outer space. It also decided to convene an international conference on new and renewable sources of energy under UN auspices in 1981 with the object of meeting future world overall energy needs.

Security Council

There are 15 members on the Security Council, five of them permanent—The People's Republic of China, France, the USSR, the United Kingdom, and the United States—and 10 elected by the General Assembly for two-year terms and ineligible for immediate reelection. As of August 1979 the ten nonpermanent members were: Bangladesh, Bolivia, Czechoslovakia, Gabon, Jamaica, Kuwait, Nigeria, Norway, Portugal and Zambia.

The council bears primary responsibility under the UN Charter for the maintenance of international peace and security. It may investigate any situation bearing the seeds of international friction. These may be brought to its attention by any UN member, by any nonmember accepting in advance the obligations of pacific settlement, by the General Assembly, or by the Secretary-General.

Having determined the existence of a threat to peace, the council may make recommendations, or may call on members to take such measures as economic sanctions or other steps short of armed force. Should these be inadequate, the council may take military action against an aggressor; all members agree under the charter to make available to the council, in accordance with agreements to be negotiated, armed forces necessary for maintaining international peace. The council also has responsibility for plans to regulate armaments.

On matters other than procedural, council decisions need an affirmative vote of nine, including all permanent members (hence the veto; abstentions do not in practice constitute a veto). On procedural matters, an affirmative vote of any nine members suffices. A UN member not on the council may take part in council discussion when it is considered that its interests are especially affected. The council presidency is held by members in monthly rotation in English alphabetical order. There is a *Committee of Experts* to advise the council on procedural and technical matters, a *Committee on Admission of New Members,* and a *Military Staff Committee,* which is composed of the chiefs of staff of the permanent members or their representatives, to advise on military matters.

Security Council Actions 1978 — mid-1979:

MIDDLE EAST—Approved on June 14, 1979, a six-month extension of the UN Interim Force in Lebanon. The resolution also called on Israel to stop its attacks on villages in southern Lebanon, and to end its support of Lebanese Christian militia.

FAR EAST—The China-Vietnam and the Cambodia-Vietnam wars were debated in February 1979, but the council was unable to take action because of the conflicting positions taken by China and the Soviet Union.

SOUTHERN AFRICA—The Council voted April 30, 1979 to condemn the Rhodesian elections and called upon member nations to maintain the economic boycott against Rhodesia. The UN plan for the independence of Namibia continued to falter. The South African-sponsored elections were denounced and the gap between Pretoria and the UN contact group on Namibia's future seemed only to get wider.

Economic and Social Council

The council makes studies and recommendations to the General Assembly on international social, economic, cultural, educational, health, and related matters. It negotiates agreements with the specialized agencies, defining their relationship with the UN, and coordinates their activities by means of consultation and recommendation.

It is composed of 54 members, 18 of whom are elected each year by the General Assembly to a three-year term. Each member has one vote, and a simple majority rules. The council works through committees, commissions, and various other subsidiary bodies. Its functional commissions include: the *Statistical Commission,* the *Population Commission,* the *Commission for Social Development,* the *Commission on Human Rights,* the *Commission on the Status of Women,* the *Commission on Narcotic Drugs* and the *Commission on Transnational Corporations.* There are also regional commissions for Europe, Asia and the Far East, Latin America, and Africa. There are a number of other related bodies, including the executive board of the children's fund (UNICEF) and the International Narcotics Control Board.

Nongovernmental agencies may also be consulted by the council.

See Membership of Principal United Nations Organs *on page 717 for list of members.*

Trusteeship Council

The council bears prime responsibility for supervision of territories placed under the UN Trusteeship System. It consists of member states administering trust territories and permanent members of the Security Council not administering territories. The present administering state is the United States (Trust Territory of the Pacific Islands). The nonadministering members are the People's Republic of China, France, the United Kingdom, and the USSR.

Voting is by simple majority. The Trusteeship Council meets once a year, usually in June.

International Court of Justice

The principal judicial organ of the UN functions in accordance with its statute, which is an integral part of the UN Charter and is based on the Statute of the Permanent Court of International Justice of the League of Nations. The court is open to all UN members, plus nonmembers who become party to the statute (at present Switzerland, Liechtenstein, and San Marino), as well as other states fulfilling certain conditions. It is not open to private individuals. The court has jurisdiction over all cases that the parties refer to it and over all matters specifically provided for in the charter or in treaties or conventions in force, including treaties that refer to the Permanent Court of International Justice. In the event of a dispute as to whether the court has jurisdiction, it decides the issue itself.

The court is composed of 15 judges of different nationalities, who are elected independently by the General Assembly and the Security Council (election in the latter does not permit the veto). Terms are for nine years. All questions are decided by a majority of judges present, nine constituting a quorum. In case of a tie, the president of the court (elected by the court for a three-year term) casts the deciding vote. The court sits at The Hague, Netherlands.

Recent Developments: The dispute between Tunisia and Libya on control of the adjacent continental shelf was submitted to the court on Dec. 1, 1978.

Secretariat

The UN's administrative spine is composed of the Secretary-General, who is appointed by the General Assembly on the recommendation of the Security Council, and "such staff as the organization may require." As chief administrative officer, the Secretary-General acts in his capacity at all meetings of the General Assembly, the Security Council, the Economic and Social Council, and the Trusteeship Council. He makes an annual report to the General Assembly and appoints the Secretariat staff. The Secretary-General is also empowered to bring before the Security Council any matter that in his opinion threatens the maintenance of international peace.

The structure of the Secretariat includes the Offices of the Secretary-General (the Executive Office of the Secretary-General, the Director-General for Economic Development, the Offices of the Under-Secretaries for Special Political Affairs, the Office of Legal Affairs, the Office of the Controller, and the Office of Personnel), the Department of Political and Security Council Affairs, the Department of Economic and Social Affairs, the Department of Trusteeship and Non-Self-Governing Territories, the Office of Public Information, the Office of Conference Services, the Office of General Services, and the UN Office in Geneva. There are also separate staffs serving subsidiary organs established by the General Assembly or the Economic and Social Council, including: the children's fund (UNICEF), the development program (UNDP), the office of the high commissioner for refugees (UNHCR), the relief and works agency for Palestine refugees (UNRWA), the institute for training and research (UNITAR), the industrial development organization (UNIDO) and trade and development (UNCTAD).

SPECIALIZED AGENCIES OF THE UNITED NATIONS

Specialized agencies are intergovernmental organizations linked to the UN by special agreement, working in partnership with it in social, scientific, and technical fields. The specialized agencies proper report annually to the Economic and Social Council. Although usually listed with them, the IAEA and GATT agencies are not, strictly speaking, specialized agencies. The former is an intergovernmental agency "established under the aegis of the UN" and reports to the General Assembly and, as appropriate, to the Security Council and the Economic and Social Council. The latter cooperates with the UN at the secretariat and intergovernmental levels.

Food and Agriculture Organization of the United Nations (FAO) *Function:* To help countries increase food production and improve distribution, to coordinate the Freedom from Hunger Campaign, and to help administer the World Food Program. *Members:* 144 countries. *Headquarters:* Rome. *Chief Officer:* Director-General Edouard Saouma (Lebanon). *Recent Developments:* International conference in Rome on world hunger problems was held July 13-20, 1979 under FAO auspices. Resolutions of the conference called for land reforms and greater participation of farmers and peasants in economic and political power.

General Agreement of Tariffs and Trade (GATT) *Function:* To establish and administer the code for orderly conduct of international trade; to assist governments to reduce customs tariffs and abolish other trade barriers; and to operate, jointly with the UN Conference on Trade and Development, the International Trade Center providing export promotion assistance for developing countries. (GATT rules govern as estimated 80 percent of international trade.) *Members:* 84 participating nations. *Headquarters:* Geneva. *Chief Officer:* Director-General Olivier Long (Switzerland).

Inter-Governmental Maritime Consultative Organization (IMCO) *Function:* To promote cooperation on technical matters affecting shipping, to encourage the highest standards of maritime safety and efficient navigation, to convene international conferences on shipping, and to draft international maritime conventions. *Members:* 107 countries plus one associate. *Headquarters:* London. *Chief Officer:* Secretary-General C.P. Srivastava (India). *Recent Developments:* The eighth session of the UN Law of the Sea Conference adjourned in a deadlock over the seabed mining issue on April 27, 1979. Developing countries have supported strict UN supervision of mineral mining on the ocean floor, while industrial nations supported a minimum of international controls.

International Atomic Energy Agency (IAEA) *Function:* To promote the use of nuclear energy for peaceful purposes; to assist in nuclear research, development, and applications; and to apply safeguards against diversion of nuclear materials to military use. *Members:* 110 countries. *Headquarters:* Vienna. *Chief Officer:* Director-General Sigvard Eklund (Sweden).

International Bank for Reconstruction and Development (World Bank; IBRD) *Function:* To further members' economic development by loans (all loans made to or guaranteed by government) and technical advice. *Members:* 133 countries. *Headquarters:* Washington, DC. *Chief Officer:* President Robert S. McNamara (United States).

International Civil Aviation Organization (ICAO) *Function:* To promote safety of international civil aviation, to provide statistical and economic information for governments and airlines, to work to reduce the red tape of customs formalities, and to help developing countries benefit from air transport. *Members:* 143 countries. *Headquarters:* Montreal. *Chief Officer:* Yves Lambert (France).

International Development Association (IDA) *Function:* To further economic development of members by providing finance on terms bearing less heavily on balance of payments than conventional loans. (Its credits have been for 50-year terms, interest free.) *Members:* 120 countries.

Headquarters: Washington, DC (IDA is an affiliate of IBRD and has the same officers and staff.)
International Finance Corporation (IFC) *Function:* To assist less developed member countries by providing risk capital, without government guarantee, for the growth of productive private enterprise. *Members:* 108 countries. *Headquarters:* Washington, DC. *Chief Officer:* Robert S. McNamara (United States). (IFC is an affiliate of IBRD.)
International Fund for Agricultural Development (IFAD) *Function:* To grant loans to promote agricultural improvement in developing countries. *Members:* 115 countries. *Headquarters:* Rome. *President:* Abelmuhsin al-Sudeary (Saudi Arabia). *Recent Developments:* With more than $1 billion in resources contributed by industrialized nations and the OPEC countries, this new agency began choosing officers and establishing lending policies and regulations in December 1977.
International Labour Organization (ILO) *Function:* To bring together government, labor, and management on pressing international labor and manpower problems; to provide governments with technical assistance, and to develop world labor standards. *Members:* 136 countries. *Headquarters:* Geneva. *Chief Officer:* Director-General Francis Blanchard (France). *Recent Developments:* The U.S. withdrew from the International Labour Organization on November 1, 1977. The move followed earlier warnings that the U.S. would pull out unless the trend toward "politicization" of the agency was halted. The financial deficit caused by American withdrawal was made up in part by additional contributions by member nations.
International Monetary Fund (Fund; IMF) *Function:* To promote international monetary cooperation and stabilization of currencies, to facilitate expansion of international trade, and to help members meet temporary difficulties in foreign payments. *Members:* 138 countries. *Headquarters:* Washington, DC. *Chief Officer:* Managing Director Jacques de Larosiere (France). *Recent Developments:* In April 1978, the IMF changed its method of setting a value for Special Drawing Rights (SDRs), the IMF's monetary standard. The value of SDRs, which serve as a kind of international money, is pegged to a basket of currencies of 16 leading trading nations. In November 1978 the U.S., in an attempt to rescue the dollar, arranged to draw $3 billion from reserves with the IMF; the U.S. would also sell $2 billion in SDRs.
International Telecommunications Union (ITU) *Function:* To promote international cooperation in radio, telegraph, telephone, and space radio communications; to be instrumental in allocating radio frequencies, and to work to establish the lowest possible charges for telecommunications. *Members:* 154 countries. *Headquarters:* Geneva. *Chief Officer:* Secretary-General Mohammed Mili (Tunisia).
United Nations Educational, Scientific and Cultural Organization (UNESCO) *Function:* To broaden the base of education in the world, to bring the benefits of science to all countries, and to encourage cultural exchange and appreciation. *Members:* 144 countries. *Headquarters:* Paris. *Chief Officer:* Director-General Amadou M'Bow. *Staff:* About 4,000.
United Nations Industrial Development Organization (UNIDO) *Function:* To encourage and extend assistance to developing countries for development, expansion and modernization of industry; to achieve full utilization of locally available natural and human resources; to provide a forum for consultation and negotiations among developing countries and between developing and industrialized countries. Administers UN Industrial Development Fund. *Headquarters:* Vienna. *Chief Officer:* Executive Director Dr. Abd-el Rahman Khene (Algeria). *Recent Developments:* Operates as an executing agency of the UN Development Programme (UNDP) until final ratification of autonomous specialized agency status. Consensus agreement and UNIDO Constitution were approved in April 1979.
Universal Postal Union (UPU) *Function:* To assure the organization and improvement of the various postal services and to promote, in the sphere, the development of international cooperation. *Members:* 158. *Headquarters:* Bern. *Chief Officer:* Director-General M.I. Sobhi (Egypt).
World Health Organization (WHO) *Function:* To direct and coordinate international health work, to help governments in public health programs, to set international drug and vaccine standards, and to promote medical research. *Members:* 151 countries. *Headquarters:* Geneva. *Chief Officer:* Director-General Dr. Halfdan Mahler (Denmark). *Recent Developments:* The annual assembly was held in Geneva May 7-25, 1979; an attempt by Arab groups to deprive Israel of voting rights and move a regional office from Alexandria, Egypt was defeated.
World Intellectual Property Organization (WIPO) *Function:* To promote and protect intellectual property, such as trademarks, industrial designs, literary and artistic works, throughout the world through new international treaties and harmonization of national legislation. *Members:* 81. *Headquarters:* Geneva. *Chief Officer:* Director-General Dr. Arpad Bogsch (United States).
World Meteorological Organization (WMO) *Function:* To promote international meteorological cooperation, especially in the establishment of a worldwide network of meteorological stations and rapid exchange of weather data, to promote standardization and publication of observations, and to further meteorological applications. *Members:* 147. *Headquarters:* Geneva. *Secretary-General:* Aksel Wiin-Nielson (Denmark). *Recent Developments:* Under the WMO program called World Weather Watch, centers have been set up in the District of Columbia, Moscow, and Melbourne to collect, process, and disseminate weather information.

UN SECRETARIES-GENERAL

Lie, Trygve Halvdan (1896-1968), Secretary-General from 1946 to 1953. Born in Oslo, Norway, the son of a carpenter, Lie earned a law degree from Oslo University in 1919 and later served as legal adviser to the Norwegian Trade Unions Federation. From 1935 to 1946 he held various Cabinet ministries, including justice, the department of shipping and supply, and foreign affairs. In the last capacity, he led the Norwegian delegation to the 1945 UN conference in San Francisco, where he headed the commission that drafted the security-council provisions of the Charter.

The rugged Norwegian was elected the first Secretary-General of the UN as a compromise candidate acceptable to both East and West. He immediately asserted himself and established the independence of the Secretary-General's office.

His strong stand on East-West issues alienated, at different times, both the United States and the Soviet Union. By endorsing UN membership for

Communist China, he angered the Americans; his stand, however, against North Korean aggression so infuriated the Russians that they refused to deal with him during the remainder of his term. Lie's resignation in 1953 was partly due to Soviet ostracism, but was also brought on by McCarthy-era claims of subversives in the Secretariat.

Hammarskjöld, Dag Hjalmar Agne Carl (1905-1961), Secretary-General from 1953 to 1961. He was born in Jonkoping, Sweden, of an aristocratic family; his father, an eminent jurist, was Sweden's Prime Minister during World War I. Hammarskjöld earned a law degree from Uppsala University in 1930 and a Ph.D. in political economy from the University of Stockholm in 1934.

In 1949 he entered the foreign ministry, where he established his reputation as an international monetary expert. He became vice-chairman of Sweden's UN delegation in 1952 and was its chairman the following year, when he was elected Secretary-General. Hammarskjöld greatly extended the scope and influence of his office. His personal missions in the cause of peace began with his visit to Peking in 1955 to secure the release of captured American fliers and ended with his 1961 Congo mission on which he died in a plane crash near Ndola, Northern Rhodesia.

He created the international peace-keeping force sent to the Middle East after the 1956 Suez crisis. Hammarskjöld's most controversial action was his insistence, against strong Soviet opposition, on maintaining the UN peace force in the Congo. All these efforts won him the Nobel Peace Prize, awarded posthumously in 1961. Publicly, the bachelor Hammarskjöld was a cool, realistic diplomat, but his diary, published as *Markings* in 1964, revealed a profoundly mystical man.

U Thant (1909-1974), Secretary-General from 1961 to 1971. Born in Pantanaw, Burma, the son of a prosperous landowner, Thant graduated from the National High School in Pantanaw and attended University College in Rangoon. He taught English and modern history at his old high school where in 1931 he became headmaster. For many years he was also an active writer on politics.

He became a member of the Burmese UN delegation in 1952 and its chairman five years later. In 1959 he was chosen vice-president of the General Assembly. After Hammarskjöld's death in

1961, Thant, known as a moderate and neutralist, was elected acting Secretary-General, and a year later he was unanimously elected to office for a full five-year term, retroactive to 1961. Thant was widely praised for his role in calming international tensions during the 1962 Cuban missile crisis, for his part in healing the secessionist Katanga breach in the Congo, and for his handling of the 1964 UN financial crisis, when France and the Communist bloc refused to pay their share of peace-keeping operations.

On the other hand, he was criticized for precipitous speed in complying with Cairo's request in 1967 that the UN emergency force be withdrawn from the Sinai peninsula. It was also remarked that while he was an outspoken critic of American policy in Vietnam, he demonstrated marked restraint toward the 1968 Soviet invasion of Czechoslovakia. In 1971 he announced his December resignation.

Waldheim, Kurt (1918), Secretary-General since January 1972. Born in Lower Austria, the son of a teacher, Waldheim earned a law degree from the University of Vienna in 1944 and joined the Austrian foreign service the following year. He headed the ministry's personnel department for four years, then in 1955, when Austria was admitted to the UN, was appointed Austria's permanent observer at the UN. Since then he has been a member of Austria's delegation at all General Assembly sessions, while also active in other high-ranking foreign ministry appointments. After four years as head of the Austrian mission in Canada he returned to Vienna in 1960, directing the political affairs section there in 1962-1964. He was Austria's UN ambassador from 1964; he left his UN duties early in 1968 to become foreign minister, returning in 1970 to the UN. In April 1971, he contested unsuccessfully in Austria's presidential election.

After election as secretary-general, Waldheim, whose repute is that of a diplomat in the classic mold rather than an "activist," told the UN that he viewed admission of the divided countries as a move toward the goal of UN universality.

In the difficult Middle East negotiations Waldheim has often met with the national leaders involved and used his office to keep peace talks alive.

Waldheim was reelected for a second five-year term in December 1976.

∎ UN GENERAL ASSEMBLY PRESIDENTS

Session	Year	President
1st	1946	Paul Henri Spaak
2nd	1947	Oswaldo Aranha
3rd	1948-49	Herbert V. Evatt
4th	1949	Carlos P. Romulo
5th	1950-51	Nasrollah Entezam
6th	1951-52	Luis Padilla Nervo
7th	1952-53	Lester B. Pearson
8th	1953-54	Mrs. Vijaya Lakshmi Pandit
9th	1954	Eelco N. van Kleffends
10th	1955	Jose Maza
11th	1956-57	Prince Wan Waithayakon
12th	1957	Sir Leslie Munro
13th	1958-59	Charles Malik
14th	1959	Victor Andres Belaunde
15th	1960-61	Frederick H. Boland
16th	1961 62	Mongi Slim
17th	1962	Muhammad Zafrulla Khan
18th	1963	Carlos Sosa Rodriguez
19th	1964-65	Alex Quaison-Sackey
20th	1965	Amintore Fanfani
21st	1966	Abdul Rahman Pazhwak
22nd	1967-68	Corneliu Manescu
23rd	1968	Emilio Arenales
24th	1969	Miss Angie Brooks
25th	1970	Edvard Isak Hambro
26th	1971	Adam Malik
27th	1972	Stanislaw Trepczynski
28th	1973	Leopoldo Benites
29th	1974	Abdelaziz Bouteflika
30th	1975	Gaston Thorn
31st	1976	Hamilton Shirley Amerasinghe
32nd	1977	Lazar Mojsov
33rd	1978	Indalecio Licvano Aguirre
34th	1979	Salim Ahmed Salim

U.S. MISSION TO UNITED NATIONS (As of September 1979)

Donald F. McHenry (Ambassador Extraordinary and Plenipotentiary) — Permanent United States Representative to the United Nations and Chairman of the Delegation to the General Assembly*

William J. vanden Heuvel—Deputy United States Representative to the United Nations

William L. Dunfey—Alternate United States Representative to the General Assembly

Howard Rosen—Alternate United States Representative to the General Assembly

Richard W. Petree (Ambassador)—Alternate United States Representative for Special Political Affairs

James Baker (Minister Counsellor) — Deputy United States Representative on the Economic and Social Council

Dr. Ruth Morgenthau—United States Representative on the Commission for Social Development of the Economic and Social Council

Edward Mezvinsky—United States Representative on the Commission on Human Rights of the Economic and Social Council

Koryne Horbal — United States Representative on the Commission on the Status of Women of the Economic and Social Council

DELEGATES TO THE GENERAL ASSEMBLY
(NON-MEMBERS OF THE UNITED STATES MISSION)

Representative Benjamin S. Rosenthal—U.S. Delegate

Representative Larry Winn, Jr.—U.S. Delegate

Esther L. Coopersmith—Public Member

MEMBERS OF THE MILITARY STAFF COMMITTEE OF THE UNITED STATES MISSION

Army:

Lt. Gen. Edward G. Meyer

Col. Frederick L. Delamain

Navy:

Vice Adm. William J. Crowe

Capt. Carl J. Lidel

Air Force:

Lt. Gen. H. M. Fish

Col. John M. Kirk

* The Secretary of State, Cyrus R. Vance, serves as ex officio Chairman when present at a session

MEMBERSHIP OF PRINCIPAL UNITED NATIONS ORGANS

SECURITY COUNCIL

Fifteen members: the 5 members shown with an asterisk are designated in the Charter as permanent; 10 members are elected for 2-year terms by the General Assembly.

Bangladesh	China*	France*	Jamaica	Nigeria	Portugal	United Kingdom*
Bolivia	Czechoslovakia	Gabon	Kuwait	Norway	USSR*	United States*
Zambia						

ECONOMIC AND SOCIAL COUNCIL

54 members: elected for 3-year terms by the General Assembly.

Algeria	Dominican Rep.	Iran	Morocco	Spain	United Arab
Argentina	Ecuador	Iraq	Netherlands	Sudan	Emirates
Barbados	Finland	Ireland	New Zealand	Sweden	United Kingdom
Brazil	France	Italy	Pakistan	Syria	United States
Cameroon	Germany (Dem. Rep.)	Jamaica	Philippines	Tanzania	Upper Volta
Central African	Germany (Fed. Rep.)	Japan	Poland	Trinidad and	Venezuela
Empire	Ghana	Lesotho	Romania	Tobago	Zambia
China	Hungary	Malta	Rwanda	Turkey	
Colombia	India	Mauritania	Senegal	Ukraine	
Cyprus	Indonesia	Mexico	Somalia	USSR	

TRUSTEESHIP COUNCIL

5 members: one (*) an administering state, and four nonadministering permanent members of the Security Council.

China	France	USSR	United Kingdom	United States*

INTERNATIONAL COURT OF JUSTICE

15 members, elected by the General Assembly for 9-year terms that end on 5 February of the year indicated. Judges are listed in order of precedence.

Sir Humphrey Waldock (UK, 1982)
   president for 3 years
Manfred Lachs (Poland, 1985)
Isaac Forster (Senegal, 1982)
André Gros (France, 1982)
Platon D. Morozov (USSR, 1988)

Nagendra Singh (India, 1982)
José Maria Ruda (Argentina, 1982)
Taslim Olawale Elias (Nigeria, 1985)
Hermann Mosler
   (Germany, Fed. Rep., 1985)
Shigeru Oda (Japan, 1985)

Salah el-Dine Tarazi (Syria, 1985)
Roberto Ago (Italy, 1988)
Richard Baxter (US, 1988)
Abdullah Ali El-Erian,
   (Egypt, 1988)
José Sette Câmara (Brazil, 1988)

ROSTER OF THE UNITED NATIONS: 1979 (As of September 1)

Member Nation	Date of Admission	Member Nation	Date of Admission	Member Nation	Date of Admission
Afghanistan	19 Nov. 1946	Germany (Fed. Rep.)	18 Sept. 1973	Oman	7 Oct. 1971
Albania	14 Dec. 1955	Ghana	8 Mar. 1957	Pakistan	30 Sept. 1947
Algeria	8 Oct. 1962	Greece	25 Oct. 1945	Panama	13 Nov. 1945
Angola	1 Dec. 1976	Grenada	17 Sept. 1974	Papua New Guinea	10 Oct. 1975
Argentina	24 Oct. 1945	Guatemala	21 Nov. 1945	Paraguay	24 Oct. 1945
Australia	1 Nov. 1945	Guinea	12 Dec. 1958	Peru	31 Oct. 1945
Austria	14 Dec. 1955	Guinea-Bissau	17 Sept. 1974	Philippines	24 Oct. 1945
Bahamas	18 Sept. 1973	Guyana	20 Sept. 1966	Poland	24 Oct. 1945
Bahrain	21 Sept. 1971	Haiti	24 Oct. 1945	Portugal	14 Dec. 1955
Bangladesh	17 Sept. 1974	Honduras	17 Dec. 1945	Qatar	21 Sept. 1971
Barbados	9 Dec. 1966	Hungary	14 Dec. 1955	Romania	14 Dec. 1955
Belgium	27 Dec. 1945	Iceland	19 Nov. 1946	Rwanda	18 Sept. 1962
Benin	20 Sept. 1960	India	30 Oct. 1945	Sao Tome and Principe	16 Sept. 1965
Bhutan	21 Sept. 1971	Indonesia	28 Sept. 1950	Saudi Arabia	24 Oct. 1945
Bolivia	14 Nov. 1945	Iran	24 Oct. 1945	Senegal	28 Sept. 1960
Botswana	17 Oct. 1966	Iraq	21 Dec. 1945	Seychelles	21 Sept. 1976
Brazil	24 Oct. 1945	Ireland	14 Dec. 1955	Sierra Leone	27 Sept. 1961
Bulgaria	14 Dec. 1955	Israel	11 May 1949	Singapore	21 Sept. 1965
Burma	19 Apr. 1948	Italy	14 Dec. 1955	Solomon Islands	19 Sept. 1978
Burundi	18 Sept. 1962	Ivory Coast	20 Sept. 1960	Somalia	20 Sept. 1960
Byelorussian SSR	24 Oct. 1945	Jamaica	18 Sept. 1962	South Africa	7 Nov. 1945
Cambodia (Kampuchea)	14 Dec. 1955	Japan	18 Dec. 1956	Spain	14 Dec. 1955
Cameroon	20 Sept. 1960	Jordan	14 Dec. 1955	Sri Lanka	14 Dec. 1955
Canada	9 Nov. 1945	Kenya	16 Dec. 1963	Sudan	12 Nov. 1956
Cape Verde	16 Sept. 1975	Kuwait	14 May 1963	Suriname	4 Dec. 1975
Central African Empire	20 Sept. 1960	Laos	14 Dec. 1955	Swaziland	24 Sept. 1968
Chad	20 Sept. 1960	Lebanon	24 Oct. 1945	Sweden	19 Nov. 1946
Chile	24 Oct. 1945	Lesotho	17 Oct. 1966	Syria	24 Oct. 1945
China	24 Oct. 1945	Liberia	2 Nov. 1945	Tanzania	14 Dec. 1961
Colombia	5 Nov. 1945	Libya	14 Dec. 1955	Thailand	16 Dec. 1946
Comoros	12 Nov. 1975	Luxembourg	24 Oct. 1945	Togo	20 Sept. 1960
Congo	20 Sept. 1960	Madagascar	20 Sept. 1960	Trinidad and Tobago	18 Sept. 1962
Costa Rica	2 Nov. 1945	Malawi	1 Dec. 1964	Tunisia	12 Nov. 1956
Cuba	24 Oct. 1945	Malaysia	17 Sept. 1957	Turkey	24 Oct. 1945
Cyprus	20 Sept. 1960	Maldives	21 Sept. 1965	Uganda	25 Oct. 1962
Czechoslovakia	24 Oct. 1945	Mali	28 Sept. 1960	Ukrainian SSR	24 Oct. 1945
Denmark	24 Oct. 1945	Malta	1 Dec. 1964	USSR	24 Oct. 1945
Djibouti	20 Sept. 1977	Mauritania	27 Oct. 1961	United Arab Emirates	9 Dec. 1971
Dominica	18 Dec. 1978	Mauritius	24 Apr. 1968	United Kingdom	24 Oct. 1945
Dominican Republic	24 Oct. 1945	Mexico	7 Nov. 1945	United States	24 Oct. 1945
Ecuador	21 Dec. 1945	Mongolia	27 Oct. 1961	Upper Volta	20 Sept. 1960
Egypt	24 Oct. 1945	Morocco	12 Nov. 1956	Uruguay	18 Dec. 1945
El Salvador	24 Oct. 1945	Mozambique	16 Sept. 1975	Venezuela	15 Nov. 1945
Equatorial Guinea	12 Nov. 1968	Nepal	14 Dec. 1955	Vietnam	20 Sept. 1977
Ethiopia	13 Nov. 1945	Netherlands	10 Dec. 1945	Western Samoa	15 Dec. 1976
Fiji	13 Oct. 1970	New Zealand	24 Oct. 1945	Yemen	30 Sept. 1947
Finland	14 Dec. 1955	Nicaragua	24 Oct. 1945	Yemen (Southern Yemen)	14 Dec. 1967
France	24 Oct. 1945	Niger	20 Sept. 1960	Yugoslavia	20 Oct. 1945
Gabon	20 Sept. 1960	Nigeria	7 Oct. 1960	Zaire	20 Sept. 1960
Gambia	21 Sept. 1965	Norway	27 Nov. 1945	Zambia	1 Dec. 1964
Germany (Dem. Rep.)	18 Sept. 1973				

REPRESENTATIVE INTERNATIONAL ORGANIZATIONS

Afro-Mauritian Common Organization (OCAM) *Formed:* 1965 *Members:* 10 African countries *Headquarters:* Bangui, Central African Empire *Secretary-General:* Sidney Moufia *Purpose:* To promote economic, technical, and cultural development of member French-speaking states within the framework of the OAU.

Recent Developments: On September 7, 1976 Gabon withdrew from the Organization, and on February 9, 1977 Seychelles became a member.

ANZUS Council *Formed:* 1951 *Members:* Australia, New Zealand, and the United States *Headquarters:* Canberra, Australia *Purpose:* This loose military alliance is pledged to respond to aggression against any of its members.

Recent Developments: At the July 1979 Canberra conference of Foreign Ministers of the three member nations, concern was voiced on the rising flow of Indo-Chinese refugees. The ministers also called for Vietnamese withdrawal from Cambodia.

Arab League (AL) *Formed:* 1945 *Members:* Algeria, Bahrain, Djibouti, Egypt, Iraq, Jordan, Kuwait, Lebanon, Libya, Mauritania, Morocco, Oman, Qatar, Saudi Arabia, Somalia, Sudan, Syria, Tunisia, United Arab Emirates, Yemen, Southern Yemen, and the PLO government. *Headquarters:* Tunis *Secretary-General:* Chedli Klibi (Tunisia) *Purpose:* To strengthen member ties and further promote Arab aspirations.

Recent Developments: The league convened on June 27, 1979 in Tunis in the first ministerial session without Egypt's participation since moving its headquarters from Cairo. All 20 members of the league have severed economic and political ties with Egypt because of the peace treaty signed with Israel.

Asian and Pacific Council (ASPAC) *Formed:* 1966 *Members:* Australia, Japan, New Zealand, Philippines, China (Taiwan), South Korea, and Thailand *Headquarters:* Bangkok, Thailand *Purpose:* To foster economic, social, and political cooperation among the non-Communist area countries. Meetings of foreign ministers of member states held annually until 1972. In 1973 it was decided to suspend future meetings. Only two regional projects sponsored by ASPAC remain functioning.

Association of Southeast Asian Nations (ASEAN) *Formed:* 1967 *Members:* Indonesia, Malaysia, the Philippines, Singapore and Thailand *Secretary-General:* Datuk Ali bin Abdullah *Purpose:* To promote economic progress and political stability in Southeast Asia; it seeks to lower trade tariffs for intraregional trade, encourage exchange programs and sharing of scientific knowledge.

Recent Developments: Meeting of foreign ministers in Kuta, Indonesia was held June 28-30, 1979. Vietnam was denounced for invasion of Cambodia and for causing unending exodus of Indo-Chinese refugees.

Bank for International Settlements (BIS) *Formed:* 1930 *Members:* Central banks of most European countries plus South Africa, United States, Australia, Japan and Canada. *Headquarters:* Basel *Manager:* Rene Larre (France) *Purpose:* To promote cooperation among central banks and provide facilities for international financial operations.

Benelux Economic Union *Formed:* 1958 *Members:* Belgium, Luxembourg, and the Netherlands *Headquarters:* Brussels *Purpose:* To achieve complete economic union of its members (as a subdivision of the EC).

Central American Common Market (CACM) *Formed:* 1960 *Members:* Costa Rica, El Salvador, Guatemala, and Nicaragua *Headquarters:* Guatemala City, Guatemala *Secretary-General:* Roberto Mayorga Cortes *Purpose:* To promote the economic integration of member nations.

Central Treaty Organization (CENTO) *Formed:* 1955 *Members:* Great Britain, Iran, and Turkey; *Associate Member:* the United States *Headquarters:* Ankara *Secretary-General:* Kamuran Gürün (Turkey) *Purpose:* A military alliance, successor to the Middle East Treaty Organization (1955 Baghdad Pact), CENTO also cooperates in regional improvements in economic, social, and technical fields.

Recent Developments: Iran announced Feb. 6, 1979 that it would withdraw from CENTO. On March 12 Pakistan withdrew from CENTO, leaving the largely symbolic alliance virtually defunct with only full-time members Turkey and Britain, with U.S. holding observer membership.

Colombo Plan for Co-operative Development in South and Southeast Asia *Formed:* 1950 *Members:* 27 countries *Headquarters:* Colombo, Sri Lanka *President:* Lal Jayewardene (Sri Lanka) *Purpose:* To aid developing countries through bilateral member agreements for the provision of capital, technical experts and training, and equipment.

Commonwealth, The (formerly British Commonwealth) *Formed:* 1931 *Members:* 41 *Headquarters:* London *Secretary-General:* Shridath Ramphal (Guyana) *Purpose:* A voluntary association of independent states and their dependencies who meet and consult of a regular basis to foster Commonwealth links and achieve a more equitable world society. All Commonwealth countries accept Queen Elizabeth II as the symbolic head of the association.

Recent Developments: Commonwealth heads of government meeting in Lusaka in August 1979 called for a cease-fire in Zimbabwe, and for a conference for a new constitution and elections supervised by Britain.

Council for Mutual Economic Assistance (COMECON) *Formed:* 1949 *Members:* Bulgaria, Cuba, Czechoslovakia, East Germany, Hungary, Mongolia, Poland, Romania, the Soviet Union and Vietnam; *Associate Member:* Yugoslavia *Headquarters:* Moscow *Secretary:* N.V. Faddeyev (Soviet Union) *Purpose:* To coordinate and integrate members' economies, under USSR leadership.

Recent Developments: Government leaders meeting June 29, 1979, agreed to proceed with intensive development of nuclear power to meet growing shortage of oil in COMECON countries.

Council of Europe *Formed:* 1949 *Members:* 21 countries *Headquarters:* Strasbourg, France *Secretary-General:* Franz Karasek (Austria) *Purpose:* To protect human rights, bring European countries closer together, and voice the views of the European public on the main political and economic questions of the day.

Recent Developments: During 1978 important conventions were adopted by the Council on extradition, on mutual assistance in criminal matters and fire arms controls. Liechtenstein was admitted as the 21st member of the Council on Nov. 23, 1978.

Eastern European Mutual Assistance Treaty (Warsaw Pact) *Formed:* 1955 *Members:* Bulgaria, Czechoslovakia, East Germany, Hungary, Poland, Romania, and the Soviet Union *Headquarters:* Moscow *Supreme Military Commander:* Marshal Viktor G. Kulikov (Soviet Union) *Purpose:* This major European military alliance is the Soviet bloc's equivalent of the North Atlantic Treaty Organization, and its forces, like NATO's, are composed of military elements from member countries.

Recent Developments: Romania refused to accept Soviet demands for an increase in defense spending at the Nov. 1978 meeting of the seven Warsaw Pact nations.

Economic Community of West African States (ECOWAS) *Formed:* 1975 *Members:* 16 countries *Headquarters:* Lagos, Nigeria *Executive Secretary:* Boubekar Diaby Ouattara (Ivory Coast) *Purpose:* To link English-speaking and French-speaking nations of West Africa in economic matters, to erase custom duties within the community, to improve trade and communications and eliminate disparities in development of member states.

European Atomic Energy Community (Euratom) *Formed:* 1958 *Members:* Belgium, France, West Germany, Italy, Luxembourg, the Netherlands, Denmark, Ireland, and Britain *Headquarters:* Brussels *Purpose:* To promote the common development of nuclear energy for peaceful purposes.

European Coal and Steel Community (ECSC) *Formed:* 1952 *Members:* Belgium, France, West Germany, Italy, Luxembourg, Britain, Ireland, Denmark and the Netherlands *Headquarters:* Luxembourg *Purposes:* To maintain a common market for coal, iron ore, and steel, and harmonize external tariffs; to abolish discriminatory pricing systems and transport rates among members, while safe-guarding continuity of employment.

European Community (EC) *Formed:* 1958 *Members:* Belgium, France, West Germany, Italy, Luxembourg, the Netherlands, Britain, Denmark, and Ireland. *Headquarters:* Brussels *President:* Roy Jenkins (Britain) *Purpose:* To abolish all internal tariffs and other trade barriers and to align external tariffs, so that there can be free movement of goods, persons, services, and capital within the EC.

Recent Developments: EC (also called the Common Market) has been a notable economic success. In 1973 EC was expanded from the original six members to include Denmark, Ireland and Britain. Greece will become a member Jan. 1, 1981 and Portugal has applied for membership. Association agreements have been signed with a number of Mediterranean countries and a full customs union with EFTA countries was achieved in 1977. On March 13, 1979 the European Monetary System linking EC's currencies went into effect. EC leaders agreed on June 22, 1979 at the Strasbourg meeting to hold the combined oil imports of the Common Market countries at their 1978 levels through 1985. The first direct elections to the European Parliament were held in June 1979. At the first session of the 410-member legislature, July 17, 1979, Simone Veil was chosen president.

European Free Trade Association (EFTA) *Formed:* 1960 *Members:* Austria, Iceland, Norway, Portugal, Sweden, and Switzerland; *Associate Member:* Finland *Headquarters:* Geneva *Secretary-General:* Charles Müller (Switzerland) *Purpose:* To maintain the elimination of internal tariffs on industrial goods (achieved at the end of 1966) and negotiate bilateral agreements on agricultural products.

Recent Developments: Once called the Outer Seven, EFTA has aimed at a lesser degree of economic integration than the European Community. A full customs union with the EC came into force July 1, 1977.

International Bureau of Weights and Measures *Formed:* 1875 *Members:* 45 countries *Headquarters:* Paris (Sevres) *Director:* Pierre Giacomo (France) *Purpose:* To ensure standardization of basic units of measure throughout the world.

International Committee of the Red Cross (ICRC) *Formed:* 1863 *Members:* 370 Swiss citizens *Headquarters:* Geneva *President:* Alexandre Hay (Switzerland) *Purpose:* To organize care for the victims of war and enforce the various Conventions on wartime practices. The ICRC constitutes, with the League of Red Cross Societies, the International Red Cross.

International Criminal Police Organization (Interpol) *Formed:* 1956 *Members:* Official police bodies in 122 countries *Headquarters:* Paris (St. Cloud) *Secretary-General:* Jean Nepote (France) *Purpose:* To ensure maximum cooperation between police authorities with the strict exclusion of political, military, religious, and racial matters. As successor to the International Criminal Police Commission, established in 1923, Interpol acts as a clearinghouse for information on international criminal activities.

Latin American Free Trade Association (LAFTA) *Formed:* 1960 *Members:* 11 Latin American countries *Headquarters:* Montevideo, Uruguay *Executive Secretary:* Daniel Mesa Bernal (Colombia) *Purpose:* To work toward the establishment of a Latin American common market.

Recent Developments: LAFTA has experienced difficulties in organizing an effective and significant diminution of international trade barriers.

Nordic Council *Formed:* 1953 *Members:* Denmark, Finland, Iceland, Norway, and Sweden *Headquarters:* Officially none; meetings are held at the various capitals. *Purpose:* To arrange cooperation among members in cultural, legal, social, and economic matters.

North Atlantic Treaty Organization (NATO) *Formed:* 1949 *Members:* Belgium, Canada, Denmark, France, West Germany, Great Britain, Greece, Iceland, Italy, Luxembourg, the Netherlands, Norway, Portugal, Turkey, and the United States *Headquarters:* Brussels *Secretary-General:* Dr. Joseph Luns (Netherlands) *Purpose:* This major Western military alliance, with prime responsibility for opposing Communist forces in Europe, is composed of elements from the armed forces of member nations.

Recent Developments: NATO members adopted long-term defense plans at summit meeting in Washington in 1978. The coordinated program calls for expenditure of $60 to $80 billion from 1979 to 1983. It sets goals for improvements in combat readiness, reinforcement capabilities, air defense systems, command communications, electronic warfare, joint supply operations, nuclear forces and joint weapon design and production. NATO defense ministers meeting in April 1979 urged that the alliance should modernize quickly its intermediate and short-range nuclear weapons in Europe. Presently there are no nuclear missiles capable of reaching the USSR stationed on Western European soil. Gen. Bernard Rogers (U.S.) replaced Gen. Alexander Haig as NATO supreme commander July 1, 1979.

Organization for Economic Cooperation and Development (OECD) *Formed:* 1961 *Members:* 24 countries, mostly in Western Europe, but also U.S., Australia, New Zealand and Japan *Headquarters:* Paris *Secretary-General:* Emile van Lennep (Netherlands) *Purpose:* To achieve economic growth and full employment and to further world economic development. As successor to the Organization for European Economic Cooperation (OEEC) that was established in 1948 to oversee Marshall Plan reconstruction, OECD has a broadened scope, having established an extensive aid program to developing countries.

Recent Developments: OECD approved $1.45 million aid package to Turkey, May 30, 1979, to shore up that country's ailing economy. At the Tokyo summit talks in June 1979 national leaders discussed the energy crisis. They agreed to set ceilings on oil imports through 1985.

Organization of African Unity (OAU) *Formed:* 1963 *Members:* All 49 independent African countries, except the white-dominated states and territories of the south *Headquarters:* Addis Ababa, Ethiopia *Secretary-General:* Edem Kodjo (Togo) *Purpose:* To promote African solidarity, coordinate policies, defend member sovereignty, and eliminate colonialism in Africa.

Recent Developments: At the annual summit of OAU nations held in Monrovia July 17-21, 1979, discord outweighed harmony. Arab nations walked out on Egyptian President Sadat's speech and open denunciations marked the debate on Tanzania's intervention in Uganda. And before passage of a resolution for a UN-supervised referendum on the future of Western Sahara, Morocco, followed by Senegal and Gabon, walked out.

Organization of American States (OAS) *Formed:* 1948 *Members:* 28 American countries *Headquarters:* Washington, D.C. *Secretary-General:* Alejandro Orfila (Argentina) *Purpose:* To promote the solidarity and defend the sovereignty of members and provide through the Pan American Union—the OAS central organ and secretariat—social, political, economic, and technical services.

Recent Developments: Dominica and St. Lucia became members of OAS in 1979. In meetings of the OAS in June 1979 to deal with the escalating war in Nicaragua, U.S. proposals for direct OAS actions were defeated. U.S. had urged that the government of Anastasio Somoza be replaced and that a OAS peace-keeping force be sent in.

Organization of Petroleum Exporting Countries (OPEC) *Formed:* 1960 *Members:* 13 oil-producing and exporting countries *Headquarters:* Vienna *Secretary-General:* Ali Muhammad Jaiddah (Qatar) *Purpose:* To coordinate policies and establish prices regarding petroleum exported to consumer nations.

Recent Developments: After raising the price of oil in December 1978 and again in March 1979, OPEC nations meeting in Geneva June 1979 agreed to a base oil charge of $18 a barrel. Members could charge a maximum of $23.15 a barrel (the spot price quickly reached $40 a barrel). With surcharges and other extras the increase represented a 60% rise in oil prices since Dec. 1978.

World Council of Churches (WCC) *Formed:* 1948 *Members:* 293 churches in 100 countries, including most major Protestant and Eastern Orthodox denominations *Headquarters:* Geneva *General Secretary:* Dr. Philip A. Potter (British West Indies) *Purpose:* To promote missionary work, facilitate common action by the churches, and maintain relations with other ecumenical organizations.

Recent Developments: During 1978, grants to black rebel groups in Africa came under increasing criticism and threatened WCC funding. On June 10, 1979, the central committee, WCC's decision-making body, voted to continue to support "anti-racism" programs that aided political movements in southern Africa.

U.S. CONTRIBUTIONS TO INTERNATIONAL ORGANIZATIONS

Source: U.S. Department of State

FISCAL YEAR 1978 (In Millions of Dollars)

Organization	Estimated Amount	Organization	Estimated Amount
United Nations and Specialized Agencies:		**Special Voluntary Programs:**	
United Nations	$118.03	Consultative Group on International	
Food and Agricultural Organization	26.71	Agricultural Research	21.40
International Atomic Energy Agency	12.72	Intergovernmental Committee for European	
International Civil Aviation Organizations	4.10	Migration	12.87
Joint Financing Program	3.11	International Atomic Energy Agency—	
International Telecommunications Union	2.21	Operational Program	4.40[3]
UNESCO	54.26[1]	Organization of American States Special	
World Health Organization	52.47[2]	Development Assistance Fund	6.10
World Meteorological Organization	2.54	Organization of American States Special	
Others	1.15	Multilateral Fund (Education and Science)	7.00
United Nations Peacekeeping Forces:		Organization of American States Special Projects	3.30
United Nations Emergency Force	47.40	Pan American Health Organization—	
United Nations Force in Cyprus	9.10	Special Voluntary Program	2.83
Inter-American Organizations:		United Nations Capital Development Fund	2.00
Organization of American States	48.05	United Nations Children Fund	25.00
Inter-American Institute of Agricultural Sciences	5.67	United Nations Decade for Women	3.00
Pan American Health Organization	20.72	United Nations Development Program	115.00
Inter-American Tropical Tuna Commission	1.60	United Nations Educational and	
Other	0.37	Training Program for South Africa	1.00
Regional Organizations:		United Nations Environment Fund	10.00
NATO Civilian Headquarters	11.54	UN/FAO World Food Program	88.90
Organization for Economic Cooperation and		United Nations Fund for Drug Abuse Control	3.00
Development	16.39	United Nations Fund for Population Activities	28.00
Others	1.14	United Nations High Commissioner for Refugees	10.71
Other International Organizations:		Special Resettlement and Relief Programs	30.60
Customs Cooperation Council	1.22	United Nations Relief and Works Agency	51.50
General Agreement on Tariffs and Trade	3.30	World Health Organization—Special Programs	3.59
Intergovernmental Committee for European Migration	3.20	World Meteorological Organization—	
International Institute for Cotton	1.35	Voluntary Assistance Program	2.00
Others	3.86	Others	4.48
		Total U.S. Contributions	**$888.89**

[1]$27.04 million appropriated in FY 1978 for FY 1977.
[2]Includes $7.28 million appropriated for prior year arrearages.
[3]Includes cash, commodities and services.

U.S. FOREIGN ECONOMIC ASSISTANCE

SOURCE: Program Data Services Division, Bureau for Program and Policy Coordination, Agency for International Development

The table below gives total U.S. foreign economic aid under the Foreign Assistance Act of 1961 and related precedent legislation—loans and grants—since 1946 and foreign aid data for fiscal year 1978.

The Agency for International Development (AID) has been the administering agency for foreign economic assistance under the Foreign Assistance Act since November 4, 1961. Agencies dealing with economic assistance programs prior to that date have been, successively: the Economic Cooperation Administration (Apr. 3, 1948–Oct. 31, 1951); the Mutual Security Agency (Nov. 1, 1951–July 31, 1953); the Foreign Operations Administration (Aug. 1, 1953–June 30, 1955); the International Cooperation Administration (July 1, 1955–Nov. 3, 1961); and the Development Loan Fund (Aug. 14, 1957–Nov. 3, 1961).

The latter two agencies operated concurrently for approximately four years until their functions were combined under the provisions of the Foreign Assistance Act of 1961.

Region and Country	Total 1946-1978 (Millions)	Fiscal Year 1978 (Millions)
GRAND TOTAL	$70,197.1	$4,086.4
Near East and South Asia	19,612.1	1,996.5
Afghanistan	337.9	5.0
Bahrain	1.2	—
Bangladesh	579.4	95.3
Cyprus	88.0	15.0
Egypt	2,765.6	750.7
Greece	1,126.3	—
India	3,849.1	60.0
Iran	600.2	—
Iraq	18.8	—
Israel	3,351.8	785.0
Jordan	1,058.9	93.0
Lebanon	97.5	20.9
Nepal	82.4	10.3
Pakistan	2,765.4	20.1
Saudi Arabia	27.4	—
Sri Lanka	96.4	23.0
Syria	352.8	90.1
Turkey	2,116.5	1.1
Yemen Arab Republic	68.2	6.8
Central Treaty Organization	55.8	0.6
Regional	172.5	19.6
Latin America	7,219.5	227.6
Argentina	137.3	—
Belize	1.0	—
Bolivia	569.4	34.3
Brazil	1,390.5	—
Chile	663.5	0.2
Colombia	919.7	—
Costa Rica	134.2	6.9
Cuba	2.8	—
Dominican Republic	353.5	1.3
Ecuador	169.9	0.8
El Salvador	109.9	8.0
Guatemala	266.3	4.5
Guyana	104.7	24.9
Haiti	141.1	8.9
Honduras	183.5	13.0
Jamaica	86.5	11.6
Mexico	77.6	—
Nicaragua	214.3	12.5
Panama	271.5	21.3
Paraguay	110.4	1.8
Peru	275.0	22.0
Suriname	4.0	—
Trinidad & Tobago	38.9	—
Uruguay	79.7	—
Venezuela	71.7	—
Regional Office for Central America & Panama	275.4	1.5
East Caribbean Regional	87.1	23.6
Regional	480.1	30.5
East Asia	14,888.6	149.8
Burma	60.0	—
Cambodia	549.7	—
China (Taiwan)	1,366.4	—
Indochina[a]	825.6	—
Indonesia	1,058.4	73.9
Japan	21.8	—
Korea	3,042.1	—
Laos	875.4	—
Malaysia	20.0	—
Philippines	677.8	52.8
Thailand	622.6	7.5
Vietnam	5,465.6	0.6
Western Samoa	*	—
Regional	303.2	15.0
Africa	3,886.4	$362.5
Algeria	3.8	—
Benin	7.6	—
Botswana	15.8	15.4

Region and Country	Total 1946-1978 (Millions)	Fiscal Year 1978 (Millions)
Burundi	$ 1.5	$ 0.1
Cameroon	40.2	12.1
Cape Verde	15.3	8.0
Central African Empire	7.0	0.6
Chad	31.7	11.2
Congo, People's Republic of	1.6	—
Djibouti, Democratic Republic of	0.1	0.1
Entente States	5.2	5.2
Ethiopia	266.4	5.2
Gabon	3.7	—
Gambia, The	2.8	1.3
Ghana	214.2	6.9
Guinea	47.7	1.8
Guinea-Bissau	3.8	1.3
Ivory Coast	13.7	0.1
Kenya	143.5	30.2
Lesotho	6.6	5.5
Liberia	210.1	5.3
Libya	137.3	—
Madagascar	9.8	—
Malawi	19.9	0.1
Mali, Republic of	55.0	10.1
Mauritania	14.3	6.0
Mauritius	0.5	0.1
Morocco	388.0	10.0
Mozambique	11.5	—
Niger	35.8	10.6
Nigeria	310.3	—
Rwanda	6.4	1.7
São Tomé and Príncipe	0.3	—
Senegal	38.7	8.7
Seychelles	0.1	—
Sierra Leone	15.8	3.0
Somali Republic	65.6	3.3
Sudan	93.2	7.6
Swaziland	13.4	12.8
Tanzania	96.6	17.2
Togo	8.5	1.3
Tunisia	366.5	20.1
Uganda	36.3	—
Upper Volta	32.0	11.4
Zaire	343.6	10.0
Zambia	40.7	30.0
Zimbabwe Rhodesia	7.0	—
Portuguese Territories	3.2	—
Central & West African Regional	146.6	9.7
East Africa Regional	34.4	0.4
Southern Africa Regional	146.8	38.8
Regional	366.0	39.3
Europe	15,822.7	352.2
Austria	726.1	—
Belgium-Luxembourg	560.0	—
Berlin	119.0	—
Denmark	280.8	—
France	3,190.3	—
Germany, Federal Republic	1,472.4	—
Iceland	60.2	—
Ireland	146.5	—
Italy	1,695.9	23.4
Malta	74.6	9.5
Netherlands	991.6	—
Norway	276.8	—
Poland	61.0	—
Portugal	486.2	300.0
Romania	12.3	12.3
Spain	602.6	7.0
Sweden	106.9	—
United Kingdom	3,834.9	—
Yugoslavia	573.9	—
Regional	550.7	—
British Oceania	0.5	0.5
Interregional	8,767.3	997.3

* Less than $50,000. — No economic assistance. [a] Prior to division into Vietnam, Cambodia, and Laos in 1955.

SELECTED FOREIGN EMBASSIES AND AMBASSADORS

SOURCE: Department of State Diplomatic List of January 1979

*Appointed Ambassador

Afghanistan: 2341 Wyoming Ave. NW, 20008
Chargé: A. Ghafar Farahi

Argentina: 1600 New Hampshire Ave. NW, 20009
Amb: Jorge A. Aja Espil

Australia: 1601 Massachusetts Ave. NW, 20036
Amb: Alan P. Renouf

Austria: 2343 Massachusetts Ave. NW 20008
Amb: Karl H. Schober

Bahamas: Suite 865, 600 New Hampshire Ave. NW, 20037
Amb: Livingston Basil Johnson

Bangladesh: 3421 Massachusetts Ave. NW, 20007
Amb: Tabarak Husain

Belgium: 3330 Garfield St. NW, 20008
Amb: Willy Van Cauwenberg

Benin: 2737 Cathedral Ave. NW, 20008
Amb: Thomas S. Boya

Bolivia: 3014 Massachusetts Ave. NW, 20008
Amb: Carlos Iturralde B.

Brazil: 3006 Massachusetts Ave. NW, 20008
Amb: João B. Pinheiro

Bulgaria: 2100 16th St. NW, 20009
Amb: Konstantin N. Grigorov

Canada: 1746 Massachusetts Ave. NW, 20036
Amb: Peter M. Towe

Chad: Suite 410, 2600 Virginia Ave. NW, 20037
Amb: Pierre Toura Gaba

Chile: 1732 Massachusetts Ave. NW, 20036
Amb: Jose Miguel Barros

China (P.R.C.): Liaison Off., 2300 Connecticut Ave. NW, 20008 Chief: Chai Zemin

Colombia: 2118 Leroy Pl. NW, 20008
Amb: Virgilio Barco

Costa Rica: 2112 S St. NW, 20008
Amb: Jose R. Echeverria

Cyprus: 2211 R St. NW, 20008
Amb: Nicos G. Dimitriou

Czechoslovakia: 3900 Linnean Ave. NW, 20008
Amb: Dr. Jaromír Johanes

Denmark: 3200 Whitehaven St. NW, 20008
Amb: Otto R. Borch

Dominican Republic: 1715 22nd St. NW, 20008
Amb: Francisco Augusto Lora

Ecuador: 2535 15th St. NW, 20009
Amb: Horacio Sevilla-Borja

Egypt: 2310 Decatur Pl. NW 20008
Amb: Dr. Ashraf A. Ghorbal

El Salvador: 2308 California St. NW, 20008
Amb: Roberto Quinonez Meza

Ethiopia: 2134 Kalorama Rd. NW, 20008
Chargé: Tibabu Bekele

Finland: 1900 24th St. NW, 20008
Amb: Jaakko Iloniemi

France: 2535 Belmont Rd. NW, 20008
Amb: Francois de Laboulaye

Germany (Federal Rep.): 4645 Reservoir Rd. NW, 20007
Amb: Berndt von Staden

German Democratic Rep.: 1717 Massachusetts Ave. NW, 20036
Amb: Dr. Horst Grunert

Ghana: 2460 16th St. NW, 20009
Amb: Dr. Alex Quaison-Sackey

Greece: 2221 Massachusetts Ave. NW, 20008
Amb: Menelas D. Alexandrakis

Guinea: 2112 Leroy Pl. NW, 20008
Amb: Ibrahima Camara

Guyana: 2490 Tracy Pl. NW, 20008
Amb: Laurence E. Mann

Honduras: Suite 408, 4301 Connecticut Ave. NW, 20008
Amb: Dr. Jose Antonio Bermudez-Milla

Hungary: 3910 Shoemaker St. NW, 20008
Amb: Ferenc Esztergalyos

India: 2107 Massachusetts Ave. NW, 20008
Amb: Nani A. Palkhivala

Indonesia: 2020 Massachusetts Ave. NW, 20036
Amb: D. Ashari

Iran: 3005 Massachusetts Ave. NW, 20008
Amb: vacant

Ireland: 2234 Massachusetts Ave. NW, 20008
Amb: Sean Donlon

Israel: 1621 22nd St. NW, 20008
Amb: Ephraim Evron

Italy: 1601 Fuller St. NW, 20009
Amb: Paolo Pansa Cedronio

Jamaica: 1666 Connecticut Ave. NW, 20009
Amb: Alfred A. Rattray

Japan: 2520 Massachusetts Ave. NW, 20008
Amb: Fumihiko Togo

Jordan: 2319 Wyoming Ave. NW, 20008
Amb: Abdullah Salah

Kenya: 2249 R St. NW, 20008
Amb: John P. Mbogua

Korea: 2370 Massachusetts Ave. NW, 20008
Amb: Yong Shik Kim

Laos: 2222 S St. NW, 20008
Chargé: Khamtan Ratanavong

Lebanon: 2560 28th St. NW, 20008
Amb: Khalil Itani

Liberia: 5201 16th St. NW, 20037
Amb: Francis A. Dennis

Lybia: 1118 22nd St. NW, 20011
Chargé: Ahmed Dia Addin Madfai

Luxembourg: 2200 Massachusetts Ave. NW, 20008
Amb: Adrien Meisch

Malawi: Bristol House, 1400 20th St. NW, 20036
Amb: Jacob T.X. Muwamba

Malaysia: 2401 Massachusetts Ave. NW, 20008
Amb: Zain Azraai

Malta: 2017 Connecticut Ave. NW, 20008
Chargé: Leslie N. Agius

Mexico: 2829 16th St. NW, 20009
Amb: Hugo B. Margain

Morocco: 1601 21st St. NW, 20009
Amb: Ali Bengelloun

Nepal: 2131 Leroy Pl. NW, 20008
Amb: Padma Bahadur Khatri

Netherlands: 4200 Linnean Ave. NW, 20008
Amb: Age R. Tammenoms Bakker

New Zealand: 37 Observatory Cir. NW, 20008
Amb: Merwyn Norrish

Nicaragua: 1627 New Hampshire Ave. NW, 20009
Amb: Vacant

Nigeria: 2201 M St. NW, 20037
Amb: Olujimi Jolaoso

Norway: 2720 34th St. NW, 20008
Amb: Soren Christian Sommerfelt

Pakistan: 2315 Massachusetts Ave. NW, 20008
Chargé: Hayat Mehdi

Panama: 2862 McGill Terr. NW, 20008
Chargé: Dr. Ricardo Bilonick

Paraguay: 2400 Massachusetts Ave. NW, 20008
Amb: Mario López Escobar

Peru: 1700 Massachusetts Ave. NW, 20036
Amb: Carlos Garcia-Bedoya

Philippines: 1617 Massachusetts Ave. NW, 20036
Amb: Eduardo Z. Romualdez

Poland: 2640 16th St. NW, 20009
Amb: Romauld Spasowski

Portugal: 2125 Kalorama Rd. NW, 20008
Amb: João Hall Themido

Romania: 1607 23rd St. NW, 20008
Amb: Nicolae Ionescu

Saudi Arabia: 1520 18th St. NW, 20036
Amb: Ali Abdallah Alireza

Senegal: 2112 Wyoming Ave. NW, 20008
Amb: André Coulbary

Singapore: 1824 R St. NW, 20009
Amb: Punch Coomaraswamy

South Africa: 3051 Massachusetts Ave. NW, 20008
Amb: Donald B. Sole

Spain: 2700 15th St. NW, 20009
Amb: José Llado

Sri Lanka: 2148 Wyoming Ave. NW, 20008
Amb: Dr. W.S. Karunaratne

Sudan: Suite 400, 600 New Hampshire Ave. NW, 20037
Amb: Omer Salih Eissa

Sweden: Suite 1200, 600 New Hampshire Ave. NW, 20037
Amb: Count Wilhelm Wachtmeister

Switzerland: 2900 Cathedral Ave. NW, 20008
Amb: Raymond Probst

Syria: 2215 Wyoming Ave. NW, 20008
Amb: Dr. Sabah Kabbani

Tanzania: 2139 R St. NW, 20008
Amb: Paul Bomani

Thailand: 2300 Kalorama Rd. NW, 20008
Amb: Klos Visessurakarn

Trinidad and Tobago: 1708 Massachusetts Ave. NW, 20036
Amb: Victor C. McIntyre

Tunisia: 2408 Massachusetts Ave. NW, 20008
Amb: Ali Hedda

Turkey: 1606 23rd St. NW, 20008
Amb: Melih Esenbel

Union of Soviet Socialist Republics: 1125 16th St. NW, 20036
Amb: Anatoliy F. Dobrynin

United Kingdom: 3100 Massachusetts Ave. NW, 20008
Amb: Sir Nicholas Hederson

Upper Volta: 5500 16th St. NW, 20011
Amb: Télesphore Yaguibou

Uruguay: 1918 F St. NW, 20006
Amb: José Pérez Caldas

Venezuela: 2445 Massachusetts Ave. NW, 20008
Amb: Dr. Ignacio Iribarren

Yugoslavia: 2410 California St. NW, 20008
Amb: Dimce Belovski

Zaire: 1800 New Hampshire Ave. NW, 20009
Amb: Kasongo Mutuale

Zambia: 2419 Massachusetts Ave. NW, 20008
Amb: Putteho M. Ngonda

ACTION

As of July 1, 1971, a number of federal volunteer service programs–the Peace Corps and its domestic equivalent, VISTA, most prominent among them–were merged into a single agency, called ACTION. It is headed by Sam Brown, former state treasurer of Colorado.

The components of the organization and their volunteer strengths as of December 31, 1978 are:

The Peace Corps, with 6,464 volunteers serving full-time in 64 developing countries. Its estimated fiscal year 1979 budget is $100 million.

Volunteers in Service to America (VISTA), with 4,290 volunteers at work full-time in programs throughout the United States. Its fiscal 1979 budget is $34 million.

The Retired Senior Volunteer Program (RSVP), which provides volunteer opportunities for elderly persons. It has 250,000 volunteers and a budget of $20.1 million.

Two other volunteer programs provide stipends to low-income senior citizens who devote 20 hours each week to in-stitutionalized children or to the homebound elderly. With an estimated FY 1979 budget of $34.9 million, ACTION supports 16,640 volunteers in the Foster Grandparent Program. Approximately 3,300 elderly men and women serve as Senior Companions, a program that has a FY 1979 budget of $7 million.

ACTION's other programs include the National Student Volunteer Program, which gives technical assistance aid to independent high school and college volunteer programs.

ACTION is also sponsoring a national demonstration project in Syracuse, N.Y., that is providing youths, ages 16 to 21, with stipended opportunities to participate in necessary community service projects. The Youth Community Service (YCS) volunteer program was developed as a model to test the concept of a national youth service. It is being funded with an $8 million discretionary grant from the Department of Labor's Youth Employment Program. The program got underway in spring 1978.

AMERICAN DIPLOMATS ABROAD

Source: U.S. Department of State   *Chargé d'Affaires.   **Ambassador-designate.

Country	Chief of Mission	Country	Chief of Mission	Country	Chief of Mission
Afghanistan	J. Bruce Amstutz*	Haiti	William B. Jones	São Tomé &	
Algeria	Ulric St. C. Haynes, Jr.	Honduras	Mari-Luci Jaramillo	Príncipe	Arthur T. Tienken
Argentina	Raul H. Castro	Hungary	Philip M. Kaiser	Saudi Arabia	John C. West
Australia	Philip H. Alston, Jr.	Iceland	Richard A. Ericson, Jr.	Senegal	Herman J. Cohen
Austria	Milton A. Wolf	India	Robert F. Goheen	Seychelles	Wilbert J. Le Melle
Bahamas	William B. Schwartz, Jr.	Indonesia	Edward E. Masters	Sierra Leone	John A. Linehan
Bahrain	Robert H. Pelletreau, Jr.	Iran	Walter Leon Cutler	Singapore	Richard F. Kneip
Bangladesh	David T. Schneider	Ireland	William V. Shannon	Solomon Isls.	Harvey J. Feldman
Barbados	Sally Angela Shelton	Israel	Samuel W. Lewis	Somalia	Donald K. Petterson
Belgium	Anne Cox Chambers	Italy	Richard N. Gardner	South Africa	William B. Edmundson
Benin	John S. Davidson*	Ivory Coast	Monteagle Stearns	Spain	Terence A. Todman
Bolivia	Paul H. Boeker	Jamaica	Loren E. Lawrence	Sri Lanka	W. Howard Wriggins
Botswana	Donald R. Norland	Japan	Michael J. Mansfield	Sudan	Donald C. Bergus
Brazil	Robert M. Sayre	Jordan	Nicholas A. Veliotes	Suriname	Nancy Ostrander
Bulgaria	Jack Perry*	Kenya	Wilbert J. Le Melle	Swaziland	Donald R. Norland
Burma	Maurice Darrow Bean	Korea	William H. Gleysteen, Jr.	Sweden	Rodney O. Kennedy-Minott
Burundi	Thomas J. Corcoran	Kuwait	Frank E. Maestrone	Switzerland	Marvin L. Warner
Cameroon	Mabel M. Smythe	Laos	George B. Roberts, Jr.*	Syria	Talcott W. Seelye
Canada	Thomas O. Enders	Lebanon	John G. Dean	Tanzania	James W. Spain
Cape Verde	Edward Marks	Lesotho	Donald R. Norland	Thailand	Morton I. Abramowitz
Central African		Liberia	Robert B. Smith	Togo	Marilyn P. Johnson
Empire	Goodwin Cooke	Libya	William L. Eagleton, Jr.*	Tonga	Anne C. Martindell
Chad	William G. Bradford	Luxembourg	James G. Lowenstein	Trinidad and	
Chile	George W. Landau	Madagascar	Robert S. Barrett*	Tobago	Irving G. Cheslaw**
China (People's		Malawi	Harold E. Horan	Tunisia	Stephen Warren Bosworth
Rep.)	Leonard Woodcock	Malaysia	Robert H. Miller	Turkey	Ronald I. Spiers
Colombia	Diego C. Asencio	Maldives	W. Howard Wriggins	Tuvalu	vacant
Comoros	Robert S. Barrett*	Mali	Patricia M. Byrne	Uganda	David Halstead*
Congo	William L. Swing	Malta	Joan M. Clark	U.S.S.R.	Thomas J. Watson, Jr.
Costa Rica	Marvin Weissman	Mauritania	E. Gregory Kryza	United Arab	
Cyprus	Galen L. Stone	Mauritius	Samuel R. Gammon	Emirates	Francois M. Dickman
Czechoslovakia	Francis J. Meehan	Mexico	Patrick J. Lucey	United Kingdom	Kingman Brewster, Jr.
Denmark	Warren D. Manshel	Morocco	Richard B. Parker	Upper Volta	Thomas D. Boyatt
Djibouti	Walter S. Clarke*	Mozambique	Willard A. De Pree	Uruguay	Lyle F. Lane**
Dominica	Sally Angela Shelton	Nauru	Philip H. Alston, Jr.	Venezuela	William H. Luers
Dominican Rep.	Robert L. Yost	Nepal	L. Douglas Heck	Western Samoa	Anne C. Martindell
Ecuador	Raymond E. Gonzalez	Netherlands	Geri M. Joseph	Yemen	George M. Lane
Egypt	Alfred L. Atherton, Jr.	New Zealand	Anne C. Martindell	Yugoslavia	Lawrence S. Eagleburger
El Salvador	Frank J. Devine	Nicaragua	Lawrence A. Pezzullo	Zaire	Allen C. Davis*
Ethiopia	Frederic L. Chapin	Niger	James K. Bishop	Zambia	Frank G. Wisner II
Fiji	John P. Condon	Nigeria	Donald B. Easum	Special Missions:	
Finland	Rozanne L. Ridgway	Norway	Louis A. Lerner	United Nations.	
France	Arthur A. Hartman	Oman	Marshall W. Wiley	U.N. (European	
Gabon	Arthur T. Tienken	Pakistan	Arthur W. Hummel, Jr.	Office)	
The Gambia	Herman J. Cohen	Panama	Ambler H. Moss, Jr.	U.N.E.S.C.O.	Esteban E. Torres
German Demo-		Papua New		O.A.S.	Gale W. McGee
cratic Rep.	David B. Bolen	Guinea	Harvey J. Feldman	N.A.T.O.	W. Tapley Bennett, Jr.
Germany, Fed.		Paraguay	Robert E. White	O.E.C.D.	Herbert Salzman
Rep. of	Walter J. Stoessel, Jr.	Peru	Harry W. Schlaudeman	I.A.E.A.	Gerard C. Smith
Ghana	Robert P. Smith	Philippines	Richard W. Murphy	European	
Greece	Robert J. McCloskey	Poland	William E. Schaufele, Jr.	Communities	Deane R. Hinton
Grenada	Sally Angela Shelton	Portugal	Richard J. Bloomfield	Ambassadors	
Guatemala	Frank V. Ortiz, Jr.	Qatar	Andrew Ivy Kilgore	at Large	Elliot L. Richardson, Gerard C.
Guinea	Oliver S. Crosby	Romania	O. Rudolph Aggrey		Smith, Henry D. Owen, W. Beverly
Guinea-Bissau	Edward Marks	Rwanda	T. Frank Crigler		Carter, Jr., Robert Krueger
Guyana	John Richard Burke	Saint Lucia	Sally Angela Shelton	Amer. Inst.	Charles Cross, Dir. (Taiwan)

BRITISH PRIME MINISTERS

Monarch and Prime Minister	Party	Served
George I, 1714–27		
Robert Walpole	Whig	1721–1727
George II, 1727–60		
Robert Walpole, Earl of Orford	Whig	1727–1742
Spencer Compton, Earl of Wilmington	Whig	1742–1743
Henry Pelham	Whig	1743–1754
Thomas Pelham-Holles,[1] Duke of Newcastle	Whig	1754–1756
William Cavendish, Duke of Devonshire	Whig	1756–1757
Thomas Pelham-Holles, Duke of Newcastle	Whig	1757–1760
George III, 1760–1820		
Thomas Pelham-Holles, Duke of Newcastle	Whig	1760–1762
John Stuart, Earl of Bute	Tory	1762–1763
George Grenville	Whig	1763–1765
Charles Watson-Wentworth, Marquis of Rockingham	Whig	1765–1766
William Pitt, Earl of Chatham	Coalition	1766–1767
Augustus Henry Fitzroy, Duke of Grafton	Whig	1767–1770
Frederick North, Lord North	Tory	1770–1782
Charles Watson-Wentworth, Marquis of Rockingham	Whig	1782
William Petty, Earl of Shelburne	Whig	1782–1783
William Henry Cavendish Bentinck, Duke of Portland	Coalition	1783
William Pitt (the Younger)	Tory	1783–1801
Henry Addington	Tory	1801–1804
William Pitt (the Younger)	Tory	1804–1806
William Wyndham Grenville,[2] Lord Grenville	Whig	1806–1807
William Henry Cavendish Bentinck, Duke of Portland	Tory	1807–1809
Spencer Perceval (assassinated)	Tory	1809–1812
Robert Banks Jenkinson, Earl of Liverpool	Tory	1812–1820
George IV, 1820–30		
Robert Banks Jenkinson, Earl of Liverpool	Tory	1820–1827
George Canning	Tory	1827
Frederick John Robinson, Viscount Goderich	Tory	1827–1828
Arthur Wellesley, Duke of Wellington	Tory	1828–1830
William IV, 1830–37		
Charles Grey, Earl Grey	Whig	1830–1834
William Lamb, Viscount Melbourne	Whig	1834
Sir Robert Peel	Tory	1834–1835
William Lamb, Viscount Melbourne	Whig	1835–1837
Victoria, 1837–1901		
William Lamb, Viscount Melbourne	Whig	1837–1841
Sir Robert Peel	Tory	1841–1846
John Russell,[3] Lord Russell	Whig	1846–1852
Edward George Geoffrey Smith Stanley, Earl of Derby	Tory	1852
George Hamilton Gordon, Earl of Aberdeen	Peelite[4]	1852–1855

Monarch and Prime Minister	Party	Served
Victoria, 1837–1901		
Henry John Temple, Viscount Palmerston	Liberal	1855–1858
Edward George Geoffrey Smith Stanley, Earl of Derby	Tory	1858–1859
Henry John Temple, Viscount Palmerston	Liberal	1859–1865
John Russell, Earl Russell	Liberal	1865–1866
Edward George Geoffrey Smith Stanley, Earl of Derby	Conservative	1866–1868
Benjamin Disraeli	Conservative	1868
William Ewart Gladstone	Liberal	1868–1874
Benjamin Disraeli, Earl of Beaconsfield	Conservative	1874–1880
William Ewart Gladstone	Liberal	1880–1885
Robert Arthur Talbot Gascoyne-Cecil, Marquis of Salisbury	Conservative	1885–1886
William Ewart Gladstone	Liberal	1886
Robert Arthur Talbot Gascoyne-Cecil, Marquis of Salisbury	Conservative	1886–1892
William Ewart Gladstone	Liberal	1892–1894
Archibald Philip Primrose, Earl of Rosebery	Liberal	1894–1895
Robert Arthur Talbot Gascoyne-Cecil, Marquis of Salisbury	Conservative	1895–1901
Edward VII, 1901–1910		
Robert Arthur Talbot Gascoyne-Cecil, Marquis of Salisbury	Conservative	1901–1902
Arthur James Balfour	Conservative	1902–1905
Sir Henry Campbell-Bannerman	Liberal	1905–1908
Herbert Henry Asquith	Liberal	1908–1910
George V, 1910–36		
Herbert Henry Asquith	Liberal	1910–1915
Herbert Henry Asquith	Coalition	1915–1916
David Lloyd George	Coalition	1916–1922
Andrew Bonar Law	Conservative	1922–1923
Stanley Baldwin	Conservative	1923–1924
James Ramsay MacDonald	Labour	1924
Stanley Baldwin	Conservative	1924–1929
James Ramsay MacDonald	Labour	1929–1931
James Ramsay MacDonald	Coalition	1931–1935
Stanley Baldwin	Coalition	1935–1936
Edward VIII, 1936 (abdicated)		
George VI, 1936–52		
Stanley Baldwin, Earl Baldwin of Bewdley	Coalition	1936–1937
(Arthur) Neville Chamberlain	Coalition	1937–1940
Winston Leonard Spencer Churchill	Coalition	1940–1945
Winston Leonard Spencer Churchill	Conservative	1945
Clement Richard Attlee	Labour	1945–1951
Winston Leonard Spencer Churchill	Conservative	1951–1952
Elizabeth II, 1952–		
Sir Winston Leonard Spencer Churchill	Conservative	1952–1955
Sir (Robert) Anthony Eden	Conservative	1955–1957
(Maurice) Harold Macmillan	Conservative	1957–1963
Sir Alec Douglas-Home	Conservative	1963–1964
(James) Harold Wilson	Labour	1964–1970
Edward Heath	Conservative	1970–1974
Harold Wilson	Labour	1974–1976
James Callaghan	Labour	1976–1979
Margaret Thatcher	Conservative	1979–

[1] Brother of Henry Pelham. [2] Son of George Grenville. [3] Lord Russell, later Earl Russell, sat in the House of Commons in his first ministry and in the House of Lords in his second. [4] On the sudden death of Sir Robert Peel in 1850, the Earl of Aberdeen became the leader of the Peelites, a coalition that supported the corn law and public reform policies of Sir Robert Peel.

THE COMMONWEALTH (September 1, 1979)

Formed in 1931, the Commonwealth is now a free association of 41 sovereign states and their dependencies.

State (date of entry)	Location	Administrative Center	Area (sq. mi.)	Population
UNITED KINGDOM*(12/31/31)	Europe	London	94,399	56,100,000
Brunei	Borneo	Bandar Seri Begawan	2,226	177,000
Dependencies				
Belize	Central America	Belmopan	8,867	145,000
Bermuda	Atlantic Ocean	Hamilton	21	57,000
British Antarctic Terr.	Antarctica	Stanley, Falkland Islands	600,000	uninhabited
British Indian Ocean Terr.	Indian Ocean	London, U.K.	29	1,400
British Virgin Islands	West Indies	Road Town	59	11,000
Cayman Islands	West Indies	George Town	100	14,000
Falkland Islands	Atlantic Ocean	Stanley	6,198	1,950
Gibraltar	Europe	Gibraltar	2.28	30,000
Hong Kong	Asia	Victoria	403	4,500,000
Montserrat	West Indies	Plymouth	40	13,000
New Hebrides†	Oceania	Vila	5,700	99,325
Pitcairn Islands	Oceania	Adamstown	18	74
St. Helena	Atlantic Ocean	Jamestown	162	6,400
Turks and Caicos Islands	West Indies	Cockburn Town (on Grand Turk)	166	6,000
West Indies Associated States				
Antigua	West Indies	St. John's	171	73,000
St. Christopher-Nevis-Anguilla	West Indies	Basseterre	155	71,500
St. Vincent	West Indies	Kingstown	150	100,000
AUSTRALIA (12/31/31)	Oceania	Canberra	2,967,909	14,248,500
Dependencies				
Ashmore & Cartier Islands	Indian Ocean	—	1.9	uninhabited
Australian Antarctic Terr.	Antarctica	—	2,362,875	uninhabited
Christmas Island	Indian Ocean	Flying Fish Cove	52	3,094
Cocos Islands	Indian Ocean	West Island	5.4	435
Coral Sea Islands	Oceania	—	8.5	3
Heard and McDonald Islands	Indian Ocean	—	113	uninhabited
Norfolk Island	Oceania	Kingston	13.3	1,913
NEW ZEALAND (12/31/31)	Oceania	Wellington	103,736	3,150,000
Dependencies				
Cook Islands	Oceania	Avarua	91	18,128
Niue	Oceania	Alofi	100	3,843
Ross Dependency	Antarctica	—	290,000	uninhabited
Tokelau Islands	Oceania	Fenuafala	3.95	1,625
BAHAMAS (7/10/73)	Atlantic Ocean	Nassau	5,382	235,000
BANGLADESH (4/18/72)	Asia	Dacca	55,126	84,700,000
BARBADOS (11/30/66)	West Indies	Bridgetown	166	265,000
BOTSWANA (9/30/66)	Africa	Gaborone	224,764	710,000
CANADA (12/31/31)	North America	Ottawa	3,851,809	23,597,600
CYPRUS (3/13/61)	Mediterranean	Nicosia	3,572	685,000
DOMINICA (11/3/78)	West Indies	Roseau	291	80,000
FIJI (10/10/70)	Oceania	Suva	7,055	610,000
GAMBIA (2/18/65)	Africa	Banjul	4,127	546,000
GHANA (3/6/57)	Africa	Accra	92,099	10,400,000
GRENADA (2/7/74)	West Indies	St. George's	133	100,000
GUYANA (5/26/66)	South America	Georgetown	83,000	820,000
INDIA (8/15/47)	Asia	New Delhi	1,269,339	635,000,000
JAMAICA (8/6/62)	West Indies	Kingston	4,244	2,200,000
KENYA (12/12/63)	Africa	Nairobi	224,960	14,200,000
KIRIBATI (7/12/79)	Oceania	Bairiki (on Tarawa)	354	50,000
LESOTHO (10/4/66)	Africa	Maseru	11,720	1,100,000
MALAWI (7/6/64)	Africa	Lilongwe	45,747	5,530,000
MALAYSIA (9/16/63)	Asia	Kuala Lumpur	128,308	12,600,000
MALTA (9/21/64)	Mediterranean	Valletta	122	330,000
MAURITIUS (3/12/68)	Indian Ocean	Port Louis	790	910,000
NAURU (1/31/68)‡	Oceania	Yaren district	7.7	7,100
NIGERIA (10/1/60)	Africa	Lagos	379,628	84,500,000
PAPUA NEW GUINEA (9/16/75)	Oceania	Port Moresby	183,540	2,910,000
SAINT LUCIA (2/22/79)	West Indies	Castries	238	111,800
SEYCHELLES (6/28/76)	Indian Ocean	Victoria	171	60,000
SIERRA LEONE (4/27/61)	Africa	Freetown	27,295	3,200,000
SINGAPORE (10/16/65)	Asia	Singapore	226	2,310,000
SOLOMON ISLANDS (7/7/78)	Oceania	Honiara	11,500	200,000
SRI LANKA (2/4/48)	Asia	Colombo	25,332	14,100,000
SWAZILAND (9/6/68)	Africa	Mbabane	6,705	500,000
TANZANIA (4/26/64)	Africa	Dar es Salaam	363,708	16,070,000
TONGA (6/4/70)	Oceania	Nuku'alofa	270	92,000
TRINIDAD AND TOBAGO (8/31/62)	West Indies	Port-of-Spain	1,980	1,175,000
TUVALU (10/1/78)‡	Oceania	Fongafale	9.78	10,000
UGANDA (10/9/62)	Africa	Kampala	91,076	12,350,000
WESTERN SAMOA (9/28/70)	South Pacific	Apia	1,133	151,800
ZAMBIA (10/24/64)	Africa	Lusaka	290,586	5,350,000

*As crown fiefdoms, the Isle of Man (227 sq. mi.; 62,000 pop.) and the Channel Islands (74 sq. mi.; 129,000 pop.) are included in the Commonwealth. ‡Secial member. †Anglo-French administration.

WORLD COMMUNIST PARTY STRENGTH

SOURCE: Richard F. Staar, (ed.), 1979 Yearbook on International Communist Affairs.
Hoover Institution Press, Stanford, CA 94305 © 1979

Country or Area	Communist Party Membership	Percent of vote; seats in legislature	Status	Sino-Soviet Dispute
Afghanistan	50,000	No elections scheduled	In power	Pro-Soviet
Albania	101,500	99.9 (1978); all 250 seats	In power	Independent
Algeria	500	— (1976)	Proscribed	Pro-Soviet
Argentina	70,000	No elections scheduled	Legal	Pro-Soviet
Australia	3,900	— (1977); no seats	Legal	Split
Austria	22,500	1.2 (1975); no seats	Legal	Pro-Soviet
Bangladesh	2,500	— (1973)	Proscribed	Split
Belgium	10,000	3.3 (1978); 4 of 212 seats	Legal	Pro-Soviet
Berlin, West	7,500	1.9 (1975); no seats	Legal	Pro-Soviet
Bolivia	500	— (1978)	Proscribed	Split
Brazil	6,000	— (1974); no seats	Proscribed	Split
Bulgaria	812,000	99.9 (1976); 272 of 400 seats	In power	Pro-Soviet
Burma	7,000	— (1974)	Proscribed	Pro-Chinese
Cambodia	10,000	100.0 (1976); all 250 seats	In power	Pro-Chinese
Canada	2,000	— (1974); no seats	Legal	Split
Chile	Unknown	Elections promised	Proscribed	Pro-Soviet
China	35,000,000	No elections	In power	—
Colombia	12,000	1.9 (1978); 3 of 311 seats	Legal	Pro-Soviet
Costa Rica	3,200	2.7 (1978); 2 of 57 seats	Legal	Pro-Soviet
Cuba	200,000	91.7 (1976); 441 of 481 seats	In power	Pro-Soviet
Cyprus	11,500	30.0 (1976); 9 of 35 Greek Cypriot seats	Legal	Pro-Soviet
Czechoslovakia	1,473,000	99.9 (1976); all 200 seats	In power	Pro-Soviet
Denmark	8,000	3.7 (1977); 7 of 179 seats	Legal	Pro-Soviet
Dominican Republic	5,000	— (1978)	Legal	Factions
Ecuador	1,000	5.1 (1978); no seats	Legal	Split
Egypt	500	— (1976); 3 of 350 seats	Proscribed	Pro-Soviet
El Salvador	225	— (1976); no seats	Proscribed	Pro-Soviet
Finland	48,000	19.0 (1975); 40 of 200 seats	Legal	Pro-Soviet
France	650,000	20.6 (1978); 86 of 491 seats	Legal	Pro-Soviet
Germany, East	2,077,262	99.9 (1976); 127 of 500 seats	In power	Pro-Soviet
Germany, West	46,400	0.3 (1976); no seats	Legal	Pro-Soviet
Greece	27,500	9.3 (1977); 11 of 300 seats	Legal	Split
Guadeloupe	3,000	— (1976); 7 of 36 seats	Legal	Pro-Soviet
Guatemala	740	— (1974); no seats	Proscribed	Pro-Soviet
Guyana	250	26.0 (1973); 14 of 53 seats	Legal	Pro-Soviet
Honduras	650	Elections scheduled 1979/80	Proscribed	Split
Hong Kong	2,000	—	Legal	Pro-Chinese
Hungary	770,000	99.6 (1975); all 352 seats	In power	Pro-Soviet
Iceland	3,000	22.9 (1978); 14 of 60 seats	Legal	Independent
India	210,000	7.1 (1977); 29 of 244 seats	Legal	Split
Indonesia	1,000	— (1971)	Proscribed	Split
Iran	1,500	— (1975)	Proscribed	Pro-Soviet
Iraq	2,000	No elections since 1958	Allowed	Pro-Soviet
Ireland	600	— (1977); no seats	Legal	Pro-Soviet
Israel	1,500	4.6 (1977); 5 of 120 seats	Legal	Pro-Soviet
Italy	1,800,000	34.4 (1976); 228 of 630 seats	Legal	Pro-Soviet
Jamaica	200	— (1976); no seats	Allowed	Pro-Soviet
Japan	350,000	10.4 (1976); 17 of 511 seats	Legal	Independent
Jordan	500	— (1967)	Proscribed	Pro-Soviet
Korea, North	1,800,000	100.0 (1977); all 579 seats	In power	Neutral
Laos	15,000	No elections scheduled	In power	Neutral
Lebanon	2,500	— (1972); no seats	Legal	Pro-Soviet
Luxembourg	600	9.0 (1974); 5 of 59 seats	Legal	Pro-Soviet
Malaysia	3,150	— (1978)	Proscribed	Pro-Chinese
Malta	100	— (1976); no seats	Legal	Pro-Soviet
Martinique	1,000	— (1976); 3 of 36 seats	Legal	Pro-Soviet
Mexico	100,000	— (1976); no seats	Legal	Pro-Soviet
Mongolia	67,000	99.9 (1973); all 336 seats	In power	Pro-Soviet
Morocco	700	— (1977); no seats	Allowed	Pro-Soviet
Nepal	6,500	— (1959)	Proscribed	Split
Netherlands	14,500	1.7 (1977); 2 of 150 seats	Legal	Pro-Soviet
New Zealand	500	0.2 (1978); no seats	Legal	Split
Nicaragua	160	— (1974)	Proscribed	Split
Norway	2,300	5.2 (1977); 2 of 155 seats	Legal	Independent
Pakistan	1,500	— (1977)	Proscribed	Pro-Soviet
Panama	500	— (1972); no seats	Allowed	Pro-Soviet
Paraguay	3,500	— (1973); no seats	Proscribed	Split
Peru	3,200	5.9 (1978); 6 of 100 seats	Legal	Split
Philippines	2,250	— (1978)	Proscribed	Split
Poland	2,758,000	99.4 (1976); 262 of 460 seats	In power	Pro-Soviet
Portugal	142,000	14.6 (1976); 40 of 263 seats	Legal	Pro-Soviet
Puerto Rico	125	— (1976); no seats	Legal	Pro-Soviet
Réunion	2,000	32.8 (1978); none in Paris	Legal	Independent

Country or Area	Communist Party Membership	Percent of vote; seats in legislature	Status	Sino-Soviet Dispute
Romania	2,747,000	99.9 (1975); all 349 seats	In power	Neutral
San Marino	300	21.1 (1978); 16 of 60 seats	Legal	Pro-Soviet
Senegal	2,000	0.32 (1978); no seats	Legal	Pro-Soviet
Singapore	500	— 1976)	Proscribed	Pro-Chinese
South Africa	Unknown	— (1977)	Proscribed	Pro-Soviet
Spain	270,000	9.2 (1977); 20 of 350 seats	Legal	Independent
Sri Lanka	6,000	1.9 (1977); no seats	Legal	Split
Sudan	3,500	— (1978); no parties	Proscribed	Pro-Soviet
Sweden	17,000	2.5 (1976); 17 of 349 seats	Legal	Split
Switzerland	5,000	2.5 (1975); 6 of 200 seats	Legal	Pro-Soviet
Syria	4,000	— (1977); 6 of 195 seats	Allowed	Pro-Soviet
Thailand	1,200	— (1976)	Proscribed	Pro-Chinese
Tunisia	100	— (1974)	Proscribed	Pro-Soviet
Turkey	2,000	— (1977)	Proscribed	Pro-Soviet
U.S.S.R.	16,300,000	99.9 (1974); all 1,517 seats CPSU-approved	In power	—
United Kingdom	25,900	0.5 (1974); no seats	Legal	Split
United States	18,000	0.2 (1976); no seats	Legal	Pro-Soviet
Uruguay	10,000	Elections scheduled 1980	Proscribed	Pro-Soviet
Venezuela	6,000	9.0 (1978); 22 of 195 seats	Legal	Factions
Vietnam	1,533,500	99.0 (1976); all 492 seats	In power	Pro-Soviet
Yugoslavia	1,629,082	— (1978); all 380 seats	In power	Independent

SOVIET LEADERS: 1979 Source: U.S. Department of State

Brezhnev, Leonid I.
General Secretary, Soviet Communist party; b. 1906

POLITBURO

FULL MEMBERS

Brezhnev, Leonid I.
Chairman of the Presidium of the Supreme Soviet (President of the Soviet Union)

Kosygin, Aleksei N.
Chairman of the Council of Ministers; b. 1904

Suslov, Mikhail A.
A secretary, Soviet Communist party (ideology, foreign affairs); b. 1902

Kirilenko, Andrei P.
A secretary, Soviet Communist party (party affairs, industry); b. 1906

Pelshe, Arvid Y.
Chairman, Party Control Commission; b. 1899

Grishin, Viktor V.
First Secretary, Moscow city party organization; b. 1914

Kunayev, Dinmukhamed A.
First Secretary, Kazakhstan Communist party; b. 1912

Shcherbitsky, Vladimir V.
First Secretary, Ukrainian Communist party; b. 1918

Andropov, Yuriy V.
KGB chief; b. 1914

Gromyko, Andrei A.
Minister of Foreign Affairs; b. 1909

Romanov, Grigory V.
First Secretary, Leningrad Oblast Party Committee; b. 1923

Ustinov, Dmitry F.
Minister of Defense; b. 1908

Chernenko, Konstantin U.
Head, General Department, Soviet Communist party Central Committee; b. 1911

CANDIDATE MEMBERS

Demichev, Pyotr N.
Minister of Culture; b. 1918

Masherov, Pyotr M.
First Secretary, Byelorussian Communist party; b. 1918

Solomentsev, Mikhail S.
Chairman of RSFSR Council of Ministers; b. 1913

Rashidov, Sharaf R.
First Secretary, Uzbek Communist party; b. 1917

Ponomaryov, Boris N.
A secretary (relations with non-ruling parties); b. 1905

Aliyev, Geidar A.
First Secretary, Azerbaidzhan Communist party; b. 1923

Kuznetsov, Vasily V.
First Deputy Chairman, Presidium of the U.S.S.R. Supreme Soviet; b. 1901

Shevardnadze, Eduard A.
Georgian Republic First Secretary; b. 1928

Tikhonov, Nikolai
First Deputy Premier; b. 1905

COMMUNIST PARTY SECRETARIAT

Brezhnev, Leonid I.; Suslov, Mikhail A.; Kirilenko, Andrei P.; Chernenko, Konstantin U.

Ponomaryov, B. N.
(candidate member of Politburo)

Dolgikh, Vladimir I.
A secretary (heavy industry); b. 1924

Rusakov, Konstantin V.
A secretary (relations with ruling Communist parties); b. 1909

Kapitonov, Ivan V.
Head, Organizational Party Work Department, Soviet Communist Party Central Committee; b. 1915

Zimyanin, Mikhail V.
A secretary (culture, propaganda); b. 1914

Gorbachev, Mikhail S.
A secretary (agriculture); b. 1931

RULERS OF CHINA: 1979 Source: Donald W. Klein, Department of Political Science, Tufts University

POLITBURO

FULL MEMBERS

Hua Guofeng (Chairman), b.c. 1920
Ye Jianying (Vice-Chairman), b. 1898
Deng Xiaoping (Vice-Chairman), b. 1904
L Xiannian (Vice-Chairman), b. 1907
Chen Yun (Vice-Chairman), b.c. 1900
Wang Dongxing (Vice-Chairman), b.c. 1910
Chen Xilian, b. 1918
Chen Yonggui, b.c. 1913

Deng Yingchao (Mrs. Zhou Enlai), b. 1903
Fang Yi, b. 1909
Geng Biao, b. 1909
Hu Yaobang, b.c. 1913
Ji Dengkui, b.c. 1930
Li Desheng, b. 1912
Liu Bocheng, b. 1892
Ni Zhifu
Nie Rongzhen, b. 1899
Peng Chong
Ulanhu, b. 1906
Wang Zhen, b. 1909
Wei Guoqing, b.c. 1914
Wu De, b.c. 1914
Xu Shiyou, b.c. 1906
Xu Xiangqian, b. 1902

Yu Qiuli, b.c. 1914
Zhang Ting-fa

STATE COUNCIL
(Premier and Vice-Premiers)

Hua Guofeng (Premier)
Bo Yibo
Chen Muhua
Chen Xilian
Chen Yonggui
Deng Xiaoping
Fang Yi
Geng Biao
Gu Mu
Ji Dengkui
Kang Shien

Li Xiannian
Wang Renzong
Wang Zhen
Xu Xiangqian
Yao Yilin
Yu Qiuli

MILITARY AFFAIRS COMMITTEE
(of the Chinese Communist Party)
(Chairman and Vice-Chairmen)

Hua Guofeng (Chairman)
Deng Xiaoping
Liu Bocheng
Nie Rongzhen
Xu Xiangqian
Ye Jianying

MILITARY AFFAIRS

U.S. WARS AND CASUALTIES
SOURCE: U.S. Department of Defense

Data prior to World War I are based, in many cases, on incomplete records. Casualty data are confined to dead and wounded personnel and therefore exclude personnel captured or missing in action who were subsequently returned to military control.

War	Branch of Service†	Number Serving	CASUALTIES Battle Deaths	Other Deaths	Not Mortal Wounds
Revolutionary War	Total	184,000–250,000	4,435	—	6,188
(1775–1783)	Army	(estimated)	4,044	—	6,004
	Navy	—	342	—	114
	Marines	—	49	—	70
War of 1812	Total	286,730	2,260	—	4,505
(1812–1815)	Army	—	1,950	—	4,000
	Navy	—	265	—	439
	Marines	—	45	—	66
Mexican War	Total	78,718	1,733	11,550	4,152
(1846–1848)	Army	—	1,721	—	4,102
	Navy	—	1	—	3
	Marines	—	11	—	47
Civil War	Total	2,213,363	140,414	224,097	281,881
(Union Forces only)*	Army	2,128,948	138,154	221,374	280,040
(1861–1865)	Navy } Marines }	84,415	2,112	2,411	1,710
			148	312	131
Spanish-American War	Total	306,760	385	2,061	1,662
(1898)	Army	280,564	369	2,061	1,594
	Navy	22,875	10	0	47
	Marines	3,321	6	0	21
World War I	Total	4,734,991	53,402	63,114	204,002
(6 April 1917–	Army	4,057,101	50,510	55,868	193,663
11 November 1918)	Navy	599,051	431	6,856	819
	Marines	78,839	2,461	390	9,520
World War II	Total	16,112,566	291,557	113,842	670,846
(7 December 1941–	Army	11,260,000	234,874	83,400	565,861
31 December 1946)††	Navy	4,183,466	36,950	25,664	37,778
	Marines	669,100	19,733	4,778	67,207
Korean War	Total	5,720,000	33,629	20,617	103,284
(25 June 1950–	Army	2,834,000	27,704	9,429	77,596
27 July 1953)	Navy	1,177,000	458	4,043	1,576
	Marines	424,000	4,267	1,261	23,744
	Air Force	1,285,000	1,200	5,884	368
Vietnam War	Total	3,300,000	47,072	10,390	303,706
(1961–7 May 1975)					

* Authoritative statistics for the Confederate Forces are not available. Estimates of the number who served range from 600,000 to 1,500,000. Based upon incomplete information, 133,821 Confederates died (74,524 in battle and 59,297 otherwise). In addition, an estimated 26,000–31,000 Confederate personnel died in Union prisons. † U.S. Coast Guard data are excluded. †† World War II hostilities declared terminated on December 31, 1946, by Presidential Proclamation.

U.S. VETERANS
SOURCE: Veterans Administration

Veterans in civil life, end of month—

Total, September 1978	29,984,000
War Veterans—Total	26,457,000
Vietnam Era—Total	8,734,000
And service in Korean Conflict	539,000
No service in Korean Conflict	8,195,000
Korean Conflict—Total (includes line 4)	5,897,000
And service in WW II	1,204,000
No service in WW II	4,693,000
World War II (includes line 7)	12,902,000
World War I	667,000
Spanish-American War	296
Service between Korean Conflict (Jan. 31, 1955) and Vietnam (Aug. 5, 1964)	3,068,000

U.S. DEFENSE EXPENDITURES
SOURCE: U.S. Office of Management and Budget

Fiscal Year	National defense[1] $ Billion	GNP $ Billion	Defense as % of GNP	Fiscal Year	National defense[1] $ Billion	GNP $ Billion	Defense as % of GNP
1960	45.2	497.3	9.1	1971	75.8	1,019.3	7.4
1961	46.6	508.3	9.2	1972	76.6	1,110.5	6.9
1962	50.4	546.9	9.2	1973	74.5	1,237.5	6.0
1963	51.5	576.3	8.9	1974	77.8	1,359.2	5.7
1964	52.7	616.2	8.6	1975	85.6	1,457.3	5.9
1965	48.6	657.1	7.4	1976	89.4	1,621.7	5.5
1966	55.9	721.1	7.8	TQ[2]	22.3	—	—
1967	69.1	774.4	8.9	1977	97.5	1,838.0	5.3
1968	79.4	829.9	9.6	1978	105.2	2,043.4	5.2
1969	79.4	903.7	8.8	1979 est[3]	114.5	2,289.4	5.0
1970	78.6	959.0	8.2	1980 est[3]	125.8	2,505.7	5.0

[1] Includes budget outlays for military activities of the Department of Defense, military assistance, atomic energy defense activities, and defense-related activities of civilian agencies. [2] See footnote 2, page 184. [3] Based on estimates in the 1980 Budget issued January 22, 1979.

NATIONAL GUARD 1978

Source: National Guard Bureau, U.S. Department of Defense

State or Area	Units*	Personnel*	State or Area	Units*	Personnel*	State or Area	Units*	Personnel*	State or Area	Units*	Personnel*
TOTAL	4,471	509,761	Idaho	40	3,780	Missouri	103	11,182	Puerto Rico	66	9,740
Alabama	203	21,248	Illinois	101	12,875	Montana	37	3,437	Rhode Island	38	4,243
Alaska	56	3,148	Indiana	111	26,149	Nebraska	45	5,403	South Carolina	108	11,816
Arizona	48	6,081	Iowa	91	9,568	Nevada	20	2,283	South Dakota	58	4,321
Arkansas	99	10,769	Kansas	93	8,780	New Hampshire	31	3,229	Tennessee	124	15,346
California	202	25,767	Kentucky	63	7,370	New Jersey	119	16,238	Texas	197	21,098
Colorado	45	4,713	Louisiana	104	10,224	New Mexico	43	4,230	Utah	53	6,065
Connecticut	58	7,291	Maine	36	4,224	New York	199	26,856	Vermont	38	3,526
Delaware	24	3,440	Maryland	68	8,567	North Carolina	139	12,704	Virginia	80	9,151
Dist. of Columbia	24	3,734	Massachusetts	121	14,972	North Dakota	37	3,613	Virgin Islands	22	835
Florida	85	9,898	Michigan	103	12,405	Ohio	148	19,220	Washington	69	8,009
Georgia	106	12,687	Minnesota	98	11,804	Oklahoma	111	10,836	West Virginia	45	4,964
Hawaii	49	5,742	Mississippi	136	13,395	Oregon	76	8,297	Wisconsin	101	12,151
						Pennsylvania	167	21,919	Wyoming	33	2,443

* Army National Guard and Air National Guard.

U.S. MILITARY PAY SCALES BY GRADE: PER MONTH (Oct.) 1978

Pay Grade	2 years or less	Over 2	Over 3	Over 4	Over 6	Over 8	Over 10	Over 12	Over 14	Over 16	Over 18	Over 20	Over 22	Over 26
Commissioned Officers														
O-10[1]	$3,298.20	$3,414.30	$3,414.30	$3,414.30	$3,414.30	$3,545.10	$3,545.10	$3,816.90	$3,816.90	$4,089.90*	$4,089.90*	$4,363.50*	$4,363.50*	$4,635.60*
O-9	2,923.20	3,000.00	3,063.60	3,063.60	3,063.60	3,141.90	3,141.90	3,272.10	3,272.10	3,545.10	3,545.10	3,816.90	3,816.90	4,089.90*
O-8	2,647.50	2,727.00	2,791.80	2,791.80	2,791.80	3,000.00	3,000.00	3,141.90	3,141.90	3,272.10	3,414.30	3,545.10	3,687.30	3,687.30
O-7	2,199.90	2,349.60	2,349.60	2,349.60	2,454.90	2,454.90	2,597.40	2,597.40	2,727.00	3,000.00	3,206.10	3,206.10	3,206.10	3,206.10
O-6	1,630.50	1,791.90	1,908.60	1,908.60	1,908.60	1,908.60	1,908.60	1,973.40	2,103.00	2,286.00	2,403.00	2,454.90	2,597.40	2,817.00
O-5	1,304.40	1,531.80	1,637.40	1,637.40	1,637.40	1,637.40	1,687.20	1,777.50	1,896.30	2,038.50	2,155.80	2,220.60	2,298.30	2,298.30
O-4	1,099.50	1,338.30	1,428.00	1,428.00	1,454.10	1,518.90	1,622.10	1,713.60	1,791.90	1,869.90	1,922.10	1,922.10	1,922.10	1,922.10
O-3	1,021.80	1,142.10	1,220.70	1,350.90	1,454.00	1,466.70	1,545.30	1,622.10	1,662.00	1,662.00	1,662.00	1,662.00	1,662.00	1,662.00
O-2	890.70	972.90	1,168.80	1,208.10	1,233.00	1,233.00	1,233.00	1,233.00	1,233.00	1,233.00	1,233.00	1,233.00	1,233.00	1,233.00
O-1	773.10	804.90	972.90	972.90	972.90	972.90	972.90	972.90	972.90	972.90	972.90	972.90	972.90	972.90
Commissioned Officers with over 4 years active service as enlisted members														
O-3	0.	0.	0.	1,350.90	1,415.40	1,466.70	1,545.40	1,622.10	1,687.20	1,687.20	1,687.20	1,687.20	1,687.20	1,687.20
O-2	0.	0.	0.	1,208.10	1,233.00	1,272.30	1,338.30	1,389.90	1,428.00	1,428.00	1,428.00	1,428.00	1,428.00	1,428.00
O-1	0.	0.	0.	972.90	1,039.20	1,077.60	1,116.60	1,155.60	1,208.10	1,208.10	1,208.10	1,208.10	1,208.10	1,208.10
Warrant Officers														
W-4	1,040.70	1,116.60	1,116.60	1,142.10	1,194.30	1,246.80	1,299.00	1,389.90	1,454.10	1,505.70	1,545.30	1,596.00	1,649.40	1,777.50
W-3	946.20	1,026.30	1,026.30	1,039.20	1,051.50	1,128.30	1,194.30	1,233.00	1,272.30	1,310.40	1,350.90	1,403.10	1,454.10	1,505.70
W-2	828.60	896.10	896.10	922.20	972.90	1,026.30	1,065.00	1,104.00	1,142.10	1,182.00	1,220.70	1,259.40	1,310.40	1,310.40
W-1	690.30	791.70	791.70	857.40	896.10	934.80	972.90	1,013.10	1,051.50	1,090.20	1,128.30	1,168.80	1,168.80	1,168.80
Enlisted Members														
E-9	0.	0.	0.	0.	0.	0.	1,182.30	1,209.30	1,236.90	1,265.40	1,293.30	1,318.50	1,388.10	1,522.80
E-8	0.	0.	0.	0.	0.	992.10	1,019.70	1,047.00	1,074.60	1,102.50	1,128.00	1,155.90	1,223.70	1,360.20
E-7	692.70	747.60	775.50	802.20	830.10	856.20	883.50	911.10	952.20	979.20	1,006.80	1,019.70	1,088.40	1,223.70
E-6	598.20	652.20	679.50	708.00	734.40	761.40	789.30	830.10	856.20	883.50	897.00	897.00	897.00	897.00
E-5	525.30	571.50	599.40	625.50	666.30	693.60	721.20	747.60	761.40	761.40	761.40	761.40	761.40	761.40
E-4	504.90	533.10	564.30	608.40	632.40	632.40	632.40	632.40	632.40	632.40	632.40	632.40	632.40	632.40
E-3	485.40	512.10	532.80	553.80	553.80	553.80	553.80	553.80	553.80	553.80	553.80	553.80	553.80	553.80
E-2	467.40	467.40	467.40	467.40	467.40	467.40	467.40	467.40	467.40	467.40	467.40	467.40	467.40	467.40
E-1	419.40	419.40	419.40	419.40	419.40	419.40	419.40	419.40	419.40	419.40	419.40	419.40	419.40	419.40

[1]While serving as Chairman of the Joint Chiefs of Staff, Chief of Staff of the Army, Chief of Naval Operations, Chief of Staff of the Air Force, or Commandant of the Marine Corps, basic pay for this grade is $5,114.70 regardless of cumulative years of service. [2]Does not apply to commissioned officers who have been credited with over 4 years' active service as enlisted members.

*Basic pay is limited to $3598.20 by Level V of the Executive Schedule. Highest Enlisted Rank, while serving as Sergeant Major of the Army, Master Chief Petty Officer of the Navy, Chief Master Sergeant of the Air Force, or Sergeant Major of the Marine Corps, basic pay for this grade is $1,851 regardless of cumulative years of service.

U.S. MILITARY PAY GRADES

SOURCE: U.S. Department of Defense

COMMISSIONED OFFICERS

Pay Grade	Army	Navy	Marines	Air Force
O–1	Second Lieutenant	Ensign	Second Lieutenant	Second Lieutenant
O–2	First Lieutenant	Lieutenant Junior Grade	First Lieutenant	First Lieutenant
O–3	Captain	Lieutenant	Captain	Captain
O–4	Major	Lieutenant Commander	Major	Major
O–5	Lieutenant Colonel	Commander	Lieutenant Colonel	Lieutenant Colonel
O–6	Colonel	Captain	Colonel	Colonel
O–7	Brigadier General	Rear Admiral (lower half)	Brigadier General	Brigadier General
O–8	Major General	Rear Admiral (upper half)	Major General	Major General
O–9	Lieutenant General	Vice Admiral	Lieutenant General	Lieutenant General
O–10	General	Admiral	General	General

WARRANT OFFICERS (All Services)

W–1	Warrant Officer	W–3	Chief Warrant Officer
W–2	Chief Warrant Officer	W–4	Chief Warrant Officer

ENLISTED PERSONNEL

Pay Grade	Army	Navy	Marines	Air Force
E–1	Private	Seaman Recruit	Private	Airman Basic
E–2	Private	Seaman Apprentice	Private First Class	Airman
E–3	Private First Class	Seaman	Lance Corporal	Airman First Class
E–4	Corporal Specialist 4	Petty Officer, Third Class	Corporal	Sergeant Senior Airman
E–5	Sergeant Specialist 5	Petty Officer, Second Class	Sergeant	Staff Sergeant
E–6	Staff Sergeant Specialist 6	Petty Officer, First Class	Staff Sergeant	Technical Sergeant
E–7	Sergeant First Class Specialist 7 Platoon Sergeant	Chief Petty Officer	Gunnery Sergeant	Master Sergeant
E–8	First Sergeant Master Sergeant	Senior Chief Petty Officer	First Sergeant Master Sergeant	Senior Master Sergeant
E–9	Command Sergeant Major Sergeant Major	Master Chief Petty Officer	Sergeant Major Master Gunnery Sergeant	Chief Master Sergeant

AMERICAN MILITARY CEMETERIES ON FOREIGN SOIL

SOURCE: The American Battle Monuments Commission

The American Battle Monuments Commission, an agency of the U. S. Government, is responsible to the people of the United States for the construction and permanent maintenance of military cemeteries and memorials on foreign soil, as well as for certain memorials on American soil. Monuments are located in Au-denarde, Belgium; Bellicourt, Aisne, France; Brest, Finistere, France; Cantigny, Somme, France; Chateau-Thierry, France; Gibraltar; Kemmel, Ypres, Belgium; Montfaucon, Meuse, France; Sommepy, Marne, France; Tours, France; Indre-et-Loire, France; and Pointe du Hoc, Calvados, France.

Cemetery	Location	Size (acres)	Burials Known	Burials Unknown	Missing Commemorated
Aisne-Marne	Belleau (Aisne), France	42.5	2,039	249	1,060
Ardennes	Neupre (Neuville-en-Condroz), Belgium	90	4,534	786	462
Brittany	St. James, France	28	4,313	97	497
Brookwood	Surrey, England	4.5	427	41	563
Cambridge	Cambridge, England	30.5	3,787	24	5,126
Epinal	Epinal, France	48	5,186	69	424
Flanders Field	Waregem, Belgium	6	347	21	43
Florence	Florence, Italy	70	4,189	213	1,409
Henri-Chapelle	Henri-Chapelle, Belgium	57	7,895	94	450
Lorraine	St. Avold, France	113.5	10,338	151	444
Luxembourg	Luxembourg City, Luxembourg	50.5	4,975	101	370
Manila	Fort Bonifacio, Philippines	152	13,462	3,744	36,279
Meuse-Argonne	Romagne, France	130.5	13,760	486	954
Netherlands	Margraten, Holland	65.5	8,195	106	1,722
Normandy	St. Laurent, France	172.5	9,079	307	1,557
North Africa	Carthage, Tunisia	27	2,601	240	3,724
Oise-Aisne	Fere-en-Tardenois, France	36.5	5,415	597	241
Rhone	Draguignan, France	12	799	62	293
St. Mihiel	Thiaucourt, France	40.5	4,036	117	284
Sicily-Rome	Nettuno, Italy	77	7,372	490	3,094
Somme	Bony, France	14	1,707	137	333
Suresnes	Seine, France	7.5	1,535	30	974

THE JOINT CHIEFS OF STAFF Source: Office of the Assistant Secretary of Defense

Chairman	From	To
Gen. Omar N. Bradley, USA	Aug. 16, 1949	Aug. 14, 1953
Adm. Arthur W. Radford, USN	Aug. 15, 1953	Ang. 14, 1957
Gen. Nathan F. Twining, USAF	Aug. 15, 1957	Sept. 30, 1960
Gen. Lyman L. Lemnitzer, USA	Oct. 1, 1960	Sept. 30, 1962
Gen. Maxwell D. Taylor, USA	Oct. 1, 1962	July 3, 1964
Gen. Earle G. Wheeler, USA	July 3, 1964	July 2, 1970
Adm. Thomas H. Moorer, USN	July 2, 1970	June 30, 1974
Gen. George S. Brown, USAF	July 1, 1974	June 30, 1978
Gen. David C. Jones, USAF	July 1, 1978	To Date

Chief of Naval Operations (Cont.)	From	To
Adm. William M. Fechteler	Aug. 16, 1951	Aug. 17, 1953
Adm. Robert B. Carney	Aug. 17, 1953	Aug. 16, 1955
Adm. Arleigh A. Burke	Aug. 17, 1955	Aug. 1, 1961
Adm. George W. Anderson	Aug. 1, 1961	July 31, 1963
Adm. David L. McDonald	Aug. 1, 1963	July 31, 1967
Adm. Thomas H. Moorer	Aug. 1, 1967	July 1, 1970
Adm. Elmo R. Zumwalt	July 1, 1970	June 30, 1974
Adm. James L. Holloway 3rd	July 1, 1974	June 30, 1978
Adm. Thomas C. Hayward	July 1, 1978	To Date

Chief of Staff, U.S. Army

Gen. of the Army

	From	To
Dwight D. Eisenhower	Nov. 19, 1945	Feb. 7, 1948
Gen. Omar N. Bradley	Feb. 17, 1948	Aug. 15, 1949
Gen. J. Lawton Collins	Aug. 16, 1949	Aug. 14, 1953
Gen. Matthew B. Ridgway	Aug. 15, 1953	June 30, 1955
Gen. Maxwell D. Taylor	June 30, 1955	June 30, 1959
Gen. Lyman L. Lemnitzer	July 1, 1959	Sept. 30, 1960
Gen. George H. Decker	Sept. 30, 1960	Sept. 30, 1962
Gen. Earle G. Wheeler	Oct. 1, 1962	July 3, 1964
Gen. Harold K. Johnson	July 3, 1964	July 3, 1968
Gen. William C. Westmoreland	July 3, 1968	July 1, 1972
Gen. Creighton W. Abrams	Oct. 16, 1972	Sept. 1974
Gen. Fred C. Weyand	Oct. 7, 1974	Oct. 1, 1976
Gen. Bernard W. Rogers	Oct. 1, 1976	July 1, 1979
Gen. Edward C. Meyer	July 1, 1979	To Date

Chief of Naval Operations

	From	To
Fleet Adm. Chester W. Nimitz	Dec. 5, 1945	Dec. 15, 1947
Adm. Louis E. Denfeld	Dec. 15, 1947	Nov. 2, 1949
Adm. Forrest P. Sherman	Nov. 2, 1949	July 22, 1951

Chief of Staff, U.S. Air Force

	From	To
Gen. Carl Spaatz	Sept. 26, 1947	April 29, 1948
Gen. Hoyt S. Vandenberg	April 30, 1948	June 29, 1953
Gen. Nathan F. Twining	June 30, 1953	June 30, 1957
Gen. Thomas D. White	July 1, 1957	June 30, 1961
Gen. Curtis E. LeMay	June 30, 1961	Jan. 31, 1965
Gen John P. McConnell	Feb. 1, 1965	Aug. 1, 1969
Gen. John D. Ryan	Aug. 1, 1969	July 31, 1973
Gen. George S. Brown	Aug. 1, 1973	June 30, 1974
Gen. David C. Jones	July 1, 1974	June 30, 1978
Gen. Lew Allen	July 1, 1978	To Date

Commandant, U.S. Marine Corps

	From	To
Gen. Lemuel C. Shepherd	Dec. 21, 1951	Dec. 31, 1955
Gen. Randolph McC. Pate	Jan. 1, 1956	Dec. 31, 1959
Gen. David M. Shoup	Jan. 1, 1960	Dec. 31, 1963
Gen. Wallace M. Greene, Jr.	Jan. 1, 1964	Dec. 31, 1967
Gen. Leonard F. Chapman, Jr.	Jan. 1, 1968	Dec. 31, 1971
Gen. Robert E. Cushman, Jr	Jan. 1, 1972	July 1, 1975
Gen. Louis H. Wilson	July 1, 1975	July 1, 1979
Gen. Robert H. Barrow	July 1, 1979	To Date

U.S. CASUALTIES IN VIETNAM Source: U. S. Department of Defense

47,072 U.S. military personnel were killed during the period 1961-1976 (June). Hospitalized wounded totaled 153,329. Casualties were highest during 1968, the year of the Tet offensive, with 14,589 killed and 46,796 wounded. Total casualties: 360,706.

TOTAL COST ESTIMATES OF AMERICAN WARS, BY RANK

Source: James L. Clayton, University of Utah. (Data in millions of dollars)

War	Original Incremental Cost[1] Constant dollars (1967)	Current dollars	Cost to Sept. 1, 1977	SERVICE-CONNECTED VETERANS' BENEFITS Total Cost Under Present Programs	INTEREST PAYMENTS ON WAR LOANS % of Original Incremental Costs	Total Cost to 1978	Estimated Current Cost (to 1978)
World War II	546,490	288,000	51,091	UKN	69	200,000	539,091
Vietnam Conflict	106,526	111,000	6,366	UKN	3	3,000	120,366
Korean Conflict	67,925	54,000	8,053	UKN	14	7,500	69,553
World War I	57,650	26,000	12,912	UKN	43	11,000	49,912
Civil War (Union Only)	6,957	3,200[4]	3,289	3,300	60	1,200	7,689
Spanish-American War	1,600	400	2,079	2,500	15	60	2,539
American Revolution	UKN	100	28	28	20	20	148
War of 1812	182	93	20	20	15	14	127
Mexican War	270	73	26	26	14	10	109

[1] Except for Korean and Vietnam conflicts, original incremental costs are outlays for national security during war years minus avg. annual outlay for preceding five years. Vietnam conflict estimate is from Dept. of Defense and represents incremental costs from 1965-77. Korean conflict estimate uses running avg. of national security outlays from 1948-1950 as a base, and then includes additional outlays over this base for 1951-52 and one-half increase for 1953 (because outlays for the Cold War increased at the same time outlays for Korean conflict declined). [2] For World War I and later wars, benefits are actual service-connected figures from 1976 Annual Report of the Veterans Admin. For earlier wars, service-connected veterans' benefits are estimated at 40% of total, the approximate ratio of service-connected to total benefits since World War I. [3] Interest costs use same formula as in footnote 1. Interest costs for wars since 1940 are rough approximations. [4] Data from Goldin and Lewis, "The Economic Cost of the American Civil War," Journal of Economic History, June 1975. Expenditures by Confederate Govt. are estimated by this study at $1.0 billion. UKN=Unknown.

VETERANS BENEFITS
Source: Veterans Administration

Benefits: In order to qualify for most benefits, veterans must have been separated from the Armed Forces under conditions other than dishonorable.

Compensation for Service-Connected Disability: Veterans disabled by injury or disease incurred or aggravated during active service in the line of duty are entitled to monthly payments ranging from $44, for a 10 percent disability, to $809 for total disability. Loss of, or loss of use of, certain limbs and organs entitles the disabled veteran to additional compensation, up to a maximum monthly payment of $2,308. Certain veterans who are at least 30 percent disabled are entitled to additional allowances for dependents.

Pension: Wartime veterans, including those of Mexican Border Service, World Wars I and II, the Korean conflict, and the Vietnam era who served 90 days or more, or—if less than 90 days—were discharged for a service-connected disability, and who are permanently and totally disabled for reasons not traceable to service, may be eligible for pension benefits. A veteran 65 years of age or older is considered totally and permanently disabled. Maximum pension payment is $295 a month for a single veteran, depending upon other income. Veterans with dependents may be entitled to higher amounts.

Medical Care: Complete care in VA hospitals, other federal hospitals, and in some cases, private hospitals is authorized under a priority system for otherwise qualified veterans who require treatment of service-connected disabilities, have compensable disabilities but require treatment of nonservice-connected disabilities, and/or have no service-connected disabilities but require medical treatment (subject to financial need and availability of facilities). Other benefits authorized when certain conditions are met include domiciliary care; outpatient medical and dental treatment in VA field stations or, in some cases, by approved private physicians; fitting and training with prosthetic appliances; medical examinations; aid for the blind; and vocational rehabilitation.

Educational Assistance—G.I. Bill: Veterans who served on active duty for more than 180 continuous days, any part of which occurred after Jan. 31, 1955, but before Jan. 1, 1977, and who (a) were released under conditions other than dishonorable, (b) were discharged for a service-connected disability or (c) continue on active duty are eligible for educational assistance for a period of 1.5 months for each month served, up to 45 months. The full 45-month entitlement is earned after 18 months' service.

War orphans and widows are eligible for similar education benefits, and education benefits are also available to wives and children of veterans who are permanently and totally disabled as the result of military service.

Educational institutions may include approved public and private secondary schools, junior or senior colleges, and vocational, scientific, or correspondence schools. Farm cooperative, on-the-job, and flight training are included. Eligibility ends ten years after release from active duty, but not later than Dec. 31, 1989.

Basic monthly payments to veterans enrolled in school courses: full time, no dependents, $311; one dependent, $370; two dependents, $422; and $26 for each additional.

A veteran who must complete elementary or high school training to qualify for higher education may receive this training without a charge against his basic entitlement.

Contributory Plan: Those who entered the service on or after Jan. 1, 1977, may participate by contributing $50 to $75 from their military pay, with a maximum contribution of $2,700. The VA then matches contributions at the rate of $2 for every $1 made by the participant. Payments from the fund may be received for school or training purposes for the number of months they contributed, or for 36 months, whichever is less.

Loans: The VA is authorized to guarantee loans to veterans. Eligible categories are veterans of World War II, Korean veterans, Vietnam veterans, servicemen on active duty, and surviving spouses of certain veterans who died from service-connected disabilities incurred during those periods of service. Loans may be for the purpose of purchasing or building a home; buying a mobile home; refinancing an existing home mortgage; purchasing a unit in a condominium; or buying a farm.

Wives of certain servicemen missing in action or captured in line of duty are eligible for one home loan guarantee. Loan guarantee benefits are available to all eligible veterans and servicemen until used.

The VA may guarantee the lender against loss of up to 60% to a maximum of $25,000 on all types of home loans except mobile home and/or lot loans, the amount of guaranty is 50% of the loan, not to exceed $17,500.

For home, farm residence or condominium loans, there are no maximums; however, there are maximums for mobile home and/or lot loans. Since these maximums vary with each transaction, veterans should consult with the VA for specific information before obligating themselves to purchase mobile homes and/or lots.

Veterans who used their entitlement before Oct. 1, 1978, may have additional entitlement available for GI home loan purposes. Veterans' maximum home loan entitlement was raised from $4,000 to $7,500 in 1950, to $12,500 in 1968 and to $17,500 in 1974. The amount of such additional entitlement is the difference between $25,000 and the amount used on prior home loans.

Insurance: Members of the uniformed services including Ready Reservists, Army and Air National Guards, ROTC members, Reservists eligible for assignment to Retired Reserves who have not received their first increment of retired pay or reached their 61st birthday, whichever is earlier; and the full-time duty cadet or midshipman at a service academy are eligible for Servicemen's Group Life Insurance. Maximum coverage is for $20,000 and premiums are deducted from service pay, except Retired Reservists, who must pay direct. Coverage continues for 120 days after discharge, within which period veterans can apply for automatic conversion of SGLI to a nonrenewable 5-year term policy under Veterans Group Life Insurance which may be converted at the end of the 5-year period to an individual policy with a commercial company. For a member totally disabled the 120-day period is extended to one year or to the end of total disability, whichever is earlier.

Dependency and Indemnity Compensation (DIC): Payments are authorized for widows, widowers, unmarried children under 18, helpless children, children between 18 and 23 who are attending an approved school, and certain parents of a serviceman or veteran who died on or after January 1, 1957, from a disease or injury incurred or aggravated in the line of duty while on active duty, active or inactive duty for training, or from a disability otherwise compensable under VA-administered laws.

Employment Preference and Reemployment Rights: Veterans are entitled to certain preference over nonveterans in obtaining federal civil service jobs, in referral to training programs and job openings by state employment offices, and in restoration to a former job in private employment or with the federal government. The Department of Labor has jurisdiction over veteran employment.

Burial: A payment of up to $300 is authorized for the person incurring burial expenses for a wartime veteran, or for a peacetime veteran who was receiving compensation or was discharged or retired for disability incurred in the line of duty. Up to $1,100 will be payable when death is due to service-connected causes.

Burial is allowed in a national cemetery (except Arlington, Va.) for veterans whose last period of service terminated honorably, and for reservists who die while performing active-duty training. The benefit applies to the deceased person's spouse, minor children, and certain unmarried adult children. Effective August 1, 1973, an interment allowance not exceeding $150, in addition to the $300 basic burial allowance, is payable when burial is in other than a national cemetery.

U.S. MILITARY AID: PROGRAM DELIVERIES: FISCAL YEARS 1950–1978

SOURCE: Office of the Assistant Secretary of Defense (figures in thousands of dollars)

	1950-78		1950-78		1950-78
Worldwide	40,971,341	Honduras	8,242	Oman	1,827
Argentina	156,198	Iceland	535	Pakistan	215,475
Australia	1,213,393	India	68,255	Panama	4,530
Austria	94,063	Indochina	8,542	Paraguay	695
Bahrain	100	Indonesia	52,186	Peru	124,554
Belgium	183,548	Iran	8,715,810	Philippines	105,927
Bolivia	1,909	Iraq	13,152	Portugal	13,694
Brazil	249,886	Ireland	579	Saudi Arabia	6,175,742
Brunei	10	Israel	5,348,530	Senegal	5
Burma	3,547	Italy	689,393	Singapore	50,501
Canada	1,273,837	Jamaica	155	South Africa	3,149
Chile	166,943	Japan	443,113	Spain	599,218
China (Taiwan)	823,992	Jordan	490,156	Sri Lanka	4
Colombia	24,404	Kenya	51,438	Sudan	47,376
Costa Rica	1,176	Korea	846,268	Suriname	1
Cuba	4,510	Kuwait	373,085	Sweden	67,042
Denmark	171,392	Lebanon	21,287	Switzerland	244,334
Dominican Republic	2,150	Liberia	3,373	Syria	1
Ecuador	26,678	Libya	29,594	Thailand	185,783
Egypt	61,684	Luxembourg	2,780	Trinidad/Tobago	85
El Salvador	3,100	Malaysia	57,086	Tunisia	8,762
Ethiopia	90,268	Mali	154	Turkey	422,530
Fiji	63	Mexico	18,411	United Arab Emirates	2,452
Finland	17	Morocco	175,042	United Kingdom	1,944,673
France	366,353	Nepal	72	Uruguay	16,856
Gabon	145	Netherlands	281,876	Venezuela	225,975
Germany	5,779,056	New Zealand	120,569	Vietnam	1,167
Ghana	342	Nicaragua	5,285	Yemen	54,708
Greece	1,072,784	Niger	8	Yugoslavia	13,606
Guatemala	24,530	Nigeria	17,550	Zaire	42,969
Haiti	992	Norway	318,338	International Organizations	439,767

NUCLEAR ARMAMENTS: UNITED STATES AND SOVIET UNION

SOURCE: International Institute for Strategic Studies, London

United States

	Type[a]	Max. range (miles)[b]	Estimated Warhead yield[c]	Number deployed July 79
LAND-BASED MISSILES				
ICBM	Titan II	7,000	5-10 MT	54
	Minuteman II	7,000	1-2 MT	450
	Minuteman III	7,500	3×170 KT	550
SRBM	Pershing	450	KT-range	108[g]
	Lance	70	KT range	36[g]
SEA-LAUNCHED MISSILES				
SLBM	Polaris A3	2,880	3×200 KT	160
	Poseidon C3	2,880	10×50 KT	496
AIR-LAUNCHED MISSILES				
ALCM	Hound Dog	600	KT range	400[h]
ALBM	SRAM	150	KT range	1,020

Soviet Union

	Type[a][d]	Max. range (miles)[b]	Estimated Warhead yield[c]	Number deployed July 79
LAND-BASED MISSILES				
ICBM	SS-9 Scarp	7,500	18-25 MT[e]	100
	SS-11 Sego	6,500	1-2 MT[e]	638
	SS-13 Savage	5,000	1 MT	60
	SS-17	6,500	5 MT[e]	100
	SS-18	6,300+	18-25 MT[e]	200
	SS-19	6,300+	5 MT[e]	300
M/IRBM	SS-4 Sandal	1,200	1 MT	500
	SS-5 Skean	2,300	1 MT	90
	SS-20	3-4,000	3×150 KT	120
SRBM	SS-1b Scud A	50	KT range	
	FROG 7	10-45	KT range	
	SS-1c Scud B	185	KT range	1300
	SS-12 Scaleboard	500	MT range	
	SS-21	65	f	
LRCM	SS-N-3 Shaddock	450	KT range	100[h]
SEA-LAUNCHED MISSILES				
SLBM	SS-N-4 Sark	350	1-2 MT	18
	SS-N-5 Serb	750	1-2 MT	60
	SS-N-6 Sawfly	1,750+	1-2 MT[e]	528
	SS-N-8	4,800	1-2 MT	266
	SS-NX-17	3,000+	1 MT[e]	12
	SS-N-18	5,000+	3×1-2 MT	144
SLCM	SS-N-3 Shaddock	450	KT range	324
AIR-LAUNCHED MISSILES				
ALCM	AS-3 Kangaroo	400	MT range	f
	AS-4 Kitchen	450	KT range	800[h]
	AS-6 Kingfish	160	KT range	f

HISTORICAL CHANGES FOR STRENGTH, 1969-1979 (MID-YEARS)

		1969	1970	1971	1972	1973	1974	1975	1976	1977	1978	1979
USA	ICBM	1,054	1,054	1,054	1,054	1,054	1,054	1,054	1,054	1,054	1,054	1,054
	SLBM	656	656	656	656	656	656	656	656	656	656	656
	Long-range bombers	560	550	505	455	442	437	432	387	373	432	431
USSR	ICBM	1,050	1,300	1,510[1]	1,527[1]	1,527[1]	1,575	1,618	1,527	1,477	1,400	1,398
	SLBM	160	280	440	560	628	720	784	845	909	1,015	1,028
	Long-range bombers	150	150	140	140	140	140	135	135	135	135	156

[a] ICBM = inter-continental ballistic missile (range over 4,000 miles); M/IRBM = medium/intermediate-range ballistic missile (500–4,000 miles); SRBM = short-range ballistic missile (under 500 miles); LRCM = long-range cruise missile (over 350 miles); SLBM = submarine-launched ballistic missile; SLCM = submarine-launched cruise missile; ALCM = air-launched cruise missile; ALBM = air-launched ballistic missile. [b] Operational range depends upon payload carried; figures are given in statute miles. [c] MT = megaton = millions tons of TNT equivalent (MT range = 1 MT or over); KT = kiloton = thousands tons of TNT equivalent (KT range = less than 1 MT); 3×, 10× = 3 warheads, 10 warheads. [d] Numerical designation of Soviet missiles are of U.S. origin; names are of NATO origin. [e] Also exists in multiple warhead mode with lesser yield per warhead. [f] Information not available. [g] Figures for systems in Europe only. [h] Estimate.

WARPLANES: UNITED STATES AND THE SOVIET UNION

AIRCRAFT	Type	United States Max. range (statute miles)	Max. speed (Mach no.)	Max. weapons load (lb.)	Number deployed (July 1979)	Type	Soviet Union Max. range (statute miles)	Max. speed (Mach no.)	Max. weapons load (lb.)	Number deployed (July 1979)
Long-range bombers	B-52 D	10,000	0.95	60,000	} 365	Tu-95 Bear	8,000	0.78	40,000	113
	B-52 G/H	12,500	0.95	70,000		Mya-4 Bison	7,000	0.87	20,000	43
Medium-range bombers	FB-111A	6,000	2.5	37,500	66	Tu-22M Backfire	5,500	2.5	20,000	80
						Tu-16 Badger	4,000	0.8	17,500	613
Strike-aircraft (incl. short-range bombers): land-based	F-4 C/D/E	1,400	2.4	16,000	} 390	Il-28 Beagle	2,500	0.81	4,850	} 3,500
	F-111 A/E	2,925	2.2/2.5	25,000		Su-7 Fitter A	900	1.7	4,500	
						Tu-22 Blinder	1,400	1.5	12,000	
						MiG-21 MF Fishbed J	1,150	2.2	2,000	
						MiG-27 Flogger D	1,800	2.5	2,880	
Strike aircraft carrier-based	F-4 J/N	1,400	2.2	16,000	} 100	Su-19A Fencer	1,800	2.3	8,000	
	A-6 E	2,000	0.9	18,000		Su-17/-20 Ftter C	1,100	1.6	5,000	
	A-7 E	2,800	0.9	20,000						

WARPLANES: NATO AND WARSAW PACT COUNTRIES

Aircraft[a]	Type[c]	NATO Operated by[d]	Max. range[e] (statute miles)	Max. speed (Mach no.)[f]	Max. weapons load (lb)	No. deployed (July 1979)	Type[g]	Warsaw Pact Operated by[d]	Max. range[e] (statute miles)	Max. speed (Mach no.)[f]	Max. weapons load (lb)	No. deployed (July 1979)
Medium-range bombers	Vulcan B2	BR	4,000	0.95	21,000	48						
Strike aircraft (incl short-range bombers)	F-104	h	1,500	2.2	4,000	n.a.[j]						
	F-4	{ BR GE }	1,400	2.4	16,000	n.a.[j]	Su-7 Fitter[i]	CZ	900	1.7	5,500	115
	Buccaneer S2	BR	2,300	0.95	8,000	50						
	Mirage IVA	FR	2,000	2.2	8,000	33	Su-20 Fitter[i]	PO	1,100	1.6	4,000	35
	Jaguar	{ BR FR }	1,000	1.1	8,000	(177)						

[a] All aircraft listed are dual-capable and many would be more likely to carry conventional than nuclear weapons. [b] Medium-range bomber = maximum range 3,500–6,000 miles, primarily designed for bombing missions. [c] Vulcan and Buccaneer are of British origin; F-104 and F-4 are of American origin; Mirage is of French origin; Jaguar is Anglo-French. [d] BR = Britain, FR = France, CZ = Czechoslovakia, HU = Hungary, PO = Poland, RU = Rumania, GE = West Germany. [e] Theoretical maximum range, with internal fuel only, at optimum altitude and speed. Ranges for strike aircraft assume no weapons load. Especially in the case of strike aircraft, therefore, range falls sharply for flights at lower altitude, at higher speed or with full weapons load (e.g. combat radius of F-104, at operational height and speed, with typical weapons load, is approximately 420 miles). [f] Mach 1 (M = 1.0) = speed of sound. [g] Warsaw Pact aircraft of Soviet origin; names (e.g. Beagle) of NATO origin. [h] The dual-capable F-104 is operated by Belgium, Canada, Denmark, West Germany, Greece, Italy, the Netherlands, Norway and Turkey, but the Canadian aircraft no longer have a nuclear role. The warheads for all of these aircraft are held in American custody. [i] Nuclear warheads for these dual-capable aircraft are held in Soviet custody. [j] The absence of figures here reflects the uncertainty as to how many of these nuclear-capable aircraft actually have a nuclear role. [k] A number of strike aircraft, such as the A-4 and Mirage III, may also be capable of carrying tactical weapons.

ACTIVE U.S. MILITARY FORCES

SOURCE: U.S. Office of Management and Budget

Description	Actual Sept. 30 1978	Estimated Sept. 30 1979	Estimated Sept. 30 1980
Military personnel (in thousands):			
End strength:			
Army	771	774	774
Navy	530	523	528
Marine Corps	191	190	189
Air Force	569	563	559
Total, Department of Defense	2,061	2,050	2,050
Average strength:			
Army	771	762	772
Navy	526	526	526
Marine Corps	191	188	189
Air Force	572	567	562
Total, Department of Defense	2,060	2,043	2,049
General purpose forces:			
Land forces:			
Army divisions	16	16	16
Marine Corps divisions	3	3	3
Tactical air forces:			
Air Force wings	26	26	26
Navy attack wings	12	12	12
Marine Corps wings	3	3	3
Naval forces:			
Attack and multipurpose carriers	13	13	13
Nuclear attack submarines	70	72	75
Other warships	166	170	181
Amphibious assault ships	64	65	63

BLACKS IN U.S. ARMED FORCES

SOURCE: U.S. Department of Defense (As of September 30, 1978)

	Officers	Enlisted	TOTAL
ARMY	6,222 (6.4%)	195,442 (29.2%)	201,664 (26.3%)
NAVY	1,371 (2.2%)	43,437 (9.4%)	44,808 (8.5%)
AIR FORCE	3,462 (3.6%)	70,027 (14.9%)	73,489 (13.0%)
MARINE CORPS	679 (3.7%)	32,842 (19.0%)	33,521 (17.6%)
TOTAL	11,734 (4.3%)	341,748 (19.3%)	353,482 (17.3%)

THE MILITARY-INDUSTRIAL COMPLEX SOURCE: Department of Defense

Companies doing more than $130,000,000 worth of business with the Department of Defense during the 1978 fiscal year, in thousands of dollars.

Rank	Company Name	1978 Contracts	% of Total	Rank	Company Name	1978 Contracts	% of Total
1.	General Dynamics Corp.	$4,153,547	6.97	32.	Amerada Hess Corp.	$325,195	0.55
2.	McDonnell Douglas Corp.	2,863,294	4.81	33.	Exxon Corp.	310,859	0.52
3.	United Technologies Corp.	2,399,789	4.03	34.	Congoleum Corp.	282,275	0.47
4.	Lockheed Corp.	2,226,431	3.74	35.	Singer Co.	281,744	0.47
5.	General Electric Co.	1,786,448	3.00	36.	Teledyne Inc.	272,281	0.46
6.	Litton Industries, Inc.	1,557,134	2.61	37.	International Tel. & Tel. Corp.	268,721	0.45
7.	Boeing Co.	1,524,454	2.56	38.	Standard Oil Co. of Calif.	243,866	0.41
8.	Hughes Aircraft Co.	1,488,558	2.50	39.	American Motors Corp.	222,602	0.37
9.	Raytheon Co.	1,306,783	2.19	40.	Bendix Corp.	220,048	0.37
10.	Grumman Corp.	1,180,032	1.98	41.	General Tire & Rubber Co.	213,341	0.36
11.	Rockwell International Corp.	890,204	1.49	42.	British Petroleum Co. Ltd.	211,054	0.35
12.	Textron Inc.	867,517	1.46	43.	Engelhard Minerals &		
13.	Chrysler Corp.	742,489	1.25		Chemicals Corp.	210,369	0.35
14.	Sperry Rand Corp.	612,020	1.03	44.	Harsco Corp.	206,320	0.35
15.	Northrop Corp.	586,049	0.98	45.	Petroleos Mexicanos	199,785	0.34
16.	RCA Corp.	565,214	0.95	46.	General Tel. & Elec. Corp.	194,516	0.33
17.	Honeywell Inc.	544,703	0.91	47.	Royal Dutch Shell Group	170,677	0.29
18.	Westinghouse Electric Corp.	539,187	0.90	48.	Mobil Corp.	168,471	0.28
19.	Martin Marietta Corp.	539,181	0.90	49.	Ret Ser Engineering Co.	167,791	0.28
20.	Fairchild Industries, Inc.	507,866	0.85	50.	Ogden Corp.	166,891	0.28
21.	American Tel. & Tel. Co.	456,634	0.77	51.	Goodyear Tire & Rubber Co.	164,560	0.28
22.	Texas Instruments Inc.	434,408	0.73	52.	Signal Companies Inc. (The)	155,527	0.26
23.	Reynolds (RJ) Industries, Inc.	421,442	0.71	53.	Coastal Corp.	154,374	0.26
24.	General Motors Corp.	419,530	0.70	54.	Hercules, Inc.	153,452	0.26
25.	Tenneco Inc.	406,971	0.68	55.	Gould, Inc.	150,779	0.25
26.	Ford Motor Co.	406,229	0.68	56.	AGIP SPA	148,653	0.25
27.	International Business			57.	North American Philips Corp.	147,293	0.25
	Machines Co.	396,443	0.67	58.	E Systems, Inc.	142,312	0.24
28.	LTV Corp.	384,439	0.65	59.	Guam Oil & Refining Co. Inc.	140,132	0.24
29.	Todd Shipyards Corp.	379,024	0.64	60.	Johns Hopkins Univ (N)	134,853	0.23
30.	FMC Corp.	360,405	0.60	61.	Chamberlain Mfg Corp.	130,247	0.22
31.	TRW Inc.	325,423	0.55	62.	Sun Co. Inc.	129,754	0.22

ARMED FORCES OF THE WORLD: 1976

SOURCE: U.S. Arms Control and Disarmament Agency (in thousands)

Country	Active-duty Military Personnel	Country	Active-duty Military Personnel	Country	Active-duty Military Personnel	Country	Active-duty Military Personnel
Afghanistan	142	El Salvador	8	Korea, Rep. of	610	Romania	220
Albania	52	Equatorial Guinea	5	Kuwait	25	Saudi Arabia	95
Algeria	85	Ethiopia	65	Laos	46	Senegal	11
Angola	35	Finland	36	Liberia	6	Singapore	35
Argentina	155	France	585	Libya	25	Somalia	31
Australia	71	German Dem. Rep.	220	Madagascar	17	South Africa	59
Austria	40	Germany, Fed. Rep.	495	Malaysia	80	Spain	368
Bangladesh	126	Ghana	20	Mali	6	Sri Lanka	18
Belgium	87	Greece	200	Mauritania	15	Sudan	50
Bolivia	22	Guatemala	14	Mexico	100	Sweden	66
Brazil	450	Guinea	10	Mongolia	25	Switzerland	25
Bulgaria	177	Guinea-Bissau	5	Morocco	90	Syria	230
Burma	210	Guyana	5	Mozambique	21	Tanzania	25
Burundi	7	Haiti	6	Nepal	32	Thailand	228
Cambodia	62	Honduras	12	Netherlands	112	Tunisia	21
Cameroon	10	Hungary	118	New Zealand	13	Turkey	460
Canada	78	India	1,440	Nicaragua	5	Uganda	25
Chad	11	Indonesia	257	Nigeria	270	U.S.S.R.	4,600
Chile	111	Iran	420	Norway	39	United Arab Emirates	27
China, People's Rep.	4,300	Iraq	190	Oman	18	United Kingdom	344
China, Rep. of	475	Ireland	14	Pakistan	604	UNITED STATES	2,000
Colombia	60	Israel	190	Panama	8	Upper Volta	10
Congo	10	Italy	432	Paraguay	15	Uruguay	28
Cuba	125	Ivory Coast	8	Peru	100	Venezuela	55
Cyprus	18	Japan	236	Philippines	140	Vietnam	637
Czechoslovakia	210	Jordan	65	Poland	435	Yemen Arab Rep.	21
Denmark	35	Kenya	9	Portugal	60	Yemen, P.D.R.	42
Dominican Republic	19	Korea, Dem. People's		Qatar	5	Yugoslavia	275
Ecuador	24	Rep.	500	Rhodesia	17	Zaire	55
Egypt	400					Zambia	17

EDUCATION: FACTS/FIGURES

EXPENDITURES FOR PUBLIC ELEMENTARY AND SECONDARY SCHOOL EDUCATION

SOURCE: National Center for Education Statistics

School year	Total	Total per pupil	School year	Total	Total per pupil
1929/1930	$ 2,316,790,000	$108	1963/1964	$21,324,993,000	$ 559
1939/1940	2,344,049,000	106	1965/1966	26,248,026,000	654
1949/1950	5,837,643,000	259	1967/1968	32,977,182,000	786
1953/1954	9,092,449,000	351	1969/1970	40,683,428,000	955
1955/1956	10,955,047,000	388	1971/1972	48,050,283,000	1,128
1957/1958	13,569,163,000	449	1973/1974	56,970,355,000	1,364
1959/1960	15,613,255,000	472	1975/1976	70,829,345,000	1,699
1961/1962	18,373,339,000	530	1976/1977	75,014,155,000	1,816
			1977/1978[1]	81,097,000,000	1,953

[1] Estimated.

HIGH SCHOOL GRADUATES   SOURCE: National Center for Education Statistics

School year	Population 17 years old	High school graduates Total	Boys	Girls	School year	Population 17 years old	High school graduates Total	Boys	Girls
1889/1890	1,259,177	43,731	18,549	25,182	1963/1964	3,001,000	2,290,000	1,121,000	1,169,000
1899/1900	1,489,146	94,883	38,075	56,808	1965/1966	3,515,000	2,632,000	1,308,000	1,324,000
1909/1910	1,786,240	156,429	63,676	92,753	1966/1967	3,518,000	2,679,000	1,331,000	1,348,000
1919/1920	1,855,173	311,266	123,684	187,582	1967/1968	3,521,000	2,702,000	1,341,000	1,361,000
1929/1930	2,295,822	666,904	300,376	366,528	1968/1969	3,622,000	2,839,000	1,408,000	1,431,000
1939/1940	2,403,074	1,221,475	578,718	642,757	1969/1970	3,825,343	2,896,000	1,433,000	1,463,000
1949/1950	2,034,450	1,199,700	570,700	629,000	1970/1971	3,859,000	3,036,000	1,506,000	1,530,000
1951/1952	2,040,800	1,196,500	569,200	627,300	1971/1972	3,957,000	3,006,000	1,490,000	1,516,000
1953/1954	2,128,600	1,276,100	612,500	663,600	1972/1973	4,024,000	3,037,000	1,501,000	1,536,000
1955/1956	2,270,000	1,414,800	679,500	735,300	1973/1974	4,096,000	3,080,000	1,515,000	1,565,000
1957/1958	2,324,000	1,505,900	725,500	780,400	1974/1975	4,210,000	3,140,000	1,541,000	1,599,000
1959/1960	2,862,005	1,864,000	898,000	966,000	1975/1976	4,216,000	3,153,000	1,572,000	1,581,000
1961/1962	2,768,000	1,925,000	941,000	984,000	1976/1977	4,206,000	3,154,000	1,548,000	1,606,000
					1977/1978[1]	4,208,000	3,160,000	1,555,000	1,605,000

[1] Estimated.

COLLEGE AND UNIVERSITY GRADUATES   SOURCE: National Center for Education Statistics

School year	All degrees	Degrees conferred Bachelor's and First Professional	Master's	Doctor's	School year	All degrees	Degrees conferred Bachelor's and First Professional	Master's	Doctor's
1869/1870	9,372	9,371	0	1	1963/1964	614,194	498,654	101,050	14,490
1889/1890	16,703	15,539	1,015	149	1965/1966	709,832	551,040	140,555	18,237
1899/1900	29,375	27,410	1,583	382	1966/1967	768,871	590,548	157,706	20,617
1909/1910	39,755	37,199	2,113	443	1967/1968	866,548	666,710	176,749	23,089
1919/1920	53,516	48,622	4,279	615	1968/1969	984,129	764,185	193,756	26,188
1929/1930	139,752	122,484	14,969	2,299	1969/1970	1,065,391	827,234	208,291	29,866
1939/1940	216,521	186,500	26,731	3,290	1970/1971	1,140,292	877,676	230,509	32,107
1949/1950	496,661	432,058	58,183	6,420	1971/1972	1,215,680	930,684	251,633	33,363
1953/1954	356,608	290,825	56,788	8,995	1972/1973	1,270,528	972,380	263,371	34,777
1955/1956	376,973	308,812	59,258	8,903	1973/1974	1,310,441	999,592	277,033	33,816
1957/1958	436,979	362,554	65,487	8,938	1974/1975	1,305,382	978,849	292,450	34,083
1959/1960	476,704	392,440	74,435	9,829	1975/1976	1,334,230	988,395	311,771	34,064
1961/1962	514,323	417,846	84,855	11,622	1976/1977	1,334,304	983,908	317,164	33,232
					1977/1978[1]	1,412,500	1,054,000	326,000	32,500

[1] Estimated.

EDUCATION AND INCOME   SOURCE: U.S. Bureau of the Census (based on 1977 data)

Income Levels	Percent of Male Income Recipients**	School Years Completed*	Income Levels	Percent of Male Income Recipients**	School Years Completed*	Income Levels	Percent of Male Income Recipients**	School Years Completed*
$1 to $999 or less	1.8	12.3	$3,500 to $3,999	2.4	9.1	$ 9,000 to $9,999	4.1	12.3
$1,000 to $1,499	1.0	9.0	$4,000 to $4,999	4.3	10.4	$10,000 to $11,999	9.1	12.5
$1,500 to $1,999	1.2	9.2	$5,000 to $5,999	4.6	11.3	$12,000 to $14,999	13.0	12.6
$2,000 to $2,499	2.2	8.5	$6,000 to $6,999	4.3	11.2	$15,000 to $19,999	18.1	12.7
$2,500 to $2,999	1.8	8.9	$7,000 to $7,999	4.5	12.1	$20,000 to $24,999	9.9	13.0
$3,000 to $3,499	2.5	9.1	$8,000 to $8,999	4.2	12.3	$25,000 and over	11.1	16.1

* Median.   ** Males 25 years old and over

LEVEL OF EDUCATION: WHITE AND BLACK ADULTS
Source: U.S. Bureau of the Census

Race and Sex	Persons 25 years old or older (1,000)	Elementary School Less than 5 years	5–7 years	8 years	High School 1–3 years	4 years	College 1–3 years	4 years or more	Median School Years Completed
Total, all races, March 1978	123,019	3.6	6.7	9.0	14.8	36.1	14.1	15.7	12.4
Male	57,922	3.9	6.9	9.0	13.5	32.1	14.9	19.7	12.5
Female	65,097	3.4	6.5	9.1	15.9	39.6	13.4	12.2	12.4
White	108,968	2.8	6.0	9.2	14.1	37.0	14.4	16.4	12.5
Male	51,619	2.9	6.2	9.2	13.0	32.7	15.2	20.7	12.6
Female	57,349	2.8	5.9	9.2	15.0	40.9	13.7	12.6	12.4
Black	11,959	9.7	12.3	8.1	22.3	29.0	11.4	7.2	11.7
Male	5,309	11.9	13.4	7.4	19.4	28.0	12.6	7.3	11.6
Female	6,650	7.9	11.5	8.7	24.5	29.7	10.5	7.1	11.7

YEARS OF SCHOOL COMPLETED 1978 (percent distribution)

EDUCATION AND INCOME
Source: U.S. Bureau of the Census

MEDIAN INCOME OF FULL-TIME YEAR-ROUND WORKERS, 25 YEARS OLD AND OVER, BY EDUCATIONAL ATTAINMENT

	Median Income, 1977 Male	Female
Elementary: Total	$ 10,509	$ 6,283
Less than 8 years	9,419	6,074
8 years	12,083	6,564
High school: Total	15,038	8,589
1 to 3 years	13,120	7,387
4 years	15,434	8,894
College: 1 or more years	18,412	11,417
5 or more years	21,941	14,338

MEDIAN INCOME OF MEN 25 YEARS OLD AND OVER, BY EDUCATIONAL ATTAINMENT

	Median Income, 1977 Black	White	All Races
Elementary: Total	$ 4,617	$ 6,520	$ 6,134
Less than 8 years	4,244	5,794	5,402
8 years	5,993	7,310	7,155
High school: Total	8,687	12,717	12,311
1 to 3 years	7,155	10,422	10,023
4 years	9,700	13,599	13,207
College: 1 or more years	12,314	16,639	16,346
5 or more years	16,797	20,288	20,108

COMPREHENSIVE EMPLOYMENT AND TRAINING ACT (CETA)

The Comprehensive Employment and Training Act Amendments of 1978, approved by the President Oct. 27 (PL 95-524), extended public service employment (PSE) and job training and initiated several new program services through FY 1982. FY 1979 operating funds were provided by a continuing resolution approved Oct. 18, 1978. Its main provisions are:

Title I: Administrative Provisions: General provisions applicable to the act. Authorizes programs through FY 1982 except for three youth programs (Part A of Title IV) and the private sector initiatives (Title VII) which are authorized only through FY 1980. Directs the Secretary of Labor to establish an Office of Management Assistance to provide prime sponsors with management and technical services to help them improve program administration.

Title II: Training, education, work experience, upgrading, retraining, and other services (Parts A, B, and C), and counterstructural public service employment (Part D) to prepare jobless persons for unsubsidized employment. Participants in training programs and services (except upgrading and retraining) must have been economically disadvantaged and either unemployed, underemployed, or in school. Participants in PSE must have been economically disadvantaged and unemployed 15 or more weeks or on welfare. PSE must be entry level and combined with training and supportive services, if available. Supplementation of wages under this title is specifically prohibited.

Title III: Programs for persons who have a particular disadvantage in the labor market, including Native Americans, migrants and other seasonal farmworkers, the handicapped, women, displaced homemakers, public assistance recipients, and other special target groups. Authorizes welfare demonstration projects, projects for middle-aged and older workers, and a program for better coordination between prime sponsors and state employment security agencies.

Title IV: The Job Corps, Summer Youth Programs, and programs enacted in the Youth Employment and Demonstration Projects Act of 1977 (except the Young Adult Conservation Corps which is still Title VIII), namely, Youth Incentive Entitlement Pilot Projects, Youth Community Conservation and Improvement Projects, and Youth Employment and Training Programs. The Job Corps and Summer Youth Program are authorized for 4 years, and the 3 new youth programs for 2.

Title V: National Commission for Employment Policy: Renames and reconstitutes the National Commission on Manpower Policy. Cabinet participation on the Commission is reduced.

Title VI: Temporary public service employment opportunities during periods of high unemployment, in sufficient number to employ 20 percent of the unemployed in excess of 4 percent unemployment, and 25 percent of the excess when national unemployment is 7 percent or higher. Participants must be unemployed at least 10 of the last 12 weeks or on welfare, and from a family whose income does not exceed the BLS lower living standard budget. At least 50 percent of the Title VI funds must be used for the employment of persons in projects. These must be limited to 18 months, but can be extended in some circumstances. Persons not employed in projects must be hired at the entry level. Funds are to be distributed to prime sponsors by formula, which for at least 85% of the title's funds is as follows: 50% based on total unemployment in a sponsor's area, 25% on unemployment over 4.5%, and 25% on unemployment over 6.5% Of the title's total funds, 2% must be reserved for programs for Native Americans.

Title VII: Authorizes a Private Sector Initiative Program (PSIP) to demonstrate the effectiveness of ways of increasing the involvment of the business community, including minority and small businesses, in employment and training activities supported by CETA, and increase private sector jobs for the economically disadvantaged. Provides funds for the establishment of private industry councils (a majority of whose members must be from the business community) which shall participate with prime sponsors in developing opportunities for economically disadvantaged persons in the private sector.

Title VIII: Provides employment and experience in various occupational skills to out-of-school young people from all social and economic backgrounds through work on conservation and other projects on federal and non-federal public lands and waters. Participants may be hired for a maximum of 12 months. Operated under agreement by Departments of Labor, Agriculture, and Interior. Authorized for 4 years, through FY 1982.

CETA ENROLLMENT IN FISCAL 1978 Type of Program	Number Enrolled & Percent of Enrollment
Public Service Employment (Total)	1,186,900 (36%)
Title I	22,500
Title II	200,900
Title VI	963,500
Vocational Ed. (Classroom) Total	625,900 (19%)
Title I	579,900
Title IV — Job Corps	46,000
On-the-Job Training (Total)	229,950 (7%)
Title I	193,700

Type of Program	Number Enrolled & Percent of Enrollment
Title III — National Contracts	22,550
— Apprentice Placements	13,698
Work Experience (Total)	729,100 (22%)
Title I	489,400
Title III — Youth	239,700
Combination of Programs (Total)	547,400 (16%)
Title I	87,400
Title III — Native Americans	110,000
— Migrants	350,000
TOTAL	**3,319,250 (100%)**

ELEMENTARY AND SECONDARY SCHOOLS

Source: National Center for Education Statistics

In the school year 1976-77, there were approximately 16,300 public school systems in the United States that included 62,600 public elementary schools and 25,400 public secondary schools. As the accompanying table indicates, the number of school districts and public elementary schools is declining, with a more rapid drop in the number of districts. However, since WWII, the number of pupils per school has risen substantially. In addition to the public schools, there are an estimated 14,200 nonpublic elementary schools and 3,800 nonpublic secondary schools in the country.

School Year	Districts	PUBLIC SCHOOLS		NONPUBLIC SCHOOLS*	
		Elementary	Secondary	Elementary	Secondary
1945–46	101,382	160,227	24,314	9,863	3,294
1949–50	83,718	128,225	24,542	10,375	3,331
1955–56	54,859	104,427	26,046	12,372	3,887
1959–60	40,520	91,853	25,784	13,574	4,061
1965–66	26,983	73,216	26,597	15,340	4,606
1970–71	17,995	65,800	25,352	14,372	3,770
1972–73	16,960	64,945	25,922	14,000†	3,700†
1973–74	16,730	65,070	25,906	14,000†	3,700†
1974–75	16,570	63,619[1]	25,697[1]	14,000†	3,700†
1975–76	16,376	63,242[1]	25,330[1]	14,000†	3,700†
1976–77	16,271	62,644[1]	25,378[1]	14,200†	3,800†

* Data for most years are partly estimated. † Estimate.
[1] Excludes special education schools for the handicapped (not reported by level).

ESTIMATED U.S. EDUCATIONAL EXPENDITURES

Source: National Center for Education Statistics

Source of funds, by level of institution and type of control	1969-70		1976-77		1977-78		1978-79	
	Amount	Percent	Amount	Percent	Amount	Percent	Amount	Percent
All levels:	(Billions)		(Billions)		(Billions)		(Billions)	
Total public and nonpublic	$70.4	100.0	$131.1	100.0	$141.2	100.0	$151.5	100.0
Federal	7.5	10.7	13.8	10.5	15.1	10.7	16.2	10.7
State	22.2	31.5	45.9	35.0	50.9	36.0	54.8	36.2
Local	22.6	32.1	37.4	28.5	40.1	28.4	42.7	28.2
All other	18.1	25.7	34.0	26.0	35.1	24.9	37.8	24.9
Elementary and secondary schools:*								
Total public and nonpublic	45.7	100.0	81.9	100.0	90.8	100.0	97.0	100.0
Federal	3.4	7.4	6.4	7.8	7.4	8.1	7.9	8.1
State	15.8	34.6	31.0	37.9	35.7	39.3	38.3	39.5
Local	21.7	47.5	35.4	43.2	38.2	42.1	40.6	41.9
All other	4.8	10.5	9.1	11.1	9.5	10.5	10.2	10.5
Total public	41.0	100.0	72.9	100.0	81.5	100.0	87.0	100.0
Federal	3.4	8.2	6.4	8.8	7.4	9.1	7.9	9.1
State	15.8	38.6	31.0	42.5	35.7	43.8	38.3	44.0
Local	21.7	52.9	35.4	48.6	38.2	46.9	40.6	46.7
All other	.1	.3	.1	.1	.2	.2	.2	.2
Total nonpublic	4.7	100.0	9.0	100.0	9.3	100.0	10.0	100.0
Federal	—	—	—	—	—	—	—	—
State	—	—	—	—	—	—	—	—
Local	—	—	—	—	—	—	—	—
All other	4.7	100.0	9.0	100.0	9.3	100.0	10.0	100.0
Institutions of higher education:								
Total public and nonpublic	24.7	100.0	49.2	100.0	50.4	100.0	54.5	100.0
Federal	4.1	16.6	7.4	15.0	7.7	15.3	8.3	15.2
State	6.4	25.9	14.9	30.3	15.2	30.1	16.5	30.3
Local	.9	3.6	2.0	4.1	1.9	3.8	2.1	3.9
All other	13.3	53.9	24.9	50.6	25.6	50.8	27.6	50.6
Total public	15.8	100.0	33.5	100.0	34.4	100.0	37.4	100.0
Federal	2.4	14.9	4.7	14.0	4.8	14.0	5.2	14.0
State	6.3	39.7	14.5	43.3	14.8	42.9	16.1	42.9
Local	.8	5.1	1.9	5.8	1.8	5.3	2.0	5.3
All other	6.3	40.3	12.4	36.9	13.0	37.8	14.1	37.8
Total nonpublic	8.9	100.0	15.7	100.0	16.0	100.0	17.1	100.0
Federal	1.7	18.8	2.7	17.0	2.9	18.3	3.1	18.3
State	.1	1.6	.4	2.3	.4	2.2	.4	2.2
Local	.1	.7	.1	.8	.1	.7	.1	.7
All other	7.0	78.9	12.5	79.9	12.6	78.8	13.5	78.8

* In addition to regular schools, these figures include other elementary and secondary schools, such as residential schools for exceptional children, Federal schools for Indians, federally operated elementary and secondary schools on posts, and subcollegiate departments of colleges.

INDEX OF U.S. COLLEGES AND UNIVERSITIES: 1978-79

This list includes all regionally accredited four-year colleges and universities in the United States that grant baccalaureate degrees. Highly specialized institutions such as schools of mortuary science, optometry, and pharmacy are not included, nor are such professional colleges as law, medicine, or theology, which generally offer only post-baccalaureate work.

Institutions are listed in standard letter-by-letter alphabetical order. For example, University of Michigan will be found under U, not M; Marshall University comes before Mars Hill College.

The explanation of the data contained in each column is as follows. Column 1: **Est** shows the founding date of the institution. Column 2: **Type/Control** shows the student body makeup (C = coed, M = primarily men, W = primarily women) and the institutional control (Ind

= independent, Pub = public, Cath = Catholic, Jewish, LDS = Latter-Day Saints, Prot = Protestant). Column 3: **UG Enroll** shows undergraduate enrollment as of fall 1978. Column 4: **% State Res** shows the percentage of the fall 1978 undergraduate enrollment that were state residents. Column 5: **Grad** shows whether graduate-level work is offered. Column 6: **Fac size** shows the number of total faculty teaching graduate and undergraduate programs as of fall 1978. Column 7: **Cmps** shows the campus setting (R = rural, S = suburban, T = college town, U = urban). Column 8: **ROTC** shows which ROTC branch has a program on campus (A = Army, N = Navy, AF = Air Force). Column 9: **Tuition** shows tuition per credit or per year for all students at private colleges or for in-state students at public colleges; X indicates campus room and board not available.

An asterisk appears where no information is available.

Name and Location	Est	Type/ Control	UG Enroll	% of State Res	Grad	Fac Size	Cmps	ROTC	Tuition
Abilene Christian University, Abilene, TX 79601	1906	C/Prot	3686	65%	G	175	T	A	$2080
Abilene Christian University at Dallas, Garland, TX 75041	1971	C/Ind	600	80%	G	40	S		2160x
Academy of The New Church, Bryn Athyn, PA 19009	1877	C/Prot	149	42%		33	S		1046
Adams State College, Alamosa, CO 81102	1921	C/Pub	1824	88%	G	121	T		680
Adelphi University, Garden City, NY 11530	1869	C/Ind	6927	89%	G	800	S		3660
Adrian College, Adrian, MI 49221	1845	C/Prot	824	78%	G	95	T		3494
Agnes Scott College, Decatur, GA 30030	1889	W/Ind	553	44%		84	S	AF	3500
Alabama A&M University, Normal, AL 35762	1875	C/Pub	3423	85%	G	500	S	A	490
Alabama State University, Montgomery, AL 36101	1874	C/Pub	4153	86%	G	244	U	AF	525
Alaska Methodist University, Anchorage, AK 99504	1957	C/Ind	106	95%	G	27	S		2540
Albany State College, Albany, GA 31705	1903	C/Pub	2166	90%		128	U	A	435
Albertus Magnus College, New Haven, CT 06511	1925	W/Cath	556	85%		52	T		3100
Albion College, Albion, MI 49224	1835	C/Prot	1818	89%		123	T		4017
Albright College, Reading, PA 19604	1856	C/Prot	1275	60%		125	S		3795
Alcorn State University, Lorman, MS 39096	1871	C/Pub	2500	92%	G	150	R	A	62824
Alderson-Broaddus College, Philippi, WV 26416	1871	C/Prot	906	44%		161	T		2678
Alfred University, Alfred, NY 14802	1836	C/Ind	1758	75%	G	176	R		4465
Allegheny College, Meadville, PA 16335	1815	C/Prot	1850	50%	G	152	T		3885
Allentown College of St Francis De Sales, Center Valley, PA 18034	1965	C/Ind	600	70%		58	R		3080
Allen University, Columbia, SC 29204	1870	C/Prot	401	80%		60	U		1500
Alliance College, Cambridge Springs, PA 16403	1912	C/Ind	209	53%		24	R		2300
Alma College, Alma, MI 48801	1886	C/Prot	1178	75%		99	T		3778
Alvernia College, Reading, PA 19607	1958	C/Cath	750	60%		80	S		1650
Alverno College, Milwaukee, WI 53215	1887	W/Cath	1165	96%		107	U		2550
American Conservatory of Music, Chicago, IL 60605	1886	C/Ind	311	90%	G	188	S		2400
American International College, Springfield, MA 01109	1885	C/Ind	1330	67%	G	115	U		3090
American Technological University, Killeen, TX 76541	1973	C/Pub	454	73%	G	44	S		1000
American University, Washington, DC 20016	1893	C/Prot	5567	9%	G	912	U		4080
Amherst College, Amherst, MA 01002	1821	C/Ind	1463	19%		150	T		5230
Anderson College, Anderson, IN 46011	1917	C/Prot	1831	47%		135	S		2600
Andrews University, Berrien Springs, MI 49104	1874	C/Prot	2026	39%	G	248	R		3450
Angelo State University, San Angelo, TX 76901	1928	C/Pub	5045	96%	G	209	T	AF	388
Anna Maria College, Paxton, MA 01612	1946	C/Cath	617	75%	G	103	S		2700
Annhurst College, Woodstock, CT 06281	1941	C/Cath	318	60%		55	R		2800
Antioch College, Yellow Springs, OH 45387	1852	C/Ind	1225	11%	G	100	T		4088
Appalachian State University, Boone, NC 28608	1899	C/Pub	8026	94%	G	550	T	A	704.50
Aquinas College, Grand Rapids, MI 49506	1922	C/Ind	1885	90%	G	122	U		3174
Arizona State University, Tempe, AZ 85281	1885	C/Pub	26,798	68%	G	1269	S	A, AF	550
Arkansas College, Batesville, AR 72501	1872	C/Prot	534	65%		44	T		1950
Arkansas State University, State University, AR 72467	1909	C/Pub	6641	88%	G	339	T	A	460
Arkansas Tech University, Russellville, AR 72801	1909	C/Pub	2541	85%	G	150	T	A	490
Armstrong College, Berkeley, CA 94704	1918	C/Ind	362	50%		48	U		1890
Armstrong State College, Savannah, GA 31406	1935	C/Pub	2854	95%	G	160	S	N	700x
Art Center College of Design, Pasadena, CA 91103	1930	C/Ind	1057	50%	G	174	S		2950
Asbury College, Wilmore, KY 40390	1890	C/Ind	1273	12%		101	T		2704
Ashland College, Ashland, OH 44805	1878	C/Prot	1629	75%	G	137	T		3782
Assumption College, Worcester, MA 01609	1917	C/Cath	1300	50%	G	100	S		2900
Athenaeum of Ohio, Cincinnati, OH 45230	1829	C/Cath	220	85%	G	52	S		2150
Athens State College, Athens, AL 35611	1822	C/Pub	1323	90%		70	T		540
Atlanta College of Art, Atlanta, GA 30309	1928	C/Ind	260	40%		30	U		2600
Atlantic Christian College, Wilson, NC 27893	1902	C/Prot	1600	80%		112	S		2014
Atlantic Union College, South Lancaster, MA 01561	1882	C/Prot	660	38%		98	T		3800
Auburn University at Montgomery, Montgomery, AL 36109	1856	C/Pub	3563	100%	G	350	S		175x
Auburn University, Auburn, AL 36830	1856	C/Pub	16,128	84%	G	1071	T	A, N, AF	600
Augsburg College, Minneapolis, MN 55454	1869	C/Prot	1751	80%		170	U		3000
Augusta College, Augusta, GA 30904	1925	C/Pub	3378	90%	G	173	U	A	520x
Augustana College, Rock Island, IL 61201	1860	C/Prot	2220	80%		179	U		3201
Augustana College, Sioux Falls, SD 57102	1860	C/Prot	1874	55%	G	188	S		3350
Aurora College, Aurora, IL 60507	1893	C/Prot	966	90%		63	S		3060
Austin College, Sherman, TX 75090	1849	C/Prot	1069	90%	G	107	S		3100
Austin Peay State University, Clarksville, TN 37040	1927	C/Pub	4636	88%	G	245	T	A	459
Averett College, Danville, VA 24541	1859	C/Prot	1077	78%	G	54	U		1525
Avila College, Kansas City, MO 64145	1916	C/Cath	1853	31%	G	199	S		2450
Azusa Pacific College, Azusa, CA 91702	1899	C/Ind	1230	85%	G	128	S		2950
Babson College, Babson Park, MA 02157	1919	C/Ind	1324	75%	G	124	S		4100
Baker University, Baldwin City, KS 66006	1858	C/Prot	889	57%		80	T		2415
Baldwin-Wallace College, Berea, OH 44017	1845	C/Prot	2656	80%	G	169	S		3909
Ball State University, Muncie, IN 47306	1918	C/Pub	14,725	92%	G	982	S	A	900
Baltimore Hebrew College, Baltimore, MD 21215	1919	C/Ind	84	96%	G	17	U		850
Baptist College at Charleston, Charleston, SC 29411	1964	C/Prot	2397	87%		100	S	AF	2750
Barat College, Lake Forest, IL 60045	1858	W/Cath	737	88%		82	S		3050
Barber-Scotia College, Concord, NC 28025	1867	C/Ind	435	61%		38	T		1600

Name and Location	Est	Type/Control	UG Enroll	% of State Res	Grad	Fac Size	Cmps	ROTC	Tuition
Bard College, Annandale, NY 12504	1860	C/Ind	700	46%		90	R		$5795
Barnard College, New York, NY 10027	1889	W/Ind	2272	50%		225	U		5300
Barrington College, Barrington, RI 02806	1900	C/Ind	516	26%		65	S		2739
Barry College, Miami, FL 33161	1940	C/Cath	1480	69%	G	159	S		2830
Bartlesville Wesleyan College, Bartlesville, OK 74003	1959	C/Prot	613	35%		49	S		1380
Bates College, Lewiston, ME 04240	1864	C/Ind	1350	15%		130	T		4850
Bayamon Central University, Bayamon, PR 00619	1961	C/Ind	2615	100%		66	S		600x
Baylor University, Waco, TX 76706	1845	C/Prot	8320	65%	G	467	U	AF	1900
Beaver College, Glenside, PA 19038	1853	C/Prot	924	69%	G	112	S		4070
Belhaven College, Jackson, MS 39202	1883	C/Prot	694	85%		58	U		1950
Bellarmine College, Louisville, KY 40205	1864	C/Cath	1619	85%	G	96	S		2250
Bellevue College, Bellevue, NE 68005	1966	C/Ind	2190	99%		77	U		1050x
Belmont Abbey College, Belmont, NC 28012	1876	C/Cath	645	27%		53	S		2278
Belmont College, Nashville, TN 37203	1951	C/Prot	1314	75%		126	U		1850
Beloit College, Beloit, WI 53511	1846	C/Ind	1005	16%		120	T		4500
Bemidji State University, Bemidji, MN 56601	1919	C/Pub	4032	94%	G	210	R		646
Benedict College, Columbia, SC 29204	1870	C/Ind	1761	90%		105	U	A	2084
Benedictine College, Atchison, KS 66002	1971	C/Cath	1006	60%		75	T		2400
Bennett College, Greensboro, NC 27420	1873	W/Ind	579	35%		56	U		1720
Bennington College, Bennington, VT 05201	1932	C/Ind	655	1%		80	R		6590
Bentley College, Waltham, MA 02154	1917	C/Ind	5691	60%	G	137	S	AF	3515
Berea College, Berea, KY 40403	1855	C/Ind	1432	38%		127	T		91
Berklee College of Music, Boston, MA 02215	1945	C/Ind	2611	20%		218	U		2750
Bernard M. Baruch College , See City U of NY, Baruch College.									
Berry College, Mount Berry, GA 30149	1902	C/Ind	1385	60%	G	98	S		2400
Bethany Bible College, Santa Cruz, CA 95066	1919	C/Prot	493	69%		31	R		2028
Bethany College, Lindsborg, KS 67465	1881	C/Prot	741	70%		61	R		2193
Bethany College, Bethany, WV 26032	1840	C/Prot	941	15%		77	R		4140
Bethany Nazarene College, Bethany, OK 73008	1899	C/Prot	1228	30%	G	85	S		1800
Bethel College, Mishawaka, IN 46544	1947	C/Prot	444	97%		37	S		2313
Bethel College, North Newton, KS 67117	1887	C/Prot	638	63%		63	T		2458
Bethel College, St Paul, MN 55112	1871	C/Prot	1864	58%		158	S		2990
Bethel College, McKenzie, TN 38201	1842	C/Ind	311	77%		36	T		2000
Bethune-Cookman College, Daytona Beach, FL 32015	1872	C/Prot	1783	84%		125	U		1767
Biola College, La Mirada, CA 90638	1908	C/Ind	2323	73%	G	161	S		2776
Birmingham-Southern College, Birmingham, AL 35204	1856	C/Prot	1256	75%		71	U	AF	2550
Biscayne College, Miami, FL 33054	1962	C/Cath	2109	65%	G	150	S		2850
Bishop College, Dallas, TX 75241	1881	C/Prot	1554	53%		112	S	A	1800
Blackburn College, Carlinville, IL 62626	1857	C/Prot	550	75%		48	R		2200
Black Hills State College, Spearfish, SD 57783	1883	C/Pub	1967	92%	G	98	T	A	864
Bloomfield College, Bloomfield, NJ 07003	1868	C/Prot	2447	99%		165	S		3110
Bloomsburg State College, Bloomsburg, PA 17815	1839	C/Pub	5546	94%	G	301	T		1040
Bluefield College, Bluefield, VA 24605	1919	C/Prot	344	68%		29	S		1500
Bluefield State College, Bluefield, WV 24701	1895	C/Pub	2747	8%		100	U		352x
Blue Mountain College, Blue Mountain, MS 38610	1873	W/Prot	340	82%		32	T		1400
Bluffton College, Bluffton, OH 45817	1899	C/Prot	640	55%		75	R		3003
Boise State University, Boise, ID 83725	1932	C/Pub	9093	34%	G	414	U	A	414
Borromeo College of Ohio, Wickliffe, OH 44092	1954	M/Cath	80	90%		25	S		2375
Boston College, Chestnut Hill, MA 02167	1863	C/Cath	10,185	52%	G	674	S		3980
Boston Conservatory of Music, Boston, MA 02215	1867	C/Ind	481	41%	G	108	U		3100
Boston State College, Boston, MA 02115	1852	C/Pub	5450	96%	G	500	U		500x
Boston University, Boston, MA 02215	1839	C/Ind	11,279	25%	G	2449	U		4800
Bowdoin College, Brunswick, ME 04011	1794	C/Ind	1316	11%		115	T		4767
Bowie State College, Bowie, MD 20715	1865	C/Pub	1877	85%	G	159	S	A	800
Bowling Green State U, Bowling Green, OH 43403	1910	C/Pub	13,951	92%	G	791	T	A, AF	1080
Bradford College, Bradford, MA 01830	1803	C/Ind	314	31%		39	S		4050
Bradley University, Peoria, IL 61625	1896	C/Ind	4554	78%	G	377	S	A	3280
Brandeis University, Waltham, MA 02154	1948	C/Ind	2846	29%	G	403	S		5900
Brenau College, Gainesville, GA 30501	1878	W/Ind	610	75%	G	74	S		2160
Brescia College, Owensboro, KY 42301	1950	C/Cath	832	91%		75	U		2000
Briar Cliff College, Sioux City, IA 51104	1930	C/Cath	1179	93%		70	U		2480
Bridgeport Engineering Institute, Bridgeport, CT 06606	1924	C/Ind	480	95%		80	S		1320
Bridgewater College, Bridgewater, VA 22812	1880	C/Prot	887	71%		78	T		2900
Bridgewater State College, Bridgewater, MA 02324	1840	C/Ind	4300	96%	G	272	T		500
Brigham Young University, Provo, UT 84602	1875	C/LDS	8522	31%	G	1300	T	A, AF	780
Brigham Young University-Hawaii Cmps, Laie, Oahu, HI 96762	1955	C/LDS	1053	35%	G	100	T		700
Brooklyn College , See City U of NY, Brooklyn College.									
Brooks Institute, Santa Barbara, CA 93108	1945	C/Ind	750	30%		32	S		1840x
Brown University, Providence, RI 02912	1764	C/Ind	5225	7%	G	471	U		5565
Bryan College, Dayton, TN 37321	1930	C/Ind	557	13%		45	R		2040
Bryant College, Smithfield, RI 02917	1863	C/Ind	2803	34%	G	145	S		2850
Bryn Mawr College, Bryn Mawr, PA 19010	1885	W/Ind	997	15%	G	216	S		5345
Bucknell University, Lewisburg, PA 17837	1846	C/Ind	3084	36%	G	252	T	A	4996
Buena Vista College, Storm Lake, IA 50588	1891	C/Prot	827	94%		58	T		3225
Butler University, Indianapolis, IN 46208	1850	C/Ind	2449	75%	G	249	S		3045
Cabrini College, Radnor, PA 19087	1957	C/Cath	429	78%		59	S		2972
Caldwell College, Caldwell, NJ 07006	1939	W/Cath	521	85%		78	S		2600
California Baptist College, Riverside, CA 92504	1950	C/Prot	763	77%		58	U		2450
California College of Arts and Crafts, Oakland, CA 94618	1907	C/Ind	930	59%	G	145	U		3450
California Institute of Technology, Pasadena, CA 91125	1891	C/Ind	801	45%	G	279	S		4705
California Institute of the Arts, Valencia, CA 91355	1883	C/Ind	501	74%	G	126	T		3750
California Lutheran College, Thousand Oaks, CA 91360	1959	C/Prot	1200	87%	G	256	S	A,AF	3200
California Polytechnic State U, San Luis Obispo, CA 93407	1901	C/Pub	14,669	98%	G	850	T	A	234
California State College, California, PA 15419	1852	C/Pub	3975	98%	G	305	T		1060
California State College, Bakersfield, CA 93309	1970	C/Pub	2272	85%	G	200	R		180
California State College, San Bernardino, CA 92407	1962	C/Pub	3063	93%	G	272	S		201
California State College, Stanislaus, Turlock, CA 95380	1957	C/Pub	2364	95%	G	222	T		200
California State Polytechnic U, Pomona, CA 91768	1938	C/Pub	12,879	88%	G	813	S	A	270

Name and Location	Est	Type/ Control	UG Enroll	% of State Res	Grad	Fac Size	Cmps	ROTC	Tuition
California State U, Chico, CA 95926	1887	C/Pub	11,440	97%	G	810	T	A	$225
California State U, Dominguez Hills, Carson, CA 90747	1960	C/Pub	5117	95%		307	U		200x
California State U, Fresno, CA 93740	1911	C/Pub	11,858	96%	G	937	U	AF	220
California State U, Fullerton, CA 92634	1957	C/Pub	16,524	97%	G	1247	S		216x
California State U, Hayward, CA 94542	1957	C/Pub	7589	97%	G	550	S		201x
California State U, Long Beach, CA 90840	1949	C/Pub	20,552	97%	G	1600	U	A, AF	200
California State U, Los Angeles, CA 90032	1947	C/Pub	18,000	95%	G	1200	U		200x
California State U, Northridge, CA 91330	1958	C/Pub	21,883	98%	G	1500	S		204x
California State U, Sacramento, CA 95819	1947	C/Pub	15,572	96%	G	1000	U		200
Calumet College, Whiting, IN 46394	1951	C/Cath	1500	60%		75	U		1200
Calvin College, Grand Rapids, MI 49506	1876	C/Prot	3948	57%	G	230	S		2670
Camden College of Arts and Sciences, See Rutgers University, Camden Campus.									
Cameron University, Lawton, OK 73501	1927	C/Pub	4717	99%		172	U	A	453.60
Campbell College, Buies Creek, NC 27506	1887	C/Prot	1790	75%	G	120	R	A	2650
Campbellsville College, Campbellsville, KY 42718	1906	C/Prot	654	76%		60	T		1980
Canisius College, Buffalo, NY 14208	1870	C/Cath	2200	95%	G	217	U	A	3200
Capital University, Columbus, OH 43209	1850	C/Prot	1894	89%	G	192	S	AF	3880
Capitol Institute of Technology, Kensington, MD 20795	1964	C/Ind	525	75%		26	S		2160x
Cardinal Glennon College, St Louis, MO 63119	1898	M/Cath	91	80%			S		1000
Cardinal Stritch College, Milwaukee, WI 53217	1937	C/Cath	597	65%	G	116	S	A	2500
Carleton College, Northfield, MN 55057	1866	C/Ind	1850	27%		168	T		4327
Carlow College, Pittsburgh, PA 15213	1929	W/Cath	792	91%		81	U		3350
Carnegie-Mellon University, Pittsburgh, PA 15213	1900	C/Ind	3880	95%	G	552	U	A, AF	4130
Carroll College, Waukesha, WI 53186	1846	C/Prot	1138	77%		110	S		3720
Carroll College of Montana, Helena, MT 59601	1909	C/Cath	1384	74%		111	T		2044
Carson-Newman College, Jefferson City, TN 37760	1851	C/Prot	1589	52%		107	T	A	2000
Carthage College, Kenosha, WI 53140	1847	C/Prot	1389	45%	G	113	U		3316
Case Western Reserve University, Cleveland, OH 44106	1826	C/Ind	3395	60%	G	1100	U		4375
Castleton State College, Castleton, VT 05735	1787	C/Pub	1832	70%	G	107	R		854
Catawba College, Salisbury, NC 28144	1851	C/Prot	1000	50%		72	S		2697.75
Cathedral Coll of Immac Conception, Douglaston, NY 11362	1914	M/Cath	108	98%		37	U		2500
Catholic University of America, Washington, DC 20064	1887	C/Cath	2700	*	G	500	S		3750
Catholic University of Puerto Rico, Ponce, PR 00731	1948	C/Cath	10,228	95%	G	426	U		35
Cedar Crest College, Allentown, PA 18104	1867	W/Prot	931	62%	G	78	S		3700
Cedarville College, Cedarville, OH 45314	1887	C/Prot	1185	50%		70	T		2230
Centenary College, Hackettstown, NJ 07840	1867	W/Ind	703	66%		67	S		3250
Centenary College of Louisiana, Shreveport, LA 71104	1825	C/Prot	830	63%	G	100	S		2200
Center for Creative Studies, Detroit, MI 48202	1926	C/Pub	1098	98%		99	U		2918
Center for Early Education, Los Angeles, CA 90048	1939	C/Pub	19	100%		9	S		65cx
Central College of Iowa, Pella, IA 50219	1853	C/Ind	1498	68%		89	T		3106
Central Connecticut State College, New Britain, CT 06050	1849	C/Pub	9337	97%	G	658	S		726
Central Methodist College, Fayette, MO 65248	1854	C/Prot	627	88%		62	T		2585
Central Michigan University, Mount Pleasant, MI 48858	1892	C/Pub	14,353	98%	G	830	T	A	820
Central Missouri State University, Warrensburg, MO 64093	1871	C/Pub	8075	97%	G	477	T	A	390
Central State University, Wilberforce, OH 45384	1887	C/Pub	2414	75%		171	S		882
Central State University, Edmond, OK 73034	1890	C/Pub	8979	95%	G	430	S	A	383.50
Central Washington University, Ellensburg, WA 98926	1891	C/Pub	5548	98%	G	332	T	AF	618
Central Wesleyan College, Central, SC 29630	1906	C/Prot	413	60%		30	R		1980
Centre College of Kentucky, Danville, KY 40422	1819	C/Ind	750	55%		64	T		3800
Chadron State College, Chadron, NE 69337	1911	C/Pub	1665	85%	G	104	T		666
Chaminade University of Honolulu, Honolulu, HI 96816	1955	C/Cath	950	65%	G	162	S		2200
Chapman College, Orange, CA 92666	1861	C/Prot	1252	70%	G	167	S		3790
Chatham College, Pittsburgh, PA 15232	1869	W/Ind	615	60%		86	U		4055
Chestnut Hill College, Philadelphia, PA 19118	1924	W/Cath	955	73%		96	S		2350
Cheyney State College, Cheyney, PA 19319	1837	C/Pub	2109	82%	G	198	R	A	950
Chicago Conservatory College, Chicago, IL 60605	1932	C/Ind	121	98%	G	100	U		2807
Chicago State University, Chicago, IL 60628	1867	C/Pub	5152	99%	G	315	U		746.50x
Christian Brothers College, Memphis, TN 38104	1871	C/Cath	1126	80%		97	U		2444
Christopher Newport College, Newport News, VA 23606	1971	C/Pub	3839	90%		201	S	A	630x
Citadel, Charleston, SC 29409	1842	M/Pub	2378	65%	G	148	U	A, N, AF	2365
City College, See City U of NY, City College.									
City U of NY, Baruch College, New York, NY 10010	1968	C/Pub	11,813	95%	G	780	U		825x
City U of NY, Brooklyn College, Brooklyn, NY 11210	1930	C/Pub	16,149	99%		1549	U		775x
City U of NY, City College, New York, NY 10031	1847	C/Pub	12,325	96%	G	800	U		850x
City U of NY, College of Staten Island, Staten Island, NY 10301	1956	C/Pub	12,647	99%	G	609	U		775x
City U of NY, Hunter College, New York, NY 10021	1870	C/Pub	14,872	97%	G	1234	U		775x
City U of NY, John Jay College, New York, NY 10019	1964	C/Pub	5345	98%	G	425	U		794.50x
City U of NY, Lehman College, Bronx, NY 10468	1931	C/Pub	9076	98%	G	679	S		825x
City U of NY, Medgar Evers College, Brooklyn, NY 11225	1969	C/Pub	3090	98%		175	U		760x
City U of NY, Queens College, Flushing, NY 11367	1937	C/Pub	13,000	99%	G	1000	U		1000x
City U of NY, York College, Jamaica, NY 11451	1967	C/Pub	3889	95%		200	U		800.25x
Claflin College, Orangeburg, SC 29115	1869	C/Ind	850	88%		65	T	A	1956
Claremont Men's College, Claremont, CA 91711	1946	C/Ind	865	60%		99	S	A	4902
Clarion State College, Clarion, PA 16214	1867	C/Pub	4900	85%	G	360	T	A	1050
Clark College, Atlanta, GA 30314	1869	C/Prot	1796	55%		134	U		1800
Clarke College, Dubuque, IA 52001	1843	W/Cath	558	71%	G	65	T		2725
Clarkson College, Potsdam, NY 13676	1896	C/Ind	3150	84%	G	219	T	A	4100
Clark University, Worcester, MA 01610	1887	C/Ind	1810	25%	G	194	U		5000
Clemson University, Clemson, SC 29631	1889	C/Pub	8925	81%	G	671	T	A, AF	850
Cleveland Institute of Art, Cleveland, OH 44106	1882	C/Ind	520	65%		71	U		2840
Cleveland State University, Cleveland, OH 44115	1964	C/Pub	14,323	94%	G	1028	U		960
Clinch Valley College of the U of VA, Wise, VA 24293	1954	C/Pub	942	91%		66	T		680
Coe College, Cedar Rapids, IA 52402	1851	C/Prot	1243	62%		104	S		3595
Cogswell College, San Francisco, CA 94108	1887	C/Pub	410	100%		53	U		1950x
Coker College, Hartsville, SC 29550	1908	C/Ind	321	88%		43	S		2769
Colby College, Waterville, ME 04901	1813	C/Ind	1671	18%		132	R		4975
Colby-Sawyer College, New London, NH 03257	1837	W/Ind	700	14%		67	R		4032

Name and Location	Est	Type/ Control	UG Enroll	% of State Res	Grad	Fac Size	Cmps	ROTC	Tuition
Colgate University, Hamilton, NY 13346	1819	C/Ind	2560	50%	G	184	T	AF	$4870
College Misericordia, Dallas, PA 18612	1924	W/Cath	1013	80%		97	S		2550
College of Boca Raton, Boca Raton, FL 33432	1936	C/Ind	480	10%		30	S		2700
College of Charleston, Charleston, SC 29401	1770	C/Pub	4137	95%		195	U		750
College of Great Falls, Great Falls, MT 59405	1932	C/Cath	1200	80%		82	T		2250
College of Idaho, Caldwell, ID 83605	1891	C/Prot	525	52%		58	R		3200
College of Insurance, New York, NY 10038	1962	C/Ind	1825	75%	G	131	U		1488
College of Mount St Joseph on the Ohio, Mt St Joseph, OH 45051	1854	W/Cath	1355	85%		100	S	A	2624
College of Mount Saint Vincent, Riverdale, NY 10471	1847	C/Ind	1228	90%		99	S		3100
College of New Rochelle, New Rochelle, NY 10801	1904	W/Cath	3248	75%	G	398	S		3000
College of Notre Dame, Belmont, CA 94002	1851	C/Ind	910	64%	G	114	S		2850
College of Notre Dame of Maryland, Baltimore, MD 21210	1848	W/Cath	653	75%		75	S		2800
College of Our Lady of the Elms, Chicopee, MA 01013	1897	W/Cath	425	65%		61	S		2450
College of Saint Benedict, Saint Joseph, MN 56374	1913	W/Cath	1622	88%		125	T		3175
College of St Catherine, St Paul, MN 55105	1905	W/Cath	2100	75%		150	U		2895
College of Saint Elizabeth, Convent Station, NJ 07961	1899	W/Cath	485	88%		83	S		2850
College of St Francis, Joliet, IL 60435	1925	C/Cath	719	90%		56	S		2570
College of St Joseph the Provider, Rutland, VT 05701	1954	C/Cath	188	71%	G	44	T		2525
College of Saint Mary, Omaha, NE 68124	1923	W/Cath	563	73%		75	U	A,AF	2916
College of Saint Rose, Albany, NY 12203	1920	C/Ind	1347	95%	G	172	U		2310
College of St Scholastica, Duluth, MN 55811	1902	C/Cath	1083	72%	G	126	U		3024
College of Saint Teresa, Winona, MN 55987	1907	W/Cath	892	97%		85	T		3117
College of Saint Thomas, St Paul, MN 55105	1885	C/Cath	2862	89%	G	245	S	AF	2800
College of Santa Fe, Santa Fe, NM 87501	1874	C/Cath	1162	80%		90	T		2130
College of Staten Island , See City U of NY, College of Staten Island.									
College of Steubenville, Steubenville, OH 43952	1946	C/Cath	599	54%		36	T		75c
College of the Atlantic, Bar Harbor, ME 04609	1969	C/Ind	138	15%		25	T		3500
College of the Holy Cross, Worcester, MA 01610	1843	C/Cath	2570	47%	G	207	S	N,AF	4312
College of the Ozarks, Clarksville, AR 72830	1834	C/Prot	602	61%		40	T	A	910
College of the Virgin Islands, St Thomas, VI 00801	1962	C/Pub	1784	70%	G	108	S		344
College of William and Mary, Williamsburg, VA 23185	1693	C/Pub	4494	70%	G	448	T	A	1076
College of Wooster, Wooster, OH 44691	1866	C/Prot	1776	48%		150	T		3990
Colorado College, Colorado Springs, CO 80903	1874	C/Ind	1873	33%	G	205	U		4200
Colorado School of Mines, Golden, CO 80401	1874	C/Pub	2085	70%	G	195	T	A	930
Colorado State University, Fort Collins, CO 80523	1870	C/Pub	15,346	75%	G	1158	T	A, AF	795
Colorado Women's College, Denver, CO 80220	1888	W/Ind	500	40%		44	U		3490
Columbia Christian College, Portland, OR 97220	1956	C/Prot	307	38%		24	U		2075
Columbia College, Chicago, IL 60605	1890	C/Ind	2916	90%		295	U		2500
Columbia College, Columbia, MO 65201	1851	C/Ind	1003	45%		71	T		2900
Columbia College, Columbia, SC 29203	1854	W/Prot	1002	92%		76	U		2400
Columbia Union College, Takoma Park, MD 20012	1904	C/Prot	865	40%		91	S		1680
Columbia University, New York, NY 10027	1754	C/Ind	2700	45%	G	500	U		5120
Columbus College, Columbus, GA 31907	1958	C/Pub	4283	88%	G	275	S	A	538x
Conception Seminary College, Conception, MO 64433	1891	M/Cath	86	48%		25	R		1270
Concord College, Athens, WV 24712	1872	C/Pub	1904	80%		97	T		364
Concordia College, Ann Arbor, MI 48105	1963	C/Ind	560	50%		52	T		1790
Concordia College, Bronxville, NY 10708	1881	C/Prot	430	65%		56	S		2305
Concordia College, Moorhead, MN 56560	1891	C/Prot	2544	66%		189	S	A	3235
Concordia College, St Paul, MN 55104	1893	C/Prot	633	65%		60	U		2340
Concordia Teachers College, River Forest, IL 60305	1894	C/Prot	1137	25%	G	100	T	AF	2456
Concordia Teachers College, Seward, NE 68434	1894	C/Prot	1137	25%	G	100	T	AF	2456
Connecticut College, New London, CT 06320	1911	C/Ind	1627	25%	G	188	S		5240
Conservatory of Music, San Juan, PR 00936	1959	C/Pub	262	97%		38	U		150x
Converse College, Spartanburg, SC 29301	1889	W/Ind	729	40%		85	U		3500
Cook College , See Rutgers University, Cook College.									
Cooper Union, New York, NY 10003	1859	C/Ind	881	78%	G	132	U		300x
Coppin State College, Baltimore, MD 21216	1900	C/Pub	2600	97%	G	150	U		570
Cornell College, Mount Vernon, IA 52314	1853	C/Ind	880	30%		104	T		4040
Cornell University, Ithaca, NY 14853	1865	C/Ind	11,978	55%	G	1620	T	A, N, AF	5256
Cornish Institute of Allied Arts, Seattle, WA 98102	1914	C/Ind	422	84%		115	U		2115
Corpus Christi State University, Corpus Christi, TX 78411	1973	C/Pub	1458	99%	G	104	U	A	300x
Covenant College, Lookout Mountain, TN 37350	1955	C/Prot	543	10%		38	S		2232
Cranbrook Academy of Art, Bloomfield Hills, MI 48013	1932	C/Ind	5	20%	G	9	S		3046
Creighton University, Omaha, NE 68178	1878	C/Cath	3171	38%	G	881	U	A	3020
Culver-Stockton College, Canton, MO 63435	1853	C/Prot	405	56%		44	T		2800
Cumberland College, Williamsburg, KY 40769	1889	C/Prot	1976	62%		60	T	A	1511
Curry College, Milton, MA 02186	1879	C/Ind	1050	52%		62	S		3900
C W Post Center of Long Island U, Greenvale, NY 11548	1954	C/Ind	7229	93%	G	635	S		3320
Daemen College, Amherst, NY 14226	1947	C/Ind	1317	95%		120	S		2950
Dakota State College, Madison, SD 57042	1881	C/Pub	841	94%		56	T		385.50
Dakota Wesleyan University, Mitchell, SD 57301	1885	C/Prot	508	72%		62	T		2285
Dallas Baptist College, Dallas, TX 75211	1898	C/Prot	960	90%		75	S	A	1500
Dana College, Blair, NE 68008	1884	C/Prot	452	40%		45	T		2970
Daniel Webster College, Nashua, NH 03060	1965	C/Ind	400	25%		25	S	AF	2850
Dartmouth College, Hanover, NH 03755	1769	C/Ind	3529	6%	G	671	R		4920
David Lipscomb College, Nashville, TN 37203	1891	C/Ind	2196	52%		117	S		1800
Davidson College, Davidson, NC 28036	1837	C/Prot	1352	30%		102	T	A	3685
Davis & Elkins College, Elkins, WV 26241	1904	C/Prot	980	25%		86	T		3275
Defiance College, Defiance, OH 43512	1850	C/Prot	800	82%		70	T		3330
Delaware State College, Dover, DE 19901	1891	C/Pub	~2153	62%		124	U		470
Delaware Valley College of Science & Agr, Doylestown, PA 18901	1896	C/Ind	1368	67%		88	R		2673
Delta State University, Cleveland, MS 38732	1924	C/Pub	2419	97%	G	168	T	A	560
Denison University, Granville, OH 43023	1831	C/Ind	2058	26%		176	R		4610
DePaul University, Chicago, IL 60604	1898	C/Cath	7726	90%	G	653	U	A,AF	2814
DePauw University, Greencastle, IN 46135	1837	C/Ind	2251	48%	G	185	T		4272
Detroit Institute of Technology, Detroit, MI 48201	1891	C/Ind	1412	84%		59	T		2344x
DeVry Institute of Technology, Phoenix, AZ 85016	1967	C/Ind	2249	22%		102	U		2245x
DeVry Institute of Technology, Chicago, IL 60618	1931	C/Ind	2191	84%		83	U		2245x

Name and Location	Est	Type/Control	UG Enroll	% of State Res	Grad	Fac Size	Cmps	ROTC	Tuition
DeVry Institute of Technology, Dallas, TX 75235	1969	C/Ind	750	61%		30	U		$2245x
Dickinson College, Carlisle, PA 17013	1773	C/Prot	1650	40%		138	T	A	4500
Dickinson State College, Dickinson, ND 58601	1918	C/Pub	1049	90%		73	T		600
Dillard University, New Orleans, LA 70122	1869	C/Prot	1217	60%		90	U	A,AF	2100
Divine Word College, Epworth, IA 52045	1932	M/Cath	94	11%		31	R		2500
Doane College, Crete, NE 68333	1858	C/Prot	662	76%		62	R		2800
Dominican College, Orangeburg, NY 10962	1952	C/Ind	1161	70%		74	S	A	2100
Dominican College of San Rafael, San Rafael, CA 94901	1890	C/Cath	427	9%	G	100	S		2889
Dominican School of Philosophy and Theology, Berkeley, CA 94709	1932	C/Cath	21	50%	G	18	O		1210
Don Bosco College, Newton, NJ 07860	1928	M/Cath	83	30%		18	R		2740
Dordt College, Sioux Center, IA 51250	1953	C/Prot	1218	28%		75	T		2600
Douglass College, See Rutgers University, Douglass College.									
Dowling College, Oakdale, NY 11769	1959	C/Ind	1500	98%	G	205	T		3000
Drake University, Des Moines, IA 50311	1881	C/Ind	4871	40%	G	340	S	AF	3680
Drew University, Madison, NJ 07940	1866	C/Prot	1558	50%	G	189	S		4330
Drexel University, Philadelphia, PA 19104	1891	C/Ind	8362	65%	G	292	U	A	3575
Drury College, Springfield, MO 65802	1873	C/Prot	973	65%	G	104	U		2650
Duke University, Durham, NC 27706	1838	C/Ind	5700	16%	G	1256	S	N, AF	4230
Duquesne University, Pittsburgh, PA 15219	1878	C/Cath	4763	85%	G	438	U	A	3555
D'Youville College, Buffalo, NY 14201	1908	C/Ind	1440	98%		119	U		2930
Earlham College, Richmond, IN 47374	1847	C/Prot	1047	20%		103	T		4490
East Carolina University, Greenville, NC 27834	1907	C/Pub	10,584	87%	G	619	R	AF	520
East Central Oklahoma State University, Ada, OK 74820	1909	C/Pub	3227	91%	G	144	S	A	350
Eastern College, St Davids, PA 19087	1932	C/Prot	708	68%		71	S		3390
Eastern Connecticut State College, Willimantic, CT 06226	1889	C/Pub	2200	95%	G	190	T		704
Eastern Illinois University, Charleston, IL 61920	1895	C/Pub	8745	98%	G	539	T		790.40
Eastern Kentucky University, Richmond, KY 40475	1906	C/Pub	11,509	84%	G	701	T	A	520
Eastern Mennonite College, Harrisonburg, VA 22801	1917	C/Prot	1056	29%		64	T		2994
Eastern Michigan University, Ypsilanti, MI 48197	1849	C/Pub	13,546	96%	G	746	T		784
Eastern Montana College, Billings, MT 59101	1927	C/Pub	3103	95%	G	186	U		519
Eastern Nazarene College, Wollaston, MA 02170	1918	C/Prot	756	32%		66	U		2530
Eastern New Mexico University, Portales, NM 88130	1934	C/Pub	2898	86%	G	175	T	A	568
Eastern Oregon State College, La Grande, OR 97850	1929	C/Pub	1516	70%	G	100	T		732
Eastern Washington University, Cheney, WA 99004	1890	C/Pub	5601	95%	G	390	T	A	618
East Stroudsburg State College, East Stroudsburg, PA 18301	1891	C/Pub	3542	81%	G	269	T	A	950
East Tennessee State University, Johnson City, TN 37601	1911	C/Pub	8487	86%	G	527	U	A	462
East Texas Baptist College, Marshall, TX 75670	1912	C/Prot	878	87%		90	S		1640
East Texas State University, Commerce, TX 75428	1889	C/Pub	5636	95%	G	456	T	AF	391
Eckerd College, St Petersburg, FL 33733	1958	C/Ind	911	30%		90	S		3995
Edgecliff College, Cincinnati, OH 45206	1935	C/Cath	951	75%		98	S		2176
Edgewood College, Madison, WI 53711	1881	C/Cath	500	70%		60	U		2600
Edinboro State College, Edinboro, PA 16412	1857	C/Pub	4800	92%	G	448	T	A	950
Eisenhower College, Seneca Falls, NY 13148	1966	C/Ind	475	65%		61	R		3925
Elizabeth City State University, Elizabeth City, NC 27909	1891	C/Pub	1600	90%		135	T		597
Elizabethtown College, Elizabethtown, PA 17022	1899	C/Prot	1683	68%		128	T		3122
Elmhurst College, Elmhurst, IL 60126	1865	C/Prot	1575	93%		120	S	AF	3220
Elmira College, Elmira, NY 14901	1855	C/Ind	2134	52%	G	179	U		3815
Elon College, Elon College, NC 27244	1889	C/Prot	2404	68%		112	T	A	2084
Embry-Riddle Aeronautical University, Daytona Beach, FL 32015	1926	C/Ind	5450	10%	G	269	U	A, N, AF	2250
Emerson College, Boston, MA 02116	1880	C/Ind	1316	45%	G	137	U		4116
Emmanuel College, Boston, MA 02115	1919	W/Cath	522	72%	G	92	U		3055
Emory and Henry College, Emory, VA 24327	1836	C/Prot	840	78%		61	R		2355
Emory University, Atlanta, GA 30322	1836	C/Ind	2900	25%	G	250	S		4095
Emporia State University, Emporia, KS 66801	1863	C/Pub	4349	95%	G	290	T		540
Erskine College, Due West, SC 29639	1839	C/Prot	660	65%		52	T		2730
Eureka College, Eureka, IL 61530	1848	C/Prot	450	88%		37	T		3050
Evangel College, Springfield, MO 65802	1955	C/Prot	1463	25%	G	90	U	A	1856
Evergreen State College, Olympia, WA 98505	1967	C/Pub	2322	77%		120	S		618
Fairfield University, Fairfield, CT 06430	1942	C/Cath	2788	50%	G	326	U		3575
Fairleigh Dickinson U, Madison, NJ 07940	1958	C/Ind	3576	80%	G	303	S		3400
Fairleigh Dickinson U, Rutherford, NJ 07070	1942	C/Ind	2914	85%	G	369	S		3400
Fairleigh Dickinson U, Teaneck, NJ 07666	1954	C/Ind	5649	85%	G	788	S		3400
Fairmont State College, Fairmont, WV 26554	1867	C/Pub	4576	94%		254	T	A, AF	348
Fashion Institute of Technology, New York, NY 10001	1944	C/Pub	3200	*		2800	U		860
Fayetteville State University, Fayetteville, NC 28301	1877	C/Pub	2125	88%		154	U	AF	592.50
Felician College, Lodi, NJ 07644	1942	W/Cath	691	99%	G	73	T		2325
Ferris State College, Big Rapids, MI 49307	1884	C/Pub	10,208	96%		673	T		804
Ferrum College, Ferrum, VA 24088	1913	C/Prot	1546	85%		81	R		2380
Findlay College, Findlay, OH 45840	1882	C/Prot	926	80%		100	T		3285
Fisk University, Nashville, TN 37203	1866	C/Ind	1108	11%	G	90	U		2850
Fitchburg State College, Fitchburg, MA 01420	1894	C/Pub	3629	97%	G	231	U	A	739
Flagler College, St Augustine, FL 32084	1968	C/Ind	745	40%		57	T		2050
Florida A&M University, Tallahassee, FL 32307	1887	C/Pub	5560	88%	G	329	T	A, N	699
Florida Atlantic University, Boca Raton, FL 33431	1961	C/Pub	4951	93%	G	317	S		780
Florida Institute of Technology, Melbourne, FL 32901	1958	C/Ind	2626	20%	G	332	S	A	2930
Florida International University, Miami, FL 33199	1965	C/Pub	6280	81%	G	630	U	A	750x
Florida Memorial College, Miami, FL 33054	1879	C/Prot	794	59%		88	U	A	2220
Florida Southern College, Lakeland, FL 33802	1885	C/Prot	1735	67%		117	U		2502
Florida State University, Tallahassee, FL 32306	1957	C/Pub	15,387	90%	G	976	U	A, AF	520
Fontbonne College, St Louis, MO 63105	1917	C/Cath	847	90%	G	117	S		2970
Fordham University, Bronx, NY 10458	1841	C/Cath	8312	86%	G	930	U	A	3430
Fort Hays State University, Hays, KS 67601	1902	C/Pub	3947	92%	G	308	T		630
Fort Lewis College, Durango, CO 81301	1911	C/Pub	2832	70%		130	T		545
Fort Valley State College, Fort Valley, GA 31030	1895	C/Pub	1778	84%	G	156	T	A	585
Fort Wright College, Spokane, WA 99204	1907	C/Cath	368	78%	G	59	S		2850
Framingham State College, Framingham, MA 01701	1839	C/Pub	3125	97%	G	150	S		800
Francis Marion College, Florence, SC 29501	1970	C/Pub	2223	99%	G	117	R	A	550x
Franklin and Marshall College, Lancaster, PA 17604	1787	C/Ind	2083	30%		137	S		4490

Name and Location	Est	Type/ Control	UG Enroll	% of State Res	Grad	Fac Size	Cmps	ROTC	Tuition
Franklin College, Franklin, IN 46131	1834	C/Ind	664	90%		51	T		$3440
Franklin Pierce College, Rindge, NH 03461	1962	C/Ind	890	6%		57	R		3675
Franklin University, Columbus, OH 43215	1902	C/Ind	4444	93%		170	U		1380x
Freed-Hardeman College, Henderson, TN 38340	1869	C/Prot	1440	37%		82	T		1840
Free Will Baptist Bible College, Nashville, TN 37205	1942	C/Prot	544	16%		27	U		1290
Fresno Pacific College, Fresno, CA 93702	1944	C/Prot	450	84%	G	63	S		2760
Friends University, Wichita, KS 67213	1898	C/Prot	908	92%		70	S		2495
Frostburg State College, Frostburg, MD 21533	1898	C/Pub	3200	93%	G	185	T	A	862
Furman University, Greenville, SC 29613	1826	C/Prot	2350	35%	G	150	S	A	3008
Gallaudet College, Washington, DC 20002	1857	C/Ind	1063	*	G	200	U		342
Gannon College, Erie, PA 16501	1944	C/Cath	3005	89%	G	231	U	A	2400
Gardner-Webb College, Boiling Springs, NC 28017	1928	C/Prot	1354	10%		88	T		2220
General Motors Institute, Flint, MI 48502	1919	C/Ind	2248	38%		144	U		1147
Geneva College, Beaver Falls, PA 15010	1848	C/Prot	1400	64%		91	T		3075
George Fox College, Newberg, OR 97132	1891	C/Prot	715	70%		71	T		3131
George Mason University, Fairfax, VA 22030	1960	C/Pub	8280	96%	G	594	S		804x
Georgetown College, Georgetown, KY 40324	1829	C/Prot	934	57%	G	84	T		2440
Georgetown University, Washington, DC 20057	1789	C/Cath	5664	7%	G	1434	S	A	4450
George Washington University, Washington, DC 20052	1821	C/Ind	6100	20%	G	1512	U		3300
George Williams College, Downers Grove, IL 60515	1890	C/Ind	727	88%	G	106	S		3436
Georgia College, Milledgeville, GA 31061	1889	C/Pub	2810	95%	G	179	T		534
Georgia Institute of Technology, Atlanta, GA 30332	1885	C/Pub	9024	54%	G	770	U	A, N, AF	694.50
Georgian Court College, Lakewood, NJ 08701	1908	W/Cath	720	91%	G	82	S		2300
Georgia Southern College, Statesboro, GA 30458	1906	C/Pub	5478	91%	G	355	T		561
Georgia Southwestern College, Americus, GA 31709	1908	C/Pub	1784	97%	G	131	T		540
Georgia State University, Atlanta, GA 30303	1913	C/Pub	13,098	93%	G	843	U	A	585x
Gettysburg College, Gettysburg, PA 17325	1832	C/Prot	1900	33%		138	T	A	4260
Glassboro State College, Glassboro, NJ 08028	1923	C/Pub	9800	97%	G	685	T		950
Glenville State College, Glenville, WV 26351	1872	C/Pub	1672	92%		96	T		330
Goddard College, Plainfield, VT 05667	1938	C/Ind	1097	14%	G	55	R		5100
Golden Gate University, San Francisco, CA 94105	1901	C/Ind	2847	80%	G	852	U		522x
Gonzaga University, Spokane, WA 99258	1887	C/Cath	1926	40%	G	224	S	A	3110
Gordon College, Wenham, MA 01984	1889	C/Prot	950	25%		65	S		2170
Goshen College, Goshen, IN 46526	1894	C/Prot	1209	37%		76	T		2945
Goucher College, Towson, MD 21204	1885	W/Ind	1039	35%	G	122	S		4180
Governors State University, Park Forest South, IL 60466	1969	C/Pub	1537	98%	G	288	S		558x
Grace Bible College, Grand Rapids, MI 49509	1945	C/Prot	216	22%		17	S		1206
Grace College, Winona Lake, IN 46590	1948	C/Prot	756	99%		44	R		2432
Graceland College, Lamoni, IA 50140	1895	C/LDS	1239	26%		101	R		2965
Grambling State University, Grambling, LA 71245	1901	C/Pub	3442	79%	G	200	T	AF	519
Grand Canyon College, Phoenix, AZ 85017	1949	C/Prot	1118	79%	U	67	U	A,AF	1728
Grand Rapids Baptist College, Grand Rapids, MI 49505	1946	C/Prot	935	47%	G	76	S		2060
Grand Valley State Colleges, Allendale, MI 49401	1960	C/Pub	6200	97%	G	375	S		828
Grand View College, Des Moines, IA 50316	1896	C/Ind	1186	90%		84	U		2090
Gratz College, Philadelphia, PA 19141	1895	C/Jewish	142	95%	G	24	U		175
Green Mountain College, Poultney, VT 05764	1834	C/Prot	447	10%		56	T		3865
Greensboro College, Greensboro, NC 27402	1838	C/Prot	658	60%		59	S		2570
Greenville College, Greenville, IL 62246	1892	C/Prot	856	62%		60	T		3003
Grinnell College, Grinnell, IA 50112	1846	C/Ind	1256	14%		117	R		4750x
Grove City College, Grove City, PA 16127	1876	C/Prot	2243	72%		119	T	AF	1970
Guilford College, Greensboro, NC 27410	1837	C/Prot	1161	45%		92	S		3212
Gustavus Adolphus College, St Peter, MN 56082	1862	C/Prot	2200	70%		255	T		3800
Gwynedd-Mercy College, Gwynedd Valley, PA 19437	1948	C/Cath	1363	91%		126	S		2650
Hamilton College, Clinton, NY 13323	1793	M/Ind	1586	60%		147	T		5175
Hamline University, St Paul, MN 55101	1854	C/Prot	1189	80%		170	U		3740
Hampden-Sydney College, Hampden-Sydney, VA 23943	1776	M/Ind	750	65%		58	R		3825
Hampshire College, Amherst, MA 01002	1965	C/Ind	1200	11%		105	T		5625
Hampton Institute, Hampton, VA 23668	1868	C/Ind	2588	39%	G	226	U	A	2490
Hannibal-LaGrange College, Hannibal, MO 63401	1858	C/Prot	450	60%		35	T		3200
Hanover College, Hanover, IN 47243	1827	C/Prot	1000	50%		73	R		2670
Harding College, Searcy, AR 72143	1924	C/Prot	2819	28%	G	148	T		2203
Hardin-Simmons University, Abilene, TX 79601	1891	C/Prot	1554	91%	G	121	U	A	1920
Harris-Stowe State College, St Louis, MO 63103	1857	C/Pub	1102	100%		66	U		350x
Hartwick College, Oneonta, NY 13820	1928	C/Ind	1422	51%		124	T		4350
Harvard and Radcliffe Colleges, Cambridge, MA 02138	1636	C/Ind	6491	12%	G	5832	U	AF	5300
Harvey Mudd College, Claremont, CA 91711	1955	C/Ind	475	60%	G	73	S	A	4940
Hastings College, Hastings, NE 68901	1882	C/Prot	730	79%		60	T		2800
Haverford College, Haverford, PA 19041	1833	M/Ind	953	19%		97	S		5600
Hawaii Loa College, Kaneohe, HI 96744	1963	C/Ind	290	40%		26	S		2100
Hawaii Pacific College, Honolulu, HI 96813	1965	C/Ind	1463	70%		62	U		1700x
Hebrew College, Brookline, MA 02146	1921	C/Ind	149	*		31	S		600
Heidelberg College, Tiffin, OH 44883	1850	C/Prot	943	75%		103	T		3980
Hellenic College, Brookline, MA 02146	1937	C/Cath	78	5%		37	S		2200
Henderson State University, Arkadelphia, AR 71923	1890	C/Pub	2611	95%	G	180	T	A	460
Hendrix College, Conway, AR 72032	1876	C/Prot	1006	85%		58	T		2177
Herbert H. Lehman College , See City U of NY, Lehman College.									
High Point College, High Point, NC 27262	1924	C/Prot	1066	55%		61	S		2325
Hillsdale College, Hillsdale, MI 49242	1844	C/Ind	960	48%		73	T		3690
Hiram College, Hiram, OH 44234	1850	C/Prot	1150	66%		80	R		4197
Hobart and William Smith Colleges, Geneva, NY 14456	1822	C/Ind	1750	50%		121	T		4850
Hofstra University, Hempstead, NY 11550	1935	C/Ind	6683	80%	G	660	S	A	3700
Hollins College, Hollins College, VA 24020	1842	W/Ind	920	37%	G	91	S		4400
Holy Apostles College, Cromwell, CT 06416	1956	C/Cath	72	25%		16	S		2300
Holy Family College, Fremont, CA 94538	1946	W/Cath	143	*		98	U		1232
Holy Family College, Philadelphia, PA 19114	1954	C/Cath	1162	99%		120	S		2150
Holy Names College, Oakland, CA 94619	1868	C/Cath	375	65%	G	101	U		2970
Holy Redeemer College, Waterford, WI 53185	1965	M/Cath	55	8%		25	R		1575
Hood College, Frederick, MD 21701	1893	W/Ind	1190	46%	G	140	T		3655

Name and Location	Est	Type/ Control	UG Enroll	% of State Res	Grad	Fac Size	Cmps	ROTC	Tuition
Hope College, Holland, MI 49423	1851	C/Prot	2371	67%		168	S		$3430
Houghton College, Houghton, NY 14744	1883	C/Prot	1229	61%		80	R		3020
Houston Baptist University, Houston, TX 77074	1960	C/Prot	1704	88%	G	131	S		2335
Howard Payne University, Brownwood, TX 76801	1889	C/Prot	1297	96%		91	T		1670
Howard University, Washington, DC 20059	1867	C/Ind	6703	34%	G	1856	U	A,AF	1765
Humboldt State University, Arcata, CA 95521	1913	C/Pub	6677	98%	G	485	T		210
Hunter College, See City U of NY, Hunter College.									
Huntingdon College, Montgomery, AL 36106	1854	C/Prot	741	75%		51	S		2050
Huntington College, Huntington, IN 46750	1854	C/Prot	741	75%		51	U		2050
Huron College, Huron, SD 57350	1883	C/Prot	314	75%		41	T		2610
Husson College, Bangor, ME 04401	1898	C/Ind	750	65%	G	35	S		2900
Huston-Tillotson College, Austin, TX 78702	1875	C/Prot	616	55%		52	U		1450
Idaho State University, Pocatello, ID 83201	1901	C/Pub	5569	95%	G	505	T	A	460
Illinois Benedictine College, Lisle, IL 60532	1887	C/Cath	1672	98%	G	111	S		1387
Illinois College, Jacksonville, IL 62650	1829	C/Ind	760	88%		60	T		2305
Illinois Institute of Technology, Chicago, IL 60616	1892	C/Ind	4002	76%	G	692	U	N,AF	3690
Illinois State University, Normal, IL 61761	1857	C/Pub	17,191	98%	G	1089	T		787.50
Illinois Wesleyan University, Bloomington, IL 61701	1850	C/Ind	1638	94%		157	T		4128
Immaculata College, Immaculata, PA 19345	1920	W/Cath	581	90%		77	S		2350
Immaculate Heart College, Los Angeles, CA 90027	1916	C/Cath	521	93%	G	64	U		3134
Incarnate Word College, San Antonio, TX 78209	1881	C/Cath	1200	81%	G	114	S	A	2100
Indiana Central University, Indianapolis, IN 46227	1902	C/Prot	1322	96%	G	190	S	A	2880
Indiana Institute of Technology, Fort Wayne, IN 46803	1930	C/Ind	430	43%		41	U	A	2565
Indiana State University, Terre Haute, IN 47809	1865	C/Pub	9738	83%	G	728	U	A	930
Indiana State University at Evansville, Evansville, IN 47712	1965	C/Pub	2863	95%		161	S		760x
Indiana University at Kokomo, Kokomo, IN 46901	1945	C/Pub	2240	98%	G	170	T		24cx
Indiana University at South Bend, South Bend, IN 46614	1922	C/Pub	4303	97%	G	330	U	A, N	597x
Indiana University, Bloomington, IN 47401	1820	C/Pub	22,816	80%	G	1486	T	A, AF	744
Indiana University Northwest, Gary, IN 46408	1959	C/Pub	3533	99%	G	279	U		786x
Indiana University of Pennsylvania, Indiana, PA 15701	1875	C/Pub	10,866	97%	G	664	T	A	1023
Indiana U-Purdue U at Fort Wayne, Fort Wayne, IN 46805	1917	C/Pub	7781	97%	G	495	U	A	900
Indiana U-Purdue U at Indianapolis, Indianapolis, IN 46202	1969	C/Pub	14,098	95%	G	2000	U	A	576
Indiana University Southeast, New Albany, IN 47150	1941	C/Pub	3490	97%		175	S		650x
Inter American U of PR, Hato Rey, PR 00919	1966	C/Prot	5908	*		270	U	A, N, AF	60cx
Inter American U of PR, San German, PR 00753	1912	C/Ind	6188	100%	G	247	U		1290
Inter American U of PR, San Juan, PR 00936	1912	C/Ind	6377	99%	G	203	U	A,AF	40c
International College, Los Angeles, CA 90024	1970	C/Ind	42	85%		97	*		2824x
Iona College, New Rochelle, NY 10801	1940	C/Ind	3500	90%	G	246	S		3060
Iowa State University, Ames, IA 50011	1858	C/Pub	19,746	81%	G	1866	T	A, N, AF	816
Iowa Wesleyan College, Mount Pleasant, IA 52641	1842	C/Prot	692	72%		55	T		3255
Ithaca College, Ithaca, NY 14850	1892	C/Ind	4550	48%	G	409	T		4244
Jackson State University, Jackson, MS 39217	1877	C/Pub	6013	92%	G	375	U	A	620
Jacksonville State University, Jacksonville, AL 36265	1883	C/Pub	5486	92%		273	T	A	500
Jacksonville University, Jacksonville, FL 32211	1934	C/Ind	1988	51%	G	128	S	N	2830
James Madison University, Harrisonburg, VA 22801	1908	C/Pub	6924	80%	G	457	T	A	850
Jamestown College, Jamestown, ND 58401	1883	C/Prot	560	55%		47	T		2790
Jarvis Christian College, Hawkins, TX 75765	1912	C/Prot	480	48%		55	R		2200
Jersey City State College, Jersey City, NJ 07305	1927	C/Pub	7700	95%	G	469	U		720
John Brown University, Siloam Springs, AR 72761	1919	C/Ind	717	25%		56	R		1900
John Carroll University, Cleveland, OH 44118	1886	C/Cath	3133	60%	G	238	S	A	2800
John F Kennedy University, Orinda, CA 94563	1964	C/Ind	120	100%	G	199	S		1650
John Jay College, See City U of NY, John Jay College.									
Johns Hopkins University, Baltimore, MD 21218	1876	C/Ind	2156	32%	G	382	U	A	4500
Johnson C Smith University, Charlotte, NC 28216	1867	C/Ind	1473	37%		85	U	A	1924
Johnson State College, Johnson, VT 05656	1828	C/Pub	957	72%	G	72	R		1141
Johnston College of the U of Redlands, Redlands, CA 92373	1969	C/Prot	140	44%		26	T		4100
John Wesley College, Owosso, MI 48867	1909	C/Prot	284	60%		25	T		2900
Judson College, Marion, AL 36756	1838	W/Prot	355	90%		43	T		1810
Judson College, Elgin, IL 60120	1963	C/Prot	434	60%		34	U		2590
Juilliard School, New York, NY 10023	1905	C/Ind	998	40%	G	200	U		3000x
Juniata College, Huntingdon, PA 16652	1876	C/Ind	1141	73%		85	T		3630
Kalamazoo College, Kalamazoo, MI 49007	1833	C/Prot	1444	70%		91	S		4194
Kansas City Art Institute, Kansas City, MO 64111	1885	C/Ind	613	30%		54	U		3840
Kansas Newman College, Wichita, KS 67213	1933	C/Cath	652	85%		54	U		2250
Kansas State University, Manhattan, KS 66502	1863	C/Pub	14,525	85%	G	3000	T	A, AF	680
Kansas Wesleyan, Salina, KS 67401	1886	C/Prot	452	83%		37	U		1960
Kean College of New Jersey, Union, NJ 07083	1855	C/Pub	9094	96%	G	716	S		660
Kearney State College, Kearney, NE 68847	1903	C/Pub	5865	98%	G	300	T	A	650
Keene State College, U of NH, Keene, NH 03431	1909	C/Pub	2700	65%	G	232	T		995
Kendall College, Evanston, IL 60204	1934	C/Prot	375	97%		34	S		2930
Kent State University, Kent, OH 44242	1910	C/Pub	15,383	93%	G	825	T	A, AF	1064
Kentucky State University, Frankfort, KY 40601	1886	C/Pub	2069	70%	G	160	T	A, AF	530
Kentucky Wesleyan College, Owensboro, KY 42301	1858	C/Prot	852	87%		73	S		2340
Kenyon College, Gambier, OH 43022	1824	C/Ind	1462	28%		120	R		4700
Keuka College, Keuka Park, NY 14478	1890	W/Ind	534	85%		55	R		4155
King College, Bristol, TN 37620	1867	C/Prot	297	36%		42	S		2660
King's College, Briarcliff Manor, NY 10510	1938	C/Ind	853	42%		64	S		3075
King's College, Wilkes-Barre, PA 18711	1946	C/Cath	1720	72%		134	U		2800
Knox College, Galesburg, IL 61401	1837	C/Ind	1042	80%		86	T	A	4310
Knoxville College, Knoxville, TN 37921	1875	C/Ind	713	24%		58	U	A, AF	1880
Kutztown State College, Kutztown, PA 19530	1866	C/Pub	4567	90%	G	277	T		1050
Ladycliff College, Highland Falls, NY 10928	1933	W/Ind	501	70%		78	T		3045
Lafayette College, Easton, PA 18042	1826	C/Ind	2081	30%		165	S	A	4550
La Grange College, La Grange, GA 30240	1831	C/Prot	847	90%	G	51	T		1890
Lake Erie College, Painesville, OH 44077	1859	W/Ind	450	48%	G	67	S		3425
Lake Forest College, Lake Forest, IL 60045	1857	C/Ind	1067	41%		93	S		4725
Lakeland College, Sheboygan, WI 53081	1862	C/Prot	595	72%		44	R		2845

Name and Location	Est	Type/Control	UG Enroll	% of State Res	Grad	Fac Size	Cmps	ROTC	Tuition
Lake Superior State College, Sault Ste Marie, MI 49783	1946	C/Pub	2280	89%		106	T	A	$870
Lamar University, Beaumont, TX 77710	1923	C/Pub	12,213	91%	G	659	U	AF	410
Lambuth College, Jackson, TN 38301	1843	C/Prot	807	84%		72	T		2320
Lander College, Greenwood, SC 29646	1872	C/Pub	1690	96%		99	T		900
Lane College, Jackson, TN 38301	1882	C/Ind	673	58%		47	T		1750
Langston University, Langston, OK 73050	1897	C/Pub	916	68%		74	R		350
Laredo State University, Laredo, TX 78040	1969	C/Pub	522	99%	G	36	U		285x
La Roche College, Pittsburgh, PA 15237	1963	C/Cath	1122	95%	G	101	S		2210
La Salle College, Philadelphia, PA 19141	1863	C/Cath	6227	80%	G	289	U	A	2970
Lawrence Institute of Technology, Southfield, MI 48075	1932	C/Ind	4860	90%		236	S		1470
Lawrence University, Appleton, WI 54911	1847	C/Ind	1184	45%		107	S		4740
Lebanon Valley College, Annville, PA 17003	1866	C/Prot	938	60%		90	T		3720
Lee College, Cleveland, TN 37311	1918	C/Prot	1313	30%		70	U		1556
Lehigh University, Bethlehem, PA 18015	1865	C/Ind	4389	45%	G	346	S	A, AF	4550
Le Moyne College, Syracuse, NY 13214	1946	C/Cath	1941	80%		160	S		3120
Lemoyne-Owen College, Memphis, TN 38126	1870	C/Ind	990	95%		62	U		2400x
Lenoir-Rhyne College, Hickory, NC 28601	1891	C/Prot	1273	70%		111	S		2461
Lesley College, Cambridge, MA 02138	1909	W/Ind	790	52%	G	60	U		3750
LeTourneau College, Longview, TX 75601	1946	C/Ind	926	11%		57	S		2536
Lewis and Clark College, Portland, OR 97219	1867	C/Ind	1880	42%	G	143	S		4300
Lewis-Clark State College, Lewiston, ID 83501	1894	C/Pub	1256	80%		100	U		370
Lewis University, Lockport, IL 60441	1930	C/Cath	2312	96%	G	179	S		2990
Limestone College, Gaffney, SC 29340	1845	C/Ind	1124	85%		77	T		2670
Lincoln Memorial University, Harrogate, TN 37752	1897	C/Ind	1067	60%		53	R		2100
Lincoln University, San Francisco, CA 94118	1919	C/Ind	220	25%	G	22	U		60cx
Lincoln University, Jefferson City, MO 65101	1866	C/Pub	2085	69%	G	189	T	A	510
Lincoln University, Lincoln University, PA 19352	1854	C/Pub	1200	52%	G	88	T		1268
Lindenwood Colleges, St Charles, MO 63301	1827	C/Prot	1403	21%	G	146	T		3080
Linfield College, McMinnville, OR 97128	1849	C/Ind	922	48%	G	104	T		3550
Livingston College, See Rutgers University, Livingston College.									
Livingstone College, Salisbury, NC 28144	1879	C/Prot	921	57%		55	T		1400
Livingston University, Livingston, AL 35470	1840	C/Pub	1059	88%	G	73	T		618
Lock Haven State College, Lock Haven, PA 17745	1870	C/Pub	2231	87%		168	T	A	1062
Loma Linda University, Loma Linda, CA 92354	1905	C/Prot	3108	69%	G	931	T		3585
Loma Linda University, La Sierra Cmps, Riverside, CA 92505	1905	C/Prot	2212	78%	G	174	S		3585
Long Island U Brooklyn Center, Brooklyn, NY 11201	1926	C/Ind	4365	80%	G	481	U		3200
Long Island U Southampton College, Southampton, NY 11968	1963	C/Ind	1410	70%	G	142	R		3290
Longwood College, Farmville, VA 23901	1839	C/Pub	2200	92%	G	153	T	A	760
Loras College, Dubuque, IA 52001	1839	C/Cath	1700	60%	G	125	U		2800
Loretto Heights College, Denver, CO 80236	1918	C/Ind	850	65%		94	S		3600
Los Angeles Baptist College, Newhall, CA 91321	1927	C/Prot	382	75%		53	S		2350
Louisiana College, Pineville, LA 71360	1906	C/Prot	1314	90%		92	T	A	1200
Louisiana State U and A&M College, Baton Rouge, LA 70803	1860	C/Pub	20,638	88%	G	1078	S	A, AF	554
Louisiana State U in Shreveport, Shreveport, LA 71105	1965	C/Pub	3103	98%	G	115	S	A	480x
Louisiana Tech University, Ruston, LA 71272	1894	C/Pub	8352	86%	G	398	T	AF	549
Loyola College, Baltimore, MD 21210	1852	C/Cath	1946	75%	G	302	S	A	2525
Loyola Marymount University, Los Angeles, CA 90045	1911	C/Cath	3629	91%	G	325	S	AF	3583
Loyola University, New Orleans, LA 70118	1912	C/Cath	3216	72%	G	303	S	A	2320
Loyola University of Chicago, Chicago, IL 60611	1870	C/Cath	8445	95%	G	1370	U	A	2890
Lubbock Christian College, Lubbock, TX 79407	1957	C/Ind	1128	66%		97	S		2016
Luther College, Decorah, IA 52101	1861	C/Prot	1999	56%		148	T		3575
Lycoming College, Williamsport, PA 17701	1812	C/Ind	1179	61%		75	S		3300
Lynchburg College, Lynchburg, VA 24501	1903	C/Prot	1774	55%	G	138	S		3100
Lyndon State College, Lyndonville, VT 05851	1911	C/Pub	1061	65%		99	R		720
Macalester College, St Paul, MN 55105	1874	C/Prot	1763	35%		149	U		4175
MacMurray College, Jacksonville, IL 62650	1846	C/Ind	743	90%		69	T		3320
Madonna College, Livonia, MI 48150	1947	C/Cath	3011	98%		132	S		1260
Maine Maritime Academy, Castine, ME 04421	1941	C/Pub	644	60%	G	60	T	N	1365
Malone College, Canton, OH 44709	1892	C/Ind	782	89%		50	S		2958
Manchester College, North Manchester, IN 46962	1889	C/Ind	1128	80%		105	T		2870
Manhattan College, Bronx, NY 10471	1853	C/Ind	4087	82%	G	310	S	AF	2950
Manhattan School of Music, New York, NY 10027	1917	C/Ind	427	55%	G	158	U		3060
Manhattanville College, Purchase, NY 10577	1841	C/Ind	801	50%	G	161	S		4290
Mankato State University, Mankato, MN 56001	1867	C/Pub	8484	87%	G	540	U		691
Mannes College of Music, New York, NY 10021	1916	C/Ind	195	61%		106	U		2050
Mansfield State College, Mansfield, PA 16933	1857	C/Pub	2501	90%	G	205	T		950
Marian College, Indianapolis, IN 46222	1851	C/Cath	748	86%		77	S		2455
Marian College of Fond du Lac, Fond du Lac, WI 54935	1936	C/Cath	479	93%	G	58	T	A	2270
Marietta College, Marietta, OH 45750	1835	C/Ind	1578	45%	G	117	T		4000
Marion College, Marion, IN 46952	1920	C/Prot	961	62%		78	S		2810
Marist College, Poughkeepsie, NY 12601	1949	C/Cath	1850	85%	G	120	S		3120
Marlboro College, Marlboro, VT 05344	1946	C/Ind	219	10%		35	R		4265
Marquette University, Milwaukee, WI 53233	1881	C/Cath	8715	49%	G	852	U	A,N	3320
Marshall University, Huntington, WV 25701	1837	C/Pub	8100	88%	G	480	U	A	340
Mars Hill College, Mars Hill, NC 28754	1856	C/Prot	1808	71%		127	T		2585
Mary Baldwin College, Staunton, VA 24401	1842	W/Ind	700	48%		60	T		3520
Mary College, Bismarck, ND 58501	1959	C/Cath	922	92%		65	S		2010
Marycrest College, Davenport, IA 52804	1939	C/Cath	708	54%	G	106	S		2975
Marygrove College, Detroit, MI 48221	1910	C/Ind	752	97%	G	56	U		2828
Maryland Institute College of Art, Baltimore, MD 21217	1826	C/Ind	622	46%	G	105	U		3300x
Marylhurst Education Center, Marylhurst, OR 97306	1893	C/Ind	850	*		80	S		2210
Marymount College, Tarrytown, NY 10591	1922	W/Cath	905	51%		113	S		3660
Marymount College of Kansas, Salina, KS 67401	1922	C/Cath	775	86%		76	T		2140
Marymount College of Virginia, Arlington, VA 22207	1950	W/Cath	852	34%		113	U		2750
Marymount Manhattan College, New York, NY 10021	1937	W/Ind	2283	90%		163	U		2840
Maryville College, St Louis, MO 63141	1827	C/Ind	1355	85%	G	100	S		2880
Maryville College, Maryville, TN 37801	1819	C/Ind	634	25%		60	T	A	2853
Mary Washington College, Fredericksburg, VA 22401	1908	C/Pub	2292	75%		145	T		870

Name and Location	Est	Type/ Control	UG Enroll	% of State Res	Grad	Fac Size	Cmps	ROTC	Tuition
Marywood College, Scranton, PA 18509	1915	W/Cath	2000	55%	G	190	S	A, AF	$1950
Massachusetts College of Art, Boston, MA 02215	1873	C/Pub	1082	85%	G	100	U		630x
Massachusetts Institute of Technology, Cambridge, MA 02139	1861	C/Ind	4291	17%	G	1700	U	A,N,AF	5300
Massachusetts Maritime Academy, Buzzards Bay, MA 02532	1891	C/Pub	850	85%		52	T		734
Mayville State College, Mayville, ND 58257	1889	C/Pub	811	80%		65	T		372
McKendree College, Lebanon, IL 62254	1828	C/Prot	805	81%		83	T	AF	3085
McMurry College, Abilene, TX 79605	1923	C/Prot	1372	89%		84	U		1560
McNeese State University, Lake Charles, LA 70609	1939	C/Pub	4626	94%	G	319	S	A	448
McPherson College, McPherson, KS 67460	1887	C/Prot	493	56%		42	R		2550
Medaille College, Buffalo, NY 14214	1875	C/Ind	1058	99%		64	U		2425x
Medgar Evers College, See City U of NY, Medgar Evers College.									
Memphis Academy of Arts, Memphis, TN 38112	1936	C/Ind	217	62%		27	U		1750
Memphis State University, Memphis, TN 38152	1912	C/Pub	16,019	93%	G	891	U	AF	448
Menlo College, Menlo Park, CA 94025	1927	C/Ind	621	56%		50	S		4250
Mercer University, Macon, GA 31207	1833	C/Ind	1910	50%	G	130	U	A	3006
Mercer University in Atlanta, Atlanta, GA 30341	1964	C/Prot	1129	97%	G	93	U		2250
Mercy College, Dobbs Ferry, NY 10522	1961	C/Ind	8000	92%		560	U		65cx
Mercy College of Detroit, Detroit, MI 48219	1941	C/Cath	2444	95%	G	214	U		2400
Mercyhurst College, Erie, PA 16501	1926	C/Ind	1300	79%	G	127	S	A	2842.50
Meredith College, Raleigh, NC 27611	1891	W/Prot	1536	85%		120	U		2350
Merrimack College, North Andover, MA 01845	1947	C/Cath	2068	80%		144	S		3380
Mesa College, Grand Junction, CO 81501	1925	C/Pub	4082	95%		155	T	A	602
Messiah College, Grantham, PA 17027	1909	C/Prot	1149	60%		108	T		2910
Methodist College, Fayetteville, NC 28301	1956	C/Prot	764	71%		48	S	A	2160
Metropolitan State College, Denver, CO 80204	1965	C/Pub	13,500	95%		596	U		513
Metropolitan State University, St Paul, MN 55101	1971	C/Pub	2055	95%		22	U		550x
Miami University, Oxford, OH 45056	1809	C/Pub	13,575	88%	G	673	T	N,AF	1120
Michigan State University, East Lansing, MI 48824	1855	C/Pub	35,645	85%	G	2607	U	A, AF	1097
Michigan Technological University, Houghton, MI 49931	1885	C/Pub	6657	85%	G	367	T	A, AF	861
Mid-America Nazarene College, Olathe, KS 66061	1964	C/Prot	1121	45%		69	S		1840
Middlebury College, Middlebury, VT 05753	1800	C/Ind	1870	7%	G	162	R		2400
Middle Tennessee State University, Murfreesboro, TN 37130	1911	C/Pub	8770	95%	G	452	T	A	0
Midland Lutheran College, Fremont, NE 68025	1883	C/Prot	757	70%		65	T		2870
Midwestern State University, Wichita Falls, TX 76308	1922	C/Pub	4020	90%	G	195	S	A	600
Miles College, Birmingham, AL 35208	1907	C/Prot	1214	90%		98	R		1120
Millersville State College, Millersville, PA 17551	1854	C/Pub	5216	96%	G	360	T	A	950
Milligan College, Milligan College, TN 37682	1866	C/Prot	776	25%		57	R		2072
Millikin University, Decatur, IL 62522	1901	C/Ind	1648	93%		121	S		3598
Millsaps College, Jackson, MS 39210	1890	C/Prot	972	74%		80	S		2639
Mills College, Oakland, CA 94613	1852	W/Ind	850	60%	G	104	U		4335
Milton College, Milton, WI 53563	1844	C/Ind	758	75%		38	R	A	3110
Milwaukee School of Engineering, Milwaukee, WI 53201	1903	C/Ind	1398	70%	G	80	U	A	3105
Minneapolis College of Art & Design, Minneapolis, MN 55404	1886	C/Ind	682	50%		60	U		3000
Minot State College, Minot, ND 58701	1913	C/Pub	2187	96%		140	T		468
Mississippi College, Clinton, MS 39058	1826	C/Prot	1855	90%	G	179	T		55c
Mississippi State University, Mississippi State, MS 39762	1878	C/Pub	9588	95%	G	813	T	A, AF	870
Mississippi University for Women, Columbus, MS 39701	1884	W/Pub	1970	75%	G	184	T		574
Mississippi Valley State University, Itta Bena, MS 38941	1946	C/Pub	2821	91%	G	186	U	AF	700
Missouri Baptist College, St Louis, MO 63141	1963	C/Prot	428	98%		37	S		1800
Missouri Institute of Technology, Kansas City, MO 64108	1931	C/Ind	740	40%		28	U		2245
Missouri Southern State College, Joplin, MO 64801	1937	C/Pub	3748	95%		189	T	A	420
Missouri Valley College, Marshall, MO 65340	1888	C/Prot	376	62%		38	T		2234
Missouri Western State College, St Joseph, MO 64507	1915	C/Pub	3686	93%		182	S	A	442
Mobile College, Mobile, AL 36613	1961	C/Prot	1002	91%		65	S	A	1400
Molloy College, Rockville Center, NY 11570	1955	W/Cath	1513	100%		143	S		3000x
Monmouth College, Monmouth, IL 61462	1853	C/Ind	675	80%		76	T	A	3480
Monmouth College, West Long Branch, NJ 07764	1933	C/Ind	3000	90%	G	214	S	A	3420
Montana College of Mineral Sci & Tech, Butte, MT 59701	1893	C/Pub	1197	83%	G	80	R		460
Montana State University, Bozeman, MT 59717	1893	C/Pub	9156	83%	G	543	T	A, AF	763
Montclair State College, Upper Montclair, NJ 07043	1908	C/Pub	11,695	95%	G	779	S	A, AF	845
Monterey Institute of Foreign Studies, Monterey, CA 93940	1955	C/Ind	89	61%	G	72	U		3300
Moore College of Art, Philadelphia, PA 19103	1844	W/Ind	500	56%		84	U		3700
Moorhead State University, Moorhead, MN 56560	1885	C/Pub	6358	76%	G	336	T		531
Moravian College, Bethlehem, PA 18018	1742	C/Ind	1263	56%		110	U		3900
Morehead State University, Morehead, KY 40351	1922	C/Pub	5429	80%	G	306	U		270
Morehouse College, Atlanta, GA 30314	1867	M/Ind	1699	36%		141	U	A, N, AF	2362
Morgan State University, Baltimore, MD 21239	1867	C/Pub	4200	75%	G	326	U	A	830
Morningside College, Sioux City, IA 51106	1889	C/Ind	1441	80%	G	114	S		3200
Morris Brown College, Atlanta, GA 30314	1881	C/Ind	1530	95%	G	150	T	AF	2080
Morris Harvey College, Charleston, WV 25304	1888	C/Ind	1685	80%		101	S		1860
Mount Holyoke College, South Hadley, MA 01075	1837	W/Ind	1913	23%	G	182	T		4550
Mount Marty College, Yankton, SD 57078	1936	C/Cath	582	46%		77	T		2580
Mount Mary College, Milwaukee, WI 53222	1913	W/Cath	1115	91%		124	S		2
Mount Mercy College, Cedar Rapids, IA 52402	1928	C/Cath	1015	90%		74	U		2830
Mount Saint Mary College, Newburgh, NY 12550	1959	C/Cath	1046	80%		80	S		2540
Mount St Mary's College, Emmitsburg, MD 21727	1808	C/Cath	1405	38%	G	83	U		2870
Mount St Mary's College, Chalon Cmps, Los Angeles, CA 90049	1925	C/Cath	944	86%	G	127	U		3055
Mount Senario College, Ladysmith, WI 54848	1962	C/Ind	422	78%		46	T		2900
Mount Union College, Alliance, OH 44601	1846	C/Prot	1020	82%		95	T		3690
Mount Vernon College, Washington, DC 20007	1875	W/Ind	461	6%		60	U		3300
Mount Vernon Nazarene College, Mt Vernon, OH 43050	1964	C/Prot	941	75%		65	T		2140
Muhlenberg College, Allentown, PA 18104	1848	C/Prot	1530	40%		117	S		4000
Mundelein College, Chicago, IL 60660	1929	W/Cath	1458	88%	G	129	U		2670
Murray State University, Murray, KY 42071	1922	C/Pub	6451	80%	G	381	T	A	520
Museum Art School, Portland, OR 97205	1909	C/Ind	160	63%		36	U		2300
Muskingum College, New Concord, OH 43762	1837	C/Prot	938	73%		96	R		3785
Nasson College, Springvale, ME 04083	1912	C/Ind	643	16%		53	R		3565
Nathaniel Hawthorne College, Antrim, NH 03440	1962	C/Ind	525	4%		60	R		3660

Name and Location	Est	Type/ Control	UG Enroll	% of State Res	Grad	Fac Size	Cmps	ROTC	Tuition
National College of Business, Rapid City, SD 57701	1941	C/Ind	1083	62%		55	U	A	$2875
National College of Education, Evanston, IL 60201	1886	C/Ind	532	65%	G	118	S		3720
National College of Education, Urban Cmps, Chicago, IL 60601	1971	C/Ind	257	100%	G	50	U		2250x
National University, San Diego, CA 92106	1971	C/Ind	2031	85%	G	259	U		3060
Nazareth College, Nazareth, MI 49074	1924	C/Ind	629	98%		64	S		3150
Nazareth College of Rochester, Rochester, NY 14610	1924	C/Ind	1408.	98%	G	142	S		3150
Nebraska Wesleyan University, Lincoln, NE 68504	1887	C/Prot	1160	84%		100	S		2819
Newark College of Arts and Sciences., See Rutgers University, Newark Campus.									
Newberry College, Newberry, SC 29108	1856	C/Prot	817	70%		67	T		2900
New College of California, San Francisco, CA 94110	1971	C/Ind	140	40%	G	20	U		2400x
New College of the U of South Florida, Sarasota, FL 33580	1960	C/Pub	508	50%		41	S		870
Newcomb College of Tulane University, New Orleans, LA 70118	1834	W/Ind	1629	26%		133	U	A, N, AF	4546
New England College, Henniker, NH 03242	1946	C/Ind	1683	15%		141	T		4150
New England Conservatory of Music, Boston, MA 02115	1867	C/Ind	508	32%	G	148	U		4305
New Hampshire College, Manchester, NH 03104	1932	C/Ind	1369	30%	G	66	S		3692
New Jersey Institute of Technology, Newark, NJ 07102	1881	C/Pub	4194	95%	G	387	U	AF	890x
New Mexico Highlands University, Las Vegas, NM 87701	1893	C/Pub	1677	85%	G	105	T		376
New Mexico Inst of Mining & Tech, Socorro, NM 87801	1889	C/Pub	814	68%	G	100	T		653
New Mexico State U, Las Cruces, NM 88003	1888	C/Pub	10,297	91%	G	800	S	A, AF	608
New School for Social Research, New York, NY 10011	1919	C/Ind	300	67%	G	125	U		3400
New School of Music, Philadelphia, PA 19103	1943	C/Ind	81	60%		46	U		2735x
New York Institute of Tech, Old Westbury, NY 11568	1955	C/Ind	10,443	95%	G	642	S		2560
New York University, New York, NY 10003	1831	C/Ind	8839	82%	G	5500	U		4520
Niagara University, Niagara University, NY 14109	1856	C/Cath	3267	80%	G	244	U	A	2970
Nicholls State University, Thibodaux, LA 70301	1948	C/Pub	5532	97%	G	233	T	A	420
Nichols College, Dudley, MA 01570	1815	C/Ind	723	50%	G	41	T		3260
Norfolk State University, Norfolk, VA 23504	1935	C/Pub	6989	80%	G	425	U	A	600
North Adams State College, North Adams, MA 01247	1894	C/Pub	2200	95%	G	190	T		650
North Carolina A&T State University, Greensboro, NC 27411	1891	C/Pub	4851	83%	G	358	U	A, AF	470
North Carolina Central University, Durham, NC 27707	1910	C/Pub	3922	90%	G	423	U	AF	527
North Carolina School of the Arts, Winston-Salem, NC 27107	1963	C/Pub	453	45%		105	U		770
North Carolina State University, Raleigh, NC 27607	1862	C/Pub	14,637	88%	G	1352	S	A, AF	558
North Carolina Wesleyan College, Rocky Mount, NC 27801	1956	C/Prot	743	74%		53	T		1970
North Central College, Naperville, IL 60540	1861	C/Prot	1100	95%		75	S		3120
North Dakota State University, Fargo, ND 58102	1890	C/Pub	6882	71%	G	570	U	A, AF	622
Northeastern Bible College, Essex Fells, NJ 07021	1950	C/Prot	380	73%	G	33	S		2258
Northeastern Illinois University, Chicago, IL 60625	1961	C/Pub	7656	99%	G	443	U		510x
Northeastern Oklahoma State U, Tahlequah, OK 74464	1846	C/Pub	4323	96%	G	220	T	A	427
Northeastern University, Boston, MA 02115	1898	C/Ind	16,405	65%	G	2183	U	A,AF	3135
Northeast Louisiana University, Monroe, LA 71201	1931	C/Pub	7630	94%	G	385	U	A	425
Northeast Missouri State University, Kirksville, MO 63501	1867	C/Pub	4499	75%	G	312	T	A	340
Northern Arizona University, Flagstaff, AZ 86011	1899	C/Pub	10,603	75%	G	526	T	AF	500
Northern Illinois University, DeKalb, IL 60115	1895	C/Pub	17,079	93%	G	1233	S	A	780
Northern Kentucky University, Highland Heights, KY 41076	1968	C/Pub	5899	90%	G	375	S	A	480x
Northern Michigan University, Marquette, MI 49855	1899	C/Pub	7603	94%	G	396	U	A	959
Northern Montana College, Havre, MT 59501	1929	C/Pub	1045	90%	G	86	R		461
Northern State College, Aberdeen, SD 57401	1901	C/Pub	2258	97%	G	110	T		595
North Georgia College, Dahlonega, GA 30533	1873	C/Pub	1511	95%		120	T	A	552
Northland College, Ashland, WI 54806	1892	C/Ind	711	35%		46	T		3120
North Park College, Chicago, IL 60625	1891	C/Prot	1212	60%	G	98	U		3387
Northrop University, Inglewood, CA 90306	1942	C/Ind	1536	18%	G	37	S		984
North Texas State University, Denton, TX 76203	1890	C/Pub	12,231	89%	G	1420	T	AF	400
Northwest Bible College, Minot, ND 58701	1934	C/Prot	180	32%		12	T		1300
Northwest Christian College, Eugene, OR 97401	1895	C/Prot	382	35%		23	U	A	1620
Northwest College, Kirkland, WA 98033	1934	C/Prot	727	55%		30	S		1060
Northwestern College, Orange City, IA 51041	1882	C/Prot	802	65%		64	R		2745
Northwestern Oklahoma State U, Alva, OK 73717	1897	C/Pub	1473	89%	G	71	T	A	415
Northwestern State U of Louisiana, Natchitoches, LA 71457	1884	C/Pub	4653	97%	G	225	T	A	500
Northwestern University, Evanston, IL 60201	1851	C/Ind	6915	32%	G	1673	S	N	5025
Northwest Missouri State University, Maryville, MO 64468	1905	C/Pub	3740	65%	G	245	T		420
Northwest Nazarene College, Nampa, ID 83651	1913	C/Prot	1218	31%	G	73	T		2325
Northwood Inst-Midland Campus, Midland, MI 48640	1959	C/Ind	1654	50%		62	S		2520
Norwich University, Northfield, VT 05663	1819	C/Ind	1459	8%	G	159	R	A, AF	3190
Notre Dame College, Manchester, NH 03104	1950	W/Cath	485	1%		62	S		2100
Notre Dame College, Cleveland, OH 44121	1922	W/Cath	585	90%		57	S		2160
Nyack College, Nyack, NY 10960	1882	C/Prot	636	50%	G	68	S		2718
Oakland City College, Oakland City, CA 47660	1885	C/Prot	526	99%		39	R		1899
Oakland University, Rochester, MI 48063	1957	C/Pub	8992	99%	G	345	S		894
Oakwood College, Huntsville, AL 35806	1896	C/Prot	1257	18%		54	U		1508
Oberlin College, Oberlin, OH 44074	1833	C/Ind	2750	12%	G	226	T		4300
Occidental College, Los Angeles, CA 90041	1887	C/Ind	1602	60%	G	154	S		4801
Oglethorpe University, Atlanta, GA 30319	1835	C/Ind	1030	48%	G	49	S		2910
Ohio Dominican College, Columbus, OH 43219	1911	C/Cath	860	85%		69	U	AF	2980
Ohio Institute of Technology, Columbus, OH 43219	1952	C/Ind	2222	40%		75	U		2245x
Ohio Northern University, Ada, OH 45810	1871	C/Prot	2126	80%		167	T		3276
Ohio State University, Columbus, OH 43210	1870	C/Pub	39,118	94%	G	3091	U	A, N, AF	975
Ohio State University, Lima, OH 45802	1961	C/Pub	865	99%		43	T	A	930x
Ohio State University, Mansfield, OH 44906	1958	C/Pub	1029	99%		48	T		930
Ohio University, Athens, OH 45701	1804	C/Pub	10,034	80%	G	817	T	A, AF	1056
Ohio Wesleyan University, Delaware, OH 43015	1841	C/Prot	2250	33%		180	T		4315
Oklahoma Baptist University, Shawnee, OK 74801	1909	C/Prot	1555	74%		113	S		1500
Oklahoma Christian College, Oklahoma City, OK 73111	1950	C/Prot	1458	49%		55	S		1480
Oklahoma City University, Oklahoma City, OK 73106	1904	C/Prot	1496	95%	G	171	S	A, AF	1936
Oklahoma Panhandle State University, Goodwell, OK 73939	1909	C/Pub	976	80%		68	R	A	474
Oklahoma State University, Stillwater, OK 74074	1890	C/Pub	19,040	90%	G	1618	U	A, AF	553
Old Dominion University, Norfolk, VA 23508	1930	C/Pub	10,768	86%	G	708	U	A	744
Olivet College, Olivet, MI 49076	1884	C/Prot	671	95%	G	52	R		3490

Name and Location	Est	Type/ Control	UG Enroll	% of State Res	Grad	Fac Size	Cmps	ROTC	Tuition
Olivet Nazarene College, Kankakee, IL 60901	1907	C/Ind	1918	40%	G	110	S		$2276
Oral Roberts University, Tulsa, OK 74171	1963	C/Ind	2503	19%	G	300	S		2110
Oregon College of Education, Monmouth, OR 97361	1856	C/Pub	2290	66%	G	200	T	AF	780
Oregon Institute of Technology, Klamath Falls, OR 97601	1946	C/Pub	2195	87%	G	207	T		779
Oregon State University, Corvallis, OR 97331	1868	C/Pub	13,916	86%	G	1122	T	A, N, AF	786
Otis Art Institute of Los Angeles County, Los Angeles, CA 90057	1918	C/Pub	85	6%	G	29	U		2940
Ottawa University, Ottawa, KS 66067	1865	C/Prot	543	50%		61	T		2616
Otterbein College, Westerville, OH 43081	1847	C/Prot	1585	89%		112	S		2412
Ouachita Baptist University, Arkadelphia, AR 71923	1885	C/Prot	1438	*	G	102	T	A	1760
Our Lady of Angels College, Aston, PA 19014	1965	W/Cath	674	70%		71	S		2200
Our Lady of Holy Cross College, New Orleans, LA 70114	1916	C/Cath	783	100%		87	S		1500
Our Lady of the Lake U of San Antonio, San Antonio, TX 78285	1896	C/Cath	1150	90%	G	130	S		2100
Pace University, New York, NY 10038	1906	C/Ind	8463	90%	G	1116	U		3000
Pace University-Coll of White Plains, White Plains, NY 10603	1923	C/Ind	1004	82%		79	S		3100
Pace University-Pleasantville/Briarcliff, Pleasantville, NY 10570	1963	C/Ind	3815	84%	G	386	S		3100
Pacific Christian College, Fullerton, CA 92631	1928	C/Prot	355	83%	G	42	U		2006
Pacific Lutheran University, Tacoma, WA 98447	1890	C/Prot	2812	72%	G	263	S		3552
Pacific Oaks College, Pasadena, CA 91105	1945	C/Ind	110	60%	G	31	U		3300x
Pacific Union College, Angwin, CA 94508	1882	C/Prot	2089	84%	G	175	R		3585
Pacific University, Forest Grove, OR 97116	1849	C/Ind	851	35%	G	106	T		3900
Paine College, Augusta, GA 30901	1882	C/Ind	817	82%		57	U		2010
Palm Beach Atlantic College, West Palm Beach, FL 33401	1968	C/Ind	580	76%		63	U		1540
Pan American University, Edinburg, TX 78539	1927	C/Pub	7815	95%	G	428	R		264
Park College, Parkville, MO 64152	1875	C/Prot	590	50%		37	S		2700
Parks College of St. Louis University, Cahokia, IL 62206	1927	C/Cath	824	45%		56	S	AF	3450
Parsons School of Design, New York, NY 10011	1896	C/Ind	1340	32%	G	235	U		4
Paul Quinn College, Waco, TX 76703	1872	C/Prot	421	71%		34	U	AF	1865
Peabody Institute of Johns Hopkins University, Baltimore, MD 21202	1857	C/Ind	250	35%	-G	104	U		4150
Pembroke State University, Pembroke, NC 28372	1887	C/Pub	2058	95%		139	R		470
Pennsylvania State U-Behrend College, Erie, PA 16510	1926	C/Pub	1510	97%	G	91	S	A	1179
Pennsylvania State U-Capitol Campus, Middletown, PA 17057	1966	C/Pub	1718	97%	G	124	S		1233
Pennsylvania State U-Univ Park Campus, University Park, PA 16802	1855	C/Pub	27,027	90%	G	1660	T	A, N, AF	1368
Pepperdine University, Malibu, CA 90265	1937	C/Prot	2049	72%	G	169	S		4576
Peru State College, Peru, NE 68421	1867	C/Pub	718	75%		52	R		650
Pfeiffer College, Misenheimer, NC 28109	1885	C/Prot	936	71%		74	R	A	2470
Philadelphia College of Art, Philadelphia, PA 19102	1876	C/Ind	1131	57%	G	170	U		4323
Philadelphia College of Bible, Philadelphia, PA 19103	1913	C/Ind	525	49%		45	U		2280
Philadelphia Coll of Textiles & Sci, Philadelphia, PA 19144	1884	C/Ind	2521	80%	G	168	S		2850
Philadelphia Coll of Performing Arts, Philadelphia, PA 19102	1870	C/Ind	340	78%	G	135	U		3600
Philander Smith College, Little Rock, AR 72203	1877	C/Prot	637	75%		61	U		1300
Phillips University, Enid, OK 73701	1906	C/Prot	1006	30%	G	121	T		2180
Piedmont College, Demorest, GA 30535	1897	C/Prot	450	70%		48	T		1498
Pikeville College, Pikeville, KY 41501	1889	C/Prot	615	78%		52	T		2100
Pine Manor College, Chestnut Hill, MA 02167	1911	W/Ind	442	17%		45	S		4515
Pittsburg State University, Pittsburg, KS 66762	1903	C/Pub	3752	71%	G	345	T	A	510.50
Pitzer College, Claremont, CA 91711	1963	C/Ind	740	45%		103	T		4670
Plymouth State College, U of NH, Plymouth, NH 03264	1871	C/Pub	3200	70%	G	150	T	A, AF	950
Point Loma College, San Diego, CA 92106	1902	C/Prot	1511	89%	G	84	U	AF	2964
Point Park College, Pittsburgh, PA 15222	1960	C/Ind	1951	85%	G	144	U	A,AF	3060
Polytechnic Institute of New York, Brooklyn, NY 11201	1854	C/Ind	2455	90%	G	348	U	A	3850
Pomona College, Claremont, CA 91711	1887	C/Ind	1362	58%		144	S		4644
Pontifical College Josephinum, Columbus, OH 43085	1888	C/Cath	94	56%	G	47	U		2164
Portland State University, Portland, OR 97207	1946	C/Pub	9552	89%	G	784	U		795x
Post College, Waterbury, CT 06708	1890	C/Ind	1446	64%		86	S		2526
Prairie View A&M University, Prairie View, TX 77445	1878	C/Pub	3848	83%	G	305	T	A, N	136
Pratt Institute, Brooklyn, NY 11205	1887	C/Ind	3133	58%	G	490	U		4100
Presbyterian College, Clinton, SC 29325	1880	C/Prot	896	67%		67	T	A	3015
Princeton University, Princeton, NJ 08540	1746	C/Ind	4422	20%	G	777	S	A	5585
Principia College, Elsah, IL 62028	1898	C/Prot	883	11%		82	R		3708
Providence College, Providence, RI 02918	1917	C/Cath	3500	38%	G	235	S	A	3342
Purdue University-Calumet Campus, Hammond, IN 46323	1951	C/Pub	5622	87%		377	U		1060x
Purdue University, West Lafayette, IN 47907	1869	C/Pub	25,146	25%	G	3749	T	A, N, AF	870
Queens College, See City U of NY, Queens College.									
Queens College, Charlotte, NC 28274	1857	W/Prot	523	64%		62	S		3175
Quincy College, Quincy, IL 62301	1859	C/Cath	1648	83%		85	S		2800
Quinnipiac College, Hamden, CT 06518	1929	C/Ind	2316	64%	G	165	S		2950
Radcliffe College, See Harvard and Radcliffe Colleges.									
Radford University, Radford, VA 24142	1913	C/Pub	4600	90%	G	290	R	A	873
Ramapo College of New Jersey, Mahwah, NJ 07430	1969	C/Pub	4022	96%		185	S		850
Randolph-Macon College, Ashland, VA 23005	1830	C/Prot	929	60%		78	T		3320
Randolph-Macon Woman's College, Lynchburg, VA 24504	1891	W/Prot	765	34%	G	80	S		3900
Reed College, Portland, OR 97202	1909	C/Ind	1120	20%	G	108	S		4990
Regis College, Denver, CO 80221	1877	C/Cath	1150	30%		95	S		3400
Regis College, Weston, MA 02193	1927	W/Cath	819	80%	G	83	S		3210
Rensselaer Polytechnic Institute, Troy, NY 12181	1824	C/Ind	4155	43%	G	345	S	A,N,AF	5000
Rhode Island College, Providence, RI 02908	1854	C/Pub	5976	90%	G	369	S		730
Rhode Island School of Design, Providence, RI 02903	1877	C/Ind	1330	10%	G	148	U		4610
Rice University, Houston, TX 77001	1891	C/Ind	2830	60%	G	476	U	A,N	2800
Rider College, Lawrenceville, NJ 08648	1865	C/Ind	4984	76%	G	314	S		2950
Rio Grande College/Community College, Rio Grande, OH 45674	1876	C/Ind	1103	94%		58	R		2230
Ripon College, Ripon, WI 54971	1851	C/Ind	936	32%		91	T	A	4116
Rivier College, Nashua, NH 03060	1933	W/Cath	1086	43%	G	108	S		2450
Roanoke College, Salem, VA 24153	1842	C/Prot	1259	50%		84	S		3245
Robert Morris College, Coraopolis, PA 15108	1921	C/Ind	4200	95%	G	179	S		2160
Roberts Wesleyan College, Rochester, NY 14624	1866	C/Prot	605	74%		90	S		2995
Rochester Institute of Technology, Rochester, NY 14623	1829	C/Ind	7766	60%	G	1247	S	A	3537
Rockford College, Rockford, IL 61101	1847	C/Ind	1600	75%	G	57	U		3275
Rockhurst College, Kansas City, MO 64110	1910	C/Cath	1247	73%	G	111	U		2680

Name and Location	Est	Type/ Control	UG Enroll	% of State Res	Grad	Fac Size	Cmps	ROTC	Tuition
Rocky Mountain College, Billings, MT 59102	1878	C/Prot	515	63%		56	S		$2093
Roger Williams College, Bristol, RI 02809	1919	C/Ind	1800	25%		211	S		2900
Rollins College, Winter Park, FL 32789	1885	C/Ind	1350	30%	G	97	T		3975
Roosevelt University, Chicago, IL 60605	1945	C/Ind	4086	90%	G	434	U		2850
Rosary College, River Forest, IL 60305	1848	C/Cath	948	90%	G	132	S		3010
Rose-Hulman Institute of Technology, Terre Haute, IN 47803	1874	M/Ind	1166	60%	G	97	T	A	3210
Rosemont College, Rosemont, PA 19010	1921	W/Cath	602	40%		84	S		3650
Russell Sage College, Troy, NY 12180	1916	W/Ind	1200	62%	G	115	U		3600
Rust College, Holly Springs, MS 38635	1866	C/Prot	723	76%		37	R	A	2125
Rutgers College, See Rutgers University, Rutgers College.									
Rutgers U, Camden Campus, Camden, NJ 08102	1925	C/Pub	3296	98%	G	179	U	A, N	1003x
Rutgers U, Cook College, New Brunswick, NJ 08903	1973	C/Pub	2885	91%		148	S	A, AF	1046
Rutgers U, Douglass College, New Brunswick, NJ 08903	1918	W/Pub	3841	95%		369	S	A, AF	1039
Rutgers U, Livingston College, New Brunswick, NJ 08903	1969	C/Ind	3795	90%		246	S	A, AF	1047
Rutgers U, Newark Campus, Newark, NJ 07102	1930	C/Pub	4887	98%	G	313	U	A, AF	998x
Rutgers U, Rutgers College, New Brunswick, NJ 08903	1766	C/Pub	11,157	93%		726	S	A, AF	1043
Sacred Heart College, Belmont, NC 28012	1892	C/Cath	307	76%		45	T	A	2360
Sacred Heart Seminary, Detroit, MI 48206	1919	M/Cath	50	100%		23	U		1150
Sacred Heart University, Bridgeport, CT 06604	1963	C/Cath	1180	99%	G	168	S		2650x
Saginaw Valley State College, University Center, MI 48710	1963	C/Pub	2938	99%	G	213	S		840
St Alphonsus College, Suffield, CT 06078	1963	M/Cath	55	92%		23	T		2900x
St Ambrose College, Davenport, IA 52803	1882	C/Cath	1818	70%	G	126	U		2910
St Andrews Presbyterian College, Laurinburg, NC 28352	1896	C/Prot	601	52%		60	T		2850
St Anselm's College, Manchester, NH 03102	1889	C/Cath	1884	99%		145	U		3300
Saint Augustine's College, Raleigh, NC 27611	1867	C/Prot	1762	61%		81	S	A	1850
St Bonaventure University, St Bonaventure, NY 14778	1855	C/Cath	2140	79%	G	140	T	A	3075
St Cloud State University, St Cloud, MN 56301	1869	C/Pub	9429	98%	G	539	U		626.70
St Edward's University, Austin, TX 78704	1881	C/Ind	1893	80%	G	101	U		2200
Saint Francis College, Fort Wayne, IN 46808	1890	C/Cath	868	80%		95	S	A	1956
St Francis College, Brooklyn, NY 11201	1858	C/Cath	3356	97%		203	U		2480
St Francis College, Loretto, PA 15940	1847	C/Cath	1127	56%	G	85	R		2946
Saint Francis de Sales College, Milwaukee, WI 53207	1856	M/Cath	78	90%		26	S		1200
St Hyacinth Seminary and Seminary, Granby, MA 01033	1927	M/Cath	60	5%		24	R		30c
St John Fisher College, Rochester, NY 14618	1948	C/Ind	3007	53%		139	S		3415
St John's College, Camarillo, CA 93010	1927	M/Cath	100	95%		25	U		2100
St John's College, Annapolis, MD 21404	1696	C/Ind	350	20%		56	T		4750
St John's College, Santa Fe, NM 87501	1696	C/Ind	270	5%	G	35	S		4800
Saint John's University, Collegeville, MN 56321	1856	M/Cath	1828	74%	G	146	R	A	2820
St John's University, Jamaica, NY 11439	1870	C/Cath	10,592	91%	G	781	U	A	2880
Saint Joseph College, West Hartford, CT 06117	1925	W/Cath	761	70%	G	97	S		3120
St Joseph's College, Rensselaer, IN 47978	1889	C/Cath	1034	35%	G	75	T		2810
St Joseph's College, North Windham, ME 04062	1915	C/Cath	500	44%		54	R		2510
St Joseph's College, Brooklyn, NY 11205	1916	C/Ind	1534	99%		120	U		2350x
St Joseph's College, Suffolk Campus, Brentwood, NY 11717	1972	C/Cath	382	100%		61	S		2360
St Joseph's College, Philadelphia, PA 19131	1851	C/Cath	2200	70%	G	160	U		2875
St Joseph Seminary College, St Benedict, LA 70457	1891	M/Cath	128	76%		30	T		3044
St Lawrence University, Canton, NY 13617	1856	C/Ind	2429	49%	G	175	R	A	4405
Saint Leo College, Saint Leo, FL 33574	1963	C/Cath	1053	50%		64	U	A	2550
St Louis Conservatory of Music, St Louis, MO 63130	1923	C/Ind	68	52%		44	U		2710x
Saint Louis University, St Louis, MO 63103	1818	C/Ind	6681	60%	G	2126	U	AF	3300
St Martin's College, Olympia, WA 98503	1895	C/Ind	781	51%		44	S		2600
Saint Mary College, Leavenworth, KS 66048	1860	W/Cath	769	70%		68	S		1950
Saint Mary of the Plains College, Dodge City, KS 67801	1952	C/Cath	616	60%		46	S		2270
Saint Mary of the Woods College, St Mary of the Woods, IN 47876	1840	W/Cath	550	44%		75	R		2795
Saint Mary's College, Moraga, CA 94575	1863	C/Cath	1447	70%	G	187	S		3426
St Mary's College, Notre Dame, IN 46556	1844	W/Cath	1839	15%		156	S		3685
Saint Mary's College, Orchard Lake, MI 48034	1885	C/Cath	191	85%		40	S		1600
Saint Mary's College, Winona, MN 55987	1912	C/Cath	1200	30%	G	95	T		2900
St Mary's College of Maryland, St Mary's City, MD 20686	1839	C/Pub	1298	92%		94	R		805
St Mary's Dominican College, New Orleans, LA 70118	1908	W/Cath	805	83%		77	U		2600
St Mary's of the Barrews Sem Coll, Perryville, MO 63775	1818	M/Cath	54	*		15	T		2982
St Mary's Seminary College, Perryville, MO 63775	1818	M/Ind	53	6%		14	T		2500
St Mary's University of San Antonio, San Antonio, TX 78284	1852	C/Cath	2337	77%	G	236	S	A	2408
Saint Meinrad College, St Meinrad, IN 47577	1890	M/Cath	193	20%		41	R		1590
Saint Michael's College, Winooski, VT 05404	1903	C/Cath	1587	12%	G	101	T	AF	3388
St Norbert College, West De Pere, WI 54178	1898	C/Cath	1559	45%		105	T	A	3125
St Olaf College, Northfield, MN 55057	1874	C/Cath	2971	60%		794	S		3595
St Patrick's College, Mountain View, CA 94042	1898	M/Cath	48	84%		16	S		1300
Saint Paul's College, Lawrenceville, VA 23868	1888	C/Prot	615	78%		50	T	A	1860
Saint Peter's College, Englewood Cliffs, NJ 07632	1975	C/Ind	*	*	G	*	S	A	2574
Saint Peter's College, Jersey City, NJ 07306	1872	C/Cath	2790	95%		315	U	A	2917
St Thomas Aquinas College, Sparkill, NY 10976	1952	C/Ind	1118	80%		67	S	A	2150
St Vincent College, Latrobe, PA 15650	1846	M/Cath	912	84%		93	R		2790
Saint Xavier College, Chicago, IL 60655	1846	C/Cath	1726	96%	G	150	U		2640
Salem College, Winston-Salem, NC 27108	1772	W/Prot	567	53%		68	S		3100
Salem College, Salem, WV 26426	1888	C/Ind	1386	25%	G	92	T		2670
Salem State College, Salem, MA 01970	1854	C/Pub	4570	98%	G	298	S		600
Salisbury State College, Salisbury, MD 21801	1925	C/Pub	3644	85%	G	183	T		780
Salve Regina College, Newport, RI 02840	1934	C/Cath	1257	51%	G	152	T		2990
Samford University, Birmingham, AL 35209	1841	C/Prot	2899	67%	G	267	S		1632
Sam Houston State University, Huntsville, TX 77340	1879	C/Pub	9326	96%	G	372	U	A	386
San Diego State University, San Diego, CA 92182	1897	C/Pub	23,512	96%	G	1702	U	AF	206
San Francisco Art Institute, San Francisco, CA 94133	1874	C/Ind	750	26%	G	63	U		3500
San Francisco Conservatory of Music, San Francisco, CA 94122	1917	C/Ind	158	56%	G	62	U		3735
San Francisco State University, San Francisco, CA 94132	1899	C/Pub	11,161	97%	G	1728	U	AF	186
Sangamon State University, Springfield, IL 62708	1969	C/Pub	2097	92%	G	211	R		500x
San Jose State University, San Jose, CA 95192	1857	C/Pub	21,426	90%	G	1685	U	A, AF	214

Name and Location	Est	Type/Control	UG Enroll	% of State Res	Grad	Fac Size	Cmps	ROTC	Tuition
Sarah Lawrence College, Bronxville, NY 10708	1928	C/Ind	774	48%	G	126	S		$5500
Savannah State College, Savannah, GA 31404	1890	C/Pub	2606	70%	G	130	U	N	580
Scarritt Coll for Christian Workers, Nashville, TN 37203	1892	C/Ind	41	24%	G	19	U		2150
School for International Training, Brattleboro, VT 05301	1964	C/Ind	39	2%	G	23	R		3486
School of the Ozarks, Point Lookout, MO 65726	1906	C/Ind	1200	70%		82	T		2440
School of the Art Inst of Chicago, Chicago, IL 60603	1866	C/Ind	934	75%	G	110	U		3536x
Scripps College, Claremont, CA 91711	1926	W/Ind	576	53%		64	S		4674
Seattle Pacific University, Seattle, WA 98119	1891	C/Prot	2048	64%	G	161	U		3063
Seattle University, Seattle, WA 98122	1891	C/Cath	2417	47%	G	276	U	A	3105
Seton Hall University, South Orange, NJ 07079	1856	C/Cath	6261	90%	G	602	S	A	2700
Seton Hill College, Greensburg, PA 15601	1882	W/Cath	880	85%		68	T		2765
Shaw University, Raleigh, NC 27611	1865	C/Ind	1263	50%		83	T		2240
Shenandoah Coll & Conservatory of Music, Winchester, VA 22601	1875	C/Prot	87	55%		110	T		2250
Shepherd College, Shepherdstown, WV 25443	1871	C/Pub	2743	60%		136	T		366
Shimer College, Mount Carroll, IL 61053	1853	C/Ind	70	50%		15	R		3000
Shippensburg State College, Shippensburg, PA 17257	1871	C/Pub	4534	94%	G	275	R		1047
Shorter College, Rome, GA 30161	1873	C/Prot	840	78%		55	U		2000
Siena College, Loudonville, NY 12211	1938	C/Cath	3054	94%		168	S	A	3055
Siena Heights College, Adrian, MI 49221	1919	C/Ind	1039	87%	G	97	U		2250
Sierra Nevada College, Incline Village, NV 89450	1969	C/Ind	272	52%		28	R		1710x
Silver Lake College, Manitowoc, WI 54220	1869	C/Cath	341	98%		49	R		2600
Simmons College, Boston, MA 02115	1899	W/Ind	1728	55%	G	289	U		4626
Simon's Rock Early College, Great Barrington, MA 01230	1964	C/Ind	212	20%		36	R		4605
Simpson College, San Francisco, CA 94134	1921	C/Prot	248	60%		30	U		2150
Simpson College, Indianola, IA 50125	1860	C/Prot	850	75%		68	T		3605
Sioux Falls College, Sioux Falls, SD 57101	1883	C/Prot	770	44%		52	U		2700
Skidmore College, Saratoga Springs, NY 12866	1922	C/Ind	2066	37%		169	S		5030
Slippery Rock State College, Slippery Rock, PA 16057	1889	C/Pub	5185	80%	G	350	R	AF	1040
Smith College, Northampton, MA 01063	1871	W/Ind	2486	25%	G	328	S		5150
Sonoma State University, Rohnert Park, CA 94928	1960	C/Pub	4135	97%	G	360	R		198
South Carolina State College, Orangeburg, SC 29117	1896	C/Pub	2898	97%	G	242	T	A	600
South Dakota School of Mines & Tech, Rapid City, SD 57701	1885	C/Pub	1552	80%	G	109	U	A	663
South Dakota State University, Brookings, SD 57006	1881	C/Pub	6115	93%	G	344	T	A, AF	740
Southeastern Louisiana University, Hammond, LA 70420	1925	C/Pub	6346	95%	G	294	T	A	750
Southeastern Massachusetts University, North Dartmouth, MA 02747	1895	C/Pub	5150	94%	G	478	S		661
Southeastern Oklahoma State U, Durant, OK 74701	1909	C/Pub	4400	71%	G	164	T		400
Southeastern University, Washington, DC 20024	1879	C/Ind	648	66%	G	110	U		60cx
Southeast Missouri State University, Cape Girardeau, MO 63701	1873	C/Pub	7877	95%	G	432	T	AF	330
Southern Arkansas University, Magnolia, AR 71753	1909	C/Pub	1760	75%	G	112	T	A	460
Southern California College, Costa Mesa, CA 92626	1920	C/Ind	580	80%		58	S		2200
Southern Connecticut State College, New Haven, CT 06515	1893	C/Pub	7641	94%	G	628	U		680
Southern Illinois U, Carbondale, IL 62901	1869	C/Pub	18,836	89%	G	3304	R	AF	859.80
Southern Illinois U, Edwardsville, IL 62026	1958	C/Pub	8474	90%	G	650	R	AF	781.50
Southern Methodist University, Dallas, TX 75275	1911	C/Prot	5481	56%	G	500	U		3460
Southern Missionary College, Collegedale, TN 37315	1892	C/Prot	1906	24%		140	T		2670
Southern Oregon State College, Ashland, OR 97520	1926	C/Pub	4177	90%	G	240	T		777
Southern Technical Institute, Marietta, GA 30011	1948	C/Pub	2330	85%		120	S	A, N, AF	508.50
Southern U and A&M Coll, Baton Rouge, LA 70813	1880	C/Pub	7231	81%	G	486	T	A, N	446
Southern U in New Orleans, New Orleans, LA 70126	1956	C/Pub	2708	99%		111	U		205.40x
Southern Utah State College, Cedar City, UT 84720	1897	C/Pub	1798	81%		113	T		564
Southern Vermont College, Bennington, VT 05201	1926	C/Ind	364	39%		32	R		2325
Southwest Baptist College, Bolivar, MO 65613	1878	C/Prot	1383	75%		92	T		2050
Southwestern Assemblies of God Coll, Waxahachie, TX 75165	1927	C/Ind	809	44%		31	T		1192
Southwestern at Memphis, Memphis, TN 38112	1848	C/Prot	1021	49%		104	U		3650
Southwestern College, Winfield, KS 67156	1885	C/Prot	628	80%		53	T		2180
Southwestern Oklahoma State U, Weatherford, OK 73096	1903	C/Pub	4143	87%	G	226	T	A	400
Southwestern Union College, Keene, TX 76059	1894	C/Prot	717	59%		70	T		3198
Southwestern University, Georgetown, TX 78626	1840	C/Pub	962	95%		77	T		2250
Southwest Missouri State University, Springfield, MO 65802	1906	C/Pub	12,067	97%	G	700	U	A	400
Southwest State University, Marshall, MN 56258	1963	C/Pub	1915	79%		105	R		600
Southwest Texas State University, San Marcos, TX 78666	1899	C/Pub	13,510	97%	G	665	T	AF	396
Spalding College, Louisville, KY 40203	1920	C/Ind	729	88%	G	98	U	AF	2000
Spelman College, Atlanta, GA 30314	1881	W/Ind	1250	25%		94	U		2080
Spertus College of Judaica, Chicago, IL 60605	1925	C/Ind	454	95%	G	23	U		1080x
Spring Arbor College, Spring Arbor, MI 49283	1873	C/Prot	845	88%		70	T		3100
Springfield College, Springfield, MA 01109	1885	C/Ind	2177	35%	G	175	S		3267
Spring Garden College, Chestnut Hill, PA 19118	1850	C/Ind	1001	87%		52	S		2900
Spring Hill College, Mobile, AL 36608	1830	C/Cath	904	30%		69	S	A	3040
Stanford University, Stanford, CA 94305	1885	C/Ind	6559	52%	G	1103	S		5595
State U of NY at Albany, Albany, NY 12222	1844	C/Pub	10,540	99%	G	810	U		960
State U of NY at Binghamton, Binghamton, NY 13901	1950	C/Pub	7809	97%	G	556	S		1005
State U of NY at Buffalo, Buffalo, NY 14214	1846	C/Pub	17,060	96%	G	1850	U		1100
State U of NY at Stony Brook, Stony Brook, NY 11794	1957	C/Pub	11,000	99%	G	1000	S		925
State U of NY College at Brockport, Brockport, NY 14420	1867	C/Pub	8201	99%	G	560	T		995
State U of NY College at Buffalo, Buffalo, NY 14222	1871	C/Pub	9451	98%	G	560	U		857
State U of NY College at Cortland, Cortland, NY 13045	1868	C/Pub	5128	98%	G	349	T		857
State U of NY College at Fredonia, Fredonia, NY 14063	1867	C/Pub	4543	97%	G	297	T	A	1005
State U of NY College at Geneseo, Geneseo, NY 14454	1867	C/Pub	4708	99%	G	311	T		845
State U of NY College at New Paltz, New Paltz, NY 12561	1885	C/Pub	4980	95%	G	350	R		1050
State U of NY College at Old Westbury, Old Westbury, NY 11568	1968	C/Pub	2283	96%		141	S		980
State U of NY College at Oneonta, Oneonta, NY 13820	1889	C/Pub	5701	98%		369	T		862
State U of NY College at Oswego, Oswego, NY 13126	1861	C/Pub	6800	97%	G	390	T		.1020
State U of NY College at Plattsburgh, Plattsburgh, NY 12901	1889	C/Pub	5595	98%	G	332	T		1000
State U of NY College at Potsdam, Potsdam, NY 13676	1816	C/Pub	3888	98%	G	291	T		1005
State U of NY College at Purchase, Purchase, NY 10577	1972	C/Pub	1950	75%		189	S		1000
State U of NY College at Utica/Rome, Utica, NY 13502	1973	C/Pub	2600	98%	G	152	U		1017x
State U of NY Coll of Envr Sci & For, Syracuse, NY 13210	1911	C/Pub	1140	85%	G	125	U		1000
State U of NY Maritime College, Bronx, NY 10465	1874	C/Pub	938	75%	G	70	S	N	1000

Name and Location	Est	Type/Control	UG Enroll	% of State Res	Grad	Fac Size	Cmps	ROTC	Tuition
Stephen F Austin State University, Nacogdoches, TX 75961	1923	C/Pub	9200	97%	G	450	T	A	$320
Stephens College, Columbia, MO 65201	1833	W/Ind	1630	23%		148	T		3675
Sterling College, Sterling, KS 67579	1887	C/Prot	534	45%		50	R		2440
Stern College for Women, New York, NY 10016	1886	W/Jewish	561	34%		347	U		3400
Stetson University, Deland, FL 32720	1883	C/Ind	1950	60%	G	138	S	A	3215
Stevens Institute of Technology, Hoboken, NJ 07030	1870	C/Ind	1410	68%	G	225	U		4325
Stillman College, Tuscaloosa, AL 35401	1876	C/Prot	645	69%		42	T	A	2972
Stockton State College, Pomona, NJ 08240	1971	C/Pub	4800	95%		230	R		952
Stonehill College, North Easton, MA 02356	1948	C/Cath	1680	70%		100	R	A	3090
Suffolk University, Boston, MA 02114	1906	C/Ind	2780	98%	G	277	U		2340
Sul Ross State University, Alpine, TX 79830	1917	C/Pub	1666	89%		128	T		268
Susquehanna University, Selinsgrove, PA 17870	1858	C/Prot	1400	46%		125	R		3826
Swarthmore College, Swarthmore, PA 19081	1864	C/Ind	1280	25%		145	S		4600
Sweet Briar College, Sweet Briar, VA 24595	1901	W/Ind	701	19%		83	R		4600
Syracuse University, Syracuse, NY 13210	1870	C/Ind	11,044	50%	G	1233	U	A, AF	4634
Tabor College, Hillsboro, KS 67063	1908	C/Prot	434	58%		55	T		2520
Talladega College, Talladega, AL 35160	1867	C/Ind	647	50%		56	T		1740
Tampa College, Tampa, FL 33609	1931	C/Ind	851	96%		65	S		1093
Tarkio College, Tarkio, MO 64491	1883	C/Prot	349	35%		35	R		2695
Tarleton State University, Stephenville, TX 76402	1899	C/Pub	2631	74%	G	156	T	A	400
Taylor University, Upland, IN 46989	1846	C/Prot	1540	30%		94	R		3155
Temple University, Philadelphia, PA 19122	1884	C/Pub	17,444	91%	G	2527	U	A	1610
Tennessee State University, Nashville, TN 37203	1912	C/Pub	4651	75%	G	293	U	AF	473
Tennessee Technological University, Cookeville, TN 38501	1915	C/Pub	5912	94%	G	376	T	A	453
Tennessee Wesleyan College, Athens, TN 37303	1857	C/Prot	453	78%		38	T		1800
Texas A&I University, Kingsville, TX 78363	1925	C/Pub	5151	90%	G	293	T	A	328
Texas A&M University, College Station, TX 77843	1876	C/Pub	25,042	89%	G	1808	T	A, N, AF	480
Texas Christian University, Fort Worth, TX 76129	1873	C/Prot	4311	55%	G	420	S	A,AF	3000
Texas College, Tyler, TX 75701	1894	C/Prot	531	60%		49	S	A	1750
Texas Lutheran College, Seguin, TX 78155	1891	C/Prot	1098	81%		77	T		2250
Texas Southern University, Houston, TX 77004	1947	C/Pub	7464	76%	G	496	U		400
Texas Tech University, Lubbock, TX 79409	1923	C/Pub	19,444	85%	G	864	U	A	560
Texas Wesleyan College, Fort Worth, TX 76105	1891	C/Prot	1504	91%		100	U	A	2640
Texas Woman's University, Denton, TX 76204	1901	W/Pub	4997	87%	G	554	T	AF	360
Thiel College, Greenville, PA 16125	1866	C/Prot	1092	77%		81	T		3438
Thomas College, Waterville, ME 04901	1894	C/Ind	910	72%	G	45	R		3290
Thomas Jefferson University, Philadelphia, PA 19107	1969	C/Ind	793	72%	G	100	U		4000
Thomas More College, Fort Mitchell, KY 41017	1921	C/Cath	1270	65%		130	S		2020
Tift College, Forsyth, GA 31029	1847	W/Prot	457	70%		43	T		1530
Tougaloo College, Tougaloo, MS 39174	1869	C/Prot	961	73%		86	S	A	1686
Touro College, New York, NY 10036	1971	C/Ind	1530	85%		230	U		3095
Towson State University, Baltimore, MD 21204	1865	C/Pub	13,499	96%	G	811	U		749
Transylvania University, Lexington, KY 40508	1780	C/Ind	783	75%		84	U		3600
Trenton State College, Trenton, NJ 08625	1855	C/Pub	7500	97%	G	500	S		900
Trevecca Nazarene College, Nashville, TN 37210	1901	C/Prot	1344	68%		75	S		1935
Trinity Christian College, Palos Heights, IL 60463	1959	C/Ind	390	85%		47	S		2570
Trinity College, Hartford, CT 06106	1823	C/Ind	1840	22%	G	167	U		4800
Trinity College, Washington, DC 20017	1897	W/Cath	600	6%	G	138	S		3400
Trinity College, Deerfield, IL 60015	1897	C/Prot	805	56%		63	S		3040
Trinity College, Burlington, VT 05401	1925	/Cath	531	73%		53	S		30
Trinity University, San Antonio, TX 78284	1869	C/Prot	2801	65%	G	290	U	A	2829
Tri-State University, Angola, IN 46703	1883	C/Ind	1298	40%		81	T		2757
Troy State University, Troy, AL 36081	1887	C/Pub	8689	85%	G	579	T	AF	585
Troy State University at Fort Rucker/Dothan, Dothan, AL 36301	1965	C/Pub	882	100%	G	71	U		810
Troy State University at Montgomery, Montgomery, AL 36104	*	C/Pub	1700	100%		154	U	AF	810
Tufts University, Medford, MA 02155	1852	C/Ind	4350	40%	G	800	S	A,N,AF	5090
Tulane University, New Orleans, LA 70118	1834	C/Ind	500	22%	G	800	U	A,N,AF	4546
Tusculum College, Greeneville, TN 37743	1794	C/Prot	448	36%		32	T		2400
Tuskegee Institute, Tuskegee, AL 36088	1881	C/Ind	3140	36%	G	374	T	A,AF	2000
Union College, Barbourville, KY 40906	1879	C/Prot	501	61%	G	68	T	A	2530
Union College, Lincoln, NE 68506	1891	C/Prot	909	25%		100	S		3350
Union College and University, Schenectady, NY 12308	1795	C/Ind	2300	70%	G	170	S		5108
Union University, Jackson, TN 38301	1825	C/Prot	1217	85%		76	S		1720
United States Air Force Academy, USAF Academy, CO 80840	1954	C/Pub	4436	5%		550	R		0
United States Coast Guard Academy, New London, CT 06320	1876	C/Pub	900	*		120	S		0
United States International U, San Diego, CA 92131	1952	C/Ind	1207	52%	G	169	S		3411
United States Merchant Marine Academy, Kings Point, NY 10024	1943	C/Pub	1100	23%		80	S		0
United States Military Academy, West Point, NY 10996	1802	C/Pub	4400	12%		550	T		0
United States Naval Academy, Annapolis, MD 21402	1845	C/Pub	4300	2%		540	S		0
United Wesleyan College, Allentown, PA 18103	1921	C/Prot	216	44%		19	U		2170
Unity College, Unity, ME 04988	1966	C/Ind	432	18%		30	R		3500
University of Akron, Akron, OH 44325	1870	C/Pub	19,360	94%	G	1045	U	A, AF	840
University of Alabama, University, AL 35486	1831	C/Pub	12,859	84%	G	952	T	A, AF	764.50
University of Alabama in Birmingham, Birmingham, AL 35294	1966	C/Pub	9628	94%	G	1417	U		771x
University of Alabama in Huntsville, Huntsville, AL 35807	1950	C/Pub	3611	98%	G	294	S		711
University of Alaska, Anchorage, AK 99504	1970	C/Pub	3009	93%	G	174	U		177x
University of Alaska, Fairbanks, AK 99701	1915	C/Pub	2961	80%	G	395	S	A	532
University of Alaska, Juneau, AK 99801	1972	C/Pub	1525	98%	G	158	R		340x
University of Albuquerque, Albuquerque, NM 87140	1889	C/Cath	2300	85%		148	S		1920
University of Arizona, Tucson, AZ 85721	1885	C/Pub	23,231	80%	G	1762	U	A, AF	550
U of Arkansas, Fayetteville, AR 72701	1871	C/Pub	11,349	85%	G	719	T	A, AF	460
U of Arkansas at Little Rock, Little Rock, AR 72204	1927	C/Pub	3728	97%	G	373	U		460x
U of Arkansas at Monticello, Monticello, AR 71655	1909	C/Pub	1612	96%		97	T		488
U of Arkansas at Pine Bluff, Pine Bluff, AR 71601	1873	C/Pub	2999	90%		174	U	A	460
University of Baltimore, Baltimore, MD 21201	1925	C/Pub	3087	94%	G	253	U		800x
University of Bridgeport, Bridgeport, CT 06602	1927	C/Ind	5265	70%	G	517	U	A	3710
University of California, Berkeley, CA 94720	1868	C/Pub	19,850	95%	G	3163	U	A, N, AF	730
University of California, Davis, CA 95616	1906	C/Pub	12,640	88%	G	1407	T	A	686

Name and Location	Est	Type/ Control	UG Enroll	% of State Res	Grad	Fac Size	Cmps	ROTC	Tuition
University of California, Irvine, CA 92664	1960	C/Pub	7668	95%	G	685	S		$717
University of California, La Jolla, CA 92093	1959	C/Pub	8514	90%	G	820	S		735
University of California, Riverside, CA 92502	1954	C/Pub	3277	97%	G	458	S	A	738
University of California, Los Angeles, CA 90024	1919	C/Pub	20,186	94%	G	2700	U	A, N, AF	738
University of California, Santa Barbara, CA 93106	1891	C/Pub	12,623	92%	G	790	S	A	702
University of California, Santa Cruz, CA 95064	1965	C/Pub	5534	90%	G	526	T		672
University of Central Arkansas, Conway, AR 72032	1907	C/Pub	4600	96%	G	252	T	A	755
University of Central Florida, Orlando, FL 32816	1963	C/Pub	10,144	96%	G	445	S	A, AF	480
University of Chicago, Chicago, IL 60637	1890	C/Ind	2670	36%	G	1040	U		675
U of Cincinnati, Cincinnati, OH 45221	1819	C/Pub	31,663	91%	G	3237	U	A, AF	4500
U of Colorado, Boulder Campus, Boulder, CO 80309	1876	C/Pub	17,000	67%	G	1200	S	A, N, AF	960
U of Colorado, Colorado Springs Cmps, Colorado Springs, CO 80907	1965	C/Pub	3212	90%	G	215	U	A	900
U of Colorado, Denver Campus, Denver, CO 80220	1938	C/Pub	5255	90%	G	429	U	A	450x
University of Connecticut, Storrs, CT 06268	1881	C/Pub	14,545	90%	G	1600	R	A, AF	498x
University of Dallas, Irving, TX 75061	1956	C/Cath	992	52%	G	99	S		1020
University of Dayton, Dayton, OH 45469	1850	C/Cath	5986	54%	G	619	S	A	2630
University of Delaware, Newark, DE 19711	1743	C/Pub	13,352	59%	G	935	T	A	2760
University of Denver, Denver, CO 80210	1864	C/Ind	4242	37%	G	600	S		950
University of Detroit, Detroit, MI 48221	1877	C/Cath	7048	85%	G	528	U	A	4170
University of Dubuque, Dubuque, IA 52001	1852	C/Prot	1028	63%		68	S		3480
University of Evansville, Evansville, IN 47702	1854	C/Prot	4206	75%	G	278	S		2750
University of Florida, Gainesville, FL 32611	1853	C/Pub	25,393	93%	G	1802	S	A, N, AF	2950
University of Georgia, Athens, GA 30602	1785	C/Pub	16,611	84%	G	1901	T	A, AF	710
University of Hartford, West Hartford, CT 06117	1877	C/Ind	6646	68%	G	618	S		753
University of Hawaii at Manoa, Honolulu, HI 96822	1907	C/Pub	15,148	85%	G	1567	U	A, AF	3580
University of Hawaii-Hilo College, Hilo, HI 96720	1970	C/Pub	2878	86%	G	212	T		507
U of Houston, Houston, TX 77004	1927	C/Pub	19,691	87%	G	1863	U	A, N	110
U of Houston at Clear Lake City, Houston, TX 77004	1971	C/Pub	2001	93%	G	226	S		354
University of Idaho, Moscow, ID 83843	1889	C/Pub	6034	81%	G	535	T	A, N	348x
University of Illinois, Chicago Circle, Chicago, IL 60680	1946	C/Pub	17,998	96%	G	1171	U	A, N, AF	438
University of Illinois, Urbana-Champaign, Urbana, IL 61801	1868	C/Pub	25,413	97%	G	2762	T	A, N, AF	885x
University of Iowa, Iowa City, IA 52242	1847	C/Pub	15,200	78%	G	1600	T	A, AF	916
University of Judaism, Los Angeles, CA 90028	1947	C/Jewish	106	80%	G	44	U		830
University of Kansas, Lawrence, KS 66045	1865	C/Pub	16,898	74%	G	1027	T	A, N, AF	2700
University of Kentucky, Lexington, KY 40506	1865	C/Pub	17,233	89%	G	1900	U	A, AF	358 10
University of La Verne, La Verne, CA 91750	1891	C/Prot	1557	98%	G	184	T		562
University of Louisville, Louisville, KY 40208	1798	C/Pub	13,318	92%	G	1472	U	AF	3340
University of Lowell, Lowell, MA 01854	1894	C/Pub	6866	93%	G	842	U	AF	570
University of Maine at Farmington, Farmington, ME 04938	1863	C/Pub	1618	85%		95	T	A	785
University of Maine at Fort Kent, Fort Kent, ME 04743	1878	C/Pub	382	79%		26	T		805
University of Maine at Machias, Machias, ME 04654	1909	C/Pub	698	80%		42	T		770
University of Maine at Orono, Orono, ME 04473	1865	C/Pub	10,083	78%	G	664	U	A	870
University of Maine at Presque Isle, Presque Isle, ME 04769	1902	C/Pub	1030	88%		86	R		920
University of Mary Hardin-Baylor, Belton, TX 76513	1845	C/Prot	1050	81%		74	S	AF	805
U of Maryland, Baltimore, MD 21201	1963	C/Pub	1504	88%	G	1051	S		1696
U of Maryland, College Park, MD 20742	1859	C/Pub	29,422	81%	G	2018	U	AF	802
U of Maryland, Baltimore County, Baltimore, MD 21228	1966	C/Pub	5000	96%	G	330	S		788
U of Maryland, Eastern Shore Campus, Princess Anne, MD 21853	1886	C/Pub	1057	66%	G	87	R		380
University of Massachusetts, Amherst, MA 01003	1863	C/Pub	19,041	93%	G	1465	T	A, AF	586
University of Massachusetts, Boston, MA 02125	1965	C/Pub	7848	96%	G	594	U		1200
University of Miami, Coral Gables, FL 33124	1925	C/Ind	9458	48%	G	1602	S	A, AF	729x
University of Michigan, Ann Arbor, MI 48109	1817	C/Pub	22,076	81%	G	2828	T	A, N, AF	3940
University of Michigan, Dearborn, MI 48128	1959	C/Pub	5957	99%	G	311	U		1174
University of Michigan, Flint, MI 48503	1956	C/Pub	3884	99%	G	198	U		832x
U of Minnesota, Duluth, MN 55812	1948	C/Pub	6450	87%	G	425	U	AF	· 882x
U of Minnesota, Minneapolis/St Paul, Minneapolis, MN 55455	1851	C/Pub	33,803	90%	G	5286	U	A, N, AF	948
U of Minnesota, Morris, MN 56267	1959	C/Pub	1471	95%		132	T		1080
University of Mississippi, University, MS 38677	1844	C/Pub	7865	74%	G	590	T	A, N, AF	1051
University of Missouri, Columbia, MO 65201	1839	C/Pub	17,297	89%	G	1610	T	A, N, AF	707
University of Missouri, Kansas City, MO 64110	1933	C/Pub	5872	88%	G	1447	U		768
University of Missouri, Rolla, MO 65401	1870	C/Pub	4741	84%	G	325	T	A	802
University of Missouri, St Louis, MO 63121	1963	C/Pub	9287	98%	G	595	U		833
University of Montana, Missoula, MT 59801	1893	C/Pub	7106	70%	G	498	T	A	412x
University of Montevallo, Montevallo, AL 35115	1896	C/Pub	2526	90%	G	175	T	AF	826
University of Nebraska, Lincoln, NE 68508	1869	C/Pub	17,222	93%	G	1259	U	A, N, AF	600
University of Nebraska at Omaha, Omaha, NE 68101	1968	C/Pub	12,906	93%	G	560	U	AF	808
University of Nevada, Las Vegas, NV 89154	1951	C/Pub	5824	85%	G	380	U		626x
University of Nevada, Reno, NV 89557	1874	C/Pub	5890	83%	G	398	U	A	720
University of New England, Biddeford, ME 04005	1953	C/Cath	406	15%		45	T		690
University of New Hampshire, Durham, NH 03824	1866	C/Ind	2399	75%	G	475	U	A, AF	3490
University of New Haven, West Haven, CT 06516	1920	C/Ind	8887	65%	G	625	T	N,AF	1150
University of New Mexico, Albuquerque, NM 87131	1889	C/Pub	17,527	92%	G	1271	U		2902
University of New Orleans, New Orleans, LA 70122	1958	C/Pub	12,033	95%	G	534	U	A	624
University of North Alabama, Florence, AL 35630	1872	C/Pub	4424	88%	G	223	S	A	524
U of North Carolina at Asheville, Asheville, NC 28801	1927	C/Pub	1446	95%		106	S		580
U of North Carolina at Chapel Hill, Chapel Hill, NC 27514	1795	C/Pub	14,025	85%	G	1745	U	N,AF	456
U of North Carolina at Charlotte, Charlotte, NC 28223	1946	C/Pub	7437	93%	G	606	U		529
U of North Carolina at Greensboro, Greensboro, NC 27412	1891	C/Pub	7082	88%	G	637	U		518
U of North Carolina at Wilmington, Wilmington, NC 28401	1947	C/Pub	3915	95%	G	242	S		603
U of North Dakota, Grand Forks, ND 58201	1883	C/Pub	7729	76%	G	645	T	A, AF	490
University of Northern Colorado, Greeley, CO 80639	1890	C/Pub	8500	80%	G	680	T	AF	645
University of Northern Iowa, Cedar Falls, IA 50613	1876	C/Pub	9127	97%	G	637	T		798
University of North Florida, Jacksonville, FL 32216	1965	C/Pub	2408	99%		155	S	A	774
University of Notre Dame, Notre Dame, IN 46556	1842	C/Cath	6800	8%	G	798	U	A,N,AF	742.50x
University of Oklahoma, Norman, OK 73069	1890	C/Pub	15,158	85%	G	752	U	A, N, AF	4130
U of Oregon, Eugene, OR 97403	1876	C/Pub	11,895	76%	G	1287	T	A	508
University of Pennsylvania, Philadelphia, PA 19104	1740	C/Ind	8000	27%	G	2500	U	A, N	800
University of Pittsburgh at Bradford, Bradford, PA 16701	1963	C/Pub	800	*		*	S		5270
									1200

Name and Location	Est	Type/Control	UG Enroll	% of State Res	Grad	Fac Size	Cmps	ROTC	Tuition
University of Pittsburgh, Johnstown, PA 15904	1927	C/Pub	2994	90%		161	S		$1566
University of Pittsburgh, Pittsburgh, PA 15260	1787	C/Pub	19,109	95%	G	2267	U	A, AF	1516
University of Portland, Portland, OR 97203	1901	C/Cath	2165	40%	G	175	U		3030
University of Puerto Rico, Cayey, PR 00633	1967	C/Pub	2601	100%		127	U	A	341
University of Puerto Rico, Mayaguez, PR 00708	1911	C/Pub	8278	99%	G	524	U	A, AF	341
University of Puerto Rico, Rio Piedras, PR 00931	1903	C/Pub	20,819	*	G	1102	U	A, AF	200
University of Puget Sound, Tacoma, WA 98416	1888	C/Prot	2771	50%	G	206	U	AF	3830
University of Redlands, Redlands, CA 92373	1909	C/Ind	1200	77%	G	183	T		4478
University of Rhode Island, Kingston, RI 02881	1892	C/Pub	9033	70%	G	830	S	A	1068
University of Richmond, Richmond, VA 23173	1830	C/Prot	2526	58%	G	318	S	A	3410
University of Rochester, Rochester, NY 14627	1850	C/Ind	4380	62%	G	1957	S	N	4994
University of St Thomas, Houston, TX 77006	1947	C/Cath	1637	80%	G	126	U		2200
University of San Diego, San Diego, CA 92110	1949	C/Cath	2326	65%	G	230	U		3654
University of San Francisco, San Francisco, CA 94117	1855	C/Cath	3460	59%	G	434	U	A	3400
University of Santa Clara, Santa Clara, CA 95053	1851	C/Cath	3600	78%	G	387	U	A	3543
U of Science and Arts of Oklahoma, Chickasha, OK 73018	1908	C/Pub	1355	90%		80	T		630
University of Scranton, Scranton, PA 18510	1888	C/Cath	3542	69%	G	220	U	A	2600
University of South Alabama, Mobile, AL 36688	1963	C/Pub	5961	77%	G	307	S	A	771
U of South Carolina, Columbia, SC 29208	1801	C/Pub	17,559	85%	G	1318	U	N,AF	732
U of South Carolina, Spartanburg, SC 29303	1967	C/Pub	2289	99%	G	176	U		630
U of South Carolina, Coastal Carolina, Conway, SC 29526	1959	C/Pub	1759	90%		125	R		630x
U of South Dakota, Springfield, SD 57062	1881	C/Pub	825	91%		69	T		734
U of South Dakota, Vermillion, SD 57069	1862	C/Pub	4362	83%	G	375	T	A	892
University of Southern California, Los Angeles, CA 90007	1880	C/Ind	15,319	80%	G	2695	U	N,AF	4708
University of Southern Colorado, Pueblo, CO 81001	1933	C/Pub	4200	88%	G	230	S	A	653
University of Southern Maine, Portland, ME 04103	1878	C/Pub	5181	89%	G	350	U	A	920
University of Southern Mississippi, Hattiesburg, MS 39401	1910	C/Pub	9140	88%	G	616	T	A, AF	680
U of South Florida, St Petersburg, FL 33701	1956	C/Pub	12,251	94%	G	950	S		15c
U of South Florida, Tampa, FL 33620	1956	C/Pub	17,041	91%	G	1059	U		800
University of Southwestern Louisiana, Lafayette, LA 70504	1898	C/Pub	11,896	88%	G	600	U	AF	440
University of Tampa, Tampa, FL 33606	1931	C/Ind	1845	25%	G	142	U	A	3500
University of Tennessee, Chattanooga, TN 37403	1886	C/Pub	5690	90%	G	283	U	A	512
University of Tennessee, Knoxville, TN 37916	1794	C/Pub	22,592	88%	G	1650	U	A, AF	558
University of Tennessee, Martin, TN 38238	1927	C/Pub	4686	92%	G	231	R	A	549
University of Tennessee, Nashville, TN 37203	1947	C/Pub	5044	98%	G	289	U		450x
U of Texas at Arlington, Arlington, TX 76019	1895	C/Pub	15,497	87%	G	790	S	A	400
U of Texas at Austin, Austin, TX 78712	1883	C/Pub	33,699	75%	G	1900	S	A, N, AF	469.60
U of Texas at El Paso, El Paso, TX 79968	1913	C/Pub	13,842	91%	G	665	U	A	360
U of Texas at San Antonio, San Antonio, TX 78275	1969	C/Pub	7020	98%	G	383	U	A	635x
University of Texas at Tyler, Tyler, TX 75701	1972	C/Pub	1242	98%	G	120	U		345x
U of the DC, Mt Vernon Square Cmps, Washington, DC 20004	1968	C/Pub	*	88%	G	1022	U		135
University of the Pacific, Stockton, CA 95211	1851	C/Ind	3719	70%	G	344	S		5245
U of Texas of the Permian Basin, Odessa, TX 79762	1969	C/Pub	887	95%	G	92	S		300
University of the Sacred Heart, Santurce, PR 00914	1939	C/Cath	5929	*		256	U		1250
University of the South, Sewanee, TN 37375	1857	C/Prot	1000	22%		105	R		4205
University of Toledo, Toledo, OH 43606	1872	C/Pub	14,171	95%	G	708	S	A	925.50
University of Tulsa, Tulsa, OK 74104	1894	C/Prot	4709	70%	G	362	U		2140
University of Utah, Salt Lake City, UT 84112	1850	C/Pub	16,845	86%	G	1358	U	A, N, AF	640.50
University of Vermont, Burlington, VT 05401	1791	C/Pub	7670	50%	G	990	S	A	1300
University of Virginia, Charlottesville, VA 22903	1819	C/Pub	10,543	65%	G	1570	U	A, N, AF	909
University of Washington, Seattle, WA 98195	1861	C/Pub	27,081	81%	G	2533	U	A, N, AF	687
University of West Florida, Pensacola, FL 32504	1963	C/Pub	4318	97%	G	308	S		743
U of Wisconsin-Eau Claire, Eau Claire, WI 54701	1916	C/Pub	9450	91%	G	531	U		794
U of Wisconsin-Green Bay, Green Bay, WI 54302	1968	C/Pub	3406	93%	G	166	U		750
U of Wisconsin-La Crosse, La Crosse, WI 54601	1909	C/Pub	7926	91%	G	777	U	A	838
U of Wisconsin-Madison, Madison, WI 53706	1849	C/Pub	25,911	82%	G	3400	U	A, N, AF	812
U of Wisconsin-Milwaukee, Milwaukee, WI 53201	1956	C/Pub	20,556	97%	G	1688	U	A	838
U of Wisconsin-Oshkosh, Oshkosh, WI 54901	1871	C/Pub	8500	97%	G	675	S	A	767
U of Wisconsin-Parkside, Kenosha, WI 53140	1965	C/Pub	5250	97%		280	S		740
U of Wisconsin-Platteville, Platteville, WI 53818	1866	C/Pub	4393	86%	G	238	T	A	850
U of Wisconsin-River Falls, River Falls, WI 54022	1874	C/Pub	4630	61%	G	279	R		802
U of Wisconsin-Stevens Point, Stevens Point, WI 54481	1894	C/Pub	8404	91%	G	550	R	A	772
U of Wisconsin-Stout, Menomonie, WI 54751	1893	C/Pub	6337	70%	G	443	T		769
U of Wisconsin-Superior, Superior, WI 54880	1893	C/Pub	1864	70%	G	200	U	AF	820
U of Wisconsin-Whitewater, Whitewater, WI 53190	1868	C/Pub	7626	90%	G	621	T	A, AF	791.50
University of Wyoming, Laramie, WY 82071	1886	C/Pub	7217	70%	G	744	T	A	434
Upper Iowa University, Fayette, IA 52142	1850	C/Ind	580	70%		50	R	A	3160
Upsala College, East Orange, NJ 07019	1893	C/Prot	1117	85%	G	85	U		3430
Urbana College, Urbana, OH 43078	1850	C/Ind	579	85%		83	T		2364
Ursinus College, Collegeville, PA 19426	1869	C/Ind	1006	66%		91	T		3600
Ursuline College, Cleveland, OH 44124	1850	W/Cath	840	95%		70	S		2300c
Utah State University, Logan, UT 84322	1888	C/Pub	7900	65%	G	1250	T	A	603
Utica College of Syracuse University, Utica, NY 13502	1946	C/Ind	1360	84%		93	S		3475
Valdosta State College, Valdosta, GA 31601	1906	C/Pub	3972	88%	G	246	U	AF	579
Valley City State College, Valley City, ND 58072	1890	C/Pub	1107	93%		66	T		588
Valparaiso University, Valparaiso, IN 46383	1859	C/Prot	3503	29%	G	360	T		3286
Vanderbilt University, Nashville, TN 37240	1872	C/Ind	6100	21%	G	1865	U	A,N	4260
Vandercook College of Music, Chicago, IL 60616	1909	C/Ind	86	75%	G	17	U		2430
Vassar College, Poughkeepsie, NY 12601	1861	C/Ind	2276	41%	G	228	S		4525
Villa Maria College, Erie, PA 16505	1925	W/Cath	617	88%		73	S	A	2750
Villanova University, Villanova, PA 19085	1842	C/Cath	5874	47%	G	524	S	N	3720
Virginia Commonwealth University, Richmond, VA 23284	1838	C/Pub	13,733	92%	G	1727	U	A	856
Virginia Intermont College, Bristol, VA 24201	1884	C/Prot	594	36%		40	U		2475
Virginia Military Institute, Lexington, VA 24450	1839	M/Pub	1310	53%		104	T	A, N, AF	2425
Virginia Polytechnic Inst & State U, Blacksburg, VA 24061	1872	C/Pub	17,498	80%	G	1400	T	A, AF	837
Virginia State College, Petersburg, VA 23803	1882	C/Pub	3787	79%	G	260	S	A	904
Virginia Union University, Richmond, VA 23220	1865	C/Ind	1178	56%		150	U	A	2190
Virginia Wesleyan College, Norfolk, VA 23502	1961	C/Prot	775	70%		55	S		2935

Name and Location	Est	Type/Control	UG Enroll	% of State Res	Grad	Fac Size	Cmps	ROTC	Tuition
Viterbo College, La Crosse, WI 54601	1890	C/Cath	1071	80%		116	U		$2830
Voorhees College, Denmark, SC 29042	1897	C/Prot	781	80%		38	T	A	1925
Wabash College, Crawfordsville, IN 47933	1832	M/Ind	850	80%		80	T		3700
Wadhams Hall Seminary-College, Ogdensburg, NY 13669	1924	M/Cath	76	87%		21	R		1900
Wagner College, Staten Island, NY 10301	1883	C/Prot	2155	80%	G	216	S	A	3530
Wake Forest University, Winston-Salem, NC 27109	1833	C/Prot	3055	45%	G	237	U	A	3300
Walla Walla College, College Place, WA 99324	1892	C/Prot	1813	40%	G	163	T		3630
Walsh College, Canton, OH 44720	1959	C/Cath	690	90%		60	S		2900
Walsh College of Acc & Bus Admin, Troy, MI 48084	1958	C/Ind	1160	100%	G	75	S		1056x
Warner Pacific College, Portland, OR 97215	1937	C/Prot	409	49%	G	42	U		2700
Warren Wilson College, Swannanoa, NC 28778	1893	C/Prot	527	30%		75	R		2600
Wartburg College, Waverly, IA 50677	1852	C/Prot	1106	65%		86	T		3163
Washburn University of Topeka, Topeka, KS 66621	1865	C/Pub	4985	97%	G	260	U	AF	764
Washington and Jefferson College, Washington, PA 15301	1781	C/Ind	1024	70%		97	T	A	4258
Washington and Lee University, Lexington, VA 24450	1749	M/Ind	1400	25%		175	T	A	3750
Washington College, Chestertown, MD 21620	1782	C/Ind	783	44%	G	68	T		3306
Washington State University, Pullman, WA 99163	1892	C/Pub	13,370	84%	G	1064	R	A, AF	886
Washington University, St Louis, MO 63130	1853	C/Ind	4431	23%	G	2277	U	A, AF	4750
Wayland Baptist College, Plainview, TX 79072	1908	C/Prot	1268	87%		67	T		1745
Waynesburg College, Waynesburg, PA 15370	1849	C/Prot	820	70%		60	T	A	3330
Wayne State College, Wayne, NE 68787	1910	C/Pub	2143	85%	G	119	T		510
Wayne State University, Detroit, MI 48202	1868	C/Pub	24,549	99%	G	2200	U		1074
Webb Institute of Naval Architecture, Glen Cove, NY 11542	1889	C/Ind	80	37%		16	S		0
Weber State College, Ogden, UT 84403	1889	C/Pub	9400	93%	G	500	U	A, AF	196
Webster College, St Louis, MO 63119	1915	C/Ind	1043	70%	G	621	S		3050
Wellesley College, Wellesley, MA 02181	1875	W/Ind	2115	26%		288	S		4650
Wells College, Aurora, NY 13026	1868	W/Ind	491	45%		70	T		4500
Wentworth Institute of Technology, Boston, MA 02115	1970	C/Ind	2079	75%		117	U		2935
Wesleyan College, Macon, GA 31201	1836	W/Prot	611	50%		61	S		3070
Wesleyan University, Middletown, CT 06457	1831	C/Ind	2400	20%	G	269	T		5550
West Chester State College, West Chester, PA 19380	1817	C/Pub	7016	89%	G	495	S		1040
West Coast U, Los Angeles, CA 90020	1909	C/Ind	734	80%	G	250	S		2040x
Western Baptist Bible College, Salem, OR 97302	1936	C/Prot	426	30%		32	T		2418
Western Carolina University, Cullowhee, NC 28723	1889	C/Pub	5368	91%	G	349	R	A	628
Western Connecticut State College, Danbury, CT 06810	1903	C/Pub	2706	90%	G	220	U		540
Western Illinois University, Macomb, IL 61455	1899	C/Pub	10,328	98%	G	741	T	A	754.50
Western Kentucky University, Bowling Green, KY 42101	1906	C/Pub	10,253	84%	G	606	T	A	500
Western Maryland College, Westminster, MD 21157	1867	C/Ind	1359	70%	G	119	T	A	3475
Western Michigan University, Kalamazoo, MI 49008	1903	C/Pub	16,868	91%	G	1034	S	A	837.50
Western Montana College, Dillon, MT 59725	1893	C/Pub	670	94%	G	45	R	A	468
Western New England College, Springfield, MA 01119	1919	C/Ind	2691	64%	G	285	S	A	2870
Western New Mexico University, Silver City, NM 88061	1893	C/Pub	1463	91%	G	75	T		370.30
Western State College of Colorado, Gunnison, CO 81230	1911	C/Pub	2843	80%	G	165	R		757
Western Washington University, Bellingham, WA 98225	1899	C/Pub	8327	88%	G	489	T		618
Westfield State College, Westfield, MA 01085	1838	C/Pub	2796	97%	G	177	S		630
West Georgia College, Carrollton, GA 30117	1933	C/Pub	4708	97%	G	281	T	A	549
West Liberty State College, West Liberty, WV 26074	1837	C/Pub	2679	65%		162	R		370
Westmar College, Le Mars, IA 51031	1890	C/Ind	646	76%		50	R		2925
Westminster Choir College, Princeton, NJ 08540	1920	C/Ind	376	36%	G	65	T		3625
Westminster College, Fulton, MO 65251	1851	M/Ind	664	45%		57	T	A	3370
Westminster College, New Wilmington, PA 16142	1852	C/Prot	1550	71%	G	140	R		3294
Westminster College, Salt Lake City, UT 84105	1875	C/Ind	1344	65%		105	S	A,N,AF	2400
Westmont College, Santa Barbara, CA 93108	1940	C/Prot	1021	75%		93	S		3800
West Texas State University, Canyon, TX 79016	1909	C/Pub	5374	93%	G	363	T	A	382
West Virginia Institute of Technology, Montgomery, WV 25136	1895	C/Pub	3005	80%		185	T	A	370
West Virginia State College, Institute, WV 25112	1891	C/Pub	3678	91%	G	195	S	A	315
West Virginia University, Morgantown, WV 26506	1867	C/Pub	14,581	59%	G	1931	T	A, AF	459
West Virginia Wesleyan College, Buckhannon, WV 26201	1890	C/Prot	1797	32%	G	131	T		2894
Wheaton College, Wheaton, IL 60187	1860	C/Prot	1970	25%	G	184	S	A	3126
Wheaton College, Norton, MA 02766	1834	W/Ind	1138	33%		125	T		5285
Wheeling College, Wheeling, WV 26003	1954	C/Cath	1031	40%		72	S		2975
Wheelock College, Boston, MA 02215	1889	W/Ind	709	41%	G	93	U		3750
Whitman College, Walla Walla, WA 99362	1859	C/Ind	1171	51%		90	T		3920
Whittier College, Whittier, CA 90608	1901	C/Ind	1340	62%	G	105	S		3800
Whitworth College, Spokane, WA 99251	1890	C/Prot	1522	46%	G	144	S		3769
Wichita State University, Wichita, KS 67208	1895	C/Pub	12,400	97%	G	800	U	A	723
Widener University, Chester, PA 19013	1821	C/Ind	1954	75%	G	131	S	A	3760
Wilberforce University, Wilberforce, OH 45384	1856	C/Prot	1026	28%		65	R		1180
Wiley College, Marshall, TX 75670	1873	C/Prot	615	99%		38	T		63c
Wilkes College, Wilkes-Barre, PA 18703	1933	C/Ind	2344	80%	G	152	U	AF	3010
Willamette University, Salem, OR 97301	1842	C/Prot	1276	54%	G	153	T		3625
William Carey College, Hattiesburg, MS 39401	1906	C/Prot	1340	65%	G	110	S		1711
William Jewell College, Liberty, MO 64068	1849	C/Prot	1410	70%		127	S		2455
William Paterson College of NJ, Wayne, NJ 07470	1855	C/Pub	9862	97%	G	601	S	AF	950x
William Penn College, Oskaloosa, IA 52577	1873	C/Prot	617	65%		52	T		3460
Williams College, Williamstown, MA 01267	1793	C/Ind	1947	17%	G	222	T		5150
William Smith College, See Hobart and William Smith Colleges.									
William Woods College, Fulton, MO 65251	1870	W/Ind	898	39%		94	T		3615
Wilmington College, New Castle, DE 19720	1967	C/Ind	683	63%	G	67	S	A	2450x
Wilmington College, Wilmington, OH 45177	1870	C/Prot	750	65%		75	T		3000
Wilson College, Chambersburg, PA 17201	1869	W/Prot	221	37%		50	T		3780
Winona State University, Winona, MN 55987	1860	C/Pub	4000	75%	G	240	T		700
Winston-Salem State University, Winston-Salem, NC 27102	1892	C/Pub	2094	93%	G	140	U	A	602
Winthrop College, Rock Hill, SC 29733	1886	C/Pub	3551	91%	G	277	U		151
Wisconsin Conservatory of Music, Milwaukee, WI 53202	1968	C/Ind	161	*	G	57	S		2300
Wittenberg University, Springfield, OH 45501	1845	C/Prot	2270	60%	G	174	S		4100
Wofford College, Spartanburg, SC 29301	1851	C/Prot	996	75%		71	U	A	3140
Woodbury University, Los Angeles, CA 90017	1884	C/Ind	1243	35%	G	58	U		2496

Name and Location	Est	Type/ Control	UG Enroll	% of State Res	Grad	Fac Size	Cmps	ROTC	Tuition
Worcester Polytechnic Institute, Worcester, MA 01609	1865	C/Ind	2388	49%	G	224	U	A	$4520
Worcester State College, Worcester, MA 01602	1874	C/Pub	3086	99%	G	207	U		650
Wright State University, Dayton, OH 45435	1967	C/Pub	10,916	98%	G	800	S	A	960
Xavier University, Cincinnati, OH 45207	1831	C/Cath	2871	80%	G	280	U	A	2860
Xavier University of Louisiana, New Orleans, LA 70125	1915	C/Cath	1797	80%	G	161	U	A	2200
Yale University, New Haven, CT 06520	1701	C/Ind	5231	10%	G	1468	U		5550
Yankton College, Yankton, SD 57078	1881	C/Prot	278	37%		43	T	A	2850
Yeshiva College, New York, NY 10016	1886	M/Ind	859	78%		347	U		3400
York College, See City U of NY, York College.									
York College of Pennsylvania, York, PA 17405	1787	C/Ind	3497	74%	G	190	S	A	2118
Youngstown State University, Youngstown, OH 44555	1908	C/Pub	13,501	91%	G	805	U	A	795

INDEX OF TWO-YEAR PRIVATE COLLEGES

Academy of Aeronautics, Flushing, NY 11371
Alabama Christian College, Montgomery, AL 36109
Alabama Lutheran Academy and College, Selma, AL 36701
Alice Lloyd College, Pippa Passes, KY 41844
Ancilla College, Donaldson, IN 46513
Anderson College, Anderson, SC 29621
Aquinas Junior College, Milton, MA 02186
Aquinas Junior College, Newton, MA 02158
Aquinas Junior College, Nashville, TN 37205
Atlanta Junior College, Atlanta, GA 30310
Bacone College, Bacone, OK 74420
Bay Path Junior College, Longmeadow, MA 01106
Becker Junior College - Leicester Campus, Leicester, MA 01524
Becker Junior College - Worcester Campus, Worcester, MA 01609
Brandywine College, Wilmington, DE 19803
Brewton-Parker College, Mt Vernon, GA 30445
Catholic University of Puerto Rico, Aguadilla, PR 00603
Catholic University of Puerto Rico, Arecibo, PR 00612
Catholic University of Puerto Rico, Guayama, PR 00654
Cazenovia College, Cazenovia, NY 13035
Center for Degree Studies, Scranton, PA 18515
Central New England College, Worcester, MA 01608
Central YMCA Community College, Chicago, IL 60606
Champlain College, Burlington, VT 05401
Chatfield College, St Martin, OH 45170
Chowan College, Murfreesboro, NC 27855
Clarke College, Newton, MS 39345
College of Boca Raton, Boca Raton, FL 33431
College of Ganado, Ganado, AZ 86508
Concordia College, Milwaukee, WI 53208
Concordia Lutheran College, Austin, TX 78705
Cottey College, Nevada, MO 64772
Crosier Seminary, Onamia, MN 56359
Culinary Institute of America, Hyde Park, NY 12538
Cumberland College of Tennessee, Lebanon, TN 37087
Davenport College of Business, Grand Rapids, MI 49502
Dean Junior College, Franklin, MA 02038
Deep Springs College, Deep Springs, CA 89010
Don Bosco Technical Institute, Rosemead, CA 91770
Donnelly College, Kansas City, KS 66102
D-Q University, Davis, CA 95616
Durham College, Durham, NC 27707
Elizabeth Seton College, Yonkers, NY 10701
Emmanuel College, Franklin Springs, GA 38639
Endicott College, Beverly, MA 01915
Felician College, Chicago, IL 60645
Fisher Junior College, Boston, MA 02116
Florida College, Temple Terrace, FL 33617
Franklin Coll (Lugano, Switzerland,) New York, NY 10021
Franklin Institute of Boston, Boston, MA 02116
Golden Valley Lutheran College, Minneapolis, MN 55422
Goldey Beacom College, Wilmington, DE 19808
Grahm Junior College, Boston, MA 02215
Grand View College, Des Moines, IA 50316
Harcum Junior College, Bryn Mawr, PA 19010
Harriman College, Harriman, NY 10926
Hartford College for Women, Hartford, CT 06105
Hilbert College, Hamburg, NY 14075
Hiwassee College, Madisonville, TN 37354
Humphreys College, Stockton, CA 95207
Inter American U of PR, Aguadilla Regional Coll, Aguadilla, PR 00603
Inter American U of PR, Arecibo Regional College, Arecibo, PR 00612
Inter American U of PR, Barranquitas Regional Coll, Barranquitas, PR 00618
Inter American U of PR, Bayamon Regional Coll, Bayamon, PR 00619
Inter American U of PR, Fajardo Regional Coll, Fajardo, PR 00648
Inter American U of PR, Guayama Regional Coll, Guayama, PR 00654
Inter American U of PR, Ponce Regional Coll, Ponce, PR 00731
Jacksonville College, Jacksonville, TX 75766

John A. Gupton College, Nashville, TN 37203
Judson Baptist College, Portland, OR 97220
Junior College of Albany, Albany, NY 12208
Kemper Military School and College, Boonville, MO 65233
Keystone Jr. College, La Plume, PA 18440
Laboure Junior College, Boston, MA 02124
Lackawanna Junior College, Scranton, PA 18503
Lasell Junior College, Newton, MA 02166
Latter-Day Saints Business College, Salt Lake City, UT 84111
Lees Junior College, Jackson, KY 41339
Lees-McRae College, Banner Elk, NC 28604
Lewis Business College, Detroit, MI 48235
Lincoln College, Lincoln, IL 62656
Lindsey Wilson College, Columbia, KY 42728
Lon Morris College, Jacksonville, TX 75766
Louisburg College, Louisburg, NC 27549
Lourdes College, Sylvania, OH 43560
Manor Junior College, Jenkintown, PA 19046
Maria College, Albany, NY 12208
Maria Regina College, Syracuse, NY 13208
Marion Military Institute, Marion, AL 36756
Martin College, Pulaski, TN 38478
Mary Holmes College, West Point, MS 39773
Marymount Palos Verdes College, Rancho Palos Verdes, CA 90274
Mater Dei College, Ogdensburg, NY 13669
Michigan Christian Junior College, Rochester, MI 48063
Miller Community College, Los Angeles, CA 90006
Mitchell College, New London, CT 06320
Montreat-Anderson College, Montreat, NC 28757
Mount Aloysius Jr College, Cresson, PA 16630
Mount Ida Junior College, Newton Centre, MA 02159
Mount Olive College, Mount Olive, NC 28365
Mount Saint Clare College, Clinton, IA 52732
Nairobi College, East Palo Alto, CA 94303
Natchez Junior College, Natchez, MS 39120
Newbury Junior College, Boston, MA 02115
New England Institute of Technology, Providence, RI 02907
Northeastern Christian Jr College, Villanova, PA 19085
North Greenville College, Tigerville, SC 29688
Northwood Inst-West Inst-Indiana Campus, West Baden, IN 47469
Ohio Valley College, Parkersburg, WV 26101
Oklahoma City Southwestern College, Oklahoma City, OK 73127
Oxford College of Emory University, Oxford, GA 30267
Paul Smith's College, Paul Smiths, NY 12970
Peace College, Raleigh, NC 27602
Peirce Junior College, Philadelphia, PA 19102
Presentation College, Aberdeen, SD 57401
Puerto Rico Junior College, Rio Piedras, PR 00928
Reinhardt College, Waleska, GA 30183
Ricks College, Rexburg, ID 83440
St Catharine College, St Catharine, KY 40061
St Gregory's College, Shawnee, OK 74801
St John's College, Winfield, KS 67156
St John's Vianney Seminary, Miami, FL 33165
St Mary's College, Raleigh, NC 27611
Saint Mary's College of O'Fallon, O'Fallon, MO 63366
St Mary's Junior College, Minneapolis, MN 55454
St Paul's College, Concordia, MO 64020
Saint Thomas Seminary Jr College, Bloomfield, CT 06002
Salem College at Clarksburg, Clarksburg, WV 26301
Schreiner College, Kerrville, TX 78028
Sheldon Jackson College, Sitka, AK 99835
Shorter College, North Little Rock, AR 72114
Sioux Empire College, Hawarden, IA 51023
Southeastern Christian College, Winchester, KY 40391
Southern Baptist College, Walnut Ridge, AR 72476
Southern Seminary Jr College, Buena Vista, VA 24416
Southwestern Christian College, Terrell, TX 75160
Southwestern Jr Coll of the Assemblies of God, Waxahachie, TX 75165

Spartanburg Methodist College, Spartanburg, SC 29301
Springfield College in Illinois, Springfield, IL 62702
Sue Bennett College, London, KY 40741
Suomi College, Hancock, MI 49930
Trocaire College, Buffalo, NY 14220
Truett-McConnell College, Cleveland, GA 30528
Union College, Cranford, NJ 07016
Valley Forge Military Jr College, Wayne, PA 19087
Vermont College, Montpelier, VT 05602
Villa Julie College, Stevenson, MD 21153
Villa Maria College of Buffalo, Buffalo, NY 14225
Waldorf College, Forest City, IA 50436
Walker College, Jasper, AL 35501

Waycross Junior College, Waycross, GA 31501
Webber College, Babson Park, FL 33827
Wentworth Military Academy & Jr Coll, Lexington, MO 64067
Wesley College, Dover, DE 19901
Westbrook College, Portland, ME 04103
West Coast Bible College, Fresno, CA 93710
White Pines College, Chester, NH 03036
Wingate College, Wingate, NC 28174
Wood Junior College, Mathiston, MS 39752
Worcester Junior College, Worcester, MA 01608
York College, York, NE 68467
Young Harris College, Young Harris, GA 30582

U.S. PUBLIC LIBRARIES WITH 1 MILLION OR MORE VOLUMES: 1974

SOURCE: U.S. Dept. of Health, Education, and Welfare, National Center for Education Statistics, **Public Library Survey, 1974.**

Library system	No. of vols.	Library system	No. of vols.
New York Public Library	8,761,899	Denver Public Library	1,488,350
Chicago Public Library	5,593,136	Dallas Public Library	1,486,146
Los Angeles Public Library	4,336,734	Public Library of Fort Wayne and Allen County (Ind.)	1,329,357
Los Angeles County Public Library	3,824,664	Minneapolis Public Library	1,303,200
Boston Public Library	3,692,569	St. Louis Public Library	1,294,251
Cleveland Public Library	3,146,982	Cuyahoga County (Ohio) Public Library	1,266,143
Cincinnati-Hamilton County Public Library	2,985,812	St. Louis County Library	1,215,126
Free Library of Philadelphia	2,925,147	San Diego Public Library	1,212,378
Queens Borough Public Library (New York)	2,901,274	Dayton and Montgomery County Public Library (Ohio)	1,207,827
Buffalo and Erie County Library System	2,839,402	Baltimore County Public Library	1,173,836
Brooklyn Public Library	2,784,153	Kansas City Public Library	1,165,505
Milwaukee Public Library	2,344,914	Columbus Public Library	1,142,852
Enoch Pratt Free Library (Baltimore)	2,282,513	Memphis and Shelby County Library	1,126,342
Detroit Public Library	2,255,266	Indianapolis-Marion County Library	1,125,375
Carnegie Library of Pittsburgh	2,120,310	Toledo-Lucas County Library	1,105,263
Public Library of Washington, D.C.	1,951,796	Public Library of Newark	1,096,139
Hawaii State Library	1,808,150	King County Library (Washington)	1,085,843
Houston Public Library	1,540,925	Library Association of Portland	1,057,667
San Francisco Public Library	1,528,602	Louisville Free Public Library	1,000,879
Seattle Public Library	1,508,950		

LARGEST LIBRARIES OF THE WORLD

MOSCOW: State V.I. Lenin Library of the USSR (founded 1862); 27,000,000 vols., 2,500,000 MSS.

WASHINGTON, D.C.: Library of Congress (founded 1800); over 72 million items; 16,466,900 vols., 31,031,500 MSS.

CAMBRIDGE, MASS.: Harvard University Library (founded 1638); 9,547,576 vols.

NEW YORK CITY: New York Public Library (founded 1895); 8,-426,680 vols., 10,245,000 MSS.

PARIS: Bibliothèque Nationale (founded 1480); 7,000,000 vols.; 155,000 MSS.

NEW HAVEN, CONN.: Yale University Library (founded 1701); 6,884,604 vols.

LONDON: British Museum (founded 1753); 6,000,000+ vols., 60,000 MSS.

URBANA, ILLINOIS: University of Illinois, Urbana-Champaign (founded 1868); 5,494,786 vols.

CHICAGO: Chicago Public Library (founded 1872); 5,069,500 vols.

BERLIN: Deutsche Staatsbibliothek (founded 1661); 4,994,170 vols.

ANN ARBOR, MICH.: University of Michigan Libraries (founded 1838); 4,917,381 vols.

BERKELEY, CALIF.: University of California, Berkeley, Calif. Library (founded 1868); 4,917,330 vols.

NEW YORK CITY: Columbia University Libraries (founded 1761); 4,716,162 vols.

PEKING: National Library of Peking (founded 1912); 4,400,000 vols.

STANFORD, CALIF.: Stanford University Libraries (founded 1891); 4,170,325 vols., 17,503,000 MSS.

LOS ANGELES: Los Angeles Public Library (founded 1872); 4,161,910 vols.

FLORENCE, ITALY: Biblioteca Nazionale Centrale (founded 1891); 4,000,000 vols.

LOS ANGELES, CALIF. University of California, Los Angeles, Calif. Library (founded 1919); 3,908,053 vols.

CHICAGO: University of Chicago Library (founded 1891); 3,-886,130 vols.

AUSTIN, TEXAS: University of Texas, Austin, Texas Library (founded 1881); 3,713,821 vols.

LOS ANGELES, CALIF.: Los Angeles County Public Library (founded 1912); 3,646,870 vols.

OXFORD: Bodleian Library (founded 1602); 3,500,000 vols., 50,000 MSS.

LARGE U.S. UNIVERSITY LIBRARIES

University	Number of Volumes	University	Number of Volumes
Harvard University	9,547,576	Princeton University	2,910,461
Yale University	6,884,604	University of Pennsylvania	2,784,260
University of Illinois (Urbana Campus)	5,494,786	Duke University	2,712,405
University of Michigan, Ann Arbor	4,917,381	Northwestern University	2,544,896
University of California at Berkeley	4,917,330	University of Washington	2,381,642
Columbia University (Main Division)	4,716,162	University of No. Car. at Chapel Hill	2,274,173
Stanford University	4,170,325	New York University	2,251,948
University of California, L.A.	3,908,053	Johns Hopkins University	2,091,315
University of Chicago	3,886,130	University of Virginia, Main Campus	2,081,003
University of Texas at Austin	3,713,821	University of Iowa	2,055,581
University of Minnesota, Minn.-St. Paul	3,363,576	University of Utah	1,944,566
Indiana University at Bloomington	3,242,300	University of Missouri, Columbia	1,882,394
University of Wisconsin, Madison	3,238,152	University of Florida	1,852,841
Cornell University	3,184,941	University of Kansas, Main Campus	1,849,096
Ohio State University, Main Campus	3,126,131	University of Southern California	1,784,192

THE REFERENCE SHELF

This list of reference books constitutes the nucleus of a reference shelf for small private, public, and organizational libraries.

Acronyms, Initialisms & Abbreviations Dictionary, ed. Ellen T. Crowley, 6th ed. (Gale Research, 1978).

American Authors, 1600-1900, ed. Stanley J. Kunitz and Howard Haycraft (H. W. Wilson Co., 1938).

American Heritage Dictionary of the English Language, ed. William Morris (American Heritage Publishing Co., Inc., and Houghton Mifflin Co., 1975).

American Men and Women of Science: The Physical and Biological Sciences, ed. The Jaques Cattell Press, 13th ed., 7 vols. (R. R. Bowker Co., 1976).

American Men and Women of Science: The Social and Behavioral Sciences, ed. The Jaques Cattell Press, 13th ed., 2 vols. (R. R. Bowker Co., 1977).

American Negro Reference Book, ed. John P. Davis (Prentice-Hall, Inc.,1966).

American Universities and Colleges, ed. W. Todd Furniss, 11th ed. (American Council on Education, 1973).

Amy Vanderbilt's Etiquette, Amy Vanderbilt, rev. ed. (Doubleday and Co.,Inc., 1972).

Baby and Child Care, Benjamin Spock, rev. ed. (Hawthorn, 1968).

Baker's Biographical Dictionary of Musicians, Theodore Baker, ed. Nicolas Slonimsky, 5th ed. (G. Schirmer, 1958; supplement, 1971).

Biographical Directory of the American Congress, 1774-1961, U.S. Congress (Government Printing Office, 1961).

Biographical Encyclopaedia and Who's Who of the American Theatre, ed. Walter Rigdon (Wm. Heineman, Ltd., 1966).

Biography Index: A Cumulative Index to Biographical Materials in Books and Magazines, annual (H. W. Wilson Co., 1946).

Black's Law Dictionary, Henry C. Black, rev. 4th ed. (West Publishing Co., 1968).

Book of the States, biennial, ed. Vincent Wilson, Jr., (American History Research Association, 1972).

Books in Print, annual, 2 vols. (R. R. Bowker Co., 1948).

Careful Writer: A Modern Guide to English Usage, Theodore M. Bernstein (Atheneum, 1965).

Chases' Calendar of Annual Events, annual, William D. Chase (Apple Tree, 1957).

Columbia Encyclopedia, ed. William H. Harris and Judith S. Levy, 4th ed. (Columbia University Press, 1975).

Columbia-Lippincott Gazetteer of the World, ed. Leon E. Seltzer et al. (Columbia University Press, 1952).

Commercial Atlas and Marketing Guide, annual (Rand McNally & Co., 1870).

Concise Dictionary of American Biography, ed. Joseph G. Hopkins (Charles Scribner's Sons, 1977).

Congress and The Nation, 1945-1964; vol. 2, 1965-1968, vol. 3, 1969-1972, vol. 4, 1972-1976, (Congressional Quarterly Service, 1965; 1969; 1973; 1977).

Congressional Directory, annual (Government Printing Office, 1935).

Contemporary Authors, ed. Clare Kinsman, semiannual (Gale Research, 1962).

Current Biography Yearbook, annual (H. W. Wilson Co., 1946).

Demographic Yearbook, annual (United Nations Statistical Office, 1949).

Dictionary of American Biography, 10 vols. and supplements. (Charles Scribner's Sons, 1974)

Dictionary of American History, ed. Michael Martin & Leonard Gelber, rev. ed.,_(Littlefield, Adams & Co., 1978).

Dictionary of Modern English Usage, Henry M. Fowler, 2nd ed., rev. by Sir Ernest Gowers (Oxford University Press, Inc., 1965).

Dictionary of Music and Musicians, George Grove, ed. Eric Blom, 5th ed., 10 vols. (St. Martin's Press, Inc., 1954; supplement, 1961).

Dictionary of National Biography, George Smith ed., 22 vols. including 1st supplement, plus 7 supplements (Oxford University Press, Inc.; 22 vols. reprinted, 1938); abridged: **Concise Dictionary of National Biography,** ed. Sir Sidney Lee, 2 vols. (Oxford University Press, Inc., 1975).

Dictionary of Quotations, Bergen Evans (Delacorte Press, 1968).

Dictionary of the Social Sciences, ed. H. F. Reading (Routledge & Kegan Paul, LTD, 1977).

Dictionary of Universal Biography, Albert M. Hyamson, 2nd rev. ed. (Routledge & Kegan Paul, LTD, 1976).

Directory of American Scholars, ed. The Jaques Cattell Press, 7th ed., 4 vols. (R. R. Bowker, 1978).

Documents of American History, 2 vols., ed. A. Commager, 9th ed. (Prentice-Hall, 1974).

Dorland's Illustrated Medical Dictionary, 25th ed. (W. B. Saunders Co., 1974).

Editor & Publisher International Yearbook, annual (Editor & Publisher, 1920).

Encyclopaedia Britannica, 30 vols. 15th ed. in (1978); 15th ed. in 30 vols. (Encyclopaedia Britannica, 1768).

Encyclopedia Americana, 30 vols. (Grolier Educational Corporation, 1979).

Encyclopedia of American Facts and Dates, ed. Gorton Carruth et al., 7th ed. (Thomas Y. Crowell Co., 1978).

Encyclopedia of American History, ed. Richard B. Morris, 5th ed. (Harper & Row, Publishers, 1976).

Encyclopedia of Associations, 13th ed., 3 vols. (Gale Research, 1979).

Encyclopedia of Chemistry, The, ed. Clifford A. Hampel and Gessner G. Hawley, 3rd ed. (Van Nostrand Reinhold Co., 1973).

Encyclopedia of Philosophy, ed. Paul Edwards, 4 vols. (The Free Press, 1973).

Encyclopedia of Physics, The, ed. Robert M. Besancon (Van Nostrand Reinhold Co., 1974).

Encyclopedia of Sports, Frank G. Menke, 6th rev. ed. (A. S. Barnes & Co., Inc., 1978).

Encyclopedia of the Biological Sciences, Peter Gray, 2nd ed. (Van Nostrand Reinhold Co., 1970).

Encyclopedia of World Art, 15 vols. (McGraw-Hill, Inc., 1959-68).

Encyclopedia of World History, ed. William L. Langer, 5th ed. (Houghton Mifflin Co., 1972).

Europa Year Book, annual 2 vols. (International Publications Service, 1959).

European Authors, 1000-1900, ed. Stanley J. Kunitz and Vineta Colby (H. W. Wilson Co., 1967).

Facts about the Presidents, Joseph N. Kane, 3rd ed. (H. W. Wilson Co., 1974).

Facts on File, annual (Facts on File, Inc., 1940).

Familiar Quotations, John Bartlett, 15th ed., rev. and enl. (Citadel Press, 1971).

Famous First Facts, Joseph N. Kane, 3rd ed. (H. W. Wilson Co., 1964).

Foundation Directory, biannual, ed. Marianna O. Lewis, 6th ed. (Foundation Center, 1977).

Future: A Guide to Information Sources, The, (World Future Society, 1977).

Granger's Index to Poetry, Edith Granger, ed. William J. Smith, 6th rev. and enl. ed. (Columbia University Press, 1962; supplement to 6th ed., 1973).

Guide to Reference Books, Eugene P. Sheehy, 9th ed. (American Library Association, 1976).

Guinness Book of World Records, ed. Norris McWhirter (Sterling, 1979).

Hammond Medallion World Atlas (Hammond Inc., 1979).

Harper Bible Dictionary, Madeleine S. and John L. Miller, 8th ed. (Harper & Row, Publishers, 1973).

Harper Encyclopedia of Science, ed. James R. Newman, rev. ed. (Harper & Row, Publishers, 1967).

Harvard Guide to American History, 2 vols., rev. ed. F. Freidel and R. K. Showman (Harvard University Press, 1974).

Historical Statistics of the United States: 1790 to 1970, 2 vols. (University of Alabama Press, 1976).

Home Book of Quotations, Burton Stevenson, 10th ed. (Dodd, Mead & Co., 1967).

Home Book of Verse, Burton E. Stevenson, 9th ed., 2 vols. (Holt, Rinehart & Winston, 1953).

International Encyclopedia of the Social Sciences, ed. David E. Sills, 17 vols. (The Macmillan Co., 1968).

International Who's Who, (International Publications Service, 1935).

Keesing's Contemporary Archives, weekly (Keesing's, London, 1931).

Literary Market Place, annual (R. R. Bowker Co., 1940).

McGraw-Hill Encyclopedia of Science and Technology, 3rd rev. ed., 15 vols. (McGraw-Hill, Inc., 1971).

Macmillan Book of Proverbs, Burton Stevenson (The Macmillan Co., 1965).

Manual of Style, Staff of the University of Chicago Press, rev. 12th ed. (University of Chicago Press, 1969).

Masterpieces of World Literature in Digest Form, ed. Frank N. Magill, 4 vols. (Harper & Row, Publishers, 1952-69).

Monthly Catalog of United States Government Publications, monthly (Government Printing Office, 1895).

Municipal Year Book, ed. International City Management Association (National Association of Counties, 1976).

National Geographic Atlas of the World, Melville B. Grovenor, 4th ed. (National Geographic Society, 1975).

Negro Almanac, ed. Harry A. Ploski and Warren Marr, rev. ed. (Bellwether Publishing, 1971).

New Acronyms and Initialisms: supplement 1977 to Acronyms and Initialisms Dictionary (Gale Research, 6th edition, 1976).

New Catholic Encyclopedia, prepared by Editorial Staff at Catholic University of America, 17 vols. (McGraw-Hill, Inc., 1967).

New Century Cyclopedia of Names, ed. Clarence L. Barnhart and William D. Halsey, 3 vols. (Prentice-Hall, Inc., 1954).

New Emily Post's Etiquette, Emily Post, rev. by Elizabeth L. Post, 12th rev. ed. (Funk & Wagnalls Co., Inc., 1975).

New Encyclopedia of the Opera, David Ewen (Hill and Wang, Inc., 1971).

New York Times Index, semimonthly and cumulated annually (The New York Times, 1851).

Oxford Classical Dictionary, ed. N. G. Hammond and H. H. Scullard, 2nd ed. (Oxford University Press, 1970).

Oxford Companion to American History, Thomas H. Johnson (Oxford University Press, Inc., 1966).

Oxford Companion to American Literature, James D. Hart, 4th ed. Oxford University Press, 1965).

Oxford Companion to Classical Literature, ed. Paul Harvey, 2nd ed. (Oxford University Press, 1937).

Oxford Companion to English Literature, ed. Paul Harvey and Dorothy Eagle, 4th ed. (Oxford University Press, Inc., 1967).

Oxford Companion to Film, ed. by Liz-Anne Bawden (Oxford University Press, Inc., 1976).

Oxford Companion to the Theatre, Phyllis Hartnoll, 3rd ed. (Oxford University Press, Inc., 1967)

Oxford Dictionary of Quotations, 2nd ed. (Oxford University Press, Inc., 1953).

Oxford English Dictionary, ed. James A. Murray et al., 13 vols. (Oxford University Press, Inc., 1933).

Peterson's Annual Guides to Graduate and Undergraduate Study, 13th ed., ed. Karen C. Hegener, 5 volumes (Peterson's Guides, 1979).

Political Handbook of the World 1977, ed. Arthur S. Banks (McGraw-Hill, 1977).

Random House Dictionary of the English Language, ed. Jess Stein (Random House, Inc., 1966).

Reader's Adviser, 12th ed., 3 vols. (R. R. Bowker Co., 1974-1977).

Reader's Encyclopedia, ed. William R. Benét, 2nd ed. (Thomas Y. Crowell Co., 1965).

Readers' Guide to Periodical Literature, 37 vols., annual (H. W. Wilson Co., 1900).

Roget's International Thesaurus, 4th ed., Peter M. Roget (Thomas Y. Crowell Co., 1977).

Shepherd's Historical Atlas, William R. Shepherd, 9th ed. (Barnes & Noble, Inc., 1964).

Statesman's Year-Book, annual (St. Martin's Press, Inc., 1864).

Statistical Abstract of the United States, annual (Government Printing Office, 1878).

Statistical Yearbook, annual (United Nations Publishing Service, 1949).

Stedman's Medical Dictionary, Thomas L. Stedman, 23rd ed. (The William & Wilkins Co., 1976).

Times Atlas of the World, comprehensive ed. (London Times/Quadrangle, 1975).

Times Atlas of World History, ed. Geoffrey Barraclough (London Times/Hammond Inc., 1979).

Timetables of History, Bernard Grun (Simon & Schuster, Inc., 1975).

Twentieth Century Authors, ed. Stanley J. Kunitz and Howard Haycraft (H. W. Wilson Co., 1942).

Twentieth Century Authors: First Supplement, ed. Stanley J. Kunitz and Howard Haycraft (H. W. Wilson Co., 1955).

Ulrich's International Periodicals Directory, 17th ed. (R. R. Bowker Co., 1977).

United States Government Organization Manual, annual (Government Printing Office, 1935).

Universal Jewish Encyclopedia and Readers Guide, ed. Isaac Landman, 11 vols. (Ktav, 1944).

Van Nostrand's International Encyclopedia of Chemical Science (Van Nostrand Reinhold Co., Inc., 1964).

Van Nostrand's Scientific Encyclopedia, 5th ed. (Van Nostrand Reinhold Co., 1976).

Webster's New Geographical Dictionary, rev. ed. (G. and C. Merriam Co., 1977).

Webster's Third New International Dictionary of the English Language, unabridged (G. and C. Merriam Co., 1976).

Who Was Who, 6 vols. (St. Martin's Press, Inc., 1897-1961).

Who Was Who in America, 7 vols. (The A. N. Marquis Co., 1897-1976).

Who Was Who in America: Historical Volume, 1607-1896 (The A. N. Marquis Co., 1963).

Who's Who, annual (St. Martin's Press, Inc., 1849).

Who's Who in America, biennial (The A. N. Marquis Co., 1899).

Who's Who in American Politics, 1977-1978, compiled by Jaques Cattell Press, 6th ed. (R. R. Bowker Co., 1977).

Who's Who of American Women, 1977-1978, 10th ed. (The A. N. Marquis Co., 1977).

Worldmark Encyclopedia of the Nations, 5 vols., ed. Moshe Y. Sachs (J. Wiley & Sons, 1976).

World of Learning, annual (International Publications Service, 1947).

World Who's Who in Science, ed. Allen G. Debus (The A. N. Marquis Co., 1968).

Yearbook of International Organizations, biennial (Union of International Publications Service, 1948).

Yearbook of the United Nations, annual (International Publications Service, 1946/47).

COMMUNICATIONS/LANGUAGE

CURRENT WORDS AND PHRASES

The following list of words and phrases consists of terms and meanings that have only recently made an appearance in English or of terms that have had some restricted usage over a period of time but are now acquiring widespread usage. Many of these words have passed the test of time and have already entered the dictionaries. Some will prove to be fleeting, and will remain only as a curious reminder of some passing vogue. The list was prepared by the staff of Laurence Urdang Inc.

ADR Abbreviation for **American Depositary Receipt,** a certificate for shares in a foreign company, issued by an American bank against such shares held by it in a foreign branch and, with a few exceptions which are traded on the N.Y.S.E., traded over the counter.

Agent Orange An herbicide used as a defoliant in the Vietnam War, held by some to cause birth defects and cancer.

Airbus a trade name for a wide-bodied airplane used chiefly as a domestic passenger carrier

airquake an explosive noise of undetermined origin heard usually in coastal communities and appearing to come from a point at some elevation above the sea.

alpha wave a brain wave, 8-12 cycles per second, associated with decreased anxiety and a state of meditation.

American Depositary Receipt. See **ADR.**

angel dust *Slang.* phencyclidine, an addictive, hallucinatory, narcotic drug. Also called **PCP.**

beefalo a source of meat, bred as one-eighth buffalo and seven-eighths beef.

beta wave a brain wave, 15-30 cycles per second, associated with problem-solving attentiveness.

bingo card a response card, bound into a periodical, containing numbers keyed to editorial or advertising matter, affording a reader the opportunity to send for further information by marking the numbers of items of interest, providing name and address, and mailing the postage-free card.

biofeedback an instrumental technique whereby a person can gain conscious information and voluntary control over bodily processes that are normally unconscious and involuntary: high blood pressure, for example, can sometimes be controlled by means of this technique

biorhythm a pattern of cyclical electrical impulses in the human body believed to be a result or an indication of intellectual, physical, and emotional states.

boomer *Informal.* a worker engaged in the building of massive oil and gas storage tanks.

breathalyzer a device for determining the alcoholic content of the bloodstream, based on the chemical analysis of a person's breath. It is used by some law enforcement agencies to test drivers suspected of intoxication.

bungee cord a piece of shock cord, with a hook fastened to each end, used for securing gear, as to a rear carrier of a bicycle.

camet an international camping card, issued by various assocations to members on payment of an additional fee, entitling holders to privileges like special insurance coverage, discounts, etc.

cardiopulmonary resuscitation. See **CPR.**

catalytic converter a device employed in an internal combustion engine for removing harmful pollutants from the exhaust before ejecting it into the atmosphere.

catch-22 a regulation or situation that is self-contradictory or that conflicts with another regulation or situation of equal force. As set forth in *Catch-22,* Joseph Heller's novel of World War II, it referred to the regulation that flight crews must report for duty unless excused for reasons of insanity, but that anyone claiming such an excuse must, by definition, be sane.

c.e.o. Abbreviation for **chief executive officer.**

CETA (see'tuh) Abbreviation for **Comprehensive Employment Training Act,** a program sponsored by the U.S. government in cooperation with local agencies to provide training and employment.

Chinese Wall (system) *Informal.* a bank's policy or practice of secrecy that prevents the interdepartmental transfer of information about customers. It is typically administered in order to maintain the confidentiality of information that may benefit one company in the acquisition of another.

cogeneration the use of waste heat to produce electrical energy.

CPR Abbreviation of **cardiopulmonary resuscitation.** A method for administering first aid to a victim of a heart attack, esp. as taught to laymen.

Delaney clause part of an amendment to the Food Additive Act of 1958 providing that "No additive should be deemed to be safe if it is found to induce cancer when ingested by man or animal."

delta wave a brain wave, 1-3 cycles per second, associated with very deep sleep.

Denver boot a device for locking onto a wheel of a car that prevents its being driven away, used by some police departments as a less expensive alternative to towing away and impounding the cars of parking violators and scofflaws. Also called **French boot.**

developmentally disabled a euphemism for **mentally retarded.**

dirigisme French. the practice, in France, of allowing the central government in Paris to direct all of the nation's business and economic affairs.

diskette. See **floppy disk.**

docudrama a presentation in the form of a play, film, television program, etc., in which historical events are dramatized and sometimes fictionalized. — docudramatist *n.*

draft (in competitive running) to run behind another runner so as to take advantage of his wind shadow. See **wind shadow.**

early exit *Informal.* (of a proficiency test) designed to offer a high-school student the opportunity to earn a diploma as much as two years earlier than a customary completion of a course of study would accord.

econobox a small- to medium-sized economical car, manufactured to sell at a low price, that sacrifices comfort and attractive design for other advantages.

equity (in package design) the advantage afforded by an established package design of being recognized by customers, regardless of how unattractive it may be.

Eurocommunism a kind of communism that recognizes human rights and certain aspects of capitalism, developed in France, Spain and Italy and at variance with Soviet-style tenets.

floppy disk a flexible plastic disk, about the size of a 45 rpm record, used for storing data in small computers and in other devices, like typesetters, that use minicomputer components. Also called **diskette.**

flubble *Comp. Tech.* a combination of a floppy disk recording medium and a magnetic bubble memory storage unit.

Foggy Bottom 1. an area in downtown Washington, D.C., where many offices of the Department of State are situated. **2.** *Figuratively.* the U.S. Department of State.

French boot. See **Denver boot.**

gasification a process for manufacturing gas for utilities and the generation of steam for industry by using pulverized coal.

gasohol a mixture of 10% alcohol and 90% unleaded gasoline, slightly more expensive than premium unleaded gasoline, said to increase mileage per gallon of cars by 5%, used to reduce consumption of gasoline in internal combustion engines.

Ginnie Mae *Informal.* Government National Mortgage Association (GNMA).

glitch *Informal.* any error or fault, or a delay, inconvenience or malfunction caused by it.

GPM Abbreviation for **graduated payment mortgage.** Also, *Informal.* Jeep.

granny gear (in a geared bicycle) a very low ratio for climbing hills with a minimum of effort.

Gulag *Figurative.* any real or imagined place of confinement.

hard-liner one who pursues a **hard line,** or firmly incisive approach to a situation.

hatchback a passenger car with a hatchlike opening at the rear that can be raised to gain access to an open storage area.

Heimlich maneuver a technique for preventing someone from choking on food by applying pressure at specific places on the body.

hog *Slang.* a large, heavy motorcycle.

holistic health the maintenance of health and the prevention of disease through such psychogenic practices and procedures as biofeedback, meditation, alternative methods of childbirth, etc.

holofiche a microfiche on which data has been recorded in the form of tiny holographic images, offering a theoretical capacity of 200 million bits of information on 20,000 individual holograms.

in the can 1. *Motion Pictures.* (of a film) completed; ready for duplication and distribution to exhibitors. 2. *Figuratively.* completed; done.

Jeep. See **GPM.**

leaded (of gasoline) containing lead tetraethyl as an anti-knock additive.

LEG Abbreviation for **liquefied energy gas.**

LNG Abbreviation for **liquefied natural gas,** natural gas cooled to –260° for storage and transportation.

LPG Abbreviation for **liquefied petroleum gas.**

meltdown 1. physical disintegration of the core of a nuclear reactor. 2. *Figurative.* any internal disintegration, as of the directorship of a company, etc.

minifloppy disk a floppy disk of reduced size, being 5¼ in. in diameter with 35–40 concentric tracks on each side. See **floppy disk.**

MIS Abbreviation for **manager of information services.**

mole *Informal.* an espionage agent.

mouse print the very small typeface used on food packages to describe the contents, showing the ingredients, weight, chemical constituents and potential harm to people, plants and animals, as required by the U.S. government.

mousse a floating, chocolate-colored mixture of crude oil and seawater, commonly formed as the result of an oil spill.

notchback a passenger car with a rear window that is nearly vertical. Also called **slantback.**

1-1/2-war capability the theoretical capability of U.S. non-nuclear conventional military forces to fight both a major war and a lesser one.

ovenable (of a paper food tray) able to withstand a temperature of 425° F, said especially of trays made for use in microwave ovens.

palimony *Informal.* a suit brought by a person for a share in the property and money of a former lover to whom the individual was not wed.

paraquat an herbicide for destroying marijuana plants, said to cause irreversible lung damage in those who smoke marijuana contaminated by it.

PCM plug-compatible manufacturer: a company that manufactures computer devices, like tape drives and terminals, that can readily be substituted for equipment offered at a higher price by the manufacturer of the mainframe computers to which they are peripheral.

PCP Another name for phencyclidine. See **angel dust.**

PBB a polybrominated biphenyl compound used as a flame retardant in the manufacture of those parts of radio and television sets that tended to overheat.

Proposition 13 legislation for limiting the amount of property tax payable to a governmental agency. (Named for the ballot proposition passed in California in June 1978 to limit taxation by amending the state constitution.)

proved reserves an estimate of the amount of oil that can be extracted economically from developed sources employing existing technology at existing costs.

psychokinesis the ability to move objects by the strength of will, without touching them.

RCH Abbreviation for **residential care home,** a neighborhood facility offering care for disabled people, typically on a small scale to allow for individual, personalized attention.

residential care home. See **RCH.**

retortable pouch a packaging container for precooked food consisting of a soft plastic and foil bag, intended to replace conventional cans and offering advantages of lightness, cheapness, shelf life equal to that of canned foods, and storage without freezing.

RONA Abbreviation for **return on net assets.**

SALT Abbreviation for **suggestive-accelerative leaning and teaching,** another term for **suggestology.**

shopping-bag lady a vagrant woman who lives in the streets of a large city, typically one who carries her few belongings in one or more large shopping bags.

Silicon Valley an area, about 40 miles south of San Francisco, characterized by a concentration of companies that manufacture silicon chips for use in computers and other electronic devices.

slantback Another name for **notchback.**

suggestive-accelerative learning and teaching Another term for **suggestology.** Abbreviation: **SALT.**

suggestology a method of classroom teaching that employs various techniques, including power of suggestion, physical calisthenics, guided imagery, role-playing, etc. Also called **SALT.**

summary seizure power the power of the Internal Revenue Service to seize property without a warrant for nonpayment of taxes.

Sunbelt a section of the United States in the southerly part, including Virginia, North Carolina, South Carolina, Georgia, Florida, Alabama, Louisiana, Tennessee, Mississippi, Arkansas, Oklahoma, Texas, New Mexico, Arizona, and southern California.

sunrise law legislation that requires a governmental agency to describe in advance its goals for every new program and to provide for periodic reviews to determine whether those goals have been accomplished.

sunset law legislation that requires a governmental agency to justify its existence periodically.

sweet spot an area in the netting of a tennis or other, similar racket designed as the optimum place where it should strike the ball.

terabit *Comp. Tech.* one trillion bits.

theta wave a brain wave, 4–7 cycles per second, associated with neural activity prior to sleep.

top-dressed (of a container of merchandise) arranged so that the better grades are at the top, concealing poorer grades below.

two-stage combustion a process for extracting oil from shale in which oil shale is vaporized with air in a liquid bed and the gas is then burned in a boiler to purify it.

Universal Product Code a pattern of lines and numbers by which information about a product may be encoded for automatic scanning by a device at the checkout counter in a supermarket that records its price for charging the consumer as well as its stock numbers, inventory, etc.

vache a lait 1. *Literally.* milking cow. 2. *Figuratively.* any source of sustenance or subvention, applied esp. to Paris as the seat of the French government's nationalized industry. Compare *vache maigre.*

vache maigre 1. *Literally.* dry cow. 2. *Figuratively.* a former source of sustenance or subvention, now dried up, applied esp. to Paris as the seat of the French government under Valérie Giscard d'Estaing, who has curtailed governmental subsidies and spending. Compare *vache a lait.*

Vietnam syndrome an attitude in U.S. government circles that diplomacy may be more effective in solving local political problems elsewhere than the use of military force, stemming from the failure of U.S. military intervention in Vietnam.

voiceprint graphic representation of a person's speech, made on a sound spectrograph, used especially for purposes of identification

Von Karman effect the effects of wind drag and turbulence created by a specific shape passing through a fluid, esp. as applied to round or oval wheel spokes of a bicycle.

warm-up suit a two-piece garment consisting of a pair of trousers, usually with close-fitting cuffs and a sweater-like top, worn by men or women for jogging and other sports activities.

wind shadow (in competitive running) an area behind a runner where the wind resistance is lowered by his forward movement.

X-body a class of car manufactured in the U.S. by General Motors, typically of medium size with an engine mounted transversely and front-wheel drive.

MOST COMMON AMERICAN SURNAMES
Source: U.S. Social Security Administration

This tabulation is based on the surnames that appear most frequently in social security records for the period of 1936 to 1973.

Rank	Surname	No. of Persons	Rank	Surname	No. of Persons	Rank	Surname	No. of Persons
1	Smith	2,382,509	21	Walker	486,498	41	Campbell	361,958
2	Johnson	1,807,263	22	Robins(on)	484,991	42	Gonzalex(ez)	360,994
3	Williams(on)	1,568,939	23	Peters(on)	479,249	43	Carter	349,950
4	Brown	1,362,910	24	Hall	471,479	44	Garcia	346,175
5	Jones	1,331,205	25	Allen	458,375	45	Evans	343,897
6	Miller	1,131,861	26	Young	455,416	46	Turner	329,752
7	Davis	1,047,848	27	Morris(on)	455,179	47	Stewart	329,581
8	Martin(ez), (son)	1,046,297	28	King	434,791	48	Collin(s)	324,680
9	Anders(on)	825,648	29	Wright	431,157	49	Parker	322,482
10	Wilson	787,825	30	Nelson	421,638	50	Edward	317,197
11	Harris(on)	754,083	31	Rodriguez	416,178	51	Murphy	311,337
12	Taylor	696,046	32	Hill	414,646	52	Cook	298,396
13	Moore	693,304	33	Baker	412,676	53	Rogers	298,288
14	Thomas	688,054	34	Richards(on)	409,262	54	Griffin, Griffith	291,862
15	White	636,185	35	Lee	409,068	55	Christian(son), Christopher	281,525
16	Thompson	635,426	36	Scott	408,439	56	Morgan	273,267
17	Jackson	630,003	37	Green	406,989	57	Cooper	269,560
18	Clark	549,107	38	Adams	406,841	58	Reed	267,589
19	Robert(s), (son)	524,688	39	Mitchell	371,434	59	Bell	267,026
20	Lewis	495,026	40	Phillips	362,013			

MAJOR WORLD LANGUAGES
Source: Kenneth Katzner, author, The Languages of the World.

Language	Speakers*	Chief Location	Language	Speakers*	Chief Location	Language	Speakers*	Chief Location
Chinese	900	China	Azerbaijani	9	USSR (Azerbaijan), Iran	Lithuanian	2.5	USSR (Lithuania)
English	325	U.S., U.K., Canada, Ireland, Australia, New Zealand	Uzbek	9	USSR (Uzbekistan)	Moldavian	2.5	USSR (Moldavia)
			Assamese	9	India (Assam)	Mongolian	2.5	Mongolia, China
Spanish	225	Spain, Latin America	Sindhi	9	Pakistan, India	Miao	2.5	China
Russian	200	USSR	Sinhalese	9	Sri Lanka	Karen	2.5	Burma
Hindi	200	India	Amharic	9	Ethiopia	Lao	2.5	Laos
Bengali	125	Bangladesh, India	Swedish	8	Sweden	Buginese	2.5	Indonesia (Celebes)
Arabic	125	Middle East, North Africa	Bulgarian	8	Bulgaria	Tigrinya	2.5	Ethiopia
Portuguese	120	Portugal, Brazil	Chuang	8	China	Tswana	2.5	South Africa, Botswana
Japanese	110	Japan	Madurese	8	Indonesia (Java, Madura)	Makua	2.5	Mozambique
German	100	Germany, Austria, Switzerland	Ibo	8	Nigeria	Turkmen	2	USSR (Turkmen SSR), Iran
French	75	France, Belgium, Switzerland, Canada, Haiti, West Africa	Galla	8	Ethiopia	Tadzhik	2	USSR (Tadzhikistan)
			Belorussian	7	USSR (Belorussia)	Gilaki	2	Iran
Punjabi	65	India (Punjab), Pakistan	Berber	7	Morocco, Algeria	Bhili	2	India
Italian	60	Italy	Malagasy	7	Malagasy Republic	Achinese	2	Indonesia (Sumatra)
Telugu	50	India (Andhra Pradesh)	Quechua	7	Peru, Bolivia	Balinese	2	Indonesia (Bali)
Korean	50	Korea	Catalan	6	Spain, France, Andorra	Bikol	2	Philippines (Luzon)
Indonesian	50	Indonesia	Malay	6	Malaysia, Singapore	Kikuyu	2	Kenya
Marathi	45	India (Maharashtra)	Khmer	6	Cambodia	Malinke	2	West Africa
Tamil	45	India (Tamil Nadu), Sri Lanka	Danish	5	Denmark	Kanuri	2	Nigeria
Javanese	45	Indonesia (Java)	Finnish	5	Finland	Guarani	2	Paraguay
Turkish	40	Turkey	Flemish	5	Belgium	Slovenian	1.5	Yugoslavia
Urdu	40	Pakistan, India	Tatar	5	USSR (Tatar ASSR)	Latvian	1.5	USSR (Latvia)
Polish	35	Poland	Kazakh	5	USSR (Kazakhstan)	Chuvash	1.5	USSR (Chuvash ASSR)
Ukrainian	35	USSR (Ukraine)	Kurdish	5	Iraq, Iran, Turkey, Syria, USSR	Kirgiz	1.5	USSR (Kirgiz SSR)
Thai	35	Thailand	Somali	5	Somalia, Ethiopia	Mazanderani	1.5	Iran
Vietnamese	35	Vietnam	Ruanda	5	Rwanda, Zaire	Baluchi	1.5	Pakistan, Iran
Persian	25	Iran, Afghanistan	Zulu	5	South Africa	Gondi	1.5	Central India
Gujarati	25	India (Gujarat)	Xhosa	5	South Africa	Shan	1.5	Burma
Kanarese	25	India (Karnataka)	Yiddish	4	U.S., USSR, Israel	Batak	1.5	Indonesia (Sumatra)
Malayalam	25	India (Kerala)	Norwegian	4	Norway	Wolof	1.5	Senegal
Burmese	25	Burma	Slovak	4	Czechoslovakia	Bambara	1.5	Mali
Bihari	20	India (Bihar)	Armenian	4	USSR (Armenia)	Ewe	1.5	Ghana, Togo
Oriya	20	India (Orissa)	Tibetan	4	Tibet	Fang	1.5	Cameroon, Gabon
Hausa	20	Nigeria, Niger	Uighur	4	China (Sinkiang), USSR	Dinka	1.5	Sudan
Romanian	18	Romania	Twi	4	Ghana	Lingala	1.5	Zaire, Congo
Serbo-Croatian	15	Yugoslavia	Sidamo	4	Ethiopia	Bemba	1.5	Zambia
			Rundi	4	Burundi	Tsonga	1.5	Mozambique
Pushtu	15	Afghanistan, Pakistan	Shona	4	Rhodesia	Aymara	1.5	Bolivia, Peru
Rajasthani	15	India (Rajasthan)	Nyanja	4	Malawi, Zambia	Breton	1	France (Brittany)
Swahili	15	East Africa	Sotho	4	South Africa, Lesotho	Macedonian	1	Yugoslavia
Dutch	13	Netherlands	Afrikaans	4	South Africa	Estonian	1	USSR (Estonia)
Sundanese	13	Indonesia (Java)	Albanian	3	Albania	Mordvin	1	USSR (Mordovian ASSR)
Hungarian	12	Hungary, Romania	Georgian	3	USSR (Georgia)	Bashkir	1	USSR (Bashkir ASSR)
Visayan	12	Philippines	Hebrew	3	Israel	Tulu	1	India (Karnataka)
Yoruba	12	Nigeria	Kashmiri	3	Kashmir	Kurukh (Oraon)	1	Eastern India
Czech	10	Czechoslovakia	Santali	3	Eastern India	Mende	1	Sierra Leone
Greek	10	Greece	Yi (Lolo)	3	China	Fon	1	Benin
Nepali	10	Nepal	Minangkabau	3	Indonesia (Sumatra)	Tiv	1	Nigeria
Tagalog	10	Philippines	Ilocano	3	Philippines (Luzon)	Ibibio	1	Nigeria
Fulani	10	West Africa	Mossi	3	Upper Volta	Luo	1	Kenya
			Ganda	3	Uganda	Kamba	1	Kenya
			Luba	3	Zaire	Sukuma	1	Tanzania
			Kongo	3	Zaire, Congo, Angola	Swazi	1	Swaziland, South Africa
			Mbundu	3	Angola	Nahuatl	1	Mexico
			Mayan	3	Mexico, Guatemala			

* In millions of speakers.

LEADING AMERICAN MAGAZINES
SOURCE: Magazine Publishers Association, Inc.

Based on average circulations per issue, 2nd six months of 1978

Rank	Magazine*	Circulation	Rank	Magazine*	Circulation
1	TV Guide	19,495,113	41	Sunset	1,372,122
2	Reader's Digest	17,978,238	42	Sport	1,269,038
3	National Geographic	10,134,530	43	Ebony	1,241,303
4	Family Circle	8,380,582	44	Nation's Business	1,186,462
5	Woman's Day	8,083,799	45	Psychology Today	1,178,516
6	Better Homes & Gardens	8,039,983	46	Bon Appetit	1,077,747
7	McCall's	6,536,728	47	House & Garden	1,073,109
8	Ladies' Home Journal	6,031,430	48	Moneysworth	1,049,827
9	National Enquirer	5,362,022	49	New Woman	1,023,054
10	Good Housekeeping	5,361,950	50	Mademoiselle	1,017,907
11	Playboy	5,248,309	51	Grit	1,009,288
12	Penthouse	4,612,958	52	Vogue	1,007,513
13	Redbook	4,463,315	52	Book Digest	1,002,903
14	Time	4,272,495	54	'Teen	974,069
15	Star, The	3,237,673	55	Discovery	968,436
16	Newsweek	2,925,694	56	Progressive Farmer	957,707
17	Cosmopolitan	2,700,364	57	Golf Digest	943,520
18	American Legion	2,598,931	58	Scouting	935,102
19	People Weekly	2,476,876	59	Family Health	933,928
20	Sports Illustrated	2,272,905	60	Junior Scholastic	913,603
21	U.S. News & World Report	2,037,177	61	Oui	907,542
22	Field & Stream	2,029,949	62	Family Handyman	880,573
23	Glamour	1,918,606	63	Co-Ed	838,954
24	Workbasket	1,845,352	64	House Beautiful	834,246
25	V.F.W. Magazine	1,830,259	65	Forum	833,328
26	Popular Science	1,822,762	66	Hot Rod	833,166
27	Midnight Globe	1,801,770	67	Apartment Life	827,059
28	Outdoor Life	1,752,056	68	Weight Watchers	822,164
29	Smithsonian	1,707,295	69	Popular Photography	820,459
30	Today's Education	1,685,507	70	Us	800,406
31	Mechanix Illustrated	1,660,484	71	Decorating & Craft Ideas	798,461
32	True Story	1,645,565	72	1,001 Decorating Ideas	787,276
33	Southern Living	1,632,619	73	Michigan Living-AAA Motor News	785,215
34	Elks	1,631,725	74	Business Week	781,072
35	Popular Mechanics	1,625,074	75	Money	774,756
36	Parents	1,517,644	76	Yankee	761,321
37	Boys' Life	1,508,788	77	Successful Farming	752,774
38	Hustler	1,508,297	78	Motor Trend	752,697
39	Seventeen	1,450,083	79	Car & Driver	742,719
40	Farm Journal	1,410,677	80	Golf	709,619

* Includes general and farm magazine members of the Audit Bureau of Circulations. Groups and comics not included.

U.S. ADVERTISING VOLUME
SOURCE: Reprinted with permission from the January 8, 1979 issue of Advertising Age. Copyright 1979 by Crain Communications Inc.

Medium	1977 Millions	1977 % of total	1978* Millions	1978* % of total	% change
Newspapers					
Total	$11,132	29.2	$12,690	29.0	+14.0
National	1,677	4.4	1,810	4.1	+ 8.0
Local	9,455	24.8	10,880	24.9	+15.0
Magazines					
Total	2,162	5.7	2,595	5.9	+20.0
Weeklies	903	2.4	1,165	2.7	+29.0
Women's	565	1.5	670	1.5	+19.0
Monthlies	694	1.8	760	1.7	+10.0
Farm publications	90	0.2	105	0.2	+14.0
Television					
Total	7,612	20.0	8,850	20.2	+16.0
Network	3,460	9.1	3,910	8.9	+13.0
Spot	2,204	5.8	2,600	5.9	+18.0
Local	1,948	5.1	2,340	5.4	+20.0
Radio					
Total	2,634	6.9	2,955	6.8	+12.0
Network	137	0.4	160	0.4	+16.0
Spot	546	1.4	610	1.4	+12.0
Local	1,951	5.1	2,185	5.0	+12.0
Direct mail	5,333	14.0	6,030	13.8	+13.0
Business publications	1,221	3.2	1,420	3.3	+16.0
Outdoor					
Total	418	1.1	465	1.1	+11.0
National	290	0.8	310	0.7	+ 7.0
Local	128	0.3	155	0.4	−21.0
Miscellaneous					
Total	7,518	19.7	8,630	19.7	+15.0
National	3,935	10.3	4,495	10.3	+15.0
Local	3,583	9.4	4,135	9.4	+15.0
Total					
National	21,055	55.2	24,045	55.0	+14.2
Local	17,065	44.8	19,695	45.0	+15.4
U.S. Grand Total	38,120	100.0	43,740	100.0	+14.7

*Preliminary

LARGEST U.S. SUNDAY NEWSPAPERS

Source: Audit Bureau of Circulations

Newspaper	Circulation*	Newspaper	Circulation*	Newspaper	Circulation*
New York News	2,328,479	Cleveland Plain Dealer	452,808	Cleveland Press	303,175
New York Times	1,435,330	St. Louis Post-Dispatch	436,930	Cincinnati Enquirer	289,575
Los Angeles Times	1,323,787	Houston Chronicle	426,685	Oklahoma City	
Chicago Tribune	1,157,870	Portland Oregonian	415,358	Sunday Oklahoman	289,126
Philadelphia Inquirer	848,592	Kansas City Star	408,007	Hartford Courant	288,186
Detroit News	828,052	Des Moines Register	406,842	Memphis Commercial Appeal	287,999
Washington Post	822,133	Phoenix Republic†	393,396	Denver Rocky Mountain News	285,109
New York Post**	741,854	Houston Post	380,159	Omaha World-Herald	278,541
Chicago Sun-Times	720,201	Baltimore Sun	365,894	St. Petersburg Times	270,926
Detroit Free Press	705,398	Indianapolis Star†	355,622	San Jose Mercury-News	261,660
Boston Globe	693,679	Boston Herald American	351,692	Buffalo Courier Express	257,219
San Francisco Chronicle-		Seattle Times	348,333	Fort Worth Star Telegram	249,852
Examiner	670,100	Dallas News	345,618	St. Paul Pioneer Press	244,719
Pittsburgh Press	666,907	Columbus Dispatch	343,589	Orange Co. (Calif.) Register	243,274
Minneapolis Tribune	608,550	Dallas Times Herald	339,787	Charlotte Observer	238,627
Miami Herald	573,879	San Diego Union†	335,943	Syracuse Herald-American	235,592
Newark Star-Ledger†	571,665	Louisville Courier-Journal		Rochester Democrat &	
Long Island Newsday	563,916	& Times	335,604	Chronicle	231,684
Philadelphia Bulletin	560,188	New Orleans Times-Picayune†	321,543	Seattle Post-Intelligencer	231,367
Milwaukee Journal	532,638	Los Angeles Herald-Examiner	319,659	Orlando Sentinel Star	231,243
Atlanta Journal & Const.	514,561	Washington Star	316,608	Tampa Tribune	228,260

* Averages for 6 months ending March 31, 1979.   ** Average for 2 months.   † Average for 3 months.

LARGEST U.S. DAILIES [1]

Source: Audit Bureau of Circulations

Newspaper	Circulation*	Newspaper	Circulation*	Newspaper	Circulation*
New York News	1,636,254	Kansas City Times	321,002	Atlanta Constitution	219,153
Los Angeles Times	1,038,942	Houston Post	320,683	Atlanta Journal	218,347
New York Times	863,532	Los Angeles Herald-Examiner	303,320	St. Petersburg Times	216,918
Chicago Tribune	783,041	Cleveland Press	303,175	Des Moines Register	216,057
Chicago Sun-Times	671,366	Kansas City Star	288,283	New Orleans Times-Picayune†	215,551
Detroit News	630,795	Dallas News	280,124	Hartford Courant	215,385
New York Post	624,287	Boston Herald American†	273,301	Orange Co. (Calif.) Register	213,538
Detroit Free Press	610,849	St. Louis Globe-Democrat	271,645	Indianapolis Star†	213,470
Washington Post	598,213	Buffalo Evening News	266,125	Memphis Commercial Appeal	208,123
Long Island Newsday	513,714	Pittsburgh Press	265,379	San Diego Union Tribune†	207,510
San Francisco Chronicle	498,100	Denver Rocky Mountain News	261,079	Columbus Dispatch	202,097
Boston Globe†	482,238	Phoenix Republic†	259,783	Orlando Sentinel Star	200,825
Philadelphia Bulletin	472,509	Seattle Times	257,383	Seattle Post-Intelligencer	198,797
Miami Herald	442,560	St. Louis Post-Dispatch	257,259	Louisville Courier-Journal	197,204
Philadelphia Inquirer	417,066	Dallas Times Herald	242,362	Tampa Tribune	192,969
Newark Star-Ledger†	406,252	Portland Oregonian	242,328	Pittsburgh Post Gazette-Sun	
Cleveland Plain Dealer	382,940	Fort Worth Star Telegram [2]	241,118	Telegraph	190,093
Baltimore Sun [2]	345,096	Omaha World Herald	234,813	Cincinnati Enquirer	189,862
Washington Star	340,150	Minneapolis Tribune	231,380	Oklahoma City Daily	
Houston Chronicle	330,639	Minneapolis Star	226,680	Oklahoman	189,847
Milwaukee Journal	329,929	Philadelphia Daily News	224,091	San Antonio Express-News	183,865

[1] Does not include Wall Street Journal, 1,632,155 circulation (National Edition).   [2] Combined morning and evening editions.
* Averages for 6 months ending March 31, 1979.   † Average for 4 months.   ‡ Average for 3 months.

WORLD'S LARGEST DAILY NEWSPAPERS

Country and Newspaper	Daily Circulation	Country and Newspaper	Daily Circulation
USSR		UNITED KINGDOM	
Pravda	10,000,000	London Daily Sun[1]	3,869,355
Izvestia	10,000,000	London Daily Mirror[1]	3,642,240
JAPAN		London Daily Express[1]	2,446,762
Yomiurii Shimbun (A.M. ed.)	8,143,583	UNITED STATES	
Asahi Shimbun (A.M. ed.)	7,272,347	New York News	1,636,254
Mainichi Shimbun (A.M. ed.)	4,600,228	Los Angeles Times	1,038,942

[1] U.K. Audit Bureau of Circulation, Ltd.

LEADING TV ADVERTISERS

Source: Television Bureau of Advertising, Inc.

Company	Total TV Expenditure (1978)	Company	Total TV Expenditure (1978)	Company	Total TV Expenditure (1978)
Procter & Gamble	$421,023,300	Nabisco, Inc.	$68,200,700	Revlon, Inc.	$36,388,900
General Foods Corp.	246,724,200	Nestle Co., Inc.	66,712,400	Eastman Kodak Co.	35,448,200
American Home		Kellogg Co.	65,465,800	Miles Laboratories Inc.	35,328,100
Products Corp.	149,857,300	Pillsbury Co.	63,498,100	Toyota Motor	
General Mills, Inc.	134,968,000	Sterling Drug, Inc.	61,341,400	Distributors, Inc.	35,218,300
General Motors	132,952,000	Kraftco Corp.	59,329,900	Quaker Oats Co.	34,065,600
Bristol-Myers Co.	127,363,300	Anheuser-Busch, Inc.	57,882,000	Nissan Motor Corp. U.S.A.	33,151,100
McDonalds Corp.	114,866,800	Gillette Co.	57,414,800	Norton Simon, Inc.	32,659,300
Ford Motor Co.	110,812,000	Esmark, Inc.	51,153,800	CPC International, Inc.	31,884,100
Lever Brothers Co.	99,568,300	Richardson Merrell, Inc.	50,079,400	Polaroid Corp.	31,861,000
Chrysler Corp.	93,663,700	J.C. Penney Co., Inc.	48,897,500	American Express Co.	31,133,300
PepsiCo, Inc.	92,500,500	Heublein, Inc.	47,245,300	RCA Corp.	30,476,200
Sears Roebuck & Co.	92,458,300	Internat'l Telephone		Mattel, Inc.	29,689,200
Coca-Cola Co.	84,537,400	& Teleg. Corp.	44,603,000	American Motors Corp.	29,186,600
Colgate-Palmolive Co.	84,479,600	Mobil Oil Co.	44,240,400	Time, Inc.	29,129,300
Warner-Lambert		Mars, Inc.	41,557,500	Volkswagenwerk A.G.	28,746,200
Pharmaceutical Co.	84,020,600	Jos. Schlitz Brewing Co.	40,622,900	Morton-Norwich	
Philip Morris, Inc.	82,331,900	The Clorox Co.	39,836,100	Products Inc.	28,701,000
American Telephone &		Chesebrough Ponds, Inc.	39,372,000	Gulf & Western	
Telegraph Co.	75,314,800	William Wrigley Jr., Co.	39,004,500	Industries, Inc.	28,233,100
Ralston Purina Co.	71,865,400	H.J. Heinz Co.	38,007,300	Hanes Corp.	28,100,200
Johnson & Johnson	71,544,400	Schering-Plough Corp.	36,629,000	Squibb Corp.	27,356,300

FORMS OF ADDRESS

Personage	Address	Social Correspondence	Salutation of Informal Letter*	Salutation of Formal Letter*
The President	The President The White House	The President and Mrs. Taylor	Dear Mr. President: or (if preferred) My dear Mr. President:[1]	Mr. President: or Sir:
The Vice-President	The Vice-President United States Senate	The Vice-President and Mrs. Taylor	Dear Mr. Vice-President: or (if preferred) My dear Mr. Vice-President:	Sir:
Chief Justice of the United States	The Chief Justice The Supreme Court	The Chief Justice and Mrs. Taylor	Dear Mr. Chief Justice: or (if preferred) My dear Mr. Chief Justice:	Sir:
Associate Justice, Supreme Court	Mr. Justice Taylor The Supreme Court	Mr. Justice Taylor and Mrs. Taylor	Dear Mr. Justice: or (if preferred) My dear Mr. Justice:	Sir:
Cabinet Member[2]	The Honorable Stephen Taylor Secretary of the Treasury (or applicable Cabinet-level department)	The Honorable The Secretary of the Treasury and Mrs. Taylor	Dear Mr. Secretary: or (if preferred) My dear Mr. Secretary:	Sir:
United States Senator[3]	The Honorable Stephen Taylor United States Senate	The Honorable Stephen Taylor and Mrs. Taylor (Dear Senator and Mrs. Taylor:) or (for a married woman senator) Mr. and Mrs. Stephen Taylor	Dear Senator Taylor: or (if preferred) My dear Senator:	Sir: or Madam:
Member, House of Representatives	The Honorable Stephen Taylor House of Representatives	The Honorable Stephen Taylor and Mrs. Taylor or (for a married woman member) Mr. and Mrs. Stephen Taylor	Dear Mr. [Mrs.] Taylor: or (if preferred) My dear Mr. [Mrs.] Taylor:	Sir: or Madam:
American Ambassador	The Honorable Stephen Taylor American Ambassador London	The Honorable The American Ambassador[4] and Mrs. Taylor (Dear Mr. Ambassador and Mrs. Taylor:) or (for a married woman ambassador) Mr. and Mrs. Stephen Taylor	Dear Mr. [Madam] Ambassador: or (if preferred) My dear Mr. [Madam] Ambassador:	Sir: or Madam:
American Chargé d'Affaires ad interim[5]	Stephen Taylor, Esquire[6] American Chargée d'Affaires ad interim (or other title)	Mr. and Mrs. Stephen Taylor	Dear Mr. Taylor: or (if preferred) My dear Mr. Taylor:	Sir:
Foreign Ambassador	His Excellency Dr.[7] Juan Luis Ortega Ambassador of Mexico	His Excellency The Ambassador of Mexico and Mrs. Ortega	Dear. Mr. [Madam] Ambassador: or (if preferred) My dear Mr. [Madam] Ambassador:	Excellency:
Secretary-General, United Nations	His Excellency Juan Luis Ortega Secretary-General of the United Nations	The Secretary-General of the United Nations and Mrs. Ortega	Dear Mr. Secretary-General: or (if preferred) My dear Mr. Secretary-General:	Sir:
Governor of a State	The Honorable Stephen Taylor Governor of Idaho or His Excellency[8] Stephen Taylor Governor of the Commonwealth of Massachusetts	The Governor of Idaho and Mrs. Taylor	Dear Governor Taylor: or (if preferred) My dear Governor:	Sir:
Mayor of a Large City	The Honorable Stephen Taylor Mayor of Baltimore	The Honorable Stephen Taylor and Mrs. Taylor	Dear Mayor Taylor: or Dear Mr. Mayor:	Sir:
Mayor of a Town	Stephen Taylor, Esquire Mayor of Newtown	The Mayor of Newtown and Mrs. Taylor	Dear Mr. Taylor:	Sir:

*"Sincerely" or "Sincerely yours" is the acceptable mode of ending both informal and formal letters to distinguished personages. [1] In the United States, "My dear Mr. President:" or "My dear Mrs. Taylor:" is a more formal salutation than "Dear Mr. President:"; however, in Great Britain, the reverse is true. [2] All but two Cabinet members use the title "Secretary": The Attorney General and the Postmaster General. Their full titles are used (e.g., on envelope: The Attorney General). [3] State senators and representatives are referred to and addressed the same way as U.S. Senators and Representatives. [4] For an American ambassador on home leave, the proper form of social address on an envelope is: "The Honorable Stephen Taylor and Mrs. Taylor," plus home address. [5] "Chargé d'affaires ad interim" is the official title given to the individual who assumes responsibility for an embassy during an ambassador's absence or change of ambassadors. [6] "Esquire" is never used, if the individual is addressed by another title, even "Mr." [7] "His Excellency" is followed by the individual's personal title, if he has one (e.g., Dr., Prince, Baron). [8] "His Excellency" is acceptable for addressing the governors of the four Commonwealths: Massachusetts, Virginia, Kentucky, and Pennsylvania; however, the State Department prefers to address all U.S. governors as "The Honorable."

U.S. POSTAL INFORMATION AND REGULATIONS   Source: U.S. Postal Service

First-Class Mail includes letters, postal cards, postcards, all matter wholly or partly in writing (except authorized additions to second-, third-, and fourth-class mail), as well as matter closed against inspection.

Kind of mail	Rate
All first-class mail weighing 12 ounces or less, except postal cards and postcards	15¢ 1st ounce & 13¢ each additional oz.
Single postal cards and postcards	10¢ each
Double postal cards and postcards (reply portion of double postcard does not have to bear postage when originally mailed)	20¢ (10¢ each portion)
Business reply mail: Cards	12¢ each
With Advance Deposit Account:	3.5¢ surcharge
Without Advance Deposit Account:	12¢ surcharge

Min. Height: 3½"; Min. Length: 5"; Max. Length: 11½"; Max. Thickness: ¼" or less; Shape: rectangular. Letters & Postcards below these specifications will not be accepted; anything above and/or weighing less than an ounce will be charged an additional 7¢. Max. Weight: 70 lbs.

Second-Class Mail includes all newspapers, magazines, and other periodicals marked as second-class mail. Within the county, the bulk rate is 2.8¢ per pound or 1.3¢ per piece. Outside the county, the non-advertising portion is charged at a rate of 13.1¢ per pound, while the non-advertising portion is charged at a rate of from 17.5¢ to 31.8¢ per pound.

Charges for copies mailed by public vary with the level of pre-sorting. Consult local postmaster. For special rates available to nonprofit organizations, publishers, and news agents, consult local postmaster.

Third-Class Mail is mailable matter that is not sent or required to be mailed as first-class mail, not entered as second-class mail, and weighs less than 16 ounces. The single piece rate is 20¢ for the first two ounces or fraction, 20¢ for the next 2 oz., and 13¢ for each additional 2 oz.

Circulars and printed matter are considered third-class mail. Certain loose enclosures relating exclusively to the book or catalogue that they accompany may be enclosed and mailed at the third-class bulk rate. Third-class mail must be prepared so that it can be easily examined. For special bulk rates for nonprofit organizations, consult local postmaster.

Special Fourth-Class Rate. A rate of 59¢ up to 1 pound or fraction, and 22¢ for each additional pound or fraction through 7 lbs., 13¢ per lb. thereafter, is provided for the following: bound books with no advertising; 16 mm films; printed music; book mss, magazine articles, and music; sound recordings; and certain other matter. The maximum size is 84 inches combined length and girth. The identification statement: Special Fourth Class Rate —Books (or other appropriate notation) must be placed conspicuously.

Fourth-Class (Parcel Post) Mail includes merchandise, printed matter, mailable live animals, and all other matter not included in first-, second-, or third-class mail. Each addressed piece must weigh 16 ounces or more but not more than 40 pounds, if mailed from one first-class post office to another. When mailed to or from a second-, third-, or fourth-class post office, the weight limit is 70 pounds. The maximum size for this class is 72 inches combined length and girth. Fourth-class mail must be wrapped or packaged for easy examination. Consult local postmaster for specification on irregular or outsize parcels and their surcharge.

Library Rate. A special library rate applies to certain items that are conspicuously marked Library Rate and show nonprofit associations or organizations in the address or return address. The postage rate is 17¢ for the first pound, 6¢ for each additional pound through 7 pounds, and 5¢ per pound thereafter.

Priority Mail (heavy pieces) is carried by air and the fastest connecting surface carriers. It is given the most expeditious handling in dispatch and delivery. Priority mail may weigh over 9 ounces, surface mail first class may weigh over 12 ounces. The upper limit is 70 pounds. It is limited to 100 inches combined in length and girth.

SPECIAL HANDLING

Third- and fourth-class only. Special handling fees (fees in addition to postage):

Weight	Fee
Not more than 10 lbs.	70¢
More than 10 lbs.	$1.25

SPECIAL DELIVERY

Special delivery fees (fees in addition to postage):

Class of Mail	Not more than 2 lbs.	2 lbs. but not more than 10 lbs.	More than 10 lbs.
First class and priority	$2.00	$2.25	$2.85
All other classes	2.25	2.85	3.25

MONEY ORDERS

Amount of money order	Amount of fee Domestic
$ 0.01 to $ 10	$ .80
$10.01 to $ 50	1.10
$50.01 to $100	1.40

INSURANCE

Fees (in addition to postage):

Liability	Fee
$ 0.01 to $ 15	$ .50
$ 15.01 to $ 50	.85
$ 50.01 to $100	1.10
$100.01 to $150	1.40
$150.01 to $200	1.75
$200.01 to $300	2.25
$300.01 to $400	2.75
Restricted delivery. (Not available for mail insured for $15 or less)	.80

C.O.D. MAIL

Consult postmaster for fees and conditions of mailing.

CERTIFIED MAIL

Fee (in addition to postage)	.80
Restricted delivery	.80

REGISTRY

Registry fees (in addition to postage):

Declared actual value	For mailers without insurance coverage	For mailers with insurance coverage
$ 0.00 to $ 100	3.00	3.00
$ 100.01 to $ 200	3.30	3.30
$ 200.01 to $ 400	3.70	3.70
$ 400.01 to $ 600	4.10	4.10
$ 600.01 to $ 800	4.50	4.50
$ 800.01 to $1,000	4.90	4.90
$1,000.01 to $2,000	5.30	4.90 + 35¢ handling per $1000 or fraction thereof

For higher values and their fees consult local postmaster.

RETURN RECEIPTS

Certified mail—numbered insured—registered
Requested at time of mailing:

Showing to whom and when delivered	$ .45
Showing to whom, when and address where delivered	.55

Requested after mailing:

Showing to whom and when delivered	2.10

INTERNATIONAL POSTAL CHARGES

LETTERS AND LETTER PACKAGES:

    Surface Mail: Canada and Mexico, 15¢ an ounce or fraction thereof; to all other countries, 20¢ for the first ounce, 36¢ for 1-2 ounces, 48¢ for 2-4 ounces, 96¢ for 4-8 ounces, $1.84 for 8-16 ounces, $3.20 for 1-2 lbs., $5.20 for 2-4 lbs. **Airmail:** Canada and Mexico, 15¢ an ounce or fraction thereof, 13¢ each additional ounce or fraction; to all other countries, 25¢-31¢ per half ounce through 2 ounces, with 21¢-26¢ for each additional ½ ounce. Consult local postmaster. **Aerogrammes:** To all countries, 22¢ each. Weight limit: 4 lbs., except to Canada, 60 lbs.

POSTCARDS:

    Surface Mail: To Canada and Mexico, 10¢, to all other countries, 14¢. **Airmail:** to Canada and Mexico, 10¢; to all other countries, 21¢.

PARCEL POST ZONE RATES

| Weight | | Zones | | | | | | |
1 lb. and not exceeding	Local	1 & 2 Up to 150 mi.	3 150 to 300 mi.	4 300 to 600 mi.	5 600 to 1,000 mi.	6 1,000 to 1,400 mi.	7 1,400 to 1,800 mi.	8 Over 1,800 mi.
2	$1.15	$1.35	$1.39	$1.56	$1.72	$1.84	$1.98	$2.22
3	1.23	1.45	1.53	1.73	1.86	2.04	2.24	2.61
4	1.29	1.56	1.65	1.82	2.00	2.23	2.50	3.00
5	1.36	1.66	1.77	1.92	2.14	2.43	2.77	3.39
6	1.42	1.71	1.84	2.01	2.28	2.62	3.03	3.78
7	1.47	1.76	1.90	2.11	2.41	2.82	3.29	4.17
8	1.51	1.80	1.97	2.20	2.55	3.02	3.56	4.56
9	1.54	1.85	2.03	2.29	2.69	3.21	3.82	4.95
10	1.57	1.89	2.10	2.39	2.83	3.41	4.08	5.34
11	1.60	1.94	2.17	2.50	3.00	3.65	4.42	5.73
12	1.64	1.98	2.22	2.56	3.09	3.77	4.57	6.12
13	1.67	2.02	2.27	2.63	3.17	3.89	4.72	6.41
14	1.70	2.05	2.32	2.69	3.25	3.99	4.86	6.62
15	1.73	2.09	2.36	2.74	3.33	4.09	4.99	6.80
16	1.76	2.13	2.41	2.80	3.40	4.19	5.11	6.98
17	1.79	2.16	2.45	2.85	3.47	4.28	5.23	7.15
18	1.82	2.20	2.49	2.91	3.54	4.37	5.34	7.31
19	1.86	2.23	2.53	2.96	3.61	4.46	5.45	7.47
20	1.89	2.27	2.58	3.01	3.67	4.54	5.55	7.62
21	1.92	2.30	2.62	3.06	3.74	4.62	5.66	7.76
22	1.95	2.34	2.66	3.14	3.85	4.78	5.80	7.90
23	1.98	2.37	2.72	3.25	3.99	4.96	6.02	8.03
24	2.01	2.44	2.80	3.35	4.12	5.13	6.24	8.16
25	2.04	2.51	2.89	3.46	4.26	5.31	6.46	8.28
26	2.07	2.58	2.97	3.56	4.39	5.48	6.68	8.40
27	2.11	2.65	3.06	3.67	4.53	5.66	6.90	8.52
28	2.14	2.72	3.14	3.77	4.66	5.83	7.12	8.63
29	2.17	2.79	3.23	3.88	4.80	6.01	7.34	8.75
30	2.20	2.86	3.31	3.98	4.93	6.18	7.56	8.85
31	2.68	3.09	3.46	4.09	5.07	6.36	7.78	9.41
32	2.71	3.12	3.49	4.19	5.20	6.53	8.00	9.51
33	2.74	3.16	3.57	4.30	5.34	6.71	8.22	9.61
34	2.77	3.19	3.65	4.40	5.47	6.88	8.44	9.80
35	2.80	3.22	3.74	4.51	5.61	7.06	8.66	10.06
36	2.83	3.28	3.82	4.61	5.74	7.23	8.89	10.32
37	2.86	3.35	3.91	4.72	5.88	7.41	9.10	10.58
38	2.89	3.42	3.99	4.82	6.01	7.58	9.32	10.84
39	2.93	3.49	4.08	4.93	6.15	7.76	9.54	11.10
40	2.96	3.56	4.16	5.03	6.28	7.93	9.76	11.36
41	2.99	3.63	4.25	5.14	6.42	8.11	9.98	11.62
42	3.02	3.70	4.33	5.24	6.55	8.28	10.20	11.88
43	3.05	3.77	4.42	5.35	6.69	8.46	10.42	12.14
44	3.08	3.84	4.50	5.45	6.82	8.63	10.64	12.40
45	3.11	3.91	4.59	5.56	6.96	8.81	10.86	12.66
46	3.14	3.98	4.67	5.66	7.09	8.98	11.08	12.92
47	3.17	4.05	4.76	5.77	7.23	9.16	11.30	13.18
48	3.20	4.12	4.84	5.87	7.36	9.33	11.52	13.44
49	3.23	4.19	4.93	5.98	7.50	9.51	11.74	13.70
50	3.27	4.26	5.01	6.08	7.63	9.68	11.96	13.96
51	3.30	4.33	5.10	6.19	7.77	9.86	12.18	14.22
52	3.33	4.40	5.18	6.29	7.90	10.03	12.40	14.48
53	3.36	4.47	5.27	6.40	8.04	10.21	12.62	14.74
54	3.39	4.54	5.35	6.50	8.17	10.38	12.84	15.00
55	3.42	4.61	5.44	6.61	8.31	10.56	13.06	15.26
56	3.45	4.68	5.52	6.71	8.44	10.73	13.28	15.52
57	3.48	4.75	5.61	6.82	8.58	10.91	13.50	15.78
58	3.51	4.82	5.69	6.92	8.71	11.08	13.72	16.04
59	3.54	4.89	5.78	7.03	8.85	11.26	13.94	16.30
60	3.57	4.96	5.86	7.13	8.98	11.43	14.16	16.56
61	3.60	5.03	5.95	7.24	9.12	11.61	14.38	16.82
62	3.64	5.10	6.03	7.34	9.25	11.78	14.60	17.08
63	3.67	5.17	6.12	7.45	9.39	11.96	14.82	17.34
64	3.70	5.24	6.20	7.55	9.52	12.13	15.04	17.60
65	3.73	5.31	6.29	7.66	9.66	12.31	15.26	17.86
66	3.76	5.38	6.37	7.76	9.79	12.48	15.48	18.12
67	3.79	5.45	6.46	7.87	9.93	12.66	15.70	18.38
68	3.82	5.52	6.54	7.97	10.06	12.83	15.92	18.64
69	3.85	5.59	6.63	8.08	10.20	13.01	16.14	18.90
70	3.88	5.66	6.71	8.18	10.33	13.18	16.36	19.16

U.S. TOWNS AND CITIES: ZIP CODES AND 1970 POPULATIONS

The following is a list of places with 6,200 or more inhabitants, according to revised final population counts of the 1970 U.S. Census. The ZIP code listed for each place is the five-digit national coding system that identifies each postal delivery area and is designed to expedite mail delivery. An asterisk indicates that there is more than one ZIP code for the town or city and that the code number applies to general delivery. To determine the exact ZIP code for a particular area within a place marked by an asterisk, consult the National Zip Code Directory or your nearest post office.

LOCATION	POPULATION	ZIP
ALABAMA		
Albertville	9,963	35950
Alexander City	12,358	35010
Andalusia	10,092	36420
Anniston	31,533	36201*
Athens	14,360	35611
Atmore	8,293	36503
Attalla	7,510	35954
Auburn	22,767	36830
Bay Minette	6,727	36507
Bessemer	33,663	35020
Birmingham	300,910	35203*
Bluff Park	12,431	35226
Brewton	6,747	36426
Center Point	15,675	35215
Chickasaw	8,447	36611
Cullman	12,601	35055
Decatur	38,044	35601*
Demopolis	7,651	36732
Dothan	36,733	36303*
Enterprise	15,591	36330
Eufaula	9,102	36027
Fairfield	14,369	35064
Florence	34,031	35630*
Fort Payne	8,435	35967
Gadsden	53,928	35901*
Gardendale	6,537	35071
Greenville	8,033	36037
Guntersville	6,491	35976
Hartselle	7,355	35640
Homewood	21,137	35209
Hueytown	8,174	35020
Huntsville	139,282	35804*
Jacksonville	7,715	36265
Jasper	10,798	35501
Lanett	6,908	36863
Leeds	6,991	35094
Midfield	6,340	35228
Mobile	190,026	36601*
Montgomery	133,386	36104*
Mountain Brook	19,509	35223
Muscle Shoals	6,907	35660
Northport	9,435	35476
Opelika	19,027	36801
Opp	6,493	36467
Ozark	13,555	36360
Phenix City	25,281	36867
Prattville	13,116	36067
Prichard	41,578	36610
Russellville	7,814	35653
Saraland	7,840	36571
Scottsboro	9,324	35768
Selma	27,379	36701
Sheffield	13,115	35660
Sylacauga	12,255	35150
Talladega	17,662	35160
Tarrant City	6,835	35217
Troy	11,482	36081
Tuscaloosa	65,773	35401*
Tuscumbia	8,828	35674
Tuskegee	11,028	36083
Vestavia Hills	8,311	35216
ALASKA		
Anchorage	49,126	99510*
Fairbanks	14,771	99701
Juneau	13,556	99801
Ketchikan	6,994	99901
Spenard	18,089	99503
ARIZONA		
Avondale	6,626	85323
Bisbee	8,329	85603
Casa Grande	10,536	85222
Chandler	13,763	85224
Douglas	12,462	85607
Flagstaff	26,117	86001
Glendale	36,228	85301*
Globe	7,333	85501
Kingman	7,312	86401
Mesa	62,853	85201*
Nogales	8,946	85621
Paradise Valley	7,155	85253
Phoenix	582,500	85026*
Prescott	13,134	86301
Scottsdale	67,823	85251*
Sierra Vista	6,689	85635
South Tucson	62,220	85713
Sun City	13,670	85351*
Tempe	63,550	85282*
Tucson	262,933	85702*
Winslow	8,066	86047
Yuma	29,007	85364
ARKANSAS		
Arkadelphia	9,841	71923
Batesville	7,209	72501
Benton	16,499	72015
Blytheville	24,752	72315
Camden	15,147	71701
Conway	15,510	72032
El Dorado	25,283	71730
Fayetteville	30,729	72701
Forrest City	12,521	72335
Fort Smith	62,802	72901*
Harrison	7,239	72601*
Helena	10,415	72342
Hope	8,830	71801
Hot Springs	35,631	71901
Jacksonville	19,832	72076
Jonesboro	27,050	72401
Little Rock	132,483	72201*
Magnolia	11,303	71753
Malvern	8,739	72104
Morrilton	6,814	72110
Newport	7,725	72112
North Little Rock	60,040	72114*
Osceola	7,204	72370
Paragould	11,840	72450
Pine Bluff	57,389	71601*
Rogers	11,050	72756
Russellville	11,750	72801
Searcy	9,040	72143
Springdale	16,783	72764
Stuttgart	10,477	72160
Texarkana	21,682	75501
Van Buren	8,373	72956
Warren	6,433	71671
West Helena	11,007	72390
West Memphis	26,070	72301
Wynne	6,696	72396
CALIFORNIA		
Alameda	70,968	94501
Alamo-Danville	14,059	94507
Albany	14,674	94706
Alhambra	62,125	91802*
Alondra Park	12,193	90249
Altadena	42,415	91001
Alum Rock	18,355	95116
Anaheim	166,408	92803*
Antioch	28,060	94509
Apple Valley	6,702	92307
Aptos	8,704	95003
Arcadia	45,138	91006
Arcata	8,985	95521
Arden-Arcade	82,492	95825
Arroyo Grande	7,454	93420
Artesia	14,757	90701
Ashland	14,810	94577
Atascadero	10,290	93422
Atherton	8,085	94025
Atwater	11,640	95301
Auburn	6,570	95603
Avocado Heights	9,810	91745
Azusa	25,217	91702
Bakersfield	69,515	93302*
Baldwin Park	47,285	91706
Banning	12,034	92220
Barstow	17,442	92311
Bell	21,836	90201
Bellflower	51,454	90706
Bell Gardens	29,308	90201
Belmont	23,538	94002
Benicia	7,349	94510
Berkeley	116,716	94701*
Beverly Hills	33,416	90213*
Bloomington	11,957	92316
Blythe	7,047	92225
Brawley	13,746	92227
Brea	18,447	92621
Broderick	9,781	95605
Buena Park	63,646	90622*
Burbank	88,871	91505*
Burlingame	27,320	94010
Calexico	10,625	92231
Camarillo	19,219	93010
Campbell	24,770	95008
Carlsbad	14,944	92008
Carmichael	37,625	95608
Carpinteria	6,982	93013
Carson	71,150	90745
Castro Valley	44,760	94546
Cerritos	15,856	90701
Cherryland	9,969	94521
Chico	19,580	95926
China Lake	11,015	93555
Chino	20,411	91710
Chula Vista	67,901	92010*
Citrus Heights	21,760	95610
Claremont	23,464	91711
Clovis	13,856	93612
Coachella	8,353	92236
Colton	20,016	92324
Commerce	10,536	90040
Compton	78,547	90220*
Concord	85,164	94520*
Corona	27,519	91720
Coronado	20,020	92118
Corte Madera	8,464	94925
Costa Mesa	72,660	92626*
Covina	30,395	91722*
Cudahy	16,998	90201
Culver City	34,451	90230
Cupertino	18,216	95014
Cypress	31,569	90630
Daly City	66,922	94015*
Davis	23,488	95616
Del Aire	11,930	90250
Delano	14,559	93215
Diamond Bar	10,576	91766
Dinuba	7,917	93618
Downey	88,442	90241*
Duarte	14,981	91010
Dublin	13,641	94566
East La Mirada	12,339	90638
East Los Angeles	105,033	90022
East Palo Alto	18,099	94303
El Cajon	52,273	92020*
El Centro	19,272	92243
El Cerrito	25,190	94530
El Encanto Hts.	6,225	93017
El Monte	69,892	91734*
El Segundo	15,620	90245
El Toro	8,654	92630
Enterprise	11,486	96001
Escondido	36,792	92025*
Eureka	24,337	95501
Fairfax	7,661	94930
Fairfield	44,146	94533
Fair Oaks	11,256	95628
Fallbrook	6,945	92028
Fillmore	6,285	93015
Florence-Graham	42,900	90001
Florin	9,646	95828
Fontana	20,673	92335
Foster City	9,522	94404
Fountain Valley	31,886	92708
Fremont	100,869	94538*
Fresno	165,972	93706*
Fullerton	85,987	92631*
Gardena	41,021	90247*

* General Delivery—for all towns so marked there is more than one zip code.

LOCATION	POPULATION	ZIP
Garden Acres	7,870	95205
Garden Grove	121,357	92640*
Gilroy	12,665	95020
Glendale	132,664	91209*
Glendora	31,380	91740
Grossmont-Mt. Helix	8,723	92041
Hacienda Heights	35,969	91745
Hanford	15,179	93230
Hawaiian Gardens	9,052	90716
Hawthorne	53,304	90250
Hayward	93,058	94544*
Hemet	12,252	92343
Hermosa Beach	17,412	90254
Highland	12,669	92346
Hillsborough	8,753	94010
Hollister	7,663	95023
Huntington Bch.	115,960	92647*
Huntington Park	33,744	90255
Imperial Beach	20,244	92032
Indio	14,459	92201
Inglewood	89,985	90306*
Irvine	20,157	92715
Isla Vista	13,441	93017
La Canada-Flintridge	20,714	91011
La Crescenta-Montrose	19,620	91214
Ladera Heights	6,535	90045
Lafayette	20,484	94549
Laguna Beach	14,550	92652*
Laguna Hills	13,676	92653
La Habra	41,350	90631
Lakeside	11,991	92040
Lakewood	83,025	90714*
La Mesa	39,178	92041
La Mirada	30,808	90638
Lamont	7,007	93241
Lancaster	32,728	93534
La Palma	9,687	90620
La Puente	31,092	91747*
Larkspur	10,487	94939
La Verne	12,965	91750
Lawndale	24,825	90260
Lemon Grove	19,690	92045
Lennox	16,121	90304
Linda	7,731	95901
Live Oak	6,443	95073
Livermore	37,703	94550
Lodi	28,691	95240
Loma Linda	6,599	92354
Lomita	19,784	90717
Lompoc	25,284	93436
Long Beach	358,879	90801*
Los Alamitos	11,346	90720
Los Altos	24,726	94022
Los Altos Hills	6,865	94022
Los Angeles	2,809,813	90053*
Los Banos	9,188	93635
Los Gatos	23,735	95030
Lynwood	43,354	90262
Madera	16,044	93637
Manhattan Beach	35,352	90266
Manteca	13,845	95336
Marina	8,343	93933
Martinez	16,506	94553
Marysville	9,353	95901
Maywood	16,996	90270
Menlo Park	26,826	94025
Merced	22,670	95340
Millbrae	20,792	94030
Mill Valley	12,942	94941
Milpitas	27,149	95035
Mira Loma	8,482	91752
Mission Viejo	11,933	92691
Modesto	61,712	95350*
Monrovia	30,562	91016
Montclair	22,546	91763
Montebello	42,807	90640
Monterey	26,302	93940
Monterey Park	49,166	91754
Moraga	14,205	94556
Morgan Hill	6,485	95037
Morro Bay	7,109	93442
Mountain View	54,304	94042*
Muscoy	7,091	92405
Napa	35,978	94558
National City	43,184	92050
Newark	27,153	94560
Newhall	9,651	91321
Newport Beach	49,422	92660*
Norco	14,511	91760
North Fair Oaks	9,740	94025
North Highlands	31,854	95660
Norwalk	91,827	90650
Novato	31,006	94947
Oakdale	6,594	95361
Oakland	361,561	94617*
Oceanside	40,494	92054
Oildale	20,879	93308
Olivehurst	8,100	95961
Ontario	64,118	91761*
Orange	77,365	92667*
Orangevale	16,493	95662
Orcutt	8,500	93454
Orinda	6,790	94563
Oroville	7,536	95965
Otay-Castle Park	15,445	92010
Oxnard	71,225	93030
Pacifica	36,020	94044
Pacific Grove	13,505	93950
Palmdale	8,511	93550
Palm Springs	20,936	92262
Palo Alto	55,835	94302*
Palos Verdes Estates	13,631	90274
Palos Verdes Pen.	38,914	90274
Paradise	14,539	95969
Paramount	34,734	90723
Pasadena	112,951	91109*
Paso Robles	7,168	93446
Petaluma	24,870	94952
Pico Rivera	54,170	90660
Piedmont	10,917	94611
Pinole	13,266	94564
Pittsburg	20,651	94565
Placentia	21,948	92670
Pleasant Hill	24,610	94523
Pleasanton	18,328	94566
Pomona	87,384	91766*
Porterville	12,602	93257
Port Hueneme	14,295	93041
Poway	9,422	92064
Rancho Cordova	30,451	95670
Red Bluff	7,676	96080
Redding	16,659	96001
Redlands	36,355	92373
Redondo Beach	57,451	90277*
Redwood City	55,686	94063*
Reedley	8,131	93654
Rialto	28,370	92376
Richmond	79,043	94802*
Ridgecrest	7,629	93555
Rio Linda	7,524	95673
Riverside	140,089	92502*
Rolling Hills Estates	6,735	90274
Rosemead	40,972	91770
Roseville	18,221	95678
Rossmoor	12,922	90720
Rowland Heights	16,881	91748
Rubidoux	13,969	92509
Sacramento	257,105	95814*
Salinas	58,896	93901*
San Anselmo	13,031	94960
San Bernardino	106,869	92403*
San Bruno	36,254	94066
San Carlos	26,053	94070
San Clemente	17,063	92672
San Diego	697,027	92101*
San Dimas	15,692	91773
San Fernando	16,571	91340*
San Francisco	715,674	94101*
San Gabriel	29,336	91776*
Sanger	10,088	93657
San Jose	445,779	95113*
San Leandro	68,698	94577*
San Lorenzo	24,633	94580
San Luis Obispo	28,036	93401
San Marino	14,177	91108
San Mateo	78,991	94402*
San Pablo	21,461	94806
San Rafael	38,977	94902*
Santa Ana	155,762	92711*
Santa Barbara	70,215	93102*
Santa Clara	87,717	95050*
Santa Cruz	32,076	95060*
Santa Fe Springs	14,750	90670
Santa Maria	32,749	93454
Santa Monica	88,289	90406*
Santa Paula	18,001	93060
Santa Rosa	50,006	95402*
Santee	21,107	92071
Saratoga	27,110	95070
Seal Beach	24,441	90740
Seaside	35,935	93955
Selma	7,459	93662
Sierra Madre	12,140	91024
Simi Valley	59,832	93065*
South El Monte	13,443	91733
South Gate	56,909	90280
South Lake Tahoe	12,921	95705
South Modesto	7,889	95350
South Pasadena	22,979	91030
South Sacramento	28,574	95823
South San Francisco	46,646	94080
South San Jose Hills	12,386	91744
South Whittier	46,641	90605
Spring Valley	29,742	92077*
Stanford	8,691	94305
Stanton	18,186	90680
Stockton	109,963	95202*
Sunnymead	6,708	92388
Sunnyvale	95,408	94088*
Susanville	6,608	96130
Temple City	31,034	91780
Thousand Oaks	35,873	91360*
Tiburon	6,209	94920
Torrance	134,968	90510*
Tracy	14,724	95376
Tulare	16,235	93274
Turlock	13,992	95380
Tustin	21,180	92680
Tustin-Foothills	26,598	92705
Ukiah	10,095	95482
Union City	14,724	94587
Upland	32,551	91786
Vacaville	21,690	95688
Vallejo	71,710	94590
Ventura (San Buenaventura)	57,964	93001*
Victorville	10,845	92392
View Park–Windsor Hills	12,268	90043
Visalia	27,268	93277
Vista	24,688	92083
Walnut Creek	39,844	94596*
Walnut Park	8,925	90255
Wasco	8,269	93280
Watsonville	14,569	95076
West Athens	13,311	90044
West Carson	15,918	90745
West Covina	68,034	91793*
West Hollywood	34,622	90069
Westminster	59,874	92683
Westmont	29,310	90047
West Puente Val.	20,733	91746
West Sacramento	12,002	95691
West Whittier	20,845	90606
Whittier	72,863	90605*
Willow Brook	32,328	90222
Woodland	20,677	95695
Yorba Linda	11,856	92686
Yuba City	13,986	95991
Yucaipa	19,284	92399

COLORADO

LOCATION	POPULATION	ZIP
Alamosa	6,985	81101
Applewood	8,214	80215
Arvada	49,083	80001*
Aurora	74,974	80010*
Boulder	66,870	80302*
Brighton	8,309	80601
Broomfield	7,261	80020
Canon City	9,206	81212
Colorado Springs	135,060	80901*
Commerce City	17,407	80022
Denver	514,678	80201*
Derby	10,206	80022
Durango	10,333	81301
Englewood	33,695	80110*
Fort Collins	43,337	80521
Fort Morgan	7,594	80701
Golden	9,817	80401
Grand Junction	20,170	81501
Greeley	38,902	80631
La Junta	7,938	81050
Lakewood	92,743	80215
Lamar	7,797	81052
Littleton	26,466	80120*
Longmont	23,209	80501

LOCATION	POPULATION	ZIP
Loveland	16,220	80537
Montrose	6,496	81401
North Glenn	27,937	80233
Pueblo	97,453	81002*
Security-Widefield	15,297	80911
Sherrelwood	18,868	80221
Sterling	10,636	80751
Stratton Meadows	6,223	80906
Thornton	13,326	80229
Trinidad	9,901	81082
Welby	6,875	80229
Westminster	19,432	80030
Wheat Ridge	29,778	80033

CONNECTICUT

LOCATION	POPULATION	ZIP
Ansonia	21,160	06401
Avon	8,352	06001
Berlin	14,149	06037
Bethel	10,945	06801
Bloomfield	18,301	06002
Branford	20,444	06405
Bridgeport	156,542	06601*
Bristol	55,487	06010
Brookfield	9,688	06804
Canton	6,868	06019
Cheshire	19,051	06410
Clinton	10,267	06413
Colchester	6,603	06415
Conning Towers—Nautilus Park	9,791	06340
Coventry	8,140	06238
Cromwell	7,400	06416
Danbury	50,781	06810
Darien	20,336	06820
Derby	12,599	06418
East Hampton	7,078	06424
East Hartford	57,583	06108
East Haven	25,120	06512
East Lyme	11,399	06333
East Windsor	8,513	06088
Ellington	7,707	06029
Enfield	46,189	06082
Fairfield	56,487	06430
Farmington	14,390	06032
Glastonbury	20,651	06033
Granby	6,150	06035
Greenwich	59,755	06830
Griswold	7,763	06351
Groton	38,244	06340
Guilford	12,033	06437
Hamden	49,357	06514
Hartford	158,017	06101*
Killingly	13,573	06241
Ledyard	14,837	06339
Litchfield	7,399	06759
Madison	9,768	06443
Manchester	47,994	06040
Mansfield	19,994	06250
Meriden	55,959	06450
Middletown	36,924	06457
Milford	50,858	06460
Monroe	12,047	06468
Montville	15,662	06353
Naugatuck	23,034	06770
New Britain	83,441	06050*
New Canaan	17,451	06840
New Fairfield	6,991	06810
New Haven	137,707	06510*
Newington	26,037	06111
New London	31,630	06320
New Milford	14,601	06776
Newtown	16,942	06470
North Branford	10,778	06471
North Haven	22,194	06473
Norwalk	79,288	06856*
Norwich	41,739	06360
Old Saybrook	8,468	06475
Orange	13,524	06477
Plainfield	11,957	06374
Plainville	16,733	06062
Plymouth	10,321	06782
Portland	8,812	06480
Prospect	6,543	06712
Putnam	8,598	06260
Ridgefield	18,188	06877
Rocky Hill	11,103	06067
Seymour	12,776	06483
Shelton	27,165	06484
Simsbury	17,475	06070
Somers	6,893	06071
Southbury	7,852	06488
Southington	30,946	06489
South Windsor	15,553	06074
Stafford	8,680	06075
Stamford	108,798	06904*
Stonington	15,940	06378
Stratford	49,775	06497
Suffield	8,634	06078
Thomaston	6,233	06787
Thompson	7,580	06277
Tolland	7,857	06084
Torrington	31,952	06790
Trumbull	31,394	06611
Vernon	27,237	06066
Wallingford	35,714	06492
Waterbury	108,033	06720*
Waterford	17,227	06385
Watertown	18,610	06795
West Hartford	68,031	06107
West Haven	52,851	06516
Weston	7,417	06880
Westport	27,318	06880
Wethersfield	26,662	06109
Willimantic	14,402	06226
Wilton	13,572	06897
Winchester	11,106	06094
Windham	19,626	06280
Windsor	22,502	06095
Windsor Locks	15,080	06096
Winsted	8,954	06098
Wolcott	12,495	06716
Woodbridge	7,673	06515

DELAWARE

LOCATION	POPULATION	ZIP
Brookside Park	7,856	19713
Claymont	6,584	19703
Dover	17,488	19901
Elsmere	8,415	19804
Newark	21,298	19702*
Wilmington	80,386	19899*
Wilmington Manor	10,134	19720

DISTRICT OF COLUMBIA

LOCATION	POPULATION	ZIP
Washington	756,510	20013*

FLORIDA

LOCATION	POPULATION	ZIP
Atlantic Beach	7,106	32233
Avon Park	6,712	33825
Azalea Park	7,367	32807
Bartow	12,891	33830
Bayshore Gardens	9,255	33507
Belle Glade	15,949	33430
Boca Raton	29,538	33432*
Boynton Beach	18,115	33435*
Bradenton	21,040	33506*
Brandon	12,749	33511
Browardale	17,444	33311
Browns Village	23,442	33142
Cape Coral	11,470	33904
Carol City	27,361	33055
Casselberry	9,438	32707
Cedar Hammock	10,820	33505
Chattahoochee	7,944	32324
Clearwater	52,074	33515*
Cocoa	16,110	32922
Cocoa Beach	9,952	32931
Collier Manor	7,202	33064
Conway	8,642	32809
Coral Gables	42,494	33134
Crestview	7,952	32536
Cutler Ridge	17,441	33157
Dania	9,013	33004
Daytona Beach	45,327	32015*
Deerfield Beach	16,662	33441
De Land	11,641	32720
Delray Beach	19,915	33444*
Dunedin	17,639	33528
Egypt Lake	7,556	33614
Eustis	6,722	32726
Fernandina Beach	6,955	32034
Fort Lauderdale	139,590	33310*
Fort Myers	27,351	33902*
Fort Pierce	29,721	33450*
Fort Walton Beach	19,994	32548
Gainesville	64,510	32601*
Goulds	6,690	33170
Gulfport	9,976	33737
Haines City	8,956	33844
Hallandale	23,849	33009
Hialeah	102,452	33010*
Holly Hill	8,191	32017
Hollywood	106,873	33022*
Homestead	13,674	33030*
Jacksonville	528,865	32201*
Jacksonville Bch.	13,326	32250
Kendall	35,497	33156
Key West	29,312	33040
Kissimmee	7,119	32741
Lake City	10,575	32055
Lake Holloway	6,227	33801
Lakeland	41,550	33802*
Lake Magdalene	9,266	33612
Lake Park	6,993	33403
Lake Wales	8,240	33853
Lake Worth	23,714	33460*
Lantana	7,126	33462
Largo	22,031	33540*
Lauderdale Lakes	10,577	33313
Lauderhill	8,465	33313
Leesburg	11,869	32748
Leto	8,458	33614
Lighthouse Point	9,071	33064
Live Oak	6,830	32060
Maitland	7,157	32751
Margate	8,867	33063
Marianna	6,741	32446
Melbourne	40,236	32901*
Merritt Island	29,233	32952
Miami	334,859	33101*
Miami Beach	87,072	33139
Miami Shores	9,425	33153
Miami Springs	13,279	33166
Mims	8,309	32754
Miramar	24,906	33023
Myrtle Grove	16,186	32506
Naples	12,042	33940*
New Smyrna Bch.	10,580	32069
North Andrews Terrace	7,082	33308
North Fort Myers	8,798	33903
North Miami	34,767	33161
North Miami Bch.	30,544	33160
North Palm Bch.	9,035	33403
Norwood	14,973	33169
Oakland Park	16,261	33334
Ocala	22,583	32670*
Opa-Locka	11,902	33054
Orange Park	7,619	32073
Orlando	99,006	32802*
Ormond Beach	14,063	32074
Palatka	9,444	32077
Palm Bay	7,176	32905
Palm Beach	9,086	33480
Palmetto	7,422	33561
Palm River—Clair Mel	8,536	33619
Panama City	32,096	32401*
Pembroke Pines	15,496	33024
Pensacola	59,507	32502*
Perrine	10,257	33157
Perry	7,701	32347
Pine Hills	13,882	32808
Pinellas Park	22,287	33565
Plantation	23,523	33317
Plant City	15,451	33566
Pompano Beach	38,587	33060*
Port Charlotte	10,769	33952
Quincy	8,334	32351
Richmond Heights	8,663	33156
Riviera Beach	21,401	33404
Rockledge	10,523	32955
St. Augustine	12,352	32084
St. Petersburg	216,159	33733*
St. Petersburg Bch.	8,024	33736
Sanford	17,393	32771
Sarasota	40,237	33578*
Satellite Beach	6,558	32901
Sebring	7,223	33870
South Miami	11,780	33143
South Miami Hts.	10,395	33157
South Patrick Shores	10,313	32901
Sunrise Golf Vill.	7,403	33313
Sweetwater Creek	19,453	33614
Tallahassee	72,624	32301*
Tampa	277,753	33602*
Tarpon Springs	7,118	33589*
Temple Terrace	7,347	33617
Tice	7,254	33905
Titusville	30,515	32780

LOCATION	POPULATION	ZIP
University	10,039	33620
Valparaiso	6,504	32580
Venice	6,648	33595*
Vero Beach	11,908	32960
Warrington	15,848	32507
West Palm Beach	57,375	33401*
West Pensacola	20,924	32502
West Winter Haven	7,716	33880
Westwood Lakes	12,811	33165
Wilton Manors	10,948	33305
Winter Haven	16,136	33880
Winter Park	21,895	32789*

GEORGIA

LOCATION	POPULATION	ZIP
Albany	72,623	31706*
Americus	16,091	31709
Athens	44,342	30601*
Atlanta	497,421	30301*
Augusta	59,864	30903*
Bainbridge	10,887	31717
Brunswick	19,585	31520
Cairo	8,061	31728
Carrollton	13,520	30117
Cartersville	10,138	30120
Cedartown	9,253	30125
Chamblee	9,127	30341
College Park	18,203	30337
Columbus	167,377	31902*
Cordele	10,733	31015
Covington	10,267	30209
Dalton	18,872	30720
Decatur	21,943	30030*
Doraville	9,157	30340
Douglas	10,195	31533
Dublin	15,143	31021
East Point	39,315	30344
Elberton	6,438	30635
Fitzgerald	8,187	31750
Forest Park	19,994	30050
Fort Valley	9,251	31030
Gainesville	15,459	30501
Griffin	22,734	30223
Hapeville	9,567	30354
Hardwick	14,047	31034
Jesup	9,091	31545
La Grange	23,301	30240
Macon	122,423	31201*
Marietta	27,216	30060*
Milledgeville	11,601	31061
Monroe	8,071	30655
Moultrie	14,400	31768
Newnan	11,205	30263*
Perry	7,771	31069
Rome	30,759	30161
Savannah	118,349	31402*
Smyrna	19,157	30080
Statesboro	14,616	30458
Swainsboro	7,325	30401
Thomaston	10,024	30286
Thomasville	18,155	31792
Thomson	6,503	30824
Tifton	12,179	31794
Toccoa	6,971	30577
Valdosta	32,303	31601
Vidalia	9,507	30474
Warner Robins	33,491	31093
Waycross	18,996	31501
Winder	6,605	30680
Windsor Forest	7,288	31406

GUAM

LOCATION	POPULATION	ZIP
Tamuning	8,230	96911

HAWAII

LOCATION	POPULATION	ZIP
Aiea	12,560	96701
Ewa Beach	7,765	96706
Hickam Housing	7,352	96824
Hilo	26,353	96720
Honolulu	324,871	96819*
Kahului	8,280	96732
Kailua	33,783	96734
Kaneohe	29,903	96744
Mokapu	7,860	96734
Nanakuli	6,506	96792
Pacific Palisades	7,846	96782
Pearl City	19,552	96782
Schofield Barracks	13,516	96786
Wahiawa	17,598	96786
Wailuku	7,979	96793
Waipahu	24,150	96797

IDAHO

LOCATION	POPULATION	ZIP
Blackfoot	8,716	83221
Boise	74,990	83701*
Burley	8,279	83318
Caldwell	14,219	83605
Coeur d'Alene	16,228	83814
Idaho Falls	35,776	83401
Lewiston	26,068	83501
Moscow	14,146	83843
Mountain Home	6,451	83647
Nampa	20,768	83651
Pocatello	40,036	83201
Rexburg	8,272	83440
Twin Falls	21,914	83301

ILLINOIS

LOCATION	POPULATION	ZIP
Addison	24,482	60101
Alsip	11,983	60658
Alton	39,700	62002
Arlington Hts.	64,884	60004*
Aurora	74,182	60507*
Barrington	8,674	60010
Bartonville	7,221	61607
Batavia	8,994	60510
Beardstown	6,222	62618
Belleville	41,699	62220*
Bellwood	22,096	60104
Belvidere	14,061	61008
Bensenville	13,396	60106
Benton	6,833	62812
Berwyn	52,502	60402
Bethalto	7,074	62010
Bloomington	39,992	61701
Blue Island	22,958	60406
Bolingbrook	8,504	60439
Bradley	9,881	60915
Bridgeview	12,522	60455
Broadview	9,623	60153
Brookfield	20,284	60513
Buffalo Grove	11,799	60090
Burbank	29,854	60459
Cahokia	20,649	62206
Calumet City	33,107	60409
Calumet Park	10,069	60643
Canton	14,217	61520
Carbondale	26,857	62901
Carpentersville	24,059	60110
Centralia	15,217	62801
Centreville	11,378	62206
Champaign	56,837	61820
Charleston	16,421	61920
Chicago	3,369,357	60607*
Chicago Heights	40,900	60411
Chicago Ridge	9,187	60415
Cicero	67,058	60650
Clarendon Hills	6,750	60514
Clinton	7,570	61727
Collinsvile	19,567	62234
Country Club Hills	6,920	60477
Crest Hill	7,460	60431
Creve Coeur	6,440	61611
Crystal Lake	14,541	60014
Danville	42,570	61832
Darien	7,789	60559
Decatur	90,397	62521*
Deerfield	18,876	60015
De Kalb	32,949	60115
Des Plaines	57,239	60016*
Dixon	18,147	61021
Dolton	25,990	60419
Downers Grove	33,588	60515
Du Quoin	6,691	62832
East Alton	7,309	62024
East Moline	20,832	61244
East Peoria	20,226	61611
East St. Louis	69,996	62201*
Edwardsville	11,070	62025
Effingham	9,458	62401
Elgin	55,691	60120
Elk Grove Village	20,346	60007
Elmhurst	48,887	60126
Elmwood Park	26,160	60635
Evanston	80,113	60204*
Evergreen Park	25,921	60642
Fairview Heights	12,577	62232
Flossmoor	8,328	60422
Forest Park	15,472	60130
Franklin Park	20,348	60131
Freeport	27,736	61032
Galesburg	36,290	61401

LOCATION	POPULATION	ZIP
Geneva	9,115	60134
Glencoe	10,675	60022
Glendale Heights	11,406	60108
Glen Ellyn	21,909	60137
Glenview	23,159	60025
Glenwood	7,416	60425
Granite City	40,685	62040
Hanover Park	11,916	60103
Harrisburg	9,535	62946
Harvey	34,636	60426
Harwood Heights	9,060	60656
Hazel Crest	10,329	60429
Herrin	9,623	62948
Hickory Hills	13,176	60457
Highland Park	32,263	60035
Hillside	8,888	60162
Hinsdale	15,918	60521
Hoffman Estates	22,238	60195
Hometown	6,729	60456
Homewood	18,871	60430
Hoopeston	6,461	60942
Jacksonville	20,553	62650
Jerseyville	7,446	62052
Joliet	78,887	60431*
Justice	9,473	60458
Kankakee	30,944	60901
Kewanee	15,762	61443
La Grange	17,814	60525
La Grange Highlands	6,842	60525
La Grange Park	15,459	60525
Lake Forest	15,642	60045
Lansing	25,805	60438
La Salle	10,620	61301
Libertyville	11,684	60048
Lincoln	17,582	62656
Lincolnwood	12,929	60645
Litchfield	7,190	62056
Lockport	9,985	60441
Lombard	34,043	60148
Loves Park	12,390	61111
Lyons	11,124	60534
Macomb	19,643	61455
Madison	7,042	62060
Marion	11,724	62959
Markham	16,117	60426
Mattoon	19,681	61938
Maywood	29,019	60153
McHenry	6,772	60050
Melrose Park	22,716	60160*
Mendota	6,902	61342
Metropolis	6,940	62960
Midlothian	15,939	60445
Moline	46,237	61265
Monmouth	11,022	61462
Morris	8,194	60450
Morton	10,419	61550
Morton Grove	26,369	60053
Mount Carmel	8,096	62863
Mount Prospect	45,228	60056
Mount Vernon	16,382	62864
Mundelein	16,128	60060
Murphysboro	10,013	62966
Naperville	22,617	60540
Niles	31,432	60648
Normal	26,396	61761
Norridge	17,113	60656
Northbrook	27,297	60062
North Chicago	47,275	60064
Northlake	14,212	60164
North Park	15,679	61111
North Riverside	8,097	60546
Oak Forest	17,870	60452
Oak Lawn	60,305	60454*
Oak Park	62,511	60303*
O'Fallon	9,365	62269
Olney	9,159	62450
Orland Park	6,391	60462
Ottawa	18,716	61350
Palatine	26,050	60067
Palos Heights	9,915	60463
Palos Hills	6,629	60465
Pana	6,326	62557
Paris	9,971	61944
Park Forest	30,864	60466
Park Ridge	42,614	60068
Pekin	31,375	61554
Peoria	126,963	61601*
Peoria Heights	7,943	61614
Peru	11,772	61354
Pontiac	10,595	61764

LOCATION	POPULATION	ZIP
Princeton	6,959	61356
Prospect Heights	13,333	60070
Quincy	45,288	62301
Rantoul	25,562	61866
Riverdale	15,806	60627
River Forest	13,402	60305
River Grove	11,465	60171
Riverside	10,432	60546
Robbins	9,641	60472
Robinson	7,178	62454
Rochelle	8,594	61068
Rock Falls	10,287	61071
Rockford	147,370	61125*
Rock Island	50,166	61201
Rolling Meadows	19,178	60008
Romeoville	12,674	60441
Roselle	6,207	60172*
St. Charles	12,945	60174
Sauk Village	7,479	60411
Schaumburg	18,730	60194
Schiller Park	12,712	60176
Skokie	68,322	60076*
South Holland	23,931	60473
South Stickney	29,900	60459
Springfield	91,753	62708*
Steger	8,104	60475
Sterling	16,113	61081
Stickney	6,601	60402
Streamwood	18,176	60103
Streator	15,600	61364
Summit	11,569	60501
Sycamore	7,843	60178
Taylorville	10,927	62568
Tinley Park	12,382	60477
Urbana	33,739	61801
Villa Park	25,891	60181
Washington	7,722	61571
Washington Park	9,524	62204
Waukegan	65,134	60085
Westchester	20,033	60153
West Chicago	10,111	60185
West End	7,554	61102
Western Springs	13,029	60558
West Frankfort	8,854	62896
Westmont	8,920	60559
West Peoria	6,873	61604
Wheaton	31,138	60187
Wheeling	14,746	60090
Wilmette	32,134	60091
Winnetka	13,998	60093
Wood Dale	8,831	60191
Woodridge	11,028	60515
Wood River	13,186	62095
Woodstock	10,226	60098
Worth	11,999	60482
Zion	17,268	60099

INDIANA

Anderson	70,787	46011*
Auburn	7,388	46706
Bedford	13,087	47421
Beech Grove	13,559	46107
Black Oak	9,624	46406
Bloomington	43,262	47401
Bluffton	8,297	46714
Brazil	8,163	47834
Carmel	6,568	46032
Cedar Lake	7,589	46303
Clarksville	13,806	47130
Columbus	26,457	47201
Connersville	17,604	47331
Crawfordsville	13,842	47933
Crown Point	10,931	46307
Decatur	8,445	46733
East Chicago	46,982	46312
East Gary	9,858	46405
Elkhart	43,152	46514
Elwood	11,196	46036
Evansville	138,764	47708*
Fort Wayne	178,021	46802*
Frankfort	14,956	46041
Franklin	11,477	46131
Gary	175,415	46401*
Goshen	17,871	46526
Greencastle	8,852	46135
Greenfield	9,986	46140
Greensburg	8,620	47240
Greenwood	11,408	46142
Griffith	18,168	46319
Hammond	107,885	46320*
Hartford City	8,207	47348

LOCATION	POPULATION	ZIP
Highland	24,947	46322
Hobart	21,485	46342
Huntington	16,217	46750
Indianapolis	746,302	46204*
Jasper	8,641	47546
Jeffersonville	20,008	47130
Kendallville	6,838	46755
Kokomo	44,042	46901
Lafayette	44,955	47902*
LaPorte	22,140	46350
Lawrence	16,917	46226
Lebanon	9,766	46052
Logansport	19,255	46947
Madison	13,081	47250
Marion	39,607	46952
Martinsville	9,723	46151
Merrillville	24,075	46410
Michigan City	39,369	46360
Mishawaka	35,517	46544
Mount Vernon	6,770	47620
Muncie	69,082	47302*
Munster	16,514	46321
New Albany	38,402	47150
New Castle	21,215	47362
Noblesville	7,548	46060
Peru	14,139	46970
Plainfield	8,211	46168
Plymouth	7,661	46563
Portage	19,127	46368
Portland	7,115	47371
Princeton	7,431	47670
Richmond	43,999	47374
Rushville	6,686	46173
Seymour	13,352	47274
Shelbyville	15,094	46176
South Bend	125,580	46624*
Speedway	14,649	46224
Tell City	7,933	47586
Terre Haute	70,335	47808*
Valparaiso	20,020	46383
Vincennes	19,867	47591
Wabash	13,379	46992
Warsaw	7,506	46580
Washington	11,358	47501
West Lafayette	19,157	47906
Whiting	7,152	46394

IOWA

Ames	39,505	50010
Ankeny	9,151	50021
Atlantic	7,306	50022
Bettendorf	22,126	52722
Boone	12,468	50036
Burlington	32,366	52601
Carroll	8,716	51401
Cedar Falls	29,597	50613
Cedar Rapids	110,642	52401*
Centerville	6,531	52544
Charles City	9,268	50616
Cherokee	7,272	51012
Clear Lake	6,430	50428
Clinton	34,719	52732
Council Bluffs	60,348	51501
Creston	8,234	50801
Davenport	98,469	52802*
Decorah	7,458	52101
Denison	6,218	51442
Des Moines	201,404	50318*
Dubuque	62,309	52001
Estherville	8,108	51334
Fairfield	8,715	52556
Fort Dodge	31,263	50501
Fort Madison	13,996	52627
Grinnell	8,402	50112
Indianola	8,852	50125
Iowa City	46,850	52240
Iowa Falls	6,454	50126
Keokuk	14,631	52632
Knoxville	7,755	50138
Le Mars	8,159	51031
Marion	18,028	52302
Marshalltown	26,219	50158
Mason City	30,379	50401
Mount Pleasant	7,007	52641
Muscatine	22,405	52761
Newton	15,619	50208
Oelwein	7,735	50662
Oskaloosa	11,224	52577
Ottumwa	29,610	52501
Pella	6,668	50219

LOCATION	POPULATION	ZIP
Perry	6,906	50220
Red Oak	6,210	51566
Sioux City	85,925	51101*
Spencer	10,278	51301
Storm Lake	8,591	50588
Urbandale	14,434	50322
Waterloo	75,533	50701*
Waverly	7,205	50677
Webster City	8,488	50595
West Des Moines	16,441	50265
Windsor Heights	6,303	50311

KANSAS

Abilene	6,661	67410
Arkansas City	13,216	67005
Atchison	12,565	66002
Chanute	10,341	66720
Coffeyville	15,116	67337
Concordia	7,221	66901
Derby	7,947	67037
Dodge City	14,127	67801
El Dorado	12,308	67042
Emporia	23,327	66801
Fort Leavenworth	8,060	66027
Fort Scott	8,967	66701
Garden City	14,790	67846
Great Bend	16,133	67530
Hays	15,396	67601
Haysville	6,483	67060
Hutchinson	36,885	67501
Independence	10,347	67301
Iola	6,493	66749
Junction City	19,018	66441
Kansas City	168,213	66110*
Lawrence	45,698	66044
Leavenworth	25,147	66048
Leawood	10,349	66206
Liberal	13,789	67901
Manhattan	27,575	66502
McPherson	10,851	67460
Merriam	10,851	66203
Mission	8,376	66205
Newton	15,439	67114
Olathe	17,917	66061
Ottawa	11,036	66067
Overland Park	79,034	66204
Parsons	13,015	67357
Pittsburg	20,171	66762
Prairie Village	28,138	66208
Pratt	6,736	67124
Roeland Park	9,974	66205
Salina	37,714	67401
Shawnee	20,482	66202*
Topeka	125,011	66601*
Wellington	8,072	67152
Wichita	276,554	67202*
Winfield	11,405	67156

KENTUCKY

Ashland	29,245	41101
Bellevue	8,847	41073
Berea	6,956	40403
Bowling Green	36,705	42101
Campbellsville	7,598	42718
Corbin	7,317	40701
Covington	52,535	41011*
Cynthiana	6,356	41031
Danville	11,542	40422
Dayton	8,751	41074
Elizabethtown	11,748	42701
Erlanger	12,676	41018
Flatwoods	7,380	41139
Florence	11,661	41042
Fort Knox	37,608	40121
Fort Mitchell	6,982	41017
Fort Thomas	16,338	41075
Frankfort	21,902	40601
Franklin	6,553	42134
Georgetown	8,629	40324
Glasgow	11,301	42141
Harrodsburg	6,741	40330
Henderson	22,976	42420
Hopkinsville	21,250	42240
Jeffersontown	9,701	40299
Lexington	108,137	40507*
Louisville	361,706	40202*
Madisonville	15,332	42431
Mayfield	10,724	42066
Maysville	7,411	41056
Middlesborough	11,878	40965

LOCATION	POPULATION	ZIP
Morehead	7,191	40351
Murray	13,537	42071
Newport	25,998	41071*
Okolona	17,643	40219
Owensboro	50,329	42301
Paducah	31,627	42001
Paris	7,823	40361
Pleasure Ridge Pk.	28,566	40258
Princeton	6,292	42445
Radcliff	7,881	40160
Richmond	16,861	40475
Russellville	6,456	42276
St. Matthews	13,152	40207
Shively	19,139	40216
Somerset	10,436	42501
Valley Station	24,471	40272
Winchester	13,402	40391

LOUISIANA

Abbeville	10,996	70510
Alexandria	41,557	71301
Baker	8,281	70714
Bastrop	14,713	71220
Baton Rouge	165,921	70821*
Bayou Cane	9,077	70360
Bogalusa	18,412	70427
Bossier City	41,595	71111*
Cooper Road	9,034	71107
Covington	7,170	70433
Crowley	16,104	70526
Denham Springs	6,752	70726
De Ridder	8,030	70634
Donaldsonville	7,367	70346
Eunice	11,390	70535
Franklin	9,325	70538
Gretna	24,875	70053
Hammond	12,487	70401
Harahan	13,037	70123
Harvey	6,347	70058
Houma	30,922	70360
Jeanerette	6,322	70544
Jefferson Heights	16,489	70121
Jennings	11,783	70546
Kenner	29,858	70062
Lafayette	68,908	70501*
Lake Charles	77,998	70601*
Leesville	8,928	71446
Little Farms	15,713	70123
Mansfield	6,432	71052
Marrero	29,015	70072
Metairie	136,477	70001*
Minden	13,996	71055
Monroe	56,374	71201*
Morgan City	16,586	70380
Natchitoches	15,974	71457
New Iberia	30,147	70560
New Orleans	593,471	70140*
Oakdale	7,301	71463
Opelousas	20,387	70570
Pineville	8,951	71360
Plaquemine	7,739	70764
Rayne	9,510	70578
Reserve	6,381	70084
Ruston	17,365	71270
St. Martinsville	7,153	70582
Scotlandville	22,599	70807
Shreveport	182,064	71102*
Slidell	16,101	70458
Springhill	6,496	71075
Sulphur	14,959	70663
Tallulah	9,643	71282
Terry Town	13,832	70053
Thibodaux	15,028	70301
Ville Platte	9,692	70586
West Monroe	14,868	71291
Westwego	11,402	70094
Winnfield	7,142	71483

MAINE

Auburn	24,151	04210
Augusta	21,945	04330
Bangor	33,168	04401
Bath	9,679	04530
Biddeford	19,983	04005
Brewer	9,300	04412
Brunswick	16,195	04011
Cape Elizabeth	7,873	04107
Caribou	10,419	04736
Falmouth	6,291	04105
Gardiner	6,685	04345
Gorham	7,839	04038

LOCATION	POPULATION	ZIP
Houlton	8,111	04730
Kittery	11,028	03904
Lewiston	41,779	04240
Limestone	10,360	04750
Lisbon	6,544	04250
Millinocket	7,742	04462
Old Town	9,057	04468
Orono	9,989	04473
Portland	65,116	04101*
Presque Isle	11,452	04769
Rockland	8,505	04841
Rumford	9,363	04276
Saco	11,678	04072
Sanford	15,812	04073
Scarborough	7,845	04074
Skowhegan	7,601	04976
South Portland	23,267	04106
Waterville	18,192	04901
Westbrook	14,444	04092
Windham	6,593	04082
Winslow	7,299	04901

MARYLAND

Aberdeen	12,375	21001
Annapolis	30,095	21401*
Arbutus	22,745	21227
Aspen Hill	16,823	20906
Avenel-Hillandale	19,520	20903
Baltimore	905,787	21233*
Bel Aire	6,307	21014
Beltsville	8,912	20705
Bethesda	71,621	20014
Birchwood City	13,514	20021
Bladensburg	7,488	20710
Bowie	35,028	20715
Brooklyn	13,896	21225
Calverton	6,543	20705
Cambridge	11,595	21613
Camp Springs	22,776	20031
Carmody Hills	6,335	20028
Catonsville	54,812	21228
Cheverly	6,808	20785
Chevy Chase	16,424	20015
Chillum	35,656	20783
Colesville	9,455	20904
College Park	26,156	20740
Columbia	8,815	21045*
Coral Hills	9,058	20027
Cumberland	29,724	21502
Defense Heights	6,775	20710
District Heights	7,659	20028
Dundalk	85,377	21222
Easton	6,809	21601
Edgemere	10,352	21219
Edgewood	8,551	21040
Ellicott City	9,435	21043
Essex	38,193	21221
Ferndale	9,929	21061
Forestville	16,188	20028
Frederick	23,641	21701
Frostburg	7,327	21532
Gaithersburg	8,344	20760
Glen Burnie	38,608	21061
Good Luck	10,584	20715
Greenbelt	18,199	20770
Hagerstown	35,862	21740
Havre de Grace	9,791	21078
Hillcrest Heights	24,037	20031
Hyattsville	14,998	20781*
Joppatowne	9,092	21085
Kemp Mill	10,037	20902
Kentland	9,649	20785
Langley Park	11,564	20787
Lanham—Seabrook	13,244	20801
Lansdowne	17,770	21227
Laurel	10,525	20810*
Lexington Park	9,136	20653
Linthicum	9,775	21090
Lutherville	24,055	21093
Maryland City	7,102	20810
Middle River	19,935	21220
Mount Rainier	8,180	20822
New Carrollton	14,870	20784
North Potomac	12,784	20854
North Takoma Pk.	7,373	20012
Overlea	13,124	21201
Owings Mills	7,360	21117
Oxon Hill	11,974	20021
Palmer Park	8,172	20785
Parkville	33,589	21234

LOCATION	POPULATION	ZIP
Pikesville	25,395	21208
Pumphrey	6,425	21090
Randalstown	33,683	21133
Randolph	13,215	20852
Reisterstown	12,568	21136
Riverside Hts.	8,941	20840
Riviera Beach	7,464	21061
Rockville	41,821	20850*
Rosedale	19,417	21237
Salisbury	15,252	21801
Seat Pleasant	7,217	20027
Severna Park	16,358	21146
Silver Spring	77,411	20907*
South Gate	9,356	21061
South Kensington	10,289	20795
South Laurel	13,345	20810
Suitland	30,355	20023
Takoma Park	18,507	20012
Towson	77,768	21204
Waldorf	7,368	20601
Walker Mill	7,103	20023
Westminster	7,207	21157
Wheaton	66,280	20902
White Oak	19,769	20904
Woodlawn	28,821	21207

MASSACHUSETTS

Abington	12,334	02351
Acton	14,770	01720
Acushnet	7,767	02743
Adams	11,772	01220
Agawam	21,717	01001
Amesbury	11,388	01913
Amherst	26,331	01002
Andover	23,695	01810
Arlington	53,524	02174
Ashland	8,882	01721
Athol	11,185	01331
Attleboro	32,907	02703
Auburn	15,347	01501
Ayer	8,283	01432*
Barnstable	19,842	02630
Bedford	13,513	01730
Bellingham	13,967	02019
Belmont	28,285	02178
Beverly	38,348	01915
Billerica	31,648	01821
Blackstone	6,566	01504
Boston	641,071	02109*
Bourne	12,636	02532
Braintree	35,050	02184
Bridgewater	11,829	02324
Brockton	89,040	02403*
Brookline	58,689	02146
Burlington	21,980	01803
Cambridge	100,361	02138
Canton	17,100	02021
Chelmsford	31,432	01824
Chelsea	30,625	02150
Chicopee	66,676	01021*
Clinton	13,383	01510
Cohasset	6,954	02025
Concord	16,148	01742
Dalton	7,505	01226
Danvers	26,151	01923
Dartmouth	18,800	02714
Dedham	26,938	02026
Dennis	6,454	02638
Dracut	18,214	01826
Dudley	8,087	01570
Duxbury	7,636	02332
East Bridgewater	8,347	02333
Easthampton	13,012	01027
East Longmeadow	13,029	01028
Easton	12,157	02334
Everett	42,485	02149
Fairhaven	16,332	02719
Fall River	96,898	02722*
Falmouth	15,942	02540*
Fitchburg	43,343	01420
Foxboro	14,218	02035
Framingham	64,048	01701
Franklin	17,830	02038
Gardner	19,748	01440
Gloucester	27,941	01930
Grafton	11,659	01519
Great Barrington	7,537	01230
Greenfield	18,116	01301
Hamilton	6,373	01936
Hanover	10,107	02339
Hanson	7,148	02341

LOCATION	POPULATION	ZIP
Harvard	12,494	01451
Haverhill	46,120	01830
Hingham	18,845	02043
Holbrook	11,775	02343
Holden	12,564	01520
Holliston	12,069	01746
Holyoke	50,112	01040
Hudson	16,084	01749
Hull	9,961	02045
Hyannis	6,847	02601
Ipswich	10,750	01938
Lawrence	66,915	01842*
Lee	6,426	01238
Leicester	9,140	01524
Leominster	32,939	01453
Lexington	31,886	02173
Lincoln	7,567	01773
Littleton	6,380	01460
Longmeadow	15,630	01106
Lowell	94,239	01853*
Ludlow	17,580	01056
Lunenburg	7,419	01462
Lynn	90,294	01901*
Lynnfield	10,826	01940
Malden	56,127	02148
Mansfield	9,939	02048
Marblehead	21,295	01945
Marlborough	27,936	01752
Marshfield	15,223	02050
Maynard	9,710	01754
Medfield	9,821	02052
Medford	64,397	02155
Medway	7,938	02053
Melrose	33,180	02176
Methuen	35,456	01844
Middleboro	13,607	02346
Milford	19,352	01757
Millbury	11,987	01527
Milton	27,190	02186
Monson	7,355	01057
Montague	8,451	01351
Natick	31,057	01760
Needham	29,748	02192
New Bedford	101,777	02740*
Newburyport	15,807	01950
Newton	91,263	02158
North Adams	19,195	01247
Northampton	29,664	01060
North Andover	16,284	01845
North Attleboro	18,665	02760*
Northboro	9,218	01532
Northbridge	11,795	01534
North Reading	11,264	01864
Norton	9,487	02766
Norwell	7,796	02061
Norwood	30,815	02062
Oxford	10,345	01540
Palmer	11,680	01069
Peabody	48,080	01960
Pembroke	11,193	02359
Pittsfield	57,020	01201
Plymouth	18,606	02360
Quincy	87,966	02169
Randolph	27,035	02368
Raynham	6,705	02767
Reading	22,539	01867
Rehoboth	6,512	02769
Revere	43,159	02151
Rockland	15,674	02370
Salem	40,556	01970
Saugus	25,110	01906
Scituate	16,973	02066
Seekonk	11,116	02771
Sharon	12,367	02067
Shrewsbury	19,196	01545
Somerset	18,088	02725
Somerville	88,779	02143
Southbridge	17,057	01550
South Hadley	17,033	01075
Southwick	6,330	01077
Spencer	8,779	01562
Springfield	163,905	01101*
Stoneham	20,725	02180
Stoughton	23,459	02072
Sudbury	13,506	01776
Swampscott	13,578	01907
Swansea	12,640	02777
Taunton	43,756	02780
Tewksbury	22,755	01876
Uxbridge	8,253	01569
Wakefield	25,402	01880
Walpole	18,149	02081

LOCATION	POPULATION	ZIP
Waltham	61,582	02154
Ware	8,187	01082
Wareham	11,492	02571
Watertown	39,307	02172
Wayland	13,461	01778
Webster	14,917	01570
Wellesley	28,051	02181
Westboro	12,594	01581
West Bridgewater	7,152	02379
Westfield	31,433	01085
Westford	10,368	01886
Weston	10,870	02193
Westport	9,791	02790
West Springfield	28,461	01089
Westwood	12,750	02090
Weymouth	54,610	02188
Whitman	13,059	02382
Wilbraham	11,984	01095
Williamstown	8,454	01267
Wilmington	17,102	01887
Winchendon	6,635	01475
Winchester	22,269	01890
Winthrop	20,335	02152
Woburn	37,406	01801
Worcester	176,572	01613*
Wrentham	7,315	02093
Yarmouth	12,033	02675

MICHIGAN

LOCATION	POPULATION	ZIP
Adrian	20,382	49221
Albion	12,112	49224
Allen Park	40,747	48101
Alma	9,611	48801
Alpena	13,805	49707
Ann Arbor	99,797	48106*
Battle Creek	38,931	49016*
Bay City	49,449	48706
Benton Harbor	16,481	49022
Berkley	21,879	48072
Beverly Hills	13,598	48010
Big Rapids	11,995	49307
Birmingham	26,170	48012*
Cadillac	9,990	49601
Carrollton	7,300	48724
Center Line	10,379	48015
Charlotte	8,244	48813
Clawson	17,617	48017
Coldwater	9,155	49036
Cutlerville	6,267	49508
Dearborn	104,199	48120*
Dearborn Heights	80,069	48127
Detroit	1,513,601	48226*
Dowagiac	6,583	49047
Drayton Plains	16,462	48020
East Detroit	45,920	48021
East Grand Rapids	12,565	49506
East Lansing	47,540	48823
Eastwood	9,682	49001
Ecorse	17,515	48229
Escanaba	15,368	49829
Farmington	10,329	48018*
Farmington Hills	48,694	48024
Fenton	8,284	48430
Ferndale	30,850	48220
Flint	193,317	48502*
Flushing	7,190	48433
Fraser	11,868	48026
Garden City	41,864	48135
Grand Haven	11,844	49417
Grand Rapids	197,649	49501*
Grandville	10,764	49418
Greenville	7,493	48838
Grosse Ile	8,306	48138
Grosse Pointe	6,637	48236
Grosse Pte. Farms	11,701	48236
Grosse Pte. Pk.	15,641	48236
Grosse Pte. Woods	21,878	48236
Hamtramck	27,245	48212
Harper Woods	20,186	48225
Hastings	6,501	49058
Hazel Park	23,784	48030
Highland Park	35,444	48203
Hillsdale	7,728	49242
Holland	26,479	49423
Holt	6,980	48842
Huntington Woods	8,536	48070
Inkster	38,595	48141
Ionia	6,361	48846
Iron Mountain	8,702	49801
Ironwood	8,711	49938
Ishpeming	8,245	49849

LOCATION	POPULATION	ZIP
Jackson	45,484	49201*
Jenison	11,266	49428
Kalamazoo	85,555	49003*
Kentwood	20,310	49508
Lakeview	11,391	49015
Lansing	131,403	48924*
Lapeer	13,444	48446
Lincoln Park	52,984	48146
Livonia	110,109	48150*
Ludington	9,021	49431
Madison Heights	38,599	48071
Manistee	7,723	49660
Marquette	21,967	49855
Marshall	7,253	49068
Melvindale	13,862	48122
Menominee	10,748	49858
Midland	35,176	48640
Monroe	23,894	48161
Mount Clemens	20,476	48043*
Mount Pleasant	20,524	48858
Muskegon	44,631	49440*
Muskegon Heights	17,304	49444
Niles	12,988	49120
Norton Shores	22,271	49441
Novi	9,668	48050
Oak Park	36,762	48237
Okemos	7,770	48864
Owosso	17,179	48867
Petoskey	6,342	49770
Plymouth	11,758	48171*
Pontiac	85,279	48056*
Portage	33,590	49081
Port Huron	35,794	48060
River Rouge	15,947	48218
Riverview	11,342	48192
Rochester	7,054	48063
Romulus	22,879	48174
Roseville	60,529	48066
Royal Oak	86,238	48067*
Saginaw	91,849	48605*
St. Clair Shores	88,093	48083*
St. Johns	6,672	48879
St. Joseph	11,042	49085
Sault Ste. Marie	15,136	49783
Southfield	69,285	48034*
Southgate	33,909	48195
South Haven	6,471	49090
Sterling Heights	61,365	48077
Sturgis	9,295	49091
Taylor	70,020	48180
Tecumseh	7,120	49286
Three Rivers	7,355	49093
Traverse City	18,048	49684
Trenton	24,127	48183
Troy	39,419	48084*
Walker	11,492	49504
Warren	179,260	48089*
Wayne	21,054	48184
Westland	86,749	48185
Westwood	9,143	49007
Wurtsmith	6,932	48753
Wyandotte	41,061	48192
Wyoming	56,560	49509
Ypsilanti	29,538	48197

MINNESOTA

LOCATION	POPULATION	ZIP
Albert Lea	19,418	56007
Alexandria	6,973	56308
Anoka	13,295	55303
Apple Valley	8,502	55124
Austin	26,210	55912
Bemidji	11,490	56601
Blaine	20,625	55433
Bloomington	81,970	55420
Brainerd	11,667	56401
Brooklyn Center	35,173	55429
Brooklyn Park	26,230	55444
Burnsville	19,940	55378
Cloquet	8,699	55720
Columbia Heights	23,837	55421
Coon Rapids	30,505	55433
Cottage Grove	13,419	55016
Crookston	8,312	56716
Crystal	30,925	55428
Duluth	100,578	55806*
East Grand Forks	7,607	56721
Eden Prairie	6,938	55344
Edina	44,046	55424
Fairmont	10,751	56031

LOCATION	POPULATION	ZIP
Faribault	16,595	55021
Fergus Falls	12,443	56537
Fridley	29,233	55432
Golden Valley	24,246	55427
Grand Rapids	7,247	55744
Hastings	12,195	55033
Hibbing	16,104	55746
Hopkins	13,428	55343
Hutchinson	8,031	55350
Internat'l Falls	6,439	56649
Inver Grove Hts.	12,148	55075
Lakeville	7,556	55044
Little Falls	7,467	56345
Mankato	30,895	56001
Maple Grove	6,275	55369
Maplewood	25,222	55109
Marshall	9,886	56258
Minneapolis	434,400	55401*
Minnetonka	35,737	55343
Moorhead	29,687	56560
Mound	7,572	55364
Mounds View	10,641	55112
New Brighton	19,507	55112
New Hope	23,180	55428
New Ulm	13,051	56073
Northfield	10,235	55057
North Mankato	7,347	56001
North St. Paul	11,950	55109
Oakdale	7,304	55109
Orono	6,787	55323
Owatonna	15,341	55060
Plymouth	18,077	55441
Red Wing	12,834	55066
Richfield	47,231	55423
Robbinsdale	16,845	55422
Rochester	53,766	55901
Roseville	34,438	55113
St. Anthony Falls	9,239	55414
St. Cloud	39,691	56301
St. Louis Park	48,922	55426
St. Paul	309,714	55101*
St. Peter	8,339	56082
Shakopee	6,876	55379
Shoreview	10,995	55112
South St. Paul	25,016	55075
Spring Lake Pk.	6,417	55432
Stillwater	10,191	55082
Thief River Falls	8,618	56701
Virginia	12,450	55792
Waseca	6,789	56093
West St. Paul	18,799	55118
White Bear Lake	23,313	55110
Willmar	12,869	56201
Winona	26,438	55987
Worthington	9,916	56187

MISSISSIPPI

Aberdeen	6,507	39730
Amory	7,236	38821
Bay St. Louis	6,752	39520
Biloxi	48,486	39530*
Brookhaven	10,700	39601
Canton	10,503	39046
Clarksdale	21,673	38614
Cleveland	13,327	38732
Clinton	7,289	39056
Columbia	7,587	39429
Columbus	25,795	39701
Corinth	11,581	38834
D'Iberville	7,288	39532
Greenville	39,648	38701
Greenwood	22,400	38930
Grenada	9,944	38901
Gulfport	40,791	39501*
Hattiesburg	38,277	39401
Indianola	8,947	38751
Jackson	153,968	39205*
Kosciusko	7,266	39090
Laurel	24,145	39440
Louisville	6,626	39339
McComb	11,969	39648
Meridian	45,083	39301
Moss Point	19,321	39563
Natchez	19,704	39120
New Albany	6,426	38652
Ocean Springs	9,580	39564
Oxford	13,846	38655
Pascagoula	27,264	39567
Pearl	12,165	39208
Petal	6,986	39465

LOCATION	POPULATION	ZIP
Picayune	10,467	39466
Southaven	8,931	38671
Starkville	11,369	39759
Tupelo	20,471	38801
Vicksburg	25,478	39180
West Gulfport	6,996	39501
West Point	8,714	39773
Yazoo City	11,688	39194

MISSOURI

Affton	24,264	63123
Arnold	17,381	63010
Ballwin	10,656	63011
Bellefontaine Neighbors	14,084	63137
Belton	12,179	64012
Berkeley	19,743	63134
Blue Springs	6,779	64015
Boonville	7,514	65233
Breckenridge Hills	7,011	63114
Brentwood	11,248	63144
Bridgeton	19,992	63044
Cape Girardeau	31,282	63701
Carthage	11,035	64836
Caruthersville	7,350	63830
Chillicothe	9,519	64601
Clayton	16,100	63105
Clinton	7,504	64735
Columbia	58,812	65201
Concord	21,217	63128
Crestwood	15,123	63126
Creve Coeur	8,967	63141
Dellwood	7,137	63135
Excelsior Springs	9,411	64024
Farmington	6,590	63640
Ferguson	28,759	63135
Festus	7,530	63028
Florissant	65,908	63033*
Fulton	12,248	65251
Gladstone	23,422	64118
Glendale	6,981	63122
Grandview	17,456	64030
Hannibal	18,698	63401
Hazelwood	14,082	63042*
Independence	111,630	64050*
Jefferson City	32,407	65101
Jennings	19,379	63136
Joplin	39,256	64801
Kansas City	507,330	64108*
Kennett	10,090	63857
Kirksville	15,560	63501
Kirkwood	31,679	63122
Ladue	10,359	64758
Lebanon	8,616	65536
Lee's Summit	16,230	64063
Lemay	40,516	63125
Liberty	13,704	64068
Maplewood	12,785	63143
Marshall	12,051	65340
Maryland Heights	8,805	63043
Maryville	9,970	64468
Mexico	11,807	65265
Moberly	12,988	65270
Neosho	7,517	64850
Nevada	9,736	64772
Normandy	6,236	63121
O'Fallon	7,018	63366
Olivette	9,156	63124
Overland	24,819	63114
Pine Lawn	6,517	63120
Poplar Bluff	16,653	63901
Raytown	33,306	64133
Richmond Hts.	13,802	63117
Rock Hill	6,815	63119
Rolla	13,571	65401
St. Ann	18,817	63074
St. Charles	31,834	63301
St. John	8,960	63114
St. Joseph	72,691	64501*
St. Louis	622,236	63166*
Sappington	10,603	63126
Sedalia	22,847	65301
Sikeston	14,699	63801
Spanish Lake	15,647	63138
Springfield	120,096	65801*
University City	47,527	63130
Warrensburg	13,125	64093
Washington	8,499	63090
Webb City	6,923	64870
Webster Groves	27,457	63119

LOCATION	POPULATION	ZIP
Wellston	7,050	63112
West Plains	6,893	65775

MONTANA

Anaconda	9,771	59711
Billings	61,581	59101*
Bozeman	18,670	59715
Butte	23,368	59701
Glendive	6,305	59330
Great Falls	60,091	59401*
Havre	10,558	59501
Helena	22,730	59601
Kalispell	10,526	59901
Lewistown	6,437	59457
Livingston	6,883	59047
Miles City	9,023	59301
Missoula	29,497	59801

NEBRASKA

Alliance	6,862	69301
Beatrice	12,389	68310
Bellevue	21,953	68005
Columbus	15,471	68601
Fremont	22,962	68025
Grand Island	32,358	68801
Hastings	23,580	68901
Kearney	19,181	68847
Lincoln	149,518	68501*
McCook	8,285	69001
Millard	7,460	68137
Nebraska City	7,441	68410
Norfolk	16,607	68701
North Platte	19,447	69101
Omaha	346,929	68108*
Plattsmouth	6,371	68048
Scottsbluff	14,507	69361
Sidney	6,403	69162
South Sioux City	7,920	68776
York	6,778	68467

NEVADA

Carson City	15,468	89701
East Las Vegas	6,501	89112
Elko	7,621	89801
Henderson	16,395	89015
Las Vegas	125,787	89114*
North Las Vegas	36,216	89030
Paradise Valley	24,477	89119
Reno	72,863	89501*
Sparks	24,187	89431
Sunrise Manor	10,886	89110
Vegas Creek	8,970	89121
Winchester	13,981	89109

NEW HAMPSHIRE

Berlin	15,256	03570
Claremont	14,221	03743
Concord	30,022	03301
Derry	11,712	03038
Dover	20,850	03820
Durham	8,869	03824
Exeter	8,892	03833
Franklin	7,292	03235
Goffstown	9,284	03045
Hampton	8,011	03842
Hanover	8,494	03755
Hudson	10,638	03051
Keene	20,467	03431
Laconia	14,888	03246
Lebanon	9,725	03766
Manchester	87,754	03101*
Merrimack	8,595	03054
Milford	6,622	03055
Nashua	55,820	03060
Portsmouth	25,717	03801
Rochester	17,938	03867
Salem	20,142	03079
Somersworth	9,026	03878

NEW JERSEY

Allendale	6,240	07401
Asbury Park	16,533	07712
Atlantic City	47,859	08401*
Audubon	10,802	08106
Barrington	8,409	08007
Bayonne	72,743	07002
Belleville	37,629	07109
Bellmawr	15,618	08031
Bergenfield	29,000	07621
Berkeley Hts. Twp.	13,078	07922

LOCATION	POPULATION	ZIP
Bernardsville	6,652	07924
Bloomfield	52,029	07003
Bloomingdale	7,797	07403
Bogota	8,960	07603
Boonton	9,261	07005
Bound Brook	10,450	08805
Brick	35,057	08723
Bridgeton	20,435	08302
Bridgewater Twp.	30,235	08807
Brigantine	6,741	08203
Browns Mills	7,144	08015
Burlington	12,010	08016
Butler	7,051	07405
Caldwell	8,677	07006
Camden	102,551	08101*
Carlstadt	6,724	07072
Carteret	23,137	07008
Cedar Grove Twp.	15,582	07009
Chatham	9,566	07928
Cherry Hill Twp.	64,395	08034*
Cinnaminson Twp.	16,962	08077
Clark Twp.	18,829	07066
Cliffside Park	18,891	07010
Cliffwood	7,056	07721
Clifton	82,437	07015*
Closter	8,604	07624
Collingswood	17,422	08108
Cranford Twp.	27,391	07016
Cresskill	8,298	07626
Delran Twp.	10,065	08075
Denville Twp.	14,045	07834
Deptford Twp.	24,232	08096
Dover	15,039	07801
Dumont	20,155	07628
Dunellen	7,072	08812
East Brunswick Twp.	34,166	08816
East Hanover Twp.	7,734	07936
East Orange	75,471	07019*
East Rutherford	8,536	07073
Eatontown	14,619	07724
Edison Twp.	67,120	08817
Elizabeth	112,654	07207*
Elmwood Park	20,511	07407
Emerson	8,428	07630
Englewood	24,985	07631*
Evesham Twp.	13,477	08053
Ewing Twp.	32,831	08618
Fairfield	6,884	07006
Fair Lawn	37,975	07410
Fairview	10,698	07022
Fanwood	8,920	07023
Florence-Roebling	7,551	08518
Florham Park	8,094	07932
Fort Lee	30,631	07024
Franklin Lakes	7,550	07417
Freehold	10,545	07728
Garfield	30,797	07026
Glassboro	12,938	08028
Glen Ridge	8,518	07028
Glen Rock	13,011	07452
Gloucester City	14,707	08030
Hackensack	36,008	07601*
Hackettstown	9,472	07840
Haddonfield	13,118	08033
Haddon Heights	9,365	08035
Haddon Twp.	18,192	08108
Haledon	6,767	07508
Hammonton	11,464	08037
Hanover Twp.	10,700	07981
Harrison	11,811	07029
Hasbrouck Hts.	13,651	07604
Hawthorne	19,173	07507
Hazlet Twp.	22,239	07730
Highland Park	14,385	08904
Hillsdale	11,768	07642
Hillside Twp.	21,636	07205
Hoboken	45,380	07030
Hopatcong	9,052	07843
Irvington	59,473	07111
Jackson Twp.	18,276	08527
Jersey City	260,350	07303*
Keansburg	9,720	07734
Kearny	37,585	07032
Kendall Park	7,412	08824
Kenilworth	9,165	07033
Keyport	7,205	07735
Kinnelon	7,600	07405
Lake Hiawatha	11,389	07034
Lake Mohawk	6,262	07871

LOCATION	POPULATION	ZIP
Lake Parsippany	7,488	07054
Lakewood	17,874	08701
Laurence Harbor	6,715	08879
Leonia	8,847	07605
Lincoln Park	9,034	07035
Linden	41,409	07036
Lindenwold	12,199	08021
Little Falls Twp.	11,727	07424
Little Ferry	9,064	07643
Livingston Twp.	30,127	07039
Lodi	25,163	07644
Long Branch	31,774	07740
Lyndhurst Twp.	22,729	07071
Madison	16,710	07940
Mahwah Twp.	10,800	07430
Manville	13,029	08835
Maple Shade	16,464	08052
Maplewood Twp.	24,932	07040
Margate City	10,576	08402
Marlton	10,180	08053
Matawan	9,136	07747
Maywood	11,087	07607
Metuchen	16,031	08840
Middlesex	15,038	08846
Middletown Twp.	54,623	07748
Midland Park	8,159	07432
Millburn Twp.	21,089	07041
Milltown	6,470	08850
Millville	21,366	08332
Montclair	44,043	07042*
Montvale	7,327	07645
Montville Twp.	11,846	07045
Moorestown	14,179	08057
Morristown	17,662	07960
Mountainside	7,520	07092
Mount Holly Twp.	12,713	08060
Neptune Twp.	27,863	07753
Newark	381,930	07101*
New Brunswick	41,885	08901*
New Milford	19,149	07646
New Providence	13,796	07974
Newton	7,297	07860
North Arlington	18,096	07032
North Bergen Twp.	47,751	07047
North Brunswick Twp.	16,691	08902
North Caldwell	6,733	07006
Northfield	8,875	08225
North Haledon	7,614	07508
North Plainfield	21,796	07060
Nutley	31,913	07110
Oakland	14,420	07436
Ocean City	10,575	08226
Oceanport	7,503	07757
Old Bridge	25,176	08857
Oradell	8,903	07649
Orange	32,566	07050*
Palisades Park	13,351	07650
Palmyra	6,969	08065
Paramus	28,381	07652
Park Ridge	8,709	07656
Parsippany-Troy Hills Twp.	55,112	07054
Passaic	55,124	07055
Paterson	144,824	07510*
Paulsboro	8,084	08066
Pennsauken Twp.	36,394	08110
Pennsville	11,014	08070
Pequannock Twp.	14,350	07440
Perth Amboy	38,798	08861*
Phillipsburg	17,849	08865
Piscataway Twp.	36,418	08854
Pitman	10,257	08071
Plainfield	46,862	07061*
Pleasantville	13,778	08232
Point Pleasant	15,968	08742
Pompton Lakes	11,397	07442
Princeton	12,311	08540
Rahway	29,114	07065*
Ramsey	12,571	07446
Raritan	6,691	08869
Red Bank	12,847	07701
Ridgefield	11,308	07657
Ridgefield Park	13,990	07660
Ridgewood	27,547	07451*
Ringwood	10,393	07456
River Edge	12,850	07661
Riverside Twp.	8,591	08075
River Vale Twp.	8,883	07675
Rochelle Pk. Twp.	6,380	07662
Rockaway	6,383	07866

LOCATION	POPULATION	ZIP
Roselle	22,585	07203
Roselle Park	14,277	07204
Rumson	7,421	07760
Runnemede	10,475	08078
Rutherford	20,802	07070*
Saddle Brook Twp.	15,975	07662
Salem	7,648	08079
Sayreville	32,508	08872
Scotch Plains Twp.	22,279	07076
Secaucus	13,228	07094
Somerdale	6,510	08083
Somers Point	7,919	08244
Somerville	13,652	08876
South Amboy	9,338	08879
South Orange	16,971	07079
South Plainfield	21,142	07080
South River	15,428	08882
Spotswood	7,891	08884
Springfield Twp.	15,740	07081
Stratford	9,801	08084
Strathmore	7,674	07747
Summit	23,620	07901
Teaneck Twp.	42,355	07666
Tenafly	14,827	07670
Tinton Falls	8,395	07724
Toms River	7,303	08753
Totowa	11,580	07512
Trenton	104,786	08608*
Union Beach	6,472	07735
Union City	57,305	07087
Union Twp.	53,077	07083
Upper Saddle River	7,949	07458
Ventnor City	10,385	08406
Verona	15,067	07044
Vineland	47,399	08360
Waldwick	12,313	07463
Wallington	10,284	07057
Wanaque	8,636	07465
Washington Twp.	10,577	07675
Wayne Twp.	49,141	07470
Weehawken Twp.	13,383	07087
West Caldwell	11,913	07006
Westfield	33,720	07091*
West Long Branch	6,845	07764
West Milford Twp.	17,304	07480
West New York	40,627	07093
West Orange	43,715	07052
West Paterson	11,692	07424
Westwood	11,105	07675
White Horse— Yardville	18,680	08620
White Meadow Lake	8,499	07866
Willingboro Twp.	43,386	08046
Woodbridge Twp.	98,944	07095
Woodbury	12,408	08096
Wood-Ridge	8,311	07075
Wyckoff Twp.	16,039	07481

NEW MEXICO

LOCATION	POPULATION	ZIP
Alamogordo	23,035	88310
Albuquerque	243,751	87101*
Artesia	10,315	88210
Carlsbad	21,297	88220
Clovis	28,495	88101
Deming	8,343	88030
Farmington	21,979	87401
Gallup	14,596	87301
Grants	8,768	87020
Hobbs	26,025	88240
Las Cruces	37,857	88001
Las Vegas	13,835	87701
Los Alamos	11,310	87544
Lovington	8,915	88260
North Valley	10,366	87114
Portales	10,554	88130
Raton	6,962	87740
Roswell	33,908	88201
Santa Fe	41,167	87501
Silver City	8,557	88061
South Valley	29,389	87105
Tucumcari	7,189	88401

NEW YORK

LOCATION	POPULATION	ZIP
Albany	115,781	12201*
Albertson	6,825	11507
Amherst Town	93,929	14226
Amityville	9,794	11701
Amsterdam	25,524	12010
Arlington	11,203	12603

LOCATION	POPULATION	ZIP
Auburn	34,599	13021
Babylon	12,897	11702*
Baldwin	34,525	11510
Baldwinsville	6,298	13027
Batavia	17,338	14020
Bayport	8,232	11705
Bay Shore	11,119	11706
Beacon	13,255	12508
Bellmore	18,431	11710
Bethpage	18,555	11714
Binghamton	64,123	13902*
Bohemia	8,926	11716
Brentwood	28,327	11717
Briarcliff Manor	6,521	10510
Brighton Town	35,065	14610
Brockport	7,878	14420
Bronxville	6,674	10708
Buffalo	462,768	14240*
Canandaigua	10,488	14424
Canton	6,398	13617
Carle Place	6,326	11514
Cedarhurst	6,941	11516
Centereach	9,427	11720
Central Islip	36,391	11722
Cheektowaga Town	113,844	14225
Cohoes	18,653	12047
Colonie	8,701	12205
Commack	24,138	11725
Copiague	19,632	11726
Corning	15,792	14830
Cortland	19,621	13045
Croton-on-Hudson	7,523	10520
Deer Park	32,274	11729
Depew	22,158	14043
De Witt	10,032	13214
Dix Hills	10,050	11746
Dobbs Ferry	10,353	10522
Dunkirk	16,855	14048
East Aurora	7,033	14052
Eastchester	23,750	10709
East Half Hollow Hills	9,691	11746
East Hills	8,624	11576
East Islip	6,861	11730
East Massapequa	15,926	11758
East Meadow	46,290	11554
East Northport	12,392	11731
East Patchogue	8,092	11772
East Rochester	8,347	14445
East Rockaway	11,795	11518
East Vestal	10,472	13850
Elmira	39,945	14902*
Elmont	29,363	11003
Elwood	15,031	11731
Endicott	16,556	13760
Endwell	15,999	13760
Fairmount	15,317	13219
Fairport	6,474	14450
Fairview	8,517	12601
Farmingdale	9,297	11735
Floral Park	18,466	11002*
Franklin Square	32,156	11010
Fredonia	10,326	14063
Freeport	40,374	11520
Fulton	14,003	13069
Garden City	25,373	11530
Garden City Park	7,488	11530
Gates Town	26,442	14606
Geddes Town	21,032	13209
Geneva	16,793	14456
Glen Cove	25,770	11542
Glens Falls	17,222	12801
Gloversville	19,677	12078
Great Neck	10,798	11022*
Greece Town	75,136	14616
Greenburgh Town	85,746	10591
Greenlawn	8,493	11740
Half Hollow Hills	12,081	11746
Hamburg	10,215	14075
Harrison Town	21,509	10528
Hartsdale	12,226	10530
Hastings-on-Hudson	9,479	10706
Hauppauge	13,957	11787
Haverstraw	8,198	10927
Hempstead	39,411	11551*
Herkimer	8,960	13350
Herricks	9,112	11040
Hewlett	6,796	11557
Hicksville	49,820	11802*
Holbrook-Holtsville	12,103	11741
Hornell	12,144	14843
Horseheads	7,989	14845
Hudson	8,940	12534
Hudson Falls	7,917	12839
Huntington	12,601	11743
Huntington Sta.	28,817	11746
Ilion	9,808	13357
Inwood	8,433	11696
Irondequoit Town	63,675	14617
Islip	7,692	11751
Ithaca	26,226	14850
Jamestown	39,795	14701
Jefferson Valley–Yorktown	9,008	10535
Jericho	14,010	11753
Johnson City	18,025	13790
Johnstown	10,045	12095
Kenmore	20,980	14217
Kingston	25,544	12401
Lackawanna	28,657	14218
Lake Grove	8,133	11755
Lancaster	13,365	14086
Larchmont	7,203	10538
Latham	9,661	12110
Lawrence	6,566	11559
Levittown	65,440	11756
Lindenhurst	28,359	11757
Little Falls	7,629	13365
Lockport	25,399	14094
Locust Grove	11,626	11791
Long Beach	33,127	11561
Loudonville	9,299	12211
Lynbrook	23,151	11563
Malone	8,048	12953
Malverne	10,036	11565
Mamaroneck	18,909	10543
Manhasset	8,541	11030
Massapequa	26,821	11758
Massapequa Pk.	22,112	11762
Massena	14,042	13662
Mattydale	8,292	13211
Mechanicville	6,247	12118
Medina	6,415	14103
Melville	6,641	11747
Merrick	25,904	11566
Middletown	22,607	10940
Mineola	21,845	11501
Monsey	8,797	10952
Mount Kisco	8,172	10549
Mount Vernon	72,778	10551*
Nanuet	10,447	10954
Nesconset	10,048	11767
Newark	11,644	14513
Newburgh	26,219	12550
New Cassel	8,721	11590
New City	27,344	10956
New Hyde Park	10,116	11040
New Rochelle	75,385	10802*
New Windsor	8,803	12550
New York City	7,895,563	10001*
Niagara Falls	85,615	14302*
North Amityville	11,936	11701
North Babylon	39,526	11703
North Bellmore	22,893	11710
North Great River	12,080	11739
North Lindenhurst	11,117	11757
North Massapequa	23,123	11758
North Merrick	13,650	11566
North New Hyde Pk.	18,154	11040
Northport	7,494	17768
North Syracuse	8,687	13212
North Tarrytown	8,334	10591
North Tonawanda	36,012	14120
North Valley Str.	14,881	11580
North Wantagh	15,053	11793
Norwich	8,843	13815
Nyack	6,659	10960
Oakdale	7,334	11769
Oceanside	35,372	11572
Ogdensburg	14,554	13669
Old Bethpage	7,084	11804
Olean	19,169	14760
Oneida	11,658	13421
Oneonta	16,030	13820
Orangetown Town	53,533	10960
Ossining	21,659	10562
Oswego	20,913	13126
Oyster Bay	6,822	11771
Patchogue	11,582	11772
Pearl River	17,146	10965
Peekskill	19,283	10566
Pelham Manor	6,673	10803
Plainedge	10,759	11714
Plainview	31,695	11803
Plattsburgh	18,715	12901
Pleasantville	7,110	10570
Port Chester	25,803	10573
Port Jefferson Sta.	7,403	11776
Port Jervis	8,852	12771*
Port Washington	15,923	11050
Potsdam	10,303	13676
Poughkeepsie	32,029	12601*
Rensselaer	10,136	12144
Riverhead	7,585	11901
Rochester	296,233	14603*
Rockville Centre	27,444	11570
Rome	50,148	13440
Ronkonkoma	7,284	11779
Roosevelt	15,008	11575
Roslyn Heights	7,242	11577
Rotterdam	25,214	12303
Rye	15,869	10580
St. James	10,500	11780
Salamanca	7,877	14779
Salina Town	38,281	13208
San Remo	8,302	11754
Saranac Lake	6,086	12983
Saratoga Springs	18,845	12866
Sayville	11,680	11782
Scarsdale	19,229	10583
Schenectady	77,958	12305*
Scotia	7,370	12302
Seaford	17,379	11783
Selden	11,613	11784
Seneca Falls	7,794	13148
Setauket	6,857	11733
Shirley	6,280	11967
Solvay	8,280	13209
South Farmingdale	20,464	11735
South Holbrook	6,700	11741
South Huntington	9,115	11746
Southport	8,685	14904
South Stony Brk.	15,329	11790
South Valley Str.	6,595	11581
South Westbury	10,978	11590
Spring Valley	18,112	10977
Stony Brook	6,391	11790
Stony Point	8,270	10980
Suffern	8,273	10901
Syosset	10,084	11791
Syracuse	197,297	13201*
Tappan	7,424	10983
Tarrytown	11,115	10591
Thornwood	6,874	10594
Tonawanda	21,898	14150
Troy	62,918	12180*
Tuckahoe	6,236	10707
Uniondale	22,077	11553
Utica	91,340	13503*
Valley Stream	40,413	11580*
Vernon Valley	7,925	11768
Vestal	8,303	13850
Wantagh	21,873	11793
Watertown	30,787	13601
Watervliet	12,404	12189
West Amityville	6,424	11701
West Babylon	12,893	11704
Westbury	15,362	11590
West Haverstraw	8,558	10993
West Hempstead	20,375	11552
West Islip	17,334	11795
Westmere	6,364	12203
West Sayville	7,386	11796
West Seneca Town	48,404	14224
Westvale	7,253	13219
White Plains	50,346	10602*
Williamsville	6,835	14221
Williston Park	9,154	11596
Woodmere	19,831	11598
Wyandanch	15,716	11798
Yonkers	204,297	10701*
Yorktown Heights	6,805	10598

NORTH CAROLINA

LOCATION	POPULATION	ZIP
Albemarle	11,126	28001
Asheboro	10,797	27203
Asheville	57,681	28801*
Boone	8,754	28607
Burlington	35,930	27215
Cary	7,686	27511
Chapel Hill	25,537	27514

LOCATION	POPULATION	ZIP
Charlotte	241,178	28202*
Clinton	7,157	28328
Concord	18,464	28025
Dunn	8,302	28334
Durham	95,438	27701*
Eden	15,871	27288
Elizabeth City	14,381	27909
Fayetteville	53,510	28302*
Forest City	7,179	28043
Gastonia	47,142	28052
Goldsboro	26,810	27530
Graham	8,172	27253
Greensboro	144,076	27420*
Greenville	29,063	27834
Henderson	13,896	27536
Hendersonville	6,443	28739
Hickory	20,569	28601
High Point	63,259	27260*
Jacksonville	16,289	28540
Kannapolis	36,293	28081
Kings Mountain	8,465	28086
Kinston	23,020	28501
Laurinburg	8,859	28352
Lenoir	14,705	28645
Lexington	17,205	27292
Lumberton	16,961	28358
Monroe	11,282	28110
Mooresville	8,808	28115
Morganton	13,625	28655
Mount Airy	7,325	27030
New Bern	14,660	28560
New River-Gieger	8,699	28540
Newton	7,857	28658
North Belmont	10,672	28012
Oxford	7,178	27565
Raleigh	123,793	27611*
Reidsville	13,636	27320
Roanoke Rapids	13,508	27870
Rocky Mount	34,284	27801
Salisbury	22,515	28144
Sanford	11,716	27330
Shelby	16,328	28150
Smithfield	6,677	27577
Statesville	20,007	28677
Tarboro	9,425	27886
Thomasville	15,230	27360
Washington	8,961	27889
Waynesville	6,488	28786
Williamston	6,570	27892
Wilmington	46,169	28402*
Wilson	29,347	27893
Winston-Salem	133,683	27102*

NORTH DAKOTA

LOCATION	POPULATION	ZIP
Bismarck	34,703	58501
Devils Lake	7,078	58301
Dickinson	12,405	58601
Fargo	53,365	58102
Grand Forks	39,008	58201
Jamestown	15,385	58401
Mandan	11,093	58554
Minot	32,290	58701
Valley City	7,843	58072
Wahpeton	7,076	58075
Williston	11,280	58801

OHIO

LOCATION	POPULATION	ZIP
Akron	275,425	44309*
Alliance	26,547	44601
Amherst	9,902	44001
Ashland	19,872	44805
Ashtabula	24,313	44004
Athens	24,168	45701
Aurora	6,549	44202
Austintown	29,393	44515
Avon	7,214	44011
Avon Lake	12,261	44012
Barberton	33,052	44203
Bay Village	18,163	44140
Beachwood	9,631	44122
Bedford	17,552	44146
Bedford Heights	13,063	44146
Bellaire	9,655	43906
Bellefontaine	11,255	43311
Bellevue	8,604	44811
Belpre	7,189	45714
Berea	22,465	44017
Bexley	14,888	43209
Blacklick Estates	8,351	43004
Blue Ash	8,324	45242

LOCATION	POPULATION	ZIP
Boardman	30,852	44512
Bowling Green	21,760	43402
Brecksville	9,137	44141
Bridgetown	13,352	45211
Broadview Heights	11,463	44141
Brooklyn	13,142	44144
Brook Park	30,774	44142
Brunswick	15,852	44212
Bryan	7,008	43506
Bucyrus	13,111	44820
Cambridge	13,656	43725
Campbell	12,577	44405
Canton	110,053	44711*
Celina	8,072	45822
Centerville	10,333	45459
Cheviot	11,135	45211
Chillicothe	24,842	45601
Churchill	7,457	44505
Cincinnati	451,455	45202*
Circleville	11,687	43113
Cleveland	750,879	44101*
Cleveland Heights	60,767	44118
Columbus	540,025	43216*
Conneaut	14,552	44030
Coshocton	13,747	43812
Covedale	6,639	45238
Cuyahoga Falls	49,678	44222*
Dayton	242,917	45401*
Deer Park	7,415	45236
Defiance	16,281	43512
Delaware	15,008	43015
Delphos	7,608	45833
Dover	11,516	44622
East Cleveland	39,600	44112
Eastlake	19,690	44094
East Liverpool	20,020	43920
Elyria	53,427	44035*
Englewood	7,885	45322
Euclid	71,552	44117
Fairborn	32,267	45324
Fairfield	14,680	45014
Fairview Park	21,681	44126
Findlay	35,800	45840
Forest Park	15,139	45405
Fort McKinley	11,536	45426
Fostoria	16,037	44830
Franklin	10,075	45005
Fremont	18,490	43420
Gahanna	12,400	43230
Galion	13,123	44833
Gallipolis	7,490	45631
Garfield Heights	41,417	44125
Geneva	6,449	44041
Girard	14,119	44420
Grandview Heights	8,460	43212
Greenville	12,380	45331
Grove City	13,911	43123
Hamilton	67,865	45012*
Heath	6,768	43055
Hilliard	8,369	43026
Hubbard	8,583	44425
Huber Heights	18,943	45424
Huron	6,896	44839
Independence	7,034	44131
Ironton	15,030	45638
Jackson	6,843	45640
Kent	28,183	44240
Kenton	8,315	43326
Kenwood	15,789	45236
Kettering	71,864	45429
Lakewood	70,173	44107
Lancaster	32,911	43130
Lebanon	7,934	45036
Lima	53,734	45801*
Lincoln Village	11,215	43228
Logan	6,269	43138
London	6,481	43140
Lorain	78,185	44052*
Louisville	6,298	44641
Loveland	7,144	45140
Lyndhurst	19,749	44124
Macedonia	6,375	44056
Madeira	6,713	45243
Mansfield	55,047	44901*
Maple Heights	34,093	44137
Marietta	16,861	45750
Marion	38,646	43302
Martins Ferry	10,757	43935
Massillon	32,539	44646
Maumee	15,937	43537
Mayfield Heights	22,139	44124

LOCATION	POPULATION	ZIP
Medina	10,913	44256
Mentor	36,912	44060
Mentor-on-the-Lake	6,517	44060
Miamisburg	14,797	45342
Middleburg Hts.	12,367	44017
Middletown	48,767	45042
Mount Healthy	7,446	45231
Mount Vernon	13,373	43050
Napoleon	7,791	43545
Newark	41,836	43055
New Philadelphia	15,184	44663
Niles	21,581	44446
North Canton	15,228	44720
North College Hill	12,363	45239
North Madison	6,882	44057
North Olmsted	34,861	44070
Northridge	10,084	45414
North Ridgeville	13,152	44035
North Royalton	12,807	44133
Norton	12,308	44203
Norwalk	13,386	44857
Norwood	30,420	45212
Oakwood	10,095	45419
Oberlin	8,761	44074
Oregon	16,563	43616
Orrville	7,408	44667
Overlook-Page Manor	19,719	45431
Oxford	15,868	45056
Painesville	16,536	44077
Parma	100,216	44129
Parma Heights	27,192	44130
Perrysburg	7,693	43551
Piqua	20,741	45356
Port Clinton	7,202	43452
Portsmouth	27,633	45662
Ravenna	11,780	44266
Reading	14,617	45215
Reynoldsburg	13,921	43068
Richmond Hts.	9,220	44143
Rittman	6,308	44270
Rocky River	22,958	44116
St. Marys	7,699	45885
Salem	14,186	44460
Sandusky	32,674	44870
Seven Hills	12,700	44131
Shaker Heights	36,306	44120
Sharonville	11,393	45241
Sheffield Lake	8,734	44054
Shelby	9,847	44875
Shiloh	11,368	45426
Sidney	16,332	45365
Silverton	6,588	45201
Solon	11,519	44139
South Euclid	29,579	44121
Springdale	8,127	45246
Springfield	81,941	45501*
Steubenville	30,771	43952
Stow	19,847	44224
Streetsboro	7,966	44240
Strongsville	15,182	44136
Struthers	15,343	44471
Sylvania	12,031	43560
Tallmadge	15,274	44278
Tiffin	21,596	44883
Toledo	383,105	43601*
Toronto	7,705	43964
Trotwood	6,997	45426
Troy	17,186	45373
Twinsburg	6,432	44087
University Hts.	17,055	44118
Upper Arlington	38,727	43221
Urbana	11,237	43078
Vandalia	10,796	45377
Van Wert	11,320	45891
Vermilion	9,872	44089
Wadsworth	13,142	44281
Wapakoneta	7,324	45895
Warren	63,494	44482*
Warrensville Hts.	18,925	44128
Washington	12,495	43160
West Carrollton	10,748	45449
Westerville	12,530	43081
Westlake	15,689	44145
Whitehall	25,263	43213
Wickliffe	21,354	44092
Willoughby	18,634	44094
Willowick	21,237	44094
Wilmington	10,051	45177
Wooster	18,703	44691
Worthington	15,326	43085

LOCATION	POPULATION	ZIP
Wyoming	9,089	45215
Xenia	25,373	45385
Youngstown	140,909	44501*
Zanesville	33,045	43701

OKLAHOMA

LOCATION	POPULATION	ZIP
Ada	14,859	74820
Altus	23,302	73521
Alva	7,440	73717
Anadarko	6,682	73005
Ardmore	21,915	73401
Bartlesville	29,683	74003
Bethany	22,694	73008
Blackwell	8,645	74631
Broken Arrow	11,787	74012
Chickasha	14,194	73018
Claremore	9,084	74017
Clinton	8,513	73601
Cushing	7,529	74023
Del City	27,133	73115
Duncan	19,718	73533
Durant	11,118	74701
Edmond	16,633	73034
Elk City	7,323	73644
El Reno	14,510	73036
Enid	44,986	73701
Guthrie	9,575	73044
Guymon	7,674	73942
Henryetta	6,430	74437
Hugo	6,585	74743
Lawton	74,470	73501*
McAlester	18,802	74501
Miami	13,880	74354
Midwest City	48,212	73110
Moore	18,761	73160
Muskogee	37,331	74401
Norman	52,117	73069*
Oklahoma City	368,377	73125*
Okmulgee	15,180	74447
Ponca City	25,940	74601
Pryor	7,057	74361
Sand Springs	10,565	74063
Sapulpa	15,159	74066
Seminole	7,878	74868
Shawnee	25,075	74801
Stillwater	31,126	74074
Tahlequah	9,254	74464
The Village	13,695	73120
Tulsa	330,350	74101*
Warr Acres	9,887	73132
Weatherford	7,959	73096
Woodward	9,412	73801
Yukon	8,411	73099

OREGON

LOCATION	POPULATION	ZIP
Albany	18,181	97321
Altamont	15,746	97601
Ashland	12,342	97520
Astoria	10,244	97103
Baker	9,354	97814
Beaverton	18,577	97005
Bend	13,710	97701
Coos Bay	13,466	97420
Corvallis	35,056	97330
Dallas	6,361	97338
Eugene	79,028	97401*
Forest Grove	8,275	97116
Gladstone	6,254	97027
Grants Pass	12,455	97526
Gresham	10,030	97030
Hillsboro	14,675	97123
Keizer	11,405	97303
Klamath Falls	15,775	97601
La Grande	9,645	97850
Lake Oswego	14,615	97034
Lebanon	6,636	97355
McMinnville	10,125	97128
Medford	28,454	97501
Milwaukie	16,444	97222
Newberg	6,507	97132
North Bend	8,553	97459
Ontario	6,523	97914
Oregon City	9,176	97045
Pendleton	13,197	97801
Portland	379,967	97208*
Roseburg	14,461	97470
St. Helens	6,212	97051
Salem	68,480	97301*
Springfield	26,874	97477
The Dalles	10,423	97058

LOCATION	POPULATION	ZIP
West Linn	7,091	97068
Woodburn	7,495	97071

PENNSYLVANIA

LOCATION	POPULATION	ZIP
Abington Twp.	62,786	19001
Aliquippa	22,277	15001
Allentown	109,871	18105*
Altoona	63,115	16603*
Ambler	7,800	19002
Ambridge	11,324	15003
Arnold	8,174	15068
Avalon	7,010	15202
Bala Cynwyd	6,483	19004
Baldwin	26,729	15208
Beaver Falls	14,375	15010
Bellefonte	6,828	16823
Bellevue	11,586	15202
Berwick	12,274	18603
Bethel Park	34,791	15102
Bethlehem	72,686	18015*
Blakely	6,391	18447
Bloomsburg	11,652	17815
Braddock	8,795	15104
Bradford	12,672	16701
Brandywine Village	11,411	19406
Brentwood	13,732	15227
Bridgeville	6,717	15017
Bristol	12,085	19007
Brookhaven	7,370	19015
Butler	18,691	16001
California	6,635	15419
Camp Hill	9,931	17011
Canonsburg	11,439	15317
Carbondale	12,808	18407
Carlisle	18,079	17013
Carnegie	10,864	15106
Carnot—Moon	13,093	15108
Castle Shannon	11,899	15234
Cedarbrook	9,980	19095
Cedar Heights	6,326	19428
Chambersburg	17,315	17201
Charleroi	6,723	15022
Chatwood	7,168	19380
Chester	56,331	19013*
Clairton	15,051	15025
Clearfield	8,176	16830
Clifton Heights	8,348	19018
Coatesville	12,331	19320
Collingdale	10,605	19023
Columbia	11,237	17512
Connellsville	11,643	15425
Conshohocken	10,195	19428
Coraopolis	8,435	15108
Corry	7,435	16407
Crafton	8,233	15205
Darby	13,729	19023
Dickson City	7,698	18519
Donora	8,825	15033
Dormont	12,856	15216
Downingtown	7,437	19335
Doylestown	8,270	18901
DuBois	10,112	15801
Dunmore	17,300	18512
Duquesne	11,410	15110
Easton	29,450	18042
East Stroudsburg	7,894	18301
Economy	7,176	15005
Elizabethtown	8,072	17022
Ellwood City	10,857	16117
Emmaus	11,511	18049
Ephrata	9,662	17522
Erie	129,231	16501*
Farrell	11,022	16121
Flourtown	9,149	19031
Folcroft	9,610	19032
Forest Hills	9,561	15221
Franklin	8,629	16323
Fullerton	7,908	18052
Gettysburg	7,275	17325
Glassport	7,450	15045
Glenolden	8,697	19036
Glenside	17,353	19038
Greensburg	17,077	15601
Green Tree	6,441	15242
Greenville	8,704	16125
Grove City	8,312	16127
Hanover	15,623	17331
Harrisburg	68,061	17105*
Hatboro	8,880	19040
Hazleton	30,426	18201

LOCATION	POPULATION	ZIP
Hellertown	6,615	18055
Hershey	7,407	17033
Hollidaysburg	6,262	16648
Home Acre-Lyndora	8,415	16045
Homestead	6,309	15120
Huntingdon	6,987	16652
Indiana	16,100	15701
Jeannette	15,209	15644
Jefferson	8,512	15344
Jefferson-Trooper	13,022	19401
Johnstown	42,476	15901*
Kingston	18,325	18704
Kittanning	6,231	16201
Lafayette Hills-Plymouth Meeting	8,275	19444
Lancaster	57,690	17604*
Lansdale	18,451	19446
Lansdowne	14,090	19050
Latrobe	11,749	15650
Lebanon	28,572	17042
Lewisburg	6,376	17837
Lewistown	11,098	17044
Lititz	7,072	17543
Lock Haven	11,427	17745
Lower Burrell	13,654	15068
Mahanoy City	7,257	17948
McKeesport	37,977	15134*
McKees Rocks	11,901	15136
Meadville	16,573	16335
Mechanicsburg	9,385	17055
Media	6,444	19063*
Middletown	9,080	17057
Millersville	6,396	17551
Milton	7,723	17847
Monaca	7,486	15061
Monessen	15,216	15062
Monongahela	7,113	15063
Monroeville	29,011	15146
Morrisville	11,309	19067
Mount Carmel	9,317	17851
Munhall	16,574	15120
Nanticoke	14,632	18634
New Brighton	7,637	15066
New Castle	38,559	16101*
New Cumberland	9,803	17070
New Kensington	20,312	15068
Norristown	38,169	19401*
Northampton	8,389	18067
North Braddock	10,838	15104
North Hills	13,096	19038
Norwood	7,229	19074
Oakmont	7,550	15139
Oil City	15,033	16301
Old Forge	9,522	18518
Oreland	9,261	19075
Palmyra	7,615	17078
Pencoyd	6,650	19004
Penn Sq.–Plymouth Valley	7,020	19401
Philadelphia	1,949,996	19104*
Phoenixville	14,823	19460
Pittsburgh	520,117	15230*
Pittston	11,113	18640*
Plains	6,606	18701
Pleasant Hills	10,409	15236
Plum	21,922	15239
Plymouth	9,536	18651
Pottstown	25,355	19464
Pottsville	19,715	17901
Prospect Park	7,250	19076
Punxsutawney	7,792	15767
Quakertown	7,276	18951
Reading	87,643	19603*
Ridley Park	9,025	19078
Roslyn	18,380	19001
St. Marys	7,470	15857
Sayre	7,473	18840
Scranton	103,564	18501*
Shamokin	11,719	17872
Sharon	22,653	16146
Sharon Hill	7,464	19079
Shenandoah	8,287	17976
Shillington	6,249	19607
Shippensburg	6,536	17257
Somerset	6,269	15501
Souderton	6,366	18964
South Williamsport	7,153	17701
State College	33,778	16801
Steelton	8,556	17113
Sunbury	13,025	17801
Swissvale	13,819	15218

LOCATION	POPULATION	ZIP
Swoyersville	6,786	18704
Tamaqua	9,246	18252
Tarentum	7,379	15084
Taylor	6,977	18517
Titusville	7,331	16354
Turtle Creek	8,308	15145
Tyrone	7,072	16686
Uniontown	16,282	15401
Vandergrift	7,889	15690
Warren	12,998	16365
Washington	19,827	15301
Waynesboro	10,011	17268
West Chester	19,301	19380
West Mifflin	28,070	15122
Westmont	6,673	15905
West Pittston	7,074	18643
West View	8,312	15229
Whitehall	16,551	15234
White Oak	9,304	15131
Wilkes-Barre	58,856	18703*
Wilkinsburg	26,780	15221
Williamsport	37,918	17701
Willow Grove	16,494	19090
Wilson	8,406	15025
Wyomissing	7,136	19610
Yeadon	12,136	19050
York	50,335	17405*

PUERTO RICO

Aguadilla	21,031	00603
Aibonito	7,582	00609
Arecibo	35,484	00612
Bayamón	147,552	00619
Cabo Rojo	7,181	00623
Caguas	63,215	00625
Carolina	94,271	00630
Cataño	26,459	00632
Cayey	21,562	00633
Cidra	6,306	00639
Coamo	12,077	00640
Comerio	6,297	00642
Fajardo	18,249	00648
Guánica	8,979	00653
Guayama	20,318	00654
Guaynabo	55,310	00657
Guarbo	6,290	00658
Hormigueros	6,531	00660
Humacao	12,411	00661
Isabela	9,515	00662
Juana Díaz	8,765	00665
Juncos	7,985	00666
Levittown	17,079	00632
Manati	13,483	00701
Mayagüez	68,872	00708
Ponce	128,233	00731
San Germán	11,613	00753
San Juan	452,749	00936*
San Lorenzo	7,702	00754
San Sebastián	7,169	00755
Trujillo Alto	18,477	00760
Utuado	11,573	00761
Vega Alta	8,688	00762
Vega Baja	17,089	00763
Yauco	12,922	00768

RHODE ISLAND

Barrington	17,554	02806
Bristol	17,860	02809
Burrillville	10,087	02830
Central Falls	18,716	02863
Coventry	22,947	02816
Cranston	74,287	02910
Cumberland	26,605	02864
East Greenwich	9,577	02818
East Providence	48,207	02914
Johnston	22,037	02919
Lincoln	16,182	02865
Middletown	29,290	02840
Narragansett	7,138	02882
Newport	34,562	02840
North Kingstown	29,793	02852
North Providence	24,337	02908
North Smithfield	9,349	02876
Pawtucket	76,984	02860*
Portsmouth	12,521	02871
Providence	179,116	02940*
Scituate	7,489	02857
Smithfield	13,468	02917
South Kingstown	16,913	02879

LOCATION	POPULATION	ZIP
Tiverton	12,559	02878
Wakefield	6,331	02880*
Warren	10,523	02885
Warwick	83,694	02887*
Westerly	17,248	02891
West Warwick	24,323	02893
Woonsocket	46,820	02895

SOUTH CAROLINA

Aiken	13,436	29801
Anderson	27,556	29621*
Beaufort	9,434	29902
Bennettsville	7,468	29512
Berea	7,186	29611
Camden	8,532	29020
Cayce	9,967	29033
Charleston	66,945	29401*
Chester	7,045	29706
Clinton	8,138	29325
Columbia	113,542	29201*
Conway	8,151	29526
Darlington	6,990	29532
Dillon	6,391	29536
Easley	11,175	29640
Florence	25,997	29501
Forest Acres	6,808	29206
Gaffney	13,253	29340
Gantt	11,386	29609
Georgetown	10,449	29440
Greenville	61,436	29602*
Greenwood	21,069	29646
Greer	10,642	29651
Hanahan	9,118	29410
Hartsville	8,017	29550
Lake City	6,247	29560
Lancaster	9,186	29720
Laurens	10,298	29360
Marion	7,435	29571
Mount Pleasant	6,879	29464
Myrtle Beach	9,035	29577
Newberry	9,218	29108
North Augusta	12,883	29841
North Charleston	53,617	29406
Orangeburg	13,252	29115
Rock Hill	33,846	29730
St. Andrews	9,202	29407
Seneca	6,382	29678
Shannontown	7,491	29150
Spartanburg	44,546	29301*
Sumter	24,555	29150
Taylors	6,831	29687
Union	10,775	29379
Wade-Hampton	17,152	29607
Walterboro	6,257	29488
West Columbia	7,838	29169

SOUTH DAKOTA

Aberdeen	26,476	57401
Brookings	13,717	57006
Huron	14,299	57350
Madison	6,315	57042
Mitchell	13,425	57301
Pierre	9,699	57501
Rapid City	43,836	57701
Sioux Falls	72,488	57101*
Vermillion	9,128	57069
Watertown	13,388	57201
Yankton	11,919	57078

TENNESSEE

Alcoa	7,739	37701
Athens	11,790	37303
Bolivar	6,674	38008
Bristol	20,064	37620
Brownsville	7,011	38012
Chattanooga	119,923	37401*
Clarksville	31,719	37040
Cleveland	20,651	37311
Columbia	21,471	38401
Cookeville	14,270	38501
Dyersburg	14,523	38024
East Ridge	21,799	37412
Elizabethton	12,269	37643
Fayetteville	7,030	37334
Franklin	9,497	37064
Gallatin	13,271	37066
Greeneville	13,722	37743
Harriman	8,734	37748
Hendersonville	14,699	37075
Humboldt	10,066	38343

LOCATION	POPULATION	ZIP
Jackson	39,996	38301
Johnson City	33,770	37601
Kingsport	31,938	37662*
Knoxville	174,587	37901*
La Follette	6,902	37766
Lake Hills– Murray Hills	7,806	37401
Lawrenceburg	8,889	38464
Lebanon	12,492	37087
Lewisburg	7,207	37091
McMinnville	10,662	37110
Martin	7,781	38237
Maryville	13,808	37801
Memphis	623,530	38101*
Milan	7,313	38358
Millington	21,177	38053
Morristown	20,318	37814
Murfreesboro	26,360	37130
Nashville	447,877	37202*
Newport	7,328	37821
Oak Ridge	28,319	37830
Paris	9,892	38242
Pulaski	6,989	38478
Red Bank	12,715	37415
Shelbyville	12,262	37160
Soddy-Daisy	7,569	37319
Springfield	9,720	37172
Tullahoma	15,311	37388
Union City	11,925	38261

TEXAS

Abilene	89,653	79604*
Alamo Heights	6,933	78209
Alice	20,121	78332
Alvin	10,671	77511
Amarillo	127,010	79105*
Andrews	8,625	79714
Angleton	9,770	77515
Arlington	90,032	76010*
Athens	9,582	75751
Austin	251,808	78767*
Balch Springs	10,464	75180
Bay City	13,445	77414
Baytown	43,980	77520*
Beaumont	117,548	77704*
Bedford	10,049	76021
Beeville	13,506	78102
Bellaire	19,009	77401
Bellmead	7,698	76704
Belton	8,696	76513
Benbrook	8,169	76126
Big Spring	28,735	79720
Bonham	7,698	75418
Borger	14,195	79007
Brenham	8,922	77833
Brownfield	9,647	79316
Brownsville	52,522	78520*
Brownwood	17,368	76801
Bryan	33,719	77801
Burkburnett	9,230	76354
Burleson	7,713	76028
Canyon	8,333	79015
Carrollton	13,855	75006*
Cleburne	16,015	76031
College Station	17,676	77840
Commerce	9,534	75428
Conroe	11,969	77301*
Copperas Cove	10,818	76522
Corpus Christi	204,525	78408*
Corsicana	19,972	75110
Crockett	6,616	75835
Crystal City	8,104	78839
Cuero	6,956	77954
Dallas	844,401	75221*
Deer Park	12,773	77536
Del Rio	21,330	78840
Denison	24,923	75020
Denton	39,874	76201
De Soto	6,617	75115
Dickinson	10,776	77539
Donna	7,365	78537
Dumas	9,771	79029
Duncanville	14,105	75116*
Eagle Pass	15,364	78852
Edinburg	17,163	78539
El Campo	9,332	77437
El Paso	322,261	79940*
Ennis	11,724	75119
Euless	19,316	76039
Falfurrias	6,375	78355

LOCATION	POPULATION	ZIP
Farmers Branch	27,492	75234
Forest Hill	8,236	76119
Fort Stockton	8,283	79735
Fort Worth	393,476	76101*
Freeport	11,997	77541
Gainesville	13,830	76240
Galena Park	10,479	77547
Galveston	61,809	77550*
Garland	81,437	75040*
Georgetown	6,395	78626
Graham	7,477	76046
Grand Prairie	50,904	75050*
Grapevine	7,023	76051
Greenville	22,043	75401
Groves	18,067	77619
Haltom City	28,127	76117
Harlingen	33,503	78550
Henderson	10,187	75652
Hereford	13,414	79045
Highland Park	10,133	75205
Hillsboro	7,224	76645
Houston	1,232,802	77052*
Huntsville	17,610	77340
Hurst	27,215	76053
Irving	97,260	75061*
Jacinto City	9,563	77029
Jacksonville	9,734	75766
Jasper	6,251	75951
Kermit	7,884	79745
Kerrville	12,672	78028
Kilgore	9,495	75662
Killeen	35,507	76541
Kingsville	28,915	78363
Lake Jackson	13,376	77566
La Marque	16,131	77568
Lamesa	11,559	79331
Lancaster	10,522	75146*
La Porte	7,149	77571
Laredo	69,024	78040*
League City	10,818	77573
Levelland	11,445	79336
Lewisville	9,264	75067*
Littlefield	6,738	79339
Lockhart	6,489	78644
Longview	45,547	75601*
Lubbock	149,101	79408*
Lufkin	23,049	75901
Marlin	6,351	76661
Marshall	22,937	75670
McAllen	37,636	78501
McKinney	15,193	75069
Mercedes	9,355	78570
Mesquite	55,131	75149*
Midland	59,463	79701*
Mineral Wells	18,411	76067
Mission	13,043	78572
Monahans	8,333	79756
Mount Pleasant	9,459	75455
Nacogdoches	22,544	75961
Nederland	16,810	77627
New Braunfels	17,859	78130
North Richland Hills	16,514	76118
Odessa	78,380	79760*
Orange	24,457	77630
Palestine	14,525	75801
Pampa	21,726	79065
Paris	23,441	75460
Pasadena	89,277	77501*
Pearland	6,444	77581
Pecos	12,682	79772
Perryton	7,810	79070
Pharr	15,829	78577
Plainview	19,096	79072
Plano	17,872	75074*
Port Arthur	57,371	77640
Portland	7,302	78374
Port Lavaca	10,491	77979
Port Neches	10,894	77651
Raymondville	7,987	78580
Richardson	48,582	75080*
Richland Hills	8,865	76118
River Oaks	8,193	77019
Robstown	11,217	78380
Rosenberg	12,098	77471
San Angelo	63,884	76901*
San Antonio	654,153	78205*
San Benito	15,176	78586
San Marcos	18,860	78666
Seguin	15,934	78155
Sherman	29,061	75090
Silsbee	7,271	77656
Slaton	6,583	79364
Snyder	11,171	79549
South Houston	11,527	77587
Stephenville	9,277	76401
Sulphur Springs	10,642	75482
Sweetwater	12,020	79556
Taylor	9,616	76574
Temple	33,431	76501
Terrell	14,182	75160
Texarkana	30,497	75501*
Texas City	38,908	77590
Tyler	57,770	75701*
Universal City	7,613	78148
University Park	23,498	75205
Uvalde	10,764	78801
Vernon	11,454	76384
Victoria	41,349	77901
Vidor	9,738	77662
Waco	95,326	76703*
Waxahachie	13,452	75165
Weatherford	11,750	76086
Weslaco	15,313	78596
West University Pl.	13,317	77005
Wharton	7,881	77488
White Settlement	13,449	76108
Wichita Falls	96,265	76307*

UTAH

LOCATION	POPULATION	ZIP
American Fork	7,713	84003
Bountiful	27,751	84010
Brigham City	14,007	84302
Cedar City	8,946	84720
Clearfield	13,316	84015
Cottonwood	8,404	84121
East Millcreek	26,579	84109
Granite Park	9,573	84115
Holladay	23,014	84117
Hunter	9,029	84120
Kearns	17,247	84118
Layton	13,603	84041
Logan	22,333	84321
Midvale	7,840	84047
Murray	21,206	84107
Ogden	69,478	84401*
Orem	25,729	84057
Price	6,218	84501
Provo	53,131	84601
Roy	14,356	84067
St. George	7,097	84770
Salt Lake City	175,885	84101*
Sandy	6,438	84070
South Ogden	9,991	84403
South Salt Lake	7,810	84115
Spanish Fork	7,284	84660
Springville	8,790	84663
Sunset	6,268	84015
Tooele	12,539	84074
Washington Terr.	7,241	84403
White City	6,402	84070

VERMONT

LOCATION	POPULATION	ZIP
Barre	10,209	05641
Bennington	14,586	05201
Brattleboro	12,239	05301
Burlington	38,633	05401
Colchester	8,776	05446
Essex	10,951	05451
Essex Junction	6,511	05452
Hartford	6,477	05047
Middlebury	6,532	05753
Montpelier	8,609	05602
Rutland	19,293	05701
St. Albans	8,082	05478
St. Johnsbury	8,409	05819
South Burlington	10,032	05401
Springfield	10,063	05156
Winooski	7,309	05404

VIRGINIA

LOCATION	POPULATION	ZIP
Alexandria	110,927	22313*
Annandale	27,405	22003
Arlington	174,284	22210*
Bailey's Crossroads	7,295	22041
Belleview	8,299	22307
Blacksburg	9,384	24060
Bon Air	10,771	23235
Bristol	20,124	24201
Buena Vista	6,425	24416
Charlottesville	38,880	22906*
Chesapeake	89,580	23320*
Christiansburg	7,857	24073
Colonial Heights	15,097	23834
Covington	10,060	24426
Dale City	13,857	22193
Danville	46,391	24541
Fairfax	22,009	22030
Falls Church	10,772	22046
Franklin	6,880	23851
Fredericksburg	14,450	22401
Front Royal	8,211	22630
Galax	6,278	24333
Groveton	11,761	22306
Hampton	120,779	23369*
Harrisonburg	14,605	22801
Highland Springs	7,345	23075
Hopewell	23,471	23860
Jefferson	25,432	22042
Lake Barcroft	11,605	22041
Lakeside	11,137	23228
Lexington	7,597	24450
Lincolnia	10,761	22313
Long Branch	21,634	22030
Lynchburg	54,083	24505*
Manassas	9,164	22110
Manassas Park	6,844	22110
Mantua	6,911	22030
Marion	8,158	24354
Martinsville	19,653	24112*
McLean	17,698	22101*
Newport News	138,177	23607*
Norfolk	307,951	23501*
North Springfield	8,631	22151
Petersburg	44,124	23803
Portsmouth	110,963	23705*
Pulaski	10,279	24301
Radford	11,596	24141
Richmond	249,431	23232*
Roanoke	92,115	24001*
Rose Hill	14,492	22310
Salem	21,982	24153
South Boston	6,889	24592
Springfield	11,613	22150*
Staunton	24,504	24401
Sterling Park	8,321	22170
Suffolk	45,024	23432*
Vienna	17,146	22180
Vinton	6,347	24179
Virginia Beach	172,106	23458*
Waynesboro	16,707	22980
West Springfield	14,143	22153
Williamsburg	9,069	23185
Winchester	19,429	22601
Woodbridge	25,412	22191*

VIRGIN ISLANDS

LOCATION	POPULATION	ZIP
Charlotte Amalie	12,220	00801

WASHINGTON

LOCATION	POPULATION	ZIP
Aberdeen	18,489	98520
Anacortes	7,701	98221
Auburn	21,653	98002
Bellevue	61,196	98009*
Bellingham	39,375	98225
Bremerton	35,307	98310
Centralia	10,054	98531
Cheney	6,358	99004
Clarkston	6,312	99403
Dishman	9,079	99213
Edmonds	23,998	98020
Ellensburg	13,568	98926
Everett	53,622	98201*
Hoquiam	10,466	98550
Kelso	10,296	98626
Kennewick	15,212	99336
Kent	16,596	98031
Kirkland	15,070	98033
Lacey	9,696	98503
Longview	28,373	98632
Lynnwood	16,919	98036
Mercer Island	19,819	98040
Moses Lake	10,310	98837
Mountlake Terr.	16,600	98043
Mount Vernon	8,804	98273
Oak Harbor	9,167	98277
Olympia	23,296	98501*
Opportunity	16,604	99214
Parkland	21,012	98444
Pasco	13,920	99301

LOCATION	POPULATION	ZIP
Port Angeles	16,367	98362
Pullman	20,509	99163
Puyallup	14,742	98371
Redmond	11,020	98052
Renton	25,878	98055
Richland	26,290	99352
Seattle	530,831	98101*
Shelton	6,515	98584
Spokane	170,516	99210*
Sunnyside	6,751	98944
Tacoma	154,407	98402*
Town and Country	6,484	99218
University Place	13,230	98416
Vancouver	41,859	98660*
Walla Walla	23,619	99362
Wenatchee	16,912	98801
Yakima	45,588	98901*

WEST VIRGINIA

LOCATION	POPULATION	ZIP
Beckley	19,884	25801
Bluefield	15,921	24701
Buckhannon	7,261	26201
Charleston	71,505	25301
Clarksburg	24,864	26301
Dunbar	9,151	25064
Elkins	8,287	26241
Fairmont	26,093	26554
Grafton	6,433	26354
Huntington	74,315	25701*
Keyser	6,586	26726
Martinsburg	14,626	25401
Morgantown	29,431	26505
Moundsville	13,560	26041
New Martinsville	6,528	26155
Nitro	8,019	25143
Parkersburg	44,208	26101
Princeton	7,253	24740
St. Albans	14,356	25177
South Charleston	16,333	25303
Vienna	11,549	26105
Weirton	27,131	26062
Weston	7,323	26452
Wheeling	48,188	26003

LOCATION	POPULATION	ZIP
WISCONSIN		
Allouez	13,753	54301
Antigo	9,005	54409
Appleton	56,377	54911
Ashland	9,615	54806
Ashwaubenon	9,323	54304
Baraboo	7,931	53913
Beaver Dam	14,265	53916
Beloit	35,729	53511
Brookfield	32,140	53005
Brown Deer	12,582	53209
Burlington	7,479	53105
Cedarburg	7,697	53012
Chippewa Falls	12,351	54729
Cudahy	22,078	53110
De Pere	13,309	54115
Eau Claire	44,619	54701
Elm Grove	7,201	53122
Fond du Lac	35,515	54935
Fort Atkinson	9,164	53538
Fox Point	7,939	53201
Franklin	12,247	53132
Germantown	6,974	53022
Glendale	13,426	53209
Green Bay	87,809	54305*
Greendale	15,089	53129
Greenfield	24,424	53220
Hales Corners	7,771	53130
Janesville	46,426	53545
Kaukauna	11,308	54130
Kenosha	78,805	53141*
Kimberly	6,131	54136
La Crosse	51,153	54601
Madison	171,769	53703*
Manitowoc	33,430	54220
Marinette	12,696	54143
Marshfield	15,619	54449
Menasha	14,836	54952
Menomonee Falls	31,697	53051
Menomonie	11,112	54751
Mequon	12,150	53092
Merrill	9,502	54452
Middleton	8,286	53562
Milwaukee	717,372	53201*
Monona	10,420	53716
Monroe	8,654	53566

LOCATION	POPULATION	ZIP
Muskego	11,573	53150
Neenah	22,902	54956
New Berlin	26,910	53151
Oak Creek	13,928	53154
Oconomowoc	8,741	53066
Oshkosh	53,082	54901
Platteville	9,599	53818
Portage	7,821	53901
Port Washington	8,752	53074
Racine	95,162	53401*
Rhinelander	8,218	54501
Rice Lake	7,278	54868
Ripon	7,053	54971
River Falls	7,238	54022
St. Francis	10,489	53207
Shawano	6,488	54166
Sheboygan	48,484	53081
Shorewood	15,576	53211
South Milwaukee	23,297	53172
Sparta	6,258	54656
Stevens Point	23,479	54481
Sturgeon Bay	6,776	54235
Sun Prairie	9,935	53590
Superior	32,237	54880
Two Rivers	13,553	54241
Watertown	15,683	53094
Waukesha	39,695	53186
Waupun	7,946	53963
Wausau	32,806	54401
Wauwatosa	58,676	53226
West Allis	71,649	53214
West Bend	16,555	53095
Whitefish Bay	17,402	53217
Whitewater	12,038	53190
Wisconsin Rapids	18,587	54494
WYOMING		
Casper	39,361	82601
Cheyenne	40,914	82001
Gillette	7,194	82716
Lander	7,125	82520
Laramie	23,143	82070
Rawlins	7,855	82301
Riverton	7,995	82501
Rock Springs	11,657	82901
Sheridan	10,856	82801

BIRTHSTONES

Source: Jewelry Industry Council

January	Garnet	July	Ruby, star ruby
February	Amethyst	August	Peridot, sardonyx
March	Aquamarine, bloodstone	September	Sapphire, star sapphire
April	Diamond	October	Opal, tourmaline
May	Emerald	November	Topaz
June	Pearl, alexandrite, moonstone	December	Turquoise, zircon

FLOWERS OF THE MONTH

Source: Society of American Florists, Alexandria, Va. in conjunction with Red Book Magazine 1977

January	Carnation	July	Larkspur (Delphinium)
February	Violet	August	Gladiolus
March	Daffodil	September	Aster
April	Sweet Pea	October	Calendula (Pot Marigold)
May	Lily of the Valley	November	Chrysanthemum
June	Rose	December	Narcissus

WEDDING ANNIVERSARY GIFTS

Anniversary	Traditional	Modern	Anniversary	Traditional	Modern
1	Paper / Plastics	Clocks	11	Steel	Fashion jewelry or accessories
2	Cotton / Calico / Straw	China	12	Silk or nylon / Linen	Pearl or colored gen
3	Leather or leatherlike items	Crystal or glass	13	Lace	Textiles / Furs
4	Fruit / Flowers / Books; also Linen / Silk or synthetic silks	Electrical appliance	14	Ivory / Agate	Gold jewelry
			15	Crystal or glass	Watch
5	Wood / Decorative home accessories	Silverware	20	China / Occasional furniture	Platinum
6	Candy or sugar / Iron	Wood	25	Silver	Silver
7	Wool / Copper, brass, or bronze	Desk set / Pen and pencil set	30	Pearl / Personal gifts	Diamond
			35	Coral / Jade	Jade
8	Bronze / Pottery / Rubber; also Electrical appliances	Linens / Lace	40	Ruby / Garnet	Ruby
			45	Sapphire	Sapphire
9	Pottery / Willow / China, glass, or crystal	Leather	50	Gold	Gold
			55	Emerald / Turquoise	Emerald
			60	Diamond / Gold	Diamond / Gold
10	Tin or aluminum	Diamond jewelry	75	Diamond / Gold	Diamond / Gold

HISTORY: ANCIENT/MODERN

PRESENT MONARCHS AND DYNASTIES

AFRICA

°*Central African Empire—Dynasty:* President Jean-Bedel Bokassa formally crowned himself emperor on December 4, 1977, in an elaborate coronation ceremony estimated to have cost $30,000,000. **Monarch:** Emperor Bokassa I **Born:** February 22, 1921 **Married:** Empress Catherine, born Catherine Dengueade. Two other wives **Children:** Prince Georges Bokassa, Prince Jean-Bedel Georges (b. 1975), St. Jean de Bokassa (b. 1977), Martine. Thirty children are reported altogether. **Heir:** Prince Jean-Bedel Georges. **Religion:** Roman Catholic.

Lesotho—Dynasty: Before independence, the people of Lesotho accepted the authority of the "Paramount Chief" of the House of Moshesh. With independence (October 1966), Moshoeshoe II of the Moshesh became head of state. **Monarch:** Moshoeshoe II ascended the throne in October 1966. In "voluntary exile" Feb.-Dec. 1970. **Born:** May 2, 1938 **Married:** Tabitha' Masentle Lerotholi Mojela **Children:** Two sons, one daughter **Heir:** Crown Prince David Letsie (b. 1963) **Religion:** Christian

Morocco—Dynasty: The Alaouite dynasty (Filali) has ruled Morocco since the 17th century. The country has been ruled by constitutional kings since independence (1956), and in 1957 King Mohammed V changed his title from "His Sherifian Majesty, the Sultan" to "His Majesty, the King of Morocco." **Monarch:** King Hassan II, son of Mohammed V, ascended the throne on March 3, 1961, following the death of his father on February 26, 1961. **Born:** July 9, 1929 **Married:** Lalla Latifa **Children:** One son and three daughters **Heir:** Crown Prince Sidi Mohammed (born 1963). **Religion:** Moslem (Sunni)

Swaziland—Dynasty: Descended from Sobhuza I, the present king succeeded as Ngwenyama (or lion) of the Swazi nation, after a 20-year regency of the Queen Mother, in 1921. The country gained independence on September 6, 1968. **Monarch:** King Sobhuza II was chosen to succeed his father upon the latter's death in December 1899, was installed as king of the Swazi nation in 1921, and was recognized as the country's king in 1967. He is the world's longest-reigning monarch. **Born:** 1899 **Married:** 100 wives **Children** 500 **Heir:** By custom, the heir to the throne is not chosen until after the death of the monarch, when the eldest son of the favored wife is proclaimed king **Religion:** Christian

ARABIA

Bahrain—Dynasty: The Emir of Bahrain, head of the powerful Bedouin Al Khalifa family, is the tenth of his family to rule in Bahrain. Succession is by primogeniture. **Monarch:** Sheikh Isa ibn Salman al Khalifa became ruler on the death of his father in 1961, and the first Emir of Bahrain on August 14, 1971, the date of Bahrain's independence. **Children:** Hamad, others **Heir:** Sheikh Hamad ibn Isa al Khalifa, defense minister, and the Emir's oldest son **Religion:** Moslem (Sunni)

Jordan—Dynasty: Hashemite cooperation with the British in World War I resulted in Abdullah Ibn Hussein's rule of British mandated Transjordan. By a 1946 treaty with Great Britan, Abdullah became the first king of the independent Hashemite kingdom of Jordan. Assassinated in 1951, Abdullah was succeeded by his son Talal, father of the present king. **Monarch:** King Hussein I (ibn Talal) ascended the throne on May 2, 1953, following the deposition of his sickly father, Talal, on August 11, 1952 **Born:** November 14, 1935 **Married:** Princess Dina Abdel Hamid (April 1955; divorced, 1957); Antoinette (Toni) Avril Gardiner (Muna al Hussein) (May 1961; divorced, 1972); Alia Toukan (1972; died 1977); Elizabeth Halaby (Nur al Hussein) (June 1978) **Children:** Three sons (Abdullah, born 1962; Faisal, born 1963; Ali, born 1976) and four daughters (Alia, born 1956; Zein, born 1968; Ayeshia, born 1968;

Haya, born 1974). Abir, an adopted daughter, was born in 1972 **Heir:** Prince Hassan, younger brother of the king **Religion:** Moslem (Sunni)

Kuwait—Dynasty: The Emir of Kuwait is the thirteenth ruler of the Al Sabah royal family. The nominated successor of the Emir must be approved by the National Assembly; succession usually alternates between the two branches of the royal family. **Monarch:** Sheikh Jabir al-Ahmad al-Jabir as-Sabah of the al-Jabir branch became Emir on the death of his cousin on Dec. 31, 1977 **Religion:** Moslem (Sunni)

Oman—Dynasty: The al Bu Said dynasty dates from 1741 when its founder, Ahmed Ibn Said, expelled the Turks from Muscat and Oman **Monarch:** Sultan Qabus ibn Said al Bu Said ascended the throne in July 1970 after overthrowing his father Said bin Taimur (1910-72) who had reigned since 1932 **Born:** November 18, 1940 **Married:** Kamilla (1976) **Heir:** Sahr bin Taimur, uncle to the Sultan **Religion:** Moslem (Ibadi)

Qatar—Dynasty: In the 19th century, the ruling Khalifa family, deposed and forced to move to Bahrain, were succeeded by the Al Thani family. The present Emir, Khalifa ibn Hamad al-Thani, is the sixth ruler. In 1972 Khalifa assumed full power. Succession is designated by family consensus **Monarch:** Sheikh Khalifa ibn Hamad al-Thani, Emir of Qatar, assumed power Feb. 22, 1972 **Born:** 1937 **Children:** Two sons—Hamad and Abd al Aziz **Heir:** Sheikh Hamad ibn Khalifa al-Thani **Religion:** Moslem (Wahabi)

Saudi Arabia—Dynasty: The kingdoms of Nejd and Hejaz and their dependencies became the Kingdom of Saudi Arabia in 1932, under King Abdul-Aziz Ibn Abdur-Rahman Al-Faisal Al Saud. His son, King Saud, ruled from 1953 to 1964, when he was deposed, and succeeded by a brother, Faisal ibn Abdul-Aziz. **Monarch:** King Khalid ibn Abdul-Aziz Al Saud ascended the throne following the assassination of Faisal on March 25, 1975 by a nephew.**Born:** 1913 **Married:** one wife **Children:** nine **Heir:** Prince Fahd ibn Abdul-Aziz, a younger brother **Religion:** Moslem (Sunni-Wahhabi sect)

ASIA

Bhutan—Dynasty: The present hereditary dynasty of Bhutan was founded in 1907 by Ugyen Dorji Wangchuk, a provincial governor, following the abolition of a dual system of government by spiritual and temporal rulers. The present king, installed in July 1972 after the death of his father Jigme Dorji Wangchuk, is his great-grandson. **Monarch:** King Jigme Singhi Wangchuk (formally crowned on June 2, 1974) **Born:** 1955 **Children:** None **Heir:** To be selected from the royal family by the National Assembly **Religion:** Buddhist (Mahayana)

Japan—Dynasty: The Meiji Restoration (1867) placed Emperor Mutsuhito and his male descendants in command of a unified Japan. During the postwar American occupation of Japan, the Emperor, a grandson of Mutsuhito, renounced any claims to divinity, becoming a symbolic ruler. **Monarch:** Emperor Hirohito ascended the throne on the death of his father, Yoshihito, on December 25, 1926; he was enthroned on November 10, 1928. **Born:** April 29, 1901 **Married:** Princess Nagako (1924) **Children:** Seven; two sons (Akihito, born 1933; Masahito, born 1935) and three daughters survive **Heir:** Crown Prince Akihito **Religion:** Shinto

Nepal—Dynasty: The Shah family has ruled the kingdom of Nepal since the middle of the 18th century; however, a hereditary prime minister from the Rana family held actual power from 1846 to 1951. The last prime minister resigned in November 1951, and King Tribhuvan assumed full control. **Monarch:** Maharajadhiraja Birendra Bir Bikram Shah Dev succeeded to the throne in January 1972 (crowned in 1975) at the death of his father, Mahendra Bir Bikram Shah Dev **Born:** 1946 **Married:** Aishwarya Rajya Lakshmi Shah Devi **Children:** One son **Heir:** Crown Prince Dependra Bir Bikram Shah Dev (b. 1971) **Religion:** Hindu

° On Sept. 21, 1979, it was announced that the Emperor and the Empire had been overthrown.

Thailand—**Dynasty:** The present ruling family of Thailand began with Rama I in 1782. His great grandson, Chulalongkorn, King Rama V, was responsible for accelerating the modernization of Thailand; his nephew is the current monarch. **Monarch:** King Bhumibol Adulyadej, or Phumiphol Aduldet (Rama IX) succeeded to the throne after the death of his elder brother, King Ananda Mahidol, on June 9, 1946; he was crowned on May 5, 1950 **Born:** December 5, 1927 **Married:** Princess Sirikit Kittiyakara (1950) **Children:** One son (Prince Vajiralongkorn, born 1952), and three daughters (Ubol Ratana, born 1951; Sirindhorn, born 1955; Chulabhorn, born 1957) **Heir:** Crown Prince Vajiralongkorn **Religion:** Buddhist (Hinayana)

EUROPE

Belgium—**Dynasty:** The ruling family of Belgium is of the Saxe-Coburg-Gotha line. After Belgian separation from the Netherlands (1830), Leopold, prince of Saxe-Coburg-Gotha, was elected hereditary King of the Belgians on June 4, 1831 as King Leopold I; he was enthroned on July 21, 1831. **Monarch:** King Baudouin I (Albert Charles Leopold Axel Marie Gustave) succeeded to the throne on July 17, 1951 on the abdication of his father, Leopold III on the previous day. **Born:** September 7, 1930 **Married:** Fabiola de Mora y Aragón (1960) **Children:** None **Heir:** Albert, Prince of Liège, brother of the king (born 1934) **Religion:** Roman Catholic

Denmark—**Dynasty:** The House of Glücksburg has ruled Denmark since King Frederik VII of the House of Oldenburg died childless in November 1863. By a treaty (1852), King Frederik VII designated as heir Prince Christian X of Schleswig-Holstein-Sonderburg-Glücksburg, who became King Christian IX on Frederik's death. **Monarch:** Queen Margrethe II succeeded to the throne on the death of her father King Frederik IX, on January 14, 1972. **Born:** April 16, 1940 **Married:** Count Henri de Laborde de Monpezat, now Prince Henrik of Denmark (1967) **Children:** Two sons: Frederik André Henrik Christian, born 1968; Joachim Holger Waldemar Christian, born 1969 **Heir:** Crown Prince Frederik **Religion:** Evangelical Lutheran

Liechtenstein—**Dynasty:** The ruling House of Liechtenstein is descended from Huc von Liechtenstein, who became hereditary ruler of the country in January 1719. **Royal Ruler:** Prince Franz Josef II succeeded at the death of his great uncle, Prince Franz de Paula, on July 25, 1938. **Born:** August 16, 1906 **Married** Countess Georgine von Wilczek (1943) **Children:** Four sons, one daughter: Prince Johannes Adam Ferdinand Alois Josef Maria Marko d'Aviano Pius (b. 1945), Prince Philipp Erasmus Alois Ferdinand Maria Sebaldus (b. 1946), Prince Nikolaus Ferdinand Maria Josef Raphael (b. 1947), Prince Franz-Josef Wenzel George Maria (b. 1962), and Princess Nora Elisabeth Maria Anunta Josefine Georgine Omnes Sancti (b. 1950) **Heir:** Crown Prince Johannes (Hans) Adam **Religion:** Roman Catholic

Luxembourg—**Dynasty:** Made a Grand Duchy in 1815, the country has been ruled by the Nassau-Braganza family, the elder line of the House of Nassau, since 1890. According to the succession agreement, Adolphe, Duke of Nassau, succeeded at the death of King William III of the Netherlands. The Grand Duchy is today ruled by the great grandson of Adolphe. **Royal Ruler:** Grand Duke Jean succeeded to the throne on the abdication of his mother, the Grand Duchess Charlotte, on November 12, 1964. **Born:** January 5, 1921 **Married:** Princess Josephine-Charlotte of Belgium, daughter of King Leopold III (1953) **Children:** Three sons and two: daughters Prince Henri Albert Gabriel Félix Marie Guillaume (b. 1955), Prince Jean Félix Marie Guillaume (b. 1957), Prince Guillaume Marie Louis Christian (b. 1963), Princess Marie Astrid Charlotte Leopoldíng Wilhelmine Ingeborg Antonia Lilane Alberta Elisabeth Anne (b. 1954), and Princess Margaretha Antonia Maria Félicité (b. 1957) **Heir:** Prince Henri **Religion:** Roman Catholic

Monaco—**Dynasty:** The House of Grimaldi has controlled the principality of Monaco since 1297. **Royal Ruler:** Prince Rainier III (Louis Henri Maxence Bertrand) succeeded his grandfather, Prince Louis II, at his death on May 9, 1949. **Born:** May 31, 1923 **Married:** Grace Patricia Kelly of Philadelphia (1956) **Children:** One son and two daughters: Prince Albert Alexandre Louis Pierre (b. 1958), Princess Caroline Louise Marguerite (b. 1957), and Princess Stéphanie Marie Elisabeth (b. 1965) **Heir:** Prince Albert **Religion:** Roman Catholic

Netherlands—**Dynasty:** The Congress of Vienna, which settled the Napoleonic Wars, created the hereditary kingdom of the Netherlands under King William I in March 1815. The present sovereign is the fifth monarch of the dynasty. **Monarch:** Queen Juliana Louise Emma Marie Wilhelmina succeeded her mother, Queen Wilhelmina, at the latter's abdication on September 4, 1948; she was enthroned on September 6, 1948. **Born:** April 30, 1909 **Married:** Prince Bernhard of Lippe-Biesterfeld (1937) **Children:** Four daughters: Princess Beatrix Wilhelmina Armgard (b. 1938), Princess Irene Emma Elisabeth (b. 1939), Princess Margriet Francisca (b. 1943) and Princess Maria Christina (b. 1947) **Heiress:** Crown Princess Beatrix **Religion:** Dutch Reformed Church

Norway—**Dynasty:** Norway was ruled by the kings of Denmark and Sweden from 1319 until its separation (1905), when Prince Carl of Denmark was elected King Haakon VII of an independent Norway. Married to Queen Maud, daughter of Edward VII of England, King Haakon VII was followed by his son, the present ruler. **Monarch:** King Olav V succeeded to the throne on the death of his father, King Haakon VII, on September 21, 1957. **Born:** July 2, 1903 **Married:** Princess Märtha, daughter of Prince Carl of Sweden (1929; d. 1954) **Children:** One son and two daughters: Prince Harald (b. 1937), Princess Ragnhild Alexandra (b. 1930), and Princess Astrid Maud Ingeborg (b. 1932) **Heir:** Crown Prince Harald **Religion:** Evangelical Lutheran

Spain—**Dynasty:** The 1947 law of succession recreated the Spanish Kingdom under the tutelage of Generalissimo Franco, who would select a successor from the royal family. The Bourbon dynasty had ruled from 1700-1808, 1814-1869, and again after 1875 until the abdication of Alfonso XIII in April 1931. In 1969 Franco named Juan Carlos, grandson of Alfonso, as heir, and after being approved by the Cortes he was entitled Prince of Spain on July 23, 1969. He was proclaimed king on November 22, 1975, following the death of Franco. **Monarch:** Juan Carlos I de Borbón y Borbón **Born:** January 5, 1938 **Married:** Princess Sofía of Greece (1962) **Children:** One son and two daughters: Prince of Asturias Felipe Juan Pablo Alfonso de Borbón y Sonderburg-Gluckberg (b. 1968), Princess Elena, Princess Cristina **Heir:** Prince Felipe **Religion:** Roman Catholic

Sweden—**Dynasty:** Jean-Baptiste-Jules Bernadotte was elected (1810) Prince Royal of Sweden and adopted by childless King Carl XIII. He ascended to the throne of Norway and Sweden in 1818 as King Carl XIV Johan. His descendant King Oscar II renounced the throne of Norway in 1905; however, the House of Bernadotte still reigns over Sweden. **Monarch:** King Carl XVI Gustav, succeeded to the throne on the death of his grandfather, King Gustav VI Adolf on September 16, 1973. King Carl's father died in 1947. **Born:** April 30, 1946 **Married:** Silvia Renate Sommerlath (1976) **Children:** Princess Victoria Ingrid Alice Desiree (b. 1977), Crown Prince Carl Philip Edmund Bertil (b. 1979) **Heir:** Crown Prince Carl Philip Edmund Bertil **Religion:** Lutheran

United Kingdom—**Dynasty:** The House of Windsor, a branch of the Saxe-Coburg and Brunswick-Lüneburg line, dates from the accession of King George V in 1910. Although of German heritage, George V abandoned the German name Wettin and adopted the surname Windsor during World War I. He was succeeded by his sons Edward VIII (the Duke of Windsor) and George VI, father of the present monarch. **Monarch:** Queen Elizabeth II succeeded her father, George VI, at his death on February 6, 1952. **Born:** April 21, 1926 **Married:** Philip Mountbatten (Duke of Edinburgh, Earl of Merioneth, Baron Greenwich, and Prince of Great Britain), the son of Prince Andrew of Greece and Denmark (1947) **Children:** Three sons and one daughter: Prince Charles Philip Arthur George (Prince of Wales and Duke of Cornwall (b. 1948), Prince Andrew Albert Christian Edward (b. 1960), Prince Edward Antony Richard Louis (b. 1964), and Princess Anne Elizabeth Alice Louise (b. 1950) **Heir:** Prince Charles **Religion:** Anglican

OCEANIA

Tonga—**Dynasty:** Tonga was unified by Taufa'ahau Tupou (George I) in 1845. The kingdom is currently ruled by his descendants. **Monarch:** King Taufa'ahau Tupou IV succeeded to the throne at the death of his mother, Queen Salote, in December 1965; he was crowned on April 7, 1967 **Born:** July 4, 1918 **Married:** Princess Halaevalu Mata'aho 'Ahome'e (1947) **Children:** Three sons, one daughter (Salote Mafile'o Pilolevu) **Heir:** Crown Prince Tapou Toa (Toufa'ahau Manumatuongo Tukuaho) (b. 1948) **Religion:** Christian

SELECTED PAST RULERS AND DYNASTIES

BRITISH RULERS

Victorious over his neighbors, Egbert of Wessex (d. 839) consolidated what was to become the first English kingdom. The British monarchy, although altered by Danish (1016) and Norman (1066) conquest, civil wars, and Cromwell's Commonwealth and weakened by constitutional restraints, still prevails.

Saxons and Danes

	Reign Dates
Egbert	802–839
Ethelwulf	839–858
Ethelbald	858–860
Ethelbert	860–c. 866
Ethelred	c. 866–871
Alfred the Great	871–c. 899
Edward the Elder	c. 899–924
Athelstan	924–939
Edmund I	939–946
Edred	946–955
Edwy	955–959
Edgar	959–975
Edward the Martyr	975–978
Ethelred II	978–1016
Edmund Ironside	1016
Canute the Dane	1016–1035
Harold I	1035–1040
Hardicanute	1040–1042
Edward the Confessor	1042–1066
Harold II	1066

Norman

William I (the Conqueror)	1066–1087
William II	1087–1100

	Reign Dates
Henry I	1100–1135
Stephen	1135–1154

Plantagenet

Henry II	1154–1189
Richard I (Lion-Heart)	1189–1199
John	1199–1216
Henry III	1216–1272
Edward I	1272–1307
Edward II	1307–1327
Edward III	1327–1377
Richard II	1377–1399

Lancaster

Henry IV (Bolingbroke)	1399–1413
Henry V	1413–1422
Henry VI	1422–1461
	1470–1471

York

Edward IV	1461–1470
	1471–1483
Edward V	1483
Richard III	1483–1485

Tudor

Henry VII	1485–1509
Henry VIII	1509–1547
Edward VI	1547–1553
Lady Jane Grey (nine days)	1553
Mary I	1553–1558
Elizabeth I	1558–1603

	Reign Dates
Stuart	
James I (VI of Scotland)	1603–1625
Charles I	1625–1649
Commonwealth	
Oliver Cromwell	1653–1658
Richard Cromwell	1658–1659
Military Rule	1659–1660
Stuart Restoration	
Charles II	1660–1685
James II	1685–1688
Interregnum	1688–1689
Orange	
William III	1689–1702
and Mary II	1689–1694
Stuart	
Anne	1702–1714
Hanover	
George I	1714–1727
George II	1727–1760
George III	1760–1820
George IV	1820–1830
William IV	1830–1837
Victoria	1837–1901
Saxe-Coburg	
Edward VII	1901–1910
Windsor (Wettin until 1917)	
George V	1910–1936
Edward VIII (325 days)	1936
George VI	1936–1952

CHINESE DYNASTIES

Hsia	c. 1994 B.C.–c. 1523 B.C.
(legendary)	
Shang	c. 1523 B.C.–c. 1027 B.C.
Chou	c. 1027 B.C.–256 B.C.
Western Chou	c. 1027 B.C.–771 B.C.
Eastern Chou	
Spring and Autumn Period	722 B.C.–481 B.C.
Warring States Period	403 B.C.–221 B.C.
Chin	221 B.C.–206 B.C.
Western Han	206 B.C.–9 A.D.
Hsin	9 A.D.–23 A.D.
Eastern Han	25–220

The Three Kingdoms	220–280
Shu	221–263
Wei	220–265
Wu	222–280
Western Tsin	266–316
Eastern Tsin	317–420
Southern and Northern Dynasties	420–581
Liu Sung	420–479
Southern Ch'i	479–502
Liang	502–557
Ch'en	557–589
Northern Wei and four minor dynasties	386–535

Sui	589–618
Tang	618–907
Five Dynasties	907–960
Later Liang	907–923
Later Tang	923–936
Later Chin	936–947
Later Han	947–951
Later Chou	951–960
Northern Sung	960–1127
Liao	916–1125
Southern Sung	1127–1279
Chin	1115–1234
Yuan	1271–1368
Ming	1368–1644
Ching (Manchu)	1644–1911

FRENCH RULERS

After the death (511) of Clovis I, the Merovingian founder of the Frankish monarchy, his kingdom was divided into Austrasia, Neustria, and Burgundy. These kingdoms were frequently at war. Dagobert I was the last active Merovingian ruler, and his descendants, called the idle kings, were completely subject to their mayors of the palace, the Carolingians, who became the actual rulers of France when Pepin the Short deposed (752) the last Merovingian king.

Carolingians

*Pepin the Short	751–768
*Charlemagne (with Carloman up to 771)	768–814
*Louis I the Pious	814–840
Charles II the Bald	840–877
Louis II the Stammerer	877–879
Louis III and Carloman	879–882
Carloman	882–884
Charles the Fat, regent	884–887
Eudes (Capetian family)	888–898
Charles III the Simple	893–922
Robert I (Capetian)	922–923
Raoul of Burgundy	923–936
Louis IV d'Outremer	936–954
Lothaire	954–986
Louis V	986–987

* King of the Franks.

Capetians

Hugh Capet	987–996
Robert II	996–1031
Henry I	1031–1060
Philip I	1060–1108
Louis VI	1108–1137
Louis VII	1137–1180
Philip II (Augustus)	1180–1223
Louis VIII	1223–1226
Louis IX (Saint)	1226–1270
Philip III	1270–1285
Philip IV	1285–1314
Louis X	1314–1316
John I (the Posthumous)	1316–1317
Philip V	1317–1321
Charles IV	1321–1328

Valois

Philip VI	1328–1350
John II	1350–1364
Charles V	1364–1380
Charles VI	1380–1422
Charles VII	1422–1461
Louis XI	1461–1483
Charles VIII	1483–1498

Valois-Orléans

Louis XII	1498–1515

Valois-Angoulême

Francis I	1515–1547

Henry II	1547–1559
Francis II	1559–1560
Charles IX	1560–1574
Henry III	1574–1589

Bourbons

Henry IV	1589–1610
Louis XIII	1610–1643
Louis XIV	1643–1715
Louis XV	1715–1774
Louis XVI	1774–1793
Louis XVII (titular)	1793–1795

First Republic	1792–1804
First Empire	
Napoleon I (Bonaparte)	1804–1814
Bourbon Restoration	
Louis XVIII	1814–1824
First Empire (100 days)	1815
Bourbons	
Charles X	1824–1830
Bourbon-Orleans	
Louis Philippe	1830–1848
Second Republic	
(Louis) Napoleon III	1848–1851
Second Empire	
(Louis) Napoleon III	1852–1870

GERMAN AND PRUSSIAN RULERS

House of Hohenzollern, Kings of Prussia

Frederick I	1701–1713	Frederick II (the Great)	1740–1786	William I (German		
Frederick William I	1713–1740	Frederick William II	1786–1797	emperor after 1871)	1861–188
		Frederick William III	1797–1840	*Frederick III	1888
		Frederick William IV	1840–1861	*William II	1888–191

* King of Prussia and Emperor of Germany.

ITALIAN RULERS

Guided by Camillo di Cavour, the House of Savoy undertook to liberate and unify the Italian peninsula, a movement known as the Risorgimento. Italy became a kingdom in 1861 and a republic in 1946.

House of Savoy
Emmanuel Philibert 1553–1580

Charles Emmanuel I	1580–1630
Victor Amadeus I	1630–1637
Charles Emmanuel II	1637–1675
Victor Amadeus II	1675–1730
Charles Emmanuel III	1730–1773
Victor Amadeus III	1773–1796
Charles Emmanuel IV	1796–1802
Victor Emmanuel I	1802–1821
Charles Felix	1821–1831

House of Savoy-Carignano
Charles Albert 1831–184

Kings of Italy
Victor Emmanuel II
(king after 1861) 1849–187
Humbert I 1878–190
Victor Emmanuel III .. 1900–194
Humbert II 1946

ROMAN EMPERORS

Successor to Julius Caesar, Octavian (also known as Augustus), became the first Roman emperor in 27 B.C. His rule began a long period (200 years) of peace, called the **Pax Romana.** Stretching westward to the British Isles and eastward to the Caucasus, the vast Roman Empire was permanently divided into West and East Empires after the death (395) of Theodosius th Great. The Western Roman Empire came to an end in 476, whe the German Odoacer deposed Romulus Augustulus. The Easter Empire, with its capital at Constantinople, was gradually sup planted by the Byzantine Empire.

Emperor

Augustus	27 B.C.–14 A.D.	Balbinus	238	Jovian	363–36
Tiberius	14–37	Gordian III	238–244	Valentinian I	364–37
Caligula	37–41	Philip the Arab	244–249	Valens	364–37
Claudius	41–54	Decius	249–251	Gratian	375–38
Nero	54–68	Hostilianus	251	Valentinian II	375–39
Galba	68–69	Gallus	251–253	Magnus Maximus	383–38
Otho	69	Volusianus	c. 251–253	Eugenius	392–39
Vitellius	69	Valerian	253–260	Theodosius I the Great	379–39
Vespasian	69–79	Gallienus	253–268	**Emperors in the East**	
Titus	79–81	Claudius II	268–270	Arcadius	395–40
Domitian	81–96	Aurelian	270–275	Theodosius II	408–45
Nerva	96–98	Tacitus	275–276	Marcian	450–45
Trajan	98–117	Florianus	276	Leo I	457–47
Hadrian	117–138	Probus	276–282	Leo II	474
Antoninus Pius	138–161	Carus	282–283	**Emperors in the West**	
Marcus Aurelius	161–180	Carinus	283–285	Honorius	395–42
Commodus	180–192	Numerianus	283–284	Constantius III	421
Pertinax	193	Diocletian	284–305	Valentinian III	425–45
Didius Julianus	193	Maximian	286–305	Petronius Maximus	455
Septimius Severus	193–211	Constantius	305–306	Avitus	455–45
Caracalla	211–217	Galerius	305–310	Majorian	457–46
Macrinus	217–218	Maxentius	306–312	Libius Severus	461–46
Elagabalus (Heliogabalus)	218–222	Constantine I the Great	306–337	Anthemius	467–47
Alexander Severus	222–235	Licinius	308–324	Olybrius	472
Maximinus	235–238	Constantine II	337–340	Glycerius	473
Gordian I	238	Constans	337–350	Julius Nepos	474–47
Gordian II	238	Constantius II	337–361	Romulus Augustulus	475–47
Pupienus	238	Magnentius	350–353		
		Julian the Apostate	361–363		

RUSSIAN RULERS

Grand Dukes of Moscow

Ivan I, Prince of Moscow	1328–1341
Ivan II, Ivanovich	1353–1359
Dmitry Donskoi	1359–1389
Vasily I Dmitrievich	1389–1425
Vasily II	1425–1462
Ivan III Vasilyevich	1462–1505
Vasily III Ivanovich	1505–1533
Ivan IV (the Terrible), tsar of Russia from 1547	1533–1584
Fyodor Ivanovich	1584–1598

Boris Godunov	1598–1605
Fyodor II	1605
False Dmitry I	1605–1606
Vasily Shuisky	1606–1610
Interregnum	1610–1613
House of Romanov	
Tsar Mikhail	1613–1645
Tsar Alexei Mikhailovich	1645–1676
Fyodor Alexeyevich	1676–1682
Peter I, the Great (with Ivan V until 1689)	1682–1725
Catherine I	1725–1727

Peter II	1727–173
Anna Ivanovna	1730–174
Ivan VI	1740–174
Elizabeth	1741–176
Peter III	1761–176
Catherine II (the Great)	1762–179
Paul I	1796–180
Alexander I	1801–182
Nicholas I	1825–185
Alexander II	1855–188
Alexander III	1881–189
Nicholas II	1894–191

SPANISH RULERS

Spain was unified by the marriage of Ferdinand of Aragon and Isabella of Castile. Alfonso XIII was exiled in 1931, when Spain became a republic. The country came under the rule of Gen. Francisco Franco in 1939. The grandson of Alfonso XIII was proclaimed king, as Juan Carlos I, on the death of Franco in 1975.

Houses of Aragon and Castile
Ferdinand II of Aragon and Isabella of Castile 1474–1504
Ferdinand II and Philip I 1504–1506
Ferdinand II and Charles I 1506–1516

Spanish Hapsburgs

Charles I (V of Holy Roman Empire)	1516–1556
Philip II	1556–1598
Philip III	1598–1621
Philip IV	1621–1665
Charles II	1665–1700

Spanish Bourbons

Philip V	1700–1724
Louis I	1724
Philip V	1724–1746
Ferdinand VI	1746–1759
Charles III	1759–1788
Charles IV	1788–1808

French King of Spain
Joseph Bonaparte 1808–181

Bourbon Restoration
Ferdinand VII 1814–183
Isabella II 1833–186

Provisional Government . 1868–187

House of Savoy
Amadeo I 1870–187

First Spanish Republic ... 1873–187

Bourbon Restoration
Alfonso XII 1875–188
Alfonso XIII 1886–193

FAMILY HISTORY IS FOR EVERYONE

Harriet Stryker Rodda, certified genealogist, lecturer and teacher; author of family histories and professional articles, including How to Climb Your Family Tree.

Everyone in America is descended from immigrant stock, no matter what the ethnic or cultural background. Even the "native American Indians" were immigrants. They just happened to arrive before the European sailors and settlers.

With the Bicentennial celebrations mostly behind us, we are facing the coming of our Tricentennial in the year 2076. By then, each of us could be an ancestor who could be a missing link to our descendants. Far too many people in this country are bemoaning the fact that they cannot complete their connections with their ancestral families because their folks left no records or they neglected to listen when stories were being told.

Families in the United States are the backbone of the nation, although they are not as stereotyped as they once were. No matter what the ethnic or cultural background, the family unit is still the core of our young, 202-year-old America. *Newsweek* declared in May 1978 "there is an underlying stability of family life that often goes unnoticed. Ninety-eight percent of all American children are raised in families, and last year 79 percent of those were living with their parents." These are the children, plus many more, who by 2076 will be asking "Who am I?", "Where did my family come from?", "When did they get here?", "How did they live?", "Why are we as we are?"

These very same questions are being asked today. The answers are not to be found easily for some, because the fore-parents left no private and often few public records of themselves. For the majority, however, most of the facts they need to answer the who, where, when, why and how are available. They can be found and the family history preserved to be passed along for years to come. "But how do I start?" is the first question.

Start with yourself. You are to be author of your family history. Your autobiography will not only inform others of the facts and facets of your life, but more importantly will reveal to you the debt you owe your family. It will show you what you would like to know about those earlier members of the family. *Who, when, where, how* and *why* will be your guides as you record yourself and your times. Add pictures to illustrate, and dig out the certificates of your birth, education, honors, marriage or anything else that will add documentation to your record. Even if you never go on to compile a family history, this autobiography may be of inestimable assistance to someone else who will take up the task where you left off.

Contact all older living members of your family. With tape recorder or pencil and notebook, get all the information on the family members they can supply. It will amaze you how much they know and how they will have contacts with relatives you have never heard of. Don't overlook the stories or traditions they may relate to you. There is a core of truth in most of them. Try not to antagonize, but tell them of your deep interest in preparing and preserving the family's history.

Check their possession of family or Bible records; ask about certificates, passports, naturalization records, pictures, letters, heirloom furniture or other items. You may want some of these, but don't be greedy. Take pictures of whatever you can and copy whatever you find in their records. But leave the original with the owner unless it is freely given to you.

Record your in-family findings. How you do this is for you to decide, but make the final record easily understandable by anyone who sees it. It should contain the time and place and from whom you received the statements so that later you won't have to wonder who told you that and where you heard it. For every statement you use in your final record, you should have some documentation to prove it. Birth, marriage, divorce, death and land ownership records are the basic public records that should be found to support your story.

Visit a good genealogical library and use their catalogs to determine whether someone in the past has written a family history or genealogy to which your family can relate. Read the local and general histories for a better understanding of where and how your people lived. See the vital records collected for researchers like you: church records, newspaper items, census records, maps, cemetery records, diaries, account books, and many, many more, including the work of genealogists whose notes on your family may have been deposited for safekeeping. Get acquainted with the publications of genealogical societies, especially those that publish genealogical records. Begin to look at some of the books on the shelves with a critical eye. Decide which of their features you like and what you would not want in your final record. Are they readable, interesting in form and format, well documented and illustrated; do they feel good in the hand; does the type of binding let them lie open readily for reading and research? Make note of those that please you so that you can refer to them when you are ready to prepare your final history.

Despite the wealth of recorded information to be found in the form of tax rolls, military records, probate, land, court and census records, not to mention church and cemetery records and the cemeteries themselves, with their informative gravestones, this information is not always easy to obtain. Help is available. Along the way you will have become acquainted with the many "how-to" books written by people who want to share their knowledge with you. You will hear and read of genealogical seminars, lectures and conferences at every level from the local historical society to the large university and the Federal Archives. Take advantage of as much of this as you can, for you will meet a vast number of people who are learning as you are, who are as eager to accomplish as you will be, and who are happy to share their knowledge with you.

Today, family history is recognized for its value in establishing a keen sense of identity. Such simple projects in elementary schools as collecting information about parents and grandparents are known to help children establish as sense of personal worth and dignity. Genealogy is no longer considered a snob hobby. It has come of age. Good hunting! Become an honored ancestor!

OUTLINE OF WORLD HISTORY

This capsule presentation of the history of the world covers the period from 4000 B.C. through 1978.

4000 B.C.—3000 B.C.

EUROPE

4000 B.C. Farmers living along **Danube River in villages** designed stone replicas of deities.

NEAR AND MIDDLE EAST

4000 B.C. Ubadians, who were settled in southern Mesopotamia, developed towns in the Tigris-Euphrates plain, laying foundation for future civilization of **Ur**. Semitic nomads from Syria and the Arabian peninsula invaded area and intermingled with Urbaidians.

3500 B.C. Sumerians, possibly from Asia, settled along the Euphrates and developed a civilization that flourished.

FAR EAST

4000 B.C. Farmers lived in villages in northern **China**.

AMERICAS

4000 B.C. Indians in North and South America, descendants of people who migrated from Asia over the Bering Strait many centuries earlier, obtained food by hunting and cultivating corn. The remains of extinct animals, such as the mastodon, as well as arrowheads and spear points found in caves at **Folsom** and **Clovis**, New Mexico, attest to the antiquity of Indians in the Americas.

AFRICA

4000 B.C. An early Negro civilization thrived in the **Sahara**. The Tassili rock paintings in southeast Algeria, which date from about 6000 B.C., portray an organized society of hunters and herders who had horses and cattle.

c. 3200 B.C. Upper and Lower **Egypt** were united by the legendary **Menes**, the first Pharaoh, who built his capital at Memphis.

3000 B.C.—2000 B.C.

EUROPE

2700-2000 B.C. Early **Helladic** culture existed on Greek mainland, and **Cycladic** culture in the Aegean islands; both noted for primitive figurines.

2500-1200 B.C. Barbarian Celts, who overran western Europe, rode horses, carried iron weapons, and were ruled by **Druids**, a priestly class.

2500-1100 B.C. **Megalithic** culture of western Europe was noted for its huge stone ceremonial constructions, such as **dolmens**, or chamber tombs, and **menhirs**, or monumental stone slabs, sometimes arranged in circles, as at **Stonehenge** in England; remains also exist at **Carnac**, Brittany.

NEAR AND MIDDLE EAST

c. 3000 B.C. **Kish**, which was situated near modern Baghdad, became leading Sumerian city in the reign of King Etana.

c. 2800 B.C. Meskiaggasher founded dynasty in **Erech**, which began to rival Kish.

2686-2181 B.C. **Old Kingdom of Egypt:** Egyptian art and architecture developed; great pyramid for Pharaoh Khufu, one of the Seven Wonders of the Ancient World, was completed (c. 2600 B.C.) at Gizeh.

c. 2650 B.C. **Gilgamesh**, hero of Sumerian legends, reigned as king of Erech.

2500 B.C. King **Lugalannemundu** of Adab briefly united Sumerian city-states; following his death, city-states fought each other for 200 years.

c. 2450 B.C. King **Eannatum** made the Sumerian city-state of Lagash supreme.

c. 2325 B.C. **Sargon the Great** ruled over vast empire in Mesopotamia and built capital at **Agade** in Akkad that had beautiful temples and palace.

2200 B.C. **Gutians**, barbarians from Iran, conquered Sumeria and destroyed Agade.

2133-1786 B.C. **Middle Kingdom of Egypt:** Egypt expanded territory southward and engaged in extensive foreign trade.

2100 B.C. **Ur-Nammu** founded last Sumerian dynasty and promulgated law code, the oldest in existence.

FAR EAST

3000-1500 B.C. **Indus valley** civilization of northern India: a sophisticated culture thrived and cities of Harappa and Mohenjo-Daro were built with courtyard houses and modern drainage systems.

c. 2205-c. 1766 B.C. **Hsia dynasty** of China: first historic Chinese dynasty thrived; horses were domesticated and rice and millet were cultivated.

AMERICAS

2500 B.C. Indians began to make pottery.

2000 B.C.—1500 B.C.

EUROPE

c. 2000-1700 B.C. **Mycenaeans**, Greek-speaking people, settled in Greece, established flourishing civilization, and traded with Crete.

c. 1900-1400 B.C. **Stonehenge**, a massive stone complex used for religious purposes, was erected on Salisbury Plain, England.

c. 1700-c. 1500 B.C. **Minoan culture** on Crete reached its zenith; magnificent Minoan palaces built at Knossos and Phaistos showed evidence of advanced engineering skills.

c. 1500 B.C. **Linear B script** existed in Crete, evidence of Mycenaean influence.

NEAR AND MIDDLE EAST

2000 B.C. **Elamites** destroyed Ur, marking end of Sumerian dominance in Mesopotamia.

c. 2000-c. 1900 B.C. **Abraham**, founder of **Judaism**, is said to have lived.

2000-1700 B.C. **Hebrews** lived as nomadic shepherds in Canaan.

1786-1567 B.C. Egypt ruled by **Hyksos kings**, who probably came from Canaan, introduced horse-drawn chariots.

1750-c. 1708 B.C. **Hammurabi** ruled Babylonia, brought most of Mesopotamia and Assyria under his control, and introduced his **law code**.

c. 1600 B.C. Babylonian dynasty destroyed by **Hittites** from Anatolia and Syria.

1567-1085 B.C. **New Kingdom in Egypt:** Hyksos kings ousted and Egyptian power and civilization reached its height.

FAR EAST

1523-1027 B.C. **Shang dynasty** ruled China, developing a high civilization characterized by specialized classes, writing, a medium of exchange, and ancestor worship.

AMERICAS

2000 B.C. By this time, Indians had permanent village settlements and were cultivating manioc, squash, maize, and beans and domesticating dogs.

1500 B.C.—1000 B.C.

EUROPE

1400 B.C. **Mycenaeans** gained supremacy of the Mediterranean, and Mycenae, in northern Peloponnesus, became major ancient city following collapse of Knossus.

c. 1200 B.C. **Trojan Wars:** Greece conquered Troy in Asia Minor.
Dorian barbarians from the north began to invade Greece, initiating Dark Ages of Greek history.

1150-1000 B.C. Greeks settled on Ionian coast of Asia Minor.

NEAR AND MIDDLE EAST

c. 1500 B.C. **Mitanni kingdom** of Hurrians (known as Horites in Old Testament) ruled much of Mesopotamia and Assyria.

1468 B.C. **Battle of Megiddo:** Egyptians, under Thutmose III, conquered Syria and part of Mesopotamia.

1292-1225 B.C. **Ramses II** ruled Egypt and completed temples at Karnak, Thebes, Luxor, and Abu-Simbel.
Moses led Hebrews out of Egypt.

1250 B.C. **Phoenicians** flourished on coasts of Syria and Lebanon, establishing great city-states of **Tyre** and **Sidon** and beginning to colonize Mediterranean coast.

c. 1250 B.C. Hebrews entered **Canaan**.

1020-1004 B.C. **Saul** became the first king of the Hebrews.

FAR EAST

1500–500 B.C. Barbarian **Aryans**, Sanskrit-speaking people from central Asia, invaded **India** and destroyed Indus valley civilization; early *Vedas*, sacred Hindu texts, were composed.

1027–256 B.C. Chou dynasty of China superseded Shang dynasty and represented the Classical Age of China with the *Five Classics*, and teachings of **Confucius**, **Lao-tze**, and **Mencius**.

AMERICAS

c. 1250 B.C. Olmecs began to settle at **San Lorenzo**, Mexico, and developed civilization with widespread influence that was famous for gigantic sculptured heads (sometimes weighing over 20 tons) and austere figurines; ceremonial center was established at **La Venta** (fl. 800–c. 400 B.C.) for jaguar cult; Stele C found at **Tres Zapotes** has date equivalent to 31 B.C. carved in Mayan calendric system.

AFRICA

1200 B.C. Negroes in Nigeria developed **Nok culture**, which became advanced civilization, noted for expressive terra-cotta sculpture, but died out c. 200 B.C.

1000 B.C.—700 B.C.

EUROPE

1000 B.C. Teutonic tribes settled northern Europe.
Latin tribes began to settle in Italy.

000–400 B.C. Etruscan people, who had probably migrated from Lydia in Asia Minor, established a high civilization in **Italy** and became maritime power.

850–600 B.C. Homeric Greece: Greeks established colonies in Italy and along Mediterranean; the *Iliad* and the *Odyssey* were probably composed by Homer, Hesiod wrote poetry, and music developed.

776 B.C. Olympic games initiated.

753 B.C. Traditional date for **founding of Rome** by Romulus and Remus.

750 B.C. Romans seized **Sabine** women at public spectacle, taking them as wives.

747 B.C. Rome taken by **Sabines**, who united with Romans as one people.

736–630 B.C. Sparta became powerful on Greek mainland.

NEAR AND MIDDLE EAST

1000–774 B.C. Phoenicians dominated the seas, perhaps sailing to Cornwall, England, for tin and probably sailing down west coast of Africa.

910–606 B.C. Assyrian Empire controlled Mesopotamia.

74–625 B.C. Phoenicia came under **Assyrian** rule.

747–728 B.C. Tiglath-Pilser III, king of Assyria, subdued Aramaean tribes in Babylonia, conquered Urartu (Armenia), and established control over Syria.

721–705 B.C. Sargon II, king of Assyria, completed conquest of Israel, exiling most Israelites.

705–681 B.C. Sennacherib, king of Assyria, destroyed Babylon and built magnificent palace at **Nineveh**.

AMERICAS

. 1000 B.C. Chavin culture in northern **Peru** began to flourish; elaborate stone ceremonial center with painted relief sculpture was erected at **Chavin de Huantar** for jaguar cult; and gold ornaments and ceramics were designed; this culture declined after 200 B.C.

AFRICA

. 800–586 B.C. Carthage, founded in North Africa by **Phoenicians**, became a wealthy commercial center.

. 750 B.C. Kushites settled in Sudan and developed high civilization, erecting palaces and pyramids; extensive archaeological remains of ironworks at **Meroë**; Kushites used elephants and traded as far as Rome and India; their last king died in 320 A.D.

700 B.C.—500 B.C.

EUROPE

. 700 B.C. Temple to Hera erected at **Olympia**.
Spartans, after a series of wars, annexed eastern part of Messenia.
Celts began to invade Spain and France.

. 660 B.C. Byzantium founded by **Megara**.

. 621 B.C. Draco codified harsh Athenian **law**.

600–300 B.C. Teutonic tribes invaded western Europe: the **Alemanni** settled on the upper Rhine, the **Franks** and **Saxons** between the Weser and the Elbe, and the **Thuringians** south of the Saxons.

594 B.C. Solon introduced constitutional and social reforms into **Athens**, establishing limited democracy.

c. 580 B.C. Thales, first Western philosopher, flourished.

566 B.C. First Roman census taken.

c. 560–510 B.C. Athens ruled by tyrants after Pisistratus seized power.

560 B.C. Croesus, wealthy king of **Lydia**, conquered Ionian cities and was defeated (546 B.C.) by Cyrus the Great.

c. 550 B.C. Temple of Artemis (Diana) erected at Ephesus.

c. 534–510 B.C. Reign of **Tarquinius Superbus**, Etruscan ruler; Etruscan supremacy ended soon after his death.

509 B.C. Traditional date for founding of the **Roman Republic**.
The **Temple of Jupiter**, on the Roman Capitol, was dedicated.

NEAR AND MIDDLE EAST

681–668 B.C. Esarhaddon, king of Assyria, reigned; at its peak Assyrian Empire extended from Iran to Egypt.

625–539 B.C. Chaldean Empire of Mesopotamia.

612 B.C. Nineveh, Assyrian capital, fell to Medes, Chaldeans, and Scythians.

606 B.C. Battle of **Carchemish** ended Assyrian Empire.

c. 605–562 B.C. Reign of **Nebuchadnezzar II**, king of Babylonia; **Babylon**, with its hanging gardens (one of Seven Wonders of Ancient World), was greatest city of its time during his reign; massive palaces, "Tower of Babel," and a temple to the god Marduk were also constructed.

586 B.C. Nebuchadnezzar took **Jerusalem**, destroying the temple of Solomon and carrying inhabitants back to Babylonia.

c. 550 B.C. Persian Empire, founded by **Cyrus the Great**, included vast areas of the Near and Middle East; Persian art and architecture flourished, and Zoroastrian religion spread.

538 B.C. Cyrus the Great conquered Babylon and returned Hebrews to Jerusalem.

525–404 B.C. Persians conquered and ruled Egypt.

521–486 B.C. Darius I (the Great), king of Persia, extended and strengthened the empire, warred with Greece, and unified Persian power in the East.

FAR EAST

c. 563–483 B.C. Gautama Buddha preached in **India**.

c. 551–479 B.C. Confucius taught in **China**.

AFRICA

c. 631 B.C. Greeks founded North African city of **Cyrene**, which became important commercial center.

500 B.C.—400 B.C.

EUROPE

500–449 B.C. Greek-Persian Wars were fought, caused by commercial rivalry between Athens and Persia; Athens became leading city-state of Greece.

500 B.C. Classical Greek civilization (drama, philosophy, and the arts) developed and flourished, declining after 300 B.C.

498 B.C. Earliest extant poem of **Pindar** was written.

490 B.C. Battle of **Marathon:** 30,000 Persians, who were sent by Darius I, landed at Marathon to march on Athens and were turned back by Athenian infantrymen under **Miltiades**.

460 B.C. Athens warred against **Peloponnesian** cities, which were allied with Sparta.

457–429 B.C. Age of **Pericles** or Golden Age of Athens: philosophy, sculpture, and painting flourished; **Parthenon** was built (447–432 B.C.) on the Acropolis.

c. 451 B.C. The Twelve Tablets: **Roman law** codified for the first time.

c. 435 B.C. Phidias completed his statue of Zeus (one of Seven Wonders of Ancient World) for temple of Olympia.

431–404 B.C. Peloponnesian War developed, growing out of Spartan-Athenian rivalry; Athens destroyed (430).

c. 411 Thucydides wrote *The Peloponnesian War*.

404–371 B.C. Sparta was leading Greek power.

NEAR AND MIDDLE EAST

490 B.C. First Persian expedition to Greece under Darius I was turned back at **Marathon**.

480–479 B.C. Second Persian expedition to Greece under **Xerxes I** was turned back at **Plataea**.

AMERICAS

c. **500 B.C.** Zapotecs established ceremonial center at Monte Albán, Mexico, which showed Olmec influence.

AFRICA

c. **500 B.C.** Kingdom of **Axum** in **Ethiopia** came into existence; palaces, temples, and carved stone obelisks were built and trade took place with Near East and India; this kingdom declined c. 700 A.D.

400 B.C.—300 B.C.

EUROPE

400–270 B.C. Rome conquered Italy, subduing Etruscans, Samnites, and Greek colonists.

399 B.C. Socrates was condemned to death and made to drink hemlock.

390 B.C. Rome sacked by **Gauls.**

c. **387 B.C.** Plato founded his **Academy** in Athens, which is considered the first university of the Western world.

359–336 B.C. Philip II of Macedon conquered Thrace, Thebes, and Athens, and attempted to unite Greece during his reign; **Demosthenes,** greatest Greek orator, warned Athenians of Macedonian aims.

336–323 B.C. Reign of **Alexander the Great** of Macedon (son of Philip II), first of the great European conquerors; Alexander extended empire to include Egypt and the Near East and invaded India.

335 B.C. Aristotle founded a school in the Lyceum at Athens known as Peripatetic from his practice of lecturing in a covered portico (*peripatos*).

323 B.C. Hellenistic Age began, during which Greek influence spread throughout Mediterranean; this age ended in 31 B.C.

NEAR AND MIDDLE EAST

c. **352 B.C.** Mausoleum at Halicarnassus in Asia Minor (one of Seven Wonders of Ancient World) was erected in memory of Mausolus of Caria.

334–330 B.C. Alexander the Great conquered Asia Minor, Phoenicia, Palestine, Egypt, and Persia and founded Alexandria.

323 B.C.–30 A.D. Ptolemies, a Greek dynasty, ruled **Egypt.**

FAR EAST

327–326 B.C. Alexander the Great and his Greek troops entered India, withdrawing after troops revolted.

325–298 B.C. Reign of **Chandragupta Maurya,** who founded Maurya dynasty and united **India.**

AFRICA

350 B.C. Meroë, Kushite capital, fell to Ethiopians and was abandoned.

300 B.C.—200 B.C.

EUROPE

300 B.C. City of Rome became a major power in Mediterranean world.

292–280 B.C. Colossus of Rhodes (one of Seven Wonders of Ancient World), a bronze statue, probably more than 100 feet tall, of the sun god, Helios, was constructed on promontory overlooking harbor.

282–272 B.C. Pyrrhus, king of Epirus, fought Romans and caused its ruin.

264–241 B.C. First Punic War: Carthage warred against Roman occupation of Sicily.

227 B.C. Rome annexed Sardinia and Corsica.

218–201 B.C. Second Punic War: **Hannibal,** the Carthaginian leader, crossed the Alps and invaded Italy; victorious Romans gained Spanish provinces and Carthaginian war fleet.

NEAR AND MIDDLE EAST

300 B.C. Alexandria, Egypt, became intellectual center of Hellenistic world until its influence ended in 50 B.C.

c. **280 B.C.** Under Ptolemy II, a **lighthouse** (one of Seven Wonders of Ancient World) was constructed on **Pharos,** Alexandria.

250 B.C. Parthian Empire, which succeeded Persian Empire, ended in 226 A.D.

FAR EAST

269–232 B.C. Emperor Asoka the Great ruled India, making Buddhism state religion.

221–207 B.C. Ch'in dynasty of China: country was unified for first time, and construction of **Great Wall** was initiated.

202 B.C. Han dynasty of China established: during lon[g] peaceful rule, Chinese realized great artistic achieve[ments], expanded territory, and introduced **Buddhism**[;] this dynasty collapsed in 220 A.D.

200 B.C.—100 B.C.

EUROPE

192–189 B.C. During **Syrian War** between Rome an[d] Seleucid kingdom, Romans acquired territory i[n] Asia Minor.

c. **150 B.C.** Polybius completed six books of his *Universa[l] History,* a political analysis of the rise of Rome.

149–146 B.C. Third **Punic War.**

146 B.C. Macedonia became a Roman province.

121 B.C. Rome conquered southeastern **Gaul,** moder[n] Provence.

NEAR AND MIDDLE EAST

192–189 B.C. Syrian War between Rome and Seleucid[s]; Antiochus III forced to give up Asia Minor.

167 B.C. Hebrew Maccabees revolted against Antiochu[s] IV, king of Syria, who had tried to Hellenize Pales[-]tine.

FAR EAST

c. **200 B.C.** *Mahabharata,* Sanskrit epic poem, began t[o] be composed and was completed c. 200 A.D.

AFRICA

149–146 B.C. Third **Punic War:** Carthage destroyed b[y] Romans, who established Roman province of Afric[a].

100 B.C.—A.D. 1

EUROPE

73–71 B.C. Spartacus led slave revolt in southern Ital[y]; Pompey crushed revolt and crucified 6,000 slaves.

63 B.C. Cicero, greatest Roman orator, exposed **Catiline** plot to seize consulship by force.

60–53 B.C. First Triumvirate: **Julius Caesar,** Pompe[y] and Marcus Licinius Crassus ruled Rome.

58–49 B.C. Gallic Wars: **Caesar's campaigns** brough[t] Gaul under Roman rule.

48 B.C. Caesar met **Cleopatra** in Egypt.

46–44 B.C. Caesar ruled Rome, which included Gau[l], Italy, part of Illyria, Macedonia, Greece, Asia Mino[r], Egypt, and part of North Africa.

44 B.C. Caesar stabbed to death in the Senate on Ides [of] March.

43–31 B.C. Second Triumvirate: **Marc Antony,** Lepidu[s] and **Octavian,** Caesar's grandnephew, ruled Rom[e].

c. **35 B.C.** Roman poets Vergil and Horace flourished.

31 B.C. Octavian defeated Antony and Cleopatra at Ac[-]tium, assuming title Augustus and becoming fir[st] Roman emperor; Augustus made Egypt a Roma[n] province.

27 B.C. Roman Empire established.

14 B.C. Pax Romana: Roman Empire began 200 years [of] peace, which ended in 192 A.D.

NEAR AND MIDDLE EAST

74–63 B.C. Third **Mithridatic War** between King Mit[h]ridates VI of Pontus and Rome, which resulted [in] further Roman conquests in Near East.

48 B.C. Cleopatra, daughter of Ptolemy XI of Egypt, wi[th] the aid of **Julius Caesar,** became Queen of Egy[pt] (47–30 B.C.).

37 B.C. Rome began to rule **Palestine;** this rule ended [in] 395 A.D.

36 B.C. Queen Cleopatra married **Marc Antony.**

30 B.C. Egypt annexed by Roman Empire, following t[he] suicides of Antony and Cleopatra.

6 or 4 B.C. Jesus born in Bethlehem.

AMERICAS

100 B.C. Paracus culture, an offshoot of Chavin civiliz[a]tion in **Peru,** flourished.

A.D. 1—A.D. 100

EUROPE

1 Christian era began.
   Gothic kingdom on the lower Vistula (Poland) d[e]veloped.

5–40 Cymbeline reigned in Britain.

9 Arminius defeated Roman commander **Varus at t[he]** Battle of Teutoburg Forest, ending Roman attemp[t] to conquer Germany.

37 Caligula made emperor of Rome by army; his cru[el] regime ended (41) with his assassination.

41–54 Reign of **Roman Emperor Claudius I,** who disenfranchised many non-Italians, annexed Mauretania, expelled Jews from Rome, and initiated Roman rule of Britain.

43 Romans ruled **Britain** until 407.

54–69 Reign of **Emperor Nero,** last of Julio-Claudian line of Roman emperors; he blamed Christians for fire that almost destroyed **(64) Rome** and rebuilt city magnificently; Roman persecution of Christians was begun, which may have caused death of **St. Peter** and **St. Paul;** Nero committed suicide.

61–62 Boadicea, British queen of Iceni (Norfolk), led revolt against Romans at Fort Londinium; defeated, she took poison.

65 Seneca, philosopher and adviser to Nero, committed suicide after he was accused of conspiracy.

69–79 Reign of **Emperor Vespasian,** who founded Flavian dynasty and erected the **Colosseum** and **Forum** in Rome.

79 Mount Vesuvius erupted, destroying Pompeii and Herculaneum.

81–96 Reign of **Emperor Domitian,** son of Vespasian, was characterized by persecution of Christians; Domitian erected **Arch of Titus** to memorialize his brother's conquest of Jerusalem.

96–180 Reign of **"the Five Good Emperors"** of Rome: Nerva, Trajan, Hadrian, Antonius Pius, and Marcus Aurelius; the empire was enlarged and great public works undertaken.

. 98 Tacitus, Roman historian, completed *Germania.*

NEAR AND MIDDLE EAST

. 28 St. John the Baptist began preaching.

. 30 Jesus crucified in Jerusalem.

. 42–60 St. Paul, one of the apostles, conducted missionary work in Asia Minor and Greece and wrote his *Epistles.*

66 Jews revolted against Roman rule in Palestine; **Titus** suppressed rebellion and destroyed (70) Jerusalem.

FAR EAST

9 Emperor Wang Mang usurped Chinese throne, initiating agrarian reforms.

25 Han dynasty held Chinese throne until 220; Buddhism was introduced during reign of **Emperor Ming-ti** (58–76), and cultural ties with India were increased.

0 Kushan kings of Grandhara began to rule in West Pakistan, establishing an empire that extended from central Asia to India; a famous school of Buddhist sculpture was organized.

100—200

EUROPE

00 For the next 375 years, Goths, Vandals, and Huns raided Roman Empire.

17 Roman Empire reached its greatest extent after **Emperor Trajan** subdued Dacia (Rumania), Armenia, and Upper Mesopotamia; Trajan's Column was erected in Rome to honor his conquests.

17–138 Reign of **Emperor Hadrian;** he standardized Roman law throughout the empire, and constructed a 73-mile-long wall named after him in Britain.

30 Pantheon built at Rome and consecrated as Christian church in 609.

160–180 Marcus Aurelius, Stoic philosopher and author of *Meditations,* ruled Roman Empire and was forced to wage numerous wars.

192–284 Roman Empire ruled by army, **"Barracks Emperors."**

96 Barbarians overran northern Britain.

NEAR AND MIDDLE EAST

132–135 Bar Kokba led Jewish revolt; defeated by Romans, Jews were barred from Jerusalem and further dispersed.

FAR EAST

00 Traditional date for beginning of **Japanese state.**

100 Funan Empire established in Cambodia.

Champa kingdom founded in South Vietnam and parts of Cambodia.

132 Indo-Scythians destroyed last traces of Hellenic rule in northern India.

150 Kanishka reigned in India.

AMERICAS

00 Teotihuacán civilization, one of America's most splendid early civilizations, developed in central Mexico; Pyramid of the Sun was as tall as 20-story building, Temple of Quetzalcoátl erected to Feather Serpent deity, and agricultural techniques advanced enough to support large urban population around huge **pyramid complex;** influence ceased when city fell c. 700 to **Chichimecs.**

200—300

EUROPE

205 British revolt against Romans was suppressed in 211.

211–217 Reign of **Emperor Caracalla,** who constructed in Rome Baths named for him.

220–238 Goths invaded Balkans, **Asia Minor,** and eastern Roman Empire.

c. 240 Franks first appeared in Europe.

c. 252 Franks, Goths, and **Alemanni** broke through borders of Roman Empire.

268 Goths sacked Athens, Corinth, and Sparta.

270–275 Emperor Aurelian consolidated empire by retreating to Danubian borders, recovered Gaul, and overthrew Queen Zenobia of Palmyra (Syria).

276 Great wall around Rome erected against barbarian attacks.

284–305 Reign of **Emperor Diocletian,** who divided empire into western part (Italy and Africa), which was governed from Milan by **Maximian;** Diocletian ruled eastern part (Near and Middle East and Egypt) from Nicomedia (now Izmit, Turkey).

NEAR AND MIDDLE EAST

200–230 Clement and Origen, Christian theologians, taught in Alexandria.

226–240 Ardashir I (or Artaxerxes) overthrew Parthian Empire; founded Neo-Persian Empire under **Sassanid dynasty.**

232 Sassanian-Roman War established **Sassanians** as major Eastern power.

c. 242 Mani, founder of Manichaeism, began to preach in Persia; he was martyred c. 276.

260 Persians under **Shapur I** captured **Roman Emperor Valerian** and Roman territory in Near and Middle East.

268 Zenobia, queen of Palmyra, conquered Syria, Mesopotamia, and parts of Egypt; Zenobia was overthrown (273) by **Roman Emperor Aurelian.**

FAR EAST

205–225 Reign of **Fan Shih-man** in Cambodia extended empire to lower Mekong River.

220 Han dynasty came to an end; China was divided and invaded for next three centuries.

265 Western Tsin (Ch'in) dynasty began, uniting China until White Huns began to invade in 317.

300—400

EUROPE

303 Diocletian harshly persecuted Christians.

306–337 Reign of **Constantine I,** first Christian emperor.

313 Edict of Milan recognized Christianity as a legal religion in Roman Empire.

325 First ecumenical council, which was convened by Constantine at **Nicaea,** voted against Arianism.

330 Constantine made **Constantinople** (now Istanbul) new capital of Roman Empire.

337 Romans fought series of wars with **Persians,** which ended (363) with loss of parts of Armenia and Mesopotamia.

c. 340 Monasticism developed in the West.

341 Wulfila began Christianizing Visigoths and resettling them (c. 348) in Balkans.

c. 350 Huns, central Asian nomads, began to invade Europe, forcing Goths westward.

360–367 Picts, Irish, and Saxons invaded Britain.

361–363 Reign of **Julian the Apostate,** who tried unsuccessfully to revive paganism.

363 Emperor Jovian restored Christianity.

379–395 Theodosius, Roman emperor, resettled Goths in empire, many of whom became soldiers.

383–407 Roman legions evacuated Britain.

390 Massacre of 7,000 following anti-Roman rebellion at Thessalonica; Theodosius did public penance before Bishop Ambrose of Milan.

395 Alaric, former head of Visigothic troops under Theodosius, became king of Visigoths and pillaged Balkans and Greece.

Roman Empire permanently partitioned.

NEAR AND MIDDLE EAST

310–379 Reign of **Shapur II** of Persia, who recovered Armenia from Romans.

337 Persians fought series of wars with **Romans**, securing (363) territory in Armenia and Mesopotamia.

378 Battle of **Adrianople**: Roman defeat left Greece unprotected from barbarians.

381 First Council of Constantinople, **second ecumenical council** convened, formalized Nicene Creed, and outlawed paganism.

387 Armenia partitioned between Rome and Persia.

399–420 Reign of **Yazdegerd I** of Persia; Christianity was tolerated initially, but later persecutions were begun in Armenia and Persia.

FAR EAST

c. 300 Funan (Cambodia) ruled by an Indian Brahman, who introduced Hindu customs, Indian legal code, and alphabet of central India.

317 China was divided into Northern and Southern dynasties; reunited in 590. Eastern Tsin dynasty ruled southern China, and capital at Nanking was established.

c. 320–c. 380 Reign of **Chandragupta I**, who established Gupta Empire that ruled India until c. 544; his reign marked the Golden Age of Hindu art and literature.

386 Northern Wei dynasty gained control of northern China, ruled until 495.

AMERICAS

300 Mayan civilization in southern **Mexico** entered its Classical Age during which its influence spread into **Guatemala** and **Honduras**; Mayans, ruled by priests, had advanced arts and science: calendar, hieroglyphic writing, and major works of stone architecture; this civilization collapsed in 900.

AFRICA

300 Kingdom of **Ghana** developed in western Sudan.

320–350 Christianity introduced into kingdom of **Axum**.

400—500

EUROPE

400 Eastern Roman Empire superseded by **Byzantine Empire**.

400–450 Europe overrun by **Goths**.

402 Roman capital moved to Ravenna.

408–450 Reign of **Theodosius II**, Byzantine emperor, who systematized (438) Roman laws (*Codex Theodosianus*) and made separation of Eastern and Western sections of empire official.

410 Alaric and Visigoths sacked **Rome**.

413–426 St. Augustine wrote *The City of God*.

432 St. Patrick began missionary work among the Irish.

445–453 Attila, king of the Huns, ruled from Hungary over Russia, Poland, and Germany, extorting concessions from Theodosius II and ravaging Balkans.

449 Angles, Saxons, and Jutes began conquest of Britain.

451 Attila, defeated at Châlons in Champagne, then invaded northern Italy, but allegedly was stopped by **Pope Leo I.**

455–475 Rome ruled by series of puppet emperors; **Ricimer**, Suebi general from central Germany, was virtual ruler of western empire until 472.

466–484 Reign of **Euric**, who established kingdom in Spain, bringing Visigothic power to its peak.

476 Odoacer, Ostrogoth chieftain, deposed **Romulus Augustulus**, last Roman emperor of the West; Odoacer was recognized as head of western empire by Zeno, Byzantine emperor.

481–511 Reign of **Clovis I**, king of the Franks, and founder of **Merovingian dynasty**, who defeated (486) Romans at Soissons, ending Roman rule in Gaul, and was converted (496) to Christianity.

493 Theodoric the Great, king of Ostrogoths, seized Ravenna, assassinated Odoacer, and established Ostrogothic kingdom in Italy.

NEAR AND MIDDLE EAST

428 Persians began to rule **Armenia**; their control ceased in 633.

491 Armenian Church separated from Byzantine and Roman churches.

FAR EAST

420 Liu Sung dynasty came to power in southern China and ruled until 479.

c. 450 Buddhism established in **Burma**.

465 By this time, White Huns had almost destroye[ ] Gupta empire in India.

479 Chi dynasty began to rule southern China; its rul[ ] ceased in 502.

AFRICA

429 Vandal kingdom established in Africa by **Gaiseri[ ]** who took his people out of Spain.

439 Gaiseric made **Carthage** Vandal capital.

476 Gaiseric concluded **treaty** with **Zeno**, who recognize[ ] Vandal rule over Roman Africa, Sicily, Sardini[ ] Corsica, and Balearic Islands.

500—600

EUROPE

500 Golden age of **Irish monastic scholarship** bega[ ] which died out c. 800.

506 Alaric II, king of Visigoths, issued *Lex Roman[ ] Visigothorum*, law code.

527–565 Reign of **Justinian**, Byzantine emperor, who w[ ] strongly influenced by his wife **Theodora**; Justini[ ] issued *Corpus Juris Civilis* (also known as the Ju[ ] tinian Code), a comprehensive code of Roman law[ ] erected public works; and recovered Africa fro[ ] Vandals and Italy from Ostrogoths.

529 Benedict of Nursia founded Monte Cassino in S[ ] biaco, Italy, first **Benedictine monastery.**

532–537 Cathedral of Hagia Sophia erected in Consta[ ] tinople.

c. 537 Traditional date of **King Arthur's death** at th[ ] Battle of Camlan.

c. 560–616 Reign of **Ethelbert**, king of Kent, who re[ ] ceived St. Augustine and was converted to Chris[ ] anity; Ethelbert made Kent supreme in Britain ar[ ] drew up first code of English laws.

563 St. Columba, an Irish missionary to Scotlan[ ] founded church and converted king of the Picts.

567 Frankish kingdom divided into Austrasia, Neustri[ ] and Burgundy.

568 Lombards, ancient German tribe, invaded norther[ ] Italy and established a kingdom that lasted ov[ ] 200 years.

584 Slavs in Balkan peninsula overran Greece and b[ ] gan to menace Byzantine Empire.

c. 585 Avars, conquering nomads from steppes of ce[ ] tral Asia, reached Danube.

590–604 Papacy of **St. Gregory I** (the Great) laid bas[ ] for later papal claims to temporal authority and i[ ] dependence and codified church music; the Gr[ ] gorian chant is named for him.

597 St. Augustine, a Roman monk, sent by Pope Grego[ ] to convert English, founded a church at Canterbur[ ] becoming (601) first Archbishop of Canterbury.

NEAR AND MIDDLE EAST

c. 500 Arabs invaded **Palestine.**

525 Yemen conquered by Abyssinians.

531–579 Reign of **Khosru I** (or Chosroes) of Pers[ ] marked political and cultural prime of Persia; Khos[ ] fought Byzantines and overthrew Abyssinian contr[ ] of Yemen.

c. 550 Migration of Turks began, which broke up (56[ ] White Hun settlements in Western Turkestan.

570 Mohammed, prophet of Islam, born.

590–628 Reign of **Khosru II** of Persia, who conquer[ ] Jerusalem, Damascus, and Egypt and restored Pe[ ] sian boundaries to those at time of Darius I.

FAR EAST

c. 550 Khmers from Chen-La state to north began to ove[ ] run Funan and made **Cambodia** (about equal[ ] Cambodia and Laos) dominant in Southeast As[ ] until c. 1400.

Japanese began to adopt **Chinese culture**, usi[ ] Chinese script and introducing Buddhism.

590 Sui dynasty began to rule China; Great Wall[ ] China was reconstructed as defense against Tur[ ] and Mongols, five million people were employed[ ] construct complex water transport system, and ci[ ] service examination was introduced; this dynas[ ] ended in 618.

600—700

EUROPE

610–641 Reign of **Heraclius**, Byzantine emperor, who r[ ] covered lands lost to Persia and then lost them[ ] Moslem Arabs at end of his reign.

613–629 Reign of **Clotair** (Lothair) **II,** Merovingian king, who reunited Frankish realm and appointed **Pepin of Landen** and **Arnulf,** bishop of Metz, (ancestors of the Carolingians) to govern Austrasia.

617 **Northumbria** became dominant kingdom in Britain.

655 **Saracens,** Arab Moslems, destroyed Byzantine fleet.

664 Saracens began series of attacks on **Constantinople.**

c. 670 **Caedmon,** English poet, wrote early English version of *Old Testament.*

679 First **Bulgarian Empire** founded by **Khan Asparuhk.**

685–695 First part of reign of **Justinian II,** Byzantine emperor, who was defeated by Arabs at Sevastopol and later deposed and exiled to Crimea.

687 **Pepin of Héristal** became ruler of all Frankish kingdoms, except Aquitaine.

NEAR AND MIDDLE EAST

c. 610 **Mohammed** began his mission as prophet of Islam.

622 Traditional date of the **Hegira,** Mohammed's flight from Mecca to Medina, that marked beginning of **Moslem Era.**

630 **Moslems** conquered **Mecca,** which became spiritual center of Islam.

633 **Islam** began conquests by taking **Syria** and **Iraq.**

639 Moslems began to conquer **Egypt.**

640 **Persia** taken by Moslems.

651–652 First edition of the *Koran* issued.

661 **Moawiya** founded **Omayyad dynasty** (caliphs of Damascus), which held caliphate until 750.

FAR EAST

c. 606–647 Reign of **King Harsha,** ruler of Kanauj in northern India, which enjoyed **Hindu renaissance** of literature, arts, and theology; Harsha received Chinese pilgrim Hsuan-Tsang.

618 **T'ang dynasty** founded in China, which annexed Korea and led successful campaigns in Mongolia, Nepal, Tibet, and Turkestan; it marked the **Golden Age of medieval China** with notable advances in astronomy and mathematics, first historical encyclopedia (801), and the development of art of printing, painting, and poetry; this dynasty ended in 906.

664 Saracens attacked Afghanistan and India.

670 **Silla** kingdom established in **Korea;** Chinese helped Koreans unite peninsula, instituting a period of prosperity and artistic achievement that lasted until 935.

AMERICAS

600 **Tiahuanaco** became a major ceremonial center near Lake Titicaca; Tiahuanacans established first unified empire that included most of **Peru;** their rule ended c. 1000.

AFRICA

698 **Carthage** fell to **Saracens,** ending Byzantine rule in North Africa.

700—800

EUROPE

700–730 *Beowulf,* oldest extant English epic, was composed.

711 **Tarik,** Berber leader of Moslems, invaded Spain, initiating **Moorish rule** in Spain, which lasted until 1492.

715–741 Reign of **Charles Martel,** son of Pepin of Héristal and grandfather of Charlemagne; as Frankish ruler, he defeated (732) Saracens at battle of Tours, halting their advance into Europe.

c. 732 **St. Bede** (the Venerable Bede) wrote his *Ecclesiastical History of the English Nation.*

751–768 **Pepin the Short,** first Carolingian king of the Franks and son of Charles Martel, defended Rome from Lombards.

756 **Papal states** began when Pepin granted lands around Ravenna to pope.

Omayyad dynasty of Córdoba came to power in Moslem Spain and was to rule until 1031.

768–814 Reign of **Charlemagne** (son of Pepin the Short), who subdued Saxony, annexed Lombardy and Bavaria, and was crowned (800) emperor of the West by Pope Leo III at Rome; Charlemagne created Palace School at his capital, Aix-la-Chapelle, which helped preserve classical and early Christian scholarship.

NEAR AND MIDDLE EAST

749 Caliph Abul Abbas overthrew Omayyads and founded **Abbasid dynasty,** which ruled until 1258.

762 Baghdad founded by Caliph Al-Mansur.

786–809 Reign of **Caliph Harun al-Rashid,** during which Baghdad became major Islamic city; this glorious period is reflected in *The Thousands and One Nights.*

FAR EAST

712 **Moslem Arabs** devastated most of northwestern **India.**

Kojiki [= records of ancient matters], sacred book of the **Shinto,** was completed.

794 **Heian period** of Japan began; during this era, Japanese began to develop their own culture and established capital at **Kyoto;** this period ended 1185.

AMERICAS

700 **Chichimec** nomads from northern Mexico invaded **Teotihuacán** civilization.

Mayan temples built at **Tikal,** in jungles of Guatemala.

AFRICA

700 **Moslem Arabs** conquered northern **Africa,** which became base for invasions of Europe.

Kingdom of **Ghana** developed as first of Sudanese empires and became wealthy trading center, extending from Timbuktu to the Atlantic.

800—900

EUROPE

c. 800 **Cynewulf,** Old English religious poet, wrote *Fates of the Apostles.*

802 The **Vikings** raided **British Isles** and by 880 had permanent settlements in Ireland and England.

803–814 Reign of **Khan Krum,** Bulgarian ruler, who captured Sofia from Byzantines and besieged Constantinople.

813–820 Reign of **Leo V,** the Armenian, who ruled Byzantium and revived iconoclasm; he defeated Bulgars and concluded 30-year truce.

827–880 **Moslems** invaded Sicily, Palermo, Messina, Rome, and Malta.

835 Vikings began to raid **Continent.**

843 Treaty of **Verdun:** the **Carolingian kingdom** was divided into three separate states: the future **France, Italy,** and **Germany** with Charles the Bald, Emperor Lothair, and Louis the German as rulers of the respective territories.

847–c. 877 **John Scotus Erigena** headed court school at Paris for Charles the Bald and wrote translations and original philosophical works.

c. 850 **Feudalism** developed in western Europe.

858 **Photius** became patriarch of Constantinople, and a schism between eastern and western churches developed during his reign.

860–869 **St. Cyril** and **St. Methodius** performed missionary work among Slavs living near Black Sea and later in Moravia; Cyril developed early **Slavic alphabet.**

862 **Rurik,** a Varangian (Viking), settled **Novgorod,** Russia; house of Rurik ruled Grand Duchy of Moscow and later all Russia until 1598.

865 **Boris I,** ruler of Bulgaria, introduced Christianity of the Greek rite.

871–899 Reign of **Alfred the Great,** king of England, who made a treaty establishing Danish territory in England and began overseeing compilation of *Anglo-Saxon Chronicle.*

882 **Oleg,** Rurik's nephew, made Kiev capital of Russia.

893–927 Reign of **Simeon I** (Tsar of the Bulgars and autocrat of the Greeks), who drove Magyars into Hungary and conquered most of Serbia; Bulgarian Empire flourished during his reign, which is considered the Golden Age of **Church Slavonic literature.**

c. 895 **Árpád,** chief of Magyars, led his people into **Hungary.**

c. 899 Medical school in **Salerno** had been established, which merged Greek, Jewish, Arabic, and Latin influences.

FAR EAST

800 **Feudalism** developed in Japan.

889 Golden Age of **Khmer** civilization, which ruled modern Cambodia, Laos, Thailand, and South Vietnam, from capital at **Angkor;** the temple complex constructed at **Angkor Wat** is one of the largest religious centers in the world; this civilization declined after 1434.

AFRICA

800 Arabs colonized **Madagascar and Zanzibar,** making expeditions into African interior for slaves for the next 200 years.

Rulers of **Kanem** developed kingdom near caravan routes of eastern Sudan.

900—1000

EUROPE

900 Danish kingdom founded by **Gorm.**

904 Saracens sacked Salonika.

906 Magyars began invading Germany, and were defeated (955) at Augsburg.

911 Rollo, Norse chieftain, received in fief the future duchy of **Normandy** from King Charles III; he was baptized (912), and his descendants included William the Conqueror.

912—960 Omayyad rule in **Spain** at its zenith under Abdu-r-Rahman III; **Córdoba** became intellectual center of Europe.

919—936 Reign of **Henry I,** the Fowler, who was considered the founder of **German realm** and recovered Lorraine for Germany.

962 Holy Roman Empire founded after Otto I, German king, united Italy and Germany; it lasted until Francis II renounced the imperial title in 1806.

976—1025 Reign of **Basil II** (Bulgar slayer), Byzantine emperor, who annexed Syria and Bulgaria, bringing empire to greatest size since the time of Justinian I.

c. 980—1015 Reign of **Vladimir I** (Saint Vladimir), duke of Kiev, who made Christianity of the Greek rite the Russian religion.

c. 985 Eric the Red established a Viking colony in **Greenland.**

987 Hugh Capet became king of **France,** beginning of the Capetian line that ruled France until 1328.

992—1025 Reign of **Boleslaus I** (the Brave), founder of the **Polish kingdom,** who brought most of the western Slavs under his rule.

997—1038 Reign of **Stephen I** (Saint Stephen), called the Apostle of Hungary, first king of **Hungary.**

NEAR AND MIDDLE EAST

969 Fatimite caliph established in Egypt; Fatimites, who captured Palestine, parts of Syria, and west Arabia, ruled until 1171.

996 Hakin, sixth Fatimite caliph, persecutor of Jews and Christians and self-proclaimed (1020) reincarnation of God, a claim still maintained by **Druses** in Syria and Lebanon; Fatimite power declined rapidly after Hakin's assassination in 1021.

999 Sultan **Mahmud of Ghazni** founded Ghaznevid dynasty, which ruled Afghanistan until c. 1155; he annexed Punjab, India; forced conversions to Islam; destroyed Hindu temples; and built a mosque, the **Celestial Bride,** at Ghazni, his capital.

FAR EAST

907 Khitan Mongols began to rule northern China, holding sway until 1123. Kingdom of the **Five Dynasties and Ten States** in China: chaos existed in China until 960.

935 Koryo kingdom established in **Korea,** in which literature was cultivated and Confucianism replaced Buddhism; this kingdom ended in 1392.

960 Sung dynasty established in China; scholarly works were composed, and drama and picaresque novel flourished; gunpowder was used for first time, and trade was carried on with India and Persia; the dynasty ruled until 1279.

986 Ghaznevids from Afghanistan began to rule Punjab, remaining there until 1001.

AMERICAS

900 Toltec civilization developed in **Mexico;** capital was established (c. 950) at **Tula,** and warrior gods were worshiped; the Toltec Indians conquered most of Mexico, before influence died out c. 1200.

AFRICA

c. 912—1043 Fatimite dynasty dominated most of northwestern Africa and the Near East; fleets raided Mediterranean, capturing Malta, Sardinia, Corsica, and Balearics.

c. 990 Great Zimbabwe civilization, probably developed by Bantu people, flourished in **Southern Rhodesia;** huge stone buildings were constructed in about the 15th century; this civilization ended c. 1750.

1000—1100

EUROPE

1000 End of the world expected throughout Christendom.

c. 1000—1010 Early edition of *Chanson de Roland* probably composed, but not transcribed for many years.

1002 Massacre of St. Brice: Danes in England were murdered and, in retaliation, raided England regularly until 1014.

1014 Knut (Canute) **II,** king of **Denmark,** became (1017) king of England and later of Norway; his kingdom was divided after his death in 1035.

1019—1054 Reign of **Yaroslav,** duke of Kiev; he drew up Russian law code, encouraged learning, erected **Cathedral of Sancta Sophia** and monastery of Lavra, and consolidated power and prestige of Kiev.

1024 Franconian house began to rule **Germany;** great imperial age ended in 1125.

1039—1056 Henry III, king of Germany and Holy Roman Emperor (1046–1056); with authority over Hungary, Poland, and Bohemia, his empire was at its height

1040 Macbeth became king of Scotland after murdering his predecessor, **Duncan;** Macbeth was killed (1057) by Malcolm, who became king until 1093.

Attempts were made to implement **Truce of God** in France, which would have prohibited war during certain seasons and times of the day.

1042—1066 Reign of **Edward the Confessor,** king of England; he began (c. 1050) construction of **Westminster Abbey.**

1054 Reciprocal excommunication of Roman and Greek Churches announced; it was **repealed** in 1965.

1063 Construction was begun on **Cathedral at Pisa,** an example of **Romanesque** style of architecture that flourished in 11th and 12th centuries.

1065—1109 Alfonso VI of Leon, king of Castile, reconquered Moorish lands, beginning with capture of Toledo in 1085.

1066 William, duke of Normandy, defeated Saxons under King Harold at the **Battle of Hastings,** ending Saxon rule in England; known as William I (the Conqueror) of England, he ordered (1086) all landed property surveyed for tax purposes and recorded in **Domesday Book.**

c. 1071 Saint Mark's Church in Venice was rebuilt in Byzantine style.

c. 1078 The White Tower, later named the **Tower of London,** was constructed.

1081 The Cid (Rodrigo Diaz) fought Moors and Spaniards; he founded and ruled Valencia until 1099

1086 Almoravides, Berber Moslems from Morocco, took over control of Islam in Spain.

c. 1088 University of Bologna founded.

1093 St. Anselm, founder of Scholasticism, became Archbishop of Canterbury.

1095 First Crusade proclaimed by Pope Urban II, who urged battle cry to be *Deus vult* [God wills it]; he established (1099) **Latin Kingdom of Jerusalem** in Syria and Palestine that endured until 1291.

1097 Construction began on the **Houses of Parliament**

NEAR AND MIDDLE EAST

c. 1000 Avicenna, Arabian philosopher and physician, wrote *Canon of Medicine.*

1055 Seljuk Turks conquered Baghdad.

1063—1072 Alp Arslan, ruler of Seljuks, conquered much of Near East and Asia Minor; he defeated Byzantine army at **Manzikert,** Armenia.

1072—1092 Reign of **Malik Shah** (son of Arslan), who was protector of **Omar Khayyam,** Persian poet and author of the *Rubáiyát.*

1096 The First Crusade began, and Crusaders captured Nicaea, Antioch, and Jerusalem, where they massacred the Moslems; Crusaders established (1099) **Latin Kingdom of Jerusalem** in Syria and Palestine which endured until 1291.

FAR EAST

c. 1020 *The Tale of Genji,* said to be the **world's first** novel, written by Lady Murasaki Shikibu in Japan

1044 King Anawratha made **Pagan, Burma,** the capital of his dynasty; it became known as the "city of thousand temples."

AMERICAS

c. 1000 Lief Ericsson allegedly discovered part of North American coast and called it **Vinland.**

Chichén Itzá, ancient Mayan city in north-central Yucatán, became **Toltec** city and was occupied until 1194.

Mixtec people, who developed high culture in Oaxaca valley of Mexico, practised picture writing.

AFRICA

c. 1000 Kano, city in northern Nigeria, began to flourish; it became leading Moslem sultanate of **Hausa States,** which were vassals of **Bornu** after 1400.

1054 Almoravides, Moslem Berber tribes, began Islamic conquest of **West Africa;** they sacked Kumbi, capital of Ghana, in 1076.

1100—1200

EUROPE

1100–1135 Reign of Henry I of England; he gained control of Normandy; his attempts to have his daughter **Matilda** succeed him caused long civil strife.

1108–1137 Reign of Louis VI (the Fat) of France, who battled with Henry I and checked German invasion.

1113–1125 Reign of Vladimir Monomakh, grand duke of Kiev; state grew in power during his reign.

1118 Order of Knights Templar founded.

1120–1220 Aristotelian philosophy introduced into the West, especially through writings of **Averroës,** Spanish-Arabian philosopher, and **Maimonides,** Hebrew scholar.

1122–1152 Suger, abbot of Saint-Denis, was leading French statesman under Louis VI and Louis VII.

1128–1185 Reign of Alfonso I Henriques of Portugal; Portugal received (1144) papal consent to be independent kingdom.

1134–1150 Western facade of **Chartres Cathedral** was built.

c. 1135 Geoffrey of Monmouth completed *History of the Kings of Britain,* major source of **Arthurian legends.**

1147 Second Crusade preached by St. Bernard of Clairvaux after Turks captured (1144) Edessa; it was led by Conrad III of Germany and Louis VII of France.

c. 1150 University of Paris came into being; **Peter Abelard** is usually regarded as its founder.

1152 Frederick I (Barbarossa), became king of Germany, and was crowned (1155) Holy Roman Emperor; he acquired land in Italy, Germany, and Poland and was drowned (1190) in Asia Minor during Third Crusade.

Louis VII annulled his marriage to **Eleanor of Aquitaine;** Henry (Plantagenet) married Eleanor.

1154–1189 Reign of Henry II (Plantagenet) of England; he appointed **Thomas à Becket** his chancellor and centralized royal administration.

1154–1213 Georgian power reached its peak in Russia, a period known as **Golden Age of Georgian literature.**

1159 John of Salisbury dedicated *Policraticus,* his treatise on government, to Thomas à Becket.

Peter Lombard, bishop of Paris, began his theological text, *Sentences.*

1162 Becket became Archbishop of Canterbury; he opposed Henry's restrictions on ecclesiastical jurisdiction, but was formally reconciled after long quarrel in 1170, only to be murdered five months later by Norman knights.

1163–1235 Cathedral of **Notre Dame** constructed in Paris.

c. 1168 Oxford University founded.

1176 Construction of **London Bridge** was begun, and completed in 1209.

Lombard League of northern Italian states defeated Barbarossa at **Legnano,** representing the first major defeat of feudal cavalry by infantry.

c. 1180 Chrestien de Troyes composed the first literary works of Arthurian legend.

1182 Jews banished from **France,** but returned in 1189.

c. 1187 *Igor's Campaign,* first notable work of **Russian** literature, was based on true account of Prince Igor's defeat and release by Cumans.

1189–1193 Third Crusade led by Barbarossa, Richard I of England, and Philip II of France.

1189–1199 Reign of Richard I (the Lionhearted), king of England; returning from Crusades, he was captured by Leopold of Austria; after release two years later, he warred against Philip II.

1190–1199 Teutonic Knights, a German military religious order, was founded.

1191 The *Nibelungenlied* first appeared.

NEAR AND MIDDLE EAST

1144 Zengi, Turkish conqueror of Syria, seized **Edessa.**

1145–1174 Reign of Nureddin, Zengi's son and Sultan of **Syria;** he ousted Crusaders from northern Syria, made (1154) **Damascus** his capital, and conquered (1171) **Egypt.**

1147–1149 Second Crusade.

1157 Seljuk Empire fell to **Khorezm shah.**

1169–1193 Reign of Saladin, sultan of Egypt; he conquered Syria and Aleppo, defeated (1187) Christians at battle of **Hattin** (near Tiberias) and took Jerusalem, and signed treaty with **Richard the Lionhearted** that allowed Christians small strip of land along Jerusalem coast.

FAR EAST

1149 Rulers of **Ghor** took over **Ghazni** in Afghanistan, which became headquarters for campaigns into India; subjugation of Upper India was completed in 1203.

1186 Kamakura era began in **Japan,** establishing rule of military warriors; **Yoritomo,** first shogun, set up centralized feudal system; China and Korea were raided; Zen Buddhism was promoted; this era ended in 1333.

c. 1190 Temujin consolidated Mongol tribes in central Asia; he assumed (1206) title **Jenghiz Khan** and led Mongol hordes in conquests of eastern Europe and western Asia.

AFRICA

c. 1174 Almohades, fierce Berber Moslems, succeeded Almoravides in Morocco and conquered other parts of North Africa, ruling area until 1550.

1200—1300

EUROPE

1202–1204 The Fourth Crusade, was led by Venetian doge, **Enrico Dandolo;** Constantinople was captured and a Latin empire established.

1204 Philip II of France took English lands north of the Loire and established **France** as a leading European power.

1209 Franciscan order founded by **Saint Francis of Assisi.**

1211 Construction began on **Rheims Cathedral.**

1215 Magna Carta, signed by **King John,** became basis of modern English constitution with its principle that the king is subject to law.

1217–1221 Fifth Crusade led by Pelasius, papal legate, was directed against Moslems in Egypt and failed.

1218 Amiens Cathedral begun.

1223 Mongols invaded Russia.

1226–1270 Reign of Louis IX (Saint Louis), a period known as **Golden Age of medieval France.**

1226–1283 Teutonic Knights subjugated Prussia and achieved commercial power.

1227 Gothic **Cathedral of Toledo,** Spain, began to be constructed.

1228–1229 Sixth Crusade; led by Frederick II, it resulted in Sultan of Egypt signing treaty that restored Jerusalem, Nazareth, and Bethlehem to Christians.

c. 1230 Salamanca University founded in Spain.

c. 1231 Cambridge University founded.

1233 The Inquisition was established when Pope Gregory IX gave Dominicans authority to investigate Albigensian heresy in southern France.

1236–1263 Reign of Alexander Nevsky in Russia, under whom country was united; he defeated (1242) Teutonic Knights at Lake Peipus, and Mongols named him **Grand Prince of Russia.**

1237–1242 Batu Khan led Mongol invasions, taking **Moscow** and most of Russia, Hungary, and Poland, and invading Germany; his empire was known as the **Golden Horde** because of brilliant tents.

1238 Kingdom of Granada became last refuge of the **Moors** until their expulsion from Spain in 1492.

1248–1254 Seventh Crusade; King Louis IX of France was its leader.

1270 Eighth Crusade; Tunis was attacked, and Louis IX died from plague.

1271 Marco Polo left Venice for **China** and other parts of the Far East; he returned in 1292 and informed Europeans of Oriental splendors.

1273 Rudolph I founded Hapsburg dynasty, which ruled
Austria until 1918.

St. Thomas Aquinas completed *Summa Theologica.*

1272–1307 Reign of Edward I of England; he systematized laws and institutions and called (1295) his
"Model Parliament," which represented all classes.

1285–1314 Reign of Philip IV (the Fair); he made
France an absolute monarchy and called (1302) the
first meeting of the Estates-General (clergy, nobility,
and townsmen) to rally against Pope Boniface VIII's
claims of papal supremacy.

1290 Jews were expelled from England; they returned
c. 1650.

NEAR AND MIDDLE EAST

1202–1204 Fourth Crusade: Crusaders took Constantinople, sacked Byzantine territories, and established
a Latin Empire.

1217–1221 Fifth Crusade; Crusaders failed in Egypt.

1218–1224 Mongols from central Asia conquered Turkestan, Afghanistan, and Persia.

1228–1229 Sixth Crusade; Sultan of Egypt signed a
treaty with Crusaders allowing free access to Jerusalem.

1245–1253 Mesopotamia and Armenia ravaged by Mongols.

1248–1253 Seventh Crusade; Crusaders massacred in
Egypt.

1250 Mamelukes, former slave-soldiers, began to rule
Egypt and checked Mongol advances; their rule
ended in 1517.

1258 Baghdad fell to Hulagu Khan, grandson of Jenghiz,
who devastated surrounding lands.

1270 Eighth Crusade; Crusaders attacked Tunis and
were turned back.

1288 Osman I, leader of Ottoman Turks, founded Ottoman dynasty, which endured until 1918.

FAR EAST

1206 Delhi Sultanate began, the first Moslem kingdom
of India; Sultan Iltutmish (1210–1235) erected famous minaret, Qutb Minar; this dynasty ended in
1398.

1220–1227 Jenghiz Khan established his capital at Kara-
korum controlling most of Ch'in Empire of northern
China; he conquered Turkestan, Afghanistan, Persia,
and southern Russia.

1221–1241 Ogotai Khan, son of Jenghiz, captured
Ghazni, Afghanistan.

1260 Yüan, Mongolian dynasty of China, founded by
Kublai Khan, grandson of Jenghiz; Kublai's attempts to conquer Japan, Southeast Asia, and Indonesia failed; Marco Polo and other westerners visited
capital at Peiping; during dynasty an advanced
postal system and extensive network of roads and
canals were created; gunpowder and printing were
introduced into Europe from China at this time;
this dynasty ended in 1368.

AMERICAS

1200 The Incas began to build empire centered at Cuzco,
Peru, and established central control over local
rulers; eventually empire extended from Quito,
Ecuador, to Rio Maule, Chile, with population c.
seven million people, who were linked by messenger
system and common language; Incan civilization
was noted for political organization and luxurious
cities; stonework in Machu Picchu, fortress city in
Andes, shows skillful engineering techniques; empire destroyed by Francisco Pizarro in 1533.

Aztecs entered the valley of Mexico, establishing
powerful political and cultural civilization and capital
(c. 1325) at Tenochtitlán (now Mexico City); Aztecs
were noted for developed social organization and
religion demanding human sacrifice; in 1519 their
population numbered about five million; Hernán
Cortés destroyed empire in 1521.

AFRICA

1200 Mali Empire developed in western Sudan, absorb-
ing Ghana and neighboring lands; King Mansa
Musa's pilgrimage (1324) to Mecca brought attention to empire's great wealth; Timbuktu grew into
center of learning and culture; Songhai began to
control region c. 1500.

1300—1400

EUROPE

1300 The Renaissance began, signaling end of Middle
Ages and beginning of modern Europe; greatest
cultural developments in European history occurred
during next 300 years.

1305 "Babylonian Captivity" began; chaos in Italy
forced Pope Clement V to desert (1309) Rome for
Avignon, France, which was the papal seat until
1377.

c. 1306 Giotto completed Arena Chapel frescoes in Pa-
dua.

1321 Death of Dante following completion of *Divine
Comedy.*

1325–1341 Reign of Ivan I (Money Bag), grand prince
of Moscow and vassal of Mongols; Russian Orthodox Church became centered in Moscow during his
reign.

1326 Ottoman Turks began invading eastern Europe.

1327–1377 Reign of Edward III of England, during
which Parliament divided into two houses, later
called Lords and Commons.

1337 Hundred Years War, which began after Edward III
claimed French crown, ended in 1453; English defeated, but French devastated by famine, plague,
and marauders who terrorized countryside.

1341 Petrarch, Italian humanist, crowned poet laureate
at Rome.

1346–1355 Reign of Stephen Dushan over Serbs, Greeks,
Bulgars, and Albanians; his rule marked height of
Serbian power.

1347–1352 Black Death, an epidemic of plague that began (1334) in Constantinople, struck Europe; within
20 years, it killed up to three quarters of population
of Europe and Asia.

1353 Giovanni Boccaccio completed the *Decameron.*

1358 French army suppressed the *Jacquerie,* a peasant
revolt protesting war taxation.

1362 William Langland wrote *Piers the Plowman.*

1370 Hanseatic League, mercantile association of German
towns, signed a treaty with Denmark giving League
a virtual trade monopoly in Scandinavia.

1378 Great Western Schism: Rome and France began
fight for control of papacy that lasted until 1417.

1379 After Parliament imposed poll tax, Wat Tyler led
peasant revolt in England.

1382 John Wycliffe directed translation of the Vulgate
Bible into English.

1386 Heidelberg University founded by Rupert I, Elector
of Palatinate.

Lithuania and Poland united under Jagiello dynasty;
Golden Age of Polish culture and power began;
this dynasty came to an end in 1572.

1387 Chaucer began to compose his *Canterbury Tales.*

1389 Turks defeated Serbs at Kossovo, and Serbia became vassal state of Turks.

1391 Ottoman Turks began conquering Byzantine lands.

1399 House of Lancaster began reign in England that
lasted until 1461.

NEAR AND MIDDLE EAST

1334 Epidemic of plague, Black Death, began in Constantinople, spreading throughout Europe and Asia
and causing extremely large number of fatalities.

1354 Ottoman Turks expanded their empire and established capital at Adrianople; by end of century
Ottomans controlled most of Balkans and Byzantine
possessions in Asia Minor.

1356–1363 Sultan Hassan mosque was constructed in
Cairo.

1392 Baghdad sacked by Tamerlane, Mongol conqueror

FAR EAST

1336 Ashikaga family began to dominate Japan, holding
sway until 1558; Ashikaga period of warfare among
feudal nobles was also a time of extraordinary economic and commercial growth.

1350 Thais from southern China established kingdom in
modern Thailand.

1353 Lao kingdom of Lan Xang (Land of a Million Elephants) established by branch of Thais in Laos.

1368 Ming dynasty began to rule China after driving out
Mongols; empire at its height extended from Burma
to Korea; European settlements made at Macao and
Canton; finest Chinese porcelain dates from this
period, which ended in 1644.

1369–1405 Reign of **Tamerlane** (or Timur), Mongol leader and conqueror of Persia, Mesopotamia, and western India; Tamerlane ravaged Georgia and captured Angora from Ottomans.

1392 Yi dynasty began to rule **Korea** and established capital at Seoul; this dynasty ended in 1919.

AFRICA

1300 **Kingdom of Ife** flourished in Nigeria; Ife, a holy city noted for its fine **bronze sculpture**, probably died out c. 1500.

1350 **Kingdom of Benin** developed in Nigeria; within a century, Benin became famous commercial center and seat of royal court; bronze plaques on king's palace depict civilization of hunters, traders, and warriors; trade was established with Portugal c. 1486; Benin had disintegrated by 1897.

1400—1500

EUROPE

1409 **Leipzig University** founded by German émigrés from Prague.

1415 **Henry V** of England defeated French in Battle of Agincourt, making England first among European powers.

1415–1460 Reign of **Prince Henry the Navigator** of Portugal, who promoted explorations along the coast of Africa.

c. 1417 **Donatello** completed his statue of St. George and the Dragon.

1419–1436 Hussite religious wars that broke out following martyrdom of **John Huss** were fought in Bohemia.

c. 1427 Thomas à Kempis, German monk, wrote The Imitation of Christ.

1429 **Joan of Arc** liberated Orléans; she was burned at the stake in Rouen in 1431.

1432 Jan van Eyck completed his altarpiece with panels portraying the Annunciation and Adoration of the Lamb.

1434 Medicis began their domination of **Florence**, which lasted until 1494 and made Florence center of Italian Renaissance.

1450 Fra Angelico completed the Annunciation.
   Vatican Library founded by Pope Nicholas V.

1453 **Constantinople** was lost to Turks, ending 1,000-year-old **Byzantine Empire**.
   Hundred Years War came to an end, and English territory on Continent was limited to Calais.

1455–1485 **Wars of the Roses:** English Houses of Lancaster and York fought for throne.

1456 **John Hunyadi,** Hungarian ruler, defeated Turks at Belgrade, preventing their conquest of Hungary for 70 years.

c. 1456 Printing of **Mazarin Bible** was completed in Mainz, Germany; it is considered earliest book printed from movable type and attributed to **Gutenberg.**

1458–1490 Reign of **Matthias Corvinus** of Hungary (son of John Hunyadi), who took (1485) Vienna and made Hungary most important state of central Europe.

1461–1483 Reign of **Louis XI,** who made France a nation by annexing Burgundy, Provence, Maine, and Anjou.

1462–1505 Reign of **Ivan III (the Great),** first national sovereign of Russia; he subjugated Novgorod and almost all Russian principalities under Moscow's rule and repudiated "Tartar Yoke"; Ivan also adopted Byzantine court ceremonials and constructed great **Kremlin palaces** and cathedrals in Moscow.

1463 **Turks** and **Venetians** began major war, in which Venetians were defeated (1479) and had to pay Turks for trading privileges.

1466 **Teutonic Knights** ceded Pomerania and West Prussia to Poland.

1469 King **Ferdinand** of Aragon married Queen **Isabella I** of Castile, initiating unification of Spain.

1473 **The Sistine Chapel** in the Vatican was built under Pope Sixtus IV.

1478 Ferdinand and Isabella instituted the **Spanish Inquisition.**

1481 **Botticelli** began his Biblical frescoes in the Sistine Chapel.

1485 **Henry VII** of England founded the House of Tudor, increased power of the **Star Chamber,** developed English navy, sponsored explorations to New World, and ended feudalism by outlawing private armies.

1488 **Bartolomeu Dias** was the first European to round the Cape of Good Hope, thus opening sea route to India.

1490 **Verrocchio's** equestrian monument of condottiere Colleoni was cast.

1492 Ferdinand and Isabella conquered Moorish kingdom of **Granada,** expelled Jews who refused to accept Catholicism, and financed **Christopher Columbus** on his first voyage to America.

1494 Treaty of **Tordesillas:** Spain and Portugal divided the New World.
   Italian Wars among Italian states and Spain began when Charles VIII of France invaded Italy; after 1559 Spain dominated Italy.

1497 **Portugal** expelled Jews who refused Catholic conversion.

1497–1498 **John Cabot** explored North American coast south of Labrador.

1497–1499 **Vasco da Gama** sailed from Lisbon to India.

1498 **Savonarola,** Dominican monk who preached against corruption in Florence, was burned at the stake.
   Leonardo da Vinci, painter, engineer, and scientist, completed the Last Supper in Milan.

1499 **Swiss independence** acknowledged by Emperor Maximilian I.

NEAR AND MIDDLE EAST

1451–1481 Reign of **Mohammed II,** Ottoman sultan; he completed conquest of Byzantine Empire by taking (1453) **Constantinople** and making it his capital; conquering most of Balkans and several Venetian possessions in Aegean islands, he was stopped (1478) at Belgrade by John Hunyadi and in Albania by Scanderbeg.

FAR EAST

1412–1443 Reign of **Ahmad Shah,** king of **Gujarat** (India), who founded city of **Ahmedabad;** Gujarat became an independent, prosperous sultanate.

1495–1530 Reign of **Baber** (or Babar), remote descendant of Tamerlane; Baber founded **Mogul Empire** of India, captured (1504) Kabul and established a kingdom in Afghanistan, and conquered most of northern India.

1498 Portuguese explorer **Vasco da Gama** landed at Calicut, India.

AMERICAS

1492–1504 **Christopher Columbus** made four voyages to America; landed on Canary Islands, Bahamas, Cuba, Hispaniola, Jamaica, Virgin Islands, Trinidad, and Honduras.

1497 **John Cabot** arrived in North America; explored coast south of Labrador.

AFRICA

1400 **Baluba Kingdom** of the Congo first emerged and eventually controlled Katanga and Kivu provinces.

1415 Portuguese began to explore **West Africa,** gradually building up profitable trade.

1482 **Diego Cão,** Portuguese explorer, discovered mouth of Congo River.

1488 **Bartolomeu Dias,** Portuguese explorer, rounded **Cape of Good Hope.**

1491 **Vasco da Gama** rounded the Cape and sailed up East African coast en route to Asia.

1500—1600

1502 **Cesare Borgia,** son of Pope Alexander VI, completed conquest of neighboring states and added them to the Papal domain.

1503 **Leonardo da Vinci** began painting the Mona Lisa.
   Alexander I, king of Poland and grand duke of Lithuania, ceded left bank of Dnieper to Ivan the Great.

1508 **Michelangelo** began to paint ceiling of **Sistine Chapel.**

1509 **Erasmus,** Dutch humanist, published The Praise of Folly.

1509–1547 Reign of **Henry VIII** of England; his first wife was **Katharine of Aragon** (m. 1509, div. 1533), mother of Mary I; second wife, **Anne Boleyn** (m. 1533, beheaded 1536), mother of Elizabeth I; third wife, Jane Seymour (m. 1536, d. 1537), mother of Edward VI; fourth wife, Anne of Cleves (m. 1540, div. 1540); fifth wife, Katharine Howard (m. 1540, beheaded 1542); sixth wife, Katharine Parr (m. 1543); Henry waged war against France and Scotland.

1513 Macchiavelli wrote *The Prince*.

Raphael painted the *Sistine Madonna*.

1515–47 Francis I ruled France; he fought Italian Wars and captured Milan at Battle of Marignano.

1515 Henry VIII appointed Thomas Wolsey cardinal and lord chancellor.

1516 Sir Thomas More, English statesman, wrote *Utopia*.

1517 Martin Luther began Protestant Reformation by posting his 95 theses against the sale of indulgences on door of Wittenberg Palace Church.

1518 Titian completed his altarpiece *Assumption of the Virgin*.

1519 Ulrich Zwingli began Reformation in Switzerland.

1519–1522 Ferdinand Magellan circumnavigated the globe.

1519–1556 Charles V, Holy Roman Emperor, ruled Spanish lands in Europe and America, as well as Hapsburg lands in central Europe; he sacked (1527) Rome and captured Pope Clement VII.

1520 Luther was declared a heretic by Pope Leo X and formally excommunicated (1521) by Edict of Worms.

1523–1560 Reign of Gustavus I (Vasa) of Sweden; he ended (1537) trade monopoly of Hanseatic League and promoted Reformation.

1524–1525 Peasants' War in Germany: revolt by south German peasants that was inspired by Lutheran religious ideas; however, Luther sided with princes.

1532 Rabelais wrote *Gargantua and Pantagruel*.

1533–1584 Reign of Ivan IV (the Terrible), first tsar of Russia; his conflicts with boyars, the powerful nobles who controlled regency, resulted in reign of terror; Ivan seized part of Livonia from Poles and concluded peace among Russia, Sweden, and Poland after much warfare.

1534 St. Ignatius Loyola founded Jesuit order, which became chief force in Roman Catholic Counter-Reformation.

Act of Supremacy: English Parliament made Henry VIII head of Church of England, initiating English Reformation.

1535 Sir Thomas More, former lord chancellor of England, was beheaded for refusing to subscribe to Act of Supremacy.

1536 Menno Simons, Dutch religious reformer, began preaching Anabaptist doctrines.

Hans Holbein, the younger, of Germany became court painter to Henry VIII.

1541–1564 John Calvin headed a theocratic state at Geneva.

1543 Nicholas Copernicus published his astronomy discoveries.

1545 Council of Trent was convened by Pope Paul III; it made internal reforms in Roman Catholic Church.

1553–1558 Reign of Mary Tudor (Bloody Mary) of England, who restored Catholicism and persecuted Protestants; she lost (1558) Calais, last English stronghold on Continent, to the French.

1555 Peace of Augsburg signed, which allowed German princes to choose Catholicism or Lutheranism, but not Calvinism, as religion of their states; Lutheranism prevailed in north; Catholicism, in south.

1556–1598 Reign of Philip II of Spain, during which Hapsburg power reached its zenith and Golden Age of Spanish art and literature was initiated.

1558–1603 Reign of Elizabeth I of England, who established (1563) Church of England and increased English power; Elizabethan Age was marked by great flowering of literature.

1559 Pope Paul IV established the Index of Forbidden Books.

1559–1567 Reign of Mary Stuart, Queen of Scots, who abdicated in favor of her son, James VI (later James I of England); she was imprisoned by Elizabeth I because of her claims to English throne.

1562 French began harsh persecution of Huguenots, French Protestants; Catherine de' Medici ordered (1572) St. Bartholomew's Day Massacre; religious wars ended in 1598.

1566 Netherlands, led by William the Silent of Orange, revolted against Spanish domination and gained independence in 1581.

1571 Battle of Lepanto: Ottoman Turks defeated in naval battle with Austrian and Holy League forces, the greatest naval battle since Actium.

1580 Montaigne began composing *Essays*.

1582 Gregorian calendar introduced.

Douay version of New Testament published.

1587 John Knox, founder of Presbyterianism in Scotland, wrote *History of the Reformation in Scotland*.

1588 Spanish Armada defeated by English fleet under Sir Francis Drake.

c. **1589** Christopher Marlowe produced *Dr. Faustus*.

1589 Henry IV founded House of Bourbon; this dynasty ruled France until 1792.

1591–1613 William Shakespeare composed his plays and poems.

1597–1625 Francis Bacon wrote his *Essays*.

1598 Henry IV of France issued the Edict of Nantes, which granted religious toleration to Huguenots.

Boris Godunov became tsar of Russia and ruled until 1605.

NEAR AND MIDDLE EAST

1501 Safavid dynasty began rule of Iran that lasted until 1736.

1512–1520 Reign of Selim I, Ottoman sultan; he defeated Mamelukes in Syria and Egypt and assumed succession to Moslem Caliphate.

1520–1566 Reign of Suleiman I (the Magnificent), Ottoman sultan; he captured Belgrade, Rhodes, and Hungary during rule, which was marked by greatest flowering of Turkish literature, art, and architecture.

1571 Turks seized Cyprus and then suffered their first major defeat from Austrian and Holy League forces at Lepanto, the greatest naval battle since Actium.

1587–1628 Reign of Abbas I, shah of Iran, who erected palace and mosque at Isfahan.

FAR EAST

1510 Portuguese conquered Goa, India.

1526 Mogul Empire that was to endure until 1857 founded in India by Baber.

1549–1552 St. Francis Xavier introduced Christianity into Japan.

1557 Portuguese settled in Macao and began trade with China.

1560–1605 Reign of Akbar the Great (grandson of Baber), who enlarged domain and founded (1569) city of Fathpur Sikri, noted for Mogul architecture, especially Jami Masjid (the Great Mosque); Akbar also encouraged Persian arts and received European traders.

1568–1582 Nobunaga, who ruled Japan as military dictator, destroyed Buddhism as political force.

1571 Spanish founded Manila and began to colonize Philippines.

1582 Hideyoshi became military dictator of Japan; he initiated unification of country and unsuccessfully invaded Korea.

1590 Portuguese landed in Taiwan, calling it Formosa.

1595 Dutch began to colonize East Indies.

AMERICAS

1500 Cabral claimed Brazil for Portugal.

1501–1502 Amerigo Vespucci explored the coast of Brazil.

1511 Spanish took Cuba and Puerto Rico, founding San Juan and settling Jamaica.

1513 Ponce de Leon discovered Florida.

Balboa discovered the Pacific.

1519 Hernán Cortés of Spain landed in Mexico; Aztecs thought Cortés was Quetzalcoatl, their god who was supposed to appear at that period; Cortés, who met Montezuma II and later imprisoned him, captured (1521) Tenochtitlán and began harsh rule of Mexico.

1523–1524 Alvarado took Guatemala and Salvador for Spain.

1524 Verrazano explored the New England coast.

1530 Portuguese colonized Brazil.

1531–1535 Francisco Pizarro subjugated Inca Empire of Peru, executing Atahuallpa and installing Manco Capac as puppet ruler; Spanish founded (1535) Lima, which became capital of viceroyalty of Peru.

1534–1541 Jacques Cartier explored St. Lawrence River, stopping at sites of Quebec and Montreal.

1539–1542 De Soto made an expedition through Florida to the Mississippi.

1540–1542 Coronado explored the **Southwest,** reaching as far as Kansas.

1551 National University of Mexico founded.

University of San Marcos founded in Lima, Peru.

1565 St. Augustine, Florida, oldest permanent settlement in the United States, was founded.

Portuguese settled **Rio de Janeiro.**

1576–1577 Martin Frobisher searched for Northwest Passage.

1579 Sir Francis Drake claimed New Albion **(California)** for England.

1580 Buenos Aires, Argentina, founded by Juan de Garay for Spain.

AFRICA

1503–1507 Leo Africanus, Spanish Moslem of Morocco, explored **Sudan;** he issued (1526) book describing **Mali** and **Songhai** kingdoms.

1508 Portuguese began to colonize **Mozambique.**

1513 Songhai Empire conquered **Hausa States.**

1520 Portuguese visited Ethiopian court.

1529 Somali war in Ethiopia began; Moslems tried to conquer Ethiopia but were defeated (1543) when Portuguese aided Somalis.

1562 Sir John Hawkins of England began **slave trade** between Africa and the Americas.

1590 Moroccan invasions destroyed **Songhai Empire.**

1600—1700

EUROPE

1603 James VI of Scotland became **James I** of England, founding **house of Stuart,** which ruled England until 1688.

1605 Guy Fawkes executed for **"Gunpowder Plot"** to blow up Parliament.

1607 Jonson completed *Volpone.*

1609 Kepler published *Astronomia Nova,* laws of orbits of planets.

1609–1631 Newspapers were started on the Continent: *Avisa Relation oder Zeitung* (1609) in Germany; the *Nieuwe Tijdingen* (1616), Antwerp; the *Gazette,* later the *Gazette de France* (1631), Paris.

1609–1610 Douay version of Old Testament published.

1611 King James version of the Bible compiled by leading English scholars.

1613 Michael Romanov, tsar of Russia, founded **Romanov dynasty,** which ruled until 1917.

1614 The Estates General met for last time until the French Revolution.

1615 Cervantes published *Don Quixote.*

1618 Thirty Years War, final great religious war, broke out in Prague; this conflict between Catholic and Protestant Europe devastated Germany.

1624 Cardinal de Richelieu became chief minister of Louis XIII; he consolidated royal authority, strengthened army, built navy, and founded (1635) **French Academy.**

1625 Grotius published *De Jure Belli ac Pacis,* pioneer work in international law.

1625–1649 Reign of Charles I of England, who was involved with conflicts over supremacy of king or parliament and summoned (1640–1641) the **Long Parliament,** which abolished the courts of High Commission and the Star Chamber; Charles was beheaded for treason.

1628 William Harvey discovered principle of blood circulation.

Petition of Right signed by Charles I; it prohibited arbitrary imprisonment, martial law, forced loans, and billeting of soldiers and sailors.

1632 Galileo published his work confirming Copernican theory of astronomy.

1640 Puritan revolution in England began; monarchists fought civil war that ended in 1649 against those who wanted republic.

1643–1715 Reign of Louis XIV (the Sun King) of France, during which royal absolutism reached a new peak; Louis allegedly said, *"L'état c'est moi";* French art and culture flourished and **Versailles palace** was constructed.

1644 Milton wrote *Areopagitica.*

1645–1664 Venetian-Turkish wars caused further decline of Ottoman power.

1648 Peace of Westphalia, which ended Thirty Years War, recognized independence of Netherlands and of Swiss cantons and sovereignty of German states.

1649 King Charles I beheaded, and England had commonwealth form of government under **Oliver Cromwell** until 1660.

1651 Hobbes published *Leviathan.*

1652 England began series of wars with **French and Dutch** that lasted until 1678 over supremacy of the seas.

1659 Spanish power in Europe ended with **Peace of Pyrennes.**

1660 Monarchy restored by **Charles II** of England; Cavalier Parliament enacted repressive measures against Puritans.

1665 Great Plague hit **London;** the following year fire virtually destroyed city.

1675 Sir Christopher Wren began St. Paul's Cathedral, London.

1682–1725 Reign of **Peter the Great** of Russia; he tried to "Westernize" Russia and established schools and a newspaper.

1683 Turkish seige of **Vienna** repulsed.

1684 Newton published his theories of motion and gravitation.

1685 Edict of Nantes revoked by Louis XIV; Protestants fled abroad.

1688 "Glorious Revolution" occurred in England; this bloodless revolution against James II ended when **William of Orange** and **Mary,** his British wife, accepted crown.

France began war against Grand Alliance of European powers that resulted in decline of French power.

1689 William and Mary began to rule England and signed **Bill of Rights,** limiting royal power; their rule ended in 1702.

1699 Peace of Karlowitz: Turkey ceded some of her conquered territories to Austria, Poland, and Venice.

NEAR AND MIDDLE EAST

1638 Turks won back **Baghdad** from Persians.

1656 Mohammed **Kuprili** became grand vizier to Mohammed IV and helped Ottoman empire regain some former power.

1699 Peace of Karlowitz: Turkey ceded Hungary, Croatia, and Slavonia to Austria; Podolia and Ukraine to Poland; and the Peloponnesus to Venice.

FAR EAST

1600 William Adams, an Englishman, arrived in Japan and imparted some technology to Japanese.

British East India Company chartered for trade in India.

1603 Ieyasu Tokugawa came to power in Japan, and his dynasty ruled until 1867; it centralized feudalism, encouraged trade, and established capital at **Tokyo; Kabuki** theater was developed.

1611 British began to send envoys to Mogul Empire and later established settlements at Surat and factories in Bengal and Madras.

1615 Dutch seized **Moluccas** (Spice Islands) from Portuguese.

1616 Manchu Tartars from Manchuria began to invade China.

1619 Dutch founded **Batavia, Java.**

1627 Japan began to exclude foreigners, allowing one Dutch trading post to remain.

1628–1658 Reign of Shah Jehan, ruler of Mogul Empire; he erected **Taj Mahal,** one of the most beautiful buildings in the world.

1636 Dutch occupied **Ceylon.**

1641–1662 Dutch controlled **Formosa.**

1644 Ch'ing dynasty in China was founded by Manchus and ruled until 1912; **Korea** became vassal state known as the "Hermit Kingdom" because of its isolation.

1661–1722 Reign of **K'ang Hsi,** Chinese emperor who consolidated empire and issued edict of toleration after Jesuit missionaries appeared.

1668 Bombay became headquarters of East India Company.

1674 Mahratta State in west central India founded by Sivaji.

1675–1708 Guru Govind Singh ruled **Sikhs** and built up their military power.

AMERICAS

1607 English founded **Jamestown,** their first permanent settlement in America; **John Smith** became leader.

1608 Champlain founded **Quebec.**

Jesuit state in **Paraguay** founded.

1620 Pilgrims arrived at **Plymouth,** Massachusetts.

1630 Massachusetts Bay colony established by **Puritans.**

1671 Danes took St. Thomas.

British settled Barbados, and Leeward and Windward Islands.

1673 Jacques **Marquette** and Louis **Joliet** explored the Mississippi.

1682 After La Salle descended Mississippi River to its mouth, **French** began to rule colonial empire in North America that extended from Quebec to New Orleans.

AFRICA

1642 French established base on **Madagascar.**

c. 1650 Slave trade from **Gold Coast** thrived until early 19th century.

1652 Dutch founded **Capetown;** Jan van Riebeeck led settlers.

1680 Germans began to colonize West Africa.

1684 English lost **Tangier** to Morocco.

1687 Arguin, Guinea, established as Brandenburgian colony.

c. 1695 Osei Tutu founded Ashanti kingdom in western Africa and established capital at Kumasi; Ashanti, noted for high-quality **gold work,** grew wealthy from slave trade.

OCEANIA

1601 Australia began to be visited by Portuguese, Spanish, and Dutch.

1642 Abel **Tasman,** Dutch navigator, discovered **New Zealand** and **Tasmania,** which was named Van Diemen's Land.

1688 William **Dampier** of England landed on northwest coast of **Australia.**

1700—1800

EUROPE

1700 **Great Northern War** began: Russia, Poland, and Denmark fought Sweden for supremacy in the **Baltic;** when war ended in 1721, Russia emerged as a major European power with "window" on the Baltic. **Philip V** became first Bourbon king of **Spain.**

1701 **Act of Settlement,** which was passed by English parliament, provided that crown would pass to **house of Hanover;** king could not be Roman Catholic.

Hohenzollerns came to power in Prussia and Germany, ruling until 1918.

War of the Spanish Succession began; Treaty of Utrecht (1713) separated thrones of France and Spain and marked rise of British and decline of French.

1705 Moscow University founded by Peter the Great.

1707 **Great Britain** formed by union of **England** and **Scotland.**

1711 Joseph **Addison** and Richard **Steele** began publishing the *Spectator* in England.

1713–1740 Reign of **Frederick William I,** king of Prussia, who became known as the soldier king because he strengthened **Prussian army.**

1714 **George I** began the **Hanoverian rule** of England; house of Hanover was succeeded (1840) by house of Wettin when Queen Victoria married.

1715 The **Age of Enlightenment** began; also known as the **Age of Reason;** Europe experienced a rich period of **philosophy** that died out after 1789.

Louis XV began to rule France, but wars and financial policy weakened government.

1733 War of Polish Succession began: Russia and Austria defeated Spain and placed Augustus III on Polish throne two years later.

1738 John **Wesley,** founder of **Methodism,** began preaching in England.

1740 War of the **Austrian Succession:** a general European war broke out after **Maria Theresa** became Hapsburg ruler; it ended in 1748.

1740–1786 Reign of **Frederick the Great,** king of Prussia, who expanded territory and made Prussia leading European military power.

1747 **Denis Diderot** and other writers began editing the *Encyclopédie.*

1748 **Montesquieu** published *Spirit of the Laws.*

c. 1750 **Industrial Revolution** had begun in England; factory system, economic specialization, and urbanization changed social structure during next century.

1755 An earthquake devastated **Lisbon,** killing 30,000.

1756 **Seven Years War** began between **England** and **France** over colonial possessions in America and India; it ended in 1763; France lost Canada and India, England became world's major colonial power.

1758 Voltaire completed *Candide.*

1760 George III began his 60-year reign in England.

1762 Jean Jacques **Rousseau** completed *Social Contract.*

1762–1796 Reign of **Catherine II (the Great)** of Russia, who promoted education, the arts, and social reforms.

1768 Major **Russo-Turkish Wars:** Russia and Turkey waged a series of wars for over a century; in 1878 Turkey was finally ousted from Crimea and much of Slavic Europe.

1769 James **Watt,** Scottish inventor, patented his **steam engine.**

1772–1795 **Poland** was partitioned among Russia, Austria, and Prussia.

1773–1774 **Pugachev** led rebellion of Russian **peasants** and **Cossacks,** causing Catherine II to institute tighter control over serfs.

1774 Louis XVI and Marie Antoinette became king and queen of France.

1776 Adam Smith published *The Wealth of Nations.*

Edward Gibbon began *The Decline and Fall of the Roman Empire.*

1785 *The Times* of London was founded by John Walter.

1789 The **French Revolution** began when Paris mob stormed the **Bastille;** third estate drafted (1791) new constitution; Louis XVI and Marie Antoinette beheaded (1793).

1790 Edmund Burke wrote *Reflections on the French Revolution.*

1791 Thomas Paine wrote *The Rights of Man,* directed against critics of French Revolution.

1798 Robert Malthus published *Essay on the Principle of Population.*

1799 Napoleon-Bonaparte staged a coup d'état in France; his conquests made France the most powerful country in Europe; Code Napoléon reformed legal system; Napoleon was exiled in 1815.

NEAR AND MIDDLE EAST

1736 Nadir Shah established Afshar dynasty in Persia; considered last of the great Asian conquerors, he conquered Afghanistan, sacked Delhi, and defeated Turks.

1768 Turkey and Russia began a century of wars, causing Turkey to lose Crimea and much of Slavic Europe to Russia.

1794 Kajar dynasty of Persia founded by Aga Mohammed; it remained in power until 1925.

1798 Napoleon Bonaparte attempted to occupy Egypt but was driven out (1801) by British and Turkish forces.

FAR EAST

1735–1796 Reign of **Emperor Ch'ien Lung,** during which Chinese empire reached its greatest territorial extent; Christian missionaries were persecuted.

1739 Nadir Shah of Persia sacked Delhi and conquered Punjab.

1757 Defeat of Nawab of Bengal by **Robert Clive** marked beginning of **British Empire in India.**

1758 Burma became an independent state with capital at Rangoon.

1782 Rama I founded Chakri dynasty in Thailand and established capital at Bangkok; this dynasty rules today.

1786 British East India Company leased the island of Penang in Malaya, first step in British domination of Malay Peninsula.

1798 Ceylon became British territory.

AMERICAS

1721 Revolts in Paraguay initiated a series of wars in Latin America for independence from Spain.

1754 French and Indian Wars started in North America; British general, James Wolfe, defeated (1759) French under Montcalm on the Plains of Abraham, Quebec, Canada, ending the wars; British dominated Canada thereafter.

1775 American Revolution began with battle of Lexington and Concord; it ended with British surrender at Yorktown in 1783.

1776 Declaration of Independence signed in Philadelphia.

1788 U.S. Constitution ratified.

1789 George Washington became first U.S. President.

1791 Canada Act: Canada was divided into Upper Canada (chiefly English) and Lower Canada (predominantly French).

AFRICA

1787 British abolitionists established colony at Freetown, which became center for British settlement of Sierra Leone.

1795–1796 Mungo Park, British explorer, explored Niger River.

1799 By this time Portuguese, French, Spanish, Danes, Dutch, and Swedes all held trading posts along West African coast and engaged in slave trade.

OCEANIA

1770 Captain James Cook claimed Cape York Peninsula, Australia, for Great Britain.

1777 Cook visited Tasmania.

1788 British established a penal colony in Sydney, Australia.

1800—1900

EUROPE

1800 Socialism developed in Europe in reaction to deplorable industrial conditions.

1801 United Kingdom was formed by union of Great Britain and Ireland.

1802 John Dalton introduced atomic theory into chemistry.
First factory law was introduced in England; it pertained to child labor.

1804 Napoleon I became emperor of France.

1806 Holy Roman Empire came to an end when Francis II renounced the imperial title.

1812 Napoleon invaded Russia, a disastrous campaign.

1814–1815 Congress of Vienna: Metternich of Austria, Talleyrand of France, Alexander I of Russia, Frederick William I of Prussia, and Castlereagh of England tried to restore European balance of power; the congress reestablished monarchies and organized German Confederation, which was dominated by Austria.

1815 Napoleon I returned from Elba and was later defeated by British and Prussian armies at Waterloo.

1821 Greeks began war with Turkey, achieving independence in 1830.

1830 July Revolution in France forced abdication of King Charles X; Louis Philippe became constitutional monarch.

1831 Russians suppressed Polish insurrection, marking beginning of "Russification" of Poland.

1837–1901 Reign of Queen Victoria of England, who married (1840) her cousin Prince Albert of Saxe-Coburg; English enjoyed era of prosperity due to industrial and colonial expansion.

1838 Chartist movement began, marking first attempt of British working classes to attain power.

1845 Friedrich Engels wrote Situation of the Working Classes in England.
Potato blight began in Ireland, which resulted by 1851 in death of about one million people from starvation and disease.

1848 Marx and Engels issued Communist Manifesto.
Revolutions broke out in France, Germany, Austria, Hungary, Bohemia, and Italy.

1848–1916 Reign of Francis Joseph, Emperor of Austria, who became (1867) ruler of Austro-Hungarian Empire.

1852–1870 Reign of Napoleon III, emperor of the Second French Empire.

1854–1856 Crimean War: Britain and France ended Russian domination of southeastern Europe.

1855–1881 Reign of Alexander II, tsar of Russia; he attempted to modernize government, emancipated (1861) serfs, and ceded (1867) Alaska to the United States; Russian literature began its most creative period.

1856 Bessemer invented process of converting iron into steel.

1859 De Lesseps began Suez Canal, which opened in 1869.
Darwin published Origin of the Species.

1859–1870 Risorgimento in Italy: a nationalist movement led by middle classes and nobility for political unification; its leaders included Mazzini, Cavour, and Giuseppe Garibaldi.

1861 Kingdom of Italy proclaimed, and Victor Emmanuel II of Sardinia became king.
Rumania formed by unification of Moldavia and Walachia.

1862 Otto von Bismarck became premier and chancellor of Germany and created German Empire.

1864 First International organized in London under leadership of Karl Marx.

1866 First permanent transatlantic cable laid by Cyrus Field.
Austro-Prussian War: Bismarck expelled Austrians from German Confederation; and established North German Confederation; Austria lost Venetia to Italy.
Nobel invented dynamite.

1867 Marx published first volume of Das Kapital.
Austro-Hungarian Empire founded: under pressure from Hungarian nationalists, Francis Joseph created dual monarchy; this empire collapsed in 1918.

1868–1894 British statesmen Benjamin Disraeli, an imperialist and Tory leader, and William Gladstone, an anti-imperialist and Liberal party leader, vied for control of prime ministry.

1870 Dogma of papal infallibility declared by Vatican Council.
Vladimir Lenin (V. I. Ulyanov), founder of modern Communism, was born.

1870–1871 Franco-Prussian War: Germans, directed by von Moltke, invaded and defeated France; French deposed Napoleon III and established Third Republic of France, which endured until 1940.
Italy incorporated Papal States, completing unification of the country.

1871 German Empire proclaimed at Versailles with William I as Emperor; north and south Germany became united into single Reich.
Paris Commune formed when Parisians refused to surrender to new regime; national troops suppressed revolutionaries.

1875 Charles Stewart Parnell, Irish nationalist leader, was elected to Parliament and began movement for Irish independence.

1878 Congress of Berlin: much of Ottoman Empire divided among Russia, Britain, and Austro-Hungarian Empire.

1881 Alexander II of Russia assassinated by member of revolutionary group called People's Will.

1882 Triple Alliance formed by Germany, Austria-Hungary, and Italy.

1885 Louis Pasteur used vaccine to prevent rabies in young boy.

1894–1906 Dreyfus Affair: Capt. Alfred Dreyfus, French Jewish military officer, was unjustly convicted of treason by a court-martial, sentenced to Devils Island, but eventually exonerated; his case divided France between left and right factions, causing (1905) separation of church and state.

1894–1917 Reign of Nicholas II, last tsar of Russia.

1895 Roentgen discovered X rays.
Marconi sent message over wireless.

1898 Zeppelin invented motor-driven airship and made first trial flight two years later.
The Curies discovered radium.

1899 First Peace Conference at The Hague established a permanent court of arbitration.

NEAR AND MIDDLE EAST

1811–1849 Reign of Mohammed Ali in Egypt extended Egyptian territory to Persian Gulf.

1854–1856 Crimean War: Britain and France backed Turkey in war with Russia that forced Russian concessions and guaranteed integrity of Ottoman Empire.

1859–1869 Suez Canal was built by De Lesseps.

c. 1870 Turkish government permitted European Jews to settle in Palestine.

1878 Congress of Berlin: Turks lost Cyprus to British, part of Asian lands to Russians, and Bosnia-Hercegovina to Austrians.

1888 European powers declared **neutrality of Suez Canal;** free passage was guaranteed to merchant and war vessels.

1892 British took over **Trucial Oman,** a region of eastern Arabia, and denied local sheiks treaty-making powers.

1894–1896 Sultan **Abdu-l-Hamid II** initiated extermination plan against Armenians; persecutions and massacres were resumed in 1915.

1896 **Young Turks,** a new national force, developed in Turkey, leading (1908) revolt against Sultan.

FAR EAST

1819 Sir **T. Stamford Raffles** secured transfer of **Singapore** to British East India Company.

1839–1842 **Opium War:** British provoked war with China and acquired commercial concessions and **Hong Kong.**

1848 **Taiping Rebellion** began in China, further weakening Ch'ing dynasty; with aid of Western powers, it was suppressed in 1865.

1853 **Commodore Perry,** an American, landed in isolationist **Japan;** the following year Japanese agreed to trade with West.

1857–1858 **Sepoy Rebellion,** or Great Mutiny: Indian soldiers revolted against British, representing first serious revolt of Indians against foreign rule.

1868 Emperor **Meiji Mutsuhito** began to rule **Japan;** he modernized country by abolishing feudalism, promoting foreign trade, and initiating industrialization and military conscription; Meiji period ended in 1912.

1887 France joined Vietnam and Cambodia as **Indo-China;** Laos was added to union in 1893.

1888 Britain completed annexation of **Burma,** making it a dependency of India.

1889 Meiji Mutsuhito issued modern **constitution for Japan.**

1894–1895 **Sino-Japanese War:** Japan became an imperial power by defeating Chinese in Korea and acquiring Formosa (Taiwan) and the Pescadores.

1898 Spain ceded **Philippines** to the United States.

1899 Western powers forced **Open Door** policy upon China by which equal trade rights for all nations were guaranteed.

AMERICAS

1801–1803 **Toussaint L'Ouverture,** martyred Haitian patriot, liberated **Santo Domingo** from the French and governed the island, thwarting Napoleon's colonial ambitions.

1803 United States purchased **Louisiana Territory** from France.

1806 **Henri Christophe,** Haitian revolutionary, elected president of Haitian republic.

1810 **Mexico** began to fight for independence from Spain.

1811 Paraguay achieved independence.

1811–1813 **Venezuela,** led by Francisco de Miranda, gained independence.

1812–1814 **War of 1812:** United States and Great Britain fought over neutrality of the seas and impressment of sailors; struggle strengthened American nationalist feelings.

1816 Argentina won independence.

1818 Chile gained independence under **José de San Martín.**

1818–1823 **Bernardo O'Higgins,** Chilean revolutionist, ruled **Chile.**

1819–1830 **Simón Bolívar,** the Liberator and greatest **Latin American hero,** defeated Spanish forces at Boyacá and was elected President of Greater Colombia (modern Colombia, Venezuela, Ecuador, and Panama).

1821 Mexicans achieved independence.

1822 Independence was won in **Brazil** and **Peru.**

1823 **Monroe Doctrine:** President James Monroe declared that the United States would neither interfere in European affairs nor tolerate European interference in American hemisphere.

1825 **Bolivia** became independent, the last Latin American country to win freedom from Spain.

1841 **Act of Union** joined Upper and Lower **Canada.**

1844 Samuel Morse transmitted message over **telegraph** from Washington to Baltimore.

1846 The **Mexican war** between United States (and Texas) and Mexico began; **Treaty of Guadalupe Hidalgo** established (1848) Rio Grande as Mexican-U.S. boundary and made New Mexico and California U.S. territory and Texas a possession.

1848 **Gold** discovered in **California.**

1861 **Civil War** (that ended in 1865) began in the United States.

1863 The **Emancipation Proclamation** ended slavery in the rebel states.

1864 **Maximilian,** Austrian archduke, became emperor of **Mexico;** he and his wife Carlotta retained power with aid of French troops; their rule was overthrown (1867) by **Benito Juárez,** an Indian, who became Mexican national hero.

1865 **War of the Triple Alliance** began: Paraguay fought against Argentina, Brazil, and Uruguay; it ended (1870) with devastation of Paraguay.

1867 **British North America Act:** Canada became a confederation.

United States purchased **Alaska** from Russia.

1868 Cubans fought **Ten Years War** for independence, being defeated by Spanish in 1878.

1876 **Porfirio Díaz** seized presidency of **Mexico** and ruled ruthlessly; he encouraged foreign capital, made Mexico prosperous but kept peasants in virtual bondage; deposed by **Madero revolution** in 1911.

1879–1884 **War of the Pacific:** Chile fought against Bolivia and Peru, securing territory from both countries; Bolivia lost sea access.

1889 Republic of **Brazil** established.

1895 Cuban poet, **José Martí,** led revolt against Spain.

1898 **Spanish-American War:** after U.S. battleship *Maine* was sunk in Havana harbor, the United States declared war on Spain and by Treaty of Paris (1898) acquired Puerto Rico, Guam, and the Philippines; the war dissolved Spanish control in Latin America.

1899 **Cuba** became an independent republic under U.S. protection.

AFRICA

1806 Britain annexed **Cape Province** in South Africa.

1807 Britain outlawed **slave trade** with France, Spain, and Portugal following suit.

1808 **Sierra Leone** became a British crown colony and administered **Gambia.**

1822 **Liberia** founded as haven for **freed American slaves;** it was declared an independent republic in 1847.

1830 French troops began conquest of Algeria.

1835 **Boers** began to leave Cape Province; the "Great Trek" established republics of Transvaal, Natal, and Orange Free State.

1841 **Dr. David Livingstone** began three decades of explorations in central Africa; he discovered (1855) Victoria Falls and his reports created interest in the "Dark Continent" and its natural resources.

1843 British annexed **Natal** after short war with Boers; it was made crown colony in 1856.

1848 British annexed **Orange Free State.**

1867–1871 **Diamonds** were discovered in South Africa, inciting diamond rush; **Kimberley** became center of diamond industry.

1874–1889 Henry Morton **Stanley** explored **Congo River.**

1876 **Leopold II,** with Stanley's aid, set up organization to exploit Congo; he founded (1885) **Congo Free State,** ruling as supreme monarch until 1908.

1878 Cetewayo led **Zulu** revolt against British that was defeated (1879) at Ulundi.

1880 **Brazzaville** founded in Congo by **French.**

1881 **Tunis** became French protectorate.

1884–1885 Germans proclaimed protectorates over **Tanganyika, Togoland, Cameroons,** and **South-West Africa.**

1886 **Gold** discovered in **Witwatersrand** in southern **Transvaal.**

1888 **Cecil Rhodes,** British diamond tycoon, gained monopoly of Kimberley diamond production; Rhodes became (1890) virtual dictator of Cape Province but resigned (1897) and thereafter developed **Rhodesia.**

1889 **Menelik II** of Ethiopia unwittingly signed Treaty of Uccialli that made Ethiopia an Italian protectorate; Italians invaded after he repudiated treaty; Menelik crushed (1896) Italians at **Aduwa.**

1891 British annexed **Nyasaland** and fought Arab slave traders.

1896 British, after a series of wars, defeated **Ashanti** kingdom and annexed it in 1901.

1899–1902 Boer War: British defeated Boers in South Africa and formed (1910) **Union of South Africa.**

OCEANIA

1803 British took possession of **Tasmania,** establishing a penal colony there.

1840 Treaty of Waitangi guaranteed Maoris in New Zealand that they would retain their land for surrendering sovereignty to British crown.

1900—1977

EUROPE

1903 Social Democrats held second party congress in London and split into **Mensheviks and Bolsheviks,** the nascent Communist party.

1904 France and England signed the **Entente Cordiale,** which became (1907) the **Triple Entente** when Russia joined.

1905 Einstein formulated theory of **relativity.**

1906 Britain launched the *Dreadnought,* first large **battleship,** signaling start of world naval buildup.

1908 Brief Balkan crisis erupted after **Austria** announced annexation of **Bosnia and Hercegovina.**

1910–1936 Reign of George V, king of Great Britain and Northern Ireland and emperor of India, was marked by **Home Rule for Ireland** (1914) and World War I.

1911 Italy declared war on Turkey and acquired Tripoli.

1912 First **Balkan War** began between Balkan countries and Turkey; a second broke out when Bulgaria attacked Serbia and Greece.

1913 European nations increased preparations for war.

1914 Assassination of **Archduke Francis Ferdinand** of Austria in Sarajevo by **Gavrilo Princip,** a member of Serbian terrorist society, sparked **World War I; Triple Entente** of France, Britain and Russia and their allies Japan, Belgium, Serbia, and Montenegro fought **Central Powers** of Germany, Austria-Hungary, and Turkey; Italy, Portugal, Rumania, and the United States later sided with Triple Entente, which with its allies achieved **victory** in 1918, when an armistice was signed. At least 10,000,000 died during war.

1915 Cunard ship *Lusitania* sunk off the coast of Ireland after attack by German submarine; 1,198 were lost.

1916 President Wilson submitted his peace proposals to warring nations.

Gregory **Rasputin,** a hedonistic mystic who influenced Russian royal family, was murdered.

1917 Bolshevik Revolution broke out in Russia; **Alexander Kerensky,** a Menshevik, headed provisional government but was overthrown by Bolshevik leader, Vladimir **Lenin.**

Balfour Declaration: Great Britain announced that Palestine should become home for Jews.

1918 Treaty of **Brest-Litovsk:** Russians signed peace treaty with Germans, losing Poland, the Ukraine, and border areas inhabited by non-Russians.

Kaiser Wilhelm abdicated, and Germans adopted **Weimar Constitution** the following year.

Austro-Hungarian Empire ended, and Austria became a republic, while Poland and Hungary proclaimed their independence.

Czechoslovakia became independent; Thomas Masaryk served as president and Eduard Beneš as foreign minister.

"Kingdom of the Serbs, Croats, and Slovenes" was proclaimed under the regency of **Peter I** of Serbia; its name was changed to **Yugoslavia** (land of southern Slavs) in 1929.

Civil War began in Russia between Reds and Whites that was complicated by Allied interventions; by end of war in 1920, Russia had been devastated.

1919 Treaty of **Versailles** ending World War I was negotiated by Woodrow Wilson (United States), Georges Clemenceau (France), David Lloyd George (England), and Vittorio Orlando (Italy).

1920 League of Nations was established in Geneva; the United States refused to join.

Northern and Southern Ireland separated; Southern Ireland became (1921) **Irish Free State** with dominion status.

1922 Russia became the **Union of Soviet Socialist Republics,** the first Communist state in the world.

Benito **Mussolini,** founder of Fascism, became premier of Italy, gradually creating dictatorship.

Major powers agreed to limit size of navies at **Washington Disarmament Conference.**

1923 Adolf **Hitler,** leader of National Socialist (Nazi) Party, led unsuccessful "Beer Hall Putsch" in Munich; during imprisonment he wrote *Mein Kampf.*

1924 A power struggle began in Russia after Lenin's death; ultimately **Joseph Stalin** was victorious and became dictator.

1928 Stalin initiated **Five Year Plan** for rapid industrialization and collectivized farms; **peasants** who refused collectivization were either sent to Siberia to perform forced labor or killed; measures caused "liquidation" of more than five million peasants.

Kellogg-Briand Pact outlawing war was signed by the United States and 62 other nations in Paris.

1929 Lateran Treaties created independent state of **Vatican City** in Rome.

1930 Worldwide **economic depression** developed, pushing many countries into bankruptcy; this disaster encouraged rise of **extremist movements.**

1931 British Commonwealth of Nations established.

Spain became a republic.

1932 Antonio **Salazar** became prime minister of **Portugal,** ruling (1936–1968) as dictator.

1933 The democratic **Weimar Republic** fell in Germany. Hitler's Nazi party won majority in *Reichstag* and the government granted him dictatorial powers; Hitler built up war economy and began to rearm Germany; he withdrew from the League of Nations and set up **concentration camps,** where, in the years that followed, over six million people (mainly Jews and Poles) died.

1935 Nuremberg Laws deprived Jews of citizenship, barred them from certain professions, and prohibited marriage between Germans and Jews.

Ethiopia, in League of Nations, brought charges against Italy; League economic sanctions against Italy did not prevent annexation (1936) of Ethiopia.

1936 Hitler repudiated Locarno Pact and sent troops into **Rhineland.**

Rome-Berlin-Tokyo Axis formed.

Spanish **Civil War** began: Republicans were backed by Communist Russia, while Nazi Germany and Fascist Italy supported Falangists; liberals from many countries fought to save republic; Falangist forces, headed by **General Francisco Franco,** were victorious by 1939.

Stalin began liquidation of his enemies with series of purge trials that lasted until 1939.

George VI became king of England after Edward VIII abdicated.

1938 Germany annexed **Austria.**

Munich Pact: French and British, led by Neville Chamberlain, appeased Hitler and allowed Germany to occupy **Sudetenland;** Germans took remainder of Czechoslovakia in 1939.

1939 Germany signed nonaggression pact with Soviet Union.

Germans invaded **Poland,** beginning **World War II.**

Russian troops invaded Poland, which was partitioned between Soviet Union and Germany.

Russians took Lithuania, Latvia, and Estonia.

Russians invaded **Finland,** defeating her the following year.

League of Nations performed its final act by expelling Soviet Union for invading Finland.

World War II broke out and developed into global conflict between **Axis** and **Allies.**

1940 Marshal Henri **Pétain** became head of French government and concluded peace treaty with Germany; Pétain set up government for unoccupied France in **Vichy,** which collaborated with Germans.

1940–1945 Winston **Churchill** was prime minister of England; his inspiring leadership helped British during dark days of war.

1941 Germany and Italy declared war on the **United States** on Dec. 11.

1942 Vidkun **Quisling** appointed by Germans to head puppet government in **Norway;** he was executed for collaboration in 1945.

1943 Mussolini's regime collapsed; **Marshal Pietro Badoglio** became prime minister, **and Italy surrendered unconditionally to Allies and declared war on Germany.**

President Roosevelt and Prime Minister Churchill held conferences at Casablanca, Cairo, and Teheran to coordinate war plans.

German defeat by Russian forces at **Stalingrad** (now Volgograd) marked turning point of war on the Eastern front.

1944 **D-Day:** Allied troops, commanded by **General Dwight D. Eisenhower,** invaded Fortress Europa at Normandy, France.

German generals staged unsuccessful attempt on Hitler's life.

U.S. and French troops liberated **Paris.**

General Charles de Gaulle established provisional government in France.

1945 **Yalta (Crimea) Conference:** Roosevelt, Churchill, and Stalin made postwar plans for German occupation and agreed to form a United Nations.

Josip Broz Tito, partisan leader, became head of Yugoslavia.

Mussolini captured and executed by Italian partisans. Hitler died in Berlin, reportedly a suicide.

Germany surrendered unconditionally to Allies; Allied Control Council set up to rule Germany and **Berlin,** both of which were divided among four powers. President Truman, Churchill, and Stalin met at **Potsdam, Germany,** to discuss control of Germany.

Clement Attlee, Labour party leader, became prime minister of England.

International War Crimes Tribunal began in Nuremberg; Nazi military and civilian leaders were tried for war crimes.

1946 **United Nations General Assembly** held its first session, in London; **Trygve Lie** of Norway became first secretary-general, holding office until 1951.

Civil war erupted in Greece between Communists and rightist government forces; Bulgaria, Albania, and Yugoslavia aided Communist guerrillas; conflict, which ended in 1949 with royalists retaining power, brought increased Western-Soviet hostility.

1946–1947 **Bulgaria** and **Rumania** proclaimed people's republics.

1947 **Cominform** was established in response to **Marshall Plan** when Communist leaders from nine countries met in Poland; it was dissolved in 1956.

1948 Communists came to power in **Hungary** and **Czechoslovakia;** Czech President Beneš resigned, and Foreign Minister Jan Masaryk was found dead.

Yugoslavia withdrew from Cominform, proclaiming its independence of Soviet influence.

European Recovery Plan (the Marshall Plan) went into effect; ERP ended in 1951.

Berlin Blockade: Soviets barred road and rail travel between Berlin and West Germany; West airlifted supplies until ban was lifted in 1949.

1949 **North Atlantic Treaty Organization** set up by the United States, Canada, and 10 European countries for collective self-defense.

Soviet Union exploded atomic bomb, ending U.S. monopoly.

Germany divided into **West Germany** (Federal Republic of Germany) and **East Germany** (German Democratic Republic).

1952 Reign of **Queen Elizabeth II** of England began.

1953 Joseph Stalin died; **Georgi Malenkov** became Soviet premier; **Nikita S. Khrushchev** elected first secretary of the Soviet Communist party's Central Committee.

Russians exploded their first **hydrogen bomb.**

Workers in East Germany staged riots that were suppressed by Soviet troops.

1954 **Geneva settlement** divided Vietnam into North and South Vietnam and recognized independence of Cambodia and Laos.

1955 **Warsaw Pact:** mutual defense treaty signed by Soviet Union, Albania, Czechoslovakia, Bulgaria, Hungary, Poland, **Rumania,** and **East Germany.**

1956 Premier Khrushchev denounced Stalin at 20th Communist Party Congress in Moscow, ushering in a period of **de-Stalinization** in Soviet Union and Eastern Europe. Workers rioted in Poznan, Poland.

Hungarian rebellion against Communist regime ruthlessly put down by Soviet troops and tanks.

1957 **Common Market:** European Economic Community established by Belgium, Netherlands, Luxembourg, West Germany, France, and Italy; its ultimate aim was political union.

Sputnik: Soviet Union launched world's first artificial earth satellite, initiating **Space Age.**

1958 Nuclear test ban negotiations began in Geneva between Western and Soviet blocs.

De Gaulle elected president of France.

Russians provoked Berlin crisis that was limited to diplomatic confrontation.

1960 Cyprus gained independence with **Archbishop Makarios** as president.

European Free Trade Association established by "Outer Seven": Austria, United Kingdom, Denmark, Norway, Portugal, Sweden, and Switzerland; Finland joined in 1961.

American U-2 plane, on photoreconnaissance mission, was shot down over Russian territory; United States agreed to suspend flights.

1961 **Berlin Wall:** East Germans erected wall between East and West Berlin, causing war scare.

Yuri A. Gagarin, Russian astronaut, was first man to orbit earth.

1963 Pope John XXIII died; Giovanni Battista Cardinal Montini elected as **Pope Paul VI.**

The United States, Soviet Union, and Great Britain signed treaty banning **nuclear tests** above ground and under water.

Fighting broke out between **Greek** and **Turkish Cypriots;** UN force is still on island to maintain order.

1964 Soviet Presidium ousted **Khrushchev** and made **Aleksei N. Kosygin** premier and **Leonid I. Brezhnev** first secretary of Communist party.

1966 De Gaulle requested **NATO** troop removal from France.

1967 Military staged coup d'état in **Greece,** installing dictatorship and driving **King Constantine II** into exile.

Britain devalued the **pound** and instituted austerity program.

1968 International monetary crises developed because of faltering British pound and French franc, but both currencies were held.

Soviet troops invaded **Czechoslovakia;** President Ludvik Svoboda and Alexander Dubcek allowed to retain posts, but Czechs had to accept Soviet troop occupation for indefinite time.

Peace talks opened in Paris between representatives of Hanoi, National Liberation Front, Saigon, and Washington to discuss **Vietnam cease-fire.**

1969 Charles de Gaulle resigned as president of France and was replaced by Georges Pompidou.

1970 **West Germany** and **USSR** signed a nonaggression pact.

Conservative leader **Edward Heath** became prime minister in England.

Violent food price riots in **Poland** led to Wladyslav Gomulka's resignation. He was replaced by Edward Gierek as the first secretary of the Communist party.

Charles De Gaulle died.

1972 **Great Britain, Ireland, and Denmark** joined the EEC.

Arab commandos disrupt the **XXth Olympic games** at Munich by taking 13 Israeli athletes hostage. The terrorists and hostages were later killed.

Terrorism rocked **Northern Ireland** in continued Protestant-Catholic conflict.

1973 **East and West Germany** established diplomatic relations, formally acknowledging their separation. Greece formally abolished the monarchy.

Western Europe was plunged into an **energy crisis** when the Arabs embargoed oil shipments to Europe, the U.S., and Japan.

1975 Western Europe experiences severe inflation and unemployment.
In Helsinki, Western and Eastern leaders signed pact at Conference on Security and Cooperation. Francisco Franco dies; Juan Carlos is proclaimed Spanish king.

1978 Pope Paul VI died; Albino Cardinal Luciani elected as Pope John Paul I, but lives only 34 days. Karol Cardinal Wojtyla of Poland elected Pope John Paul II.

MIDDLE EAST

1900 Ibn Saud began to conquer Arabia, which became (1932) kingdom of Saudi Arabia.

1901 Persians discovered petroleum, causing increased rivalry in the area between Russia and England.

1914 British declared Egypt a protectorate, which it remained until 1922.

1916 British Colonel T. E. Lawrence (Lawrence of Arabia) led Arab military campaigns against Turks, hoping for independent Arab states.

1919 Kemal Ataturk organized Turkish Nationalist party and began to form army; he was elected (1923) president of newly founded Turkish republic and began "Westernization" of country, abolishing (1923) caliphate and ruling until 1938.

1920 Syria and Lebanon became French mandates; their independence was recognized when they were admitted to United Nations in 1945.
Palestine, including Jordan, became British mandate; three-way struggle among Jews, Arabs, and British developed, lasting until 1948.

1921 Reza Shah Pahlavi, who staged coup d'etat in Persia, eventually ruled as dictator; changed (1935) name of country to Iran; abdicated in 1941.

1936 Farouk became king of Egypt.

1941 Mohammed Reza Shah Pahlevi became shah of Iran.

1945 The Arab League, an association of Arab states, was formed for economic unity and as opposition to establishment of Jewish state in Palestine.

1946 Iran protested to UN Security Council the presence of Russian troops in Azerbaijan province; this incident, which ended the following year, was the first crisis of the Cold War.
Kingdom of Jordan proclaimed.

1948 State of Israel achieved independence after bitter struggle; David Ben-Gurion first prime minister.

1948–1949 Arab-Israeli war ended in defeat of Arab League forces.

1951–1953 Iran oil industry nationalized by Prime Minister Mohammed Mossadegh.

1952 Gamal Abdel Nasser led army coup against King Farouk; Nasser was elected (1956) president of Egypt and promoted Arab unity.

1956 Suez Crisis: when Nasser nationalized Suez Canal, Israel, Britain, and France attacked Egypt but withdrew after UN Emergency Task-Force entered conflict.

1958 United Arab Republic formed by unification of Egypt and Syria; Syria withdraws in 1961.
Lebanon accused U.A.R. of intervention; President Eisenhower dispatched troops to area.
Iraqi monarchy overthrown in bloody coup led by General Kassem.
British paratroopers landed in Jordan to prevent pro-Nasser take-over.

1960 U.A.R., with Russian aid, began construction of a new Aswan Dam.

1961 Kuwait achieved independence.

1962 Kurdish tribes in northern Iraq rebelled, demanding independent state. Revolt is crushed in 1975.
Adolf Eichmann, chief administrator of Nazi program for exterminating Jews, was tried and executed by Israel.
Yemen monarchy overthrown; civil war broke out between republicans, who were supported by Egyptians, and royalists, backed by Saudi Arabia.

1963 British protectorate of Federation of South Arabia formed by union of Aden and Aden Federation; terrorist groups worked for unification with Yemen; the area achieved independence in 1968 as Southern Yemen.

1965 West Germany established diplomatic relations with Israel, causing most Arab nations to sever ties with West Germany.

1967 Arab-Israeli war: six-day conflict broke out after Nasser closed Gulf of Aqaba to Israeli ships; Israelis defeated Arabs and occupied Sinai peninsula and Jerusalem.

1968 President Abdul Rahman Arif of Iraq was ousted in bloodless coup led by former premier Ahmed Hassan al-Bakr, who later assumed premiership.
Israel attacked Lebanese airport in Beirut in retaliation for Arab attack on El Al airplane at Athens.

1969 Despite world condemnation, Iraqi Revolutionary Court executed some 40 persons.

1970 Nasser died in Cairo; succeeded by Anwar Sadat.
Palestinian commandos held 54 passengers of three hijacked planes as hostages in Jordan.
Civil war broke out between Jordanian army and Palestinian guerrilla groups.

1973 Large-scale fighting once again broke out between Israel and the Arab nations. The war ended in an inconclusive cease-fire.
The Arabs embargoed the shipment of oil to the U.S., Europe, and Japan, and boosted prices.

1974 The organization of petroleum exporting countries (OPEC) ended its oil embargo.

1975 Civil war raged in Lebanon between Christians and Moslems. Israel and Egypt signed Sinai disengagement pact. Suez Canal reopened.

1976 Cease-fire achieved in Lebanon.

1978 Egyptian President Sadat and Israeli Premier Begin agreed to peace treaty at Camp David, Maryland.

FAR EAST

1904–1905 Russo-Japanese War: Russia's fleet was destroyed, and Japan's victory gained her recognition as world power.

1907 Mohandas Gandhi organized his first campaign of civil disobedience in Africa; he returned (1915) to India and supported England during World War I, hoping to attain Indian independence.

1910 Japan annexed Korea.

1911 Chinese Revolution: Sun Yat-sen forced Manchu emperor to abdicate and served briefly as president of Chinese Republic.

1917 War developed in China between Kuomintang, Sun Yat-sen's party of the Republic, and "war lords" of the national government in the North; Kuomintang established capital in Canton.

1919 Amritsar Massacre: hundreds of Indian nationalists were fired upon and killed by British.

1921 Chinese Communist party founded and became allied (1923) with Kuomintang.

1926 Chiang Kai-shek led Nationalist army in capture of Hankow, Shanghai, and Nanking; he drove (1927) Chinese Communists from Shanghai, initiating long civil war between Kuomintang forces and Communists.

1927 Mao Tse-tung, one of the founders of the Chinese Communist party, led peasant uprising in Hunan province.

1931 Japanese invaded Manchuria and set up Manchukuo, a puppet state.
Mao Tse-tung elected chairman of Soviet Republic of China.

1934–1935 Mao Tse-tung led Red Army on Long March (6,000 miles) from Kiangsi province north to new headquarters at Yenan.

1937 Burma became independent of India.
Japanese invaded northern China and fought war that continued until 1945.
Gandhi's long fasts forced some Indian states to grant democratic reforms.

1940 Japanese established puppet government in Nanking and signed military alliance with Germany and Italy.

1941 Japan bombed Pearl Harbor, captured Singapore, Philippines, and other areas of the Pacific, initiating World War II in the Pacific and drawing United States into war.

1945 United States dropped atomic bombs on Hiroshima and Nagasaki, marking the beginning of the Nuclear Age; as a result, Japan surrendered, ending World War II.

Korea was divided into Russian and American occupation zones; partition was formalized in 1948 when country became **North Korea** (Democratic People's Republic of Korea) and **South Korea** (Republic of Korea), which were separated by 38th parallel.

Vietnamese nationalists began demands for independence from France; war broke out; **Ho Chi Minh**, founder of Communist party in Vietnam, led Viet Minh forces.

Indonesian nationalists led by **Sukarno** began to fight Dutch for independence.

1946 **Philippines** granted independence by the **United States.**

1947 **India** and **Pakistan** became separate independent dominions; **Jawaharlal Nehru** became prime minister of Hindu state of India and **Mahomed Ali Jinnah,** governor general of Moslem state of Pakistan; bloody rioting broke out after partition, causing the death of millions of Hindus and Moslems.

1948 Gandhi assassinated by Hindu fanatic.

Communists began guerrilla warfare in Malaya that lasted over a decade.

1949 **Chinese People's Republic** headed by Mao Tse-tung established government at Peking, after defeating **Chiang Kai-shek,** whose **Nationalist government** was forced to **Taiwan** (Formosa).

1950 Sukarno elected president of the Republic of **Indonesia.**

Korean war broke out when North Koreans invaded South Korea; United Nations force under U.S. command intervened.

Chinese Communists invaded **Tibet** and sent troops to aid **North Koreans.**

1951 Armistice talks began at **Panmunjon** to end Korean war.

1954 Battle of **Dienbienphu:** Crushing French defeat ended her control in Indo-China; **Vietnam** divided at 17th parallel, with **Ho Chi Minh** as president of North Vietnam; Cambodia and Laos became independent.

1955 A U.S. military advisory group took over training of **South Vietnamese** army.

Premier **Ngo Dinh Diem** became president of **South Vietnam.**

1957 Federation of Malaya gained independence.

1959 Communist Chinese suppressed uprising in **Tibet.** Communist **Pathet Lao** forces began civil war in Laos; a temporary cease-fire was secured (1961) in Geneva. **China and India** begun a series of border wars.

1961 India forcibly annexed Portuguese **Goa, Damão,** and **Diu.**

United States sent guerrilla warfare specialists to train **South Vietnamese** soldiers.

1962 Neutralist government set up in Laos under **Prince Souvanna Phouma,** but Pathet Lao continued sporadic fighting in North.

1963 **Federation of Malaysia** created by union of Federation of Malaya, Singapore, Sarawak, and North Borneo; the union suffered infiltration by Indonesian guerrillas until 1966; **Singapore** seceded (1965) and became independent.

Diem regime in South Vietnam overthrown; government changed hands frequently until military regime of **Nguyen Cao Ky** took over in 1965.

1964 **China exploded her first atomic bomb.**

France recognized Communist China.

Nehru died in India and was succeeded by **Lal Bahadur Shastri.**

1965 United States began bombing **North Vietnam.**

After an abortive Communist coup in **Indonesia,** the army slaughtered at least 100,000 Communists; Indonesia withdrew from United Nations.

India and Pakistan fought over Kashmir.

1966 Communist China initiated **"cultural revolution"** aimed at ideological conformity of party leaders.

Sukarno forced to yield power to **Suharto,** who outlawed Communist party.

Indira Gandhi, Nehru's daughter, became prime minister of India after Shastri's death.

1967 Communist China exploded first hydrogen bomb.

South Vietnam: first national election; Nguyen Van Thieu president and Nguyen Cao Ky vice-president.

1968 **North Korea** seized *Pueblo,* U.S. Navy intelligence ship, holding its officers and crew for 11 months.

Peace talks for Vietnam cease-fire began in Paris between representatives of Hanoi, National Liberation Front, Saigon, and Washington.

President Johnson ordered halt to bombing of North Vietnam.

1969 **Soviet and Chinese forces** fought on the Manchurian border over a disputed island in the Ussuri River.

Nixon administration withdrew 25,000 troops from **Vietnam.**

1970 Prince **Sihanouk** was deposed as chief of state in **Cambodia.** He was replaced by Gen. Lon Nol.

U.S. and South Vietnamese troops invaded **Cambodia.**

1971 Communist China admitted to **U.N.; Nationalist Chinese** (Taiwan) ousted.

East Pakistan became independent state of **Bangladesh** after bloody civil war.

1972 President Nixon visits Peking and Moscow.

1973 U.S. and South Vietnamese signed cease-fire agreement with North Vietnamese and Vietcong. Fighting continued through Indochina.

1975 The thirty year Indochina war ended with the military collapse of U.S.-backed **South Vietnam** and **Cambodia.**

1976 Communist Chinese leader **Mao Tse-tung** dies.

1977 **Morarji R. Desai** became prime minister of India on defeating Mrs. Gandhi in election.

AMERICAS

1901 President **William McKinley** assassinated by anarchist; **Theodore Roosevelt** became President and held office until 1909.

1903 **Panama,** with U.S. assistance, revolted against Colombia and gained independence.

Orville and Wilbur Wright made their first **airplane** flight near Kitty Hawk, North Carolina.

1910 **Francisco Madero** led **Mexican Revolution** against President Diaz; after Madero's assassination, **Francisco** (Pancho) **Villa, Emiliano Zapata,** and **Venustiano Carranza** continued revolution; Mexico's constitution was enacted 1917.

1914 Panama Canal opened.

1916–1924 U.S. troops occupied **Dominican Republic.**

1917 United States entered World War I on side of Allies.

1929 **Stock Market** crash in the United States initiated the **Great Depression;** during height of depression, 12 million people were unemployed.

1932–1935 Chaco War: Bolivia and **Paraguay** fought exhausting war over disputed Chaco plain.

1933 President **Franklin D. Roosevelt** was inaugurated; he enacted **New Deal** legislation aimed at improving social and economic conditions in the U.S.

1938 Mexico nationalized foreign oil companies.

1941–1945 United States in World War II: after Japanese bombed **Pearl Harbor,** December 7, 1941, the United States declared war; Nazi Germany and Fascist Italy declared war on the United States; war was terminated after defeat of German army and surrender of Japanese after atomic bombing of Hiroshima and Nagasaki.

1942 Enrico Fermi achieved first self-sustaining nuclear chain reaction.

1944 Bretton Woods (New Hampshire) Conference established the **International Bank for Reconstruction** and the **International Monetary Fund.**

Dumbarton Oaks, Washington, D.C., Conference: the United States, Great Britain, and Soviet Union laid plans for an **international organization.**

1945 Roosevelt died and was succeeded by **Harry S Truman.**

United Nations Charter signed at San Francisco.

United States made first **atom bomb** test at Los Alamos, New Mexico, warned Japan of her complete destruction unless she surrendered, and dropped atomic bombs on **Hiroshima** and **Nagasaki.**

1946 Juan Perón elected president of Argentina; he established totalitarian regime and an ultranationalistic program that ultimately ruined economy, and was deposed (1955) by miltary coup.
Churchill gave "iron curtain" speech at Fulton, Missouri, warning of Soviet expansionism.

1948 Truman won upset Presidential victory; he initiated overseas military and economic aid to contain Communism and became leader in NATO formation.
Organization of American States (OAS) founded for hemispheric unity and mutual defense.

1949 U.S. Senate ratified NATO treaty, establishing collective self-defense among Western powers.

1950 United States in UN Security Council charged North Korea with invading South Korea and initiated military intervention against aggressors with General MacArthur as UN Commander.

1952 Fulgencio Batista seized power in Cuba.
United States exploded its first hydrogen bomb.

1954 General Alfredo Stroessner staged coup in Paraguay; in spite of opposition, he remains in power.
Brown v. *Board of Education:* U.S. Supreme Court outlawed racial segregation in public schools, initiating civil rights movement.

1957 François Duvalier elected president of Haiti; his harsh rule included reign of terror.

1958 Explorer I: United States successfully launched her first artificial satellite.

1959 Fidel Castro came to power in Cuba; he gradually linked country with Soviet bloc and proclaimed (1961) loyalty to Communism.

1960 John F. Kennedy elected U.S. President.

1961 United States severed relations with Cuba.
Bay of Pigs: U.S.-trained Cuban exiles' invasion of Cuba ended disastrously.
Charter of the Alliance for Progress signed in Punta del Este, Uruguay; it was aimed at increasing economic and social development in Latin America with U.S. aid.

1962 The United States and Soviet Union appeared on the brink of war when Soviet missiles were discovered on Cuba; President Kennedy forced Khrushchev to have them dismantled.
John H. Glenn was first American to orbit earth.

1963 President Kennedy assassinated in Dallas, Texas, November 22; Lyndon Baines Johnson sworn in as President and defeated Barry M. Goldwater in 1964.

1964 Panamanians staged anti-U.S. riots.

1965 U.S. marines landed in Dominican Republic.
President Johnson signed Medicare and war on poverty legislation.
Race riots ravaged Los Angeles suburb of Watts.

1966 Guyana became independent.

1967 Race riots wasted Newark, Detroit, and other cities.

1968 Frank Borman, William A. Anders, and James A. Lovell, Jr., were first men to orbit the moon.
Dr. Martin Luther King, Jr. and Senator Robert Kennedy were assassinated in the United States.
Richard M. Nixon won U.S. Presidential contest.
Military coup deposed Peruvian President Fernando Belaúnde Terry.
Pierre Elliott Trudeau succeeded to Canadian premiership.

1969 U.S. astronaut Neil A. Armstrong became first man to walk on the Moon.

1970 U.S. student protests against the Viet Nam war resulted in the killing of four students by National Guard at Kent State, Ohio, and of two students by police at Jackson State, Miss.
Trudeau invoked the War Measures Act in Canada after the murder of Quebec Labor Minister Pierre Laporte by the Quebec Liberation Front.
Salvador Allende was elected president of Chile and Luis Echeverría Alvarez of Mexico.

1971 Wage-price freeze enacted by Nixon administration.

1972 Governor Wallace seriously injured in attempted assassination while campaigning in Maryland.
Watergate burglars apprehended in Democratic National Headquarters; "Watergate" begins.
Richard M. Nixon reelected president.

1973 Spiro T. Agnew resigned from the vice-presidency; Gerald R. Ford named to replace Agnew. "Watergate" dominates American political scene.
Salvador Allende Gossens, Marxist President of Chile, overthrown and reportedly committed suicide.
Juan Perón returned from exile to become Argentine president.

1974 Juan Perón died in Buenos Aires; His wife,Vice-President Isabel Perón assumes the presidency.
Richard M. Nixon resigned from the presidency; Gerald R. Ford succeeds to the office.

1975 Surinam and Grenada attained independence.
U.S. suffered severe economic recession.

1976 Argentine military junta deposed Mrs. Perón.
José López Portillo elected to Mexican presidency.
Jimmy Carter elected U.S. President.

1977 President Carter and Panamanian leader Torrijos signed treaty for the cession to Panama of the Canal Zone and the canal.

AFRICA

1906 Algeçiras Conference recognized predominance of French and Spanish interests in Morocco but also assured protection of German interests.

1908 Belgium annexed Congo Free State, calling it Belgian Congo.

1910 Union of South Africa formed from former British colonies of Cape of Good Hope and Natal, Orange Free State, and Transvaal.

1911 Germans sent gunboat *Panther* to Morocco as show of force.

1912 African partition among European powers was completed; only Ethiopia and Liberia remained independent.

1914 World War I in Africa: British and French troops occupied German colonies of Togoland and the Cameroons.

1920 Former German colonies became League mandates under Great Britain (Tanganyika, parts of Togoland and Cameroons), Belgium (Ruanda-Urundi), France (parts of Togoland and Cameroons), and Union of South Africa (South-West Africa).
Most of Kenya became British crown colony.
Abd-el-Krim, leader of Riff tribes of Morocco, began fight against Spanish and French rule in Africa; early successes followed by his defeat and deportation (1926) by combined Franco-Spanish troops.

1923 Rhodesia was divided into Southern and Northern Rhodesia and placed under British rule.

1930 Emperor Haile Selassie ascended Ethiopian throne.

1935 Italy invaded Ethiopia, causing Haile Selassie to flee country; League of Nations issued economic sanctions to no avail.

1946 India broke diplomatic relations with Union of South Africa because of her treatment of Indian minority.

1948 Apartheid: D. F. Malan made apartheid in Union of South Africa a political issue; the policy was aimed at perpetuating supremacy of white minority.

1951 Rising African nationalism achieved first victory with independence of Libya.

1952 Mau Mau, secret terrorist organization in Kenya, began bloody campaign to oust white settlers; British declared state of emergency that lasted until 1960.

1954 Algerian nationalists formed National Liberation Front and began terrorist campaign against French; war ended with Algeria gaining independence in 1962.

1956 Tunisia gained independence from France with Habib Bourguiba as premier.

1960 Immediately after Republic of the Congo achieved independence, civil war broke out; political struggle within central government developed between Patrice Lumumba, premier, and Joseph Kasavubu, head of state; UN peace-keeping force entered dispute; when Lumumba was seized by army and murdered (1961), Moise Tshombe became premier.
African nationalism reached peak of success when 16 nations gained freedom and African nations made up one third of UN membership.

1961 Dag Hammarskjöld, UN secretary-general, killed in plane crash on mission to **Congo.**
Union of South Africa became a republic; later left British Commonwealth.

1963 Jomo Kenyatta became Kenya's first premier.

1964 Tanzania formed by unification of Tanganyika and Zanzibar; **Julius K. Nyerere** became first president. Nyasaland became independent state of **Malawi;** Northern Rhodesia gained independence as **Zambia.**

1965 Mohammed Ben Bella, Algerian premier, overthrown by **Col. Houari Boumédiene.**
Rhodesia unilaterally declared independence from Great Britain.
President **Kasavubu** dismissed Tshombe and his government; **General Mobutu,** commander of Congolese National army, seized power.

1966 Kwame Nkrumah's government in **Ghana** toppled by military coup; **Nkrumah** went into exile.
United Nations terminated South Africa's mandate over **South-West Africa** and proclaimed UN administration over country.

1967 Tshombe held in custody in **Algeria** while Congo sought his extradition, in order to execute him; Congolese troops engaged rebel forces in Kisangani and Bukavu. Tshombe died (1969) in Algeria.
Republic of Biafra proclaimed when eastern province of **Nigeria** seceded; Nigerian government sent troops and blockaded province, causing widespread famine throughout 1968/69.
Dr. **Christiaan Barnard** performed first human heart transplant in Cape Town, South Africa.

1969 Pope **Paul VI** became the first pope to visit Africa when he flew to Kampala, Uganda to attend an African episcopal symposium meeting.
Portugal utilized 40% of her national budget and 120,000 troops to quell rebels in territories of Angola, Mozambique, and Portuguese Guinea.

1970 Surrender of secessionist **Biafra** on January 12 ended the 31-month civil war in Nigeria.

1973 A drought-induced famine cripples much of western Africa.

1975 Mozambique, Cape Verde, São Tomé and Príncipe, and Angola gained independence, ending centuries-old Portuguese colonial empire.

1976 Proponents of black majority rule wage guerrilla war against white regime in **Rhodesia.**

1977 Ethiopia and Somalia made war over disputed Ogaden region.

1978 Belgian and French paratroopers repelled Angola-based rebel invasion of Shaba province of **Zaire.**

OCEANIA

1901 Commonwealth of **Australia** formed by unification of Australia and Tasmania.

1907 New Zealand attained dominion status.

1959 Hawaii became a U.S. state.

1962 Western Samoa obtained independence.

1968 Nauru became an independent republic.

1970 Fiji and Tonga gained independence.

1975 Papua New Guinea achieved independence.

1978 Solomon Islands and Tuvalu gained independence.

ARCTIC AND ANTARCTICA

1908-1909 E. H. Shackleton's expedition to **Antarctica** failed to reach South Pole.

1909 Robert E. Peary discovered **North Pole.**

1911 Roald Amundsen reached South Pole.

1926 Richard E. Byrd flew over North Pole.

1928 Byrd established Little America, in Antarctica.

1955-1958 Edmund Hillary and Vivian Fuchs from Great Britain led overland crossing of **Antarctica.**

1957-1958 During the International Geophysical Year, many nations participated in studies of Antarctica and the Arctic.

1958 Nautilus, U.S. nuclear submarine, was first ship to cross **North Pole** under ice pack.

1959-1960 Treaty accepted by 12 nations, including the United States, reserved **Antarctica** for scientific research and recognized no existing national claims to territory in area.

1967 Peter J. Barrett and geologists from New Zealand discovered bone fragment and plant fossils embedded beneath icy surface of **Antarctica** indicating that Antarctica formerly had warmer climate.

1968-1969 First overland crossing of the **North Pole** by foot and dog sled. Royal Geographic Society of Britain's 3,600-mile expedition, encompassing more than 15 months, reached Pole in April 1969.

SEVEN WONDERS OF THE ANCIENT WORLD

The **Great Pyramid of Khufu** (or Cheops)—the world's largest pyramid located at Gizeh near Cairo. Built of limestone blocks, it originally stood 756 feet square, 482 feet high and covered 13 acres.

The **Hanging Gardens of Bablyon**—luxurious gardens which added to the glamorous atmosphere of Mesopotamia's most important ancient city.

The **Mausoleum at Halicarnassus**—a magnificent sepulcher in Asia Minor constructed of white marble richly decorated with sculpture and erected (c. 352 B.C.) in memory of Mausolus of Caria.

The **Artemision at Ephesus**—great temple built (c. 550

B.C.) as a center of worship for the nature-goddess Artemis.

The **Colossus of Rhodes**—large bronze statue (height about 100 feet) of the sun god Helios situated in the harbor of Rhodes and thought to be built by Chares of Rhodes between 292 and 280 B.C.

The **Olympian Zeus by Phidias**—built for the temple of Olympia (c. 435 B.C.); it consisted of a majestic bearded figure wearing a mantle and seated upon a huge ornamented throne.

The **Pharos at Alexandria**—celebrated lighthouse (estimated height: 200–600 feet) built by Ptolemy II (c. 280 B.C.) on the peninsula of Pharos.

WORLD BIOGRAPHY

Abd-el-Krim, c. 1882-1963, Moroccan Rif leader and national hero.

Abdullah, 1882–1951, assassinated first Hashemite king of Jordan.

Abrams, Creighton W., Jr., 1914-1974, American general in Vietnam.

Abruzzi, Duca degli (Luigi Amedeo), 1873–1933, Italian explorer of the Arctic (1899–1900).

Acheson, Dean G., 1893-1971, U.S. Secretary of State (1949-52) who helped to establish NATO.

Adams, Samuel, 1722–1803, American patriot, signer of Declaration of Independence, and firebrand of Boston Tea Party.

Addams, Jane, 1860–1935, American social worker and co-founder of Hull House.

Adenauer, Konrad, 1876–1967, German statesman, postwar chancellor, and architect of West German recovery.

Aga Khan III, 1877-1957, fabulously wealthy Moslem leader and statesman.

Agnelli, Giovanni, 1921–   , Italian industrialist and chairman of FIAT.

Agrippina the Younger, A.D. c. 16-59, Nero's mother, who contrived his accession to the throne.

Aguinaldo, Emilio, c. 1869–1964, Filipino revolutionary against Spain and the United States.

Akbar, 1542–1605, greatest Mogul emperor of India.

Alanbrooke, Viscount (Alan F. Brooke), 1883-1963, British general, W.W. II chief of imperial general staff.

Alaric I, c. 370–410, Visigothic ruler who devastated southern Europe.

Albert, Prince, 1819–61, German-born consort of Victoria of England.

Albuquerque, Afonso de, 1453–1515, Portuguese admiral and founder of Portuguese empire in the East.

Alcibiades, c. 450–404 B.C., Athenian statesman and general in Peloponnesian War.

Alexander (III) the Great, 356–323 B.C., king of Macedon, Greek conqueror, and one of the greatest generals of all time.

Alexius I (Alexius Comnenus), 1048–1118, emperor who restored Byzantine military and political power.

Allen, Ethan, 1738–89, American Revolutionary hero, leader of Green Mountain Boys.

Allende (Gossens), Salvador, 1908–73, President of Chile (1970–73); advocated democratic socialism.

Altgeld, John P., 1847–1902, German-born American political leader and social reformer.

Amin Dada, Idi, 1925– , Ugandan president (1971–79).

Amundsen, Roald, 1872–1928, Norwegian polar explorer, first to reach the South Pole (December 14, 1911).

Andrada e Silva, José Bonifácio de, 1763–1838, Brazilian statesman, chief founder of independent Brazil.

Andrassy, Julius (Count), 1823–90, Hungarian statesman and first constitutional premier (1867–71).

Andreotti, Giulio, 1919– , Italian premier (1972-73, 1976–79).

Andropov, Yuri V., 1914– , head of Soviet secret police, ambassador to Hungary during 1956 uprising.

Anthony, Susan B., 1820–1906, American reformer and suffragette leader.

Antonescu, Ion, 1882–1946, Rumanian dictator (1940–44), executed as a war criminal.

Antony, Mark, c. 83-80 B.C., Roman politician and soldier who allied himself with Cleopatra and defied Rome.

Arafat, Yasir, 1929– , leader of the Palestine Liberation Organization.

Arnold, Benedict, 1741–1801, American Revolutionary general and traitor.

al-Assad, Hafez, 1928– , Syrian president (1971–).

Astor, John Jacob, 1763–1848, American merchant and fur trader, the richest man in America at his death.

Astor, Lady (Nancy W.), 1879–1964, American-born British political leader, first woman member of Parliament.

Astor, William W. (Viscount), 1848–1919, Anglo-American financier and philanthropist.

Atahualpa, d. 1533, Inca (ruling chief) of Peru, executed by Pizarro.

Ataturk, Kemal (b. Mustafa Kemal), 1881–1938, father of modern Turkey and president (1923–1938).

Attila, d. 453, Hun leader, conqueror of eastern Europe.

Attucks, Crispus, c. 1723–70, American Negro patriot killed by British in Boston Massacre.

Augustus (Octavius), 63 B.C.–14 A.D., first Roman emperor; he defeated Antony and returned Rome from military dictatorship to constitutional rule.

Aurangzeb, 1618–1707, Mogul Indian emperor who brought his empire to its greatest expanse.

Auriol, Vincent, 1884–1966, first president (1947–54) of French Fourth Republic.

Austin, Stephen F., 1793–1836, American leader of colonization in Texas.

Ayub Khan, Mohammad, 1907-74, Pakistani military leader who became (1958) president and resigned (1969).

Babar, c. 1482-1530, founder of Mogul empire in India.

Babeuf, François N., 1760–97, executed French revolutionary, philosophical forerunner of Marx.

Badoglio, Pietro, 1871–1956, Italian field marshal in Ethiopia, premier after fall of Mussolini.

Baffin, William, c. 1584–1622, British arctic explorer, for whom Baffin Island and Baffin Bay are named.

Bakunin, Mikhail, 1814–76, militant Russian anarchist, expelled from First International by Marxists.

Balboa, Vasco Núñez de, c. 1475–1519, beheaded Spanish conquistador, discoverer of Pacific Ocean.

Bancroft, George, 1800–91, American statesman and historian, founder of U.S. Naval Academy.

Banneker, Benjamin, 1731–1806, American Negro colonial astronomer, mathematician, and inventor.

Barry, John, 1745-1803, Irish-born naval commander during the American Revolution; considered to be the "Father of the American Navy."

Barton, Clara, 1821–1912, American humanitarian, organizer of the American Red Cross.

Baruch, Bernard M., 1870–1965, American financier and government economic adviser.

Batista y Zaldívar, Fulgencio, 1901-73, Cuban dictator (president 1940-44, 1952-59), overthrown by Castro.

Batu Khan, d. 1255, Mongol leader of Golden Horde.

Beauregard, Pierre G. T., 1818–93, American Confederate general.

Beaverbrook, Lord (William Maxwell Aitken), 1879–1964, Canadian-born British statesman and publisher.

Begin, Menachem, 1913– , Israeli prime minister.

Belisarius, c. 505-565, Byzantine general under Justinian.

Bellinghausen, Fabian von, 1778–1852, Russian admiral and discoverer (1819-21) of Antarctica.

Ben Bella, Ahmed, 1918– , Algerian revolutionary, elected (1962) premier and deposed (1965) by Boumédienne.

Beneš, Eduard, 1884–1948, Czechoslovak president.

Ben-Gurion, David, 1886–1973, Israeli statesman, first prime minister (beginning in 1948).

Benjamin of Tudela, d. 1173, Jewish traveler and author of an itinerary of his trip (1159–73) to China.

Bennett, James Gordon, Jr., 1841-1918, American publisher who financed Stanley's trip to find Livingstone.

Bentinck, Lord William C., 1774–1839, British statesman, appointed (1833) first governor-general of British India.

Beria, Lavrenti P., 1899–1953, executed Soviet secret police chief under Stalin.

Bering, Vitus J., 1681–1741, Russian-backed Danish discoverer (1728) of Bering Strait.

Bernadotte, Count (Folke), 1895–1948, Swedish internationalist, UN mediator in Palestine until assassinated.

Betancourt, Romulo, 1908– , progressive Venezuelan president (1945-48, 1959-64).

Bevan, Aneurin, 1897–1960, British political leader, developer of England's socialized medicine system.

Bevin, Ernest, 1881–1951, British labor leader and Labour government foreign minister (1945–51).

Bhave, Acharya Vinoba, 1895– , foremost Indian advocate of nonviolent (Gandhian) social revolution.

Bhutto, Zulfikar Ali, 1928–79, Pakistani president (1971–73) and prime minister (1973–77). Overthrown (1977) and executed in 1979.

Biddle, F.ancis B., 1886–1968, American jurist, U.S. Attorney General (1941–45).

Bismarck, Otto von, 1815–98, German statesman who unified Germany under Prussian leadership.

Blackstone, Sir William, 1723–80, English jurist, first professor of English law at Oxford University.

Bloomer, Amelia J., 1818–94, American reformer, devoted to women's rights.

Blücher, Gebhard L. von, 1742–1819, Prussian field marshal who helped Wellington defeat Napoleon at Waterloo.

Blum, Léon, 1872–1950, French Socialist statesman, Popular Front organizer, and writer.

Boleyn, Anne, c. 1507–36, beheaded second wife of Henry VIII of England, mother of Elizabeth I.

Bolívar, Simón, 1783–1830, South American revolutionary who liberated much of the continent from Spanish rule.

Bonaparte, Joseph, 1768–1844, eldest brother of Napoleon I, ineffective king of Naples and Spain.

Bonaparte, Napoleon see Napoleon Bonaparte.

Booth, John Wilkes, 1838–65, egomaniacal American actor, assassin of Abraham Lincoln.

Booth, William, 1829–1912, English religious leader, founder and first general of Salvation Army.

Borgia, Caesar, c. 1475–1507, Italian Renaissance ecclesiastic and statesman; brother of Lucretia Borgia.

Borgia, Lucretia, 1480–1519, famous figure of Italian Renaissance, daughter of Pope Alexander VI.

Bormann, Martin L., 1900–1945, German Nazi leader.

Bosch, Juan, 1909– , progressive Dominican leader.

Botha, Louis, 1862–1919, Boer soldier and first prime minister (1910–19) of Union of South Africa.

Bougainville, Louis Antoine de, 1729–1811, French navigator, leader of scientific expeditions in South Pacific.

Boumédiene, Houari, 1927–78, Algerian revolutionary, deposed (1965) Ben Bella.

Bourguiba, Habib, 1903– , Tunisian independence leader and first premier (subsequently president).

Boycott, Charles C., 1832–97, English land agent in Ireland whose ruthlessness led his workers to "boycott" him.

Braddock, Edward, 1695–1755, British general in French and Indian Wars.

Bradley, Omar N., 1893– , U.S. Army WW II general, later chairman of joint chiefs of staff.

Braille, Louis C., 1809–52, French inventor of Braille system of printing and writing for the blind.

Brandt, Willy, 1913– , West German chancellor (1969-74), leader of Social Democratic party.

Brauchitsch, Walther von, 1881–1948, German WW II general.

Brezhnev, Leonid I., 1906– , Soviet Communist party leader, successor to Khrushchev; Chairman of the Presidium of the Supreme Soviet (1977–).

Brian Boru, c. 940–1014, Irish king who broke Norse power in Ireland.

Briand, Aristide, 1862–1932, French statesman, chief architect of antiwar Kellogg-Briand Pact (1928).

Brown, John, 1800–59, hanged American abolitionist whose raid at Harpers Ferry stunned North and South.

Bryan, William Jennings, 1860–1925, American political leader, greatest orator of his day.

Brzezinski, Zbigniew, 1928– , foreign affairs adviser to President Carter (1977–).

Bulganin, Nikolai A., 1895-1975, Soviet Communist leader and premier (1955–58).

Bullitt, William C., 1891–1967, American diplomat, first American ambassador to USSR (1933–36).

Bunche, Ralph J., 1904–1971, American Negro government official and UN mediator.

Bundy, McGeorge, 1919–   , American professor, Presidential adviser, and Ford Foundation head.

Bunker, Ellsworth, 1894–   , American business executive and diplomat.

Burghley, William Cecil (Baron), 1520–98, English statesman, influential adviser to Elizabeth I for 40 years.

Burgoyne, John, 1722–92, British statesman and general in American Revolution.

Burke, Edmund, 1729–97, English political writer and statesman, proponent of conservatism.

Burnside, Ambrose E., 1824–81, American Union general.

Burton, Sir Richard F., 1821–90, English writer, orientalist, and discoverer (1858) of Lake Tanganyika.

Byrd, Richard E., 1888–1957, American admiral and polar explorer, first to fly over the North Pole (1926).

Caesar, Julius, c. 102–44 B.C., Roman statesman and general who enlarged and pacified Rome's provinces.

Cagliostro, Alessandro (Giuseppe Balsamo), 1743–95, Italian adventurer.

Callaghan, James, 1912–   , Labour prime minister of Great Britain (1976–79).

Calles, Plutarco E., 1877–1945, Mexican Revolutionary statesman and president (1924–28).

Campesino, El (Valentin Gonzáles), c. 1909–   , Spanish Republican soldier in the civil war (1936–39).

Canaris, Wilhelm, 1887–1945, German WW II admiral and intelligence chief who opposed Hitler.

Cárdenas, Lázaro, 1895–1970, Mexican president (1934–40) and revolutionary general.

Cardigan, Earl of (James T. Brudenell), 1797–1868, British Crimean War general who led disastrous cavalry attack at Balaklava, immortalized in Tennyson's "The Charge of the Light Brigade."

Carnegie, Andrew, 1835–1919, Scottish-American iron and steel tycoon and philanthropist.

Carnot, Lazare, 1753–1823, French revolutionary general.

Carpini, Giovanni de Piano, c. 1180–1252, Italian monk who produced a full record of Mongol life from missionary experiences in Central Asia.

Carranza, Venustiano, 1859–1920, Mexican revolutionary leader who arranged Zapata's assassination.

Casanova de Seingalt, Giovanni G., 1725-98, Venetian adventurer and author.

Castelo Branco, Humberto, 1900–67, Brazilian revolutionary president.

Castiglione, Baldassare (Conte), 1478–1529, Italian Renaissance statesman and author.

Castlereagh, Robert S. (Viscount), 1769–1822, Irish-born British foreign secretary, and organizer of successful coalition against Napoleon I.

Castro, Fidel, 1927–   , Cuban Communist premier who wrested power from Fulgencio Batista in 1959.

Catherine de' Medici, 1519–89, queen of France who helped to plan (1572) French Protestant massacre on Saint Bartholomew's Day.

Catherine II, 1729–96, forceful German-born empress and tsarina of Russia, also known as Catherine the Great.

Cato the Elder (Cato the Censor), 234–149 B.C., Roman statesman and moralist.

Cavell, Edith, 1865–1915, English nurse executed by Germans during WW I.

Cavour, Camillo Benso (conte di), 1810–61, Italian statesman, leader in unifying Italy under house of Savoy.

Ceausescu, Nicolae, 1918–   , Romanian head of state.

Černik, Oldřich, 1921–   , liberal Czechoslovak Communist premier during 1968 Soviet invasion.

Chamberlain, (A.) Neville, 1869–1940, British prime minister who signed (1938) Munich Pact with Hitler.

Chang Tso-lin, 1873–1928, Chinese general, warlord of Manchuria.

Charcot, Jean B., 1867–1936, French neurologist and explorer in the Antarctic.

Chase, Salmon P., 1808–73, American abolitionist, statesman, and Secretary of the Treasury under Lincoln.

Chateaubriand, François R. (vicomte de), 1768–1848, French diplomat and romantic writer.

Cheops (or Khufu), fl. c. 2680 B.C., king of Egypt, builder of great pyramid at Gizeh.

Chiang Kai-shek, 1887–1975, Chinese Nationalist leader whose government was driven (1950) from mainland China to island of Taiwan.

Chiang Kai-shek, Madame (Soong Mai-ling), 1896–   , politically active wife of the Chinese Nationalist leader.

Ch'ien Lung (Hung-li), 1711–99, fourth emperor of Ching dynasty who greatly extended borders of China.

Chou En-lai see Zhou Enlai.

Christophe, Henri, 1767–1820, Haitian revolutionary and self-proclaimed king (Henri I).

Churchill, Sir Winston L. S., 1874–1965, British prime minister, soldier, author, and war leader.

Ciano, Galeazzo, 1903–44, Italian Fascist foreign minister who helped create Rome-Berlin Axis, executed by Mussolini—his father-in-law.

Cid, El, d. c. 1099, Spanish national hero, whose real name was Rodrigo (or Ruy) Díaz de Vivar.

Clarendon, Earl of (Edward Hyde), 1609–74, English statesman, historian, and adviser to Charles II.

Clark, Charles Joseph 1939–   , Conservative prime minister of Canada (1979–   ).

Clay, Henry, 1777–1852, American statesman, author of Compromise of 1850.

Clemenceau, Georges, 1841–1929, French statesman (the "Tiger"), twice premier (1906–09, 1917–20).

Cleopatra, 69–30 B.C., Ptolemaic queen of Egypt, one of the great romantic figures of all time.

Clinton, De Witt, 1769–1828, American statesman, Presidential nominee (1812), sponsor of Erie Canal.

Cobden, Richard, 1804–65, British statesman, advocate (after 1849) of peace and international conferences.

Coen, Jan P., 1587–1629, Dutch colonial governor, founder of Dutch East Indian empire.

Coke, Sir Edward, 1552–1634, one of the most eminent English jurists in history.

Colbert, Jean B., 1619–83, French statesman under Louis XIV, successful practitioner of mercantilism.

Columbus, Christopher, 1451–1506, Italian-born discoverer of America for Spain (1492).

Constantine V (Constantine Copronymus), 718–775, iconoclastic Byzantine emperor (741–775).

Constantine VI, b. c. 770, Byzantine emperor (780–797), blinded by Irene, his mother and successor.

Constantine XI (Constantine Palaeologus), d. 1453, last Byzantine emperor (1449–53).

Cook, James (Captain), 1728–79, English explorer along coasts of Australia and New Zealand.

Cooper, Peter, 1791–1883, American inventor, industrialist, and philanthropist.

Corday, Charlotte, 1768–93, aristocratic French Revolution sympathizer who assassinated Jean Paul Marat.

Cornwallis, Charles (Marquess), 1738–1805, English general in American Revolution.

Cortés, Hernán, 1485–1547, Spanish conquistador in Mexico who toppled Aztec empire of Montezuma.

Coty, René, 1882–1962, last president of French Fourth Republic.

Cox, James M., 1870–1957, American political leader, U.S. Presidential candidate (1920), and journalist.

Cranmer, Thomas, 1489–1556, English churchman, adviser to Henry VIII.

Cripps, Sir Stafford, 1889–1952, British statesman and diplomat, chancellor of exchequer after WW II.

Croesus, d. c. 547 B.C., king of Lydia; his name has become synonym for wealth.

Cromwell, Oliver, 1599–1658, English general and statesman, lord protector of England (1653–58).

Crump, Edward H., 1876–1954, American political boss in Tennessee.

Cuauhtémoc, d. c. 1525, Aztec emperor executed by Cortés.

Cunard, Sir Samuel, 1787–1865, Canadian pioneer of regular transatlantic steam navigation (Cunard Line).

Curtis, Cyrus H. K., 1850–1933, American publisher and philanthropist.

Curzon, George N. (Marquess), 1859–1925, British statesman and viceroy of India.

Cyrano de Bergerac, Savinien, 1619–55, French poet and duelist romanticized by Edmond Rostand's drama.

Dalai Lama, 1935–   , theocratic ruler of Tibet, ousted (1959) by Chinese invasion of his country.

Danton, Georges J., 1759–94, French statesman and a leading figure of French Revolution.

Darius I (the Great), d. 486 B.C., king of Persia (521–486 B.C.) who consolidated Persian power in the East.

Darlan, Jean F., 1881–1942, assassinated French admiral, vice-premier of Vichy government.

Darnley, Lord (Henry S.), 1545–67, claimant to English throne, second husband of Mary Queen of Scots.

Davis, Angela, 1944–   , former university lecturer and black political activist acquitted in controversial political murder trial in 1972.

Davis, Jefferson, 1808–89, American statesman, president of Southern Confederacy.

Davitt, Michael, 1846–1906, Irish revolutionary and land reformer.

Dayan, Moshe, 1915–   , Israeli statesman, soldier, and hero of 1967 June War.

Debs, Eugene V., 1855–1926, American Socialist leader, Presidential candidate (1900, 1904, 1908, 1912, 1920).

De Gasperi, Alcide, 1881–1954, Italian premier (1945–53), organizer of Christian Democratic party.

de Gaulle, Charles, 1890–1970, French general and controversial nationalist president (1959–69).

Deng Xiaoping, 1904– , Chinese Communist Politburo vice-chairman (1977–).

Dassai, Morarji, 1895– , Indian prime minister (1977–79).

De Soto, Hernando, c. 1500–42, Spanish conquistador and explorer in what is now United States.

Dessalines, Jean J., c. 1758–1806, emperor of Haiti, born a slave.

De Valera, Eamon, 1882–1975, long-time Irish prime minister and president.

Dewey, George, 1837–1917, American admiral, hero of battle of Manila.

Dewey, Thomas E., 1902–71, governor of New York (1942–54), Republican Presidential candidate (1944, 1948).

Dias, Bartolomeu, d. 1500, Portuguese navigator, first European to round (1488) the Cape of Good Hope.

Díaz, Porfirio, 1830–1915, Mexican president (1876–1911), whose ruthless rule fostered revolution.

Díaz Ordaz, Gustavo, 1911-79, progressive Mexican president (1964-70) and lawyer.

Diefenbaker, John G., 1895–1979, Conservative prime minister of Canada (1957–63).

Diem, Ngo Dinh, 1901–63, assassinated South Vietnamese president.

Dimitrov, Georgi, 1882–1949, Bulgarian Communist premier (1946–49), acquitted of Reichstag fire.

Dirksen, Everett M., 1896–1969, U.S. Senator (Ill., first elected 1950) and Republican minority leader.

Dix, Dorothea L., 1802–87, American social reformer, champion of specialized treatment for the mentally ill.

Djilas, Milovan, 1911– , Yugoslavian political leader and intellectual, frequently imprisoned by Tito.

Dobrynin, Anatoly F., 1919– , Soviet ambassador to U.S.

Dollfuss, Engelbert, 1892–1934, Austrian chancellor assassinated by Austrian Nazis.

Douglas, Stephen A., 1813–61, American statesman who opposed (1860) Lincoln for Presidency.

Douglass, Frederick, c. 1817–95, American Negro abolitionist leader.

Drake, Sir Francis, c. 1540–96, first Englishman to circumnavigate the earth (1577–80).

Dreyfus, Alfred, 1859–1935, French soldier whose treason trial (and ultimate exoneration) was a *cause célèbre*.

Du Barry, Madame (Jeanne B.), 1743–93, mistress of Louis XV of France, guillotined during French Revolution.

Dubcek, Alexander, 1921– , liberal Czechoslovak Communist party secretary during 1968 Soviet invasion.

Du Bois, William E. B., 1868–1963, American Negro editor, author, exponent of equality for the Negro.

Duclos, Jacques, 1896– , French Communist leader.

Dulles, Allen W., 1893–1969, U.S. public official, director of CIA (1953–61).

Dulles, John Foster, 1888–1959, U.S. Secretary of State (1953–59), architect of "containing Communism" policy.

Duong Van Minh ("Big Minh"), 1916– , South Vietnamese general.

Duvalier, François, 1907–71, Haitian dictator.

Dzerzhinsky, Felix E., 1877–1926, Russian Bolshevik politician, organizer of Soviet secret police.

Earhart, Amelia, 1898–1937, pioneering American aviatrix who disappeared on a round-the-world flight.

Early, Jubal A., 1816–94, American Confederate general.

Eban, Abba, 1915– , Israeli diplomat and statesman.

Ebert, Friedrich, 1871–1925, first president (1919–25) of the German republic.

Echeverría Álvarez, Luis, 1922– , President of Mexico (1970–76).

Eden, Sir Anthony R. A. (Earl of Avon), 1897–77, British statesman, Conservative prime minister (1955–57).

Edinburgh, Duke of (Philip Mountbatten), 1921– , consort of Elizabeth II of Great Britain.

Eichmann, Adolf, 1906–62, German Nazi official executed by Israel for crimes against the Jewish people and humanity.

Elizabeth I, 1533–1603, queen of England during the great age of British expansion and exploration.

Ellsworth, Lincoln, 1880–1951, American explorer, the first man to fly over Antarctic (1935).

Emin Pasha (Eduard Schnitzer), 1840–92, German physician, colonial administrator, and explorer of Sudan.

Emmet, Robert, 1778–1803, executed Irish patriot.

Engels, Friedrich, 1820–95, German Socialist, co-founder with Karl Marx of modern Communism.

Enver Pasha, 1881–1922, Turkish general and political leader.

Erlander, Tage F., 1901– , Swedish Social Democratic premier (1946–69).

Ervin, Samuel J., Jr., 1896– , U.S. Senator from North Carolina (1954–1974).

Eshkol, Levi, 1895–1969, Israeli prime minister (1963-69)

Essex, Earl of (Robert Devereux), 1567–1601, favorite of Elizabeth I of England who signed his death warrant.

Fanfani, Amintore, 1908– , Italian statesman and premier (1958-59, 1960-63).

Farouk I, 1920–65, king of Egypt (1936–52), forced to abdicate (1952) by military coup.

Fawkes, Guy, 1570–1606, English Roman Catholic conspirator involved in scheme to blow up Parliament.

Fish, Hamilton, 1808–93, American statesman, one of the ablest of U.S. Secretaries of State.

Foch, Ferdinand, 1851–1929, French marshal, commander (1918) of British, French, and American armies.

Ford, Henry, 1863–1947, American industrialist, pioneer automobile manufacturer.

Forrestal, James V., 1892–1949, U.S. Secretary of the Navy (1944–47) and first Secretary of Defense (1947–49).

Fox, Charles J., 1749–1806, British statesman, orator, and liberal reformer.

Francis (Franz) Ferdinand, 1863–1914, Austrian archduke whose assassination precipitated WW I.

Franco, Francisco, 1892–1975, leader of rebel forces in Spanish Civil War (1936–39) and dictator of Spain (1937–75).

Frank, Anne, 1929–45, Dutch Jewish girl killed by the Nazis; her diary made her posthumously famous.

Franklin, Benjamin, 1706–90, outstanding American statesman, also printer, scientist, and writer.

Fraser, John Malcolm, 1930– , Australian prime minister (1975–).

Frederick William, 1620–88, "Great Elector" of Brandenburg, who laid the base of the state of Prussia.

Frémont, John C., 1813–90, American explorer, soldier, and politician, a controversial figure of history.

Frobenius, Leo, 1873-1938, German archaeologist and authority on prehistoric African art and culture.

Fugger, Jacob (Jacob the Rich), 1459–1525, German merchant prince.

Fukuda, Takeo, 1905– , Japanese premier (1976–78).

Fulbright, J. William, 1905– , U.S. Senator (Ark., 1945-1974), chairman of Senate Foreign Relations Committee from 1959.

Gage, Thomas, 1721–87, English general in America whose orders led to battles of Lexington and Concord.

Gallatin, Albert, 1761–1849, American statesman and financier.

Gama, Vasco da, c. 1469–1524, Portuguese navigator, first European to journey to India by sea (1497–99).

Gambetta, Léon, 1838–82, French republican statesman.

Gamelin, Maurice G., 1872–1958, French general, leader of Allied forces at WW II's outbreak.

Gandhi, Indira, 1917– , Indian prime minister (1966–77), daughter of Jawaharlal Nehru, and first woman ever elected to head the government of a major power.

Gandhi, Mohandas K., 1869–1948, Indian ascetic who advocated nonviolent resistance to secure independence of India from Great Britain.

Garibaldi, Giuseppe, 1807–82, Italian patriot and soldier who fought for Italy's unification.

Garrison, William Lloyd, 1805–79, American abolitionist and social reformer.

Garvey, Marcus, 1887–1940, American Negro nationalist leader.

Giap, Vo Nguyen, 1912– , North Vietnamese statesman and victor at Dienbienphu in 1954.

Giscard d'Estaing, Valery, 1926– , French president since 1974.

Glubb, Sir John B. (Glubb Pasha), 1897– , British commander of Arab Legion of Jordan.

Gneisenau, August (Graf Neithardt von), 1760–1831, Prussian field marshal in Napoleonic Wars.

Godfrey of Bouillon, c. 1058–1100, crusader, ruler of Jerusalem.

Godunov, Boris, c. 1551–1605, Russian tsar, adviser to Ivan the Terrible.

Goebbels, Paul J., 1897–1945, German Nazi propagandist, master of mass psychology.

Goering, Hermann W., 1893–1946, German Nazi leader, early supporter of Hitler, and head of Luftwaffe.

Goldwater, Barry M., 1909– , U.S. Senator (Ariz.), unsuccessful Republican Presidential candidate (1964).

Gompers, Samuel, 1850–1924, American labor leader, founder and president (1886–94, 1896–1924) of AFL.

Gomulka, Wladyslav, 1905– , Polish Communist Party leader.

Gordon, Charles G. (Chinese Gordon), 1833–85, British soldier and administrator killed by Moslems at Khartoum.

Gottwald, Klement, 1896–1953, Czechoslovak Communist leader, who ushered Communism into his country.

Gowon, Yakubu, 1934– , Nigerian head of state who opposed the unsuccessful secession of the late 1960s.

Greeley, Horace, 1811–72, American newspaper publisher (New York *Tribune*) and Presidential candidate (1872).

Grenville, Sir Richard, c. 1542–91, English naval hero against Spanish.

Gresham, Sir Thomas, c. 1519–79, English financier who gave his name to economic principle: "bad money drives out good."

Grey, Lady Jane, 1537–54, queen of England for nine days, succeeded by Mary I.

Gromyko, Andrei A., 1909– , Soviet foreign minister and ambassador.

Grotius, Hugo, 1583–1645, Dutch jurist and humanist, considered the founder of international law.

Guevara, Che (Ernesto), 1928–67, Argentine-born Cuban guerrilla leader killed in Bolivia.

Gwyn, Nell (Eleanor), 1650–87, English actress, mistress of Charles II.

Haig, Alexander Meigs, Jr., 1924– , U.S. Army General; Chief of Staff of the White House (1973-74).

Haile Selassie, 1892–1975, emperor of Ethiopia (1930–74).

Hale, Nathan, 1755–76, American Revolutionary patriot, hanged by the British without trial as a spy.

Halsey, William F., 1882–1959, American WW II admiral in Pacific.

Hamilton, Alexander, 1755–1804, American Federalist statesman, first Secretary of the Treasury.

Hammurabi, fl. 1792–1750 B.C., king of Babylonia; his code of laws is one of the greatest of ancient codes.

Hannibal, 247–c. 182 B.C., Carthaginian general, great military opponent of Rome (Second Punic War).

Harriman, W. Averell, 1891– , American diplomat, U.S. representative (1968) at Vietnam peace talks.

Harun-al-Rashid, c. 764–809, famous caliph of Baghdad under whom the Abbasid empire reached its apogee.

Hastings, Warren, 1732–1818, controversial first governor-general of British India.

Hawkins, Sir John, 1532–95, Elizabethan sea dog, knighted for his actions in defeat of Spanish Armada.

Hay, John, 1838–1905, American author and statesman, who formulated the Open Door policy toward China.

Haya de la Torre, Victor Raúl, 1895–1979, Peruvian leader, advocate of Latin-American nationalist revolutions.

Hearst, William Randolph, 1863–1951, American journalist and publisher, innovator in mass-appeal newspapers.

Heath, Edward R. G., 1916– , British Conservative prime minister (1970–74).

Henry, Patrick, 1736–99, American orator and patriot, who worked to have Bill of Rights added to the Constitution.

Herodotus, c. 484–c. 425 B.C., Greek historian and traveler considered the father of history.

Herzl, Theodor, 1860–1904, Hungarian writer, founder of modern Zionism.

Hess, Rudolf, 1894– , erratic German Nazi leader, imprisoned (1946) for life as a war criminal.

Heydrich, Reinhard, 1904–42, German Nazi police official ("the Hangman") whose assassination by Czech patriots led to Lidice massacre.

Heyerdahl, Thor, 1914– , Norwegian explorer-ethnologist, substantiated the diffusionist theory of anthropology with his trans-pacific raft journeys.

Hidalgo y Costilla, Miguel, 1753–1811, executed Mexican national hero and priest.

Hillary, Sir Edmund P., 1919– , New Zealand mountain climber; first to reach summit of Mt. Everest (1953).

Hillel, fl. 30 B.C.–10 A.D., Jewish scholar; many of Christ's teachings resemble Hillel's sayings.

Hillman, Sidney, 1887–1946, Lithuanian-born American labor leader.

Himmler, Heinrich, 1900–45, terroristic Nazi chief of SS and Gestapo.

Hindenburg, Paul von, 1847–1934, German president (1925–34) who appointed Hitler as chancellor.

Hitler, Adolf, 1889–1945, founder of German Nazism and infamous tyrant who precipitated WW II.

Ho Chi Minh, c. 1890–1969, Vietnamese Communist leader and national hero; first president of North Vietnam.

Hoover, J. Edgar, 1895–1972, American administrator, director of FBI (1924–72).

Horthy de Nagybanya, Nicholas, 1868–1957, Hungarian admiral and political leader.

Houphouët-Boigny, Félix, 1905– , president of Ivory Coast, leader of former French Africa.

Houston, Samuel, 1793–1863, American frontier hero and Texan statesman.

Howe, Julia Ward, 1819–1910, American social reformer and writer of "The Battle Hymn of the Republic."

Howe, Richard (Earl), 1726–99, admiral and commander (1776–78) of British fleet in American Revolution.

Howe, William (Viscount), 1729–1814, English general in American Revolution.

Hoxha, Enver 1908– , Albanian Communist leader.

Hua Guofeng (Kuo-feng), 1921– , Chinese Communist premier and Politburo chairman (1976–).

Hull, Cordell, 1871–1955, U.S. Secretary of State (1933–44), recipient (1945) Nobel Peace Prize.

Hunyadi, John, c. 1385–1456, Hungarian national hero, resistance leader against Turks.

Ibn Saud, c. 1880–1953, founder (1932) and first king of Saudi Arabia.

Ikhnaton, d. c. 1354 B.C., pharaoh of Egypt who established perhaps the world's first monotheistic religion.

Iqbal, Mohammad, 1873–1938, Moslem leader, national hero of Pakistan.

Irene, 752–803, repressive Byzantine empress who had her son blinded.

Isabella I, 1451–1504, queen of Spain who supported the 1492 New World voyage of Columbus.

Jabotinsky, Vladimir, 1880-1940, Russian-born Zionist leader.

Jackson, Stonewall (Thomas J.), 1824–63, American Confederate general.

Jaurès, Jean, 1859–1914, assassinated French Socialist leader and historian.

Jenghiz (also Genghis) Khan, c. 1167–1227, brilliant Mongol conqueror, ruler of a vast Asian empire.

Jinnah, Mohammad Ali, 1876–1948, founder and first governor-general of Pakistan (1947–48).

Joan of Arc, c. 1412–31, French saint and national heroine, burned at the stake for heresy.

Joffre, Joseph J. C., 1852–1931, French WW I marshal.

John III (John Sobieski), 1620-96, king of Poland, champion of Christian Europe against Turks.

Jones, John Paul, 1747–92, Scottish-born American naval hero of American Revolution.

Jordan, Vernon E., Jr., 1935– , civil rights leader and executive director of the National Urban League.

Josephine, 1763–1814, empress of the French (1804–09), first wife of Napoleon I.

Joyce, William (Lord Haw-Haw), 1906–46, executed Anglo-American Nazi propagandist.

Juárez, Benito, 1806–72, Mexican Indian president, revered by Mexicans as great political figure.

Juin, Alphonse, 1888–1967, French soldier and marshal.

Justinian I, 483–565, Byzantine emperor (527–65) whose accomplishment was codification of Roman law.

Kadar, Janos, 1912– , Hungarian Communist premier who sided with Soviets in 1956 Hungarian revolt.

Kamenev, Lev B., 1883–1936, Soviet Communist leader executed during 1936 Moscow purges.

Karamanlis, Constantine, 1907– , twice Greek premier, proponent of economic improvement.

Kasavubu, Joseph, c. 1910–69, first president of the Congo.

Kassem, Abdul Karim, 1914–63, executed Iraqi general who overthrew (1958) monarchy and became premier.

Kaunda, Kenneth, 1924– , Zambian president, proponent of Gandhian principles.

Kefauver, (C.) Estes, 1903–63, U.S. Senator (Tenn., 1949–63), supporter of civil rights legislation.

Kekkonen, Urho K., 1900– , Finnish president (beginning 1956).

Kennedy, Edward M., 1932– , U. S. Senator (Mass., (1962–), brother of John F. and Robert F. Kennedy.

Kennedy, Robert F., 1925–68, assassinated U.S. Senator (N.Y., 1965–68), brother of slain President John F. Kennedy under whom he was U.S. Attorney General.

Kenyatta, Jomo, c. 1893–1978, first Kenyan president, an early African nationalist leader.

Kerensky, Aleksandr F., 1881–1970, exiled Russian revolutionary premier (1917), overthrown by Bolsheviks.

Khomeini, Ayatollah Ruhollah, 1900– , Moslem religious leader who led Iranian Revolution of 1979.

Khrushchev, Nikita S., 1894–1971, Soviet Communist leader, deposed (1964) as premier.

Kidd, Captain (William), c. 1645–1701, British privateer hanged for murder and piracy.

Kiesinger, Kurt G., 1904– , West German chancellor (1966–69), advocate of reconciliation with Eastern Europe.

Kim Il Sung, 1912– , first premier of Communist North Korea.

King, Martin Luther, Jr., 1929–68, assassinated American Negro rights leader and Nobel Prize winner.

King, (W. L.) Mackenzie, 1874–1950, liberal Canadian prime minister (1921–30, 1935–48).

Kissinger, Henry A., 1923– , chief foreign affairs adviser to President Nixon, and leading authority on international relations and national defense policy. U.S. Secretary of State (1973–77).

Kitchener, Horatio H. (Earl), 1850–1916, British field marshal during the imperial era.

Kittikachorn, Thanom, 1911– , Thai premier and minister of defense (1963–73).

Knox, Henry, 1750–1806, American patriot and Revolutionary general, U.S. Secretary of War (1785–94).

Konev, Ivan S., 1897–1973, Soviet WW II field marshal, commander (1955–60) of Warsaw Pact military forces.

Konoye, Prince Fumimaro, 1891–1945, Japanese premier who allied Japan with Axis.

Koo, (V. K.) Wellington, 1887– , Chinese statesman elected (1957) to International Court of Justice at The Hague.

Kornilov, Lavr G., 1870–1918, Russian anti-Bolshevik general.

Kosciusko, Thaddeus, 1746–1817, Polish general who fought for patriot cause in American Revolution.

Kossuth, Louis, 1802–94, exiled Hungarian revolutionary leader.

Kosygin, Aleksei N., 1904– , Soviet Communist premier, successor to Khrushchev.

Kropotkin, Prince (Peter), 1842–1921, Russian anarchist who championed peasantry but opposed Bolshevism.

Kruger, S. J. Paulus (Paul Kruger), 1825–1904, South African pioneer, soldier, farmer, and statesman.

Krupp, Alfred, 1812–87, German armaments magnate known as the "Cannon King."

Krupp, Alfred (von Bohlen and Halbach), 1907–67, German industrialist and imprisoned war criminal.

Kublai Khan, c. 1215–94, Mongol emperor, founder of Yüan dynasty in China.

Kun, Bela, 1886–c. 1939, Hungarian Communist dictator.

Kutuzov, Mikhail I., 1745–1813, Russian field marshal, victor over Napoleon I.

Ky, Nguyen Cao, 1930– , South Vietnamese general and political leader.

Lafayette, Marquis de, 1757–1834, French statesman and general who served in American Revolution.

La Follette, Robert M., 1855–1925, U.S. Senator (Wis., 1906–25), Progressive Party Presidential candidate (1924).

LaFontaine, Sir Louis H., 1807–64, distinguished French-Canadian statesman.

LaGuardia, Fiorello H., 1882–1947, U.S. Congressman (1916, 1923–33) and reform mayor of New York City (1934–45), affectionately known as the "Little Flower."

Laing, Alexander G., 1793–1826, Scottish soldier and explorer who was murdered by Arabs near Timbuktu.

Langton, Stephen, c. 1155–1228, English archbishop who acted with barons to obtain Magna Carta's signing.

Largo Caballero, Francisco, 1869–1946, Spanish Socialist leader and premier (1936–37).

Laski, Harold J., 1893–1950, English political scientist, economist, author, and lecturer.

Lassalle, Ferdinand, 1825–64, a founder of German Socialist movement, killed in a duel over a love affair.

Lattre de Tassigny, Jean de, 1889–1952, French general who fought in Indo-China.

Laval, Pierre, 1883–1945, executed French politician and foreign minister of Vichy government.

Lawrence, Thomas E. (Lawrence of Arabia), 1888–1935, British scholar and Middle East soldier-adventurer.

Leahy, William D., 1875–1959, American diplomat and WW II admiral.

Leclerc, Jacques P. (comte de Hauteclocque), 1902–47, French WW II general who later served in Indo-China.

Lee, Henry, 1756–1818, American cavalry leader in the Revolution; known as Light-Horse Harry Lee.

Lee, Robert E., 1807–70, brilliant American Confederate commander in chief.

Lee Kuan Yew, 1923– , Singaporean Socialist prime minister.

Lehman, Herbert H., 1878–1963, liberal U.S. Senator (N.Y.), opponent of Senator Joseph R. McCarthy.

Lemnitzer, Lyman L., 1899– , American general, NATO commander (1963-1969).

Lenin, Vladimir I., 1870–1924, Russian revolutionary statesman, founder of Bolshevism and U.S.S.R.

Leo Africanus, c. 1465–1550, Moorish traveler in Africa and the Near East.

Lesseps, Ferdinand (Vicomte de), 1805–94, French diplomat and engineer who conceived idea of Suez Canal.

Lewis, John L., 1880–1969, important American labor spokesman, head of UMW and CIO.

Liaquat Ali Khan, 1895–1951, assassinated Moslem leader and first prime minister (1947–51) of Pakistan.

Liebknecht, Karl, 1871–1919, murdered German Communist leader.

Lin Piao, 1907–1971, Chinese Communist leader and political heir to Mao.

Lipton, Sir Thomas J., 1850–1931, Scottish merchant and yachtsman.

Litvinov, Maxim M., 1876–1951, Soviet statesman, proponent of Soviet cooperation with Western powers.

Liu Shao-ch'i, c. 1898-1974, Chinese Communist leader who fell from grace in "cultural revolution" (1966-67).

Livingston, Edward, 1764–1836, American jurist and statesman, U.S. Secretary of State under Andrew Jackson.

Livingston, Robert R., 1746–1813, American Revolutionary political leader who negotiated Louisiana Purchase.

Livingstone, David, 1813–73, Scottish medical missionary, abolitionist, and African explorer.

Lodge, Henry Cabot, 1850–1924, conservative U.S. Senator (Mass., 1893–1924).

Lodge, Henry Cabot, Jr., 1902– , U.S. Senator, ambassador, and Vietnam peace negotiator.

Long, Huey P., 1893–1935, assassinated American political demagogue in Louisiana.

López Portillo, José, 1920- , Mexican president (1976-).

Low, Sir David, 1891–1963, British cartoonist, famous for caricatures.

Lübke, Heinrich, 1894–1972, West German administrator and president.

Luce, Henry R., 1898–1967, American publisher, founder of Time, Inc.

Luckner, Felix, Graf von, 1881-1966, German WW I naval commander, nicknamed "the Sea Devil."

Lumumba, Patrice E., 1925–61, murdered first prime minister (1960) of Republic of the Congo.

Luthuli, Albert J., 1898-1967, South African Zulu leader and Nobel Prize winner.

Luxemburg, Rosa, c. 1870–1919, Polish-born German Communist leader, murdered while being taken to prison.

MacArthur, Douglas, 1880–1964, distinguished American general in WW II, recalled (1951) from Korea for insubordination.

Maccabee, Judas, d. c. 161 B.C., Jewish military leader who opposed foreign rule in Judea.

McCarthy, Eugene J., 1916– , U.S. Senator (Minn.) who became nationally prominent for his opposition to American participation in Vietnam war.

McCarthy, Joseph R., 1908-57, U.S. Senator (Wis.) known for his charges of Communism in government.

McClellan, George B., 1826–85, American Union general.

McCormick, Robert R., 1880–1955, American publisher (Chicago *Tribune*), famous for his isolationist views.

McGill, James, 1744–1813, Scottish-born Canadian fur trader and university founder.

Machado, Gerardo, 1871–1939, repressive Cuban president (1925–33).

Machiavelli, Niccolò, 1469–1527, Florentine diplomat and political philosopher, an outstanding Renaissance figure.

Macmillan, M. Harold, 1894– , conservative British prime minister (1957–63).

McNamara, Robert S., 1916– , U.S. Secretary of Defense under Presidents Kennedy and Johnson.

Madero, Francisco I., 1873–1913, assassinated Mexican revolutionist and president (1911–13).

Magellan, Ferdinand, c. 1480–1521, Portuguese leader of first expedition to circumnavigate the earth (1519-22).

Magsaysay, Ramón, 1907–57, president of the Philippines (1953–57) who campaigned against the Huk rebels.

Mahan, Alfred T., 1840–1914, American naval officer and historian.

Mahdi, title claimed by Mohammed Ahmed, 1844–85, Moslem religious leader in Anglo-Egyptian Sudan.

Mahmud of Ghazni, c. 971–1030, Afghan emperor and conqueror.

Makarios III, 1913–77, Cypriot Greek Orthodox archbishop, first president (elected 1960) of Cyprus.

Malan, Daniel F., 1874–1959, Afrikaner prime minister of South Africa.

Malcolm X (b. Malcolm Little), 1925–65, assassinated American Negro separatist leader.

Malenkov, Georgi M., 1902– , Soviet Communist successor to Stalin (1953-55), expelled (1964) from party.

Malinovsky, Rodion Y., 1898–1967, Soviet marshal and minister of defense.

Malraux, André, 1901–76, French man of letters and political figure, minister of culture under de Gaulle.

Mannerheim, Baron Carl G. E., 1867–1951, Finnish field marshal, later president (1944–46).

Mansur, d. 775, Abbasid caliph (754–775), founder of Baghdad.

Mao Zedong (Tse-tung), 1893–1976, founder of Communist China, leader of radical wing of international Communism.

Marat, Jean Paul, 1743–93, French revolutionary stabbed to death in his bath by Charlotte Corday.

Marcos, Ferdinand E., 1917– , Filipino president.

Maria Theresa, 1717–80, popular Hapsburg empress, queen of Bohemia and Hungary.

Marie Antoinette, 1755–93, guillotined queen of France, wife of Louis XVI.

Marion, Francis ("the Swamp Fox"), c. 1732–95, American guerrilla leader in the Revolution.

Marlborough, Duke of (John Churchill), 1650–1722, English general and statesman.

Martí, José, 1853–95, Cuban poet and patriot, leader of Cuban struggle for independence.

Marx, Karl H., 1818–83, German philosopher, proponent of modern Communism, author of *Das Kapital*.

Masaryk, Jan, 1886–1948, Czechoslovak statesman whose "suicide" mysteriously followed Communist coup.

Masaryk, Thomas G., 1850–1937, Czechoslovak statesman, founder and president (1918–35) of Czechoslovakia.

Massey, Vincent, 1887–1967, Canadian diplomat and governor-general.

Mata Hari (Margaretha G. Zelle), 1876–1917, Dutch dancer executed by the French as a WW I German spy.

Matteotti, Giacomo, 1885–1924, murdered Italian Socialist leader, opponent of Mussolini.

Matthias Corvinus, c. 1443–90, king of Hungary (1458–90) and of Bohemia (1478–90), crusader against Turks.

Mawson, Sir Douglas, 1882–1958, English-born Australian geologist who charted antarctic coast.

Maximilian, 1832–67, Austrian archduke and emperor of Mexico (1864–67), executed by the forces of Juarez.

Mazarin, Jules, 1602–61, French statesman and Roman Catholic cardinal.

Mazzini, Giuseppe, 1805–72, Italian patriot and revolutionary who figured in Italy's unification.

Mboya, Tom (Thomas J.), 1930–69, Kenyan political leader, instrumental in securing independence for his country.

Medici, Cosimo de', 1389–1464, Florentine merchant prince and first Medici ruler of Florence.

Medici, Lorenzo de' (Lorenzo the Magnificent), 1449–92, Florentine statesman, Renaissance patron of the arts.

Meir, Golda, 1898–1978, Israeli prime minister (1969–74).

Mendès-France, Pierre, 1907– , French premier (1954–55), who opposed Charles de Gaulle's return to power.

Menelik II, 1844–1913, emperor of Ethiopia after 1899, who expanded and modernized his country.

Metaxas, John, 1871–1941, Greek general and dictator.

Metternich, Clemens W. N. L., Fürst von, 1773–1859, Austrian foreign minister and arbiter of Europe.

Mikhailovich, Draja (Dragoljub), c. 1893–1946, executed Yugoslav soldier, foe of Tito.

Miki, Takeo, 1907– , Japanese prime minister (1974-76).

Mikoyan, Anastas I., 1895–1978, Soviet Communist leader.

Mindszenty, Cardinal (Jozsef), 1892–1975, Hungarian Roman Catholic prelate who sought asylum in U.S. legation after Hungarian uprising (1956).

Minuit, Peter, c. 1580–1638, director general (1626–31) of New Netherland, who purchased Manhattan for $24.

Mirabeau, Honoré G. R., comte de, 1749–91, French revolutionary who favored a strong constitutional monarchy.

Mitchell, Billy (William), 1879–1936, American general, demoted for criticism of U.S. military leaders.

Mobuto Sese Seko, 1930– , Zairean president who deposed (1960) Patrice Lumumba.

Mohammad Reza Pahlavi, 1919– , shah of Iran (1941–1979).

Mohammed V, 1910–61, sultan of Morocco (1927–53), first king (1957–61) of independent Morocco.

Moi, Daniel arap, 1924– , Kenyan president (1978–).

Molotov, Vyacheslav M., 1890– , Soviet Communist leader whose political fortunes waned in post-Stalin era.

Moltke, Helmuth J. L., Graf von, 1800–91, Prussian field marshal, victor in Franco-Prussian War.

Mongkut (Rama IV), 1804–68, king of Siam, a main character in 1944 book, *Anna and the King of Siam*.

Monnet, Jean, 1888–1979, French political economist who conceived idea of the Common Market.

Montcalm, Louis de (Marquis de Saint-Véran), 1712–59, French general in French and Indian Wars, defeated and killed in Battle of Quebec.

Montezuma, c. 1480–1520, murdered Aztec emperor who defied Cortés.

Montgomery, Bernard L. (1st Viscount Montgomery of Alamein), 1887–1976, distinguished British WW II field marshal.

More, Sir Thomas, 1478–1535, English author (*Utopia*) and statesman, celebrated as a Roman Catholic martyr.

Morelos y Pavón, José M., 1765–1815, executed Mexican leader in revolution against Spain.

Morgan, Daniel, 1736–1802, American Revolutionary general, victor in the Carolina campaign.

Morgan, Sir Henry, c. 1635–88, English buccaneer, later acting governor of Jamaica.

Morgan, J. P. (John Pierpont), 1837–1913, American banker who built his family's fortunes into a financial colossus.

Morgenthau, Henry, Jr., 1891–1967, U.S. Secretary of the Treasury (1934–45).

Morris, Gouverneur, 1752–1816, American Revolutionary statesman who advocated centralized government.

Morris, Robert, 1734–1806, "financier of the American Revolution," signer of Declaration of Independence.

Mossadegh, Mohammed, 1880–1967, deposed and imprisoned Iranian premier (1951–53) who attempted to nationalize Iran's British-controlled oil industry.

Mountbatten, Lord Louis, 1900–79, British WW II admiral who commanded in both the Atlantic and Pacific.

Muñoz Marin, Luis, 1898– , long-time governor of Puerto Rico, energetic supporter of its commonwealth status.

Mussolini, Benito ("Il Duce"), 1883–1945, Italian dictator 1922–45), founder of Fascism, ally of Adolf Hitler.

Mutsuhito (Meiji), 1852–1912, Japanese emperor (1867–1912) during whose reign feudalism came to an end.

Nadir Shah, 1688–1747, shah of Iran, perhaps the last great Asiatic conqueror.

Nagy, Imre, c. 1895–1958, Hungarian Communist premier (1953–55), executed after the 1956 uprising.

Nansen, Fridtjof, 1861–1930, Norwegian arctic explorer, statesman, and Nobel Peace Prize winner (1922).

Napoleon Bonaparte (Napoleon I), 1769–1821, Corsican-born emperor of the French (1804–15).

Napoleon III (Louis Napoleon Bonaparte), 1808–73, emperor of the French (nephew of Napoleon I).

Nasser, Gamal Abdel, 1918–70, Egyptian leader of Arab unification, became (1956) first president of Egypt.

Nebuchadnezzar, d. 562 B.C., king of Babylonia and destroyer of Jerusalem (586 B.C.).

Necker, Jacques, 1732–1804, Swiss-born French financier and statesman, father of Madame de Staël.

Negrin, Juan, 1891–1956, Spanish Socialist premier (1937–39), who fled from his country after the civil war.

Nehru, Jawaharlal, 1889–1964, first prime minister of India, guided country during early years of independence.

Nelson, Lord (Horatio), 1758–1805, English admiral in Napoleonic Wars, killed during victory at Trafalgar.

Nenni, Pietro, 1891– , Italian Socialist leader.

Ne Win, 1911– , Burmese general and prime minister, leader of 1962 coup against U Nu.

Newman, Cardinal (John Henry), 1801–90, English prelate, a founder (1833) of Oxford Movement.

Ney, Michel, 1769–1815, executed marshal of France, commander at Waterloo.

Nightingale, Florence, 1820–1910, English nurse in Crimean War, founder of modern nursing.

Nimeiry, Jaafar Muhammad al, 1929– , Sudanese president (1971–).

Nimitz, Chester W., 1885–1966, American admiral who headed Pacific naval forces throughout WW II.

Nkrumah, Kwame, 1909–1972, former dictatorial prime minister of Ghana, deposed in 1966.

Nobel, Alfred B., 1833–96, Swedish inventor of dynamite who established annual philanthropic prizes.

Nobile, Umberto, 1885–1978, Italian aeronautical engineer, arctic explorer, and pilot.

Norris, George W., 1861–1944, U.S. Senator (Neb.).

Norstad, Lauris, 1907– , U.S. general, supreme commander (1956–63) of Allied Powers in Europe.

Nostradamus (Michel de Nostredame), 1503-66, French astrologer and physician.

Novotny, Antonin, 1904-1975, Czechoslovak leader eight months before 1968 Soviet invasion.

Nu, U, 1907– , Burmese Socialist premier overthrown in 1962 coup.

Nyerere, Julius K., 1921– , African statesman in Tanganyika, elected (1962) first president of Tanzania.

Oates, Titus, 1649–1705, English fabricator of Popish Plot (1678).

Obregón, Alvaro, 1880–1928, assassinated Mexican revolutionary general and president (1920–24).

Ochs, Adolph S., 1858–1935, American publisher of *The New York Times* and a director (1900–35) of the Associated Press.

O'Connell, Daniel (the Liberator), 1775–1847, Irish political leader whose nationalism affected Ireland's history.

O'Connor, Thomas P. (Tay Pay), 1848–1929, Irish journalist and nationalist who aided cause of Irish Home Rule.

O'Higgins, Bernardo, 1778–1842, Chilean revolutionary and dictator (1817–23) who died in exile in Peru.

Ohira, Masayoshi, 1910– , Japanese premier (1978–).

Ojukwu, C. Odumegwu, 1933– , leader of Biafra's unsuccessful war of secession in the late 1960s.

Oppenheimer, J. Robert, 1904–67, American physicist who led research effort culminating in atom bomb.

Orlando, Vittorio Emanuele, 1860–1952, Italian jurist and premier (1917–19), one of the "Big Four" at WW I Paris Peace Conference.

Osman I, 1259–1326, founder of Ottoman dynasty who inaugurated a policy of religious toleration.

Oswald, Lee Harvey, 1939–63, President John F. Kennedy's assassin; murdered in Dallas jail by Jack Ruby.

Owen, Robert, 1771–1858, British social reformer, socialist, and cooperative-movement pioneer.

Paderewski, Ignace J., 1860–1941, Polish statesman, composer, and popular classical pianist.

Paley, William S., 1901–   , American radio and television executive.

Palmer Nathaniel B., 1799-1877, American sea captain, ship designer and Antarctic explorer.

Pandit, Madame (Vijaya L.), 1900–   , Indian diplomat and president of UN General Assembly (1953–54).

Pankhurst, Emmeline (née Goulden), 1858–1928, revered English woman suffragist.

Papadreou, George, 1919–   , Greek premier, seized power in April 1967 and was overthrown in Nov. 1973.

Papandreou, George, 1888–1968, Greek premier, opponent of King Constantine and military junta.

Papen, Franz von, 1879–1969, German chancellor, diplomat under Hitler, acquitted by Nuremberg tribunal.

Park Chung Hee, 1917–   , South Korean president.

Park, Mungo, 1771–1806, Scottish explorer of Niger River and western Africa.

Parnell, Charles S., 1846–91, magnetic Irish nationalist leader, "uncrowned king of Ireland."

La Pasionaria (Dolores Ibarruri), 1895-   , Spanish revolutionist and a founder of Spain's Communist party.

Patiño, Simón I., 1868–1947, Bolivian tin king, reputed to have been one of world's wealthiest men.

Patterson, Joseph M., 1879–1946, American publisher of first successful U.S. tabloid, Daily News.

Patton, George S., Jr., 1885–1945, brilliant but controversial American WW II general ("Old Blood and Guts").

Paulus, Friedrich, 1890-1957, German field marshal who surrendered (1943) to Russians at Stalingrad.

Peabody, George, 1852-1938, American banker and philanthropist who fought for Negro education.

Pearson, Lester B., 1897–1972, Liberal prime minister of Canada (1963–68).

Peary, Robert E., 1856–1920, American rear admiral and first man to reach the North Pole (April 6, 1909).

Peel, Sir Robert, 1788–1850, British reformist statesman, organizer of London police force.

Pendergast, Thomas J., 1872–1945, American political boss in Missouri.

Pérez Jiménez, Marcos, 1914–   , Venezuelan dictator and army officer.

Pericles, c. 495–429 B.C., democratic Athenian statesman, great patron of the arts.

Perkins, Frances, 1882–1965, U.S. Secretary of Labor during New Deal era, first woman cabinet member.

Perón, Juan D., 1895–1974, Argentine general and dictator (President 1946-55; 1973-74).

Perry, Oliver H., 1785–1819, American naval hero (Battle of Lake Erie) in War of 1812.

Pershing, John J. (Jack), 1860–1948, American WW I general, AEF commander in chief.

Pétain, Henri P., 1856–1951, French marshal, head of Vichy France (1940–42).

Pham Van Dong, 1906–   , Vietnamese premier, a founder of the Vietminh.

Philby, Harold St. J. B., 1885–1960, British explorer, author and adviser to King Ibn Saud of Saudi Arabia.

Philip II, 382–336 B.C., father of Alexander the Great.

Pilsudski, Joseph, 1867–1935, Polish general and authoritarian premier (1926–28, 1930–35).

Pizarro, Francisco, c. 1476–1541, rapacious Spanish conquistador, conqueror of Peru.

Podgorny, Nikolai V., 1903–   , Chairman of the Presidium of the Supreme Soviet (1965–77).

Poincaré, Raymond, 1860–1934, French president (1913–20) and advocate of harsh punishment for Germany after WW I.

Polo, Marco, c. 1254–c. 1324, Venetian traveler, favorite of Mongol Emperor Kublai Khan, and author of remarkably accurate Asian travelogue.

Pompadour, Madame, 1721–64, French mistress of Louis XV and his confidante until her death.

Pompey (the Great), 106–48 B.C., assassinated Roman general and statesman, rival of Caesar.

Pompidou, Georges J. R., 1911–74, French president (1969–1974).

Potemkin, Grigori A., 1739–91, eccentric Russian field marshal, a favorite of Catherine the Great.

Primo de Rivera, José A., 1903–36, Spanish founder of fascist Falange, executed by Loyalists after outbreak of Spanish Civil War.

Primo de Rivera, Miguel, 1870–1930, Spanish general and dictator (1923–30), father of José Primo de Rivera.

Princip, Gavrilo, 1895–1918, Serbian political agitator and hero, assassin (1914) of Archduke Francis Ferdinand.

Przhevalsky, Nikolai M., 1839–88, Russian geographer and explorer in central Asia and the Russian Far East.

Pugachev, Emelyan I., d. 1775, beheaded Russian leader who posed as Peter III in peasant rebellion (1773–75).

Pulaski, Casimir, c. 1748–79, Polish military commander in American Revolution, mortally wounded at Savannah.

Pulitzer, Joseph, 1847–1911, Hungarian-born publisher who established annual prizes for American letters.

Pu Yi, Henry, 1906–67, last emperor (1908–12) of China, later emperor of Japanese puppet state of Manchukuo.

el-Qaddafi, Muammar, 1938–   , Libyan head of state since 1969.

Quezon, Manuel L., 1878–1944, first president of Philippines (1935–44), led it to independence.

Quisling, Vidkun, 1887–1945, executed Norwegian Fascist leader who helped Germany conquer his country.

Radek, Karl, 1885–1939?, Russian Communist leader and journalist, purged by Stalin.

Raeder, Erich, 1876–1960, German WW II admiral who disagreed with Hitler on strategy.

Raffles, Sir Thomas S. B., 1781–1826, British East Indian administrator, founder of Zoological Society of London.

Raglan, Lord (Fitzroy J. H. Somerset), 1788–1855, British general in Napoleonic and Crimean wars.

Rahman, Tunku Abdul, Prince, 1903-1973, first prime minister of Malaya (1957-1970).

Randolph, Edmund, 1753–1813, first U.S. Attorney General (1789–94), figure at Constitutional Convention (1787).

Rasmussen, Knud J. V., 1879–1933, Danish explorer of Greenland and the Arctic.

Rasputin, Grigori Y., 1872–1916, Russian libertine monk, a notorious influence on Nicholas II's court.

Rathenau, Walter, 1867–1922, assassinated German industrialist, idealistic social theorist, and statesman.

Rayburn, Sam (Samuel T.), 1882–1961, U.S. Congressman (Tex.), long-time Democratic House speaker.

Récamier, Madame (Juliette), 1777–1849, French beauty who presided over a salon of notables.

Reid, Ogden M., 1882–1947, American newspaper publisher.

Revere, Paul, 1735–1818, American Revolutionary patriot immortalized by Longfellow's poem.

Reza Shah Pahlavi, 1877–1944, shah of Iran (1925-41) who gained independence for his country.

Rhee, Syngman, 1875–1965, authoritarian president (1948–60) of Republic of (South) Korea.

Rhodes, Cecil J., 1853–1902, British statesman and business magnate in South Africa who set up Rhodes scholarships; Rhodesia was named for him.

Ribbentrop, Joachim von, 1893–1946, Anglophobic Nazi foreign minister (1938–45).

Ricci, Matteo, 1552–1610, Italian missionary and geographer in China, a favorite at the Chinese court.

Richelieu, Cardinal (Armand J.), duc de, 1585–1642, French prelate and statesman, founder of French Academy.

Riis, Jacob A., 1849–1914, Danish-American social reformer and journalist.

Rizal, José, 1861–96, Filipino patriot, author, poet, physician; his martyrdom inspired anti-Spanish revolt.

Robert I (Robert the Bruce), 1274–1329, king of Scotland who freed his country from England's grip.

Robert Guiscard, c. 1015–85, Norman conqueror of southern Italy.

Robespierre, Maximilien M. I., 1758–94, guillotined French revolutionary associated with the Reign of Terror.

Rob Roy (Robert MacGregor), 1671–1734, Scottish outlaw who figures in Scott's novel Rob Roy.

Rochambeau, Count (Jean B.), 1725–1807, French marshal in American Revolution.

Rockefeller, John D., 1839–1937, American oil tycoon and philanthropist, a founder of University of Chicago.

Rockefeller, Nelson A., 1908–79, governor of New York (1959–73), Vice-President of U.S. (1974–1977).

Rodino, Peter W., 1909–   , chairman of the House Judiciary Committee which considered the impeachment of President Nixon in 1974.

Rokossovsky, Konstantin, 1896–1968, Soviet marshal, symbol of Russian influence in Poland (1949-56).

Rommel, Erwin, 1891–1944, German field marshal in Africa ("the Desert Fox") and France (1940–44).

Romulo, Carlos P., 1900–   , Filipino statesman, president of UN General Assembly (1949).

Ronne, Finn, 1899–   , Norwegian-born American explorer and geographer.

Root, Elihu, 1845–1937, U.S. Secretary of State (1905–09), an architect of League of Nations; Nobel Peace Prize winner (1912).

Rosecrans, William S., 1818–98, American Union general.

Ross, James C., 1800–62, British rear admiral and polar explorer.

Rothschild, Guy, Baron de, 1909– , descendant of the prominent French banking family and head of the Banque Rothschild.

Rothschild, Meyer A., 1743–1812, German founder (in Frankfurt) of international banking house of Rothschild.

Rundstedt, Karl R. G. von, 1875–1953, German WW II field marshal and supreme commander in West (1942–45).

Rusk, (D.) Dean, 1909– , U.S. Secretary of State under Presidents Kennedy and Johnson.

Russell, Richard B., 1897–1971, conservative U.S. Senator (Ga., first elected 1933).

Sadat, Anwar, 1918– , Egyptian president since 1970.

Sage, Russell, 1816–1906, American tycoon whose widow established (1907) Russell Sage Foundation.

Saladin, c. 1137–93, Moslem warrior and sultan of Egypt, major opponent of Crusaders.

Salazar, Antonio de Oliveira, 1889–1970, long-time Portuguese dictator (beginning in 1932).

Salomon, Haym, 1740–85, American Revolutionary patriot and financier.

Sandracottus (Greek for Chandragupta), fl. c. 321–c. 298 B.C., Indian emperor, founder of the Maurya dynasty.

Sanger, Margaret, 1879–1966, American founder of the birth-control movement.

San Martín, José de, 1778–1850, South American revolutionary, protector of Peru (1821–22).

Santa Anna, Antonio L. de, 1794–1876, Mexican general at Alamo and in Mexican War, several times president.

Santander, Francisco de Paula, 1792–1840, Colombian revolutionary and political leader.

Sarnoff, David, 1891–1971; Russian-born American pioneer in radio and television.

Savonarola, Girolamo, 1452–98, executed Florentine religious reformer.

Saxe, Comte de (Maurice), 1696–1750, French marshal, one of the greatest generals of his era.

Scanderbeg (George Castriota), c. 1404–68, Albanian national hero who led his people against Turks.

Schacht, Hjalmar H. G., 1877–1970, German president of Reichsbank (1923–30, 1933–39), acquitted by Nuremberg tribunal.

Schlieffen, Alfred, Graf von, 1833–1913, German field marshal whose battle strategy was reflected in both WW I and II.

Schmidt, Helmut, 1918– , West German chancellor since 1974.

Schuman, Robert, 1886–1963, French premier (1947–48) who worked to promote a European community.

Schurz, Carl, 1829–1906, German-born U.S. Secretary of the Interior (1877–81), newspaper editor, and reformer.

Schuschnigg, Kurt von, 1897–1977, Austrian chancellor (1934–38) imprisoned by Nazis until 1945.

Scipio Africanus Major, c. 234–183 B.C., Roman general, victor over Hannibal in Punic Wars.

Scott, Dred, c. 1795–1858, American slave and central figure in law case argued (1856–57) before U.S. Supreme Court.

Scott, Robert F., 1868–1912, British naval officer and antarctic explorer.

Scott, Winfield, 1786–1866, American army commander (1841–61), and Mexican War hero.

Scripps, Edward W., 1854–1926, American newspaper publisher.

Senghor, Léopold S., 1906– , African statesman and poet, first president of independent Senegal.

Sennacherib, d. 681 B.C., king of Assyria (705–681 B.C.) and conqueror who was murdered by his sons.

Seward, William H., 1801–72, U.S. Secretary of State, purchaser (1867) of Alaska ("Seward's folly").

Sforza, Ludovico, c. 1451–1508, duke of Milan (1494–99), Renaissance prince, patron of Leonardo da Vinci.

Shackleton, Sir Ernest H., 1874–1922, Irish-born British explorer whose antarctic expedition (1907–09) crossed within 100 miles of the South Pole.

Shaftesbury, Earl of (Anthony A. Cooper), 1801–85, leading English social reformer who advocated government action to reduce misery caused by Industrial Revolution.

Sharett, Moshe, 1894–1965, Israeli prime minister (1953–55), Ben-Gurion's closest associate in promoting an independent Jewish state.

Shastri, Shri L. B., 1904–66, prime minister of India (1964–66), disciple of Gandhi.

Shays, Daniel, c. 1747–1825, American Revolutionary soldier, leader of Shays's Rebellion (1786–87) of financially depressed small farmers in Massachusetts.

Sheridan, Philip H., 1831–88, American Union general, observer with Prussian army in Franco-Prussian War.

Sherman, William Tecumseh, 1820–91, American Union general who practiced war of attrition in the South.

Smith, Ian Douglas, 1919– , Rhodesian prime minister (1964–79).

Smith, John, c. 1580–1631, English adventurer and colonial leader; Pocahontas probably saved his life.

Smith, Walter Bedell, 1895–1961, U.S. WW II general, ambassador to USSR (1946–49), CIA head (1950–53).

Smuts, Jan C., 1870–1950, South African prime minister twice, WW II field marshal, and a UN organizer.

Snorri Sturluson, 1178–1241, Icelandic chieftain and historian, leading light in medieval Norse literature.

Somoza, Anastasio, 1896–1956, assassinated dictator of Nicaragua (1937–47, 1950–56).

Soong, T. V., 1894–1971, Harvard-educated Chinese statesman.

Sorge, Richard, 1895–1944, executed German spy for USSR in Japan.

Souphanouvong, Prince, 1902– , Laotian politician, leader of leftist Pathet Lao forces. President since 1975.

Soustelle, Jacques, 1912– , French author and statesman.

Souvanna Phouma, Prince, 1901– , Laotian neutralist prime minister (1962–75).

Spaak, Paul Henri, 1899–1972, Belgian statesman and Socialist leader, first president of UN general assembly (1946), and secretary-general of NATO (1957–61).

Spartacus, d. 71 B.C., Thracian gladiator and leader of Italian slave revolt, killed in battle.

Speke, John H., 1827–64, English explorer in Africa and discoverer (1858) of Lake Tanganyika.

Springer, Axel C., 1912– , powerful German publisher.

De Staël, Germaine, 1766–1817, French-Swiss writer and intellectual leader.

Stalin, Joseph V. (b. J. V. Dzhugashvili), 1879–1953, Russian Communist dictator.

Stambuliski, Alexander, 1879–1923, murdered Bulgarian premier (1919–23) and agrarian reformer.

Stanley, Sir Henry M., 1841–1904, Anglo-American adventurer, journalist, and empire builder, who was commissioned (1871) by the *New York Herald* to find David Livingstone in Africa.

Stanton, Edwin M., 1814–69, U.S. Secretary of War under Presidents Lincoln and Andrew Johnson.

Stavisky, Serge A., 1886–1934, French swindler, chief figure in scandal that rocked France (1934).

Stefansson, Vilhjalmur, 1879–1962, Canadian-born Icelandic ethnologist and arctic explorer.

Stepinac, Cardinal (Aloysius), 1898–1960, Yugoslav Roman Catholic prelate convicted (1946) by Tito government of Nazi collaboration but released (1951).

Steuben, Baron von (Friedrich W.), 1730–94, Prussian general in American Revolution.

Stevens, Thaddeus, 1792–1868, U.S. Congressman (Pa., 1849–53, 1859–68) active during Civil War and Reconstruction, devoted to Negro betterment.

Stevenson, Adlai E., 1900–65, eloquent American lawyer, Presidential candidate (1952, 1956), and U.S. ambassador to UN (1961–65).

Stimson, Henry L., 1867–1950, U.S. Secretary of War (1911–13, 1940–45) and Secretary of State (1929–33).

Stolypin, Piotr A., 1862–1911, Russian premier and minister of interior (1906–11).

Stowe, Harriet Beecher, 1811–96, American humanitarian whose novel *Uncle Tom's Cabin* was a factor in bringing about the Civil War.

Strabo, b. c. 63 B.C., Greek geographer, historian, and traveler.

Stresemann, Gustav, 1878–1929, German foreign minister dedicated to regaining world friendship for post-WW I Germany, and sharer of 1926 Nobel Peace Prize.

Stroessner, Alfredo, 1913– , repressive Paraguayan general and president.

Stuart, Charles Edward, 1720–88, claimant (Bonnie Prince Charlie) to English throne.

Stuyvesant, Peter, c. 1610–72, autocratic Dutch director general of New Netherland (beginning 1647).

Suárez González, Adolfo, 1932– , Spanish premier (1976-).

Sucre, Antonio J. de, 1795–1830, South American revolutionary and military commander, associate of Bolívar.

Suharto, 1921– , Indonesian general and chief executive who overthrew (1965) Sukarno.

Sukarno, 1902–70, independence leader and dictatorial first president of republic of Indonesia (1945–66).

Sukhe-Bator, 1893–1923, Mongolian political leader who helped set up Mongolian People's Revolutionary party.

Suleiman I (the Magnificent), 1494–1566, Ottoman sultan under whom Ottoman Empire reached its height.

Sulla, Lucius C., 138–78 B.C., notorious Roman general and dictator.

Sully, Maximilien de B., duc de, 1560–1641, French statesman and closest adviser to Henry IV of France.

Sun Yat-sen, 1866–1925, Chinese revolutionary founder of the Chinese republic and of the Kuomintang.

Suslov, Mikhail A., 1902– , Soviet ideologist.

Suvarov, Aleksandr V., 1729–1800, revered Russian marshal in French Revolutionary Wars (1798–99).

Svoboda, Ludvík, 1895– , Communist president of Czechoslovakia during 1968 Soviet invasion.

Taft, Robert A., 1889–1953, conservative U.S. Senator who helped write Taft-Hartley Labor Act.

Talleyrand, Charles M. de, 1754–1838, French statesman and diplomat.

Tamerlane, c. 1336–1405, cruel Mongol conqueror of Asia, subject of a play by Christopher Marlowe.

Tanaka, Kakuei, 1918– , self-made businessman and premier of Japan (1972-74).

Taraki, Nur Mohammad, 1917–79, president of Afghanistan (1978-79).

Tasman, Abel Janszoon, c. 1603–59, Dutch explorer who discovered (1642) Tasmania.

Teng Hsiao-ping see Deng Xiaoping.

Tetzel, Johann, c. 1465-1519, German Roman Catholic preacher who was attacked by Martin Luther.

Thatcher, Margaret, 1925– , British Conservative prime minister (1979–).

Themistocles, c. 525-c. 460 B.C., Athenian statesman and naval commander.

Theodora, d. 548, Byzantine empress, joint ruler with her husband, Justinian I.

Thiers, Adolphe, 1797–1877, French statesman, journalist, and historian of the Revolution and Bonaparte.

Thieu, Nguyen Van, 1923– , South Vietnamese president (1967-75), instrumental in 1963 overthrow of Diem.

Thomas, Norman M., 1884–1968, American Socialist leader, lecturer, and writer; frequent Socialist Party Presidential candidate after 1928.

Thomas à Becket, Saint, c. 1118–70, martyred English archbishop (Canterbury).

Thomson, Roy H., (1st Baron Thomson of Fleet), 1894–1976, Canadian-born British publisher.

Thorez, Maurice, 1900–64, French Communist leader, vice premier (1946–47).

Thurmond, (J.) Strom, 1902– , conservative U.S. Senator (S.C.), States' Rights Presidential candidate (1948).

Tilden, Samuel J., 1814–86, Democratic Presidential candidate (1876 against Rutherford B. Hayes).

Tirpitz, Alfred von, 1849–1930, German WW I admiral, advocate of unrestricted submarine warfare.

Tito, Marshal (b. Josip Broz), 1892– , unorthodox Yugoslav Communist leader since 1945.

Togliatti, Palmiro, 1893–1964, Italian Communist leader and party founder in his country.

Togo, Heihachiro, Count, 1847–1934, Japanese admiral and naval hero of Russo-Japanese War.

Tojo, Hideki, 1884–1948, Japanese general and prime minister (1941–44), executed by Allies as a war criminal.

Torquemada, Tomás de, 1420–98, severe Spanish Dominican who headed Spanish Inquisition.

Touré, Sékou, 1922– , African left-wing political leader, first president of Republic of Guinea.

Toussaint L'Ouverture, François D., c. 1744–1803, Haitian patriot and martyr who thwarted French colonial aims.

Trotsky, Leon, 1879–1940, exiled Soviet revolutionary and a principal founder of USSR.

Trudeau, Pierre E., 1919– , French-Canadian Liberal prime minister (1968-79) and lawyer.

Trujillo Molina, Rafael L., 1891–1961, murdered president (1930–38, 1942–60) of Dominican Republic.

Trung Trac, fl. 39-43 A.D., Vietnamese national heroine who led a revolt against China.

Tshombe, Moise K., 1919–69, Congolese political leader of Katanga, which he proclaimed (1960) independent.

Tubman, Harriet, c. 1820–1913, slave-born American abolitionist and Underground Railroad "conductor."

Tubman, William V. S., 1895–1971, long-time Liberian president.

Tukhachevsky, Mikhail N., 1893–1937, Soviet marshal who helped to modernize and mechanize Red Army.

Tupac Amaru, c. 1742–81, Indian national hero of Peru, executed leader of antigovernment rebellion (1780).

Turner, Nat, 1800–31, executed American leader of slave rebellion (1831, Southampton Co., Va.).

Tutankhamen, fl. c. 1350 B.C., Egyptian pharaoh whose tomb revealed new knowledge of XVIII dynasty life.

Tweed, Boss (William M.), 1823–78, American politician and Tammany leader, who defrauded New York City.

Tyler, Wat, d. 1381, English leader of great peasant rebellion (1381) over labor conditions.

Tz'u Hsi, 1834–1908, dowager empress of China who encouraged Boxer Rebellion (1898–1900).

Ulbricht, Walter, 1893–1973, Communist who became (1960) East German head of state.

Vance, Cyrus R., 1917– , American lawyer, government official, and Secretary of State since 1977.

Vanderbilt, Commodore (Cornelius), 1794–1877, American railroad magnate, founder of Vanderbilt University.

Vargas, Getúlio D., 1883–1954, Brazilian statesman and president (1930–45, 1951–54).

Venizelos, Eleutherios, 1864–1936, Cretan-born Greek statesman and reformer.

Verwoerd, Hendrik F., 1901–66, assassinated South African prime minister (1958–66), proponent of apartheid.

Victoria, 1819–1901, longest reigning English monarch in history (64 years), who ruled during the height of the British Empire's prestige.

Videla, Jorge Rafael, 1925– , Argentine general and president (1976–).

Villa, Pancho (b. Doroteo Arango), c. 1877–1923, assassinated Mexican bandit and revolutionary.

Visconti, Gian C., c. 1351–1402, Italian duke of Milan who reformed and centralized the government.

Vishinsky, Andrei Y., 1883–1954, Soviet jurist and diplomat, foreign minister (1949-53) of USSR.

Volstead, Andrew J., 1860–1947, American legislator, author (1919) of Volstead (alcohol prohibition) Act.

Voroshilov, Kliment Y., 1881-1969, Soviet general and statesman, close associate of Stalin.

Vorster, Balthazar J., 1915– , South African prime minister (1966-78) and lawyer.

Wainwright, Jonathan M., 1883–1953, American general who in World War II defended Bataan and Corregidor.

Waldheim, Kurt, 1918– , Austrian career diplomat and Secretary General of the United Nations (1972–).

Wallace, George C., 1919– , American conservative politician, third party Presidential candidate (1968).

Washington, Booker T., 1856-1915, Black American educator, organizer (1881) of Tuskegee Institute; author.

Wavell, Archibald P. (Earl), 1883–1950, British field marshal and viceroy of India (1943–47).

Webb, Beatrice (née Potter), 1858–1943, English Socialist economist; she and her husband, Sidney J. Webb (1859–1947), were leading figures in Fabian Society and building British Labour party.

Webster, Daniel, 1782–1852, American statesman, a leading political figure, noted orator, and Whig luminary.

Weizmann, Chaim, 1874–1952, Russian-born scientist, Zionist leader, and first president of Israel (1948–52).

Welles, Sumner, 1892–1961, American diplomat and statesman, specialist in Latin American affairs.

Westmoreland, William C., 1914– , American general in Vietnam.

White, William A., 1868–1944, American author and editor (1895–1944) of Emporia (Kans.) *Gazette.*

Wilkes, Charles, 1798–1877, American naval officer and discoverer of area in Antarctic named Wilkes Land.

Willkie, Wendell L., 1892–1944, American industrialist and anti-isolationist political leader, Republican Presidential candidate (1940).

Wilson, J. Harold, 1916– , Labour prime minister (1964-1970, 1974–76), of Great Britain.

Wingate, Orde C., 1903–44, British WW II general, who demonstrated effectiveness of guerrilla warfare.

Wolfe, James, 1727–59, British victor against French in battle of Quebec (Plains of Abraham).

Wollstonecraft, Mary, 1759–97, English feminist whose writings inspired the American women's rights movement.

Wolsey, Cardinal (Thomas), c. 1473–1530, English prelate and favorite of Henry VIII.

Wrangel, Baron Ferdinand von, 1796–1870, Russian naval officer, arctic explorer, governor of Russian Alaska.

Wrangel, Baron (Piotr N.), 1878–1928, Russian anti-Bolshevik general and exile who died at Brussels.

Wyszynski, Cardinal (Stefan), 1901– , Polish prelate often in conflict with Gomulka government.

Xenophon, c. 430 B.C.–c. 355 B.C., Greek historian who led retreat of "Ten Thousand" Greek mercenaries from Persia (401 B.C.).

Yamamoto, Isoroku, 1884–1943, Japanese admiral who masterminded (1941) attack on Pearl Harbor.

Yamani, Ahmed Zaki, 1930– , Saudi Arabian oil minister; leading figure in Arab and OPEC oil activities.

Yamashita, Tomoyuki, 1888–1946, Japanese general defeated (1945) by General MacArthur's invasion of Philippines, hanged in Manila as a war criminal.

Yoshida, Shigeru, 1878–1967, Japanese Liberal prime minister (1946-54).

Yüan Shih-kai, 1859–1916, dictatorial president of China (1912-16) who declared (1916) himself emperor.

Zaharoff, Sir Basil (b. Basileios Zacharias), 1850–1936, Turkish-born British financier and munitions manufacturer.

Zapata, Emiliano, c. 1879–1919. Mexican revolutionary.

Zenger, John Peter, 1697–1746, German-American journalist whose libel trial and acquittal furthered freedom of the press in America.

Zhdanov, Andrei A., 1896–1948, murdered Soviet Communist leader who fostered extreme nationalism.

Zhou Enlai, 1898–1976, Chinese Communist premier and foreign minister (1949-76).

Zhukov, Georgi K., 1896-1974, Soviet marshal who defeated Germans at Stalingrad and occupied Berlin.

Zinoviev, Grigori E., 1883–1936, Russian Communist leader executed by Stalin after the first spectacular purge trial.

SCIENTISTS AND MATHEMATICIANS

Ampère, André Marie, 1775–1836, French physicist, discovered, 1820, the left-hand and right-hand rules of the magnetic field about a current-carrying wire.

*****Archimedes,** c. 287–212 B.C., Greek mathematician.

Aston, Francis William, 1877–1945, English chemist and physicist, developed, 1919, the mass spectrograph.

Avogadro, Amedeo, 1776–1856, Italian physicist, put forth a hypothesis in which equal volumes of all gasses at the same temperature and pressure contain the same number of molecules.

Becquerel, Antoine Henri, 1852–1908, French physicist.

Bernoulli, Daniel, 1700–82, Dutch-Swiss mathematician, 1738, advanced the kinetic theory of gases and fluids.

Berzelius, Jons Jakob, 1779–1848, Swedish chemist, introduced chemical symbols and chemical radical theory.

Bethe, Hans Albrecht, 1906– , German-born American physicist, proposed, 1938, the nuclear mechanism by which stars obtain their energy.

*****Bohr, Niels,** 1885–1962, Danish physicist.

Brahe, Tycho, 1546–1601, Danish astronomer.

Carnap, Rudolf, 1891–1970, German-born American philosopher of science, founded logical positivism.

Cavendish, Henry, 1731–1810, English chemist and physicist, discovered, 1766, hydrogen; devised, 1798, a gravitational method for weighing the Earth.

Charles, Jacques Alexandre César, 1746–1823, French physicist, discovered, 1787, the law governing the expansion and contraction of gases with changes in temperature.

Cockcroft, John Douglas, 1897–1967, English nuclear physicist, with E. T. S. Walton, constructed (c. 1932), the first atomic particle accelerator.

Compton, Arthur Holly, 1892–1962, American physicist, discovered, 1923, that X-rays scattered by diffraction in crystals have their wavelengths lengthened, the Compton effect; discovered, c. 1930, that cosmic rays consist of particles.

*****Copernicus (Mikolaj Kopernik),** 1473–1543, Polish astronomer.

Coulomb, Charles Augustin de, 1736–1806, French engineer and physicist, established the law describing the attraction and repulsion of electric charges.

*****Crick, Francis H. C.,** 1916– , English biophysicist.

Ctesibius, 2d century B.C., Greek engineer, invented the water clock, force pump, and air as motive force.

Curie, Marie, 1867–1934, and Pierre, 1859–1906, French chemists, isolated, 1898, the first radioactive element —radium.

*****Darwin, Charles,** 1809–1882, English naturalist.

Davy, Humphry, 1778–1829, English chemist, established the electrical nature of chemical affinity.

*****Descartes, René,** 1596–1650, French mathematician.

Dewar, James, 1842–1923, British chemist and physicist, liquified, 1898, and solidified, 1899, hydrogen.

Dirac, Paul Adrien Maurice, 1902– , English physicist, in 1920s, unified relativity and quantum theories, and unified wave mechanics and special relativity; proposed, 1930–31, antiparticles.

Dubos, René, 1901– , French microbiologist and environmentalist in America.

Edison, Thomas Alva, 1847–1931, prolific American inventor. Discovered "Edison effect."

*****Einstein, Albert,** 1879–1955, American physicist (born Germany).

Euler, Leonhard, 1707–83, Swiss mathematician and physicist, produced work in astronomy, mechanics, hydrodynamics, and optics; founded higher mathematics.

Fahrenheit, Gabriel Daniel, 1686–1736, German physicist, developed temperature scale that bears his name.

*****Faraday, Michael,** 1791–1867, English chemist, physicist.

Fermat, Pierre de, 1601–65, French mathematician, discovered analytic geometry; founded modern theory of numbers and the calculus of probabilities.

Fermi, Enrico, 1901–54, Italian-born American physicist.

Fischer, Emil, 1852–1919, German chemist, especially noted for his work on structure of sugars.

Fourier, Jean Baptiste Joseph, 1768–1830, French mathematician, discovered, c. 1822, the theorem governing periodic oscillation.

Franklin, Benjamin, 1706–90, American statesman and scientist, discovered, 1752, the electrical nature of lightning; proposed the one-fluid theory of electricity.

Gabor, Dennis, 1900–79, Hungarian-born British physicist known for the development of holography.

*****Galileo Galilei,** 1564–1642, Italian scientist.

*****Gauss, Karl F.,** 1777–1855, German mathematician.

Gay-Lussac, Joseph Louis, 1778–1850, French chemist, discovered, 1809, the law of combining volumes.

Gibbs, Josiah Willard, 1839–1903, American physicist, founded, 1876–78, chemical thermodynamics.

Grzimek, Bernhard, 1909– , Polish zoologist and wildlife conservationist.

Guericke, Otto von, 1602–86, German physicist and engineer, invented the first vacuum pump and used it, (c. 1650) to demonstrate atmospheric pressure.

Haber, Fritz, 1868–1934, German chemist, developed, 1900–1911, a process for "fixing" atmospheric nitrogen in chemical compounds.

Hall, James, 1761–1832, British geologist and chemist, founded, c. 1797, experimental geology, geochemistry.

Halley, Edmund, 1656–1742, English astronomer, calculated orbits of many comets.

*****Heisenberg, Werner Karl,** 1901–1976, German physicist.

Helmont, Jan Baptista Van, 1577–1644, Flemish physician and alchemist, initiated quantitative biochemistry.

Hero of Alexandria, c. 1st century, Greek engineer, invented principle of the steam engine; extended Archimedes' principle of the lever.

*****Hertz, Heinrich,** 1857–94, German physicist.

Herzberg, Gerhard, 1904– , Canadian physicist ·known for his work on electronic structure and molecular geometry.

Hilbert, David, 1862–1943, German mathematician, formulated, 1899, the first set of axioms for geometry.

Hubble, Edwin Powell, 1889–1953, American astronomer, discovered, 1929, the universal recession of galaxies.

Humboldt, Friedrich Wilhelm Heinrich Alexander von, 1769–1859, established, c. 1830–1859, geophysics.

Janssen (or Jansen), Zacharias, 1580–c. 1638, Dutch optician, invented, c. 1590, the microscope.

Jensen, Arthur Robert, 1923– , educational psychologist. His view is that intelligence is primarily inherited.

Kamerlingh Onnes, Heike, 1853–1926, Dutch physicist, established, 1882, cryogenics.

Kapitza, Peter, 1894– , Soviet physicist, research contributed to Soviet space achievements.

Kelvin, Lord (William Thompson), 1826–1907, British physicist, made advances in thermodynamics and thermometry.

*****Kepler, Johannes,** 1571–1630, German astronomer.

Khorana, Har Gobind, 1922– , Indian organic chemist, synthesized functioning gene, 1976.

Landau, Lev Davidovich, 1908–68, Russian physicist, developed mathematical theory explaining behavior of superfluid helium at temperatures near absolute zero.

LaPlace, Pierre Simon, 1749–1827, French astronomer and mathematician, put forth, 1796, the nebular hypothesis of the origin of the solar system.

°**Lavoisier, Antoine,** 1743–94, French chemist.

Lawrence, Ernest Orlando, 1901–58, American physicist, constructed, 1930, the first cyclotron.

Leakey, Louis, 1903-72, **Mary,** 1913- , and **Richard,** 1944- , Anglo-Kenyan anthropologists, discovered important fossil remains of early hominids.

Lee, Tsung-Dao, 1926– , Chinese-born American physicist, with Yang refuted the law of parity.

Leeuwenhoek, Anton van, 1632–1723, Dutch microscopist and the father of microbiology.

*****Leibniz, Gottfried,** 1646–1716, German mathematician, philosopher.

Levene, Phoebus Aaron Theodore, 1869–1940, Russian-born American chemist, discovered, 1909, the nucleic acids RNA and, 20 years later, DNA.

Lévi-Strauss, Claude, 1908– , French anthropologist, leader of the structuralist school of ethnology.

Liebig, Justus von, 1803–73, German chemist, established, c. 1831, quantitative organic chemical analysis.

Lowell, Percival, 1855–1916, American astronomer, 1930, discovered Pluto.

Mach, Ernst, 1838–1916, Austrian physicist, psychologist, and philosopher of science, influential in the development of logical positivism.

Marshak, Robert E., 1916– , American nuclear physicist who helped to develop the first atomic bomb.

°**Maxwell, James C.,** 1831–79, English physicist.

*****Mendel, Gregor Johann,** 1822–84, Austrian founder of genetics.

Mead, Margaret, 1901–78, American anthropologist noted for her studies in primitive and contemporary cultures.

---

* See listing in "Landmarks of Science," pp. 338–339.

*Mendeleyev, Dmitri Ivanovich, 1834—1907, Russian chemist.

Michelson, Albert Abraham, 1852–1931, German-born American physicist, developed the interferometer, which measured, 1881 and 1887, the velocity of light and proved the nonexistence of ether in space.

Mohorovicic, Andrija, 1857–1936, Croatian geophysicist, discovered, 1909, the ("Moho".) discontinuity that marks the bottom of the Earth's crust.

Mössbauer, Rudolf Ludwig, 1929– , German-born American physicist, discovered, 1958, the recoilless emission and absorption of gamma rays by atoms in crystals.

*Napier, John, 1550–1617, Scottish mathematician.

*Newton, Isaac, 1642–1727, English mathematician.

Ochoa, Severo, 1905– , Spanish-born American biochemist, synthesized, 1955, ribonucleic acid (RNA).

Ostwald, Wilhelm, 1853–1932, German chemist, was chief founder, beginning in 1887, of physical chemistry.

Pascal, Blaise, 1623–62, French scientist, mathematician, and religious philosopher, founded the modern theory of probability and the law of hydrostatic pressure (Pascal's law).

Pauling, Linus Carl, 1901– , American chemist, developed, 1939, the theory of the chemical bond.

*Planck, Max, 1858–1947, German physicist.

Priestley, Joseph, 1733–1804, English theologian and scientist, discovered, 1774, oxygen.

Raman, Chandrasekhara Vankata, 1888–1970, Indian physicist, discovered, 1928, the change in wavelength and frequency of monochromatic light passing through a transparent medium.

Riemann, Georg F. B., 1826–66, German mathematician, developed non-Euclidian system of geometry representing elliptic space.

*Rutherford, Lord (Ernest), 1871–1937, British physicist, born in New Zealand.

*Schroedinger, Erwin, 1887–1961, Austrian physicist.

Seaborg, Glenn T., 1912– , American chemist, led, 1941–c. 1951, the group that discovered the transuranium elements americium, curium, berkelium, californium, einsteinium, fermium, plutonium, mendelevium and nobelium.

Stanley, Wendell Meredith, 1904–71, American biochemist, crystallized, 1935, the tobacco mosaic virus, thus demonstrating that matter may have both living and nonliving forms.

Steno, Nicolaus (Niels Stensen), 1638–86, Danish anatomist and Catholic prelate, recognized the nature of fossils.

Szilard, Leo, 1898–1964, Hungarian-born American physicist, proved, 1939, with Walter Zinn, the possibility of self-sustaining nuclear fission; worked, 1942, with Enrico Fermi, on development of first nuclear reaction.

Tsvett (or Tswett), Mikhail Semenovich, 1872–1919, Italian-born Russian botanist, discovered, 1906, chromatography.

Urey, Harold Clayton, 1893– , American chemist, discovered, 1931, heavy hydrogen (deuterium).

Volta, Alessandro, 1745–1827, Italian physicist, invented the first electric cell and electric battery.

Von Neumann, John, 1903–57, Hungarian-born American mathematician, was a founder of the mathematical theory of games and contributed to computer theory.

Walton, Ernest Thomas Sinton, 1903– , Irish physicist, constructed, 1929, the first atomic particle accelerator.

*Watson, James Dewey, 1928– , American biochemist.

Wegener, Alfred Lothar, 1880–1930, German meteorologist and geophysicist, postulated theory of continental drift.

Wiener, Norbert, 1894–1964, American mathematician, contributed to development of computers; founded cybernetics.

Wigner, Eugene Paul, 1902– , Hungarian-born American physicist, accomplished pioneering work in nuclear structure.

*Wilkins, Maurice H. F., 1916– , British biophysicist.

Yang, Chen Ning, 1922– , Chinese-born American physicist. See Lee.

Yukawa, Hideki, 1907– , Japanese physicist who predicted the existence of mesons.

PHILOSOPHERS, THEOLOGIANS, AND RELIGIONISTS

Abelard, Peter (1079–1142), French philosopher.

Abravanel, Isaac (1437–1508), Jewish theologian.

Adler, Felix (1851–1933), German-American Ethical Culture movement founder.

Alexander of Hales (d. 1245), English scholastic philosopher.

Ambrose, Saint (c. 340–397), bishop of Milan.

Anaxagoras (c. 500–c. 428 B.C.), Greek philosopher.

Anaximander (c. 611–c. 547 B.C.), Greek philosopher.

Anaximenes (6th cent. B.C.), Greek philosopher.

Anselm, Saint (c. 1033–1109), Italian founder of scholasticism.

Anthony, Saint (c. 251–c. 350), Egyptian father of Christian monasticism.

Antisthenes (c. 444 B.C.–after 371 B.C.), Greek philosopher.

Aristotle (384–322 B.C.), Greek philosopher.

Arius (c. 256–336), Libyan theologian.

Arminius, Jacobus (1560–1609), Dutch Reformed theologian.

Augustine, Saint (354–430), North African Doctor of the Church.

Averroës (1126–98), Spanish-Arabian philosopher.

Avicenna (980–1037), Arabian philosopher.

Ayer, Alfred Jules (1910–), British philosopher.

Baal-Shem-Tov (1700–60), Jewish founder of modern Hasidism.

Bacon, Francis (1561–1626), English philosopher.

Bacon, Roger (c. 1214–c. 1294), English philosopher.

Balthasar, Hans Urs von (1905–), German theologian.

Barth, Karl (1886–1968), Swiss Protestant theologian.

Bentham, Jeremy (1748–1832), English philosopher, founder of utilitarianism.

Berdyaev, Nicholas (1874–1948), Russian philosopher.

Berengar of Tours (c. 1000–c. 1088), French theologian.

Bergson, Henri (1859–1941), French philosopher.

Berkeley, George (1685–1753), Anglo-Irish philosopher.

Bernard of Clairvaux, Saint (c. 1090–1153), French mystic.

Bernard of Cluny (fl. 1150), Anglo-French monk.

Bernardine of Siena, Saint (1380–1444), Italian preacher.

Biddle, John (1615–62), English founder of Unitarianism.

Boehme, Jakob (1575–1624), German religious mystic.

Boethius (c. 475–525), Roman philosopher.

Bonaventure, Saint (1221–74), Italian scholastic theologian.

Bonhoeffer, Dietrich (1906–45), German theologian.

Brunner, Emil (1889–1966), Swiss Protestant theologian.

Bruno, Giordano (1548–1600), Italian philosopher.

Buber, Martin (1878–1965), German-Israeli philosopher.

Büchner, Ludwig (1824–99), German philosopher.

Bultmann, Rudolf (1884–1976), German existentialist theologian.

Cabrini, Mother Francesca (1850–1917), Italian-born American nun and first American saint.

Calvin, John (1509–64), French Protestant theologian.

Carnap, Rudolf (1891–1970), German-American philosopher.

Cassirer, Ernst (1874–1945), German philosopher.

Comte, Auguste (1798–1857), French positivist philosopher.

Cranmer, Thomas (1489–1556), English churchman.

Croce, Benedetto (1866–1952), Italian philosopher.

Democritus (c. 460–c. 370 B.C.), Greek philosopher.

Descartes, René (1596–1650), French philosopher.

Dewey, John (1859–1952), American philosopher.

Diderot, Denis (1713–84), French philosopher.

Diogenes (c. 412–323 B.C.), Greek Cynic philosopher.

Duns Scotus, John (c. 1266–1308), Scottish theologian.

Eckhart, Meister (c. 1260–c. 1328), German theologian.

Edwards, Jonathan (1703–58), American theologian.

Emerson, Ralph Waldo (1803–82), American transcendentalist.

Empedocles (c. 495–c. 435 B.C.), Greek philosopher.

Engels, Friedrich (1820–95), German social philosopher.

Enrique Tarancón, Vicente Cardinal (1907–), Spanish religious reformer.

Epictetus (c. 50–c. 138), Phrygian Stoic philosopher.

Epicurus (341–270 B.C.), Greek philosopher.

Erigena, John Scotus (c. 810–c. 877), Irish philosopher.

Fichte, Johann G. (1762–1814), German philosopher.

Fox, George (1624–91), English founder of Society of Friends.

George, Henry (1839–97), American economic theorist.

Ghazali, al (c. 1058-1111), Islamic philosopher.

Gilson, Etienne (1884–1978), French philosopher.

Gorton, Samuel (c. 1592–1677), Anglo-American religious founder.

Graham, Billy (1918–), American evangelist.

Groote, Gerard (1340–84), Dutch ecclesiastical reformer.

Guardini, Romano (1885–1968), Italian-born German Catholic theologian.

Hegel, Georg W. F. (1770–1831), German philosopher.

Heidegger, Martin (1889–1976), German philosopher.

*See listing in "Landmarks of Science"

Heraclitus (c. 535–c. 475 B.C.), Greek philosopher.

Hobbes, Thomas (1588–1679), English philosopher.

Hooker, Richard (c. 1554–1600), English theologian.

Hume, David (1711–76), Scottish philosopher.

Hus, Jan (c. 1369–1415), Czech religious reformer.

Husserl, Edmund (1859–1938), German philosopher, founder of phenomenology.

Huxley, Thomas H. (1825–95), English agnostic philosopher.

Ignatius of Loyola, Saint (1491–1556), Spanish founder of the Jesuits.

James, William (1842–1910), American philosopher.

Jansen, Cornelis (1585–1638), Dutch Roman Catholic theologian.

Jaspers, Karl (1883–1969), German philosopher and psychopathologist.

John of the Cross, Saint (1542–91), Spanish mystic.

Kant, Immanuel (1724–1804), German metaphysical philosopher.

Kierkegaard, Soren (1813–55), Danish philosopher.

Knox, John (c. 1514–72), Scottish founder of Presbyterianism.

Küng, Hans (1928–), Swiss Roman Catholic theologian.

Laing, R. D. (1927–), Scottish existentialist psychoanalyst, writer, and social critic.

Law, William (1686–1761), English churchman and mystic.

Leibniz, Gottfried W., Baron von (1646–1716), German philosopher.

Locke, John (1632–1704), English philosopher.

Lombard, Peter (c. 1100–c. 1160).Italian theologian.

Lonergan, Bernard J. F. (1904–), Canadian theologian and Thomist philosopher.

Lucretius (c. 99–c. 55 B.C.), Roman philosopher-poet.

Luther, Martin (1483–1546), German Protestant leader.

Mahesh Yogi, Maharishi (1911?–), Hindu guru.

Maimonides (1135–1204), Spanish-Jewish philosopher.

Malthus, Thomas R. (1766–1834), English economic and social philosopher.

Marcel, Gabriel (1889–1973), French philosopher.

Marcus Aurelius (121–180), Stoic philosopher.

Marias, Julián (1914–), Spanish philosopher.

Maritain Jacques (1882–1973), French Neo-Thomist philosopher.

Marx, Karl (1818–83), German social philosopher.

Mather, Cotton (1663–1728), American Puritan minister.

Mather, Increase (1639–1723), American Puritan minister.

May, Rollo (1909–), American humanistic psychoanalyst-philosopher.

Melanchthon, Philip (1497–1560), German theologian.

Mencius (c. 371–c. 288 B.C.), Chinese sage.

Mill, John Stuart (1806–73), English philosopher and economist.

Molina, Luis (1535–1600), Spanish Jesuit theologian.

Moore, George E. (1873–1958), English philosopher.

Murray, John (1741–1815), English founder of American Universalist denomination.

Nestorius (d. c. 451), Byzantine theologian.

Newman, John Henry, Cardinal (1801–90), English philosopher.

Nicholas of Cusa (c. 1401–46), German humanist.

Niebuhr, H. Richard (1894–1962), American theologian.

Niebuhr, Reinhold (1892–1971), American theologian.

Nietzsche, Friedrich W. (1844–1900), German philosopher.

Origen (c. 185–c. 254), Egyptian Christian philosopher.

Parmenides (b. c. 514 B.C.), Greek philosopher.

Pascal, Blaise (1623–62), French philosopher and mathematician.

Peirce, Charles S. (1839–1914), American philosopher.

Philo (c. 20 B.C.–A.D. c. 50), Alexandrian Jewish philosopher.

Plato (c. 427–c. 347 B.C.), Greek philosopher.

Plotinus (c. 205–270), Egyptian Neoplatonist philosopher.

Protagoras (c. 480–c. 410 B.C.), Greek Sophist.

Rapp, George (1757–1847), German-American Harmony Society founder.

Rousseau, Jean Jacques (1712–78), French philosopher.

Royce, Josiah (1855–1916), American philosopher.

Russell, Bertrand (1872–1970), British philosopher and mathematician.

Santayana, George (1863–1952), American philosopher.

Savonarola, Girolamo (1452–98), Italian religious reformer.

Schelling, Friedrich W. J. von (1775–1854), German philosopher.

Schopenhauer, Arthur (1788–1860), German philosopher.

Schweitzer, Albert (1875–1965), Alsatian philosopher and theologian.

Seneca (c. 3 B.C.–A.D. 65), Roman philosopher.

Seton, Elizabeth Ann Bayley (1774–1821), 1st U.S.-born canonized saint.

Shaftesbury, Anthony Ashley Cooper, 3d earl of (1671–1713), English philosopher.

Smith, Adam (1723–90), Scottish economist and philosopher.

Socrates (469–399 B.C.), Greek philosopher.

Spencer, Herbert (1820–1903), English philosopher of evolution.

Spinoza, Baruch (1632–77), Dutch philosopher.

Suso, Heinrich (c. 1295–1366), German mystic.

Suzuki, Daisetz Teitaro (1870–1966), Japanese Buddhist scholar.

Swedenborg, Emanuel (1688–1772), Swedish theologian and mystic.

Taylor, Jeremy (1613–67), English theologian.

Teilhard de Chardin, Pierre (1881–1955), French Jesuit scientist-theologian.

Thales (c. 636–c. 546 B.C.), Greek philosopher.

Theresa, Saint (1515–82), Spanish mystic.

Thomas Aquinas, Saint (1225–74), Italian philosopher and Doctor of the Church.

Tillich, Paul (1886–1965), German-born American theologian.

Tyndale, William (c. 1494–1536), English Bible translator.

Ussher, James (1581–1656), Irish prelate and scholar.

Veblen, Thorstein (1857–1929), American economic and social philosopher.

Vico, Giovanni B. (1668–1744), Italian philosopher and historian.

Watts, Isaac (1674–1748), English clergyman and hymn writer.

Wesley, John (1703–91), English founder of Methodism.

Whitehead, Alfred North (1861–1947), English philosopher and mathematician.

William of Occam (d. c. 1349), English philosopher.

Williams, Roger (c. 1603–83), Anglo-American clergyman.

Winebrenner, John (1797–1860), American founder of Churches of God in North America.

Wise, Stephen (1874–1949), American reform rabbi and Zionist leader.

Wittgenstein, Ludwig (1889–1951), Austrian philosopher.

Woodbridge, Frederick J. E. (1867–1940), American philosopher.

Wyclif, John (c. 1328–84), English reformer.

Zeno of Citium (c. 334–c. 262 B.C.), Greek philosopher, founder of Stoicism.

Zoroaster (628–551 B.C.), Persian prophet.

Zwingli, Huldreich (1484–1531), Swiss Protestant reformer.

MEN OF MEDICINE AND PHYSIOLOGY

Abulcasis, or Abu Khasim, fl. 11th century, Arabian physician, author of the *Tasrif* (collection), a detailed account of surgery and medicine of his day.

Addison, Thomas, 1793–1860, English physician, discoverer of the malady of the suprarenal cortex, known as Addison's disease.

Allbutt, Thomas Clifford, 1836–1925, English physician, invented, 1866, the clinical thermometer.

Avicenna, or Ibn Sina, A.D. 980–1037, Arabian physician and philosopher, wrote the *Canon of Medicine*, most famous textbook of medicine until the 17th century.

Baer, Karl Ernst von, 1792–1876, Estonian biologist, founded, 1827–37, embryology.

Banting, Frederick G., 1891–1941, Canadian physician, with Charles Best, discovered, 1921, the use of insulin in diabetic therapy.

Barnard, Christiaan N., 1923– , South African surgeon, performed, 1967, first transplant of a human heart.

Beaumont, William, 1785–1853, American physician, first to describe, 1822, the process of digestion.

Behring, Emil Adolf von, 1854–1917, German bacteriologist noted for work on diphtheria antitoxin.

Berger, Johannes (Hans), 1873–1941, German neurologist, invented, 1929, the electroencephalograph.

Bernard, Claude, 1813–78, French physiologist, considered founder of experimental medicine.

Best, Charles Herbert, 1899–1978, Canadian physiologist, with Frederick Banting discovered, 1921, the use of insulin in diabetic therapy.

Bichat, Marie François Xavier, 1771–1802, French physician, founded, 1800, histology, the study of living tissues.

Blalock, Alfred, 1899–1964, American surgeon, with Helen B. Taussig introduced, 1944, corrective heart surgery enabling survival of "blue babies."

Braun, Heinrich Friedrich Wilhelm, 1862–1934, German surgeon, introduced, 1905, procaine (Novocain) into clinical use.

Bright, Richard, 1789–1858, English physician, first to describe, 1827, the kidney disease known as Bright's disease.

Canano, Giovanni Battista, 1515–79, Italian anatomist, first to describe, c. 1547, venous valves.

Carrel, Alexis, 1873–1944, French-American surgeon, developed methods for transplanting blood vessels; invented, with Charles A. Lindbergh, a mechanical heart.

Cohn, Ferdinand Julius, 1828–98, German botanist, founded, c. 1872, science of bacteriology.

Cooley, Denton A., 1920– , American surgeon, pioneer in cardiovascular surgery.

De Bakey, Michael Ellis, 1908– , American surgeon, developed artificial heart.

De Forest, Lee, 1873–1961, American inventor, invented, 1907, the electrical high-frequency surgical knife.

Dick, George F., 1881–1967, and Gladys H. Dick, isolated, 1923, the scarlet fever toxin.

Domagk, Gerhard, 1895–1964, German chemist, used, c. 1932, the first sulfa drug (prontosil) in therapy.

Eberth, Karl Joseph, 1835–1926, German pathologist, discovered, 1880, the typhoid bacillus.

Edelman, Gerald M., 1929– , American biochemist, deciphered, 1969, the structure of gamma globulin.

Ehrlich, Paul, 1854–1915, German bacteriologist and pathologist, developed, 1897, the differential blood count; established, 1892–94, serology and immunology; established, 1909, chemotherapy.

Eijkman, Christiaan, 1858–1930, Dutch bacteriologist, proved, 1896, that beriberi is a deficiency disease, thus leading to discovery of the first vitamin.

Einthoven, Willem, 1860–1927, Dutch physiologist, invented, 1903, the electrocardiograph.

Ermengem, Émile P. M. van, 1851–1932, Belgian bacteriologist, discovered, 1897, the food-poisoning bacillus.

Fabricius, Hieronymus, or Geronimo Fabrizio, 1537–1619, Italian anatomist, discovered, 1603, venous valves.

Fauchard, Pierre, 1678–1761, French dentist, founder of modern dentistry; described pyorrhea.

Finlay, Carlos Juan, 1833–1915, Cuban physician, first to suggest mosquitoes might be carriers of yellow fever.

Fleming, Alexander, 1881–1955, Scottish bacteriologist, discovered, 1928, penicillin.

Fleming, Lady Amalia, 1909– , British bacteriologist, physician, civil libertarian.

Flourens, Marie J. P., 1794–1867, French physiologist, distinguished the three main parts of the brain.

Freud, Sigmund, 1856–1939, Austrian psychiatrist, founded, c. 1895, psychoanalysis.

Funk, Casimir, 1884–1967, Polish-American biochemist, discovered, 1912, the first vitamin.

Gaffky, Georg T. A., 1850–1918, German bacteriologist, proved, 1884, that *Bacillus typhosus*, discovered by Eberth, is cause of typhoid fever.

Galen, Claudius, c. A.D. 130–c. 200, Greco-Roman physician, systematized medical knowledge of his day; made first scientific dissections.

Goldberger, Joseph, 1874–1929, American public health physician, discovered, 1915, the cure for pellagra.

Golgi, Camillo, 1844–1926, Italian physician, established, 1870–1909, the science of neuroanatomy.

Good, Robert, 1922– , American pediatrician; pioneer in fields of immunology and cancer research.

Gross, Robert E., 1905– , performed, 1938, first surgery for congenital heart disease.

Hales, Stephen, 1677–1761, English physiologist and clergyman, first to demonstrate, c. 1705, blood pressure.

Haller, Albrecht von, 1708–77, Swiss physiologist and anatomist, established physiology as a branch of science.

Harvey, William, 1578–1657, English physician, discovered, 1628, the circulation of the blood.

Helmholtz, Hermann Ludwig Ferdinand von, 1821–94, German physicist and physiologist, invented, 1851, the modern type of ophthalmoscope.

Hench, Philip S., 1896–1965, American physician, introduced, 1949, the use of ACTH in the treatment of disease.

Herophilus, fl. 300 B.C., Egyptian-Greek physician and anatomist, distinguished sensory and motor nerves.

Hippocrates of Cos, c. B.C. 460–c. 370, Greek physician, "Father of Medicine," took medicine from the realm of superstition to that of disciplined observation.

Holmes, Oliver Wendell, 1809–94, American physician and author, recognized, 1843, contagious nature of puerperal fever and advocated antiseptic techniques.

Hunter, John, 1728–93, Scottish surgeon, raised surgery from a technical treatment mode to a branch of scientific medicine.

Ivanovski, Dmitri Iosifovich, 1864–1920, Russian botanist, discovered, 1892, filterable viruses, thus establishing virology.

Janssen, Zacharias, fl. late 16th–early 17th cent., Dutch spectacle maker, invented, c. 1590, the microscope.

Jenner, Edward, 1749–1823, English physician, introduced, 1796, the technique of vaccination against disease.

Kitasato, Shibasaburo, 1852–1931, Japanese bacteriologist, discovered, 1894, the bubonic plague causative bacillus.

Klebs, Edwin T. A., 1834–1913, German-American bacteriologist, discovered, 1875, pneumococcus, the bacillus causative of lobar pneumonia; discovered, 1883–84, the diphtheria causative bacillus.

Koch, Robert, 1843–1910, German bacteriologist, set forth criteria for establishing the etiology of a disease; introduced, 1877, staining of bacteria with aniline dyes; established, 1882, the identity of the tuberculosis causative cholera.

Laënnec, René T. H., 1781–1826, French physician, invented, 1816, the stethoscope.

Landsteiner, Karl, 1868–1943, Austrian-American pathologist, established, 1900, the basis for blood grouping; isolated, 1908, the poliomyelitis virus; discovered, 1940, the Rh factor.

Lister, Joseph, 1827–1912, English surgeon, introduced, 1865, antisepsis into surgical procedure.

Löffler, Friedrich A. J., 1852–1915, German pathologist, discovered, 1883–84, the diphtheria causative bacillus.

Long, Crawford Williamson, 1815–78, American surgeon, introduced, 1842, the use of ether in surgery.

Magnus-Levy, Adolf, 1865–1955, German physiologist, developed, 1893, the method for measuring the basal metabolic rate.

Malpighi, Marcello, 1628–94, Italian anatomist, discovered, 1661, that capillaries are vein-artery junctions.

Mesmer, Friedrich (or Franz) Anton, c. 1733–1815, Austrian physician, introduced, c. 1778, the use of hypnotism in medicine.

Metchnikoff, Élie, 1845–1916, Russian biologist, introduced theory of phagocytosis, i.e., the defensive nature of blood cells.

Minot, George Richards, 1885–1950, American physician, discovered, 1926, the liver extract treatment for anemia.

Morgan, Thomas Hunt, 1886–1945, American geneticist, discovered and demonstrated, c. 1907, the role of chromosomes in heredity.

Nitze, Max, 1848–1906, German surgeon and urologist, constructed, 1877, first cystoscope, with the aid of an instrument maker named Leiter.

Paracelsus (Theophrastus Bombastus von Hohenheim), c. 1493–1541, Swiss chemist, alchemist, and physician, established, 1526, chemotherapy.

Paré, Ambroise, 1510 or 1517–90, French surgeon, introduced modern surgery, including the tying-off of arteries to control bleeding.

Pasteur, Louis, 1822–95, French chemist and bacteriologist, discovered (1880–1885) methods for inoculation and vaccination against anthrax, rabies, and chicken cholera.

Perthes, Georg Clemens, 1869–1927, German surgeon, noted, 1903, effects of X rays on cancerous growths.

Plenciz, Marcus Antonius von, 1705–1786, Viennese physician, published, 1762, the germ theory of disease.

Pylarino, James, or Giacomo, 1659–1715, Italian physician, inoculated, 1701, three Turkish children with smallpox exudate in first attempt at immunization.

Reed, Walter, 1851–1902, American surgeon, studied the etiology of yellow fever and reported, 1901, that the disease was caused by a filterable virus transmitted by the mosquito.

Rhazes, or Rasis, c. A.D. 860–c. 925, Persian physician, first to differentiate, c. 910, measles and smallpox.

Roentgen, Wilhelm Conrad, 1845–1923, German physicist, discovered, 1895, X rays.

Roux, Pierre Paul Émile, 1853–1933, French physician and bacteriologist, with A. E. J. Yersin, demonstrated, 1888, that the diphtheria bacillus produces a toxin.

Rush, Benjamin, c. 1745–1813, American physician, established, 1786, first free dispensary in U.S.

Sabin, Albert Bruce, 1906– , Russian-American bacteriologist, 1957, produced an oral vaccine for poliomyelitis.

Sakel, Manfred J., 1900–1957, Austro-American psychiatrist, introduced, 1929, insulin shock treatment of schizophrenia.

Salk, Jonas Edward, 1914–   , American virologist, introduced, 1954, hypodermic vaccine for poliomyelitis.

Sanctorius, 1561–1636, Italian physician, described, c. 1626, the first use of the clinical thermometer in the diagnosis of disease.

Schick, Bela, 1877–1967, Hungarian-American pediatrician, developed, 1913, a test for determining susceptibility to diphtheria.

Schleiden, Matthias Jakob, 1804–1881, German botanist, founded, 1838, cytology.

Schwann, Theodor, 1810–1882, German anatomist, founder, 1839, of cell theory as applied to animals.

Semmelweis, Ignaz P., 1818–65, Hungarian physician, obstetrician, independently identified, c. 1850, puerperal (childbed) fever as an infectious disease.

Servetus, Michael, 1511–1553, Spanish physician and theologian, described, 1546, pulmonary circulation.

Sherrington, Charles Scott, 1857–1952, English physiologist, established, 1906–1940, neurophysiology.

Spallanzani, Lazzaro, 1729–99, Italian naturalist, performed, 1768, experiments that led to the discrediting of the doctrine of spontaneous generation.

Steptoe, Patrick C., 1913–   , British gynecologist, performed first successful laboratory-conceived human birth (1978).

Swammerdam, Jan, 1637–80, Dutch naturalist, discovered, 1658, red blood cells.

Takamine, Jokichi, 1854–1922, Japanese chemist working in U.S., isolated, 1901, crystalline epinephrine (adrenalin), the first hormone known in pure form.

Taussig, Helen Brooke, 1898–   , American physician, with Alfred Blalock, introduced, 1944, corrective heart surgery enabling survival of "blue babies."

Vesalius, Andreas, 1514–64, Flemish anatomist, published, 1543, first anatomical text based entirely on observation.

Virchow, Rudolf L. K., 1821–1902, German pathologist, founder, c. 1855, of cellular pathology.

Waksman, Selman Abraham, 1888–1973, Russian-American bacteriologist, discovered, 1943, streptomycin and its use in tuberculosis therapy.

Wassermann, August von, 1866–1925, German bacteriologist, developed, 1906, specific test for syphilis.

Wells, Horace, 1815–48, American dentist, first to use, 1844, nitrous oxide as an anesthetic in surgery.

Wiley, Harvey Washington, 1844–1930, American chemist, led fight for U.S. Pure Food Law of 1906.

Wundt, Wilhelm Max, 1832–1920, German psychologist, established, 1878, the first laboratory for experimental psychology, bringing mind into the realm of science.

Yersin, Alexandre Émile John, 1863–1943, French bacteriologist, discovered, 1888, the diphtheria toxin; discovered, 1894, *Pasteurella pestis*, the bubonic plague causative bacillus.

NOTABLES OF ART AND ARCHITECTURE

Aalto, Alvar (1898–1976), Finnish architect and designer.

Agostino di Duccio (1418–1498), Florentine sculptor.

Albers, Josef (1888–1976), German-American painter.

Alberti, Leone B. (1404–72), Italian architect and painter.

Alma-Tadema, Sir Lawrence (1836–1912), English painter.

Angelico, Fra (c. 1400–55), Florentine painter.

Antonello da Messina (c. 1430–79), Italian painter.

Apelles (fl. 330 b.c.), Greek painter.

Apollodorus (fl. 430–400 b.c.), Athenian painter.

Archipenko, Alexander (1887–1964), Ukrainian-American sculptor.

Arp, Jean (1887–1966), French sculptor and painter.

Asplund, Erik Gunnar (1885–1940), Swedish architect.

Audubon, John J. (d. 1851), American artist and ornithologist.

Avery, Milton (1893–1965), American painter.

Bacon, Francis (1910–   ), English painter.

Baldovinetti, Alessio, (c. 1425–99), Florentine painter.

Balla, Giacomo (1871–1958), Italian futurist painter.

Barlach, Ernst (1870–1938), German sculptor.

Barthé, Richmond (1901–   ), American sculptor.

Bartolomeo, Fra (1475–1517), Italian painter.

Baskin, Leonard (1922–   ), American sculptor.

Baziotes, William (1912–63), American painter.

Bearden, Romare (1914–   ), American realistic painter.

Beardsley, Aubrey (1872–98), English illustrator.

Beckmann, Max (1884–1950), German painter.

Bellini, Giovanni (c. 1430–1516), Venetian painter.

Bellows, George W. (1882–1925), American painter.

Benjamin, Asher (1773–1845), American architect.

Benton, Thomas Hart (1889–1975), American painter.

Berlage, Hendrik P. (1856–1934), Dutch architect.

Bernini, Giovanni Lorenzo (1598–1680), Italian architect.

Bertola, Harry (1915–78), American sculptor and designer.

Bierstadt, Albert (1830–1902), American Western painter.

Bingham, George Caleb (1811–79), American genre painter.

Boccioni, Umberto (1882–1916), Italian futurist painter.

Böcklin, Arnold (1827–1901), Swiss painter.

Bonheur, Rosa (1822–99), French painter.

Bonnard, Pierre (1867–1947), French painter.

Borromini, Francesco (1559–1677), Italian architect.

Bosch, Hieronymus (c. 1450–1516), Flemish painter.

Botticelli, Sandro (c. 1444–1510), Florentine painter.

Boucher, François (1703–70), French painter.

Boudin, Eugène L. (1824–98), French painter.

Bouts, Dierick (c. 1420–75), Dutch painter.

Brady, Mathew B. (c. 1823–96), American photographer.

Bramante, Donato (1444–1514), Italian architect.

Brancusi, Constantin (1876–1957), Rumanian sculptor.

Braque, Georges (1882–1963), French painter.

Breuer, Marcel (1902–   ), Hungarian-born American architect and designer.

Bronzino, Il (1503–72), Florentine mannerist painter.

Brouwer, Adriaen (c. 1606–38), Flemish painter.

Bruegel, Pieter, the elder (c. 1525–69), Flemish genre painter.

Brunelleschi, Filippo (1377–1446), Florentine architect.

Bulfinch, Charles (1763–1844), American architect.

Burne-Jones, Sir Edward (1833–98), English painter.

Calder, Alexander (1898–1976), American sculptor.

Canaletto (1697–1768), Venetian painter.

Candela, Felix (1910–   ), Mexican architect.

Caravaggio, Michelangelo M. da (1573–1610), Italian painter.

Carracci, Annibale (1560–1609), Bolognese painter.

Carracci, Lodovico (1555–1619), Bolognese painter.

Cartier-Bresson, Henri (1908–   ), French photographer.

Cassatt, Mary (1845–1926), American painter.

Castagno, Andrea del (c. 1423–57), Florentine painter.

Catlin, George (1796–1872), American painter.

Cellini, Benvenuto (1500–71), Italian sculptor and metalsmith.

Cézanne, Paul (1839–1906), French painter.

Chagall, Marc (1889–   ), Russian painter.

Chardin, Jean Baptiste (1699–1779), French painter.

Chippendale, Thomas (1718–79), English cabinetmaker.

Chirico, Giorgio de (1888–1978), Italian painter.

Christo (1935–   ), Bulgarian-born American artist.

Cimabue, Giovanni (d. c. 1302), Florentine painter.

Claude Lorrain (1600–82), French landscape painter.

Cole, Thomas (1801–48), English-born American painter.

Constable, John (1776–1837), English painter.

Copley, John Singleton (1738–1815), American portrait painter.

Cornelius, Peter von (1783–1867), German painter.

Corot, Jean B. C. (1796–1875), French landscape painter.

Correggio, Antonio (1494–1534), Italian painter.

Costa, Lucio (1902–   ), Brazilian architect.

Courbet, Gustave (1819–77), French painter.

Cox, Kenyon (1856–1919), American painter and critic.

Cranach, Lucas, the elder (1472–1553), German painter.

Curry, John S. (1897–1946), American painter.

Dali, Salvador (1904–   ), Spanish surrealist painter.

Daubigny, Charles F. (1817–78), French landscape painter.

Daumier, Honoré (1808–79), French painter.

David, Gerard (c. 1460–1523), Flemish painter.

David, Jacques L. (1748–1825), French painter.

Davis, Stuart (1894–1964), American painter.

Decamps, Alexandre G. (1803–60), French painter.

Degas, Edgar (1834–1917), French painter and sculptor.

de Kooning, Willem (1904–   ), Dutch-born American painter.

Delacroix, Ferdinand V. E. (1798–1863), French painter.

Delaunay, Robert (1885–1941), French painter.

Della Robbia, Luca (c. 1400–82), Florentine sculptor.

Demuth, Charles (1883–1935), American watercolorist.

Derain, André (1880–1954), French painter.

Dine, Jim (1935–   ), American neosurrealist artist.

Dix, Otto (1891–1969), German painter and draughtsman.

Doesburg, Theo van (1883–1931), Dutch painter.

Donatello (c. 1386–1466), Italian sculptor.

Dongen, Kees van (1877–1968), Dutch painter.

Dou, Gerard (1613–75), Dutch painter.

Dubuffet, Jean (1901–), French painter.

Duccio di Buoninsegna (fl. 1278–1319), Italian painter.

Duchamp, Marcel (1887–1968), French painter.

Dufy, Raoul (1877–1953), French painter and illustrator.

Dürer, Albecht (1471–1528), German painter and engraver.

Eakins, Thomas (1844–1916), American painter.

Eiffel, Alexandre G. (1832–1923), French engineer.

Elisofon, Eliot (1911–73), American photographer.

Ensor, James (1860–1949), Belgian painter and etcher.

Epstein, Sir Jacob (1880–1959), American-born English sculptor.

Ernst, Max (1891–1976), German painter.

Evergood, Philip (1901–1973), American painter.

Eyck, Hubert van (c. 1370–1426), Flemish painter.

Eyck, Jan van (c. 1390–1441), Flemish painter.

Fabritius, Carel (1622–54), Dutch painter.

Feininger, Lyonel (1871–1956), American painter and illustrator.

Flagg, Ernest (1857–1947), American architect.

Flandrin, Hippolyte J. (1809–64), French painter.

Fouquet, Jean (c. 1420–1480), French painter.

Fragonard, Jean-Honoré (1732–1806), French painter.

Frasconi, Antonio (1919–), South American-born woodcut artist in U.S.

Friesz, Othon (1879–1949), French painter.

Fuller, George (1822–84), American painter.

Fuller, (Richard) Buckminster (1895–), American architect and engineer.

Fuseli, Henry (1741–1825), Anglo-Swiss painter and draughtsman.

Gabo, Naum (1890–1977), Russian sculptor and architect.

Gainsborough, Thomas (1727–88), English painter.

Gaudi i Cornet, Antonio (1852–1926), Spanish architect.

Gauguin, Paul (1848–1903), French painter.

Gentile da Fabriano (c. 1370–1427), Italian painter.

Gentileschi, Orazio (c. 1562–1647), Tuscan painter.

Gérard, François P. S., Baron (1770–1837), French painter.

Géricault, Jean Louis A. T. (1791–1824), French painter.

Gérôme, Jean Léon (1824–1904), French painter.

Ghiberti, Lorenzo (c. 1378–1455), Florentine sculptor.

Ghirlandaio, Domenico (1449–94), Florentine painter.

Giacometti, Alberto (1901–66), Swiss sculptor and painter.

Gilbert, Cass (1859–1934), American architect.

Giordano, Luca (1632–1705), Italian painter.

Giorgio, Francesco di (1439–1502), Italian architect, painter, and sculptor.

Giorgione (c. 1478–1510), Venetian painter.

Giotto (c. 1266–c. 1337), Florentine painter.

Giovanni di Paulo (c. 1403–83), Italian painter.

Glackens, William J. (1870–1938), American painter.

Gleizes, Albert L. (1881–1953), French cubist painter.

Goes, Hugo van der (d. 1482), Flemish painter.

Gogh, Vincent van (1853–90), Dutch postimpressionist painter.

Gorky, Arshile (1904–48), Armenian-born American painter.

Goya y Lucientes, Francisco José de (1746–1828), Spanish painter and etcher.

Goyen, Jan van (1596–1656), Dutch landscape painter.

Greco, El (c. 1541–1614), Cretan painter in Spain.

Greuze, Jean Baptiste (1725–1805), French painter.

Gris, Juan (1887–1927), Spanish cubist painter.

Grooms, Red (1937–), American painter.

Gropius, Walter (1883–1969), German-American architect.

Gropper, Wiliam (1897–1977), American painter and cartoonist.

Grosz, George (1893–1959), German-American caricaturist and painter.

Grunewald, Mathias (c. 1475–1528), German painter.

Guardi, Francesco (1712–93), Venetian painter.

Guston, Philip (1913–), Canadian-born American painter.

Hals, Franz (c. 1580–1666), Dutch portrait painter.

Hartley, Marsden (1877–1943), American painter.

Harunobu, Suzuki (1725–70), Japanese color-print artist.

Hassam, Childe (1859–1935), American painter and etcher.

Hennebique, François (1842–1921), French architect.

Henri, Robert (1865–1929), American painter.

Hicks, Edward (1780–1849), American painter.

Hilliard, Nicholas (1537–1619), English miniaturist.

Hobbema, Meindert (1638–1709), Dutch landscape painter.

Hockney, David (1937–), English painter.

Hodler, Ferdinand (1853–1918), Swiss painter.

Hofmann, Hans (1880–1966), German-American painter.

Hogarth, William (1697–1764), English painter, satirist, and engraver.

Hokusai, Katsushika (1760–1849), Japanese wood engraver.

Holbein, Hans, the younger (c. 1497–1543), German-Swiss painter.

Homer, Winslow (1836–1910), American painter.

Hooch, Pieter de (c. 1629–after 1677), Dutch painter.

Hopper, Edward (1882–1967), American painter.

Houdon, Jean A. (1741–1828), French neoclassic sculptor.

Indiana, Robert (1928–), American pop artist.

Ingrès, Jean A. D. (1780–1867), French painter.

Inman, Henry (1801–46), American painter.

Inness, George (1825–1894), American landscape painter.

Jackson, William H. (1843–1942), American artist and pioneer photographer.

Jacobsen, Arne (1902–1971), Danish architect.

Jenney, William Le Baron (1832–1907), American architect.

John, Augustus Edwin (1879–1961), British painter.

Johns, Jasper (1930–), American pop artist.

Johnson, Philip C. (1906–), American architect.

Jones, Inigo (1573–1652), English architect.

Jordaens, Jacob (1593–1678), Flemish baroque painter.

Kandinsky, Wassily (1866–1944), Russian abstract painter.

Kano Motonobu (c. 1476–1559), Japanese artist.

Kaufmann, Angelica (1741–1807), Swiss painter and etcher.

Kepes, György (1906–), Hungarian-born artist.

Kirchner, Ernst L. (1880–1938), German painter and graphic artist.

Kiyonaga (1752–1815), Japanese woodcut designer.

Klee, Paul (1879–1940), Swiss painter and graphic artist.

Klimt, Gustav (1862–1918), Austrian painter.

Kokoschka, Oskar (1886–), Austrian expressionist painter.

Kollwitz, Käthe S. (1867–1945), German graphic artist and sculptor.

Kuhn, Walt (1880–1949), American painter.

Kuniyoshi, Yasuo (c. 1892–1953), Japanese-born American painter.

Kupka, Frank (1871–1957), Czech painter and illustrator.

Lachaise, Gaston (1882–1935), French-born American sculptor.

La Farge, John (1835–1910), American painter.

Lancret, Nicolas (1690–1743), French rococo painter.

Landseer, Sir Edwin H. (1802–73), English animal painter.

La Tour, Georges de (1593–1652), French painter.

Lawrence, Jacob (1917–), American painter.

Lawrence, Sir Thomas (1769–1830), English portrait painter.

Le Corbusier (1887–1965), Swiss-born French architect.

Ledoux, Claude N. (1736–1806), French architect.

Léger, Fernand (1881–1955), French painter.

Lehmbruck, Wilhelm (1881–1919), German sculptor.

L'Enfant, Pierre C. (1754–1825), French-American architect and engineer.

Leonardo da Vinci (1452–1519), Italian painter, sculptor, and architect.

Lescaze, William (1896–1969), Swiss-born American architect.

Leutze, Emanuel (1816–68), German-American painter of Anglo-American history.

Levine, Jack (1915–), American painter.

Lichtenstein, Roy (1923–), American pop artist.

Lipchitz, Jacques (1891–1973), Lithuanian-born French sculptor.

Lippi, Fra Filippo (c. 1406–69), Italian painter.

Lippo, Filippino (c. 1457–1504), Italian painter.

Lippold, Richard (1915–), American sculptor and engineer.

Lochner, Stephan (d. 1451), German religious painter.

Lombardo, Pietro (c. 1435–1515), Venetian architect.

Lorenzetti, Ambrogio (d. c. 1348), Sienese painter.

Lucas van Leyden (1494–1533), Dutch painter and engraver.

Luini, Bernardino (c. 1480–1532), Italian painter.

Luks, George B. (1867–1933), American painter.

Lysippus (4th cent. B.C.), Greek sculptor.

Mabuse, Jan de (c. 1478–c. 1533), Flemish painter.

Macke, August (1887–1914), German painter.

McKim, Charles F. (1847–1909), American architect.

Magritte, René (1898–1967), Belgian surrealist painter.

Maillol, Aristide (1861–1944), French sculptor and painter.

Manet, Edouard (1832–83), French painter.

Mansart, François (1598–1666), French architect.

Mansart, Jules H. (1646–1708), French architect.

Mantegna, Andrea (1431–1506), Italian painter of the Paduan school.

Marc, Franz (1880–1916), German painter.

Marisol (1930–), Venezuelan-American sculptor.

Marsh, Reginald (1898–1954), French-born American painter.
Martini, Simone (c. 1283–1344), Sienese painter.
Masaccio (1401–c. 1428), Florentine painter.
Massys, Quentin (c. 1466–1530), Flemish painter.
Matisse, Henri (1869–1954), French painter and sculptor.
Maurer, Alfred H. (1868–1932), American painter.
Meissonier, Jean L. E. (1815–91), French military painter.
Memling, Hans (c. 1430–94), German-born Flemish painter.
Mendelsohn, Eric (1887–1953), German architect.
Mestrovic, Ivan (1883–1962), Yugoslav sculptor.
Michelangelo Buonarroti (1475–1564), Italian sculptor, painter, and architect.
Mies van der Rohe, Ludwig (1886–1969), German-American architect.
Millais, Sir John E. (1829–96), English painter.
Millet, Jean F. (1814–75), French painter.
Miró, Joan (1893–), Spanish surrealist painter.
Modigliani, Amadeo (1884–1920), Italian painter.
Mondrian, Piet (1872–1944), Dutch painter.
Monet, Claude (1840–1926), French impressionist painter.
Moore, Henry (1898–), English sculptor.
Moreau, Gustave (1826–98), French painter.
Morisot, Berthe (1841–95), French impressionist painter.
Moronobu, Hishikawa (c. 1618–c. 1694), Japanese painter.
Morris, William (1834–96), English artist, printer, and poet.
Morse, Samuel F. B. (1791–1872), American artist and inventor.
Moses, Grandma (Anna Mary R. Moses) (1860–1961), American primitive painter.
Motherwell, Robert (1915–), American painter.
Munch, Edvard (1863–1944), Norwegian painter.
Murillo, Bartholomé E. (c. 1617–82), Spanish painter.
Muybridge, Eadweard (1830–1904), English photographer.
Myron (5th cent. B.C.), Greek sculptor.
Nash, John (1752–1835), English architect.
Nash, Paul (1889–1946), English painter and wood engraver.
Neel, Alice (1900–), American painter.
Nervi, Pier Luigi (1891–1979), Italian architect.
Neutra, Richard (1892–1970), American architect.
Nevelson, Louise (1900–), Russian-born American sculptor.
Nicholson, Ben (1894–), English abstract painter.
Niemeyer, Oscar (1907–), Brazilian architect.
Noguchi, Isamu (1904–), American sculptor.
Noland, Kenneth (1924–), American color-field painter.
Nolde, Emil (1867–1956), German expressionist painter.
O'Keeffe, Georgia (1887–), American painter.
Oldenburg, Claes (1929–), Swedish-born American pop artist.
Olmsted, Frederick L. (1822–1903), American landscape architect.
Orley, Bernard van (c. 1491–1542), Flemish painter.
Orozco, José C. (1883–1949), Mexican mural painter.
Ostade, Adriaen van (1610–85), Dutch genre painter.
Palladio, Andrea (1508–80), Italian architect.
Parks, Gordon (1912–), American photographer.
Parmigiano (1503–40), Italian mannerist painter.
Parrhasius (fl. c. 400 B.C.), Greek painter.
Parrish, Maxfield (1870–1966), American illustrator.
Patinir, Joachim de (d. 1524), Flemish landscape and religious painter.
Paxton, Sir Joseph (1803–65), English architect.
Peale, Charles Willson (1741–1827), American painter.
Peale, James (1749–1831), American portrait painter.
Peale, Raphaelle (1774–1825), American portrait painter.
Peale, Rembrandt (1778–1860), American portrait painter.
Pearlstein, Philip (1924–), American realist painter.
Pechstein, Max (1881–1955), German expressionist painter.
Pei, I(eoh) M(ing) (1917–), Chinese-born American architect.
Perrault, Claude (1613–88), French architect.
Perugino (c. 1445–c. 1523), Umbrian painter.
Pevsner, Antoine (1886–1962), Russian sculptor and painter.
Phidias (c. 500–c. 432 B.C.), Greek sculptor.
Phyfe, Duncan (c. 1768–1854), Scottish-born cabinetmaker.
Picasso, Pablo (1881–1973), Spanish painter and sculptor in France.
Piero della Francesca (c. 1420–92), Italian painter.
Piero di Cosimo (1462–1521), Florentine painter.
Pinturicchio (c. 1454–1513), Umbrian painter.
Piranesi, Giovanni B. (1720–78), Italian architect.
Pisanello (c. 1395–c. 1455), Italian medalist and painter.
Pisano, Andrea (c. 1290–c. 1348), Italian sculptor.
Pisano, Giovanni (c. 1250–after 1314), Italian architect.

Pisano, Nicola (c. 1220–between 1278 and 1287), Italian sculptor.
Pissarro, Camille (1830–1903), French impressionist painter.
Pollaiuolo, Antonio (c. 1429–98), Florentine goldsmith, painter, sculptor, and engraver.
Pollock, Jackson (1912–56), American painter.
Polyclitus the elder (fl. c. 450–c. 420 B.C.), Greek sculptor.
Polygnotus (fl. c. 460–447 B.C.), Greek painter.
Poussin, Nicolas (1594–1665), French painter.
Praxiteles (fl. c. 370–c. 330 B.C.), Greek sculptor.
Prendergast, Maurice B. (1859–1924), American painter.
Primaticcio, Francesco (1504–70), Italian painter.
Prud'hon, Pierre Paul (1758–1823), French painter.
Puvis de Chavannes, Pierre (1824–98), French mural painter.
Pyle, Howard (1853–1911), American painter, illustrator and writer.
Quercia, Jacopo della (c. 1374–1438), Italian sculptor.
Raeburn, Sir Henry (1756–1823), Scottish portrait painter.
Raphael Santi (1483–1520), Italian Renaissance painter.
Rauschenberg, Robert (1925–), American pop artist.
Ray, Man (1890–1976), American painter and photographer.
Redon, Odilon (1840–1916), French painter.
Reinhardt, Ad (1913–67), American painter.
Rembrandt Harmenszoon van Rijn (1606–69), Dutch painter and etcher.
Remington, Frederic (1861–1909), American painter and sculptor.
Renoir, Pierre A. (1841–1919), French impressionist painter.
Reynolds, Sir Joshua (1723–92), English portrait painter; first president of Royal Academy of Arts.
Ribera, Jusepe (c. 1590–1652), Spanish baroque painter.
Rivera, Diego (1886–1957), Mexican muralist.
Rivers, Larry (1923–), American pop artist.
Rodin, Auguste (1840–1917), French sculptor.
Romney, George (1734–1802), English portrait painter.
Rosa, Salvator (1615–73), Italian baroque painter.
Rosenquist, James (1933–), American pop artist.
Roszak, Theodore (1907–), Polish-born American sculptor.
Rothko, Mark (1903–70), Russian-born American abstract expressionist painter.
Rouault, Georges (1871–1958), French painter.
Rousseau, Henri (1844–1910), French primitive painter.
Rubens, Peter Paul (1577–1640), Flemish painter.
Rudolph, Paul (1918–), American architect.
Ruisdael, Jacob van (c. 1628–82), Dutch painter and etcher.
Ryder, Albert P. (1847–1917), American painter.
Saarinen, Eero (1910–61), Finnish-American architect.
Saarinen, Eliel (1873–1950), Finnish-American architect.
Saint-Gaudens, Augustus (1848–1907), Irish-born American sculptor.
Samaras, Lucas (1936–), Greek collage artist.
Sargent, John Singer (1856–1925), American painter.
Sarto, Andrea del (1486–1531), Florentine painter.
Sassetta (c. 1400–1450), Sienese painter.
Schongauer, Martin (1430–1491), German engraver and painter.
Scopas (fl. 4th cent. B.C.), Greek sculptor.
Scorel, Jan van (1495–1562), Dutch painter.
Segal, George (1924–), American sculptor.
Seurat, Georges (1859–91), French neoimpressionist painter.
Shahn, Ben (1898–1969), American painter and graphic artist.
Signac, Paul (1863–1935), French neoimpressionist painter.
Signorelli, Luca (c. 1441–1523), Italian painter of the Umbrian school.
Siqueiros, David A. (1898–1974), Mexican muralist.
Sisley, Alfred (1839–99), French landscape painter.
Sloan, John (1871–1951), American painter and etcher.
Sloane, Eric (1910–), American landscape painter.
Sluter, Claus (d. 1406), Flemish sculptor.
Smith, David (1906–65), American sculptor.
Soleri, Paolo (1919–), Italian architect.
Soutine, Chaim (1894–1943), Russian-born French painter.
Steen, Jan (1626–79), Dutch genre painter.
Steichen, Edward (1879–1973), Luxembourg-born American photographer.
Stella, Joseph (1877–1946), Italian-born American painter.
Stieglitz, Alfred (1864–1946), American photographer.
Stone, Edward Durell (1902–78), American architect.
Stoss, Veit (c. 1445–1533), German sculptor.
Stuart, Gilbert (1755–1828), American portrait painter.
Stuart, James (1713–88), English architect and painter.
Sullivan, Louis Henry (1856–1924), American architect.

Sutherland, Graham (1903–   ), English painter.
Tamayo, Rufino (1899–   ), Mexican painter.
Tange, Kenzo (1913–   ), Japanese architect.
Tanguy, Yves (1900–55), French surrealist painter.
Tchelitchew, Pavel (1898–1957), Russian-American painter.
Teniers, David, the younger (1610–90), Flemish genre painter.
Ter Borch, Gerard (1617–81), Dutch painter.
Terbrugghen, Hendrick (1588–1629), Dutch painter.
Thoma, Hans (1839–1924), German painter and lithographer.
Thorvaldsen, Albert B. (1770–1844), Danish sculptor.
Tiepolo, Giovanni B. (1696–1770), Venetian painter.
Tiffany, Louis C. (1848–1933), American artist and decorative designer.
Tinguely, Jean (1925–   ), Swiss sculptor.
Tintoretto (1518–94), Venetian painter.
Titian (c. 1490–1576), Venetian painter.
Toulouse-Lautrec, Henri de (1864–1901), French painter and lithographer.
Trumbull, John (1756–1843), American painter.
Tura, Cosmé (c. 1430–95), Italian painter.
Turner, Joseph M. W. (1775–1851), English landscape painter.
Uccello, Paolo (c. 1396–1475), Florentine painter.
Utamaro, Kitagawa (1753–1806), Japanese color-print artist.
Utrillo, Maurice (1883–1955), French painter.
Utzon, Joern (1918–   ), Danish architect.
Van Dyck, Sir Anthony (1599–1641), Flemish portrait painter.
Vasari, Giorgio (1511–74), Italian architect, painter, and writer.

Vaux, Calvert (1824–95), English-born American landscape architect.
Velázquez, Diego R. de S. y (1599–1660), Spanish painter.
Velde, Henri van de (1863–1957), Belgian designer and architect.
Vermeer, Jan (1632–75), Dutch genre and landscape painter.
Veronese, Paolo (1528–88), Italian painter.
Verrocchio, Andrea del (1435–88), Florentine sculptor.
Vigée-Lebrun, Elisabeth (1755–1842), French painter.
Vignola, Giacomo da (1507–73), Italian architect.
Viollet-le-Duc, Eugène E. (1814–79), French architect.
Vlaminck, Maurice de (1876–1958), French painter.
Vos, Cornelis de (1584–1651), Flemish painter.
Vuillard, Edouard (1868–1940), French painter.
Warhol, Andy (1930?–   ), American pop artist.
Watteau, Antoine (1684–1721), French painter.
Wedgwood, Josiah (1730–95), English potter.
Wesselmann, Tom (1931–   ), American pop artist.
West, Benjamin (1738–1820), American historical painter.
Westermann, H. C. (1922–   ), American pop sculptor.
Weyden, Roger van der (c. 1400–64), Flemish painter.
Whistler, James A. McN. (1834–1903), American painter and etcher.
White, Stanford (c. 1853–1906), American architect.
Witz, Conrad (fl. c. 1434–c. 1447), German painter.
Wood, Grant (1891–1942), American painter.
Wren, Sir Christopher (1632–1723), English architect.
Wright, Frank Lloyd (1869–1959), American architect.
Wyeth, Andrew N. (1917–   ), American painter.
Wyeth, Newell Convers (1882–1945), American painter and illustrator.
Zorach, William (1887–1966), Lithuanian-born American sculptor.

NOVELISTS, DRAMATISTS, POETS, AND OTHER WRITERS

Adams, Henry (1838–1918), American biographer, historian, and novelist.
Addison, Joseph (1672–1719), English essayist and poet.
Aeschylus (525–456 B.C.), Athenian tragedian.
Aesop (c. 620–c. 560 B.C.), Greek fabulist.
Agee, James (1909–55), American essayist and journalist.
Agnon (b. Czaczkes), Shmuel Y. (1888–1970), Polish-born Israeli novelist.
Aiken, Conrad (1889–1973), American novelist and poet.
Alarcón, Pedro Antonio de (1833–91), Spanish novelist.
Albee, Edward (1928–   ), American dramatist.
Alcott, Louisa May (1832–88), American novelist.
Aldington, Richard (1892–1962), English poet and novelist.
Aleichem, Sholom (Solomon Rabinowitz) (1859–1916), Russian-born Yiddish writer.
Algren, Nelson (1909–   ), American novelist.
Amado, Jorge (1912–   ), Brazilian novelist.
Ambler, Eric (1909–   ), English suspense novelist.
Amis, Kingsley (1922–   ), English novelist.
Andersen, Hans Christian (1805–75), Danish poet and fairy tale writer.
Anderson, Maxwell (1888–1959), American dramatist.
Anderson, Robert (1917–   ), American dramatist.
Anderson, Sherwood (1876–1941), American novelist.
Andreyev, Leonid (1871–1919), Russian writer.
Andric, Ivo (1892–1975), Yugoslav novelist.
Anouilh, Jean (1910–   ), French dramatist.
Apollinaire, Guillaume (Wilhelm Apollinaris de Kostrowitzky) (1880–1918), French poet.
Apuleius, Lucius (fl. 2d cent. A.D.), Latin romance writer.
Aragon, Louis (1897–   ), French novelist and poet.
Arden, John (1930–   ), English dramatist.
Ariosto, Ludovico (1474–1533), Italian epic and lyric poet.
Aristophanes (c. 448–after 388 B.C.), Athenian comic poet.
Arnold, Matthew (1822–88), English poet and critic.
Arrabel (Terán), Fernando (1932–   ), Spanish dramatist.
Asch, Sholem (1880–1957), Polish-born Yiddish novelist.
Auchincloss, Louis (1917–   ), American novelist.
Auden, W(ystan) H(ugh) (1907–73), Anglo-American poet.
Austen, Jane (1775–1817), English novelist.
Azuela, Mariano (1873–1952), Mexican novelist.
Bacon, Francis (1561–1626), English essayist.
Bagnold, Enid (1889–   ), English dramatist.
Baldwin, James (1924–   ), American novelist and essayist.
Balzac, Honoré de (1799–1850), French novelist.
Barrie, Sir James M. (1860–1937), British playwright.
Barth, John (1930–   ), American novelist.
Baudelaire, Charles (1821–67), French poet and critic.
Beaumarchais, Pierre A. C. de (1732–99), French dramatist.

Beaumont, Francis (c. 1584–1616), English dramatist.
Beauvoir, Simone de (1908–   ), French novelist and essayist.
Beckett, Samuel (1906–   ), Irish-French dramatist.
Bede (c. 673–735 A.D.), Old English historian.
Beerbohm, Sir Max (1872–1956), English parodist.
Behan, Brendan (1923–64), Irish dramatist.
Behn, Aphra (1640–89), English novelist and dramatist.
Behrman, S. N. (1893–1973), American playwright.
Belloc, Hilaire (1870–1953), British poet, essayist, satirist, and historian.
Bellow, Saul (1915–   ), Canadian-American novelist.
Benchley, Robert (1889–1945), American humorist.
Benét, Stephen Vincent (1898–1943), American poet, novelist, and short story writer.
Bennett, Arnold (1867–1931), English novelist.
Bernanos, Georges (1888–1948), French novelist.
Bernstein, Carl (1944–   ), American journalist and author.
Berryman, John (1914–72), American poet.
Betjeman, John (1906–   ), English poet.
Betti, Ugo (1892–1953), Italian poet and dramatist.
Bierce, Ambrose (1842–1914?), American short story writer and journalist.
Bishop, Elizabeth (1911–   ), American poet.
Bjornson, Bjornstjerne (1832–1910), Norwegian novelist.
Blackmur, R(ichard) P. (1904–65), American critic and poet.
Blake, William (1757–1827), English poet.
Blasco-Ibáñez, Vicente (1867–1928), Spanish novelist.
Boccaccio, Giovanni (1313–75), Italian poet and storyteller.
Bodenheim, Maxwell (1893–1954), American poet.
Bogan, Louise (1897–1970), American poet.
Boileau-Despréaux, Nicolas (1636–1711), French literary critic and poet.
Böll, Heinrich (1917–   ), German novelist.
Bolt, Robert (1924–   ), English dramatist.
Borges, Jorge Luis (1899–   ), Argentine poet.
Boswell, James (1740–95), Scottish biographer and diarist.
Bowen, Elizabeth (1899–1973), Anglo-Irish novelist.
Bowles, Paul (1910–   ), American novelist.
Boyle, Kay (1903–   ), American novelist.
Bradbury, Ray (1920–   ), American science fiction writer.
Braine, John (1922–   ), English novelist.
Brecht, Bertolt (1898–1956), German dramatist and poet.
Breton, André (1896–1966), French surrealistic writer.
Bridges, Robert (1844–1930), English poet.
Brontë, Charlotte (1816–55), English novelist.
Brontë, Emily (1818–48), English novelist.
Brooke, Rupert (1887–1915), English poet.
Brooks, Van Wyck (1886–1963), American critic.

Brophy, Brigid (1929–   ), English novelist and critic.
Brown, John Mason (1900–69), American critic and biographer.
Browne, Sir Thomas (1605–82), English author and physician.
Browning, Elizabeth Barrett (1806–61), English poet.
Browning, Robert (1812–89), English poet.
Bryant, William Cullen (1794–1878), American poet.
Buchan, John (1875–1940), British novelist and historian.
Bullins, Ed (1935–   ), American dramatist.
Bunin, Ivan (1870–1953), Russian novelist.
Bunyan, John (1628–88), English allegorist.
Burgess, Anthony (1917–   ), English novelist and critic.
Burns, Robert (1759–96), Scottish poet.
Burroughs, Edgar Rice (1875–1950), American novelist.
Burroughs, William (1914–   ), American novelist.
Butler, Samuel (1835–1902), English novelist and essayist.
Byron, Lord (George Gordon) (1788–1824), English poet.
Cabell, James Branch (1879–1958), American novelist.
Caedmon (fl. 670 A.D.), Old English poet.
Calderón de la Barca, Pedro (1600–81), Spanish dramatist.
Calisher, Hortense (1911–   ), American novelist.
Callimachus (fl. c. 265 B.C.), Greek poet and critic.
Camoes, Luis de (1524?–80), Portuguese poet.
Camus, Albert (1913–60), French essayist, novelist, and dramatist.
Capek, Karel (1890–1938), Czech playwright.
Capote, Truman (1924–   ), American novelist.
Carew, Thomas (c. 1595–c. 1639), English poet.
Carlino, Lewis John (1932–   ), American dramatist.
Carlyle, Thomas (1795–1881), Anglo-Scottish essayist, critic, translator, and historian.
Carroll, Lewis (Charles Lutwidge Dodgson) (1832–98), English novelist.
Cary, Joyce (1888–1957), English novelist.
Cassill, R(onald) V(erlin) (1919–   ), American novelist, short story writer, and essayist.
Castiglione, Baldassare (1478–1529), Italian social critic.
Cather, Willa (1876–1947), American novelist.
Catton, Bruce (1899–1978), American historian.
Catullus, Caius Valerius (c. 84 B.C.–c. 54 B.C.), Roman poet.
Céline, Louis Ferdinand (1894–1961), French novelist.
Cervantes Saavedra, Miguel de (1547–1616), Spanish novelist.
Chandler, Raymond (1888–1959), American detective story writer.
Chateaubriand, François R. (1768–1848), French novelist.
Chaucer, Geoffrey (c. 1340–1400), English poet.
Chayefsky, Paddy (1923–   ), American dramatist.
Cheever, John (1912–   ), American novelist and short story writer.
Chekhov, Anton (1860–1904), Russian dramatist.
Chesterton, G(ilbert) K(eith) (1874–1936), English novelist, poet, biographer, and essayist.
Chikamatsu, Monzaemon (1653–1725), Japanese dramatist.
Christie, Agatha (1891–1976), English mystery writer.
Ciardi, John (1916–   ), American poet and critic.
Cicero, Marcus Tullius (106–43 B.C.), Roman essayist.
Claudel, Paul (1868–1955), French poet and dramatist.
Cocteau, Jean (1889?–1963), French novelist and film-maker.
Coleridge, Samuel Taylor (1772–1834), English poet.
Colette (Sidonie Gabrielle Collette) (1873–1954), French novelist.
Collins, Wilkie (1824–89), English novelist.
Collins, William (1721–59), English poet.
Colum, Padraic (1881–1972), Irish-American poet, dramatist, and novelist.
Compton-Burnett, Ivy (1892–1969), English novelist.
Congreve, William (1670–1729), English dramatist.
Connolly, Cyril (1903–74), English critic and editor.
Conrad, Joseph (1857–1924), Polish-born English novelist.
Cooper, James Fenimore (1789–1851), American novelist.
Corneille, Pierre (1606–84), French dramatist.
Coward, Sir Noël (1899–1973), English dramatist, composer, lyricist, and autobiographer.
Cowley, Abraham (1618–67), English poet.
Cowper, William (1731–1800), English poet.
Cozzens, James Gould (1903–78), American novelist.
Crabbe, George (1754–1832), English poet.
Crane, Hart (1899–1932), American poet.
Crane, Stephen (1871–1900), American novelist.
Crashaw, Richard (c. 1612–49), English poet.
cummings, e. e. (1894–1962), American poet.
Cunha, Euclides da (1866–1909), Brazilian writer.
Cynewulf (fl. c. early 9th cent.), Old English poet.

D'Annunzio, Gabriele (1863–1938), Italian poet.
Dante (Alighieri) (1265–1321), Italian poet.
Daudet, Alphonse (1840–97), French novelist, poet, and short story writer.
Day Lewis, C(ecil) (1904–72), Anglo-Irish poet.
Defoe, Daniel (c. 1660–1731), English novelist.
Dekker, Thomas (1572?–1632?), English dramatist.
Delaney, Shelagh (1939–   ), English dramatist.
De la Mare, Walter (1873–1956), English novelist and poet.
De la Roche, Mazo (1885–1961), Canadian novelist.
Demosthenes (c. 384–322 B.C.), Greek orator.
De Quincey, Thomas (1785–1859), English essayist.
De Vries, Peter (1910–   ), American novelist.
Dickens, Charles (1812–70), English novelist.
Dickey, James (1923–   ), American poet and critic.
Dickinson, Emily (1830–86), American poet.
Diderot, Denis (1713–84), French encyclopedist, novelist, dramatist, satirist, and critic.
Didion, Joan (1934-   ), American novelist.
Dinesen, Isak (Karen Blixen) (1885–1962), Danish writer.
Donleavy, J(ames) P(atrick) (1926–   ), American-born, Irish novelist.
Donne, John (1572–1631), English poet and essayist.
Doolittle, Hilda ("H.D.") (1886–1961), American poet.
Dos Passos, John (1896–1970), American novelist.
Dostoyevsky, Feodor (1821–81), Russian novelist.
Doyle, Sir Arthur Conan (1859–1930), English detective story and romance writer.
Dreiser, Theodore (1871–1945), American novelist.
Drexler, Rosalyn (1926–   ), American dramatist.
Dryden, John (1631–1700), English poet and dramatist.
Dumas, Alexandre (fils) (1824–95), French dramatist.
Dumas, Alexandre (père) (1802–70), French novelist and dramatist.
Duras, Marguerite (1914–   ), French novelist.
Durrell, Lawrence (1912–   ), British novelist and poet.
Durrenmatt, Friedrich (1921–   ), Swiss dramatist.
Eberhart, Richard (1904–   ), American poet.
Ehrenburg, Ilya (1891–1967), Russian novelist.
Eliot, George (Mary Ann Evans) (1819–80), English novelist.
Eliot, T(homas) S(tearns) (1888–1965), American-born British poet, dramatist, and critic.
Ellison, Ralph (1914–   ), American novelist.
Emerson, Ralph Waldo (1803–82), American essayist and poet.
Erasmus, Desiderius (c. 1466–1536), Dutch humanist.
Euripides (c. 480–406 B.C.), Greek tragic poet.
Farrell, James T. (1904–79), American novelist.
Faulkner, William (1897–1962), American novelist.
Feuchtwanger, Lion (1884–1958), German novelist.
Fielding, Henry (1707–54), English novelist.
FitzGerald, Edward (1809–83), English translator.
Fitzgerald, F. Scott (1896–1940), American novelist.
Flaubert, Gustave (1821–80), French novelist.
Fleming, Ian (1908–64), English secret agent novelist.
Fletcher, John (1579–1625), English dramatist.
Ford, Ford Madox (Ford Madox Hueffer) (1873–1939), English poet, novelist, critic, and essayist.
Ford, John (1586–c. 1640), English dramatist.
Forster, E(dward) M(organ) (1879–1970), English novelist.
Foster, Paul (1931–   ), American dramatist.
France, Anatole (Jacques Anatole Thibault) (1844–1924), French novelist and satirist.
Friedman, Bruce Jay (1930–   ), American novelist.
Friel, Brian (1929–   ), Irish dramatist.
Frisch, Max (1911–   ), Swiss dramatist.
Froissart, Jean (c. 1337–1410?), French chronicler.
Frost, Robert (1874–1963), American poet.
Fry, Christopher (1907–   ), English dramatist.
Fuentes, Carlos (1928–   ), Mexican short story writer.
Galsworthy, John (1867–1933), English novelist.
Garcia Lorca, Federico (1898–1936), Spanish poet.
Garcia Márquez, Gabriel José (1928–   ), Colombian writer.
Gardner, Erle Stanley (1889–1970), American detective story writer.
Garland, Hamlin (1860–1940), American novelist.
Gaskell, Elizabeth (1810–65), English novelist and biographer.
Gay, John (1685–1732), English playwright and poet.
Gelber, Jack (1932–   ), American dramatist.
Genet, Jean (1910–   ), French novelist and dramatist.
George, Stefan (1868–1933), German poet.
Ghelderode, Michel de (1898–1962), Belgian dramatist.
Gibbon, Edward (1737–94), English historian.
Gide, André (1869–1951), French novelist.

Gilroy, Frank D. (1925–   ), American dramatist.
Ginsberg, Allen (1926–   ), American poet.
Giono, Jean (1895–1970), French novelist.
Giraudoux, Jean (1882–1944), French dramatist.
Gissing, George (1857–1903), English novelist.
Glasgow, Ellen (1873–1945), American novelist.
Godwin, William (1756–1836), English novelist and political philosopher.
Goethe, Johann Wolfgang von (1749–1832), German novelist.
Gogol, Nikolai (1809–52), Russian novelist.
Golding, William (1911–   ), English novelist.
Goldman, James (1927–   ), American dramatist.
Goldoni, Carlo (1707–93), Italian dramatist.
Goldsmith, Oliver (1730?–74), English essayist and dramatist.
Goodman, Paul (1911–1972), American writer and pacifist.
Gorey, Edward (1925–   ), American writer and artist.
Gorki, Maxim (Aleksey Maximovich Pyeshkov) (1868–1936), Russian novelist, dramatist, and short story writer.
Grass, Günter (1927–   ), German novelist.
Graves, Robert (1895–   ), English poet and novelist.
Gray, Thomas (1716–71), English poet.
Greene, Graham (1904–   ), English novelist.
Gregory, Lady Augusta (1859–1932), Irish dramatist.
Grimm, Jakob (1785–1863), German folklorist.
Grimm, Wilhelm (1786–1859), German folklorist.
Gunther, John (1901–70), American political writer.
Hafiz (Shams-ud-Din-Mohammed) (d. 1389?), Persian poet.
Haley, Alex (1921–   ), American historian.
Hammett, Dashiell (1894–1961), American novelist.
Hamsun, Knut (1859–1952), Norwegian novelist.
Hansberry, Lorraine (1930–65), American dramatist.
Hardy, Thomas (1840–1928), English novelist.
Harris, Joel Chandler (1848–1908), American short story writer.
Harte, Bret (1836–1902), American short story writer.
Hauptmann, Gerhart (1862–1946), German dramatist, novelist, and poet.
Hawthorne, Nathaniel (1804–64), American novelist.
Hazlitt, William (1778–1830), English essayist.
Hecht, Ben (1894–1964), American journalist and author.
Heine, Heinrich (1797–1856), German poet.
Heller, Joseph (1923–   ), American novelist.
Hellman, Lillian (1905–   ), American dramatist and author.
Hemingway, Ernest (1899–1961), American novelist.
Henry, O. (William Sydney Porter) (1862–1910), American short story writer.
Herbert, George (1593–1633), English poet.
Herder, Johann G. von (1744–1803), German poet.
Herodotus (c. 484–c. 425 B.C.), Greek historian.
Herrick, Robert (1591–1674), English poet.
Hersey, John (1914–   ), American novelist and journalist.
Hesiod (fl. c. 8th cent. B.C.), Greek poet.
Hesse, Hermann (1877–1962), German novelist.
Heyward, DuBose (1885–1940), American novelist.
Heywood, Thomas (1574?–1641), English dramatist.
Hochhuth, Rolf (1931–   ), German dramatist.
Hoffmann, E(rnst) T(heodor) A(madeus) (1776–1822), German novelist and short story writer.
Hölderlin, Johann C. F. (1770–1843), German poet.
Homer (before 700 B.C.), Greek epic poet.
Hopkins, Gerard Manley (1844–89), English poet.
Horace (65 B.C.–8 B.C.), Latin poet.
Horovitz, Israel (1939–   ), American dramatist.
Housman, A. E. (1859–1936), English poet.
Howard, Sidney (1891–1939), American dramatist.
Howe, Irving (1920–   ), American historian and critic.
Hughes, Langston (1902–67), American poet.
Hugo, Victor (1802–85), French novelist.
Huxley, Aldous (1894–1963), English novelist and essayist.
Huxtable, Ada Louise (1921–   ), American journalist and architecture critic.
Ibsen, Henrik (1828–1906), Norwegian dramatist.
Inge, William (1913–73), American dramatist.
Ionesco, Eugène (1912–   ), French dramatist.
Irving, Washington (1783–1859), American short story writer, historian, and biographer.
Isherwood, Christopher (1904–   ), Anglo-American novelist and dramatist.
Jackson, Shirley (1919–65), American novelist.
James, Henry (1843–1916), American novelist.
Jarrell, Randall (1914–65), American poet and novelist.
Jeffers, Robinson (1887–1962), American poet.

Jellicoe, Ann (1927–   ), English dramatist and director.
Jewett, Sarah Orne (1849–1909), American novelist.
Johnson, Samuel (1709–84), English critic, essayist, lexicographer, poet, and biographer.
Jones, James (1921–77), American novelist.
Jones, LeRoi (Imamu Baraka) (1934–   ), American dramatist.
Jonson, Ben (1572–1637), English dramatist and poet.
Joyce, James (1882–1941), Irish novelist.
Juvenal (1st–2d cent. A.D.), Roman satirical poet.
Kafka, Franz (1883–1924), German novelist.
Kawabata, Yasunari (1899–1972) Japanese novelist.
Kazantzakis, Nikos (c. 1883–1957), Greek novelist.
Keats, John (1795–1821), English poet.
Keller, Gottfried (1819–90), Swiss novelist.
Kempton, J. Murray (1918–   ), American journalist and social critic.
Kennedy, Adrienne (1932–   ), American dramatist.
Kerouac, Jack (1922–69), American novelist.
Kesey, Ken (1935–   ), American novelist.
Kingsley, Charles (1819–75), English novelist.
Kingsley, Sidney (1906–   ), American playwright.
Kipling, Rudyard (1865–1936), British poet and novelist.
Kleist, Heinrich von (1777–1811), German dramatic poet.
Knowles, John (1926–   ), American novelist.
Koestler, Arthur (1905–   ), Hungarian-born English novelist and essayist.
Kopit, Arthur (1937–   ), American dramatist.
Kyd, Thomas (1558–94), English dramatist.
La Fontaine, Jean de (1621–95), French fabulist and poet.
Lagerkvist, Pär (1891–1974), Swedish novelist.
Lagerlof, Selma (1858–1940), Swedish novelist.
Lamartine, Alphonse (1790–1869), French poet.
Lamb, Charles (1775–1834), English essayist.
Langland, William (c. 1332–c. 1440), English poet.
Lanier, Sidney (1842–81), American poet.
Lardner, Ring (1885–1933), American short story writer.
La Rochefoucauld, François, duc de (1613–80), French classical writer, maximist, and epigrammatist.
Lash, Joseph (1909–   ), American biographer.
Lawrence, D(avid) H(erbert) (1885–1930), English novelist.
Laxness, Halldor (1902–   ), Icelandic novelist.
Lear, Edward (1812–88), English humorist.
Leavis, F(rank) R(aymond) (1895–1978), English critic.
Le Carré, John (David J. M. Cornwell) (1931–   ), English spy novelist.
Lee, Robert E. (1918–   ), American playwright.
Leopardi, Giacomo (1798–1837), Italian poet.
Lermontov, Mikhail Y. (1814–41), Russian novelist.
Lessing, Doris (1919–   ), English novelist.
Lessing, Gotthold E. (1729–81), German dramatist.
Lewis, C(live) S(taples) (1898–1963), Anglo-Irish critic, spiritual writer, and novelist.
Lewis, Sinclair (1885–1951), American novelist.
Lewis, Wyndham (1886–1957), English novelist.
Lind, Jakov (1927–   ), Anglo-Austrian novelist.
Lindsay, Vachel (1879–1931), American poet.
Livy (59 B.C.–17 A.D.), Roman historian.
London, Jack (1876–1916), American novelist.
Longfellow, Henry Wadsworth (1807–82), American poet.
Lope de Vega Carpio, Félix (1562–1635), Spanish poet.
Lord, Walter (1917–   ), American historical novelist.
Lovelace, Richard (1618–57?), English poet.
Lowell, Amy (1874–1925), American poet and critic.
Lowell, James Russell (1819–91), American poet.
Lowell, Robert (1917–77), American poet and translator.
Lucian (c. 125–after 180), Greek satirist.
Lucretius (c. 99–c. 55 B.C.), Roman poet.
Macaulay, Thomas Babington (1800–59), English historian, essayist, and critic.
McCarthy, Mary (1912–   ), American novelist and literary critic.
McCullers, Carson (1917–67), American novelist.
Machiavelli, Niccoló (1469–1527), Italian political essayist.
MacLeish, Archibald (1892–   ), American poet.
McNally, Terrence (1939–   ), American dramatist.
Maeterlinck, Maurice (1862–1949), Belgian dramatist.
Mailer, Norman (1923–   ), American novelist and essayist.
Malamud, Bernard (1914–   ), American novelist.
Mallarmé, Stéphane (1842–98), French poet.
Malory, Sir Thomas (d. 1471), English Arthurian romance writer.
Malraux, André (1901–76), French man of letters.
Mann, Heinrich (1871–1950), German novelist.
Mann, Thomas (1875–1955), German novelist.
Mansfield, Katherine (1888–1923), British short story writer.

Manzoni, Alessandro (1785–1873), Italian novelist.
Marcus, Frank (1928–　), English dramatist.
Marlowe, Christopher (1564–93), English dramatist.
Marquand, John P. (1893–1960), American novelist.
Marsh, Ngaio (1899–　), New Zealand detective story writer.
Martial (c. 40–c. 104 A.D.), Roman epigrammatic poet.
Marvell, Andrew (1621–78), English poet.
Masefield, John (1878–1967), English poet.
Massinger, Philip (1583–1640), English dramatist.
Masters, Edgar Lee (1869–1950), American poet and biographer.
Maugham, W(illiam) Somerset (1874–1965), English novelist.
Maupassant, Guy de (1850–93), French novelist and short story writer.
Mauriac, François (1885–1970), French novelist.
Maurois, André (1885–1967), French biographer.
Melville, Herman (1819–91), American novelist.
Menander (c. 342 B.C.–c. 291 B.C.), Greek dramatist.
Mencken, H(enry) L(ouis) (1880–1956), American satirist, editor, critic, and philologist.
Meredith, George (1828–1909), English novelist and poet.
Mérimée, Prosper (1803–70), French novelist, dramatist, and poet.
Michener, James (1907–　), American novelist.
Millay, Edna St. Vincent (1892–1950), American poet.
Miller, Arthur (1915–　), American dramatist.
Miller, Henry (1891–　), American novelist.
Milne, A(lan) A(lexander) (1882–1956), English poet, dramatist, and children's author.
Milton, John (1608–74), English poet.
Mistral, Frédéric (1830–1914), French Provençal poet.
Mistral, Gabriela (1889–1957), Chilean poet.
Molière, Jean Baptiste (Jean Baptiste Poquelin) (1622–73), French dramatist.
Molnar, Ferenc (1878–1952), Hungarian dramatist.
Montaigne, Michel Eyquem de (1533–92), French essayist.
Moore, George (1852–1933), Irish novelist.
Moore, Marianne (1887–1972), American poet.
Moore, Thomas (1779–1852), Irish poet.
Moravia, Alberto (1907–　), Italian novelist.
More, Sir Thomas (1478–1535), English humanist.
Morison, Samuel Eliot (1887–1976), American historian.
Morley, Christopher (1890–1957), American novelist.
Morris, William (1834–96), English poet.
Murdoch, Iris (1919–　), British novelist.
Musset, Alfred de (1810–57), French dramatist and poet.
Nabokov, Vladimir (1899–1977), Russian-American novelist.
Neruda, Pablo (1904–73), Chilean poet.
Nerval, Gérard de (Gérard Labrunie) (1808–55), French poet, translator, and short story writer.
Nevins, Allan (1890–1971), American historian.
Norris, Frank (1870–1902), American novelist.
Novalis (Friedrich von Hardenberg) (1772–1801), German poet.
Oates, Joyce Carol (1938–　), American novelist.
O'Casey, Sean (1884–1964), Irish dramatist.
O'Connor, Flannery (1925–64), American novelist and short story writer.
O'Connor, Frank (Michael O'Donovan) (1903–66), Irish short story writer.
Odets, Clifford (1906–63), American dramatist.
O'Faoláin, Seán (1900–　), Irish novelist.
O'Flaherty, Liam (1897–　), Irish novelist.
O'Hara, John (1905–70), American novelist.
Omar Khayyam (fl. 11th cent.), Persian poet.
O'Neill, Eugene (1888–1953), American dramatist.
Orwell, George (Eric Blair) (1903–50), British novelist and essayist.
Osborne, John (1929–　), English dramatist.
Ovid (43 B.C.–18 A.D.), Latin poet.
Parker, Dorothy (1893–1967), American poet, short story writer, satirist, and critic.
Pasternak, Boris (1890–1960), Russian poet and novelist.
Pater, Walter (1839–94), English essayist and critic.
Paton, Alan (1903–　), South African novelist.
Pavese, Cesare (1908–50), Italian novelist.
Peacock, Thomas Love (1785–1866), English novelist.
Pepys, Samuel (1633–1703), English diarist.
Perelman, S(idney) J(oseph) (1904–　), American humorist.
Perse, St. John (Alexis St. Léger) (1887–1975), French poet.
Petrarch (1304–74), Italian poet and humanist.
Petronius (d. c. 66 A.D.), Roman satirist.
Peyrefitte, Roger (1907–　), French novelist.
Pindar (c. 518–438 B.C.), Greek lyric poet.
Pinero, Sir Arthur Wing (1855–1934), English dramatist.

Pinter, Harold (1930–　), English dramatist.
Pirandello, Luigi (1867–1936), Italian dramatist.
Plath, Sylvia (1932–63), American poet and novelist.
Plautus (c. 254 B.C.–184 B.C.), Roman comic poet.
Plutarch (c. 46–c. 120 A.D.), Greek biographer.
Poe, Edgar Allan (1809–49), American poet, short story writer, and critic.
Pope, Alexander (1688–1744), English poet.
Porter, Katherine Anne (1890–　), American short story writer and novelist.
Pound, Ezra (1885–1972), American poet and critic.
Powell, Anthony (1905–　), English novelist.
Priestley, J(ohn) B(oynton) (1894–　), English novelist, dramatist, and critic.
Pritchett, V(ictor) S(awdon) (1900–　), English novelist and critic.
Proust, Marcel (1871–1922), French novelist.
Purdy, James (1923–　), American novelist.
Pushkin, Aleksandr (1799–1837), Russian poet.
Queneau, Raymond (1903–　), French novelist.
Quintilian (c. 35–95 A.D.), Roman rhetorician.
Rabe, David (1940–　), American playwright.
Rabelais, François (c. 1490–1553), French satirist.
Racine, Jean (1639–99), French dramatist.
Ransom, John Crowe (1888–1974), American poet and critic.
Rattigan, Terence (1911–77), English dramatist.
Reade, Charles (1814–84), English novelist and dramatist.
Remarque, Erich Maria (1897–1970), German-American novelist.
Rice, Elmer (1892–1967), American dramatist.
Richards, I. A. (1893–1979), British poet and critic.
Richardson, Jack (1935–　), American dramatist.
Richardson, Samuel (1689–1761), English novelist.
Richler, Mordecai (1931–　), Canadian novelist.
Richter, Conrad (1890–1968), American novelist.
Rilke, Rainer Maria (1875–1920), German poet.
Rimbaud, Arthur (1854–91), French poet.
Robinson, Edwin Arlington (1869–1935), American poet.
Roethke, Theodore (1908–63), American poet.
Rolland, Romain (1866–1944), French novelist.
Rolvaag, O(le) E(dvart) (1876–1931), Norwegian-American novelist.
Romains, Jules (1885–1972), French novelist.
Ronsard, Pierre de (c. 1524–85), French poet.
Rossetti, Christina (1830–94), English poet.
Rossetti, Dante G. (1828–82), English poet and translator.
Rostand, Edmond (1868–1918), French dramatist and poet.
Roth, Phillip (1933–　), American novelist.
Ruskin, John (1819–1900), English critic and essayist.
Russell, George ("A.E.") (1867–1935), Irish poet.
Sachs, Nelly (1891–1970), German-born Swedish poet.
Sagan, Françoise (1935–　), French novelist.
Sainte-Beuve, Charles A. (1804–69), French critic.
Saint-Exupéry, Antoine de (1900–44), French writer.
Saki (Hector H. Munro) (1870–1916), English short story writer.
Salinger, J(erome) D(avid) (1919–　), American novelist.
Sand, George (Amandine A. L. Dupin, baronne Dudevant) (1804–76), French novelist.
Sandburg, Carl (1878–1967), American poet.
Santayana, George (1863–1952), American philosopher, poet, and essayist.
Sappho (fl. early 6th cent. B.C.), Greek lyric poet.
Saroyan, William (1908–　), American novelist, dramatist, and short story writer.
Sartre, Jean Paul (1905–　), French philosopher, novelist, and dramatist.
Sayers, Dorothy L. (1893–1957), English novelist.
Schiller, Friedrich von (1759–1805), German dramatist.
Schisgal, Murray (1926–　), American dramatist.
Schlegel, Friedrich von (1772–1829), German philosopher, critic, and writer.
Schnitzler, Arthur (1862–1931), Austrian dramatist and novelist.
Schwartz, Delmore (1913–66), American poet.
Scott, Sir Walter (1771–1832), Scottish novelist.
Seferis, George (1900–71), Greek poet.
Seneca, Lucius Annaeus (c. 3 B.C.–65 A.D.), Roman dramatist and philosopher.
Senghor, Léopold S. (1906–　), Senegalese poet, essayist.
Shakespeare, William (1564–1616), English dramatist and poet.
Shange, Ntozake (1948–　), American dramatist and poet.
Shapiro, Karl (1913–　), American poet, critic, and editor.
Shaw, George Bernard (1856–1950), Irish dramatist.

Shaw, Irwin (1913–   ), American novelist.
Shelley, Mary Wollstonecraft (1797–1851), English novelist.
Shelley, Percy Bysshe (1792–1822), English poet.
Shepard, Sam (1943–   ), American playwright.
Sheridan, Richard Brinsley, (1751–1816), Irish-born dramatist.
Sherwood, Robert E. (1896–1955), American dramatist.
Sholokhov, Mikhail (1905–   ), Russian novelist.
Sidney, Sir Philip (1554–86), English poet and essayist.
Sienkiewicz, Henryk (1846–1916), Polish novelist.
Sillanpää, Frans E. (1888–1964), Finnish novelist.
Silone, Ignazio (1900–78), Italian novelist.
Simenon, Georges (1903–   ), Franco-Belgian novelist.
Simon, Neil (1927–   ), American playwright.
Sinclair, Upton (1878–1968), American novelist.
Singer, Isaac Bashevis (1904–   ), Polish-born Yiddish American novelist and short story writer.
Sitwell, Dame Edith (1887–1964), English poet and critic.
Sitwell, Sir Osbert (1892–1969), English poet and essayist.
Sitwell, Sacheverell (1897–   ), English poet and essayist.
Smollett, Tobias (1721–71), Scottish-born novelist.
Snow, C(harles) P(ercy) (1905–72), English critic and novelist.
Solzhenitsyn, Aleksandr I. (1918–   ), Russian novelist.
Sontag, Susan (1933–   ), American critic and novelist.
Sophocles (c. 496–406 B.C.), Greek tragic poet.
Southey, Robert (1774–1843), English poet.
Spark, Muriel (1918–   ), Scottish novelist, short story writer, poet, and biographer.
Spender, Stephen (1909–   ), English poet.
Spengler, Oswald (1880–1936), German historian.
Spenser, Edmund (1552?–99), English poet.
Spigelgass, Leonard (1908–   ), American playwright.
Steegmuller, Francis (1906–   ), American biographer.
Steele, Sir Richard (1672–1729), English essayist.
Stein, Gertrude (1874–1946), American poet, novelist, critic, and autobiographer.
Steinbeck, John (1902–68), American novelist.
Stendhal (Marie Henri Beyle) (1783–1842), French novelist.
Sterne, Laurence (1713–68), English novelist.
Stevens, Wallace (1879–1955), American poet.
Stevenson, Robert Louis (1850–94), Scottish-born English novelist.
Stoker, Bram (1847–1912), Irish-born novelist.
Stone, I. F. (1907–   ), American journalist and editor.
Stoppard, Tom (1937–   ), English dramatist.
Strindberg, August (1849–1912), Swedish dramatist.
Styron, William (1925–   ), American novelist.
Sudermann, Hermann (1857–1928), German dramatist.
Swados, Harvey (1920–1972), American novelist, short story writer, and essayist.
Swift, Jonathan (1667–1745), English satirist, poet, and essayist.
Swinburne, Algernon Charles (1837–1909), English poet.
Symonds, John Addington (1840–93), English cultural historian, critic, and translator.
Symons, Arthur (1865–1945), English poet and critic.
Synge, John Millington (1871–1909), Irish dramatist and poet.
Tacitus (c. 55–c. 117 A.D.), Roman historian.
Tagore, Sir Rabindranath (1861–1941), Indian poet, novelist, and essayist.
Taine, Hippolyte (1828–93), French critic and historian.
Tarkington, Booth (1869–1946), American novelist.
Tasso, Torquato (1544–95), Italian poet.
Tate, Allen (1899–1979), American poet and critic.
Taylor, Samuel (1912–   ), American playwright.
Teichmann, Howard (1916–   ), American dramatist.
Tennyson, Alfred (1809–92), English poet.
Thackeray, William Makepeace (1811–63), English novelist.
Theocritus (fl. c. 270 B.C.), Greek poet.
Thomas, Dylan (1914–53), Anglo-Welsh poet.
Thompson, Francis (1859–1907), English poet.
Thoreau, Henry David (1817–62), American essayist.

Thucydides (c. 460–c. 400 B.C.), Greek historian.
Thurber, James (1894–1961), American humorist.
Tolkien, J(ohn) R(onald) R(euel) (1892–1973), English novelist and critic.
Tolstoy, Leo (1828–1910), Russian novelist.
Toynbee, Arnold (1889–1975), English historian.
Traven, B. (Traven Torsvan) (1890–1969), American expatriate novelist.
Trollope, Anthony (1815–82), English novelist.
Trumbo, Dalton (1905–76), American screenwriter.
Turgenev, Ivan (1818–83), Russian novelist.
Tutuola, Amos (1920–   ), Nigerian writer.
Twain, Mark (Samuel L. Clemens) (1835–1910), American novelist and humorist.
Undset, Sigrid (1882–1949), Norwegian novelist.
Updike, John (1932–   ), American novelist and poet.
Valéry, Paul (1871–1945), French poet and critic.
van Itallie, Jean-Claude (1936–   ), Belgian-born American dramatist.
Van Doren, Mark (1894–1972), American poet and critic.
Vergil (70–19 B.C.), Roman poet.
Verne, Jules (1828–1905), French novelist.
Vidal, Gore (1925–   ), American novelist and critic.
Vigny, Alfred de (1797–1863), French dramatist.
Villon, François (1431–c. 1463), French poet.
Voltaire, François M. A. de (1694–1778), French novelist, dramatist, critic, and poet.
Vonnegut, Kurt, Jr. (1922–   ), American novelist.
Wain, John (1925–   ), English poet and novelist.
Waller, Edmund (1606–87), English poet.
Walpole, Horace (1717–97), English man of letters.
Walton, Izaak (1593–1683), English essayist.
Ward, Douglas Turner (1930–   ), American dramatist.
Warren, Robert Penn (1905–   ), American novelist, poet, and critic.
Wassermann, Jakob (1873–1934), Austrian novelist.
Waugh, Evelyn (1903–66), English novelist and satirist.
Webster, John (c. 1580–c. 1625), English dramatist.
Webster, Noah (1758–1843), American lexicographer.
Weidman, Jerome (1913–   ), American novelist.
Weiss, Peter (1916–   ), German-born Swedish dramatist.
Wells, H(erbert) G(eorge) (1866–1946), English novelist, essayist, and historian.
Werfel, Franz (1890–1945), Austrian novelist.
Wescott, Glenway (1901–   ), American novelist and critic.
Wesker, Arnold (1932–   ), English novelist.
West, Nathanael (Nathan Weinstein) (1903–40), American novelist.
Wharton, Edith (1862–1937), American novelist.
White, E(lwyn) B(rooks) (1899–   ), American essayist.
White, Patrick (1912–), Australian novelist.
Whitman, Walt (1819–92), American poet.
Whittier, John Greenleaf (1807–92), American poet.
Wilbur, Richard (1921–   ), American poet.
Wilde, Oscar (1854–1900), Irish dramatist.
Wilder, Thornton (1897–1975), American novelist and dramatist.
Williams, Tennessee (1914–   ), American dramatist.
Williams, William Carlos (1883–1963), American poet.
Wilson, Edmund (1895–1972), American writer and literary critic.
Wolfe, Thomas (1900–38), American novelist.
Woodward, Robert (1944–   ), American journalist.
Woolf, Virginia (1882–1941), English novelist.
Wordsworth, William (1770–1850), English poet and critic.
Wright, Richard (1908–60), American novelist.
Wyatt, Sir Thomas (1503–42), English poet.
Wylie, Elinor (1885–1928), American poet and novelist.
Xenophon (c. 430–c. 355 B.C.), Greek historian.
Yeats, William Butler (1865–1939), Irish poet.
Yevtushenko, Yevgeny (1933–   ), Russian poet.
Zola, Emile (1840–1902), French novelist.
Zweig, Stefan (1881–1942), Austrian novelist, poet, and biographer.

NOTABLES OF THE MUSICAL WORLD

Abbado, Claudio (1933–   ), Italian conductor.
Addinsell, Richard (1904–77), English film composer.
Adler, Kurt (1905–   ), American opera director.
Ailey, Alvin, Jr. (1931–   ), American choreographer.
Albanese, Licia (1913–   ), Italian-American soprano.
Albéniz, Isaac (1860–1909), Spanish pianist and composer.
Amara, Lucine (1927–   ), American soprano.
Amram, David (1930–   ), American composer.
Anderson, Marian (1902–   ), American contralto.

Ansermet, Ernest (1883–1969), Swiss conductor.
Antheil, George (1900–59), American composer.
Antonio (1921–   ), Spanish dancer.
Arnold, Malcolm (1921–   ), English composer.
Arpino, Gerald (1928–   ), American choreographer.
Arrau, Claudio (1903–   ), Chilean pianist.
Ashton, Sir Frederick (1906–   ), English choreographer.
Auber, Daniel F. E. (1782–1871), French operatic composer.

Auer, Leopold (1845–1930), Hungarian violinist-teacher.
Auric, Georges (1899–   ), French composer.
Babbitt, Milton (1916–   ), American composer.
Babin, Victor (1908–   ), Russian-American pianist.
Bach, Carl P. E. (1714–88), German composer.
Bach, Johann C. (1735–82), German composer.
Bach, Johann Sebastian (1685–1750), German composer.
Bach, Wilhelm F. (1710–84), German composer.
Bachauer, Gina (1913–76), Greek pianist.
Bachaus, Wilhelm (1884–1969), German pianist.
Badura-Skoda, Paul (1927–   ), Austrian pianist.
Baker, Janet (1933–   ), British mezzo-soprano.
Balanchine, George (1904–   ), American choreographer.
Balfe, Michael (1808–70), Irish operatic composer.
Barber, Samuel (1910–   ), American composer.
Barbirolli, Sir John (1899–1970), English conductor.
Barenboim, Daniel (1942–   ), Israeli pianist and conductor.
Bartók, Béla (1881–1945), Hungarian composer.
Baryshnikov, Mikhail (1948–   ), Russian ballet dancer.
Bastianini, Ettore (1923–67), Italian operatic baritone.
Beecham, Sir Thomas (1879–1961), English conductor.
Beethoven, Ludwig van (1770–1827), German composer.
Bellini, Vincenzo (1801–35), Italian operatic composer.
Bennett, Robert Russell (1894–   ), American composer.
Berg, Alban (1885–1935), Austrian composer.
Berganza, Teresa (1935–   ), Spanish mezzo-soprano.
Berlin, Irving (1888–   ), American popular composer.
Berlioz, Hector (1803–69), French composer.
Berman, Lazar (1930–   ), Russian pianist.
Bernstein, Leonard (1918–   ), American composer, conductor, and pianist.
Bettis, Valerie (1920–   ), American choreographer.
Biggs, E. Power (1906–77), English-American organist.
Bing, Rudolf (1902–   ), Austrian-English operatic manager.
Bizet, Georges (1838–75), French composer.
Björling, Jussi (1911–60), Swedish tenor.
Bliss, Sir Arthur (1891–1975), English composer.
Blitzstein, Marc (1905–64), American composer.
Bloch, Ernest (1880–1959), Swiss-American composer.
Boccherini, Luigi (1743–1805), Italian composer.
Boehm, Karl (1894–   ), German conductor.
Boito, Arrigo (1842–1918), Italian composer and librettist.
Borkh, Inge (1921–   ), German soprano.
Borodin, Aleksandr (1833–87), Russian composer.
Boulanger, Nadia (1887–   ), French composer and teacher.
Boulez, Pierre (1925–   ), French composer and conductor.
Boult, Sir Adrian (1889–   ), English conductor.
Brahms, Johannes (1833–97), German composer.
Brailowsky, Alexander (1896–1976), Russian pianist.
Bream, Julian (1933–   ), English guitarist and lutenist.
Britten, Benjamin (1913–76), English composer.
Browning, John (1933–   ), American pianist.
Bruch, Max (1838–1920), German composer.
Bruckner, Anton (1824–96), Austrian composer.
Bülow, Hans von (1830–94), German pianist and conductor.
Bumbry, Grace (1937–   ), American mezzo-soprano.
Butler, John (1920–   ), American choreographer.
Buxtehude, Dietrich (1637–1707), Swedish composer.
Cage, John (1912–   ), American composer.
Caldwell, Sarah (1928–   ), American opera conductor.
Callas, Maria (1923–77), Greek-American soprano.
Carreras, José (1946–   ), Spanish operatic tenor.
Caruso, Enrico (1873–1921), Italian operatic tenor.
Casadesus, Robert (1899–72), French pianist.
Casals, Pablo (1876–1973), Spanish cellist and conductor.
Chabrier, Alexis E. (1841–94), French composer.
Chaliapin, Feodor (1873–1938), Russian operatic bass.
Charpentier, Gustave (1860–1956), French composer.
Chausson, Ernest (1855–99), French composer.
Chávez, Carlos (1899–1978), Mexican composer.
Cherubini, Luigi (1760–1842), Italian composer.
Chopin, Frédéric (1810–49), Polish composer.
Christoff, Boris (1919–   ), Bulgarian bass.
Cimarosa, Domenico (1749–1801), Italian composer.
Cleva, Fausto (1902–   ), Italian-American conductor.
Cliburn, Van (1934–   ), American pianist.
Clifford, John (1947–   ), American dancer.
Copland, Aaron (1900–   ), American composer.
Corelli, Arcangelo (1653–1713), Italian composer.
Corelli, Franco (1924–   ), Italian dramatic tenor.
Couperin, François (1668–1733), French composer.
Crespin, Régine (1927–   ), French dramatic soprano.
Creston, Paul (1906–   ), American composer.
Cunningham, Merce (1922?–   ), American choreographer.
Curtin, Phyllis (c. 1930–   ), American operatic singer.
Dallapiccola, Luigi (1904–75), Italian pianist and composer.

D'Amboise, Jacques (1934–   ), American ballet dancer.
Damrosch, Leopold (1832–85), German conductor.
Damrosch, Walter (1862–1950), German-American conductor and composer.
Danilova, Alexandra (1906–   ), Russian ballerina.
Debussy, Claude (1862–1918), French composer.
De Lavallade, Carmen (1931–   ), American dancer.
Délibes, Léo (1836–91), French composer.
Delius, Frederick (1862–1934), English composer.
Della Casa, Lisa (1921–   ), Swiss lyric soprano.
Dello Joio, Norman (1913–   ), American composer.
Del Mar, Norman (1919–   ), English conductor.
De Mille, Agnes (1908–   ), American choreographer.
Del Monaco, Mario (1915–   ), Italian dramatic tenor.
De los Angeles, Victoria (1923–   ), Spanish lyric soprano.
Diaghilev, Sergei (1872–1929), Russian ballet impresario.
Di Stefano, Giuseppe (1921–   ), Italian lyric tenor.
Dittersdorf, Karl D. von (1739–99), Austrian composer.
Dobbs, Mattiwilda (1925–   ), American coloratura soprano.
Dohnanyi, Ernst von (1877–1960), Hungarian composer, pianist, and conductor.
Dolin, Anton (1904–   ), English ballet choreographer.
Domingo, Placido (1941–   ), Spanish opera tenor.
Donizetti, Gaetano (1797–1848), Italian composer.
Dorati, Antal (1906–   ), Hungarian-American conductor.
Dukas, Paul (1865–1935), French composer.
Duncan, Isadora (1878–1927), American dancer.
Dunham, Katherine (1910–   ), American choreographer.
Dvorak, Antonin (1841–1904), Czech composer.
Eglevsky, André (1917–77), Russian-born American dancer.
Elgar, Sir Edward (1857–1934), English composer.
Ellington, Duke (1899–1974), American composer.
Elman, Mischa (1891–1967), Russian-American violinist.
Enesco, Georges (1881–1955), Rumanian composer.
Entremont, Philippe (1934–   ), French pianist and conductor.
Falla, Manuel de (1876–1946), Spanish composer.
Farrar, Geraldine (1882–1967), American operatic soprano.
Farrell, Eileen (1920–   ), American dramatic soprano.
Farrell, Suzanne (1945–   ), American ballerina.
Fauré, Gabriel (1845–1924), French composer.
Feuermann, Emanuel (1902–42), Polish-American cellist.
Fiedler, Arthur (1894–1979), American conductor.
Fischer-Dieskau, Dietrich (1925–   ), German baritone.
Flagstad, Kirsten (1895–1962), Norwegian soprano.
Flotow, Friedrich von (1812–83), German operatic composer.
Fokine, Michel (1880–1942), Russian-American dancer.
Fonteyn, Dame Margot (1919–   ), English ballerina.
Foss, Lukas (1922–   ), German-born American composer.
Foster, Stephen (1826–64), American song writer.
Francescatti, Zino (1905–   ), French violinist.
Franck, César (1822–90), Belgian-French composer.
Frescobaldi, Girolamo (1583–1643), Italian composer.
Friml, Rudolf (1879–1972), Czech-American composer.
Furtwängler, Wilhelm (1886–1954), German conductor.
Gades, Antonio (1936–   ), Spanish dancer.
Galli-Curci, Amelita (1882–1963), Italian-American soprano.
Garden, Mary (1877–1967), Scottish-American soprano.
Gatti-Casazza, Giulio (1869–1940), Italian opera manager.
Gedda, Nicolai (1925–   ), Swedish operatic tenor.
Gershwin, George (1898–1937), American composer.
Gieseking, Walter (1895–1956), German pianist.
Gigli, Beniamino (1890–1957), Italian tenor.
Gilels, Emil (1916–   ), Russian pianist.
Ginastera, Alberto (1916–   ), Argentinian composer.
Glazunov, Aleksandr (1865–1936), Russian composer.
Glière, Reinhold (1875–1956), Russian composer.
Glinka, Mikhail (1804–57), Russian composer.
Gluck, Christoph W. von (1714–87), German composer.
Gobbi, Tito (1915–   ), Italian operatic baritone.
Godowsky, Leopold (1870–1938), Polish pianist.
Goldmark, Karl (1830–1915), Hungarian composer.
Goldovsky, Boris (1908–   ), Russian-American conductor.
Goldsand, Robert (1911–   ), Austrian-American pianist.
Golschmann, Vladimir (1893–1972), French-American conductor.
Goossens, Sir Eugene (1893–1962), English conductor.
Gould, Glenn (1932–   ), Canadian pianist.
Gould, Morton (1913–   ), American conductor.
Gounod, Charles (1818–93), French composer.
Graham, Martha (1893?–   ), American choreographer.
Grainger, Percy (1882–1961), Australian-American pianist and composer.
Greco, Jose (1918–   ), Italian-born American dancer.
Gretchaninov, Aleksandr (1864–1956), Russian composer.

Grieg, Edvard (1843–1907), Norwegian composer.
Grofé, Ferde (1892–1972), American musician.
Gueden, Hilde (1917–), Austrian operatic lyric soprano.
Halévy, Jacques (1799–1862), French operatic composer.
Hammerstein, Oscar, II (1895–1960), American lyricist.
Handel, George Frideric (1685–1759), German composer.
Hanson, Howard (1896–), American composer.
Harris, Roy (1898–), American composer.
Hart, Lorenz (1895–1943), American lyricist.
Haydée, Marcia (1937–), Brazilian ballerina.
Haydn, Franz Joseph (1732–1809), Austrian composer.
Heifetz, Jascha (1901–), Russian-American violinist.
Helpmann, Robert (1909–), Australian-born English choreographer.
Henze, Hans Werner (1926–), German composer.
Herbert, Victor (1859–1924), Irish-American musician.
Hess, Dame Myra (1890–1965), English pianist.
Hindemith, Paul (1895–1963), German-American composer.
Hines, Jerome (1921–), American operatic bass.
Hofmann, Joseph (1876–1957), Polish-American pianist.
Holst, Gustav (1874–1934), English composer.
Honegger, Arthur (1892–1955), Swiss-French composer.
Horne, Marilyn (1934–), American mezzo-soprano.
Horowitz, Vladimir (1904–), Russian-American pianist.
Humperdinck, Engelbert (1854–1921), German composer.
Humphrey, Doris (1895–1958), American choreographer.
Hurok, Sol (1888–1974), Russian-American impresario.
Ibert, Jacques (1890–1962), French composer.
Indy, Vincent d' (1851–1931), French composer.
Ippolitov-Ivanov, Mikhail (1859–1935), Russian composer.
Istomin, Eugene (1925–), American pianist.
Iturbi, José (1895–), Spanish-American pianist.
Ives, Charles (1874–1954), American composer.
Jamison, Judith (1944–), American dancer.
Jeritza, Maria (1887–), Austrian-American soprano.
Joffrey, Robert (1930–), American ballet director.
Kabalevsky, Dmitri (1904–), Russian composer.
Karajan, Herbert von (1908–), Austrian conductor.
Kempff, Wilhelm (1895–), German pianist.
Kern, Jerome (1885–1945), American popular composer.
Khachaturian, Aram (1903–1978), Russian composer.
Kidd, Michael (1919–), American choreographer.
Kiepura, Jan (1902–66), Polish tenor.
Kipnis, Alexander (1891–1978), Russian-American bass.
Kleiber, Erich (1890–1956), Austrian conductor.
Klemperer, Otto (1885–1973), German conductor.
Kodály, Zoltán (1882–1967), Hungarian composer.
Kogan, Leonid (1924–), Russian violinist.
Kondrashin, Kyril (1914–), Russian conductor.
Kostelanetz, André (1901–), Russian-American conductor.
Koussevitzky, Serge (1874–1951), Russian-American conductor.
Kreisler, Fritz (1875–1962), Austrian-American violinst.
Krips, Josef (1902–1974), Austrian conductor.
Kubelik, Rafael (1914–), Czech conductor and composer.
Kunz, Erich (1909–), Austrian singer.
Lalo, Edouard (1823–92), French composer.
Lambert, Constant (1905–51), English composer.
Landowska, Wanda (1877–1959), Polish-French harpsichordist and pianist.
Lehár, Franz (1870–1948), Hungarian composer.
Lehmann, Lilli (1848–1929), German operatic soprano.
Lehmann, Lotte (1888–1976), German-American soprano.
Leinsdorf, Erich (1912–), Austrian-American conductor.
Leoncavallo, Ruggiero (1858–1919), Italian composer.
Lerner, Alan Jay (1918–), American lyricist.
Lewis, Henry (1932–), American conductor.
Lhevinne, Joseph (1874–1944), Russian-American pianist.
Lhevinne, Rosina (1880–1976), Russian-American pianist.
Limón, José (1908–72), Mexican-American choreographer.
Lind, Jenny (1820–87), Swedish soprano.
Liszt, Franz (1811–86), Hungarian composer.
Loewe, Frederick (1904–), Viennese-born American composer.
London, George (1920–), Canadian bass baritone.
Lorengar, Pilar (1931?–), Spanish lyric soprano.
Loring, Eugene (1914–), American choreographer.
Lully, Jean B. (1632–87), French operatic composer.
Lympany, Moura (1916–), English pianist.
Maazel, Lorin (1930–), American conductor.
McBride, Patricia (1942–), American ballerina.
McCormack, John (1884–1945), Irish-American tenor.
McCracken, James (1926–), American dramatic tenor.
MacDowell, Edward (1861–1908), American composer.
Mahler, Gustav (1860–1911), Austrian composer.
Makarova, Natalia (1940–), Russian ballerina.

Markevich, Igor (1912–), Russian-Swiss conductor.
Markova, Dame Alicia (1910–), English ballerina.
Martinelli, Giovanni (1885–1969), Italian-American tenor.
Martinon, Jean (1910–76), French conductor and composer.
Mascagni, Pietro (1863–1945), Italian operatic composer.
Massenet, Jules (1842–1912), French operatic composer.
Massine, Léonide (1896–1979), Russian-American choreographer.
Mehta, Zubin (1936–), Indian conductor.
Melba, Dame Nellie (c. 1859–1931), Australian soprano.
Melchior, Lauritz (1890–1973), Danish heroic tenor.
Mendelssohn, Felix (1809–47), German composer.
Mengelberg, Josef W. (1871–1951), Dutch conductor.
Mennin, Peter (1923–), American composer.
Menotti, Gian-Carlo (1911–), Italian-American composer.
Menuhin, Yehudi (1916–), American violinist.
Merrill, Robert (1919–), American operatic baritone.
Merriman, Nan (1920–), American mezzo-soprano.
Meyerbeer, Giacomo (1791–1864), German composer.
Milanov, Zinka (1906–), Yugoslavian operatic soprano.
Milhaud, Darius (1892–1974), French composer.
Milstein, Nathan (1904–), Russian violinist.
Mitchell, Arthur (1934–), American ballet dancer.
Mitropoulos, Dimitri (1896–1960), Greek-American conductor.
Moffo, Anna (c. 1935–), American soprano.
Moiseiwitsch, Benno (1890–1963), Russian-English pianist.
Moiseyev, Igor (1906–), Russian choreographer.
Monteux, Pierre (1875–1964), French-American conductor.
Monteverdi, Claudio (1567–1643), Italian composer.
Moore, Douglas (1893–1969), American operatic composer.
Moore, Grace (1901–47), American soprano.
Morini, Erica (c. 1905–), Austrian-American violinist.
Moussorgsky, Modest (1839–81), Russian composer.
Mozart, Wolfgang Amadeus (1756–91), Austrian composer.
Münch, Charles (1891–1968), French conductor.
Münchinger, Karl (1915–), German conductor.
Munsel, Patrice (1925–), American operatic soprano.
Muzio, Claudia (1889–1936), Italian operatic soprano.
Neway, Patricia (c. 1923–), American soprano.
Nicolai, Otto (1810–49), German composer.
Nielsen, Carl (1865–1931), Danish composer.
Nijinsky, Vaslav (1890–1950), Russian ballet dancer.
Nikolais, Alwin (1912–), American dancer.
Nilsson, Birgit (1918–), Swedish dramatic soprano.
Novaes, Guiomar (1895–1979), Brazilian pianist.
Nureyev, Rudolf (1938–), Russian ballet dancer.
Offenbach, Jacques (1819–80), French composer.
Oistrakh, David (1908–74), Russian violinist.
Orff, Carl (1895–), German composer.
Ormandy, Eugene (1899–), Hungarian-born American conductor.
Ozawa, Seiji (1935–), Japanese conductor.
Paderewski, Ignace J. (1860–1941), Polish pianist and composer.
Paganini, Niccolò (1782–1840), Italian violinist.
Palestrina, Giovanni P. da (c. 1525–94), Italian composer.
Pavarotti, Luciano (1935–), Italian opera singer.
Pavlova, Anna (c. 1882–1931), Russian ballerina.
Peerce, Jan (1904–), American tenor.
Pergolesi, Giovanni B. (1710–36), Italian composer.
Peters, Roberta (1930–), American coloratura soprano.
Petit, Roland (1924–), French choreographer and dancer.
Piatigorsky, Gregor (1903–76), Ukrainian-American cellist.
Pinza, Ezio (1892–1957), Italian-American basso.
Piston, Walter (1894–1976), American composer.
Pizzetti, Ildebrando (1880–1968), Italian composer.
Plisetskaya, Maya (1925–), Russian ballerina.
Ponchielli, Amilcare (1834–86), Italian composer.
Pons, Lily (1904–76), French-American coloratura soprano.
Ponselle, Rosa (1897–), American operatic soprano.
Porter, Cole (1893–1964), American composer and lyricist.
Poulenc, Francis (1899–1963), French composer.
Previn, André (1929–), German-American conductor.
Price, Leontyne (1927–), American dramatic soprano.
Primrose, William (1904–), Scottish-American violist.
Prokofiev, Sergei (1891–1953), Russian composer.
Puccini, Giacomo (1858–1924), Italian operatic composer.
Purcell, Henry (1659–95), English composer and organist.
Queler, Eve (1936–), American conductor.
Rabin, Michael (1936–1972), American violinist.
Rachmaninoff, Sergei (1873–1943), Russian composer.
Ravel, Maurice (1875–1937), French composer.
Reiner, Fritz (1888–1963), Hungarian-American conductor.
Reisenberg, Nadia (1905–), Russian-American pianist.
Resnik, Regina (1924–), American mezzo-soprano.

Respighi, Ottorino (1879–1936), Italian composer.
Reszke, Edouard de (1853–1917), Polish bass.
Reszke, Jan de (1850–1925), Polish tenor.
Ricci, Ruggiero (1918–), American violinist.
Richter, Sviatoslav (1914–), Russian pianist.
Rimsky-Korsakov, Nikolai (1844–1908), Russian composer.
Robbins, Jerome (1918–), American choreographer.
Robeson, Paul (1898–1976), American bass.
Rodgers, Richard (1902–), American popular composer.
Rodzinski, Artur (1894–1958), Polish-American conductor.
Romberg, Sigmund (1887–1951), Hungarian-American operetta composer.
Rorem, Ned (1923–), American composer.
Rose, Leonard (1918–), American cellist.
Rosenthal, Moriz (1862–1946), Polish pianist.
Rossini, Gioacchino (1792–1868), Italian composer.
Rostropovitch, Mstislav (1927–), Russian cellist.
Roussel, Albert (1869–1937), French composer.
Rózsa, Miklos (1907–), Hungarian-American composer.
Rubinstein, Anton (1829–94), Russian pianist and composer.
Rubinstein, Artur (1886–), Polish-American pianist.
Rysanek, Leonie (1926–), Austrian dramatic soprano.
St. Denis, Ruth (1877?–1968), American dancer.
Saint-Saëns, Camille (1835–1921), French composer.
Sargent, Sir Malcolm (1895–1967), English conductor.
Satie, Erik (1866–1925), French composer.
Scarlatti, Alessandro (c. 1660–1725), Italian composer.
Scarlatti, Domenico (1685–1757), Italian composer.
Scherman, Thomas (1917–79), American conductor.
Schipa, Tito (1889–1965), Italian operatic tenor.
Schippers, Thomas (1930–77), American conductor.
Schmidt-Isserstedt, Hans (1900–1973), German conductor.
Schnabel, Artur (1882–1951), Austrian-American pianist.
Schneider, Alexander (1908–), Russian-American violinist.
Schoenberg, Arnold (1874–1951), Austrian composer.
Schubert, Franz (1797–1828), Austrian composer.
Schuller, Gunther (1925–), American composer.
Schuman, William (1910–), American composer.
Schumann, Clara (1819–96), German pianist and composer.
Schumann, Elisabeth (1885–1952), German soprano.
Schumann, Robert (1810–56), German composer.
Schumann-Heink, Ernestine (1861–1936), Austrian-American contralto.
Schwarzkopf, Elisabeth (1915–), German lyric soprano.
Scotti, Antonio (1866–1936), Italian operatic baritone.
Scotto, Renata (1936–), Italian soprano.
Scriabin, Aleksandr (1872–1915), Russian composer.
Seefried, Irmgard (1919–), German soprano.
Segovia, Andrés (1893–), Spanish guitarist.
Serkin, Rudolph (1903–), Czech-born American pianist.
Sessions, Roger (1896–), American composer.
Shaw, Robert (1916–), American choral conductor.
Shawn, Ted (1891–1972), American dancer.
Shostakovich, Dmitri (1906–1975), Russian composer.
Sibelius, Jean (1865–1957), Finnish composer.
Siepi, Cesare (1923–), Italian operatic bass.
Sills, Beverly (1929–), American coloratura soprano.
Slezak, Leo (1873–1946), Czech tenor.
Smallens, Alexander (1899–1972), Russian-born American conductor.
Smetana, Bedřich (1824–84), Czech composer.
Solomon (1902–), English pianist.
Solti, Georg (1912–), Hungarian conductor.
Somes, Michael (1917–), English ballet dancer.
Sousa, John Philip (1854–1932), American bandmaster and composer.
Sowerby, Leo (1895–1968), American organist.
Spivakovsky, Tossy (1907–), Russian-American violinist.
Steber, Eleanor (1916–), American operatic soprano.
Steinberg, William (1899–1978), German conductor.
Steiner, Max (1888?–1971), Austrian-American composer.
Stern, Isaac (1920–), Russian-born American violinist.
Stevens, Risë (1913–), American mezzo-soprano.

Stich-Randall, Teresa (c. 1928–), American soprano.
Stokowski, Leopold (1882–1977), English-born American conductor.
Straus, Oscar (1870–1954), Austrian operetta composer.
Strauss, Johann (1804–49), Austrian composer.
Strauss, Johann, Jr. (1825–99), Austrian composer.
Strauss, Richard (1864–1949), German composer.
Stravinsky, Igor (1882–1971), Russian composer.
Sullivan, Sir Arthur (1842–1900), English composer.
Sutherland, Joan (1926–), Australian soprano.
Swarthout, Gladys (1904–69), American mezzo-soprano.
Szell, Georg (1897–1970), Hungarian-born American conductor.
Szigeti, Joseph (1892–1973), Hungarian violinist.
Tagliavini, Ferruccio (1913–), Italian lyric tenor.
Tallchief, Maria (1925–), American ballerina.
Tauber, Richard (1892–1948), Austrian tenor.
Taylor, Deems (1885–1966), American music critic.
Taylor, Paul (1930–), American choreographer.
Tchaikovsky, Piotr Ilich (1840–93), Russian composer.
Tebaldi, Renata (1922–), Italian lyric soprano.
Te Kanawa, Kiri (1946–), New Zealand mezzo-soprano.
Telemann, Georg P. (1681–1767), German composer.
Tetley, Glen (1926–), American choreographer.
Tetrazzini, Luisa (1871–1940), Italian coloratura soprano.
Tharp, Twyla (1941–), American choreographer.
Thebom, Blanche (1918–), American mezzo-soprano.
Theodorakis, Mikis (1925–), Greek composer.
Thomas, Ambroise (1811–96), French operatic composer.
Thomas, John Charles (1891–1960), American baritone.
Thomson, Virgil (1896–), American composer and critic.
Tibbett, Lawrence (1896–1960), American baritone.
Toscanini, Arturo (1867–1957), Italian conductor.
Tourel, Jennie (1910–73), Canadian operatic soprano.
Traubel, Helen (1899–1972), American soprano.
Troyanos, Tatiana (1938–), American mezzo-soprano.
Tucker, Richard (c. 1914–75), American dramatic tenor.
Tudor, Antony (1909–), English choreographer.
Tureck, Rosalyn (1914–), American pianist.
Ulanova, Galina (1910–), Russian ballerina.
Varèse, Edgard (1885–1965), French-American composer.
Varnay, Astrid (1918–), Swedish dramatic soprano.
Vaughan Williams, Ralph (1872–1958), English composer.
Verdi, Giuseppe (1813–1901), Italian composer.
Verrett, Shirley (c. 1933–), American mezzo-soprano.
Vickers, Jon (1926–), Canadian operatic tenor.
Villa-Lobos, Heitor (1887–1959), Brazilian composer.
Villella, Edward (1936–), American ballet dancer.
Vishnevskaya, Galina (1926–), Russian soprano.
Vivaldi, Antonio (c. 1675–1741), Italian composer.
von Stade, Frederica (1945–), American mezzo-soprano.
Wagner, Richard (1813–83), German composer.
Walter, Bruno (1876–1962), German-American conductor.
Walton, Sir William (1902–), English composer.
Warren, Leonard (1911–60), American baritone.
Watts, André (1946–), American pianist.
Weber, Carl M. von (1786–1826), German composer.
Webern, Anton von (1883–1945), Austrian composer.
Weidman, Charles (1901–75), American choreographer.
Weill, Kurt (1900–50), German-American composer.
Weingartner, Felix (1863–1942), Austrian conductor.
Weissenberg, Alexis (1929–), French pianist.
Welitsch, Ljuba (1913–), Bulgarian soprano.
Whiteman, Paul (1890–1967), American jazz conductor.
Wilde, Patricia (1928–), Canadian ballerina.
Wolf, Hugo (1860–1903), Austrian composer of lieder.
Wolf-Ferrari, Ermanno (1876–1948), German-Italian operatic composer.
Wunderlich, Fritz (1930–66), German lyric tenor.
Wuorinen, Charles (1938–), American composer.
Youmans, Vincent (1898–1946), American composer.
Youskevitch, Igor (1912–), Russian ballet dancer.
Zimbalist, Efrem (1889–), Russian-American violinist.
Zukerman, Pinchas (1948–), Israeli-American violinist.

FILM DIRECTORS

FRANCE

Allégret, Yves (1907–): The Proud and the Beautiful, Oasis, Germinal.

Becker, Jacques (1906–60): Casque d'Or, Montparnasse 19, The Hole.

Bresson, Robert (1901–): Les Dames du Bois de Boulogne, Pickpocket, The Trial of Joan of Arc.

Camus, Marcel (1912–): Black Orpheus, Le Chant du Monde.

Carné, Marcel (1909–): Quai des Brumes, Les Enfants du Paradis, Terrain Vague.

Cayatte, André (1909–): *Avant de Déluge, Le Passage du Rhin, La Vie Conjugale, La Raison d'état.*

Chabrol, Claude (1930–): *Les Cousins, A Double Tour, Landru, Une Partie de plaisir, Violette Nozière.*

Christian-Jaque (1904–): *La Chartreuse de Parme, Fanfan la Tulipe.*

Clair, René (1898–): *Sous les Toits de Paris, À Nous la Liberté, And Then There Were None.*

Clément, René (1913–): *Forbidden Games, Gervaise, Is Paris Burning?*

Clouzot, Henri-Georges (1907–77): *The Wages of Fear, Diabolique, La Vérité.*

Cocteau, Jean (1889–1963): *The Blood of a Poet, Beauty and the Beast, Orpheus.*

De Broca, Philippe (1933–):*Cartouche, That Man from Rio, King of Hearts.*

Delannoy, Jean (1908–): *La Symphonie Pastorale, La Princesse de Clèves.*

Demy, Jacques (1931–): *Lola, The Umbrellas of Cherbourg.*

Duvivier, Julien (1896–1967): *Poil de Carotte, Un Carnet de Bal, The Little World of Don Camillo.*

Godard, Jean-Luc (1930–): *Breathless, La Chinoise, Weekend.*

Guitry, Sacha (1885–1957): *La Poison, Désiré, Assassins et Voleurs.*

Malle, Louis (1932–): *Les Amants; Viva Maria!; Le Voleur; Lacombe, Lucien, Pretty Baby.*

Marker, Chris (1921–): *Cuba Sí!, Joli Mai.*

Melville, Jean-Pierre (1917–73): *Les Enfants Terribles, Le Doulos.*

Ophuls, Max (1902–57): *La Ronde, Madame De, Lola Montès.*

Pagnol, Marcel (1895–1974): *César, Angèle, Topaze.*

Renoir, Jean (1894–1979): *The Crime of M. Lange, La Grande Illusion, The Diary of a Chambermaid.*

Resnais, Alain (1922–): *Hiroshima, Mon Amour; Last Year at Marienbad; La Guerre Est Finie; Providence.*

Tati, Jacques (1908–): *Jour de Fête, Mr. Hulot's Holiday, Mon Oncle, Traffic.*

Truffaut, François (1932–): *The 400 Blows, Stolen Kisses, Bed and Board, Jules et Jim, The Wild Child, Day for Night, The Story of Adèle H., Small Change.*

Vadim, Roger (1928–): *And God Created Woman, Les Liaisons Dangereuses, Barbarella.*

Varda, Agnes (1928–): *Cléo from 5 to 7, Le Bonheur.*

Vigo, Jean (1905–34): *Zéro de Conduite, L'Atalante.*

GERMANY

Fassbinder, Rainer W. (1946–): *Fox and His Friends, Mother Küsters Goes to Heaven.*

Harlan, Veit (1899–1964): *Kreutzer Sonata, Jew Süss.*

Herzog, Werner (1942–): *Aguirre: the Wrath of God, The Mystery of Kaspar Hauser, Stroszek, Woyzeck.*

Käutner, Helmut (1908–): *The Captain from Kopenick, The Wonderful Years, The Redhead.*

Murnau, Friedrich W. (1899–1931): *Nosferatu, Faust, Sunrise.*

Pabst, Georg W. (1885–1967): *The Joyless Street, Kameradschaft, The Threepenny Opera.*

Riefenstahl, Leni (1902–): *Triumph of the Will, Olympiad 1936.*

GREAT BRITAIN

Anderson, Michael (1920–): *The Naked Edge, The Quiller Memorandum.*

Asquith, Anthony (1902–68): *The Importance of Being Earnest, The Net, The Yellow Rolls-Royce.*

Clayton, Jack (1921–): *Room at the Top, The Innocents, The Great Gatsby.*

Cornelius, Henry (1913–58): *Passport to Pimlico; Genevieve; I Am a Camera.*

Crichton, Charles (1910–): *The Lavender Hill Mob, Battle of the Sexes, The Third Secret.*

Hamer, Robert (1911–63): *Kind Hearts and Coronets, The Scapegoat, School for Scoundrels.*

Lean, David (1908–): *Great Expectations, The Bridge on the River Kwai, Lawrence of Arabia, Dr. Zhivago, Ryan's Daughter.*

Lester, Richard (1932–): *A Hard Day's Night, Help!*

Mackendrick, Alexander (1912–): *The Man in the White Suit, The Ladykillers, The Sweet Smell of Success.*

Olivier, Sir Laurence (1907–): *Henry V, Hamlet, Richard III, Othello.*

Powell, Michael (1905–): *One of Our Aircraft Is Missing, The Red Shoes, Tales of Hoffmann.*

Reed, Sir Carol (1906–76): *Odd Man Out, The Third Man, Oliver!*

Reisz, Karel (1926–): *Saturday Night and Sunday Morning, Morgan, Isadora, The Gambler.*

Richardson, Tony (1928–): *Look Back in Anger, The Entertainer, A Taste of Honey, Tom Jones.*

Schlesinger, John (1926–): *A Kind of Loving, Billy Liar, Darling, Midnight Cowboy, Sunday, Bloody Sunday.*

ITALY

Antonioni, Michelangelo (1912–): *L'Avventura, La Notte, Red Desert, Blow-Up, Zabriskie Point.*

Camerini, Mario (1895–): *I Promessi Sposi, Wife for a Night.*

Comencini, Luigi (1916–): *The Mill on the Po; Bread, Love, and Dreams; Mariti in Citta.*

De Santis, Giuseppe (1917–): *Bitter Rice, Rome Eleven O'Clock, Anna.*

De Sica, Vittorio (1902–74): *The Bicycle Thief, Umberto D, Two Women.*

Fellini, Federico (1920–): *La Strada, Nights of Cabiria, La Dolce Vita, 8½, Fellini Satyricon, Amarcord.*

Germi, Pietro (1914–74): *Divorce, Italian Style; Seduced and Abandoned.*

Monicelli, Mario (1915–): *The Organizer, Casanova 70.*

Pasolini, Pier Paolo (1922–75): *Accattone, Mamma Roma, The Gospel According to St. Matthew, Salo.*

Pontecorvo, Gillo (1919–): *Kapo, The Battle of Algiers.*

Rossellini, Roberto (1906–77): *Open City, Stromboli, Il Generale Della Rovere, The Rise of Louis XIV.*

Visconti, Luchino (1906–76): *Rocco and His Brothers, The Leopard, The Stranger, The Damned, Death in Venice, The Innocent.*

Wertmuller, Lina (1929–): *Swept Away, All Screwed Up, Seven Beauties.*

Zampa, Luigi (1905–): *City on Trial, The Woman of Rome.*

Zeffirelli, Franco (1922–): *The Taming of the Shrew, Romeo and Juliet.*

SWEDEN

Bergman, Ingmar (1918–): *The Seventh Seal, Wild Strawberries, Virgin Spring, Persona, The Passion of Anna, The Magic Flute, Face to Face, Cries and Whispers.*

Sjöberg, Alf (1903–): *Miss Julie, Barabbas, The Judge.*

Sjöström, Victor (1879–1960): *He Who Gets Slapped, The Scarlet Letter.*

Stiller, Mauritz (1883–1928): *The Story of Gösta Berling, Hotel Imperial, The Street of Sin.*

UNITED STATES

Allen, Woody, (1935–), *Annie Hall, Interiors, Manhattan.*

Altman, Robert (1925–): *M*A*S*H, Nashville, Buffalo Bill and the Indians, 3 Women, A Wedding.*

Bogdanovich, Peter (1939–): *Targets, The Last Picture Show, What's Up Doc?, Saint Jack.*

Brooks, Richard (1912–): *The Brothers Karamazov, Cat on a Hot Tin Roof, In Cold Blood, Looking for Mr. Goodbar.*

Capra, Frank (1897–): *It Happened One Night, You Can't Take It with You, A Hole in the Head.*

Cassavetes, John (1929–): *Shadows, A Child Is Waiting, Faces.*

Chaplin, Charles (1889–1977): *The Gold Rush, City Lights, Modern Times, The Great Dictator, Limelight.*

Coppola, Francis Ford (1939–): *The Godfather I & II, The Conversation, Apocalypse Now.*

Cukor, George (1899–): *Dinner at Eight, Camille, The Women, A Star Is Born, My Fair Lady.*

Curtiz, Michael (1888–1962): *Casablanca, Mildred Pierce.*

Dassin, Jules (1911–): *The Naked City, Rififi, He Who Must Die, Never on Sunday.*

De Mille, Cecil B. (1881–1959): *The King of Kings, Samson and Delilah, The Greatest Show on Earth.*

Donen, Stanley (1924–): *Seven Brides for Seven Brothers, Funny Face, Charade, Two for the Road.*

Flaherty, Robert (1884–1951): *Nanook of the North, Moana, Louisiana Story.*

Fleischer, Richard (1916–): *20,000 Leagues under the Sea, Compulsion, The Boston Strangler.*

Fleming, Victor (1883–1949): *Captains Courageous, The Wizard of Oz, Gone with the Wind.*

Ford, John (1895–1973): *Stagecoach, The Grapes of Wrath, The Quiet Man, Mogambo.*

Frankenheimer, John (1930–): *Birdman of Alcatraz, The Manchurian Candidate, Grand Prix, Black Sunday.*

Goulding, Edmund (1891–1959): *Grand Hotel, The Razor's Edge, Nightmare Alley.*

Griffith, D. W. (1875–1948): *The Birth of a Nation, Intolerance, Orphans of the Storm.*

Hawks, Howard (1896–1977): *Scarface, Twentieth Century, Bringing Up Baby, The Big Sleep.*

Hitchcock, Alfred (1899–): *The 39 Steps, Strangers on a Train, Rear Window, North by Northwest, Family Plot.*

Huston, John (1906–): *The Maltese Falcon, The Treasure of the Sierra Madre, The African Queen.*

Kazan, Elia (1909–): *A Streetcar Named Desire, Viva Zapata!, On the Waterfront, East of Eden.*

King, Henry (1891–): *Stella Dallas, State Fair, The Gunfighter.*

Kramer, Stanley (1913–): *Inherit the Wind, Judgment at Nuremberg, Guess Who's Coming to Dinner?*

Kubrick, Stanley (1928–): *Paths of Glory, Lolita, Dr. Strangelove, 2001, Clockwork Orange, Barry Lyndon.*

Le Roy, Mervyn (1900–): *I Am a Fugitive from a Chain Gang, Quo Vadis, Gypsy.*

Lubitsch, Ernst (1892–1947): *The Love Parade, Design for Living, Angel, Ninotchka.*

Lucas, George (1944–): *American Graffiti, Star Wars.*

Lumet, Sidney (1924–): *Long Day's Journey into Night, The Pawnbroker, The Seagull, Murder on the Orient Express, Network, Equus, The Wiz.*

McCarey, Leo (1898–1969): *The Awful Truth, Going My Way, An Affair to Remember.*

Mankiewicz, Joseph L. (1909–): *All About Eve, Julius Caesar, Suddenly Last Summer, Cleopatra.*

Milestone, Lewis (1895–): *All Quiet on the Western Front, Of Mice and Men, A Walk in the Sun.*

Nichols, Mike (1931–): *Who's Afraid of Virginia Woolf?, The Graduate, Catch 22, Carnal Knowledge.*

Peckinpah, Sam (1925–): *The Wild Bunch, Straw Dogs, Junior Bonner.*

Penn, Arthur (1922–): *The Miracle Worker, Mickey One, Bonnie and Clyde, Alice's Restaurant.*

Perry, Frank (1930–): *David and Lisa, Diary of a Mad Housewife, Last Summer.*

Preminger, Otto (1906–): *Laura, The Moon Is Blue, The Man with the Golden Arm, Anatomy of a Murder.*

Ray, Nicholas (1911–79): *Knock on Any Door, Rebel without a Cause, Johnny Guitar, In a Lonely Place.*

Ritt, Martin (1920–): *Edge of the City; The Long, Hot Summer; Hud; The Brotherhood; Sounder; The Front.*

Rossen, Robert (1908–66): *Body and Soul, All the King's Men, The Hustler.*

Scorsese, Martin (1942–): *Mean Streets, Alice Doesn't Live Here Anymore, Taxi Driver, New York, New York, The Last Waltz.*

Silverstein, Elliot (1927–): *Cat Ballou, The Happening, A Man Called Horse.*

Siodmak, Robert (1900–73): *The Spiral Staircase, The Dark Mirror, The Killers.*

Spielberg, Steven (1947–): *The Sugarland Express, Jaws, Close Encounters of the Third Kind.*

Sternberg, Josef von (1894–1969): *The Blue Angel, Morocco, Shanghai Express.*

Stevens, George (1904–75): *A Place in the Sun, Shane, Giant, The Diary of Anne Frank.*

Stroheim, Erich von (1885–1957): *Merry Go Round, Greed, The Merry Widow.*

Sturges, Preston (1898–1959): *The Great McGinty, Sullivan's Travels, Hail the Conquering Hero.*

Vidor, King (1894–): *The Big Parade, Northwest Passage, Duel in the Sun, War and Peace.*

Walsh, Raoul (1892–): *Thief of Bagdad, They Drive by Night, The Naked and the Dead.*

Warhol, Andy (1927?–): *Chelsea Girls, Lonesome Cowboys, Blue Movie.*

Welles, Orson (1915–): *Citizen Kane, The Magnificent Ambersons, Touch of Evil, The Trial.*

Wellman, William (1896–1975): *Nothing Sacred, The Story of G. I. Joe, The High and the Mighty.*

Wilder, Billy (1906–): *The Lost Weekend, Sunset Boulevard, Stalag 17, Some Like It Hot.*

Wood, Sam (1883–1949): *A Night at the Opera; A Day at the Races; Goodbye, Mr. Chips; Our Town.*

Wyler, William (1902–): *Wuthering Heights, Mrs. Miniver, The Best Years of Our Lives, Ben Hur.*

Zinnemann, Fred (1907–): *High Noon, From Here to Eternity, The Nun's Story, A Man for All Seasons.*

USSR

Alexandrov, Grigori (1903–): *Jazz Comedy, Circus, Volga Volga.*

Bondarchuk, Sergei (1922–): *Destiny of a Man, War and Peace, The Steppe.*

Chukrai, Grigori (1921–): *The Forty-First, Ballad of a Soldier, Clear Sky.*

Donskoi, Mark (1897–): *The Maxim Gorki Trilogy, The Rainbow.*

Dovzhenko, Alexander (1894–1956): *Arsenal, Earth, Life in Blossom.*

Eisenstein, Sergei (1898–1948): *Potemkin, Alexander Nevsky, Ivan the Terrible.*

Gerasimov, Sergei (1906–): *Young Guard, And Quiet Flows the Don.*

Kalatosow, Mikhail (1903–1973): *The First Echelon, The Cranes Are Flying.*

Pudovkin, Vsevolod (1893–1953): *Mother, Storm over Asia, The Deserter.*

Pyryev, Ivan (1901–68): *The Wealthy Bride, The Idiot.*

Romm, Mikhail (1901–71): *Boule de Suif, Nine Days of One Year.*

OTHER COUNTRIES

Buñuel, Luis (1900–), Spain: *Evil Eden, Nazarin, Viridiana, Belle de Jour, Las Olvidados, Tristana, The Discrete Charm of the Bourgeoisie.*

Cacoyannis, Michael (1922–), Greece: *Stella, Electra, Zorba the Greek.*

Cavalcanti, Alberto (1897–), Brazil: *Dead of Night, Champagne Charlie, Monster.*

Costa-Gavras, Henri (1933–), Greece: *Z, The Confession.*

Dreyer, Carl Theodore (1889–1968), Denmark: *Joan of Arc, Vampyr, Day of Wrath, Gertrud.*

Fábri, Zoltán (1917–), Hungary: *Professor Hannibal, Twenty Hours, Late Season.*

Ford, Alexander (1908–), Poland: *The Young Chopin, Kings of the Teutonic Order.*

Forman, Milos (1932–), Czechoslovakia: *Loves of a Blonde, The Fireman's Ball, One Flew Over the Cuckoo's Nest, Hair.*

Ivens, Joris (1898–), Netherlands: *Zuyderzee, Spanish Earth.*

Jancso, Miklos (c. 1922–), Hungary: *The Round Up, The Red and the White.*

Kadar, Jan (1918–79), Czechoslovakia: *The Shop on Main Street, The Angel Levine, Adrift, Lies My Father Told Me.*

Kinugasa, Teinosuke (1898–), Japan: *Gate of Hell, The White Heron.*

Kurosawa, Akira (1910–), Japan: *Rashomon, Seven Samurai, Ikiru, The Lower Depths.*

Lang, Fritz (1890–1976), Austria: *Metropolis, M, The 1,000 Eyes of Dr. Mabuse.*

Lindtberg, Leopold (1902–), Switzerland: *The Last Chance, Four in a Jeep, The Village.*

McLaren, Norman (1914–), Canada: *Blinkity-Blank; Dots, Loops.*

Menzel, Jiri (1938–), Czechoslovakia: *Closely Watched Trains, Capricious Summer.*

Mizoguchi, Kenji (1898–1956), Japan: *Ugetsu, The Princess Yang, Street of Shame.*

Nemec, Jan (1936–), Czechoslovakia: *Diamonds of the Night, A Report on the Party and the Guests, The Martyrs of Love.*

Polanski, Roman (1933–), Poland: *Knife in the Water, Repulsion, Rosemary's Baby, Chinatown, The Tenant.*

Ray, Satyajit (1921–), India: *The Apu Trilogy, The Music Room, Devi, The Chess Players.*

Saura, Carlos (1932–), Spain: *The Hunt, Cousin Angelica, Cria!*

Teshigahara, Hiroshi (1927–), Japan: *Pitfall, Woman in the Dunes.*

Torre-Nilsson, Leopoldo (1924–), Argentina: *The House of the Angel, The Hand in the Trap, Summer Skin.*

Wajda, Andrzej (1926–), Poland: *Kanal, Ashes and Diamonds, Fury Is a Woman.*

BIOGRAPHY

CELEBRITIES: PAST AND PRESENT

The Almanac celebrity list includes well-known personalities of stage, screen, radio, and television, as well as notables of other popular worlds. Entries indicate the celebrity's birthplace.

Aaron, Hank Mobile, Ala., 1934
Abbott, George Forestville, N.Y. 1887
Abel, Walter St. Paul, Minn., 1898
Ace, Goodman Kansas City, Mo., 1899
Acuff, Roy Maynardsville, Tenn., 1907
Adams, Don New York City, 1927
Adams, Edie Kingston, Pa., 1929
Adams, Joey New York City, 1911
Adams, Julie Waterloo, Iowa, 1928
Addams, Charles Westfield, N. J., 1912
Addams, Dawn Felixstowe, Eng., 1930
Adderley, Cannonball Tampa, 1928-75
Adjani, Isabelle Paris, 1956
Adler, Larry Baltimore, 1914
Adler, Luther New York City, 1903
Adler, Stella New York City, 1902
Alberghetti, Anna Maria Pesaro, Italy, 1936
Albert, Eddie Rock Island, Ill., 1908
Albertson, Jack Malden, Mass., 1910
Albright, Lola Akron, O., 1925
Alda, Alan New York City, 1936
Alda, Robert New York City, 1914
Alexander, Ben Goldfield, Nev., 1911-69
Allen, Dick Chewton, Pa., 1942
Allen, Fred Boston, 1894-1956
Allen, Gracie San Francisco, 1906-64
Allen, Mel Birmingham, Ala., 1913
Allen, Steve New York City, 1921
Allen, Woody New York City, 1935
Allison, Fran La Porte City, Iowa, 1924?
Allyson, June New York City, 1923
Alpert, Herb Los Angeles, 1935
Ameche, Don Kenosha, Wis., 1908
Ames, Ed Boston, 1929
Ames, Leon Portland, Ind., 1903
Ames, Nancy Washington, D. C., 1937
Amory, Cleveland Nahant, Mass., 1917
Amsterdam, Morey Chicago, 1912
Anderson, Judith Adelaide, Austral., 1898
Anderson, Michael, Jr. London, 1943
Andersson, Bibi Stockholm, 1935
Andersson, Harriet Stockholm, 1932
Andress, Ursula, Berne, Switz., 1936
Andretti, Mario Trieste, 1940
Andrews, Dana Collins, Miss., 1912
Andrews, Julie Walton-on-Thames, Eng., 1935
Andrews, LaVerne Minneapolis, 1915–67
Andrews, Maxine Minneapolis, 1918
Andrews, Patty Minneapolis, 1920
Angeli, Pier Sardinia, 1932-71
Anka, Paul Ottawa, Can., 1941
Annabella La Varenne-St. Hilaire, Fr., 1910
Ann-Margret Valsjobyn, Sweden, 1941
Arbuckle, "Fatty" Smith Center, Kans., 1887-1933
Arcaro, Eddie Newport, Ky., 1916
Arden, Elizabeth Ontario, 1891-1966
Arden, Eve Mill Valley, Cal., 1912
Arkin, Alan New York City, 1934
Armstrong, Louis New Orleans, 1900-71
Arnaz, Desi Santiago, Cuba, 1917
Arness, James Minneapolis, 1923
Arno, Peter New York, 1904-68
Arnold, Eddy Henderson, Tenn., 1918
Arnold, Edward New York, 1890-1956
Arquette, Cliff Toledo, O., 1905-74
Arthur, Beatrice New York, 1926
Arthur, Jean New York City, 1908
Ashcroft, Peggy London, 1907
Ashe, Arthur Richmond, Va., 1943
Ashley, Elizabeth Ocala, Fla., 1940
Asner, Edward Kansas City, Kans., 1929
Astaire, Adele Omaha, Neb., 1898
Astaire, Fred Omaha, Neb., 1899
Astor, Mary Quincy, Ill., 1906
Atkins, Chet Luttrell, Tenn., 1924
Attenborough, Richard Cambridge, Eng., 1923
Aumont, Jean-Pierre Paris, 1913
Austin, Tracy Palos Verdes, Cal., 1962
Autry, Gene Tioga, Tex., 1907
Avalon, Frankie Philadelphia, 1940
Avedon, Richard New York City, 1923
Ayres, Lew Minneapolis, 1908

Aznavour, Charles Paris, 1924
Bacall, Lauren New York City, 1924
Baccaloni, Salvatore Rome, 1900-69
Bacharach, Burt Kansas City, Mo., 1929
Backe, John Akron, O., 1932
Backus, Jim Cleveland, 1913
Baer, Max Omaha, 1909-59
Baez, Joan New York City, 1941
Bailey, Mildred Washington, 1903-51
Bailey, Pearl Newport News, Va., 1918
Bainter, Fay Los Angeles, 1893-1963
Baird, Bil Grand Island, Neb., 1904
Baker, Carroll Johnstown, Pa., 1935
Baker, Diane Hollywood, Cal., 1940?
Baker, Josephine St. Louis, 1906-75
Baker, Kenny Monrovia, Cal., 1912
Balenciaga, Cristobal Guetaria, Sp., 1895-1972
Ball, Lucille Jamestown, N. Y., 1911
Ballard, Kaye Cleveland, 1926
Balmain, Pierre St.-Jean-de-Maurienne, Fr., 1914
Balsam, Martin New York City, 1919
Bancroft, Anne New York City, 1931
Bankhead, Tallulah Huntsville, Ala., 1903-68
Bara, Theda Cincinnati, 1890-1955
Barber, Red Columbus, Miss., 1908
Bardot, Brigitte Paris, 1934
Barker, Lex Rye, N. Y., 1919-73
Barnes, Binnie London, 1906
Barrault, Jean-Louis Vesinet, Fr., 1910
Barrie, Wendy London, 1913–78
Barry, Gene New York City, 1921
Barrymore, Diana New York, 1922-60
Barrymore, Ethel Phila., 1879-1959
Barrymore, John Phila., 1882-1942
Barrymore, John Blyth Beverly Hills, Cal., 1932
Barrymore, Lionel Phila. 1878-1954
Barthelmess, Richard New York, 1895-1963
Bartholomew, Freddie London, 1924
Bartok, Eva Budapest, 1926
Basehart, Richard Zanesville, O., 1914
Basie, Count Red Bank, N. J., 1904
Bass, Alfie London, 1921
Bassey, Shirley Cardiff, Wales, 1937
Bates, Alan Allestree, Eng., 1934
Baxter, Anne Michigan City, Ind., 1923
Baxter, Warner Columbus, O., 1893-1951
Bean, Orson Burlington, Vt., 1928
Beaton, Cecil London, 1904
Beatty, Clyde Bainbridge, O., 1905-65
Beatty, Warren Richmond, Va., 1938
Bechet, Sidney New Orleans, 1897-1959
Beene, Geoffrey Haynesville, La., 1927
Beery, Noah Kansas City, Mo., 1883-1946
Beery, Noah, Jr., New York City, 1916
Beery, Wallace Kansas City, Mo., 1886-1949
Begley, Ed Hartford, Conn., 1901-70
Belafonte, Harry New York City, 1927
Belasco, David San Francisco, 1854-1931
Bel Geddes, Barbara New York, 1922
Bel Geddes, Norman Adrian, Mich., 1893-1958
Bellamy, Ralph Chicago, 1904
Belmondo, Jean-Paul Neuilly-sur-Seine, Fr., 1933
Belushi, John Chicago, 1949
Benchley, Robert Worcester, Mass., 1889-1945
Bendix, William New York, 1906-64
Benjamin, Richard New York City, 1939
Bennett, Constance New York, 1914-65
Bennett, Joan Palisades, N. J., 1910
Bennett, Richard Indiana, 1873-1944
Bennett, Tony New York City, 1926
Benny, Jack Waukegan, Ill. 1894-1974
Benzell, Mimi Bridgeport, Conn., 1924-70
Berg, Gertrude New York, 1900-66
Bergen, Candice Beverly Hills, Cal., 1946

Bergen, Edgar Chicago, 1903-78
Bergen, Polly Knoxville, Tenn., 1930
Berger, Senta Vienna, 1941
Bergerac, Jacques Biarritz, Fr., 1927
Bergman, Ingrid Stockholm, 1917
Bergner, Elisabeth Vienna, 1900
Berkeley, Busby Los Angeles, 1895-1976
Berle, Milton New York City, 1908
Berlin, Irving Russia, 1888
Berman, Pandro S. Pittsburgh, 1905
Berman, Shelley Chicago, 1926
Bernardi, Herschel New York City, 1923
Bernhardt, Sarah Paris, 1844-1923
Bernie, Ben Bayonne, N.J., 1893-1943
Bickford, Charles Cambridge, Mass., 1889-1967
Bikel, Theodore Vienna, 1924
Birney, David Washington, 1940
Bishop, Joey New York City, 1918
Bissell, Richard Dubuque, Iowa, 1913-77
Bisset, Jacqueline Weybridge, Eng., 1944
Black, Karen Park Ridge, Ill., 1942
Blackman, Honor London, 1929
Blackmer, Sidney Salisbury, N. C., 1898-1973
Blaine, Vivian Newark, N. J., 1924
Blair, Janet Altoona, Pa., 1921
Blair, Linda Westport, Conn., 1959
Blake, Robert Nutley, N.J., 1938
Blakeley, Ronee Idaho, 1946
Blass, Bill Fort Wayne, Ind., 1922
Blocker, Dan Bowie Co., Tex., 1929-72
Blondell, Joan New York City, 1912
Bloom, Claire London, 1931
Blue, Ben Montreal, 1901-75
Blue, Vida Mansfield, La., 1949
Blyth, Ann New York City, 1928
Bogarde, Dirk London, 1921
Bogart, Humphrey New York, 1899-1957
Boland, Mary Phila., 1885-1965
Bolger, Ray Dorchester, Mass., 1904
Bond, Sheila New York City, 1928
Bond, Ward Denver, 1904-60
Bono, Sonny Detroit, 1940
Boone, Pat Jacksonville, Fla., 1934
Boone, Richard Los Angeles, 1917
Booth, Shirley New York City, 1909
Borge, Victor Copenhagen, 1909
Borgnine, Ernest Hamden, Conn., 1917
Bosley, Tom Chicago, 1927
Bourke-White, Margaret New York City, 1906-71
Bow, Clara New York, 1905-65
Bowes, "Major" San Francisco, 1874-1946
Bowie, David Brixton, Eng., 1947
Bowman, Lee Cincinnati, 1914
Boyd, Stephen Belfast, Northern Ireland, 1928-77
Boyd, William Cambridge, O., 1898-1972
Boyer, Charles Figeac Lot, Fr., 1899–1978
Bracken, Eddie New York City, 1920
Bradshaw, Terry Shreveport, La., 1948
Brady, Alice New York, 1892-1939
Brady, Scott New York City, 1924
Brand, Neville Kewanee, Ill., 1921
Brando, Marlon Omaha, Neb., 1924
Brasselle, Keefe Lorain, O., 1923
Brazzi, Rossano Bologna, Italy, 1916
Brel, Jacques Brussels, 1929-78
Brennan, Walter Lynn, Mass., 1894-1974
Brenner, David Philadelphia, 1945
Brent, George Dublin, 1904-79
Brewer, Teresa Toledo, O., 1931
Brice, Fanny New York, 1891-1951
Bridges, Lloyd San Leandro, Cal., 1913
Brinkley, David Wilmington, N. C., 1920
Brisson, Frederick Copenhagen, 1917
Britt, Mai Lidingo, Swed., 1936
Brock, Lou El Dorado, Ark., 1939
Broderick, Helen Phila., 1890-1959
Bronson, Charles, Ehrenfeld, Pa., 1922
Brooks, Donald New York City, 1928
Brooks, Geraldine New York, 1925-77
Brooks, Mel New York City, 1926
Brothers, Joyce New York City, 1928

Broun, Heywood New York, 1888-1939
Broun, Heywood Hale New York, 1918
Brown, Georgia London, 1933
Brown, Helen Gurley Portland, Me., 1922
Brown, James Augusta, Ga., 1930?
Brown, Jim Manhasset, N. Y., 1936
Brown, Joe E. Holgate, O., 1892-1973
Brown, Vanessa Vienna, 1928
Brubeck, Dave Concord, Cal., 1920
Bruce, Carol Great Neck, N. Y., 1919
Bruce, Nigel Mexico, 1895-1953
Bruce, Virginia Minneapolis, 1910
Bryant, Anita Barnsdall, Okla., 1940
Brynner, Yul Sakhalin, 1917
Buchanan, Edgar Humansville, Mo., 1903-79
Buchanan, Jack Scotland, 1891-1957
Buchholz, Horst Berlin, 1933
Buchwald, Art Mount Vernon, N. Y., 1925
Buckley, William F. New York City, 1925
Bujold, Genevieve Montreal, 1942
Burke, Billie Washington, D.C., 1884-1970
Burnett, Carol Dallas, 1934
Burns, George New York City, 1896
Burr, Raymond New Westminster, Can., 1917
Burrows, Abe New York City, 1910
Burstyn, Ellen Detroit, Mich., 1932
Burton, Richard Pontrhydyfen, Wales, 1925
Busch, August A., Jr. St. Louis, 1899
Bushman, Francis X. Norfolk, 1883-1966
Butterworth, Charles South Bend, Ind., 1897-1946
Buttons, Red New York City, 1919
Buzzi, Ruth Westerly, R. I., 1936
Byington, Spring, Colorado Springs, 1893-1971
Byrd, Charlie Chuckatuck, Va., 1925
Caan, James New York City, 1939
Cabot, Sebastian London, 1918-77
Cabot, Susan Boston, 1927
Caen, Herb Sacramento, Cal., 1916
Caesar, Irving New York City, 1895
Caesar, Sid Yonkers, N. Y., 1922
Cagney, James New York City, 1904
Cahn, Sammy New York City, 1913
Caine, Michael London, 1933
Caldwell, Zoë Melbourne, Austral., 1933
Calhern, Louis New York, 1895-1956
Calhoun, Rory Los Angeles, 1923
Callan, Michael Philadelphia, 1935
Calloway, Cab Rochester, N. Y., 1907
Cambridge, Godfrey New York, 1933-76
Cameron, Rod Calgary, Can., 1912
Campbell, Glen near Delight, Ark., 1938
Campbell, Mrs. Patrick London, 1865-1940
Cannon, Dyan Tacoma, Wash., 1938?
Canova, Judy Jacksonville, Fla., 1916
Cantinflas Mexico City, 1911
Cantor, Eddie New York, 1892-1964
Cantrell, Lana Sydney, Austral., 1944
Capp, Al New Haven, Conn., 1909
Capucine Toulon, Fr., 1935?
Cardin, Pierre near Venice, 1922
Cardinale, Claudia Tunis, 1940
Carew, Rod Gatun, C.Z., 1945
Carey, Macdonald Sioux City, Iowa, 1913
Carlin, George New York City, 1938
Carlisle, Kitty New Orleans, 1914
Carmichael, Hoagy Bloomington, Ind., 1899
Carmines, Al Hampton, Va., 1937
Carne, Judy Northampton, Eng., 1939
Carney, Art Mt. Vernon, N. Y., 1918
Carnovsky, Morris St. Louis, 1897
Carol, Martine Paris, 1920-67
Caron, Leslie Paris, 1931
Carr, Vikki El Paso, Tex., 1942
Carradine, John New York City, 1906
Carrillo, Leo Los Angeles, 1881-1961
Carroll, Diahann New York City, 1935
Carroll, Earl Pittsburgh, 1893-1948
Carroll, Leo G. Weedon, Eng., 1892-1972
Carroll, Madeleine West Bromwich, Eng., 1906
Carroll, Nancy New York, 1906-65
Carroll, Pat Shreveport, La., 1927

Carson, Jack Carman, Can., 1910-63
Carson, Johnny Corning, Iowa, 1925
Carter, Billy Plains, Ga., 1937
Carter, Jack New York City, 1923
Cash, Johnny Kingsland, Ark., 1932
Cass, Peggy Boston, 1925
Cassavetes, John New York, 1929
Cassidy, Jack New York City, 1927-76
Cassini, Oleg Paris, 1913
Castle, Irene New Rochelle, N.Y., 1893-1969
Cauthen, Steve Covington, Ky., 1960
Cavett, Dick Gibbon, Neb., 1936
Cerf, Bennett New York City, 1898-1971
Chakiris, George Norwood, O., 1933
Chamberlain, Richard Beverly Hills, Cal., 1935
Chamberlain, Wilt Philadelphia, 1936
Champion, Gower Geneva, Ill., 1921
Champion, Marge Hollywood, Cal., 1925
Chancellor, John Chicago, 1927
Chandler, Jeff New York, 1918-61
Chanel, "Coco" Issoire, Fr., 1883-1971
Chaney, Lon Colorado Springs, 1883-1930
Chaney, Lon, Jr. Oklahoma City, 1915-73
Channing, Carol Seattle, 1921
Chaplin, Charles London, 1889–1977
Chaplin, Geraldine Santa Monica, Cal. 1944
Chaplin, Sydney Los Angeles, 1926
Charisse, Cyd Amarillo, Tex., 1923
Charles, Ray Albany, Ga., 1932
Chase, Chevy New York City, 1943
Chase, Ilka New York City, 1905–78
Chatterton, Ruth New York, 1893-1961
Chekhov, Michael Russia, 1891-1955
Cher El Centro, Cal., 1946
Chevalier, Maurice Paris, 1888-1972
Child, Julia Pasadena, Cal., 1912
Christian, Linda Tampico, Mexico, 1923
Christie, Julie Chukua, India, 1941
Christopher, Jordan Akron, O., 1941
Cilento, Diane Brisbane, Austral., 1933
Claire, Ina Washington, D. C., 1895
Clark, Bobby Springfield, O., 1888-1960
Clark, Dane New York City, 1915
Clark, Dick Mt. Vernon, N. Y., 1929
Clark, Fred Lincoln, Cal., 1914-68
Clark, Petula Ewell, Eng., 1932
Clark, Roy Meherrin, Va., 1933
Clayburgh, Jill New York City, 1944
Clift, Montgomery Omaha, 1920-66
Clooney, Rosemary Maysville, Ky., 1928
Cobb, Irvin S. Paducah, Ky., 1876-1944
Cobb, Lee J. New York City, 1911-76
Coburn, Charles Macon, Ga., 1877-1961
Coburn, James Laurel, Neb., 1928
Coca, Imogene, Philadelphia, 1908
Coco, James New York City, 1929
Cohan, George M. Providence, R.I., 1878-1942
Cohen, Myron Grodno, Poland, 1902
Colbert, Claudette Paris, 1905
Colby, Anita Washington, D. C., 1914
Cole, Nat "King" Montgomery, Ala., 1919-65
Coleman, Ornette Fort Worth, Tex., 1930
Collingwood, Charles Three Rivers, Mich., 1917
Collins, Dorothy Windsor, Can., 1926
Collins, Joan London, 1933
Collins, Judy Seattle, 1939
Collyer, "Bud" New York, 1908-69
Colman, Ronald Richmond, Eng., 1891-1959
Colonna, Jerry Boston, 1905
Comaneci, Nadia Onesti, Romania, 1961
Comden, Betty New York City, 1919
Como, Perry Canonsburg, Pa., 1913
Condon, Eddie Goodland, Ind., 1905-73
Conklin, Peggy Dobbs Ferry, N. Y., 1912
Connelly, Marc McKeesport, Pa., 1890
Connery, Sean Edinburgh, 1930
Connolly, Walter Cincinnati, 1887-1940
Connors, Chuck New York City, 1921
Connors, Jimmy St. Louis, 1952
Connors, Mike Fresno, Cal., 1925
Conrad, William Louisville, Ky., 1920

Conried, Hans Baltimore, 1917
Conte, Richard New York City 1914-75
Conway, Tom Russia, 1904-67
Coogan, Jackie Los Angeles, 1914
Cook, Joe Chicago, 1890-1959
Cooke, Alistair Manchester, Eng., 1908
Cooney, Joan Ganz Phoenix, 1929
Cooper, Alice Phoenix, 1948
Cooper, Gary Helena, Mont., 1901-61
Cooper, Gladys Lewisham, Eng., 1888-1971
Cooper, Jackie Los Angeles, 1922
Coote, Robert London, 1909
Corey, Wendell Dracut, Mass., 1914-68
Corio, Ann Hartford, Conn., 1914?
Cornell, Katharine Berlin, 1898-1974
Cosby, Bill Philadelphia, 1937
Cosell, Howard Winston-Salem, N.C., 1920
Costello, Lou Paterson, N.J., 1906-59
Cotten, Joseph Petersburg, Va., 1905
Coulouris, George Manchester, Eng., 1903
Courrèges, André Pau, Fr., 1923
Courtenay, Tom Hull, Eng., 1937
Cousins, Norman Union Hill, N. J., 1912
Cousteau, Jacques Yves St. André-de-Cubzac, Fr., 1910
Cox, Wally Detroit, 1924-73
Crabbe, Buster Oakland, Cal., 1909
Crain, Jeanne Barstow, Cal., 1925
Craven, Frank Boston, 1878-1948
Crawford, Broderick Philadelphia, 1911
Crawford, Joan San Antonio, 1908-77
Cregar, Laird Phila., 1916-44
Crenna, Richard Los Angeles, 1927
Croce, Jim Philadelphia, Pa., 1943-73
Cronkite, Walter St. Joseph, Mo., 1916
Cronyn, Hume London, Can., 1911
Crosby, Bing Tacoma, Wash., 1904–77
Crosby, Bob Spokane, Wash., 1913
Crouse, Russel Findlay, O., 1893-1966
Csonka, Larry Stow, O., 1946
Cugat, Xavier Barcelona, 1900
Cukor, George New York City, 1899
Cullen, Bill Pittsburgh, 1920
Culp, Robert Berkeley, Cal., 1930
Cummings, Robert Joplin, Mo., 1910
Curtis, Tony New York City, 1925
Curtiz, Michael Budapest, 1888-1962
Dahl, Arlene Minneapolis, 1927
Dailey, Dan New York City, 1915-78
Daly, John Johannesburg, South Africa, 1914
Damone, Vic New York City, 1928
Dana, Bill Quincy, Mass., 1924
Dandridge, Dorothy Cleveland, 1924-65
Daniels, Bebe Dallas, 1901-71
Daniels, Billy Jacksonville, Fla., 1914?
Danton, Ray New York City, 1931
Darcel, Denise Paris, 1925
Darin, Bobby New York City, 1936-73
Darnell, Linda Dallas, 1921-65
Darren, James Philadelphia, 1936
Darrieux, Danielle Bordeaux, Fr., 1917
Darvas, Lilli Budapest, 1906-74
Darvi, Bella Sosnowiec, Poland, 1928
Darwell, Jane Palmyra, Mo., 1880-1967
da Silva, Howard Cleveland, 1909
Dauphin, Claude Corbeil, Fr., 1903-78
Davenport, Harry New York 1866-1949
Davenport, Nigel Cambridge, Eng., 1928
Davidson, John Pittsburgh, Pa., 1941
Davies, Marion New York, 1897-1961
Davis, Bette Lowell, Mass., 1908
Davis, Joan St. Paul, Minn., 1908-61
Davis, Mac Lubbock, Tex., 1942
Davis, Meyer Ellicott City, Md., 1895-1976
Davis, Miles Alton, Ill., 1927
Davis, Ossie Cogdell, Ga., 1921
Davis, Sammy, Jr. New York City, 1925
Day, Dennis New York City, 1917
Day, Doris Cincinnati, 1924
Day, Laraine Roosevelt, Utah, 1920
Dean, Dizzy Lucas, Ark., 1911-74
Dean, James Fairmount, Ind., 1931-55
DeCamp, Rosemary Prescott, Ariz., 1914
De Carlo, Yvonne Vancouver, Can., 1924
Dee, Frances Los Angeles, 1907
Dee, Ruby Cleveland, 1923?
Dee, Sandra Bayonne, N. J., 1942

De Fore, Don Cedar Rapids, Iowa, 1916
De Haven, Gloria Los Angeles, 1925
de Havilland, Olivia Tokyo, 1916
Dekker, Albert New York, 1905-68
De Laurentiis, Dino Torre Annunziata, Italy, 1919
Delon, Alain Scéaux, Fr., 1935
Del Rio, Dolores Durango, Mex., 1905
DeLuise, Dom Brooklyn, N.Y., 1933
Demarest, William St. Paul, 1892
De Mille, Cecil B. Ashfield, Mass., 1881-1959
Dempsey, Jack Manassa, Colo., 1895
Deneuve, Catherine Paris, 1943
De Niro, Robert New York City, 1943
Dennis, Sandy Hastings, Neb., 1937
Denny, Reginald Richmond, Eng., 1891-1967
Denver, John Roswell, N.M., 1943
Dern, Bruce Chicago, 1936
Desmond, Johnny Detroit, 1921
Devine, Andy Flagstaff, Ariz., 1905-77
Dewhurst, Colleen Montreal, 1926
de Wilde, Brandon New York, 1942-72
De Wolfe, Billy Wollaston, Mass. 1907-74
Diamond, Neil Brooklyn, N.Y., 1941
Dickinson, Angie Kulm, N. D., 1931
Dietrich, Marlene Berlin, 1904
Dietz, Howard New York City, 1896
Diller, Phyllis Lima, O., 1917
Dillman, Bradford San Francisco, 1930
Di Maggio, Joe San Francisco, 1914
Dior, Christian Granville, Fr., 1905-57
Disney, Walt Chicago, 1901-66
Dixon, Jeane Medford, Wis., 1918
Dolly, Jenny Hungary, 1892-1941
Dolly, Rosie Hungary, 1892-1970
Donahue, Troy New York City, 1937
Donat, Robert Manchester, Eng., 1905-59
Donlevy, Brian Portadown, Ire., 1899-1972
Donovan (Leitch) Glasgow, 1946
Dors, Diana Swindon, Eng., 1931
Dorsey, Jimmy Mahonoy Plane, Pa., 1904-57
Dorsey, Tommy Mahonoy Plane, Pa., 1905-56
Douglas, Jack New York City, 1908
Douglas, Kirk Amsterdam, N. Y., 1918?
Douglas, Melvyn Macon, Ga., 1901
Douglas, Michael New Brunswick, N.J., 1944
Douglas, Mike Chicago, 1925
Douglas, Paul Phila., 1907-59
Downs, Hugh Akron, O., 1921
Drake, Alfred New York City, 1914
Drake, Betsy Paris, 1923
Draper, Paul Florence, Italy, 1909
Draper, Ruth New York, 1884-1956
Dressler, Marie Canada, 1869-1933
Dreyfuss, Richard New York City, 1947
Dru, Joanne Logan, W. Va., 1923
Duchin, Eddy Boston, 1909-51
Duchin, Peter New York City, 1937
Duff, Howard Bremerton, Wash., 1917
Duke, Doris New York City, 1912
Duke, Patty New York City, 1946
Dullea, Keir Cleveland, 1939
Dunaway, Faye Tallahassee, Fla., 1941
Duncan, Sandy Henderson, Tex., 1946
Dunn, James New York, 1906-67
Dunne, Irene Louisville, Ky., 1904
Dunnock, Mildred Baltimore, 1906
Durante, Jimmy New York City, 1893
Durbin, Deanna Winnipeg, Can., 1922
Durocher, Leo West Springfield, Mass., 1906
Duryea, Dan White Plains, N.Y., 1907-68
Duse, Eleanora Italy, 1858-1924
Duvall, Robert San Diego, Cal., 1931
Dylan, Bob Duluth, Minn., 1941
Eagels, Jeanne Kansas City, Mo., 1894-1929
Eastwood, Clint San Francisco, 1933
Ebsen, Buddy Orlando, Fla., 1908
Eddy, Nelson Providence, R.I., 1901-67
Eden, Barbara San Francisco, 1936
Edwards, Ralph Merino, Colo., 1913
Edwards, Vince New York City, 1928
Egan, Richard San Francisco, 1923

Eggar, Samantha London, 1940
Ekberg, Anita Malmö, Swed., 1931
Eldridge, Florence New York City, 1901
Elliot, Cass Arlington, Va., 1943?-74
Elliott, Bob Boston, 1923
Elliott, Maxine Rockland, Me., 1868-1940
Emerson, Faye Elizabeth, N. J., 1917
Erickson, Leif Alameda, Cal., 1914
Erving, Julius Roosevelt, N.Y., 1950
Erwin, Stuart Squaw Valley, Cal., 1903-67
Esposito, Phil Sault Ste. Marie, Ont., 1942
Evans, Bergen Franklin, O., 1904-78
Evans, Dale Uvalde, Tex., 1912
Evans, Madge New York City, 1909
Evans, Maurice Dorchester, Eng., 1901
Evert-Lloyd, Chris Fort Lauderdale, Fla., 1954
Ewell, Tom Owensboro, Ky., 1909
Fabray, Nanette San Diego, Cal., 1920
Fadiman, Clifton New York City, 1904
Fairbanks, Douglas Denver, 1883-1939
Fairbanks, Douglas, Jr. New York, 1909
Faith, Percy Toronto, 1908-76
Falk, Peter New York City, 1927
Farber, Barry Baltimore, 1930
Farrell, Glenda Enid, Okla., 1904-71
Farrow, Mia Los Angeles, 1945
Faulk, John Henry Austin, Tex., 1913
Fawcett-Majors, Farrah Corpus Christi, Tex., 1947
Fay, Frank San Francisco, 1897-1961
Faye, Alice New York City, 1915
Feiffer, Jules New York City, 1929
Feldman, Marty London, 1933
Feldon, Barbara Pittsburgh, 1939
Feliciano, José Larez, P. R., 1945
Feller, Bob Van Meter, Iowa, 1918
Fernandel Marseilles, 1903-71
Ferrer, José Santurce, P. R., 1912
Ferrer, Mel Elberon, N. J., 1917
Fidrych, Mark Northboro, Mass., 1955
Field, Betty Boston, 1918-73
Fields, Dorothy Allenhurst, N. J., 1905
Fields, Gracie Rochdale, Eng., 1898
Fields, Totie Hartford, Conn., 1931-78
Fields, W. C. Phila., 1879-1946
Finch, Peter London, 1916-77
Finney, Albert Salford, Eng., 1936
Fischer, Bobby Chicago, 1943
Fisher, Eddie Philadelphia, 1928
Fitzgerald, Barry Dublin, 1888-1961
Fitzgerald, Ella Newport News, Va., 1918
Fitzgerald, Geraldine Dublin, 1914
Flack, Roberta Black Mountain, N. C., 1940
Fleming, Rhonda Los Angeles, 1923
Fletcher, Louise Birmingham, Ala., 1934
Flynn, Errol Tasmania, 1909-59
Foch, Nina Leyden, Neth., 1924
Fonda, Henry Grand Island, Neb., 1905
Fonda, Jane New York City, 1937
Fonda, Peter New York City, 1939
Fontaine, Frank Haverhill, Mass., 1920-78
Fontaine, Joan Tokyo, 1917
Fontanne, Lynn Woodford, Eng., 1887?
Ford, Glenn Quebec, 1916
Ford, Tennessee Ernie Bristol, Tenn., 1919
Forsythe, John Penns Grove, N. J., 1918
Fosse, Bob Chicago, 1927
Foster, Jodie Los Angeles, 1962
Foxx, Redd St. Louis, 1922
Foy, Eddie, Jr. New Rochelle,N.Y., 1910
Frampton, Peter Beckenham, Eng., 1950
Franciosa, Anthony New York City, 1928
Francis, Arlene Boston, 1908
Francis, Connie Newark, N. J., 1938
Francis, Kay Oklahoma City, 1905-68
Franklin, Aretha Memphis, Tenn., 1942
Frazier, Walt Atlanta, 1945
Freberg, Stan Pasadena, Cal., 1926
Freed, Arthur Charleston, S. C., 1894
Friedan, Betty Peoria, Ill., 1921
Friendly, Fred W. New York City, 1915
Fröbe, Gert Planitz, Ger., 1913
Froman, Jane St. Louis, 1911
Frost, David Tenterden, Eng., 1939
Funt, Allen New York City, 1914

Furness, Betty New York City, 1916
Gabel, Martin Philadelphia, 1912
Gable, Clark Cadiz, O., 1901-60
Gabor, Eva Budapest, 1926?
Gabor, Zsa Zsa Budapest, 1923?
Gallico, Paul New York City, 1897-1976
Gam, Rita Pittsburgh, 1928
Garagiola, Joe St. Louis, 1926
Garbo, Greta Stockholm, 1906
Gardiner, Reginald Wimbledon, Eng., 1903
Gardner, Ava Smithfield, N. C., 1922
Garfield, John New York, 1913-52
Garfunkel, Arthur New York City, 1941
Gargan, William, New York City, 1905-79
Garland, Judy Grand Rapids, Minn., 1922-69
Garner, Erroll Pittsburgh, 1921-77
Garner, James Norman, Okla., 1928
Garner, Peggy Ann Canton, O., 1932
Garroway, Dave Schenectady, N.Y., 1913
Garson, Greer County Down, Northern Ireland, 1908
Gassman, Vittorio Genoa, Italy, 1922
Gavin, John Los Angeles, 1928
Gaxton, William San Francisco, 1893-1963
Gaynor, Janet Philadelphia, 1906
Gaynor, Mitzi Chicago, 1931
Gazzara, Ben New York City, 1930
Geer, Will Frankfort, Ind., 1902-78
Genn, Leo London, 1905-78
Gentry, Bobbie Chickasaw Co., Miss., 1944
George, Gladys Patten, Me., 1904-54
George, Grace New York, 1879-1961
Gernreich, Rudi Vienna, 1922
Gershwin, George New York, 1898-1937
Gershwin, Ira New York City, 1896
Gerulaitis, Vitas Brooklyn, 1954
Getty, J. Paul Minneapolis, 1892-1976
Getz, Stan Philadelphia, 1927
Ghostley, Alice Eve, Mo., 1926
Giannini, Giancario La Spezia, Italy, 1942
Gibbs, Georgia Worcester, Mass., 1923?
Gielgud, John London, 1904
Gilbert, Billy Louisville, Ky., 1894-1971
Gilbert, John Logan, Utah, 1895-1936
Gilford, Jack New York City, 1913?
Gillespie, Dizzy Cheraw, N. C., 1917
Gingold, Hermione London, 1897
Gish, Dorothy Massillon, O., 1898-1968
Gish, Lillian Springfield, O., 1899
Givenchy, Hubert Beauvais, Fr., 1927
Gleason, Jackie New York City, 1916
Gleason, James New York, 1886-1959
Gobel, George Chicago, 1920
Goddard, Paulette Great Neck, N. Y., 1911
Godfrey, Arthur New York City, 1903
Goldberg, Rube San Francisco, 1883-1970
Golden, Harry New York City, 1902
Goldwyn, Samuel Warsaw, 1882-1974
Gonzales, Pancho Los Angeles, 1928
Goodman, Benny Chicago, 1909
Goodman, Dody Columbus, O., 1929
Goodson, Mark Sacramento, Cal., 1915
Goolagong, Evonne Barellan, Australia, 1951
Gordon, Ruth Wollaston, Mass., 1896
Goren, Charles Philadelphia, 1901
Goring, Marius Isle of Wight, 1912
Gormé, Eydie New York City, 1932
Gould, Chester Pawnee, Okla., 1900
Gould, Elliott New York City, 1939
Goulding, Ray Lowell, Mass., 1922
Goulet, Robert Lawrence, Mass., 1933
Grable, Betty St. Louis, 1916-73
Graham, Sheilah London, 1905?
Graham, Virginia Chicago, 1912
Grahame, Gloria Los Angeles, 1929
Granger, Farley San José, Cal., 1925
Granger, Stewart London, 1913
Grant, Cary Bristol, Eng., 1904
Grant, Lee New York City, 1927
Gray, Barry Red Lion, N. J., 1916
Gray, Dolores Chicago, 1930
Grayson, Kathryn, Winston-Salem, N. C., 1923
Graziano, Rocky New York City, 1922

Killy, Jean-Claude St.-Cloud, Fr.,1943
King, Alan New York City, 1927
King, Alexander Vienna, 1900-65
King, Billie Jean Long Beach, Cal.,1943
King, Carole New York City, 1941
King, Dennis Coventry, Eng., 1897-1971
Kirk, Lisa Brownsville, Pa., 1925
Kirsten, Dorothy Montclair, N.J., 1919
Kitt, Eartha North, S.C., 1928
Klein, Calvin New York City, 1942
Klein, Robert New York City, 1942
Klemperer, Werner Cologne, Ger., 1920
Klugman, Jack Philadelphia, 1922
Knievel, Evel Butte, Mont., 1938
Knight, Gladys Atlanta, 1944
Knotts, Don Morgantown, W. Va., 1924
Knox, Alexander Strathroy, Can., 1907
Korbut, Olga Grodno, Russia, 1956
Korda, Alexander Hungary, 1893-1956
Korman, Harvey Chicago, 1927
Koufax, Sandy New York City, 1935
Kovacs, Ernie Trenton, N.J., 1919-62
Kramer, Jack Las Vegas, Nev., 1921
Kramer, Stanley New York City, 1913
Krasna, Norman New York City, 1909
Kristofferson, Kris Brownsville, Tex., 1936
Krupa, Gene Chicago, 1909-73
Kuralt, Charles Wilmington, N.C., 1934
Kwan, Nancy Hong Kong, 1939
Ladd, Alan Hot Springs, Ark., 1913-64
Lahr, Bert New York, 1895-1967
Laine, Frankie Chicago, 1913
Lake, Veronica Lake Placid, N.Y., 1919-73
Laker, Freddie Canterbury, Eng., 1922
Lamarr, Hedy Vienna, 1915
Lamas, Fernando, Buenos Aires, 1920
Lamour, Dorothy New Orleans, 1914
Lancaster, Burt New York City, 1913
Lanchester, Elsa Lewisham, Eng., 1902
Landau, Martin New York City, 1925?
Landers, Ann Sioux City, Iowa, 1918
Landi, Elissa Venice, 1904-48
Landis, Carole Fairchild, Wis., 1919-48
Landon, Michael New York City, 1937
Lane, Abbe New York City, 1935
Langdon, Harry Council Bluffs, Iowa, 1884-1944
Lange, Hope Redding Ridge, Conn., 1933
Langella, Frank Bayonne, N. J., 1940
Langford, Frances Lakeland, Fla., 1914?
Langtry, Lily Jersey, Eng., 1852-1929
Lansbury, Angela London, 1925
Lanza, Mario Philadelphia, 1921-59
La Rosa, Julius New York City, 1930
Lasser, Louise New York, 1941
Lauder, Harry Scotland, 1870-1950
Laughton, Charles Scarborough, Eng., 1899-1962
Laurel, Stan Ulverson, Eng., 1890-1965
Laurents, Arthur New York City, 1918
Laurie, Piper Detroit, 1932
Lawford, Peter London, 1923
Lawrence, Carol Melrose Park, Ill., 1934
Lawrence, Gertrude London, 1898-1952
Lawrence, Mary Wells Youngstown, 1928
Lawrence, Vicki Los Angeles, 1949
Leachman, Cloris Des Moines, 1926
Learned, Michael Washington, 1939
Lederer, Francis Prague, 1906
Lee, Brenda Atlanta, 1944
Lee, Gypsy Rose Seattle, 1914-70
Lee, Peggy Jamestown, N. D., 1920
Le Gallienne, Eva London, 1899
Legrand, Michel Paris, 1932
Lehrer, Tom New York City, 1928
Leigh, Janet Merced, Cal., 1927
Leigh, Vivien India, 1913-67
Leighton, Margaret Barnt Green, Eng., 1922-76
Lembeck, Harvey New York City, 1923
Lemmon, Jack Boston, 1925
Lennon, John Liverpool, Eng., 1940
Lenya, Lotte Vienna, 1900
Leonard, Sheldon New York City, 1907
Leslie, Joan Detroit, 1925
Levant, Oscar Pittsburgh, 1906-72
Levene, Sam Russia, 1905
Levenson, Sam New York City, 1911

Levine, Joseph E. Boston, 1905
Lewis, Jerry Newark, N. J., 1926
Lewis, Joe E. New York City, 1902?-71
Lewis, Ramsey Chicago, 1935
Lewis, Robert Q. New York City, 1921
Lewis, Shari New York City, 1934
Lewis, Ted Circleville, O., 1891-1971
Liberace West Allis, Wis., 1919
Lightfoot, Gordon Orillia, Can., 1938
Lillie, Beatrice Toronto, 1898
Lindfors, Viveca Uppsala, Swed., 1920
Lindsay, Howard Saratoga, N.Y., 1889-1968
Lindsay, Margaret Dubuque, Iowa, 1910
Linkletter, Art Moose Jaw, Can., 1912
Lippmann, Walter New York, 1889-1974
Lisi, Virna Ancona, Italy, 1937
Little, Rich Ottawa, Can., 1938
Littlewood, Joan London, 1916
Litvak, Anatole Kiev, Russ., 1902
Livingstone, Mary Seattle, 1909
Lloyd, Harold Burchard, Neb., 1893-1971
Lockhart, Gene London, Can., 1891-1957
Lockhart, June New York City, 1925
Lockwood, Margaret Karachi, Pakistan, 1916
Loesser, Frank New York, 1910-69
Logan, Ella Glasgow, 1913-69
Lollobrigida, Gina Subiaco, Italy, 1928
Lom, Herbert Prague, 1917
Lombard, Carole Fort Wayne, Ind., 1908-42
Lombardi, Vince New York, 1913-70
Lombardo, Guy London, Can., 1902-77
London, Julie Santa Rosa, Cal., 1926
Loos, Anita Sissons, Cal., 1893
Lopez, Nancy Torrence, Cal., 1957
Lopez, Trini Dallas, 1937
Lopez, Vincent New York, 1895-1975
Lord, Jack New York City, 1930
Loren, Sophia Rome, 1934
Lorre, Peter Hungary, 1904-64
Louis, Joe near Lafayette, Ala., 1914
Louise, Anita New York, 1917-70
Louise, Tina New York City, 1937
Lovejoy, Frank New York, 1912-62
Lowe, Edmund San Jose, Cal., 1892-1971
Loy, Myrna Helena, Mont., 1905
Lubitsch, Ernst Berlin, 1892-1947
Luboff, Norman Chicago, 1917
Luce, Clare Boothe New York City, 1903
Lugosi, Bela Lugos, Hung., 1888-1956
Lukas, Paul Budapest, 1894-1971
Lulu Glasgow, 1948
Lumet, Sidney Philadelphia, 1924
Lund, Art Salt Lake City, 1920
Lund, John Rochester, N. Y., 1913
Lundigan, William Syracuse, 1914-75
Lunt, Alfred Milwaukee, 1892-1977
Lupino, Ida London, 1918
Lynde, Paul Mt. Vernon, O., 1926
Lynley, Carol New York City, 1942
Lynn, Diana Los Angeles, 1926-71
Lynn, Loretta Butcher Hollow, Ky., 1932?
Lyon, Sue Davenport, Iowa, 1946
Lyons, Leonard New York City, 1906-76
MacArthur, Charles Scranton, Pa., 1895-1956
MacArthur, James Los Angeles, 1937
McBride, Mary Margaret Paris, Mo., 1899-1976
McCallum, David Scotland, 1933
McCambridge, Mercedes Joliet, Ill., 1918
McCardell, Claire Frederick, Md. 1905-58
McCarey, Leo Los Angeles, 1898-1969
McCartney, Paul Allerton, Eng., 1942
McClure, Doug Glendale, Cal., 1938
McCormick, Myron Albany, Ind., 1907-62
McCrea, Joel Los Angeles, 1905
McDaniel, Hattie Wichita, 1895-1952
MacDonald, Jeanette Phila., 1906-65
McDowell, Malcolm Leeds, Eng., 1943
McEnroe, John New York City, 1959
McGavin, Darren San Joaquin Valley, Cal., 1922
McGraw, Ali Westchester Co., N. Y., 1939

McGuire, Biff New Haven, Conn., 1927
McGuire, Dorothy Omaha, Neb. 1919
McHugh, Frank Homestead, Pa., 1898
McHugh, Jimmy Boston, 1896-1969
McKelway, St. Clair Charlotte, N. C., 1905
McKenna, Siobhan Belfast, 1922
MacKenzie, Gisele Winnipeg, Can., 1927
McKuen, Rod Oakland, Calif. 1933
McLaglen, Victor Tunbridge Wells, Eng., 1886-1959
MacLaine, Shirley Richmond, Va., 1934
MacLane, Barton Columbia, S.C., 1902-68
McLean, Don New Rochelle, N.Y., 1945
McLuhan, Marshall Edmonton, Can., 1911
MacMahon, Aline McKeesport, Pa., 1899
McMahon, Ed Detroit, 1923
MacMurray, Fred Kankakee, Ill., 1908
McNair, Barbara Chicago, 1937?
McNeill, Don Galena, Ill., 1907
McNellis, Maggi Chicago, 1917
McQueen, Butterfly Tampa, Fla., 1911
McQueen, Steve Indianapolis, 1930
MacRae, Gordon East Orange, N. J., 1921
MacRae, Sheila London, 1923?
Madison, Guy Bakersfield, Cal., 1922
Magnani, Anna Rome, 1908-73
Maharis, George New York City, 1928
Main, Marjorie Acton, Ind., 1890-1975
Mainbocher Chicago, 1890-1976
Makeba, Miriam Prospect Township, South Africa, 1932
Malbin, Elaine New York City, 1932
Malden, Karl Chicago, 1914
Malina, Judith Kiel, Ger., 1926
Malone, Dorothy Chicago, 1930
Malone, Nancy New York City, 1935
Mamoulian, Rouben Tiflis, Russ., 1897
Mancini, Henry Cleveland, 1924
Mangano, Silvana Rome, 1930
Manilow, Barry New York City, 1946
Mann, Herbie New York City, 1930
Mannes, Marya New York City, 1904
Mansfield, Jayne Bryn Mawr, Pa., 1933-67
Mantle, Mickey Spavinaw, Okla., 1931
Mantovani, Annunzio Venice, 1905
Marceau, Marcel Strasbourg, Fr., 1923
March, Fredric Racine, Wis., 1897-1975
March, Hal San Francisco, 1920-70
Marciano, Rocky Boston, 1924-69
Margo Mexico City, 1920
Marlowe, Hugh Philadelphia, 1911
Marsh, Jean London, 1934
Marshall, E. G. Owatonna, Minn., 1910
Marshall, Herbert London, 1890-1966
Marshall, Penny New York City, 1942
Martin, Dean Steubenville, O., 1917
Martin, Dick Battle Creek, Mich., 1927
Martin, Mary Weatherford, Tex., 1913
Martin, Steve Waco, Tex., 1945
Marvin, Lee New York City, 1924
Marx, Chico New York, 1891-1961
Marx, Groucho New York, 1895-1977
Marx, Harpo New York, 1893-1964
Masina, Giulietta Bologna, Italy, 1925?
Mason, Jackie Sheboygan, Wis., 1931
Mason, James Huddersfield, Eng., 1909
Mason, Pamela Westgate, Eng., 1918
Massey, Raymond Toronto, 1896
Mastroianni, Marcello Fontana Liri, Italy, 1924
Mathis, Johnny San Francisco, 1935
Matthau, Walter New York City, 1920
Mature, Victor Louisville, Ky., 1916
Mauldin, Bill Mountain Park, N. M., 1921
Maxwell, Elsa Keokuk, Iowa, 1883-1963
Maxwell, Marilyn Clarinda, Iowa, 1922-72
May, Elaine Philadelphia, 1932
Mayehoff, Eddie Baltimore, 1914
Mayer, Louis B. Minsk, Russ., 1885-1957
Mayo, Virginia St. Louis, 1928
Mays, Willie Westfield, Ala., 1931
Meadows, Audrey Wuchang, China, 1922?
Meadows, Jayne Wuchang, China, 1920?
Medford, Kay New York City, 1920

Meek, Donald Glasgow, 1880-1946
Meeker, Ralph Minneapolis, 1920
Melton, James Moultrie, Ga., 1904-61
Mendes, Sergio Niteroi, Brazil, 1941?
Menjou, Adolphe Pittsburgh, 1890-1963
Menken, Helen New York, 1902-66
Mercer, Johnny Savannah, Ga., 1909-76
Mercouri, Melina Athens, 1925
Meredith, Burgess Cleveland, 1908
Merkel, Una Covington, Ky., 1903
Merman, Ethel New York City, 1909
Merrick, David St. Louis, 1912
Merrill, Dina New York City, 1925
Merrill, Gary Hartford, Conn., 1915
Merrill, Robert New York City, 1919
Mesta, Perle Sturgis, Mich., 1891-1975
Middleton, Ray Chicago, 1907
Midler, Bette Honolulu, 1945(?)
Mielziner, Jo Paris, 1901-76
Miles, Sarah Ingatestone, Eng., 1941
Miles, Vera Boise City, Okla., 1929
Milland, Ray Neath, Wales, 1908
Miller, Ann Chireno, Tex., 1919
Miller, Glenn Clarinda, Iowa, 1909-44
Miller, Marilyn Findlay, O., 1898-1936
Miller, Mitch Rochester, N.Y., 1911
Miller, Roger Erick, Okla., 1936
Millett, Kate St. Paul, 1934
Mills, Hayley London, 1946
Mills, John Felixstowe, Eng., 1908
Mills, Juliet London, 1941
Mimieux, Yvette Los Angeles, 1939
Mineo, Sal New York City, 1939-76
Mingus, Charlie Nogales, Ariz., 1922-79
Minnelli, Liza Los Angeles, 1946
Minnelli, Vincente Chicago, 1913
Minnesota Fats New York City, 1903?
Miranda, Carmen Portugal, 1917-55
Mitchell, Cameron Dallastown, Pa., 1918
Mitchell, Joni Ft. MacLeod. Can., 1943
Mitchell, Martha Pine Bluff, Ark., 1918-76
Mitchell, Thomas Elizabeth, N.J., 1892-1962
Mitchum, Robert Bridgeport, Ct., 1917
Mix, Tom El Paso, Tex., 1880-1940
Monk, Thelonius Rocky Mount, N. C., 1918
Monroe, Earl Philadelphia, 1944
Monroe, Marilyn Los Angeles, 1926-62
Monroe, Vaughan Akron, O., 1912-73
Montalban, Ricardo Mexico City, 1920
Montand, Yves Monsummano, Italy, 1921
Montgomery, Elizabeth Hollywood, Cal., 1933
Montgomery, Robert Beacon, N. Y., 1904
Moore, Constance Sioux City, Iowa, 1922
Moore, Dick Los Angeles, 1925
Moore, Garry Baltimore, 1915
Moore, Grace Del Rio, Tenn., 1901-47
Moore, Mary Tyler New York City, 1937
Moore, Melba New York City, 1945
Moore, Terry Los Angeles, 1929
Moore, Victor Hammonton, N.J., 1876-1962
Moorehead, Agnes Clinton, Mass., 1906-74
Moreau, Jeanne Paris, 1928
Moreno, Rita Humacao, P. R., 1931
Morgan, Frank New York, 1890-1949
Morgan, Helen Danville, Ill., 1900-41
Morgan, Henry New York City, 1915
Morgan, Jane Newton, Mass., 1924
Morgan, Ralph New York, 1883-1956
Morgan, Russ Scranton, Pa., 1904-69
Mori, Hanae Shimane, Japan, 1926
Morison, Patricia New York City, 1915
Morley, Robert Somley, Eng., 1908
Morris, Chester New York, 1919-70
Morris, Wayne Los Angeles, 1914-59
Morse, Robert Newton, Mass., 1931
Morton, Craig Flint, Mich., 1943
Morton, "Jelly Roll" New Orleans, 1885-1941
Moss, Arnold New York City, 1910
Mostel, Zero New York City, 1915-77
Mowbray, Alan London, 1897-1969
Muhammed Ali (Cassius Clay) Louisville, Ky., 1942
Mulhare, Edward County Cork, Ire., 1928
Mull, Martin Chicago, 1943

Muni, Paul Lemberg, Pol., 1895-1967
Murdoch, Rupert Melbourne, 1931
Murphy, Audie Kingston, Tex., 1924-71
Murray, Arthur New York City, 1895
Murray, Don Hollywood, Cal., 1929
Murray, Jan New York City, 1917
Murray, Kathryn Jersey City, N. J., 1906
Murray, Ken New York City, 1903
Murray, Mae Portsmouth, Va., 1885-1965
Murrow, Edward R. Greensboro, N.C., 1908-65
Musial, Stan Donora, Pa., 1920
Myerson, Bess New York City, 1924
Nabors, Jim Sylacauga, Ala., 1932?
Nader, Ralph Winsted, Conn., 1934
Nagel, Conrad Keokuk, Iowa, 1897-1970
Naish, J. Carrol New York City, 1900-73
Naldi, Nita New York, 1899-1961
Namath, Joe Beaver Falls, Pa., 1943
Nash, Ogden Rye, N.Y., 1902-71
Natwick, Mildred Baltimore, 1908
Nazimova, Alla Yalta, Russ., 1879-1945
Neagle, Anna London, 1904
Neal, Patricia Packard, Ky., 1926
Neff, Hildegarde Ulm, Ger., 1925
Nelson, Barry Oakland, Cal., 1920
Nelson, Harriet Des Moines, 1912?
Nelson, Ozzie Jersey City, 1907-75
Nelson, Willie Abbott, Tex., 1933
Nero, Peter New York City, 1934
Newhart, Bob Chicago, 1929
Newley, Anthony London, 1931
Newman, Edwin New York, 1919
Newman, Paul Cleveland, 1925
Newman, Phyllis Jersey City, N. J., 1935
Newmar, Julie Los Angeles, 1935
Newton, Wayne Roanoke, Va., 1944
Newton-John, Olivia Cambridge, Eng., 1948
Nichols, Mike Berlin, 1931
Nicholson, Jack Neptune, N.J., 1937
Nicklaus, Jack Columbus, Ohio 1940
Nimoy, Leonard Boston, 1932
Niven, David Kirriemuir, Scot., 1910
Nizer, Louis London, 1902
Nolte, Nick Omaha, 1941
Normand, Mabel Boston, 1894-1930
North, Sheree Los Angeles, 1933
Novak, Kim Chicago, 1933
Novarro, Ramon Durango, Mex., 1899-1968
Novello, Ivor Cardiff, Wales, 1893-1951
Nugent, Elliott Dover, O., 1899
Nuyen, France Marseilles, 1939
Nyad, Diana New York City, 1949
Oakie, Jack Sedalia, Mo., 1903-78
Oberon, Merle Hobart, Tasmania, 1915
Obolensky, Serge Tsarskoe Selo, Russ., 1890-1978
O'Brian, Hugh Rochester, N.Y., 1930
O'Brien, Edmond New York City, 1915
O'Brien, Margaret San Diego, 1937
O'Brien, Pat Milwaukee, 1899
Ochs, Phil El Paso, Tex., 1940-76
O'Connell, Arthur New York City, 1908
O'Connor, Carroll New York City, 1924
O'Connor, Donald Chicago, 1925
O'Connor, Una Belfast, 1881-1959
O'Day, Anita Chicago, 1920
O'Hara, Jill Warren, Pa., 1947
O'Hara, Maureen Milltown, Ire., 1921
O'Herlihy, Dan Wexford, Ire., 1919
O'Keefe, Dennis Fort Madison, Iowa, 1910-68
Oland, Warner Umea, Swed., 1880-1938
Oliver, Edna May Malden, Mass., 1883-1942
Olivier, Laurence Dorking, Eng., 1907
Onassis, Aristotle Smyrna, Turkey, 1906-75
Onassis, Christina New York City, 1950
O'Neal, Patrick Ocala, Fla., 1927
O'Neal, Ryan Los Angeles, 1941
O'Neal, Tatum Los Angeles, 1963
Ono, Yoko Tokyo, 1933
Opatoshu, David New York City, 1918
Orbach, Jerry New York City, 1935
Orbison, Roy Texas, 1936
Orlando, Tony New York City, 1944
Osmond, Donny, Ogden, Utah, 1957
Osmond, Marie Ogden, Utah, 1959
O'Sullivan, Maureen Boyle, Ire., 1911

O'Toole, Peter Connemarra, Ire., 1932
Ouspenskaya, Maria Russia, 1876-1949
Owens, Buck Sherman, Tex., 1929
Paar, Jack Canton, O., 1918
Pacino, Al New York City, 1940
Page, Geraldine Kirksville, Mo., 1924
Page, Patti Claremore, Okla., 1927
Paige, Janis Tacoma, Wash., 1922
Paige, "Satchel" Mobile, Ala., 1906?
Palance, Jack Lattimore Mines, Pa., 1920
Paley, William S. Chicago, 1901
Pallette, Eugene Winfield, Kans., 1889-1943
Palmer, Arnold Latrobe, Pa., 1929
Palmer, Betsy East Chicago, Ind., 1929
Palmer, Lilli Posen, Poland, 1914
Papas, Irene Chiliomodion, Gr., 1926
Papp, Joseph New York City, 1921
Parker, Eleanor Cedarville, O., 1922
Parker, Fess Fort Worth, Tex., 1927
Parker, Suzy San Antonio, Tex., 1933
Parks, Bert Atlanta, 1915
Parnis, Mollie New York City, 1909
Parsons, Estelle Lynn, Mass., 1927
Parton, Dolly nr. Sevierville, Tenn., 1946
Paulsen, Pat South Bend, Wash., 1930?
Paxinou, Katina Piraeus, Gr., 1900
Payne, John Roanoke, Va., 1912
Peale, Norman Vincent Bowersville, Ohio, 1898
Pearl, Minnie Centerville, Tenn., 1912
Peck, Gregory La Jolla, Cal., 1916
Pelé Três Coracoes, Brazil, 1941
Pendleton, Nat Davenport, Iowa, 1899-1967
Peppard, George Detroit, 1932
Perkins, Anthony New York City, 1932
Perrine, Valerie Galveston, Tex., 1943
Perry, Antoinette Denver, 1888-1946
Persoff, Nehemiah Jerusalem, 1920
Peters, Bernadette New York City, 1948
Peters, Jean Canton, O., 1926
Peters, Susan Spokane, 1921-52
Peterson, Oscar Montreal, 1925
Piaf, Edith Paris, 1912-63
Piazza, Ben Little Rock, Ark., 1934
Piazza, Marguerite New Orleans, 1926
Pickens, Slim Kingsberg, Cal., 1919
Pickford, Mary Toronto, 1893-1979
Plcon, Molly New York City, 1898
Pidgeon, Walter East St. John, Can., 1897
Pleasance, Donald Worksop, Eng., 1921
Pleshette, Suzanne New York City, 1937
Plimpton, George New York City, 1927
Plowright, Joan Scunthorpe, Eng., 1929
Plummer, Christopher Toronto, 1929
Podesta, Rosana Tripoli, Libya, 1934
Poitier, Sidney Miami, Fla., 1924
Pollard, Michael J. Passaic, N. J., 1939
Ponti, Carlo Milan, 1913
Portman, Eric Halifax, Eng., 1903-69
Porter, Cole Peru, Ind., 1893-1964
Post, Mrs. Merriweather Springfield, Ill., 1887-1973
Poston, Tom Columbus, O., 1927
Powell, Dick Mountain View, Ark., 1904-63
Powell, Eleanor Springfield, Mass., 1912
Powell, Jane Portland, Ore., 1929
Powell, William Pittsburgh, 1892
Power, Tyrone Cincinnati, 1913-58
Powers, Stefanie Hollywood, Cal., 1942
Premice, Josephine New York City, 1926
Prentiss, Paula San Antonio, Tex., 1939
Presley, Elvis Tupelo, Miss., 1935-77
Preston, Robert Newton, Mass., 1918
Price, Leontyne Laurel, Miss., 1927
Price, Vincent St. Louis, 1911
Primus, Pearl Trinidad, B.W.I., 1919
Prince, Harold New York City, 1928
Prinze, Freddie New York City, 1954-77
Provine, Dorothy Deadwood, S. D., 1937
Prowse, Juliet Bombay, 1936
Pucci, Emilio Naples, 1914
Purdom, Edmund London, 1926
Purviance, Edna Nevada, 1894-1958
Quant, Mary London, 1934
Quayle, Anthony Ainsdale, Eng., 1913
Quinn, Anthony Chihuahua, Mex., 1915
Quintero, José Panama, 1924

Radziwill, Lee New York City, 1933
Raft, George, New York City, 1903
Raines, Ella Snoqualmie Falls, Wash., 1921
Rains, Claude London, 1889-1967
Raitt, John Santa Ana, Cal., 1917
Rambeau, Marjorie San Francisco, 1889-1970
Rand, Sally Hickory, Mo., 1904?-79
Randall, Tony Tulsa, Okla., 1920
Rathbone, Basil South Africa, 1892-1967
Rather, Dan Wharton, Tex., 1931
Ratoff, Gregory Russia, 1893-1961
Ray, Aldo Pen Argyl, Pa., 1926
Ray, Johnny Dallas, Ore., 1927
Raye, Martha Butte, Mont., 1916
Raymond, Gene New York City, 1908
Reagan, Ronald, Tampico, Ill., 1911
Reasoner, Harry Dakota City, Iowa, 1923
Reddy, Helen Melbourne, Australia, 1941
Redford, Robert Santa Monica, Cal., 1937
Redgrave, Lynn London, 1943
Redgrave, Michael Bristol, Eng., 1908
Redgrave, Vanessa London, 1937
Reed, Donna Iowa, 1921
Reed, Rex Fort Worth, 1940?
Reed, Willis Hico, La., 1942
Reese, Della Detroit, 1932
Reeves, Steve Glasgow, Mont., 1926
Reid, Wallace St. Louis, 1890-1923
Reiner, Carl New York City, 1922
Reiner, Rob Beverly Hills, Calif., 1947
Reinhardt, Max Austria, 1873-1943
Remick, Lee Quincy, Mass., 1935
Rennie, Michael Bradford, Eng., 1909-71
Rey, Fernando La Coruña, Spain, 1917
Reynolds, Burt Waycross, Ga., 1936
Reynolds, Debbie El Paso, Tex., 1932
Rice, Jim Anderson, S.C., 1953
Rich, Buddy New York City, 1917
Rich, Irene Buffalo, N. Y., 1897
Richardson, Ralph Cheltenham, Eng., 1902
Rickles, Don New York City, 1926
Riddle, Nelson Hackensack, N. J., 1921
Rigg, Diana Doncaster, Eng., 1938
Ringling, Charles McGregor, Iowa, 1864-1926
Ritchard, Cyril Sydney, Austral., 1897-1977
Ritter, Tex Murvaul, Tex., 1907-74
Ritter, Thelma New York, 1905-69
Rivera, Chita Washington, D. C., 1933
Rivers, Joan New York City, 1937?
Roach, Hal Elmira, N. Y., 1892
Robards, Jason, Jr. Chicago, 1922
Robbins, Harold New York City, 1916
Robertson, Cliff La Jolla, Cal., 1925
Robertson, Dale Oklahoma City, 1923
Robeson, Paul, Princeton, N.J., 1898-1976
Robinson, "Bojangles" Richmond, Va., 1878-1949
Robinson, Edward G. Bucharest, 1893-1973
Robinson, Jackie Cairo, Ga., 1919-72
Robinson, Sugar Ray Detroit, 1921
Robson, Flora South Shields, Eng., 1902
Rockwell, Norman New York City, 1894-1978
Rogers, Buddy Olathe, Kans., 1904
Rogers, Ginger Independence, Mo., 1911
Rogers, Roy Cincinnati, 1912
Rogers, Will Oologah, Okla., 1879-1935
Rogers, Will, Jr. New York City, 1911
Roland, Gilbert Juarez, Mexico, 1905
Roman, Ruth Boston, 1924
Rome, Harold Hartford, Conn. 1908
Romero, Cesar New York City, 1907?
Ronstadt, Linda Tucson, Ariz., 1946
Rooney, Mickey New York City, 1920
Rooney, Pat New York, 1880-1962
Rose, Billy New York, 1899-1966
Rose, David London, 1910
Rose, Pete Cincinnati, 1942
Ross, Diana Detroit, 1944
Ross, Katharine Hollywood, Cal., 1943
Ross, Lanny Seattle, 1906
Roth, Lillian Boston, 1910
Rowan, Dan Okla., 1926
Rowlands, Gena Cambria, Wis., 1936

Rozelle, Pete South Gate, Cal., 1914
Rubenstein, Helena Poland, 1882?-1965
Rudd, Paul Boston, 1940
Ruggles, Charles Los Angeles, 1892-1970
Rule, Janice Norwood, O., 1931
Runyon, Damon Manhattan, Kans., 1884-1946
Rush, Barbara Denver, 1929
Russell, Jane Lake Bemidji, Minn., 1921
Russell, Lillian Clinton, Iowa, 1861-1922
Russell, Nipsey Atlanta, 1924?
Russell, "Pee Wee" St. Louis, 1906-69
Russell, Rosalind Waterbury, Conn., 1911-76
Ruth, "Babe" Baltimore, 1895-1948
Rutherford, Ann Toronto, 1924
Rutherford, Margaret London, 1892-1972
Ryan, Peggy Long Beach, Cal., 1924
Ryan, Robert Chicago, 1913-73
Rydell, Bobby Philadelphia, 1942
Sablon, Jean Nogent-sur-Marne, Fr., 1909
Sabu Mysore, India, 1924-63
Safer, Morley Toronto, 1931
Sahl, Mort Montreal, 1927
Saint, Eva Marie Newark, N. J., 1929
St. John, Jill Los Angeles, 1940
Saint Laurent, Yves Oran, Algeria, 1936
Saint-Subber, Arnold Washington, D. C., 1918
Sainte-Marie, Buffy Saskatchewan, 1942
Sakall, "Cuddles" Budapest, 1884-1955
Sales, Soupy Wake Forest, N. C., 1926?
Sanders, George St. Petersburg, Russ., 1906-72
Sanders, Col. Harland Henryville, Ind., 1890
Sarnoff, Dorothy New York City, 1919
Sarnoff, Robert New York City, 1918
Sarrazin, Michael Quebec, Can., 1940
Sassoon, Vidal London, 1928
Savalas, Telly Garden City, N. Y., 1924
Scali, John Canton, Ohio, 1918
Schary, Dore Newark, N. J., 1905
Schell, Marla Vienna, 1926
Schell, Maximilian Vienna, 1930
Schildkraut, Joseph Vienna, 1895-1964
Schiff, Dorothy New York, 1903
Schneider, Romy Vienna, 1938
Schulz, Charles Minneapolis, 1922
Schwarzenegger, Arnold Graz, Austria, 1947
Scofield, Paul King's Norton, Eng., 1922
Scott, George C. Wise, Va., 1927
Scott, Hazel Port of Spain, Trin., 1920
Scott, Lisbeth Scranton, Pa., 1922
Scott, Martha Jamesport, Mo., 1914
Scott, Randolph Orange Co., Va., 1903
Scott, Zachary, Austin, Tex., 1914-65
Scourby, Alexander New York City, 1913
Scruggs, Earl Flint Hill, N.C., 1924-79
Searle, Ronald Cambridge, Eng., 1920
Seaver, Tom Fresno, Cal., 1944
Seberg, Jean Marshalltown, Iowa, 1938-79
Sedaka, Neil Brooklyn, 1939
Seeger, Pete New York City, 1919
Segal, Erich Brooklyn, N.Y., 1937
Segal, George New York City, 1934
Sellers, Peter Southsea, Eng., 1925
Selznick, David O. Pittsburgh, 1902-65
Sennett, Mack Danville, Can., 1880-1960
Serban, Andrei Bucharest, 1943
Sevareid, Eric Velva, N. D., 1912
Seymour, Dan Chicago, 1915
Shankar, Ravi Benares, India, 1920
Sharif, Omar Cairo, 1933
Shatner, William Montreal, 1931
Shaw, Artie New York City, 1910
Shaw, Robert Westhoughton, Eng., 1927-78
Shawn, Dick Buffalo, N. Y., 1929?
Shearer, Moira Dunfermline, Scot., 1926
Shearer, Norma Montreal, 1905
Shearing, George London, 1919
Shepherd, Jean Chicago, 1923
Sheridan, Ann Denton, Tex., 1916?-67
Sherman, Allan Chicago, 1924-73
Shields, Brooke New York City, 1965

Shire, Talia Long Island, N.Y., 1947
Shoemaker, Willie El Paso, 1931
Shore, Dinah Winchester, Tenn., 1917
Short, Bobby Danville, Ill., 1936
Shrimpton, Jean High Wycombe, Eng., 1942
Shriner, Herb Toledo, O., 1918-70
Shubert, Lee Syracuse, N.Y., 1875-1953
Shulman, Max St. Paul, Minn., 1919
Shumlin, Herman Atwood, Colo., 1898-1979
Sidney, Sylvia New York City, 1910
Signoret, Simone Wiesbaden, Ger., 1921
Silverman, Fred New York City, 1937
Silvers, Phil New York City, 1911
Sim, Alastair Edinburgh, 1900-76
Simmons, Jean London, 1929
Simon, Carly, New York City, 1945
Simon, Paul Queens, N.Y., 1941
Simon, Simone Marseilles, 1914
Simonetta Rome, 1922
Simpson, Adele New York City, 1903
Simpson, O. J., San Francisco, 1947
Sinatra, Frank Hoboken, N. J., 1915
Sinatra, Frank, Jr. Jersey City, 1944
Sinatra, Nancy Jersey City, N. J., 1940
Sissle, Noble Indianapolis, 1889-1975
Skelton, Red Vincennes, Ind., 1913
Skinner, Cornelia Otis Chicago, 1901-79
Skinner, Otis Cambridge, Mass., 1858-1943
Skulnik, Menasha Warsaw, 1898-1970
Slezak, Walter Vienna, 1902
Smith, Alexis Penticton, Can., 1921
Smith, Bessie Chattanooga, 1894-1937
Smith, C. Aubrey London, 1863-1948
Smith, Howard K. Ferriday, La., 1914
Smith, Kate Greenville, Va., 1909
Smith, Maggie Ilford, Eng., 1934
Smith, Roger South Gate, Cal., 1932
Smothers, Dick New York City, 1938
Smothers, Tommy New York City, 1937
Snodgress, Carrie Park Ridge, Ill., 1945
Snowdon, Lord (Antony Armstrong-Jones) London, 1930
Sommer, Elke Berlin, 1941
Sondergaard, Gale Litchfield, Minn., 1907
Sondheim, Stephen New York City, 1930
Sothern, Ann Valley City, N. D., 1909
Spacek, Sissy Quitman, Tex., 1949
Sparks, Ned Guelph, Can., 1884-1957
Spassky, Boris V. Leningrad, 1937
Spewack, Bella Bucharest, 1899
Spiegel, Sam Jaroslau, Poland, 1904?
Spitalney, Phil Russia, 1890-1970
Spitz, Mark Modesto, Calif., 1950
Spivak, Lawrence E. New York City, 1900
Spock, Benjamin N. Haven, Ct., 1903
Springsteen, Bruce Freehold, N. J., 1949
Stack, Robert Los Angeles, 1919
Stafford, Jo Coalinga, Cal., 1918
Stallone, Sylvester New York City, 1946
Stamp, Terence London, 1940
Stang, Arnold Chelsea, Mass., 1925
Stanislavsky, Könstantin Moscow, 1863-1938
Stanley, Kim Tularosa, N. M., 1925
Stanton, Frank Muskegon, Mich., 1908
Stanwyck, Barbara New York City, 1907
Stapleton, Jean New York City, 1923
Stapleton, Maureen Troy, N. Y., 1925?
Starr, Ringo Dingle, Eng., 1940
Staubach, Roger Cincinnati, 1942
Steele, Tommy London, 1936
Steiger, Rod Westhampton, N. Y., 1925
Stein, Jules C. South Bend, Ind., 1896
Steinberg, Saul Rumania, 1914
Steinem, Gloria Toledo, O., 1936
Stengel, Casey Kansas City, Mo., 1891-1975
Sterling, Jan New York City, 1923
Sternberg, Josef von Vienna, 1894-1969
Stevens, Connie New York City, 1938
Stevens, Inger Stockholm, 1934-70
Stevens, Kaye Pittsburgh, 1935
Stevens, Mark Cleveland, 1922
Stevens, Stella Yazoo City, Miss., 1938
Stewart, James Indiana, Pa., 1908
Stewart, Rod London, 1945
Stickney, Dorothy Dickinson, N. D., 1900
Stockwell, Dean Hollywood, Cal., 1936
Stone, Ezra New Bedford, Mass., 1917

Stone, Irving San Francisco, 1903
Stone, Lewis Worcester, Mass., 1879-1953
Straight, Beatrice Long Island, N.Y., 1918
Strasberg, Lee Austria-Hungary, 1901
Strasberg, Susan New York City, 1938
Streisand, Barbra New York City, 1942
Stritch, Elaine Detroit, 1925
Stroheim, Erich von Vienna, 1885-1957
Stromberg, Hunt Louisville, 1894-1968
Strudwick, Shepperd Hillsboro, N. C., 1907
Struthers, Sally Portland, Ore., 1948
Sturges, Preston Chicago, 1898-1959
Styne, Jule London, 1905
Sullavan, Margaret Norfolk, 1911-60
Sullivan, Barry New York City, 1912
Sullivan, Ed New York City, 1902-74
Sullivan, Francis L. London, 1903-56
Summer, Donna Boston, 1948
Susann, Jacqueline Philadelphia, 1923-74
Susskind, David Brookline, Mass., 1920
Sutherland, Donald St. John, Can., 1934
Suzuki, Pat Cressy, Cal., 1931
Swanson, Gloria Chicago, 1899
Swarthout, Gladys Deepwater, Mo., 1904-69
Syms, Sylvia London, 1934
Talbot, Lyle Pittsburgh, 1902
Talmadge, Norma Jersey City, N.J., 1897-1957
Tamblyn, Russ Los Angeles, 1934
Tamiroff, Akim Baku, Russ., 1901-72
Tandy, Jessica London, 1909
Tanguay, Eva Marbleton, Can., 1878-1947
Tatum, Art Toledo, O., 1910-56
Taurog, Norman Chicago, 1899
Taylor, Elizabeth London, 1932
Taylor, James Boston, 1948
Taylor, June Chicago, 1918
Taylor, Laurette New York, 1884-1946
Taylor, Robert Filley, Neb., 1911-69
Taylor, Rod Sydney, Austral., 1930
Teagarden, Jack Vernon, Tex., 1905-64
Temple, Shirley Santa Monica, Cal., 1928
Templeton, Alec Cardiff, Wales, 1910-63
Templeton, Fay Little Rock, 1865-1939
Ter-Arutunian, Rouben Tiflis, Russ., 1920
Terry, Ellen Coventry, Eng., 1848-1936
Terry-Thomas London, 1911
Thalberg, Irving New York, 1899-1939
Thaxter, Phyllis Portland, Me., 1921
Thomas, Danny Deerfield, Mich., 1914
Thomas, John Charles Meyersdale, Pa., 1892-1960
Thomas, Lowell Woodington, O., 1892
Thomas, Marlo Detroit, 1937
Thomas, Richard New York City, 1951
Thompson, Sada Des Moines, 1929
Thorndike, Sybil Gainsborough, Eng., 1882-1976
Thorpe, Jim Prague, Okla., 1888-1953
Thulin, Ingrid Sollefta, Sweden, 1929
Tierney, Gene New York City, 1920
Tiffin, Pamela Oklahoma City, 1942
Tilden, William Phila., 1893-1953
Tillstrom, Burr Chicago, 1917
Tiny Tim (Herbert Khaury) New York City, 1923?
Tiomkin, Dmitri Russia, 1899
Todd, Ann Hartford, Eng., 1910
Todd, Mike Minneapolis, 1907-58
Todd, Richard Dublin, 1919
Toler, Sidney Warrensburg, Mo., 1874-1947
Tomlin, Lily Detroit, 1936
Tone, Franchot Niagara Falls, N.Y., 1905-68
Toomey, Regis Pittsburgh, 1902
Toren, Marta Sweden, 1926-57
Torme, Mel Chicago, 1925
Torn, Rip Temple, Tex., 1931
Torre, Joe Brooklyn, 1940
Tors, Ivan Budapest, 1916
Tracy, Spencer Milwaukee, 1900-67
Travers, Mary Louisville, Ky., 1936
Travolta, John Englewood, N.J., 1954

Treacher, Arthur Brighton, Eng., 1894-1975
Tremayne, Les London, 1913
Trevor, Claire New York City, 1909
Trigère, Pauline Paris, 1912
Truex, Ernest Kansas City, 1889-1973
Tryon, Tom Hartford, Conn., 1926
Tucker, Forrest Plainfield, Ind., 1919
Tucker, Sophie Russia, 1888-1966
Tufts, Sonny Boston, 1911-70
Tunney, Gene New York City, 1897-1978
Turner, Lana Wallace, Ida., 1921
Turpin, Ben New Orleans, 1874-1940
Tushingham, Rita Liverpool, Eng., 1942
Twelvetrees, Helen New York, 1908-58
Twiggy (Leslie Hornby) London, 1949
Uggams, Leslie New York City, 1943
Ullmann, Liv Tokyo, 1939
Ulric, Lenore Milwaukee, 1894-1970
Unitas, John Pittsburgh, 1933
Uris, Leon Baltimore, 1924
Ustinov, Peter London, 1921
Vaccaro, Brenda New York City, 1939
Valenti, Jack Houston, 1921
Vallee, Rudy Island Pond, Vt., 1901
Valli, Alida Pola, Italy, 1921
Valli, Frankie Newark, N.J., 1937
Vallone, Raf Tropea, Italy, 1918
Van Buren, Abigail Sioux City, Iowa, 1919
Van Cleef, Lee Somerville, N. J., 1925
Vanderbilt, Alfred G. London, 1912
Vanderbilt, Amy Staten Island, N. Y., 1908-74
Vanderbilt, Gloria New York City, 1924
Van Doren, Mamie Rowena, S. D., 1933
Van Dyke, Dick West Plains, Mo., 1925
Van Fleet, Jo Oakland, Cal., 1922
Van Heusen, Jimmie Syracuse, N. Y., 1913
Van Vooren, Monique Brussels, 1933
Vaughan, Sarah Newark, N. J., 1924
Vaughn, Robert New York City, 1932
Veidt, Conrad Berlin, 1893-1943
Velez, Lupe Mexico, 1908-44
Vera-Ellen Cincinnati, O., 1926
Verdon, Gwen Culver City, Cal., 1925
Vereen, Ben Miami, 1946
Vernon, Jackie New York City, 1928
Vilas, Guillermo Mar del Plata, Arg., 1952
Vinton, Bobby Canonsburg, Pa., 1935
Vitti, Monica Rome, 1933
Voight, Jon Yonkers, N. Y., 1938
Von Furstenberg, Betsy Neiheim-Heusen, Ger., 1932
Von Fürstenberg, Diane Brussels, Belg., 1946
Von Sydow, Max Lund, Sweden, 1929
Wagner, Robert Detroit, 1930
Walker, Clint Hartford, Ill., 1927
Walker, Nancy Philadelphia, 1922
Walker, Robert Salt Lake City, 1919-51
Wallace, DeWitt St. Paul, Minn., 1889
Wallace, Irving Chicago, 1916
Wallace, Mike Brookline, Mass., 1918
Wallach, Eli New York City, 1915
Waller, "Fats" New York, 1904-43
Wallis, Hal B. Chicago, 1899
Walters, Barbara Boston. 1931
Wanger, Walter San Francisco, 1894-1968
Warden, Jack Newark, N. J., 1920
Warfield, William West Helena, Ark., 1920
Waring, Fred Tyrone, Pa., 1900
Warner, Jack L. London, Can., 1892-1978
Warwicke, Dionne Orange, N. J., 1941
Washington, Dinah Tuscaloosa, Ala., 1924-64
Waters, Ethel Chester, Pa., 1900-77
Wayne, David Traverse City, Mich., 1914
Wayne, John Winterset, Iowa, 1907-79
Weaver, Dennis Joplin, Mo., 1925
Weaver, Fritz Pittsburgh, 1926
Webb, Clifton Indianapolis, 1891-1966
Webb, Jack Santa Monica, Cal., 1920
Welch, Raquel La Jolla, Cal., 1942
Weld, Tuesday New York City, 1943
Welk, Lawrence Strasburg, N. D., 1903
Welles, Orson Kenosha, Wis., 1915
Werner, Oskar Vienna, 1922
West, Adam Walla Walla, Wash., 1938?

West, Mae New York City, 1892
Wheeler, Bert Paterson N.J., 1895-1968
White, George New York, 1890-1968
White, Josh Greenville, S.C., 1908-69
White, Pearl Greenridge, Mo., 1889-1938
Whiting, Margaret Detroit, 1924
Whitmore, James White Plains, N. Y., 1921
Whitty, Dame May Liverpool, 1865-1948
Widmark, Richard Sunrise, Minn., 1914
Wilde, Cornel New York City, 1918
Wilder, Billy Vienna, 1906
Wilder, Gene Milwaukee, 1935
Wilding, Michael Westcliff, Eng., 1912-79
William, Warren Aitkin, Minn., 1895-1948
Williams, Andy Wall Lake, Iowa, 1930
Williams, Emlyn Glanrafon, Wales, 1905
Williams, Esther Inglewood, Cal., 1923
Williams, Hank Georgiana, Ala., 1923-53
Williams, Joe Cordele, Ga., 1918
Williams, Paul Omaha, 1944?
Williams, Robin Chicago, 1952
Williams, Roger Omaha, Neb., 1926
Williams, Ted San Diego, 1918
Williamson, Nicol Hamilton, Scot., 1938
Wills, Chill Seagoville, Tex., 1903-78
Willson, Meredith Mason City, Iowa, 1902
Wilson, Don Lincoln, Neb., 1900
Wilson, Earl Rockford, O., 1907
Wilson, Flip Jersey City, N. J., 1933
Wilson, Julie Omaha, Neb., 1925
Wilson, Marie Anaheim, Cal., 1917-72
Wilson, Nancy Chillicothe, O., 1937
Winchell, Paul New York City, 1923
Winchell, Walter New York, 1897-1972
Windsor, Duchess of (Wallis Warfield Simpson) Blue Ridge Summit, Pa., 1896
Windsor, Duke of Richmond Park, Eng., 1894-1972
Winkler, Henry New York City, 1947
Winninger, Charles Athens, Wis., 1884-1969
Winters, Jonathan Dayton, O., 1925
Winters, Shelley St. Louis, Ill., 1923
Withers, Jane Atlanta, 1926
Wolfit, Donald Newark-on-Trent, Eng., 1902-68
Wonder, Stevie Detroit, 1951
Wong, Anna May Los Angeles, 1907-61
Wood, Natalie San Francisco, 1939
Wood, Peggy New York City, 1892-1978
Woodward, Joanne Thomasville, Ga., 1930
Woollcott, Alexander Phalanx, N.J., 1887-1963
Woolley, Monty New York, 1888-1962
Worth, Irene Nebraska, 1916
Wray, Fay Alberta, Can., 1907
Wright, Martha Seattle, 1926
Wright, Teresa New York City, 1918
Wyatt, Jane Campgaw, N. J., 1912
Wyler, Gretchen Oklahoma City, 1932
Wyman, Jane St. Joseph, Mo., 1914
Wynette, Tammy Tupelo, Miss., 1942
Wynn, Ed Philadelphia, 1886-1966
Wynn, Keenan New York City, 1916
Wynter, Dana London, 1930?
Yarborough, Glenn Milwaukee, 1930
Yarrow, Peter New York City, 1938
York, Dick Fort Wayne, Ind., 1928
York, Michael Fulmer, Eng., 1942
York, Susannah London, 1942
Young, Gig St. Cloud, Minn., 1917-78
Young, Loretta Salt Lake City, 1913
Young, Robert Chicago, 1907
Young, Roland London, 1887-1953
Young, Sheila Birmingham, Mich., 1950
Young, Victor Chicago, 1900-56
Youngman, Henny London, 1906?
Yurka, Blanche St. Paul, 1887-1974
Zanuck, Darryl F., Wahoo, Neb., 1902
Zeffirelli, Franco Florence, Italy, 1923
Zetterling, Mai Sweden, 1925
Ziegfeld, Florenz Chicago, 1869-1932
Zimbalist, Efrem, Jr. New York, 1913
Zolotow, Maurice New York City, 1913
Zorina, Vera Berlin, 1917

ARTS: POPULAR/CLASSICAL

ALL-TIME MOVIE MONEYMAKERS

SOURCE: *Variety*

The following list includes all feature films that have grossed $19 million or more domestically (U. S. and Canada), as of Jan. 1, 1979. The film title is followed by the name of the director, producer, production company, and release year.

Film	Gross
Star Wars (G. Lucas; G. Kurtz; 20th; 1977)	$164,765,000
Jaws (S. Spielberg; Zanuck/Brown; Universal; 1975)	121,254,000
The Godfather (F. F. Coppola; A. Ruddy; Par; 1972)	86,275,000
Grease (R. Kleiser; R. Stigwood/A. Carr; Par; 1978)	83,091,000
The Exorcist (W. Friedkin; W. P. Blatty; WB; 1973)	82,200,000
The Sound of Music (R. Wise; 20th; 1965)	79,000,000
The Sting (G. R. Hill; T. Bill, M. & J. Phillips; Univ; 1973)	78,889,000
Close Encounters of the Third Kind (S. Spielberg; J. & M. Phillips; Col; 1977)	77,000,000
Gone With The Wind (V. Fleming; D. Selznick; MGM-UA; 1939)	76,700,000
Saturday Night Fever (J. Badham; R. Stigwood; Par; 1977)	71,463,000
One Flew Over The Cuckoo's Nest (M. Forman; S. Zaentz/M. Douglas; UA; 1975)	59,000,000
Smokey and the Bandit (H. Needham; M. Engelberg; Univ; 1977)	57,259,000
American Graffiti (G. Lucas; F. F. Coppola; Univ; 1973)	55,886,000
Rocky, (J. Avildsen; Chartoff/Winkler; UA; 1976)	54,000,000
National Lampoon's Animal House (J. Landis; M. Simmons/I. Reitman; Univ; 1978)	52,368,000
Love Story (A. Hiller; H. Minsky; Par; 1970)	50,000,000
Towering Inferno (J. Guillermin; I. Allen; 20th; 1975)	50,000,000
Jaws II (J. Szwarc; Zanuck/Brown; Univ; 1978)	49,299,000
The Graduate (M. Nichols; L. Turman; Avco Embassy; 1968)	49,078,000
Doctor Zhivago (D. Lean; C. Ponti; MGM-UA; 1965)	46,550,000
Butch Cassidy and Sundance Kid (G. R. Hill; J. Foreman; 20th; 1969)	46,039,000
Airport (G. Seaton; R. Hunter; Univ; 1970)	45,300,000
The Ten Commandments (C. B. DeMille; Par; 1956)	43,000,000
Heaven Can Wait (W. Beatty; Par; 1978)	42,517,000
The Poseidon Adventure (R. Neame; I. Allen; 20th; 1972)	42,000,000
Mary Poppins (R. Stevenson; W. Disney; BV; 1964)	41,000,000
Goodbye Girl (H. Ross; R. Stark; Warners; 1977)	41,000,000
Blazing Saddles (M. Brooks; M. Hertzberg; WB; 1974)	37,200,000
A Star is Born (F. Pierson; J. Peters; WB; 1976)	37,100,000
King Kong (J. Guillermin; D. DeLaurentiis; Par; 1976)	36,915,000
MASH (R. Altman; I. Preminger; 20th; 1970)	36,720,000
Ben-Hur (W. Wyler; S. Zimbalist; MGM-UA; 1959)	36,650,000
Earthquake (M. Robson; Univ; 1974)	36,250,000
Young Frankenstein (M. Brooks; M. Gruskoff; 20th; 1975)	34,600,000
Fiddler On The Roof (N. Jewison; UA; 1971)	34,010,000
Billy Jack (T. Frank; M. Solti; WB; 1971)	32,500,000
Hooper (H. Needham; B. Reynolds/L. Gordon; Warners; 1978)	31,500,000
The Deep (P. Yates; P. Guber; Columbia; 1977	31,300,000
Oh, God! (C. Reiner; J. Weintraub; Warners; 1977)	31,000,000
Godfather Part II (F. F. Coppola; Coppola/Fredrickson/Roos; Par; 1974)	30,073,000
All The President's Men (A. Pakula; W. Coblenz; WB; 1976)	30,000,000
Silver Streak (A. Hiller; E. Milkis/T. Miller; 20th; 1976)	28,850,000
Thunderball (T. Young; Eon; UA; 1965)	28,530,000
Trial of Billy Jack (F. Laughlin; D. Cramer; T-1/WB; 1974)	28,516,000
Patton (F. Schaffner; F. McCarthy; 20th; 1970)	28,100,000
What's Up Doc? (P. Bogdanovich; WB; 1972)	28,000,000
The Omen (R. Donner; H. Bernhard; 20th; 1976)	27,851,000
Snow White (animated; W. Disney; RKO/BV; 1937)	26,750,000
Wilderness Family (S. Raffill; A. Dubs; PIE; 1976)	26,649,000
Funny Girl (W. Wyler; R. Stark; Col; 1968)	26,325,000
The French Connection (W. Friedkin; P. D'Antoni/Schine-Moore; 20th; 1971)	26,315,000
Cleopatra (J. Mankiewicz; W. Wanger; 20th; 1963)	26,000,000
Airport 1975 (J. Smight; W. Fry; Universal; 1974)	25,805,000
Guess Who's Coming To Dinner (S. Kramer; Col; 1968)	25,500,000
Foul Play (C. Higgins; Miller/Milkis; Par; 1978)	25,065,000
The Jungle Book (W. Reitherman; W. Disney; BV; 1967)	25,000,000
The Way We Were (S. Pollack; R. Stark; Col; 1973)	25,000,000
Revenge of the Pink Panther (B. Edwards; UA; 1978)	25,000,000
The Bad News Bears (M. Ritchie; S. Jaffe; Par; 1976)	24,888,000
2001: A Space Odyssey (S. Kubrick; MGM-UA; 1968)	24,100,000
The Enforcer (J. Fargo; R. Daley; WB; 1976)	24,000,000
Around World in 80 Days (M. Anderson; M. Todd; UA; 1956)	23,120,000
The Longest Yard (R. Aldrich; A. Ruddy; Par; 1974)	23,017,000
In Search of Noah's Ark (J.L. Conway; C.E. Sellier Jr.; Sunn; 1977)	23,000,000
Goldfinger (G. Hamilton; Eon; UA; 1964)	22,860,000
Bonnie and Clyde (A. Penn; W. Beatty; WB; 1967)	22,700,000
Papillon (F. J. Schaffner; R. Dorfmann; AA; 1973)	22,500,000
Dog Day Afternoon (S. Lumet; M. Bregman/M. Elfand; WB; 1975)	22,500,000
Deliverance (J. Boorman; WB; 1972)	22,400,000
Midway (J. Smight; W. Mirsch; Universal; 1976)	22,329,000
Shampoo (H. Ashby; W. Beatty; Col; 1975)	22,000,000
Murder By Death (R. Moore; R. Stark; Col; 1976)	22,000,000
The Spy Who Loved Me (L. Gilbert; A. Broccoli; UA; 1977)	22,000,000
Jeremiah Johnson (S. Pollack; J. Wizan; WB; 1972)	21,600,000
Up In Smoke (L. Adler; Adler/Lombardo; Par; 1978)	21,271,000
The Love Bug (R. Stevenson; W. Walsh; BV; 1969)	21,000,000
Silent Movie (M. Brooks; M. Hertzberg; 20th; 1976)	21,000,000
A Bridge Too Far (R. Attenborough; J.E. Levine/R.P. Levine; UA; 1977)	21,000,000
It's A Mad, Mad, Mad, Mad World (S. Kramer; UA; 1963)	20,800,000
Summer of '42 (R. Mulligan; R. Roth; WB; 1971)	20,500,000
Midnight Cowboy (J. Schlesinger; J. Hellman; UA; 1969)	20,325,000
The Dirty Dozen (R. Aldrich; K. Hyman; MGM-UA; 1967)	20,300,000
Cabaret (B. Fosse; C. Feuer; AA; 1972)	20,250,000
Magnum Force (T. Post; R. Daley; WB; 1973)	20,100,000
Three Days of the Condor (S. Pollack; S. Schneider; Par; 1975)	20,014,000
Valley of the Dolls (M. Robson; D. Weisbart; 20th; 1967)	20,000,000
The Odd Couple (G. Saks; H. W. Koch; Par; 1968)	20,000,000
Return of the Pink Panther (B. Edwards; UA; 1975)	20,000,000
The End (B. Reynolds; L. Gordon; UA; 1978)	20,000,000
Diamonds Are Forever (G. Hamilton; Eon; UA; 1971)	19,620,000
The Pink Panther Strikes Again (B. Edwards UA; 1976)	19,500,000
The Cheap Detective (R. Moore; R. Stark; Col; 1978)	19,500,000
West Side Story (R. Wise; J. Robbins; Mirisch/7 Arts; UA; 1961)	19,450,000
You Only Live Twice (L. Gilbert; Eon; UA; 1967)	19,400,000
Murder on the Orient Express (S. Lumet; J. Brabourne/R. Goodwin; Par; 1974)	19,124,000
To Sir, With Love (J. Clavell; Col; 1967)	19,100,000
Easy Rider (D. Hopper; Pando/Raybart; Col; 1969)	19,100,000
Swiss Family Robinson (K. Annakin; W. Disney; BV; 1960)	19,000,000
Bullitt (P. Yates; P. D'Antoni; WB; 1969)	19,000,000
Funny Lady (H. Ross; R. Stark; Col; 1975)	19,000,000

LONGEST BROADWAY RUNS
Source: *VARIETY*

Play	Perfor-mances	Play	Perfor-mances	Play	Perfor-mances
Fiddler on the Roof	3,242	Oh! Calcutta!	1,316	Kiss and Tell	962
Life with Father	3,224	Angel Street	1,295	Anna Lucasta	957
Tobacco Road	3,182	Lightnin'	1,291	Annie*	941
Grease*	3,083	Promises, Promises	1,281	The Moon is Blue	924
Hello, Dolly!	2,844	The King and I	1,246	Bells Are Ringing	924
My Fair Lady	2,717	Cactus Flower	1,234	Beatlemania	914
Man of La Mancha	2,329	Sleuth	1,222	Luv	902
Abie's Irish Rose	2,327	1776	1,217	Can-Can	895
Oklahoma!	2,212	Equus	1,209	Carousel	890
Pippin	1,944	Guys and Dolls	1,200	Hats Off to Ice	890
South Pacific	1,925	Cabaret	1,166	Fanny	888
Magic Show	1,920	Mister Roberts	1,157	Follow the Girls	882
Harvey	1,775	Annie Get Your Gun	1,147	The Bat	878
Hair	1,742	The Seven Year Itch	1,141	Camelot	873
The Wiz	1,661	Butterflies Are Free	1,128	My Sister Eileen	866
Born Yesterday	1,642	Pins and Needles	1,108	White Cargo	864
A Chorus Line*	1,635	Plaza Suite	1,097	No, No, Nanette	861
Mary, Mary	1,572	Kiss Me Kate	1,071	Song of Norway	860
The Voice of the Turtle	1,557	Don't Bother Me I Can't Cope	1,065	A Streetcar Named Desire	855
Barefoot in the Park	1,532	Pajama Game	1,063	Comedy in Music	849
Mame	1,503	The Teahouse of the August		You Can't Take It with You	837
Same Time, Next Year*	1,452	Moon	1,027	La Plume de Ma Tante	835
Arsenic and Old Lace	1,444	Damn Yankees	1,019	Three Men on a Horse	835
The Sound of Music	1,443	Never Too Late	1,007	The Subject Was Roses	832
How To Succeed in Business		Mummenschanz*	1,000	That Championship Season	820
without Really Trying	1,417	Any Wednesday	984	Inherit the Wind	806
Hellzapoppin	1,404	A Funny Thing Happened on		The Prisoner of Second Avenue	798
The Music Man	1,375	the Way to the Forum	964	No Time for Sergeants	796
Funny Girl	1,348	The Odd Couple	964	Fiorello!	795

* As of July 25, 1979. Figures reflect consecutive performances.

MAJOR WORLD DANCE GROUPS

Source: The Dance Collection, Library & Museum of the Performing Arts, Lincoln Center, New York

Dates in parentheses indicate the founding year.

AMSTERDAM: The Dutch National Ballet (1961); *Director:* Rudi van Dantzig.

BOSTON: Boston Ballet (1964); *Director:* E. Virginia Williams.

BRUSSELS: Ballets du Vingtième Siècle (1960); *Director:* Maurice Béjart.

CHICAGO: Chicago Ballet (1970); *Directors:* Ruth Page, Frederic Franklin; *Artistic Advisor:* Robert Joffrey.

COPENHAGEN: Royal Danish Ballet (1771); *Director:* Henning Kronstam.

GLASGOW: Scottish Ballet (1969); *Dir.:* Peter Darrell.

THE HAGUE: Nederlands Dans Theater (1959); *Artistic Director:* Jiří Kylián.

HAVANA: Ballet Nacional de Cuba (1948); *Director:* Alicia Alonzo.

HOUSTON: Houston Ballet (1968); *Artistic Director:* Ben Stevenson.

LENINGRAD: Kirov Ballet (1783); *Director:* Oleg Vinogradov.

LONDON:
Festival Ballet (1950); *Director:* Beryl Grey, C.B.E.
Royal Ballet, Covent Garden (formerly Sadler's Wells Ballet) (1931); *Director:* Norman Morrice.
Ballet Rambert (1926); *Directors:* Dame Marie Rambert, John Chesworth.
London Contemporary Dance Theatre (1969); *Director:* Robert Cohan.

MELBOURNE: Australian Ballet (1962); *Director:* Dame Peggy van Praagh.

MOSCOW: Bolshoi Ballet (c. 1820); *Director:* Stanislav Louchin; *Artistic Director:* Yuri Grigorovich.

NEW YORK CITY:
Nikolais Dance Theatre (1948); *Director:* Alwin Nikolais.
American Ballet Theatre (1939); *Directors:* Lucia Chase, Oliver Smith.

Alvin Ailey American Dance Theatre (1958); *Director:* Alvin Ailey.

The Joffrey Ballet (1954); *Artistic Director:* Robert Joffrey.

The Dance Theatre of Harlem (1969); *Directors:* Arthur Mitchell and Karel Shook.

Eliot Feld Ballet (1974); *Director:* Eliot Feld.

Martha Graham Dance Company (1930); *Director:* Martha Graham.

Merce Cunningham and Dance Group (1952); *Director:* Merce Cunningham.

New York City Ballet (1948); *Dance Masters:* George Balanchine, Jerome Robbins, John Taras.

Paul Taylor Dance Company (1954); *Director:* Paul Taylor.

Twyla Tharp Foundation (1965); *Artistic Director:* Twyla Tharp.

PARIS: Paris Opera Ballet (1671); *Director:* Raymond Franchetti.

PHILADELPHIA: Pennsylvania Ballet (1964); *Director:* Barbara Weisberger; *Artistic Director:* Benjamin Harkarvy.

PITTSBURGH: Pittsburgh Ballet Theatre (1970); *Artistic Director:* Patrick Frantz.

SAN FRANCISCO: San Francisco Ballet (1937); *Directors:* Lew Christensen and Michael Smith.

STOCKHOLM: Royal Swedish Ballet (1773); *Artistic Director:* Ivo Cramer.

STUTTGART: Stuttgart Ballet (c. 1760); *Director:* Marcia Haydée.

TORONTO: National Ballet of Canada (1951); *Director:* Alexander Grant.

WASHINGTON (CONN.): Pilobolus Dance Theater (1971); *Manager:* Mark Ross.

WASHINGTON (D.C.): Washington Ballet (1962); *Director:* Mary Day.

WINNIPEG: Royal Winnipeg Ballet (1939); *Artistic Director:* Arnold Spohr.

POPULAR DISCOGRAPHY

Note: Numeral and hyphen preceding record label indicate multi-disc album, the numeral indicating the number of discs.

STANDARD POP

Herb Alpert & Tijuana Brass—You Smile/A&M 3620; **Paul Anka**—His Best/U. Artists LA922-H; **Frankie Avalon**—Venus/De-Lite 2020; **Burt Bacharach**—Greatest Hits/A&M 3661; **Tony Bennett**—Tony/Harmony KH 32171; **Glen Campbell**—Wichita Lineman/Capitol SM 513; **Captain & Tennille**—Love Will Keep Us Together/A&M SP4552; **Carpenters**—Singles/A&M 3601; **Nat "King" Cole**—Best/Capitol SKAO-2944; **Ray Conniff**—Harmony/Columbia KC-32553; **Bing Crosby**—Feels Good/London 679; **John Denver**—Greatest Hits/Victor CPL1-0374; **Neil Diamond**—Greatest Hits/MCA 2106; **José Feliciano**—Fireworks/RCA LSP 4370; **Four Seasons**—2nd Vault of Golden Hits/Philips 600-221; **Bobbie Gentry**—Fancy/Capitol ST-428; **Tom Jones**—Greatest Hits/Paramount XPAS 71062; **Peggy Lee**/Arc. Folk. 294; **Henry Mancini**—Country Gentlemen/Victor APL1-0270; **Barry Manilow**—Greatest Hits/2-Arista 8601; **Mantovani**—Greatest Hits, Vol. 1/London XPS 906; **Johnny Mathis**—All-Time Greatest Hits/2-Columbia PG 31345; **Mabel Mercer (w. Bobby Short)**—At Town Hall/2-Atlantic S-604; **Hugo Montenegro**—Hugo in Wonderland/Victor APL1-0413; **Olivia Newton-John**—Totally Hot/MCA 3067; **Tony Orlando & Dawn**—Prime Time/Bell 1317; **Donny & Marie Osmond**—New Season/Polydor 6083; **Pointer Sisters**—That's a Plenty/Blue Thumb 48; **Frank Sinatra**—Come Fly with Me/Capitol SY 4528; **Kate Smith**—At Carnegie Hall/Camden CAS-2587; **Barbra Streisand**—Greatest Hits Vol. 2/Columbia FC-35679; **Dionne Warwicke**—Very Best of/U. Artists LA 337-G; **Andy Williams**—Solitaire/Columbia KC-32383; **Nancy Wilson**—Best/Capitol SKAO-2947.

ROCK 'N' ROLL

ABBA—Greatest Hits/Atlantic 18189; **Badfinger**—Ass/Capitol SW 3411; **The Band**—Best/Capitol ST-11553; **Beach Boys**—Good Vibrations/Reprise 2223; **Beatles**—Rubber Soul/Apple ST 2442; **Bee Gees**—Best, Vol. 2/Atlantic RSO SO-875; **Blood, Sweat & Tears**—Greatest Hits/Columbia KC-31170; **Boston**—Epic PE 34188; **David Bowie**—Space Oddity/RCA LSP-4813; **Chicago**/2-Columbia C2-30110; **Joe Cocker**/A&M 4368; **Alice Cooper**—Welcome to my Nightmare/Atlantic SD 18130; **Cream**—Best of/Atco SD 33-291; **Crosby, Stills, Nash & Young**—Déjà Vu/Atlantic SD 7200; **Doors**/Elektra 74007; **Double Live Gonzo**/2-Epic KEZ-35069; **Eagles**—Hotel California/Asylum 7E 103; **Earth, Wind & Fire**—Best of, Vol. 1/Columbia FC-35647; **Fleetwood Mac**—Rumours/Warner Bros. BSK 3010; **Peter Frampton**—Comes Alive/A&M SP 3703; **Jimi Hendrix**—Are You Experienced?/Reprise S-6261; **Jefferson Starship**—Red Octopus/Grunt BFL1-0999; **Jethro Tull**—War Child/Chrysalis 1067; **Elton John**—Greatest Hits/MCA 2128; **Carole King**—Tapestry/Ode 77009; **Kiss**—Alive/Casablanca NBLP 7020; **Led Zeppelin**—Four/Atlantic 7208; **Meat Loaf**—Bat Out of Hell/Epic PE-34974; **Bette Midler**/Atlantic 7270; **Steve Miller**—Greatest Hits 1974-78/Capitol S00-11872; **Mothers of Invention**—We're Only in it for the Money/Verve 65045; **Randy Newman**—Little Criminals/Warner Bros. 3079; **Elvis Presley**—Elvis/RCA APL1-0283; **Queen**—News of the World/Elektra 112; **Gerry Rafferty**—City to City/U. Artists LA840-H; **Rolling Stones**—Some Girls/Roll. Stones Rec. 39108; **Santana**—Abraxas/Columbia KC-30130; **Boz Scaggs**—Silk Degrees/Columbia PC 33920; **Sex Pistols**—Never Mind the Bollocks/Warner Bros. K-3147; **Simon & Garfunkel**—Bridge over Troubled Water/Columbia KCS-9914; **Southside Johnny & The Asbury Jukes**—Hearts of Stone/Epic JE-35488; **Rod Stewart**—Best/2-Mercury 7507; **Donna Summer**—Live & More/2-LCasablanca 7119; **T. Rex**/Reprise 6440; **Village People**—Macho Man/Casablanca 7096; **The Who**—Tommy/2-Polydor PD2 9502; **Wings**—Greatest/Capitol S00-11905; **Neil Young**—After the Gold Rush/Reprise S-6383; **Warren Zevon**—Excitable Boy/Asylum 118.

FOLK AND FOLK-ROCK

Hoyt Axton—Life Machine/A&M 3604; **Joan Baez**—Blessed Are/2-Vanguard VSD 6570/1; **Jackson Browne**—For Everyman/Asylum 5067; **Leonard Cohen**—Songs of/Columbia CS 9533; **Judy Collins**—Whales & Nightingales/Elektra 75010; **Jim Croce**—Photographs & Memories/ABC 835; **Desire**/Columbia PC 33893; **Bob Dylan**—Blonde on Blonde/2-Columbia C2S-841, **Jack Elliott**/Vanguard 79151; **Kinky Friedman**—Sold American/Vanguard 79333; **Gathering at the Earl of Old Town**—Various/Mount. 670; **Bob Gibson**—Where I'm Bound/Elektra 7239; **Steve Goodman**—Somebody Else's Troubles/Buddah 5121; **Arlo Guthrie**—Washington County/Reprise 6411; **Woody Guthrie**—Dust Bowl Ballads/Folkways 5212; **Tim Hardin**—I/Verve Folk. FTS 3004; **George Harrison**—All Things Must Pass/3-Apple STCH 639; **Richie Havens**—Portfolio/Stormy Forest 6013; **Fred Holstein**—Chicago & Other Ports/Philo PH 1030; **Ian & Sylvia**—Best/2-

Columbia CG-32516; **Michael Johnson**—The Michael Johnson Album/EMI SW-17002; **Bonnie Koloc**—Close-Up/Epic PE-34184; **Leo Kottke**—Ice Water/Capitol ST 11262; **Leadbelly**—Huddie Ledbetter/Fantasy 24715; **Gordon Lightfoot**—Gord's Gold/2-Reprise 2RS 2237; **Melanie**—Candles in the Rain/Buddah BDS-5060; **Joni Mitchell**—Court & Spark/Elek. Asylum 7E 1001; **Maria Muldaur**—Sweet Harmony/Reprise MS 2235; **Harry Nilsson**—Nilsson Schmilsson/RCA LSP-4515; **Oliver (Bill Swofford)**—Good Morning Starshine/Crewe CR 1333; **Jim Post**—Slow to 20/Fantasy 9408; **John Prine**—Bruised Orange/Asylum 139; **Linda Ronstadt**—Greatest Hits/Asylum 1092, Simple Dreams/Asylum 104; **Rotary Connection**—Peace/Cadet-Concept LPS 318; **Leon Russell**—Will o' the Wisp/Shelter SR 2138; **Buffy Sainte-Marie**—It's My Way!/Vanguard VSD 79142; **Carly Simon**—Best/Elektra 7E-1048; **Skymonters (w. Hamid Hamilton Camp)**/Elektra 75073; **Bruce Springsteen**—Born to Run/Columbia PC-33795; **Cat Stevens**—Foreigner/A&M 4391; **James Taylor**—Mud Slide Slim/Warner Bros. BS-2561; **Dave Van Ronk**—Songs for Aging Children/Cadet 50044.

RHYTHM AND BLUES, SOUL, GOSPEL

Big Bill Broonzy—Blues/Encore 22017; **James Brown**—Reality/Polydor 6039; **Ray Charles**—Genius Sings the Blues/Atlantic SD 8052; **Sam Cooke**—You Send Me/Camden ACS1 0445; **Bo Diddley**—Greatest/Checker 8034; **Fats Domino**—Very Best/U. Artists LA 233-G; **Sleepy John Estes**—Broke & Hungry/Delmark 608; **Roberta Flack**—Killing Me Softly/Atlantic 7271; **Aretha Franklin**—With Everything I Feel in Me/Atlantic SD 18116; **B.B. King**—Best/ABC 724; **Gladys Knight & the Pips**—Knight Time/Soul 741; **Taj Mahal**—Mo Roots/Columbia KC 33051; **Curtis Mayfield**—Curtis in Chicago/Curtom 8018; **Mighty Clouds of Joy**—It's Time/Dunwich 50177; **Wilson Pickett**—Greatest Hits/2-Atlantic 2-501; **Lou Rawls**—She's Gone/Bell 1318; **Otis Redding**—Tell the Truth/Atco SD 33-333; **Smokey Robinson & Miracles**—195772/2-Tamia 320; **Sly & Family Stone**—Fresh/Epic KE-32134; **Bessie Smith**—Empty Bed Blues/Columbia G 30450; **Supremes (w. Diana Ross)**—Where Did Our Love Go?/Motown 621; **Sweet Inspirations**—Sweet Sweet Soul/Atlantic SD 8253; **Temptations**—Greatest Hits, Vol. 2/Gordy 5 954; **Muddy Waters**—Live/Chess 50012; **Stevie Wonder**—Songs in the Key of Life/2-Tamia 13-340C2.

JAZZ

Amanda Ambrose—Amanda/Dunwich 668; **George Benson**—Bad Benson/CTI 6045; **Dave Brubeck**—Greatest Hits/Columbia CS-9284; **John Coltrane**—My Favorite Things/Atlantic 1361; **Miles Davis**—Kind of Blue/Columbia PC 8163; **Ella Fitzgerald**—Best/Reprise S 6354; **Erroll Garner**—Misty/Mercury 60662; **Stan Getz (w. Charlie Byrd)**—Jazz Samba/Verve 68432; **Dizzy Gillespie**—Groovin' High/Savoy 12020; **Benny Goodman**—1938 Carnegie Hall Jazz Concert/2-Columbia OSL-160; **Woody Herman**—Woody/Cadet 845; **Earl Hines**—Tea for Two/Black Lion BL-112; **Billie Holiday**—Lady Day/Columbia CL-637; **Scott Joplin**—Ragtime, Vol. 3/Biograph 1010Q; **Roland Kirk**—Gifts & Messages/Mercury S 90939; **Chuck Mangione**—Chase the Clouds Away/A&M 4518; **Charles Mingus**—Mingus Dynasty/Columbia CL 1440; **Modern Jazz Quartet**—Best/Atlantic 1546; **Wes Montgomery**—Best/Verve 68714; **Jelly Roll Morton**—King of New Orleans Jazz/Victor LPM 1649; **Oliver Nelson**—Blues & the Abstract Truth/Impulse 5; **Charlie Parker**—On Dial, Vol. 1/Spotlite 101; **Oscar Peterson**—Newport Years/Verve 8828; **Django Reinhardt**—Djangology/Victor LPM 2319; **Sonny Rollins (w. Max Roach)**—Freedom Suite/2-Milestone 47007; **Art Tatum**—Essential/Verve 68433; **Lennie Tristano (w. George Russell)**—Crosscurrents/Capitol M-11060; **Sarah Vaughan**—Golden Hits/Mercury 60645; **Fats Waller**—One Never Knows, Do One?/Victor LPM 1503; **Lester Young**—Essential/Verve 68398.

COUNTRY AND WESTERN

Bill Anderson—Bill/MCA 320; **Lynn Anderson**—Greatest Hits/Columbia KC 31641; **Eddy Arnold**—Best, Vol. 3/RCA LSP 4844; **Chet Atkins**—Mr. Atkins, Guitar Picker/Camden CASX 2464(e); **Jimmy Buffett**—Changes in Latitudes, Changes in Attitudes/ABC 990; **Johnny Cash**—Greatest/Columbia CS-9478; **Jimmy Dean**—Favorite Son/Harmony 11270; **Flatt & Scruggs**—Greatest Hits/Columbia CS 9370; **Crystal Gayle**—Crystal/U. Artists UA-LA614-G; **Wanda Jackson**—Country Keepsakes/Capitol ST 11161; **Waylon Jennings**—Ol' Waylon/RCA AFL1-2317; **Loretta Lynn**—Greatest Hits, Vol. 2/MCA 420; **Jody Miller**—Country Girl/Epic KE-33349; **Willie Nelson**—Stardust/Columbia JC-35305; **Dolly Parton**—Here You Come Again/RCA AFL1-2544; **Charley Pride**—Pride of America/Victor APL1-0757; **Johnny Rodriguez**—Hits/Mercury SRM1-1078; **Carl Smith**—Country on My Mind/Columbia CS-9688; **Statler Bros.**—Best/Mercury 1037; **Hank Williams**—Greatest Hits/2-MGM S-4755; **Bob Wills**—Anthology/Columbia KG 32416; **Tammy Wynette**—My Man/Epic KE 31717.

CLASSICAL DISCOGRAPHY

OPERA

Beethoven—Fidelio: Klemperer/3-Angel S-3625; **Bellini**—Norma: Callas/3-Angel S-3615; **Berg**—Wozzeck: Böhm/2-DGG 2707023; **Bizet**—Carmen: Troyanos, Solti, London Phil./3-London 13115; **Debussy**—Pelléas et Mélisande: Ansermet/London 1379; **Donizetti**—Lucia di Lammermoor: Sutherland/London 25702; **Flotow**—Martha (highlights): Berlin Mun. Op./Angel S-36236; **Gilbert & Sullivan**—The Yeoman of the Guard: Gilbert & Sullivan Festival Orch./BSAF MIC BB 25l09; **Gluck**—Orfeo ed Euridice: Fasano/3-RCA LSC-6169; **Gounod**—Faust: Gedda/4-Angel S-3622; **Leoncavallo**—Pagliacci: Corelli/2-Angel S-3618; **Mascagni**—Cavalleria Rusticana: Del Monaco/3-London 1213; **Massenet**—Manon: Sills-Gedda/4-ABC ATS-20007; **Mozart**—Marriage of Figaro: Klemperer/4-EMI Odeon 1c 191-02134/7; Don Giovanni: Klemperer/4-Angel S-3700; The Magic Flute: Böhm/3-DG-2709017; **Moussorgsky**—Boris Godunov: Christoff/4-Angel S-3633; **Puccini**—La Bohème: Tebaldi/2-London 1208; Tosca: Price/2-London 1284; Madama Butterfly: De los Angeles/3-Angel S-3604; **Rossini**—The Barber of Seville: Leinsdorf/4-RCA 6143; **Schoenberg**—Moses and Aaron: Gielen/2-Philips 6700084; **R. Strauss**—Der Rosenkavalier: Solti/4-London 1435; **Verdi**—Rigoletto: MacNeil/3-Angel S-3718; La Traviata: Moffo/3-RCA LSC-6154; Aida: Price/3-RCA 6198; Otello: Del Monaco/3-London 1324; Falstaff: Gobbi/3-Angel S-3552; La Forza del Destino/Angel S-3604; **Wagner**—Gotterdämmerung: Nilsson/6-London 1604.

SYMPHONY

Beethoven—Complete Symphonies, 1-9: Karajan/8-DG 2721001; **Berlioz**—Symphonie Fantastique: Munch/RCA LSC-2608; **Bizet**—Symphony No. 1: Ansermet/London 6208; **Brahms**—Complete Symphonies 1-4: Szell/3-Columbia D3S-758; **Bruckner**—No. 4: Klemperer/Angel S-36245; No. 9: Mehta/London 6462; **Copland**—Symphony No. 3: Bernstein/Columbia MS-6954; **Dvořák**—Nos. 7-9: Szell/3-Columbia D3S-814; **Franck**—Symphony in D minor: Monteux/RCA LSC-2514; **Haydn**—Nos. 93-104: Dorati/3-London STS 15319-15324; **Mahler**—No. 1: Giulini/DG 2707097; No. 4: Reiner/RCA 2364; No. 9: Walter/2-Odyssey Y2-30308; **Mendelssohn**—Nos. 4-5: Munch/RCA LSC-2221; **Mozart**—Nos. 25,29: Marriner/Argo ZRG-706; Nos. 32, 35, 38: Boehm/DG 138112; Nos. 40,41: Klemperer/Angel S-36183; **Nielsen**—No. 5: Bernstein/Columbia MS-6414; **Prokofiev**—Classical Symphony, Lt. Kijé and "Three Oranges" Suites: Ormandy/Columbia MS-6545; **Saint-Saëns**—No. 3: Munch/RCA LSC-2341; **Schubert**—Nos. 5,8: Walter/Columbia MS-6218; No. 9: Szell/Angel S-36044; **Schumann**—Complete Symphonies, 1-4: Bernstein/3-Columbia D3S-725; **Shostakovich**—No. 2: Ormandy/Columbia MS-6124; **Sibelius**—No. 5: Bernstein/Columbia MS-6749; **Stravinsky**—Symphony in Three Movements: Ansermet/London MS-6190; **Tchaikovsky**—No. 4: Monteux/RCA 2369; No. 6: Ormandy/Columbia MS-6160; **Vaughan Williams**—No. 9: Boult/Everest 3006.

ORCHESTRAL AND CHORAL

Bach—Brandenburg Concertos: Harnoncourt/Telefunken S-9459/60; Cantatas 56 & 169: Saar Ch. Orch./Nonesuch 71142; Suites for Orchestra: Casals/2-Columbia M2S-755; **Bartók**—Concerto for Orchestra: Bernstein/Columbia MS-6140; Hungarian Sketches: Reiner/RCA VICS 1620; Music for Strings, Percussion and Celesta: Boulez/Columbia MS-7206; **Beethoven**—Overtures: Karajan/2-DG 2707046; **Copland**—Appalachian Spring; El Salon Mexico: Bernstein/Columbia MS-6355; Billy the Kid; Rodeo: Bernstein/Columbia MS-6175; **Debussy**—La Mer; Nocturnes: Giulini/Angel S-35977; Images pour Orchestre: Boulez/Columbia MS-7362; **Dvořák**—Slavonic Dances: Szell/Columbia MS-7208; **Elgar**—Enigma Variations; Cockaigne Overture: Barbirolli/Angel S-36120; **Falla**—Three Cornered Hat & La Vida Breve Dances: Reiner/RCA 2230; **Gershwin**—An American in Paris; Rhapsody in Blue: Bernstein/Columbia MS-6091; **Handel**—Concerti Grossi Op. 6: Leppard/Mercury 9124; Water Music and Royal Fireworks Suites: Szell/London 6236; **Hindemith**—Symphonic Metamorphoses of Themes by Weber; Mathis der Maler: Ormandy/Columbia MS-6562; **Kodály**—Háry János Suite; Dances from Galánta: Kertész/London 6417; **Liszt**—A Faust Symphony; Les Preludes: Bernstein/2-Columbia MG-699; **Mendelssohn**—A Midsummer Night's Dream: Klemperer/Angel S-3588l; **Mozart**—Eine Kleine Nachtmusik; Serenade No. 9: Szell/Columbia MS-7273; **Moussorgsky-Ravel**—Pictures at an Exhibition: Ansermet/London 6177; **Orff**—Carmina Burana: Thomas & Cleveland Orch. Chorus & Boys' Choir/Columbia M-33172; **Ravel**—Daphnis et Chloe: Ansermet/London 6456; La Valse; Menuet Antique; Ma Mère l'Oye: Boulez/Columbia M-32838Q; **Respighi**—The Pines of Rome; The Fountains of Rome: Reiner/RCA LSC-2436; **Rimsky-Korsakov**—Scheherazade: Rostropovich/Angel S-37061(Q); **Rossini**—Overtures: Toscanini/Victrola 1274; **Smetana**—Moldau; Bartered Bride Dances: Szell/Odyssey Y-30049; **J. Strauss**—Waltzes: Ormandy/Columbia MS-6217; **R. Strauss**—Also sprach Zarathustra, Don Juan & Till Eulenspiegel: Solti/London 6978; **Stravinsky**—The

Firebird: Stokowski/London 21026; Le Sacre du Printemps: Bernstein/Columbia MS-6010; **Tchaikovsky**—The Nutcracker: Ansermet/London 2203; Romeo and Juliet; Francesca da Rimini: Munch/RCA VICS-1197; The Sleeping Beauty: Previn/3-Angel SX 3812(Q); **Wagner**—Siegfried Idyll; Overtures: Walter/Columbia MS-6507.

SOLOS WITH ORCHESTRA

Bach—Clavier Concertos Nos. 1,2: Kirkpatrick/DG ARC 198013; Violin Concertos Nos. 1, 2; Concerto for 2 Violins: David and Igor Oistrakh/DG 138820; **Bartók**—Piano Concertos Nos. 2,3: Anda/DG 138111; **Beethoven**—Piano Concertos Nos. 1-5: Ashkenazy/4-London 2404; Violin Concerto: Stern/Columbia MS-6093; **Berg**—Violin Concerto: Grumiaux/Philips 900194; **Berlioz**—Harold in Italy: Menuhin/Angel S-36123; **Brahms**—Piano Concerto No. 2: Richter/RCA LSC-2466; Violin Concerto: Heifetz/RCA LSC-1903; Double Concerto: Oistrakh-Rostropovich/Angel S-36032; **Bruch**—Violin Concerto No. l: Stern/Columbia MS-7003; **Chopin**—Piano Concerto Nos. 1,2; Andante: Rubinstein/2-RCA VCS-7091; **Dvořák**—Cello Concerto: Starker/Mercury 90303; **Grieg**—Piano Concerto: Rubinstein/RCA LSC-2566; **Lalo**—Symphonie Espagnole; **Liszt**—Piano Concertos Nos. 1,2: Richter/Philips 835474; **Mendelssohn**—Violin Concerto: Francescatti/Columbia MS-6758; **Mozart**—Horn Concertos Nos. 1-4; Rondo K.371: Civil/Philips 6500325; Piano Concertos Nos. 25,27: Gulda/DG 2530642; Violin Concertos Nos. 3,4: Francescatti/Columbia MS-6063; **Paganini**—Violin Concertos Nos. 1,2: Gitlis/Turn. 34203; **Poulenc**—Organ Concerto: Duruflé (w. Gloria: Carteri)/Angel S-35953; **Prokofiev**—Piano Concertos Nos. 3,4: Browning/RCA 3019; **Rachmaninoff**—Piano Concerto No. 2: Ashkenazy/London 6390; **Saint-Saëns**—Cello Concertos Nos. 1,2, etc.: Walevska/Philips 6500459; **Schumann**—Cello Concerto: Rostropovich/DG 138674; Piano Concerto: Rubinstein/RCA LSC-2997; **Sibelius**—Violin Concerto: Heifetz/RCA LSC-2435; **Tchaikovsky**—Piano Concerto No. l: Cliburn/RCA LSC-2252; Violin Concerto: Zuckerman/Columbia MS-7313; **Vivaldi**—The Four Seasons: Virtuosi di Roma/Angel S-35877.

CHAMBER MUSIC

Bartók—Quartets Nos. 1-6: Juilliard Quartet/3-Columbia D3S-717; **Beethoven**—Quartets (complete): Amadeus Quartet/4-DG 2721006; "Archduke" Trio: Stern-Rose-Istomin/Columbia MS-6819; Violin Sonatas (complete): Grumiaux-Haskil/Philips 6733001; **Berg**—Lyric Suite: RCA/Juilliard Quartet/RCA 2531; **Brahms**—Quartet Op. 34: Previn, Yale Quartet/Angel S-36928; Trio Op. 40: Tuckwell-Perlman-Ashkenazy/London 6628; Violin Sonatas: Szeryng, Rubinstein/2-RCA LSC-2619/20; **Debussy** and **Ravel**—Quartets: Juilliard Quartet/Columbia M-30650; **Dvořák**—Quartets Nos. 2,6: Janáček Quartet/London 6394; Piano Quintet: Curzon/Vienna Phil. Quartet/London 6357; **Haydn**—Quartets Op. 76, Nos. 2,5: Hungarian Quartet/Turnabout 34012; Quartets Op. 77, Nos. 1,2: Amadeus Quartet/DG 138980; **Hindemith**—Kleine Kammermusik: Boston Symphony Players/RCA 3166; **Mendelssohn**—Octet: Laredo, et al/Columbia MS-6848; **Mozart**—Quartets Nos. 14-19: Italiano/3-Philips S-C 71AX301; Piano Quartets: Horszowski, Budapest/Columbia MS-6683; Quintets K. 515,516: Primrose, Griller/Vanguard S-158: Quintet, K. 581, Trio K. 498: De Peyer, Melos Ensemble/Angel S-36241; **Schubert**—Octet: Melos Ensemble/Angel S-36529; Quartets Nos. 12,14: Amadeus Quartet/DG 138048; "Trout" Quintet: Marlboro Players/Vanguard 71145; **Schumann**—Piano Quintet: Serkin, Budapest/2-Columbia M2S-734: **Stravinsky**—L'Histoire du Soldat: Cocteau, Markevitch/Philips 90046.

SOLO INSTRUMENTAL

Bach—Goldberg Variations: Leonhardt/Vanguard S-175; Well-tempered Clavier, Bk. 1: Kirkpatrick/2-DG ARC 2708006; Sonatas and Partitas for Violin: Grumiaux/3-Philips 835198/200; Organ Music: Walcha/DG 198305; **Beethoven**—Piano Sonatas 8,14,23: Kempff/DG 139300; 17,21: Brendel/Turnabout 34394; 28,31: Serkin/Columbia M 31239; 30,32: Backhaus/London CS-6246; **Chopin**—Ballades: Rubinstein/RCA LSC-2370; Mazurkas: Novaes/Vox 57920; Nocturnes: Rubinstein/RCA LSC-7050; Scherzos: Rubinstein/RCA LSC-2368; Sonatas Nos. 2,3: Rubinstein/RCA 3194; **Debussy**—Piano Music (complete): W. Haas/5-Philips 5-012; **Liszt**—Sonata in B minor; Piano Music: Curzon/London 6371; **Mendelssohn**—Songs without Words: Novaes/Turnabout 34245; **Mozart**—Piano Sonatas (complete), Fantasy K. 475, Rondo K. 494: Klein/6-Vox SVBX 5428/9; **Rachmaninoff**—Preludes, etc.: Weissenberg—RCA 7069; **Ravel**—Piano Music: De Larrocha/Columbia 30115; **Scarlatti**—Sonatas: Kirkpatrick/DG ARC-2533072; **Schubert**—Sonata in A; Wanderer Fantasy: Richter/Angel S-36150; Sonata in D; Impromptus: Curzon/London 6416; Sonata in A, Op. Posth.: Serkin/Columbia MS-6849; **Schumann**—Carnaval; Fantasia, Op. 17: Arrau/Philips 802746; **Scriabin**—Piano Sonatas 3,4,5,9: Ashkenazy/London 6920.

LEADING OPERA COMPANIES
SOURCE: Central Opera Service

WORLD OPERA COMPANIES (exclusive of U.S.)

AMSTERDAM: **Nederlandse Operastichting;** *Manager:* J.H. de Roo.

BARCELONA: **Gran Teatro del Liceo;** *General Director:* Juan A. Pamias.

BAYREUTH: **Bayreuther Festspiele;** *Director:* Wolfgang Wagner.

BELGRADE: **Srpsko Narodno Pozoriste;** *Director:* D. Djurdjevic.

BERLIN: **(West) Deutsche Oper;** *Director:* Siegfried Palm. **(East) Deutsche Staatsoper;** *General Director:* Hans Pischner. **(East) Komische Oper;** *Director:* Joachim Herz.

BRUSSELS: **Théâtre Royal de la Monnaie;** *Director:* Maurice Huisman.

BUCHAREST: **Romanian Opera;** *Director:* Petre Codreanu.

BUDAPEST: **Magyar Allami Operahaz & Erkel Theater (Hungarian State Opera);** *Director:* Miklos Lukacs.

BUENOS AIRES: **Teatro Colon.**

COLOGNE: **Bühnen der Stadt Köln;** *Director:* Michael Hampe, *Music Director:* John Pritchard.

COPENHAGEN: **Det kongelige Teater;** *Manager:* Niels Moeller.

DRESDEN: **Staatsoper Dresden;** *Director:* Horst Seeger.

DUSSELDORF/DUISBURG: **Deutsche Oper am Rhein;** *Director:* Grischa Barfuss.

EDINBURGH: **Edinburgh Festival;** *Director:* John Drummond.

FLORENCE: **Teatro Comunale & Maggio Fiorentino;** *Music Director:* Riccardo Muti.

FRANKFURT: **Stadtische Buhnen;** *Director:* Michael Gielen.

GENEVA: **Grand Theatre de l'Opera;** *General Director:* Jean-Claude Riber; *Director Designate:* Hugues Gall.

GLASGOW: **Scottish Opera;** *General Director:* Peter Ebert.

GLYNDEBOURNE: **Festival Opera;** *Chairman:* George W. Christie.

HAMBURG: **Staatsoper;** *Dir. & Chief conductor:* Christoph von Dohnányi.

HELSINKI: **Finnish National Opera;** *General Manager:* J. Raiskinen.

LEIPZIG: **Staedtische Theater;** *Director Opera:* Karl Kayser.

LENINGRAD: **Kirov Opera & Ballet Theatre;** *Director:* Yuri Temirkanov.

LONDON: **D'Oyly Carte Ltd.;** *Musical Director:* Royston Nash. **Royal Opera, Covent Garden;** *General Administrator:* John Tooley. **English National Opera Ltd.;** *Managing Director:* Lord Harewood.

MARSEILLE: **Opera Municipal;** *Director:* R. Giovaninetti.

MILAN: **Teatro alla Scala;** *Music Director:* Claudio Abbado; *Gen. Mgr.:* Carlo Mania Badini

MONTE CARLO: **L'Opera de Monte-Carlo;** *Director:* Guy Grinda

MOSCOW: **Bolshoi Theatre of the USSR;** *Director:* Giorgy Ivanov.

MUNICH: **Bayerische Staatsoper;** *Director:* August Everding. **Theater am Gartnerplatz;** *Director:* Kurt Pscherer.

NAPLES: **Teatro San Carlo;** *Acting General Manager:* Adriano Falvo.

OSLO: **Den Norske Opera (The Norwegian Opera);** *Director:* Aase Nordmo-Loevberg.

OTTAWA: **Ottawa Festival Opera;** *Administrator:* Andrée Gingras.

PARIS: **Theatre National de l'Opera;** *Administrator:* Rolf Liebermann.

PRAGUE: **National Theatre & Smetana Theatre & Tyl Theatre;** *Director:* Premysl Koci.

RIO DE JANEIRO: **Opera Estaveldo Teatro Municipal;** *Director:* Edmundo Barreto Pintos.

ROME: **Teatro dell'Opera;** *Gen. Mgr.:* Luca di Schieane

SALZBURG: **Salzburg Festival;** *Director:* Dr. Otto Sertl. **Easter Festival;** *Director:* Herbert von Karajan.

SOFIA: **Bulgarian National Opera;** *Director:* Dimitar Petkov.

STOCKHOLM: **Kungliga Teatern;** *General Manager:* Folke Abenius.

STRASBOURG: **L'Opera du Rhin;** *Artistic Director:* Alain Lombard.

STUTTGART: **Wurttembergisches Staatstheater;** *Music Director:* Silvio Varviso.

SYDNEY: **Australian Opera;** *General Manager:* Peter Hemmings.

TEL AVIV: **Israel National Opera;** *Director:* Simha Evan Zohar.

TORONTO: **Canadian Opera Company;** *General Director:* Lotfi Mansouri.

VANCOUVER: **Vancouver Opera Association;** *General Manager:* Hamilton McClymont.

VENICE: **Teatro La Fenice;** *General Manager:* Gianmario Vianello.

VERONA: **Arena di Verona;** *Artistic Director:* Luciano Chailly.

VIENNA: **Staatsoper;** *Director:* Egon Seefehlner. **Volksoper;** *Director:* Karl Donsh.

WARSAW: **Teatr Wielki (Grand Theatre Warsaw);** *Artistic Director:* Antoni Wicherek.

ZURICH: **Opernhaus Zurich;** *General Manager:* Klaus Helmut Drese.

AMERICAN OPERA COMPANIES

BALTIMORE: **Baltimore Opera Company;** *General Manager:* Robert Collinge.

BOSTON: **Opera Company of Boston;** *Artistic Director:* Sarah Caldwell.

CENTRAL CITY: **Central City Opera House Association;** *Artistic Director:* Robert Darling.

CHARLESTON: **Spoleto Festival USA;** *General Manager:* James Kearney.

CHICAGO: **Lyric Opera of Chicago;** *General Manager:* Carol Fox.

CINCINNATI: **Cincinnati Opera Association;** *General Manager:* James de Blasis.

DALLAS: **Dallas Civic Opera;** *General Manager:* Plato Karayanis.

DAYTON/TOLEDO: **Dayton/Toledo Opera Associations;** *General Director:* Lester Freedman.

DETROIT: **Michigan Opera Theater;** *General Director:* David Di Chiera.

DISTRICT OF COLUMBIA: **Washington Opera, Inc.;** *General Manager:* Gary Fifield.

FORT WORTH: **Fort Worth Opera Association;** *General Manager:* Rudolf Kruger.

GLENS FALLS: **Lake George Opera Company;** *General Director:* David Lloyd.

HARTFORD: **Connecticut Opera Association, Inc.;** *General Manager:* William Warden.

HONOLULU: **Hawaii Opera Theatre;** *General Manager:* Robert C. Bickley.

HOUSTON: **Houston Grand Opera Association;** *General Director:* R. David Gockley.

KANSAS CITY (MO.): **Lyric Opera of Kansas City;** *General Manager:* Russell Patterson.

LOUISVILLE: **Kentucky Opera Association;** *Artistic Director:* Moritz Bomhard.

MEMPHIS: **Memphis Opera Theatre;** *General Director:* Kenneth Caswell.

MIAMI: **Greater Miami Opera Association;** *General Manager:* Robert Herman.

MILWAUKEE: **Florentine Opera Company;** *General Manager:* Robert Caulfield.

NEW ORLEANS: **New Orleans Opera;** *General Director:* Arthur Cosenza.

NEW YORK: **Goldovsky Opera Theatre;** *Artistic Director:* Boris Goldovsky. **Metropolitan Opera Association;** *Executive Director:* Anthony A. Bliss. **New York City Opera;** *General Director:* Beverly Sills.

NEWARK: **New Jersey State Opera;** *Artistic Director:* Alfred Silipigni.

NORFOLK: **Virginia Opera Association;** *Artistic Director:* Peter Mark.

OMAHA: **Opera/Omaha;** *General Manager:* Martha Elsberry.

PHILADELPHIA: **Opera Company of Philadelphia;** *General Manager:* Edward Corn.

PITTSBURGH: **Pittsburgh Opera Company;** *Manager:* Vincent Artz.

PORTLAND (ORE.): **Portland Opera Association;** *General Director:* Stefan Minde.

PROVIDENCE: **Artists Internationale;** *Artistic Director:* Ken Russell Slade.

ST. LOUIS: **Opera Theater of St. Louis;** *General Manager:* Richard Gaddes.

ST. PAUL: **Minnesota Opera Company;** *Artistic Director:* H. Wesley Balk.

SAN DIEGO: **San Diego Opera Association;** *Artistic Director:* Tito Copobianco.

SAN FRANCISCO: **San Francisco Opera Association;** *General Director:* Kurt Herbert Adler. **Spring Opera Theatre;** *General Director:* Kurt Herbert Adler. **Western Opera Theatre;** *Manager:* Robert Bailey.

SANTA FE: **Santa Fe Opera;** *General Director:* John O. Crosby.

SEATTLE: **Seattle Opera Association, Inc.;** *General Director:* Glynn Ross.

TUCSON: **Arizona Opera Company;** *General Director:* James Sullivan.

TULSA: **Tulsa Opera Company;** *General Manager:* Edward Purrington.

MAJOR SYMPHONY ORCHESTRAS OF THE UNITED STATES AND CANADA

SOURCE: American Symphony Orchestra League

Atlanta Symphony Orchestra
1280 Peachtree Street, NE, Atlanta, Georgia 30309
Mus. Dir.: Robert Shaw
Gen. Mgr.: Stephen Sell

Baltimore Symphony Orchestra
5204 Roland Ave., Baltimore, MD 21210
Mus. Dir.: Sergiu Comissiona
Gen. Mgr.: Joseph Leavitt

Boston Symphony Orchestra
301 Massachusetts Ave., Symphony Hall
Boston, Massachusetts 02115
Mus. Dir.: Seiji Ozawa
Exec. Dir.: Thomas W. Morris

Buffalo Philharmonic Orchestra
26 Richmond Avenue, Buffalo, New York 14222
Mus. Dir.: Julius Rudel
Co-Mgrs.: Michael Bielski & Ruth Spero

Chicago Symphony Orchestra
220 South Michigan Avenue, Chicago, Illinois 60604
Mus. Dir.: Sir Georg Solti
Exec. V. Pres. & Gen. Mgr.: John S. Edwards

Cincinnati Symphony Orchestra
1241 Elm Street, Cincinnati, Ohio 45210
Mus. Dir.: Walter Susskind
Gen. Mgr.: Steven I. Monder
Manager: Judith Arron

Cleveland Orchestra
11001 Euclid Avenue, Cleveland, Ohio 44106
Mus. Dir.: Lorin Maazel
Gen. Mgr.: Kenneth Haas

Dallas Symphony Orchestra
P.O. Box 26207, Dallas, Texas 75226
Mus. Dir.: Eduardo Mata
Mng. Dir.: Leonard D. Stone

Denver Symphony Orchestra
1615 California Street, Denver, Colorado 80202
Mus. Dir.: Gaetano Delogu
Exec. Dir.: Carlos Wilson

Detroit Symphony Orchestra
Ford Auditorium
20 Auditorium Drive, Detroit, Michigan 48226
Mus. Dir.: Antal Dorati

Honolulu Symphony Orchestra
1000 Bishop Street, Suite 901
Honolulu, Hawaii 96813
Mus. Dir.: Donald Johanos
V. Pres. & Gen. Mgr.: Robert C. Bickley

Houston Symphony Orchestra
615 Louisiana, Houston, TX 77002
Prin. Guest Cond.: Michael Palmer
Gen. Mgr.: Michael J. Woolcock

Indianapolis Symphony Orchestra
4600 Sunset Ave., Indianapolis, IN 46208
Mus. Dir.: John Nelson
Gen. Mgr.: Fritz Kumb

Kansas City Philharmonic Orchestra
200 W. 14th St., Kansas City, MO 64105
Mus. Dir.: Maurice Peress
Gen. Mgr.: David Kent

Los Angeles Philharmonic Orchestra
135 N. Grand Ave., Los Angeles, CA 90012
Mus. Dir.: Carlo Maria Giulini
Exec. Dir.: Ernest Fleischmann

Milwaukee Symphony Orchestra
Performing Arts Center
929 North Water St., Milwaukee, WI 53202
Mus. Dir.: Kenneth Schermerhorn
Gen. Mgr.: Richard Thomas

Minnesota Orchestra
1111 Nicollet Mall, Minneapolis, MN 55403
Mus. Dir.: Neville Marriner
President: Richard M. Cisek

Montreal Symphony Orchestra
Place des Arts
Montreal, Quebec H2X 1Y9 Canada
Mus. Dir.: Charles Dutoit
Mng. Dir.: John C. Goodwin

National Symphony Orchestra
J. F. Kennedy Center for the Performing Arts
Washington, DC 20566
Mus. Dir.: Mstislav Rostropovich
Mng. Dir.: Oleg Lobanov
Manager: Robert Noerr

New Jersey Symphony Orchestra
213 Washington St., 16th Floor
Newark, NJ 07101
Mus. Dir.: Thomas Michalak
Gen. Mgr.: Kenneth R. Meine

New Orleans Philharmonic Symphony Orchestra
203 Carondelet St., Suite 903
New Orleans, LA 70130
Mus. Dir.: Leonard Slatkin
Exec. Dir. & V.P.: James D. Hicks

New York Philharmonic Orchestra
Avery Fisher Hall
65th St. and Broadway
New York, NY 10023
Mus. Dir.: Zubin Mehta
Exec. V.P. & Mng. Dir.: Albert K. Webster

North Carolina Symphony Orchestra
Memorial Auditorium, P.O. Box 28026
Raleigh, NC 27611
Art. Dir.: John Gosling
Gen. Mgr.: Ralph O. Guthrie

Philadelphia Orchestra
1420 Locust St., Philadelphia, PA 19102
Mus. Dir.: Euguene Ormandy
Exec. Dir.: Seymour L. Rosen

Pittsburgh Symphony Orchestra
Heinz Hall for the Performing Arts
600 Penn Avenue, Pittsburgh, PA 15222
Mus. Dir.: André Previn
Mng. Dir.: Marshall W. Turkin

Rochester Philharmonic Orchestra
20 Grove Pl., Rochester, NY 14605
Mus. Dir.: David Zinman
Gen. Mgr.: Tony H. Dechario

Saint Louis Symphony Orchestra
718 N. Grand Blvd., St. Louis, MO 63103
Mus. Dir.: Leonard Slatkin
Exec. Dir.: David Hyslop
Manager: James M. Cain

San Antonio Symphony Orchestra
109 Lexington Ave., Suite 207
San Antonio, TX 78205
Mus. Dir.: Francois Huybrechts
Manager & Mng. Dir.: Nat Greenberg

San Francisco Symphony Orchestra
107 War Memorial Veterans' Bldg.
San Francisco, CA 94102
Mus. Dir.: Edo de Waart
Exec. Dir.: Peter Pastreich

Seattle Symphony Orchestra
305 Harrison St., Seattle, WA 98109
Mus. Dir.: Rainer Miedel
Gen. Mgr.: Lanham Deal

Syracuse Symphony Orchestra
Suite 40, Civic Center, 411 Montgomery St.
Syracuse, NY 13202
Mus. Dir.: Christopher Keene

Toronto Symphony Orchestra
215 Victoria St.
Toronto, Ontario M5B 1V1 Canada
Mus. Dir.: Andrew Davis
Mng. Dir.: Walter Homburger

Utah Symphony Orchestra
55 W. First S., Salt Lake City, UT 84101
Mus. Dir.: Maurice Abravanel
Exec. Dir.: Herold L. Gregory

Vancouver Symphony Orchestra
873 Beatty St.
Vancouver, B.C. V6B 2M6 Canada
Mus. Dir.: Kazuyoshi Akiyama
Gen. Mgr.: Michael Allerton

PROFESSIONAL RESIDENT AND REPERTORY THEATERS

Source: Actors' Equity Association. The following resident and repertory groups are member companies of the League of Resident Theatres or use the L.O.R.T. contract.

ABINGDON (VA): **Barter Theatre;** P.O. Box 250 Abingdon, VA 24210

ALLENTOWN (PA): **Free Hall Theatre Company;** J.I. Rodale Theatre, 837 Linden St., Allentown, Pa 18101

AMHERST (MA): **The Commonwealth Stage;** Rm. 125 B, Fine Arts Center, U. of Mass., Amherst, MA 01003

ANCHORAGE (AK): **Alaska Repertory Theatre;** 523 W. 8th Ave., Suite 110, Anchorage, AK 99501

ARROW ROCK (MO): **Arrow Rock Lyceum Theatre;** Arrow Rock, MO 63520 (Summer)

ATLANTA (GA): **Alliance Theatre Company;** 1280 Peachtree St., N.E., Atlanta, GA 30309

BALTIMORE (MD): **Center Stage;** 700 N. Calvert St., Baltimore, MD 21202

BERKELEY (CA): **Berkeley Repertory Theatre;** 2980 College Ave., Berkeley, CA 94707

BOSTON (MA): **Boston Repertory Theatre;** 1 Boylston Pl., Boston, MA 02116

BUFFALO (NY): **Studio Arena Theatre;** 710 Main St., Buffalo, NY 14202

CHAPEL HILL (NC): **Playmakers Repertory Company;** 103 South Bldg., U. of N.C., Chapel Hill, NC 27514

CHICAGO (IL): **Goodman Theatre Company;** 200 S. Columbus Dr., Chicago, IL 60603

CINCINNATI (OH): **Playhouse in the Park;** P.O. Box 6537, Cincinnati, OH 45206

CLEVELAND (OH): **The Cleveland Playhouse;** 2040 E. 86th St., Cleveland, OH 44106

  Center Repertory Theatre; 1630 Euclid Ave., Cleveland, OH 44115

COHOES (NY): **Cohoes Music Hall;** 58 Remsen St., Cohoes, NY 12047

COSTA MESA (CA): **South Coast Repertory Theatre;** 655 South Town Center Dr., Costa Mesa, CA 92626

DALLAS (TX): **Theatre 3, Inc.;** 2800 Routh St., Dallas TX 75201

EVANSTON (IL): **The North Light Repertory Theatre, Inc,;** 927 Noyes, Evanston, IL 60201

HARTFORD (CT): **Hartford Stage Company;** 50 Church St., Hartford, CT 06103

HORSE CAVE (KY): **Horse Cave Theatre;** P.O. Box 215, Horse Cave, KY 42749 (Summer)

HOUSTON (TX): **Alley Theatre;** 615 Texas Ave., Houston, TX 77002

HUNTINGTON STATION (NY): **The Performing Arts Foundation; PAF Playhouse,** 185 Second St., Huntington Station, NY 11746

INDIANAPOLIS (IN): **Indiana Repertory Theatre;** 411 E. Michigan St., Indianapolis, IN 46204

KANSAS CITY (MO): **Missouri Vanguard Theatre** (Spring); **Missouri Repertory Theatre** (Summer); U. of Missouri at Kansas City, 5100 Rockhill Rd., Kansas City, MO 64110

KNOXVILLE (TN): **Department of Speech and Theatre;** 206 McClung Tower, U. of Tennessee, Knoxville, TN 37916

LAKE PLACID (NY): **Center for Music, Drama, and Art;** Saranac Ave. at Fawn Ridge, Lake Placid, NY 12946

LAKEWOOD (OH): **Great Lakes Shakespeare Festival;** Lakewood Civic Auditorium, Franklin Blvd. & Bunts Rd., Lakewood, OH 44107 (Summer)

LEWISTON (ME): **Bates Summer Theatre;** Bates College, Lewiston, ME 04240 (Summer)

LOS ANGELES (CA): **Mark Taper Forum** (Center Theatre Group); 135 N. Grand Ave., Los Angeles, CA 90012

  L.A. Free Shakespeare Festival; P.O. Box 1951, Los Angeles, CA 90028

LOS GATOS (CA): **California Actors Theatre;** P.O. Box 1355, Los Gatos, CA 95030

LOUISVILLE (KY): **Actors Theatre of Louisville;** 316-320 W. Main St., Louisville, KY 40202

MADISON (NJ): **New Jersey Shakespeare Festival;** Drew U., Madison, NJ 07940 (Summer & Fall)

MIAMI (FL): **Players State Theatre;** Coconut Grove Playhouse, 3500 Main Hwy., Miami, FL 33133

MIDDLETOWN (VA): **The Wayside Theatre;** P.O. Box 260, Middletown, VA 22645

MILWAUKEE (WI): **Milwaukee Repertory Theatre;** Performing Arts Center, 929 N. Water St., Milwaukee, WI 53202

MINNEAPOLIS (MN): **Cricket Theatre;** 345 13th Ave. N.E., (University at 13th), Minneapolis, MN 55413

  The Guthrie Theater; 725 Vineland Pl., Minneapolis, MN 55403

MISSOULA (MT): **Montana Repertory Theatre;** U. of Mont., Missoula, MT 59812

MONMOUTH (ME): **The Theater at Monmouth;** Cumston Hall, Monmouth, ME 04295 (Summer)

NASHVILLE (TN): **The Advent Theater;** 1202 17th Ave. S., Nashville, TN 37212

NEW HAVEN (CT): **Long Wharf Theatre;** 222 Sargent Dr., New Haven, CT 06511

  Yale Repertory Theatre; Yale School of Drama, New Haven, CT 06520

NEW YORK (NY): **The Acting Company;** 420 W. 42nd St., 3rd Fl., New York, NY 10036

  Chelsea Theatre Center; 511 W. 54th St., New York, NY 10019

  The Negro Ensemble Company; St. Mark's Playhouse, 133 Second Ave., New York, NY 10003

  New York Shakespeare Festival; (Delacorte and Mobil Theatres), The Public Theatre, 425 Lafayette St., New York, NY 10003 (Summer)

  The Playhouse Repertory Theatre; Century Theatre; 235 W. 46th St., New York, N.Y. 10036

  The Roundabout Theatre Company; 333 W. 23rd St., New York, NY 10011

PARK FOREST (IL): **Illinois Theatre Center;** 400 Lakewood Blvd., Park Forest, IL 60466

PHILADELPHIA (PA): **The Philadelphia Drama Guild;** 220 S. 16th St., Philadelphia, PA 19102

PITTSBURGH (PA): **Pittsburgh Public Theatre;** Suite 1150, 300 6th Ave. Bldg., Pittsburgh, PA 15222

PORTSMOUTH (NH): **Theatre By The Sea;** 91 Market St., Portsmouth, NH 03801

PRINCETON (NJ): **McCarter Theatre Company, Inc.;** P.O. Box 526, Princeton U., Princeton, NJ 08540

PROVIDENCE (RI): **Trinity Square Repertory Company;** 201 Washington St., Providence, RI 02903

RICHMOND (VA): **American Revels Company of Richmond;** 114 W. Broad St., Richmond, VA 23220

  Virginia Museum Theatre; Boulevard & Grove Ave., Richmond, VA 22331

ROCHESTER (MI): **Meadow Brook Theatre;** Oakland U., Rochester, MI 48063

ROCHESTER (NY): **Genesee Valley Arts Foundation;** 168 Clinton Ave. South, Rochester, NY 14604

ST. LOUIS (MO): **Repertory Theatre of Loretto-Hilton;** 130 Edgar Rd., St. Louis, MO 63119

ST. PAUL (MN): **Actors Theatre of St. Paul;** 2115 Summit Ave., St. Paul, MN 55105

SAN DIEGO (CA): **Old Globe Theatre;** P.O. Box 2171, San Diego, CA 92112

SAN FRANCISCO (CA): **American Conservatory Theatre;** 450 Geary St., San Francisco, CA 94102

SARASOTA (FL): **Asolo Theatre Festival;** P.O. Box Drawer E, Sarasota, FL 33578

SEATTLE (WA): **Seattle Repertory Theatre;** P.O. Box B, Queen Anne Sta., Seattle Center, Seattle, WA 98109

  A Contemporary Theatre; 709 First Ave. W., Seattle, WA 98119 **Intiman Theatre;** Box 4246, Seattle, WA 98104

STAMFORD (CT): **Hartman Theatre Company;** 61 Atlantic St., Stamford, CT 06910

SYRACUSE (NY): **Syracuse Stage;** University Regent Theatre, 820 E. Genesee St., Syracuse, NY 13210

TUCSON (AZ): **Arizona Civic Theatre;** 120 W. Broadway, Tucson, AZ 85701

WASHINGTON (DC): **Arena Stage;** Sixth and M Sts. S.W., Washington, DC 20024

  Folger Theatre Group; 201 E. Capitol St. S.E., Washington, DC 20003

WATERFORD (CT): **Eugene O'Neill Memorial Theatre Center;** P.O. Box 206, Waterford, CT 06385

WEST SPRINGFIELD (MA): **Stage/West;** 1511 Memorial Ave., W. Springfield, MA 01089

ART MUSEUMS

WORLD

AMSTERDAM: Rijksmuseum (1808); Collections: 16th/
17th-century Dutch paintings and drawings by Rembrandt, Hals, Vermeer, and others.
Stedelijk Museum (1895); Collections: Impressionist
to modern paintings and sculpture, including works of
van Gogh, Chagall, and Dubuffet.

ANTWERP: Koninklijk Museum voor Schone Kunsten
(Royal Museum of Fine Arts) (1890); Collections:
Dutch, Flemish, and French old masters, including
Van Eyck, Van der Weyden, Memling, Rubens, Rem-
brandt, and Hals; 19th/20th-century Belgian art.

BERLIN: National-Galerie (1876); Collections: European paintings and sketches from the 18th century to
the present.

BRUSSELS: Musée des Beaux-Arts (1892); Collections:
Old and new masters, drawings, and sculpture.

BUDAPEST: Magyar Nemzeti Museum (Hungarian
tional Museum) (1802); Collections. Archaeological
finds; medieval to contemporary art; coins and historical objects.
Szépmüveszéti Museum (Museum of Fine Arts)
(1896); Collections: Egyptian and Greco-Roman antiquities; Hungarian and foreign old masters; sculpture, drawings, and engravings.

CAIRO: Coptic Museum (1908); Collections: Art treasures of early Christian culture in Egypt.
Museum of Islamic Art (1881); Collections: Islamic
painting, sculpture, ceramics, and applied arts (7th
to 19th century).

CALCUTTA: Indian Museum (1814); Collections: Indian art from prehistoric to Moslem times; Indian and
Persian paintings; and Tibetan banners.

DRESDEN: National Gallery (1846); Collections: Italian, Dutch, Flemish, and German old and new masters,
including Rembrandt, Correggio, Titian, Rubens, Van
Dyck, Veronese, and del Sarto.

FLORENCE: Galleria dell'Accademia (1784); Collections: The most complete collection of Michelangelo's
statues in Florence, as well as paintings by Tuscan
masters of the 13th to 16th centuries.
Galleria degli Uffizi (16th century); Collections: The
world's finest collection of Italian Renaissance painting.

THE HAGUE: Keninklijk Kabinet van Schilderijen
(Mauritshuis) (Royal Picture Gallery) (1820); Collec-
tions: Dutch and German art; excellent Vermeers and
Rembrandts.

ISTANBUL: Museum of the Seraglio of Topkapi (Built
mid-15th century); Collections: Sultans' treasure; Chinese and Japanese porcelain; enamels, embroidery,
miniatures, and precious stones.

JERUSALEM: Museum of Archaeology and Art (1965);
Collections: Works concerning the Bible and Middle
Eastern history; features the Billy Rose Art Garden and
the Shrine of the Book.

LENINGRAD: Hermitage (1764); Collections: More
than 2.5 million objets d'art, including gold artifacts
from Helleno-Scythian times, jewelry of the tsars,
French impressionist paintings, old and new masters.
State Russian Museum (1898); Collections: Exhibits
numbering 250,000 of Russian art, sculpture, drawings, coins, and medals.

LONDON: The British Museum; Collections: Extensive
collections spanning man's art and culture from neolithic age to present, including the Elgin Marbles.
National Gallery (1857); Collections: A superb collection from the 12th century to the present.
Tate Gallery (1897); Collections: British painting from
the 16th century to the present, including works by
Blake, Constable, Turner; French impressionists and
modern sculpture.
Victoria and Albert Museum (1852); Collections: Fine
and applied art of all countries, periods, and styles;
ceramics, textile, sculpture, woodwork, paintings,
prints, and drawings.

MADRID: El Prado (1819); Collections: Italian, Flemish, Dutch, and Spanish Renaissance paintings; classical, Renaissance, and baroque sculpture; includes a
large collection of Murillo, Goya, El Greco, Rubens,
Bosch, Van Dyck, da Vinci, and Tintoretto.

MEXICO CITY: Museo Nacional de Antropologia (1865);
Collections: Anthropological, ethnological, and archaeological collections relating to Mexico.

MOSCOW: State Tretyakov Gallery (1856); Collectie
A rich collection of 40,000 Russian icons; Russian
Soviet sculpture, graphics and paintings, dating f
the 11th century to the present.

MUNICH: Alte Pinakothek (1836); Collections: Germ
Dutch, Flemish, Italian, Spanish, and French mast

NEW DELHI: National Museum of India (1949); (
lections: Indian and Central Asian treasures that (
from 3000 B.C. to the present; sculpture, painti
manuscripts, miniatures, and crafts.

PARIS: Galerie du Jeu de Paume (1920); Collectie
Including examples by Monet, Cézanne, van Go
Renoir, Degas, Pissarro, and Gaugin.
Musée Guimet; Collections: The finest European
lection of oriental painting, sculpture, and applied a
Musée du Louvre (1793); Collections: Oriental, Eg
tian, Roman, and Greek antiquities, medieval, Ren
sance, and modern sculpture and painting.
Musee National d'Art Moderne (1943) (Centre
tional d'Art et de Culture Georges Pompidou); (
lections: 20th-century paintings and sculpture.
Musée de l'Orangerie (1853); Collections: A group
Utrillos, Cézannes, Monets, and others, exhibited in
atmosphere of a collector's apartment.
Musée Rodin (1916); Collections: The sculptor's w
and collection are displayed in a home and garden.

ROME: Borghese Art Gallery (c. 1616); Collectie
Classical and baroque sculpture and painting.

ROTTERDAM: Museum Boymans-van Beunin
(1847); Collections: European art from the 15th c
tury to the present, including Van Eyck, Breughel
Elder, Hals, Rembrandt, van Ruisdael, Hobbema,
bens, Titian, Watteau, and Boucher.

SAO PAULO: Museu de Arte Contemporânea (194
Collections: Nearly 1,700 works by such modern m
ters as Kandinsky, Léger, and the early cubists.
Museu de Arte de São Paulo (1947); Collections
panoramic view of Western art from gothic times to
present; paintings by Hals, Raphael, Renoir, Toulo
Lautrec, and Rembrandt are included.

TAIPEI: National Palace Museum (1925); Collectie
Examples of Chinese art from the Shang to the Ch
dynasty that were brought to Taipei from the M
land during the Communist revolution.

TORONTO: Royal Ontario Museum at Toronto (19
Collections: Art and archaeological objects from
Americas, Africa, Polynesia, ancient Egypt, Rome
Greece; Chinese, Japanese, Islamic, and Indian
European art from all ages.

VIENNA: Kunsthistorisches Museum (Museum of I
Arts) (1891); Collections: Egyptian, Greek, Etrusc
Roman, and Cyprian antiquities; excellent Breu
collection; French, Dutch, Italian, and German Ren
sance and baroque art.

UNITED STATES

BALTIMORE: Baltimore Museum of Art (1914); Col
tions: Epstein and Jacobs collections of old mas
and sculpture; 19th/20th-century French paint
sculpture, graphics; Toulouse-Lautrec posters; (
temporary American art; Oriental art and mosaics.
Walters Art Gallery (1931); Collections: More t
25,000 objects, of which the Byzantine and medi
examples are noteworthy; classical art of Greece, Rc
Egypt, medieval to 19th-century European art.

BOSTON: Isabella Steward Gardner Museum (19
Collections: American and European painting
sculpture, from classical times to the 20th century.
Museum of Fine Arts (1870); Collections: Ex
tionally fine collection of prints, Oriental art, de
rative arts; Egyptian, Greek, and Roman art; old m
ters and 19th-century French paintings.

BUFFALO: Buffalo Fine Arts Academy, Albright-K
Art Gallery (1862); Collections: 19th-century Am
can and French painting and 18th-century Eng
painting; sculpture (3000 B.C. to the present).

CAMBRIDGE: Harvard University, Fogg Art Muse
(1895); Collections: Oriental and Western art f
ancient times to the present; representative collect
of painting, sculpture, prints, and drawings, includ
Italian primitives and Chinese jades and bronzes.

CHICAGO: Art Institute of Chicago (1879); Collectie
Major periods of Western art and primitive and m
ental art.
University of Chicago, Oriental Institute Muse
(1919); Collections: More than 70,000 objects

represent the art, religion, and daily life of ancient Egypt, Nubia, Assyria, Babylonia, Persia, Palestine, Syria, Anatolia, Libya, and Cyprus.

CINCINNATI: **Cincinnati Art Museum** (1881); *Collections:* Sculpture, painting, and ceramics of Egypt, Greece, Rome; Near Eastern and Far Eastern art; 19th/20th-century European and American art; primitive art from Oceania, Africa, and the Americas.

CLEVELAND: **Cleveland Museum of Art** (1913); *Collections:* Art from many cultures and periods, including old masters and modern paintings, sculpture, prints, drawings, porcelain, metalwork, and furniture.

COLUMBUS: **Columbus Gallery of Fine Arts** (1878); *Collections:* Schumacher Collection of old masters; Howald Collection of modern French and American painting; major collection of the art of George Bellows; South Pacific primitives.

DALLAS: **Dallas Museum of Fine Arts** (1903); *Collections:* Ancient, pre-Columbian, African sculpture, Japanese, European and American art.

DETROIT: **Detroit Institute of Arts** (1885); *Collections:* Art from many cultures, dating from prehistoric times to the present, including Italian medieval and Renaissance sculpture, 17th-century Dutch paintings, and French-Canadian art.

DISTRICT OF COLUMBIA: **Corcoran Gallery of Art** (1859); *Collections:* American painting, sculpture, and drawing from the 18th century to the present; Dutch, Flemish, French and English painting.
Hirshhorn Museum and Sculpture Garden (1974); *Collections:* Joseph Hirshhorn's private modern art collection valued at over $1 million.
National Gallery of Art (1937); *Collections:* Mellon, Kress, and Widener collections of old masters; Rosenwald Collection of prints and drawings; Garbisch Collection of American primitive paintings; East Building (1978) contains permanent and changing exhibits of painting and sculpture.
Phillips Collection (1918); *Collections:* Modern art, especially 19th/20th-century American and European works.
Smithsonian Institution, Freer Gallery of Art (1906); *Collections:* Near and Far Eastern art and artifacts, 19th/20th-century American art, including the Peacock Room entirely decorated by Whistler.

FORT WORTH: **Amon Carter Museum of Western Art** (1961); *Collections:* Western paintings and sculpture, includes Frederic Remington and Charles Russell.
Kimball Art Museum (1972); *Collections:* masterpieces from ancient times to cubism.
Fort Worth Art Museum (1961); *Collections:* 20th century paintings and sculpture.

HARTFORD: **Wadsworth Atheneum** (1842); *Collections:* European and American painting from 1400 to the present, including medieval and Renaissance European tapestries; early South and Central American art.

HOUSTON: **Museum of Fine Arts of Houston** (1900); *Collections:* Paintings, sculpture, and decorative arts covering most periods of history, including Renaissance painting, classical art and sculpture, and American art.

KANSAS CITY (MO.): **William Rockhill Nelson Gallery and Atkins Museum of Fine Arts** (1926); *Collections:* Oriental art, especially Chinese; classical, European, and American painting, sculpture, and decorative arts.

LOS ANGELES: **Los Angeles County Museum of Art** (1961); *Collections:* Major periods of European and American art; Oriental art.

MERION STATION (PA.): **Barnes Foundation** (1922); *Collections:* European Renaissance and 20th-century American painting; African sculpture and Chinese art.

MINNEAPOLIS: **Minneapolis Institute of Arts** (1914); *Collections:* Oriental and pre-Columbian art; American and European painting and sculpture.
Walker Art Center (1972); *Collections:* 20th century art, changing exhibits.

NEWARK: **Newark Museum** (1909); *Collections:* American painting and sculpture from all periods; Oriental art, emphasizing the expression of Tibet.

NEW HAVEN: **Yale Center for British Art** (1977); *Collections:* British paintings, prints and drawings.

NEW ORLEANS: **Isaac Delgado Museum of Art** (1910); *Collections:* Kress Collection of Renaissance painting; Hyams Collection of the Barbizon school; contemporary European and American painting, sculpture, and drawings; Howard Collection of Greek vases.

NEW YORK CITY: **Brooklyn Museum** (1893); *Collections:* Egyptian, Near and Far Eastern art; Renaissance and medieval painting; American painting from all periods and 19th/20th-century European art; primitive art and artifacts from Oceania, Africa, the Far East, and South America.
Frick Collection (1935); *Collections:* European painting, sculpture, prints, and drawings from the 14th century to the 1800s that constitute the former personal treasures of Henry Clay Frick; Limoges enamels, French and Chinese porcelains, and period furniture.
Jewish Museum (1904); *Collections:* This largest exhibit of Judaica in the Western Hemisphere is housed in the former Felix Warburg mansion.
Metropolitan Museum of Art (1870); *Collections:* Comprehensive collections that cover 5,000 years of history and represent the arts of Egypt, Babylonia, Assyria, Greece, Rome, Near and Far East, Europe, pre-Columbian culture, and the United States; Robert Lehman collection of European paintings and drawings; includes the Cloisters in Fort Tryon Park.
Museum of Modern Art (1929); *Collections:* One of the foremost collections of 19th/20th-century American and European painting, sculpture, prints, photographs, posters, and films.
Pierpont Morgan Library (1924); *Collections:* Old master drawings, Rembrandt etchings, and manuscripts.
Solomon R. Guggenheim Museum (1937); *Collections:* Impressionist to contemporary painting and sculpture, including the world's largest collection of Kandinsky's work; paintings and sculpture by Picasso, Chagall, Klee, Brancusi, and Modigliani.
Whitney Museum of American Art (1930); *Collections:* American paintings, sculpture, drawings, and prints; the 20th-century American art housed ranges from realism to abstract expressionism.

PASADENA (CALIF.): **Norton Simon Museum of Art at Pasadena** (1974); *Collections:* European paintings spanning six centuries; modern sculpture garden; Indian and South Asian bronzes and stone figures.

PHILADELPHIA: **Philadelphia Museum of Art** (1875); *Collections:* Dutch, Flemish, French, American, and Italian masters; cubist and postcubist art; Far Eastern and Near Eastern art; Pennsylvania Dutch folk art; tapestries, silver, china, and period rooms.
University of Pennsylvania, University Museum (1887); *Collections:* Archaeological finds of Near East, Egypt, the Mediterranean, and the Americas; ethnology of Africa, Oceania, and art of China, pre-1000 A.D.

PITTSBURGH: **Carnegie Institute, Museum of Art** (1896); *Collections:* American and European painting and sculpture, including old masters and impressionists; international collection of modern art.

SAN FRANCISCO: **California Palace of the Legion of Honor** (1924); *Collections:* European and American painting, sculpture, and decorative arts; Egyptian and Greek antiquities.
M. H. De Young Memorial Museum (1895); *Collections:* European and American art from ancient times to 1850; Oriental and South Pacific art, including the Avery Brundage Collection of Asian art; Kress Collection of European old masters, Flemish tapestries; art of pre-Columbian Central, South, and North American Indians.
San Francisco Museum of Modern Art (1921); *Collections:* Contemporary painting, sculpture, drawings, prints, photography, and decorative arts from Europe, the United States, and Latin America.

SAN MARINO (CALIF.): **Henry E. Huntington Library and Art Gallery** (1919); *Collections:* Eighteenth-century British portraits and French sculpture; 15th/16th-century Italian and Flemish paintings; 18th/19th-century French and British decorative arts, and Renaissance bronzes.

SEATTLE: **Seattle Art Museum** (1917); *Collections:* Chinese, Japanese, Indian, and Near Eastern art; Egyptian, Greek, Roman antiquities; European Renaissance painting, sculpture, and porcelain, including the Kress Collection; Northwest Indian and pre-Columbian primitive art.

TOLEDO: **Toledo Museum of Art** (1901); *Collections:* European art from classical times to the 20th century; American painting and decorative arts.

WORCESTER (MASS.): **Worcester Art Museum** (1896); *Collections:* American, European, and Oriental art—ancient through contemporary; painting, sculpture, prints, decorative arts; early American and Italian art.

THE REVIEWS: 1978/79

BOOKS

It was America's year for the Nobel Prize in Literature. Isaac Bashevis Singer, whose Yiddish prose is translated into English, became the eighth United States author to be given the award.

A milestone of another sort occurred between August 1978 and mid-July 1979. It was the year of three Popes. In fact, Peter Hebblethwaite's *The Year of Three Popes* was one of nearly a dozen books published about John Paul I, John Paul II and their predecessor, Paul VI. Others of relevance included two by the two more recent pontiffs themselves — *Illustrissimi: Letters of Pope John Paul I* and a book of verse by Pope John Paul II, *Easter Vigil and Other Poems.*

Much closer to home, former President Ford and his wife handed out their own memoirs. First was Betty Ford's *The Times of My Life*, written with Chris Chase. Later came Gerald Ford's *A Time to Heal*. Neither caused a run on bookstores.

Americans may not be much concerned with the presidency, but they are intent upon themselves. Christopher Lasch's *The Culture of Narcissism: American Life in an Age of Diminishing Expectations* was a surprise best seller.

There is no denying that Americans seek self-gratification with considerable dedication. One title catering successfully to that drive was *How to Get Whatever You Want Out of Life* by everybody's favorite (and our most ubiquitous) psychology booster Dr. Joyce Brothers. Another woman with a far-flung audience promised a lot with *The Ann Landers Encyclopedia: A to Z — Improve Your Life Emotionally, Medically, Sexually, Socially and Spiritually.*

Fitness was one of the year's bywords, but while joggers still galloped in herds across the countryside and through the cityscape, a few publishers noticed that the interest in running stumbled and turned toward walking. Some people didn't think there would be enough to say about walking to fill one book, but more than seven books appeared on walking during the year. However, walking didn't move books as quickly as running did, even though one by John Man exhorted: *Walk! It Could Change Your Life*. In the end, the slothful were rewarded when a paperback spoof plopped onto the field, *The Non-Runner's Book* by Vic Ziegel and Lewis Grossberger.

And there was roller skating. This booming fad led our fellow citizens to purchase skates. costing $200 and up, and many of the more open-handed were the hoped-for buyers for the swarm of books such as *The Complete Book of Roller Skating* by Ann-Victoria Phillips.

The biggest diet book in many years was named after a town in New York State where the author practices medicine. *The Complete Scarsdale Diet* by Herman Tarnower, M.D. and Samm Sinclair Baker sold hundreds of thousands of copies in hardcover. A man who is not a doctor, Nathan Pritikin, claims nevertheless to have discovered a regimen enabling many of his converts to live healthier and longer. Accord-ingly, *The Pritikin Program for Diet and Exerci* by Nathan Pritikin with Patrick McGrady, J drew fervent adherents. So did *How to Flatt Your Stomach* by Coach Jim Everroad, a pape back first self-published by the author in 197 then released early in 1978 by a commerci publisher. Its sales finally soared during the pa year as innumerable copies were snapped by hopeful tummy trimmers. A diet parody paperback attracted readers with a sense humor, who bought *The Dieter's Guide Weight Loss During Sex* by Richard Smith.

Once the body and the mind were on t mend, attention could be paid to the out trappings with books such as *Dressing Rig* by Charles Hix with Brian Burdine, *The Pow Look* by Egon von Furstenberg and *Looki Terrific: Express Yourself Through the Langua of Clothing* by Emily Cho and Linda Grover.

But people did look beyond themselves. was a heavy year for celebrity autobiographi Lauren Bacall, Sophia Loren, Charlton Hesto Dirk Bogard, Gene Tierney, Joan Fontaine a many others made voyeurs of us all. Lilli Palm did it too, but she used an autobiographic novel called *The Red Raven* to divulge fac about an early love. Christina Crawford told about life with mother, Joan Crawford, *Mommie Dearest*. One movie star wrote n about himself, but about his concern for t dying Old West in the *Outlaw Trail: A Journ Through Time* by Robert Redford.

Political figures, too, earned an audienc William Manchester wrote *American Caesc Douglas MacArthur 1880-1964*, and Arthur N Schlesinger, Jr. provided *Robert Kennedy a His Times*. RFK's son wrote a biography, tc but not as one might expect about his fath The subject for Robert Francis Kennedy, Jr. w an Alabama justice: *Judge Frank M. Johnso Jr.* Edmund Morris elicited enthusiastic reviev with his carefully researched *The Rise of The dore Roosevelt*. Judge John J. Sirica brought v Watergate in his account of the period intend *To Set the Record Straight*. Lester David open a keyhole showing a former White House Fam with *The Lonely Lady of San Clemente: T Story of Pat Nixon*. Another former First Lad one with apparently timeless allure, inspir *Jacqueline Bouvier Kennedy Onassis* by Steph Birmingham and the racier *Jackie Oh!* by Kit Kelley. Kelley's biography sold more copies a presumably made her publisher more money.

Eyebrows were raised by the staggering re ords established for paperback rights. In nc fiction *Linda Goodman's Love Signs* (Fawcet brought Harper & Row $2,250,000. In fictic Mario Puzo's *Fools Die* brought the sar amount. With $300,000 for paperback rights *The Godfather*, the total paid to Putnam by Ne American Library was $2,550,000.

Among other fiction titles was William Styrox first novel in 12 years, *Sophie's Choice*. Ju Blume, a popular author for younger reade published *Wifey*, her first novel for adul The lure of Indian lore gave us a pair of nove both many pages long and years in the making.

Ruth Beebe Hill's fiction was the dramatica authentic *Hanta Yo*, while Anna Lee Wal offered *Sacajawea*. The latter was something a best selling breakthrough, a large-sized pap back priced at $8.95.

James Michener was not deserted by his fans when he delivered a fictionalized saga of the American East Coast. *Chesapeake* covered the years of the bay's environs from 1583 to 1978. Herman Wouk's sequel to *The Winds of War* was a major success, as *War and Remembrance* traced the course of World War II from the attack on Pearl Harbor to the Japanese surrender. *The Coup* was John Updike's vision of contemporary Africa. An original paperback assembled a number of Updike's previously uncollected stories for *Too Far to Go*, which was adapted into a critically acclaimed television special. More short works of fiction, 61 of them by one of our country's greatest authors, were published, and *The Stories of John Cheever* went on to disprove the notion that such collections don't sell. It also went on to collect the National Book Critics Circle Award and the Pulitzer Prize for fiction. William Wharton flew off with applause for his imaginative first novel called *Birdie*, which took as its unlikely subject a man who thinks he is a canary.

—**Robert Dahlin**

SELECTED BEST SELLERS: 1978-79

FICTION

Title	Author	Publisher
War and Remembrance	Herman Wouk	Little, Brown
Chesapeake	James Michener	Random House
The Matarese Circle	Robert Ludlum	Richard Marek
Good as Gold	Joseph Heller	Simon & Schuster
The Stories of John Cheever	John Cheever	Knopf
Hanta Yo	Ruth Beebe Hill	Doubleday
Fools Die	Mario Puzo	Putnam
The Third World War	General Sir John Hackett, et al	Macmillan
Sophie's Choice	William Styron	Random House
Overload	Arthur Hailey	Doubleday
Evergreen	Belva Plain	Delacorte
Shibumi	Trevanian	Crown
SS-GB	Len Deighton	Knopf
Second Generation	Howard Fast	Houghton Mifflin
The Far Pavilions	M. M. Kaye	St. Martin's Press
Dubin's Lives	Bernard Malamud	Farrar, Straus & Giroux
The Coup	John Updike	Knopf
Eye of the Needle	Ken Follett	Arbor House
The Empty Copper Sea	John D. MacDonald	Lippincott
The Sixth Commandment	Lawrence Sanders	Putnam
Bright Flows the River	Taylor Caldwell	Doubleday
Prelude to Terror	Helen MacInness	Harcourt Brace Jovanovich
The Island	Peter Benchley	Doubleday

NONFICTION

The Complete Scarsdale Diet	Herman Tarnower, M.D., and Samm Sinclair Baker	Rawson, Wade
Lauren Bacall by Myself	Lauren Bacall	Knopf
Mommie Dearest	Christina Crawford	Morrow
A Distant Mirror: The Calamitous Fourteenth Century	Barbara W. Tuchman	Knopf
In Search of History: A Personal Adventure	Theodore H. White	Harper & Row
Cruel Shoes	Steve Martin	Putnam
How to Prosper During the Coming Bad Years	Howard J. Ruff	Times Books
Sophia, Living and Loving: Her Own Story	A. E. Hotchner	Morrow
American Caesar: Douglas MacArthur, 1880-1964	William Manchester	Little, Brown
The Pritikin Program for Diet and Exercise	Nathan Pritikin with Patrick McGrady, Jr.	Grosset & Dunlap
The Powers That Be	David Halberstam	Knopf
The Bronx Zoo	Sparky Lyle and Peter Golenbock	Crown
Linda Goodman's Love Signs	Linda Goodman	Harper & Row
Robert Kennedy and His Times	Arthur M. Schlesinger, Jr.	Houghton Mifflin
Time for Truth	William E. Simon	Reader's Digest

THEATER

A fleet of Broadway musicals lost millions of dollars. Serious drama made a re-entry into the marketplace. The Vivian Beaumont Theater at Lincoln Center announced it would re-open under new management and a six-man directorate. And, despite a newspaper strike, which dampened the beginning of the season, by the end of the year Broadway had set a new high for box office grosses.

According to *Variety*, theater receipts for 1978-79 escalated to $125,686,072 from a previous high for 1977-78 of $103,846,494. However, profits had to be measured against inflation, rising costs of production and ticket prices.

The year's best play was "The Elephant Man" by Bernard Pomerance, an American living in London. This extraordinary study of a grotesque circus freak's adoption and seduction by society received both a Tony Award and a New York Drama Critics prize as Best Play, as well as winning awards for director Jack Hofsiss and actress Carole Shelley, playing opposite two exceptional actors, newcomer Philip Anglim in the title role and Kevin Conway as a sympathetic doctor. Discoverer and co-producer of the work, which moved from Off Broadway to a long run on Broadway, was Richmond Crinkley, the new head of the Beaumont Theater.

The theme of the incapacitated hero was also reflected in other works. Brian Clark's "Whose Life Is It Anyway?", a British import, focused on a sculptor, paralyzed from the neck down as the result of an auto accident. For his performance in this challenging role, Tom Conti was deservedly named Best Actor by the Tony voters.

In "Wings," Arthur Kopit wrote a stark, poetic drama about a stroke victim, a former aviatrix, played by Constance Cummings, who tied with Miss Shelley for Tony acting honors. Off Broadway at the Negro Ensemble Company, Steve Carter offered "Nevis Mountain Dew," a sensitive portrait of a black businessman who suffers polio and is confined to an iron lung.

Sam Shepard's "Buried Child," about a bizarre middle American family in the process of disintegration, was awarded the Pulitzer Prize for drama. Shepard was also represented by "Seduced," a pop cartoon taking off from the life of Howard Hughes. Late in the season, there were two excellent new plays — Lanford Wilson's lovely midwestern romance "Talley's Folley" (starring Judd Hirsch) and Michael Weller's buoyant "Loose Ends," about the survivors of the Sixties.

"Getting Out" was an arresting first play about an ex-convict's problems of readjustment by a new woman writer, Marsha Norman. This seemed to be a breakthrough season for women playwrights. Ntozake Shange matched "For Colored Girls" with "Spell #7." Elizabeth Swados presented her lilting musical version of "Alice in Wonderland" in concert and also an explosive rock adaption of Michael Herr's Vietnam journal, "Dispatches." Other interesting women writers were Susan Miller, Beth Henley and Olwen Wymark, the last two co-winners of the new play competition at the Actors Theater

of Louisville, which first produced "Getting Out." This year the Actors Theater also gave Broadway "Lone Star" and "Pvt. Wars," two rollicking one-act comedies by James McLure.

Tennessee Williams was represented by "A Lovely Sunday for Creve Coeur," a gentle look at Southern womanhood, and Arthur Miller returned with a revival of "The Price." Thomas Babe's "Taken in Marriage," about a family of women, was elevated by the performances of Meryl Streep, Elizabeth Wilson and Dixie Carter among others.

Luis Valdez's "Zoot Suit," a rare Hispanic show on Broadway, was weighted down by its social consciousness. From Ireland came Stewart Parker's "Spokesong," about the Irish rebellion, and from England came Peter Terson's "Good Lads at Heart," an insightful look inside a reform school. Simon Gray's "The Rear Column" was a thoughtful investigation of history in Africa, "Bedroom Farce," a sprightly romantic comedy by Alan Ayckbourn. Poland provided Tadeuz Kantor's "Dead Class" and Japan sent Kobo Abe's "The Little Elephant Is Dead," two striking pieces of experimental theater.

Offsetting the liveliness of the dramatic season was the poverty of the musical season. Standing far ahead of other offerings was "Sweeney Todd: the Demon Barber of Fleet Street," a murderous musical about cutthroat revenge, with imaginative music and lyrics by Stephen Sondheim and direction by Harold Prince. Most musical honors were won by "Sweeney," including Best Musical Actor and Actress, Len Cariou and Angela Lansbury.

"They're Playing Our Song" was a two-character musical about songwriters by Neil Simon, Marvin Hamlisch and Carole Bayer Sager, starring Lucie Arnaz and Robert Klein. "Whoopee" and "Tip-Toes" were revitalized relics from the Goodspeed Opera House in Connecticut. "Eubie" was a tribute to the ageless Eubie Blake. Among the musical disappointments were "Carmelina" by Alan Jay Lerner and Burton Lane, Michael Bennett's "Ballroom," Jerry Herman's "The Grand Tour" and Richard Rodgers "I Remember Mama" (with Liv Ullmann making her musical debut).

Among other outstanding performances were Irene Worth, buried up to her neck in earth in Andrei Serban's revival of Samuel Beckett's modern classic, "Happy Days"; Henry Fonda as a Supreme Court justice in the hackneyed "First Monday in October"; Alec McCowen in his virtuoso one-man reading of "St. Mark's Gospel."

The unpredictable Joseph Papp aroused critics and audiences with the formation of a black-Hispanic Shakespeare acting company, as represented by "Julius Caesar" and "Coriolanus." Robert Kalfin's Chelsea Theater Center returned, healthily, with Max Frisch's "Biography" and "Strider," an adaptation from Tolstoy, starring Gerald Hiken as a woeful Russian horse. Other animals in season included "The Enchanted Pig" by Charles Ludlam and Bob Carroll's "Salmon Show," a monodrama that told us far more than we ever thought we wanted to know about the spawning habits of salmon.

— Mel Gussow

MUSIC

A widely-mourned ending as well as some important beginnings marked the 1978-79 classical music season.

In Boston, Arthur Fiedler succumbed to a cardiac arrest after 50 years at the helm of the Boston Pops, closing a remarkable era in which the white-haired maestro introduced a wide variety of music to countless audiences of all ages. Although he had performed continuously before New England audiences since 1929 and had made his first RCA Victor recording in 1935, Fiedler reached the climax of his career on July 4, 1976, when his concert next to the Charles River thrilled millions on television.

In Philadelphia, another career neared a close, albeit voluntarily, with the announcement that Eugene Ormandy would step down as musical director of the Philadelphia Orchestra after 44 years in the post. It came as no surprise that Riccardo Muti, who had been groomed for the post in recent years, was announced as Ormandy's successor.

In New York, Zubin Mehta began a reign as music director of the New York Philharmonic with a performance of Mahler's First Symphony that brought down the house. Mehta's successor in Los Angeles, Carlo Maria Giulini, opened his tenure with a similarly received rendition of Beethoven's Ninth Symphony.

The New York City Opera announced that Julius Rudel, its music director of 20 years, would leave his post at the end of the season. Soprano Beverly Sills, long the company's leading vocal light, will assume the music directorship. Miss Sills was scheduled to close her own illustrious vocal career with a farewell recital in the fall.

Symphony orchestras, which Leonard Bernstein in a rare moment of pessimism once relegated to to the category of musical museums, remained as vital as ever. Three new orchestras were born: the Orchestra of Illinois, with a membership largely drawn from the Lyric Opera; the Orchestra in Los Angeles, which promised to usher in a "new era in American music" under two film composers; and the portentously titled Orchestra of the 20th Century, which began its life in New York with a program of Stravinsky, Berio and Elliot Carter. As for established orchestras, they received a powerful shot in the arm with a record contribution of $10.8 million from the National Endowment for the Arts.

New music and its composers continued to suffer the punishment of critics and audiences who found little or nothing enjoyable about it. The *New York Times* created a stir by publishing an op-ed article by a midwestern history professor who called contemporary composers "absurdists" and defied music lovers to name even a handful of compositions written in the last decade.

Defenders shot back that any art that looks back invites self-extinction. Composers made their own case by offering a bumper crop of new works performed in cities and on university campuses across the nation.

Among the compositions that impressed first-time listeners were Samuel Barber's Third Essay for Orchestra, played by Mehta and the New York Philharmonic; Alan Hovhaness's Symphony No. 36 for flute and orchestra and Gunther Schuller's Contrabassoon Concerto, both performed the same evening by the National Symphony Orchestra; William Schuman's "In Sweet Music" drawn from an earlier Schuman song and played by the Chamber Music Society of Lincoln Center; Jacob Druckman's Viola Concerto, performed by the Philharmonic under James Levine; and George Rochberg's three "Concord" quartets, introduced at the University of Pennsylvania.

Other notable new works came from the pens of Ullyses Kay, Henry Brant, Milton Babbitt, Marvin Feinsmith, Gene Gutche, Howard Boatwright, Leon Kirchner, Malcolm Arnold, Easley Blackwood, Wendel Browning, William T. McKinley, John Downey, Luciano Berio and Frank Droto.

On the opera scene, the big new works were Dominick Argento's "Miss Havisham's Fire," introduced by the New York City Opera, and Michael Tippett's "The Ice Break," heard in its U.S. premiere by the Opera Company of Boston. Argento's score, with its echoes of earlier 20th century composers, was adjudged a misfire. But Tippett's work impressed listeners as one of his finest, full of color and violence.

The opera-going public, ever hungry for familiar masterpieces, feasted on such praiseworthy productions as the Metropolitan Opera's "Otello," "Tannhauser," and "Don Pasquale"; the Lyric Opera of Chicago's "Faust" and "Girl of the Golden West"; the Houston Grand Opera's "La Traviata"; Dallas Civic Opera's "Flying Dutchman"; San Francisco Opera's "Werther" and New York City Opera's "Andrea Chenier."

A Michigan revival of Louis Gruenberg's "The Emperor Jones" exposed the dated quality of this 1933 opera. In New York, a radical production of "Flying Dutchman" provoked a *Time* magazine comment that "Anti-Wagner has finally arrived at the Metropolitan Opera . . ."

On the other hand, Schubert's "Alfonso and Estrella" and Massenet's "Sapho," revived in Detroit and New York respectively, demonstrated that there is musical gold left in some of the dusty scores of yesteryear.

Television, once a musical wasteland, provided some of the liveliest listening of the season by presenting major orchestral concerts from New York, Los Angeles, Chicago, Detroit, Pittsburgh, Boston and Berlin. Cable stations made arrangements to tie in with a Chicago FM radio station to carry concerts by six major orchestras and four opera companies.

Although televised symphony concerts were "not exactly riveting" to watch, as one critic put it, there was excellent viewing in the Met's "Otello," "Bartered Bride," "Tosca" and "Louisa Miller."

Other noteworthy events included:

A concert tour of mainland China by the Boston Symphony Orchestra.

Seventieth birthday celebrations for composer Elliot Carter in New York and Olivier Messiaen in Parowan, Utah, which named a nearby peak "Mt. Messiaen."

A concert by flutist James Galway, one of the season's brightest solo stars, at which the audience overflowed onstage.

—Henry Wallhauser

TELEVISION

It was a chaotic year for TV in general, and a particularly painful one for two of the networks. Both CBS and NBC lost profits during the 1978-79 season; the former's dropped slightly — 2 percent, the latter's took a nose dive — 50 percent, thus reversing the automatic ascent of recent years.

NBC made most of the TV news during the 78-79 season, but probably would rather not have done so. The causes for diminished profits were many, led by a massive failure in the prime-time ratings war. NBC finished third in ratings for a fourth year in a row. During the mid-fall season, President Fred Silverman, after successful stints at CBS and ABC, tried to apply his magic programming touch, but at midseason he had to cancel all of the new season's series; the second season was not much better.

Problems came from many directions. Vital affiliates began switching from NBC to ABC, often giving ABC vital VHF outlets, leaving NBC with weaker UHFs. Some markets that defected included Minneapolis, Indianapolis, and Dayton.

The "Tonight Show," one of NBC's pillars of profit, was threatened when Johnny Carson sought to leave before his contract expired. He was persuaded to stay, but his dissatisfaction was made known to everyone, and rumors of a move to ABC persisted.

Other NBC stalwarts, including the "Today Show" and the "NBC Evening News," lost significant ground to ABC. NBC was reduced to hoping for a return to its former good ratings position. Another promise which might be harder to keep is for NBC to be in first place by Christmas, 1980.

ABC's profit picture was happy again, showing an increase of 13 percent. The overall numbers for the year put ABC's profits at $187 million, CBS's at $136 million, and NBC's at $51 million. Profit losses for both CBS and NBC were indicative of their overzealous efforts to catch top-dog ABC. They used up profits in paying for the development of new programs.

The chaotic 78-79 season was reflected in the prime-time scheduling, which at times resembled a berserk game of shuffleboard. Shows were rearranged all over.

The scheduling madness reached a peak in February, during a ratings "sweep" month, when long-suffering viewers, abused all year by poor choices in programing, were subjected to killing competition in which the top shows of the year went head to head. On one giddy Sunday night, the networks squared off with an extravagant biography of Elvis Presley (ABC) against two Oscar-winning films — "Gone With the Wind" (CBS) and "One Flew Over the Cuckoo's Nest" (NBC).

Unlike recent years, there was no distinctive programming trend to the season as the networks backed off from the sex and violence content that had sparked protests in previous years. Comedy was the dominant factor, although the TV year was perhaps best described by one observer as "the season of So What?"

Of the 21 new shows that hit the air in September, 4 survived. The biggest success was "Mork and Mindy," which launched Robin Williams to mega-stardom. ABC also scored with "Roots II," its lavish sequel to Alex Haley's family saga.

Noteworthy failures included Mary Tyler Moore, who bombed in two efforts at a variety show; NBA basketball; and "Battlestar Galactica," the most expensive and loudest crash-landing of the year.

The year's chaos spilled over a bit into the world of public television where persistent financial and scheduling problems inspired a number of suggested solutions. PBS decided to go to a "core" schedule, with two hours of national programming four nights a week. The whole system was to be restructured with three separate programming services established.

In addition, public television underwent the comprehensive scrutiny of a second Carnegie Commission, whose book-length recommendations called for more funds, more insulation from political pressure and a new programming mechanism designed to encourage more diversity.

Much was made of the ever-expanding technology of the video world. The networks debunked any fears of fragmentation of their mass audience, but constant talk of inroads by cable systems, "superstations," and video cassettes and discs indicated a growing concern.

The 78-79 season was a bullish year for cable, with expansion impressive enough to have the ratings master, the Nielsen company, considering including cable stations in its survey. Cable's association with superstations — strong independent stations hooked up by communications satellites to various cable outlets — had some industry people talking about an eventual cable TV network. But the cable industry was probably nearing a crossroads; aside from sports and movies, it cried out for original programming.

One change that did not take place in 1978-79 was a re-write of the Communications Act of 1934. In fact, the two-year effort of California Congressman, Lionel Van Deerlin, was finally abandoned when he conceded the industry opposition to his re-write bill was too much to overcome.

The Justice Department managed to hit television with one suit that seemed to unite everyone — viewers and broadcasters alike — in opposition. It sued the National Association of Broadcasters over its rules limiting the number of commercials. The Justice Department said that was unfair restraint of trade. Nobody understood how more commercials could be considered fair in any way.

— Bill Carter

FILMS

Vietnam and a new, "serious" Woody Allen were the biggest news in a generally facetious movie season (the sort of year in which a *Dracula* parody, *Love at First Bite* was one of the big money-makers).

Allen's artistic maturation was the most heartening development. Sensing that his reliance on one-liners, sight gags and Jewish jokes had become a limitation, he absented himself from the screen altogether in *Interiors* to enforce the discipline of a relentless focus on a group of characters. The resulting production (described by some critics as Ingmar Bergman's first American movie) seemingly equated humorlessness with seriousness.

If *Interiors* smacked too much of an exercise, it suggested that Allen's next film, hopefully combining the formal control of *Interiors* with the mixture of moods in *Annie Hall*, might really be something. This expectation was fulfilled in *Manhattan*, perhaps the first film in which Allen has truly spoken with his own voice and in which what was on the screen matched the thoughtful and articulate personality that came through in interviews.

The Deer Hunter also excited critical interest. This surprisingly ambitious film recalled Norman Mailer's 1967 novel *Why We Are in Vietnam* in its linkage of the male hunting mystique to a belligerent foreign policy (again demonstrating the tendency of the screen to lag behind literature by about a dozen years in theme and treatment). Intelligent handling made the film a success; Universal resisted the temptation to cut the three-hour-plus running time and revived the road show, reserved ticket policy to lend the film an aura of importance.

Sunday *New York Times* "think pieces" berating the movie as racist and anti-Vietnamese unwittingly illuminated its merits. Unlike the schematic *Coming Home*, in which the three protagonists represent not merely themselves but varying degrees of political consciousness toward the war, in *The Deer Hunter* neither political activists nor the career military ever appear. The emphasis is entirely on two-year draftees who become disillusioned without ever becoming radicalized.

A favorite pre-Oscar night theory was that *The Deer Hunter* and *Coming Home* would divide the message picture enthusiasts and give Best Picture honors to Warren Beatty's frivolous but popular *Heaven Can Wait*, a remake of 1941's *Here Comes Mr. Jordan*. It soon became apparent that there was enough unresolved anti-Vietnam sentiment to go around for ten movies.

Undoubtedly boosted by interest in *The China Syndrome* coincident with the Three Mile Island nuclear accident, Jane Fonda won a second Oscar for *Coming Home*. In one of the more ambiguous and ironic of public events, erstwhile Hawk John Wayne, so soon to die of cancer, appeared amid a standing ovation to present the Best Picture award to *The Deer Hunter*.

Largely overlooked at Oscar time was *Days of Heaven*; the choice of the New York Film Critics but too cold for general acceptance except as a *Barry Lyndon*-ish objet d'art.

The more typical fare was aimed at the adolescent market in taste if not in years. *Superman* carried on the *Star Wars* tradition of uniting ambitious production values and juvenile content to become the big hit of Christmas 1978. The summer's commercial blockbuster, *Moonraker*, refashioned James Bond for the *Superman/Star Wars* market, while minimizing Bond's super-stud attributes.

Not since the youth revolt cycle of 1969-71 were there so many teen-aged characters on the screen. *Animal House* looked to be the major trend-setter, suggesting that a raid of *National Lampoon* and *Saturday Night Live* for performers and material could be expected. *Breaking Away* explored the world of non-college youth. There was a minor cycle of gang pictures, notably *The Warriors* (which actually provoked violence and vandalism in and near theaters showing it). *More American Graffiti*, the sequel to George Lucas' 1973 original, seemed in danger of getting lost amid all the unofficial derivations.

Anyone wishing to feel nostalgic for 1968 already had *Hair*, which Milos Forman's airy, inventive direction made as good as any film version could possibly be.

One of the more unusual features was *Movie, Movie*, a pastiche of 1930's Warner Bros. productions that did absolutely nothing to prevent straight-faced unneeded remakes of *The Champ*, *National Velvet* and *Dracula*.

John Carpenter became a cult favorite with *Halloween* (saturation-released during Halloween week), a low-budget shocker combining references to *Psycho* (Jamie Lee Curtis is Janet Leigh's daughter) and *The Thing*.

Male-female passion (once such a central subject of Hollywood films) disappeared so totally from native movies as a primary subject that Visconti's elegant, slow-moving *The Innocent* (posthumously completed and released) seemed more important than it was. At a time when few foreign films were succeeding, unclothed Laura Antonelli made such an impression that her previous pictures were re-released or dusted off for export to the U.S.

With heterosexuality in full retreat on the screen, gay activists protested with demonstrations and near riots William Friedkin's *Cruising*, filmed on location in Greenwich Village.

Peter Bogdanovich returned with a small film, *Saint Jack*, but Robert Altman's stock sank to a new low after *Quintet*.

Among the notable shifts and upheavals, Alan Ladd, Jr., left Fox to form an Orion Pictures-type company financed by Warners. Donald Rugoff lost control of Cinema 5 to West Coast Theater magnate William Forman, and Pauline Kael left as film critic for *The New Yorker* to work with Warren Beatty's production company but was rumored to be ready to come back.

Possibly the biggest industry news of all in its ultimate implications was that the MCA Disco-Vision system went on sale in its Atlanta test market, offering feature films on an LP-sized disc.

— Stephen Handzo

PRIZES/AWARDS

THE HALL OF FAME FOR GREAT AMERICANS

Elected 1900:
John Adams
John James Audubon
Henry Ward Beecher
William Ellery Channing
Henry Clay
Peter Cooper
Jonathan Edwards
Ralph Waldo Emerson
David Glasgow Farragut
Benjamin Franklin
Robert Fulton
Ulysses Simpson Grant
Asa Gray
Nathaniel Hawthorne
Washington Irving
Thomas Jefferson
James Kent
Robert E. Lee
Abraham Lincoln
Henry Wadsworth Longfellow
Horace Mann
John Marshall
Samuel Finley Breese
  Morse
George Peabody
Joseph Story
Gilbert Charles Stuart
George Washington
Daniel Webster
Eli Whitney

Elected 1905:
John Quincy Adams
James Russell Lowell
Mary Lyon
James Madison
Maria Mitchell
William Tecumseh
  Sherman
John Greenleaf Whittier
Emma Willard
Elected 1910:
George Bancroft
Phillips Brooks
William Cullen Bryant
James Fenimore Cooper
Oliver Wendell Holmes
Andrew Jackson
John Lothrop Motley
Edgar Alan Poe
Harriet Beecher Stowe
Frances Elizabeth Willard
Elected 1915:
Louis Agassiz
Daniel Boone
Rufus Choate
Charlotte Saunders Cushman
Alexander Hamilton
Joseph Henry
Mark Hopkins
Elias Howe
Francis Parkman

Elected 1920:
Samuel Langhorne
  Clemens
James Buchanan Eads
Patrick Henry
William Thomas Green
  Morton
Alice Freeman Palmer
August Saint-Gaudens
Roger Williams
Elected 1925:
Edwin Booth
John Paul Jones
Elected 1930:
Matthew Fontaine
  Maury
James Monroe
James Abbott McNeill
  Whistler
Walt Whitman
Elected 1935:
Grover Cleveland
Simon Newcomb
William Penn
Elected 1940:
Stephen Collins Foster
Elected 1945:
Sidney Lanier
Thomas Paine
Walter Reed
Booker T. Washington

Elected 1950:
Susan B. Anthony
Alexander Graham Bell
Josiah Willard Gibbs
William Crawford Gorgas
Theodore Roosevelt
Woodrow Wilson
Elected 1955:
Thomas Jonathan Jackson
George Westinghouse
Wilbur Wright
Elected 1960:
Thomas Alva Edison
Edward Alexander MacDowell
Henry David Thoreau
Elected 1965:
Jane Addams
Oliver Wendell Holmes, Jr.
Sylvanus Thayer
Orville Wright
Elected 1970:
Albert Abraham Michelson
Lillian Wald
Elected 1973:
Louis Dembitz Brandeis
George Washington Carver
Franklin Delano Roosevelt
John Philip Sousa
Elected 1976:
Clara Barton
Luther Burbank
Andrew Carnegie

NOBEL PRIZE WINNERS

PHYSIOLOGY AND MEDICINE

Year	Winner and Life Dates	Nationality	Achievement
1901	Emil A. von Behring (1854–1917)	German	Serum therapy, especially for work on dipththeria antitoxin.
1902	Ronald Ross (1857–1932)	British	Discovery of the life cycle of the malaria parasite.
1903	Niels R. Finsen (1860–1904)	Danish	Treatment of skin diseases with concentrated light rays, especially lupus vulgaris (skin tuberculosis).
1904	Ivan P. Pavlov (1849–1936)	Russian	Work on the physiology of digestion.
1905	Robert Koch (1843–1910)	German	Work on tuberculosis and the scientific development of bacteriology.
1906	Camillo Golgi (c.1843–1926)	Italian	Their study of the nervous system and of cell distribution.
	Santiago Ramón y Cajal (1852–1934)	Spanish	
1907	Charles L. A. Laveran (1845–1922)	French	Study of protozoa-caused disease.
1908	Paul Ehrlich (1854–1915)	German	Their work on immunology including the introduction of quantitative methods.
	Élie Metchnikoff (1845–1916)	Russian	
1909	E. Theodor Kocher (1841–1917)	Swiss	Work on the physiology, pathology, and surgery of the thyroid gland.
1910	Albrecht Kossel (1853–1927)	German	Contributions to the knowledge of cell chemistry.
1911	Allvar Gullstrand (1862–1930)	Swedish	For his work on ocular dioptrics, the refraction of light through the eye.
1912	Alexis Carrel (1873–1944)	American (b. France)	Development of vascular suture and surgical transplantation of blood vessels and organs.
1913	Charles R. Richet (1850–1935)	French	Work on anaphylaxis.
1914	Robert Bárány (1876–1936)	Austrian	Study of physiology and pathology of the inner ear.
1919	Jules J. P. V. Bordet (1870–1961)	Belgian	Discoveries in the field of immunity.
1920	S. August Krogh (1874–1949)	Danish	Discovering the mechanism that regulates blood-capillary action.
1922	Archibald V. Hill (1886–1977)	English	Discoveries concerning heat produced by muscular activity.
	Otto F. Meyerhof (1884–1951)	American (b. Germany)	Establishing the correlation between oxygen and lactic acid in muscle.
1923	Frederick G. Banting (1891–1941)	Canadian	Their production of insulin and demonstration of its value in combating diabetes.
	John J. R. Macleod (1876–1935)	British	
1924	Willem Einthoven (1860–1927)	Dutch	Invention of the electrocardiograph.
1926	Johannes A. G. Fibiger (1867–1928)	Danish	Experimental work in cancer.
1927	Julius Wagner-Jauregg (1857–1940)	Austrian	Discovery of malarial therapy in paralysis.
1928	Charles J. H. Nicolle (1866–1936)	French	Work on typhus.
1929	Christiaan Eijkman (1858–1930)	Dutch	Discovering vitamin B.
	Frederick G. Hopkins (1861–1947)	English	Discovering vitamin A.
1930	Karl Landsteiner (1868–1943)	American (b. Austria)	Discovery of human blood groups.
1931	Otto H. Warburg (1883–1970)	German	Discovery of the character and action mode of the respiratory enzyme.
1932	Edgar C. Adrian (1889–1977)	English	Studies on the physiology of the nervous system, especially the function of neurons.
	Charles S. Sherrington (1857–1952)	English	

Year	Name	Nationality	Description
1933	Thomas H. Morgan (1866–1945)	American	Discovering the functions of chromosomes in heredity.
1934	George R. Minot (1885–1950)	American	Their discoveries that administering liver extract increases activity in the bone-marrow where red cells are formed.
	William P. Murphy (1892–)	American	
	George H. Whipple (1878–1976)	American	
1935	Hans Spemann (1869–1941)	German	Discovery of the organizer effect in embryonic development.
1936	Henry H. Dale (1875–1968)	English	Their discoveries of the chemical transmission of nerve impulses.
	Otto Loewi (1873–1961)	American (b. Germany)	
1937	Albert von Szent-Györgyi (1893–)	American (b. Hungary)	Studies of metabolism and the effects of vitamins A and C.
1938	Corneille J. F. Heymans (1892–1968)	Belgian	Discovery of the influence of the carotid sinus on respiration rate.
1939	Gerhard Domagk (1895–1964)	German	Discovering prontosil, the first sulfa drug.
1943	C. P. Henrik Dam (1895–1976)	Danish	Discovering vitamin K.
	Edward A. Doisy (1893–)	American	Discovery of the chemical nature of vitamin K.
1944	E. Joseph Erlanger (1874–1965)	American	Work on the highly differentiated functions of single nerve fibers.
	Herbert S. Gasser (1888–1963)	American	
1945	Alexander Fleming (1881–1955)	British	The discovery of penicillin and its curative properties in infections including those of the heart, syphilis, and certain types of pneumonia.
	Howard W. Florey (1898–1968)	British (b. Australia)	
	Ernst B. Chain (1906–1979)	British (b. Germany)	
1946	Hermann Joseph Muller (1890–1967)	American	Discovering the influence of X rays in genetics.
1947	Carl F. Cori (1896–)	American (b. Czechoslovakia)	Their research on carbohydrate metabolism and enzymes.
	Gerty T. Cori (1896–1957)	American (b. Czechoslovakia)	
	Bernardo A. Houssay (1887–1971)	Argentine	Discovery of the role of the pituitary hormone in sugar metabolism.
1948	Paul H. Müller (1899–1965)	Swiss	Discovering the insect-killing properties of DDT.
1949	Walter R. Hess (1881–1973)	Swiss	Discovering how certain parts of the brain control body organs.
	Antonio de Egas Moniz (1874–1955)	Portuguese	Discovery of the therapeutic value in certain psychoses of prefrontal lobotomy.
1950	Philip S. Hench (1896–1965)	American	Their research in hormones including the discovery of cortisone and its antidisease effects.
	Edward C. Kendall (1886–1972)	American	
	Tadeus Reichstein (1897–)	Swiss (b. Poland)	
1951	Max Theiler (1899–1972)	American (b. South Africa)	Developing the yellow-fever vaccine.
1952	Selman A. Waksman (1888–1973)	American (b. Russia)	Work in the discovery of streptomycin and its value in treating tuberculosis.
1953	Fritz A. Lipmann (1899–)	American (b. Germany)	Their biochemical studies on cell metabolism, including the discovery of coenzyme A.
	Hans A. Krebs (1900–)	British (b. Germany)	
1954	John F. Enders (1897–)	American	Their successful growth of polio viruses in cultures of tissues and discovery of more effective methods of polio detection.
	Thomas H. Weller (1915–)	American	
	Frederick C. Robbins (1916–)	American	
1955	A. Hugo T. Theorell (1903–)	Swedish	Discoveries of the nature of oxidation enzymes.
1956	D. W. Richards (1895–1973)	American	Developing a technique of inserting a catheter through a vein into the heart to chart its interior and to diagnose circulatory ailments.
	André F. Cournand (1895–)	American (b. France)	
	Werner Forssmann (1904–1979)	German	
1957	Daniel Bovet (1907–)	Italian (b. Switzerland)	Developing muscle-relaxing drugs used in surgery.
1958	George W. Beadle (1903–)	American	Discovery that genes transmit hereditary traits.
	Edward L. Tatum (1909–1975)	American	
	Joshua Lederberg (1925–)	American	Experiments establishing that sexual recombination of bacteria results in exchange of genetic material.
1959	Severo Ochoa (1905–)	American (b. Spain)	Their synthesis of ribonucleic acid (RNA) and deoxyribonucleic acid (DNA), organic compounds that carry hereditary characteristics, in genetics.
	Arthur Kornberg (1918–)	American	
1960	F. Macfarlane Burnet (1899–)	Australian	Their discovery of acquired immunity, that is, that an animal can be made to accept foreign tissues.
	Peter B. Medawar (1915–)	British (b. Brazil)	
1961	Georg von Békésy (1899–1972)	American (b. Hungary)	Work on the mechanism of the inner ear.
1962	Francis H. C. Crick (1916–)	English	Their determining the molecular structure of deoxyribonucleic acid (DNA) and its significance for information transfer in living material.
	Maurice H. F. Wilkins (1916–)	British	
	James D. Watson (1928–)	American	
1963	Alan L. Hodgkin (1914–)	English	Their research on nerve cells and on how electrical charges pass through nerve membranes by means of a sodium-potassium exchange.
	Andrew F. Huxley (1917–)	English	
	John C. Eccles (1903–)	Australian	
1964	Konrad E. Bloch (1912–)	American (b. Germany)	Their discovery of the mechanism and control of cholesterol metabolism.
	Feodor Lynen (1911–1979)	German	
1965	Francois Jacob (1920–)	French	Their discovery of the regulatory processes in body cells that contribute to genetic control of enzymes and virus synthesis.
	Andre M. Lwoff (1902–)	French	
	Jacques L. Monod (1910–1976)	French	
1966	Charles B. Huggins (1901–)	American (b. Canada)	Discoveries concerning hormonal treatment of prostate-gland cancer.
	Francis P. Rous (1879–1970)	American	Discovery of a cancer virus.
1967	Haldan K. Hartline (1903–)	American	Their discoveries pertaining to the eye's primary chemical and physiological processes, including work on color reception.
	George Wald (1906–)	American	
	Ragnar A. Granit (1900–)	Swedish (b. Finland)	
1968	Robert W. Holley (1922–)	American	Their discovery of the process by which enzymes, consisting of a sequence of amino acids, determine a cell's function in genetic development.
	H. Gobind Khorana (c.1922–)	American (b. India)	
	Marshall W. Nirenberg (1927–)	American	
1969	Max Delbrück (1906–)	American (b. Germany)	Their discoveries concerning the replication mechanism and the genetic structure of viruses.
	Alfred D. Hershey (1908–)	American	
	Salvador E. Luria (1912–)	American (b. Italy)	
1970	Bernard Katz (1911–)	British (b. Germany)	Their discoveries on the nature of the substances found at the end of nerve fibers.
	Ulf von Euler (1905–)	Swedish	
	Julius Axelrod (1912–)	American	
1971	Earl W. Sutherland (1915–1974)	American	Discoveries concerning the mechanisms of the action of hormones.
1972	Gerald M. Edelman (1929–)	American	Research into the chemical structure of antibodies (Conducted independently).
	Rodney R. Porter (1917–)	English	
1973	Konrad Lorenz (1903–)	Austrian	Research into ethology.
	Nikolaas Tinbergen (1906–)	English (b. Netherlands)	
	Karl von Frisch (1886–)	German (b. Austria)	
1974	Albert Claude (1899–)	American	Research which helped create the science of cell biology.
	Christian Rene de Duve (1917–)	Belgian	
	George Emil Palade (1912–)	American	

Year	Winner and Life Dates	Nationality	Achievement
1975	David Baltimore (1938–)	American	Discoveries concerning the interaction between tumor viruses and the genetic material of the cell.
	Renato Dulbecco (1914–)	American (b. Italy)	
	Howard M. Temin (1935–)	American	
1976	Baruch S. Blumberg (1925–)	American	Discoveries concerning new mechanisms for the origin and dissemination of infectious diseases.
	Daniel C. Gajdusek (1923–)	American	
1977	Rosalyn S. Yalow (1921–)	American	Developed analytic radioimmunoassay technique utilizing isotopes for diagnostic purposes.
	Roger C. L. Guillemin (1924–)	American (b. France)	Their use of radioimmunoassay in pituitary hormone research.
	Andrew V. Schally (1927–)	American (b. Poland)	
1978	Werner Arber (1929–)	Swiss	Discoveries and studies on the restriction enzymes' linkage control of genes on chromosomes.
	Daniel Nathans (1928–)	American	
	Hamilton Smith (1931–)	American	

CHEMISTRY

Year	Winner and Life Dates	Nationality	Achievement
1901	Jacobus H. van't Hoff (1852–1911)	Dutch	Discovering laws of chemical dynamics and osmotic pressure in solutions.
1902	Emil H. Fischer (1852–1919)	German	Synthesizing sugars and purines.
1903	Svante A. Arrhenius (1859–1927)	Swedish	Originating the theory of ionization.
1904	William Ramsay (1852–1916)	British	Discovering helium, neon, xenon, and krypton.
1905	Adolf von Baeyer (1835–1917)	German	Research in organic dye stuffs, especially hydroaromatic compounds.
1906	Henri Moissan (1852–1907)	French	Isolation of the element fluorine; development of the electric furnace.
1907	Eduard Buchner (1860–1917)	German	Discovering cell-free fermentation.
1908	Ernest Rutherford (1871–1937)	British	Artificial disintegration of elements; chemistry of radioactive elements.
1909	Wilhelm Ostwald (1853–1932)	German	Work on catalysts, chemical equilibria, and rate of chemical reactions.
1910	Otto Wallach (1847–1931)	German	Pioneer work in the field of alicyclic compounds.
1911	Marie S. Curie (1867–1934)	French (b. Poland)	Discovering radium and polonium.
1912	F. A. Victor Grignard (1871–1935)	French	Discovering the reagent that is named after him.
	Paul Sabatier (1854–1941)	French	Process of hydrogenating organic compounds.
1913	Alfred Werner (1866–1919)	Swiss (b. Germany)	Study of the linkage of atoms in molecules.
1914	Theodore W. Richards (1868–1928)	American	Determining the atomic weights of many elements.
1915	Richard M. Willstätter (1872–1942)	German	Research into plant pigments, especially chlorophyll.
1918	Fritz Haber (1868–1934)	German	Process of synthesizing ammonia from nitrogen and hydrogen.
1920	Walther Nernst (1864–1941)	German	Application of thermodynamics to chemistry.
1921	Frederick Soddy (1877–1956)	British	Research into radioactive substances and isotopes.
1922	Francis W. Aston (1877–1945)	British	Discovering many isotopes by use of the mass spectrograph.
1923	Fritz Pregl (1869–1930)	Austrian	Invention of methods of microanalysis of organic substances.
1925	Richard A. Zsigmondy (1865–1929)	German (b. Austria)	Clarifying the nature of colloid solutions.
1926	Theodor Svedberg (1884–1971)	Swedish	Work on colloids.
1927	Heinrich O. Wieland (1877–1957)	German	Studies of bile acids.
1928	Adolf O. R. Windaus (1876–1959)	German	Work defining a group of sterols (including cholesterol) and their connection to vitamins.
1929	Sir Arthur Harden (1865–1940)	British	Investigations into the fermentation of sugar and fermentative enzymes.
	Hans von Euler-Chelpin (1873–1964)	Swedish (b. Germany)	
1930	Hans Fischer (1881–1945)	German	Research into the constitution of hemin (coloring matter of blood) and chlorophyll.
1931	Carl Bosch (1874–1940)	German	Their invention and development of chemical high pressure methods.
	Friedrich Bergius (1884–1949)	German	
1932	Irving Langmuir (1881–1957)	American	Investigations of the fundamental properties of absorbed films and surface chemistry.
1934	Harold C. Urey (1893–)	American	Discovering heavy hydrogen, which he called deuterium.
1935	Frédéric Joliot-Curie (1900–58)	French	Their synthesizing of new radioactive elements, including radioactive nitrogen and phosphorus.
	Irène Joliot-Curie (1897–1956)	French	
1936	Peter J. W. Debye (1884–1966)	American (b. Netherlands)	Studies of the structure of molecules, dipole moments, and the diffraction of electrons and X rays in gases.
1937	Walter N. Haworth (1883–1950)	British	Research into carbohydrates and vitamin C.
	Paul Karrer (1889–1971)	Swiss (b. Russia)	Chemical anlysis of vitamins A and B$_2$.
1938	Richard Kuhn (1900–67)	Austrian	Work on carotinoids and vitamins.
1939	Adolf F. J. Butenandt (1903–)	German	Studying the chemistry of sex hormones, determining the chemical structure of the female hormone (progestin), and isolating the male hormone (androsterone).
	Leopold Ruzicka (1887–1976)	Swiss (b. Yugoslavia)	Work on polymethylenes and higher terpenes.
1943	Georg von Hevesy (1885–1966)	Hungarian	Using isotopes as tracer elements in chemistry.
1944	Otto Hahn (1879–1968)	German	Discovery of the fission of heavy atomic nuclei.
1945	Artturi I. Virtanen (1895–1973)	Finnish	Work on plant synthesis of nitrogen compounds; development of a new method of making silage.
1946	James B. Sumner (1887–1955)	American	Discovering the crystallizability of enzymes.
	John H. Northrop (1891–)	American	Their preparation of enzymes and virus proteins in pure form.
	Wendell M. Stanley (1904–1971)	American	
1947	Robert Robinson (1886–1975)	British	Research on plant substances, especially alkaloids.
1948	Arne W. K. Tiselius (1902–1971)	Swedish	Devising new methods of separating and detecting colloids and serum proteins.
1949	William F. Giauque (1895–)	American (b. Canada)	Studies of the properties of substances at extremely low temperatures.
1950	Otto P. H. Diels (1876–1954)	German	Developing a method of synthesizing organic compounds of the diene group.
	Kurt Alder (1902–58)	German	
1951	Edwin M. McMillan (1907–)	American	Their work in the field of synthetic transuranium elements.
	Glenn T. Seaborg (1912–)	American	
1952	Archer J. P. Martin (1910–)	British	Advancing the use of paper partition chromatography (a method of separating and identifying chemical substances).
	Richard L. M. Synge (1914–)	British	
1953	Hermann Staudinger (1881–1965)	German	Work in the nature of giant molecules.

Year	Winner and Life Dates	Nationality	Achievement
1954	Linus C. Pauling (1901–)	American	Studies in molecular structure, especially the nature of the bonding of atoms in molecules.
1955	Vincent du Vigneaud (1901–1978)	American	Work on pituitary hormones and the first synthesis of a polypeptide hormone.
1956	Cyril N. Hinshelwood (1897–1967)	British	Parallel but independent research into the kinetics of
	Nikolai N. Semenov (1896–)	Russian	certain chemical reactions.
1957	Alexander R. Todd (1907–)	British	Studies of the compounds that are the components of nucleic acid.
1958	Frederick Sanger (1918–)	British	Isolating and identifying the amino acid components of the insulin molecule.
1959	Jaroslav Heyrovsky (1890–1967)	Czech	Developing polarography (an electrochemical method of analysis).
1960	Willard F. Libby (1908–)	American	Development of the "atomic time clock" (for determining geological age by measuring the amount of radioactive carbon-14 in organic objects).
1961	Melvin Calvin (1911–)	American	Establishing the chemical reactions that occur during photosynthesis.
1962	Max F. Perutz (1914–)	British (b. Austria)	Discovering the molecular structure of hemoglobin
	John C. Kendrew (1917–)	British	and myoglobin.
1963	Karl Ziegler (1898–1973)	German	Changing simple hydrocarbons into complex molecu-
	Giulio Natta (1903–1979)	Italian	lar substances.
1964	Dorothy C. Hodgkin (1910–)	British	Discovery of the structure of biochemical substances, notably penicillin and vitamin B_{12}.
1965	Robert B. Woodward (1917–1979)	American	Development of fundamental techniques for synthesis of complicated organic compounds, notably chlorophyll and sterols.
1966	Robert S. Mulliken (1896–)	American	Fundamental work on chemical bonds and the electronic structure of molecules by the molecular orbital method.
1967	Manfred Eigen (1927–)	German	Studies of extremely fast chemical reactions effected
	Ronald G. W. Norrish (1897–1978)	English	by disturbing equilibrium by very short energy
	George Porter (1920–)	English	pulsations.
1968	Lars Onsager (1903–76)	American (b. Norway)	Discovery of the reciprocal relations between voltage and temperature that are fundamental for the thermodynamics of irreversible processes, such as those in living cells.
1969	Derek H. R. Barton (1918–)	British	Independent studies of conformation analysis: how
	Odd Hassel (1897–)	Norwegian	certain compounds react when their three-dimensional molecular shape is known.
1970	Luis F. Leloir (1906–)	Argentinian (b. France)	Discovery of sugar nucleotides and their role in the biosynthesis of carbohydrates.
1971	Gerhard Herzberg (1904–)	Canadian (b. Germany)	Study of electronic structure, geometry of molecules.
1972	Dr. Christian Boehmer Anfisen (1916–)	American	Research relating to the chemical structure of a com-
	Dr. Stanford Moore (1913–)	American	plex protein known as ribonuclease.
	Dr. William Howard Stein (1911–)	American	
1973	Ernst Otto Fischer (1918–)	German	Research into how organic and metallic atoms can
	Geoffrey Wilkinson (1921–)	British	merge.
1974	Paul J. Flory (1910–)	American	For his work in macromolecules.
1975	John W. Cornforth (1917–)	English (b. Australia)	For contributions to stereochemistry — the study of
	Vladimir Prelog (1906–)	Swiss (b. Yugoslavia)	how the properties of a chemical compound are affected by the exact arrangement of their atoms in three-dimension space.
1976	William N. Lipscomb, Jr. (1920–)	American	For studies on the structure and bonding mechanisms of "boranes".
1977	Ilya Prigogine (1917–)	Belgian (b. Russia)	Theoretical work explaining contradictory biological process whereby increased growth and structural complexity on the molecular level are promoted while energy is dissipated.
1978	Peter Mitchell (1920–)	English	Study of energy reception of human cells.

PHYSICS

Year	Winner and Life Dates	Nationality	Achievement
1901	Wilhelm C. Roentgen (1845–1923)	German	Discovering X rays.
1902	Hendrik A. Lorentz (1853–1928)	Dutch	Their research into the influence of magnetism upon
	Pieter Zeeman (1865–1943)	Dutch	radiation.
1903	Antoine H. Becquerel (1852–1908)	French	Discovery of spontaneous radioactivity.
	Pierre Curie (1859–1906)	French	Their study of the radiation phenomena that were
	Marie S. Curie (1867–1934)	French (b. Poland)	discovered by Becquerel.
1904	John W. S. Rayleigh (1842–1919)	British	Discovering argon.
1905	Philipp E. A. Lenard (1862–1947)	German (b. Hungary)	Experiments with cathode rays.
1906	Joseph J. Thomson (1856–1940)	British	Investigations on how gases conduct electricity.
1907	Albert A. Michelson (1852–1931)	American (b. Germany)	Developing optical measuring instruments; spectroscopic and meteorological investigations.
1908	Gabriel Lippmann (1845–1921)	French (b. Luxembourg)	Color photography.
1909	Guglielmo Marconi (1874–1937)	Italian	Their separate but parallel development of the wire-
	Karl F. Braun (1850–1918)	German	less telegraph.
1910	Johannes D. van der Waals (1837–1923)	Dutch	Work on an equation relating gases and liquids.
1911	Wilhelm Wien (1864–1928)	German	Discoveries of the laws governing heat radiation.
1912	Nils G. Dalén (1869–1937)	Swedish	Their invention of automatic gas regulators, for turning acetylene buoys, beacons, and railway lights on and off.
1913	Heike Kamerlingh-Onnes (1853–1926)	Dutch	Experiments with the properties of matter at low temperatures, leading to helium liquefaction.
1914	Max von Laue (1879–1960)	German	Employing crystals to diffract X rays.
1915	William H. Bragg (1862–1942)	British	Their use of X rays to determine the structure of
	Lawrence Bragg (1890–1971)	British	crystals.
1917	Charles G. Barkla (1877–1944)	British	Discovery of X-ray radiation of elements.
1918	Max K. E. L. Planck (1858–1947)	German	Formulation of the quantum theory.
1919	Johannes Stark (1874–1957)	German	Discovery of the splitting of spectral lines in an electrical field.

Year	Winner and Life Dates	Nationality	Achievement
1920	Charles É. Guillaume (1861–1938)	French (b. Switzerland)	Discovering anomalies in nickel-steel alloys.
1921	Albert Einstein (1879–1955)	American (b. Germany)	Contributing to theoretical physics: especially for the discovery of photoelectric-effect law.
1922	Niels H. D. Bohr (1885–1962)	Danish	Studies of the structure of atoms and their radiation.
1923	Robert A. Millikan (1868–1953)	American	Work on electrons and the photoelectric effect.
1924	Karl M. G. Siegbahn (1886–1978)	Swedish	Discoveries in X-ray spectroscopy.
1925	James Franck (1882–1964)	German	Their discovery of the laws governing the impact of an electron on an atom.
	Gustav Hertz (1887–1975)	German	
1926	Jean B. Perrin (1870–1942)	French	Work on the discontinuous structure of matter; discovery of sedimentation equilibrium.
1927	Arthur H. Compton (1892–1962)	American	Discovering the Compton effect (the change in wavelength of X rays colliding with electrons).
	Charles T. R. Wilson (1869–1959)	British	Discovery of the cloud chamber method of tracking paths of electrically charged particles.
1928	Owen W. Richardson (1879–1959)	British	Study of electron emission from heated bodies; formulation of the law governing such emission.
1929	Louis-Victor de Broglie (1892–)	French	Discovering the wave nature of electrons.
1930	Chandrasekhara V. Raman (1888–1970)	Indian	Light diffusion research; discovery of Raman effect.
1932	Werner Heisenberg (1901–1976)	German	Creating a quantum mechanics; new discoveries in the study of hydrogen.
1933	Erwin Schrödinger (1887–1961)	Austrian	For their development of new useful forms of atomic theory.
	Paul A. M. Dirac (1902–)	British	
1935	James Chadwick (1891–1971)	British	Discovery of the neutron.
1936	Victor F. Hess (1883–1964)	American (b. Austria)	Discovering cosmic radiation.
	Carl D. Anderson (1905–)	American	Discovery of the positron.
1937	Clinton J. Davisson (1881–1958)	American	Their discovery of the diffraction of electrons by crystals.
	George P. Thomson (1892–1975)	British	
1938	Enrico Fermi (1901–54)	American (b. Italy)	Work on radioactive elements, including artificial ones produced by neutron bombardment.
1939	Ernest O. Lawrence (1901–58)	American	Inventing the cyclotron.
1943	Otto Stern (1888–1969)	American (b. Germany)	Studies related to the magnetic properties of atoms; discovery of the magnetic moment of the proton.
1944	Isidor Isaac Rabi (1898–)	American (b. Austrian)	Discovery of resonance method of recording the magnetic properties of atomic nuclei.
1945	Wolfgang Pauli (1900–58)	American (b. Austrian)	Discovering the exclusion principle governing the quantum state of electrons in an atom.
1946	Percy Williams Bridgman (1882–1961)	American	Work in the field of high-pressure physics.
1947	Edward V. Appleton (1892–1965)	British	Investigations of the physics of the upper atmosphere; discovery of the so-called Appleton layer.
1948	Patrick M. S. Blackett (1897–1974)	British	Improvement of the Wilson cloud chamber method and resulting discoveries in nuclear physics and cosmic rays.
1949	Hideki Yukawa (1907–)	Japanese	Theoretical deductions of the existence of mesons.
1950	Cecil F. Powell (1903–69)	British	Photographic method of tracking nuclear particles.
1951	Sir John D. Cockcroft (1897–1967)	British	Their pioneer work in transmuting atomic nuclei with artificially accelerated atomic particles.
	Ernest T. S. Walton (1903–)	Irish	
1952	Felix Bloch (1905–)	American (b. Switzerland)	Developing the nuclear resonance method for precision measurements of atomic nuclei magnetic fields.
	Edward M. Purcell (1912–)	American	
1953	Frits Zernike (1888–1966)	Dutch	Inventing the phase-contrast microscope.
1954	Max Born (1882–1970)	British (b. Germany)	Basic research in quantum mechanics and modern nuclear physics.
	Walther Bothe (1891–1957)	German	Development of the coincidence method for measuring time.
1955	Willis E. Lamb, Jr. (1913–)	American	Discoveries concerning the fine structure of the hydrogen spectrum.
	Polykarp Kusch (1911–)	American (b. Germany)	Precise measurement of the electron's electromagnetic properties.
1956	John Bardeen (1908–)	American	Their work on developing the transistor, a device which replaced electronic tubes in many applications.
	Walter H. Brattain (1902–)	American	
	William B. Shockley (1910–)	American (b. England)	
1957	Tsung-Dao Lee (1926–)	American (b. China)	Their disproving of the law of parity conservation in nuclear physics.
	Chen Ning Yang (1922–)	American (b. China)	
1958	Pavel A. Cherenkov (1904–)	Russian	Discovering the Cherenkov effect (radiated electrons accelerate in water to speeds greater than that of light in the same medium).
	Ilya M. Frank (1908–)	Russian	
	Igor Y. Tamm (1895–1971)	Russian	
1959	Emilio G. Segrè (1905–)	American (b. Italy)	Discovery of the antiproton, a particle of mass identical to the proton but of opposite charge.
	Owen Chamberlain (1920–)	American	
1960	Donald A. Glaser (1926–)	American	Inventing the bubble chamber to study subatomic particles.
1961	Robert Hofstadter (1915–)	American	Investigations of atomic nuclei; discoveries relating to the structure of nucleons.
	Rudolf L. Moessbauer (1929–)	German	The method named for him of producing and measuring recoil-free gamma rays.
1962	Lev D. Landau (1908–68)	Russian	Pioneering studies on condensed gases, especially liquid helium.
1963	Eugene P. Wigner (1902–)	American (b. Hungary)	Contributions to nuclear and theoretical physics.
	Maria Goeppert-Mayer (1906–1972)	American (b. Poland)	Their discoveries regarding atomic nucleus shell structure.
	J. Hans D. Jensen (1907–1973)	German	
1964	Charles H. Townes (1915–)	American	Their fundamental research in quantum electronics that led to development of the maser-laser principle.
	Nikolai G. Basov (1922–)	Russian	
	Aleksander M. Prokhorov (1916–)	Russian	
1965	Richard P. Feynman (1918–)	American	Research in quantum electrodynamics that contributed to the understanding of elementary particles in high-energy physics.
	Julian S. Schwinger (1918–)	American	
	Sin-itiro Tomonaga (1906–1979)	Japanese	
1966	Alfred Kastler (1902–)	French	Discovery and development of optical methods for studying Herzian resonances in atoms.

Year	Winner and Life Dates	Nationality	Achievement
1967	Hans A. Bethe (1906–)	American (b. Germany)	Contributions to the theory of nuclear reaction; discoveries concerning the energy production of stars.
1968	Luis W. Alvarez (1911–)	American	Contributions to the physics of subatomic particles and techniques for their detection.
1969	Murray Gell-Mann (1929–)	American	Major theoretical insights into the interrelationships of elementary particles, including the theoretical model that he calls "The Eight-fold Way."
1970	Louis Néel (1904–)	French	Discoveries about ferromagnetism and antiferromagnetism; basic work in magneto-hydrodynamics.
	Hannes Alfvén (1908–)	Swedish	
1971	Dennis Gabor (1900–1979)	British (b. Hungary)	Inventor of the three-dimensional, lensless system of photography known as holography.
1972	John Bardeen (1908–)	American	Joint development of a theory explaining the phenomenon of superconductivity.
	Leon Cooper (1930–)	American	
	John Robert Schrieffer (1931–)	American	
1973	Leo Esaki (1925–)	Japanese	Research into how electrons tunnel through conductors to become superconductors.
	Ivar Giaever (1929–)	American	
	Brian D. Josephson (1940–)	British	
1974	Sir Martin Ryle (1918–)	British	For their pioneering work in radio astrophysics.
	Anthony Hewish (1924–)	British	
1975	James Rainwater (1918–)	American	Discovery of the connection between collective motion and particle motion in the atomic nucleus and the development of the theory of the structure of the atomic nucleus based on this connection.
	Aage N. Bohr (1922–)	Danish	
	Ben R. Mottelson (1926–)	Danish (b. U.S.)	
1976	Burton Richter (1931–)	American	For independent discovery of a new subatomic particle, known as "psi" or "J".
	Samuel C.C. Ting (1936–)	American	
1977	John H. Van Vleck (1899–)	American	For their contributions to the development of modern electronic solid state circuitry and basic theories of magnetism and conduction.
	Philip W. Anderson (1924–)	American	
	Sir Nevill F. Mott (1905–)	British	
1978	Pyotr Kapitsa (1894–)	Russian	Pioneer work in low-temperature physics.
	Arno A. Penzias (1933–)	American (b. Germany)	Discovery of cosmic microwave background radiation, further support for the Big Bang theory.
	Robert W. Wilson (1936–)	American	

ECONOMIC SCIENCE

Year	Winner and Life Dates	Nationality	Achievement
1969	Ragnar Frisch (1895–1973)	Norwegian	Their development of econometrics: mathematical models in the analysis of economic processes.
	Jan Tinbergen (1903–)	Dutch	
1970	Paul Anthony Samuelson (1915–)	American	Deriving new theorems; devising new applications.
1971	Simon Kuznets (1901–)	American (b. Russia)	Development of concept of using GNP as measure of national economic growth.
1972	Kenneth J. Arrow (1921–)	American	Contributions to equilibrium theory and welfare theory.
	John R. Hicks (1904–)	English	
1973	Wassily Leontief (1906–)	American (b. Russia)	For the development of "input-output" analysis.
1974	Gunnar Myrdal (1898–)	Swedish	Work on the theory of money and the interdependence of economic, social, and institutional phenomena.
	Friedrich A. von Hayek (1899–)	British (b. Austria)	
1975	Leonid V. Kantorovich (1912–)	Russian	Independent contributions to the theory of optimum allocation of resources.
	Tjalling C. Koopmans (1910–)	American (b. Netherlands)	
1976	Milton Friedman (1912–)	American	For achievements in the fields of consumption analysis, monetary history and theory; demonstration of the complexity of stabilization policy.
1977	Bertil Ohlin (1899–1979)	Swedish	For their contribution to international trade theory.
	James Meade (1907–)	English	
1978	Herbert Simon (1916–)	American	Research in the decision-making process within economic organizations.

LITERATURE

1901 René F. A. Sully-Prudhomme (1839–1907), French
1902 Theodor Mommsen (1817–1903), German
1903 Björnstjerne Björnson (1832–1910), Norwegian
1904 Frédéric Mistral (1830–1914), French
     José Echegaray (1832–1916), Spanish
1905 Henryk Sienkiewicz (1846–1916), Polish
1906 Giosuè Carducci (1835–1907), Italian
1907 Rudyard Kipling (1865–1936), British
1908 Rudolf C. Eucken (1846–1926), German
1909 Selma Lagerlöf (1858–1940), Swedish
1910 Paul J. L. Heyse (1830–1914), German
1911 Maurice Maeterlinck (1862–1949), Belgian
1912 Gerhart Hauptmann (1862–1946), German
1913 Rabindranath Tagore (1861–1941), Indian
1915 Romain Rolland (1866–1944), French
1916 Verner von Heidenstam (1859–1940), Swedish
1917 Karl A. Gjellerup (1857–1919), Danish
     Henrik Pontoppidan (1857–1943), Danish
1919 Carl F. G. Spitteler (1845–1924), Swiss
1920 Knut Hamsun (1859–1952), Norwegian
1921 Anatole France (1844–1924), French
1922 Jacinto Benavente y Martínez (1866–1954), Spanish
1923 William Butler Yeats (1865–1939), Irish
1924 Wladyslaw S. Reymont (c. 1867–1925), Polish
1925 George Bernard Shaw (1856–1950), British (b. Ireland)
1926 Grazia Deledda (1875–1936), Italian
1927 Henri Bergson (1859–1941), French
1928 Sigrid Undset (1882–1949), Norwegian (b. Denmark)
1929 Thomas Mann (1875–1955), German
1930 Sinclair Lewis (1885–1951), American
1931 Erik A. Karlfeldt (1864–1931), Swedish
1932 John Galsworthy (1867–1933), English
1933 Ivan A. Bunin (1870–1953), Russian
1934 Luigi Pirandello (1867–1936), Italian
1936 Eugene O'Neill (1888–1953), American
1937 Roger Martin du Gard (1881–1958), French
1938 Pearl S. Buck (1892–1973), American

1939 Frans E. Sillanpää (1888–1964), Finnish
1944 Johannes V. Jensen (1873–1950), Danish
1945 Gabriela Mistral (1889–1957), Chilean
1946 Hermann Hesse (1877–1962), Swiss (b. Germany)
1947 André Gide (1869–1951), French
1948 T. S. Eliot (1888–1965), British (b. United States)
1949 William Faulkner (1897–1962), American
1950 Bertrand A. W. Russell (1872–1970), British
1951 Pär F. Lagerkvist (1891–1974), Swedish
1952 François Mauriac (1885–1970), French
1953 Sir Winston Churchill (1874–1965), British
1954 Ernest Hemingway (1899–1961), American
1955 Halldór K. Laxness (1902–), Icelandic
1956 Juan Ramón Jiménez (1881–1958), Spanish
1957 Albert Camus (1913–60), French
1958 Boris L. Pasternak (1890–1960), Russian
1959 Salvatore Quasimodo (1901–68), Italian
1960 Saint-John Perse (1887–1975), French
1961 Ivo Andrić (1892–1975), Yugoslav
1962 John Steinbeck (1902–68), American
1963 Giorgos Seferis (1900–71), Greek
1964 Jean Paul Sartre (1905–), French
1965 Mikhail A. Sholokov (1905–), Russian
1966 Samuel Y. Agnon (1888–1970), Israeli (b. Poland)
     Nelly Sachs (1891–1970), Swedish (b. Germany)
1967 Miguel Angel Asturias (1899–1974), Guatemalan
1968 Yasunari Kawabata (1899–1972), Japanese
1969 Samuel Beckett (1906–), Irish (res. France)
1970 Aleksandr Solzhenitsyn (1918–), Russian
1971 Pablo Neruda (1904–1973), Chilean
1972 Heinrich Böll (1917–), German
1973 Patrick White (1912–), Australian
1974 Eyvind Johnson (1900–76), Swedish
     Edmund Martinson (1904–1978), Swedish
1975 Eugenio Montale (1896–), Italian
1976 Saul Bellow (1915–), American
1977 Vicente Aleixandre (1898–), Spanish
1978 Isaac Bashevis Singer (1904–), American (b. Poland)

PEACE

1901 Jean H. Dunant (1828–1910), Swiss
 Frédéric Passy (1822–1912), French
1902 Élie Ducommun (1833–1906), Swiss
 Charles A. Gobat (1843–1914), Swiss
1903 William R. Cremer (1828–1908), English
1904 Institute of International Law
1905 Bertha von Suttner (1843–1914), Austrian
1906 Theodore Roosevelt (1858–1919), American
1907 Ernesto T. Moneta (1833–1918), Italian
 Louis Renault (1843–1918), French
1908 Klas P. Arnoldson (1844–1916), Swedish
1909 August M. F. Beernaert (1829–1912), Belgian
 Paul H. Benjamin Estournelles de Constant (1852–1924), French
1910 International Peace Bureau
1911 Tobias M. C. Asser (1838–1913), Dutch
 Alfred H. Fried (1864–1921), Austrian
1912 Elihu Root (1845–1937), American
1913 Henri La Fontaine (1854–1943), Belgian
1917 International Red Cross Committee
1919 Woodrow Wilson (1856–1924), American
1920 Léon Bourgeois (1851–1925), French
1921 Hjalmar Branting (1860–1925), Swedish
 Christian L. Lange (1869–1938), Norwegian
1922 Fridtjof Nansen (1861–1930), Norwegian
1925 Sir J. Austen Chamberlain (1863–1937), British
 Charles G. Dawes (1865–1951), American
1926 Aristide Briand (1862–1932), French
 Gustav Stresemann (1878–1929), German
1927 Ferdinand E. Buisson (1841–1932), French
 Ludwig Quidde (1858–1941), German
1929 Frank B. Kellogg (1856–1937), American
1930 Nathan Söderblom (1866–1931), Swedish
1931 Jane Addams (1860–1935), American
 Nicholas Murray Butler (1862–1947), American
1933 Norman Angell (c. 1872–1967), British
1934 Arthur Henderson (1863–1935), British
1935 Carl von Ossietzky (1889–1938), German

1936 Carlos Saavedra Lamas (1880–1959), Argentine
1937 E. A. R. Cecil (1864–1958), British
1938 Nansen International Office for Refugees
1944 International Red Cross Committee
1945 Cordell Hull (1871–1955), American
1946 John R. Mott (1865–1955), American
 Emily Balch (1867–1961), American
1947 Friends Service Council (British)
 American Friends Service Committee (American)
1949 Sir John Boyd Orr (1880–1971), British
1950 Ralph J. Bunche (1904–71), American
1951 Léon Jouhaux (1879–1954), French
1952 Albert Schweitzer (1875–1965), Alsatian
1953 George C. Marshall (1880–1959), American
1954 Office of the UN High Commissioner for Refugees
1957 Lester B. Pearson (1897–1972), Canadian
1958 Father Georges H. Pire (1910–69), Belgian
1959 Philip J. Noel-Baker (1889–), British
1960 Albert J. Luthuli (1899–1967), South African
1961 Dag Hammarskjöld (1905–61), Swedish
1962 Linus C. Pauling (1901–), American
1963 International Red Cross Committee
 League of Red Cross Societies
1964 Martin Luther King, Jr. (1929–68), American
1965 UNICEF (UN Children's Fund)
1968 René Cassin (1887–1976), French
1969 International Labor Organization
1970 Norman E. Borlaug (1914–), American
1971 Willy Brandt (1913–), German
1973 Henry A. Kissinger (1923–), American
 Le Duc Tho (1910–), Vietnamese
1974 Eisaku Sato (1901–75), Japanese
 Sean McBride (1904–), Irish
1975 Andrei D. Sakharov (1921–), Russian
1976 Mairead Corrigan (1944–), Northern Irish
 Betty Williams (1943–), Northern Irish
1977 Amnesty International
1978 Menachem Begin (1913–), Israeli
 Anwar el-Sadat (1918–), Egyptian

PULITZER PRIZES

LOCAL INVESTIGATIVE REPORTING

1953 Edward J. Mowery
 (New York World-Telegram & Sun)
1954 Alvin Scott McCoy
 (Kansas City [Mo.] Star)
1955 Roland Kenneth Towery
 (Cuero [Tex.] Record)
1956 Arthur Daley (N.Y. Times)
1957 Wallace Turner and William Lambert
 (Portland Oregonian)
1958 George Beveridge
 (Evening Star, Washington, D.C.)
1959 John Harold Brislin
 (Scranton [Pa.] Tribune and Scrantonian)
1960 Miriam Ottenberg
 (Evening Star, Washington, D.C.)
1961 Edgar May
 (Buffalo [N.Y.] Evening News)
1962 George Bliss
 (Chicago [Ill.] Tribune)
1963 Oscar O'Neal Griffin, Jr.
 (Pecos [Tex.] Enterprise)
1964 James V. Magee, Albert V. Gaudiosi, and Frederick A. Meyer
 (Philadelphia [Pa.] Bulletin)
1965 Gene Goltz
 (Houston [Tex.] Post)
1966 John A. Frasca
 (Tampa [Fla.] Tribune)
1967 Gene Miller
 (Miami [Fla.] Herald)
1968 J. Anthony Lukas
 (New York Times)
1969 Albert L. Delugach
 Denny Walsh
 (St. Louis Globe-Democrat)

1970 Harold Eugene Martin
 ([Montgomery] Alabama Journal)
1971 William Hugh Jones
 (Chicago [Ill.] Tribune)
1972 Richard Cooper and John Machacek (Rochester [N.Y.] Times Union)
1973 The Sun Newspapers, Omaha, Nebraska
1974 Arthur M. Petacque
 Hugh F. Hough
 (The Chicago Sun-Times)
1976 The Chicago [Ill.] Tribune
1977 Acel Moore and Wendell Rawls, Jr. (The Philadelphia [Pa.] Inquirer)
1978 Anthony R. Dolan (Stamford [Conn.] Advocate)
1979 Gilbert M. Gaul and Elliot G. Jaspin
 (Pottsville [Pa.] Republican)

GENERAL LOCAL REPORTING

1953 Providence (R.I.) Journal and Evening Bulletin
1954 Vicksburg (Miss.) Sunday Post-Herald
1955 Mrs. Caro Brown
 (Alice [Tex.] Daily Echo)
1956 Lee Hills
 (Detroit [Mich.] Free Press)
1957 Salt Lake (Utah) Tribune
1958 Fargo (N.D.) Forum
1959 Mary Lou Werner
 (Evening Star, Washington, D.C.)
1960 Jack Nelson
 (Atlanta [Ga.] Constitution)
1961 Sanche de Gramont
 (New York Herald Tribune)
1962 Robert D. Mullins
 (Deseret News, Salt Lake City, Utah)
1963 Sylvan Fox, Anthony Shannon, and William Longgood
 (New York World-Telegram & Sun)

1964 Norman C. Miller, Jr.
 (Wall Street Journal)
1965 Melvin H. Ruder
 (Hungry Horse News, Columbia Falls, Mont.)
1966 Los Angeles (Calif.) Times staff
1967 Robert V. Cox
 (Chambersburg [Pa.] Public Opinion)
1968 Detroit (Mich.) Free Press
1969 John Fetterman
 (Louisville [Ky.] Times and Courier-Journal)
1970 Thomas Fitzpatrick
 (Chicago [Ill.] Sun-Times)
1971 Akron [Ohio] Beacon Journal
1972 Timothy Leland, Gerald M. O'Neill, Stephen A. Kurjan, and Ann Desantis (Boston Globe)
1973 Chicago Tribune
1974 William Sherman
 (New York Daily News)
1976 Gene Miller (Miami [Fla.] Herald)
1977 Margo Huston (The Milwaukee [Wis.] Journal)
1978 Richard Whitt (Louisville [Ky.] Courier-Journal)
1979 San Diego (Calif.) Evening Tribune

NATIONAL REPORTING

1948 Bert Andrews
 (New York Herald Tribune)
 Nat S. Finney
 (Minneapolis [Minn.] Tribune)
1949 C. P. Trussel
 (New York Times)
1950 Edwin O. Guthman
 (Seattle [Wash.] Times)
1952 Anthony Leviero
 (New York Times)
1953 Don Whitehead (AP)
1954 Richard Wilson
 (Cowles Newspapers)

1955 Anthony Lewis
(*Washington* [D.C.] *Daily News*)
1956 Charles L. Bartlett
(*Chattanooga* [Tenn.] *Times*)
1957 James Reston
(*New York Times*)
1958 Relman Morin (AP)
Clark Mollenhoff
(*Des Moines* [Iowa] *Register & Tribune*)
1959 Howard Van Smith
(*Miami* [Fla.] *News*)
1960 Vance Trimble
(Scripps-Howard Newspaper Alliance)
1961 Edward R. Cony
(*Wall Street Journal*)
1962 Nathan G. Caldwell and
Gene S. Graham
(*Nashville Tennessean*)
1963 Anthony Lewis
(*New York Times*)
1964 Merriman Smith (UPI)
1965 Louis M. Kohlmeier
(*Wall Street Journal*)
1966 Haynes Johnson
(*Evening Star, Wash., D.C.*)
1967 Monroe W. Karmin and
Stanley W. Penn
(*Wall Street Journal*)
1968 Howard James
(*Christian Science Monitor*)
Nathan K. Kotz (*Des Moines* [Iowa] *Register*)
1969 Robert Cahn
(*Christian Science Monitor,* Boston, Mass.)
1970 William J. Eaton
(*Chicago* [Ill.] *Daily News*)
1971 Lucinda Franks and Thomas
Powers (UPI)
1972 Jack Anderson (Columnist)
1973 Robert Boyd and Clark Hoyt
(Knight Newspapers)
1974 James R. Polk
(*Washington Star News*)
Jack White
(*Providence Journal-Bulletin*)
1975 Donald L. Barlett and
James B. Steele (*The Philadelphia Inquirer*)
1976 James Risser (*Des Moines* [Iowa] *Register*)
1977 Walter Mears (AP)
1978 Gaylord Shaw (*Los Angeles* [Calif.] *Times*)
1979 James Risser
(*Des Moines* [Iowa] *Register*)

INTERNATIONAL CORRESPONDENCE
1948 Paul W. Ward
(*Sun,* Baltimore, Md.)
1949 Price Day
(*Sun,* Baltimore, Md.)
1950 Edmund Stevens
(*Christian Science Monitor,* Boston, Mass.)
1951 Keyes Beech
(*Chicago* [Ill.] *Daily News*)
Homer Bigart
Marguerite Higgins
(*New York Herald Tribune*)
Relman Morin (AP)
Fred Sparks
(*Chicago* [Ill.] *Daily News*)
Don Whitehead (AP)
1952 John M. Hightower (AP)
1953 Austin Wehrwein
(*Milwaukee* [Wis.] *Journal*)
1954 Jim G. Lucas
(Scripps-Howard Newspaper Alliance)
1955 Harrison E. Salisbury
(*New York Times*)

1956 William Randolph Hearst,
Jr., Kingsbury Smith, and
Frank Coniff
(International News Service)
1957 Russell Jones (UPI)
1958 *New York Times*
1959 Joseph Martin and Philip
Santora (New York *Daily News*)
1960 A. M. Rosenthal
(*New York Times*)
1961 Lynn Heinzerling (AP)
1962 Walter Lippmann
(*New York Herald Tribune Syndicate*)
1963 Hal Hendrix
(*Miami* [Fla.] *News*)
1964 Malcolm W. Browne (AP)
David Halberstam
(*New York Times*)
1965 J. A. Livingston
(*Philadelphia Bulletin*)
1966 Peter Arnett (AP)
1967 R. John Hughes
(*Christian Science Monitor,* Boston, Mass.)
1968 Alfred Friendly
(*Washington* [D.C.] *Post*)
1969 William Tuohy
(*Los Angeles Times*)
1970 Seymour M. Hersh
(free-lance reporter)
1971 Jimmie Lee Hoagland
(*Washington* [D.C.] *Post*)
1972 Peter R. Kann
(*Wall Street Journal*)
1973 Max Frankel
(*New York Times*)
1974 Hedrick Smith
(*The New York Times*)
1975 William Mullen and
Ovie Carter
(*The Chicago Tribune*)
1976 Sydney H. Schanberg
(*The New York Times*)
1978 Henry Kamm (*The New York Times*)
1979 Richard Ben Cramer
(*Philadelphia* [Pa.] *Inquirer*)

EDITORIAL WRITING
1917 *New York Tribune*
1918 *Courier-Journal,* Louisville, Ky.
1920 Harvey E. Newbranch
(*Evening World-Herald,* Omaha, Nebr.)
1922 Frank M. O'Brien
(*New York Herald*)
1923 William Allen White
(*Emporia* [Kans.] *Gazette*)
1924 *Boston* (Mass.) *Herald*
Special prize: Frank I. Cobb
(*World,* New York, N.Y.)
1925 *Charleston* (S.C.) *News and
Courier*
1926 Edward M. Kingsbury (*New
York Times*)
1927 F. Lauriston Bullard (*Boston*
[Mass.] *Herald*)
1928 Grover Cleveland Hall
(*Montgomery* [Ala.] *Adver-
tiser*)
1929 Louis Isaac Jaffe
(*Norfolk Virginian-Pilot*)
1931 Charles S. Ryckman
(*Fremont* [Nebr.] *Tribune*)
1933 *Kansas City* (Mo.) *Star*
1934 E. P. Chase
(*Atlantic News Telegraph*)
1936 Felix Morley
(*Washington* [D.C.] *Post*)
George B. Parker
(Scripps-Howard Newspaper Alliance)
1937 John W. Owens
(*Sun,* Baltimore, Md.)

1938 W. W. Waymack
(*Register and Tribune,* Des Moines, Iowa)
1939 Ronald G. Callvert
(*Oregonian,* Portland, Ore.)
1940 Bart Howard
(*St. Louis Post-Dispatch*)
1941 Reuben Maury
(*Daily News, N.Y.*)
1942 Geoffrey Parsons
(*New York Herald Tribune*)
1943 Forrest W. Seymour
(*Register and Tribune,* Iowa)
1944 Henry J. Haskell
(*Kansas City* [Mo.] *Star*)
1945 George W. Potter
(*Providence* [R.I.] *Journal-Bulletin*)
1946 Hodding Carter
(*Delta Democrat-Times,* Greenville, Miss.)
1947 William H. Grimes
(*Wall Street Journal*)
1948 Virginius Dabney
(*Richmond* [Va.] *Times-Dispatch*)
1949 John H. Crider
(*Boston* [Mass.] *Herald*)
Herbert Elliston
(*Washington* [D.C.] *Post*)
1950 Carl M. Saunders
(*Jackson* [Mich.] *Citizen Patriot*)
1951 William Harry Fitzpatrick
(*New Orleans* [La.] *States*)
1952 Louis LaCoss
(*St. Louis Globe-Democrat*)
1953 Vermont C. Royster
(*Wall Street Journal*)
1954 Don Murray
(*Boston* [Mass.] *Herald*)
1955 Royce Howes
(*Detroit* [Mich.] *Free Press*)
1956 Lauren K. Soth
(*Des Moines* [Iowa] *Register
and Tribune*)
1957 Buford Boone
(*Tuscaloosa* [Ala.] *News*)
1958 Harry S. Ashmore
(*Arkansas Gazette*)
1959 Ralph McGill
(*Atlanta* [Ga.] *Constitution*)
1960 Lenoir Chambers
(*Norfolk Virginian-Pilot*)
1961 William J. Dorvillier
(*San Juan* [P.R.] *Star*)
1962 Thomas M. Storke
(*Santa Barbara News-Press*)
1963 Ira B. Harkey, Jr.
(*Pascagoula* [Miss.] *Chronicle*)
1964 Hazel Brannon Smith
(*Lexington* [Miss.] *Adver-
tiser*)
1965 John R. Harrison
(*Gainesville* [Fla.] *Sun*)
1966 Robert Lasch
(*St. Louis Post-Dispatch*)
1967 Eugene Patterson
(*Atlanta* [Ga.] *Constitution*)
1968 John S. Knight
(Knight Newspapers)
1969 Paul Greenberg
(*Pine Bluff* [Ark.] *Commercial*)
1970 Philip L. Geyelin
(*Washington* [D.C.] *Post*)
1971 Horance G. Davis, Jr.
(*Gainesville* [Fla.] *Sun*)
1972 John Strohmeyer (*Bethlehem*
[Pa.] *Globe-Times*)
1973 Roger B. Linscott
(*Berkshire Eagle* [Pittsfield, Mass.])
1974 F. Gilman Spencer
(*Trenton Trentonian*)

1975　John Daniell Maurice
(*Charleston Daily Mail*)

1976　Philip P. Kerby (*The Los Angeles* [Calif.] *Times*)

1977　Warren Lerude, Foster Church, Norman F. Cardoza (*The Reno* [Nev.] *Evening Gazette* and *Nevada State Journal*)

1978　Meg Greenfield (*The Washington* [D.C.] *Post*)

1979　Edwin M. Yoder, Jr. (*The Washington* [D.C.] *Star*)

CARTOONS

1922　Rollin Kirby
(*World*, New York, N.Y.)

1924　Jay Norwood Darling
(*New York Tribune*)

1925　Rollin Kirby
(*World*, New York, N.Y.)

1926　D. R. Fitzpatrick
(*St. Louis Post-Dispatch*)

1927　Nelson Harding
(*Brooklyn* [N.Y.] *Daily Eagle*)

1928　Nelson Harding
(*Brooklyn Daily Eagle*)

1929　Rollin Kirby
(*World*, New York, N.Y.)

1930　Charles R. Macauley
(*Brooklyn* [N.Y.] *Daily Eagle*)

1931　Edmund Duffy
(*Sun*, Baltimore, Md.)

1932　John T. McCutcheon
(*Chicago* [Ill.] *Tribune*)

1933　Harold M. Talburt
(*Washington* [D.C.] *Daily News*)

1934　Edmund Duffy
(*Sun*, Baltimore, Md.)

1935　Ross A. Lewis
(*Milwaukee* [Wis.] *Journal*)

1937　Clarence D. Batchelor
(*Daily News*, New York, N.Y.)

1938　Vaughn Shoemaker
(*Chicago* [Ill.] *Daily News*)

1939　Charles G. Werner
(*Daily Oklahoman*, Oklahoma City, Okla.)

1940　Edmund Duffy
(*Sun*, Baltimore, Md.)

1941　Jacob Burck
(*Times*, Chicago, Ill.)

1942　Herbert L. Block
(NEA Service)

1943　Jay Norwood Darling
(*New York Herald Tribune*)

1944　Clifford K. Berryman
(*Evening Star*, Washington, D.C.)

1945　William (Bill) Mauldin
(United Features Syndicate)

1946　Bruce Alexander Russell
(*Los Angeles* [Calif.] *Times*)

1947　Vaughn Shoemaker
(*Chicago* [Ill.] *Daily News*)

1948　Reuben L. (Rube) Goldberg
(*Sun*, New York, N.Y.)

1949　Lute Pease
(*Newark* [N.J.] *Evening News*)

1950　James T. Berryman
(*Evening Star*, Washington, D.C.)

1951　Reginald W. Manning
(*Arizona Republic*, Phoenix)

1952　Fred L. Packer
(*New York* [N.Y.] *Mirror*)

1953　Edward D. Kuekes
(*Cleveland Plain Dealer*)

1954　Herbert L. Block
(*Washington* [D.C.] *Post & Times-Herald*)

* Amateur photographer.

1955　Daniel R. Fitzpatrick
(*St. Louis Post-Dispatch*)

1956　Robert York
(*Louisville* [Ky.] *Times*)

1957　Tom Little
(*Nashville Tennessean*)

1958　Bruce M. Shanks
(*Buffalo Evening News*)

1959　William (Bill) Mauldin
(*St. Louis Post-Dispatch*)

1961　Carey Orr
(*Chicago* [Ill.] *Tribune*)

1962　Edmund S. Valtman
(*Hartford* [Conn.] *Times*)

1963　Frank Miller
(*Des Moines* [Iowa] *Register*)

1964　Paul Conrad
(*Denver* [Colo.] *Post*)

1966　Don Wright
(*Miami* [Fla.] *News*)

1967　Patrick B. Oliphant
(*Denver* [Colo.] *Post*)

1968　Eugene Gray Payne
(*Charlotte* [N.C.] *Observer*)

1969　John Fischetti
(*Chicago* [Ill.] *Daily News*)

1970　Thomas F. Darcy
(*Newsday*, Garden City, NY)

1971　Paul Conrad
(*Los Angeles* [Calif.] *Times*)

1972　Jeffrey K. MacNelly (*Richmond* [Va.] *News Leader*)

1974　Paul Szep
(*The Boston Globe*)

1975　**Garry Trudeau**
(Universal Press Syndicate)

1976　Tony Auth (*The Philadelphia* [Pa.] *Inquirer*)

1977　Paul Szep (*The Boston* [Mass.] *Globe*)

1978　Jeffrey K. MacNelly (*Richmond* [Va.] *News Leader*)

1979　Herbert L. Block
(*The Washington* [D.C.] *Post*)

PHOTOGRAPHY

1942　Milton Brooks
(*Detroit* [Mich.] *News*)

1943　**Frank Noel (AP)**

1944　**Frank Filan (AP)**
Earle L. Bunker
(*World-Herald*, Omaha, Nebr.)

1945　Joe Rosenthal (AP)

1947　Arnold Hardy°

1948　Frank Cushing
(*Boston* [Mass.] *Traveler*)

1949　Nathaniel Fein
(*New York Herald Tribune*)

1950　Bill Crouch
(*Oakland* [Calif.] *Tribune*)

1951　Max Desfor (AP)

1952　John Robinson and Don Ultang (*Des Moines* [Iowa] *Register and Tribune*)

1953　William M. Gallagher
(*Flint* [Mich.] *Journal*)

1954　Mrs. Walter M. Schau°

1955　John L. Gaunt, Jr.
(*Los Angeles* [Calif.] *Times*)

1956　*Daily News*, New York, N.Y.

1957　Harry A. Trask
(*Boston* [Mass.] *Traveler*)

1958　William C. Beall
(*Washington* [D.C.] *Daily News*)

1959　William Seaman
(*Minneapolis* [Minn.] *Star*)

1960　Andrew Lopez (UPI)

1961　Yasushi Nagao
(*Mainichi Newspapers*, Tokyo, Japan)

1962　Paul Vathis (AP)

1963　Hector Rondon
(*La Republica*, Caracas, Venezuela)

1964　Robert H. Jackson
(*Dallas* [Tex.] *Times Herald*)

1965　**Horst Faas (AP)**

1966　Kyoichi Sawada (UPI)

1967　**Jack R. Thornell (AP)**

1968　Rocco Morabito
(*Jacksonville* [Fla.] *Journal*)
Toshio Sakai (UPI)

1969　**Edward T. Adams (AP)**
Moneta Sleet, Jr. (*Ebony*)

1970　**Steve Starr (AP)**
Dallas Kinney
(*Palm Beach* [Fla.] *Post*)

1971　John Paul Filo (Kent [Ohio] State University student)°
Jack Dykinga
(*Chicago* [Ill.] *Sun-Times*)

1972　Horst Fass and Michael Laurent (Associated Press) Dave Kenerly (United Press International)

1973　**Huynh Cong Ut (AP)**
Brian Lanker (*Topeka* [Kans.] *Capital-Journal*)

1974　Slava Veder (AP)
Anthony K. Roberts (AP)

1975　Gerald H. Gay
(*The Seattle Times*)
Matthew Lewis
(*Washington Post*)

1976　Stanley Forman (*The Boston* [Mass.] *Herald-American*); *Louisville* [Ky.] *Courier-Journal and Times*

1977　Stanley Forman (*The Boston* [Mass.] *Herald-American*); Neal Ulevich (AP); Robin Hood (*The Chattanooga* [Tenn.] *News-Free Press*)

1978　J. Ross Baughman (AP); John W. Blair (free-lance, UPI Indianapolis [Ind.] bureau)

1979　Thomas J. Kelly 3d (*Pottstown* [Pa.] *Mercury*); the photographic staff of *The Boston* (Mass.) *Herald-American*

MERITORIOUS PUBLIC SERVICE

1918　*New York Times*

1919　*Milwaukee* (Wis.) *Journal*

1921　*Boston* (Mass.) *Post*

1922　*World*, New York, N.Y.

1923　*Memphis* (Tenn.) *Commercial Appeal*

1924　*World* (New York, N.Y.)

1926　*Enquirer Sun* (Columbus, Ga.)

1927　*Canton* (Ohio) *Daily News*

1928　*Indianapolis* (Ind.) *Times*

1929　*Evening World*, New York, N.Y.

1931　*Atlanta* (Ga.) *Constitution*

1932　*Indianapolis* (Ind.) *News*

1933　*New York World-Telegram*

1934　*Medford* (Ore.) *Mail Tribune*

1935　*Sacramento* (Calif.) *Bee*

1936　*Cedar Rapids* (Iowa) *Gazette*

1937　*St. Louis* (Mo.) *Post-Dispatch*

1938　*Bismarck* (N.D.) *Tribune*

1939　*Miami* (Fla.) *Daily News*

1940　*Waterbury* (Conn.) *Republican and American*

1941　*St. Louis* (Mo.) *Post-Dispatch*

1942　*Los Angeles* (Calif.) *Times*

1943　*World-Herald*, Omaha, Nebr.

1944　*New York Times*

1945　*Detroit* (Mich.) *Free Press*

1946　*Scranton* (Pa.) *Times*

1947　*Sun*, Baltimore, Md.

1948　*St. Louis* (Mo.) *Post-Dispatch*

1949　*Nebraska State Journal*

1950　*Chicago* (Ill.) *Daily News* and *St. Louis Post-Dispatch*

1951　*Miami* (Fla.) *Herald* and *Brooklyn* (N.Y.) *Eagle*

1952　*St. Louis* (Mo.) *Post-Dispatch*

1953 News Reporter (Whiteville, N.C.) and Tabor City (N.C.) Tribune
1954 Newsday, Garden City, N.Y.
1955 Columbus (Ga.) Ledger and Sunday Ledger-Enquirer
1956 Watsonville (Calif.) Register-Pajaronian
1957 Chicago (Ill.) Daily News
1958 Arkansas Gazette, Little Rock
1959 Utica (N.Y.) Observer-Dispatch and Utica Daily Press
1960 Los Angeles (Calif.) Times
1961 Amarillo (Tex.) Globe-Times
1962 Panama City (Fla.) News-Herald
1963 Chicago (Ill.) Daily News
1964 St. Petersburg (Fla.) Times
1965 Hutchinson (Kans.) News
1966 Boston (Mass.) Globe
1967 Courier Journal (Louisville, Ky.) and Milwaukee (Wis.) Journal
1968 Riverside (Calif.) Press-Enterprise
1969 Los Angeles (Calif.) Times
1970 Newsday, Garden City, N.Y.
1971 Winston-Salem [N.C.] Journal & Sentinel
1972 The New York Times
1973 The Washington Post
1974 Newsday, Garden City, N.Y.
1975 Boston (Mass.) Globe
The Xenia (Ohio) Daily Gazette
1976 The Anchorage [Alaska] Daily News
1977 Lufkin (Tex.) News
1978 Philadelphia [Pa.] Inquirer
1979 Point Reyes (Calif.) Light

FEATURE WRITING

1979 Jon D. Franklin (The Baltimore [Md.] Evening Sun)

SPECIAL CITATIONS FOR JOURNALISM

1938 Edmonton (Alberta) Journal, for its editorial leadership in defense of the freedom of the press in the Province of Alberta, Canada.
1941 New York Times, for the public educational value of its foreign news reporting, exemplified by its scope, excellence of writing and presentation, and supplementary background information, illustration, and interpretation.
1944 Byron Price, Director of the Office of Censorship, for the creation and administration of the newspaper and radio codes during World War II.
1944 William Allen White, for his interest and service during his membership on the Advisory Board of Columbia University's School of Journalism.
1945 The cartographers of the American press, whose maps of the war fronts helped notably to clarify and increase public information on military progress.
1947 Columbia University and the Graduate School of Journalism, for their efforts to maintain and advance the high standards governing the Pulitzer Prize awards. The St. Louis Post-Dispatch, for its unswerving adherence to the public and professional ideals of its founder.

1948 Dr. Frank Diehl Fackenthal, a scroll indicating appreciation of his interest and service during the past years.
1951 Cyrus L. Sulzberger of the New York Times for his exclusive interview with Archbishop Stepinac.
1952 Max Kase of the New York Journal-American for his exclusive exposures of bribery and other forms of corruption in the popular American sport of basketball.
1952 Kansas City (Mo.) Star for coverage of the great regional floods of 1951 in Kansas and northwestern Missouri—a distinguished example of editing and reporting, as well as providing advance information that achieved maximum public protection.
1953 New York Times, for the section of its Sunday edition headed "Review of the Week," which for 17 years had been affording enlightenment and intelligent commentary.
1958 Walter Lippmann, nationally syndicated columnist of the New York Herald Tribune, for the wisdom, perception, and high sense of responsibility with which he commented for many years on national and international affairs.
1964 Gannett Newspapers, Rochester, N.Y.
1976 Professor John Hohenberg, expressing appreciation for his services for 22 years as Administrator of the Pulitzer Prizes and for his achievements as teacher and journalist
1978 Richard L. Strout, Washington, D.C. reporter for The Christian Science Monitor for 56 years and columnist for The New Republic since 1958, in recognition and appreciation of his thoughtful reporting and sharp analysis on events in the nation's capital.

BIOGRAPHY OR AUTOBIOGRAPHY

1917 Julia Ward Howe, by Laura E. Richards and Maude Howe Elliott, assisted by Florence Howe Hall
1918 Benjamin Franklin, Self-Revealed, by William Cabell Bruce
1919 The Education of Henry Adams, by Henry Adams
1920 The Life of John Marshall by Albert J. Beveridge
1921 The Americanization of Edward Bok, by Edward Bok
1922 A Daughter of the Middle Border, by Hamlin Garland
1923 The Life and Letters of Walter H. Page, by Burton J. Hendrick
1924 From Immigrant to Inventor, by Michael Idvorsky Pupin
1925 Barrett Wendell and His Letters, by M. A. DeWolfe Howe
1926 The Life of Sir William Osler, by Harvey Cushing

1927 Whitman, by Emory Holloway
1928 The American Orchestra and Theodore Thomas, by Charles Edward Russell
1929 The Training of an American: The Earlier Life and Letters of Walter H. Page, by Burton J. Hendrick
1930 The Raven, by Marquis James
1931 Charles W. Eliot, by Henry James
1932 Theodore Roosevelt, by Henry F. Pringle
1933 Grover Cleveland, by Allan Nevins
1934 John Hay, by Tyler Dennett
1935 R. E. Lee, by Douglas S. Freeman
1936 The Thought and Character of William James, by Ralph Barton Perry
1937 Hamilton Fish, by Allan Nevins
1938 Pedlar's Progress, by Odell Shepard, and Andrew Jackson (2 volumes), by Marquis James
1939 Benjamin Franklin, by Carl Van Doren
1940 Woodrow Wilson, Life and Letters (Volumes VII and VIII), by Ray Stannard Baker
1941 Jonathan Edwards, by Ola Elizabeth Winslow
1942 Crusader in Crinoline, by Forrest Wilson
1943 Admiral of the Ocean Sea, by Samuel Eliot Morison
1944 The American Leonardo: The Life of Samuel F. B. Morse, by Carleton Mabee
1945 George Bancroft: Brahmin Rebel, by Russell Blaine Nye
1946 Son of the Wilderness, by Linnie Marsh Wolfe
1947 The Autobiography of William Allen White
1948 Forgotten First Citizen: John Bigelow, by Margaret Clapp
1949 Roosevelt and Hopkins, by Robert E. Sherwood
1950 John Quincy Adams and the Foundations of American Foreign Policy, by Samuel Flagg Bemis
1951 John C. Calhoun: American Portrait, by Margaret Louise Coit
1952 Charles Evans Hughes, by Merlo J. Pusey
1953 Edmund Pendleton 1721–1803, by David J. Mays
1954 The Spirit of St. Louis, by Charles A. Lindbergh
1955 The Taft Story, by William S. White
1956 Benjamin Henry Latrobe, by Talbot Faulkner Hamlin
1957 Profiles in Courage, by John F. Kennedy
1958 George Washington (Volumes I–VI), by Douglas Southall Freeman; Volume VII, by Mary Wells Ashworth and John Alexander Carroll
1959 Woodrow Wilson, American Prophet, by Arthur Walworth
1960 John Paul Jones, by Samuel Eliot Morison

1961 *Charles Sumner and the Coming of the Civil War*, by David Donald

1963 *Henry James* (Volumes II and III), by Leon Edel

1964 *John Keats*, by Walter Jackson Bate

1965 *Henry Adams* (3 volumes), by Ernest Samuels

1966 *A Thousand Days*, by Arthur M. Schlesinger, Jr.

1967 *Mr. Clemens and Mark Twain*, by Justin Kaplan

1968 *Memoirs (1925–1950)*, by George F. Kennan

1969 *The Man from New York: John Quinn and His Friends*, by Benjamin Lawrence Reid

1970 *Huey Long*, by T.H. Williams

1971 *Robert Frost: The Years of Triumph*, by L. R. Thompson

1972 *Eleanor and Franklin*, by Joseph P. Lash

1973 *Luce and His Empire*, by W. A. Swanberg

1974 *O'Neill, Son and Artist*, by Louis Sheaffer

1975 *The Power Broker: Robert Moses and the Fall of New York*, by Robert A. Caro

1976 *Edith Wharton: A Biography*, by R.W.B. Lewis

1977 *A Prince of Our Disorder*, by John E. Mack

1978 *Samuel Johnson*, by Walter Jackson Bate

1979 *Days of Sorrow and Pain: Leo Baeck and the Berlin Jews*, by Leonard Baker

DRAMA

1918 *Why Marry?*, by Jesse Lynch Williams

1920 *Beyond the Horizon*, by Eugene O'Neill

1921 *Miss Lulu Bett*, by Zona Gale

1922 *Anna Christie*, by Eugene O'Neill

1923 *Icebound*, by Owen Davis

1924 *Hell-Bent for Heaven*, by Hatcher Hughes

1925 *They Knew What They Wanted*, by Sidney Howard

1926 *Craig's Wife*, by G. Kelly

1927 *In Abraham's Bosom*, by Paul Green

1928 *Strange Interlude*, by Eugene O'Neill

1929 *Street Scene*, by Elmer L. Rice

1930 *The Green Pastures*, by Marc Connelly

1931 *Alison's House*, by Susan Glaspell

1932 *Of Thee I Sing*, by George S. Kaufman, Morrie Ryskind, and Ira Gershwin (with music by George Gershwin)

1933 *Both Your Houses*, by Maxwell Anderson

1934 *Men in White*, by Sidney Kingsley

1935 *The Old Maid*, by Zoe Akins

1936 *Idiot's Delight*, by Robert E. Sherwood

1937 *You Can't Take It with You*, by Moss Hart and George S. Kaufman

1938 *Our Town*, by Thornton Wilder

1939 *Abe Lincoln in Illinois*, by Robert E. Sherwood

1940 *The Time of Your Life*, by William Saroyan°

1941 *There Shall Be No Night*, by Robert E. Sherwood

1943 *The Skin of Our Teeth*, by Thornton Wilder

1945 *Harvey*, by Mary Chase

1946 *State of the Union*, by Russel Crouse and Howard Lindsay

1948 *A Streetcar Named Desire*, by Tennessee Williams

1949 *Death of a Salesman*, by Arthur Miller

1950 *South Pacific*, by Richard Rodgers, Oscar Hammerstein II, and Joshua Logan

1952 *The Shrike*, by Joseph Kramm

1953 *Picnic*, by William Inge

1954 *The Teahouse of the August Moon*, by John Patrick

1955 *Cat on a Hot Tin Roof*, by Tennessee Williams

1956 *Diary of Anne Frank*, by Albert Hackett and Frances Goodrich

1957 *Long Day's Journey into Night*, by Eugene O'Neill

1958 *Look Homeward, Angel*, by Ketti Frings

1959 *J. B.*, by Archibald MacLeish

1960 *Fiorello!*, book by Jerome Weidman and George Abbott, music by Jerry Bock, and lyrics by Sheldon Harnick

1961 *All the Way Home*, by Tad Mosel

1962 *How to Succeed in Business Without Really Trying*, by F. Loesser and A. Burrows

1965 *The Subject Was Roses*, by Frank D. Gilroy

1967 *A Delicate Balance*, by Edward Albee

1969 *The Great White Hope*, by Howard Sackler

1970 *No Place to Be Somebody*, by Charles Gordone

1971 *The Effect of Gamma Rays on Man-in-the-Moon Marigolds*, by Paul Zindel

1973 *That Championship Season*, by Jason Miller

1975 *Seascape*, by Edward Albee

1976 *A Chorus Line*, conceived, choreographed and directed by Michael Bennett; book by James Kirkwood & Nicholas Dante; music by Marvin Hamlisch; lyrics by Edward Kleban.

1977 *The Shadow Box*, by Michael Cristofer

1978 *The Gin Game*, by Donald L. Coburn

1979 *Buried Child*, by Sam Shepard

HISTORY

1917 *With Americans of Past and Present Days*, by His Excellency J. J. Jusserand, Ambassador of France to the U.S.

1918 *A History of the Civil War, 1861–1865*, by James Ford Rhodes

1920 *The War with Mexico* (2 volumes), by Justin H. Smith

1921 *The Victory at Sea*, by William Sowden Sims in collaboration with Burton J. Hendrick

1922 *The Founding of New England*, by James Truslow Adams

1923 *The Supreme Court in United States History*, by Charles Warren

1924 *The American Revolution—A Constitutional Interpretation*, by Charles Howard McIlwain

1925 *A History of the American Frontier*, by F. L. Paxson

1926 *The History of the United States* (Volume VI: *The War for Southern Independence*), by Edward Channing

1927 *Pinckney's Treaty*, by Samuel Flagg Bemis

1928 *Main Currents in American Thought*, 2 volumes, by Vernon Louis Parrington

1929 *The Organization and Administration of the Union Army, 1861–1865*, by Fred Albert Shannon

1930 *The War of Independence*, by Claude H. Van Tyne

1931 *The Coming of the War: 1914*, by Bernadotte E. Schmitt

1932 *My Experiences in the World War*, by John J. Pershing

1933 *The Significance of Sections in American History*, by Frederick J. Turner

1934 *The People's Choice*, by Herbert Agar

1935 *The Colonial Period of American History*, by Charles McLean Andrews

1936 *The Constitutional History of the United States*, by Andrew C. McLaughlin

1937 *The Flowering of New England*, by Van Wyck Brooks

1938 *The Road to Reunion, 1865–1900* by Paul Herman Buck

1939 *A History of American Magazines* by Frank Luther Mott

1940 *Abraham Lincoln: The War Years*, by Carl Sandburg

1941 *The Atlantic Migration, 1607–1860, by Marcus Lee Hansen*

1942 *Reveille in Washington*, by Margaret Leech

1943 *Paul Revere and the World He Lived In*, by Esther Forbes

1944 *The Growth of American Thought*, by Merle Curti

1945 *Unfinished Business*, by Stephen Bonsal

1946 *The Age of Jackson*, by Arthur M. Schlesinger, Jr.

1947 *Scientists Against Time*, by James Phinney Baxter III

1948 *Across the Wide Missouri*, by Bernard DeVoto

1949 *The Disruption of American Democracy*, by Roy Franklin Nichols

1950 *Art and Life in America*, by Oliver W. Larkin

1951 *The Old Northwest: Pioneer Period, 1815–1840*, by R. Carlyle Buley

1952 *The Uprooted*, by Oscar Handlin

1953 *The Era of Good Feelings*, by George Dangerfield

1954 *A Stillness at Appomattox*, by Bruce Catton

1955 *Great River: The Rio Grande in North American History*, by Paul Horgan

1956 *The Age of Reform*, by Richard Hofstadter

° Declined.

1957 *Russia Leaves the War: Soviet-American Relations, 1917–1920,* by George F. Kennan

1958 *Banks and Politics in America—From the Revolution to the Civil War,* by Bray Hammond

1959 *The Republican Era: 1869–1901,* by Leonard D. White, with the assistance of Jean Schneider

1960 *In the Days of McKinley,* by Margaret Leech

1961 *Between War and Peace: The Potsdam Conference,* by Herbert Feis

1962 *The Triumphant Empire: Thunder-Clouds Gather in the West 1763–1766,* by Lawrence H. Gipson

1963 *Washington: Village and Capital, 1800–1878,* by Constance McLaughlin Green

1964 *Puritan Village: The Formation of a New England Town,* by Sumner Chilton Powell

1965 *The Greenback Era,* by Irwin Unger

1966 *Life of the Mind in America From the Revolution to the Civil War,* by Perry Miller

1967 *Exploration and Empire,* by William H. Goetzmann

1968 *The Ideological Origins of the American Revolution,* by Bernard Bailyn

1969 *Origins of the Fifth Amendment,* by Leonard W. Levy

1970 *Present at the Creation: My Years in the State Department,* by Dean Acheson

1971 *Roosevelt: The Soldier of Freedom,* by James MacGregor Burns

1972 *Neither Black Nor White,* by Carl M. Degler

1973 *People of Paradox: An Inquiry Concerning the Origin of American Civilization,* by Michael Kammen

1974 *The Americans,* by Daniel J. Boorstin

1975 *Jefferson and His Time,* by Dumas Malone

1976 *Lamy of Santa Fe,* by Paul Horgan

1977 *The Impending Crisis,* by David M. Potter

1978 *The Invisible Hand: The Managerial Revolution in American Business,* by Alfred D. Chandler

1979 *The Dred Scott Case,* by Don E. Fehrenbacher

PRIZES IN LETTERS

FICTION

1918 *His Family,* by Ernest Poole

1919 *The Magnificent Ambersons,* by Booth Tarkington

1921 *The Age of Innocence,* by Edith Wharton

1922 *Alice Adams,* by B. Tarkington

1923 *One of Ours,* by Willa Cather

1924 *The Able McLaughlins,* by Margaret Wilson

1925 *So Big,* by Edna Ferber

1926 *Arrowsmith,* by S. Lewis

1927 *Early Autumn,* by Louis Bromfield

1928 *The Bridge of San Luis Rey,* by Thornton Wilder

1929 *Scarlet Sister Mary,* by Julia Peterkin

1930 *Laughing Boy,* by Oliver LaFarge

1931 *Years of Grace,* by Margaret Ayer Barnes

1932 *The Good Earth,* by Pearl S. Buck

1933 *The Store,* by T. S. Stribling

1934 *Lamb in His Bosom,* by Caroline Miller

1935 *Now in November,* by Josephine Winslow Johnson

1936 *Honey in the Horn,* by Harold L. Davis

1937 *Gone With the Wind,* by Margaret Mitchell

1938 *The Late George Apley,* by John Phillips Marquand

1939 *The Yearling,* by Marjorie Kinnan Rawlings

1940 *The Grapes of Wrath,* by John Steinbeck

1942 *In This Our Life,* by Ellen Glasgow

1943 *Dragon's Teeth,* by Upton Sinclair

1944 *Journey in the Dark,* by Martin Flavin

1945 *A Bell for Adano,* by John Hersey

1947 *All the King's Men,* by Robert Penn Warren

1948 *Tales of the South Pacific,* by James A. Michener

1949 *Guard of Honor,* by James Gould Cozzens

1950 *The Way West,* by A. B. Guthrie, Jr.

1951 *The Town,* by Conrad Richter

1952 *The Caine Mutiny,* by Herman Wouk

1953 *The Old Man and the Sea,* by Ernest Hemingway

1955 *A Fable,* by Wm. Faulkner

1956 *Andersonville,* by MacKinlay Kantor

1958 *A Death in the Family,* by James Agee

1959 *The Travels of Jaimie McPheeters,* by Robert Lewis Taylor

1960 *Advise and Consent,* by Allen Drury

1961 *To Kill a Mockingbird,* by Harper Lee

1962 *The Edge of Sadness,* by Edwin O'Connor

1963 *The Reivers,* by Wm. Faulkner

1965 *The Keepers of the House,* by Shirley Ann Grau

1966 *Collected Short Stories,* by Katherine Ann Porter

1967 *The Fixer,* by Bernard Malamud

1968 *The Confessions of Nat Turner,* by William Styron

1969 *House Made of Dawn,* by M. Scott Momaday

1970 *Collected Stories,* by Jean Stafford

1972 *Angel of Repose,* by Wallace Stegner

1973 *The Optimist's Daughter,* by Eudora Welty

1975 *The Killer Angels,* by Michael Shaara

1976 *Humboldt's Gift,* by Saul Bellow

1978 *Elbow Room,* by James Allan McPherson

1979 *The Stories of John Cheever*

POETRY

1918 *Love Songs,* by Sara Teasdale

1919 *Old Road to Paradise,* by Margaret Widdemer

1919 *Corn Huskers,* by Carl Sandburg

1922 *Collected Poems,* by Edwin Arlington Robinson

1923 *The Ballad of the Harp-Weaver; A Few Figs from Thistles;* eight sonnets in *American Poetry, 1922, A Miscellany,* by Edna St. Vincent Millay

1924 *New Hampshire: A Poem with Notes and Grace Notes,* by Robert Frost

1925 *The Man Who Died Twice,* by Edwin Arlington Robinson

1926 *What's O'Clock,* by Amy Lowell

1927 *Fiddler's Farewell,* by Leonora Speyer

1928 *Tristram,* by Edwin Arlington Robinson

1929 *John Brown's Body,* by Stephen Vincent Benét

1930 *Selected Poems,* by Conrad Aiken

1931 *Collected Poems,* by Robert Frost

1932 *The Flowering Stone,* by George Dillon

1933 *Conquistador,* by Archibald MacLeish

1934 *Collected Verse,* by Robert Hillyer

1935 *Bright Ambush,* by Audrey Wurdemann

1936 *Strange Holiness,* by Robert P. Tristram Coffin

1937 *A Further Range,* by Robert Frost

1938 *Cold Morning Sky,* by Marya Zaturenska

1939 *Selected Poems,* by John Gould Fletcher

1940 *Collected Poems,* by Mark Van Doren

1941 *Sunderland Capture,* by Leonard Bacon

1942 *The Dust Which Is God,* by William Rose Benét

1943 *A Witness Tree,* by Robert Frost

1944 *Western Star,* by Stephen Vincent Benét

1945 *V-Letter and Other Poems,* by Karl Shapiro

1947 *Lord Weary's Castle,* by Robert Lowell

1948 *The Age of Anxiety,* by W. H. Auden

1949 *Terror and Decorum,* by Peter Viereck

1950 *Annie Allen,* by Gwendolyn Brooks

1951 *Complete Poems,* by Carl Sandburg

1952 *Collected Poems,* by Marianne Moore

1953 *Collected Poems 1917–1952,* by Archibald MacLeish

1954 *The Waking, Poem 1933–1953,* by Theodore Roethke

1955 *Collected Poems,* by Wallace Stevens

1956 *Poems—North & South,* by Elizabeth Bishop

1957 *Things of This World,* by Richard Wilbur

1958 *Promises: Poems 1954–56,* by Robert Penn Warren

1959 *Selected Poems 1928–1958,* by Stanley Kunitz

1960 *Heart's Needle,* by W. D. Snodgrass

1961 *Times Three: Selected Verse from Three Decades*, by Phyllis McGinley
1962 *Poems*, by Alan Dugan
1963 *Pictures from Breughel*, by William Carlos Williams
1964 *At the End of the Open Road*, by Louis Simpson
1965 *77 Dream Songs*, by John Berryman
1966 *Selected Poems*, by Richard Eberhart
1967 *Live or Die*, by Anne Sexton
1968 *The Hard Hours*, by A. Hecht
1969 *Of Being Numerous*, by George Oppen
1970 *Untitled Subjects*, by Richard Howard
1971 *The Carrier of Ladders*, by William S. Merwin
1972 *Collected Poems*, by James Wright
1973 *Up Country*, by Maxine Winokur Kumin
1974 *The Dolphin*, by R. Lowell
1975 *Turtle Island*, by G. Snyder
1976 *Self-Portrait in a Convex Mirror*, by John Ashbery
1977 *Divine Comedies*, by James Merrill
1978 *Collected Poems*, by Howard Nemerov
1979 *Now and Then*, by Robert Penn Warren

GENERAL NONFICTION

1962 *The Making of the President 1960*, by Theodore H. White
1963 *The Guns of August*, by Barbara W. Tuchman
1964 *Anti-intellectualism in American Life*, by R. Hofstadter
1965 *O Strange New World*, by Howard Mumford Jones
1966 *Wandering Through Winter*, by Edwin Way Teale
1967 *The Problem of Slavery in Western Culture*, by David Brion Davis
1968 *The Story of Civilization* (Volume X), by Will and Ariel Durant
1969 *So Human An Animal*, by Rene Jules Dubos
The Armies of the Night, by Norman Mailer
1970 *Gandhi's Truth*, by Erik H. Erikson
1971 *The Rising Sun*, by John Toland
1972 *Stilwell and the American Experience in China, 1911–1945*, by Barbara Tuchman
1973 *Fire in the Lake: The Vietnamese and the Americans in Vietnam*, by Frances Fitz-Gerald, and *Children of Crisis*, by Dr. Robert Coles
1974 *The Denial of Death*, by Ernest Becker

1975 *Pilgrim at Tinker Creek*, by Annie Dillard
1976 *Why Survive? Being Old in America*, by Robert N. Butler
1977 *Beautiful Swimmers: Watermen, Crabs and the Chesapeake Bay*, by William W. Warner
1978 *The Dragons of Eden*, by Carl Sagan
1979 *On Human Nature*, by Edward O. Wilson

CRITICISM/COMMENTARY

1970 Ada Louise Huxtable of *The New York Times* for distinguished architecture criticism
Marquis Childs of the *St. Louis (Mo.) Post-Dispatch* for distinguished commentary from Washington, D.C.
1971 Harold C. Schonberg, *The New York Times'* senior music critic
William A. Caldwell, *The [Hackensack, N.J.] Record*, for "Simeon Stylites," a column on local affairs, written daily for more than 40 years.
1972 Frank Peters, Jr., *St. Louis (Mo.) Post Dispatch*
1973 Ronald Powers, *Chicago Sun-Times* and David S. Broder, *Washington Post*
1974 Emily Genauer, *Newday* Edwin A. Roberts, *National Observer*
1975 Mary McGrory, *The Washington Star* and Roger Ebert, *Chicago Sun Times*
1976 Alan M. Kriegsman, *The Washington [D.C.] Post* Walter W. (Red) Smith, *The New York Times*
1977 William McPherson, *The Washington Post;* George F. Will, Washington Post Writers Group
1978 Walter Kerr, *The New York Times;* William Safire, *The New York Times*
1979 Paul Gapp, *The Chicago Tribune;* Russell Baker, *The New York Times*

SPECIAL CITATIONS

1944 *Oklahoma!,* by Richard Rodgers and Oscar Hammerstein II
1957 Kenneth Roberts, a special citation for his historical novels which long contributed to the creation of greater interest in early American history
1960 Garrett Mattingly for *The Armada*
1961 *American Heritage Picture History of the Civil War*
1973 *George Washington*, by James Thomas Flexner

1976 Scott Joplin, for his contributions to American music
1977 Alex Haley for *Roots*
1978 E. B. White for his contributions to *The New Yorker* and his general enrichment of the American language

PRIZES IN MUSIC

1943 William Schuman: *Secular Cantata No. 2, A Free Song*
1944 Howard Hanson: *Symphony No. 4, Opus 34*
1945 Aaron Copland: *Appalachian Spring*
1946 Leo Sowerby: *The Canticle of the Sun*
1947 Charles Ives: *Symph. No. 3*
1948 Walter Piston: *Symph. No. 3*
1949 Virgil Thomson: *Louisiana Story*
1950 Gian-Carlo Menotti: *The Consul*
1951 Douglas S. Moore: *Giants in the Earth*
1952 Gail Kubik: *Symphony Concertante*
1954 Quincy Porter: *Concerto for Two Pianos and Orchestra*
1955 Gian-Carlo Menotti: *The Saint of Bleecker Street*
1956 Ernst Toch: *Symphony No. 3*
1957 Norman Dello Joio: *Meditations on Ecclesiastes*
1958 Samuel Barber: the score of *Vanessa*
1959 John La Montaine: *Concerto for Piano and Orchestra*
1960 Elliott Carter: *Second String Quartet*
1961 Walter Piston: *Symph. No. 7*
1962 Robert Ward: *The Crucible*
1963 Samuel Barber: *Piano Concerto No. 1*
1966 Leslie Bassett: *Variations for Orchestra*
1967 Leon Kirchner: *Quartet No. 3*
1968 George Crumb: *Echoes of Time and the River*
1969 Karel Husa: *String Quartet No. 3*
1970 Charles W. Wuorinen: *Time's Encomium*
1971 Mario Davidovsky: *Synchronisms No. 6 for Piano and Electronic Sound*
1972 Jacob Druckman: *Windows*
1973 Elliot Carter: *String Quartet No. 3*
1974 Donald Martino: *Notturno*
1975 Dominick Argento: *From the Diary of Virginia Wolff*
1976 Ned Rorem: *Air Music*
1977 Richard Wernick: *Visions of Terror and Wonder*
1978 Michael Colgrass: *Déja Vu for Percussion Quartet and Orchestra*
1979 Joseph Schwantner: *Aftertones of Infinity*

OTHER PRIZES AND AWARDS

ACHIEVEMENT

ALL-AMERICA CITY AWARDS (1978–79) for Community Involvement Through Citizen Action, sponsored by the National Municipal League:

Charlottesville, Virginia; Haverhill, Massachusetts; La-Moure, North Dakota; Mesa, Arizona; Roanoke Valley, Virginia; Rockville, Maryland; Roswell, New Mexico; Southbridge, Massachusetts; Southfield, Michigan; Vincennes, Indiana; Winona, Minnesota.

WOMEN OF THE YEAR AWARDS (1979) for outstanding achievement by women in their fields, presented by *Ladies' Home Journal Magazine*:

Women of the Decade (selected by *Journal* readers from past recipients): Marian Anderson; Joan Ganz Cooney; Betty Ford; Helen Hayes; Katherine Hepburn; Barbara Jordan; Elisabeth Kubler-Ross; Sylvia Porter; Beverly Sills; Barbara Walters; Margaret Mead (Posthumous award).

PUBLIC SERVICE

AMERICAN JEWISH COMMITTEE (1979):

Herbert H. Lehman Award in human relations:
Jack Nash

Institute of Human Relations Mass Media Award:
Bill Moyers

MEDALS OF FREEDOM awarded by the President of the United States, for exceptionally meritorious contributions to national security, world peace, or to cultural or other significant public or private endeavors. The most recent recipients are:

I.W. Abel, President, United Steelworkers of America
John Bardeen, Co-recipient, Nobel Prize in physics in 1956 and 1972
Irving Berlin, composer
Norman Ernest Borlaug, agricultural scientist and 1970 Nobel Prize winner
Gen. Omar N. Bradley, Ret., former Chairman of the Joint Chiefs of Staff
Adm. Arleigh A. Burke, Ret., former Chief of Naval Operations
Alexander Calder (dec.), sculptor
Bruce Catton (dec.), writer and editor
Joe DiMaggio, retired ballplayer, New York Yankees
Ariel and Will Durant, writers and winners of the 1968 Pulitzer Prize
Arthur Fiedler (dec.), conductor, Boston Pops Orchestra
Henry Jacob Friendly, Judge of U.S. Circuit Court of Appeals
Arthur Goldberg, former U.S. Ambassador to the United Nations, former Justice on the U.S. Supreme Court, U.S. representative at European security conference.
Lady Bird Johnson, wife of the late President Lyndon B. Johnson
Rev. Dr. Martin Luther King, Jr., (dec.), Black civil rights activist
Archibald MacLeish, poet and winner of the 1932 and 1959 Pulitzer Prizes
Dr. Margaret Mead (dec.), anthropologist, writer and social theorist
James A. Michener, author and winner of the 1947 Pulitzer Prize
Georgia O'Keeffe, artist
Nelson A. Rockefeller (dec.), Vice President of the United States
Norman Rockwell (dec.), illustrator
Dr. Jonas E. Salk, developer of vaccine against poliomyelitis
Jouett Shouse, donor of the Wolf Trap Farm Park for the Performing Arts
Lowell Thomas, author, radio and television commentator
James Dewey Watson, educator, biochemist, and winner of the Nobel Prize in medicine and physiology in 1962

TEACHER OF THE YEAR (1979) awarded by the Chief State School Officers, the *Encyclopaedia Britannica*, and the *Ladies' Home Journal*: Marilyn Williams (Willy) Black, Hanover, New Hampshire

SCIENCE

NATIONAL ACADEMY OF SCIENCES AWARDS (1979):

Richard Lounsbery Award for Biology and Medicine: Michael S. Brown; Joseph L. Goldstein
Alexander Agassiz Medal: Henry Melson Stommel
Daniel Giraud Elliot Medal: G. Arthur Cooper; Richard Evans Grant
Benjamin Apthorp Gould Prize: Prof. Irwin Ira Shapiro
Jessie Stevenson Kovalenko Medal: Prof. Henry G. Kunkel
James Murray Luck Award for Excellence in Scientific Reviewing: Prof. Alan Robison
Gilbert Morgan Smith Medal in Phycology: William Randolph Taylor
J. Lawrence Smith Medal: Ralph B. Baldwin
James Craig Watson Medal: Charles T. Kowal
U.S. Steel Foundation Award in Molecular Biology: Prof. Mark Ptashne
N.A.S. Award in Chemical Sciences: Linus Pauling
N.A.S. Award for Environmental Quality: Alexander Hollaender
N.A.S. Public Welfare Medal: Cecil H. & Ida M. Green
N.A.S. Award for Distinguished Service: Mary Brown Bullock; Anne Keatley

NATIONAL MEDAL OF SCIENCE, the highest award for outstanding achievement in science and engineering in the United States (1976):

Morris Cohen, Cambridge, Massachusetts
Kurt Otto Friedricks, New York, New York
Peter C. Goldmark, Stamford, Connecticut
Samuel A. Goudsmit, Stony Brook, New York
Roger Guillemin, San Diego, California
H.S. Gutowsky, Chicago, Illinois
Erwin W. Mueller (posthumous award)
Keith Roberts Porter, Boulder, Colorado
Efraim Racker, Ithaca, New York
Frederick D. Rossini, Houston, Texas
Verner E. Suomi, Madison, Wisconsin
Henry Taube, Stanford, California
George E. Uhlenbeck, New York, New York
Hassler Whitney, Princeton, New Jersey
Edward O. Wilson, Cambridge, Massachusetts

WESTINGHOUSE SCIENCE TALENT SEARCH (1979): high school student scholarship competition conducted by Science Service, Inc., sponsored by Westinghouse Educational Foundation and the Westinghouse Corporation:

$12,000: Ron Keeva Unz, North Hollywood, Calif.
$10,000: David Nathan Shykind, Silver Spring, Md.
Eileen Chang, Forest Hills, N.Y.
$7,500: David John LePoire, Holland, Mich.
Geoffrey Campbell Frank, Starkville, Mo.
Gregory Bret Sorkin, New York, N.Y.
$5,000: Michael Urciuoli, Bayside, N.Y.
Julia Elizabeth Little, St. Albans, W. Va.
Ernest Mingway Moy, Dix Hills, N.Y.
Ashfaq Abdulrehman Munshi, New York, N.Y.

JOURNALISM

CLAUDE BERNARD SCIENCE JOURNALISM AWARDS (1978) awarded by the National Society for Medical Research of Washington, D.C.

Newspapers: Bruce DeSilva, *Providence* (R.I.) *Sunday Journal*
Honorable Mention: Cristine Russell, *The Washington Star*
Magazines: Joan Arehart-Treichel, *New York Magazine*
Honorable Mention: Peter Gwynne with Tony Clifton, Mary Hager, Sharon Begley and Barbara Gastel, *Newsweek*; Albert Rosenfeld, *Saturday Review*

NIEMAN FELLOWSHIPS (1979-80) for working Journalists—(Harvard University):

James Boyd; Stanley J. Foreman; William Grant; Michael Kirk; Jonathan Larsen; Paul Lieberman; Lynda McDonnell; Acel Moore; Judith Nicol; Judith Stoia; Jan Stucker; Robert Timberg

SIGMA DELTA CHI AWARDS (1978) for distinguished service in print and broadcast journalism:

Newspapers:

General Reporting: Pamela Zekman, Zay N. Smith, James R. Frost and Eugene Pesek, *Chicago Sun-Times*
Editorial Writing: Philip R. Goldsmith, *The Philadelphia Inquirer*
Washington Correspondence: Joseph Albright, Cox Newspapers
Foreign Correspondence: Charles A. Krause, *The Washington Post*
News Photography: Norman Y. Lono, *Philadelphia* (Pa.) *Daily News*
Editorial Cartooning: James Mark Borgman, *Cincinnati* (Ohio) *Enquirer*
Public Service: *Chicago Sun-Times*

Magazines:

Reporting: Tony Green, *Philadelphia* Magazine
Public Service: *New West*

Radio:

Reporting: WGST Newsradio 92, Atlanta, Ga.
Public Service KXL Radio, Portland, Ore.
Editorializing: KYW Newsradio, Philadelphia, Pa.

Television:

Reporting: Steve Howell and John Britton, KCST-TV, San Diego, California
Public Service: WCCO-TV, Minneapolis, Minnesota
Editorializing: Peter Kohler, WCBS-TV, New York, N.Y.
Research in Journalism: John Hohenberg, University of Tennessee, Knoxville

ARTS

AMERICAN ACADEMY AND INSTITUTE OF ARTS AND LETTERS AWARDS (1979):

Academy-Institute Gold Medal: I. M. Pei (Architecture), Archibald MacLeish (Poetry).

Academy-Institute Award for Distinguished Service to the Arts: Lloyd Goodrich

ACADEMY-INSTITUTE AWARDS:

In Literature: Arlene Croce, Barry Hannah, James McConkey, John N. Morris, Robert M. Pirsig, Richard Poirier, Philip Schultz, Dave Smith

In Art: Fletcher Benton, Randall Deihl, Anne Healy, Wolf Kahn, Arthur Levine

In Music: Paul Chihara, Vivian Fine, Robert Starer, Morton Subotnick

SPECIAL AWARDS:

American Academy in Rome Fellowship in Creative Writing: Joseph Caldwell

Arnold W. Brunner Memorial Prize in Architecture: Charles W. Moore

E. M. Forster Award: Bruce Chatwin

Charles Ives Scholarships: Robert Beaser, Susan Blaustein, Marilyn S. Bliss, Carl Brenner, David B. Goodman, Tobias Picker

Charles Ives Award: The Charles Ives Society

Goddard Lieberson Fellowships: Gerald Levinson and Bruce MacCombie

The Award of Merit for the Novel: William H. Gass

Richard and Hinda Rosenthal Foundation Awards: Diane Johnson and Nicholas Isaak

Harold D. Vursell Memorial Award: Wallace Fowlie

Marjorie Peabody Waite Award: James Still

Morton Dauwen Zabel Award: Richard Gilman

Art

NATIONAL ACADEMY OF DESIGN PRIZES (1979):

Benjamin Altman Prizes: Landscape — Sidney Laufman ($3,000); John Maxwell ($1,500); Figure — Robert Gwathmey ($3,000); Bruce Currie ($1,500)

Emil and Dines Carlsen Award: Jules Kirschenbaum ($1,000)

Andrew Carnegie Prize: Cornelis Ruthenberg ($1,000)

Adolph and Clara Obrig Prize: Karl E. Fortess ($600)

Aldro T. Hibbard Memorial Award: Gregory Gillespie ($200)

Paul Puzinas Memorial Award: Bridget Rutenberg ($200)

Isaac N. Maynard Prize: Zygmunt Menkes ($150)

Salmagundi Club Prize: Joseph De Martini ($100)

Thomas B. Clarke Prize: Selina Trieff ($500)

S. J. Wallace Truman Prize: Mark D. Sherwin ($850)

Julius Hallgarten Prizes: Charles H. Cecil ($400); Annamarie Dunne ($300); Hilary H. Holmes ($200)

Edwin Palmer Memorial Prize: Reuben Tam ($2,000)

Thomas R. Proctor Prize: Joseph Solman ($500)

Certificate of Merit: Aurora Dias Jorgensen

Sculpture Awards:

Artists Fund Prize: Nina Winkel ($400)

Helen Foster Barnett Prize: Greg Wyatt ($500)

Dessie Greer Prize: Elisabeth Gordon Chandler ($100)

N.A.D. Gold Medal: Albert Wein

Elizabeth N. Watrous Gold Medal: Chaim Gross ($350)

Ellin P. Speyer Prize: Cleo Hartwig ($400)

Certificates of Merit: Nathaniel Kaz; Edmond Amateis; Ernest Moreaon; Neil Estern; Bruno Mankowski

Graphic Art Awards:

Anonymous Prize: Charles S. Klabunde ($100)

Cannon Prize: Antonio Frasconi ($400)

Ralph Fabri Prize: Gerson Leiber ($200)

William H. Leavin Prize: Martin Levine ($100)

Certificate of Merit: Ray Wiley

Watercolor Awards:

Frank and Annie Shikler Prize: Sal Grasso ($250)

Walter Biggs Memorial Award: Robert Crowl ($200)

Adolph and Clara Obrig Prizes: Vladimir Shatalow ($450); Don Stone ($300)

William A. Paton Prize: Barbara Weldon ($1,000)

Certificates of Merit: Reeve Schley III; Harold Frank; Oscar Velasquez

Literature

AMERICAN BOOKSELLERS ASSOCIATION AWARD (1979):

Irita Van Doren Award: Louis Epstein, former ABA President and founder of Pickwick Bookstore chain

BANCROFT PRIZES (1979) presented by Columbia University for books of exceptional merit and distinction in American history, American diplomacy, and the international relations of the United States:

Christopher Thorne, *Allies of a Kind: The United States, Britain and the War Against Japan, 1941-1945*

Anthony F. C. Wallace, *Rockdale: The Growth of an American Village in the Early Industrial Revolution*

THE BOLLINGEN PRIZE IN POETRY (1977-78) an award of $5,000 given by Yale University Library: W. S. Merwin

NATIONAL BOOK AWARDS (1979) presented by the American Academy and Institute of Arts and Letters:

Fiction: *Going After Cacciato*, Tim O'Brien

Contemporary Thought: *The Snow Leopard*, Peter Matthiessen

Biography and Autobiography: *Robert Kennedy and His Times*, Arthur M. Schlesinger, Jr.

History: *Intellectual Life in the Colonial South, 1585-1763*, Richard Beale Davis

Poetry: *Mirabell: Books of Numbers*, James Merrill

Children's Literature: *The Great Gilly Hopkins*, Katherine Paterson

Translation: *The Complete Posthumous Poetry*, Cesar Vallejo, by Clayton Eshleman and Jose Rubia Garcia

NEWBERY-CALDECOTT MEDALS (1979) presented by the American Library Association for the most distinguished American books in the children's field:

John Newbery Medal: *The Westing Game*, Ellen Raskin

Randolph Caldecott Medal: *The Girl Who Loved Wild Horses*, Paul Goble

POETRY SOCIETY OF AMERICA PRIZES (1978-79):

Bernice Ames Memorial Award: Alice McIntyre

Gordon Barber Memorial Award: Geraldine C. Little

Melville Crane Award: Andrew Welsh

Gertrude B. Claytor Award: Isabel Nathaniel

Gustav Davidson Memorial Award: Ulrich Troubetzkoy & Richard Frost (shared)

Mary Carolyn Davies Award: Ulrich Troubetzkoy

Alice Fay di Castagnola Award: No award

Emily Dickinson Award: Mildred Nash

Consuelo Ford Memorial Award: Joan LaBombard

Cecil Hemley Award: Geraldine C. Little

Elias Lieberman Student Poetry Award: Catherine Talmadge

John Masefield Memorial Award: Gary Miranda

Alfred Kreymborg Memorial Award: Elizabeth Spires

Poetry Society of America First Prize: Alfred Dorn

Poetry Society of America Second Prize: Grace Morton

Shelley Memorial Award: Hayden Carruth

Celia B. Wagner Memorial Award: Ona Siporin

William Carlos Williams Award: Back Roads Press

Music

GRAMMY AWARDS (1978) given by the National Academy of Recording Arts and Sciences:

Record of the Year: "Just the Way You Are" (Billy Joel)

Album of the Year: "Saturday Night Fever" (The Bee Gees, David Shire, Yvonne Elliman, Tavares, Kool & The Gang, K.C. & The Sunshine Band, MFSB, Trammps, Walter Murphy, Ralph MacDonald)

Song of the Year: "Just the Way You Are" (Billy Joel)

Best New Artist of the Year: A Taste of Honey

Best Pop Vocal Performance, Female: "You Needed Me" (Anne Murray)

Best Pop Vocal Performance, Male: "Copacabana (At The Copa)" (Barry Manilow)

Best Pop Vocal Performance, Group: "Saturday Night Fever" (The Bee Gees)

Best Pop Instrumental Performance: "Children of Sanchez" (Chuck Mangione Group)

Best Jazz Vocal Performance: "All Fly Home" (Al Jarreau)

Best Jazz Performance by a Soloist: "Montreux '77 — Oscar Peterson Jam" (Oscar Peterson)

Best Jazz Performance, Group: "Friends" (Chick Corea)

Best Jazz Performance, Big Band: "Live in Munich" (Thad Jones and Mel Lewis)

Best Rhythm & Blues Vocal Performance, Female: "Last Dance" (Donna Summer)

Best Rhythm & Blues Vocal Performance, Male: "On Broadway" (George Benson)

Best Rhythm & Blues Instrumental Performance: "Runnin' " (Earth, Wind & Fire)

Best Rhythm & Blues Song: "Last Dance" (Paul Jabara, songwriter)

Best Gospel Performance, Contemporary or Inspirational: "What a Friend" (Larry Hart)

Best Country Vocal Performance, Female: "Here You Come Again" (Dolly Parton)

Best Country Vocal Performance, Male: "Georgia On My Mind" (Willie Nelson)

Best Country Vocal Performance, Group: "Mammas, Don't Let Your Babies Grow Up to Be Cowboys" (Waylon Jennings & Willie Ntlson)

Best Country Instrumental Performance: "One O'Clock Jump" (Asleep At The Wheel)

Best Recording for Children: "The Muppet Show" (Jim Henson)

Best Comedy Recording: "A Wild and Crazy Guy" (Steve Martin)

Best Cast Show Album: "Ain't Misbehavin' " (Thomas Z. Shepard, producer)

Album of the Year, Classical: "Brahms: Concerto for Violin in D Major" (Itzhak Perlman with Carlo Maria Giulini, conducting the Chicago Symphony; Christopher Bishop, producer)

Best Opera Recording: Lehar, "The Merry Widow" (Julius Rudel, conductor, New York City Opera Orchestra & Chorus; George Sponhaltz & John Coveney, producers)

Television and Radio

EMMY AWARDS (1978–79): major awards presented by the Academy of Television Arts and Sciences:

Limited Series: "Roots: The Next Generations"

Special (Drama or Comedy): "Friendly Fire"

Drama series: "Lou Grant"

Actor (limited series): Peter Strauss, "The Jericho Mile"

Actress (limited series): Bette Davis, "Strangers: A Story of a Mother and Daughter"

Actor (drama series): Ron Leibman, "Kaz"

Actress (drama series): Mariette Hartley, "The Incredible Hulk"

Actor (comedy series): Carroll O'Connor, "All in the Family"

Actress (comedy series): Ruth Gordon, "Taxi"

Supporting actor (drama series): Stuart Margolin, "The Rockford Files"

Supporting actress (drama series): Kristy McNichol, "Family"

Supporting actor (single drama performance, limited series): Marlon Brando, "Roots: The Next Generations"

Supporting actress (single drama performance, limited series): Esther Rolle, "Summer of My German Soldier"

Directing (comedy series): Noam Pitnik, "Barney Miller"

Writing (comedy series): Alan Alda, "M°A°S°H"

Writing (limited series): Patrick Nolan and Michael Mann, "The Jericho Mile"

1978 GEORGE FOSTER PEABODY

BROADCASTING AWARDS

Radio

CBS News, New York City: "World News Roundup"

The National Radio Theatre of Chicago: "Chicago Radio Theatre" dramas

WMUK, "Kalamazoo, Mich.: "Super Summer Arts Festival" live dramas.

WABE-FM, Atlanta, Georgia: "The Eyewitness Who Wasn't"

NBC Radio, New York City: "Second Sunday" series

National Public Radio, Washington, D.C.: "Dialogues on a Tightrope: an Italian Mosaic"

WOCB, West Yarmouth, Mass.: "The Last Voyage of Cap'n Bill"

Jewish Theological Seminary of America: "The Eternal Light"

Personal Awards

Bob Keeshan

Richard S. Salant

Television

Jim Henson Associates, Inc.: "The Muppets"

Titus Productions, Inc., and NBC-TV: "Holocaust"

The Baptist Radio And TV Commission, Ft. Worth, Tex.: "A River to the Sea"

WDVM-TV, Washington, D.C.: "Your Health and Your Wallet"

WENH-TV, Durham, N.H.: "Arts in New Hampshire"

CBS News, New York City: "The Battle for South Africa"

Tomorrow Entertainment/Medcom Company and the CBS Television Network: "The Body Human: The Vital Connection"

Survival Anglia Ltd./World Wildlife Fund and the NBC Television Network: "Mysterious Castles of Clay"

KGO-TV, San Francisco, Calif.: "Old Age: Do Not Go Gentle"

WDVM-TV, Washington, D.C.: "Race War in Rhodesia"

KQED, San Francisco, Calif.: "Over Easy"

Four D Productions/Trisene Corporation, Hollywood, Cal., and the ABC Television Network: "Barney Miller"

Newsweek Broadcasting, New York City: "Cartoon-A-Torial"

KHET, Honolulu, Hawaii: "Damien"

CBS News, New York City: "30 Minutes"

MTM Productions, Hollywood, Cal., and CBS-TV, New York City: "Lou Grant"

WAVE-TV, Louisville, Ky.: "Whose Child Is This?"

WQED, Pittsburgh, Pa.: "A Connecticut Yankee in King Arthur's Court"

ACADEMY AWARD WINNERS

Year	Best Picture	Best Actor	Supporting Actor	Best Actress	Supporting Actress	Best Director
1978	"The Deer Hunter"	Jon Voight "Coming Home"	Christopher Walken "The Deer Hunter"	Jane Fonda "Coming Home"	Maggie Smith "California Suite"	Michael Cimino "The Deer Hunter"
1977	"Annie Hall"	Richard Dreyfuss "The Goodbye Girl"	Jason Robards "Julia"	Diane Keaton "Annie Hall"	Vanessa Redgrave "Julia"	Woody Allen "Annie Hall"
1976	"Rocky"	Peter Finch "Network"	Jason Robards "All the President's Men"	Faye Dunaway "Network"	Beatrice Straight "Network"	John G. Avildsen "Rocky"
1975	"One Flew Over the Cuckoo's Nest"	Jack Nicholson "One Flew Over the Cuckoo's Nest"	George Burns "The Sunshine Boys"	Louise Fletcher "One Flew Over the Cuckoo's Nest"	Lee Grant "Shampoo"	Milos Forman "One Flew Over the Cuckoo's Nest"
1974	"The Godfather, Part II"	Art Carney "Harry and Tonto"	Robert DeNiro "The Godfather, Part II"	Ellyn Burstyn "Alice Doesn't Live Here Anymore"	Ingrid Bergman "Murder on the Orient Express"	Francis Ford Coppola "The Godfather, Part II"
1973	"The Sting"	Jack Lemmon "Save the Tiger"	John Houseman "The Paper Chase"	Glenda Jackson "A Touch of Class"	Tatum O'Neal "Paper Moon"	George Roy Hill "The Sting"
1972	"The Godfather"	Marlon Brando "The Godfather"	Joel Grey "Cabaret"	Liza Minnelli "Cabaret"	Eileen Heckart "Butterflies Are Free"	Bob Fosse "Cabaret"
1971	"The French Connection"	Gene Hackman "The French Connection"	Ben Johnson "The Last Picture Show"	Jane Fonda "Klute"	Cloris Leachman "The Last Picture Show"	William Friedkin "The French Connection"
1970	"Patton"	George C. Scott "Patton"	John Mills "Ryan's Daughter"	Glenda Jackson "Women in Love"	Helen Hayes "Airport"	Franklin Schaffner "Patton"
1969	"Midnight Cowboy"	John Wayne "True Grit"	Gig Young "They Shoot Horses, Don't They?"	Maggie Smith "The Prime of Miss Jean Brodie"	Goldie Hawn "Cactus Flower"	John Schlesinger "Midnight Cowboy"
1968	"Oliver!"	Cliff Robertson "Charly"	Jack Albertson "The Subject Was Roses"	Katharine Hepburn "The Lion in Winter" Barbra Streisand "Funny Girl"	Ruth Gordon "Rosemary's Baby"	Sir Carol Reed "Oliver!"
1967	"In the Heat of the Night"	Rod Steiger "In the Heat of the Night"	George Kennedy "Cool Hand Luke"	Katharine Hepburn "Guess Who's Coming to Dinner?"	Estelle Parsons "Bonnie and Clyde"	Mike Nichols "The Graduate"
1966	"A Man for All Seasons"	Paul Scofield "A Man for All Seasons"	Walter Matthau "The Fortune Cookie"	Elizabeth Taylor "Who's Afraid of Virginia Woolf?"	Sandy Dennis "Who's Afraid of Virginia Woolf?"	Fred Zinnemann "A Man for All Seasons"
1965	"The Sound of Music"	Lee Marvin "Cat Ballou"	Martin Balsam "A Thousand Clowns"	Julie Christie "Darling"	Shelley Winters "A Patch of Blue"	Robert Wise "The Sound of Music"
1964	"My Fair Lady"	Rex Harrison "My Fair Lady"	Peter Ustinov "Topkapi"	Julie Andrews "Mary Poppins"	Lila Kedrova "Zorba the Greek"	George Cukor "My Fair Lady"
1963	"Tom Jones"	Sidney Poitier "Lilies of the Field"	Melvyn Douglas "Hud"	Patricia Neal "Hud"	Margaret Rutherford "The V.I.P.s"	Tony Richardson "Tom Jones"
1962	"Lawrence of Arabia"	Gregory Peck "To Kill a Mockingbird"	Ed Begley "Sweet Bird of Youth"	Anne Bancroft "The Miracle Worker"	Patty Duke "The Miracle Worker"	David Lean "Lawrence of Arabia"
1961	"West Side Story"	Maximilian Schell "Judgment at Nuremberg"	George Chakiris "West Side Story"	Sophia Loren "Two Women"	Rita Moreno "West Side Story"	Jerome Robbins, Robert Wise "West Side Story"
1960	"The Apartment"	Burt Lancaster "Elmer Gantry"	Peter Ustinov "Spartacus"	Elizabeth Taylor "Butterfield 8"	Shirley Jones "Elmer Gantry"	Billy Wilder "The Apartment"
1959	"Ben-Hur"	Charlton Heston "Ben-Hur"	Hugh Griffith "Ben-Hur"	Simone Signoret "Room at the Top"	Shelley Winters "The Diary of Anne Frank"	William Wyler "Ben-Hur"
1958	"Gigi"	David Niven "Separate Tables"	Burl Ives "The Big Country"	Susan Hayward "I Want to Live"	Wendy Hiller "Separate Tables"	Vincente Minnelli "Gigi"
1957	"The Bridge on the River Kwai"	Alec Guinness "The Bridge on the River Kwai"	Red Buttons "Sayonara"	Joanne Woodward "The Three Faces of Eve"	Miyoshi Umeki "Sayonara"	David Lean "The Bridge on the River Kwai"
1956	"Around the World in 80 Days"	Yul Brynner "The King and I"	Anthony Quinn "Lust for Life"	Ingrid Bergman "Anastasia"	Dorothy Malone "Written on the Wind"	George Stevens "Giant"
1955	"Marty"	Ernest Borgnine "Marty"	Jack Lemmon "Mister Roberts"	Anna Magnani "The Rose Tattoo"	Jo Van Fleet "East of Eden"	Delbert Mann "Marty"
1954	"On the Waterfront"	Marlon Brando "On the Waterfront"	Edmond O'Brien "The Barefoot Contessa"	Grace Kelly "The Country Girl"	Eva Marie Saint "On the Waterfront"	Elia Kazan "On the Waterfront"

Year	Best Picture	Best Actor	Supporting Actor	Best Actress	Supporting Actress	Best Director
1953	"From Here to Eternity"	William Holden "Stalag 17"	Frank Sinatra "From Here to Eternity"	Audrey Hepburn "Roman Holiday"	Donna Reed "From Here to Eternity"	Fred Zinnemann "From Here to Eternity"
1952	"The Greatest Show on Earth"	Gary Cooper "High Noon"	Anthony Quinn "Viva Zapata!"	Shirley Booth "Come Back, Little Sheba"	Gloria Grahame "The Bad and The Beautiful"	John Ford "The Quiet Man"
1951	"An American in Paris"	Humphrey Bogart "The African Queen"	Karl Malden "A Streetcar Named Desire"	Vivian Leigh "A Streetcar Named Desire"	Kim Hunter "A Streetcar Named Desire"	George Stevens "A Place in the Sun"
1950	"All About Eve"	Jose Ferrer "Cyrano de Bergerac"	George Sanders "All About Eve"	Judy Holliday "Born Yesterday"	Josephine Hull "Harvey"	Joseph L. Mankiewicz "All About Eve"
1949	"All the King's Men"	Broderick Crawford "All the King's Men"	Dean Jagger "Twelve O'Clock High"	Olivia de Havilland "The Heiress"	Mercedes McCambridge "All the King's Men"	Joseph L. Mankiewicz "A Letter to Three Wives"
1948	"Hamlet"	Laurence Olivier "Hamlet"	Walter Huston "The Treasure of the Sierre Madre"	Jane Wyman "Johnny Belinda"	Claire Trevor "Key Largo"	John Huston "The Treasure of the Sierra Madre"
1947	"Gentleman's Agreement"	Ronald Colman "A Double Life"	Edmund Gwenn "Miracle on 34th Street"	Loretta Young "The Farmer's Daughter"	Celeste Holm "Gentleman's Agreement"	Elia Kazan "Gentleman's Agreement"
1946	"The Best Years of Our Lives"	Fredric March "The Best Years of Our Lives"	Harold Russell "The Best Years of Our Lives"	Olivia de Havilland "To Each His Own"	Anne Baxter "The Razor's Edge"	William Wyler "The Best Years of Our Lives"
1945	"The Lost Weekend"	Ray Milland "The Lost Weekend"	James Dunn "A Tree Grows in Brooklyn"	Joan Crawford "Mildred Pierce"	Anne Revere "National Velvet"	Billy Wilder "The Lost Weekend"
1944	"Going My Way"	Bing Crosby "Going My Way"	Barry Fitzgerald "Going My Way"	Ingrid Bergman "Gaslight"	Ethel Barrymore "None But the Lonely Heart"	Leo McCarey "Going My Way"
1943	"Casablanca"	Paul Lukas "Watch on the Rhine"	Charles Coburn "The More the Merrier"	Jennifer Jones "The Song of Bernadette"	Katina Paxinou "For Whom the Bell Tolls"	Michael Curtiz "Casablanca"
1942	"Mrs. Miniver"	James Cagney "Yankee Doodle Dandy"	Van Heflin "Johnny Eager"	Greer Garson "Mrs. Miniver"	Teresa Wright "Mrs. Miniver"	William Wyler "Mrs. Miniver"
1941	"How Green Was My Valley"	Gary Cooper "Sergeant York"	Donald Crisp "How Green Was My Valley"	Joan Fontaine "Suspicion"	Mary Astor "The Great Lie"	John Ford "How Green Was My Valley"
1940	"Rebecca"	James Stewart "The Philadelphia Story"	Walter Brennan "The Westerner"	Ginger Rogers "Kitty Foyle"	Jane Darwell "The Grapes of Wrath"	John Ford "The Grapes of Wrath"
1939	"Gone with the Wind"	Robert Donat "Goodbye, Mr. Chips"	Thomas Mitchell "Stagecoach"	Vivien Leigh "Gone with the Wind"	Hattie McDaniel "Gone with the Wind"	Victor Fleming "Gone with the Wind"
1938	"You Can't Take It with You"	Spencer Tracy "Boys Town"	Walter Brennan "Kentucky"	Bette Davis "Jezebel"	Fay Bainter "Jezebel"	Frank Capra "You Can't Take It with You"
1937	"The Life of Emile Zola"	Spencer Tracy "Captains Courageous"	Joseph Schildkraut "The Life of Emile Zola"	Luise Rainer "The Good Earth"	Alice Brady "In Old Chicago"	Leo McCarey "The Awful Truth"
1936	"The Great Ziegfeld"	Paul Muni "The Story of Louis Pasteur"	Walter Brennan "Come and Get It"	Luise Rainer "The Great Ziegfeld"	Gale Sondergaard "Anthony Adverse"	Frank Capra "Mr. Deeds Goes to Town"
1935	"Mutiny on the Bounty"	Victor McLaglen "The Informer"	—	Bette Davis "Dangerous"	—	John Ford "The Informer"
1934	"It Happened One Night"	Clark Gable "It Happened One Night"	—	Claudette Colbert "It Happened One Night"	—	Frank Capra "It Happened One Night"
1932–33	"Cavalcade"	Charles Laughton "The Private Life of Henry VIII"	—	Katharine Hepburn "Morning Glory"	—	Frank Lloyd "Cavalcade"
1931–32	"Grand Hotel"	Wallace Beery "The Champ" Fredric March "Dr. Jekyll and Mr. Hyde"	—	Helen Hayes "The Sin of Madelon Claudet"	—	Frank Borzage "Bad Girl"
1930–31	"Cimarron"	Lionel Barrymore "A Free Soul"	—	Marie Dressler "Min and Bill"	—	Norman Taurog "Skippy"
1929–30	"All Quiet on the Western Front"	George Arliss "Disraeli"	—	Norma Shearer "The Divorcee"	—	Lewis Milestone "All Quiet on the Western Front"
1928–29	"Broadway Melody"	Warner Baxter "In Old Arizona"	—	Mary Pickford "Coquette"	—	Frank Lloyd "The Divine Lady"
1927–28	"Wings"	Emil Jannings "The Last Command" "The Way of All Flesh"	—	Janet Gaynor "Seventh Heaven" "Street Angel" "Sunrise"	—	Frank Borzage "Seventh Heaven" Lewis Milestone "Two Arabian Knights"

Theater

ANTOINETTE PERRY (TONY) AWARDS (1978–79) presented by the League of New York Theaters under authorization from the American Theater Wing:

Best Play: "The Elephant Man"

Best Musical: "Sweeney Todd"

Best Score: Stephen Sondheim, "Sweeney Todd"

Best Actor, Play: Tom Conti, "Whose Life Is It Anyway?"

Best Actress, Play: Constance Cummings, "Wings"; Carole Shelley, "The Elephant Man" (tie)

Best Actor, Musical: Len Cariou, "Sweeney Todd"

Best Actress, Musical: Angela Lansbury, "Sweeney Todd"

Best Featured Actor, Play: Michael Gough, "Bedroom Farce"

Best Featured Actress, Play: Joan Hickson, "Bedroom Farce"

Best Featured Actor, Musical: Henderson Forsythe, "The Best Little Whorehouse in Texas"

Best Featured Actress, Musical: Carlin Glynn, "The Best Little Whorehouse in Texas"

Best Director, Play: Jack Hofsiss, "The Elephant Man"

Best Director, Musical: Harold Prince, "Sweeney Todd"

Best Scenic Designer: Eugene Lee, "Sweeney Todd"

Best Costume Designer: Franne Lee, "Sweeney Todd"

Best Lighting Designer: Roger Morton, "The Crucifer of Blood"

Best Choreographer: Michael Bennett and Bob Avian, "Ballroom"

Special Tony Awards: Henry Fonda; The Eugene O'Neill Theater Center, Waterford, Conn.; The American Conservatory Theater, San Francisco, Calif.; Walter F. Diehl, president, International Association of Theatrical Stage Employees and Motion Picture Operators

Lawrence Langer Award: Richard Rodgers

OBIE (OFF BROADWAY) AWARDS (1978–79):

Best Play: "Josephine," Michael McClure

Sustained Achievement: Al Carmines

Distinguished Performances: Mary Alice, "Nongogo" and "Julius Caesar"; Philip Anglim, "The Elephant Man"; Joseph Buloff, "The Price"; Constance Cummings, "Wings"; Fred Gwynne, "Grand Magic"; Judd Hirsch, "Talley's Folly"; Marcel Rosenblatt, "Vienna Notes"; Meryl Streep, "Taken in Marriage"; Elizabeth Wilson, "Taken in Marriage"

Distinguished Direction: Maria Irene Fornes, "Eyes on the Harem"; Jack Hofsiss, "The Elephant Man"

Sets and Lighting (Design): Theatre X, "A Fierce Longing"; Jennifer Tipton, *Public Theatre*

Playwriting: Rosalyn Drexler, "The Writer's Opera"; Susan Miller, "Nasty Rumours and Final Remarks"; Richard Nelson, "Vienna Notes"; Bernard Pomerance, "The Elephant Man"; Sam Shepard, "Buried Child"

Special Citations: Gordon Chater, Richard Wherett, and Steve J. Spears, "The Elocution of Benjamin"; JoAnne Akalaitis, Ellen McElduff, and David Warrilop, "Southern Exposure"; Tadeusz Kantor, "The Dead Class"; The Negro Ensemble Company for sustained excellence of ensemble acting; The French Department of NYU for its Samuel Beckett Festival

Films

CANNES INTERNATIONAL FILM FESTIVAL (1979):

Best Film: "Apocalypse Now," Francis Ford Coppola, and "The Tin Drum," Volker Schlöndorf (tie)

Best Actress: Sally Field, "Norma Rae"

Best Actor: Jack Lemmon, "The China Syndrome"

NEW YORK FILM CRITICS AWARDS (1978):

Best Film: "The Deer Hunter"

Best Director: Terence Malick, "Days of Heaven"

Best Actor: Jon Voight, "Coming Home"

Best Actress: Ingrid Bergman, "Autumn Sonata"

Best Supporting Actor: Christopher Walken, "The Deer Hunter"

Best Supporting Actress: Maureen Stapleton, "Interiors"

Best Screenplay: "An Unmarried Woman," by Paul Mazursky

Best Foreign-language Film: "Bread and Chocolate"

MISS AMERICA

Year	Winner
1921	Margaret Gorman, Washington, D.C.
1922–23	Mary Campbell, Columbus, Ohio
1924	Ruth Malcolmson, Philadelphia, Pennsylvania
1925	Fay Lamphier, Oakland, California
1926	Norma Smallwood, Tulsa, Oklahoma
1927	Lois Delaner, Joliet, Illinois
1933	Marion Bergeron, West Haven, Connecticut
1935	Henrietta Leaver, Pittsburgh, Pennsylvania
1936	Rose Coyle, Philadelphia, Pennsylvania
1937	Bette Cooper, Bertrand Island, New Jersey
1938	Marilyn Meseke, Marion, Ohio
1939	Patricia Donnelly, Detroit, Michigan
1940	Frances Marie Burke, Philadelphia, Pennsylvania
1941	Rosemary LaPlanche, Los Angeles, California
1942	Jo-Caroll Dennison, Tyler, Texas
1943	Jean Bartel, Los Angeles, California
1944	Venus Ramey, Washington, D.C.
1945	Bess Myerson, New York City, N.Y.
1946	Marilyn Buferd, Los Angeles, California
1947	Barbara Walker, Memphis, Tennessee
1948	BeBe Shopp, Hopkins, Minnesota
1949	Jacque Mercer, Litchfield, Arizona
1951	Yolande Betbeze, Mobile, Alabama
1952	Coleen Kay Hutchins, Salt Lake City, Utah
1953	Neva Jane Langley, Macon, Georgia
1954	Evelyn Margaret Ay, Ephrata, Pennsylvania
1955	Lee Meriwether, San Francisco, California
1956	Sharon Ritchie, Denver, Colorado
1957	Marian McKnight, Manning, South Carolina
1958	Marilyn Van Derbur, Denver, Colorado
1959	Mary Ann Mobley, Brandon, Mississippi
1960	Lynda Lee Mead, Natchez, Mississippi
1961	Nancy Fleming, Montague, Michigan
1962	Maria Fletcher, Asheville, North Carolina
1963	Jacquelyn Mayer, Sandusky, Ohio
1964	Donna Axum, El Dorado, Arkansas
1965	Vonda Kay Van Dyke, Phoenix, Arizona
1966	Deborah Irene Bryant, Overland Park, Kansas
1967	Jane Anne Jayroe, Laverne, Oklahoma
1968	Debra Dene Barnes, Moran, Kansas
1969	Judith Anne Ford, Belvidere, Illinois
1970	Pamela Anne Eldred, Birmingham, Michigan
1971	Phyllis Ann George, Denton, Texas
1972	Laurie Lea Schaefer, Columbus, Ohio
1973	Terry Anne Meeuwsen, DePere, Wisconsin
1974	Rebecca Ann King, Denver, Colorado
1975	Shirley Cothran, Fort Worth, Texas
1976	Tawney Elaine Godin, Yonkers, N.Y.
1977	Dorothy Kathleen Benham, Edina, Minnesota
1978	Susan Perkins, Columbus, Ohio
1979	Kylene Baker, Galax, Virginia
1980	Cheryl Prewitt, Ackerman, Mississippi

THE DIRECTORY

SOCIETIES AND ASSOCIATIONS

Information abstracted from listings in the 1979 edition of the **Encyclopedia of Associations**, which includes details on more than 13,000 organizations. Used by permission of the publisher, Gale Research Company, Book Tower, Detroit, Michigan 48226

Academy of Applied Science, 65 India Wharf, Boston, MA 02110; **Membership:** 300

Academy of Motion Picture Arts and Science, 8949 Wilshire Blvd., Beverly Hills, CA 90211; **Membership:** 4,035

Academy of Political Science, 2852 Broadway, New York, NY 10025; **Membership:** 11,000

Actors Equity Association, 1500 Broadway, New York, NY 10036; **Membership:** 22,000

Adult Education Association of the United States, 810 18th St. NW, Washington DC 20006; **Membership:** 3,000

Advertising Club of New York, Three W. 51st St., New York, NY 10019; **Membership:** 300

Aerospace Industries Association of America, 1725 De Sales St. NW, Washington DC 20036; **Membership:** 60 companies

African-American Institute, 833 United Nations Plaza, New York, NY 10017

AFS (American Field Service) International Exchange, 313 East 43rd St., New York, NY 10017; **Membership:** 100,000

Air Force Association, 1750 Pennsylvania Ave. NW, Washington DC 20006; **Membership:** 155,000

Air Pollution Control Association: P.O. Box 2861, Pittsburgh, PA 15230; **Membership:** 6,600

Alcoholics Anonymous, 468 Park Ave. S., New York, NY 10016; **Membership:** 1,000,000

Amateur Athletic Union of the United States, 3400 West 86th St., Indianapolis, IN 46268; **Membership:** 331,000

American Academy of Arts and Letters, 633 West 155th St., New York, NY 10032; **Membership:** 250

American Academy of Arts and Sciences, 165 Allandale St., Boston, MA 02130; **Membership:** 2,300

American Academy of Political and Social Sciences, 3937 Chestnut St., Philadelphia, PA 19104; **Membership:** 14,000

American Alliance for Health, Physical Education, and Recreation, 1201 16th St. NW, Washington DC 20036; **Membership:** 50,000

American Anthropological Association, 1703 New Hampshire Ave. NW, Washington DC 20009; **Membership:** 10,000

American Antiquarian Society, 185 Salisbury St., Worcester, MA 01609; **Membership:** 320

American Anti-Vivisection Society, 1903 Chestnut St., Philadelphia, PA 19103

American Arbitration Association, 140 West 51st St., New York, NY 10020

American Association for the Advancement of Science, 1515 Massachusetts Ave. NW, Washington DC 20005; **Membership:** 128,000

American Association of Advertising Agencies, 200 Park Ave., New York, NY 10017; **Membership:** 440

American Association of Blood Banks, 1828 L St. NW, Washington DC 20036; **Membership:** 7,200

American Association of Community and Junior Colleges, National Center for Higher Education, 1 Dupont Circle NW, Washington DC 20036; **Membership** 1,507

American Association of Retired Persons, 1909 K St. NW, Washington DC 20049; **Membership:** 11,000,000

American Association of University Professors, 1 Dupont Circle NW, Washington DC 20036; **Membership:** 72,200

American Assiocation of University Women, 2401 Virginia Ave. NW, Washington DC 20037; **Membership:** 190,885

American Astronomical Society, 211 FitzRandolph Rd., Princeton, NJ 08540; **Membership:** 3,500

American Automobile Association, 8111 Gatehouse Rd., Falls Church, Va. 22042; **Membership:** 19,500,000

American Bankers Association, 1120 Connecticut Ave. NW, Washington DC 20036; **Membership:** 13,600 banks and trust companies

American Bar Association, 1155 East 60th St., Chicago, IL 60637; **Membership:** 220,000

American Bible Society, 1865 Broadway, New York, NY 10023; **Membership:** 290,000

American Camping Association, Bradford Woods, Martinsville, IN 46151; **Membership:** 6,000

American Cancer Society, 777 Third Ave., New York, NY 10017; **Membership:** 2,500,000 with 56 divisions and 3,000 county units

American Chemical Society, 1155 16th St. NW, Washington DC 20036; **Membership:** 115,000

American Civil Liberties Union, 22 E. 40th St., New York, NY 10016; **Membership:** 275,000

American Classical League, Miami University, Oxford, OH 45056; **Membership:** 3,000

American College of Hospital Administrators, 840 N. Lake Shore Dr., Chicago, IL 60611

American College of Physicians, 4200 Pine St., Philadelphia, PA 19104; **Membership:** 36,900

American College of Surgeons, 55 E. Erie St., Chicago, IL 60611; **Membership:** 39,000

American Conservation Association Inc., 30 Rockefeller Plaza, New York, NY 10020

American Contract Bridge League, 2200 Democrat Rd., Memphis, TN 38132; **Membership:** 200,000 in 5,000 clubs

American Council on Education, 1 Dupont Circle, Washington DC 20036; **Membership:** 1,294 and 234 affiliates

American Council for Judaism, 309 Fifth Ave., New York, NY 10016; **Membership:** 20,000

American Council of Learned Societies, 345 E. 46th St., New York, NY 10017; **Membership:** 42 organizations

American Council of Life Insurance, 1850 K St. NW, Washington DC 20006; **Membership:** 425 companies

American Council on Schools and Colleges, P.O. Box 1252, York, PA 17405; **Membership:** 201 institutions

American Council on the Teaching of Foreign Languages, Two Park Ave., New York, NY 10016; **Membership:** 2,000

American Dental Association, 211 E. Chicago Ave., Chicago, IL 60611; **Membership:** 131,000 in 484 societies

American Diabetes Association, 600 Fifth Ave., New York, NY 10020; **Membership:** 125,000 in 68 state organizations

American Diatetic Association, 430 N. Michigan Ave., Chicago, IL 60611; **Membership:** 36,203 in 52 state groups

American Economic Foundation, 51 E. 42nd St., New York, NY 10017; **Membership:** 18,000

American Farm Bureau Federation, 225 Touhy Ave., Park Ridge, IL 60068; **Membership:** 2,895,357

American Federation of Arts, 41 E. 65th St., New York, NY 10021; **Membership:** 3,000

American Federation of Labor and Congress of Industrial Organizations, 815 16th St. NW, Washington DC 20006; **Membership:** 13,600,000 in 106 organizations

American Federation of Teachers, 11 Dupont Circle NW, Washington DC 20036; **Membership:** 475,000

American Federation of Television and Radio Artists, 1350 Ave. of the Americas, New York, NY 10019; **Membership:** 29,500 in 33 locals

American Forestry Association, 1319 18th St. NW, Washington DC 20036; **Membership:** 79,000

American Friends of the Middle East, 1717 Massachusetts Ave. NW, Washington DC 20036

American Friends Service Committee, 1501 Cherry St., Philadelphia, PA 19102; **Membership:** 10 regional Offices

American Geographical Society, Broadway at 156th St., New York, NY 10032; Membership 2,400

American Geological Institute, 5205 Leesburg Pike, Falls Church, VA 22041; **Membership:** 18 societies

American Geophysical Union, 1909 K St. NW, Washington DC 20006; **Membership:** 12,000

American Geriatrics Society, 10 Columbus Circle, New York, NY 10019; **Membership:** 8,000

American Group Psychotherapy Association, 1995 Broadway, 14th Floor, New York, NY 10023; **Membership:** 3,000 in 22 societies

American Heart Association, 7320 Greenville Ave., Dallas, TX 75231; **Membership:** 112,000 in 55 affiliates and 127 chapters

American Historical Association, 400 A St. SE, Washington DC 20003; **Membership:** 14,500

American Home Economics Association, 2010 Massachusetts Ave. NW, Washington DC 20036; **Membership:** 52,000 in 52 associations

American Horse Shows Association, 598 Madison Ave., New York, NY 10022; **Membership:** 19,675

American Horticulture Society, Mt. Vernon, VA 22121; **Membership:** 33,000

American Hospital Association, 840 N. Lake Shore Dr., Chicago, IL 60611; **Membership:** 31,500

American Humane Association, 5351 Roslyn, Englewood, CO 80111; **Membership:** 2 million in 1,500 societies

American Institute of Aeronautics and Astronautics, 1290 Ave. of the Americas, New York, NY 10019; **Membership:** 25,000 in 68 sections and 110 student branches

American Institute of Architects, 1735 New York Ave. NW, Washington DC 20006; **Membership:** 26,000

American Institute of Biological Sciences, 1401 Wilson Blvd., Arlington, VA 22209; **Membership:** 10,000

American Institute of Certified Public Accountants, 1211 Ave. of the Americas, New York, NY 10036; **Membership:** 136,000

American Institute of Chemists, 7315 Wisconsin Ave. NW, Washington DC 20014; **Membership:** 5,000 in 30 state groups

American Institute of Interior Designers, (See American Society of Interior Designers)

American Institute of Nutrition, 9650 Rockville Pike, Bethesda, MD 20014; **Membership:** 1,600

American Institute of Physics, 335 E. 45th St., New York, NY 10017; **Membership:** nine national societies

American Jewish Committee, % Institute of Human Relations, 165 E. 56th St., New York, NY 10022; **Membership:** 42,000 in 80 chapters

American Jewish Congress, 15 E. 84th St., New York, NY 10028; **Membership:** 300 groups

American Kennel Club, 51 Madison Ave., New York, NY 10010; **Membership:** 406 associations

American Law Institute, 4025 Chestnut St., Philadelphia, PA 19104; **Membership:** 2,300

American Legion, 700 N. Pennsylvania St., Indianapolis, IN 46206; **Membership:** 2.7 million in 58 state departments

American Legion Auxiliary, 777 N. Meridian St., Indianapolis, IN 46204; **Membership:** 1 million

American Library Association, 50 E. Huron St., Chicago, IL 60611; **Membership:** 33,000

American Lung Association, 1740 Broadway, New York, NY 10019; **Membership:** 7,500

American Management Associations, 135 W. 50th St., New York, NY 10020; **Membership:** 67,000

American Mathematical Society, P.O. Box 6248, Providence, RI 02940; **Membership:** 16,403

American Medical Assocation, 535 N. Dearborn St., Chicago, IL 60610; **Membership:** 206,905

American Ministerial Association, P.O. Box 1252, York, PA 17405; **Membership:** 58,700

American National Red Cross, 17th and D Sts. NW, Washington DC 20006; **Membership:** 33,065,741 in 3,128 chapters

American National Theatre and Academy, 245 W. 52nd St., New York, NY 10019

American Newspaper Publishers Association, 11600 Sunrise Valley Dr., Reston, VA 22091; **Membership:** 1,286 daily newspapers

American Numismatic Association, P.O. Box 2366, Colorado Springs, CO 80901; **Membership:** 34,000 individuals and 1,000 clubs

American Numismatic Society, 1814 Broadway betw. 155th and 156th St., New York, NY 10032; **Membership:** 1,842

American Nurses' Association, 2420 Pershing Rd., Kansas City, MO 64108; **Membership:** 200,000 in 53 state groups

American Optometric Association, 7000 Chippewa St., St. Louis, MO 63119; **Membership:** 20,216

American Ornithologists' Union, National Museum of Natural History, Smithsonian Institution, Washington DC 20560; **Membership:** 4,000

American Osteopathic Association, 212 E. Ohio St., Chicago, IL 60611; **Membership:** 13,002 in 54 state groups

American Personnel and Guidance Association, 1607 New Hampshire Ave. NW, Washington DC 20009; **Membership:** 41,000

American Pharmaceutical Association, 2215 Constitution Ave. NW, Washington DC 20037; **Membership:** 52,000

American Philatelic Society, P.O. Box 800, State College, PA 16801; **Membership:** 44,000

American Philological Association, Dept. of Classics, University of Colorado, Boulder, CO 80309; **Membership:** 2,800

American Philosophical Society, University of Delaware, Newark, DE 19711; **Membership:** 6,000

American Physical Society, 335 E. 45th St., New York, NY 10017; **Membership:** 30,000

American Podiatry Association, 20 Chevy Chase Circle NW, Washington DC 20015; **Membership:** 6,800 in 52 state groups

American Political Science Association, 1527 New Hampshire Ave. NW, Washington DC 20036; **Membership:** 15,000

American Power Boat Association, 22811 Greater Mack, St. Clair Shores, MI 48080; **Membership:** 6,000 in 300 clubs

American Psychiatric Association, 1700 18th St. NW, Washington DC 20009; **Membership:** 25,000

American Psychoanalytic Association, 1 E. 57th St., New York, NY 10022; **Membership:** 2,530

American Psychological Association, 1200 17th St. NW, Washington DC 20036; **Membership:** 40,000

American Public Health Assocation, 1015 18th St. NW, Washington DC 20036; **Membership:** 45,000

American Radio Relay League, 225 Main St., Newington, CT 06111; **Membership:** 167,000 in 2,000 clubs

American Social Health Association, 260 Sheridan Ave., Suite 307, Palo Alto, CA 94306; **Membership:** 2,000

American Society for the Prevention of Cruelty to Animals, 441 E. 92nd St., New York, NY 10028; **Membership:** 3,627

American Society of Civil Engineers, 345 E. 47th St., New York, NY 10017; **Membership:** 77,000

American Society of Composers, Authors, and Publishers, 1 Lincoln Plaza, New York, NY 10023; **Membership:** 23,000

American Society of Interior Designers, 730 Fifth Ave., New York, NY 10019; **Membership:** 10,000 in 45 chapters

American Society of Mechanical Engineers, 345 E. 47th St., New York, NY 10017; **Membership:** 76,000 in 177 sections

American Society of Newspaper Editors, Box 551, 1350 Sullivan Trail, Easton, PA 18042; **Membership:** 800

American Society of Travel Agents, 711 Fifth Ave., New York, NY 10022; **Membership:** 16,000 worldwide

American Sociological Association, 1772 N St. NW, Washington DC 20036; **Membership:** 14,000

American Speech and Hearing Association, 10801 Rockville Pike, Rockville, MD 20852; **Membership:** 30,000

American Statistical Association, 806 15th St. NW, Washington DC 20005; **Membership:** 13,000

American Thoracic Society, 1740 Broadway, New York, NY 10019; **Membership:** 7,500

American Trucking Associations, 1616 P St. NW, Washington DC 20036; **Membership:** 51 organizations

American Veterans Committee, 1333 Connecticut Ave. NW, Washington DC 20036; **Membership:** 25,000

American Veterinary Medical Association, 930 N. Meacham Rd., Schaumburg, IL 60196; **Membership:** 28,000

American Woman's Association, Time-Life Building, Suite 3909, 1271 Ave. of the Americas, New York, NY 10020

American Youth Hostels, Inc., National Campus, Delaplane, VA 22025; **Membership:** 70,000 in 30 local councils

Americans for Democratic Action, 1411 K St. NW, Washington DC 20005; **Membership:** 65,000 in 20 state groups

AMVETS, 1710 Rhode Island Ave. NW, Washington DC 20036; **Membership:** 150,000

Ancient Order of Hibernians in America, Box 700, Riverdale Station, Bronx, NY 10471; **Membership:** 191,000

Anti-Defamation League of B'nai B'rith, 315 Lexington Ave., New York, NY 10016; **Membership:** 26 regional offices

Appalachian Mountain Club, 5 Joy St., Boston, MA 02108; **Membership:** 23,000

Archaeological Institute of America, 53 Park Place, Eighth Fl., New York, NY 10007; **Membership:** 6,500

Army and Navy Union, U.S.A., 1391 Main St., P.O. Box 537, Lakemore, OH 44250; **Membership:** 5,000

Arthritis Foundation, 3400 Peachtree Rd. NE, Atlanta, GA 30326; **Membership:** 73 chapters

Associated Councils of the Arts, 507 Seventh Ave., New York, NY 10018

Association for the Study of Afro-American Life and History, 1401 14th St. NW, Washington DC 20005; **Membership:** 30,000

Association of American Colleges, 1818 R St. NW, Washington DC 20009; **Membership:** 700 institutions

Association on American Indian Affairs, Inc., 432 Park Ave. S., New York, NY 10016

Association of American Railroads, American Railroads Bldg., 1920 L St. NW, Washington DC 20036; **Membership:** 240

Association of American Universities, 1 Dupont Circle NW, Suite 730, Washington DC 20036; **Membership:** 50 university presidents

Association of Chairmen of Departments of Mechanics, % R.T. Shields, Dept. of Theoretical and Applied Mechanics, 216 Talbot Laboratory, Urbana, IL 61801; **Membership:** 98

Association of Governing Boards of Universities and Colleges, 1 Dupont Circle NW, Suite 720, Washington DC 20036; Membership: 19,000

Association of Junior Leagues, 825 Third Ave., New York, NY 10022; Membership: 122,000 in 235 leagues

Audit Bureau of Circulations, 123 N. Wacker Dr., Chicago, IL 60606; Membership: 4,500

Authors League of America, 234 W. 44th St., New York, NY 10036; Membership: 7,200

Benevolent and Protective Order of Elks, 2750 Lake View Ave., Chicago, IL 60614; Membership: 1,640,000 in 2,230 lodges

Bide-A-Wee Home Association, 410 E. 38th St., New York, NY 10016

Big Brothers of America, 220 Suburban Station Bldg., Philadelphia, PA 19103; Membership: 370 local agencies

Blue Cross Association, 840 N. Lake Shore Dr., Chicago, IL 60611; Membership: 76 Blue Cross plans

B'nai B'rith International, 1640 Rhode Island Ave. NW, Washington DC 20036; Membership: 500,000 in 3,500 groups

Boys' Clubs of America, 771 First Ave., New York, NY 10017

Boy Scouts of America, North Brunswick, NJ 08902; Membership: 4,718,138 scouts and adult leaders

Brand Names Foundation, 477 Madison Ave., New York, NY 10022; Membership: 500

Brookings Institution, 1775 Massachusetts Ave. NW, Washington DC 20036

Camp Fire Girls, 4601 Madison Ave., Kansas City, MO 64112; Membership: 750,000

CARE (Cooperative for American Relief Everywhere), 660 First Ave., New York, NY 10016; Membership: 25 agencies

Catholic Daughters of America, 10 W. 71st St., New York, NY 10023; Membership: 180,000 in 45 state groups

Catholic War Veterans of U.S.A., 2 Massachusetts Ave. NW, Washington DC 20001; Membership: 50,000

CCCO, An Agency for Military and Draft Counseling, 2016 Walnut St., Rm. 300, Philadelphia, PA 19103

Chamber of Commerce of the United States, 1615 H St. NW, Washington DC 20062; Membership: 3,600 chambers of commerce and trade associations, 69,000 business firms and individuals

Chautauqua Literary and Scientific Circle, Chautauqua, NY 14722; Membership: 1,100

Children's Aid Society, 105 E. 22nd St., New York, NY 10010

Child Study Association of America, 853 Broadway, New York, NY 10003; Membership: 400

College English Association, Kean College of New Jersey, Union, NJ 07083; Membership: 2,500 in 25 groups

College Entrance Examination Board, 888 Seventh Ave., New York, NY 10019; Membership: 2,403 colleges, universities, secondary schools, school systems and educational associations

Colonial Dames XVII Century, National Society, 1300 New Hampshire Ave. NW, Washington DC 20036; Membership: 8,500

Committee for Economic Development, 477 Madison Ave., New York, NY 10022; Membership: 200 trustees

Common Cause, 2030 M St. NW, Washington DC 20036; Membership: 225,000

The Conference Board, 845 Third Ave., New York, NY 10022; Membership: 4,000 organizations

Conference on Jewish Material Claims against Germany, 15 E. 26th St., New York, NY 10010; Member Organizations: 23

CORE (Congress of Racial Equality), 200 W. 135th St., New York, NY 10030

Cooperative League of the U.S.A., 1828 L St. NW, Washington DC 20036; Membership: 161 organizations

Correspondance Chess League of America, P.O. Box l24, Algonquin, IL 60102; Membership: over 1,200. Affiliated with the International Correspondance Chess League

Council for the Advancement and Support of Education, 1 Dupont Circle NW, Washington DC 20036; Membership: 9,000

Council of Better Business Bureaus, 1150 17th St. NW, Washington DC 20036; Membership: 1,000 in 150 member bureaus

Council on Foreign Relations, 58 E. 68th St., New York, NY 10021; Membership: 1,796 in 37 local groups

Council of Graduate Schools in the United States, 1 Dupont Circle NW, Washington DC 20036; Membership: 361

Council on International Educational Exchange, 777 United Nations Plaza, New York, NY 10017; Membership: 172 North American institutions

Country Music Association, 7 Music Circle N., Nashville, TN 37203; Membership: 5,000

Credit Union National Association, Inc., P.O. Box 431, Madison, WI 53701; Membership: 22,606 credit unions

Daughters of the American Revolution, National Society, 1776 D St. NW, Washington DC 20006; Membership: 207,202

Democratic National Committee, 1625 Massachusetts Ave. NW, Washington DC 20036; Membership: 360

Disabled American Veterans, 3725 Alexandria Pike, Cold Spring, KY 41076; Membership: 545,000

Dramatists Guild, 234 W. 44th St., New York, NY 10036

Ducks Unlimited, Inc., P.O. Box 66300, Chicago, IL 60666; Membership: 250,000

Ecological Society of America, Library 3131, The Evergreen State College, Olympia, WA 98505; Membership: 5,700

English-Speaking Union of the United States, 16 E. 69th St., New York, NY 10021; Membership: 33,000 in 81 branches

Entomological Society of America, 4603 Calvert Rd., College Park, MD 20740; Membership: 7,300

Epilepsy Foundation of America, 1828 L St. NW, Suite 406, Washington DC 20036; Membership: 161 affiliates in 50 states

Experiment in International Living, United States Headquarters, Brattleboro, VT 05301; Membership: national offices in 70 other countries and 10 regional U.S. offices

Eye-Bank for Sight Restoration, 210 E. 64th St., New York, NY 10021

Federation of American Scientists, 307 Massachusetts Ave. NE, Washington DC 20002; Membership: 6,000

Fellowship of Reconciliation, Box 271, Nyack, NY 10960; Membership: 25,238 in 100 groups

Fleet Reserve Association, 1303 New Hampshire Ave. NW, Washington DC 20036; Membership: 138,776

Foreign Policy Association, 345 E. 46th St., New York, NY 10017

Foster Parents Plan, 155 Plan Way, Warwick, RI 02887

Fraternal Order of Eagles, 2401 W. Wisconsin Ave., Milwaukee, WI 53233; Membership: 750,000 in 50 state groups

Garden Club of America, 598 Madison Ave., New York, NY 10022; Membership: 13,000

General Federation of Women's Clubs, 1734 N St. NW, Washington DC 20036; Membership: 10 million in 45 countries

General Society of Mayflower Descendants, 4 Winslow St., Plymouth, MA 02360; Membership: 18,075 in 51 state groups

Gideons International, 2900 Lebanon Road, Nashville, TN 37214; Membership: 58,000 in 112 countries

Girl Scouts of the U.S.A., 830 Third Ave., New York, NY 10022; Membership: 3,140,000 in 348 local groups

Girls Clubs of America, 205 Lexington Ave., New York, NY 10016; Membership: 215,000

Group Health Association of America, 1717 Massachusetts Ave. NW, Washington DC 20036; Membership: 1,000

Guide Dog Foundation for the Blind, Inc., 109-19 72nd Ave., Forest Hills, NY 11375

Hadassah, the Women's Zionist Organization of America, 50 W. 58th St., New York, NY 10019; Membership: 335,000 in 1,500 chapters and groups

Health Insurance Institute, 1850 K St. NW, Washington DC 20006; Membership: 324 companies

Helicopter Association of America, 1156 15th St. NW, Suite 610, Washington DC 20005; Membership: 668 firms

Humane Society of the United States, 2100 L St. NW, Washington DC 20037; Membership: 70,000

Imperial Council of the Ancient Arabic Order of Nobles of the Mystic Shrine, 323 N. Michigan Ave., Chicago, IL 60601; Membership: 1 million

Independent Order of Odd Fellows, 5618 Wilson Blvd., Arlington, VA 22205; Membership: 1.2 million

Indian Rights Association, 1505 Race St., Philadelphia, PA 19102; Membership: 2,500

Institute of International Education, 809 United Nations Plaza, New York, NY 10017

International Air Transport Association, P.O. Box 550, International Aviation Sq., 1000 Sherbrooke St. W, Montreal, PQ, Canada H3A 2R4; Membership: 106 airlines

International College of Surgeons, 1516 Lake Shore Dr., Chicago, IL 60610; Membership: 14,000

International Game Fish Association, 3000 E. Las Olas Blvd., Fort Lauderdale, FL 33316; Membership: 10,000

International Student Service, 291 Broadway, New York, NY 10007; Membership: 190 local groups

Italian-American War Veterans of the U.S., 115 S. Meridian Rd., Youngstown, OH 44509; Membership: 8,500 in 110 posts

Izaak Walton League of America, 1800 N. Kent St., Suite 806, Arlington, VA 22209; Membership: 50,000

Jewish War Veterans of the U.S.A., 1712 New Hampshire Ave. NW, Washington DC 20009; Membership: 105,000

Junior Achievement, 550 Summer St., Stamford, CT 06901; Membership: 245,000

Kiwanis International, 101 E. Erie St., Chicago, IL 60611; **Membership:** 289,731 in 7,132 clubs

Knights of Columbus, Columbus Plaza, New Haven, CT 06507; **Membership:** 1,283,301

Knights of Pythias, Pythian Bldg., Rm. 201, 47 N. Grant St., Stockton, CA 95202; **Membership:** 200,000 in 55 domains

Knights Templar of the U.S.A., 14 E. Jackson Blvd., Suite 1700, Chicago, IL 60604; **Membership:** 365,000

League of Women Voters of the U.S., 1730 M St. NW, Washington, DC 20036; **Membership:** 135,000 in 1,345 leagues

Leukemia Society of America, Inc., 211 E. 43rd St., New York, NY 10017; **Membership:** 51 local groups

Lions International, 300 22nd, Oak Brook, IL 60521; **Membership:** 1,230,000

Little League Baseball, Williamsport, PA 17701; **Membership:** 10,951 leagues

Loyal Order of Moose, Mooseheart, IL 60539; **Membership:** 1,564,039 in 4,062 lodges and chapters

March of Dimes (The National Foundation), 1275 Mamaroneck Ave., White Plains, NY 10605

Marine Corps League, 933 N. Kenmore St., Suite 321, Arlington, VA 22201; **Membership:** 20,000

Masonic Service Association of the U.S., 8120 Fenton St., Silver Spring, MD 20910; **Membership:** 43 grand lodges

Mensa, American Mensa Ltd., 1701 W. 3d St., Brooklyn, NY 11223; **Membership:** 29,000 in 125 groups

Modern Language Association of America, 62 Fifth Ave., New York, NY 10011; **Membership:** 30,000

Modern Woodmen of America, 1701 First Ave., Rock Island, IL 61201; **Membership:** 510,000 in 1,000 local groups

Motor Vehicle Manufacturers Association of the United States, 300 New Center Bldg., Detroit, MI 48202; **Membership:** 11 manufacturers

Muscular Dystrophy Associations of America, Inc., 810 Seventh Ave., New York, NY 10019; **Membership:** 28,000 in 214 chapters

National Academy of Television Arts and Sciences, 110 W. 57th St., New York, NY 10019; **Membership:** 10,000

National Aeronautic Association, 821 15th St. NW, Washington DC 20005; **Membership:** 160,000

National Amputation Foundation, 12-45 150th St., Whitestone, NY 11357; **Membership:** 5,200 veterans

National Association for Hearing and Speech Action, 814 Thayer Ave., Silver Spring, MD 20910; **Membership:** 2,000 in 180 groups

National Association for Mental Health, 1800 N. Kent St., Rosslyn, VA 22209; **Membership:** 850 groups

National Association for Retarded Citizens, 2709 Ave. E East, Arlington, TX 76011; **Membership:** 275,000 in 1,800 local groups

National Association for Stock Car Auto Racing, 1801 Volusia Ave., Daytona Beach, FL 32015; **Membership:** 18,000

National Association for the Advancement of Colored People, 1790 Broadway, New York, NY 10019; **Membership:** 450,673

National Association of Blue Shield Plans, 211 East Chicago Ave., Chicago, IL 60611; **Membership:** 72 medical care plans

National Association of Broadcasters, 1771 N St. NW, Washington DC 20036; **Membership:** 6,000

National Association of Colored Women's Clubs, 5808 16th St. NW, Washington DC 20011; **Membership:** 45,000

National Association of Intercollegiate Athletics, 1221 Baltimore, Kansas City, MO 64106; **Membership:** 515 members and 32 groups

National Association of Manufacturers, 1776 F St., Washington DC 20006; **Membership:** 13,000

National Association of Negro Business and Professional Women's Clubs, 201 Dryden Bldg., Suite 201, Flint, MI 48503; **Membership:** 3,000 in 300 groups

National Association of Social Workers, 1425 H St. NW, Washington DC 20005; **Membership:** 75,000

National Association of State Universities and Land Grant Colleges, 1 Dupont Circle NW, Suite 710, Washington DC 20036; **Membership:** 141 colleges and universities

National Association of Theatre Owners, 1500 Broadway, New York, NY 10036; **Membership:** 10,000

National Audubon Society, 950 Third Ave., New York, NY 10022; **Membership:** 395,000 plus 162 affiliated groups

National Automobile Dealers Association, 8400 Westpark Dr., McLean, VA 22101; **Membership:** 21,000

National Board of Review of Motion Pictures, 210 E. 68th St., New York, NY 10021; **Membership:** 100

National Braille Association, Inc., Catholic Schools Office, 345 Adams St., Brooklyn, NY 11201; **Membership:** 2,700

National Campers and Hikers Association, Inc., 7172 Transit Rd., Buffalo, NY 14221; **Membership:** 200,000

National Catholic Educational Association, 1 Dupont Circle NW, Suite 350, Washington DC 20036; **Membership:** 14,225

National Civil Service League, 5530 Wisconsin Ave. NW, Suite 1600, Washington DC 20015; **Membership:** 3,000

National Collegiate Athletic Association, U.S. Hwy. 50 and Nall Ave., PO Box 1906, Shawnee Mission, KS 66222; **Membership:** 855 colleges and allied organizations

National Conference of Catholic Charities, 1346 Connecticut Ave. NW, Washington DC 20036; **Membership:** 3,000

National Conference of Christians and Jews, 43 W. 57th St., New York, NY 10019; **Membership:** 70 regional groups

National Conference on Social Welfare, 22 W. Gay St., Columbus, OH 43215; **Membership:** 4,500

National Congress of American Indians, 1430 K St. NW, Washington DC 20005; **Membership:** representing 450,000 Indians

National Congress of Parents and Teachers, 700 N. Rush St., Chicago, IL 60611; **Membership:** 6,403,854

National Council of Churches of Christ in the U.S.A., 475 Riverside Dr., New York, NY 10027; **Membership:** 39,980,443 in 31 denominations

National Council of Farmer Cooperatives, 1129 20th St. NW, Washington DC 20036; **Membership:** 3 million in 154 cooperative associations

National Council of Jewish Women, 15 E. 26th St., New York, NY 10010; **Membership:** 100,000

National Council of Negro Women, 1346 Connecticut Ave. NW, Washington DC 20036; **Membership:** 4 million in 167 local groups within 25 national affiliated organizations

National Council of State Garden Clubs, 824 N. Biltmore Ave., Clayton, MO 63105; **Membership:** 365,680

National Council of Women of the United States, 345 E. 46th St., New York, NY 10017

National Council on Crime and Delinquency, Continental Plaza, 411 Hackensack Ave., Hackensack, NJ 07601; **Membership:** 60,000

National Democratic Club, 52 E. 41st St., New York, NY 10017; **Membership:** 1,200

National Easter Seal Society for Crippled Children and Adults, 2023 W. Ogden Ave., Chicago, IL 60612; **Membership:** 52 state units with 1,400 local societies

National Education Association, 1201 16th St. NW, Washington DC 20036; **Membership:** 1,600,800; 53 state and 9,000 local affiliated groups

National Farmers Union (Farmers Educational and Cooperative Union of America), P.O. Box 39251, Denver, CO 80239; **Membership:** 250,000 farm families in 3,000 groups

National Federation of the Blind, P.O. Box 4422 Baltimore, MD 21227; **Membership:** 50,000

National Federation of Business and Professional Women's Clubs, Inc., 2012 Massachusetts Ave. NW, Washington DC 20036; **Membership:** 170,000

National Federation of Music Clubs, 310 S. Michigan Ave., Suite 1936, Chicago, IL 60604; **Membership:** 500,000 in 4,500 clubs

National 4-H Council, 150 N. Wacker Dr., Chicago, IL 60606

National Genealogical Society, 1921 Sunderland Pl. NW, Washington DC 20036; **Membership:** 3,500

National Geographic Society, 17th & M Sts. NW, Washington DC 20036; **Membership:** 9,500,000

National Grange, 1616 H St. NW, Washington DC 20006; **Membership:** 525,000 in 5,500 groups

National Hairdressers and Cosmetologists Assoc., Inc., 3510 Olive St., St. Louis, MO 63103; **Membership:** 71,000

National Health Council, Inc., 1740 Broadway, New York, NY 10019; **Membership:** 85 organizations

National Institute of Social Sciences, 622 Third Ave., New York, NY 10017; **Membership:** 1,000

National Jewish Welfare Board, 15 E. 26th St., New York, NY 10010; **Membership:** 370 Jewish community centers and YM-YMHAs

National League of Cities, 1620 Eye St. NW, Washington DC 20006; **Membership:** 15,000 municipal governments in 49 states

National Legal Aid and Defender Association, 2100 M St. NW, Suite 601, Washington DC 20037; **Membership:** 8,000 individuals; 2,000 organizations

National Medical Association, Inc., 1720 Massachusetts Ave. NW, Washington DC 20036; **Membership:** 8,000

National Multiple Sclerosis Society, 205 E. 42nd St., New York, NY 10017; **Membership:** 370,000 in 160 chapters

National Municipal League, 47 E. 68th St., New York, NY 10021; **Membership:** 6,500

National Newspaper Publishers Association, 770 National Press Bldg., Washington DC 20004; **Membership:** 161 publishers

National Organization for Women (NOW), Suite 1048, 425 13th St. NW, Washington DC 20004; **Membership:** 77,000

National Parks and Conservation Association, 1701 18th St. NW, Washington DC 20009; **Membership:** 45,000

National Press Club, National Press Bldg., 529 14th St. NW, Room 1380, Washington DC 20045; **Membership:** 4,734

National Railway Historical Society, P.O. Box 2051, Philadelphia, PA 19103; **Membership:** 10,000

National Rifle Association of America, 1600 Rhode Island Ave. NW, Washington DC 20036; **Membership:** 1,200,000

National Safety Council, 444 N. Michigan Ave., Chicago, IL 60611; **Membership:** 15,000

National Small Business Association, 1604 K St. NW, Washington DC 20036; **Membership:** 40,000

National Society for the Prevention of Blindness, 79 Madison Ave., New York, NY 10016; **Membership:** 321

National Tax Association-Tax Institute of America, 21 E. State St., Columbus, OH 43215; **Membership:** 2,500

National Urban League, 500 E. 62nd St., New York, NY 10021; **Membership:** 50,000 in 107 local groups

National Wildlife Federation, 1412 16th St. NW, Washington DC 20036; **Membership:** 3.5 million

National Woman's Christian Temperance Union, 1730 Chicago Ave., Evanston, IL 60201; **Membership:** 250,000

Newspaper Guild, The, 1125 15th St. NW, Washington DC 20005; **Membership:** 33,500 in 80 locals

Optimist International, 4494 Lindell Blvd., St. Louis, MO 63108; **Membership:** 120,000

Order of Ahepa (American Hellenic Educational Progressive Association), 1422 K St. NW, Washington DC 20005; **Membership:** 25,000 in 430 groups

Order of the Eastern Star, General Grand Chapter, 1618 New Hampshire Ave. NW, Washington DC 20009; **Membership:** 3 million

Overseas Press Club of America, 55 E. 43rd St., New York, NY 10017; **Membership:** 1,600

Parkinson's Disease Foundation, William Black Medical Research Bldg., Columbia Presbyterian Medical Center, 640 W. 168th St., New York, NY 10032

P.E.N. American Center, 156 Fifth Ave., New York, NY 10010

Photographic Society of America, 2005 Walnut St., Philadelphia, PA 19103; **Membership:** 18,700

Planned Parenthood–World Population (Planned Parenthood Federation of America), 810 Seventh Ave., New York, NY 10019; **Membership:** 189 organizations

Polish Legion of American Veterans, U.S.A., 3134 S. 17th St., Milwaukee, WI 53215; **Membership:** 15,000 in 114 posts

Public Relations Society of America, 845 Third Ave., New York, NY 10022; **Membership:** 8,700 executives

Puppeteers of America, Apt. 501, 2311 Connecticut Ave., Washington DC 20008; **Membership:** 2,500 in 35 guilds

Republican National Committee, 310 First St. SE, Washington DC 20003; **Membership:** 162

Rotary International, 1600 Ridge Ave., Evanston, IL 60201; **Membership:** 818,000

Save-The-Redwoods League, 114 Sansome St., Room 605, San Francisco, CA 94104; **Membership:** 55,000

Screen Actors Guild, 7750 Sunset Blvd., Hollywood, CA 90046; **Membership:** 35,700

Society for the Advancement of Education, 1860 Broadway, New York, NY 10023; **Membership:** 3,000

Society of Automotive Engineers, 400 Commonwealth Dr., Warrendale, PA 15096; **Membership:** 30,000 in 52 groups

Society of the Cincinnati, 2118 Massachusetts Ave. NW, Washington DC 20008; **Membership:** 2,600 in 14 groups

Sons of the American Revolution, National Society, 2560 Huntington Ave., Suite 302, Alexandria, VA 22303; **Membership:** 21,000

Soroptimist International of the Americas, Inc., 1616 Walnut St., Philadelphia, PA 19103; **Membership:** 31,000 in 1,062 groups

Southern Christian Leadership Conference, 330 Auburn Ave. NE, Atlanta, GA 30303; **Membership:** 80 chapters

Speech Communication Association, 5205 Leesburg Pike, Falls Church, VA 22041; **Membership:** 9,000

Sports Car Club of America, Box 22476, Denver, CO 80222; **Membership:** 21,000

Supreme Council, Ancient Accepted Scottish Rite of Freemasonry, Northern Jurisdiction, 33 Marrett Rd., Lexington, MA 02173; **Membership:** 513,355 in 113 groups

Supreme Council 33°, Ancient Accepted Scottish Rite of Freemasonry, Southern Jurisdiction, 1733 16th St. NW, Washington DC 20009; **Membership:** 653,000

Transportation Association of America, 1100 17th St. NW, Washington DC 20036; **Membership:** 1,000

UNICEF, 331 E. 38th St., New York, NY 10016; **Membership:** 90

United Cerebral Palsy Associations, 66 E. 34th St., New York, NY 10016; **Membership:** 291 affiliates

United Daughters of the Confederacy, 328 North Blvd., Richmond, VA 23220; **Membership:** 35,000

United Federation of College Teachers, 260 Park Ave. S., 8th Floor, New York, NY 10010; **Membership:** 1,000

United Jewish Appeal, Inc., 1290 Ave. of the Americas, New York, NY 10019; **Membership:** 9 regional groups

United Nations Association of the United States of America, 300 E. 42nd St., New York, NY 10017; **Membership:** 31,000 in 200 chapters

United Negro College Fund, 500 E. 62nd St., New York, NY 10021; **Membership:** 39 private accredited four-year colleges; 2 graduate and professional schools

United States Catholic Conference, 1312 Massachusetts Ave. NW, Washington DC 20005

United States Independent Telephone Association, 1801 K St. NW, Suite 1201, Washington DC 20006; **Membership:** 2,015

The United States Jaycees, 4 W. 21st St., PO Box 7, Tulsa, OK 74102; **Membership:** 370,000 in 51 state groups

United States National Student Association, 2115 S St. NW, Washington DC 20008; **Membership:** 400 colleges and universities

United States Olympic Committee, 1750 E. Boulder St., Colorado Springs, CO 80909; **Membership** 43

United States Power Squadrons, P.O. Box 30423, Raleigh, NC 27612; **Membership:** 88,000

United Way of America, 801 N. Fairfax St., Alexandria, VA 22314; **Membership:** 2,289 local united funds, community chests and welfare councils

USO (United Service Organizations), 1146 19th St. NW, Washington D.C. 20036

Variety Clubs International, 58 W. 58th St., Suite 23-C, New York, NY 10019; **Membership:** 10,000 in 41 groups

Veterans of Foreign Wars of the U.S., V.F.W. Bldg., Kansas City MO 64111; **Membership:** 1,850,000 in 10,000 groups; ladies auxiliary numbers 580,000 in 6,855 groups

Volunteers of America, 340 W. 85th St., New York, NY 10024; **Membership:** 44 state groups

The Wilderness Society, 1901 Pennsylvania Ave. NW, Washington DC 20006; **Membership:** 70,000

Wildlife Society, 7101 Wisconsin Ave. NW, Suite 611, Washington DC 20014; **Membership:** 7,500

Women Strike for Peace, 145 S. 13th St., Philadelphia, PA 19107

Women's American ORT (Organization for Rehabilitation through Training), 1250 Broadway, New York, NY 10001; **Membership:** 135,000 in 1,089 chapters

Women's International League for Peace and Freedom, 1213 Race St., Philadelphia, PA 19107; **Membership:** 110 branches

Workmen's Benefit Fund of the U.S.A., 714 Seneca Ave., Brooklyn, NY 11227; **Membership:** 36,000 in 125 groups

Workmen's Circle, 45 E. 33rd St., New York, NY 10016; **Membership:** 60,000 in 340 groups

World Future Society, 4916 St. Elmo Ave., Washington DC 20014; **Membership:** 45,000 in 60 groups

Writers Guild of America, East, 22 W. 48th St., New York, NY 10036; **Membership:** 2,100

Writers Guild of America, West, 8955 Beverly Blvd., Los Angeles, CA 90048; **Membership:** 4,600

Young Democratic Clubs of America, % Democratic National Committee, 1625 Massachusetts Ave. NW, Washington DC 20036; **Membership:** 1 million in 4,000 groups

Young Men's and Young Women's Hebrew Association, 1395 Lexington Ave., New York, NY 10028; **Membership:** 9,600

Young Men's Christian Associations of the U.S.A., National Council, 291 Broadway, New York, NY 10007; **Membership:** 8,670,000 in 1,842 associations

Young Republican National Federation, 310 First St. SE, Washington DC 20003; **Membership:** 300,000 in 4,000 groups

Young Women's Christian Association of the U.S.A., 600 Lexington Ave., New York, NY 10022; **Membership:** 2,476,000 in 4,628 local groups

Zionist Organization of America, 4 E. 34th St., New York, NY 10016; **Membership:** 130,000 in 600 groups

RELIGION: FAITHS/FOLLOWERS

MAJOR WORLD RELIGIONS

JUDAISM

The religion of the Jewish people is the world's oldest great monotheism and the parent religion of both Christianity and Islam. The name derives from the Latin *Judaeus* and the Hebrew *Yehudhi*, meaning *descendant of Judah*, who was the fourth son of Jacob.

The founder of Judaism was Abraham, who lived about 1500 B.C. and made a covenant with God that he and his descendants, as the Chosen People, would carry the message of one God to the world. The new nation was given structure by Moses, who in the 13th century B.C. led the Israelites out of slavery in Egypt, received the Ten Commandments from God on Mt. Horeb (Sinai), and brought his people to the edge of the land of Canaan, which had been promised to Abraham as part of the covenant.

Once in the Promised Land, the Israelites built a temple, established a priesthood, and began offering sacrifices in accordance with the teachings of Moses—practices that survived the 6th-century Babylonian Exile. But in A.D. 70, when the temple in Jerusalem was destroyed by the Roman army, sacrificial worship was supplanted by study and prayers in synagogues.

Although Judaism has no specific creeds, its sacred writings consist of laws, prophecies, and traditions that reflect 3,500 years of spiritual experience. The principal text is the Torah, or Pentateuch, which consists of the first five books of the Bible. The rest of the Hebrew Bible, known to Christians as the Old Testament, includes the Psalms and writings of the major and minor prophets.

Another authoritative work is the Talmud, a collection of laws that includes the Mishna, a Hebrew compilation of the Oral Law (in Hebrew), and the Gemara, a collection of comments (in Aramaic) on the Mishna by rabbis. There are actually two Talmuds, one that emanated from Palestine in the 5th century and one from Babylonia a century later.

The basis of Judaism is belief in the living God who is transcendent, omnipotent, and just, and who reveals himself to mankind. The faith rests on the words of Deuteronomy 6:4: "Hear, O Israel, the Lord our God, the Lord is One."

For Jews the oneness of God implies the brotherhood of men, and religious knowledge is considered inseparable from the ethical injunction "to do justly, and love mercy, and to walk humbly with thy God." Judaism's elaborate system of laws and rituals, such as dietary regulations, is designed to give sacred meaning to every aspect of daily life.

Jews have an ordained clergy and observe the Sabbath, which runs from sunset Friday to sunset Saturday and is observed with services of prayer and readings in local synagogues. Major festivals include Pesach (Passover, celebrating the Exodus), Shabuoth (Pentecost), Rosh Hashana (New Year), Yom Kippur (Day of Atonement), and Sukkoth (Feast of Tabernacles).

Judaism has generated numerous internal sects and movements, including the Sadduccees and Pharisees during the early Christian era. In the 12th century, Maimonides tried to relate Judaism to Western philosophy, especially that of Aristotle. Modern religious movements developed from Moses Mendelssohn, a rationalist of the 18th-century Enlightenment, and Hasidism, which preaches piety and mysticism.

Present-day American Judaism is divided among three major denominations. The Orthodox stresses strict adherence to the Torah. Reform Jews, in the tradition of Mendelssohn, have repudiated legalism and emphasize the compatibility of Judaism with secular liberal values. Conservative Judaism reflects a middle road—acceptance of the Torah but also a willingness to adapt it to modern conditions. In recent years a Reconstructionist movement, which was originated by Mordecai M. Kaplan and developed out of the Conservative wing, has stressed Judaism as an evolving religious civilization.

Since the destruction of their nation in A.D. 70, Jews have dreamed of once again having their own state. The first Zionist Congress was held (1897) in Basle and, in the wake of the Nazi holocaust that took the lives of six million Jews, the State of Israel came into being in 1948. Although the religious significance of the state's existence is not yet clear, the Six-Day War of 1967 nonetheless made many non-Israeli Jews realize how closely they are involved with Israel both in their cultural and religious lives.

MOSES (c. 1350–1250 B.C.)

According to Biblical accounts, the great lawgiver of Jewish monotheism was born probably in Egypt to slave parents, Amram and Jochebed, of the tribe of Levi. Because of an Egyptian law requiring newborn male Hebrew children to be killed, his mother is said to have hid him in a basket among the reeds of the Nile River. Found by one of Pharaoh's daughters, he was raised by her with Jochebed as his nurse.

As a young man Moses became interested in the cause of his people and had to flee to Midian after slaying an Egyptian whom he had discovered beating a Hebrew. Finding refuge as a shepherd for Jethro, a local priest, Moses married his daughter Zipporah.

While tending sheep one day at Mt. Horeb, Moses had a vision of God in a bush that burned but was not consumed, and he experienced a call to return to Egypt to liberate his people. With the aid of his brother Aaron, he aproached the Pharaoh (probably Ramses II: reigned c. 1292 to 1225 B.C.), who acceded to the Exodus of the Hebrews after a series of 10 plagues, the last of which took the life of his firstborn son. The Pharaoh subsequently changed his mind, pursued the Hebrews, and his army was drowned in the Red Sea, but the Israelites miraculously escaped.

Moses led his people across the Sinai desert to Mt. Horeb (Sinai), where he received the Ten Commandments from God in the form of two tablets, which he smashed on the ground when he discovered his Hebrews worshiping a Golden Calf. Later he prepared two new tablets and placed them in the most sacred section of the Tabernacle, a portable sanctuary that was set up according to divine instructions. He also taught the Hebrews a complete legal code, organized a judicial system, and spelled out sacrificial practices.

Moses spent 40 years leading his people in the wilderness, never entering the promised land of Canaan—a privilege that went to his chosen successor, Joshua. Moses' great achievement, however, was the development of a system of morality and law applicable to all aspects of daily life.

CHRISTIANITY

Christianity developed among first-century Jews out of the conviction that Jesus of Nazareth, who lived from about c. 4 B.C. to A.D. 29, was the long-awaited Hebrew Messiah. . . . The name Jesus is Greek for the Hebrew Joshua, a name meaning Savior, while Christ derives from the Greek Christos, meaning Messiah, or Anointed.

The Christian Bible includes the Hebrew Bible, which is called the Old Testament, and the New Testament, which contains 27 additional books and was formalized by the 4th century. Central are the four Gospels of Matthew, Mark, Luke, and John, which describe the life and teachings of Jesus. Some Christians also accept the 14-book appendix to the Authorized Version of the Old Testament, known as the Apocrypha, as canonical.

The essence of traditional Christian theology is that Jesus was the Son of God who came to save the world, was crucified, resurrected, and will come again to judge mankind. The core of the Christian ethic is the commandment: "Thou shalt love the Lord thy God with all thy heart and thy neighbor as thyself."

A turning point in Christian history occurred at the Council of Jerusalem in A.D. 49 when St. Paul convinced other church leaders to spread the faith to non-Jews. Early Christians endured severe persecution, but in

A.D. 313 Constantine I officially tolerated Christianity in the Roman Empire.

Fundamental theological issues such as the divinity of Jesus Christ were thrashed out at a series of ecumenical councils during the first eight centuries. Doctrinal statements emanated from these councils, such as the Nicene Creed and the teaching of the Trinity, which asserts that God has appeared to man as the Father, the Son, and the Holy Ghost.

In 1054 Christianity was split into a Western or Roman Catholic Church, which acknowledges the pope—the bishop of Rome—as Christ's supreme vicar on earth, and the Eastern Orthodox Churches, which recognize the patriarch of Constantinople as the preeminent ecclesiastical figure. In the 16th century the Roman Catholic Church was further divided by the Protestant Reformation. The ecumenical movement of this century has now shifted momentum toward a quest for unity among Christian churches. An important development was the founding in 1948 of the World Council of Churches, which has more than 220 Protestant and Orthodox churches as members.

ROMAN CATHOLICISM

Roman Catholicism is the form of Christianity practiced by those who recognize the authority of the pope—the bishop of Rome—as the successor of Peter and vicar of Christ on Earth. The great majority of Catholics follow the Western or Latin Rite, but there are also a number of Eastern or Uniate churches, including the Byzantine and Armenian rites, that exercise a considerable degree of autonomy.

The Roman Catholic Church claims to be the "One Holy, Catholic and Apostolic Church." Although it acknowledges the Old and New Testaments and the Apocrypha, it also asserts that teachings disclosed in only seminal form to the Apostles have subsequently germinated and flowered in the Christian Community and have been formulated by General Councils and/or the pope. Recent examples of articles of faith include the doctrines of papal infallibility (1870) and the Assumption of the Virgin Mary (1950).

The basis of the Church's claim to sanctity is its authority to offer the sacrifice of the Mass, the Eucharist, that reenacts and re-presents Christ's sacrifice in behalf of man's sins. There are six other recognized sacraments: baptism, confirmation, confession and penance, matrimony, ordination, and extreme unction.

The key figure in the church hierarchy is the bishop, who has the power to confirm and ordain. The members of the College of Cardinals serve as the pope's privy councillors and also have the responsibility of electing new popes. The central administrative body of the church is the Curia Romana, which is located in Rome and organized around a varying number of sacred "congregations."

Priests are divided into "secular," or diocesan, clergy and "regular" clergy, who belong to religious orders living under a "rule." Since the 12th century, celibacy has been required of both types of clergy.

Following the 16th-century Protestant Reformation, the Church entered a period of retrenchment that was characterized by sharply defined standards of orthodoxy. Since the First Vatican Council, which ended in 1870, the papacy has been exceptionally strong. The Second Vatican Council (1962–65), however, produced significant changes, and the Church is now undergoing a period of uncertainty and flux that is marked by demands for increased power for laymen and priests and serious questioning of such traditions as clerical celibacy and papal authority.

EASTERN ORTHODOXY

The term Eastern Orthodox refers to those churches and their offspring that, for a variety of cultural, political, and theological reasons, split with Rome in A.D. 1054. These churches regard themselves as the true heirs of the early Christian Church and define their theological unity by acceptance of the decrees of the first seven ecumenical (general) councils that were held from A.D. 325 to 787.

The Eastern communion is a fellowship of autonomous churches consisting of the ancient patriarchates of Constantinople, Alexandria, Antioch, and Jerusalem, as well as the Orthodox churches of Cyprus, Russia, Rumania, Yugoslavia, Greece, Bulgaria, Georgia, Albania, Finland, and Czechoslovakia. The leader is the Ecumenical Patriarch of Constantinople, who is regarded as "first among equals" but whose direct authority is limited to the affairs of his own church, whose members are for the most part located in Europe and the Americas.

Eastern Orthodox theology is grounded in Greek philosophy rather than Roman law, and its creeds are important more as acts of worship than as standards of belief. Great reverence is shown for the writings of the church fathers, including Saints Basil the Great, Gregory Nazianzen, and John Chrysostom.

In addition to rejecting the authority of the pope, Eastern Orthodoxy disagrees with the Roman Catholic Church by rejecting the Nicene Creed's *Filioque*, which asserts that the Holy Spirit proceeds "from the Son" as well as from the Father. Orthodoxy also has no indulgences and pays honor to Mary as the mother of God but rejects the Roman dogma of Immaculate Conception. It reveres relics and icons but bans all "graven images," except the crucifix.

Orthodox priests may marry before but not after ordination, although monks must remain celibate and bishops are chosen from among the celibate clergy. The liturgy of Eastern Orthodox churches is sung, and great emphasis is placed on fasting. Eastern Orthodox church structures, which are normally square, feature a solid screen that separates the sanctuaries and the edifices' main bodies. They are often elaborately decorated with gilded icons and other works of art.

The fact that a majority of Orthodox believers now live in Communist-controlled areas has cut into the vitality of Orthodoxy, but nonetheless many of its churches—including the Russian one—are active in the World Council of Churches. Relations with Rome have greatly improved, and Ecumenical Patriarch Athenagoras I has had several dramatic meetings with Pope Paul VI, including one on the Mount of Olives in Jerusalem.

PROTESTANTISM

In a broad sense *Protestantism* is a generic term for most Western Christian churches that are not Roman Catholic or Eastern Orthodox. In a narrower connotation, it designates those churches and their heirs that came into being after the 16th-century Protestant Reformation.

The Reformation was sparked by Martin Luther, an Augustinian monk who challenged the papal practice of dispensing indulgences; with the support of German princes, he established a separate church. In addition to the Lutheran, there are at least three other Protestant traditions. The Reformed, or Calvinistic, tradition developed in Switzerland and led to the formation of Presbyterian and related churches. Anglicanism, which is represented in the United States by the Episcopal Church and originated in England, was the parent of Methodism. Numerous "free" or "independent" churches have also developed, including the Baptist and others that exercise a congregational system of government.

The fundamental philosophical characteristics of the reformers were the rejection of the authority of Rome, belief in the Bible as the only source of revelation, recognition of the "priesthood of all believers," and the assertion that salvation is the result of faith rather than good works or the dispensations of a church. Protestantism's characteristic individualism led to the development of religious liberty in many areas, but also contributed to denominational fragmentation.

Protestant churches permit ministers to marry, and even those that have bishops tend to concentrate governing powers in lay boards. Liturgies generally emphasize preaching and Bible reading rather than elaborate ritual; however, some traditions—notably the Anglo-Catholic wing of Anglicanism—are highly liturgical.

The modern ecumenical movement has developed out of Protestantism, and, except for fundamentalist churches (and thereby most Baptist churches), the major Protestant denominations tend to be involved in organizations such as the World Council of Churches. Mergers have been common in recent years, and nine major American denominations are in the process of negotiating a merger that would create a single, 25-million-member church.

JESUS (c. 4 B.C.–A.D. 29)

The founder of Christianity was born in Bethlehem to Mary, the wife of Joseph, who was a carpenter from Nazareth. Little is known about his early life. According to the Gospels, at the age of about 30 he was baptized by his cousin John the Baptist and began to preach, soon gathering a band of 12 disciples.

Jesus, who preached a message of repentance, made repeated attacks on Pharisees and scribes, the rulers of

Judaism. He couched his teachings in parables that could be understood by the masses and reinforced his words with extraordinary deeds that included healing the sick, raising the dead, and changing water into wine at the marriage feast of Cana.

After three years of preaching, Jesus set out for Jerusalem with his disciples for the celebration of Passover. He created a disturbance by throwing the money changers out of the Temple. Meanwhile, the Roman Governor Pontius Pilate, who was sensitive to Jewish nationalist threats, became alarmed. The authorities induced one of the disciples, Judas Iscariot, to betray Jesus. Following a Last Supper with his followers in which the Eucharist, or Lord's Supper, was symbolically enacted, Jesus was arrested in the Garden of Gethsemane.

He was tried for the treasonous charge of calling himself the Messiah and was crucified under a sign reading "Jesus of Nazareth, King of the Jews." The Gospels report, however, that three days later when Mary Magdalene went to the tomb she found it empty. An angel announced that Jesus had been resurrected; according to the Book of Acts, he appeared to his disciples, remained on earth 40 days, and then ascended into heaven.

Orthodox Christian theology asserts that Jesus was God made man and the second Person of the Trinity. The calendar of the Christian Church revolves around the events of his life, beginning with Advent—the preparation for his coming—and concluding with his Resurrection, Ascension, and the reception of the Holy Spirit by the church.

The discovery in 1947 of the Dead Sea Scrolls in a cave above the waters of the northwest Dead Sea in a section known as Qumran provided information about a pacifist and ascetic community generally identified with the Essene Jewish sect.

Some scholars attempted to link Jesus with the "Teacher of Righteousness," an Essene figure who would be "raised up" by God after death. A more general consensus now is that such ties are tenuous and that the scrolls are important primarily for their information about cultural conditions of the early Christian era, especially Palestinian Judaism and the background of John the Baptist.

ISLAM

Islam is the religion founded by the prophet Mohammed (c. A.D. 570–632) in 622 at Yathrib (now Medina) in Arabia. The Arabic word *Islam* means *submission to God,* and followers call themselves Moslems.

Mohammed was a caravan conductor and Mecca shopkeeper of the Koreish tribe who experienced a prophetic call at the age of 40. After founding his religion, he also acted as a governor, general, and judge. Mohammed is regarded as the "Seal of the Prophets"—the last in a series of messengers from God, consisting of Adam, Noah, Abraham, Moses, and Jesus.

The sacred text of Islam is the Koran (*Quran* in Arabic), which means *reading* and contains the revelations of Mohammed over a period of 20 years; it also deals with manners, religious laws, and morals. It has been supplemented by the Sunna, a collection of Traditions (moral sayings and anecdotes), and both are reinforced by the principle of Ijma, which states the belief that a majority of Moslems cannot agree in error. The Koran, the Sunna, and the Ijma are the three foundations of Islam.

Islam is radically theistic, and the essence of its creed is simply stated: "There is no God but Allah, and Mohammed is the messenger [or prophet] of Allah." Mohammed rejected the trinitarianism of Christianity, but he incorporated a number of Judeo-Christian concepts into his system. For example, the creed states: "I believe in God, his Angels, his Books and his Messengers, the Last Day, the Resurrection from the dead, Predestination by God, Good and Evil, the Judgment, the Balance, Paradise and Hell-fire."

There is no professional priesthood in Islam, and followers are expected to refrain from drinking wine. In addition to acceptance and recital of the creed, there are four duties required of the devout: prayer, fasting during the lunar month of Ramadan, giving alms, and a pilgrimage to the holy city of Mecca—if at all possible.

Moslems pray five times a day—at dawn, noon, midafternoon, dusk, and at night. The prayers, which consist primarily of thanksgiving and praise of Allah, are performed facing Mecca and involve traditional physical postures. The principal public service takes place at midday on Friday, usually in a mosque.

Early disputes over the "caliph," or successor of Mohammed, led to sectarian divisions within Islam. The most important were the Sunnites, Shiites, and Khawarij, who differed over matters of ceremony and law. Other modern movements have included the Babis and the Wahabis.

Islam is a missionary religion, though Moslems do not regard Jews and Christians as pagans and have normally permitted them to keep practicing their faiths after conquests. In centuries past, Moslem armies took over large sections of India and once came within 100 miles of Paris.

The principal areas of Islamic influence today are the Middle East, North Africa, and western Asia, and there are substantial communities in the Philippines, Indonesia, and Malaysia. It is currently increasing rapidly in African countries south of the Sahara.

Considerable theological activity has gone on during this century toward discrediting such Islamic practices as polygamy, slavery, and intolerance, thus making Islam more acceptable under modern conditions.

MOHAMMED (c. 570–A.D. 632)

The founder of Islam was born in Mecca in Arabia, the son of a poor merchant from the ruling tribe of Koreish. Both his parents died shortly after his birth, and he was raised by a grandfather and later an uncle. As a youth he was a shepherd and worked as a conductor of trading caravans.

Following his marriage at the age of 24 to the wealthy widow Khadija, who was 15 years his senior, Mohammed settled down in Mecca as a prosperous merchant and began devoting himself to the contemplative life. At the age of 40 in the cave of Mount Hira, north of Mecca, he had a vision, in which he was commanded to preach. This revelation and subsequent ones were recorded in the Koran, the sacred book of the Moslems.

Mohammed's first converts were his wife and children, and he began to collect other followers slowly and secretly, because of his many enemies. He taught belief in only one God, Allah, and preached heaven and hell and divine judgment.

When he began to operate openly, he aroused considerable hostility; some of his followers had to seek sanctuary in Abyssinia because of persecution. In 622 he himself barely escaped assassination and fled to Yathrib, which was later renamed Medina. Moslems regard this flight, the hegira, as the beginning of Islam and the start of their calendar.

Mohammed became the absolute ruler of Yathrib, where he founded his model theocratic state. He built the first mosque, changed the direction of prayers from Jerusalem to Mecca, and instituted the fast month of Ramadan and the practice of tithing. Relations with Christians and Jews deteriorated, but eventually he made treaties granting them freedom of worship in return for taxes. He initiated warfare with the Meccans, eventually gaining control of all of Arabia.

His private life has been the source of much attention, especially his frequent marriages—often politically inspired—and troubles with his harem. He basically led a simple and unpretentious life, however, and in 632 died in the arms of his last favorite wife, Ayesha.

HINDUISM

Known to its followers as *Santana Dharma* (the Eternal Religion), Hinduism is the religion of the majority of Indians today. It has developed gradually over a period of 5,000 years, making it possibly the world's oldest faith.

Hinduism has no ecclesiastical organization, and there are no beliefs or practices universal to all Hindus. It is polytheistic in the extreme, with literally hundreds of thousands of gods and some forms of animal life worshiped. The principal gods are Brahma, the unapproachable creative spirit, and the two popular gods, Siva and Vishnu—both of which have spawned innumerable cults.

Hindus emphasize the divinity of the soul and the harmony of all religions. Life is seen as a series of lives in which a man's position is determined by his *Karma,* or deeds, in previous lives. The social "caste" into which he is born is thus an indication of his spiritual status. The ultimate goal is to be released from the cycle of rebirths in various human and animal forms through absorption by the absolute. Asceticism and the discipline of Yoga are practiced to help achieve this release.

Hinduism has no fixed canon of sacred books. The principal text is the Veda (Vedic word meaning *divine knowledge*), a collection of 1,200 hymns and incantations addressed to various deities, including those of fire and wind. Some of this material is believed to date from the arrival of the Aryans in India c. 1500 B.C. More philosophical works that have also gained wide acceptance include the *Brahamanas*, the *Upanishads*, and the poem "Bhagavad-Gita" (Sanskrit for Song of the Lord).

For the ordinary man, Hinduism involves careful observance of food and marriage rules, pilgrimages to sacred rivers and shrines, participation in festivals, and worship in the temples and shrines that are found in every village. Entry to ultimate truth comes not from the acceptance of certain dogmas but from worship and religious experience.

Over the centuries Hinduism has produced numerous reform movements, including Buddhism and Sikhism. Modern social and cultural conditions are also bringing about modification of the caste system and other changes such as increased social status for women.

BUDDHISM

Buddhism is the way of life based on the teachings of Siddhartha Gautama, an Indian prince who lived in the sixth century B.C. and came to be known as the Buddha (Sanskrit for *enlightened one*).

Dissatisfied with the formalism of the Hinduism of his day and vowing to find an explanation for evil and human suffering, the prince left his family and wandered as a hermit for six years in search of a truth that would liberate mankind. He found it after seven weeks of meditation under a bo (pipal or sacred fig) tree (the tree of enlightenment) and began preaching and sending missionaries forth to spread his discovery.

The Buddha taught that the path beyond sorrow and suffering was the "middle way" between austerity and sensuality. He spoke of "four noble truths": existence involves suffering, suffering results from craving, craving can be destroyed, and such destruction of desire is obtainable by following the "noble eightfold path." The steps of this path are right views, right desires, right speech, right conduct, right livelihood, right endeavor, right mindfulness, and right meditation.

The Buddha did not speak of God, and his teachings constitute, in the ordinary Western sense, more of a philosophy and system of ethics than a religion. Buddhism affirms the law of Karma, by which a person's actions in life determine his status in future incarnations. The object of the Buddhist life is to achieve Nirvana, a condition of enlightenment and detachment from the world by which the cycle of successive rebirths comes to an end.

The simple life of the Buddha and his followers gave way after his death to the creation of monasteries, shrines, and temples; however, Buddhism eventually split into numerous branches. The two major ones today are Mahayana (greater vehicle) Buddhism, which is practiced in China, Korea, and Japan and has an elaborate theology in which the Buddha is regarded as a divine savior, and Hinayana (lesser vehicle) Buddhism, which is concentrated in Southeast Asia and preserves the earlier monastic traditions. Zen Buddhism, a Japanese variation of Mahayana Buddhism, stresses contemplation, while the Lamaism of Tibet represents a mixture of Buddhism with local demonolatry.

BUDDHA (c. 563–483 B.C.)

The founder of Buddhism, known as the Buddha or "Enlightened One," was born into a military caste in Lumbini, near the Himalayas in southern Nepal. Estimates of the precise year range from 624 to 466 B.C.

His original name was Siddhartha Gautama (or Gotama), and legend holds that his father, a rajah, had been warned at his birth that Siddhartha would become either a universal ruler or a universal teacher. Preferring the former course, the father took pains to prevent him from seeing any unpleasant aspects of life that might influence him to renounce the world.

Riding through the royal park one day when he was 29 years old, however, Siddhartha saw human misery for the first time in the form of an old man, a diseased man, a corpse, and a wandering religious mendicant. Resolving to solve the riddle of human suffering, he left his wife and newborn son and spent the next six years as a wandering hermit and ascetic.

His austere living failed to bring illumination, and he became an ordinary mendicant. One day he sat under a bo tree in the village of Buddh Gaya in northern India and resolved not to rise until he had found enlightenment. He stayed 49 days, resisting temptations by Mara, the Buddhist devil, and was finally rewarded with the "bliss of emancipation," or Nirvana. Suffering, he concluded, was caused by attachment to the world and could only be eliminated through mental discipline and correct living.

Two merchants heard his teachings and became his first lay disciples. Later he preached a sermon to five monks with whom he had shared his ascetic quest, and they were ordained as the first members of the Sangha, the Buddhist monastic order. He returned home briefly and converted his family, thereafter spending the rest of his life teaching among neighboring tribes and organizing monks to spread the message of life lived according to the "middle way" between the extremes of pleasure-seeking and self-mortification.

He died at the age of 80 in the lap of Ananda, his favorite disciple, and his last words were said to have been: "Decay is inherent in all component things. Work out your own salvation with diligence."

SHINTOISM

The ancestral religion of Japan, Shinto developed out of primitive nature and ancestor worship sometime before the sixth century, when written records first appeared. The term *Shinto* is the Chinese equivalent of *the way of the gods*, and came into use at that time to distinguish it from the Buddhism that was then being imported from the Chinese mainland.

Shinto is essentially a set of customs and rituals rather than an ethical or moral system. Followers participate in festivals and pilgrimages, and great emphasis is placed on ceremonial purity and bodily cleanliness. Many Shintoists are also practicing Buddhists.

The religion has a complex pantheon of *kami*, or deities, the most exalted of whom is the sun-goddess known as Ruler of Heaven. Other objects of veneration include deified emperors, guardian family spirits, national heroes, and the divinities of trees, rivers, villages, and water sources.

Shrines ranging from small wayside god-houses to great national sanctuaries have been constructed and dedicated to these deities. Each Shinto home also has a "god-shelf" on which is placed a miniature wooden shrine holding tablets bearing beloved ancestors' names.

TAOISM

The chief rival to Confucianism in influencing Chinese philosophy and culture, Taoism actually consists of two movements: a philosophy (Tao Chia) and a religion (Tao Chiao). Both derive from the philosopher Lao-tze, who, according to tradition, lived in the sixth century B.C.

The term *Tao* has been translated as *way, road,* and even *being*. The book *Tao-teh-king*, attributed to Lao-tze, states that "the eternal Tao cannot be put into words, nor can the unchanging name be given a definition."

Philosophical Taoism espoused a radical naturalism that urged the acceptance of "all things in their natural state" and deplored passion, unnecessary invention, artificial ceremonies, and government activities such as war and taxation. Virtue was cast in passive and feminine terms. "There is nothing softer and weaker than water, and yet there is nothing better for attacking hard and strong things," was one of its precepts.

Tao Chia declined by the fourth century, partly because of the excessive assimilation of Buddhism, but its spirit of simplicity and harmony has contributed to such Chinese customs as tea drinking.

Religious Taoism originated in the first century under the leadership of Chang Tao-lin, a popular religious leader who healed the sick and founded large numbers of monasteries, nunneries, and temples. His work was continued in the next four centuries by Wei Po-yang and Ko Hung, both philosophers, and by K'ou Ch'ien-chih, who organized elaborate ceremonies and fixed the names of its multifarious deities.

Taoism has been marked by a proliferation of sects and societies. Since a brief period of state patronage during the T'ang dynasty (618–907), it has been a religion of the semiliterate.

LAO-TZE OR LAO-TZU (b. c. 604 B.C.)

The reputed founder of Taoism is usually said to have been born in 604 B.C. in Honan province, China, though confusion about his historical identity and whether there even was such a person has existed since early times. The name means simply "the old philosopher."

According to Chinese tradition, he was born as Li Erh, lived as a recluse, and became an archivist in the Chou court. He was said to have met his younger contemporary Confucius in 517 and to have rebuked him for his pride and ambition. When he retired in his old age, Lao-tze supposedly journeyed westward and was never heard from again.

Legend says that as he was about to pass out of Honan the gatekeeper asked him to write down his views of the Tao and that in response he created the Tao-teh-king, the text of which became the basis of Taoist philosophy and religion.

Scholars now date the anthology in the mid-third century. It is a remarkable collection that is thought to have been built on Indian legends, especially those about Buddha; however, the work is Chinese in texture and emphasizes ethics and politics.

Living according to Tao (literally Way or Being) involved submission to natural actions and avoidance of all formality and artificiality. It emphasized the virtues of passivity and harmony in an effort to maintain "the original simplicity of human nature." Modern religious Taoism, however, has become highly institutionalized and marked by numerous gods, the use of magic and superstition, and an emphasis on earthly blessings such as wealth and long life.

CONFUCIANISM

More a religious philosophy or ethical system than a religion in the strict sense, Confucianism is known to the Chinese as *Ju Chaio* (teachings of the scholars) and was the dominant force in Chinese thought, education, and government for 2,000 years.

Its founder was Confucius (c. 551–c. 479 B.C.), who was not so much an original thinker as a teacher and compiler of wisdom from the past. His sayings, together with those of Mencius and other disciples, have been collected in the *Wu Ching (Five Classics)*, and the *Shih Shu (Four Books)*, the latter of which includes the *Analects*—the sayings of Confucius.

The central concept of Confucian ethics is *jen*, which originally signified benevolence on the part of rulers but was broadened to encompass the supreme virtue of love and goodness: "that by which a man is a man." Confucianism teaches that man is good and possesses free will and that virtue is its own reward.

There are no churches, clergy, or creeds in Confucianism, and its founder was far more interested in making this world more human than in contemplating the supernatural. Nevertheless, he believed in Heaven—although it

was often interpreted in naturalistic terms—and encouraged the Chinese custom of ancestor-worship as a sign of gratitude and respect. Temples were built for this purpose and sacrificial rites performed in them.

From A.D. 125 to 1905 Confucianism dominated Chinese education, and members of the mandarin class of civil servants were appointed to government posts on the basis of examinations in the Confucian classics. This system had the effect of permitting many individuals from humble backgrounds to rise to prominence, and it placed a premium on the moral basis of the ruler and ruled. At the same time, its emphasis on book learning at the expense of natural science, for example, proved a liability in modern times.

Confucianism went into a period of decline following the elimination of the examination system (1905) and of the sacrificial rites (1911), but its ideas continued to play a part in the thought of some Chinese leaders, including Sun Yat-sen (1866–1925).

CONFUCIUS (551–479 B.C.)

The name of the founder of Confucianism and China's most prominent teacher and philosopher is a Latinized version of the Chinese K'ung Fu-tse.

Little reliable data is available about his life, although it is known that he was born in the feudal province of Lu, now Shantung, probably into an impoverished noble family. His father died when he was three, and he was evidently self-educated and as a young man earned his living keeping accounts.

Confucius became perhaps the most learned man of his day, but he was at heart a reformer rather than a scholar, a pragmatist rather than an intellectual. He was shocked by the constant warfare that went on between various states and by the suffering that aristocratic rulers brought upon the masses. He dedicated his life to relieving this suffering through governmental reforms, including the reduction of taxes, more humane punishments, and a system of statecraft that was based on mutual moral responsibilities between the ruler and the ruled.

His lifelong ambition was to occupy a governmental post from which he could implement his reforms, and for a short period he was apparently administrator of justice in his native province. Clashes with the nobility, however, forced him out of office and into voluntary exile.

At the age of 55, Confucius began touring neighboring states speaking to the feudal lords about his ideas. He was received as a scholar, but none of the rulers were willing to put his ideas into practice. He returned home to concentrate on teaching, in which he was successful; some of his students achieved positions of authority that Confucius himself had been unable to reach.

ESTIMATED MEMBERSHIP OF THE PRINCIPAL RELIGIONS OF THE WORLD*

SOURCE: Reprinted with permission from the 1976 BRITANNICA BOOK OF THE YEAR, copyright 1976, Encyclopaedia Britannica, Inc., Chicago, Ill.

Religions	No. Amer.[1]	So. Amer.	Europe[2]	Asia	Africa	Oceania[3]	World
Total Christian	229,006,000	164,884,000	354,894,600	87,683,000	101,144,100	17,155,000	954,766,700
Roman Catholic	131,596,500	154,067,000	174,141,000	45,285,000	32,314,500	3,200,000	540,704,000
Eastern Orthodox	4,120,000	55,000	63,900,600	1,781,000	16,442,000[4]	355,000	86,653,600
Protestant[5]	93,289,500	10,762,000	116,833,000	40,617,000	52,367,600[6]	13,600,000	327,509,100
Jewish	6,653,725	686,700	3,489,750	3,089,150	359,465	75,000	14,353,790
Muslim[7]	242,100	195,300	8,370,000	430,267,000	99,073,500	66,000	538,213,900
Zoroastrian[8]	250	—	—	229,650	480	—	230,380
Shinto[9]	60,000	92,000	—	60,004,000	—	—	60,156,000
Taoist[10]	16,000	12,000	—	30,375,700	—	—	30,403,700
Confucian[10]	96,000	85,000	30,000	185,850,700	500	42,000	186,104,300
Buddhist[11]	150,500	190,300	222,000	249,296,500	2,000	16,000	249,877,300
Hindu[12]	75,000	533,000	350,000	522,184,500	490,550	640,000	524,273,050
Totals	236,299,675	166,678,300	367,356,350	1,568,980,200	201,070,595	17,994,000	2,558,379,120

* Religious statistics are directly affected by war and persecution; e.g., recent events in Uganda, Bangladesh, and Cyprus alter the estimates of religious affiliation substantially. World refugees approximate 18,000,000. [1] Includes Central America and the West Indies. [2] Includes the U.S.S.R., in which the effect of a half century of official Marxist ideology upon religious adherence is much disputed. The same difficulty in estimating continuing religious adherence obtains in other nations with officially Marxist establishments. [3] Includes New Zealand and Australia as well as islands of the South Pacific. [4] Including Coptic Christians, chiefly found in Egypt and Ethiopia. [5] Protestant statistics outside Europe usually include "full members" only, rather than all baptized persons, and are not comparable to those of ethnic religions or churches counting all adherents. [6] Including many sects and cults of recent appearance and rapid growth. [7] The chief base of Islam is still ethnic, although some missionary work is now carried on in Europe and America. In countries where Islam is the state religion, minority religions are frequently persecuted and statistics are scarce. [8] Zoroastrians are found in Iran and India. [9] A Japanese ethnic religion, Shinto has declined markedly since the Japanese emperor gave up claim to divinity (1947). In contrast to Japanese branches of Buddhism, Shinto does not survive well among emigrants outside the homeland. Japanese religious statistics are problematical because adherents frequently are related to several different religions simultaneously. [10] Figures on China are highly speculative, since the abiding effects of the Maoist-Marxist revolution upon religion are yet to be measured. [11] Buddhism has produced several modern renewal movements which have gained adherents in Europe and America, areas not formerly ethnic-Buddhist. [12] Hinduism's strength in India has been enhanced by nationalism, and modern Hinduism has also developed renewal movements that have reached into Europe and America for converts.

THE POPES

In the list below, the name of each pope is given, with, if known, his family name and birthplace, and the dates of his pontificate. The dates of the early popes are uncertain.

St. Peter (Simon, son of Jona); Bethsaida in Galilee; c.42–c.67
St. Linus; Tuscany; c.67–c.79
St. Anacletus or St. Cletus; Rome; c.79–c.92
St. Clement I (Clement of Rome); c.92–c.101
St. Evaristus; Asia Minor; c.99–c.107
St. Alexander I; Rome; c.107–c.116
St. Sixtus I; Rome; c.116–c.125
St. Telesphorus; Greece; c.125–c.138
St. Hyginus; Greece; 138–142
St. Pius I; Venetia; 142–155
St. Anicetus; Syria; 155–166
St. Soterus or St. Soter; Campania; c.166–c.174
St. Eleutherius or St. Eleuterius; Greece; c.174–c.189
St. Victor I; Africa; c.189–c.199
St. Zephyrinus; Rome; 199–217
St. Callistus I or St. Calixtus I; Rome; c.217–c.222
St. Urban I; Rome; 222–230
St. Pontianus or St. Pontian; Rome; 230–235
St. Anterus; Greece; c.235
St. Fabian; Rome; 236–250
St. Cornelius; Rome; 251–253
St. Lucius I; Rome; 253–254
St. Stephen I; Rome; 254–257
St. Sixtus II; Greece; 257–258
St. Dionysius; 259–268
St. Felix I; Rome; 269–274
St. Eutychian or St. Eutychianus; Tuscany; 275–283
St. Caius or St. Gaius; Dalmatia; 283–296
St. Marcellinus; Rome; 296–304
St. Marcellus I; Rome; 308–309
St. Eusebius; Greece; c.309–c.310
St. Melchiades or Meltiades or Miltiades; Africa; 311–314
St. Sylvester I; Rome; 314–335
St. Marcus or St. Mark; Rome; 10 months, 336
St. Julius I; Rome; 337–352
Liberius; Rome; 352–366
St. Damasus I; Spain; 366–384
St. Siricius; Rome; 384–399
St. Anastasius I; Rome; 399–401
St. Innocent I; Latium; 401–417
St. Zozimus or St. Zosimus; Greece; 417–418
St. Boniface I; Rome; 418–422
St. Celestine I; Campania; 422–432
St. Sixtus III; Rome; 432–440
St. Leo I (the Great); Tuscany; 440–461
St. Hilary or St. Hilarius; Sardinia; 461–468
St. Simplicius; Latium; 468–483
St. Felix II; Rome; 483–492
St. Gelasius I; Africa; 492–496
Anastasius II; Rome; 496–498
St. Symmacus or St. Symmachus; Sardinia; 498–514
St. Hormisdas; Frosinone; 514–523
St. John I; Tuscany; 523–526
St. Felix III; Rome; 526–530
Boniface II; Rome; 530–532
John II; Rome; 533–535
St. Agapitus or St. Agapetus; Rome; 535–536
St. Silverius; Campania; 536–537
Vigilius; Rome; 537–555
Pelagius I; Rome; 556–561
John III; Rome; 561–574
Benedict I; Rome; 575–579
Pelagius II; Rome; 579–590
St. Gregory I (the Great); Rome; 590–604
Sabinianus or Sabinian; Tuscany; 604–606
Boniface III; Rome; 9 months, 607
St. Boniface IV; 608–615
St. Deusdedit I or St. Adeodatus I; Rome; 615–618
Boniface V; Naples; 619–c.625
Honorius I; Campania; 625–638
Severinus; Rome; 4 months, 640
John IV; Dalmatia; 640–642
Theodore I; Greece?; 642–649
St. Martin I; Umbria?; 649–655
St. Eugene I or St. Eugenius I; Rome; 654–657[a]
St. Vitalian; Latium; 657–672
Adeodatus II or Deusdedit II; Rome; 672–676
Donus I; Rome; 676–678
St. Agatho or St. Agathonus; Sicily; 678–681
St. Leo II; Sicily; 682–683
St. Benedict II; Rome; 684–685
John V; Syria; 685–686
Conon; 686–687
St. Sergius I; Palermo; 687–701
John VI; Greece; 701–705
John VII; Greece; 705–707
Sisinnius; Syria; 2 months, 708

Constantine; Syria; 708–715
St. Gregory II; Rome; 715–731
St. Gregory III; Syria; 731–741
St. Zachary or St. Zacharias; Greece; 741–752
Stephen II; Rome; 752–757
St. Paul I; Rome; 757–767
Stephen III; Sicily; 768–772
Adrian I or Hadrian I; Rome; 772–795
St. Leo III; Rome; 795–816
Stephen IV; Rome; 816–817
St. Paschal I or St. Pascal I; Rome; 817–824
Eugene II or Eugenius II; Rome; 824–827
Valentine; Rome; 2 months, 827
Gregory IV; Rome; 827–844
Sergius II; Rome; 844–847
St. Leo IV; Rome; 847–855
Benedict III; 855–858
St. Nicholas I (the Great); Rome; 858–867
Adrian II; Rome; 867–872
John VIII; Rome; 872–882
Marinus I or Martin II; Rome; 882–884
St. Adrian III; Rome; 884–885
Stephen V; Rome; 885–891
Formosus; Rome; 891–896
Boniface VI; Rome; one month, 896
Stephen VI; Rome; 896–897
Romanus; 4 months, 897
Theodore II; Rome; one month, 897
John IX; Tivoli; 898–900
Benedict IV; Rome; 900–903
Leo V; 3 months, 903
Sergius III; Rome; 904–911
Anastasius III; Rome; 911–913
Lando; Rome; 913–914
John X (John of Tossignano); Emilia-Romagna; 914–928
Leo VI; Rcme; 8 months, 928
Stephen VII; Rome; 928–931
John XI; 931–c.935
Leo VII; Rome; 936–939
Stephen VIII; Rome; 939–942
Marinus II or Martin III; Rome; 942–946
Agapitus II or Agapetus II; Rome; 946–955
John XII (Octavian); Latium; 955–964[b]
Leo VIII; Rome; 963–965[b]
Benedict V; Rome; 2 months; 964[b]
John XIII; Rome; 965–972
Benedict VI; Rome; 973–974
Benedict VII; Rome; 974–983
John XIV (Peter Canepanova); 983–984
John XV; Rome; 985–996
Gregory V (Bruno of Carinthia); Germany; 996–999
Sylvester II (Gerbert); France; 999–1003
John XVII (John Sicco); Rome; 7 months, 1003
John XVIII (Fasanus); Rome; 1003–09
Sergius IV (Peter Buccaporci); Rome; 1009–12
Benedict VIII (Theophylactus); 1012–24
John XIX (Romanus); Latium; 1024–c.32
Benedict IX (Theophylactus); 1032–44[c]
Sylvester III (John); Rome; 2 months, 1045
Benedict IX; 2 months, 1045
Gregory VI (John Gratian); Rome; 1045–46
Clement II (Suidger, Lord of Morsleben and Hornburg); Germany; 1046–47
Benedict IX; 1047–48
Damascus II (Poppo); Germany; 2 months, 1048
St. Leo IX (Bruno of Egisheim); Germany; 1048–54
Victor II (Gebhard); Germany; 1055–57
Stephen IX (Frederick); France; 1057–58
Nicholas II (Gerard); France; 1058–61
Alexander II (Anselmo da Baggio); Milan; 1061–73
St. Gregory VII (Hildebrand); Tuscany; 1073–85
Victor III (Dauferius; Desiderius); Campania; 1086–87
Urban II (Odo of Châtillon-sur-Marne); France; 1088–99
Paschal II or Pascal II (Rainerius); Latium; 1099–1118
Gelasius II (John of Gaeta); Latium; 1118–19
Callistus II or Calixtus II (Guido of Burgundy); France; 1119–24
Honorius II (Lambert Scannabecchi); Emilia-Romagna; 1124–30
Innocent II (Gregory Papareschi); Rome; 1130–43
Celestine II (Guido of Castellis); Ancona; 1143–44
Lucius II (Gerardo Caccianemici); Bologna; 1144–45
Eugene III (Bernard); Pisa; 1145–53
Anastasius IV (Conrad de Suburra); Rome; 1153–54
Adrian IV (Nicholas Breakspear); England; 1154–59
Alexander III (Roland Bandinelli); Siena; 1159–81
Lucius III (Ubaldus Allucingolus); Lucca; 1181–85
Urban III (Uberto Crivelli); Milan; 1185–87
Gregory VIII (Alberto de Morra); Benevento; 2 months, 1187
Clement III (Paolo Scolari); Rome; 1187–91
Celestine III (Giacinto Bobo); Rome; 1191–98
Innocent III (Lothar of Segni); Latium; 1198–1216
Honorius III (Cencio Savelli); Rome; 1216–27
Gregory IX (Hugo, Count of Segni); Latium; 1227–41

Celestine IV (Goffredo Castiglioni); Milan; 2 months, 1241
Innocent IV (Sinibaldo Fieschi); Genoa; 1243–54
Alexander IV (Rainaldo, Count of Segni); Latium; 1254–61
Urban IV (Jacques Pantaléon); France; 1261–64
Clement IV (Guy Fulcodi); France; 1265–68
Gregory X (Tedaldo Visconti); Emilia-Romagna; 1271–76
Innocent V (Peter of Tarentaise); Savoy; 5 months, 1276
Adrian V (Ottobono Fieschi); Genoa; 2 months, 1276
John XXI (Petrus Juliani or Petrus Hispanus); Portugal; 1276–77
Nicholas III (Giovanni Gaetano Orsini); Rome; 1277–80
Martin IV (Simon de Brie); France; 1281–85
Honorius IV (Jacobus Savelli); Rome; 1285–87
Nicholas IV (Girolamo Masci); Ascoli; 1288–92
St. Celestine V (Peter of Morrone); Abruzzi e Molise; 5 months, 1294
Boniface VIII (Benedetto Gaetani); Latium; 1294–1303
Benedict XI (Niccolo Boccasini); Venetia; 1303–04
Clement V (Bertrand de Got); France; 1305–14
John XXII (Jacques Duèse); France; 1316–34
Benedict XII (Jacques Fournier); France; 1334–42
Clement VI (Pierre Roger); France; 1342–52
Innocent VI (Etienne Aubert); France; 1352–62
Urban V (Guillaume de Grimoard); France; 1362–70
Gregory XI (Pierre Roger de Beaufort); France; 1370–78
Urban VI (Bartolomeo Prignano); Naples; 1378–89
Boniface IX (Pietro Tomacelli); Naples; 1389–1404
Innocent VII (Cosimo de' Migliorati); Abruzzi e Molise; 1404–06
Gregory XII (Angelo Correr); Venice; 1406–15
Martin V (Oddo Colonna); Abruzzi; 1417–31
Eugene IV (Gabriel Condulmaro); Venice; 1431–47
Nicholas V (Tommaso Parentucelli); Liguria; 1447–55
Callistus III or Calixtus III (Alfonso Borgia); Spain; 1455–58
Pius II (Enea Silvio Piccolomini); Siena; 1458–64
Paul II (Pietro Barbo); Venice; 1464–71
Sixtus IV (Francesco Della Rovere); Liguria; 1471–84
Innocent VIII (Giovanni Battista Cibo); Genoa; 1484–92
Alexander VI (Rodrigo Borgia); Spain; 1492–1503
Pius III (Francesco Todeschini Piccolomini); Siena; 2 months, 1503
Julius II (Giuliano Della Rovere); Liguria; 1503–13
Leo X (Giovanni de' Medici); Florence; 1513–21
Adrian VI (Adrian Florensz Dedal); Utrecht; 1522–23
Clement VII (Giulio de' Medici); Florence; 1523–34
Paul III (Alessandro Farnese); Rome; 1534–49
Julius III (Giovanni Maria Ciocchi del Monte); Rome; 1550–55
Marcellus II (Marcello Cervini); Siena; 2 months, 1555

Paul IV (Gian Pietro Carafa); Avellino; 1555–59
Pius IV (Giovanni Angelo de' Medici); Milan; 1559–65
St. Pius V (Antonio Ghislieri); Alessandria; 1556–72
Gregory XIII (Ugo Boncompagni); Bologna; 1572–85
Sixtus V (Felice Peretti); Astoli-Piceno; 1585–90
Urban VII (Giovanni Battista Castagna); Rome; one month, 1590
Gregory XIV (Niccolo Sfondrati); Milan; 1590–91
Innocent IX (Giovanni Antonio Facchinetti); Bologna; 2 months, 1591
Clement VIII (Ippolito Aldobrandini); Pesaro e Urbino, 1592–1605
Leo XI (Alessandro de' Medici); Florence; one month, 1605
Paul V (Camillo Borghese); Rome; 1605–21
Gregory XV (Alessandro Ludovisi); Bologna; 1621–23
Urban VIII (Maffeo Barberini); Florence; 1623–44
Innocent X (Giovanni Battista Pamphili); Rome; 1644–55
Alexander VII (Fabio Chigi); Siena; 1655–67
Clement IX (Giulio Rospigliosi); Tuscany; 1667–69
Clement X (Emilio Altieri); Rome; 1670–76
Innocent XI (Benedetto Odescalchi); Lombardy; 1676–89
Alexander VIII (Pietro Vito Ottoboni); Venice; 1689–91
Innocent XII (Antonio Pignatelli); Bari; 1691–1700
Clement XI (Giovanni Francesco Albani); Pesaro e Urbino; 1700–1721
Innocent XIII (Michelangelo dei Conti); Rome; 1721–24
Benedict XIII (Pietro Francesco Orsini); Bari; 1724–30
Clement XII (Lorenzo Corsini); Florence; 1730–40
Benedict XIV (Prospero Lambertini); Bologna; 1740–58
Clement XIII (Carlo Rezzonico); Venice; 1758–69
Clement XIV (Giovanni Vincenzo Antonio Ganganelli); Emilia-Romagna; 1769–74
Pius VI (Giovanni Angelo Braschi); Emilia-Romagna; 1775–99
Pius VII (Barnaba Chiaramonti); Emilia-Romagna; 1800–23
Leo XII (Annibale Della Genga); Spoleto; 1823–29
Pius VIII (Francesco Saverio Castiglioni); Ancona; 1829–30
Gregory XVI (Bartolomeo Alberto-Mauro-Cappellari); Venetia; 1831–46
Pius IX (Giovanni M. Mastai Ferretti); Ancona; 1846–78
Leo XIII (Gioacchino Pecci); Latium; 1878–1903
St. Pius X (Giuseppe Melchiorre Sarto); Treviso; 1903–14
Benedict XV (Giacomo Della Chiesa); Genoa; 1914–22
Pius XI (Achille Ratti); Milan; 1922–39
Pius XII (Eugenio Pacelli); Rome; 1939–58
John XXIII (Angelo Giuseppe Roncalli); Lombardy; 1958–63
Paul VI (Giovanni Battista Montini); Lombardy; 1963–1978
John Paul I (Albino Luciani), Venetia; 34 days, 1978
John Paul II (Karol Wojtyla); Wadowice, Poland; 1978–

ᵃ He was elected during the exile of St. Martin I, who had been banished to Crimea for his condemnation of the Monothelite heresy.
ᵇ There is confusion about the legitimacy of claims to the pontificate by Leo VIII and Benedict V. John XII was deposed on Dec. 4, 963. If his deposition was invalid, Leo was an antipope. If it was valid, Leo was the legitimate pope, and Benedict was an antipope.
ᶜ If the triple deposition of Benedict IX (in 1044, in 1046, and again in 1048) was illegitimate, Sylvester III, Gregory VI, and Clement II were antipopes.

CALENDAR OF RELIGIOUS HOLIDAYS: 1979–1980

SOURCE: Yearbook of American and Canadian Churches 1979. ⓒ copyright 1979, by the National Council of the Churches of Christ in the United States of America.

1st Sunday in Advent	Dec. 2, 1979	Ascension Day	May 15
1st Day of Hanukkah	Dec. 15	1st Day of Shavuot	May 21
Christmas	Dec. 25	Whitsunday (Pentecost)	May 25
New Year's Eve (Watch Night)	Dec. 31	Trinity Sunday	June 1
New Year's Day	Jan. 1, 1980	Children's Sunday	June 8
Twelfth Night: Epiphany Eve	Jan. 5		
Epiphany	Jan. 6	Father's Day	June 15
Week of Prayer for Christian Unity	Jan. 18 to 25	The Transfiguration	Aug. 6
(Missionary Day)		(also last Sunday after Epiphany)	
Presentation of Jesus in the Temple	Feb. 2	Labor Sunday	Aug. 31
Brotherhood Week	Feb. 17 to 24	1st Day of Rosh Hashanah	Sep. 11
The Transfiguration	Feb. 17		
Ash Wednesday	Feb. 20		
1st Sunday in Lent	Feb. 24	Yom Kippur	Sep. 20
Purim	Mar. 2	1st Day of Sukkot	Sep. 25
		Shemini Atzeret	Oct. 2
The Annunciation	Mar. 25	Simhat Torah	Oct. 3
Holy Week	Mar. 30-Apr. 5	World Communion Sunday	Oct. 5
Palm Sunday	Mar. 30		
Passion Sunday	Mar. 30		
1st Day of Passover	Apr. 1	Thanksgiving Day (Canada)	Oct. 13
Maundy Thursday	Apr. 3	Reformation Sunday	Oct. 26
Good Friday	Apr. 4	Reformation Day	Oct. 31
Easter Eve	Apr. 5	All Saint's Day	Nov. 1
Easter (Latin)	Apr. 6	All Soul's Day	Nov. 2
Easter (Orthodox)	Apr. 6		
May Fellowship Day	May 2		
National Family Week	May 4 to 11	World Community Day	Nov. 7
Rural Life Sunday	May 11	Stewardship Day	Nov. 9
(Rogation Sunday, 6th after Easter)		Bible Sunday	Nov. 23
Festival of the Christian Home	May 11	Thanksgiving Sunday (U.S.)	Nov. 23
(Mother's Day)		Thanksgiving Day (U.S.)	Nov. 27

COLLEGE OF CARDINALS

Source: 1980 Catholic Almanac. Data as of June 30, 1979.

The cardinals are bishops chosen by the pope to serve as his principal advisers in the central administration of church affairs; those under the age of 80 are electors of the pope. Collectively, they form the Sacred College of Cardinals.

The college evolved gradually during the first 11 centuries from the synods of Roman clergy. The first cardinals, in about the sixth century, were priests of the leading churches of Rome who assisted the Holy See in directing church affairs.

Name	Office or Dignity	Nationality	Created
Ahumada, Ernesto Corripio	Archbishop of Mexico City	Mexican	1979
Alfrink, Bernard	Former Archbishop of Utrecht	Dutch	1960
Antonelli, Ferdinando		Italian	1973
Aponte Martinez, Luis	Archbishop of San Juan	Puerto Rican	1973
Aramburu, Juan Carlos	Archbishop of Buenos Aires	Argentinian	1976
Arns, Paulo Evaristo	Archbishop of Sao Paolo	Brazilian	1973
Bafile, Corrado	Prefect of Sacred Congregation for Causes of Saints	Italian	1976
Baggio, Sebastiano	Prefect of Sacred Congregation for Bishops	Italian	1969
Ballestrero, Anastasio, O.C.D.	Archbishop of Turin	Italian	1979
Barbieri, Antonio, M.	Former Archbishop of Montevideo	Uruguayan	1958
Baum, William W.	Archbishop of Washington, D.C.	American	1976
Benelli, Giovanni	Archbishop of Florence	Italian	1977
Bengsch, Alfred	Archbishop-Bishop of Berlin	German	1967
Beras Rojas, Octavio Antonio	Archbishop of Santo Domingo	Dominican	1976
Bertoli, Paolo	Chamberlain of Holy Roman Church	Italian	1969
Brandao Vilela, Avelar	Archbishop of Sao Salvador	Brazilian	1973
Bueno y Monreal, Jose M.	Archbishop of Seville	Spanish	1958
Caggiano, Antonio	Former Archbishop of Buenos Aires	Argentinian	1946
Caprio, Giuseppe	President of Administration of Patrimony of the Holy See	Italian	1979
Carberry, John	Archbishop of St. Louis	American	1969
Carpino, Francesco	Referendary of Sacred Congregation of Bishops	Italian	1967
Carter, Gerald Emmett	Archbishop of Toronto	Canadian	1979
Casariego, Mario	Archbishop of Guatemala	Guatamalan	1969
Casaroli, Agostino	Secretary of State	Italian	1979
Cé, Marco	Patriarch of Venice	Italian	1979
Ciappi, Mario Luigi	Pro-Theologian of the Pontifical Household	Italian	1977
Civardi, Ernesto		Italian	1979
Cody, John P.	Archbishop of Chicago	American	1967
Colombo, Giovanni	Archbishop of Milan	Italian	1965
Confalonieri, Carlo	Dean of College of Cardinals	Italian	1958
Cooke, Terence	Archbishop of New York	American	1967
Cooray, Thomas B.	Former Archbishop of Colombo in Ceylon	Sri Lankan	1965
Cordeiro	Archbishop of Karachi	Pakistani	1973
Darmojuwono, Justin	Archbishop of Semarang	Indonesian	1967
De Araujo Sales, Eugenio	Archbishop of Rio de Janeiro	Brazilian	1969
Dearden, John	Archbishop of Detroit	American	1969
de Furstenberg, Maximilien		Dutch	1967
di Jorio, Alberto		Italian	1958
Duval, Leon-Etienne	Archbishop of Algiers	Algerian	1965
Ekandem, Dominic	Bishop of Ikot Ekpene	Nigerian	1976
Enrique y Tarancon, Vicente	Archbishop of Madrid	Spanish	1969
Etchegaray, Roger	Archbishop of Marseilles	French	1979
Felici, Pericle	Prefect Supreme Tribunal of Apostolic Signatura	Italian	1967
Flahiff, George	Archbishop of Winnipeg	Canadian	1969
Florit, Ermenegildo	Former Archbishop of Florence	Italian	1965
Freeman, James Darcy	Archbishop of Sydney	Australian	1973
Gantin, Bernardin	President of Pontifical Commission for Justice and Peace	Beninese	1977
Garrone, Gabriele M.	Prefect of the Sacred Congregation for Catholic Education	French	1967
Gonzales Martin, Marcelo	Archbishop of Toledo	Spanish	1973
Gouyon, Paul	Archbishop of Rennes	French	1969
Gray, Gordon	Archbishop of St. Andrews and Edinburgh	Scottish	1969
Guerri, Sergio	Pro-President of the Pontifical Commission for Vatican City State	Italian	1969
Guyot, Jean	Former Archbishop of Toulouse	French	1973
Hoeffner, Joseph	Archbishop of Cologne	German	1969
Hume, Basil	Archbishop of Westminster	English	1976
Jubany Arnau, Narciso	Archbishop of Barcelona	Spanish	1973
Kim Sou Hwan, Stephan	Archbishop of Seoul	Korean	1969
Knox, James	Prefect of Sacred Congregation for the Discipline of the Sacraments and Divine Worship	Australian	1973
Koenig, Franz	Archbishop of Vienna, President of Secretariat for Non-Believers	Austrian	1958
Krol, John	Archbishop of Philadelphia	American	1967
Landazuri Ricketts, Juan	Archbishop of Lima	Peruvian	1962
Leger, Paul	Former Archbishop of Montreal	Canadian	1953
Lekai, Laszlo	Archbishop of Esztergom	Hungarian	1976

Name	Office or Dignity	Nationality	Created
Lorscheider, Aloisio	Archbishop of Fortaleza	Brazilian	1976
Macharski, Franciszek	Archbishop of Krakow	Polish	1979
Malula, Joseph	Archbishop of Kinshasa	Zairean	1969
Manning, Timothy	Archbishop of Los Angeles	American	1973
Marella, Paolo	Sub-Dean of College of Cardinals; Arch-priest of Vatican Basilica	Italian	1959
Marty, François	Archbishop of Paris	French	1969
Maurer, Jose	Archbishop of Sucre	Bolivian	1967
McCann, Owan	Archbishop of Cape Town	So. African	1965
Medeiros, Humberto	Archbishop of Boston	American	1973
Miranda y Gomez, Miguel	Former Archbishop of Mexico City	Mexican	1969
Motta, Carlos Carmelo de Vasconcellos	Archbishop of Aparecida	Brazilian	1946
Mozzoni, Umberto	President of Pontifical Commission for Sancturaries of Pompei and Loreto	Italian	1973
Munoz Duque, Anibal	Archbishop of Bogota	Colombian	1973
Munoz Vega, Pablo	Archbishop of Quito	Ecuadorian	1969
Nasalli Rocca di Corneliano, Mario		Italian	1969
Nsubuga, Emmanuel	Archbishop of Kampala	Ugandan	1976
O'Boyle, Patrick	Former Archbishop of Washington	American	1967
Oddi, Silvio		Italian	1969
O'Fiaich, Tomas	Archbishop of Armagh	Irish	1979
Otunga, Maurice	Archbishop of Nairobi	Kenyan	1973
Palazzini, Pietro		Italian	1973
Pappalardo, Salvatore	Archbishop of Palermo	Italian	1973
Parecattil, Joseph	Archbishop of Ernakulam	Indian	1969
Parente, Pietro		Italian	1967
Paupini, Giuseppe	Major Penitentiary	Italian	1969
Pellegrino, Michele	Former Archbishop of Turin	Italian	1967
Philippe, Paul	Prefect of Sacred Congregation for Oriental Churches	French	1973
Picachy, Lawrence Trevor	Archbishop of Calcutta	Indian	1976
Pignedoli, Sergio	President of Secretariat for Non-Christians	Italian	1973
Pironio, Eduardo	Prefect of Sacred Congregation for Religious and Secular Institutes	Argentinian	1976
Poletti, Ugo	Vicar General of Rome	Italian	1973
Poma, Antonio	Archbishop of Bologna	Italian	1969
Primatesta, Raul	Archbishop of Cordoba	Argentinian	1973
Quintero, Jose	Archbishop of Caracas	Venezuelan	1961
Ratzinger, Joseph	Archbishop of Munich and Freising	German	1977
Razafimahatrata, Victor	Archbishop of Tananarive	Madagascan	1976
Renard, Alexandre	Archbishop of Lyons	French	1967
Ribeiro, Antonio	Patriarch of Lisbon	Portuguese	1973
Righi-Lambertini, Egano		Italian	1979
Rosales, Julio	Archbishop of Cebu	Filipino	1969
Rossi, Agnelo	Prefect of the Sacred Congregation for the Evangelization of Peoples	Brazilian	1965
Rossi, Opilio	President of Pontifical Council for Laity and Committee for the Family	Italian	1976
Roy, Maurice	Archbishop of Quebec	Canadian	1965
Rubin, Wladislaw	Secretary-General of Synod of Bishops	Polish	1979
Rugambwa, Laurean	Archbishop of Dar-es-Salaam	Tanzanian	1960
Salazar Lopez, Jose	Archbishop of Guadalajara	Mexican	1973
Samore, Antonio	Librarian and Archivist of Holy Roman Church	Italian	1967
Satowaki, Joseph Asajiro	Archbishop of Nagasaki	Japanese	1979
Scherer, Alfredo	Archbishop of Porto Alegre	Brazilian	1969
Schröffer, Joseph		German	1976
Sensi, Giuseppe M.		Italian	1976
Seper, Franjo	Prefect of Sacred Congregation for Doctrine of Faith	Yugoslavian	1965
Shehan, Lawrence	Former Archbishop of Baltimore	American	1965
Sidarouss, Stephanos Coptic	Patriarch of Alexandria	Egyptian	1965
Silva Henriquez, Raul	Archbishop of Santiago	Chilean	1962
Sin, Jaime L.	Archbishop of Manila	Filipino	1976
Siri, Giuseppe	Archbishop of Genoa	Italian	1953
Slipyj, Josyf	Archbishop of Lwow	Ukranian	1965
Suenens, Leo	Archbishop of Mechelen-Brussels	Belgian	1962
Taofinu'u, Pius	Bishop of Samoa and Tokelau	Samoan	1973
Thiandoum, Hyacinthe	Archbishop of Dakar	Senegalese	1976
Tomasek, Frantisek	Archbishop of Prague	Czech	1976
Trinh Van-Can, Joseph-Marie	Archbishop of Hanoi	Vietnamese	1979
Ursi, Corrado	Archbishop of Naples	Italian	1967
Vagnozzi, Egidio	President of the Prefecture of the Holy See's Economic Affairs	Italian	1967
Volk, Hermann	Bishop of Mainz	German	1973
Willebrands, Johannes	Archbishop of Utrecht, President of Secretariat for the Union of Churches	Dutch	1969
Wyszynski, Stefan	Archbishop of Gniezno and Warsaw	Polish	1953
Zoungrana, Paul	Archbishop of Ouagadougou	Upper Voltese	1965

U.S. RELIGIOUS BODIES

SOURCE: Yearbook of American and Canadian Churches 1978, by Constant H. Jacquet. Copyright © 1979, by the National Council of the Churches of Christ in the United States of America

This directory of American religious denominations includes only those with a membership of 50,000 or more. Membership and other data are for 1977-78 unless otherwise noted.

African Methodist Episcopal Church This church began (1787) in Philadelphia when members of St. George's Methodist Episcopal Church withdrew as a protest against color segregation. In 1816 the denomination was started, led by Rev. Richard Allen. Membership: 1,950,000; Gen. Sec., Dr. Richard A. Chappelle, Sr., P.O. Box 183, St. Louis, MO 63107

African Methodist Episcopal Zion Church The A.M.E. Zion Church is an independent body, having withdrawn (1796) from the John Street Methodist Church of New York City. Membership: 1,083,391; Gen. Sec., Herman L. Anderson, P.O. Box 1401, Charlotte, NC 28232

American Baptist Association A fellowship of regular and independent missionary Baptist churches distributed throughout the United States, with their greatest strength in the South. Their national fellowship was formed in 1905. Membership: 1,350,000; Headquarters: 4605 N. State Line Ave., Texarkana, TX 75501

American Baptist Churches in the U.S.A. Formerly known as the Northern Baptist Convention, this body of Baptist churches changed the name to American Baptist Convention at the annual meeting in Boston, May 24, 1950. In 1972 American Baptist Churches in the U.S.A. was adopted as the new name. Membership: 1,304,088; National Office: Valley Forge, PA 19481

The American Carpatho-Russian Orthodox Greek Catholic Church This body is a self-governing diocese that is in communion with the Ecumenical Patriarchate of Constantinople. In 1938 the late Patriarch Benjamin I canonized the Diocese in the name of the Orthodox Church of Christ. Membership: 100,000 (1976); Headquarters: Johnstown, PA 15906

The American Lutheran Church This body was organized during a constituting convention at Minneapolis, MN, April 22-24, 1960. It combined the following three church bodies: American Lutheran Church (ALC), The Evangelical Lutheran Church (ELC), and United Evangelical Lutheran Church (UELC). The union brought together major Lutheran church bodies of different national heritage—German (ALC), Norwegian (ELC), Danish (UELC). Headquarters of the new church were established (January 1, 1961) at Minneapolis. On Feb. 1, 1963, the Lutheran Free Church (LFC) merged with the American Lutheran Church. Membership: 2,390,076; Headquarters: 422 S. 5th St., Minneapolis, MN 55415

The Antiochian Orthodox Christian Archdiocese of North America In 1975 the Antiochian Orthodox Christian Archdiocese of New York and North America merged with the Antiochian Orthodox Archdiocese of Toledo, Ohio with dependencies in N.A. under this name. Formerly the Syrian Antiochian Orthodox Archdiocese of New York and North America, this body is a member of the Orthodox Church under the jurisdiction of the Patriarch of Antioch. Membership: 152,000; Headquarters: 358 Mountain Rd., Englewood, NJ 07631

Apostolic Overcoming Holy Church of God A Negro body incorporated (1919) in Alabama. It is evangelistic in purpose and emphasizes sanctification, holiness, and divine healing. Membership: 75,000 (1956); Sec., Mrs. Juanita Arrington, 514 10th Ave. W., Birmingham, AL 35204

Armenian Apostolic Church of America This church was under the jurisdiction of the Etchmiadzin See (now in Soviet Armenia) from 1887 to 1933, when a division occurred over the church's condition in Soviet Armenia. One group remained independent until 1957 when it came under the jurisdiction of the Holy See of Cilicia in Lebanon. Membership: 125,000 (1972); Headquarters: 138 E. 39th St., New York, NY 10016

Armenian Church of America: Diocese of the (Including Diocese of California) The American branch of the Ancient Church of Armenia was established in America in 1889. Diocesan organization is under the jurisdiction of the Holy See of Etchmiadzin, Armenia, USSR. Membership: 326,500; Headquarters: 630 Second Ave., New York, NY 10016

Assemblies of God An evangelical, missionary fellowship which grew out of the Pentecostal revivals at the turn of this century. The organization is composed of self-governing churches which constitute 55 districts and seven foreign language branches. The founding meetings of the denomination were held (1914) in Hot Springs, AR. Membership: 1,283,892; Headqarters: 1445 Boonville Ave., Springfield, MO 65802

Baptist General Conference This body has operated as a Conference since 1879; its first church was organized in 1852. It has a ministry through 752 churches and six boards of operation. Membership: 120,222; Headquarters: 1233 Central St., Evanston, IL 60201

Baptist Missionary Associaton of America A group of regular Baptist churches organized in associational capacity in Little Rock (1950) as North American Baptist Association. Name changed (1969) to Baptist Missionary Association of America. There are several state and numerous local associations of cooperating churches. In theology these churches are evangelical, missionary, fundamental, and in the main premillennial. Membership: 218,361; Rec. Sec.: Rev. Ralph Cottrell, P.O. Box 2866, Texarkana, AK 75501

Buddhist Churches of America Organized in 1914 as the Buddhist Mission of North America, this body was incorporated in 1942 under the present name and represents the Jodo Shinshu Sect of Buddhism in this country. Membership: 60,000 (1976); Headquarters: 1710 Octavia St., San Francisco, CA 94109

Bulgarian Eastern Orthodox Church (Diocese of N. & S. America and Australia) The Holy Synod of the Bulgarian Eastern Orthodox Church established for its Bulgarian Christians in North and South America and Australia an Eastern Orthodox Mission in 1907, which became (1938) Episcopate and was officially registered (1947) as a Canonical Archdiocese. Membership: 86,000 (1971); Headquarters: NY Diocese, 312 W. 101st St., New York, NY 10025

The Christian and Missionary Alliance An evangelical, evangelistic and missionary movement, organized (1887) by Rev. A.B. Simpson, in New York. It stresses "the deeper Christian life and consecration to the Lord's service." Membership: 152,841; Headquarters: 350 N. Highland Ave., Nyack, NY 10960

Christian Church (Disciples of Christ) Started on the American frontier at the beginning of the 19th century as a movement to unify Christians, this body drew its major inspiration from Thomas and Alexander Campbell in western Pennsylvania and Barton W. Stone in Kentucky. Developing separately the "Disciples," under Alexander Campbell and the "Christians," led by Stone, merged in Lexington, Ky. in 1832. Membership: 1,256,849; Headquarters: 222 S. Downey Ave., Box 1968, Indianapolis, IN 46206

Christian Churches and Churches of Christ The fellowship has its origins in the American movement to "restore the New Testament church in doctrine, ordinances and life" initiated by Thomas and Alexander Campbell, Walter Scott and Barton W. Stone in the early 1900's. Membership: 1,044,842; No general organization

The Christian Congregation, Inc. Original incorporation, March 10, 1887; revised incorporation, October 29, 1898. The New Commandment, John 13:34-35, is the bond of fellowship in creative ethical activism. Membership: 80,411; Gen. Supt.: Rev. Ora W. Eads, 804 W. Hemlock St., LaFollette, TN 37766

Christian Methodist Episcopal Church In 1870 the General Conference of the M.E. Church, South, approved the request of its colored membership for the formation of a separate ecclesiastical body, which became the Colored Methodist Episcopal Church. The Christian Methodist Episcopal Church became the official name on January 3, 1956. Membership: 466,718 (1965); Sec., Rev. N. Charles Thomas, 664 Vance Ave., Memphis, TN 38126

Christian Reformed Church in North America A group of Dutch Calvinists that dissented (1857) from the Reformed Church in America and was strengthened by later accessions from the same source and by immigration. Doctrines: The Heidelberg Catechism (1563), the Canons of Dort (1618-19), and the Belgic Confession (1561). Membership: 210,088; Office Address: 2850 Kalamazoo Ave. S.E., Grand Rapids, MI 49508

The Church of Christ, Scientist (Christian Scientists) The Church of Christ, Scientist was founded in 1879 when Mrs. Mary Baker Eddy and 15 students met and voted to "organize a church designed to commemorate the word and works of our Master, which should reinstate primitive Christianity and its lost element of healing." Membership: not given; Headquarters: Christian Science Church Center, Boston, MA 02115

The Church of God This body was inaugurated by Bishop A.J. Tomlinson, who served (1903-43) as General Overseer, and many groups of the Pentecostal and Holiness Movement stem from it. It is episcopal in administration, evangelical in doctrines of justification by faith, sanctification as a second work of grace, and of the baptism of the Holy Ghost, speaking with other tongues, miracles of healing. Membership: 75,890; Headquarters: 2504 Arrow Wood Drive, S.E., Huntsville, AL 35803

Church of God (Anderson, IN) This body is one of the largest of the groups that have taken the name "Church of God." It originated about 1880 and emphasizes Christian unity. Membership: 171,947; Headquarters: Box 2420, Anderson, IN 46011

Church of God (Cleveland, TN) America's oldest Pentecostal church began (1886) as an outgrowth of the holiness revival under the name Christian Union. Reorganized (1902) as the Holiness Church, the church adopted (1907) the name Church of God. Its doctrine is fundamental and Pentecostal; it maintains a centralized form of government and a missionary program. Membership: 377,765; Headquarters: Keith St. at 25th NW, Cleveland, TN 37311

The Church of God in Christ Organized in Arkansas in 1895 by Charles Harrison Mason and incorporated in 1897. Membership: 425,000 (1965); Headquarters: 938 Mason St., Memphis, TN 38126

The Church of God in Christ, International Organized in 1969 in Kansas City, MO, by 14 bishops of the Church of God in Christ of Memphis, TN. The doctrine is the same, but the separation came because of a disagreement over polity and governmental authority. Membership: 501,000 (1971); Headquarters: 170 Adelphi St., Brooklyn, NY 11025

The Church of God of Prophecy Organized in 1886 at Barney Creek Meeting House, Monroe Co., TN, and reorganized in 1902 at Camp Creek, NC, this church formally adopted the name Church of God, but since 1952 the name Church of God of Prophecy has been used for secular purposes and in order to avoid confusion with other similarly named organizations. Membership: 65,801 (1976); Headquarters: Bible Place, Cleveland, TN 37311

The Church of Jesus Christ of Latter-Day Saints (Mormons) was organized (April 6, 1830) at Fayette, NY, by Joseph Smith. Its members consider the Bible, Book of Mormon, Doctrine and Covenants, and the Pearl of Great Price to be the word of God. Their belief is summed up in 13 Articles of Faith written by Joseph Smith. Membership: 2,486,261; Headquarters: 50 East North Temple St., Salt Lake City, UT 84111

Church of the Brethren German pietists-anabaptists founded (1708) under Alexander Mack, Schwarzenau, Germany, entered the colonies in 1719 and settled at Germantown, PA. They have no creed other than the New Testament, hold to principles of nonviolence, temperance, and voluntarism, and emphasize religion in life. Membership: 177,534; Headquarters: Church of the Brethren General Offices, 1451 Dundee Ave., Elgin, IL 60120

Church of the Nazarene One of the larger holiness bodies, it was organized (1908) in Pilot Point, TX. It is in general accord with the early doctrines of Methodism and emphasizes entire sanctification as a second definite work of grace. Membership: 455,648; Headquarters: 6401 The Paseo, Kansas City, MO 64131

Churches of Christ This body is made up of a large group of churches, formerly reported with the Disciples of Christ but reported separately since the Religious Census (1906). They are strictly congregational and have no organization larger than the local congregation. Membership: 2,500,000

Community Churches, National Council of The result of a 1946 merger between the all-black Biennial Council of Community Churches and an association of white churches with the same name as the present body, the NCCC is a non-creedal fellowship of theologically ecumenical Protestant churches with congregational self-government. Membership: 125,000; Central Office: 89 E. Wilson Bridge Rd., Worthington, OH 43085

Congregational Christian Churches, National Association of Organized (1955) in Detroit by delegates from Congregational Christian Churches committed to continuing the Congregational way of faith and order in church life. It has no doctrinal requirements. Participation by member churches is voluntary. Membership: 95,000; Headquarters: P.O. Box 1620, Oak Creek, WI 53154

Conservative Baptist Association of America Organized (May 17, 1947) at Atlantic City, NJ, the association regards the Old and New Testaments as the divinely inspired Word of God and as infallible and of supreme authority. Each church is independent and autonomous. Membership (1976): 300,000; Headquarters: Geneva Rd., P.O. Box 66, Wheaton IL 60187

Cumberland Presbyterian Church An outgrowth of the Great Revival of 1800, the Cumberland Presbytery was organized on February 4, 1810, in Dickson County, TN, by three Presbyterian ministers, Revs. Finis Ewing, Samuel King, and Samuel McAdow. Membership: 93,200; Headquarters: Box 4149, 1978 Union Ave., Memphis, TN 38104

The Episcopal Church This body entered the colonies with the earliest settlers (Jamestown, VA, 1607) as the Church of England. It became autonomous and adopted its present name in 1789. It is an integral part of the Anglican Communion. In 1967 the General Convention adopted "The Episcopal Church" as an alternate name for the Protestant Episcopal Church in the United States. Membership: 2,818,830; Headquarters: 815 Second Ave., New York, NY 10017

ACTIVE EPISCOPAL BISHOPS IN THE U.S.

Note: MB, Missionary Bishop; Address: Right Reverend

Headquarters Staff: Presiding Bishop, John M. Allin; Exec. Vice-Pres., Milton L. Wood; Exec. for Education for Ministry, Richard B. Martin; Suffragan Bishop for the Armed Forces, Charles L. Burgreen; 815 Second Ave., New York, NY 10017

Alabama: Furman C. Stough, 521 N. 20th St., Birmingham, AL 35203

Alaska: David E. Cochran, Box 441, Fairbanks, AK 99707

Albany: Wilbur E. Hogg, 62 S. Swan St., Albany, NY 12210

Arizona: Joseph M. Harte, 110 W. Roosevelt St., Phoenix, AZ 85003

Arkansas: Christoph Keller, Jr., 300 W. 17th St., P.O. Box 6120, Little Rock, AR 72206

Atlanta: Bennett J. Sims, 2744 Peachtree Rd. NW, Atlanta, GA 30305

Bethlehem: Lloyd E. Gressle, 826 Delaware Ave., Bethlehem, PA 18015

California: C. Kilmer Myers, 1055 Taylor St., San Francisco, CA 94108

Central Florida: William H. Folwell, 324 N. Interlachen Ave., Box 790, Winter Park, FL 32789

Central Gulf Coast: George M. Murray, 3809 Old Shell Rd., Box 8395, Mobile, AL 36608

Central New York: Ned Cole, Jr., 310 Montgomery St., Syracuse, NY 13203

Central Pennsylvania: Dean T. Stevenson, 221 N. Front St., P.O. Box W, Harrisburg, PA 17108

Chicago: James W. Montgomery, 65 E. Huron St., Chicago, IL 60611

Colorado: William C. Frey, Box M, Capitol Hill Sta., Denver, CO 80218

Connecticut: Morgan Porteus, 1335 Asylum Ave., Hartford, CT 06105

Dallas: A. Donald Davies, 1630 Garrett St., Dallas, TX 75206

Delaware: William H. Clark, 2020 Tatnall St., Wilmington, DE 19802

East Carolina: Hunley A. Elebash, 305 S. 3rd St., Wilmington, NC 28401

Eastern Oregon: William B. Spofford, Jr., 1336 W. Glacier, Redmond, OR 97756

Easton: Moultrie Moore, Box 1027, Easton, MD 21601

Eau Claire: Stanley H. Atkins, 510 S. Farwell St., Eau Claire, WI 54701

Erie: Donald J. Davis, 145 W. 6th St., Erie, PA 16501

Florida: Frank S. Cerveny, 325 Market St., Jacksonville, FL 32202

Fond du Lac: William H. Brady, Box 149, Fond du Lac, WI 54935

Georgia: G. Paul Reeves, 611 E. Bay St., Savannah, GA 31401

Hawaii: Edmond L. Browning, Queen Emma Square, Honolulu, HI 96813

Idaho: Hanford L. King, Jr., Box 936, Boise, ID 83701

Indianapolis: Edward W. Jones, 1100 W. 42nd St., Indianapolis, IN 46208

Iowa: Walter C. Righter, 225 37th St., Des Moines, IA 50312

Kansas: Edward C. Turner, Bethany Pl., Topeka, KS 66612

Kentucky: David B. Reed, 421 S. 2nd St., Louisville, KY 40202

Lexington: Addison Hosea, 530 Sayre Ave., Lexington, KY 40508

Long Island: Robert Campbell Witcher, 36 Cathedral Ave., Garden City, NY 11530

Los Angeles: Robert C. Rusack, 1220 W. 4th St., Los Angeles, CA 90017

Louisiana: James B. Brown, P.O. Box 15719, New Orleans, LA 70175

Maine: Frederick B. Wolf, 143 State St., Portland, ME 04101

Maryland: David K. Leighton, Sr., 105 W. Monument St., Baltimore, MD 21230

Massachusetts: John B. Coburn, 1 Joy St., Boston, MA 02108

Michigan: H. Coleman McGehee, Jr., 4800 Woodward Ave., Detroit, MI 48201

Milwaukee: Charles T. Gaskell, 804 E. Juneau Ave., Milwaukee, WI 53202

Minnesota: Robert M. Anderson, 309 Clifton Ave., Minneapolis, MN 55403

Mississippi: Duncan M. Gray, Jr., Box 1636, Jackson, MS 39205

Missouri: William A. Jones, Jr., 1210 Locust St., St. Louis, MO 63103

Montana: Jackson E. Gilliam, 303 Horsky Block, Helena, MT 59601

Nebraska: James Daniel Warner, 200 N. 62nd St., Omaha, NB 68132

Nevada: Wesley Frensdorff, 2930 W. 7th St., Reno, NV 89503

New Hampshire: Philip A. Smith, 63 Green St., Concord, NH 03301

New Jersey: Albert W. Van Duzer, 808 W. State St., Trenton, NJ 08618

New York: Paul Moore, Jr., 1047 Amsterdam Ave., New York, NY 10025

Newark: George E. Rath, 24 Rector St., Newark, NJ 07102

North Carolina: Thomas A. Fraser, Jr., Box 17025, Raleigh, NC 27609

North Dakota: George T. Masuda, 809 8th Ave., S., Fargo, ND 58102

Northern California: John L. Thompson, Jr., Box 161268, Sacramento, CA 95816

Northern Indiana: William C.R. Sheridan, 117 N. Lafayette Blvd., South Bend, IN 46601

Northern Michigan: William A. Dimmick, 131 E. Ridge St., Marquette, MI 49855

Northwest Texas: Willis R. Henton, Box 1067, Lubbock, TX 79408

Ohio: John H. Burt, 2230 Euclid Ave., Cleveland, OH 44115

Oklahoma: Gerald N. McAllister, Box 1098, Oklahoma City, OK 73101

Olympia: Robert H. Cochrane, 1551 Tenth Ave., E., Seattle, WA 98102

Oregon: Matthew P. Bigliardi, Box 467, Portland, OR 97034

Panama and the Canal Zone: Lemuel B. Shirley (MB), P.O. Box R, Balboa, CZ

Pennsylvania: Lyman C. Ogilby, 1700 Market St., Philadelphia, PA 19103

Pittsburgh: Robert B. Appleyard, 325 Oliver Ave., Pittsburgh, PA 15222

Puerto Rico: Francisco Reus-Fróylán (MB), P.O. Box C, Saint Just, PR 00750

Quincy: Donald J. Parsons, 3601 N. North St., Peoria, IL 61604

Rhode Island: Frederick H. Belden, 275 N. Main St., Providence, RI 02903

Rio Grande: Richard M. Trelease, Jr., P.O. Box 4130, Albuquerque, NM 87106

Rochester: Robert R. Spears, Jr., 935 East Ave., Rochester, NY 14607

San Diego: Robert M. Wolterstorff, 2728 Sixth Ave., San Diego, CA 92103

San Joaquin: Victor M. Rivera, 4159 E. Dakota Ave., Fresno, CA 93726

South Carolina: Gray Temple, 1020 King St., Drawer 2127, Charleston, SC 29403

South Dakota: Walter H. Jones, P.O. Box 517, Sioux Falls, SD 57101

Southeast Florida: James L. Duncan, 525 NE 15th St., Miami, FL 33132

Southern Ohio: John M. Krumm, 412 Sycamore St., Cincinnati, OH 45202

Southern Virginia: Claude C. Vaché, 600 Talbot Hill Rd., Norfolk, VA 23505

Southwest Florida: E. Paul Hayes, P.O. Box 20899, St. Petersburg, FL 33742

Southwestern Virginia: William H. Marmion, P.O. Box 2068, Roanoke, VA 24009

Spokane: Leigh A. Wallace, Jr., 245 E. 13th Ave., Spokane, WA 99202

Springfield: Albert W. Hillestad, 821 S. 2nd St., Springfield, IL 62704

Tennessee: William E. Sanders, P.O. Box 3807, Knoxville, TN 37917

Texas: James M. Richardson, 520 San Jacinto St., Houston, TX 77002

Upper South Carolina: George M. Alexander, P.O. Box 1789, Columbia, SC 29202

Utah: E. Otis Charles, 231 E. First St. S., Salt Lake City, UT 14111

Vermont: Robert S. Kerr, Rock Point, Burlington, VT 05401

Virgin Islands: Edward M. Turner (MB), P.O. Box 1589, St. Thomas, U.S. VI 00801

Virginia: Robert B. Hall, 110 W. Franklin St., Richmond, VA 23220

Washington: John T. Walker, Episcopal Church House, Mt. St. Alban, Washington, DC 20016

West Missouri: Arthur A. Vogel, 415 W. 13th St., Kansas City, MO 64105

West Texas: Scott Field Bailey, P.O. Box 6885, San Antonio, TX 78209

West Virginia: Robert P. Atkinson, 1608 Virginia St. E., Charleston, WV 25311

Western Kansas: William Davidson, P.O. Box 1383, Salina, KS 67401

Western Massachusetts: Alexander D. Stewart, 37 Chestnut St., Springfield, MA 01103

Western Michigan: Charles E. Bennison, 2600 Vincent Ave., Kalamazoo, MI 49001

Western New York: Harold B. Robinson, 1114 Delaware Ave., Buffalo, NY 14209

Western North Carolina: William G. Weinhauer, P.O. Box 368, Black Mountain, NC 28711

Wyoming: Bob Gordon Jones, 104 S. 4th St., P.O. Box 1007, Laramie, WY 82070

The Evangelical Covenant Church of America This church has its roots in historical Christianity. It emerged in the Protestant Reformation, the Biblical instruction of the Lutheran State Church of Sweden, and the spiritual awakenings of the 19th century. The denomination was organized (1885) in Chicago; prior to 1957 it was named the Evangelical Mission Covenant Church of America. Membership: 74,060; Headquarters: 5101 N. Francisco Ave., Chicago, IL 60625

The Evangelical Free Church of America Organized in Boone, IA, in the 1880s, as the Swedish Evangelical Free Mission. The Evangelical Free Church Association merged (June 1950) with this group, and the merged body is known as The Evangelical Free Church of America. Membership: 100,000; Headquarters: 1515 E. 66th St., Minneapolis, MN 55423

Evangelical Lutheran Churches, Association of Organized in Chicago at a December 3-4, 1976, meeting of regional synods of former affiliates to the Missouri Synod and several independent congregations, the AELC is doctrinally conservative and adheres to traditionalist Lutheran creeds and emphasizes Biblical fundamentalism and evangelical service. Membership: 106,684; Temporary Headquarters: 12015 Manchester Rd., St. Louis, MO 63131

Free Methodist Church of North America This body grew out of a movement in the Genesee Conference of the Methodist Episcopal Church, about 1850, toward a more original Methodism. It was organized in 1860. Membership: 69,134; Headquarters: 901 College Ave., Winona Lake, IN 46590

Free Will Baptists This evangelical group of Baptists was organized (1727) by Paul Palmer in North Carolina. Another similar fellowship of churches (teaching the same doctrines of free grace, free will, and free salvation) was organized (June 30, 1780) in New Hampshire by Benjamin Randall. The General Conference of Free Will Baptists was organized in 1827; it continued to exist after the main body of churches merged with the Northern Baptist Convention, October 5, 1911. It was reorganized (1935) as The National Association of Free Will Baptists in Nashville, Tennessee. Membership: 216,831; National Offices: 1134 Murfreesboro Rd., Nashville, TN 37217

Friends United Meeting (The Five Years Meeting of Friends) This body was formed (1902) by 11 Yearly Meetings entering into a loose confederation. Since that time two of the original Yearly Meetings have withdrawn (Kansas and Oregon), and two American Yearly Meetings and three Yearly Meetings outside the United States have joined. It now consists of 15 Yearly Meetings. In 1965 the name was changed to Friends United Meeting. Membership: 65,384; Presiding Clerk, Walter Schutt, 101 Quaker Hill Dr., Richmond, IN 47374

The General Association of Regular Baptist Churches Founded (May 1932) in Chicago by a group of churches that had withdrawn from the Northern Baptist Convention (now the American Baptist Churches in the U.S.A.) because of doctrinal differences. Its Confession of Faith, which it requires all churches to subscribe to, is the old historic New Hampshire Confession of Faith with a premillennial ending applied to the last article. Membership: 235,918; Headquarters: 1300 N. Meacham Rd., Schaumburg, IL 60195

General Baptists (General Association of) An Arminian group of Baptists first organized (1607) by John Smyth and Thomas Helwys in England, and transplanted to the colonies in 1714. It died out along the seaboard, but was revived (1823) in the Midwest by Rev. Benoni Stinson. Membership: 72,030; Exec. Sec., Rev. Glen O. Spence, Box 537, Poplar Bluff, MO 63901

Greek Orthodox Archdiocese of North and South America Greek-speaking Orthodox Christians have parishes in the United States, Canada, and Central and South America, which are under the jurisdiction of the Ecumenical Patriarchate of Constantinople (Istanbul). Membership: 1,950,000; Headquarters: 8-10 E. 79th St., New York, NY 10021

Independent Fundamental Churches of America Organized (1930) at Cicero, IL, by representatives of various independent churches. Membership: 87,582; Headquarters: P.O. Box 250, 1860 Mannheim Rd., Westchester, IL 60153

International Church of the Foursquare Gospel An evangelistic missionary body organized (1927) by Aimee Semple McPherson. The parent church is Angelus Temple in Los Angeles, organized (1923) with mission stations and meeting places in 30 foreign countries. Membership: 89,215 (1963); Headquarters: Angelus Temple, 1100 Glendale Blvd., Los Angeles, CA 90026

Jehovah's Witnesses It is the belief of Jehovah's Witnesses that they adhere to the oldest religion on earth: the worship of Almighty God revealed in his Bible as Jehovah. All of Jehovah's Witnesses are considered to be ministers of the gospel and have no human leader. Their Yearbook shows them active (1977) in 216 countries, where there are approximately 2,223,538 such ministers preaching, teaching the people of all nations that God's word is true and that their only hope is in the Kingdom of Jehovah under Christ Jesus, which has been established to rule over Earth and replace all governments. There are 7,438 congregations and 554,018 ministers in the United States; Headquarters: 124 Columbia Heights, Brooklyn, NY 11201

Jewish Congregations Jews arrived in the colonies before 1650. The first congregation is recorded (1654) in New York City, the Shearith Israel (Remnant of Israel). Membership of Jewish congregations in the U.S.: 5,775,935

CONGREGATIONAL AND RABBINICAL ORGANIZATIONS

*Union of American Hebrew Congregations (Reform): 838 Fifth Ave., New York, NY 10021; Pres., Rabbi Alexander M. Schindler

*United Synagogue of America (Conservative): 155 Fifth Ave., New York, NY 10010; Pres., Simon Schwartz; Exec. Vice Pres., Rabbi Benjamin Kreitman

*Union of Orthodox Jewish Congregations of America: 116 E. 27th St., New York, NY 10016; Pres. Harold Jacobs; Exec. Vice Pres., Rabbi Pinchas Stolper

*Central Conference of American Rabbis (Reform): 790 Madison Ave., New York, NY 10021; Pres., Rabbi Eli Pilchik; Exec. Vice-Pres., Rabbi Joseph Glaser

Rabbinical Alliance of America (Orthodox): 156 Fifth Ave., New York, NY 10011; Pres. Rabbi David B. Hollander

*The Rabbinical Assembly (Conservative): 3080 Broadway, New York, NY 10027; Pres., Saul I. Teplitz; Exec. Vice-Pres., Rabbi Wolfe Kelman

*Rabbinical Council of America, Inc. (Orthodox): 220 Park Ave., So., New York, NY 10003; Pres., Berard Rosenweig; Exec. Vice-Pres., Rabbi Israel Klavan

Union of Orthodox Rabbis of the United States and Canada: 235 E. Broadway, New York, NY 10002; Pres., Rabbi Moshe Feinstein, Chpn., Rabbi Symcha Elberg

*Synagogue Council of America: 432 Park Ave., So., New York, NY 10016; Pres., Rabbi Saul I. Teplitz; Exec. Vice-Pres., Rabbi Henry Siegman

*Synagogue Council of America represents the organizations starred above

Lutheran Church in America This body was organized (1962) by consolidation of the American Evangelical Lutheran Church (1874); the Augustana Evangelical Lutheran Church (1860); the Finnish Evangelical Lutheran Church (1890); and the United Lutheran Church in America (1918). The new body began to function formally on January 1, 1963. Membership: 2,967,168; Headquarters: 231 Madison Ave., New York, NY 10016

The Lutheran Church–Missouri Synod This body, second largest Lutheran church in America, was organized (1847) and holds to an unwavering confessionalism coupled with a strong outreach in ministry. It is the leader in the conservative Lutheran group. Membership: 2,673,321; Headquarters: 500 N. Broadway, St. Louis, MO 63102

Mennonite Church The largest group of the Mennonites, who began arriving in the U.S. as early as 1683, settled in Germantown, PA, and derives their name from Menno Simons, their outstanding leader, b. 1496. Membership: 96,609; 528 E. Madison St., Lombard, IL 60148

Moravian Church in America (Unitas Fratrum) In 1735 Moravian missionaries of the pre-Reformation faith of John Hus came to Gerogia, in 1740 to Pennsylvania, and in 1753 to North Carolina. They established the Moravian Church, which is broadly evangelical, liturgical, with an episcopacy as a spiritual office and in form of government "conferential." NORTHERN PROVINCE: Headquarters: 69 W. Church St., P.O. Box 1245, Bethlehem, PA 18018; Membership: 32,511. SOUTHERN PROVINCE: Headquarters: 459 S. Church St., Winston-Salem, NC 27108; Membership: 20,957

National Baptist Convention of America This is the "unincorporated" body of National Baptists. Organized in 1880. Membership: 2,668,799 (1956); Corr. Sec., Albert E. Chew, 2823 N. Houston, Ft. Worth, TX 76106

National Baptist Convention, U.S.A., Inc. The older and parent convention of black Baptists, this body is to be distinguished from the National Baptist Convention of America, usually referred to as the "unincorporated" body. Membership: 5,500,000 (1958); Pres., Rev. J.H. Jackson, 405 E. 31st St., Chicago, IL 60616

National Baptist Evangelical Life and Soul Saving Assembly of U.S.A. Organized in 1921 by A.A. Banks as a charitable, educational, and evangelical organization. Membership: 57,674 (1951); Headquarters: 441-461 Monroe Ave., Detroit, MI 48226

National Primitive Baptist Convention, Inc. A group of Baptists having associations, state conventions, and a National Convention (organized 1907). Membership: 250,000; Headquarters: P.O. Box 2355, Tallahassee, FL 32304

North American Old Roman Catholic Church A body with the doctrine of the Old Catholics in right and succession of Catholic orders. Knott Missal used for Masses. Pontificale used for all Order Rights. Not under Papal jurisdiction. Membership: 60,214; Presiding Bishop: Most Rev. John E. Schweikert, 4200 N. Kedvale Ave., Chicago, IL 60641

Orthodox Church in America The Russian Orthodox Greek Catholic Church of America entered Alaska in 1792 before its purchase by the United States in 1867. Its canonical status of independence (autocephaly) was granted by its Mother Church, the Russian Orthodox Church, on April 10, 1970. Membership: 1,000,000; Sec. to the Metropolitan: Serge Troubetzkoy, P.O. Box 675, Syosset, NY 11791

Pentecostal Church of God of America, Inc. Organized (1919) at Chicago, the first convention was held in October, 1933. Membership: 110,670. Headquarters: Messenger Plaza, 211 Main St., Joplin, MO 64801

Pentecostal Holiness Church, International This body grew out of the holiness movement (1895-1900) in the South and Middle West. It is premillennial in belief, emphasizes Christian perfection as taught by John Wesley, and believes in the Pentecostal baptism with the Holy Spirit, accompanied by glossolalia. Membership: 74,108 (1972); Headquarters: P.O. Box 12609, Oklahoma City, OK 73112

Plymouth Brethren An orthodox and evangelical movement to unite Christians from various denominations which began in the British Isles in the 1820's. In the 1840's the movement divided. The smaller "Exclusive branch" stresses the interdependency of congregations. The "Open branch" stresses congregational independency. Membership: 74,000; No general organization

Polish National Catholic Church of America After a long period of dissatisfaction with Roman Cathoic administration and ideology, accompanied by a strong desire for religious freedom, this body was organized in 1897. Membership: 282,411 (1960); Headquarters: 529 E. Locust St., Scranton, PA 18505

Presbyterian Church in America This body was formed December 4-7, 1973, in Birmingham, AL, as the result of an act of separation from the Presbyterian Church in the U.S. The PCA has the intent of restoring purity of faith and practice and is committed to the Reformed Faith as set forth in the Westminster Confession and Catechisms. Membership: 73,899; Stated Clk., Rev. Morton H. Smith, Box 256, Clinton, MS 39056

Presbyterian Church in the U.S. This body is a branch of the Presbyterian Church established (1861) in separate existence. Membership: 869,693; Office of General Assembly: 341 Ponce de Leon Ave. NE, Atlanta, GA 30308

Primitive Baptists A large group of Baptists, located mainly in the South, who are opposed to all centralization and to modern missionary societies. Membership: 72,000 (1950); Headquarters: Cayce Publ. Co., S. Second St., Thornton, AR 71766

Progressive National Baptist Convention, Inc. This body held its organizational meeting at Cincinnati (1961). The first annual session was held in Philadelphia (1962). Membership: 521,692 (1967); Gen. Sec., Dr. S.S. Hodges, 3907 Georgia Ave. NW, Washington DC 20011

Reformed Church in America This body was established (1628) by the earliest Dutch settlers of New York as the Reformed Protestant Dutch Church. It is evangeli-

cal in theology, Presbyterian in government, and has 896 churches. Membership: 211,486; Headquarters: 475 Riverside Drive, New York, NY 10027

Reorganized Church of Jesus Christ of Latter Day Saints A division among the Latter-Day Saints occurred on the death (1844) of Joseph Smith, Jr. His son, Joseph Smith III, became presiding officer of this group, which has established headquarters at Independence, MO. Membership: 186,414; Headquarters: The Auditorium, P.O. Box 1059, Independence, MO 64051

The Roman Catholic Church The largest single body of Christians in the United States, the Roman Catholic Church is under the spiritual leadership of His Holiness the Pope. Its establishment in America dates back to the priests who accompanied Columbus on his second voyage to the New World. A settlement, later discontinued, was made at St. Augustine, Fla. The continuous history of this Church began (1634) at St. Mary's, in Maryland. Membership: 49,836,176. The following information has been furnished by the editor of The Official Catholic Directory for 1979, published by P.J. Kenedy & Sons, P.O. Box 729, New York, NY 10022

VISIBLE HEAD OF THE CHURCH

His Holiness the Pope, Bishop of Rome, Vicar of Jesus Christ, Successor of St. Peter, Prince of the Apostles, Supreme Pontiff of the Universal Church, Patriarch of the West, Primate of Italy, Archbishop and Metropolitan of the Roman Province and Sovereign of Vatican City. ROMAN CATHOLIC HIERARCHY: Supreme Pontiff, His Holiness Pope John Paul II. APOSTOLIC DELEGATE IN THE UNITED STATES: Most Rev. Jean Jadot, 3339 Massachusetts Ave. NW, Washington, DC 20008

BISHOPS AND ARCHBISHOPS

Archdiocese of Anchorage, Alaska–Most Rev. Francis T. Hurley; Diocese of Fairbanks, Alaska–Most Rev. Robert L. Whelan; Diocese of Juneau, Alaska–Vacant

Archdiocese of Atlanta, GA–Most Rev. Thomas A. Donnellan; Diocese of Charlotte, NC–Most Rev. Michael J. Begley; Diocese of Charleston, SC–Most Rev. Ernest L. Unterkoefler; Diocese of Raleigh, NC–Most Rev. F. Joseph Gossman; Diocese of Savannah, GA–Most Rev. Raymond W. Lessard.

Archdiocese of Baltimore, MD–Most Rev. William D. Borders; Diocese of Arlington, VA–Most Rev. Thomas J. Welsh; Diocese of Richmond, VA–Most Rev. Walter F. Sullivan; Diocese of Wheeling-Charleston, WV–Most Rev. Joseph H. Hodges; Diocese of Wilmington, DE–Most Rev. Thomas J. Mardaga.

Archdiocese of Boston, MA–His Eminence Humberto Cardinal Medeiros; Diocese of Burlington, VT–Most Rev. John A. Marshall; Diocese of Fall Riv— MA–Most Rev. Daniel A. Cronin; Diocese of Manchester, NH–Most Rev. Odore J. Gendron; Diocese of Portland, ME–Most Rev. Edward C. O'Leary; Diocese of Springfield, MA–Most Rev. Joseph F. Maguire; Diocese of Worcester, MA–Most Rev. Bernard J. Flanagan.

Archdiocese of Chicago, IL–His Eminence John Cardinal Cody; Diocese of Belleville, IL–Most Rev. William M. Cosgrove; Diocese of Joliet, IL–Most Rev. Romeo Blanchette; Diocese of Peoria, IL–Most Rev. Edward W. O'Rourke; Diocese of Rockford, IL–Most Rev. Arthur J. O'Neill; Diocese of Springfield, IL–Most Rev. Joseph A. McNicholas.

Archdiocese of Cincinnati, OH–Most Rev. Joseph L. Bernadin; Diocese of Cleveland, OH–Most Rev. James A. Hickey; Diocese of Columbus, OH–Most Rev. Edward J. Herrmann; Diocese of Steubenville, OH–Most Rev. Albert H. Ottenwell; Diocese of Toledo, OH–Most Rev. John A. Donovan; Diocese of Youngstown, OH–Most Rev. James W. Malone.

Archdiocese of Denver, CO–Most Rev. James V. Casey; Diocese of Cheyenne, WY–Most Rev. Joseph H. Hart; Diocese of Pueblo, CO–Most Rev. Charles A. Buswell.

Archdiocese of Detroit, MI–His Eminence John Cardinal Dearden; Diocese of Gaylord, MI–Most Rev. Edmund C. Szoka; Diocese of Grand Rapids, MI–Most Rev. Joseph M. Breitenbeck; Diocese of Kalamazoo, MI–Most Rev. Paul V. Donovan; Diocese of Lansing, MI–Most Rev. Kenneth J. Povish; Diocese of Marquette, MI–Most Rev. Mark F. Schmitt; Diocese of Saginaw, MI–Most Rev. Francis F. Reh.

Archdiocese of Dubuque, IA–Most Rev. James J. Byrne; Diocese of Davenport, IA–Most Rev. Gerald F. O'Keefe; Diocese of Des Moines, IA–Most Rev. Maurice J. Dingman; Diocese of Sioux City, IA–Most Rev. Frank H. Greteman.

Archdiocese of Hartford, CT–Most Rev. John F. Whealon; Diocese of Bridgeport, CT–Most Rev. Walter W. Curtis; Diocese of Norwich, CT–Most Rev. Daniel P. Reilly; Diocese of Providence, RI–Most Rev. Louis E. Gelineau.

Archdiocese of Indianapolis, IN–Most Rev. George J. Biskup; Diocese of Evansville, IN–Most Rev. Francis R. Shea; Diocese of Fort Wayne-South Bend, IN–Most Rev. William E. McManus; Diocese of Gary, IN–Most Rev. Andrew G. Grutka; Diocese of Lafayette in Indiana, IN–Most Rev. Raymond J. Gallagher.

Archdiocese of Kansas City, KS–Most Rev. Ignatius J. Strecker; Diocese of Dodge City, KS–Most Rev. Eugene J. Gerber; Diocese of Salina, KS–Most Rev. Cyril J. Vogel; Diocese of Wichita, KS–Most Rev. David M. Maloney.

Archdiocese of Los Angeles, CA–His Eminence Timothy Cardinal Manning; Diocese of Fresno, CA–Most Rev. Hugh A. Donohoe; Diocese of Monterey, CA–Most Rev. Harry A. Clinch; Diocese of Orange, CA–Most Rev. William R. Johnson; Diocese of San Bernardino, CA–Most Rev. Phillip F. Stralina; Diocese of San Diego, CA–Most Rev. Leo T. Maher.

Archdiocese of Louisville, KY–Most Rev. Thomas J. McDonough; Diocese of Covington, KY–Most Rev. Richard H. Ackerman; Diocese of Memphis, TN–Most Rev. Carroll T. Dozier; Diocese of Nashville, TN–Most Rev. James D. Niedergeses; Diocese of Owensboro, KY–Most Rev. Henry Soenneker.

Archdiocese of Miami, FL–Most Rev. Edward A. McCarthy; Diocese of Orlando, FL–Most Rev. Thomas J. Grady; Diocese of Pensacola-Tallahassee, FL–Most Rev. Rene H. Gracida; Diocese of St. Augustine, FL–Most Rev. Paul F. Tanner; Diocese of St. Petersburg, FL–Vacant

Archdiocese of Milwaukee, WI–Most Rev. Rembert G. Weakland, O.S.B.; Diocese of Green Bay, WI–Most Rev. Aloysius J. Wycislo; Diocese of La Crosse, WI–Most Rev. Frederick W. Freking; Diocese of Madison, WI–Most Rev. Cletus F. O'Donnell; Diocese of Superior, WI–Most Rev. George A. Hammes.

Archdiocese of Newark, NJ–Most Rev. Peter L. Gerety; Diocese of Camden, NJ–Most Rev. George H. Guilfoyle; Diocese of Paterson, NJ–Most Rev. Frank J. Rodimer; Diocese of Trenton, NJ–Most Rev. George W. Ahr.

Archdiocese of New Orleans, LA–Most Rev. Philip M. Hannan; Diocese of Alexandria-Shreveport, LA–Most Rev. Lawrence P. Graves; Diocese of Baton Rouge, LA–Most Rev. Joseph V. Sullivan; Diocese of Houma-Thibodaux, LA–Most Rev. Warren L. Boudreaux; Diocese of Lafayette, LA–Most Rev. Gerard L. Frey; Diocese of Birmingham, AL–Most Rev. Joseph G. Vath; Diocese of Mobile, AL–Most Rev. John L. May; Diocese of Biloxi, MS–Most Rev. Joseph Lawson Howse; Diocese of Jackson, MS–Most Rev. Joseph B. Brunini.

Archdiocese of New York, NY–His Eminence Terence Cardinal Cooke; Diocese of Albany, NY–Most Rev. Howard J. Hubbard; Diocese of Brooklyn, NY–Most Rev. Francis J. Mugavero; Diocese of Buffalo, NY–Most Rev. Edward D. Head; Diocese of Ogdensburg, NY–Most Rev. Stanislaus J. Brzana; Diocese of Rochester, NY–Most Rev. Matthew H. Clark Diocese of Rockville Centre, NY–Most Rev. John R. McGann; Diocese of Syracuse, NY–Frank J. Harrison.

Archdiocese of Oklahoma City, OK–Most Rev. Charles A. Salatka; Diocese of Little Rock, AR–Most Rev. Andrew J. McDonald; Diocese of Tulsa, OK–Most Rev. Eusebius Beltran.

Archdiocese of Omaha, NB–Most Rev. Daniel E. Sheehan; Diocese of Grand Island, NB–Most Rev. Lawrence J. McNamara; Diocese of Lincoln, NB–Most Rev. Glennon P. Flavin.

Archdiocese of Philadelphia, PA–His Eminence John Cardinal Krol; Diocese of Allentown, PA–Most Rev. Joseph McShea; Diocese of Altoona-Johnstown, PA–Most Rev. James J. Hogan; Diocese of Erie, PA–Most Rev. Alfred M. Watson; Diocese of Greensburg, PA–Most Rev. William G. Connare; Diocese of Harrisburg, PA–Most Rev. Joseph T. Daley; Diocese of Pittsburgh, PA–Most Rev. Vincent M. Leonard; Diocese of Scranton, PA–Most Rev. J. Carroll McCormick.

Archdiocese of Portland, OR–Most Rev. Cornelius M. Power; Diocese of Baker, OR–Most Rev. Thomas J. Connolly; Diocese of Boise, ID–Most Rev. Sylvester W. Treinen; Diocese of Great Falls, MT–Most Rev. Thomas J. Murphy; Diocese of Helena, MT–Most Rev. Elden F. Curtiss.

Archdiocese of St. Louis, MO–His Eminence John Cardinal Carberry; Diocese of Jefferson City, MO–Most Rev. Michael F. McAuliffe; Diocese of Kansas City-St. Joseph, MO–Most Rev. John J. Sullivan; Diocese of Springfield-Cape Girardeau, MO–Most Rev. Bernard F. Law.

Archdiocese of St. Paul and Minneapolis, MN–Most Rev. John R. Roach; Diocese of Bismarck, ND–Most Rev. Hilary B. Hacker; Diocese of Crookston, MN–Most Rev. Victor H. Balke; Diocese of Duluth, MN–Most Rev. Paul F. Anderson; Diocese of Fargo, ND–Most Rev. Justin A. Driscoll; Diocese of New Ulm, MN–Most Rev. Raymond A. Lucker; Diocese of Rapid City, SD–Most Rev. Harold J. Dimmerling; Diocese of St. Cloud, MN–Most Rev. George H. Speltz; Diocese of Sioux Falls, SD–Most Rev. Paul V. Dudley; Diocese of Winona, MN–Most Rev. Loras J. Watters.

Archdiocese of San Antonio, TX–Most Rev. Francis J. Furey; Diocese of Amarillo, TX–Most Rev. Lawrence M. DeFalco; Diocese of Austin, TX–Most Rev. Vincent M. Harris; Diocese of Beaumont, TX–Most Rev. Bernard J. Ganter; Diocese of Brownsville, TX–Most Rev. John J. Fitzpatrick; Diocese of Corpus Christi, TX–Most Rev. Thomas J. Drury; Diocese of Dallas, TX–Most Rev. Thomas Tschoepe; Diocese of Fort Worth, TX–Most Rev. John J. Cassata; Diocese of Galveston-Houston, TX–Most Rev. John L. Morkovsky; Diocese of San Angelo, TX–Most Rev. Stephen A. Leven.

Archdiocese of San Francisco, CA–Most Rev. John R. Quinn; Diocese of Agana, Guam–Most Rev. Felixberto C. Flores; Diocese of Honolulu, HI–Most Rev. John J. Scanlan; Diocese of Oakland, CA–Most Rev. John S. Cummins; Diocese of Reno-Las Vegas, NV–Most Rev. Norman F. McFarland; Diocese of Sacramento, CA–Most Rev. Alden J. Bell; Diocese of Salt Lake City, UT–Most Rev. Joseph L. Federal; Diocese of Santa Rosa, CA–Most Rev. Mark J. Hurley; Diocese of Stockton, CA–Most Rev. Merlin J. Guilfoyle.

Archdiocese of Sante Fe, NM–Most Rev. Robert F. Sanchez; Diocese of El Paso, TX–Most Rev. Patrick F. Flores; Diocese of Gallup, NM–Most Rev. Jerome J. Hastrich; Diocese of Phoenix, AZ–Most Rev. James S. Rausch; Diocese of Tucson, AZ–Most Rev. Francis J. Green.

Archdiocese of Seattle, WA–Most Rev. Raymond G. Hunthausen; Diocese of Spokane, WA–Most Rev. Lawrence H. Welsh; Diocese of Yakima, WA–Most Rev. William S. Skylstad.

Archdiocese of Washington, DC–His Eminence William Cardinal Baum; Prelature of the Virgin Islands–Most Rev. Edward J. Harper, C.SS.R.

Archeparchy (Byzantine) of Philadelphia, PA–Most Rev. Joseph M. Schmondiuk; Eparchy of St. Nicholas in Chicago, IL–Most Rev. Jaroslav Gabro; Diocese of Stamford, CT–Vacant.

Archdiocese of Pittsburgh, PA–Most Rev. Stephen Kocisko; Eparchy of Parma, OH–Most Rev. Emil Mihalik; Eparchy of Passaic, NJ–Most Rev. Michael J. Dudick.

MARONITES

Dioceses of St. Maron, Detroit, MI & Brooklyn, NY–Most Rev. Francis Zayek.

MELKITES

Exarchy for the Melkites, West Newton, MA–Most Rev. Joseph Tawil.

Russian Orthodox Church in the U.S.A., Patriarchal Parishes of the This autonomous body is the direct canonical successor of the Orthodox Catholic mission established (1793) in Alaska by the Russian Orthodox Church and is under the spiritual jurisdiction of the Patriarch of Moscow and All Russia. Membership: 51,500 (1977); Headquarters: St. Nicholas Patriarchal Cathedral, 15 E. 97th St., New York, NY 10029

The Russian Orthodox Church Outside Russia (Formerly The Russian Orthodox Church Abroad) This body was organized (1920) to unite the missions and parishes of the Russian Orthodox Church outside of Russia. The governing body was set up in Constantinople; in November 1950, it came to the United States. This church emphasizes being true to the old traditions of the Russian Church, but it does not compromise with official church leaders in Moscow "since that would amount to being under the influence and direction of a godless State." Membership: 55,000 (1955); Headquarters: 75 E. 93rd St., New York, NY 10028

The Salvation Army An international religious & charitable organization with a military government, first set up (1865) by General William Booth in England and introduced (1880) into America. Membership: 396,238; Headquarters: 120-130 W. 14th St., New York, NY 10011

Serbian Eastern Orthodox Church for the U.S.A. and Canada Membership: 65,000 (1967); Headquarters: 5701 N. Redwood Dr., Chicago, IL 60631

Seventh-day Adventists This Protestant body developed out of an interdenomination movement that appeared in the early 19th century, stressing the imminence of the Second Advent of Christ. Seventh-day Adventists were not formally organized until 1863. Taking the Bible as their sole rule of faith and practice, they are evangelical, holding to the full inspiration of the Scriptures and the deity of Christ. They believe in the personal, imminent, and premillennial return of Christ, and in the observance of the seventh day as the Sabbath. Membership: 522,317; Headquarters: 6840 Eastern Ave. NW, Washington DC 20012

Southern Baptist Convention Southern Baptists withdrew (1845) from the General Missionary Convention, when in 1845, Baptists in Northern states resolved to exclude slaveholders from missionary ranks, and formed the Southern Baptist Convention, the largest U.S. Protestant denomination. Membership: 12,917,992; Executive Committee Offices: 460 James Robertson Pkwy., Nashville, TN 37219

Syrian Orthodox Church of Antioch (Archdiocese of the U.S.A. and Canada) An archdiocese in America in a direct eclesiastical line of the Syrian Orthodox Church. Membership: 50,000 (1972); Archbishop: Mar-Athanasius Y. Samuel, 293 Hamilton Pl, Hackensack, NJ 07601

Triumph the Church and Kingdom of God in Christ (International) The Triumph Church, as this body is more commonly known, was founded in 1902. It was incorporated in Washington DC, in 1918. Membership: 54,307 (1972); Headquarters: 213 Farrington Ave., Atlanta, GA 30318

Ukrainian Orthodox Church in the U.S.A., This body was formally organized in the United States in 1919. Archbishop John Theodorovich arrived from Ukraine in 1924. Membership: 87,745 (1966); Headquarters: South Bound Brook, NJ 08880

Unitarian Universalist Association This association is the consolidated body of the former American Unitarian Association and the Universalist Church of America. The Unitarian movement arose in Congregationalism in the 18th century and produced (1825) the American Unitarian Association. In 1865 a national conference was organized. The philosophy of Universalism originated with the doctrine of universal salvation in the first century, and was brought to America in the 1700s. Universalists were first formally organized in 1793. In 1961 the Unitarian and Universalist bodies were consolidated to become the present association. The movement is non-creedal. Membership: 180,240; Pres., Dr. Paul N. Carnes; Headquarters: 25 Beacon St., Boston, MA 02108

United Church of Christ This body results from a union (1957) of the Evangelical and Reformed Church and the General Council of the Congregational Christian Churches. The union was completed (1961) when the constitution was adopted in Philadelphia. Membership: 1,785,652; Headquarters: 297 Park Ave. S., New York, NY 10010

The United Free Will Baptist Church A body that was organized in 1870. Membership: 100,000 (1952); Headquarters: Kinston College, 1000 University St., Kinston, NC 28501

The United Methodist Church The church was formed (1968) in Dallas by the union of The Methodist Church and The Evangelical United Brethren Church, which shared a common historical and spiritual heritage. The Methodist movement began in 18th-century England under John Wesley, but the Christmas Conference of 1784 in Baltimore is the date on which the organized Methodist Church was founded. It was there that Francis Asbury was elected the first bishop in this country. The Evangelical United Brethren Church was formed (1946) with the merger of the Evangelical Church and the Church of the United Brethren in Christ, both of which began in Pennsylvania in the evangelistic movement of the 18th and early 19th centuries. Membership: 9,785,534; Sec. of Gen. Conference, Dr. J.B. Holt, Perkins School of Theology, Southern Methodist University, Dallas, TX 75222

METHODIST BISHOPS IN U.S.

Allen, L. Scott, Charlotte, NC; Alton, Ralph T., Indianapolis, IN; Ammons, Edsel A., Detroit, MI; Armstrong, A. James, Aberdeen, SD; Ault, James M., Valley Forge, PA; Blackburn, Robert M., Raleigh, NC; Bryan, Monk, Lincoln, NB; Cannon, William R., Atlanta, GA; Carleton, Alsie H., Albuquerque, NM; Carroll, Edward G., Boston, MA; Choy, Wilbur W.Y., Seattle, WA; Clymer, Wayne K., Minneapolis, MN; Crutchfield, Finis A., Houston, TX; DeWitt, Jesse R., Sun Prairie, WI; Dixon, Ernest T., Topeka, KS; Finger, H. Ellis, Jr., Knoxville, TN; Golden, Charles F., Los Angeles, CA; Goodrich, Robert E., Jr., St. Louis, MO; Goodson, W. Kenneth, Richmond, VA; Hicks, Kenneth W., Little Rock, AR; Hodapp, Leroy C., Springfield, IL; Hunt, Earl G., Jr., Nashville, TN; Loder, Dwight E., Columbus, OH; Lovern, J. Chess, San Antonio, TX; Mathews, James K., Washington, DC; McDavid, Joel D., Lakeland, FL; Milhouse, Paul W., Oklahoma City, OK; Nichols, Roy C., Pittsburgh, PA; Robertson, Frank L., Louisville, KY; Sanders, Carl J., Birmingham, AL; Shamblin, J. Kenneth, New Orleans, LA; Stokes, Mack B., Jackson, MS; Stowe, W. McFerrin, Dallas, TX; Stuart, R. Marvin, San Francisco, CA; Thomas, James S., Canton, OH; Tuell, Jack M., Portland, OR; Tullis, Edward L., Columbia, SC; Ward, W. Ralph, Rye, NY; Warman, John B., Harrisburg, PA; Washburn, Paul A., Chicago, IL; Webb, Lance, Des Moines, IA; Wertz, D. Frederick, Charleston, WV; Wheatley, Melvin E., Jr., Denver, CO; White, C. Dale, Princeton, NJ; Yeakel, Joseph, Syracuse, NY

United Pentecostal Church International Pentecostal Church, Inc., and Pentecostal Assemblies of Jesus Christ merged (1945) at St. Louis. Membership: 420,000; Headquarters: 8855 Dunn Rd., Hazelwood, MO 63042

The United Presbyterian Church in the United States of America The United Presbyterian Church of North America and The Presbyterian Church in the U.S.A. united at a General Assembly in Pittsburgh, Pa. in 1958. The moderator is the presiding officer of the General Assembly, the supreme governing body.

The Presbyterian Church in the United States of America dated from the first presbytery organized (1706) in Philadelphia.

The United Presbyterian Church of North America was formed (1858) when the Associate Reformed Presbyterian Church and the Associate Presbyterian Church united. Membership: 2,561,234; Headquarters: Office of the General Assembly, 475 Riverside Dr., Rm. 1201, New York, NY 10027

The Wesleyan Church This body originated through the uniting of the Pilgrim Holiness Church (1897) and The Wesleyan Methodist Church of America (1943) at a merging conference held in June 1968. It emphasizes Scriptural truth concerning the new birth, the entire sanctification of believers, and the personal return of Christ. Membership: 97,859; Headquarters: P.O. Box 2000, Marion, IN 46952

Wisconsin Evangelical Lutheran Synod This body was organized (1850) in Wisconsin and subscribes to the confessional writings of the Lutheran Church. Membership: 401,489; Pres., Rev. Oscar Naumann, 3512 W. North Ave., Milwaukee, WI 53208

DISASTERS/CATASTROPHES

MAJOR DISASTERS

This list encompasses both natural disasters and such "technological" catastrophes as rail and aircraft crashes (50 or more deaths), shipwrecks (200 or more deaths), and mine accidents (50 or more deaths). Some other calamities that resulted in fewer fatalities are also cited because of their recentness and/or significance. The list is worldwide in scope.

Year	Type of Disaster	Place	Remarks
64 A.D.	Fire	Rome	Fire destroyed most of Rome; Christians were blamed and executed as arsonists
79 A.D.	Volcanic eruption	Pompeii and Herculaneum, Italy	Mount Vesuvius erupted, destroying both cities; more than 2,000 dead
80 A.D.	Epidemic	Rome	Anthrax killed thousands
250–265	Epidemic	Roman Empire	Bubonic plague killed thousands
444	Epidemic	Great Britain	Bubonic plague claimed thousands
526	Earthquake	Antioch, Syria	Shock results killed 250,000 (?)
542	Epidemic	Roman Empire	Bubonic plague killed tens of thousands
558	Epidemic	Europe, Asia, and Africa	Bubonic plague and smallpox pandemic killed millions; 5,000–10,000 died daily in Constantinople
681	Earthquake	Tosa, Japan	Three-square-mile area submerged
740–744	Epidemic	Constantinople	Bubonic plague killed 200,000 (?)
772	Epidemic	Chichester, England	Disease killed 34,000 (?)
856	Earthquake	Corinth, Greece	Disaster killed 45,000 (?)
869	Earthquake	Sanriku coast, Japan	Shock followed by tidal wave; thousands killed
954	Epidemic	Scotland	Bubonic plague killed 40,000 (?)
1038	Earthquake	Shansi, China	Recorded deaths: 23,000
1057	Earthquake	Chihli, China	Earthquake killed 25,000 (?)
1228	Flood	Friesland, Holland	Killed 100,000 (?)
1290	Earthquake	Chihli, China	September 27; 100,000 (?) victims
1293	Earthquake	Kamakura, Japan	May 20; 30,000 (?) lives lost
1340s	Epidemic	Asia and Europe	"The Black Death," bubonic plague pandemic, is said to have killed 25 million
1361	Earthquake	Kotyi, Japan	Thousands killed by quakes
1382–85	Epidemic	Ireland	Bubonic plague claimed thousands
1407	Epidemic	London	Bubonic plague killed 30,000 (?)
1456	Earthquake	Naples	December 5; 30,000–40,000 killed
1491	Fire	Dresden	City almost destroyed
1499–1500	Epidemic	London	Bubonic plague and other scourges killed 30,000 (?)
1528	Epidemic	Italy	July; typhus killed 21,000 (?)
1531	Earthquake	Lisbon	January 26; 30,000 (?) killed
1545	Epidemic	Cuba	Typhus killed 250,000 (?)
1556	Earthquake	Shensi Province, China	January 24; quake killed more than 800,000, the largest number of fatalities from one earthquake in recorded history
1560	Epidemic	Brazil	Smallpox killed several million
1603	Epidemic	London	Bubonic plague killed more than 30,000
1618	Epidemic	Naples	Diphtheria fatal for 8,000 (?)
1624	Fire	Oslo	City destroyed
1625	Epidemic	London	Bubonic plague claimed 35,000
1628	Epidemic	Lyons, France	Typhus killed 60,000 (?)
1631	Volcanic eruption	southern Italy	Mount Vesuvius erupted, followed by earthquake and tidal wave; more than 4,000 dead
1642	Flood	China	Fatalities: 300,000 (?)
1665	Epidemic	London	Bubonic plague killed more than 70,000
1666	Fire	London	September 2–6; "The Great Fire" destroyed about 14,000 buildings, leaving 200,000 homeless
1669	Volcanic eruption	Catania, Italy	Mt. Etna erupted, killing 20,000 (?)
1672	Epidemic	Lyons, France	Bubonic plague killed 60,000 (?)
	Epidemic	Naples	In six months bubonic plague claimed 400,000 (?)
1693	Earthquake	Catania, Italy	January 11; 60,000 died
1694	Fire	Warwick, England	Destroyed more than half of city
1703	Storm	England	November 26–27; "Great Storm" killed 8,000 (?)
	Earthquake	Tokyo	December 30; earthquake killed 200,000 (?)
1711	Epidemic	Germany and Austria	Bubonic plague; more than 500,000 fatalities
	Marine	Egg Island, Labrador	August 23; 8 English transports wrecked; 900 (?) deaths
1716	Earthquake	Algiers	Earthquake killed 20,000 (?)
1720	Epidemic	Marseilles	Bubonic plague killed 50,000–60,000
1728	Fire	Copenhagen	City nearly destroyed
1737	Cyclone	Calcutta	October 7–11; earthquake followed tornado, killing 300,000 (?)
1741	Epidemic	Cadiz, Spain	Yellow fever fatal for 10,000 (?)
1752	Fire	Moscow	Destroyed about 18,000 houses
1755	Earthquake	Lisbon	November 1; quake, fire, and tidal waves killed 60,000 (?)
1759	Earthquake	Baalbek, Lebanon	October 30; death toll: 30,000
1783	Earthquake	southern Italy and Sicily	February 5–March 28; a series of six quakes claimed 50,000 (?)
	Volcanic eruption	Iceland	June 8; Mount Skaptar erupted, killing one fifth of the population
1787	Flood	eastern India	Storm drove seas 20 miles inland; 10,000 (?) fatalities
1792	Earthquake	Hizen, Japan	Earthquake killed 15,000 (?)
	Epidemic	Egypt	Bubonic plague; 800,000 (?) victims
1793	Epidemic	Philadelphia	Yellow fever killed 5,000 (?)
1797	Earthquake	Cuzco, Peru and Quito, Ecuador	February 4; quake killed 40,000 (?)

Year	Type of Disaster	Place	Remarks
1800	Epidemic	Spain	Yellow fever claimed 80,000 (?)
1802	Epidemic	Santo Domingo	Yellow fever killed 29,000 (?) of Napoleon's soldiers
1810	Epidemic	Cadiz and Barcelona, Spain	Yellow fever fatal for 25,000 (?)
1815	Volcanic eruption	Sumbawa Island, Indonesia	April 5; Tamboro erupted, followed by whirlwinds and tidal waves; 12,000 (?) fatalities
1816–19	Epidemic	Ireland	Typhus lessened population by one fourth
1822	Earthquake	Aleppo, Syria	September 5; quake claimed 22,000 (?) victims
1826–37	Epidemic	continental Europe	Cholera pandemic killed millions; 900,000 (?) Europeans died in 1831 alone
1828	Earthquake	Echigo, Japan	December 28; quake killed 30,000 (?)
1831	Marine	off Cape May, New Jersey	July 9; immigrant vessel Lady Sherbrooke sank; 263 dead
1833	Marine	in the Atlantic between England and Quebec	May 11; Lady of the Lake struck iceberg; 215 dead
1834	Fire	London	October 16; Houses of Parliament and part of city burned
1835	Fire	New York City	December 16; 700 buildings destroyed; damage: $20 million
1840–62	Epidemic	worldwide	Cholera pandemic claimed millions
1841	Earthquake	Shinano, Japan	Quake killed 12,000 (?)
1842	Fire	Hamburg, Germany	May 4–7; much of the city destroyed; damage: $35 million
1845–48	Famine	Ireland	Potato crop failure; over 750,000 died of starvation and hundreds of thousands left the country
1846	Fire	Quebec	June 12; theater burned; 200 (?) dead
1847–48	Epidemic	London	Influenza killed 15,000 (?)
1849	Fire	St. Louis	May 17; 15 blocks of the city destroyed; damage: $3.5 million
1850	Marine	off Margate, England	March 29; Royal Adelaide wrecked; 400 (?) lost
1851–55	Epidemic	England	Tuberculosis killed an average of 51,000 a year
1852	Marine	off South Africa	February 26; British troopship Birkenhead wrecked; 454 dead
1853	Marine	off Scotland	September 29; immigrant ship Annie Jane wrecked; 348 dead
1854	Marine	in the Atlantic between London and Philadelphia	March; City of Glasgow vanished; 450 lost
	Marine	in the Atlantic near Grand Banks	September 27; U.S.S. Arctic sank; 350 (?) dead
	Marine	off New Jersey coast	November 13; immigrant ship New Era wrecked; more than 300 dead
1855	Mine	Coalfield, Virginia	Coal mine exploded; 55 dead
1856	Rail	near Philadelphia	July 17; train wrecked; 66 fatalities
	Hurricane	Ile Dernière, Louisiana	August 10–11; tropical storm destroyed the island, killing more than 400
1857	Blizzard	U.S. eastern seaboard	January 17–19; this violent storm caused widespread damage
	Marine	in the Atlantic between New York and Havana	September 12; Central America sank; 400 (?) dead
1858	Marine	in the Atlantic between Hamburg and New York City	September 13; Austria burned; 471 dead
1859	Marine	off Ireland	April 27; Pomona wrecked; 400 (?) lost
	Marine	in the Irish Sea	October 25; Royal Charter wrecked; 450 (?) dead
1860	Marine	on Lake Michigan	September 8; excursion steamer Lady Elgin and lumbership Augusta collided; 300 (?) dead
1863	Epidemic	England	Scarlet fever killed more than 30,000
	Fire	Santiago, Chile	December 8; Church of Campania burned, killing over 2,000
1863–75	Epidemic	worldwide	Cholera pandemic; in 1866 Prussia lost 120,000 (?) and Austria, 110,000
1864	Rail	near St. Hilaire, Canada	June 29; train ran through open switch; 90 (?) dead
	Rail	near Shohola, Pennsylvania	July 15; two-train collision; 65 dead
	Cyclone	Calcutta	October 1; most of city destroyed by storm; 70,000 (?) dead
1865	Marine	Memphis, Tennessee	April 27; river streamer Sultana exploded and sank; 1,400 (?) dead
1866	Fire	Portland, Maine	July 4; city almost destroyed by fire; damage: $10 million
	Fire	Quebec	October 13; about 2,500 buildings destroyed
1867	Mine	Winterpock, Virginia	April 3; coal mines exploded, killing 69
	Marine	St. Thomas, West Indies	October 29; Rhone, Wye, and many small vessels wrecked in storm; 1,000 (?) dead
1868	Earthquake	Peru and Ecuador	August 13–15; quake killed 25,000 (?); damage: $300 million
1869	Mine	Plymouth, Pennsylvania	September 6; coal mine fire killed 110
1870	Marine	off Finistère, France	September 6; English warship Captain foundered; 472 fatalities
1871	Fire	Chicago	October 8–9; 3.5 sq. miles destroyed and 250 (?) dead from "Mrs. O'Leary's cow kicking over lantern"; damage $200 million
	Fire	Michigan and Wisconsin	October 8–14; more than 1 million acres of forest consumed; 1,000 (?) dead, mostly in Peshtigo, Wis.
1872	Fire	Boston	November 9–11; more than 600 buildings burned; damage: $75 million
	Marine	in the Atlantic	About November 25; Nova Scotian Mary Celeste abandoned; 10 lost
1873	Marine	off Nova Scotia	April 1; British steamer Atlantic wrecked; 481 dead
1875	Earthquake	Venezuela and Colombia	May 16; quake killed 16,000 (?)
1876	Cyclone	Bakarganj, India	October 31; storm and subsequent wave killed 200,000 (?)
	Fire	Brooklyn, New York	December 5; Conway's Theater burned; 300 (?) dead
	Rail	Ashtabula River, Ohio	December 29; train derailed as iron bridge collapsed in snowstorm; 91 dead
1877	Fire	St. John, New Brunswick, Canada	June 20; this Canadian fire killed 100; damage: $12.5 million
1878	Epidemic	southern United States	Yellow fever claimed 14,000 (?)
	Marine	on the Thames, London	September 3; British Princess Alice sank; 700 (?) dead
1881	Typhoon	China and Indo-China	October 8; violent storm plus tidal wave killed 300,000 (?)
	Fire	Vienna	December 8; Ring Theater burned; more than 600 dead
1882	Cyclone	Bombay	June 5; storm and subsequent tidal wave killed 100,000 (?)
	Rail	near Tchery, Russia	July 13; train derailed; more than 150 dead
1883	Fire	Berdichev, Russia	January 13; theater fire killed more than 150
	Mine	Braidwood, Illinois	February 16; coal mine flooded; 69 drowned
	Earthquakes	Ischia, Tyrrhenian Sea	July 28 and August 3; these two quakes killed 2,000 (?)

Year	Type of Disaster	Place	Remarks
1883	Volcanic eruption	Sunda Strait, Indonesia	August 26–28; Krakatoa erupted, destroying two thirds of the island; 36,419 dead and many missing after the greatest eruption of modern times.
1883–94	Epidemic	worldwide	Cholera pandemic killed millions
1884	Mine	Crested Butte, Colorado	January 24; coal mine exploded; 59 dead
	Tornado	central United States	February 18–19; series of tornadoes destroyed 10,000 (?) buildings and killed 800 (?)
	Mine	Pocahontas, Virginia	March 13; coal mine explosion killed 112
	Earthquake	Colchester, England	April 22; quake destroyed the city
1886	Blizzard	central United States	January 6–13; Kansas was hardest hit; 70 (?) dead
	Earthquake	Charleston, S.C.	August 31; quake caused severe damage and killed 60
1887	Flood	Honan, China	Yellow River overflowed; more than 900,000 dead
	Fire	Paris	May 25; Opéra Comique burned, killing 200 (?)
	Rail	Chatsworth, Illinois	August 10; train wrecked by collapse of burning bridge; 81 dead
	Fire	Exeter, England	September 4; theater burned; 200 (?) dead
1888	Blizzard	U.S. eastern seaboard	March 11–14; blizzard paralyzed major cities of Northeast, and killed more than 400; damage: several million dollars
	Rail	Mud Run, Pennsylvania	October 10; locomotive hit standing train; more than 50 dead
1889	Flood	Johnstown, Pennsylvania	May 31; this legendary American deluge killed more than 2,000
1889–90	Epidemic	worldwide	Influenza pandemic affected about 40 percent of the globe's population
1891	Mine	Mount Pleasant, Pennsylvania	January 27; coal mine exploded; 109 dead
	Marine	off Gibraltar	March 17; British steamer **Utopia** sank; 574 dead
	Rail	near Basel, Switzerland	June 14; trains collided; 100 (?) dead
	Earthquake	Mino-Owari, Japan	October 28; quake killed 10,000 (?)
1892	Mine	Krebs, Oklahoma	January 7; coal mine exploded; 100 dead
1893	Hurricane	southern United States and Caribbean	August 23–30; tropical storm devastated Charleston, S.C., and Savannah, Ga.; 1,000 (?) dead
1894	Fire	Hinckley, Minnesota	September 1; more than 160,000 acres of forest burned
1895	Marine	near Gibraltar	March 14; Spanish cruiser **Reina Regenta** foundered; 400 dead
	Mine	Red Canyon, Wyoming	March 20; coal mine exploded, killing 60
1896	Tornado	St. Louis	May; storm that devastated city killed 306; damage: $13 million
	Earthquake	Sanriku coast, Japan	June; quake and tidal wave killed 27,000 (?)
	Mine	Pittston, Pennsylvania	June 28; coal mine cave-in; 58 dead
	Rail	Atlantic City, New Jersey	July 30; train wrecked; 60 dead
1898	Marine	Havana	February 15; U.S. battleship **Maine** exploded; more than 260 dead
	Marine	near Sable Island, off Nova Scotia	July 4; French **La Bourgogne** and British **Cromartyshire** collided; 560 lost
	Marine	in the Atlantic off U.S. coast	November 26; **Portland** wrecked during storm; 200 (?) dead
1898–1908	Epidemic	China and India	Bubonic plague killed 3 (?) million
1900	Fire	Hull and Ottawa, Canada	April 26; conflagration damage: $10 million
	Mine	Scofield, Utah	May 1; coal mine exploded; 200 dead
	Fire	Hoboken, New Jersey	June 30; pier burned and 300 died; damage: over $4.6 million
	Hurricane	Texas	August 27–September 15; storm was followed by storm tide that inundated Galveston Island; 6,000 (?) dead
1901	Fire	Jacksonville, Florida	May 3; damage: $10 million
1902	Volcanic eruption	Martinique, West Indies	May 8; Mont Pelée erupted, totally destroying the city of St. Pierre and killing more than 30,000
	Mine	Coal Creek, Tennessee	May 19; coal mine exploded, killing 184
	Mine	Johnstown, Pennsylvania	July 10; coal mine exploded; 112 dead
	Fire	Birmingham, Alabama	September 20; church burned; 115 dead
1903	Flood	Heppner, Oregon	Flood destroyed this town and killed more than 250
	Mine	Hanna, Wyoming	June 30; coal mine explosion and fire killed 169
	Rail	Laurel Run, Pennsylvania	December 23; train crashed into fallen timber; 75 (?) dead
	Fire	Chicago	December 30; Iroquois Theater burned; 600 (?) victims
1904	Mine	Cheswick, Pennsylvania	January 25; coal mine exploded; 179 dead
	Fire	Baltimore	February 7–8; 75 city blocks burned; damage: $85 million
	Fire	Toronto	April 19; damage: $12 million
	Marine	New York City	June 15; steamer **General Slocum** burned in East River; more than 1,000 dead
	Marine	Rockall Reef, Scotland	June 28; **Norge** wrecked; more than 600 dead
	Rail	Eden, Colorado	August 7; train wreck killed 96
	Rail	New Market, Tennessee	September 24; train wrecked; 56 dead
1905	Mine	Virginia City, Alabama	February 26; coal mine exploded; 112 dead
1906	Mine	Courrières, France	March 10; explosion fatal for 1,060
	Earthquake	San Francisco	April 18; fire followed famous 'Frisco quake, which together killed 700 (?) and left more than 250,000 homeless; damage: $524 million
	Typhoon	Hong Kong	September 19; tropical cyclone claimed 50,000 (?)
	Rail	Washington, D.C.	December 30; train wrecked; 53 dead
1907	Mine	Stuart, West Virginia	January 29; coal mine exploded; 84 dead
	Mine	Monongah, West Virginia	December 6; coal mines exploded, killing 361
	Mine	Jacobs Creek, Pennsylvania	December 19; coal mine exploded; 239 dead
	Epidemic	India	Bubonic plague killed 1.3 million
1908	Fire	Boyertown, Pennsylvania	January 13; Rhoades Opera House burned; more than 100 dead
	Fire	Collinwood, Ohio	March 4; school burned, killing more than 160
	Mine	Hanna, Wyoming	March 28; coal mine exploded; 59 lost
	Fire	Chelsea, Massachusetts	April 12; city destroyed by fire; damage: $17 million
	Mine	Marianna, Pennsylvania	November 28; coal mines exploded; 154 killed
	Earthquake	southern Italy and Sicily	December 28; quake rendered one million (?) homeless and took lives of 100,000 (?)
	Mine	Switchback, West Virginia	December 29; coal mine exploded; 50 dead
1909	Mine	Switchback, West Virginia	January 12; coal mine exploded; 67 dead
	Fire	Acapulco	February 15; Flores Theater burned; 250 (?) dead
	Hurricane	Louisiana and Mississippi	September 14–21; this tropical storm killed 350
	Mine	Cherry, Illinois	November 13; coal mine fire killed 259
1909–18	Epidemic	China and India	Bubonic plague fatal for 1.5 million (?)
1910	Mine	Primero, Colorado	January 31; coal mine exploded; 75 dead

Year	Type of Disaster	Place	Remarks
	Rail	Wellington, Washington	March 1; avalanche swept two trains into canyon; 96 dead
	Rail	Green Mountain, Iowa	March 21; train wrecked; 55 dead
	Mine	Palos, Alabama	May 5; coal mine exploded; 90 dead
	Mine	Starkville, Colorado	October 8; coal mine exploded; 56 dead
	Mine	Delagua, Colorado	November 8; coal mine explosion and fire killed 79
1910–11	Epidemic	Manchuria	Pneumonic plague killed 60,000 (?)
1911	Flood	China	Yangtze River overflowed; 100,000 (?) dead
	Fire	New York City	March 25; Triangle Shirtwaist Factory holocaust claimed 145
	Mine	Throop, Pennsylvania	April 7; coal mine burned; 72 dead
	Mine	Littleton, Alabama	April 8; coal mine exploded; 128 dead
	Mine	Briceville, Tennessee	December 9; coal mine explosion killed 84
1912	Marine	off Spain	March 5; Spanish Principe de Asturias wrecked; 500 dead
	Mine	McCurtain, Oklahoma	March 20; coal mine exploded; 73 dead
	Mine	Jed, West Virginia	March 26; coal mine exploded; 83 dead
	Marine	in the North Atlantic	April 15; "unsinkable" British Titanic struck an iceberg and sank; 1,500 (?) dead
	Marine	off Japan	September 28; Japanese Kichemaru sank; 1,000 lost
1913	Tornado	Omaha	March 23; storm fatal for 100 (?); damage: $3.5 million
	Flood	Ohio and Indiana	March 25–27; Ohio and Indiana Rivers overflowed; 700 (?) dead
	Mine	Finleyville, Pennsylvania	April 23; coal mine exploded; 96 dead
	Mine	Dawson, New Mexico	October 22; coal mine exploded, killing 263
1914	Mine	Eccles, West Virginia	April 28; coal mines exploded; 183 dead
	Marine	St. Lawrence River	May 29; Canadian Pacific Empress of Ireland collided with collier and sank; 1,024 dead
	Fire	Salem, Massachusetts	June 25–26; conflagration destroyed 1,700 (?) buildings; damage: $14 million
	Mine	Royalton, Illinois	October 27; coal mine exploded; 52 dead
1915	Earthquake	central Italy	January 13; quake killed 30,000 (?)
	Mine	Layland, West Virginia	March 2; coal mine exploded; 112 dead
	Marine	off coast of Ireland	May 7; Lusitania sank after attack by German submarine; 1,198 dead
	Rail	near Gretna, Scotland	May 22; three trains crashed; 227 killed
	Marine	Chicago River, Chicago	July 24; excursion boat Eastland capsized in port; 800–900 dead
	Epidemic	Serbia	Summer; typhus claimed 150,000 (?)
	Hurricane	Texas and Louisiana	August 5–25; tropical storm followed by storm tide; 275 (?) dead
	Hurricane	Gulf Coast	September 22–October 1; in large area of Louisiana, 90 percent of the buildings were destroyed; more than 250 dead
1916	Marine	in the Mediterranean	February 26; French cruiser Provence sank; 3,100 (?) dead
	Fire	Paris, Texas	March 21; fire destroyed 1,440 structures; damage: $11 million
	Tornado	Arkansas	June 5; series of twisters claimed 100 (?)
	Explosion	Jersey City, New Jersey	July 30; German sabotage (explosion and fire) on Black Tom Island killed 4; damage: more than $14 million
	Marine	off China	August 29; Hsin Yu sank; 1,000 (?) dead
1917	Explosion	Chester, Pennsylvania	April 10; munitions-plant blast killed 125
	Mine	Hastings, Colorado	April 27; coal mine exploded; 121 dead
	Mine	Clay, Kentucky	August 4; coal mine exploded; 62 dead
	Fire	Halifax, Nova Scotia	December 6; S.S. Mont Blanc and Belgian relief ship Imo collided and exploded, with resulting fire consuming one square mile of the city; more than 1,400 dead
	Rail	near Modane, France	December 12; troop train derailed near entrance to Mont Cenis tunnel; 550 (?) dead
1917–19	Epidemic	worldwide	Influenza pandemic killed 20–30 million
1917–21	Epidemic	Russia	Typhus killed 2.5–3 million
1918	Marine	Barbados, West Indies	March 4; U.S.S. Cyclops lost at sea; 280 fatalities
	Rail	Ivanhoe, Indiana	June 22; two trains collided; 85 dead
	Rail	near Nashville, Tennessee	July 9; head-on collision killed 100 (?)
	Marine	Tokayama Bay, Japan	July 12; Japanese battleship Kawachi exploded; 500 (?) dead
	Earthquake	Puerto Rico	October 11; sea wave followed quake, causing severe damage; 116 dead
	Fire	Minnesota and Wisconsin	October 13–15; death toll: 1,000 (?); damages from the forest fires: $100 million
	Rail	Brooklyn, New York	November 1; derailment at Malbone St. tunnel; 100 (?) dead
1919	Marine	in the Strait of Messina	January 17; French Chaonia wrecked; 460 dead
	Mine	Wilkes-Barre, Pennsylvania	June 5; coal powder explosion killed 92
	Fire	San Juan, Puerto Rico	June 20; Mayaguez Theater burned, killing 150
	Tornado	Fergus Falls, Minnesota	June 22; storm killed 59; damages: $3.5 million
	Hurricane	Florida, Louisiana, and Texas	September 2–15; cyclone killed 287
1920s	Epidemic	India	Bubonic plague claimed 2 (?) million
1920	Blizzard	New England	March 5–6; this severe snowstorm considered comparable with "Blizzard of '88"
	Earthquake	Kansu, China	December 16; quake destroyed 10 cities and killed 180,000 (?)
1921	Epidemic	India	Cholera claimed 500,000 (?)
	Marine	off Swatow, South China Sea	March 18; Hong Kong wrecked on rocks; 1,000 (?) dead
	Aircraft	near Hull, England	August 24; British dirigible ZR-2 broke in two; 62 dead
	Explosion	Oppau, Germany	September 21; ammonium nitrate blast killed 600 (?)
1922	Fire	Smyrna, Asia Minor	September 13; city almost destroyed; hundreds dead; damage: $100 million
	Mine	Spangler, Pennsylvania	November 6; coal mine exploded; 77 dead
	Mine	Dolomite, Alabama	November 22; coal mine explosion killed 90
1923	Mine	Dawson, New Mexico	February 8; coal mine exploded; 120 dead
	Mine	Kemmerer, Wyoming	August 14; coal mine exploded; 99 dead
	Earthquake	Tokyo and Yokohama	September 1; quake followed by fire destroyed most of both Japanese cities; 200,000 (?) dead
	Fire	Berkeley, California	September 17; fire destroyed more than 600 buildings; damage: $12.5 million
	Aircraft	in the Mediterranean or Sahara Desert	December 21; French dirigible Dixmude disappeared; 50 (?) lost
1924	Epidemic	India	Cholera death toll: 300,000 (?)
	Mine	Castle Gate, Utah	March 8; coal mine exploded; 171 dead

Year	Type of Disaster	Place	Remarks
1924	Mine	Benwood, West Virginia	April 28; coal mine explosion killed 119
	Tornado	Lorain and Sandusky, Ohio	June 28; twister killed 85; damage: $12 million
1925	Mine	Sullivan, Indiana	February 20; coal mine exploded; 52 dead
	Tornado	Missouri, Illinois, and Indiana	March 18; tornado killed 689; damage: $17 million
	Mine	Coal Glen, North Carolina	May 27; coal mine exploded; 53 dead
	Rail	Hackettstown, New Jersey	June 16; train derailed at highway crossing; 50 dead
	Mine	Acemar, Alabama	December 10; coal mine exploded; 53 dead
1926–30	Epidemic	India	Smallpox claimed 423,000 (?)
1926	Mine	Wilburton, Oklahoma	January 13; coal mine explosion killed 91
	Hurricane	Florida and Alabama	September 11–22; 243 dead
1927	Mine	Everettville, West Virginia	April 30; coal mine exploded; 97 dead
	Tornado	Arkansas and Missouri	May 9; 92 dead from storm
	Tornado	St. Louis	September 29; death toll: 90; damage: $40 million
1928	Flood	Santa Paula, California	March 13; St. Francis Dam collapsed; 450 dead
	Mine	Mather, Pennsylvania	May 19; coal mine explosion killed 195
	Flood	southern Florida	September 6–20; hurricane caused Lake Okeechobee to overflow; 1,836 lives lost
	Marine	off the Virginia Capes	November 12; British steamer Vestris sank; 110 (?) dead
1929	Fire	Cleveland	May 15; hospital burned; 125 suffocations from poisonous fumes
	Mine	McAlester, Oklahoma	December 17; coal mine exploded; 61 dead
1930	Fire	Columbus	April 21; Ohio State Penitentiary burned, killing 317 convicts
	Earthquake	Naples	July 23–25; shock results killed 1,883 and injured 10,000 (?)
	Hurricane	Dominican Republic	September 3; storm fatalities: 2,000 (?)
	Aircraft	Beauvais, France	October 5; British dirigible R-101 crashed; 47 dead
	Mine	Millfield, Ohio	November 5; coal mine exploded; 82 dead
1931	Flood	Yangtze River, China	July–August; flood waters of Yangtze leave over 2 million homeless and 140,000 dead
1932	Tornado	southern United States	March 21–22; tornadoes hit five states; at least 362 dead
	Mine	Moweaqua, Illinois	December 23; coal mine exploded; 54 dead
	Earthquake	Kansu, China	December 26; quake killed 70,000 (?)
1933	Earthquake	Sanriku coast, Japan	March 3; quake killed more than 2,500
	Earthquake	Long Beach, California	March 10; quake claimed 115 lives; damage: $40 million
	Aircraft	New Jersey coast	April 4; U.S. dirigible Akron II crashed; 73 dead
1934	Fire	Hakodate, Japan	March 22; fire destroyed city; 1,500 dead (?)
	Marine	off New Jersey	September 8; luxury liner Morro Castle burned; 134 dead
	Typhoon	Honshu, Japan	September 21; storm killed 4,000 (?); damage: $50 million
	Mine	Wrexham, Wales	September 22; coal mine exploded; 265 dead
1935	Epidemic	Uganda	Bubonic plague killed 2,000 (?)
	Earthquake	India and Pakistan	May 31; quake killed more than 50,000
	Hurricane	southern Florida	August 29–September 10; storm killed 408; damage: up to $50 million
	Hurricane	Haiti	October 22; storm and flood fatalities: more than 2,000
1936	Tornado	southern United States	April 5–6; series of twisters, mostly in Mississippi and Georgia, killed 455; damage: $21 million
1937	Fire	Antung, Manchuria	February 13; theater burned, killing 658
	Explosion	New London, Texas	March 19; natural gas explosion destroyed school; more than 400 dead
	Aircraft	Lakehurst, New Jersey	May 6; German zeppelin Hindenburg exploded; 36 dead
	Rail	near Patna, India	July 16; Delhi-Calcutta express derailed; 107 dead
1938	Aircraft	Bogotá, Colombia	July 24; military stunt plane crashed into grandstand, killing 53
	Hurricane	Long Island and lower New England	September 10–22; this storm killed 600; damage: $50–500 million
	Rail	near Kishinev, Rumania	December 25; two-train collision killed 100 (?)
1939	Earthquake	Chile	January 24; quake killed 40,000 (?)
	Marine	off New Hampshire	May 23; U.S. submarine Squalus sank; 26 dead
	Marine	in the Irish Sea	June 1; British submarine Thetis sank; 99 lost
	Marine	off Indochina	June 15; French submarine Phenix sank; 63 dead
	Flood	Tientsin, China	July–August; millions rendered homeless and thousands dead
	Fire	Langunillas, Venezuela	November 14; oil town built over Lake Maracaibo destroyed
	Rail	near Magdeburg, Germany	December 22; two trains collided; 132 dead
	Rail	near Freidrichshafen, Germany	December 22; train wrecked; 99 dead
	Earthquake	Anatolia, Turkey	December 27; series of shocks and subsequent floods devastated about 60,000 square miles; more than 30,000 dead
1940	Mine	Bartley, West Virginia	January 10; coal mine exploded; 91 dead
	Rail	Osaka, Japan	January 29; two trains collided; 200 (?) dead
	Mine	St. Clairsville, Ohio	March 16; coal mine exploded; 72 dead
	Mine	Portage, Pennsylvania	July 15; coal mine explosion killed 63
	Blizzard	U.S. Northeast and Midwest	November 11–12; one of the most destructive snowstorms ever caused 144 deaths; damage: $6 million
1941	Marine	off Maine	June 16; U.S. submarine O-9 sank in test dive; 33 fatalities
1942	Marine	New York City	February 9; French liner Normandie burned at pier; 1 dead
	Tornado	U.S. South and Midwest	March 17; twister killed 111
	Mine	Honkeiko Colliery, Manchuria	April 26; worst mine disaster in history; 1,549 dead
	Mine	Osage, West Virginia	May 12; coal mine exploded; 56 dead
	Marine	off England	October 2; British Curacao rammed and sunk by Queen Mary; more than 330 dead
	Cyclone	Bengal, India	October 16; storm fatalities: 40,000 (?)
	Fire	Boston	November 28; Cocoanut Grove night club burned; 492 dead
1943	Mine	Red Lodge, Montana	February 27; coal mine exploded; 74 dead
	Rail	Philadelphia	September 6; "Congressional Limited" derailed; 80 dead
	Rail	near Lumberton, North Carolina	December 16; two trains collided; 72 dead
1944	Earthquake	San Juan, Argentina	January 15; quake killed 5,000 (?)
	Rail	Leon Province, Spain	January 16; train wrecked inside tunnel; 500–800 dead
	Rail	near Salerno, Italy	March 2; train stalled in tunnel, suffocating 526
	Mine	Belmont, Ohio	July 5; coal mine fire claimed 66
	Fire	Hartford, Connecticut	July 6; circus "big top" burned, killing 168
	Marine	Port Chicago, California	July 18; two ammunition ships exploded; 322 dead
	Aircraft	Freckleton, England	August 23; U.S. bomber crashed into school; more than 70 dead

Year	Type of Disaster	Place	Remarks
	Hurricane	U.S. eastern seaboard	September 9–16; storm killed 46; damage: $50–500 million
	Fire	Cleveland	October 20; liquid gas tanks exploded, setting fire to 50-block area and killing 130; damage: $10 million
	Rail	near Ogden, Utah	December 31; two sections of "Pacific Limited" collided; 50 dead
1945	Marine	off Danzig	January 30; German passengership **Wilhelm Gustloff** loaded with refugees and hospital ship **General Steuben** sunk by Soviet submarine; 6,800 lives lost in world's largest marine disaster
	Rail	Cazadero, Mexico	February 1; train struck from rear by freight train; 100 (?) dead
	Marine	Bari, Italy	April 9; U.S.S. **Liberty** exploded in harbor; 360 dead
	Tornado	Oklahoma and Arkansas	April 12; twister killed 102; damage: $4 million
	Aircraft	New York City	July 28; U.S. bomber crashed into Empire State Building; 13 dead
1946	Rail	near Aracaju, Brazil	March 20; train wreck killed 185
	Earthquake	Dutch Harbor, Alaska	April 1; subterranean quake caused tidal waves that hit Hawaiian Islands, Aleutians, and the West Coast; 173 dead in Hawaii alone and damage there $25 million
	Fire	Atlanta	December 7; Winecoff Hotel burned; 119 dead
	Aircraft	near Shanghai	December 25; three China Air Transport planes crashed, separately, in fog; at least 71 dead
1947	Marine	off Athens	January 19; Greek ship **Himera** struck mine and sank; 392 lost
	Aircraft	Bogotá, Colombia	February 15; Avianca DC-4 crashed into Mount Tablazo; 53 fatalities
	Mine	Centralia, Illinois	March 25; coal mine exploded; 111 dead
	Tornado	Texas, Oklahoma, and Kansas	April 9; twister killed 167; damage: $10 million
	Explosion	Texas City, Texas	April 16; S.S. **Grandcamp** blew up, destroying most of city and killing 561; damage: $67 million
	Aircraft	Leesburg, Virginia	June 13; Pennsylvania Central DC-4 crashed; 50 dead
	Explosion	Cadiz, Spain	August 18; dockyard exploded; 147 dead
	Epidemic	Egypt	September–December; cholera killed 10,276
	Hurricane	Florida and Gulf coasts	September 4–21; storm fatalities: 51; damage: $50–500 million
	Typhoon	Honshu, Japan	September 15–19; storm plus floods killed 2,000 (?)
	Aircraft	Bryce Canyon, Utah	October 24; United DC-6 crashed into hillside; 52 dead
	Fire	Bar Harbor, Maine	October 25; forest fire on Mount Desert Island burned large part of famous summer resort; damage: $30 million
1948	Marine	in the Inland Sea, Japan	January 28; freighter **Joo Maru** struck mine and sank; 250 dead
	Earthquake	Fukui, Japan	June 28; quake destroyed most of city; more than 5,000 dead
	Explosion	Ludwigshafen, Germany	July 28; blast and fire at I. G. Farben chemical works killed more than 200; damage: $6 million
	Aircraft	French West Africa	August 1; Air France plane disappeared on flight from Martinique; 53 lost
	Explosion	Hong Kong	September 22; chemical warehouse blast and fire killed 135
1949	Marine	off southern China	January 27; Chinese **Taiping** and collier collided and sank; more than 600 dead
	Fire	Effingham, Illinois	April 5; St. Anthony's Hospital burned; 74 dead
	Aircraft	Puerto Rico	June 7; U.S. Strato Freight crashed into water; 54 dead
	Earthquake	Ecuador	August 5; shock razed 50 towns; 100,000 (?) homeless and 6,000 (?) dead; damage: $20 million
	Marine	Toronto	September 17; Canadian **Noronic** burned at pier; 130 (?) dead
	Rail	Nowy Dwor, Poland	October 22; Danzig-Warsaw express derailed; 200 (?) dead
	Cyclone	southeastern India	October 27; storm fatalities: 1,000 (?)
	Typhoon	Philippine Islands	October 31–November 2; storm killed 1,000 (?)
	Aircraft	Washington, D.C.	November 1; Bolivian fighter plane and Eastern DC-4 collided over airport; 55 dead
1950	Marine	in the Thames estuary, England	January 12; British submarine **Truculent** rammed by Swedish tanker; more than 60 dead
	Aircraft	near Cardiff, Wales	March 12; British Avro Tudor V crashed; 80 dead
	Rail	near Tangua, Brazil	April 6; train plunged into Indios River; 108 dead
	Rail	near Jasidih, India	May 7; Punjab mail train crash killed 81
	Fire	Rimouski, Quebec	May 7; blaze left 2,000 homeless; damage: $12 million
	Trolley	Chicago	May 25; trolley and gas truck collided; 34 dead
	Aircraft	in Lake Michigan	June 24; Northwest DC-4 crash claimed 58
	Flood	Anhwei Province, China	August 14; cataclysm inundated more than five million acres, leaving 10 million homeless and killing 500
	Earthquake	Assam, India	August 15; quake killed 1,500 (?) and devastated area of about 30,000 miles
	Aircraft	Cairo	August 31; TWA Constellation crashed; 55 dead
	Hurricane	Florida	October 13–19; Miami struck and four dead; damage: $5–50 million
	Aircraft	Grenoble, France	November 13; Canadian Curtiss-Reid DC-4 crashed; 58 dead
	Rail	Richmond Hill, New York	November 22; commuter train rammed by another; 79 dead
	Blizzard	U.S. Northeast	November 25; this storm killed 100 (?)
1951	Tornado	Comoro Islands	January 4; more than 500 victims
	Rail	Woodbridge, New Jersey	February 6; commuter train plunged through overpass; 84 dead
	Aircraft	in the North Atlantic	March 23; U.S.A.F. plane wreckage found off Ireland; 53 lost
	Marine	off Isle of Wight	April 16; British submarine **Affray** sank; 75 dead
	Earthquake	Jacuapa, El Salvador	May 6; fatalities numbered more than 1,000
	Mine	Easington, England	May 29; coal mine explosion killed 81
	Rail	Nova Iguaca, Brazil	June 7; train and gasoline truck collided; 54 dead
	Aircraft	Rocky Mountain National Park, Colorado	June 30; United DC-6 crashed; 50 dead
	Flood	Kansas and Missouri	July 2–19; the most severe floods in American history killed 41 and left 200,000 homeless; damage: $1 billion
	Aircraft	near Decoto, California	August 24; United DC-6B crashed; 50 dead
	Flood	Manchuria	August 28; deluge caused extensive damage; 5,000 (?) dead or missing
	Typhoon	Philippine Islands	December 9–10; fatalities: 724
	Aircraft	Elizabeth, New Jersey	December 16; nonscheduled plane plunged into river after take-off from Newark Airport; 56 dead
	Mine	West Frankfort, Illinois	December 21; coal mine exploded; 119 dead

Year	Type of Disaster	Place	Remarks
1952	Rail	near Rio de Janeiro	March 4; two trains crashed; 119 dead
	Tornado	Mississippi Valley	March 21–22; twisters killed 229
	Aircraft	Moscow	March 27; two Soviet planes collided over Tula Airport; 70 dead
	Aircraft	San Juan, Puerto Rico	April 11; Pan Am DC–4 crashed; 52 dead
	Marine	in the Atlantic	April 26; U.S. destroyer-minesweeper **Hobson** and aircraft carrier **Wasp** collided; Hobson sank; 176 dead
	Aircraft	northern Brazil	April 29; Pan Am Stratocruiser crashed in jungle; 50 dead
	Rail	near Rzepin, Poland	July 9; train wrecked; 160 dead
	Earthquake	southern California	July 21; quake killed 14; damage: $60 million
	Bus	near Waco, Texas	August 4; two buses collided; 28 dead
	Rail	Harrow-Wealdstone, England	October 8; two trains collided with a third; 112 dead
	Typhoon	Luzon, Philippine Islands	October 22; this tropical cyclone left 1,000 (?) dead or missing; damage: $50 million
	Aircraft	near Elmendorf A.F.B., Alaska	November 23; U.S.A.F. plane crashed; 52 dead
	Aircraft	in Moses Lake, Washington	December 20; after takeoff, U.S.A.F. plane crashed and caught fire; 87 dead
1953	Marine	off Pusan, South Korea	January 9; South Korean liner sank in heavy seas; 249 dead
	Flood	northern Europe	January 31–February 1; floods devastated North Sea coastal areas; more than 2,000 dead
	Trolley	Mexico City	February 21; two trolley cars collided; more than 60 dead
	Earthquake	eastern Iran	February 22; town of Trud destroyed; 1,000 dead
	Earthquake	northwestern Turkey	March 18; quake killed 1,200 (?)
	Tornado	Waco, Texas	May 11; series of twisters killed 114
	Tornado	Michigan and Ohio	June 8; tornado series killed 142
	Tornado	central Massachusetts	June 9; storm killed 92; damage: $52 million
	Aircraft	near Tokyo	June 18; U.S.A.F. plane crashed; 129 fatalities
	Aircraft	off Wake Island	July 12; nonscheduled plane crashed in Pacific, killing 58
	Marine	near New Caledonia	August 1; French **Monique** vanished in South Pacific; 120 lost
	Tornado	Vicksburg, Mississippi	December 5; tornado killed 38; damage: $25 million
	Rail	near Waiouru, New Zealand	December 24; Wellington-Auckland express plunged into stream; 155 dead
1954	Rail	near Karachi, Pakistan	January 21; mail express wrecked; 60 dead
	Rail	near Seoul, South Korea	January 31; train wreck killed 56
	Marine	off Quonset Point, Rhode Island	May 26; U.S. aircraft carrier **Bennington** exploded and burned; 103 dead
	Flood	Kazvin District, Iran	August 1; flash flood killed 2,000 (?)
	Hurricane	U.S. eastern seaboard	August 25–31; storm fatalities numbered 60; damage: $50–500 million
	Rail	Negros Island, Philippines	September 2; train wrecked; 55 dead
	Earthquake	Orléansville, Algeria	September 9–12; quake killed 1,600 (?)
	Marine	in Tsugaru Strait, Japan	September 26; Japanese ferry **Toya Maru** sank; 1,172 dead
	Rail	east of Hyderabad, India	September 28; express train plunged from bridge; 137 dead
	Hurricane	U.S. eastern seaboard	October 5–18; this hurricane took 95 lives; damage: $50–500 million
1955	Fire	Yokohama, Japan	February 16–17; home for aged burned, killing 100 (?)
	Aircraft	Honolulu	March 22; U.S. Navy plane hit cliff; 66 dead
	Rail	near Guadalajara, Mexico	April 3; train plunged into canyon; 300 (?) dead
	Tornado	Kansas, Missouri, Oklahoma, and Texas	May 25; series of tornadoes killed 115
	Hurricane	U.S. eastern seaboard	August 7–21; storm and floods, which took 184 lives, caused more damage than any series of storms on record in America: between $500 million and $5 billion
	Aircraft	near Edelweiler, West Germany	August 11; two U.S.A.F. planes collided in midair; 66 dead
	Hurricane	Mexico and West Indies	September 22–28; more than 750 lives lost; extensive damage
	Flood	Pakistan and India	October 4; claiming more than 1,700 lives, this deluge devastated about 5.6 million crop acres valued at $63 million
	Aircraft	near Laramie, Wyoming	October 6; United DC–4 crashed in mountains; 66 dead
1956	Aircraft	Malta	February 18; British Lancaster bomber crashed; 50 dead
	Aircraft	near Cairo	February 20; Transport Aeriens Intercontinentaux DC–6B crashed; 52 dead
	Earthquake	northern Afghanistan	June 10–17; series of shocks caused 2,000 (?) deaths
	Aircraft	in the Atlantic, south of New York City	June 20; Venezuelan Super-Constellation crashed; 74 dead
	Aircraft	Grand Canyon, Arizona	June 30; TWA Super-Constellation and United DC–7 collided in midair; 128 dead
	Marine	off Massachusetts	July 25; Italian **Andrea Doria** and Swedish **Stockholm** collided in fog, sinking the **Doria**; 50 (?) dead or missing
	Typhoon	Chekiang, China	August 1; storm and subsequent floods killed more than 2,000
	Explosion	Cali, Colombia	August 7; seven truckloads of dynamite exploded, killing more than 1,200 and destroying town; damage: $40 million
	Mine	Marcinelle, Belgium	August 8; coal mine fire claimed 263
	Rail	near Secunderabad, India	September 21; two trains plunged into river as bridge collapsed; 121 dead
	Aircraft	in the Atlantic, north of the Azores	October 10; U.S.A.F. plane disappeared; 59 lost
	Rail	Marudaiyar River, India	November 23; express train derailed; 143 dead
	Aircraft	near Vancouver, Canada	December 9; Trans-Canada North Star crashed; 62 dead
1957	Fire	Warrenton, Missouri	February 17; home for aged burned; 72 dead
	Aircraft	in the Pacific	March 21; U.S.A.F. transport disappeared; 67 lost
	Blizzard	Midwest	March 22–25; storm claimed 21 lives; damage: $5–6 million
	Tornado	Kansas and Missouri	May 18–21; twister killed 40 (?); damage: in the millions of dollars
	Hurricane	Texas to Alabama	June 25–28; storm killed 390; damage: $50–500 million
	Earthquake	Caspian Coast, Iran	July 2; quake killed more than 1,500 and rendered more than 10,000 homeless
	Marine	in the Caspian Sea	July 14; USSR **Eshghabad** ran aground in storm; 270 dead
	Aircraft	off Netherlands New Guinea	July 16; KLM Super-Constellation crashed in sea; 57 dead
	Aircraft	Quebec	August 11; Maritime Central DC–4 charter crashed; 79 dead

Year	Type of Disaster	Place	Remarks
	Rail	near Kendal, Jamaica	September 1; train plunged into ravine; 175 (?) dead
	Rail	near Montgomery, West Pakistan	September 29; express train crashed into standing train; 250 dead
	Earthquake	Outer Mongolia	December 2; quake fatal for 1,200 (?)
	Rail	near London	December 4; two-train collision killed 92
	Aircraft	near Bolívar, Argentina	December 8; Aerolineas Argentina DC-4 crashed; 62 dead
	Earthquake	western Iran	December 13 and 15–17; quake killed 1,392
1958	Mine	near Asansoi, India	February 19; coal mine exploded; more than 180 dead
	Marine	near Istanbul	March 1; Turkish ferry Uskudar sank; 238 dead
	Rail	Santa Cruz, Brazil	March 7; two trains collided; 67 dead
	Rail	near Rio de Janeiro	May 8; two-train collision killed 128
	Aircraft	Casablanca	May 18; Sabena DC-6B crashed; 65 dead
	Aircraft	in the Atlantic, west of Ireland	August 14; KLM Super-Constellation crashed; 99 dead
	Typhoon	Tokyo	September 21; at least 681 killed
	Typhoon	Honshu, Japan	September 27–28; storm killed 679; many missing; extensive damage
	Aircraft	Kanash, USSR	October 17; Aeroflot TU-104 crashed; 65 dead
	Fire	Chicago	December 1; parochial school burned; 95 dead
	Fire	Bogotá, Colombia	December 16; department store conflagration caused 84 deaths
1959	Aircraft	New York City	February 3; American Electra crashed in the East River; 65 dead
	Rail	Java	May 28; train derailed, spilling into ravine and killing 92
	Rail	São Paulo, Brazil	June 5; two trains collided; 60 (?) dead
	Aircraft	near Milan	June 26; TWA Super-Constellation exploded in storm; 68 dead
	Typhoon	Fukien coast, China	August 20; storm claimed 2,334 lives
	Typhoon	Honshu, Japan	September 26–27; tropical cyclone killed more than 4,400
	Hurricane	Jalisco and Colima, Mexico	October 27–28; storm caused mudslides and floods; 1,000 (?) dead
	Flood	Frejus, France	December 2; Malpasset Dam collapsed; 412 victims
1960	Aircraft	near Wilmington, North Carolina	January 6; National DC-6B "disintegrated" in flight; 34 dead
	Aircraft	near Richmond, Virginia	January 18; Capitol Viscount crashed into swampy ravine; 50 dead
	Mine	Coalbrook, South Africa	January 21; coal mine cave-in and explosion killed more than 400
	Aircraft	near La Paz, Bolivia	February 5; Lloyd Aereo Boliviano DC-4 crashed; 56 dead
	Mine	Zwickau, East Germany	February 22; explosion killed 123
	Aircraft	Rio de Janeiro	February 25; U.S. Navy plane and Real DC-3 collided; 61 victims
	Earthquake	Agadir, Morocco	February 29 and March 1; quakes followed by tidal waves destroyed city; 20,000 (?) dead
	Aircraft	near Tell City, Indiana	March 17; Northwest Electra exploded in flight; 63 dead
	Tornado	Oklahoma and Arkansas	May 5; tornadoes killed 29
	Rail	Leipzig, East Germany	May 15; two trains collided; 59 dead
	Earthquake	Chile, Japan, and Hawaii	May 22–29; series of earthquakes, volcanic eruptions, landslides, and tsunami caused widespread devastation; in Chile, more than 2,000 dead and damage: $550 million; in Hawaii, 61 dead and damage: $22 million; in Japan, 138 dead and damage: $50 million
	Fire	Guatemala City	July 14; hospital burned; 225 (?) dead
	Aircraft	near Dakar, Senegal	August 29; Air France Super-Constellation plunged into sea; 63 dead
	Hurricane	South and northeast United States	September 10; hurricane killed 30
	Aircraft	Agaña, Guam	September 18–19; World DC-6B exploded; 78 dead
	Aircraft	Boston	October 4; Eastern Electra crashed into harbor after takeoff; 62 dead
	Cyclone	East Pakistan	October 10 and 31; fatalities from cyclones (6,000) and tidal waves (4,000)
	Fire	Amude, Syria	November 13; movie house burned; 152 deaths
	Rail	Pardubice, Czechoslovakia	November 14; two trains collided; 110 dead
	Aircraft	New York City	December 16; United DC-8 and TWA Super Constellation collided in mid-air over Staten Island, New York; 134 dead
	Fire	Brooklyn Navy Yard	December 19; fire swept aircraft carrier; 50 dead
1961	Aircraft	Berg, Belgium	February 15; Sabena Boeing 707 crashed; 73 dead, including 18 American figure skaters
	Aircraft	Nuremberg, West Germany	March 28; Czechoslovak Ilyushin-18 crashed; 52 dead
	Marine	in the Persian Gulf	April 8; British ship Dara burned; more than 200 dead
	Floods	Midwest United States	Early May; floods caused deaths of 25
	Typhoon	East Pakistan	May 9; cyclone plus tidal waves killed 2,000 (?)
	Aircraft	Ghadames, Libya	May 10; Air France Starliner crashed; 79 dead
	Marine	off Mozambique	July 8; Portuguese Save burned and exploded; 227 dead
	Mine	Dolna Suce, Czechoslovakia	July 8; coal gas explosion killed 108
	Aircraft	Casablanca	July 12; Czechoslovak Ilyushin-18 crashed; 72 dead
	Aircraft	near Chicago	September 1; TWA Constellation crashed in a field; 78 dead
	Aircraft	Shannon, Ireland	September 10; Presidential DC-6 charter crashed; 83 dead
	Hurricane	Southwest and Midwest United States	September 10–14; hurricane and associated tornadoes and floods caused deaths of 46
	Aircraft	Rabat, Morocco	September 12; Air France Caravelle crashed, killing 77
	Typhoon	Japan	September 16–17; storm killed 185; extensive damage
	Aircraft	Chicago	September 17; Northwest Electra struck high tension line and crashed; 37 dead
	Rail	west of Calcutta, India	October 20; express train derailed; more than 50 dead
	Hurricane	Belize, British Honduras	October 31; hurricane devastated city, causing 250 (?) deaths and damage: $150 million
	Aircraft	near Richmond, Virginia	November 8; chartered Imperial Constellation crashed in woods; 77 dead
	Hurricane	southern Mexico	November 14; hurricane killed at least 330
	Fire	Niteroi, Brazil	December 17; circus tent burned, killing more than 320
	Rail	Catanzaro, Italy	December 23; train fell into gorge; 69 dead

Year	Type of Disaster	Place	Remarks
1962	Rail	Woerden, Netherlands	January 8; two trains collided; 91 dead
	Avalanche	Mt. Huscaran, Peru	January 10; Andean avalanche buried more than 3,000
	Mine	Voelklingen, West Germany	February 7; coal mine exploded; 298 dead
	Aircraft	New York City	March 1; American 707 plunged into Jamaica Bay; 95 dead
	Aircraft	near Douala, Cameroon	March 4; British Caledonian DC-7C crashed in jungle; 111 dead
	Hurricane	Atlantic coast of United States	March 6-7; windstorm and associated high tides caused 35 deaths
	Aircraft	in the western Pacific	March 16; Flying Tiger Super-Constellation charter disappeared; 107 lost
	Rail	Tokyo	May 3; three trains collided; 163 dead
	Aircraft	near Centerville, Iowa	May 22; Continental Boeing 707 exploded in flight; 45 dead
	Rail	Voghera, Italy	May 31; two trains collided; 63 dead
	Aircraft	Paris	June 3; Air France Boeing 707 crashed; 130 killed
	Aircraft	Guadeloupe, West Indies	June 22; Air France Boeing 707 crashed; 113 dead
	Aircraft	Bombay	July 7; Alitalia DC-8 crashed; 94 dead
	Rail	Dumraon, India	July 21; two trains collided; 69 dead
	Earthquake	northwestern Iran	September 1; quake killed more than 10,000
	Flood	Barcelona	September 27; flash flood killed more than 470
	Hurricane	Pacific coast of United States	October 12-13; near-hurricane winds and floods killed 40
	Cyclone	Thailand	October 27; hurricane toll: 769 dead and 142 missing; damage: $19 million
	Aircraft	Lima, Peru	November 27; Varig Boeing 707 crashed; 97 dead
	Aircraft	in the Amazon jungle, Brazil	December 14; Panair Do Brasil Constellation crashed; 50 dead
	Flood	northern Europe	December 31; winter-storm floods caused 309 deaths in Germany and took lives in other countries
1963	Aircraft	Ankara	February 1; Turkish Air Force plane and Lebanese Viscount collided; 95 dead
	Aircraft	Everglades, Florida	February 12; Northwest Boeing 720-B crashed; 43 dead
	Volcanic eruption	Bali	March 18; Mount Agung erupted, forcing 78,000 to flee homes; 1,584 deaths recorded
	Marine	in the Atlantic, east of Boston	April 10; Thresher, U.S. Navy nuclear submarine, sank; 129 dead in navy's worst peacetime submarine disaster
	Cyclone	Bay of Bengal, East Pakistan	May 28-29; hurricane and tidal waves took lives of 22,000 (?)
	Aircraft	in the Pacific, off Alaska	June 3; Northwest DC-7 charter crashed; 101 dead
	Earthquake	Skopje, Yugoslavia	July 26; quake killed 1,100 (?)
	Aircraft	near Bombay	July 28; wreckage found of United Arab Comet; 62 dead
	Aircraft	Zurich	September 4; Swissair Caravelle crashed; 80 dead
	Hurricane	Caribbean	October 1-9; cyclone killed 4,000 (?) in Cuba and Haiti
	Flood	near Belluno, Italy	October 9; landslides and flooding, near Vaiont Dam, resulted in death for more than 2,000
	Fire	Indianapolis, Indiana	October 31; explosion and fire at Coliseum; 74 dead
	Rail	near Yokohama	November 9; two Japanese trains hurtled into derailed freight train; at least 162 dead
	Mine	Omuta, Japan	November 9; coal mine exploded; 446 dead
	Flood	Haiti	November 14-15; deluges and landslides killed 500 (?)
	Fire	near Norwalk, Ohio	November 23; fire at nursing home for aged; 63 dead
	Aircraft	Montreal	November 29; Trans-Canada DC-8F crashed; 118 dead
	Aircraft	near Elkton, Maryland	December 8; Pan Am Boeing 707 crashed into a field; 81 dead
1964	Rail	Altamirano, Argentina	February 1; two trains collided; 70 dead
	Aircraft	near New Orleans, Louisiana	February 25; Eastern DC-8 crashed into Lake Pontchartrain; 58 dead
	Aircraft	near Innsbruck, Austria	February 29; British Eagle International Britannia turboprop crashed, killing 83
	Aircraft	near Lake Tahoe, California	March 1; nonscheduled carrier plane crashed; 85 dead
	Earthquake	Alaska	March 27; earthquake was responsible for 114 deaths
	Aircraft	Clark A.F.B., Philippines	May 11; U.S. military transport crashed; 75 dead
	Floods	northern Montana	June 8-9; floods were responsible for 36 deaths
	Aircraft	near Fengyuan, Taiwan	June 20; Chinese Civil Air Patrol plane crashed; 57 dead
	Rail	near Oporto, Portugal	July 26; train wreck killed 94
	Bridge	near Caracas, Venezuela	August 23; 50 (?) killed in collapse of bridge over Caroni Falls
	Aircraft	near Granada, Spain	October 2; Union Transports Africains DC-6 crashed; 80 dead
	Hurricane	southern Louisiana	October 3; hurricane and associated tornadoes killed 36
	Floods	mainly California, Oregon, and Washington	Late December; floods responsible for 45 deaths
1965	Aircraft	in the Andes, Chile	February 6; Chilean Airline DC-6B crashed; 87 dead
	Aircraft	near New York	February 8; Eastern DC-7B crashed in Atlantic; 84 dead
	Earthquake	near Santiago, Chile	March 28; quake killed 400 (?); damage: $200 million
	Aircraft	in the Strait of Gibraltar	March 31; Iberia Convair charter crashed; 50 dead
	Aircraft	near Damascus	April 10; Royal Jordanian plane crashed; 54 dead
	Tornadoes	Midwest United States	April 11; tornadoes killed 272
	Cyclone	Barisal, East Pakistan	May 12; storm killed 12,000 to 20,000; millions homeless
	Aircraft	near Cairo	May 20; Pakistan International Boeing 707 crashed; 119 dead
	Mine	Bihar State, India	May 28; coal mine accident; more than 400 dead
	Mine	Kyushu, Japan	June 1; accident killed 236
	Mine	Kakanj, Yugoslavia	June 7; gas explosion claimed 108
	Aircraft	near El Toro, California	June 25; military plane hit mountain; 84 dead
	Aircraft	British Columbia	July 8; Canadian Pacific DC-6B crashed; 52 dead
	Explosion	near Searcy, Arkansas	August 9; explosion and fire at missile site killed 53
	Hurricane	southern United States	September 8-10; hurricane killed 88
	Rail	near Durban, South Africa	October 4; train derailed; 81 dead
	Aircraft	near Cincinnati, Ohio	November 8; American Boeing 727 crashed into hill; 58 dead
	Marine	in the Caribbean	November 13; Panamanian cruise ship Yarmouth Castle caught fire and sank; 89 dead
	Rail	near Toungoo, Burma	December 9; two trains collided, killing 76
	Cyclone	Karachi, Pakistan	December 15; cyclone killed 10,000 (?)
1966	Flood	Rio de Janeiro	January 11-13; deluge and landslides killed more than 300
	Aircraft	in the French Alps	January 24; Air India 707 crashed into Mont Blanc; 117 dead
	Marine	Chandpur Port, East Pakistan	January 30; Pakistani launch and steamer collided; 80 dead
	Marine	near Belawan, Indonesia	February 2; Indonesian oil tanker sank; 89 lost
	Aircraft	Tokyo	February 4; Boeing 727 plunged into Tokyo Bay; 133 dead

Year	Type of Disaster	Place	Remarks
	Tornadoes	Mississippi and Alabama	March 3; tornadoes killed 58
	Aircraft	Honshu, Japan	March 5; BOAC Boeing 707 caught fire and crashed into Mount Fujiyama; 124 dead
	Rail	Lumding Junction, India	April 20; train exploded, killing 55
	Aircraft	near Ardmore, Oklahoma	April 22; military charter plane crashed; 83 dead
	Rail	Bombay	June 13; two-train collision claimed 60
	Earthquake	eastern Turkey	August 19; quake killed 2,529, rendering 108,000 (?) homeless
	Aircraft	Belgrade	August 31; British Airways Ltd. Britannia turboprop crashed during landing; 96 dead
	Hurricane	Caribbean and Mexico	September 25–October 1; cyclone fatal for at least 200
	Marine	in the Gulf of Tonkin	October 26; U.S. aircraft carrier Oriskany caught fire; 43 lost
	Marine	in Kosi River, India	October 26; Indian vessel sank; more than 100 dead
	Flood	Arno Valley, Italy	November 3–4; overflow of Arno River, which killed 113, destroyed priceless art treasures in Florence and elsewhere
	Aircraft	Bratislava, Czechoslovakia	November 24; TABSO Bulgarian Ilyushin–18 crashed; 82 dead
	Marine	in the Sea of Crete	December 8; Greek ferry Heraklion sank in storm; 217 dead
1967	Flood	Rio de Janeiro and São Paulo states, Brazil	January–March; heavy rain floods killed more than 600
	Missile	Cape Kennedy, Florida	January 27; the three-man crew of Apollo 1 spacecraft, were killed in a flash fire at the launching pad.
	Fire	Tasmania	February 7–9; forest fire killed 52; damage: $11.2 million
	Aircraft	Nicosia, Cyprus	April 20; Swiss Globe Britannia turboprop charter crashed while landing; 126 dead
	Tornadoes	northeastern Illinois	April 21; tornadoes killed 55
	Fire	Brussels	May 22; Innovation department store burned; 322 lost their lives
	Aircraft	in the French Pyrenees	June 3; British Air Ferry Ltd. DC–6 charter crashed into Mont Canigou; 88 dead
	Aircraft	Stockport, England	June 4; British Midland charter DC–4 crashed; 72 dead
	Rail	Langenweddingen, East Germany	June 6; train collided with gasoline truck and exploded; 82 dead
	Aircraft	near Hendersonville, North Carolina	July 19; Piedmont Boeing 727 and private plane collided; 82 dead
	Marine	off Vietnam	July 25; U.S. aircraft carrier Forrestal crippled by fire; 134 dead
	Earthquake	Venezuela	July 30–31; quake, ranging from the Andes to Caribbean, killed 277; damage in Caracas alone: $15 million
	Fire	U.S. Northwest and British Columbia	August–September; millions of acres of forest consumed
	Aircraft	southern Turkey	October 12; BEA Comet crashed; 67 dead
	Rail	London	November 5; express train derailed; 53 dead
	Aircraft	near Cincinnati, Ohio	November 20; TWA Convair 880 crashed near airport; 70 dead
	Flood	Lisbon	November 26; fatality toll: 457
	Bridge	near Pt. Pleasant, West Virginia	December 15; bridge collapsed; 46 dead
1968	Marine	in the eastern Mediterranean	January 26; Israeli submarine Dakar sank; 69 dead
	Marine	in the western Mediterranean	January 27; French submarine Minerve went down; 52 lost
	Aircraft	Guadeloupe, West Indies	March 5; Air France Boeing 707 crashed; 63 dead
	Aircraft	Atlantic Ocean off Wales	March 24; Irish International Viscount crashed; 61 dead
	Marine	Wellington Harbor	April 10; New Zealand ferry Wahine crashed and sank; 51 dead
	Aircraft	near Windhoek, South-West Africa	April 20; South African Boeing 707 crashed; 123 dead
	Aircraft	near Dawson, Texas	May 3; Braniff Electra crashed; 85 dead
	Tornadoes	Midwest United States	May 15; tornadoes killed 71
	Marine	in the Atlantic, southwest of the Azores	May 27; U.S. nuclear submarine Scorpion sank; 99 lost
	Flood	Gujarat, India	August 8–14; floods killed 1,000 (?)
	Earthquake	northeastern Iran	August 31; quake killed 12,000 (?)
	Aircraft	off the French Riviera	September 11; Air France Caravelle crashed; 95 dead
	Mine	near Mannington, West Virginia	November 20; coal mine exploded and caught fire; 78 dead
	Aircraft	off Caracas, Venezuela	December 12; Pan Am Boeing 707 crashed; 51 dead
1969	Floods	southern California	January 25–29; floods killed 95
	Aircraft	La Coruba, Venezuela	March 16; VIASA DC–9 crashed near Maracaibo; 154 dead
	Aircraft	Aswan Airport, Egypt	March 20; United Arab IL–18 crashed while landing; 91 dead
	Mine	Barroteran, Mexico	March 31; gas mine exploded; 156 dead
	Cyclone	Dacca, East Pakistan	April 15; storm killed 500 (?)
	Marine	in the South China Sea	June 2; U.S. destroyer Frank E. Evans sliced in two by the Australian carrier Melbourne; 74 assumed dead
	Aircraft	near Monterrey, Mexico	June 4; Mexican Airways Boeing 727 crashed; 79 dead
	Rail	near Benares, India	June 21; train plunged off tracks into river bed; 75 dead
	Rail	Jaipur, India	July 15; freight train rammed standing passenger train; 85 dead
	Hurricane	Mississippi and Louisiana	August 17; Hurricane Camille killed 200 (?)
	Floods	Virginia	August 23; floods killed 100 (?)
	Aircraft	near Indianapolis, Indiana	September 9; small plane and Allegheny DC–9 collided; 83 dead
	Aircraft	near Danang	September 20; Air Vietnam DC–4 crashed; 77 dead
	Aircraft	near La Paz, Bolivia	September 26; Lloyd Aereo Boliviano DC–6 crashed in the Andes; 74 dead
1970	Rail	near Buenos Aires	February 4; commuter train struck by express train; 236 killed
	Avalanche	Val d'Isère, France	February 10; worst snowslide in French history killed 42 at youth hostel
	Aircraft	in the Caribbean	February 15; Dominican DC–9 crashed, killing 102
	Marine	in the Mediterranean	March 4; French submarine Eurydice exploded, sank; 57 dead
	Earthquake	Kutahya, Turkey	March 28; quake toll: more than 1,000
	Aircraft	Casablanca, Morocco	April 1; Royal Air Maroc Caravelle jetliner crashed; 61 killed
	Explosion	Osaka, Japan	April 8; serial gas-main blasts killed 73; 300 injured
	Avalanche	Saint-Gervais, France	April 16; snowslide hit tuberculosis sanatorium, killing 72

Year	Type of Disaster	Place	Remarks
	Flood	Oradea, Rumania	May 11–23; 200 (?) killed; more than 225 towns destroyed
	Earthquake	northern Peru	May 31; quake plus floods and landslides killed 30,000 (?)
	Aircraft	Barcelona	July 4; British charter Comet jet crashed during landing approach, killing all 112 aboard
	Aircraft	Toronto	July 5; Air Canada DC-8 crashed north of Toronto International Airport; 108 killed
	Bus	New Delhi	July 22; 25 buses, 5 taxis, and an army vehicle swept into narrow gorge by floods; 600 dead
	Marine	near Nevis Island	August 1; ferry Christina sank; 125 (?) dead
	Aircraft	near Cuzco, Peru	August 9; Peruvian Electra crashed; 100 dead
	Fire	Saint-Laurent-du-Pont, France	November 1; fire in a dance hall killed 146
	Cyclone	East Pakistan, delta region	November 12; storm and floods killed 500,000 (?)
	Aircraft	Huntington, West Virginia	November 14; Southern Airways DC-9 carrying the Marshall Univ. football team exploded while landing; 75 killed
1971	Aircraft	Moscow	January 1; Aeroflot Il-18 crashed during takeoff; 90 killed
	Marine	near Dungeness, England	January 13; freighter hit submerged wreckage; 21 lost
	Earthquake	Los Angeles area	February 9; quake killed 64, of these, 43 were at V.A. hospital
	Tornado	Mississippi and Louisiana	February 21; storm killed 115
	Avalanche	Lima, Peru	February 19; Andean avalanche killed 600 (?)
	Earthquake	Bingol, Turkey	May 23; quake killed 800
	Aircraft	Belgrade	May 23; Yugoslav TU-134A crashed at Rijeka Airport; 78 killed
	Rail	Wuppertal, West Germany	May 28; two trains collided; 47 schoolchildren killed
	Aircraft	Honshu, Japan	July 30; Japanese airliner struck by fighter plane over Japanese Alps; 162 dead
	Aircraft	Alaska	September 4; Alaska Airlines 727 crashed into a mountain in the Tongass National Forest; all 111 passengers killed
	Fire	Seoul, S. Korea	December 25; explosion and fire at hotel; 163 dead
1972	Flood	Buffalo Creek, W. Virginia	February 26; coal mine waste waters caused a makeshift dam to collapse; 118-dead
	Aircraft	United Arab Emirates	March 14; Danish Sterling Airways charter crashed near Dubai; all 112 passengers killed
	Poisoning	Iraq	March–April; outbreak of mercury poisoning; over 100 dead
	Earthquake	Iran	April 10; 45 villages leveled; over 5,000 dead
	Mine	Kellogg, Idaho	May 2; fire in the Sunshine Silver Mine; 91 miners dead
	Aircraft	Palermo, Italy	May 6; Alitalia DC-8 struck a mountainside in bad weather; all 115 passengers killed
	Marine	near Buenos Aires, Argentina	May 11; Liberian tanker Tien Chee and British cargo ship Royalston Grange collide; 83 lost at sea
	Fire	Osaka, Japan	May 13; Sennichi department store gutted by flames; 115 killed
	Mine	Northwest Rhodesia	June 6; explosion in Wankie Colliery Co. coal mine; 427 dead
	Flood	Rapid City, S. Dakota	June 10; flash flooding caused over $120 million damage; 226 dead, 124 missing
	Hurricane	Eastern United States	June 10–20; Florida, Maryland, Pennsylvania, New York, and Virginia declared disaster areas; $1.7 billion damage; 134 dead
	Rail	Soissons, France	June 17; falling rocks in a tunnel cause derailment; 107 dead
	Aircraft	London	June 18; BEA Trident crashed on takeoff; 118 dead
	Flood	Luzon Island, Philippines	June-August; Typhoon Rita and six weeks of rain caused landslides and burst dams; 427 dead
	Aircraft	East Berlin	August 14; Interflug Ilyushin-62 crashed on takeoff; 156 dead
	Rail	Saltillo, Mexico	October 6; speeding passenger train jumped its tracks; 204 dead
	Aircraft	Krasnaya Polyana, USSR	October 14; Aeroflot Ilyushin-62 crashed; 176 dead
	Aircraft	Canary Islands	December 3; Spanish charter plane exploded; 155 dead
	Earthquake	Managua, Nicaragua	December 23; worst earthquake in Nicaraguan history; leveled 70% of the city; 10,000 dead
	Aircraft	near Miami	December 29; Eastern Airlines Tristar jetliner crashed into Everglades; 98 dead
1973	Aircraft	Kano, Nigeria	January 22; Boeing 707 jet carrying 200 Moslems from a pilgrimage to Mecca crashed in thick fog; 176 dead
	Epidemic	Bangladesh	Reported March 1; smallpox swept country, killing at least 1,000
	Flood	Western Tunisia	March 31; week-long rains flooded Mejerda River; 150 dead
	Aircraft	Basel, Switzerland	April 10; British charter carrying women on a one-day shopping trip crashed in snowstorm; 104 killed
	Marine	Dacca coast	May 5; two riverboats collided; 250 dead
	Storms	Indonesian Islands	Reported June 16; spring storms took 1,650 lives, including those of 1,500 fishermen
	Aircraft	Paris	July 11; Brazilian Boeing 707 crashed in an emergency landing at Orly; 122 dead
	Aircraft	Boston	July 31; Delta jetliner crashed in fog on landing at Logan Airport; 88 dead
	Earthquake	central Mexico	August 28; earthquake and rains killed 527; 200,000 homeless
	Fire	Kumamoto, Japan	November 29; fire hit department store which had no fire escape chutes; 101 dead; 84 injured
	Marine	Ecuador coast	December 24; overloaded ferryboat capsized, killing 200
1974	Aircraft	Pago Pago, Samoa	January 31; Pan Am jet crashed on landing; 92 dead
	Fire	Sao Paulo, Brazil	February 1; a faulty air conditioner caused a flash fire to sweep a modern bank, killing 189 people in 25 minutes
	Famine	Sahel, West Africa	Reported March 3; 100,000 persons were estimated dead and millions starving due to drought in this sub-Sahara region
	Aircraft	Paris	March 3; Turkish DC-10 crashed on takeoff from Orly; 346 dead
	Aircraft	Leningrad	April 27; Soviet Ilyushin 18 crashed on takeoff; 108 killed
	Aircraft	Bali, Indonesia	April 27; Pan Am 707 crashed on landing; 107 dead
	Marine	Bangladesh coast	May 1; motor launch capsized; 250 dead
1975	Aircraft	Saigon, South Vietnam	April 4; U.S. Air Force C-5A transport jet carrying South Vietnamese orphans to U.S. crashed on takeoff; 155 dead
	Famine	East Africa	Reported May 25; drought since October 1974 in Ethiopia and Somalia; 40,000 dead
	Aircraft	New York	June 24; Eastern Airlines Boeing 727 crashed on landing at Kennedy International Airport; 113 dead
	Flood	northern India	July; month-long monsoon rains caused flooding; 300 dead

Year	Type of Disaster	Place	Remarks
	Marine	near Canton, China	August 3; two ferries collided on Hsi River; 500 (?) drowned
	Aircraft	near Agadir, Morocco	August 3; charter Boeing 707 hit mountainside; 188 dead
	Aircraft	Damascus, Syria	August 20; Czechoslovak airliner, a Soviet built Ilyushin 62, crashed while landing; 126 dead
	Flood	eastern India	August-September; monsoon rains cause flooding and spread of cholera; 450 (?) dead
	Earthquake	Lice, Turkey	September 6; earthquake leaves 2,312 dead, 3,372 injured
	Mine	near Dhanbad, India	December 27; coal mine explosion caused flooding of mine; 372 believed dead
1976	Aircraft	Saudi Arabia	January 1; Middle East Airlines Boeing 707 crashed; 82 dead
	Earthquake	Guatemala	February 4; earthquake toll estimated 22,419 dead, 74,105 injured and 1 million homeless
	Aircraft	Erivan, USSR	March 5; Soviet Il-18 crashed; 120 dead
	Earthquake	Friuli region of Italy	May 6; earthquake in northeast Italy; more than 1,000 dead
	Earthquake	Indonesia	June 26 and July 14; successive quakes, the first on West New Guinea caused mudslides, which left 443 dead, 3,000 missing; the second quake in Bali left 600 dead, 3,400 injured
	Earthquake	Tangshan area of China	July 28; two major quakes devastated industrial city of Tangshan; casualities estimated to be about 700,000, the second worst disaster in recorded history
	Flood	Big Thompson River, Colo.	July 31; vacationers and campers caught in flash flood in canyon; 138 dead, 5 missing
	Earthquake	southern Philippines	August 17; earthquake hit Mindanao and neighboring islands, 8,000 (?) dead or missing and 175,000 homeless
	Aircraft	near Zagreb, Yugoslavia	September 10; Yugoslav charter jet DC-10 and British Airlines Trident collided in world's worst midair collision; 176 dead
	Aircraft	near Isparta, Turkey	September 19; Turkish Boeing 727 hit mountain; 155 dead
	Flood	La Paz, Mexico	October 1; earthen dam broke after heavy rains; 630 dead
	Aircraft	Santa Cruz, Bolivia	October 15; Boeing 707 cargo plane crashed in downtown Santa Cruz; 100 dead
	Earthquake	Van Province, Turkey	November 24; earthquake; estimated 4,000 dead
1977	Rail	Granville, Australia	January 18; Sydney-bound commuter train derailed; 82 dead
	Earthquake	Bucharest, Romania	March 4; earthquake leaves 1,541 dead, 11,275 injured and 80,000 homeless
	Aircraft	Tenerife, Canary Islands	March 27; Pan American 747 and KLM 747 jumbo jets collide on runway; 579 dead in worst disaster in aviation history
	Tornado	near Dacca, Bangladesh	April 1; tornado struck Madaripur district; about 900 dead
	Fire	Southgate, Kentucky	May 28; supper club fire; 161 dead, 129 injured
	Flood	Johnstown, Pennsylvania	July 19-20; nine-inch rainfall caused flash flood; over 70 dead
	Flood	Toccoa, Georgia	November 6; dam broke, killing 39
	Storm	Andhra Pradesh, India	November 19; cyclone caused tidal wave killing 20,000
	Aircraft	Funchal, Madeira	November 19; Portuguese 727 crashed on landing; 130 dead
	Aircraft	Johore Strait, Malaysia	December 4; Malaysian 737 crashed after hijacking; 100 dead
	Earthquake	Kerman Province, Iran	December 20; earthquake hit rural villages; over 520 dead
1978	Aircraft	near Bombay, India	January 1; Air India 747 exploded and crashed; 213 dead
	Aircraft	near Sofia, Bulgaria	March 16; Bulgarian airliner crashed; 73 dead
	Tornado	Orissa, India	April 16; storm killed 400 to 500 in six villages
	Construction	St. Marys, West Virginia	April 27; scaffolding on cooling tower collapsed; 51 dead
	Explosion	near Tarragona, Spain	July 11; propylene gas truck exploded at tourist camp; 200 dead
	Bus	Lac d'Argent, Quebec	41 drown as bus plunges into lake 50 miles from Montreal, Canada
	Explosion	Beirut, Lebanon	August 13; blast destroyed building, killing 150 to 200
	Fire	Abadan, Iran	August 20; arsonist-set theater fire killed 430
	Earthquake	Tabas, Iran	September 16; major quake; estmated 25,000 dead
	Aircraft	San Diego, California	September 25; Pacific Southwest 727 jet and private plane collided in midair; 150 dead
	Marine	Bay of Bengal	April 4; fleet of cargo boats lost in storm; 1,000 dead
	Mass suicide	Jonestown, Guyana	November 18; mass poisoning and murder in American religious commune; over 900 dead
	Aircraft	Leh, India	November 19; Indian Air Force transport crashed; 78 killed
	Storm	Sri Lanka and India	November 23; cyclone leveled 500,000 buildings; over 1,500 dead
	Aircraft	Colombo, Sri Lanka	November 25; charter Icelandic DC-8 jet crashed in thunderstorm; 183 dead
	Aircraft	Tyrrhenian Sea	December 23; Alitalia DC-9 jet ditched at sea; 103 believed drowned
1979	Earthquake	eastern Iran	January 16; quake killed 199
	Volcanic eruption	Central Java	February 21; 175 dead after inhaling poisonous gases
	Aircraft	near Moscow	March 17; Tupalev 141 airliner caught fire and crashed; 90 dead
	Tornado	Texas and Oklahoma	April 10; twisters struck border area; 60 dead, over 800 injured
	Earthquake	Yugoslavia and Albania	April 15; shocks hit coastal area; 129 reported dead, 1,500 injured and 80,000 homeless
	Aircraft	Chicago	May 25; American Airlines DC-10 crashed on takeoff after losing engine; 272 passengers and 3 persons on ground killed in worst accident in U.S. aviation history
	Aircraft	Sumatra, Indonesia	July 11; domestic airliner crashed into mountain; 61 dead
	Fire	Saragossa, Spain	July 13; hotel fire; 80 dead
	Bus	Lugezi, Tanzania	July 14; overcrowded bus fell into Lake Victoria; 60 dead
	Tidal wave	Lomblem, Indonesia	July 17; death toll estimated at 539
	Flood	Morvi, India	August 11; dam broke causing flood; 1,335 dead
	Aircraft	over Ukraine	Reported August 17; collision of two Soviet Aeroflot jet liners; 173 dead
	Rail	Bangkok, Thailand	August 21; commuter train and freight train collided; over 65 dead
	Hurricane	Dominican Republic	September 1; Hurricane David ravaged Hispanola; 1,000 dead and 150,000 homeless
	Rail	Stalac, Yugoslavia	September 13; freight train rammed train filled with army recruits; over 50 dead

SPORTS

CONTENTS:

PAN AMERICAN GAMES — 1979 CHAMPIONS

SOURCE: U.S. Olympic Committee

ARCHERY
Men's Individual—Rodney Baston, USA
Men's Team—USA
Women's Individual—Lynette Johnson, USA
Women's Team—USA

BOXING
Light Flyweight—Hector Ramirez, Cuba
Flyweight—Albert Mercado, Puerto Rico
Bantamweight—Jackie Beard, USA
Featherweight—Bernard Taylor, USA
Lightweight—Adolfo Horta, Cuba
Light Welterweight—Lemuel Steeples, USA
Welterweight—Andres Aldama, Cuba
Light Middleweight—Jose Molina, Puerto Rico
Middleweight—Jose Gomez, Cuba
Light Heavyweight, Tony Tucker, USA
Heavyweight—Teofilo Stevenson, Cuba

CYCLING
100 km. Team Road Race—USA
Individual Road Race—Carlos Cardet, Cuba
Kilometer Time Trial—Gordon Singleton, Canada
4,000 m. Pursuit—Claude Langlois, Canada
4,000 m. Team Pursuit—Chile
Scratch Sprint—Gordon Singleton, Canada

DIVING—SEE PAGE 993

EQUESTRIAN
Show Jumping—Jet Run (Michael Matz), USA
Show Jumping, Team—USA
Dressage—Keen (Hilda Gurney), USA
Dressage, Team—USA

FENCING
Epee—Mario de Brelaz, Argentina
Team Epee—USA
Sabre—Manuel Oritz, Cuba
Team Sabre—Cuba
Foil (Men)—Heriberto Gonzalez, Cuba
Team Foil (Men)—Cuba
Foil (Women)—Del Risco, Cuba
Team Foil (Women)—Cuba

GYMNASTICS (MEN)
Team—Cuba
All-Around—Sergio Suarez, Cuba
Floor Exercises—Sergio Suarez, Cuba
Pommel Horse—Roberto Richard, Cuba
Long Horse Vault—Sergio Suarez, Cuba
Parallel Bars—Roberto Richard, Cuba
Horizontal Bars—Jorge Roche, Cuba
Rings—Jorge Roche, Cuba

GYMNASTICS (WOMEN)
Team—Canada
All-Around—Monica Goermann, Canada
Floor Exercises—Jenine Creek, USA
Side Horse Vault—Jackie Cassello, USA
Uneven Parallel Bars—Monica Goermann, Canada
Balance Beam—Sherry Hawco, Canada

JUDO
60 kilos—Luiz Shinohara, Brazil
65 kilos—Guillermo Nelson, Cuba
71 kilos—Brad Farron, Canada
78 kilos—Louis Hanny, Canada
86 kilos—Carlos Cunha, Brazil
95 kilos—Carlos Pacheco, Brazil
Over 95 kilos—Jose Ibanez, Cuba
Open Class—Osvaldo Simoes, Brazil

ROLLER SKATING (MEN)
500 m. Against Clock—Kenneth Sutton, USA
500 m. Pairs—Kenneth Sutton, U.S.A.
3,000 m. Pack Style—Raul Subiledt, Argentina
5,000 m. Pack Style—Tom Peterson, USA
10,000 m. Pack Style—Tom Peterson, USA
20,000 m. Cross-Country—Tom Peterson, USA
10,000 m. Relay—Peterson-Chris Snyder, USA

ROLLER SKATING (WOMEN)
500 m. Against Clock—Nora Vega, Argentina
500 m. Pairs—Nora Vega, Argentina
3,000 m. Pack Style—Nora Vega, Argentina
5,000 m. Pack Style—Claudia Rodriguez, Argentina
5,000 m. Relay—Vega and Rodriguez, Argentina

ROLLER SKATING, ARTISTIC
Singles, Men—Fred Morante, USA
Singles, Women—Natalie Dunn, USA
Pairs Skating—R. Coleman-P. Jones, USA
Dancing—F. Arsenault-D. Littel, USA

ROWING
Single Sculls—Ricardo Ibarra, Argentina
Double Sculls—Canada
Pairs without Coxswain—Canada
Pairs with Coxswain—Brazil
Fours without Coxswain—Cuba
Fors with Coxswain—Cuba
Quadruple Sculls—Cuba
Eights with Coxswain—USA

SWIMMING—SEE PAGE 993

TENNIS
Men's Singles—Mel Purcell, USA
Women's Singles—Susie Hagey, USA
Men's Doubles—Purcell-Andy Kohlberg, USA
Women's Doubles—Hagey-Ann Hendricksson, USA
Mixed Doubles—M. Noriega-J. Boveda, Venezuela

TRACK AND FIELD (MEN)

100 m. Dash—Silvio Leonard, Cuba
200 m. Dash—Silvio Leonard, Cuba
400 m. Dash—Tony Darden, USA
800 m. Run—James Robinson, USA
1,500 m. Run—Donald Paige, USA
5,000 m. Run—Matt Centrowitz, USA
10,000 m. Run—Rodolfo Gomez, Mexico
Marathon—Radames Gonzalez, Cuba
20 km. Walk—Daniel Bautista, Mexico
50 km. Walk—Raul Gonzalez, Mexico
110 m. Hurdles—Renaldo Nehemiah, USA
400 m. Hurdles—James Walker, USA
3,000 m. Steeplechase—Henry Marsh, USA
4 x 100 m. Relay—USA
4 x 400 m. Relay—USA
Decathlon—Bob Coffman, USA
High Jump—Franklin Jacobs, USA
Long Jump—Joao de Oliveira, Brazil
Triple Jump—Joao de Oliveira, Brazil
Pole Vault—Bruce Simpson, Canada
Shot Put—David Laut, USA
Discus Throw—Mac Wilkins, USA
Javelin Throw—Duncan Atwood, USA
Hammer Throw—Scott Neilson, Canada

TRACK AND FIELD (WOMEN)

100 m. Dash—Evelyn Ashford, USA
200 m. Dash—Evelyn Ashford, USA
400 m. Dash—Sharon Dabney, USA

800 m. Run—Essie Kelley, USA
1,500 m. Run—Mary Decker, USA
3,000 m. Run—Jan Merrill, USA
100 m. Hurdles—Deby LaPlante, USA
4 x 100 m. Relay—USA
4 x 400 m. Relay—USA
Pentathlon—Diane Jones, Canada
High Jump—Louise Ritter, USA
Long Jump—Kathy McMillan, USA
Shot Put—Maria Sarria, Cuba
Discus Throw—Carmen Romero, Cuba
Javelin Throw—Maria Colon, Cuba

WEIGHTLIFTING

52 kilos—Francisco Casamayor, Cuba
56 kilos—Daniel Nunez, Cuba
60 kilos—Victor Perez, Cuba
67 kilos—Mario Ricardo, Cuba
75 kilos—Robert Urrutia, Cuba
82.5 kilos—Julio Echenique, Cuba
90 kilos—Daniel Zayas, Cuba
100 kilos—Alberto Blanco, Cuba
110 kilos—Mark Cameron, USA
Over 110 kilos—Thomas Stock, USA

YACHTING

470 Class—USA (Steve Cuchiaro, helmsman)
Snipe Class—USA (Mark Reynolds, helmsman)
Soling Class—USA (David Curtis, helmsman)
Laser Class—Canada (Terry Neilson, helmsman)
Lightning Class—Brazil (Mario Buck Up, helmsman)

TEAM SPORTS

Baseball—Cuba
Basketball (Men)—USA
Basketball (Women)—Cuba
Field Hockey—Argentina

Roller Hockey—Argentina
Soccer—Brazil
Softball (Men)—Canada
Softball (Women)—USA

Volleyball (Men)—Cuba
Volleyball (Women)—Cuba
Water Polo—USA

THE OLYMPICS

THE SUMMER OLYMPIC GAMES

Sites	Year	Total Events	Total Nations	Total Athletes	Sites	Year	Total Events	Total Nations	Total Athletes
I Athens	1896	42	13	285	XIV London	1948	138	59	4,468
II Paris	1900	60	20	1,066	XV Helsinki	1952	149	69	5,867
III St. Louis	1904	67	11	496	XVI Melbourne	1956	145	67	3,184
IV London	1908	104	22	2,059	XVI Stockholm*	1956	3	29	154
V Stockholm	1912	106	28	2,541	XVII Rome	1960	150	84	5,396
VII Antwerp	1920	154	29	2,606	XVIII Tokyo	1964	163	94	5,565
VIII Paris	1924	137	44	3,092	XIX Mexico City	1968	172	109	6,082
IX Amsterdam	1928	120	46	3,015	XX Munich	1972	194	121	8,500
X Los Angeles	1932	124	37	1,408	XXI Montreal	1976	198	89	9,564[1]
XI Berlin	1936	142	49	4,069	XXII Moscow	1980			
					XXIII Los Angeles	1984			

* Equestrian Games only. [1] Includes officials.

1976 SUMMER OLYMPICS MEDAL TABLE

	Gold (1st)	Silver (2d)	Bronze (3d)	Total		Gold (1st)	Silver (2d)	Bronze (3d)	Total
U.S.S.R.	47	43	35	125	Jamaica	1	1	0	2
East Germany	40	24	25	89	North Korea	1	1	0	2
United States	34	35	25	94	Norway	1	1	0	2
West Germany	10	12	17	39	Mexico	1	0	1	2
Japan	9	6	10	25	Trinidad & Tobago	1	0	0	1
Poland	8	6	11	25	Canada	0	5	6	11
Bulgaria	7	8	9	24	Belgium	0	3	3	6
Cuba	6	4	3	13	Netherlands	0	2	3	5
Romania	4	9	14	27	Portugal	0	2	0	2
Hungary	4	5	12	21	Spain	0	2	0	2
Finland	4	2	0	6	Australia	0	1	4	5
Sweden	4	1	0	5	Iran	0	1	1	2
Britain	3	5	5	13	Mongolia	0	1	0	1
Italy	2	7	4	13	Venezuela	0	1	0	1
Czechoslovakia	2	2	4	8	Brazil	0	0	2	2
France	2	2	4	8	Austria	0	0	1	1
Yugoslavia	2	3	3	8	Bermuda	0	0	1	1
New Zealand	2	1	1	4	Pakistan	0	0	1	1
South Korea	1	1	4	6	Puerto Rico	0	0	1	1
Switzerland	1	1	2	4	Thailand	0	0	1	1
Denmark	1	0	2	3					

MEDALISTS AT MONTREAL: 1976
1st (gold), 2nd (silver), 3rd (bronze)

ARCHERY
Men's (July 30)
Darrell Pace, U.S. 2,571 points*
Hiroshi Michinaga, Japan
Carlo Ferrari, Italy
Women's (July 30)
Luann Ryon, U.S. 2,499 points*
Valentina Kovpan, U.S.S.R.
Zebinisso Rustamova, U.S.S.R.

BASKETBALL
Men's Team Championship (July 27)
U.S.
Yugoslavia
U.S.S.R.
Women's Team Championship (July 26)
U.S.S.R.
U.S.
Bulgaria

BOXING
Lightflyweight (July 31)
Jorge Hernandez, Cuba
Byong Uk Li, N. Korea
Payao Pooltarat, Thailand
Orlando Maldonado, Puerto Rico
Flyweight (July 31)
Leo Randolph, U.S.
Ramon Duvalon, Cuba
David Torosyan, U.S.S.R.
Leszek Blazynski, Poland
Bantamweight (July 31)
Yong Jo Gu, N. Korea
Charles Mooney, U.S.
Patrick Cowdell, Britain
Viktor Rybakov, U.S.S.R.
Featherweight (July 31)
Angel Herrera, Cuba
Richard Nowakowski, East Germany
Leszek Kosedowski, Poland
Juan Paredes, Mexico
Lightweight (July 31)
Howard Davis, U.S.
Simion Cutov, Romania
Vasily Solomin, U.S.S.R.
Ace Rusevski, Yugoslavia
Light Welterweight (July 31)
Ray Leonard, U.S.
Andres Aldama, Cuba
Vladimir Kolev, Bulgaria
Kazimier Szczerba, Poland
Welterweight (July 31)
Jochen Bachfeld, East Germany
Pedro Gamarro, Venezuela
Reinhard Skricek, West Germany
Victor Zilberman, Romania
Light Middleweight (July 31)
Jerzy Rybicki, Poland
Tadija Kacar, Yugoslavia
Viktor Savchenko, U.S.S.R.
Rolando Garbey, Cuba
Middleweight (July 31)
Michael Spinks, U.S.
Rufat Riskiyev, U.S.S.R.
Luis Martinez, Cuba
Alec Nastac, Romania
Light Heavyweight (July 31)
Leon Spinks, U.S.
Sixto Soria, Cuba
Costica Dafinoiu, Romania
Janusz Gortat, Poland
Heavyweight (July 31)
Teofilo Stevenson, Cuba
Mircea Simon, Romania
John Tate, U.S.
Clarence Hill, Bermuda

* Olympic record.

MEN'S CANOEING
Kayak Singles, 500 meters (July 30)
Vasile Diba, Romania 1:46.41
Zoltan Sztanity, Hungary
Rudiger Helm, East Germany
Kayak Pairs, 500 meters (July 30)
East Germany 1:35.87
U.S.S.R.
Romania
Kayak Singles, 1,000 meters (July 31)
Rudiger Helm, East Germany 3:48.20
Geza Csapo, Hungary
Vasile Diba, Romania
Kayak Pairs, 1,000 meters (July 31)
U.S.S.R. 3:29.01
East Germany
Hungary
Kayak Fours, 1,000 meters (July 31)
U.S.S.R. 3:08.69
Spain
East Germany
Canadian Singles, 500 meters (July 30)
Aleksandr Rogov, U.S.S.R. 1:59.23
John Wood, Canada
Matija Ljubek, Yugoslavia
Canadian Pairs, 500 meters (July 30)
U.S.S.R. 1:45.81
Poland
Hungary
Canadian Singles, 1,000 meters (July 31)
Matija Ljubek, Yugoslavia 4:09.51
Vasily Yurchenko, U.S.S.R.
Tamas Wichmann, Hungary
Canadian Pairs, 1,000 meters (July 31)
U.S.S.R. 3:52.76
Romania
Hungary

WOMEN'S CANOEING
Kayak Singles, 500 meters (July 30)
Carola Zirzow, East Germany 2:01.05
Tatyana Korshunova, U.S.S.R.
Klara Rajnai, Hungary
Kayak Pairs, 500 meters (July 30)
U.S.S.R. 1:51.15
Hungary
East Germany

CYCLING
1,000-meter Time Trial (July 19)
Klaus-Jürgen Grunke, East Germany
1:05.93
Michel Vaarten, Belgium
Niels Fredborg, Denmark
Individual Pursuit (July 22)
Gregor Braun, W. Germany 4:47.61
Herman Ponsteen, Netherlands
Thomas Huschke, East Germany
Team Pursuit (July 24)
West Germany 4:21.06
U.S.S.R.
Britain
Road Race (July 26)
Bernt Johansson, Sweden
4 hrs, 46:52
Giuseppe Martinelli, Italy
Mieczysl Nowicki, Poland
100-Kilometer Time Trial (July 18)
U.S.S.R. 2 hrs., 8:53
Poland
Denmark
Sprint (July 24)
Anton Tkac, Czechoslovakia
Daniel Morelon, France
Hans-Jürgen Goeschke, East Germany

EQUESTRIAN
Individual 3-Day Event (July 25)
Edmund Coffin, U.S. 114.99 points
John Plumb, U.S.
Karl Schultz, West Germany
Team 3-Day Event (July 25)
U.S. 441.00 points
West Germany
Australia
Grand Prix Dressage Individual (July 30)
Christine Stueckelberger, Switzerland
1,486.00 points
Harry Boldt, West Germany
Reiner Klimke, West Germany
Grand Prix Dressage Team (July 29)
West Germany 5,155.00 points
Switzerland
U.S.
Grand Prix Jumping Individual (July 27)
Alwin Schockemoehle, West Germany
0.00 points
Michel Vaillancourt, Canada
Francois Mathy, Belgium
Grand Prix Jumping Team (August 1)
France 40.00 points
West Germany
Belgium

MEN'S FENCING
Individual Foil (July 21)
Fabio Dal Zotto, Italy
Aleksandr Romankov, U.S.S.R.
Bernard Talvard, France
Team Foil (July 25)
West Germany
Italy
France
Individual Epee (July 23)
Alexander Pusch, West Germany
Jürgen Hehn, West Germany
Györző Kulcsar, Hungary
Team Epee (July 29)
Sweden
West Germany
Switzerland
Individual Saber (July 22)
Viktor Krovopuskov, U.S.S.R.
Vladimir Nazlymov, U.S.S.R.
Viktor Sidyak, U.S.S.R.
Team Saber (July 27)
U.S.S.R.
Italy
Romania

WOMEN'S FENCING
Individual Foil (July 24)
Ildiko Schwarczenberger, Hungary
Maria Collino, Italy
Yelena Belova, U.S.S.R.
Team Foil (July 28)
U.S.S.R.
France
Hungary

FIELD HOCKEY
Team Championship (July 30)
New Zealand
Australia
Pakistan

MEN'S GYMNASTICS
Parallel Bars (July 23)
Sawao Kato, Japan 19.675
Nikolai Andrianov, U.S.S.R.
Mitsuo Tsukahara, Japan

Long Horse Vault (July 23)
Nikolai Andrianov, U.S.S.R. 19.450
Mitsuo Tsukahara, Japan
Hiroshi Kajiyama, Japan

All-Around (July 21)
Nikolai Andrianov, U.S.S.R. 58.25
Sawao Kato, Japan
Mitsuo Tsukahara, Japan

Pommeled Horse (July 23)
Zoltan Magyar, Hungary 19.700
Eizo Kenmotsu, Japan
Nikolai Andrianov, U.S.S.R.

Rings (July 23)
Nikolai Andrianov, U.S.S.R. 19.650
Aleksandr Dityatin, U.S.S.R.
Danut Grecu, Romania

Horizontal Bars (July 23)
Mitsuo Tsukahara, Japan 19.675
Eizo Kenmotsu, Japan
Eberhard Gienger, West Germany

Team Competition (July 20)
Japan 576.8
U.S.S.R.
East Germany

Floor Exercises (July 23)
Nikolai Andrianov, U.S.S.R. 19.450
Vladimir Marchenko, U.S.S.R.
Peter Kormann, U.S.

WOMEN'S GYMNASTICS

All-Around (July 21)
Nadia Comaneci, Romania 79.275
Nelli Kim, U.S.S.R.
Lyudmila Turishcheva, U.S.S.R.

Floor Exercises (July 22)
Nelli Kim, U.S.S.R. 19.850
Lyudmila Turishcheva, U.S.S.R.
Nadia Comaneci, Romania

Balance Beam (July 22)
Nadia Comaneci, Romania 19.950
Olga Korbut, U.S.S.R.
Teodora Ungureanu, Romania

Uneven Parallel Bars (July 22)
Nadia Comaneci, Romania 20.000
Teodora Ungureanu, Romania
Marta Egervari, Hungary

Side Horse Vault (July 22)
Nelli Kim, U.S.S.R. 19.800
Lyudmila Turishcheva, U.S.S.R.
Carola Dombeck, East Germany

Team Competition (July 19)
U.S.S.R. 390.35
Romania
East Germany

HANDBALL

Men's Team Championship (July 28)
U.S.S.R.
Romania
Poland

Women's Team Championship (July 28)
U.S.S.R.
East Germany
Hungary

JUDO

Lightweight (July 30)
Hector Rodriguez, Cuba
Eunkyung Chang, South Korea
Felice Mariani, Italy
Jozsef Tuncsik, Hungary

Light Middleweight (July 29)
Vladimir Nevzorov, U.S.S.R.
Koji Kuramoto, Japan
Patrick Vial, France
Marian Talaj, Poland

Middleweight (July 28)
Isamu Sonoda, Japan
Valery Dvoinikov, U.S.S.R.
Youngchul Park, South Korea
Slavko Obadov, Yugoslavia

Light Heavyweight (July 28)
Kazuhiro Ninomiya, Japan
Ramaz Kharshiladze, U.S.S.R.
David Starbrook, Britain
Juerg Roethlisberger, Switzerland

Heavyweight (July 26)
Sergei Novikov, U.S.S.R.
Günther Neureuther, West Germany
Allen Coage, U.S.
Sumio Endo, Japan

Open Class (July 31)
Haruki Uemura, Japan
Keith Remfry, Britain
Shota Chochishvili, U.S.S.R.
Jeaki Cho, South Korea

MODERN PENTATHLON

Individual (July 22)
Janusz Pyciak-Peciak, Poland
5,520 points
Pavel Lednyov, U.S.S.R.
Jan Bartu, Czechoslovakia

Team (July 22)
Britain 15,559
Czechoslovakia
Hungary

MEN'S ROWING

Single Sculls (July 25)
Pertti Karppinen, Finland 7:29.03
Peter Kolbe, West Germany
Joachim Dreifke, East Germany

Double Sculls (July 25)
Norway 7:13.20
Britain
East Germany

Quadruple Sculls (July 25)
East Germany 6:18.65
U.S.S.R.
Czechoslovakia

Pairs With Coxswain (July 25)
East Germany 7:58.99
U.S.S.R.
Czechoslovakia

Pairs Without Coxswain (July 25)
East Germany 7:23.31
U.S.
West Germany

Fours With Coxswain (July 25)
U.S.S.R. 6:40.22
East Germany
West Germany

Fours Without Coxswain (July 25)
East Germany 6:37.42
Norway
U.S.S.R.

Eights With Coxswain (July 25)
East Germany 5:58.29
Britain
New Zealand

WOMEN'S ROWING

Single Sculls (July 24)
Christine Scheiblich, East
Germany 4:05.56
Joan Lind, U.S.
Yelena Antonova, U.S.S.R.

Double Sculls (July 24)
Bulgaria 3:44.36
East Germany
U.S.S.R.

Quadruple Sculls (July 24)
East Germany 3:29.99
U.S.S.R.
Romania

Pairs Without Coxswain (July 24)
Bulgaria 4:01.22
East Germany
West Germany

Fours With Coxswain (July 24)
East Germany 3:45.08
Bulgaria
U.S.S.R.

Eights with Coxswain (July 24)
East Germany 3:33.32
U.S.S.R.
U.S.

SHOOTING

Free Pistol (July 18)
Uwe Potteck, East Germany
573 points*
Harald Vollmar, East Germany
Rudolf Dollinger, Austria

Rapid Fire Pistol (July 23)
Norbert Klaar, East Germany
597 points*
Jürgen Wiefel, East Germany
Roberto Ferraris, Italy

Small Bore Rifle, Prone (July 19)
Karlheinz Smieszek, West Germany
599*
Ulrich Lind, West Germany
Gennady Lushchikov, U.S.S.R.

Small Bore Rifle, 3 Positions (July 21)
Lanny Bassham, U.S. 1,162 points
Margaret Murdock, U.S.
Werner Seibold, West Germany

Moving Target (July 23)
Aleksandr Gazov, U.S.S.R.
579 points*
Aleksandr Kedyarov, U.S.S.R.
Jerzy Greszkiewicz, Poland

Skeetshooting (July 24)
Josef Panacek, Czechoslovakia
198 points†
Eric Swinkels, Netherlands
Wieslaw Gawlikowski, Poland

Trapshooting (July 20)
Donald Haldeman, U.S. 190 points
Armando Marques, Portugal
Ubaldesc Baldi, Italy

SOCCER

Team Championship (July 31)
East Germany
Poland
U.S.S.R.

MEN'S SWIMMING

100-Meter Freestyle (July 25)
Jim Montgomery, U.S. 0:49.99*
Jack Babashoff, U.S.
Peter Nocke, West Germany

200-Meter Freestyle (July 19)
Bruce Furniss, U.S. 1:50.29*
John Naber, U.S.
Jim Montgomery, U.S.

400-Meter Freestyle (July 22)
Brian Goodell, U.S. 3:51.93*
Tim Shaw, U.S.
Vladimir Raskatov, U.S.S.R.

1,500-Meter Freestyle (July 20)
Brian Goodell, U.S. 15:02.40*
Robert Hackett, U.S.
Stephen Holland, Australia

* Olympic record. † Equals Olympic record.

100-Meter Backstroke (July 19)
John Naber, U.S. 0:55.49*
Peter Rocca, U.S.
Roland Matthes, East Germany

200-Meter Backstroke (July 24)
John Naber, U.S. 1:59.19*
Peter Rocca, U.S.
Daniel Harrigan, U.S.

100-Meter Breaststroke (July 20)
John Hencken, U.S. 1:03.11*
David Wilkie, Britain
Arvydas Juozaitis, U.S.S.R.

200-Meter Breaststroke (July 24)
David Wilkie, Britain 2:15.11*
John Hencken, U.S.
Rick Colella, U.S.

100-Meter Butterfly (July 21)
Matt Vogel, U.S. 0:54.35
Joe Bottom, U.S.
Gary Hall, U.S.

200-Meter Butterfly (July 18)
Michael Bruner, U.S. 1:59.23*
Steven Gregg, U.S.
William Forrester, U.S.

400-Meter Individual Medley (July 25)
Rod Strachan, U.S. 4:23.68*
Tim McKee, U.S.
Andrei Smirnov, U.S.S.R.

800-Meter Freestyle Relay (July 21)
U.S. 7:23.22*
U.S.S.R.
Britain

400-Meter Medley Relay (July 22)
U.S. 3:42.22*
Canada
West Germany

WOMEN'S SWIMMING

100-Meter Freestyle (July 19)
Kornelia Ender, East Germany
0:55.65*
Petra Priemer, East Germany
Enith Brigitha, Netherlands

200-Meter Freestyle (July 22)
Kornelia Ender, East Germany
1:59.26*
Shirley Babashoff, U.S.
Enith Brigitha, Netherlands

400-Meter Freestyle (July 20)
Petra Thuemer, East Germany
4:09.89*
Shirley Babashoff, U.S.
Shannon Smith, Canada

800-Meter Freestyle (July 25)
Petra Thuemer, East Germany
8:37.14*
Shirley Babashoff, U.S.
Wendy Weinberg, U.S.

100-Meter Backstroke (July 21)
Ulrike Richter, East Germany
1.01.83*
Birgit Treiber, East Germany
Nancy Garapick, Canada

200-Meter Backstroke (July 25)
Ulrike Richter, East Germany 2:13.43*
Birgit Triber, East Germany
Nancy Garapick, Canada

100-Meter Breaststroke (July 24)
Hannelore Anke, East Germany
1:11.16*
Lyubov Rusanova, U.S.S.R.
Marina Koshevaya, U.S.S.R.

200-Meter Breaststroke (July 21)
Marina Koshevaya, U.S.S.R.
2:33.35*
Marina Yurchenya, U.S.S.R.
Lyubov Rusanova, U.S.S.R.

100-Meter Butterfly (July 22)
Kornelia Ender, East Germany
1:00.13*
Andrea Pollack, East Germany
Wendy Boglioli, U.S.

200-Meter Butterfly (July 19)
Andrea Pollack, East Germany
2:11.41*
Ulrike Tauber, East Gerany
Rosemarie Gabriel, East Germany

400-Meter Individual Medley (July 24)
Ulrike Tauber, East Germany
4:42.77*
Cheryl Gibson, Canada
Becky Smith, Canada

400-Meter Freestyle Relay (July 25)
U.S. 3:44.82*
East Germany
ˉnada

400-Meter Medley Relay (July 18)
East Germany 4:07.95*
U.S.
Canada

MEN'S DIVING

Springboard (July 22)
Phil Boggs, U.S. 619.52 points
Franco Cagnotto, Italy
Aleksandr Kosenkov, U.S.S.R.

Platform (July 27)
Klaus DiBiasi, Italy 600.51 points*
Greg Louganis, U.S.
Vladimir Aleinik, U.S.S.R.

WOMEN'S DIVING

Springboard (July 20)
Jennifer Chandler, U.S.
506.19 points
Christa Kohler, East Germany
Cynthia McIngvale, U.S.

Platform (July 26)
Yelena Vaitsekhovskaya, U.S.S.R.
406.49 points
Ulrika Knape, Sweden
Deborah Wilson, U.S.

MEN'S TRACK & FIELD

100-Meter Dash (July 24)
Hasely Crawford, Trinidad
& Tobago 10.06
Donald Quarrie, Jamaica
Valery Borzov, U.S.S.R.

200-Meter Dash (July 26)
Donald Quarrie, Jamaica 20.23
Millard Hampton, U.S.
Dwayne Evans, U.S.

400-Meter Dash (July 29)
Alberto Juantorena, Cuba 44.26
Fred Newhouse, U.S.
Herman Frazier, U.S.

800-Meter Run (July 25)
Alberto Juantorena, Cuba 1:43.50*
Ivo Vandamme, Belgium
Rick Wohlhuter, U.S.

1,500-Meter Run (July 31)
John Walker, New Zealand
3:39.17
Ivo Vandamme, Belgium
Paul Wellmann, West Germany

5,000-Meter Run (July 30)
Lasse Viren, Finland 13:24.76*
Richard Quax, New Zealand
Klaus Hildenbrand, West Germany

10,000-Meter Run (July 26)
Lasse Viren, Finland 27:40.38
Carlos Sousa Lopes, Portugal
Brendan Foster, Britain

Marathon (July 31)
Waldemar Cierpinski, East
Germany 2 hrs. 9:55*
Frank Shorter, U.S.
Karel Lismont, Belgium

110-Meter Hurdles (July 28)
Guy Drut, France 13.30
Alejandro Casanas, Cuba
Willie Davenport, U.S.

400-Meter Hurdles (July 25)
Edwin Moses, U.S. 47.64*
Michael Shine, U.S.
Yevgeny Gavrilenko, U.S.S.R.

3,000-Meter Steeplechase (July 28)
Anders Gärderud, Sweden
8:08.20*
Bronislaw Malinowski, Poland
Frank Baumgartl, East Germany

400-Meter Relay (July 31)
U.S. 0:38.33
East Germany
U.S.S.R.

1,600-Meter Relay (July 31)
U.S. 2:58.65
Poland
West Germany

20-Kilometer Walk (July 23)
Daniel Bautista, Mexico 1 hr. 24:40.6*
Hans Reimann, East Germany
Peter Frenkel, East Germany

Long Jump (July 29)
Arnie Robinson, U.S. 27' 4¾"
Randy Williams, U.S.
Frank Wartenberg, East Germany

Triple Jump (July 30)
Viktor Saneyev, U.S.S.R.
56' 8¾"
James Butts, U.S.
João Oliveira, Brazil

High Jump (July 31)
Jacek Wszola, Poland 7' 4½"*
Greg Joy, Canada
Dwight Stones, U.S.

Pole Vault (July 26)
Tadeusz Slusarski, Poland 18' ½"†
Antti Kalliomaki, Finland
Dave Roberts, U.S.

Shot Put (July 24)
Udo Beyer, East Germany 69' 6.7"*
Yevgeny Mironov, U.S.S.R.
Aleksandr Baryshnikov, U.S.S.R.

Discus Throw (July 25)
Mac Wilkins, U.S. 221' 5.4"*
Wolfgang Schmidt, East Germany
John Powell, U.S.

Javelin Throw (July 26)
Miklos Nemeth, Hungary 310' 4½"*
Hannu Siitonen, Finland
Gheorghe Megelea, Romania

Hammer Throw (July 28)
Yuri Sedykh, U.S.S.R. 254' 4"*
Alexei Spiridonov, U.S.S.R.
Anatoly Bondarchuk, U.S.S.R.

Decathlon (July 30)
Bruce Jenner, U.S. 8,618 points*
Guido Kratschmer, West Germany
Nikolai Avilov, U.S.S.R.

WOMEN'S TRACK & FIELD

100-Meter Dash (July 25)
Annegret Richter, West Germany
11.01*
Renate Stecher, East Germany
Inge Helten, West Germany

---

* Olympic record.   † Equals Olympic record.

200-Meter Dash (July 28)

Baerbel Eckert, East Germany 22.37*
Annegret Richter, West Germany
Renate Stecher, East Germany

400-Meter Dash (July 29)

Irena Szewinska, Poland 49.29*
Christina Brehmer, East Germany
Ellen Streidt, East Germany

800-Meter Run (July 26)

Tatyana Kazankina, U.S.S.R.
1:54.94*
Nikolina Chtereva, Bulgaria
Elfi Zinn, East Germany

1,500-Meter Run (July 30)

Tatyana Kazankina, U.S.S.R.
4:5.48
Gunhild Hoffmeister, East Germany
Ulrike Klapezynski, East Germany

100-Meter Hurdles (July 29)

Johanna Schaller, East Germany
12.77
Tatyana Anisimova, U.S.S.R.
Natalya Lebedeva, U.S.S.R.

400-Meter Relay (July 31)

East Germany 42.55*
West Germany
U.S.S.R.

1,600-Meter Relay (July 31)

East Germany 3:19.23*
U.S.
U.S.S.R.

Long Jump (July 23)

Angela Voigt, East Germany 22' 2½"
Kathy McMillan, U.S.
Lydia Alfeyeva, U.S.S.R.

High Jump (July 28)

Rosemarie Ackermann, East
Germany 6' 4"*
Sara Simeoni, Italy
Yordanka Blagoeva, Bulgaria

Shot Put (July 31)

Ivanka Khristova, Bulgaria 69' 5"*
Nadezhda Chizhova, U.S.S.R.
Helena Fibingerova, Czechoslovakia

Discus Throw (July 29)

Evelin Schlaak, East Germany
226' 4½"*
Maria Vergova, Bulgaria
Gabriele Hinzmann, East Germany

Javelin Throw (July 24)

Ruth Fuchs, East Germany 216' 4"*
Marion Becker, West Germany
Kathryn Schmidt, U.S.

Pentathlon (July 26)

Siegrun Siegl, East Germany
4,745 points
Christine Laser, East Germany
Burglinde Pollak, East Germany

VOLLEYBALL

Men's (July 30)

Poland
U.S.S.R.
Cuba

Women's (July 30)

Japan
U.S.S.R.
South Korea

WATER POLO

Team Championship (July 27)

Hungary
Italy
Netherlands

* Olympic record.

WEIGHTLIFTING

Flyweight (July 18)

Aleksandr Voronin, U.S.S.R.
533.5 lbs.°
Gyorgy Koszegi, Hungary
Mohammad Nassiri, Iran

Bantamweight (July 19)

Norair Nurikian, Bulgaria
577.5 lbs.°
Grzegorz Cziura, Poland
Kenkichi Ando, Japan

Featherweight (July 19)

Nikolai Kolesnikov, U.S.S.R.
627 lbs.°
Georgi Todorov, Bulgaria
Kazumasa Harai, Japan

Leightweight (July 21)

Zbigniew Kaczmarek, Poland
676.5 lbs.
Pyotr Korol, U.S.S.R.
Daniel Senet, France

Middleweight (July 22)

Yordan Mitkov, Bulgaria 737 lbs.
Vartan Melitosyan, U.S.S.R.
Peter Wenzel, East Germany

Light Heavyweight (July 24)

Valery Shary, U.S.S.R. 803 lbs.
Blagoi Blagoev, Bulgaria
Trendafil Stoichev, Bulgaria

Middle Heavyweight (July 26)

David Rigert, U.S.S.R. 841.5 lbs.
Lee James, U.S.
Atanas Chopev, Bulgaria

Heavyweight (July 26)

Valentin Khristov, Bulgaria 880 lbs.*
Yuri Zaitsev, U.S.S.R.
Krastio Semerdjiev, Bulgaria

Super Heavyweight (July 27)

Vasily Alexeyev, U.S.S.R. 968 lbs.°
Gerd Bonk, East Germany
Helmut Losch, East Germany

FREE-STYLE WRESTLING

Paperweight (July 31)

Khassan Issaev, Bulgaria
Roman Dmitriyev, U.S.S.R.
Akira Kudo, Japan

Flyweight (July 31)

Yuji Takada, Japan
Aleksandr Ivanov, U.S.S.R.
Hae-Sup Jeon, South Korea

Bantamweight (July 31)

Vladimir Yumin, U.S.S.R.
Hans-Dieter Bruchert, East Germany
Massao Arai, Japan

Featherweight (July 31)

Jung-Mo Yang, South Korea
Zeveg Oidov, Mongolia
Gene Davis, U.S.

Lightweight (July 31)

Pavel Pinigin, U.S.S.R.
Lloyd Keaser, U.S.
Yasaburo Sugawara, Japan

Welterweight (July 31)

Jiichiro Date, Japan
Mansour Barzegar, Iran
Stanley Dziedzic, U.S.

Middleweight (July 31)

John Peterson, U.S.
Viktor Novozhilov, U.S.S.R.
Adolf Seger, West Germany

Light Heavyweight (July 31)

Levan Tediashvili, U.S.S.R.
Benjamin Peterson, U.S.
Stelica Morcov, Romania

Heavyweight (July 31)

Ivan Yaryagin, U.S.S.R.
Russell Hellickson, U.S.
Dimo Kostov, Bulgaria

Super Heavyweight (July 31)

Soslan Andiyev, U.S.S.R.
Jozsef Balla, Hungary
Ladislau Simon, Romania

GRECO-ROMAN WRESTLING

Paperweight (July 24)

Alexei Shumakov, U.S.S.R.
Gheorghe Berceanu, Romania
Stefan Angelov, Bulgaria

Flyweight (July 24)

Vitaly Konstantinov, U.S.S.R.
Nicu Ginga, Romania
Koichiro Hirayama, Japan

Bantamweight (July 24)

Pertti Ukkola, Finland
Ivan Frgic, Yugoslavia
Farkhat Mustafin, U.S.S.R.

Featherweight (July 24)

Kazimierz Lipien, Poland
Nelson Davidyan, U.S.S.R.
Laszlo Reczi, Hungary

Lightweight (July 24)

Suren Nalbandyan, U.S.S.R.
Stefan Rusu, Romania
Heinz-Helmut Wehling, East
Germany

Welterweight (July 24)

Anatoly Bykov, U.S.S.R.
Vitezslav Macha, Czechoslovakia
Karlheinz Helbing, West Germany

Middleweight (July 24)

Momir Petkovic, Yugoslavia
Vladimir Cheboksarov, U.S.S.R.
Ivan Kolev, Bulgaria

Light Heavyweight (July 24)

Valery Rezantsev, U.S.S.R.
Stoyan Ivanov, Bulgaria
Czeslaw Kwiecinski, Poland

Heavyweight (July 24)

Nikolai Balboshin, U.S.S.R.
Kamen Goranov, Bulgaria
Andrzej Skrzylewski, Poland

Super Heavyweight (July 24)

Aleksandr Kolchinsky, U.S.S.R.
Aleksandr Tomov, Bulgaria
Roman Codreanu, Romania

YACHTING

Finn Class (July 27)

East Germany 35.40 points
U.S.S.R.
Australia

Flying Dutchman (July 27)

West Germany 34.7 points
Great Britain
Brazil

Tempest (July 27)

Sweden 14 points
U.S.S.R.
U.S.

Soling (July 27)

Denmark 46.7 points
U.S.
East Germany

470 Class (July 27)

West Germany 42.4 points
Spain
Australia

Tornado (July 27)

Great Britain 18.00 points
U.S.
West Germany

SUMMER OLYMPIC CHAMPIONS
NOTE: An asterisk * denotes Olympic record.

SWIMMING AND DIVING (Men)

Year	Champion and Country	Time
100 Meter Free Style		**Min./Sec.**
1896	Alfred Hajos, Hungary	1:22.2
1904	Zoltan de Halmay, Hungary (100 yds.)	1:02.8
1908	Charles Daniels, United States	1:05.6
1912	Duke Kahanamoku, United States	1:03.4
1920	Duke Kahanamoku, United States	1:01.4
1924	John Weissmuller, United States	59.0
1928	John Weissmuller, United States	58.6
1932	Yasuji Miyazaki, Japan	58.2
1936	Ferenc Csik, Hungary	57.6
1948	Walter Ris, United States	57.3
1952	Clarke Scholes, United States	57.4
1956	Jon Hendricks, Australia	55.4
1960	John Devitt, Australia	55.2
1964	Donald A. Schollander, United States	53.4
1968	Michael Wenden, Australia	52.2
1972	Mark Spitz, United States	51.2
200 Meter Free Style		
1968	Michael Wenden, Australia	1:55.2
1972	Mark Spitz, United States	1:52.8
400 Meter Free Style		
1896	Paul Neumann, Austria (500 m.)	8:12.6
1904	Charles Daniels, United States (440 yds.)	6:16.2
1908	Henry Taylor, Great Britain	5:36.8
1912	George Hodgson, Canada	5:24.4
1920	Norman Ross, United States	5:26.8
1924	John Weissmuller, United States	5:04.2
1928	Albert Zorilla, Argentina	5:01.6
1932	Clarence Crabbe, United States	4:48.4
1936	Jack Medica, United States	4:44.5
1948	William Smith, United States	4:41.0
1952	Jean Boiteux, France	4:30.7
1956	Murray Rose, Australia	4:27.3
1960	Murray Rose, Australia	4:18.3
1964	Donald A. Schollander, United States	4:12.2
1968	Michael Burton, United States	4:09.0
1972	Bradford Cooper, Australia	4:00.3
1,500 Meter Free Style		**Min./Sec.**
1896	Alfred Hajos, Hungary (1,200 m.)	18:22.2
1900	John Jarvis, Great Britain (1,000 m.)	13:40.2
1904	Emil Rausch, Germany (1,609 m.)	27:18.2
1908	Henry Taylor, Great Britain	22:48.4
1912	George Hodgson, Canada	22:00.0
1920	Norman Ross, United States	22:23.2
1924	Andrew Charlton, Australia	20:06.6
1928	Arne Borg, Sweden	19:51.8
1932	Kusuo Kitamura, Japan	19:12.4
1936	Noboru Terada, Japan	19:13.7
1948	James P. McLane, United States	19:18.5
1952	Ford Konno, United States	18:30.0
1956	Murray Rose, Australia	17:58.9
1960	John Konrads, Australia	17:19.6
1964	Robert Windle, Australia	17:01.7
1968	Michael Burton, United States	16:38.9
1972	Michael Burton, United States	15:52.6
100 Meter Backstroke		
1904	Walter Brack, Germany (100 yds.)	1:16.8
1908	Arno Bieberstein, Germany	1:24.6
1912	Harry Hebner, United States	1:21.2
1920	Warren Kealoha, United States	1:15.2
1924	Warren Kealoha, United States	1:13.2
1928	George Kojac, United States	1:08.2
1932	Masaji Kiyokawa, Japan	1:08.6
1936	Adolph Kiefer, United States	1:05.9
1948	Allen Stack, United States	1:06.4
1952	Yoshinobu Oyakawa, United States	1:05.4
1956	David Thiele, Australia	1:02.2
1960	David Thiele, Australia	1:01.9
1964	Not on Program	
1968	Roland Matthes, East Germany	58.7
1972	Roland Matthes, East Germany	56.6
200 Meter Backstroke		
1900	Ernest Hoppenberg, Germany	2:47.0
1964	Jed R. Graef, United States	2:10.3
1968	Roland Matthes, East Germany	2:09.6
1972	Roland Matthes, East Germany	2:02.8
100 Meter Breaststroke		
1968	Donald McKenzie, United States	1:07.7
1972	Nobutaka Taguchi, Japan	1:04.9
200 Meter Breaststroke		
1908	Frederick Holman, Great Britain	3:09.2
1912	Walter Bathe, Germany	3:01.8
1920	Haken Malmroth, Sweden	3:04.4
1924	Robert Skelton, United States	2:56.6
1928	Yoshiyuki Tsuruta, Japan	2:48.8
1932	Yoshiyuki Tsuruta, Japan	2:45.4
1936	Tetsuo Hamuro, Japan	2:41.5
1948	Joseph Verdeur, United States	2:39.3
1952	John Davies, Australia	2:34.4
1956	Masaru Furukawa, Japan	2:34.7
1960	William Mulliken, United States	2:37.4
1964	Ian O'Brien, Australia	2:27.8
1968	Felipe Muñoz, Mexico	2:28.7
1972	John Hencken, United States	2:21.5
100 Meter Butterfly		
1968	Douglas Russell, United States	55.9
1972	Mark Spitz, United States	54.3*
200 Meter Butterfly		
1956	William Yorzyk, United States	2:19.3
1960	Michael Troy, United States	2:12.8
1964	Kevin Berry, Australia	2:06.6
1968	Carl Robie, United States	2:08.7
1972	Mark Spitz, United States	2:00.7
200 Meter Individual Medley		
1968	Charles Hickcox, United States	2:12.0
1972	Gunnar Larsson, Sweden	2:07.2*
400 Meter Individual Medley		
1964	Richard W. Roth, United States	4:45.4
1968	Charles Hickcox, United States	4:48.4
1972	Gunnar Larsson, Sweden	4:32.0
400 Meter Free Style Relay		
1964	United States	3:33.2
1968	United States	3:31.7
1972	United States	3:26.4*
400 Meter Medley Relay		
1960	United States	4:05.4
1964	United States	3:58.4
1968	United States	3:54.9
1972	United States	3:48.2
800 Meter Free Style Relay		
1908	Great Britain	10:55.6
1912	Australia	10:11.2
1920	United States	10:04.4
1924	United States	9:53.4
1928	United States	9:36.2
1932	Japan	8:58.2
1936	Japan	8:51.5
1948	United States	8:31.1
1952	United States	8:31.1
1956	Australia	8:23.6
1960	United States	8:10.2
1964	United States	7:52.1
1968	United States	7:52.3
1972	United States	7:38.8
Springboard Diving		**Points**
1908	Albert Zurner, Germany	85.50
1912	Paul Guenther, Germany	79.23
1920	Louis Kuehn, United States	675.00
1924	Albert C. White, United States	696.40
1928	Pete Desjardins, United States	185.04
1932	Michael Galitzen, United States	161.38
1936	Richard Degener, United States	163.57
1948	Bruce Harlan, United States	163.64
1952	David Browning, United States	205.29
1956	Robert L. Clotworthy, United States	159.56
1960	Gary Tobian, United States	170.00
1964	Kenneth R. Sitzberger, United States	159.90
1968	Bernard Wrightson, United States	170.15
1972	Vladimir Vasin, USSR	594.09
High Diving		
1904	Dr. G. E. Sheldon, United States	12.75
1908	Hjalmar Johansson, Sweden	83.75
1912	Erik Adlerz, Sweden	73.94
1920	Clarence Pinkston, United States	100.67
1924	Albert C. White, United States	97.46
1928	Pete Desjardins, United States	98.74
1932	Harold Smith, United States	124.80
1936	Marshall Wayne, United States	113.58
1948	Dr. Samuel Lee, United States	130.05
1952	Dr. Samuel Lee, United States	156.28
1956	Joaquin Capilla, Mexico	152.44
1960	Robert Webster, United States	165.56
1964	Robert Webster, United States	148.58
1968	Klaus DiBiasi, Italy	164.18
1972	Klaus DiBiasi, Italy	504.12

SWIMMING AND DIVING (Women)

100 Meter Free Style
	Min./Sec.
1912—Fanny Durack, Australia	1:22.2
1920—Ethelda Bleibtrey, United States	1:13.6
1924—Ethel Lackie, United States	1:12.4
1928—Albina Osipowich, United States	1:11.0
1932—Helene Madison, United States	1:06.8
1936—Hendrika Mastenbroek, Netherlands	1:05.9
1948—Greta Andersen, Denmark	1:06.3
1952—Katalin Szoke, Hungary	1:06.8
1956—Dawn Fraser, Australia	1:02.0
1960—Dawn Fraser, Australia	1:01.2
1964—Dawn Fraser, Australia	59.5
1968—Margo Jan Henne, United States	1:00.0
1972—Sandra Neilson, United States	58.6

200 Meter Free Style
1968—Deborah Meyer, United States	2:10.5
1972—Shane Gould, Australia	2:03.6

400 Meter Free Style
1920—Ethelda Bleibtrey, United States (300 m.)	4:34.0
1924—Martha Norelius, United States	6:02.2
1928—Martha Norelius, United States	5:42.4
1932—Helene Madison, United States	5:28.5
1936—Hendrika Mastenbroek, Netherlands	5:26.4
1948—Ann Curtis, United States	5:17.8
1952—Valeria Gyenge, Hungary	5:12.1
1956—Lorraine Crapp, Australia	4:54.6
1960—S. Chris Von Saltza, United States	4:50.6
1964—Virginia Duenkel, United States	4:43.3
1968—Deborah Meyer, United States	4:31.8
1972—Shane Gould, Australia	4:19.0

800 Meter Free Style
1968—Deborah Meyer, United States	9:24.0
1972—Keena Rothhammer, United States	8:53.7

100 Meter Backstroke
1924—Sybil Bauer, United States	1:23.2
1928—Marie Braun, Netherlands	1:22.0
1932—Eleanor Holm, United States	1:19.4
1936—Dina Senff, Netherlands	1:18.9
1948—Karen Harup, Denmark	1:14.4
1952—Joan Harrison, South Africa	1:14.3
1956—Judy Grinham, Great Britain	1:12.9
1960—Lynn Burke, United States	1:09.3
1964—Cathy Ferguson, United States	1:07.7
1968—Kaye Hall, United States	1:06.2
1972—Melissa Belote, United States	1:05.8

200 Meter Backstroke
1968—Lillian (Pokey) Watson, United States	2:24.8
1972—Melissa Belote, United States	2:19.2

100 Meter Butterfly
1956—Shelley Mann, United States	1:11.0
1960—Carolyn Schuler, United States	1:09.5
1964—Sharon Stouder, United States	1:04.7
1968—Lynn McClements, Australia	1:05.5
1972—Mayumi Aoki, Japan	1:03.3

200 Meter Butterfly
1968—Ada Kok, Netherlands	2:24.7
1972—Karen Moe, United States	2:15.6

100 Meter Breaststroke
1968—Djurdjica Bjedov, Yugoslavia	1:15.8
1972—Cathy Carr, United States	1:13.6

200 Meter Breaststroke
1924—Lucy Morton, Great Britain	3:33.2
1928—Hilde Schrader, Germany	3:12.6
1932—Clare Dennis, Australia	3:06.3
1936—Hideko Maehata, Japan	3:03.6
1948—Nelly Van Vliet, Netherlands	2:57.2
1952—Eva Szekely, Hungary	2:51.7
1956—Ursula Happe, Germany	2:53.1
1960—Anita Lonsbrough, Great Britain	2:49.5
1964—Galina Prozumenshikova, USSR	2:46.4
1968—Sharon Wichman, United States	2:44.4
1972—Beverly Whitfield, Australia	2:41.7

400 Meter Free Style Relay
1912—Great Britain	5:52.8
1920—United States	5:11.6
1924—United States	4:58.8
1928—United States	4:47.6
1932—United States	4:38.0
1936—Netherlands	4:36.0
1948—United States	4:29.2
1952—Hungary	4:24.4
1956—Australia	4:17.1
1960—United States	4:08.9
1964—United States	4:03.8
1968—United States	4:02.5
1972—United States	3:55.2

400 Meter Medley Relay
1960—United States	4:41.1
1964—United States	4:33.9
1968—United States	4:28.3
1972—United States	4:20.7

200 Meter Individual Medley
1968—Claudia Kolb, United States	2:24.7
1972—Shane Gould, Australia	2:23.1*

400 Meter Individual Medley
1964—Donna de Varona, United States	5:18.7
1968—Claudia Kolb, United States	5:08.5
1972—Gail Neall, Australia	5:03.0

Springboard Diving
	Points
1920—Aileen Riggin, United States	539.90
1924—Elizabeth Becker, United States	474.50
1928—Helen Meany, United States	78.62
1932—Georgia Coleman, United States	87.52
1936—Marjorie Gestring, United States	89.27
1948—Victoria Draves, United States	108.74
1952—Patricia McCormick, United States	147.30
1956—Patricia McCormick, United States	142.36
1960—Ingrid Kramer, Germany	155.81
1964—Ingrid Engle-Kramer, Germany	145.00
1968—Sue Gossick, United States	150.77
1972—Micki King, United States	450.03

High Diving
1912—Greta Johansson, Sweden	39.90
1920—Stefani Fryland-Clausen, Denmark	34.60
1924—Caroline Smith, United States	33.20
1928—Elizabeth Pinkston, United States	31.60
1932—Dorothy Poynton, United States	40.26
1936—Dorothy Poynton Hill, United States	33.93
1948—Victoria Draves, United States	68.87
1952—Patricia McCormick, United States	79.37
1956—Patricia McCormick, United States	84.85
1960—Ingrid Kramer, Germany	91.28
1964—Lesley Bush, United States	99.80
1968—Milena Duchkova, Czechoslovakia	109.59
1972—Ulrika Knape, Sweden	390.00

TRACK AND FIELD (Men)

100 Meter Dash
	Sec.
1896—Thomas E. Burke, United States	12.0
1900—Francis W. Jarvis, United States	10.8
1904—Archie Hahn, United States	11.0
1908—Reginald E. Walker, South Africa	10.8
1912—Ralph C. Craig, United States	10.8
1920—Charles W. Paddock, United States	10.8
1924—Harold M. Abrahams, Great Britain	10.6
1928—Percy Williams, Canada	10.8
1932—Eddie Tolan, United States	10.3
1936—Jesse Owens, United States	10.3
1948—Harrison Dillard, United States	10.3
1952—Lindy J. Remigino, United States	10.4
1956—Bobby J. Morrow, United States	10.5
1960—Armin Hary, Germany	10.2
1964—Robert L. Hayes, United States	10.0
1968—James Hines, United States	9.9*
1972—Valery Borzov, USSR	10.1

200 Meter Dash
1900—John W. B. Tewksbury, United States	22.2
1904—Archie Hahn, United States	21.6
1908—Robert Kerr, Canada	22.6
1912—Ralph C. Craig, United States	21.7
1920—Allan Woodring, United States	22.0
1924—Jackson V. Scholz, United States	21.6
1928—Percy Williams, Canada	21.8
1932—Eddie Tolan, United States	21.2
1936—Jesse Owens, United States	20.7
1948—Melvin Patton, United States	21.1
1952—Andrew W. Stanfield, United States	20.7
1956—Bobby J. Morrow, United States	20.6
1960—Livio Berruti, Italy	20.5
1964—Henry Carr, United States	20.3
1968—Tommie Smith, United States	19.8*
1972—Valery Borzov, USSR	20.0

400 Meter Dash
1896—Thomas E. Burke, United States	54.2
1900—Maxwell W. Long, United States	49.4
1904—Harry I. Hillman, United States	49.2
1908—Wyndham Halswelle, Great Britain	50.0
1912—Charles D. Reidpath, United States	48.2
1920—Bevil G. D. Rudd, South Africa	49.6
1924—Eric H. Liddel, Great Britain	47.6
1928—Ray Barbuti, United States	47.8
1932—William A. Carr, United States	46.2
1936—Archie Williams, United States	46.5
1948—Arthur Wint, Jamaica	46.2
1952—George Rhoden, Jamaica	45.9
1956—Charles L. Jenkins, United States	46.7

1960—Otis Davis, United States	44.9
1964—Michael D. Larrabee, United States	45.1
1968—Lee Evans, United States	43.8*
1972—Vince Matthews, United States	44.7

800 Meter Run   **Min./Sec.**

1896—Edwin H. Flack, Australia	2:11.0
1900—Alfred E. Tysoe, Great Britain	2:01.4
1904—James D. Lightbody, United States	1:56.0
1908—Melvin W. Sheppard, United States	1:52.8
1912—James E. Meredith, United States	1:51.9
1920—Albert G. Hill, Great Britain	1:53.4
1924—Douglas G. A. Lowe, Great Britain	1:52.4
1928—Douglas G. A. Lowe, Great Britain	1:51.8
1932—Thomas Hampson, Great Britain	1:49.8
1936—John Woodruff, United States	1:52.9
1948—Malvin Whitfield, United States	1:49.2
1952—Malvin Whitfield, United States	1:49.2
1956—Thomas W. Courtney, United States	1:47.7
1960—Peter Snell, New Zealand	1:46.3
1964—Peter Snell, New Zealand	1:45.1
1968—Ralph Doubell, Australia	1:44.3
1972—Dave Wottle, United States	1:45.9

1,500 Meter Run

1896—Edwin H. Flack, Great Britain	4:33.2
1900—Charles Bennett, Great Britain	4:06.2
1904—James D. Lightbody, United States	4:05.4
1908—Melvin W. Sheppard, United States	4:03.4
1912—Arnold N. S. Jackson, Great Britain	3:56.8
1920—Albert G. Hill, Great Britain	4:01.8
1924—Paavo Nurmi, Finland	3:53.6
1928—Harry E. Larva, Finland	3:53.2
1932—Luigi Beccali, Italy	3:51.2
1936—Jack E. Lovelock, New Zealand	3:47.8
1948—Henry Eriksson, Sweden	3:49.8
1952—Joseph Barthel, Luxembourg	3:45.2
1956—Ronald Delany, Ireland	3:41.2
1960—Herbert Elliott, Australia	3:35.6
1964—Peter Snell, New Zealand	3:38.1
1968—Kipchoge Keino, Kenya	3:34.9*
1972—Pekka Vasala, Finland	3:36.3

5,000 Meter Run

1912—Hannes Kolehmainen, Finland	14:36.6
1920—Joseph Guillemot, France	14:55.6
1924—Paavo Nurmi, Finland	14:31.2
1928—Willie Ritola, Finland	14:38.0
1932—Lauri Lehtinen, Finland	14.30.0
1936—Gunnar Hockert, Finland	14:22.2
1948—Gaston Reiff, Belgium	14:17.6
1952—Emil Zatopek, Czechoslovakia	14:06.6
1956—Vladimir Kuts, USSR	13.39.6
1960—Murray Halberg, New Zealand	13:43.4
1964—Robert K. Schul, United States	13:48.8
1968—Mohamed Gammoudi, Tunisia	14:05.0
1972—Lasse Viren, Finland	13:26.4

10,000 Meter Run

1912—Hannes Kolehmainen, Finland	31:20.8
1920—Paavo Nurmi, Finland	31:45.8
1924—Willie Ritola, Finland	30:23.2
1928—Paavo Nurmi, Finland	30:18.8
1932—Janusz Kusocinski, Poland	30:11.4
1936—Ilmari Salminen, Finland	30:15.4
1948—Emil Zatopek, Czechoslovakia	29:59.6
1952—Emil Zatopek, Czechoslovakia	29:17.0
1956—Vladimir Kuts, USSR	28:45.6
1960—Petr Bolotnikov, USSR	28:32.2
1964—William Mills, United States	28:24.4
1968—Naftali Temu, Kenya	29:27.4
1972—Lasse Viren, Finland	27:38.4*

Marathon   **Hr./Min./Sec.**

1896—Spyros Loues, Greece	2:58:50.0
1900—Michel Theato, France	2:59:45.0
1904—Thomas J. Hicks, United States	3:28:53.0
1908—John J. Hayes, United States	2:55:18.4
1912—Kenneth McArthur, South Africa	2:36:54.8
1920—Hannes Kolehmainen, Finland	2:32:35.8
1924—Albin Stenroos, Finland	2:41:22.6
1928—A. B. El Ouafi, France	2:32:57.0
1932—Juan Zabala, Argentina	2:31:36.0
1936—Kitei Son, Japan	2:29:19.2
1948—Delfo Cabrera, Argentina	2:34:51.6
1952—Emil Zatopek, Czechoslovakia	2:23:03.2
1956—Alain Mimoun, France	2:25:00.0
1960—Abebe Bikila, Ethiopia	2:15:16.2
1964—Abebe Bikila, Ethiopia	2:12:11.2
1968—Mamo Wolde, Ethiopia	2:20:26.4
1972—Frank Shorter, United States	2:12:19.7

110 Meter Hurdles   **Sec.**

1896—Thomas P. Curtis, United States	17.6
1900—Alvin E. Kraenzlein, United States	15.4

1904—Frederick W. Schule, United States	16.0
1908—Forrest Smithson, United States	15.0
1912—Frederick W. Kelley, United States	15.1
1920—Earl J. Thompson, Canada	14.8
1924—Daniel C. Kinsey, United States	15.0
1928—Sydney Atkinson, South Africa	14.8
1932—George Saling, United States	14.6
1936—Forrest Towns, United States	14.2
1948—William Porter, United States	13.9
1952—Harrison Dillard, United States	13.7
1956—Lee Q. Calhoun, United States	13.5
1960—Lee Q. Calhoun, United States	13.8
1964—Hayes W. Jones, United States	13.6
1968—Willie Davenport, United States	13.3
1972—Rod Milburn, United States	13.2*

400 Meter Hurdles

1900—John W. B. Tewksbury, United States	57.6
1904—Harry L. Hillman, United States	53.0
1908—Charles J. Bacon, United States	55.0
1920—Frank F. Loomis, United States	54.0
1924—F. Morgan Taylor, United States	52.6
1928—Lord David Burghley, Great Britain	53.4
1932—Robert Tisdall, Ireland	51.8
1936—Glenn Hardin, United States	52.4
1948—Roy Cochran, United States	51.1
1952—Charles Moore, United States	50.8
1956—Glenn A. Davis, United States	50.1
1960—Glenn A. Davis, United States	49.3
1964—Warren (Rex) Cawley, United States	49.6
1968—David Hemery, Great Britain	48.1
1972—John Akii-Bua, Uganda	47.8

3,000 Meter Steeplechase   **Min./Sec.**

1920—Percy Hodge, Great Britain	10:00.4
1924—Willie Ritola, Finland	9:33.6
1928—Toivo A. Loukola, Finland	9:21.8
1932—Volmari Iso-Hollo, Finland	10:33.4
(3,460 meters—extra lap by official error)	
1936—Volmari Iso-Hollo, Finland	9:03.8
1948—Thore Sjostrand, Sweden	9:04.6
1952—Horace Ashenfelter, United States	8:45.4
1956—Chris Brasher, Great Britain	8:41.2
1960—Zdzislaw Krzyszkowiak, Poland	8:34.2
1964—Gaston Roelants, Belgium	8:30.8
1968—Amos Biwott, Kenya	8:51.0
1972—Kipchoge Keino, Kenya	8:23.6

20,000 Meter Walk   **Hr./Min./Sec.**

1956—Leonid Spirine, USSR	1:31:27.4
1960—Vladimir Golubnichy, USSR	1:34:07.2
1964—Kenneth Matthews, Great Britain	1:29:34.0
1968—Vladimir Golubnichy, USSR	1:33:58.4
1972—Peter Frenkel, East Germany	1:26:42.4

50,000 Meter Walk

1932—Thomas W. Green, Great Britain	4:50:10.0
1936—Harold Whitlock, Great Britain	4:30:41.4
1948—John A. Ljunggren, Sweden	4:41:52.0
1952—Giuseppe Dordoni, Italy	4:28:07.8
1956—Norman Read, New Zealand	4:30:42.8
1960—Donald Thompson, Great Britain	4:25:30.0
1964—Abdon Pamich, Italy	4:11:12.4
1968—Christoph Kohne, East Germany	4:20:13.6
1972—Bernd Kannenberg, West Germany	3:56:11.6*

400 Meter Relay   **Sec.**

1912—Great Britain (D. H. Jacobs, H. M. Macintosh, Victor d'Arcy, William Applegarth)	42.4
1920—United States (Charles Paddock, Jackson Scholz, Morris Kirksey, Loren Murchison)	42.2
1924—United States (Louis Clarke, Francis Hussey, Loren Murchison, Alfred Leconey)	41.0
1928—United States (Frank Wykoff, James Quinn, Charles Borah, Henry Russell)	41.0
1932—United States (Robert Kiesel, Emmett Toppino, Hector Dyer, Frank Wykoff)	40.0
1936—United States (Jesse Owens, Ralph Metcalfe, Foy Draper, Frank Wykoff)	40.0
1948—United States (Norwood Ewell, Lorenzo Wright, Harrison Dillard, Mel Patton)	40.3
1952—United States (Dean Smith, Harrison Dillard, Lindy J. Remigino, Andrew Stanfield)	40.1
1956—United States (Ira Murchison, Leamon King, Thane Baker, Bobby J. Morrow)	39.5
1960—Germany (Bernd Cullman, Armin Hary, Walter Mahlendorf, Martin Lauer)	39.5
1964—United States (Otis Paul Drayton, Gerald Ashworth, Richard Stebbins, Robert Hayes)	39.0
1968—United States (Charles Greene, Melvin Pender, Ronnie Ray Smith, James Hines)	38.2
1972—United States (Larry Black, Robert Taylor, Gerald Tinker, Eddie Hart)	38.2*

1,600 Meter Relay	Min./Sec.
1908—United States (William F. Hamilton, Nathan J. Cartmell, John Taylor, Melvin W. Sheppard)	3:29.4
1912—United States (Melvin W. Sheppard, Edward F. Lindberg, James E. Meredith, Charles D. Reidpath)	3:16.6
1920—Great Britain (Robert Lindsay, Guy Butler, John Ainsworth-Davies, Cecil Griffiths)	3:22.2
1924—United States (C. S. Cochran, William E. Stevenson, J. O. McDonald, Allen Helffrich)	3:16.0
1928—United States (George Baird, Fred Alderman, Emerson Spencer, Ray Barbuti)	3:14.2
1932—United States (Ivan Fuqua, Edgar Ablowich, Karl Warner, William Carr)	3:08.2
1936—Great Britain (Frederick Wolff, Godfrey Rampling, William Roberts, Arthur Brown)	3:09.0
1948—United States (Cliff Bourland, Art Harnden, Roy Cochran, Malvin Whitfield)	3:10.4
1952—Jamaica (Herbert McKenley, Leslie Laing, Arthur Wint, George Rhoden)	3:03.9
1956—United States (Charles Jenkins, Louis Jones, Jesse Mashburn, Thomas Courtney)	3:04.8
1960—United States (Jack Yerman, Earl Young, Glenn Davis, Otis Davis)	3:02:2
1964—United States (Ollan Cassell, Michael Larrabee, Ulis Williams, Henry Carr)	3:00.7
1968—United States (Vincent Matthews, Ronald Freeman, Lawrence James, Lee Evans)	2:56.1*
1972—Kenya (Charles Asafi, Hezahiah Nyamau, Robert Ouko, Julius Sang)	2:59.8

Pole Vault	Height
1896—William W. Hoyt, United States	10' 9¾"
1900—Irving K. Baxter, United States	10' 9 9/10"
1904—Charles E. Dvorak, United States	11' 6"
1908—Albert C. Gilbert, United States Edward T. Cook, Jr., United States	12' 2"
1912—Harry S. Babcock, United States	12' 11½"
1920—Frank K. Foss, United States	12' 5 9/16"
1924—Lee S. Barnes, United States	12' 11½"
1928—Sabin W. Carr, United States	13' 9¾"
1932—William Miller, United States	14' 1⅞"
1936—Earle Meadows, United States	14' 3¼"
1948—O. Guinn Smith, United States	14' 1¼"
1952—Robert Richards, United States	14' 11¼"
1956—Robert Richards, United States	14' 11½"
1960—Donald Bragg, United States	15' 5⅛"
1964—Fred M. Hansen, United States	16' 8¾"
1968—Robert Seagren, United States	17' 8½"
1972—Wolfgang Nordwig, East Germany	18' ½"*

High Jump	
1896—Ellery Clark, United States	5' 11¼"
1900—Irving K. Baxter, United States	6' 2⅝"
1904—Samuel Jones, United States	5' 11"
1908—Harry Porter, United States	6' 3"
1912—Almer Richards, United States	6' 4"
1920—Richmond Landon, United States	6' 4¼"
1924—Harold Osborn, United States	6' 5 15/16"
1928—Robert W. King, United States	6' 4⅜"
1932—Duncan McNaughton, Canada	6' 5⅝"
1936—Cornelius Johnson, United States	6' 7 15/16"
1948—John Winter, Australia	6' 6"
1952—Walter Davis, United States	6' 8¼"
1956—Charles E. Dumas, United States	6' 11¼"
1960—Robert Shavlakadze, USSR	7' 1"
1964—Valery Brumel, USSR	7' 1¾"
1968—Richard Fosbury, United States	7' 4¼"
1972—Juri Tarmak, USSR	7' 3¾"

Long Jump	Distance
1896—Ellery Clark, United States	20' 10"
1900—Alvin Kraenzlein, United States	23' 6⅞"
1904—Myer Prinstein, United States	24' 1"
1908—Francis Irons, United States	24' 6½"
1912—Albert Gutterson, United States	24' 11¼"
1920—William Pettersson, Sweden	23' 5½"
1924—DeHart Hubbard, United States	24' 5½"
1928—Edward Hamm, United States	25' 4¾"
1932—Edward Gordon, United States	25' ¾"
1936—Jesse Owens, United States	26' 5⅜"
1948—Willie Steel, United States	25' 8"
1952—Jerome Biffle, United States	24' 10"
1956—Gregory C. Bell, United States	25' 8¼"

1960—Ralph H. Boston, United States	26' 7¾"
1964—Lynn Davies, Great Britain	26' 5¾"
1968—Robert Beamon, United States	29' 2¼"**
1972—Randy Williams, United States	27' ½"

Triple Jump	
1896—James B. Connolly, United States	45' 0"
1900—Myer Prinstein, United States	47' 4¼"
1904—Myer Prinstein, United States	47' 0"
1908—Timothy Ahearne, Great Britain	48' 11¼"
1912—Gustaf Lindblom, Sweden	48' 5⅛"
1920—Vilho Tuulos, Finland	47' 6⅞"
1924—Archibald Winter, Australia	50' 11⅛"
1928—Mikio Oda, Japan	49' 10 13/16"
1932—Chuhei Nambu, Japan	51' 7"
1936—Naoto Tajima, Japan	52' 5⅞"
1948—Arne Ahman, Sweden	50' 6¼"
1952—Adhemar Ferreira da Silva, Brazil	53' 2½"
1956—Adhemar Ferreira da Silva, Brazil	53' 7½"
1960—Jozef Schmidt, Poland	55' 1¾"
1964—Jozef Schmidt, Poland	55' 3¼"
1968—Viktor Saneyev, USSR	57' ¾"*
1972—Viktor Saneyev, USSR	56' 11"

16-Pound Shot Put	
1896—Robert Garrett, United States	36' 9¾"
1900—Richard Sheldon, United States	46' 3½"
1904—Ralph Rose, United States	48' 7"
1908—Ralph Rose, United States	46' 7½"
1912—Patrick McDonald, United States	50' 4"
1920—Ville Porhola, Finland	48' 7¼"
1924—Clarence Houser, United States	49' 2½"
1928—John Kuck, United States	52' 13/16"
1932—Leo Sexton, United States	52' 6 3/16"
1936—Hans Woellke, Germany	53' 1¾"
1948—Wilbur Thompson, United States	56' 2"
1952—Wm. Parry O'Brien, Jr., United States	57' 1½"
1956—Wm. Parry O'Brien, Jr., United States	60' 11"
1960—William Nieder, United States	64' 6¾"
1964—Dallas C. Long, United States	66' 8¼"
1968—James Randel Matson, United States	67' 4¾"
1972—Wladyslaw Komar, Poland	69' 6"

Discus Throw	
1896—Robert Garrett, United States	95' 7½"
1900—Rudolf Bauer, Hungary	118' 2 9/10"
1904—Martin Sheridan, United States	128' 10½"
1908—Martin Sheridan, United States	134' 2"
1912—Armas Taipale, Finland	145' 9/16"
1920—Elmer Niklander, Finland	146' 7"
1924—Clarence Houser, United States	151' 5¼"
1928—Clarence Houser, United States	155' 2⅘"
1932—John Anderson, United States	162' 4 ⅞"
1936—Kenneth Carpenter, United States	165' 7½"
1948—Adolfo Consolini, Italy	173' 2"
1952—Sim Iness, United States	180' 6½"
1956—Alfred A. Oerter, United States	184' 10½"
1960—Alfred A. Oerter, United States	194' 2"
1964—Alfred A. Oerter, United States	200' 1½"
1968—Alfred A. Oerter, United States	212' 6½"
1972—Ludwick Danek, Czechoslovakia	211' 3½"

16-Pound Hammer Throw	
1900—John Flanagan, United States	167' 4"
1904—John Flanagan, United States	168' 1"
1908—John Flanagan, United States	170' 4¼"
1912—Matthew McGrath, United States	179' 7½"
1920—Patrick Ryan, United States	173' 5⅝"
1924—Frederick Tootell, United States	174' 10¼"
1928—Patrick O'Callaghan, Ireland	168' 7½"
1932—Patrick O'Callaghan, Ireland	176' 11⅛"
1936—Karl Hein, Germany	185' 4¼"
1948—Imre Nemeth, Hungary	183' 11½"
1952—Jozsef Csermak, Hungary	197' 11¾"
1956—Harold V. Connolly, United States	207' 3½"
1960—Vasiliy Rudenkov, USSR	220' 1¾"
1964—Romuald Klim, USSR	228' 9½"
1968—Gyula Zsivotzky, Hungary	240' 8"
1972—Anatol Bondarchuk, USSR	247' 8"

Javelin Throw	
1908—Erik Lemming, Sweden	179' 10½"
1912—Erik Lemming, Sweden	198' 11¼"
1920—Jonni Myyra, Finland	215' 9¾"
1924—Jonni Myyra, Finland	206' 6"¾
1928—Erik Lundquist, Sweden	218' 6¼"
1932—Matti Jarvinen, Finland	238' 7"
1936—Gerhard Stock, Germany	235' 8 5/16"
1948—Tapio Rautavaara, Finland	228' 10½"
1952—Cyrus Young, United States	242' ¾"
1956—Egil Danielson, Norway	281' 2¼"
1960—Viktor Tsibulenko, USSR	277' 8¾"
1964—Pauli Nevala, Finland	271' 2¼"
1968—Janis Lusis, USSR	295' 7¼"
1972—Klaus Wolfermann, West Germany	296' 10"

Decathlon	Points
1912—Hugo Wieslander, Sweden	7724.49
1920—Helge Lovland, Norway	6804.35
1924—Harold Osborn, United States	7710.77
1928—Paavo Yrjola, Finland	8053.29
1932—James Bausch, United States	8462.23
(Old point system, 1912 through 1932)	
1936—Glenn Morris, United States	7900.00
1948—Robert Mathias, United States	7139.00
1952—Robert Mathias, United States	7887.00
1956—Milton G. Campbell, United States	7937.00
1960—Rafer Johnson, United States	8392.00
(Revised point system, 1936 through 1960)	
1964—Willi Holdorf, Germany	7887.00
(New scoring system)	
1968—William Toomey, United States	8193.00
1972—Nikolai Avilov, USSR	8454.00

TRACK AND FIELD (Women)

100 Meter Dash	Sec.
1928—Elizabeth Robinson, United States	12.2
1932—Stanislawa Walasiewicz, Poland	11.9
1936—Helen Stephens, United States	11.5
1948—Francina Blankers-Koen, Netherlands	11.9
1952—Marjorie Jackson, Australia	11.5
1956—Betty Cuthbert, Australia	11.5
1960—Wilma Rudolph, United States	11.0
1964—Wyomia Tyus, United States	11.4
1968—Wyomia Tyus, United States	11.0
1972—Renate Stecher, East Germany	11.1

200 Meter Dash	
1948—Francina Blankers-Koen, Netherlands	24.4
1952—Marjorie Jackson, Australia	23.7
1956—Betty Cuthbert, Australia	23.4
1960—Wilma Rudolph, United States	24.0
1964—Edith McGuire, United States	23.0
1968—Irena Kirszenstein Szewinska, Poland	22.5
1972—Renate Stecher, East Germany	22.4

400 Meter Dash	
1964—Betty Cuthbert, Australia	52.0
1968—Colette Besson, France	52.0
1972—Monika Zehrt, East Germany	51.1

800 Meter Run	Min./Sec.
1928—Linda Radke-Batschauer, Germany	2:16.8
1960—Ljudmila Shevcova-Lysenko, USSR	2:04.3
1964—Ann Packer, Great Britain	2:01.1
1968—Madeline Manning, United States	2:00.9
1972—Hildegard Falck, West Germany	1:58.6

400 Meter Relay	Sec.
1928—Canada	48.4
1932—United States	47.0
1936—United States	46.9
1948—Netherlands	47.5
1952—United States	45.9
1956—Australia	44.5
1960—United States	44.5
1964—Poland	43.6
1968—United States	42.8
1972—West Germany	42.8

80 Meter Hurdles	
1932—Mildred Didrikson, United States	11.7
1936—Trebisonda Valla, Italy	11.7
1948—Francina Blankers-Koen, Netherlands	11.2
1952—Shirley Strickland de la Hunty, Australia	10.9
1956—Shirley Strickland de la Hunty, Australia	10.7
1960—Irina Press, USSR	10.8
1964—Karin Balzer, Germany	10.5
1968—Maureen Caird, Australia	10.3*

100 Meter Hurdles	
1972—Annelie Erhardt, East Germany	12.6*

High Jump	Height
1928—Ethel Catherwood, Canada	5' 3"
1932—Jean Shiley, United States	5' 5¼"

1936—Ibolya Csak, Hungary	5' 3"
1948—Alice Coachman, United States	5' 6⅛"
1952—Esther Brand, South Africa	5' 5¾"
1956—Mildred McDaniel, United States	5' 9¼"
1960—Iolanda Balas, Rumania	6' ¼"
1964—Iolanda Balas, Rumania	6' 2¾"
1968—Miloslava Rezkova, Czechoslovakia	5' 11¾"
1972—Ulrika Meyfarth, West Germany	6' 3½"

Long Jump	Distance
1948—Olga Gyarmati, Hungary	18' 8¼"
1952—Yvette Williams, New Zealand	20' 5¾"
1956—Elizbieta Krzeskinska, Poland	20' 9¾"
1960—Vyera Krepkina, USSR	20' 10¾"
1964—Mary Rand, Great Britain	22' 2"
1968—Viorica Viscopoleanu, Rumania	22' 4½"*
1972—Heidemarie Rosendahl, West Germany	22' 3"

Discus Throw	
1928—Helena Konopacka, Poland	129' 11⅞"
1932—Lillian Copeland, Unted States	133' 2"
1936—Gisela Mauermayer, Germany	156' 3 3/16"
1948—Micheline Ostermeyer, France	137' 6½"
1952—Nina Romaschkova, USSR	168' 8½"
1956—Olga Fikotova, Czechoslovakia	176' 1½"
1960—Nina Ponomareva, USSR	180' 8¼"
1964—Tamara Press, USSR	187' 10¾"
1968—Lia Manoliu, Rumania	191' 2½"
1972—Faina Melnik, USSR	218' 7"

8-Lb./13-Oz. Shot Put	
1948—Micheline Ostermeyer, France	45' 1½"
1952—Galina Zybina, USSR	50' 1½"
1956—Tamara Tishkyevich, USSR	54' 5"
1960—Tamara Press, USSR	56' 9¾"
1964—Tamara Press, USSR	59' 6"
1968—Margitta Gummel, East Germany	64' 4"
1972—Nadezhda Chizhova, USSR	69'

Javelin Throw	
1932—Mildred Didrikson, United States	143' 4"
1936—Tilly Fleischer, Germany	148' 2¾"
1948—Herma Bauma, Austria	149' 6"
1952—Dana Zatopekova, Czechoslovakia	165' 7"
1956—Inessa Janzeme, USSR	176' 8"
1960—Elvira Ozolina, USSR	183' 8"
1964—Mihaela Penes, Rumania	198' 7½"
1968—Angela Nemeth, Hungary	198' ½"
1972—Ruth Fuchs, East Germany	209' 7"

Pentathlon	Points
1964—Irina Press, USSR	5,246
1968—Ingrid Becker, West Germany	5,098
1972—Mary Peters, Britain	4,801*

WEIGHTLIFTING

Light Heavyweight	Total
1948—Stanley Stanczyk, United States	920¼
1952—Trofim Lomakin, USSR	920¼
1956—Tommy Kono, United States	986¼
1960—Ireneusz Palinski, Poland	975¼
1964—Rudolf Plyukfeider, USSR	1,047
1968—Boris Selitsky, USSR	1,067
1972—Leif Jenssen, Norway	1,118.8*

Middle Heavyweight	
1952—Norbert Schemansky, United States	980¾
1956—Arkady Vorobiev, USSR	1,019¼
1960—Arkady Vorobiev, USSR	1,041¼
1964—Vladimir Golovanov, USSR	1,072½
1968—Kaarlo Kangasniemi, Finland	1,138½
1972—Andon Nikolv, Bulgaria	1,157.4*

Heavyweight	
1948—John Davis, United States	997½
1952—John Davis, United States	1,013¾
1956—Paul Anderson, United States	1,102
1960—Yury Vlasov, USSR	1,184¼
1964—Leonid Zhabotinsky, USSR	1,262
1968—Leonid Zhabotinsky, USSR	1,259½
1972—Yan Talts, USSR	1,278.7

WRESTLING (Free Style)

Year Champion and Country	Year Champion and Country	Year Champion and Country
Middleweight		
1948—Glen Brand, United States	1956—Nikoli Nikolov, Bulgaria	1964—Prodan Gardjev, Bulgaria
1952—David Cimakuridze, USSR	1960—Hasan Gungor, Turkey	1968—Boris Gurevitch, USSR
		1972—Levan Tediashvili, USSR
Light Heavyweight		
1948—Henry Wittenberg, United States	1956—Ghalam Takhiti, Iran	1964—Aleksandr Medved, USSR
1952—Wiking Palm, Sweden	1960—Ismet Atli, Turkey	1968—Ahmet Ayuk, Turkey
		1972—Ben Peterson, U.S.
Heavyweight		
1948—Gyula Bobis, Hungary	1956—Hamil Kaplan, Turkey	1964—Aleksandr Ivanitsky, USSR
1952—Arsen Mekokishvili, USSR	1960—Wilfried Dietrich, Germany	1968—Aleksandr Medved, USSR
		1972—Ivan Yarygin, USSR

THE WINTER OLYMPIC GAMES

Sites	Year	Sites	Year
I Chamonix	1924	VII Cortina	1956
II St. Moritz	1928	VIII Squaw Valley	1960
III Lake Placid	1932	IX Innsbruck	1964
IV Garmisch-Partenkirchen	1936	X Grenoble	1968
V St. Moritz	1948	XI Sapporo	1972
VI Oslo	1952	XII Innsbruck	1976
		XIII Lake Placid	1980

1976 WINTER OLYMPICS MEDAL TABLE

	Gold (1st)	Silver (2d)	Bronze (3d)	Total		Gold (1st)	Silver (2d)	Bronze (3d)	Total
USSR	13	6	8	27	Switzerland	1	3	1	5
East Germany	7	5	7	19	Italy	1	2	1	4
U.S.A.	3	3	4	10	Canada	1	1	1	3
West Germany	2	5	3	10	Liechtenstein	0	2	0	2
Norway	3	3	1	7	Sweden	0	0	2	2
Finland	2	4	1	7	United Kingdom	1	0	0	1
Austria	2	2	2	6	Czechoslovakia	0	1	0	1
Netherlands	1	2	3	6	France	0	0	1	1

INNSBRUCK WINNING MEDALISTS: 1976   (* denotes Olympic record)

ALPINE SKIING (Men)
Downhill
Franz Klammer, Austria
Bernhard Russi, Switzerland
Herbert Plank, Italy
Giant Slalom
Heini Hemmi, Switzerland
Ernst Good, Switzerland
Ingemar Stenmark, Sweden
Slalom
Piero Gros, Italy
Gustavo Thoeni, Italy
Willy Frommelt, Liechtenstein

ALPINE SKIING (Women)
Downhill
Rosi Mittermaier, West Germany
Brigitte Totschnig, Austria
Cynthia Nelson, U.S.A.
Giant Slalom
Kathy Kreiner, Canada
Rosi Mittermaier, West Germany
Danielle Debernard, France
Slalom
Rosi Mittermaier, West Germany
Claudia Giordani, Italy
Hanni Wenzel, Liechtenstein

NORDIC SKIING AND JUMPING (Men)
15-kilometer cross-country
Nikolai Bajukov, U.S.S.R.
Evgeny Beliaev, U.S.S.R.
Arto Koivisto, Finland
30-kilometer cross-country
Sergei Saveliev, U.S.S.R.
William Koch, U.S.A.
Ivan Garanin, U.S.S.R.
50-kilometer cross-country
Ivar Formo, Norway
Gert-Dietmar Klause, East Germany
Ben Soedergren, Sweden
4x10-kilometer cross-country relay
Finland (Pitkaenen, Mieto,
   Teaurajärvi, Koivisto)
Norway
U.S.S.R.
70-meter special jump
Hans-Georg Aschenbach, East Germany
Jochen Danneberg, East Germany
Karl Schnabl, Austria
90-meter special jump
Karl Schnabl, Austria
Anton Innauer, Austria
Henry Glass, East Germany
Nordic combined
Ulrich Wehling, East Germany
Urban Hettich, West Germany
Konrad Winkler, East Germany

NORDIC SKIING (Women)
5-kilometer cross-country
Helena Takalo, Finland
Raisa Smetanina, U.S.S.R.
Nina Baldicheva, U.S.S.R.
10-kilometer cross-country
Raisa Smetanina, U.S.S.R.
Helena Takalo, Finland
Galina Kulakova, U.S.S.R.
4x5-kilometer cross-country relay
U.S.S.R. (Baldicheva, Amosova,
   Smetanina, Kulakova)
Finland
East Germany

BIATHLON
20-kilometer individual
Nikolai Kruglov, U.S.S.R.
Heikki Ikola, Finland
Aleksandr Elizarov, U.S.S.R.
40-kilometer relay
U.S.S.R. (Elizarov, Biakov,
   Kruglov, Tihonov)
Finland
East Germany

HOCKEY
U.S.S.R. (5 wins, 0 losses)
Czechoslovakia (3 wins, 2 losses)
West Germany (2 wins, 3 losses)

BOBSLEDDING
Two-man
East Germany (Meinhard Nehmer,
   Bernhard Germeshausen)
West Germany
Switzerland
Four-man
East Germany (Nehmer, Babok,
   Germeshausen, Lehmann)
Switzerland
West Germany

LUGE
Single Seat (Men)
Detlef Guenther, East Germany
Josef Fendt, West Germany
Hans Rinn, East Germany
Twoseaters (Men)
East Germany (Hans Rinn,
   Norbert Hahn)
West Germany
Austria
Single seat (Women)
Margit Schumann, East Germany
Ute Ruehrold, East Germany
Elisabeth Demleitner, West Germany

FIGURE SKATING
Men
John Curry, United Kingdom
Vladimir Kovalev, U.S.S.R.
Toller Cranston, Canada
Women
Dorothy Hamill, U.S.A.
Dianne de Leeuw, Netherlands
Christine Errath, East Germany
Pairs
U.S.S.R. (Irina Rodnina,
   Aleksandr Zaitsev)
East Germany (Romy Kermer,
   Rolf Oesterreich)
East Germany (Manuela Gross,
   Uwe Kagelmann)
Ice Dancing
U.S.S.R. (Lyudmila Pakhomova,
   Aleksandr Gorshkov)
U.S.S.R. (Irina Moiseyeva,
   Andrey Minenkov)
U.S.A. (Colleen O'Connor,
   Jim Millns)

SPEED SKATING (Men)
500-meter
Evgeny Kulikov, U.S.S.R., 39.17*
Valery Muratov, U.S.S.R.
Dan Immerfall, U.S.A.
1,000-meter
Peter Mueller, U.S.A., 1:19.32*
Jorn Didriksen, Norway
Valery Muratov, U.S.S.R.
1,500-meter
Jan Egil Storholt, Norway, 1:59.38*
Yuri Kondakov, U.S.S.R.
Hans van Helden, Netherlands
5,000-meter
Sten Stensen, Norway, 7:24.48
Piet Kleine, Netherlands
Hans van Helden, Netherlands
10,000-meter
Piet Kleine, Netherlands, 14:50.59*
Sten Stensen, Norway
Hans van Helden, Netherlands

SPEED SKATING (Women)
500-meter
Sheila Young, U.S.A., 42.76*
Cathy Priestner, Canada
Tatiana Averina, U.S.S.R.
1,000-meter
Tatiana Averina, U.S.S.R., 1:28.43*
Leah Poulos, U.S.A.
Sheila Young, U.S.A.
1,500-meter
Galina Stepanskaya, U.S.S.R., 2:16.58*
Sheila Young, U.S.A.
Tatiana Averina, U.S.S.R.
3,000-meter
Tatiana Averina, U.S.S.R., 4:45.19*
Andrea Mitscherlich, East Germany
Lisbeth Korsmo, Norway

WINTER OLYMPIC CHAMPIONS

ALPINE SKIING (Men)

Downhill

1948—Henri Oreiller, France
1952—Zeno Colo, Italy
1956—Toni Sailer, Austria
1960—Jean Vuarnet, France
1964—Egon Zimmermann, Austria
1968—Jean Claude Killy, France
1972—Bernhard Russi, Switzerland

Giant Slalom

1952—Stein Eriksen, Norway
1956—Toni Sailer, Austria
1960—Roger Staub, Switzerland
1964—Francois Bonlieu, France
1968—Jean Claude Killy, France
1972—Gustavo Thoeni, Italy

Slalom

1948—Edi Reinalter, Switzerland
1952—Othmar Schneider, Austria
1956—Toni Sailer, Austria
1960—Ernst Hinterseer, Austria
1964—Josef Stiegler, Austria
1968—Jean Claude Killy, France
1972—Francisco Fernandez Ochoa, Spain

ALPINE SKIING (Women)

Downhill

1948—Hedi Schlunegger, Switzerland
1952—Trude Jochum-Beiser, Austria
1956—Madeleine Berthod, Switzerland
1960—Heidi Biebl, Germany
1964—Christl Haas, Austria
1968—Olga Pall, Austria
1972—Marie Therese Nadig, Switzerland

Giant Slalom

1952—Andrea Mead Lawrence, United States
1956—Ossi Reichert, Germany
1960—Yvonne Ruegg, Switzerland
1964—Marielle Goitschel, France
1968—Nancy Greene, Canada
1972—Marie Therese Nadig, Switzerland

Slalom

1948—Gretchen Fraser, United States
1952—Andrea Mead Lawrence, United States
1956—Renee Colliard, Switzerland
1960—Anne Heggtveigt, Canada
1964—Christine Goitschel, France
1968—Marielle Goitschel, France
1972—Barbara Cochran, United States

NORDIC SKIING AND JUMPING (Men)

15-Kilometer Cross-Country

1924—Thorleif Haug, Norway
1928—Johan Grottumsbraaten, Norway
1932—Sven Utterstrom, Sweden
1936—Erik-August Larsson, Sweden
1948—Martin Lundstrom, Sweden
1952—Hallgeir Brenden, Norway
1956—Hallgeir Brenden, Norway
1960—Hakon Brusveen, Norway
1964—Eero Mantyranta, Finland
1968—Harald Groenningen, Norway
1972—Sven-Ake Lundback, Sweden

30-Kilometer Cross-Country

1956—Veikko Hakulinen, Finland
1960—Sixten Jernberg, Sweden
1964—Eero Mantyranta, Finland
1968—Franco Nones, Italy
1972—Vyacheslav Vedenin, USSR

50-Kilometer Cross-Country

1924—Thorleif Haug, Norway
1928—Per Erik Hedlund, Sweden
1932—Veli Saarinen, Finland
1936—Elis Viklund, Sweden
1948—Nils Karlsson, Sweden
1952—Veikko Hakulinen, Finland
1956—Sixten Jernberg, Sweden
1960—Kalevi Hamalainen, Finland
1964—Sixten Jernberg, Sweden
1968—Ole Ellefsaeter, Norway
1972—Paal Tyldum, Norway

4 x 10-Kilometer Cross-Country Relay

1936—Finland
1948—Sweden
1952—Finland
1956—USSR
1960—Finland
1964—Sweden
1968—Norway
1972—USSR

70-Meter Special Jump

1964—Veikko Kankkonen, Finland
1968—Jiri Raska, Czechoslovakia
1972—Yukio Kasaya, Japan

90-Meter Special Jump

1924—Jacob T. Thambs, Norway
1928—Alfred Andersen, Norway
1932—Birger Ruud, Norway
1936—Birger Ruud, Norway
1948—Petter Hugsted, Norway
1952—Arnfinn Bergmann, Norway
1956—Antti Hyvarinen, Finland
1960—Helmut Recknagel, Germany
1964—Toralf Engan, Norway
1968—Vladimir Beloussov, USSR
1972—Wojiech Fortuna, Poland

Nordic Combined

1924—Thorleif Haug, Norway
1928—Johan Grottumsbraaten, Norway
1932—Johan Grottumsbraaten, Norway
1936—Oddbjorn Hagen, Norway
1948—Heikki Hasu, Finland
1952—Simon Slattvik, Norway
1956—Sverre Stenersen, Norway
1960—Georg Thoma, Germany
1964—Tormod Knutsen, Norway
1968—Franz Keller, West Germany
1972—Ulrich Wehling, East Germany

NORDIC SKIING (Women)

5-Kilometer Cross-Country

1964—Claudia Boyarskikh, USSR
1968—Toini Gustafsson, Sweden
1972—Galina Koulacova, USSR

10-Kilometer Cross-Country

1952—Lydia Wideman, Finland
1956—Lyubov Kozyreva, USSR
1960—Marija Gusakova, USSR
1964—Claudia Boyarskikh, USSR
1968—Toini Gustafsson, Sweden
1972—Galina Koulacova, USSR

15-Kilometer Relay

1956—Finland
1960—Sweden
1964—USSR
1968—Norway
1972—USSR

BIATHLON

20-Kilometer Individual

1960—Klas Lestander, Sweden
1964—Vladimir Melanin, USSR
1968—Magnar Solberg, Norway
1972—Magnar Solberg, Norway

40-Kilometer Relay

1968—USSR
1972—USSR

HOCKEY

1920—Canada
1924—Canada
1928—Canada
1932—Canada
1936—Great Britain
1948—Canada
1952—Canada
1956—USSR
1960—United States
1964—USSR
1968—USSR
1972—USSR

BOBSLEDDING

Two-Man
- 1932—United States
- 1936—United States
- 1948—Switzerland
- 1952—Germany
- 1956—Italy
- 1964—Great Britain
- 1968—Italy
- 1972—West Germany

Four-Man
- 1924—Switzerland
- 1928—United States (5-Man)
- 1932—United States
- 1936—Switzerland
- 1948—United States
- 1952—Germany
- 1956—Switzerland
- 1964—Canada
- 1968—Italy
- 1972—Switzerland

LUGE

Single seat (Men)
- 1964—Thomas Kohler, Germany
- 1968—Manfred Schmid, Austria
- 1972—Wolfgang Scheidel, East Germany

Twoseater (Men)
- 1964—Austria
- 1968—East Germany
- 1972—Italy, East Germany (tie)

Single seat (Women)
- 1964—Ortrun Enderlein, Germany
- 1968—Erica Lechner, Italy
- 1972—Anna M. Muller, East Germany

FIGURE SKATING

Men
- 1908—Ulrich Salchow, Sweden
- 1920—Gillis Grafstrom, Sweden
- 1924—Gillis Grafstrom, Sweden
- 1928—Gillis Grafstrom, Sweden
- 1932—Karl Schafer, Austria
- 1936—Karl Schafer, Austria
- 1948—Richard Button, United States
- 1952—Richard Button, United States
- 1956—Hayes Alan Jenkins, United States
- 1960—David W. Jenkins, United States
- 1964—Manfred Schnelldorfer, Germany
- 1968—Wolfgang Schwartz, Austria
- 1972—Ondrej Nepela, Czechoslovakia

Women
- 1908—Madge Syers, Great Britain
- 1920—Magda Julin-Mauroy, Sweden
- 1924—Heima von Szabo-Planck, Austria
- 1928—Sonja Henie, Norway
- 1932—Sonja Henie, Norway
- 1936—Sonja Henie, Norway
- 1948—Barbara Ann Scott, Canada
- 1952—Jeanette Altwegg, Great Britain
- 1956—Tenley Albright, United States
- 1960—Carol Heiss, United States
- 1964—Sjoukje Dijkstra, Netherlands
- 1968—Peggy Fleming, United States
- 1972—Beatrix Schuba, Austria

Pairs
- 1908—Germany-Anna Hubler, Heinrich Burger
- 1920—Finland-Ludovika & Walter Jakobsson
- 1924—Austria-Helene Engelman, Alfred Berger
- 1928—France-Andree Joly, Pierre Brunet
- 1932—France-Andree & Pierre Brunet
- 1936—Germany-Maxie Herber, Ernst Baier
- 1948—Belgium-Micheline Lannoy, Pierre Baugniet
- 1952—Germany-Ria & Paul Falk
- 1956—Austria-Elisabeth Schwartz, Kurt Oppelt
- 1960—Canada-Barbara Wagner, Robert Paul
- 1964—USSR-Ludmila Beloussova, Oleg Protopopov
- 1968—USSR-Ludmila Beloussova, Oleg Protopopov
- 1972—USSR-Irina Rodnina, Alexei Ulanov

SPEED SKATING (Men)

500-Meters
- 1924—Charles Jewtraw, United States, 44.0
- 1928—Clas Thunberg, Finland and Bernt Evensen, Norway (tie), 43.4
- 1932—John A. Shea, United States, 43.4
- 1936—Ivar Ballangrud, Norway, 43.4
- 1948—Finn Helgesen, Norway, 43.1
- 1952—Ken Henry, United States, 43.2
- 1956—Yevgeni Grishin, USSR, 40.2
- 1960—Yevgeni Grishin, USSR, 40.2
- 1964—Terry McDermott, United States, 40.1
- 1968—Erhard Keller, West Germany, 40.3
- 1972—Erhard Keller, West Germany, 39.4

1,500-Meters
- 1924—Clas Thunberg, Finland, 2:20.8
- 1928—Clas Thunberg, Finland, 2:21.1
- 1932—John A. Shea, United States, 2:57.5
- 1936—Charles Mathisen, Norway, 2:19.2
- 1948—Sverre Farstad, Norway, 2:17.6
- 1952—Hjalmar Andersen, Norway, 2:20.4
- 1956—Yevgeni Grishin and Yuri Mikhailov, USSR (tie), 2:08.6
- 1960—Roald Aas, Norway and Yevgeni Grishin, USSR (tie), 2:10.4
- 1964—Ants Anston, USSR, 2:10.3
- 1968—Cornelis Verkerk, Netherlands, 2:03.4
- 1972—Ard Schenk, Netherlands, 2:02.9

5.000-Meters
- 1924—Clas Thunberg, Finland, 8:39
- 1928—Ivar Ballangrud, Norway, 8:50.5
- 1932—Irving Jaffee, United States, 9:40.8
- 1936—Ivar Ballangrud, Norway, 8:19.6
- 1948—Reidar Liaklev, Norway, 8:29.4
- 1952—Hjalmar Andersen, Norway, 8:10.6
- 1956—Boris Shilkov, USSR, 7:48.7
- 1960—Viktor Kosichkin, USSR, 7:51.3
- 1964—Knut Johannesen, Norway, 7:38.4
- 1968—F. Anton Maier, Norway, 7:22.4*
- 1972—Ard Schenk, Netherlands, 7:23.6

10,000-Meters
- 1924—Julien Skutnabb, Finland, 18:04.8
- 1928—(ice thawed, event cancelled)
- 1932—Irving Jaffee, United States, 19:13.6
- 1936—Ivar Ballangrud, Norway, 17:24.3
- 1948—Ake Seyffarth, Sweden, 17:26.3
- 1952—Hjalmar Andersen, Norway, 16:45.8
- 1956—Sigvard Ericsson, Sweden, 16:35
- 1960—Knut Johannessen, Norway, 15:46.6
- 1964—Jonny Nilsson, Sweden, 15:50.1
- 1968—Johnny Hoeglin, Sweden, 15:23.6
- 1972—Ard Schenk, Netherlands, 15:01.3

SPEED SKATING (Women)

500-Meters
- 1960—Helga Haase, Germany, 45.9
- 1964—Lydia Skoblikova, USSR, 45.0
- 1968—Ludmila Titova, USSR, 46.1
- 1972—Anne Henning, United States, 43.3

1,000-Meters
- 1960—Klara Guseva, USSR, 1:34.1
- 1964—Lydia Skoblikova, USSR, 1:33.2
- 1968—Carolina Geijssen, Netherlands, 1:32.6
- 1972—Monika Pflug, West Germany, 1:31.4

1,500-Meters
- 1960—Lydia Skoblikova, USSR, 2:25.2
- 1964—Lydia Skoblikova, USSR, 2:22.6
- 1968—Kaija Mustonen, Finland, 2:22.4
- 1972—Dianne Holum, United States, 2:20.8

3,000-Meters
- 1960—Lydia Skoblikova, USSR, 5:14.3
- 1964—Lydia Skoblikova, USSR, 5:14.9
- 1968—Johanna Schut, Netherlands, 4:56.2
- 1972—Stien Kaiser-Baas, Netherlands, 4:52.1

BASEBALL

BASEBALL GOVERNMENT

Office of the Commissioner: 75 Rockefeller Plaza, New York City 10019

Prior to 1920, major league baseball was governed by a three-man commission. However, in that year, following the ''Black Sox'' scandal of the 1919 World Series, the office of baseball commissioner was created. The first commissioner was Kenesaw M. Landis (1921–44); he was succeeded by Albert B. Chandler (1945–51), Ford C. Frick (1951–65), William D. Eckert (1965–69), and the current commissioner, Bowie Kuhn (1969–   ).

THE NATIONAL LEAGUE: One Rockefeller Plaza, Suite 1602, New York City 10020. Organized in 1876.

President: Charles S. Feeney Vice-President: **John J. McHale**

Club	President	1979 Manager
Atlanta Braves	R. E. (Ted) Turner	Bobby Cox
Chicago Cubs	William J. Hagenah, Jr.	Herman Franks, Joey Amalfitano
Cincinnati Reds	Richard Wagner	Sparky Anderson, John McNamara
Houston Astros	Talbot M. Smith	Bill Virdon
Los Angeles Dodgers	Peter O'Malley	Tom Lasorda
Montreal Expos	J. J. McHale	Dick Williams
New York Mets	Mrs. Lorinda de Roulet	Joe Torre
Philadelphia Phillies	R. R. M. Carpenter, III	Dan Ozark, Dallas Green
Pittsburgh Pirates	Daniel M. Galbreath	Chuck Tanner
St. Louis Cardinals	August A. Busch, Jr.	Ken Boyer
San Diego Padres	Ballard Smith	Roger Craig
San Francisco Giants	Robert A. Lurie	Joe Altobelli, Dave Bristol

THE AMERICAN LEAGUE: 280 Park Ave., New York City 10017 Founded in 1900.

Chairman: Joseph E. Cronin President: **Leland S. MacPhail, Jr.** Vice-Pres.: **Calvin R. Griffith**

Club	President	1979 Manager
Baltimore Orioles	Jerry C. Hoffberger	Earl Weaver
Boston Red Sox	Mrs. Jean Yawkey	Don Zimmer
California Angels	Gene Autry	Jim Fregosi
Chicago White Sox	Bill Veeck	Don Kessinger, Tony LaRussa
Cleveland Indians	Gabe Paul	Jeff Torborg, Dave Garcia
Detroit Tigers	J. E. Fetzer	Les Moss, Sparky Anderson
Kansas City Royals	Ewing Kauffman	Whitey Herzog
Milwaukee Brewers	Allan Selig	George Bamberger
Minnesota Twins	Calvin Griffith	Gene Mauch
New York Yankees	George Steinbrenner	Bob Lemon, Billy Martin
Oakland Athletics	Charles O. Finley	Jim Marshall
Seattle Mariners	Lester Smith, Danny Kaye	Darrell Johnson
Texas Rangers	Bradford G. Corbett	Pat Corrales
Toronto Blue Jays	Peter Bavasi	Roy Hartsfield

MAJOR LEAGUE RECORDS: 1900–1979

BATTING

Highest Batting Average, Lifetime: .367, Ty Cobb (AL), 1905–1928; .358, Rogers Hornsby (NL), 1915–1937.

Highest Batting Average, Season: .424, Rogers Hornsby, St. Louis (NL), 1924; .420, George Sisler, St. Louis (AL), 1922.

Most Years Led League in Batting: 12, Ty Cobb, Detroit (AL), 1907–1915, 1917–1919; 8, Honus Wagner, Pittsburgh (NL), 1900, 1903–1904, 1906–1909, 1911.

Most Years Batting .300 or More: 23, Ty Cobb, Detroit and Philadelphia (AL), 1906–1928; 17, Honus Wagner, Louisville and Pittsburgh (AL), 1897–1913; 17, Stan Musial, St. Louis (NL), 1942–1944, 1946–1958, 1962.

Most Hits: 4,191, Ty Cobb (AL), 1905–1928; 3,630, Stan Musial (NL), 1941–1944, 1946–1963.

Most Hits, Season: 257, George Sisler, St. Louis (AL), 1920; 254, Lefty O'Doul, Philadelphia (NL), 1929; 254, Bill Terry, New York (NL), 1930.

Most Consecutive Games Batted Safely: 56, Joe DiMaggio, New York (AL), 1941; 44, Pete Rose, Cincinnati (NL), 1978

Most Consecutive Games Played: 2,130, Lou Gehrig, New York (AL), 1925-39; 1,117, Billy Williams, Chicago (NL), 1963–70.

Most Runs: 2,244, Ty Cobb (AL), 1905–1928; 2,174, Babe Ruth, Boston (AL), New York (AL), Boston (NL), 1914–1935.

Most Runs, Season: 177, Babe Ruth, New York (AL), 1921; 158, Chuck Klein, Philadelphia (NL), 1930.

Most Consecutive Years 100 or More Runs: 13, Lou Gehrig, New York (AL), 1926–1938; 13, Hank Aaron, Milwaukee and Atlanta (NL), 1955–1967.

Most Runs Batted In, Lifetime: 2,297, Hank Aaron, 1954–1976; 2,204, Babe Ruth, 1914–1935.

Most Runs Batted In, Season: 190, Hack Wilson, Chicago (NL), 1930; 184, Lou Gehrig, New York (AL), 1931.

Highest Slugging Percentage, Lifetime: .690, Babe Ruth, Boston and New York (AL), Boston (NL); .634, Ted Williams, Boston (AL).

Most Home Runs, Lifetime: 755, Hank Aaron, Milwaukee and Atlanta (NL), Milwaukee (AL), 1954–1976; 714, Babe Ruth, Boston and New York (AL), Boston (NL).

Most Home Runs, Season: 61, Roger Maris, New York (AL), 1961, 162-game schedule; 60, Babe Ruth, New York (AL), 1927, 154-game schedule.

Most Years League Home-Run Leader: 12, Babe Ruth (AL), 1918–1919, 1920–1921, 1923–1924, 1926–1931; 7, Ralph Kiner, Pittsburgh (NL), 1946–1952.

Most Years 20 or More Home Runs: 19, Henry Aaron (NL); 17, Willie Mays (NL); 16, Babe Ruth (AL).

Most Grand Slam Home Runs, Lifetime: 23, Lou Gehrig, New York (AL); 17, Willie McCovey, San Francisco, San Diego (NL).

Most Grand Slam Home Runs, Season: 5, Ernie Banks, Chicago (NL), 1955; 5, Jim Gentile, Baltimore (AL), 1961.

Most Bases on Balls, Season: 170, Babe Ruth, New York (AL), 1923; 162, Ted Williams, Boston (AL), 1947, 1949.

Fewest Strikeouts, Lifetime (7,000 or More At Bats): 114, Joe Sewell (AL); 173, Lloyd Waner (NL).

Most Consecutive Games without Strikeouts: 98, Nelson Fox, Chicago (AL), 1958; 77, Lloyd Waner (NL), 1941.

Most Pinch Hits, Lifetime: 145, Manny Mota (NL).

Most Stolen Bases, Lifetime: 938, Lou Brock (NL); 892, Ty Cobb (AL).

Most Stolen Bases, Season: 118, Lou Brock, St. Louis (NL), 1974, 162-game schedule; 96, Ty Cobb, Detroit (AL), 1915, 154-game schedule.

PITCHING

Most Games Won, Lifetime: 511, Cy Young (NL–AL); 416, Walter Johnson (AL).

Most Games Won, Season: 41, Jack Chesbro, New York (AL), 1904; 39, Ed Walsh, Chicago (AL), 1908.

Most Years 20-or-More-Game Winner: 16, Cy Young (NL–AL), 1891–1904, 1907–1908; 13, Christy Mathewson (NL), 1901, 1903–1914; 13, Warren Spahn (NL), 1947, 1949–1951, 1953–1954, 1956–1961, 1963; 12, Walter Johnson (AL), 1910–1919, 1924–1925.

Most Consecutive Games Won, Lifetime: 24, Carl Hubbell, New York (NL), 16 in 1936, 8 in 1937; 17, John Allen, Cleveland (AL), 2 in 1936, 15 in 1937; 17, Dave McNally, Baltimore (AL), 2 in 1968, 15 in 1969.

Most Consecutive Games Won, Season: 19, Rube Marquard, New York (NL), 1912; 17, ElRoy Face, Pittsburgh (NL), 1959.

Most Shutout Games, Lifetime: 113, Walter Johnson (AL); 90, Grover Alexander (NL).

Most Shutout Games, Season: 16, Grover Alexander, Philadelphia (AL), 1916; 13, Jack Coombs, Philadelphia (AL), 1910; 13, Bob Gibson, St. Louis, 1968.

Most Consecutive Shutout Games, Season: 6, Don Drysdale, Los Angeles (NL), 1968; 5, Harris White, Chicago (AL), 1904.

Most Consecutive Shutout Innings, Season: 58, Don Drysdale, Los Angeles (NL), 1968; 56, Walter Johnson, Washington (AL), 1913; 46½, Carl Hubbell, New York (NL), 1933.

Lowest Earned Run Average, Season: 1.01, Hubert Leonard, Boston (AL), 1914; 1.04, Three Finger Brown, Chicago (NL), 1906.

Most Consecutive Years Lowest Earned Run Average: 5, Sandy Koufax, Los Angeles (NL), 1962–1966; 4, Lefty Grove, Philadelphia (AL), 1929–1932.

Highest Won-Lost Percentage, Lifetime (100 or More Decisions): .690, Whitey Ford, New York (AL), 1950–1967.

Highest Won-Lost Percentage, Season (15 or More Decisions): .947, ElRoy Face, Pittsburgh (NL), 1959.

Most Strikeouts, Lifetime: 3,508, Walter Johnson (AL); 3,117, Bob Gibson, St. Louis (NL).

Most Strikeouts, Season: 383, Nolan Ryan, California (AL), 1973; 382, Sandy Koufax, Los Angeles (NL), 1965.

Most Strikeouts in 9-Inning Game: 19, Steve Carlton, St. Louis (NL), 1969; 19, Tom Seaver, New York (NL), 1970; 19, Nolan Ryan, California (AL), 1974, 1977.

Most Games Won, Relief Pitcher, Lifetime: 123, Hoyt Wilhelm (NL-AL), 1952-70; 114, Lindy McDaniel (NL-AL), 1955-73.

MAJOR LEAGUE BASEBALL ALL-TIME LEADERS[1]

BATTING

SEASONS
James McGuire	26
Eddie Collins	25
Bobby Wallace	25
Ty Cobb	24
Hank Aaron	23
Brooks Robinson	23
Rabbit Maranville	23
Rogers Hornsby	23
Stan Musial	22
Tris Speaker	22
Mel Ott	22
Babe Ruth	22
Bill Dahlen	22
Jimmie Dykes	22
Cap Anson	22
Phil Cavarretta	22
Harry Davis	22
Willie Mays, Al Kaline	22
Harmon Killebrew	22

GAMES
Hank Aaron	3,298
Ty Cobb	3,033
Stan Musial	3,026
Willie Mays	2,992
Brooks Robinson	2,896
Carl Yastrzemski	2,862
Al Kaline	2,834
Eddie Collins	2,826
Frank Robinson	2,808
Tris Speaker	2,789
Honus Wagner	2,785
Mel Ott	2,730
Rabbit Maranville	2,670
Pete Rose	2,668
Lou Brock	2,616
Luis Aparicio	2,599
Paul Waner	2,549
Ernie Banks	2,528
Sam Crawford	2,517

BATTING AVERAGE
Ty Cobb	.367
Rogers Hornsby	.358
Joe Jackson	.356
Ed Delahanty	.346
Willie Keeler	.345
Ted Williams	.344
Tris Speaker	.344
Billy Hamilton	.344
Dan Brouthers	.342
Babe Ruth	.342
Harry Heilmann	.342
Pete Browning	.341
Bill Terry	.341
George Sisler	.340
Lou Gehrig	.340
Jesse Burkett	.340
Nap Lajoie	.339

AT BATS
Hank Aaron	12,364
Ty Cobb	11,429
Stan Musial	10,972
Willie Mays	10,881
Pete Rose	10,824
Brooks Robinson	10,654
Carl Yastrzemski	10,447
Honus Wagner	10,427
Lou Brock	10,332
Luis Aparicio	10,230
Tris Speaker	10,208
Al Kaline	10,116
Rabbit Maranville	10,078
Frank Robinson	10,006
Eddie Collins	9,949
Vada Pinson	9,645
Nap Lajoie	9,589
Sam Crawford	9,579
Jake Beckley	9,476

RUNS
Ty Cobb	2,244
Babe Ruth	2,174
Hank Aaron	2,174
Willie Mays	2,062
Stan Musial	1,949
Lou Gehrig	1,888
Tris Speaker	1,881
Mel Ott	1,859
Frank Robinson	1,829
Eddie Collins	1,818
Ted Williams	1,798
Charlie Gehringer	1,773

HITS
Ty Cobb	4,191
Hank Aaron	3,771
Stan Musial	3,630
Tris Speaker	3,515
Honus Wagner	3,430
Pete Rose	3,372
Eddie Collins	3,311
Willie Mays	3,283
Nap Lajoie	3,251
Paul Waner	3,152
Cap Anson	3,081
Lou Brock	3,023

DOUBLES
Tris Speaker	793
Stan Musial	725
Ty Cobb	724
Honus Wagner	651
Nap Lajoie	650
Hank Aaron	624
Pete Rose	612
Paul Waner	603
Charlie Gehringer	574
Carl Yastrzemski	565
Harry Heilmann	542
Rogers Hornsby	541

TRIPLES
Sam Crawford	312
Ty Cobb	297
Honus Wagner	252
Jake Beckley	246
Roger Connor	227
Tris Speaker	224
Fred Clarke	219
Dan Brouthers	212
Paul Waner	190
Joe Kelley	189
Bid McPhee	189
Eddie Collins	186

HOME RUNS
Hank Aaron	755
Babe Ruth	714
Willie Mays	660
Frank Robinson	586
Harmon Killebrew	573
Mickey Mantle	536
Jimmie Foxx	534
Ted Willams	521
Willie McCovey	520
Eddie Mathews	512
Ernie Banks	512
Mel Ott	511
Lou Gehrig	493
Stan Musial	475
Willie Stargell	461
Billy Williams	426
Duke Snider	407
Carl Yastrzemski	404
Al Kaline	399
Frank Howard	382
Orlando Cepeda	379
Norm Cash	377
Rocky Colavito	374
Gil Hodges	370
Ralph Kiner	369
Reggie Jackson	369

TOTAL BASES
Hank Aaron	6,838
Stan Musial	6,134
Willie Mays	6,066
Ty Cobb	5,863
Babe Ruth	5,793
Frank Robinson	5,373
Tris Speaker	5,101
Lou Gehrig	5,059
Mel Ott	5,041
Jimmie Foxx	4,956
Honus Wagner	4,888
Ted Williams	4,884

EXTRA BASE HITS
Hank Aaron	1,477
Stan Musial	1,377
Babe Ruth	1,356
Willie Mays	1,323
Lou Gehrig	1,190
Frank Robinson	1,186
Ty Cobb	1,139
Tris Speaker	1,132
Jimmie Foxx	1,117
Ted Williams	1,117
Mel Ott	1,071
Carl Yastrzemski	1,025

BASES ON BALLS
Babe Ruth	2,056
Ted Williams	2,018
Mickey Mantle	1,734
Mel Ott	1,708
Carl Yastrzemski	1,639
Eddie Yost	1,614
Stan Musial	1,599
Harmon Killebrew	1,559
Lou Gehrig	1,508
Eddie Collins	1,503
Willie Mays	1,464
Jimmie Foxx	1,452
Eddie Mathews	1,444

STOLEN BASES
Lou Brock	938
Ty Cobb	892
Eddie Collins	743
Max Carey	738
Honus Wagner	720
Bert Campaneris	628
Joe Morgan	601
Maury Wills	586
Luis Aparicio	506
Clyde Milan	494
Jimmy Sheckard	460
Sherry Magee	441

RUNS BATTED IN
Hank Aaron	2,297
Babe Ruth	2,204
Lou Gehrig	1,990
Ty Cobb	1,954
Stan Musial	1,951
Jimmie Foxx	1,921
Willie Mays	1,903
Mel Ott	1,860
Ted Williams	1,839
Al Simmons	1,827
Frank Robinson	1,812
Honus Wagner	1,732

STRIKEOUTS
Willie Stargell	1,851
Lou Brock	1,730
Mickey Mantle	1,710
Harmon Killebrew	1,699
Bobby Bonds	1,640
Reggie Jackson	1,606
Dick Allen	1,556
Frank Robinson	1,532
Willie McCovey	1,527
Willie Mays	1,526
Eddie Mathews	1,487
Frank Howard	1,460

PITCHING

SEASONS
Early Wynn	23
Jack Quinn	23
Cy Young	22
Sad Sam Jones	22
Red Ruffing	22
Herb Pennock	22
Hoyt Wilhelm	21
Walter Johnson	21
Warren Spahn	21
Eppa Rixey	21
Waite Hoyt	21
Ted Lyons	21

WINS
Cy Young	511
Walter Johnson	416
Christy Mathewson	373
Grover Alexander	373
Warren Spahn	363
Pud Galvin	361
Kid Nichols	360
Tim Keefe	343
John Clarkson	327
Eddie Plank	327
Mickey Welch	311

COMPLETE GAMES
Cy Young	751
Pud Galvin	639
Tim Keefe	554
Walter Johnson	531
Kid Nichols	531
Mickey Welch	525
John Clarkson	488
Old Hoss Radbourn	479
Tony Mullane	464
Jim McCormick	462
Gus Weyhing	448

INNINGS PITCHED
Cy Young	7,377
Pud Galvin	5,959
Walter Johnson	5,924
Warren Spahn	5,246
Grover Alexander	5,189
Kid Nichols	5,067
Tim Keefe	5,043
Christy Mathewson	4,781
Mickey Welch	4,784
Robin Roberts	4,689
Gaylord Perry	4,592

SHUTOUTS
Walter Johnson	113
Grover Alexander	90
Christy Mathewson	83
Cy Young	77
Eddie Plank	64
Warren Spahn	63
Ed Walsh	58
Three Finger Brown	58
Pud Galvin	57

STRIKEOUTS
Walter Johnson	3,508
Gaylord Perry	3,141
Bob Gibson	3,117
Nolan Ryan	2,909
Tom Seaver	2,887
Jim Bunning	2,855
Cy Young	2,819
Mickey Lolich	2,812
Ferguson Jenkins	2,770

BASES ON BALLS
Early Wynn	1,775
Bob Feller	1,764
Bobo Newsom	1,732
Nolan Ryan	1,646
Amos Rusie	1,637
Gus Weyhing	1,569
Red Ruffing	1,541
Bump Hadley	1,442
Warren Spahn	1,434

EARNED RUN AVERAGE
Ed Walsh	1.82
Addie Joss	1.88
Three Finger Brown	2.06
Monte Ward	2.10
Christy Mathewson	2.13
Rube Waddell	2.16
Walter Johnson	2.17
Orval Overall	2.24
Tommy Bond	2.25

[1]At start of 1980 season.

HALL OF FAME

ELECTED FOR MERITORIOUS SERVICE

Barrow, Edward, manager and executive
Bulkeley, Morgan G., first National League president
Cartwright, Alexander J., formulated first baseball rules
Chadwick, Henry, first reporter and keeper of records
Comiskey, Charles A., player, manager, and executive
Conlan, Jocko, National League umpire
Connolly, Thomas, American League umpire
Cummings, William A., early pitcher, said to have invented the curve ball
Evans, William, American League Umpire
Frick, Ford C., National League president and commissioner
Giles, Warren C., general manager and National League pres.
Griffith, Clark C., player, manager, and executive
Harridge, William, American League president
Harris, Stanley (Bucky), player, manager, executive
Hubbard, Robert C. (Cal), American League umpire
Huggins, Miller J., manager
Johnson, Byron Bancroft, first American League president
Klem, William, National League umpire
Landis, Kenesaw M., first commissioner of baseball
Lopez, Alfonso R., manager
Mack, Connie, manager and executive
Mac Phail, Larry, executive
McCarthy, Joseph, manager
McGraw, John J., player and manager
McKechnie, William B., manager
Rickey, W. Branch, manager and executive
Robinson, Wilbert, player and manager
Spalding, Albert G., early pitcher and organizer of the National League
Stengel, Charles D., player and manager
Weiss, George, general manager
Wright, George, early player
Wright, Harry, early player and manager

PITCHERS	Years	Won	Lost
Alexander, Grover Cleveland	1911–1930	373	208
Bender, Charles (Chief)	1903–1925	212	128
Brown, Mordecai (Three-Finger)	1903–1916	239	130
Chesbro, John	1899–1909	199	128
Clarkson, John	1882–1894	328	175
Coveleski, Stanley	1912–1928	215	141
Dean, Jerome (Dizzy)	1930–1947	150	83
Faber, Urban (Red)	1914–1933	254	212
Feller, Robert	1936–1956	266	162
Ford, Edward (Whitey)	1950–1967	236	106
Galvin, James (Pud)	1879–1892	361	309
Gomez, Vernon (Lefty)	1930–1943	189	102
Grimes, Burleigh	1916–1934	270	212
Grove, Robert (Lefty)	1925–1941	300	141
Haines, Jesse	1918–1937	210	158
Hoyt, Waite	1918–1938	237	182
Hubbell, Carl	1928–1943	253	154
Johnson, Walter (Big Train)	1907–1927	416	279
Joss, Adrian (Addie)	1902–1910	160	97
Keefe, Timothy	1880–1893	346	225
Koufax, Sanford	1955–1966	165	87
Lemon, Robert	1941–1958	207	128
Lyons, Theodore	1923–1946	260	230
Marquard, Richard (Rube)	1908–1925	201	177
Mathewson, Christopher	1900–1916	373	188
McGinnity, Joseph (Iron Man)	1899–1908	247	142
Nichols, Charles (Kid)	1890–1906	360	202
Pennock, Herbert	1912–1934	240	162
Plank, Edward	1901–1917	325	190
Radbourne, Charles (Old Hoss)	1880–1891	308	191
Rixey, Eppa	1912–1933	266	251
Roberts, Robin	1948–1966	286	245
Ruffing, Charles (Red)	1924–1947	273	225
Rusie, Amos	1889–1901	246	174
Spahn, Warren	1942–1965	363	245
Vance, Arthur (Dazzy)	1915–1935	197	140
Waddell, George (Rube)	1897–1910	193	140
Walsh, Edward (Big Ed)	1904–1917	195	126
Welch, Mickey	1880–1892	308	209
Wynn, Early	1939–1963	300	244
Young, Denton (Cy)	1890–1911	511	315

ELECTED FROM NEGRO LEAGUES

Bell, James (Cool Page)
Charleston, Oscar
Dihigo, Martin
Gibson, Joshua
Irvin, Monte

Johnson, William (Judy)
Leonard, Walter (Buck)
Lloyd, John Henry (Pop)
Paige, Leroy (Satchel)

BATTERS	Years	Average
Anson, Adrian (Cap)	1876–1897	.339
Appling, Lucius B. (Luke)	1930–1950	.310
Averill, H. Earl	1929–1941	.318
Baker, J. Frank (Home Run)	1908–1922	.307
Bancroft, Dave	1915–1930	.279
Banks, Ernest	1953–1971	.274
Beckley, Jake	1888–1907	.309
Berra, Lawrence (Yogi)	1946–1965	.285
Bottomley, James	1922–1937	.310
Boudreau, Louis	1938–1952	.295
Bresnahan, Roger	1897–1915	.279
Brouthers, Dennis (Dan)	1879–1904	.349
Burkett, Jesse	1890–1905	.342
Campanella, Roy	1948–1957	.276
Carey, Max	1910–1929	.285
Chance, Frank	1898–1914	.297
Clarke, Fred	1894–1915	.315
Clemente, Roberto	1955–1972	.317
Cobb, Tyrus	1905–1928	.367
Cochrane, Gordon (Mickey)	1925–1937	.320
Collins, Edward	1906–1930	.333
Collins, James	1895–1908	.294
Combs, Earle	1924–1935	.325
Connor, Roger	1880–1897	.325
Crawford, Samuel (Wahoo)	1899–1917	.309
Cronin, Joseph	1926–1945	.302
Cuyler, Hazen (Kiki)	1921–1938	.321
Delahanty, Edward	1888–1903	.346
Dickey, William	1928–1946	.313
DiMaggio, Joseph	1936–1951	.325
Duffy, Hugh	1888–1906	.330
Evers, John	1902–1929	.270
Ewing, William (Buck)	1880–1897	.311
Flick, Elmer	1898–1910	.315
Foxx, James	1925–1945	.325
Frisch, Frank	1919–1937	.316
Gehrig, Henry (Lou)	1923–1939	.340
Gehringer, Charles	1924–1942	.320
Goslin, Leon (Goose)	1921–1938	.316
Greenberg, Henry	1930–1947	.313
Hafey, Charles (Chick)	1924–1937	.317
Hamilton, William	1888–1901	.344
Hartnett, Charles (Gabby)	1922–1941	.297
Heilmann, Harry	1914–1932	.342
Herman, William	1931–1947	.304
Hooper, Harry	1909–1925	.281
Hornsby, Rogers (Rajah)	1915–1937	.358
Jennings, Hugh	1891–1918	.314
Keeler, William (Wee Willie)	1892–1910	.345
Kelley, Joe	1891–1908	.321
Kelly, George	1915–1932	.297
Kelly, Michael (King)	1878–1893	.313
Kiner, Ralph	1946–1955	.279
Lajoie, Napoleon	1896–1916	.339
Lindstrom, Fred	1924–1939	.311
McCarthy, Thomas	1884–1896	.294
Manush, Henry (Heinie)	1923–1939	.330
Mantle, Mickey	1951–1968	.298
Maranville, Walter (Rabbit)	1912–1935	.258
Mathews, Eddie	1952–1968	.271
Mays, Willie	1951–1973	.302
Medwick, Joseph (Ducky)	1932–1948	.324
Musial, Stan	1941–1963	.331
O'Rourke, James	1876–1904	.314
Ott, Melvin	1926–1947	.304
Rice, Edgar (Sam)	1915–1934	.322
Robinson, Jack	1947–1956	.311
Roush, Edd	1913–1931	.323
Ruth, George (Babe)	1914–1935	.342
Schalk, Raymond	1912–1929	.253
Sewell, Joseph	1920–1933	.312
Simmons, Al	1924–1944	.334
Sisler, George	1915–1930	.340
Speaker, Tris	1907–1928	.344
Terry, William	1923–1936	.341
Thompson, Samuel L.	1885–1906	.336
Tinker, Joseph	1902–1916	.264
Traynor, Harold (Pie)	1920–1937	.320
Wagner, John (Honus)	1897–1917	.329
Wallace, Roderick (Bobby)	1894–1918	.267
Waner, Lloyd (Little Poison)	1927–1945	.316
Waner, Paul (Big Poison)	1926–1945	.333
Ward, John Montgomery	1878–1894	.283
Wheat, Zachary	1909–1927	.317
Williams, Theodore	1939–1960	.344
Wilson, Hack	1923–1934	.307
Youngs, Ross (Pep)	1917–1926	.322

1979 MAJOR LEAGUE STANDINGS

NATIONAL LEAGUE

Eastern Division

	W.	L.	Pct.	G.B.
Pittsburgh	98	64	.605	—
Montreal	95	65	.594	2
St. Louis	86	76	.531	12
Philadelphia	84	78	.519	14
Chicago	80	82	.494	18
New York	63	99	.389	35

Western Division

	W.	L.	Pct.	G.B.
Cincinnati	90	71	.559	—
Houston	89	73	.549	1½
Los Angeles	79	83	.488	11½
San Francisco	71	91	.438	19½
San Diego	68	93	.422	22
Atlanta	66	94	.413	23½

AMERICAN LEAGUE

Eastern Division

	W.	L.	Pct.	G.B.
Baltimore	102	57	.642	—
Milwaukee	95	66	.590	8
Boston	91	69	.569	11½
New York	89	71	.556	13½
Detroit	85	76	.528	18
Cleveland	81	80	.503	22
Toronto	53	109	.327	50½

Western Division

	W.	L.	Pct.	G.B.
California	88	74	.543	—
Kansas City	85	77	.525	3
Texas	83	79	.512	5
Minnesota	82	80	.506	6
Chicago	73	87	.456	14
Seattle	67	95	.414	21
Oakland	54	108	.333	34

1979 ALL-STAR GAME — Seattle, July 17

NATIONAL LEAGUE

	ab	r	h	bi
Lopes, 2b	3	0	1	0
Morgan, 2b	1	1	0	0
Parker, rf	3	0	1	1
Garvey, 1b	2	1	0	0
Perry, p	0	0	0	0
Sambito, p	0	0	0	0
Reynolds, ss	2	0	0	0
Schmidt, 3b	3	2	2	1
Cey, 3b	1	0	0	0
Parrish, 3b	0	0	0	0
Foster, lf	1	0	1	1
Matthews, lf	2	0	0	0
Mazzilli, cf	1	1	1	2
Winfield, cf-lf	5	1	1	1
Boone, c	2	1	1	0
Carter, c	2	0	1	1
Bowa, ss	2	0	0	0
LaCoss, p	0	0	0	0
Hernandez, ph	1	0	0	0
Sutter, p	0	0	0	0
Carlton, p	0	0	0	0
Brock, ph	1	0	1	0
Andujar, p	0	0	0	0
Clark, ph	1	0	0	0
Rogers, p	0	0	0	0
Rose, 1b	2	0	0	0
Total	**35**	**7**	**10**	**7**

AMERICAN LEAGUE

	ab	r	h	bi
Smalley, ss	3	0	0	0
Grich, 2b	1	0	0	0
Brett, 3b	3	1	0	0
Nettles, 3b	1	0	1	0
Baylor, lf	4	2	2	1
Kern, p	0	0	0	0
Guidry, p	0	0	0	0
Singleton, ph	1	0	0	0
Rice, lf	5	0	1	0
Lynn, cf	1	1	1	2
Lemon, cf	2	1	0	0
Yastrzemski, 1b	3	0	2	1
Burleson, ss	2	1	0	0
Porter, c	3	0	1	0
Downing, c	1	0	1	0
White, 2b	2	0	0	0
Bochte, 1b	1	0	1	1
Ryan, p	0	0	0	0
Cooper, ph	0	0	0	0
Stanley, p	0	0	0	0
Kemp, ph	1	0	0	0
Clear, p	0	0	0	0
Jackson, ph	1	0	0	0
Total	**35**	**6**	**10**	**5**

National League	2	1	1	0	0	1	0	1	1—7
American League	3	0	2	0	0	1	0	0	0—6

E—Schmidt. DP—American 2. LOB—National 8, American 9. 2B—Foster, Baylor, Schmidt, Winfield, Porter, Rice. 3B—Schmidt. HR—Lynn, Mazzilli. S—Bochte. SF—Parker.

National	IP	H	R	ER	BB	SO
Carlton	1	2	3	3	1	0
Andujar	2	2	2	1	1	0
Rogers	2	0	0	0	0	2
Perry*	0	3	1	1	0	0
Sambito	⅔	0	0	0	1	0
LaCoss (W)	1⅓	1	0	0	0	0
Sutter	2	2	0	0	2	3

American	IP	H	R	ER	BB	SO
Ryan	2	5	3	3	1	2
Stanley	2	1	1	0	0	0
Clear	2	1	1	1	0	0
Kern (L)	2⅔	2	2	2	3	2
Guidry	⅓	0	0	0	1	0

*Pitched to 3 batters in 6th
HBP—by Andujar (Lemon). WP—Andujar. Balk—Kern. T—3:11. A—58,905.

1979 PLAYOFF RESULTS

NATIONAL LEAGUE

	Game No.			
	One	Two	Three	Four
Pittsburgh	5	3	7	—
Cincinnati	2	2	1	—

AMERICAN LEAGUE

	Game No.			
	One	Two	Three	Four
Baltimore	6	9	3	8
California	3	8	4	0

1979 WORLD SERIES BOX SCORES

FIRST GAME: Memorial Stadium, October 10

PITTSBURGH (NL)

	ab	r	h	bi
Moreno, cf	5	0	0	0
Foli, ss	5	1	1	0
Parker, rf	5	1	4	0
B. Robinson, lf	5	1	1	0
Stargell, 1b	5	1	1	2
Madlock, 3b	3	0	0	0
Nicosia, c	4	0	0	0
Garner, 2b	4	0	2	0
Kison, p	0	0	0	0
Rooker, p	1	0	0	0
Sanguillen, ph	1	0	0	0
Romo, p	0	0	0	0
Lacy, ph	1	0	0	0
D. Robinson, p	0	0	0	0
Stennett, ph	1	0	1	0
Jackson, p	0	0	0	0
Total	**40**	**4**	**11**	**4**

BALTIMORE (AL)

	ab	r	h	bi
Bumbry, cf	4	1	1	0
Belanger, ss	3	1	0	0
Singleton, rf	3	0	1	0
Murray, 1b	2	1	1	0
Lowenstein, lf	4	1	0	1
Roenicke, lf	0	0	0	0
DeCinces, 3b	3	1	1	2
Smith, 2b	2	0	1	0
Dauer, 2b	1	0	1	0
Dempsey, c	4	0	0	0
Flanagan, p	4	0	0	0
Total	**30**	**5**	**6**	**3**

Pittsburgh	0	0	0	1	0	2	0	0	1—4
Baltimore	5	0	0	0	0	0	0	0	x—5

E—Garner, Foli, Stargell, Decinces 2, Belanger. DP—Pittsburg 1. LOB—Pittsburgh 10, Baltimore 8. 2B—Parker, Garner. HR—DeCinces, Stargell. SB—Murray. S—Bumbry.

Pittsburgh	IP	H	R	ER	BB	SO
Kison (L, 0-1)	⅓	3	5	4	2	0
Rooker	3⅔	2	0	0	1	2
Romo	1	0	0	0	2	0
D. Robinson	2	0	0	0	1	1
Jackson	1	1	0	0	0	1
Baltimore						
Flanagan (W, 1-0)	9	11	4	2	1	7

WP—Kison. Time—3:18. Attendance—53,735.

SECOND GAME: Memorial Stadium, October 11

PITTSBURGH (NL)

	ab	r	h	bi
Moreno, cf	5	0	1	0
Foli, ss	4	0	1	0
Parker, rf	4	0	1	0
Stargell, 1b	4	1	1	0
Milner, lf	3	1	1	0
B. Robinson, ph	1	0	1	0
Alexander, lf	0	0	0	0
Madlock, 3b	4	0	2	1
Ott, c	3	1	1	1
Garner, 2b	2	0	1	0
Blyleven, p	2	0	0	0
Easler, ph	0	0	0	0
D. Robinson, p	0	0	0	0
Sanguillen, ph	1	0	1	1
Tekulve, p	0	0	0	0
Total	**33**	**3**	**11**	**3**

BALTIMORE (AL)

	ab	r	h	bi
Bumbry, cf	5	0	0	0
Belanger, ss	3	0	0	0
Crowley, rf	0	0	0	0
T. Martinez, p	0	0	0	0
Stanhouse, p	0	0	0	0
Singleton, rf	4	1	1	0
Murray, 1b	3	1	3	2
DeCinces, 3b	4	0	0	0
Lowenstein, lf	3	0	1	0
Smith, 2b	4	0	0	0
Dempsey, c	3	0	1	0
Palmer, p	2	0	0	0
Kelly, ph	0	0	0	0
Garcia, ss	1	0	0	0
Total	**32**	**2**	**6**	**2**

Pittsburgh	0	2	0	0	0	0	0	0	1—3
Baltimore	0	1	0	0	1	0	0	0	0—2

E—Parker, DeCinces, Foli. DP—Pittsburgh 3, Baltimore 2. LOB—Pittsburgh 7, Baltimore 8. 2B—Murray. HR—Murray. SF—Ott.

Pittsburgh	IP	H	R	ER	BB	SO
Blyleven	6	5	2	2	2	1
D. Robinson (W, 1-0)	2	1	0	0	3	2
Tekulve (S, 1)	1	0	0	0	0	2
Baltimore						
Palmer	7	8	2	2	2	3
T. Martinez	1*	1	0	0	0	1
Stanhouse (L, 0-1)	1	2	1	1	1	0

*Pitched to one batter in the ninth.
WP—Palmer. Time—3:13. Attendance—53,739.

THIRD GAME: Three Rivers Stadium, October 12

BALTIMORE	ab	r	h	bi		PITTSBURGH	ab	r	h	bi
Garcia, ss	4	2	4	4		Moreno, cf	4	1	2	0
Ayala, lf	2	1	2	2		Foli, ss	4	0	0	0
Bumbry, cf	2	1	1	0		Parker, rf	3	0	0	1
Singleton, rf	5	0	2	1		B. Robinson, lf	4	0	1	0
Murray, 1b	4	0	0	0		Stargell, 1b	4	2	2	0
DeCinces, 3b	5	0	0	1		Madlock, 3b	4	0	1	1
Roenicke, cf-lf	5	0	1	0		Nicosia, c	4	1	1	0
Dauer, 2b	5	1	1	0		Garner, 2b	4	0	1	2
Dempsey, c	5	2	2	0		Candelaria, p	1	0	1	0
McGregor, p	3	1	0	0		Romo, p	1	0	0	0
						Jackson, p	0	0	0	0
						Lacy, ph	1	0	0	0
						Tekulve, p	0	0	0	0
Total	**40**	**8**	**13**	**8**		**Total**	**34**	**4**	**9**	**4**

Baltimore   0 0 2   5 0 0   1 0 0—8
Pittsburgh   1 2 0   0 0 1   0 0 0—4

E—Foli, Stargell. LOB—Baltimore 9, Pittsburgh 4. 2B—Garcia, Moreno 2, Garner, Dauer, Stargell, Dempsey. 3B—Garcia. HR—Ayala. SF—Parker.

	IP	H	R	ER	BB	SO
Baltimore—McGregor (W, 1-0)	9	9	4	4	0	6
Pittsburgh—Candelaria (L, 0-1)	3*	8	6	5	2	2
Romo	3⅓	5	2	2	1	4
Jackson	⅓	0	0	0	0	0
Tekulve	2	0	0	0	0	1

*Pitched to four batters in the fourth.
HBP—by Romo (Bumbry). Balk—McGregor.
Time—2:51. Attendance—50,848.

FOURTH GAME: Three Rivers Stadium, October 13

BALTIMORE	ab	r	h	bi		PITTSBURGH	ab	r	h	bi
Bumbry, cf	5	1	1	1		Moreno, cf	5	0	2	1
Garcia, ss	5	2	2	2		Foli, ss	4	2	3	0
Belanger, ss	0	0	0	0		Parker, rf	5	0	2	1
Singleton, rf	5	0	3	1		Stargell, 1b	5	1	3	1
Murray, 1b	5	1	0	0		Milner, lf	3	1	2	1
DeCinces, 3b	1	1	0	0		D. Robinson, p	0	0	0	0
Roenicke, lf	3	0	0	0		Tekulve, p	0	0	0	0
Lowenstein, lf	2	1	1	2		Easler, ph	1	0	0	0
Dauer, 2b	3	0	1	0		Madlock, 3b	3	1	2	0
Smith, 2b	0	1	0	0		Ott, c	5	0	1	2
Skaggs, 3b	3	1	1	0		Garner, 2b	4	1	2	0
Dempsey, c	0	1	0	0		Bibby, p	3	0	0	0
Crowley, ph	1	0	1	2		Jackson, p	0	0	0	0
D. Martinez, p	0	0	0	0		B. Robinson, lf	1	0	0	0
Stewart, p	1	0	0	0						
May, ph	1	0	0	0						
Stone, p	0	0	0	0						
Kelly, ph	1	0	1	0						
Stoddard, p	1	0	1	1						
Total	**37**	**9**	**12**	**9**		**Total**	**39**	**6**	**17**	**6**

Baltimore   0 0 3   0 0 0   0 6 0—9
Pittsburgh   0 4 0   0 1 1   0 0 0—6

E—Madlock. DP—Baltimore 2, Pittsburgh 3. LOB—Baltimore 6, Pittsburgh 10. 2B—Madlock, Ott, Garcia, Singleton, Stargell, Milner, Parker, Lowenstein, Crowley. HR—Stargell. SB—DeCinces.

	IP	H	R	ER	BB	SO
Baltimore—D. Martinez	1⅓	6	4	4	0	0
Stewart	2⅔	4	0	0	1	0
Stone	2	4	2	2	2	2
Stoddard (W, 1-0)	3	3	0	0	1	3
Pittsburgh—Bibby	6⅓	7	3	2	2	7
Jackson	⅔	0	0	0	0	0
D. Robinson	⅓	2	3	3	1	0
Tekulve (L, 0-1)	1⅔	3	3	3	2	1

Time—3:48. Attendance—50,883.

FIFTH GAME: Three Rivers Stadium, October 14

BALTIMORE	ab	r	h	bi		PITTSBURGH	ab	r	h	bi
Garcia, ss	4	0	0	0		Moreno, cf	4	1	0	0
Ayala, lf	1	0	0	0		Foli, ss	4	2	2	3
Bumbry, cf	1	0	0	0		Parker, rf	4	1	2	1
Singleton, rf	4	0	0	0		B. Robinson, lf	4	0	1	0
Murray, 1b	4	0	0	0		Stargell, 1b	3	1	1	1
Roenicke, cf-lf	4	1	1	0		Madlock, 3b	4	1	4	1
DeCinces, 3b	4	0	2	0		Nicosia, c	4	0	0	0
Dauer, 2b	3	0	0	0		Garner, 2b	4	1	2	1
Lowenstein, ph	1	0	1	0		Rooker, p	1	0	0	0
Dempsey, c	3	0	2	0		Lacy, ph	1	0	1	0
Crowley, ph	1	0	0	0		Blyleven, p	1	0	0	0
Flanagan, p	1	0	0	0						
Kelly, ph	1	0	0	0						
Stoddard, p	0	0	0	0						
T. Martinez, p	0	0	0	0						
Stanhouse, p	0	0	0	0						
Total	**32**	**1**	**6**	**0**		**Total**	**34**	**7**	**13**	**7**

Baltimore   0 0 0   0 1 0   0 0 0—1
Pittsburgh   0 0 0   0 0 2   2 3 x—7

E—Garner, Stoddard, Stanhouse. DP—Pittsburgh 2. LOB—Baltimore 7, Pittsburgh 9. 2B—B. Robinson, Roenicke, Parker, Dempsey. 3B—Foli. S—B. Robinson, Blyleven. SF—Stargell.

	IP	H	R	ER	BB	SO
Baltimore—Flanagan (L, 1-1)	6	6	2	2	1	6
Stoddard	⅔	2	2	1	0	0
T. Martinez	⅓*	2	1	1	0	0
Stanhouse	1	3	2	2	2	0
Pittsburgh—Rooker	5	3	1	1	2	2
Blyleven (W, 1-0)	4	3	0	0	1	3

*Pitched to one batter in the eighth.
Time—2:54. Attendance—50,920.

SIXTH GAME: Memorial Stadium, October 16

PITTSBURGH	ab	r	h	bi		BALTIMORE	ab	r	h	bi
Moreno, cf	5	1	3	1		Garcia, ss	3	0	1	0
Foli, ss	5	1	2	0		Kelly, ph	1	0	0	0
Parker, rf	4	0	1	1		Belanger, ss	0	0	0	0
Stargell, 1b	4	0	0	1		Ayala, lf	3	0	0	0
Milner, lf	3	0	0	0		Crowley, ph	1	0	0	0
Tekulve, p	1	0	0	0		Stoddard, p	1	0	0	0
Madlock, 3b	4	0	1	0		Singleton, rf	4	0	3	0
Ott, c	4	1	2	0		Murray, 1b	4	0	0	0
Garner, 2b	3	1	2	0		DeCinces, 3b	4	0	0	0
Candelaria, p	2	0	0	0		Roenicke, cf	2	0	0	0
Lacy, ph	1	0	0	0		Bumbry, cf	1	0	0	0
B. Robinson, lf	0	0	1	0		Dauer, 2b	2	0	1	0
						Smith, 2b	1	0	1	0
						Dempsey, c	3	0	1	0
						Palmer, p	2	0	0	0
						Lowenstein, lf	1	0	0	0
Total	**35**	**4**	**10**	**4**		**Total**	**32**	**0**	**7**	**0**

Pittsburgh   0 0 0   0 0 0   2 2 0—4
Baltimore   0 0 0   0 0 0   0 0 0—0

E—Bumbry. DP—Pittsburgh 2. LOB—Pittsburgh 10, Baltimore 5. 2B—Foli, Garner. SF—Stargell, B. Robinson.

	IP	H	R	ER	BB	SO
Pittsburgh—Candelaria (W, 1-1)	6	6	0	0	0	2
Tekulve (S, 2)	3	1	0	0	0	4
Baltimore—Palmer (L, 0-1)	8	10	4	4	3	5
Stoddard	1	0	0	0	0	0

HBP—by Palmer (Garner). Time—2:30. Attendance—53,739.

SEVENTH GAME: Memorial Stadium, October 17

PITTSBURGH	ab	r	h	bi		BALTIMORE	ab	r	h	bi
Moreno, cf	5	1	3	1		Bumbry, cf	3	0	0	0
Foli, ss	4	0	1	0		Garcia, ss	3	0	1	0
Parker, rf	4	0	0	0		Ayala, ph	1	0	0	0
B. Robinson, lf	4	1	1	1		Crowley, ph	1	0	0	0
Stargell, 1b	5	1	4	2		Stoddard, p	0	0	0	0
Madlock, 3b	3	0	0	0		Flanagan, p	0	0	0	0
Nicosia, c	4	0	0	0		Stanhouse, p	0	0	0	0
Garner, 2b	3	1	1	0		T. Martinez, p	0	0	0	0
Bibby, p	1	0	0	0		D. Martinez, p	0	0	0	0
Sanguillen, ph	1	0	1	0		Singleton, rf	3	0	0	0
D. Robinson, p	0	0	0	0		Murray, 1b	4	0	0	0
Jackson, p	1	0	0	0		Lowenstein, lf	2	0	0	0
Tekulve, p	0	0	0	0		Roenicke, lf	2	0	0	0
						DeCinces, 3b	4	0	2	0
						Dempsey, c	4	0	0	0
						Kelly, ph	1	0	0	0
						Dauer, 2b	3	1	1	1
						McGregor, p	1	0	0	0
						May, ph	0	0	0	0
						Belanger, ss	0	0	0	0
Total	**36**	**4**	**10**	**4**		**Total**	**30**	**1**	**4**	**1**

Pittsburgh   0 0 0   0 0 2   0 0 2—4
Baltimore   0 0 1   0 0 0   0 0 0—1

E—Lowenstein, Garcia. DP—Baltimore 1. LOB—Pittsburgh 10, Baltimore 6. 2B—Stargell 2, Garner. HR—Dauer, Stargell. S—Foli.

	IP	H	R	ER	BB	SO
Pittsburgh—Bibby	4	3	1	1	0	3
D. Robinson	⅔	1	0	0	1	0
Jackson (W, 1-0)	2⅔	0	0	0	1	2
Tekulve (S, 3)	1⅔	0	0	0	1	2
Baltimore—McGregor (L, 1-1)	8	7	2	2	2	2
Stoddard	⅓	1	1	1	0	0
Flanagan	0*	1	1	0	0	0
Stanhouse	0*	1	0	0	0	0
T. Martinez	0*	0	0	0	0	0
D. Martinez	⅔	0	0	0	0	0

*Pitched to one batter in the ninth.
HBP—by T. Martinez (Parker), by D. Martinez (B. Robinson). Time—2:54. Attendance—53,733.

1979 CLUB AND INDIVIDUAL RECORDS

NATIONAL LEAGUE

Club Batting

Club	Pct.	R.	H.
St. Louis	.278	731	1,594
Pittsburgh	.272	775	1,541
Chicago	.268	706	1,494
Philadelphia	.266	683	1,453
Montreal	.264	701	1,445
Cincinnati	.264	731	1,445
Los Angeles	.263	739	1,443
Houston	.256	583	1,382
Atlanta	.256	669	1,389
New York	.250	593	1,399
San Francisco	.246	672	1,328
San Diego	.242	603	1,316

Individual Batting

Leaders—360 or More At Bats

Players — Club	Pct.	R.	H.
Hernandez, St. Louis	.344	116	210
Rose, Philadelphia	.331	90	208
Knight, Cincinnati	.318	64	175
Garvey, Los Angeles	.315	92	204
Horner, Atlanta	.314	66	153
Templeton, St. Louis	.314	105	211
Parker, Pittsburgh	.310	109	193
Winfield, San Diego	.308	97	184
Parrish, Montreal	.307	83	167
Matthews, Atlanta	.304	97	192

Club Pitching

Club	ERA.	IP.	H.	SO.
Montreal	3.14	1,447	1,379	813
Houston	3.19	1,448	1,278	854
Pittsburgh	3.41	1,493	1,424	904
Cincinnati	3.58	1,440	1,415	773
San Diego	3.69	1,453	1,438	779
St. Louis	3.73	1,487	1,449	788
Los Angeles	3.83	1,444	1,425	811
New York	3.84	1,483	1,486	819
Chicago	3.88	1,447	1,500	933
Philadelphia	4.16	1,441	1,455	787
San Francisco	4.16	1,436	1,484	880
Atlanta	4.18	1,408	1,496	779

Individual Pitching

Leaders—162 or More Innings

Pitcher — Club	W.	L.	ERA.	IP.
Richard, Houston	18	13	2.71	292
Hume, Cincinnati	10	9	2.76	163
Schatzeder, Montreal	10	5	2.83	162
Hooton, Los Angeles	11	10	2.97	212
J. Niekro, Houston	21	11	3.00	264
Rogers, Montreal	13	12	3.00	249
Forsch, Houston	11	6	3.03	178
Lee, Montreal	16	10	3.04	222
Perry, San Diego	12	11	3.05	233
Seaver, Cincinnati	16	6	3.14	215

Pitching Leaders

VICTORIES		STRIKEOUTS	
J. Niekro (Hou.)	21	Richard (Hou.)	313
P. Niekro (Atl.)	21	Carlton (Phila.)	213
Carlton (Phila.)	18	P. Niekro (Atl.)	208
Reuschel (Chi.)	18	Blyleven (Pitt.)	172
Richard (Chi.)	18		

Batting Leaders

RUNS		HITS	
Hernandez (St.L.)	116	Templeton (St.L.)	211
Moreno (Pitt.)	110	Hernandez (St.L.)	210
Lopes (L.A.)	109	Rose (Phila.)	208
Parker (Pitt.)	109	Garvey (L.A.)	204
Schmidt (Phila.)	109		

HOME RUNS		RUNS BATTED IN	
Kingman (Chi.)	48	Winfield (S.D.)	118
Schmidt (Phila.)	45	Kingman (Chi.)	115
Winfield (S.D.)	34	Schmidt (Phila.)	114
Horner (Atl.)	33	Garvey (L.A.)	110

AMERICAN LEAGUE

Club Batting

Club	Pct.	R.	H.
Boston	.283	841	1,567
Kansas City	.282	851	1,596
California	.281	866	1,563
Milwaukee	.280	807	1,552
Minnesota	.278	764	1,544
Texas	.278	750	1,549
Chicago	.275	730	1,505
Detroit	.269	770	1,446
Seattle	.269	711	1,490
New York	.266	734	1,443
Baltimore	.261	757	1,401
Cleveland	.258	760	1,388
Toronto	.251	613	1,362
Oakland	.239	573	1,276

Individual Batting

Leaders—360 or More At Bats

Players — Club	Pct.	R.	H.
Lynn, Boston	.333	116	177
Brett, Kansas City	.329	119	212
Downing, California	.326	87	166
Rice, Boston	.325	117	201
Oliver, Texas	.323	69	159
Molitor, Milwaukee	.322	88	188
Lezcano, Milwaukee	.321	84	152
Kemp, Detroit	.318	88	156
Lemon, Chicago	.318	79	177
Bochte, Seattle	.316	81	175

Club Pitching

Club	ERA.	IP.	H.	SO.
Baltimore	3.28	1,434	1,279	786
New York	3.83	1,432	1,446	731
Texas	3.86	1,437	1,371	773
Boston	4.03	1,431	1,487	731
Milwaukee	4.03	1,439	1,563	580
Minnesota	4.13	1,444	1,590	721
Chicago	4.10	1,409	1,365	675
Detroit	4.27	1,423	1,429	802
California	4.34	1,436	1,463	820
Kansas City	4.45	1,448	1,477	640
Cleveland	4.57	1,431	1,502	781
Seattle	4.58	1,438	1,567	736
Oakland	4.74	1,429	1,606	727
Toronto	4.81	1,417	1,537	611

Individual Pitching

Leaders—162 or More Innings

Pitcher — Club	W.	L.	ERA.	IP.
Guidry, New York	18	8	2.78	236
John, New York	21	9	2.96	276
Eckersley, Boston	17	10	2.99	246
Flanagan, Baltimore	23	9	3.08	265
Morris, Detroit	17	7	3.28	197
Caldwell, Milwaukee	16	6	3.29	235
McGregor, Baltimore	13	6	3.35	174
Koosman, Minnesota	20	13	3.38	263
Baumgarten, Chicago	13	8	3.54	190
Zahn, Minnesota	13	7	3.57	169
Frost, California	16	10	3.57	239

Pitching Leaders

VICTORIES		STRIKEOUTS	
Flanagan (Balt.)	23	Ryan (Calif.)	223
John (N.Y.)	21	Guidry (N.Y.)	201
Koosman (Minn.)	20	Flanagan (Balt.)	190
Guidry (N.Y.)	18	Jenkins (Tex.)	164

Batting Leaders

RUNS		HITS	
Baylor (Calif.)	120	Brett (K.C.)	212
Brett (K.C.)	119	Rice (Bos.)	201
Rice (Bos.)	117	Bell (Tex.)	200
Lynn (Bos.)	116	Lansford (Calif.)	189

HOME RUNS		RUNS BATTED IN	
Thomas (Milw.)	45	Baylor (Calif.)	139
Rice (Bos.)	39	Rice (Bos.)	130
Lynn (Bos.)	39	Thomas (Milw.)	123
Baylor (Calif.)	36	Lynn (Bos.)	122

ALL-TIME WORLD SERIES RESULTS

Year	Winner	Games Won	Lost	Loser	Year	Winner	Games Won	Lost	Loser
1903	Boston (AL)	5	3	Pittsburgh (NL)	1942	St. Louis (NL)	4	1	New York (AL)
1905	New York (NL)	4	1	Philadelphia (AL)	1943	New York (AL)	4	1	St. Louis (NL)
1906	Chicago (AL)	4	2	Chicago (NL)	1944	St. Louis (NL)	4	2	St. Louis (AL)
1907	Chicago (NL)	4	0	Detroit (AL)	1945	Detroit (AL)	4	3	Chicago (NL)
1908	Chicago (NL)	4	1	Detroit (AL)	1946	St. Louis (NL)	4	3	Boston (AL)
1909	Pittsburgh (NL)	4	3	Detroit (AL)	1947	New York (AL)	4	3	Brooklyn (NL)
1910	Philadelphia (AL)	4	1	Chicago (NL)	1948	Cleveland (AL)	4	2	Boston (NL)
1911	Philadelphia (AL)	4	2	New York (NL)	1949	New York (AL)	4	1	Brooklyn (NL)
1912	Boston (AL)	4	3	New York (NL)	1950	New York (AL)	4	0	Philadelphia (NL)
1913	Philadelphia (AL)	4	1	New York (NL)	1951	New York (AL)	4	2	New York (NL)
1914	Boston (NL)	4	0	Philadelphia (AL)	1952	New York (AL)	4	3	Brooklyn (NL)
1915	Boston (AL)	4	1	Philadelphia (NL)	1953	New York (AL)	4	2	Brooklyn (NL)
1916	Boston (AL)	4	1	Brooklyn (NL)	1954	New York (NL)	4	0	Cleveland (AL)
1917	Chicago (AL)	4	2	New York (NL)	1955	Brooklyn (NL)	4	3	New York (AL)
1918	Boston (AL)	4	2	Chicago (NL)	1956	New York (AL)	4	3	Brooklyn (NL)
1919	Cincinnati (NL)	5	3	Chicago (AL)	1957	Milwaukee (NL)	4	3	New York (AL)
1920	Cleveland (AL)	5	2	Brooklyn (NL)	1958	New York (AL)	4	3	Milwaukee (NL)
1921	New York (NL)	5	3	New York (AL)	1959	Los Angeles (NL)	4	2	Chicago (AL)
1922	New York (NL)	4	0	New York (AL)	1960	Pittsburgh (NL)	4	3	New York (AL)
1923	New York (AL)	4	2	New York (NL)	1961	New York (AL)	4	1	Cincinnati (NL)
1924	Washington (AL)	4	3	New York (NL)	1962	New York (AL)	4	3	San Francisco (NL)
1925	Pittsburgh (NL)	4	3	Washington (AL)	1963	Los Angeles (NL)	4	0	New York (AL)
1926	St. Louis (NL)	4	3	New York (AL)	1964	St. Louis (NL)	4	3	New York (AL)
1927	New York (AL)	4	0	Pittsburgh (NL)	1965	Los Angeles (NL)	4	3	Minnesota (AL)
1928	New York (AL)	4	0	St. Louis (NL)	1966	Baltimore (AL)	4	0	Los Angeles (NL)
1929	Philadelphia (AL)	4	1	Chicago (NL)	1967	St. Loius (NL)	4	3	Boston (AL)
1930	Philadelphia (AL)	4	2	St. Louis (NL)	1968	Detroit (AL)	4	3	St. Louis (NL)
1931	St. Louis (NL)	4	3	Philadelphia (AL)	1969	New York (NL)	4	1	Baltimore (AL)
1932	New York (AL)	4	0	Chicago (NL)	1970	Baltimore (AL)	4	1	Cincinnati (NL)
1933	New York (NL)	4	1	Washington (AL)	1971	Pittsburgh (NL)	4	3	Baltimore (AL)
1934	St. Louis (NL)	4	3	Detroit (AL)	1972	Oakland (AL)	4	3	Cincinnati (NL)
1935	Detroit (AL)	4	2	Chicago (NL)	1973	Oakland (AL)	4	3	New York (NL)
1936	New York (AL)	4	2	New York (NL)	1974	Oakland (AL)	4	1	Los Angeles (NL)
1937	New York (AL)	4	1	New York (NL)	1975	Cincinnati (NL)	4	3	Boston (AL)
1938	New York (AL)	4	0	Chicago (NL)	1976	Cincinnati (NL)	4	0	New York (AL)
1939	New York (AL)	4	0	Cincinnati (NL)	1977	New York (AL)	4	2	Los Angeles (NL)
1940	Cincinnati (NL)	4	3	Detroit (AL)	1978	New York (AL)	4	2	Los Angeles (NL)
1941	New York (AL)	4	1	Brooklyn (NL)	1979	Pittsburgh (NL)	4	3	Baltimore (AL)

THE ALL-STAR GAMES

Year	Site	Winner	Score	Year	Site	Winner	Score
1933	Comiskey Park, Chicago	American	4-2	1959	Forbes Field, Pittsburgh	National	5-4
1934	Polo Grounds, New York	American	9-7		Memorial Coliseum, L.A.	American	5-3
1935	Municipal Stadium, Cleveland	American	4-1	1960	Municipal Stadium, Kansas City	National	5-3
1936	Braves Field, Boston	National	4-3		Yankee Stadium, New York	National	6-0
1937	Griffith Stadium, Washington	American	8-3	1961	Candlestick Park, San Francisco[4]	National	5-4
1938	Crosley Field, Cincinnati	National	4-1		Fenway Park, Boston[5]	Tie	1-1
1939	Yankee Stadium, New York	American	3-1	1962	D.C. Stadium, Washington	National	3-1
1940	Sportsman's Park, St. Louis	National	4-0		Wrigley Field, Chicago	American	9-4
1941	Briggs Stadium, Detroit	American	7-5	1963	Municipal Stadium, Cleveland	National	5-3
1942	Polo Grounds, New York	American	3-1	1964	Shea Stadium, New York	National	7-4
1943	Shibe Park, Philadelphia*	American	5-3	1965	Metropolitan Stadium,		
1944	Forbes Field, Pittsburgh*	National	7-1		Bloomington, Minnesota	National	6-5
1945	Not played	—	—	1966	Busch Stadium, St. Louis[6]	National	2-1
1946	Fenway Park, Boston	American	12-0	1967	Anaheim Stadium, California[7]	National	2-1
1947	Wrigley Field, Chicago	American	2-1	1968	Houston Astrodome[8]	National	1-0
1948	Sportsman's Park, St. Louis	American	5-2	1969	R. F. Kennedy Stadium, Wash.	National	9-3
1949	Ebbets Field, Brooklyn	American	11-7	1970	Riverfront Stadium, Cincinnati[8]	National	5-4
1950	Comiskey Park, Chicago[1]	National	4-3	1971	Tiger Stadium, Detroit	American	6-4
1951	Briggs Stadium, Detroit	National	8-3	1972	Atlanta, Georgia[8]	National	4-3
1952	Shibe Park, Philadelphia[2]	National	3-2	1973	Kansas City, Missouri	National	7-1
1953	Crosley Field, Cincinnati	National	5-1	1974	Pittsburgh, Pennsylvania	National	7-2
1954	Municipal Stadium, Cleveland	American	11-9	1975	Milwaukee, Wis.	National	6-3
1955	Milwaukee County Stadium[3]	National	6-5	1976	Veterans Stadium, Philadelphia	National	7-1
1956	Griffith Stadium, Washington	National	7-3	1977	Yankee Stadium, New York	National	7-5
1957	Busch Stadium, St. Louis	American	6-5	1978	San Diego Stadium	National	7-3
1958	Memorial Stadium, Baltimore	American	4-3	1979	Seattle Kingdome	National	7-6

* A night game. [1] Fourteen-inning game. [2] Game called at the end of the fifth inning because of rain. [3] Twelve-inning game. [4] Ten-inning game. [5] Game called in the ninth inning because of rain. [6] Ten-inning game. [7] Fifteen-inning game. [8] First All-Star game played indoors.

MODERN FRANCHISE CHANGES IN MAJOR LEAGUES

NATIONAL LEAGUE

Year	New Team	How Created
1953	Milwaukee Braves	Formerly, Boston Braves
1958	Los Angeles Dodgers	Formerly, Brooklyn Dodgers
1958	San Francisco Giants	Formerly, New York Giants
1962	New York Mets	Expansion team
1962	Houston Astros†	Expansion team
1966	Atlanta Braves	Formerly, Milwaukee Braves
1969	Montreal Expos	Expansion team
1969	San Diego Padres	Expansion team

AMERICAN LEAGUE

Year	New Team	How Created
1954	Baltimore Orioles	Formerly, St. Louis Browns
1955	Kansas City Athletics	Formerly, Philadelphia Athletics
1961	Minnesota Twins	Formerly, Washington Senators
1961	Washington Senators*	Expansion team
1961	Los Angeles Angels	Expansion team
1965	California Angels	Formerly, Los Angeles Angels
1968	Oakland Athletics	Formerly, Kansas City Athletics
1969	Kansas City Royals	Expansion team
1969	Seattle Pilots	Expansion team
1970	Milwaukee Brewers	Formerly, Seattle Pilots
1972	Texas Rangers	Formerly, Washington Senators
1977	Seattle Mariners	Expansion team
1977	Toronto Blue Jays	Expansion team

† Originally Colts, then Colt-45's. * New Washington Senators.

AMERICAN LEAGUE PENNANT WINNERS

Year	Club	Won	Lost	%	Manager
1901	Chicago	83	53	.610	Clark Griffith
1902	Philadelphia	83	53	.610	Connie Mack
1903	Boston	91	47	.659	James Collins
1904	Boston	95	59	.617	James Collins
1905	Philadelphia	92	56	.622	Connie Mack
1906	Chicago	93	58	.616	Fielder Jones
1907	Detroit	92	58	.613	Hugh Jennings
1908	Detroit	90	63	.588	Hugh Jennings
1909	Detroit	98	54	.645	Hugh Jennings
1910	Philadelphia	102	48	.680	Connie Mack
1911	Philadelphia	101	50	.669	Connie Mack
1912	Boston	105	47	.691	J. Garland Stahl
1913	Philadelphia	96	57	.627	Connie Mack
1914	Philadelphia	99	53	.651	Connie Mack
1915	Boston	101	50	.669	William Carrigan
1916	Boston	91	63	.591	William Carrigan
1917	Chicago	100	54	.649	Clarence Rowland
1918	Boston	75	51	.595	Edward Barrow
1919	Chicago	88	52	.629	William Gleason
1920	Cleveland	98	56	.636	Tris Speaker
1921	New York	98	55	.641	Miller Huggins
1922	New York	94	60	.610	Miller Huggins
1923	New York	98	54	.645	Miller Huggins
1924	Washington	92	62	.597	Stanley Harris
1925	Washington	96	55	.636	Stanley Harris
1926	New York	91	63	.591	Miller Huggins
1927	New York	110	44	.714	Miller Huggins
1928	New York	101	53	.656	Miller Huggins
1929	Philadelphia	104	46	.693	Connie Mack
1930	Philadelphia	102	52	.662	Connie Mack
1931	Philadelphia	107	45	.704	Connie Mack
1932	New York	107	47	.695	Joseph McCarthy
1933	Washington	99	53	.651	Joseph Cronin
1934	Detroit	101	53	.656	Gordon Cochrane
1935	Detroit	93	58	.616	Gordon Cochrane
1936	New York	102	51	.667	Joseph McCarthy
1937	New York	102	52	.662	Joseph McCarthy
1938	New York	99	53	.651	Joseph McCarthy
1939	New York	106	45	.702	Joseph McCarthy
1940	Detroit	90	64	.584	Delmar Baker
1941	New York	101	53	.656	Joseph McCarthy
1942	New York	103	51	.669	Joseph McCarthy
1943	New York	98	56	.636	Joseph McCarthy
1944	St. Louis	89	65	.578	James Sewell
1945	Detroit	88	65	.575	Stephen O'Neill
1946	Boston	104	50	.675	Joseph Cronin
1947	New York	97	57	.630	Stanley Harris
1948	Cleveland	97	58	.626	Louis Boudreau
1949	New York	97	57	.630	Charles Stengel
1950	New York	98	56	.636	Charles Stengel
1951	New York	98	56	.636	Charles Stengel
1952	New York	95	59	.617	Charles Stengel
1953	New York	99	52	.656	Charles Stengel
1954	Cleveland	111	43	.721	Alfonso Lopez
1955	New York	96	58	.623	Charles Stengel
1956	New York	97	57	.630	Charles Stengel
1957	New York	98	56	.636	Charles Stengel
1958	New York	92	62	.597	Charles Stengel
1959	Chicago	94	60	.610	Alfonso Lopez
1960	New York	97	57	.630	Charles Stengel
1961	New York	109	53	.673	Ralph Houk
1962	New York	96	66	.593	Ralph Houk
1963	New York	104	57	.646	Ralph Houk
1964	New York	99	63	.611	Lawrence Berra
1965	Minnesota	102	60	.630	Sabath Mele
1966	Baltimore	97	63	.606	Henry Bauer
1967	Boston	92	70	.568	Richard Williams
1968	Detroit	103	59	.636	Mayo Smith
1969	Baltimore	109	53	.673	Earl Weaver
1970	Baltimore	108	54	.667	Earl Weaver
1971	Baltimore	101	57	.639	Earl Weaver
1972	Oakland	93	62	.600	Dick Williams
1973	Oakland	94	68	.580	Dick Williams
1974	Oakland	90	72	.556	Alvin Dark
1975	Boston	95	65	.594	Darrell Johnson
1976	New York	97	62	.610	Billy Martin
1977	New York	100	62	.617	Billy Martin
1978	New York	100	63	.613	Bob Lemon
1979	Baltimore	102	57	.642	Earl Weaver

NATIONAL LEAGUE PENNANT WINNERS

Year	Club	Won	Lost	%	Manager
1880	Chicago	67	17	.798	Adrian C. Anson
1881	Chicago	56	28	.667	Adrian C. Anson
1882	Chicago	55	29	.655	Adrian C. Anson
1883	Boston	63	35	.643	John F. Morrill
1884	Providence	84	28	.750	Frank C. Bancroft
1885	Chicago	87	25	.777	Adrian C. Anson
1886	Chicago	90	34	.726	Adrian C. Anson
1887	Detroit	79	45	.637	W. H. Watkins
1888	New York	84	47	.641	James J. Mutrie
1889	New York	83	43	.659	James J. Mutrie
1890	Brooklyn	86	43	.667	Wm. H. McGunnigle
1891	Boston	87	51	.630	Frank G. Selee
1892	Boston	102	48	.680	Frank G. Selee
1893	Boston	86	43	.667	Frank G. Selee
1894	Baltimore	89	39	.695	Edward H. Hanlon
1895	Baltimore	87	43	.669	Edward H. Hanlon
1896	Baltimore	90	39	.698	Edward H. Hanlon
1897	Boston	93	39	.705	Frank G. Selee
1898	Boston	102	47	.685	Frank G. Selee
1899	Brooklyn	88	42	.677	Edward H. Hanlon
1900	Brooklyn	82	54	.603	Edward H. Hanlon
1901	Pittsburgh	90	49	.647	Fred C. Clarke
1902	Pittsburgh	103	36	.741	Fred C. Clarke
1903	Pittsburgh	91	49	.650	Fred Clarke
1904	New York	106	47	.693	John McGraw
1905	New York	105	48	.686	John McGraw
1906	Chicago	116	36	.763	Frank Chance
1907	Chicago	107	45	.704	Frank Chance
1908	Chicago	99	55	.643	Frank Chance
1909	Pittsburgh	110	42	.724	Fred Clarke
1910	Chicago	104	50	.675	Frank Chance
1911	New York	99	54	.647	John McGraw
1912	New York	103	48	.682	John McGraw
1913	New York	101	51	.664	John McGraw
1914	Boston	94	59	.614	George Stallings
1915	Philadelphia	90	62	.592	Patrick Moran
1916	Brooklyn	94	60	.610	Wilbert Robinson
1917	New York	98	56	.636	John McGraw
1918	Chicago	84	45	.651	Fred Mitchell
1919	Cincinnati	96	44	.686	Patrick Moran
1920	Brooklyn	93	61	.604	Wilbert Robinson
1921	New York	94	59	.614	John McGraw
1922	New York	93	61	.604	John McGraw
1923	New York	95	58	.621	John McGraw
1924	New York	93	60	.608	John McGraw
1925	Pittsburgh	95	58	.621	William McKechnie
1926	St. Louis	89	65	.578	Rogers Hornsby
1927	Pittsburgh	94	60	.610	Owen Bush
1928	St. Louis	95	59	.617	William McKechnie
1929	Chicago	98	54	.645	Joseph McCarthy
1930	St. Louis	92	62	.597	Charles Street
1931	St. Louis	101	53	.656	Charles Street
1932	Chicago	90	64	.584	Charles Grimm
1933	New York	91	61	.599	William Terry
1934	St. Louis	95	58	.621	Frank Frisch
1935	Chicago	100	54	.649	Charles Grimm
1936	New York	92	62	.597	William Terry
1937	New York	95	57	.625	William Terry
1938	Chicago	89	63	.586	Charles Hartnett
1939	Cincinnati	97	57	.630	William McKechnie
1940	Cincinnati	100	53	.654	William McKechnie
1941	Brooklyn	100	54	.649	Leo Durocher
1942	St. Louis	106	48	.688	William Southworth
1943	St. Louis	105	49	.682	William Southworth
1944	St. Louis	105	49	.682	William Southworth
1945	Chicago	98	56	.636	Charles Grimm
1946	St. Louis	98	58	.628	Edwin Dyer
1947	Brooklyn	94	60	.610	Burton Shotton
1948	Boston	91	62	.595	William Southworth
1949	Brooklyn	97	57	.630	Burton Shotton
1950	Philadelphia	91	63	.591	Edwin Sawyer
1951	New York	98	59	.624	Leo Durocher
1952	Brooklyn	96	57	.627	Charles Dressen
1953	Brooklyn	105	49	.682	Charles Dressen
1954	New York	97	57	.630	Leo Durocher
1955	Brooklyn	98	55	.641	Walter Alston
1956	Brooklyn	93	61	.604	Walter Alston
1957	Milwaukee	95	59	.617	Fred Haney
1958	Milwaukee	92	62	.597	Fred Haney
1959	Los Angeles	88	68	.564	Walter Alston
1960	Pittsburgh	95	59	.617	Daniel Murtaugh
1961	Cincinnati	93	61	.604	Fred Hutchinson
1962	San Francisco	103	62	.624	Alvin Dark
1963	Los Angeles	99	63	.611	Walter Alston
1964	St. Louis	93	69	.574	John Keane
1965	Los Angeles	97	65	.599	Walter Alston
1966	Los Angeles	95	67	.586	Walter Alston
1967	St. Louis	101	60	.627	Albert Schoendienst
1968	St. Louis	97	65	.599	Albert Schoendienst
1969	New York	100	62	.617	Gil Hodges
1970	Cincinnati	102	60	.630	Sparky Anderson
1971	Pittsburgh	97	65	.599	Danny Murtaugh
1972	Cincinnati	95	59	.617	Sparky Anderson
1973	New York	82	79	.509	Lawrence Berra
1974	Los Angeles	102	60	.630	Walter Alston
1975	Cincinnati	108	54	.667	Sparky Anderson
1976	Cincinnati	102	60	.630	Sparky Anderson
1977	Los Angeles	98	64	.605	Tom Lasorda
1978	Los Angeles	95	67	.586	Tom Lasorda
1979	Pittsburgh	98	64	.605	Chuck Tanner

NATIONAL LEAGUE BATTING CHAMPIONS

Year	Player and Club	Percent
1876	Roscoe Barnes, Chicago	.404
1877	Jim White, Boston	.385
1878	Abner Dalrymple, Milwaukee	.356
1879	Cap Anson, Chicago	.407
1880	George Gore, Chicago	.365
1881	Cap Anson, Chicago	.399
1882	Dan Brouthers, Buffalo	.367
1883	Dan Brouthers, Buffalo	.371
1884	James O'Rourke, Buffalo	.350
1885	Roger Connor, N.Y.	.371
1886	King Kelly, Chicago	.388
1887	Cap Anson, Chicago	.421
1888	Cap Anson, Chicago	.343
1889	Dan Brouthers, Boston	.373
1890	John Glasscock, N.Y.	.336
1891	Wm. Hamilton, Philadelphia	.338
1892	Dan Brouthers, Brooklyn, and Clarence Childs, Cleveland	.335
1893	Hugh Duffy, Boston	.378
1894	Hugh Duffy, Boston	.438
1895	Jesse Burkett, Cleveland	.423
1896	Jesse Burkett, Cleveland	.410
1897	Willie Keeler, Baltimore	.432
1898	Willie Keeler, Baltimore	.379
1899	Ed Delahanty, Philadelphia	.408
1900	Honus Wagner, Pittsburgh	.381
1901	Jesse Burkett, St. Louis	.382
1902	Clarence Beaumont, Pittsburgh	.357
1903	Honus Wagner, Pittsburgh	.355
1904	Honus Wagner, Pittsburgh	.349
1905	Cy Seymour, Cincinnati	.377
1906	Honus Wagner, Pittsburgh	.339
1907	Honus Wagner, Pittsburgh	.350
1908	Honus Wagner, Pittsburgh	.354
1909	Honus Wagner, Pittsburgh	.339
1910	Sherwood Magee, Philadelphia	.331
1911	Honus Wagner, Pittsburgh	.334
1912	Henry Zimmerman, Chicago	.372
1913	Jake Daubert, Brooklyn	.350
1914	Jake Daubert, Brooklyn	.329
1915	Larry Doyle, New York	.320
1916	Hal Chase, Cincinnati	.339
1917	Edd Roush, Cincinnati	.341
1918	Zack Wheat, Brooklyn	.335
1919	Edd Roush, Cincinnati	.321
1920	Rogers Hornsby, St. Louis	.370
1921	Rogers Hornsby, St. Louis	.397
1922	Rogers Hornsby, St. Louis	.401
1923	Rogers Hornsby, St. Louis	.384
1924	Rogers Hornsby, St. Louis	.424
1925	Rogers Hornsby, St. Louis	.403
1926	Gene Hargrave, Cincinnati	.353
1927	Paul Waner, Pittsburgh	.380
1928	Rogers Hornsby, Boston	.387
1929	Lefty O'Doul, Philadelphia	.398
1930	Bill Terry, New York	.401
1931	Chick Hafey, St. Louis	.349
1932	Lefty O'Doul, Brooklyn	.368
1933	Chuck Klein, Philadelphia	.368
1934	Paul Waner, Pittsburgh	.362
1935	Arky Vaughan, Pittsburgh	.385
1936	Paul Waner, Pittsburgh	.373
1937	Joe Medwick, St. Louis	.374
1938	Ernie Lombardi, Cincinnati	.342
1939	Johnny Mize, St. Louis	.349
1940	Debs Garms, Pittsburgh	.355
1941	Pete Reiser, Brooklyn	.343
1942	Ernie Lombardi, Boston	.330
1943	Stan Musial, St. Louis	.357
1944	Dixie Walker, Brooklyn	.357
1945	Phil Cavaretta, Chicago	.355
1946	Stan Musial, St. Louis	.365
1947	Harry Walker, St. Louis-Philadelphia	.363
1948	Stan Musial, St. Louis	.376
1949	Jackie Robinson, Brooklyn	.342
1950	Stan Musial, St. Louis	.346
1951	Stan Musial, St. Louis	.355
1952	Stan Musial, St. Louis	.336
1953	Carl Furillo, Brooklyn	.344
1954	Willie Mays, New York	.345
1955	Richie Ashburn, Philadelphia	.338
1956	Hank Aaron, Milwaukee	.328
1957	Stan Musial, St. Louis	.351
1958	Richie Ashburn, Philadelphia	.350
1959	Hank Aaron, Milwaukee	.355
1960	Dick Groat, Pittsburgh	.325
1961	Roberto Clemente, Pittsburgh	.351
1962	Tommy Davis, Los Angeles	.346
1963	Tommy Davis, Los Angeles	.326
1964	Roberto Clemente, Pittsburgh	.339
1965	Roberto Clemente, Pittsburgh	.329
1966	Matty Alou, Pittsburgh	.342
1967	Roberto Clemente, Pittsburgh	.357
1968	Pete Rose, Cincinnati	.335
1969	Pete Rose, Cincinnati	.348
1970	Rico Carty, Atlanta	.366
1971	Joe Torre, St. Louis	.363
1972	Billy Williams, Chicago	.333
1973	Pete Rose, Cincinnati	.338
1974	Ralph Garr, Atlanta	.353
1975	Bill Madlock, Chicago	.354
1976	Bill Madlock, Chicago	.339
1977	Dave Parker, Pittsburgh	.338
1978	Dave Parker, Pittsburgh	.334
1979	Keith Hernandez, St. Louis	.344

NATIONAL LEAGUE HOME RUN CHAMPIONS

Year	Player and Club	Home Runs
1876	George Hall, Phila. Athletics	5
1877	George Shaffer, Louisville	3
1878	Paul Hines, Providence	4
1879	Charles Jones, Boston	9
1880	James O'Rourke, Boston	6
	Harry Stovey, Worcester	6
1881	Dan Brouthers, Buffalo	8
1882	George Wood, Detroit	7
1883	William Ewing, New York	10
1884	Ed Williamson, Chicago	27
1885	Abner Dalrymple, Chicago	11
1886	Arthur Richardson, Detroit	11
1887	Roger Connor, New York	17
	Wm. O'Brien, Washington	17
1888	Roger Connor, New York	14
1889	Sam Thompson, Philadelphia	20
1890	Tom Burns, Brooklyn	13
	Mike Tiernan, New York	13
1891	Harry Stovey, Boston	16
	Mike Tiernan, New York	16
1892	Jim Holliday, Cincinnati	13
1893	Ed Delahanty, Philadelphia	19
1894	Hugh Duffy, Boston	18
	Robert Lowe, Boston	18
1895	Bill Joyce, Washington	17
1896	Ed Delahanty, Philadelphia	13
	Sam Thompson, Philadelphia	13
1897	Nap Lajoie, Philadelphia	10
1898	James Collins, Boston	14
1899	John Freeman, Washington	25
1900	Herman Long, Boston	12
1901	Sam Crawford, Cincinnati	16
1902	Tom Leach, Pittsburgh	6
1903	James Sheckard, Brooklyn	9
1904	Harry Lumley, Brooklyn	9
1905	Fred Odwell, Cincinnati	9
1906	Tim Jordan, Brooklyn	12
1907	David Brain, Boston	10
1908	Tim Jordan, Brooklyn	12
1909	John Murray, New York	7
1910	Fred Beck, Boston	10
	Frank Schulte, Chicago	10
1911	Frank Schulte, Chicago	21
1912	Henry Zimmerman, Chicago	14
1913	Cliff Cravath, Philadelphia	19
1914	Cliff Cravath, Philadelphia	19
1915	Cliff Cravath, Philadelphia	24
1916	Davis Robertson, New York	12
	Cy Williams, Chicago	12
1917	Davis Robertson, New York	12
	Gavvy Cravath, Philadelphia	12
1918	Gavvy Cravath, Philadelphia	8
1919	Gavvy Cravath, Philadelphia	12
1920	Cy Williams, Philadelphia	15
1921	George Kelly, New York	23
1922	Rogers Hornsby, St. Louis	42
1923	Cy Williams, Philadelphia	41
1924	Jack Fournier, Brooklyn	27
1925	Rogers Hornsby, St. Louis	39
1926	Hack Wilson, Chicago	21
1927	Hack Wilson, Chicago	30
	Cy Williams, Philadelphia	30
1928	Hack Wilson, Chicago	31
	Jim Bottomley, St. Louis	31
1929	Chuck Klein, Philadelphia	43
1930	Hack Wilson, Chicago	56
1931	Chuck Klein, Philadelphia	31

NATIONAL LEAGUE HOME RUN CHAMPIONS (Cont.)

Year	Player and Club	Home Runs	Year	Player and Club	Home Runs
1932	Chuck Klein, Philadelphia	38	1954	Ted Kluszewski, Cincinnati	49
	Mel Ott, New York	38	1955	Willie Mays, New York	51
1933	Chuck Klein, Philadelphia	28	1956	Duke Snider, Brooklyn	43
1934	Mel Ott, New York	35	1957	Hank Aaron, Milwaukee	44
	Rip Collins, St. Louis	35	1958	Ernie Banks, Chicago	47
1935	Wally Berger, Boston	34	1959	Eddie Mathews, Milwaukee	46
1936	Mel Ott, New York	33	1960	Ernie Banks, Chicago	41
1937	Mel Ott, New York	31	1961	Orlando Cepeda, San Francisco	46
	Joe Medwick, St. Louis	31	1962	Willie Mays, San Francisco	49
1938	Mel Ott, New York	36	1963	Hank Aaron, Milwaukee	44
1939	Johnny Mize, St. Louis	28		Willie McCovey, San Francisco	44
1940	Johnny Mize, St. Louis	43	1964	Willie Mays, San Francisco	47
1941	Dolph Camilli, Brooklyn	34	1965	Willie Mays, San Francisco	52
1942	Mell Ott, New York	30	1966	Hank Aaron, Atlanta	44
1943	Bill Nicholson, Chicago	29	1967	Hank Aaron, Atlanta	39
1944	Bill Nicholson, Chicago	33	1968	Willie McCovey, San Francisco	36
1945	Tommy Holmes, Boston	28	1969	Willie McCovey, San Francisco	45
1946	Ralph Kiner, Pittsburgh	23	1970	Johnny Bench, Cincinnati	45
1947	Ralph Kiner, Pittsburgh	51	1971	Willie Stargell, Pittsburgh	48
	Johnny Mize, New York	51	1972	Johnny Bench, Cincinnati	40
1948	Ralph Kiner, Pittsburgh	40	1973	Willie Stargell, Pittsburgh	44
	Johnny Mize, New York	40	1974	Mike Schmidt, Philadelphia	36
1949	Ralph Kiner, Pittsburgh	54	1975	Mike Schmidt, Philadelphia	38
1950	Ralph Kiner, Pittsburgh	47	1976	Mike Schmidt, Philadelphia	38
1951	Ralph Kiner, Pittsburgh	42	1977	George Foster, Cincinnati	52
1952	Ralph Kiner, Pittsburgh	37	1978	George Foster, Cincinnati	40
	Hank Sauer, Chicago	37	1979	Dave Kingman, Chicago	48
1953	Eddie Mathews, Milwaukee	47			

NATIONAL LEAGUE RUNS BATTED IN CHAMPIONS

Year	Player and Club	RBI	Year	Player and Club	RBI
1920	Rogers Hornsby, St. Louis	94	1949	Ralph Kiner, Pittsburgh	127
	George Kelly, New York	94	1950	Del Ennis, Philadelphia	126
1921	Rogers Hornsby, St. Louis	126	1951	Monte Irvin, New York	121
1922	Rogers Hornsby, St. Louis	152	1952	Hank Sauer, Chicago	121
1923	Irish Meusel, New York	125	1953	Roy Campanella, Brooklyn	142
1924	George Kelly, New York	136	1954	Ted Kluszewski, Cincinnati	141
1925	Rogers Hornsby, St. Louis	143	1955	Duke Snider, Brooklyn	136
1926	Jim Bottomley, St. Louis	120	1956	Stan Musial, St. Louis	109
1927	Paul Waner, Pittsburgh	131	1957	Hank Aaron, Milwaukee	132
1928	Jim Bottomley, St. Louis	136	1958	Ernie Banks, Chicago	129
1929	Hack Wilson, Chicago	159	1959	Ernie Banks, Chicago	143
1930	Hack Wilson, Chicago	190	1960	Hank Aaron, Milwaukee	126
1931	Chuck Klein, Philadelphia	121	1961	Orlando Cepeda, San Francisco	142
1932	Don Hurst, Philadelphia	143	1962	Tommy Davis, Los Angeles	153
1933	Chuck Klein, Philadelphia	120	1963	Hank Aaron, Milwaukee	130
1934	Mel Ott, New York	135	1964	Ken Boyer, St. Louis	119
1935	Wally Berger, Boston	130	1965	Deron Johnson, Cincinnati	130
1936	Joe Medwick, St. Louis	138	1966	Hank Aaron, Atlanta	127
1937	Joe Medwick, St. Louis	154	1967	Orlando Cepeda, St. Louis	111
1938	Joe Medwick, St. Louis	122	1968	Willie McCovey, San Francisco	105
1939	Frank McCormick, Cincinnati	128	1969	Willie McCovey, San Francisco	126
1940	Johnny Mize, St. Louis	137	1970	Johnny Bench, Cincinnati	148
1941	Dolf Camilli, Brooklyn	120	1971	Joe Torre, St. Louis	137
1942	Johnny Mize, New York	110	1972	Johnny Bench, Cincinnati	125
1943	Bill Nicholson, Chicago	128	1973	Willie Stargell, Pittsburgh	119
1944	Bill Nicholson, Chicago	122	1974	Johnny Bench, Cincinnati	129
1945	Dixie Walker, Brooklyn	124	1975	Greg Luzinski, Philadelphia	120
1946	Enos Slaughter, St. Louis	130	1976	George Foster, Cincinnati	121
1947	Johnny Mize, New York	138	1977	George Foster, Cincinnati	149
1948	Stan Musial, St. Louis	131	1978	George Foster, Cincinnati	120
			1979	Dave Winfield, San Diego	118

AMERICAN LEAGUE BATTING CHAMPIONS

Year	Player and Club	Percent	Year	Player and Club	Percent
1901	Nap Lajoie, Phila	.422	1923	Harry Heilmann, Detroit	.403
1902	Ed Delahanty, Wash.	.376	1924	Babe Ruth, New York	.378
1903	Nap Lajoie, Cleve.	.355	1925	Harry Heilmann, Detroit	.393
1904	Nap Lajoie, Cleve.	.381	1926	Henry Manush, Detroit	.378
1905	Elmer Flick, Cleve.	.306	1927	Harry Heilmann, Detroit	.398
1906	George Stone, St. Louis	.358	1928	Goose Goslin, Washington	.379
1907	Ty Cobb, Det.	.350	1929	Lew Fonseca, Cleveland	.369
1908	Ty Cobb, Det.	.324	1930	Al Simmons, Philadelphia	.381
1909	Ty Cobb, Det.	.377	1931	Al Simmons, Philadelphia	.390
1910	Ty Cobb, Detroit	.385	1932	Dale Alexander, Detroit-Boston	.367
1911	Ty Cobb, Detroit	.420	1933	Jimmy Foxx, Philadelphia	.356
1912	Ty Cobb, Detroit	.410	1934	Lou Gehrig, New York	.363
1913	Ty Cobb, Detroit	.390	1935	Buddy Myer, Washington	.349
1914	Ty Cobb, Detroit	.368	1936	Luke Appling, Chicago	.388
1915	Ty Cobb, Detroit	.369	1937	Charley Gehringer, Detroit	.371
1916	Tris Speaker, Cleveland	.386	1938	Jimmy Foxx, Boston	.349
1917	Ty Cobb, Detroit	.383	1939	Joe DiMaggio, New York	.381
1918	Ty Cobb, Detroit	.382	1940	Joe DiMaggio, New York	.352
1919	Ty Cobb, Detroit	.384	1941	Ted Williams, Boston	.406
1920	George Sisler, St. Louis	.407	1942	Ted Williams, Boston	.356
1921	Harry Heilmann, Detroit	.394	1943	Luke Appling, Chicago	.328
1922	George Sisler, St. Louis	.420	1944	Lou Boudreau, Cleveland	.327

AMERICAN LEAGUE BATTING CHAMPIONS (Cont.)

Year	Player and Club	Percent	Year	Player and Club	Percent
1945	George Sternweiss, New York	.309	1963	Carl Yastrzemski, Boston	.321
1946	Mickey Vernon, Washington	.353	1964	Tony Oliva, Minnesota	.323
1947	Ted Williams, Boston	.343	1965	Tony Oliva, Minnesota	.321
1948	Ted Williams, Boston	.369	1966	Frank Robinson, Baltimore	.316
1949	George Kell, Detroit[1]	.343	1967	Carl Yastrzemski, Boston	.326
1950	Billy Goodman, Boston	.354	1968	Carl Yastrzemski, Boston	.301
1951	Ferris Fain, Philadelphia	.344	1969	Rod Carew, Minnesota	.332
1952	Ferris Fain, Philadelphia	.327	1970	Alex Johnson, California[2]	.329
1953	Mickey Vernon, Washington	.337	1971	Tony Oliva, Minnesota	.337
1954	Bobby Avila, Cleveland	.341	1972	Rod Carew, Minnesota	.318
1955	Al Kaline, Detroit	.340	1973	Rod Carew, Minnesota	.350
1956	Mickey Mantle, New York	.353	1974	Rod Carew, Minnesota	.364
1957	Ted Williams, Boston	.388	1975	Rod Carew, Minnesota	.359
1958	Ted Williams, Boston	.328	1976	George Brett, Kansas City	.333
1959	Harvey Kuenn, Detroit	.353	1977	Rod Carew, Minnesota	.388
1960	Pete Runnels, Boston	.320	1978	Rod Carew, Minnesota	.333
1961	Norm Cash, Detroit	.361	1979	Fred Lynn, Boston	.333
1962	Pete Runnels, Boston	.326			

[1] Kell won the batting championship with an average of .3429; Ted Williams of Boston was second with .3427. [2] Johnson won the batting championship with an average of .3289; Carl Yastrzemski of Boston was second with .3286.

AMERICAN LEAGUE HOME RUN CHAMPIONS

Year	Player and Club	Home Runs	Year	Player and Club	Home Runs
1901	Nap Lajoie, Philadelphia	13	1940	Hank Greenberg, Detroit	41
1902	Ralph Seybold, Philadelphia	16	1941	Ted Williams, Boston	37
1903	Buck Freeman, Boston	13	1942	Ted Williams, Boston	36
1904	Harry Davis, Philadelphia	10	1943	Rudy York, Detroit	34
1905	Harry Davis, Philadelphia	8	1944	Nick Etten, New York	22
1906	Harry Davis, Philadelphia	12	1945	Vern Stephens, St. Louis	24
1907	Harry Davis, Philadelphia	8	1946	Hank Greenberg, Detroit	44
1908	Sam Crawford, Detroit	7	1947	Ted Williams, Boston	32
1909	Ty Cobb, Detroit	9	1948	Joe DiMaggio, New York	39
1910	J. Garland Stahl, Boston	10	1949	Ted Williams, Boston	43
1911	Franklin Baker, Philadelphia	9	1950	Al Rosen, Cleveland	37
1912	Franklin Baker, Philadelphia	10	1951	Gus Zernial, Chicago-Philadelphia	33
1913	Franklin Baker, Philadelphia	12	1952	Larry Doby, Cleveland	32
1914	Franklin Baker, Philadelphia	8	1953	Al Rosen, Cleveland	43
	Sam Crawford, Detroit	8	1954	Larry Doby, Cleveland	32
1915	Robert Roth, Chi.-Cleve.	7	1955	Mickey Mantle, New York	37
1916	Wally Pipp, New York	12	1956	Mickey Mantle, New York	52
1917	Wally Pipp, New York	9	1957	Roy Sievers, Washington	42
1918	Clarence Walker, Philadelphia	11	1958	Mickey Mantle, New York	42
	Babe Ruth, Boston	11	1959	Rocky Colavito, Cleveland	42
1919	Babe Ruth, Boston	29		Harmon Killebrew, Washington	42
1920	Babe Ruth, New York	54	1960	Mickey Mantle, New York	40
1921	Babe Ruth, New York	59	1961	Roger Maris, New York	61
1922	Ken Williams, St. Louis	39	1962	Harmon Killebrew, Minnesota	48
1923	Babe Ruth, New York	41	1963	Harmon Killebrew, Minnesota	45
1924	Babe Ruth, New York	46	1964	Harmon Killebrew, Minnesota	49
1925	Bob Meusel, New York	33	1965	Tony Conigliaro, Boston	32
1926	Babe Ruth, New York	47	1966	Frank Robinson, Baltimore	49
1927	Babe Ruth, New York	60	1967	Harmon Killebrew, Minnesota	44
1928	Babe Ruth, New York	54		Carl Yastrzemski, Boston	44
1929	Babe Ruth, New York	46	1968	Frank Howard, Washington	44
1930	Babe Ruth, New York	49	1969	Harmon Killebrew, Minnesota	49
1931	Babe Ruth, New York	46	1970	Frank Howard, Washington	44
	Lou Gehrig, New York	46	1971	Bill Melton, Chicago	33
1932	Jimmy Foxx, Philadelphia	58	1972	Dick Allen, Chicago	37
1933	Jimmy Foxx, Philadelphia	48	1973	Reggie Jackson, Oakland	32
1934	Lou Gehrig, New York	49	1974	Dick Allen, Chicago	32
1935	Jimmy Foxx, Philadelphia	36	1975	Reggie Jackson, Oakland	36
	Hank Greenberg, Detroit	36		George Scott, Milwaukee	36
1936	Lou Gehrig, New York	49	1976	Graig Nettles, New York	32
1937	Joe DiMaggio, New York	46	1977	Jim Rice, Boston	39
1938	Hank Greenberg, Detroit	58	1978	Jim Rice, Boston	46
1939	Jimmy Foxx, Boston	35	1979	Gorman Thomas, Milwaukee	45

AMERICAN LEAGUE RUNS BATTED IN CHAMPIONS

Year	Player and Club	RBI	Year	Player and Club	RBI
1920	Babe Ruth, New York	137	1936	Hal Trosky, Cleveland	162
1921	Babe Ruth, New York	171	1937	Hank Greenberg, Detroit	183
1922	Ken Williams, St. Louis	155	1938	Jimmie Foxx, Boston	175
1923	Babe Ruth, New York	131	1939	Ted Williams, Boston	145
1924	Goose Goslin, Washington	129	1940	Hank Greenberg, Detroit	150
1925	Bob Meusel, New York	138	1941	Joe DiMaggio, New York	125
1926	Babe Ruth, New York	145	1942	Ted Williams, Boston	137
1927	Lou Gehrig, New York	175	1943	Rudy York, Detroit	118
1928	Lou Gehrig, New York	142	1944	Vern Stephens, St. Louis	109
	Babe Ruth, New York	142	1945	Nick Etten, New York	111
1929	Al Simmons, Philadelphia	157	1946	Hank Greenberg, Detroit	127
1930	Lou Gehrig, New York	174	1947	Ted Williams, Boston	114
1931	Lou Gehrig, New York	184	1948	Joe DiMaggio, New York	155
1932	Jimmie Foxx, Philadelphia	169	1949	Ted Williams, Boston	159
1933	Jimmie Foxx, Philadelphia	163		Vern Stephens, Boston	159
1934	Lou Gehrig, New York	165	1950	Vern Stephens, Boston	144
1935	Hank Greenberg, Detroit	170		Walt Dropo, Boston	144

AMERICAN LEAGUE RUNS BATTED IN CHAMPIONS (Cont.)

Year	Player and Club	RBI	Year	Player and Club	RBI
1951	Gus Zernial, Chicago-Philadelphia	129	1965	Rocky Colavito, Cleveland	108
1952	Al Rosen, Cleveland	105	1966	Frank Robinson, Baltimore	122
1953	Al Rosen, Cleveland	145	1967	Carl Yastrzemski, Boston	121
1954	Larry Doby, Cleveland	126	1968	Ken Harrelson, Boston	109
1955	Ray Boone, Detroit	116	1969	Harmon Killebrew, Minnesota	140
	Jackie Jensen, Boston	116	1970	Frank Howard, Washington	126
1956	Mickey Mantle, New York	130	1971	Harmon Killebrew, Minnesota	119
1957	Roy Sievers, Washington	114	1972	Richie Allen, Chicago	113
1958	Jackie Jensen, Boston	122	1973	Reggie Jackson, Oakland	117
1959	Jackie Jensen, Boston	112	1974	Jeff Burroughs, Texas	118
1960	Roger Maris, New York	112	1975	George Scott, Boston	109
1961	Roger Maris, New York	142	1976	Lee May, Baltimore	109
1962	Harmon Killebrew, Minnesota	126	1977	Larry Hisle, Minnesota	119
1963	Dick Stuart, Boston	118	1978	Jim Rice, Boston	139
1964	Brooks Robinson, Baltimore	118	1979	Don Baylor, California	139

MOST NO-HITTERS IN A LIFETIME

4, Sandy Koufax, Los Angeles (NL), 1962, 1963, 1964, 1965.
4, Nolan Ryan, California (AL), 1973, 1973, 1974, 1975.
3, Cy Young, Boston (NL-AL), 1897, 1904, 1908.
3, Bob Feller, Cleveland (AL), 1940, 1946, 1951.
3, Jim Maloney, Cincinnati (NL), 1965 (2), 1969

NO-HITTERS OF TEN OR MORE INNINGS

Year	Pitcher	Clubs Playing	Score
1884	Samuel Kimber	Brooklyn–Toledo (AA)	0–0
1906	Harry McIntire	Brooklyn–Pittsburgh (NL)	0–1
1908	George Wiltse	New York-Philadelphia (NL)	1–0
1917	Fred Toney	Cincinnati–Chicago (NL)	1–0
1959	Harvey Haddix	Pittsburgh–Milwaukee (NL)*	0–1
1965	Jim Maloney	Cincinnati–New York (NL)	0–1
1965	Jim Maloney	Cincinnati–Chicago (NL)	1–0

* Perfect game for 12 innings. Lost in 13th.

PERFECT GAMES

1880	John Richmond	Worcester–Cleveland (NL)	1–0
1880	John Ward	Providence–Buffalo (NL)	5–0
1904	Cy Young	Boston–Philadelphia (AL)	3–0
1908	Addie Joss	Cleveland–Chicago (AL)	1–0
1917	Ernie Shore*	Boston–Washington (AL)	4–0
1922	Charles Robertson	Chicago–Detroit (AL)	2–0
1956	Don Larsen†	New York (AL)–Brooklyn (NL)	2–0
1964	Jim Bunning	Philadelphia–New York (NL)	6–0
1965	Sandy Koufax	Los Angeles–Chicago (NL)	1–0
1968	Jim Hunter	Oakland–Minnesota (AL)	4–0

* Babe Ruth, the starting pitcher. was ejected from the game by the umpire after walking the first batter. Ernie Shore relieved him, the base-runner was thrown out trying to steal second base, and Shore retired the next 26 batters to complete a perfect game. † The only World Series perfect game.

CY YOUNG AWARD

Year	Pitcher
BOTH MAJOR LEAGUES	
1956	Don Newcombe, Dodgers (NL)
1957	Warren Spahn, Boston (NL)
1958	Bob Turley, New York (AL)
1959	Early Wynn, Chicago (AL)
1960	Vernon Law, Pittsburgh (NL)
1961	Whitey Ford, New York (AL)
1962	Don Drysdale, Los Angeles (NL)
1963	Sandy Koufax, Los Angeles (NL)
1964	Dean Chance, Los Angeles (AL)
1965	Sandy Koufax, Los Angeles (NL)
1966	Sandy Koufax, Los Angeles (NL)
NATIONAL LEAGUE	
1967	Mike McCormick, San Francisco
1968	Bob Gibson, St. Louis
1969	Tom Seaver, New York
1970	Bob Gibson, St. Louis
1971	Ferguson Jenkins, Chicago
1972	Steve Carlton, Philadelphia
1973	Tom Seaver, New York
1974	Mike Marshall, Los Angeles
1975	Tom Seaver, New York
1976	Randy Jones, San Diego
1977	Steve Carlton, Philadelphia
1978	Gaylord Perry, San Diego
AMERICAN LEAGUE	
1967	Jim Lonborg, Boston
1968	Denny McLain, Detroit
1969	Denny McLain, Detroit
	Mike Cuellar, Baltimore
1970	Jim Perry, Minnesota
1971	Vida Blue, Oakland
1972	Gaylord Perry, Cleveland
1973	Jim Palmer, Baltimore
1974	James Hunter, Oakland
1975	Jim Palmer, Baltimore
1976	Jim Palmer, Baltimore
1977	Sparky Lyle, New York
1978	Ron Guidry, New York

MAJOR LEAGUE NO-HIT GAMES SINCE 1968

Year	Pitcher	Clubs Playing	Score	Year	Pitcher	Clubs Playing	Score
1968	Tom Phoebus	Baltimore–Boston (AL)	6–0	1973	Nolan Ryan	California–Kansas City (AL)	3–0
1968	Jim Hunter	Oakland–Minnesota (AL)	4–0	1973	Nolan Ryan	California–Detroit (AL)	6–0
1968	George Culver	Cincinnati–Philadelphia (NL)	6–1	1973	Jim Bibby	Texas–Oakland (AL)	6–0
1968	Gaylord Perry	San Francisco–St. Louis (NL)	1–0	1973	Phil Niekro	Atlanta–San Diego (NL)	9–0
1968	Ray Washburn	St. Louis–San Francisco (NL)	2–0	1974	Steve Busby	Kansas City–Milwaukee (AL)	2–0
1969	Bill Stoneman	Montreal–Philadelphia (NL)	6–0	1974	Dick Bosman	Cleveland–Oakland (AL)	4–0
1969	Jim Maloney	Cincinnati–Houston (NL)	10–0	1974	Nolan Ryan	California–Minnesota (AL)	4–0
1969	Don Wilson	Houston–Cincinnati (NL)	4–0	1975	Nolan Ryan	California–Baltimore (AL)	1–0
1969	Jim Palmer	Baltimore–Oakland (AL)	8–0	1975	Ed Halicki	San Francisco–New York (NL)	6–0
1969	Ken Holtzman	Chicago–Atlanta (NL)	3–0	1975	Vida Blue, Glenn Abbott, Paul Lindblad, Rollie Fingers	Oakland–California (AL)	5–0
1969	Bob Moose	Pittsburgh–New York (NL)	4–0				
1970	Dock Ellis	Pittsburgh–San Diego (NL)	2–0	1976	Larry Dierker	Houston–Montreal (NL)	6–0
1970	Clyde Wright	California–Oakland (AL)	4–0	1976	John Odom, Francisco Barrios	Chicago–California (AL)	2–1
1970	Bill Singer	Los Angeles–Philadelphia (NL)	5–0	1976	John Candelaria	Pittsburgh–St. Louis (NL)	2–0
1970	Vida Blue	Oakland–Minnesota (AL)	6–0	1976	John Montefusco	San Francisco–Atlanta (NL)	9–0
1971	Ken Holtzman	Chicago–Cincinnati (NL)	1–0	1977	Jim Colborn	Kansas City–Texas (AL)	6–0
1971	Rick Wise	Philadelphia–Cincinnati (NL)	4–0	1977	Dennis Eckersley	Cleveland–California (AL)	1–0
1971	Bob Gibson	St. Louis–Pittsburgh (NL)	11–0	1977	Bert Blyleven	Texas–California (AL)	6–0
1972	Burt Hooton	Chicago–Philadelphia (NL)	4–0	1978	Bob Forsch	St. Louis–Philadelphia (NL)	5–0
1972	Milt Pappas	Chicago–San Diego (NL)	8–0		Tom Seaver	Cincinnati–St. Louis (NL)	4–0
1972	Bill Stoneman	Montreal–New York (NL)	7–0	1979	Ken Forsch	Houston–Atlanta (NL)	6–0
1973	Steve Busby	Kansas City–Detroit (AL)	3–0				

PITCHERS WITH BEST WON-AND-LOST PERCENTAGES (162 or More Innings)

NATIONAL LEAGUE				AMERICAN LEAGUE			
Year Pitcher and Club	Won	Lost	Per-cent	Year Pitcher and Club	Won	Lost	Per-cent
1939—Paul Derringer, Cincinnati	25	7	.781	1939—Lefty Grove, Boston	15	4	.789
1940—Fred Fitzsimmons, Brooklyn	16	2	.889	1940—Schoolboy Rowe, Detroit	16	3	.842
1941—Elmer Riddle, Cincinnati	19	4	.826	1941—Lefty Gomez, New York	15	5	.750
1942—Larry French, Brooklyn	15	4	.789	1942—Ernie Bonham, New York	21	5	.808
1943—Mort Cooper, St. Louis	21	8	.724	1943—Spud Chandler, New York	20	4	.833
1944—Ted Wilkes, St. Louis	17	4	.810	1944—Tex Hughson, Boston	18	5	.783
1945—Harry Brecheen, St. Louis	15	4	.789	1945—Hal Newhouser, Detroit	25	9	.735
1946—Murry Dickson, St. Louis	15	6	.714	1946—Dave Ferriss, Boston	25	6	.806
1947—Larry Jansen, New York	21	5	.808	1947—Allie Reynolds, New York	19	8	.704
1948—Harry Brecheen, St. Louis	20	7	.741	1948—Jack Kramer, Boston	18	5	.783
1949—Preacher Roe, Brooklyn	15	6	.714	1949—Ellis Kinder, Boston	23	6	.793
1950—Sal Maglie, New York	18	4	.818	1950—Vic Raschi, New York	21	8	.724
1951—Preacher Roe, Brooklyn	22	3	.880	1951—Bob Feller, Cleveland	22	8	.733
1952—Hoyt Wilhelm, New York	15	3	.833	1952—Bobby Shantz, Philadelphia	24	7	.774
1953—Carl Erskine, Brooklyn	20	6	.769	1953—Ed Lopat, New York	16	4	.800
1954—Johnny Antonelli, New York	21	7	.750	1954—Sandy Consuegra, Chicago	16	3	.842
1955—Don Newcombe, Brooklyn	20	5	.800	1955—Tommy Byrne, New York	16	5	.762
1956—Don Newcombe, Brooklyn	27	7	.794	1956—Whitey Ford, New York	19	6	.760
1957—Bob Ruhl, Milwaukee	18	7	.720	1957—Dick Donovan, Chicago	16	6	.727
1958—Warren Spahn, Milwaukee	22	11	.667	Tom Sturdivant, New York	16	6	.727
Lew Burdette, Milwaukee	20	10	.667	1958—Bob Turley, New York	21	7	.750
1959—El Roy Face, Pittsburgh	18	1	.947	1959—Bob Shaw, Chicago	18	6	.750
1960—Ernie Broglio, St. Louis	21	9	.700	1960—Jim Perry, Cleveland	18	10	.643
1961—Johnny Podres, Los Angeles	18	5	.783	1961—Whitey Ford, New York	25	4	.862
1962—Bob Purkey, Cincinnati	23	5	.821	1962—Ray Herbert, Chicago	20	9	.690
1963—Ron Perranoski, Los Angeles	16	3	.842	1963—Whitey Ford, New York	24	7	.774
1964—Sandy Koufax, Los Angeles	19	5	.792	1964—Wally Bunker, Baltimore	19	5	.792
1965—Sandy Koufax, Los Angeles	26	8	.765	1965—Jim Grant, Minnesota	21	7	.750
1966—Juan Marichal, San Francisco	25	6	.806	1966—Sonny Siebert, Cleveland	16	8	.667
1967—Dick Hughes, St. Louis	16	6	.727	1967—Joel Horlen, Chicago	19	7	.731
1968—Steve Blass, Pittsburgh	18	6	.750	1968—Denny McLain, Detroit	31	6	.836
1969—Tom Seaver, New York	25	7	.781	1969—Jim Palmer, Baltimore	16	4	.800
1970—Bob Gibson, St. Louis	23	7	.767	1970—Mike Cuellar, Baltimore	24	8	.750
1971—Tug McGraw, New York	11	4	.733	1971—Dave McNally, Baltimore	21	5	.807
1972—Steve Carlton, Philadelphia	27	10	.730	1972—James Hunter, Oakland	21	7	.750
1973—Tommy John, Los Angeles	16	7	.696	1973—James Hunter, Oakland	21	5	.808
1974—Tommy John, Los Angeles	13	3	.813	1974—Mike Cuellar, Baltimore	22	10	.688
1975—Al Hrabosky, St. Louis	13	3	.813	1975—Roger Moret, Boston	14	3	.824
1976—Steve Carlton, Philadelphia	20	7	.741	1976—Wayne Garland, Baltimore	20	7	.741
1977—John Candelaria, Pittsburgh	20	5	.800	1977—Paul Splittorff, Kansas City	16	6	.727
1978—Gaylord Perry, San Diego	21	6	.778	1978—Ron Guidry, New York	25	3	.893
1979—Tom Seaver, Cincinnati	16	6	.727	1979—Mike Caldwell, Milwaukee	16	6	.727

PITCHERS WITH LOWEST-EARNED-RUN AVERAGES (162 or More Innings)

NATIONAL LEAGUE			AMERICAN LEAGUE		
Year Pitcher and Club	Innings Pitched	ERA	Year Pitcher and Club	Innings Pitched	ERA
1945 .... Hank Borowy, Chicago	122	2.14	1945 .... Hal Newhouser, Detroit	313	1.81
1946 .... Howie Pollet, St. Louis	266	2.10	1946 .... Hal Newhouser, Detroit	293	1.94
1947 .... Warren Spahn, Boston	290	2.33	1947 .... Spud Chandler, New York	128	2.46
1948 .... Harry Brecheen, St. Louis	233	2.24	1948 .... Gene Bearden, Cleveland	230	2.43
1949 .... Dave Koslo, New York	212	2.50	1949 .... Mel Parnell, Boston	295	2.78
1950 .... Jim Hearn, St. Louis-New York	134	2.49	1950 .... Early Wynn, Cleveland	214	3.20
1951 .... Chet Nichols, Boston	156	2.88	1951 .... Saul Rogovin, Detroit-Chicago	217	2.78
1952 .... Hoyt Wilhelm, New York	159	2.43	1952 .... Allie Reynolds, New York	244	2.07
1953 .... Warren Spahn, Milwaukee	266	2.10	1953 .... Eddie Lopat, New York	178	2.43
1954 .... John Antonelli, New York	259	2.29	1954 .... Mike Garcia, Cleveland	259	2.64
1955 .... Bob Friend, Pittsburgh	200	2.84	1955 .... Billy Pierce, Chicago	206	1.97
1956 .... Lew Burdette, Milwaukee	256	2.71	1956 .... Whitey Ford, New York	226	2.47
1957 .... John Podres, Brooklyn	196	2.66	1957 .... Bobby Shantz, New York	173	2.45
1958 .... Stu Miller, San Francisco	182	2.47	1958 .... Whitey Ford, New York	219	2.01
1959 .... Sam Jones, San Francisco	271	2.82	1959 .... Hoyt Wilhelm, Baltimore	226	2.19
1960 .... Mike McCormick, San Francisco	253	2.70	1960 .... Frank Baumann, Chicago	185	2.68
1961 .... Warren Spahn, Milwaukee	263	3.01	1961 .... Dick Donovan, Washington	169	2.40
1962 .... Sandy Koufax, Los Angeles	184	2.54	1962 .... Hank Aguirre, Detroit	216	2.21
1963 .... Sandy Koufax, Los Angeles	311	1.88	1963 .... Gary Peters, Chicago	243	2.33
1964 .... Sandy Koufax, Los Angeles	223	1.74	1964 .... Dean Chance, Los Angeles	278	1.65
1965 .... Sandy Koufax, Los Angeles	336	2.04	1965 .... Sam McDowell, Cleveland	273	2.18
1966 .... Sandy Koufax, Los Angeles	323	1.73	1966 .... Gary Peters, Chicago	205	1.98
1967 .... Phil Niekro, Atlanta	207	1.87	1967 .... Joel Horlen, Chicago	258	2.06
1968 .... Bob Gibson, St. Louis	305	1.12	1968 .... Luis Tiant, Cleveland	258	1.60
1969 .... Juan Marichal, San Francisco	300	2.10	1969 .... Dick Bosman, Washington	193	2.19
1970 .... Tom Seaver, New York	291	2.81	1970 .... Diego Segui, Oakland	162	2.56
1971 .... Tom Seaver, New York	286	1.76	1971 .... Vida Blue, Oakland	312	1.82
1972 .... Steve Carlton, Philadelphia	346	1.98	1972 .... Luis Tiant, Boston	179	1.91
1973 .... Tom Seaver, New York	290	2.08	1973 .... Jim Palmer, Baltimore	296	2.40
1974 .... Buzz Capra, Atlanta	217	2.28	1974 .... James Hunter, Oakland	318	2.49
1975 .... Randy Jones, San Diego	288	2.24	1975 .... Jim Palmer, Baltimore	323	2.09
1976 .... John Denny, St. Louis	207	2.52	1976 .... Mark Fidrych, Detroit	250	2.34
1977 .... John Candelaria, Pittsburgh	231	2.34	1977 .... Frank Tanana, California	241	2.54
1978 .... Craig Swan, New York	207	2.43	1978 .... Ron Guidry, New York	274	1.74
1979 .... J. Rodney Richard, Houston	292	2.71	1979 .... Ron Guidry, New York	236	2.78

LONGEST GAMES IN THE MAJOR LEAGUES

Innings	Teams	Date	Innings	Teams	Date
26	Brooklyn 1, Boston 1, NL	May 1, 1920	24	Houston 1, New York 0, NL	April 15, 1968
25	St. Louis 4, New York 3, NL	Sept. 11, 1974	23	Brooklyn 2, Boston 2, NL	June 27, 1939
24	Philadelphia 4, Boston 1, AL	Sept. 1, 1906	23	San Francisco 8, New York 6, NL	May 31, 1964
24 ...	Detroit 1, Philadelphia 1, AL	July 21, 1945			

MOST-VALUABLE-PLAYER AWARD SOURCE: Baseball Writers' Association of America

NATIONAL LEAGUE

Year	Player	Club
1931	Frank Frisch	St. Louis
1932	Chuck Klein	Philadelphia
1933	Carl Hubbell	New York
1934	Dizzy Dean	St. Louis
1935	Gabby Hartnett	Chicago
1936	Carl Hubbell	New York
1937	Joe Medwick	St. Louis
1938	Ernie Lombardi	Cincinnati
1939	Bucky Waters	Cincinnati
1940	Frank McCormick	Cincinnati
1941	Dolph Camilli	Brooklyn
1942	Mort Cooper	St. Louis
1943	Stan Musial	St. Louis
1944	Marty Marion	St. Louis
1945	Phil Cavarretta	Chicago
1946	Stan Musial	St. Louis
1947	Bob Elliott	Boston
1948	Stan Musial	St. Louis
1949	Jackie Robinson	Brooklyn
1950	Jim Konstanty	Philadelphia
1951	Roy Campanella	Brooklyn
1952	Hank Sauer	Chicago
1953	Roy Campanella	Brooklyn
1954	Willie Mays	New York
1955	Roy Campanella	Brooklyn
1956	Don Newcombe	Brooklyn
1957	Hank Aaron	Milwaukee
1958	Ernie Banks	Chicago
1959	Ernie Banks	Chicago
1960	Dick Groat	Pittsburgh
1961	Frank Robinson	Cincinnati
1962	Maury Wills	Los Angeles
1963	Sandy Koufax	Los Angeles
1964	Ken Boyer	St. Louis
1965	Willie Mays	San Francisco
1966	Roberto Clemente	Pittsburgh
1967	Orlando Cepeda	St. Louis
1968	Bob Gibson	St. Louis
1969	Willie McCovey	San Francisco
1970	Johnny Bench	Cincinnati
1971	Joe Torre	St. Louis
1972	Johnny Bench	Cincinnati
1973	Pete Rose	Cincinnati
1974	Steve Garvey	Los Angeles
1975	Joe Morgan	Cincinnati
1976	Joe Morgan	Cincinnati
1977	George Foster	Cincinnati
1978	Dave Parker	Pittsburgh

AMERICAN LEAGUE

Year	Player	Club
1931	Lefty Grove	Philadelphia
1932	Jimmy Foxx	Philadelphia
1933	Jimmy Foxx	Philadelphia
1934	Mickey Cochrane	Detroit
1935	Hank Greenberg	Detroit
1936	Lou Gehrig	New York
1937	Charley Gehringer	Detroit
1938	Jimmy Foxx	Boston
1939	Joe DiMaggio	New York
1940	Hank Greenberg	Detroit
1941	Joe DiMaggio	New York
1942	Joe Gordon	New York
1943	Spud Chandler	New York
1944	Hal Newhouser	Detroit
1945	Hal Newhouser	Detroit
1946	Ted Williams	Boston
1947	Joe DiMaggio	New York
1948	Lou Boudreau	Cleveland
1949	Ted Williams	Boston
1950	Phil Rizzuto	New York
1951	Yogi Berra	New York
1952	Bobby Shantz	Philadelphia
1953	Al Rosen	Cleveland
1954	Yogi Berra	New York
1955	Yogi Berra	New York
1956	Mickey Mantle	New York
1957	Mickey Mantle	New York
1958	Jackie Jensen	Boston
1959	Nelson Fox	Chicago
1960	Roger Maris	New York
1961	Roger Maris	New York
1962	Mickey Mantle	New York
1963	Elston Howard	New York
1964	Brooks Robinson	Baltimore
1965	Zoilo Versalles	Minnesota
1966	Frank Robinson	Baltimore
1967	Carl Yastrzemski	Boston
1968	Denny McLain	Detroit
1969	Harmon Killebrew	Minnesota
1970	John (Boog) Powell	Baltimore
1971	Vida Blue	Oakland
1972	Dick Allen	Chicago
1973	Reggie Jackson	Oakland
1974	Jeff Burroughs	Texas
1975	Fred Lynn	Boston
1976	Thurman Munson	New York
1977	Rod Carew	Minnesota
1978	Jim Rice	Boston

ROOKIE-OF-THE-YEAR AWARD

NATIONAL LEAGUE

Year	Player and Position	Club
1949	Don Newcombe, pitcher	Brooklyn
1950	Sam Jethroe, outfielder	Boston
1951	Willie Mays, outfielder	New York
1952	Joe Black, pitcher	Brooklyn
1953	Jim Gilliam, second baseman	Brooklyn
1954	Wally Moon, outfielder	St. Louis
1955	Bill Virdon, outfielder	St. Louis
1956	Frank Robinson, outfielder	Cincinnati
1957	Jack Sanford, pitcher	Philadelphia
1958	Orlando Cepeda, first baseman	San Francisco
1959	Willie McCovey, first baseman	San Francisco
1960	Frank Howard, outfielder	Los Angeles
1961	Billy Williams, outfielder	Chicago
1962	Ken Hubbs, second baseman	Chicago
1963	Pete Rose, second baseman	Cincinnati
1964	Richie Allen, third baseman	Philadelphia
1965	Jim Lefebvre, second baseman	Los Angeles
1966	Tommy Helms, third baseman	Cincinnati
1967	Tom Seaver, pitcher	New York
1968	Johnny Bench, catcher	Cincinnati
1969	Ted Sizemore, second baseman	Los Angeles
1970	Carl Morton, pitcher	Montreal
1971	Earl Williams, catcher	Atlanta
1972	Jon Matlack, pitcher	New York
1973	Gary Mathews, outfielder	San Francisco
1974	Bake McBride, outfielder	St. Louis
1975	John Montefusco, pitcher	San Francisco
1976	Pat Zachry, pitcher	Cincinnati
	Butch Metzger, pitcher	San Diego
1977	Andre Dawson, outfielder	Montreal
1978	Bob Horner, third baseman	Atlanta

AMERICAN LEAGUE

Year	Player and Position	Club
1949	Roy Sievers, outfielder	St. Louis
1950	Walt Dropo, first baseman	Boston
1951	Gil McDougald, third baseman	New York
1952	Harry Byrd, pitcher	Philadelphia
1953	Harvey Kuenn, shortstop	Detroit
1954	Bob Grim, pitcher	New York
1955	Herb Score, pitcher	Cleveland
1956	Luis Aparicio, shortstop	Chicago
1957	Tony Kubek, infielder-outfielder	New York
1958	Albie Pearson, outfielder	Washington
1959	Bob Allison, outfielder	Washington
1960	Ron Hansen, shortstop	Baltimore
1961	Don Schwall, pitcher	Boston
1962	Tom Tresh, infielder-outfielder	New York
1963	Gary Peters, pitcher	Chicago
1964	Tony Oliva, outfielder	Minnesota
1965	Curt Blefary, outfielder	Baltimore
1966	Tommie Agee, outfielder	Chicago
1967	Rod Carew, second baseman	Minnesota
1968	Stan Bahnsen, pitcher	New York
1969	Lou Piniella, outfielder	Kansas City
1970	Thurman Munson, catcher	New York
1971	Chris Chambliss, infielder	Cleveland
1972	Carlton Fisk, catcher	Boston
1973	Al Bumbry, outfielder	Baltimore
1974	Mike Hargrove, first baseman	Texas
1975	Fred Lynn, outfielder	Boston
1976	Mark Fidrych, pitcher	Detroit
1977	Eddie Murray, first baseman	Baltimore
1978	Lou Whitaker, second baseman	Detroit

ROBERTO CLEMENTE AWARD

Ability, sportsmanship, character, community involvement, humanitarianism, contribution to team and baseball

1971 Willie Mays, San Francisco	1974 Willie Stargell, Pittsburgh	1977 Rod Carew, Minnesota
1972 Brooks Robinson, Baltimore	1975 Lou Brock, St. Louis	1978 Greg Luzinski, Philadelphia
1973 Al Kaline, Detroit	1976 Pete Rose, Cincinnati	1979 Andre Thornton, Cleveland

BASEBALL STADIUMS

AMERICAN LEAGUE

	Seating	Field Distances			Wall Heights		
		LF	CF	RF	LF	CF	RF
Baltimore (Memorial Stadium)	52,860	309'	405'	309'	14'	7'	14'
Boston (Fenway Park)	33,538	315'	390'	302'	37'	17'	3–5'
California (Anaheim Stadium)	43,250	333'	404'	333'	8'	8'	8'
Chicago (Comiskey Park)	44,492	352'	445'	352'	9'	17'	9'
Cleveland (Municipal Stadium)	76,713	320'	400'	320'	9'	8'	9'
Detroit (Tiger Stadium)	53,676	340'	440'	325'	9'	9'	9'
Kansas City (Royals Stadium)	40,760	330'	410'	330'	12'	12'	12'
Milwaukee (County Stadium)	54,192	320'	402'	315'	8'	10'	10'
Minnesota (Metropolitan Stadium)	45,919	343'	402'	330'	12'	8'	8'
New York (Yankee Stadium)	57,545	312'	417'	310'	7'	7'	8'
Oakland (Oakland Coliseum)	50,000	330'	400'	330'	8'	8'	8'
Seattle (Kingdome)	59,438	316'	410'	316'	11½'	11½'	11½'
Texas (Arlington Stadium)	41,097	330'	400'	330'	11'	11'	11'
Toronto (Exhibition Stadium)	43,737	330'	400'	330'	12'	12'	12'

NATIONAL LEAGUE

	Seating	Field Distances			Wall Heights		
		LF	CF	RF	LF	CF	RF
Atlanta (Atlanta Stadium)	52,194	330'	402'	330'	6'	6'	6'
Chicago (Wrigley Field)	37,741	355'	400'	353'	11½'	11½'	11½'
Cincinnati (Riverfront Stadium)	51,880	330'	404'	330'	12'	12'	12'
Houston (Astrodome)	45,000	340'	406'	340'	10'	10'	10'
Los Angeles (Dodger Stadium)	56,000	330'	395'	330'	8'	8'	8'
Montreal (Olympic Stadium)	60,476	325'	404'	325'	12'	12'	12'
New York (Shea Stadium)	55,300	341'	410'	341'	8'	8'	8'
Philadelphia (Veterans Stadium)	60,515	330'	408'	330'	12'	12'	12'
Pittsburgh (Three Rivers Stadium)	50,230	335'	400'	335'	10'	10'	10'
San Diego (San Diego Stadium)	51,362	330'	420'	330'	17'	17'	17'
San Francisco (Candlestick Park)	58,000	335'	410'	335'	12'	12'	12'
St. Louis (Busch Memorial Stadium)	50,222	330'	414'	330'	10½'	10½'	10½'

MINOR LEAGUE BASEBALL AFFILIATIONS: 1979

American League	Class AAA	Class AA	National League	Class AAA	Class AA
Baltimore	Rochester (IL)	Charlotte (SL)	Atlanta	Richmond (IL)	Savannah (SL)
Boston	Pawtucket (IL)	Bristol (EL)	Chicago	Wichita (AA)	Midland (TL)
California	Salt Lake City (PCL)	El Paso (TL)	Cincinnati	Indianapolis (AA)	Nashville (SL)
Chicago	Iowa (AA)	Knoxville (SL)	Houston	Charleston (IL)	Columbus (SL)
Cleveland	Tacoma (PCL)	Chattanooga (SL)	Los Angeles	Albuquerque (PCL)	San Antonio (TL)
Detroit	Evansville (AA)	Montgomery (SL)	Montreal	Denver (AA)	Memphis (SL)
Kansas City	Omaha (AA)	Jacksonville (SL)	New York	Tidewater (IL)	Jackson (TL)
Milwaukee	Vancouver (PCL)	Holyoke (EL)	Philadelphia	Oklahoma City (AA)	Reading (EL)
Minnesota	Toledo (IL)	Orlando (SL)	Pittsburgh	Portland (PCL)	Buffalo (EL)
New York	Columbus (IL)	West Haven (EL)	St. Louis	Springfield (AA)	Arkansas (TL)
Oakland	Ogden (PCL)	Waterbury (EL)	San Diego	Hawaii (PCL)	Amarillo (TL)
Seattle	Spokane (PCL)		San Francisco	Phoenix (PCL)	Shreveport (TL)
Texas	Tucson (PCL)	Tulsa (TL)			
Toronto	Syracuse (IL)				

(AA) American Association, (IL) International League, (PCL) Pacific Coast League, (EL) Eastern League, (SL) Southern League, (TL) Texas League.

NATIONAL COLLEGIATE BASEBALL CHAMPIONSHIPS

SOURCE: NCAA

Year	Champion	Coach	Runner-up	Outstanding Player
1970	Southern California	Rod Dedeaux	Florida State	Gene Ammann (Florida State)
1971	Southern California	Rod Dedeaux	Southern Illinois	Jerry Tabb (Tulsa)
1972	Southern California	Rod Dedeaux	Arizona State	Russ McQueen (USC)
1973	Southern California	Rod Dedeaux	Arizona State	Dave Winfield (Minnesota)
1974	Southern California	Rod Dedeaux	Miami (Fla.)	George Mike (USC)
1975	Texas	Cliff Gustafson	South Carolina	Mickey Reichenbach (Texas)
1976	Arizona	Jerry Kindall	Eastern Michigan	Steve Powers (Arizona)
1977	Arizona State	Jim Brock	South Carolina	Bob Horner (Arizona State)
1978	Southern California	Rod Dedeaux	Arizona State	Rod Boxberger (USC)
1979	Cal. State-Fullerton	Augie Garrido	Arkansas	Tony Hudson (Cal. State)

BASKETBALL

PROFESSIONAL BASKETBALL GOVERNMENT

National Basketball Association (NBA): Olympic Tower, 645 5th Ave., New York City 10022. **Commissioner:** Lawrence F. O'Brien. Founded in 1946, the NBA today consists of 22 teams.

ATLANTIC DIVISION	President	Coach
Boston Celtics	Red Auerbach	Bill Fitch
New York Knicks	Michael Burke	Red Holzman
New Jersey Nets	Alan Cohen	Kevin Loughery
Philadelphia 76ers	F. Eugene Dixon	Billy Cunningham
Washington Bullets	Abe Pollin	Dick Motta

CENTRAL DIVISION	President	Coach
Atlanta Hawks	Mike Gearon	Hubie Brown
Cleveland Cavaliers	Nicholas Mileti	Stan Albeck
Detroit Pistons	William Davidson	Dick Vitale
Houston Rockets	Ray Patterson	Del Harris
Indiana Pacers	Sam Nassi	Bob Leonard
San Antonio Spurs	Angelo Drossos	Doug Moe

MIDWEST DIVISION	President	Coach
Chicago Bulls	William Wirtz	Jerry Sloan
Denver Nuggets	Carl Scheer	Donnie Walsh
Kansas City Kings	Paul Rosenberg	Cotton Fitzsimmons
Milwaukee Bucks	James Fitzgerald	Don Nelson
Utah Jazz	Sam Battistone	Tom Nissalke

PACIFIC DIVISION	President	Coach
Golden State Warriors	Franklin Mieuli	Al Attles
Los Angeles Lakers	Jerry Buss	Jack McKinney
Phoenix Suns	Richard Bloch	John MacLeod
Portland Trail Blazers	Lawrence Weinberg	Jack Ramsay
Seattle SuperSonics	Samuel Schulman	Lenny Wilkens
San Diego Clippers	Irv Levin	Gene Shue

THE NBA CHAMPIONS

Season	Eastern Conference (W–L)	Western Conference (W–L)	Playoff Champions (W–L)
1957/58	Boston Celtics (49–23)	St. Louis Hawks (41–31)	St. Louis Hawks (4–2) over Boston
1958/59	Boston Celtics (52–20)	St. Louis Hawks (49–23)	Boston Celtics (4–0) over Minneapolis
1959/60	Boston Celtics (59–16)	St. Louis Hawks (46–29)	Boston Celtics (4–3) over St. Louis
1960/61	Boston Celtics (57–22)	St. Louis Hawks (51–28)	Boston Celtics (4–1) over St. Louis
1961/62	Boston Celtics (60–20)	Los Angeles Lakers (54–26)	Boston Celtics (4–3) over Los Angeles
1962/63	Boston Celtics (58–22)	Los Angeles Lakers (53–27)	Boston Celtics (4–2) over Los Angeles
1963/64	Boston Celtics (59–21)	San Francisco Warriors (48–32)	Boston Celtics (4–1) over San Francisco
1964/65	Boston Celtics (62–18)	Los Angeles Lakers (49–31)	Boston Celtics (4–1) over Los Angeles
1965/66	Philadelphia 76ers (55–25)	Los Angeles Lakers (45–35)	Boston Celtics (4–3) over Los Angeles
1966/67	Philadelphia 76ers (68–13)	San Francisco Warriors (44–37)	Philadelphia 76ers (4–2) over San Francisco
1967/68	Philadelphia 76ers (62–20)	St. Louis Hawks (56–26)	Boston Celtics (4–2) over Los Angeles
1968/69	Baltimore Bullets (57–25)	Los Angeles Lakers (55–27)	Boston Celtics (4–3) over Los Angeles
1969/70	New York Knickerbockers (60–22)	Los Angeles Lakers (46–36)	New York Knicks (4–3) over Los Angeles
1970/71	Baltimore Bullets (42–40)	Milwaukee Bucks (66–16)	Milwaukee Bucks (4–0) over Baltimore
1971/72	New York Knickerbockers (48–34)	Los Angeles Lakers (69–13)	Los Angeles Lakers (4–1) over New York
1972/73	New York Knickerbockers (57–25)	Los Angeles Lakers (60–22)	New York (4–1) over Los Angeles
1973/74	Boston Celtics (56–26)	Milwaukee Bucks (59–23)	Boston (4–3) over Milwaukee
1974/75	Washington Bullets (60–22)	Golden State Warriors (48–34)	Golden State (4–0) over Washington
1975/76	Boston Celtics (54–28)	Phoenix Suns (42–40)	Boston Celtics (4–2) over Phoenix
1976/77	Philadelphia 76ers (50–32)	Los Angeles Lakers (53–29)	Portland Trail Blazers (4–2) over Phila.
1977/78	Philadelphia 76ers (55–27)	Portland Trail Blazers (58–24)	Washington Bullets (4–3) over Seattle
1978/79	Washington Bullets (54–28)	Seattle SuperSonics (52–30)	Seattle (4–1) over Washington

TOP NBA SCORERS

Season	Player and Team	Points	Game Avg.	Season	Player and Team	Points	Game Avg.
1957/58	George Yardley, Detroit	2,001	27.8	1968/69	Elvin Hayes, San Diego	2,327	28.4
1958/59	Bob Pettit, St. Louis	2,105	29.2	1969/70	Jerry West, Los Angeles	2,309	31.2
1959/60	Wilt Chamberlain, Philadelphia	2,707	37.6	1970/71	Lew Alcindor, Milwaukee	2,596	31.7
1960/61	Wilt Chamberlain, Philadelphia	3,033	38.4	1971/72	Kareem Abdul-Jabbar, Milwaukee	2,822	34.8
1961/62	Wilt Chamberlain, Philadelphia	4,029	50.4	1972/73	Nate Archibald, Kansas City-Omaha	2,719	34.0
1962/63	Wilt Chamberlain, San Francisco	3,586	44.8	1973/74	Bob McAdoo, Buffalo	2,261	30.6
1963/64	Wilt Chamberlain, San Francisco	2,948	36.5	1974/75	Bob McAdoo, Buffalo	2,831	34.5
1964/65	Wilt Chamberlain, Philadelphia	2,534	34.7	1975/76	Bob McAdoo, Buffalo	2,427	31.1
1965/66	Wilt Chamberlain, Philadelphia	2,649	33.5	1976/77	Pete Maravich, New Orleans	2,273	31.1
1966/67	Rick Barry, San Francisco	2,775	35.6	1977/78	George Gervin, San Antonio	2,232	27.2
1967/68	Dave Bing, Detroit	2,142	27.1	1978/79	George Gervin, San Antonio	2,365	29.6

TOP NBA FIELD GOAL PERCENTAGE

Season	Pct.	Player and Team	Season	Pct.	Player and Team
1957/58	.452	Jack Twyman, Cincinnati	1968/69	.583	Wilt Chamberlain, Los Angeles
1958/59	.490	Ken Sears, New York	1969/70	.559	Johnny Green, Cincinnati
1959/60	.477	Ken Sears, New York	1970/71	.587	Johnny Green, Cincinnati
1960/61	.509	Wilt Chamberlain, Philadelphia	1971/72	.649	Wilt Chamberlain, Los Angeles
1961/62	.519	Walt Bellamy, Chicago	1972/73	.727	Wilt Chamberlain, Los Angeles
1962/63	.528	Wilt Chamberlain, San Francisco	1973/74	.547	Bob McAdoo, Buffalo
1963/64	.527	Jerry Lucas, Cincinnati	1974/75	.539	Don Nelson, Boston
1964/65	.510	Wilt Chamberlain, Philadelphia	1975/76	.561	Wes Unseld, Washington
1965/66	.540	Wilt Chamberlain, Philadelphia	1976/77	.579	Kareem Abdul-Jabbar, Los Angeles
1966/67	.683	Wilt Chamberlain, Philadelphia	1977/78	.578	Bobby Jones, Denver
1967/68	.595	Wilt Chamberlain, Philadelphia	1978/79	.584	Cedric Maxwell, Boston

TOP NBA FREE THROW PERCENTAGE

Season	Pct.	Player and Team	Season	Pct.	Player and Team
1957/58	.904	Dolph Schayes, Syracuse	1968/69	.864	Larry Siegfried, Boston
1958/59	.932	Bill Sharman, Boston	1969/70	.898	Flynn Robinson, Milwaukee
1959/60	.892	Dolph Schayes, Syracuse	1970/71	.859	Chet Walker, Chicago
1960/61	.921	Dolph Schayes, Syracuse	1971/72	.894	Jack Marin, Baltimore
1961/62	.896	Bill Sharman, Boston	1972/73	.902	Rick Barry, Golden State
1962/63	.881	Larry Costello, Syracuse	1973/74	.902	Ernie DiGregorio, Buffalo
1963/64	.853	Oscar Robertson, Cincinnati	1974/75	.904	Rick Barry, Golden State
1964/65	.877	Larry Costello, Philadelphia	1975/76	.923	Rick Barry, Golden State
1965/66	.881	Larry Siegfried, Boston	1976/77	.945	Ernie DiGregorio, Buffalo
1966/67	.903	Adrian Smith, Cincinnati	1977/78	.924	Rick Barry, Golden State
1967/68	.873	Oscar Robertson, Cincinnati	1978/79	.947	Rick Barry, Houston

NBA REBOUND LEADERS

Season	Rebs.	Player and Team	Season	Rebs.	Player and Team
1957/58	1564	Bill Russell, Boston	1968/69	1712	Wilt Chamberlain, Los Angeles
1958/59	1612	Bill Russell, Boston	1969/70	1386	Elvin Hayes, San Diego
1959/60	1941	Wilt Chamberlain, Philadelphia	1970/71	1493	Wilt Chamberlain, Los Angeles
1960/61	2149	Wilt Chamberlain, Philadelphia	1971/72	1572	Wilt Chamberlain, Los Angeles
1961/62	2052	Wilt Chamberlain, Philadelphia	1972/73	1526	Wilt Chamberlain, Los Angeles
1962/63	1946	Wilt Chamberlain, San Francisco	1973/74	1463	Elvin Hayes, Capital
1963/64	1930	Bill Russell, Boston	1974/75	1077	Wes Unseld, Washington
1964/65	1878	Bill Russell, Boston	1975/76	1383	Kareem Abdul-Jabbar, Los Angeles
1965/66	1943	Wilt Chamberlain, Philadelphia	1976/77	1090	Kareem Abdul-Jabbar, Los Angeles
1966/67	1957	Wilt Chamberlain, Philadelphia	1977/78	1288	Truck Robinson, New Orleans
1967/68	1952	Wilt Chamberlain, Philadelphia	1978/79	1444	Moses Malone, Houston

NBA ASSIST LEADERS

Season	Asst.	Player and Team	Season	Asst.	Player and Team
1957/58	463	Bob Cousy, Boston	1968/69	772	Oscar Robertson, Cincinnati
1958/59	557	Bob Cousy, Boston	1969/70	683	Len Wilkens, Seattle
1959/60	715	Bob Cousy, Boston	1970/71	832	Norm Van Lier, Cincinnati
1960/61	690	Oscar Robertson, Cincinnati	1971/72	747	Jerry West, Los Angeles
1961/62	899	Oscar Robertson, Cincinnati	1972/73	910	Nate Archibald, Kansas City-Omaha
1962/63	825	Guy Rodgers, San Francisco	1973/74	663	Ernie DiGregorio, Buffalo
1963/64	868	Oscar Robertson, Cincinnati	1974/75	650	Kevin Porter, Washington
1964/65	861	Oscar Robertson, Cincinnati	1975/76	661	Don Watts, Seattle
1965/66	847	Oscar Robertson, Cincinnati	1976/77	685	Don Buse, Indiana
1966/67	908	Guy Rodgers, Chicago	1977/78	837	Kevin Porter, New Jersey
1967/68	702	Wilt Chamberlain, Philadelphia	1978/79	1099	Kevin Porter, Detroit

NBA FINAL STANDINGS: 1978-79

EASTERN CONFERENCE

ATLANTIC DIVISION	Won	Lost	Pct.	G.B.
Washington Bullets	54	28	.659	—
Philadelphia 76ers	47	35	.573	7
New Jersey Nets	37	45	.451	17
New York Knicks	31	51	.378	23
Boston Celtics	29	53	.354	25

CENTRAL DIVISION	Won	Lost	Pct.	G.B.
San Antonio Spurs	48	34	.585	—
Houston Rockets	47	35	.573	1
Atlanta Hawks	46	36	.561	2
Cleveland Cavaliers	30	52	.366	18
Detroit Pistons	30	52	.366	18
New Orleans Jazz	26	56	.317	22

WESTERN CONFERENCE

MIDWEST DIVISION	Won	Lost	Pct.	G.B.
Kansas City Kings	48	34	.585	—
Denver Nuggets	47	35	.573	1
Indiana Pacers	38	44	.463	10
Milwaukee Bucks	38	44	.463	10
Chicago Bulls	31	51	.378	17

PACIFIC DIVISION	Won	Lost	Pct.	G.B.
Seattle SuperSonics	52	30	.634	—
Phoenix Suns	50	32	.610	2
Los Angeles Lakers	47	35	.573	5
Portland Trail Blazers	45	37	.549	7
San Diego Clippers	43	39	.524	9
Golden State Warriors	38	44	.463	14

NBA PLAYOFFS: 1979

EASTERN CONFERENCE

FIRST ROUND: Philadelphia over New Jersey (2–0) Atlanta over Houston (2–0)
SEMIFINALS: San Antonio over Philadelphia (4–3) Washington over Atlanta (4–3)
FINALS: Washington over San Antonio (4–3)

WESTERN CONFERENCE

FIRST ROUND: Los Angeles over Denver (2–1) Phoenix over Portland (2–1)
SEMIFINALS: Seattle over Los Angeles (4–1) Phoenix over Kansas City (4–1)
FINALS: Seattle over Phoenix (4–3)

CHAMPIONSHIP SERIES

Seattle 4   Washington 1

(Mostly Valuable Player—D. Johnson, Seattle)

May 20 — Washington 99, Seattle 97
May 24 — Seattle 92, Washington 82
May 27 — Seattle 105, Washington 95
May 29 — Seattle 114, Washington 112
June 1 — Seattle 97, Washington 93

Scoring Leader: Williams, Seattle ..... 143 pts.
Scoring Average: Williams 28.6
Rebounds: Sikma, Seattle 74
Assists: J. Johnson, Seattle 35
Field Goals Made: Williams 56
Free Throws Made: Williams 31

NBA INDIVIDUAL LEADERS: NBA INDIVIDUAL LEADERS: 1978-79

SCORING

Minimum: 70 games played or 1400 points

	Games	FG.	FT.	Pts.	Avg.		Games	FG.	FT.	Pts.	Avg.
Gervin, San Ant.	80	947	471	2,365	29.6	Erving, Phila.	78	715	373	1,803	23.1
Free, San Diego	78	795	654	2,244	28.8	Drew, Atlanta	79	650	495	1,795	22.7
M. Johnson, Milw.	77	820	332	1,972	25.6	McGinnis, Denver	76	603	509	1,715	22.6
McAdoo, Boston	60	596	295	1,487	24.8	Williamson, N.J.	74	635	373	1,643	22.2
Malone, Houston	82	716	599	2,031	24.8	Kenon, San Ant.	81	748	295	1,791	22.1
Thompson, Den.	76	693	439	1,825	24.0	Russell, Cleve.	74	603	417	1,623	21.9
Westphal, Phoenix	81	801	339	1,941	24.0	Hayes, Wash.	82	720	349	1,789	21.8
Abdul-Jabbar, L.A.	80	777	349	1,903	23.8	Birdsong, K.C.	82	741	296	1,778	21.7
Gilmore, Chicago	82	753	434	1,940	23.7	King, N.J.	82	710	349	1,769	21.6
Davis, Phoenix	79	764	340	1,868	23.6	Robinson, Phoenix	69	566	324	1,456	21.1

FIELD GOAL PERCENTAGE

Minimum: 300 FG made

	FG	Attempted	Pct.
Maxwell, Boston	472	808	.584
Abdul-Jabbar, Los Angeles	777	1347	.577
Unseld, Washington	346	600	.577
Gilmore, Chicago	753	1310	.575
Nater, San Diego	357	627	.569

FREE THROW PERCENTAGE

Minimum: 125 FT made

	FT	Attempted	Pct.
Barry, Houston	160	169	.947
Murphy, Houston	246	265	.928
Brown, Seattle	183	206	.888
Smith, Denver	159	180	.883
Sobers, Indiana	298	338	.882

REBOUNDS

Minimum: 70 games or 800 rebounds

	G	Off.	Def.	Total	Avg.
Malone, Houston	82	587	857	1444	17.6
Kelley, New Orleans	80	303	723	1026	12.8
Abdul-Jabbar, Los Angeles	80	207	818	1025	12.8
Gilmore, Chicago	82	293	750	1043	12.7
Sikma, Seattle	82	232	781	1013	12.4

ASSISTS

Minimum: 70 games or 400 assists

	G	No.	Avg.
Porter, Detroit	82	1099	13.4
Lucas, Golden State	82	762	9.3
Nixon, Los Angeles	82	737	9.0
Ford, Kansas City	79	681	8.6
Westphal, Phoenix	81	529	6.5

STEALS

Minimum: 70 games or 125 steals

	G	No.	Avg.
Carr, Detroit	80	197	2.46
Jordan, New Jersey	82	201	2.45
Nixon, Los Angeles	82	201	2.45
Walker, Cleveland	55	130	2.36
Ford, Kansas City	79	174	2.20

BLOCKED SHOTS

Minimum: 70 games or 100 blocked shots

	G	No.	Avg.
Abdul-Jabbar, Los Angeles	80	316	3.95
Johnson, New Jersey	78	253	3.24
Rollins, Atlanta	81	254	3.14
Parish, Golden State	76	217	2.86
Tyler, Detroit	82	201	2.45

NBA ALL-STAR TEAMS: 1978-79

First Team

Player, Club	Position
Marques Johnson, Milwaukee	F
Elvin Hayes, Washington	F
Moses Malone, Houston	C
George Gervin, San Antonio	G
Paul Westphal, Phoenix	G

Second Team

Player, Club	Position
Walter Davis, Phoenix	F
Bobby Dandridge, Washington	F
Kareem Abdul-Jabbar, Los Angeles	C
Lloyd Free, San Diego	G
Phil Ford, Kansas City	G

NBA ALL-ROOKIE TEAMS: 1978-79

First Team

Player, Club

Phil Ford, Kansas City
Mychal Thompson, Portland
Ron Brewer, Portland
Reggie Theus, Chicago
Terry Tyler, Detroit

Second Team

Player, Club

John Long, Detroit
Mike Mitchell, Cleveland
Maurice Cheeks, Philadelphia
Rick Robey, Boston
*(5 players tied)

*Wayne Cooper, Golden State
Purvis Short, Golden State
George Johnson, Milwaukee
Winford Boynes, New Jersey
Freeman Williams, San Diego

NBA ROOKIE OF THE YEAR

Year	Player	Year	Player
1952–53	Don Meineke, Fort Wayne	1966–67	Dave Bing, Detroit
1953–54	Ray Felix, Baltimore	1967–68	Earl Monroe, Baltimore
1954–55	Bob Pettit, Milwaukee	1968–69	Wes Unseld, Baltimore
1955–56	Maurice Stokes, Rochester	1969–70	Lew Alcindor, Milwaukee
1956–57	Tom Heinsohn, Boston	1970–71	Dave Cowens, Boston, and
1957–58	Woody Sauldsberry, Philadelphia		Geoff Petrie, Portland
1958–59	Elgin Baylor, Minneapolis	1971–72	Sidney Wicks, Portland
1959–60	Wilt Chamberlain, Philadelphia	1972–73	Bob McAdoo, Buffalo
1960–61	Oscar Robertson, Cincinnati	1973–74	Ernie DiGregorio, Buffalo
1961–62	Walt Bellamy, Chicago	1974–75	Keith Wilkes, Golden State
1962–63	Terry Dischinger, Chicago	1975–76	Alvan Adams, Phoenix
1963–64	Jerry Lucas, Cincinnati	1976–77	Adrian Dantley, Buffalo
1964–65	Willis Reed, New York	1977–78	Walter Davis, Phoenix
1965–66	Rick Barry, San Francisco	1978–79	Phil Ford, Kansas City

NBA COACH OF THE YEAR

Year	Coach, Team	Year	Coach, Team
1962–63	Harry Gallatin, St. Louis	1970–71	Dick Motta, Chicago
1963–64	Alex Hannum, San Francisco	1971–72	Bill Sharman, Los Angeles
1964–65	Red Auerbach, Boston	1972–73	Tom Heinsohn, Boston
1965–66	Dolph Schayes, Philadelphia	1973–74	Ray Scott, Detroit
1966–67	Johnny Kerr, Chicago	1974–75	Phil Johnson, Kansas City–Omaha
1967–68	Richie Guerin, St. Louis	1975–76	Bill Fitch, Cleveland
1968–69	Gene Shue, Baltimore	1976–77	Tom Nissalke, Houston
1969–70	Red Holzman, New York	1977–78	Hubie Brown, Atlanta
		1978–79	Cotton Fitzsimmons, Kansas City

NBA PODOLOFF TROPHY WINNERS (Most Valuable Player)

Year	Player, Team	Year	Player, Team
1955–56	Bob Pettit, St. Louis	1967–68	Wilt Chamberlain, Philadelphia
1956–57	Bob Cousy, Boston	1968–69	Wes Unseld, Baltimore
1957–58	Bill Russell, Boston	1969–70	Willis Reed, New York
1958–59	Bob Pettit, St. Louis	1970–71	Lew Alcindor, Milwaukee
1959–60	Wilt Chamberlain, Philadelphia	1971–72	Kareem Abdul-Jabbar, Milwaukee
1960–61	Bill Russell, Boston	1972–73	Dave Cowens, Boston
1961–62	Bill Russell, Boston	1973–74	Kareem Abdul-Jabbar, Milwaukee
1962–63	Bill Russell, Boston	1974–75	Bob McAdoo, Buffalo
1963–64	Oscar Robertson, Cincinnati	1975–76	Kareem Abdul-Jabbar, Los Angeles
1964–65	Bill Russell, Boston	1976–77	Kareem Abdul-Jabbar, Los Angeles
1965–66	Wilt Chamberlain, Philadelphia	1977–78	Bill Walton, Portland
1966–67	Wilt Chamberlain, Philadelphia	1978–79	Moses Malone, Houston

1979 NBA FIRST ROUND COLLEGE DRAFT

	Team	Player	College		Team	Player	College
1.	Los Angeles	Earvin Johnson	Michigan State	12.	Portland	Jimmy Paxson	Dayton
2.	Chicago	David Greenwood	U.C.L.A.	13.	Indiana	Dudley Bradley	North Carolina
3.	New York	Bill Cartwright	San Francisco	14.	Los Angeles	Brad Holland	U.C.L.A.
4.	Detroit	Greg Kelser	Michigan State	15.	Detroit	Phil Hubbard	Michigan
5.	Milwaukee	Sidney Moncrief	Arkansas	16.	Philadelphia	Jim Spanarkel	Duke
6.	Seattle	James Bailey	Rutgers	17.	Houston	Lee Johnson	E. Texas State
7.	Seattle	Vinnie Johnson	Baylor	18.	Kansas City	Reggie King	Alabama
8.	New Jersey	Calvin Natt	N.E. Louisiana	19.	San Antonio	Wiley Peck	Mississippi State
9.	New York	Larry Demic	Arizona	20.	Utah	Larry Knight	Chicago Loyola
10.	Detroit	Roy Hamilton	U.C.L.A.	21.	New York	Sly Williams	Rhode Island
11.	New Jersey	Cliff Robinson	U.S.C.	22.	Phoenix	Kyle Macy	Kentucky

BASKETBALL HALL OF FAME

Springfield, Massachusetts

Player	Year Elected
Paul Arizin	1977
Elgin Baylor	1976
John Beckman	1972
Bennie Borgmann	1961
Joseph Brennan	1974
Wilt Chamberlain	1979
Charles (Tarzan) Cooper	1976
Bob Cousy	1970
Bob Davies	1969
Forrest DeBernardi	1961
H. G. (Dutch) Dehnert	1968
Paul Endacott	1971
Harold (Bud) Foster	1964
Max (Marty) Friedman	1971
Joe Fulks	1977
Lauren (Laddie) Gale	1976
Tom Gola	1975
Robert (Ace) Gruenig	1963
Cliff Hagan	1977
Victor Hanson	1960
Nat Holman	1964
Chuck Hyatt	1959
William Johnson	1976
Edward (Moose) Krause	1975
Bob Kurland	1961
Joe Lapchick	1966
Hank Luisetti	1959
Branch McCracken	1960
Jack McCracken	1962
Ed Macauley	1960
George Mikan	1959
Charles (Stretch) Murphy	1960
H. O. (Pat) Page	1962
Bob Pettit	1970
Andy Phillip	1961
Jim Pollard	1977
Col. John Roosma	1961
John (Honey) Russell	1964
Bill Russell	1974

	Year
Dolph Schayes	1972
Ernest Schmidt	1973
John Schommer	1959
Barney Sedran	1962
Bill Sharman	1975
Christian Steinmetz	1961
John (Cat) Thompson	1962
Robert (Fuzzy) Vandivier	1974
Edward Wachter	1961
John Wooden	1960

Coach	Year Elected
A. J. (Red) Auerbach	1968
Sam Barry	1979
Ernest Blood	1960
Howard Cann	1967
Dr. H. Clifford Carlson	1959
Ben Carnevale	1969
Everett Dean	1966
Edgar Diddle	1971
Bruce Drake	1972
Amory (Slats) Gill	1967
Ed Hickey	1979
Howard Hobson	1965
Hank Iba	1968
A. F. (Doggie) Julian	1967
Frank Keaney	1960
George Keogan	1961
Ward Lambert	1960
Harry Litwack	1975
Ken Loeffler	1964
A. C. (Dutch) Lonborg	1972
John McLendon	1979
Frank McGuire	1976
Dr. Walter Meanwell	1959
Ray Meyer	1979
Pete Newell	1979
Adolph Rupp	1968
Leonard Sachs	1961
John Wooden	1972

	Year
George Hepbron	1960
George Hoyt	1961
Matthew Kennedy	1959
John Nucatola	1977
Ernest Quigley	1961
David Tobey	1961
David Walsh	1961

Contributor	Year Elected
Dr. Forrest (Phog) Allen	1959
Clair Bee	1967
Walter Brown	1965
John Bunn	1964
Bob Douglas	1971
Jim Enright	1979
Harry Fisher	1973
Edward Gottlieb	1971
Dr. Luther Gulick	1959
Edward Hickox	1959
Paul (Tony) Hinkle	1965
Ned Irish	1964
William Jones	1964
Emil Liston	1974
Bill Mokray	1965
Ralph Morgan	1959
Frank Morgenweck	1962
Dr. James Naismith	1959
John O'Brien	1961
Harold Olsen	1959
Maurice Podoloff	1973
H. V. Porter	1960
William Reid	1963
Elmer Ripley	1972
Lynn St. John	1962
Abe Saperstein	1970
Arthur Schabinger	1961
Amos Alonzo Stagg	1959
Chuck Taylor	1968
Oswald Tower	1959
Arthur Trester	1961
Clifford Wells	1971

NBA ALL-STAR GAMES

Year	Result	Site	Year	Result	Site	Year	Result	Site
1951	East 111, West 94	Boston	1961	West 153, East 131	Syracuse	1970	East 142, West 135	Philadelphia
1952	East 108, West 91	Boston	1962	West 150, East 130	St. Louis	1971	West 108, East 107	San Diego
1953	West 79, East 75	Ft. Wayne	1963	East 115, West 108	Los Angeles	1972	West 112, East 110	Los Angeles
1954	East 98, West 93	New York	1964	East 111, West 107	Boston	1973	East 104, West 84	Chicago
1955	East 100, West 91	New York	1965	East 124, West 123	St. Louis	1974	West 134, East 123	Seattle
1956	West 108, East 94	Rochester	1966	East 137, West 94	Cincinnati	1975	East 108, West 102	Phoenix
1957	East 109, West 97	Boston	1967	West 135, East 120	San Francisco	1976	East 123, West 109	Philadelphia
1958	East 130, West 118	St. Louis	1968	East 144, West 124	New York	1977	West 125, East 124	Milwaukee
1959	West 124, East 108	Detroit	1969	East 123, West 112	Baltimore	1978	East 133, West 125	Atlanta
1960	East 125, West 115	Philadelphia				1979	West 134, East 129	Detroit

ALL-TIME NBA LEADERS

SOURCE: National Basketball Association

At start of 1979/80 season

Top Scorers

Player	Years	Games	FG	FT	Rebounds	Assists	Points	Average	Career Span
Wilt Chamberlain	14	1,045	12,681	6,057	23,924	4,643	31,419	30.1	1960-73
Oscar Robertson	14	1,040	9,508	7,694	7,804	9,887	26,710	25.7	1961-74
John Havlicek	16	1,270	10,513	5,369	8,007	6,114	26,395	20.8	1963-78
Jerry West	14	932	9,016	7,160	5,376	6,238	25,192	27.0	1961-74
Elgin Baylor	14	846	8,693	5,763	11,463	3,650	23,149	27.4	1959-72
Kareem Abdul-Jabbar	10	773	9,144	3,853	11,460	3,440	22,141	28.6	1970-79
Hal Greer	15	1,122	8,504	4,578	5,665	4,540	21,586	19.2	1959-73
Elvin Hayes	11	897	8,530	4,189	12,971	1,798	21,249	23.7	1969-79
Walt Bellamy	14	1,043	7,914	5,113	14,241	2,544	20,941	20.1	1962-75
Bob Pettit	11	792	7,349	6,182	12,849	2,369	20,880	26.4	1955-65
Dolph Schayes	16	1,059	6,135	6,979	11,256	3,072	19,249	18.2	1949-64
Gail Goodrich	13	1,031	7,431	4,319	3,279	4,805	19,181	18.6	1966-79
Chet Walker	13	1,032	6,876	5,079	7,314	2,126	18,831	18.2	1963-75
Dave Bing	12	901	6,962	4,403	3,420	5,397	18,327	20.3	1967-78
Lou Hudson	13	890	7,392	3,156	3,926	2,432	17,940	20.2	1967-79
Len Wilkens	15	1,077	6,189	5,394	5,030	7,211	17,772	16.5	1961-75
Bailey Howell	12	950	6,515	4,740	9,383	1,853	17,770	18.7	1960-71
Rick Barry	9	722	6,927	3,675	4,932	3,749	17,529	24.3	1966-79
Earl Monroe	12	875	6,745	3,586	2,760	3,527	17,076	19.5	1968-79
Bob Cousy	14	924	6,168	4,624	4,786	6,955	16,960	18.4	1951-70

Most Games Played

John Havlicek	1,270
Paul Silas	1,172
Hal Greer	1,122
Len Wilkens	1,077
Dolph Schayes	1,059
Johnny Green	1,057
Don Nelson	1,053
Leroy Ellis	1,048
Wilt Chamberlain	1,045
Walt Bellamy	1,043

Most Field Goals Made

Wilt Chamberlain	12,681
John Havlicek	10,513
Oscar Robertson	9,508
Kareem Abdul-Jabbar	9,144
Jerry West	9,016
Elgin Baylor	8,693
Elvin Hayes	8,530
Hal Greer	8,504
Walt Bellamy	7,914
Gail Goodrich	7,431

Most Field Goals Attempted

John Havlicek	23,930
Wilt Chamberlain	23,497
Elgin Baylor	20,171
Oscar Robertson	19,620
Jerry West	19,032
Elvin Hayes	18,920
Hal Greer	18,811
Bob Pettit	16,872
Kareem Abdul-Jabbar	16,600
Bob Cousy	16,468

Most Assists

Oscar Robertson	9,887
Len Wilkens	7,211
Bob Cousy	6,955
Guy Rodgers	6,917
Jerry West	6,238
John Havlicek	6,114
Dave Bing	5,397
Norm Van Lier	5,217
Walter Frazier	5,032
Gail Goodrich	4,805

Highest Scoring Average (400 Games Minimum)

	G.	FG	FTM	Pts.	Avg.
Wilt Chamberlain	1,045	12,681	6,057	31,419	30.1
Kareem Abdul-Jabbar	773	9,144	3,853	22,141	28.6
Bob McAdoo	525	5,665	3,075	14,405	27.4
Elgin Baylor	846	8,693	5,763	23,149	27.4
Jerry West	932	9,016	7,160	25,192	27.0
Bob Pettit	792	7,349	6,182	20,880	26.4
Oscar Robertson	1,040	9,508	7,694	26,710	25.7
Pete Maravich	615	5,943	3,473	15,359	25.0
Rick Barry	722	6,927	3,675	17,529	24.3
Elvin Hayes	897	8,530	4,189	21,249	23.7

Most Minutes Played

Wilt Chamberlain	47,859
John Havlicek	46,471
Oscar Robertson	43,886
Bill Russell	40,726
Hal Greer	39,789
Walt Bellamy	38,940
Len Wilkens	38,064
Elvin Hayes	37,558
Jerry West	36,571
Nate Thurmond	35,875

Highest Field Goal Percentage (2000 FG Minimum)

	FGA	FGM	Pct.
Artis Gilmore	3,661	2,027	.554
Kareem Abdul-Jabbar	16,600	9,144	.551
George Gervin	4,695	2,537	.540
Wilt Chamberlain	23,497	12,681	.540
Clifford Ray	3,915	2,066	.528
Walt Bellamy	15,340	7,914	.516
David Thompson	4,563	2,343	.513
Paul Westphal	7,067	3,618	.512
Bob McAdoo	11,132	5,665	.509
Wes Unseld	7,520	3,817	.508

Highest Free Throw Percentage (1200 FTM Minimum)

	FTA	FTM	Pct.
Rick Barry	4,090	3,675	.899
Calvin Murphy	3,087	2,730	.884
Bill Sharman	3,557	3,143	.884
Mike Newlin	2,428	2,098	.864
Fred Brown	1,581	1,364	.863
Larry Siegfried	1,945	1,662	.854
Flynn Robinson	1,881	1,597	.849
Dolph Schayes	8,273	6,979	.844
Jack Marin	2,852	2,405	.843
Larry Costello	2,891	2,432	.841

Most Free Throws Made

Oscar Robertson	7,694
Jerry West	7,160
Dolph Schayes	6,979
Bob Pettit	6,182
Wilt Chamberlain	6,057
Elgin Baylor	5,763
Len Wilkens	5,394
John Havlicek	5,369
Walt Bellamy	5,113
Chet Walker	5,079

Most Free Throws Attempted

Wilt Chamberlain	11,862
Oscar Robertson	9,185
Jerry West	8,801
Dolph Schayes	8,273
Bob Pettit	8,119
Walt Bellamy	8,088
Elgin Baylor	7,391
Len Wilkens	6,973
John Havlicek	6,589
Chet Walker	6,384

Most Rebounds

Wilt Chamberlain	23,924
Bill Russell	21,620
Nate Thurmond	14,464
Walt Bellamy	14,241
Elvin Hayes	12,971
Jerry Lucas	12,942
Bob Pettit	12,849
Wes Unseld	12,002
Paul Silas	11,921
Elgin Baylor	11,463

Most Personal Fouls

Hal Greer	3,855
Dolph Schayes	3,664
Walt Bellamy	3,536
Bailey Howell	3,498
Bill Bridges	3,375
Len Wilkens	3,285
John Havlicek	3,281
Tom Sanders	3,044
Paul Silas	2,985
Elvin Hayes	2,942

NCAA CONFERENCE CHAMPIONS: 1978-79

Conference	Champion	CONFERENCE RECORD Won	Lost	Pct.	REGULAR SEASON Won	Lost	Pct.	Conf. Runner Up	Won	Lost
Atlantic Coast	North Carolina	9	3	.750	23	5	.821	Virginia	7	5
	Duke	9	3	.750	22	7	.759			
Big Eight	Oklahoma	10	4	.714	20	9	.690	Kansas, Kansas State,		
								Missouri	8	6
Big Sky	Weber State	10	4	.714	24	8	.750	Idaho St., No. Arizona	8	6
Big Ten	Michigan State	13	5	.722	21	6	.778	Ohio State	12	6
	Purdue	13	5	.722	23	7	.767			
	Iowa	13	5	.722	20	7	.741			
East Coast (E)	Temple	10	0	1.000	25	3	.893	St. Joseph's, LaSalle	9	2
East Coast (W)	Bucknell	11	5	.688	18	9	.667	Lafayette	8	8
Eastern-8	Villanova	9	1	.900	15	13	.536	W. Virginia, Rutgers	7	3
Ivy League	Pennsylvania	13	1	.929	21	5	.808	Columbia	10	4
Metro-7	Louisville	9	1	.900	23	7	.767	Florida State	7	3
Mid-American	Toledo	13	3	.813	20	7	.741	Ohio	10	6
	Central Michigan	13	3	.813	19	7	.731			
Missouri Valley	Indiana State	16	0	1.000	29	0	1.000	New Mexico State	11	5
Ohio Valley	Eastern Kentucky	9	3	.750	21	7	.750	W. Kentucky, Middle Tenn., Morehead St., Tennessee Tech.	7	5
Pacific Coast	Pacific	11	3	.786	15	11	.577	Utah St., Fresno St.	9	5
Pacific-10	U.C.L.A.	15	3	.833	23	4	.852	So. California	14	4
Southeastern	Louisiana State	14	4	.778	22	5	.815	Tennessee	12	6
Southern	Appalachian State	11	3	.786	23	5	.821	Furman	9	3
Southland	Lamar	9	1	.900	22	8	.733	Louisiana Tech, S.W. Louisiana	6	4
Southwest	Arkansas	13	3	.813	23	4	.852	Texas A & M	11	5
	Texas	13	3	.813	21	7	.750			
Sun Belt	South Alabama	10	0	1.000	20	6	.769	UNC-Charlotte, South Florida	6	4
West Coast	San Francisco	12	2	.857	21	6	.778	Pepperdine	10	4
Western	Brigham Young	10	2	.833	20	7	.741	Utah	9	3

INDEPENDENTS (NCAA DIV. I)

Team	Won	Lost	Team	Won	Lost	Team	Won	Lost
Syracuse	25	3	Va. Commonwealth	20	5	North Carolina A & T	20	7
Georgetown	24	4	Marquette	21	6	Rhode Island	20	8
DePaul	22	4	Mercer	21	6	Nevada-Las Vegas	20	8
N.E. Louisiana	23	5	Wagner	21	6	N.C.-Wilmington	19	8
Iona	23	5	Old Dominion	21	6	St. Bonaventure	19	8
Notre Dame	22	5	Tennessee State	20	6	Boston College	21	9
Detroit	22	5	Connecticut	21	7			

NATIONAL COLLEGE TOURNAMENT CHAMPIONS

NCAA (Division I)

Year	Champion	Year	Champion
1950	City College of New York	1965	UCLA
1951	Kentucky	1966	Texas Western
1952	Kansas	1967	UCLA
1953	Indiana	1968	UCLA
1954	La Salle	1969	UCLA
1955	San Francisco	1970	UCLA
1956	San Francisco	1971	UCLA
1957	North Carolina	1972	UCLA
1958	Kentucky	1973	UCLA
1959	California	1974	N.C. State
1960	Ohio State	1975	UCLA
1961	Cincinnati	1976	Indiana
1962	Cincinnati	1977	Marquette
1963	Loyola (Chicago)	1978	Kentucky
1964	UCLA	1979	Michigan State

NIT

Year	Champion	Year	Champion
1950	City College of New York	1965	St. John's
1951	Brigham Young	1966	Brigham Young
1952	La Salle	1967	Southern Illinois
1953	Seton Hall	1968	Dayton
1954	Holy Cross	1969	Temple
1955	Duquesne	1970	Marquette
1956	Louisville	1971	North Carolina
1957	Bradley	1972	Maryland
1958	Xavier of Ohio	1973	Virginia Tech
1959	St. John's	1974	Purdue
1960	Bradley	1975	Princeton
1961	Providence College	1976	Kentucky
1962	Dayton	1977	St. Bonaventure
1963	Providence College	1978	Texas
1964	Bradley	1979	Indiana

NCAA (Division II)

Year	Champion	Year	Champion
1975	Old Dominion	1977	Tenn.-Chattanooga
1976	Puget Sound	1978	Cheyney St. (Pa.)
		1979	North Alabama

NCAA (Division III)

Year	Champion	Year	Champion
1975	LeMoyne Owen	1977	Wittenberg
1976	Scranton	1978	North Park (Chicago)
		1979	North Park (Chicago)

1979 COLLEGE ALL-AMERICA SELECTIONS

Associated Press (A), United Press (U), NBA Coaches (N), Sporting News (S); First Team (1), Second Team (2)

Player	Height	School	Class	Selected by	NBA Draft by
Larry Bird	6'9"	Indiana State	Senior	A1, U1, N1, S1	Boston
Earvin Johnson	6'8"	Michigan State	Sophomore	A1, U1, N1, S1	Los Angeles
David Greenwood	6'9"	U.C.L.A.	Senior	A1, U1, N1, S2	Chicago
Bill Cartwright	7'1"	San Francisco	Senior	A1, U2, N1, S1	New York
Sidney Moncrief	6'4"	Arkansas	Senior	A1, U2, N1, S2	Milwaukee
Mike Gminski	6'11"	Duke	Junior	A2, U1, N2, S2	—
Mike O'Koren	6'7"	North Carolina	Junior	U2, N2, S1	—
Calvin Natt	6'5"	Northeast Louisiana	Senior	A2, N2, S2	New Jersey
James Bailey	6'9"	Rutgers	Senior	N2, S1	Seattle
Darrell Griffith	6'4"	Louisville	Junior	U2, S1	—
Darnell Valentine	6'2"	Kansas	Sophomore	N2, S2	—
Jim Spanarkel	6'5"	Duke	Senior	U1	Philadelphia
Reggie King	6'6"	Alabama	Senior	A2	Kansas City
Vinnie Johnson	6'1"	Baylor	Senior	A2	Seattle
Ronnie Lester	6'2"	Iowa	Junior	A2	—
Kelly Tripucka	6'6"	Notre Dame	Sophomore	U2	—

NCAA DIVISION I BASKETBALL RECORDS
SOURCE: N.C.A.A. Basketball Guide

INDIVIDUAL

Scoring Average (Career) : 44.2, Maravich, LSU, 1968–70
Scoring Average (Season) : 44.5, Maravich, LSU, 1970
Scoring (Game) : 100 points, Selvy, Furman, 1954
Field Goals Attempted (Season) : 1168, Maravich, LSU, 1970
Field Goal Percentage (Season) : .699, Senser, West Chester, 1977
Free Throws Attempted (Season) : 444, Selvy, Furman, 1954
Free Throw Percentage (Season) : .944, Gibson, Marshall, 1978
Rebounds (Season) : 734, Dukes, Seton Hall, 1953
Rebounds Per Game (Season) : 25.6, Slack, Marshall, 1955

TEAM

Points Per Game (Season) : 110.5, Nevada-Las Vegas, 1976
Field Goals Per Game (Season) : 46.3, Nevada-Las Vegas, 1976
Field Goal Percentage (Season) : .547, Maryland, 1975
Free Throw Percentage (Season) : .809, Ohio State, 1970
Least Points Allowed Per Game (Season) : 32.5, Oklahoma State, 1948

WOMEN'S BASKETBALL

WOMEN'S PROFESSIONAL LEAGUE (WBL) — 1979 FINAL STANDINGS

EASTERN DIVISION	Won	Lost	Pct.	G.B.	WESTERN DIVISION	Won	Lost	Pct.	G.B.
Houston Angels	26	8	.765	—	Chicago Hustle	21	13	.618	—
New York Stars	19	15	.559	7	Iowa Cornets	21	13	.618	—
Dayton Rockettes	12	22	.353	14	Minnesota Fillies	17	17	.500	4
New Jersey Gems	9	25	.265	17	Milwaukee Does	11	23	.324	10

Playoffs: Houston over New York (2–0); Iowa over Chicago (2–1)
Championship: Houston over Iowa (3–2)

A.I.A.W. COLLEGIATE CHAMPIONS — 1979
SOURCE: Association for Intercollegiate Athletics for Women

LARGE COLLEGES

Eastern Finals: 1. Tennessee; 2. Fordham; 3. Rutgers; 4. Long Beach State
Southern Finals: 1. Old Dominion; 2. Maryland; 3. Valdosta State; 4. Kansas State
Central Finals: 1. Louisiana Tech; 2. Northwestern; 3. Kansas; 4. Connecticut State
Western Finals: 1. U.C.L.A.; 2. Wayland Baptist; 3. Brigham Young; 4. Oregon State
National Championship: Old Dominion 75, Louisiana Tech 65

SMALL COLLEGES

National Champions: 1. South Carolina State; 2. Dayton; 3. Niagara; 4. Tuskegee Institute; 5. Tougaloo (Miss.); 6. High Point (N.C.)

OTHER 1979 BASKETBALL CHAMPIONS

N.A.I.A. Tournament: Drury College (Missouri)
National AAU: Men — Joliet (Illinois) Christian Youth Center
                      Women — Anna's Bananas (Los Angeles)
NWIT Tournament: Women — South Carolina

PROFESSIONAL FOOTBALL

NATIONAL FOOTBALL LEAGUE
410 Park Avenue, New York City 10022.   Commissioner: Pete Rozelle.

NATIONAL FOOTBALL CONFERENCE (George Halas, Pres.)

Eastern Division	Chief Executive	Coach
Dallas Cowboys	Clint W. Murchison, Jr.	Tom Landry
New York Giants	Wellington T. Mara	Ray Perkins
Philadelphia Eagles	Leonard H. Tose	Dick Vermeil
St. Louis Cardinals	William V. Bidwill	Bud Wilkinson
Washington Redskins	Edward B. Williams	Jack Pardee

Central Division		
Chicago Bears	George Halas, Sr.	Neill Armstrong
Detroit Lions	William Clay Ford	Monte Clark
Green Bay Packers	Dominic Olejniczak	Bart Starr
Minnesota Vikings	Max Winter	Bud Grant
Tampa Bay Buccaneers	Hugh Culverhouse	John McKay

Western Division		
Atlanta Falcons	Rankin M. Smith, Jr.	Leeman Bennett
Los Angeles Rams	Steve Rosenbloom	Ray Malavasi
New Orleans Saints	John W. Mecom, Jr.	Dick Nolan
San Francisco 49ers	Edward J. DeBartolo, Jr.	Bill Walsh

AMERICAN FOOTBALL CONFERENCE (Lamar Hunt, Pres.)

Eastern Division	Chief Executive	Coach
Baltimore Colts	Robert Irsay	Ted Marchibroda
Buffalo Bills	Ralph C. Wilson, Jr.	Chuck Knox
Miami Dolphins	Joseph Robbie	Don Shula
New England Patriots	William H. Sullivan	Ron Erhardt
New York Jets	James Kensil	Walt Michaels

Central Division		
Cincinnati Bengals	John Sawyer	Homer Rice
Cleveland Browns	Arthur B. Modell	Sam Rutigliano
Houston Oilers	K. S. Adams, Jr.	O. A. Phillips
Pittsburgh Steelers	Art Rooney	Chuck Noll

Western Division		
Denver Broncos	Gerald Phipps	Bob Miller
Kansas City Chiefs	Lamar Hunt	Marv Levy
Oakland Raiders	Al Davis	Tom Flores
San Diego Chargers	Eugene V. Klein	Don Coryell
Seattle Seahawks	Elmer Nordstrom	Jack Patera

PROFESSIONAL FOOTBALL HALL OF FAME (Canton, Ohio)

MEMBERS

Lance Alworth, Wide Receiver, San Diego Chargers, 1962–70.

Cliff Battles, Back, 1932, Boston Braves; 1933–36, Boston Redskins; 1937, Washington Redskins.

Sammy Baugh, Quarterback, Washington Redskins, 1937–52.

Chuck Bednarik, Center and Linebacker, Philadelphia Eagles, 1949–62.

Bert Bell, Founder, Philadelphia Eagles, 1933, and Head Coach; Commissioner, National Football League, 1946–59.

Raymond Berry, End, Baltimore Colts, 1955–67.

Charles W. Bidwill, Founder, Chicago Cardinals, 1933–47

Jim Brown, Fullback, Cleveland Browns, 1957–65.

Paul E. Brown, Head Coach, Cleveland Browns, 1946–62; Cincinnati Bengals, 1968–75.

Roosevelt Brown, Tackle, N.Y. Giants, 1953–65.

Dick Butkus, Linebacker, Chicago Bears, 1965–73.

Tony Canadeo, Backfield, Green Bay Packers, 1940–52.

Joe Carr, Founder, Columbus Panhandles, 1904; Organizer, National Football League, 1920; President of League, 1921–39.

Guy Chamberlin, Head Coach, Halfback, End, Canton Bulldogs, Decatur Staleys, Cleveland Bulldogs, Frankford Yellowjackets, Chicago Cardinals, 1918–28.

Jack Christiansen, Defensive Back, Detroit Lions, 1951–58.

Dutch Clark, Quarterback and Head Coach, Portsmouth (O.) Spartans, Detroit Lions, Cleveland Rams, 1931–42.

George Connor, Tackle, Defensive Tackle, Linebacker, Chicago Bears, 1948–55.

Jimmy Conzelman, Head Coach, Halfback, Executive, Decatur Staleys, Rock Island Independents, Milwaukee Badgers, Detroit Panthers, Providence Steam Rollers, Chicago Cardinals, 1920–48.

Art Donovan, Tackle, 1950, Baltimore Colts; 1951, New York Yanks; 1952, Dallas Texans; 1953–61, Baltimore Colts.

Paddy Driscoll, Halfback and Head Coach, Chicago Cardinals and Chicago Bears, 1919–31, 1941–68.

Bill Dudley, Halfback, Pittsburgh Steelers, Detroit Lions, Washington Redskins, 1942, 1945–53.

Turk Edwards, Tackle, Washington Redskins, 1932–40.

Weeb Ewbank, Head Coach, 1954–62 Baltimore Colts; 1963–73, New York Jets.

Tom Fears, End, Los Angeles Rams, 1948–56.

Ray Flaherty, End and Head Coach, New York Giants, New York Yankees, Boston & Washington Redskins, Chicago Hornets, 1928–49.

Len Ford, Defensive End, Los Angeles Dons, Cleveland Browns, Green Bay Packers, 1948–58.

Daniel J. Fortmann, M.D., Guard, Chicago Bears, 1936–46.

Bill George, Middle Linebacker, Chicago Bears, 1952–65.

Frank Gifford, Halfback, New York Giants, 1952–60, 1962–64.

Otto Graham, Quarterback, Cleveland Browns, 1946–55.

Red Grange, Halfback, Chicago Bears, New York Yankees, 1925–37.

Forrest Gregg, Tackle, 1956, 1958–70, Green Bay Packers; 1971, Dallas Cowboys.

Lou Groza, Tackle, Kicker, Cleveland Browns, 1946–67.

Joe Guyon, Halfback, Canton Bulldogs, Cleveland Indians, Oorang Indians, Rock Island Independents, Kansas City Cowboys, New York Giants, 1919–27.

George Halas, Founder, Head Coach, End, Decatur Staleys (1920) which became the Chicago Bears; retired as Bears' head coach in 1968.

Ed Healey, Tackle, Rock Island Independents, Chicago Bears, 1920–27.

Mel Hein, Center, New York Giants, 1931–45.

Pete Henry, Tackle, Canton Bulldogs, Akron, New York Giants, Pottsville Maroons, Staten Island Stapletons, 1920–30.

Arnie Herber, Halfback, Green Bay Packers, New York Giants, 1930–41, 1944–45.

Bill Hewitt, End, 1932–36, Chicago Bears; 1936–39, Philadelphia Eagles; 1943, Philadelphia-Pittsburgh.

Clarke Hinkle, Fullback, Green Bay Packers, 1932–41.

Elroy Hirsch, End, 1946–48, Chicago Rockets (AAFC); 1949–57, Los Angeles Rams; Rams' club executive, 1960–68.

Cal Hubbard, Tackle, New York Giants, Green Bay Packers, Pittsburgh Pirates, 1927–36.

Lamar Hunt, Founder, American Football League, 1959. Owner, Dallas Texans, 1960–1962, Kansas City Chiefs, 1963 to present.

Don Hutson, End, Green Bay Packers, 1935–45.

Walt Kiesling, Player-Coach, Duluth Eskimos, Pottsville Maroons, Boston Braves, Chicago Cardinals, Chicago Bears, Green Bay Packers, Pittsburgh Steelers, Philadelphia-Pittsburgh, Chicago-Pittsburgh, 1926–61.

Frank (Bruiser) Kinard, Tackle, 1938–43, Brooklyn Dodgers; 1944, Brooklyn Tigers; 1946–47, New York Yankees.

Curly Lambeau, Founder, Head Coach, Halfback, Green Bay Packers, 1919–49; also Head Coach of Chicago Cardinals and Washington Redskins, 1950–54.

Dick Lane, Defensive Back, Los Angeles Rams, Chicago Cardinals, Detroit Lions, 1952–65.

Yale Lary, Defensive Back, Detroit Lions, 1952–53, 1956–64.

Dante Lavelli, End, Cleveland Browns, 1946–56.

Bobby Layne, Quarterback, Chicago Bears, New York Bulldogs, Detroit Lions, Pittsburgh Steelers, 1948–62.

Alphonse (Tuffy) Leemans, Fullback, New York Giants, 1937–43

Vince Lombardi, Head Coach, 1959–67, Green Bay Packers; 1969, Washington Redskins.

Sid Luckman, Quarterback, Chicago Bears, 1939–50.

Link Lyman, Tackle, Canton Bulldogs, Cleveland Bulldogs, Chicago Bears, 1922–34.

Tim Mara, Founder, New York Giants, 1925.

Gino Marchetti, Defensive End, Dallas Texans, 1952; Baltimore Colts, 1953–1964–1966.

George P. Marshall, Founder, Washington Redskins (as Boston Braves) in 1932.

Ollie Matson, Halfback, Chicago Cardinals, 1952, 1954–1958, Los Angeles Rams, 1959–1962, Detroit Lions, 1963, Philadelphia Eagles, 1964–1966.

George McAfee, Halfback, Chicago Bears, 1940–41, 1945–50.

Hugh McElhenny, Halfback, San Francisco 49ers, Minnesota Vikings, New York Giants, Detroit Lions, 1952–64.

John Blood McNally, Halfback, Milwaukee Badgers, Duluth Eskimos, Pottsville Maroons, Green Bay Packers, Pittsburgh Steelers, 1925–39.

Mike Michalske, Guard, New York Yankees, Green Bay Packers, 1926–37.

Wayne Millner, End, 1936, Boston Redskins; 1937–41, 1945 Washington Redskins.

Ron Mix, Tackle, Los Angeles-San Diego Chargers, 1960–69, Oakland Raiders, 1971.

Lenny Moore, Running Back, Baltimore Colts, 1956–67.

Marion Motley, Fullback, 1946–53, Cleveland Browns; 1955, Pittsburgh Steelers.

Bronko Nagurski, Fullback and Tackle, Chicago Bears, 1930–37, 1943.

Earl (Greasy) Neale, Head Coach, Philadelphia Eagles, 1941–50.

Ernie Nevers, Fullback and Head Coach, Duluth Eskimos, Chicago Cardinals, 1926–31, 1939.

Ray Nitschke, Linebacker, Green Bay Packers, 1958–72

Leo Nomellini, Defensive Tackle, San Francisco 49ers, 1950–63.

Steve Owen, Player-Coach, Kansas City Cowboys, New York Giants, 1924–53.

Ace Parker, Quarterback, Brooklyn Dodgers, 1937–1941, Boston Yanks, 1945, New York Yankees (AAFC), 1946.

Jim Parker, Tackle, Baltimore Colts, 1957–67.

Joe Perry, Fullback, San Francisco 49ers, Baltimore Colts, 1949–63.

Pete Pihos, End, Philadelphia Eagles, 1947–55.

Hugh (Shorty) Ray, National Football League technical adviser and supervisor of officials, 1938–56.

Dan Reeves, Founder, Cleveland Rams, 1941 (moved to Los Angeles in 1946).

Andy Robustelli, Defensive End, 1951–55, Los Angeles Rams; 1956–64, New York Giants.

Art Rooney, Founder, Pittsburgh Steelers, 1933.

Gale Sayers, Running Back, 1965–1971, Chicago Bears.

Joe Schmidt, Linebacker, Detroit Lions, 1953–65.

Bart Starr, Quarterback, Green Bay Packers, 1956–71.

Ernie Stautner, Defensive End, Pittsburgh Steelers, 1950–63.

Ken Strong, Halfback, Staten Island Stapletons, New York Giants, New York Yankees, 1929–37, 1939, 1944–47.

Joe Stydahar, Tackle, Chicago Bears, 1936–42, 1945–46. Head

Coach of Los Angeles Rams, 1950–51; Head Coach of Chicago Cardinals, 1953–54.

Jim Taylor, Fullback, Green Bay Packers, New Orleans Saints, 1958–67.

Jim Thorpe, Halfback, Canton Bulldogs, Pine Village (Ind.) A. A., Oorang Indians, Toledo Maroons, Rock Island Independents, New York Giants, 1915–26; President of American Professional Football Association, forerunner of N.F.L., 1920.

Y. A. Tittle, Quarterback, 1948–50, Baltimore Colts; 1951–60, San Francisco 49ers; 1961–64, New York Giants.

George Trafton, Center, Chicago Bears, 1920–32.

Charley Trippi, Halfback-Quarterback, 1947–55, Chicago Cardinals.

Emlen Tunnell, Halfback, New York Giants, Green Bay Packers, 1946–61.

Clyde (Bulldog) Turner, Center, Chicago Bears, 1940–52.

Johnny Unitas, Quarterback, Baltimore Colts, 1956–72, San Diego Chargers, 1973.

Norm Van Brocklin, Quarterback, 1949–57, Los Angeles Rams; 1958–60, Philadelphia Eagles.

Steve Van Buren, Halfback, Philadelphia Eagles, 1944–51.

Bob Waterfield, Quarterback, Cleveland and Los Angeles Rams, 1945–52; Head Coach of Rams, 1960–62.

Bill Willis, Guard, 1946–53, Cleveland Browns.

Larry Wilson, Defensive Back, St. Louis Cardinals, 1960–72

Alex Wojciechowicz, Center and Linebacker, 1938–46, Detroit Lions; 1946–50, Philadelphia Eagles.

THE NFL CONFERENCE CHAMPIONS

AMERICAN CONFERENCE (formerly NFL Eastern)

Year	Team	Won	Lost	Tied	Coach
1978	Pittsburgh	14	2	0	Chuck Noll
1977	Denver	12	2	0	Red Miller
1976	Oakland	13	1	0	John Madden
1975	Pittsburgh	12	2	0	Chuck Noll
1974	Pittsburgh	10	3	1	Chuck Noll
1973	Miami	12	2	0	Don Shula
1972	Miami*	14	0	0	Don Shula
1971	Miami*	10	3	1	Don Shula
1970	Baltimore*	11	2	1	Don McCafferty
1969	Cleveland*	10	3	1	Blanton Collier
1968	Cleveland*	10	4	0	Blanton Collier
1967	Dallas	9	5	0	Tom Landry
1966	Dallas	10	3	1	Tom Landry
1965	Cleveland	11	3	0	Blanton Collier
1964	Cleveland	10	3	1	Blanton Collier
1963	New York	11	3	0	Allie Sherman
1962	New York	12	2	0	Allie Sherman
1961	New York	10	3	1	Allie Sherman
1960	Philadelphia	10	2	0	Buck Shaw
1959	New York	10	2	0	Jim Howell
1958	New York*	9	3	0	Jim Howell
1957	Cleveland	9	2	1	Paul Brown
1956	New York	8	3	1	Jim Howell
1955	Cleveland	9	2	1	Paul Brown
1954	Cleveland	9	3	0	Paul Brown
1953	Cleveland	11	1	0	Paul Brown
1952	Cleveland	8	4	0	Paul Brown
1951	Cleveland	11	1	0	Paul Brown

NATIONAL CONFERENCE (formerly NFL Western)

Year	Team	Won	Lost	Tied	Coach
1978	Dallas	12	4	0	Tom Landry
1977	Dallas	12	2	0	Tom Landry
1976	Minnesota	11	2	1	Bud Grant
1975	Dallas	10	4	0	Tom Landry
1974	Minnesota	10	4	0	Bud Grant
1973	Minnesota	12	2	0	Bud Grant
1972	Washington*	11	3	0	George Allen
1971	Dallas*	11	3	0	Tom Landry
1970	Dallas	10	4	0	Tom Landry
1969	Minnesota*	12	2	0	Bud Grant
1968	Baltimore*	13	1	0	Don Shula
1967	Green Bay	9	4	1	Vince Lombardi
1966	Green Bay	12	2	0	Vince Lombardi
1965	Green Bay*	10	3	1	Vince Lombardi
1964	Baltimore	12	2	0	Don Shula
1963	Chicago	11	1	2	George Halas
1962	Green Bay	13	1	0	Vince Lombardi
1961	Green Bay	11	3	0	Vince Lombardi
1960	Green Bay	8	4	0	Vince Lombardi
1959	Baltimore	9	3	0	Weeb Ewbank
1958	Baltimore	9	3	0	Weeb Ewbank
1957	Detroit*	8	4	0	George Wilson
1956	Chicago	9	2	1	Paddy Driscoll
1955	Los Angeles	8	3	1	Sid Gillman
1954	Detroit	9	2	1	Buddy Parker
1953	Detroit	10	2	0	Buddy Parker
1952	Detroit*	9	3	0	Buddy Parker
1951	Los Angeles	8	4	0	Joe Stydahar

* Won divisional playoff.

NFL FINAL 1978 STANDINGS

AMERICAN FOOTBALL CONFERENCE

EASTERN DIVISION

	W	L	T	Pct.	Pts.	OP
New England	11	5	0	.688	358	286
*Miami	11	5	0	.688	372	254
N.Y. Jets	8	8	0	.500	359	364
Buffalo	5	11	0	.313	302	354
Baltimore	5	11	0	.313	239	421

CENTRAL DIVISION

	W	L	T	Pct.	Pts.	OP
Pittsburgh	14	2	0	.875	356	195
*Houston	10	6	0	.625	283	298
Cleveland	8	8	0	.500	334	356
Cincinnati	4	12	0	.250	252	284

WESTERN DIVISION

	W	L	T	Pct.	Pts.	OP
Denver	10	6	0	.625	282	198
Oakland	9	7	0	.563	311	283
San Diego	9	7	0	.563	355	309
Seattle	9	7	0	.563	345	358
Kansas City	4	12	0	.250	243	327

*Wild card qualifiers.

NATIONAL FOOTBALL CONFERENCE

EASTERN DIVISION

	W	L	T	Pct.	Pts.	OP
Dallas	12	4	0	.750	384	208
*Philadelphia	9	7	0	.563	270	250
Washington	8	8	0	.500	273	283
St. Louis	6	10	0	.375	248	296
N.Y. Giants	6	10	0	.375	264	298

CENTRAL DIVISION

	W	L	T	Pct.	Pts.	OP
Minnesota	8	7	1	.531	294	306
Green Bay	8	7	1	.531	249	269
Detroit	7	9	0	.438	290	300
Chicago	7	9	0	.438	253	274
Tampa Bay	5	11	0	.313	241	259

WESTERN DIVISION

	W	L	T	Pct.	Pts.	OP
Los Angeles	12	4	0	.750	316	245
*Atlanta	9	7	0	.563	240	290
New Orleans	7	9	0	.438	281	298
San Francisco	2	14	0	.125	219	350

*Wild card qualifiers.

NATIONAL FOOTBALL LEAGUE RECORDS   Source: Elias Sports Bureau

Through 1978 season; includes all performances in American Football League (1960–69)

Most Points, Lifetime: 2,002, George Blanda, Chicago Bears, Baltimore, Houston, Oakland

Most Points, Season: 176, Paul Hornung, Green Bay, 1960

Most Points, Game: 40, Ernie Nevers, Chicago Cards vs. Chicago Bears, November 28, 1929

Most Touchdowns, Lifetime: 126, Jim Brown, Cleveland

Most Touchdowns, Season: 23, O. J. Simpson, Buffalo, 1975.

Most Yards Gained Rushing, Lifetime: 12,312, Jim Brown, Cleveland, 1957–65

Most Yards Gained Rushing, Season: 2,003, O. J. Simpson, Buffalo, 1973

Most Yards Gained Rushing, Game: 275, Walter Payton, Chicago vs. Minnesota, Nov. 20, 1977

Highest Average Gain Rushing, Lifetime: 5.22, Jim Brown, Cleveland

Highest Average Gain Rushing, Season: 9.94, Beattie Feathers, Chicago, 1934; 6.87, Bobby Douglass, Chicago, 1972

Most Touchdowns Rushing, Lifetime: 106, Jim Brown, Cleveland

Most Touchdowns Rushing, Season: 19, Jim Taylor, Green Bay, 1962

Most Passes Completed, Lifetime: 3,686, Fran Tarkenton, Minnesota, New York Giants, Minnesota

Most Passes Completed, Season: 345, Fran Tarkenton, Minnesota, 1978

Most Passes Completed, Game: 37, George Blanda, Houston, 1964

Passing Percent (Attempts-Completions), Lifetime: 59.61, Ken Stabler, Oakland

Passing Percent (Attempts-Completions), Season: 70.33, Sammy Baugh, Washington, 1945

Most Yards Gained Passing, Lifetime: 47,003, Fran Tarkenton, Minnesota, New York Giants, Minnesota

Most Yards Gained Passing, Season: 4,007, Joe Namath, New York Jets, 1967

Most Yards Gained Passing, Game: 554, Norm Van Brocklin, Los Angeles, 1951

Most Touchdown Passes, Lifetime: 342, Fran Tarkenton, Minnesota, New York Giants, Minnesota

Lowest Interception Percent, Lifetime: 3.31, Roman Gabriel, Los Angeles, Philadelphia

Receptions, Most Yards Gained, Lifetime: 11,834, Don Maynard, New York Giants, New York Jets, St. Louis

Receptions, Most Yards Gained, Season: 1,746, Charlie Hennigan, Houston, 1961

Receptions, Most Touchdowns, Lifetime: 99, Don Hutson, Green Bay

Receptions, Most Touchdowns, Season: 17, Don Hutson, Green Bay, 1942; 17, Elroy Hirsch, Los Angeles, 1951; 17, Bill Groman, Houston, 1961

Most Receptions, Lifetime: 649, Charley Taylor, Washington

Interceptions, Most Touchdowns from, Lifetime: 9, Ken Houston, Houston, Washington

Most Points After Touchdown, Lifetime: 943, George Blanda, Chicago Bears, Baltimore, Houston, Oakland

Most Points After Touchdown, Season: 64, George Blanda, Houston, 1961

Most Consecutive Points After Touchdown: 234, Tommy Davis, San Francisco, 1959–65

Most Field Goals, Lifetime: 335, George Blanda, Chicago Bears, Baltimore, Houston, Oakland

Most Field Goals, Season: 34, Jim Turner, New York Jets, 1968

Most Field Goals, Game: 7, Jim Bakken, St. Louis vs. Pittsburgh, September 24, 1967

Longest Field Goal: 63 yards, Tom Dempsey, New Orleans vs. Detroit, November 8, 1970

Most Consecutive Field Goals: 16, Jan Stenerud, Kansas City, 1969; Don Crockroft, Cleveland, 1974-75, Garo Yepremian, Miami, 1978

Longest Punt: 98, Steve O'Neal, New York Jets, 1969

Highest Punting Average, Lifetime: 45.10, Sammy Baugh, Washington; 44.68, Tommy Davis, San Francisco

Most Punt Returns, Lifetime: 258, Em Tunnell, New York Giants and Green Bay

Punt Returns, Most Yardage Gained, Lifetime: 2,209, Em Tunnell, New York Giants and Green Bay

Punt Returns, Highest Average, Season: 23.00, Herb Rich, Baltimore, 1950

Kickoff Returns, Most Yards Gained, Lifetime: 6,922, Ron Smith, Chicago, Atlanta, Los Angeles, San Diego, Oakland

Kickoff Returns, Highest Average Yardage Gained, Lifetime: 30.56, Gale Sayers, Chicago

Kickoff Returns, Highest Average Yardage Gained, Season: 41.06, Travis Williams, Green Bay, 1967

Most Seasons, Active Player: 26, George Blanda, Chicago Bears, Baltimore, Houston, Oakland

Most Games Played, Lifetime: 340, George Blanda, Chicago Bears, Baltimore, Houston, Oakland

Most Seasons NFL Champion Team: 11, Green Bay, 1929-1931, 1936, 1939, 1944, 1961-1962, 1965-1967.

Team, Most Consecutive Victories, Regular Season: 17, Chicago Bears, 1933-1934

Most Fumbles, Season: 17, Dan Pastorini, Houston, 1973

Most Fumbles, Game: 7, Len Dawson, Kansas City, 1964

NATIONAL FOOTBALL LEAGUE STARS: BY YEARS

PASSERS	Passes	Comp	Yards	Tds	Inter.
1978—Roger Staubach, Dallas (NFC)	413	231	3,190	25	16
1977—Bob Griese, Miami (AFC)	307	180	2,252	22	13
1976—Ken Stabler, Oakland (AFC)	291	194	2,737	27	17
1975—Ken Anderson, Cincinnati (AFC)	377	228	3,169	21	11
1974—Ken Anderson, Cincinnati (AFC)	328	213	2,667	18	10
1973—Roger Staubach, Dallas Cowboys (NFC)	286	179	2,428	23	15
1972—Norm Snead, New York Giants (NFC)	325	196	2,307	17	12
1971—Bob Griese, Miami (AFC)	263	145	2,089	19	9
1970—John Brodie, San Francisco (NFC)	378	223	2,941	24	10
1969—C. A. (Sonny) Jurgensen, Wash. (NFL)	442	274	3,102	22	15
1968—Earl Morrall, Baltimore (NFL)	317	182	2,909	26	17
1967—C. A. (Sonny) Jurgensen, Wash. (NFL)	508	288	3,747	31	16
1966—Len Dawson, Kansas City (AFL)	284	159	2,527	26	10
1965—John Hadl, San Diego (AFL)	348	174	2,798	20	21
1964—Len Dawson, Kansas City (AFL)	354	199	2,879	30	18
1963—Y. A. Tittle, New York (NFL)	367	221	3,145	36	14
1962—Len Dawson, Dallas (AFL)	310	189	2,759	29	17
1961—George Blanda, Houston (AFL)	362	187	3,330	36	22

PASSERS	Passes	Comp	Yards	Tds	Inter.
1960—Jack Kemp, Los Angeles (AFL)	406	211	3,018	20	25
1959—Charles Conerly, N.Y.	194	113	1,706	14	4
1958—Eddie LeBaron, Wash.	145	79	1,365	11	10
1957—Tommy O'Connell, Cleveland	110	63	1,229	9	8
1956—Eddie Brown, Chicago	168	96	1,667	11	12
1955—Otto Graham, Cleveland	185	98	1,721	15	8
1954—Norman Van Brocklin, L.A.	260	139	2,637	13	21
1953—Otto Graham, Clev.	258	167	2,722	11	9
1952—Norman Van Brocklin, L.A.	205	113	1,736	14	17
1951—Bob Waterfield, L.A.	176	88	1,566	13	10
1950—Norman Van Brocklin, L.A.	233	127	2,061	18	14
1949—Sammy Baugh, Wash.	255	145	1,903	18	14
1948—Tommy Thompson, Phila.	246	141	1,965	25	11
1947—Sammy Baugh, Wash.	354	210	2,938	25	15
1946—Bob Waterfield, L.A.	251	127	1,747	18	17
1945—Sid Luckman, Chicago	217	117	1,725	14	10
1944—Frank Filchock, Washington	147	84	1,139	13	9
1943—Sammy Baugh, Wash.	239	133	1,754	23	19
1942—Cecil Isbell, Green Bay	268	146	2,021	24	14
1941—Cecil Isbell, Green Bay	206	117	1,479	15	11
1940—Sammy Baugh, Washington	177	111	1,367	12	10
1939—Parker Hall, Clev.*	208	106	1,227	9	13
1938—Ed Danowski, N.Y.	129	70	848	8	8
1937—Sammy Baugh, Washington*	171	81	1,127	7	14
1936—Arnie Herber, Green Bay	173	77	1,239	9	13
1935—Ed Danowski, N.Y.	113	57	794	9	9

* First year in League

RUSHERS

	Yards	Att.	TDs
1978—Earl Campbell, Houston (AFC)*	1,450	302	13
1977—Walter Payton, Chicago (NFC)	1,852	339	14
1976—O. J. Simpson, Buffalo (AFC)	1,503	290	8
1975—O. J. Simpson, Buffalo (AFC)	1,817	329	16
1974—Otis Armstrong, Denver (AFC)	1,407	263	9
1973—O. J. Simpson, Buffalo (AFC)	2,003	332	12
1972—O. J. Simpson, Buffalo (AFC)	1,251	292	6
1971—Floyd Little, Denver (AFC)	1,133	284	6
1970—Larry Brown, Washington (NFC)	1,125	237	5
1969—Gale Sayers, Chicago (NFL)	1,032	236	8
1968—Leroy Kelly, Cleveland (NFL)	1,239	248	16
1967—Jim Nance, Boston (AFL)	1,216	269	7
1966—Jim Nance, Boston (AFL)	1,458	299	11
1965—Jim Brown, Cleveland (NFL)	1,544	289	17
1964—Jim Brown, Cleveland (NFL)	1,446	280	7
1963—Jim Brown, Cleveland (NFL)	1,863	291	12
1962—Jim Taylor, Green Bay (NFL)	1,474	272	19
1961—Jim Brown, Cleveland (NFL)	1,408	305	8
1960—Jim Brown, Cleveland (NFL)	1,257	215	9
1959—Jim Brown, Cleveland	1,329	290	14
1958—Jim Brown, Cleveland	1,527	257	17
1957—Jim Brown, Cleveland*	942	202	9
1956—Rick Casares, Chicago Bears	1,126	234	12
1955—Alan Ameche, Baltimore*	961	213	9
1954—Joe Perry, San Francisco	1,049	173	8
1953—Joe Perry, San Francisco	1,018	192	10
1952—Dan Towler, Los Angeles	894	156	10
1951—Eddie Price, New York Giants	971	271	7
1950—Marion Motley, Cleveland*	810	140	3
1949—Steve Van Buren, Philadelphia	1,146	263	11
1948—Steve Van Buren, Philadelphia	945	201	10
1947—Steve Van Buren, Philadelphia	1,008	217	13
1946—Bill Dudley, Pittsburgh	604	146	3
1945—Steve Van Buren, Philadelphia	832	143	15
1944—Bill Paschal, New York	737	196	9
1943—Bill Paschal, New York*	572	147	10
1942—Bill Dudley, Pittsburgh*	696	162	5
1941—Clarence Manders, Brooklyn	486	111	6
1940—Byron White, Detroit	514	146	5
1939—Bill Osmanski, Chicago Bears*	699	121	7
1938—Byron White, Pittsburgh*	567	152	4
1937—Cliff Battles, Washington	874	216	6
1936—Alphonse Leemans, New York*	830	206	2
1935—Doug Russell, Chicago Cardinals	499	140	0

RECEIVERS

	No.	Yards	TDs
1978—Rickey Young, Minnesota (NFC)	88	704	5
1977—Lydell Mitchell, Baltimore (AFC)	71	620	4
1976—MacArthur Lane, Kansas City (AFC)	66	686	1
1975—Chuck Foreman, Minnesota (NFC)	73	691	9
1974—Lydell Mitchell, Baltimore (AFC)	72	544	2
1973—Harold Carmichael, Philadelphia (NFC)	67	1,116	9
1972—Harold Jackson, Philadelphia (NFC)	62	1,048	4
1971—Fred Biletnikoff, Oakland (AFC)	61	929	9
1970—Dick Gordon, Chicago (NFC)	71	1,026	13
1969—Dan Abramowicz, New Orleans (NFL)	73	1,015	7
1968—Lance Alworth, San Diego (AFL)	68	1,312	10
1967—George Sauer, New York (AFL)	75	1,189	6
1966—Lance Alworth, San Diego (AFL)	73	1,383	13
1965—Dave Parks, San Francisco (NFL)	80	1,344	12
1964—Charley Hennigan, Houston (AFL)	101	1,546	8
1963—Lionel Taylor, Denver (AFL)	78	1,101	10
1962—Bobby Mitchell, Washington (NFL)	72	1,384	11
1961—Lionel Taylor, Denver (AFL)	100	1,176	4
1960—Raymond Berry, Baltimore, (NFL)	74	1,298	10
1959—Raymond Berry, Baltimore	66	959	14
1958—Raymond Berry, Baltimore	56	794	9
1957—Billy Wilson, San Francisco	52	757	6
1956—Billy Wilson, San Francisco	60	889	5
1955—Pete Pihos, Philadelphia	62	864	7
1954—Pete Pihos, Philadelphia	60	872	10
1953—Pete Pihos, Philadelphia	63	1,049	10
1952—Mac Speedie, Cleveland	62	911	5
1951—Elroy Hirsch, Los Angeles	66	1,495	17
1950—Tom Fears, Los Angeles	84	1,116	7
1949—Tom Fears, Los Angeles	77	1,013	9
1948—Tom Fears, Los Angeles*	51	698	4
1947—Jim Keane, Chicago Bears	64	910	10
1946—Jim Benton, Los Angeles	63	981	6
1945—Don Hutson, Green Bay	47	834	9
1944—Don Hutson, Green Bay	58	866	9
1943—Don Hutson, Green Bay	47	776	11
1942—Don Hutson, Green Bay	74	1,211	17
1941—Don Hutson, Green Bay	58	738	10
1940—Don Looney, Philadelphia*	58	707	4
1939—Don Hutson, Green Bay	34	846	6
1938—Gaynell Tinsley, Chi. Cards	41	516	1
1937—Don Hutson, Green Bay	41	552	7
1936—Don Hutson, Green Bay	34	536	8
1935—Tod Goodwin, New York	26	432	4

*First year in League

PUNTERS

	Att.	Avg.
1978—Pat McInally, Cincinnati (AFC)	91	43.1
1977—Ray Guy, Oakland (AFC)	59	43.3
1976—Marv Bateman, Buffalo (AFC)	86	42.8
1975—Ray Guy, Oakland (AFC)	68	43.8
1974—Ray Guy, Oakland (AFC)	74	42.2
1973—Jerrel Wilson, Kansas City (AFC)	80	45.5
1972—Jerrel Wilson, Kansas City (ACF)	66	44.8
1971—Dave Lewis, Cincinnati (AFC)	72	44.8
1970—Dave Lewis, Cincinnati (AFC)*	79	46.2
1969—David Lee, Baltimore (NFL)	57	45.3
1968—Jerrel Wilson, Kansas City (AFL)	63	45.1
1967—Bob Scarpitto, Denver (AFL)	105	44.9
1966—Bob Scarpitto, Denver (AFL)	76	45.8
1965—Gary Collins, Cleveland (NFL)	65	46.7
1964—Bobby Walden, Minnesota (NFL)	72	46.4
1963—Yale Lary, Detroit (NFL)	35	48.9
1962—Tommy Davis, San Francisco (NFL)	48	45.6
1961—Yale Lary, Detroit (NFL)	52	48.4
1960—Jerry Norton, St. Louis (NFL)	39	45.6
1959—Yale Lary, Detroit	45	47.1
1958—Sam Baker, Washington	48	45.4
1957—Don Chandler, New York	60	44.6
1956—Norm Van Brocklin, Los Angeles	48	43.1
1955—Norm Van Brocklin, Los Angeles	60	44.6
1954—Pat Brady, Pittsburgh	66	43.2
1953—Pat Brady, Pittsburgh	80	46.9
1952—Horace Gillom, Cleveland Browns	61	45.7
1951—Horace Gillom, Cleveland Browns	73	45.5
1950—Fred Morrison, Chicago Bears*	57	43.3
1949—Mike Boyda, N.Y. Bulldogs*	56	44.2
1948—Joe Muha, Philadelphia	57	47.3
1947—Jack Jacobs, Green Bay	57	43.5
1946—Roy McKay, Green Bay	64	42.7
1945—Roy McKay, Green Bay	44	41.2
1944—Frank Sinkwich, Detroit	45	41.0
1943—Sammy Baugh, Washington	50	45.9
1942—Sammy Baugh, Washington	37	48.2
1941—Sammy Baugh, Washington	30	48.7
1940—Sammy Baugh, Washington	35	51.4
1939—Parker Hall, Cleveland Rams*	58	40.8

TOTAL POINTS

	TDs	XP	FG	Points
1978—Frank Corral, Los Angeles (NFC)	0	31	29	118
1977—Errol Mann, Oakland (AFC)	0	39	20	99
1976—Tony Linhart, Baltimore (AFC)	0	49	20	109
1975—O. J. Simpson, Buffalo (AFC)	23	0	0	138
1974—Chester Marcol, Green Bay (NFC)	0	19	25	94
1973—David Ray, Los Angeles (NFC)	0	40	30	130
1972—Chester Marcol, Green Bay (NCF)*	0	29	33	128
1971—Garo Yepremian, Miami (ACF)	0	33	28	117
1970—Fred Cox, Minnesota (NFC)	0	35	30	125
1969—Jim Turner, New York (AFL)	0	33	32	129
1968—Jim Turner, New York (AFL)	0	43	34	145
1967—Jim Bakken, St. Louis (NFL)	0	36	27	117
1966—Gino Cappelletti, Boston (AFL)	6	35	16	119
1965—Gale Sayers, Chicago (NFL)*	22	0	0	132
— Gino Capelletti, Boston (AFL)	9	27	17	132
1964—Gino Cappelletti, Boston (AFL)	7	36	25	155
1963—Gino Cappelletti, Boston (AFL)	2	35	22	113
1962—Gene Mingo, Denver (AFL)	4	32	27	137
1961—Gino Cappelletti, Boston (AFL)	8	48	17	147
1960—Paul Hornung, Green Bay (NFL)	15	41	15	176
1959—Paul Hornung, Green Bay	7	31	7	94
1958—Jim Brown, Cleveland Browns	18	0	0	108
1957—Sam Baker, Washington	1	29	14	77
— Lou Groza, Cleveland Browns	0	32	15	77
1956—Bobby Layne, Detroit	5	33	12	99
1955—Doak Walker, Detroit	7	27	9	96
1954—Robert Walston, Philadelphia	11	36	4	114
1953—Gordon Soltau, San Francisco	6	48	10	114
1952—Gordon Soltau, San Francisco	7	34	6	94
1951—Elroy Hirsch, Los Angeles	17	0	0	102
1950—Doak Walker, Detroit*	11	38	8	128
1949—Pat Harder, Chicago Cardinals	8	45	3	102
— Gene Roberts, New York Giants	17	0	0	102
1948—Pat Harder, Chicago Cardinals	6	53	7	110
1947—Pat Harder, Chicago Cardinals	7	39	7	102
1946—Ted Fritsch, Green Bay	10	13	9	100
1945—Steve Van Buren, Philadelphia	18	2	0	110
1944—Don Hutson, Green Bay	9	31	0	85
1943—Don Hutson, Green Bay	12	36	3	117
1942—Don Hutson, Green Bay	17	33	1	138
1941—Don Hutson, Green Bay	12	20	1	95
1940—Don Hutson, Green Bay	7	15	0	57
1939—Andy Farkas, Washington	11	2	0	68
1938—Clarke Hinkle, Green Bay	7	7	3	58
1937—Jack Manders, Chicago Bears	5	15	8	69
1936—Earl (Dutch) Clark, Detroit	7	19	4	73
1935—Earl (Dutch) Clark, Detroit	6	16	1	55

NATIONAL FOOTBALL LEAGUE ALL-TIME LEADERS

Rushing Yardage		Pass Receptions		Points		Interceptions	
12,312	Jim Brown	649	Charley Taylor	2,002	George Blanda	79	Emlen Tunnell
10,776	O. J. Simpson	633	Don Maynard	1,380	Jim Bakken	78	Paul Krause
8,597	Jim Taylor	631	Raymond Berry	1,368	Jim Turner	68	Night Train Lane

TEAM DEPARTMENTAL CHAMPIONS

Total Yards Gained		Yards Rushing		Yards Passing		Points Scored	
1978–New England (AFC)	5,965	1978–New England (AFC)	3,165	1978–San Diego (AFC)	3,375	1978–Dallas (NFC)	384
1977–Dallas (NFC)	4,812	1977–Chicago (NFC)	2,811	1977–Buffalo (AFC)	2,530	1977–Oakland (AFC)	351
1976–Baltimore (AFC)	5,236	1976–Pittsburgh (AFC)	2,971	1976–Baltimore (AFC)	2,933	1976–Baltimore (AFC)	417
1975–Buffalo (AFC)	5,467	1975–Buffalo (AFC)	2,974	1975–Cincinnati (AFC)	3,241	1975–Buffalo (AFC)	420
1974–Dallas (NFC)	4,983	1974–Pittsburgh (AFC)	2,417	1974–Washington (NFC)	2,978	1974–Oakland (AFC)	355
1973–Los Angeles (NFC)	4,906	1973–Buffalo (AFC)	3,088	1973–Philadelphia (NFC)	3,236	1973–Dallas (AFC)	388
1972–Miami (AFC)	5,036	1972–Miami (AFC)	2,960	1972–New York Jets (AFC)	2,777	1972–Miami (AFC)	385
1971–Dallas (NFC)	5,035	1971–Miami (AFC)	2,429	1971–San Diego (AFC)	3,134	1971–Dallas (NFC)	406
1970–Oakland (AFC)	4,829	1970–Dallas (NFC)	2,300	1970–San Francisco (NFC)	2,923	1970–San Francisco (NFC)	352
1969–Dallas (NFL)	5,122	1969–Dallas (NFL)	2,276	1969–Oakland (AFL)	3,271	1969–Minnesota (NFL)	379
1968–Oakland (AFL)	5,696	1968–Chicago (NFL)	2,377	1968–San Diego (AFL)	3,623	1968–Oakland (AFL)	453
1967–New York (AFL)	5,152	1967–Cleveland (NFL)	2,139	1967–New York (AFL)	3,845	1967–Oakland (AFL)	468
1966–Dallas (NFL)	5,145	1966–Kansas City (AFL)	2,274	1966–New York (AFL)	3,464	1966–Kansas City (AFL)	448
1965–San Francisco (NFL)	5,270	1965–Cleveland (NFL)	2,331	1965–San Francisco (NFL)	3,487	1965–San Francisco (NFL)	421
1964–Buffalo (AFL)	5,206	1964–Green Bay (NFL)	2,276	1964–Houston (AFL)	3,527	1964–Baltimore (NFL)	428
1963–San Diego (AFL)	5,153	1963–Cleveland (NFL)	2,639	1963–Baltimore (NFL)	3,296	1963–New York (NFL)	448
1962–New York (AFL)	5,005	1962–Buffalo (AFL)	2,480	1962–Denver (AFL)	3,404	1962–Green Bay (NFL)	415
1961–Houston (AFL)	6,288	1961–Green Bay (NFL)	2,350	1961–Houston (AFL)	4,392	1961–Houston (AFL)	513
1960–Houston (AFL)	4,936	1960–St. Louis (NFL)	2,356	1960–Houston (AFL)	3,203	1960–New York (AFL)	382
1959–Baltimore	4,458	1959–Cleveland	2,149	1959–Baltimore	2,753	1959–Baltimore	374
1958–Baltimore	4,539	1958–Cleveland	2,526	1958–Pittsburgh	2,752	1958–Baltimore	381
1957–Los Angeles	4,143	1957–Los Angeles	2,142	1957–Baltimore	2,388	1957–Los Angeles	307
1956–Chicago Bears	4,537	1956–Chicago Bears	2,468	1956–Los Angeles	2,419	1956–Chicago Bears	363
1955–Chicago Bears	4,316	1955–Chicago Bears	2,388	1955–Philadelphia	2,472	1955–Cleveland	349
1954–Los Angeles	5,187	1954–San Francisco	2,498	1954–Chicago Bears	3,104	1954–Detroit	337
1953–Philadelphia	4,811	1953–San Francisco	2,230	1953–Philadelphia	3,089	1953–San Francisco	372
1952–Cleveland	4,352	1952–San Francisco	1,905	1952–Cleveland	2,566	1952–Los Angeles	349
1951–Los Angeles	5,506	1951–Chicago Bears	2,408	1951–Los Angeles	3,296	1951–Los Angeles	392
1950–Los Angeles	5,420	1950–New York Giants	2,336	1950–Los Angeles	3,709	1950–Los Angeles	466
1949–Chicago Bears	4,873	1949–Philadelphia	2,607	1949–Chicago Bears	3,055	1949–Philadelphia	364
1948–Chicago Cards	4,705	1948–Chicago Cards	2,560	1948–Washington	2,861	1948–Chicago Cards	395
1947–Chicago Bears	5,053	1947–Los Angeles	2,171	1947–Chicago Bears	3,336	1947–Chicago Bears	363
1946–Los Angeles	3,793	1946–Green Bay	1,765	1946–Los Angeles	2,080	1946–Chicago Bears	289
1945–Washington	3,549	1945–Cleveland Rams	1,714	1945–Washington	1,857	1945–Philadelphia	272
1944–Chicago Bears	3,239	1944–Philadelphia	1,661	1944–Washington	2,021	1944–Philadelphia	267
1943–Chicago Bears	4,045	1943–Phil-Pitt	1,730	1943–Chicago Bears	2,310	1943–Chicago Bears	303
1942–Chicago Bears	3,900	1942–Chicago Bears	1,881	1942–Green Bay	2,407	1942–Chicago Bears	376
1941–Chicago Bears	4,265	1941–Chicago Bears	2,263	1941–Green Bay	2,002	1941–Chicago Bears	396
1940–Green Bay	3,400	1940–Chicago Bears	1,818	1940–Washington	1,887	1940–Washington	245
1939–Chicago Bears	3,988	1939–Chicago Bears	2,043	1939–Chicago Bears	1,965	1939–Chicago Bears	298
1938–Green Bay	3,037	1938–Detroit	1,893	1938–Washington	1,536	1938–Green Bay	223
1937–Green Bay	3,201	1937–Detroit	2,074	1937–Green Bay	1,398	1937–Green Bay	220
1936–Detroit	3,703	1936–Detroit	2,885	1936–Green Bay	1,629	1936–Green Bay	248
1935–Chicago Bears	3,454	1935–Chicago Bears	2,096	1935–Green Bay	1,449	1935–Chicago Bears	192
1934–Chicago Bears	3,750	1934–Chicago Bears	2,847	1934–Green Bay	1,165	1934–Chicago Bears	286
1933–New York Giants	2,970	1933–Boston Redskins	2,260	1933–New York	1,348	1933–New York Giants	244
1932–Chicago Bears	2,755	1932–Chicago Bears	1,770	1932–Chicago Bears	1,013	1932–Green Bay	152

Since 1952 based on net yards.

NFC CHAMPIONSHIP GAMES

Year	Date		Winner-Loser	Score	Year	Date	Winner-Loser	Score
1978	Jan. 7,	1979	Cowboys-Rams	28-0	1955	Dec. 26	Browns-Rams	38-14
1977	Jan. 1,	1978	Cowboys-Vikings	23-6	1954	Dec. 26	Browns-Lions	56-10
1976	Dec. 26		Vikings-Rams	24-13	1953	Dec. 27	Lions-Browns	17-16
1975	Jan. 4,	1976	Vikings-Rams	14-10	1952	Dec. 28	Lions-Browns	17-7
1974	Dec. 29		Cowboys-Rams	37-7	1951	Dec. 23	Rams-Browns	24-17
1973	Dec. 30		Vikings-Cowboys	27-10	1950	Dec. 24	Browns-Rams	30-28
1972	Dec. 31		Redskins-Cowboys	26-3	1949	Dec. 18	Eagles-Rams	14-0
1971	Jan. 2,	1972	Cowboys-49ers	14-3	1948	Dec. 19	Eagles-Cardinals	7-0
1970	Jan. 3,	1971	Cowboys-49ers	17-10	1947	Dec. 28	Cardinals-Eagles	28-21
1969	Jan. 4,	1970	Vikings-Browns	27-7	1946	Dec. 15	Bears-Giants	24-14
1968	Dec. 29		Colts-Browns	34-0	1945	Dec. 16	Rams-Redskins	15-14
1967	Dec. 31		Packers-Cowboys	21-17	1944	Dec. 17	Packers-Giants	14-7
1966	Jan. 1,	1967	Packers-Cowboys	34-27	1943	Dec. 26	Bears-Redskins	41-21
1965	Jan. 2,	1966	Packers-Browns	23-12	1942	Dec. 13	Redskins-Bears	14-6
1964	Dec. 27		Browns-Colts	27-0	1941	Dec. 21	Bears-Giants	37-9
1963	Dec. 29		Bears-Giants	14-10	1940	Dec. 8	Bears-Redskins	73-0
1962	Dec. 30		Packers-Giants	16-7	1939	Dec. 10	Packers-Giants	27-0
1961	Dec. 31		Packers-Giants	37-0	1938	Dec. 11	Giants-Packers	23-17
1960	Dec. 26		Eagles-Packers	17-13	1937	Dec. 12	Redskins-Bears	28-21
1959	Dec. 27		Colts-Giants	31-16	1936	Dec. 13	Packers-Redskins	21-6
1958	Dec. 28		Colts-Giants	23-17*	1935	Dec. 15	Lions-Giants	26-7
1957	Dec. 29		Lions-Browns	59-14	1934	Dec. 9	Giants-Bears	30-13
1956	Dec. 30		Giants-Bears	47-7	1933	Dec. 17	Bears-Giants	23-21

* Sudden death

AFC CHAMPIONSHIP GAMES

Year	Date	Winner-Loser	Score
1978	Jan. 7, 1979	Steelers-Oilers	34-5
1977	Jan. 1, 1978	Broncos-Raiders	20-17
1976	Dec. 26	Raiders-Steelers	24-7
1975	Jan. 4, 1976	Steelers-Raiders	16-10
1974	Dec. 29	Steelers-Raiders	24-13
1973	Dec. 30	Dolphins-Raiders	27-10
1972	Dec. 31	Dolphins-Steelers	21-17
1971	Jan. 2, 1972	Dolphins-Colts	21-0
1970	Jan. 3, 1971	Colts-Raiders	27-17
1969	Jan. 4, 1970	Chiefs-Raiders	17-7
1968	Dec. 29	Jets-Raiders	27-23
1967	Dec. 31	Raiders-Oilers	40-7
1966	Jan. 1, 1967	Chiefs-Bills	31-7
1965	Dec. 26	Bills-Chargers	23-0
1964	Dec. 26	Bills-Chargers	20-7
1963	Jan. 5, 1964	Chargers-Patriots	51-10
1962	Dec. 23	Chiefs-Oilers	20-17
1961	Dec. 24	Oilers-Chargers	10-3
1960	Jan. 1, 1961	Oilers-Chargers	24-16

THE SUPER BOWL GAMES

1967 January 15 at the Memorial Coliseum, Los Angeles

Green Bay Packers (NFL) .... 7 7 14 7—35
Kansas City Chiefs (AFL) .... 10 10 0 0—10

GB—McGee, 37, pass from Starr (Chandler, kick).
KC—McClinton, 7, pass from Dawson (Mercer, kick).
GB—J. Taylor, 14, run (Chandler, kick).
KC—FG, Mercer, 31.
GB—E. Pitts, 5, run (Chandler, kick).
GB—McGee, 13, pass from Starr (Chandler, kick).
GB—E. Pitts, 1 foot, run (Chandler, kick).

1968 January 14 at the Orange Bowl, Miami

Green Bay Packers (NFL) .... 3 13 10 7—33
Oakland Raiders (AFL) .... 0 7 0 7—14

GB—FG, Chandler, 39.
GB—FG, Chandler, 20.
GB—Dowler, 62, pass from Starr (Chandler, kick).
Oak—Miller, 23, pass from Lamonica (Blanda, kick).
GB—FG, Chandler, 43.
GB—Anderson, 2, run (Chandler, kick).
GB—FG, Chandler, 31.
GB—Adderley, 60, interception (Chandler, kick).
Oak—Miller, 23, pass from Lamonica (Blanda, kick).

1969 January 12 at the Orange Bowl, Miami

New York Jets (AFL) .... 0 7 6 3—16
Baltimore Colts (NFL) .... 0 0 0 7— 7

NY—Snell, 4, run (J. Turner, kick).
NY—FG, J. Turner, 32.
NY—FG, J. Turner, 30.
NY—FG, J. Turner, 9.
Balt—Hill, 1, run (Michaels, kick).

1970 January 11 at Tulane Stadium, New Orleans

Kansas City Chiefs (AFL) .... 3 13 7 0—23
Minnesota Vikings (NFL) .... 0 0 7 0— 7

KC—FG, Stenerud, 48.
KC—FG, Stenerud, 32.
KC—FG, Stenerud, 25.
KC—Garrett, 5, run (Stenerud, kick).
Minn—Osborn, 4, run (Cox, kick).
KC—Taylor, 46, pass from Dawson (Stenerud, kick).

1971 January 17 at the Orange Bowl, Miami

Baltimore Colts (AFC) .... 0 6 0 10—16
Dallas Cowboys (NFC) .... 3 10 0 0—13

Dal—FG, Clark, 14.
Dal—FG, Clark, 30.
Balt—Mackey, 75, pass from Unitas (kick blocked).
Dal—Thomas, 7, pass from Morton (Clark, kick).
Balt—Nowatzke, 2, run (O'Brien, kick).
Balt—FG, O'Brien, 32.

1972 January 16 at Tulane Stadium, New Orleans

Dallas Cowboys (NFC) .... 3 7 7 7—24
Miami Dolphins (AFC) .... 0 3 0 0— 3

Dal—FG, Clark, 9.
Dal—Alworth, 7, pass from Staubach (Clark, kick).
Mia—FG, Yepremian, 31.
Dal—D. Thomas, 3, run (Clark, kick).
Dal—Ditka, 7, pass from Staubach (Clark, kick).

1973 January 14 at Memorial Coliseum, Los Angeles

Miami Dolphins (AFC) .... 7 7 0 0—14
Washington Redskins (NFC) .... 0 0 0 7— 7

Mia—Twilley 28, pass from Griese (Yepremian kick)
Mia—Kiick, 1 run (Yepremian kick)
Wash—Bass 49, fumble recovery return (Knight kick).

1974 January 13 at Rice Stadium, Houston

Miami Dolphins (AFC) .... 14 3 7 0—24
Minnesota Vikings (NFC) .... 0 0 0 7— 7

Mia—Csonka 5 run (Yepremian kick)
Mia—Kiick 1 run (Yepremian kick)
Mia—FG Yepremian 28
Mia—Csonka 2 run (Yepremian kick)
Minn—Tarkenton 4 run (Cox kick)

1975 January 12 at Tulane Stadium, New Orleans

Pittsburgh Steelers (AFC) .... 0 2 7 7—16
Minnesota Vikings (NFC) .... 0 0 0 6— 6

Pitt.—Safety (White downed Tarkenton in end zone)
Pitt.—Harris 12 run (Gerela kick)
Minn.—T. Brown recovered blocked punt (kick failed)
Pitt.—L. Brown 4 pass from Bradshaw (Gerela kick)

1976 January 18 at the Orange Bowl, Miami

Pittsburgh Steelers (AFC) .... 7 0 0 14—21
Dallas Cowboys (NFC) .... 7 3 0 7—17

Dal—D. Pearson, 29, pass from Staubach (Fritsch kick)
Pitt—Grossman, 7, pass from Bradshaw (Gerela kick)
Dal—FG, Fritsch, 36
Pitt—Safety (Harrison blocked Hoopes attempted punt)
Pitt—FG, Gerela, 36
Pitt—FG, Gerela, 18
Pitt—Swann, 64, pass from Bradshaw (kick failed)
Dal—P. Howard, 34, pass from Staubach (Fritsch kick)

1977 January 9 at the Rose Bowl, Pasadena

Oakland Raiders (AFC) .... 0 16 3 13—32
Minnesota Vikings (NFC) .... 0 0 7 7—14

Oak—FG, Mann, 24
Oak—Casper, 1, pass from Stabler (Mann kick)
Oak—Banaszak, 1, run (kick failed)
Oak—FG, Mann, 40
Minn—S. White, 8, pass from Tarkenton (Cox kick)
Oak—Banaszak, 2, run (Mann kick)
Oak—Brown, 75, interception (kick failed)
Minn—Voigt, 13, pass from Lee (Cox kick)

1978 January 15 at the Louisiana Superdome, New Orleans

Dallas Cowboys (NFC) .... 10 3 7 7—27
Denver Broncos (AFC) .... 0 0 10 0—10

Dal—Dorsett, 3, run (Herrera kick)
Dal—FG, Herrera, 35
Dal—FG, Herrera, 43
Den—FG, Turner, 47
Dal—Johnson, 45, pass from Staubach (Herrera kick)
Den—Lytle, 1, run (Turner kick)
Dal—Richards, 29, pass from Newhouse (Herrera kick)

1979 January 21 at the Orange Bowl, Miami

Pittsburgh Steelers (AFC) .... 7 14 0 14—35
Dallas Cowboys (NFC) .... 7 7 3 14—31

Pitt—Stallworth, 28, pass from Bradshaw (Gerela kick)
Dal—Hill, 39, pass from Staubach (Septien kick)
Dal—Hegman, 37, run with recovered fumble (Septien kick)
Pitt—Stallworth, 75, pass from Bradshaw (Gerela kick)
Pitt—Bleier, 7, pass from Bradshaw (Gerela kick)
Dal—FG, Septien, 27
Pitt—Harris, 22, run (Gerela kick)
Pitt—Swann, 18, pass from Bradshaw (Gerela kick)
Dal—DuPree, 7, pass from Staubach (Septien kick)
Dal—Johnson, 4, pass from Staubach (Septien kick)

1978 NFL ALL-PRO TEAM   (Selected by The Associated Press)

Offense

Running backs	— Earl Campbell, Houston
	— Delvin Williams, Miami
Wide receivers	— Lynn Swann, Pittsburgh
	— Wesley Walker, New York Jets
Quarterback	— Terry Bradshaw, Pittsburgh
Tackles	— Leon Gray, New England
	— Dan Dierdorf, St. Louis
Guards	— John Hannah, New England
	— Bob Kuechenberg, Miami
Center	— Mike Webster, Pittsburgh
Tight end	— Dave Casper, Oakland
Place Kicker	— Pat Leahy, New York Jets
Punter	— Ray Guy, Oakland

Defense

Ends	— Jack Youngblood, Los Angeles
	— Al Baker, Detroit
Tackles	— Randy White, Dallas
	— Louie Kelcher, San Diego
Middle linebacker	— Randy Gradishar, Denver
Outside linebackers	— Jack Ham, Pittsburgh
	— Robert Brazile, Houston
Cornerbacks	— Louis Wright, Denver
	— Willie Buchanon, Green Bay
Free Safety	— Cliff Harris, Dallas
Strong Safety	— Ken Houston, Washington
Return specialist	— Rick Upchurch, Denver

1979 NATIONAL FOOTBALL LEAGUE DRAFT

First Two Choices of Each Team, Position Played and Order of Selection

Atlanta	Don Smith, de, Miami, Fla. (17)	Minnesota	Ted Brown, rb, North Carolina State (16)
	Pat Howell, g, USC (49)		Dave Huffman, c, Notre Dame (43)
Baltimore	Barry Krauss, lb, Alabama (6)	New England	Rick Sanford, db, South Carolina (25)
	Kim Anderson, db, Arizona State (69)		Bob Golic, lb, Notre Dame (52)
Buffalo	Tom Cousineau, lb, Ohio State (1)	New Orleans	Russell Erxleben, k, Texas (11)
	Jerry Butler, wr, Clemson (5)		Reggie Mathis, lb, Oklahoma (38)
Chicago	Dan Hampton, dt, Arkansas (4)	N. Y. Giants	Phil Simms, qb, Morehead State (7)
	Al Harris, de, Arizona State (9)		Ernest Gray, wr, Memphis State (36)
Cincinnati	Jack Thompson, qb, Washington State (3)	N. Y. Jets	Marty Lyons, de, Alabama (14)
	Charles Alexander, rb, Louisiana State (12)		Mark Gastineau, de, E. Central Okla. St. (41)
Cleveland	Willis Adams, wr, Houston (20)	Oakland	Willie Jones, lb, Florida State (42)
	Lawrence Johnson, db, Wisconsin (40)		Ira Matthews, rb, Wisconsin (144)
Dallas	Robert Shaw, c, Tennessee (27)	Philadelphia	Jerry Robinson, lb, UCLA (21)
	Aaron Mitchell, db, Nevada-Las Vegas (55)		Petey Perot, g, NW Louisiana (48)
Denver	Kelvin Clark, t, Nebraska (22)	Pittsburgh	Greg Hawthorne, rb, Baylor (28)
	Bruce Radford, de, Grambling (78)		Zack Valentine, lb, East Carolina (56)
Detroit	Keith Dorney, t, Penn State (10)	St. Louis	Ottis Anderson, rb, Miami, Fla. (8)
	Ken Fantetti, lb, Wyoming (37)		Theotis Brown, rb, UCLA (35)
Green Bay	Eddie Lee Ivery, rb, Georgia Tech (15)	San Diego	Kellen Winslow, te, Missouri (13)
	Steve Atkins, rb, Maryland (44)		Clifford Thrift, lb, E. Central Okla. St. (74)
Houston	Mike Stensrud, td, Iowa State (31)	San Francisco	James Owens, wr, UCLA (29)
	Jesse Baker, de, Jacksonville (Ala.) St. (50)		Joe Montana, qb, Notre Dame (83)
Kansas City	Mike Bell, de, Colorado State (2)	Seattle	Manu Tuiasosopo, dt, UCLA (18)
	Steve Fuller, qb, Clemson (23)		Joe Norman, lb, Indiana (45)
Los Angeles	George Andrews, lb, Nebraska (19)	Tampa Bay	Greg Roberts, lb, Oklahoma (33)
	Kent Hill, t, Georgia Tech (26)		Gordon Jones, wr, Pittsburgh (34)
Miami	Jon Giesler, t, Michigan (24)	Washington	Don Warren, te, San Diego State (104)
	Jeff Toews, t, Washington (53)		Rich Milot, lb, Penn State (184)

NATIONAL FOOTBALL LEAGUE STADIUMS

AMERICAN FOOTBALL CONFERENCE

Team	Stadium	Capacity
Baltimore	Memorial Stadium	60,020
Buffalo	Rich Stadium	80,020
Cincinnati	Riverfront Stadium	56,200
Cleveland	Cleveland Stadium	79,891
Denver	Mile High Stadium	76,000
Houston	Astrodome	50,000
Kansas City	Arrowhead Stadium	78,198
Miami	Orange Bowl	76,000
New England	Schaefer Stadium (Foxboro, Mass.)	61,279
N. Y. Jets	Shea Stadium	60,000
Oakland	Oakland-Alameda Co. Coliseum	54,615
Pittsburgh	Three Rivers Stadium	50,350
San Diego	San Diego Stadium	53,000
Seattle	Kingdome	64,752

NATIONAL FOOTBALL CONFERENCE

Team	Stadium	Capacity
Atlanta	Atlanta-Fulton Co. Stadium	60,498
Chicago	Soldier Field	57,359
Dallas	Texas Stadium	65,100
Detroit	Pontiac Silverdome	80,638
Green Bay	Lambeau Field	56,267
	Milwaukee Co. Stadium	55,896
Los Angeles	Memorial Coliseum	93,000
Minnesota	Metropolitan Stadium	48,446
New Orleans	Louisiana Superdome	71,300
N. Y. Giants	Giants Stadium (E. Rutherford, N.J.)	76,500
Philadelphia	Veterans Stadium	66,000
St. Louis	Busch Memorial Stadium	51,392
San Francisco	Candlestick Park	61,246
Tampa Bay	Tampa Stadium	71,600
Washington	Robert F. Kennedy Stadium	55,004

1978 CANADIAN FOOTBALL LEAGUE FINAL STANDINGS

EASTERN CONFERENCE	W	L	T	PF	PA	Pts.
Ottawa Rough Riders	11	5	0	395	261	22
Montreal Alouettes	8	7	1	331	295	17
Hamilton Tiger-Cats	5	10	1	225	403	11
Toronto Argonauts	4	12	0	234	389	8

WESTERN CONFERENCE	W	L	T	PF	PA	Pts.
Edmonton Eskimos	10	4	2	452	301	22
Calgary Stampeders	9	4	3	381	311	21
Winnipeg Blue Bombers	9	7	0	371	351	18
B. C. Lions	7	7	2	359	308	16
Saskatchewan Roughriders	4	11	1	330	459	9

Conference Semifinals: Montreal 35-Hamilton 20, Calgary 38-Winnipeg 4
Conference Finals: Montreal 21-Ottawa 16, Edmonton 26-Calgary 13
Championship (Grey Cup): Edmonton 20-Montreal 13

CANADIAN FOOTBALL LEAGUE CHAMPIONS (GREY CUP)

Year	Champion	Year	Champion	Year	Champion	Year	Champion
1951	Ottawa	1958	Winnipeg	1965	Hamilton	1972	Hamilton
1952	Toronto	1959	Winnipeg	1966	Saskatchewan	1973	Ottawa
1953	Hamilton	1960	Ottawa	1967	Hamilton	1974	Montreal
1954	Edmonton	1961	Winnipeg	1968	Ottawa	1975	Edmonton
1955	Edmonton	1962	Winnipeg	1969	Ottawa	1976	Ottawa
1956	Edmonton	1963	Hamilton	1970	Montreal	1977	Montreal
1957	Hamilton	1964	British Columbia	1971	Calgary	1978	Edmonton

COLLEGE FOOTBALL

RECORD OF THE MAJOR COLLEGE BOWL GAMES

ROSE BOWL Pasedena, California (January)

Year	Result	Year	Result	Year	Result
1902	Michigan 49, Stanford 0	1936	Stanford 7, Southern Methodist 0	1958	Ohio State 10, Oregon 7
1916	Washington State 14, Brown 0	1937	Pittsburgh 21, Washington 0	1959	Iowa 38, California 12
1917	Oregon 14, Pennsylvania 0	1938	California 13, Alabama 0	1960	Washington 44, Wisconsin 8
1918	Mare Island Marines 19, Camp Lewis 7	1939	So. California 7, Duke 3	1961	Washington 17, Minnesota 7
1919	Great Lakes 17, Mare Island Marines 0	1940	So. California 14, Tennessee 0	1962	Minnesota 21, UCLA 3
		1941	Stanford 21, Nebraska 13	1963	So. California 42, Wisconsin 37
		1942*	Oregon State 20, Duke 16		
1920	Harvard 7, Oregon 6	1943	Georgia 9, UCLA 0	1964	Illinois 17, Washington 7
1921	California 28, Ohio State 0	1944	Southern California 29, Washington 0	1965	Michigan 34, Oregon State 7
1922	Washington and Jefferson 0, California 0			1966	UCLA 14, Michigan State 12
1923	So. California 14, Penn State 3	1945	So. California 25, Tennessee 0	1967	Purdue 14, So. California 13
1924	Navy 14, Washington 14	1946	Alabama 34, So. California 14	1968	So. California 14, Indiana 3
1925	Notre Dame 27, Stanford 10	1947	Illinois 45, UCLA 14	1969	Ohio State 27, Southern California 16
1926	Alabama 20, Washington 19	1948	Michigan 49, Southern California 0		
1927	Alabama 7, Stanford 7			1970	So. California 10, Michigan 3
1928	Stanford 7, Pittsburgh 6	1949	Northwestern 20, California 14	1971	Stanford 27, Ohio State 17
1929	Georgia Tech 8, California 7	1950	Ohio State 17, California 14	1972	Stanford 13, Michigan 12
1930	So. California 47, Pittsburgh 14	1951	Michigan 14, California 6	1973	So. California 42, Ohio State 17
1931	Alabama 24, Washington State 0	1952	Illinois 40, Stanford 7	1974	Ohio State 42, So. California 21
1932	So. California 21, Tulane 12	1953	So. California 7, Wisconsin 0	1975	So. California 18, Ohio State 17
1933	So. California 35, Pittsburgh 0	1954	Michigan State 28, UCLA 20	1976	UCLA 23, Ohio State 10
1934	Columbia 7, Stanford 0	1955	Ohio State 20, So. California 7	1977	So. California 14, Michigan 6
1935	Alabama 29, Stanford 13	1956	Michigan State 17, UCLA 14	1978	Washington 27, Michigan 20
		1957	Iowa 35, Oregon State 19	1979	So. California 17, Michigan 10

* Played at Durham, North Carolina.

ORANGE BOWL Miami, Florida (January)

Year	Result	Year	Result	Year	Result
1933	Miami (Fla.) 7, Manhattan 0	1948	Georgia Tech 20, Kansas 14	1964	Nebraska 13, Auburn 7
1934	Duquesne 33, Miami (Fla.) 7	1949	Texas 41, Georgia 28	1965	Texas 21, Alabama 17
1935	Bucknell 26, Miami (Fla.) 0	1950	Santa Clara 21, Kentucky 13	1966	Alabama 39, Nebraska 28
1936	Catholic Univ. 20, Mississippi 19	1951	Clemson 15, Miami (Fla.) 14	1967	Florida 27, Georgia Tech 12
1937	Duquesne 13, Miss. State 12	1952	Georgia Tech 17, Baylor 14	1968	Oklahoma 26, Tennessee 24
1938	Auburn 6, Michigan State 0	1953	Alabama 61, Syracuse 6	1969	Penn State 15, Kansas 14
1939	Tennessee 17, Oklahoma 0	1954	Oklahoma 7, Maryland 0	1970	Penn State 10, Missouri 3
1940	Georgia Tech 21, Missouri 7	1955	Duke 34, Nebraska 7	1971	Nebraska 17, Louisiana State 12
1941	Miss. State 14, Georgetown 7	1956	Oklahoma 20, Maryland 6	1972	Nebraska 38, Alabama 6
1942	Georgia 40, Texas Christian 26	1957	Colorado 27, Clemson 21	1973	Nebraska 40, Notre Dame 6
1943	Alabama 37, Boston College 21	1958	Oklahoma 48, Duke 21	1974	Penn State 16, Louisiana State 9
1944	LSU 19, Texas A&M 14	1959	Oklahoma 21, Syracuse 6	1975	Notre Dame 13, Alabama 11
1945	Tulsa 26, Georgia Tech 12	1960	Georgia 14, Missouri 0	1976	Oklahoma 14, Michigan 6
1946	Miami (Fla.) 13, Holy Cross 6	1961	Missouri 21, Navy 14	1977	Ohio State 27, Colorado 10
1947	Rice 8, Tennessee 0	1962	Louisiana State 25, Colorado 7	1978	Arkansas 31, Oklahoma 6
		1963	Alabama 17, Oklahoma 0	1979	Oklahoma 31, Nebraska 24

SUGAR BOWL

New Orleans, Louisiana (January)

Year	Result	Year	Result	Year	Result
		1946	Oklahoma A & M 33, St. Mary's (Calif.) 13	1962	Alabama 10, Arkansas 3
1935	Tulane 20, Temple 14	1947	Georgia 20, North Carolina 10	1963	Mississippi 17, Arkansas 13
1936	Texas Christian 3, Louisiana State 2	1948	Texas 27, Alabama 7	1964	Alabama 12, Mississippi 7
1937	Santa Clara 21, Louisiana State 14	1949	Oklahoma 14, North Carolina 6	1965	Louisiana State 13, Syracuse 10
		1950	Oklahoma 35, Louisiana State 0	1966	Missouri 20, Florida 18
1938	Santa Clara 6, Louisiana State 0	1951	Kentucky 13, Oklahoma 7	1967	Alabama 34, Nebraska 7
1939	Texas Christian 15, Carnegie Tech 7	1952	Maryland 28, Tennessee 13	1968	Louisiana State 20, Wyoming 13
1940	Texas A&M 14, Tulane 13	1953	Georgia Tech 24, Mississippi 7	1969	Arkansas 16, Georgia 2
1941	Boston College 19, Tennessee 13	1954	Georgia Tech 42, West Va. 19	1970	Mississippi 27, Arkansas 22
1942	Fordham 2, Missouri 0	1955	Navy 21, Mississippi 0	1971	Tennessee 34, Air Force 13
1943	Tennessee 14, Tulsa 7	1956	Georgia Tech 7, Pittsburgh 0	1972	Oklahoma 40, Auburn 22
1944	Georgia Tech 20, Tulsa 18	1957	Baylor 13, Tennessee 7	1972 (Dec.) Oklahoma 14, Penn State 0	
1945	Duke 29, Alabama 26	1958	Mississippi 39, Texas 7	1973 (Dec.) Notre Dame 24, Alabama 23	
		1959	Louisiana State 7, Clemson 0	1974 (Dec.) Nebraska 13, Florida 10	
		1960	Mississippi 21, Louisiana State 0	1975 (Dec.) Alabama 13, Penn State 6	
		1961	Mississippi 14, Rice 6	1977	Pittsburgh 27, Georgia 3
				1978	Alabama 35, Ohio State 6
				1979	Alabama 14, Penn State 7

COTTON BOWL

Dallas, Texas (January)

Year	Result	Year	Result	Year	Result
1937	Texas Christian 16, Marquette 6	1950	Rice 27, North Carolina 13	1965	Arkansas 10, Nebraska 7
1938	Rice 28, Colorado 14	1951	Tennessee 20, Texas 14	1966	Louisiana State 14, Arkansas 7
1939	St. Mary's (Calif.) 20, Texas Tech 13	1952	Kentucky 20, Texas Christian 7	1966 (Dec.) Georgia 24, SMU 9	
1940	Clemson 6, Boston College 3	1953	Texas 16, Tennessee 0	1968	Texas A&M 20, Alabama 16
1941	Texas A&M 13, Fordham 12	1954	Rice 28, Alabama 6	1969	Texas 36, Tennessee 13
1942	Alabama 29, Texas A&M 21	1955	Georgia Tech 14, Arkansas 6	1970	Texas 21, Notre Dame 17
1943	Texas 14, Georgia Tech 7	1956	Mississippi 14, TCU 13	1971	Notre Dame 24, Texas 11
1944	Randolph Field 7, Texas 7	1957	Texas Christian 28, Syracuse 27	1972	Penn State 30, Texas 6
1945	Oklahoma A & M 34, Texas Christian 0	1958	Navy 20, Rice 7	1973	Texas 17, Alabama 13
		1959	Air Force 0, Texas Christian 0	1974	Nebraska 19, Texas 3
1946	Texas 40, Missouri 27	1960	Syracuse 23, Texas 14	1975	Penn State 41, Baylor 20
1947	Louisiana State 0, Arkansas 0	1961	Duke 7, Arkansas 6	1976	Arkansas 31, Georgia 10
1948	So. Methodist 13, Penn St. 13	1962	Texas 12, Mississippi 7	1977	Houston 30, Maryland 21
1949	So. Methodist 21, Oregon 13	1963	Louisiana State 13, Texas 0	1978	Notre Dame 38, Texas 10
		1964	Texas 28, Navy 6	1979	Notre Dame 35, Houston 34

SUN BOWL
El Paso, Texas (J = January, D = December)

Year	Result	Year	Result	Year	Result
1936J	H.-Simmons 14, N.M. State 14	1950J	Tex. Western 33, Georgetown 20	1964D	Georgia 7, Texas Tech 0
1937J	H.-Simmons 34, Tex. Mines 6	1951J	W. Tex. St. 14, Cincinnati 13	1965D	Texas Western 13, TCU 12
1938J	West Virginia 7, Texas Tech 6	1952J	Texas Tech 25, Col. Pacific 14	1966D	Wyoming 28, Florida State 20
1939J	Utah 26, New Mexico 0	1953J	Col. Pacific 26, Miss. Southern 7	1967D	Texas-El Paso 14, Miss. 7
1940J	Catholic U. 0, Arizona St. 0	1954J	Tex. Western 37, Miss. So. 14	1968D	Auburn 34, Arizona 10
1941J	W. Reserve 26, Arizona St. 13	1955J	Tex. Western 47, Florida St. 20	1969D	Nebraska 45, Georgia 6
1942J	Tulsa 6, Texas Tech 0	1956J	Wyoming 21, Texas Tech 14	1970D	Georgia Tech 17, Texas Tech 9
1943J	2nd Air Force 13, H.-Simmons 7	1957J	George Wash. 13, Texas W. 0	1971D	LSU 33, Iowa State 15
1944J	Southwestern 7, New Mexico 0	1958J	Louisville 34, Drake 20	1972D	N. Carolina 32, Texas Tech 28
1945J	Southwestern 35, U. Mexico 0	1958D	Wyoming 14, H.-Simmons 6	1973D	Missouri 34, Auburn 17
1946J	New Mexico 34, Denver 24	1959D	N.M. State 28, N. Tex. State 8	1974D	Miss. State 26, N. Carolina 24
1947J	Cincinnati 18, Virginia Tech 6	1960D	N.M. State 20, Utah State 13	1975D	Pittsburgh 33, Kansas 19
1948J	Miami (Ohio) 13, Texas Tech 12	1961D	Villanova 17, Wichita 9	1977J	Texas A & M 37, Florida 14
1949J	W. Virginia 21, Texas Mines 12	1962D	W. Texas St. 15, Ohio U. 14	1977D	Stanford 24, LSU 14
		1963D	Oregon 21, SMU 14	1978D	Texas 42, Maryland 0

GATOR BOWL
Jacksonville, Florida (J = January, D = December)

Year	Result	Year	Result	Year	Result
1946J	Wake Forest 26, S. Carolina 14	1956D	Georgia Tech 21, Pittsburgh 14	1967D	Penn State 17, Florida St. 17
1947J	Oklahoma 34, N.C. State 13	1957J	Tennessee 3, Texas A & M 0	1968D	Missouri 35, Alabama 10
1948J	Maryland 20, Georgia 20	1958D	Mississippi 7, Florida 3	1969D	Florida 14, Tennessee 13
1949J	Clemson 24, Missouri 23	1960J	Arkansas 14, Georgia Tech 7	1971J	Auburn 35, Mississippi 28
1950J	Maryland 20, Missouri 7	1960D	Florida 13, Baylor 12	1971D	Georgia 7, N. Carolina 3
1951J	Wyoming 20, Wash. & Lee 7	1961D	Penn State 30, Georgia Tech 15	1972D	Auburn 24, Colorado 3
1952J	Miami (Fla.) 14, Clemson 0	1962D	Florida 17, Penn State 7	1973D	Texas Tech 28, Tennessee 19
1953J	Florida 14, Tulsa 13	1963D	N. Carolina 35, Air Force 0	1974D	Auburn 27, Texas 3
1954J	Texas Tech 35, Auburn 13	1965J	Florida St. 36, Oklahoma 19	1975D	Maryland 13, Florida 0
1954D	Auburn 33, Baylor 13	1965D	Georgia Tech 31, Texas Tech 21	1976D	Notre Dame 20, Penn State 9
1955D	Vanderbilt 25, Auburn 13	1966D	Tennessee 18, Syracuse 12	1977D	Pittsburgh 34, Clemson 3
				1978D	Clemson 17, Ohio State 15

TANGERINE BOWL
Orlando, Florida (J = January, D = December)

Year	Result	Year	Result	Year	Result
1947J	Catawba 31, Maryville 6	1958J	E. Texas St. 10, So. Miss. 9	1968D	Richmond 49, Ohio U. 42
1948J	Catawba 7, Marshall 0	1958D	E. Texas St. 26, Missouri Va. 7	1969D	Toledo 56, Davidson 33
1949J	Murray St. 21, Sul Ross St. 7	1960J	Middle Tenn. 21, Presbyterian 12	1970D	Toledo 40, William & Mary 12
1950J	St. Vincent 7, Emory & Henry 6	1960D	Citadel 27, Tennessee Tech 0	1971D	Toledo 28, Richmond 3
1951J	Mor. Harvey 35, Emory & Henry 14	1961D	Lamar 21, Middle Tennessee 14	1972D	Tampa 21, Kent State 18
1952J	Stetson 35, Arkansas St. 20	1962D	Houston 49, Miami (Ohio) 21	1973D	Miami (Ohio) 16, Florida 7
1953J	E. Texas St. 33, Tenn. Tech 0	1963D	W. Kentucky 27, Coast Guard 0	1974D	Miami (Ohio) 21, Georgia 10
1954J	E. Texas St. 7, Arkansas St. 7	1964D	E. Carolina 14, Massachusetts 13	1975D	Miami (Ohio) 20, S. Carolina 7
1955J	Nebraska (Omaha) 7, E. Ken. 6	1965D	E. Carolina 31, Maine 0	1976D	Okla. State 49, Brigham Young 21
1956J	Juniata 6, Missouri Valley 6	1966D	Morgan St. 14, West Chester 6	1977D	Florida St. 40, Texas Tech 17
1957J	W. Texas St. 20, So. Miss. 13	1967D	Tenn. (Martin) 25, West Chester 8	1978D	N. Carolina St. 30, Pittsburgh 17

BLUEBONNET BOWL
Houston, Texas (December)

Year	Result	Year	Result	Year	Result
1959	Clemson 23, TCU 7	1965	Tennessee 27, Tulsa 6	1972	Tennessee 24, LSU 17
1960	Texas 3, Alabama 3	1966	Texas 19, Mississippi 0	1973	Houston 47, Tulane 7
1961	Kansas 33, Rice 0	1967	Colorado 31, Miami (Fla.) 21	1974	N.C. State 31, Houston 31
1962	Missouri 14, Georgia Tech 10	1968	SMU 28, Oklahoma 27	1975	Texas 38, Colorado 21
1963	Baylor 14, LSU 7	1969	Houston 36, Auburn 7	1976	Nebraska 27, Texas Tech 24
1964	Tulsa 14, Mississippi 7	1970	Alabama 24, Oklahoma 24	1977	USC 47, Texas A & M 28
		1971	Colorado 29, Houston 17	1978	Stanford 25, Georgia 22

LIBERTY BOWL
Memphis, Tennessee* (December)

Year	Result	Year	Result	Year	Result
1959	Penn State 7, Alabama 0	1965	Mississippi 13, Auburn 7	1972	Georgia Tech 31, Iowa State 30
1960	Penn State 41, Oregon 12	1966	Miami (Fla.) 14, Virginia Tech 7	1973	N.C. State 31, Kansas 18
1961	Syracuse 15, Miami (Fla.) 14	1967	N.C. State 14, Georgia 7	1974	Tennessee 7, Maryland 3
1962	Oregon St. 6, Villanova 0	1968	Mississippi 34, Virginia Tech 17	1975	USC 20, Texas A & M 0
1963	Mississippi St. 16, N.C. State 12	1969	Colorado 47, Alabama 33	1976	Alabama 36, UCLA 6
1964	Utah 32, West Virginia 6	1970	Tulane 17, Colorado 3	1977	Nebraska 21, N. Carolina 17
		1971	Tennessee 14, Arkansas 13	1978	Missouri 20, LSU 15

*Philadelphia 1960-1964, Atlantic City 1965

PEACH BOWL
Atlanta, Georgia (December)

Year	Result	Year	Result	Year	Result
1968	LSU 31, Florida State 27	1971	Mississippi 41, Georgia Tech 18	1975	W. Virginia 13, N.C. State 10
1969	W. Virginia 14, S. Carolina 3	1972	N.C. State 49, W. Virginia 13	1976	Kentucky 21, N. Carolina 0
1970	Arizona St. 48, N. Carolina 26	1973	Georgia 17, Maryland 16	1977	N.C. State 24, Iowa State 14
		1974	Vanderbilt 6, Texas Tech 6	1978	Purdue 41, Georgia Tech 21

FIESTA BOWL
Tempe, Arizona (December)

Year	Result	Year	Result	Year	Result
1971	Arizona St. 45, Florida St. 38	1973	Arizona St. 28, Pittsburgh 7	1976	Oklahoma 41, Wyoming 7
1972	Arizona St. 49, Missouri 35	1974	Okla. St. 16, Brigham Young 6	1977	Penn State 42, Arizona St. 30
		1975	Arizona St. 17, Nebraska 14	1978	Arkansas 10, UCLA 10

NATIONAL COLLEGE FOOTBALL CHAMPIONS

The college football team selected each year by The Associated Press poll of sportswriters and the United Press International poll of football coaches is unofficially recognized as national champion. Where the polls disagree, both teams are given.

Year	Champion	Year	Champion	Year	Champion	Year	Champion
1924	Notre Dame	1938	Texas Christian	1952	Michigan State	1965	Alabama
1925	Dartmouth	1939	Texas A&M	1953	Maryland	1966	Notre Dame
1926	Stanford	1940	Minnesota	1954	Ohio State	1967	Southern California
1927	Illinois	1941	Minnesota		UCLA	1968	Ohio State
1928	Southern California	1942	Ohio State	1955	Oklahoma	1969	Texas
1929	Notre Dame	1943	Notre Dame	1956	Oklahoma	1970	Texas—Nebraska
1930	Notre Dame	1944	Army	1957	Auburn-Ohio State	1971	Nebraska
1931	Southern California	1945	Army	1958	Louisiana State	1972	Southern California
1932	Michigan	1946	Notre Dame	1959	Syracuse	1973	Notre Dame
1933	Michigan	1947	Notre Dame	1960	Minnesota	1974	Oklahoma—USC
1934	Minnesota	1948	Michigan	1961	Alabama	1975	Oklahoma
1935	Southern Methodist	1949	Notre Dame	1962	Southern California	1976	Pittsburgh
1936	Minnesota	1950	Oklahoma	1963	Texas	1977	Notre Dame
1937	Pittsburgh	1951	Tennessee	1964	Alabama	1978	Alabama-USC

COLLEGE FOOTBALL CONFERENCE CHAMPIONS

ATLANTIC COAST		BIG EIGHT		BIG TEN		IVY LEAGUE	
Year	Champion	Year	Champion	Year	Champion	Year	Champion
1962	Duke	1962	Oklahoma	1962	Wisconsin	1962	Dartmouth
1963	No. Carolina State	1963	Nebraska	1963	Illinois	1963	Dartmouth-Princeton
1964	No. Carolina State	1964	Nebraska	1964	Michigan	1964	Princeton
1965	Duke	1965	Nebraska	1965	Michigan State	1965	Dartmouth
1966	Clemson	1966	Nebraska	1966	Michigan State	1966	Dartmouth-Harvard-Princeton
1967	Clemson	1967	Oklahoma	1967	Indiana-Purdue		
1968	No. Carolina State	1968	Kansas-Oklahoma		Minnesota	1967	Yale
1969	South Carolina	1969	Missouri	1968	Ohio State	1968	Yale-Harvard
1970	Wake Forest		Nebraska	1969	Ohio State-Michigan	1969	Princeton-Yale
1971	North Carolina	1970	Nebraska	1970	Ohio State		Dartmouth
1972	North Carolina	1971	Nebraska	1971	Michigan	1970	Dartmouth
1973	No. Carolina State	1972	Oklahoma	1972	Ohio State-Michigan	1971	Cornell-Dartmouth
1974	Maryland	1973	Oklahoma	1973	Michigan-Ohio State	1972	Dartmouth
1975	Maryland	1974	Oklahoma	1974	Michigan-Ohio State	1973	Dartmouth
1976	Maryland	1975	Nebraska	1975	Ohio State	1974	Yale-Harvard
1977	North Carolina		Oklahoma	1976	Michigan-Ohio State	1975	Harvard
1978	Clemson	1976	Colorado	1977	Michigan-Ohio State	1976	Yale-Brown
			Oklahoma	1978	Michigan St.-Michigan	1977	Yale
			Oklahoma State			1978	Dartmouth
		1977	Oklahoma				
		1978	Nebraska-Oklahoma				

MISSOURI VALLEY		PACIFIC TEN		SOUTHEASTERN		SOUTHERN	
Year	Champion	Year	Champion	Year	Champion	Year	Champion
1962	Tulsa	1962	Southern California	1962	Mississippi	1962	VMI
1963	Cincinnati-Wichita	1963	Washington	1963	Mississippi	1963	Virginia Tech
1964	Cincinnati	1964	Oregon State	1964	Alabama	1964	West Virginia
1965	Tulsa		Southern California	1965	Alabama	1965	West Virginia
1966	North Texas-Tulsa	1965	UCLA	1966	Georgia	1966	William & Mary
1967	North Texas	1966	Southern California		Alabama		East Carolina
1968	Memphis State	1967	Southern California	1967	Tennessee	1967	West Virginia
1969	Memphis State	1968	Southern California	1968	Georgia	1968	Richmond
1970	Louisville	1969	Southern California	1969	Tennessee	1969	Richmond
1971	North Texas	1970	Stanford	1970	Louisiana State		Davidson
1972	Louisville-Drake-	1971	Stanford	1971	Alabama	1970	William & Mary
	West Texas	1972	Southern California	1972	Alabama	1971	Richmond
1973	North Texas-Tulsa	1973	Southern California	1973	Alabama	1972	East Carolina
1974	Tulsa	1974	Southern California	1974	Alabama	1973	East Carolina
1975	Tulsa	1975	UCLA-California	1975	Alabama	1974	VMI
1976	Tulsa-N. Mexico State	1976	Southern California	1976	Georgia	1975	Richmond
1977	West Texas State	1977	Washington	1977	Alabama	1976	East Carolina
1978	New Mexico State	1978	Southern California	1978	Alabama	1977	VMI-Tenn.-Chattanooga
						1978	Tenn.-Chattanoga Furman

MID-AMERICAN		SOUTHWEST		WESTERN		PACIFIC COAST	
Year	Champion	Year	Champion	Year	Champion	Year	Champion
1962	Bowling Green	1962	Texas	1963	New Mexico	1969	San Diego State
1963	Ohio University	1963	Texas	1964	New Mexico-Utah	1970	Long Beach State
1964	Bowling Green	1964	Arkansas		Arizona	1971	Long Beach State
1965	Miami (Ohio)	1965	Arkansas	1965	Brigham Young	1972	San Diego State
	Bowling Green	1966	Southern Methodist	1966	Wyoming	1973	San Diego State
1966	Miami (Ohio)	1967	Texas A&M	1967	Wyoming	1974	San Diego State
	Western Michigan	1968	Texas-Arkansas	1968	Wyoming	1975	San Jose State
1967	Toledo-Ohio U.	1969	Texas	1969	Arizona State	1976	San Jose State
1968	Ohio University	1970	Texas	1970	Arizona State	1977	Fresno State
1969	Toledo	1971	Texas	1971	Arizona State	1978	Utah State
1970	Toledo	1972	Texas	1972	Arizona State		San Jose State
1971	Toledo	1973	Texas	1973	Arizona-Ariz. State		
1972	Kent State	1974	Baylor	1974	Brigham Young		
1973	Miami (Ohio)	1975	Texas-Texas A&M-Arkansas	1975	Arizona State		
1974	Miami (Ohio)			1976	Wyoming		
1975	Miami (Ohio)	1976	Houston-Texas Tech		Brigham Young		
1976	Ball State	1977	Texas	1977	Arizona State		
1977	Miami (Ohio)	1978	Houston		Brigham Young		
1978	Ball State			1978	Brigham Young		

1978 REGULAR SEASON RECORDS OF MAJOR COLLEGE FOOTBALL TEAMS

Team	W	L	T	Team	W	L	T	Team	W	L	T
Air Force	3	8	0	Kansas	1	10	0	Richmond	3	8	0
Alabama	10	1	0	Kansas State	4	7	0	Rutgers	9	2	0
Arizona	5	6	0	Kentucky	4	6	1	San Diego State	4	6	0
Arizona State	8	3	0	Louisiana State	8	3	0	San Jose State	6	5	0
Arkansas	9	2	0	Louisville	7	3	0	South Carolina	5	5	1
Army	4	6	1	Maryland	9	2	0	Southern California	10	1	0
Auburn	6	4	1	Memphis State	4	7	0	Southern Methodist	4	6	1
Baylor	3	8	0	Miami (Fla.)	6	5	0	Southern Mississippi	7	4	0
Boston College	0	10	0	Michigan	10	1	0	Stanford	7	4	0
Brigham Young	8	3	0	Michigan State	8	3	0	Syracuse	3	8	0
Brown	6	3	0	Minnesota	5	6	0	Temple	6	3	1
California	6	5	0	Mississippi	5	6	0	Tennessee	5	5	1
Cincinnati	5	6	0	Mississippi State	6	5	0	Texas	8	3	0
Citadel	5	6	0	Missouri	7	4	0	Texas A & M	7	4	0
Clemson	10	1	0	Navy	8	3	0	Texas Christian	2	9	0
Colgate	3	8	0	Nebraska	9	2	0	Texas-El Paso	1	11	0
Colorado	6	5	0	Nevada-Las Vegas	7	4	0	Texas Tech	7	4	0
Colorado State	5	6	0	New Mexico	7	5	0	Tulane	4	7	0
Columbia	3	5	1	New Mexico State	6	5	0	Tulsa	9	2	0
Cornell	5	3	1	North Carolina	5	6	0	U.C.L.A.	8	3	0
Dartmouth	6	3	0	North Carolina State	8	3	0	Utah	7	3	0
Duke	4	7	0	North Texas State	9	2	0	Utah State	7	4	0
East Carolina	8	3	0	Northwestern	0	10	1	Vanderbilt	2	9	0
Florida	4	7	0	Notre Dame	8	3	0	Villanova	5	6	0
Florida State	8	3	0	Ohio State	7	3	1	Virginia	2	9	0
Furman	8	3	0	Oklahoma	10	1	0	Virginia Military	3	8	0
Georgia	9	1	1	Oklahoma State	3	8	0	Virginia Tech	4	7	0
Georgia Tech	7	3	0	Oregon	2	9	0	Wake Forest	1	10	0
Harvard	4	4	1	Oregon State	3	7	1	Washington	7	4	0
Hawaii	6	5	0	Pacific	4	8	0	Washington State	3	7	1
Holy Cross	7	4	0	Pennsylvania	2	6	1	West Virginia	2	9	0
Houston	9	2	0	Pennsylvania State	11	0	0	Wichita State	4	7	0
Illinois	1	8	2	Pittsburgh	8	3	0	William & Mary	5	5	1
Indiana	4	7	0	Princeton	2	5	2	Wisconsin	5	4	2
Iowa	2	9	0	Purdue	8	2	1	Wyoming	5	6	0
Iowa State	8	3	0	Rice	2	9	0	Yale	5	2	2

1978 FINAL COLLEGE FOOTBALL RANKINGS

ASSOCIATED PRESS

1. Alabama	11. Arkansas
2. Southern California	12. Michigan State
3. Oklahoma	13. Purdue
4. Penn State	14. U.C.L.A.
5. Michigan	15. Missouri
6. Clemson	16. Georgia
7. Notre Dame	17. Stanford
8. Nebraska	18. N. Carolina State
9. Texas	19. Texas A & M
10. Houston	20. Maryland

UNITED PRESS INTERNATIONAL

1. Southern California	11. Houston
2. Alabama	12. U.C.L.A.
3. Oklahoma	13. Purdue
4. Penn State	14. Missouri
5. Michigan	15. Georgia
6. Clemson	16. Stanford
Notre Dame	17. Navy
8. Nebraska	18. Texas A & M
9. Texas	19. Arizona State
10. Arkansas	N. Carolina State

MAJOR COLLEGE FOOTBALL STADIUMS (40,000 or more seats)

Team (Stadium) Location	Capacity	Team (Stadium) Location	Capacity
Air Force (Falcon) A. F. Academy, Colo.	46,600	Northwestern (Dyche) Evanston, Ill.	48,500
Alabama (Denny) University, Ala.	59,000	Notre Dame (Notre Dame) South Bend, Ind.	59,000
Arizona (Arizona) Tucson, Ariz.	57,000	Ohio State (Ohio) Columbus, Ohio	83,100
Arizona State (Sun Devil) Tempe, Ariz.	70,000	Oklahoma (Owen Field) Norman, Okla.	71,000
Arkansas (Razorback) Fayetteville, Ark.	43,500	Oklahoma State (Lewis) Stillwater, Okla.	50,500
Army (Michie) West Point, N.Y.	41,600	Oregon (Autzen) Eugene, Ore.	42,000
Auburn (Jordan Hare) Auburn, Ala.	61,200	Oregon State (Parker) Corvallis, Ore.	41,000
Baylor (Baylor) Waco, Tex.	48,000	Pennsylvania (Franklin Field) Philadelphia, Pa.	60,500
California (Memorial) Berkeley, Cal.	76,700	Pennsylvania State (Beaver) University Park, Pa.	76,000
Clemson (Memorial) Clemson, S.C.	53,000	Pittsburgh (Pitt) Pittsburgh, Pa.	56,500
Colorado (Folsom) Boulder, Colo.	52,000	Princeton (Palmer) Princeton, N.J.	45,700
Duke (Wallace Wade) Durham, N.C.	44,000	Purdue (Ross-Ade) West Lafayette, Ind.	69,200
Florida (Florida Field) Gainesville, Fla.	62,000	Rice (Rice) Houston, Tex.	70,000
Florida State (Campbell) Tallahassee, Fla.	40,500	San Diego State (San Diego) San Diego, Cal.	53,000
Georgia (Sanford) Athens, Ga.	59,200	South Carolina (Williams-Brice) Columbia, S.C.	54,400
Georgia Tech (Grant Field) Atlanta, Ga.	58,100	Stanford (Stanford) Stanford, Cal.	86,300
Hawaii (Aloha) Honolulu, Hawaii	50,000	Tennessee (Neyland) Knoxville, Tenn.	80,200
Illinois (Memorial) Champaign, Ill.	71,200	Texas (Memorial) Austin, Tex.	80,000
Indiana (Memorial) Bloomington, Ind.	52,300	Texas A & M (Kyle Field) College Station, Tex.	54,000
Iowa (Kinnick) Iowa City, Iowa	60,000	Texas Christian (TCU-Amon Carter) Fort Worth, Tex.	46,000
Iowa State (Cyclone) Ames, Iowa	50,000	Texas Tech (Jones) Lubbock, Tex.	47,000
Jackson State (Miss. Memorial) Jackson, Miss.	46,000	Tulsa (Skelly) Tulsa, Okla.	40,200
Kansas (Memorial) Lawrence, Kans.	51,500	Va. Polytechnic Inst. (Lane) Blacksburg, Va.	40,000
Kansas State (KSU) Manhattan, Kans.	42,000	Washington (Husky) Seattle, Wash.	58,900
Kentucky (Commonwealth) Lexington, Ky.	58,000	Wisconsin (Camp Randall) Madison, Wis.	77,200
Louisiana State (Tiger) Baton Rouge, La.	75,000	Yale (Yale Bowl) New Haven, Conn.	70,800
Maryland (Byrd) College Park, Md.	45,000		
Memphis State (Liberty Bowl) Memphis, Tenn.	50,100	**OTHER STADIUMS USED BY MAJOR COLLEGE TEAMS**	
Michigan (Michigan) Ann Arbor, Mich.	101,700	Astrodome, Houston (Houston, Texas Southern)	50,000
Michigan State (Spartan) East Lansing, Mich.	76,000	Cotton Bowl, Dallas	72,000
Minnesota (Memorial) Minneapolis, Minn.	56,700	Los Angeles Memorial Coliseum (USC,UCLA)	93,000
Missouri (Faurot Field) Columbia, Mo.	60,000	Louisiana Superdome, New Orleans (Tulane)	71,300
Nebraska (Memorial) Lincoln, Neb.	76,400	Orange Bowl, Miami (Miami, Fla.)	76,000
North Carolina (Kenan) Chapel Hill, N.C.	47,000	Texas Stadium, Irving (Southern Methodist)	65,100
North Carolina State (Carter) Raleigh, N.C.	44,000	Veterans Stadium, Philadelphia (Temple)	66,000

THE HEISMAN MEMORIAL TROPHY: Awarded annually to the nation's outstanding college football player.

Year	Player and College	Year	Player and College	Year	Player and College
1937	Clint Frank, Yale	1951	Dick Kazmaier, Princeton	1965	Mike Garrett, Southern California
1938	Davey O'Brien, Texas Christian	1952	Billy Vessels, Oklahoma	1966	Steve Spurrier, Florida
1939	Nile Kinnick, Iowa	1953	John Lattner, Notre Dame	1967	Gary Beban, UCLA
1940	Tom Harmon, Michigan	1954	Alan Ameche, Wisconsin	1968	O. J. Simpson, USC
1941	Bruce Smith, Minnesota	1955	Howard Cassady, Ohio State	1969	Steve Owens, Oklahoma
1942	Frank Sinkwich, Georgia	1956	Paul Hornung, Notre Dame	1970	Jim Plunkett, Stanford
1943	Angelo Bertelli, Notre Dame	1957	John Crow, Texas A&M	1971	Pat Sullivan, Auburn
1944	Les Horvath, Ohio State	1958	Pete Dawkins, Army	1972	Johnny Rogers, Nebraska
1945	Felix Blanchard, Army	1959	Billy Cannon, Louisiana State	1973	John Capelletti, Penn State
1946	Glenn Davis, Army	1960	Joe Bellino, Navy	1974	Archie Griffin, Ohio State
1947	John Lujack, Notre Dame	1961	Ernie Davis, Syracuse	1975	Archie Griffin, Ohio State
1948	Doak Walker, Southern Methodist	1962	Terry Baker, Oregon State	1976	Tony Dorsett, Pittsburgh
1949	Leon Hart, Notre Dame	1963	Roger Staubach, Navy	1977	Earl Campbell, Texas
1950	Vic Janowicz, Ohio State	1964	John Huarte, Notre Dame	1978	Billy Sims, Oklahoma

COLLEGE FOOTBALL COACH OF THE YEAR (American Football Coaches Ass'n)

Year	Coach and College	Year	Coach and College	Year	Coach and College
1938	Bill Kern, Carnegie Tech	1952	Biggie Munn, Michigan State	1966	Tom Cahill, Army
1939	Eddie Anderson, Iowa	1953	Jim Tatum, Maryland	1967	John Pont, Indiana
1940	Clark Shaughnessy, Stanford	1954	Red Sanders, UCLA	1968	Joe Paterno, Penn State
1941	Frank Leahy, Notre Dame	1955	Duffy Daugherty, Michigan State	1969	Bo Schembechler, Michigan
1942	Bill Alexander, Georgia Tech	1956	Bowden Wyatt, Tennessee	1970	Darrell Royal, Texas
1943	Amos Alonzo Stagg, Pacific	1957	Woody Hayes, Ohio State		Charlie McLendon, La. State
1944	Carroll Widdoes, Ohio State	1958	Paul Dietzel, Louisiana State	1971	Paul Bryant, Alabama
1945	Bo McMillin, Indiana	1959	Ben Schwartzwalder, Syracuse	1972	John McKay, Southern California
1946	Earl H. Blaik, Army	1960	Murray Warmath, Minnesota	1973	Paul Bryant, Alabama
1947	Fritz Crisler, Michigan	1961	Paul Bryant, Alabama	1974	Grant Teaff, Baylor
1948	Bennie Oosterbaan, Michigan	1962	John McKay, Southern California	1975	Frank Kush, Arizona State
1949	Bud Wilkinson, Oklahoma	1963	Darrell Royal, Texas	1976	Johnny Majors, Pittsburgh
1950	Charlie Caldwell, Princeton	1964	Ara Parseghian, Notre Dame	1977	Don James, Washington
1951	Chuck Taylor, Stanford	1965	Tommy Prothro, UCLA	1978	Joe Paterno, Penn State

OUTLAND AWARDS: Awarded annually to the nation's leading college football lineman.

Year	Player, College, Pos.	Year	Player, College, Pos.	Year	Player, College, Pos.
1946	George Connor, Notre Dame, T	1957	Alex Karras, Iowa, T	1968	Bill Stanfill, Georgia, T
1947	Joe Steffy, Army, G	1958	Zeke Smith, Auburn, G	1969	Mike Reid, Penn State, DT
1948	Bill Fischer, Notre Dame, G	1959	Mike McGee, Duke, T	1970	Jim Stillwagon, Ohio State, LB
1949	Ed Bagdon, Michigan St., G	1960	Tom Brown, Minnesota, G	1971	Larry Jacobson, Nebraska, DT
1950	Bob Gain, Kentucky, T	1961	Merlin Olsen, Utah State, T	1972	Rich Glover, Nebraska, MG
1951	Jim Weatherall, Oklahoma, T	1962	Bobby Bell, Minnesota, T	1973	John Hicks, Ohio State, T
1952	Dick Modzelewski, Maryland, T	1963	Scott Appleton, Texas, T	1974	Randy White, Maryland, DT
1953	J. D. Roberts, Oklahoma, G.	1964	Steve DeLong, Tennessee, T	1975	Leroy Selmon, Oklahoma, DT
1954	Bill Brooks, Arkansas, G	1965	Tommy Nobis, Texas, G	1976	Ross Browner, Notre Dame, DT
1955	Calvin Jones, Iowa, G	1966	Lloyd Phillips, Arkansas, T	1977	Brad Shearer, Texas, DT
1956	Jim Parker, Ohio State, G	1967	Ron Yary, Southern Cal, T	1978	Greg Roberts, Oklahoma, G

1978 COLLEGE ALL-AMERICA SELECTIONS

OFFENSIVE TEAM

Receivers	Emanuel Tolbert, SMU (AP,FWAA,WC)
	Kellen Winslow, Missouri (UPI,AFCA,WC)
	Jerry Butler, Clemson (AP)
	Kirk Gibson, Oklahoma St. (UPI)
	Gordon Jones, Pittsburgh (AFCA)
	Mark Brammer, Michigan St. (FWAA)
Tackles	Keith Dorney, Penn State (AP,UPI,AFCA,FWAA,WC)
	Kelvin Clark, Nebraska (AP,AFCA,FWAA,WC)
	Matt Miller, Colorado (UPI)
Guards	Pat Howell, USC (AP,UPI,AFCA,FWAA,WC)
	Greg Roberts, Oklahoma (AP,UPI,AFCA,FWAA,WC)
	Jim Ritcher, N. Carolina St. (AP,AFCA)
Centers	Dave Huffman, Notre Dame (UPI,FWAA,WC)
Quarter-backs	Chuck Fusina, Penn State (AP,UPI,AFCA,FWAA,WC)
	Rick Leach, Michigan (AFCA)
Running backs	Billy Sims, Oklahoma (AP,UPI,AFCA,FWAA,WC)
	Charles White, USC (AP,UPI,AFCA,FWAA,WC)
	Charles Alexander, LSU (AFCA,FWAA,WC)
	Ted Brown, N. Carolina St. (AP,UPI)
Kickers	Matt Bahr, Penn State (UPI,WC)
	Tony Franklin, Texas A&M (FWAA)

DEFENSIVE TEAM

Linemen	Al Harris, Arizona St. (AP,UPI,AFCA,FWAA,WC)
	Bruce Clark, Penn State (AP,UPI,AFCA,FWAA)
	Hugh Green, Pittsburgh (AP,UPI,WC)
	Mike Bell, Colorado St. (AFCA,FWAA,WC)
	Matt Millen, Penn State (UPI,WC)
	Reggie Kinlaw, Oklahoma (UPI,WC)
	Marty Lyons, Alabama (AP)
	Dan Hampton, Arkansas (AFCA)
	Jimmy Walker, Arkansas (FWAA)
Linebackers	Bob Golic, Notre Dame (AP,UPI,AFCA,FWAA,WC)
	Jerry Robinson, UCLA (AP,UPI,AFCA,FWAA,WC)
	Tom Cousineau, Ohio State (AP,UPI,AFCA,WC)
	John Corker, Oklahoma (AP)
	Ken Fantetti, Wyoming (FWAA)
Defensive backs	Johnnie Johnson, Texas (AP,UPI,AFCA,FWAA,WC)
	Kenny Easley, UCLA (AP,UPI,FWAA,WC)
	Jeff Nixon, Richmond (AP,AFCA,FWAA,WC)
	Pete Harris, Penn State (UPI)
	Henry Williams, San Diego St. (AFCA)
Punter	Russell Erxleben, Texas (FWAA,WC)

Selections by (AP) Associated Press, (UPI) United Press International, (AFCA) American Football Coaches Association, (FWAA) Football Writers Association of America, (WC) Walter Camp Foundation

NATIONAL CHAMPIONSHIP GAMES

Year	NCAA Division I-AA
1978	Florida A&M 35, Massachusetts 28

Year	NCAA Division II
1975	Northern Michigan 16, Western Kentucky 14
1976	Montana State 24, Akron 13
1977	Lehigh 33, Jacksonville (Ala.) State 0
1978	Eastern Illinois 10, Delaware 9

Year	NCAA Division III
1975	Wittenberg 28, Ithaca 0
1976	St. Johns (Minn.) 31, Towson State 28
1977	Widener 39, Wabash 36
1978	Baldwin-Wallace 24, Wittenberg 10

Year	NAIA Division I
1975	Texas A & I 37, Salem (W. Va.) 0
1976	Texas A & I 26, Central Arkansas 0
1977	Abilene Christian 24, Southwestern Oklahoma State 7
1978	Angelo State (Tex.) 34, Elon (N.C.) 14

Year	NAIA Division II
1975	Texas Lutheran 34, California Lutheran 8
1976	Westminster (Pa.) 20, Redlands 13
1977	Westminster (Pa.) 17, California Lutheran 9
1978	Concordia (Minn.) 7, Findlay (Ohio) 0

HOCKEY

HOCKEY GOVERNMENT

The National Hockey League (NHL): 960 Sun Life Building, Montreal, Quebec. President: John A. Ziegler, Jr. Chairman of the Board: William W. Wirtz. Organized in 1917. The NHL expanded to 21 teams in 1979 with the Edmonton Oilers, Hartford Whalers, Quebec Nordiques and Winnipeg Jets joining the league.

PRINCE OF WALES CONFERENCE
JAMES NORRIS DIVISION

	Pres./Owner	Coach
Detroit Red Wings	Bruce A. Norris	Bobby Kromm
Los Angeles Kings	Lou Baumeister	Bob Berry
Hartford Whalers	Howard L. Baldwin	Don Blackburn
Montreal Canadiens	Morgan McCammon	Bernie Geoffrion
Pittsburgh Penguins	Vincent J. Bartimo	John Wilson

CHARLES F. ADAMS DIVISION

	Pres./Owner	Coach
Boston Bruins	Paul A. Mooney	Fred Creighton
Buffalo Sabres	Seymour H. Knox III	Scotty Bowman
Minnesota North Stars	George Gund III	Glen Sonmor
Quebec Nordiques	Marcel Aubut	Jacques Demers
Toronto Maple Leafs	Harold E. Ballard	Floyd Smith

CLARENCE CAMPBELL CONFERENCE
CONN SMYTHE DIVISION

	Pres./Owner	Coach
Chicago Black Hawks	William W. Wirtz	Eddie Johnston
Colorado Rockies	Armand Pohan	Don Cherry
Edmonton Oilers	Peter Pocklington	Glen Sather
St. Louis Blues	Emile Francis	Barclay Plager
Vancouver Canucks	Frank A. Griffiths	Harry Neale
Winnipeg Jets	Michael Gobuty	Tom McVie

LESTER PATRICK DIVISION

	Pres./Owner	Coach
Atlanta Flames	Thomas G. Cousins	Al MacNeil
New York Islanders	John O. Pickett, Jr.	Al Arbour
New York Rangers	William M. Jennings	Fred Shero
Philadelphia Flyers	Edward M. Snider	Pat Quinn
Washington Capitals	Abe Pollin	Dan Belisle

NATIONAL HOCKEY LEAGUE RECORDS   At start of 1979/80 season

Most Goals, Lifetime: 786, Gordie Howe, Detroit Red Wings.

Most Goals, One Season: 76, Phil Esposito, Boston Bruins, 1970/71.

Most Assists, One Season: 102, Bobby Orr, Boston Bruins, 1970/71.

Most Points, One Game: 10, Darryl Sittler, Toronto Maple Leafs, February 7, 1976.

Most Victories, One Season: 60, Montreal Canadiens, 1976/77.

Longest Winning Streak: 14 games, Boston Bruins, 1929/30.

Most Goals, One Season: 399, Boston Bruins, 1970/71.

Most Shutouts by a Goaltender: 103, Terry Sawchuk, Detroit, Boston, Toronto, Los Angeles, N.Y. Rangers.

Most Penalty Minutes, One Season: 472, Dave Schultz, Philadelphia Flyers, 1974/75.

Most Seasons: 25, Gordie Howe, Detroit Red Wings, 1946/47 through 1970/71.

Most Games, Including Playoffs, Lifetime: 1,841, Gordie Howe, Detroit Red Wings.

Most Goals, Including Playoffs, Lifetime: 853, Gordie Howe, Detroit Red Wings.

Most Assists, Including Playoffs, Lifetime: 1,114, Gordie Howe, Detroit Red Wings.

Most Points, Including Playoffs, Lifetime: 1,967, Gordie Howe, Detroit Red Wings.

Most Penalty Minutes, Including Playoffs, Lifetime: 2,678 Dave Schultz, Philadelphia Flyers, Los Angeles Kings, Pittsburgh Penguins, Buffalo Sabres.

Most Consecutive Games: 883, Garry Unger, Toronto Maple Leafs, Detroit Red Wings, St. Louis Blues, 1967/68–1978/79.

Most Consecutive Complete Games by Goaltender: 502, Glenn Hall, Detroit Red Wings and Chicago Black Hawks, 1955/56 through 1962/63.

Most Shutouts by a Goaltender, One Season: 22, George Hainsworth, Montreal Canadiens, 1928/29.

Longest Shutout Sequence by a Goaltender: 461 Minutes 29 Seconds, Alex Connell, Ottawa Senators, 1927/28.

Most Goals, One Game: 7, Joe Malone, Quebec Bulldogs, January 31, 1920.

Most Assists, One Game: 7, Billy Taylor, Detroit Red Wings, March 16, 1947.

Most Penalties, One Game: 9, Jim Dorey, Toronto Maple Leafs, October 16, 1968; Dave Schultz, Pittsburgh Penguins, April 6, 1978.

Most Penalty Minutes, One Game: 67, Randy Holt, Los Angeles Kings, March 11, 1979.

Most Goals in One Period: 4, Harvey (Busher) Jackson, Toronto Maple Leafs, November 20, 1934; Max Bentley, Chicago Black Hawks, January 28, 1943; Clint Smith, Chicago Black Hawks, March 4, 1945; Gordon (Red) Berenson, St. Louis Blues, November 7, 1968.

Fastest Opening Goal: 6 seconds, Henry Boucha, Detroit Red Wings, January 28, 1973; Jean Pronovost, Pittsburgh Penguins, March 25, 1976.

Fastest Two Goals: 4 seconds, Nels Stewart, Montreal Maroons, January 3, 1931.

Fastest Three Goals: 21 seconds, Bill Mosienko, Chicago Black Hawks, March 23, 1952.

NHL CHAMPIONS

Season	Regular Season	Stanley Cup
1950/51	Detroit Red Wings	Toronto Maple Leafs
1951/52	Detroit Red Wings	Detroit Red Wings
1952/53	Detroit Red Wings	Montreal Canadiens
1953/54	Detroit Red Wings	Detroit Red Wings
1954/55	Detroit Red Wings	Detroit Red Wings
1955/56	Montreal Canadiens	Montreal Canadiens
1956/57	Detroit Red Wings	Montreal Canadiens
1957/58	Montreal Canadiens	Montreal Canadiens
1958/59	Montreal Canadiens	Montreal Canadiens
1959/60	Montreal Canadiens	Montreal Canadiens
1960/61	Montreal Canadiens	Chicago Black Hawks
1961/62	Montreal Canadiens	Toronto Maple Leafs
1962/63	Toronto Maple Leafs ...	Toronto Maple Leafs
1963/64	Montreal Canadiens	Toronto Maple Leafs
1964/65	Detroit Red Wings	Montreal Canadiens
1965/66	Montreal Canadiens	Montreal Canadiens
1966/67	Chicago Black Hawks ...	Toronto Maple Leafs
1967/68	Montreal Canadiens* ..... Philadelphia Flyers†	Montreal Canadiens
1968/69	Montreal Canadiens* ..... St. Louis Blues†	Montreal Canadiens
1969/70	Chicago Black Hawks* .... St. Louis Blues†	Boston Bruins
1970/71	Boston Bruins* .... Chicago Black Hawks†	Montreal Canadiens
1971/72	Boston Bruins* .... Chicago Black Hawks†	Boston Bruins
1972/73	Montreal Canadiens* ..... Chicago Black Hawks†	Montreal Canadiens
1973/74	Boston Bruins* .... Philadelphia Flyers†	Philadelphia Flyers
1974/75	Montreal Canadiens ..... Buffalo Sabres Philadelphia Flyers Vancouver Canucks	Philadelphia Flyers
1975/76	Montreal Canadiens ..... Boston Bruins Philadelphia Flyers Chicago Black Hawks	Montreal Canadiens
1976/77	Montreal Canadiens ..... Boston Bruins Philadelphia Flyers St. Louis Blues	Montreal Canadiens
1977/78	Montreal Canadiens ..... Boston Bruins New York Islanders Chicago Black Hawks	Montreal Canadiens
1978/79	Montreal Canadiens ..... Boston Bruins New York Islanders Chicago Black Hawks	Montreal Canadiens

* East Division. † West Division.

NHL FINAL STANDINGS: 1978/79

CAMPBELL CONFERENCE

PATRICK DIVISION

	W	L	T	Pts.	GF	GA
NY Islanders	51	15	14	116	358	214
Philadelphia	40	25	15	95	281	248
NY Rangers	40	29	11	91	316	292
Atlanta	41	31	8	90	327	280

SMYTHE DIVISION

	W	L	T	Pts.	GF	GA
Chicago	29	36	15	73	244	277
Vancouver	25	42	13	63	217	291
St. Louis	18	50	12	48	249	348
Colorado	15	53	12	42	210	331

WALES CONFERENCE

ADAMS DIVISION

	W	L	T	Pts.	GF	GA
Boston	43	23	14	100	316	270
Buffalo	36	28	16	88	280	263
Toronto	34	33	13	81	267	252
Minnesota	28	40	12	68	257	289

NORRIS DIVISION

	W	L	T	Pts.	GF	GA
Montreal	52	17	11	115	337	204
Pittsburgh	36	31	13	85	281	279
Los Angeles	34	34	12	80	292	286
Washington	24	41	15	63	273	338
Detroit	23	41	16	62	252	295

STANLEY CUP PLAYOFFS: 1979

Preliminary Round (Best-of-three series)
NY Rangers over Los Angeles: 2–0
Philadelphia over Vancouver: 2–1
Pittsburgh over Buffalo: 2–1
Toronto over Atlanta: 2–0

Quarter Finals (Best-of-seven series)
NY Rangers over Philadelphia: 4–1
NY Islanders over Chicago: 4–0
Boston over Pittsburgh: 4–0
Montreal over Toronto: 4–0

Semi-Finals (Best-of-seven series)
NY Rangers over NY Islanders: 4–2
Montreal over Boston: 4–3
Finals (Best-of-seven series)
Montreal over NY Rangers: 4–1

STANLEY CUP CHAMPIONS

Season	Champions	Manager	Season	Champions	Manager
1978–79	Montreal Canadiens	Irving Grundman	1948–49	Toronto Maple Leafs	Conn Smythe
1977–78	Montreal Canadiens	Sam Pollock	1947–48	Toronto Maple Leafs	Conn Smythe
1976–77	Montreal Canadiens	Sam Pollock	1946–47	Toronto Maple Leafs	Conn Smythe
1975–76	Montreal Canadiens	Sam Pollock	1945–46	Montreal Canadiens	Tommy Gorman
1974–75	Philadelphia Flyers	Keith Allen	1944–45	Toronto Maple Leafs	Conn Smythe
1973–74	Philadelphia Flyers	Keith Allen	1943–44	Montreal Canadiens	Tommy Gorman
1972–73	Montreal Canadiens	Hector Blake	1942–43	Detroit Red Wings	Jack Adams
1971–72	Boston Bruins	Milt Schmidt	1941–42	Toronto Maple Leafs	Conn Smythe
1970–71	Montreal Canadiens	Sam Pollock	1940–41	Boston Bruins	Art Ross
1969–70	Boston Bruins	Milt Schmidt	1939–40	New York Rangers	Lester Patrick
1968–69	Montreal Canadiens	Sam Pollock	1938–39	Boston Bruins	Art Ross
1967–68	Montreal Canadiens	Sam Pollock	1937–38	Chicago Black Hawks	Bill Stewart
1966–67	Toronto Maple Leafs	Punch Imlach	1936–37	Detroit Red Wings	Jack Adams
1965–66	Montreal Canadiens	Sam Pollock	1935–36	Detroit Red Wings	Jack Adams
1964–65	Montreal Canadiens	Sam Pollock	1934–35	Montreal Maroons	Tommy Gorman
1963–64	Toronto Maple Leafs	Punch Imlach	1933–34	Chicago Black Hawks	Tommy Gorman
1962–63	Toronto Maple Leafs	Punch Imlach	1932–33	New York Rangers	Lester Patrick
1961–62	Toronto Maple Leafs	Punch Imlach	1931–32	Toronto Maple Leafs	Conn Smythe
1960–61	Chicago Black Hawks	Tommy Ivan	1930–31	Montreal Canadiens	Cecil Hart
1959–60	Montreal Canadiens	Frank Selke	1929–30	Montreal Canadiens	Cecil Hart
1958–59	Montreal Canadiens	Frank Selke	1928–29	Boston Bruins	Art Ross
1957–58	Montreal Canadiens	Frank Selke	1927–28	New York Rangers	Lester Patrick
1956–57	Montreal Canadiens	Frank Selke	1926–27	Ottawa Senators	Dave Gill
1955–56	Montreal Canadiens	Frank Selke	1925–26	Montreal Maroons	Eddie Gerard
1954–55	Detroit Red Wings	Jack Adams	1924–25	Victoria Cougars	Lester Patrick
1953–54	Detroit Red Wings	Jack Adams	1923–24	Montreal Canadiens	Leo Dandurand
1952–53	Montreal Canadiens	Frank Selke	1922–23	Ottawa Senators	Tommy Gorman
1951–52	Detroit Red Wings	Jack Adams	1921–22	Toronto St. Pats	Charlie Querrie
1950–51	Toronto Maple Leafs	Conn Smythe	1920–21	Ottawa Senators	Tommy Gorman
1949–50	Detroit Red Wings	Jack Adams	1919–20	Ottawa Senators	Tommy Gorman

NHL SCORING LEADERS

Season	Player and Team	Points	Season	Player and Team	Points
1947/48	Elmer Lach, Montreal	61	1963/64	Stan Mikita, Chicago	89
1948/49	Roy Conacher, Chicago	68	1964/65	Stan Mikita, Chicago	87
1949/50	Ted Lindsay, Detroit	78	1965/66	Bobby Hull, Chicago	97
1950/51	Gordie Howe, Detroit	86	1966/67	Stan Mikita, Chicago	97
1951/52	Gordie Howe, Detroit	86	1967/68	Stan Mikita, Chicago	87
1952/53	Gordie Howe, Detroit	95	1968/69	Phil Esposito, Boston	126
1953/54	Gordie Howe, Detroit	81	1969/70	Bobby Orr, Boston	120
1954/55	Bernie Geoffrion, Montreal	75	1970/71	Phil Esposito, Boston	152
1955/56	Jean Beliveau, Montreal	88	1971/72	Phil Esposito, Boston	133
1956/57	Gordie Howe, Detroit	89	1972/73	Phil Esposito, Boston	130
1957/58	Dickie Moore, Montreal	84	1973/74	Phil Esposito, Boston	145
1958/59	Dickie Moore, Montreal	96	1974/75	Bobby Orr, Boston	135
1959/60	Bobby Hull, Chicago	81	1975/76	Guy Lafleur, Montreal	125
1960/61	Bernie Geoffrion, Montreal	95	1976/77	Guy Lafleur, Montreal	136
1961/62	Bobby Hull, Chicago	84	1977/78	Guy Lafleur, Montreal	132
1962/63	Gordie Howe, Detroit	86	1978/79	Brian Trottier, NY Islanders	134

NHL SCORING LEADERS: 1978/79

Player	Pos.	Team	G	A	Pts.	Player	Pos.	Team	G	A	Pts.
Brian Trottier	C	NY Islanders	47	87	134	Dave Taylor	RW	Los Angeles	43	48	91
Marcel Dionne	C	Los Angeles	59	71	130	Clark Gilles	LW	NY Islanders	35	56	91
Guy Lafleur	RW	Montreal	52	77	129	Dennis Maruk	C	Washington	31	59	90
Mike Bossy	RW	NY Islanders	69	57	126	Darryl Sittler	LW	Toronto	36	51	87
Bob MacMillan	LW	Atlanta	37	71	108	Butch Goring	C	Los Angeles	36	51	87
Guy Chouinard	C	Atlanta	50	57	107	Rick Middleton	RW	Boston	38	48	86
Denis Potvin	D	NY Islanders	31	70	101	Lanny McDonald	RW	Toronto	43	42	85
Bernie Federko		St. Louis	31	64	95	Gilbert Perreault	C	Buffalo	27	58	85

NHL ALL-TIME SCORING LEADERS

Player (Team)	Seasons	Games	Goals	Assists	Points	Scoring Percentage
Gordie Howe (Detroit)	25	1,687	786	1,023	1,809	1.072
Phil Esposito (Chicago, Boston, N.Y. Rangers)	16	1,161	676	816	1,492	1.285
Stan Mikita (Chicago)	21	1,377	539	921	1,460	1.060
Johnny Bucyk (Detroit, Boston)	23	1,540	556	813	1,369	.889
Alex Delvecchio (Detroit)	24	1,549	456	825	1,281	.827
Norm Ullman (Detroit, Toronto)	20	1,410	490	739	1,229	.872
Jean Beliveau (Mtl. Canadiens)	20	1,125	507	712	1,219	1.084
Jean Ratelle (N.Y. Rangers, Boston)	19	1,167	452	705	1,157	.991
Bobby Hull (Chicago)	15	1,036	604	549	1,153	1.113
Frank Mahovlich (Toronto, Detroit, Mtl. Canadiens)	18	1,181	533	570	1,103	.934
Henri Richard (Mtl. Canadiens)	20	1,256	358	688	1,046	.833
Rod Gilbert (N.Y. Rangers)	18	1,065	406	615	1,021	.959
Andy Bathgate (N.Y. Rangers, Toronto, Detroit, Pittsburgh Penguins)	17	1,069	349	624	973	.910
Maurice Richard (Mtl. Canadiens)	18	978	544	421	965	.987
Bobby Orr (Boston, Chicago)	12	657	270	645	915	1.393
Bobby Clarke (Philadelphia Flyers)	10	773	270	598	868	1.123
Yvan Cournoyer (Mtl. Canadiens)	16	968	428	435	863	.892
Dean Prentice (N.Y. Rangers, Boston, Detroit, Pittsburgh Penguins, Minnesota)	22	1,378	391	469	860	.624
Dave Keon (Toronto)	15	1,062	365	493	858	.808
Ted Lindsay (Detroit, Chicago)	17	1,068	379	472	851	.797
Jacques Lemaire (Montreal Canadiens)	12	853	366	469	835	.978
Red Kelly (Detroit, Toronto)	20	1,316	281	542	823	.625
Bernie Geoffrion (Mtl. Canadiens, N.Y. Rangers)	16	883	393	464	791	1.278
Guy Lafleur (Mtl. Canadiens)	8	603	355	461	816	1.353
Pit Martin (Detroit, Boston, Chicago)	17	1,101	324	485	809	.735
Ken Hodge (Chicago, Boston, N.Y. Rangers)	14	881	328	472	800	.908
Marcel Dionne (Detroit, Los Angeles)	8	619	327	464	791	1.278
Gilbert Perreault (Buffalo)	9	673	300	463	763	1.134
Garry Unger (Toronto, Detroit, St. Louis)	12	893	377	352	729	.816
Murray Oliver (Detroit, Boston, Toronto, Minnesota)	17	1,127	274	454	728	.646
Bob Nevin (Toronto, N.Y. Rangers, Minnesota, Los Angeles)	18	1,128	307	419	726	.644
George Armstrong (Toronto)	21	1,187	296	417	713	.601
Vic Hadfield (N.Y. Rangers, Pittsburgh Penguins)	16	1,002	323	389	712	.711
Doug Mohns (Boston, Chicago, Minnesota, Atlanta, Washington)	22	1,390	248	462	710	.511
Bobby Rousseau (Mtl. Canadiens, Minnesota, N.Y. Rangers)	15	942	245	458	703	.736
Pete Mahovlich (Detroit, Mtl. Canadiens, Pittsburgh Penguins)	14	780	271	431	702	.900
Darryl Sittler (Toronto)	9	653	288	397	685	1.049
Phil Goyette (Mtl. Canadiens, N.Y. Rangers, St. Louis Blues, Buffalo)	16	941	207	467	674	.716
Jean Pronovost (Pittsburgh, Atlanta)	11	828	344	326	670	.809
Red Berenson (Mtl. Canadiens, NY Rangers, St. Louis, Detroit)	17	987	261	397	658	.667
Dennis Hull (Chicago)	14	959	303	351	654	.682
Wayne Cashman (Boston)	13	777	225	418	643	.828
Bob Pulford (Toronto, Los Angeles)	16	1,079	281	362	643	.596

NATIONAL HOCKEY LEAGUE TROPHY WINNERS

HART TROPHY For Most Valuable Player

1955/56 Jean Beliveau, Montreal	1963/64 Jean Beliveau, Montreal	1971/72 Bobby Orr, Boston
1956/57 Gordie Howe, Detroit	1964/65 Bobby Hull, Chicago	1972/73 Bobby Clarke, Philadelphia
1957/58 Gordie Howe, Detroit	1965/66 Bobby Hull, Chicago	1973/74 Phil Esposito, Boston
1958/59 Andy Bathgate, New York	1966/67 Stan Mikita, Chicago	1974/75 Bobby Clarke, Philadelphia
1959/60 Gordie Howe, Detroit	1967/68 Stan Mikita, Chicago	1975/76 Bobby Clarke, Philadelphia
1960/61 Bernie Geoffrion, Montreal	1968/69 Phil Esposito, Boston	1976/77 Guy Lafleur, Montreal
1961/62 Jacques Plante, Montreal	1969/70 Bobby Orr, Boston	1977/78 Guy Lafleur, Montreal
1962/63 Gordie Howe, Detroit	1970/71 Bobby Orr, Boston	1978/79 Brian Trottier, N.Y. Islanders

VENZINA TROPHY For Best Goalie Record

1960/61 Johnny Bower, Toronto	1967/68 Lorne Worsley and Rogatien Vachon, Montreal	1973/74 Bernie Parent, Philadelphia and Tony Esposito, Chicago
1961/62 Jacques Plante, Montreal		1974/75 Bernie Parent, Philadelphia
1962/63 Glenn Hall, Chicago	1968/69 Glenn Hall and Jacques Plante, St Louis	1975/76 Ken Dryden, Montreal
1963/64 Charlie Hodge, Montreal		1976/77 Ken Dryden and Michel Larocque, Montreal
1964/65 Terry Sawchuk and Johnny Bower, Toronto	1969/70 Tony Esposito, Chicago	
	1970/71 Ed Giacomin and Gilles Villemure, New York	1977/78 Ken Dryden and Michel Larocque, Montreal
1965/66 Lorne Worsley and Charlie Hodge, Montreal		1978/79 Ken Dryden and Michel Larocque, Montreal
1966/67 Denis DeJordy and Glenn Hall, Chicago	1971/72 Tony Esposito and Gary Smith, Chicago	
	1972/73 Ken Dryden, Montreal	

JAMES NORRIS TROPHY For Best Defenseman

1955/56 Doug Harvey, Montreal	1963/64 Pierre Pilote, Chicago	1971/72 Bobby Orr, Boston
1956/57 Doug Harvey, Montreal	1964/65 Pierre Pilote, Chicago	1972/73 Bobby Orr, Boston
1957/58 Doug Harvey, Montreal	1965/66 J. Laperriere, Montreal	1973/74 Bobby Orr, Boston
1958/59 Tom Johnson, Montreal	1966/67 Harry Howell, New York	1974/75 Bobby Orr, Boston
1959/60 Doug Harvey, Montreal	1967/68 Bobby Orr, Boston	1975/76 Denis Potvin, N.Y. Islanders
1960/61 Doug Harvey, Montreal	1968/69 Bobby Orr, Boston	1976/77 Larry Robinson, Montreal
1961/62 Doug Harvey, New York	1969/70 Bobby Orr, Boston	1977/78 Denis Potvin, N.Y. Islanders
1962/63 Pierre Pilote, Chicago	1970/71 Bobby Orr, Boston	1978/79 Denis Potvin, N.Y. Islanders

FRANK J. SELKE TROPHY For Best Defensive Forward

1977/78	Bob Gainey, Montreal	1978/79	Bob Gainey, Montreal

CALDER TROPHY For Best Rookie

1952/53	Lorne Worsley, New York	1961/62	Bobby Rousseau, Montreal	1970/71	Gil Perreault, Buffalo
1953/54	Camille Henry, New York	1962/63	Kent Douglas, Toronto	1971/72	Ken Dryden, Montreal
1954/55	Ed Litzenberger, Chicago	1963/64	Jacques Laperriere, Montreal	1972/73	Steve Vickers, N. Y. Rangers
1955/56	Glenn Hall, Detroit	1964/65	Roger Crozier, Detroit	1973/74	Denis Potvin, N. Y. Islanders
1956/57	Larry Regan, Boston	1965/66	Brit Selby, Toronto	1974/75	Eric Vail, Atlanta
1957/58	Frank Mahovlich, Toronto	1966/67	Bobby Orr, Boston	1975/76	Bryan Trottier, N.Y. Islanders
1958/59	Ralph Backstrom, Montreal	1967/68	Derek Sanderson, Boston	1976/77	Willie Plett, Atlanta
1959/60	Billy Hay, Chicago	1968/69	Danny Grant, Minnesota	1977/78	Mike Bossy, N. Y. Islanders
1960/61	Dave Keon, Toronto	1969/70	Tony Esposito, Chicago	1978/79	Bobby Smith, Minnesota

LADY BYNG TROPHY For Sportsmanship

1952/53	Red Kelly, Detroit	1961/62	Dave Keon, Toronto	1970/71	Johnny Bucyk, Boston
1953/54	Red Kelly, Detroit	1962/63	Dave Keon, Toronto	1971/72	Jean Ratelle, New York
1954/55	Sid Smith, Toronto	1963/64	Ken Wharram, Chicago	1972/73	Gil Perrault, Buffalo
1955/56	Earl Reibel, Detroit	1964/65	Bobby Hull, Chicago	1973/74	John Bucyk, Boston
1956/57	Andy Hebenton, New York	1965/66	Alex Delvecchio, Detroit	1974/75	Marcel Dionne, Detroit
1957/58	Camille Henry, New York	1966/67	Stan Mikita, Chicago	1975/76	Jean Ratelle, Boston
1958/59	Alex Delvecchio, Detroit	1967/68	Stan Mikita, Chicago	1976/77	Marcel Dionne, Los Angeles
1959/60	Don McKenney, Boston	1968/69	Alex Delvecchio, Detroit	1977/78	Butch Goring, Los Angeles
1960/61	Red Kelly, Toronto	1969/70	Phil Goyette, St. Louis	1978/79	Bob MacMillan, Atlanta

CONN SMYTHE TROPHY For Most Valuable Player in Stanley Cup Playoffs

1965	Jean Beliveau, Montreal	1970	Bobby Orr, Boston	1975	Bernie Parent, Philadelphia
1966	Roger Crozier, Detroit	1971	Ken Dryden, Montreal	1976	Reggie Leach, Philadelphia
1967	Dave Keon, Toronto	1972	Bobby Orr, Boston	1977	Guy Lafleur, Montreal
1968	Glenn Hall, St. Louis	1973	Yvan Cournoyer, Montreal	1978	Larry Robinson, Montreal
1969	Serge Savard, Montreal	1974	Bernie Parent, Philadelphia	1979	Bob Gainey, Montreal

NHL ALL-STAR TEAMS: 1979

First Team			Second Team		
Goal	Ken Dryden	Montreal	Goal	Chico Resch	N.Y. Islanders
Defense	Denis Potvin	N.Y. Islanders	Defense	Serge Savard	Montreal
Defense	Larry Robinson	Montreal	Defense	Borje Salming	Toronto
Center	Bryan Trottier	N.Y. Islanders	Center	Marcel Dionne	Los Angeles
Right Wing	Guy Lafleur	Montreal	Right Wing	Mike Bossy	N.Y. Islanders
Left Wing	Clark Gilles	N.Y. Islanders	Left Wing	Bill Barber	Philadelphia

NHL ALL-STAR GAME RESULTS

Prior to 1969 the All-Star Game between the chosen team and the holder of the Stanley Cup.

Year	Score	Location	Year	Score	Location
1979	no game played		1964	All-Stars 3, Toronto 2	Toronto
1978	Prince of Wales 3, Campbell 2	Buffalo	1963	All-Stars 3, Toronto 3	Toronto
1977	Prince of Wales 4, Campbell 3	Vancouver	1962	Toronto 4, All-Stars 1	Toronto
			1961	All-Stars 3, Chicago 1	Chicago
1976	Prince of Wales 7, Campbell 5	Philadelphia	1960	All-Stars 2, Montreal 1	Montreal
			1959	Montreal 6, All-Stars 1	Montreal
1975	Prince of Wales 7, Campbell 1	Montreal	1958	Montreal 6, All-Stars 3	Montreal
			1957	All-Stars 5, Montreal 3	Montreal
			1956	All-Stars 1, Montreal 1	Montreal
1974	West 6, East 4	Chicago	1955	Detroit 3, All-Stars 1	Detroit
1973	East 5, West 4	New York	1954	All-Stars 2, Detroit 2	Detroit
1972	East 3, West 2	Minnesota	1953	All-Stars 3, Montreal 1	Montreal
1971	West 2, East 1	Boston	1952	1st Team 1, 2nd Team 1	Detroit
1970	East 4, West 1	St. Louis	1951	1st Team 2, 2nd Team 2	Toronto
1969	East 3, West 3	Montreal	1950	Detroit 7, All-Stars 1	Detroit
1968	Toronto 4, All-Stars 3	Toronto	1949	All-Stars 3, Toronto 1	Toronto
1967	Montreal 3, All-Stars 0	Montreal	1948	All-Stars 3, Toronto 1	Chicago
1965	All-Stars 5, Montreal 2	Montreal	1947	All-Stars 4, Toronto 3	Toronto

FINAL WORLD HOCKEY ASSOCIATION RESULTS: 1978/79

	Won	Lost	Tied	Pts.	GF	GA		Won	Lost	Tied	Pts.	GF	GA
Edmonton	48	30	2	98	340	266	Cincinnati	33	41	6	72	274	284
Quebec	41	34	5	87	288	271	Birmingham	32	42	6	70	286	311
Winnipeg	39	35	6	84	307	306	Indianapolis*	5	18	2	12	78	130
New England	37	34	9	83	298	287	*Team disbanded Dec. 1978						

WHA CHAMPIONSHIP PLAYOFFS: 1979

Quarter Final (Best-of-three series)	Semi-Finals (Best-of-seven series)	Final (Best-of-seven series)
New England over Cincinnati: 2–1	Winnipeg over Quebec: 4–0	Winnipeg over Edmonton: 4–2
	Edmonton over New England: 4–3	

WHA SCORING LEADERS: 1978/79

Player	Team	GP	G	A	Pts.	Player	Team	GP	G	A	Pts.
Cloutier	Quebec	77	75	54	129	Bernier	Quebec	65	36	46	82
Ftorek	Cincinnati	80	39	77	116	Leduc	Quebec	74	35	41	76
Gretzky	Edmonton	80	46	64	110	Rogers	New England	80	27	45	72
Mark Howe	New England	77	42	65	107	MacDonald	Edmonton	80	34	37	71
Nilsson	Winnipeg	78	39	68	107	Thomas	Cincinnati	80	32	39	71
Lukowich	Winnipeg	80	65	34	99	Callighen	Edmonton	71	31	39	70
Tardif	Quebec	74	41	55	96	Hislop	Cincinnati	80	30	40	70
Lacroix	New England	78	32	56	88	Chipperfield	Edmonton	55	32	37	69
Sullivan	Winnipeg	80	46	40	86	Marsh	Cincinnati	80	43	23	66
Ruskowski	Winnipeg	75	20	66	86	Keon	New England	79	22	43	65

HOCKEY HALL OF FAME

Source: N.H.L.

Players	Players	Players	Builders
Sidney Abel	Ebenezer Goodfellow	A. Joseph Primeau	Thomas "Frank" Ahearn
John Adams	Michael Grant	J. R. Marcel Pronovost	John "Bunny" Ahearne
C. J. "Syl" Apps	W. "Shorty" Green	Harvey Pulford	Sir Montague Allen
George Armstrong	Silas Griffis	H. G. "Bill" Quackenbush	Harold Ballard
I. W. "Ace" Bailey	George Hainsworth	Frank Rankin	John Bickell
Donald Bain	Glenn Hall	C. E. "Chuck" Rayner	George Brown
Hobart Baker	Joseph Hall	Kenneth Reardon	Walter Brown
Martin Barry	Douglas Harvey	Henri Richard	Frank Buckland
Andrew Bathgate	George Hay	J. H. Maurice Richard	Frank Calder
Jean Beliveau	W. M. "Riley" Hern	George Richardson	Angus Campbell
Clinton Benedict	Bryan Hextall	Gordon Roberts	Clarence Campbell
Douglas Bentley	Harry Holmes	Arthur Ross	Joseph Cattarinich
Maxwell Bentley	C. Thomas Hooper	Blair Russel	Joseph "Leo" Dandurand
Hector "Toe" Blake	G. R. "Red" Horner	J. D. "Jack" Ruttan	Francis Dilio
Richard Boon	M. G. "Tim" Horton	Terrance Sawchuk	George Dudley
Emile "Butch" Bouchard	Gordon Howe	Fred Scanlan	James Dunn
Frank Boucher	Sydney Howe	Milton Schmidt	Dr. John Gibson
George "Buck" Boucher	Harry Howell	D. "Sweeney" Schriner	Thomas Gorman
John Bower	J. B. "Bouse" Hutton	Earl Seibert	Charles Hay
Russell Bowie	Harry Hyland	Oliver Seibert	James Hendy
Francis Brimsek	J. D. "Dick" Irvin	Edward Shore	Foster Hewitt
H. L. "Punch" Broadbent	H. "Busher" Jackson	A. C. "Babe" Siebert	William Hewitt
W. E. "Turk" Broda	E. "Moose" Johnson	Harold Simpson	Fred Hume
Billy Burch	Ivan "Ching" Johnson	Alfred Smith	Thomas Ivan
Harold Cameron	Thomas Johnson	R. "Hooley" Smith	William Jennings
F. M. "King" Clancy	Aurel Joliat	Thomas Smith	Gen. John Kilpatrick
Aubrey "Dit" Clapper	G. "Duke" Keats	R. "Barney" Stanley	George Leader
Sprague Cleghorn	L. P. "Red" Kelly	John Stewart	Robert LeBel
Neil Colville	T. S. "Teeder" Kennedy	Nelson Stewart	Thomas Lockhart
Charles Conacher	Elmer Lach	Bruce Stuart	Paul Loicq
Alex Connell	E. C. "Newsy" Lalonde	Hod Stuart	Maj. Frederic McLaughlin
William Cook	Jean Laviolette	F. "Cyclone" Taylor	Hon. Hartland Molson
Arthur Coulter	Hugh Lehman	C. R. "Tiny" Thompson	Francis Nelson
William Cowley	Percy LeSeur	Col. Harry J. Trihey	Bruce Norris
S. R. "Rusty" Crawford	Robert "Ted" Lindsay	Georges Vezina	James Norris, Sr.
John Darragh	D. "Mickey" MacKay	John Walker	James D. Norris
A. M. "Scotty" Davidson	Joseph Malone	Martin Walsh	William Northey
Clarence "Hap" Day	Sylvio Mantha	Harry Watson	John O'Brien
Alex Delvecchio	John Marshall	Ralph "Cooney" Weiland	Frank Patrick
Cyril Denneny	Fred "Steamer" Maxwell	Harry Westwick	Allan Pickard
Gordon Drillon	Frank McGee	Fred Whitcroft	Samuel Pollock
Charles Drinkwater	William McGimsie	Gordon Wilson	Sen. Donat Raymond
Thomas Dunderdale	George McNamara	Roy Worters	John Robertson
William Durnan	Richard Moore		Claude Robinson
M. A. "Red" Dutton	Patrick Moran	**Referees**	Philip Ross
C. H. "Babe" Dye	Howie Morenz	William Chadwick	Frank Selke
Arthur Farrell	William Mosienko	Chaucer Elliott	Frank Smith
Frank Foyston	Frank Nighbor	Robert Hewitson	Conn Smythe
Frank Frederickson	E. Reginald Noble	Fred "Mickey" Ion	Lord Stanley of Preston
William Gadsby	Harry Oliver	Michael Rodden	Capt. James Sutherland
Charles Gardiner	Bobby Orr	J. Cooper Smeaton	Anatoli Tarasov
Herbert Gardiner	Lester Patrick	R. A. "Red" Storey	Lloyd Turner
James Gardner	Tommy Phillips	Frank Udvari	William Tutt
J. A. Bernard Geoffrion	J. A. Pierre Pilote		Carl Voss
Eddie Gerard	Didier "Pit" Pitre	**Builders**	Fred Waghorne
H. L. "Billy" Gilmour	J. Jacques Plante	Charles Adams	Arthur Wirtz
F. X. "Moose" Goheen	Walter "Babe" Pratt	Weston Adams	William Writz

NATIONAL COLLEGIATE HOCKEY CHAMPIONS

1956	Michigan	1962	Michigan Tech	1968	Denver	1974	Minnesota
1957	Colorado College	1963	North Dakota	1969	Denver	1975	Michigan Tech
1958	Denver	1964	Michigan	1970	Cornell	1976	Minnesota
1959	North Dakota	1965	Michigan Tech	1971	Boston Univ.	1977	Wisconsin
1960	Denver	1966	Michigan State	1972	Boston Univ.	1978	Boston Univ.
1961	Denver	1967	Cornell	1973	Wisconsin	1979	Minnesota

SOCCER

NORTH AMERICAN SOCCER LEAGUE: 1979 FINAL STANDINGS

NATIONAL CONFERENCE

Eastern Division	Won	Lost	Pts.	Goals For	Ag'st
New York Cosmos	24	6	216	84	52
Washington Diplomats	19	11	172	68	50
Toronto Metros	14	16	133	52	65
Rochester Lancers	15	15	132	43	57

Central Division	Won	Lost	Pts.	For	Ag'st
Minnesota Kicks	21	9	184	67	48
Dallas Tornado	17	13	152	53	51
Tulsa Roughnecks	14	16	139	61	56
Atlanta Chiefs	12	18	121	59	61

Western Division	Won	Lost	Pts.	For	Ag'st
Vancouver Whitecaps	20	10	172	54	34
Los Angeles Aztecs	18	12	162	62	47
Seattle Sounders	13	17	125	58	52
Portland Timbers	11	19	112	50	75

AMERICAN CONFERENCE

Eastern Division	Won	Lost	Pts.	Goals For	Ag'st
Tampa Bay Rowdies	19	11	169	67	46
Ft. Lauderdale Strikers	17	13	165	75	65
Philadelphia Fury	10	20	111	55	60
New England Tea Men	12	18	110	41	56

Central Division	Won	Lost	Pts.	For	Ag'st
Houston Hurricane	22	8	187	61	46
Chicago Sting	16	14	159	70	62
Detroit Express	14	16	133	61	56
Memphis Rogues	6	24	73	38	74

Western Division	Won	Lost	Pts.	For	Ag'st
San Diego Sockers	15	15	140	59	55
California Surf	15	15	140	53	56
Edmonton Drillers	8	22	88	43	78
San Jose Earthquake	8	22	86	41	74

LEADING SCORERS

	Games	Goals	Assists	Pts.
Oscar Fabbiani, Tampa Bay	26	25	8	58
Giorgio Chinaglia, New York	27	26	5	57
Gerd Mueller, Ft. Lauderdale	25	19	17	55
David Robb, Philadelphia	30	16	20	52
Jeff Bourne, Atlanta	29	18	15	51

LEADING SCORERS

	Games	Goals	Assists	Pts.
Karl-Heinz Granitza, Chicago	30	20	10	50
Teofilo Cubillas, Ft. Lauderdale	30	16	18	50
Alan Willey, Minnesota	29	21	7	49
Dennis Tueart, New York	27	16	16	48
Laurie Abrahams, California/Tulsa	25	18	9	45

LEADING GOALKEEPERS

	Games	Saves	Goals Ag'st	Avg.
Phil Parkes, Vancouver	29	99	29	0.965
Victor Nogueira, Atlanta	17	79	20	1.26
Zeljko Bilecki, Tampa Bay	17	93	22	1.28
Mike Ivanov, Seattle	28	149	39	1.39
Bill Irwin, Washington	28	134	42	1.45

LEADING GOALKEEPERS

	Games	Saves	Goals Ag'st	Avg.
Paul Hammond, Houston	29	215	44	1.46
Volkmar Gross, San Diego/Minnesota	24	137	38	1.604
Kevin Keelan, New England	25	133	40	1.6057
Colin Boulton, Los Angeles/Tulsa	30	109	49	1.6059
Tino Lettieri, Minnesota	16	95	25	1.63

AWARD WINNERS

Most Valuable Player — Johan Cruyff, Los Angeles
Coach of the Year — Timo Liekoski, Houston
Offensive Player of the Year — Johan Cruyff, Los Angeles
Defensive Player of the Year — John Dempsey, Philadelphia; Nick Mijatovic, Rochester

Rookie of the Year — Larry Hulcer, Los Angeles
Top Scorer — Oscar Fabbiani, Tampa Bay
Top Goalkeeper — Phil Parkes, Vancouver
Top North American Player — Rick Davis, New York
Goal of the Year — Oscar Fabbiani, Tampa Bay

NASL PLAYOFFS

National Conference

Vancouver over Dallas
Los Angeles over Washington
Tulsa over Minnesota
New York over Toronto

Vancouver over Los Angeles
New York over Tulsa

Vancouver over New York

American Conference

Philadelphia over Houston
Tampa Bay over Detroit
Chicago over Ft. Lauderdale
San Diego over California

Tampa Bay over Philadelphia
San Diego over Chicago

Tampa Bay over San Diego

CHAMPIONSHIP (SOCCER BOWL 1979) — Vancouver 2, Tampa Bay 1

NASL ALL-STAR TEAMS: 1979

Position	First Team	Second Team	Honorable Mention
Goalkeeper	Phil Parkes, Vancouver	Paul Hammond, Houston	Alan Mayer, San Diego
Defender	Carlos Alberto, New York	Marinho, New York	Steve Litt, Minnesota
Defender	Bruce Wilson, Chicago	John Gorman, Tampa Bay	Bobby Smith, San Diego
Defender	Wim Rijsbergen, New York	Mihalj Keri, Los Angeles	Willem Suurbier, Los Angeles
Defender	Mike Connell, Tampa Bay	Bob Lenarduzzi, Vancouver	Artur, New England
Midfielder	Franz Beckenbauer, New York	Teofilo Cubillas, Ft. Lauderdale	Rodney Marsh, Tampa Bay
Midfielder	Johan Neeskens, New York	Vladislav Bogicevic, New York	Alan Hudson, Seattle
Midfielder	Ace Ntsoelengoe, Minnesota	Alan Ball, Vancouver	Gerry Daly, New England
Forward	Johan Cruyff, Los Angeles	Oscar Fabbiani, Tampa Bay	Jorgen Kristensen, Chicago
Forward	Trevor Francis, Detroit	Karl-Heinz Granitza, Chicago	Steve Wegerle, Tampa Bay
Forward	Giorgio Chinaglia, New York	Gerd Mueller, Ft. Lauderdale	Dennis Tueart, New York

1978 WORLD CUP CHAMPIONSHIP

Games played in Argentina, June 1 – June 25
Qualified for First Round: Argentina, Austria, Brazil, France, Germany (West), Hungary, Iran, Italy, Mexico, Netherlands, Peru, Poland, Scotland, Spain, Sweden, Tunisia.
Advanced to Second Round: Argentina, Austria, Brazil, Germany (West), Italy, Netherlands, Peru, Poland.
Third Place Game: Brazil 2, Italy 1   **Championship Game:** Argentina 3, Netherlands 1

OTHER CHAMPIONSHIPS (1979)

American Soccer League .... Sacramento
Major Indoor League .... New York Arrows
NCAA Division I (1978) .... San Francisco
NCAA Division II (1978) .... Seattle Pacific
NCAA Division III (1978) .... Lock Haven State

NAIA (1978) .... Quincy
English Association Cup .... Arsenal
English First Division .... Liverpool
European Cup .... Nottingham Forest, England
European Winners Cup .... Barcelona, Spain

GOLF

TOTAL MONEY-WINNING LEADERS: 1978   Source: P.G.A.

Official Money shall be awarded to individual prize winners in major tournaments and such other events as the Tournament Policy Board may designate, even if part of the tournament is canceled provided; however, that Official Money shall not be awarded, in any team competition or a pro-am tournament (but Official Money will be awarded in a major tournament for individuals even if held concurrently with a pro-am tournament). The scale of Official Money will be determined from time to time by the Tournament Policy Board.

Rank	Name	Winnings	Rank	Name	Winnings	Rank	Name	Winnings
1.	Tom Watson	$362,429	18.	Bruce Lietzke	$113,905	34.	Jack Renner	$73,396
2.	Gil Morgan	267,459	19.	Tom Weiskopf	110,311	35.	Gibby Gilbert	72,758
3.	Andy Bean	267,241	20.	Fuzzy Zoeller	109,055	36.	Bob Gilder	72,515
4.	Jack Nicklaus	256,672	21.	Ben Crenshaw	108,305	37.	Barry Jaeckel	72,421
5.	Hubert Green	247,406	22.	Mac McLendon	107,299	38.	George Burns	71,498
6.	Lee Trevino	228,723	23.	Lou Graham	105,617	39.	Jerry McGee	71,228
7.	Hale Irwin	191,666	24.	Miller Barber	101,989	40.	John Schroeder	70,707
8.	Bill Kratzert	183,681	25.	Howard Twitty	92,409	41.	Bobby Wadkins	70,426
9.	Gary Player	177,336	26.	Jim Simons	90,218	42.	Rex Caldwell	68,451
10.	Jerry Pate	172,999	27.	Ed Sneed	86,510	43.	David Graham	66,909
11.	Tom Kite	161,370	28.	Ron Funseth	83,731	44.	Phil Hancock	66,460
12.	John Mahaffey	153,520	29.	Jerry Heard	79,511	45.	Larry Nelson	65,686
13.	Lee Elder	152,198	30.	Ray Floyd	77,595	46.	Dave Stockton	65,016
14.	Andy North	150,398	31.	Jay Haas	77,176	47.	J. C. Snead	63,561
15.	Mark Hayes	146,456	32.	Grier Jones	76,930	48.	Craig Stadler	63,486
16.	Lon Hinkle	138,388	33.	Bob Murphy	73,598	49.	Dave Eichelberger	63,405
17.	Bill Rogers	114,206				50.	Victor Regalado	62,621

THE BRITISH OPEN

Year	Winner	Score	Year	Winner	Score	Year	Winner	Score
1860	Willie Park	174	1895	John H. Taylor	322	1937	Henry Cotton	290
1861	Tom Morris	163	1896	*Harry Vardon	316 (157)	1938	R. A. Whitcombe	295
1862	Tom Morris	163	1897	Harold H. Hilton	314	1939	Richard Burton	290
1863	Willie Park	168	1898	Harry Vardon	307	1940–1945 No championships played		
1864	Tom Morris	160	1899	Harry Vardon	310	1946	Sam Snead	290
1865	Andrew Strath	162	1900	John H. Taylor	309	1947	Fred Daly	293
1866	Willie Park	169	1901	James Braid	309	1948	Henry Cotton	294
1867	Tom Morris	170	1902	Alexander Herd	307	1949	*Bobby Locke	283 (135)
1868	Tom Morris, Jr.	154	1903	Harry Vardon	300	1950	Bobby Locke	279
1869	Tom Morris, Jr.	157	1904	Jack White	296	1951	Max Faulkner	285
1870	Tom Morris, Jr.	149	1905	James Braid	318	1952	Bobby Locke	287
1871	No championship played		1906	James Braid	300	1953	Ben Hogan	282
1872	Tom Morris, Jr.	166	1907	Arnaud Massy	312	1954	Peter Thomson	283
1873	Tom Kipp	179	1908	James Braid	291	1955	Peter Thomson	281
1874	Mungo Park	159	1909	John H. Taylor	295	1956	Peter Thomson	286
1875	Willie Park	166	1910	James Braid	299	1957	Bobby Locke	279
1876	Robert Martin	176	1911	Harry Vardon	303	1958	Peter Thomson	278 (139)
1877	Jamie Anderson	160	1912	Edward (Ted) Ray	295	1959	Gary Player	284
1878	Jamie Anderson	157	1913	John H. Taylor	304	1960	Kel Nagle	278
1879	Jamie Anderson	169	1914	Harry Vardon	306	1961	Arnold Palmer	284
1880	Robert Ferguson	162	1915–1919 No championships played		1962	Arnold Palmer	276
1881	Robert Ferguson	170	1920	George Duncan	303	1963	*Bob Charles	277
1882	Robert Ferguson	171	1921	*Jock Hutchison	296 (150)	1964	Tony Lema	279
1883	*Willie Fernie	159	1922	Walter Hagen	300	1965	Peter Thomson	285
1884	Jack Simpson	160	1923	Arthur G. Havers	295	1966	Jack Nicklaus	282
1885	Bob Martin	171	1924	Walter Hagen	301	1967	Roberto De Vicenzo	278
1886	David Brown	157	1925	James M. Barnes	300	1968	Gary Player	289
1887	Willie Park, Jr.	161	1926	Robert T. Jones, Jr.	291	1969	Tony Jacklin	280
1888	Jack Burns	171	1927	Robert T. Jones, Jr.	285	1970	*Jack Nicklaus	283 (72)
1889	*Willie Park, Jr.	155 (158)	1928	Walter Hagen	292	1971	Lee Trevino	278
1890	John Ball	164	1929	Walter Hagen	292	1972	Lee Trevino	278
1891	Hugh Kirkaldy	166	1930	Robert T. Jones, Jr.	291	1973	Tom Weiskopf	276
	(Championship extended from		1931	Tommy D. Armour	296	1974	Gary Player	282
	36 to 72 holes)		1932	Gene Sarazen	283	1975	*Tom Watson	279 (71)
1892	Harold H. Hilton	305	1933	*Denny Shute	292 (149)	1976	Johnny Miller	279
1893	William Auchterlonie	322	1934	Henry Cotton	283	1977	Tom Watson	268
1894	John H. Taylor	326	1935	Alfred Perry	283	1978	Jack Nicklaus	281
			1936	Alfred Padgham	287	1979	Severiano Ballesteros	283

* Winner in playoff, figures in parentheses indicate playoff scores.

THE MASTERS

Year	Winner	Score	Year	Winner	Score	Year	Winner	Score
1936	Horton Smith	285	1952	Sam Snead	286	1966	Jack Nicklaus*	288
1937	Byron Nelson	283	1953	Ben Hogan	274	1967	Gay Brewer	280
1938	Henry Picard	285	1954	Sam Snead*	289	1968	Bob Goalby	277
1939	Ralph Guldahl	279	1955	Cary Middlecoff	279	1969	George Archer	281
1940	Jimmy Demaret	280	1956	Jack Burke	289	1970	Billy Casper*	279
1941	Craig Wood	280	1957	Doug Ford	283	1971	Charles Coody	279
1942	Byron Nelson*	280	1958	Arnold Palmer	284	1972	Jack Nicklaus	286
1946	Herman Keiser	282	1959	Art Wall	284	1973	Tommy Aaron	283
1947	Jimmy Demaret	281	1960	Arnold Palmer	282	1974	Gary Player	278
1948	Claude Harmon	279	1961	Gary Player	280	1975	Jack Nicklaus	276
1949	Sam Snead	282	1962	Arnold Palmer*	280	1976	Ray Floyd	271
1950	Jimmy Demaret	283	1963	Jack Nicklaus	286	1977	Tom Watson	276
1951	Ben Hogan	280	1964	Arnold Palmer	276	1978	Gary Player	277
			1965	Jack Nicklaus	271	1979	Fuzzy Zoeller*	280

* Won in playoff.

THE UNITED STATES OPEN Source: U. S. Golf Association

Year	Site	Winner	Score	Year	Site	Winner	Score
1895	Newport, R.I.	Horace Rawlins	173	1937	Birmingham, Mich.	Ralph Guldahl	281
1896	Southampton, N.Y.	James Foulis	152	1938	Denver, Colo.	Ralph Guldahl	284
1897	Wheaton, Ill.	Joe Lloyd	162	1939	W. Conshohocken, Pa.	Byron Nelson	284*
1898	S. Hamilton, Mass.	Fred Herd	328	1940	Cleveland, Ohio	Lawson Little	287*
1899	Baltimore, Md.	Willie Smith	315	1941	Ft. Worth, Texas	Craig Wood	284
1900	Wheaton, Ill.	Harry Vardon	313	1942–1945 No Competition Held			
1901	S. Hamilton, Mass.	Willie Anderson	331*	1946	Cleveland, Ohio	Lloyd Mangrum	284*
1902	Garden City, N.Y.	Lawrence Auchterlonie	307	1947	Clayton, Mo.	Lew Worsham	282*
1903	Springfield, N.J.	Willie Anderson	307°	1948	Los Angeles, Calif.	Ben Hogan	276
1904	Golf, Ill.	Willie Anderson	303	1949	Medinah, Ill.	Cary Middlecoff	286
1905	S. Hamilton, Mass.	Willie Anderson	314	1950	Ardmore, Pa.	Ben Hogan	287*
1906	Lake Forest, Ill.	Alex Smith	295	1951	Birmingham, Mich.	Ben Hogan	287
1907	Philadelphia, Pa.	Alex Ross	302	1952	Dallas, Texas	Julius Boros	281
1908	S. Hamilton, Mass.	Fred McLeod	322*	1953	Oakmont, Pa.	Ben Hogan	283
1909	Englewood, N.J.	George Sargent	290	1954	Springfield, N.J.	Ed Furgol	284
1910	St. Martins, Pa.	Alex Smith	298*	1955	San Francisco, Calif.	Jack Fleck	287*
1911	Wheaton, Ill.	John J. McDermott	307*	1956	Rochester, N.Y.	Cary Middlecoff	281
1912	Buffalo, N.Y.	John J. McDermott	294	1957	Toledo, Ohio	Dick Mayer	282°
1913	Brookline, Mass.	Walter Hagen	290	1958	Tulsa, Okla.	Tommy Bolt	283
1914	Blue Island, Ill.	Francis Ouimet (A)	304*	1959	Mamaroneck, N.Y.	Bill Casper, Jr.	282
1915	Springfield, N.J.	Jerome D. Travers (A)	297	1960	Englewood, Colo.	Arnold Palmer	280
1916	Minneapolis, Minn.	Charles Evans, Jr. (A)	286	1961	Birmingham, Mich.	Gene Littler	281
1917–1918 No Competion Held				1962	Oakmont, Pa.	Jack Nicklaus	283*
1919	West Newton, Mass.	Water Hagen	301*	1963	Brookline, Mass.	Julius Boros	293*
1920	Toledo, Ohio	Edward Ray	295	1964	Washington, D.C.	Ken Venturi	278
1921	Chevy Chase, Md.	James M. Barnes	289	1965	St. Louis, Mo.	Gary Player	282*
1922	Glencoe, Ill.	Gene Sarazen	288	1966	San Francisco, Calif.	Bill Casper, Jr.	278*
1923	Inwood, N.Y.	Robert T. Jones, Jr. (A)	296°	1967	Springfield, N.J.	Jack Nicklaus	275
1924	Birmingham, Mich.	Cyril Walker	297	1968	Rochester, N.Y.	Lee Trevino	275
1925	Worcester, Mass.	William Macfarlane	291*	1969	Houston, Texas	Orville Moody	281
1926	Columbus, Ohio	Robert T. Jones, Jr. (A)	293	1970	Chaska, Minn.	Tony Jacklin	281
1927	Oakmont, Pa.	Tommy Armour	301*	1971	Ardmore, Pa.	Lee Trevino	280*
1928	Mateson, Ill.	Johnny Farrell	294*	1972	Pebble Beach, Calif.	Jack Nicklaus	290
1929	Mamaroneck, N.Y.	Robert T. Jones, Jr. (A)	294*	1973	Oakmont, Pa.	John Miller	279
1930	Minneapolis, Minn.	Robert T. Jones, Jr. (A)	287	1974	Mamaroneck, N.Y.	Hale Irwin	287
1931	Toledo, Ohio	Billy Burke	292*	1975	Medinah, Ill.	Lou Graham	287*
1932	Flushing, N.Y.	Gene Sarazen	286	1976	Duluth, Ga.	Jerry Pate	277
1933	Glen View, Ill.	John G. Goodman (A)	287	1977	Tulsa, Okla.	Hubert Green	278
1934	Ardmore, Pa.	Olin Dutra	293	1978	Denver, Colo.	Andy North	285
1935	Oakmont, Pa.	Sam Parks, Jr.	299	1979	Toledo, Ohio	Hale Irwin	284
1936	Springfield, N.J.	Tony Manero	282				

(A) Amateur. °Won Playoff

PGA CHAMPIONSHIP Source: P. G. A.

Year	Winner	Score	Year	Winner	Score	Year	Winner	Score
1916	James M. Barnes	1 up	1938	Paul Runyan	8 & 7	1959	Bob Rosburg	277
1917–1918 No Competition Held			1939	Henry Picard	1 up	1960	Jay Hebert	281
1919	James M. Barnes	6 & 5	1940	Byron Nelson	1 up	1961	Jerry Barber	277*
1920	Jock Hutchison	1 up	1941	Vic Ghezzi	1 up	1962	Gary Player	278
1921	Walter Hagen	3 & 2	1942	Sam Snead	2 & 1	1963	Jack Nicklaus	279
1922	Gene Sarazen	4 & 3	1943	No Competition Held		1963	Bobby Nichols	271
1923	Gene Sarazen	1 up	1944	Bob Hamilton	1 up	1965	Dave Marr	280
1924	Walter Hagen	2 up	1945	Byron Nelson	4 & 3	1966	Al Geiberger	280
1925	Walter Hagen	6 & 5	1946	Ben Hogan	6 & 4	1967	Don January	281*
1926	Walter Hagen	5 & 3	1947	Jim Ferrier	2 & 1	1968	Julius Boros	281
1927	Walter Hagen	1 up	1948	Ben Hogan	7 & 6	1969	Ray Floyd	276
1928	Leo Diegel	6 & 5	1949	Sam Snead	3 & 2	1970	Dave Stockton	279
1929	Leo Diegel	6 & 4	1950	Chandler Harper	4 & 3	1971	Jack Nicklaus	281
1930	Tommy Armour	1 up	1951	Sam Snead	7 & 6	1972	Gary Player	281
1931	Tom Creavy	2 & 1	1952	Jim Turnesa	1 up	1973	Jack Nicklaus	277
1932	Olin Dutra	4 & 3	1953	Walter Burkemo	2 & 1	1974	Lee Trevino	276
1933	Gene Sarazen	5 & 4	1954	Chick Harbert	4 & 3	1975	Jack Nicklaus	276
1934	Paul Runyan	1 up	1955	Doug Ford	4 & 3	1976	Dave Stockton	281
1935	Johnny Revolta	5 & 4	1956	Jack Burke	3 & 2	1977	Lanny Wadkins	282*
1936	Denny Shute	3 & 2	1957	Lionel Hebert	2 & 1	1978	John Mahaffey	276*
1937	Denny Shute	1 up	1958	Dow Finsterwald	276	1979	Dave Graham	272*

°Won Playoff

THE CANADIAN OPEN

Year	Winner	Score	Year	Winner	Score	Year	Winner	Score
1950	Jim Ferrier	271	1960	Art Wall, Jr.	269	1970	Kermit Zarley	279
1951	Jim Ferrier	273	1961	Jacky Cupit	270	1971	Lee Trevino	275*
1952	John Palmer	263	1962	Ted Kroll	278	1972	Gay Brewer	275
1953	Dave Douglas	273	1963	Doug Ford	280	1973	Tom Weiskopf	278
1954	Pat Fletcher	280	1964	Kel Nagle	277	1974	Bobby Nichols	270
1955	Arnold Palmer	265	1965	Gene Littler	273	1975	Tom Weiskopf	274*
1956	Doug Sanders (A)	273	1966	Don Massengale	280	1976	Jerry Pate	267
1957	George Bayer	271	1967	Bill Casper	279°	1977	Lee Trevino	280
1958	Wesley Ellis, Jr.	267	1968	Bob Charles	274	1978	Bruce Lietzke	283
1959	Doug Ford	276	1969	Tommy Aaron	275°	1979	Lee Trevino	281

(A) Amateur. °Won Playoff

PROFESSIONAL GOLF'S LEADING MONEY WINNERS, 1935-1978

Year	Player	Winnings	Year	Player	Winnings	Year	Player	Winnings
1935	Johnny Revolta	$ 9,543.00	1949	Sam Snead	$31,593.83	1964	Jack Nicklaus	113,284.50
1936	Horton Smith	7,682.00	1950	Sam Snead	35,758.83	1965	Jack Nicklaus	140,752.14
1937	Harry Cooper	14,138.69	1951	Lloyd Mangrum	26,088.83	1966	Billy Casper	121,944.92
1938	Sam Snead	19,534.49	1952	Julius Boros	37,032.97	1967	Jack Nicklaus	188,998.08
1939	Henry Picard	10,303.00	1953	Lew Worsham	34,002.00	1968	Billy Casper	205,168.67
1940	Ben Hogan	10,655.00	1954	Bob Toski	65,819.81	1969	Frank Beard	175,223.93
1941	Ben Hogan	18,358.00	1955	Julius Boros	63,121.55	1970	Lee Trevino	157,037.00
1942	Ben Hogan	13,143.00	1956	Ted Kroll	72,835.83	1971	Jack Nicklaus	244,490.50
1943	No statistics compiled		1957	Dick Mayer	65,835.00	1972	Jack Nicklaus	320,542.26
1944	Byron Nelson	37,967.69	1958	Arnold Palmer	42,607.50	1973	Jack Nicklaus	308,362.00
1945	Byron Nelson	63,335.66	1959	Art Wall, Jr.	52,167.60	1974	Johnny Miller	353,021.00
1946	Ben Hogan	42,556.16	1960	Arnold Palmer	75,262.85	1975	Jack Nicklaus	298,149.00
1947	Jimmy Demaret	27,936.83	1961	Gary Player	64,540.45	1976	Jack Nicklaus	266,426.00
1948	Ben Hogan	32,112.00	1962	Arnold Palmer	81,448.33	1977	Tom Watson	310,653.00
			1963	Arnold Palmer	$128,230.00	1978	Tom Watson	362,429.00

RYDER CUP MATCHES (PROFESSIONALS)

Year	Played at	Results	Year	Played at	Results
1927	Worcester C.C., Worcester, Mass.	U.S. 9½–Britain 2½	1959	Eldorado C.C., Palm Desert, Calif.	U.S. 8½–Britain 3½
1929	Moortown, England	Britain 7 –U.S. 5	1961	Royal Lytham and St. Anne's Golf Club, St. Anne's-On-The-Sea, England	U.S. 14½–Britain 9½
1931	Scioto C.C., Columbus, Ohio	U.S. 9 –Britain 3			
1933	Southport & Ainsdale Courses, England	Britain 6½–U.S. 5½	1963	East Lake C.C., Atlanta, Georgia	U.S. 23 –Britain 9
1935	Ridgewood C.C., Ridgewood, N.J.	U.S. 9 –Britain 3	1965	Royal Birkdale Golf Club, Southport, England	U.S. 19½–Britain 12½
1937	Southport & Ainsdale Courses, England	U.S. 8 –Britain 4	1967	Champions Golf Club, Houston	U.S. 23½–Britain 8½
	Ryder Cup Matches not held during World War II years.		1969	Royal Birkdale Golf Club, Southport, England	U.S. 16–Tie –Britain 16
1947	Portland Golf Club, Portland, Oregon	U.S. 11 –Britain 1	1971	Old Warson Country Club, St. Louis, Mo.	U.S. 18½–Britain 13½
1949	Ganton Golf Course, Scarborough, England	U.S. 7 –Britain 5	1973	Muirfield, Scotland	U.S. 18 –Britain 13
1951	Pinehurst C.C., Pinehurst, N.C.	U.S. 9½–Britain 2½	1975	Laurel Valley Golf Club, Ligonier, Pa.	U.S. 21 –Britain 11
1953	Wentworth, England	U.S. 6½–Britain 5½	1977	Royal Lytham and St. Annes Golf Club, England	U.S. 12½–Britain 7½
1955	Thunderbird Ranch and C.C., Palm Springs, Calif.	U.S. 8 –Britain 4	1979	Greenbrier Hotel Resort, White Sulphur Sprs., W.Va.	U.S. 17 –Europe 11
1957	Lindrick Golf Club, Yorkshire, England	Britain 7½–U.S. 4½			

PGA HALL OF FAME
SOURCE: P.G.A.

Member	Year Elected	Member	Year Elected	Member	Year Elected
Willie Anderson	1940	Johnny Farrell	1961	Byron Nelson	1953
Tommy Armour	1940	Doug Ford	1975	Francis Ouimet	1940
Jim Barnes	1940	Vic Ghezzi	1965	Henry Picard	1961
Patty Berg	1977	Ralph Guldahl	1963	Johnny Revolta	1963
Julius Boros	1974	Walter Hagen	1940	Paul Runyan	1959
Mike Brady	1960	Chick Harbert	1968	Gene Sarazen	1940
Billy Burke	1966	Chandler Harper	1969	Denny Shute	1957
Jack Burke, Jr.	1975	Dutch Harrison	1962	Alex Smith	1940
Harry Cooper	1959	Ben Hogan	1953	Horton Smih	1958
Bobby Cruickshank	1967	Jock Hutchison, Sr.	1959	MacDonald Smith	1954
Jimmy Demaret	1960	Bobby Jones	1940	Sam Snead	1953
Roberto De Vicenzo	1978	Lawson Little	1961	Jerry Travers	1940
Leo Diegel	1955	Lloyd Mangrum	1964	Walter Travis	1940
Ed Dudley	1964	John McDermott	1940	Craig Wood	1956
Olin Dutra	1962	Fred McLeod	1960	Babe Zaharias	1977
Chick Evans	1940	Cary Middlecoff	1974		

WORLD AMATEUR TEAM CHAMPIONSHIPS
SOURCE: U. S. Golf Association

Year	Men's Champion	Women's Champion	Site
1958	Australia	—	St. Andrews, Scotland
1960	United States	—	Ardmore, Pa.
1962	United States	—	Kanawa, Japan
1964	Great Britain & Ireland	—	Rome, Italy
		France	St. Germain, France
1966	Australia	United States	Mexico City, Mexico
1968	United States	United States	Melbourne, Australia
1970	United States	United States	Madrid, Spain
1972	United States	United States	Buenos Aires, Argentina
1974	United States	United States	LaRomana, Dominican Rep.
1976	Great Britain & Ireland	United States	Algarve, Portugal
1978	United States	Australia	Pacific Harbour, Fiji

LPGA TOTAL MONEY WINNERS: 1978

Source: L.P.G.A.

Rank	Name	Amount	Rank	Name	Amount	Rank	Name	Amount
1.	Nancy Lopez	$189,813	18.	Debbie Austin	$44,768	34.	Mary Mills	$31,460
2.	Pat Bradley	118,057	19.	Sandra Palmer	44,498	35.	Janet Coles	30,750
3.	Jane Blalock	117,768	20.	Betsy King	44,092	36.	Sandra Spuzich	24,305
4.	JoAnne Carner	108,092	21.	Pat Meyers	43,639	37.	Sharon Miller	23,457
5.	Donna C. Young	95,993	22.	Gloria Ehret	42,470	38.	Kathy McMullen	23,223
6.	Hollis Stacy	95,800	23.	Jerilyn Britz	39,397	39.	Kathy Martin	23,004
7.	Sandra Post	92,118	24.	Alexandra Reinhardt	37,831	40.	Barbara Barrow	21,438
8.	Sally Little	84,895	25.	Laura Baugh	37,469	41.	Murle Breer	21,143
9.	Amy Alcott	75,516	26.	Joyce Kazmierski	37,323	42.	Vivian Brownlee	20,804
10.	Penny Pulz	71,011	27.	Pam Higgins	36,600	43.	Peggy Conley	19,733
11.	Debbie Massey	70,211	28.	Betty Burfeindt	35,143	44.	Beth Solomon	18,024
12.	Kathy Whitworth	67,855	29.	Shelley Hamlin	34,494	45.	Roberta A. Speer	17,584
13.	Jan Stephenson	66,033	30.	Dot Germain	33,590	46.	Marlene Floyd	16,825
14.	Silvia Bertolaccini	53,935	31.	Beth Stone	32,856	47.	M. J. Smith	16,233
15.	Judy T. Rankin	51,306	32.	Mary Dwyer	32,488	48.	Marlene Hagge	15,837
16.	Jo Ann Washam	45,407	33.	Donna H. White	32,214	49.	Patty Hayes	15,711
17.	Kathy Postlewait	45,066				50.	Jo Ann Prentice	15,609

LEADING LPGA MONEY WINNERS BY YEAR, 1948–1978

Year	Player	Amount	Year	Player	Amount	Year	Player	Amount
1948	Babe Zaharias	$ 3,400.00*	1958	Beverly Hanson	12,639.55	1968	Kathy Whitworth	48,379.50
1949	Babe Zaharias	4,650.00*	1959	Betsy Rawls	26,774.39	1969	Carol Mann	49,152.50
1950	Babe Zaharias	14,800.00*	1960	Louise Suggs	16,892.12	1970	Kathy Whitworth	30,235.01
1951	Babe Zaharias	15,087.00*	1961	Mickey Wright	22,236.21	1971	Kathy Whitworth	41,181.75
1952	Betsy Rawls	14,505.00	1962	Mickey Wright	21,641.99	1972	Kathy Whitworth	65,063.99
1953	Louise Suggs	19,816.25	1963	Mickey Wright	31,269.50	1973	Kathy Whitworth	82,864.25
1954	Patty Berg	16,011.00	1964	Mickey Wright	29,800.00	1974	JoAnne Carner	87,094.04
1955	Patty Berg	16,492.34	1965	Kathy Whitworth	28,658.00	1975	Sandra Palmer	76,374.51
1956	Marlene Hagge	20,235.50	1966	Kathy Whitworth	33,517.50	1976	Judy Rankin	150,734.28
1957	Patty Berg	16,272.00	1967	Kathy Whitworth	32,937.50	1977	Judy Rankin	122,890.44
						1978	Nancy Lopez	189,813.83

* Approximate Figure

WOMEN'S OPEN CHAMPIONSHIP

Source: U.S. Golf Association

Year	Site	Winner	Score	Year	Site	Winner	Score
1946	Spokane, Wash.	Patty Berg	5 & 4	1963	Cincinnati, Ohio	Mary Mills	289
1947	Greensboro, N.C.	Betty Jameson	295*	1964	Chula Vista, Calif.	Mickey Wright	290*
1948	Northfield, N.J.	Babe Zaharias	300	1965	Northfield, N.J.	Carol Mann	290
1949	Landover, Md.	Louise Suggs	291	1966	Minneapolis, Minn.	Sandra Spuzich	297
1950	Wichita, Kans.	Mildred Zaharias	291	1967	Hot Springs, Va.	Catherine Lacoste (A)	294
1951	Atlanta, Ga.	Betsy Rawls	293	1968	Fleetwood, Pa.	Susie Berning	289
1952	Philadelphia, Pa.	Louise Suggs	284	1969	Pensacola, Fla.	Donna Caponi	294
1953	Rochester, N.Y.	Betsy Rawls	302*	1970	Muskogee, Okla.	Donna Caponi	287
1954	Peabody, Mass.	Babe Zaharias	291	1971	Erie, Pa.	JoAnne Carner	288
1955	Wichita, Kans.	Fay Crocker	299	1972	Mamaroneck, N.Y.	Susie Berning	299
1956	Duluth, Minn.	Kathy Cornelius	302*	1973	Rochester, N.Y.	Susie Berning	290
1957	Mamaroneck, N.Y.	Betsy Rawls	299	1974	LaGrange, Ill.	Sandra Haynie	295
1958	Bloomfield Hills, Mich.	Mickey Wright	290	1975	Northfield, N.J.	Sandra Palmer	295
1959	Pittsburg, Pa.	Mickey Wright	287	1976	Springfield, Pa.	JoAnne Carner	292*
1960	Worcester, Mass.	Betsy Rawls	292	1977	Chaska, Minn.	Hollis Stacy	292
1961	Springfield, N.J.	Mickey Wright	293	1978	Indianapolis, Ind.	Hollis Stacy	289
1962	Myrtle Beach, S.C.	Murle Lindstrom	301	1979	Fairfield, Conn.	Jerilyn Britz	284

(A) Amateur.   *Won Playoff

LPGA CHAMPIONSHIP

Source: L.P.G.A.

Year	Winner	Score	Year	Winner	Score	Year	Winner	Score
1955	Beverly Hanson	4 & 3	1963	Mickey Wright	294	1971	Kathy Whitworth	288
1956	Marlene Hagge	291*	1964	Mary Mills	278	1972	Kathy Ahern	293
1957	Louise Suggs	285	1965	Sandra Haynie	279	1973	Mary Mills	288
1958	Mickey Wright	288	1966	Gloria Ehret	282	1974	Sanda Haynie	288
1959	Betsy Rawls	288	1967	Kathy Whitworth	284	1975	Kathy Whitworth	288
1960	Mickey Wright	292	1968	Sandra Post	294*	1976	Betty Burfeindt	287
1961	Mickey Wright	287	1969	Betsy Rawls	293	1977	Chako Higuchi	279
1962	Judy Kimball	282	1970	Shirley Englehorn	285*	1978	Nancy Lopez	275
						1979	Donna Caponi Young	279

*Won Playoff

LPGA HALL OF FAME

Source: L.P.G.A.

Member	Year Elected	Member	Year Elected	Member	Year Elected
Patty Berg	1951	Babe Zaharias	1951	Kathy Whitworth	1975
Betty Jameson	1951	Betsy Rawls	1960	Sandra Haynie	1977
Louise Suggs	1951	Mickey Wright	1964	Carol Mann	1977

U.S. AMATEUR CHAMPIONSHIP WINNERS

SouRCE: U.S. Golf Association

1895 Charles B. Macdonald	1915 Robert A. Gardner	1936 John W. Fischer	1959 Jack Nicklaus
1896 H. J. Whigham	1916 Charles Evans, Jr.	1937 John Goodman	1960 Deane R. Beman
1897 H. J. Whigham	1917–1918 No Competition	1938 William P. Turnesa	1961 Jack Nicklaus
1898 Findlay S. Douglas	1919 S. Davidson Herron	1939 Marvin H. Ward	1962 Labron Harris, Jr.
1899 H. M. Harriman	1920 Charles Evans, Jr.	1940 Richard D. Chapman	1963 Deane R. Beman
1900 Walter J. Travis	1921 Jesse P. Guilford	1941 Marvin H. Ward	1964 William C. Campbell
1901 Walter J. Travis	1922 Jess W. Sweetser	1942–1945 No Competition	1965 Robert J. Murphy, Jr.
1902 Louis N. James	1923 Max R. Marston	1946 S. E. (Ted) Bishop	1966 Gary Cowan
1903 Walter J. Travis	1924 Robert T. Jones, Jr.	1947 R. H. (Skee) Riegel	1967 Robert B. Dickson
1904 H. Chandler Egan	1924 Robert T. Jones, Jr.	1948 William P. Turnesa	1968 Bruce Fleisher
1905 H. Chandler Egan	1926 George Von Elm	1949 Charles R. Coe	1969 Steven Melnyk
1906 Eben M. Byers	1927 Robert T. Jones, Jr.	1950 Sam Urzetta	1970 Lanny Wadkins
1907 Jerome D. Travers	1928 Robert T. Jones, Jr.	1951 Billy Maxwell	1971 Gary Cowan
1908 Jerome D. Travers	1929 Harrison R. Johnston	1952 Jack Westland	1972 Marvin Giles
1909 Robert A. Gardner	1930 Robert T. Jones, Jr.	1953 Gene Littler	1973 Craig Stadler
1910 William C. Fownes, Jr.	1931 Francis Ouimet	1954 Arnold Palmer	1974 Jerome Pate
1911 Harold H. Hilton	1932 C. Ross Somerville	1955 E. Harvie Ward, Jr.	1975 Fred Ridley
1912 Jerome D. Travers	1933 George T. Dunlap, Jr.	1956 E. Harvie Ward, Jr.	1976 Bill Sander
1913 Jerome D. Travers	1934 Lawson Little	1957 Hillman Robbins, Jr.	1977 John Fought
1914 Francis Ouimet	1935 Lawson Little	1958 Charles R. Coe	1978 John Cook
			1979 Mark O'Meara

WOMEN'S AMATEUR CHAMPIONSHIP WINNERS

SouRCE: U.S. Golf Association

1951 Dorothy Kirby	1958 Anne Quast	1965 Jean Ashley	1972 Mary Budke
1952 Jacqueline Pung	1959 Barbara McIntire	1966 JoAnne Carner	1973 Carol Semple
1953 Mary Faulk	1960 JoAnne Gunderson	1967 Mary Lou Dill	1974 Cynthia Hill
1954 Barbara Romack	1961 Anne Quast Decker	1968 JoAnne Carner	1975 Beth Daniel
1955 Patricia Lesser	1962 JoAnne Gunderson	1969 Catherine Lacoste	1976 Donna Horton
1956 Marlene Stewart	1963 Anne Quast Welts	1970 Martha Wilkinson	1977 Beth Daniel
1957 JoAnne Gunderson	1964 Barbara McIntire	1971 Laura Baugh	1978 Cathy Sherk
			1979 Carolyn Hill

THE WALKER CUP (Men Amateur Golfers)

SouRCE: U.S. Golf Association

Year	Results	Site	Year	Results	Site
1922	U.S. 8, Great Britain 4	Southampton, N.Y.	1953	U.S. 9, Great Britain 3	Marion, Mass.
1923	U.S. 6, Great Britain 5	St. Andrews, Scotland	1955	U.S. 10, Great Britain 2	St. Andrews, Scotland
1924	U.S. 9, Great Britain 3	Garden City, N.Y.	1957	U.S. 8, Great Britain 3	Minneapolis, Minn.
1926	U.S. 6, Great Britain 5	St. Andrews, Scotland	1959	U.S. 9, Great Britain 3	Muirfield, Scotland
1928	U.S. 11, Great Britain 1	Wheaton, Ill.	1961	U.S. 11, Great Britain 1	Seattle, Wash.
1930	U.S. 10, Great Britain 2	Sandwich, England	1963	U.S. 12, Great Britain 8	Turnberry, Scotland
1932	U.S. 8, Great Britain 1	Brookline, Mass.	1965	U.S. 11, Great Britain 11	Baltimore, Md.
1934	U.S. 9, Great Britain 2	St. Andrews, Scotland	1967	U.S. 13, Great Britain 7	Sandwich, England
1936	U.S. 9, Great Britain 0	Clementon, N.J.	1969	U.S. 10, Great Britain 8	Milwaukee, Wis.
1938	Great Britain 7, U.S. 4	St. Andrews, Scotland	1971	Great Britain 13, U.S. 11	St. Andrews, Scotland
1947	U.S. 8, Great Britain 4	St. Andrews, Scotland	1973	U.S. 14, Great Britain 10	Brookline, Mass.
1949	U.S. 10, Great Britain 2	Mamaroneck, N.Y.	1975	U.S. 15½, Great Britain 8½	St. Andrews, Scotland
1951	U.S. 6, Great Britain 3	Southport, England	1977	U.S. 16, Great Britain 8	Southampton, N.Y.
			1979	U.S. 15½, Great Britain 8½	Muirfield, Scotland

THE CURTIS CUP (Women Amateur Golfers)

SouRCE: U.S. Golf Association

Year	Results	Site	Year	Results	Site
1932	U.S. 5½, British Isles 3½	Wentworth, England	1960	U.S. 6½, British Isles 2½	Worksop, England
1934	U.S. 6½, British Isles 7½	Chevy Chase, Md.	1962	U.S. 8, British Isles 1	Colorado Sprs., Colo.
1936	U.S. 4½, British Isles 4½	Gleneagles, Scotland	1964	U.S. 10½, British Isles 7½	Porthcawl, South Wales
1938	U.S. 5½, British Isles 3½	Manchester, Mass.	1966	U.S. 13, British Isles 5	Hot Springs, Va.
1948	U.S. 6½, British Isles 2½	Southport, England	1968	U.S. 10½, British Isles 7½	Newcastle, No. Ireland
1950	U.S. 7½, British Isles 1½	Williamsville, N.Y.	1970	U.S. 11½, British Isles 6½	West Newton, Mass.
1952	British Isles 5, U.S. 4	Muirfield, Scotland	1972	U.S. 10, British Isles 8	Western Gailes, Scotland
1954	U.S. 6, British Isles 3	Ardmore, Pa.	1974	U.S. 13, British Isles 5	San Francisco, Calif.
1956	British Isles 5, U.S. 4	Sandwich Bay, England	1976	U.S. 11½, British Isles 6½	St. Annes-On-Sea, Eng.
1958	British Isles 4½, U.S. 4½	West Newton, Mass.	1978	U.S. 12, British Isles 6	Rye, N.Y.

OTHER GOLF CHAMPIONS

Year	NCAA Team	NCAA Individual	Women's Intercollegiate
1968	Florida	Grier Jones, Oklahoma State	Gail Sykes, Odessa (Texas)
1969	Houston	Bob Clark, California (L.A.) State	Jane Bastanchury, Arizona State
1970	Houston	John Mahaffey, Houston	Cathy Gaughan, Arizona State
1971	Texas	Ben Crenshaw, Texas	Shelley Hamlin, Stanford
1972	Texas	Ben Crenshaw & Tom Kite, Texas	Ann Laughlin, Miami (Florida)
1973	Florida	Ben Chrenshaw, Texas	Bonnie Lauer, Michigan State
1974	Wake Forest	Curtis Strange, Wake Forest	Mary Budke, Oregon State
1975	Wake Forest	Jay Haas, Wake Forest	Barbara Barrow, San Diego State
1976	Oklahoma State	Scott Simpson, Southern California	Nancy Lopez, Tulsa
1977	Houston	Scott Simpson, Southern California	Cathy Morse, Miami (Florida)
1978	Oklahoma State	David Edwards, Oklahoma State	Deborah Petrizzi, Texas-Austin
1979	Ohio State	Gary Hallberg, Wake Forest	Kyle O'Brien, Southern Methodist

TENNIS

United States Tennis Association (USTA); 51 East 42nd Street, New York 10017. President: W. E. Hester Jr. Executive Secretary: Michael J. Burns.

USTA NATIONAL CHAMPIONS (U.S. Open since 1968)

Men's Singles

1924	Bill Tilden (U.S.A.)	1938	Don Budge (U.S.A.)	1952	Frank Sedgman (Australia)	1966	Fred Stolle (Australia)
1925	Bill Tilden (U.S.A.)	1939	Bobby Riggs (U.S.A.)	1953	Tony Trabert (U.S.A.)	1967	John Newcombe (Australia)
1926	Rene Lacoste (France)	1940	Don McNeill (U.S.A.)	1954	Vic Seixas (U.S.A.)	1968	Arthur Ashe (U.S.A.)
1927	Rene Lacoste (France)	1941	Bobby Riggs (U.S.A.)	1955	Tony Trabert (U.S.A.)	1969	Rod Laver (Australia)
1928	Henri Cochet (France)	1942	Ted Schroeder (U.S.A.)	1956	Ken Rosewall (Australia)	1970	Ken Rosewall (Australia)
1929	Bill Tilden (U.S.A.)	1943	Joe Hunt (U.S.A.)	1957	Mal Anderson (Australia)	1971	Stan Smith (U.S.A.)
1930	John Doeg (U.S.A.)	1944	Frank Parker (U.S.A.)	1958	Ashley Cooper (Australia)	1972	Ilie Nastase (Romania)
1931	Ellsworth Vines (U.S.A.)	1945	Frank Parker (U.S.A.)	1959	Neale Fraser (Australia)	1973	John Newcombe (Australia)
1932	Ellsworth Vines (U.S.A.)	1946	Jack Kramer (U.S.A.)	1960	Neale Fraser (Australia)	1974	Jimmy Connors (U.S.A.)
1933	Fred Perry (England)	1947	Jack Kramer (U.S.A.)	1961	Roy Emerson (Australia)	1975	Manuel Orantes (Spain)
1934	Fred Perry (England)	1948	Pancho Gonzales (U.S.)	1962	Rod Laver (Australia)	1976	Jimmy Connors (U.S.A.)
1935	Wilmer Allison (U.S.A.)	1949	Pancho Gonzalez (U.S.A.)	1963	Rafael Osuna (Mexico)	1977	Guillermo Vilas (Argentina)
1936	Fred Perry (England)	1950	Art Larsen (U.S.A.)	1964	Roy Emerson (Australia)	1978	Jimmy Connors (U.S.A.)
1937	Don Budge (U.S.A.)	1951	Frank Sedgman (Australia)	1965	Manuel Santana (Spain)	1979	John McEnroe (U.S.A.)

Men's Doubles

1924	Howard Kinsey–Robert Kinsey	1943	Jack Kramer–Frank Parker
1925	Vinnie Richards–R. Norris Williams	1944	Don McNeill–Bob Falkenburg
1926	Vinnie Richards–R. Norris Williams	1945	Gardnar Mulloy–Bill Talbert
1927	Bill Tilden–Frank Hunter	1946	Gardnar Mulloy–Bill Talbert
1928	George Lott–John Hennessey	1947	Jack Kramer–Ted Schroeder
1929	George Lott–John Doeg	1948	Gardnar Mulloy–Bill Talbert
1930	George Lott–John Doeg	1949	Jack Bromwich–William Sidwell
1931	Wilmer Allison–John Van Ryn	1950	Jack Bromwich–Frank Sedgman
1932	Ellsworth Vines–Keith Gledhill	1951	Frank Sedgman–Ken McGregor
1933	George Lott–Lester Stoefen	1952	Vic Seixas–Mervyn Rose
1934	George Lott–Lester Stoefen	1953	Rex Hartwig–Mervyn Rose
1935	Wilmer Allison–John Van Ryn	1954	Vic Seixas–Tony Trabert
1936	Don Budge–Gene Mako	1955	Kosei Kamo–Atsushi Miyagi
1937	Gottfried von Cramm–Henner Henkel	1956	Lew Hoad–Ken Rosewall
1938	Don Budge–Gene Mako	1957	Neale Fraser–Neale Fraser
1939	Adrian Quist–Jack Bromwich	1958	Alex Olmedo–Ham Richardson
1940	Jack Kramer–Ted Schroeder	1959	Neale Fraser–Roy Emerson
1941	Jack Kramer–Ted Schroeder	1960	Neale Fraser–Roy Emerson
1942	Gardnar Mulloy–Bill Talbert	1961	Chuck McKinley–Dennis Ralston

1962	Rafael Osuna–Antonio Palafox
1963	Chuck McKinley–Dennis Ralston
1964	Chuck McKinley–Dennis Ralston
1965	Roy Emerson–Fred Stolle
1966	Roy Emerson–Fred Stolle
1967	John Newcombe–Tony Roche
1968	Stan Smith–Bob Lutz
1969	Ken Rosewall–Fred Stolle
1970	Nikki Pilic–Pierre Barthes
1971	John Newcombe–Roger Taylor
1972	Cliff Drysdale–Roger Taylor
1973	Owen Davidson–John Newcombe
1974	Bob Lutz–Stan Smith
1975	Jimmy Connors–Ilie Nastase
1976	Marty Riessen–Tom Okker
1977	Bob Hewitt–Frew McMillan
1978	Stan Smith–Bob Lutz
1979	John McEnroe–Peter Fleming

Women's Singles

1924	Helen Wills (U.S.A.)	1943	Pauline Betz (U.S.A.)
1925	Helen Wills (U.S.A.)	1944	Pauline Betz (U.S.A.)
1926	Molla Bjurstedt Mallory (U.S.A.)	1945	Sarah Palfrey Cooke (U.S.A.)
1927	Helen Wills (U.S.A.)	1946	Pauline Betz (U.S.A.)
1928	Helen Wills (U.S.A.)	1947	Louise Brough (U.S.A.)
1929	Helen Wills (U.S.A.)	1948	Margaret Osborne du Pont (U.S.A.)
1930	Betty Nuthall (England)	1949	Margaret Osborne du Pont (U.S.A.)
1931	Helen Wills Moody (U.S.A.)	1950	Margaret Osborne du Pont (U.S.A.)
1932	Helen Hull Jacobs (U.S.A.)	1951	Maureen Connolly (U.S.A.)
1933	Helen Hull Jacobs (U.S.A.)	1952	Maureen Connolly (U.S.A.)
1934	Helen Hull Jacobs (U.S.A.)	1953	Maureen Connolly (U.S.A.)
1935	Helen Hull Jacobs (U.S.A.)	1954	Doris Hart (U.S.A.)
1936	Alice Marble (U.S.A.)	1955	Doris Hart (U.S.A.)
1937	Anita Lizana (Chile)	1956	Shirley Fry (U.S.A.)
1938	Alice Marble (U.S.A.)	1957	Althea Gibson (U.S.A.)
1939	Alice Marble (U.S.A.)	1958	Althea Gibson (U.S.A.)
1940	Alice Marble (U.S.A.)	1959	Maria Bueno (Brazil)
1941	Sarah Palfrey Cooke (U.S.A.)	1960	Darlene Hard (U.S.A.)
1942	Pauline Betz (U.S.A.)	1961	Darlene Hard (U.S.A.)

1962	Margaret Smith (Australia)
1963	Maria Bueno (Brazil)
1964	Maria Bueno (Brazil)
1965	Margaret Smith (Australia)
1966	Maria Bueno (Brazil)
1967	Billie Jean King (U.S.A.)
1968	Virginia Wade (England)
1969	Margaret Smith Court (Australia)
1970	Margaret Court (Australia)
1971	Billie Jean King (U.S.A.)
1972	Billie Jean King (U.S.A.)
1973	Margaret Court (Australia)
1974	Billie Jean King (U.S.A.)
1975	Chris Evert (U.S.A.)
1976	Chris Evert (U.S.A.)
1977	Chris Evert (U.S.A.)
1978	Chris Evert (U.S.A.)
1979	Tracy Austin (U.S.A.)

Women's Doubles

1924	Mrs. Hazel Wightman–Helen Wills
1925	Mary K. Browne–Helen Wills
1926	Elizabeth Ryan–Eleanor Goss
1927	Mrs. Kathleen McKane Godfree–Ermyntrude Harvey
1928	Mrs. Hazel Wightman–Helen Wills
1929	Mrs. Phoebe Watson–Mrs. L. R. C. Michell
1930	Betty Nuthall–Sarah Palfrey
1931	Betty Nuthall–Mrs. Eileen Whittingstall
1932	Helen Jacobs–Sarah Palfrey
1933	Betty Nuthall–Freda James
1934	Helen Jacobs–Sarah Palfrey
1935	Helen Jacobs–Mrs. Sarah Palfrey Fabyan
1936	Mrs. Marjorie Van Ryn–Carolin Babcock
1937	Mrs. Sarah Palfrey Fabyan–Alice Marble
1938	Mrs. Sarah Palfrey Fabyan–Alice Marble
1939	Mrs. Sarah Palfrey Fabyan–Alice Marble
1940	Mrs. Sarah Palfrey Fabyan–Alice Marble
1941	Mrs. Sarah Palfrey Cooke–Margaret Osborne
1942	Louise Brough–Margaret Osborne
1943	Louise Brough–Margaret Osborne
1944	Louise Brough–Margaret Osborne
1945	Louise Brough–Margaret Osborne
1946	Louise Brough–Margaret Osborne
1947	Louise Brough–Margaret Osborne
1948	Louise Brough–Mrs. Margaret Osborne duPont
1949	Louise Brough–Mrs. Margaret Osborne duPont
1950	Louise Brough–Mrs. Margaret Osborne duPont
1951	Shirley Fry–Doris Hart

1952	Shirley Fry–Doris Hart
1953	Shirley Fry–Doris Hart
1954	Shirley Fry–Doris Hart
1955	Louise Brough–Mrs. Margaret Osborne duPont
1956	Louise Brough–Mrs. Margaret Osborne duPont
1957	Louise Brough–Mrs. Margaret Osborne duPont
1958	Jeanne Arth–Darlene Hard
1959	Jeanne Arth–Darlene Hard
1960	Maria Bueno–Darlene Hard
1961	Darlene Hard–Lesley Turner
1962	Darlene Hard–Maria Bueno
1963	Robyn Ebbern–Margaret Smith
1964	Billie Jean Moffitt–Mrs. Karen Susman
1965	Carole Graebner–Nancy Richey
1966	Maria Bueno–Nancy Richey
1967	Mrs. Billie Jean King–Rosemary Casals
1968	Maria Bueno–Margaret Smith Court
1969	Darlene Hard–Françoise Durr
1970	Margaret Smith Court–Judy Tegart Dalton
1971	Rosemary Casals–Judy Tegart Dalton
1972	Françoise Durr–Betty Stove
1973	Mrs. Margaret Smith Court–Virginia Wade
1974	Billie Jean King–Rosemary Casals
1975	Mrs. Margaret Smith Court–Virginia Wade
1976	Linky Boshoff–Ilana Kloss
1977	Betty Stove–Martina Navratilova
1978	Billie Jean King–Martina Navratilova
1979	Betty Stove–Wendy Turnbull

ALL-ENGLAND CHAMPIONS, WIMBLEDON (Open competition since 1968)

Men's Singles

Year	Champion	Year	Champion	Year	Champion
1926	Jean Borotra (France)	1948	Bob Falkenburg (U.S.A.)	1964	Roy Emerson (Australia)
1927	Henri Cochet (France)	1949	Ted Schroeder (U.S.A.)	1965	Roy Emerson (Australia)
1928	Rene Lacoste (France)	1950	Budge Patty (U.S.A.)	1966	Manuel Santana (Spain)
1929	Henri Cochet (France)	1951	Dick Savitt (U.S.A.)	1967	John Newcombe (Australia)
1930	Bill Tilden (U.S.A.)	1952	Frank Sedgman (Australia)	1968	Rod Laver (Australia)
1931	Sid Wood (U.S.A.)	1953	Vic Seixas (U.S.A.)	1969	Rod Laver (Australia)
1932	Ellsworth Vines (U.S.A.)	1954	Jaroslav Drobny (Egypt)	1970	John Newcombe (Australia)
1933	John Crawford (Australia)	1955	Tony Trabert (U.S.A.)	1971	John Newcombe (Australia)
1934	Fred Perry (England)	1956	Lew Hoad (Australia)	1972	Stan Smith (U.S.A.)
1935	Fred Perry (England)	1957	Lew Hoad (Australia)	1973	Jan Kodes (Czechoslovakia)
1936	Fred Perry (England)	1958	Ashley Cooper (Australia)	1974	Jimmy Connors (U.S.A.)
1937	Don Budge (U.S.A.)	1959	Alex Olmedo (U.S.A.)	1975	Arthur Ashe (U.S.A.)
1938	Don Budge (U.S.A.)	1960	Neale Fraser (Australia)	1976	Bjorn Borg (Sweden)
1939	Bobby Riggs (U.S.A.)	1961	Rod Laver (Australia)	1977	Bjorn Borg (Sweden)
1946	Yvon Petra (France)	1962	Rod Laver (Australia)	1978	Bjorn Borg (Sweden)
1947	Jack Kramer (U.S.A.)	1963	Chuck McKinley (U.S.A.)	1979	Bjorn Borg (Sweden)

Men's Doubles

Year	Champions	Year	Champions	Year	Champions
1929	Wilmer Allison–John Van Ryn	1950	Jack Bromwich–Adrian Quist	1965	John Newcombe–Tony Roche
1930	Wilmer Allison–John Van Ryn	1951	Ken McGregor–Frank Sedgman	1966	Ken Fletcher–John Newcombe
1931	John Van Ryn–George Lott	1952	Ken McGregor–Frank Sedgman	1967	Bob Hewitt–Frew McMillan
1932	Jean Borotra–Jacques Brugnon	1953	Lew Hoad–Ken Rosewall	1968	John Newcombe–Tony Roche
1933	Jean Borotra–Jacques Brugnon	1954	Rex Hartwig–Mervyn Rose	1969	John Newcombe–Tony Roche
1934	George Lott–Lester Stoefen	1955	Rex Hartwig–Lew Hoad	1970	John Newcombe–Tony Roche
1935	John Crawford–Adrian Quist	1956	Lew Hoad–Ken Rosewall	1971	Rod Laver–Roy Emerson
1936	George Hughes–Charles Tuckey	1957	Gardnar Mulloy–Budge Patty	1972	Bob Hewitt–Frew McMillan
1937	Don Budge–Gene Mako	1958	Sven Davidson–Ulf Schmidt	1973	Jim Connors–Illie Nastase
1938	Don Budge–Gene Mako	1959	Neale Fraser–Roy Emerson	1974	John Newcombe–Tony Roche
1939	Bobby Riggs–Elwood Cooke	1960	Rafael Osuna–Dennis Ralston	1975	Vitas Gerulatis–Sandy Mayer
1946	Jack Kramer–Tom Brown	1961	Neale Fraser–Roy Emerson	1976	Brian Gottfried–Raul Ramirez
1947	Jack Kramer–Bob Falkenburg	1962	Fred Stolle–Bob Hewitt	1977	Ross Case–Geoff Masters
1948	Jack Bromwich–Frank Sedgman	1963	Rafael Osuna–Antonio Palafox	1978	Bob Hewitt–Frew McMillan
1949	Pancho Gonzalez–Frank Parker	1964	Bob Hewitt–Fred Stolle	1979	John McEnroe–Peter Fleming

Women's Singles

1926	Kathleen M. Godfree (England)	1948	Louise Brough (U.S.A.)	1964	Maria Bueno (Brazil)
1927	Helen Wills (U.S.A.)	1949	Louise Brough (U.S.A.)	1965	Margaret Smith (Australia)
1928	Helen Wills (U.S.A.)	1950	Louise Brough (U.S.A.)	1966	Billie Jean King (U.S.A.)
1929	Helen Wills (U.S.A.)	1951	Doris Hart (U.S.A.)	1967	Billie Jean King (U.S.A.)
1930	Helen Wills Moody (U.S.A.)	1952	Maureen Connolly (U.S.A.)	1968	Billie Jean King (U.S.A.)
1931	Cecile Aussem (Germany)	1953	Maureen Connolly (U.S.A.)	1969	Ann Haydon Jones (England)
1932	Helen Wills Moody (U.S.A.)	1954	Maureen Connolly (U.S.A.)	1970	Margaret S. Court (Australia)
1933	Helen Wills Moody (U.S.A.)	1955	Louise Brough (U.S.A.)	1971	Evonne Goolagong (Australia)
1934	Dorothy Round (England)	1956	Shirley Fry (U.S.A.)	1972	Billie Jean King (U.S.A.)
1935	Helen Wills Moody (U.S.A.)	1957	Althea Gibson (U.S.A.)	1973	Billie Jean King (U.S.A.)
1936	Helen Hull Jacobs (U.S.A.)	1958	Althea Gibson (U.S.A.)	1974	Chris Evert (U.S.A.)
1937	Dorothy Round (England)	1959	Maria Bueno (Brazil)	1975	Billie Jean King (U.S.A.)
1938	Helen Wills Moody (U.S.A.)	1960	Maria Bueno (Brazil)	1976	Chris Evert (U.S.A.)
1939	Alice Marble (U.S.A.)	1961	Angela Mortimer (England)	1977	Virginia Wade (England)
1946	Pauline Betz (U.S.A.)	1962	Karen Hantze Susman (U.S.A.)	1978	Martina Navratilova (U.S.A.)
1947	Margaret Osborne (U.S.A.)	1963	Margaret Smith (Australia)	1979	Martina Navratilova (U.S.A.)

Women's Doubles

Year	Champions	Year	Champions	Year	Champions
1926	Elizabeth Ryan–Mary K. Browne	1948	Louise Brough–Margaret Osborne duPont	1963	Maria Bueno–Darlene Hard
1927	Elizabeth Ryan–Helen Wills	1949	Louise Brough–Margaret Osborne duPont	1964	Margaret Smith–Lesley Turner
1928	Phoebe Watson–Peggy Saunders	1950	Louise Brough–Margaret Osborne duPont	1965	Maria Bueno–Billie Jean Moffitt
1929	Phoebe Watson–Peggy Saunders Mitchel			1966	Maria Bueno–Nancy Richey
1930	Elizabeth Ryan–Helen Wills Moody	1951	Shirley Fry–Doris Hart	1967	Billie Jean King–Rosemary Casals
1931	Mrs. D. C. Shepherd-Baron–Phyllis Mudford King	1952	Shirley Fry–Doris Hart	1968	Billie Jean King–Rosemary Casals
1932	D. Metaxa–J. Sigart	1953	Shirley Fry–Doris Hart	1969	Margaret S. Court–Judy Tegart
1933	Elizabeth Ryan–Rene Mathieu	1954	Louise Brough–Margaret Osborne duPont	1970	Billie Jean King–Rosemary Casals
1934	Elizabeth Ryan–Rene Mathieu	1955	Angela Mortimer–Anne Shilcock	1971	Billie Jean King–Rosemary Casals
1935	Kay Stammers–Freda James	1956	Angela Buxton–Althea Gibson	1972	Billie Jean King–Betty Stove
1936	Kay Stammers–Freda James	1957	Althea Gibson–Darlene Hard	1973	Billie Jean King–Rosemary Casals
1937	Rene Mathieu–A. M. Yorke	1958	Maria Bueno–Althea Gibson	1974	Peggy Michel–Evonne Goolagong
1938	Alice Marble–Sarah Palfrey Fabyan	1959	Jeanne Arth–Darlene Hard	1975	Kazuko Sawamatsu–Ann Kiyomura
1939	Alice Marble–Sarah Palfrey Fabyan	1960	Maria Bueno–Darlene Hard	1976	Chris Evert–Martina Navratilova
1946	Louise Brough–Margaret Osborne	1961	Karen Hantze–Billie Jean Moffitt	1977	Helen G. Cawley–Joanne Russell
1947	Doris Hart–Patricia Canning Todd	1962	Karen Hantze Susman–Billie Jean Moffitt	1978	Wendy Turnbull–Kerry Reid
				1979	Billie Jean King–Martina Navratilova

WIGHTMAN CUP

Year	Result	Year	Result	Year	Result
1925	Great Britain 4, United States 3	1947	United States 7, Great Britain 0	1963	United States 6, Great Britain 1
1926	United States 4, Great Britain 3	1948	United States 6, Great Britain 1	1964	United States 5, Great Britain 2
1927	United States 5, Great Britain 2	1949	United States 7, Great Britain 0	1965	United States 5, Great Britain 2
1928	Great Britain 4, United States 3	1950	United States 7, Great Britain 0	1966	United States 4, Great Britain 3
1929	United States 4, Great Britain 3	1951	United States 6, Great Britain 1	1967	United States 6, Great Britain 1
1930	Great Britain 4, United States 3	1952	United States 7, Great Britain 0	1968	Great Britain 4, United States 3
1931	United States 5, Great Britain 2	1953	United States 7, Great Britain 0	1969	United States 5, Great Britain 2
1932	United States 4, Great Britain 3	1954	United States 6, Great Britain 1	1970	United States 4, Great Britain 3
1933	United States 4, Great Britain 3	1955	United States 6, Great Britain 1	1971	United States 4, Great Britain 3
1934	United States 5, Great Britain 2	1956	United States 5, Great Britain 2	1972	United States 5, Great Britain 2
1935	United States 4, Great Britain 3	1957	United States 6, Great Britain 1	1973	United States 5, Great Britain 2
1936	United States 4, Great Britain 3	1958	Great Britain 4, United States 3	1974	Great Britain 6, United States 1
1937	United States 6, Great Britain 1	1959	United States 4, Great Britain 3	1975	Great Britain 5, United States 2
1938	United States 5, Great Britain 2	1960	Great Britain 4, United States 3	1976	United States 5, Great Britain 2
1939	United States 5, Great Britain 2	1961	United States 6, Great Britain 1	1977	United States 7, Great Britain 0
1946	United States 7, Great Britain 0	1962	United States 4, Great Britain 3	1978	Great Britain 4, United States 3

DAVIS CUP CHALLENGE ROUND (No matches in 1910, 1915–18, and 1940–45)

Year	Result	Year	Result	Year	Result
1906	British Isles 5, United States 0	1932	France 3, United States 2	1959	Australia 3, United States 2
1907	Australasia 3, British Isles 2	1933	Great Britain 3, France 2	1960	Australia 4, Italy 1
1908	Australasia 3, United States 2	1934	Great Britain 4, United States 1	1961	Australia 5, Italy 0
1909	Australasia 5, United States 0	1935	Great Britain 5, United States 0	1962	Australia 5, Mexico 0
1911	Australasia 5, United States 0	1936	Great Britain 3, Australia 2	1963	United States 3, Australia 2
1912	British Isles 3, Australasia 2	1937	United States 4, Great Britain 1	1964	Australia 3, United States 2
1913	United States 3, British Isles 2	1938	United States 3, Australia 2	1965	Australia 4, Spain 1
1914	Australasia 3, United States 2	1939	Australia 3, United States 2	1966	Australia 4, India 1
1919	Australasia 4, British Isles 1	1946	United States 5, Australia 0	1967	Australia 4, Spain 1
1920	United States 5, Australasia 0	1947	United States 4, Australia 1	1968	United States 4, Australia 1
1921	United States 5, Japan 0	1948	United States 5, Australia 0	1969	United States 5, Rumania 0
1922	United States 4, Australasia 1	1949	United States 4, Australia 1	1970	U.S. 5, W. Germany 0
1923	United States 4, Australasia 1	1950	Australia 4, United States 1	1971	United States 3, Rumania 2
1924	United States 5, Australia 0	1951	Australia 3, United States 2	1972	United States 3, Rumania 2
1925	United States 5, France 0	1952	Australia 4, United States 1	1973	Australia 5, United States 0
1926	United States 4, France 1	1953	Australia 3, United States 2	1974	South Africa defeated
1927	France 3, United States 2	1954	United States 3, Australia 2		India, by default
1928	France 4, United States 1	1955	Australia 5, United States 0	1975	Sweden 3, Czechoslovakia 2
1929	France 3, United States 2	1956	Australia 5, United States 0	1976	Italy 4, Chile 1
1930	France 4, United States 1	1957	Australia 3, United States 2	1977	Australia 3, Italy 1
1931	France 3, Great Britain 2	1958	United States 3, Australia 2	1978	U.S. 4, Great Britain 1

OTHER FOREIGN CHAMPIONSHIPS (Open competition since 1969)

	AUSTRALIAN	CANADIAN	FRENCH	ITALIAN
Men's Singles	**Men's Singles**	**Men's Singles**	**Men's Singles**	**Men's Singles**
1967	Roy Emerson	Manuel Santana	Roy Emerson	Martin Mulligan
1968	Bill Bowrey	Ramanathan Krishnan	Ken Rosewall	Tom Okker
1969	Rod Laver	Cliff Richey	Rod Laver	John Newcombe
1970	Arthur Ashe	Rod Laver	Jan Kodes	Ilie Nastase
1971	Ken Rosewall	John Newcombe	Jan Kodes	Rod Laver
1972	Ken Rosewall	Ilie Nastase	Andres Gimeno	Manuel Orantes
1973	John Newcombe	Tom Okker	Ilie Nastase	Ilie Nastase
1974	Jimmy Connors	Guillermo Vilas	Bjorn Borg	Bjorn Borg
1975	John Newcombe	Manuel Orantes	Bjorn Borg	Raul Ramirez
1976	Mark Edmondson	Guillermo Vilas	Adriano Panatta	Adriano Panatta
1977	Roscoe Tanner	Jeff Borowiak	Guillermo Vilas	Vitas Gerulaitis
1978	Vitas Gerulaitis	Eddie Dibbs	Bjorn Borg	Bjorn Borg
1979	Guillermo Vilas	Bjorn Borg	Bjorn Borg	Vitas Gerulaitis
Women's Singles	**Women's Singles**	**Women's Singles**	**Women's Singles**	**Women's Singles**
1967	Nancy Richey	Kathy Harter	Françoise Durr	Lesley Turner
1968	Billie Jean King	Peaches Bartkowicz	Nancy Richey	Lesley Turner Bowrey
1969	Margaret Smith Court	Faye Urban	Margaret Smith Court	Julie Heldman
1970	Margaret Smith Court	Margaret Smith Court	Margaret Smith Court	Billie Jean King
1971	Margaret Smith Court	Françoise Durr	Evonne Goolagong	Virginia Wade
1972	Virginia Wade	Evonne Goolagong	Billie Jean King	Linda Tuero
1973	Margaret Court	Evonne Goolagong	Margaret Court	Evonne Goolagong
1974	Evonne Goolagong	Chris Evert	Chris Evert	Chris Evert
1975	Evonne Goolagong	Marcie Louie	Chris Evert	Chris Evert
1976	Evonne Goolagong	Mima Jausovec	Sue Barker	Mima Jausovec
1977	Kerry Reid	Regina Marsikova	Mima Jausovec	Janet Newberry
1978	Evonne Goolagong	Regina Marsikova	Virginia Ruzici	Regina Marsikova
1979	Chris O'Neill	Laura DuPont	Chris Evert Lloyd	Tracy Austin

THE GRAND SLAM OF TENNIS

Winners of the Australian, French, British and United States Championships in the same season.

Year	Champions	Country	Event
1938	Don Budge	United States	Men's Singles
1951	Frank Sedgman–Ken McGregor	Australia	Men's Doubles
1953	Maureen Connolly	United States	Women's Singles
1960	Maria Bueno	Brazil	Women's Doubles*
1962	Rod Laver	Australia	Men's Singles
1963	Margaret Smith–Ken Fletcher	Australia	Mixed Doubles
1967	Owen Davidson	Australia	Mixed Doubles*
1969	Rod Laver	Australia	Men's Singles
1970	Margaret Smith Court	Australia	Women's Singles

*Won in Australia with a different doubles partner.

COLLEGIATE SINGLES CHAMPIONS

Year	Man	School	Woman	School
1966	Charles Pasarell	U.C.L.A.	Cecilia Martinez	San Francisco State
1967	Bob Lutz	Southern California	Patsy Rippy	Odessa Jr. College
1968	Stan Smith	Southern California	Emilie Burrer	Trinity
1969	Joaquin Loyo-Mayo	Southern California	Emilie Burrer	Trinity
1970	Jeff Borowiak	U.C.L.A.	Laura DuPont	North Carolina
1971	Jimmy Connors	U.C.L.A.	Pam Richmond	Arizona State
1972	Dick Stockton	Trinity	Janice Metcalf	Redlands
1973	Alex Mayer	Stanford	Janice Metcalf	Redlands
1974	John Whitlinger	Stanford	Carrier Meyer	Marymount
1975	Bill Martin	U.C.L.A.	Stephanie Tolleson	Trinity
1976	Bill Scanlon	Trinity	Barbara Hallquist	Southern California
1977	Matt Mitchell	Stanford	Barbara Hallquist	Southern California
1978	John McEnroe	Stanford	Jeanne DuVall	U.C.L.A.
1979	Kevin Curran	Texas	Kathy Jordan	Stanford

FEDERATION CUP
Women's International Team Competition
SOURCE: U.S.T.A.

Year	Final Round Results	Year	Final Round Results
1963	United States, 2, Australia 1	1971	Australia 3, Great Britain 0
1964	Australia 2, United States 1	1972	South Africa 2, Great Britain 1
1965	Australia 2, United States 1	1973	Australia 3, South Africa 0
1966	United States 3, West Germany 0	1974	Australia 2, United States 1
1967	United States 2, Great Britain 0	1975	Czechoslovakia 3, Australia 0
1968	Australia 3, Netherlands 0	1976	United States 2, Australia 1
1969	United States 2, Australia 1	1977	United States 2, Australia 1
1970	Australia 3, West Germany 0	1978	United States 2, Australia 1
		1979	United States 3, Australia 0

1979 TOP MONEY WINNERS (to Sept. 28)

MEN

1.	John McEnroe, United States	$486,885
2.	Bjorn Borg, Sweden	485,442
3.	Jimmy Connors, United States	407,305
4.	Peter Fleming, United States	227,112
5.	Vitas Gerulaitis, United States	217,902
6.	Eddie Dibbs, United States	189,311
7.	Roscoe Tanner, United States	171,932
8.	Guillermo Vilas, Argentina	156,086
9.	Wojtek Fibak, Poland	147,403
10.	Gene Mayer, United States	133,294

WOMEN

1.	Martina Navratilova, United States	$440,984
2.	Chris Evert Lloyd, United States	374,632
3.	Tracy Austin, United States	308,110
4.	Diane Fromholtz, Australia	188,374
5.	Wendy Turnbull, Australia	186,963
6.	Betty Stove, Netherlands	133,106
7.	Sue Barker, England	128,269
8.	Virginia Wade, England	106,050
9.	Rosemary Casals, United States	104,001
10.	Greer Stevens, South Africa	95,532

WORLD CHAMPIONSHIP TENNIS (WCT) FINALS: 1979

Singles—John McEnroe   Doubles—John McEnroe - Peter Fleming   Challenge Cup (Dec. 1978) — Ilie Nastase

OTHER 1979 TENNIS CHAMPIONS

NCAA DIVISION I
  Singles — Kevin Curren, Texas
  Doubles — Erick Iskersky - Ben McKown, Trinity (Texas)
  Team — U.C.L.A.
  Runner-Up — Trinity (Texas)

NCAA DIVISION II
  Singles — Arjun Fernando, Southern Illinois (Edwardsville)
  Doubles — Juan Farrow-Arjun Fernando, Southern Illinois (Edwardsville)
  Team — Southern Illinois (Edwardsville)
  Runner-Up — San Diego

NCAA DIVISION III
  Singles — Mark Tappan, Redlands (Calif.)
  Doubles — Mike Capelouto - Ken Whitmer, Redlands (Calif.)
  Team — Redlands (Calif.)
  Runnnr-Up — Gustavus Adolphus (Minn.)

AIAW (LARGE COLLEGE)
  Singles — Kathy Jordan, Stanford
  Doubles — Kathy Jordan - Alycia Moulton, Stanford
  Team — Southern California
  Runner-Up — Stanford

AIAW (SMALL COLLEGE)
  Singles — Phyllis Blackwell, Tennessee-Chattanooga
  Doubles — Elizabeth Sharp - Kathy Kolankiewicz, Tennessee-Chattanooga
  Team — Tennessee-Chattanooga
  Runner-Up — College of Charleston (S.C.)

NAIA Team — Atlantic Christian (N.C.)

JUNIOR COLLEGES — Team
  Men — Odessa College (Texas)
  Women — Odessa College (Texas)

JAMES E. SULLIVAN MEMORIAL TROPHY
Sportsmanship — Outstanding Amateur Athlete

Year	Athlete	Sport	Year	Athlete	Sport
1930	Bobby Jones	Golf	1954	Mal Whitfield	Track & Field
1931	Bernard Berlinger	Track & Field	1955	Harrison Dillard	Track & Field
1932	James Bausch	Track & Field	1956	Patricia McCormick	Diving
1933	Glenn Cunningham	Track & Field	1957	Bobby Morrow	Track & Field
1934	Bill Bonthron	Track & Field	1958	Glenn Davis	Track & Field
1935	Lawson Little	Golf	1959	Parry O'Brien	Track & Field
1936	Glen Morris	Track & Field	1960	Rafer Johnson	Track & Field
1937	Don Budge	Tennis	1961	Wilma Rudolph Ward	Track & Field
1938	Donald Lash	Track & Field	1962	Jim Beatty	Track & Field
1939	Joe Burk	Rowing	1963	John Pennel	Track & Field
1940	Greg Rice	Track & Field	1964	Don Schollander	Swimming
1941	Leslie MacMitchell	Track & Field	1965	Bill Bradley	Basketball
1942	Cornelius Warmerdam	Track & Field	1966	Jim Ryun	Track & Field
1943	Gilbert Dodds	Track & Field	1967	Randy Matson	Track & Field
1944	Ann Curtis	Swimming	1968	Debbie Meyer	Swimming
1945	Doc Blanchard	Football	1969	Bill Toomey	Track & Field
1946	Arnold Tucker	Football	1970	John Kinsella	Swimming
1947	John Kelly, Jr.	Rowing	1971	Mark Spitz	Swimming
1948	Robert Mathias	Track & Field	1972	Frank Shorter	Track & Field
1949	Richard Button	Skating	1973	Bill Walton	Basketball
1950	Fred Wilt	Track & Field	1974	Rick Wohlhuter	Track & Field
1951	Bob Richards	Track & Field	1975	Tim Shaw	Swimming
1952	Horace Ashenfelter	Track & Field	1976	Bruce Jenner	Track & Field
1953	Sammy Lee	Diving	1977	John Naber	Swimming
			1978	Tracy Caulkins	Swimming

AUTO RACING

THE HISTORY OF THE MILE RECORD

DATE	DRIVER	CAR	AMERICAN TIME	AVG.	WORLD'S TIME	AVG.
12/18/98	Chasseloup-Laubat	Jeantaud			57.000	39.24
1/17/99	Camille Jenatzy	Jamais Contente Jeantzy			54.000	41.42
1/17/99	Chasseloup-Laubat	Jeantaud			51.500	43.69
1/27/99	Camille Jenatzy	Jamais Contente Jeantzy			44.800	49.40
3/4/99	Chasseloup-Laubat	Jeantaud			38.400	58.25
4/29/99	Camille Jenatzy	Jamais Contente Jeantzy			34.400	65.79
4/13/02	Serpollet	Serpollet			29.800	76.06
8/5/02	W. K. Vanderbilt	Mors			29.400	76.08
11/5/02	H. Fournier	Mors			29.200	76.60
11/17/02	Augieres	Mors			29.000	77.13
3/17/03	Rigolly	Gorbron-Brillie			26.800	83.46
11/5/03	A. Duray	Gobron-Brillie			26.400	84.73
1/12/04	Henry Ford	Ford "999"	39.40	91.370		
1/22/04	W. K. Vanderbilt	Mercedes	39.00	92.307		
3/31/04	Rigolly	Gobbron-Brillie			23.600	94.78
5/12/04	De Caters	Mercedes			23.000	97.26
7/21/04	Rigolly	Gobron-Brillie			21.600	103.56
11/13/04	Victor Hemery	Darracq			21.400	104.53
12/30/04	Barras	Darracq			20.400	109.65
1/24/05	Arthur MacDonald	Napier	34.40	104.65		
1/25/05	H. L. Bowden	Mercedes	32.80	109.75		
1/26/06	Fred Marriott	Stanley (Steam)	28.20	127.659		
11/8/09*	Victor Hemery	Benz			17.761	125.914*
3/16/10	Barney Oldfield	Benz	27.33	131.724		
4/23/11	Bob Burman	Benz	25.40	141.732		
6/24/14	L. G. Hornsted	Benz			29.01	124.095
2/12/19	Ralph DePalma	Packard	24.02	149.875		
4/27/20	Tom Milton	Duesenberg	23.07	156.046		
5/17/22	K. Lee Guinness	Sunbeam			27.87	129.171
6/26/24	J. G. Parry-Thomas	Leyland-Thomas			27.75	129.730
7/6/24	Rene Thomas	Delage			25.12	143.312
7/12/24	E. A. D. Eldridge	Fiat			24.675	145.897
9/25/24	Capt. M. Campbell	Sunbeam			24.630	146.163
7/21/25	Capt. M. Campbell	Sunbeam			23.878	150.766
4/27/26	J. G. Parry-Thomas	Thomas Special			21.419	168.075
4/28/26	J. G. Parry-Thomas	Thomas Special			21.099	170.624
2/4/27	Capt. M. Campbell	Napier-Campbell			20.663	174.224
3/29/27	Maj. H. O. D. Seagrave	Sunbeam	17.665	203.790	17.665	203.790
2/19/28	Capt. M. Campbell	Napier-Campbell	17.395	206.956	17.395	206.956
4/22/28	Ray Keech	White Triplex	17.345	207.552	17.345	207.552
3/11/29	Maj. H. O. D. Seagrave	Irving-Napier	15.56	231.446	15.56	231.446
2/5/31	Sir Malcolm Campbell	Napier-Campbell	14.65	245.086	14.65	246.086
2/24/32	Sir Malcolm Campbell	Napier-Campbell	14.175	253.96	14.175	253.96
2/22/33	Sir Malcolm Campbell	Napier-Campbell	13.23	272.109	13.23	272.109
3/7/35	Sir Malcolm Campbell	Bluebird Special	13.01	276.82	13.01	276.82
9/3/35	Sir Malcolm Campbell	Bluebird Special	11.96	301.13	11.96	301.13
11/19/37	Capt. G. E. T. Eyston	Thunderbolt No. 1	11.56	311.42	11.56	311.42
8/27/38	Capt. G. E. T. Eyston	Thunderbolt No. 1	10.42	345.5	10.42	345.5
9/15/38	John Cobb	Railton	10.28	350.2	10.28	350.2
9/16/38	Capt. G. E. T. Eyston	Thunderbolt No. 1	10.07	357.5	10.07	357.5
8/23/39	John Cobb	Railton	9.76	368.9	9.76	368.9
9/16/47	John Cobb	Railton-Mobil Special	9.1325	394.2	9.1325	394.2
8/5/63	Craig Breedlove	Spirit of America	8.8355	407.45	8.8355	407.45
10/2/64	Tom Green	Wingfoot Express	8.7125	413.20	8.7125	413.20
10/5/64	Art Arfons	Art Arfons Green Monster	8.2945	434.02	8.2945	434.02
10/13/64	Craig Breedlove	Spirit of America	7.6805	468.719	7.6805	468.719
10/15/64	Craig Breedlove	Spirit of America	6.8405	526.277	6.8405	526.277
10/27/64	Art Arfons	Art Arfons Green Monster	6.7075	536.71	6.7075	536.71
11/2/65	Craig Breedlove	Spirit of America–Sonic I	6.485	555.127	6.485	555.127
11/7/65	Art Arfons	Art Arfons Green Monster	6.244	576.553	6.244	576.553
11/15/65	Craig Breedlove	Spirit of America–Sonic I	5.994	600.601	5.994	600.601
10/23/70	Gary Gabelich	Blue Flame	5.784	622.407	5.784	622.407
9/9/79	Stan Barrett	The Budweiser Rocket	5.637	638.637	5.637	638.637

* Records above this point for World's Time were made over the flying kilometer, the recognized distance in the early years.
NOTE: The above records are the average of two runs made in opposite directions within one hour.

FORMULA 1 GRAND PRIX CHAMPIONS
SOURCE: Sports Car Club of America

Year	Champion	Car	Nationality
1950	Giuseppe Farina	Alfa Romeo	Italy
1951	Juan Manuel Fangio	Alfa Romeo	Argentina
1952	Alberto Ascari	Ferrari	Italy
1953	Alberto Ascari	Ferrari	Italy
1954	Juan Manuel Fangio	Mercedes & Maserati	Argentina
1955	Juan Manuel Fangio	Mercedes	Argentina
1956	Juan Manuel Fangio	Lancia	Argentina
1957	Juan Manuel Fangio	Maserati	Argentina
1958	Mike Hawthorn	Ferrari	Great Britain
1959	Jack Brabham	Cooper	Australia
1960	Jack Brabham	Cooper	Australia
1961	Phil Hill	Ferrari	USA
1962	Graham Hill	BRM	Great Britain
1963	Jim Clark	Lotus	Great Britain
1964	John Surtees	Ferrari	Great Britain
1965	Jim Clark	Lotus	Great Britain
1966	Jack Brabham	Brabham	Australia
1967	Denis Hulme	Brabham	New Zealand
1968	Graham Hill	Lotus	Great Britain
1969	Jackie Stewart	Matra	Great Britain
1970	Jochen Rindt	Lotus	Austria
1971	Jackie Stewart	Tyrrell	Great Britain
1972	Emerson Fittipaldi	Lotus	Brazil
1973	Jackie Stewart	Tyrrell	Great Britain
1974	Emerson Fittipaldi	McLaren	Brazil
1975	Niki Lauda	Ferrari	Austria
1976	James Hunt	McLaren	Great Britain
1977	Niki Lauda	Ferrari	Austria
1978	Mario Andretti	Lotus	USA
1979	Jody Scheckter	Ferrari	South Africa

UNITED STATES GRAND PRIX, WATKINS GLEN, N.Y.
SOURCE: Sports Car Club of America

Year	Winner	Car	Year	Winner	Car
1959*	Bruce McLaren	Cooper	1969	Jochen Rindt	Lotus
1960**	Stirling Moss	Lotus	1970	Emerson Fittipaldi	Lotus
1961	Ines Ireland	Lotus	1971	Francois Cevert	Tyrrell
1962	Jim Clark	Lotus	1972	Jackie Stewart	Tyrrell
1963	Graham Hill	BRM	1973	Ronnie Peterson	Lotus
1964	Graham Hill	BRM	1974	Carlos Reutemann	Brabham
1965	Graham Hill	BRM	1975	Niki Lauda	Ferrari
1966	Jim Clark	Lotus	1976	James Hunt	McLaren
1967	Jim Clark	Lotus	1977	James Hunt	McLaren
1968	Jackie Stewart	Matra	1978	Carlos Reutemann	Ferrari
			1979	Gilles Villeneuve	Ferrari

* Held at Sebring   ** Held at Riverside

UNITED STATES GRAND PRIX WEST, LONG BEACH, CALIF.
SOURCE: Sports Car Club of America

Year	Winner	Car	Year	Winner	Car
1976	Clay Regazzoni	Ferrari	1978	Carlos Reutemann	Ferrari
1977	Mario Andretti	Lotus	1979	Gilles Villeneuve	Ferrari

SPORTS CAR CLUB OF AMERICA SERIES CHAMPIONS
SOURCE: Sports Car Club of America

Citicorp Can-Am® Challenge

Year	Champion	Car
1966	John Surtees	Lola
1967	Bruce McLaren	McLaren M6A
1968	Denis Hulme	McLaren M6A
1969	Bruce McLaren	McLaren M8B
1970	Denis Hulme	McLaren M8D
1971	Peter Revson	McLaren M8F
1972	George Follmer	Porsche 917/10
1974	Mark Donohue	Porsche 917/30
1973	Jackie Oliver	Shadow
1975–1976	(no series)	
1977	Patrick Tambay	Lola T-333CS
1978	Alan Jones	Lola T-333CS

Robert Bosch/VW Gold Cup

Year	Champion	Car
1971	Bill Scott	Royale
1972	Bill Scott	Royale
1973	Bertil Roos	Tui BH3
1974	Elliott Forbes-Robinson	Lynn
1975	Eddie Miller	Lola T-324
1976	Tom Bagley	Zink Z-11
1977	Bob Lazier	Lola T-324
1978	Bill Alsup	Argo

Trans-Am® Championship

Year	Champion	Car
1972	George Follmer	Javelin
1973	Peter Gregg	Chevrolet
1974	Peter Gregg	Porsche
1975	John Greenwood	Chevrolet
1976	George Follmer	Porsche
1977 Category I	Bob Tullius	Jaguar
Category II	Ludwig Heimrath	Porsche
1978 Category I	Bob Tullius	Jaguar
Category II	Greg Pickett	Corvette
1979 Category I	Gene Bothello	Corvette
Category II	John Paul	Porsche

Pro Rally Series

Year	Champion	Car
1973	Scott Harvey/Wayne Zitkus	Dodge Colt
1974	Gene Henderson/Ken Pogue	Jeep Cherokee
1975	John Buffum/Vicki Dykema	Ford Escort
1976	Hendrik Blok/Erick Hauge	Dodge Colt
1977	John Buffum/''Vicki''	TR-7
1978	John Buffum/Doug Shepherd	TR-7

Rabbit/Bilstein Cup

Year	Champion	Car
1976	Paul Hacker	Scirocco
1977	Bill Deters	Scirocco
1978	Gary Benson	Rabbit

INDIANAPOLIS 500
SOURCE: Jack C. Fox, *The Indianapolis 500* (1967), and other sources

Year	Winner	Chassis	Engine	Cylinders	Mph	Gross	Second Place
1920	Gaston Chevrolet	Frontenac	Frontenac	4	88.16	$ 93,550	Rene Thomas
1921	Tommy Milton	Frontenac	Frontenac	8	89.62	$ 86,650	Roscoe Sarles
1922	Jimmy Murphy	Duesenberg	Miller	8	94.48	$ 70,575	Harry Hartz
1923	Tommy Milton	Miller	Miller	8	90.95	$ 83,425	Harry Hartz
1924	L. L. Corum, Joe Boyer	Duesenberg	Duesenberg	8	98.23	$ 86,850	Earl Cooper
1925	Peter DePaolo	Duesenberg	Duesenberg	8	101.13	$ 87,750	Dave Lewis
1926	Frank Lockhart	Miller	Miller*	8	95.885[1]	$ 88,100	Harry Hartz
1927	George Souders	Duesenberg	Duesenberg*	8	97.545	$ 89,850	Earl DeVore
1928	Lou Meyer	Miller	Miller*	8	99.482	$ 90,750	Lou Moore
1929	Ray Keech	Miller	Miller*	8	97.585	$ 95,150	Lou Meyer
1930	Billy Arnold	Summers	Miller†	8	100.448	$ 97,600	Shorty Cantlon
1931	Lou Schneider	Stevens	Miller	8	96.629	$ 81,800	Fred Frame
1932	Fred Frame	Wetteroth	Miller†	8	104.144	$ 93,900	Howdy Wilcox 2d
1933	Lou Meyer	Miller	Miller	8	104.162	$ 54,450	Wilbur Shaw
1934	Bill Cummings	Miller	Miller†	4	104.863	$ 83,775	Mauri Rose
1935	Kelly Petillo	Wetteroth	Offenhauser	4	106.240	$ 78,575	Wilbur Shaw
1936	Lou Meyer	Stevens	Miller	4	109.069	$ 82,525	Ted Horn
1937	Wilbur Shaw	Shaw	Offenhauser	4	113.580	$ 92,135	Ralph Hepburn
1938	Floyd Roberts	Wetteroth	Miller	4	117.200	$ 91,075	Wilbur Shaw
1939	Wilbur Shaw	Maserati	Maserati*	8	115.035	$ 87,050	Jimmy Snyder
1940	Wilbur Shaw	Maserati	Maserati*	8	114.277	$ 85,525	Rex Mays
1941	Floyd Davis, Mauri Rose	Wetteroth	Offenhauser	4	115.117	$ 90,925	Rex Mays
1946	George Robson	Adams	Sparks*	6	114.820	$115,450	Jimmy Jackson
1947	Mauri Rose	Deidt	Offenhauser†	4	116.338	$137,425	Bill Holland
1948	Mauri Rose	Deidt	Offenhauser†	4	119.814	$171,075	Bill Holland
1949	Bill Holland	Deidt	Offenhauser†	4	121.327	$179,050	Johnnie Parsons
1950	Johnnie Parsons	Kurtis Kraft	Offenhauser	4	124.002[2]	$201,135	Bill Holland
1951	Lee Wallard	Kurtis Kraft	Offenhauser	4	126.244	$207,650	Mike Nazaruk
1952	Troy Ruttman	Kuzma	Offenhauser	4	128.922	$230,100	Jim Rathmann
1953	Bill Vukovich	Kurtis Kraft 500A	Offenhauser	4	128.740	$246,300	Art Cross
1954	Bill Vukovich	Kurtis Kraft 500A	Offenhauser	4	130.840	$269,375	Jimmy Bryan
1955	Bob Sweikert	Kurtis Kraft 500C	Offenhauser	4	128.209	$270,400	Tony Bettenhausen
1956	Pat Flaherty	Watson	Offenhauser	4	128.490	$282,052	Sam Hanks
1957	Sam Hanks	Epperly	Offenhauser	4	135.601	$300,252	Jim Rathmann
1958	Jimmy Bryan	Epperly	Offenhauser	4	133.791	$305,217	George Amick
1959	Rodger Ward	Watson	Offenhauser	4	135.857	$338,100	Jim Rathmann
1960	Jim Rathmann	Watson	Offenhauser	4	138.767	$369,150	Rodger Ward
1961	A. J. Foyt	Watson	Offenhauser	4	139.130	$400,000	Eddie Sachs
1962	Rodger Ward	Watson	Offenhauser	4	140.293	$426,152	Len Sutton
1963	Parnelli Jones	Watson	Offenhauser	4	143.137	$494,031	Jim Clark
1964	A. J. Foyt	Watson	Offenhauser	4	147.350	$506,625	Rodger Ward
1965	Jim Clark	Lotus	Ford‡	8	151.388	$628,399	Parnelli Jones
1966	Graham Hill	Lola	Ford‡	8	144.317	$691,809	Jim Clark
1967	A. J. Foyt	Coyote	Ford‡	8	151.207	$737,109	Al Unser
1968	Bobby Unser	Eagle	Ford‡**	8	152.882	$809,627	Dan Gurney
1969	Mario Andretti	Hawk	Ford‡**	8	156.867	$805,127	Dan Gurney
1970	Al Unser	P. J. Colt	Ford‡**	8	155.749	$1,000,002	Mark Donohue
1971	Al Unser	P. J. Colt	Ford‡**	8	157.735	$1,001,604	Peter Revson
1972	Mark Donohue	McLaren	Offenhauser	8	162.962	$1,011,846	Al Unser
1973	Gordon Johncock	Eagle	Offenhauser	4	159.014	$1,006,105	Billy Vukovich
1974	Johnny Rutherford	McLaren	Offenhauser	4	158.589	$1,015,686	Bobby Unser
1975	Bobby Unser	Eagle	Offenhauser	4	149.213[3]	$1,001,322	Johnny Rutherford
1976	Johnny Rutherford	McLaren	Drake-Offenhauser	4	148.7[4]	$1,038,776	A. J. Foyt
1977	A. J. Foyt	Coyote	Foyt	8	161.331	$1,116,807	Tom Sneva
1978	Al Unser	Lola	Cosworth	8	161.363	$1,145,255	Tom Sneva
1979	Rick Mears	Penske	Cosworth	8	155.899	$1,271,954	A. J. Foyt

*Supercharged. **Turbocharged. †Front drive. ‡ Rear engine. [1]400 miles. [2]345 miles; all other races at 500 miles. [3]Race stopped at 435 miles due to rain. [4]Race stopped at 255 miles due to rain. [5]Winner's share.

NATIONAL RACING CHAMPIONS—USAC*

1902	Harry Harkness	1920	Gaston Chevrolet	1939	Wilbur Shaw	1962	Rodger Ward
1903	Barney Oldfield	1921	Thomas Milton	1940	Rex Mays	1963	A. J. Foyt
1904	George Heath	1922	James Murphy	1941	Rex Mays	1964	A. J. Foyt
1905	Victor Hemery	1923	Eddie Hearne	1946	Ted Horn	1965	Mario Andretti
1906	Joe Tracy	1924	James Murphy	1947	Ted Horn	1966	Mario Andretti
1907	Eddie Bald	1925	Peter DePaolo	1948	Ted Horn	1967	A. J. Foyt
1908	Louis Strang	1926	Harry Hartz	1949	Johnnie Parsons	1968	Bobby Unser
1909	George Robertson	1927	Peter DePaolo	1950	Henry Banks	1969	Mario Andretti
1910	Ray Harroun	1928	Louis Meyer	1951	Tony Bettenhausen	1970	Al Unser
1911	Ralph Mulford	1929	Louis Meyer	1952	Chuck Stevenson	1971	Joe Leonard
1912	Ralph DePalma	1930	Billy Arnold	1953	Sam Hanks	1972	Joe Leonard
1913	Earl Cooper	1931	Louis Schneider	1954	Jimmy Bryan	1973	Roger McCluskey
1914	Ralph DePalma	1932	Bob Carey	1955	Bob Sweikert	1974	Bobby Unser
1915	Earl Cooper	1933	Louis Meyer	1956	Jimmy Bryan	1975	A. J. Foyt
1916	Dario Resta	1934	Bill Cummings	1957	Jimmy Bryan	1976	Gordon Johncock
1917	Earl Cooper	1935	Kelly Petillo	1958	Tony Bettenhausen	1977	Tom Sneva
1918	Ralph Mulford	1936	Mauri Rose	1959	Rodger Ward	1978	Tom Sneva
1919	Howard Wilcox	1937	Wilbur Shaw	1960	A. J. Foyt	1979	A. J. Foyt
		1938	Floyd Roberts	1961	A. J. Foyt		

* USAC founded 1956.

1978 USAC NATIONAL CHAMPIONSHIP DRIVER STANDINGS

Pos.	Driver/Hometown	Races	Points	Pos.	Driver/Hometown	Races	Points
1.	Tom Sneva, Spokane, Wash.	18	4,153	24.	Mike Mosley, Fallbrook, Calif.	7	483
2.	Al Unser, Albuquerque, N.M.	16	4,031	25.	Roger Mears, Bakersfield, Calif.	1	400
3.	Gordon Johncock, Phoenix, Ariz.	17	3,548	26.	Bobby Olivero, Lakewood, Calif.	4	360
4.	Johnny Rutherford, Ft. Worth, Tex.	18	3,067	27.	Al Loquasto, Easton, Pa.	7	321
5.	A. J. Foyt, Houston, Tex.	18	3,024	28.	Joe Saldana, Lincoln, Nebr.	8	314
6.	Wally Dallenbach, Basalt, Colo.	18	2,966	29.	Gary Bettenhausen, Monrovia, Ind.	9	294
7.	Steve Krisiloff, Dana Pt., Calif.	18	2,874	30.	Spike Gehlhausen, Jasper, Ind.	17	188
8.	Danny Ongais, Costa Mesa, Calif.	17	2,662	31.	Larry Cannon, Oakwood, Ill.	6	184
9.	Rick Mears, Bakersfield, Calif.	11	2,171	32.	Larry Rice, Linden, Ind.	2	180
10.	Pancho Carter, Brownsburg, Ind.	10	1,206	33.	Jerry Karl, Manchester, Pa.	8	104
11.	Tom Bagley, Centre Hall, Pa.	17	1,188	34.	Jerry Sneva, Spokane, Wash.	6	62
12.	Bobby Unser, Albuquerque, N.M.	16	1,122	35.	Roger McCluskey, Tucson, Ariz.	7	61
13.	Larry Dickson, Marietta, Ohio	8	1,121	36.	Phil Threshie, Alamo, Calif.	6	45
14.	Johnny Parsons, Speedway, Ind.	14	978	37.	Todd Gibson, Richwood, Ohio	4	34
15.	George Snider, Bakersfield, Calif.	7	766	38.	Vern Schuppan, Whyalla, Australia	3	26
16.	Tom Bigelow, Whitewater, Wis.	12	764		Bob Harkey, Indianapolis, Ind.	2	26
17.	Mario Andretti, Nazareth, Pa.	8	681	40.	Bill Vukovich, Coarsegold, Calif.	2	20
18.	Dick Simon, San Juan Capistrano, Calif.	13	670	41.	Roger Rager, Mound, Minn.	1	15
19.	Jim McElreath, Arlington, Tex.	11	573		Eldon Rasmussen, Indianapolis, Ind.	1	15
20.	Salt Walther, Dayton, Ohio	12	562	43.	John Mahler, Newport Beach, Calif.	1	10
21.	Cliff Hucul, Prince George, Br. Col.	8	519		Bubby Jones, Danville, Ill.	1	10
22.	Lee Kunzman, Guttenberg, Iowa	3	513	45.	Chuck Gurney, Livermore, Calif.	1	6
23.	Sheldon Kinser, Bloomington, Ind.	13	495				

1978 USAC TOP MONEY WINNERS

		Total				Total
1.	Al Unser, Albuquerque, N.M.	$591,599	11.	Pancho Carter, Brownsburg, Ind.		$114,410
2.	Tom Sneva, Spokane, Wash.	341,396	12.	Tom Bagley, Centre Hall, Pa.		101,835
3.	A. J. Foyt, Houston, Tex.	285,590	13.	Tom Bigelow, Whitewater, Wis.		95,067
4.	Johnny Rutherford, Ft. Worth, Tex.	247,478	14.	Johnny Parsons, Speedway, Ind.		89,566
5.	Danny Ongais, Costa Mesa, Calif.	221,316	15.	Gary Bettenhausen, Monrovia, Ind.		76,815
6.	Gordon Johncock, Phoenix, Ariz.	211,382	16.	Sheldon Kinser, Bloomington, Ind.		76,534
7.	Rick Mears, Bakersfield, Calif.	157,900	17.	Salt Walther, Dayton, Ohio		69,721
8.	Wally Dallenbach, Basalt, Colo.	149,261	18.	Larry Dickson, Marietta, Ohio		68,410
9.	Steve Krisiloff, Dana Pt., Calif.	131,480	19.	George Snider, Bakersfield, Calif.		67,424
10.	Bobby Unser, Albuquerque, N.M.	119,976	20.	Dick Simon, San Juan Capistrano, Calif.		67,278

USAC ROOKIE OF THE YEAR

1971	George Eaton	1974	Duane Carter, Jr.	1977	Danny Ongais
1972	Mike Hiss	1975	Spike Gehlhausen	1978	Tom Bagley
1973	Tom Sneva	1976	Rick Mears	1979	Tony Bettenhausen, Jr.

1979 DAYTONA-LE MANS 24-HOUR ENDURANCE RACES

	Drivers	Laps	Car	Avg. Speed (Mph)
DAYTONA:	1. Ted Field — Danny Ongais — Hurley Haywood (U.S.)	684 (2,626 mi.)	Porsche	109.249
	2. John Morton — Tony Adamowicz (U.S.)	635	Ferrari	
LE MANS:	1. Bill and Don Whittington (U.S.) — Klaus Ludwig (West Germany)	306 (2,592 mi.)	Porsche	107.99
	2. Paul Newman and Dick Barbour (U.S.) — Rolf Stommelen (West Germany)	299	Porsche	

STOCK CAR RACING

SOURCE: The National Association for Stock Car Auto Racing, Inc.

RESULTS OF 1978 WINSTON CUP GRAND NATIONAL SEASON

EVENT-LOCATION	DATE	FIRST	SECOND
WINSTON WESTERN 500 Riverside, Calif.	Jan. 22	Cale Yarborough Oldsmobile	Benny Parsons Chevrolet
DAYTONA 500 Daytona Beach, Fla.	Feb. 19	Bobby Allison Ford	Cale Yarborough Oldsmobile
RICHMOND 400 Richmond, Va.	Feb. 26	Benny Parsons Chevrolet	Lennie Pond Chevrolet
CAROLINA 500 Rockingham, N.C.	Mar. 5	David Pearson Mercury	Bobby Allison Ford
ATLANTA 500 Atlanta, Ga.	Mar. 19	Bobby Allison Ford	Dave Marcis Chevrolet
SOUTHEASTERN 500 Bristol, Tenn.	Apr. 2	Darrell Waltrip Chevrolet	Benny Parsons Oldsmobile
REBEL 500 Darlington, S.C.	Apr. 9	Benny Parsons Chevrolet	Darrell Waltrip Chevrolet
STALEY 400 N Wilkesboro, N.C.	Apr. 16	Darrell Waltrip Chevrolet	Richard Petty Dodge
VIRGINIA 500 Martinsville, Va.	Apr. 23	Darrell Waltrip Chevrolet	Neil Bonnett Dodge
WINSTON 500 Talladega, Ala.	May 14	Cale Yarborough Oldsmobile	Buddy Baker Oldsmobile
MASON-DIXON 500 Dover, Del.	May 21	David Pearson Mercury	Cale Yarborough Oldsmobile
WORLD 600 Charlotte, N.C.	May 28	Darrell Waltrip Chevrolet	Donnie Allison Chevrolet
MUSIC CITY USA 420 Nashville, Tenn.	June 6	Cale Yarborough Oldsmobile	Lennie Pond Chevrolet
NAPA RIVERSIDE 400 Riverside, Calif.	June 11	Benny Parsons Chevrolet	Richard Petty Dodge
GABRIEL 400 Brooklyn, Mich.	June 18	Cale Yarborough Oldsmobile	David Pearson Mercury
FIRECRACKER 400 Daytona Beach, Fla.	July 4	David Pearson Mercury	Cale Yarborough Oldsmobile
NASHVILLE 420 Nashville, Tenn.	July 15	Cale Yarborough Oldsmobile	Darrell Waltrip Chevrolet
COCA-COLA 500 Pocono, Pa.	July 30	Darrell Waltrip Chevrolet	David Pearson Mercury
TALLADEGA 500 Talladega, Ala.	Aug. 6	Lennie Pond Oldsmobile	Donnie Allison Oldsmobile
CHAMPION SPARK PLUG 400 Brooklyn, Mich.	Aug. 20	David Pearson Mercury	Cale Yarborough Oldsmobile
VOLUNTEER 500 Bristol, Tenn.	Aug. 26	Cale Yarborough Oldsmobile	Benny Parsons Oldsmobile
SOUTHERN 500 Darlington, S.C.	Sept. 4	Cale Yarborough Oldsmobile	Darrell Waltrip Chevrolet
CAPITAL CITY 400 Richmond, Va.	Sept. 10	Darrell Waltrip Chevrolet	Bobby Allison Ford
DELAWARE 500 Dover, Del.	Sept. 17	Bobby Allison Ford	Cale Yarborough Oldsmobile
OLD DOMINION 500 Martinsville, Va.	Sept. 24	Cale Yarborough Oldsmobile	Darrell Waltrip Chevrolet
WILKES 400 N. Wilkesboro, N.C.	Oct. 1	Cale Yarborough Oldsmobile	Darrell Waltrip Chevrolet
NAPA NATIONAL 500 Charlotte, N.C.	Oct. 8	Bobby Allison Ford	Darrell Waltrip Chevrolet
AMERICAN 500 Rockingham, N.C.	Oct. 22	Cale Yarborough Oldsmobile	Bobby Allison Ford
DIXIE 500 Atlanta, Ga.	Nov. 5	Donnie Allison Chevrolet	Richard Petty Chevrolet
LOS ANGELES TIMES 500 Ontario, Calif.	Nov. 19	Bobby Allison Ford	Cale Yarborough Oldsmobile

NASCAR CHAMPIONS

WINSTON CUP GRAND NATIONAL

1964—Richard Petty, Randleman, N.C. (Plymouth)
1965—Ned Jarrett, Camden, S.C. (Ford)
1966—David Pearson, Spartanburg, S.C. (Dodge)
1967—Richard Petty, Randleman, N.C. (Plymouth)
1968—David Pearson, Spartanburg, S.C. (Ford)
1969—David Pearson, Spartanburg, S.C. (Ford)
1970—Bobby Isaac, Catawba, N.C. (Dodge)
1971—Richard Petty, Randleman, N.C. (Plymouth)
1972—Richard Petty, Randleman, N.C. (Plymouth-Dodge)
1973—Benny Parsons, Ellerbe, N.C. (Chevrolet)
1974—Richard Petty, Randleman, N.C. (Dodge)
1975—Richard Petty, Randleman, N.C. (Dodge)
1976—Cale Yarborough, Timmonsville, S.C. (Chevrolet)
1977—Cale Yarborough, Timmonsville, S.C. (Chevrolet)
1978—Cale Yarborough, Timmonsville, S.C. (Oldsmobile)

1978 WINSTON CUP GRAND NATIONAL STANDINGS

Driver	Points	Starts	Wins	Top 5	Top 10	Money Won
1. Cale Yarborough	4841	30	10	23	24	$530,751
2. Bobby Allison	4367	30	5	14	22	335,635
3. Darrell Waltrip	4362	30	6	19	20	343,367
4. Benny Parsons	4350	30	3	15	21	288,458
5. Dave Marcis	4335	30	0	14	24	178,725
6. Richard Petty	3949	30	0	11	17	215,491
7. Lennie Pond	3794	28	1	11	19	160,627
8. Dick Brooks	3769	30	0	5	17	131,474
9. Buddy Arrington	3626	30	0	1	7	112,959
10. Richard Childress	3566	30	0	1	12	108,106
11. J. D. McDuffie	3255	30	0	1	6	86,856
12. Neil Bonnett	3129	30	0	7	12	155,875
13. Tighe Scott	3110	29	0	0	7	83,745
14. Frank Warren	3036	30	0	0	0	68,172
15. Dick May	2936	28	0	0	2	65,290

1979 WINSTON CUP GRAND NATIONAL (to Oct. 1)

EVENT	DATE	WINNER	EVENT	DATE	WINNER
WINSTON WESTERN 500	Jan. 14	Darrell Waltrip	TEXAS 400	June 3	Darrell Waltrip
DAYTONA 500	Feb. 18	Richard Petty	NAPA RIVERSIDE 400	June 10	Bobby Allison
CAROLINA 500	Mar. 4	Bobby Allison	GABRIEL 400	June 17	Buddy Baker
RICHMOND 400	Mar. 11	Cale Yarborough	FIRECRACKER 400	July 4	Neil Bonnett
ATLANTA 500	Mar. 18	Buddy Baker	NASHVILLE 420	July 14	Darrell Waltrip
NORTHWESTERN BANK 400	Mar. 25	Bobby Allison	COCA-COLA 500	July 30	Cale Yarborough
SOUTHEASTERN 500	Apr. 1	Dale Earnhardt	TALLADEGA 500	Aug. 5	Darrell Waltrip
REBEL 500	Apr. 8	Darrell Waltrip	CHAMPION SPARK PLUG 400	Aug. 19	Richard Petty
VIRGINIA 500	Apr. 22	Richard Petty	VOLUNTEER 500	Aug. 25	Darrell Waltrip
WINSTON 500	May 6	Bobby Allison	SOUTHERN 500	Sept. 3	David Pearson
MUSIC CITY 420	May 12	Cale Yarborough	CAPITAL CITY 400	Sept. 9	Bobby Allison
MASON-DIXON 500	May 20	Neil Bonnett	CRC CHEMICALS 500	Sept. 16	Richard Petty
WORLD 600	May 27	Darrell Waltrip	OLD DOMINION 500	Sept. 23	Buddy Baker

THOROUGHBRED RACING

SOURCE: *American Racing Manual*, 1979 ed. Reproduced with permission of the copyright owner, Daily Racing Form, Inc.

HIGHEST ANNUAL PAYOFF ODDS

Date	Winner	Track	Payoff Odds	Date	Winner	Track	Payoff Odds
1948 Sept. 30	Buddie Bones	Rockingham Park	192–1	1963 Aug. 12	Ivalinda	Arlington Park	190–1
1949 Sept. 20	Luxuriant	Narragansett Park	282–1	1964 Dec. 11	Wilson Hill Doll	Bay Meadows	279–1
1950 Oct. 30	Minnix	Lincoln Downs	253–1	1965 June 5	Blunt Edge	Cahokia Downs	142–1
1951 Sept. 27	Royal Marvel	Rockingham Park	183–4	1966 Oct. 7	Dutch Wrackateer	Narragansett Park	186–1
1952 Sept. 16	Rock House	Woodbine Park	214–1	1967 May 26	Mambo Rhythm	Seminole Downs	214–1
1953 Aug. 28	Can It Yes	Exhibition Park	253–1	1968 June 24	Waverley Steps	Woodbine	396–1
1954 Nov. 10	Ruff Mate	Pimlico Race Course	209–1	1969 Sept. 24	Judes Song	Latonia	241–1
1955 May 27	Gold Champ	Suffolk Downs	144–1	1970 May 7	Corpus Delicti	Fort Erie	175–1
1956 July 24	Buster Bell	Charles Town	203–1	1971 Apr. 1	Moonlight City	Portland Meadows	169–1
1957 Aug. 27	Miss Profit	Detroit Race Course	172–1	1972 Nov. 16	Norton	Churchill Downs	190–1
1958 Mar. 22	Whisk Tru	Bowie Race Course	231–1	1973 Sept. 28	Cedars Crown	Detroit Race Course	256–1
1959 June 5	Janie Brown	Thistledown	168–1	1974 Mar. 17	Campus Bright	Yakima Meadows	156–1
1960 Nov. 4	Kamal Bey	Laurel Race Course	175–1	1975 Sept. 1	Second Ticking	Narragansett Park	147–1
1961 Sept. 29	Djebonita	Bay Meadows	259–1	1976 Sept. 21	Tiger Red K	Columbus	188–1
1962 July 20	Wee Highway	Delaware Park	170–1	1977 Mar. 10	Black Ticket	Fonner Park	259–1
1963 Sept. 13	Confiancita	El Comandant	201–1	1978 Nov. 21	Golden Rubies	Churchill Downs	246–1

STRAIGHT MUTUEL PAYOFFS RECORD

Tabulation based on a $2 straight mutuel ticket

Horse	Track and Date	Payoff	Horse	Track and Date	Payoff
Wishing Ring, Latonia, June 17, 1912		$1,885.50	Nanamay, Tanforan, April 14, 1932		$602.20
Augeas, Agua Caliente, February 14, 1933		840.00	Zombro, Charles Town, December 5, 1933		590.00
Muzetta W., Lexington, May 7, 1910		830.70	Cadeau, Pimlico, May 7, 1913		577.10
King Jack, Agua Caliente, January 8, 1933		820.00	Escohigh, Tropical Park, December 29, 1937		571.00
Trycook, Hagerstown, May 19, 1934		810.00	Luxuriant, Narragansett Park, September 20, 1949		566.80
Fincastle, Havana, December 19, 1923		702.60	Welga, Douglas Park, May 29, 1916		560.40
Lt. Wm. J. Murray, Havana, February 11, 1923		696.00	Wilson Hill Doll, Bay Meadows, December 11, 1964		559.80
Miss Fountain, Havana, February 9, 1930		685.60	Mad Scramble, Bay Meadows, April 22, 1941		530.80
Playmay, Santa Anita Park, February 4, 1938		673.40	Djebonita, Bay Meadows, September 29, 1961		520.80
Fleetglow, Green Mountain, May 9, 1968		658.80	Black Ticket, Fonner Park, March 10, 1977		520.50
Meadow Money, Lincoln Fields, June 5, 1941		652.40	Cedars Crown, Detroit Race Course, September 28, 1973		514.20
			Minnix, Lincoln Downs, October 30, 1950		508.80

THE TRIPLE CROWN

Only eleven three-year-olds have managed to win the celebrated Triple Crown of American Racing—the Kentucky Derby, the Preakness Stakes, and the Belmont Stakes:

1919—Sir Barton	1943—Count Fleet
1930—Gallant Fox	1946—Assault
1935—Omaha	1948—Citation
1937—War Admiral	1973—Secretariat
1941—Whirlaway	1977—Seattle Slew
	1978—Affirmed

The following horses won two of the three great races: Cloverbrook (1877), Duke of Magenta (1878), Grenada (1880), Saunterer (1881), Belmar (1895), Man o' War (1920), Pillory (1922), Zev (1923), Twenty Grand (1931), Burgoo King (1932), Bold Venture (1936), Johnstown (1939), Bimelech (1940), Shut Out (1942), Pensive (1944), Capot (1949), Middleground (1950), Native Dancer (1953), Nashua (1955), Needles (1956), Tim Tam (1958), Carry Back (1961), Chateaugay (1963), Northern Dancer (1964), Kauai King (1966), Damascus (1967), Forward Pass (1968), Majestic Prince (1969), Canonero II (1971), Riva Ridge (1972), Little Current (1974), Spectacular Bid (1979).

LEADING MONEY-WINNING THOROUGHBRED HORSES

Year	Horse	Age	Starts	1st	2d	3d	Amount Won	Year	Horse	Age	Starts	1st	2d	3d	Amount Won
1924	Sarazen	3	12	8	1	1	$ 95,640	1951	Counterpoint	3	15	7	2	1	250,525
1925	Pompey	2	10	7	2	0	121,630	1952	Crafty Admiral	4	16	9	4	1	277,225
1926	Crusader	3	15	9	4	0	166,033	1953	Native Dancer	3	10	9	1	0	513,425
1927	Anita Peabody	2	7	6	0	1	111,905	1954	Determine	3	15	10	3	2	328,700
1928	High Strung	2	6	5	0	0	153,590	1955	Nashua	3	12	10	1	1	752,550
1929	Blue Larkspur	3	6	4	1	0	153,450	1956	Needles	3	8	4	2	0	440,850
1930	Gallant Fox	3	10	9	1	0	308,275	1957	Round Table	3	22	15	1	3	600,383
1931	Top Flight	2	7	7	0	0	219,000	1958	Round Table	4	20	14	4	0	662,780
1932	Gusto	3	16	4	3	2	145,940	1959	Sword Dancer	3	13	8	4	0	537,004
1933	Singing Wood	2	9	3	2	2	88,050	1960	Bally Ache	3	15	10	3	1	455,045
1934	Cavalcade	3	7	6	1	0	111,235	1961	Carry Back	3	16	9	1	3	565,349
1935	Omaha	3	9	6	1	2	142,255	1962	Never Bend	2	10	7	1	2	402,969
1936	Granville	3	11	7	3	0	110,295	1963	Candy Spots	3	12	7	2	1	604,481
1937	Seabiscuit	4	15	11	2	2	168,580	1964	Gun Bow	4	16	8	4	2	580,100
1938	Stagehand	3	15	8	2	3	189,710	1965	Buckpasser	2	11	9	1	0	568,096
1939	Challedon	3	15	9	2	3	184,535	1966	Buckpasser	3	14	13	1	0	669,078
1940	Bimelech	3	7	4	2	1	110,005	1967	Damascus	3	16	12	3	1	817,941
1941	Whirlaway	3	20	13	5	2	272,386	1968	Forward Pass	3	13	7	2	0	546,674
1942	Shut Out	3	12	8	2	0	238,872	1969	Arts and Letters	3	14	8	5	1	555,604
1943	Count Fleet	3	6	6	0	0	174,055	1970	Personality	3	18	8	2	1	444,049
1944	Pavot	2	8	8	0	0	179,040	1971	Riva Ridge	2	9	7	0	0	503,263
1945	Busher	3	13	10	2	1	273,735	1972	Droll Role	4	19	7	3	4	471,633
1946	Assault	3	15	8	2	3	424,195	1973	Secretariat	3	12	9	2	1	860,404
1947	Armed	6	17	11	4	1	376,325	1974	Chris Evert	3	8	5	1	2	551,063
1948	Citation	3	20	19	1	0	709,470	1975	Foolish Pleasure	3	11	5	4	1	716,278
1949	Ponder	3	21	9	5	2	321,825	1976	Forego	6	8	6	1	1	491,701
1950	Noor	5	12	7	4	1	346,940	1977	Seattle Slew	3	7	6	0	0	641,370
								1978	Affirmed	3	11	8	2	0	901,541

THE KENTUCKY DERBY (THREE-YEAR-OLDS) Distance: 1¼ miles (Churchill Downs, Ky.)

Year	Winner	Jockey	Net to Winner	Time	Second
1937	War Admiral	C. Kurtsinger	52,050	2:03½	Pompoon
1938	Lawrin	E. Arcaro	47,050	2:04⅘	Dauber
1939	Johnstown	J. Stout	46,350	2:03⅗	Challedon
1940	Gallahadion	C. Bierman	60,150	2:05	Bimelech
1941	Whirlaway	E. Arcaro	61,275	2:01⅖	Staretor
1942	Shut Out	W. D. Wright	64,225	2:04⅖	Alsab
1943	Count Fleet	J. Longden	60,275	2:04	Blue Swords
1944	Pensive	C McCreary	64,675	2:04⅕	Broadcloth
1945	Hoop Jr.	E. Arcaro	64,850	2:07	Pot o' Luck
1946	Assault	W. Mehrtens	96,400	2:06¾	Spy Song
1947	Jet Pilot	E. Guerin	92,160	2:06¾	Phalanx
1948	Citation	E. Arcaro	83,400	2:05⅖	Coaltown
1949	Ponder	S. Brooks	91,600	2:04⅕	Capot
1950	Middleground	W. Boland	92,650	2:01¾	Hill Prince
1951	Count Turf	C. McCreary	98,050	2:02⅗	Royal Mustang
1952	Hill Gail	E. Arcaro	96,300	2:01⅗	Sub Fleet
1953	Dark Star	H. Moreno	90,050	2:02	Native Dancer
1954	Determine	R. York	102,050	2:03	Hasty Road
1955	Swaps	W. Shoemaker	108,400	2:01⅘	Nashua
1956	Needles	D. Erb	123,450	2:03⅘	Fabius
1957	Iron Liege	W. Hartack	107,950	2:02⅕	Gallant Man
1958	Tim Tam	I. Valenzuela	116,400	2:05	Lincoln Road
1959	Tomy Lee	W. Shoemaker	119,650	2:02⅕	Sword Dancer
1960	Venetian Way	W. Hartack	114,850	2:02⅖	Bally Ache
1961	Carry Back	J. Sellers	120,500	2:04	Crozier
1962	Decidedly	W. Hartack	119,650	2:00⅖	Roman Line
1963	Chateaugay	B. Baeza	108,900	2:01⅘	Never Bend
1964	Northern Dancer	W. Hartack	114,300	2:00	Hill Rise
1965	Lucky Debonair	W. Shoemaker	112,000	2:01⅕	Dapper Dan
1966	Kauai King	D. Brumfield	120,500	2:02	Advocator
1967	Proud Clarion	R. Ussery	119,700	2:00⅗	Barbs Delight
1968	Forward Pass	I. Valenzuela	122,600	2:02⅕	Francie's Hat
1969	Majestic Prince	W. Hartack	113,200	2:01⅘	Arts & Letters
1970	Dust Commander	M. Manganello	127,800	2:03⅖	My Dad George
1971	Canonero II	G. Avila	145,500	2:03⅕	Jim French
1972	Riva Ridge	Ron Turcotte	140,300	2:01.8	No Le Hace
1973	Secretariat	Ron Turcotte	155,050	1:59⅖	Sham
1974	Cannonade	Angel Cordero, Jr.	274,000	2:04	Hudson County
1975	Foolish Pleasure	Jacinto Vasquez	209,600	2:02	Avatar
1976	Bold Forbes	Angel Cordero, Jr.	217,700	2:01¾	Honest Pleasure
1977	Seattle Slew	Jean Cruguet	214,700	2:02⅕	Run Dusty Run
1978	Affirmed	Steve Cauthen	186,900	2:01⅕	Alydar
1979	Spectacular Bid	Ron Franklin	228,650	2:02⅖	General Assembly

THE PREAKNESS STAKES (THREE-YEAR-OLDS) Distance 1-3/16 miles (Pimlico, Md.)

Year	Winner	Jockey	Net to Winner	Time	Second
1937	War Admiral	C. Kurtsinger	45,600	1:58⅖	Pompoon
1938	Dauber	M. Peters	51,875	1:59⅘	Cravat
1939	Challedon	G. Seabo	53,710	1:59⅘	Gilded Knight
1940	Bimelech	F. A. Smith	53,230	1:58⅗	Mioland
1941	Whirlaway	E. Arcaro	49,365	1:58⅘	King Cole
1942	Alsab	B. James	58,175	1:57	tie
1943	Count Fleet	J. Longden	43,190	1:57⅖	Blue Swords
1944	Pensive	C. McCreary	60,075	1:59⅕	Platter
1945	Polynesian	W. D. Wright	66,170	1:58⅖	Hoop Jr.
1946	Assault	W. Mehrtens	96,620	2:01⅖	Lord Boswell
1947	Faultless	D. Dodson	98,005	1:59	On Trust
1948	Citation	E. Arcaro	91,870	2:02⅖	Vulcan's Forge
1949	Capot	T. Atkinson	79,985	1:56	Palestinian
1950	Hill Prince	E. Arcaro	56,115	1:59⅕	Middleground
1951	Bold	E. Arcaro	83,110	1:56⅖	Counterpoint
1952	Blue Man	C. McCreary	86,135	1:57⅖	Jampol
1953	Native Dancer	E. Guerin	65,200	1:57⅘	Jamie K.
1954	Hasty Road	J. Adams	91,600	1:57⅖	Correlation
1955	Nashua	E. Arcaro	67,550	1:54⅗	Saratoga
1956	Fabius	W. Hartack	84,250	1:58⅖	Needles
1957	Bold Ruler	E. Arcaro	65,250	1:56⅕	Iron Liege
1958	Tim Tam	I. Valenzuela	97,900	1:57⅕	Lincoln Road
1959	Royal Orbit	W. Harmatz	136,200	1:57	Sword Dancer
1960	Bally Ache	R. Ussery	121,000	1:57⅗	Victoria Park
1961	Carry Back	J. Sellers	126,200	1:57⅘	Globemaster
1962	Greek Money	J. L. Rotz	135,800	1:56⅕	Ridan
1963	Candy Spots	W. Shoemaker	127,500	1:56⅕	Chateaugay
1964	Northern Dancer	W. Hartack	124,200	1:56⅘	The Scoundrel
1965	Tom Rolfe	R. Turcotte	128,100	1:56⅕	Dapper Dan
1966	Kauai King	D. Brumfield	129,000	1:55⅗	Stupendous
1967	Damascus	W. Shoemaker	141,500	1:55⅕	In Reality
1968	Forward Pass	I. Valenzuela	142,700	1:56⅘	Out of the Way
1969	Majestic Prince	W. Hartack	129,500	1:55¾	Arts & Letters
1970	Personality	E. Belmonte	151,300	1:56⅕	My Dad George
1971	Canonero II	G. Avila	137,400	1:54	Eastern Fleet
1972	Bee Bee Bee	Eldon Nelson	135,000	1:55.4	No Le Hace
1973	Secretariat	Ron Turcotte	129,900	1:54⅖	Sham
1974	Little Current	Miguel Rivera	156,500	1:54⅖	Neapolitan Way
1975	Master Derby	Darrel McHarque	158,100	1:56⅖	Foolish Pleasure
1976	Elocutionist	John Lively	129,700	1:55	Play the Red
1977	Seattle Slew	Jean Cruguet	138,600	1:54⅖	Iron Constitution
1978	Affirmed	Steve Cauthen	136,200	1:54⅖	Alydar
1979	Spectacular Bid	Ron Franklin	165,300	1:54⅕	Golden Act

THE BELMONT STAKES (THREE-YEAR-OLDS)   Distance: 1½ miles.

Year	Winner	Jockey	Net to Winner	Time	Second
1936	Granville	J. Stout	29,800	2:30	Mr. Bones
1937	War Admiral	C. Kurtsinger	38,020	2:28⅜	Sceneshifter
1938	Pasteurized	J. Stout	34,530	2:29⅞	Dauber
1939	Johnstown	J. Stout	37,020	2:29⅗	Belay
1940	Bimelech	F. A. Smith	35,030	2:29⅗	Your Chance
1941	Whirlaway	E. Arcaro	39,770	2:31	Robert Morris
1942	Shut Out	E. Arcaro	44,520	2:29½	Alsab
1943	Count Fleet	J. Longden	35,340	2:28⅕	Fairy Manhurst
1944	Bounding Home	G. L. Smith	55,000	2:32½	Pensive
1945	Pavot	E. Arcaro	52,675	2:30½	Wildlife
1946	Assault	W. Mehrtens	75,400	2:30⅘	Natchez
1947	Phalanx	R. Donoso	78,900	2:29⅗	Tide Rips
1948	Citation	E. Arcaro	77,700	2:28⅕	Better Self
1949	Capot	T. Atkinson	60,900	2:30⅕	Ponder
1950	Middleground	W. Boland	61,350	2:28⅗	Lights Up
1951	Counterpoint	D. Gorman	82,000	2:29	Battlefield
1952	One Count	E. Arcaro	82,400	2:30⅕	Blue Man
1953	Native Dancer	E. Guerin	82,500	2:28⅗	Jamie K.
1954	High Gun	E. Guerin	89,000	2:30⅘	Fisherman
1955	Nashua	E. Arcaro	83,700	2:29	Blazing Count
1956	Needles	D. Erb	83,600	2:29⅘	Career Boy
1957	Gallant Man	W. Shoemaker	77,300	2:26⅗	Inside Tract
1958	Cavan	P. Anderson	73,440	2:30⅕	Tim Tam
1959	Sword Dancer	W. Shoemaker	93,525	2:28⅖	Bagdad
1960	Celtic Ash	W. Hartack	96,785	2:29⅗	Venetian Way
1961	Sherluck	B. Baeza	104,900	2:29½	Globemaster
1962	Jaipur	W. Shoemaker	109,550	2:28⅘	Admiral's Voyage
1963	Chateaugay	B. Baeza	101,700	2:30⅕	Candy Spots
1964	Quadrangle	M. Ycaza	110,850	2:28⅘	Roman Brother
1965	Hail to All	J. Sellers	104,150	2:28⅖	Tom Rolfe
1966	Amberoid	W. Boland	117,700	2:29⅗	Buffle
1967	Damascus	W. Shoemaker	104,950	2:28⅘	Cool Reception
1968	Stage Door Johnny	H. Gustines	117,700	2:27⅕	Forward Pass
1969	Arts and Letters	B. Baeza	104,050	2:28⅘	Majestic Prince
1970	High Echelon	J. L. Rotz	115,000	2:34	Needles n Pens
1971	Pass Catcher	W. Blum	97,710	2:30⅖	Jim French
1972	Riva Ridge	Ron Turcotte	93,540	2:28	Ruritania
1973	Secretariat	Ron Turcotte	90,720	2:24	Twice a Prince
1974	Little Current	Miguel Rivera	101,970	2:29¼	Jolly Johu
1975	Avatar	W. Shoemaker	116,160	2:28	Foolish Pleasure
1976	Bold Forbes	Angel Cordero, Jr.	117,000	2:29	McKenzie Bridge
1977	Seattle Slew	Jean Cruguet	109,080	2:29⅗	Run Dusty Run
1978	Affirmed	Steve Cauthen	110,580	2:26⅘	Alydar
1979	Coastal	Ruben Hernandez	161,400	2:28⅗	Golden Act

WORLD THOROUGHBRED RACING RECORDS

Distance	Horse, age, weight	Track	Date	Time
¼ mi.	Big Racket, 4, 114	Hipodromo de las Americas, Mexico City	Feb. 5, 1945	:20⅘
2½ f.	Tie Score, 5, 115	Hipodromo de las Americas, Mexico City	Feb. 5, 1946	:26⅘
⅜ mi.	Atoka, 6, 105	Butte, Mont.	Sept. 7, 1906	:33½
3½ f.	Tango King, 6, 116	Northlands Park, Canada	April 22, 1978	:38⅘
½ mi.	Norgor, 9, 118	Ruidoso Downs, Ruidoso, N.M.	Aug. 14, 1976	:44¾
4½ f.	Kathryn's Doll, 2, 111	Turf Paradise, Phoenix, Ariz.	April 9, 1967	:50⅖
	Dear Ethel, 2, 114	Miles Park, Louisville, Ky.	July 4, 1967	:50⅖
	Scott's Poppy, 2, 118	Turf Paradise, Phoenix, Ariz.	Feb. 22, 1976	:50⅖
⅝ mi.	Zip Pocket, 3, 122	Turf Paradise, Phoenix, Ariz.	April 22, 1967	:55⅗
5½ f.	Zip Pocket, 3, 129	Turf Paradise, Phoenix, Ariz.	Nov. 19, 1967	1:01⅗
5¾ f.	Last Freeby, 4, 116	Timonium, Md.	July 20, 1974	1:07⅕
¾ mi	Grey Papa, 6, 112	Longacres, Seattle, Wash.	Sept. 4, 1972	1:07⅕
6½ f.	Best Hitter, 4, 114	Longacres, Seattle, Wash.	Aug. 24, 1973	1:13⅖
⅞ mi.	Triple Bend, 4, 123	Hollywood Park, Inglewood, Calif.	May 6, 1972	1:19⅘
1 mi.	Dr. Fager, 4, 134	Arlington Park, Arlington Heights, Ill.	Aug. 24, 1968	1:32⅕
1 mi. 70 yd.	Aborigine, 6, 119	Penn National, Pa.	Aug. 20, 1978	1:37⅕
1¹⁄₁₆ mi.	Swaps, 4, 130	Hollywood Park, Inglewood, Calif.	June 23, 1956	1:39
1⅛ mi.	Tentam, 4, 118	Saratoga, Saratoga Springs, N.Y.	Aug. 10, 1973	1:45⅘
	Secretariat, 3, 124	Belmont Park, Elmont, N.Y.	Sept. 15, 1973	1:45⅖
1⅜ mi.	Toonerville, 5, 120	Hialeah Park, Hialeah, Fla.	Feb. 7, 1976	1:51⅘
1¼ mi.	Double Discount, 4, 116	Santa Anita, Arcadia, Calif.	Oct. 9, 1977	1:57⅖
1⅝ mi.	Roberto, 3, 122	York, England	Aug. 15, 1972	2:07
1¾ mi.	Cougar II, 6, 126	Hollywood Park, Inglewood, Calif.	April 29, 1972	2:11
1½ mi.	Fiddle Isle, 5, 124	Santa Anita Park, Arcadia, Calif.	Mar. 21, 1970	2:23
1⁹⁄₁₆ mi.	Lone Wolf, 5, 115	Keeneland, Lexington, Ky.	Oct. 31, 1961	2:37⅗
1⅝ mi.	Red Reality, 6, 113	Saratoga, Saratoga Springs, N.Y.	Aug. 23, 1972	2:37⅘
	Malwak, 5, 110	Saratoga, Saratoga Springs, N.Y.	Aug. 22, 1973	2:37⅘
1¾ mi.	Noor, 5, 117	Santa Anita Park, Arcadia, Calif.	March 4, 1950	2:52⅘
1⅞ mi.	El Moro, 8, 116	Delaware Park, Wilmington, Del.	July 22, 1963	3:11⅕
2 mi.	Polazel, 3, 142	Salisbury, England	July 8, 1924	3:15
2¹⁄₁₆ mi.	Midafternoon, 4, 126	Jamaica, Jamaica, N.Y.	Nov. 15, 1956	3:29¾
2⅛ mi.	Ceinturion, 5, 119	Newbury, England	Sept. 29, 1923	3:35
2³⁄₁₆ mi.	Santiago, 5, 112	Narragansett Park, Pawtucket, R.I.	Sept. 27, 1941	3:51⅘
2¼ mi.	Dakota, 4, 116	Lingfield, England	May 27, 1927	3:37⅗
2⅜ mi.	Pamroy, 4, 120	Goodwood Park, Sussex, England	Aug. 1, 1973	4:10⅗
2½ mi.	Miss Grillo, 6, 118	Pimlico, Baltimore, Md.	Nov. 12, 1948	4:14⅗
2⅝ mi.	Girandole, 4, 126	Goodwood Park, Sussex, England	July 31, 1975	4:38⅖
2¾ mi.	Shot Put, 4, 126	Washington Park, Homewood, Ill.	Aug. 14, 1940	4:48⅘
2⅞ mi.	Bosh, 5, 100	Tijuana, Mexico	Mar. 8, 1925	5:23
3 mi.	Farragut, 5, 113	Agua Caliente, Mexico	Mar. 9, 1941	5:15

HARNESS RACING

Source: The U.S. Trotting Association

LEADING MONEY-WINNERS

TROTTERS			PACERS		
Year	Horse	Amount Won	Year	Horse	Amount Won
1949	Bangaway	$74,438.81	1949	Good Time	$88,766.17
1950	Proximity	87,175.00	1950	Scottish Pence	73,387.00
1951	Pronto Don	80,850.44	1951	Tar Heel	66,629.58
1952	Sharp Note	101,625.70	1952	Good Time	110,299.10
1953	Newport Dream	94,933.31	1953	Keystoner	59,131.23
1954	Katie Key	84,867.50	1954	Red Sails	66,615.00
1955	Scott Frost	186,101.00	1955	Adios Harry	98,900.00
1956	Scott Frost	85,851.00	1956	Adios Harry	129,912.00
1957	Hoot Song	114,877.00	1957	Torpid	113,982.00
1958	Emily's Pride	118,830.00	1958	Belle Acton	167,887.00
1959	Diller Hanover	149,897.00	1959	Bye Bye Byrd	199,933.00
1960	Su Mac Lad	159,662.00	1960	Bye Bye Byrd	187,612.00
1961	Su Mac Lad	245,750.00	1961	Adios Butler	180,250.00
1962	Duke Rodney	206,113.00	1962	Henry T. Adios	220,302.00
1963	Speedy Scot	244,403.00	1963	Overtrick	208,833.00
1964	Speedy Scot	235,710.00	1964	Race Time	199,292.00
1965	Dartmouth	252,348.00	1965	Bret Hanover	341,784.00
1966	Noble Victory	210,696.00	1966	Bret Hanover	407,534.00
1967	Carlisle	231,243.00	1967	Romulus Hanover	277,636.00
1968	Nevele Pride	427,440.00	1968	Rum Customer	355,618.00
1969	Lindy's Pride	323,997.00	1969	Overcall	373,150.00
1970	Fresh Yankee	359,002.00	1970	Most Happy Fella	387,239.00
1971	Fresh Yankee	293,950.00	1971	Albatross	558,009.00
1972	Super Bowl	436,258.00	1972	Albatross	459,921.00
1973	Spartan Hanover	262,023.00	1973	Sir Dalrae	307,354.00
1974	Delmonica Hanover	252,165.00	1974	Armbro Omaha	357,146.00
1975	Savoir	351,385.00	1975	Silk Stockings	336,312.00
1976	Steve Lobell	357,005.00	1976	Keystone Ore	539,759.00
1977	Green Speed	584,405.00	1977	Governor Skipper	522,148.00
1978	Speedy Somolli	362,404.00	1978	Abercrombie	703,260.00

HARNESS HORSE OF THE YEAR

Year	Horse	Gait	Year	Horse	Gait
1951	Pronto Don	trotter	1965	Bret Hanover	pacer
1952	Good Time	pacer	1966	Bret Hanover	pacer
1953	Hi-Lo's Forbes	pacer	1967	Nevele Pride	trotter
1954	Stenographer	trotter	1968	Nevele Pride	trotter
1955	Scott Frost	trotter	1969	Nevele Pride	trotter
1956	Scott Frost	trotter	1970	Fresh Yankee	trotter
1957	Torpid	pacer	1971	Albatross	pacer
1958	Emily's Pride	trotter	1972	Albatross	pacer
1959	Bye Bye Byrd	pacer	1973	Sir Dalrae	pacer
1960	Adios Butler	pacer	1974	Delmonica Hanover	trotter
1961	Adios Butler	pacer	1975	Savoir	trotter
1962	Su Mac Lad	trotter	1976	Keystone Ore	pacer
1963	Speedy Scot	trotter	1977	Green Speed	trotter
1964	Bret Hanover	pacer	1978	Abercrombie	pacer

THE HAMBLETONIAN (THREE-YEAR-OLD TROTTERS)

Year	Purse	Winner	Second	Winning Driver	Fastest Heat
1949	69,791.08	Miss Tilly	Volume	Fred Egan	2:01¾
1950	75,209.12	Lusty Song	Star's Pride	Delvin Miller	2:02
1951	95,263.93	Mainliner	Spennib	Guy Crippen	2:02¾
1952	87,637.55	Sharp Note	Hit Song	Bion Shively	2:02⅗
1953	117,117.98	Helicopter	Morse Hanover	Harry M. Harvey	2:01¾ (a)
1954	106,830.68	Newport Dream	Princess Rodney	Adelbert Cameron	2:02⅖
1955	86,863.32	Scott Frost	(1)	Joe O'Brien	2:00⅜
1956	100,603.99	The Intruder	Valiant Rodney	Ned F. Bower	2:01⅖
1957	111,126.25	Hickory Smoke	Hoot Song	John F. Simpson, Sr.	2:00⅛
1958	106,719.24	Emily's Pride	Little Rocky	Flave T. Nipe	1:59⅗
1959	125,283.98	Diller Hanover	Tie Silk	Frank Ervin	2:01½
1960	147,481.94	Blaze Hanover	Quick Song	Joe O'Brien	1:59⅗(b)
1961	131,573.01	Harlan Dean	Caleb	James W. Arthur	1:58⅖
1962	116,612.78	A. C.'s Viking	Isaac	Sanders Russell	1:59⅘
1963	115,549.28	Speedy Scot	Floris	Ralph N. Baldwin	1:57⅖(c)
1964	115,281.40	Ayres	Big John	John F. Simpson	1:56⅗ (R)
1965	122,245.56	Egyptian Candor	Armbro Flight	Adelbert Cameron	2:03½(d)
1966	122,540.00	Kerry Way	Polaris	Frank Ervin	1:58⅘
1967	122,650.00	Speedy Streak	Keystone Pride	Adelbert Cameron	2:00
1968	116,190.00	Nevele Pride	Keystone Spartan	Stanley Dancer	1:59¾
1969	124,910.00	Lindy's Pride	The Prophet	Howard Beissinger	1:57⅗
1970	143,630.00	Timothy T.	Formal Notice	John F. Simpson, Jr.	1:58⅗(e)
1971	129,770.00	Speedy Crown	Savoir	Howard Beissinger	1:57⅖
1972	119,090.00	Super Bowl	Delmonica Hanover	Stanley Dancer	1:56⅖(R)
1973	144,710.00	Flirth	Florinda	Ralph Baldwin	1:57.1
1974	160,150.00	Christopher T.	Nevele Diamond	Wm. Haughton	1:58.3
1975	232,192.00	Bonefish	Yankee Bambino	Stanley Dancer	1:59
1976	263,524.00	Steve Lobell	Zoot Suit	Wm. Haughton	1:56.2(R)
1977	284,000.00	Green Speed	Texas	Wm. Haughton	1:55⅜ (R)
1978	241,000.00	Speedy Somolli	Briscoe Hanover	Howard Beissinger	1:55(R)
1979	300,000.00	Legend Hanover	Chiola Hanover	George Sholty	1:56½

(1) Galophone and Leopold Hanover divided second and third monies. (a) By Morse Hanover. (b) By Quick Song and Hoot Frost. (c) By Floris. (d) By Armbro Flight. (e) By Formal Notice. (R) Record.

THE KENTUCKY FUTURITY (THREE-YEAR-OLD TROTTERS)

Year	Purse	Winner	Second	Winning Driver	Fastest Heat
1951	66,659.57	Ford Hanover	Candy Man	John F. Simpson, Sr.	2:01⅗
1952	66,231.89	Sharp Note	Duke of Lullwater	Bion Shively	2:00
1953	67,485.05	Kimberly Kid	Faber Hanover	Thomas S. Berry	2:00⅗
1954	63,121.84	Harlan	Pronto Boy	Delvin Miller	2:01
1955	62,702.60	Scott Frost	Home Free	Joe O'Brien	2:00⅗
1956	53,731.74	Nimble Colby	Barlow Hanover	Ralph N. Baldwin	2:02
1957	50,460.00	Cassin Hanover	Storm Cloud	Fred Egan	2:02⅕
1958	53,330.00	Emily's Pride	Senator Frost	Flave T. Nipe	1:59⅕ (a)
1959	53,810.00	Diller Hanover	Tie Silk	Ralph N. Baldwin	2:01⅕
1960	64,040.00	Elaine Rodney	Quick Song	Clint T. Hodgins	1:58⅗
1961	59,330.00	Duke Rodney	Caleb	Eddie T. Wheeler	1:58½(b)
1962	55,230.00	Safe Mission	Impish	Joe O'Brien	1:59½
1963	61,128.82	Speedy Scot	Florlis	Ralph N. Baldwin	1:57⅕
1964	57,096.21	Ayres	Dashing Rodney	John F. Simpson, Sr.	1:58¼
1965	65,133.93	Armbro Flight	Noble Victory	Joe O'Brien	1:59⅗
1966	61,602.18	Governor Armbro	Gay Sam	Joe O'Brien	2:00⅗
1967	58,642.36	Speed Model	Rocket Speed	Arthur L. Hult	1:59⅗(c)
1968	57,397.00	Nevele Pride	Snow Speed	Stanley F. Dancer	1:57 (R)
1969	64,757.00	Lindy's Pride	Nevele Major	Howard Beissinger	1:59
1970	76,351.00	Timothy T.	Paris Air	John F. Simpson, Jr.	1:59⅖
1971	63,415.00	Savoir	Keystone Hilliard	James Arthur	1:58⅕
1972	56,210.00	Super Bowl	Spartan Hanover	Joe O'Brien	1:59
1973	64,174.00	Arnie Almahurst	Knightly Way	Joe O'Brien	1:59½
1974	100,000.00	Waymaker	Dancing Party	John Simpson, Jr.	1:58⅕
1975	100,000.00	Noble Rogue	Exclusive Way	William Herman	1:59 (d)
1976	100,000.00	Quick Pay	Steve Lobell	Peter Haughton	1:59
1977	100,000.00	Texas	Cold Comfort	William Herman	1:57⅗
1978	100,000.00	Doublemint	Way to Gain	Peter Haughton	1:58⅗

(a) By Senator Frost. (b) By Caleb. (c) By Rocket Speed. (d) By Exclusive Way. (R) Record.

WORLD HARNESS RACING RECORDS

Age	Record	Horse	Driver	Track	Year
TROTTERS: MILE TRACK					
All Ages	1:54⅘	Nevele Pride	Stanley Dancer	Indianapolis, Ind.	1969
2-year-old	1:57 (r)	Briscoe Hanover	James Miller	Du Quoin, Ill.	1977
3-year-old	1:55 (r)	Speedy Somolli	Howard Beissinger	DuQuoin, Ill.	1978
	1:55 (r)	Florida Pro	George Sholty	DuQuoin, Ill.	1978
4-year-old	1:54⅘	Nevele Pride	Stanley Dancer	Indianapolis, Ind.	1969
TROTTERS: HALF-MILE TRACK					
All Ages	1:56⅘ (r)	Nevele Pride	Stanley Dancer	Saratoga Springs, N.Y.	1969
2-year-old	2:00½ (r)	Ayres	John Simpson	Delaware, Ohio	1963
3-year-old	1:58⅗ (r)	Songcan	George Sholty	Delaware, Ohio	1972
4-year-old	1:56⅘ (r)	Nevele Pride	Stanley Dancer	Saratoga Springs, N.Y.	1969
PACERS: MILE TRACK					
All Ages	1:52	Steady Star	Joe O'Brien	Lexington, Ky.	1971
2-year-old	1:54⅛ (r)	Jade Prince	Jack Kopas	Lexington, Ky.	1976
	1:54⅕	Fulla Strikes	Joe O'Brien	Inglewood, Calif.	1976
3-year-old	1:52⅖ (r)	Falcon Almahurst	Wm. Haughton	Lexington, Ky.	1978
4-year-old	1:52	Steady Star	Joe O'Brien	Lexington, Ky.	1971
PACERS: HALF-MILE TRACK					
All Ages	1:55⅗ (r)	Falcon Almahurst	Wm. Haughton	Delaware, Ohio	1978
2-year-old	1:58⅘ (r)	Columbia George	Roland Beaulieu	Yonkers, N.Y.	1969
	1:58⅘ (r)	J. R. Skipper	Greg Wright	Delaware, Ohio	1972
	1:58⅘ (r)	Armbro Ranger	Stanley Dancer	Cicero, Ill.	1975
	1:58⅘ (r)	Scarlett Skipper	Wm. Herman	Louisville, Ky.	1978
	1:58⅘ (r)	Mostest Yankee	C. Abbatiello	Westbury, N.Y.	1978
3-year-old	1:55⅖ (r)	Falcon Almahurst	Wm. Haughton	Delaware, Ohio	1978
4-year-old	1:55⅗ (r)	Albatross	Stanley Dancer	Delaware, Ohio	1972
TROTTERS: FIVE-EIGHTHS MILE					
All Ages	1:57⅜(r)	Dream of Glory	Stan Bayless	Cicero, Ill.	1976
2-year-old	2:01 (r)	Starlark Hanover	David Wade	Wilkes-Barre, Pa.	1973
	2:01 (r)	Green Speed	Wm. Haughton	Philadelphia, Pa.	1976
3-year-old	1:58⅛(r)	Speedy Somolli	Howard Beissinger	Meadow Lands, Pa.	1978
	1:58⅛(r)	Florida Pro	George Sholty	Philadelphia, Pa.	1978
	1:58⅛(r)	Speedy Somolli	Howard Beissinger	Meadow Lands, Pa.	1978
4-year-old	1:57⅜(r)	Green Speed	Wm. Haughton	Chicago, Ill.	1978
PACERS: FIVE-EIGHTHS MILE					
All Ages	1:54⅗(r)	Albatross	Stanley Dancer	Cicero, Ill.	1972
		Governor Skipper	John Chapman	Montreal, Canada	1977
		Rambling Willie	Robert Farrington	Wilmington, Del.	1977
2-year-old	1:57 (r)	Wellwood Hanover	Peter Haughton	Philadelphia, Pa.	1977
3-year-old	1:54½(r)	Governor Skipper	John Chapman	Montreal, Canada	1977
4-year-old	1:54⅗(r)	Albatross	Stanley Dancer	Cicero, Ill.	1972

(r) Record made in race. Other records were set in time trials.

HARNESS RACING DOLLAR EARNINGS

Pacers, All-Time			Trotters, All-Time			Drivers, All-Time		
Rank	Horse	Winnings	Rank	Horse	Winnings	Rank	Winning Driver	Winnings
1.	Rambling Willie	$1,860,887	1.	Bellino II	$1,960,945*	1.	William Haughton	$27,158,057
2.	Albatross	1,201,470	2.	Une de Mai	1,660,627*	2.	Herve Filion	25,810,950
3.	Governor Skipper	1,039,756	3.	Savoir	1,365,145	3.	Delmer Insko	21,456,233
4.	Rum Customer	1,001,548	4.	Fresh Yankee	1,294,252	4.	Stanley Dancer	20,463,446
5.	Cardigan Bay	1,000,837	5.	Eleazar	1,037,735*	5.	Carmine Abbatiello	19,409,540
6.	Bret Hanover	922,616	6.	Roquepine	956,161*	6.	John Chapman	18,766,936
7.	Laverne Hanover	868,557	7.	Green Speed	953,013	7.	Joe O'Brien	17,574,887
8.	Handle With Care	809,689	8.	Wayne Eden	925,000	8.	William Gilmour	15,634,557
9.	Overcall	784,006	9.	Timothy T.	897,000	9.	Lucien Fontaine	15,457,933
10.	Abercrombie	752,639	10.	Su Mac Lad	885,005	10.	Ben Webster	13,337,311

BOXING

AMATEUR BOXING CHAMPIONS

1978 WORLD	CLASS	1979 NATIONAL AAU
Teofilo Stevenson, Cuba	Heavyweight (over 178 lbs.)	Tony Tubbs, Santa Monica, Calif.
Sixto Soria, Cuba	Light Heavyweight (178 lbs.)	Tony Tucker, Grand Rapids, Mich.
Jose Gomez, Cuba	Middleweight (165 lbs.)	Alex Ramos, Bronx, N.Y.
Viktor Savchenko, USSR	Light Middleweight (156 lbs.)	Jeff Stoudemire, Cleveland, Ohio
Valeriy Rachkov, USSR	Welterweight (147 lbs.)	Donald Curry, Ft. Worth, Tex.
Valeriy Lvov, USSR	Light Welterweight (139 lbs.)	Lemuel Steeples, St. Louis, Mo.
Davidson Andeh, Nigeria	Lightweight (132 lbs.)	Davey Armstrong, Santa Monica, Calif.
Angel Herrera, Cuba	Featherweight (125 lbs.)	Bernard Taylor, Charlotte, N.C.
Adolfo Horta, Cuba	Bantamweight (119 lbs.)	Jackie Beard, Jackson, Tenn.
Henryk Srednicki, Poland	Flyweight (112 lbs.)	Harold Petty, St. Louis, Mo.
Stephen Mushioki, Kenya	Light Flyweight (106 lbs.)	Richard Sandoval, Pomona, Calif.

PROFESSIONAL BOXING CHAMPIONS
To September 16, 1979

DIVISION	WORLD BOXING ASSOCIATION (WBA)	WORLD BOXING COUNCIL (WBC)
Heavyweight		Larry Holmes, Easton, Pa.
Light Heavyweight	Victor Galindez, Argentina	Matthew Saad Muhammad, Phila., Pa.
Middleweight	Vito Antuofermo, Italy	Vito Antuofermo
Jr. Middleweight	Masashi Kudo, Japan	Maurice Hope, United Kingdom
Welterweight	Jose Cuevas, Mexico	Wilfredo Benitez, Puerto Rico
Jr. Welterweight	Antonio Cervantes, Colombia	Kim Sang-Hyun, S. Korea
Lightweight	Ernesto Espana, Venezuela	Jim Watt, Scotland
Jr. Lightweight	Sammy Serrano, Puerto Rico	Alexis Arguello, Nicaragua
Featherweight	Eusebio Pedroza, Panama	Danny Lopez, Los Angeles, Calif.
Jr. Featherweight	Ricardo Cordona, Venezuela	Wilfredo Gomez, Panama
Bantamweight	Jorge Lujan, Panama	Lupe Pintor, Mexico
Flyweight	Betulio Gonzalez, Venezuela	Park Chan-hee, S. Korea
Jr. Flyweight	Yoko Gushiken, Japan	Kim Sung-Jun, S. Korea

HEAVYWEIGHT CHAMPIONSHIP FIGHTS IN WHICH TITLE CHANGED HANDS

Date	Site	Winner	Weight (age)	Citizen	Loser	Weight (age)	Rounds	Referee
July 8, 1889[a]	Richburg, Miss.	John L. Sullivan, 198	(30)	U.S.	Jake Kilrain, 185	(30)	75	John Fitzpatrick
Sept. 7, 1892	New Orleans	James J. Corbett, 178	(26)	U.S.	John L. Sullivan, 212	(33)	21	Prof. John Duffy
Mar. 17, 1897	Carson City, Nev.	Bob Fitzsimmons, 167	(34)	England	James J. Corbett, 183	(30)	KO 14	George Siler
June 9, 1899	Coney Island	[b]James J. Jeffries, 206	(24)	U.S.	Bob Fitzsimmons, 167	(37)	KO 11	George Siler
Feb. 23, 1906	Los Angeles	[c]Tommy Burns, 180	(24)	Canada	Marvin Hart, 188	(29)	20	James J. Jeffries
Dec. 26, 1908	Sydney, Australia	Jack Johnson, 196	(30)	U.S.	Tommy Burns, 176	(27)	KO 14	Hugh McIntosh
April 5, 1915	Havana, Cuba	Jess Willard, 230	(33)	U.S.	Jack Johnson, 205½	(37)	KO 26	Jack Welch
July 4, 1919	Toledo	Jack Dempsey, 187	(24)	U.S.	Jess Willard, 245	(37)	KO 3	Ollie Pecord
Sept. 23, 1926	Philadelphia	[d]Gene Tunney, 189	(28)	U.S.	Jack Dempsey, 190	(31)	10	Pop Reilly
June 12, 1930	New York	[h]Max Schmeling, 188	(24)	Germany	Jack Sharkey, 197	(27)	4	Jim Crowley
June 21, 1932	Long Island City	Jack Sharkey, 205	(29)	U.S.	Max Schmeling, 188	(26)	15	Gunboat Smith
June 29, 1933	Long Island City	Primo Carnera, 260½	(26)	Italy	Jack Sharkey, 201	(30)	KO 6	Arthur Donovan
June 14, 1934	Long Island City	Max Baer, 209½	(25)	U.S.	Primo Carnera, 263¼	(27)	KO 11	Arthur Donovan
June 13, 1935	Long Island City	Jim Braddock, 193¾	(29)	U.S.	Max Baer, 209½	(26)	15	Jack McAvoy
June 22, 1937	Chicago	Joe Louis, 197¼	(23)	U.S.	Jim Braddock, 197	(31)	KO 8	Tommy Thomas
June 22, 1949	Chicago	[e]Ezzard Charles, 181¾	(27)	U.S.	Joe Walcott, 195½	(35)	15	Davey Miller
Sept. 27, 1950	New York	[f]Ezzard Charles, 184½	(29)	U.S.	Joe Louis, 218	(36)	15	Mark Conn
July 18, 1951	Pittsburgh	Joe Walcott, 194	(37)	U.S.	Ezzard Charles, 182	(30)	KO 7	Buck McTiernan
Sept. 23, 1952	Philadelphia	[g]Rocky Marciano, 184	(29)	U.S.	Joe Walcott, 196	(38)	KO 13	Charley Daggert
Nov. 30, 1956	Chicago	Floyd Patterson, 182¼	(21)	U.S.	Archie Moore, 187¾	(42)	KO 5	Frank Sikora
June 26, 1959	New York	Ingemar Johansson, 196	(26)	Sweden	Floyd Patterson, 182	(24)	KO 3	Ruby Goldstein
June 20, 1960	New York	Floyd Patterson, 190	(25)	U.S.	Ingemar Johansson, 193¾	(27)	KO 5	Arthur Mercante
Sept. 25, 1962	Chicago	Sonny Liston, 214	(28)	U.S.	Floyd Patterson, 189	(27)	KO 1	Frank Sikora
Feb. 25, 1964	Miami Beach	Cassius Clay, 210	(22)	U.S.	Sonny Liston, 218	(30)	KO 7	Barney Felix
March 4, 1968	New York	[i]Joe Frazier, 204½	(24)	U.S.	Buster Mathis, 243½	(23)	KO 11	Arthur Mercante
April 27, 1968	Oakland, Calif.	[i]Jimmy Ellis, 197	(28)	U.S.	Jerry Quarry, 195	(22)	15	Elmer Costa
Feb. 16, 1970	New York	[i]Joe Frazier, 205	(26)	U.S.	Jimmy Ellis, 201	(29)	KO 5	Tony Perez
Jan. 22, 1973	Kingston, Jamaica	George Foreman, 217½	(25)	U.S.	Joe Frazier, 214	(29)	TKO 2	Arthur Mercante
Oct. 30, 1974	Zaire, Africa	Muhammad Ali, 216	(32)	U.S.	George Foreman, 220	(25)	KO 8	Zach Clayton
Feb. 15, 1978	Las Vegas	Leon Spinks, 197½	(24)	U.S.	Muhammad Ali, 224½	(36)	15	David Pearl
Sept. 15, 1978	New Orleans	Muhammad Ali, 221	(36)	U.S.	Leon Spinks, 201	(25)	15	Locien Joubert

[a] Last bareknuckle heavyweight title fight. [b] Jim Jeffries retired in March 1905 for lack of opposition. He named Marvin Hart and Jack Root as the leading contenders; they fought on July 3, 1905, and Hart knocked out Root in the 12th round. [c] Burns claimed title after beating Hart. [d] Tunney retired in July 1928. [e] On March 1, 1949, Joe Louis retired; the NBA named Charles champion after he defeated Walcott. [f] Charles became undisputed champion by beating Louis, who had come out of retirement. [g] Marciano retired as champion in April 1956. [h] Won on a foul. [i] Immediately after a Federal Grand Jury had indicted Clay (also known as Muhammad Ali) on May 9, 1967, for refusing to accept induction into the Army, his title was vacated by the World Boxing Association and the New York State Athletic Commission. The WBA then staged an eight-man tournament, won by Ellis, to crown a successor. Frazier eventually earned recognition in New York and several other states and later defeated Ellis.

BOXING CHAMPIONS   Source: World Boxing Association

LIGHT HEAVYWEIGHT DIVISION

1903–05	Bob Fitzsimmons
1905–12	"Philadelphia" Jack O'Brien
1912–16	Jack Dillon
1916–20	Battling Levinsky
1920–22	Georges Carpentier
1922–23	Battling Siki
1923–25	Mike McTigue
1925–26	Paul Berlenbach
1926–27	Jack Delaney
1927	Mike McTigue
1927–29	Tommy Loughran
1930	Jimmy Slattery
1930–34	Maxie Rosenbloom
1934–35	Bob Olin
1935–39	John Henry Lewis
1939	Melio Bettina
1939–41	Billy Conn
1941	Anton Christoforidis (NBA)
1941–48	Gus Lesnevich
1948–50	Freddie Mills
1950–52	Joey Maxim
1952–61	Archie Moore
1961–63	Harold Johnson
1963–65	Willie Pastrano
1965–66	Jose Torres
1966–68	Dick Tiger
1968–71	Bob Foster
1971–72	Vicente Rondon
1972–73	Bob Foster
1973–78	Victor Galindez
1978–79	Mike Rossman (WBA)
1979	Victor Galindez (WBA)

MIDDLEWEIGHT DIVISION

1891–97	Bob Fitzsimmons
1897-1907	Tommy Ryan
1908	Stanley Ketchel
1908	Billy Papke
1908–10	Stanley Ketchel
1913	Frank Klaus
1913–14	George Chip
1914–17	Al McCoy
1917–20	Mike O'Dowd
1920–23	Johnny Wilson
1923–26	Harry Greb
1926	Tiger Flowers
1926–31	Mickey Walker
1931–41	Title in dispute
1941–47	Tony Zale
1947–48	Rocky Graziano
1948	Tony Zale
1948–49	Marcel Cerdan
1949–51	Jake LaMotta
1951	Ray Robinson, Randy Turpin
1951–52	Ray Robinson
1953–55	Bobo Olson
1955–57	Ray Robinson
1957	Gene Fullmer, Ray Robinson
1957–58	Carmen Basilio
1958–60	Ray Robinson
1959–62	Gene Fullmer (NBA)
1960–61	Paul Pender
1961–62	Terry Downes
1962	Paul Pender
1962–63	Dick Tiger
1963–65	Joey Giardello
1965–66	Dick Tiger
1966–67	Emile Griffith
1967	Nino Benvenuti
1967–68	Emile Griffith
1968–70	Nino Benvenuti
1970–77	Carlos Monzon
1977–78	Rodrigo Valdes
1978–79	Hugo Corro
1979–	Vito Antuofermo

WELTERWEIGHT DIVISION

1901	Rube Ferns
1901–04	Joe Walcott
1904	Dixie Kid
1904–06	Joe Walcott
1906–07	Honey Mellody
1907–15	Mike (Twin) Sullivan
1915–19	Ted Lewis
1919–22	Jack Britton
1922–26	Mickey Walker
1926–27	Pete Latzo
1927–29	Joe Dundee
1929–30	Jackie Fields

1930	Young Jack Thompson
1930–31	Tommy Freeman
1931	Young Jack Thompson
1931–32	Lou Brouillard
1932–33	Jackie Fields
1933	Young Corbett 3d
1933–34	Jimmy McLarnin
1934	Barney Ross
1934–35	Jimmy McLarnin
1935–38	Barney Ross
1938–40	Henry Armstrong
1940–41	Fritzie Zivic
1941–46	Freddie Cochrane
1946	Marty Servo
1946–51	Ray Robinson
1951	Johnny Bratton (NBA)
1951–54	Kid Gavilan
1954–55	Johnny Saxton
1955	Tony DeMarco
1955–56	Carmen Basilio
1956	Johnny Saxton
1956–57	Carmen Basilio
1958	Virgil Akins
1958–60	Don Jordan
1960–61	Benny (Kid) Paret
1961	Emile Griffith
1961–62	Benny (Kid) Paret
1962–63	Emile Griffith
1963	Luis Rodriguez
1963–66	Emile Griffith
1966–69	Curtis Cokes
1969–70	Jose Napoles
1970–71	Billy Backus
1971–72	Jose Napoles
1972–76	Angel Espada
1976–	Jose Cuevas (WBA)

LIGHTWEIGHT DIVISION

1901–08	Joe Gans
1908–10	Battling Nelson
1910–12	Ad Wolgast
1912–14	Willie Ritchie
1914–17	Freddie Welsh
1917–25	Benny Leonard
1925	Jimmy Goodrich
1925–26	Rocky Kansas
1926–30	Sammy Mandell
1930	Al Singer
1930–33	Tony Canzoneri
1933–35	Barney Ross
1935–36	Tony Canzoneri
1936–38	Lou Ambers
1938–39	Henry Armstrong
1939–40	Lou Ambers
1940–41	Lew Jenkins
1941–42	Sammy Angott
1943–47	During this period of dispute the National Boxing Association and the New York State Athletic Commission recognized different lightweight champions. Title holders, according to the N.Y. Commission, were Beau Jack and Bob Montgomery, and, according to the NBA, Sammy Angott, Juan Zurita, and Ike Williams. The issue was decided in August 1947 when Williams beat Montgomery.
1947–51	Ike Williams
1951–52	Jimmy Carter
1952	Lauro Salas
1952–54	Jimmy Carter
1954	Paddy DeMarco
1954–55	Jimmy Carter
1955–56	Wallace (Bud) Smith
1956–62	Joe Brown
1962–65	Carlos Ortiz
1965	Ismael Laguna
1965–68	Carlos Ortiz
1968–69	Carlos (Teo) Cruz
1969–70	Mando Ramos
1970	Ismael Laguna
1970–71	Ken Buchanan
1971–72	Mando Ramos
1972–73	Chango Carmona
1973–78	Roberto Duran
1979	Ernesto Espana (WBA)

FEATHERWEIGHT DIVISION

1904	Abe Attell
1904–08	"Brooklyn" Tommy Sullivan
1908–12	Abe Attell

1912–23	Johnny Kilbane
1923	Eugene Criqui
1923–25	Johnny Dundee
1926–27	Louis (Kid) Kaplan
1927–28	Benny Bass
1928	Tony Canzoneri
1928–29	Andre Routis
1929–32	Battling Battalino
1932	Tommy Paul (NBA)
1932	Kid Chocolate (NY)
1933–36	Freddie Miller
1936–37	Petey Sarron
1937–38	Henry Armstrong
1938–40	Joey Archibald
1940–41	Harry Jeffra
1941	Joey Archibald
1941–42	Chalky Wright
1942–48	Willie Pep
1948–49	Sandy Saddler
1949–50	Willie Pep
1950–57	Sandy Saddler
1957–59	Kid Bassey
1959–63	Davey Moore
1963–64	Sugar Ramos
1964–67	Vicente Saldivar
1968	Raul Rojas
1968	Sho Saijyo
1969	Johnny Famechon
1969–70	Vicente Saldivar
1970–71	Kuniaki Shibata
1971–72	Clemente Sanchez
1972–74	Ernesto Marcell
1974–77	Alexis Arguello
1977	Rafael Ortega
1977–78	Celio Lastra
1978–	Eusebio Pedroza (WBA)

BANTAMWEIGHT DIVISION

1936	Tony Marino
1936–37	Sixto Escobar
1937–38	Harry Jeffra
1938–40	Sixto Escobar
1940–42	Lou Salica
1942–47	Manuel Ortiz
1947	Harold Dade
1947–50	Manuel Ortiz
1950–52	Vic Toweel
1952–54	Jimmy Carruthers
1954–56	Robert Cohen
1956–57	Mario D'Agata
1957–59	Alphonse Halimi
1959–60	Joe Becerra
1961–65	Eder Jofre
1965–68	Masahiko (Fighting) Harada
1968–69	Lionel Rose
1969–70	Ruben Olivares
1970–71	Chucho Castillo
1971–72	Ruben Olivares
1972–73	Enrique Pinder
1973–74	Arnold Taylor
1974–77	Alfonso Zamora
1977–	Jorge Lujan (WBA)

FLYWEIGHT DIVISION

1938–43	Peter Kane
1943–48	Jackie Paterson
1948–50	Rinty Monaghan
1950	Terry Allen
1950–52	Dado Marino
1952–54	Yoshio Shirai
1954–60	Pascual Perez
1960–62	Pone Kingpetch
1962–63	Masahiko (Fighting) Harada
1963	Pone Kingpetch
1963–64	Hiroyuki Ebihara
1964–65	Pone Kingpetch
1965–66	Salvatore Burruni
1966	Horacio Accavallo
1966	Walter McGowan
1966–69	Chartchai Choinoi
1969	Hiroyuki Ebihara
1969–70	Bernabe Villacampo
1970	Berkrek Chartvanchai
1970–71	Masao Ohba
1971–72	Bertulio Gonzales
1972–73	Masao Ohba
1973–74	Chatchai Chionoi
1974–75	Erbito Salavarria
1976	Alfonso Lopez
1976–78	Gutty Espadas
1978–	Betulio Gonzalez (WBA)

TRACK AND FIELD

1979 NCAA INDOOR CHAMPIONSHIPS

60-Yard Dash
1. Curtis Dickey, Texas A & M, 6.15
2. Harvey Glance, Auburn
3. Terry Carter, Kent State

600-Yard Run
1. Anthony Tufariello, Villanova, 1:09.41
2. Lester Mickens, Kansas
3. Joe Coombs, Alabama

1,000-Yard Run
1. Don Paige, Villanova, 2:07.27
2. Greg Canty, Virginia
3. Todd Harbour, Baylor

One-Mile Run
1. Suleiman Nyambui, Texas-El Paso, 3:57.89
2. Sydney Maree, Villanova
3. Amos Korir, Villanova

Two-Mile Run
1. Suleiman Nyambui, Texas-El Paso, 8:37.87
2. Jim Stintzi, Wisconsin
3. Mark Nuggleton, Arkansas

Three-Mile Run
1. Mike Musyoki, Texas-El Paso, 13:21.6
2. Hillary Tuwei, Richmond
3. George Buckheit, Bucknell

60-Yard Hurdles
1. Renaldo Nehemiah, Maryland, 6.90
2. Garnett Edwards, West Virginia
3. Terron Wright, Memphis State

One-Mile Relay
1. Villanova, 3:15.52
2. Kansas
3. Southern University

Two-Mile Relay
1. Nebraska, 7:31.9
2. Western Michigan
3. Harvard

Distance Medley Relay
1. Tennessee, 9:47.1
2. Brigham Young
3. Villanova

High Jump
1. Jim Pringle, Florida, 7'2¾"
2. Bob Peterson, Idaho
3. Mike Lattany, Michigan

Long Jump
1. Larry Myrcks, Mississippi Coll. 25'10¾"
2. Greg Artis, Middle Tenn. State
3. Mike Pleasant, Oklahoma

Triple Jump
1. Bob Cannon, Indiana, 54'8¼"
2. Paul Jordan, Tennessee
3. Keith Connor, Texas-El Paso

Pole Vault
1. Geoff Stiles, Harvard, 17'3"
2. Jeff Buckingham, Kansas
3. Brian Goodman, Washington State

35 lb.—Weight Throw
1. Scott Neilson, Washington, 71'5½"
2. Ed Kania, Dartmouth
3. Ken Jansson, Dartmouth

Shot Put
1. Mark Baughman, Houston, 62'7¾"
2. John Marks, Southern Illinois
3. Jeff Braun, Wisconsin

TEAM STANDINGS
1. Villanova, 52
2. Texas-El Paso, 51
3. Auburn, 27
4. Tennessee, Kansas, 24
6. Maryland, 22
7. Harvard, 16
8. Dartmouth, Indiana, Missouri, 14

1979 NCAA OUTDOOR CHAMPIONSHIPS

100—Meter Dash
1. Jerome Deal, Texas-El Paso, 10.19
2. James Sanford, Southern California
3. Harvey Glance, Auburn

200—Meter Dash
1. Greg Foster U.C.L.A., 20.22
2. LaMonte King, Calif.-Irvine
3. Don Coleman, Oregon

400—Meter Dash
1. Kasheef Hassan, Oregon State, 45.18
2. Leslie Kerr, Texas A & M
3. Ronnie Harris, Tennessee

800—Meter Run
1. Don Paige, Villanova, 1:46.18
2. Jack McIntosh, Western Michigan
3. David Omwansa, Southern California

1,500—Meter Run
1. Don Paige, Villanova, 3:39.20
2. Todd Harbour, Baylor
3. Kipsubai Koskei, New Mexico

5,000—Meter Run
1. Sydney Maree, Villanova, 13:20.63
2. Rudy Chapa, Oregon
3. Adrian Leek, East Tenn. State

10,000—Meter Run
1. Suleiman Nyambui, Texas-El Paso, 28:01.30
2. Mike Musyoki, Texas-El Paso
3. Alberto Salazar, Oregon

3,000—Meter Steeplechase
1. Henry Rono, Washington State, 8:17.92
2. Amos Korir, Villanova
3. Hillary Tuwei, Richmond

110—Meter Hurdles
1. Renaldo Nehemiah, Maryland, 12.91
2. Dan Oliver, Ohio State
3. James Walker, Auburn

400—Meter Hurdles
1. James Walker, Auburn, 48.68
2. Dennis Otono, Mississippi State
3. Bart Williams, Cal. Poly-San L. Obispo

400—Meter Relay
1. Southern California, 39.35
2. Auburn
3. Louisiana State

1,600—Meter Relay
1. Louisiana State, 3:03.67
2. Texas
3. Florida State

High Jump
1. Nat Page, Missouri, 7'4½"
2. James Frazier, Arizona
3. Jeff Woodward, Alabama

Long Jump
1. Larry Myricks, Mississippi Coll., 26'7¼"
2. LaMonte King, Calif.-Irvine
3. Ned Armour, San Diego State

Triple Jump
1. Nate Cooper, Villanova, 56′1¼″
2. Dennis Ivory, Maryland
3. Robert Cannon, Indiana

Pole Vault
1. Paul Pilla, Arkansas State, 17′4¼″
2. Randy Hall, Texas A & M
3. Jon Warner, U.C.L.A.

Discus Throw
1. Bradley Cooper, Florida State, 209′9″
2. Svein Walvik, Texas-El Paso
3. Tim Fox, Oregon State

Hammer Throw
1. Scott Neilson, Washington, 237′3″
2. Richard Olsen, Texas-El Paso
3. Thommie Sjoholm, Texas-El Paso

Javelin Throw
1. Tom Sinclair, Washington, 261′3″
2. Mike Juskus, Glassboro State
3. Jari Keihas, Brigham Young

Shot Put
1. David Laut, U.C.L.A., 66′11½″
2. Hans Almatrom, Texas-El Paso
3. Steve Summers, Washington

TEAM STANDINGS
1. Texas-El Paso, 64
2. Villanova, 48
3. U.C.L.A., 36
4. Auburn, 30
5. Oregon, 28
6. Washington, 26
7. Southern California, 25½
8. Maryland, Louisiana State, 22
10. Washington State, 21

1979 AAU INDOOR CHAMPIONSHIPS

MEN'S EVENTS

60—Yard Dash
1. Steve Riddick, Philadelphia Pioneer Club, 6.14
2. Houston McTear, Muhammad Ali T.C.
3. Steve Williams, Athletic Attic

600—Yard Run
1. Mike Solomon, Philadelphia Pioneer Club, 1:12.4
2. Fred Sowerby, D.C. International
3. Stan Vinson, Univ. of Chicago T.C.

1,000—Yard Run
1. Evans White, Prairie View A & M, 2:08.4
2. Mark Belger, Athletic Attic
3. Mark Lech, Northeastern

One—Mile Run
1. Steve Scott, Irvine T.C., 4:01.4
2. Steve Lacy, Wisconsin T.C.
3. Craig Masback, N.Y. Pioneer Club

Three—Mile Run
1. Marty Liquori, Athletic Attic, 13:14.7
2. Bill Donakowski, New York A.C.
3. Robbie Perkins, New York A.C.

60—Yard Hurdles
1. Renaldo Nehemiah, Maryland, 6.94
2. Dedy Cooper, Bay Area Striders
3. Kerry Bethel, Philadelphia Pioneer Club

One—Mile Relay
1. D.C. International, 3:15.7
2. Philadelphia Pioneer Club
3. Howard University

Two—Mile Relay
1. New York Athletic Club, 7:35.8
2. Univ. of Chicago Track Club
3. Adelphi University

Sprint Medley Relay
1. Philadelphia Pioneer Club, 2:02.7
2. D.C. International
3. Philadelphia Pioneer "B" Team

Two—Mile Walk
1. Todd Scully, Shore A.C., 12:40
2. Jim Heiring, Univ. of Chicago T.C.
3. Dan O'Connor, New York A.C.

High Jump
1. Benn Fields, Philadelphia Pioneer Club, 7′4¾″
2. Franklin Jacobs, Fairleigh Dickinson Univ.
3. James Frazier, Univ. of Arizona

Long Jump
1. Larry Myricks, Mississippi Coll., 26′2″
2. Alfred Ogunfeyimi (Nigeria), Ohio Univ.
3. Theo Hamilton, Maccabi Union T.C.

Triple Jump
1. Ron Livers, Philadelphia Pioneer Club, 54′9¾″
2. Tommy Haynes, N.Y. Pioneer Club
3. Milan Tiff, Tobias Striders

Pole Vault
1. Dan Ripley, Norwalk, Calif., 18′1″
2. Earl Bell, Jonesboro, Arkansas
3. Ralph Haynie, Tobias Striders

35 lb.—Weight Throw
1. Ed Kania, Dartmouth Coll., 71′5″
2. Emmitt Berry, Maccabi Union T.C.
3. Boris Djerassi, New York A.C.

Shot Put
1. Colin Anderson, Univ. of Chicago T.C., 67′5¾″
2. Bruno Pauletto, Canada
3. Peter Shmock, Tobias Striders

WOMEN'S EVENTS

60—Yard Dash
1. Evelyn Ashford, Maccabi Union, 6.71
2. Brenda Morehead, Tennessee State Univ.
3. Laren Hodges, Texas Woman's Univ.

220—Yard Dash
1. Chandra Cheeseborough, Tenn. State Univ., 23.93
2. Gwen Gardner, Los Angeles Mercurettes
3. Rosalyn Bryant, Muhammad Ali T.C.

440—Yard Dash
1. June Griffith, Adelphi University, 54.2
2. Yolanda Rich, Southern California Cheetahs
3. Sherrie Howard, Los Angeles Mercurettes

880—Yard Run
1. Wendy Knudson, Athletes International, 2:07.3
2. Karel Jones, Atoms T.C.
3. Joetta Clark, Brooklyn, N.Y.

One—Mile Run
1. Francie Larrieu, Los Angeles, Calif., 4:39.2
2. Jan Merrill, Age Group A.A.
3. Debbie Heald, Golden Bear T.C.

Two—Mile Run
1. Julie Brown, Los Angeles Naturite T.C., 9:46.1
2. Jan Merrill, Age Group A.A.
3. Cindy Bremser, Madison, Wis.

60—Yard Hurdles
1. Candy Young, Beaver Falls, Pa., 7.50
2. Deby LaPlante, Englewood, N.J.
3. Rhonda Brady, Tennessee State Univ.

640—Yard Relay
1. Tennessee State University, 1:10.6
2. Los Angeles Mercurettes
3. Los Angeles Naturite Track Club

880–Yard Medley Relay
1. Tennessee State University, 1:44.5
2. Flashette Track Club
3. Grambling

One–Mile Relay
1. Prairie View A & M, 3:43
2. Atoms Track Club
3. Tennessee State University

One–Mile Walk
1. Chris Shea, Georgetown, 6:58.9
2. Susan Brodock, Southern Calif. Roadrunners
3. Christine Sakelarios, Southern Calif. Roadrunners

1979 AAU OUTDOOR CHAMPIONSHIPS

MEN'S EVENTS

100–Meter Dash
1. James Sanford, Tobias Striders, 10.07
2. Harvey Glance, Athletic Attic
3. Emmit King, Pioneer A.C.

200–Meter Dash
1. Dwayne Evans, Phoenix, Ariz., 20.28
2. Don Coleman, Operation PUSH A.C.
3. Cliff Wiley, D.C. International

400–Meter Dash
1. Willie Smith, Athletic Attic, 45.10
2. Tony Darden, Philadelphia Pioneers
3. Bill Green, Palo Alto, Calif.

800–Meter Run
1. James Robinson, Inner City A.C., 1:45.9
2. Agberto Guimares, Brazil
3. Mike White, Bay Area Striders

1,500–Meter Run
1. Steve Scott, Sub-Four T.C., 3:36.4
2. Don Paige, Athletic Attic
3. Todd Harbour, Baylor Univ.

5,000–Meter Run
1. Matt Centrowitz, Athletic Attic, 13:40.8
2. Wilson Waigwa, Philadelphia Pioneers
3. Herb Lindsay, Univ. of Chicago T.C.

10,000–Meter Run
1. Craig Virgin, St. Louis T.C., 27:39.4
2. Ric Rojas, Colorado T.C.
3. Frank Shorter, Colorado T.C.

3,000–Meter Steeplechase
1. Henry Marsh, Athletics West, 8:33.1
2. Bill McCullough, Santa Monica T.C.
3. Greg Meyer, Greater Boston T.C.

110–Meter Hurdles
1. Renaldo Nehemiah, D.C. International, 13.19
2. Dedy Cooper, Bay Area Striders
3. Charles Foster, Philadelphia Pioneers

400–Meter Hurdles
1. Edwin Moses, Pomona, Calif., 47.89
2. Quentin Wheeler, Maccabi T.C.
3. James Walker, Auburn T.C.

High Jump
1. Louise Ritter, Texas Woman's Univ., 6'1"
2. Paula Girven, Univ. of Maryland
3. Pam Spencer, Los Angeles Naturite T.C.

Long Jump
1. Kathy McMillan, Tenn. State Univ., 21'3"
2. Jody Anderson, Los Angeles Naturite T.C.
3. Martha Watson, Club International

Shot Put
1. Trixi Philipp, West Germany, 56'11"
2. Maren Seidler, San Jose Stars
3. Marcia Mecklenburg, Sports West

5,000–Meter Walk
1. Dan O'Connor, New York A.C., 21:46.6
2. Peter Timmons, New York A.C.
3. Martin Kraft, Motor City Striders

20,000–Meter Walk
1. Neal Pyke, Sequoia Sports Club, 1 hr., 27:11
2. Todd Scully, Shore A.C.
3. Chris Banaen, Univ. of Chicago, T.C.

50,000–Meter Walk
1. Marco Evoniuk, Colorado T.C., 4 hrs., 10:33
2. Vince O'Sullivan, Hunter College
3. Karl Johansen, Club Northwest

High Jump
1. Franklin Jacobs, Athletic Attic, 7'4¾"
2. Benn Fields, Philadelphia Pioneers
3. Reynoldo Brown, Operation PUSH A.C.

Long Jump
1. Larry Myricks, Mississippi Coll., 27'2"
2. Carl Lewis, Willingboro (N.J.) T.C.
3. Randy Williams, Maccabi T.C.

Triple Jump
1. Ron Livers, Philadelphia Pioneers, 57'7½"
2. Willie Banks, Tobias Striders
3. James Butts, Muhammad Ali T.C.

Pole Vault
1. Mike Tully, International Amateur A.A., 18'½"
2. Billy Olson, Maccabi T.C.
3. Greg Woepse, San Jose State

Discus Throw
1. Mac Wilkins, Athletics West, 231'10"
2. Ken Stadel, Tobias Striders
3. Knut Hjeltnes, Bay Area Striders

Hammer Throw
1. Scott Neilson, Canada, 236'5"
2. Boris Djerassi, New York A.C.
3. Andy Bessette, New York A.C.

Javelin Throw
1. Duncan Atwood, Athletics West, 268'7"
2. Rod Ewaliko, Athletics West
3. Bill Schmidt, Knoxville T.C.

Shot Put
1. David Laut, Los Angeles, Calif., 69'3¼"
2. Al Feuerbach, Athletics West
3. Colin Anderson, Univ. of Chicago T.C.

WOMEN'S EVENTS

100–Meter Dash
1. Evelyn Ashford, Maccabi T.C., 11.01
2. Brenda Morehead, Tennessee State T.C.
3. Chandra Cheeseborough, Tennessee State T.C.

200–Meter Dash
1. Evelyn Ashford, Maccabi T.C., 22.07
2. Valerie Brisco, Los Angeles Naturite T.C.
3. Brenda Morehead, Tennessee State T.C.

400–Meter Dash
1. Patricia Jackson, Prairie View A & M, 52.37
2. Sharon Dabney, Clippers T.C.
3. Sherri Howard, Los Angeles Mercurettes

800–Meter Run
1. Essie Kelley, Prairie View A & M, 2:02.3
2. Julie Brown, Los Angeles Naturite T.C.
3. Madeline Manning, Oral Roberts T.C.

1,500–Meter Run
1. Francie Larrieu, Pacific Coast Club, 4:04.6
2. Mary Decker, Eugene, Ore.
3. Julie Brown, Los Angeles Naturite T.C.

3,000–Meter Run
1. Francie Larrieu, Pacific Coast Club, 8:53.8
2. Jan Merrill, Age Group A.A.
3. Julie Brown, Los Angeles Naturite T.C.

10,000–Meter Run
1. Mary Shea, Cardinal Gibbons H.S., 32:52.5
2. Joan Benoit, Liberty A.C.
3. Amy Laffoon, Colorado State

100–Meter Hurdles
1. Deby LaPlante, KCBQ T.C., 12.86
2. Candy Young, Beaver Falls, Pa.
3. Stephanie Hightower, Ohio State

400—Meter Hurdles
1. Edna Brown, Temple, 57.60
2. Debra Melrose, Prairie View A & M
3. Debbie Esser, Iowa State

400—Meter Relay
1. Tennessee State Track Club, 43.68
2. Los Angeles Mercurettes
3. Los Angeles Naturite Track Club

800—Meter Medley Relay
1. Prairie View A & M, 1:38.2
2. Los Angeles Naturite Track Club
3. Tennessee State T.C.

1,600—Meter Relay
1. Prairie View A & M, 3:32.8
2. New York Police Athletic League
3. Colorado Flyers

3,200—Meter Relay
1. Oral Roberts Track Club, 8:31.4
2. Los Angeles Naturite Track Club
3. Sports West

5,000—Meter Walk
1. Sue Brodock, Southern Calif. Roadrunners, 24:07.6
2. Paula Cash, California
3. Chris Sakelarios, Southern Calif. Roadrunners

10,000—Meter Walk
1. Sue Brodock, Southern Calif. Roadrunners, 50:32.6
2. Sue Liers, Island T.C.
3. Chris Sakelarios, Southern Calif. Roadrunners

High Jump
1. Debbie Brill, Pacific Coast Club, 6'4"
2. Louise Ritter, Texas Woman's Univ.
3. Pam Spencer, Los Angeles Naturite T.C.

Long Jump
1. Kathy McMillan, Tennessee State T.C., 21'3¼"
2. Jane Frederick, Pacific Coast Club
3. Pat Johnson, Wisconsin United

Discus Throw
1. Lynne Winbigler, Oregon T.C., 189'5"
2. Lorna Griffin, Sports West
3. Ria Stalman, Sports West

Javelin Throw
1. Kate Schmidt, Pacific Coast Club, 206'1"
2. Cathy Sulinski, Millbrae Lions T.C.
3. Lynn Cannon, Millbrae Lions T.C.

Shot Put
1. Maren Seidler, San Jose Stars, 62'7¾"
2. Ann Turbyne, Gilly's Gym
3. Kathy Devine, Texas A.C.

1979 AAU DECATHLON CHAMPIONSHIPS

1. Bob Coffman, Hurricane T.C., 8154
2. John Crist, unattached
3. John Whitson, Sun Land T.C.

AMERICAN TRACK AND FIELD RECORDS

SOURCE: Track & Field News

Event	Men's Record	Name, Year	Women's Record	Name, Year
100—Meter Dash	9.95 sec.	Jim Hines, 1968	10.97 sec.	Evelyn Ashford, 1979
200—Meter Dash	19.83 sec.	Tommie Smith, 1968	21.83 sec.	Evelyn Ashford, 1979
300—Meter Dash	32.40 sec.	Ken Randle, 1975	—	
400—Meter Dash	43.86 sec.	Lee Evans, 1968	50.62 sec.	Rosalyn Bryant, 1976
600—Meter Run	1 min., 15.5 sec.	Rob Cassleman, 1974	—	
800—Meter Run	1 min., 43.9 sec.	Rick Wohlhuter, 1974	1 min., 57.9 sec.	Madeline Jackson, 1976
1,000—Meter Run	2 min., 13.9 sec.	Rick Wohlhuter, 1974	—	
1,500—Meter Run	3 min., 33.1 sec.	Jim Ryun, 1967	4 min., 2.6 sec.	Jan Merrill, 1976
One—Mile Run	3 min., 51.1 sec.	Jim Ryun, 1967	4 min., 23.8 sec.	Mary Decker, 1979
2,000—Meter Run	5 min., 1.4 sec.	Steve Prefontaine, 1975	—	
3,000—Meter Run	7 min., 37.7 sec.	Rudy Chapa, 1979	8 min., 42.6 sec.	Jan Merrill, 1978
5,000—Meter Run	13 min., 15.1 sec.	Marty Liquori, 1977	15 min., 35.5 sec.	Kathy Mills, 1978
10,000—Meter Run	27 min., 39.4 sec.	Craig Virgin, 1979	33 min., 15.1 sec.	Peg Neppel, 1977
15,000—Meter Run	43 min., 39.8 sec.	Bill Rodgers, 1977	—	
20,000—Meter Run	58 min., 15.0 sec.	Bill Rodgers, 1977	—	
25,000—Meter Run	1 hr., 14 min., 12 sec.	Bill Rodgers, 1979	—	
30,000—Meter Run	1 hr., 31 min., 50 sec.	Bill Rodgers, 1979	—	
Marathon	2 hr., 9 min., 55 sec.	Bill Rodgers, 1975	2 hr., 35 min., 41 sec.	Joan Benoit, 1979
One—Hour Run	12 miles, 997 yards	Bill Rodgers, 1979	—	
20—Kilometer Walk	1 hr., 30 min., 10 sec.	Larry Young, 1972	(10km) 50 min., 32.6 sec.	Sue Brodock, 1979
50—Kilometer Walk	4 hr., 13 min., 36 sec.	Bob Kitchen, 1972	—	
110—Meter Hurdles	13.00 sec.	Renaldo Nehemiah, 1979	(100m) 12.86 sec.	Deby LaPlante, 1979
400—Meter Hurdles	47.45 sec.	Edwin Moses, 1977	56.61 sec.	Mary Ayres, 1977
3,000—Meter Steeplechase	8 min., 19.3 sec.	Doug Brown, 1978	—	
4 X 100—Meter Relay	38.03 sec.	National Team, 1972	42.87 sec.	National Team, 1968
4 X 200—Meter Relay	1 min., 20.3 sec.	Southern California, 1978	1 min., 32.6 sec.	National Team, 1979
4 X 400—Meter Relay	2 min., 56.1 sec.	National Team, 1968	3 min., 22.8 sec.	National Team, 1976
4 X 800—Meter Relay	7 min., 10.4 sec.	Chicago Track Club, 1973	8 min., 19.9 sec.	National Team, 1979
4 X 1,500—Meter Relay	14 min., 46.3 sec.	National Team, 1979	—	
Sprint Medley Relay	3 min., 15.2 sec.	Kansas, 1967	—	
Distance Medley Relay	9 min., 31.8 sec.	Kansas State, 1972	—	
High Jump	2.32m (7'7¼")	Dwight Stones, 1976	1.93m (6'4")	Louise Ritter, 1979
Long Jump	8.90m (29'2½")	Bob Beamon, 1968	6.90m (22'7½")	Jodi Anderson, 1978
Triple Jump	17.24m (56'6¾")	James Butts, 1978	—	
Pole Vault	5.70m (18'8¼")	Dave Roberts, 1976	—	
Shot Put	21.85m (71'8½")	Terry Albritton, 1976	19.09m (62'7¾")	Maren Seidler, 1979
Discus Throw	70.86m (232'6")	Mac Wilkins, 1976	58.26m (191'2")	Lorna Griffin, 1979
Hammer Throw	71.90m (235'11")	Ed Burke, 1967	—	
Javelin Throw	91.44m (300')	Mark Murro, 1970	69.32m (227'5")	Kate Schmidt, 1977
Pentathlon			4708 points	Jane Frederick, 1979
Decathlon	8617 points	Bruce Jenner, 1976		

WORLD TRACK AND FIELD RECORDS

SOURCE: Track & Field News

Men's Event	Time/Distance	Name (Country)	Date
100–Meter Dash	9.95 sec.	Jim Hines (United States)	10/14/68
200–Meter Dash	19.83 sec.	Tommie Smith (United States)	10/16/68
400–Meter Dash	43.86 sec.	Lee Evans (United States)	10/18/68
800–Meter Run	1 min., 42.4 sec.	Sebastian Coe (United Kingdom)	7/5/79
1,000–Meter Run	2 min., 13.9 sec.	Rick Wohlhuter (United States)	7/30/74
1,500–Meter Run	3 min., 32.1 sec.	Sebastian Coe (United Kingdom)	8/15/79
One–Mile Run	3 min., 49 sec.	Sebastian Coe (United Kingdom)	7/17/79
2,000–Meter Run	4 min., 51.4 sec.	John Walker (New Zealand)	6/30/76
3,000–Meter Run	7 min., 32.1 sec.	Henry Rono (Kenya)	6/27/78
5,000–Meter Run	13 min., 8.4 sec.	Henry Rono (Kenya)	5/13/78
10,000–Meter Run	27 min., 22.5 sec.	Henry Rono (Kenya)	6/11/78
20,000–Meter Run	57 min., 24.2 sec.	Jos Hermens (Netherlands)	5/1/76
25,000–Meter Run	1 hr., 14 min., 12 sec	Bill Rodgers (United States)	2/21/79
30,000–Meter Run	1 hr., 31 min., 30.4 sec.	Jim Adler (United Kingdom)	9/5/70
Marathon	2 hr., 8 min., 34 sec.	Derek Clayton (Australia)	5/30/69
One–Hour Run	13 miles, 24 yards	Jos Hermens (Netherlands)	5/1/76
20–Kilometer Walk	1 hr., 23 min., 32 sec.	Daniel Bautista (Mexico)	5/14/77
30–Kilometer Walk	1 hr., 49 min., 54 sec.	Raul Gonzalez (Mexico)	5/19/78
50–Kilometer Walk	3 hr., 52 min., 24 sec.	Raul Gonzalez (Mexico)	5/19/78
Two–Hour Walk	16 miles, 1637 yards	Raul Gonzalez (Mexico)	5/19/78
110–Meter Hurdles	13.00 sec.	Renaldo Nehemiah (United States)	5/6/79
400–Meter Hurdles	47.45 sec.	Edwin Moses (United States)	6/11/77
3,000–Meter Steeplechase	8 min., 5.4 sec.	Henry Rono (Kenya)	4/8/78
4 X 100–Meter Relay	38.03 sec.	United States	9/3/77
4 X 200–Meter Relay	1 min., 20.3 sec.	United States	5/27/77
4 X 400–Meter Relay	2 min., 56.1 sec.	United States	10/20/68
4 X 800–Meter Relay	7 min., 8.6 sec.	West Germany	8/13/66
4 X 1,500–Meter Relay	14 min., 38.8 sec.	West Germany	8/16/77
High Jump	2.34m (7'8")	Vladimir Yashchenko (U.S.S.R.)	6/16/78
Long Jump	8.90m (29'2½")	Bob Beaman (United States)	10/18/68
Triple Jump	17.89m (58'8¼")	Joao Oliveira (Brazil)	10/15/75
Pole Vault	5.70m (18'8¼")	Dave Roberts (United States)	6/22/76
Shot Put	22.15m (72'8")	Udo Beyer (East Germany)	7/6/78
Discus Throw	71.16m (233'5")	Wolfgang Schmidt (East Germany)	8/9/78
Hammer Throw	80.32m (263'6")	Karl Hans Riehm (West Germany)	8/6/78
Javelin Throw	94.58m (310'4")	Miklos Nemeth (Hungary)	7/26/76
Decathlon	8617 points	Bruce Jenner (United States)	7/30/76

Women's Event	Time/Distance	Name (Country)	Date
100–Meter Dash	10.88 sec.	Marlies Gohr (East Germany)	7/1/77
200–Meter Dash	21.71 sec.	Marita Koch (East Germany)	6/10/79
400–Meter Dash	48.60 sec.	Marita Koch (East Germany)	8/4/79
800–Meter Run	1 min., 54.9 sec.	Tatyana Kazankina (U.S.S.R.)	7/26/76
1,000–Meter Run	2 min., 30.6 sec.	Tatyana Providokhina (U.S.S.R.)	8/21/78
1,500–Meter Run	3 min., 56.0 sec.	Tatyana Kazankina (U.S.S.R.)	6/28/76
One–Mile Run	4 min., 22.1 sec.	Natalia Maracescu (Romania)	1/27/79
2,000–Meter Run	5 min., 25.5 sec.	Maricica Puica (Romania)	5/19/79
3,000–Meter Run	8 min., 27.1 sec.	Lyudmila Bragina (U.S.S.R.)	8/7/76
5,000–Meter Run	15 min., 8.8 sec.	Loa Olafsson (Denmark)	5/31/78
10,000–Meter Run	31 min., 45.4 sec.	Loa Olafsson (Denmark)	4/6/78
Marathon	2 hr., 34 min., 48 sec.	Christa Vahlensieck (West Germany)	9/11/77
100–Meter Hurdles	12.48 sec.	Grazyna Rabsztyn (Poland)	6/10/78, 6/18/79
400–Meter Hurdles	54.89 sec.	Marina Makeyeva (U.S.S.R.)	7/27/79
4 X 100–Meter Relay	42.09 sec.	East Germany	6/10/79, 8/5/79
4 X 200–Meter Relay	1 min., 30.8 sec.	Ukraine	7/29/79
4 X 400–Meter Relay	3 min., 19.2 sec.	East Germany	7/31/76
4 X 800–Meter Relay	7 min., 52.3 sec.	U.S.S.R.	8/16/76
High Jump	2.01m (6'7")	Sara Simeoni (Italy)	8/31/78
Long Jump	7.09m (23'3¼")	Vilma Bardauskiene (U.S.S.R.)	8/31/78
Shot Put	22.32m (73'2¾")	Helena Fibingerova (Czechoslovakia)	8/20/77
Discus Throw	70.72m (232')	Evelin Jahl (East Germany)	8/12/78
Javelin Throw	69.52m (228'1")	Ruth Fuchs (East Germany)	6/13/79
Pentathlon	4839 points	Nadyezhda Tkachenko (U.S.S.R.)	9/18/77

BOWLING

1979 LEADING MONEY WINNERS (to Aug. 15)

Source: P.B.A.

Bowler	Tournaments	Amount	Bowler	Tournaments	Amount
1. Mark Roth, North Arlington, N.J.	19	$79,474	11. Bill Spigner, Hamden, Conn.	24	33,448
2. Earl Anthony, Kent, Wash.	23	76,990	12. Gary Dickinson, Ft. Worth, Tex.	23	33,400
3. Marshall Holman, Medford, Ore.	22	70,085	13. Larry Laub, Santa Rosa, Calif.	19	33,270
4. George Pappas, Charlotte, N.C.	22	53,675	14. Steve Cook, Roseville, Calif.	24	31,755
5. Joe Berardi, Pearl River, N.Y.	23	51,755	15. Butch Soper, Whittier, Calif.	25	29,955
6. Ed Ressler, Bethlehem, Pa.	26	50,261	16. Cliff McNealy, San Lorenzo, Calif.	20	28,365
7. Dick Ritger, River Falls, Wis.	15	49,670	17. Ernie Schlegel, Vancouver, U.S.A.	23	28,205
8. Johnny Petraglia, Staten Island, N.Y.	17	43,499	18. Guppy Troup, Savannah, Ga.	25	27,585
9. Tommy Hudson, Akron, Ohio	24	34,470	19. Dan Roche, Downey, Calif.	25	27,225
10. Jeff Mattingly, Tacoma, Wash.	25	34,010	20. Fred Conner, Mar Vista, Calif.	24	27,179

PBA TOP-MONEY WINNERS, 1959–1978

Year	Bowler	Winnings	Year	Bowler	Winnings
1959	Dick Weber	$ 7,672	1969	Billy Hardwick	64,160
1960	Don Carter	22,525	1970	Mike McGrath	52,049
1961	Dick Weber	26,280	1971	John Petraglia	85,065
1962	Don Carter	49,972	1972	Don Johnson	56,648
1963	Dick Weber	46,333	1973	Don McCune	69,000
1964	Bob Strampe	33,592	1974	Earl Anthony	99,585
1965	Dick Weber	47,675	1975	Earl Anthony	107,585
1966	Wayne Zahn	54,720	1976	Earl Anthony	110,883
1967	Dave Davis	54,165	1977	Mark Roth	105,583
1968	Jim Stefanich	$67,375	1978	Mark Roth	134,500

BOWLING CHAMPIONS

BPAA U.S. Open (Formerly All-Star)	ABC Masters	PBA National Championship	A.B.C. Classic All-Events
1962 .... Dick Weber	1962 .... Billy Golembiewski	1962 .... Carmen Salvino	1962 .... Jack Winters
1963 .... Dick Weber	1963 .... Harry Smith	1963 .... Billy Hardwick	1963 .... Tom Hennessey
1964 .... Bob Strampe	1964 .... Billy Welu	1964 .... Bob Strampe	1964 .... Billy Hardwick
1965 .... Dick Weber	1965 .... Billy Welu	1965 .... Dave Davis	1965 .... Tom Hennessey
1966 .... Dick Weber	1966 .... Bob Strampe	1966 .... Wayne Zahn	1966 .... Les Schissler
1967 .... Les Schissler	1967 .... Lou Scalia	1967 .... Dave Davis	1967 .... Bob Strampe
1968 .... Jim Stefanich	1968 .... Pete Tountas	1968 .... Wayne Zahn	1968 .... Jim Stefanich
1969 .... Billy Hardwick	1969 .... Jim Chestney	1969 .... Mike McGrath	1969 .... Larry Lichstein
1970 .... Bobby Cooper	1970 .... Don Glover	1970 .... Mike McGrath	1970 .... Bob Strampe
1971 .... Mike Lemongello	1971 .... Jim Godman	1971 .... Mike Lemongello	1971 .... Gary Dickinson
1972 .... Don Johnson	1972 .... Bill Beach	1972 .... John Guenther	1972 .... Teata Semiz
1973 .... Mike McGrath	1973 .... Dave Soutar	1973 .... Earl Anthony	1973 .... Jimmy Mack
1974 .... Larry Laub	1974 .... Paul Colwell	1974 .... Earl Anthony	1974 .... Jim Godman
1975 .... Steve Neff	1975 .... Ed Ressler	1975 .... Earl Anthony	1975 .... Bobby Meadows
1976 .... Paul Moser	1976 .... Nelson Burton, Jr.	1976 .... Paul Colwell	1976 .... Gary Fust
1977 .... John Petraglia	1977 .... Earl Anthony	1977 .... Tommy Hudson	1977 .... Dick Ritger
1978 .... Nelson Burton, Jr.	1978 .... Frank Ellenburg	1978 .... Warren Nelson	1978 .... Bill Beach
1979 .... Joe Berardi	1979 .... Doug Myers	1979 .... Mike Aulby	1979 .... N. Burton, Jr.

BOWLER OF THE YEAR

Selected by Bowling Writers Association of America

MEN

1956	Bill Lillard, Chicago, Ill.
1957	Don Carter, St. Louis, Mo.
1958	Don Carter, St. Louis, Mo.
1959	Ed Lubanski, Detroit, Mich.
1960	Don Carter, St. Louis, Mo.
1961	Dick Weber, St. Louis, Mo.
1962	Don Carter, St. Louis, Mo.
1963	Dick Weber, St. Louis, Mo.
1964	Billy Hardwick, San Mateo, Calif.
1965	Dick Weber, St. Louis, Mo.
1966	Wayne Zahn, Atlanta, Ga.
1967	Dave Davis, Phoenix, Ariz.
1968	Jim Stefanich, Joliet, Ill.
1969	Billy Hardwick, Louisville, Ky.
1970	Nelson Burton, Jr., St. Louis, Mo.
1971	Don Johnson, Akron, Ohio
1972	Don Johnson, Akron, Ohio
1973	Don McCune, Munster, Ind.
1974	Earl Anthony, Tacoma, Wash.
1975	Earl Anthony, Tacoma, Wash.
1976	Earl Anthony, Tacoma, Wash.
1977	Mark Roth, Staten Island, N.Y.
1978	Mark Roth, N. Arlington, N.J.

WOMEN

1956	Anita Cantaline, Detroit, Mich.
1957	Marion Ladewig, Grand Rapids, Mich.
1958	Marion Ladewig, Grand Rapids, Mich.
1959	Marion Ladewig, Grand Rapids, Mich.
1960	Sylvia Wene, Philadelphia, Pa.
1961	Shirley Garms, Palatine, Ill.
1962	Shirley Garms, Palatine, Ill.
1963	Marion Ladewig, Grand Rapids, Mich.
1964	LaVerne Carter, St. Louis, Mo.
1965	Betty Kuczynski, Chicago, Ill.
1966	Joy Abel, Chicago, Ill.
1967	Mildred Martorella, Rochester, .N.Y.
1968	Dotty Fothergill, N. Attleboro, Mass.
1969	Dotty Fothergill, N. Attleboro, Mass.
1970	Mary Baker, Central Islip, N.Y.
1971	Paula Sperber, Miami, Fla.
1972	Patty Costello, New Carrollton, Md.
1973	Judy Soutar, Kansas City, Mo.
1974	Betty Morris, Stockton, Calif.
1975	Judy Soutar, Kansas City, Mo.
1976	Patty Costello, Scranton, Pa.
1977	Betty Morris, Stockton, Calif.
1978	Donna Adamek, Monrovia, Calif.

1979 LEADING WOMEN'S MONEY WINNERS (to Oct. 1) — WPBA Events and U.S. Open
SOURCE: W.P.B.A.

	Bowler	Amount		Bowler	Amount
1.	Pam Buckner, Reno, Nevada	$15,975	9.	Dianna Silva, Albuquerque, N.M.	$8,000
2.	Pat Costello, Union City, Calif.	15,110	10.	Kathy Wodka, New London, Conn.	7,830
3.	Virginia Norton, South Gate, Calif.	12,313	11.	Patty Costello, Scranton, Pa.	6,955
4.	Betty Morris, Stockton, Calif.	11,630	12.	Barbara Thorberg, Florissant, Mo.	5,650
5.	Donna Adamek, Monrovia, Calif.	9,835	13.	Edith Burroughs, Akron, Ohio	5,515
6.	Vesma Grinfelds, San Francisco, Calif.	9,610	14.	Judy Soutar, Kansas City, Mo.	5,440
7.	Bev Ortner, Tucson, Arizona	8,998	15.	Kottie Kemp, Las Vegas, Nevada	5,050
8.	Nikki Gianulias, Vallejo, Calif.	8,212			

WOMEN'S BOWLING CHAMPIONS

	U.S. Open (Formerly All-Star)	WIBC Queens Tournament	WPBA National Championship
1961	Phyllis Notaro	Janet Harman	Shirley Garms
1962	Shirley Garms	Dorothy Wilkinson	Stevie Balogh
1963	Marion Ladewig	Irene Monterosso	Janet Harman
1964	LaVerne Carter	D.D. Jacobson	Betty Kuczynski
1965	Ann Slattery	Betty Kuczynski	Helen Duval
1966	Joy Abel	Judy Lee	Judy Lee
1967	Gloria Bouvia	Mildred Martorella	Betty Mivalez
1968	Dotty Fothergill	Phyllis Massey	Dotty Fothergill
1969	Dotty Fothergill	Ann Feigel	Dotty Fothergill
1970	Mary Baker	Mildred Martorella	Bobbe North
1971	Paula Sperber	Mildred Martorella	Patty Costello
1972	Lorrie Koch	Dotty Fothergill	Patty Costello
1973	Mildred Martorella	Dotty Fothergill	Betty Morris
1974	Pat Costello	Judy Soutar	Pat Costello
1975	Paula Sperber	Cindy Powell	Pam Rutherford
1976	Patty Costello	Pam Rutherford	Patty Costello
1977	Betty Morris	Dana Stewart	Vesma Grinfelds
1978	Donna Adamek	Loa Boxberger	Toni Gillard
1979	Dianna Silva	Donna Adamek	

1978 LEADING MONEY WINNERS — WOMEN
SOURCE: W.P.B.A.

	Bowler	Amount		Bowler	Amount
1.	Donna Adamek, Monrovia, Calif.	$31,000	6.	Pat Costello, Union City, Calif.	$16,305
2.	Vesma Grinfelds, San Francisco, Calif.	29,600	7.	Judy Souter, Kansas City, Mo.	16,130
3.	Virginia Norton, South Gate, Calif.	26,125	8.	Toni Gillard, Beverly, Ohio	12,705
4.	Betty Morris, Stockton, Calif.	18,750	9.	Edie Jo Neal, Miami, Florida	12,665
5.	Cheryl Robinson, Van Nuys, Calif.	16,620	10.	Bev Ortner, Tucson, Arizona	8,910

CHESS
SOURCE: U.S. Chess Federation

WORLD CHAMPIONSHIPS

Year	Winner, Country	Year	Winner, Country	Year	Winner, Country
1886	Wilhelm Steinitz, Austria	1921	Jose Capablanca, Cuba	1958	Mikhail Botvinnik, USSR
1889	Wilhelm Steinitz, Austria	1927	Alexander Alekhine, France	1960	Mikhail Tal, USSR
1891	Wilhelm Steinitz, Austria	1929	Alexander Alekhine, France	1961	Mikhail Botvinnik, USSR
1892	Wilhelm Steinitz, Austria	1934	Alexander Alekhine, France	1963	Tigran Petrosian, USSR
1894	Emanuel Lasker, Germany	1935	Max Euwe, Netherlands	1966	Tigran Petrosian, USSR
1897	Emanuel Lasker, Germany	1937	Alexander Alekhine, France	1969	Boris Spassky, USSR
1907	Emanuel Lasker, Germany	1948	Mikhail Botvinnik, USSR	1972	Bobby Fischer, US
1908	Emanuel Lasker, Germany	1951	Mikhail Botvinnik, USSR	1975	Anatoly Karpov, USSR
1909	Emanuel Lasker, Germany	1954	Mikhail Botvinnik, USSR	1978	Anatoly Karpov, USSR
1910*	Emanuel Lasker, Germany	1957	Vassily Smyslov, USSR		

* Two championship matches held in 1910. Lasker won both.

U.S. NATIONAL CHAMPIONSHIPS

UNOFFICIAL CHAMPIONS							
1857-71	Paul Morphy	1894	Jackson Showalter	1942	Samuel Reshevsky	1963	Bobby Fischer
1871-76	George Mackenzie	1894	Albert Hodges	1944	Arnold Denker	1964	Bobby Fischer
1876-80	James Mason	1895	Jackson Showalter	1946	Arnold Denker	1965	Bobby Fischer
1880-89	George Mackenzie	1896	Jackson Showalter	1946	Samuel Reshevsky	1966	Bobby Fischer
1889-90	S. Lipschutz	1896	Jackson Showalter	1948	Herman Steiner	1968	Larry Evans
1890	Jackson Showalter	1897	Harry Pillsbury	1951	Larry Evans	1969	Samuel Reshevsky
1990-91	Max Judd	1898	Harry Pillsbury	1952	Larry Evans	1972	Robert Byrne
1891	Jackson Showalter	1909	Frank Marshall	1954	Arthur Bisguier	1973	Lubomir Kavalek and John Grefe
		1923	Frank Marshall	1958	Bobby Fischer		
		1936	Samuel Reshevsky	1959	Bobby Fischer	1974	Walter Browne
CHAMPIONS		1938	Samuel Reshevsky	1960	Bobby Fischer	1975	Walter Browne
1892	Jackson Showalter	1940	Samuel Reshevsky	1961	Bobby Fischer	1977	Walter Browne
1892	S. Lipschutz	1941	Samuel Reshevsky	1962	Larry Evans	1978	Lubomir Kavalek

SWIMMING AND DIVING

1979 NCAA CHAMPIONS

DIVISION I

50 yd. Freestyle	Rowdy Gaines, Auburn
100 yd. Freestyle	Andy Coan, Tennessee
200 yd. Freestyle	Andy Coan, Tennessee
500 yd. Freestyle	Brian Goodell, UCLA
1,650 yd. Freestyle	Brian Goodell, UCLA
100 yd. Backstroke	Carlos Berrocal, Alabama
200 yd. Backstroke	Peter Rocca, Calif.–Berkeley
100 yd. Breaststroke	Graham Smith, Calif.–Berkeley
200 yd. Breaststroke	Graham Smith, Calif.–Berkeley
100 yd. Butterfly	Par Arvidsson, Calif.–Berkeley
200 yd. Butterfly	Par Arvidsson, Calif.–Berkeley

200 yd. Indiv. Medley	Graham Smith, Calif.–Berkeley
400 yd. Indiv. Medley	Brian Goodell, UCLA
400 yd. Freestyle Relay	Tennessee
800 yd. Freestyle Relay	Florida
400 yd. Medley Relay	Calif.–Berkeley
One Meter Dive	Greg Louganis, Miami (Fla.)
Three Meter Dive	Matt Chelich, Michigan
Team	California–Berkeley
DIVISION II Team	Northridge (Calif.) State
DIVISION III Team	Johns Hopkins

1979 AIAW CHAMPIONS (Large College)

50 yd. Freestyle	Sue Hinderaker, USC
100 yd. Freestyle	Gail Amundrud, Arizona State
200 yd. Freestyle	Gail Amundrud, Arizona State
500 yd. Freestyle	Jo Clark, Stanford
1,650 yd. Freestyle	Jo Clark, Stanford
50 yd. Backstroke	Linda Jezek, Stanford
100 yd. Backstroke	Linda Jezek, Stanford
200 yd. Backstroke	Linda Jezek, Stanford
50 yd. Breaststroke	Allison Grant, Arizona State
100 yd. Breaststroke	Renee Laravie, Florida
200 yd. Breaststroke	Debbie Rudd, USC
50 yd. Butterfly	Joan Pennington, Texas–Austin
100 yd. Butterfly	Joan Pennington, Texas–Austin

200 yd. Butterfly	Diane Johannigman, Houston
100 yd. Indiv. Medley	Joan Pennington, Texas–Austin
200 yd. Indiv. Medley	Joan Pennington, Texas–Austin
400 yd. Indiv. Medley	Diane Girard, Texas–Austin
200 yd. Freestyle Relay	Arizona State
400 yd. Freestyle Relay	Arizona Sate
800 yd. Freestyle Relay	Florida
200 yd. Medley Relay	Stanford
400 yd. Medley Relay	Stanford
One Meter Dive	Janet Thorburn, SMU
Three Meter Dive	Janet Thorburn, SMU
Team	Florida

1979 AAU SHORT COURSE SWIMMING CHAMPIONS

MEN

100 yd. Freestyle	David McCagg, Florida Aquatics
200 yd. Freestyle	David Larson, Florida Aquatics
500 yd. Freestyle	Brian Goodell, Mission Viejo
1,650 yd. Freestyle	Brian Goodell, Mission Viejo
100 yd. Backstroke	Robert Jackson, West Valley A.T.
200 yd. Backstroke	Jesse Vassallo, Mission Viejo
100 yd. Breaststroke	Steve Lundquist, Tallman Pools S.T.
200 yd. Breaststroke	Steve Lundquist, Tallman Pools S.T.
100 yd. Butterfly	Robert Placak, UCLA
200 yd. Butterfly	Glynn Perry, Florida Aquatics
200 yd. Indiv. Medley	Jesse Vassallo, Mission Viejo
400 yd. Indiv. Medley	Jesse Vassallo, Mission Viejo
400 yd. Freestyle Relay	Florida Aquatics
800 yd. Freestyle Relay	Florida Aquatics
400 yd. Medley Relay	Longhorn Aquatics

WOMEN

100 yd. Freestyle	Cynthia Woodhead, Riverside A.A.
200 yd. Freestyle	Cynthia Woodhead, Riverside A.A.
500 yd. Freestyle	Tracy Caulkins, Nashville A.C.
1,650 yd. Freestyle	Kim Linehan, Sarasota Sharks
100 yd. Backstroke	Linda Jezek, Mission Viejo
200 yd. Backstroke	Linda Jezek, Mission Viejo
100 yd. Breaststroke	Tracy Caulkins, Nashville A.C.
200 yd. Breaststroke	Patty Spees, Pleasant Hill S.C.
100 yd. Butterfly	Jill Sterkel, unattached
200 yd. Butterfly	Mary Meagher, Lakeside S.C.
200 yd. Indiv. Medley	Tracy Caulkins, Nashville A.C.
400 yd. Indiv. Medley	Tracy Caulkins, Nashville A.C.
400 yd. Freestyle Relay	Nashville Aquatic Club
800 yd. Freestyle Relay	Mission Viejo
400 yd. Medley Relay	Nashville Aquatic Club

1979 AAU LONG COURSE SWIMMING CHAMPIONS

MEN

100 m. Freestyle	Rowdy Gaines, Florida Aquatics
200 m. Freestyle	Rowdy Gaines, Florida Aquatics
400 m. Freestyle	Brian Goodell, Mission Viejo
1,500 m. Freestyle	Brian Goodell, Mission Viejo
100 m. Backstroke	Bob Jackson, West Valley Aquatics
200 m. Backstroke	Steve Barnicoat, Mission Viejo
100 m. Breaststroke	Bill Barrett, Cinci Pepsi Marlins
200 m. Breaststroke	John Simons, DeAnza S.C.
100 m. Butterfly	Grant Ostlund, Florida Aquatics
200 m. Butterfly	Steve Gregg, Conquistador Aquatics
200 m. Indiv. Medley	Jesse Vassallo, Mission Viejo
400 m. Indiv. Medley	Jesse Vassallo, Mission Viejo
400 m. Freestyle Relay	Florida Aquatics
800 m. Freestyle Relay	Florida Aquatics
400 m. Medley Relay	Longhorn Aquatics

WOMEN

100 m. Freestyle	Cynthia Woodhead, Riverside A.A.
200 m. Freestyle	Cynthia Woodhead, Riverside A.A.
400 m. Freestyle	Cynthia Woodhead, Riverside A.A.
800 m. Freestyle	Kim Linehan, Longhorn Aquatics
1,500 m. Freestyle	Kim Linehan, Longhorn Aquatics
100 m. Backstroke	Linda Jezek, Mission Viejo
200 m. Backstroke	Linda Jezek, Mission Viejo
100 m. Breaststroke	Torry Blazey, Florida Aquatics
200 m. Breaststroke	Tracy Caulkins, Nashville A.C.
100 m. Butterfly	Mary Meagher, Lakeside S.C.
200 m. Butterfly	Mary Meagher, Lakeside S.C.
200 m. Indiv. Medley	Tracy Caulkins, Nashville A.C.
400 m. Indiv. Medley	Tracy Caulkins, Nashville A.C.
400 m. Freestyle Relay	Pleasant Hill
800 m. Freestyle Relay	Mission Viejo
400 m. Medley Relay	Longhorn Aquatics

1979 AAU INDOOR DIVING CHAMPIONS

MEN

One Meter	Greg Louganis, Mission Viejo
Three Meter	Greg Louganis, Mission Viejo
Platform	Kent Vossler, Ohio State
Team	Kimball Divers (Ann Arbor, Mich.)

WOMEN

One Meter	Cynthia Potter, Summers Divers
Three Meter	Carrie Finneran, Ohio State
Platform	Barb Weinstein, Kimball Divers
Team	SMU Summers Divers (Dallas, Tex.)

1979 AAU OUTDOOR DIVING CHAMPIONS

MEN

One Meter	Greg Louganis, Mission Viejo
Three Meter	Greg Louganis, Mission Viejo
Platform	Greg Louganis, Mission Viejo
Team	Kimball Divers

WOMEN

One Meter	Kelly McCormick, Mission Viejo
Three Meter	Michele Hain, Summers Divers
Platform	Kit Salness, Mission Viejo
Team	Summers Divers

1979 AAU INDOOR AND OUTDOOR SYNCHRONIZED SWIMMING CHAMPIONS

SOLO — Linda Shelley (Santa Clara Aquamaids)   **Duet** — Michelle Barone, Linda Shelley (Santa Clara Aquamaids)
TEAM — Santa Clara Aquamaids (Tami Allen, Michelle Barone, Suzanne Cameron, Kathy Kish, Becky Price, Linda Shelley, Holly Spencer)

1979 PAN AMERICAN GAMES CHAMPIONS

MEN

100m. Freestyle — David McCagg, Ft. Myers, Fla.
200m. Freestyle — Rowdy Gaines, Winter Haven, Fla.
400m. Freestyle — Brian Goodell, Mission Viejo, Calif.
1500m. Freestyle — Brian Goodell, Mission Viejo, Calif.
100m. Backstroke — Bob Jackson, San Jose, Calif.
200m. Backstroke — Peter Rocca, Orinda, Calif.
100m. Breaststroke — Steve Lundquist, Jonesboro, Ga.
200m. Breaststroke — Steve Lundquist, Jonesboro, Ga.
100m. Butterfly — Bob Placak, San Rafael, Calif.
200m. Butterfly — Craig Beardsley, Harrington Park, N. J.
200m. Indiv. Medley — Jesse Vassallo, Mission Viejo, Calif.
400m. Indiv. Medley — Jesse Vassallo, Mission Viejo, Calif.
400m. Freestyle Relay — United States
800m. Freestyle Relay — United States
400m. Medley Relay — United States
Springboard Diving — Greg Louganis, Mission Viejo, Calif.
Platform Diving — Greg Louganis, Mission Viejo, Calif.

WOMEN

100m. Freestyle — Cynthia Woodhead, Riverside, Calif.
200m. Freestyle — Cynthia Woodhead, Riverside, Calif.
400m. Freestyle — Cynthia Woodhead, Riverside, Calif.
800m. Freestyle — Kim Linehan, Sarasota, Fla.
100m. Backstroke — Linda Jezek, Los Altos, Calif.
200m. Backstroke — Linda Jezek, Los Altos, Calif.
100m. Breaststroke — Tami Paumier, Columbia, Md.
200m. Breaststroke — Anne Gagnon, Canada
100m. Butterfly — Jill Sterkel, Hacienda Hts., Calif.
200m. Butterfly — Mary Meagher, Louisville, Ky.
200m. Indiv. Medley — Tracy Caulkins, Nashville, Tenn.
400m. Indiv. Medley — Tracy Caulkins, Nashville, Tenn.
400m. Freestyle Relay — United States
400m. Medley Relay — United States
Springboard Diving — Denise Christensen, Tucson, Ariz.
Platform Diving — Barbara Weinstein, Cincinnati, Ohio
Synchronized Swimming — Solo: Helen Vanderberg, Canada;
Duet: Vanderberg and Kelly Kryszka; Team: United States

WORLD SWIMMING RECORDS (September 4, 1979)

MEN'S EVENTS

Event	Time	Name	Country	Date	
100 meter freestyle	0:49.44	Jonty Skinner	South Africa	August	1976
200 meter freestyle	1:49.83	Sergey Kopliakov	USSR	April	1979
400 meter freestyle	3:51.41	Vladimir Salnikov	USSR	April	1979
800 meter freestyle	7:56.49	Vladimir Salnikov	USSR	March	1979
1500 meter freestyle	15:02.40	Brian Goodell	United States	July	1976
400 meter freestyle relay	3:19.74	Babashoff, Gaines, McCagg, Montgomery	United States	August	1978
800 meter freestyle relay	7:20.82	Furniss, Forrester, Gaines, Hackett	United States	August	1978
100 meter breaststroke	1:02.86	Gerald Mörken	West Germany	August	1977
200 meter breaststroke	2:15.11	David Wilkie	United Kingdom	July	1976
100 meter butterfly	0:54.18	Joe Bottom	United States	August	1977
200 meter butterfly	1:59.23	Mike Bruner	United States	July	1976
100 meter backstroke	0:55.49	John Naber	United States	July	1976
200 meter backstroke	1:59.19	John Naber	United States	July	1976
200 meter individual medley	2:03.29	Jesse Vassallo	United States	July	1979
400 meter individual medley	4:20.05	Jesse Vassallo	United States	August	1978
400 meter medley relay	3:42.22	Naber, Hencken, Vogel, Montgomery	United States	July	1976

WOMEN'S EVENTS

Event	Time	Name	Country	Date	
100 meter freestyle	55.41	Barbara Krause	East Germany	July	1978
200 meter freestyle	1:58.23	Cynthia Woodhead	United States	Sept.	1979
400 meter freestyle	4:06.28	Tracey Wickham	Australia	August	1978
800 meter freestyle	8:24.62	Tracey Wickham	Australia	August	1978
1500 meter freestyle	16:04.49	Kim Linehan	United States	August	1979
400 meter freestyle relay	3:43.43	Caulkns, Elkins, Sterkle, Woodhead	United States	August	1978
100 meter breaststroke	1:10.31	Julia Bogdanova	USSR	August	1978
200 meter breaststroke	2:28.36	Lina Kachushite	USSR	April	1979
100 meter butterfly	59.46	Andrea Pollack	East Germany	July	1978
200 meter butterfly	2:07.01	Mary T. Meagher	United States	August	1979
100 meter backstroke	1:01.51	Ulrike Richter	East Germany	June	1976
200 meter backstroke	2:11.93	Linda Jezek	United States	August	1978
200 meter individual medley	2:14.07	Tracy Caulkins	United States	August	1978
400 meter individual medley	4:40.83	Tracy Caulkins	United States	August	1978
400 meter medley relay	4:07.95	Richter, Anke, Pollack, Ender	East Germany	July	1976

WORLD FRESHWATER FISHING RECORDS

Source: International Game Fish Association (All tackle records, as of June 1, 1979)

Species	Weight	Where Caught	Date	Angler
Bass, Largemouth	22 lbs. 4 oz.	Montgomery Lake, Ga.	June 2, 1932	George W. Perry
Bass, Redeye	8 lbs. 3 oz.	Flint River, Ga.	Oct. 23, 1977	David A. Hubbard
Bass, Rock	3 lbs.	York River, Ontario	Aug. 1, 1974	Peter Gulgin
Bass, Smallmouth	11 lbs. 15 oz.	Dale Hollow Lake, Ky.	July 9, 1955	David L. Hayes
Bass, Spotted	8 lbs. 15 oz.	Smith Lake, Ala.	Mar. 18, 1978	Philip C. Terry, Jr.
Bass, White	5 lbs. 6 oz.	Grenada Lake, Miss.	Apr. 21, 1979	William C. Mulvihill
Bass, Whiterock	20 lbs.	Savannah R., Ga.	May 5, 1977	Don Raley
Bass, Yellow	2 lbs. 4 oz.	Lake Monroe, Ind.	Mar. 27, 1977	Donald L. Stalker
Bluegill	4 lbs. 12 oz.	Ketona Lake, Ala.	Apr. 9, 1950	T. S. Hudson
Bowfin	19 lbs. 12 oz.	Lake Marion, S.C.	Nov. 5, 1972	M. R. Webster
Buffalo, Bigmouth	56 lbs.	Lock Loma L., Mo.	Aug. 19, 1976	W. J. Long
Buffalo, Smallmouth	32 lbs. 8 oz.	Sardis Res., Miss.	Oct. 22, 1977	Eddie O'Daniel
Bullhead, Black	8 lbs.	Lake Waccabuc, N.Y.	Aug. 1, 1951	Kani Evans
Carp	55 lbs. 5 oz.	Clearwater Lake, Minn.	July 10, 1952	Frank J. Ledwein
Catfish, Blue	97 lbs.	Missouri River, S.D.	Sept. 16, 1959	Edward B. Elliott
Catfish, Channel	58 lbs.	Santee-Cooper Res., S.C.	July 7, 1964	W. B. Whaley
Catfish, Flathead	79 lbs. 8 oz.	White Riv., Ind.	Aug. 13, 1966	Glenn T. Simpson
Catfish, White	10 lbs. 5 oz.	Raritan R., N.J.	June 23, 1976	Lewis W. Lomerson
Char, Arctic	29 lbs. 11 oz.	Arctic River, N.W.T.	Aug. 21, 1968	Jeanne P. Branson
Crappie, Black	5 lbs.	Santee-Cooper Res., S.C.	Mar. 15, 1957	Paul E. Foust
Crappie, White	5 lbs. 3 oz.	Enid Dam, Miss.	July 31, 1957	Fred L. Bright
Dolly Varden	32 lbs.	L. Pend Oreille, Idaho	Oct. 27, 1949	N. L. Higgins
Drum, Freshwater	54 lbs. 8 oz.	Nickajack Lake, Tenn.	Apr. 20, 1972	Benny E. Hull
Gar, Alligator	279 lbs.	Rio Grande, Texas	Dec. 2, 1951	Bill Valverde
Gar, Longnose	50 lbs. 5 oz.	Trinity River, Texas	July 30, 1954	Townsend Miller
Grayling, American	5 lbs. 15 oz.	Katseyedie R., N.W.T.	Aug. 16, 1967	Jeanne P. Branson
Kokanee	6 lbs. 9¾ oz.	Priest L., Idaho	June 9, 1975	Jerry Verge
Muskellunge	69 lbs. 15 oz.	St. Lawrence R., N.Y.	Sept. 22, 1957	Arthur Lawton
Perch, White	4 lbs. 12 oz.	Messalonskee Lake, Me.	June 4, 1949	Mrs. Earl Small
Perch, Yellow	4 lbs. 3½ oz.	Bordentown, N.J.	May 1865	Dr. C. C. Abbot
Pickerel, Chain	9 lbs. 6 oz.	Homerville, Ga.	Feb. 17, 1961	Baxley McQuaig, Jr.
Pike, Northern	46 lbs. 2 oz.	Sacandaga Res., N.Y.	Sept. 15, 1940	Peter Dubuc
Redhorse, Silver	4 lbs. 2 oz.	Gasconade Riv., Mo.	Oct. 5, 1974	C. Larry McKinney
Salmon, Atlantic	79 lbs. 2 oz.	Tana River, Norway	1928	Henrik Henriksen
Salmon, Chinook	93 lbs.	Kelp Bay, Alaska	June 24, 1977	Howard C. Rider
Salmon, Chum	27 lbs. 3 oz.	Raymond Cove, Alaska	June 11, 1977	Robert A. Jahnke
Salmon, Coho or Silver	31 lbs.	Cowichan Bay, B.C.	Oct. 11, 1947	Mrs. Lee Hallberg
Salmon, Landlocked	22 lbs. 8 oz.	Sebago Lake, Maine	Aug. 1, 1907	Edward Blakely
Sauger	8 lbs. 12 oz.	Lake Sakakawea, N.D.	Oct. 6, 1971	Mike Fischer
Shad, American	9 lbs. 2 oz.	Enfield, Conn.	Apr. 28, 1973	Edward P. Nelson
Sturgeon, White	360 lbs.	Snake River, Idaho	Apr. 24, 1956	Willard Cravens
Sunfish, Green	2 lbs. 2 oz.	Stockton Lake, Mo.	June 18, 1971	Paul M. Dilley
Sunfish, Redbreast	1 lb. 8½ oz.	Suwanee R., Fla.	Apr. 30, 1977	Tommy D. Cason, Jr.
Sunfish, Redear	4 lbs. 8 oz.	Chase City, Va.	June 19, 1970	Maurice E. Ball
Trout, Brook	14 lbs. 8 oz.	Nipigon River, Ontario	July 1916	Dr. W. J. Cook
Trout, Brown	35 lbs. 15 oz.	Nahuel Huapi, Arg.	Dec. 16, 1952	Eugenio Cavaglia
Trout, Cutthroat	41 lbs.	Pyramid Lake, Nev.	Dec. 1925	John Skimmerhorn
Trout, Golden	11 lbs.	Cook's Lake, Wyo.	Aug. 5, 1948	Chas. S. Reed
Trout, Lake	65 lbs.	Great Bear Lake, N.W.T.	Aug. 8, 1970	Larry Daunis
Trout, Rainbow, Stlhd. or Kamloops	42 lbs. 2 oz.	Bell Island, Alaska	June 22, 1970	David R. White
Trout, Sunapee	11 lbs. 8 oz.	Lake Sunapee, N.H.	Aug. 1, 1954	Ernest Theoharis
Trout, Tiger	17 lbs.	L. Michigan, Wis.	Aug. 2, 1977	Edward Rudnicki
Walleye	25 lbs.	Old Hickory L., Tenn.	Aug. 1, 1960	Mabry Harper
Warmouth	2 lbs.	Sylvania, Ga.	May 4, 1974	Carlton Robbins
Whitefish, Lake	13 lbs.	Great Bear L., N.W.T.	July 14, 1974	Robert L. Stintsman
Whitefish, Mountain	5 lbs.	Athabasca R., Alberta	June 3, 1963	Orville Welch

WORLD SALTWATER FISHING RECORDS

Source: International Game Fish Association (All tackle records, as of June 1, 1979)

Species	Weight	Where Caught	Date	Angler
Albacore	74 lbs. 13 oz.	Arguineguin, Canary Islands	10/28/73	Olof Idegren
Amberjack (Greater)	149 lbs.	Bermuda	6/21/64	Peter Simons
Barracuda (Great)	83 lbs.	Lagos, Nigeria	1/13/52	K. J. W. Hackett
Bass (Black Sea)	8 lbs. 12 oz.	Oregon Inlet, N.C.	4/21/79	Joe W. Mizelle, Jr.
Bass (Giant Sea)	563 lbs. 8 oz.	Anacapa Island, Calif.	8/20/68	James D. McAdam, Jr.
Bass (Striped)	72 lbs.	Cuttyhunk, Mass.	10/10/69	Edward J. Kirker
Bluefish	31 lbs. 12 oz.	Hatteras Inlet, N.C.	1/30/72	James M. Hussey
Bonefish	19 lbs.	Zululand, South Africa	5/26/62	Brian W. Batchelor
Bonito (Atlantic)	10 lbs. 4 oz.	Block Island, R.I.	10/21/78	Daniel Vaccaro
Bonito (Pacific)	23 lbs. 8 oz.	Victoria, Seychelles	2/19/75	Mrs. Anne Cochain
Cobia	110 lbs. 5 oz.	Mombasa, Kenya	9/8/64	Eric Tinworth
Cod	98 lbs. 12 oz.	Isles of Shoals, N.H.	6/8/69	Alphonse J. Bielevich
Dolphin	87 lbs.	Papagayo Gulf, Costa Rica	9/25/76	Manuel Salazar
Drum (Black)	113 lbs. 1 oz.	Lewes, Del.	9/15/75	Gerald M. Townsend
Drum (Red)	90 lbs.	Rodanthe, N.C.	11/7/73	Elvin Hooper
Flounder (Summer)	22 lbs. 7 oz.	Montauk, N.Y.	9/15/75	Charles Nappi
Jack (Crevalle)	51 lbs.	Lake Worth, Fla.	6/20/78	Stephen V. Schwenk
Jewfish	680 lbs.	Fernandina Beach, Fla.	5/20/61	Lynn Joyner
Kawakawa	21 lbs.	Kilauea, Kauai, Hawaii	8/21/75	E. John O'Dell
Mackerel (King)	90 lbs.	Key West, Fla.	2/16/76	Norton I. Thomton
Marlin (Atlantic Blue)	1282 lbs.	St. Thomas, Virgin Is.	8/6/77	Larry Martin
Marlin (Black)	1560 lbs.	Cabo Blanco, Peru	8/4/53	Alfred C. Glassell, Jr.
Marlin (Pacific Blue)	1153 lbs.	Ritidian Point, Guam	8/21/69	Greg D. Perez
Marlin (Striped)	417 lbs.	Cavalli Is., New Zealand	1/14/77	Phillip Bryers
Marlin (White)	174 lbs. 3 oz.	Vitoria, Brazil	11/1/75	Otavio Cunha Reboucas
Permit	51 lbs. 8 oz.	Lake Worth, Fla.	4/28/78	William M. Kenney

SALTWATER FISHING RECORDS (Continued)

Species	Weight	Where Caught	Date	Angler
Pollock	46 lbs. 7 oz.	Brielle, N.J.	5/26/75	John Tomes Holton
Pompano (African)	41 lbs. 8 oz.	Fort Lauderdale, Fla.	2/15/78	Wayne Sommers
Roosterfish	114 lbs.	LaPaz, Mexico	6/1/60	Abe Sackheim
Runner (Rainbow)	33 lbs. 10 oz.	Clarion Island, Mexico	3/14/76	Ralph A. Mikkelsen
Sailfish (Atlantic)	128 lbs. 1 oz.	Luanda, Angola	3/27/74	Harm Steyn
Sailfish (Pacific)	221 lbs.	Santa Cruz Island, Galapagos Is.	2/12/47	C. W. Stewart
Seabass (White)	83 lbs. 12 oz.	San Felipe, Mexico	3/31/53	L. C. Baumgardner
Seatrout (Spotted)	16 lbs.	Mason's Beach, Va.	5/28/77	William Katko
Shark (Blue)	437 lbs.	Catherine Bay, Australia	10/2/76	Peter Hyde
Shark (Hammerhead)	703 lbs.	Jacksonville Beach, Fla.	7/5/75	H. B. "Blackie" Reasor
Shark (Porbeagle)	465 lbs.	Padstow, Cornwall, England	7/23/76	Jorge Potier
Shark (Shortfin Mako)	1061 lbs.	Mayor Island, New Zealand	2/17/70	James B. Penwarden
Shark (Thresher)	739 lbs.	Tutukaka, New Zealand	2/17/75	Brian Galvin
Shark (Tiger)	1780 lbs.	Cherry Grove, S.C.	6/14/64	Walter Maxwell
Shark (White)	2664 lbs.	Ceduna, Australia	4/21/59	Alfred Dean
Skipjack (Black)	14 lbs. 8 oz.	Cabo San Lucas, Mexico	5/24/77	Lorraine Carlton
Snook	53 lbs. 10 oz.	Rio de Parasmina, Costa Rica	10/18/78	Gilbert Ponzi
Spearfish	79 lbs. 5 oz.	Madeira Islands	5/25/79	Ronald Eckert
Swordfish	1182 lbs.	Iquique, Chile	5/7/53	L. Marron
Tanguigue	85 lbs. 6 oz.	Rottnest I., West Australia	5/5/78	Barry Wrightson
Tarpon	283 lbs.	Lake Maracaibo, Venezuela	3/19/56	M. Salazar
Tautog	21 lbs. 6 oz.	Cape May, New Jersey	6/12/54	R. N. Sheafer
Trevally (Giant)	116 lbs.	Pago Pago, Amer. Samoa	2/20/78	William G. Foster
Tuna (Atlantic Bigeye)	375 lbs. 8 oz.	Ocean City, Md.	8/26/77	Cecil Browne
Tuna (Blackfin)	42 lbs.	Bermuda	6/2/78	Alan J. Card
Tuna (Bluefin)	1235 lbs.	North Lake, P.E.I., Canada	10/17/78	Michael MacDonald
Tuna (Dog-tooth)	189 lbs. 2 oz.	Dar es Salaam, Tanzania	11/12/78	L. J. Samaros
Tuna (Longtail)	65 lbs.	Port Stephens, N.S.W., Australia	4/20/78	Michael James
Tuna (Pacific Bigeye)	435 lbs.	Cabo Blanco, Peru	4/17/57	Dr. Russel V. A. Lee
Tuna (Skipjack)	40 lbs.	Baie du Tambeau, Mauritius	4/19/71	Joseph R. P. Caboche, Jr.
Tuna (Southern Bluefin)	220 lbs. 7 oz.	Tasman I., Tasmania, Australia	6/10/78	Stanley Gibbon
Tuna (Yellowfin)	388 lbs. 12 oz.	San Benedicto I., Mexico	4/1/77	Curt Wiesenhutter
Tunny (Little)	27 lbs.	Key Largo, Fla.	4/20/76	William E. Allison
Wahoo	149 lbs.	Cat Cay, Bahamas	6/15/62	John Pirovano
Weakfish	19 lbs. 8 oz.	Trinidad, West Indies	4/13/62	Dennis B. Hall
Yellowtail (California)	50 lbs.	Alijos Rocks, Mexico	6/5/78	Jerry Reid
Yellowtail (Southern)	111 lbs.	Bay of Islands, New Zealand	6/11/61	A. F. Plim

WRESTLING

1979 NAT'L AAU FREESTYLE CHAMPIONS

105.5 lbs.—Bob Weaver, New York A.C.
114.5 lbs.—Tom Dursee, New York A.C.
125.5 lbs.—Joe Corso, Hawkeye W.C.
136.5 lbs.—Andre Metzger, Oklahoma
149.5 lbs.—Chuck Yagla, Hawkeye W.C.
163 lbs.—Leroy Kemp, Wisconsin W.C.
180.5 lbs.—Dan Lewis, Fullerton W.C.
198 lbs.—Laurent Soucie, Wisconsin W.C.
220 lbs.—Russ Hellickson, Wisconsin W.C.
Heavyweight—Greg Wojciechowski, Ohio W.C.
Outstanding Wrestler—Chuck Yagla
Team—New York Athletic Club

1979 NAT'L AAU GRECO-ROMAN CHAMPIONS

105.5 lbs.—Greg Williams, S.F. Peninsula Grapplers
114.5 lbs.—Raymond Pavia, U.S. Air Force
125.5 lbs.—Bruce Thompson, Rosemount, Minn.
136.5 lbs.—Hachiro Oishi, New York A.C.
149.5 lbs.—Abdul Raheem-Ali, Minnesota W.C.
163 lbs.—John Matthews, Michigan W.C.
180.5 lbs.—Daniel Chandler, Minneapolis, Minn.
198 lbs.—Frank Andersson, Sweden
220 lbs.—Brad Rheingans, Minnesota W.C.
Heavyweight—Greg Wojciechowski, Toledo, Ohio
Outstanding Wrestler—John Matthews
Team—Minnesota Wrestling Club

1979 NCAA CHAMPIONS

DIVISION I

118 lbs.—Gene Mills, Syracuse
126 lbs.—Randy Lewis, Iowa
134 lbs.—Darryl Burley, Lehigh
142 lbs.—Dan Hicks, Oregon State
150 lbs.—Bruce Kinseth, Iowa
158 lbs.—Kelly Ward, Iowa State
167 lbs.—Mark Churella, Michigan

177 lbs.—Mark Lieberman, Lehigh
190 lbs.—Eric Wais, Oklahoma State
Heavyweight—Fred Bohna, U.C.L.A.
Team—Iowa

Division II Team—Bakersfield State

Division III Team—Trenton State

1979 WORLD CUP CHAMPIONS

105.5 lbs.—Roman Dmitriyev, U.S.S.R.
114.5 lbs.—Anatoliy Beloglazov, U.S.S.R.
125.5 lbs.—Bozaliy Ibragimov, U.S.S.R.
136.5 lbs.—Tim Cysewski, U.S.A.
149.5 lbs.—Chuck Yagla, U.S.A.
163 lbs.—Leroy Kemp, U.S.A.

180.5 lbs.—Hasan Zangiyev, U.S.S.R.
198 lbs.—Hasan Ortseyev, U.S.S.R.
220 lbs.—Ivan Yarygin, U.S.S.R.
Heavyweight—Jimmy Jackson, U.S.A.
Teams—1. U.S.S.R., 2. U.S.A., 3. Japan, 4. Cuba,
5. Pan-Africa

OTHER SPORTS

ARCHERY
1978 World Field Champions
FREESTYLE
Men—Darrell Pace, Cincinnati, Ohio
Women—Anna Marie Lehmann,
W. Germany
BAREBOW
Men—Anders Rosenberg, Sweden
Women—Suizuko Kobuchi, Japan
1978 U.S. Target Champions
Men—Darrell Pace, Cincinnati, Ohio
Women—Luann Ryon, Riverside, Calif.
1979 Nat'l Field Archery Champions
FREESTYLE
Men's Open—John Foze, Florida
Women's Open—Marita Gilmer, Minnesota
Men's Amateur—Donald Allen, Iowa
BAREBOW
Men's Open—Verlyn Owens, Nevada
Women's Open—Peggy Grubb, California
Men's Amateur—Frank Foxwell, Conn.
BOWHUNTER
Men's Open—James Revis, Oklahoma
Women's Open—Ida Revis, Oklahoma
1979 U.S. Indoor Target Champions
Men—Rodney Baston, Baton Rouge, La.
Women—Janet Dohrman, E. Stroudsburg,
Pa.
1978 Distance Record
1113 yds., 1 ft., 1 in.—Arlyne Rhode,
Mahomet, Ill.

BADMINTON (1979)
U.S. National Champions
Men's Singles—Chris Kinard, Pasadena,
Calif.
Women's Singles—Pam Brady, Flint, Mich.
Men's Doubles—Jim Poole, Westminster,
Calif.-Mike Walker, Manhattan Beach,
Calif.
Women's Doubles—Judianne Kelly, Costa
Mesa, Calif.-Pam Brady
Mixed Doubles—Mike Walker-Judianne
Kelly
AIAW Champions
Singles—Carrie Morrison, Ariz. St.
Doubles—Tracy McDonald-Carrie Theis,
U.C.L.A.
Team—Arizona State
World Champions
Men's Singles—Liem Swie King, Indonesia
Women's Singles—Lene Koeppen, Den.
Men's Doubles—Hadinata Christian-Abe
Chandra, Indonesia
Women's Doubles—Emiko Ueno-Yoshiko
Yonekura, Japan

BIATHLON (1979)
20km—Klaus Seibert, E. Germany
10km—Frank Ullrich, E. Germany
U.S. Nat'l Champion
(20 km)—Ken Alligood, Anchorage, Alaska
(10 km)—Lyle Nelson, Olympic Valley,
Calif.

BILLIARDS
1979 World Open Pocket—Mike Sigal,
Towson, Md.
1978 World 3-Cushion—Raymond Ceule-
mans, Belgium
1978 U.S. Women's Open Pocket—Jean
Balukas, Brooklyn, N.Y.
1978 National 8-Ball— Men: Mike
Carrella; Women: Catherine Stephens

BOBSLEDDING (1979)
World 4-Man—W. Germany
World 2-Man—Switzerland

CANOEING (1979)
U.S. Champions — KAYAK
Singles (500m.)—Terry White, Amherst,
Mass.

Women—Linda Dragan, Washington, D.C.
Singles (100m.)—Terry White
Women's Singles (5000m.)—Ann Turner,
St. Charles, Ill.
Singles (10,000m.)—Brent Turner,
St. Charles, Ill.
Tandem (500m.)—Steve Kelly, Inwood
(N.Y.) C.C.-Brent Turner
Women's Tandem—Leslie Klein, Amherst,
Mass.-Ann Turner
Tandem (1000m.)—S. Kelley-B. Turner
Women's Tandem (5000m.)—Sue Turner,
St. Charles, Ill.-Jean Campbell, Webster
Groves, Mo.
13 miles—Brent Turner
Tandem—Turner-Kelly
Women—A. Turner
Women's Tandem—A. Turner-L. Klein
U.S. Champions — CANOE
Singles (500m.)—Roland Muhlen,
Cincinnati, Ohio
Singles (1000m.)—R. Muhlen
Singles (10,000m.)—Kurt Doberstein,
Lombard, Ill.
Tandem (500m.)—Jay Kearney, Lexington,
Ky.-Jay Batlick, Seattle, Wash.
Tandem (1000m.)—Blaise Staneck, New
York-Kurt Doberstein
Tandem (10,000m.)—Bruce and Berry
Merritt, Washington, D.C.
U.S. Slalom and Wildwater Champions
Canoe Slalom—David Hearn, Garrett Park,
Md.
Canoe Wildwater—Chuck Lyda, Olympic
Valley, Calif.
Kayak Slalom—Daniel Isbister, Bel Air,
Md.
Women—Linda Harrison, Newark, Del.
Kayak Wildwater—Dan Schnurrenberger,
Silver Spring, Md.
Women—Cathy Hearn, Garrett Park, Md.

CROSS-COUNTRY (1978)
National AAU Champions
Men—Greg Meyer, Boston, Mass.
Women—Julie Brown, Northridge, Calif.
Men's Team—Mason Dixon A.C.
Women's Team—Liberty A.C.
National Collegiate Champions
NCAA Div. I—Alberto Salazar, Oregon
Team—Texas-El Paso
NCAA Div. II—James Schankel, Calif.
Poly-San Luis Obispo
Team—Calif. Poly-San Luis Obispo
NCAA Div. III—Dan Henderson, Wheaton
Team—North Central (Ill.)
NAIA—Kelly Jensen, So. Oregon State
Team—Pembroke State
AIAW (Women's)—Mary Decker, Colorado
Team—Iowa State
1979 World Champions
Men—John Treacy, Ireland
Women—Grete Waitz, Norway
Highest U.S. Finishers
Men—Craig Virgin, Lebanon, Ill. (13th)
Women—Jan Merrill, New London, Conn.
(7th)

CURLING
1979 World Champion—Norway
1978 U.S. Champion—Superior, Wis.
Women—Wisconsin

CYCLING (1979)
World Champions (Professional)
Sprint—Koichi Nakano, Japan
Road—Jan Raas, Neth.
Tour de France (1979)
Bernard Hinault, France
U.S. Champions — ROAD RACING
Senior—Steve Wood, Albuquerque, N.M.
Women—Connie Carpenter, Berkeley,
Calif.
U.S. Champions — TRACK RACING
Sprint—Leigh Barczewski, W. Allis, Wis.
Women—Sue Novara, Flint, Mich.

Pursuit—Dave Grylls, Grosse Pte., Mich.
Women—Connie Carpenter, Berkeley,
Calif.
Point Race—Gus Pipenhagen,
Northhbrook, Ill.
Women—Mary Jane Reoch, Philadelphia,
Pa.
World Champions (Amateur) (1978)
Sprint—Anton Tkac, Czech.
Women—Galina Tsareva, USSR
Pursuit—Detlef Mackha, E. Ger.
Women—Keetie van Oosten-Hage, Neth.
Team—E. Ger.
Road—Gilbert Glaus, Switz.
Women—Beate Habetz, W. Ger.
Kilometer—Lothar Thoms, E. Ger.
Point Race—Noel Dejonckheere, Belg.

DOGS
Best-in-Show Winners
1979 Westminster (N.Y.)—Ch. Oak Tree's
Irishtocrat (Irish Water Spaniel); Mrs.
Ann Snelling, Ottawa, Ontario; 3,154
entries
1979 International (Chicago)—Ch. Lou-
Gins Kiss Me Kate (standard poodles);
Terri Meyers and Jack and Paula Phelan,
Manhattan, Ill.
1978 Boardwalk (Atlantic City)—Ch.
Sporting Fields Clansman (whippet);
Dionne and Mr. and Mrs. James Butt;
3,127 entries
1979 Westchester (Tarrytown, N.Y.)—Ch.
Cozy's Mischief Maker (Lakeland terrier);
Satcheko Takada, Malibu, Calif.; 2,955
entries
1979 Bucks County (Pa.)—Ch. Laurwyn's
Banner (wire-haired pointer), Patricia
Laurans, Newtown, Conn.; 2,721 entries

FENCING (1979)
World Champions
Foil—Aleksandr Romankov, USSR
Epee—Philippe Riboud, France
Sabre—Vladimir Lazimyov, USSR
Women's Foil—Cornelia Hanisch, W. Ger.
Foil Team—USSR
Epee Team—USSR
Sabre Team—USSR
Women's Foil Team—USSR
U.S. Champions
Foil—Michael Marx, Portland, Ore.
Epee—Tim Glass, San Antonio, Tex.
Sabre—P. Westbrook, N.Y. Fencers Club
Women's Foil—Jana Angelakis, Peabody,
Mass.
Foil Team—Fencing Acad. of Michigan
Epee Team—U.S. Mod. Pentathlon Train-
ing Center
Sabre Team—N.Y. Fencers Club
Women's Foil Team—Salle Csiszar
National Collegiate Champions
Foil—Andy Bonk, Notre Dame
Epee—Carlo Sangini, Cleveland State
Sabre—Yuri Rabinovich, Wayne State
Team—Wayne State
**Nat'l Intercollegiate Fencing
Association Champions — MEN**
Foil—Rich Pantel, Princeton
Team—Princeton
Epee—Chris Hanson, Pennsylvania
Team—Pennsylvania
Sabre—Paul Friedberg, Pennsylvania
Team—Pennsylvania
Overall Team—Princeton
WOMEN
Joy Ellington, San Jose State
Team—1. San Jose State; 2. Penn State

GYMNASTICS (1979)
Nat'l AAU Champions — MEN
All Around—Peter Korman, New York A.C.
Floor Exercise—Steve Elliott, Nebraska
Pommel Horse—Dave Stoldt, Illini
Rings—Jim Hartung, Nebraska
Vault—Ron Galimore, Iowa State

OTHER SPORTS (Cont.)

Parallel Bars—Mike Nadour, A.I.A.
Horizontal Bar—Al Kwiatkowski,
unattached
Team—New York Athletic Club

Nat'l AAU Championships — WOMEN
All-Around—Jackie Cassello, M.G.
Gymnastics
Floor Exercise—Kathy Johnson, Olympia
T.C.
Vault—Jackie Cassello
Balance Beam—Kathy Johnson
Uneven Parallel Bars—Shari Mann,
M.G. Gymnastics
Team—Olympia Training Center

NCAA Champions
Division I
All Around—Kurt Thomas, Indiana State
Floor Exercise—Mike Wilson, Oklahoma
Pommel Horse—Mike Burke, Northern
Illinois
Rings—Kirk Mango, Northern Illinois
Vault—Les Moore, Oklahoma
Parallel Bars—Kurt Thomas
High Bar—Kurt Thomas
Team—Nebraska
Div. II Team—Illinois-Chicago Circle

AIAW (Women's) Nat'l Champions
Floor Exercise—Marcy Levine, Penn State
Vault—Barbie Myslak, Cal. State-
Fullerton
Balance Beam—Kolleen Casey, S.W.
Missouri State
Uneven Parallel Bars—Barbie Myslak
All Around—Kolleen Casey
Team—Cal. State-Fullerton

U.S. Federation Women's Champions
Overall—Leslie Pyfer
Floor Exercise—Heidi Anderson
Vault—Christa Canary
Balance Beam—Heidi Anderson
Uneven Parallel Bars—Marcia Frederick-
Tracee Talavera
NAIA Team—Wisconsin-Oshkosh

HANDBALL

1979 U.S. Handball Ass'n Champions
Singles—Naty Alvarado, Hisperia, Calif.
Doubles—Marty Decatur, New York-Stuffy
Singer, Los Angeles
Masters Singles (over 40)—Jim McKee,
Memphis, Tenn.
Masters Doubles—Marty Goffstein-Ron
Earl, San Jose, Calif.
Golden Masters Singles (over 50)—Jack
Briscoe, St. Louis, Mo.
Golden Masters Doubles—Alvis Grant,
Dallas, Tex.-Chuck Harris, Kansas
City, Mo.
Super Masters Doubles (over 60)—Lee
Shinn-Ralph Stapper, Salem, Ore.

HORSESHOE PITCHING

1978 World Champions
Men—Walter Williams, Chino, Calif.
Women—Opal Reno, Lucasville, Ohio

HORSE SHOWS (1978)

National Horse Show Champions
Working Hunter Champion—Ruxton, August
A. Busch, Jr. and Cismont Manor Farm
Conformation Hunter Champion—Stocking
Stuffer, Mr. & Mrs. August Busch, Jr.
Grand Hunter Champion—Ruxton

National Horse Show Equitation Champions
Saddle Seat (Good Hands)—Mary Lou
Gallagher, Tulsa, Okla.
ASPCA Trophy (Maclay)—Michael Sasso,
Wilmington, Del.
The Nations Cup—U.S. Equestrian Team

ICE SKATING (1979)

World Figure Skating Champions
Men—Vladimir Kovalev, USSR
Women—Linda Fratianne, Northridge,
Calif.

Pairs—Tai Babilonia, Mission Hills,
Calif.-Randy Gardner, Los Angeles,
Calif.
Dance—Natalia Lininchuk/Grennadi Karpo-
nosov, USSR

U.S. Figure Skating Champions
Men—Charles Tickner, Littleton, Colo.
Women—Linda Fratianne, Northridge, Cal.
Pairs—Tai Babilonia, Mission Hills, Cal.-
Randy Gardner, Los Angeles, Cal.
Dance—Stacey Smith-John Summers,
Wilmington, Del.

World Speed Skating Champions
Men—Eric Heiden, Madison, Wis.
Women—Beth Heiden, Madison, Wis.
Sprint—Eric Heiden
Women's Sprint—Beth Heiden
Junior—Eric Heiden
Women—Beth Heiden

U.S. Speed Skating Champions
Outdoor—Erik Henriksen, Champaign, Ill.
Women—Gretchen Byrne, Syracuse, N.Y.
Indoor—Bill Lanigan, Teaneck, N.J.
Women—Patti Lyman, Boulder, Colo.

**North American Speed Skating
Championships**
Outdoor—Erik Henriksen, Champaign, Ill.
Women—Pat Durnin, Winnipeg, Man.
Indoor—Gaetan Boucher, Quebec, Canada
Women—Cathy Turnbull, Saskatchewan,
Canada

JUDO (1979)

National AAU Champions—MEN
132 Lbs.—Keith Nakasone, Honolulu,
Hawaii
143 Lbs.—James Martin, Wheeling, Ill.
156 Lbs.—Steven Seck, Chatsworth, Calif.
172 Lbs.—Brett Barron, San Mateo, Calif.
189 Lbs.—Leo White, Seaside, Calif.
Under 209 Lbs.—Miguel Tudela, Los
Angeles, Calif.
Over 209 Lbs.—Dewey Mitchell,
Tuscaloosa, Ala.
Open Division—Shawn Gibbons, St.
Petersburg, Fla.

National AAU Champions—WOMEN
106 Lbs.—Mary Lewis, E. Berne, N.Y.
114 Lbs.—Robin Takemori, Alexandria,
Va.
123 Lbs.—Monica Emmerson, Daly City,
Calif.
134 Lbs.—Anne Marie Fuller, Salem, Ore.
145 Lbs.—Dolores Brodie, Los Angeles,
Calif.
Under 158 Lbs.—Christine Penick, Los
Angeles, Calif.
Over 158 Lbs.—Margaret Castro, New
York City
Open Div.—Barbara Fest, Boston, Mass.

JUNIOR COLLEGES (1978-79)

Nat'l J.C. Champions — Men's Div.
Baseball—Middle Georgia Coll.
Basketball—Three Rivers (Mo.) C.C.
Bowling—Niagara County (N.Y.) C.C.
Cross-Country—Southwestern Michigan
Coll.
Decathlon—Jeff Montpas, Mesa (Ariz.)
C.C.
Football—Iowa Central C.C.
Golf—Broward C.C., Central (Fla.)
Gymnastics—Odessa Coll. (Tex.)
Ice Hockey—S.U.N.Y. at Canton (N.Y.)
Judo—Glendale (Calif.) C.C.
Lacrosse—Suffolk County (N.Y.) C.C.
Marathon—Dave Magness, Lane (Ore.)
C.C.
Skiing (Alpine)—Champlain Coll. (Vt.)
Skiing (Nordic)—Vermont Tech. Coll.
Skiing (Combined)—Vermont Tech. Coll.
Soccer—Ulster County (N.Y.) C.C.
Swimming—Indian River C.C. (Fla.)
Tennis—Odessa Coll. (Tex.)
Track & Field (Indoor and Outdoor)—
New Mexico J.C.
Wrestling—Lakeland (Ohio) C.C.

Nat'l J.C. Champions—Women's Div.
Basketball—Northern Oklahoma Coll.
Bowling—Erie (N.Y.) C.C.
Cross Country—Dodge City (Kans.) C.C.
Field Hockey—Essex (Md.) C.C.
Golf—Palm Beach (Fla.) J.C.
Gymnastics—Odessa Coll. (Tex.)
Skiing—(Alpine & Combined)—Central
Oregon C.C.
Swimming—Indian River (Fla.) C.C.
Tennis—Odessa Coll. (Tex.)
Track & Field—Mesa (Ariz.) C.C.
Volleyball—Kellogg (Mich.) C.C.

KARATE

1979 Nat'l AAU Champions
MEN'S KATA
Int.—Dennis Zamudio, Fla. Gold Coast
Adv.—Alberto Pena, Metropolitan
Weapons—Glen Hart, New England
MEN'S KUMITE
Int.—Patrick Gentempo, New Jersey
Open—Tokay Hill, Ohio
WOMEN'S KATA
Int.—Gwen Hoffman, New Jersey
Adv.—Vicki Johnson, Central
Weapons—Katherine Loakopolos,
Metropolitan
WOMEN'S KUMITE
Int.—Rhonda Hansen, New Jersey
Adv.—Andrea Clark, Metropolitan

LACROSSE (1979)

NCAA Div. I—Johns Hopkins
NCAA Div. II—Adelphi
Women's Lacrosse Ass'n—Penn State

LUGE (1979)

World Champions
Singles—Dettlef Guenther, E. Germany
Women—Melitta Sollmann, E. Germany
Doubles—Hans Brandner-Balthasar
Schwarm, W. Germany
World Cup Champions
Singles—Hans Rinn, E. Germany
Women—Margit Schumann, E. Germany
Nat'l AAU Champions
Singles—Frank Masley, Newark, Del.
Women—Donna Burke, L. Placid, N.Y.
Doubles—Gary Schmeusser, Wilmington,
Del.-Ty Danco, Pepper Pike, Ohio

MARATHON

1979 Boston Marathon—Bill Rodgers,
Melrose, Mass.
1978 N.Y. City Marathon—Bill Rodgers
Women—Joan Benoit, Cape Elizabeth, Me.
1979 National AAU Champions
Men—Tom Antczak, Rockford, Ill.
Team—Greater Boston Track Club
Women—Sue Petersen, Seniors T.C.
Team—Terlingua T.C. (Houston)

MODERN PENTATHLON
   (1979)

World Champion—Robert Nieman,
Hinsdale, Ill.
World Team Champion—United States
U.S. Champion—Lt. Michael Burley,
Beria, Ohio
Women—Kimberly Dunlop, Tallahassee,
Fla.

MOTORCYCLING (1979)

AMA National Champions
125 cc Motocross—Broc Glover, El Cajon,
Calif.
250 cc Motocross—Bob Hannah, Carson
City, Nev.
500 cc Motocross—Danny LaPorte, Yucca
Valley, Calif.
Toyota Supercross Series—Bob Hannah
U.S. Road Racing—750 Expert Class—
Richard Schlachter, Old Lyme, Ct.
Superbike Production—Wes Cooley,
Mission Viejo, Calif.

OTHER SPORTS (Cont.)

Lightweight—Freddie Spencer, Shreveport, La.
Novice—Alan Collins, Saratoga, Calif.
Sidecar—Larry Coleman, Chicago, Ill.
Grand National (1978)—Jay Springsteen, Lapeer, Mich.

PADDLEBALL (1979)

Nat'l Four-Wall Champions
Singles—Marty Hogan, San Diego, Calif.
Women (1978)—Grace Louwsma, Ann Arbor, Mich.
Doubles—R. P. Valenciano, Flint, Mich.-Dick Jury, Lansing, Mich.
Women—Judy Shirley, Ann Arbor, Mich.-Grace Louwsma

PADDLE TENNIS

U.S. National Doubles Champions
Men (1979)—Sol Hauptman-Jeff Fleitman, Brooklyn, N.Y.
Women (1978)—Annabel Rogan, Pacific Palisades, Calif.-Nena Perez, Venice, Calif.
Mixed Doubles (1978)—Doris Castaneda-Rick Beckendorf, Los Angeles, Calif.
U.S. National Clay Court Champions
Men (1978)—Jeff Fleitman-Steve Geller, Brooklyn, N.Y.
Women (1978)—Debbie Samuels-Dinah Day, New York, N.Y.
Mixed Doubles (1978)—Debbie Samuels and Steve Geller

PARACHUTING

1978 World Championship Team—Canada
1979 U.S. Champions
Overall—Cheryl Stearns
Women—Cheryl Stearns
Accuracy—Dwight Reynolds
Women—Cheryl Stearns
Style—Maurice Fernandez
Women—Cheryl Stearns
4-Man Relative Work—Tesseract
8-Man Relative Work—Mirror Image
10-Man Relative Work—Visions

PENTATHLON (1979)

National Women's Indoor Champion —
Themis Zambrzycki, Brigham Young Univ./Brazil
National Women's Outdoor Champion —
Jane Frederick, unattached

PLATFORM TENNIS (1978-79)

U.S. National Doubles Champions
Men—Clark Graebner, Green's Farm, Ct.-Doug Russell, New York, N.Y.
Women—Yvonne Hackenberg, Kalamazoo, Mich.-Linda Wolf, New Canaan, Ct.
Mixed—Hilary Hilton, Glen Ellyn, Ill.-Doug Russell

POLO (1979)

U.S. Open—Retama
Gold Cup—Retama
America Cup—Boca Raton
Continental Cup—Oak Brook
Delegate's Cup—Twin Cities
National President's Cup—Joy Farm
Butler Handicap—Oak Brook
Collegiate—U. of California—Davis

POWERBOATING (1979)

Unlimited Hydroplane
Gold Cup—Atlas Van Lines, Bill Muncey, driver
U.S. Offshore Champion—Betty Cook, Newport Beach, Calif.
1978 World Champion—Nicholas Cosentino, Italy

POWERLIFTING (1979)

Nat'l AAU Champions
52 kilos—Chuck Dunbar
56 kilos—Robert Lech

60 kilos—George Hummel
67.5 kilos—Clyde Wright
75 kilos—Mike Bridges
82.5 kilos—Walter Thomas
90 kilos—Roger Estep
100 kilos—Larry Pacifico
110 kilos—John Kuc
125 kilos—Larry Kidney
Superheavyweight—Paul Wrenn

QUARTER HORSE RACING (1979)

Race—Winner and Jockey
All American Futurity—Pie in the Sky, Danny Cordoza
All American Derby—Dickeys Fireman, Donald Knight
Rainbow Derby—Black Sable, Steve Treasure
Kansas Futurity—Favorite Past Time, Harley Crosby
Rainbow Futurity—Streakin Six, Danny Cordoza
Kindergarten Futurity—Easy Angel, Billy Hunt

RODEO (1978)

World Champions
All-Around—Tom Ferguson, Miami, Okla.
Saddle Bronc Riding—Joe Marvel, Battle Mountain, Nev.
Bareback Bronc Riding—Jack Ward, Springdale, Ark.
Bull Riding—Butch Kirby, Alba, Tex.
Steer Wrestling—Tom Ferguson, Miami, Okla.
Calf Roping—Dave Brock, Pueblo, Colo.
Steer Roping—Kenny Call, Newhall, Calif.
Team Roping—Brad Smith, Prescott, Ariz. and George Richards, Humboldt, Ariz.
Women's Barrel Racing—Lynn McKenzie, Shreveport, La.

ROLLER SKATING

World Champions (1978)
Singles—Thomas Nieder, W. Germany
Women—Natalie Dunn, Bakersfield, Cal.
Dance—Fleurette Arsenault-Dan Littel, East Meadow, N.Y.
Mixed Pairs—Pat Jones-Robbie Coleman, Memphis, Tenn.
U.S. Champions (1979)
Singles—Michael Glatz, San Diego, Calif.
Women—Moana Pitcher, San Diego, Calif.
Figures—Bob Calzone, Maumee, Ohio
Women—Rita Drago, Hammonton, N.J.
Speed—Curtis Cook, Orchards, Wash.
Women—Linda Swain, High Point, N.C.

ROWING

1979 World Champions
MEN:
Single Sculls—Pertti Karppinen, Finland
Double Sculls—Norway
Pairs with Coxswain—East Germany
Pairs without Coxswain—East Germany
4s with Coxswain—East Germany
8s—East Germany
WOMEN:
Single Sculls—Sanda Toma, Rumania
Double Sculls—E. Germany
4s with Coxswain—U.S.S.R.
Pairs without Coxswain—E. Germany
8s—U.S.S.R.
1978 U.S. Champions
Singles—Jim Dietz, N.Y.A.C.
Singles, Dash—Jim Dietz
Double Sculls—Greg Stone-Tiff Wood, Harvard
Pairs with Coxswain—Tom Woodman-Philip Stekl-John Chatzky, Pennsylvania
Pairs without Coxswain—Sean Colgan-Bruce Ibbetson, Pennsylvania
4s with Coxswain—Pennsylvania
4s without Coxswain—Cornell/Potomac B.C.
Quadruple Sculls—New York A.C.
8s—Pennsylvania/Penn A.C.

1979 Intercollegiate Champions

IRA Varsity—Brown
IRA Freshman—Wisconsin
IRA Second Varsity—Northeastern
IRA Jim Ten Eyck Trophy—Wisconsin
Harvard-Yale—Harvard
Adams Cup—Harvard
Copley Cup—Harvard
Eastern Women's—Yale
Thames Challenge Cup—Leander Club, Britain
Ladies' Challenge Plate—Yale Jr. Varsity
1979 The Boat Race (Cambridge-Oxford)—Oxford series: Cam: 68, Oxf: 56, 1 tie)
1979 Grand Challenge Cup (Henley)—Thames Tradesmen's and London Rowing Clubs (combined team)
1978 Nile Int'l Festival—Univ. of Washington

RUGBY

1978 Five Nations Tournament—Wales
1978 South Africa Currie Cup—Northern Transvaal
1979 U.S. Nat'l Club Champion—Old Blue R.F.C., Oakland, Calif.
U.S. vs Canada
(1977) Canada 17, U.S. 6
(1978) U.S. 12, Canada 7
(1979) Canada 19, U.S. 12

SHOOTING

1979 U.S. National Outdoor Champions
Men's Pistol—SP4 Darius R. Young, Winterburn, Canada
Women's Pistol—SP4 Ruby E. Fox, Parker, Ariz.
Smallbore Rifle (Prone)—David P. Weaver, Oil City, Pa.
Smallbore Rifle (Position)—Lt. Col. Lones W. Wigger, Ft. Benning, Ga.
High Power Rifle—Carl R. Bernosky, Gordon, Pa.
1979 U.S. National Indoor Champions
Conv. Rifle—Karen Monez, Wanda Jewell, Ft. Benning, Ga.
Int'l Rifle—Lones Wigger, Ft. Benning, Ga.
Women—Karen Monez
Conv. Pistol—Thomas Woods, Ft. Benning, Ga.
Women—Norma Puryear, N. Canton, Ohio
1979 Grand Amer. Trapshooting Champions
Men—Dean Shanahan, Dubuque, Iowa
Women—Debbie Moore, Nepanoch, N.Y.
1979 NRA Int'l Skeet Champions
Men—Matt Dryke, Ft. Benning, Ga.
Women—Joan Elkins, Naples, Fla.
Junior—Jeff Sizemore, Corpus Christi, Tex.

SKIING

1978-79 World Cup Champions
Overall—Peter Luescher, Switzerland
Women—Annemarie Proell Moser, Austria
Highest U.S. Qualifiers
Overall—(3rd) Phil Mahre, White Pass, Wash.
Women—(4th) Cindy Nelson, Lutsen, Minn.
Downhill, Women—(4th) Cindy Nelson
Slalom—(2nd) Phil Mahre
Women—(13th) Abbi Fisher, South Conway, N.H.
Giant Slalom, Women—(6th) Heidi Preuss, Lakeport, N.H.
1979 U.S. Nordic Champions
Combined—Mike Devecka, Sandy, Ore.
Jumping (Sr.)—Jeff Davis, Steamboat Springs, Colo.
Jumping (Jr.)—Jon Denney, Duluth, Minn.
Men's Cross-Country
15km.—Bill Koch, Guilford, Vt.
30km.—Tim Caldwell, Putney, Vt.
50km.—Stan Dunklee, Brattleboro, Vt.
Women's Cross-Country
7.5km.—Alison Owen-Spencer, Anchorage, Alaska

OTHER SPORTS (Cont.)

10km.—Alison Owen-Spencer
20km.—Beth Paxson, Charlotte, Vt.
1979 Middlebury Winter Carnival
Men—Vermont
Women—Middlebury
Cross-Country 15km.—Craig Ward,
Saranac Lake, N.Y.
Women 15km.—Judy Rabinowitz,
Fairbanks, Alaska
1979 Collegiate Champions
Slalom—Per Nicholaysen, Utah
Giant Slalom—Chris Mikell, Vermont
Jumping—Roger Holden, Vermont
Cross-Country—Svein Arne Olsen, Utah
Team—Colorado
1978 AIAW (Women's) Nat'l Champions
Slalom—Fran Malindzak, Northern
Michigan
Giant Slalom—Sara McNealus, Middlebury
Alpine Combined—Fran Malindzak
Cross-Country (7.5km.)—Britta Kjellstrand,
Alaska-Anchorage
Team—Middlebury

SOFTBALL

1979 Amateur Softball Ass'n Champions
Men's Fast Pitch—McArdle Pontiac-
Cadillac, Midland, Mich.
Women—Sun City Saints, Sun City, Ariz.
Men's Slow Pitch—Nelco Manufacturing,
Oklahoma City, Okla.
Women—Bob Hoffman Dots, Miami, Fla.
Industrial Slow Pitch—Sikorsky,
Stamford, Ct.
Women—Philip Morris, Richmond, Va.
16" Slow Pitch—Bobcats, Chicago, Ill.
Men's Class A Fast Pitch—Joaquin
Construction, Modesto, Calif.
Women—Astros, San Diego, Calif.
Men's Class A Slow Pitch—Clark and
Sons, Providence, R.I.
Women—Northside Knights, Cincinnati,
Ohio
Men's Class A Industrial Slow Pitch—
Leslie Fay, Wilkes-Barre, Pa.
Men's Church Slow Pitch—Grace Metho-
dist Blacks, Oklahoma City, Okla.
Women—Mt. Hermon Methodist, Graham,
N.C.
Modified Fast Pitch—Clinica, Miami
Beach, Fla.

SQUASH RACQUETS (1979)

North American Open—Sharif Khan,
Toronto, Canada
Women's Int'l Open—Heather McKay,
Toronto, Canada
U.S. Women's Open—Heather McKay
World Pro Championship—Sharif Khan
U.S. Mixed Doubles—Carol Thesieres,
Bryn Mawr, Pa.-Gilbert Mateer,
Bethlehem, Pa.

SQUASH TENNIS

1979 U.S. Nat'l Champion—Pedro
Bacallao, Princeton Club

TABLE TENNIS

1979 World Champions
Singles—Seiji Ono, Japan
Women—Ge Xinai, P.R. China
Doubles—Dragutin Surbek-Anton
Stipancic, Yugoslavia

Women—Zhang Li-Zhang Deying,
P.R. China
Mixed Doubles—Ge Xinai-Liang Geliang,
P.R. China
Men's Team—Hungary
Women's Team—P.R. China
1979 U.S. Open Champions
Singles—Milan Orlowski, Czech.
Women—Lee Ki Won, S. Korea
Doubles—Josef Dvoracek-Jindrich Pansky,
Czech.
Women—Shoko Takahashi-Kayo Kawahi-
gashi, Japan
Mixed Doubles—Jacques Secretin-Claude
Bergeret, France
Men's Team—Czechoslovakia
Women's Team—Japan

TRAMPOLINE & TUMBLING

1979 Nat'l AAU Champions
MEN
Trampoline—Stuart Ransom, Lafayette,
La.
Tumbling—Dickie Bivins, Newark, N.J.
Double Mini-Tramp—Stuart Ransom
Synchronized Trampoline—Ron Seibert,
Geneva, Ohio and Stuart Ransom
WOMEN
Trampoline—Karen Kernan, Livingston,
N.J.
Tumbling—Nancy Quattrocki, Chicago
Double Mini-Tramp—Karen Kernan
Synchronized Trampoline—Mary
Rugheimer, Bozeman, Mont. and
Karen Kernan

VOLLEYBALL (1979)

U.S. Volleyball Ass'n Champions
Men's Open—Nautilus Pacific, Long
Beach, Calif.
Women's Open—Fireside Mavericks, Los
Angeles, Calif.
Men's Senior—Vessel's Quartermaster,
Long Beach, Calif.
Women's Senior—Fireside Mavericks,
Los Angeles, Calif.
NCAA—U.C.L.A.
NAIA—Graceland College (Iowa)
AIAW—Utah State (1978)
Int'l Volleyball Ass'n Champion—Tucson
Sky

WATER POLO (1979)

World Cup—Hungary
Women—United States
1978 NCAA Champion—Stanford
Nat'l AAU Outdoor Champions
Men—Newport (Calif.)
Women—Seal Beach (Calif.)
Nat'l AAU Indoor Champions
Women—Long Beach, California

WATER SKIING (1979)

U.S. Open Champions
Overall—Ricky McCormick, Winter Haven,
Fla.
Women—Karin Roberge, San Diego, Calif.
Slalom—Bob LaPoint, Castro Valley, Calif.
Women—Cindy Todd, Pierson, Fla.
Tricks—Ricky McCormick

Women—Karin Roberge
Jumping—Sammy Duvall, Greenville, S.C.
Women—Cindy Todd
World Champions
Overall—Joel McClintock, Canada
Women—Cindy Todd, Pierson, Fla.
Team—United States

WEIGHTLIFTING

1978 World Champions
52 kilos—Kanybek Osmonaliev, USSR
56 kilos—Daniel Nunez, Cuba
60 kilos—Nikolai Kolesnikov, USSR
67½ kilos—Yanko Rusev, Bulgaria
75 kilos—Roberto Urrutia, Cuba
82½ kilos—Yurik Vardanian, USSR
90 kilos—Rolf Milser, W. Germany
100 kilos—David Rigert, USSR
110 kilos—Yuriy Zaitsev, USSR
Over 110 kilos—Jurgen Heuser, E.
Germany
Team—USSR
1979 Nat'l AAU Champions
52 kilos—Jon Chappell
56 kilos—Pat Omori
60 kilos—Phil Sanderson
67½ kilos—Dave Jones
75 kilos—Dave Reigle
82½ kilos—Tom Hirtz
90 kilos—Jim Curry, Jr.
100 kilos—Kurt Setterburg
110 kilos—Mark Cameron
Over 110 kilos—Tom Stock

YACHTING

1977 America's Cup—US (Courageous;
Ted Turner, skipper) over Australia
(Australia; Noel Robins, skipper) 4–0
1978 Yachtsman of the Year—Buddy
Melges, Zenda, Wis.
1978 Yachtswoman of the Year—Bonnie
Shore, Newport, R.I.
U.S. Yacht Racing Union
Men—1979 (Mallory Cup)—Glenn Darden,
Ft. Worth, Tex.
Women—1979 (Adams Trophy)—Allison
Jolly, St. Petersburg, Fla.
Junior—1979 (Sears Cup)—Bill Lynn, Jr.,
Rye, N.Y.
Single-handed—1979 (O'Day Trophy)—
Peter Commette, Mantiloking, N.J.
Club—1979 (Prince of Wales Trophy)—
Dr. John W. Jennings, St. Petersburg,
Fla.
1979 Bemis Cup—John Shedder, Alamitos
Bay, Calif.
1979 Smythe Cup—Baird Lobree, Coconut
Grove, Fla.
Other Races (1979)
Admiral's Cup—Tenacious
Block Island Race—Inverness
Lipton Cup—Obsession
Marblehead-Halifax—Recluta
Miami-Nassau—Tenacious
Nassau Cup—Illusion
SORC Championship—Williwaw
Trans-Pacific—Arriba
Two Ton Championship—Iorama
World Soloing—Robby Haines, San Diego,
Calif.
World 5.5 Meter—Frank Tolhurst,
Australia

POPULARITY OF DOG BREEDS

SOURCE: American Kennel Club

	Breed	1978 Registrations		Breed	1978 Registrations
1.	Poodle	101,100	11.	Shetland Sheepdog	24,668
2.	Doberman Pinscher	81,964	12.	Lhasa Apso	22,330
3.	German Shepherd	61,783	13.	Collie	22,032
4.	Cocker Spaniel	58,719	14.	Yorkshire Terrier	21,913
5.	Labrador Retriever	43,500	15.	Siberian Husky	20,650
6.	Beagle	36,920	16.	English Springer Spaniel	19,131
7.	Golden Retriever	34,249	17.	Pekingese	18,892
8.	Dachshund	33,660	18.	Brittany Spaniel	18,418
9.	Miniature Schnauzer	33,534	19.	Great Dane	16,600
10.	Irish Setter	30,839	20.	Pomeranian	15,870

OBITUARIES

Acheampong, Ignatius K., 47, deposed President of Ghana (1972-78) convicted by a military tribunal of the new revolutionary regime of squandering government funds; executed in Accra, Ghana, June 16, 1979.

Akuffo, Gen. Frederick W. K., 42, recently deposed military chief of Ghana, executed with five other officers convicted of abuse of power by the Armed Forces Revolutionary Council, in Accra, Ghana, June 26, 1979.

Allyn, John, 61, owner of the Chicago White Sox (1969-75) whose sale of his majority interest in that baseball team to outside investors prevented its moving to Seattle, in Chicago, Ill., April 29, 1979.

Almond, Lt. Gen. Edward M. ("Ned"), 86, chief of staff to Gen. Douglas MacArthur (1946-50) who led the Army's 10th Corps in the amphibious landing at Inchon and in other actions during the Korean War, in San Antonio, Texas, June 11, 1979.

Baroody, Jamil M., 73, Saudi Arabia's spokesman in the United Nations since 1948, considered the "dean" of the UN delegates, in New York City, March 4, 1979.

Bartlett, Dewey F., 59, one-term Republican Senator from Oklahoma (1973-79) who was an outspoken proponent of a strong U.S. military posture and a strong NATO, in Tulsa, Okla., March 1, 1979.

Barzani, Mustafa, 76, flamboyant Kurdish nationalist leader who led an unsuccessful war (1960-75) with alleged U.S. and Iranian help for regional autonomy from Iraq, in Washington, D.C., March 1, 1979.

Bayh, Marvella H., 46, wife of U.S. Senator Birch Bayh (D.-Ind.), who toured the nation as a special representative of the American Cancer Society since discovering her own terminal illness in 1975, in Washington, D.C., April 24, 1979.

Beltran, Pedro Gerardo, 81, former premier of Peru and publisher of Lima's *La Prensa;* an advocate of a free press in developing countries, he was jailed in 1956 by the ruling military junta, in Lima, February 16, 1979.

Bennett, William A.C., 78, former premier of British Columbia (1952-72) and leader of the Social Credit party, in Kelowna, B.C. (Canada), February 23, 1979.

Bernstein, Theodore M., 74, assistant managing editor of *The New York Times* (1951-69) and popular writer and authority on the use of the English language, in New York City, June 27, 1979.

Bertoia, Harry, 63, Italian-born sculptor and designer best known for his now-classic diamond-shaped chair suspended in a steel cradle, in Barton, Pa., November 6, 1978.

Bhutto, Zulfikar Ali, 51, Pakistani political leader who became President (1971) after disastrous war with India over Bangladesh; he later became Premier, but was deposed by the army in 1977 and subsequently convicted of ordering the death of a political foe, executed in Rawalpindi, Pakistan, April 4, 1979.

Boumedienne, Houari, 53, President of Algeria since 1965 and one of the Third World's most well-known spokesmen, in Algiers, December 27, 1978.

Bousseif, Ahmed Ould, 45, military officer appointed Prime Minister of Mauritania by Pres. Mustapha Ould Salek in April 1979, killed when his military plane crashed, May 27, 1979.

Breckinridge, John B., 65, three-term Kentucky congressman (1973-78) who was chairman of the Congressional Rural Caucus and an advocate of a strong national defense, in Lexington, Ky., July 29, 1979.

Brent, George, 75, well-known stage and screen actor ("The Fighting 69th," "Jezebel," "Dark Victory") of the 1930s and 40s, in Solana Beach, Calif., May 26, 1979.

Brown, Gen. George S., 60, Air Force commander and chairman of the Joint Chiefs of Staff (1974-78) whose tenure was marked by his often controversial remarks about Jews, Israel and U.S. allies, in Washington, D.C., December 5, 1978.

Brundage, Percival F., 87, budget director under President Eisenhower (1956-58) noted for his efforts to secure a record peacetime budget of $73.5 billion for U.S. missile development in the woke of Sputnik, in Ridgewood, N.J., July 16, 1979.

Buchanan, Edgar, 76, veteran actor best known for his rustic yet sly Western characters in over 100 films and four television series, including the long-running "Petticoat Junction;" in Palm Desert, Calif., April 4, 1979.

Buzhardt, J. Fred, 54, attorney and special counsel for President Nixon in his Watergate defense, who spent 20 years in public life as aide to Sen. Strom Thurmond and former Defense Secretary Melvin Laird, in Hilton Head Island, S.C., December 16, 1978.

Capehart, Homer E., 82, Indiana businessman and three-term Republican Senator (1944-62) who was a forceful opponent of the Roosevelt and Truman Administrations, in Indianapolis, Ind., September 3, 1979.

Carnes, Paul N., 58, minister and president of the Unitarian Universalist Association of North America since 1977 in Boston, Mass., March 17, 1979.

Carroll, John, 72, actor of the 1930s, best known for his role as Zorro in that continuing film series and once considered a rival as America's heartthrob to Clark Gable, in Hollywood, Calif., April 24, 1979.

Cassidy, Ted, 46, towering 6'9" actor best known for his television roles as Lurch the butler in "The Addams Family" and Bigfoot in "The Six Million Dollar Man," in Los Angeles, Calif., January 16, 1979.

Chain, Dr. Ernst B., 73, Berlin-born British biochemist who shared the 1945 Nobel Prize in Medicine with physicians Howard W. Florey and Alexander Fleming for development of penicillin, in Ireland, August 14, 1979.

De Chirico, Giorgio, 90, Italian painter *(Melancholy and Mystery of a Street, The Great Metaphysician)* who created modern school of metaphysical art, in Rome, Italy, November 20, 1978.

Clore, Sir Charles, 74, British financier reputed to be the wealthiest man in England — with a personal fortune estimated at $70 to $120 million —, owner of such lucrative properties as London's famous Selfridges department store, in London, July 26, 1979.

Cochran, Col. Philip G., 69, American fighter pilot commander in North Africa and Burma during World War II, he was inspiration for two characters created by Milton Coniff in the syndicated comic strips "Terry and the Pirates" and "Steve Canyon," in Geneseo, N.Y., August 25, 1979.

Coe, Fred, 64, television producer and director ("Mr. Peepers," "Playhouse 90," "Peter Pan") responsible for some of the best live drama during television's "Golden Age" of the 1950s and early 60s, in Los Angeles, April 29, 1979.

Compton, Fay, 84, British actress whose distinguished career spanned 70 years, noted for her 1925 performance opposite John Barrymore in *Hamlet* and in vehicles by Noel Coward and J. M. Barrie *(Blithe Spirit, Peter Pan)*, in London, December 12, 1978.

Costello, Dolores, 73, silent screen actress best known for her 1926 performance opposite John Barrymore in *The Sea Beasts,* whom she later married but divorced in 1935; in Fallbrook, Calif., March 1, 1979.

Cousteau, Philippe, 39, French oceanographer and cinematographer who filmed and produced several underwater documentaries in association with his father, famed oceanographer Jacques-Yves Cousteau, after the seaplane he was piloting crashed and sank off Alverca, Portugal, June 28, 1979.

Crockett, James, 63, horticulturist whose television series "Crockett's Victory Garden" was watched by over 4 million American home gardeners, in Jamaica, July 11, 1979.

Dasburg, Andrew, 92, American abstract painter and a pioneer of the Cubist school in the decades preceding World War I, in Taos, N.M., August 13, 1979.

Dauphin, Claude, 75, French actor who appeared on Broadway *(No Exit* (1946), *The Happy Time* (1950) and in over 80 films, the most recent being "Madame Rosa" (1978), in Paris, France, November 17, 1978.

De Guingand, Maj. Gen. Sir Francis, 79, chief of staff to Britain's Field Marshall Viscount Montgomery and a leading architect of the Allied victory in World War II, in Cannes, France, June 29, 1979.

Dehnert, Henry ("Dutch"), 81, Hall of Fame basketball player with the original Celtics team credited with developing the 'pivot' play, in Far Rockaway (Queens), N.Y., April 20, 1979.

De Rochemont, Louis, 79, producer of numerous documentary films for nearly 30 years ("House on Ninety-Second Street", "Windjammer"), who originated and produced the March of Time newsreel series (1934-43), in Newington, N.H., December 23, 1978.

Diefenbaker, John G., 83, Prime Minister of Canada (1957-63) and a leader of the Progressive Conservative party; also a member of the House of Commons since 1940, in Ottawa, Canada, August 16, 1979.

Diaz Ordaz, Gustavo, 68, President of Mexico (1964-70) who ordered troops and police to suppress student protesters in Mexico City in 1968, resulting in over 100 deaths, in Mexico City, July 15, 1979.

Douglas, Aaron, 79, leading painter of the Harlem Renaissance in the 1920s, called the "father of Black American art" for pioneering the use of African iconography in his work, in Nashville, Tenn., February 2, 1979.

Dubs, Adolph, 58, U.S. Ambassador to Afghanistan, killed in crossfire between police and Moslem terrorists who had kidnapped him, in Kabul, Afghanistan, February 14, 1979.

Du Vigneaud, Dr. Vincent, 77, biochemist who won the Nobel Prize in 1955 for his work in the isolation and synthesis of hormones, in White Plains, N.Y., December 11, 1978.

Eaton, Cyrus S., 95, self-made millionaire industrialist who was an early champion of establishing trade and other relations with the Soviet Union, and advocated scientific and cultural exchanges between East and West to lessen Cold War tensions, in Northfield, Ohio, May 9, 1979.

Eberle, Ray, 60, Big Band singer with the Glenn Miller Orchestra who recorded many popular tunes in the 1930s, later singing with the Tex Beneke band in the 1940s, in Douglasville, Ga., August 25, 1979.

Ellis, Don, 44, jazz trumpeter, bandleader and composer known for his experimentation with various musical forms, in North Hollywood, Calif., December 17, 1978.

Farrell, James T., 75, novelist whose *Studs Lonigan* trilogy — about lower-class Irish-American life in his native Chicago — made him a dominant figure among American realistic writers of the 1930s, in New York City, Aug. 22, 1979.

Feathers, Beattie, 69, All-American running back for the Chicago Bears (1934-37) and member of the National Football Hall of Fame; he set an unbroken record for rushing — averaging 9.9 yards per carry; in Winston-Salem, N.C., March 10, 1979.

Fiedler, Arthur, 84, conductor of the Boston Pops Orchestra for nearly 50 years and one of America's most popular musical figures, whose combinations of both classical and pop tunes brought pleasure to an entire generation of music lovers, in Brookline, Mass., July 10, 1979.

Fields, Gracie, 81, beloved British actress-singer, Dame Commander of the Order of the British Empire, whose long career spanned music hall, theater, television and stage. She died at her home in Capri, Italy, September 27, 1979.

Flanner, Janet, 86, correspondent for *The New Yorker* who for nearly 50 years under the byline "Genet" wrote the regular "Letter From Paris" column, profiling such diverse notables as Adolph Hitler, Henri Matisse and Queen Mary, in New York City, November 27, 1978.

Flatt, Lester, 64, veteran country singer-guitarist and star of the Grand Ole Opry, whose partnership with banjo-player Earl Scruggs as the bluegrass duo Flatt and Scruggs spanned 25 years, in Nashville, Tenn., May 11, 1979.

Focke, Heinrich, 88, German aviation pioneer whose FW-61 helicopter made the first free flight of a rotary-wing aircraft in 1936, in Bremen, West Germany, February 25, 1979.

Foran, Dick, 69, veteran actor who was one of the first "singing cowboys;" his film credits include "The Petrified Forest," "My Little Chickadee," "Fort Apache" and "Donovan's Reef," in Panorama City, Calif., August 10, 1979.

Forssmann, Dr. Werner, 73, medical researcher whose work on intra-veinous therapy showing that a catheter inserted into a vein at the elbow could be safely guided all the way to the heart won him the 1956 Nobel Prize in Medicine, in Schopfheim, West Germany, June 6, 1979.

Franzblau, Dr. Rose N., 77, psychologist who wrote the popular syndicated advice column "Human Relations" for over 25 years (1951-76), in New York City, September 2, 1979.

Frings, Joseph Cardinal, 91, Archbishop of Cologne (1942-69) who denounced Nazi persecution of the Jews from his pulpit during World War II, appointed Cardinal in 1946, in Cologne, West Germany, December 17, 1978.

Furey, Rev. Francis J., 74, Roman Catholic Archbishop of San Antonio (1969-79) and a leading supporter of social causes among Hispanic-Americans, in San Antonio, Texas, April 23, 1979.

Galante, Carmine, 69, reputed New York crime boss who had promised to take over all of that city's crime "families," shot in an apparent underworld dispute, in Brooklyn, N.Y., July 12, 1979.

Galento, Tony ("Two-Ton"), 69, heavyweight boxer of the 1930s who knocked down Joe Louis in a June 28, 1939 championship bout which he subsequently lost; famous for his motto, "I'll moider da bum," of a heart attack in Livingston, N.J., July 22, 1979.

Gargan, William D., 73, actor noted for his tough-guy detective roles in the 1930s and 40s who courageously relearned to speak after surgery for cancer of the larynx removed his vocal chords in 1960, aboard a San Diego-bound airline flight from New York, February 17, 1979.

Garin, Georges, 66, French chef who pioneered "la nouvelle cuisine," and owner of the famous *Chez Garin* restaurant on Paris' Left Bank, in Toulon, France, announced May 22, 1979.

Gathings, E.C. ("Took"), 75, conservative Democratic congressman from Arkansas (1939-69) known for his influence on farm legislation and his opposition to civil rights measures, in West Memphis, Ark., May 2, 1979.

Gehlen, Reinhard, 77, Nazi spymaster on the Russian Front during World War II who later became the first chief of West Germany's intelligence service (1955-68), in Lake Starnberg, West Germany, June 8, 1979.

Geismar, Maxwell D., 69, literary critic, author and editor of many anthologies; best known for his trilogy tracing the course of the modern American novel (1890-1940), and for his espousal of many radical causes, in Harrison, N.Y., July 24, 1979.

Giles, Warren, 82, former president of the Cincinnati Reds and president of Baseball's National League for 18 years, in Cincinnati, Ohio, February 7, 1979.

Gordon, Max, 86, Broadway producer of such long-running hits as *Born Yesterday, My Sister Eileen, Junior Miss* and *The Solid Gold Cadillac,* in New York City, November 2, 1978.

Goudsmit, Samuel, A., 76, physicist who co-discovered the electron's spin with George Uhlenbeck in 1925, and head of the Allied scientific team which sought information on German plans for the atomic bomb during World War II, in Reno, Nev., December 4, 1978.

Griffith, Corrine, 73, actress who as "orchid of the screen" starred in Hollywood's early silent films, and the author of the popular memoir, *Papa's Delicate Condition,* in Santa Monica, California, July 13, 1979.

Grosvenor, Robert George, fifth Duke of Westminster, 68, head of one of Britain's wealthiest families, whose landholdings were estimated at $1 billion, near Enniskillen in Northern Ireland, February 19, 1979.

Haekkerup, Per, 63, Danish political figure who since 1945 served as Foreign Minister and then Finance Minister in successive Social Democratic governments under Premier Jens Otto Krag, in Copenhagen, March 13, 1979.

Haley, Jack, 79, mellow stage and screen comedian who played the Tin Woodsman in the 1939 American classic, "The Wizard of Oz," in Los Angeles, June 6, 1979.

Halsman, Philippe, 73, internationally-known portrait photographer whose famous subjects included Albert Einstein, Winston Churchill, John F. Kennedy, Ingrid Bergman and Marilyn Monroe, in New York City, June 25, 1979.

Hartnell, Sir Norman, 78, official dressmaker to Queen Elizabeth II and a member of the Incorporated Society of London Dressmakers, in Windsor, England, June 8, 1979.

Hathaway, Donny, 33, Grammy Award-winning pop and blues singer; a suspected suicide, in New York City, January 13, 1979.

Haya de la Torre, Victor Raul, 84, political leader and elder statesman of Latin American nationalism, whose American Popular Revolutionary Alliance (Apra) party dominated politics in Peru for many years; in Lima, Peru, August 2, 1979.

Hayward, Max, 54, translator and foremost British scholar on contemporary Russian literature, who brought proscribed Soviet writers such as Pasternak, Solzhientsyn, Nadezhda Mandelstam and Andrei Sinyavsky to the attention of the English-speaking world, in Oxford, England, May 18, 1979.

Hilton, Conrad N., 91, hotel entrepreneur and chairman of the multi-billion dollar Hilton Hotels and Hilton International corporate empire, in Santa Monica, Calif., January 3, 1979.

Hodge, Al, 66, actor who portrayed the Green Hornet on radio (1936-43) and later became one of television's first stars as "Captain Video" (1950-56), in New York City, March 19, 1979.

Hood, Darla, 48, the dark-eyed, curly-haired female member of the "Our Gang" comedy troupe of the 1930s, appearing in over 132 Our Gang pictures from 1935 to 1942, in Canoga Park, California, June 13, 1979.

Hoveida, Amir Abbas, 59, Prime Minister of Iran (1965-77) and a close political advisor to Shah Reza Mohammed Pahlavi, executed by order of the revolutionary Islamic court in Tehran, Iran, April 7, 1979.

Hoyt, Palmer, 82, retired editor and publisher of the *Denver Post* (1948-71) who championed freedom of the press and objective reporting, in Denver, Colorado, June 25, 1979.

Hutton, Barbara, 66, Woolworth heiress whose personal misfortunes earned her the nickname "poor little rich girl;" married seven times, her husbands included royalty from Russia, Lithuania, Prussia and Laos, and actor Cary Grant, in Los Angeles, May 11, 1979.

Hutton, Jim, 45, youthful-looking actor and light romantic-comedy lead in over a dozen films, best known for his portrayal of amateur sleuth Ellery Queen in the 1975-76 NBC-TV series, in Los Angeles, June 2, 1979.

Johnson, Ching, 81, National Hockey League Hall of Fame star with the original New York Rangers, whose defensive playing helped that team win two Stanley Cup championships (1927-28, 1932-33), in Silver Springs, Md., July 16, 1979.

Johnson, Sam Houston, 64, younger brother of President Lyndon Baines Johnson, whose depiction of the President in his 1969 book, *My Brother Lyndon,* aroused LBJ's ire, in Austin, Texas, December 11, 1978.

Jones, Preston, 43, playwright and author of *A Texas Trilogy,* which was successfully produced in Dallas, Washington, D.C., and on Broadway in 1976; in Dallas, Texas, September 19, 1979.

Joos, Kurt, 78, German choreographer whose ballets were noted for their compassion and social consciousness; his *The Green Table* (1932) is perhaps the most acclaimed anti-war ballet, in Heilbronn, West Germany, May 22, 1979.

Di Jorio, Alberto Cardinal, 95, oldest member of the Roman Catholic Church's College of Cardinals, in Rome, Italy, September 5, 1979.

Kadar, Jan, 61, Hungarian-born Czech expatriate film director who won an Oscar in 1965 for his film, "The Shop on Main Street," about Jewish-Gentile relations in Nazi-occupied Prague; in Los Angeles, June 1, 1979.

Kardelj, Edvard, 69, leading theoretician of Yugoslavia's ruling Communist party and a close associate of Marshall Tito, in Ljubljana, Yugoslavia, February 10, 1979.

Karpis, Alvin, 71, bank-robbing leader of the Ma Barker Gang in the 1930s, when he was "Public Enemy No. 1;" arrested by J. Edgar Hoover in 1936, he spent the next 33 years in Federal prisons until he was paroled in 1969; in Torremolinos, Spain, August 26, 1979.

Kasznar, Kurt, 66, versatile stage and screen character actor who appeared on Broadway in *The Sound of Music* and *Barefoot in the Park;* his film credits include "My Sister Eileen" and "A Farewell to Arms," in Santa Monica, Calif., August 6, 1979.

Kelly, Emmett, 80, America's foremost circus clown, whose tattered hobo Weary Willie delighted audiences for over 40 years, including 14 years with Ringling Bros. and Barnum & Bailey Circus (1942-56); in Sarosota, Florida, March 28, 1979.

Kenton, Stan, 67, Big Band leader, jazz composer and pianist of the 1930s and 40s; a controversial musician, his arrangements were marked by strong brass ensembles and experimental use of Afro-Cuban themes; in Hollywood, Calif., August 25, 1979.

Khue, Trinh Nhu Cardinal, 79, Vietnamese Roman Catholic Archbishop of Hanoi, in Hanoi, Vietnam, November 28, 1978.

Kilian, Victor, 88, veteran character actor of stage and screen, best known recently for his 1976 portrayal of the senile grandfather — the "Fernwood Flasher" — in the television soap opera spoof, "Mary Hartman, Mary Hartman"; in Hollywood, Calif., March 11, 1979.

Knowles, Dr. John H., 52, president of the Rockefeller Foundation since 1972; a leading figure in American medicine, he was an outspoken critic of high medical fees and unnecessary surgery, in Boston, Mass., March 6, 1979.

Kuznetsov, Anatoly, 49, prominent Soviet writer who defected to Britain in 1969, best known for his 1966 book, *Babi Yar*, recounting the German massacre of Jews outside Kiev during World War II, in London, June 13, 1979.

Larsen, Roy E., 80, vice-president of Time, Inc., who, along with founders Henry R. Luce and Burton Hadden, directed the publishing empire's business concerns for over 50 years; in Fairfield, Conn., September 9, 1979.

Lasswell, Harold D., 76, political scientist best known for his application of psychological principles to the study of politics, in New York City, December 18, 1978.

Lavalle, Gen. John D., 62, U.S. Air Force commander in Southeast Asia who was relieved of duty after ordering unauthorized bombing raids against North Vietnam in 1971 and 1972, in Fairfax, Va., July 10, 1979.

Leonetti, Tommy, 50, singer best known for his stint on the 1957-58 "Your Hit Parade" television show, in Houston, Tex., Sept. 15, 1979.

Lewis, "Duffy," 91, Boston Red Sox outfielder who played on three World Series championship teams (1912, 1915 and 1916), and played Fenway Park's sloping outfield so well it was nicknamed "Duffy's Cliff," in Salem, N.H., June 17, 1979.

Little, Lou, 85, Columbia University's football coach (1930-56) whose underdog 1934 team upset Stamford in that year's Rose Bowl game, in Delray Beach, Fla., May 28, 1979.

Lucas, Bill, 43, vice-president of the Atlanta Braves and the highest-ranking black official in professional baseball, in Atlanta, Ga., May 5, 1979.

Lynen, Feodor, 68, winner of the 1964 Nobel Prize in Medicine; a pioneer in research on fatty acids, he was director of biochemistry at the Max Planck Institute, in Munich, West Germany, August 8, 1979.

La Malfa, Ugo, 75, deputy Prime Minister of Italy and leader of the small Republican Party, who had served in eight post-war governments, in Rome, March 26, 1979.

Manion, Clarence E., 83, host of the Manion Forum radio show (1954-79) and former dean of the University of Notre Dame Law School, in South Bend, Ind., July 28, 1979.

Marcuse, Herbert, 81, German-born Marxian philosopher and author of *One Dimensional Man* (1964), whose theories influenced a generation of radical activists in the 1960s, in Starnberg, West Germany, July 29, 1979.

Marques, Rene, 59, Puerto Rican writer best known for his play *The Oxcart* and his novel *The Evening of Man*, in San Juan, Puerto Rico, March 22, 1979.

Massine, Léonide, 83, one of the great ballet choreographers of the century, who began as a dancer with the *Ballets Russes* and was much influenced by its director, Serge Diaghilev, in Cologne, West Germany, March 16, 1979.

Maudling, Reginald, 61, former Conservative Chancellor of the Exchequer who twice lost contests for party leadership that would have made him Prime Minister of Britain, in London, February 14, 1979.

McCoy, Van, 39, songwriter and performer best known for his 1975 Grammy Award-winning hit disco song, "The Hustle," in Englewood, N.J., July 6, 1979.

McDonald, David J., 76, president of the United Steelworkers of America (1952-65) and a major figure in the American labor movement who led his union through the bitter 1959-60 national steel strike; in Palm Springs, Calif., August 8, 1979.

McIntyre, James Francis Cardinal, 93, Roman Catholic Archbishop of Los Angeles (1948-70), considered one of the most conservative and controversial prelates in the American Church, in Los Angeles, July 16, 1979.

McNeil, Adm. William J., 78, Assistant Secretary of Defense (1949-59) and fiscal chief known for his budget-trimming policies during the Cold War era; in Bethesda, Md., August 30, 1979.

Mead, Margaret, 76, noted anthropologist whose 1928 *Coming of Age in Samoa* popularized social anthropology and made her famous; curator emeritus of the American Museum of Natural History, she served as president of the American Association for the Advancement of Science since 1974, in New York City, November 15, 1978.

Meir, Golda, 80, Israel's elder stateswoman who served as Prime Minister (1969-74) and was a founder of the Labor party; in Jerusalem, December 8, 1978.

Merrit, Dr. Hiram H., 78, pioneer neurologist who co-developed the anti-epilepsy drug Dilantin in 1936 with Dr. Tracy J. Putnam, in New York City, January 9, 1979.

Meyer, André, 81, French-born investment banker and financial wizard who headed the influential New York-based Lazard Frères & Co., for 33 years, in Lausanne, Switzerland, September 9, 1979.

Milk, Harvey, 48, member of San Francisco's Board of Supervisors and that body's first avowed homosexual, shot by former Supervisor Dan White, in San Francisco, November 27, 1978.

Miller, Don C., 77, All-American right halfback and member of the four-man backfield of Notre Dame's 1922-24 football team, nicknamed the "Four Horsemen," in Cleveland, Ohio, July 28, 1979.

Mingus, Charles, 56, noted jazz bassist, band leader and composer known for his fervent, free-form harmonies and technical sophistication, in Cuernavaca, Mexico, January 5, 1979.

Mohr, Senator Alberto Fuentes, 56, leader of Guatemala's moderate leftist opposition party, assassinated in Guatemala City, Jan. 25, 1979.

Mohsen, Zuheir, 43, military chief of the Palestine Liberation Organization and head of the Syrian-backed As Saiqa guerrilla faction; shot in an apparent ambush in Cannes, France, July 26, 1979.

Monnet, Jean, 90, French financier and father of the European Economic Community and a major proponent of European Union, in Houjarray, France, March 16, 1979.

Monsarrat, Nicholas, 69, British sailor-turned-author who wrote the bestselling novel, *The Cruel Sea* (1951), in London, August 7, 1979.

Moriarty, Joseph V. ("Newsboy"), 68, long-time gambling boss of Hudson County, New Jersey; convicted in 1973 on gambling-conspiracy charges, in Jersey City, N.J., February 24, 1979.

Morris, Joe Alex, Jr., 51, award-winning foreign correspondent for the Los Angeles *Times,* killed in a crossfire while covering the revolution in Iran, in Tehran, February 10, 1979.

Mountbatten, Louis, Earl of Burma, 79, member of Britain's Royal Family who was Allied Commander-in-Chief in Southeast Asia during World War II and served as the last British Viceroy of India; killed along with three companions by a terrorist bomb set by the IRA aboard his fishing boat, at sea near Mullaghmore, Ireland, August 27, 1979.

Moscone George R., 49, liberal two-term Democratic Mayor of San Francisco, California, shot by former city Supervisor Dan White, in San Francisco, November 27, 1978.

Munson, Thurman, 32, catcher and team captain of the New York Yankees who was named Most Valuable Player in the American League in 1970; when the single-engine plane he was piloting crashed near Canton, Ohio, August 2, 1979.

Muzrukov, Boris G., 74, designer of the Soviet T-34 tank used in World War II, announced in Moscow, January 31, 1979.

Nagy, Ferenc, 75, the last non-Communist Premier of Hungary (1946-May, 1947), in Washington, D.C., June 12, 1979.

Natta, Giulio, 76, Italian chemist who won the Nobel Prize in Chemistry in 1963 for his contribution to research in macromolecular chemistry and the development of new high polymer plastics, in Bergamo, Italy, May 2, 1979.

Nervi, Pier Luigi, 87, award-winning Italian architect famous for his pioneering use of reinforced concrete in new structural design techniques, in Rome, Italy, January 9, 1979.

Neto, Dr. Agostino A., 56, Marxist poet and physician who became the first President of Angola in 1975; in Moscow, USSR, September 10, 1979.

Newhouse, Samuel I., 84, millionaire newspaper magnate whose multi-billion dollar empire was one of the largest in the U.S.; an "absentee" owner, he left each of his newspapers with its own editorial independence, in New York City, August 29, 1979.

Novaes, Guiomar, 83, diminutive five-foot-tall Brazilian pianist who was considered one of the foremost virtuosi of the keyboard in her time, in Sao Paulo, Brazil, March 7, 1979.

Ocampo, Victoria, 88, Argentine writer, editor of the international literary journal *Sur,* and literary *grand dame* of Latin America jailed briefly by the Perón regime in 1953 for "subversion," in Buenos Aires. January 27, 1979.

Ohlin, Bertil, 80, Swedish economist who won the 1977 Nobel Prize in Economics for his contribution to international trade theory; he served as Minister of Trade (1944-45) in the wartime Socialist-Liberal government, in Sweden, August 3, 1979.

O'Malley, Walter F., 75, owner of the Los Angeles Dodgers, who moved that baseball team from Brooklyn after the 1957 season, opening up the West Coast to major league baseball; in Rochester, Minn., August 9, 1979.

Ottaviani, Alfredo Cardinal, 88, conservative Roman Catholic prelate who headed the Vatican's Holy Office under Popes Pius XII and John XIII, in the Vatican, Rome, August 3, 1979.

Parks, Gordon, Jr., 44, director of "Super Fly" and other black-oriented films of the 1970s — and son of photographer Gordon Parks; in a plane crash near Nairobi, Kenya, April 3, 1979.

Parsons, Talcott, 76, professor of sociology at Harvard University (1927-73) and a scholar of social thought and theory who educated three generations of sociologists, in Munich, West Germany, May 8, 1979.

Partridge, Eric, 85, noted lexicographer at Oxford University who was the recognized expert on slang, catch phrases, clichés and other specialized uses of the English language, in southwest England, June 1, 1979.

Pérez Alfonzo, Juan, 75, former Venezuelan oil minister widely regarded as the founder of the Organization of Petroleum Exporting Countries group in the 1960s, in Washington, D.C., Sept. 3, 1979.

Petra, Yahya, 62, King of Malaysia since 1975 — a ceremonial head of state under the constitution; in Kuala Lumpur, Malaysia, March 28, 1979.

Pickford, Mary, 86, "America's Sweetheart" and Hollywood's first great film star of the silent era; she won an Oscar in 1929 for her performance in "Coquette," one of the first "talkies," in Santa Monica, Calif., May 29, 1979.

Pospelov, Pyotr N., 80, major theoretician of the Soviet Communist Party during the Cold War and longtime editor of *Pravda,* announced in Moscow, April 24, 1979.

Potofsky, Jacob S., 84, president of the powerful Amalgamated Clothing Workers of America (1946-72) noted for his ability to mediate inter-union disputes, in New York City, August 5, 1979.

Prouvost, Jean, 93, Frances' leading newspaper publisher for over 50 years, whose empire included the dailies *Paris-Soir* and *Le Figaro,* as well as *Paris-Match* magazine, outside Paris, October 17, 1978.

Rand, Sally, 75, renowned fan dancer and striptease artist whose debut at the 1933 Chicago World's Fair shocked public opinion and delighted audiences; in Glendora, Calif., August 31, 1979.

Randolph, A. Phillip, 90, black labor leader and a founder of the modern civil rights movement who organized the Brotherhood of Sleeping Car Porters in the 1930s — the first all-black union in the AFL; he later forced both the Roosevelt and Truman Administrations to end discriminatory practices in government and the military services, in New York City, May 16, 1979.

Ray, Nicholas, 67 film director noted for such critical and popular successes as "Johnny Guitar," "Rebel Without a Cause," "They Live by Night," and "55 Days at Peking;" in New York City, June 16, 1979.

Renoir, Jean, 84, French-born film director and son of Impressionist painter Pierre Auguste Renoir, best known for classics like "The Grand Illusion" (1937) and "The Rules of the Game" (1939), in Los Angeles, February 12, 1979.

Rhys, Jean, 84, British novelist best known for her 1966 book, *Wide Sargasso Sea,* exploring the theme of female loneliness in a male-dominated world; in Exeter, England, May 14, 1979.

Richards, I(vor) A(rmstrong), 86, British educator, writer and literary critic who influenced a generation of British and American scholars, in Cambridge, England, September 7, 1979.

Riperton, Minnie, 31, singer and songwriter best known for her 1974 hit, "Loving You," in Los Angeles, July 12, 1979.

Rockefeller, Nelson A., 70, former Vice-President and four-term Governor of New York (1958-73), scion of the Rockefeller family fortune whose political career included an unsuccessful 1968 bid for the White House, in New York City, January 26, 1979.

Rockwell, Norman, 84, one of America's most popular artists, best known for his cover illustrations for *The Saturday Evening Post* (1916-63) which evoked nostalgia for smalltown Americana, in Stockbridge, Mass., November 8, 1978.

Rosenbloom, Carroll, 72, owner of the Los Angeles Rams football team since 1972, who was known for his often heated disagreements with sports officials; drowned off Golden Beach, Florida, April 2, 1979.

Ryan, Elizabeth ("Bunny"), 87, famous tennis pro who won a record 19 Wimbledon titles between 1914 and 1934, recognized as one of the best doubles players in the game; in Wimbledon, England, July 6, 1979.

Ryan, Leo J., 53, three-term liberal Democratic Congressman from suburban San Francisco, California; killed in an ambush near Kaituma, Guyana, while on a trip to investigate the People's Temple commune at Jonestown, Nov., 17, 1978.

Saltonstall, Leverett, 86, Massachusetts GOP leader for four decades, serving as Governor (1938-44) and later elected to the U.S. Senate (1944-66); in Dover, Mass., June 17, 1979.

Sardi, Eugenia Pallera, 89, Italian-born restaurateur who with husband Melchiorre established Sardi's, the famous Broadway theater-district restaurant, in New York City, November 17, 1978.

Saville, Victor, 83, British director and producer whose credits during his 40-year film career in London and Hollywood include "Goodbye, Mr. Chips," "Evergreen," "Green Dolphin Street" and "Dr. Jekyll and Mr. Hyde," in London, May 8, 1979.

Sawyer, Charles, 92, Cincinnati civic leader who served as President Truman's Secretary of Commerce (1948-53) and ordered the 1952 federal seizure of the nation's steel mills, an action that was overturned by the Supreme Court; in Palm Beach, Fla., April 7, 1979.

Seaton, George, 68, producer, director and screenwriter who won an Oscar in 1947 for his screenplay for "Miracle on 34th Street;" he also wrote and directed the 1969 film, "Airport," in Los Angeles, July 28, 1979.

Seberg, Jean, 40, film actress of the 1950s and 60s ("Saint Joan," "Bonjour Tristesse") whose later life was marked by tragedy; she became the target of a smear campaign by the FBI because of her support to black nationalist causes; an apparent suicide in Paris, France, September 8, 1979.

Shumlin, Herman, 80, leading producer-director of serious dramatic fare on Broadway for nearly 40 years (*Grand Hotel* (1930), *The Children's Hour* (1934), *Inherit the Wind* (1955), *The Deputy* (1964)); in New York City, June 14, 1979.

Sigcau, Chief Botha, 65, president of the Xhosa Republic of the Transkei since it was granted independence by South Africa in 1976; in Umtata, Transkei, December 1, 1978.

Simonov, Konstantin, 63, Soviet author best known for his novels and reportage on World War II, including his *Days and Nights* (1944), about the battle of Stalingrad; announced in Moscow, August 28, 1979.

Simons, Col. Arthur D., 60, Green Beret commander who led a 1970 raid into North Vietnam in an unsuccessful attempt to free American POW's, and was decorated by President Nixon; in Dallas, Texas, May 21, 1979.

Skinner, Cornelia Otis, 78, actress, author and playwright famous for her satirical sense of humour, which she displayed in her many stage roles since the 1930s, and in her best-selling 1942 memoir which she co-authored with Emily Kimbrough, *Our Hearts Were Young and Gay;* in New York City, July 9, 1979.

Smith, W. Eugene, 60, renowned photojournalist for over 40 years, serving as a combat photographer for both *Life* and *Newsweek* during World War II; also known for his more recent photo documentary, *Minimata,* on the effects of industrial pollution on a small Japanese fishing village, in Tucson, Ariz., October 15, 1978.

Soo, Jack, 63, actor best remembered for his portrayal of Nick Yamana, the dour-faced detective on the "Barney Miller" television series, in Los Angeles, January 11, 1979.

Southwell, Paul, 66, Prime Minister of St. Kitts-Nevis, one of the West Indies Associated States in the British Commonwealth; in St. Lucia, May 18, 1979.

Stafford, Jean, 63, short-story writer and novelist who won a Pulitzer Prize in 1970 for her *Collected Stories,* in White Plains, N.Y., March 26, 1979.

Stewart, Bill, 37, television correspondent for ABC-TV News since 1974, killed by National Guard soldiers in Managua, Nicaragua, while covering the civil war in that country, June 21, 1979.

Still, William Grant, 83, dean of black classical composers whose 1931 "Afro American Symphony" drew on the black spiritualist tradition and is regarded as the first work of its kind by a black composer, in Los Angeles, December 3, 1978.

Svoboda, Ludvik, 83, President of Czechoslovakia (1968-75) during the 1968 Soviet invasion and a member of the liberal reform wing of the Czech CP; he was also a much-decorated hero of both World Wars, in Prague, Czechoslovakia, September 20, 1979.

Swanson, Howard, 71, composer whose works were performed by the country's leading symphony orchestras and by major concert artists, in New York City, November 12, 1978.

Sykes, Sir Richard, 58, Britain's Ambassador to the Netherlands, killed by suspected IRA gunmen in The Hague, March 22, 1979.

Taleghani, Ayatollah Syed Mahmoud, 68, moderate Iranian religious leader and a key aide to the Ayatollah Khomeini; in Tehran, September 10, 1979.

Tate, Allen, 79, poet, critic and teacher, best known for his *Ode to the Confederate Dead;* a founder of the New Criticism school, he was a major figure in the Southern literary renaissance, in Nashville, Tenn., February 9, 1979.

Teitelbaum, Rabbi Joel, 92, spiritual leader of 150,000 members of the Satmar and Neturei Karta Hasidic sects of Orthodox Judaism in the U.S. and Israel; in New York City, August 19, 1979.

Todman, William S., 62, television producer who with partner Mark Goodson introduced such landmark audience-participation game shows as "What's My Line?", "The Price is Right" and "I've Got a Secret," in New York City, July 29, 1979.

Tomonaga, Shinichero, 73, Japanese scientist who won the 1965 Nobel Prize in physics for research on the nature of elementary particles in high-energy physics, in Tokyo, Japan, July 8, 1979.

Tugwell, Rexford Guy, 88, member of President Franklin D. Roosevelt's original "Brain Trust" who served as undersecretary of Agriculture (1934) and headed the Rural Resettlement Administration (1934-35) and was one of FDR's chief New Deal advisors; in Santa Barbara, California, July 21, 1979.

Tunney, Gene, 80, undefeated world heavyweight boxing champion (1926-28) who defeated Jack Dempsey twice and later pursued a successful career as a corporate executive, in Greenwich, Conn., November 7, 1978.

Vance, Vivian, 66, actress and co-star with Lucille Ball in the "I Love Lucy" (1951-59) and "The Lucy Show" (1962-65) television series, in Belvedere, Calif., August 17, 1979.

Velasco Ibarra, José María, 86, controversial political figure in Ecuador for over 40 years, he was elected President five times between 1938 and 1968, but was overthrown by the military four times; in Quito, Ecuador, March 30, 1979.

Vicious, Sid (John Simon Richie), 21, British 'punk' rock star of the Sex Pistols, accused of the stabbing murder of his girl friend Nancy Spungen; of an overdose of heroin in New York City, February 2, 1979.

Villot, Jean Cardinal, 73, French cleric and and theologian who served as Vatican Secretary of State under three Popes since 1969; in Vatican City, Rome, March 9, 1979.

Waltari, Mika, 70, Finnish author who wrote the 1945 international best seller, *The Egyptian,* in He'sinki, Finland, August 26, 1979.

Wayne, John, 72, the "Duke" who starred in over 200 films during a career spanning 50 years, winning the Academy Award for his 1969 performance in "True Grit;" he was considered one of the last true American heroes, in Los Angeles, June 11, 1979.

Weybright, Victor, 75, publisher who founded New American Library in 1947 — the first U.S. paperback book company, in New York City, November 3, 1978.

Wilding, Michael, 66, British stage and screen actor of the 1940s and 50s ("Under Capricorn," "Stage Fright") whose greatest notoriety came when he married actress Elizabeth Taylor, her second husband (1952-57); in Chichester, England, July 8, 1979.

Wills, Chill, 76, raspy-voiced character actor who appeared in hundreds of movies, best remembered as the voice of Francis, the talking mule in the famous comedy film series, in Encino, Calif., December 15, 1978.

Woodward, Robert Burns, 62, science professor at Harvard University who won the 1965 Nobel Prize in Chemistry for his work in determining the molecular structure of such complex organic compounds as penicillin; in Cambridge, Mass., July 8, 1979.

Wright, John Cardinal, 70, Vatican's chief administrator of clergy since 1969 and the highest-ranking American in the Roman Catholic Church; in Cambridge, Mass., August 10, 1979.

Zeller, André, 81, one of four retired French generals — including Maurice Challe, Edmond Jouhoud, and Raoul Salan — who staged unsuccessful 1961 *coup d'état* against French Pres. Charles deGaulle in Algeria; in Paris, France, September 18, 1979.

INDEX